GUIDE TO

FRENCH LITERATURE
Beginnings to 1789

Guide to French Literature

Beginnings to 1789

1789 to the Present

GUIDE TO
FRENCH, LITERATURE
Beginnings to 1789

ANTHONY LEVI

St-J

ST. JAMES PRESS
DETROIT   LONDON   WASHINGTON DC

Gale Research International Ltd.
PO Box 699
Cheriton House
North Way
Andover
Hants SP10 5YE

or

Gale Research Inc.
835 Penobscot Bldg.
Detroit, MI 48226-4094

ST JAMES PRESS is an imprint of Gale Research International Ltd.
An Affiliated Company of Gale Research Inc.

A CIP catalogue record for this book is available from the British Library.

ISBN 1-55862-159-8

Typeset by Data Text (UK), Tunbridge Wells, England
Printed in the United States of America

The paper used in this publication meets the minimum requirements of American National Standard for Information Sciences – Permanence Paper for printed Library materials, ANSI Z39.48-1984 ∞™

Published simultaneously in the United Kingdom and the United States of America

I(T)P™

The trademark **ITP** is used under license.

FOR

PETER and GILLIAN

CONTENTS

ABOUT THE AUTHOR

Professor Anthony Levi, born in 1929, regards himself as much as a cultural historian as a critic whose primary concern is the literature of France. After studying mathematics, he took *magna cum laude* Roman degrees in philosophy and theology, specializing in canon law, as well as a first at Oxford in German and French. The Oxford University Press published his successful D. Phil. thesis *French Moralists: The Theory of the Passions: 1585–1649* in 1964. From 1952 to 1955 he lived in Munich and both during those years and subsequently travelled widely in Europe, studying in France for the academic year 1963–64, after which he returned to teach at Oxford, specializing in the French renaissance.

In 1965 he was appointed Reader in French at the University of Warwick, holding the post concurrently with the Oxford lectureship. After appointment to a personal chair at Warwick, Professor Levi was appointed Buchanan Professor of French Language and Literature in the University of Saint Andrews, a post which he held until taking premature retirement in 1988. He has taught in New York and Washington DC, lectured widely in the US, in continental Europe, Australia, and New Zealand, and held fellowships in Washington, Canberra, Saint Petersburg, and Florence.

His *Religion in Practice* was published by the Oxford University Press in 1971 and translated into French, Italian, and Polish. In the same year he edited Erasmus's *Praise of Folly* for Penguin Classics. "His assessment of the work's intellectual climate is masterly," wrote Margaret Mann Phillips in *The Times Literary Supplement*. Professor Levi, well known as a reviewer, is the editor of the two volumes of Erasmus's satires for the Toronto University Press edition of *The Collected Works of Erasmus*, and has edited two collections of essays and published numerous papers in French and English collections. Oxford University Press is publishing his edition of Pascal's *"Pensées" and other texts* and Yale University Press his *An Intellectual History of the northern Renaissance*.

Anthony Levi is married with two daughters and lives in Scotland.

ACKNOWLEDGEMENTS

It is impossible to convey adequate thanks to the innumerable teachers, students, colleagues, librarians, and other friends to whom I am indebted for their patient help, particularly those who read drafts of entries. My wife is, and will no doubt remain, the only other person to have read every word in both volumes. Her criticism has been invaluable, but I have also been lucky in having two daughters ending school and starting university who, in connection with their own work, were exactly the right age to ask the right questions at the right time. Apart, however, from Daniel Kirkpatrick, quite special gratitude must be expressed to Philippe Barbour, the editor from Gale Research International, which took over St. James Press as an imprint from the beginning of 1992, to my research assistant, Alison Andrews, and to my two copy-editors, Ruth Sharman and Olive Classe.

8 March 1993   Anthony Levi

LIST OF ENTRIES

Jean-François Regnard
Mathurin Régnier
Nicolas-Anne-Edme Rétif de la Bretonne
Jean-François-Paul de Gondi, cardinal de Retz
Antoine Rivaroli, known as comte de Rivarol
Pierre de Ronsard
Jean Rotrou
Jean-Jacques Rousseau

Donatien-Alphonse-François, marquis de Sade
Jean Duvergier de Hauranne, abbé de Saint-Cyran
Charles de Marquetel de Saint-Denis, seigneur de Saint-
    Evremond
Louis de Rouvroy, duc de Saint-Simon
François de Sales
La Satire Ménippée
Paul Scarron
Maurice Scève

Georges de Scudéry
Madeleine de Scudéry
Michel-Jean Sedaine
Marie de Rabutin-Chantal, marquise de Sévigné
Charles Sorel, sieur de Soigny

Gédéon Tallemant des Réaux
François l'Hermite, known as Tristan l'Hermite
Pontus de Tyard

Honoré d'Urfé

Luc de Clapiers, marquis de Vauvenargues
Théophile de Viau
Vincent Voiture
François-Marie Arouet, known as Voltaire

_____

CHRONOLOGY

1498   Accession of Louis XII (1462–1515). Having divorced the childless Saint Jeanne de France (1464–1505), in 1499 he marries Anne de Bretagne (1477–1514), 22-year-old widow of Charles VIII (1470–98). The heir presumptive is François d'Angoulême (1494–1547) likely to be displaced by a still unborn male heir in the direct line

His father died in 1496; his mother is the ambitious and mercenary Louise de Savoie (1476–1531), his elder sister Marguerite d'Angoulême (1492–1549), later queen of Navarre

Anne de Bretagne had eight pregnancies but no male heir. Two daughters survived infancy: Claude de France (1499–1524), who in 1506 married François, the heir presumptive; and Renée (1510–75), duchess of Ferrara from 1534

1512–17   Fifth Lateran Council

1514   Death of Anne de Bretagne. Louis XII, still hoping for a male heir, marries at 52 the 18-year-old sister of Henry VIII, Mary Tudor. He dies 1 January 1515

1515   Accession of François d'Angoulême, François I. For his seven children by Claude de France, born 1515, 1516, 1518 (the dauphin), 1519 (to become Henri II), 1520, 1522, and 1523, see index under Claude de France

1516   Concordat of Bologna signed between François I and Leo X. Zwingli (1484–1531) starts preaching in Zurich against veneration of relics

Charles of Austria (1500–1558) becomes Charles I of Spain, king of Castile, Aragon, and Naples

1517   Peace of Cambrai (11 March) temporarily secures territorial advantages won by France in Italy, and French diplomatic ascendancy over the emperor, England, and the papacy

Luther (1483–1546) attacks attribution to the souls of the dead of indulgences granted in exchange for money

1519   Charles I of Spain elected emperor Charles V

1520   English and French meeting at Field of the Cloth of Gold

The bull *Exsurge Domine* (15 June) condemns Luther. It is followed by his excommunication on 3 January 1521 and condemnation by the Paris theology faculty on 15 April

1521   War breaks out between the French and the imperial forces in alliance with Charles V Guillaume Briçonnet (1472–1534), bishop of Meaux, calls Jacques Lefèvre d'Etaples (?1450–1536) to his diocese to organize its evangelical reform

1521–23   Reorganization and centralization of French fiscal system. Loans raised for first time by public subscription

1525–26   25 February 1525: defeat of François I at Pavia. Heavy death toll amongst French nobility. François I imprisoned in Madrid. Harsh terms, including surrender of Burgundy and delivery of two sons as hostages, imposed for release on 17 March 1526

1526   League of Cognac (22 May) allies anti-imperial forces: France, the papacy, Venice, Florence, and Francesco Sforza, duke of Milan. During the ensuing war, France loses its territory in Italy

1527   Sack of Rome by imperial troops

Execution of Semblançay, former général des finances, to whom the king and his mother owed money

1529   April: *Grande Rebeine* in Lyons, when placards posted inciting rebellion against speculators, thought responsible for high price of bread. Riots and looting brutally suppressed

3 August: peace of Cambrai ("Peace of the Ladies"). France buys back Burgundy, surrenders all Italian claims, and gives up towns in the north-east. Royal princes returned from Spain

1533   After mounting tension between the court and the Paris theology faculty, Gérard Roussel (1480–1555), the university rector, Nicolas Cop, the acting principal of Sainte-Barbe, Andrea de Gouvea, and Jean Calvin (1509–64), flee Paris

28 October: the 15-year-old prince Henri, later to become Henri II, marries the pope's niece, the 12-year-old Catherine de Medici. Of the seven children born of the marriage (on whom see index under Catherine de Medici), three were to become kings of France, François II, Charles IX, and Henri III. The death of the

fourth son, François d'Anjou, in 1584 will leave Protestant Henri de Navarre, later Henri IV, heir presumptive

1534   17–18 October: during the night "placards," printed sheets denouncing the Mass, posted throughout Paris, and in Orléans, Blois, Amboise, Tours, and Rouen. A further document attacking the Mass distributed on 13 January 1535

1535   21 January: expiatory procession in Paris. Six dissidents burnt

16 July: edict of Coucy pardons prisoners and exiles whose sedition is solely religious, but demands abjuration within six months. Penalty for relapsing is hanging

1536   French invade Savoy. Forced to retreat, they successfully defend Provence by a scorched earth policy

Imperial forces defeated in north France

10 August: sudden death of dauphin, almost certainly from natural causes, although Montecuculli is executed for poisoning

1538   May-June: the new pope, Alessandro Farnese, Paul III, comes to Nice, where he meets the emperor four times and François I twice. A ten-year truce is signed. The emperor and François I exchange warm greetings at Aigues-Mortes in July

Royal policy on the repression of heresy intensifies

1539–40   November-January: the emperor crosses France at the king's invitation in order to reach the Spanish Netherlands without a dangerous sea journey

1540   May: Lazare de Baïf (1496–1547): unsuccessful mission to Haguenau to negotiate with the Schmalkaldic league of six schismatic princes and ten cities

1541   Reform of the *gabelle* system of taxing salt production by compulsory purchase. Rebellion of those whose living depended on salt mining

The French ambassador to Turkey and an envoy to Venice murdered by imperial troops as they sail down the Po

1542   12 July: François I, promised massive Turkish support, declares war on the emperor

1544   18 September: treaty of Crépy-en-Laonnais ends wars with emperor Charles V. Huge loans raised from Lyons bankers at 16%, against rates of 5% to a peak of 8% available to the public

1545   9 September: death of Charles d'Orléans, leaving François with two surviving children, Henri, dauphin since 1536, and Marguerite de France

1545–63   Council of Trent

1546   October: Anne d'Heilly, duchesse d'Etampes (1508–80), the king's mistress since about 1527, urges an Anglo-French alliance, with risk of break with Rome on the English model

1547   31 March: death of François I. Accession of his 27-year-old son Henri II, whose 48-year-old mistress, Diane de Poitiers, was to further the rise of the Guise family, the junior branch of the house of Lorraine, against the court faction headed by the duchesse d'Etampes

1548   October: Jeanne d'Albret (1528–72) marries Antoine de Bourbon, duc de Vendôme (1518–62). She was to inherit the throne of Navarre from Marguerite d'Angoulême, her mother, in 1549, and passes it on to her son, born in 1553 and eventually to become Henri IV

François (1544–60), eldest son of Henri II and Catherine de Medici, betrothed to Mary Stuart, Queen of Scots (1542–87), daughter of James V of Scotland and Marie de Guise

1552   Henri II invades Lorraine and occupies the principal towns of the three great bishoprics, Toul, Metz, and Verdun

1555–56   Charles V abdicates the imperial throne in favour of his brother Ferdinand I and renounces the Spanish throne in favour of his son Philip II

1559   2 April: Treaty of Cateau-Cambrésis between Henri II and Philip II leaves Lorraine to France but restores independence to Savoy. Contains secret anti-Protestant clauses; Spanish supremacy accepted in Italy; the duke of Savoy to marry Marguerite de France, sister of Henri II, and Philip II, widower of Mary Tudor, to marry Elisabeth de France, the king's daughter

26 May: first synod of French Protestant church opens in Paris

10 July: Henri II dies, fatally injured by comte de Montgomery (1530–74) at jousting tournament in honour of double marriage. Calvinism has by now spread into aristocracy, notably to members of Bourbon-Condé and Châtillon-Coligny families

Accession of François II. Although he is 15 and has attained his majority, the weakness of his mind makes a council of government necessary. France is ruled not, as custom demands, by princes of the blood, but by the maternal uncles of the queen, Mary Stuart: François de Lorraine, second duc de Guise (1519–63) and Charles de Guise, cardinal de Lorraine (1524–74)

23 December: burning of magistrate Anne du Bourg for outspoken, public recommendation of toleration for Protestants

1560   February-March: Conjuration d'Amboise, Protestant plot to arrest the Guise influence. The conspiracy is leaked, and put down with summary beheadings, hangings, and drownings

30 June: Michel de l'Hôpital formally appointed chancellor

5 December: death of François II

Postponement of execution, then reprieve of Louis I de Bourbon, prince de Condé (1530–69) sentenced on 26 November for fomenting uprising in south with his brother, Antoine de Bourbon, king of Navarre and father of the future Henri IV. Protestantism has acquired a strong political dimension

Accession of 10-year-old Charles IX, brother of late king. Regency of his mother, Catherine de Medici.

1561   September: Colloque de Poissy between Catholics led by Cardinal de Lorraine, including six cardinals, 40 bishops, a dozen doctors of theology, and as many canonists, and Huguenots led by Théodore de Bèze, with 12 ministers and a score of laypeople. No agreement was reached; sectarian disturbances increase

1562   7 January: Michel de l'Hôpital advocates separation of religious from political affiliations.

17 January: edict of January ordering Protestants to give up buildings and not to assemble in cities bestows legal recognition on Protestants. Paris parlement for that reason resists registration of edict

Sunday 1 March: Wassy. François de Guise, passing with retainers through Wassy on his way to lunch, finds some 1,200 Huguenots holding a service within the town. His men attack, leaving 74 dead and 100 wounded. Sectarian massacres, eventually by both sides, become frequent

François de Guise welcomed in Paris where, on 20 March, he brings an armed force in spite of a prohibition by Catherine de

Medici. The provost of merchants offers him two million livres and an army of 20,000 men. Orléans declares itself for the Huguenots. The parlements declare the Huguenots to be rebels, and Guise re-takes Rouen, sacking it

December: defeat of Huguenots near Dreux. There are at least 6,000 deaths

1563–98   Religious wars, traditionally but misleadingly divided into eight discrete civil wars: i) 1562–63 ii) 1567–68 iii) 1568–70 iv) 1573 v) 1575 vi) 1577 vii) 1580 and viii) 1585–98. During periods of relative calm, clashes of marauding bands, aggrieved peasants, and touchy nobles remain continuous

1563   18 February: François de Guise assassinated at the siege of Orléans by a Huguenot

18 March: peace of Amboise published, less favourable to Huguenots than edict of January, but still recognizing them as a religious group. Orléans restored to the crown

15 September: Charles IX, although not yet 14, declared of age, to prevent the appointment of Condé, senior prince of the blood, as lieutenant-general of France

1564   The court tours France, exploring possibility of a league of Catholic princes. Suppression of Calvinism not yet ruled out. Emergence of a "politique" party dedicated to a pragmatic political solution dates from this period

1567   The Huguenots renew hostilities. La Rochelle, its port affording invaluable access to foreign allies, becomes a Huguenot stronghold

1568   23 March: peace of Longjumeau

Third war intensifies hostilities. L'Hôpital dismissed and all edicts of toleration revoked. The future Henri III put in charge of the army

1569   13 March: Huguenots defeated at Jarnac. Condé surrenders, but is immediately shot. Huguenot defeat at Moncontour, leads to peace of Saint-Germain

Full freedom of worship for Huguenots still felt likely to lead to territorial split in France

1570   8 August: peace signed at Saint-Germain. La Rochelle, Cognac, Montauban, and La Charité made into safe towns for Protestants

1572   9 June: death of Jeanne d'Albret, queen of Navarre, where Salic law did not apply

18 August: her son, now Henri, king of Navarre, marries sister of Charles IX, Marguerite. Paris filled with Huguenot nobility for the festivities

Friday 22 August: sniper's bullet, fired by a Guise follower, wounds Coligny. The king sends his surgeon, Ambrose Paré

Sunday 24 August: feast of Saint Bartholomew. An armed band murders Coligny. Other armed groups set about slaughtering Huguenots, and the massacre is echoed in the provinces. Degree of premeditation and coordination is disputed

Henri I de Bourbon, prince de Condé, son of Louis I killed at Jarnac, is spared, but later with Henri de Navarre forced to abjure. There are several thousand deaths in Paris

1573   The fourth religious war consists of the Catholic attempts to reduce the Huguenot strongholds of La Rochelle and Sancerre

June: Henri, the king's eldest surviving brother and heir presumptive to the French throne, becomes king of Poland. Peace is signed in La Rochelle

1574   The start of the fifth religious war is normally dated from 10 March, after a general rising on 23 February. Alençon, the king's youngest brother, has become leader of the politiques. Catherine puts three armies in the field, in the west, the south-east, and Normandy. Montgomery is captured and executed

30 May: death of Charles IX. Henri III returns from Poland to assume French crown. His brother, François d'Alençon, the new heir presumptive, becomes François d'Anjou

Catherine de Medici, regent until the return of Henri III, declares a truce, and meanwhile pays the wages of the Huguenot garrison at La Rochelle

1575   13 February: Henri III crowned at Reims. Next day he marries Louise de Vaudémont, princesse de Lorraine (1553–1601)

10 October: at Dormans, Henri de Guise is victor against the Huguenots, but is himself wounded in the face. He is henceforward known as "le Balafré (scar-face)," a nickname already used of his father. In November a truce is agreed

1576   Friday 3 February: Navarre escapes from surveillance, reaching Alençon in time for the Protestant service on Sunday 5th. No attempt is made to pursue him, and he abjures Catholicism a few days later

6 May: edict of Beaulieu grants freedom of worship to Huguenots, except in immediate vicinity of Paris. Amnesties are granted, and eight towns of refuge nominated. But the only parlement to ratify the edict is Paris, and the slaughter of Huguenots continues sporadically

A League is formed for the defence of Catholicism, claiming from its members an allegiance superior to that which they owe to the crown. It is inspired by the Guise family (on which see index)

The king, to avert too great a swing of power to the Guise family, assumes headship of the League

6 December: all sections of the Estates General, convoked at Blois, are favourable to the League

1577   The sixth religious war is dominated by the return of Anjou to the Catholic cause and his victories at La Charité and Issoire, in both of which the inhabitants were massacred. Mayenne (1554–1611), brother of Guise, in charge of royal forces in west, takes Brouage, and so controls La Rochelle harbour

17 September: treaty concluded at Bergerac

1580   Navarre's seizure of Cahors re-opens hostilities for seventh religious war

November: peace is signed at Fleix

1584   10 June: death of Anjou makes Protestant Henri de Navarre heir presumptive to the French throne. The only alternative appears to involve Spanish domination through Guise family, or break-up of kingdom

1585   2 January: League and king of Spain agree to vest the French succession in the Cardinal de Bourbon (1523–90), younger brother of Navarre's father. League can claim France's allegiance north of a line from Angers to Lyons. Even in west and south, Huguenots in minority. By an edict of 19 July they become an outlawed sect

The king attempts to reassert his authority, sending armies under Mayenne to Guyenne, under Biron to Saintonge, under Joyeuse to Gascony, and under Epernon to Provence. Montmorency is left in charge of Languedoc

9 September: Pope Sixtus V issues bull declaring Navarre and Condé incapable of succeeding to the throne, absolving all vassals from allegiance

The sixteen districts of Paris have secretly appointed some 40 representatives to an

1587   intended governing body known as the "Seize," totally subservient to the League

20 October: Navarre, forced to fight at Coutras, wins pitched battle for Huguenots for first time in wars, against army twice the size of his own. A week later Guise scores a victory at Anneau near Chartres

1588   February: Guise presents the king with demands to pursue strongly anti-Huguenot policies and enters Paris in spite of king's prohibition. With Catherine he calls on king at Louvre

Plots on king's life

11 May: 4,000 Swiss mercenaries under Biron are summoned into Paris by king. On 12 May the populace erects barricades to isolate the detachments, which surrender. The king flees to Chartres on 13th, while Catherine de Medici and Guise are conferring. Guise in complete charge of Paris

11 July: the king agrees to most of Guise's conditions, and to convoke the Estates on 16 October. Overwhelming support at Estates for League

23 December: the king at Blois sends for Guise and his brother, the cardinal. The duke is murdered immediately on entering king's antechamber, his brother executed next day. The bodies are burnt to leave no relics. The cardinal de Bourbon is imprisoned, as are the new duc de Guise, Charles prince de Joinville (1571–1640), son of the recently murdered Henri; Michel Marteau de la Chapelle from the Seize; and the archbishop of Lyons. Countrywide surge of support for League

1589   5 January: death of Catherine de Medici

The Sorbonne announces that the king has forfeited all right to the crown; only Bordeaux, Caen, Blois, Tours, Saumur, and some small towns of lower Loire remain faithful to king

15 February: Mayenne enters Paris at head of a powerful force and assumes leadership of League. The king's only remaining hope is negotiation with Henri de Navarre against League

24 May: the pope threatens the king with excommunication unless he releases the imprisoned prelates

2 August: Henri III, his army reinforced by 14,000 mercenaries, dies of stab wound on eve of projected attack on Paris, recognizing Navarre as his heir

Navarre judges that immediate conversion to Catholicism would alienate too many of his followers to secure him the throne. Some Catholics immediately accept him; others retire from army

Henri withdraws with 7,000 men to Normandy, followed by Mayenne with 30,000, but holds his own at Arques on 21 September. He gains ground as Le Mans, Bayeux, and Lisieux acknowledge him. By end of year his position is no longer hopeless

1590   14 March: Navarre routs League forces at Ivry, sparing the French, but massacring foreign auxiliaries. He might have taken Paris, but prefers siege to pillage

10 May: death of cardinal de Bourbon. No supporter of the League now has vestige of a claim to Henri III's succession

August: the young duc de Guise escapes from captivity at Tours

September: famine in Paris during the siege. The city saved only by the brilliant generalship of the duke of Parma. However, he quarrels with the League leaders and returns home in November. Relations between Mayenne and the Spanish faction have become strained. When Parma dies in 1592, the League has no further hope of winning the war by superior generalship

1591   19 April: Chartres surrenders to the king, but Henri forced to raise siege of Rouen

1592   Mayenne calls meeting of Estates General in Paris for January 1593. The Spaniards urge claims to French throne of infanta, granddaughter of Henri II, excluded only by treaty and medieval Salic legal codes

1593   The Estates refuse strong arguments in favour of the infanta, and negotiations take place with the king

18 May: Henri de Navarre writes to the archbishops expressing desire to be "instructed" in Catholicism

25 July: Henri IV absolved by archbishop of Bourges, pending remission of the excommunication by the pope. He hears Mass at Saint-Denis

18 September: Lyons rises against Nemours, governing the town for the League, and imprisons him

31 July-31 October: the power of the League dissolves during the three-month truce granted by the king

1594   27 February: consecration of Henri IV at Chartres, since Reims, the traditional location, still in League hands

6 March: departure of Mayenne from Paris; peaceable entry of Henri IV on 22nd. Complex arrangements made for financial

compensation. Paris costs 2,000,000 livres; Rouen and other towns surrendered by Villars, 3,500,000; Guise receives 4,000,000 livres and Villars 500,000. Henri IV has at times less than a week's funding available, but organizes tax exemptions

Later in 1594 attempt on the king's life leads to expulsion of the Jesuits, wrongly thought openly to have taught that circumstances can legitimize tyrannicide, but parlements implement the expulsion only patchily and spasmodically

1595–97   Open warfare on French territory between Spain and France, ending with the capitulation of Amiens 25 September 1597

1598   Mercoeur surrenders Brittany to the king for 4,000,000 livres

13 April: promulgation of edict of Nantes conceding to French Calvinists complete freedom of conscience, extensive rights of public worship, and access to all public offices. The Calvinists allowed control of 200 named safe towns. The edict is intended to be only a provisional measure. Registered 1599 by Paris parlement, only later and with restrictions by the others

May: treaty of Vervins with Spain reinstates provisions of Cateau-Cambrésis

1599   10 April: death of king's mistress Gabrielle d'Estrées. Marguerite de Valois, Henri IV's childless wife, accepts annulment of her marriage, granted 17 December

1600   5 October: marriage of Henri IV and Marie de Medici (1573–1642)

Military use of modern artillery to occupy Bresse and Savoy

1601   27 September: birth of future Louis XIII (1601–43) assures succession in direct line

Bresse, Bugey, Gex, and Valromey incorporated into France

1603   Recall to France of the Jesuits

1604   The "Paulette" formally turns judicial offices and administrative posts into hereditable property

1607   Franco-Venetian alliance securing the Valtelline pass, 100 kilometres of the upper Adda valley, from Spanish control. It allowed overland access between Lombardy and Austria, and was key to European political dominance

1610   14 May: assassination of Henri IV and accession of Louis XIII (1601–43). See index under Henri IV on his children and their marriages. Gaston d'Anjou, later d'Or-

léans (1608–60), was heir presumptive from 1611 to 1638, when the future Louis XIV was born. Next in line was Henri, prince de Condé (1588–1646), son of Henri IV's cousin and father of Louis "le grand" Condé (1621–86)

1614   Uprising of princes led by Condé and Nevers (d.1637)

Last meeting of Estates General before 1789. Majority of Louis XIII

1615   Marriage of Louis XIII to Anne of Austria, the Spanish infanta (1601–66) and of the king's sister Elisabeth (1602–44) to Philip IV of Spain (1605–65)

1616   September: Condé, dangerously popular in Paris, is arrested, and Richelieu (1585–1642) given charge of foreign affairs

1617   Louis XIII at 16½ seizes personal power under tutelage of 39-year-old duc de Luynes (1578–1621), who was made duke and peer. Marie de Medici, the queen mother confined to Blois

1618   Outbreak of Thirty Years War

1619   Escape from Blois of Marie de Medici, given governorship of landlocked Anjou to curtail overseas communication. Condé restored to favour

1620   Marie de Medici seeks to return to power, and joins conspiracy of nobles, including Epernon, Mayenne, Longueville, and Soissons. Louis XIII has support of rest of country

8 August: skirmish at Ponts-de-Cé on 8 August, and surrender of château of Angers on 9th, lead to conclusion of peace on 10th

Louis, still personal ruler of Béarn where edict of Nantes does not apply, forcibly incorporates Béarn and lower Navarre into France, restoring Catholicism

1621   2 April: Luynes made Connétable. Open war between royal and Protestant forces. Louis XIII forced to raise siege of Montauban, but overall victor

25 April: treaty of Madrid restores status quo after erection by Spaniards of forts in Valtelline

1622   5 September: Richelieu made cardinal

19 October: victorious anti-Huguenot campaign marked by needless atrocities leads to peace of Montpellier. Huguenots keep Montauban and La Rochelle as cities of refuge. Ascendancy of Richelieu begins. The queen's first miscarriage leaves the king's brother, Gaston, still heir presumptive

1624 Richelieu appointed to king's council in April, chief minister in August

1625 Richelieu's proposals for radical administrative reform

1626 Promulgation of harsh anti-duelling edict. The queen's second miscarriage makes Gaston's marriage important. Any male issue of Gaston would remove Condé's reversionary rights

6 August: attempt to which Gaston and the queen were privy on life of Richelieu, whose power increases. Execution of Chalais (b.1599) as conspirator. The two sons of Henri IV by Gabrielle d'Estrées, César de Vendôme and his brother Alexandre, the Grand Prior of Knights of Malta, imprisoned; flight to Lorraine of duchesse de Chevreuse; Gaston raised to duchy of Orléans, given pension, and married to wealthy Marie de Bourbon-Montpensier

December: assembly of notables summoned to inaugurate Richelieu's administrative reforms

1627 14 May: fashionable duel involving principals and four seconds, one of whom was killed. Two of those involved, Bouteville and Chapelles, beheaded despite protests from nobility on 22 June

4 June: the duchesse d'Orléans dies giving birth to "La grande Mademoiselle"

1627–28 29 October: capitulation of La Rochelle after siege

1629 Edict of Alès pardons Protestants who had regrouped in south

1630 Monday 11 November: Day of Dupes. Richelieu intrudes on private interview between Marie de Medici, who now loathes him, and Louis XIII, rightly supposing that the queen mother was at the least demanding his dismissal. Louis XIII reduced to pallor, Richelieu and the queen mother to tears. Richelieu, who believes he is disgraced, is sent for by the king, and re-affirmed in favour. Some of his opponents, including Michel de Marillac (1563–1632), keeper of the seals, and the maréchal de Bassompierre (1579–1646), imprisoned. Marillac's brother, Louis, commanding the army in Italy, executed for embezzlement

1631 Orléans deserts his mother, seeks reconciliation with Richelieu, hesitates about raising an army, and flees to Lorraine in March

The queen mother escapes from banishment at Compiègne and leaves France for good

August: Richelieu raised to duché-pairie.

Appalling harvest leads to popular uprisings.

Disturbances in Languedoc follow introduction of direct taxation in place of contributions through the provincial Estates, convoked for 12 December by the governor, Condé's brother-in-law, Henry II de Montmorency (1595–1632). Toulouse parlement refuses to register taxation edict

1632 3 January: secret marriage of Gaston d'Orléans to Marguerite, princesse de Lorraine, sister of the duke of Lorraine

Montmorency joins Orléans and queen mother in planning an uprising in the south coordinated with invasion from Lorraine. Orléans moves prematurely in mid-June, fails to win over Dijon, and Toulouse parlement does not support Montmorency, wounded and taken prisoner at Castelnaudary on 1 September, executed on 30 October. Orléans, still heir presumptive, is pardoned, escapes from Tours, and remains two years in exile in Brussels

1633 France takes control of Lorraine, annexing it in 1634

1635 19 May: provoked by Spain, France formally sends herald to Brussels to proclaim declaration of war

Foundation by Richelieu of Académie française. The chancellor, Pierre Séguier (1588–1672), increasingly controls France's internal affairs. The surintendants de finance, Bullion and Bouthillier, little more than functionaries. Richelieu postpones internal reforms to strengthen France's international position. Condé puts himself in service of Spain

1636 Most severe to date of the recurrent financial crises which keep campaigns short and brutal. Agricultural yields fall, but price of goods increases. Peasantry taxed to starvation, and war funded from creation of offices for sale

1637 King's confessor, Père Caussin, removed largely for insisting on king's duty to alleviate plight of people

1638 Birth of a dauphin. A second son, Philippe, was to be born in 1640. Spanish infanta born within days of dauphin. Both Richelieu and the Spanish minister Olivares (1587–1645), immediately see solution to Europe's problems in marriage of Louis XIV and Maria-Teresa. It will take place in 1660

1639 Revolt of the Nu-Pieds, provoked by the threat to bring panning of high-class white salt in lower Normandy into compulsory state purchase regime of the gabelle. The peasant uprising turned into an organized army of 20,000, and spread round Avranches

1640   Exaction of 4,000,000 livres from Assembly of the Clergy. Louis d'or introduced

1641   The sovereign courts stripped of right to take notice of affairs of state, administrative or financial matters, or questions of government. Revolt of comte de Soissons, with Vendôme, Guise, and Bouillon, Turenne's older brother. Soissons killed at battle of La Marfée. Widespread resentment at taxation level

30 December: Mazarin (1602–61) made cardinal

1642   Attempt by Cinq-Mars (1620–42), the king's intimate young companion, to make peace with Spain, necessarily displacing Richelieu. Orléans, no longer heir presumptive, was to be put on throne. Cinq-Mars and a confidant, François-Auguste de Thou (1607–42), beheaded at Lyons 12 September

Louis XIII, gravely ill, starts to rely on Mazarin
Richelieu dies 4 December

1643   14 May: death of Louis XIII. The parlement rejects agreed provisions for government by Council in favour of regency of Anne of Austria, who retains Mazarin, Richelieu's successor

A dissident cabal formed against Mazarin by "Les Importants" is defeated, and Mazarin's relationship with the queen mother becomes increasingly intimate. It is generally accepted that they were lovers

Victory at Rocroi for 21-year-old Enghien, Condé's son, whose generalship destroys the Spanish infantry. His victories continue: at Fribourg (1644), Nördlingen (1645), the surrender of Dunkirk on 11 October 1646, and Lens (1648)

1648   Turenne (1611–75) victorious at Sommershausen

Treaty of Westphalia ends Thirty Years War

Opening in Paris of first Fronde, essentially result of exactions by central government. Enghien, who had now succeeded to the Condé title, is called on to restore order in Paris

Two members of the parlement are arrested, but popular uprising puts barricades in streets during night of 26–27 August. The queen regent flees first to Rueil and then to Saint-Germain, where a capitulatory declaration is registered on 24 October. The court briefly returns to Paris

1649   The party of Condé, his brother Conti, and his sister Anne de Longueville now makes demands inconsistent with royal authority. Condé himself still sides with the crown, but his brother, sister, her lover, that is the future La Rochefoucauld, Retz, Beaufort, and Bouillon head the rebels in Paris while Longueville raises Normandy. Turenne attempts to join them, but his troops are bought by Mazarin, and he flees to Holland. Condé blockades Paris for the crown from 6 January 1649, and by 4 March the rebels are ready to treat. Treaty of Rueil registered on 1 April

1650   Condé's demands exorbitant and behaviour of his friends, the "petits-maîtres," offensive

18 January: Mazarin has Condé, Conti, and Longueville arrested. Mme de Longueville flees to Normandy before joining Turenne at Stenay. Normandy is subdued, and the court succeeds in imposing order except at first in Bordeaux and Provence

1651   Orléans and Retz, allied to Mazarin's enemies, now demand release of the princes. Mazarin leaves Paris on night of 6–7 February and releases the princes in Le Havre on 13th. They had been removed from Vincennes to Marcoussis, near Limours, and then to Le Havre, in case their release became objective for invaders. The queen mother is practically a rebel prisoner in Paris, and Mazarin takes refuge at Brühl, near Cologne. Condé momentarily in command of almost all of France. Retz urges his arrest or murder, and allies himself politically with the queen mother and all other anti-Condé forces

21 August: Retz and Condé, each supported by armed followers, come to Paris parlement. La Rochefoucauld nearly murders Retz

Charges against Condé are withdrawn

7 September: Louis XIV's majority declared two days after his 13th birthday, turning hostility to Mazarin, now the king's minister, into treason

Condé in open revolt seeks support from Spain. Mazarin, recalled, reaches Poitiers on 29 January 1652. Orléans has joined the rebels. Turenne and Bouillon rally to the court

1652   Turenne occupies Saint-Denis with 12,000 men, threatening Condé's 6,000 at Saint-Cloud. Condé forced to fight in the Faubourg Saint-Antoine. Remnants of his force admitted to Paris on 2 July, but order cannot be restored. Support for rebels melts

6 August: a royal decree moves the parlement to Pontoise

Mazarin again withdraws from France to make pacification easier, and an amnesty is accorded

The court is able to return to Paris 21 October; Orléans retires to Blois; Retz is arrested; and the parlement is again ordered not to concern itself with questions of state, administration, or finance

1653   Mazarin's return to Paris. Condé retires to Holland. Within months the whole of France returns to the royal allegiance.

Foucquet (1615–80) made surintendant des finances

1659   Treaty of the Pyrenees finally ends hostilities. Louis XIV to marry the infanta, and Condé to return to the government of Burgundy

1660   June: marriage of Louis XIV to his first cousin, Maria-Teresa, infanta of Spain

Death of Gaston d'Orléans

1661   Marriage of Henrietta of England with Philippe d'Orléans, the king's brother

9 March: death of Mazarin

November: birth of dauphin, the only son of Louis XIV and Maria-Teresa

Beginning of the personal government of Louis XIV. It means only that no chief minister is formally appointed. In fact Colbert exercises supreme political power, then Louvois. Only late in the reign does Louis XIV originate political policy decisions. His glorification is itself a political tool designed by Colbert, chiefly but not exclusively for internal consumption. Centrally organized thurification of a sun-king equipped with the trappings of grandeur was a successful political means of promoting national identity and external respect

Louis XIV kept Mazarin's ministers: Séguier as chancellor; Le Tellier for war; Lionne for sea-power, maritime trade, and foreign affairs; and Foucquet for finance. Colbert establishes central control over all the organs of French culture through a system of academies, permissions, censures, and patronage. He inherits the Académie française but reorganizes and at least attempts to professionalize it in 1673; founds Académie des Inscriptions et des Médailles (1663); Académie des Sciences (1669); and promotes academies for painting and sculpture, for dance, for music, and for architecture. The Gobelins manufactory requires authority for each tapestry design, and is set to producing all furnishings required for the royal residences. A French academy is founded in Rome in 1666. For system of government see index under Louis XIV

1661   At the instigation of Colbert, the surintendant des finances, Foucquet, from whose practices Mazarin must have profited, and whose literary patronage surpassed that of the court, indicted for corruption, tried, and sentenced to banishment and the confiscation of his property, increased by Louis XIV to life imprisonment. He had entertained the king at his magnificent new property at Vaux-le-Vicomte on 17 August and was arrested at Nantes on 5 September. Colbert has other financiers tried. Some are condemned to death, although none is executed. Over 4,000 heavily fined

1667–68   Louis XIV's Dutch campaign, known as the "war of devolution," in pursuit of his claim that Maria-Teresa, as the only surviving child of her father's first marriage had inherited the Low Countries and Franche-Comté. The dangers of French territorial ambitions are obvious to all Europe. The campaign ends with the treaty of Aix-la-Chapelle, which gives France much of Flanders in exchange for surrendering Franche-Comté

1672–78   War between France and the united Dutch provinces. France had on 31 December 1671 made the treaty of Dover with England against the Dutch, England's nominal allies, and had placed heavy duties on Dutch goods entering France, which leads to tariff war

21 May 1672: Louis XIV leaves Charleroi for Maastricht with 80,000 men to link with Condé's army of 40,000, making for Maastricht from Sedan. The "crossing of the Rhine" takes place at Tolhuis ford on the branch of the Rhine known as the Waal, which flows south of Arnhem after the split below Emmerich. The Dutch form an alliance with Spain, the empire, and Denmark. The French re-take Franche-Comté. Turenne is killed in 1675

1678   Treaty of Nijmegen ends war and returns Franche-Comté to France

1680   28 January: marriage of dauphin to Marie-

Anne-Victoire, 19-year-old sister of Maximilian II, elector of Bavaria

1681   Assembly of the clergy leads to Gallican declaration of March 1682

1682   6 August: birth of dauphin's heir, the duc de
Bourgogne

1683   6 September: death of Colbert. Influence of
François-Michel le Tellier, marquis de
Louvois (1641–91), secretary of state for
war from 1662, increasingly important
over previous ten years, now unchallenged. He inclines to policies of territorial
aggrandizement by war rather than Colbert's cultivation of industry and commerce. He favoured the court's move from
the Louvre to Versailles and furthered the
disastrous revocation of the edict of Nantes
Death of Maria-Teresa

1684   January: secret marriage of Louis XIV to Mme
de Maintenon (1635–1719), governess of
three of king's seven children by Mme de
Montespan

1685   17 October: revocation of the edict of Nantes.
Some 200 edicts between 1665 and 1685
had already imposed increasing constraints but revocation entails the exile of
ministers, the closing of schools and, in
spite of a prohibition on emigration, the
move into exile of tens of thousands

1688   War of League of Augsburg. The league was
a defensive alliance formed against
France. Louis XIV at this date openly
intends to acquire military dominance in
Europe, independence of Gallican
church, and the emperor's position for
himself or his son. Allied with Denmark
and James II of England, Louis XIV
starts military operations on the Rhine,
while the emperor gains territory from
the Turks in eastern Europe

29 October: William of Orange sails for
England and Philippsburg falls to the
French. William enters London on 28
December. James II flees and reaches
France 4 January 1689. England from
being an ally had become an enemy

1689   Devastation of Palatinate on advice of Louvois. Heidelberg, Mannheim, Speier, and
Worms are sacked; Ledenburg and
Oppenheim are burnt, and large tracts of
country ravaged

Rivalry of France and England in India and
America now established

12 May: signature of Grand Alliance between
Holland and the emperor

1691–97 Death of Louvois. The harvests of 1692 and

1693 aggravate personal and corporate
penury, but war continues spasmodically
until peace of Ryswyck in 1697. France
cedes virtually all conquered territories
except Strasbourg

1701–14 War of the Spanish Succession against Austria,
England, and the United Provinces.
Charles II of Spain died in 1700 without
issue, leaving the kingship of Spain to the
second grandson of Louis XIV, the duke of
Anjou (1683–1746), who becomes Philip
V of Spain. Marlborough begins his series
of successful campaigns. By 1713 peace
of Utrecht, France concedes Newfoundland, Hudson's Bay, and the whole Saint
Lawrence basin; Philip V keeps Spain, but
renounces all rights to succeed to French
territory, surrendering Gibraltar and
Menorca; France is excluded from Italian
peninsula and Netherlands

1707   Intensification of peasant uprisings in France.
Famines

1709   Particularly harsh winter

1713   Anti-Jansenist constitution *Unigenitus* signed

1715   1 September: death of Louis XIV. Louis XIV
and Maria-Teresa had only one son, the
dauphin Louis de Bourbon, who married
Maria-Anna of Bavaria in 1680. She had
died in 1690. The dauphin himself had
died in April 1711, before his father, leaving the three children of his marriage: the
duc de Bourgogne, who died with his wife,
Marie-Adélaïde de Savoie, and his eldest
son, of an unidentified fever in February
1712, after being heir apparent for a year;
the duc d'Anjou, who had become Philip
V of Spain; and Charles, duc de Berry,
who died in 1714, before Louis XIV. Louis
XIV's great-grandson, the duc de
Bretagne, had died in March 1712, leaving
as direct heir the duc de Bourgogne's
second son, duc d'Anjou after Philip V's
accession to the Spanish throne, and now
Louis XV (1710–74)

Louis XIV's provision for a council of regency
is overthrown by Philippe d'Orléans, his
nephew, made unconditional regent
through the lavish use of bribery and
promises. Guillaume Dubois (1656–
1743), cardinal from 11 September 1726,
appointed minister

1716   Creation of Law's bank, made the royal bank in
1718

1717   Philip V plots overthrow of regent. The invasion of Spain by France in 1719 leads to
peace

1720 Law's bankruptcy. 85,000 deaths from plague in Marseilles. Famine and intense social turmoil

1722 9 January: exchange of princesses. Louis XV to marry Spanish infanta, and Philip V's heir to marry regent's daughter. Dubois made prime minister

1723 Majority of Louis XV. Consequent resignation of regent 16 February. His death 2 December. Ministry of Bourbon (1692–1740), grandson of "le grand" Condé. The six-year-old infanta is at once returned to Spain

1725 Marriage of 15-year-old Louis XV to the impoverished and low-born, but charming, healthy, and Catholic 22-year-old Maria Leszczynska, daughter of the ex-king of Poland. After three girls, a boy is born on 4 September 1729 (d. 1765), father of Louis XVI. There were in all seven children of the marriage

1726 André-Hercule Fleury (1653–1743), the king's tutor, becomes first minister. Disgrace of Bourbon

1733 War of the Polish succession begins. Austria and Russia oppose the claims of Stanislaus Leszczynski. France sends a small force which is annihilated, and Fleury seeks vengeance by invading Austrian territory in Italy. The war ends 1735, although treaty of Vienna dates only from 1738. Leszczynski compensated with Lorraine for loss of throne. Lorraine erected into a kingdom, to revert to France on Leszczynski's death, which occurs in 1766

1735 After intermission of several years, recommencement of sporadic popular uprisings in French provinces, mostly on account of starvation, itself exacerbated by poor transport facilities

1741 Start of War of the Austrian Succession on death of emperor Charles VI. Franco-Prussian alliance

1745 French victory at Fontenoy

1748 Treaty of Aix-la-Chapelle scarcely profits France

1754 23 August: birth of future Louis XVI, son of dauphin and Maria Josepha of Saxony

1755 I November: Lisbon earthquake. Estimated 30,000 deaths

1756–63 Seven Years War. France, having repudiated its alliance with Prussia in favour of Austria, loses much of its colonial empire in Canada, the West Indies, and India to England. Louisiana is ceded to Spain. Peace of Paris ends war in 1763

1757 Assassination attempt on Louis XV by Robert-François Damiens, a former servant, alarms court and administration

1758 Duc de Choiseul (1719–85) foreign secretary and effectively chief minister

1764 Dissolution of the Jesuit order in France. Abolition by Clement XIV follows in 1773

1765 Death of dauphin

1770 Marriage of third son of dauphin, now himself dauphin and future Louis XVI, to Marie-Antoinette of Lorraine, archduchess of Austria (1755–93)

24 December: disgrace of Choiseul, principally for forcing through war taxation after peace of 1763, obliging parlements and provincial Estates to form their dangerous defensive alliance against the crown

1771 Choiseul replaced by duc de Maupeou (1714–92), assisted by the abbé Terray (1715–78) for finance, and by the duc d'Aiguillon (1720–88). Maupeou's brief is to break the resistance of the parlements. He discharges and exiles the members of the Paris parlement 20 January 1771, appointing new parlement with no political authority. The sale of judicial offices is abolished, and councils are established with jurisdiction superior to that of the parlements. The new system, unworkable, will be revoked in 1774, but further crystallizes the conflict of rights between crown and nation

1774 10 May: death of Louis XV. Accession of his grandson as Louis XVI. On advice of Maurepas (1701–81), appointment of Turgot (1727–81) as finance minister. Turgot impressed by "physiocrat" doctrines and dedicated to free trade in grain and liberal economic reform. Turgot's dismissal 12 May 1776

1775–83 American War of Independence, joined by France against Britain

1776 Jacques Necker appointed to fulfil the financial function of Turgot's office, now divided into two

1781 19 May 1781: Necker resigns. From this date on finance ministers do not last long. Joly de Fleury, Lefèvre d'Ormesson, and Calonne cover in succession the years to 8 April 1787. Debt is horrific, taxation unbearable, and the political system could be saved only through the reform of social and financial privilege

More and more frequent and desperate expedients are found. Loménie de Brienne,

Malesherbes, and Necker come and go as ministers while France slides into anarchy

1788   The winter of 1788 is especially hard. There is scarcely money to pay troops to keep order. France has no constitution, and the body from which one has to emerge is a medieval forum for the clash of three different sectional interests, nobility, clergy, and tiers état, each petitioning absolute royal authority

1789   Meeting place for the Estates General finally fixed at Versailles. Weeks are taken up with procedural questions. The central one, whether the three estates might meet together, is finally the pivotal point on which hinged the outbreak of conflict

By 2 July the Estates has turned itself into a national assembly and vested in itself sovereign power. By concentrating defensive forces in and round Paris, the court authorities have determined the geographical location of the demonstration that there is no force left in France capable of keeping order. That demonstration is the taking of the Bastille on 14 July.

INTRODUCTION

1. GESTATION AND PURPOSE OF THE *GUIDE*

The primary purpose of this introduction is to discuss the methodological presuppositions of the whole two-volume *Guide to French Literature*, as promised in the introduction to the volume already published, devoted to French literature after 1789. Together with the life-and-works format adopted for the *Guide*, this introduction considers therefore the criteria the *Guide* uses for the evaluation of literary quality, and for the *Guide*'s inclusions and exclusions. Each of the volumes carries its own short preface, intended to do service as a brief manual on the use of the *Guide*. In this volume, which necessarily and often repeatedly uses technical administrative, legal, and ecclesiastical terms, a glossary has also been provided.

Although the *Guide* is everywhere written in the third person, and aims accordingly in the first instance at providing accurate information together with judgements as authoritative as they could be made, it was never intended to be entirely impersonal. The format and method finally adopted emerged only slowly during the *Guide*'s gestation and a process of constant consultation between publisher and author. We hoped that the life-and-works entries, followed by full lists of the publications of each of about 300 authors, would satisfy most reference needs, provide an acceptable amount of original literary analysis of major texts, and link both texts and authors to their own literary culture and that of their period.

The work is about twice as long as the single volume originally projected, its 326 alphabetical entries over two volumes built up ring by ring from a core, and chosen from an initial list of well over 1,000 potential entry titles. It was the roughly even density of treatment desirable in the entries which in the end governed the length of each entry, and the final number which could be accommodated. The decision to rely on an extensive and detailed general index to link the major authors and texts to a wider cultural context, which we hoped would lead to a deeper understanding of the texts and smooth over too abrupt a distinction between those authors who were made the subject of personal entries and those who were not, was arrived at comparatively late, but made into the keystone which holds the arch together.

Academics generally defend the inseparability of research and teaching on the grounds that excellence in teaching can derive only from continuous research. That argument is the wrong way round. It is more nearly true that excellence in research, especially in the humanities, depends on continuous teaching. At least in the humanities, only the teacher is normally in immediate contact with the reactions of a public capable of making instantly clear what are the questions to which it wants to know the answers, and the nature of those questions helps powerfully to indicate the direction research should take. Although the *Guide* is in no sense a textbook, it was born of the classroom. It is partly a belated attempt to answer an unending stream of real or implied questions. Many of those questions were reducible to generally polite requests to explain why individual authors were on the syllabus, or individual works considered interesting enough for governments, public and private institutions, and charities everywhere to pour huge sums of money into courses of education based on them, especially as we lived in a world with other calls on resources, and not short of starving mouths to feed.

In so far as the *Guide* had a single moment of conception, it was during a lecture. I was giving the lecture, and it was on the Italian neoplatonism, mostly deriving from Plotinus, which it is necessary to know about in order to understand much 16th-century French literature. It was ordinarily believed that in the convention created in Medici Florence love was so idealized as not only to represent a moral striving towards spiritual perfection, but also to exclude the normal physical sexual relationships which were ordinarily thought to prevent a higher fulfilment. Chastity was still the Church's spiritual ideal, and no troubadour's lady was ever his wife. It occurred to me while lecturing that "Platonic" love had actually been invented by Marsilio Ficino (1433–99), who first used the term, in order morally to rehabilitate instinctive sexual activity.

He legitimized ordinary physical and emotional relationships by regarding them, no doubt dressed up in quasi-mythological clothing, as perhaps even necessary first steps to the beatifying perfection of the love of God. If that was the real meaning of his 1469 *In Convivium Platonis de amore commentarium*, then Platonic love was the sign of a quite new attitude in European culture towards manifestations of human nature and instinct, certainly at odds with the Christian spirituality current in late 15th-century Paris and protected by the fashionable theology of scholastic orthodoxy, whose "nominalism" was aimed primarily at protecting the complete independence of God from his creation, and the arbitrariness of his moral order.

That discovery took conventional literary history much nearer to the centre of cultural history, itself one strand of what we call social history, and demanding much greater contextualization of the literary text for an understanding not only of its purpose, but also of its meaning, than had hitherto been thought necessary or, according to some critics, even relevant. The discovery, not just about the significance of Ficino, but about the need to examine as carefully as possible the cultural circumstances of the composition of a literary text in order to understand both its meaning and its function in promoting and reflecting cultural development, was then extensively bench-tested over 20 years of teaching, on many texts, in many countries, including the UK and the US, in publications in French and English, and at innumerable international conferences.

The *Guide* reflects the method which the original discovery seemed to impose. We may not as a community of educators have got the focuses of interest quite right, but some decades of teaching experience lie behind the view that the reason we have to teach and study literature is that the literary examination of real or possible forms of human experience not only helps us to understand and control our own personal experience, but also teaches us how the literary text investigates present, past, and potential human attitudes and ways of behaviour; how and under what pressures in which literature plays any part they change and develop; and what part literature has played in the alteration of the values of a whole culture.

Because the *Guide*, although it draws on virtually innumerable sources, is ultimately the work of one person, a particular effort is everywhere made to point out where and why its judgements suggest the modification of a received traditional view or a current consensus, as for instance on the subjects of 17th-century *préciosité* or the *Querelle des anciens et des modernes*, to both of which it devotes individual entries. In the course of the *Guide*'s preparation it emerged that many more texts were inadequately understood than had seemed likely, and that seriously distorting perspectives were still being imposed on the overall history of French literature. In particular, the historical role of French literature since about AD 1500 in the cultural history not only of France, but initially of the western European and then of the wider worlds, seemed to call for new examination.

The *Guide* reveals and analyses in its treatment of the 16th century the connection between French literary culture and the quite new way of regarding human nature and experience which appeared in France during the reign of François I (1515–47). Literature began to play a cultural role in France which, in the wake of the utilization of movable type, speedily modified its social function. Well before the end of the 15th century, printed texts, still primarily serving the multiplication of texts for liturgical use, even when ostensibly disseminating knowledge or multiplying writings of ancient authors, also began to carry heavy ideological loadings, exalting or denigrating the texts and values of pagan and Patristic antiquity or the spiritual orthodoxy of contemporary Parisian scholastics.

Literature quickly came to explore moral values and educational ideals in a quite new way and, also in a new way, to open them for immediate and widespread discussion. The new technology of printing, backed up by the economics of book fairs, created a forum which, by very shortly after the beginning of the 16th century, ensured that the same text was read simultaneously and within days of printing in all the widespread literary centres of Europe. Such a text might perhaps discuss a utopian society or satirize an existing concept of sovereignty, promote another devotion to a miraculous shrine, or insidiously restrain itself to the evangelical values of the *New Testament*. By soon after 1500 literature throughout Europe had almost suddenly become a major force in the promotion of cultural change.

2. NORMS AND FUNCTION OF THE *GUIDE*

The cultural history of France differs in important respects from that of each of the other linguistically defined western European literatures, but few attempts have been made to define the direction of the overall thrust of the literary investigation in French of public and private attitudes, values, and forms of experience. The *Guide* hopes, in the light of the historical information now available, to contribute to a new such attempt. The need is immediately clear from the way categories are still used by literary historians. No critical label can be expected to have an indefinite useful life, as critics and classrooms eventually generalize and simplify all the categories, but the current usage of such terms as "renaissance," "baroque," "enlightenment," and especially "classical" with reference to the literature of France has become so loose as to make those terms virtually unemployable as historical categories without rigorous definition on each occasion. The *Guide* avoids some of them altogether.

"Baroque" is used in the *Guide* of any manifestation of exuberant cultural optimism in France between the end of the 16th-century religious wars and perhaps the Fronde, although the term can meaningfully still be applied to Foucquet's patronage until 1661. "Renaissance" refers essentially to the period in France roughly co-terminous with the 16th century, although in the following pages it has generally been kept for the more buoyantly confident first half of the century. The terms "classical" and "enlightenment" have as far as possible been avoided altogether. The presuppositions implied in the use of the term "classical" are almost wholly misleading, and the resonances a term like "enlightenment" carries of faded ideologies and moral approbations makes its use offensive as well as disinformative.

"Reformation" is probably the most difficult of the historical categories. It is normally accorded a capital initial and taken to denote, if not a single event, a series of homogenous religious occurrences, but there was little underlying homogeneity, and there is no agreement about what constitute "reformed" spiritualities, liturgical practices, or theological doctrines. "Reformation," with its upper case initial, and in spite of distasteful lingering overtones of moral, spiritual, theological, and sometimes liturgical cleansing, can scarcely now be avoided to designate the early 16th-century movement of a number of Christian communities into schism, although the dates, occasions, subsequent doctrinal changes, and locations of the schisms are widely disparate, and although the original 16th-century use of the term was limited to the ecclesiastical re-structuring of Lutheran communities under the inspiration of Calvin, and not before the early 1640s.

A great deal of work on individual authors and particular aspects or periods of French literature is available, some of it in English and clearly inspired by the needs of anglophone readers and students. However, students of English are brought up in an environment dominated by a background philosophy of literature and criticism quite different from that which normally dominates the study of other vernacular literatures. The study of English and American literature has for many years included a consideration of critical theory, becoming perhaps dangerously preoccupied with its own methodology, and has been conducted against a succession of theoretical backgrounds, each of which has laid emphasis on different canonical authors, different literary qualities, different genres, and different techniques of analysis. In France the predominant emphasis has been more historical, fostering a tradition in which biographical information has been used as a critical tool.

The difference of critical philosophies is so great that some of the most esteemed anglophone institutions of higher education advise students against combining the study of English with that of other literatures, including French, studied in their vernaculars. Once translated into English, French literary texts can be absorbed into literature syllabuses dominated by the approach to English literary studies. There is now, however, an identifiable need for anglophone guides to the literatures of other European languages not uniquely based on applying the critical philosophies of schools of English. Continental European literatures are often taught in history departments in the US. Elsewhere in the anglophone world the original difference of culture and language commands an approach to European literature other than English which emphasizes the historical and geographical perspectives and cultural background within which any given text needs to be understood. It is for instance important for anglophone students correctly to evaluate in exactly what lay the audacity of a tragedy like Hugo's *Hernani*. The famous ternary opening line was only token provocation. But any understanding of romantic tragedy requires some knowledge of the new staging possibilities opened up by gas lighting, and the reasons why it was thought desirable to make verse tragedy a down-market popular entertainment. One of the functions envisaged for the *Guide* is to provide that sort of knowledge.

For at least half a century the few overall surveys, generally of smaller scope than that of the *Guide*, concerned however tangentially with the history of France's literary culture, have invariably consisted of entries normally syndicated between busy academics. The result is that individual critics and historians have seemed constantly to be fighting their individual corners. Specialist reviews have been founded, and international conferences held, to cater for the study of several score of individual authors. The emergence of a coordinated overall historical view of how and why French literary culture developed, and what works are chiefly important for its development, has on that account been inhibited, and the critical evaluation of individual texts has been distorted. It is partly because the correction of that distortion demands a unicity of viewpoint which will even out the individual enthusiasms ineradicable from works of multiple authorship that the *Guide* has been written by a single author.

The production of a *Guide* arranged in alphabetical order, chiefly of individual authors, seems to presuppose the existence of a canon of acknowledged great writers, however necessarily mutable its content. The *Guide*, by giving detailed references in the general index to a host of writers to whom individual entries are not devoted, as well as to patrons, publishers, editors, and other non-writers important in the context of the history of French literary culture, deliberately blurs the edges of any canonical list. There can never be any finally agreed list of great authors, as the criterion by which they are selected is itself subject to development, but the process of canon formation, essential to the educational world of syllabuses and examinations, and to publishers' needs for a measure of agreement, must be considered. A section of this Introduction is devoted to it.

The criteria used in the *Guide* have generated a list of entries which does not depart significantly far from what might have been produced by counting the column-inches devoted to French writers in other works of reference and selecting those with the highest averages. What may well strike critics or historians as unexpected is the way the *Guide*'s own literary criterion of the imaginative power of a work to illuminate human experience supports common evaluative judgements in the critical portions of its entries. Modified evaluations are indeed proposed, but the *Guide*, using its own evaluative principles, more often, if not always for the conventional reasons, confirms the consensus reached by the countless historians, critics, teachers, examiners, literary journalists, editors, reviewers, students, publishers, translators, and readers who, in this context and over many years, constitute the public.

The *Guide* contends that no literary work can be really major if it does not seek to shed light on some form of public or private human experience. There is no "great tradition," in the sense given to that well-known phrase by the critic with whom it is chiefly associated, and fine writing does not necessarily make great literature. The function of the critic is to make clear how, as well as how far, any given work succeeds or fails in illuminating and evaluating what is occurring in our lives and in the world. The function of the literary historian is to record and account for the outstanding successes. To be of major signifi-

cance, a work of literature must investigate the meaning of some private or corporate experience in the light of a coordinated vision which attempts to understand it, perhaps examining the possibility that it should be seen, understood, or felt in some new way, or even implicitly or explicitly urging changes in the way we see the world and organize our affairs. Literature, as the *Guide* makes clear, is for that reason often subversive of established attitudes. It provides, among other things, a social mechanism for detecting, imaginatively examining, and sometimes articulating or promoting new ways of thinking and feeling. Great authors are often those who have early sensed the undercurrent which will end by changing a whole society's perception of its world, and who have examined what may be the results of an emerging shift in sensibility.

The view that a major literary work must in some way examine the values which underlie, or might desirably or undesirably be made to underlie, our perception of ourselves and of the world, will no doubt appear commonplace to many. It may seem bizarre to those who either regard literature as no more than refined entertainment, or think that its "appreciation" requires some particularly developed or unusual aesthetic sensitivity. It does not, although the perception of a text's underlying moral vision may require critical guidance which must sometimes rely on a methodical contextualization to define and account for it. It is the process of contextualization in the *Guide* which has repeatedly shown how the accepted understanding of a text requires revision.

The function of literature only normally depends on the presence of a reader. There are works like Saint-Simon's *Mémoires*, intended for publication only posthumously if at all, or like Mme de Sévigné's *Lettres*, Diderot's *Jacques le fataliste*, and what are referred to as Retz's *Mémoires*, meant for communication only to intimate friends, immediate family, or very small groups, or like Tallemant des Réaux's hugely undervalued *Les Historiettes*, abandoned after apparent preparation for publication, whose literary status is scarcely affected by non-publication during the author's lifetime. The literary status of works not intended for publication at all, like Diderot's *Le Neveu de Rameau*, Sade's *Les 120 Journées de Sodome*, or Stendhal's *Journal*, is governed by quite different considerations. Although different norms have prevailed, it is not immediately apparent why authors should be judged on what they chose not to publish, although that category includes works like Rimbaud's *Les Illuminations* and Kafka's two best-known novels. Indeed, the view appears defensible that there is in addition a category of documents unpublished by their authors sufficiently private for posterity to have no right to read them. Sade's *120 Journées de Sodome* or even Stendhal's *Journal* might be thought to belong to it.

What endows the work of great authors with its merit is generally the strength, coherence, originality, and power of the focused evaluative way of perceiving the world, which we refer to as the moral vision which is implied, whether or not we approve of the ethical values involved. Indeed, in this context moral vision has no necessary connection with ethical values at all. If a poet writes and then publishes a sonnet about a tree, we are being invited to look at the tree in a particular way, or for a particular reason, and the selection by the poet of what features of the tree are of interest to him throws some light on his experience and, if the poem is successful enough, on ours. It implies some form of moral vision. But no literary work, poem or prose, distant from ourselves in time or culture can be understood, and still less critically evaluated, without some awareness of the nature of the experiences, values, attitudes, or forms of behaviour with which it is concerned, and how it regards them, or what its moral vision is.

Any elucidation of that depends partly on features within the text itself, often capable of being decoded without further explanation, but partly also on the text's relationship to the society in which it was produced and for which it was written. That often, even generally, involves a consideration of the historical circumstances of its composition, or "contextualization," a term which means much more than merely setting a series of works in the context of a life. It is true that it is important for the understanding of a text to know whether it was written for publication, for fame or gain or fun, or whether a poet has hired his services to a patron of whose love he sings, whose lady he courts, or for whose flattery he is rewarded, but to situate a work in a life means more than attempting to relate the actual author to the literary persona, or to relate fictional incidents, poetic idealizations, and dramatic characters to real people the author can be shown to have known.

Contextualization also often entails a knowledge of political circumstance, social gossip, the ordinary intellectual, literary contexts in which works were produced. It is not, either, simply a matter of background information, although the success or failure of a play can send us looking for non-literary as well as literary reasons which might explain it. Background information is often essential to gauge how daring a text is, how serious, how satirical, or whether there are elements of deliberate or undeliberate flamboyance in a text. Contextuality is a matter in the end of setting an author's works in the context of the times as well as the life, and the term both means and requires the adduction of all information about the biographical, social, political, and cultural contexts which assist in understanding the codes of communication used in any given literary text, the sole end to which the process should be directed. If it is disconcerting to find critics unaware of the meaning of a text because they are unfamiliar with the intellectual world it inhabits, it can be wearisome to find unnecessary historical detail ousting the properly literary analysis of the text to which it should be subordinated.

The practical difficulty arises, as all teachers of literature at university level can confirm, not only because the modern world is making demands such that English-speaking students ordinarily acquire less and less of the cultural background needed to understand the writers discussed in this volume, but also because there no longer exists any uniform stock of cultural experience common to an age-group such as previously could be taken for granted, like a knowledge of the workings of feudal society, of the four gospels, of the major teachings of the Christian councils, of Homer, and of the Oedipus myth. It has become increasingly difficult to know how much needs to be explained. The *Guide* has sought, when in doubt, to risk providing superfluous information to some users rather than bewildering others.

3. CONTEXTUALIZATION AND THE LITERATURE OF THE PAST

The pre-Revolution authors in this volume have produced texts that we have retrospectively regarded as literature or on which, as some recent critics would say, we have for ideological reasons imposed literary status. By investigating the values by which their society lived, their texts often gained a place among the chief agents articulating or examining its experience, and so promoting its cultural development, changing contemporary personal and social values and, always tentatively, ushering in new ways of thinking and feeling. The historical process of cultural change, in so far as it is dependent on or powered by literary culture, invariably begins with hesitant explorations of experimental values and attitudes, and often creates new literary genres, like the Christian epic or the comédie-ballet of the 17th century or infuses new life into old ones, as in the 16th century with the antique models taken for verse from Anacreon or for satire from Lucian; or adapts existing forms for its purposes— as with the dramatic tragi-comédie or heroic adventure novel of the early 17th century in France, the 18th-century epistolary novel, or 19th-century Romantic tragedy—appropriate to the modified values being investigated.

Even before the 19th and 20th centuries, with newspapers, magazines, then cinema, radio, and television, and their revolutions in systems of transport and communication, there were naturally non-literary forums in which patterns of behaviour were discussed, evaluated, and changed. But there was a date at which it first became possible for the European literary imagination to test whether persons not of elevated social status could be accepted as fictional or dramatic vehicles for tragic emotion, a date somewhere between Shakespeare's *Romeo and Juliet* and Racine's *Andromaque* at which the emotion of love itself could be regarded as tragic, and a date at which Europeans began to regard majestic natural phenomena, like high mountains, raging storms, and rushing rivers, as manifestations of an environment which was more uplifting than menacing. Literature no doubt reflected such changes of sensibility. More importantly, it increasingly became a principal engine powering both the general modification of moral vision and an awareness that it was taking place.

It is because literary greatness should not be denied to a text which incorporated a vision of human experience which once did catch a modification of previously accepted ways of thinking and feeling, as for instance without doubt did the texts of Rabelais, Montaigne, Pierre Corneille, and Voltaire, that a case should be made on behalf of the literary value of a series of works whose status recent generations have questioned. In spite of what appears to modern readers as sentimentality, real literary status should not lightly be denied to such hugely popular works, each with a once powerful and original moral vision, as Fénelon's *Télémaque* or Bernardin de Saint-Pierre's *Paul et Virginie*, for much the same reason as it should not be withdrawn from the more sentimental works of Dickens in English. Can the literary value with which these texts were once invested now be detected from within the texts themselves? Can the literary qualities of texts change as they come to relate differently to the preoccupations of later generations? We have lost touch, apparently for good, with the refined, elegant, anonymous 1820 volume of *Méditations poétiques*, in fact by Lamartine, for so long taken as the anthologist's ideal poet. Has Lamartine's verse ceased to be great poetry; or was it always a mistake to think of it in those terms; or is it still a great literary achievement?

Whatever the different literary qualities of *Télémaque*, *Paul et Virginie*, and the *Méditations poétiques* actually were, they are still there, locked into the text in the way the authors communicate a consciousness of the novelty and even daring of what is being attempted, although the literary form adopted by Bernardin de Saint-Pierre interestingly suggests a waning confidence in the vision incorporated into the text. It is improbable that after some new era of restraint a generation yet to be born will again find Lamartine's destruction of reticence in the parade of gentle forms of personal melancholy daring, or that future generations will again be stimulated by Fénelon's extended parable designed to point a 12-year-old towards the virtuous exercise of real power. But that does not deprive either the *Méditations poétiques* or *Télémaque* of interest, significance, or literary quality.

Sue and Dumas or, in the pre-Revolutionary period, Gomberville and La Calprenède were not fastidious, profound, or subtle writers, but the power of their novels, as well as the reasons for their popularity, are still perceptible. However crudely their effects were achieved for what was clearly a down-market readership, their works still manifest a powerfully organized, fresh moral vision and warrant consideration as great literary achievements, even if they are no longer likely to move us or hold us in excited suspense. Mme de Lafayette and Marivaux, Balzac and Zola went deeper, and are regarded as authors of important works of literature whose power we can still directly feel. The way in which our own moral vision interacts with that of the literary text from some earlier period is not a certain, instant guide to the literary power of that text.

For nearly two centuries, Pascal was overwhelmingly regarded as the brilliant satirist and polemicist of the *Lettres provinciales*. They are undoubtedly of the highest literary order, moving from the most amusing gentle satire to incandescent rage, inspired with a forceful moral vision superbly focused and conveyed in exquisitely balanced prose, but the material discussed is becoming too remote from our own debates; publishers' sales figures suggest that fewer people are making the effort; but no one would suggest that any falling off in public interest is due to an initial misjudgment about the literary value of the text. It was in 1842, only just after the height of the French romantic movement, that Victor Cousin drew attention to the agonized text with which Pascal's name has been primarily associated ever since, the *Pensées*. The French romantics had reflected a new interest in anguished appraisals of the cosmic status of the human race just when the mentally tortured Kierkegaard was beginning to be known in the informed German philosophical circles with which Victor Cousin was acquainted. Cousin's reaction switched attention from the Pascal of the controlled and brilliant prose of the *Lettres provinciales* to the author of the confused and terrifying text we know as Pascal's *Pensées.*

In spite of the possibly unrecognized theological difficulties with which the text demands confrontation for its proper understanding, the *Pensées* has increased in public esteem ever since, although its literary value cannot have altered. Pascal is acknowledged at least to be among the two or three greatest writers of 17th-century France, but it is only the spiritual and theological contextualization of each work which makes its meaning clear. It requires technical theological knowledge to identify the problems Pascal was trying to solve, and to understand the light he was trying to project on to an experience governed by theological assumptions it is now no longer possible to make, some subtle and complex, like those concerning the theology of grace, others more picturesque, as that God had revealed through Moses that the world was 6,000 years old.

The entry on Pascal naturally attempts to provide the required guidance to the working of his texts, but the example of Pascal vividly illustrates both why we cannot trust our own immediate

reaction as an indication of the literary power of a text, and how, nevertheless, that power must depend on the strength with which a text can be shown to illuminate, or to have illuminated, its readers' understanding of human experience. Where the assumptions in moral theology or the theology of grace are as technical as they are in Pascal, the need for critical guidance is clear. In a different way, the real power of Sue or Dumas, Gomberville and La Calprenède, even Mme de Lafayette, Marivaux, Balzac, and Zola can today normally be perceived by anglophone students only after professional guidance about the nature of the societies in which these authors were writing; what values, attitudes and power relationships were being supposed; and what light was being shed on them.

An uninformed or cursory reading of Rabelais cannot reveal to the casual reader who is not a specialist in the demotic literature of 16th-century France more than the surface eighth of the iceberg, although the text might be so obviously incomprehensible as to convey to the reader that it contained much more than any simple reading could communicate. Again the entry on Rabelais provides the necessary keys with which to decode the brilliant but densely allusive text and, like that on Montaigne or d'Aubigné, illustrates both the meaning of contextual criticism and its ordinary indispensability. In the same way *Télémaque*, *Paul et Virginie*, and Lamartine's *Méditations poétiques* can be shown to have had a literary quality by a historian well enough acquainted with the societies for which Fénelon, Bernardin de Saint-Pierre, and Lamartine wrote. In other words, while we may directly feel the power of some texts distant in time or culture, any serious evaluation of their power and literary merit must depend on detailed contextual evaluation.

Fénelon's *Télémaque* raises other matters which require mention in this context. One of the more interesting indications of the power of *Télémaque* is the enduring admiration for it of adults as sophisticated in questions of political organization as Montesquieu. Texts written for children, including those of La Fontaine's *Fables* genuinely written for the young dauphin or later for his son, the duc de Bourgogne, can not only be just as imaginatively powerful as texts written for adults, but the need to avoid subtleties of characterization and the possibility of relying more firmly on simple incongruity, as both Fénelon and La Fontaine do, can actually enhance the literary effect.

Again *Télémaque* has often been criticized for being badly written, and the concept of "good writing" needs to be confronted. It appears to have little to do with literary quality, except in the sense that any great writer must communicate his vision through the composition of text and the manipulation of words, and that "good writing" is any that successfully communicates the imaginative power of its author. Great writers do not however necessarily need fine ears, a sense of style, compositional skills, or honed techniques. The rules established by Malherbe for correctness in the composition of French verse, and used by him in criticism of the work of Ronsard and Desportes, reduce poetic composition to such acrostic complexity as to make the communication of feeling an intrusion, if not an impossibility. The stylistic rules decreed by Malherbe were intended to make poetry appropriate only for formal purposes, laments or encomia, preferably on public occasions. It is as easy now to laugh at his personal pomposity and bad manners as at his pedantic poetic norms, but we should remember that very early in the 17th century there was some point in trying to establish a normative correct usage in French, and that Malherbe chose to try to impose one for poetry, leaving correct prose taste to be established by Guez de Balzac. It is certainly clear that some late 16th-century looseness needed pruning back. What Malherbe shows us is that any attempt to lay down antecedent rules for successful literary composition is bound to end in ridicule.

In prose Vauvenargues is at least one outstanding example of a major author who by no criterion can be said to have written well. He had had no formal academic training, but he did have a very trenchant mind. We know that the first edition of his book is badly written; we have the copy with Voltaire's improvements in the margin; and we have Vauvenargues's text incorporating Voltaire's improvements in readiness for the posthumous second edition. Vauvenargues himself knew that he had much to say but lacked what was regarded as the literary skill of proper style with which to say it. If Voltaire had not instantly realized that, he would never have taken Vauvenargues under his protection in the way he did.

It could well be argued that Jean-Jacques Rousseau did not publish a single text that was even averagely well written. Rousseau himself saw that *Du Contrat social* needed rewriting. The text is inconsistently argued and, as it stands, contains elements from English liberalism which are not compatible with the reliance Rousseau places on the Huguenot concept of the inalienable sovereignty of the people and on the concept of the general will. The work contains other internal incompatibilities. The *Discours sur l'inégalité* sometimes demands to be understood as the history of the rise of inequality, and sometimes simply as a non-historical explanatory metaphor for it. *Julie; ou, La Nouvelle Héloïse* starts as a novel and turns into a survey of contemporary society, while *Emile; ou, De l'éducation* is a treatise on education which turns into a Bildungsroman with a long interpolated lyrical section on natural religion. Not one of these major works is satisfactorily composed.

Yet there was virtually no form of human experience whose nature this self-educated misanthropist did not investigate from a point as near absolute intellectual independence as, after wide reading, he could attain. His major works contain extraordinarily potent considerations about all the most important areas of human experience, including the conduct of his own life, analyses of the principal emotional states, disquisitions about the ethics of love, discussions about happiness, about education, about religion, and about social organization, all painfully thought through almost from scratch. The strength of moral vision is incomparable, and the illumination of experience intense. There is of course also the famous new way of looking at the physical phenomena of nature which we call pre-romantic.

There are obsessively recurrent patterns of personal behaviour and choice in the way Rousseau lived his life which help to define the meaning and explain the imaginative power of his work. He paid very heavily for his intellectual independence. In the appropriate entry an effort is made to analyse the source of the imaginative power of his texts, and to explain the nature of his literary importance. The biography offers some important clues, while the literary, social, and political situations in Rousseau's France offer others. What the *Guide* has to consider, however, is just how imaginatively powerful were the texts communicating his ideas and feelings, however imperfect their literary expression, and why a whole generation could so swiftly and so wholeheartedly endorse them.

The criteria of literary quality cannot therefore be limited to considerations of stylistic refinement or cultivated taste, but must centre in the power of an author's imagination in the specific society in which and for which the text was composed. This means that the perception of the literary value of a text invariably requires effort, and very often knowledge, on the part of the reader. However, the ultimate touchstone of the highest literary quality must include public acknowledgement because, no matter how difficult it may be to define or to establish, a major literary work will eventually be recognized as the product or echo of a way of thinking and feeling which recognizably differs from what preceded it, involving fresh attitudes and values, and a new understanding of human experience imaginatively stimulating to a wide public.

4. PRINCIPLES OF THE *GUIDE*

Before going on to consider further the methodology of the *Guide* in the light of the assumptions just presented, and drawing attention to some of the conclusions which appear to emerge from the present volume, there are four matters which should briefly be mentioned:

Firstly, French literary culture was generated by the society which in turn it nourished. During the years shortly before and after 1500, vernacular literary culture in France underwent a sea change as it began to investigate alternatives to medieval ways of looking at human activities, in which the highest spiritual perfection invariably demanded the abnegation of instinctive behaviour. In a technical sense it is possible at the same date to speak of the inception of a new literary culture dependent on the dissemination of the printed book. From around 1500, we also have available increasing amounts of important information, with more chance that documents will still be available, and more reliable statistics. On the other hand the literary culture becomes less involved with feudal power struggles and civil wars, and the underlying institutions of French society come to need less explaining for contemporary anglophone readers than did the application of Salic feudal codes which sometimes governed the legitimacy of claims to 16th-century thrones. There is therefore a difference of balance within individual entries as the dates move forward, and publication history, for instance, often increases in importance relative to personal biography.

Secondly, in this pre-Revolution volume the rules limiting individual author entries to writers in the imaginative genres have been slightly more relaxed than in the volume devoted to the later period, simply because it is likely to be more convenient to users of the *Guide* to be able to find information about humanism and philosophical and theological positions under authors like Lefèvre d'Etaples, Budé, Calvin, Bodin, Descartes, Gassendi, Malebranche, and Bayle rather than have to use the index and find the information scattered through entries on individual authors who wrote in the imaginative genres. There are entries under certain still meaningful headings such as "Pléiade," "Cartesianism," "Commedia dell'arte," "préciosité," "Querelle des anciens et des modernes," "Philosophes," and "Encyclopédie," but where the categories have already acquired their own historiography, as have "renaissance," "Reformation," "Protestant," "classical," and "enlightenment," the essays such entries would have required seemed too far removed from the actual writers and texts which are the subject of this volume, and to whose understanding and evaluation all further information provided is intended to be ancillary. Entries have, however, been included on the three most important journals of the ancien régime, *Le Mercure (Galant/de France)*, *Le Journal des Savants*, and *La Gazette*. The whole subject of Jansenism is treated in the four entries "Jansenism," "Port-Royal," Saint-Cyran, and Nicole.

Thirdly, although the *Guide* is intended for a wide range of potential users, many of whose needs will be only occasional, it is intended also to be more than a simple reference book. While it has aimed to include all the essential information which might usually be sought from the background reading normally recommended for first degree French literature courses throughout the anglophone world, it has been written in the knowledge that some of its potential users will have easy full-time access to well-stocked university libraries, while for others it may be the only easily accessible work containing information in English about the great writers and works of the literature of France. The risk has always been that one category of user would find the *Guide* too detailed for a quick overview, while others may find its coverage of specific texts or topics still too sparse. The compromise has been to offer at least single-paragraph analyses of all important texts, particularly those unlikely to be prescribed for detailed study in universities or to be generally available for reading outside them, and to offer users neither unsupported general impressions nor aesthetic judgements, but dated facts and important samples from major texts which are also always translated. No information is consciously presupposed in the *Guide* which is not commonly assumed to be available to students of the humanities throughout the English-speaking world.

Finally, the general index itself has been designed as an integral part of the *Guide* rather than as a simple list of references. Not only do the cross-references it provides serve to shade the edges of what might wrongly be assumed to be the agreed canon of authors to whom individual entries have been devoted, giving access to virtually as much information about some who are excluded, like Conrart or Quinault, as to some who are included, but the general index is also intended to turn an alphabetic dictionary of authors and major groupings and reviews into a selective encyclopedia of French literary culture. The index changes the nature of the *Guide*. What it does *not* contain are references to an author's own entry, as that would mean virtually repeating in the index what is already contained in the body of the text. The individual index entries under Racine, therefore, only mention topics which relate to entries other than his own.

5. THE LIST OF ENTRIES AND THE PROCESS OF CANON FORMATION

The criteria for including and excluding individual authors from any alphabetically organized guide must seem to presuppose the existence of some agreed list from which the entries are selected. Syllabuses generate a demand for texts which are suitable for educational purposes and cheaply available, and texts suitable for educational purposes are made cheaply available for the syllabuses which prescribe them. The resulting vortex both distorts and accelerates the process of canon formation, and allows the educational context to play in it a role which is not altogether desirable.

We are unlikely today to regard the cultivation of literature as it used to be regarded, primarily important either because it enables us to stand back from the day-to-day realities of our society and view its economic hurly-burly from on high with serene detachment, or because it has been endowed by our ancestors or

our peers with a literary value which instructs our minds and purifies our hearts. The real reason for distinguishing literature from other popular reading material must have to do with the light it sheds on our experience and the power with which it enables us to envisage different ways of understanding and modifying it. We should also probably add the interest of the historical results achieved by literary texts in the development of the culture of our society.

The difficulty today is that the authors and texts most written about and on which attention is ever more exclusively focused are those on the educational syllabuses. This does not necessarily mean the authors and texts of the highest literary merit, but merely those most frequently prescribed for study, and therefore most closely read, most intensely discussed, and most frequently lectured on. There are today, of course, also other pressure points intensified by the system of literary prizes, but generated by critics with fixed responses, publishers with balance sheets, authors with livings to earn, and agents with clients to promote. But even the writers considered in this pre-Revolution volume have largely been divided into those given star status and commonly prescribed, and those not given star status and for the most part still unobtainable in affordable modern editions.

Of course, major French authors are still widely read for their intrinsic qualities, and many people who are neither teaching nor studying need or want to know something about some of the authors, their texts, or their backgrounds. But the concentration of interest on authors commonly prescribed for study has come to exaggerate their relative importance within the whole canon. Dramatists, in particular, have always had to keep down the length of their pieces to fit into the varying durations allocated at different dates to a theatrical performance. It is probable that the pantheon contains for that reason a disproportionate number of dramatists, the brevity of whose texts attracts the compilers of syllabuses, although a script for stage performance, like a musical score, cannot be complete without a stage interpretation. Indeed, much of what we regard as 17th-century French drama ought more properly to be considered only in relation to the elaborate staging for which it was written, including music and dancing with which it blended to become what was often court entertainment. It is also impossible today for any student in the French-speaking or English-speaking worlds to acquire reasonably-priced modern editions of sufficient 17th-century dramatic texts not by Pierre Corneille, Molière, or Racine to write a paper on what was probably the richest of all periods in the French theatre.

Other constraints exert pressure on the demand for texts, the ultimate determinant of their availability: the difficulty of finding sufficient time for reading; the need in order to read successfully to master mental worlds alien to our own; and the unlikelihood that the richest and densest texts of the ancien régime can be understood on a casual first reading. As a result very long texts, like Proust's *A la recherche du temps perdu*, do not figure on syllabuses as often as they deserve, and are read less widely within the pool of those with literary interests than they should be. They would crowd out too much else. Everyday demands do not allow time to plough through such lengthy authors as Rabelais, especially if the alternatives include other authors from such perceptibly different cultures as Tolstoy and Thomas Mann. The nature of the guidance required for the principal writers is indicated in the relevant *Guide* entry, but most anglophone readers will need properly annotated editions, especially for authors, like Gide, who demand for their comprehension familiarity with a complex cultural background. It requires quite detailed guidance for most readers, even francophone, to assess such matters as the degree of stylization in Ronsard's sonnets, the presence of irony in Rabelais, the relevance to particular personal or social events of Molière's plays, and the sets of private or public constraints operative on Racine's decision to give up writing for the stage to get on with what he considered his principal career as a courtier.

It remains true, however, that it is frequently about the authors who are not read that it is most necessary to provide information. Information about Madeleine de Scudéry, who discusses love in the ten-volume novels *Le Grand Cyrus* and *Clélie*, is vital for the understanding of Mme de Lafayette's often prescribed *La Princesse de Clèves*. Much in Racine's frequently prescribed *Andromaque* depends on the audience's recollection of the same words coming from the mouth of the same actress in Thomas Corneille's *Timocrate*, which virtually never appears even on specialist syllabuses. The *Guide* leans as far as seems reasonable in the direction of correcting distortions in the pantheon created by the vortex phenomenon of syllabus construction, while attempting not to neglect the specific demands for texts of definite provenance, such as texts by women writers, for texts in different genres, for texts written from different religious, political, and philosophical points of view and, in the post-Revolution volume, for texts not written by authors born in metropolitan France and for short texts by living authors.

There are few more sensitive indicators to the values held in a society than its imaginative texts, and the selection of entries in the *Guide* has kept in mind not only current academic requirements, but also the way in which literary history opens up an understanding of the inner history of a society's cultural development. At the end of the original 1637 text of Pierre Corneille's *Le Cid*, the audience was to be left in no doubt that the heroine, Chimène, was after a decent but unspecified interval to marry the hero, Rodrigue, although he had just honourably killed her father in a duel. In 1648 Corneille changed the title from tragi-comédie to tragédie, and in 1660 he removed from the play the couplet which made the marriage certain, leaving it in doubt. The boldness of 1637, exploring the possibility that even after he had killed her father Rodrigue's extraordinary merit allowed Chimène to marry him is dropped in 1660. The *Guide* offers analyses of texts by different authors to show how and why the exuberant optimism of Corneille's 1637 ending, in spite of the imposition of the delay before the marriage, had become less acceptable in 1660, but a proper understanding of the play depends on more than that.

Corneille changes a feudal pitched battle in his Spanish original into a duel. Richelieu had lost an elder brother, Henri, in a duel against the marquis de Thémines in April 1619, and in 1626 he issued a severe edict against duelling. As a matter of fact, Corneille, devout Catholic that he was, approved of the edict. In 1627, to the protests of most of the nobility, after a very public duel in the smart Place Royale in which one of the six participants had been killed, two of the others, inveterate duellers, were chased, caught, tried, and beheaded. But when, in 1637, Corneille had to put an obligation of honour on Rodrigue to fight the duel in which he would kill Chimène's father, he knew he could still count on the sympathy of the audience. Furthermore, Corneille sheltered behind a Spanish setting. France had just been at war with Spain, at whose service Condé had put himself, but the values shared by the aristocratic castes in both countries in 1637 clearly outweighed any nationalistic feelings of belligerent animosity. The play was a runaway success.

6. LIFE AND WORKS: CONTEXTUALITY

In critical and historical study, the contextualization of a literary work is an attempt to discover its meaning. Some schools of criticism, always concerned with English literature, in which the exercise of "practical criticism" is not at all the same as the analogous French "explication de texte (explanation of the text)," have contended that the text stands alone, its meaning always self-referentially contained within itself, discoverable only by a rigidly exclusive attention to the words it comprises. The author's intentions, if knowable, are irrelevant. Others shudder at the idea that a text has a single discernible meaning, thinking that what turns words into literature are tensions, ambivalences, ambiguities, echoes, resonances, or exclusions. Happily we are not here concerned with such theoretical debates, except in so far as they must be referred to in the justification of the *Guide*'s methodology, and in particular the life-and-works format it has adopted.

Some of the purely incidental functions of the systematic contextualization of works and authors in the *Guide* do not call for much comment. Contextualization, for instance, allows some account to be given of the social, political, or religious background from which important literary works emanated, thereby generating an alertness in readers to moments when a text was covertly taking a controversial position, making a political allusion, adopting an ironic register, or perfunctorily drawing on a stock of commonplaces. It alerts readers to the importance of the fact that from 1611, when he was three, to 1638, when his sister-in-law, Anne of Austria, gave birth to a male heir later to become Louis XIV, Gaston d'Orléans, by turns craven and arrogant, petulant and generous, but debauched, power-hungry, rebellious, never loyal, and seldom dignified, was the heir presumptive to the throne of France. He, therefore, rightly never considered himself likely to be held responsible for his own treachery, even when those who supported him were executed. The major works of drama and fiction of the 1630s require for their understanding an awareness that legitimate sovereignty seemed likely to fall into the hands of a worthless, inconstant, and incompetent monarch. Contextualization also allows some sense of the changing social background of literary culture to emerge, of the webs at the centre of literary life and the functioning of the patronage system, of the social decline of the feudal aristocracy, of the way the state came to control activity in all the arts, and of the growth of political liberalism.

The placing of a literary work in its social context can change its meaning. The elements of reticence and openness of Saint-Simon's *Mémoires* take on a different significance if he did intend them to be posthumously published. The context shows not only how daring was Cyrano de Bergerac's *La Mort d'Agrippine* in 1653, but how careful Cyrano had been to allow for the transmission of original sin from Adam to the inhabitants of the moon. Laclos's life shows that *Les Liaisons dangereuses* cannot bear the meaning so often put on it. It was intended here to be a defence of Rousseau's educational ideas, not an attractive study of techniques of seduction, although the reader will not be particularly surprised to learn that Laclos was an artillery officer, used to thinking up strategic campaigns. There is scarcely a single author among the three hundred to whom individual entries have been assigned whose works do not demand to be seen in a quite new light as a result of the contextualization generally, but not exclusively, provided in the "Life" section of each entry.

Perhaps most authors put into their works quasi-allusions to persons and events which the general reader is not intended to notice, and perhaps, as often in Rabelais, there are private jokes of the author written in to amuse no one but himself. Sainte-Beuve included in published work private messages for Hugo's wife. The lives of authors are not intended here to be directly linked to the works, as if the literary text were covert autobiography. They are intended to sketch in the background of friendships, enmities, love affairs, jealousies, ambitions, economic pressures, and particularly the all-important social background and official constraints from which the texts emerged. Only Montesquieu's personal history makes clear how he wished to atone for the anonymous scurrility of the *Lettres persanes* with the tongue-in-cheek orthodoxy of a work on the Roman empire which manages to avoid reference to the rise of Christianity and how, having failed to obtain the ambassadorship or similar office he wanted, he then spent most of the next 12 years composing his masterly *De l'Esprit des lois* with affected digressions to disguise the radicalness of his thought. Casual reading suggests that the work rambles. Contextualizing it reveals 19 different amanuenses at work on the manuscripts. That book was very carefully written indeed.

By splitting life and works sections in the individual entries, it has been made easier for those users who wish to go straight to the critical account of any work in which they are interested. The biographical essays offer information which is intended to help in the understanding of the works, but which is generally not essential for those who need perhaps to know only a date, a plot, the correct spelling of a character's name. Occasionally, as with Bayle, some knowledge of the biography is indispensable to an interpretation of the texts. Sometimes, when an author suffered symptoms of a terminal illness, it is important for an understanding of the texts that we should know what, in those extreme circumstances, was that author's greatest concern.

What is perhaps Chénier's most important poem was written probably within 48 hours of his death. Pascal probably did say just before his death that he would have written his *Lettres provinciales* even more strongly if he had to write them again. It would shed much light on the meaning of *Les Essais* if we knew what La Boétie's last words to Montaigne actually meant. We would know more how to understand the enigmatic Bayle if the deathbed declaration of Christian orthodoxy had itself been somewhat less enigmatic. More often, however, than what was said in the knowledge of proximate death, it is the repeated imaginative patterns, or the focuses of imaginative interest to which the texts return, which most illumine the meaning of the individual texts themselves.

The same imaginative pattern recurs through all the works of Flaubert's maturity, in which hopes of high achievement are raised and frustrated; in most of Stendhal's works where determined young men so often fall in love with elder women; and in Beckett, where the perpetual subject is the limitation of what human beings can possibly hope to achieve. The great plays of Pierre Corneille first performed between 1637 and 1643 all examine the same heroic values. All of Racine's plays from

Andromaque on are centrally concerned with the catastrophic effects of female passion. The repeated imaginative patterns in the work of any author throw light on each of that author's works individually, and the repeated focus of imaginative interest is often explained by some knowledge of the biographical and historical circumstances: biographical with Stendhal and Beckett, historical with Flaubert, Corneille, and Racine. These are only a few of the better-known examples. The focus of imaginative interest of virtually every one of the authors given individual entries in the *Guide*, and therefore the actual meaning of the individual works, becomes clearer when set into the context of the author's biography, historical period, and whole literary corpus.

The *Guide* offers more contextual information than is usual or, indeed, precedented, and it seemed essential not to allow it to clog up the critical treatment. Equally, however, the contextual information from the beginning yielded results too important for it to be omitted. Two reasonably striking examples may be considered, of which the first, from Balzac, although it comes from the post-1789 period, warrants mention here firstly because the text, *Le Père Goriot*, frequently appears on examination syllabuses and is very widely known, and secondly because the *Guide* Balzac entry, one of the first to be written, was among those which led to the adoption of contextualization as the key to its methodology. It was the changes in understanding and evaluation imposed by the systematic application of a contextual method which led to the reliance on the general index.

Unless *Le Père Goriot* is set in its context, and the circumstances of its composition are taken into account, it is difficult to make sense of it as a novel in itself. Indeed, with its abandoned elements of plot, bewildering shifts of focus, structurally distracting side-plots, its inadequacy as straight narrative fiction, its looseness of episodic construction, and its implausible because only inchoate characterization, and in spite of its huge energy and almost crushing imaginative power, it could reasonably be asked where its greatness as a novel actually lies.

To answer that question it helps to know that Balzac was still dazed by what he had announced as a great discovery when bursting into the flat of his sister Laure, that by recycling his characters from novel to novel he could, as he ironically told his sister, limit to one, Delphine de Nucingen, the number of new evil women he was going to have to introduce into *Le Père Goriot*. His fascination for such characters had earlier been remarked on. Once he had had the idea of a series of novels in which the same characters, or at least names, would recur, the seedy boarding house offered him the chance to include a core cast for the whole social panorama he had begun to project. It could contain its whirling social mixture of inhabitants, some on the way up and others on the way down, with room for the shabby genteel and the thrustingly ambitious, the crooked, the cruel, the shy and lonely, and the old and pathetic, the broke and the reasonably well off. Through the dwellers in the boarding house, insights could be offered into the styles of life and norms of behaviour adopted in the aristocratic world of the Beauséants, the bureaucratic life of Poiret, and the banking environment of Nucingen.

There are moments of prodigious skill. The description of the squalid boarding house exactly mirrors the moral shabbiness of its inmates, emphasized in a hundred sordid little details about the automatic reactions they exhibit in their daily lives. There is an almost surprising delicacy in the treatment of the repellent

Mlle Michonneau's feelings, offended by Vautrin's flippancy at envisaging her as a cemetery Venus, the "Vénus du Père-Lachaise," and in the complex nature of the criminal and scheming Vautrin's intellectual and moral superiority over the other inhabitants of the boarding house, as well as in the treatment of his feelings for Rastignac.

But Balzac was taking fiction down-market. He was about to become the first French author ever to publish a novel in a dozen daily instalments in a newspaper, *La vieille fille* in Girardin's newly founded (1 July 1836) and cheap *La Presse* in October and November 1836, and *Goriot* was itself to be serialized in four episodes for the *Revue de Paris*. Balzac started writing in September 1834 and wanted to be in Vienna with Evelina Hanska for the first anniversary of their love-making on 26 January. The four episodes appeared on 14 and 18 December 1834, 18 January and 1 February 1835, so Balzac was late, and writing in a tearing hurry under even more pressure than usual. He had had to spend two days with Laure de Berny, his former mistress, now dying of heart trouble, and to content himself with writing to Mme Hanska on 26 January. He finally travelled to Vienna on 9 May, thanks to an advance from his publisher, and stayed until 4 June.

The central character, Rastignac, absorbs the character "Massiac" whom he was in the original manuscript going to meet, about three-quarters of the way through the first of the four parts to which the novel was reduced from the six parts marked out by Balzac but squeezed into the four instalments. Balzac did not know how the story was going to finish when he began it; but his notes demonstrate that he set out with the intention of a simple story line in which Goriot would ruin himself and "die like a dog," having given all he had to his two daughters. Balzac, while writing, revising, correcting, and making additions, changed the focus of the novel to make Rastignac its central figure. Numerous extra layers of text were added, chiefly on proof after the copy had been set for the *Revue de Paris*; he knew that he wanted to start an open-ended panoramic description of society, but did not know that the title "comédie humaine" would be used as a marketing device; he was borrowing characters and incidents from his mental stock-pot, from earlier published material, sometimes his own, sometimes not, but probably including imprecise reminiscences of *King Lear*, played once in January and twice in June 1828 at the Paris Odéon by the Drury Lane company; and he had to invent a way of writing a novel specifically for serialization.

It is no doubt possible to enjoy reading *Le Père Goriot*, or even to study it, without knowing anything more than the text contains because, at least in this example, there are so many loose ends that the text positively offers itself as a part of something bigger, which is what it became while Balzac wrote it, gradually planting in the characters for re-use and development elsewhere. Had his published work ceased after *Goriot* we might reasonably have speculated whether he would have gone on to write a series of novels following Rastignac through what would probably have turned out, given what Balzac reveals in *Goriot* itself about his imagination, the ups and downs of life, certainly with spells of wealth and poverty. What gives *Le Père Goriot* its literary quality is not fine writing, profundity of psychological insight, delicacy of nuance in the depiction, but the quality and power of the imagination behind the text, perhaps only in the case of an author as powerful as Balzac discernible from a single hastily written novel, and even then much assisted by awareness at least of the fact that the novel was, unusually at the time, written for serialization.

The second instance of a change in understanding demanded by the *Guide*'s routine contextualization concerns the Querelle du Cid, the controversy following the first night of Corneille's *Le Cid*, and emerges from the entries on Corneille himself and from those on Mairet and Georges de Scudéry. Chapelain tells us on 22 January 1637 that the play had been running for a fortnight. It was played by the Marais company with an enthusiastic Montdory in the lead. Since first nights were always on Fridays or Sundays, Sunday 4 January seems marginally more likely as the date than the alternative possibilities on the 2nd or the 9th. In 1635 Richelieu had forced letters patent on a somewhat unwilling group who used to meet weekly at Conrart's house, turning them into the Académie française, with the intention of asking them to produce an official grammar and a dictionary of the language. That winter Corneille played *L'Illusion comique*, inspired by two similar plays probably of 1632 entitled *La Comédie des comédiens*, one by Gougenot for the Hôtel de Bourgogne, and the other, which may have been derived from it but may also have been written in simultaneous rivalry, by Scudéry for the Marais company.

Corneille was known to be mercenary, but he also did not hide the fact that he regarded himself as socially superior to other dramatists who depended on patrons and the theatre for their living, excusing himself to his social peers in *La Comédie des comédiens* for dabbling in the theatre at all. *Le Cid*'s success was such that Corneille within two or three weeks asked the company for a further 100 livres. It is likely that he was turned down and on that account decided to publish his play, thereby removing the staging monopoly from the Marais company. The privilège for the publication is dated 21 January, and the achevé d'imprimer, when it was put on sale, was 23 March. The next day Corneille's father was ennobled. In the meanwhile, about 20 February, Corneille had published his early poem, the *Excuse à Ariste* which, perhaps innocently, contained the lines,

Je ne dois qu'à moi seul toute ma renommée,
Et pense toutefois n'avoir point de rival
A qui je fasse tort en le traitant d'égal

(I owe all my fame to myself alone,/And yet I believe I have no rival/To whom I do wrong in treating him as my equal).

The only author who had any right to call himself France's greatest dramatist at that date was Mairet, on whose *La Sophonisbe* Corneille's play may well have been drawing, and whose declining fortunes and failure to conquer the place in Richelieu's esteem enjoyed by Bensserade had embittered him. He was staying on an estate near Le Mans belonging to his patron, the comte de Belin, and very early in April published a short, violent, and personal poem occupying two sheets of paper, replying not to *Le Cid* but to *L'Excuse*, and entitled *L'Auteur du vrai Cid espagnol à son traducteur françois sur une lettre en vers qu'il a faict, intitulée "Excuse à Ariste"*. At almost exactly the same date as Mairet, but without any possible collusion, Scudéry in Paris uncharacteristically challenged Corneille to an academic debate in his *Observations sur Le Cid*, which he persistently referred to as a tragedy, although Corneille was calling it a tragi-comédie.

Corneille, who had hitherto been on good terms with both Mairet and Scudéry, refused to reply on the level of Scudéry's theoretical debate, but published in a *Lettre apologétique*, addressed to Scudéry about the middle of May, an attack on Mairet based on his humble origins and current impoverishment. Scarron was among the members of the literary world outraged by Corneille's *Lettre*, and Mairet now counter-attacked, henceforth aiming not at the poem but at the play, and Scudéry wrote a formal appeal to the Académie sometime between 4 and 13 June. The text was submitted to the arbitration of the Académie after Corneille on 13 June had given the coolest of possible consents, without which the Académie had no right to advert to the matter. Corneille had no choice if he wished to retain Richelieu's goodwill.

Scudéry had not failed to enter Richelieu's inner circle for want of trying. He was neither a member of the Académie nor one of Richelieu's five dramatists (Rotrou, l'Estoille, Corneille, Boisrobert, and Colletet), but he had in 1635 written a lost or abandoned epic in honour of Richelieu, as well as the 1633 *Le Temple, poème à la gloire du Roi et de M. le cardinal duc de Richelieu*, and the 1634 *Discours de la France à Mgr le cardinal duc de Richelieu après son retour de Nancy*. Scudéry intended his 1638 *L'Amour tyrannique* to be virtually a demonstration of how *Le Cid* should have been written, and it won Richelieu's enthusiastic approval. Scudéry called it a tragi-comédie, although Sarrazin argues that it was a tragedy. It seems, given the context, likely that the Querelle du Cid was set up by Scudéry to ingratiate himself with Richelieu by finding something with which to get the Académie off the ground, and that Mairet first intervened in the debate about the play only after Corneille's *Lettre* to Scudéry. Mairet was finally ordered to cease his attacks on Corneille by Richelieu, using Boisrobert as an intermediary, on 5 October 1637. The contextualization puts the whole Querelle in a light quite different from that in which it is ordinarily seen.

7. IMAGINATIVE POWER AND LINGUISTIC REGISTER

The final step in the methodological justification for the *Guide*'s approach to its task must concern the criterion of imaginative power. If contextualizing a work or an author helps generally towards a more accurate understanding of meaning, then imaginative power measures the strength with which a text illuminates some form of human experience. "Measure" does not mean calibrate, but there has to be some way of distinguishing even well-wrought stories or television serials, often ingeniously put together and capable of engaging the emotions as well as the interest of a reader or a viewer, from work which makes a serious attempt to appraise forms of human behaviour, codes, principles and attitudes, if only by clarifying rather than condoning or condemning them.

Examples are invidious, and it is no part of the *Guide*'s intention to denigrate reading matter which makes no pretence to be more than light entertainment. The *Guide*'s function does not include taking part in a debate about any sort of material for which literary status has not been claimed, even if it is of the kind sometimes regarded as sufficiently dangerous in its social effects possibly to warrant restrictions on availability. But sex and violence can play as prominent a role in serious literature as in light or erotic fiction intended merely to distract or divert. There is no litmus test to distinguish what is escapist

from what is imaginatively probing, or what is pure pornography from what is literary; whether a work is mere fantasy or genuinely derives from a creative imagination is a matter for discussion. But any justification of the *Guide*'s methodology must at least advert to the criterion by which the literary material it discusses can be distinguished from the reading material which it does not. There may be a rough consensus about who the great authors are, but there is no consensus about why they are in the pantheon, only a range of wobbly criteria which uncertainly distinguish their work from everything else that is published.

Ultimately the public decides whether or not its world has been illuminated or expanded and therefore enriched by literary texts. It is not the function of a work of literature to recommend or condemn attitudes or forms of behaviour. If it does so, it promotes or impedes them, but loses its power to illuminate and clarify. Historians are wary of the moral and other ideological viewpoints which can be implied by critical judgements. Even those approaches to criticism whose ideological independence has been most vigorously flaunted have been criticized for other inadequacies. Psychoanalytical criticism has itself been criticized for removing the intellectually creative element from the product of the literary imagination; deconstructive criticism for removing from a text all clearly defined, univocal meaning; and structuralist criticism for seeing texts as coded statements more interesting for their codes than for their statements.

All forms of criticism implying an ideology other than that necessarily implied in the act of criticism itself have shown themselves vulnerable to criticism, although all those mentioned above, and many others, have in recent years been found of interest. They all touch the position in which texts do not have meanings, or have an indefinite multiplicity of meanings. There are of course major texts with layers of controlled ambivalence, but the view that texts are the richer for the number of meanings which can be read into them reduces literature to no more than an initial stimulus to personal fantasy. It undermines both the nature of literature and the function of criticism. Ultimately it trivializes literature by causing intelligent criteria of literary value to evaporate, leaving as literature any text about which any group of initiates can be persuaded to enthuse. The history of literary criticism in France is littered with examples of the dead ends into which the view has led that texts do not have meanings, univocal even when multiple, obscure, or heavily encoded. Literary theory is itself not often of much help to literary critics. It sometimes still skirts a position in which it could deny the legitimacy of the critic's necessary function, because it involves an act of evaluation which, by placing the critic above and beyond the activity being evaluated, implies what to some theorists is an unacceptable ideology.

The resolution of the problem of the critics and historians can scarcely fail to involve some concept like that here referred to as imaginative power. It is the function of the critic to discern it, explain where it lies, how any given text communicates it, and how it is exercised. Is the moral guilt of an individual ever as far beyond personal control as that of Racine's Phèdre? Very often, and for understandable reasons, authors themselves, concerned with shaping their imaginative vision, are not good at explaining what it is. Racine said in his preface that he was portraying the passions in ways clearly alien to what the play actually does do. The imaginative vision which a poet or a novelist chooses to explore in a work of literature is created only as the work progresses, and cannot generally be expressed by the writer otherwise than through the work.

It is the critic's function, not the poet's, to analyse and evaluate the vision, and to explain its mode of communication. What readers, teachers, and students derive from literary historians and critics is guidance on the way the imaginative power is manifested, the vision communicated, and the new understanding of our experience suggested. The point of literature in the end has always been that, by helping us to understand our experience and become aware of its potential, it has given us greater power to manage, control, expand, and change it. There is nothing else to distinguish it from non-literature. Something of what that implies emerges from the concluding sections of this introduction, which also attempts to provide a sequential literary context for some of the authors arranged alphabetically in the body of the *Guide*'s text, and to make clear any major conclusions in literary history towards which the *Guide* seems to be pointing the way.

8. THE CHRONOLOGY OF FRENCH LITERARY CULTURE

a) The 16th century

During the whole of the period with which this volume is concerned, the literature of France was carried by a deep tide running underneath all sorts of eddies and whirls towards an understandably tentative investigation of the possibility that human instinct might be trusted as a guide to both virtue and what virtue would inevitably bring with it, happiness. The literary investigation naturally concentrated on the potential of instinct in the best possible circumstances of birth, breeding, education, and natural endowment, with leading characters of unimaginably heroic moral and physical stature. There are many examples in which the subject of the investigation is made clear. In French the most famous is the Thélème episode from Rabelais's *Tiers livre*, which derives its opening principle from Erasmus.

The 15th century had ended in French intellectual history with scarcely a crack in the prevailing Parisian scholastic orthodoxy. The ideal of Christian virtue involved the abnegation of instinct; the "state of perfection" embraced by those seeking spiritual fulfilment to the exclusion of all other ends involved vows of poverty, chastity, and obedience; and the very few married female saints in the calendar who were not martyrs were bundled under the rubric "nec virgo, nec martyr (neither a virgin nor a martyr)."

The moral law was seen as a promulgation of the divine will, and the goodness of an action was not antecedent to God's law, but flowed only from the divinely instituted moral order. It followed that Christian perfection involved conformity to a moral law whose derivation was potentially arbitrary. Religious perfection was extrinsic to any human aspiration to moral fulfilment. God rewarded if, as, and how he saw fit. It is true that God had established by his "potestas ordinata (regulatory power)" an order entrusted to his Church in which those would be saved who kept the law or even, as the faithful were told consolingly by their pastors, who did what lay within them. But God need not have bound himself in this way; Ockham went as far as to wonder whether God might have rewarded those who sinned and condemned those who loved him; and no one could know whether they had done all that lay within

them. The characteristic devotional practices invented in the late 15th century were all devices for making psychologically tolerable the repetition of identical acts, the rosary, the stations of the cross, the angelus, or the performance of onerous ones, like pilgrimages.

Chantry bequests, indulgences, and prayers for the dead all implied that the status of the dead was not solely determined by their moral state at the moment of death. How, then, could the Christian be assured of salvation? Devout Christianity in France had come to involve intense spiritual strain and anguished doubts about salvation, already alleviated east of the Rhine by the long development of the "devotio moderna (modern devotion)," on the whole a resolutely non-humanist movement led by the Brethren of the Common Life who educated Erasmus. Inevitably, the quest for spiritual reassurance bred hordes of superstitious attitudes and practices. Punctilious observances of rites and practices easily took precedence over interior moral conversion. Rome, it is true, was the primatial see, doctrinal as well as jurisdictional, and claimed the right to pronounce on matters of doctrine, but the French commonly held that a general council of the Church had superior authority. The infallibility of the magisterium was not in doubt, but whether or not the primatial see held the magisterium was certainly disputed by the 15th-century French "conciliar" theologians. The custodian of ecclesiastical orthodoxy which had both defined and enforced it from the 13th century onwards was in fact the theology faculty of the university of Paris.

The distinction between Rome's doctrinal and its jurisdictional primacy is immensely important in the history of French literature. Firstly, Lutheranism, like Anglicanism, was a schism, not a heresy, at least at first. As late as 1541 the theological differences could still have been overcome and adequate political good will could have ended the Lutheran schism that year at Ratisbon. We do not know which, if any, of Luther's 40 propositions condemned at Rome in *Exsurge, Domine* on 15 June 1520 were considered heretical. The bull did not say so. Jansenism, on the other hand was a heresy, but never a schism. Ecclesiastical jurisdiction and the status of the Gallican church were never questioned during that dispute. Secondly, whenever it wished to invoke non-spiritual penalties, the Church itself and the Paris theology faculty referred the matter to the courts of the parlements, whose judgements might, however, be overturned by the supreme authority of the king.

The new beginnings of French vernacular literary culture can be situated at about the moment at which the wave began to break, and the seething social and religious rebellion against late medieval Christianity invaded France. Luther's flamboyant revolt at the brash new institution at Wittenberg was at first only another of the isolated incidents in which combustion burst into flame, always a long way from Paris. There had been Wyclif and Hus, with whose names that of Luther had at first been linked, and there were soon to be the very radical religious revolutions of the Swiss cantons.

The earliest French authors given individual entries in the *Guide* were writing within a year or two of 1500, a moment which marks something very like a real point of discontinuity in the literary culture's development. Before that year comparatively little had been published in the vernacular. Printing was a novelty, still in 1500 overwhelmingly devoted to the production of books for liturgical use. In spite of the glories of medieval French literature, it needs to be written about and analysed in a quite different way from all that came later. In 1500 France's unification was scarcely stable, and its organization was still largely feudal. Indeed, it was scarcely until the 1559 Traité de Cateau-Cambrésis that properly defined nation-states emerged in Europe.

Imaginative literature can be so sensitive an indicator of the tensions existing in the interior of a society that it is unusually important when considering it to avoid the misleading models imposed by the conventional categories. In view of the looseness of the terms as used in modern English, it is inappropriate in so exact a context as this to employ the terms Reformation and Protestant in any senses other than their original and precise ones. In the modern English sense, there is no agreement about what was reformed, how successfully, why, by whom, or where. If Reformation is taken simply to mean schism, then it must be applied to all three of Canterbury, Zurich, and Wittenberg, and can mean nothing except the refusal to accept a particular power relationship with Rome, involving jurisdiction rather than doctrine, a relationship which France, too, on several occasions only just avoided breaking.

More difficult still is the need, if strict propriety is to be observed, to avoid the term "renaissance." The early 16th-century admirers of antique literary texts claimed that they were inaugurating the rebirth, or re-flowering, of an educational ideal; they rallied to the trumpet call of "bonae literae (good learning)"; and they created the need for some way of referring to the millennium between the barbarian destruction of the remnants of Rome's empire and their own cultivation of what they took to be the antique ideal of human development. The term invented for what happened between Augustine and the generation of Erasmus was the "middle" or dark ages, sometimes called Gothic, and the result is that, precisely used, the term "middle ages" or "medieval" must imply sharing the assumption that something which had once flourished had, around 1500, been re-created.

But for half a century scholars have been patiently demonstrating that, except for an accelerated interest in reading antique and Christian texts in the original languages, nothing was. We are left with the term "renaissance" to define a cultural event which occurred in northern Europe most intensely between about 1500 and not much after 1550, but about whose nature there is still no general agreement. The term "medieval" now simply denotes the whole of the period from late antiquity until about 1500, or perhaps 1450 south of the Alps, without implying anything at all about its culture. In the *Guide* the terms "Reform" and "Reformation" are used in the usual way, although the more correct "schism" is generally preferred to denote the rejection of the Roman claim to exercise jurisdiction as the primatal see. France always deferred to Rome as the ultimate authority in the definition of doctrinal orthodoxy, although the routine behaviour of the Paris faculty certainly usurped the primatial prerogative. An attempt has been made in the *Guide* to observe neutrality about the initial meaning of the term "renaissance," although suggestions are proffered about the nature of the underlying event. The students of the antique, Erasmus and Budé, More and Fisher, Busleyden, Beatus, and Reuchlin can now be seen heavily to have promoted themselves and one another, and largely to have generated a sense of excited innovation for which there was not in 1520 enough real warrant.

France's literary culture at least reflects, and may partially have powered, the changes that took place in the way of perceiving and feeling human experience during the 300 years with which the present volume is concerned. This section of the Introduction, not itself intended to be an introductory guide to the *Guide*'s entries, points to the principal of these shifts in sensibility. In 1500 there was not yet any sane expression of public disbelief either in God or in the immortality of the soul. Indeed, the word "atheist," applied for instance to Luther by Montaigne, meant someone who acted as if God did not exist by disregarding his law, not yet someone who believed that the universe was necessary, eternal, and uncreated. Through the literary culture it is possible to trace the slow, tortuous, and tentative emergence of the possibility that human intellection, while still generally considered a spiritual activity, could in the late 18th century be regarded as capable of being generated by a highly enough organized physical being without a separate informing spiritual principle or soul. Descartes's great rearguard action on behalf of the spirituality of the soul in the end failed, but it is sufficiently important for an entry to have been devoted to him, as well as that on Cartesianism, although Descartes himself did not except frivolously write in the imaginative genres.

Unsurprisingly, more imaginatively important is the investigation into the compatibility of emotional love, and physical sexual relationships, with the highest forms of moral and spiritual perfection. The upgrading of instinctive affection in this way invariably went with a strong feminism, ironically more pronounced in male authors like Fontenelle and Fénelon than in female authors like Madeleine de Scudéry and Mme de Lafayette. In this context attention should be called to the often great difficulty in establishing the literary registers of important texts. It is only recently that the ironic nature of the texts of Somaize and the abbé de Pure (see: Préciosité) has been established. In an age when sets of aristocratic young women were beginning to vie with one another to conquer the most dashing cavaliers, the little coterie of précieuses, nearly all of whom in the end married, affected, in the manner of the Sapho of Madeleine de Scudéry's *Clélie*, to see in the refusal of all physical relationships the only remedy against male tyranny. Part of the *Guide*'s task is to chart the reader through the whirlpools of irony and affectation.

Early French humanism was concerned almost uniquely with the application of the ancient languages to the task of undermining the authority of the Latin Vulgate version of the scriptures, although Lefèvre d'Etaples, the most important of the French humanists, an Aristotelian with a piety formed in the 15th century, also edited, in the sense of having printed, the major neoplatonist mystical texts. Budé was more a legal scholar and an archaeologist of Greek antiquity than what we would today call a humanist. François I had failed to establish a "trilingual" foundation on the model of what was being attempted at Oxford, Cambridge, Louvain, Alcala, and elsewhere, an enterprise for which Budé's enthusiasm may have been less pronounced than was Erasmus's clear reluctance to go anywhere near Paris. When in the end the simple royal lecteurships of 1529–30 were finally established, they did, however late in the day, show a strong emphasis on Greek and Hebrew, both taught in Latin until Pierre de la Ramée became the first lecteur royal to use the vernacular in the early 1550s.

It was Marsilio Ficino, author of a Platonic theology on the immortality of the soul, whose "*De amore*," the *In Convivium Platonis de amore commentarium* of 1469, provided the basically Plotinian mythologized philosophy in which earthly love was the first step towards final beatification in the union with God. Here was a view which allowed human emotion to be compatible with, and indeed to lead to, the soul's final and eternal beatitude and it not surprisingly swept through Italy and France, creating the "trattato d'amore (treatise on love)" as its vehicle. It was the foundation for an immensely optimistic exploration of what cultivated human effort might achieve; it upgraded the status of women from mere objects of male desire; the basic neoplatonism for some years obsessed Colet and through him gained an association with Saint Paul, whose first convert at Athens the fourth-century neoplatonist Pseudo-Areopagite was thought to be; it fitted easily into the neoplatonist inheritance of Augustine; it allowed for four different forms of divine rapture, so associating the erotic rapture with that of poetry and music, themselves linked through their numbers and ratios to the harmony of the spheres and made capable of putting the soul, disturbed by its passions, back in harmony with God and his creation; it made Plato the defender of Christianity and revived the old idea that he had picked up traces of the Mosaic revelation in Egypt; and it linked love, poetry, music, and contemplation with virtue, happiness, and religious fulfilment.

Ficinian Platonism was obviously useful in upgrading the status of the arts and of human emotion, all of which were linked with the human aspiration to harmony with nature and God. The elevation of love to a spiritually enriching emotion not dependent on the idealization of its object also brought with it the first serious attempts at upgrading the role of women in society in what we know as the Querelle des femmes. Women's domestic role needed no longer to be culturally confined by housewifely commitments or as untouchable hypostases of the male aspiration to chivalric and moral perfection. Covert and overt references to Ficino replace in Marguerite d'Angoulême the more austere neoplatonist spirituality which derived from Nicolas of Cusa and which she imbibed from Lefèvre's doctrine, transmitted to her through Guillaume Briçonnet's letters.

Following the attempt by Erasmus and others to improve the theological status of the Greek Father, Origen, thoroughly neoplatonist, believing in free will, the non-eternity of hell, and the ultimate salvation of the pagans, Marguerite reversed her earlier belief that pagans would inevitably be damned. The defence of pagan virtue by Erasmus, and even by Lefèvre d'Etaples, and the theologians' attempt to substitute the authority of Origen for that of Augustine are at the heart of the cultural movement of the early 16th century. Erasmus is clearly followed by Rabelais, who bases his idea of Thélème on the principles laid down in Erasmus's second *Hyperaspistes* letter to Luther. The problem was that there was no possible orthodox way of reconciling any autonomous human power of self-determination to good, free will in the full sense, with a non-heretical theory of grace, if Christian belief in anything like its totality was strictly necessary for salvation, and if, therefore, apparent pagan virtue was unauthentic, a view very weakly defended, but still strongly held by the 17th-century Jansenists, and secularized among others by La Rochefoucauld.

Elements of Ficino are to be found not only in the work of Rabelais, but also in that of Scève, Peletier du Mans, Héroët, and Pontus de Tyard, clearly entering France through Italianate Lyons. Substantial portions of Rabelais's third and fourth books are inspired by Ficino, and a new examination of Ficino's utilization by the whole corpus of 16th-century French authors is urgently needed. It would throw powerful illumination on the interior history of the move in early 16th-century France to repudiate the arbitrary observances and the repression of instinct called for by late 15th-century Christianity, and to replace it with a sometimes giddy confidence in human potential.

Where the repudiation of the 15th-century understanding of human nature and its relationship to God was less optimistic, there was naturally no recourse to the neoplatonist matrix of Ficino. For the removal of a religion based on sacraments and observances in favour of a strict insistence on interior conversion, there was the remorselessly logical Calvin, still combining a 15th-century distrust of human nature with a strict spirituality of moral conversion, now enforced by ecclesiastical structures and civil penalties of relentless intransigence.

The history of French literary culture in the mid-16th century is traditionally dominated by the emergence of the Pléiade. As a group the Pléiade never existed, as the entry devoted to it makes clear, but the *Guide* has felt obliged to devote individual entries to most of the poets and dramatists named at different times by Ronsard, or after his death by his biographer, in the changing list of seven poets with whom Ronsard early in his life had wished to be associated. This has meant excluding the poets known as the "grands rhétoriqueurs," always a term of derision, whose acrostic techniques of versification were of some historical but no literary interest. For the rhétoriqueurs, poetry was a court game. It was Clément Marot, the son of one of them, who almost systematically substituted antique verse forms for those of the rhétoriqueurs, and whose epigrammatic wit, at its best refined and delicate, showed a new sort of poetic sensibility, as was acknowledged by Ronsard and du Bellay, though rather grudgingly.

This might have been for religious reasons. Marot was inclined to the "Lutheran" Christianity of interior conversion and simplified observances, and was forced into exile on that account, and to recantation as a condition of return. In the earlier part of the century he shared with Etienne Dolet, the admirer of Cicero, author of the large Ciceronian dictionary, the two-volume *Commentarii linguae latinae* (1536–38), a religious attitude inclined towards Lutheranism and an admiration for Latin rather than Greek antiquity. Dolet was a fervent advocate of enriching the French language by imitating Cicero and translating into it, and resented Erasmus's mocking association of Budé with the printer Josse Bade in the 1528 *Ciceronianus*. Ronsard, du Bellay, and Baïf, the nucleus of the new school of poets which started to emerge in 1549, were on the other hand savagely intent on asserting their own poetic originality, were strongly Catholic, admired Greek antiquity, and were taught by the Erasmian Dorat, whose interest in antique literature was more moral than linguistic, and who was himself a disciple of Erasmus.

Du Bellay did not live long enough to develop his full poetic potential, and he left behind the earlier literary ideals he had shared with Ronsard, who was himself undoubtedly, above all for the *Hymnes* rather than the sonnets, the towering poet of the 16th century. It is difficult to resist the feeling that Ronsard's achievement would have been even greater had he continued to live in a time when it was possible to take an optimistic view of human destiny and the conduct of human affairs. He became uncomfortable as the court poet celebrating royal strategies, and the polemical poems attacking Huguenot opponents are not his best verse. He ended his life disconsolate, and in comparative isolation.

The optimistic literary explorations of human potential which had characterized the earlier part of the century stopped abruptly with the outbreak of the religious wars. The tone became defensive and, although the moral doctrines did not change very much, their expression took on strongly stoic accents. The relativism of Montaigne's *Les Essais* demonstrates a link between scepticism and stoic indifference, the only rational attitude possible in a world in which no knowledge of the ultimate truths appeared attainable. There was a link between scepticism and stoicism in antiquity. It was tightened by the way in which the antique texts were transmitted to the 16th century, and was clearly re-forged by the Dutch humanist Justus Lipsius. The religious disputes left political positions entrenched but theological certainties eroded and, while the moral ideals of virtue, following nature, and rational control remained, they were more often borrowed from stoic authors, Seneca or Epictetus, than from the Platonizing mid-century authors, and tinged with a stoic vocabulary, emphasizing such passive virtues as constancy and patience.

The greatest prose writer of the period covered by the religious wars was certainly Montaigne, still curiously misunderstood. The publicly announced self-portrait was a pretence, disguising the more urgent and pressing real need assuaged by *Les Essais* for the intimate companionship of which La Boétie's death had deprived Montaigne. To understand the literary registers of *Les Essais*, it is essential to take into account the truer if unintentional and unselfconscious self-portrait of the *Journal de voyage en Italie*, in which Montaigne reveals himself as bustling, intolerably over-energetic for his companions, and insatiably curious, quite likely to climb a mountain to see what the stones were like on top, or to interrogate the first passing Italian peasant about cooking methods. It is the *Journal* which shows us how personal a book *Les Essais* becomes as it progresses not only through the three states of the text at which it was printed, but through a process of accumulating anecdote and comment, which continued often daily between editions. In spite of the predominating note sounded by Montaigne's relativist cast of mind, and of his repudiation of Ficinian fineries on sexual relationships, which for Montaigne were either a pleasure or a duty but never a stepping-stone to spiritual perfection, Montaigne only half conceals a real zest for living, a mental curiosity from which a type of optimism is inseparable.

The greatest poet of the religious wars, d'Aubigné, presents an enigma of a different kind. His great poem, *Les Tragiques*, like Montaigne's *Les Essais*, can be understood only in its context, but unhappily we do not know how much of it was written while the wars were still in progress, exactly what was added later, whether any of it was written for publication at all, and why d'Aubigné did publish it, but only 25 years after the fighting was over, when the rest of France had picked up again where the exuberant optimism of the mid-16th century had been cut off. The presumption must be that d'Aubigné resented the new climate of Catholic victory, and became determined to publish a testimony to the forgotten bitternesses and hatreds. It contains a very strong expression of outrage.

b) The 17th century

The neostoicism died away through the works of du Vair, Charron—whose entry in these pages is due to his reputation and historical importance, but not to the literary quality of any-

thing he wrote—and Malherbe, who somewhat ostentatiously appointed himself the saviour and custodian of the language and versification of France. He managed to command a certain respect in that role, as did Balzac as the arbiter of prose and, associated with both, Chapelain, later the important mediator of patronage. Colbert's reliance on Chapelain allowed Chapelain to enjoy the sort of thurification at which the young Boileau was wittily and bitingly to scoff before he, in turn, became a self-satisfied and tedious mouthpiece for the rearguard admirers of antiquity, semi-Jansenist in spirituality, and the pompous denigrator of women's role in society.

The first half of the 17th century is for clear but regrettable reasons little studied; clear because it was a period during which France's culture was striding forward to catch up with the rest of Europe, where the optimism of the mid-16th century had not been halted by the terrible experience of the French civil wars; regrettable, because of the sheer audacity and overwhelming energy of the imaginative investigations of the period. In the rest of Europe the pastoral had been flourishing while France was at war, and the pastoral setting has always been used to emphasize the natural innocence of the instinctive behaviour which occurs within it. Unfortunately, literary works whose exploration of experience is optimistic in tone are generally less tautly and less tightly written than, for instance, the great tragedies of antiquity, or even the best ones of the 17th century.

The preferred genre of the early 17th century becomes the novel, of which we have the fascinating but immensely long and loosely structured examples of Gomberville, La Calprenède, and Madeleine de Scudéry, whose imaginative thrusts towards an examination of the heroic combination of happiness and virtue are achievements of great vigour. We have only a highly probable idea of what Madeleine de Scudéry wrote, and what her brother contributed to their joint novels, but *Clélie*, which we can safely suppose to be Madeleine's own work, explores a quite unrealistic but intensely powerful view of love, and reflects and promotes in its series of portraits a quite new refinement and delicacy in French society, whose roots, however, were no doubt to be found in the Hôtel de Rambouillet.

In the literary culture of France in the first half of the 17th century, the four authors of really towering importance in the optimistic examination of human experience were François de Sales, Descartes, Honoré d'Urfé, and Pierre Corneille, whose optimistic effrontery in *Le Cid* in proposing that Rodrigue's merit is such as to allow Chimène to agree to marry him immediately after he has killed her father has already been mentioned. François de Sales, the author of an early handbook of lay piety, allowing make-up and dancing, and including a chapter on marital intercourse, "de l'honnêteté du lit nuptial," omitted as indecent in the unending 19th-century editions, and of a long but meandering treatise on the love of God, is sometimes mentioned for his elaborate metaphors about animals, particularly partridges, and natural history generally. They are long-winded, genial, and never entirely serious. What is serious is that here, for the first time, a doctor of the Church and one of the foremost ascetical and mystical theologians of post-medieval times erects a Christian spirituality wholly on the natural instinct to love God. Impeccably orthodox, Sales finds authority in Augustine for his sacralization of human nature, while his documented direction of Jeanne-Françoise de Chantal, the widow who with François de Sales founded the Visitation order, shows him to have been intensely exigent in his spiritual demands.

Descartes's attempt to unite all that is non-empirically knowable into one logical system, which would support belief in the spirituality and immortality of the soul, basing it on self-justifying metaphysical certainty and leading to all three of health, happiness and virtue was, not surprisingly, never finished. Given its initial supposition, the cogency of the system is remarkable, even if there is no single element in it which, strictly speaking, is new. The basic presuppositions are neoplatonist. What is breath-taking is the sheer audacity of supposing that it was possible to discover an irrefutable philosophic system which would infallibly lead to both virtue and happiness.

D'Urfé is another author whose imaginative daring is remarkable although, properly to evaluate it, it is necessary to trace the evolution of his moral vision through the three volumes of the *Epîtres morales* in order to understand the real thrust of the endless analyses of forms of love in *L'Astrée*, one of the truly great works ushering in what has often been thought of as the golden age of French literature. The *Epîtres* progressively shed their neostoic elements to revert to the Ficinian perspectives in which the love of another human being is the first rung on the ladder leading to the love of God. *L'Astrée*, stripped of its immense digressions and anecdotes, concerns three couples, the central pair, Astrée and Céladon, flanked on the one hand by a couple for whom love starts by excluding desire, and on the other by a couple for whom love is reducible to it. The novel ends with the triple marriage, and the moral could not be clearer. A sexual union is not only not any obstacle to virtue and happiness, but possibly even its necessary, and at any rate its usual condition.

The refining activity in French society of the Hôtel de Rambouillet has often been commented on. Its political influence was greater than many literary historians have supposed, but its only corporate literary production, the *Guirlande de Julie*, to which the *Guide* devotes an entry, is composed of unrelievedly atrocious verse. However Voiture, its most important resident poet and a member of its inner circle, was a much better poet than the satirical Boileau, whose notion of the sublime could find no room for him. To understand exactly what was being achieved amid the practical joking of the Hôtel, it helps much to observe how what we might call the legitimate theatre was beginning to establish itself, largely at first with the help of patrons like the comte de Belin and Richelieu, although also of the king, Louis XIII, and his brother, Gaston d'Orléans. The interest of Hardy is very largely historical, but Rotrou, Théophile de Viau, Racan, Tristan, and Mairet were all imaginatively important authors involved in the immense transformation of French cultural life. Some of the important new plays, or parts of them, were read at the Hôtel.

With Richelieu, chief minister from 1624, also begin the sumptuous theatrical entertainments, often later designed primarily for the court. Not enough is yet known about their staging, but it is reasonable to assume that from the mid-1630s the path of what was to become opera diverged from the straight theatre staged at the Hôtel de Bourgogne, originally too small for the elaborate stage machinery often later used for productions of the Marais company. Racinian tragedy, although played at court, may well have been developed from a tradition affected by the physical and economic constraints imposed by the size and shape of the Hôtel de Bourgogne, to which Racine moved when he broke with Molière late in 1665. The performances staged by Richelieu in the Palais-Cardinal (now the Palais-Royal) which he had had built, and in which he had included two theatres, were certainly elaborate and costly. What is clear is that some of the texts we regard as literature depended for performance on little more than bravura declaration, while other texts played different and sometimes comparatively minor roles in combination with astonishing stage effects, changes of scenery, music, and dancing in collaborative entertainments.

The texts of Desmarets de Saint-Sorlin for Richelieu, and of Bensserade chiefly for the court, were not intended to achieve their effect independently of the other theatrical arts. Molière was edged out of tragedy by the reputation of the Hôtel de Bourgogne, and out of elaborate machine pieces by the physical constraints imposed by the unrestored larger theatre, by now dilapidated, in the Palais-Royal, and was therefore obliged to rely on the social satire at which he excelled. He certainly used both music and dance. In fact, much work remains to be done on 17th-century drama in Paris. The traditional contrast between Racine and Pierre Corneille simply dissolves in the light of the work of Thomas Corneille, which forms a bridge between that of his elder brother and that of the ambitious young courtier, Racine, whose talent, while great, does not really merit the soaring isolation accorded to it by works of literary history. In comparison, neither his rival Pradon, nor Thomas Corneille, to whose work Racine's makes frequent allusion and who was the author of by far the greatest theatrical success of the century, the popular and powerful *Timocrate*, has been given his due. Thomas Corneille in particular is one of the century's undervalued dramatists.

The mention of the dramatic rivalries of the 17th century takes us straight to the heart of its essential cultural debate, which finally crystallized into the *Querelle des anciens et des modernes*. The debate about whether the aesthetic norms of antiquity were preferable to the elegant refinements of taste generated by salon society and partly catered for by the pensioned burners of incense to the glories of the reign of Louis XIV organized by Colbert is tangential to the real issue, which was the perfectibility of human nature and human society. On the spiritual and theological levels the defenders of perfectibility were strongly opposed by the writers of Port-Royal, who wrongly regarded themselves as the monopolistic inheritors of the Augustinian tradition, and whose views were characterized by an extreme distrust of human nature. The "anciens," or defenders of the aesthetic norms in the Querelle, were led by Racine and Boileau, and vigorously opposed by Thomas Corneille, his partner Donneau de Visé at the *Mercure Galant* (q.v.), Pradon and, most provocatively, by Perrault, whose *Contes* have to be seen in the context of the Querelle.

The use of the term "Zeitgeist" has rightly been discredited as nebulous or, what to many historians is even worse, Hegelian. There is, however, something that might be described as pre-articulate public opinion, if that phrase were not so cumbersome and did not suggest that there were some process by which surges of feeling were refined into intellectually coherent statements of position. It may indeed be so, but comparatively minute shifts in a shared public reaction are commonly discerned with apparent simultaneity by thousands of journalists, broadcasters, and political commentators. The changed perception operates mysteriously, no doubt in the same way as the partridges in a covey convey to one another a sense of approaching danger which enables them to fly at the same moment in exactly the same direction.

The rise and decline in waves of optimism and doubt operate rather like the birds, and do not depend on "influences," a word so doubtful in any literary application that it scarcely appears in the *Guide*. Not only are passively undergone influences seldom susceptible of easy proof but, even when they have been established beyond reasonable doubt, they help little in assessing the imaginative processes of the author or the literary interest of the text. Authors can deliberately derive elements in the expression of their imaginative experience from other authors, and it can be helpful for the critic to know of their affiliation to literary groups or predecessors. But the establishment of a possible passive "influence" has so often been misused as a substitute for historical or critical analysis as to have eroded its utility as a critical tool.

The 17th-century diminution of enthusiasm for optimistic cultural exploration can in retrospect be seen to have originated in France before ever the heroic adventure novel had reached its zenith, in the neoplatonist spirituality untransformed by Ficino and derived from the Pseudo-Areopagite by Bérulle, Condren, and Bérulle's Oratorian chaplain and disciple, Gibieuf, whose theology was repudiated by Jansen, who none the less derived important elements from it. As usual, the spirituality emerged before the theology erected to protect it. There is very little evidence that Jansen's theology, incorporated in the 1640 *Augustinus*, ever inspired the austere and deeply anguished spirituality of his close friend, Saint-Cyran, which it none the less protected.

To the spirituality of Saint-Cyran, which he thought to be more genuinely orthodox than it was, Pascal added an entirely new adroitness in the manipulation of the French language. Every one of the *Lettres provinciales* is a masterpiece, and what we refer to as the *Pensées*—not Pascal's title—contains insights of immense brilliance into the more terrifying aspects of human experience and the insignificant but appalling cosmic destiny of the individual human being. Pascal rather unfairly reproached the Jesuits for a trivialization of properly Christian norms of behaviour derived from their teaching on grace which, in Lessius's form of debased Molinism in which Pascal encountered it, was certainly heterodox, but he was reacting almost as strongly to exuberant Jesuit optimism about human nature as he was to Jesuit norms used in dispensing sacramental absolution. His own theory of grace made it impossible for him to complete the work of apologetic in view of which the most important of the fragments in the *Pensées* were jotted down.

Richelieu's death in 1642, followed by that of Louis XIII in 1643, brought no immediate cultural change, but the final revolts of the parlements, which were seeking to be more than mere courts of justice, and the feudal aristocracy, who were striving to wrest power from Anne of Austria, the regent, and from her minister, Mazarin, who seems certainly also to have been her lover, soon announced themselves in the separate uprisings known together as the Fronde. Peace was restored by 1652, and there followed a decade during which, in Paris at least, a certain cultural liberalism appears momentarily to have halted the relentless march towards the nationalization of all cultural enterprise. This was the decade of préciosité. Molière returned to Paris only at its end. It did, however, see the composition of one of the century's unregarded masterpieces of moral writing, a gallery of short sharp historical portraits of the famous, written with malicious humour and a focused moral vision, *Les Historiettes* of Tallemant des Réaux, beautifully edited in French, but regrettably not at present available in English.

Then in 1661 Mazarin died and, although Louis XIV declared that he would no longer have a chief minister, Colbert, a brilliant, rather unsmiling administrator, in fact toppled Foucquet and the financiers. Thereafter he virtually governed France in the name of the king, the extravagance of whose court life Colbert gave the impression of loftily, or perhaps calculatingly, indulging, in the end, and in spite of the ruinous expense, allowing even the move from the Louvre to Versailles. He not only organized the system of literary and other artistic patronage, but scarcely disguised the comparative austerity of his personal taste.

With the crown virtually the only source of patronage left, France's literary culture underwent a change. For the Fronde we have, not memoirs, in spite of the title which has stuck to Retz's tour de force, but what were much more the personal apologies of Retz and La Rochefoucauld. Bossuet became the court prelate, useful for knowing how to keep his place without subservience and to assert his authority without offending, for allying Gallican principles with an ability to keep relations between Paris and Rome more or less in kilter, for disposing of the king's discarded mistresses, and for furnishing the higher aristocracy with tutors for their children. The quietist affair took the course it did largely because Fénelon's refined and aristocratic spiritual discernment and superior intelligence became a real threat to Bossuet's bluntly uncomprehending peasant conservatism. Behind an apparently esoteric dispute in mystical theology a new refinement was gaining strength in which the cultivation of the individual was reasserting itself against the bludgeon of mass conformity.

The major authors of Colbert's ascendancy did, however, almost necessarily include gifted amateurs from the nobility, who often did not publish, or only surreptitiously and anonymously, or pseudo-anonymously connived at publication: Mme de Sévigné, Mme de Lafayette, Retz, La Rochefoucauld. La Fontaine, Racine, Boileau, and Bossuet lived on the fringes of the nobility, and La Bruyère was simply a slightly downtrodden member of the Condé household. Their writings—satires, poems, fables, maxims, portraits, letters, "nouvelles," "caractères," and drama, scenes from which were commonly played or read in the salons—all belonged to the shorter literary genres, often polished, perceptive, exquisite, and refined, sometimes dense and anguished but, except for the stage pieces, seldom demanding long spans of attention. The use of the term "classical" to describe the literature produced between Foucquet's fall and Colbert's death in 1683 has been misleading, serving simply to obscure what was at stake in an astonishingly penetrating and powerful body of brief literary works, but exaggerating the importance of some authors, like Furetière, and marginalizing that of others, particularly Pradon and Thomas Corneille.

c) The 18th century

Before the end of the 17th century the victory of the partisans of the "modernes" in the Querelle, led by Perrault, was assured, in literature as in painting. There is a new note of social concern in the work of La Bruyère and Fénelon, an agnosticism in Bayle, and an elegant cynicism in Fontenelle, all of which mark a shift in imaginative interest. The optimism which had been held back, first by the influential spirituality associated with Port-Royal and then by the canons of taste favoured by Boileau, broke out exuberantly again, most spectacularly in the re-writing of the

Iliad according to contemporary taste by Houdar de la Motte in 1714. The renewed exuberance exacted its price. What are normally considered the wrong-headed policies of the flamboyant Louvois were adopted, the country bankrupted itself in the Dutch wars after his death, and the effects of the revocation of the Edict of Nantes were clearly ruinous for France's economic welfare.

In spite of Voltaire, known during the 18th century itself as above all a dramatist and a poet, dramatic activity, as represented for instance first by Marivaux, and then by Nivelle de la Chaussée, Sedaine, and Diderot, was changing the imaginative register. Bourgeois characters were becoming the vehicles at least for pathos if not for tragedy itself. Between Marivaux, forced to earn a living by writing for the reinstalled Italian company, and Beaumarchais, for whom writing plays was never much more than a serious hobby, servants became more skilful and ingenious than the nobles they served. It is arguable that Beaumarchais's comic brilliance was never shown to better effect than in his 1773–74 underrated *Mémoires contre Goëzmann*. Again, Marivaux's plays need to be put in context, with his failures with the French company set against the increasing boldness with which the servant class in the plays written for the Italians move from mimicking their employers' relationships and speaking in patois to regarding their employers as social equals and intellectual inferiors. In Marivaux's novels, the ease with which a character is moved to tears can indicate nobility of birth in *La Vie de Marianne*, while *Le Paysan parvenu* suggests that it is possible to start from the bottom of the social scale and arrive near its summit. Prévost tests the reader's ability to accept, in a parody of the chivalresque novel, the fundamental innocence of the Chevalier des Grieux, and even of Manon Lescaut, in spite of everything they do in the name of their passion for one another.

It is against the examination of society's class structure that must be seen the new imaginative preoccupation with forms of political organization of which the two most monumental achievements are Montesquieu's apparently rambling *De l'Esprit des lois* and Rousseau's internally inconsistent *Du Contrat social*. Voltaire was the clever and rich epigrammatic wit, essentially conservative and monarchist, brilliantly wielding his weapon of ridicule, and capable of real compassion as well as fearsome prejudice, always clearer about what was wrong or foolish than about what might be substituted for it, and to the end hesitant about the need for a belief in immortality and in remuneration after death in order to maintain society in a state of law and order. Rousseau, on the other hand, poor, self-taught, and republican,was much the more radical thinker, who imaginatively pursued with dogged resolution ways of convincing himself and others that humanity was naturally virtuous, and that only proper education and social organization were necessary for universal happiness.

The rise of atheism in 18th-century France was much slower and more hesitant than is often realized. The anonymously published 1721 *Lettres persanes* of Montesquieu might wrongly have been interpreted as blasphemous and atheistic if their light-hearted and frivolous tone had not saved them. In fact the Cartesian defence of immortality founded on the spirituality of the soul had to be abandoned when it became clear from Locke that it was not totally unbelievable that purely material beings might be so organized as to possess the power of thought. The Christian apologists then looked to the Epicureanism of Gassendi for a defence of their position and, if it is undeniable that formal materialism made strong progress during the 18th century in France, philosophically the Christian position on the immortality of an immaterial soul even as envisaged by Descartes had not been surrendered by the outbreak of the Revolution.

The role played by Diderot in the movement of ideas is ambiguous, partly because so much of what he wrote was not destined by him to be published, and may not contain any precise expression of his view, partly because his literary register is sometimes singularly difficult to determine, and partly because he was determinedly practical, and that meant getting the *Encyclopédie* actually published, and no doubt prudently omitting or disguising some of the opinions it might otherwise have expressed. In addition, we do not know how many of the unsigned articles were written by him. He clearly did not get as far in converting Catherine II of Russia to political liberalism as he thought he had. We know that Diderot's novel *La Religieuse* was never much more than a practical joke, that *Jacques le fataliste* was an elaborate amusement for the European monarchs who paid Grimm to write fortnightly from Paris with gossip and news, and that *Le Neveu de Rameau*, never intended for anyone other than himself to see, neither needed nor contained the two consistent points of view commentators have ceaselessly tried to read into the words of each of the two characters in the dialogue.

The Revolution itself finally broke out as the result of a series of misjudgements, and while the literary culture was exploring many avenues of constitutional reform, there was no very strong public desire in 1789 totally to do away either with the monarchy or with the Church, although the public function of each was everywhere being reconsidered. By the death of Rousseau in 1778 a serious social disturbance in France seemed unavoidable. As far as the literary exploration of human perfectibility was concerned, the idyll was for the time being suspended, never really to return, in spite of Chateaubriand, Constant, and Lamartine. Its final expression was perhaps in Bernardin de Saint-Pierre's *Paul et Virginie*, less confident in tone than Rousseau's *Emile; ou, De l'éducation* or *Julie; ou, La nouvelle Héloïse*. In 1789 the greatest of Chénier's poems had not been written. Much of Sade and Rétif de la Bretonne, both of whose works clearly played therapeutic roles for the psyches of their authors, was still to come. The establishment of a science of man founded on the congruence of instinct, virtue, and happiness which had inspired cultural endeavour for 300 years had turned out to be a chimera.

France in 1794, at the end of the Terror, was not in quite so bad a state as it had been 300 years earlier; some of the refinement, the civilized reflexes conquered during that period would quickly be recovered. There was political unification. But 1789 is a melancholy moment to end a volume. France's rich literary culture had not in the end enabled the country to achieve a stable and acceptable society and less progress towards the understanding and control of human experience had been achieved than generations had hoped for.

A.L.

PREFACE

The index to this volume of the *Guide* has been designed in such a way as to link the individual entries with conventional narrative literary history, and with cultural history generally. It is intended to enable users of the *Guide* to relate writers, including those without their own entries, as well as other culturally important figures, including patrons, monarchs, musicians, ministers, and book-sellers, to other figures, movements, and groupings with which they were associated, including the important salons, stage companies, and religious, literary, and artistic groups with which they came into contact. Even more than in the volume of the *Guide* devoted to post-Revolutionary French literature, it has proved virtually impossible to subject literary texts to critical analysis without taking account of their political, social, religious, and ideological content and context. The meaning of the texts is changed by such facts as whether or not they were intended for publication.

Individual entries have again been reserved in principle for authors of imaginative literature, and for institutions, reviews, and movements connected with it but, as explained in the Introduction, the nature and development of French literary culture before the Revolution seemed to impose the inclusion of more entries than originally envisaged on theological and philosophical topics and authors. However, the index has been used to smooth out some of the anomalies created by the inclusions and exclusions among the alphabetical entries. It indicates in what connection authors and themes occur outside articles devoted individually to them, and mediates virtually as much information about, for instance, Valentin Conrart or the Académie française as if individual entries had been devoted to them.

In the centuries to whose literature this volume is devoted, it is often necessary for the reader to be aware of the real and potential power relationships in French society. When the duc d'Anjou died in 1584, the heir presumptive became the Protestant Henri de Navarre, but in 1585 the pope declared him incapable of the succession and absolved his vassals of all allegiance. The whole of the literature of the ensuing decade, most of it produced by those with at least connections at court or with Henri de Navarre, requires for its understanding an awareness of the fragile political situation. After the pope's intervention, it was not as clear as we suppose that Henri de Navarre's claim to the throne outweighed that of his father's younger brother. Later, the literature of the first half of the 17th century can scarcely be read without an awareness that the king's frivolous, licentious, and ambitious brother, Gaston d'Anjou, to become Gaston d'Orléans, was heir presumptive from 1611 to 1638, or that the Condé family's waning political ambitions would be adversely affected by the marriage into which Richelieu calculatedly pushed Gaston. In order to show its importance, specimen information of this sort has been included in the chronology.

The political background simply changes our understanding of the novels of Madeleine de Scudéry, the *Mémoires* of La Rochefoucauld and the work of Retz known by the same title, as the loyalties and betrayals of the Fronde explain much in the texts of Mme de Sévigné and Mme de Lafayette. The general index is intended to make available an exposition of the whole political background, with an account of friendships, allegiances and obligations of honour, relationships to the court, and to the centre of power, Colbert rather than Louis XIV. It is possible that the aristocratic literature of the second half of the 17th century was conditioned more than has been realized by the toppling of the financiers in 1661 and the reduction of patronage to that exercised principally by Colbert. Narrative literary history could scarcely have presented the sort of panoramic view of French literary culture which the *Guide*'s combination of critical analysis, biographical information, and background material made available through the general index has sought to achieve.

The final section of the Introduction has given some indication of where the charts proposed by the *Guide* to help readers understand complex texts with confusing resonances are new. In view, however, of disputes about whether dramatic texts were written for performance or not, and of the way the terms "tragédie," "tragi-comédie," and "comédie-ballet" were actually used, some care has been exercised in giving dates of performance as well as of publication, where either or both were applicable and ascertainable, as well as the author's own description of the genre to which a literary text belongs, "tragédie" or "tragi-comédie," "roman" or "nouvelle." To read the text of a Molière "comédie-ballet" as if it were straight farce or social satire can only lead to bewilderment. *Le Bourgeois Gentilhomme* is not a very good play if there is no music or dancing. More difficult, naturally, is the detection of literary register in a text like that of Mme de Sévigne's *Lettres*, where the spontaneity is not always uncontrived. The portions of the entries devoted to critical analysis pay more attention than may have been expected to the essential question of the literary registers of the major texts. Were La Fontaine or Perrault writing only, or also, or not at all, for children?

The practice of the post-Revolution volume of the *Guide* has been modified in the light of the nature of the material in the present volume. The length of entries more approximately reflects a judgement about the literary importance of the subject although length of treatment has had also to reflect the number and the complexity of the biographical details needed for an understanding of the works. Diderot may have more columns than Rousseau, but he is not the greater author. Background material has more often been isolated in special entries.

During the whole of three centuries religious disputes were so important in the cultural life of France that more attention than might have been expected has been devoted to the precise theological and religious issues which were at stake. Users of the *Guide* interested, for instance, in Pascal may well find that the entries under Saint-Cyran, Port-Royal, Jansenism, and Nicole provide helpful background material, while those interested in Boileau may well find the general index and the entry on the *Querelle des anciens et des modernes* of assistance. The entry on préciosité contains material of relevance for virtually all the major authors of the second half of the 17th century.

The general complexity of the cultural life of France between 1500 and 1800 has throughout exerted pressure to devote space to expounding the background to the major texts at the expense of multiplying entries on individual authors. No literary historian is likely to approve exactly of the balance struck, but regret should be expressed that some poets had to be omitted, Lemaire de Belges, Sponde, and Chassignet in particular; and that room could not be found for des Masures and du Bartas, for more preachers, and above all for the great spiritual directors, Jeanne-Françoise de Chantal, Olier, Surin, and Rancé among others. Bourdaloue is absent only because there is no reliable edition of more than a handful of the sermons; the engaging, prolix, but muddle-headed Jean-Pierre Camus only because in all manner of genres he wrote over 150 works, but none of them well enough to serve as more than illustrations of the sort of thing that others were doing better.

Dates and Discrepancies

In this volume the problems of dating largely concern dramatic texts. Given the custom of challenging with plays on the same subjects as rivals, of parodying plays still successfully running, and the wholesale plundering of plots and even texts which went on, it is sometimes very important to know exact dates. The interpretation of Rabelais's *Gargantua* clearly depends on whether it was published before or after the "placards" of October 1534, and the entries in the *Encyclopédie* can scarcely be understood without reference to the date at which they appeared and what they might have been replying to. Quite precise dates of composition are needed for an understanding of the component parts of what we call the *Satire Ménippée*, and the meaning of the text of *Manon Lescaut* could still change if the currently accepted hypothesis about the date of composition turned out to be wrong.

It is also necessary to know the precise circumstances of publication in order to form a credible view of whether publication in book form was intended or half intended, and whether anonymity or pseudonymity was wholly or partly an affectation. It considerably alters our understanding of Bayle to realize how improbable it was that he wrote the *Avis aux refugiés*. On such matters as much information as possible has been given, although not always in the lists of publications. Mostly the facts were complex enough to warrant treatment in the "works" section of the entry, and occasionally under "life" but, given the exceptional importance in the 17th and 18th centuries of the dates and circumstances of publication, as much detail as possible has always been provided, including notes drawing attention to place names known to be false.

Notes

– Accents are omitted on upper case letters, except in the names of authors at the head of an entry (e.g. HÉROËT)
– Diphthongs are printed as double vowels (e.g. *oeuvre*)
– For the purposes of alphabetical arrangement, the *Guide* follows the usual convention in counting the prefixes "Le," "La," "Les," "Du," and "Des" as the opening part of a name, whether or not they are prefixes, as in "du Bellay," which precedes "Duclos." "De," "d'," "von," and "van" are ignored for purposes of placing within an alphabetical arrangement. Jean de Mairet is therefore placed under "M," but Guillaume du Vair under "D." "De la" is always split, so that the entry for François, duc de la Rochefoucauld appears as "La Rochefoucauld, François, duc de."

A

ALEMBERT, Jean-Baptiste le Rond d', 1717–1783.

Philosophe, mathematician, and scientist.

LIFE

D'Alembert, born in November 1717, was the illegitimate child of the well-known literary hostess, the marquise de Tencin, who abandoned him at birth on the steps of the church of Saint-Jean-le-Rond, near Notre-Dame in Paris. His father was the high-ranking Louis Camus, Chevalier Destouches, married, a lieutenant-général in the artillery, and a friend of Fénelon. He was abroad when the infant was born and never acknowledged paternity, but provided for the child's upkeep and, on his death in 1726, left the nine-year-old boy a modest 1,200 livres a year, having sent him to a boarding school from the age of four and arranged for his education at the Jansenist (q.v.) Collège des Quatre Nations from the age of 12. The foundling is said to have been baptized by a police commissioner, and at the age of about six months was placed with the wife of a glazier, a Mme Rousseau, with whom he was to stay until he was 47. She was astonished by his childhood precocity, but never realized that he had become eminent.

He was enrolled at the Collège under the name of Daremberg and wished to be known as Jean-Baptiste Lerond, but finally accepted the name by which he has become known. He was a brilliant and hard-working pupil, exceptionally good at Greek and Latin, and urged by his masters to take up theology. Under their direction he wrote a commentary on Saint Paul's epistle to the Romans before graduating in 1735, at the normal age of 18. He then studied law for two years, becoming a barrister in 1738. He lived frugally, studied in his room, and scarcely went out except to the theatre. He did not practise as a barrister, but for a while studied medicine, although it soon became clear to him that his real interest lay in mathematics, which he began to study on his own. Some of the theorems he proved had in fact been established earlier and more elegantly, although d'Alembert believed himself to have been their originator.

In 1739 he presented a mathematical paper to the Académie des Sciences, following it later in 1741 with a paper on the refraction of solid bodies and fluid mechanics which won the praise of the celebrated mathematician, Clairaut. In that year he became a member of the Académie des Sciences as "adjoint" in astronomy, rising to "associé géomètre" in 1746, in 1756 to "pensionnaire," in 1765 to "titulaire," and in 1768 to "pensionnaire géomètre." In 1746 he was elected to the Berlin academy, and in 1748 became a member of the Royal Society. After the two early papers, his principal scientific works were the 1743 *Traité de dynamique*, on the physics of motion, but in which he also discussed the degree of probability to be ascribed to accepted truths and developed the principle in dynamics which

has ever since been called after him; the 1744 *Traité de l'équilibre et du mouvement des fluides*; the 1746 *Réflexions sur la cause générale des vents* dedicated to Frederick the Great; the 1747 *Recherches sur les cordes vibrantes*; the 1749 *Recherches sur la précession des équinoxes et sur la mutation de l'axe de la terre*; and in 1751–2 the *Essai sur une nouvelle théorie sur la résistance des fluides*. All belong to the realm of applied mathematics and physics which still came together as mechanics, as do the *Opuscules mathématiques* written between 1761 and 1780. By considering at length the problems posed by two objects of equal mass subject to equal but opposite forces, d'Alembert partly succeeded in reducing problems in dynamics to terms of statics.

D'Alembert was already an established if still promising young scientist when he was first associated with the *Encyclopédie* (q.v.) in December 1745, when payments are recorded to him and to Gua de Malves, before Diderot and d'Alembert were each in February 1746 assigned 1,200 livres from the 18,000 livres put at the disposal of Gua de Malves. It was in 1746 that d'Alembert was introduced into the salon of Mme Geoffrin, which carried on the functions for liberal Paris men of letters previously exercised by that of Mme de Tencin. Artists were received on Mondays and men of letters on Wednesdays. Politics and religion were not discussed. Mme Geoffrin claimed to have discovered d'Alembert, whose gifts for mimicry and parody delighted her, and whom she initiated into the social life of Paris.

By 1748, however, d'Alembert had also come very close to the marquise du Deffand, whom he had met in 1743 when visiting président Hénault, and whom he called on daily. D'Alembert was already the lion of her salon when in 1751 he published the celebrated *Discours préliminaire* to the *Encyclopédie*. In 1754 she succeeded in having him elected to the Académie française, on 28 November, at his third attempt. The duchesse de Chaulnes was campaigning against him for the election of the abbé Trublet, who had by now fallen out with Voltaire and had to wait until 1761. At his reception on 18 December d'Alembert read the *Discours préliminaire*. He was to become the Académie's perpetual secretary from 1772, in succession to Duclos, and to engage in a series of campaigns to have like-minded encyclopédistes elected, including Marmontel, Condillac, Suard, Malesherbes, and Condorcet.

Mme du Deffand was losing her sight, and engaged Julie de Lespinasse, born in 1732, to keep her company and read to her. Julie, like d'Alembert illegitimate, was not totally without money and when, in 1764, she quarrelled with Mme du Deffand, walked out, and started her own salon 100 metres down the road, she was considerably helped by friends and soon came to have about 11,500 livres a year, not enough to make her rich but enough to allow her to spend extravagantly on her wardrobe and keep a staff of four. It was in April 1754 that d'Alembert saw her at Mme du Deffand's. He swiftly fell in love with her and in 1764, when he was 47, moved to the apartment underneath hers, which was on two floors, undertaking secretarial duties for her. In 1765 she nursed d'Alembert through a serious illness, but was herself in love with the Spanish marquis de Mora, born in Saragossa on 19 April 1744, married and commissioned in the army just before his 13th birthday, and at 20 a widower and father of two children. D'Alembert never knew how much Julie loved Mora, and while d'Alembert's love for her was clearly passionate, her feelings for him, to his lasting disappointment, never went beyond those of close friendship. He had written her portrait in 1771 accusing her of frigidity. In 1776 Julie died in d'Alembert's arms begging forgiveness, and he discovered what for only when, as her executor, he found out about her love for Mora, who had died in 1774.

The intimacy of d'Alembert's friendship for Mme du Deffand was already cooling when, in the spring of 1760, Mme du Deffand was spiteful about d'Alembert in a letter to Voltaire, who then wrote in reply. Mme du Deffand had both letters read out to her assembled guests without knowing that d'Alembert was in the room. He laughed the incident off, but was hurt by it, and attempted to get his own back by denouncing to Voltaire what he portrayed as Mme du Deffand's support for Palissot's 1760 play *Les Philosophes*. Voltaire wrote to ask her whether she had really been protecting Palissot, and Mme du Deffand's reply shows that she knew that the trouble had been stirred up by d'Alembert, with whom she then quarrelled. Her final break with Julie de Lespinasse in 1764 was the result of her discovery that, for some years, d'Alembert, sometimes with Marmontel or Turgot and others, had been meeting Julie privately in her upstairs room for an hour or two, before coming down to Mme du Deffand's own salon.

In 1762, and again the following year, d'Alembert turned down an invitation from Frederick the Great to become president of the Berlin academy in succession to Maupertuis, although he was granted a small pension, and did spend a few weeks at Potsdam in 1763. He also declined an invitation in 1762 from Catherine II to become tutor to her son, the czarevitch Paolo, at a salary of 100,000 livres, with an invitation to bring as many of his friends as he wished to be accommodated at the Russian court, but he was none the less in 1764 made a member of the Saint Petersburg academy of science. He was also made a member of the Bologna academy. David Hume was to leave him a legacy of £200. D'Alembert's only other recorded journey was in 1756, when he spent a fateful six weeks with Voltaire at Les Délices, of which the result was the very long article on Geneva in volume seven of the *Encyclopédie*, which gave too much prominence to too many of Voltaire's own propagandist views, and eventually led to d'Alembert's withdrawal from the enterprise.

D'Alembert's initial association with the project for the *Encyclopédie* dates from 1745, and he appears at first to have been subordinate to Gua de Malves, but to have had a first appointment senior, and certainly by a few weeks prior, to Diderot's. It may have been through Gua de Malves, who would have known d'Alembert from the Académie des Sciences, that d'Alembert first met the virtually unknown Diderot. We do not know the precise circumstances of Gua de Malves's withdrawal from the editorship, but he formally resigned on 3 August 1747 and d'Alembert signed a contract on 16 October to edit the work jointly with Diderot, both of them to receive 144 livres a month,

although Diderot's payments were to go on for over three years and d'Alembert's for just under a year and a half, and Diderot's were to be supplemented by a lump sum on the appearance of the first volume. D'Alembert was later to gloss over the plain seniority for Diderot implied in these arrangements, and Diderot had begun to mistrust d'Alembert by the mid-1750s, although d'Alembert, in addition to the *Discours préliminaire*, contributed a new prefatory manifesto to the third volume, which appeared late in 1753.

D'Alembert often acted as though he were in charge of the project, and the fact that he thought of himself in that light is obvious from his letters to Voltaire, with whom his friendship was intimate from the end of 1752. Diderot meanwhile regarded him as responsible merely for the entries on mathematical and related topics, as already seemed to have been envisaged in the prospectus, delayed by Diderot's imprisonment at Vincennes in 1749 but issued in November 1750, limiting d'Alembert's responsibilities by mentioning him only "quant à la partie mathématique (with regard to the mathematical portion)" of the work. D'Alembert not only contributed some 450 articles in all, including "Collèges," attacking the Jesuits, in volume 3, and "Convulsionnaires," attacking the Jansenists, in volume 4, but he was also responsible, on account of his standing in the scientific world, for securing the collaboration of some of the better-known contributors.

For volume 7, however, published in October 1757, along with the article on geometry, and one on probability entitled "Gageure" and later much attacked, d'Alembert wrote his fateful article on Geneva, heavily influenced by his six-week stay at Les Délices with Voltaire in 1756. The article was inordinately long, four double-column pages against three fifths of a column for England and just over a column for Spain. It was aggressively tactless, and very nearly caused a diplomatic incident by managing to praise the Genevan church for reducing Christianity to a system different from deism only in its admiration for Christ, so alienating the whole spectrum of religious opinion from devout Catholic to severe Calvinist. Grimm immediately realized that the article was a mistake.

It advocated for a whole column the establishment of a theatre in Geneva, so venting a particular grievance of Voltaire and giving rise to Rousseau's famous attack in the 1758 *Lettre à d'Alembert sur les spectacles*, which brought about the final rupture between Rousseau and Voltaire. Reaction at Geneva was intense enough to lead to the formation of a committee to obtain a retractation, but Diderot merely dissociated himself from d'Alembert's views, virtually disowning them in letters to Tronchin. By January 1758 d'Alembert had announced his intention of withdrawing from the *Encyclopédie*, obviously supposing that the project would therefore collapse. Voltaire now urged everyone to withdraw, and Rousseau urged Diderot to withdraw if d'Alembert did. In fact Turgot, Marmontel, and Duclos did withdraw with d'Alembert, and it is almost certain that the further difficulties placed in the path of the undertaking arose from the article on Geneva. Diderot felt that d'Alembert had "deserted" when he did withdraw, after hesitating, partly for financial reasons, until the middle of 1758. D'Alembert did, however, continue to defend the aims of the *Encyclopédie*, and to contribute technical articles. Diderot's *Rêve de d'Alembert* was not in any sense intended for d'Alembert, and it was not written for publication.

Sometimes personally and sometimes together with the philosophe (q.v.) movement generally, d'Alembert was attacked in a series of anonymous pamphlets, in Moreau's 1757 *Nouveau Mémoire pour servir à l'histoire des Cacouacs*, in a series of ironic *Petites lettres sur de grands philosophes*, by the Jesuit *Journal de Trévoux*, and in the general defence of its value and belief by the church party. D'Alembert himself triumphed when, after the Jesuits had been suppressed as an order in France in November 1764 by the king, heavily supported by the Jansenist parlement, in the wake of the bankruptcies following the speculations of Père La Valette, their superior in Martinique, and their refusal to accept Choiseul's compromise in their constitutional arrangements, he could publish his anonymous 1765 *Mémoire sur la destruction des Jésuites*. D'Alembert continued to publish scientific and mathematical works, but his interests veered to philosophy and literature.

As early as 1753 he had published his *Essai sur la société des gens de lettres avec les grands*, on the need of writers for independence and the evils of the system of patronage. He translated parts of Tacitus, and in 1759 brought out his *Essai sur les éléments de philosophie ou sur les principes des connaissances humaines*, containing important "éclaircissements." In 1764 appeared his final set of *Mélanges de philosophie, d'histoire et de littérature*, to which he had continually added since the original 1753 version, and of which four volumes had been published in 1759. Inspired by the example of Fontenelle's work as secretary of the Académie des Sciences, d'Alembert wrote brief accounts of the lives and works of the 80 members of the Académie française who had died between 1700 and 1770. He also developed Rameau's musical system in the 1752 *Eléments de musique théorique et pratique*.

D'Alembert came to be looked on as the leader of the philosophe movement after the death of Voltaire in 1778. His frugality of life was dictated more by taste than by lack of means, although he occasionally felt financial constraints. He managed to support his foster-mother, Mme Rousseau, in her old age, and helped a number of young students to complete their studies. He had a reputation for combining malice of tongue with benevolence of heart, and delicacy with plain speaking. After Julie de Lespinasse's death, d'Alembert frequented the salons of Mme Helvétius and Mme Necker, as well as that of Condorcet's beautiful young wife. He himself received three times a week. He died in Paris on 29 October 1783.

WORKS

Apart from the papers read at the Académie des Sciences or at the Académie française, the correspondence, and the collections of éloges and essays, d'Alembert's writing was mostly confined to such occasional pieces as the entries for the *Encyclopédie*. The essence of his scientific method and his philosophical thought is contained in the single work for which, apart from the article on Geneva for the seventh volume of the *Encyclopédie*, he is remembered, the *Discours préliminaire* published in front of the first volume on 28 June 1751. It is in three parts, of which the third is the prospectus drawn up by Diderot, incorporated, at d'Alembert's own insistence, into the whole. The first part is devoted to "la généalogie des sciences (the genealogy of the sciences)" which d'Alembert stressed in his 1759 "avertissement," had nothing to do with the ordering of the sciences according to their logical relationships with one another, what the ancient

world and then the renaissance knew as "the circle of the disciplines." The second part concerned "l'histoire philosophique des progrès de l'esprit humain depuis la renaissance des lettres (the philosophical history of the progress of the human mind from the renaissance of letters)."

The original 1751 text, however modified by the 1759 avertissement, did envisage expounding in the first part as far as possible "l'ordre et enchaînement des connaissances humaines (the order and connections of the types of human knowledge)." The formulation is important because, although d'Alembert goes on to substitute Leibnizian for Cartesian and Newtonian mechanics, the idea of a logical ordering of the disciplines was Descartes's leading inspiration. It came from antiquity, notably Quintilian and Martianus Capella, and was taken up by Lull, and then such 16th-century authors as Budé, Melanchthon, Pierre de la Ramée, and Jacques Peletier du Mans. The term "encyclopédie" is used by Rabelais, and in French, Latin or Greek it appears in Budé, Nizolio, Pontus de Tyard, Vitruvius, Gyraldi, and Guy Le Fèvre de la Boderie. The idea of reorganizing the disciplines had been everywhere in the renaissance, and culminated in the huge philosophical effort of Descartes. Earlier than Amyot, who avoided the word when translating Plutarch, it had for a short time been modish to refer to the original Greek notion of the circle of the disciplines, what Budé calls the encyclopedia. D'Alembert distinguished between the *Encyclopédie*'s desire to indicate the general principles which form the basis of each of the disciplines, including the liberal and mechanical arts, and the intention to deal with the most essential details of the content of each. The two parts of the *Discours*, as expounded at its opening, would be devoted respectively to the encyclopedic aspect, of foundations and logical connections, and to the catalogue of disciplines, arts, and trades.

In fact d'Alembert immediately refuses to keep distinct the historical development of the disciplines and their intrinsic connections. In spite of the theorizing, the *Encyclopédie* was conceived more as a guide to factual, theoretical, and practical knowledge than as an attempt to demonstrate, as Descartes had attempted to demonstrate, the interconnection of the disciplines.

Pour peu qu'on ait réfléchi sur la liaison que les découvertes ont entre elles, il est facile d'apercevoir que les sciences et les arts se prêtent mutuellement des secours, et qu'il y a par conséquent une chaîne qui les unit. Mais s'il est souvent difficile de réduire à un petit nombre de règles ou de notions générales, chaque science ou chaque art en particulier, il ne l'est pas moins de renfermer dans un système qui soit un, les branches infiniment variées de la science humaine.

Le premier pas que nous ayons à faire dans cette recherche, est d'examiner, qu'on nous permette ce terme, la généalogie et la filiation de nos connaissances, les causes qui ont dû les faire naître et les caractères qui les distinguent; en un mot, de remonter jusqu'à l'origine et à la génération de nos idées

(One has only to have reflected on the connections which discoveries have with one another, and it is easy to see that the sciences and the arts assist one another, and that consequently they are linked together by a chain. But just as it is often difficult to reduce each individual science or art to a small number of general rules or ideas, so it is not less difficult to enclose in a unified system the infinitely varied branches of human knowledge.

The first step we have to take in this quest is to examine, if we may be allowed to use the term, the genealogy and filiation of our forms of knowledge, the causes which gave them birth and the characteristics which distinguish them; in a word, to go back to the origin and the formation of our ideas).

The accent is to be put, not on the renaissance and Cartesian need to organize the disciplines in the light of their logical dependence on one another, already by the mid-18th century obviously impossible, but on a general historical introduction to the advance of the human mind towards the arts and the theoretical and practical sciences to which the *Encyclopédie* will be the guide.

D'Alembert now launches straight into an attack on innate ideas, which were still sometimes accepted "tant la vérité a de peine à reprendre sa place quand les préjugés ou le sophisme l'en ont chassé (so hard is it for truth to regain its position when prejudice or sophistry have driven it out)." D'Alembert argues that our knowledge must come through our senses, as the scholastics had thought. But by the late 18th century it was impossible philosophically to defend the soul's immortality in the way the Aristotelian scholastics had done, if all knowledge depended on the senses. What it is difficult to know is how explicitly d'Alembert was adverting to that fact, especially since his argument goes on much as had that of Descartes, establishing the initial certainty about the existence of the self, however, not on self-awareness, but on sensation. The argument runs almost in parallel with that of Descartes in its attempt at least to establish sensation as the basis for our knowledge of ourselves, of the external world, and of others, although this is not a metaphysical treatise, and none of the difficulties is squarely confronted.

As is no doubt to be expected in what is a manifesto at the outset of so vast an undertaking as the *Encyclopédie*, d'Alembert affirms more than he argues, and he dismisses the need for argument almost impatiently. "C'est aux philosophes de juger… Pour me renfermer dans mon sujet… (It is for the philosophers to judge… To keep myself to my own subject…)," D'Alembert argues his ethical values from "l'agrément et l'avantage (the pleasure and the advantage)." From the existence of other people the need for an ethic is immediately apparent. Not everyone can draw the same advantages from the community, although all have the same right to them. D'Alembert now follows with the much-criticized statement which, he later claimed, had been misunderstood:

Un droit si légitime est donc bientôt enfreint par ce droit barbare d'inégalité, appelé loi du plus fort, dont l'usage semble nous confondre avec les animaux, et dont il est pourtant si difficile de ne pas abuser

(So legitimate a right is therefore soon curtailed by the barbaric right of inequality, called the law of the strongest, whose adoption seems to put us among the animals, and which it is none the less so difficult not to abuse).

The argument was about whether d'Alembert had regarded inequality itself, or merely recourse to the law of the strongest, as barbaric.

In a prefatory manifesto of this sort it was clearly necessary to tread with care and, although the passage to follow was probably not intended to be especially provocative, there is a clear implication that the principal truths of religion and morals depend on sensation before they depend on revelation. It is almost certain that the full consequences of d'Alembert's position were not intended to be immediately obvious when he wrote

Il est donc évident que les notions purement intellectuelles du vice et de la vertu, le principe et la nécessité des lois, la spiritualité de l'âme, l'existence de Dieu et nos devoirs envers lui, en un mot les vérités dont nous avons le besoin le plus prompt et le plus indispensable, sont le fruit des premières idées réfléchies que nos sensations occasionnent

(It is therefore obvious that the purely intellectual concepts of vice and virtue, the principle of and the need for laws, the spiritual nature of the soul, the existence of God and our duties towards him, in a word the truths we need most immediately and most indispensably, are the fruit of our first reflective ideas occasioned by our sensations).

The undertow of deep scepticism set up by the reverberating implications of passages like that were not instantly obvious, but religious truth was being down-graded in favour of instinctive and natural drives, abilities, and processes. The wide-eyed innocence of tone in what is an apparently innocuous summary of accepted but perfectly orthodox modern thinking is disarming, and the reader in search of what, in the modern English sense, an encyclopedia might be expected to contain, would not complain of having been subjected to anything exceptionable. Elsewhere we are told of the absolute need for a revealed religion, but again the restrictions, while apparently innocuous, are deeply subversive: "elle se borne à ce qu'il nous est absolument nécessaire de connaître ([revealed religion] is limited to what it is absolutely necessary for us to know)." There is a great deal in Scripture which no one pretended it was absolutely necessary for us to know.

We know that d'Alembert pitched his register just about where he wanted it to be. Those with noses professionally cultivated to sniff out irreligion would certainly find what was there, as they did, but d'Alembert would be able to say that he had not actually written anything irreligious, as he, too, did. After all, there was nothing he could not defend as obvious, even platitudinous, in the text just quoted, and the dependence on perception was anyway in accordance with the scholastic doctrine that man's knowledge depends on his senses. The devout party was not going to allow itself to be pinned into a defence of innate ideas and Descartes, the dangers of whose reliance on reason had by the mid-18th century become clear, as had the vulnerability of his whole epistemology and his non-empirical approach to scientific investigation. The subversive potential of the *Discours préliminaire* comes almost entirely from the all-pervading tone and the assumptions rather than from any particular statement which is made.

It would not be surprising if d'Alembert, like Diderot, Grimm, and Voltaire, later came to think that the Geneva article had become over-confident, and gone too far in allowing what was at best a latent deism to emerge into the light of day. Confronted as the encyclopédistes were, after the article's publication, with the choice between producing a circumspect catalogue of what was known within the arts and sciences, but without religious innuendoes, and abandoning the enterprise altogether, two views did in fact emerge. Diderot wanted to finish his encyclopedia. D'Alembert, for whom subversion had had a higher position in the hierarchy of aims, preferred to give up, or at any rate stick to mathematics, as he thereafter did.

The art and interest of the *Discours préliminaire* lies almost wholly in the tone. Few of its paragraphs yield their meaning at first reading; the direction of the argument is never very clear; there are digressions and lyrical interpolations; the language is so lofty as to touch a level of generality at which it sounds impressive but says almost nothing; d'Alembert manages to convey the perfectly accurate impression that he is writing about one thing, in fact the supremacy of science and empirical investigation, while pretending to write about another, the way the branches of knowledge arose and fit together. The statements are given the appearance of logical flow, but the lyrical buoyancy with which the sublimity of astronomy is proclaimed carries, if analysed, the unmistakable innuendo that the mysteries of the universe are better solved by geometry and mechanics than by recourse to *Genesis*.

The first part of the *Discours* purports to be cautious in its assumptions, and does indeed work towards a description of the concerns of the individual disciplines and an introduction to the way in which the work intends to reconcile the encyclopedic with the alphabetical order. The branches of knowledge are divided according to the faculties of the soul on which they depend—memory, reason, and imagination. D'Alembert here draws on a whole variety of earlier classifications, deriving chiefly from the Spanish physician Huarte, but with all sorts of subsequent channels of transmission possible, notably including Bacon and Pascal. The second part of the *Discours* is quite different in tone, clearer, concerned now to show the progress of the human race, and to warn the theologians off the territory of the empirical sciences. There is a eulogy of Bacon, and the general tone is strongly reminiscent of that portion of Voltaire's *Lettres philosophiques* dealing with English philosophers. Almost all the statements are too summary to be accurate and, as in Voltaire, gross exaggeration is built into the style. Descartes is praised for having thrown off the principle of authority in philosophy.

On the whole the *Discours préliminaire* was a smoke-screen, a philosophical statement necessarily camouflaged in high-sounding language, but which insinuated rather than stated its real content. Its function as an introduction to the *Encyclopédie* was fulfilled by incorporating into it as its third part Diderot's prospectus. Its own lofty generalizations, put into obscure long sentences in sometimes convoluted syntax, announced something of great importance, but it is impossible to infer from it more than a little of the philosophy which, when he wrote the *Discours*, d'Alembert himself only hoped the *Encyclopédie* might contain.

PUBLICATIONS

Collections

Mélanges de littérature, d'histoire et de philosophie, vols. 1–4, 1759, vol. 5, 1767

Opuscules mathématiques, 8 vols., 1761–80
Oeuvres posthumes, 2 vols., 1799
Oeuvres philosophiques, historiques et littéraires, 18 vols., 1805
Oeuvres, 5 vols., 1821–22
Oeuvres et correspondance inédites, 1887

Scientific works

Traité de dynamique, 1743
Traité de l'équilibre et du mouvement des fluides, 1744
Réflexions sur la cause générale des vents, 1746
Recherches sur les cordes vibrantes, 1747
Recherches sur la précession des équinoxes et sur la mutation de l'axe de la terre, 1749
Essai sur une nouvelle théorie sur la résistance des fluides, 1751–52
Recherches sur différents points importants du système du monde, 3 vols., 1754–65
Opuscules mathématiques, 8 vols., 1761–80
Mémoire sur la théorie mathématique de l'inoculation, 1761

Other

Discours préliminaire de l'"Encyclopédie", 1751; modern edition 1965; English translation 1912
Eléments de musique théorique et pratique suivants les principes de M Rameau, 1752
Essai sur la société des gens de lettres avec les grands, 1753
Mélanges de littérature, d'histoire et de philosophie, 1753; 4 vols., 1759, vol. 5, 1767; English translation of 1759 edition, 1764
Sur la destruction de Jésuites en France, 1765; English translation 1866
Histoire des membres de l'Académie française, morts depuis 1700 jusqu'à 1770, 6 vols., 1779; as *Select Eulogies*, 2 vols., 1699

Biographical and critical studies

Grimsley, R., *Jean D'Alembert*, [in English] 1963
Briggs, J.M. jr., *D'Alembert: philosophy and mechanics in the 18th Century*, 1964

ALENÇON, Marguerite d': see **MARGUERITE D'ANGOULÊME**

ANGOULÊME, Marguerite d': see MARGUERITE D'ANGOULÊME

AUBIGNÉ, Théodore Agrippa d', 1552–1630.

Poet and historian.

LIFE

D'Aubigné's father, Jean, seigneur de Brie, came from a Protestant family and married the poet's mother, Catherine de l'Estang, dame des Landes-Guinemer, whose family were Catholic, on 2 June 1550. She died giving birth to d'Aubigné on 8 February 1552. She had a reputation for learning, and her son inherited from her a Greek text of Saint Basil which she had annotated. In 1553 his father married Anne de Limur, who had Agrippa, said to be so-called from the Latin for "aegre partus (born with bitterness)", brought up by his cousin Michelle Joly, daughter of his father's sister and wife of Aubin d'Abbeville, at Archiac, and then near Pons, in the château of Antoinette d'Albret, wife of the guardian of the future Henri IV. D'Aubigné says that his father chose to save his life rather than his mother's, and that his step-mother found the manner in which his father was rearing him too expensive. Most of the early biography derives essentially from d'Aubigné's own *Sa Vie à ses enfants*, unpublished during his lifetime. The first reasonably reliable edition, based on a manuscript of the *Mémoires* which was plainly defective and which was subsequently destroyed in the 1871 Louvre fire, dates only from 1854.

Since he had become the best-known military figure on the Protestant side during the religious wars and his biographers have had to rely on his own memoirs, accounts of d'Aubigné's life and deeds have become contaminated with a considerable mythology. D'Aubigné tells us that his father had the Protestant Jean Cottin brought back from exile to be his tutor, and that he was harsh. In fact Cottin later went mad and in 1569 was condemned to be burnt by the Rouen parlement. The best modern biography simply repeats d'Aubigné's claim that at six he could read Latin, Greek, and Hebrew, and that at seven and a half he was translating Plato's *Crito*, without mentioning that we have only his word for it. D'Aubigné admits to having had "a little help" with the Plato, and says his father promised to have it published. He also claims when he was six to have had a vision of a white-robed woman who came into the room, opened the curtains, and kissed him coldly.

More probable is the account of a journey to Paris with his father and a score of horsemen in 1560, when d'Aubigné was eight and a half. They passed through Amboise during the fair, and d'Aubigné's father could still recognize the heads of his colleagues, some of whom had been beheaded, and others hanged or drowned in the Loire, after the failed "conjuration" in March to topple the Guise family from power. D'Aubigné says that his father caused a disturbance, and putting his hand to his head told the child that he would not spare it until the deaths had been avenged, and that he would curse d'Aubigné if he spared his own head.

In 1561 the Colloque de Poissy between Catholics led by the cardinal de Lorraine and Protestants led by Théodore de Bèze was held at the instigation of the chancellor Michel de l'Hôpital, and in January 1562 an edict allowed Protestant freedom of worship outside city walls. In March at Wassy the duc de Guise and his men heard Protestants singing hymns in a barn, and attacked them, killing 650 and wounding another 200. In April d'Aubigné was sent to Paris to study with the eminent Hebraist Matthieu Béroalde. On 2 April Condé, at the head of a Huguenot army, had taken Orléans, heralding the outbreak of the first War of Religion, and on 26 and 27 May the Huguenots were expelled from Paris.

D'Aubigné accompanied Béroalde's small party which was waylaid and robbed by a band under capitaine d'Achon, a Catholic later to be taken prisoner at Dreux, and then held captive by d'Aubigné's father at Orléans. D'Aubigné himself gives an extraordinarily colourful account of the incident. He tells of condemnations to burning, of having a horror of the Mass greater than that of death by fire, of dancing, violins, the inquisitor, supper, the executioner, prayers, kisses, extortion, and a guide to take them at midnight to the road to Montargis, less only the 180 livres they had had hidden in their shoes and their valuables, including the 10-year-old d'Aubigné's silver-handled sword and silver-buckled belt. They were received at Montargis by Renée de France, the duchess of Ferrara, who had retired there in 1560. D'Aubigné says she sat him down beside her for three days to hear "ses jeunes discours sur le mespris de la mort (his youthful reflections on contempt for death)." Then, after a month at Gien, the party arrived at Orléans, where d'Aubigné's father was second-in-command. He had them lodged in the house of the L'Estoile family, whose son Pierre, author of the famous diary, had been a pupil of Béroalde.

D'Aubigné was ill with the plague, which killed, he says, 30,000 people in Orléans, including the doctor and Béroalde's wife. At the end of June Catherine de Medici had had a series of meetings with Condé, but they failed, and on 20 September 1562 Condé concluded the treaty of Hampton Court with Elizabeth of England, who was to invade France and hold the Normandy ports. On 19 December the Catholic army was victorious over the Huguenots at the battle of Dreux, at which Condé was taken prisoner by the Catholics and Montmorency by the Huguenots. The Huguenots also lost Rouen, where Antoine de Bourbon, duc de Vendôme, king of Navarre by virtue of his marriage to Jeanne d'Albret and father of Henri IV, was mortally wounded fighting on the Catholic side. A Bourbon, he had been made lieutenant-general of France by Catherine de Medici. Regent from the accession of her second son, Charles IX, Catherine had hoped, by promoting the converted king of Navarre and by releasing from captivity his brother, the Protestant Louis de Bourbon, prince de Condé, to counter-balance the power of the unpopular Catholic Guise family from Lorraine.

D'Aubigné now recounts a picturesque episode in which he is reprehended by his father for neglecting his studies, but by January 1563 he was helping to defend Orléans against the Catholic siege. In February François, duc de Guise, was assassinated by Poltrot de Méré, and on 12 March the Paix d'Amboise returned Orléans to the king. An edict of 19 March took back some of the liberties accorded to the Protestants in January 1562. D'Aubigné's father, one of the negotiators of the peace, had been given the judicial office of maître des requêtes, but was to die at Amboise later that year of an infection in a wound received during the siege. Before he died he reminded d'Aubigné of what he had said at Amboise in 1560, recommending to his son zeal in religion, love of knowledge, and loyalty in friendship. D'Aubigné notes that he had to renounce the income his father had left on account of his father's debts, but that he was kept on the inheritance from his mother.

Aubin d'Abbeville left him for another year with Béroalde before sending him to Geneva at the age of 13 when, d'Aubigné proudly writes, he could read unpointed Hebrew texts, that is texts without any printed indication of the vowels. D'Aubigné was still indignant that his academic skills were underestimated at Geneva, where, he says, in spite of Bèze's indulgence, his other teachers ill-treated him. He says he remained two years in Geneva before, without telling his family, he went off to Lyons. In fact the Genevan records show that a 15-year-old Italian was condemned in May 1566 to be drowned in the Rhône for attempted sodomy with d'Aubigné and another co-pupil at the college. Both victims were subjected to long interrogations, and it must have been some consequence of that experience which drove d'Aubigné to depart abruptly and secretively, although it may not have been until the end of the year. In Lyons he worked at mathematics and magic with an adventurer, Loys d'Arza, he says for nine months, until he ran out of money. He tells us that he was on the point of suicide when he met the messenger with money for him on the way to Geneva.

To his annoyance, his guardian kept him at his books during the second religious war of 1567–68. At the start of the third war in September 1568 d'Aubigné, who says his clothes were removed from him every night, escaped through the window in his night-shirt to join a band of companions, and was finally allowed by a captain to join a group of soldiers. They overcame a small company of Catholics, and d'Aubigné bagged an arquebus, but refused to take clothes. His colourfully telescoped account of the whole campaign includes moments of very sharp focus in a great blur of military impressions. It recounts vividly his defeat of family efforts to retrieve him. D'Aubigné was obviously a venturesome youth. In his maturity he was a memorialist of outstanding ability. The verve and skill of his fictionalized autobiographical narrative already put him very high in the ranks of authors of narrative fiction.

He fought at the sieges of Angoulême and Pons, was present at Jarnac, where Condé was killed, and fought again at La Roche-Abeille in his old age, when he wrote *Sa Vie à ses enfants* plainly still relishing the sheer vigour of his undiscriminating commitment to physical violence, although now aware of the moral shortcomings it entailed. He was seriously ill in 1570. He recalls at 70 that at 18 he had already regretted his failure to punish a soldier under his command who had needlessly killed an elderly peasant. His account of the third war is in fact understated, and he was, in view of the risk he ran and the haphazard prospects of his survival, not surprisingly thought to have perished. On even the most sober interpretation of the story of his youth, the antecedent chances of his getting through it alive were remote. On one occasion he was one of five survivors out of a troop of 80. Since Jarnac and La Roche-Abeille, he had distinguished himself at Archiac, Cognac, and Pons. By 8 August 1570, when the peace of Saint-Germain was signed, he was an ensign in the first company of the regiment of Asnières, who had captained the troop which d'Aubigné had first joined in September 1568. Protestants were admitted to public office, and given the four towns of La Rochelle, Cognac, Montauban, and La Charité. Marguerite de Valois, daughter of Catherine de Medici, was to marry Henri de Navarre.

D'Aubigné, now aged 18, had to fight a court case against cousins to win back possession of the property left to him by his mother. His account of that incident in *Sa Vie à ses enfants* has the same fundamentally histrionic properties as the most boldly conceived passages in *Les Tragiques*. It is so dramatically heightened in colour as to communicate wryness as he looked back from old age. Having got his hands on his scant wealth, he baldly writes, he fell in love with Diane de Salviati. She was the niece of Ronsard's Cassandre. That made him want to write verse, he tells us just as simply, so he composed *Le Printemps*. In 1572 he was given a commission as captain in the army raised by Coligny in support of the Prince of Orange, but he could not gather his company together in time. He was in Paris for the wedding of Henri de Navarre with Marguerite de Valois on 18 August, and wounded a serjeant who tried to stop him from seconding a friend in a duel. He fled Paris on that account just three days before the St Bartholomew's Day massacre on 24 August.

Only Sancerre and La Rochelle were now firm centres of Protestant resistance, and d'Aubigné, having sent men to Sancerre, had not the means himself to get to La Rochelle. He did, however, think his father had left him papers linking the disgraced ex-chancellor, Michel de l'Hôpital, to the Amboise conspiracy, and Diane's father, the Sieur de Talcy, offered to get them redeemed for 30,000 livres. D'Aubigné says he burnt them to avoid the temptation of using them for blackmail—"I burnt them for fear that they would burn me"—and this gesture impelled Diane's father to offer him his daughter's hand. The flattering light in which d'Aubigné shows himself in this passage awakes suspicion, as does the inherent improbability of Michel de l'Hôpital's involvement in the Amboise conspiracy, but the episode can scarcely have been simply made up. D'Aubigné may of course have been mistaken about what the papers proved.

Within days he claims that he was nearly killed again in an incident in which he ran after an assailant with a sword snatched from a kitchen boy and in slippers, which shows him to have been impetuous to the point of foolhardiness. He thought he was dying, got back to Talcy, and was looked after by Diane. His mother's family, who had attempted to take his estates, now tried to have him arrested. D'Aubigné tells us that he forced the arresting procurator at pistol point to renounce his Catholicism, and that Diane's uncle, the Chevalier de Salviati, broke off his relationship with Diane on grounds of poverty and religion. The probability is that the unfaithful Diane, of whose inconstancy d'Aubigné complains in *Le Printemps*, herself initiated the rupture, and that d'Aubigné is tardily refusing in his memoirs to accuse her of infidelity. The most poignant parts of *Le Printemps* were written after the break, which left d'Aubigné exhausted and ill.

La Rochelle fell on 26 June 1573. In July the edict of Boulogne allowed liberty of conscience to Protestants, but public Protestant services only in some towns, and on 19 August Sancerre fell. D'Aubigné was called to court to join the suite of Henri de Navarre for the festivities in honour of the Polish mission, which had come officially to offer the Polish crown to the duc d'Anjou. Anjou was later to become Henri III of France. His brother, François de Valois, was to succeed to the Anjou title. In the early part of 1574 d'Aubigné, loyal to the now Catholic Henri de Navarre, was sent by him in the interest of furthering any possible conciliation to fight in the Catholic royal army with Guillaume de Hautemer, seigneur de Fervacques. Fervacques was Matignon's principal lieutenant and notoriously the lover of the widow of François de Carnavalet (a corruption of Kern-venoy), a circumstance which was later the subject of a serious quarrel, however picturesquely narrated, between Fervacques and d'Aubigné. There are signs of understandable embarrass-ment as d'Aubigné recounts this part of his story. He did not take an oath in the Catholic army, and tried to negotiate with the Huguenot captain, Montgomery. Montgomery had been the cause of the accidental death of Henri II in the 1559 tournament, and this was ultimately the reason, in spite of the safety he had been promised, for his trial and execution at the instigation of Catherine de Medici, the widow of Henri II and mother of Henri III, after the defeat on 25 May 1574 of the Huguenot troops in Normandy.

In the early part of 1574 at least two plots for the escape from court of Henri de Navarre and François de Valois, the fourth son of Henri II and Catherine and still duc d'Alençon, were foiled. Two conspirators, La Môle, the lover of Marguerite, daughter of Catherine de Medici and wife of Henri de Navarre, and Concon-nato, were tortured and beheaded. Montmorency and Cossé were sent to the Bastille for complicity. By the date of the death of Charles IX, on 30 May 1574, d'Aubigné was back in Paris, although he was still fighting with the Catholic troops under Guise at Dormans on 10 October 1575 against Catherine's fourth son, now duc d'Anjou, who had finally succeeded in escaping from court on 15 September 1575. On 4 February 1576 Henri de Navarre, aided by Jean de Beaumanoir, marquis de Lavardin, d'Aubigné, and Fervacques, escaped while hunting at Senlis and returned to captain the Huguenot troops again at Alençon, which he reached in time to attend the Sunday service on 5 February. Navarre's personal property was sent after him and no attempt was made to bring him back. In June he abjured Catholicism at Niort.

From this point on, d'Aubigné remained Henri de Navarre's trusted friend and follower until, as Henri IV, he abjured Protes-tantism at Saint-Denis on 25 July 1593. D'Aubigné's life, *Les Tragiques*, and his prose, all show him to have had more military virtues than courtly ones, in spite of the attractions courtly life had once briefly held for him. He was loyal, brave, frank, and impetuous, but he also had a vivid imagination, a gift for seeing everything in strong primary colours, without subtleties or half-tints, and for simplifying issues. He was quarrelsome, vigorous, ardent, and obstinate. His religion, like his heart, was simple, passionate, and massively honest. It is characteristic of his bluff forthrightness that when, after a particularly bitter quarrel with Henri de Navarre late in 1586, he wondered whether to desert him for the Catholic side, he should have read Catholic apolo-getic literature, notably, but not only, Campion and Bellarmine, both of whom were Jesuits. He was prepared to give himself as wholeheartedly to the Catholic cause as he had to the Protestant, but decided that there were no intellectual grounds for changing sides, and in due course patched up the quarrel with Henri de Navarre and resumed his military commitment to the Huguenot struggle. His tastes were plain, and if his attitudes were histri-onic or boastful and his behaviour apt to be coarse, he could also be chivalrous, although never obsequious. Indeed, he was proud of his independence, and could mistake stubbornness for honesty.

He was not shocked by cruelty. His plain, strong Protestant-ism suited his taste for the dramatic, and he needed its awe-somely unbending moral constraints to keep his passionate temperament in check. He says that he admired Campion's elo-

quence and Bellarmine's method and openness, but it is doubtful whether his mind was pliable or resilient enough to be impressed by the theological sophistication of either. When he did put theological considerations down on paper he always reduced to simple issues what were often complex problems. He preferred the straightforward biblical simplicity of Calvinist spirituality. It did not shock him that whole companies or even populations were put to the sword, or that death was an ordinary penalty for failure. His quest for military distinction was remorseless. He was never squeamish. It is important for an understanding of d'Aubigné's literary output that we should not think of him either as inhibited by evangelical scruple or as incapable of repentance. His literary imagination was the prod-uct of a hugely energetic temperament constrained by firmly uncompromising moral intransigence.

D'Aubigné's own account of his life is too dramatized to serve as the basis of a biographical summary. It does not ade-quately convey the style of his domestic life: half gentleman and half farmer, he was as comfortable sleeping on straw in a barn with the dogs as sitting at the head of the table of a seigneurial household. Henri de Navarre sent him on a number of missions. On 6 December 1576, reporting on Catholic troop concentra-tions in the north, he was at Blois for the opening of the Estates. There only a swift change of clothes and prompt flight saved him from arrest, and he composed a speech in favour of the peace sought by the ordinary citizenry, while the nobility and the clergy wanted first of all religious unity, which meant war.

A month later, in January 1577 at Marmande, d'Aubigné and La Noue, with 15 horsemen, charged into a company of 600 troops. On 23 January he was the first to try to scale the wall of Saint-Macaire and was hit by fire from an arquebus. He quite expected death, and seems almost to have taken unnecessary risks involving its possibility. Then in April he was sent to Péze-nas to find out whether Montmorency Damville, the governor of Languedoc and Catholic ally of Henri de Navarre, was trying to negotiate a separate peace with Henri III. He discovered that among the Catholic captains of Henri de Navarre were several who could not be relied on, including Lavardin. By talking too freely about what he had discovered he caused sufficient bitter-ness among Henri's captains to incur his own disgrace. Several attempts were made on his life and he was again severely wounded fighting before he retired to the governorship of Casteljaloux, west of Agen, in June 1577.

It was in 1577 that d'Aubigné began to compose *Les Tragiques*. The peace of Bergerac of 17 September 1577 had ended hostilities for the moment, and d'Aubigné left the service of Henri de Navarre, with whom he was in temporary disgrace, intending to enter that of John Casimir, the Calvinist son of Fre-derick III, the elector palatine, who had raised troops to fight in France with the Huguenots. On the way home he met Suzanne de Lezay, later to become his wife, and although he still con-spired in the Huguenot interest, he remained at home, wrote a long elegy turning his back on life at court, and spent a year at Landes-Guinemer writing *Les Tragiques*. He was called back by Henri de Navarre for discussions with Catherine de Medici in February 1579, and that October joined two other Protestant nobles, Prinçay and du Bouchet, in a conspiracy to deliver Limoges to the Protestants. D'Aubigné, already in the town square, at the last moment suspected a plot and escaped. His companions were executed within hours.

Overtures from Henri de Navarre were eventually accepted,

and in the renewed fighting of 1580 d'Aubigné, with 15 companions, took the château of Montaigu, although later in the summer an attempt to take Blaye was foiled. Later in the year, too, d'Aubigné's half-brother, his father's son by Anne de Limur, was killed at Montaigu. Montaigu was finally given back into Catholic hands by virtue of the peace of Fleix, signed on 26 November 1580. For the next two years d'Aubigné's public activity was once again mostly diplomatic. He carried out negotiations or fulfilled courtly functions at the highest level on behalf of Navarre and the Protestant interest. He was apparently now equally accustomed to the breath-taking risks he was perpetually running whenever there was fighting, to the important diplomatic negotiations involving the future of France in which he was from time to time engaged, and to the massive and dangerous intrigues and betrayals within and between the courts and armies of France, as the nobles, generals and representatives of the great dynastic families struggled often single-mindedly for personal power.

On 6 June 1583 d'Aubigné's marriage contract with Suzanne de Lezay was signed. Her dowry included the estate of Surimeau and that of Mursay, about eight kilometres north of Niort, where the couple were to live. Some difficulty had been made by the bride's family, the Vivonnes, about d'Aubigné's vulnerable titles to nobility, and Henri de Navarre had written to Suzanne de Lezay on d'Aubigné's behalf. D'Aubigné acted as intermediary between the royal court, to which Henri's wife had returned early in 1582, and Henri himself, who became the legitimate heir to the throne when his wife's brother, François de Valois, duc d'Anjou, died on 10 June 1584. The formation of the League, inspired by the Guise family, was hastened in the effort to prevent the throne falling into Huguenot hands. For some time in 1585 Henri III sought to integrate the Protestant army into his own to fight against the League. D'Aubigné strongly opposed the proposal and prevailed against Turenne. The treaty of Nemours marked a pact between Henri III and the League, and anti-Protestant measures were tightened.

War had broken out again by the autumn of 1585, and in October Condé failed to take Angers. D'Aubigné escaped, although he had been reported dead to his wife, to whom his hat and sword had been returned. After spending the winter at Mursay, he raised a regiment and in March 1586 took the Ile d'Oléron, of which he became governor and where, in July, he splendidly received Henri de Navarre. At the end of that month d'Aubigné was cut off by Catholic troops and taken captive by Saint-Luc. Allowed by Saint-Luc to go on parole to La Rochelle, d'Aubigné was warned by him not to return, as Saint-Luc had orders to hand him over to Henri III, who was intent on his execution. Quixotically d'Aubigné did return, although he expected to be executed. Saint-Luc found means of saving him until he was freed in an exchange of prisoners in November. It was now that, following a new quarrel with Henri de Navarre, d'Aubigné decided to study the religious arguments on the Catholic side, but disillusion merely reinforced his Protestant commitment.

In 1587 Henri de Navarre, who had just lost an illegitimate infant daughter, came to rely again on d'Aubigné, who took part in May and June in the capture of Maillezais and Saint-Maixent, soon to be re-taken by Joyeuse with horrifying brutality. On 20 October d'Aubigné again fought in the battle of Coutras. On 12 May 1588, the day of the barricades, Paris rose in favour of the duc de Guise, who had been forbidden entry to the city but rode through it unarmed, and Henri was forced to take refuge at Chartres. Later in the year the Protestant assembly at La Rochelle reorganized the political and financial structure of the Huguenot party, and on 23 and 24 December Henri III had the duc de Guise and his young brother, the cardinal, assassinated at Blois, leaving the duc de Mayenne as sole leader of the League.

Catherine de Medici, exhausted by her mediation between Henri III and the League during 1588, had become ill before the end of the year. She died on 5 January 1589, shortly after hearing of the Guise murders, rightly surmising that Henri III had not yet secured his position. In fact, apart from Bordeaux and the Loire towns, most of France rallied to the support of the League. Henri had the Guise bodies burnt to avoid the existence of relics. On 31 December d'Aubigné had received the capitulation of the small town of Maillezais, whose governorship seemed to him a mean reward for his services. During the first months of 1589 an alliance between the royal troops and the Protestants against the League became a condition for the survival of Henri III, but it was only during April that Henri de Navarre and Henri III, temporarily residing at Tours, met at Plessis-lez-Tours, promulgating an agreement on 30 April, and joining forces to repulse Mayenne's army on 8 May. Sixtus V excommunicated Henri III for the murder of the cardinal, not the duc, de Guise, and withheld absolution until the release of the archbishop of Lyons and the cardinal de Bourbon, arrested immediately after the murders.

In June and July of that summer d'Aubigné continued to fight with Henri de Navarre, sometimes obviously relishing the whole mixture of death-defying danger, courage, physical exertion, the test of skill, and the resultant glory. On 1 August he was taunted by an opponent who knew that there was a wide ditch between them. Finding himself with no choice but to attempt to leap the ditch, he spurred his horse and took his enemy prisoner back to the king's camp. That evening Henri III had been stabbed in the abdomen by Jacques Clément and, although the injury did not at first seem serious, he died in the night. Henri de Navarre was de iure king of France, although only by becoming a Catholic again could he hope to secure peace, and a succession that would otherwise have to be fought over between the League and the Huguenots. Even conversion might well have alienated the Huguenots without conciliating the League. Some of the nobles present, including Biron and d'Aumont, recognized Henri de Navarre as king. Others, like d'Epernon, withdrew their forces from the army. Mayenne proclaimed the still imprisoned cardinal de Bourbon as Charles X. The cardinal was committed to d'Aubigné's charge at Maillezais on 6 September, before being transferred to Fontenay-le-Comte on 15 October.

D'Aubigné was with Henri de Navarre immediately after the victory at Arques on 21 September 1589. Henri had recovered from political and strategic positions which at first looked hopeless, and had the support of most of the nobility by the end of 1589. He won the decisive battle of Ivry on 14 March 1590, although d'Aubigné was still skirmishing in Poitou at the end of the year. On 10 May the cardinal de Bourbon died, leaving the League with no pretender to the throne, just as Henri was beginning to implement his decision to reduce Paris by siege rather than battle. D'Aubigné took part in the nocturnal attack on the faubourgs on 27 July, but Paris, which was being quickly starved to death, was relieved by Alessandro Farnese, duke of Parma, the most distinguished strategist of the whole campaign, early in September. Henri's position was none the less strengthened during 1591, and that November d'Aubigné took part in the siege of Rouen, the last important town held by the League in the north. Fighting continued, with d'Aubigné at Henri's side at Rouen and skirmishing again in Poitou in July. Lack of funds caused Henri to abandon the siege at Rouen, but the resolution of the situation through Henri's conversion to Catholicism grew increasingly inevitable. News of Parma's death reached Paris on 4 December, removing the League's last real hope.

While the League held its estates general in Paris in January 1593 to choose a Catholic king, d'Aubigné was at the synod called at Saint-Maixent to elaborate the principles which were later to govern the edict of Nantes. In July he vainly tried to dissuade the king from the proposed abjuration of Protestantism, which took place at Saint-Denis on 25 July. On 27 February 1594 Henri IV was anointed king at Chartres, with a triumphant entry into Paris on 22 March. In June d'Aubigné attended the Protestant assembly at Sainte-Foy. On 17 September 1595, Suzanne de Lezay died, leaving her husband a son, Constant, and two daughters, Marie and Louise. D'Aubigné was also to have an illegitimate son, Nathan, born early in 1601.

In January 1595, the civil war over, war broke out with Philip II of Spain, whose troops were still occupying Burgundy. D'Aubigné, whose role in Protestant affairs was increasingly prominent, was with the king at the siege of La Fère at the end of the year. The Spaniards, removed from Burgundy, made an attack in Picardy and took Amiens on 11 March 1597. Henri IV took it back on 25 September, and in 1598, on 13 April, the edict of Nantes officially put an end to the Wars of Religion. On 2 May, the peace of Vervins was signed with Spain. The sudden death on 10 April 1599 of Gabrielle d'Estrées, mistress of Henri IV and mother of his children César and Alexandre de Vendôme, and the removal of the fear that Henri might marry her, now allowed his first wife, Marguerite de Valois, to consent to an annulment, granted by the Pope on 17 December. Henri thereupon married Marie de Medici. She was to give birth in 1601 to the future Louis XIII, so assuring the succession.

On 4 May 1600 Jacques Davy du Perron, bishop of Evreux, and from 1604 cardinal, had held a public religious debate at Fontainebleau with Duplessis-Mornay, accused of falsifying quotations in his book on the Eucharist. Duplessis-Mornay refused to return on the second day, but d'Aubigné and du Perron continued private discussions in Paris later in the month. D'Aubigné also wrote a letter to "Madame," the king's sister, Catherine de Bourbon, who had married a Catholic, encouraging her not herself to become a Catholic. In 1601 he was briefly in Paris, and began L'Histoire universelle. Then in 1606 he turned down an invitation from Henri IV to preside over the tournament to be held on the occasion of the dauphin's baptism. In December of the following year d'Aubigné boasted about having obstructed an attempt to find common religious ground between Catholics and Protestants.

The following years saw the marriages of his three legitimate children and continued activity by him in the Protestant cause. He was briefly in Paris with Henri IV at the end of 1609. After Henri's assassination in 1610, Protestant resistance to the queen regent focused round Condé. In October 1615 d'Aubigné became a maréchal de camp in his army, but Condé made his peace with the court in May 1616, leaving d'Aubigné in debt and now without a pension. He had the first edition of Les Tragiques clandestinely printed at Maillé. On 1 September Condé was arrested, and fighting broke out between the inhabit-

ants of La Rochelle, advised by d'Aubigné, and on the other side d'Epernon, the province's governor. In January 1617 d'Aubigné composed the first two books of the Avantures du baron de Faeneste, ridiculing d'Epernon's army. They were published in the same year. In spite of the cover date of 1616, the achevé d'imprimer of the first volume of the Histoire universelle is 31 March 1618. In that year d'Aubigné ceded to his son Constant the lieutenancy of Maillezais. The life Constant lived there was scandalous enough for d'Aubigné to eject him in February 1619. Constant was to catch his wife, Anne Marchant, in the act of committing adultery, and kill her.

D'Aubigné himself, after long negotiations with the court had fallen through, sold Maillezais and nearby Dognon, where he had built a fort, to Rohan, and lent him money in exchange for a large pension. He remained Rohan's lieutenant at Maillezais, where he repulsed an attempt by Constant to take it back. Failing to get a privilège for the Histoire universelle, d'Aubigné none the less published his second volume, as also the third book of the Avantures du baron de Faeneste. On 2 January 1620, the Histoire universelle was condemned to be burnt. That year none of the Protestant nobility joined the uprising initiated by Marie de Medici in April against Luynes, Connétable and favourite of Louis XIII, except Rohan, Soubise, and d'Aubigné. The king made peace with his mother in August, and d'Aubigné, with a warrant out for his arrest, more serious than that issued when the Histoire universelle was condemned, fled to Geneva. In 1621 Louis XIII was briefly at war again with the Protestants of his kingdom. D'Aubigné wrote a series of pamphlets, and advised on the fortification of Berne. On 24 April 1623, at the age of 71, he married Renée Burlamachi, widow of César Balboni, and bought a property in Switzerland. He was offered the captaincy of the French troops in the Venetian army, but Louis XIII imposed a veto on the appointment. The second edition of Les Tragiques probably dates from 1623, and in 1624 Constant d'Aubigné came to Geneva and was reconciled with his father.

In 1626, with the place-name Amsterdam, the three-volume second edition of the Histoire universelle was published at Geneva. Constant d'Aubigné was imprisoned on the orders of the court at Bordeaux in September, but was released in time to marry the Catholic Jeanne de Cardilhac, daughter of the prison governor. In 1635 the couple would have a daughter, Françoise, the future Mme de Maintenon. In 1630 d'Aubigné's Petites Oeuvres meslées was published in Geneva. In March or April appeared the fourth volume of the Avantures du baron de Faeneste, sufficiently scandalous for the printer to have been imprisoned. On 9 May d'Aubigné died.

WORKS

It was Sainte-Beuve who first drew attention to the grandeur of the conception of d'Aubigné's epic poem Les Tragiques, uneven, stylized, but with an extraordinary power drawn from its baroque vision of man's activities viewed against a background of uncontainable forces clashing with cosmic violence throughout the universe. D'Aubigné's imagination is vigorous, visual, and dramatic, so that he can quite naturally describe background paintings on the vaults of heaven depicting human activity in terms of the struggle between divine and satanic forces. A strong, simplified, harsh moral vision permeates the description of what occurs on earth.

The story of the religious wars, their righteousness, the devastation they caused, the simpering effeminacy of the Catholic court, the upright manliness of the Huguenot warriors, the foreign derivation of its presiding witch, Catherine de Medici, are simple strands charged with huge amounts of imaginative energy. The poem distorts the balance of rights and wrongs with the equivalent of the elongated distortion of baroque perspective in painting. It is often tasteless in its flagrant appeal to the reader's least subtle emotions, but the vivid brightness of the colour, wiping out any shadow and dispensing with any attempt at delicacy, and the pointed sharpness of its focus overwhelm the reader with force. Even when the images are not particularly successful poetically, when the narrative drags, or the repetitiousness becomes wearing, the reader's interest is kept alive by the overwhelming sense of indignant, malicious moral certitude.

D'Aubigné's earliest work, *Le Printemps*, first published in 1874, consists firstly of 100 sonnets to Diane entitled "L'Hécatombe à Diane," punning on the fact that Hecate is a manifestation of Diana and that in Greek "hekaton" means a hundred, to which he added 20 sets of stances in different metres and rhythms, and a number of odes. The collection is distinguished by little more than a tendency to violence in the imagery. Sometimes clever or epigrammatic, occasionally allusive or learned, the sonnets are normally Petrarchan, an individualized assemblage of devices separately all to be found at this date frequently enough elsewhere, and by no means always sufficiently felt to be elevated into more than elegant conceits. The following sonnet contrasts statements about nature in the first quatrain and the first tercet with statements about the poet's emotions in the second quatrain and second tercet. The poem is held together by its commonplace contrasts between heat and cold, fire and water, hard and soft, while a number of words serve primarily to pad out the syllable count.

Je voyoy' que le ciel après tant de chaleurs
Prodigeoit mille pleurs sur la terre endurcye,
Puis je voyoy' comment sa rigueur amollie
Faisoit naistre de là le printemps et les fleurs.

J'arrose bien ainsi et trempe de mes pleurs
Le sein de ma deesse, et ma force affoiblie,
Mes yeux fondus en eau, ces breches de ma vie,
M'ont attendry, Madame, et noyé mes ardeurs.

Des neiges, des frimatz, et mesmes des orages
La terre esclost son fruict, et ses riches ouvrages
Qu'un doux air puis appres flatte de ses souspirs.

Hélas! je souffre bien les enuieuses guerres
Des cieux, des ventz, les froids, les pluyes et les tonnerres
Mais je ne voy' ny fleurs, ny printemps, ny zephirs!

(I saw that after so much heat the sky/Showered a thousand tears on the hardened earth,/Then I saw how once its harshness had been softened/The earth brought forth the spring and the flowers.//So I sprinkle well and soak with my tears/The bosom of my goddess, and my enfeebled strength,/My eyes melted into water, those breaches in my life,/Have moved me, Madame, and drowned my fires.//From snows, winter hoar, and even storms/The earth produces its fruit, and its rich works/Which a milder air after-

wards then caresses with its sighs.//Alas! I must suffer the hostile clashes/Of skies, winds, cold, rain and thunder/But I see neither flowers, nor spring, nor soft breezes!).

Most of these poems were written when d'Aubigné was 19 or 20. Although we know he was strongly attracted to Diane Salviati, he did not need to have been in order to write a well-turned sonnet like this one, based on well-worked-out antitheses, with no more than a touch of violence in the images of thunder, storm and warfare. Wistfulness is the predominating sentiment.

There are gratifying signs that, in the wake of *Les Tragiques*, d'Aubigné's prose works are beginning to attract some of the attention they deserve, but his name is still above all associated with his great, uneven, seven-book poem. The "Aux lecteurs" announces that the poem is intended not to instruct but to move, and d'Aubigné, who in his confessedly autobiographical *Sa Vie à ses enfants* writes of himself in the third person, here so confuses first and third persons that it is reasonable to assume that "I" means d'Aubigné, and not an invented poet other than the real writer of the poem. The first book, "Misères," is, he tells us, a "tableau piteux du Royaume en general, d'un style bas et tragique, n'excedant que fort peu les lois de la narration (a grievous picture of the kingdom in general, in a low, tragic style, not going far beyond ordinary narrative)." It is preceded by a preface from the author to his book. The poem proper is in alexandrines. Its exordium is a prayer, and the muse invoked is not the muse of poetry, but Melpomene, the muse of tragedy, "en sa vive fureur (in her living fury)."

France is immediately depicted as a giant whose humours are in conflict with one another. This is the first example of the immensely powerful images which run through the poem; often, as here, because of an attitude struck, a formal pose described, or a visual stylization, they are oddly static. The effect is achieved partly because the imagery overflows from the physiology of the giant into the moral physiognomy of France in a confusion of words. Blood, people, nobles, king, melancholy, infection all tumble out in a surging, uncontrolled medley. From the beginning there is a gruesome lack of fastidiousness. D'Aubigné describes how the giant,

Aussi foible que grand n'enfle plus que son ventre.
Ce ventre dans lequel tout se tire, tout entre,
Ce faux dispensateur des communs excremens
N'envoye plus aux bords les justes alimens:
Des jambes et des bras les os sont sans moelle,
Il ne va plus en haut pour nourrir la cervelle
Qu'un chime venimeux dont le cerveau nourri
Prend matiere et liqueur d'un champignon pourri.
Ce grand geant changé en une horrible beste
A sur ce vaste corps une petite teste,
Deux bras foibles pendans, des-ja secs, des-ja morts,
Impuissans de nourrir et defendre le corps;
Les jambes sans pouvoir porter leur masse lourde
Et à gauche et à droit font porter une bourde

(As weak as he is tall inflates only its belly./That belly into which everything is drawn, everything goes,/That traitrous dispenser of what should be discharged into the blood/No longer furnishes the limbs with their proper nourishment:/The bones of legs and arms have no marrow,/[And] rising on high to nourish the brain/Is only a poisonous digestive juice; when nourished with it, the brain/Takes the consistency of liquid, like a rotten mushroom./This great giant changed into a horrible animal/Has a tiny head on its vast body,/Two weak arms hanging, already withered, already dead,/Incapable of nourishing and defending the body;/The legs, unable to carry their heavy load/Both to left and to right need to be supported by crutches). (Lines 149–62)

This is the first of many sustained metaphors, unusually well worked through, although with repetition and what, even for the late 16th century, was dubious taste, leaning heavily to the macabre. The image is striking, and shows d'Aubigné's preference for vigour over charm. The language is not always effective in its repetitiveness. The repeated "ce" does make the image more vivid, but the choice between "cerveau/cervelle" is dictated by rhyme and syllable count, and the use of the verb "nourrir" for the second time, presumably to rhyme with the striking "pourri," betrays a disdain for mere elegance.

Another strong metaphor immediately follows, less garish but scarcely less vivid. France is a boat (lines 179–90) with hostile troops at prow and poop. D'Aubigné occasionally coins new words from Greek, such as "discrasie (δυσκρασια)" for the imbalance of humours in the giant—although that word had already been used by Rabelais—and the victor of the war on the boat is still "autochire," killed by his own hand (from αυτό-χειρ). The robustness of language and vision goes with authentic humanist learning. The poet goes on to address the French in the second person, "You…," and then returns to moralizing comment before addressing, in the singular, the stylized peasant with white hair who is a hundred years old,

Mais je te plains, rustic, qui, ayant la journee
Ta pantelante vie en rechignant gaignee
Reçois au soir les coups, l'injure et le tourment,
Et la fuite et la faim, injuste payement.
Le païsan de cent ans, dont la teste chenuë
Est couverte de neige, en suivant sa charrue
Voit galopper de loin l'argolet outrageux,
Qui d'une rude main arrache les cheveux,
L'honneur du vieillard blanc, piqué de son ouvrage
Par qui la seule faim se trouvoit au village

(But I pity you, rustic, who all day/Have grimly gained your panting livelihood/And receive in the evening blows, curses and suffering,/Flight and hunger, inequitable reward./The hundred-year-old peasant, whose white head/Is covered in snow, while following his plough/Sees far off the galloping destroying horseman,/Who with a rough hand tears hair/And honour from the white old man, proud of his work/By which only hunger came to the village). (Lines 257–66)

Here there is a deliberate attempt at poetic effect in the alliteration "fuite/faim," and an imagery as exaggerated as it is visually stylized, like a baroque statue carved to be looked at from below. Some time later (line 371) the poet is formally identified with the author—"Car mes yeux sont tesmoins du subjet de mes vers (For my eyes have witnessed the subject of my poem)"—before a digression taking the example of a man dying, like France, of hunger. Part of the polemical strength of the poem is its constant exploitation of the patriotic theme, and the reiteration of France/François. The invective against Henri III becomes harsh. Against his mother, the Florentine and therefore foreign "Jesabel," Catherine de Medici, it is even more withering. Towards the end of "Misères" the attack concentrates on Catherine, on the Cardinal of Lorraine, adding the pope, "cet ancien loup, romain (that old Roman wolf)," and on the Jesuits—"ô vermine espagnolle (O Spanish vermin)." The book ends in a prayer of over 100 lines.

The second book, "Princes," is said in the "Aux lecteurs" to be "d'un style moyen mais satyrique (ordinary style, but satirical)." It is the great of the world who cause the miseries of its people. D'Aubigné in this book spends some time discussing his own technique in the poem, and it seems certain that the bulk of "Princes" belongs among the earlier parts of the poem to have been composed, most probably dating from the late 1570s, although the text as we have it is more than tinged with self-recrimination at d'Aubigné's own momentary temptation during the 1570s to succumb to the delights of the Valois court he excoriates. It is much more probable that d'Aubigné added overlays to his poem than that he revised it for fastidious imaginative consistency shortly before publication, and it reads throughout as if, as must have been the case, parts have been inserted into an original.

Initially impelled, no doubt, by the impact made on his mind by the Saint Bartholomew's Day massacre, which he escaped only because he had had to flee Paris after killing the serjeant, D'Aubigné must have been writing, if not simply to exorcize his own ineradicable anger, then for the benefit of a few like-minded and highly literate acquaintances. It is necessary to assume either that he had not any particular readership in mind but was addressing virtually himself alone; or that those he sought to move, at first intended to see his poem quite soon after it was written, and certainly before 1616, were co-religionaries not themselves responsible for the mass civilian murders or for the implementations of scorched earth policies which the prosecution of the wars entailed; or were those who continued to be guilty of imposing military victory through the starvation of besieged populations. He was not therefore writing merely for Protestant army captains, whose literacy can often at best have been doubtful, and whose bitter resolution d'Aubigné could not have hoped to move by evocations of rural misery, or even of patriotism, but for members of the small educated Protestant aristocracy, with its courtiers, functionaries, and ministers, hostile to Spanish domination and Italian interference, whether or not inspired by Rome, and at least open to those humane considerations conspicuously present in d'Aubigné's poem, but absent from the conduct of the wars.

D'Aubigné certainly wished to extract the maximum effect by exciting emotional sympathy with those who had most suffered from the wars in which they had no part, whose crops had been burnt in order that they should starve, or stolen to feed armies; those who had been besieged into famine, or simply put to death because the place they lived in was taken by the other side with a hostile religious affiliation. We actually have no evidence that the poem was written for publication at all, although we know that large portions of it were read by Henri de Navarre before the assassination of Henri III in 1589, and that some portions must have been written later. We also know that d'Aubigné himself did subsequently have the poem published in 1616, and that he added to it between 1616 and 1623. Its appeal as published must therefore have been intended to be retrospective, a memorial to what took place, and an indication of how, in d'Aubigné's view, the memory of it all should be preserved much more than a quarter of a century later, when the succession was assured and residual religious bitterness was being contained. The poem can only be understood if it is remembered that much must have been written in what was tantamount to incandescent rage, shortly after the events which provoked it, but that publication in 1616 demanded that the poem should be a commemoration, not a call to action.

Hence, particularly in "Princes," the overlay of reflection and the dwelling on poetic intention, hence the powerful reiteration of "Je veux (I intend)" of the opening lines, which read as if they had been added after the real beginning of the book at line nine, although there is no actual evidence that they were written later. The attack on flattery was a renaissance commonplace, particularly associated with Erasmus. The bitterly satirical remarks about Henri III's bodyguard as a bunch of young homosexuals is another commonplace, a myth whose foundations have been exaggerated, but which fits in well with d'Aubigné's admiration for the rougher virtues of the male warrior and with his posture of contempt for all things Spanish and Italian. After the invective in turn against the three sons of Catherine de Medici who survived into d'Aubigné's own adolescence—Charles IX, Henri III and the duc d'Alençon—d'Aubigné, in a development which has been seen as fictionalized autobiography and occupies the final third of the book, describes the corruptive effect of the court on the well-brought-up young man who is sent there by his father.

The third book, "La Chambre dorée," said in the "Aux lecteurs" to be in the same style as the second, opens with the splendid although not entirely original conception of God on the throne of judgement, before whom allegorized or personified pleaders appear. They include earthly justice, piety, peace, and the angelic chorus. The focus narrows as God concentrates more and more closely on the Valois court, with its monstrous list of attendants, including avarice, ambition, anger, drunkenness, vengeance, stupidity, ignorance, passion, hatred, and vanity, and stretching to 27 allegorical figures in all. The book concludes with a prayer for vengeance.

The fourth book, "Les Feux," "d'un style tragique moyen (of a medium tragic style)," is generally considered on account of its long list of martyrs to be the weakest of the seven. The scene returns to heaven at the opening of the fifth book, "Les Fers," "du style tragicque eslevé, plus poëtic et plus hardi que les autres (in an elevated tragic style, more poetic and audacious than the others)." The core of the book is the account of the 1572 massacre, but beforehand Satan appears in front of the divine throne. He arrives disguised as the angel of light referred to in II Corinthians, xi, 14, a text of great importance in the history of 16th-century spirituality since its use by Erasmus. Slowly Satan turns back into a snake:

Lors le trompeur trompé d'asseuré devint blesme,
L'enchanteur se trouva desenchanté luy-mesme.
Son front se seillonna, ses cheveux herissés,
Ses yeux flambants dessous les sourcils refroncés…
La bouche devint pasle: un changement estrange
Luy donna front de diable et osta celuy d'ange.
L'ordure le flestrit, tout au long se respend.
La teste se descoëffe et se change en serpent…

Il tomba sur la voute, où son corps s'alongeant,
De diverses couleurs et venin se chargeant,
Le ventre jaunissant, et noirastre la queuë,
Pour un ange trompeur mit un serpent en veuë

(When the deceiver deceived from confident became pale,/ The magician found his magic dispelled./His forehead became furrowed, his hair stood on end,/His eyes flaming under frowning brows…/The mouth became pale: a strange change/Gave him the forehead of a devil and took away that of an angel./Filth sullied him, and spread all over him./The head was uncovered and turned into a snake's…/ He fell on the vault [of heaven], where his body, stretching out,/Took on different colours and a poisonous power,/ The belly yellowed, the tail blackened,/And in place of a deceiving angel a snake was revealed). (From lines 53–74)

D'Aubigné's most powerful poetic effects can be demonstrated only with extracts of several scores of lines, since they so often depend on syntactical repetitions or other cumulative procedures. The above brief extract does, however, contain characteristic word-play in the first two lines and concentration of "t" sounds in the first two and of "s" sounds in the second two lines. It shows the visual character of d'Aubigné's poetic imagination. He does not shrink from "ordure," less politely translated "excrement," has a poetic scruple about the hair that an angel has but a snake does not, needs a weak half-line about a "strange change," and has a poetic inversion in the penultimate line, with an antithesis in the last one. The third line from the end leaves a problem unsolved. D'Aubigné needs a single verb to describe how the snake takes on stripes and poison, both of which are traditional and necessary accoutrements. It is not careful poetry, but it is vigorous, and its imagery is effective because it is so energetic.

Satan wagers that he can break, corrupt, and seduce God's faithful. He starts by possessing Catherine de Medici, and then creates the Tuileries. D'Aubigné's description is the better for being unusually succinct, its details selectively chosen to evoke the splendour of

…colomnes parfaites,
De pavillons hautains, de folles girouëttes,
De domes accomplis, d'escaliers sans noyaux,
Fenestrages dorés, pilastres et portaux,
De sales, cabinets, de chambres, galeries,
En fin d'un tel project que sont les Tuilleries

(…perfect columns,/Lofty pavilions, crazy weathervanes,/Skilfully built domes, spiral staircases,/Gilded window-frames, pilasters and portals,/Halls, rooms to live in and to sleep in, galleries,/In a word, a project like the Tuileries). (Lines 199–204)

If hell was in turmoil, so was heaven. The angels visit earth and, on their return, paint on the vaults of heaven what is happening below. D'Aubigné is naturally using the fiction that the universe is enclosed in a sphere with a vaulted heaven on top and hell underneath. Fifty lines or so are devoted to describing each of the paintings. The whole concept of angels magnifying earthly events into paintings on the vaults of heaven itself is characteristic in its grandeur of d'Aubigné's imagination at its most powerful. The book ends with the account of the poet's apocalyptic vision and the ocean's complaint at the blood and debris of war swept into it by the rivers of France.

The sixth and seventh books—"Vengeances," referred to as "théologien et historial (theological and historical)" and "Jugement," "d'un style eslevé, tragicque (elevated and tragic)"—are less powerful than "Les Fers." "Vengeances" is devoted to the persecutors of the true faithful from the earliest days of the Old Testament, and is generally thought to have been among the earlier parts of the poem to have been written. The first persecutor was Cain, the first martyr, Abel. There is a poetic intensity in the description of Cain's obsessive state of guilt, quite simply achieved with the help of play on sounds and simple rhetorical devices.

Il avoit peur de tout, tout avoit peur de lui.
Car le Ciel s'affeubloit du manteau d'une nue
Si tost que le transi au Ciel tournoit la veuë;
S'il fuyoit au desert, les rochers et les bois
Effrayés abbayoyent au son de ses abois.
Sa mort ne peut avoir de mort pour recompense,
L'Enfer n'eut point de morts à punir cette offense,
Mais autant que de jours il sentit de trepas;
Vif il ne vescut point, mort il ne mourut pas;
Il fuit d'effroy transi, troublé, tremblant et blesme,
Il fuit de tout le monde, il s'enfuit de soy-mesme

(He was afraid of everything, everything was afraid of him./For heaven wrapped itself in the mantle of a cloud/As soon as the terrified fugitive looked at heaven;/If he fled to the desert, the rocks and the woods/Bayed in terror at the sound of his bayings./His death could not have death for its reward/[Since] hell had no deaths to punish that offence/But he experienced death every day that he lived;/Alive, he did not live, dead, he did not die;/He fled convulsed with fear, troubled, trembling, and pale,/He fled from everyone, he fled from himself). (Lines 192–202)

The punishment of other persecutors is gruesome, too, but the poem ends peacefully with the faithful transfigured in their final vindication. This is poetically less moving than the contemptuous dismissal in "Princes" of

…les hermaphrodits, monstres effeminez,
Corrompus, bourdeliers, et qui estoyent mieux nez
Pour valets des putains que seigneurs sur les hommes

(…hermaphrodites, effeminate/Corrupt, brothel-crawling monsters, better born/To be servants of tarts than superiors of men). (Lines 667–9)

The poem impresses above all by the force of its imaginative energy, the violence of its invective, and the intensity of the moral outrage it communicates. It is uneven, and there are dull moments as well as clumsy images. It is also lacking in unity, since not all its sections are consistent with the commemorative character it had had to assume by the time it was published. Yet its strength lies in the preservation of an indignation that is locked into the text even though its cause had long abated when the final touches were put to it. As a poetic expression, however clumsy, of imaginative energy, it achieves an overwhelming

power that is too easily obscured by any critical analysis of its techniques.

The *Histoire universelle*, like *Les Tragiques*, is a work of religious commitment. D'Aubigné spent much of 30 years writing it, largely because he felt that the religious wars had ended in defeat, and that the edict of Nantes was a humiliation. The *Confession catholique du sieur de Sancy* may have been begun as early as 1597 and not finished until as late as 1617, although most of it was written by 1600. It was, at least originally, a pamphlet intended to rally Protestant sentiment against conversion to Catholicism, and d'Aubigné never dared to publish it. The *Histoire* on the other hand is not a pamphlet but an interpretation of what happened, written with what d'Aubigné intended to be sufficient moral vigour to justify his point of view, and finished by about 1612. D'Aubigné knew that there was no chance of a privilège for the violently polemical *Les Tragiques*, whose 1616 publication was therefore anonymous. It was actually signed "L.B.D.D." (Le Bouc du désert: "the scapegoat"). He did on the other hand want a privilège for its counterpart, the opening books of the *Histoire*, of whose authorship he was proud. Arrangements for publication were made in 1616, but no permission had been received when the printing of the first volume was finished on 31 March 1618.

D'Aubigné postponed distribution, started the second volume, and very nearly obtained his privilège for the first. Unhappily the commissioners were prevented by troop movements from getting to Maillé, where printing had taken place, and d'Aubigné went ahead without one, finishing the second volume in 1619 and the third at Saint-Jean-d'Angély in the spring of 1620, in debt on account of the expenses incurred during Condé's rising and of the loss of his pension. The three volumes of the first edition were dated 1618, 1618, and 1620, but the first two had already been condemned to be burnt by a decree of 2 January 1620. D'Aubigné's arrest was ordered, although the danger was not as serious as that consequent on the warrant issued after the defeat of Rohan and Soubise on 7 August 1620, when d'Aubigné managed to escape to Geneva.

D'Aubigné makes it quite clear, not only in explicit statement, that his history was not intended to be polemical, but only a fair account of what had taken place. It is not therefore presented as a work of the imagination. It throws much light on the biography, on the attitudes taken in *Les Tragiques*, and on the events referred to in the poem. The *Confession catholique du sieur de Sancy* was not published until 1660 in the *Recueil de diverses pièces servant à l'Histoire de Henri III*, and it was republished in the same *Recueil* in 1662, 1663, and then 1693 and 1699.

The first two parts of *Les Avantures du Baron de Faeneste* were published in 1617, the third part in 1619, and the fourth in 1630, when the printer was imprisoned. The text, a series of comic dialogues, is d'Aubigné's most important work in prose. Its satirical aim is much the same as that of *Sancy*, to discredit Catholicism and ridicule the vanities of court life. Polemic gives way to farce, and the relationship between Faeneste and Enay is here modelled more on that between Cervantes's Don Quixote and Sancho Panza than on that between Rabelais's Pantagruel and Panurge. Spanish picaresque novels were being translated into French immediately on their appearance, and in 1623 Sorel's *Francion* inaugurated the vogue for the realist satirical novel in France. Faeneste is everything that d'Aubigné was not, all froth and boasting, the descendant of Plautus's "Miles gloriosus," the coward, the courtier, the charlatan, and the Catholic.

His attempts to convert Enay are a comic transposition of those of Monsieur le Convertisseur in *Sancy*.

Faeneste enjoys war because it lets him live off the peasants, pillage, maraud, steal, eat for nothing, and be lodged. The text visibly moves towards the novel form, although it is weighed down for most modern readers by the Gascon spelling, which incidentally can scarcely be produced in translation. Gascon has no "v" sound, so Faeneste says "Je beux" for "Je veux (I want)," but d'Aubigné also writes "v" for standard French "b," so that "bottes (boots)" is written "vottes." No doubt that piles on the fun made of Gascons trying to pronounce "v," but it makes the parodic quality of the text difficult to illustrate in English. Gascon makes other changes, too, so that "village" is written "bilaye." The humour itself is subdued, as in the list of six things in which it is dangerous to take appearance for the reality, which is what Faeneste is always doing: profit, pleasure, friendship, honour, service of one's king or country, and religion. Naturally, most is made of religion, and its appearance, hypocrisy.

D'Aubigné also wrote often moving meditations on the psalms in poetic prose. These were written particularly in the immediate aftermath of his first wife's death, but also for Henri de Navarre, and in 1626 to prepare a friend, and ultimately himself, for death. His final *Petites oeuvres meslées* is a collection of religious poetry and meditations published in the year of his death in 1630. It includes psalm translations in "vers mesurés," some of which date back to 1600, but which are interesting mostly as experiments.

PUBLICATIONS

Collections

Oeuvres complètes, 6 vols., 1873–92
Oeuvres, Bibliothèque de la Pléiade, 1969

Verse

Les Tragiques, 1616; 4 vols., 1962–65
Le Printemps, 1874
Petites oeuvres meslées, 1630

Other

Histoire universelle, 3 vols., 1616–20; 10 vols., 1886–1909; 5 vols., 1981–91
Les Avantures du baron de Faeneste, 1st and 2nd parts, 1617; 3rd part, 1619; 4th part, 1630
Confession catholique du sieur de Sancy, in *Recueil de diverses pièces servant à l'histoire de Henri III*, 1660
Mémoires, 1731
Sa Vie à ses enfants, 1928

Biographical and critical studies

Garnier, A., *Agrippa d'Aubigné et le parti protestant*, 3 vols., 1928
Plattard, Jean, *Agrippa d'Aubigné. Une figure de premier plan dans nos lettres de la renaissance*, 1931
Buffum, Imbrie, *Agrippa d'Aubigné's "Les Tragiques." A Study in the baroque style in poetry*, 1951
Sauerwein, Henry A., *Agrippa d'Aubigné's "Les Tragiques." A Study in structure and poetic method*, 1953
Galzy, Jeanne, *Agrippa d'Aubigné*, 1965
Bailbé, Jacques, *Agrippa d'Aubigné, poète des Tragiques*, 1968
Randall, Catherine, *Subverting the System. D'Aubigné and Calvinism*, 1990

B

BAÏF, Jean-Antoine de, 1532–1589.

Poet and translator.

LIFE

Baïf was the illegitimate child of a Venetian mother, about whom nothing is known. His father, Lazare de Baïf, born into the Anjou aristocracy at the minuscule two-bedroomed château des Pins, near La Flèche, in about 1496, had in about 1516 accompanied Christophe de Longueil to Rome. He studied Greek there for several years at the newly founded Quirinal College under Musurus and Lascaris, to whom he was later to write in Greek. Considered by his contemporaries only just inferior to Budé as a Greek scholar, he must have made some effort to study law before turning resolutely to the study of Greek literature and, in the wake of Budé, to Greek social history. In 1526 he published a work on Greek clothing, *De re vestiaria*, a commentary on the law *Vestis* (*ff. de auro et argento legato*, *Digest*, xxxiv, ii, 23–25). It was dedicated to Jean de Guise, the first Guise cardinal of Lorraine, and was admired by Erasmus.

An understanding of Baïf's own career, and the early history of the group of poets surrounding Ronsard, not quite congruent with the kernel of the Pléiade (q.v.), depends to an unusual extent on a knowledge of his background and upbringing, and the interpretation of his father's activities. Lazare de Baïf, a protonotary apostolic from 1527 and the holder thereafter of two abbacies, was also to publish a work on Greek vases, *De vasculorum materiis ac varietate*, dedicated to the chancellor Antoine du Bourg, in 1531, and another on the navies of antiquity, the *De re navali* of 1536, dedicated to François I. Lazare de Baïf also published a rhymed translation of Sophocles's *Electra* in 1537, translated the first four of Plutarch's *Lives*, may have written a lost treatise on architecture, and helped Robert Estienne with his 1531 *Thesaurus linguae latinae*. Baïf's father was therefore an active and accomplished humanist.

In 1525 he had joined the household of Jean de Lorraine, the first cardinal de Lorraine, brother of Claude, the first duc de Guise. He took part in the peasants' war in Alsace, returned to Lyons, and then to his humanist activities, before leaving for Venice on 25 June 1529 as the resident ambassador of François I. The centre of a humanist circle in Venice, Lazare de Baïf had as his secretary from May 1530 Pierre Bunel of Toulouse. Baïf himself was born in February 1532. At the beginning of 1534 his father was at his own request recalled to Paris, where he had built for himself a superb mansion in the rue des Fossés-Saint-Victor just outside the town wall and the moat, near both the principal colleges and the abbaye de Saint-Victor. The abbey possessed a famous library, which was open to the public and from which it was possible to borrow books; its catalogue was caricatured by Rabelais. The site of the mansion was later acquired by English

Catholic refugee nuns, the canonesses of St Augustine, in whose convent George Sand was to be educated. Opposite the mansion and just inside the town wall was the collège de Boncourt, where Jean Galland, Ronsard's friend and executor, succeeded his great-uncle as principal. Ronsard had a house in the grounds. He also owned a house next or very near to the Baïf mansion.

The importance of Lazare de Baïf's preoccupations becomes clear in the light of the social relationship after his death in 1547 between his mansion and Ronsard's two houses. Ronsard obtained permission from François I to have a door pierced in the town wall for ease of communication with Baïf, and the Academy of Painting and Music formally founded in 1570 very closely involved Ronsard, in one of whose houses it also met. "Baïf's academy," formalized in 1570 and extended into what was institutionalized as the Académie du Palais in the mid-1570s, continued the original cooperation between Baïf and Ronsard in setting out to develop the French language and restore French literature through the imitation of antique poets and the re-introduction of their poetic genres.

If Lazare de Baïf was essentially a devotee of Greek-based humanism in the mould of Budé, then there is a plausible continuity between the early and scholarly poetic collaboration of Ronsard and Baïf under Dorat at Coqueret, Baïf's Académie de Poésie et Musique, and the Académie du Palais. If this were to be generally recognized, then the movement of cultural, literary, musical, and educational reform in the mid-16th century which centred on Ronsard and Baïf would have to be seen as more closely connected than is usually thought with the "encyclopedic" educational theory and quasi-mythological neoplatonist structures of such authors as Tyard and Peletier du Mans. The Greek-based humanism of the educational reform and its relationship to the enthusiasms of Budé and Erasmus may need to be even more firmly acknowledged, while the idea that du Bellay's *Deffence et illustration de la langue françoise* can be regarded as the manifesto of a group of poets subsequently known as the "Pléiade" may be even more fragile than has already been apparent for some time.

While still in Venice, Lazare de Baïf had been appointed on 17 November 1530 a conseiller clerc at the Paris parlement. He took the oath on 27 March 1534, soon after his return to France, in 1538 became maître des requêtes in the royal household, and in 1540 took Ronsard with him as a secretary on his mission to Hagenau to re-assure the German Protestants of the good-will of François I. No contemporary sources speak highly of his abilities as a diplomat, but he plainly enjoyed the confidence of the king and was sent on further missions, for instance to Champagne in May 1542, and to Languedoc and Poitou in 1544. He died during the late summer or autumn of 1547. The inventory of the contents of the château des Pins is dated 8 November. Baïf himself tells us that his father carefully arranged from his earliest youth for his son's determinedly humanist education, choosing as tutors Charles Estienne, a former pupil of Lazarro Buonamici and gifted teacher, for Latin, and the Cretan Ange Vergèce, better known for his calligraphy than for his humanism, for Greek. Baïf himself always had a remarkably clear hand. When, in May 1540, Baïf's father went on his mission to Hagenau, the eight-year-old Baïf was sent to board for four years with Jacques Toussaint, pupil and friend of Budé and one of the royal lecturers in Greek.

From 1544 to 1547 Baïf lived at home, with Dorat, his tutor, a member of his father's household. On 5 June 1544 Ronsard's father died, and Ronsard came to Paris, tonsured, 20, and seeking a career no longer at court, but in the world of letters. His mother was a cousin of Baïf's father, to whom Ronsard had acted as secretary at Hagenau, and he now joined Baïf as Dorat's pupil in the Rue des Fossés-Saint-Victor. Baïf, barely adolescent, was already advanced in Greek, while Ronsard had been encouraged by Peletier du Mans in writing French odes in the manner of Horace. We do not know through what mixture of luck, patronage, and astuteness Dorat was made principal of the obscure collège de Coqueret, one of the smallest of the 30 or so which constituted the university, and little more than the house of a regent master allowed to teach publicly. It was still owned by a former principal, Robert Dugast, who had been stripped of all academic privileges by the faculty of arts as a consequence of a number of complaints from regent teachers deriving, it appears, almost entirely from his meanness. Dugast was restored as principal in 1551, and Dorat was not necessarily in charge of the financial administration. He appears to have been primarily the institution's director of studies, and was almost certainly appointed for the academic year starting in the autumn of 1547. He took with him his two pupils from the Rue des Fossés-Saint-Victor, soon to be joined by du Bellay.

Lazare de Baïf's dispositions in favour of his illegitimate son were incomplete on his death. Baïf inherited the mansion, the château des Pins, and a small house in Anjou, but nothing had been done to exchange the abbacies or the post of maître des requêtes into transferable assets. One of his aunts legally and vainly contested his right to the furniture in the château des Pins, and with his second aunt Baïf appears to have had no contact at all. He was to live chiefly as a private scholar and poet in Paris, the academies funded at least partly from royal patronage.

The two accounts of the way in which at Coqueret Ronsard studied until 2 a.m. and then woke Baïf to take over the candle when he went to bed, are given by Binet in his *Vie de Ronsard*, and by Jacques Velliard in his *Laudatio funebris*. The parsimoniously shared candle comes from Binet, but it is more likely that the subject of joint study was Greek and the shortage was of Greek texts. Of the two, Ronsard, whose humanist foundations were less secure, was plainly from the beginning the superior poet, although Baïf later recounted the success among his friends of his own earliest verses. A first sonnet, adapted from a set of Greek distichs by Claude Rammile, was published in 1549, and a second sonnet together with six Greek distichs appeared with Ronsard's 1550 *Odes*. Other youthful work of Baïf survives, often originally intended as contributions to communal undertakings and sometimes experimental, as in the case of his first narrative poem, *Le Ravissement d'Europe*, imitated from Moschos and published in 1552.

Baïf's poetic output is none the less generally considered to have started with *Les Amours de Jan-Antoine de Baïf*, published two months after the first edition of Ronsard's *Amours*, with a

privilège of 10 December 1552. By this date Baïf was universally known as "le docte (the learned)" Baïf, and often by his friends as "Toinet." The poems were re-entitled "Les Amours de Méline" in the 1573 *Euvres en rime*, and Baïf tells us that "Méline," unlike the later Francine of the 1555 *Quatre livres de l'Amour de Francine*, had no model in real life. In his 1552 volume, Baïf is nearer to Tyard in his mixture of sonnets and lyrical pieces in various forms than to du Bellay or than to Ronsard, whose 1555 *Continuation des amours*, in praise of Marie, Baïf seems to be challenging in his Francine cycle. In fact Baïf had been disappointed at the poor public reception accorded to the Méline poems and, to escape the pangs of envy, had gone to Poitiers early in 1554 with Jacques Tahureau du Mans, three years older than Baïf himself. There had certainly been some kind of quarrel with Ronsard, perhaps based partly on a misinterpretation of poses struck by Baïf, to which perhaps envy was not altogether foreign. In Poitiers Baïf found Jean de la Péruse, whom he had known in Paris at the collège de Boncourt, and it was there that he met not only "Francine," Françoise de Gennes, but a whole new group of young poets, including Jean Vauquelin de la Fresnaye, who was to become a firm friend, and Scévole de Sainte-Marthe.

It is Guy de Bruès who tells us that Baïf and Ronsard were reconciled in what must have been late 1555 or early 1556, by which date Baïf had been forced to accept the failure of his collections of love poetry and, for that matter, the success of Ronsard's. Baïf spent the early months of 1556 staying at Loudun and then Tronchet, near Le Mans, with the humanist lawyer, Jacques Morin, a conseiller first at the Turin and then at the Paris parlement. Baïf was working on the translation of Giovanni Francesco Pico della Mirandola's *De imitatione*, apparently published as *Traitté de l'Imagination* in 1557 with a dedication to Morin. He also stayed with Vauquelin de la Fresnaye in Normandy. Back in Paris he published in 1558, no doubt in hope of reward, a *Chant de joie* to celebrate the dauphin François's marriage to Mary, Queen of Scots, on 24 April.

In April 1560 Baïf visited Ronsard at la Possonnière and took him to the wedding of a cousin of Ronsard's Marie at Saint-Cosme-lez-Tours, at which his own "Francine" was to be present. Our account of the whole episode comes from a delightful pastoral poem by Ronsard, "Le Voiage de Tours, ou les amoureus Thoinet et Perrot" printed in the first part of Ronsard's 1560 *Oeuvres*, with a privilège of 25 September. Thoinet and Perrot are naturally Baïf and Ronsard, but the pastoral narrative is so stylized, with so many implied as well as quasi-explicit allusions to Theocritus, and the need for a poem of reconciliation aptly culminating in a shared misfortune is so obvious, that it is difficult to know how far this account of the wedding can be taken as a historical narrative of events. Marion lets Perrot down as Francine lets down Thoinet and, after their entertainment by "Phelipot le gaillard," Ronsard's cousin, at which they were feasted "jusques au soir bien tard (until very late at night)," the poem has the two shepherds improbably sleeping

Sous des saules plantés le long d'une praerie

(under willows planted along the side of a meadow).

That is not impossible in April, but it is difficult to imagine Baïf and Ronsard not having slept in some corner of Phelipot's château at Beaumont-la-Ronce, or dancing at a wedding, as the poem implies, in the clothes they had been wearing while they slept overnight in a field. The whole pattern of military and economic life, and of marine trade, as indicated by the dates at which insurance policies were taken out, the known instances of flooding, and the incidence of plague, all suggest that the French climate was already in 1600 getting colder and wetter, reversing a 300-year-old trend, and that in April unpleasantly wintry conditions were still to be expected in the Loire valley. That the poem has some basis in fact seems plain from the accumulation of realistic details, and both the itinerary which we are given and the chronological position in Ronsard's life of a final meeting with Marie before the "Elégie à Marie" of October 1560 make it practically certain that the incident had some historical basis. But the poem is far too pastorally stylized to yield the sort of biographical evidence which critics, biographers, and historians have tried to extract from it.

From late in 1562 Baïf spent six months at the Council of Trent, from which he returned by way of northern Italy. He must have been part of the suite of one of the 40 French bishops sent to represent France, and is quite likely to have been in the service of the cardinal of Lorraine, who arrived in Trent on 15 November 1562. He needed what employment was available to him. It was not easy to become an official poet to king, court, or important benefactor. During the all-important 1550s, under Henri II, the court poets were Lancelot de Carles and Mellin de Saint-Gelais, who felt momentarily threatened by Ronsard, and who was asked by Michel de l'Hôpital to ensure favour at court for Ronsard and his friends. Michel de l'Hôpital also advised the young generation of Ronsard and his friends to cultivate Carles and Saint-Gelais, to cultivate them alone, and to avoid shocking conservative taste. It was through Saint-Gelais that court favour was bestowed also on Dorat and Tahureau, and du Bellay wrote no fewer than five epitaphs on him. References in Baïf's poetry suggest that he, too, assiduously courted Saint-Gelais's favour, and that through Saint-Gelais the cardinal of Lorraine accepted Baïf's dedications without, however, bestowing on the poet any of the 2,000 benefices of which, according to the historian of the Council of Trent, he annually had the patronage.

Up to 1555 most of Baïf's poems had been addressed to friends. Thereafter they were overwhelmingly dedicated individually to potential benefactors, among them two dozen high administrative officials, a dozen members of the hereditary aristocracy, half a dozen influential court ladies, and a variety of lesser channels of influence—astrologers, doctors, secretaries, tutors, and librarians. Baïf liberally distributed copies of his works, often with a quatrain or a Latin epigram to the recipient, offering poetic services for rewards. He did not easily let slip opportunities to commemorate the births, engagements, trivial pursuits, marriages, campaigns, victories, diplomatic triumphs, and deaths which could occasion reward or patronage, and those are the poems—rather than the ones we remember today, endlessly recited, memorized, and copied—of which manuscripts survive.

No doubt Baïf turned his begging and his complaints about poverty and the trials of the poetic condition into a literary game, accepting less hardship than Marot with less lightness of heart, but he needed an income which his Muse was not providing. He had been tonsured before his father's death in 1547, and therefore soon after attaining the canonical age of 13, but his first benefices did not come until he received four, which he then exchanged, between 1564 and 1567. François II had granted

him a pension, continued by Charles IX and Henri III, while Charles IX in particular proved an important patron, especially in the establishment of the Académie de Poésie et Musique and in giving Baïf a household appointment as secrétaire. Towards 1570 he had an illegitimate child called Guillaume, subsequently legitimized, as Baïf himself had been. We know nothing of the mother except that she continued to keep up social relationships with Baïf's friends, which suggests that she may well have been living with Baïf in his father's mansion. It is perfectly reasonable to speculate that it was the need for an income from ecclesiastical benefices which kept Baïf from marrying his son's mother; it is not unlikely, but there is no evidence.

Well before the pursuit of patronage brought Baïf ecclesiastical benefices he was receiving a pension from François II and Catherine de Medici, dating therefore from 1559 or 1560. From the 1558 Chant de joie he published nothing until 1567, when he produced the didactic poem Le Premier Livre des Meteores, dedicated to Catherine de Medici, largely derived from Pontano's Metereorum liber and from Tyard's L'Univers. It was originally followed by a poem Presages d'Orpheus sur les tremblemens de terre, deriving from the Corpus hermeticum via the Greek Anthology. In 1567, too, Baïf published a free adaptation of Plautus's Miles gloriosus, entitled Le Brave, in octosyllabic verse. It was played on Tuesday, 28 January 1567 at the Hôtel de Guise in front of Catherine de Medici and Charles IX, who had commanded the performance. It finally realized Baïf's ambition to bring antique drama to the French stage which he had years before abandoned to sing the praises of the imaginary "Méline." The intermissions were filled by songs complimenting the royal family, written by, among others, Ronsard, Belleau, and Desportes.

Towards 1570 Baïf's activities were mainly directed towards the founding of the Académie de Poésie et Musique, to some extent modelled in its aims and methods on the Italian academies of about 1540, of which the most famous are probably Sperone Speroni's Accademia degli Infiammati at Padua, which was the background to his 1542 Dialogo delle lingue e della retorica, and the Accademia Fiorentina at Florence. At Florence Giovanni de' Bardi initiated the "riforma melodrammatica," a movement of musical reform through return to the antique, incorporating his views into a Discorso...sopra la Musica antica, e'l cantar bene. The speech starts with a reference to that harmony of which Pythagoras and then Plato said the world was composed, and it insists on the ethically elevating properties and psychological powers of good music. In practice the proposed reform meant accommodating musical time to the long and short feet of the poems to be set, uniting "measured" verse to "measured" music, and it led in Italy, where Bardi's associates preferred strict observance of antique monody to the homophony in part settings generally preferred in France, to the emergence of both opera and oratorio. Baïf even alludes, in a poem to Charles IX probably written in 1571, to an attempt at "measured" choreography, with a single step to a single note, a jump to a double note, and a posture at the cadence.

Catherine de Medici had been explicitly reminded of the original patronage of her ancestors Cosimo and Lorenzo in founding Ficino's Platonic academy at Careggi in the dedications of both Pierre de la Ramée's 1567 Prooemium mathematicum and Philibert de l'Orme's 1568 Premier tome de l'architecture. La Ramée, in particular, both relates his whole project for educational reform in the 1551 Oratio pro philosophica disciplina to the "encyclopedic" ideal which inspired Tyard, and extends it to the advocacy of measured verse in the 1562 edition of the *Gramere*. The 1572 edition mentions Baïf's experiments, and Mersenne's account of Baïf's academy, derived from information supplied by the aged Mauduit and improbably contained in the 1623 *Quaestiones celeberrimae in Genesim...*, emphasizes that music and poetry there, in spite of the prominence given to them, were none the less regarded as belonging to the whole neoplatonist encyclopedia of morally elevating arts and sciences, much as Tyard, Peletier and La Ramée had envisaged it after Budé, himself drawing on Martianus Capella and Aulus Gellius.

There is some evidence that, while such members of the university as Galland and Pibrac wholeheartedly supported Baïf, the university as a corporate body was sensitive to the possibility that Baïf's academy might be about to usurp its own monopolistic teaching privileges, a further confirmation that its aims actually did extend beyond the reform of music and poetry, or the organization of a series of concerts under royal patronage. As earlier, in the matter of the foundation in 1530 of the royal lecturerships that were to become the Collège Royal and then the Collège de France, the conservative reaction of the university was forcing all that was most innovative in the humanist approach to education and the development of the disciplines outside its own gates. In an analogous way the court's conservative reaction to Ronsard, du Bellay, and their group of poetic innovators must be ascribed to a feeling that went deeper than simple offence taken at the group's brashly confrontatory attitudes.

Surviving evidence about the activities, membership, and proceedings of Baïf's academy is disappointingly slight and sometimes contradictory. We know, however, that it also met elsewhere than in Baïf's house, that Baïf was quite lavishly subsidized by Charles IX, and that Henri III not only continued Baïf's pension but also contributed funds for the academy as late as 1585, just before the outbreak of the final religious war. Henri III's Académie du Palais was therefore not its replacement but its organic extension, and for a period the two bodies had a largely common membership, including Ronsard, Baïf, Tyard, Pibrac, Desportes, and du Perron. There can, however, be little doubt that Baïf's own specialized interest was the revival of antiquity's close union of poetry and music, as presupposed by Plato and, especially, Plutarch, and consisting for Baïf of the attempt to accommodate the length of each note to the length of the verse syllables, and that his aim necessarily clashed with late medieval polyphonic practice in which loosely overlapping melodic lines obscured the words. For Baïf the meaning of the words should strive for the same effect which the unified sound of music and verse was also intended to produce. Unfortunately, his treatises *De la prononciation françoise* and *De l'Art metric; ou, De la façon de composer en vers* have not survived.

Baïf's other concern at about the time of the establishment of the Académie de Poésie et Musique was the production of his 1573 four-volume collected *Euvres en rime*, with an autobiographical dedication in alexandrines to Charles IX and a privilège of 26 July 1571. The volumes contained nine books of "Poëmes," nine of "Amours," five of "Jeux," and five of "Passetems." The second volume, printed first, was dedicated to the duc d'Anjou, the future Henri III. In spite of the care which Baïf had lavished on them, the *Euvres*, which included a free adaptation of Sophocles's *Antigone* and a translation of Terence's

L'Eunuque, were not particularly successful, and there was no second printing. Worse, Baïf had, logically enough, prolonged his preoccupation with the importance of the length of syllables, rather than their accentuation, into a projected reform of orthography.

His intention was to make visibly obvious the different sounds in the language, an undertaking which took meaning from the way in which the union of music and poetry was conceived. He started, however, by publishing a verse collection in 1574 without any reference to music. The *Etrénes de Poézie fransoęze an vers mezurés*, with 29 signs, plus accents, in the alphabet, lost most of its meaning when deprived of its relationship to a musical setting, and appears to have robbed Baïf of the serious consideration to which he felt his verse was entitled. Baïf incidentally makes it quite clear that there was no agreement in 16th-century France about the length of syllables. The systems of Bèze—almost without long syllables—Meigret, Peletier, Jacques de la Taille, and Baïf are in fundamental disagreement. In consequence, it was naturally impossible to win acceptance for any form of quantitative versification.

The collection itself contains a series of official odes to very highly placed personages and a series of laborious translations into dactylic hexameters from Hesiod, Pythagoras, and Simonides (attributed to Phocylides), surprisingly collected into a single volume. Baïf was to publish further court odes, sometimes individually in plaquettes with ordinary spelling, in the hope of rewards or patronage, and also the work on which he finally counted to vindicate his poetic reputation, the *Mimes, enseignemens et proverbes* of which 164 six-line strophes were published in 1576, augmented to 819 in 1581. A posthumous edition, due to Mauduit, extended to 1,246 strophes of six lines, or 7,476 lines of verse. There had been, especially towards the beginning of the religious wars, a strongly defensive vogue for moral aphorisms distilling practical wisdom, moral precepts, educational maxims, and stoic attitudes with which to face adversity. Baïf's collection belongs to that tradition, except that the "mimes" are no longer the comic dialogues of antiquity, but have largely been reduced to moral aphorisms, the "sentences" for which Pasquier so admired the text of Montaigne's *Les Essais*, and which are still strewn throughout the plays of Pierre Corneille.

In 1577 Baïf published his Latin *Carmina*, perhaps in a final effort to conquer a poetic reputation in the neo-Latin field where, after the success in advancing the vernacular to which he had himself contributed, there were now fewer rivals. In fact the collection did little to further his reputation. Much that Baïf did publish must have cost immense amounts of time and labour, but it is to be assumed that we have lost translations of at least one play each by Euripides, Sophocles, Aristophanes, and Terence, and probably also two large volumes of odes and other poems which du Verdier claims in the 1585 *Bibliothèque Françoise* to have seen written in Baïf's hand, as well as a translation of Epictetus, some "chansonettes," two of Plutarch's moral treatises, and two dialogues of Lucian, some of which were included in the 1571 privilège.

An autograph manuscript in the Bibliothèque Nationale contains a psalter in measured verse completed, Baïf writes, at 11 a.m. on 24 November 1573, and dedicated to Gregory XIII; the first 68 psalms, also in measured verse, finished in 1569 and published in 1888; a psalter in ordinary rhymed verse, finished on 20 January 1587 and published in 1963; and 176 "chansonnettes" from a collection missing eight leaves which contained an additional 26 pieces. Of the chansonnettes, five were published in a collection of 23 Baïf pieces by Jacques Mauduit with his own music in the 1586 *Chansonnettes mesurées*; seven more from the manuscript were posthumously published with music by Claude Le Jeune in *Le Printemps* of 1603. All the chansonnettes in the manuscript were published in facsimile with a transcription in ordinary orthography in 1964. If Mersenne is to be believed, we have also lost all but the two psalms he prints of a complete psalter in measured Latin verse by Baïf.

Baïf's position in the religious wars was clearly aligned with the legitimate monarchy against the League, and with the Catholics against the Protestants. He had once been enthusiastic about the Saint Bartholomew's Day massacres, and the unfinished psalter is headed *Psautier commencé en intention de servir aux bons catholiques contre les Psalmes de haeretiques* (intended for the use of good Catholics against the psalms of the heretics). The reference is above all to Marot. But towards the end of his life, Baïf's views were those of the moderate "politiques," which had been those of Michel de l'Hôpital, and which in the end prevailed. Baïf was gratified by the award of the silver Apollo of the Toulouse Jeux Floraux on 3 May 1586, making him the successor of his deceased friend and rival, Ronsard, who had received the equivalent award on 3 May 1554. The citation made clear that Baïf was regarded by the Toulouse masters as the greatest living French poet. However, he had to wait. When the masters heard that Baïf was by royal command to produce a translation of the psalter, they decided to have the statue of Apollo exchanged for one of David giving thanks to God. He is sculpted with an open psalter, a lyre on the ground, and the dead Goliath at his feet.

The award might have been expected to go to Desportes, a frequent caller at the Baïf house in the Rue des Fossés-Saint-Victor. Both, with Ronsard, had celebrated on 24 September 1581, for rich reward, the wedding of the most favoured of all the "mignons," Anne de Joyeuse, to Marguerite de Vaudémont, the queen's sister. Desportes and Baïf were left to mourn his death at 26 on the field at Coutras on 20 October 1587, and Baïf's *Epitafes de feu Monseigneur Anne de Ioieuse, beau frere du Roy, duc pair et amiral de France, gouverneur de Normandie*, consisting of a dedication, 35 alexandrine sonnets, and 14 Latin hexameters, was the last work he himself published, although the sonnets appeared the same year in an anonymous collection of *Prieres* with nine alexandrine translations or paraphrases from the *Book of Job*.

Baïf had been ill and had aged prematurely. On 11 September 1587 he gave his house to Jeanne du Bignon, wife of Antoine Patu, and by a will of the same date he made Guillaume Patu his heir, providing he carried the Baïf name and arms. There is confirmatory evidence that Jeanne de Bignon had been his mistress and that Guillaume was his son. He himself died towards the end of October 1589.

WORKS

Of all the poets associated by Ronsard with himself in the lists of seven contemporary poets which he referred to in the "Epistre au lecteur" of the 1563 *Trois livres du Recueil des nouvelles Poësies* as the modern "Pléiade," (q.v.) Baïf may well have been the most learned. Unambitious, not in any real sense mercenary,

laborious, apt to be short-tempered, and generally uninspired, he was none the less a powerful theoretician of verse and language, and he certainly had the most vigorously original mind in Ronsard's group, whose best organizer, most wide-ranging experimentalist, and boldest theoretician he also was. Himself originally an interesting, if not important lyric poet in the generally Petrarchan and Anacreontic traditions as they had developed by the mid-16th century, he also experimented successfully with the use of the flexible alexandrine in the sonnet form he helped to pioneer; with the writing of verse specifically intended to be set to music, from which it therefore takes part of its meaning; with attempts to replace medieval polyphony with syllabic homophony, in which each voice sang the same syllable at the same time; and with the verse adaptation of antique drama.

He made several French versions of the psalms, experimented with an astonishing variety of metrical patterns, including a 15-syllable line, with the caesura after the seventh syllable, and explored a reform of orthography and the possible establishment of quantitative verse, "vers mesurés à l'antique (measured verse in the antique style)," in French, although the French language does not distinguish in the systematic Latin way between long and short vowels. The verse which Baïf wrote to be set to music for court entertainments took him incidentally to a more important achievement. The most important of the musicians with whom he collaborated included Jacques Mauduit, the composer of the special five-part requiem for Ronsard's academic memorial service on the morning of 24 February 1586, and Joachim Thibault de Courville. In his collaboration particularly with them, but also with others, Baïf was one of the great originators of the ambitious "ballets de cour," which were to be later so important in the emergence of opera.

Baïf's greatest historical importance, however, must lie in his various attempts to base practical artistic creativity, and particularly the setting of measured verse to measured music, on the neoplatonist assumptions of the morally and even religiously elevating effects to be expected from the union of poetry and music. They had already been elaborated theoretically by such predecessors as Pontus de Tyard and Jacques Peletier du Mans, and Baïf draws on the well-known renaissance list of the supernatural "effects" of which music had shown itself capable. The existence of Baïf's academy of poetry and music makes clear that the neoplatonist concord of ratios in the minds of God and man, in the harmonies of the spheres and the motions of the planets, and underlying both the harmonies and no doubt the rhythms of music and the metres of poetry, was thought capable of being understood in a way that was not merely metaphorical.

Héroët had tested in his verse the possible coincidence of the psychology of love with the built-in moral and spiritual enrichment of love conceived on the model of Ficinian neoplatonism. La Ramée had sought to overcome the hostility between medieval dialectic and humanist rhetoric and tested his actual renaissance educational reform against the marriage of philosophy and eloquence symbolized, together with the encyclopedic organization of the disciplines, in Martianus Capella's *De nuptiis Mercurii et philologiae*. In the same way Baïf was testing the actual effects of joining certain sorts of verse to certain sorts of music against Peletier's and Tyard's neoplatonist and partly metaphorically intended account of the mathematical structure of the universe.

Ultimately the myth of the mathematical ratios underlying the mind of God and the world-soul derives from Plato's *Timaeus* in which the Creator, having divided the world-soul into harmonic intervals, created individual human souls in the same way, so that the harmony of the universe is organically related to the harmonic proportions built into the structure of the human soul. Since the passions, defined as irrational by the earliest stoics, obviously in the psychological order disturb interior peace, harmony, and concord, the Platonic myth of harmonic proportions becomes very nearly congruent with the commonplace psychological analysis of emotional phenomena according to which passion disturbs peace of soul. Once again renaissance humanism is relying on the power of the Ficinian vision to join the actual psychology of the human emotional or intellectual experience, which it more or less plausibly explains in what is an only semi-mythological register, to a religiously and morally elevated state defined in terms which make it consistent with orthodox Christian spirituality.

Baïf's literary importance undoubtedly lies chiefly in his vision of the function of literature and therefore also of the norms which should govern its production. His own verse is sometimes not without real poetic interest. Since, however, it is often only half of a composite words-and-music creation; since it is often avowedly an experimentation with an admittedly controversial view about poetic rhythms, metres and structures and the desirability of a return to the antique through syllabic homophony in music; since its effect is also partially dependent on the reader's willingness to assimilate a new alphabet of signs; since the proportion of his total output which consists in translations or paraphrases suggests a lack of inventiveness which is also borne out in his original pieces; and since neither contemporaries nor subsequent critics have ever spoken warmly about his perhaps over-laborious and over-lengthy poetic works themselves, his literary stature must continue to depend on his early association with Ronsard as both collaborator and rival, and the power of the later vision of a morally enriching union of poetry and music which he devoted so much of his life to implementing.

The letters patent and statutes of Baïf's academy do not reveal the generally neoplatonist assumptions behind the relationships it envisaged between God, the human soul, the universe, the mathematical proportions governing each, music, poetry, the restoration of the antique, the reorganization of education according to the encyclopedic harmony of the disciplines, the psychology of the human passions, and the nature of human moral and religious perfection. Even in their practical aims, however, something is betrayed of the grandeur of the conception which was shared, with whatever differences of emphasis, between Baïf and Tyard, Peletier, and La Ramée. The letters patent declare that

> ...il importe grandement pour les moeurs... que la Musique courante et usitée... soit retenuë sous certaines loix, dautant que la pluspart des esprits des hommes se conforment et comportent, selon qu'elle est; de façon que où la Musique est desordonnée, là volontiers les moeurs sont dépravez, et où elle est bien ordonnée, la sont les hommes bien moriginez... depuis trois ans en ça ils [Baïf and Courville] auroient avec grande estude et labeur assiduel unanimement travaillé pour l'advancement du langage François, à remettre sus, tant la façon de la Poësie, que la

mesure et reglement de la Musique anciennement usitée par les Grecs et Romains,...et...dés cette heure...ils auroient desia parachevé quelques essays de Vers mesurez mis en Musique, mesurée selon les loix à peu prés des Maîtres de la Musique du bon et ancien âge

(...it is of great importance for moral standards that ordinary and customary music should be constrained by certain laws, more especially because the majority of people's minds conform and accommodate themselves to those constraints; so that, where music is uncontrolled, there, too, moral standards are likely to be depraved, and wherever it is properly controlled, people's behaviour is well ordered...for the last three years they [Baïf and Courville] have worked with one mind in great study and continuous effort for the advancement of the French language and for the restoration not only of the sort of poetry but also of the rhythm and laws of the music practised in antiquity by the Greeks and Romans,... and... even now... they have already achieved success in several experiments with measured verse set to music measured approximately according to the laws of the masters of music of the good and antique age).

Built into the letters patent are therefore the ideas of the morally elevating effects of music, the aim of advancing the French language, and the not here explicitly connected purpose of restoring the measured verse, set to measured music, as it had been in Greece and Rome. The academy was to include composers, singers, and listeners, not only to serve as a nursery for poets and musicians. The statutes which follow are introduced by a paragraph which repeats that the perfection of music consists in the transformation of speech into song with harmony and melody. Voice, notes, and harmony should strive to achieve the effect intended by the words,

> renouvellant aussi l'ancienne façon de composer Vers mesurez pour y accommoder le chant pareillement mesuré selon l'Art Metrique

(also renewing the antique way of composing measured verse to accommodate to it song similarly measured according to the art of metre).

The regulations which follow are very detailed, prescribing two-hour concerts of measured verse and music every Sunday, with payment of subscriptions, and specifying generally how the academy's affairs should be conducted. It is from Mersenne's 1623 *Quaestiones celeberrimae in Genesim...*, with information passed on by Mauduit, that we learn that the aim of Baïf's academy included physical as well as spiritual well-being, and included the cultivation of the whole encyclopedia (μεγαλοδιδάσκαλος) of natural sciences. Mersenne does not, he says, deal in detail with the "other disciplines, especially languages, music, poetics, geography, the other parts of mathematics, and painting, which promote the good of the mind," therefore implying that they must have been included in the academy's vision. Mersenne also mentions military art, bodily exercises, and such arts as are concerned with dress, gardens, food, and money.

The 1552 *Amours*, which in 1573 became *Les Amours de*

Méline, is a mixture in two books of sonnets, of which only one is in alexandrines, and of lyric poems in other forms, in all 42 sonnets and 32 chansons. Baïf is driven by no particular experience, and the tone of the collection is light, almost frivolous. There are 15 poems inspired by Italian predecessors and contemporaries, of which only three come directly from Petrarch. Four poems are imitated from pieces in the *Greek Anthology*, several more from Tibullus, Propertius, and Ovid, and a number from Catullus and his neo-Latin imitators. In a number of instances Baïf trawled first in waters, like the epigrams of Marullus, in which Ronsard's catch was to be much richer, but from the beginning he mixed frank eroticism with his more delicate idealizations of love.

> Ça, sans plus me recourir,
>   Fai mourir
> Tous mes senz, ô douce folle.
> Baise moy, vien apaiser
>   D'un baiser
> La chaude amour qui m'affole

(There, without asking me again, / Make die / All my senses, O sweet mad woman. / Kiss me, come and assuage / With a kiss / The hot love which is sending me mad).

The real experience behind the 1555 *L'Amour de Francine*, and the desire to rival Ronsard and du Bellay, drove Baïf to a much closer imitation of the Italian poets in general, and to a much greater reliance on Petrarch himself, of about 30 of whose poems Baïf provides close imitations. There are 248 sonnets in all, with 23 in decasyllables and the big majority now in alexandrines. Eleven sonnets are imitated from Bembo and nine from Sannazaro. We do not know whether Baïf's two books of sonnets and two of chansons came out before Ronsard's *Continuation des Amours* in the summer of 1555, although Baïf still regarded their rivalry as unresolved. However, the very closeness of Baïf's imitations betrays the lack of inventiveness which condemned him to the laborious complexities of so many of his later poetic undertakings.

Even in this collection the poses and attitudes artificially struck intrude through the close dependence on the Italian and antique models, and the imitations of Horace and Catullus lose by their prolixity. There are too many occasions when a single line of Virgil is expanded into six or eight by Baïf. For *Le Brave* Baïf transposed Plautus's characters to France, and exchanged Orléans for Ephesus, Nantes for Athens, although for the sake of a joke in the text he left Plautus's Indian elephants indigenous to England. The octosyllabic form is deliberately medieval.

Baïf's real inventiveness was in only a technical sense poetic, being concerned chiefly with metre and versification. Having assisted powerfully in the importation of the flexible alexandrine into the love sonnet, Baïf invented the 15-syllable line of seven plus eight syllables.

> Je veu donner aux François / un vers de plus libre accordance,
> Pour le joindre au lut sonné / d'une moins contrainte cadance
> (*Hippocrene*, II, ii)

(I want to give the French / a line which runs more freely, //

To join it to the plucking of the lute / with a less constrained cadence).

The lengths of vowel sounds in French, not so distinctive as the lengths of Latin vowels, cannot support the same sort of quantitative verse. Most French speakers would need guidance with the prosody of the following lines taken from a chansonnette, and transcribed fom Baïf's personal orthography:

> Mŏi quī sūis tŏut fēu păr ămōur tŏut ēn fēu,
> C'ăi-jĕ dīt crāintīf, rĕdŏublēr jĕ pōurrāis,
> D'ēllĕ m'āpprŏchānt, dĕ să fīèvrĕ l'ārdēur
> Cōntrĕ mŏn ārdēur

(I, who am all fire, through love all on fire, / Said I timidly, I could now redouble, / When I come near her, the ardour of her fever / Against my ardour).

Even at his best, Baïf's poetry lacks the lyrical or elegiac intensity of the best verse of his contemporaries:

> Hier, cueillant ceste rose en autonne fleurie,
> Je my devant mes yeux nostre esté qui s'enfuit,
> Et l'autonne prochain, et l'hyver qui le suit,
> Et la fin trop voisine à nostre chere vie.
>
> La voyant aujourduy languissante et fletrie,
> Un regret du passé à plorer me conduit.
> La raison que mon dueil pour un temps a seduit,
> Juge que cet exemple à plaisir nous convie.
>
> Belle, que vous et moy serons bien à reprendre,
> Hé, si le bien present nous dedaignons de prendre
> Tant que, voyans le jour, icy nous demourons.
>
> Las, Helas! chaque hyver les ronces effeuillissent,
> Puis de fueille nouvelle au printemps reverdissent,
> Mais sans revivre plus une fois nous mourons!

(Yesterday, picking this autumn-flowering rose, / I called before my eyes our summer which slips by, / And autumn approaching, and the winter which follows it, / And the end to our cherished life, only too close. // Seeing it today, drooping and withered, / A regret for the past brings me to tears. / Reason, which my grief has momentarily beguiled, / Judges that this example [the withered rose] invites us to joy. // My beauty, ali, how guilty you and I will be / If we disdain to grasp present good / While, seeing the light of day, we live here [on earth]. // Alas, alas! each winter the brambles lose their leaves, / Then become green again with new leaf in spring, / But we don't come to life again; we die once and for all).

PUBLICATIONS

Collections

Euvres en rime, 5 vols., 1881–90

Verse

Le Ravissement d'Europe, 1552
Les Amours de Jan-Antoine de Baïf, 1552

Quatre livres de l'Amour de Francine, 1555

Chant de joie du jour des espousailles de François, Roi Daufin, et Marie, roine d'Ecosse, 1558

Epitaphium in mortem Henrici Gallorum Regis, 1560

Le Brave, 1567

Le Premier Livre des Meteores, 1567

Euvres en rime, 1573

De profectione et adventu Henrici Regis Polnorum Augusti in regnum suum Ode, 1574

Complainte sur le trespas de feu roy Charles IX, 1574

Etrénes de Poézie fransoëze an vers mezurés, 1574

Premiere salutation au roy sur son avenement a la couronne de France, 1575

Seconde salutation au roy sur son avenement a la couronne de France, 1575

Epistre au roy, 1575

Mimes, enseignemens et proverbes, 1576; augmented 1581

Carminum liber I, 1577

Medanis, poema elegiacum, 1577

Orphei seu Mercurii ter maximi prognostica a Terrae motibus, 1586

Chansonnettes mesurées, 1586

Epitafes de feu monseigneur Anne de Ioieuse, 1587

Prieres, 1587

Paraphrase sur les sept pseaumes penitenciels, 1587

Psautier (Metrische Bearbeitung), 1888

Le Psautier de 1857, 1963

Chansonnettes, 2 vols., 1964

Biographical and critical studies

Augé-Chiquet, Mathieu, *La Vie, les idées et l'oeuvre de Jean-Antoine de Baïf*, 1909

Chamard, Henri, *Histoire de la Pléiade*, 4 vols., 1930–40

BALZAC, Jean-Louis Guez de, 1597–1654.

Social and political moralist, letter-writer.

LIFE

Balzac's father's pretensions to membership of the minor aristocracy have been regarded as exaggerated, but were taken seriously enough for him to have been admitted to positions from which it was possible to exercise real political influence. He first became secretary to Roger de Bellegarde, the Grand Ecuyer, and then principal secretary to his relation by marriage, the duc d'Epernon, France's senior peer and a "mignon" of Henri III, whose reconciliation with Henri IV Guillaume Guez organized in 1596. In 1588 Balzac's father had married Marie de Nesmond, from one of the most prominent families in Angoulême, and later established himself as a land-owner and owner of paper-mills in Angoulême. He became mayor of the town and an écuyer in 1612, and échevin from 1622 until his death on 20 September 1650. He owned what was regarded as the town's finest house. Marie de Medici stayed there after her rescue from Blois, from January to 29 August 1619, and Anne of Austria stayed in July 1650.

The village of Balzac, of which Guillaume Guez owned the seigneurie, together with those of Roussines and Puy-de-Neuville, was about six kilometres outside the town. Our writer, who had a brother and a sister, had no real claim to call himself after the village where the family had a small country house, but the name suggested a connection with the illustrious Balzac d'Entragues family. The Guez family itself was well-to-do, it belonged to a land-owning social class whose wealth, however, was derived from expanding industry. Essentially, Guillaume Guez belonged to the upper bourgeoisie which aspired to join the aristocracy and aped the feudal, conservative, royalist, and Catholic habits, prejudices, and values of its social superiors from the noblesse d'épée.

Balzac, the eldest child, was baptized on 1 June 1597. His talent was precocious enough for his date of birth to be important, and disputes based on what he said about it have revealed important variations in the ways of computing year-dates on the basis of stated intervals rather than dated documents in the early 17th century. Ages were sometimes computed as years already accomplished and sometimes as years to have been accomplished at the next birthday, and intervals since or before an event sometimes include the base year, but sometimes do not, so that we might, if we knew, have today to say, for "x years ago" mentioned in a 17th-century letter, "x–1 years ago." It is now generally accepted that Balzac was deliberately casual when referring to his age, but that he was born shortly before his baptism, that is in May 1597. The godfather was Epernon, after whom Balzac was named Jean-Louis, and the place of the godmother, the duke's mother, was taken by her daughter, Mme de Rouilhat.

Balzac was as a matter of course sent to the Jesuit college at Angoulême for the classes of grammar, and then to their college at Poitiers for rhetoric, possibly finishing with his philosophy classes at the Collège Royal de Sainte-Marthe in Paris. On the assassination of Henri IV the regent promised the Jesuits the return of their Collège de Clermont in Paris, but they lost their lawsuit against the university in 1611 and Clermont was not re-opened until 1618. It may well be that Balzac's formal education stopped with rhetoric, as Père Garasse, who taught him at Poitiers, declared. Balzac was to remain all his life close to his former teachers, and his achievement was to reflect a particular feature of their humanist educational style, which was the treatment of the letter as a rhetorical exercise, intended to present a position in moral philosophy, politics, or literature.

Balzac obtained a privilège on 14 December 1614 for a series of official pieces published in 1615, the *Harangues, Panégyriques au Roy sur l'ouverture de ses Estats, et à la Reine, sur l'heureux succès de sa Régence*. He then travelled to Holland with Théophile de Viau, the protégé of Epernon's eldest son, the duc de Candale, but he may already have been there before, since he knew Baudius, who died on 22 August 1613, when Théophile, too, may well also have been in Holland. The most probable hypothesis is that Balzac made two journeys to Holland, perhaps the first at least in someone's suite. In fact we know little of what Balzac did between 1613 and 1618, except that with Théophile he was on the student roll at the University of Leiden on 8 May 1615. Théophile was back in Paris that summer. Before Balzac left Leiden he wrote a *Discours politique sur l'Estat des Païs Bas*, a diatribe against tyranny which Heinsius was to publish behind his back in 1638. The subsequent obscure allusion by Théophile to one or more incidents involving Balzac in Holland in either or both of sodomy and theft was not taken seriously in the 17th century, and is almost certainly an allusion to some sort of boisterous joke. Even Tallemant, who seldom deliberately avoids scandal where he can find something for the *Historiettes*, went out of his way to say that everyone regarded it as nonsense.

By 1616 Balzac had probably returned to Paris. In 1618 he was in Metz with Epernon, who was quarrelling with Luynes. It was under the tutelage of Luynes, who was made a duke and peer on Concini's murder in 1617 and later became Connétable of France, that Louis XIII had emerged from the regency, but Luynes, for a period the most prominent person in the kingdom, overreached himself. He had married not, as had been expected, Mlle de Verneuil, the illegitimate daughter of Henri IV, but Marie de Rohan-Montbazon, later to remarry and become better known as the duchesse de Chevreuse, famed for her beauty, capacity for intrigue, and hostility to Richelieu. When the king's stammer made him unable to preside effectively over the Council, in which Epernon was picking a quarrel with the keeper of the seals, Guillaume du Vair, Luynes took over. It was he who, in January 1619, pushed Louis XIII into bed with his wife and virtually forced him to consummate his marriage. Louis XIII would have had an heir much earlier if Mme de Chevreuse and Mlle de Verneuil had not joined Anne of Austria in a game which involved sliding along the gallery in the Louvre late in Lent 1622. The pregnant queen fell and had a miscarriage.

In December 1617 the Assembly of Notables, an enlargement of the Council consisting of 11 deputies for the clergy, 13 nobles, of whom four were Protestant, and 27 members of the magistracy, met in Rouen. There was a quarrel over precedence between nobles and magistrates which pitted du Vair against Epernon as leaders of their respective factions. The magistrates maintained that they should take precedence over those whom they had the right to try, the noblesse d'épée that the magistrates belonged to the third estate. For a variety of reasons Epernon was also bitter against Luynes, partly because Epernon's Gascons had been excluded on Luynes's advice from the Guards regiment, and partly because Henri de Gondi had been promoted to a red hat promised for ten years to Epernon's son, Louis de la Valette. Epernon had to leave hurriedly for Metz, of which he was governor, to cool his heels. There Balzac wrote on his behalf a violent letter to du Vair, worse for being insufferably patronizing, accusing du Vair of corruption, mercenariness, and above all the "vaine gloire (vainglory)" which cares about "les petites differences qui ont esté introduites au hazard pour la distinction des qualitez (the little differences which have been introduced here and there to distinguish between qualities [of birth])."

The letter was printed in 1618, and Balzac was to repent it, but neither Luynes nor du Vair ever forgot it. It blocked any political future for the ambitious and socially pretentious young Balzac, who also wrote on Epernon's behalf three letters to the king, dated 17 January, 7 February and 20 June 1619, all printed, with alterations, in the *Mercure François* (q.v.). In January 1619 Balzac was with Epernon and his third son, the archbishop of Toulouse, when they contrived the escape to Angoulême of the

portly Marie de Medici, who had to climb out of a window and down a ladder to get out of the castle at Blois. Since both Marie de Medici and Epernon, being governors of provinces, disposed of troops and strongholds, it seemed to Luynes that only Richelieu, whom Marie de Medici trusted but whom Luynes had sent to exile in Avignon, could avert a civil war. He successfully concluded negotiations. Marie de Medici, staying in the Guez house, was given the governorship of Anjou, her debts were paid off, and Epernon was restored to favour.

Balzac said that the regularity of the prospective life made him turn down the post of secretary to Marie de Medici but, had it not been for the letter to du Vair, the star of the family would have been in the ascendant. Marie de Medici and Epernon were the godparents of Balzac's niece, his sister's daughter, at her baptism on 19 July. Richelieu, Bérulle, the cardinal de la Rochefoucauld, and Boisrobert all came to Angoulême to invite Marie de Medici back to court, and Richelieu visited the village of Balzac at least twice. It was in April 1619 that Richelieu's elder brother Henri du Plessis-Richelieu was killed by Charles de Lauzières, marquis de Thémines, in a duel at Angoulême. In July 1618 the Siti brothers had been executed, one of them for a crime no worse than having copied a treasonable pamphlet, and on 14 June Théophile was exiled. Secretaries could pay heavily for the miscalculations of their protectors, and that may have helped to persuade Balzac not to ally his fortunes too closely to those of Epernon, whom he did not follow when he left Angoulême. After the episode of the Epernon letter, Richelieu never trusted him.

In the winter of 1619–20, Balzac himself appears to have been in love with a young Huguenot neighbour of whom we know nothing. He made overtures to remind Richelieu of his existence in May 1620, but the piece he was commissioned to write on behalf of Marie de Medici in August 1620 was found by Richelieu and others too violent to use, and in the autumn Balzac disappeared to Rome acting as an agent of Epernon's son, the future cardinal de la Valette, a sinecure which allowed him to keep a prudently low profile. He may have accompanied Sébastien Bouthillier, sent by Richelieu and the queen mother to work on obtaining a cardinal's hat for Richelieu, and remained in Rome about 18 months, until he left on 5 April 1622; it is a period in his life of which we know very little. He appears to have replaced abandoned political ambitions by hopes of ecclesiastical preferment, but those, too, were to be left unsatisfied. He said he returned to France older than his father, and took a cure at the fashionable resort of Pougues in the autumn of 1622, spending the rest of the time until 1624 in his native region, the hermit of la Charente, as he called himself, referring to the region just to the north of Angoulême. From 1624 he was historiographe de France with a pension of 4,000 livres.

At the end of May 1624 Balzac's *Premières Lettres* appeared, the edition prepared by Boisrobert. The six books of Aretino's letters published between 1537 and 1557 had re-established the vernacular letter as a literary form in renaissance Europe, while Erasmus's vast correspondence, for the most part hurriedly dashed off, had none the less been written with publication in mind. Balzac's collection was rapturously received, with 16 authentic editions in 18 years, and 20 counterfeit editions known before the big posthumous edition of 1665. Balzac became known as a unique stylist, the "unico eloquente." Jean-Pierre Camus wrote that henceforward a letter from Balzac was received in the capital with the reverence normally accorded to an encyclical letter from the pope. Canonization, wrote one cynic, is too slight an honour. There has to be an apotheosis. In 1625 Jean de Lannel wrote of Balzac's letters that he could not believe they had been written by a mortal. French eloquence would die with their author. Immortality is better assured by his pen than by statues of bronze. The letters have made the further study of good letters otiose, and its author's ability is one of the miracles of the age. In fact it was the political and social situations in France which made the letter the peculiarly appropriate form to replace the political, social or moral discourse for which the oral forums had been abolished, and which had not yet been replaced by the formal treatise or dissertation defending a thesis.

Du Vair and Luynes had both died in 1621, but Balzac did not visit Paris until pressed by Boisrobert. He was there from the end of 1624 until spring or summer of 1625 and from early in 1626 until 1628. The letters were intended to be controversial, especially IX, XI, and XIV which form the kernel of the first edition, and positions held in the consequent debate were taken in at least 30 documents, especially in what touched Balzac's disputes with Père Garasse and Théophile. However, neither in his 1619 *Rabelais Réformé* nor in the 1623 *Doctrine curieuse des beaux esprits du temps* against Théophile and the sceptical tradition does Garasse really aim his attack at Balzac, and the former pupil was reconciled to his old master through the mediation of Le Roy de Gomberville in April 1625, although not before Balzac had written to his brother a very harsh letter about Garasse, *A Hydaspe*, and Garasse had replied with the *Lettre du sieur Hydaspe...sous le nom de Sacrator*, written before the spring of 1524.

The attack on Balzac by Père Goulu, general of the Feuillants—"Phyllarque"—is more important, because it raised the whole question of Balzac's ambiguity. He was understood, and then both welcomed and attacked, as a propagator of what has been called "modernism," accused of ruining the traditional foundations of monarchical power, of developing a cynical view in politics, and of propagating a religious scepticism which, none the less, he camouflaged with a carefully orthodox tone, remembering his ultramontane origins with Epernon, defending the integrity of Catholic doctrine, attacking the Reform, and showing outrage at the carefree libertinism of a Théophile.

It was Balzac's enigmatic rationalism which provoked the strongest reactions, while his personality attracted a whole young generation. He cultivated a sickly disposition and an ashen countenance and, always too cold, huddled in front of a fire, but at the same time he was acutely aware of all bodily sensation, with wild eyes and an imperious temperament. The classical rhetoric and the erudition were deployed in the interests of discarding classical models. Balzac was irreverent without being disrespectful, thoughtful and reflective where others, like Saint-Amant and Théophile, were simply impatient of constraint. In a way analogous to that of Malherbe in poetry, Balzac was reacting against a university-based, purely academic erudition but also, sometimes for personal reasons, against the authoritative examples offered by du Vair and Coëffeteau.

In September 1625, already endorsed by Malherbe, Balzac was attacked by the abbé de Crosilles. His contempt for his adversary, "a slave in revolt," provoked annoyance, and Sorel made fun of Balzac in the second, 1626 edition of the *Vraie histoire comique de Francion*. Balzac did not appear to be worried, but there was a more serious confrontation with the Feuillant Frère André de Saint-Denis whose innocent-sounding manu-

script, *Conformité de l'Eloquence de M. de Balzac avec celle des plus grands personnages du temps présent et du passé*, had circulated from about 1625, and contained the serious proof that Balzac had pillaged the antique authors he affected to despise. Balzac wrote an *Apologie pour M. de Balzac* which was signed by his friend François Ogier and published in 1627 with the original attack. Tallemant says that Ogier, asked whether he would pronounce the funeral oration when Balzac died, declined on the grounds that Balzac would say he had written that himself, too.

Goulu's reputation as a bon viveur and a good companion was considerable, but he enjoyed polemic and, since he was the grandson of Dorat and the son of the professor of Greek at the Collège de France whom Ronsard and Belleau had helped to appoint, he had a strong background in the classics. His attack in the 1627 *Lettres de Phyllarque à Ariste* was very firmly based in a defence of classical culture, although it also took in Balzac's vanity, and his care for his comfort. In addition there was an attack from a different direction. A young lawyer, libertin and freelance soldier from Cognac, Bernard de Javerzac, who had frequented the milieu in which Théophile was well known, wrote a *Discours d'Aristarque à Nicandre* intended as an attack on Goulu, although it also made criticisms of Balzac. Balzac's replies to these attacks appeared only in 1644 as *Relations à Menandre*, but there is clearly something we do not know about the dispute with Javerzac. His *Discours* scarcely attacked Balzac, and could have been ignored; Balzac had asked to see it before publication, so knew that it was coming; it had privileged access to information concerning Théophile in Holland; its publication was unaccountably delayed; and both Javerzac and Balzac lived as though in a state of siege. Armed men came looking for Javerzac, and he was in fact beaten up in his room at about 9 a.m. on 2 August 1628.

Balzac was protected by Gaston d'Orléans, and Javerzac wrote an account of the incident in the *Discours d'Aristarque à Calidoxe sur ce qui s'est passé entre lui et Balzac*, which elicited a facetious reply from Balzac's camp, also printed in 1628, *La défaite du Paladin Javerzac par les amis, alliés et confédérés du Prince des feuilles*. Goulu left his reply to Javerzac to his secretary, who wrote a letter *Achates à Pamémon pour le défense de Phyllarque*, but then himself wrote a second volume of *Lettres de Phyllarque à Ariste* against Balzac. The polemic diminished in intensity, but pamphlets were still being published in 1630. It left Balzac clearly linked with Malherbe, and supported by Racan, Faret, and Vaugelas against the possibly free-thinking but erudite academic humanists like Peiresc and the du Puy brothers. He had broken with Nicolas Bourbon, who had taught him to admire the Romans, before 1628 but, in spite of his modernism, Balzac, like his friend and supporter Descartes, remained an admirer of the achievements of the Romans.

From 1628 Balzac was almost permanently at home in Angoulême, intervening in the literary life of Paris only through books and letters. Late in 1631 he published *Le Prince*, a text he had been preparing for years, and which had gone through different forms, focuses and changes of title. He had come to Paris at the end of 1630, hoping that his prefatory flattering portrait of Louis XIII would at least bring him preferment. In fact, it much displeased Richelieu, and Balzac returned to Angoulême disappointed. The work had been announced by Jean Silhon in his dedication to Richelieu of Balzac's 1627 edition of the *Lettres*. Balzac had considered two other models for his prince, the prince of Wales and the duc de Guise, before settling on Louis XIII, and the final work, of which the posthumous *Aristippe* would also have been part, was to have had three parts and to include, following *Le Prince*, a panoramic historical section called "Jugement," and another devoted to "Le Ministre." The work would have amounted to a full treatise on the philosophy of politics and government. In the end Balzac fell between two parties, those on the one hand of Richelieu and the king and, on the other, of Gaston d'Orléans and the queen mother.

Balzac wrote two important letters to Richelieu. The first, which may have been published, and was certainly known, by August 1630, sets out the plan for the three-part work. But late in 1630 Mantua was lost, the king fell gravely ill, and the plot against Richelieu on the "Journée des dupes" failed on 11 November. The reconciliation of the two parties had become impossible. Marie de Medici was exiled to Compiègne, and Balzac's second letter, dated 3 March 1631 and pleading with Richelieu to heal his rift with the queen mother, probably accompanied the text of *Le Prince*. Richelieu did not admit that there was a rift, and told Boisrobert that he thought Balzac a fool. At best Balzac had indeed behaved with astonishing naivety. A letter to Descartes shows that he toyed with the idea of exile before slipping back to Angoulême.

The ensuing dispute was chiefly literary rather than political. A *Discours sur le Livre de Balzac intitulé le Prince, et sur deux lettres suivantes* appeared in December 1631. There was another pamphlet war, with partisans of Balzac replying three times to hostile publications. Politically Balzac had alienated both sides, and as the rift became more and more bitter, with the party of the queen mother unable to save Marillac, with the death of his brother at Châteaudun, the defeat of the duc de Lorraine, and the failure of Balzac's former protectors to save Montmorency from execution on 30 October 1632, Balzac himself was again left stranded in a political desert. Criticisms of his inability to produce sustained discourse began to be heard. He had become a master of baroque prose, but only in a limited number of small genres, and his concerns, while widespread and including literature, history, social and personal attitudes and values, politics, and government, notably still excluded religion. The most important quality of his prose was the intellectual vigour to which the early letters gave expression.

A series of letters between Conrart, Chapelain, and Balzac suggests that Balzac might, had he wished, have been one of the founding members of the Académie, but that he feared the conformism which the new body would be required to enforce, not least on its members. He was in fact a member at least from 1636, although it was early understood that he would not attend, and his status at the beginning is not entirely clear. In the 1634 octavo of *Le Prince* the initial portrait of Louis XIII disappeared, and the rest was better ordered into 32 chapters, forming two sections, devoted respectively to the interior and the external successes of the royal policies. The work's thrust became clearer, although the text remained scarcely altered. Only late, in 1638, did Chapelain introduce Balzac to the Hôtel de Rambouillet (see: *Guirlande de Julie*) where, although he was only a year older than Voiture, his name was linked to the staid and formal literary tastes of Conrart and Chapelain and opposed to that of the more frivolous madrigalists. He got on well with Montauzier, but his relationship with Voiture was never short of antagonistic.

To add to Balzac's misfortunes, his financial situation began to deteriorate, partly on account of the general economic situation and of arrears in the payment of his pension, but partly because his works brought him nothing, and he had disdained the ordinary quest for patrons. The dedication of his Latin poems to Christina of Sweden had brought a gratification only to Ménage, who wrote the preface. The decline of the aristocracy was already in any case causing great difficulties to writers who depended on patronage, and the victorious Richelieu's hostility to Balzac was working strongly to Balzac's disadvantage. On 1 April 1635 the bishop of Lisieux solicited for Balzac the priory of Saint-Paul de Boutteville, without success. Balzac himself was constrained to observe the formalities demanded by the world of patronage, in spite of his obvious distaste for it. Rejected by Richelieu in the early and mid-1630s, he succeeded in renewing relationships with the Epernon and Valette familes in the later years of the decade. He mourned the death of Candale, Epernon's son, and received acquaintances loosely associated with the Cinq-Mars conspiracy against Richelieu. Political constraints made him turn at this period to the formality of Latin, in which contemporary political allusions could more easily remain disguised in references to the heroes, villains, and tyrants of antiquity.

The deaths of Richelieu and Louis XIII allowed Balzac's indignation to explode. His sights were again set on political objectives, as he compared the deceased Richelieu to the worst of the antique tyrants. Balzac's sympathies were with the rebels of the Fronde, but he had gradually become cautious, and the *Socrate Chrestien* of 1652 ends with a letter to Mme de Longueville's nephew as well as one protesting Balzac's devotion to the new king. During the last months of 1653 Balzac was ill. From spring 1652 he had had himself taken to the Capuchines in Angoulême, where he spent some months daily expecting death before finally dying on 8 February 1654.

WORKS

Balzac's literary reputation in his lifetime was grounded firmly in the modernity of his style and attitudes. In 1627 he sent Philippe Cospeau, the bishop of Nantes, a copy of the letter he had written on behalf of Epernon to du Vair in 1618. Du Vair was keeper of the seals, and had a wide reputation as a forensic orator and a neostoic philosopher. He was well over 60. Balzac exaggerates his youth at the time, when he says he was 19, but on no calculation can he have been older than his early twenties, and he had had no more than secondary formal education when he risked writing

Monsieur,

Ayant appris ce qui vous arriva dernierement avec Messieurs les Ducs et Pairs où vous vous laissastes tellement emporter à vostre passion qu'on ne croyait plus que ce fust vous qui parlassiez avec si peu de modestie en la presence du Roy, et de l'autre costé considerant les tesmoignages advantageux que la renommé a tousjours rendu de vostre vertu, il faut que vous me permettiez, s'il vous plaist, de vous dire là-dessus, ou que vous vous estes estudié toute vostre vie à tromper le monde, ou que vous n'avez pu conserver à la Cour les intentions que vous y avez apportées

(Sir,

Having learnt what recently happened to you with their
lordships the dukes and peers, when you allowed yourself
to be so carried away by your passion that people could no
longer believe it was you who spoke with so little modesty
in the presence of the king; and considering on the other
hand the favourable witness fame has always borne to your
virtue, you must permit me, if you will, to say to you that
either you have striven all your life to deceive, or that you
have not been able to keep at court the intentions you
brought there…).

The tone is trenchant, irreverent, and in fact gets more pointed
still. The style is formally classical, although the rhetoric is
clearly baroque is its unbalanced complexity, but the political
risk taken by a young man writing in such terms to the country's
senior judicial officer is breathtaking. A generation of young
iconoclasts may well have admired the daring, but in fact the letter betrays an immaturity of judgement which Balzac never outgrew, although his cultivation of linguistic purity was an attempt
to conceal it. It was not only the official reaction to that letter,
bad luck, and being caught between two camps which thwarted
all Balzac's political, ecclesiastical, administrative, and in the
end also financial ambitions. It was in addition the lack of diplomatic judgement which the letter shows.

By 1618 the almost hysterical atmosphere of the Catholic
revival, which resulted in the military action against Béarn and
eventually against La Rochelle, was already discernible in
France, but there was no real possibility, so soon after the resolution of the religious wars, either that Epernon and the party of
the noblesse d'épée which had once provided captains for the
forces of Henri III could win, even with the help of the queen
mother and the king's brother, a struggle for power, even against
a Luynes who had overreached himself as badly as the future
connétable had, or that any victorious statesman successful in
reaching the position which Richelieu went on to achieve would
ever trust the author of a public letter which started like that.
Balzac was to go on to learn prudence, and to make his style
more concise. But his political instincts were to continue to mis-
direct him.

The early letters include many that are unremarkable, like a
purely formal but elaborately couched note of 16 September
1622 congratulating Richelieu on his elevation to the sacred college. Few modern readers find it easy to understand the fascination of the cynical, shoulder-shrugging content of letters
composed at this date in such a highly formal style, with elaborate and complex syntax, but also with wildness of metaphor.
While Montaigne refused to write in the classical mould, in
favour of the intimacy of a form which would reflect the confid-
ing content of his book, Balzac uses the inflation of classical
rhetoric as a way of demonstrating its function for him of empty
ornamentation. Balzac alludes much in the major letters to
Théophile. Lettre XIV starts with these words addressed to Père
Garasse about his outspoken attack against often imaginary
atheists in the *Doctrine curieuse*:

Je vous l'ay dit mille fois: je me contente que le serein me
face mal aux yeux, sans qu'il faille que j'aille voir des
laides, et que je lise des sottises. Et neantmoins pour
m'obliger fort vous m'avez condamné à passer dix jours

sur vostre gros volume, dont je n'ay jamais pensé trouver
la fin quoy que je la souhaitasse comme le port apres la
tempeste. A n'en point mentir j'estime bien plus le silence
des Chartreux, que l'eloquence de cette sorte de gens, et il
me semble qu'hors du service de l'Eglise, et la necessité du
commerce, le Pape et le Roy leur devroient deffendre le
Latin et le François, dont ils veulent faire deux langues barbares

(I have told you a thousand times: it is enough that I have
an affliction which makes my eyes hurt, without having to
go and see ugly women, and read idiocies. And none the
less to win my strong devotion you condemned me to
spend ten days over your large volume, whose end I
thought I should never see, though I longed for it like port
after storm. I am not lying when I say I prefer the silence
of the Carthusians to the eloquence of those sorts of people,
indeed it seems to me that except for the service of the
Church and the needs of business, the pope and the king
should forbid them to use Latin and French, which they
want to turn into two barbaric tongues).

Even if we allow that the date and circumstances of composition
account for the gratingly abrasive tone, the invective humour
lies wholly in the tension between elevated pomposity of style,
and witty irreverence of content. The rather stilted metaphors
are still striven for, but the style suits the serious congratulatory
tone for which it was developed, and amusingly contrasts with
the writer's resentful seething at Père Garasse's book.

Silhon's 1627 prefatory letter to the second collection of
Lettres, written for Richelieu, makes clear the rules of the genre:

…en entretenant un particulier, M. de Balzac fait des
leçons à tout le monde; et…parmy la beauté des compli-
mens, et les gentillesses de la raillerie, il traite souvent des
matieres les plus relevées, et des secrets les plus importans
de la Philosophie

(in talking to an individual, M. de Balzac has something to
teach everyone; and…among the fineness of the compliments and the gentle touches of mockery, he often treats of
the most elevated matters, and of the most important matters of philosophy).

The letters naturally afford us an inside view of contemporary
history, but this is not what was considered remarkable about
them. The published letters were an artificial genre. Not all
available letters were published, and some that were answer
others that may never even have been written, and would certainly not have been seen by those for whose eyes Balzac's supposed replies were intended. Some are clearly set pieces about
the joys of country life, spiced, like a famous letter to Jacques de
la Motte Aigron of 4 September 1622, with a little gossip about
what is going on.

Balzac wrote enough about political and moral philosophy in
Le Prince and *Socrate chrestien* for it to be possible to use these
works as landmarks in the evolving way in which their subjects
were treated, although neither work puts forward a properly
coherent thesis. Both, indeed, are clearly extended versions of
the shorter genres, like the letter, in which Balzac's writing is
shown off at its best. His opinions are not powerfully or origi-

nally expressed, and are at best of historical interest at a moment when French culture was beginning to establish strict and stable aesthetic norms in the middle of the exuberance which followed the ending of the wars. More successful than either of the longer works are the numerous but brief posthumously collected *Entretiens*, of which the latest editor lists 41, many originally published, like so much else of Balzac's work, in one or other of the collected editions.

The political philosophy of *Le Prince*, like the Christian morality of the *Socrate chrestien*, suffers from being sententious, commonplace, and written in long, inflated periods. The *Socrate chrestien* does little more than state with the gravity appropriate to a ritual solemnity the fact that the Christian Socrates despises human vanities and believes in Christ crucified, which means observance of the norms imposed by faith. The gravity of tone hollowly celebrates an absence of content. None the less, once this is clear, Balzac's views do have an important historical interest, particularly because of the representative but changing roles which Balzac, like Malherbe, had assumed for his generation. Like Malherbe, for instance, Balzac grew steadily stricter in his reactionary views about Montaigne and, particularly, Ronsard.

Ultimately Balzac's importance, like Malherbe's, is to have moved on from the unreflective and ultimately irresponsible libertinism of Théophile to articulate the severe aesthetic canons which, when extended into the realms of morality, formed the nucleus for one of the two sharply contrasting visions which were shortly to clash, more in the disputes between Jansenists (q.v.) and Jesuits than in those between partisans of the "anciens" and those of the "modernes" in the Querelle des anciens et des modernes (q.v.). Here, for instance, is Balzac at an uncertain date, but probably very near the end of his life, perhaps as late as 1652, on Ronsard, recalling what he had written for Chapelain about "un grand Personnage," Montaigne:

Ce Poëte [Ronsard] si celebre et si admiré a ses defauts et ceux de son Temps, comme j'ay dit autrefois d'un grand Personnage [Montaigne]. Ce n'est pas un Poëte bien entier, c'est le commencement et la matiere d'un Poëte. On voit, dans ses Oeuvres, des parties naissantes, et à-demi animées, d'un corps qui se forme, et qui se fait, mais qui n'a garde d'estre achevé. C'est une grande source, il le faut avoüer; mais c'est une source trouble et boüeuse; une source où non seulement il y a moins d'eau que de limon, mais où l'ordure empesche de couler l'eau. Du naturel, de l'imagination, de la facilité, tant qu'on veut; mais peu d'ordre, peu d'oeconomie, point de choix

(This poet [Ronsard], so famous and so admired, has his own faults, and those of his time, as I once said of another great author [Montaigne]. He is not a fully rounded poet, but has the beginnings and the material of a poet. Inchoate parts can be seen in his works, half brought to life, of a body still being formed, being made, but which is not nearly finished. It must be conceded that it is a great well spring, but it is a muddy and unclear spring, a spring in which not only is there less water than silt, but the dirt stops the water from flowing. There is natural vigour, imagination, fluency of composition, in plenty, but little order, little economy, no discrimination).

Balzac goes on to talk about out-of-place philosophy, mathematics where it should not be, Latin and Greek coarsely and ridiculously travestied, bad translations instead of good imitations, and Pindar and Anacreon "escorchez tous vifs (flayed alive)." That is a baroque statement of classical taste awaiting Boileau for its canonical formulation.

PUBLICATIONS

[For the many short pamphlets in whose authorship Balzac had or may have had some part, see the Beugnot Bibliographie, 1967, with 1969 Supplément, and the pamphlets listed by Jehasse, below]

Collections

Les Oeuvres de Monsieur de Balzac, 1627 (and augmented 1628, 1630, 1633, 1642, before the 2-volume folio of 1665)

Prose in French

Harangues panégyriques, 1615
Lettres du Sieur de B, 1624
Apologie pour M. de B., 1627
Lettres de M. de B. Seconde partie, 2 vols., 1636 (preface signed 1627); critical edition, 2 vols., 1933–34; as *The Letters of Mounsieur de Balzac* (omits four letters referring to Protestants), 1634, augmented 1639, 4 vols.
Le Prince, 1631; as *The Prince*, 1648
Discours sur une tragédie de M. Heinsius intitulée "Herodes infanticida", 1636
Le Barbon, 1648
La harangue célèbre faite à la reyne sur sa régence, 1649
Socrate chrestien, 2 vols., 1652
Les Entretiens de feu M. de B., 1657; critical edition, 2 vols., 1972
Aristippe; ou, De la Cour, 1658; as *Aristippus*, 1659

Prose and verse in Latin

Ventus et fumus, 1613
I.L.B. epistolarum liber unus, 1637
I.L.G.B. carminum libri tres, 1650
Versus in obitum Petri Piteani, 1652

Biographical and critical studies

Guillaumie, Gaston, *J.L. Guez de Balzac et la prose française*, 1927
Watter, P., *Jean Louis Guez de Balzac's "Le Prince": a reevaluation* (Journal of the Warburg and Courtauld Institutes, 1957)
Sutcliffe, F.E., *Guez de Balzac et son temps. Littérature et politique*, 1959
Brooks, H.F., *Deliciarum arbiter: Guez de Balzac the Critic* (Thesis), Baltimore 1966
Zuber, R., *Les Belles Infidèles et la formation du goût classique. Perrot d'Ablancourt et Guez de Balzac*, 1968
Jehasse, Jean, *Guez de Balzac et le génie romain 1597–1645*, 1977

29

Guez de Balzac. Bibliographie générale, 1967
——————*Guez de Balzac. Bibliographie génerale. Supplément I, 1969*

BAYLE, Pierre, 1647–1706.

Scholar, critic, and journalist.

LIFE

The first life of Bayle was written by his young admirer, Desmaizeaux, at the head of the first volume of the 1730 fifth edition of the *Dictionnaire historique et critique*. They had met in 1699 in Rotterdam. Although Bayle gave Desmaizeaux a final present of books just three months before he died, their correspondence, while frequent, never became intimate. The biography, of which an English sketch had appeared in 1708, is hagiographically stilted and formal, but very well informed about the facts. The family was Calvinist, and Bayle's father, born on 3 March 1609, studied theology in his native Montauban before being admitted to the ministry in 1637 and appointed to the church at Le Carla, where in 1643 he married Jeanne de Bruguière, of somewhat higher social standing and related to the local aristocracy. The first child of the marriage was Jacob, born on 31 August 1644; Bayle was born on 18 November 1647; and a final child, Joseph, was born on 11 June 1656. Bayle's father remained pastor at Le Carla until he died on 30 March 1685. He appears to have been devout, disorganized, unambitious, and not at all given to assiduity.

The south-west generally was poor, and the Calvinist communities had been steadily drained of their richest members, who had left in a steady and ambitious stream for the north. The church at Le Carla had no glass in the windows, and it is not certain that the presbytery was protected against the cold. The family had a maid and a 12-year-old boy as servants and ate well enough off the land, but were without money. Bayle attended the church primary school, learned some Latin from the age of about 10 from his father, with whom he also started Greek at 12. Jacob, the eldest of the brothers, was in his final school class in 1661 at Puylaurens, about 50 kilometres east of Toulouse, where the Montauban academy had been moved in 1660.

There was difficulty in finding the money to send Bayle to finish his secondary schooling, and Jacob seems to have been reduced to extremes even of student poverty and indebtedness while he studied theology. Something appears to have happened in 1666 to enable his father to send Bayle, aged 18, to Puylaurens that February, still at that age needing two years to complete his humanities, and therefore at least four years behind the children of the rich in his schooling. Since the availability of money dictated the pace of education, he may still not have been

the oldest in his class. Shortage of money meant a further interruption in the winter of 1666–1667, although, presumably thanks to what had been achieved at home, Bayle had by then finished his humanities; Joseph's humanities were for similar reasons to be delayed into his twenties. Bayle himself seems to have stayed at home for nearly two years, then to have spent four months in 1668 with an uncle at Saverdun. Jacob was admitted to the ministry on 20 September 1668, and that November the 21-year-old Bayle was finally able to return to Puylaurens to finish school with his philosophy classes.

Joseph could not follow him until November 1676, when he, too, was 20. All three of the boys were intended almost automatically to embrace the Calvinist ministry. Not only were they bred to it, but there was little else they could do without coming well down in social rank and frustrating the high value put on education by their family and social environment from their earliest youth. Bayle's only occupations at home in his late teens, apart from his passion for quail hunting, must have been study, using the few books he could get hold of, and the making and receiving of visits, with the gossip which necessarily filled them and which we know from his letters that Bayle found tedious. Social life was not made livelier by the paucity of the Calvinist families to which it was virtually restricted, more numerous only further to the south. It was impossible to get a coach or carriage anywhere near Le Carla until halfway through the 18th century. Only mules and horses could manage the boulder-strewn hills and badly made roads.

There was no regular source of news or comment other than the expensive gazettes, and it may well be that it was the dearth of information about the outside world which from this period onwards occasioned Bayle virtually to hoard accurate facts, and gave rise to what was almost to be his later obsession with news and reviews. His brothers reacted in different ways, but Bayle himself acquired a passion for voracious reading and doubtless disorganized study, so overwhelming that he developed what was certainly also a temperamental inclination to remain unambitious, never interested in a family life of his own, a career, the exploitation of the fame he acquired, or more than the most modest comfort. He appears never to have noticed mountains, lakes, the picturesque, or any scenery; there is no reliable record of any infatuation; and he never described the towns he passed through or lived in, noting at most the temperature, the humidity, or his dislike of the cuisine. He preferred warmer climates to those he had to endure.

When he left Le Carla again in November 1668, Bayle was never in fact to return. His Calvinism was both domestic, acquired at home, and dynastic, in the sense that, since there were almost no converts to Calvinism, it was handed on from one generation to the next. The affiliation was by divine election; for the period during which Bayle was a Catholic he had to break with his family. The French synods of Alès in 1620 and Charenton in 1623 had registered the 1619 anti-liberal decrees of Dordrecht, and the theological studies of Bayle's father had started in 1629 in the classically based but strict Calvinist atmosphere of Montauban, whose orthodoxy was regulated by the French synods which had adopted the Dordrecht norms. Bayle's elder brother, Jacob, who would undergo arrest in June 1685 and die in prison that November rather than recant at the revocation of the Edict of Nantes, wrote home in 1665 noting, as perfectly normal, the exclusion of Jean-Robert Chouet from the ministry on grounds, not of his well-known Cartesianism, but because he shared Amyraut's liberal Saumur theology of predestination, and was therefore suspect of Arminianism.

Three months after Bayle's return to Puylaurens, on 19 February 1669, he arrived at the Jesuit college at Toulouse as a day-boy, and there on 19 March, exactly a month later, he became a Catholic, reverting to Calvinism only 17 months later. The motive can scarcely have been material, although Bayle received a pension from the bishop of Rieux and could no doubt have eventually expected a modest benefice. His family considered him a renegade, and almost certainly shared the belief that Catholics could not be saved, particularly not once they had been shown the light of the gospel. It seems probable that Bayle had had serious doubts about the Calvinist position at Puylaurens and himself taken the initiative to move to Toulouse, and we know he read through various works of theological controversy. What we do not know is whether his Calvinist beliefs had already been shaken before he did so, or whether they alone prompted his conversion. In any case, it seems more appropriate to think in terms of a change of intellectual conviction than of any interior conversion. Having, for reasons of whatever order, decided that his Calvinist allegiance was mistaken, Bayle rectified his error without obvious signs of emotional upheaval, returning, as he notes, next day to his classes.

Bayle's diary, the *Calendarium carlananum*, tells us that he left Toulouse on 19 August 1670 for Mazères, about 50 kilometres to the south-east, perhaps five kilometres from Saverdun and twenty from Le Carla. There, two days later, he abjured Catholicism in the presence of his Saverdun uncle, Laurent Rivals, and his brother Jacob from Le Carla, and fled to Geneva, where he arrived on Tuesday 2 September. The penalties in France against Calvinists who, in the official language, "relapsed" into Calvinism after conversion to Catholicism were harsh, and increased in severity throughout the century, with decrees in 1663, 1665, and 1679 before the revocation of the Edict of Nantes. By 1670 they included exile.

Bayle may well have decided on his abjuration before defending his philosophy theses in July. His notebooks tell us that he had been vigorously defending Aristotelian scholasticism against Descartes and Gassendi, but his new change of conviction, often thought to have been precipitated by the incompatibility of the Cartesian physics Bayle is presumed to have held and the doctrine of transsubstantiation, seems from the *Calendarium* and such apologetic works of the period as Bossuet's partly Port-Royal (q.v.) inspired 1670 *L'Exposition de la doctrine catholique* to have been really occasioned by rather wider considerations, including the whole of Catholic Eucharistic theology, ecclesiastical infallibility, and the entire general style of Jesuit devotion, with its tendency to exploit the role of the tangible and sensible in representing the spiritual and the real.

For Bayle, the role of infallible authority in the discernment of religious truth was ultimately replaced by the recourse to direct religious experience, widely if often tacitly accepted on both sides of the schism during the northern renaissance, quite clearly by Zwingli, but also notably by the Jesuits on the Catholic side of the schism. The correction of his original intellectual error had seemed to have been put right, with as much conviction but no greater fervour on this occasion than on the previous one. Bayle's deviation from Calvinist orthodoxy made it difficult for him to obtain employment while he continued his studies in a Geneva overflowing with students in search of tutorships, but the solid foundations and fluency in Latin with which he had been provided in Toulouse also stood Bayle in good stead. Apparently recommended by Louis Tronchin, a liberal professor at the Geneva academy, Bayle was taken on as tutor by Michel de Normandie, Tronchin's brother-in-law and one of the members of Geneva's governing Petit Conseil. Jacques Basnage, from a well-to-do family and six years younger than Bayle, one of whose closest friends he was to become, was a paying boarder in the same household.

In Geneva, where Bayle had few duties in return for bed and board and occasionally, until the summer of 1671 when the family became again too poor, received money from home, he was won over to Cartesian physics, largely by Chouet at his public conferences and by Louis Tronchin, who was Chouet's uncle, while he continued his studies at the academy. He concentrated more on languages than on theology, as they presented a surer way of earning a living, and he was taken on as tutor to boys of seven, nine, and eleven by a family of authentic but impoverished aristocrats, the Dohnas, at Coppet. The Geneva academy had entered on a decline, partly because the stricter Swiss cantons were having doubts about the rigour of its orthodoxy, and partly because the controversy between the Saumur liberals and the rigorous conservatives had led to a general diminution of enthusiasm. Bayle tried to make his pupils speak only Latin, and they did not enjoy the tuition. Fifty years later the youngest recalled the occasion on which, by accurate positioning and correct timing, he dodged the new book which Bayle threw at him for having forgotten the meaning of a word. It went straight into the fire. For the first time in his life Bayle also found himself in the company of educated and intelligent women, and in an environment to which international news travelled fast.

The impoverished family at Coppet offered Bayle little money and no future. He was actively seeking a safe opportunity to return to France, when Basnage found him a tutorship at Rouen with the Calvinist La Rive family. Bayle left Coppet on 29 May 1674 and, travelling through Lyons and Paris, reached Rouen on 15 June. Because of the danger of being uncovered as a relapsed convert, he spelled his name "Bêle." He had no money, no completed professional training, could not return home, and did not see any prospect of a career other than as a semi-menial member of someone's household. The La Rive boy was not interested in study; Basnage was at the orthodox Calvinist academy at Sedan; Bayle was bored with the three months he had to spend in the country with his charge from that August. He tried for a post in Paris and thought about London, but had not sufficient money to go. The informative correspondence with his young brother, Joseph, began, and Bayle had his portrait painted at his mother's insistent request, although it had not yet arrived at Le Carla when she died on 21 March 1675.

Bayle did obtain a tutorship in the family of Jean de Beringhen in Paris, where the two youngest boys of the 63-year-old conseiller at the parlement de Paris, only nine and eleven, had two tutors. It was rather like Coppet, a job leading nowhere with the indisciplined children of impoverished aristocracy. Bayle spent six months in Paris. In spite of complaints at his cloistered life he was presented to Conrart, Ménage, and Huet and attended, no doubt with his pupils, Thomas Corneille's *Circé*, but he was too discouraged to allow his name to go forward when Basnage alerted him to a vacancy arising at Sedan out of a retirement. In the end Bayle yielded to persuasion, but found that the election was not the formality which Basnage had promised. He was, however, appointed, and started teaching on 11 November 1675.

Pierre Jurieu, ten years his senior, was professor of theology and Hebrew, and was anxious for Bayle's appointment in order to defeat the choice of a local candidate which, given the diminutive salary, would otherwise have been automatic. With a predecessor still alive and drawing 400 livres a year, Bayle was offered only 250 livres, although his lodging and board alone cost 300 livres. Even with the strictest economy and some help from private fees, Bayle had to borrow from Jurieu. His predecessor died at the end of 1676, and Bayle was drawing the full 400 livres from his second year at Sedan. There were five hours of teaching a day. Bayle learned from Le Carla that inquiries were being made about him. He arranged to have himself registered as living in England, but the danger of deportation remained real. At Sedan only Jurieu knew about his past. He had, however, now at least achieved a modest social status and professional rank, and for the time being he had in Jurieu a kind and welcoming friend. It was only later that Jurieu was to show himself vindictive, imperious, and more than a little paranoid.

Jurieu had no children, but lived with his wife and three female relations. Bayle became virtually the family's adopted son. He grew, as he later admitted, blind to the prejudice and trickery with which Jurieu persecuted the Calvinist theologian Claude Pajon, who taught that God did not intervene in the universe after its initial creation, so that there could be no direct action of the Holy Spirit on individual souls, and the mediation of secondary causes, the preaching of the word, was required. Pajon was accused of teaching a double human participation in the work of conversion, that of the preacher of the word, and the cooperation of those who heard it. Pajon steered a course clear of the full Arminianism of Amyraut by regarding conversion as an event, even if only an act of knowledge, but Bayle, in spite of what he said later, was from very early on convinced of the dangers of Pajon's doctrine of divine non-intervention into human affairs.

Bayle complained that he was inadequately informed about the world at large, and sought a correspondent in the literary world of Paris. We find, however, that in November 1674 he had already read Malebranche's *De la recherche de la vérité*, of which only three volumes had been published; that by 1675 he had read early work by the still unknown Richard Simon; and that in 1679 he was reading Spinoza's *Tractatus*, although that work had already been for some time circulating among the students at Sedan. Bayle spent the summer of 1679 in Paris, and what he there discovered, or perhaps felt, prepared him for what came none the less as a shock when, in an anticipation of the revocation of Edict of Nantes, the academy of Sedan was closed down in July 1681. By then Bayle had for a long time been contemplating the prospect of earning a living in England or Holland.

When the blow fell, Bayle moved in with the Jurieu family until September, to save the cost of bed and board. Jurieu, although minister of Sedan, and therefore with a non-academic income and duties to his flock and under no direct legal ban, was warned to leave, and saw all round him his co-religionaries imprisoned for trivial reasons. He accepted the parish of Rouen, where he was installed before the winter. Bayle went to Paris, intending to spend the winter with Basnage or Jurieu when, through the good offices of an ex-pupil, he was invited to take the chair of philosophy and history at an institute of higher studies to be created at Rotterdam by Adriaan van Paets, later ambassador to London, of whom Bayle was to become a protégé. Jurieu, whose prominence made him a quarry for the French regime, felt it wiser not to go to Rouen, but accepted a post at the academy of Rotterdam, which Bayle helped to arrange, as well as a pastorship in the town. Bayle himself arrived there on 30 October 1681 and began teaching on 5 December. He was to continue for 12 years. He had with him three unpublished texts, written during his last two years at Sedan: a satirical harangue put into the mouth of the maréchal de Luxembourg, a dissertation defending the Cartesian notion of extension against an attack by a Jesuit; and a letter on the comet which had appeared in 1680 and which Bayle had originally destined for the *Mercure Galant* (q.v.).

From the beginning there was some tension between Jurieu's dignity and the tolerance of his Dutch hosts. Jurieu felt superior, and insufficiently recognized. He quarrelled with van Paets, who had been to some pains to procure his appointment. None of the French influx regarded the need to beg as tolerable, although it was part of the Dutch academic system, and salaries were exiguous. Bayle, however, got on well. His unostentatious and unambitious modesty made him at home in Holland. His salary rose quickly from 300 to 500 florins a month, but the fees of the pension at which he lodged, admittedly providing a French cuisine, rose as well, from 400 to 450 florins. He was expected to lecture without notes, but he taught for only three hours a week, one of philosophy and two of history, reducing to two hours at some date no later than 1684. In fact the academy was a gesture of Dutch kindness to the French exiles. It could not hope to rival the established Dutch universities or to offer a culture or professional training the equal of theirs. It attracted therefore only a local clientele, small merchants or impecunious immigrants.

Bayle met the Dutch printer and bookseller Reinier Leers, a member of the Walloon church, more liberal than orthodox in its Calvinism, as soon as he arrived in Rotterdam. Leers published under his own name, but also under the imprint "à Cologne, chez Pierre Marteau" used too by other Dutch publishers. On 11 March 1682 he published a considerably reworked and augmented but anonymous version of Bayle's *Lettre sur la comète* (*Lettre à M. L.A.D.C. Docteur de Sorbone Où il est prouvé par plusieurs raisons tirées de la Philosophie et de la Theologie, que les Cometes ne sont pas le présage d'aucun malheur. Avec plusieurs Reflexions Morales et Politiques, et plusieurs Observations historiques; et la refutation de quelques erreurs populaires. A Cologne, chez Pierre Marteau M.DC.LXXXII.*) Leers quickly divulged the authorship, and the book was well received, even in France, where it did not attract any unfavourable attention from the censors. Eighteen months later, in 1683, a still anonymous second edition appeared as *Pensées diverses sur la comète*. This was the much augmented edition on which later controversy would be based.

Between the two editions of the *Comète* Bayle wrote in a fortnight a refutation of the Gallican ex-Jesuit Père Louis Maimbourg's 1682 *Histoire du Calvinisme*. The pope had had Maimbourg dismissed from the Jesuits for Gallicanism, and Louis XIV gave him a pension of 3,000 livres and an apartment at the abbaye Saint-Victor. Bayle's understandably anonymous *Critique générale de l'histoire du calvinisme de M. Maimbourg* was published by Wolfgang at Amsterdam under the imprint "à Villefranche, chez Pierre le Blanc," with a second augmented edition in November. The anonymity was pierced and the name of the author soon revealed. The book was burnt in Paris in March 1683. Bayle was naturally worried for the safety and well-being of his family, and encouraged his younger brother to adopt a false name whenever he came to Paris.

Bayle appears to have been acting as reader, scout, and proof corrector for Leers, and it may well have been Leers's idea to have the *Critique générale* published in Amsterdam. From 1682 onwards Bayle seems at least to have had no serious financial worries, and he would be able to face the future with some confidence even when he lost his right to teach in 1693. He was able to afford a year and a half effectively without stipend, to travel for two months, and to take the waters at Aix when he was ill, probably from overwork, in 1687–88, and he even left a modest sum on his death. No doubt Leers would not have let him down after the spectacular success of the *Dictionnaire*, and no doubt Bayle ceased to take on the lowlier chores initially assumed during his association with Leers, but he certainly steered manuscripts to the printer during his early years in Holland, and had advance knowledge of the contents of volumes published by Leers.

When Mme van Paets had died in March 1682 she had left Bayle 2000 florins to buy books, although the money had to be used to settle his younger brother's debts, without payment of which Joseph would have been prevented from leaving Geneva and would have lost a desirable tutorship with a Paris family related to the Bayles. Joseph was to die on 9 May 1684 after a short illness. It took a week for the news to reach Bayle. Bayle's anonymity had been widely enough breached for it to be regarded as scandalous that one of the best pens of French Protestantism should be forced to live so modestly, and Bayle was offered a more lucrative appointment at Franeker. He turned it down politely, alleging his health and especially his propensity to migraine. In fact he liked Rotterdam, with its large French-speaking community, and preferred a minimal standard of comfort, with leisure to write, to the onus of a proper university teaching post.

He may, furthermore, in the summer of 1684 already have been contemplating a different sort of change. The Saumur librarian, Henry Desbordes, now a publisher in Amsterdam, had in March 1684 published in a volume devoted to Descartes's philosophy the *Dissertation sur l'essence des corps* which Bayle had brought with him from Sedan. Desbordes, in collaboration with a Catholic doctor in France, Nicolas de Blégny, who had himself edited the first medical journal, a monthly, from 1679 to 1682, had produced two issues of a *Mercure Savant* early in 1684. Desbordes now proposed to Bayle cooperation on a new monthly journal, and *Les Nouvelles de la République des Lettres* started to appear anonymously in the spring of 1684. The anonymity, never very serious, was dropped in 1685, and the editor's name appeared in that March, with a dedication to the magistrates of Rotterdam. Success was instantaneous, particularly before January 1685, after which administrative regulation demanded that the review should be sent to France by ordinary post rather than freighted in bulk, considerably increasing the cost.

The closeness of Bayle's relationship with Jurieu diminished by degrees, but quite speedily, between 1681 and 1683. It is possible that Jurieu became jealous. Bayle's reply to Maimbourg was considerably more successful than Jurieu's own, and Bayle was no longer submitting his work for Jurieu's opinion before publication. There was, however, no question yet of a break. At Le Carla, Jacob had married the daughter of a Montauban minister, signing the contract on 23 November 1682. Early in 1685 Bayle's father died, and on 10 June Jacob was imprisoned at nearby Pamiers, then moved, first to Toulouse and finally to Bordeaux, where he died on 12 November, after the lettre de cachet ordering his release had already been signed. Under the revocation's conditions, by the date of his death he had the right to leave France.

After the mass exile of Protestants following the revocation, Jurieu at first continued to hold monarchist views and, buoyed up by the Book of Revelation, even to hope for the conversion to Protestantism of Louis XIV. He then changed his mind, had recourse to the 16th-century Protestant views on the rights of the people and their release from all obligation of loyalty to tyrants, and encouraged militant support for the enemies of Louis XIV, that is the Dutch, abetted by the English, so consummating the rupture between the Protestantism and the Frenchness of the communities in exile, and for ever precluding a change of heart at Versailles—however unlikely—at least as long as Louvois was in charge. Bayle, on the other hand, continued to address moderate Catholic opinion in France, seeking not a tolerance in the sense limited to a willingness to endure, but a tolerance which involved a real respect for the conscience of the individual. His view was already discernible in the second part of the *Critique générale* of March 1685. A few months later he did everything he could to disseminate Paets's exhortation to English Protestants to obey James II in spite of his Catholicism, so creating as an ideal a reciprocity of tolerances, French for Calvinism in France to be seen as counter-weighted by the loyalty of Protestants to a Catholic king in England, and in 1686 Bayle published *Ce que c'est que la France toute catholique sous le règne de Louis le Grand*.

Bayle multiplied his activities, issuing pamphlets that were, like the impassioned plea for tolerance of October 1686, the *Commentaire philosophique*, only pseudo-anonymous. Jurieu replied with his *Des droits des deux souverains en matière de religion* of 1687, to which Bayle replied briefly in the third part of the *Commentaire*, dated 30 May 1687. He was, however, exhausted, and had had to give up the *Nouvelles* and his teaching in February. He did not start to teach again until the spring of 1688. He may towards the end of 1687 have asked the pastor Abbadie to find him a teaching post in Berlin. Although Bayle's stipend continued to be paid, he had himself to pay his substitute.

Basnage had been forced out of France by the revocation and was at Rotterdam in 1691, finally, in spite of opposition from Jurieu, becoming a Walloon pastor in that town. He remained a monarchist, rather than a populist of the Jurieu type, but did not go as far as Bayle in the advocacy of a simple respect for conscience in matters of religion. Bayle resumed their friendship and got to know Basnage's brother, Henri Basnage de Beauval, the author of the 1684 treatise *La Tolérance des religions*, and from October 1687 the editor of *L'Histoire des ouvrages des savans* published by Leers. At that date Bayle thought that his own *Nouvelles* had been abandoned for good. It was in fact to be continued by Jacques Bernard. Paets had died in October 1686, but not before introducing Bayle to the rich Quaker merchant Benjamin Furly, through whom Bayle met Locke and, much later, Shaftesbury. Bayle was himself absent from Rotterdam only for the two months from 8 August 1687 terminating in the cure at Aix, and must have met many of his co-nationals, driven out by the revocation. Almost all passed through Rotterdam, which was also the port for England, whether to cross the Channel or to move on to other destinations within Holland or beyond.

It was in 1687 that Daniel de Larroque came to Rotterdam. Bayle had known his father and got to know the son, whose book had been published by Leers in 1683. Larroque went to England, from where he supplied Bayle with information for the *Nouvelles*, and then to Hanover in 1689 as secretary to the English ambassador. It is probable that he left with Bayle the first draft of what we know as Bayle's anonymously published *L'Avis important aux Réfugiez sur leur prochain retour en France*, which appeared in mid-April 1690 "à Amsterdam, chez Jacques le Censeur." It was printed by Moetjens at The Hague. Moetjens's reader, one Louis, said that the entire manuscript was in Bayle's writing, although it is not clear how he knew, and the *Avis* continues the argument of one of Bayle's pamphlets which had appeared early in 1689, the *Réponse d'un nouveau converti à la lettre d'un réfugié*. Bayle strenuously and always denied having written the *Avis*, and the general assumption that he was lying rests on evidence which is altogether too slender for comfort. Larroque abjured a year after leaving Holland, and returned to France, where he was involved in several polemics and the composition of *L'Ombre de Scarron*, a scurrility for which booksellers were hanged. He was imprisoned, released on Bossuet's advice, and finally employed by the department of foreign affairs.

The *Avis* questions Jurieu's new identification of the Protestant religious interest with the political advantage of the Dutch, and it has been less than conclusively argued that Bayle miscalculated, touched up Larroque's *Avis* with the intention of refuting it, but desisted when it became clear that the weight of refugee opinion clearly turned out to be for the sovereignty of the people, the House of Orange, and the English revolution, and against Bayle's own monarchist attachment to Louis XIV and the hope of being allowed to return to France under renewed tolerance. Since we know that Bayle is at least alleged to have copied out the text, the unresolved questions are: firstly, whether Larroque or someone else was the real author; secondly, how, if at all, Bayle modified the text; and thirdly, why he colluded in the publication. The matter concerns more than the history of Bayle's intellectual opinions and literary strategies.

When Jurieu suspected Bayle of authorship, the war of personal invective and multiple anonymous pamphlets between Bayle and Jurieu began. Jurieu, who had a strong political motive for tarring Bayle with the authorship of the *Avis* and thereby discrediting his political stance within the Calvinist community, accused Bayle of being an enemy of William III, a lackey of Versailles and, in religion, a Socinian, a deist, then an atheist, the terms not just to be understood as insulting invective rather than theological accusation, since Jurieu did for some years ostentatiously drop the accusation of atheism. Some of Bayle's pamphlets were published in the *Oeuvres diverses*, and most of those by Jurieu are available, but the texts thrown up by the whole war, which had over half a dozen participants and lasted throughout 1691, have never been published, and some of the broadsheets have been lost.

In 1693 there was a municipal coup d'état at Rotterdam and the republicans were ousted in favour of Orangist supporters. The friends of van Paets were removed and Bayle lost his post on 30 October. He stayed in Rotterdam, supported by Leers. Basnage, in November 1690, had already announced in the *Histoire des ouvrages des savans* that a Project was being prepared for a *Dictionnaire*, without naming an author. Printing of the Project began in December 1692. About half the entries were to be devoted to antiquity, but since most of what was subsequently added was about modern subjects, the proportion of articles devoted to antiquity dropped to under 25%. The *Dictionnaire* itself had begun almost as a supplement to Louis Moreri's 1674 *Grand Dictionnaire historique*, whose fifth edition of 1688 had contained three volumes. Bayle started by wanting to correct some of the entries bearing upon Roman history and mythology.

The polemic with Jurieu spluttered into life again early in 1694, when Jurieu denounced Bayle at Rotterdam. Bayle published an *Addition aux Pensées diverses* and on 2 March 1694 a virulent pamphlet, *Nouvelle hérésie dans la morale, touchant la haine du prochain, prêchée par M. Jurieu*. By this time, however, we now know that Holland had received a request from London for Bayle's dismissal before the upset on the Rotterdam council, and that they said nothing, taking only steps to examine the 10-year-old *Pensées sur la comète* and finding, as they expected, nothing. Jurieu had apparently been running a spy ring in France on behalf of London. It was uncovered by the French authorities in 1696, and there were hangings in Paris, Brest, Saint-Malo and La Rochelle, eight or ten in all. Jurieu thought Basnage responsible for uncovering the network, and knew, of course, that Basnage tended to share Bayle's French loyalism.

The first of the two folio volumes of the *Dictionnaire historique et critique*, A to G, was printed by August 1695, but not put on sale until the second volume was ready, with an index by Gédéon Huet, and the set went on sale on 24 October 1696, the only one of Bayle's works published, in accordance with a condition of the privilège, over the author's name. Bayle declined offers of generosity in return for a dedication, particularly from England and probably because of the loyalty he still felt to France. In France, bookseller publishers who presumed that the work contained only the sort of material normally found in dictionaries applied for a privilège. The chancellor had the work read by Renaudot, whose report was so unfavourable that not only was no privilège granted but the work's importation was forbidden. Renaudot's report was leaked, and a copy was sent by a friend to Bayle and by an enemy to Jurieu. Jurieu made the report the basis of a pamphlet, to which Bayle hurriedly replied.

The Calvinist authorities courteously asked for some modifications in future editions. Bayle gave the appearance of unhurried compliance and published a pamphlet in which he announced his intention of making them, and no further action was taken. Bayle also offered to set out as well as he could replies to the Manichaean point of view he had expounded, "if the Consistory would be good enough to let him have them." The second edition, published on 27 December 1701 in three volumes, with the celebrated "Eclaircissements (explanations)," deliberately included alterations as well as additions, so that purchasers needed a whole new set, rather than just a supplement. The first edition had sold out. Bayle continued after 1701 to work at the *Dictionnaire*, but it was no longer his major preoccupation. He compiled his *Réponse aux questions d'un Provincial*, of which the first volume appeared in 1703, and in 1704 he published the *Continuation des Pensées diverses*, preferring atheism to idolatry.

In 1698 Bayle had made the acquaintance at Rotterdam of Lord Ashley, Anthony Ashley Cooper, the future Shaftesbury, to whom, a little later, Bayle would recommend Desmaizeaux, the ex-pastor and itinerant tutor who was to become his biographer.

In the winter of 1702 or 1703 Bayle fell into a canal on leaving church and, since he could not swim, subsequently said that he had supposed he would drown. Someone had heard the splash and he was saved, but he appears not even to have shouted for help. On 12 February Bayle registered a will making Basnage, with whom relationships seem slightly to have cooled, his universal heir. He spent his time now answering adversaries, either in journals or in further volumes of *Réponse aux questions d'un Provincial*, although he did not answer Jurieu's final attack, the 1706 *Le Philosophe de Rotterdam, accusé, atteint et convaincu*, which much contributed to the *Dictionnaire*'s reputation for heterodoxy after Bayle's death. From 1699 Jacques Bernard, a former collaborator with Jean Le Clerc on the *Bibliothèque universelle* and then editor at The Hague of his own *Lettres historiques* from 1692 to 1698, had resurrected the *Nouvelles de la République des Lettres*. It was he who led the attack sustained by Bayle during the last years of his life on grounds that were not theological, and Bernard's subsequent nomination to a pastorship at Leiden in 1705 appears to have owed something to his attack on Bayle. The attack by Isaac Jaquelot, a Cartesian inclined towards Arminianism, was aimed at Bayle's demonstration of the incompatibility of rationality with belief in revealed truth, which eventually compelled Jaquelot to abandon any attempt to defend Calvin's doctrine on predestination. Le Clerc was an Arminian professor at Amsterdam, who disliked Jurieu even more than he disliked Bayle, whose doctrine, however, he regarded as more dangerous for being less absurd.

In the autumn of 1705, more or less as habitually at the onset of winter, Bayle began to cough. This time, however, the cough did not clear up in the spring. Tuberculosis set in. Bayle seems to have regarded death as already inevitable, and did nothing except avoid company, since it was talking that made him cough. There are two slightly different accounts of the time of his death, but it is clear that Bayle died alone, in his room, more probably on the late afternoon of 27 December 1706 than on the following morning.

Works

Shortly before Bayle died, his friend, the Rotterdam minister André Terson, wrote to ask him to set down in writing a declaration of belief that would remove any scandal after his death. Bayle replied jocularly, quoting Horace and Martial, but without complying. There is very strong evidence, however, that he also wrote a note, perhaps within hours of his death:

> Je sens que je n'ai plus que quelques moments à vivre; je meurs en Philosophe Chrétien, persuadé et pénétré des bontés et de la miséricorde de Dieu et vous souhaite un bonheur parfait

> (I feel that I have only moments left to live; I die a Christian philosopher, persuaded and convinced of the goodness and mercies of God, and wish you perfect happiness).

Written by a Calvinist accused of atheism who obviously delighted in irreverence and in the contradictions he could everywhere establish between different accounts of the same event, between natural and supernatural explanations of it, and between incompatible conclusions drawn from the same evidence, that statement was pounced on and pored over by the enlightenment. Was it a statement of belief? In what? In immortality? Which was more important, that Bayle thought of himself as a Christian or that he called himself a philosopher? Did he imply a belief in his personal immortality?

The works have been interpreted as diversely as the statement at the hour of death, and for the same reasons. Was this powerful, original, courageous, and honest mind a sincere Christian believer, a sincere disbeliever, or a committed or a reluctant doubter? Was he a liberal Calvinist, or the founding father of a new and enlightened type of European thought liberated from the tyrannical pressure of belief in a religious revelation? To capture Bayle for the Christian or the anti-Christian camp mattered in the 18th century, and indeed for a long time after that. Only recently has the interpretation of the works moved into an arena in which reasonably dispassionate analysis can at least be hoped for.

Since, however, the problem that confronts the reader of Bayle is the general one of literary register, with Bayle, even more than with the subjects of most of the other entries in this volume, the pattern of biographical facts provides a necessary check on what the works may be taken to imply. Given the contradictory interpretations which extend well into the 20th century, there is not yet complete agreement about how much of what the works contain is insinuation, how much caution, how much subversion, mischievousness, genuine but reluctant doubt, genuine and also provocative doubt, or sheer curiosity about facts, about the nature of evidence, or about the possibility of certainty.

Two things seem probable from the beginning. Firstly, there is enough evidence to suppose that all the participants in apparently intellectual debates among French Calvinists in Holland after the revocation of the Edict of Nantes were aware of the political implications of their seemingly theological positions for the justification of conflicting political attitudes and activities; and secondly, there is no one body of doctrine or philosophical or theological method that Bayle is teaching. His interest is, at least initially, in discovering what is the case. There is actually every reason to suppose that Bayle moved from an initial interest in historical fact in the projected *Dictionnaire* to an almost exclusive interest in speculative matters in the printed text, especially of the second edition. But the famous double columns of sometimes subversive notes underneath a few straightforward lines of uncontroversial text are at least at the outset prompted by a desire to set down the facts, or the evidence, in an effort to weigh it up and get to the truth.

The first work is already vintage Bayle. The *Pensées diverses sur la comète*, to use the abbreviated title of the second edition (*Pensées diverses écrites à un docteur de Sorbonne à l'occasion de la Comete qui parut au mois de decembre 1680*) is not about the 1680 appearance of Halley's comet. It is not the genuine collection of letters written by a Roman Catholic it purports to be, and it is not intended to "desabuser entierement ceux qui persistent à s'imaginer, que les Cometes presagent de grands malheurs (to disabuse totally those who persist in thinking that comets foretell great disasters)." In the second edition the text is divided into chapters, and admits in chapter VII that no one believes anyway that comets presage disasters. The preface to the third edition, dated 1 June 1699, is at least relatively honest about the circumstances of the work's composition and publication, and explains its bantering tone with reference to the original intention to write in a style suited to the *Mercure Galant* (q.v.).

How seriously was the banter to be taken in 1682, before anyone knew that the work was intended for the *Mercure Galant*, if indeed that is the real explanation of the style? The first letter of the first edition announces that there is no good reason to suppose that anything can be foretold from comets, clearly insinuating that this is not the only area of belief in which superstitions can occur. Bayle then demolishes in order the authority of poets, who can conjure up eclipses and shipwrecks whenever it suits them, and of historians, where he borrows some cynicism from La Mothe le Vayer. Then, in chapter VII, the fictional letter-writer implies that universal consensus and tradition are worthless, and should yield to rational evidence. Malebranche had stated that firmly and openly. Bayle's daring is in putting that view to the readership his tone envisages and invites. His Catholic letter-writer quotes Pascal on caution lest theological authority should poach on the territory of reason.

A score of pages in, and no reader can really tell what Bayle is insinuating. It had all been openly stated by the most orthodox theologians, but only in the context of serious academic debate. By the thirteenth chapter the letter-writer is ponderously affirming that vapour has as much difficulty in going down as in going up. Whatever system is adopted, that of Ptolemy, of Copernicus, or of Tycho Brahé, there is cosmic movement round a common centre. Certainly, but that was rather like inviting the reader to forget for the moment about divine revelation, supposed to demand a Ptolemaic explanation of heavenly happenings, and saying that it did not, for the moment, matter whether or not you accepted it. The Church was naturally sensitive about arguments based on any suspension of belief in its teaching. Bayle was living in Protestant Holland, and was not risking more than he accurately calculated he would get away with, but the whole of the essence of the book, and of the technique Bayle was to develop, is already there. It chiefly remains to see where, how, and why he uses the technique, checking any tentative conclusions against the known facts that he lived and died within a community of French Calvinists in Holland, and that at no point in his life had he shown any reluctance to pursue abstract intellectual truth, whatever its consequences. The only proven or indeed likely duplicity was in the constantly playful anonymity.

Some more technical arguments from physics in the original *Lettre* were suppressed in the 1683 *Pensées*, and Bayle has a malicious repertoire of mocking examples of popular credulity and bizarre ecclesiastical rulings, and cannot resist listing, in fact for the reader's amusement but apparently to demonstrate his letter-writer's point, the ordinances of French provincial councils forbidding the reading of almanacks. Bayle's letter-writer then takes up an assortment of superstitions, apparently picking out a selection of suitable items from Bayle's repertoire of facts about curious beliefs, linked only by the ease with which pagan and Christian attitudes towards them either are or should be distinguished. An account of events following the comets of 1665 gives scope for some comment on contemporary politics. The tone of the text certainly becomes more serious as Bayle's letter-writer piles argument on argument to demonstrate, with occasional Latin quotations, firstly that idolatry is a worse state than atheism, and, secondly that atheists can be virtuous. The sanction of a reward or punishment after death is, according to Bayle's letter-writer, simply not necessary to ensure virtuous behaviour in this life, and the cohesiveness of society which depends on it.

The real difficulty in the interpretation of the text comes when the letter-writer argues that the literal understanding of scripture can be imposed by the Church even when it makes God seem to human eyes manifestly unjust and that, when that happens, human understanding must defer to transcendent norms of holiness and justice it cannot understand. But there is no revelation that God uses comets as a sign of his punishment to come. In fact the text constitutes a very powerful argument against the literal understanding of the texts on which Calvinists based their understanding of predestination, but it is not couched in a form in which its tenor can be pinned down in a statement. The letter-writer starts by saying that "les Peres et les Conciles ont donné à ces paroles de l'Ecriture, *indurabo cor Pharaonis* (*Exodus*, VII, 3) une interprétation trés-éloignée de ce qu'elles signifient litéralement; et cela, parce qu'il est manifeste que le sens litéral choqueroit les perfections de Dieu (The Fathers and Councils have given these words of scripture, *I shall harden Pharaoh's heart*, a sense very distant from that which they mean literally; and they do so because the literal sense would clash with the divine perfections)."

We start therefore with the example of the solid tradition of the Church, which has refused to take literally God's statement "I shall harden Pharaoh's heart," since it would be manifestly unjust of God deliberately to deprive Pharaoh of any chance of not sinning by releasing the children of Israel. Having established from tradition that the Church refused to postulate this apparent injustice of God, the text (chapter 225) continues,

Si nous avions une revelation expresse qui nous asseurast, que l'intention du St. Esprit a été que ces paroles fussent prises dans toute la rigueur de la lettre, l'Eglise ne manqueroit d'y deferer, imposant silence à la raison, et lui remontrant, que puis que Dieu qui est la reigle et la source de la saincteté et de la justice, nous déclare qu'il a endurci le coeur de Pharao au pied de la lettre, cet endurcissement est un acte qui ne choque ni sa sincérité, ni sa justice, ni sa saincteté

(If we had an express revelation to assure us that the intention of the Holy Spirit was that these words should be taken in a rigorously literal sense, the Church would not fail to defer to it, imposing silence on reason, and showing it that, since God, who is the rule and source of holiness and justice, declares to us that he literally hardened Pharaoh's heart, that hardening is an act which does not clash with his sincerity, or justice, or holiness).

But the Councils and the Fathers decided that God could not have meant those words to be taken literally. What is Bayle, through his letter-writing, actually implying? That God's revelation has always to be understood in relation to the norms of justice we understand; which is what "the Councils and the Fathers" thought, and which precludes any strict Calvinist belief in predestination? Or that God, himself the source of all morality, has established norms which we cannot understand and to which we, like the Church, must of course defer? Or does he simply, and as if without noticing, send live electricity down the uninsulated line, telling us to make of it what we will? When he goes on to say that we should not accept comets as miraculous manifestations of the divine will because, unless we had a clearly revealed assurance that God used comets to announce his indignation, that would be against reason, Bayle is clearly re-establishing ambiguity, leaving the live wire uninsulated.

Dieu ne fait point de miracles non seulement inutiles, mais aussi contraires à sa sincérité, à sa saincteté, à sa justice, et à sa bonté. Car si selon l'esprit de l'Eglise, toute interpretation de l'Ecriture qui attribué à Dieu des actions manifestement contraires à l'idée que nous avons de ses vertus, est fausse, sans qu'il nous soit permis d'alleguer que Dieu a des droits que nous ne connoissons pas, et qui s'accordent avec ses autres vertus d'une maniere que nous ne connoissons pas, le droit, par exemple, d'endurcir Pharao, litéralement parlant; si, dis-je, cela est ainsi, on peut soûtenir que tout miracle qui est manifestement contraire à l'idée que nous avons des vertus de Dieu, est faux, sans qu'il faille avoir égard, pendant qu'on n'est pas asseuré du fait, à des fins cachées, ou à des droits inconnus que Dieu peut avoir: car s'il étoit nécessaire d'avoir ces égards, nous serions réduits au plus étrange Pyrrhonisme qui fut jamais

(God does not perform miracles that are not only useless, but also contrary to his sincerity, his holiness, his justice, and his goodness. For if, according to the spirit of the Church, every interpretation of scripture is false which attributes to God actions manifestly contradictory to the ideas which we have of his virtues, and we are not permitted to hold that God has rights we know nothing about, and which accord with his other virtues in ways we do not understand, such as the right, understood literally, to harden Pharaoh; if, I say, all that is so, then we can hold that every miracle which manifestly contradicts the idea we have of the divine virtues is false, without needing to take into account the hidden ends or unknown rights which God might have until they have been established: for if we had to respect them [God's hidden ends not yet established as existing] we should be reduced to the most extraordinary Pyrrhonism which ever existed).

It is not unimportant about that passage that Bayle allows the workings of his mind to be so visibly apparent. There is no attempt at fine writing, not even any effort to turn thought processes into properly presented argument, just the raw processing of thought. The syntax, here deliberately smoothed in translation in the interests of intelligibility, is that of mental processes, not of expository prose.

The importance of Bayle's 1682 *Critique générale du Calvinisme de M. Maimbourg* lies in the argument for toleration. On the Catholic side, Nicole, whose Jansenist (q.v.) doctrine of grace had effects in practice similar to those flowing from some sorts of Calvinist theology, had changed the controversial ground in his 1671 *Préjugés légitimes contre les Calvinistes*, calling on the Calvinists to justify the legitimacy of their church. Maimbourg had gone further, virtually threatening the revocation of the Edict of Nantes in his 1682 *Histoire du Calvinisme*. Bayle takes his stand on tolerance in the positive sense of respect for the individual conscience, to be elaborated in the 1686 *Commentaire philosophique* on the gospel phrase "compelle intrare (force them to come in)," which Bayle shows cannot possibly be used as a justification for forced conversion. Bayle published a supplementary *Nouvelles lettres critiques* in 1685 just before the appearance of Locke's very different Latin letter on toleration of 1685.

Bayle's monthly review, the *Nouvelles de la République des Lettres*, which ran under his direction from March 1684 to Feb-ruary 1687, contained ten or twelve six- or eight-page articles a number and was modelled on the *Journal des Savants* (q.v.). Some were serious contributions to scientific or philosophical discussion, but there was also a gazette element, items about elections to the Académie française, for instance, or obituaries. In three years there were 256 book reviews, about half of them devoted to works on philosophy or religion, 43 to works of history, 18 to new classical editions, and only half a dozen to literary works. Bayle gives disproportionate space to works that appeared in Holland, and almost limits himself to what appeared in Latin and French. He made a deliberate effort to please the non-learned with gossip and some humour, and gave authors the right to reply to reviews of their works.

The work for which Bayle is chiefly remembered is the *Dictionnaire historique et critique*. It is almost a map of Bayle's own unsatisfied quest for religious certainty, implying both theological and philosophical knowledge, thereby differing from both Descartes and Locke, who kept the two forms of knowledge and the two disciplines distinct, but not from Malebranche or Spinoza, who did not. Bayle also wanted additionally to satisfy a purely historical curiosity. The *Dictionnaire*, however, is even further away from a simple exposition of Bayle's thought than the *Pensées sur la comète*, and does not expound any doctrine, or even systematically any method, from which it is possible to draw more than general conclusions.

Bayle was clearly conscious of the historical and speculative difficulties confronting a believing Calvinist around the turn of the century, and he knew that those he had left unresolved were bound to become the most serious. The mischievous delight in opposing irreconcilable authorities is there, and Bayle relishes the theological absurdities he straight-facedly quotes. In significance as well as in date, although not in the author's intention, the *Dictionnaire* undoubtedly stands on the threshold of the French enlightenment. But in view of its utilization by historians as a quarry of tendencies and innuendoes to be developed by other writers later on, it is important firstly to note that the *Dictionnaire*, particularly when used in conjunction with Moreri's *Le grand dictionnaire historique; ou, Le Mélange curieux de l'histoire sainte et profane*, originally published in 1674 but frequently thereafter republished in augmented editions, is still a seriously helpful research tool into antique, renaissance, and more modern views and thinkers. The *Dictionnaire* is called on a dozen times, for instance, by Sainte-Beuve for historical details included in his *Port-Royal*, and even since the second world war Tallemant's editor has on a score of occasions found in the *Dictionnaire* useful facts and pointers about people who lived in the first half of the 17th century. The Bibliothèque Nationale discovered in the mid-1960s that it was wearing out two sets a year, mostly no doubt for that three-quarters of the *Dictionnaire* which Voltaire found of no interest, because of merely antiquarian import and without subversive potential.

Bayle was also clearly conscious of the refinement in manners and social behaviour of his own generation:

encore que notre siècle ne soit pas plus chaste que les autres, il est du moins plus poli et plus honnête pour l'extérieur. Les loix de la bienséance sont à présent plus sévères et plus étendues qu'elles n'ont jamais été. Jamais les Auteurs qui ont voulu plaire au beau monde n'ont été obligé d'écrire si honnêtement (even if our century is not more chaste than others, it is at least more refined and polished on the outside. The rules of propriety are stricter and more extensive now than they have ever been. Authors who have wanted to please fashionable society have never been obliged to write with such respect for the decencies).

As Bayle proceeds to justify the terse statements that run across the page in the immensely long double-column footnotes, we catch his delight at making asides, and simply in speculating. He recommends books, especially if they are scholarly, saying of Athenaeus's *Dipnosophistes* that it contains "a whole miscellany of facts and quotations;" heaps on facts himself if they happen to interest him, such as that Gryphiander had written a book on the phoenix in 1618; and puts in comments: "I am grateful to the Germans for not lightening their works with digressions." Bayle even grumpily laments in his asides that not enough importance is attached any longer to putting a date right, to correcting a point of geography or of grammar, or to elucidating some obscure passage in an ancient author. Indeed, things have got so bad that the publisher of Mme Dacier's translations of Homer will no longer print the Greek text alongside the translation: 'Il appréhende sans doute que la vue des caractères Grecs n'épouvante les Lecteurs (He is no doubt afraid the sight of Greek characters will scare readers away)."

The obsessive pursuit of truth runs right through the *Dictionnaire*, certainly less tendentiously than the association of religion with superstition, greed, quibbling, and fanaticism in the background of the *Pensées sur la comète*. Bayle is at enormous pains to disentangle the true from the false in the accusations against Luther, and in another of the more celebrated articles the fifth note makes it clear that his entry, "Marcionites," seeking to discover whether or not they were persecuted, is intended as an example of nosing out and weighing up evidence before coming to a conclusion: "J'ai voulu donner ici un échantillon de ce travail pour encourager à l'entreprise de cet ouvrage ceux qui en seront capables (I wanted to give here a specimen of this [type of] work to encourage those capable of it to undertake it)." It is only in his 16th note ("P") on the entry "Mahomet" that Bayle gets round to expressing his loathing for war.

He dislikes fanaticism and intolerance, but is subversive primarily in withholding respect where it was normally bestowed. Almost everything he says can be matched from undoubtedly firmly believing forerunners, like Erasmus and Montaigne. It is true that when Saint Bernard blamed on the sins of the crusaders the non-fulfilment of his prophecies Bayle can remark, "Il n'y a point d'imposteur, qui ne se puisse cacher derrière ce retranchement (There is no impostor who cannot take refuge behind that cop-out)," but he disliked pretence and sham, and knew enough about the history of theology to have conceived a distaste for Saint Bernard's treatment of Abelard. He observes that zeal is not measured by austerity, and it is only the context, a discussion of Japanese bonzes in the notes to the article "Japon," which makes it sound subversive to say that there are "comparaisons" to be made with Christian monks:

le célibat mal observé, les tromperies cachées sous les apparences d'une morale rigide, le profit des enterrements, le secours envoyé aux âmes séparées du corps

(celibacy badly observed, trickeries concealed behind the

façade of a strict moral code, profit from burials, help sent to souls separated from the body).

Bayle's strongest weapon is common sense, but he uses it to question and to imply, and its effectiveness derives from the fact that the comments are all in the reader's mind. He has not set out to ruin religious belief, but does end up sometimes wondering just how it can be maintained, and the pressure can be felt as it forces his mind to interrogate the pathways that lead to pantheism or deism. The Old Testament, in the notes on the article "Rimini," is adduced to show against Descartes that God does deceive human beings, and various miracles, such as that of Jonah and the whale, are recounted alongside parallel mythological stories, leaving the reader to draw whatever conclusions he wishes. It is not at all clear that Bayle drew one quite so crassly as most of his commentators suppose.

Bayle did not disbelieve in miracles any more than Montaigne or Erasmus. Bayle is much more likely to have been looking for a commonsense doctrine of biblical inspiration compatible with the sort of critical exegesis being applied by Richard Simon, seeking to allow the status of divine inspiration to the scriptural canon while regarding some of the matter in it as intended otherwise than literally, perhaps allegorically, metaphorically, or as revelatory of a content that did not entail either the literal truth of the Jonah story or the elevation of Abraham, who incestuously married his half-sister, into a moral paradigm. Bayle was also obviously ready to admit the corruption of the inspired text, instancing for instance the double account of the sparing of Saul's life by David. Bayle has no doubts about the great and sublime truths, the general doctrines of scripture.

Christianity survived the discovery that Copernicus and Galileo had been right, and it is likely that an earlier sensitivity to the literary register of the scriptural books would have postponed, weakened, or even prevented the widespread secularization of European culture, just as a less implacable reaction from the Tridentine and first Vatican councils might have better served the purposes of evangelization than what happened. The point, however, is that it is simply anachronistic to suppose that Bayle either did cause or wished to cause the enlightment secularization of European thought. To suppose any such thing is simply incompatible with any real contextualization of the *Dictionnaire*'s composition and publication, and it goes flatly against the meaning the text communicates to anyone who understands its register and can see what the life affirms. We are still half a century early for Voltaire, and it is not necessary to be a cultural determinist to realize that cynical boutades buried in a work as learned as the *Dictionnaire* needed a long period of incubation and a complex process of interaction with other forces and ideas before some sort of methodical distillation could form the basis for a plausible system which might command widespread acceptance. Even with the ineptitude of orthodox response to Bayle, which must have hastened the spread of any inherently subversive elements in his thought, their formal systematization was to attract no substantial support for at least very nearly a century, perhaps even not before Comte.

There are apparently subversive remarks scattered throughout the notes, the most sensitive sets of notes generally being held to include, apart from those already mentioned, those on the entries "David," "Epicure," "Hobbes," "Leucippe," "Mahomet," "Manichéens," "Origène," "Pauliciens," "Pyrrhon," "Rorarius," "Rufin," and, perhaps above all, "Spinoza," the shining example for Bayle of a "virtuous atheist." Pagans, virtuous with no thought of reward, tower as examples over Christians in pursuit of personal salvation. Society is bound not by virtue but by law. There is nothing very new in hammering home the contrast, routinely made during the preceding two centuries, between the values of the Sermon on the Mount and those of the Christian warrior princes.

Much more damaging in the medium term to Christian orthodoxy is the constant splintering of Descartes's arguments, which demanded matter wherever there was extension, and sharply distinguished men with souls from animals without souls. Cartesianism by the late 1690s was a last and insecure bastion protecting the immortality of the soul against the inroads of Locke's thinking matter. That is why the celebrated fifth note ("E") to Bayle's *Dictionnaire* entry on Rorarius is so important. It implies the impossibility of distinguishing humans from animals by the functions of the soul:

il est sûr que la même âme, qui dans les enfants ne fait que sentir, médite et raisonne d'une manière solide dans un homme fait; et que la même âme, qui fait admirer sa raison et son esprit dans un grand homme, ne ferait que radoter dans un vieillard, qu'extravaguer dans un fou, que sentir dans un enfant

(it is certain that the same soul which in children causes only sensation, meditates and reasons solidly in a mature adult; and that the same soul, whose reason and intelligence are to be admired in an adult, would only babble in an aged person, rave in a madman, and register sensation in a child).

But the greatest problem is not the immortality of the soul, nor the inspiration of scripture, it is the problem of evil. Bayle sees the difficulty of reconciling divine omnipotence with divine bounty. Religiously, the easiest exit is fideism. We do not and cannot know the purposes of God, the source of all justice and rectitude and therefore, by definition, never in contradiction with them. But that solution does not satisfy our demands for a rational comprehension of our experience. Intellectually, the most promising ways out are pantheism, which avoids the need for creation, since the cosmos is a manifestation, not a creation of God, or Manichaeanism, which at least avoids the need for the creation of evil, or the capacity for evil, which coexists with God. Bayle sees the great metaphysical problems, allows us to see him wrestling with them, knows that he has found no solution, and can only make a series of asides, setting out the difficulties, some obvious absurdities, and considerations people have overlooked. The mistake is to look for a system, either in the thought or in the presentation. That same powerfully disordered mind is at work in the *Dictionnaire* as was clear in the *Pensées*, in which the structure of the argument scarcely matters, which is as well, since pencil and paper are needed for the average reader to work it out.

There remains the possibility that Bayle, dimly aware of the destructive power of his own common sense, and overwhelmed at his impotence to resolve the important questions to which he sought answers, able only on a small scale to marshal a few facts and insights, was relieved that he could take refuge behind unanswered question marks. The power of his writing is quite clearly in the importance of the questions he raises and the common assumptions he derides, not in any answers at which later readers may have thought he should have arrived.

PUBLICATIONS

Collections

Recueil de quelques pièces curieuses concernant la philosophie de Mr Descartes, 1684
Oeuvres diverses, 4 vols., 1727; augmented 1737; photographic reproduction in 1964–68, with fifth volume 1982
Choix de la correspondance inédite, 1890

Philosophy and theology

Lettre à M.L.A.D.C., docteur de Sorbonne: Où il est prouvé par plusieurs raisons tirées de la Philosophie et de la Théologie que les comètes ne sont point le présage d'aucun malheur. Avec plusieurs réflexions morales et politiques et plusieurs observations historiques et la réfutation de quelques erreurs populaires, 1682; augmented as *Pensées diverses écrites à un docteur de Sorbonne à l'occasion de la comète qui parut au mois de Décembre 1680*, 1683; critical edition 2 vols., 1911; as *Miscellaneous Reflections*, 1708
Critique générale de l'histoire du Calvinisme de M. Maimbourg, 1682; continued in a series of *Nouvelles lettres* from 1685
Ce que c'est que la France toute catholique sous le règne de Louis le Grand, 1686; modern edition 1973
Commentaire philosophique sur ces paroles de Jésus-Christ: Contrains-les d'entrer; où l'on prouve par plusieurs raisons démonstratives qu'il n'y a rien de plus abominable que de faire les conversions par la contrainte, et où l'on réfute tous les sophismes des convertisseurs à contrainte, et l'apologie que saint Augustin a faite des persécutions. Traduit de l'Anglais du sieur Jean Fox de Bruggs, 3 parts, 1686–87; augmented by a *Supplément* of 1688; as *A Philosophical Commentary*, 1708
Réponse d'un nouveau converti à la lettre d'un réfugié, 1689
Avis important aux réfugiez sur leur prochain retour en France, 1690 [Bayle's authorship unlikely; traditionally attributed to Bayle, but strongly and persistently repudiated by him], 1690; augmented 1692
[There is no reliable list of the pamphlets and broadsheets issued by Bayle in the course of the controversy of 1691: the surviving texts are in the *Oeuvres diverses*]
Projet et fragments d'un Dictionnaire historique, 1692
Dictionnaire historique et critique, 2 vols., 1696; augmented in 3 vols., 1702; as *A Historical and critical Dictionary*, 1710; 10 vols., 1734–41; in *Selections*, 1952; another anthology 1965
Eclaircissements sur certaines choses répandues dans ce dictionnaire, 1701
Réponse aux questions d'un Provincial, 4 vols., 1704–06
Continuation des pensées diverses…à l'occasion de la comète, 2 vols., 1704.
Entretiens de Maxime et de Thêmiste, 1706

Biographical and critical studies

Desmaizeaux, P., *La Vie de Pierre Bayle*, 1730

Delvolvé, Jean, *Religion, critique, et philosophie positive chez Pierre Bayle*, 1906

Robinson, Howard, *Bayle, the Skeptic*, 1931

Labrousse, Elisabeth, *Pierre Bayle*, 2 vols., 1964

——*Bayle* (in English), 1983

Rex, W.E., *Essays on Pierre Bayle and Religious Controversy*, 1965

Sandberg, K.C., *At the Crossroads of Faith and Reason; an Essay on Pierre Bayle*, 1966

Brush, Craig, *Montaigne and Bayle*, 1966

BEAUMARCHAIS, Pierre-Augustin Caron de, 1732–1799.

Financier, dramatist, and memorialist.

LIFE

Beaumarchais should be taken seriously in his repeated assertion that he was not a man of letters: "Je n'ai pas le mérite d'être auteur (I have not the honour of being a writer)," if only because it is exuberant amateurism which explains the strengths and defects of the plays, and the attitude of the professionals of the world of letters to their author. Beaumarchais was primarily a businessman, and his main concern was his career as a financier, with the political entanglements which it entailed, and which no doubt gave him a sense of importance. He was also deeply devoted to his family, despite his numerous liaisons, and to promoting the well-being of society.

Writing for the stage was a diversion, in which he could permit himself to base sophisticated comedies of manners on what were basically exaggerated commedia dell' arte (q.v.) plots, to include in his plays dangerously forthright social satire and private vengeance, and even to incur failure by trying to realize Diderot's dramatic theories on the stage. He intended to make money writing for the stage, but found even more important functions for his plays. His activity was more involved in the world's affairs than Voltaire's had been, and his sense of injustice even fiercer, but his targets were of less central public concern, his irony was less controlled, and his aim less sure.

He was born on 24 January 1732 above his father's watch shop. His father, André-Charles Caron, who was born in 1698, had been in the army. In 1722, after converting from Protestantism to Catholicism, he had become a master watch-maker, and married Marie-Louise Pichon, by whom he had 15 children. Beaumarchais was the seventh of these, and the only boy to survive, with two elder and three younger sisters. His father, never particularly successful, was none the less cultivated. He invented a dredging machine for the governor of Madrid, and wrote well. The family read, made music, and enjoyed the theatre. Beaumarchais's favourite sister, Marie-Julie, never married, and also wrote. In 1784 she published *L'Existence réfléchie; ou, Coup d'oeil moral sur le prix de la vie.*

From 1742 to 1745 Beaumarchais attended a local trade school, the Ecole des métiers d'Alfort, learned a little Latin, and worked at watch-making until, in 1749, his father, tired of Beaumarchais's petty thefts of watches whose private sale financed his amours, and the time he took off from his duties to write songs, sent him away from home. He yielded to the pleas of friends of the family to take him back. Beaumarchais then dutifully interested himself in watch-making, and in July 1753 laboriously perfected a new escapement mechanism, by which the unwinding of the watch-spring transmitted movement to the hands in such a way as to give a more accurate reading of the time. It also enabled him to make watches small and thin enough to fit into a ring. The invention took time, ingenuity, and dexterity, and the experiments and sketches must have been to some extent directed by Beaumarchais's father, but the result so impressed Lepaute, the king's watch-maker and a colleague of the father, that he used the new mechanism in a clock, and published the discovery as his own in the *Mercure* (q.v.) for September.

However determined, skilful, articulate, and audacious he may have been, Beaumarchais must also have had the support of his father in sending to the Secretary of the Académie des Sciences a box containing, under seals, the successive stages of his mechanism; in demanding from the minister of the king's household a confrontation with Lepaute, who refused it; in asking for a police enquiry, which also was refused; in writing again to the Académie on 13 November, requesting arbitration and clearly setting out step by step with irrefutable evidence what had happened between Lepaute and himself; and in writing a letter of protest to the *Mercure* on 15 November. On 23 February 1754, the Académie adjudicated in his favour. He was made for life and so, incidentally, was his father, whose business had not been prospering.

Beaumarchais was invited to court to demonstrate his invention to Louis XV and Mme de Pompadour. The Carons advertised the thinness and tininess of their watches in the *Mercure* for June 1755. Beaumarchais further perfected his escapement and had a new dispute with a Swiss, Romilly. In June 1755 the Académie adjudicated equal rights to each and, about this time, Madeleine-Catherine Aubertin, Mme Franquet, brought a watch into the shop to be repaired. Her husband was controller of the royal table, and Beaumarchais soon found himself wearing a sword and preceding the roast as it was brought in to be set before the king. Mme Franquet's husband was elderly and ill, and Beaumarchais bought his office from him on 9 November 1755. When Franquet died on 3 January 1756, Beaumarchais's relationship with the widow became closer, and on 27 November he married her. She was about 10 years older than he was. From 1757, Pierre-Augustin Caron added "de Beaumarchais" to his name, after a small property his wife had inherited.

She died during the night of 29 September 1757 after eight days of fever. Since the marriage contract was not registered until 11 October, presumably in haste after an unanticipated death, Beaumarchais inherited nothing except his wife's debts and a series of law-suits with her family, who disputed Beaumarchais's entitlement to her legacy. For two or three years he was in financial difficulties, although he made progress at court, got to know the banker husband of Mme de Pompadour, Le Normand d'Etiolles, and began to be friendly with the king's daughters, Adélaïde, Victoire, Sophie, and Louise, over whose music-making he presided, teaching them to use his new pedalled harp. In 1758 Beaumarchais's mother died, and perhaps in 1759 he got to know Le Normand's uncle, Pâris-Duverney, one of the four brothers who dominated French banking. Pâris-Duverney had the contract for supplying the army with food, clothes and equipment. He also had enemies at court, who prevented the king from taking official notice of the Ecole Militaire which Duverney had built on the Champ-de-Mars. It was through the king's daughters that, on 18 August 1760, Beaumarchais contrived to arrange for a royal visit to the military academy. Duverney, grateful, made Beaumarchais an associate in affairs of which we know nothing but which were patently lucrative. The escapement had brought him to court, and the court had brought him to money.

We know that from 1760 Beaumarchais was lending his father money and paying him a pension, and that in December 1761 his father gave up his business. In the same month Beaumarchais bought for 55,000 livres, of which Duverney provided 50,000, the post of conseiller secrétaire du roi, which ennobled him. He tried to buy the high-yielding post of grand maître des eaux et forêts for 560,000 livres, also advanced by Duverney, but had to withdraw on the objections of the other Grand Masters and content himself with a post of lieutenant général des chasses, a judicial appointment with jurisdiction over the king's hunting territory, for which Beaumarchais took the oath on 11 September 1763. In that year he also bought a large house in the rue de Condé for his father, his two youngest sisters, and himself. Something of his taste for domestic comedy, and for Diderot's theatre, is to be explained by the strength of the links which bound him to his family. He looked after his father, and he had his elder sister Marie-Josèphe's husband appointed architect to the king of Spain. When she was widowed and retired to a convent with her two children, Beaumarchais paid the pensions, and it was he who provided a dowry for his niece, Jeanne-Marguerite's daughter.

He also had a strong sense of the dramatic, demonstrated by producing his father from an adjoining room one evening, after gossip had been going round about the way he had been sent away from home, and by contriving to humiliate a courtier who once in exalted company set out to put him to shame by asking him to have a look at his watch, which had gone wrong. Beaumarchais, having warned his adversary of his clumsiness, contrived to drop and break it.

During the period from 1757 to 1763 Beaumarchais was already writing his "parades," cheeky little after-supper low-style curtain raisers, generally obscene, to be played on 4 November for the feast day of Saint Charles, the patron saint of Le Normand, at Etiolles, as well as the two slight pieces *Colin et Colette*, a "paysannerie," and *Les Députés de la Halle et du Gros-Caillou*, a "poissard," and the "Parades" proper, mixtures of burlesque and parody of the sort originally written to tempt passers-by into the fairground booths for more substantial entertainment: *Les Bottes de sept lieues*, *Jean-Bête à la foire*, *Léandre marchand d'agnus* and *Zizabelle mannequin*.

At the same time Beaumarchais was also compensating for his missing education, reading the French classics, and learning to translate the Latin ones. It was probably Diderot's 1757 *Le Fils naturel*, with the *Entretiens*, and *Le père de famille*, published in 1758, which stimulated Beaumarchais to write *Eugénie; ou, La Vertu malheureuse*, of which the first plan dates back, with the *Essai sur le genre dramatique sérieux*, to 1759. Beaumarchais himself maintained that he began both play and *Essai* at this date—eight years before they appeared in 1767—

on being moved by *Le Père de famille* in 1759. Just as in the 18th century the encyclopédiste (q.v.) literature of serious philosophical reflection was preceded by an apparently much more radical but also much less seriously meant literature of blasphemy, so elevated and even sentimental comedy could proceed from the same pen as Beaumarchais's earlier witty little scatalogical dramatic pieces.

Beaumarchais fought one duel to which the king did not advert, and there was a projected second duel with a M. de Sablières, to whom he had lent money. Both sisters living in the rue de Condé were being courted, and Beaumarchais's father was thinking of remarriage. It was more or less understood that Beaumarchais himself would marry Pauline Le Breton, although his attentions to her were not undeflected while he sent someone out to look at the vast but neglected estates in Dominica which would be her dowry. On Good Friday, 20 April 1764, Beaumarchais left for Spain, ostensibly to see to the marriage of his elder sister Marie-Louise to Durand, a French merchant in Madrid, but actually as an agent for Duverney, for whom he was carrying 160,000 livres and with whom he sought to win important concessions for the exploitation of the Spanish overseas territories. Duverney's consortium wanted contracts to supply slaves, to provision the army, and to colonize Louisiana and make Sierra Morena fertile by proper irrigation. Beaumarchais travelled without haste, stopping at Tours, Bordeaux, and Bayonne. Ten years later he makes it seem as if he travelled urgently to rescue "Lisette" from the acute distress in which a second walk-out by her fiancé José Calvijo y Fajardo had left her. There is no mention of any intention to marry Durand, nor any suggestion that Lisette in 1764 was already 33. The fourth *Mémoire contre Goëzman* contains much dramatized comic fiction.

Part of the difficulty of keeping track of exactly what Beaumarchais was doing comes from his own four books of *Mémoires* of 1773–74, which certainly dramatize and simplify what actually happened in order to achieve the effect he wanted ten years later. However, his account in *Année 1764, Fragment de mon voyage d'Espagne* is at least based on a diary kept at the time, however much the events narrated might subsequently have been distorted. Beaumarchais had two sisters living in Madrid, Marie-Josèphe, Mme Guilbert, and Marie-Louise, staying with a correspondent of her father whose fortune she expected to inherit. The correspondent died and Lisette thought of marrying Clavijo as soon as he had established himself. She appears to have been his mistress. He became royal archivist and director of the philosophical and literary review *Pensador* and broke off the engagement, whereat Lisette proposed to marry Durand.

It looks as if Beaumarchais had found Lisette in Madrid in a social situation which would not further his negotiations on behalf of the consortium, and much preferred Clavijo as a brother-in-law. Lisette on this hypothesis got engaged to him a third time and, after he had found medical reasons to delay, even a fourth. In fact Lisette married neither Clavijo nor Durand, and no-one knows what happened to her, even where or when she died. Beaumarchais had shown determination and ingenuity. In the *Mémoire*, he was going to show his powers of re-structuring a situation to suit the interpretation of events which most favoured him ten years later, and the text is a brilliant dramatization, incorporating only occasional elements of truth. In Madrid he met failure, in spite of offering the Marquise de La Croix, with whom he was living, to the king as a mistress. He left Madrid on 22 March 1765, and in May sold his office as conseiller secrétaire for 70,000 livres.

In 1764 Beaumarchais had written a sketch for a long poem on optimism, already showing the same yearning of an obviously comic genius for success in the more serious literary genres that can be found in Voltaire. The letters from Spain had been vivid, with an eye for the incongruous. Meanwhile things had not gone well in Dominica. Pauline Le Breton, refusing to accompany Beaumarchais there, broke off the engagement in February to marry elsewhere. Beaumarchais's father had remarried in January. During the summer Beaumarchais, still associated with Duverney, began the commercial exploitation of the forest of Chinon, destined to lead him into much difficulty. Meanwhile Sedaine's success with *Le Philosophe sans le savoir* of 1765 encouraged Beaumarchais to dig *Eugénie*, the first play to be entitled "drame," out of his papers. It was hissed at its first performance at the Théâtre-Français on 29 January 1767, but established itself when Beaumarchais instantly re-wrote the fourth and fifth acts. The plot was inspired by Lesage's *Le Diable boiteux*, but the censor had insisted on moving the action from France to England. The five manuscripts show how frequently Beaumarchais modified the text. The play was translated into Italian and German in 1768, and adapted as *The School for Rakes* in 1769. Only the second 1767 edition is preceded by the *Essai*, and the title is shortened to the simple *Eugénie*.

On 11 April 1768 Beaumarchais was to marry a rich widow, Geneviève-Madeleine Wattebled, Mme Lévêque, whose husband had been garde général des Menus-Plaisirs. She was to bear Beaumarchais a child, Augustin, on 14 December. His stepmother and Pauline Le Breton's husband had both died during the year, but Beaumarchais, himself now established as the father of an adored child, could not resist returning to the theatre with a serious drama about a commercial failure and a clandestine paternity, *Les Deux Amis; ou, Le Négociant de Lyon*, played on 13 January 1770, dropped by the company after eleven performances, and the butt of a number of popular jokes. Like its predecessor this piece had its title modified several times and evolved through different stages attested by various manuscripts. Beaumarchais, however, learnt the lesson. His next play was not a serious drama, but was a frivolity elaborated from a lost parade, and incorporated songs brought back from Spain and imported from Italy. As a comic opera it was turned down by the Italian company in 1772 but, re-written, it was accepted by the French company in the following January. It was only to be played two years later, and was then called *Le Barbier de Séville*.

A daughter, Aimable-Eugénie, who lived only a few days, was born on 7 March 1770, but in November 1770 Beaumarchais's wife died. Her money had been used for an annuity, so there was no inheritance. For the purposes of the timber enterprise in the forest of Chinon, Beaumarchais, constrained by his lieutenancy to employ a nominee, had used the name of his valet, César Lesueur, only to find it difficult to disembarrass himself of him. Lesueur deceived him, but Beaumarchais's subsequent treatment of him was coarsely bullying. The more considerable difficulty, however, was the relationship of intense dislike between Beaumarchais and La Blache, heir of Pâris-Duverney from whom Beaumarchais had borrowed most of the necessary capital. A document was accordingly drawn up in Beaumarchais's handwriting and signed by Duverney on 1 April

1770. As a result of re-calculating investments and loans Duverney agreed in it that he owed Beaumarchais 15,000 livres, and engaged himself to make Beaumarchais an interest-free loan of 75,000 livres for eight years. Beaumarchais was ill for nearly two months in June, but Pâris-Duverney died on 17 July 1770, before the provisions of the document had been put into effect. The comte de La Blache contested the document's undoubted authenticity, wished to establish that Beaumarchais was a crook, refused to pay the 15,000 livres, and took the matter to court. Beaumarchais made the mistake of drawing the king's daughters into the affair, and they had to disavow any knowledge of it. Beaumarchais won the case in 1772, but appeals delayed final victory, and wealth, until 31 July 1778.

Beaumarchais's son died in October 1772 and then, on 11 February 1773, there was a disagreeable fracas with the duc de Chaulnes, a fierce eccentric of illustrious lineage, huge strength, and violent temper. His mistress, the actress Mlle Mesnard, whom he used to beat, left him for Beaumarchais. He appeared not to mind this until he unpredictably went berserk, called on Mlle Mesnard, found her talking to a friend of Beaumarchais, discovered that Beaumarchais was sitting in court, and irrupted into the proceedings declaring he was about to kill him. He was made to wait, but there was difficulty about procuring swords suitable for duelling, there were scuffles and fist fighting, and servants tried to restrain the enraged duke, who rolled with them in the gutter. The police took him away and he was imprisoned. Beaumarchais that evening gave a reading of *Le Barbier de Séville* and played the harp.

However, Beaumarchais, although found innocent of causing an affray, was imprisoned by ministerial edict from 26 February to 8 May, during which period La Blache's appeal succeeded on the basis of a report commissioned from a lawyer with an appointment to the parlement, Charles Goëzman. Beaumarchais was allowed out of prison under escort and wrote numerous letters, but twice had to bribe Goëzman's wife to get an interview. The bribes were returned, with the exception of 15 louis which Mme Goëzman said had gone to her husband's secretary, presumably because La Blache had capped them. He had obviously pressed his advantage while Beaumarchais was in jail. Beaumarchais did not get the important interview, lost his case on 6 April, and by implication was declared a forger.

He was condemned to pay 56,300 livres, five years' interest, and costs. La Blache caused his goods to be seized and his family thrown out of his house while he was still in prison, where he not surprisingly fell ill. Turning down his father's advice to accept what providence had in store, he counterattacked with a letter to Mme Goëzman of 21 April asking for the return of his 15 louis. On his release he let it be widely known how Goëzman sold his interviews. Goëzman applied in vain for a lettre de cachet to have Beaumarchais imprisoned, and then accused him of an attempt to corrupt. On 10 July Beaumarchais was summoned to appear before the court. The law allowed for any penalty on conviction short of death; trial was in secret; the judge needed to give no reasons. Goëzman's lawyer colleagues had every reason to defend his integrity.

Beaumarchais, as resourceful as the Figaro of *Barbier*, had recourse to public opinion, as Pascal had done with the *Lettres provinciales*. Later that year, on 5 September, 18 November, and 15 December, aided by his father, sister, in-laws, particularly the Lépines, his sister Madeleine-Françoise and her husband, with whom he was staying, and a small group of friends, Beaumarchais issued his first three *Mémoires* against Goëzman, who was then himself compelled to appear before the court. There were intermediate documents, but on 10 February 1774 Beaumarchais published what is normally accounted the fourth *Mémoire*. On 26 February he went to hear the verdict, apparently prepared to commit suicide if it went against him. He was sentenced to a reprimand which the judges did not dare formally administer. They left the building by a side door. The *Mémoires* were condemned. Mme Goëzman was also reprimanded, Goëzman himself condemned. Conti held a celebration in honour of Beaumarchais. The *Mémoires* were a huge success. Thousands of copies of each had been sold, culminating in the sale of 10,000 copies of the fourth in three days. On 5 March they were publicly burnt. On 17th, Beaumarchais won his case against the corruption charge.

The old parlements had been abolished by Louis XV in January 1771 to be replaced by courts run by administrative appointees, the "parlements Maupeou," supported by Voltaire, and potentially a sensible reform. What was missing was a pool of trained judges, and it is arguable that the case won by Beaumarchais was against the new system for the administration of justice. At the beginning of his reign Louis XVI was to reverse the reform. Beaumarchais's fly-sheets were written and re-written very carefully indeed, and are exquisitely straight-faced comedy, prodigiously effective polemic. Mme du Barry had the second *Mémoire* acted out in front of Louis XV, who is reported to have burst out laughing at the ridicule piled on his new parlement.

Beaumarchais discovered that Goëzman had once signed a baptism certificate with a false name to disguise a clandestine paternity, and the Théâtre-Français immediately resurrected *Eugénie*. The public applauded frenetically at the appropriate place, where the court case is mentioned. Beaumarchais wanted to carry through his victory by getting *Barbier* staged, but Goëzman's friends obtained an injunction. Goethe in Frankfurt gave a reading of the fourth *Mémoire*, which inspired his *Clavigo*, and the series was the success of the Vienna season. It is ultimately for his role in the prosecution of Beaumarchais that Goëzman, twenty years later, was guillotined. Beaumarchais himself started to live with Marie-Thérèse de Miller-Mawlas, whom he was to marry only in 1786, when their daughter was nine.

In the meanwhile he took refuge in London while things quietened down in Paris. He wrote home to the king, who was displeased by the public tumult, and was rewarded with a mission to buy off a French adventurer, who had available for purchase a publication about Mme du Barry, *Les Mémoires secret d'une femme publique*. When he returned to Paris, Louis XV was already dead, but Beaumarchais was able to get himself charged with a new mission by Louis XVI to buy off another pamphlet, this time on the reasons for the royal sterility. By and large Beaumarchais's own account of the episode, which certainly contained lies which got bigger from day to day, has to be rejected. The pamphlet existed and was not written by Beaumarchais, who merely fabricated with increasing elaboration a dashing adventure story, and succeeded in his aim, which was not to suppress the pamphlet's English and Dutch editions, but to have it accepted in Paris that he had rendered an important service to the crown, for which he deserved recognition. The adventure included a mysterious episode in a wood on the way to Vienna, where the police, accurately supposing that Beaumarchais's

story could not be true, put him under house arrest for the month it took to resolve the matter.

Beaumarchais was back in Paris by October 1774, and in November the official reprimand was withdrawn. *Le Barbier de Séville* was approved by the censor, Crébillon fils, on 29 December 1774. The permis d'imprimer is dated 31 January 1775. Two four-act texts were approved in 1773 and 1774, but Beaumarchais had drawn *Barbier* out to five acts, and the play failed at its premiere on 23 February 1775. Beaumarchais immediately reduced it to the four acts we know and moved the present act II, scene viii, out of the first act to where it now is. Only the third 1775 edition prints the definitive text.

There were further confidential missions in London, some simply to make diplomatic reports on the government of George III. Beaumarchais also put up a project to provision the American insurgents, for which France and Spain each supplied him with 1,000,000 livres. He opened the company of Roderigue, Hortalez et Cie, for which he took large premises in the Marais in 1776, and started to gather together a considerable fleet, based on Le Havre, Nantes, La Rochelle, Bordeaux, and Marseilles. There was inevitably strong English protest, but enough material was clandestinely shipped to equip 25,000 men. Unhappily the boats returned without the promised tobacco and salted fish, and had it not been for a third million from the government, Roderigue, Hortalez et Cie would have been ruined. Despite Beaumarchais's repeated, understandable, and energetic protests, the American Congress decided to regard Beaumarchais's shipments as a gift from the French government.

Eventually the French government did take over the company's operations, leaving Beaumarchais to operate on his own account, but payments were still slow. He received 2,500,000 livres, but in bills of exchange payable three years later, in a currency rapidly being devalued, and the French tax farmers made sure that his American tobacco did not fetch the anticipated price. The English blockade, too, was expensive. Beaumarchais's flagship, once *L'Hippopotame* but renamed by him the *Fier Rodrigue*, armed with 60 cannon, was requisitioned and helped to defeat the English. Beaumarchais was politely thanked. In the end he appears to have made money from his American operations, although not as much as he should have done, or as soon, given how much he had done for the cause of American independence.

In view of his life story and the invention of Figaro as he appears in *Barbier*, it is not really surprising to discover that Beaumarchais was not essentially mercenary. He was a businessman, interested in making money, but he also had, together with a sense of family, a strong commitment towards his country, and towards the general furtherance of liberal progress. He was concerned that France should emerge with honour from America's struggle for independence, and that America should succeed in winning it. It is doubtful whether or not he begrudged the meagre return from his mostly American operations from 1776 to 1783. He spent 21,044,191 livres, and received 21,092,515, profiting less than 50,000 livres from the whole colossal undertaking. He dreamt of reopening the eastern route for the spice trade, and later proposed something analogous to the present Panama canal. He was interested in balloons, was present at the ascents of the Montgolfier brothers, worked with a mechanic on a flying machine, and assisted with the construction of a manoeuvrable balloon.

It was not solely for commercial reasons that, after the death of Panckoucke, he took over the great Kehl edition of Voltaire. He admired Voltaire, supported what he stood for, and probably enjoyed both the risk and the intrigue involved. The edition would have to be printed abroad, and the French authorities would have to be relied on to connive at permitting the importation of an edition they would have officially to prohibit. Beaumarchais behaved in characteristic fashion, founded a firm, paid 160,000 francs to Panckoucke's estate for the manuscripts, bought the type from the English printer Baskerville, acquired three paper factories, and appointed a manager, a proof-reader, and Condorcet for the annotation. The prospectus was issued in 1781, and the edition came out very slowly, from 1783 to 1790. Having counted on 5,000 subscribers, Beaumarchais found only 2,500. He lost half a million livres.

Meanwhile he was also beginning to have trouble with the Théâtre-Français about author's fees. He had given Eugénie to the company free of all fees, but there had been initial difficulties at the end of 1775, after Barbier, and on 6 January 1777, the day after his daughter Eugénie was born, he wrote again to the company, requesting accounts. He had been asked by Richelieu, one of the four directors appointed to oversee the company, to reach agreement, when one author, whose play had produced 12,000 livres, found himself receiving nothing, but owing money to the company, which was also trying to organize a "failure" for Barbier, after which the players would then own outright the acting monopoly. A failure occurred whenever a play brought in less than 800 livres in summer or 1,200 in winter. On 3 July 1777 and again on 18 January 1778 Beaumarchais held a meeting of dramatists which elected a committee to follow up the matter of the accountability of the Théâtre-Français to the authors whose plays it staged. In principle, from 1757 an author received a ninth of the box-office takings, but this was so calculated as to reduce it by half, and the frequency of failures was driving some of the better-known dramatists to the Théâtre des Italiens, the only other alternative being the "Foire" (Fair)." The result of Beaumarchais's efforts was the foundation of the "Société des auteurs dramatiques," an organization almost wholly ineffective until the monopoly of the players' company was broken in 1791, during the Revolution.

Beaumarchais's activities at this period ran concurrently. In 1778 he was still being victorious over La Blache at Aix. The fight with the English coincided with that against the actors, the edition of Voltaire with efforts to do something to staunch the loss of money from Chinon, and America had to be supplied with provisions. In 1783 Beaumarchais needed a million livres from the French government, wrote to the American Congress demanding payment, travelled to London on business, and managed to get Le Mariage de Figaro on to at least a private stage. A first draft had been ready since 1778, but the piece was not played publicly until 1784. Its hectic intrigue reflects the pace of Beaumarchais's daily life. In 1777, the year of the birth of his daughter by Mlle de Miller-Mawlas, a Mme de Godeville attempted to usurp her place in Beaumarchais's life, and she was followed by the more successful "Mlle Ninon." Meanwhile there were the philanthropic activities to care about, particularly the advancement of the cause of Protestant rehabilitation.

Socially, feeling was moving faster in France than was generally realized at the time, although it explains why the preoccupations of the Figaro of Mariage are different from those of the Figaro of Barbier. The undertow of social satire in the second play is so strong as to appear downright subversive. The censor

passed Le Mariage de Figaro and the players were glad to accept it, but the king was told that it was dangerous and demanded to have it read in his presence. The text was bolder than the one we have, with the action in France, the Bastille mentioned by name, and further sharp liberties taken. The king, listening to Figaro's famous monologue, swore that the comedy would never be played. Beaumarchais toned down the text, removed the action to Spain, asked for another censor, and began a campaign of salon readings such that the worlds of elegance and literature got to know the play well, at least by reputation. The second censor turned it down, but a court performance was called for, probably by the comte d'Artois in an effort to force the king's hand. More and more people were admitted to the rehearsals. The fashionable audience had already gathered for the private court performance on 13 June 1783 when a courier forbidding it arrived from the king. Another private performance was arranged, this time at Gennevilliers, the home of the comte de Vaudreuil. Louis XVI permitted it, and the most elegant part of the court attended. More than half a dozen censors passed the text, and Beaumarchais read it in front of a quasi-tribunal.

The king, being told that the play would fail, finally allowed it. The performance on 27 April 1784 took five hours. The queue formed ten hours before the curtain rose. Duchesses dined in the theatre to be sure of their places. When the box office faltered, Beaumarchais gave the proceeds of the 50th performance to the Institute for indigent nursing mothers. Controversy was prolonged but sharp. The king had Beaumarchais committed to the prison of Saint-Lazare from 8 to 13 March 1785, only to find him resisting release until he had been properly accused and tried. On 22 March he resigned his lieutenant-general's post. In the end peace was contrived, and Beaumarchais was invited to watch the queen play Rosine in Barbier at the Trianon on 19 August, with the comte d'Artois as Figaro. Paisiello had already turned the play into an opera in 1782. The first night of Mozart's Le Nozze di Figaro was on 1 May 1786.

In 1785 Beaumarchais dreamt up yet another way of improving at a stroke the public lot and his private purse. He founded a company to provide Paris with running water, thereby annoying important bankers who had other schemes. Since it was essential to them that the value of Beaumarchais's shares should be kept low, so favouring investment in the national loans they were floating, they paid Mirabeau to write a pamphlet attacking his scheme. Beaumarchais's reply brought forth a bitter attack from Mirabeau to which Calonne, the finance minister, asked Beaumarchais not to reply. Earlier in the year the 30 volumes of the Kehl edition of Voltaire which had so far appeared were suppressed. It was the year in which Beaumarchais's fortunes changed, and began to decline. He did, however, finish the libretto of Tarare, bringing Gluck's pupil, Salieri, from Vienna to write the music under his direction. By the time the opera had its premiere on 8 June 1787, Beaumarchais was under considerable pressure from a new quarter.

In 1781 his attention had been drawn by his friend the prince of Nassau-Siegen to the fate of Mme Kornman, married at 15 with a dowry of 360,000 livres to a banker from Alsace who connived at her liaison with Daudet de Jossan, who was able to put rewarding business in his way. When her lover became a minister, her husband had her locked up, although she was pregnant, because she would not release her dowry to him. Beaumarchais had her freed, but little happened until Kornman met a lawyer called Bergasse, who immediately saw the profit to be gained by getting Kornman to play the martyred husband. The 1787 *Mémoire sur une question d'adultère* was signed by Kornman but written by Bergasse, who turned Beaumarchais into a symbol of the ancien régime, maliciously distorting everything he had ever done, starting with the old allegation that he had stolen someone else's escapement for his watches. There was a war of more than 400 pamphlets, most of them now directed against Beaumarchais. Kornman and Bergasse were, however, condemned for calumny on 2 April 1789. They did none the less destroy Beaumarchais's credibility by using him as a symbol of all that the on-rushing Revolution was against. He deliberately slowed the rhythm of performances of *Figaro* to lower his profile.

The magnificent house he was having built near the Bastille did not help him. It cost 1,663,000 livres and was pulled down in 1818. During and after 1789, Beaumarchais made considerable efforts to ensure the goodwill of the Revolutionary authorities, although his genuinely liberal sympathies did not save him from harassment or bring him any more public credit than did *La Mère coupable*, written in the winter of 1791–92, accepted by the Théâtre-Français and then withdrawn from it, to be played at the recently opened Marais on 26 June 1792. Beaumarchais wrote to the chief of police about safeguarding his house and, in the spring of 1789, was elected president of his district. On 15 July he led an armed force of 24 into the Bastille and in August was charged with supervising its demolition. Although he gave his district 12,000 livres in August, he was denounced, and only re-instated as a member of the Assembly after carefully refuting all the accusations against him. In 1790 he gave another 6,000 livres to a Lyons charity, and lodged without remuneration 800 provincial representatives sent to the Fête de la Fédération on 14 July from the 83 départements.

Beaumarchais had envisaged going to America to get his debts paid when, towards the end of 1791, he heard of the possibility of acquiring from Holland arms which France badly needed for the looming war with Austria. He was offered 60,000 guns. Did he see a way of making a profit, doing a public service, or palliating the new hostility being shown towards him? He must have known how dangerously he was acting, although arms trading was still lucrative. Austria had only sold the guns on condition that they should be removed from Europe, and Holland was reluctant to license their export, but on 3 April 1792 Beaumarchais was given assignats for 500,000 livres, already worth only 300,000, against a security whose capitalized value was 745,000 livres. In his last months on the throne Louis XVI probably offered him a ministerial portfolio.

However, the gun deal leaked out, and Beaumarchais was publicly accused on 4 June of storing 60,000 guns in Paris. On 7 June he replied, on 26 June *La Mère coupable* had its first performance, in July a new contract with the government was signed in respect of the arms deal, and on 11 August his house and garden were searched. He was then made a low offer for the guns by people he could not trust, but who had clearly done a deal with a minister, with a threat to his life if he did not sell. He did not sell, and was arrested on 23 August 1792. On 29 August he was locked up in a batch of 192 detainees in 18 small rooms. His life was clearly in danger. It was saved because Mlle Ninon from Aix—Amélie Houret, now the comtesse de la Marinaie—with whom Beaumarchais's liaison had continued, had obtained his release. It happened with four days to spare before the September massacres.

He remained an official suspect, and therefore in danger of being picked up and executed, but hid no farther away than Versailles, and continued with his arms deal. He was given a passport and was in Le Havre by 22 September, in London on 2 October, and on 10 October in Holland to conclude matters, but his life was threatened and he fled to London, where he learnt that in France he had been formally indicted on 23 November. To prevent the return to France on which he was intent, much more likely to have led to the guillotine than to rehabilitation, a friend who had lent him money had Beaumarchais imprisoned in London for debt. He managed to repay the debt, returned to France with his six self-justificatory *Epoques* and, with unheard-of temerity, had 6,000 copies printed. They were full of counter-revolutionary views, ridiculed Marat, and once again were successful.

The indictment was lifted for two months on 10 February 1793, and Beaumarchais was back in Paris four days later. In May his innocence was recognized, and he was given a formal mission to buy the guns, received a passport, and was given the necessary money. He was unwell, and travelled through Switzerland at the end of June, was refused permission to land in England on 4 August, and was sent back to Ostend on 16 August. There he was ill for three months. In December the revolutionary tribunal, the Comité de salut public, acknowledged that he had been sent abroad by the government and was therefore not an émigré. Then that decree was rescinded, and from 14 March 1794, Beaumarchais was again on the list of émigrés.

On 5 July Beaumarchais's wife, daughter, and sister Julie were imprisoned. They were saved by the fall of Robespierre less than three weeks later, and released on 8 August, although Julie was overlooked, and had to stay in prison for another four months. On 15 August there was a formal divorce, obligatory for the wives of émigrés. Beaumarchais offered himself as a peace envoy in Holland but was turned down, and spent his exile in Germany, mostly in Hamburg with the large émigré community. On 6 October the English got hold of the guns and took them to England. There followed a long campaign by Beaumarchais to be allowed back into France, successful only under the Directory. He returned to Paris on 5 July 1796. The splendid house was a wreck, and both his family and he had known a period of real privation. On 10 July his daughter Eugénie married André-Toussaint Delarue. On the following 30 April Beaumarchais and his ex-wife remarried, and on 5 May 1797 he was acclaimed at a revival of *La Mère coupable* in the theatre of the Rue Feydeau. Later that year he was allowed back into his house, but Talleyrand refused him a passport to America, where he had hoped to be ambassador.

In January 1798 a decree ruled that he was the state's creditor, and then another in April that he was its debtor. Julie died on 9 May. Financially Beaumarchais's situation was now difficult. He continued to pour out mémoires on various topics and kept up a series of love letters to Amélie Houret de la Marinaie. Two letters on Voltaire and Jesus published in the *Journal de Paris* for April 1799 were not well received. The Catholic restoration had already begun. Beaumarchais died in his sleep during the night of 17 to 18 May 1799.

In spite of the huge losses he had from time to time amassed, and an official debt to the state at the moment of death, Beaumarchais endowed Eugénie with 659,000 livres, and left 20,000 livres a year, which meant 1,000,000 livres for his wife. Behind both the American and the Dutch involvements there must have been powerful financial forces at work, seeking to tap the potential profitability of both situations. It looks just possible that Beaumarchais, imitating his own comic creation, Figaro, did finally finish on top. He once calculated that *Mariage* had cost him in expenses, suppers, and presents 37,440 livres 10 sols, and that it had brought him in 41,499 livres, 19 sols after 65 performances. His biographers note that he could be insensitive, vulgar, and mean, but that he had charm, energy, great verve, and luck.

WORKS

Beaumarchais's pen was not sure. The real masterpieces, the four *Mémoires contre Goëzman*, *Le Barbier de Séville*, and *Le Mariage de Figaro* were all re-written with other people's help. There are examples of draft sentences for the *Mémoires* where Beaumarchais's text, too dry, was much improved by Julie, or too prolix, and finally adjusted effectively by Beaumarchais himself. Some of the jokes in *Barbier* were supplied by others, and the comedy as initially played had one act more than the plot warranted. *Le Mariage* loses its verve with the sharp turn to solemnity in the social satire after two acts, although it recaptures it in the glorious final scenes. All of the major texts were the product of cooperation, revision, and tireless re-writing. The plays were tested in private readings and the *Mémoires* went through detailed revisions in family privacy. It is not unusual to find up to half a dozen versions of a Beaumarchais text in successive revisions. Nothing is as spontaneous as it seems.

Beaumarchais's latest editor, Pierre Larthomas, prints under the rubric "Théâtre de société" six early pieces as probably genuine. They all belong to the fairground derivatives of *commedia dell' arte* (q.v.), the genuinely popular theatre of renaissance Europe with stereotyped characters. Paris had two annual fairs, those of Saint-Germain and Saint-Laurent, whose clowns, acrobats, circus acts, contortionists, and players of farces offered for a period the main alternative to the formal declamatory rhetoric of the legitimate tragic stage, although for most of the 18th century the Italian company presented something in between, livelier, less pretentious, less ostentatiously high-brow, and more entertaining. It was the Italian company which was the more fashionable with the young aristocrats, and in the course of the eighteenth century a vogue developed for adapting the fairground farces for country house performance, and in particular the brief sketches, full of coarse humour and licentious jokes, with kicks, sticks, tricks, and masks, presented by the charlatans to attract customers into the booths. Some of the best dramatists of the century wrote for the Italian company, and some even for the fairground. Aping with sophistication in refined surroundings the scatology, vulgarity, and patois of the mob became an elegant pastime of the wealthy and well bred. In 1756 Gueulette catered for it in his three-volume *Théâtre des Boulevards; ou, Recueil des Parades*, and other authors published their own similar but less well-known collections.

Beaumarchais's early pieces were put on after dinner at Etiolles, probably between 1760 and 1763. Their social historical interest is greater than their literary significance, but some of the imaginative inventiveness of the later comedies can already be found in them in an inchoate state. There was a theatre at Etiolles with proper stage machinery, and gifted aristocratic amateurs played parts, together with hired actors from among the

best on the professional stage. *Colin et Colette* is the slightest of sketches, in which real peasants start off the evening after a stage quarrel by offering a bouquet to the seigneur, while *Les Députés de la Halle et du Gros-Caillou* is a "poissard" (literally: "fishwife's sketch") with the traditional names of the characters probably taken from the best-known example of the genre, Vadé's *Racoleurs*, played at the Foire Saint-Germain in 1756, or from his 1758 *Catéchisme*. Gros-Caillou is a district of Paris, near the present Invalides, then being developed. The play is again a compliment to the audience, in the form of a fish-wife's quarrel, ending with a song of which Beaumarchais almost certainly wrote the music.

The other four pieces are "Parades" only in form. They were created for the châteaux, not the fairs to which, for instance, the title of one, *Jean-Bête à la foire*, alludes. The characters are standardized, derived from the Italians, but by now naturalized: the bourgeois or noble father Cassandre, his daughters Isabelle and Columbine, Léandre the handsome young man who wants to marry Isabelle against her father's will, and the servants Gilles, Cassandre's valet made up with white flour, and Arlequin, Léandre's roguish man wearing a black mask. The plots are all stratagems, with deceit, intrigue, disguise, and victory for the lovers. Beaumarchais did not have further to look for the matrix behind the later plays, although his public comedies were models of considered restraint compared with the unscripted obscenity of gesture expected in the parades.

These early pieces contain deplorable puns, deliberately distorted proverbs, neologisms and expressions formed by association, all of which allow Beaumarchais some audaciously obscene double-entendres. There are two bawdy jokes hidden in apparently innocent, if otherwise rather pointless phrases from the last speech of Gilles in the "Annonces" before the parade about seven-league boots, whose title is that of a Perrault fairy-story. "Being in Persia" is also an allusion to a proverb in which the words "en perce" refer only literally to the broaching of a cask of wine, and providing "it" with a respectable correlative scarcely turns "putting it there" into a proper euphemism. Beaumarchais had the advantage of having been trained in the company of ordinary boys learning an ordinary trade in his father's workshop. His licentious allusions are authentic, even if they often seem gratuitously added like condiments to the text.

In *Les Bottes de sept lieues* Isabelle and Léandre, tired of their nocturnal meetings, decide to elope. Cassandre and his servant Gilles arrive with a suitcase containing an inheritance of 60,000 livres. Gilles is left to look after it, and also to keep an eye on Isabelle. Léandre and Arlequin, who has overheard everything, arrive equipped with enormous boots, posing as travellers just back from visiting the Grand Mogul.

Léandre says he has forgotten to bring a letter from Rome and puts on his boots to go and get it. Arlequin borrows a trick from Molière, and Gilles is duped into going off to care for his dying mother. Léandre, back from Rome, lends Gilles the boots; Arlequin, showing him how to tie up the laces, binds him tight and goes off with Léandre, Isabelle and the money. Cassandre returns to see what has happened and Beaumarchais produces the first of his remarkable coups de théâtre. Léandre and Arlequin return without their disguises, but with Isabelle and the money, announce to Cassandre that they caught the robbers, and have brought back Isabelle and the money. Cassandre recompenses Léandre by giving him the hand of Isabelle. The cast turn to the audience and sing a vaudeville. It has been pointed out that it is not difficult to see how the same matrix can be used for *Le Barbier de Séville* by the substitution of Bartholo's absence for Cassandre's, of Bazile for Gilles, Figaro for Arlequin, Rosine for Isabelle, and Almaviva for Léandre.

The *Essai sur le genre dramatique sérieux* purports to bring to the theatre an amateur's impatience with professional conservatism. It is a manifesto which develops Diderot's views about the theatre, but builds on Beaumarchais's own deeply bourgeois sentimentality. Essentially, Beaumarchais separates the "drame sérieux" more completely from the antithetically coupled heroic tragedy and entertaining comedy than Diderot had done. The watch-word is authenticity. What happens on the stage should correspond to what happens in life, and what is required is

la peinture touchante d'un malheur domestique, d'autant plus puissante sur nos coeurs qu'il semble nous menacer de plus près

(the touching depiction of a domestic misfortune, acting more powerfully on our emotions because it threatens us more closely).

Beaumarchais sees the domestic "drame" producing a potentially more powerful moral effect than the classical genres, and his clear preference for prose merely forces further the basic principle that the audience should be elevated to higher moral standards by the lessons it learns from watching scenes on the stage analogous to those its members undergo in their own lives. Prose enhances the realism.

Beaumarchais's "drame" is neither "tragi-comédie," nor "tragédie bourgeoise" nor "comédie larmoyante." It does not, that is, seek to move without elevating. After denying that he is a "writer," Beaumarchais gives the source of *Eugénie* as Lesage's *Le Diable boiteux*, and refers directly to Diderot and Richardson, as well as to stage pieces by Voltaire, Nivelle de la Chaussée, Mme Graffigny, and Sedaine. The *Essai*, although prolix, makes its points forcibly. Beaumarchais was responding to the imaginative needs of the theatre-going public in a new and still, in spite of Diderot, audacious way, and he sets out the corresponding dramatic theory with clarity, logic, and conviction.

Eugénie, with the copious stage directions that befit the authentically domestic atmosphere, is generally thought to suffer from the over-use of the multiple, sudden, and inadequately motivated reversals of fortune on which Beaumarchais will later depend for more brilliant comic effects in *Barbier* and *Mariage*. Eugénie, who is pregnant, thinks she has been secretly married to her lover, Lord Clarendon, but the ceremony in his château had been faked and he is in fact preparing to marry an heiress. He is naturally anxious that Eugénie should not announce to her father that she is married, but she begins to suspect that something is wrong, and in the third act tells her father about her marriage. A valet, Drink, who had intercepted a letter and knows about the proposed marriage as well as the faked one, inadvertently betrays the true situation to Eugénie's father. Eugénie's brother, Sir Charles, now appears. Clarendon saves his life from assassins. Eugénie's aunt intends to force Clarendon to marry Eugénie properly. Sir Charles challenges Clarendon to a duel, but has broken his sword. Clarendon repents and marries Eugénie, whose father ends the play with the admonition, "N'oubliez donc jamais qu'il n'y a de vrais biens sur la terre que dans l'exercice de la vertu (Don't forget that there is no true good to be had on earth except in the practice of virtue)."

Beaumarchais in the *Essai* had foreseen the objection that his genre sérieux would be more successful in the provinces than in the corruption of the capital. *Les Deux Amis; ou, Le Négociant de Lyon* failed in Paris, but was successful abroad and in such mercantile centres as Lyons, Marseilles, and Rouen. The piece was endlessly re-worked, and the title Beaumarchais decided on is the fifth he gave it. It abolishes the silent stage business between the acts of *Eugénie* and sticks more closely to the formula of the *Essai*. Beaumarchais thought it "le plus fortement composé de mes ouvrages (the most strongly composed of my works)." The plot is more unified than that of *Eugénie*, with a financial intrigue reinforced from the beginning by an amorous one. Beaumarchais has recourse here, as so often, to the theme of a secret marriage, to a recognition, and to a defence of the dignity of the illegitimate.

A rich Lyons businessman, Aurelly, is posing as the uncle and guardian of Pauline, who is in fact his daughter. He lives with his friend Mélac *père*, a tax official who has brought Pauline up. Mélac *fils* and Pauline are in love, but Pauline is also loved by Saint-Alban, the tax farmer who is Mélac's superior. Aurelly has between Pauline and himself 1,100,000 livres deposited with his Paris lawyer, Préfort. Just before a debt of Aurelly's for 600,000 livres matures, the lawyer dies, and the transfer of funds cannot be made. Without Aurelly's knowledge, Mélac puts together the 600,000 livres, taking 500,000 from the tax funds, and adding 100,000 of his own which had been destined for the setting up of his son. Saint-Alban announces his arrival to look at the books, finds 500,000 missing and, like Aurelly, who thinks he still has 500,000 livres lying in Paris after the payment of his debt, suspects that Mélac has misappropriated the money. Pauline consents to parting with her 300,000 livres, and Aurelly, unconsciously mirroring his friend's good turn to him, gives Saint-Alban a draft on Préfort for the missing 500,000 livres. Everything could now be easily arranged if Pauline agreed to marry Saint-Alban, but she does not have to. Mélac's cashier, Dabins, explains the situation to Saint-Alban, who is so moved by Aurelly's generosity that he himself lends the necessary 600,000 livres until Préfort's affairs are settled and the money becomes available. He also renounces Pauline in favour of Mélac *fils*.

Les Deux Amis failed in Paris. It has been criticized because Beaumarchais undoubtedly did not develop his intrigue to its full potential. Aurelly, after all, aspired to join the aristocracy and had bought letters of nobility. His commercial colleagues were jealous. His social climbing could have been used by the author to make him less worthily dull. The plot is also improbable. Lawyers' deaths do not drive wealthy merchants whose funds are briefly unavailable to the brink of suicide. The heroism in the play is inadequately motivated, and is just a moral example rather than a dramatic necessity. As in *Eugénie* the final scenes are weak and the dialogue becomes too dense for an audience to follow as the intrigue is so suddenly unravelled.

The *Mémoires contre Goëzman* is a major satirical work, its stature due not least to the two contradictory constraints acting on its composition. A great deal was at stake for Beaumarchais. He had to rouse public opinion in his support, and he had to avoid alienating the parlement, composed of Goëzman's colleagues and much disliked by the public. He deploys considerable virtuosity in flattering the parlement while calling it to account at the bar of public satisfaction, with banter his most powerful weapon. He may have inherited from Voltaire an admiration for Pascal's *Lettres provinciales*. Like Voltaire, he used them as a model, and makes a point of referring to them in the third *Mémoire*. The four *Mémoires* are the *Mémoire à consulter* printed by Claude Simon, the *Supplément au Mémoire à consulter*, printed by Quillau, the *Addition au Supplément du Mémoire à consulter*, printed by Jacques-Gabriel Clousier, and the *Quatrième mémoire à consulter* from the same printer. The pamphlets were burned by the public executioner for "expressions et imputations téméraires, scandaleuses et injurieuses à la magistrature en général, à aucun de ses membres, et diffamatoires envers différents particuliers (expressions and imputations which are temerarious, scandalous and injurious to the magistracy in general, and to one of its members, and defamatory of different individuals)."

The first *Mémoire* is a reasonably restrained exposition of the facts, obstinately insisting in rotund periods on exactly what happened. Initial obsequious tribute is paid to the judges, their intelligence, and their integrity. The musical structure of antithetical phrases in paragraphs ending with cadences, like the short snatches of comic dialogue, clearly echoes the Pascal of the eleventh and subsequent *Lettres*, as do the carefully simplified and slanted presentations of precisely what is at stake. Not from Pascal are the remaining prolixity, the self-indulgent exclamation marks, and the rows of rhetorical questions. Early classical has moved into rococo. The first *Mémoire* ends with a series of "réflexions," openly accusing Mme Goëzman of selling interviews with her husband, but the most powerful passages rely wholly on insinuation. Beaumarchais cheats a little with the list of 22 visits to Goëzman in pursuit of his audience, as in the list of seven people involved in the chain along which the money for the alleged corruption passed, but it is difficult to answer his conclusion:

Voilà donc, de M. Goëzman à moi, une chaîne de sept personnes, dont il prétend que je tiens le premier chaînon comme corrupteur, et lui le dernier comme incorruptible

(There, then, between M. Goëzman and me, is a chain of seven people, whose first link he alleges I hold as corruptor, and he the last as incorruptible).

The *Supplément* or second memoir also uses Pascal, making much of chicanery on plain meanings. Lejay, the almost illiterate book-seller who spent a month in prison for a false declaration dictated to him by the Goëzman faction, had been used to carry the bribe. Beaumarchais quotes from the irretractable deposition of Mme Goëzman, who ought to have known better, and for whom Beaumarchais supplies the underlining:

Je déclare que jamais Lejay ne m'a présenté d'argent pour gagner le suffrage de mon mari, qu'on sait bien être incorruptible, mais qu'il *sollicitait* seulement des *audiences* pour le sieur de Beaumarchais

(I declare that Lejay has never given me money to win the vote of my husband, who is known to be incorruptible, but that he merely *requested audiences* for M. de Beaumarchais).

That is probably true, but it remains enormously damaging, and

Beaumarchais simply remarks that the statement cuts the knot. It is the confrontation in this memoir between Mme Goëzman and Beaumarchais, after the account of the humiliation which Mme Lejay, even more illiterate than her husband, had had to undergo in court, that Mme du Barry had dramatized and played before the king. Beaumarchais's account of the confrontation sparkles with malicious ingenuity as he uncovers the slips, trips, and plain lapses of memory in his adversary, and then shows how absurd are her conclusions. At each attempt she makes to unravel the threads, Beaumarchais shows her fastening herself more tightly. Devastatingly polite, he offers her compliments whose barbs she is too stupid to notice, and then traps into which she pitches herself headlong. He condescendingly explains the court procedure "pour l'instruction de ceux qui sont assez heureux pour n'avoir pas encore été dénoncés par M. Goëzman sur des audiences payées à sa femme,…(for the information of those fortunate enough not yet to have been denounced by M. Goëzman for interviews paid for to his wife,…)."

The fourth of the *Mémoires*, much admired by Voltaire, is generally considered the finest. It starts with several pages in the form of a prayer to the supreme being, saying that if the writer had the choice of trials on earth, he would choose precisely his present enemies to inflict on him the tribulations which would prove him. He would even like the same judges, who would rather expel from their number any wrong-doer they found there than render any number of equivocal judgements. He returns to the single testimony against him, and to Mme Goëzman's affirmation that what could be bought was not a judgement but an interview. That, however, as he points out, is not corruption. Mme Goëzman could scarcely admit that she sold her husband's judgements but, not seeing the trap, she had in her deposition formally destroyed her husband's accusation against Beaumarchais. By the date of the fourth memoir, Beaumarchais was clearly going to win his case, and he unleashed unsuspected reserves of irony, for instance at the sheer greed with which the interview's cost was quadrupled, and then rose exponentially. The rhetoric is annihilating. Beaumarchais borrows from Voltaire the description of Goëzman acting as godfather at the baptism of the child whose paternity he disavowed and whose mother he repudiated, "and you, his good friends, it would be interesting to see how you would go about excusing his honest pleasures."

What we know as *Le Barbier de Séville; ou, La Précaution inutile* started life as a private entertainment, an "intermède" called *Le Sacristain*. Most of this text has been lost, but the relationship is clear. An elderly doctor Batholo has married the young Pauline, whose name is replaced by Rosine in later drafts and who dreams of Lindor, a pupil of the organist Bazile who appears first as a soldier and then as a monk. Some of the exchanges survived into the final text of *Barbier*. Between the intermède and the comedy came a lost opéra-comique *Le Barbier de Séville*, turned down by the Italian company in 1772, probably because there was not enough music. The comedy itself went through two four-act drafts before the five-act version, which had to be cut back again to the four acts we now have after the first performance. No-one knows how Beaumarchais came on the name Figaro for a Spaniard, although he hesitated at first over "Figuaro." The plot is commonplace, and commedia dell' arte in origin. Beaumarchais must, however, have remembered Molière's *L'Ecole des femmes*.

The strength of the play as we have it derives partly from the removal of the material which clogged up the action of the first performance, and results to some extent from the cat-calls of the first-night audience. The local colour is almost derisorily stage-Spanish, but Beaumarchais has now ostentatiously abandoned any pursuit of realism. This is a comedy with songs, the characters are again caricatures. Almaviva opens the play, standing in the street, waiting for Rosine to appear at her window. Figaro comes on singing. He is known to the count as an attractively ingenious rogue, as the count is known to Figaro as a grand and powerful womanizer. Inside the house, Bartholo, a doctor, has under lock and key the ward he wants to marry. Figaro recounts to Almaviva, who insists on being called Lindor, a traditional lover's name, the amusing reversals of fortune he has undergone, side-swiping at various of Beaumarchais's enemies, like those who think that business and letters cannot go together, and theatrical claques.

Rosine and Bartholo appear at the window and Rosine lets drop a letter to Almaviva which she pretends is a song given her by her music master and which she sends the suspicious Bartholo to retrieve while she exchanges brief remarks with "Lindor" through the open window. Almaviva thinks Rosine is married to Bartholo. Figaro tells him that she is not but soon will be, and that the story of her marriage has been spread round by Bartholo to keep her safe. Figaro, intoxicated with language, describes Bartholo euphoniously:

C'est un beau, gros, court, jeune vieillard, gris pommelé, rusé, rasé, blasé, qui guette, et furette, et gronde, et geint tout à la fois

(He's a fine, fat, short, young old man, grizzled, crafty, smooth-faced, blasé, who spies, and pries, and scolds, and whines, all at the same time).

Originally the list of decriptive words was much longer, and commented on Bartholo's sexual proclivities. The words left in are there as much for the sound as the sense.

Figaro, who is also Bartholo's factotum, immediately sees a chance to profit from Almaviva's obsession. He promises to fix everything and tells Almaviva to pretend his regiment has billeted him on Bartholo. He should appear a little drunk, to lull suspicion, and bring a little gold, "C'est le nerf de l'intrigue (It's the sinews of a plot)." Act two is set in Rosine's room, where Figaro teasingly lets Rosine know that the Lindor who interests her is also interested in her. The audience has meanwhile learnt that Bartholo has fixed the wedding for the next day. Bartholo does not at first suspect that Figaro is drugging the whole household, imagining he is just increasing his bill for medical services. There is a great deal of farce. L'Eveillé (Wide-awake) appears yawning. Figaro hides, but pokes his head out from time to time, when Bazile calls, warning Bartholo that Almaviva is in Séville. Bazile not only caricatures himself as a music teacher, but he also parodies, with Bartholo, Figaro's role with Almaviva. He will see that Almaviva is kept away but, like Figaro, he needs more money if the wedding is to be assured.

At this point in the play Bartholo's mind is wholly alert. Rosine draws the attention of the audience to the fact that he misses nothing, and suspects that the dropped song was a letter. He finds ink on her finger and a sheet of paper missing. Almaviva calls, but has to go away on finding that Bartholo is exempt from lodging the military. Rosine succeeds in exchanging the letter he slips her for a perfectly innocent one which Bartholo manages to wrest from her. At the end of act two, she is on friendly terms again with Bartholo. At the start of act three Almaviva appears in a new disguise as a pupil of Bazile's. He has a new ruse, and there is much farcical play with Bartholo's deafness and Almaviva's asides. Almaviva pretends that Bazile is ill, but has intercepted a letter from Rosine to Lindor. When he gives Rosine her music lesson Bartholo carelessly falls momentarily asleep. He is so successfully taken in by Bazile's substitute, whom he believes to be on his side, that he refuses to allow Bazile to reveal that the substitute is not his pupil.

There is much display of wit by Figaro, but the brilliance of the wit is incidental to the comic effect, almost entirely achieved by the rapidity with which the essentially tragic device of reversals of fortune is used with increasingly bewildering frequency as the play comes to its climax and denouement. The plot does not stand up to analysis, but the audience simply has no time to register anything more than who, for the moment, is winning, Bartholo or Almaviva. By the time a witty remark has been disentangled in the audience, the situation on the stage has changed again. Bazile turns up perfectly well, but is bribed to go away again, as he is bribed again to sign the marriage document between Almaviva and Rosine, without really knowing whether he is signing the right piece of paper. At one moment Bartholo has virtually won, when Rosine thinks that Lindor has betrayed her to Almaviva and agrees to marry Bartholo. It is almost otiose to list the number of reversals, but it is the pace at which they occur which constitutes Beaumarchais's most original contribution to comic writing for the stage.

There are over 30 reversals of fortune in the much more elaborate but less purely light-hearted play of which the correct title is *La Folle Journée; ou, Le Mariage de Figaro*. It is a long piece. Manuscript indications show that Beaumarchais calculated it to take two hours, thirty-nine minutes, setting a slow pace by modern standards. The first performance lasted from 5.30 p.m. to 10 p.m., and no short piece was given beforehand or afterwards. The professionals of the theatre did not welcome the play, any more than they had liked *Barbier*, although their chief objection was not to the insolent tone of the social criticism, but to the immorality of the count. It is noticeable that, though an element of salaciousness is re-introduced on the subject of the "droit du seigneur," the title of a recently revived play by Voltaire, also to be used by one of Beaumarchais's censors, Desfontaines, who probably derived from Beaumarchais and Voltaire, Beaumarchais never leaves the the comtesse alone with Chérubin in the darkness of the last act. Suzanne was brought in to act II scene vi so that the comtesse should not be alone with him. Beaumarchais went out of his way to avoid the speculations about the comtesse's moral integrity which actually became the focus of critical reaction to this play.

Beaumarchais himself was not happy with the last two acts, or with Figaro's long monologue in the third scene of the final act. He preferred the lighter, less controversial register of the first two acts, which is where the reversals of fortune are most thickly crammed together, and the satire of judicial process in the third. It is in the first act that Figaro decides on his plan. The reversals make a second plan necessary, but its execution prevents the carrying out of the first one. The contrivers of the intrigue for the last two acts, in which it slows down, are the comtesse and Suzanne. They turn a pure situation comedy into something deeper, although the two halves do not fit perfectly together. Yet it was essential to penetrate below the froth churned up by the thwarting of Figaro's ingenuities, and the plunge into seriousness, even if dramatically clumsy, makes the play a great deal more effective, as if the audience had to be reminded that, underneath the wit and the farce, there did indeed lie comedy. Figaro's monologue is an integral part of the play, although it has no single gist and is superfluous to the intrigue. For Mozart's libretto, which required an altogether different perspective, da Ponte cut the play back to four acts, and the text of his fourth act is weakened by the Viennese emasculation of Figaro's monologue.

It is useless to try to link the characters of *Le Mariage de Figaro* to the other two plays of the trilogy in which characters of the same names occur in the same relationships. The three plays are written on quite different comic registers. It is to misunderstand the play even to attempt to analyse the characters as they are presented in *Mariage* alone, since Beaumarchais is not interested in anything but broad brush strokes in his characterization, and the society in which the play is set is not only unreal, but also impossible. Suzanne is the niece of the drunken peasant Antonio, but she has had music lessons, can play the guitar, and is the chief lady-in-waiting to the comtesse. Not even Rousseau went as far in dissociating social attainment from class. Figaro is part valet, part concierge, part steward, who looks down on the servants. He runs the domestic affairs of the household, but his lord has tyrannical rights over him which could never anywhere have been compatible with Figaro's more elevated functions.

Beaumarchais boasted in his preface of the "disconvenance sociale (social incongruity)" he had introduced into the play, but the examples he gave show that he meant socially unacceptable behaviour, not socially unimaginable situations. He may well have felt justified in depicting as "la risée de ses valets (the laughing-stock of his servants)"

un seigneur assez vicieux pur vouloir prostituer à ses caprices tout ce qui lui est subordonné, pur se jouer dans ses domaines de la pudicité de toutes ses jeunes vassales

(an overlord evil enough to want to prostitute to his whims everyone who is his subordinate, and on his estates take advantage of the modesty of all his young female vassals),

but he did not bother to try to make the impossible reconciliation between that sort of master-servant relationship and Almaviva's other relationship with his concierge, in the 18th-century sense of manager or factor rather than the 20th-century sense of janitor.

The play, as usual, was much improved by other people's comments, notably those of Sedaine. Some bad jokes were removed, along with routine attacks on the clergy, the name of Gusman, too obviously Goëzman, and the mention by name of the Bastille. The prurience was toned down. Figaro no longer speaks of his intention to "désusanizer" Suzanne, incidentally coining a word in a way which, like so much else in Beaumarchais's plays, is inescapably reminiscent of Molière. If a passage cut from *Barbier* is now in the text of *Mariage*, the opening of *Mariage*, too similar to that of *Barbier*, was changed. The provision of a legitimate father for Figaro is now accomplished more simply than in the original act IV, where Bartholo, Bazile, and Antonio all proposed themselves as husbands for Marceline. The register of the whole comedy was appreciably lightened by the changes made in the drafts.

As the text stands, the play opens with Figaro and Suzanne almost quarrelling about the residence offered them by the comte for after their marriage. We only slowly learn that it puts Suzanne too close to Almaviva's reach, and that he intends to re-establish his droit du seigneur before the wedding. The Figaro we meet is much more serious, clever, and committed than the character of the same name in *Barbier*, but some characteristics are the same. Suzanne knows the man she is marrying: "De l'intrigue, et de l'argent, te voilà dans ta sphère (Plotting and money, there you are in your element)." In the second scene, Figaro announces his first plan:

Attention sur la journée, Monsieur Figaro! D'abord avancer l'heure de votre petite fête, pour épouser plus sûrement; écarter une Marceline qui de vous est friande en diable; empocher l'or et les présents; donner le change aux petites passions de M. le comte; étriller rondement monsieur du Bazile...

(Pay attention to today's programme, Monsieur Figaro! First bring forward the time of your little celebration, to be surer of marrying; get rid of a Marceline who wants to eat you alive; pocket the gold and the presents; thwart the little passions of M. le comte; give monsieur du Bazile a good thrashing...).

Marceline and Bartholo now have a scene in which the count is described accurately enough by Bartholo as "libertin par ennui, jaloux par vanité (a womanizer out of boredom, and jealous out of vanity)," and in which reference is made to Emmanuel, the child Marceline says she bore Bartholo. She wants Bartholo's help to marry, if not him, then Figaro:

Jamais fâché, toujours en belle humeur; donnant le présent à la joie, et s'inquiétant de l'avenir tout aussi peu que du passé; sémillant, généreux...

(Never angry, always good-humoured; devoting the present to joy and caring about the future as little as about the past; vivacious, generous...).

Marceline goes on to coin aphorisms with surprising skill. Women, she says, must say to themselves, "Be beautiful, if you can, good if you want; but be calculating, you have to be." Bartholo and Marceline quarrel with Suzanne in polite sarcasms. Chérubin appeals to Suzanne for help. He is the count's first page, just dismissed for having been found with Suzanne's cousin, Fanchette. Beaumarchais uses the occasion to allow Chérubin to describe the comtesse: "qu'elle est noble et belle! mais qu'elle est imposante (how noble and beautiful she is, but how awesome)." Chérubin envies Suzanne her chance to dress and undress the comtesse "pin by pin," and snatches from her a ribbon the comtesse wears at night.

The comte comes in, and is apparently alone with Suzanne. There is much farcical business as he moves round the room, while Chérubin tries to stay hidden behind furniture. The comte has been made ambassador to London and wants to take his valet and his valet's wife with him. Bazile is heard coming in, and the comte, too, needs to hide behind the furniture. Bazile, however, remarks on how Chérubin makes eyes at the comtesse at table, and the comte, furious, rises, denounces Chérubin, confirms his dismissal, and, moments later, discovers him in the room. He forbids the marriage of Figaro to Suzanne, but the comtesse, Figaro, and a host of villagers come in, asking the comte solemnly to confirm his renunciation of the droit du seigneur. Chérubin is forgiven providing he leaves straight away. The first act ends with Figaro working out a plan to allow Chérubin to stay.

Everything is now in place. The audience knows all it needs to know about all the characters and their relationships. It knows Figaro's plans, and the comte's, and it even knows that Figaro will win. It is left uncertain only about what obstacles will arise and how they will be surmounted. Act one certainly fulfils the classic function of exposition, even if Figaro's mission is partly self-imposed. With act two the development begins. The comtesse wants Suzanne to tell her everything. "He wanted to seduce you?" "Oh! que non! Monseigneur n'y met pas tant de façons avec sa servante: il voulait m'acheter (Oh! certainly not! Monseigneur doesn't beat around the bush with his maid. He wanted to buy me)." When Suzanne mentions Chérubin and the ribbon, the stage directions note that the comtesse replies once smiling, and twice "rêvant (dreaming)." She knows her husband is jealous not through love—"Il ne m'aime plus du tout (he no longer loves me at all)"—but solely through pride. Figaro comes in. The comte is going to have his vengeance on Suzanne for refusing him. Figaro is to be a courier for the new ambassador, Suzanne his counsellor, and the comte will decide in favour of Marceline's claims on Figaro, who now needs a new plan.

It is daring and dangerous. He has given Bazile a note for transmission to the comte warning him that a gallant is seeking to see the comtesse at that evening's wedding feast. Elegantly and truthfully he explains to the comtesse that there are few women's honour he would have put at risk in that way, "crainte de rencontrer juste (for fear of being right)." Chérubin is to be dressed up as Suzanne. When it comes to hatching a plot, says Suzanne, trust Figaro! As he says himself, "Deux, trois, quatre à la fois; bien embrouillées, qui se croisent. J'étais né pour être courtisan (Two, three, four at once, thoroughly mixed up, interlocking. I was born to be a courtier)." Figaro has a number of these aphoristic replies throughout the play. When Chérubin comes in, Suzanne teases him into singing in front of the comtesse, before whom his clothes are arranged in female fashion and his quasi-feminine physical charms are commented on. The comtesse retrieves her ribbon. Suzanne has momentarily disappeared with Chérubin's coat and Chérubin has no collar and bare arms, when the comte walks in, having received the note set up by Figaro. Chérubin just has time to hide.

Suzanne returns and she too hides. The comte does not believe that it is Suzanne who is in the side-room. He leaves, taking the comtesse with him, and locking the door on the situation. Chérubin gallantly kisses Suzanne, who is clearly attracted to him, and bravely jumps out of the window while Suzanne is terrified for him. The comtesse is as surprised as the comte when, on their return, they find Suzanne but no Chérubin. The story the comtesse had made up turns out to be true, and the comte is humiliated. He is obliged to ask pardon for the blustering and bullying, but still has the better of Figaro, who does not know that the comte has been told the true provenance of the note. *But* the gardener, the drunken Antonio, Suzanne's uncle, arrives to complain about the way his flower-bed has been trampled, *but* Figaro says it was he who jumped, *but* Antonio hands him the piece of paper he had dropped, *but* it turns out to be

Chérubin's warrant as an officer, and the comte refuses to order the wedding. Marceline arrives to claim Figaro on the grounds that he had once borrowed money from her and promised to repay or marry her, *but* Bazile arrives and says he has a right to marry Marceline. The act ends with the comtesse concealing the ribbon in her corsage.

So far the comedy has been held together by the unbelievable pace of the reversals of fortune. From the third act the undertow is felt immediately, firstly in the confrontation between the comte and Figaro. The droit du seigneur ceases to be entirely funny, and the absurd court scene edges into real social satire, although the play is still apparently about whether or not the comte will succeed in imposing his rights, and Figaro succeed in marrying Suzanne without yielding on the droit du seigneur. The danger from Marceline is easily despatched, if with obtrusive sentimentality. Figaro turns out to be the lost Emmanuel, Marceline's son by Bartholo, and in the last two acts the plot turns centrally on the comtesse's vindication of her right to be correctly treated by her husband. The shortened but still lengthy monologue by Figaro, mostly a reflection on the vagaries of destiny as he wittily surveys his life to date, almost fulfils the function of a slow movement, giving food for serious thought before the hilarious and hectic ending. Its dramatic function is also, naturally, to remind the audience that what has been made fun of was not in the end completely frivolous at all.

The play ends with the comtesse and Suzanne dressed in one another's clothes, successfully deceiving the comte and Figaro in the dark. The farce of mistaken identities is exploited with ingenuity. Figaro is on his knees before the woman whom he takes to be the comtesse, but who is really Suzanne, and the comte expresses his sentiments to the woman he thinks is Suzanne but who is really his wife. Beaumarchais is careful, and the comte says to the woman he takes to be Suzanne about his wife, "Je l'aime beaucoup; mais trois ans d'union rendent l'hymen si respectable! (I love her very much, but three years together make marriage so respectable!)." He thought the other person with the comtesse was Chérubin, but it turns out finally to have been Fanchette, and all, naturally, having been explained, the play ends in a song, largesse to the happy couple, and a wedding to come.

L'Autre Tartuffe; ou, La Mère coupable is an attempt to do something new again, to blend comedy and the "drame." It is historically important because it provides an important link between 18th-century gaiety and the melodrama of Pixérécourt, whose dramatic techniques are already discernible. The complicated intrigue actually shows only that the exploitation of hectic reversals of fortune requires a frothy and light-hearted comic register and is incompatible with any real attempt to move the audience. Figaro and Suzanne are still in the service of the comte and comtesse. Léon is the son of Chérubin and the comtesse, and Florestine the illegitimate daughter of the comte. Bégearss, an Irish major and former embassy secretary, plots to marry Florestine and inherit the comte's fortune. He plans to send Figaro and Léon to the east and shut the comtesse up in a convent. Bégearss is disgraced, the comte discovers everything, and the ending is sentimental.

Beaumarchais was officially considered subversive by Sarcey as late as 1871. Political remarks and references to freedom of the press still had to be removed from *Mariage*, and for at least three quarters of the 19th century the play was a political weapon. Beaumarchais's reputation for hostility to the established order outweighed in public awareness his counter-revolutionary sentiments. For a properly balanced assessment France had to wait for Sainte-Beuve in 1852 but, in spite of Sainte-Beuve, the *Mémoires contre Goëzman* remain an under-estimated masterpiece.

PUBLICATIONS

Collections

Oeuvres complètes, 7 vols., 1809
Oeuvres complètes, 1973
Oeuvres, Bibliothèque de la Pléiade, 1988
Théâtre. Lettres relatives à son théâtre, Bibliothèque de la Pléiade, 1934
Théâtre de Beaumarchais [*Le Barbier de Séville, Le Mariage de Figaro, La Mère coupable*], edited by M. Rat, 1950
Théâtre complet de Beaumarchais, 1952
Théâtre complet, Parades, Lettres relatives à son théâtre, Bibliothèque de la Pléiade, 1957
Théâtre, edited by R. Pomeau, 1965
Théâtre, edited by J.-P. de Beaumarchais, 1980

Plays

Le Barbier de Séville; ou, La Précaution inutile (produced 1775), 1775; as *The Barber of Seville*, 1776; same title, 1964
Eugénie (produced 1767), 1762; with *Essai sur le genre dramatique sérieux*, 1767; as *The School for Rakes*, 1769
Les Deux Amis; ou, Le Négociant de Lyon (produced 1770), 1770; as *The Two Friends*, 1800
La Folle Journée; ou, Le Mariage de Figaro (produced 1784), 1785; as *The Follies of a Day; or, The Marriage of Figaro* 1785; as *The Marriage of Figaro*, 1964
L'Autre Tartuffe; ou, La Mère coupable (produced 1792), 1794; as *Frailty and Hypocrisy*, 1804
The Complete Figaro Plays, 1983
Tarare (produced 1787), 1787; as *Axur, King of Ormus*, 1813

Other

Mémoire à consulter, 1773
Supplément au Mémoire à consulter, 1773
Addition au Supplément du Mémoire à consulter, 1773
Requête d'atténuation, 1773
Quatrième mémoire à consulter, 1774
Mémoires, 1774
Mémoires, 4 vols., 1830
Correspondance, edited by Brian N. Morton 1969ff. (4 vols. to 1778)

Biographical and critical studies

La Brenellerie, Gudin de, *Histoire de Beaumarchais*, 1801–09
Loménie, Louis de, *Beaumarchais et son temps*, 2 vols., 1855
Lintilhac, Eugène, *Beaumarchais et son oeuvre*, 1897
Kite, Elizabeth S., *Beaumarchais and the War of American Independence*, 1918
Johnson, Margaret L., *Beaumarchais and his Opponents*, 1936
Scherer, Jacques, *La Dramaturgie de Beaumarchais*, 1954
Pomeau, René, *Beaumarchais, l'homme et l'oeuvre*, 1956

Ratermanius, J.-B. and Irwin, W.R., *The Comic Style of Beaumarchais*, 1961
Cox, Cynthia, *The Real Figaro*, 1962
Sungolowski, Joseph, *Beaumarchais* (in English), 1974
Descotes, M., *Les Grands Rôles du théâtre de Beaumarchais*, 1974
Grendel, Frédéric, *Beaumarchais, the Man who was Figaro*, 1977
Boussel, P., *Beaumarchais, le Parisien universel*, 1983
Conesa, G., *La Trilogie de Beaumarchais*, 1985

Bibliography

Cordier, H., *Bibliographie des oeuvres de Beaumarchais*, 1883

BELLEAU, Rémy, 1528–1577.

Poet.

LIFE

Very little is known of Belleau's early life. The family belonged to the lower nobility, and an epitaph tells us that Belleau was born at Nogent-le-Rotrou, about 60 kilometres east of Alençon. The next certain thing known about him is that from approximately 1550 he was being kept by Chretophle de Choiseul, the abbot of Mureaux, just to the west of Paris, whom in 1560 he was to thank for "feeding and maintaining" him for ten years. It was to Choiseul that Belleau was to dedicate the 1556 translation of Anacreon that brought him fame, although his first published verse, an ode and a sonnet, had appeared early in 1553 at the front of the *Cantiques* of Nicolas Denisot, with a further sonnet in the same year at the head of the *Amours* of Olivier de Magny.

In 1553 Belleau was at the Collège de Boncourt, presumably still a student. Etienne Pasquier relates in his *Recherches de la France* that Belleau and Jean de la Péruse, who was to die in 1554, played the principal roles in Jodelle's *Cléopâtre* when it was staged at Boncourt, for the carnival of 1553. The probability is that Belleau had also played the part at the earlier performance before Henri II at the Hôtel de Reims, the residence of Charles de Guise, archbishop of Reims and cardinal of Lorraine, perhaps to celebrate Charles's brother's victory in relieving the siege of Metz on the preceding 1 January. When, in the late 1555 *Hymne de Henri II*, Ronsard revised the list of six poets with whom he wished to be regarded as forming a group, while replacing Guillaume des Autelz with Jacques Peletier du Mans, he also replaced the name of the now dead Jean de la Péruse with that of Belleau, whose translation of the Anacreon poems recently discovered by Henri Estienne had not yet appeared.

At Boncourt Belleau had been a pupil of Muret. He knew Greek, was friendly with Dorat and close to Ronsard, and attended Pierre de la Ramée's lectures. If it was Ronsard who inaugurated the Pléiade (q.v.) vogue for Anacreontic verse, it seems none the less likely that Belleau started his translation of what we now recognize to be the pseudo-Anacreontic poems in 1554, as soon as the Estienne text appeared, although his volume was not published before the second half of 1556. Belleau's preliminary epistre to Mureaux is dated 15 August 1556, and Ronsard added an elegy to the same patron. The volume also included original poems by Belleau, the "quelques petites hymnes de son invention." Belleau was translating straight from the Greek, with no obvious dependence on the Latin translations available, but it has been shown that he quite closely imitated Ronsard.

Belleau's second volume was the 1565 *La Bergerie*, which appeared in the same year as Ronsard's volume with the same title. In December 1556 Belleau had taken up arms to follow the duc de Guise to Italy in the cavalry regiment commanded by the marquis d'Elbeuf, Guise's younger brother, returning only in October 1557. Thereafter he published a number of single poems, the *Ode au duc de Guise* in 1558 on the taking of Calais, the *Epithalame* of 1559 on the marriage of Charles de Lorraine and Claude de France, and the *Chant pastoral de la paix* of the same year, inspired by the *Damon* of Naugerius, all three of which were reprinted with modifications in *La Bergerie*. Belleau also published an ode at the head of Pasquier's *Recherches* of 1560, mentioning the death of du Bellay, with whom Belleau had formed a close friendship on du Bellay's return from Rome, and for whom he also published the *Chant pastoral sur la mort de Ioachim du Bellay Angevin* in the same year. That poem was to be divided into two and re-published in the 1572 edition of *La Bergerie*.

Belleau appears for a time to have been attracted towards the Reform, and in 1561 published anonymously three allegorical poems, "L'innocence prisonnière," "L'innocence triomphante," and "La Vérité fugitive," to celebrate the release of Condé, the Huguenot chief, on 13 June. Condé had been imprisoned on account of his implication in the Amboise "conjuration" of March 1560. Persuaded by Ronsard to abandon his sympathy for the Huguenot cause, Belleau was invited by René de Lorraine, marquis d'Elbeuf and general of the galleys, that is, the fleet, to become in 1563 tutor to his son, Charles, aged seven. Belleau lived in consequence from 1563 to 1566 at the Château de Joinville in Bassigny, on the left bank of the Marne, just over halfway between Paris and Strasbourg. It was the home of the dowager Antoinette de Bourbon, duchesse de Guise, quite near the Lorraine border. Belleau dedicated *La Bergerie*, a mixture of prose and verse inspired by Sannazaro's *Arcadia*, to his pupil.

In 1566 René de Lorraine died, and 18 days later his wife died of grief. Belleau published his octosyllabic *Larmes* in 14-line strophes later in the same year. He continued to base his life on Joinville, but was now more frequently in Paris, where, for instance, he was part of the celebrated committee which appointed Nicolas Goulu royal professor of Greek on 15 September 1567 in succession to his father-in-law, Dorat. He had written an ode for the fifth act of Baïf's *Le Brave*, which had been played during the preceding January, and which he may have attended. In 1572 the second edition of *La Bergerie* split the work into two "days" dedicated respectively to Belleau's former pupil and to Louis de Lorraine, the future archbishop of Reims and cardinal de Guise. The second, and disordered, "day" draws on a large number of sources, and experiments with a number of new forms. The Huguenot sympathies are removed

from the Condé poems and some of the poems are now biblical. The volume contains translations not only from the Bible, but also from Aratus.

Then in 1576 Belleau published his *Les Amours et nouveaux eschanges des pierres precieuses*, including a paraphrase of the Book of Ecclesiastes, of which he had read four chapters to Charles IX at Fontainebleau in 1573, and eclogues inspired by the *Song of Songs*. It is here that Belleau pub. .ed the blasons—endowing minutely described small insects, animals, fruits, and precious stones with hermetic qualities—for which he is probably best known.

Belleau died in Paris on 6 March 1577, aged 49, at the Hôtel de Guise. Ronsard, Baïf, Desportes, and Jamyn attended the funeral, and a "Tombeau" was published in Belleau's honour in the same year. His comedy *La Reconnue*, partly derived from Plautus and likely to have derived from the period of Belleau's Huguenot sympathies, and the translations of Aratus's *Phaenomena* were published with the rest of his works by Belleau's friends in the *Oeuvres poétiques* of 1578.

WORKS

Of all the poets associated with Ronsard, Belleau has the reputation of being the least lyrical, in the sense of being less given than any of the others to the direct inspiration of personal feeling, although the strength of his religious commitment is clear. Belleau invariably controlled sentiment with a strong restraining filter, needed to depend heavily on models, neo-Latin as well as antique, although he seldom resorted to mere pastiche, and was at his best at the translations which make up about a quarter of his output and also surreptitiously occur within the original compositions. Belleau's published volumes are disordered, and his verse, which has a domesticated quality, often relies heavily on intrusively obvious stylistic devices. It is not always clearly a genuine product of the poetic imagination, and is notable for the sentimental use of diminutives, for being sensuous rather than elevated, and neither refined nor elegant. Belleau was, however, immensely erudite, above all a craftsman of metre and language, who excelled himself in the meticulous description of objects, and when indulging his gentle feeling for nature.

What attracted Ronsard and Belleau to the pseudo-Anacreontic poems discovered by Henri Estienne was their natural, unsophisticated, but refined sensuality and grace. The language used by Belleau makes clear that he depends very closely on Ronsard, and he is also more prolix than the original Greek. Not particularly faithful to the original, Belleau's language is notably less sentimental in 1556 than it later becomes. The verse is only minor, devoted to such matters as comparing love's effects to those of a bee sting in "L'Amour picqué d'une mouche à miel." Its strongest quality is charm. About half the Anacreon volume is devoted to more original compositions, although Belleau still follows Ronsard in his development of the celebratory blason, or detailed description of a small object.

Ronsard had dedicated to Belleau poems on the frog, the hornet, and the ant. Belleau replied with his poem on the butterfly, published by Ronsard in *Le Bocage* of 1554. Ronsard also published Belleau's blasons "L'Heure," "La Cerise," and "L'Escargot" in the 1555 *Continuation des amours*. In his 1556 volume, Belleau adds another six blasons, "Le Coral,"

"L'Huître," "Le Pinceau," "L'Ombre," "La Tortue," and "Le Ver luisant de nuict." The metres, like the subjects, are light, with verses of six or eight lines of seven or eight syllables, and Belleau sticks closely to Ronsard's understanding of the genre, with hyperbolic praise for the humblest qualities, erudite and popular terminology mingled together, frequent diminutives, and a mixture of narration, realism, and fantasy. He describes the butterfly:

Est-il peintre que la Nature?
Tu contrefais une peinture
Sur tes aelles si proprement,
Qu'à voir ton beau bigarrement,
On diroit que le pinceau mesme
Auroit d'un artifice extresme
Peint de mile et mille fleurons
Le crespe de tes aellerons.
Ce n'est qu'or fin dont tu te dores,
Qu'argent, qu'azur…

(Is there any painter like nature?/You imitate a painting/On your wings so perfectly,/That to look at your rainbow colouring/One would say that a real brush/With extraordinary skill/Had painted thousands and thousands of flowerlets/On the silk of your winglets./You are adorned only with fine gold,/With silver, with blue…).

As first published, *La Bergerie*, containing a mixture of prose and verse, is scarcely unified except by its bucolic setting. It starts with a description of the château de Joinville. Three pictures in the gallery at the end of the terrace provide pretexts for inserting three of the previously published poems. Then a tapestry has verses embroidered round its edges, the 32 alexandrines of 1565 extended to 222 in 1572, as the volume continues its mixture of descriptions and poems. The love verse is on the whole lifeless, a seemingly inexhaustible re-working of the Italian Petrarchists, especially Bembo, Ariosto and Tebaldeo, with other pieces taking their inspiration obviously and directly from Pontano and Jean Second. Even the rustic descriptions have their literary sources, notably in Amyot's 1559 translation of Longus's *Amours pastorales de Daphnis et Chloé*, but there is a realism of often accumulated detail which brings Belleau's pages to life, and a colourful precision which allows the printed text to mediate an almost visual impact.

The second edition is even more loosely unified than the first, almost all of whose texts are now lengthened. Belleau also added the descriptive poems on April and May. The much-anthologized "Avril" is generally considered Belleau's best poem. There are thirteen stanzas, of which the first six start with the name of the month which is being addressed.

Avril, l'honneur et des bois
    Et des mois,
Avril, la douce espérance
Des fruits qui, sous le coton
    Du bouton,
Nourissent leur jeune enfance;

Avril, l'honneur des prés verts,
    Jaunes, pers,
Qui d'une humeur bigarrée,
Emaillent de mille fleurs

De couleurs
Leur parure diaprée.…

(April, honour of the woods/And of the months,/April, the sweet hope/Of the fruits which, beneath the fluff/Of the bud/Nourish their young childhood;//April, honour of the meadows, green,/Yellow, blue-green,/Who in a many-hued mood,/Enamel with a thousand flowers/Of diverse colours/Their variegated apparel…).

The second day of *La Bergerie* in its second edition narrates a stroll with a friend in the garden at Joinville, which offers pretexts for different sorts of prose and verse description, narration, readings, and conversation, irritatingly improbable in the proposed setting. Belleau plunders the whole of Second's *Basia*, and introduces the marine eclogue into his second day. He also draws on Biblical inspiration, partly for the universally disliked "Amours de David et de Bersabée," considered by most critics as a simple lapse of taste, but also to paraphrase, somewhat verbosely, some of Job's Lamentations.

Belleau's final volume continues the exploitation of the Biblical inspiration, often sentimentalizing it, and contains the 21 poems in a variety of metres celebrating the quasi-magical powers of precious stones. The idea is antique, and Belleau had many forerunners, whose often childish superstitions about the properties of jewels he maintains. It was in these poems that Belleau's contemporaries saw his greatest originality, and it may well be true that his creation of myths to explain the birth of the magical properties attributed to precious stones shows his imagination at its most vigorous.

The two-volume posthumous *Oeuvres poétiques* of 1578 also contains the unrevised text of the comedy *La Reconnue*. A young girl, Antoinette, leaves her convent when she is converted to the Reform, and in 1562 falls captive to a young captain, Rodomont. When he is called to serve the king at Le Havre, Antoinette is given into the custody of one of his cousins, a rich, old, and childless lawyer, to whose advances she will not respond. Another lawyer, but young and known only as "L'Amoureux (the lover)," falls in love with her. His valet, Potiron, saves the day. Rodomont, thought dead, returns; Antoinette's father is discovered in a client of the elderly lawyer; he insists that she choose her own husband, and she chooses L'Amoureux. Largesse is distributed to everyone, and the end is happy. The comedy, in rhyming octosyllables, is badly constructed, unmotivated, and almost without true dialogue, with each character addressing the audience in turn. None the less it has come a long way from earlier farces, has dropped the medieval coarseness, and is humanist in the sense of deriving from Plautus's *Casina*. There is a historically interesting attempt to emphasize the Frenchness of the play, which was also written with Italian models in mind. There is also some satirical social and moral comment in the comic realism on such matters as the cost of living and what is for supper.

PUBLICATIONS

Collections

Oeuvres poétiques, 2 vols., 1578
Oeuvres, 2 vols., 1877

Verse

Les Odes d'Anacreon Teien, traduites de Grec en François…
  ensemble quelques petites hymnes de son invention, 1556
Ode à Mgr le duc de Guyse à son retour de Calais, 1558
Chant pastoral de la paix, 1559
Epithalame sur le mariage de Mgr le duc de Lorraine et de
  Madame Claude, fille du Roy, 1559
Chant pastoral sur la mort de Ioachim du Bellay, 1560
La Bergerie, 1565
Larmes sur le trespas de Mgr René de Lorraine et de Madame
  Louise de Rieux. Ensemble le tombeau de Mgr François de
  Lorraine, duc de Guise, 1566
Les Amours et nouveaux eschanges des pierres precieuses,
  vertus et proprietez d'icelles. Discours de la vanité, pris de
  l'Eccleiaste. Eclogues sacrées, prise du Cantique des Can-
  tiques, 1576
La Reconnue [verse comedy], 1577

Biographical and critical studies

Eckhardt, Alexandre, *R. Belleau, sa vie, sa "Bergerie", étude*
  historique et critique, 1917
Chamard, Henri, *Histoire de la Pléiade,* 4 vols., 1939–40
Delacourcelle, Doris, *Le Sentiment de l'art dans la "Bergerie"*
  de R. Belleau, 1945

BENSSERADE, Isaac de, 1613–1691.

Poet, dramatist, author of ballets de cour.

LIFE

Bensserade at first signed his name Bensseradde, and at the end
of his life Benserade, the form in which it appears in the *Regis-
tres de l'Académie Française.* The abbé Paul Tallemant, however, the cousin of Gédéon Tallemant des Réaux, the author of
the *Historiettes,* reverted to the spelling used between 1641 and
the 1670s for the two-volume *Oeuvres* of Bensserade in 1697, to
which he appended a "Discours sommaire" of Bensserade's life;
modern critical usage is uncertain. There was already during the
17th century some dispute about Bensserade's ancestry, and
even the date of birth is uncertain. Bensserade was baptized in
the fashionable Marais district of Paris on 5 November 1613.
Tallemant, who disliked him, suggests twice in his *Historiettes*
that Bensserade's mother was notoriously loose in her behaviour, while both he and his cousin maintain that she was related
to the Richelieu family. Paul Tallemant reports in the "Discours
sommaire" that Bensserade was related to the Richelieus
through the La Porte family to which his mother belonged, and
that Bensserade was born in 1612, at Lions-la-Fôret in Normandy. He was indeed almost certainly Norman, and may well
have been of Protestant parentage.

The *Mercure Galant* (q.v.) published an obituary tracing
Bensserade's noble ancestry back to the 15th century, but his
successor at the Académie française, Etienne Pavillon, was publicly reserved about that in his speech of acceptance. Ménage
had been sceptical, but dropped any public expression of doubt
when Bussy-Rabutin wrote to Bensserade's enemy, Furetière,
on 4 May 1686, asking him not to say that Bensserade, "homme
de naissance (of noble birth)," "s'étoit acquis quelque réputation
pendant le regne du mauvais goût; car outre que cette proposition est fausse, elle seroit encore criminelle (had acquired some
reputation for himself during the reign of bad taste; because that
statement is not only false, but it would also be criminal)." The
question of Bensserade's birth had therefore got caught up in literary warfare even before his death. To question his nobility in
the 1680s was equivalent to taking sides with the partisans of the
"anciens" in the Querelle des anciens et des modernes (q.v.),
although Bayle could not be more doubtful about it in the article
on the poet in the 1697 *Dictionnaire historique et critique,* in
which he thought it worth while to dispute Moreri's view of
Bensserade's ancestry, based on Paul Tallemant's "Discours," in
the 1674 *Grand Dictionnaire historique.*

Bensserade's later fame has generated curiosity about his origins, and the evidence is scant enough to make obvious how it
has been embellished. Unhappily, investigation into the historical lineage of such snatches of a biography of Bensserade as can
plausibly be reconstructed is more fascinating than fruitful, and
what we actually know is very little. Almost certainly minor
aristocrats from the noblesse de robe, Bensserade's family must
have settled in Paris, and they were ambitious enough to send
him to the Collège de Navarre. Paul Tallemant tells us in the
"Discours" that Bensserade's father died while he was young,
that the inheritance was not worth the lawsuits. In the *Historiettes,* his cousin notes somewhat sneeringly that Richelieu gave
Bensserade a pension of only 600 livres, but would not see his
mother "à cause de sa mauvaise vie (on account of her loose way
of life)." Segrais says the pension was for Bensserade's studies.
It must have had something to do with the dedication of Bensserade's first tragedy, *Cléopâtre,* to the cardinal in 1636, and the
pension probably dated from that year.

Tallemant des Réaux said of Bensserade that "il a du génie,
mais il ne sçait rien (he has genius but no knowledge)," and Chapelain's *Liste de quelques gens de lettres françois vivans en
1662* marks against Bensserade's name "a peu de sçavoir (has
little learning)," a view often repeated and not contradicted
during his long life. He spent much time at the theatre, mostly at
the Hôtel de Bourgogne with Henri de Conflans, the marquis
d'Armentières, and fell in love with the wife of the company's
male lead. Originally Nicole Gassot, she was already an actor's
widow when, in 1630, she married Bellerose, and she was herself an actress. It was for her that Bensserade wrote *Cléopâtre,*
first played in 1635 and published the year after. His comedy
Iphis et Ianthe, with a plot borrowed from Ovid, had already
been presented at the Hôtel, probably as early as February 1634.
It was published in 1636, with a title page dated 1637.

Cléopâtre was probably a deliberate challenge to Mairet's
Marc-Antoine; ou, La Cléopâtre put on by the Marais troupe and
written with a strong male part for Montdory. Mairet's play
seems to have been performed towards the end of the 1634–35
season, and Bensserade's only later in 1635. Bensserade went
on to write another tragedy, *La Mort d'Achille et la dispute de
ses armes,* played late in 1635 without, apparently, any great

success, but published in 1636 with a dedication to Louis XIII. The plot comes more from Hardy than from Homer. It was followed by the tragi-comédie *Gustaphe; ou, L'Heureuse Ambition*, which was put on at the Hôtel late in 1636 and published, with a dedication to La Hunaudaye, in 1637. Then came the tragedy *Méléagre*, probably played late in 1639. The privilège is for December 1640, and the achevé d'imprimer is dated 28 January 1641. The play was dedicated to the marquis de Brézé, Richelieu's nephew, but again failed to make the hoped-for success, and Bensserade gave up writing for the theatre, although he may in 1642 have put into verse d'Aubignac's *La Pucelle d'Orléans*. For a period before Brézé was killed at Orbitello in 1646, Bensserade was a generously treated companion-secretary, with perquisites and large gifts in addition to a further 3,000 livres a year of pension.

He had been introduced into the Hôtel de Rambouillet (see: *Guirlande de Julie*) about 1634. He appears to have been in love with either Marguerite Vion, Mme de Saintot, the sister of Vion d'Alibray—she certainly used the familiar "tu" with him—which is what Sarrazin implies in Voiture's *Pompe funèbre* or, more probably, with her eldest daughter, Anne, later Mme de Givry, which is what the *Historiettes* tell us. Anne de Saintot was just 16. Bensserade published in Courbé's 1639 *Recueil de divers rondeaux* an invitation to her to write him a rondeau, and one duly appears in the same collection, possibly written for Anne by a friend. After the quarrel of the sonnets, in which one of Bensserade's was pitted against one of Voiture's, had ended on Christmas Day 1649, Bensserade's reputation as a writer of light verse was to soar. His name was linked by his near-contemporaries with those of Voiture and Pierre Corneille as the trio of great poets of the 17th century.

Before 1651 he was the author of only four of the 999 attributable pieces in the recueils published since 1639. Between 1652 and 1669 there were 61 recueils, of which 42 contained work by Bensserade, who contributed in all 244 of the 4,814 attributable pieces. He more or less retired with the *Ballet de Flore* of 1669 and, from 1670 to 1691 only 28 of the total of 724 attributable pieces are certainly his. Shortly after his death the fifth volume of Barbin's *Recueil* published 128 of his poems, which boosted his relative prominence. Of those 128 pieces, 52 had appeared in other collections, 35 were extracted from ballets and 18 were selected from his *Métamorphoses d'Ovide en rondeaux*. He had been made a member of the Académie française in 1674, but his real importance in the literary history of France lies in his verse contributions to two dozen ballets de cour from 1651 onward.

One consequence of Bensserade's friendship with Mme de Saintot was his acquaintance with the Pascal family. He exchanged stances with Jacqueline Pascal, whom he addressed as Amarante, when she was only 13. Voiture had written anxiously from Brussels early in 1634 to inquire who was the new red-headed poet at the Hôtel de Rambouillet. Since Bensserade is not thereafter heard of at the Hôtel, it would not be surprising if Voiture had elbowed him out as a possible rival on his return. However, socially his reputation was for forthright wit, without any of Voiture's delicacy or finesse, and it may also well have been that his taste was simply too unrefined for him to be one of the Hôtel's poets. His compliments were heavy, although suitable for the relative solemnity of an elaborate court entertainment. Bensserade's natural haunt was the cabaret, where his reputation for not paying bills caused him trouble. Paul Talle-

ment says that "sa familiarité même avait quelque chose d'impérieux (he was imperious even in friendship)," and his wit was often malicious and hurtful. In many ways Bensserade came to represent the more ponderous official side of the court's frivolity; he was not, like Voiture, occasionally clumsy, but already in the period before Voiture's death in 1648 brusquely heavy-handed.

On Richelieu's death, for instance, Bensserade had launched an epigram which alienated the sympathy of the minister's favourite niece, the widowed Mme de Combalet, now elevated as the duchesse d'Aiguillon, her husband, the marquis de Combalet, Luynes's nephew, having been killed at Montpellier in 1622. Mindful of the pension he had lost, Bensserade tried to put matters right with the duchesse, but his versified compliments did not succeed. The impression is that, before final success at court, Bensserade was too unrefined in his attitudes to women, to money, and to versifying to arouse much response other than distaste among those who were cultivating a real refinement in both manners and literature. It seems unlikely that he was invited to contribute to the *Guirlande de Julie* (q.v.), although Paul Tallemant attributed to him one of the three pieces signed "B" and normally considered to have been by Arnauld de Briotte, the son of Arnauld d'Andilly.

Happily for Bensserade the queen mother found him amusing and gave him a pension of 1,500 livres, to which Mazarin added 2,000 livres. He also received 4,000 livres to go to Sweden on behalf of the queen mother on a visit of diplomatic courtesy after Christina of Sweden had escaped assassination; this might have been intended as a full ambassadorship. Tallemant tells us that Bensserade did not go but kept the money, and Scarron was amusing about the cancellation of the mission, whose date is also uncertain. It may have been as early as 1645 and cannot have been later than 1653. After Brézé's death, Bensserade was largely dependent on the queen mother, to whom he rendered important services, but Mazarin, short of poets on his side, also rewarded Bensserade generously. In the end Bensserade accumulated so many ecclesiastical benefices that his biographers have been unable to keep track of his income which, during the period of ballet scenarios, became vast.

He did, however, have a liaison with Catherine-Gilonne de Goyon-Matignon, who had married François de Silly, comte de la Rocheguyon. She had been widowed at 26 in 1628, and in 1648 rumours were circulating in the gazettes about a possible marriage to Bensserade, whom she provided with a house, a carriage, three laquais and a silver table-service, a much-mentioned symbol of financial ease in the 17th century. Tallemant's malice concentrates its venom as he recounts that Mme de la Rocheguyon and Bensserade fell out, "et insensiblement les trois laquais furent reduits à un, et le carrosse s'esvanoüit (and gradually the three lackeys were reduced to one and the carriage disappeared)." Tallement also took pleasure in recounting other misfortunes of Bensserade. "Il a de la vivacité d'esprit, mais il a une présomption enragée, et souvent il luy est arrivé de dire des sottises en pensant dire de plaisantes choses (He has a lively intelligence, but a lunatic presumptuousness, and it has often happened that he has said something rude when he was trying to be funny)." None the less he was to ingratiate himself particularly with yet another generous patron when Philippe d'Orléans became old enough to control his own affairs, and Bensserade contrived life tenure of an apartment in the Palais-Royal.

When, late in 1648, Bensserade sent a copy of the new edition of his *Paraphrases sur les IX leçons de Job* to the comtesse de Brégy, and she showed round the "Sonnet de Job," there was more than a merely playful rift between its champions and those who in indignation had dug out one of Voiture's half-dozen sonnets as a better example of the genre. The "Jobelins" included Conti, Conrart, Scarron, Chevreau, Segrais, La Mesnardière and the Princesse palatine. The "Uranistes," supporters of Voiture's *Sonnet d'Uranie*, led by Mme de Longueville, included Mme de Sablé, Madeleine de Scudéry, Mme de Saintot, Sarazin, Desmarets de Saint-Sorlin, and the Hôtel de Rambouillet group. There were some notorious abstainers, like Balzac, Chapelain, Costar, and Ménage. The neutrals were called "Tobistes" because Mlle Roche-du-Maine, being for Bensserade but unable to remember whom his sonnet was about, made a wild stab at the various sounds involved and said she was on the side of "Tobie." The interest of the semi-frivolous contest split in the end into pro- and anti-Mazarin camps. Meanwhile there was a flood of literary comments and epigrams on the affair. Finally, since nobody else would adjudicate, the dispute was submitted to the Caen academy, who came down in favour of Voiture's sonnet. Bensserade wrote a gracious letter to Mme de Longueville, but his own fame was now sealed. Loret's *Muse Historique* for 5 November 1650 testifies to Bensserade's celebrity even before his first ballet de cour.

It was before the first ballets, too, that Bensserade had his first brush with the queen's maids-in-waiting, the "filles de la reine," whose side he often took in their amorous, marital, and political enterprises, but to whom he also wrote scandalously lewd or offensive verses. There is nothing either funny or clever in the nine quatrains Bensserade published in 1652 on the marriage of Mlle de Saint-Michel. The poems to the maids-in-waiting are on the whole simply coarse, referring to a dozen by name, remarking on their girth, age, or whatever unattractive features came to mind. Bensserade was repaid in several ways, mostly in verse, and often with reference to his physical odour which is quite frequently and unpleasantly remarked on.

Revenez, revenez, beau faiseur de chansons.
La reine a commandé que l'on vous les pardonne,
Pourvu que votre rousse et puante personne
Change pendant l'esté plus souvent de chaussons

(Come back, come back, fine maker of songs,/The queen has commanded us to forgive you for them,/Provided that your ginger-haired and smelly person/Changes socks/ [literally: slippers] more frequently during the summer).

Tallemant does quote one genuinely kind and disinterested act, when Bensserade got Gombauld's pension renewed, but Bensserade seems on the whole to have been deservedly disliked for his coarseness, his vulgarity, his crude avarice, the ease with which he confused wit with offensiveness, and his generally predatory attitude to women.

After 1651 he was almost wholly taken up with court entertainments, although his court function went beyond the ballets. When the court travelled, he was sometimes in charge of making detailed arrangements for the accommodation of grandees, and we occasionally find him alone with the king, his immediate family, and perhaps Mazarin. It is almost surprising to find how high his reputation was with the authorities, for whom admittedly he undertook some delicate negotiations. His "gratifica-

tion" of 1,500 livres from the beginning until 1673 was more an indication of court favour than of literary merit. When Henrietta of England, "Madame" since her marriage to Philippe d'Orléans in 1661, went to negotiate the treaty of Dover with her brother Charles II in 1670, Bensserade accompanied her, more as a courtier than as a poet. Pellisson was the historiographer.

Something of Bensserade's situation can be gathered from the fact that, when he succeeded to Chapelain's place in the Académie française, incidentally receiving 17 votes on the first ballot on 5 April 1674 from the 19 members present (Furetière, Desmarets, Charpentier, Cotin, Fléchier, François Tallemant—who was the brother of the author of the *Historiettes*—Paul Tallemant, Segrais, Le Clerc, Mézeray, Pellisson, Dangeau, Racine, Doujat, Boyer, Quinault, Testu, Corneille, and Perrault), he was himself sent to solicit the approval of the king, the Académie's protector since 1672, after the second and unanimous ballot. The inference must be that he was closer to the king than any of the members of the Académie. Retz and Colbert attended the reception on 17 May, when Bensserade extolled the king but omitted the customary eulogy of his predecessor, Chapelain. He was to be an assiduous attender, was twice directeur in 1676 and became chancelier on 3 July 1680.

He was a supporter of La Fontaine's candidacy, but caused much offence with a satirical description of the members of the Académie in 1684, read on 2 January 1685. It was rather in the manner of earlier verses written for the dancers of his ballets, and full of allusions to the academicians' personal circumstances and physical peculiarities. Furetière, who had satirized Bensserade in the 1665 *Roman bourgeois* and had thereafter been harassed by him with malice but without wit, replied with both in the second and third *Factums* of 1688. Opinion ran strongly against Bensserade, defended however by Bussy-Rabutin in the letter of 4 May 1686 to Furetière, and by Charpentier. Bensserade's reputation needed salvaging for the sake of the partisans of the "modernes" in the Querelle. Furetière had already returned to the attack, once answering Bussy's letter on 20 May 1686, and then twice in his *Couches de l'Académie* of 1687.

Bensserade's standing can also be assessed from the reception of his *Métamorphoses d'Ovide en rondeaux* of 1676. The king had ordered it for the education of the dauphin, and it was a magnificent example of book-making. The quarto volume had a frontispiece by Lebrun, engraved by Sébastien Le Clerc, with a two-page letter from Lebrun explaining his allegory. A double rondeau is addressed to the king, and an épître to the dauphin, a preface, an extract from the privilège and even the errata are put into rondeaux. There are then 224 rondeaux, printed only on odd-numbered pages, one to a page, with on the facing page an engraving by Le Clerc or François Chauveau, underneath which is a French summary of the story in question, and Ovid's Latin original. The work ends with an acrostic pair of rondeaux containing the name of Mme de Ludres, the king's mistress from 1676 until Mme de Montespan heard about her in 1677 and obliged her to retire to a convent. The sumptuous book had taken at least three years to prepare and appears to have cost close to 20,000 livres, quite apart from what may have been paid to Bensserade, whose rondeaux were universally condemned. Ménage, naturally Furetière, Paul Tallemant, Boileau, Mme de Sévigné, and the *Mercure Historique et Politique* all dismissed Bensserade's work slightingly, despite its provenance. Only Perrault was complimentary.

In 1678 Bensserade published his *Fables d'Esope en quatrains, dont il y a une partie au labyrinthe de Versailles*. This again was a royal command, and it commemorates the maze at Versailles where the fountains played on 39 groups illustrative of the *Fables* of Aesop. Le Nôtre had executed the project after the king had selected the episodes from Aesop. The explanatory inscriptions were in quatrains—which explains Bensserade's choice of form—with gold letters inscribed on bronze plaques. Bensserade now spent most of his time at a country house he owned at Gentilly, although he kept the apartment in the Palais-Royal. He frequented the salon of Marie-Anne Mancini, now duchesse de Bouillon, and was on friendly terms with La Fontaine, Mme Deshoulières and her daughter, Ménage, Segrais, Pradon, and the ageing Pierre Corneille, the now somewhat out-of-date members of the party of the "modernes," still aligned to fight a battle which had been won.

In Bensserade's final years, his preoccupations became largely religious. He translated the little office of the Virgin Mary and the *Book of Psalms*. He died at Gentilly in the night of 19–20 October 1691, having been operated on for a stone which had been troubling him for some time and had finally induced a fever.

WORKS

Bensserade's literary importance rests chiefly on his contributions to court entertainments, as well, of course, as on the not inconsiderable if also not particularly distinguished role he played in the literary life of his century. From 1651 to 1669 he had practically the monopoly of script-writing for the royal ballets danced at the Louvre, Fontainebleau and latterly at Versailles, and it is not reasonable to base any estimate of his literary interest on either his early dramatic writing or on his published poetry, which on the whole lacks the grace, elegance, and refinement which could make such unpretentious pieces poetically effective. Too much of Bensserade's published verse is a mere jeu d'esprit, like the series of 20 sonnets addressed alternately to the beauty and the ugliness of parts of the anatomy. He relies much too heavily on rhetorical and syntactical devices for his effects, and a great deal of what has been published is simply too trivial to be of real interest, its poetic content not much more elevated than that of Loret's *Muse Historique*.

Bensserade's malicious allusions are more suited to his cooperation with Lulli, where the stage compliments made to the characters representing grand mythological personages were obviously intended, and interpreted, as picturesque flattery of the principal characters at court. Although some of the ballet writing is skilful, the satirical and allusive techniques appropriate to the ballet libretti fell flat in the realm of galant verse. Yet even as a poet Bensserade was esteemed by his peers, even if more for his wit than for his taste. He was praised, and prized, for the galanteries of his verses, and Sercy, whose living depended on his judgement of the public's literary tastes, relied quite heavily on pieces by Bensserade, "le plus illustre autheur de la cour (the most celebrated author of the court)" for his recueils.

Historically, the most important of Bensserade's poems is that which so outraged opinion among habitués of the Hôtel de Rambouillet that Anne de Bourbon on their behalf disinterred one of Voiture's sonnets to oppose to it as an example of galant verse.

The matter did cause real differences of opinion to appear, in spite of the Fronde, during 1649, before the matter was finally settled in favour of Voiture. Bensserade's subject was dictated by the fact that he was sending Mme de Brégy a copy of his Job paraphrases.

> Job de mille tourments atteint
> Vous rendra sa douleur connue,
> Et raisonnablement il craint
> Que vous n'en soyez point émue.
>
> Vous verrez sa misère nue;
> Il s'est lui-même ici dépeint;
> Accoutumez-vous à la vue
> D'un homme qui souffre et se plaint.
>
> Bien qu'il eut d'extrêmes souffrances,
> On voit aller des patiences
> Plus loin que la sienne n'en alla.
>
> Il souffrit des maux incroyables,
> Il s'en plaignit, il en parla:
> J'en connais de plus misérables

(Job, afflicted by a thousand torments/Will make his sorrows known to you,/And reasonably he fears/That you will not be moved by them.// You will see his naked wretchedness;/He has depicted himself here;/Accustom yourself to the sight/Of a man who suffers and groans.// Although his sufferings were extreme,/There are feats of patience that go/Further than his went.// He suffered from unbelievable ills,/He complained of them, he spoke of them:/I know worse ones still).

One sentence goes into each quatrain and each tercet, but the versifying shows no great skill, the hyperbolic expression of sentiment is reminiscent of stale baroque, and the sonnet cannot have cost a great deal of poetic effort. Its importance lay in its effrontery. Here was the embattled lover, court poet, and defender of the arch-enemy Mazarin, comparing himself in the cause of love, and not to his disfavour, with the Biblical symbol of suffering and patience. Mme de Brégy might have been proud to have attracted Bensserade's attention, but it would have been better not, in the political circumstances, to have flaunted it.

Bensserade's early dramas were not highly considered at the time, and are now universally regarded as weak both poetically and dramatically. His gift was to amuse his contemporaries, sometimes with allusions that were often pointed and sometimes hurt, and also no doubt to flatter the great. He outlived Voiture by so long that it is difficult to compare their financial success stories, but Bensserade's was even more lucrative than Chapelain's. His obvious careerism was undoubtedly and outstandingly efficacious. However, even if the court verse is discounted, with its rather graceless forms of amusing and half-sardonic galanterie, its more wounding endeavours at satire, its successful poems of erotic play and overt flattery—as for example to the king on the subject of the women who attracted his attention—together with the literary politics and the personal allegiances which, more than taste, aligned Bensserade with the "modernes," we are none the less left with an important achievement. The court ballets are skilled and poetic entertainments, and the verse which Benserrade contributed to the total effect is certainly the best he wrote.

The ballet de cour as a genre has as its immediate antecedent the "ballet-mascarade," made up with no pretention to dramatic interest of unconnected pieces of dance, acrobatics, and pantomime, sometimes interspersed with episodes of farce. It flourished from near the beginning of the century, was easily put together, providing cheap, mobile, and often very nearly improvised entertainment for grand houses. It still betrayed its medieval origins, and developed alongside the mythological and pastoral "ballet-comique," with which it merged to produce the "ballet à entrées." Tirades and récits began to be sung. Serious and comic "entrées" alternated, and the semblance of a plot, or at least a central theme, developed.

Dramatic interest, however, then dropped off, no doubt taken over by the straight comedies and tragedies which began to be played, and the classic 17th-century French ballet à entrées consists of virtually self-contained sections, each beginning with its own récit, the whole ending in a grand ballet, generally danced even later on, after professionals predominated during the body of the entertainment, by the nobles alone, gorgeously clad and moving in strict and sometimes complex patterns. This was the model in about 1630. Dance, gesture, and mime took the place of words to express action. The abbé de Pure was to complain in his 1658 *Idée des spectacles* that the story of a ballet had to be put into sung récits, or printed as verse in programmes. C.-F. Ménestrier still refers to ballet as "comédie muette (silent comedy)" or "peinture parlante (animated pictures)" in the 1682 *Des Ballets anciens et modernes selon les règles du théâtre.*

Bensserade's early ballets do not depend on elaborate stage machinery of the type introduced by Torelli for Richelieu's *Ballet de la Prospérité des armes de France* of 1641. They resemble the earlier ballets à entrées, and have only a single, simple setting. It was from 1658, when Lulli took over the monopoly of the music for the ballets, that magnificent settings and quick changes of scenery became regular. The ballets were originally played by the noble company alone, but from about 1630 professionals were introduced for the more demanding sung roles, and some of the grotesque or buffoon entrées are introduced expressly to make way for hired actors or acrobats. From *La Raillerie* in 1659, Bensserade even uses professional female dancers, and his "livrets" rely increasingly on sung récits.

The professional musicians play the overture on stage, before climbing up into the scaffolding at the side of the stage, from where they can see the dancers with whom they have to keep time. Occasionally they form part of the action and are dressed in appropriate costumes. Louis XIV himself did not disdain dancing the roles of even the most lowly characters in even the most dignified entertainments.

Bensserade was not the first to seek associations between the characters represented by the members of the court and the personal lives and attributes of the courtiers who played them, although the systematization of those associations was no doubt the foundation of his permanent career success. It also raised the ballet "livret" to the status of a literary genre although, in view of the personal associations with the lives, loves, and heroic deeds of the aristocratic players, the bare text more obviously requires decoding in the light of the circumstances of its composition and presentation than do other literary texts in any way remote from the circle in and for which they are generated.

Bensserade's first ballet was the "Ballet de Cassandre," whose text was published in 1651 as *Mascarade en forme de Ballet, dansé par le Roi au Palais-Cardinal*, played on 26 February 1651 with a part for the young king, presumably to distract him from the gloomy political situation at court. Anne of Austria had just been obliged to consent to Mazarin's exile. There were at least four performances, with an announcement in the *Gazette* (q.v.) and a notice in Loret's *Muse Historique*, as well as a brief comment by Madeleine de Scudéry in a letter of 2 March 1651 to Godeau. We know very little about the performance, who danced, who wrote the music, and who organized everything. There were nine professional dancers, 20 nobles, and 15 entrées. There is already in Bensserade's text an allusion to the personal qualities of those dancing the roles, to the ugliness of the marquis de Genlis and the erudition of the marquis de Montglas.

The second ballet, *Ballet royal de la Nuit...*, also for carnival, was danced on 23 February 1653 and published the same year. There are four parts and 43 entrées. Loret had to queue to see it, obtained a very poor seat, and had to base his description of what happened on the programme, although he was given a place in the parterre for 6 March. Renaudot wrote a long description in the *Gazette*. There were more than half a dozen performances, with decor and machinery by Torelli, and the young king danced six roles, including that of the sun. The lavishness was a landmark. Torelli starts with a countryside and seascape. The moon, dressed in a black robe studded with crescents and stars, wearing a bat for a hat, enters on a cloud drawn by an owl, accompanied by the 12 yellow-skirted hours of the night, wearing owl hats and butterfly wings. The seventh entrée changes to a street scene, and the fourteenth to a yard in which the maimed and lame are healed. At the opening of part two, Venus comes down in a machine. Later there is a witches' sabbath, later still a house on fire, and after that Aurora appears in the air in a chariot surrounded by the hours of the day and by dawn, sprinkling dew from an urn. Mostly, however, the scenes are realistic, with for example lovers shopping.

Bensserade wrote the "vers pour les personnages," that is the allusive dialogue, and five récits. He is at his best in the high style, where he varies the metrical patterns and subverts allegorical solemnity with humour. When the king first appears, there is a complicated stanza about time, clocks and quadrants. These four lines are as applicable to his majesty as they are to time:

Elle avance toûjours, et jamais ne recule
Chacun de ses momens fait qu'on la reconnoist,
Et jette un tel éclat qu'il seroit ridicule
    De demander quelle heure c'est ...

(It always moves forwards, and never goes back./Each of its moments proclaims its identity,/And projects such brightness that it would be ridiculous/To ask what time it is...).

It is a constant theme of Bensserade that the young monarch can look forward to future conquests in love and battle. Venus must hurry if she is to catch him before Mars, the god of war. There is charm, even grace, in the outdated baroque conceits, as the court ladies are admonished to run as quickly as the wind to catch him. He can run faster. What the rising sun says can also be understood of the king:

Sans doute j'apartiens au monde à qui je sers,

Je ne suis point à moi, je suis à l'Univers,
Je lui dois les rayons qui couronnent ma Tête;
C'est à moi de regler mon temps et mes saisons,
Et l'ordre ne veut pas que mon plaisir m'arreste
    Dans toutes mes maisons

(Without doubt I belong to the world which I serve,/I am not my own, I belong to the universe,/I owe it the rays which crown my head;/It is for me to regulate my time and my seasons,/And order does not require that my pleasure should detain me/In all my houses).

The verse is not strong, but the effrontery is now harnessed to imposing effect, and the fantasy confined by the relatively formal alexandrines does not lack an appropriate grandiloquence. It is still pastiche, but serves very well for an adolescent king dancing a ballet, particularly when there are 24 lesser aristocrats to be alluded to under the rising sun. Bensserade sticks carefully to court jokes, about Genlis's ugliness again, Créquy's well-known stupidity, Hesselin's pretentious entertaining, La Meilleraye's flat nose; he skirts insensitivity. In the case of the duke of York he approaches downright indignation at the treatment of Charles I. Bensserade is finding the mixture of satire, real flattery, and mock pomposity that made him so successful a provider of court entertainment. He did not frighten the great. He might bludgeon with coarseness, but he was not going to cut deep like Molière.

It has always to be remembered that we are dealing with a text, a single element in a performance, which had not only to fit in with all the rest but also to follow strict rules of at least social propriety, understood in the sense of what court etiquette demanded in the order of flattery. Queen Victoria was not the only monarch it was easy not to amuse, and Bensserade often touched the outskirts of lèse-galanterie. The duchesse d'Aiguillon had punished him for it once, the regent's maids-in-waiting a second time, and the Hôtel de Rambouillet had taught him that sensitivity was a suit he was not strong in. He had to calculate his audacities.

The *Ballet des Proverbes, dansé par le Roy, le 17 février 1654* was published the same year, with twice as many professional dancers as nobles, and 23 entrées illustrating as many proverbs. The *Ballet de Nopces de Pelée, et de Thétis, comédie italienne, dansé par le roi en 1654*, published the same year, is a series of ballet interludes danced in the interval of *Le Nozze di Peleo e Theti*, Mazarin's third attempt to introduce Italian opera into France. Loret had a good seat for the first performance; the entertainment lasted four hours; and the king danced three times a week from 14 April to 4 May. Bensserade made no real effort to relate the ballets to the opera. That would have to wait for Molière. Choreography, complicated and formal dance and patterns, and costumes, always glorious, rich, but leaving unencumbered legs to dance on, were by Saint-Aignan.

Also danced by the king in 1654, at the end of November, was the *Ballet du Temps*, to be followed by the *Ballet des Plaisirs* in February 1655, and the *Ballet des Bien-Venus* in May, performed for the wedding festivities of Mazarin's niece and Alphonse d'Este. The king paid, but did not on this occasion himself dance. Normally he did. In all, Bensserade collaborated in two dozen of these court entertainments, not always contributing all the verse, but not, again, changing his style. The *Ballet royal des Muses* contains, in its forthright eulogy of the king, a plain statement of the position of the "modernes" in the Querelle but, in spite of its allusions, Bensserade's verse does not succeed even here.

Superbe Antiquité, dont si mal à propos
Le Siecle trop long-temps a souffert les reproches,
Et qui voulez toûjours à l'égard des Heros,
Que les plus éloignez ternissent les plus proches;
Si vous en avez eu, nous en avons aussi
Et la chose entre nous doit estre égale ici

(Proud antiquity, whose/Reproaches our century has borne unjustly and too long,/And who want always, with regard to heroes,/That those farthest off dull the glory of those nearest to us;/If you had some, so too have we/And the matter should be equal between us).

Bensserade's other verse continued in its own direction. The 15-line "Errata" in rondeau form to the *Métamorphoses* contains, apart from the line "Dans ce volume" twice, eight lines ending in "-ables" and five in "-tion." The book is essentially a book of engravings with commentaries in rondeau form, rather than rondeaux illustrated by engravings. His ballet verses are his most successful, because the form precludes the poeticization of emotion, and his verse always lacked feeling.

PUBLICATIONS

Collections

Les Oeuvres de Monsieur de Bensserade, 2 vols., 1697
Poésies de Benserade, 1875

Plays

La Cleopatre de Bensseradde, Tragedie (produced 1635), 1636
La Mort d'Achille et la Dispvte de ses Armes, Tragedie (produced 1635), 1636
Iphis et Iante, Comedie (produced 1634), 1636, dated 1637
Gustaphe; ou, L'Hevrevse Ambition, Tragi-comedie (produced 1636), 1637
Meleagre, Tragedie (produced 1639), 1641
La Pucelle d'Orléans, Tragedie, Paris, 1642 [authorship doubtful]

Ballets

Mascarade en forme de Ballet (Cassandre), dansé par le Roi au Palais-Cardinal, le 26 Février 1651, 1651
Ballet royal de la Nuit, divise en quatre parties, ou quatre veilles, et dansé par Sa Majesté, le 23 février 1653, 1653
Ballet des Proverbes, dansé par le Roy le 17 février 1654, 1654
Ballet des Nopces de Pelée, & de Thetis, comédie italienne, dansé par le roi en 1654, 1654
Ballet du Temps, dansé par le Roy le dernier jour de novembre 1654, 1654
Ballet des Plaisirs, dansé par Sa Majesté, le 4e jour de febvrier 1655, 1655
Le Grand Ballet des Bien-Venus, dansé à Compiègne, le 30 may 1655, par ordre exprès du Roy, 1655 [undated]
Le Ballet de la Revente des habits du ballet et comédie [1655?]

Ballet de Psyché ou de la Puissance de l'Amour, dansé par Sa Majesté, le 16ᵉ jour de janvier 1656, 1656

Amour malade, ballet du Roy, dansé par Sa Majesté, le 17ᵉ jour de janvier 1657, 1657

Ballet royal d'Alcidiane, divisé en trois parties, dansé par Sa Majesté, le 14 de febvrier 1658, 1658

Ballet de la Raillerie, dansé par Sa Majesté, le 19 février 1659, 1659

Ballet royal de l'Impatience, dansé par Sa Majesté, le 19 febvrier 1661, 1661

Ballet des Saisons, dansé à Fontainebleau par Sa Majesté, le 23 juillet 1661, 1661

Vers du ballet royal dansé par Leurs Majestez entre les actes de la grande tragédie de l' "Hercule amoureux," avec la traduction du prologue et des argumens de chaque acte, 1662

Ballet des Arts, dansé par Sa Majesté, le 8 janvier 1663, 1663

Les Nopces de vilage, mascarade ridicule, dansé par Sa Majesté à son chasteau de Vincennes, 1663

Les Amours déguisez, ballet du Roy, dansé par Sa Majesté au mois de février 1664, 1664

Les Plaisirs de l'Isle enchantée, Course de bague faite par le Roy à Versailles, le 6 may 1664 [the verses are by Bensserade], 1664

Ballet royal de la Naissance de Vénus, dansé par Sa Majesté, le 26 de janvier 1665, 1665

Ballet des Muses, dansé par Sa Majesté à son chasteau de S. Germain en Laye, le 2 décembre 1666, 1666

Le Carnaval, mascarade royale, dansée par Sa Majesté, le 18 janvier 1668, 1668

Ballet royal de Flore, dansé par Sa Majesté, le mois de février 1669, 1669

Le Triomphe de l'Amour, Ballet dansé devant Sa Majesté à Saint-Germain-en-Laye, le…jour de janvier 1681, 1681

Recueils in which appeared poems by Bensserade not included in his Oeuvres

Airs et Vaudevilles de Cour dédiez à Son Altesse Royale Mademoiselle, 1665

Les Chevilles de Mᵉ Adam, menuisier de Nevers, 1644

Les Délices de la Poésie galante, des plus célèbres Autheurs du Temps, 1663
    Seconde partie, 1664
    Troisième partie, 1667

Elogia Julii Mazarini Cardinalis, 1666

L'Eslite des Bouts-rimez de ce temps. Première partie, 1649

La Fine Galanterie du Temps, 1661

Nouveau recueil de plusieurs et diverses Pièces galantes de ce temps, 1665

Nouveau recueil de poésies des plus célèbres autheurs du temps, 1653

Nouveau recueil des plus belles poésies contenant: Le Triomphe d'Aminte, 1654

Nouveau recueil de vers mis en chant à la fin duquel sont tous les airs nouveaux, jusqu'à l'an 1670, n.d.

Les Plaisirs de la Poésie galante, gaillarde et amoureuse, n.d.

Poésies choisies de Messieurs Corneille, Bensserade, de Scudéry, Boisrobert…, et plusieurs autres, 1653 [referred to as *Recueil de Sercy*]
    Seconde partie, 1653
    Quatrième partie, 1658

    Cinquième partie, 1660

Ramas de Poësies vieilles et nouvelles où l'on a joint en vers héroïques l'expédition du Prince d'Orange en Angleterre, 1689

Recueil de ce qui s'est fait de plus considérable sur les conquestes du Roy en Hollande par les meilleurs esprits de ce temps, n.d. [1673]

Recueil de diverses poésies choisies des sieurs: La Ménardière, Brébeuf, Segrets, du Ryer, Rotrou, Bensserade…, 1660

Recueil de diverses poésies des plus célèbres autheurs de ce temps, Tome II, 1652

Recueil de diverses poésies des plus célèbres autheurs de ce temps. Revue, corrigé et augmenté, 1654

Recueil de divers rondeaux, 1639

Recueil de plusieurs pièces d'Eloquence et de Poësies présentées à l'Académie françoise. 1689, 1695

Recueil de Poësies diverses dédié à Monseigneur le Prince de Conty, par M. de La Fontaine. Tome II, 1671

Recueil de quelques pièces nouvelles et galantes, tant en Prose qu'en Vers, 1663
    Seconde partie (avec reimpression de la première), 1667

Recueil des plus beaux vers qui ont esté mis en chant, 1661
    Seconde et nouvelle partie, 1668
    Troisième partie, n.d.

Recueil des plus Epigrammes des Poëtes françois depuis Marot jusqu'à présent, Tome premier, 1698

Recueil de Vers choisis, 1693

Le Tableau de la Vic et du Gouvernement de Messieurs les Cardinaux Richelieu et Mazarin, et de Monsieur Colbert, représenté en diverses Satyres et Poësies ingénieuses, 1693

Vaudevilles de Cour dédiez à Madame. Tome second, 1666

Other

Ode sur la grossesse de la reyne, 1638

Paraphrases sur les IX leçons de Job, 1638

Lettre en vers et en prose à M. le chevalier de Lorraine, 1672

Métamorphoses d'Ovide en rondeaux, 1676

Fables d'Esope en quatrains, dont il y a une partie au labyrinthe de Versailles, 1678; as *Aesop at court; or, The Labyrinth of Versailles,* 1768

Biographical and critical studies

Silin, Charles I., *Benserade and his Ballets de cour,* 1940

BERNARDIN DE SAINT-PIERRE, Jacques-Henri, 1737–1814.

Naturalist and novelist.

LIFE

Bernardin de Saint-Pierre belongs to that group of French writers, much larger than is often imagined, who, having been praised perhaps excessively, but certainly for the wrong reasons, have virtually had their names deleted from the canon, as critics and historians have discovered that the emperor's clothes were not visible as advertised. Bernardin de Saint-Pierre's complex personality is undoubtedly difficult to understand, and as an author he has been treated with increasing dismissiveness by important critics. The editor of the 1965 "Bibliothèque de la Pléiade" *Paul et Virginie*—"one of the most mediocre and most widely read books of French literature"—devoted two viciously invective pages to explaining why he detested its author, while even the more restrained and perceptive editor of the 1966 Garnier Flammarion text felt it necessary to point out that it incurred today "the virtually unanimous contempt of historians, editors and critics." Yet there was well over an edition a year in France alone during the text's first one and a half centuries of existence, and few educated French citizens even today can have escaped reading it. There has to be a case to be made out for its literary merit that has escaped its denouncers.

Surprisingly, little is known about the Bernardin de Saint-Pierre family. It was bourgeois, pretentiously tracing its ancestry back to the 16th century, and well-to-do enough to have Jacques-Henri, born on 19 January 1737 at Le Havre, instructed at first by the local curé at Caen. From an atmosphere of pious exaltation and imaginative excitement, both stimulated by the *Lives of the Saints* and *Robinson Crusoe*, he was to turn to a hatred of the Church. At 12 he embarked on a sailing ship bound for Martinique and captained by one of his mother's brothers. He returned detesting the sea and having, he said, nearly died of homesickness. It was when he returned home and was sent to the Jesuit school at Caen that he conceived his dislike of priests, discipline, and an ordered community life, although he still dreamed of becoming a missionary and a martyr. In fact he moved to the famous Jesuit college at Rouen, which he left in 1757 with a prize in mathematics.

From 1757 until 1758, when it was closed, Bernardin de Saint-Pierre spent a year at the Ecole des Ponts et Chaussées, and then had to move to the military school at Versailles, where he obtained a commission as a military engineer. The Seven Years War had been in progress since 1756, and in 1760 he was sent to join the victorious Rhine army under the command of the comte de Saint-Germain. Touchy and unable to tolerate the discipline and corporate existence of the engineers, he was soon sent back penniless to France where, by a piece of luck, he won money in a lottery. The following year saw another setback when he was appointed to Malta as engineer-geographer. He forgot to take his commission with him, was refused recognition, subjected to ragging, and forced to return home, destitute. He gave mathematics lessons and, having decided to emigrate, forged a chimerical genealogy for himself, called himself chevalier, and in 1762 set out for Holland, where he helped a French refugee to run a newspaper.

Even earlier in his extraordinary career, but especially from this point onwards, Bernardin Saint-Pierre's biographers have been reduced to reporting unverified or improbable hearsay about his life. We do, however, know that he made his way to Saint Petersburg, where he is said to have arrived with only 13 ducats. He became a sub-lieutenant in the engineering corps at Moscow, which was commanded by a Frenchman, du Bosquet, got to know the grand master of the artillery, Villebois, and obtained the protection of the French ambassador, the baron de Breteuil. He dreamt of establishing a company to seek a passage to the Indies through Russia, and of founding an ideal republic on the shores of Lake Aral. In 1763 Catherine II commissioned him as a captain and awarded him 1,500 livres, and du Bosquet took him to Finland to organize a defence system.

When Bernardin de Saint-Pierre got back to Saint Petersburg, Villebois had been disgraced, and Bernardin de Saint-Pierre left Russia for Warsaw. He is improbably said, while in Holland, to have turned down the hand of the sister-in-law of the editor of the journal on which he had been working, to have been presented by Villebois to Catherine II as a possible replacement for her then favourite, Gregori Orloff, to have refused Orloff's protection on his return from Finland, and to have refused the hand of du Bosquet's niece in marriage. He was certainly in Warsaw in 1764, active in the interests of the Radziwill party supported by France and Austria against the Poniatowski party supported by the invading Russians. He was arrested, probably had undertaken espionage work, and fell in love with a Polish princess, Marie Mesnik. We do not know how close their relationship became, but it embarrassed Marie, who terminated it, but never forgot him.

In January and February 1765 Bernardin de Saint-Pierre visited Vienna, where the French ambassador declined the offer of his services, and in April he was in Dresden, where something like an elopement took place and he found a protector in the holder of the tobacco monopoly, whose eldest daughter, Virginie, he reputedly declined to marry. Since the tobacco monopolist, Taubenheim, was unmarried, this story seems unlikely, but it has been conjectured that masonic connections explain the ease with which protectors everywhere appeared, as well as prospective brides. It is reported that at this point he both did and, more probably, did not get offered a commission by Frederick II. He certainly returned to France in November. His father had died, and he visited Le Havre, but received no inheritance, everything having been left to his step-mother. He appears to have spent a period virtually destitute in Paris, but at the end of 1767, under the cover of a commission as engineer captain in the Ile de France, now Mauritius, he was sent to Madagascar with the secret mission of contributing to the reestablishment of Fort Dauphin.

He set sail on 18 February 1768, quarrelled with the head of the Madagascar mission and refused to disembark, carrying on to Mauritius, where he was employed in a civilian capacity, repairing buildings. The island was a centre of intrigue, with immense luxury co-existing with extreme misery and fierce cruelty. Bernardin Saint-Pierre was quickly involved in a series of disputes, particularly with the island's "intendant," M. Poivre, who had directed his interests towards natural history, but whose wife he had tried to seduce. An official report notes that he lived meagrely, and repaid the 1,500 livres of debts with which he had left France. He left Mauritius, disillusioned, in December 1770, and arrived back in France in June 1771. Destitute again, he stayed at first in the Tuileries with Breteuil, with whom he soon quarrelled, and was reduced to cadging to eke out his half pay. He began to frequent Mlle de Lespinasse and to get to know the leading philosophes (q.v.), from whom, however, he slowly parted company between 1775 and 1779, although he was to conserve and cultivate his relationship with Jean-Jacques Rousseau, on whose life and works he left fragments of a book.

In 1773 Merlin published Bernardin de Saint-Pierre's *Voyage à l'Ile-de-France* in the form of letters to a friend. In spite of its fresh exoticism and the efforts on its behalf of the encyclopédistes, with whom he was still friendly, the work was an only moderate success, and led to a court case with the publisher. From 1773 also dates a manuscript, "De la Royauté et des Rois," which Bernardin de Saint-Pierre did not publish, but which contains a pseudo-mystical theory of monarchy in rebuttal of Helvétius. In 1775 Bernardin de Saint-Pierre underwent a crisis of religious fervour and made a retreat at La Trappe. Meanwhile, from 1773, he worked with Rousseau's encouragement on what were to become the *Etudes de la nature* while also seeking patronage and employment, moving to an attic in the Faubourg Saint-Victor in 1781. From 1779 he spent much time and energy fighting on behalf of a brother who had been imprisoned for treason in the Bastille, and who gradually went mad before dying in 1791.

The first three volumes of the *Etudes de la nature* were finished in December 1783 and published in December 1784, an extraordinary assembly of scientific, moral, sociological, economic, and educational ideas, almost a shorter one-man solution to the problems to which the encyclopédistes were addressing themselves, but differing from them markedly in its total commitment to the idea of a divine providence, and in its sometimes puerile exaggerations of the way providence operated in the world. The *Etudes* brought immediate fame to Bernardin de Saint-Pierre. The third edition of the *Etudes* appeared in four volumes in 1787. It contained the immensely and immediately successful "pastorale," as its author called it, *Paul et Virginie*, and put an end to its author's financial tribulations. The vogue it enjoyed was extraordinary. "Virginie" became a hair-style; scenes from the novel were endlessly painted, engraved, etched, and carved; 300 non-authorized editions have been counted, together with translations into a dozen languages. In 1789 Bernardin de Saint-Pierre published a continuation called *Voeux d'un solitaire* and in the following year *La Chaumière indienne*. By this date he was in sympathy with the Revolution and a member of the assembly of his district, but was incurring ridicule in the scientific community, particularly, and in spite of some agreement, with theories concerning the melting of the polar ice caps and the distortion of the earth's spherical shape by longitudinal extension at the poles.

In July 1792 Bernardin de Saint-Pierre was appointed Intendant of the Jardin des Plantes, the Paris botanical gardens, at a salary of 10,800 livres with his own accommodation, and it was he who installed the zoo there. He was elected to the new national Convention which in September 1792 took the place of the old Assembly, but he refused to serve in any elective capacity. His post was suppressed in June 1793 and the Convention voted him a compensation of 3,000 livres. On 27 October 1793 he married Félicité Didot, the daughter of the publisher of the *Etudes*, and moved with his wife to Essonnes, just south of Paris. The couple were to have three children, Virginie, born in 1794, Paul, who died in infancy, and another son, also called Paul, born in 1798. Félicité was to die the following year, after a marriage that had not been happy.

In 1794 Bernardin de Saint-Pierre had been appointed professor of moral philosophy at the newly established Ecole Normale Supérieure at a salary of 12,000 livres with supplementary allowances, but the school was closed after a year, although its professors continued to received a salary. Bernardin de Saint-Pierre was then made a member of the Institut, where he received a second salary. At its meetings he strongly defended, against the atheists, a deist position. After the death of his first

wife he married again, in 1800, the 20-year-old Désirée de Pelleporc, this time quite happily. In 1802 a child, Bernardin, was born, but he was to die when he was two. Politically Bernardin de Saint-Pierre now moved again. A royalist until 1791, and then a revolutionary patriot until 1802, he rallied to Napoleon, who much admired *Paul et Virginie*, a copy of which he had with him during his Italian campaign. Napoleon was to give Bernardin de Saint-Pierre a pension during the empire, and he became a personal friend of Joseph Bonaparte, to whose wife his own was invited to become a lady-in-waiting.

In 1806 Bernardin de Saint-Pierre returned to strictly orthodox Catholic practice, and was made a member of the Legion d'Honneur. From 1803 he had been a member of the Académie Française, and in 1807 he became its president. His colleagues at the Institut prevented his nomination to the senate. The *Harmonies de la nature*, started in 1790, was finished in 1812. Bernardin de Saint-Pierre died on 21 January 1814 at Eragny-sur-Oise, two days after his 77th birthday.

He had clearly been difficult to get on with, cantankerous and quirky, and the accusations that he had earned money by working secretly for an unpleasant regime, and that he condoned appallingly brutal social habits while sentimentalizing his exotic reminiscences are undoubtedly true. He was plainly cranky, possibly even unstable, certainly touchy, harsh in his judgements, unyielding in his attitudes, and erratic in his sometimes remarkable intuitions and analytic conclusions. He was a visionary, a dilettante, given to ferocious exaggeration, imaginative exaltation, commitments that were too firm, and intellectual procedures that were too slipshod. It is probably even true that he did not write well and was sensitive only to a private selection of moral attitudes and social values. But many of these were shared by others of his generation and, whatever his personal faults and idiosyncracies, he daringly, even provocatively, explored a new way of feeling and a new series of moral attitudes, touching a chord which immediately and strongly reverberated in the popular imagination, and he must at least on that account be acknowledged as an important literary figure.

The pastorale *Paul et Virginie* started off by presenting a new way of looking at the world and at human reactions and attitudes, no doubt building on that of the Rousseau he admired, which instantly caused the moral and literary sensibilities of the pre-Revolutionary generation to vibrate in sympathy. The imaginative vigour, now no longer instantly apparent, is locked into the text in much the same way as the strength of Lamartine's imagination is for ever encapsulated in his first collection of verse. It can be seen to be present, even though we no longer share his reactions and attitudes, or sympathize with his cultivation of feelings. It is probably a matter as much of posthumous biography as of literary history that the advanced sensibility once represented by Bernardin de Saint-Pierre survived through the Revolution, the Empire, and the Restoration, but that gradually, in the course of the 19th century, the literary status of *Paul et Virginie* diminished. What had once been an imaginatively daring exploration of new values and ways of feeling was slowly demoted to a stereotyped model of virtuous behaviour for the edification of juvenile readers. The phenomenon by which a text gradually ceases to be of literary interest to later generations, but may still remain educationally important to them, may in essence be the proper concern only of sociologists, but it should not be entirely neglected by literary critics and historians.

WORKS

The two-volume *Voyage à l'Isle de Bourbon, au Cap de Bonne-Espérance, etc., avec des observations nouvelles sur la nature et sur les hommes, par un officier du Roi* published in letter form by Bernardin de Saint-Pierre in 1773 was probably intended to have been extended to include the "petit ouvrage (short text)" which was to become the pastorale *Paul et Virginie*, had the initial success of *Le Voyage* been less mediocre. The indulgence in the lushness of an exotic setting was new, like the luxuriating in the enchantment of names of mountains and rivers, and the evocation of colours, bird-songs, and odours, even if the letter form itself must owe something to Rousseau's 1761 *Julie; ou, La Nouvelle Héloïse*. Bernardin de Saint-Pierre describes, catalogues, and classifies the sites, flora, and fauna of Mauritius. Leconte de Lisle, who came from the island, and the harshness of whose criticism was legendary, was to feel moved by the charm as well as the precision of Bernardin de Saint-Pierre's descriptions of the customs and countryside.

However, we know from his letters that Bernardin de Saint-Pierre suffered in fact from the harshness of the landscape, its lack of the very greenery in which his descriptions exult. What he wrote home was "Ici le paysage est sans verdure, les promenades sans arbres (here the countryside has no green growth, the walks are without trees)," so that the exotic descriptions, however accurate a possibly nostalgic Leconte de Lisle found them, must be supposed to contain a good deal of imaginative effort.

Quand le soleil était descendu à l'horizon, ses rayons, brisés par les troncs des arbres, divergeaient dans les ombres de la forêt en larges gerbes lumineuses qui produisaient le plus majestueux effet. Quelquefois son disque paraissait à l'extremité d'une avenue et la rendait tout étincelant de lumière. Le feuillage des arbres, éclairés en dessous de ses rayons safranés, brillait des feux de la topaze et de l'émeraude; leurs troncs moussus et bruns paraissaient changés en colonne de bronze antique

(When the sun had sunk to the horizon, its rays, broken by the trunks of the trees, fanned out into the shadows of the forest in broad luminous sheaves, producing the most majestic effect. Sometimes its disc appeared at the end of an avenue and made it sparkle with light. The leaves on the trees lit from below by its saffron rays gleamed with the flames of topaz and emerald; their moss-covered brown trunks appeared to have been changed into a column of antique bronze).

That description is quite remarkable for the precision with which the play of light and colour is reproduced in a dazzling pattern of similes, metaphors, and implied metaphors.

From the early drafts of the "petit ouvrage," to the final text of the pastorale, the text of *Paul et Virginie* underwent a series of painstaking alterations which resulted not only in the imaginative embroidering of the actual historical events that inspired the novel, but also in the increasing emphasis on the conflicts of moral attitudes, so that the idyll becomes weighed down by its overlay of moral demonstration. The essential event in which the story culminates is the refusal of Virginie, the young heroine, to save herself from drowning in a shipwreck by taking off her clothes and throwing herself into the arms of a sailor who could then swim with her to the shore. A huge wave comes:

A cette terrible vue le matelot s'élança seul à la mer; et Virginie, voyant la mort inévitable, posa une main sur ses habits, l'autre sur son coeur, et levant en haut les yeux sereins, parut un ange qui prend son vol vers les cieux

(At this terrible sight the sailor threw himself alone into the sea; and Virginie, seeing death unavoidable, held her clothes down with one hand, laid the other on her heart and, lifting her tranquil eyes on high, appeared as an angel about to take flight to heaven).

We know that the story of the shipwreck of the *Saint-Géran* on 17 August 1744 was modified to fit Bernardin de Saint-Pierre's conflict between the idyllic myth of a world in which human harmony with nature made instinct and virtue reciprocally dependent on one another, and actual civilized humanity, in which the achievement of virtue was incompatible with the satisfaction of instinct. It is in the interest of sharpening this conflict that Bernardin de Saint-Pierre changed the story as recounted by the survivors. What happened when the ship went down was that the chaplain gave absolution and blessed those about to die, who then sang the hymns to the Virgin, "Salve, Regina" and "Ave, maris stella." To emphasize the dislocation of values that is imposed by civilized convention and epitomized by Virginie's refusal to strip off her clothes and throw herself into the sailor's arms, preferring the preservation of her modesty to the conservation of her life, Bernardin de Saint-Pierre alters the historical event, to send those about to drown to their deaths shouting "Vive le roi (Long live the king)."

However reluctant Bernardin de Saint-Pierre may have been to allow in 1787 that instinct led to confidence in God, the constraint of his own substituted ending to the account given by the old man who is telling the story to the novel's first-person narrator is clear. There is certainly implied criticism of the conditioning which led the men about to drown to behave as is described.

Nous en étions si près que, malgré le bruit des flots, nous entendîmes le sifflet du maître qui commandait la manoeuvre, et les cris des matelots, qui crièrent trois fois VIVE LE ROI! car c'est le cri des Français dans les dangers extrêmes, ainsi que dans les grandes joies: comme si, dans les dangers, ils appelaient leur prince à leur secours, ou comme s'ils voulaient témoigner alors qu'ils sont prêts à périr pour lui

(We were so near that, in spite of the noise of the waves, we heard the whistle of the captain who was giving instructions to the crew, and the shouts of the sailors who shouted out three times "Long live the king!" for that is the cry of the French in extreme dangers, as in great joys: as if, when in danger, they called their prince to their aid, or as if they wanted to show then that they are ready to die for him).

The stilted patriotic reaction is not exactly condemned, but it is intended to strike the reader as forced, the product not of instinct at all, but of instilled virtue, like that of Virginie.

Bernardin de Saint-Pierre's other changes to the story involved the alteration of the date to Christmas, and bringing the wreck nearer to the island so that the end could at least be heard from land. In fact the *Saint-Géran* went down well out to sea, and its sinking was not reported until three days later. There may have been an actual model for Virginie who drowned on her way back from a European education after a shipboard idyll on the *Saint-Géran*. The changes all increase the extent to which the reader is moved by the unnatural constraints of a virtue which, in clear conflict with nature and inclination, entails Virginie's useless death, seen to be incurred as a direct result of her social conditioning.

Even critics well disposed towards Bernardin de Saint-Pierre are inclined to feel that he spoiled a charming love idyll in a simple natural setting with too heavy an overlay of moral comment as the text proceeded from its original status as an appendix to the *Voyage* towards incorporation in the four-volume second edition of the *Etudes de la nature*, and from a purely aesthetic point of view they are doubtless correct. The didactic and pointed moralizing does not increase the reader's pleasure, but it does disturb the unity of tone. It does, however, also make Bernardin de Saint-Pierre's point clearer. As we have it now, *Paul et Virginie* starts with a description of a tropical island given by someone who, after two paragraphs, refers to himself as "I." This narrator asks an old man whom he meets to recount what he can remember, for

l'homme même le plus dépravé par les préjugés du monde aime à entendre parler du bonheur que donnent la nature et la vertu

(even the person most depraved by the prejudices of the world likes to hear about the happiness conferred by nature and virtue).

The old man then tells the story of M. de la Tour, who had come to the island with a woman whom, because he was not a noble, he had had to marry privately and without a dowry in France. M. de la Tour goes off to Madagascar to buy some black slaves, but dies of fever, leaving his wife pregnant. Mme de la Tour meets on the island a solitary woman, Marguerite, with a small boy called Paul, and herself has a baby which she calls Virginie. Marguerite's slave, Dominique, marries Mme de la Tour's black maid. The old man moralizes a great deal as he tells his tale, but all in the small earthly paradise of the two homes is natural, happy, and virtuous. Paul and Virginie were brought up together and, as infants, did not wear clothes. They were not taught to read or write, or to know anything other than what it was immediately necessary for them to know.

Bernardin de Saint-Pierre does not reason clearly and is no theologian, but the old man takes the reader a long way towards sympathizing with the possibility that, if left undisturbed, nature might lead humanity to physical, moral, and intellectual heights unattained and even undreamt of in civilized society. Virtue, it is true, requires "effort over ourselves for the good of others in order to please God," and evil exists, although it can be overcome. Human beings might be born equal, but their social functions can differ. All this is neither asserted as a philosophical truth nor excessively sentimentalized. The old man has a very simple conviction which, according to him, was borne out in the upbringing of Paul and Virginie.

Bernardin de Saint-Pierre was considered for the post of tutor to the dauphin shortly after *Paul et Virginie* appeared, and he was then made a professor of moral theology on the strength of it, but there is no real attempt in the book to argue the old man's position. The reader is merely implicitly invited to consider the possibility that his view, however philosophically vague or theo-logically dangerous, could actually be more or less right, and that nature and instinct really might, if left untrammelled, lead to happiness and virtue. His views are enshrined in the book's central myth, and the writing incorporates some impressively lush descriptive writing, but there are naturally also didactic passages, making explicit the implications of the myth for domestic behaviour, attitudes to material possessions, social organization, class, slavery, institutions of all sorts, the origins of language, and the nature of emotional love.

Bernardin de Saint-Pierre is at least thorough in applying the essential basic assumptions throughout the major realms of primitive human activity. There is neither logical reasoning nor sentimentality of any intensity in the exceedingly powerful suggestion that nature might itself be a more trustworthy moral guide than philosophy, theology, or social convention.

De temps en temps madame de la Tour lisait publiquement quelque histoire touchante de l'ancien ou du nouveau Testament. Ils raisonnaient peu sur ces livres sacrés; car leur théologie était tout en sentiment, comme celle de la nature, et leur morale toute en action, comme celle de l'Evangile. Ils n'avaient point des jours destinés aux plaisirs et d'autres à la tristesse. Chaque jour était pour eux un jour de fête, et tout ce qui les environnait un temple divin, où ils admiraient sans cesse une Intelligence infinie, toute-puissante, et amie des hommes…Voilà comme ces femmes, forcées par le malheur de rentrer dans la nature, avaient développé en elles-mêmes et dans leurs enfants ces sentiments que donnent la nature pour nous empêcher de tomber dans le malheur

(From time to time Madame de la Tour would read out loud some moving story from the old or new Testament. They reasoned little about these sacred books, since their theology, like nature's, consisted in feelings, and their morality, like the Gospel's, in actions. They did not have days set aside for pleasure and others for mourning. Every day was a feast day for them, and all that surrounded them a divine temple, in which they ceaselessly admired an infinite, omnipotent Intelligence, beneficent to humanity…That is how these women, forced by misfortune to return to nature, had developed in themselves and their children those feelings which nature gives to prevent us from falling into unhappiness).

The naivety of the narrative in both style and content touches parable. Virginie begins to feel embarrassment when she falls in love with Paul, and it starts to thunder: an event in the natural order parallels and comments on an emotional occurrence. Virginie is eventually called back by a rich imperious aunt to Paris, where her values are corrupted by class, wealth, civilization, education, fashion, and everything that can be brought into conflict with primitive nature. The governor arrives with a symbolic bag of money sent from Paris for the preparations for the journey. The old man teaches Paul to read and write so that he can correspond with Virginie. No book gives Paul more pleasure than Fénelon's *Télémaque*. Virginie is unhappy in Paris and the text of the novel interrupts the old man's narrative to allow him directly to address a paragraph to the two young people, and then turns into a dialogue set out as in a drama between Paul and the old man. The dialogue is in fact a moral sermon.

From time to time in the text, the narrator had intruded with his "I." It is after the long dialogue lesson given by the old man to Paul that the old man reports Virginie's return and death. When she had shown herself unwilling to marry the spouse destined for her, her aunt had disinherited her and sent her back to Mauritius in the stormy season. Paul dies two months after Virginie, and his mother a week after that. Mme de la Tour survives only by a month. The old man ends his account with an apostrophe to the characters in his story and turns away with tears in his eyes, while the narrator admits to having cried during the course of the story. Not even the tears are simple sentimentality, however. Bernardin de Saint-Pierre certainly put them there to indicate that a readiness to be moved is itself a sign of virtue.

PUBLICATIONS

Collections

Oeuvres complètes, 12 vols., 1818
Oeuvres posthumes, 2 vols., 1833
The Works of Saint-Pierre, 2 vols., 1846

Prose

Voyage à l'Ile de France, 2 vols., 1773; as *A Voyage to the Island of Mauritius*, 1775
Etudes de la nature, 3 vols., 1784 (includes *L'Arcadie*)
Etudes de la nature, 4 vols., 1787 (includes *Paul et Virginie*); as *Studies of Nature*, 5 vols., 1796 [Many of the component elements of the *Etudes* have also been issued separately in translation]
Paul and Mary [first English translation of *Paul et Virginie*], 2 vols., 1789
Voeux d'un solitaire, 1789
La Chaumière indienne, 1791; as *The Indian Cottage*, 1791
Mémoire sur la nécessité de joindre une ménagerie au Jardin national des plantes de Paris, 1792
Voyage en Silésie, 1807
La Mort de Socrate, drame, etc., 1808
Harmonies de la nature, 3 vols., 1815; as *Harmonies of Nature*, 3 vols., 1815
Correspondance de Bernardin de Saint-Pierre, 3 vols., 1826
La Vie et les ouvrages de Jean-Jacques Rousseau, 1907

Biographical and critical studies

Souriau, M., *Bernardin de Saint-Pierre d'après ses manuscrits*, 1905
Mornet, D., *Le Sentiment de la nature en France de J.-J. Rousseau à B. De Saint-Pierre*, 1907
Trahard, P., *Les Maîtres de la sensibilité française au XVIIIe siècle*, 4 vols., 1933
Simon, J., *Bernardin de Saint-Pierre; ou, Le Triomphe de Flore*, 1967

BODIN, Jean, 1529/1530–1596.

Philosopher, historian, and political theorist.

"La plus forte tête que l'ancien régime ait vu paraître en France (The strongest mind to have appeared in pre-Revolutionary France)" is one way in which a modern critic has described Bodin, and the claim, while probably not sustainable, is not quite absurd, either. Bayle thought him "one of the cleverest men to have lived in 16th-century France," and that if this claim erred, it was on the side of modesty. Bodin was an extraordinarily powerful thinker over a wider range of subjects than is usually remembered. The reasons for the eclipse of his reputation have been catalogued by his 1951 editor, Pierre Mesnard, and it seems certain that a more balanced history of the literary, political, and religious culture of 16th-century France will produce a reassessment which will attribute to Bodin again the importance accorded to him by Bayle, still an important source of biographical information.

Bodin was born at Angers three years after the death of Machiavelli, to whose theory of statecraft his own was strongly opposed. His father was a master-tailor, to whom his mother, Catherine Dutertre, bore in all four children. Notaried acts of 1546 and 1566 show that the family belonged to the body of modestly affluent trained Angers tradespeople, with other members of which its children intermarried. In 1566 Bodin is referred to as noble, and as a member of the Paris bar. He had therefore achieved a higher social position than that of his immediate family. Angers was, from shortly after Bodin's birth to the outbreak of the religious wars in 1562, a prosperous commercial and intellectual centre, with a university built up round a celebrated law faculty. De Thou's report that Bodin became a Carmelite was until recently controverted, but is now regarded as certainly correct. It happened at an age sufficiently young for Bodin's vows subsequently to have been annulled on grounds of youth.

At an unknown date Bodin attracted the patronage of the bishop of Angers, from 1540 Gabriel Bouvery, son of a rich merchant and financier, and of Guillemine Poyet, sister of the chancellor of François I. The bishop was a person of vast culture, with Greek and Hebrew, whose protection had proved more attractive to Guillaume Postel than a royal lecturership. Bodin's early education must have been in Angers. In 1545 he was sent as a Carmelite to the order's house in Paris, where he stayed until at least 1547. His later acquaintance with Greek, Jewish, and Arabian neoplatonism, with Aristotelianism, the Bible and the Talmud, together with Bouvery's known interests and Bodin's later homage to François I as a patron of learning, suggest that he must at this time have attended the courses of the royal lecturers which had been given since 1530.

There is substantial evidence that Bodin was made to appear before the parlement in Paris, suspected of Lutheranism. Two Franciscans and three Carmelites, including Bodin, were convicted of heresy on 7 August 1548. One of the five, Florent Venot, was burnt alive on 9 July 1549. Bodin must have abjured, and almost certainly owed his deliverance to the bishop of Angers, acting through the cardinal of Lorraine, bishop of Paris. The annulment of Bodin's vows in 1548–49 seems probably to have been a way of protecting him from further molestation. From about 1550 Bodin was studying law at Toulouse. Much in his biography remains conjectural, but it is possible that he may have spent up to two years in Geneva, and may even have been the "Jehan Boudin" who married the twice-widowed Typhaine Renaud there on 25 August 1552. It has been suggested that, if he was at Geneva, the burning of Michel Servet in 1553 may well have been the reason why he left Calvin's citadel. It was in 1553 that Bodin finished his translation of Oppian's poems on hunting, the *Commentarius in Oppiani de venatione* fulsomely dedicated to Bouvery in a letter dated from Paris in February 1555.

Bodin was in Toulouse again, entrusted as a "hallebardier" with at least one course of law lectures in the late 1550s, a normal apprenticeship for aspiring professors. Before his death Bodin demanded the destruction of five manuscripts dating from this period, which he regarded as superseded by what became his most famous work, the *Six livres de la république*, and which were presumably the notes from which he lectured. They were the "De imperio," "De jurisdictione," "De legis actionibus," "De decretis," and "De judiciis." The view which held sway up to and including 1941, although controverted as early as 1933, that Bodin in 1554 supported Etienne Forcadel against the humanist lawyer Jacques Cujas for the chair of Roman law at Toulouse is now fully discredited. Forcadel was wrongly supposed to have been a follower of the mos italicus of legal teaching, based on the casuistic adaptation of Roman law of which Bartolo di Sassoferrato had been the leading exponent, while Cujas was thought to be the authentic representative of the mos gallicus, based on the elucidation of the texts of the antique codes. The rivalry at this date appears to have been invented later on to explain the feud between Cujas and Bodin which broke out after the publication of the *République*.

Towards the end of his academic period Bodin, hoping to be appointed principal of the new humanist Collège de l'Esquille at Toulouse, delivered in 1559 an important address, the *Oratio de instituenda in republica juventute ad senatum populumque tolosatum*. The foundation was to have been an important college of liberal arts to be planned, together with a new Jesuit institution, at Toulouse, on the partial analogy of earlier trilingual institutions (see: Budé) elsewhere in Europe, and notably at Oxford, Cambridge, and Louvain. Money was to come from the suppression by the king in 1551 of eight disused boarding houses belonging to the law faculty. Bodin's address is an important document in the history of humanist legal reform as well as in the development of Bodin's thought. It called for a systematic exposition of the law, later sketched by Bodin himself, along the lines laid down by Pierre de la Ramée, in the *Iuris universi distributio*, first published in 1578 but written many years previously, probably before 1561. The view adopted in that work links the 1559 *Oratio* to the 1566 version of the *Methodus ad facilem historiarum cognitionem*, in which three distinct layers can be detected in the second edition of 1572.

It is possible that Bodin's 1559 discourse had connected the projected college, and his own desired nomination as principal, too closely with the protection of the Du Faur family. In fact the college was not completed. When the reaction to the treaty of Cateau-Cambrésis made Toulouse unsafe in 1559, and Bodin understood that his bid for the new college had failed, he moved in 1560 to Paris. For a moment in 1561, in spite of the warning signalled by the Colloque de Poissy in that year, it seemed as if the new regent, Catherine de Medici, might lead France into a further phase of cultural expansion and political peace, but the religious wars which broke out in 1562 soon seemed inevitable.

Before they did break out, Bodin was registered at the Paris bar. He signed in June 1562 the oath of Catholic loyalty required of all legal officers, although his Parisian lawyer friend Bautru des Matras, his friend's father who was a judge at Anjou, and the later Protestant leader La Noue all refused. Experience at the Paris bar brought home to Bodin that more depended on practical skills of advocacy than on an exact knowledge of the texts and interpretation of the legal codes. Paris was still dependent on customary law, to which the *Codex iuris civilis* of Roman law, accepted as primary in Toulouse and Bourges, was regarded merely as a complement.

Cujas became increasingly devoted to Roman law and textual study, while Bodin's concerns veered into practical considerations and the adaptation of constitutional theory. With Hotman and Le Roy, Bodin began to follow the example of François Connan in reducing Roman law to the perspectives of universal jurisprudence. He published the *Methodus*, followed in 1568 by *La Réponse aux paradoxes de Monsieur de Malestroict* on topics we refer to as inflation and the money supply. Bodin was furnishing a testimony to his fitness for the financial administration, whose officers were traditionally drawn from the Paris bar.

He was duly promoted, and appears to have been somewhat over-eager in his defence of the royal rights, over which he was given charge, in the Normandy forests. He regarded the king's dominion as inalienable, but only over the usage of the forests, which he thought themselves belonged to the people. In 1571, as maître des requêtes and conseiller, he joined the staff of the duc d'Alençon, then the younger of the king's surviving brothers, and shortly to emerge at the head of the party of "Mécontents" as it developed into the Politiques. Bodin, once suspect of Lutheranism, and again very possibly a Calvinist for a period, was very nearly murdered at the massacre of 1572, although the exact circumstances are not known. Bodin helped with the speeches and accompanied the party which went to Metz when the Polish representatives came to invite the duc d'Anjou to take the Polish crown.

Bodin was well placed on the death of Charles IX, to whom he had become close. The Polish king returned as Henri III, and Bodin's former employer, Alençon, succeeded to the Anjou title. Henri III relied on Bodin for information about the customs and institutions of other countries, and of antiquity. Whether or not he was a widower, on 25 February 1576 Bodin married Françoise Trouillart, widow of a contrôleur, Claude Guyart, to whose office of procurator at Laon he duly succeeded in 1577 or 1578. He had been elected a député for the Tiers Etat at the 1576 Estates General at Blois. In that year he published the highly successful *Les six livres de la république*, dedicated to Guy du Faur de Pibrac, but had also been elected president of the assembly of Blois, to lead the opposition to the expenditure that would be occasioned by the wars bound to follow any attempt by Henri III to impose Catholicism on his kingdom. His attempt to leave the edicts of pacification in force failed. In 1577 Bodin published his diary of the Estates, the *Recueil de tout ce qui s'est négocié en la compagnie du Tiers Etat de France, en l'Assemblée générale des trois estats, assignés par le Roy en la ville de Bloys au 15 novembre 1576.*

Bodin's function at court was now obscure, but he had certainly had access to confidential reports from representatives of the French administration abroad, and had discussed confidential matters of state with foreign diplomats in France. The success of the *République* was such that the English ambassador reported on it, and a Latin translation of 1586 was swiftly followed by translations into Italian, Spanish, and German. There were six French editions in four years. Bodin now published the *Iuris universi distributio* (Lyons 1578, Cologne 1580, Prague 1582) to assert against Hotman, Baudouin and others his right to be regarded as Connan's legitimate successor as the leading lawyer of his school, and republished (1578) his answer to Malestroict. To a set of remarks on the fourth book of the *République*, Bodin replied in 1581 with the *Apologie de René Herpin contre les attaques d'Augier Ferrier*, and he continued to be employed on diplomatic missions. The 1580 *Démonomanie des sorciers*, written against the German J. Wier's suggestion that most witchcraft was trickery, represented sorcery as a real danger to society and was a procedural guide to the prosecution of witches. It is sometimes thought to mark a falling off in Bodin's mental powers.

Bodin probably went to England with Alençon in 1581 and accompanied him to the Low Countries in 1584, shortly before his death, which left the Protestant Henri de Navarre the natural successor to the throne. Sentiment polarized, and about two thirds of France came under the control of the League. Bodin was suspected by the Catholic extremists. In 1577 the Paris Carmelites inquired into the annulment of his vows nearly 30 years previously. The *République* was much too moderate for League sentiment, and the *Démonomanie* provoked accusations of dabbling in the occult. Bodin's house was searched on 3 June 1587. Laon went over to the League in 1588 after the Guise assassinations, and Bodin went over to it with the Paris parlement, partly out of his principle of not resisting strong popular movements. It has been suggested that he thought the victory of the League might lead to the downfall of the monarchy and the advent of democracy, but there is no evidence.

Laon returned to the obedience of Henri IV on 2 August 1594. Bodin was then 64, and had become discredited. He was attacked by the Jesuit Père Possevin in 1593, and led a diminishingly public life, content to teach his three children. Bayle says that both sons died young and that the daughter became insane but lived to be more than 80. The *Universae naturae theatrum* of 1596 is a disconsolate work, resigned to the failures of human history, the impenetrability of divine mysteries, and the small consolation afforded by meditation on the order behind the natural history of the physical world. Bodin is thought to have written the syncretist *Colloquium heptaplomeres de abditis rerum sublimium arcanis* about 1593. Seven wise men of different religions discuss their doctrines. Natural religion has the greatest philosophical appeal; Judaism occupies a moderate central position; and Catholicism is the most convenient. The dialogue was published fully only in 1857. A French translation which appears to have been made soon after Bodin's death was published in 1984.

WORKS

The 1559 *Oratio* is of interest not primarily for Bodin's proposed system of legal training, which followed later in his *Iuris universi distributio*, but on account of the nature of the appeal to the Toulouse senate and people. François I, said Bodin, had restored in France all that had been lost in Greece. Budé is praised for the expulsion from Paris of barbarism and François I for his grandiose project for a trilingual college for 600 students at the Hôtel de Nesle, eventually scaled down to the royal lecturerships. Bodin emphasizes the civilizing role of France and at least insinuates that political supremacy must go hand in hand with cultural advance if, indeed, it does not depend on it. The rhetorical register is clear, and Bodin's oratory is skilled. It is difficult to understand how the orator of this discourse was the failure at the bar that he is said to have been.

From France he moves his subject to Toulouse, addressing an audience of which each member knew about the humanist fame of the Collège de Guyenne at rival Bordeaux. From liberal arts Bodin proceeds to social organization and law; and from the general basis for prosperity to education. Then he mentions a list of towns ending with Nîmes, where François I had recently instigated proposals for an important humanist foundation. The citizens are shamed by a recitation of the support given elsewhere, even in empty Switzerland, to liberal education. The appeal to local patriotism is strong, and Bodin strikes fear into the heart of any parent who contemplates sending a child to Paris. The knock-about rhetoric is too long-winded to quote at what would be necessary length, and the *Oratio* was in Latin, but the point is Bodin's thorough commitment to legal studies as a humane discipline, the really essential humane discipline for a civilized provincial community aiming at prosperity and national, even international, standing. The best jurists, writes Bodin, are those

> iustitiae naturam non instabilem illam, et ad hominum voluntates mutabilem, sed aeterna lege definitam clare intuerentur; qui legum vim ac majestatem poenitus perspicerent; qui normam aequitatis perite tractarent; qui iuris ortum ac stirpem diligenter, et ab ultimo principio repeterent; qui legumlatorum ac iurisconsultorum omnem historiam, et antiquitatis cognitionem accurate traderent;... qui denique artem universam suis finibus circumscriberent, generibus notarent, partibus distribuerent, verbis designarent, exemplis illustrarent

(who clearly understand that justice is not that unstable rule pliable to the human will, but is determined by eternal law; who truly grasp what makes the strength and majesty of the laws; who eruditely treat of the norm of equity; who penetrate assiduously to the origin and derivation of the law as far as its first principles; who transmit to us the whole history of legislators and lawyers, and who hand on accurately a knowledge of antiquity... who, finally, enclose the whole art of law within its boundaries, note its varieties, divide it into its parts, give it its vocabulary, and illustrate it with examples).

Bodin had shown himself familiar with the precise circumstances of the Toulouse administration. His plan for legal studies is in the *Iuris universi distributio* which he did not for the moment publish. It shows Bodin's debt to Connan, and moves legal studies firmly in the direction of universal synthesis, or comparative law. Budé, Alciati, and Connan had removed from legal studies the idea that lawyers needed to be barbarians. The *Distributio* subordinates the teaching of Roman law to the general end of jurisprudence, defined as

> ars tribuendi suum cuique, ad tuendam hominum societatem, et quia virtus est mentis, in sceleratos etiam cadit,

qui prudenter iudicent, quo quaeque modo constituenda
civitas est, quid quemque cuique dare facere oporteat

(the art of rendering to each what is due, with the aim of
preserving human society; which art, since it is a virtue of
the mind, can be found even in the evil, who judge prudently why and how their association is to be regulated,
and what it is appropriate for each member to give or do).

Bodin divides his treatment of law into four parts: law, equity,
application of the law, and the duty of the judge. Law, defined
by the Aristotelian scholastics as a rational regulation for the
common good, promulgated by the appropriate authority,
although, for other scholastics, it proceeded from the divine will
rather than God's reason, is defined by Bodin like the neostoic
spark of divine reason, as a ray of divine goodness and prudence. Bodin then goes on to consider natural law and positive
human law, but always with the general purpose of legal systems
in view, rather than a simple elucidation of the meaning of the
texts.

More important than either the *Oratio* or the *Distributio*, and
perhaps more important even than the more celebrated *Les six
livres de la république*, is the *Methodus ad facilem historiarum
cognitionem*, first published in 1566 with an important preface
of 1 February addressed to Jean Tessier, president of the chambre des enquêtes, and rewritten for its second edition in 1572.
The text appears to have been worked on at least three times, so
that, of the proemium and ten chapters, the seventh chapter
appears to be the conclusion of an interior philosophical and
religious struggle reflecting the early studies in Paris, and the
sixth, closely connected with the 1566 preface and considerations of constitutional law, to reflect the period of teaching at
Toulouse. The last two chapters reflect Bodin's quarrel with the
German legal schools and with Cujas. The work is as concerned
with law as it is with history, although it remains a handbook for
students on how to judge historical evidence.

The real originality of the *Methodus* is the radical way in
which it looks to historical study to furnish the tools with which
to reform constitutional law. For Bodin by 1566, and probably
earlier, the aim is a systematic assessment of legal systems by
means of a comparison and synthesis of the data revealed by the
study of history. In the *Methodus* Bodin works out in the eighth
chapter, "Of universal time," the chronology he needs, only
after, in the fifth, "Of the right judgement of history," beginning
to examine the underlying sociological rules for the evolution of
societies, which will include in chapter six, "On the constitution
of republics," a whole series of determining influences which
have acted on societies in different times and places. His plan is
no less than to found constitutional theory on the study of the
history of societies, and on the structures underlying the development of societies as revealed by their histories.

Such a goal was bound to bring Bodin into conflict with
Cujas. Both belonged to the mos gallicus, believing not just in
the Bartolist mos italicus which had contrived the adaptation of
antique legislation to contemporary circumstances by the utilization of casuist devices, but in the uncovering of antique legislation in the circumstances in which it was enacted and
enforced. The difficulty came when Bodin found Cujas's
approach inimical to any appreciation of why antique legislation, once understood, might need to be shown to have lost its
applicability and need to be replaced by constitutional and other

law based on the study of historical events and patterns.

Bodin is in effect turning away from Lutheranism in his reading of history, attributing much less importance to the old
Roman empire of which the remnant was a Protestant Germany
hostile to a Catholic France, and settling for what amounts to a
deism in religion allied to political, nationalistically based
Catholicism. The prefatory letter of 1566 makes Bodin's point
most clearly. He does not deny the need for glossators, but holds
that they merely exercised their ingenuity to tease meanings out
of texts and thereby neglected their true function. Under the
name of civil law, the glossators, with great learning, as Bodin
admits, have transmitted the law of a single state,

Omitto quam sit absurdum, ex Romanis legibus, quae
paulo momento mutabiles fuerunt, de universo iure statu-
ere velle: praesertim cum edictorum ac legum infinita mul-
titudine… ac subinde veteres novis renascentibus sublatae
fuerint. Quinetiam Justiniani pene ius, omne a consequen-
tibus Imperatoribus abrogatum videmus

(I leave out how absurd it is to want to establish universal
law from Roman laws which were constantly subject to
slight changes, particularly in view of the infinite multitude
of new edicts and laws,… and the old laws were suppressed as those taking their place were reborn. We see
even that almost the whole code of Justinian was abrogated
by later emperors).

Bodin goes on to refer to the absurdities surviving in many
laws, continuing to complain at having Roman laws of different
periods presented as a single body of law. He himself has, he
says, taken Plato's advice, and put together all the laws from at
least the most famous republics and attempted to choose the
best. Bodin, in other words, still following the mos gallicus, has
sought to understand antique legislation in its context, and then
to systematize and universalize what is best in it, obviously
without the contradictions and incompatibilities which the glossators, ignorant of the social context of the laws, had had to use
so much ingenuity to explain away. Bodin has taken much from
elsewhere as well as from Rome, and now insists on the need to
have seen the law in practice, to have worked at the bar, to
understand the whole subject. He quotes almost verbatim his
own text from the *Oratio* quoted above. The real attack on Cujas
comes in what might be called the peroration of the prefatory
letter:

quod ab iis sperari non debet, quos nemo de iure consulere
velit: qui se grammaticos malunt quam jurisconsultos
haberi: qui falsam scientiae, nullam aequitatis opinionem
induerunt: qui syllabarum momentis Rempublicam servari,
judicia constitui, lites dirimi putant. quae sane pestis gram-
maticalis, in intimos omnium disciplinarum aditus usque
eo serpere coepit, ut pro philosophis, oratoribus, mathe-
maticis, theologis: minutos de schola grammaticos ferre
cogamur

(Nothing can be hoped for from those whom no one would
consult about law; who would rather be taken for grammarians than for lawyers; from those who cover up ignorance
of law with a facade of false learning; who think that by
mere syllables the state can be saved, the law constituted,
and disputes regulated. This pest of grammar has begun to

eat into the heart of all the disciplines so that we have to put up with bad grammarians scarcely out of school posturing as philosophers, orators, mathematicians, and theologians).

That was aimed at Cujas, the worst of the four types of lawyer, the academic archaeologist of texts. Those who depend on practice alone do not fare much better. The third class of lawyer includes Connan and combines a practical knowledge of the application of law in the courts with an academic understanding of the texts. Best of all is the class that Bodin evidently regards as his own, which joins practice and academic understanding with philosophy and a literary culture. To some extent he was only marginally more radical than Hotman and Baudouin in his theory, although Bodin went a long way further towards the practical implementation of his views.

Les six livres de la république, published in 1576 and written in French for popular accessibility, incorporates historical and contemporary evidence not only from the sources mentioned in the prefatory letter to the *Methodus*, but also from England, Scandinavia, Poland, and Venice. Essentially the whole work elaborates the sixth chapter of the *Methodus*. Bodin's catalogue of foreign and antique, even exotic constitutional arrangements is impressive, and his erudition is crushing. The book's real merit is to take a stance against Machiavelli's series of formulae for gaining and maintaining power, by insisting on the standpoint of right, and therefore also raising the question of legitimacy of sovereignty. The attack on Machiavelli is forthright. Those who have spoken of the affairs of the world with no knowledge of the laws and of public right "ont profané les sacrez mystères de la Philosophie politique (have profaned the sacred mysteries of political philosophy)."

Bodin deals in *La République* with six principal topics. Firstly, "L'Etat, une extension de l'image de la famille (the state, an extension of the image of the family)," draws on the vulnerably unsophisticated analogy between domestic and civic or national administration. This concept makes national sovereignty an elevation of private domestic authority, and was to invite Bodin's opponents, like the Calvinist Althusius in his 1603 *Politica*, not only to insist on greater limits to monarchical sovereignty, but to propose abolishing it altogether in favour of the inalienable sovereignty of the people, understood in the manner transmitted in Calvin's Geneva to be taken up by Rousseau. The parallelism between the private and the public had earlier supported a long development in the *Oratio*, where already the basic political unit had been considered to be not the individual but the family. Bodin is absolutist without being totalitarian. Althusius thought that that view was inconsistent. It does of course rely on the operation of feeling, judgement, or good will supplied by the "law-giver" so prominent in 18th-century constitutional theory. Bodin uses paternalistic feeling to attack Aristotle's endorsement of the legitimacy of slavery.

The second topic is sovereignty, the source in any community of positive law. Sovereign power allows declarations of war to be made, treaties of peace to be signed, officials to be appointed. It provides the ultimate appeal in any community, is the source of mercy, and confers the right to mint money and to raise levies in taxation. It confers the powers to

donner loi à tous en général et à chacun en particulier, sans le consentement de plus grand, ni de pareil, ni de moindre que soi

(to impose law on everyone in general and on each individual in particular, without the consent of any superior, equal or inferior to itself).

That meant, naturally, that European states were sovereign, freed from any superior authority of emperor or pope, and was the theoretical expression of the de facto situation, which was made the foundation of European law in the 1648 treaty of Westphalia.

Under the heading of absolute power, Bodin reviews the traditional forms of government, democracy, aristocracy, and monarchy (see: Montesquieu). Bodin rejects full democracy as impractical to achieve, and unworkable in operation. The totality of citizens cannot itself corporately manage its affairs. Government by the few is preferable, but requires the achieving of a difficult balance. Best seems to Bodin to be monarchy, with the monarch constrained by the laws of nature. The monarch for Bodin is the actual possessor of power, not merely its repository, and the monarch is not bound to the citizens by a contract. Bodin does not favour the sharing of authority between king, nobles, and people, assuming it would guarantee conflict until one of the other forms of government prevailed. In practice Bodin favours the French monarchy, with parlements acting only as courts and the Estates with powers of petition and complaint alone.

For the limits of power, Bodin relies on natural and divine laws.

Quant aux lois divines et naturelles, tous les princes de la terre y sont sujets et n'est en leur puissance d'y contrevenir s'ils ne veulent être coupables de lèse-majesté divine, faisant la guerre à Dieu.... Si la justice est le fait de la loi, la loi l'oeuvre du prince, le prince est l'image de Dieu, il faut par même suite de raison que la loi du prince soit faite au modèle de la loi de Dieu

(As to divine and natural laws, all the princes of the earth are subject to them, and it is not in their power to contravene them without becoming guilty of lèse-majesté [treason] towards God, and making war on God.... If justice derives from law, and the law is the work of the prince, the prince is the image of God, and by the same chain of reasoning the law of the prince must be modelled on the law of God).

Bodin insists that the prince should keep his word, respect private property, and not tax according merely to his convenience. Since, however, there are no sanctions, it is easy to see why Althusius needed to go further.

Fifthly, Bodin introduces the theory that government should be adapted to people, places, and times, but does not seriously suggest that forms of government should be adapted to different climates, as Montesquieu notoriously was to do, and Cardano already had done in the 1545 *De animorum immortalitate*. The idea that religion might legitimately be adapted to climates was naturally dangerous, since it attacked the monopoly of divine revelation claimed by the Church, but climatic influence on legal systems and individual temperaments was being openly discussed in the second half of the 16th century. Charron was to be heavily dependent on Bodin's treatment of the subject.

Finally, Bodin is in *La République* an advocate of religious toleration. The existence of Protestantism should be admitted, and the king should place himself above religious disputes. Bodin repudiates the use of force to impose religious unity.

The seven sages who discuss their religious problems so openly in the *Colloquium heptaplomeres* represent different religious attitudes and traditions which Bodin's dialogue examines with a distinctly syncretist bias. The dialogue was far too dangerous to publish, but there is no evidence that Bodin wrote it for publication. On the other hand he did not stipulate that the manuscript should be burnt, together with his early course notes. It would not be unreasonable to assume that Bodin's state of mind was timidly inclined to deism.

He may well have been undecided, but he can scarcely have been firmly committed to Catholic orthodoxy. All we know for certain is that he asked to be buried in the Franciscan church at Laon, and that was what happened. The *Heptaplomeres* makes out a disconcertingly good case for the merits of Judaism, and emphasizes the importance of natural religion. The conclusion, if there were one, might reasonably have been an external Catholic observance with quite a number of mental reservations. The dialogue is naturally important for Bodin's biography, but it is also a fascinatingly erudite speculative study in comparative religion, devised for his private interest by one of the most astute historical, legal, and political thinkers of the late 16th century.

PUBLICATIONS

Collection

Oeuvres philosophiques de Jean Bodin, edited by Pierre Mesnard, 1951

Philosophical and legal

Oratio de instituenda in republica iuventute, 1559
Methodus ad facilem historiarum cognitionem, 1566; in French, 1941; as *Method for the easy comprehension of history*, 1945
Réponse au paradoxe de M. de Malestroit, 1568; English translation, 1946
Les six livres de la république, 1576; as *The six books of a commonweale*, 1606
Iuris universi distributio, 1578
Apologie de René Herpin contre les attaques d'Augier Ferier, 1581
De la démonomanie des sorciers, 1580; in Latin, *De magorum demonomania libri IV*, 1581
Universae naturae theatrum, 1596; in French, 1597
Colloquium heptaplomeres de rerum sublimium arcanis abditis, 1857; early French translation, *Colloque entre sept sçavans qui sont de differens sentimens des secrets cachez des choses relevées*, 1984

Other

Oppiani de venatione libri IIII, 1555
Recueil de tout ce qui s'est négocié en la compagnie du Tiers Estat de France, 1577

Biographical and critical studies

Chauviré, R., *Jean Bodin, auteur de la République*, 1914
Moreau-Reibel, M., *Jean Bodin et le droit public*, 1933
Brown, J.L., *The Methodus of Jean Bodin. A critical study*, 1939
Franklin, J.L., *Jean Bodin and the 16th-century Revolution in the Methodology of Law and History*, 1963

BOILEAU-DESPRÉAUX, Nicolas, 1636–1711.

Poet and critic.

LIFE

Boileau, known even during his lifetime as Despréaux to distinguish him from the rest of his family, was the 15th child of his father, Gilles, a well-to-do Parisian lawyer. Gilles owned a house in the fashionable Enclos du Palais, as well as a small country estate at Crosnes, and had had eight children from a first marriage to Charlotte Brochart. He was a barrister ("commis au greffe"), from 1618 at the court of the Parlement de Paris and from 1633 at the Conseil de la Grand'Chambre. On 15 April 1630, at 46, he married the 20-year-old Anne de Niélé, daughter of another lawyer, by whom he had five children, of whom Boileau, born on 1 November 1636, was the fifth. Boileau's mother died on 16 May 1638. Like his father, he pretended to be of noble birth. In fact false papers of nobility were drawn up by Haudiquer, a professional forger of such documents who was sent to the galleys in 1701. Boileau's father in fact owed his success largely to the protection of Pomponne de la Bellièvre and to his two marriages into the interrelated world of the higher magistracy.

Boileau later complained about the misery of his childhood, much of which he said he spent in a wind-swept roof hut on top of the house. He went to school first at the Collège d'Harcourt; after his third year, never robust, he had to be operated on for the stone, and apparently suffered pain until he was 40. Probably in 1648 and after the operation, he was sent to the Collège de Beauvais, finishing school in 1652. He had written the sketch for a tragedy, read the modern poets and novelists, and begun to write verse. For four years he studied law, becoming a barrister on 4 December 1656, but gave up legal practice soon after the death of his father on 2 February 1657.

He may have contemplated an ecclesiastical career, perhaps as the result of an unhappy emotional affair with the niece, Marie Poncher, of the prior of Saint-Paterne in the diocese of Beauvais. She became a nun in 1662, and in the same year Boileau accepted the tonsure, and the clerical status it conferred. It entitled him to hold benefices, and some years later, when Marie Poncher's uncle died, Boileau obtained the priory, with an income of 800 livres. His father had died in 1657 leaving him 12,000 écus, of which he invested a third in Lyons municipal bonds to yield 1,500 livres a year, which ensured financial comfort for the rest of his life. He continued to live in the family house, now belonging to his elder brother, Jérôme, high-spending barrister much given to gambling.

The second brother, Pierre de Puymorin, was a member of the dissolute household of Gaston d'Orléans, and then steward of the king's amusements. He is said to have been good at making organ noises. His brother Gilles, five years older than Boileau, had started to publish in 1653 and was to prepare the way for Boileau in the world of letters, at least until the break between them in 1665. In 1656 Gilles had attacked Ménage, and the successful fight of Chapelain, backed by Colbert, to have him elected to the Académie française in 1659, when he was only 28, was widely regarded as a scandal. Jacques, one year older than Boileau, was to become a priest in 1661 and a Sorbonne doctor in 1662. He was a close friend of Brienne, and joined the chapter at Sens in 1671, remaining there as dean until 1694, when he returned to the Sainte-Chapelle in Paris.

Boileau appears to have tried his hand at "galant" verse, but by 1657, according to Le Verrier, he had sketched out what was to become the first *Satire*. The text was to be completely altered before its definitive publication in 1701. In 1666, the year of the earliest surviving version, first published surreptitiously, probably in a Rouen *Recueil contenant plusieurs discours libres et moraux en vers*, and then, modified, in the authentic *Satires du sieur D**** which repudiated the Rouen text, it contained an attack on Foucquet, said to have been penned between March and September 1661, repeated the current scurrilous accusations against Condé and Conti of incest with their sister, the duchesse de Longueville, and threw in for good measure a quip at writers who must be Pellisson, Bensserade, and Montauzier. The authentic 1666 edition omitted further outspoken attacks on the sexual orientations of various members of the entourage of the king's brother, but it remains quite clear that Boileau, like most of the magistracy, had, from at the latest 1659, leaned heavily towards Colbert against Foucquet and the remnants of the feudal aristocracy. The whole literary world knew the patronage which Chapelain, who often acted as an agent for Colbert, had bestowed on both Gilles Boileau and his younger brother. Allusions to Boileau's subsequent ingratitude are not infrequent.

It also seems more than likely that Boileau was closely associated both with the circle of Furetière, Cotin, and Patru which surrounded Marolles and the household of César d'Estrées, and with that of the abbé d'Aubignac and his purist friends, hostile to préciosité, the exaggerated language of galanterie, and to the influence of women on literature, as well as to the old-fashioned scholarly approach to letters of the Académie. He was certainly protected by the Montmort family. The Marolles circle included in particular Habert de Montmort's intimate friend, Maulévrier, whose *Carte du Royaume des Précieuses* launched the attack on préciosité. The circle was in general Cartesian (q.v.), given to irony and satire, but also devoted to the cultivation of the power of distinguishing the true from the false which, according to the opening of Descartes's *Discours de la méthode*, is "proprement ce qu'on nomme le bon sens ou la raison (properly what is called good sense or reason)," in the name of which, for instance, Furetière condemned "le Prince Galimatias" in the 1658 *Nouvelle allégorique*, making Bon Sens the prime minister of the Princesse Rhétorique.

Reason, in the company frequented by Boileau, denoted what for him were the immutable norms of taste which, because they were dictated by reason, should always and everywhere obtain. It was Sorel, Furetière's opponent, who complained in his *Description de l'île de portraiture* that legitimate criticism was turning into satirical attack. Furetière, Gilles Boileau—notably

in his 1656 attack on Ménage, the *Avis à M. Ménage sur son Eglogue intitulée Christine*—and Cotin, in his *Ménagerie*, prepared Boileau himself for his career as a satirist and as an opponent of the precious, over-refined, over-subtle analysis of sentiment in inflated language, ballooning rhetoric, and overstretched metaphor. Boileau came to disapprove outspokenly of everything that, however bitingly ironic, was not precise, accurate, elevated, and sublime.

Cotin had explained in his *Lettre à M. Truffier, maître des comptes à Paris*, published in the *Oeuvres galantes* of 1663, that satire was a form of moral poetry, as it had been in antiquity. It should not mention names, nor seek to wound, a view from which Boileau was to depart only cautiously in material intended for publication. With Chapelain, Furetière, and Sauval, Boileau was now at the centre of a small group hostile to the spirit of galanterie favoured by Foucquet. He was also at the literary fringe of a political cabal, directed against Foucquet and such other financiers as Jacquier and Monnerot by Colbert and the duchesse de Chevreuse, which was active between Mazarin's death in March 1661 and Foucquet's fall that September. It is highly probable that Boileau was the author of the satire *A ceux qui ont fait des vers contre le Roy* which circulated in Paris in 1662, justifying repressive measures against writers critical of the court and, with d'Aubignac's circle and Mlle Desjardins, Boileau seems to have applauded Molière's *Les Précieuses ridicules* in 1659. Together with a sonnet, "Sur la mort d'une parente," Boileau published in the 1663 *Délices de la poésie galante* his "Stances sur *L'Ecole des femmes*," partly directed against Corneille's jealousies. The *Discours au Roi*, placed now at the head of the *Satires*, must have been begun in 1662.

It was in 1663 that Chapelain, having himself received 3,000 livres, wrote the celebrated sonnet comparing Louis XIV to Mars, Jupiter, and the sun. Neither Boileau nor his brother Gilles was on the list of "gratifiés," on whose compilation Chapelain was consulted by Colbert, mostly because satire was not a genre which easily lent itself to singing the king's glories. Boileau wrote what we know as *Satire VII*, "Muse, changeons de style…(Muse, let us change our subject…)," to indicate that he had learnt the lesson: encomiastic verse in honour of monarchs is better retributed than satire. The satire, which included an attack on Chapelain, was a popular success and, perhaps on its account, Boileau was introduced to the free-thinking goodliving gourmand companionship at the cabaret La Croix blanche in the Rue de Bercy, where he met Chapelle. In the same year Boileau met Racine, who had sent him his *Thébaïde*, and Molière, to whom *Satire II* is addressed and whom Boileau also met at La Croix blanche. Dating from 1664 are *Satire V*, re-written to be read by Dangeau before the king, who was gaming at the time but whom it is said to have pleased; *Satire IV*, attacking reason as if it were an illness and dedicated to La Mothe le Vayer; *Satire V*, aimed at the pretentiousness of the aristocracy and maintaining that virtue is the only true honour; and *Satire VI*, on Paris.

Boileau's break with his brother Gilles came in 1665. The two, together with other wits of La Croix blanche, including probably Furetière, Chapelle, and Racine, had parodied parts of Corneille's *Le Cid* in a lampoon about Chapelain's wig, the *Chapelain décoiffé*, written in late August 1664, and it was probably the two brothers who followed it with a parody of the famous "stances" from Corneille's play, this time called *Colbert enragé*. By February 1665 Boileau was being received by the

Duplessis-Guénégauds at the Hôtel de Nevers, hostile to Colbert. His political affiliation had changed, but Gilles made amends to Chapelain and Colbert after the parodies, quite probably by blaming his brother, and appeared on the 1665 list of gratifiés in consequence. The brothers were to remain enemies until shortly before the death of Gilles in 1669. *Satire III*, "Le Repas ridicule," harshly deriding absurd gastronomic fastidiousness, was finished only at the end of December 1665.

It was the publication of an unauthorized version of the *Satires* early in 1666 that drove Boileau himself to take out a privilège on 6 March 1666. First intended as poems of moral comment for private circulation, it was through them that Boileau finally hoped, in vain, to attract royal patronage. Barbin immediately printed all seven that existed, and Boileau became the subject of a number of satires on account of the attitudes he had adopted, some of which were thought by his contemporaries to be either disloyal or hypocritical or simply too partisan. Boileau was still considered by those who knew of him to be an angry young man, scoffing with wit and mockery at anyone or anything he disliked, occasionally going too far, as in the ridiculing of Chapelain or on occasion in the apparently random choice of victim.

He had incurred the rage of Montauzier, and the authors hostile to him included Quinault, the abbé de Pure, Boursault, and Cotin. The most important pamphlets, sometimes of corporate authorship, directed against him included the probably collective *Bastonnade*, signed by Perrin and dedicated to Montauzier; the *Discours satyrique au cynique Despréaux*, likely to have been written by Cotin, primarily attacking Boileau's purist attachment to formal perfection and published before July; the *Satire des satires*, composed in its briefer, original form in July 1666, probably by Edme Boursault, the close friend of Donneau de Visé, and reproaching Boileau with his Latin models; and the *Critique désintéressée sur les Satyres du temps*, almost certainly written after the *Satire des satires* by Boileau's former friend, Cotin. But it was Boileau's disrespect for the new poetry protected by the court, his flouting of authority in matters of culture, and the extension of satire into matters of literature rather than morals, that was chiefly and menacingly held against Boileau.

It was probably in 1666 that he wrote the first sketch for what we know as the *Dialogue des héros de romans*, originally one among several "Dialogues des morts." He must have been thinking of publishing it when, in 1671, he took out a privilège for "several dialogues," and he is also reported to have abandoned publication in October 1676 of a dialogue against Latin verse, of which he had written occasional fragments. During the following year began his association with Guillaume de Lamoignon, the premier président of the parlement de Paris. In October he wrote the *Satire IX*, "A son esprit," defending himself against the attacks of 1666. It was read to their enjoyment in the presence of Mme Scarron—the future Mme de Maintenon—and Mme de la Sablière, and published on its own in 1668. The first version had contained angry remarks about Gilles. *Satire VIII*, "De l'homme," and the *Discours sur la satire* appeared in the 1668 octavo *Satires du sieur D****. In 1668, too, appeared the *Dissertation sur Joconde* on La Fontaine's poem, which, however, may have been by Gilles.

By the time his brother died in 1669, Boileau himself had begun to write in a tone calmer than that of the satires. He had begun to frequent the grander literary salons, was received by Mme de Lafayette and by La Rochefoucauld and, at 33, he had become the protégé of Mme de Montespan and of her sister Mme de Thianges, and a friend of their brother, the duc de Vivonne. He was esteemed by the Cartesian and pacifist clientèle of the Hôtel de Lamoignon, which included Bossuet as well as a number of Jesuits, among whom were Bourdaloue, Rapin and Bouhours. It was there that the aesthetics of art as the imitation of nature was worked out, and where Boileau's *Satire VIII*, "De l'homme," published individually in 1668, and *Le Lutrin* with its Jansenist (q.v.) sympathies, were conceived. The anti-Colbert and to some extent pro-Jansenist atmosphere of the Hôtel de Lamoignon is important in view of the way in which the literary, generally cultural, social, religious, and political camps were beginning to divide.

About this time Boileau renounced the benefice of Saint-Paterne, which he did not need, and which it began to look unseemly for him to hold. Racine, on friendly terms with Port-Royal (q.v.) again since 1669, had given up his benefices by 1674, coincidentally the year of the "conversion" of Mme de Thianges. The first *Epître*, probably discussed in a small group before presentation to the king, was written in 1669 and dedicated to Louis XIV on publication in 1670, when it prefaced the fable *L'Huître et les plaideurs*, which urged proposals to reform the judicial system. The fable was replaced in 1672, although the *Epître II*, written soon after 1674, salvaged the fable only reluctantly abandoned. It may well be that, after the end of the Dutch war and the peace of Aix-la-Chapelle in 1668, Boileau was in 1669 seeking to urge the king to follow Colbert's politics of peace as against the quest for further military glories urged by Louvois, who, disastrously for France, was to be Colbert's successor, as flamboyant in his cultural preferences as in his foreign policy.

On 11 August 1671 the amusing Cartesian skit on academic conservatism, the *Arrêt burlesque*, appeared, to be acknowledged as his work by Boileau only in 1701. On 9 March 1672 Boileau read parts of the *Art poétique* and *Le Lutrin* to Retz, and in August, either cynically following his interest or having genuinely changed his mind, he published the *Epître IV*, dedicated to the king and celebrating the glorious crossing of the Rhine on 12 June. He had taken his inspiration from the *Mercure galant* (q.v.), which had printed a joke about marrying the god of the Rhine to the goddess of the Seine. The borrowing caused real amusement in the opposition ranks, particularly on the part of Desmarests de Saint-Sorlin, Lignières, and, apparently, Bussy-Rabutin. Boileau was also presented to Condé. Racine and he were to be protected by Condé against the duc de Nevers, who in fact behaved magnanimously, after the affair of the sonnets provoked by Racine's *Phèdre* in 1677. Boileau's presentation to the king, by Vivonne, finally took place in January 1674, after which Boileau was awarded, although not immediately paid, a pension of 2,000 livres.

The death of Chapelain in 1674 removed the obstacle to the granting by Colbert to Boileau of a privilège for his complete works. They appeared in a quarto volume on 10 July, and included the first publication of *L'Art poétique*, probably conceived as early as 1669–70 but not finished until 1673; the first publication of the first four "chants" of *Le Lutrin*, the burlesque mock epic about the dispute arising from the positioning of a lectern in the Sainte-Chapelle in August 1667 which Lamoignon had challenged Boileau to write, and of which fragments had appeared without authorization in 1673 and which was first published in its full six cantos in 1683; the first publication of the translation of the *Traité du sublime*, attributed to Longinus, begun by Gilles Boileau before his death and probably finished by his brother in 1662; and the first publication of the two new *Epîtres* now known as II and III. *Epître III*, on deference to public opinion, was dedicated to Antoine Arnauld, who had hoped to convert to Catholicism the Protestant pastor, Jean Claude. *Epître V*, dedicated to Guilleragues, was published separately in December 1674. By the following year Boileau was sufficiently well-known as a literary arbiter to appear with Racine in the "Chambre du Sublime," the arrangement of wax figures given by Mme de Thianges to her nephew, the duc du Maine, son of Louis XIV and Mme de Montespan. It was also early in 1675 that Boileau composed the *Epître IX*, dedicated to the marquis de Seignelay, Colbert's son, but not published until the *Oeuvres diverses* of 1683.

1677 was the year of Racine's *Phèdre* and the serious literary and at bottom social disturbance of which it was the eruption. The immediate aftermath in Boileau's literary production was the *Epître VII* to Racine, written in February 1677. Boileau had wrongly been thought to have had some part in writing the obscene sonnet against the duc de Nevers (see: Racine). In fact it was by Nantouillet, Guilleragues and others, who, with the duchesse de Mazarin and the duchesse de Bouillon, were on Pradon's side of the cabal, with Montauzier. The sonnet's rhymes were those used in an attack on the Racine play wrongly supposed to have been written by Nevers. A threat announced over dinner by the duc d'Aumont made it seem wise for Racine and Boileau to take temporary refuge in Gourville's quarters in the Hôtel de Condé, and it was Condé himself who smoothed matters over. The *Epître*, which mentions the names of half a dozen grandee protectors including Condé and Colbert, like *Epître VI* and *Epître VIII*, was not published until 1683.

It may be that, to help matters settle down, Boileau decided, or was encouraged, to rest in the country. In July 1677 he was staying with his nephew, Nicolas Dongois, at Hautisle, near La Roche-Guyon, where he wrote *Epître VI* to the advocate general Chrétien-François de Lamoignon, son of the first president. The sycophantic *Epître VIII* was written to thank the king for Boileau's appointment, jointly with Racine, as royal historiographer, announced in the *Mercure galant* for October 1677. The salary was 6,000 livres, and the duties to celebrate the historic achievements of the royal reign. Mme de Sévigné wrote to her cousin, Bussy-Rabutin, on 13 October that Boileau had also been told to drop everything else. This is quite likely to have been the case in view of the social disturbance occasioned by the activities of both Boileau and Racine, culminating in the insults, and perhaps even scuffles, following the affair of the *Phèdre* sonnets. From this date Racine also abandoned writing for the stage. Boileau and he shared 12,000 livres to equip themselves to follow the king in his campaigns.

From about 1674, date of the publication of the *Art poétique* with its attack on Desmarests's *Clovis*, of the reception of Huet at the Académie française on 13 August, with the strongly pro-moderne interventions of Quinault and Charles Perrault, and of the opening of the competitions of the academy of painting to Biblical as well as mythological subjects, there was a cohesive party of modernes, as well as an underlying philosophy (See: Querelle des anciens et des modernes). The appearance in the 1674 *Oeuvres* of Boileau's translation of the treatise *On the sublime* attributed to Longinus, and the publication in 1675 of Racine's preface to his *Iphigénie*, made the divergence of views

between the two camps become even clearer and, since the original pagan author of the *Traité du sublime* praised the lofty nobility of style in *Genesis* as well as in Homer, the link forged in the Hôtel de Lamoignon between the Augustinian party and the anciens was made public. For all their classical learning, the Jesuits, patronized by Foucquet, had represented the values and attitudes of baroque, and in the affair of Pascal's *Lettres provinciales* had not only shown an exuberance of style regarded by Pascal as "extravagant" but had also admitted the evolution of moral values, to which the Augustinians were firmly opposed, as the partisans of the anciens were to the mutability of aesthetic norms.

To judge from his presentation to Louis XIV, the granting of a pension, and the according of the privilège for the 1674 *Oeuvres diverses*, Boileau's position had changed. His nomination to the post of historiographer in 1677 further advanced him along the path which he had then chosen. He attended court, cultivated Mme de Montespan and Mme de Thianges, and found himself in agreement with Bossuet, not an original theologian, but with decided views on most matters and a definite position in favour of the partisans of the anciens. Boileau followed the king in 1678 to Holland and in 1681 to Alsace, but he appears to have lost interest in carrying out his historiographical duties, and in 1692 his pension was reduced further than that of Racine. In 1683 both authors collaborated on a carnival ballet—receiving, if the *Gazette de Leyde* for 16 March is to be believed, 10,000 livres each—and on a comedy played at Versailles at midnight on 2 March by the company of the Comédie-Française.

From October 1683 Boileau lived in the Cloître Notre-Dame as a tenant of one of the canons, although he spent his days at the Palais-Royal. The *Oeuvres diverses* of 1683 contained the *Epîtres VI, VII, VIII,* and *IX* and the fifth and sixth "chants" of *Le Lutrin*. In the same year Boileau was refused election to the Académie française because he would not visit Quinault, as custom required, although there had earlier been a brief reconciliation. He was in fact admitted on Louis XIV's insistence on 1 July 1684, and did thereafter visit Quinault. The admission of La Fontaine had been held up by the king until that of Boileau was agreed. In 1685 Boileau became a member of the academy of inscriptions and medals, and bought his house at Auteuil, in the Rue des Garennes, for 8,000 livres. He was to sell it again in 1709 to his friend Le Verrier.

It was on 27 January 1687 that Boileau got up to interrupt the reading at the Académie by the abbé Lavau of Charles Perrault's poem *Le Siècle de Louis le Grand*, and had to be restrained by Huet. In the summer of 1687 Boileau lost his voice, recovering it early in 1688, but apparently not on account of a cure he had taken in the autumn. In 1688 the *Dialogue des héros de romans* was published in Holland in the second volume of *Le Retour des pièces choisies; ou, Bigarrures curieuses*. The first authorized publication was in the posthumous *Oeuvres complètes* of 1713. After his retirement to Auteuil, Boileau began to cultivate the image of himself as the repository of all true literary wisdom in France, and indeed successfully during his own lifetime to invent that legend of his own literary eminence, at least as the codifier of immutable literary canons, which imposed itself on French education until the 20th century.

The 1693 poem to the king, the *Ode sur la prise de Namur*, exalted the style of Pindar, and was accompanied by an Avis au lecteur replying to the three volumes of Charles Perrault's *Par-*

allèles des anciens et des modernes with their *Lettre à M. Despréaux en lui envoyant le présent livre.* Perrault replied with his *Lettre à M. D*** touchant la préface de son Ode sur Namur,* and in 1694 Boileau published in a further edition of his *Oeuvres diverses* his nine *Réflexions critiques sur quelques passages de Longin,* together with the *Ode, Satire X* against women, and eight epigrams. Perrault replied in March 1694 with an *Apologie des femmes.* Arnauld, in exile in Brussels, liked the satire, although Bossuet and the Paris Jansenists thought it irreligious and, partly on Arnauld's initiative, the reconciliation of Boileau and Perrault was brought about. They embraced at the Académie on 30 August 1694. Arnauld had died on the eighth.

On 23 October 1697 Boileau obtained a privilège for three new *Epîtres, X, XI,* and *XII,* the last on the love of God, written in 1696. They were published on 8 January 1698 by D. Thierry, after an earlier unauthorized edition. Boileau's landlord in the Cloître Notre-Dame died on 21 September 1698 and Boileau moved to become the tenant of a close neighbour. He also became friendly with Claude Brossette, a Lyons lawyer, to whom he gave permission to publish an annotated edition of his work. It appeared posthumously in 1716. Boileau's friendship with Racine also flourished, and he enjoyed the company of Racine's children, even after Racine's death in 1699. But from about 1690 Boileau's health had deteriorated and he had virtually withdrawn from the court.

In 1701 Boileau issued a further edition of his *Oeuvres diverses,* now containing in addition to the earlier editions a new preface, *Satire XI* on honour, the *Ode sur les Anglais,* epigrams, Latin poems, the *Arrêt burlesque,* the *Lettres à M. d'Ericeyra et à Perrault,* Boivin's *Remarques* on the *Traité du sublime,* some Latin translations of Boileau's works, and the *Lettre d'Arnauld à Perrault.* An unfavourable notice in the Jesuit *Journal de Trévoux* led to a dispute, and Boileau wrote the Jansenistically inspired *Satire XII* on equivocation but, fearing the retaliation, decided four times not to attempt to publish it. He does not appear to have felt strongly about Augustinianism, although most of those who, like Racine, shared his literary tastes tended to side with the Jansenists in the religious disputes. An account of his wrangle with the Jesuits appeared in 1706.

In that year Boileau had a fall from which he never really recovered. By 1709 he was complaining of deafness, blindness, and an inability to walk. In January 1711 he did make an attempt to publish *Satire XII.* A privilège was promised and Thierry started to print. Boileau corrected the proofs, and the cardinal de Noailles interceded with the king. Nevertheless, the king's Jesuit confessor, Le Tellier, succeeded in having publication forbidden. On 13 March 1711 Boileau died of a bronchial infection. He was 74. *Satire XII* was printed and circulating in Paris the same month. There was an edition of the *Oeuvres complètes* of 1713, either by Valincour and Renaudot or by Le Verrier. Brossette's two-volume 1716 edition contains for the first time *Satire XII* and with some other additional material, including the *Dissertation sur la Joconde* [*sic*], first published in the works of La Fontaine, but here with *Joconde*'s article in the wrong gender.

A great deal of what is known of Boileau's life comes from his own letters, mostly written during his last years. His enemies jeered at his sexual incapacity, presumably the result of a genital injury incurred during the schoolboy operation. He was obviously excitable, by turns elated and depressed, and his tenacious spitefulness is related to a general obsessiveness. He could cer-

tainly be disloyal and may have been devious to the point of duplicity. He was clearly ambitious for status and reputation, but never quite overcame a youthful iconoclasm. Towards the end of his life, as he shaded in the image of himself he had formed and wished to project, he began to assert his independence as well as his authority. Moral rigour attracted him, but he was a courtier as well as a critic and he enjoyed belonging for most of his life to a series of interlocking coteries.

WORKS

When Boileau first sketched *Satire I,* probably in 1657, the great Latin satirists had recently become a vogue in Paris, but Boileau's text, which drew on them, must have undergone a whole series of transformations between its first sketch and the authorized publication of 1666, after what Boileau referred to as the "édition monstrueuse" of the same year. Boileau falsely accused the unauthorized text of not being authentic, a simple tactic which allowed him to disavow anything which caused too strong a reaction, or one from an undesired quarter. In fact the unauthorized text is remarkable for its vigour, its malice, its allusiveness, and its realism. The poet affects to be a naive observer of the Paris scene, "La Cour et la Ville (The Court and the Town),″ while in fact addressing a closed society which would, for instance, understand the insinuation accusing the duchesse de Longueville of incest with her two brothers, Condé and Conti, in the two lines

L'inceste me fait peur, et je hais l'homicide: L'adultère et le vol allarment mes esprits

(Incest frightens me, and I hate murder:/Adultery and theft chill my humours).

A great deal of the mordant aggressiveness of the early satires depends on the reader's knowing who or what is being alluded to, and whether what is at stake is personal animosity or something as trivial as a convenient rhyme. Boileau was never technically more than competent as a versifier, although he enjoyed puns. He filled in lines with repetitions, allowing too much bombast and too many adjectives, and plainly placing many adverbs merely to boost the syllable count. The irony of *Satire I* in the unauthorized version is biting but unfocused, hitting out unpredictably at financiers, lawyers, philistines, the ambitious, and homosexuals ready to believe in God only on their deathbeds. The authorized version trims some of the burlesque and focuses the attack, concentrating more on political and moral targets, although Boileau still clearly plays on the tension between himself, as he was known to those to whom he recited, and the personality affected by the poet: "Je suis rustique et fier, et j'ai l'âme grossière (I am countrified and proud, and I have a coarse soul).″ The author, who did not at first intend to publish the satires, but took the opportunity provided by the printing of the untrammelled version in the "édition monstrueuse," cannot have wished to have been taken as speaking here in his own name.

The vivid but comic low-life realism of the initial description of Paris in *Satire VI* draws on a whole tradition starting with Juvenal, dragging in the abbé de Pure presumably for precise reasons we do not know, unless simply for the rhyme obscure/ Pure:

Qui frappe l'air, bon Dieu! de ces lugubres cris?
Est-ce donc pour veiller qu'on se couche à Paris?…
Ce n'est pas tout encor. Les souris et les rats,
Semblent pour m'éveiller, s'entendre avec les chats,
Plus importuns pour moi, durant la nuit obscure,
Que jamais, en plein jour, ne fut l'Abbé de Pure

(Who is disturbing the air, good heavens, with these
mournful cries?/Do people go to bed in Paris in order to
stay awake?/…And that is not all. The mice and rats seem
to have come to an agreement with the cats to keep me
awake,/More of a nuisance to me in the darkness of the
night,/Than ever in broad daylight was the abbé de Pure).

The abbé de Pure was to have his name substituted inappositely
for that of Ménage in the later *Satire II*. He was, we know, in the
opposite camp, but either Boileau is being unusually obsessive,
or some sort of riposte is being made to a remark or an action we
do not know about. The half-line, "And that is not all," is a good
example of Boileau's limping poetic technique. Its purpose is
simply to get "rats" to the end of the line, where the word
rhymes with the name of their traditional enemies, "chats." An
ironically incongruous switch to high-style language takes place
with a pseudo-epic account of trivial inconvenience when the
noisy locksmith turns out to have been chosen for the poet's
neighbour by "the heavens in their fury (le Ciel en courroux)."

The list of names of mediocre poets from *Satire VII* was occasionally altered by Boileau in different editions, almost as if to
demonstrate that his choice of targets was not entirely serious,
any more than the poet's request to his muse to change his style
from moralist to thurifer of the great was other than ironic.
Satire II, addressed to Molière, is a playful tribute from Boileau
to his senior. Boileau is conscious of his own penchant for
cliché, but there is an underlying challenge. Although Boileau,
even if his taste was nowhere near as sure as he allowed himself
to think, must have known that there are weak lines in Molière,
he seems to wonder whether his own will stand comparison, perhaps not realizing that they will not. *Satire IV* is not much more
earnest, although it singles out different sorts of character, the
"Pédant," the "Galant," and the "Libertin," for lampooning,
much as La Bruyère was to do, and then throws in Chapelain by
name.

Neither *Satire V*, which is a rhetorical homily on the moral
nature of true nobility, nor *Satire III*, the delightful send-up of
farcical gourmets, is of great importance, but *Satire IX*, even if
it is obviously not great poetry, none the less returns to literary
criteria and raises important questions about the nature of
poetry. The inflated language merely points up the heavy sarcasm. The poet addresses his mind:

Phébus a-t-il pour vous applani le Parnasse?
Et ne scavez-vous pas, que sur ce mont sacré,
Qui ne vôle au sommet tombe au plus bas dégré:
Et qu'à moins d'estre au rang d'Horace ou de Voiture
On rampe dans la fange avec l'abbé de Pure

(Has Phoebus smoothed the way to Parnassus for you?/
And don't you know that on this sacred mountain/He who
fails to fly to the top falls to the very bottom?/And that
unless you can rank with Horace or Voiture/You slither in
the mud with the abbé de Pure).

The verse is doggerel but the bathos amusing, like the ironic use
of elevated poetic style in the first line to state what is necessary
for poetry before the choice of down-to-earth terms to describe
in deliberately atrocious verse what happens if you are not
Horace or Voiture. As an object of contempt the abbé de Pure
makes a convenient rhyme for Voiture, not one of the "poètes
coquets," but certainly a representative of the modern poetry
identified with the Chambre bleue (see: *Guirlande de Julie*) and,
by extension, with Montauzier. The comparison of Voiture with
Horace is grotesque.

Satire VIII shows Boileau at his most subtle, keeping his literary register ambiguous throughout. There is direct speech,
comedy, and if not irony, then certainly paradox, but it is never
quite clear how far the underlying affirmations are serious. How
far, it asks, should humanity seek to control its affairs by the
application of naked rationality? Like Pascal, Boileau, although
for different reasons, is ultimately unwilling either to affirm an
unlimited trust in reason or to abandon it. Lamoignon, whose
interests and entourage the satire reflects, relished the company
of Jansenists and Jesuits, and also of doubters, while himself a
"dévot" and member of the Compagnie du Saint-Sacrement.

In 1663 a violently satirical anonymous pamphlet known as
Le Livre abominable was circulating, directed against Colbert,
the queen mother, and Mazarin, who had died in 1661. It
accused Colbert of irreligion and Machiavellian cynicism, suggesting that he was in league with the Jesuits, who were in fact
to be associated with his entourage just as they had been with
Foucquet's. It may have been written largely by Chapelle and
perhaps even partly by Molière, whose *Tartuffe* it must have
influenced. Its composition is unlikely not to have involved
habitués of La Croix blanche, although Boileau was not implicated by more than association.

The collective *Chapelain décoiffé* certainly originated in La
Croix blanche. Boileau may in later life have played down his
part in the text's production. Chapelle, Racine, Furetière, and
Gilles Boileau were also involved in its composition. Written in
dramatic form for three characters, almost certainly soon after
the list of "gratifications" was announced on 22 August 1664, it
is an amusing skit of perhaps a dozen pages on Corneille's *Le
Cid*. It was printed for the first time in the 1665 *Nouveau Recueil
de plusieurs et diverses pièces galantes de ce temps*, after the
appearance of another anonymous pamphlet, *La Clémence de
Colbert*, of January 1665, to which it alludes. Chapelain, whose
ancient wig was as much a joke as his renowned stinginess, was
livid with Boileau, whom he suspected of originating the
parody, in which his wig is torn from his head by an author, La
Serre, not on the list of gratifiés. Chapelain calls on his "pupil,"
Cassaigne, to avenge him. Cassaigne, who had received a pension, then declaims a close parody of Rodrigue's famous
"stances."

Auteur, Perruque, honneur, argent,
Impitoyable loi, cruelle tyrannie,
Je vois gloire perduë, ou pension finie.
D'un côté je suis lâche, et de l'autre indigent

(Author, wig, honour, money,/Merciless law, cruel tyranny,/I see my reputation lost, or my pension withdrawn./
One way I'm a coward, the other a beggar).

The same formula, a parody of *Le Cid*, this time wholly in

stances, although irregular, was used for the *Colbert enragé*, written after Colbert had failed to obtain a death sentence at the condemnation of Foucquet on 20 December 1664. The provenance is contested and the piece not very funny at all, but it seems at least probable that it was written by Boileau and his brother Gilles. *La Clémence de Colbert* of January suggests the coming reconciliation of Gilles with Colbert, which resulted in Gilles's pension in 1665 and the break between the brothers. The authorship of the *Dissertation sur Joconde* is still disputed. Boileau certainly said in 1702 to Brossette that he was the author, and this view has found strong academic support. The evidence, however, suggests that the real author was probably Gilles.

The *Dialogue des héros de romans*, sketched in 1666, was probably re-written in 1670–71 in the manner of Lucian, and published as "Dialogue des morts," unknown to Boileau, in 1688, in the second volume of the *Retour des pièces choisies; ou, Bigarrures curieuses*. The first authorized edition was in the posthumous *Oeuvres complètes* of 1713. The *Dialogue* is a conversation between Minos, Pluton, Diogene, and various heroes. Madeleine de Scudéry's popular Cyrus is summoned to lead Pluton's troops, and arrives sighing with love, conscious only of the galant's servitude. Quinault's Thomiris appears reciting the opening lines of *La Mort de Cyrus* and looking for the tablets on which he has that morning written a madrigal for "le charmant Ennemi que j'aime (the charming enemy I love)." Madeleine de Scudéry's Horatius comes in singing his love for Clélie, leaving after repeating his couplet four times, and Clélie herself enters to explain the famous Carte de Tendre. The excesses of the galant style are, of course, caricatured, and the allusions, satire, and literary attitudes give interest to the dialogue. Like Boileau's own satires, and so much else in 17th-century French literature—Mme de Sévigné's letters, La Rochefoucauld's *Maximes*, and Mme de Lafayette's *La Princesse de Montpensier*—the *Dialogue* was never intended for publication and, like the Carte de Tendre itself, it is little more than a party game.

The *Arrêt burlesque* is an amusing lampoon of an official decree. It had appeared anonymously in 1671 and was published over Boileau's name in 1701, from which year a manuscript dated 11 August is known. It is again little more than an amusing game which none the less tells us a good deal about how the social and cultural lives of Paris were being conducted. Boileau appears to have drawn up the *Arrêt* with the help of Racine and of the Orientalist popularizer of Gassendi, Bernier. It ridicules the theology faculty's attempt to proscribe the Cartesianism by then associated with Port-Royal, where it was popular and, since beast-machines had no souls, justified experiments on animals involving vivisection. Aristotelianism, however, remained the official teaching. In 1675 the University of Angers, and in 1678 Caen, had issued decrees against Cartesianism, as had the Oratorians in whose ranks the new doctrine, like the Jansenism originally nurtured in the Oratory by Bérulle, Condren, and Gibieuf, was winning too many adherents to please the authorities. In 1685 a decree of Louis XIV was again to forbid the teaching of Cartesianism, and in 1699 Edme Pourchot, rector of the University of Paris from 1692 to 1694 and professor of philosophy, was reported to the chancellor for the Cartesian views being taught in faculty of medicine.

The *Arrêt* forbids the admission of Reason to the university, deplores the removal of authority over the nervous system from the heart to the brain, and annuls the authority given to the blood to

voiturer par tout le corps, avec plein pouvoir audit Sang d'y vaguer, errer et circuler impunément par les veines et arteres, n'ayant autre droit ni titre pour faire lesdites vexations que la seule Experience, dont le témoignage n'a jamais esté reçû dans lesdites Ecôles

(journey throughout the body, with full power to the aforesaid Blood to roam, wander, and circulate with impunity through the veins and arteries, without other right or title to commit such stated aggravations than Experience alone, whose evidence has never been admissible in the aforesaid Schools).

The document is little more than a riposte to the mild harassment of Port-Royal after the Paix de l'Eglise of 1668 under the pretence of defending the official Aristotelianism against the inroads of the philosophies of Gassendi and Descartes. If irregular cures are made with quinine and other drugs unknown to the ancients, the doctors are authorized to restore fevers, and Reason is forbidden access on pain of being declared Jansenist. A reference to Alexander the Great, "acquirer of Asia, Europe, Africa, and other places," "de querelleuse memoire (of quarrelsome memory)," suggests that Boileau's own views on the importance of peace go beyond those of Colbert and are in harmony with Lamoignon's feelings.

Epître I, addressed to the king, is of interest for its deliberate mixture of formal and intimate styles, used here as a device to assert independence by implication while formally adopting an attitude of servile flattery. *Epître III* and *Epître IX* plead rather pompously for individuals to free themselves from the restraints on personal independence imposed by social conformism, while *Epître IV*, written in July and August 1672 to celebrate French victories in the Dutch war, may not so much mark a departure from previous pacificism as constitute a possible attempt to imbue Boileau's verse with something of an epic quality, in a cause which could do him no harm at court. Some contemporaries, like Lignières, were shocked at what they regarded as a failed effort to achieve a grave tone by adopting complicated rhymes. It is likelier that the whole piece is deliberate pastiche, not much more than elevated doggerel, composed with the amused and successful intention of taking in the court. *Epître IV* does, however, contain a roll call of some of the wounded, including Vivonne and Nantouillet, in a list which also mentions Nogent, who was killed, in spite of the fact that the poem seems otherwise to stay on a level with the mock heroic *Le Lutrin*. A list of real dead and wounded blended into a mock heroic pastiche might not have seemed totally incongruous to readers of the *Mercure galant*, which at any rate commonly juxtaposed such materials. The later *Epître VII*, written to encourage Racine after *Phèdre*, *Epître VI*, addressed to Lamoignon's son during Boileau's summer exile at Hautisle, and *Epître VIII*, thanking the king for the post of historiographer, are all conventional occasional pieces.

L'Art poétique was submitted to Patru for detailed revision before it was published. The doctrine is that emanating corporately from the Hôtel de Lamoignon, from Patru, who supervised the work's gestation, from Père Rapin, and from the abbé Claude Fleury, whose exposition in the unpublished *Lettre sur Homère*, written in 1665, Boileau misunderstood and weakened, but followed step by step. Fleury had understood that what was at stake was not so much an aesthetic as a way of life, simple, natural, austere. What he had been against was refinement, elegance, that which took society away from natural simplicity. For Boileau the debate never penetrated below the surface level of aesthetic effects.

L'Art poétique gained much from being read aloud. Mme de Sévigné writes of three such readings and there are other testimonies to similar occasions. The text was known well before publication in 1674. César-Pierre Richelet, author of the 1680 dictionary, had a copy by 1672, when he published his *Traité de versification*. The content can be criticized as unoriginal, codifying the tradition of Malherbe, Balzac, Mainard, d'Aubignac, and Chapelain, insisting on the norm of solidly conservative taste, and the criteria of the Latin and Greek classics, and elevating them not only above the preciousness of the madrigals of galanterie but also above any imaginative vigour. It was only in his later years that Boileau imagined he had revealed to his compatriots the true literary heritage which he thought they had been in danger of jettisoning. In fact *L'Art poétique* is a long, pompous, and derivative statement in favour of the natural, the elevated, the unornamented and the sublime, enlivened by the malice of its boutades, but important also on account of the way it relates a spectrum of literary attitudes to their focus. Boileau had translated the treatise on the sublime attributed to Longinus. Rapin had transposed the aesthetic criterion to the ethical plane in his *Du grand ou du sublime dans les moeurs*. Neither realized that the changes in literary fashion to which they were opposed reflected, if often with exaggeration or distortion, an underlying cultural movement of increased refinement, trust in nature, and confidence in progress.

L'Art poétique ought to have been harsher than it is on the exploitation of love as a tragic emotion. Only in private was Boileau prepared to say what Mme de Sévigné, at least, knew he thought, which is that it could not be done. Having herself recounted what she preferred about Corneille in the context of discussing Racine's *Bajazet*, she wrote to her daughter on 16 March 1672, "Despréaux en dit encore plus que moi (Despréaux goes even further on the subject than I do)." Rapin, who disliked the monotony of the alexandrine, reports that Boileau, too, scoffed at it as "psalmody," a term of opprobrium used of boring authors in *L'Art poétique*, itself written in alexandrines. *L'Art poétique* says nothing about the alexandrine. Its boldness is confined to intransigence on the subject of the modern epic, and especially that which draws on divine intervention, "le merveilleux chrétien." Boileau had recently been irritated by an uncomplimentary allusion to *Epître IV* prefacing a new edition of Desmarests de Saint-Sorlin's *Clovis* in 1673, this preface itself perhaps being a reply to the doctrine of *L'Art poétique*, known to Desmarests from its salon readings. Boileau's poem has to be understood primarily as a personally motivated intervention in the Querelle des anciens et des modernes.

There are four "chants." The first starts off with half a dozen lines in a high style which is intended to be totally serious,

C'est en vain qu'au Parnasse un temeraire Auteur
Pense de l'Art des Vers atteindre la hauteur.
S'il ne sent point du Ciel l'influence secrete,
Si son astre en naissant ne l'a formé Poëte…

(It is in vain that too bold an author/Thinks he can achieve on Parnassus the summit of the art of verse./If he does not feel the secret influence of heaven/If his star did not form him into a poet at his birth…).

Very soon, however, the exordium ends with a reference to Horace's *Ars poetica*, and remarks about the refined authors of galant literature follow almost perfunctory lines of deference to Malherbe and Racan. The rule for every author should be "Bon sens" and "Raison." The norms which are laid down are banal enough—"N'offrez rien au Lecteur que ce qui peut lui plaire (Offer the reader only that which can please him)"—with elementary instructions about such matters as pauses and vowels when writing verse. There are recommended models, like Marot's "élegant badinage (elegant witticisms)," and attacks, as on burlesque, about which everyone by 1674 was in agreement, and on "l'extravagance aisée," using the word which Pascal had notoriously exploited in the *Lettres provinciales* against Jesuit baroque.

It should not be held too forcibly against Boileau that the brief history of French literature in the middle of the first chant of *L'Art poétique* so completely misunderstands the merits of the culture of the French renaissance; his attitudes were not uncommon in his generation, although they were by no means universally shared. Historically after Marot came Ronsard, of whose linguistic and poetic innovations Malherbe had so strongly disapproved. Ronsard "broüilla tout (ruined everything)" on account of "sa Muse en François parlant Grec et Latin (his Muse talking Greek and Latin in French)," but "Enfin Malherbe vint (Malherbe finally came)," and reduced his Muse "aux regles du devoir (to the rules of duty)." Malherbe purified the language again, and Boileau pleads for correctness with a couple of pages of commonplaces.

The second chant starts by laying down rules for the minor poetic genres—idyll, eclogue, elegy, ode, sonnet, and epigram—with Boileau closely following Guillaume Colletet's 1668 *L'Art poétique*. He throws in a derogatory remark about Voiture's famous "Sonnet à Uranie," and mounts a sustained attack on galant poetry. Whereas Cotin and then Fleury had dismissed the elegant poetic "point" which Boileau says the French imported from Italy, he himself offers a long tirade against it only to end by allowing it. He is clearly more interested in achieving the effect of magisterial exposition than in advocating a properly thought-out poetic theory, or even a manual of practice.

The most important chant is the third, mainly devoted to tragedy, with the criteria of pity and terror taken from Aristotle and those of "pleasing and touching" from Horace. The versification is still weak, and the maxims for theatrical success now read almost as if they had in fact been taken from a manual. Boileau writes of the unities

Nous voulons…
Qu'en un Lieu, qu'en un jour, un seul Fait accompli
Tienne jusqu'à la fin le Theatre rempli

(We want…/In a single place, in a single day, a single completed action/That keeps the stage occupied until it ends).

Boileau follows Rapin's *Reflexions sur la Poetique d'Aristote et sur les ouvrages des Poëtes anciens et modernes* in preferring the "vraisemblable" to the "vrai" (see: Corneille)

Jamais au Spectateur n'offrez rien d'incroyable.
Le Vrai peut quelquefois n'estre pas vraisemblable,
Une merveille absurde est pour moy sans appas.
L'esprit n'est point ému de ce qu'il ne croit pas

(Never offer the public anything unbelievable./What is true can sometimes not be probable,/What is marvellous but absurd is for me without charm./The mind is not moved by what it does not believe).

The Greek tragedians, Aeschylus, Sophocles, and Euripides, are placed above the Latins, and Boileau launches into his attack on the medieval mystery plays, and on the exploitation of love in the pastoral, objecting more to its refinement and improbability than to the underlying exploration of the trustworthiness of natural impulse. When he moves on to the novels, *Clélie* and *Le Grand Cyrus* are attacked by name. Boileau laments the draining of vigour from the antique epic before making the strong attack on the "merveilleux chrétien" which has become the point of the whole poem. There is an assault on Tasso and, after Boileau has returned to antique comedy, a plea to "follow nature." The chant ends with a passage on Molière in which Boileau deplores the occasions on which Molière has "quitté pour le bouffon, l'agreable et le fin (put aside for farce what is pleasant and delicate)." It is the Molière of *Le Misanthrope* of whom Boileau approves: he might have held the prize for his art,

Si, moins ami du peuple en ses doctes peintures,
Il n'eust point fait souvent grimacer ses figures

(If, pandering less to the mob in his learned portraits, he had not often distorted his characters).

Most of Boileau's remarks, whether prescriptive or critical, derive from ordinary, moderate common sense, but behind the continual appeal to "le bon sens" lies his fear of the ephemeral, fashionable, and exaggerated, together with the perpetual ideal of the noble, the elevated, the dignified, and the sublime.

Boileau was neither a great poet nor a great critic. The early satires are sharp, pointed, and effective, but their author's importance resides primarily in the part he played in the literary life of his generation, holding a rearguard position, and contriving to impose himself as its spokesman, almost instinctively choosing his personal friends and enemies from the appropriate literary camps. He was not the best spokesman available for the position he represented, but he had the instinct, ambition, and guile of the courtier, and turned his mastery of the bombastic commonplace into a real asset. His confidence in his own achievement has imprinted itself on posterity, and his works are brief, accessible, often amusing, and sometimes clever. Paradoxically feared in his time for his outspokenness, although so often afraid to speak his own mind, and incapable of complexity or subtlety, he offers in his work traditional and easy access to all that was most reactionary in acceptable literary taste during the 1660s and 1670s. Still no doubt overestimated as regards his intrinsic importance, he remains an imposing literary personality. The danger is that his judgements, which are superficial, and aesthetic rather than moral, should be taken as an indication of what was really happening in the rich cultural life of his generation.

PUBLICATIONS

Collections

Oeuvres diverses, 1674, revised 1683, 1692
Oeuvres diverses, 2 vols. (quarto and duodecimo editions), 1701

Oeuvres posthumes, 1711
Oeuvres de N. B. D. (edited by Valincour and Renaudot), 1713
Oeuvres de N. B. D. (edited by Brossette), 2 vols., 1716
Oeuvres complètes, 7 vols., 1932–43
Oeuvres complètes, Bibliothèque de la Pléiade, 1966
Works, 3 vols., 1711–13

Verse

Satires (I–VII), 1666; with *Satires VIII–IX*, 1668
Epître au Roi (Epître I), no date (1669)
Satire VIII, 1668
Epître au Roy (Epître IV), 1672
Epître à M. de Guilleragues (Epître V), 1674
Ode sur la prise de Namur, 1693
Dialogue ou Satire X, 1694
Epistres nouvelles (X, XI, XII), 1698
Satire XII, 1711
Le Lutrin, poème héroï-comique, 1822
Satires, in English, 1904
Les premières satires de Boileau, edited by A. Adam (*Satires I–IX*), 1941

Other

Requeste des maistres és arts, professeurs et régens de l'université de Paris, présentée à la cour souveraine du Parnasse. Ensemble l'arrest intervenu sur la dite requeste, 1671
Traité du sublime; ou, Du merveilleux dans le discours, traduit du grec de Longin, 1694
Lettres familières, 3 vols., 1770

Biographical and critical studies

Bray, René, *Boileau, l'homme et l'oeuvre*, 1942
Adam, Antoine, *Histoire de la littérature française au XVIIe siècle*, 5 vols., 1949–56
Brody, Jules, *Boileau and Longinus*, 1958
Clarac, Pierre, *Boileau*, 1964
White, Julian Eugene Jr., *Boileau* (in English), 1969
Pocock, Gordon, *Boileau and the Nature of Neo-classicism*, 1980

BOSSUET, Jacques-Bénigne, 1627–1704.

Orator, bishop, and religious controversialist.

LIFE

Although Bossuet was undoubtedly a great orator, it is difficult to avoid the impression that his most serious interest was power. He amassed and enjoyed it; he was indifferent to its outward accoutrements, but subservient to its reality. By nature he was conformist and by instinct on the side of authority. He liked stability and order. His abilities were considerable and enabled him to acquire the influence which led to power, although his more grandiose ambitions, like a re-union of the churches, were thwarted. His achievement was greater than is sometimes acknowledged, although it was primarily of a political rather than a literary or theological order; it involved making himself at ease as a bourgeois among grands seigneurs, the reliable tool of those who needed the services of an influential court prelate, a respected ecclesiastic with a foot in the world of letters, but not so pliable as to lose credibility.

He was employed by Louis XIV to teach his son and deal with his discarded mistresses, to organize the ecclesiastical component of his absolutist rule, and to contain clerical dissidence from whatever quarter it threatened. He was fittingly rewarded for the appearance of decorum he conferred on court proceedings during the ascendancy of Mme de Montespan, and for not needing to be told too often what was expected of him. From his peasant origins he derived both bluntness and craftiness. He was proud of both characteristics.

But if he was not a schemer, he was also not a thinker, or a theologian, or a historian, or a writer of distinction, refinement, or subtlety, and at no point in his life did he demonstrate perceptiveness of vision, originality of thought, or imaginative idealism of a realistic order. Insensitive to the point of ruthlessness from the beginning of his career to its end, he was jovial, a bon viveur, and only a tendency to domineer and a perpetual need to vindicate himself betrayed a lack of assurance beneath the apparently robust confidence with which he faced the world.

Bossuet was born on 27 September 1627, of ancient Burgundian peasant stock, the seventh child in a family which had slowly risen to the ranks of the noblesse de robe. The family had been wheelwrights, but by the mid-16th century had, in the person of Bossuet's great grandfather, achieved noble status through the purchase and exercise of an administrative office. Bossuet's grandfather, Jacques, who died in 1637, was a counsellor at the parlement of Dijon, and in 1612 mayor of that town, independently enough minded to support Henri de Navarre, dynastically the legitimate successor to the throne, when all Burgundy was solidly behind the Catholic League and the Guise interests. Bossuet's father also belonged to the magistracy, was procureur général of the parlement, roughly suppressed social unrest as échevin in 1630, and was in 1638 promoted to the parlement of Metz, where he acquired a reputation for intrigue, was friendly with the governor and the Protestant minister, and became a leader of the Compagnie du Saint-Sacrement, formally founded in 1630, but in process of formation from 1627.

The Compagnie, known as the "cabale des dévots," was primarily devotional and charitable, exercising in many ways a hugely beneficial influence on care for the poor and the sick, but it also organized the political infiltration of the civil administration to achieve religious purposes. It counted some of the highest members of the aristocracy among its members, was intensely secretive, privately pressed for exemplary sentences like mutilations and burnings after successful prosecutions for heresy and blasphemy, and sought to by-pass the hierarchical channels of Church government. It was often behind the defence of the public interests of Catholicism, as in the exclusion of Protestants from public office and the enforcement both of the anti-duelling edicts and of the onerous abstention from work on the numerous feast-days. It was behind the suppression of

Molière's *Le Tartuffe*, as well as the efforts to extirpate Jansenism (q.v.) in France. Mazarin suppressed it in 1666.

Bossuet was a member, and owed his rapid ascent to its support. His mother, Marguerite Mochet, had also come from a family which had been peasant but had achieved bourgeois status. She had married in 1618. There were 10 children, of whom four died young. Two of the girls married into the magistracy and one became a religious. Bossuet's eldest brother, Claude (1620–68), became a canon of Toul, and the second brother, Antoine (1624–99), became successively treasurer of the Etats de Bourgogne, maître des requêtes, and intendant de justice at Soissons. Antoine's two children, Louis, who married and had a daughter, and a second Jacques-Bénigne, an abbé who in 1716 became bishop of Troyes, were both to live with Bossuet in his episcopal palace at Meaux. Louis was a counsellor of the parlement of Metz before becoming a maître des requêtes in Paris.

On his mother's death, Bossuet's father (c. 1592–1677) bought Bossuet a canonry at Metz and himself took orders, finally succeeding his own son as archdeacon of Metz when Bossuet became dean of the chapter. When his parents moved to Metz, Bossuet and his brother, Antoine, were left in the charge of his uncle Claude, mayor of Dijon. Bossuet was educated at the Jesuit Collège des Godrans, where his companions nicknamed him "Bos suetus aratro (ox accustomed to the plough)." He was already a plodder. He did well at school, and at the age of 10 received the tonsure from Sébastien Zamet, the bishop of Langres, recently ousted by his protégé, the abbé de Saint-Cyran, as spiritual director of Port-Royal (q.v.) and very closely associated with the Compagnie du Saint-Sacrement.

In 1642 Bossuet went to Paris to complete his studies at the Collège de Navarre, where he was taught by Nicolas Cornet, who would play an important part in the Jansenist dispute. His father obtained the canonry in the Metz chapter for him while he was still 15. He graduated as a master of arts in 1644, defended his initial thesis on 25 January 1648, took his baccalauréat in theology after three more years and then, in the accustomed way, took orders during the two years before he could begin to study for his licentiate. He composed a *Méditation sur la brièveté de la vie*, was ordained sub-deacon at Langres in 1648, deacon at Metz in 1649, and priest on 16 March 1652. On 16 May 1652 he defended his doctoral theses, taking part, apparently on behalf of the Principal of the Collège de Navarre, in a protest against the pre-eminence accorded to the Sorbonne on the occasion of doctoral awards in theology. In the licentiate he was placed third to Rancé and the prior of the Sorbonne. While preparing for the priesthood, Bossuet had put himself under the spiritual direction of Vincent de Paul, a fellow-member of the Compagnie and in the process of establishing at Saint-Lazare the seminary for his new congregation. He was to be canonized in 1737.

The influence of Vincent de Paul may well have been important in turning Bossuet away from the chair of theology he was offered at the Collège de Navarre, and in his decision to return to the canonry at Metz. An academic career in Paris was a real possibility, Bossuet was not short of powerful protection. He was received at the Hôtel de Rambouillet, now in its final decline, and his exceedingly rich cousin, François Bossuet, whose notorious financial dealings worried even Mazarin, introduced him to the Du Plessis-Guénégauds and to the entourage of the regent, Anne of Austria. At Metz, which had large Protestant and Jewish communities, and where Bossuet became successively archdeacon of Sarrebourg and then, in 1654, of the cathedral chapter, he devoted himself to preaching, controversy, and obtaining conversions. His father had bought him a house. He notably engaged in a dispute about the orthodoxy of the Catholic concepts of grace with the Protestant pastor, Paul Ferry, a close friend of his father. Ferry and Bossuet attended one another's sermons, and Bossuet composed a *Réfutation du Catéchisme de Paul Ferry*.

Even if it was a sense of vocation that took Bossuet back to Metz, his activity there seems to have been chiefly oratorical and polemical rather than, in the sense of Vincent de Paul, pastoral. An early feeling of indignation at the unequal distribution of this world's goods, imbibed from John Chrysostom and expressed in a 1652 sermon, was quickly to give way to the exploitation of the poor as potential beneficiaries of the virtuous almsgiving of the rich in the 1659 sermon on the "Eminente dignité des pauvres." The famine of the winter following the failed harvest of 1661 was to be the occasion not for anger at the prodigal consumption at court festivities or for analysis of the causes of social distress, but for pointing to the wrath of God aimed at unregenerate and ungrateful humanity. When Metz's contribution to Condé's coffers was increased by his procureur, Bossuet, by personally arguing the matter with Condé, managed to have the new assessment reduced. His apostolic activity seems to have consisted chiefly in acting in concert with his cell of the Compagnie. Bossuet engaged himself in preventing access for Protestant pastors to the Protestant sick in the Metz hospital, and put obstacles in the way of the reconstruction of the Protestant church in the town. The governor of Metz, his father's friend the maréchal de Schomberg, married to the proverbially beautiful Marie de Hautefort, was a member of the Compagnie.

It was the Compagnie who recalled Bossuet to Paris in February 1659, although there was a convenient pretext in a lawsuit which the Metz chapter then had to fight in Paris. He had not been lost from sight, and had been in Paris from July 1656 to late in 1657, had preached the panegyric on Saint Thomas in front of half a dozen bishops, on Saint Joseph before Cardinal Barberini and more than a score of prelates, and on Saint Theresa in the presence of Monsieur, the king's brother. On his return to Paris, the Lenten course he preached in 1661 to the Carmelites was talked about, and led to the invitation to preach the court's Lenten sermons in 1662. The Compagnie knew that it was about to be dissolved, and Bossuet was one of the eight charged with ensuring the preservation of its secret archives. When the Compagnie founded the séminaire des Missions in order to be able to continue publicly its more acceptable activities, it was Bossuet who preached the inaugural sermon.

On his return to Paris, Bossuet had already preached the first two of his surviving "oraisons funèbres (funeral orations)", on Yolande de Monterby in 1656 and Henri de Gornay in 1658. The appropriate form of such pulpit oratory had long been established. In Paris Bossuet's first big occasion was a course of Lenten sermons preached for the Minims in 1660, still perceptibly influenced by Vincent de Paul's exhortations to him to remove all obvious rhetorical embellishments. He was hesitant before adducing the example of Plato and cultivated for a period a style of plain narrative simplicity, dispensing with the traditional and obvious divisions of his material. Then his oratorical skills can be seen developing during the 1660s, the line becoming more pliable, smoother, as allusions and references give way to sermons constructed as massive blocks of streamlined rhetorical development. In 1662 he was to preach the oraison funèbre of Père Bourgoing, and then in 1663 that of Nicolas Cornet.

Privately, Bossuet gave the impression of superciliousness and ironic distance together with the desire to ingratiate himself with as many people as possible. His demeanour was supple and his attitudes adaptable. When the suffragan bishop of Metz, Pierre Bédacier, died on 19 October 1660, Bossuet certainly resorted to trickery in an attempt to vindicate his right to the priory of Gassicourt. The other claimants took the matter to law and won. Only through a compromise did Bossuet eventually acquire the benefice. He was also embarrassed by the ultramontane sympathies of the Compagnie du Saint-Sacrement. It showed a global hostility to Jansenism (q.v.) and Gallicanism, with which Bossuet was inclined to sympathize, as well as for Protestantism, for which Bossuet felt no sympathy at all.

When in 1663 Gabriel Drouet de Villeneuve defended ultramontane theses in the Sorbonne and the faculty was invited by the parlement to register its disapproval, the ultramontane doctors from Olier's Saint-Sulpice were against the rejection. Bossuet went so far in their direction as to demand the censure of the presiding procureur. He left his place and disorder followed. When he learned subsequently what he should already have realized, that the court, notoriously Gallican, had not been pleased by his behaviour, Bossuet retreated, and absented himself on a preaching engagement when the vote was retaken. A contemporary document reports "il se ménagea extraordinairement (he handled his situation with extraordinary tact)." It was the first of a series of lessons which he learned not to forget. Louis XIV needed preachers in the grand style, not priests who would draw attention to people dying of hunger on the steps of the Louvre. Bossuet had proved his reliability in this respect as well. Since he had also achieved considerable success in converting notable Protestants like Turenne and the marquis de Dangeau, he was marked out for preferment. It helped that he was more interested in real power than in its visible trappings. He would several times be passed over for sees which carried peerages, but about 1665 outward recognition of his standing began to be conferred when he became the personal assistant to Hardouin de Péréfixe, the archbishop of Paris.

Earlier, while still serving his court apprenticeship, he had thought to please the queen mother's party at the court's Lenten sermons in 1662 by calling the king discreetly to order on the subject of his mistress, Françoise-Louise de la Baume le Blanc de la Vallière, already no doubt suffering pangs of repentance in spite of her undoubted devotion to the king, and perhaps already foreseeing the usurpation of her position as the king's mistress by Mme de Montespan. The king had ridden after her to the convent at Chaillot where she had fled, and brought her angrily back to court. Mazarin had died in March 1661, and Louis XIV had not been joking when he proclaimed his intention to run the country without naming a chief minister. What he kept, however, were more the trappings than the realities of political power, although he intended to be in charge of his private affairs, at least, and ostentatiously missed one of Bossuet's veiled but monitory sermons. Bossuet noted the fact in the margin of his manuscript, and probably modified in advance of delivery the tenor of the Palm Sunday sermon "Sur le devoir des Rois (On the duties of kings)" in which the king, subject to God alone, is exempt from the considerations which apply only to his subjects.

At first, Bossuet was resolutely anti-Jansenist, as befitted the early ultramontane inclinations, but when, at the archbishop's request, he held discussions with Arnauld, Nicole, and Sacy about Arnauld's *La Perpetuité de la foi* and the possible revision of the Jansenist translation of the New Testament, the "Mons" version, his hostility melted, with the result that the nuntius Bargellini tried to get the bulls delayed appointing Bossuet to the see of Condom. It was too late, though—the choice of the French government made on 10 September 1669 had been ratified by a papal consistory of 2 June 1670. Bossuet was felt by the nunciature to have let down ultramontane hopes, and his dossier accordingly remained marked "C.M.P." (catholicus mollior politicus), which is ecclesiastical jargon for political unreliability. Bossuet would have liked to end with a united anti-Protestant front in the Gallican church.

His support from 1664 for Gallican manoeuvres, which pleased the court and could not have displeased Arnauld, had severely damaged his standing with the Roman authorities, aware of Bossuet since the 1663 backdown after his Sorbonne protest. In 1664, recently elected dean of the Metz chapter, he had met with a dismissive response when he had been to see the nuntius in an attempt to clear his name. On the day of his installation as dean he himself installed his father in the post of archdeacon, which he was vacating. He seems to have been oddly tactless in his attempts to reform the Benedictine abbey of Sainte-Glossinde, where the abbess, Louise de Foix, wrapped him up in procedural wrangles and aroused the indignation of the regional aristocracy against him. He lacked the patience, subtlety, and urbanity required for success in ecclesiastical politics. His way of handling disputes involving the Paris theology faculty was found in Rome to be distastefully coarse as well as headstrong. Alexander VII had to refuse to endorse one of Bossuet's over-precipitate censures.

Bossuet had preached the oraison funèbre of Anne of Austria in 1667, although the text has been lost. He spent much of the rest of that year at Dijon and Metz, where his father was dying. On 16 November 1669 he preached the funeral oration of Henriette de France, the text of which he published, as he was to publish the texts of the remaining five he was to deliver. It was Bossuet who was chosen to preach the funeral oration of Henriette d'Angleterre on 21 August 1670. A fortnight later, on 5 September, he was appointed tutor to the Dauphin, and in the following year, on 8 June 1671, he was received into the Académie française. He was assiduous at court and, although careful to temper his demeanour and his judgements to the company he was in, he plainly got on easily with some of the great ladies of "la cour" (the court), especially Mme de Montespan and her sister, Mme de Thianges, and of "la ville" (the town), like Mme de Sablé and Mme de Lafayette. In the literary world his tastes were on the side of severity, formality, and the antique. The overwhelming impression he made was of remaining sufficiently uncommitted to anyone to be able to please everyone.

It was Bossuet who smoothed things over when Mlle de la Vallière retired to become a Carmelite in 1674, having been rejected by the king in favour of Mme de Montespan, and it was Bossuet whom the king charged in 1676 with preparing Mme de Montespan to receive the news that she, too, was being rejected when, partly through the agency of Mme Scarron, the king was reconciled to his wife. It is only from 1678 that Françoise d'Aubigné, Scarron's widow and tutor to Mme de Montespan's three children by Louis XIV, was known as the marquise de Maintenon. In 1684 she was to marry the king privately, in the presence only of Harlay, the archbishop of Paris, and Louvois. Bossuet's métier as court ecclesiastic now took over for a period from other aspects of his career. The Louvre Lenten course of 1662 had been a setback, and Bossuet undertook comparatively little formal preaching for the next decade—Advent at the Louvre in 1665, Lent at Saint-Germain in 1666, Advent at Saint-Thomas-du-Louvre in 1668, Advent at Saint-Germain in 1669, and little else apart from the three funeral orations between 1667 and 1670. When he did preach, it was loftily to take the side of the devout party at court, that of Anne d'Autriche, against the worldliness of that side of Louis XIV so skilfully flattered by Molière, the court of frivolities and festivities in the 1660s.

Bossuet had resigned as canon and dean of Metz immediately on being appointed bishop of Condom, about 100 kilometres west of Toulouse. He had hesitated before accepting the post of tutor to the dauphin, but finally agreed on 5 September 1670, only days before his consecration as bishop of Condom on 21st. When he was installed as bishop, he had already decided to be a courtier rather than a pastor. There was a touch of maliciousness in Charpentier's reference to Bossuet's satisfaction "of heart and countenance" in the discourse of reception into the Académie. Bossuet devoted his speech of thanks to a simple eulogy of the king. His income was now about 50,000 livres. He resigned his see in 1672 on account of the predicted incompatibility between the administration of the diocese with the tutorship, but he had his salary as tutor and three benefices, Gassicourt, du Plessis-Grimoult, and Saint-Lucien at Beauvais. He wrote to the maréchal de Bellefonds, "Je perdrais plus de la moitié de mon esprit, si j'étais à l'étroit dans mon domestique (I would lose more than half of my intellectual abilities if I was pinched for my domestic expenditure)." It is not unlikely that there was a conflict within him between the priest who preached without rhetorical elaboration at the Carmelite profession of Louise de la Vallière on 4 June 1675 and the prelate who liked to spend lavishly, live well, and enjoy the confidence of princes.

In 1675 Bossuet required considerable tact to handle the delicate matter of the king's relationship with Mme de Montespan, which had been brought to a head when she was refused Communion on account of her flagrant relationship with the king. Bossuet also made representations on behalf of the country's citizens, reduced to misery by what were ultimately the king's wars. He agreed that the scandal involving Mme de Montespan was public, and that a public separation was therefore required if Louis XIV and Mme de Montespan were to be admitted to Communion, and thereby fulfil their Easter duty as Catholics. Everyone seems to have given a little ground, if only temporarily. Mme de Montespan talked to Bossuet about changing her ways, and for a while she abandoned residence at court. Louis XIV took Bossuet's admonitions momentarily to heart, but then abruptly changed his mind. Having achieved the miracle of a separation, Bossuet seems not to have intervened too stridently in the subsequent arrangement which, even at first, scarcely appeared to observe the decencies, and finally abandoned any pretence. Mme de Maintenon was to say that she had foreseen that Bossuet would be used as a dupe: "Il a beaucoup d'esprit, mais il n'a pas l'esprit de la cour (He has much understanding, but he doesn't understand the court)." He has been accused of conniving, and of letting himself be silenced by the chimera of a red hat, or perhaps the see of Paris. But Louis XIV was irritated, and Bossuet spent most of 1676 away from the court.

He had taken his preceptorial duties seriously, and produced a whole series of treatises for the use of his pupil, who could hardly have been less rewarding to teach—apathetic, slovenly, imperious, and irritable. Some of what Bossuet wrote at this time can scarcely have been intended for his pupil, falling between a pedagogical and a speculative or even polemical register. His *Traité du libre arbitre, Logique*, and *Traité de la conaissance de Dieu et de soi-même* are too advanced to have been suitable for the dauphin, but not original or penetrating enough to contribute to moral or religious debate. It was Bossuet who was ultimately responsible for organizing the production of the edition of the classics "ad usum Delphini (for the use of the dauphin)" whose volumes came to be known as "delphins," but he also continued to write in the context of a dialogue with the Protestants, still seeking and making converts, but also holding conferences with the pastor Claude. He believed on the whole in cultivating friendly relations with leading Protestants, although his treatment of the Protestant communities in the diocese of Meaux after the revocation of the edict of Nantes was harsh and, if he repeatedly tried to narrow the areas of disagreement, there was never any possibility that Bossuet would yield ground he considered essential.

From 1674 until his departure for Meaux, Bossuet also regularly received a group of ecclesiastics and men of letters for sessions of Bible study. It was here that Fénelon came to Bossuet's attention. Other participants at various dates included Fléchier, Mabillon, Fleury, Renaudot, Cordemoy, the mathematician Sauveur, and La Bruyère. Even Pellisson came. Although Bossuet was on terms of close friendship with Perrault, too, Fontenelle regarded Bossuet's group of friends at Versailles as the kernel of the party of the "anciens" in the Querelle des anciens et des modernes (q.v.). Until Bossuet's 1694 attack on the theatre, he had been virtually the spokesman for Racine. After 1694, and even more after Boileau's publication of his 12th épître, *Sur l'amour de Dieu*, on 8 January 1698, Bossuet was to be very close to Boileau. He had created for himself a considerable power of patronage, strongly influencing admission to the Académie française, and placing a whole series of his friends and disciples as tutors in great houses. The abbé de Cordemoy owed Bossuet his place as lecteur to the dauphin, and it was Bossuet who placed the Orientalist Galland in his post as secretary of the cabinet, Fleury as tutor of Conti and his brother, La Bruyère as tutor to Condé's son, Valincour in the household of the comte de Toulouse, the Cartesian Malézieu as tutor to the duc du Maine, and Sauveur in that of the dauphine.

On 8 March 1680 the dauphin married Marie-Anne de Bavière at Châlons. Bossuet's duties were over, although he was given the honorific title of chaplain to the dauphin's wife. On the way back from the wedding he left the royal party to console the dying La Rochefoucauld. He was now impatient for a diocese, and said so, but was passed over for Châlons and Beauvais, both of which carried peerages. On 2 May 1681, he was appointed bishop of Meaux.

On 9 November Bossuet took on the difficult task of delivering the opening address to the assembly of the clergy, *Sur l'unité de l'Eglise*, the only sermon other than the funeral orations which he published. The Gallican church was close to rupture with Innocent XI in Rome, the exact point of contention at that moment being the "régale," the royal right to nominate to vacant benefices, which also involved the right claimed by the king to keep them vacant and purloin their revenues, and the pope's right not to issue the necessary bulls to royal nominees. The task of reconciliation seemed impossible. Bossuet, still in pursuit of an anti-Protestant alliance between Gallicans and ultramontanes, inclined to the Gallican position, although he favoured concessions to Rome. He was felt to have let down the ultramontane party when the four articles agreed by the assembly were proclaimed at the session of 19 March 1682. A compromise was patched up only in 1693.

Bossuet had taken possession of his diocese in February 1682, and preached there with acclaim on Ash Wednesday. He was at the peak of his successful career as an ecclesiastic, lived well, but was devoted to hard work. He had a country house as well as the episcopal palace, and he received the highest members of the court. It was here that he slept in a garden building, wrapped in his famous bear-skin, leaving the main house to the unecclesiastical behaviour of his nephew's wife. Released, however, from the constant subservience of function and pliability of attitude into which life as the dauphin's tutor had more or less successfully constrained him, Bossuet appears to have become harsher, more self-righteous, and less charming. He was impatient of jurisdictional niceties when dealing with the ancient monastic houses within his diocese over which he had no legitimate authority.

Even those close to Bossuet at this period talk of a disdainful, sometimes contemptuous attitude, and it seems clear that he relished his power, an increasing amount of which came from his friendship with Louvois, without resenting the modesty of his episcopal rank. He was not censorious towards his family, whose members he dispensed from the ordinary observance of abstinence, and he turned a blind eye to the conduct of his nephew, the abbé Bossuet, son of Bossuet's brother Antoine and future bishop of Troyes, and his role as lover of the wife of Louis, Antoine's other son, who also lived under Bossuet's roof. The behaviour of Antoine's own wife, whose lover was the abbé de Choisy, was sufficiently scandalous for Antoine Bossuet to have considered committing her to a convent. There was even gossip about himself in 1676, but the chances are that we would have heard a lot more about any real foundation for it.

Bossuet thought of himself as a great controversialist, a great theologian, and a Church Father, and that is how he was treated and how he behaved. He consciously behaved as if he were the Augustine of his age. Politically, he still dreamed of re-union with theologically defeated Protestants, condemned the Jansenist five propositions, but disliked the Jesuits, and felt sympathy for Arnauld and Nicole. His attitudes, at least, were moderate, and his applause for the revocation of the edict of Nantes in 1695 was no more than perfunctory, but his works never show any real grasp of the intellectual issues at stake in any of the disputes in which he was involved, Jansenist, Gallican, or quietist. He did, however, at the height of his powers preach the funeral orations of Marie-Thérèse, the queen of France, on 1 September 1683, of Anne de Gonzague de Clèves, princesse palatine and mother of the duchesse d'Enghien, on 9 July 1685, of Michel Le Tellier, chancellor and Louvois's father, on 25 January 1686, and finally of le Grand Condé himself, on 10 March 1687. The funeral orations were naturally pieces of some solemnity, constructed according to the stylized conventions of the genre. Other sermons, for which we have only often incomplete notes, were prepared with care, although Bossuet did not adhere to any set, memorized text when delivering them.

After about 1690 Bossuet's life became harder. France itself had lost the culturally disagreeable but restraining guidance of Colbert in 1683, and Louis XIV delivered the country to the disastrous flamboyance of Louvois. The catastrophic revocation of the edict of Nantes set the tone for the economic ruin that was to follow, soon redoubled by the unaffordable War of the Spanish Succession. The court, it is true, was now at Versailles, and being reformed by Mme de Maintenon. After being obviously reserved about Bossuet, she now made him her most trusted counsellor, allowing him, through her, to dictate policy to Noailles, from 1695 archbishop of Paris. None the less, his Protestant opponents and his Jansenist one-time friends increased the pressures on Bossuet, and he became increasingly pugnacious in his opposition to much stronger and subtler thinkers, like Spinoza and Malebranche, whose views threatened the certainties on which his whole career had depended. In a famous letter to Nicole of 7 December 1691, Bossuet, a previous strong defender of Cartesianism who had encouraged Huet to remain faithful to it, mounted a strong attack on a system he had discovered only as late in the day as this to lead to the views then currently being propagated by Spinoza and Malebranche.

The Protestants, too, had remustered their arguments after Bossuet's 1688 *Histoire des Variations des Eglises protestantes*, and instead of challenging Bossuet on historical detail, which they might well have done, they began to regard the modifications in their position as a sign of vitality, taking over the ground already won by the partisans of the "modernes" in the literary Querelle des anciens et des modernes. Bossuet's discussions with Leibniz about reunification with the Protestants, although in fact they were broken off by Leibniz on instructions from the German princes, could not actually have led anywhere. On all sides Bossuet found waters too deep for him. He had genuinely deluded himself not only about the unshakeable foundations of his major ideological positions, but about his own abilities as a theologian, philosopher, spiritual director, and even ecclesiastical politician. Arnauld began to remark on Bossuet's smallness of spirit. By 1700 the assembly of the clergy plainly found the domineering tendency of the ageing bishop of Meaux intolerable. Bossuet began to discover that he was less heeded by the royal administration, and he was irritated when Pontchartrain, chancellor from 1699, made him submit his attack on Richard Simon, the Biblical critic, for censorship in the ordinary way.

From his 1694 *Traité de la concupiscence*, which condemned all poetry, all diversion, and all laughter as unchristian, Bossuet's mental processes, always leaning towards intransigence, took him outside the range of serious interest, literary, theological, or spiritual. The 1694 *Maximes et Réflexions sur la Comédie* was intended primarily to settle Bossuet's account with Molière, although he added in Pierre Corneille and Racine. Both the 1694 works are violent and exaggerated, and attempt to defend preposterous positions by augmented recourse to thunderous prose. By chicanery, persistence, and obstinacy, Bossuet was to succeed in having Fénelon condemned and, he thought, through Fénelon, the Jesuits. In fact Bossuet understood nothing about either mystical theology or religious psychology. The 1671 *Exposition de la doctrine de l'Eglise catholique*, written as early as 1667, had been a highly skilful accommodation of orthodox Catholic doctrine to Protestant susceptibilities, although regarded by both sides as softening the doctrinal difficulties. The 1688 *Histoire des Variations des Eglises protestantes* grew out of the earlier work, but already showed a diminished skill, since the arguments were so easily turned against Bossuet.

With the *Discours sur l'histoire universelle*, Bossuet consciously assumed the mantle of Augustine, drew heavily on the *De civitate dei*, regarded history as directed by providence, but reduced the story of the human race to an apologetic for the direction of affairs by a firm authority. Augustine's own great tour de force had derived its importance primarily from the need to accomplish a synthesis between the neoplatonism left over from the Greco-Roman philosophical legacy in late fourth-century Milan and the newly forged definitions both of the trinity of persons sharing one nature in God and of the duality of natures in the single person of Christ. Bossuet had no such cultural miracle to perform, and Augustine's mantle is almost grotesquely too big for him although, like Augustine, he attempted in his writings to combat heresy, to defend sound theological views, write a theology of history, compose works of moral philosophy, and compile works of devotion. The posthumous *Politique tirée de l'Ecriture sainte* was to be an attack on the natural law school of political philosophers who, like Grotius, or for that matter Aquinas, regarded natural law as anterior to positive divine legislation. With hindsight, Bossuet's writings can be shown to have manifested a gradual relapse into a merely instinctive defence of firm, stable, and assured authority, repressing heterodoxy and dissidence, and imposing order at whatever cost to justice.

When the sheets of Richard Simon's *Histoire critique du Vieux Testament* were sent to Bossuet early in 1678, Simon had already received the backing of important theological opinion and, although he was later to be expelled from the Oratorian congregation for his book, he had obtained a privilège. It is true Simon admitted that Moses could not himself have written all the Pentateuch, but he held that it was composed by scribes writing under his supervision, so that Mosaic authorship was kept still quasi-intact. Arnauld had sent Bossuet the sheets. Bossuet read only the preface and the table of contents before rushing the same day to denounce the work to Le Tellier as impious, and Le Tellier's police seized all copies. Simon after all had applied ordinary critical methods to sacred texts, and that for Bossuet was enough to undermine the foundations of true religion.

It has to be asked whether, even at this comparatively early date, Bossuet's instant recourse to the secular power did not show an incipient sense of his own intellectual inadequacy, whose realization must surely be seen as the real tragedy of his last decade, as he came more and more to rely on the old certainties of his student days. Was it really appropriate for an influential bishop to call on Le Tellier's police to suppress Simon's view that miracles could be metaphors, while for Bossuet revelation demanded that they should have been events?

Bossuet had already had recourse to the civil power to have the conferences of the abbé de Launoy stopped in 1676. These meetings had been devoted to the discussion of matters of ecclesiastical doctrine and discipline, in a spirit of freedom which for Bossuet undermined the authority of the Church. It was again to the chancellor Boucherat that Bossuet denounced Ellies du Pin in 1691 for the first volumes of the *Bibliothèque des auteurs ecclésiastiques*, which seemed to Bossuet to speak too freely of the Fathers of the Church, and even to allow a certain evolution in a doctrine which, if revealed, had to be immutable. In 1702 again, on the publication in March that year of Richard Simon's translation of the New Testament, Bossuet pressed for Noailles's censure of 15 September. At Bossuet's instigation the theologian who had originally approved the translation was also suspended. Bossuet himself published two instructions against the translation in August 1703. One of the reasons why Bossuet had to clash with Fénelon was that Fénelon understood something of the psychological mechanisms of religious experience, and could discount them, while Bossuet simply needed the rock of firmly grounded reasoning and unshakable authority to keep him upright. The subtlety, delicacy, and sharpness with which Fénelon could defend esoteric doctrine simply infuriated him.

From 1692 Bossuet had again spent rather more time in Paris and with the court. He was chaplain to the duchesse de Bourgogne, a counsellor of state, grand-maître of the Collège de Navarre, and custodian of the privileges of the university. He was writing works of piety for the religious of his diocese and other highly born women, none of whose lives of prayer created problems, and with Leibniz he was trying once again to come to a position from which Protestants might be persuaded to accept Catholic views on the relatively few controverted issues. Then in 1695 he discovered the link between Fénelon and Mme Guyon. She was influential at court, with views about spiritual passivity which persuaded Bossuet that she was mad. He had consecrated Fénelon archbishop of Cambrai. There were four suffragan bishops, vast revenues, and a title to go with that see. Fénelon, obviously more spiritually gifted and of an altogether higher degree of intellectual refinement than Bossuet, wrote the *Maximes des saints* partly to justify what appeared to be a new mystical doctrine. Bossuet felt this threat to his position keenly for two reasons which had not previously applied to his controversies.

The challenge to his position came from someone he regarded as a disciple and protégé, and it involved the most intimate of religious experiences of which he had neither personal nor vicarious experience, advanced forms of prayer, associated with spiritual doctrines which, whether in the northern mystics like Ruysbroeck or Harphius, or in the quietist Molinos, condemned in 1687, appeared to be associated with, and seemed probably to lead to, heresy. Bossuet was forced to argue against Fénelon's ideal of the disinterested love of God that "on ne peut se désintéresser jusqu'à perdre dans un seul acte, quel qu'il soit, la volonté d'être heureux, pour laquelle on veut toutes choses (no one can be disinterested to the point of losing in a single act, whatever it be, the will to be happy, on account of which all things are willed)." He goes on to say that charity itself can will nothing except to "jouir de Dieu (to derive pleasure from God)." This position is merely the other horn of a dilemma imposed by the debasement of scholastic faculty psychology inherited by the 17th century, and it must be seen in the context more fully discussed in the entries on Descartes and Fénelon, but it does reduce Bossuet to the historically crass position of making the highest forms of the traditionally disinterested love of God a by-product of the quest for personal satisfaction, a position which Rome carefully refused to uphold for him.

About the mental balance of Mme Guyon, Bossuet may have been right. She had submitted her doctrine to a panel of three judges, Bossuet, Noailles, still bishop of Châlons, and Tronson, who met at Issy over a period of some months from 1694 to 1695. Fénelon was not on trial, although he was consulted by the panel and must have helped in the redaction of the final 34 articles in April 1695, which were harsh on Mme Guyon. Bossuet then tried to explain what he thought the articles meant in his *Instruction sur les Etats d'Oraison*, sending Fénelon a copy before himself consecrating Fénelon archbishop of Cambrai on

10 July 1695. It was only after his consecration that Fénelon reflected indignantly on the treatment given to Mme Guyon, and on his own spiritual progress achieved on the basis of her insights. His *Explication des maximes des saints* actually appeared before Bossuet's *Instruction*. When it was suggested that Fénelon's book should be submitted for doctrinal scrutiny, he appealed to Rome, and it was then that Bossuet sent his nephew to secure the condemnation of 12 March 1699. It came in as gentle a form as Rome could give it, a brief and not a bull, avoiding the term "heretical," and even qualifying the mild "erroneous." It did not satisfy either Bossuet or Louis XIV. In the meantime Bossuet had published his pamphlet *La Relation sur le quiétisme* of June 1698, Fénelon issued a *Réponse*, Bossuet his *Remarques sur la Réponse*, and Fénelon finally published his *Réponse aux remarques*.

From 1699 Bossuet's health began to give way. There was no longer any prospect of the sees of Paris or Lyons, and hopes of the red hat were receding. Bossuet wanted a see for his nephew, but the abbé's reputation had not withstood the informed gossip. In November 1703 Bossuet was taken ill at Sèvres and had to be brought back to Paris by carriage. An operation for kidney stone had been advised but declined. Bossuet's doctors prolonged his life for about a year. He died after some weeks of pain in the early hours of 12 April 1704.

WORKS

Bossuet's claim to consideration in a literary context naturally centres on his sermons, but some attention must also be paid to the speculative, polemical, and devotional writings, and to the way in which he exercised the powerful influence bestowed on him by the position of social and ecclesiastical respect he had acquired for himself. He achieved a large measure of control over tutorial appointments in the private households of the great, over the formation and promotion of literary coteries, over the arrangement and blocking of candidacies for the Académie française, and over the dissemination and inhibition of expressions of political, theological, and philosophical opinion. He freely wielded his moral and religious authority in all the domains of civil and ecclesiastical administration, using Gallican or ultramontane centres of power, as suited him best.

His influence over opinion and policy was, in other words, out of all proportion to the abilities he had and the offices he held. His powers of literary patronage, in particular, should not be underestimated. He could, at least until about 1690 or shortly thereafter, promote or destroy budding careers, advance particular doctrines, contribute heavily towards the formation and implementation of public policy and, by playing Versailles off against Rome, adjust the conduct of religious affairs and theological debate largely to suit the interests he had made his own.

Because Bossuet's literary importance was not solely, or even chiefly, established by what he wrote or preached, much that concerns it has been considered in the section of this entry devoted to his life. It remains to examine his published work, which goes from sometimes ill-considered pamphlets of instant polemic to fully elaborated treatises of sustained argument, and much of which was first published only posthumously. Even the texts of the single sermon and the six funeral orations which Bossuet himself published are not polished literary pieces. They bear much the same relationship to the sermon as the notes of a sonata might do to a performance, except that musical interpretations normally stick to the printed text, while it is virtually certain that Bossuet in the pulpit, providing his own material, not only varied his pace and intensity and added gestures and silences, to warm up his congregation before his rotund oratorical style took him to the soaring heights of lyricism of which he was capable, but that he did not say all the words, or nothing but the words, that we can now read. The texts that we have been left are certain to have been touched up. We do not even have as much in the way of contemporary accounts of his preaching as we do of the preaching of those who came slightly later than the peak period of Bossuet's pulpit activity—Bourdaloue, Fléchier, Mascaron, or Massillon, for instance.

Some things none the less are quite clear. Bossuet accommodated himself easily to the lofty generalities and sublime tones called for in pulpit oratory on those moving and solemn occasions when it is the preacher's function to lead a congregation through a not too specific panegyric of the virtues of the eminent deceased towards a meditation on one of the great Christian truths. When the congregation is dismissed, it must be both satisfied with the commemorative honour paid to the defunct and the dignity and pertinence of the moral truths proposed for its own reflection, and struck with sufficient awe for each of its members to meditate on the personal implications of the unavoidable encounter with death so recently undergone by the public figure whose earthly life has just ended. Bossuet not only progressively departed further from the old subdivisions which inhibited free lyrical development, but his simple, direct, and down-to-earth vocabulary tied the oratory to the reality of the recent death. What had happened was a real event, one that would happen to each person present, and not just an excuse for freely ascending oratorical flights which could leave the listeners more elevated than moved. The sublime had to be tinged with awe and remain in contact with biographical fact.

The first of six funeral oration scripts which Bossuet published is that of Henriette de France, known in British history as Queen Henrietta Maria. The oration itself was the culminating point in a whole display of funeral pomp for the daughter of Henri IV and widow of Charles I. She had tried and failed to win England back to Catholicism, and retired to France in 1644. Her husband was beheaded in 1649, her son Charles II failed to recover his kingdom in 1651, and her sons were forced to leave France in 1657 as the result of an agreement between Mazarin and Cromwell. The English restoration took place in 1660, and her daughter married Philippe d'Orléans in 1661. Henriette spent four further years in England, returned to France in 1665, and died on 10 September 1669. She founded the monastery at Chaillot where she was buried and where Bossuet preached. Mme de Motteville drew up a memoir on Henriette's life for Bossuet's use in preparing his sermon.

His text omits certain colourful episodes from the memoir, like Henriette's plan to escape pursuit by scuttling the ship carrying her to France, and it concentrates on the edifying side of Henriette's on the whole faithfully depicted character. The ceremony, and sermon, were arranged by Henriette's daughter, known as Henriette d'Angleterre, about to make a diplomatic visit to her brother Charles II in England, which explains Bossuet's discretion about some diplomatic aspects of the mother's career, seen first as an episode in the history of mankind directed by God, with each of its episodes governed by divine providence.

The sermon dwells also on the utility of suffering and failure, but it insists as well on the princely rank of its subject: the French monarchs have always been the support of the Catholic church. The monarch must promote the reign of God. If he does not, the result is anarchy. The sermon was directed at Charles II, Henriette's son, and praises both him and the English people, encouraging Henriette d'Angleterre to work for the union of the kingdom of her brother Charles II with that of her brother-in-law, Louis XIV. The unity of Catholicism aids the internal unity of kingdoms as well as the unification between them, and the disunity and variations in Protestantism announce the break-up of the political body. The treatment comes from Bossuet, preaching sincerely to the "old court" group, associated with the regency of Anne of Austria, but the political theme must have been imposed, both with respect to the union of England and France and to the unitive force of Catholicism.

The text's paradigm is discernible. There is a short exordium. Henriette turned both extreme happiness and extreme distress to her spiritual advantage, using moments of happiness to do good and moments of distress to work out her own Christian salvation. Both come from God. Life and fortune are variable. The first part remembers the expectations, Catholicism and virtues of Henriette, recalling her work for union and for conversions to Catholicism, and hoping that her daughter and her daughter's husband will continue her work. The second part takes up two-thirds of the sermon and contains Bossuet's reading of history. The English revolution has its root cause in the schism. Bossuet recalls the heroic efforts of Henriette to save the English royalty and deplores her exile, after showering compliments on her daughter and her noble demeanour in adversity. Charles II is praised. The brief conclusion consists of the expression of hope for the future. The sermon, Robinet's *Gazette* recorded with disapproval, lasted one and a half hours. Even allowing for some exaggeration, that means a very slow delivery, not much above 100 words a minute, compared with the 180 words a minute that would today be regarded as normal on a solemn occasion in a large hall with amplification.

The style is classical, but permeated also with Biblical reminiscences. It is possible that Bossuet intended his congregation to recognize half a dozen lines virtually following the opening of Tacitus's *Annales*, but it is much more likely that he is simply modelling himself on Tacitus. The grandeur of the text lies in its unified and lofty tone, although it is at the same time what it pretends to be—an adequate celebration of the life of the dead Henriette, and an exhortation to admire the Christian virtues she displayed—and what it does not pretend to be, which is a strong political warning to Henriette's son, Charles II, that salvation lies only in the double unification, of England with France, and of England within itself, which means a return to Catholicism's binding force. These aims and themes are twined together until they blend inseparably into one another, but Bossuet does not despise recounting in narrative detail the events on which he relies, even switching to the narrative present to create an element of suspense.

The difficulty is to convey something of the much-admired elevation of tone, which derives its effect from the counterpoint with examples and allusions which are entirely down to earth. The rhetorical devices are effective but simple, most usually antitheses and parallel syntactical constructions. The trouble is that the text is a script. It may well be, indeed certainly was, "un des chefs-d'oeuvre de la littérature classique (one of the masterpieces of classical literature)," but it is nearly unreadable, because it was not meant to be read. As a written literary text, it does not score highly for its skill, grandeur, and beauty. As written, it is a coded political message from his sister, who immediately had it published, to Charles II, to whom she was about to come on a diplomatic mission, opportunistically masquerading as a panegyric of their dead mother.

It is the punctuation which gives it away. In the best modern edition, the second paragraph has 35 lines, comprising five sentences whose approximate lengths in lines are five, eighteen, two, two, and eight. The eighteen-line sentence is printed with one colon and thirteen semi-colons. In other words the text is printed as a script. The punctuation indicates not semantic syntactical units, but the pauses in spoken discourse. The semi-colons indicate speech intervals and, if the text is analysed as literature, it becomes clear why the sentence is almost incomprehensible at first reading. There is a main verb at the very beginning, with sixteen direct objects in apposition, many of which are qualified by adjectival clauses and at least one of which is the object of another unrelated subject as well. In other words, the script is written and punctuated in the syntax not of the written but of the spoken language. Properly delivered, it would have been very effective indeed. The grandeur was in the sermon, to whose content and phrasing the script gives us only an approximate guide.

A year later, on 30 June 1690, immediately after her journey to visit her brother, Charles II, the daughter of Henriette de France, Henriette-Anne d'Angleterre, wife of Philippe d'Orléans, son of Anne d'Autriche, died at the age of just 26. Bossuet preached a funeral oration on 21 August. It is often considered his best. The occasion was unusually solemn. The church was heavily draped in black, and ornamented with images, real skeletons, sculptures, and allegories of death. It was the earliest, or at least one of the earliest, of such funeral decorations in a French church. The *Gazette* for 30 August 1670 describes in detail both the decoration, undertaken at the king's command, and the ceremonial. Nothing like it had previously been seen in France, reported the *Gazette*. Henriette d'Angleterre had been born in Exeter, England, in 1644, and had lived without splendour until her marriage to Philippe d'Orléans in 1661. She had then been a rival of Mlle de la Vallière for the affections of Louis XIV. Mme de Lafayette wrote her life, but this time Bossuet did not need a memoir. He had been her confessor at the end of her life, and had assisted her on her deathbed. He relates in a letter, perhaps addressed to his brother, Antoine, how he was fetched to Saint-Cloud in the middle of the night at the request of his dying penitent. He was with her for an hour before she lost consciousness and died, and it had been Bossuet who had informed Philippe d'Orléans of his wife's death and given the king an account of her end.

Of all the funeral orations, this one gives least biographical detail. It is not unnaturally that in which the emotion is most directly communicated. Bossuet speaks throughout in the first person, whether singular or plural, "I" or "we." This time the problem was not to encode a political message, or in any difficulty in moving the congregation by evoking the memory of a beautiful young princess whose childhood and adolescence had been unenviable. The sermon was addressed to Condé, generally thought to be a doubter in all matters concerning religion. The problem was to treat delicately enough what needed to be alluded to, and still produce a solemn and elevated account which would be both true and also morally edifying. The sermon had to avoid any appearance of naive ignorance about things that everyone in the congregation knew, or it would have become empty ritual, while yet referring to Henriette's relationships with the king and with her husband only in terms of delicacy and discretion, in order to keep the tone elevated and fulfil the ceremonial function of commemoration.

Bossuet also needed to gloss over the trouble which had broken out about the behaviour of the canon who had arrived before him at the deathbed, given viaticum and performed the last rites, and subsequently issued an account of the death which provoked widespread criticism and had been the subject of at least two anonymous pamphlets in 1670. The canon also gave a funeral oration which openly denounced Henriette's life at court as that of a public sinner. The difficulty is clear from what Mme de Lafayette tells us of Henriette's last words to her husband:

Hélas! Monsieur, vous ne m'aimez plus il y a longtemps; mais cela est injuste: je ne vous ai jamais manqué

(Alas, Monsieur, for a long time you have no longer loved me; but that is unjust: I have never failed in my duty to you).

The oration is general enough nearly to have become a simple sermon on death. The Louvre Lenten course had contained one on that subject, and the oration, like the sermon, moves from the wretchedness of life on earth to the grandeur of the soul's everlasting destiny, but is naturally more concrete and concise. The fragments left by Pascal are notably more forceful on human wretchedness than on human grandeur, but Bossuet, who may have known them even before their publication in 1670, had a pastoral end in view and was always careful to put only a restrained emphasis on any consideration which might lead to despair, and to strengthen not only the idea of the initial vocation to grace, but also that of the all-important grace of final perseverance, which allowed even the most "Augustinian" spiritualities to allow cooperation with grace during life, while reserving to God's arbitrary will the decision whether or not to bestow the only important supernatural gift, which is that of dying in a state of grace, and so attaining to salvation.

What we have is still a script, but its delivery posed less acute problems than that on which Henriette's mother's oration had been based. The dynamics seem at the opening to have preceded the words. There is a brief reference to the oration of the previous year; then three statements terminating in exclamation marks; then four progressively longer rhetorical questions; and finally the statement of the only theme which Bossuet finds possible, "Vanité des vanités, et tout est vanité (Vanity of vanities, and all is vanity)." Nothing can be taken for granted, not health, not pleasure, not vitality, not riches, or beauty, or honour, or life itself. The end of the exordium is clearly signified, "These are the truths which I have to treat of," before an equally clear launch into the oration's development. However high her birth, and Bossuet does not stint in his description of the elevation of the "maison de France," Henriette's heart and mind were even higher. Considering her life at court, Bossuet is almost histrionic:

O mort, éloigne-toi de notre pensée, et laisse-nous tromper pour un peu de temps la violence de notre douleur par le souvenir de notre joie!

(O death, go from our minds, and let us briefly beguile the violence of our grief with the memory of our joy!).

It is difficult to believe that the dynamic markings did not come first. Only these needed to be fixed precisely in advance. A practised orator could expect the cadenced and balanced syntactical rhythms to occur to him spontaneously, while actually preaching.

The text continues to follow its speech rhythms, immensely long coordinate clauses much more easily comprehensible to the ear than the eye. After his recollection of "la grandeur et la gloire (greatness and glory)," Bossuet returns to the triumph of death, the serious religious content of his discourse, culminating in the celebrated, if histrionic

Considérez, Messieurs, ces grandes puissances que nous regardons de si bas. Pendant que nous tremblons sous leur main, Dieu les frappe pour nous avertir…O nuit désastreuse! o nuit effroyable, où retentit tout à coup, comme un éclat de tonnerre, cette étonnante nouvelle: MADAME se meurt, MADAME est morte! Qui de nous ne se sentit frappé à ce coup, comme si quelque tragique accident avait désolé sa famille? Au premier bruit d'un mal si étrange, on accourut à Saint-Cloud de toutes parts; on trouve tout consterné, excepté le coeur de cette princesse. Partout on entend des cris, partout on voit la douleur et le désespoir, et l'image de la mort. Le roi, la reine, Monsieur, toute la cour, tout le peuple, tout est abattu, tout est désespéré

(Consider, gentlemen, these great powers which we look at from so far beneath them. While we are trembling under their hand, God strikes them to warn us…O disastrous night! O terrifying night, during which there suddenly resounded, like a clap of thunder, the stupefying news: MADAME is dying, MADAME is dead! Which of us did not feel stricken by this blow, as if some tragic accident had ravaged our family? At the first rumour of that dreadful illness, people ran to Saint-Cloud from all sides; everything is consternation except the heart of the princess. Everywhere cries are heard, everywhere grief and despair are seen, and the image of death. The king, the queen, Monsieur, all the court, all the people, all is dejection, all is despair).

God strikes the great for the instruction of the weak. Bossuet's climax, the repetition of "O…night", mimics the famous lyrical outburst in the Easter "Exsultet" in which the author breaks out "O happy fault," contemplating the redemption which undid Adam's sin. After his dramatic echo "dying/dead", Bossuet inserts a rhetorical question before changing to a clipped rhythm, the present tense, and the impersonal "on," before the final list ends with the four times repeated "all."

Bossuet continues by developing the contrast between the princess alive in the morning and dead in the evening, and dwells on Henriette's virtues. The hint of criticism, the allusion to her relationship with her husband and with other men, for which the congregation must have been waiting, is deft, discreet, rapid, adequate, and ambiguously subjunctive:

…et si quelque chose manquait encore à son bonheur, elle eût tout gagné par sa douceur et par sa conduite

(and if there was something still lacking to her happiness, she would/could/might have achieved everything by her gentleness and by her conduct).

Bossuet has succeeded in saying everything and nothing, and nobody in the congregation can have been sure how much or how little he actually had said.

The first part of the oration ends with its emphasis on the dead body, and the second moves on to the eternal soul. It is here that Bossuet develops the theme of final perseverance, a grace to whose bestowal Henriette's death offered testimony. It seems at least probable that, between Bossuet's arrival and her death an hour later, Henriette gave Bossuet an emerald. All accounts agree that she knew she was dying and was in full possession of her senses as she composed herself to die. In an emotional account of the death, of the call for the sacraments, the eagerness to confess, to be given viaticum, Bossuet refers directly to the last words which the whole congregation knew she had spoken to her husband, but which Bossuet does not quote. He has said enough, and in a strongly lyrical passage silently invites the congregation into complicity.

Rappelez en votre pensée ce qu'elle dit à MONSIEUR. Quelle force! Quelle tendresse! O paroles qu'on voyait sortir de l'abondance d'un coeur qui se sent au-dessus de tout, paroles que la mort présente, et Dieu plus présent encore, ont consacrés, sincère production d'une âme qui, tenant au ciel, ne doit plus rien à la terre que la vérité, vous vivrez éternellement dans la mémoire des hommes, mais surtout vous vivrez éternellement dans le coeur de ce grand prince. MADAME ne peut plus résister aux larmes qu'elle lui voit répandre. Invincible par tout autre endroit, ici elle est contrainte de céder. Elle prie MONSIEUR de se retirer, parce qu'elle ne veut plus sentir de tendresse que pour ce Dieu crucifié qui lui tend les bras. Alors qu'avons-nous vu? qu'avons-nous ouï? Elle se conformait aux ordres de Dieu; elle lui offrait ses souffrances en expiation de ses fautes; elle professait hautement la foi catholique, et la résurrection des morts, cette précieuse consolation des fidèles mourants

(Recall to your minds what she said to MONSIEUR. What strength! What tenderness! O words which we saw coming from the fullness of a heart which feels itself above everything, words which the presence of death, and even more the presence of God, have consecrated, the sincere expression of a soul which, belonging to heaven, no longer owes to earth anything but truth, you will live eternally in the memory of humans, but above all you will live eternally in the heart of this great prince. MADAME cannot withstand the tears she sees him shed. Unconquerable from any other quarter, here she must yield. She asks MONSIEUR to withdraw since she no longer wishes to feel love except for this crucified God who stretches out his arms towards her. What then have we seen? what have we heard? She was obeying God's orders; she offered him her sufferings in expiation of her faults; she firmly professed the Catholic faith, and the resurrection of the dead, that precious consolation of the dying faithful).

The question that must be addressed is not whether such a

funeral celebration should ever have been held, or such a panegyric ever preached, but what is the nature of Bossuet's achievement. He is inviting his congregation to draw edification from
the words of a dying woman reproaching her husband for his
infidelities and affirming that she had herself never let him
down. He is drawing attention to the fact that everyone knew
what she actually said, and by implication what it actually
meant. The modern reader is, as so often, eavesdropping on the
privileged proceedings of a tightly organized group, understandable only in the light of a shared experience to which we are not
privy.

The canon's funeral oration had been brutal about a final
repentance after a life of sin. Mascaron, on the other hand, presented Henriette's death as the supernatural enhancement of a
life of natural virtue: "Voilà de quelle manière l'Esprit de Dieu
a fait servir les nobles inclinations de ce coeur dans la nature aux
effets merveilleux de la grâce (That is how the Holy Spirit used
the noble natural inclinations of that heart for the miraculous
effects of grace)." Bossuet steers a middle course. Was he
merely lending himself to a hollow sham, dithyrambically spinning lofty imaginings to distract from a sordid reality, or did he
believe what he was saying?

He was naturally doing both, but blending both together with
so much skill that no one could conceivably have unravelled the
strands. He knew that enough had been said to remind everyone
present of the realities of Henriette's court life, her beginnings
in poverty, the strained relationship with her mother-in-law,
Anne of Austria, the brilliant marriage in which neither she nor
her husband was privately expected to confine sexual partnership to the other, the amorous intrigues with Vardes and Guiche,
the seriousness of political purpose in the interests of France
when she negotiated the treaty of Dover with her brother,
Charles II, and the final pious demise. The reference to strength
and tenderness is the bridge: that is how, Bossuet almost openly
tells his congregation, he proposes, for the purpose of encomiastic fiction, to regard Henriette's last words to Philippe d'Orléans. He then addresses the words themselves in a long
sentence whose theatricality must have been intended to be perceived.

Like Montaigne, or La Bruyère, Bossuet can rely on his
public, powerfully assisted by seeing themselves surrounded by
skeletons, drapes, and images of death, to connive, as also in the
passage about Henriette's conquest by the prince's tears, which
everyone must have known to have been on a register of deco-
rous fantasy. Bossuet is using the present tense, always for him
a sign of heightened artificiality. But the end, when Henriette
asks her husband to withdraw so that she may seek consolation
from the crucifix alone? There is an unlikely rumour that she
was poisoned, and we do not know what she was dying of. However, that she wanted to die peacefully and prayerfully seems not
at all unlikely. Was that why her husband withdrew? Bossuet
echoes that question when he switches to the rhetorical questions in the first person and the past tense. Well may he ask what
have we seen, and what have we heard. Who can say? He is
defying his congregation to deny him connivance. And just what
does the sign-off imply? The immortality of the soul may well
console a Christian at the moment of death, but few, then or now,
can have found in the idea of bodily resurrection "the precious
consolation of the dying faithful." Bossuet is surely announcing
that the ritual has now been observed, and the sermon can end
on a note of sincere piety:

Changeons maintenant de langage…disons que [la mort] a
mis fin aux plus grands périls dont une âme chrétienne peut
être assaillie. Et, pour ne point parler ici des tentations
infinies qui attaquent à chaque pas la faiblesse humaine,
quel péril n'eût point trouvé cette princesse dans sa propre
gloire?…

(Let us change theme…let us say that death has put an end
to the greatest dangers by which a Christian soul can be
assailed. And, not to speak here of the infinite temptations
which at each step attack human weakness, what danger
would the princess not have found in her own glory?…).

Each of the *Oraisons funèbres* has its own particular interest,
and together the collection constitutes one of the major monuments of late 17th-century literature in France, although the orations are both less finished as literary texts and more finely
wrought products of literary craftsmanship than is sometimes
supposed. The temptation is to assume that their merit lies in
their outmoded lyricism. In fact it is to be found in the extraordinary skill with which Bossuet extricates himself from the
manifest constraints imposed by the genre, and the oratorical
feats which they wrested from him. That is one reason why they
have survived, while the 200 sermons, only one of which was
published by Bossuet himself, are not widely held in such high
regard.

The interest of Bossuet's other works is not literary, or for that
matter philosophical or theological. As a thinker Bossuet was
seldom original or powerful, but his historical importance is
massive, not only because his views covered so wide a range of
topics and were defended with such determination and political
skill, but also because they came at the last moment when it was
possible inside the educated international European community
to make so intransigent a restatement of an unyieldingly reactionary absolutism in the face of Protestantism, libertinism, or
any form of liberalism. Additional importance accrues to Bossuet's views because of his full-scale last-ditch defence of a
human history caused not by the interaction of human forces,
but directed by divine providence.

In much the same way Bossuet was the last pre-enlightenment
Catholic theologian who both achieved externally accorded
authority for his views, and regarded the eternal destiny of the
individual human being as determined by the arbitrary decision
of a divinity to whose decrees the individual was subject without
being able to influence them by his own moral self-determining
choice. By flattering Louis XIV's absolutist political ambitions,
and remaining adequately Gallican in his views, Bossuet created
a penumbra in which he came near to assuming an analogous
absolutism in France on matters pertaining to religion, which
necessarily included intellectual debate generally.

It is for these reasons that Bossuet's doctrine requires to be
discussed as a whole, and as a historical phenomenon. Unlike
his model, Augustine, whose intellectual achievement was of an
altogether different order of magnitude, Bossuet was at heart a
popularizer of safe, reliable, unimaginative, conservative positions, who required order to be imposed, but who was over-
inclined to confuse his own firm moral ground with legitimate
authority. At best, it can be claimed that his early anti-Protestant
polemic showed a certain dialectical brilliance that was later to
be blunted, and that in youth at least he was open to such new
currents of thought as Cartesianism.

The *Discours sur l'histoire universelle* started off as a synopsis of world history for the dauphin, to which was added a history of religion, and then an account of the rise and fall of empires and political systems. This in turn gave rise to a view of history as ruled by divine providence, which Bossuet then made explicit. As finished towards the end of 1679 and published in 1681, the *Discours* had three parts: the initial chronology from Adam to Charlemagne, the "Suite de la Religion," which was the story of Christianity, and the reflections on the rise and fall of empires. Bossuet accepted the already obsolete calculation, based on the number of generations between Adam and Jesus recorded in the Bible, which put the creation of the world in 4,004 B.C.

It was after publication that Bossuet started to use his view of history for apologetic purposes. He left alone the first, chronological part, but turned the second, on Christianity, into a defence of Christianity against Spinoza's denial of the divine inspiration of the Bible. The third part was turned into a defence against the libertins, who were using historical events and processes to deny the world's government by divine providence. In this form the *Discours* was published again in 1700. Bossuet was working on a third version when he died. The pedagogical plan had been to establish a world chronology into which to fit the foundation of Christianity as an enduring religion and the rise and fall of secular powers, showing secondary human causes subordinate to the overall divine plan for the human race. The whole concept owed much to Augustine's survey in the *De civitate dei* of the secular culture which had preceded him, to Augustine's later insistence on the determining influence exercised by God on corporate and individual human destinies, to Arnauld's theology and anti-Protestant polemic in the *Perpétuité de la foi*, and to Bossuet's concept of his own role as the Augustine of his times, defending orthodoxy against attacks from whichever angle they came.

Bossuet's conception of Christianity in the second part of his book, stripped of the immediate defence against Spinoza, has a certain exalted grandeur and lyrical intensity.

Cette Eglise toujours attaquée et jamais vaincue est un miracle perpétuel et un témoignage éclatant de l'immutabilité des conseils de Dieu

(This Church, always attacked and never conquered, is a continual miracle and a brilliant manifestation of the immutability of God's counsels).

Bossuet relies on Herodotus and Xenophon for much pagan history, is better informed when he comes to the Greeks, but esteems the Roman empire above all others. He does not avoid touches of grandiosity. The rhetoric of oratory has now permeated into the prose.

De tous les peuples du monde, le plus fier et le plus hardi, mais tout ensemble le plus réglé dans ses conseils, le plus constant dans ses maximes, le plus avisé, le plus laborieux et enfin le plus patient, a été le peuple Romain

(Of all the peoples in the world, the proudest and most daring, but also the best regulated in its policies, the most constant in its moral codes, the wisest, the most hard-working, and finally the most patient, was the Roman people).

The 1688 *Histoire des Variations des Eglises protestantes* was quite evidently published as simply anti-Protestant apologetic. The problem for Bossuet was how to recognize the one true Church which the Protestants agreed had been founded by Jesus. Bossuet's criterion was doctrinal immutability, any claim to which the Protestants swiftly abandoned, challenging the criterion itself, rather than Bossuet's claims that it was a characteristic unique to the Church of Rome. Whatever efforts he may make to understand their individual personalities, Bossuet clearly sees the generality of Protestant leaders as too proud and independent to submit to doctrinal authority and prefer what he regards as a universal consensus to their own view. The weakness of Bossuet's own position lies much more in his inability to tackle the various forms of Protestantism on the authenticity of religious experience, of which he nowhere in his writings shows real understanding, than in his line on the historical variations in Catholic teaching, which his whole religious culture made him unable to see. What gives life and interest to Bossuet's book is no more than his passionate conviction that he is right, together with his determination to convince his opponents that they are wrong.

Bossuet did not finish his *Politique tirée de l'Ecriture Sainte*, published only posthumously. It is important chiefly for the deductions he makes from the initial denial that there is such a thing as natural law, anterior to the law of God as promulgated by revelation. The project dated from the 1670s, and a version was communicated to the duc de Beauvillier for the education of the duc de Bourgogne in 1692. Bossuet laid the work aside during the dispute with Fénelon, but worked on it again in 1700 and, especially, the following year. His nephew published it in 1709. Essentially, the doctrine of natural law as it developed from Aquinus to Grotius limited the arbitrary power of absolute monarchs, and even bound God by the structure of his own creation.

The important point for Bossuet was the need, after original sin, for a positive law-giving authority. Human reason was not, after Adam's sin, to be trusted. Civil and political order had to be imposed by force, since agreement was no longer to be expected. The source from which it might have derived had been corrupted. Bossuet is concerned to defend the monarch's absolute power, restrained by custom and tradition, rather than any unbridled arbitrary power, even if he also admits that his view justifies slavery and the right of conquest, and adduces examples of acceptable behaviour from the patriarchs of the Old Testament. His view was indignantly attacked for its absolutism by Boulainvilliers in the *Lettres sur les Parlements*, written between 1710 and 1712, although, like the rest of Boulainvilliers's work, published only after his death in 1722.

PUBLICATIONS

[The numerous editions of selections from Bossuet's works have not been listed. None of the complete editions is satisfactory, but the standard editions are indicated below, together with all editions published during Bossuet's lifetime. The items pertaining to the controversy on prayer are listed in a separate category]

Collections

Oeuvres complètes, 31 vols., 1862–66
Oeuvres oratoires, 7 vols., 1928–29

Correspondance de Bossuet, 15 vols., 1909–25
Oraisons funèbres, 1961
Oeuvres, Bibliothèque de la Pléiade, 1961

Pulpit oratory

Oraison funèbre de Henriette-Marie de France, 1669
Oraison funèbre de Henriette-Anne d'Angleterre, 1670
Sermon prononcé à la profession de Mme de la Vallière, 1675
Sermon presché à l'ouverture de l'assemblée générale du clergé de France ("Sur l'unité de l'Eglise"), 1682
Oraison funèbre de Marie-Thérèse d'Autriche, 1683; as *Funeral Oration of Maria Theresa of Austria*, 1683
Oraison funèbre de [la]...princesse Anne de Gonzague de Clèves, 1685
Oraison funèbre de...seigneur messire Michel Le Tellier, 1686
Oraison funèbre [du]...prince Louis de Bourbon, prince de Condé, 1687

Theological, historical, and polemical

Réfutation du catéchisme du Sr. Paul Ferry, ministre de la religion prétendue réformée, 1655
Exposition de la doctrine de l'Eglise catholique, 1671; as *An Exposition of the Doctrine of the Catholic Church*, 1672
Discours sur l'histoire universelle, 1681; revised 1682; revised 1704; as *A Discourse on the History of the Whole World*, 1686
Conférence avec M. Claude, ministre de Charenton, 1682; as *Conference with Mr Claude*, 1687
Traité de la communion sous les deux espèces, 1682
Lettre pastorale...aux nouveaux catholiques, 1686
Histoire des variations des églises protestantes, 1688; as *History of the Variations of the Protestant Churches*, 1742
Catéchisme, 3 vols., 1687
Avertissement aux protestants: premier, 1689
    second, 1689
    troisième, 1689
    quatrième, 1690
    cinquième, 1690
    sixième, 1691
L'Apocalypse, avec une explication, 1689
Explication de quelques difficultés sur les prières de la Messe, 1689
Défense de l'"Histoire des variations", 1691
Maximes et réflexions sur la comédie, 1694
Instruction pastorale sur les promesses de l'Eglise, 1700
Seconde instruction pastorale sur les promesses de Jésus-Christ, 1701; as *A Pastoral Instruction on the Promises of Christ to his Church*, 1825
Politique tirée...de l'Ecriture sainte, 1709; as *The Political Science drawn from the Holy Scriptures*, 1826

Controversy on prayer

Ordonnance et instruction pastorale...sur les états d'oraison, 1695
Declaratio circa librum "Explication des maximes des saints", 1697
Summa doctrinae libri cui titulus "Explication des maximes des saints", 1697
De nova quaestione tractatus tres, 1698

Divers écrits ou mémoires sur le livre intitulé "Explication des maximes des saints", 1698
Relation sur le quiétisme, 1698
Remarques sur la réponse...à la "Relation sur le quiétisme", 1698
Réponse...à quatre lettres de Mgr l'archevesque de Cambray, 1698
Réponse aux "Préjugés décisifs", 1699
Lettre à M. l'évesque de Saint-Omer, 1699
Mandement de M. l'évesque de Meaux, 1699
Les passages éclaircis; ou, Réponse au livre intitulé "Les principales propositions du livre des maximes des saints justifiés", 1699

Biographical and critical studies

Ledieu, abbé, *Mémoire et journal sur la vie et les oeuvres de Bossuet*, 4 vols., 1857–59
Rébelliau, A., *Bossuet historien du protestantisme*, 1892
—————*Bossuet*, 1900
Bremond, Henri, *Bossuet*, 3 vols., 1909
Truc, G., *Bossuet et le classicisme religieux*, 1934
Calvet, J., *Bossuet, l'homme et l'oeuvre*, 1941
Martimort, A.-G., *Le Gallicanisme de Bossuet*, 1953
Truchet, J., *La Prédication de Bossuet*, 2 vols., 1960
Goyet, T., *L'Humanisme de Bossuet*, 2 vols., 1965

Bibliography

Urbain, C., *Bibliographie critique de Bossuet*, 1899

BRANTÔME, Pierre de Bourdeille, seigneur de, c.1540–1614.

Memorialist.

LIFE

Pierre de Bourdeille came from an ancient Périgord family of courtiers and soldiers, in which the eldest sons were generally made sénéchals of Périgord and the younger sons commendatory abbés of Brantôme in the Dordogne. He was the third son of François de Bourdeille, whose life he was to write. Through his mother, he was a Vivonne. An elder brother had been killed in 1553 when Hesdin was taken by Emmanuel Philibert, about to become duke of Savoy, and it was in 1556 that Henri II conferred the abbacy on the third Bourdeille son, from then on known as Brantôme.

Born about 1540, the future Brantôme was brought up by a grandmother, the sénéchale of Poitou, at the court of Marguerite de Navarre. When his mother died in 1549, Brantôme was sent early to one of the Paris colleges, and then went to study civil law at Poitiers, one of three faculties to which Parisian students were usually sent while the Paris law faculty was still prohibited from teaching the subject, which some centuries earlier had taken too many students away from theology. Destined for a military career, Brantôme finished his studies knowing no Greek and only, he says, a little Latin.

At the age of 20 Brantôme went to Italy, where the young French nobility could not only see for themselves the splendours of the Italian renaissance, wonder at its buildings, visit its courts, and admire its decorative and visual arts, but could also learn to converse in Spanish, the language of the conquerors of Pavia, as well as Italian. As early as 1560 Brantôme was keeping a note-book, jotting down amorous adventures about which he heard, or notes about duels, who fought them and why, unworried about blending fiction, hearsay, and experience. In Rome he met the cardinal de Guise and his youngest brother, François, grand prior of the knights of Malta, accompanying them to Naples and its "plaisirs délicieux (sweet pleasures)."

The highly connected 20-year-old called to greet the maréchal de Brissac in Lombardy before returning to France, where he was present at the court mascarade at Amboise just before the "conjuration" of 1560. His association with the Guise family became closer. The family, on whom the index should be consulted, included two members nicknamed "le Balafré" after wounds they received; two who were cardinals of Lorraine; and two cardinals de Guise. As a family the Guises lost influence when Catherine de Medici became regent in 1560, but they reasserted their power with a new generation led by Henri de Lorraine, the third duc de Guise, who was to be assassinated on the orders of Henri III in 1588.

The immensely powerful Claude de Lorraine, first duc de Guise, had had twelve children, and leadership of the family devolved on to François de Lorraine, second duc de Guise, the first "Balafré," and Charles de Guise, cardinal de Lorraine, and therefore the uncle of the five children to survive the Balafré in 1563. Those children included Louis de Guise, later cardinal de Lorraine, and Henri, his brother, the third duc de Guise, with whom the cardinal Louis was to be assassinated at the instigation of Henri III in 1588. The niece of the first Balafré, Mary Stuart, queen of Scots, who was married to François II, had become queen of France in 1559. It was at the removal of the heir presumptive, later Charles IX, from the influence of the Guise family during Mary's reign as queen of France that the abortive conjuration d'Amboise was partly aimed in March 1560.

Although a sickly and incapable child of 15 on his father's death, François II had attained the legal age of majority, and on his accession no regent could be appointed. For the time being, the Guise relations of his queen defeated the boy king's mother, Catherine de Medici, for de facto control of France. It was momentarily possible that the Guise family might have urged the claims of their niece to the English throne against Elizabeth, and Catherine, hoping to ward off the Guise ascendancy, at this date firmly favoured a moderate political solution in France, allowing toleration of the Protestants, with whom she was prepared to ally herself, and friendly relations with England.

The most immediate consequence of the death of François II on 5 December 1560 was to prevent the execution of Condé, the Protestant nearest the throne, condemned on 26 November to an execution fixed for 10 December. The regency belonged by custom to the king of Navarre, who had made it over to the queen-mother for the duration of the minority of Charles IX, born in 1550 and formally to be declared to have attained his majority in 1563. Catherine was naturally inclined at first to favour the interests of Henri de Navarre. When Mary, François II's widow, no longer a useful political tool, was sent back to Scotland to reclaim her father's Scottish throne, Brantôme was in her suite. He returned to France in 1562, when the religious wars offered an impoverished nobility a new function, and a chance to remake lost fortunes. In 1562 Brantôme fought on the winning side at Blois, and was with the victorious Guise at the siege of Rouen and the battle of Dreux. He was with Catherine de Medici's forces when the English were driven from Le Havre in 1563.

By the time Brantôme returned to Paris in 1564, François de Guise had been assassinated by the Huguenot Jean Poltrot de Méré outside Orléans in February 1563, and the grand prior had died. Brantôme followed the court to Bar-le-Duc and entered the service of Philip II of Spain, who was organizing his expedition to Morocco. Brantôme returned through Lisbon, met the infanta of Portugal, set sail for Bayonne, and went on to Madrid, where he met the duke of Alba. Philip II's third wife, the young Elisabeth de Valois, daughter of Catherine de Medici and Henri II, had borne Philip his favourite daughter, the infanta Isabelle, and Brantôme appears to have been charged by her with the preliminary soundings which led to the 1565 conference of Bayonne, at which Elisabeth de Valois, her mother, and Catherine de Medici, her grandmother, might meet with a view to strengthening the Franco-Spanish alliance and implementing the secret anti-Protestant religious clauses of the 1559 treaty of Cateau-Cambrésis. Agreement was finally subverted by Catherine's hope to keep a balance of power between Spain and England. Brantôme attended the conference, and continued to take notes on the gossip, and on the behaviour patterns, especially of Europe's highest-born women.

Brantôme now followed the French court, enjoying the company of the maids-of-honour, about whom his fond aunt, Mme de Dampierre, kept him well informed. In 1565 Brantôme negotiated the marriage of his aunt's daughter, Claude-Catherine de Clermont-Dampierre, widow of the baron d'Annebaut et de Retz, to Albert de Gondi, sieur du Perron, the future maréchal de Retz. The maréchale was destined to play a distinguished part in French literary life at the end of the wars. Brantôme went on to take part in the successful 1565 expedition led by Garcia de Toledo, viceroy of Sicily, to relieve Malta, where the forts of Saint-Angelo and Saint-Michel were still being besieged by the Turks. Brantôme then sailed with his close friend Philippe Strozzi, the French commander and grandson of the Italian general, throughout the Mediterranean, to divert the attentions of Philip II while more serious action against Spain was to be undertaken in the Netherlands. He then travelled again extensively in Italy, taking fencing lessons at Milan, and meeting Marguerite de France, daughter of François I and Claude de France and wife of Emmanuel-Philibert, duke of Savoy.

Brantôme was clearly a courtier, attracted to military life, and a professional diplomat, but he was also at heart an adventurer. His opinions can only be described as moderate, "politique," like those of Anjou, but he saw no discredit in selling his diplomatic services. When finally he did have to choose between loyalty to Catherine de Medici and loyalty to Henri III, he chose the mother rather than the son. Officially there had been peace after the religious war which ended with the peace of Amboise of

1565, but in 1567 an unsuccessful attempt was made by Protestant forces to take Charles IX hostage at Meaux, and what is rather misleadingly known as the second war began. It traduces the historical reality to separate the religious hostilities into the traditional seven discrete wars. Brantôme now fought with the army of Catherine de Medici's third son, the Anjou who was to become Henri III, taking part in the successful battle of Saint-Denis, at which Montmorency, the 75-year-old Connétable, was mortally wounded. He then pursued the Protestants, led by Henri de Navarre's uncle, Louis de Bourbon, prince de Condé, Coligny, d'Andelot, and La Noue, through Champagne and Lorraine.

After the 1568 peace of Longjumeau, signed on 23 March, which ended the second war, Brantôme gave up his military career and lived for a period at Péronne. He was a close friend of Théligny, La Noue's son, who was about to become Coligny's son-in-law, so that ties of personal fellowship crossed the boundaries imposed by military hostilities. Brantôme gave up his Catholicism, without apparently formally becoming a Protestant. However, he did for a period commit himself militarily to the Protestant cause. Hostilities simmered on, and a plan to seize Condé and Coligny at Noyers in Burgundy was foiled when they successfully reached La Rochelle, a port important for its communications with England, and where, therefore, the Huguenot leaders were congregating. The third war is considered to have broken out when Michel de l'Hôpital finally retired to his estate at Vignay, near Etampes, having refused to sign an anti-Huguenot document; he formally resigned as chancelier only some years later. Brantôme was with the Catholic forces of Henri d'Anjou on 13 March 1569 when, with Tavannes and Biron commanding, they defeated Coligny, d'Andelot, and La Noue at Jarnac while they were waiting for Condé to arrive. When Condé did come with the Huguenot cavalry he was routed and, after his personal surrender, was killed when Montesquiou, the captain of Anjou's guard, shot him, possibly on the orders of Anjou.

Brantôme, having apparently saved Montesquiou from recrimination or worse, looked helplessly on as the Protestant forces ravaged Périgord and seized the château de Brantôme among others. He received the prince of Orange and Louis de Nassau, and offered himself to Coligny at La Rochelle to lead an army to the Netherlands. When he heard the news of the Saint Bartholomew's Day massacre on 24 August 1572 he was at Brouage, 40 kilometres south of La Rochelle, and was horrified both at the massacre and at what he supposed was the king's complicity, but his commitment changed again, and in 1573 he none the less took part in the siege of La Rochelle with the young duc de Guise, Henri, who gave him a sword of honour as a souvenir. Brantôme was at court when Charles IX died, and was among those who welcomed Henri III back from Poland in 1574. He was to treat on the king's behalf with La Noue, who had agreed to negotiate with the Huguenots of La Rochelle for Charles IX, and found himself at one moment in the difficult situation of being both the king's emissary and the elected leader of the La Rochelle Huguenots. It is only against the rapidly changing political background that it is possible to understand Brantôme's feelings and behaviour. It is unlikely that he sold his military commitment, or was persuaded by any change in his personal religious conviction.

It is probable that the massacre of August 1572 grew out of a plan by the Guises only for the murder of Coligny, but that the fire had been lit which instantly turned into an unquenchable conflagration. That, however, was also the propaganda version put out by Catherine, although it was also what the Spanish ambassador reported. Navarre and Henri de Bourbon, now prince de Condé, survived at the cost of abjuration, but the other Huguenot nobles who were in the Louvre were dragged into the courtyard and killed, and deaths amounted to several thousands in Paris alone. Peace was signed in La Rochelle after the election in June 1573 of Henri d'Anjou to the Polish throne. His brother, François d'Alençon, already established as leader of the politique faction and now heir presumptive to the French throne, at this point openly aligned himself with the Huguenots, no doubt on grounds of personal ambition, since there was not yet any reason to suppose that the line of Charles IX, born in 1550, would not in due course be continued.

The Guises by 1574 were again largely perceived as half foreign, and fear at the probable results of Catherine's policy attached opprobrium to her Italian origins. French patriotism seemed to dictate the link-up between Protestants and legitimists headed by François d'Alençon, soon to become Anjou. L'Hôpital, and the maréchaux Montmorency, Damville, and Cossé, were behind the new alliance of forces, which also had the backing of La Noue and the young Turenne. In March 1574 a scheme was mounted to get Alençon and Navarre away from court, and to start a general insurrection. When it failed, and Montgomery was executed after being captured in the Normandy fighting, a fresh plot was set on foot at Vincennes. It was betrayed, and d'Alençon's intimate, La Môle, was tortured and beheaded on 30 April. Montmorency and Cossé were sent to the Bastille on 4 May. No serious attempt was at first made to interfere with Montmorency's brother, the powerful Damville, in the south. When Damville heard of the order for his own arrest, he immediately assumed greater personal powers, summoned the estates of Languedoc to Montpellier, where he was more popular than in Toulouse, its normal meeting place, and worked for three years with the Huguenots although, unlike his brothers, he never ceased to be a Catholic.

In 1575 Henri III, having finally decided not to lead an open attack on Damville, left Avignon on 20 January, was crowned at Reims on 13 February, and on 14 February married Louise de Vaudémont of the house of Lorraine. Guise made overtures to Navarre, hoping to get him separated from Anjou, as Alençon had become, and to prepare an alliance for any eventual quarrel with Henri III. Then on the night of 25 September 1575 Anjou, possibly abetted by his mother, escaped to join La Noue and Turenne in Poitou. Condé immediately sent an army under Thoré from the Vosges to join them. It was intercepted by Guise with twice the numbers; and at the confrontation at Dormans he received the face wound which earned him his father's "Balafré" nickname. Brantôme accompanied Catherine de Medici in pursuit of her son to Chambord, and a series of meetings was arranged near Blois, and then near Loches. Cossé and Montmorency were released to negotiate with Anjou, and Brantôme followed Marguerite de Valois, the daughter of Henri II, who had married Henri de Navarre in August 1572 and would eventually be repudiated by him, back to the south-west. Brantôme was to rely on her advice and patronage, and was to write as if he aspired to be her lover.

It is not difficult to see why Brantôme chose to follow first Catherine and then Anjou, but it cost him the favour of Henri III, who passed over him for what was considered the family post of sénéchal of Périgord when his brother André de Bourdeille died in 1582. Brantôme left the king's service altogether, and appeared only in the entourage of the king's mother. In the early summer of 1584, on the death of Anjou, whose chamberlain he had become, Brantôme even considered offering his services, together with plans of the coastal and frontier towns of the west and south-west, to Philip of Spain, who would not stint signs of his gratitude. He was to be pleased that he had not.

In the autumn of 1584 Brantôme's horse slipped and rolled over on top of him. For 18 months he had to keep first to his bed and then to his room. He was crippled for life, and began to write, with little but his memory of personal experiences and his notebooks to go on. He repented his idea of only weeks previously:

> Possible si je fusse venu au bout de mes attentes et propositions, j'eusse fait plus de mal à ma patrie que n'a jamais faict renegat d'Alger à la sienne: dont j'en fusse esté maudit à perpetuité des dieux et des hommes

> (It is possible that if I had carried through my expectations and projects I would have done more damage to my country than any Algerian traitor did to his; for which I would have been cursed for ever by gods and men).

Brantôme exaggerated his importance but, in view of denials that he was in any sense a moralist, and in view of the general underestimation of his literary interest, it is important to see how in that reflection self-interest, self-importance, patriotism, nobility of sentiment, and a need for self-esteem all conflict. The reasons he alleges for having refused an invitation to work for Guise, no doubt transmitted by Marguerite de Valois, are less complex. Brantôme knew that Guise would not show loyalty.

After his accident Brantôme moved very little from the château de Matha, which belonged to his brother's widow, Jacquette de Montbrun, to whose projects for remarriage he was always opposed. He did visit Catherine de Medici at Cognac in January 1587, and stay briefly in Paris, where old friends were now scattered between the three camps, League, Politiques, and Huguenots. He had to save his sister-in-law from Condé's troops in 1587, remained in the country throughout the difficult year for France of 1588, but attended the baptism of Guise's posthumous child in Paris on 7 February 1589. He then definitively retired to his estates, leaving only for Usson to greet Marguerite de Valois, who scarcely needed to encourage him to write, and who dedicated to him her own *Mémoires*, intending them to be the raw material for her own biography by Brantôme.

Brantôme's final years were occupied by troubles in the administration of his abbey, the loss of his niece, Mme Aubeterre, in September 1593, and that of his sister-in-law in June 1598. He wrote for her a funeral oration and a prose and verse "Tombeau." He felt keenly the loss also of his youthful vigour and the disappointments caused by his ambition, his illness, his poverty, and his approaching senility. He did however retain sufficient energy to build near Brantôme the splendid château de Richemont and to erect his own tombstone. He died on 5 July 1614, a knight of the Order of Saint John.

He had begun to write before his accident. His military experiences are contained in the *Discours sur les couronels* of 1575, and the *Discours sur les duels* dates from sometime after 1578. The major works appear to have been begun, in the sense of

redacted in dictation to his secretaries, the two Mathaud brothers, on the basis of anecdotes and jottings from the notebooks, only as Brantôme recovered from his injury. He referred to dictating what he called a "recueil d'aucuns discours, devis, contes, histoires etc (a collection of certain conversations, tales, stories, adventures etc)." He boasted of always making corrections in his own hand. The *Capitaines étrangers* were not finished before 1590, but the two-volume *Dames*, divided by their first editor into *Les Dames illustres* and *Les Dames galantes*, were finished, and probably for the most part written first. The manuscript of Brantôme's biography of his father is dated 1600.

In Brantôme's will, dated 1613, he announced his desire to have his works both published and attributed. He left money for the printing of the five velours-bound volumes, engagingly suggesting that, if he did not leave enough money, he thought the books good enough for booksellers to print them at their own expense. In them would be found "de belles choses comme contes, histoires, discours et beaux mots qu'on ne desdaignera, s'il me semble bien, si on y a mis une fois la veue (fine things like stories, adventures, conversations and pithy sayings, which will not be cast aside, so I believe, once they have been looked at)," and he did not want to be deprived "de ma peine et de la gloire qui m'est deue (of my effort and of the esteem due to me)." He wanted a folio, of which the first copy should be dedicated to Marguerite de Valois.

His will was neglected. Only in 1665 did a great-nephew publish a duodecimo of the *Memoires* at Leiden. However, and importantly, about 1646 the Dupuy brothers had had a copy made of Brantôme's papers, and some manuscripts, left to the king in 1662, had been published by Le Laboureur in his 1659 *Additions aux Memoires de Castelnau*, and were known to Mme de Lafayette and La Rochefoucauld before they had ever appeared in their own name. The first proper eight-volume edition was published at Leiden in 1665–66.

WORKS

Brantôme was a covert braggart. He was a Gascon who wrote for publication under his own name and wanted that name highlighted, preserved, and remembered, but only for what it revealed about him when he was gone. He willingly boasted about his role in affairs, and exaggerated the importance, interest, humour, or veracity of whatever he related. It has taken social historians to show how, as a memorialist, he exaggerated the corruption, violence, and cruelty of the Valois court. Life was not as full either of conspiracies, wickednesses, betrayals, and punishments or of lecherous pursuits, trivial pastimes, and petty sexual rivalries and ambitions as he knew he was successfully suggesting for the amusement of what he assumed in 1590 would be a posterity of cultivated courtiers, who would understand him. Few of them had a chance to.

Brantôme was, perhaps unconsciously and at least inconsistently, writing in the ironic manner which would have been recognized by and would have amused Marguerite de Valois or the dead François d'Anjou. Even when, nearly a century later, Mme de Lafayette relied on Brantôme for the depiction of Henri II's court, she knew exactly how to transpose the register back into credibility for the small literary salon coteries which she assumed would constitute her own readership. Modern literary critics have undervalued Brantôme mostly because they have too often taken him at his face value, rather than as the shrewd observer of ambitious and libido-driven behaviour, masquerading as an entertainer, which he actually was.

The masquerade is a good one, but it was not intended to deceive as it has. It is for instance simply untrue to say that Brantôme was not in the French sense a "moraliste." He was brilliantly capable, under the smokescreen of frivolity, of indicating the ambition and the strong need for self-assertion which he admired, and if it seems that "he was not a psychologist of developed powers," that is because he communicates psychological insights, which can be annihilating in their implications, through innuendo, inference, and insinuation rather than outright comment. He much admired Anne de Bretagne, but he leaves no doubt that everything she did was governed by her desire to maintain and, if possible, augment her regal power. He did not comment on the ethics of the behaviour he observed, but his whole constellation of attitudes makes clear his contempt for the low, the cowardly, the treacherous, and the ignoble, tendencies towards which he had probably had to fight against within himself. He has in fact a highly focused system of values which acts as a prism. Licentious behaviour, if it is refined, amuses him, and he retails it with relish, without blushes, savouring the details. He is not amused by cowardice, and he does not talk about it.

Brantôme has so often been misleadingly compared to Montaigne that it is better to avoid any risk of adding to the confusion. If, after his accident, he quite quickly recalled at longhand dictation speed the episodes of a life which had been too full for reflection, he did not, like Montaigne, start an intimate personal conversation daily with an unknown interlocutor, adding short fragments to his discourse all the time. Brantôme did have a personal library, almost wholly of modern authors, but what he shared with Montaigne was a quite insatiable curiosity, not a need to probe the meaning of his experience. Brantôme's speculative digressions on details of dress or circumstance seldom irritate by holding up the generally predictable end of an anecdote, but they communicate Brantôme's immensely enthusiastic interest in his subjects.

Brantôme did criticize his neighbour, Montaigne, for having changed his pen for a sword which suited him less well. He did not think his own exchange in the opposite direction was a mistake. The accident no doubt prompted him to turn to writing, but everything we know about his intention to write, and especially his will, suggests that he had always hoped to undertake the sort of reflection on his observation of other people's behaviour which was bound to result in a written text. The critics' mistake has been to suppose that for Brantôme "memory replaces life." On the contrary, for Brantôme memory was a necessary continuation, retrospective deepening, and consequent completion of the experience of life, even if he ironically idealized the court and its chivalric ideals while flippantly mocking both by reducing the standard motivation to be found at court to ambition, power lust, and the pursuit of sexual gratification. He clearly enjoys his own flamboyance. The pity is that he was writing for people he knew, depended on material he could not publish in his lifetime, and would not therefore be read until any readership which would instantly have understood the teasing was mostly dead. Mme de Lafayette removes the teasing from her background accounts of life at the court of Henri II.

Brantôme himself attributed more importance to his *Dames* than to his other manuscripts, and it is the second volume of the

Dames, now usually entitled *Les Dames galantes*, which has excited most attention. The first is more obviously indebted to Boccaccio. The totally matter-of-fact style throughout makes it clear that the intention is more to amuse than to titillate, but the presentation of the text as sophisticated licentiousness is obvious from the contents, comprising seven discourses: "Sur les dames qui font l'amour et leurs maris cocus (On women who make love, and their cuckolded husbands);" "Sur le sujet qui contente plus en amours, ou le toucher, ou la veue, ou la parolle (On which gives most pleasure in love, touch, sight, or speech);" "Sur la beauté de la belle jambe et la vertu qu'elle a (On the beauty of a pretty leg, and on the power it has);" "Sur l'amour des dames vieilles, et comme aucunes l'ayment autant que les jeunes (On the love of elderly women, and how some love it as much as the young);" "Sur ce que les belles et honnestes dames ayment les vaillans hommes, et les braves hommes ayment les dames courageuses (How beautiful and honest women love valiant men, and brave men love courageous women);" "Sur ce qu'il ne faut jamais parler mal des dames, et la consequence qui en vient (How one should never speak ill of women, and the consequences which come from so doing);" and "Sur les femmes mariées, les vefves et les filles, à sçavoir desquelles les unes sont plus chaudes à l'amour que les autres (On married women, widows and young girls, and which warm more easily to love than the others)."

Having in this way provocatively set up seven categories of subject matter for his more or less salacious anecdotes, a few of which he no doubt already had in his notebook, Brantôme must have cast about for more in each category. He took them where he could find them, making some up: "J'ai ouy dire que… (I have heard tell that…)." Most of the antique classical material came from handbooks, and over a score of sources have been identified. Some passages are translated, or plagiarized, or simply incorporated, and if much comes from Boccaccio, the single most important model for Brantôme was Marguerite de Navarre's *Heptaméron*. A good deal really does come from Brantôme's experience, and its disordered inclusion on account of some association in Brantôme's mind acts almost as a guarantee of the spontaneity with which he is writing. He exhibits the workings of indeliberate memory, like Joyce, rather than ordering them, like Proust.

On the subject of whether women love warriors, Brantôme starts with a provocative paragraph about Venus, goddess of love, who could have had her pick at Jupiter's court of well-behaved and well-brought-up young men with whom to cuckold her husband, "that good fellow, Vulcan." Why did she choose Mars, "coming straight from war, dirty, sweaty, black," "sentant mieux son soldat de guerre que son mignon de coeur (smelling more of the fighting soldier than the court charmer)," perhaps even bleeding, to make love with her without cleaning and perfuming himself. Irreverently disrespectful and flippantly full of contrast, the opening is witty, amusing, and not at all as devoid of psychological interest as it is made to sound. The reader is invited to confront what we conspire not to remember, that perfumery is not the strongest ingredient in the stimulation of sexual desire.

But what goes to reduce even Venus to the level of common experience obviously goes for mortals, too, and there follow three classical illustrations of Brantôme's thesis, in one of which Brantôme is clearly embarrassed by the double tradition which makes the Amazon queen Penthesilea arrive at Troy both before and after the death of Hector. Then come confirmatory examples from Boccaccio and the third volume of Bandello's 1565 *Histoires tragiques*. At this point Brantôme attempts to draw a conclusion. Audacity in war goes with audacity in love, and is therefore a sign of attractiveness, not that women want men who are "effrontez et hardis, impudents et sots (disrespectful and bold, presumptuous and stupid)." What is required is the *juste milieu*. While on the subject, and as if to remind the reader that he is not a professional scribbler—"Je ne scay rien de bien escrire (I do not know anything about writing well)"—Brantôme throws in a story about a boldness carried too far which does not illustrate his argument at all.

The anecdotes continue, two about the sexual tastes of Elizabeth of England, which will have gone the rounds amusing Brantôme's friends, one from the *Cent nouvelles nouvelles*, and a series starting "J'ai cogneu/j'ai ouy faire/j'ai ouy dire (I knew/ I have heard of/I have heard tell of…)." The anecdotes, however, are interspersed with queries, speculative answers, generalizations, and a groping for something which will explain the sorts of behaviour under review.

Or, il y a une demande: pourquoy les femmes ayment tant ces vaillants hommes? Et, comme j'ay dit au commencement, la vaillance a cette vertu et force de se faire aymer à son contraire. Davantage c'est une certaine inclination naturelle qui pousse les dames pour aymer la generosité, qui est certainement cent fois plus aymable que la couardise: aussi toute vertu se fait plus aymer que le vice

(But there is a question: why do women love these valiant men so much? And, as I said to begin with, valour has this virtue and power to make itself loved by its contrary. But rather there is a certain natural inclination which impels women to love magnanimity, which is certainly a hundred times more lovable than cowardice: because any virtue is more lovable than vice).

The urbane, refined titillation of some of the anecdotes is no doubt self-indulgent, and intended sardonically to amuse, but the ethic is fastidious in more important ways than the merely sexual.

In that comment, penned between 1585 and 1590, there is a reference to a natural, and therefore instinctive, inclination, which appears to be ethically perfective and is justified by reference to the merit of its object. "Générosité" is used here, as again more than once later in Brantôme's chapter, in the sense in which Descartes would use it in the context of the definitive Cartesian ethic of 1649. The upgrading of human instinct to make happiness, instinctive gratification, and virtue coincide with one another is already appearing outside the moral philosophy treatises at the very moment of the apogee in Du Vair of the neostoic moral philosophy it was going to displace. The tentative ethical conclusions are that much more impressive because they are accompanied by a perfect lack of hypocrisy in the open discussion of sexual matters. The reason why women are not drawn to old men is not that they lack increased desires, but that they are afflicted with decreased powers. By discussing matters such as that, Brantôme creates an atmosphere of uninhibitedly honest openness of discussion in which the focus of his moral vision sporadically becomes very powerful.

It is seldom more intense than at the end of this fifth discourse when Brantôme relates the death of his niece, his brother's eldest daughter, Mme Aubeterre, almost as if he is modelling his text on the sudden intrusion of serious meditation on a Christian death in the middle of Rabelais's otherwise mostly flippant and irreverent *Quart livre*. Without the moral visions explored in Brantôme's works, but also in those of Rabelais and Marguerite de Navarre, we should be left with much that was amusing, clever, even mentally agile and energetic, but not with writings of any literary power approaching that of the works which we now have. There are other conteurs, memorialists, and moralists, especially compilers of encyclopaedic collections, in 16th-century France, but they do not often have the moral vision which turns Brantôme from a racy raconteur into a memorialist of much more serious literary importance than is often realized.

PUBLICATIONS

Collections

Memoires de messire Pierre de Bourdeille seigneur de Brantosme, 8 vols., 1665–1666
Memoires… contenant les vies des hommes illustres et grands capitaines étrangers de son temps; les vies des hommes illustres et grands capitaines français de son temps, 4 vols., 1699
Oeuvres du seigneur de Brantôme, 15 vols., 1740
Oeuvres complètes du seigneur de Brantôme, 8 vols., 1822
Oeuvres… selon le plan de l'auteur, 13 vols., 1858–1893
Oeuvres complètes, 11 vols., 1864–1882

Editions of single works

Discours sur les duels, 1887
Poésies inédites, 1880
Recueil d'aulcunes rymes de mes jeunes amours, 1927
Vie des dames illustres françaises et étrangères, 1868
Les Dames galantes, 1960; as *The Lives of Gallant Ladies*, 2 vols., 1908

Biographical and critical studies

Lalanne, L., *Brantôme, sa vie et ses écrits*, 1896
Crucy, Fr., *Brantôme*, 1934

BUDÉ, Guillaume, 1468–1540.

Scholar and humanist.

LIFE

Guillaume Budé was the foremost humanist scholar of the French renaissance, the founder of Greek studies in France, and the chief instigator of what subsequently turned out to be the most important development in French educational reform in the first half of the 16th century. In so far as the French renaissance can, and probably must, be seen in terms of a confluence of evangelicalism and classical humanism, which led both to evangelical humanism and, away from Paris, to the religious schism, Budé's activities, writings, and aims must be taken to represent one part of the early contribution of French classical humanist learning to the wave of cultural optimism which swept into France from late 15th-century Italy.

Budé was born on 26 January 1468 into a family from Auxerre. Earlier, we know of a pair of brothers of whom one, Guillaume, bought wine for the royal table, while the other, Jean, married into a family which sold it. Both brothers were ennobled 1399, and one of Jean's administrative posts in the royal chancery was handed down through his son Dreux to Dreux's son Jean, Budé's father. This Jean's career was erratic. Louis XI sent him on a diplomatic mission to Dijon on the death of Charles the Bold in 1477, but he later lost his post in a series of scandals and lawsuits, although it was restored to his eldest son, Dreux, Budé's brother.

Budé's father was himself educated, and owned the rare luxury of a collection of books, all in Latin and some, together with those on liturgy, theology, and medicine, on such humanist subjects as history and moral philosophy. He held three seigneuries near Paris, Villiers-sur-Marne, Yerres, and Marly-la-Ville, but his wife, the daughter of a royal secretary and treasurer under Charles VI and Charles VII, also bore him 18 children between 1455 and 1480. Budé's eldest brother, Dreux (1455–1528), received, on his father's death in 1502, half the estate, including the seigneuries of Yerres and Marly, as well as the chancery post. Dreux ceded the Marly property to Budé, who himself received one 12th of his father's estate in 1502, and the same share of his mother's when she died in 1506. When Dreux himself died in 1528, he left an estate worth 50,000 livres, to be divided between 12 heirs.

Budé was the fourth son. His post as secrétaire du roi was probably a gift from the king granted as a favour to Budé's father. It could be removed, did not ennoble, and could not be sold or left to an heir. Budé received it partly owing to the good offices in 1497 of the chancellor Guy de Rochefort, who may also have mediated Fausto Andrelini's dedication to Budé of his 1496 De influentia syderum. We know that two of Budé's brothers entered the Church and were taken to Troyes in 1494 by Jacques Raguier, their first cousin and bishop of Troyes from 1484 to 1518. One of the two ecclesiastics among the brothers, Etienne, born in 1459, died in 1501, earlier than his parents, leaving Budé a horse. Budé was closest among his brothers to the other ecclesiastic, Louis (1470–1517), only two years younger than himself, with whom he appears to have studied Greek, and whom he seems from his letter headings often to have visited at Troyes.

Among the siblings there were two ecclesiastics, five office-holders, and four sisters who married office-holders. Two of the ten sons died in infancy. The offices held by Budé's father and grandfather, as by most of the other family members we know about, included at least an archival component, and involved the drafting of records, but they explain Budé's professional aspirations and career more easily than his devotion to the pursuit of antiquarian learning. It is no doubt on account of the archival habit of mind that we have so many details of Budé's family, inscribed in the breviary of his brother Jean (1463–1522).

We know that Budé studied law, probably from 1483 to 1486,

at Orléans, one of the universities, with Bourges, Poitiers and Toulouse, offering Parisians the qualification for an administrative career. The teaching of civil law was banned in Paris, where the vocational orientation of the degree had been taking too many students away from theology. Budé was later disparaging about the legal teaching he received, and may never have finished his course, although his later interest in Roman law, which was still technically in force in the southern half of France, may derive from his years at Orléans. On his return to Paris, we are told by Louis le Roy, Budé's biographer in the year of his death, Budé devoted himself "to the pleasures of youth," including hunting and falconry. Years later Budé wrote a treatise on falconry, De venatione, interpolated in 1530 into the De philologia, first published in 1532, in order to demonstrate to François I, who had virtually no Latin, that any subject could be treated in that language. It was the first of Budé's works to be translated into French, and Louis le Roy's translation, the Traitté de la Vénerie, was finally published in 1861.

There are many anecdotes about the suddenness of Budé's turn to intense study around 1491, which made him one of the earliest full-time scholars outside the ranks of the clergy. Something like a religious conversion is reasonably well attested, and Budé's habits of study certainly led early in the new century to constant and sharply painful headaches, and to recurrent states of severe anxiety. He could later not recall having had more than three consecutive nights of good sleep. The symptoms Budé described suggest migraine, but were accompanied by throat swelling, difficulties in breathing, emaciation, moroseness, and signs of premature ageing.

The symptoms began about the period round 1505 when Budé married Roberte le Lieur, who bore him at least 12 children, of whom eight survived infancy. In 1505 Budé was 37, and he later wrote to Thomas More, mentioning on 9 September 1518 that his wife was not quite 27. If the marriage was as early as 1505, and it cannot have been much later, Budé's wife must have been 13. Again, there is a book of hours which tells us that Roberte came from a family of book-owning, educated, office-holding administrators. She was wealthy, whether she was the daughter of the sieur de Maillemans or of the other possibility, who was a rich Paris merchant. She was, like several of her children, to become a Calvinist after Budé's death.

When Budé turned from his life of leisure to his life of study the revival in Greek studies north of the Alps had scarcely begun. During the late middle ages there had been desultory ecclesiastical exhortations and decrees favouring the teaching of eastern languages, mostly in the interests of converting the heathen. By the late 15th century Ficino's Latin Plato, Plotinus and Corpus Hermeticum had adapted Greek thought to its immensely important role in providing western culture with a conceptual structure which heavily upgraded human instinct, and underpinned the movement promoting the hugely important convergence of happiness and virtue and making normal sexual activity potentially conducive to both. Almost no Greek was taught in Paris or Oxford. At best incompetent scraps of teaching might occasionally be had from left-over Greek speakers from the Council of Florence. The real impetus for the sudden sprouting of Greek studies must have been theological. Greek and Hebrew studies could undermine the stranglehold of the scholastics on the interpretation of the Vulgate Latin text of scripture, and there were very important religious reasons for doing that in and around the year 1500.

Schism was of course not in fact avoided, but it would have been if properly evangelical values had been capable of finding new roots which simply by-passed the irresolvable dilemmas imposed by late 15th-century scholastic categories. What has come to be known as the "tri-lingual" educational reform had become urgent. At Cambridge colleges were founded and chairs endowed for the teaching of Greek. At Oxford, Wolsey used the revenues of suppressed monasteries for his intended trilingual foundation, Cardinal's College, subsequently renamed Christ Church. Corpus Christi College was founded at Oxford with the same emphasis on Latin, Greek, and Hebrew, like the university of Alcala in Spain, founded by Jiménez de Cisneros, and Busleyden's trilingual college at Louvain. Leo X's Roman college for Greek studies and the college which Lascaris tried to found in Milan for the French were similarly humanist in intention. The hostility of the Paris theology faculty stopped any such foundation in Paris, although Budé was to come quite near to assisting François I to make one.

It was pre-eminently to the study of Greek that Budé turned in the last decade of the 15th century. Robert Gaguin and Jean Heynlin had picked up some elements of Greek from Gregory Tiphernas, and themselves with Tardif had taught Reuchlin, who gave lessons in Greek at Poitiers and Orléans before becoming internationally famous as a Hebraist in Cologne, where his celebrated dispute with the scholastics about the Talmud took place. Budé did get some help from George Hermonymus of Sparta, from whom Erasmus, Reuchlin, Lefèvre d'Etaples, and Beatus Rhenanus also at different times took lessons, about which Erasmus and Beatus were both scathing. Budé claimed to have learnt nothing from him.

Hermonymus was a competent copyist, but Paris's first Greek teacher of any distinction was Jan Lascaris, who was, however, only briefly in Paris for two short periods. Budé did have lessons from him but was, in the end, like Erasmus and as he himself boasted, self-taught. The Greek manuscripts of which Lascaris took charge at Blois were later combined with the collection at Fontainebleau in Budé's charge. At about the same time as More and Erasmus were practising their Greek by translating Lucian together in London, Budé was demonstrating his mastery of Greek by publishing his first translations into Latin from Plutarch and Saint Basil, in 1503 the *De placitis decretisque philosophorum naturalibus, De fortuna Romanorum*, and in 1505 the *Tria opuscula: De tranquillitate et securitate animi cui accessit epistola Basilii magni de vita per solitudinem transigenda; De fortuna Romanorum; De fortuna vel virtute Alexandri*. The choice of texts from Plutarch's *Moralia* reflects an interest in the choice between active and contemplative life, such as Budé must himself have experienced.

We do not know when or why Budé left the service of Louis XII. It may have been on the occasion of his father's death in 1502, or his mother's in 1506, or on his marriage in 1505 or 1506. He re-entered the service of François I in 1521, but in between undertook missions and performed duties for the new king, who had succeeded in 1515. A chance remark shows Budé on what was obviously official business in Venice in 1501, and he travelled with a French delegation to the papal court. Although he saw the great towns as far south as Rome, Budé complained that he got only a glimpse, with no time to tarry.

The Plutarch translations were from manuscript, since the Aldine editio princeps of the *Moralia* appeared only in 1509, and they may, like those of Erasmus and More, have been practices, or demonstrations of competence. What is puzzling is the fact that Budé's next works were purely antiquarian. Erasmus had acquired Greek, partly driven by Colet, in order to translate the New Testament, and his *Novum Instrumentum* was published in 1516. It is difficult to explain Budé's conversion to antiquarian Greek studies before the turn of the century if there was no ultimate theological objective. Lefèvre d'Etaples, roughly contemporaneous, who wrote prefaces for Budé's 1505 volume which appeared on 15 October, and for a new edition of the *De placitis* of the following March (1506 new style), may have undertaken the study of Greek simply to teach Aristotle, but he very swiftly turned to the mystics, the Fathers, and the translation of scripture. Budé's works of antiquarian philology may have been a passionate hobby. He was later not to repudiate but to turn away from them in the 1535 *De transitu Hellenismi ad christianismum*.

Delayed by bad health, Budé's first major work of scholarship was published by Josse Bade on 17 November 1508, the *Annotationes in quattuor et viginti Pandectarum libros*, dedicated to the chancellor, Jean de Ganay. It was a commentary with notes on the self-contained first 24 books of Justinian's codification of Roman law, also known as the *Digest*. Budé was to comment on later sections of the *Digest* in the 1526 *Annotationes posteriores*. Roman law had more or less been lost until its recovery as a unifying force and a politically useful tool in the 11th century, when it was rediscovered, updated, and exploited in the imperial interest at Bologna by Irnerius, Accursius, and their fellow-glossators. The ban on teaching civil law in Paris had also been partly inspired by the joint hostility in 1219 of papal and French authorities to the claim of the German emperors to a universal "imperium (sovereignty)" over the whole of the territory governed from ancient Rome.

The 16th-century renewal of interest in Roman law inaugurated by Budé and Alciati, who taught law from 1518 in Avignon and then throughout northern Italy, opposed the "mos gallicus (French style)" to the "mos italicus (Italian style)" associated with the 14th-century Bartolo di Sassoferrato, who interpreted Roman law in such a way as to adapt it to late medieval political realities. He was harshly attacked by Valla who, like Budé, was more interested in the texts of Roman law than in its application to the period in which they themselves lived. It is tempting to compare Lefèvre d'Etaples, who went back to the text of Aristotle to combat scholastic philosophy, and Erasmus, who went back to the text of scripture to defeat the scholastic theologians, with Budé, who went back to the text of Roman law to controvert the glossators who had distorted it. The crucial difference is that both Lefèvre and Erasmus always had, or quickly developed, a practical reformatory ambition which Budé lacked.

Louis XII died on 1 January 1515 (new style), and was succeeded by François I, son of Charles d'Orléans and Louise de Savoie. Budé's most famous work, the *De asse et partibus eius* on Greek weights, measures, and money, left the press on the following 15 March, dated 1514 (old style). While the text was in press Budé added an epilogue indicating that he was available for the service of the new king if an office was forthcoming. He wished to further the study of classical antiquity in France and, if it is possible that he was concerned to vindicate the independence of the French revival of interest in classical languages and literatures from what had happened in Italy, he was notwithstanding notably less hostile to the Italian humanists and their Ciceronianism than were some of his contemporaries.

But in defending France against the charge of merely importing from Italy what he looked on as a revival of classical studies, Budé does contribute to constructing an affinity between Greek and Paris parallel to that which the Italians established between ancient Rome and modern Rome. The parallel is important because it is merely the secular dimension of the attempt, clear, for example, in Jacques Lefèvre d'Etaples, to give the French church apostolic authority by deriving its tradition from Saint Paul, through his first convert, Denis, at the Areopagus in Athens, identified with the neoplatonist pseudo-Denys, known also as the Pseudo-Areopagite, author of the *Celestial Hierarchies*, and also with Denis the first martyr of France. That chain would allow the French church deriving from Peter quasi-equal status with the primatial Petrine see of the Roman church.

Although in 1517 Budé was recruited by his cousin, Etienne Poncher, chancellor of France in all but name from 1512 to 1515, and Guillaume Petit, the king's Dominican confessor and bishop of Troyes from 1518, to mediate between Erasmus and François I, whom they hoped to persuade to found a trilingual college in Paris, they succeeded only in obtaining from 1529 the appointment of the "lecteurs royaux (royal readers)" who, until his disgrace in 1538, were under the general supervision of François's almoner, Jacques Colin. The first lecteurs were teaching by March 1530, but Budé himself was not in the end closely concerned with the implementation of the project.

Budé, with his private income, philological interests, and sometime diplomatic status, was never connected with any of the Paris colleges and, as far as we know, never consented to take pupils, although he was approached by Christophe de Longueil, the devotee of Cicero ridiculed by Erasmus in the *Ciceronianus*. The opposition of the scholastics in the university ensured that the royal lecteurs, the kernel of what became the Collège de France, stayed outside the formal degree-granting system, from which they faced sometimes intense hostility. By 1530 Pierre Danès and Jacques Toussaint were holding chairs of Greek, Agazio Guidacerio and François Vatable, chairs of Hebrew, and Oronce Finé a chair of mathematics. A third chair of Hebrew was founded for Paul Paradis in 1531, and Barthélemy Latomus was appointed reader in Italian in 1534. Of these seven early lecteurs, only Toussaint is known to have been close to Budé.

It was in 1519 that Budé presented to the king his *De l'institution du prince*, the manual of advice taken from ancient history but written in the vernacular in deference to the king's ignorance of Latin. It was not published until 1547, when it appeared in three slightly different versions, with the titles chosen by the printers. Erasmus's *Institutio principis christiani*, a much more ambitious work, had been published in 1516, and it is likely that Budé did not wish to appear to compete with Erasmus. The manuscript was presented to the king just before Budé's first mission on his behalf, to meet representatives of Charles V at Montpellier. Budé must have resumed some functions at court because, after congratulating himself in 1518 on having been absent from court for 12 years, he complained in 1519 of the nuisance of having to take up residence in Paris again.

Budé wrote about 50 letters to mostly foreign humanists between 1516 and 1520, and about 100 to humanists, mostly in France, after 1520, when in May and June he attended with Thomas More the meeting between François I and Henry VIII at the Field of the Cloth of Gold, with the French and English

each on territory of their own just outside Calais. In the following year, Budé was made a maître des requêtes on 21 August, having been elected prévot of the Paris merchants on 16 August. That year he also became king's librarian at Fontainebleau, a post with no specific duties which was created for him. The meeting at the Field of the Cloth of Gold was a failure, since Henry VIII went on immediately to meet the emperor on English territory at Calais, and within two years England and France were at war. Budé, meanwhile, had followed the court to Amboise, Blois, Romorantin, Dijon, Autun, Troyes, and Reims.

Relations between Budé and Erasmus began to be strained as Erasmus quarrelled with Lefèvre d'Etaples and, as the schism took hold, allowed his feelings for France to become increasingly glacial, no doubt at least partly on account of the power and intransigence of the Paris theologians. The French humanists were incensed when the character Nosoponus in Erasmus's *Ciceronianus*, a satirical dialogue apparently aimed at Longueil, had unfavourably compared Budé's Latin style with that of the printer Josse Bade. Longueil disliked Erasmus, and had disadvantageously compared him with Budé. Epigrams were coined in France against Erasmus, Budé replied to no more letters and, although Erasmus omitted the comparison of Budé with Bade in his March 1529 second edition, he did not succeed in appeasing the resentment.

During the 1520s Budé spent much time acquitting himself of his official duties. In September 1523 and from October to December 1524, he was at Lyons. After the battle of Pavia and the capture of François I, Budé's relations with the chancellor, Antoine Duprat, apparently soured. Duprat seems to have exaggerated the royal powers in ecclesiastical matters in a manner detrimental to those of the parlement, conceded by the 1516 concordat. He arrogated to himself, with the support of Louise de Savoie and the pope, the archbishopric of Sens and the abbacy of the Benedictine abbey of Saint-Benoît-sur-Loire on the death of Etienne Poncher on 23 February 1525. The parlement, to which Budé belonged as a maître des requêtes, sought to curtail the encroachment of the royal prerogative in all domains and supported the election by the monks of Poncher's nephew, François, but lost. Duprat became a cardinal in 1527, and François Poncher, imprisoned for sedition in 1526, died in Vincennes in 1532.

Budé, who was inclined to side with the royalists, seems, whether or not on account of his conflict of interests, to have ceased to follow the court in its peregrinations. He was to become the close adviser of Duprat's successor in 1535, Guillaume Poyet, but the period of his strongest influence over François I was from October 1527 until March 1529. His role as an administrator and adviser has in the past been underestimated, although it is true he was forever complaining that court duties kept him away from his studies and his family. Partly for reasons of political commitment and belief, he chose to be identified with the policy of François I, which in minor ways he helped to implement, as it swung against the religious innovators. By 1526 the parlement had obtained the power to approve all books before they were submitted even to the faculty of theology, and there is no reason to suppose that Budé at that date regarded innovatory theology as anything other than a cause of civil disorder. He was a member of the special commission in April 1529 which sentenced the headstrong Berquin to life imprisonment. It was Berquin's appeal to the parlement on 17 April which resulted in the condemnation to burning, pronounced at 10 a.m. in the absence from Paris of the king and his mother and implemented at midday.

In the last five years of his life Budé showed himself clearly hostile to the reformers. The *De transitu* renounced Hellenism as an end in itself, and its preface as well as its text congratulated François on his firm reaction to the blasphemous placards posted up and down the kingdom on the night of 17–18 October 1534. It was while accompanying the court on a royal visit to Normandy that Budé fell terminally ill in July 1540. He returned to die in Paris on 22 August, surrounded by his family.

WORKS

Budé was a solitary man, a late developer who reached a crisis in his mid-20s when his temperamental seriousness clashed with the life of leisure such as was enjoyed by the richer members of the minor aristocracy which Budé never aspired to join. The drinking, hunting, and falconry in which his private means allowed him to indulge gave way to an adulthood which oscillated between diplomatic service and the life of a studious recluse. His antiquarian studies and his mastery of Greek were not directed to seriously religious or moral ends, in spite of the celebrated digressions in the major works of scholarship. The digressions of the *De asse* show that, while Budé may have shared the social concerns evident in the essays which Erasmus added to the Froben 1515 and subsequent editions of the *Adages* at numbers ending in -500 and -000, he did not feel them as strongly or urge them so vigorously.

His digressions must be regarded as an element of personal and original thought offered diffidently and made acceptable, Budé must have felt, by being sandwiched between slabs of irrefutable scholarship. The personal element in Budé's work became stronger and, in the end, when the schism had become well entrenched in the Alps and east of the Rhine, and Budé recognized that no synthesis of Hellenism and evangelical Christianity was possible, he turned his back on pure scholarship. Like Lefèvre d'Etaples and Erasmus, he found evangelicalism more relevant and important to his life and his society than classical humanism, particularly in the antiquarian way in which he had earlier cultivated it.

The limits of Budé's thought distinguish him at the outset from the majority of his fellow humanists. Politically he embraced a concept of kingship which allowed little power to the nobility and none at all to anyone else. The *De asse* advocates a form of government in which the happiness of the people is wholly dependent on the kindness of the prince, and the sagacity of the advice he receives. Although as a maître des requêtes Budé was a member of the Paris parlement, his sympathies lay with the king's efforts to impose his own sovereign authority on that body.

In an analogous way, the strong sympathies which Budé expressed for the cultivation of "bonae literae (good learning)" were never integrated into a project for educational reform in a way which made clear how the study of ancient languages could enrich the experience or even improve the mind of the individual. Budé at first affirmed that they did before, in the *De transitu*, apparently holding that they did not. He ended in a purely verbal resolution of what has been referred to as his "pervasive confusion." It is true that Budé does not offer or allow of any coherent moral, religious, philosophical, or theological basis for his posi-

tions, that his theoretical reflections about education never amounted to an integrated programme for reform, and that the confusion of thought is mirrored by the style and structure of his works. What his intellectual positions do show, even if erratically adopted in response to particular circumstances, and irreconcilable when taken together, are the unconfident and tentative origins of the serious pursuit of Greek studies at Paris.

Much of Budé's *Annotationes... in quattuor et viginti Pandectarum libros*, published in November 1508, is devoted to textual criticism, showing how the original Roman texts had become corrupted, often thereby leading the medieval lawyers into ingenious but erroneous efforts to harmonize "tituli," or rubrics, which had simply been misread by a copyist, misunderstood by a glossator, or never been in force contemporaneously with one another. Budé is almost shockingly prepared to concede that Justinian's jurists, led by Tribonian, had let occasional incompatibilities between the laws escape their attention. He sets Roman law into its context, shows how it developed and, already at this date, in his long discussion of the Roman "senatus" favours the contemporary French arrangement whereby the chancellor, as the representative of the king, rather than the parlement, exercises royal power. The Romans had different needs and a different arrangement.

In mid-14th-century Perugia Bartolo di Sassoferrato had reintroduced the concept of an equity overriding positive law in the interests of natural justice and common sense into the vocabulary of jurisprudence, so in effect allowing lip-service to be paid to the immutability of a code of laws which was none the less made to adapt to changing values and circumstances. Yet Budé inveighed heavily against Bartolo's "mos italicus," because it relied on distorting the actual meaning of the codified legislation, in spite of the way in which its end result, to allow Roman law to be adapted to the needs of the newly emerging Italian city states, converged with Budé's aim of replacing a legislative system whose obsolete nature he painstakingly laid bare. He was later to admit that he had been intemperate in his attacks on those of his contemporaries who followed Bartolo even after he had alerted them to the textual problems in the interpretation of Justinian's codification of antique legislation.

Budé's 1515 *De asse et partibus eius* again uses a law of the Digest as a point of departure, and is aimed at uncovering the worth of the measures and coinage of antiquity, and the slow erosion of the coinage's value. Budé's contemporaries also regarded it as a florilegium of classical sayings. Budé derived much from the elder Pliny, and something from the scholarship of Ermalao Barbaro, the humanist adversary of Pico della Mirandola who, in perfect humanist style, had defended what the humanists saw as the barbaric style and syntax of scholastic Latin. Budé's own prolix style is normally thought inelegant to the point of unreadability, heavy with the sort of laboured circumlocution which referred to Jesus as "Hercules" and to nonhumanists as dwelling in "Cimmerian darkness," after a people on whom, according to Homer, the sun never shone. Even Budé's firmest defenders admit the disorganization of his presentation and the clumsiness of his Latin.

Yet, in spite of serious errors about some individual coins and measures, the learning is impressive, the conclusions on the value of ancient coins as measured by their gold or silver content remarkably accurate, and even the style was much admired, for instance by Thomas More. Budé was often favourably compared to Erasmus, and it is true that his cumbersome digressions, filling about a third of his text, do very tentatively speculate on wealth in Budé's own society, on the abuse of ecclesiastical possessions, and on social injustices. Budé thought the level of taxation excessive, the hiring of foreign mercenaries extravagant, and was heavily critical of the government of Louis XII and of his minister, cardinal Georges d'Amboise. Louis XII's death on 1 January 1515 was an event which Budé regarded as a misfortune only for very few.

The notion of the community of property, at the head of Erasmus's *Adages* and the foundation of More's *Utopia*, was little more than a commonplace, emphasizing the unimportance of worldly possessions. When in 1516 the English humanist Thomas Lupset, associated with the circle of Colet, Grocyn, and Latimer, brought to Budé Linacre's translation from Galen, the present of two dogs from Thomas More, and the Louvain 1516 edition of *Utopia*, Budé wrote to Lupset two letters, the first of which was used to preface the second edition of *Utopia*, which Lupset was seeing through the press of Gilles de Gourmont in Paris in 1517. Budé's second letter to Lupset was used to preface Linacre's translation from Galen, the 1519 *Galeni methodus melendi, vel de morbis curandis*, but the first is Budé's strongest statement of his belief in equality of possessions, his love of peace, and his contempt for money.

More's retention of Budé's letter in subsequent editions except the second Froben edition of 1518 is less an acquiescence by More in Budé's interpretation of the ideological content of his work, although that interpretation may well have been correct, than a gesture of recognition, like the flowery rhetorical compliments which More, as also Erasmus and Vives, accorded to Budé. Budé's correspondence with the anti-French Richard Pace, with Lascaris, Tunstall, and other scholars shows that Budé had been adopted into what was virtually a loose, if assiduously self-promoting association of major European humanists, linked mostly by a copious correspondence. Budé's correspondence with Guillaume de Croy's tutor, Juan Luis Vives, whom he met in Paris in 1519, is particularly intimate.

On the question of the cultural independence of France from Italy, bound up in his mind with the question of the ultimate right to dispose of the wealth of the Gallican church, Budé was firmly nationalistic although, like Erasmus, he hoped for much support for international humanism from Leo X, successor to Erasmus's warrior pope, Julius II. The final section of the *De asse* is a long dialogue between Budé and his great friend François Deloynes, who tries to dissuade Budé from abandoning the active for the contemplative life. It is interrupted by news of the accession of François I, and is generally read as an expression by Budé of his readiness to serve, if a suitable position were to be found for him as an administrator or a diplomat. In private correspondence he made clear his expectation of an important post.

Budé's 1519 text, known from the title of the edition printed in 1547 as *De l'institution du prince*, is largely another florilegium of adages about government culled above all from Plutarch and the Bible, but also from Pliny, Aristotle, Suetonius, Lucan, Homer, Livy, and others. In the struggle for temporal power in the Gallican church, Budé was firmly on the side of the king against on the one hand the pope, and on the other the parlement, which suspected a collusion between king and pope. Budé's principles, like his ambitions, were moving in the direction of a still qualified royal absolutist government in which he undoubtedly saw a place for himself, alongside the philosopher-king. He clearly looked forward to an enlightened royal patronage of the arts, and dreamt of establishing French primacy in eloquence and learning. It was at least partly Erasmus's attitude to France which lay behind the touchiness of Budé's letters to him and led to the final break, partly precipitated by Budé's last letter to Erasmus, dated 22 April 1527, in which Budé complained to Erasmus about the attitude to the French expressed in his published works.

The *De contemptu rerum fortuitarum libri tres* is generally dated mid-1520, although the first known copy appears to date from Cologne in 1521. The subject combined the spiritual commonplace considerations on contempt for the world, as taken up among others by Petrarch and Erasmus's early *De contemptu mundi*, probably of 1488, with the fashionable stoicism deriving from the opening sentences of Epictetus's *Manual*, that our true good had to be in our power, and that any object of our desire which was not in our power, not being our true good, deserved only to be despised. Budé takes something from Plutarch's *De tranquillitate et securitate animi*, which he had translated 15 years before. He had written to Vives in August 1519 about his life in the country, his financial worries, and his family, insisting on his preference for rural tranquillity, another classical topos chiefly associated with Horace, over life at court. He intended to write about these matters. The *De contemptu*, addressed to his successful elder brother, Dreux, reflects his disappointment about not in fact achieving high office, disserts about the active and contemplative lives in a tone of resignation, and is self-congratulatory on Budé's victory over his headaches. The gifts of fortune are illusory; the powerful are unjust; and the neglect of letters is the fault of princes.

Budé did receive the posts he had hoped for, and wrote little more in the vein of the factitious *De contemptu*. His administrative and judicial roles precluded much serious study, but in 1526 he published the *Annotationes posteriores in Pandectas* to complete his commentary on the Digest, and in 1529 the *Commentarii linguae graecae*, a lexicographical thesaurus with some 7,000 entries on points of Greek usage, with about 500 on Latin. Published in Paris, it was to be reprinted as early as 1530 in Cologne, Basle, and Venice. Enlarged in 1548, it was to be the basis for Henri Estienne's celebrated Greek-Latin *Thesaurus graecae linguae*, in six folio volumes, of 1572.

In November 1532 Budé published the dialogue on eloquence *De philologia libri duo* and its attached *De studio literarum, recte ac commode instituendo*. It is primarily here that Budé collects explicitly together important strands in his humanism which had been scattered throughout what he had written from the beginning of his career. He regards the liberal arts as accomplishing what Aulus Gellius had identified with "humanitas" and defined in the *Noctes atticae* (xiii, 17) as "eruditio institutioque in bonas artes (the learning and teaching of the good [liberal] arts)," but Budé, inspired by Martianus Capella's late fourth-century *De nuptiis Philologiae et Mercurii (The Marriage of Philology and Mercury)*, goes beyond Aulus Gellius. Martianus Capella's work on the marriage of Philologia and Mercury is used by Budé, and subsequently by a whole series of important French renaissance writers and educational reformers of whom Pierre de la Ramée is probably the most important, to upgrade humanist rhetoric at the expense of scholastic dialectic.

Budé had defended in the *De asse* the reduction of all the liberal arts to philosophy. In the *Commentarii* and the *De philologia*, the study of "philology," that is the writings of classical antiquity, however strongly biased towards language rather than literature, replaces the study of philosophy, or the dialectic promoted by scholastic logic. Mercury represents eloquence, so that the use of the *De nuptiis* allows Budé to sketch a theoretical basis for the need which he had felt from the beginning to anchor an educational reform in classical studies. Others were to use the literature of classical antiquity to promote elegance of expression over the style developed by the scholastics for their dialectic and disputations. For reasons to be explained by the rise of scholastic forms of debate during the intervening middle ages, Budé replaced Cicero's philosophy as the source and epitome of all learning with philology, the study of classical antiquity. He made much the same point by playing in the *De studio* on the affinity between "ratio (reason)" and "oratio (discourse)," both of which translate the Greek λόγοσ, meaning a spoken or written word as well as reason or wisdom. Budé also argues with Valla against Jerome that at the beginning of John's gospel λόγοσ must imply the relationship of generation with God the Father.

Budé himself was the first northern humanist seriously to link the liberal arts together according to the antique ideal of an encyclopedia in the sense of a circular organization of interdependent disciplines, referred to by Quintilian as an encyclopedia in both Greek and Latin in the *Institutio oratoria* (I, x, 1), an εγχύχλιοσ παιδεία or "orbis doctrinae (circle of doctrine)." Budé himself goes little further towards a scheme for educational reform than giving the primacy of the disciplines to philology in an architecturally structured unity. The reference to architecture suggests that he is remembering Vitruvius, who had described architecture as an "encyclios disciplina (circular discipline)." Budé's key text is in the *De l'institution*, where he speaks of the disciplines

desquelles les bonnes lettres font profession, faisans d'icelles une perfection des arts liberaux et sciences politiques qu'on appelle en grec, "Encyclopedia" qui veult autant dire…erudition circulaire, ayans les dictes sciences et disciplines connexité mutuelle et coherence de doctrine et affinité d'estude qui ne se doibt ny peult bonnement separer ny destruire par distinction de faculté ou profession

(professed by good letters [liberal studies], making of them a perfection of liberal arts and political sciences which in Greek are called "Encyclopedia," which means…circular learning, the sciences and disciplines mentioned having between them a reciprocal connection, and doctrinal cohesion, and mutual implication which cannot and should not be sundered or destroyed by any distinction of faculty or calling).

It is important in any assessment of Budé's last large-scale work, the 1535 *De transitu Hellenismi ad christianismum libri III*, to bear in mind the important distinctions between reformation, excommunication, schism, and heresy, no one of which necessarily implied any of the others. It is possible that schism was only one of a number of possible solutions to the social problems caused by religious reformation and was, in England and perhaps in Germany, at first more a declaration of religious autonomy than a rejection of the teaching authority of the Roman see. Schism was an attractive solution in territory shielded from Paris, much more concerned about heresy than

schism, and much more than Rome the defender of traditional belief, by the Alps, and it accordingly took hold most firmly in Switzerland, which could be reached from Paris only with difficulty, through Strasbourg or Lyons. In France in 1535 there were heretical stirrings, as shown by the famous placards against the Mass of 17–18 October 1534, but there were only ever fleeting attempts at territorially-based schism. There were not before 1535 worshipping Christian communities in France not in communion with Rome. The first outspoken published work of theological heterodoxy was Calvin's *Christiani religionis institutio* of March 1536, published in Basle, and it was not published in French translation until the Geneva 1541 edition.

The privilege of the *De transitu* dates from February 1534, that is before the placards occasioned the change of policy of François I towards those whose attitudes to the Church's sacramental system were redolent of "Lutheranism." The preface, congratulating François on his prompt response to the placards, like the reflection on the episode of the placards in the text itself, was necessarily added subsequently. Budé had always been inclined to dismissiveness towards any connection between the study of antique literature and Christian values, and he was often explicit about its non-existence. Even the *De studio* allows only a doubtful propedeutic utility to the study of antique literature, and even that is taken back by the condemnation of what Budé calls Hellenism in the *De transitu*. The approach, if not the style, is humanist. Antique authors are quoted as authorities and antique myths used as illustrations, but we need the insights of revelation to derive nourishment from the study of the pagan writers of antiquity, and the nourishment we receive is in the order of human prudence. Budé correctly sees the frivolity of those humanists who see in antique authors examples merely of fine writing and elegance of expression, but he refuses to make the connection which Erasmus attempted between what he early considered the barbarous Latin of the scholastics and what he thought of as their theological contentiousness.

Budé links the philosophies of antiquity with the reception of novel religious doctrines and, although he does not refer to Luther, he comes out strongly in favour of free will and the possibility of an autonomous self-determining moral choice by which the individual becomes responsible for the soul's ultimate destiny. In spite of his own epoch's "literae restitutae (restored [humanist] letters)," the religious factions were bitterly attacking one another. Budé goes out of his way to repudiate the Lutheran doctrine of justification by faith. The reformers are blamed for a general relaxation of behaviour and a rebellion against all authority, although Budé tries hard to drive a wedge between learned humanist reform and the thirst for total liberty among the masses. The text, which is a cross between a sociological analysis of religious disquiet and an exhortation to individuals to concentrate on the pursuit of true Christian virtue, rests in fact on a serious late medieval Christian piety, shorn of superstitious elements, and dressed up in humanist garb, but with a spiritual foundation itself not widely different from that of Gerson a century earlier.

PUBLICATIONS

Collections

Opera omnia, 2 vols., 1557

Philosophical, moral, and academic works

Annotationes in quattuor et viginti Pandectarum libros, 1508
De asse et partibus eius libri quinque, 1515; French summary, 1522
De contemptu libri fortuitarum libri tres, 1521
Annotationes posteriores in Pandectas, 1526
Commentarii linguae graecae, 1529
De philologia libri duo, 1532
De studio literarum recte et commode instituendo, 1532
De transitu Hellenismi ad christianismum libri tres, 1535; modern edition with French translation, 1973
Forensia, 1544
De l'institution du prince, 1547

Other

Plutarchi de placitis philosophorum, De fortuna Romanorum, 1503
Tria opuscula: De tranquillitate et securitate animi cui accessit epistola Basilii magni de vita per solitudinem transigenda: De fortuna Romanorum; De fortuna vel virtute Alexandri; 1505
Plutarchi Cheronei, 1505
Epistolae, 1520; augmented 1522
Aristotele de mundo libellus....Philonis Iudaei itidem de mundo libellus, 1526

Biographical and critical studies

Budé, Eugène de, *Vie de Guillaume Budé, fondateur du Collège de France (1467–1640)*, 1884
Delaruelle, Louis, *Guillaume Budé, les origines, les débuts, les idées maîtresses*, 1907
——*Répertoire analytique et chronologique de la correspondance de Guillaume Budé*, 1907
Plattard, Jean, *Guillaume Budé et les origines de l'humanisme en France*, 1923
McNeil, David O., *Guillaume Budé and Humanism in the Reign of Francis I*, 1975

BUFFON, Georges-Louis Leclerc, comte de, 1707–1788.

Scientist, man of letters.

LIFE

Buffon's connection with French literature is not wholly limited to the famous short treatise which he delivered verbally at his reception into the Académie française on 25 August 1753 and which we now know as the *Discours sur le style*, however intrinsically important and subsequently influential that work turned out to be. Buffon was also the greatest of the French natural sci-

entists of the 18th century to devote works of literary imagination to scientific research. He much furthered the process by which scientific discovery was entering the realm of literary discussion.

Buffon's conclusions were based on accurate and well-informed research but, although he accepted ecclesiastical authority, his work showed a cautious awareness of the revolutionary change in human attitudes and behaviour to which scientific discovery was leading. He wrote in a way which was knowledgeable but also comprehensible, generative of powerful hypotheses and always aware of the wider cultural context in which scientific discovery had to be set. He is the most imaginatively powerful 18th-century French author to have contributed substantially to the development of the biological sciences, because he was aware of how directly that development was affecting the understanding of human nature and destiny, and of the reverberating echoes which the life sciences, as we now call them, were having in social and political thought. His synthetic grasp of what was being discovered hugely stimulated an urgent literary exploration of the repercussions of scientific discovery on human values and behaviour.

Buffon, born on 7 September 1707 at Montbard, was the son of Benjamin-François Leclerc de Buffon, a counsellor of the Dijon parlement, and of Mlle de Marlin. Buffon went to school with the Jesuits at Dijon before being sent to study law at Angers but, after fighting a duel with an Englishman, had to return in 1730 to Dijon, where he was hastily despatched with another young Englishman, the duke of Kingston, and his tutor, Hickmann, an entomologist, on a two-year tour of the south of France, Switzerland, and Italy. The party started out on 3 November 1730 and was in Rome when Buffon was recalled by the death of his mother on 1 August 1731. He rejoined Kingston and Hickmann in Paris in 1732, visited England, and was back at Montbard on 27 September, inheriting a substantial property from his mother on reaching the age of 25 in that month. On 30 December his father married one of his relatives, Antoinette Nadault, born in 1709. Buffon was enduringly bitter to find himself two years older than his stepmother, who was to live until 1770.

From the age of 25 Buffon devoted himself, mostly at Montbard, to his scientific work, although from 1734 he did spend some time in Paris, where he frequented La Popelinière, Holbach, Mme d'Epinay, and Mme Dupin. He was later to get to know Mme Necker well. He did not, however, play any great part in salon life. Already on 27 December 1733 he was appointed adjoint or associate in mechanics at the Académie des Sciences, and further honours were to accumulate. On 16 March 1739 he became an adjoint in botany, and on 13 June of the same year an associate in the same subject. On 24 June 1744 he was made the Académie's permanent treasurer. He had meanwhile published in French translation Stephen Hales's 1727 *Vegetable Staticks* and 1733 *Haemostaticks* as *La Statique des végétaux et analyse de l'air* in 1735 and Isaac Newton's papers on fluxions and the arithmetic of infinities from the mid-1660s as *Méthode des fluxions et des suites infinies* in 1740, taking Newton's side against Leibniz in the debates about calculus.

In 1739 Buffon succeeded Du Fay as Intendant of the Jardin et Cabinet du Roi, the botanical garden later to become the zoo and Jardin des Plantes. He enlarged and developed the garden, often advancing money from his own resources in a way later to cause much trouble to his heirs. It was he who introduced the pharmaceutical plants and the animals. Henceforward he spent four months every year in Paris, and the rest in Montbard, where he was visited by Henry of Prussia and the king of Sweden. Catherine II of Russia sent magnificent presents, and received Buffon's son with much honour.

Buffon's early papers had been devoted to mathematics, physics, and agriculture. It was only from the date of his appointment to the Jardin du Roi that he dedicated himself totally to those aspects of science encompassed in the *Histoire naturelle, générale et particulière*. He became a member of the Royal Societies of London and Edinburgh, and of the academies of St Petersburg, Berlin, and Dijon, and of the institute of Bologna. On 1 July 1753 he was elected to the Académie française in succession to Languet de Gergy, the archbishop of Sens, whose eulogy he unconventionally left to a paragraph at the end of his discourse of reception, the famous discourse on style. Louis XV made him a count in 1773 by elevating the Buffon property into a comté, and also had the *Histoire naturelle* printed at the Imprimerie royale.

There had been a second duel with an Englishman during a visit to London in 1739, in which Buffon was wounded by a cousin of Lord Grandisson. At Montbard he was in charge of the forges which produced about 400 tonnes of iron a year and employed 400 workers. He was also involved in various other industrial projects involving applied sciences. On 21 September 1752 Buffon married the 20-year-old Marie-Françoise de Saint-Belin Malain, by whom he had one child in 1764. He was deeply attached to his wife and much upset when she died in 1769. His father did not die until he was 93 in 1775. Buffon's son, Georges-Louis-Marie, an army officer attached to the entourage of the duc d'Orléans, was to be guillotined on 10 July 1793.

Buffon's reputation in his day was probably second only to those of Voltaire and Rousseau, but he was inevitably in different ways both over- and under-estimated. Although he contributed only one article, "Nature," published in 1765, to the *Encyclopédie* (q.v.), and was generally friendly to that undertaking's objectives, both d'Alembert and Voltaire laughed at his rotund, pompous, rather out-of-date style, his reliance on others for experimentation and field-work, and his aloofness from the struggle in which the philosophes (q.v.) were engaged. He was the butt of a number of amusing epigrams. He was also delated for heresy. The first three volumes of the *Histoire* appeared in 1749 to universal acclaim, but were criticized by the abbé de Lignac in his *Lettres à un Américain* and above all in the *Nouvelles ecclésiastiques*. The Sorbonne condemned 14 propositions relative to Buffon's suggestion that the earth might be 60,000 years old. Buffon submitted, signing a declaration that he renounced any view which was in contradiction with the narrative of Moses, repeating his abjuration in the *Epoques de la nature*. In fact, his original notes had estimated the age of the earth at 2,993,280 years.

The over-valuation of Buffon became clear in the 19th-century reaction to it. His literary style was considered by some "theatrical and turgid," and his mind far too ready to produce a synthesis that went well beyond the observable facts. His mineralogy was weak, his anthropology inadequate. In fact the poetry of his descriptive style, the grandeur and breadth of his hypotheses, the sharpness of his intuitions, the remarkable accuracy of some of his predictions, and the pioneering work in palaeontology and geology, and on the origin of species show him to have had a faculty of imaginative synthesis of the highest order. He also had a powerfully poetic vision of the world. The pendulum has swung, and the criticisms of the 19th century about how often Buffon was wrong have been replaced by admiration for the number of times he was right. He not only popularized imaginative scientific writing, but he directed his contemporaries towards the right questions, and indicated in important cases the general direction in which the answers were to be found.

The *Histoire naturelle* was intended to be little less than an encyclopedia of the natural sciences, an "Histoire complète et scientifique de la nature." Buffon had several principal collaborators, L.-J. Daubenton, who wrote on natural history for the *Encyclopédie*, and later P. Guéneau de Montbéliard, the abbé G.C.L.A. Bexon, Faujas de Saint-Fond, André Thouin, and C.N.S. Sonnini de Manoncourt. The first three volumes, which were entitled *Terre, Histoire de l'homme*, appeared in 1749; then came 12 volumes of *Quadrupèdes vivipares* in 1753–67, with the anatomy sections by Daubenton; the nine volumes of *L'Histoire des oiseaux*, written with the help of Bexon and Guéneau de Montbéliard, in 1770 to 1783; the five volumes of *L'Histoire des minéraux*, written with the help of André Thouin, from 1783 to 1788; and the seven volumes of supplements from 1774 to 1789. The whole collection of 36 volumes was completed by B.G.E. de Lacépède, who extended the work to 44 quarto volumes published from 1749 to 1804. The first edition is much coveted for the beauty of its plates. The fifth supplementary volume of 1778 contains what is regarded as Buffon's masterpiece, the *Epoques de la nature*.

Buffon toiled at his great work for forty years, invariably at his desk from 6 a.m. until midday and from 5 p.m. until 7 p.m., whether at Montbard or in Paris. His whole life-style was the product of the order which he advocated in the *Discours sur le style* and to which the *Histoire naturelle* gave expression. He was 81 when, having refused an operation, he died in Paris on 15 April 1788.

WORKS

The *Discours sur le style* delivered at the Académie on 25 August 1753 is not quite so casual as Buffon allowed it to be believed. Grimm, commenting on the substitution of a discourse on how to write for the customary eulogy of the new member's predecessor, maliciously noted, having read the reply to Buffon's *Discours*, how badly the Académie needed a writing master. The reply had been made by François-Augustin Paradis de Moncrif, chiefly notorious for his light-hearted if erudite history of cats.

Buffon's *Discours* was not a comprehensive treatise on writing, but it was the product of some reflection. He had already had to issue some instructions to his collaborators about how the *Histoire naturelle* was to be written. He took the view that the content of a work passed into the public domain, but its style remained the author's.

Le style n'est que l'ordre et le mouvement qu'on met dans ses pensées

(Style is only the order and movement one puts into one's thoughts).

He goes on to maintain that movement, in the statement quoted, itself proceeds from order. Indeed the whole of the *Histoire naturelle* is in a sense an attempt to give an ordered explanation to the universe, although Buffon's botanical categories clashed severely with those of his senior contemporary, the Swede Carl von Linné, which were clearer and more comprehensive, but also because of their exactness more vulnerable.

In so far as the *Discours sur le style* can be reduced to a doctrine, it teaches the need for clarity and logic in all expository discourse, demanding clearly inter-related parts. There has to be a plan, and it is in the perception of the underlying structure of a work that feeling is generated, and that the pleasure of reading it and its power of persuasion both lie:

La chaleur naîtra de ce plaisir, se répandra partout et donnera la vie à chaque expression: tout s'animera de plus en plus, le ton s'élèvera, les objets prendront de la couleur, et le sentiment se joignant à la lumière l'augmentera, la portera plus loin, la fera passer de ce qu'on dit à ce que l'on va dire, et le style deviendra intéressant et lumineux

(Warmth will be generated by this pleasure, will spread throughout and will give life to each expression: everything will come increasingly to life, the tone will intensify, objects will take on more colour, and feeling added to understanding will increase it, carry it further, make the transition from what is being said to what is about to be said, and the style will become interesting and luminous).

That doctrine does more to illuminate the difficulties of writing expository prose than it does to resolve general questions of literary composition, where a plan is very often a hindrance or, if not, no more than a preliminary scaffolding, bearing as much relationship to the shape of the work as scaffolding does to the appearance of the finished building. The point, however, is not immediately whether Buffon is right or wrong, but whether he is trying to lay down general principles of any sort, whether deduced or induced, or merely reflecting on his own experience. Interpreted as an attempt to draw the consequences from a set of principles, the *Discours* would instantly have been felt to be over half a century out of date on the day it was pronounced, an inadequate attempt to systematize Boileau's rhetorical principles. But it is a lot more than that. It explains how from a basis of scientific exposition Buffon could find himself synthesizing information about the universe in the most imaginatively exciting ways, how a certain type of poetic imagination could function for Michelet, for instance, or Teilhard de Chardin, or Lévi-Strauss, stimulated to produce lyrical flights only on the basis of the mental effort entailed in mastering large amounts of exact factual material. In the famous phrase, generally misquoted and almost always misunderstood, "Le style, c'est de l'homme même," Buffon is saying that the style proceeds from the quality of the mind that produces it, not that we can infer the character of the writer from the style used.

Buffon attacks mere ornamentation and an unnecessarily technical vocabulary and is obviously attracted to an elevated, oratorical tone. The historian and critic Nisard once pointed out that the word "noble" occurred as frequently in the writings of Buffon as "grand" in the writings of Bossuet and "aimable" in those of Fénelon. Parts of the *Epoques de la nature* were written 18 times, until the effect was what Buffon strove for. "Not as

natural as all that!" was what Voltaire said on reading the *Histoire naturelle*. There was more to writing than Buffon is often taken to suggest. The writer himself must have taste and feeling, as well as a plan:

Bien écrire, c'est à la fois bien penser, bien sentir, et bien rendre: c'est avoir en même temps de l'esprit, de l'âme et du goût

(To write well is at the same time to think well, to feel properly, and to express yourself appropriately: it means having at the same time intelligence, sensibility, and taste).

Scientifically, Buffon was cautious. There might, he at first thought, be a very small number of original species from which all the others derived. He still believed in indestructible organic molecules rather than entities whose future development was programmed, and reacted against Linné's categorizations of species. For Buffon, each species had to have been separately created by God, although he later came to allow more variation through climate or feeding habits, reducing the number of separate species and slowly yielding to evidence from the new world. He insisted that classifications were themselves the work not of the creator of species but of the human mind seeking to categorize them. For Buffon the principle of classification is the relationship of particular types of animal to human beings. The wolf and the tiger are savage, and belong to different categories from those of the domesticated dog and cat. Only later did Buffon come to a categorization based on external physical and internal anatomical features. The only real order in the natural world remained for Buffon that imposed by God, and not the categories projected into it by the human mind.

He guessed at the idea of natural selection in zoology before Lamarck and Darwin. His own really important personal contribution to the great compilation, which he ended up by virtually editing on the basis of information supplied to him by his numerous correspondents, had to do with the slowness with which causal chains brought about developments in species, and with geological eras which divide the earth's history into seven epochs.

Buffon's own view altered visibly as he proceeded. His original commitment to the divine creation of each individual species yielded to an increasing emphasis on human happiness as God's goal in creation. Transformist views developed as he came to realize the significance of the relationships between specimens belonging to the same species, but with individual differences found in locations widely distant from one another. In the end, he wondered if there was any permanent, universal order, and he skirted pantheism by appearing to imply that nature itself fulfilled the functions once attributed to God.

PUBLICATIONS

[*Not only are there many editions of the Oeuvres complètes, but there are also many selections and abridgements*]

Collections

Oeuvres complètes, 25 vols., 1774–78
Oeuvres philosophiques, 1954 [with Buffon bibliography]

Science

Histoire naturelle générale et particulière, avec la description du Cabinet du Roi, 44 vols., 1749–1804; translated into English 1775 (6 vols.), 1785 (9 vols.), 1792 (10 vols.), 1831 (4 vols.)
Les Epoques de la nature, 1962

Other

Discours sur le style, 1753

Translations

Hales, Stephen, *La Statique des végétaux et l'analyse de l'air*, 1735
Newton, Isaac, *La Méthode des fluxions et les suites infinies*, 1740

Biographical and critical studies

Dimier, L., *Buffon*, 1919
Roule, L., *Buffon et la description de la nature*, 1924

BUSSY, Roger de RABUTIN, comte de, 1618–1693.

Memorialist, letter-writer, author of pen-sketches.

LIFE

Bussy was proud to be able to trace his family back to his mid-12th-century noble ancestor Mayeul de Rabutin, about his discovery of whom he wrote to his cousin, Mme de Sévigné, who replied with some satisfaction on 22 July 1685. On 14 February 1687, having seen the 1681 second edition of Moreri's *Grand Dictionnaire historique*, she wrote again that Mayeul, from one of the oldest Burgundy families, had been alive in 1147. The Rabutin family had split into the senior line, seigneurs de Chantal, to which Mme de Sévigné belonged, and the junior, the seigneurs de Bussy. Bussy's great-grandfather, Christophe I de Rabutin, was Mme de Sévigné's great-great-grandfather. Bussy's first wife, Gabrielle de Toulongeon, whose mother, Françoise de Rabutin, was a daughter of saint Jeanne-Françoise, Mère de Chantal, founder of the Order of the Visitation, was also a sister of Mme de Sévigné's father. Bussy was therefore doubly connected to Mme de Sévigné, who was to play so great a part in his life and correspondence.

It is a measure of the aristocratic rank which Bussy's family wished to have respected that neither Bussy's father, Léonor, nor his uncle, Hugues, to be grand prior of the knights of Malta from 1645, was willing to sign the marriage contract of Celse-Bénigne de Rabutin, baron de Chantal, with Marie de Coulanges, mother of the future Mme de Sévigné, from a rich family

for whom a Rabutin marriage was a socially desirable aspiration. Bussy's father, Léonor, a noted military leader whose position of mestre de camp Bussy was to take over in 1638, had married Diane de Cugnac, and Bussy was born on 13 April 1618, at Epiry in Burgundy.

Made very young a knight of Malta, Bussy was sent to the Jesuit school at Autun and then to the Paris Collège de Clermont. On 6 August 1633 he was already in charge of a company in his father's regiment. He took part in the Lorraine campaign of 1634, was present at the siege of Lamothe-en-Blaizy, at Neufchâteau in 1635, at the taking of Corbie in 1636, and at Landrecies in 1637. Mestre de camp in place of his father from 12 March 1638, Bussy took part in the years which followed in the campaigns in the north-east during the final years of the Thirty Years War. In 1638, he was presented at court, where his adventures began with a duel in which he killed his adversary and he was forced to flee. It was Henri de Bourbon, prince de Condé, to be succeeded in 1646 by his son Louis, le grand Condé, known before 1646 as the duc d'Enghien, who arranged matters for Bussy.

Bussy led his regiment in the army commanded by Enghien at the sieges of Thionville in 1639 and of Arras in 1640. A series of satirical songs draws attention to the notoriety of his liaisons and duels. In 1641, while he was on garrison duty at Moulins and occupied by his liaison with the comtesse de Busset, members of his regiment were caught up in salt-tax evasion. Bussy was held responsible. His regiment was disbanded, and he himself was sent to the Bastille for five months. He was released in exchange for a fine of 600,000 livres, for which, however, no receipt was ever issued. It is not unlikely that his cousin was in love with him, although it was not until much later that any intimacy crept into their correspondence. It is unlikely that they did not frequent company in which they often met in the year following Bussy's release. Bussy, however, married the wealthy Gabrielle de Toulongeon on 28 April 1643, using her money to buy himself the post of lieutenant in the light cavalry of Enghien.

Bussy's father died on 8 March 1645, and Bussy inherited the post of lieutenant governor of the Nivernais, of which the capital was Nevers. He also became a conseiller d'état. He went back to the front after Nördlingen and was at the siege of Heilbronn in September. In the next year, he was with Enghien in Flanders, distinguished himself at the siege of Mardyck, and was present at the capture of Furnes and Dunkirk. At the end of 1646 his wife died, leaving him three daughters. He served with his former commander, who had now succeeded to the Condé title, in the unsuccessful Catalonian campaign in the summer of 1647 which failed to take the town of Lerida, and in 1648 fought again in Flanders.

Bussy's mother was urging him to remarry, and he was persuaded by a monk of the Order of Mercy, called Père Clément, that a wealthy young widow was deeply attached to him. Tallemant mentions the monk, but was not believed until the editor of Bussy's *Mémoires* found his existence confirmed. The printer had merely erased all mention of him. Marie de Bonneau, born in 1629 into an ennobled family of successful merchants, had married Jean-Jacques de Beauharnais, seigneur de Miramion, on 26 April 1645. He died on 2 November, leaving her a widow at 16, four and a half months pregnant with Marguerite de Beauharnais, born on 7 March 1646, and herself to marry on 22 June 1660, at the age of 14. Her mother was in fact to devote her life to works of piety. Bussy was at Flanders with Condé and returned to bear news of the taking of Ypres in May 1648 to the king. Bussy, who had become sceptical, was again persuaded by a letter he received on 24 May from Père Clément, who posed as Mme de Miramion's confessor and obtained 6,000 livres for his trouble; he was correctly led to believe that Mme de Miramion's family were pressing her to marry another suitable candidate, in fact Louis-François Lefèvre, sieur de Caumartin, a conseiller de parlement who was to become Intendant of Champagne in 1667. Bussy was given to understand that she wanted him to abduct her.

Absurdly in the circumstances, and catastrophically, that is what Bussy did on 7 August 1648, near the Pont Saint-Cloud, having been tipped off by Père Clément that Mme de Miramion would be returning from Mass through the Bois de Boulogne. Tallemant and Bussy do not agree about what happened next, but it is clear that, not privy to what Bussy thought was going on, the lady screamed, that operations were coordinated by Bussy's brother Guy, that Bussy did not hear the screams, and that the unfortunate woman was taken away in a carriage for a 125-kilometre ride to the château de Launay near Sens, owned by Bussy's uncle, the grand prior. Mme de Miramion's mother defended her daughter with a sword she snatched from a retainer and with which she injured someone's arm, and later on took Bussy to law. As soon as Bussy had realized that Mme de Miramion had not wanted him to abduct her, he had had her taken home, and at no point did she actually suffer more than fright, however horrific. There was a court case, and Condé intervened to save Bussy from serious trouble, but Bussy, this time generally thought to have gone too far, had started to store up real trouble for himself.

He had also missed the battle of Lens, but he did accompany Condé in his march on Paris, was present at the battle of Charenton in 1649, and during the Fronde stayed faithful to Condé more out of loyalty than out of conviction. However, when Condé, released from prison, asked Bussy to resign in favour of Condé's favourite, Guitaut, Bussy made his submission to the king, alienating Condé in a way that would not be forgiven. Anne of Austria promoted him maréchal de camp on 19 October 1651, restoring to him the governorship of the Nivernais. Bussy raised a regiment of cavalry and regiment of infantry, defeated Condé, took Montrond for the king, and suppressed the Fronde in the Nivernais, after which he sought out Mazarin at Bouillon and accompanied him back to Paris, having served at the sieges of Château-Porcien and, in January 1653, of Vervins.

Bussy had meanwhile married again in May 1650. His wife was Louise de Rouville. On 31 August 1653 Bussy bought the post of mestre de camp of the royal light cavalry, and went to serve during the siege of Sainte-Menehould under Turenne, with whom he did not get on. At court his liaison with the 35-year-old Mme de Montglas was publicly acknowledged. Her name had previously been linked with at least two other partners and she had been married since 1645. The liaison was to last until Bussy's imprisonment in 1665. On his return to the army, Bussy served with Conti and was promoted lieutenant general on 4 May 1654. That year, with Conti, he apparently composed the *Carte du pays de Braquerie* satirizing the wives of the aristocracy. No doubt picking up the vogue in the first year in which a group of women allowed themselves to be referred to as "précieuses" (q.v.), Bussy himself was one of the first to use the word in the sense it had acquired in 1654 when alluding to Mme

de la Trousse on 17 August, and it occurs in the same sense in the *Carte du pays de Braquerie*.

In the following year Bussy was again with Turenne and achieved glory at Landrecies. He was, however, ambushed at the siege of Valenciennes in 1656, and Turenne had scoffed publicly at Bussy's military exploits, as Mme de Sévigné teased him in a letter of 14 July 1655. Bussy's financial affairs were now plunging him into real difficulties. His regiment had been dissolved, and he had been obliged to sell his office as governor of the Nivernais. To equip himself for the sieges of Cambrai, Saint-Venant, and Mardyck he had had to negotiate with Foucquet, whom he plausibly believed to be in love with his cousin, Mme de Sévigné, about terms for the surrender of his office as mestre de camp.

By 1658 he was desperate, and his relationship with Mme de Sévigné degenerated swiftly when her uncle, the abbé de Coulanges, who advised her about her affairs, made difficulties about a loan to Bussy which he thought might reasonably have come from the legacy of 30,000 livres which Mme de Sévigné, like Bussy, had recently received on the death of her uncle Jacques de Neuchèze, the bishop of Chalon and uncle of Bussy's first wife. Her refusal to lend the money led to a serious break between them. Mme de Montglas finally allowed him to raise 6,000 livres "on her diamonds," and Bussy took part in the battle of the Dunes, where he captured a regiment of infantry. Turenne, frightened of Bussy's tongue, tried to belittle Bussy's exploits in order to make his undeniably caustic comments count for less. Bussy, furious at his cousin, was a little later, perhaps early in 1662, to write her portrait, maliciously pointing to defects in her character, although stopping short of hinting at a liaison to which unfounded rumours had given rise when what were in fact perfectly innocent letters to Foucquet from her were found among Foucquet's private correspondence after his arrest.

It was in 1659 that Bussy was taken by the duc de Nevers to spend the end of Holy Week at the château de Roissy with the duc de Vivonne, whose mother-in-law owned it, with the future cardinal le Camus, the marquis de Vardes, who was Bussy's wife's cousin, and the notorious marquis de Manicamp. They spent Good Friday, Holy Saturday, and part of Easter Sunday there. Bussy almost certainly took part in making pen-sketches of prominent women at court, and probably in obscene parodies of elements of the Holy Week liturgy. There was a scandal anyway, and Bussy, with plenty of enemies, a notoriously sharp tongue, and no powerful protection, was an easy scapegoat. Whatever he had done was magnified by speculation. He was exiled to his estates and allowed back to Paris, but not to court, only in November. Permission to attend court was withheld until October 1660, after he had been present at the ceremonial entry into Paris of the king and queen on 26 August 1660. While he was at Bussy he wrote out and no doubt elaborated some of the portraits he had improvised at Roissy.

It was not until 1662 that Bussy is known to have read out some of the pen-sketches, now stitched together into *L'Histoire amoureuse des Gaules*. He even lent the manuscript for 48 hours to Mme de la Baume. In May 1663 Bussy spent five days at Saint-Fargeau with Mademoiselle, the daughter of Gaston d'Orléans, brother of Louis XIII, who had come back to visit the place where, with her small court, she had been exiled after the Fronde. On his return from Paris, Bussy heard that his portraits had become "assez public (quite public)," but believed Mme de la Baume's insistent denial that she had shown the manuscript to anyone. In August he campaigned again in Lorraine. It was in 1664 that Mme de Sourdis brought Bussy proofs that he had been betrayed by Mme de la Baume, with whom Mme de Sourdis had quarrelled. Bussy was enraged and a scene followed, after which Mme de la Baume became bitterly hostile to Bussy. The king is recorded to have voiced displeasure to Le Tellier about Bussy on account of things he had been saying. That, as we can see now, must have been a reference to what was contained in the *Histoire amoureuse*. Le Tellier reassured Bussy that the king was no doubt alluding to old indiscretions, while François de Beauvillier, comte de Saint-Aignan, Bussy's most stalwart friend, who also had daily access to the king, assured Bussy that the calumnies against him were not believed.

In 1664 Bussy wrote his verse *Maximes d'amour*, which amused the king and his brother, and at the beginning of 1665 the king ratified Bussy's election to the Académie française. His discourse on reception in January was not well thought of. He did not yet know that not much later than the end of January *L'Histoire amoureuse des Gaules* was circulating, although he was able to follow the king on a brief pilgrimage to Chartres two days later. It used to be thought that a signed edition of *L'Histoire amoureuse des Gaules*, printed in Liège, had been published early in 1665, but what then circulated may have been manuscript copies. The oldest extant editions give neither date, place, nor author, although in 1665 one was printed in Liège. The first to carry Bussy's name was apparently not printed until 1666. It also substituted the real names for the fictional ones used in Bussy's autograph manuscript.

On the evening of 26 March 1665 Bussy, aware that trouble was impending, gave his autograph manuscript to Saint-Aignan to show to the king, who kept it for four days. The king then received Bussy, who thought the matter was closed. Next day, however, the king received a letter from a woman complainant, identified by the Venetian ambassador as Mme de la Baume, whom he received for several hours. He was apparently then convinced that Bussy had subsequently added to the text he had been shown. François d'Aubusson, duc de La Feuillade, was enraged by what Bussy had written about him. It appeared that Mme de la Baume had interpolated a number of injurious passages into Bussy's manuscript. It would not have been out of character. Her numerous liaisons were such that her husband had had her imprisoned with a lettre de cachet and, with the connivance of her lover the marquis de Villeroy, she wrote an anonymous letter to Mlle de la Vallière informing her of Louis XIV's liaison with Mme de Monaco. The duc d'Enghien wrote a scathing letter about her in 1665.

On 2 April Condé wrote to the queen of Poland that things did not look good for Bussy, although he had not read Bussy's text, which it was difficult to get hold of. The comtesse de Soissons spoke to the king attacking Bussy, who on 12 April drew up a solemn declaration, to be given by Saint-Aignan to the king, that he had not shown lack of respect to the king, the queen, the queen mother, the king's brother or his wife, or to any persons of the royal blood. None the less Bussy was arrested on 16 April and kept in solitary confinement in the Bastille. What had counted chiefly against him was the hostility of Condé, as well as his poor relations with Turenne, the negotiation conducted with Foucquet, who certainly until about 1657 felt more love than friendship for Mme de Sévigné, and what he had said about the king's mistress, Mlle de la Vallière. At his interrogation of 19 April Bussy was questioned by Le Tardieu, the lieutenant of

police, about any disrespect for Louis XIV and about anything he may have written about Condé. Two letters, one from Marigny and the other from the Venetian ambassador, suggest that it was remarks about Condé that were the real cause of contention, and Guy Patin on 28 April reported that the complaint behind the arrest had come from Condé. Bussy's capitulation to the royal forces in 1651, when at Condé's request he was made to resign his military command to Guitaut, had not pleased Condé and, now that Condé and the king were reconciled, his honour as a prince of the blood involved that of the king himself.

Much remains mysterious, and it seems fairly clear that Bussy was blamed for interpolations, one of which, concerning the legate Chigi and the duchesse de Créquy, could not have been written before July 1664, and for satirical pamphlets in which he had had no hand. The accusations of caustic comments about the comtesse de Soissons and about Madame, the duchesse d'Orléans, are particularly puzzling, since Bussy mentions neither. But there were high-born persons at whose expense Bussy was thought to have exercised his taste for scandal and scurrility, like Henriette d'Angleterre. Louis XIV had indeed himself to be satisfied that Bussy was not the author of any mordant remarks about him, his mother, or his sister-in-law. The accusation of comments about the queen mother appears, on account of the known virtue of her behaviour, incredible to the point of being absurd. Her conduct had never occasioned gossip. A great deal was being pinned on to Bussy because scandalous gossip about those closest to the king had reached such proportions that a perpetrator had to be found or invented, and punished. Bussy had imprudently behaved in such a way as almost to cast himself for the role of sacrificial victim. It is therefore exceedingly unlikely that the text printed at Liège, or any text ever printed, is free from contamination by those wishing to harm him, or merely interested in making more mischief. Bussy never recognized any edition, and we are probably not now reading what Bussy actually wrote.

Bussy defended himself in a long letter of 12 September 1665 to Saint-Aignan. Mme de Montglas dropped him. In December he was made to resign his post as mestre de camp of the light cavalry. In February 1666 Bussy heard of a scurrilous pamphlet about to be published over his name by Foppens of Brussels and succeeded in getting Colbert to set up an investigation which resulted in two arrests. On 16 May he was allowed out of the Bastille to be operated on by Dalancé for a fistula. He remained with Dalancé, where Mme de Sévigné visited him on a number of occasions, calling finally to say goodbye before she left for Brittany with the abbé de Coulanges on 12 August. On 10 August Bussy was authorized to retire to Bussy. He left Paris on 6 September. He was allowed to come back to Paris briefly in 1672 and 1676, and in 1681 was let back definitively. In 1682, allowed to attend the lever du roi, he had the impression that his disgrace had been lifted. When, a week later, he discovered that he was wrong, he went back to Bussy, appearing in Paris again, and briefly at court, in the winter of 1687–88. Apart from two months in the spring of 1690, he spent the rest of his life in Burgundy.

Of Bussy's three daughters by Gabrielle de Toulongeon, Diane-Jacqueline joined the Visitation, and Charlotte became a Benedictine nun. Louise-Françoise caused him much distress after the death of her first husband, the marquis de Coligny. Bussy disapproved of the projected remarriage to La Rivière, whom he considered a fraud and a peasant, and Mme de

Coligny's marriage to him in June 1681 was clandestine. Bussy then abducted his daughter, who had a secret confinement. Bussy's son-in-law took him to court for abduction. The court sent Louise back to La Rivière and Bussy was virtually ruined. On his appearance at the royal court in the winter of 1687–88, Bussy was accorded a pension of 4,000 livres. He had four children by his second marriage, Amé-Nicolas, who succeeded to the title, Roger-Celse, the bishop of Luçon, Marie-Thérèse, who married the marquis de Montataire, and Louise-Françoise-Léonore, who became a Benedictine nun.

Bussy's relationship with Mme de Sévigné was very close from the time when she may have been in love with him, in the early 1640s, to the break in 1658. In 1655, the year after the emergence of the group of aristocratic young women acknowledging the term "précieuses," and two years before she was allowed back to court after her part in the Fronde, Mlle de Montpensier held what we should regard as a house-party at Saint-Fargeau, attended by the comtesse de Maure, Mlle de Vandy, Mme de Montglas, who was Bussy's mistress, Mme de Lavardin, and Mme de Sévigné, with one or two others who stayed more briefly. It was probably from this or some similar party that the idea of putting together a series of portraits derived.

Madeleine de Scudéry, protected by Foucquet, was multiplying recognizable portraits of highly placed individuals in the final volumes of *Clélie*, and Mlle de Montpensier was certainly assembling her famous collection of 59 *Divers portraits*, of which she herself composed 16, by the winter of 1657. The sumptuously bound book appeared in its limited edition at Caen early in 1659, and was quickly followed by the commercial exploitation of the portrait when Barbin and Sercy published a collection of 500 of them in the *Recueil de portraits et éloges en vers et en prose*, whose achevé d'imprimer was 25 January 1659. The portrait of Mme de Sévigné in *Clélie* under the name of Clarinte, princesse d'Erice, was certainly recognized by Costar, Saint-Pavin, Ménage, and Mme de Lafayette, and it is understandable that Bussy should have written a maliciously satirical portrait of his cousin after their quarrel in 1658. He later acknowledged that he had been peevish to take such exception to the refusal of the loan.

There is a series of half a dozen letters between Bussy and his cousin in the early 1640s, and about a dozen from the mid-1650s, and the correspondence picks up again from the mid-1670s. His *Mémoires* show him as a vigorous defender of his cousin's reputation in spite of the quarrel. After it, Mme de Montglas, an old friend of the marquise, negotiated a reconciliation. Bussy promised to destroy his spiteful portrait of the marquise, who quickly found in his support in the matter of her letters to Foucquet a reason for forgiving her cousin. In 1663, when Bussy needed money to get to the siege of Marsal, Mme de Sévigné guaranteed a loan of 2,000 livres, and in 1664 she stayed with him in Burgundy, later recalling, in a letter of 26 July 1668, the pleasant time they spent together. But the portrait had not been effectively removed from Bussy's manuscript, and it duly appeared, to Mme de Sévigné's horror, in the *Histoire amoureuse*. On Bussy's arrest, his cousin had not joined the other women who called at the Bastille to wave to him, but she was the first to visit him after the fistula operation. He had to wait six months for a reply to the letter he wrote on 21 November 1666, after which there was a year's hesitation before the old intimacy took over again, drawing out the best in both correspondents.

In his exile Bussy wrote his *Mémoires* and a large number of letters, as well as a *Histoire en abrégé de Louis le Grand*. He died of a heart attack at Autun on 9 April 1693.

WORKS

The respect accorded by his contemporaries to Bussy contrasts sufficiently with the way his malicious and titillating *Histoire amoureuse des Gaules* has been ignored or disparaged by all but the most recent historians to make it clear that the 17th century in France was less worried by scurrility, providing it was the product of elegant if caustic wit and refined literary judgement, than subsequent critics have been. Bussy, in exile on his estates, still imposed himself as the supreme judge of Parisian literary taste. Contemporaries saw in him a new "arbiter elegantiae (judge of elegance)," playing a role comparable to that of Petronius in late antiquity. Perrault wrote,

> Nous avons parmi nous un auteur de même nature que Pétrone, qui narre avec autant de netteté et plus de politesse que cet arbitre des élégances
>
> (We have amongst us an author of the same sort as Petronius, who narrates with as much clarity as and more polish than that judge of taste).

The elegance and lucidity of Bussy's style were universally acknowledged. Saint-Evremond spoke fulsomely of his "grâce négligée, libre et originale, qu'on ne saurait imiter (free, original, and unaffected grace, impossible to imitate)," although he had come to dislike the author. Bussy had foretold the success of La Bruyère's *Les Caractères* when it first appeared in 1688. In the 1689 fourth edition La Bruyère links Bussy-Rabutin with Bouhours as an example of how to write. The Jesuits, conscious of their lack of any writer of sufficient brilliance, vainly invited Bussy to reply on their behalf to Pascal's *Lettres provinciales*. The *Histoire amoureuse des Gaules* quickly became famous. Samuel Pepys was reading it on 1 May 1666.

It is still apparently necessary to warn the modern reader that Bussy did not set out to shock, or to spread scandal. The literary interest of the *Histoire amoureuse des Gaules* derives from the way it deploys wit and malice to divert Mme de Montglas with an unravelling of the complicated social games being played by members of the court, mostly high-born persons whom they both knew, and whose lives, when the males were not called away to do battle, were spent largely in what amounted to elaborate charades. Bussy is more interested in the underlying spitefulness, vanity, power rivalries, in the motives behind public displays of galanterie, coquettishness or prudery, than in scandal-mongering. He is interested in authentic virtue and restraint, as well as in what drove a Mme d'Olonne from being a prude to becoming an outrageously barefaced purveyor of sexual favours, for which the tariff was a subject of public comment.

A perfectly innocent woman might have several "amants" for each of whom she was perhaps not the unique "maîtresse." The terms implied something more than normal friendship, but almost invariably less than a sexual liaison, generally a form of more or less flirtatious game, in which the chief rules to be respected were those of rank. Bussy wrote frankly and with almost frightening penetration, inferring from individual instances a typology of the court behaviour of his time, and writing what actually is, although Bussy would never have used so pretentious an expression, an inchoate anthropology of the small, privileged, and exclusive group which was the French royal court at the beginning of the second half of the 17th century. He is particularly alert to the psychological motivations, power rivalries, and defensive strategies generated inside the group from which his detached insight, promoting rule-breaking impudence, brought about his exclusion.

The *Histoire amoureuse des Gaules* is invaluable for its sociological history, but it also gives a brilliantly observed and sharply understood depiction of the nature and force of the proprieties, and the patterns of behaviour, licence, and constraint developed within a society whose chief unbreakable rule was still the one Bussy broke, respect for the hierarchy conferred by blood, not by merit. It must be remembered that the whole French court knew about the sexual tastes and changing arrangements of most of its members, and that its most virtuous ladies, like Mme de Sévigné, could have a robust taste for bawdy jokes. Far from emerging as "a man of disagreeable character, an unscrupulous libertine, arrogant, fatuously conceited… caustic and slanderous," in the words actually written in the second half of the 20th century to describe a Bussy at worst pompous, ill-considered, or impetuous, Bussy shows himself discerning of the admirable where it is to be found, and also capable of affection, loyalty, and the energetic pursuit of what he thinks right. Until very recently one of the few critics to understand Bussy was Sainte-Beuve, who wrote a particularly fascinating comparison of the retailing of the behaviour of the great by Bussy, the aristocrat, and Tallemant, the bourgeois. Saint-Simon, who hated Louis XIV, despised Bussy, who vainly toadied to him in an effort to achieve rehabilitation.

Exactly what Bussy was doing can well be illustrated by a comparison between a letter he wrote to Mme de Sévigné while with the army on 7 October 1655, a few weeks after the house-party at Saint-Fargeau, and its satirical adaptation four years later in the portrait included in *L'Histoire amoureuse des Gaules*. Trying successfully to be amiable, Bussy wrote on 7 October 1655,

Je ne pense pas qu'il y ait au monde une personne plus généralement estimée que vous… il n'y a point de femme à votre âge plus aimable ni plus vertueuse que vous. Je connais des princes du sang, des princes étrangers, des grands seigneurs façon de prince, des grands capitaines, des ministres d'Etat, des gentilshommes, des magistrats et des philosophes qui fileraient, si vous les laissiez faire, pour vous. A moins qu'en vouloir à la liberté des cloîtres, vous ne sauriez aller plus loin

(I do not think there is a woman in the world more generally esteemed than you… there is no woman of your age more worthy of love or more virtuous than you. I know princes of the blood, foreign princes, great lords with princely ways, great captains, ministers of state, noblemen, judges and philosophers, who would take fire for you if you let them. Unless you hanker to enslave the cloister also, you can go no further).

After the quarrel, the portrait is malicious, but not bad-tempered.

Avec tant de feu, il n'est pas étrange que le discernement soit médiocre… La gaieté des gens la préoccupe; elle ne jugera pas si l'on entend ce qu'elle dit: la plus grande marque d'esprit qu'on lui peut donner, c'est d'avoir de l'admiration pour elle; elle aime l'encens; elle aime être aimée, et, pour cela, elle sème afin de recueillir; elle donne de la louange pour en recevoir. Elle aime généralement tous les hommes; quelque âge, quelque naissance et quelque mérite qu'ils aient, et de quelque profession qu'ils soient… Entre les hommes elle aime mieux un amant qu'un ami; et, parmi les amants, les gais que les tristes

(With so much fire it is not strange that her [power of] discernment is middling… Amusing people is what she is interested in; she will not worry whether you understand what she is saying: the greatest sign of intelligence you can show her is to admire her; she enjoys adulation; she loves to be loved, and to that end she sows so that she can reap; she gives praise in order to receive it. She likes all men generally, whatever their age, whatever their birth, whatever their merit, and whatever their profession… Among men, she prefers those who court her to those who just offer friendship; and between those who pay court, those who are cheerful to those who are sad).

That is a portrait with hard edges, shrewd, piercing, not kind, even waspish, but certainly true, and not fundamentally unkind. Bussy takes no moral stance, and to see someone as clearly as was necessary to write like that Bussy must have drawn on a foundation of affection, whose existence he communicates. The remarks get sharper. Bussy writes that his cousin's ardour, "at least according to her late husband," was all in her mind. Mme de Sévigné made up for the coldness of her temperament, and Bussy believes that she was physically faithful to her husband.

Je crois que la foi conjugale n'a point été violée: si l'on regarde l'intention c'est une autre chose. Pour en parler franchement, je crois que son mari s'est tiré d'affaire devant les hommes, mais je le tiens un sot devant Dieu. Cette belle, qui veut être à tous les plaisirs, a trouvé un moyen sûr, à ce qu'il lui semble, pour se réjouir sans qu'il en coûte rien à sa réputation: elle s'est faite amie de quatre ou cinq prudes, avec lesquelles elle va en tous les lieux du monde

(I believe that conjugal fidelity was never actually violated: but it is another matter if you look at the intention. To speak openly, I believe her husband's honour was saved before men, but I think she made a fool of him before God. This beautiful woman, who wants to partake of every pleasure, has found a guaranteed way, it seems to me, to enjoy herself without it costing her reputation anything: she has made herself the friend of four or five prudes, with whom she goes all over the place).

The portrait is etched with precision, and the edge of bitterness to which the circumstances of its composition gave rise does not obscure either Bussy's power-driven understanding of his subject or the quasi-anthropological focus of his interest. How do people contrive to appear what at a deeper level they might not want to be, but without conscious hyocrisy?

The interest of Bussy's portraits for Mme de Montglas, for Mme de la Baume and her friends, for the world of the French court, was to point to a particular person known by everyone, analyse not only the performance but also the underlying motivations, comment on the stratagems, and draw generalized anthropological conclusions on the behaviour of those belonging to the select group of persons admitted to the court. Even when Bussy first read from his manuscript, he probably did not anticipate a total final audience extending into three figures. We are not exactly eavesdropping, as we are on Mme de Sévigné's letters to her daughter, parts of which were quite private, but parts of which might have been intended to be communicated to perhaps a dozen, conceivably a score, of her daughter's family and close friends. Bussy did read extracts to a wider audience of intimates on whom he thought he could rely. But he never intended his manuscript to be either copied or published.

The inspiration came consciously from Petronius—much admired by Bussy's early friend, Saint-Evremond—whose *Satiricon* had recently been translated by the captain of Condé's guards, and Bussy may himself have been involved in an abandoned translation of the same work. He explained to Saint-Aignan that his intention had been to write a novel, "une histoire, ou plutôt un roman satirique (a novel, or rather a satirical tale)." His own portraits, part fiction, part observation, part rumour, contain more delicacy of feeling and greater insight than Petronius ever showed, along with the lubricious interest. Bussy unstintingly admires Mlle de Montpensier, for example, and discerns with exact nuances of understanding the difference between good and bad behaviour, and how one can be disguised as the other.

The narration of Mme d'Olonne's scandalous promiscuity revealed nothing that was not generally known. No one deemed likely to see the text when it was written, or even copied, could fail to penetrate the poetic names given to the succession of lovers. Even when the text was printed, those likely to read it would either possess the key to the characters, or could easily find it out. What interests Bussy is the manner and the motive of the behaviour. His account of Angélie's (Mme de Châtillon's) reaction to the declaration of Amédé (duc de Nemours) is too long to be quoted at sufficient length, but it is a small gem in its depiction of Mme de Châtillon's elation, her desire, and her knowledge of her duty to herself, of the rules of the social group constituting the French court, and of her need to uphold her reputation, still at that date more or less intact. The embarrassed result of the clashing constraints is communicated with exactitude and finesse, as is the feeling of Demura (the comtesse de Maure), who intruded by mistake, thought that matters had progressed further than was in fact the case, and tried to withdraw, but whose obvious understanding of the situation was then used by Nemours as a lever to extract Mme de Châtillon's consent.

In a few years' time, Mme de Lafayette would take for granted the focus of interest in Bussy's analysis on the ways in which court society accommodated its rules to its behaviour. *L'Histoire amoureuse des Gaules* is brief, and its effort to divert Mme de Montglas and a few others is probably too obvious for it ever to be placed on the very highest literary level. But it is among the minor masterpieces of the narrative literature of the century. The historical fascination of its anthropology of court conduct is a bonus.

PUBLICATIONS

[*Note: A great deal of material has in the past been falsely or uncertainly attributed to Bussy-Rabutin*]

Collection

Oeuvres meslées de messire Roger de Rabutin, comte de Bussy, 3 vols., 1711

Fiction

Histoire amoureuse des Gaules, 1665; modern editions, 1967; edited by Roger Duchêne, 1993

Other

Discours sur le bon usage des adversités…à ses enfants, 1694
Les mémoires de messire Roger de Rabutin, comte de Bussy, lieutenant-général des armes du roy et mestre de camp général de la cavalerie légère, 2 vols., 1696; modern edition, 2 vols., 1856
Histoire en abrégé de Louis le Grand, 1699
Correspondance, 6 vols., 1858–59
Histoire généalogique de la maison de Rabutin, 1866

Biographical and critical studies

Gailly, Gérard, *Bussy-Rabutin, sa vie, ses oeuvres et ses amies*, 1909
Orieux, J., *Bussy-Rabutin, le libertin galant homme*, 1958
Duchêne, Jacqueline, *Bussy-Rabutin*, 1992

C

CALPRENÈDE: see **LA CALPRÈNEDE**

CALVIN, Jean, 1509–1564.

Theologian and moralist.

LIFE

Strictly, Calvin's name was Cauvin, Latinized into Calvinus and Gallicized back into Calvin. Little is known of his mother, Jeanne Lefranc, except that she had a reputation for piety, and that she died during Calvin's childhood. His father, Gérard, was a minor legal officer at Noyon, on the border between Picardy and the Ile-de-France, and an agent for the collection of taxes. At the same time he held a more important civil post in church service as secretary of the bishopric and the steward of the cathedral chapter. Calvin had an elder brother, Charles, a priest who died excommunicated for heresy in 1537, another brother, Antoine, and a sister, Marie. The family was on terms of close friendship with the bishop, Charles de Hangest, two of whose four nephews later became Calvinists. The two nephews of the bishop whom Calvin knew as a boy became priests.

Calvin was born on 10 July 1509. His father's connections strongly indicated ecclesiastical careers for his sons, and Calvin, whose early schooling was at the Noyon Collège des Capettes, acquired his first benefice in 1521—the year in which he became 12—immediately after being tonsured. The income financed his studies. Six years later, in 1527, Calvin also acquired the parish of Saint-Martin de Martheville. Just 14, Calvin was sent in August 1523 to Paris in the charge of the tutor engaged for the Hangest boys. Calvin went to the Collège de la Marche, where his Latin teacher was Mathurin Cordier, a pedagogical reformer and theoretician and author of a textbook on spoken Latin, who later moved to the Collège de Navarre, then to Nevers and Bordeaux, before becoming what would later be called a Protestant, principal of the colleges at Neuchâtel and then at Lausanne. He died in Geneva where, in 1550, Calvin dedicated to him his commentary on Saint Paul's first epistle to the Thessalonians.

The following year, 1524, Calvin was moved to the Collège de Montaigu, where he remained as a boarder until 1528, when he graduated master of arts. The institution, austerely reformed by Standonck, had been in the charge of Noël Beda from 1504 to 1513, and was under Pierre Tempête from 1514 to 1528. Strict and litigious, Tempête continued to impose Standonck's discipline and the external forms of his spirituality—meditation, examination of conscience, fraternal admonition, spiritual reading, and corporal mortification—without however apparently preserving the spirituality of the devotio moderna which had originally dictated them.

Calvin belonged to the college of fee-paying pupils, still constrained to regularity of religious observance and academic performance, but not to uniform, menial tasks, ascetic practices, or the vow of obedience required from the poor students, all destined for the priesthood. Calvin attended the lecture-commentary classes covering the arts syllabus in the normal way, but had his own, no doubt shared, repetitor at home, as the system demanded. Although Calvin was following only the undergraduate syllabus, that is arts, there is no reason to suppose that he did not share the commitment of the institution to which he belonged to a religious reform based on austerity and a strict code of behaviour.

Montaigu was the college which became the headquarters of the scholastic defenders of traditional observances, as the split in the university grew between the colleges determined at all costs to retain the religious status quo, whatever reforms were needed within it, and those which were more open to the humanist study of the learned languages, allowing access to the original texts of scripture. The colleges determined to preserve the old forms of teaching and strict adherence to traditional forms of scholastic theology included three of the four colleges which only or also taught the graduate discipline of theology, the exception being the Thomist Dominicans at Saint-Jacques. It was the humanist colleges, led by Sainte-Barbe, which chiefly served students from the Iberian peninsula, which were more often open not only to the study of antique literature as well as of Greek language, but also what were conceived of as "Lutheran" religious ideas, which excluded, along with superstitious practices of all sorts, a religious observance dependent on merit, guilt, and the autonomous power in human nature of moral self-determination.

The religious turbulence in the university during the 1520s was considerable, and the suddenness of Calvin's subsequent conversion suggests that he probably conformed as an arts student to the attitudes obtaining at Montaigu. College allegiances were at this date strong, and the ideological differences between Montaigu and Sainte-Barbe were paralleled by robust student battles to tip the sewage in the lane against the wall of the other college by altering the camber of the alley-way between them. Luther's 95 theses had been posted at Wittenberg on 31 October 1517. The dispute, involving an appeal to Leo X, was at first limited to the subject of indulgences, by which the state of the dead was thought to be affected by something other than their moral state at the moment of death. In 1519 Johannes Eck, vice-chancellor of Ingolstadt and canon of Eichstädt, disputed at Leipzig on 27–28 June with Carlstadt about grace and free will and on 4–8 July with Luther on the primacy of the episcopal see of Rome. Both Eck and Luther agreed to submit the disputed propositions to the faculties of Paris, Louvain, and Cologne.

The documents arrived in Paris on 20 January 1520, but the faculty waited for Rome's bull condemning Luther, *Exsurge Domine*, of 15 June 1520, and Luther's excommunication of 3 January 1521, before giving its decision against Luther on 15 April 1521. Only four of the Leipzig propositions submitted to Paris were among the 40 statements of Luther condemned by Rome, and Rome's condemnation had not said which, if any, were heretical. None the less, Beda had become syndic of the Paris theology faculty in the autumn of 1520, and on 3 August 1521 the parlement forbade the reading of Luther's books. From the burning of Luther's books at Louvain and Cologne, Luther's appeal to a General Council on 17 November 1520, and his burning of the bull excommunicating him on 10 December 1520, it is reasonable to speak of a Lutheran schism, although schism actually dated only from the existence of the first Lutheran communities with their own distinctive form of worship.

The terms "reformed" and "reformation" were first used of a rigorist reform of existing Lutheran communities, so that it is difficult to know precisely what is meant when the term "reformation" is used in connection with Luther's own activity. No single identifiable group had any monopoly of reforming activity, and the presence, absence, nature, and intensity of reformatory endeavour has little to do with membership of any particular Christian community. Even the term "Protestant" came too late to be of help to modern historians. It is first attested in French as an adjective in 1546 and as a noun in 1585. The terms, except for "schism" denoting the acknowledged break-off of communion between two communities, and "communion" denoting an acknowledged fellowship of institutional organization and discipline, are too ideologically loaded to be helpful in connection, for instance, with Calvin's biography.

In 1528 Calvin's father, having quarrelled with the cathedral chapter at Noyon and been excommunicated, thought it better for Calvin henceforward to study law, with a view no doubt to non-ecclesiastical office. Since the teaching of civil law—one of the four graduate disciplines, with canon law, medicine, and theology—was still forbidden in Paris, Calvin theoretically had the choice of Bourges, Orléans, Poitiers, and Toulouse. He spent some months, probably the academic year 1528–29, at Orléans, where he learned some Greek from Melchior Wolmar and was taught by Pierre de l'Estoile, who represented his bishop at the anti-Lutheran provincial council of Sens, presided over by the chancellor, Antoine Duprat, in February 1528. For the academic year starting in 1529 Calvin went to Bourges, where he was taught by the celebrated jurist, Andrea Alciati, and joined by Melchior Wolmar, invited to Bourges by the university's new patron, Marguerite d'Angoulême. Calvin's first published work was a preface to a friend's 1531 *Antapologia* on behalf of L'Estoile, who had been attacked by Alciati. It was probably written a year or so before Calvin went to Paris in May 1531 to see it through the press.

In Paris he heard that his father was grievously ill. He died on 26 May, still excommunicated, and Calvin's brother Charles, himself also excommunicated, had to engage in humiliating negotiations for a posthumous absolution and burial in consecrated ground. Calvin now spent some time in Paris, probably after a brief visit to Orléans, moving from one set of private lodgings to a second, before settling at the Collège Fortet. In April 1532 Calvin published at his own expense his commentary on Seneca's *De clementia* which he also edited. That made him short of money. Charles fell behind on the monthly payments he owed Calvin, who was accordingly forced to borrow from his friend Nicolas Cop, and from the author of the *Antapologia*, Nicolas Duchemin, "Amice mi, mea vita carior (my friend, dearer to me than my life)," as he had addressed him in May 1531. In the summer of 1532, Calvin also was unwell. On his recovery, he returned to Orléans, almost certainly for the whole of the academic year 1532–33. On 23 August 1533 he attended a meeting of the canons of Noyon to organize prayers for the cessation of the plague.

The year 1533 was momentous in the religious life of France (see: Marguerite d'Angoulême). Gérard Roussel, who was almoner to Marguerite d'Angoulême, now queen of Navarre, and a former colleague of Lefèvre d'Etaples at Meaux, had already in 1531 been accused of preaching heresy in his Lenten sermons given at Marguerite's invitation and in her presence. He was ordered in future to give advance notice of whatever he intended to say. In 1533 he was invited to preach the Lenten sermons at the Louvre in the presence of Marguerite, and the strongly interior nature of their spirituality, which was widely applauded, drew down further denunciations from members of the faculty. On 12 May Beda had a list of 12 propositions alleged to be held by Roussel which Beda considered suspect of heresy. François I set up a commission and invited the faculty to submit complaints, at which the faculty, calling on the king at Fontainebleau, attempted to withdraw its accusations. Beda was banished from Paris and Roussel confined to Marguerite's household, while the king went to meet the pope in the south.

In early October, students at the Collège de Navarre put on a ribald skit in which a queen was depicted with Mégère, the fury Megaera—a pun on Roussel's name. The queen, according to Calvin, was represented as accepting the gospels from Mégère, reading them, and then, under their influence, abandoning her good habits to persecute the poor and the innocent. Marguerite had the piece suppressed and the college raided. Two of its senior members were detained for examination. The conservative portion of the university was by now bubbling with resentment, and the faculty went so far as to proscribe the second edition of Marguerite's anonymous *Miroir de l'âme pécheresse*. The university's rector, Nicolas Cop, called the faculties together. Excuses were made. Marguerite's book had been banned only because it touched on religion but lacked the ecclesiastical authorization which thereby became necessary. The theologians backed down, and an apology was sent to the king in the name of the university, with a declaration by 58 theologians that they had never read the poem which gave the book its title, and had neither approved nor disapproved of it. On 1 November the rector preached at the solemn opening Mass for the new academic year.

Cop preached not a sermon, but a homily, itself a provocative gesture. That it was the feast of All Saints, with its gospel the passage from Matthew containing the eight beatitudes, played into his hands. He used the Lefèvre translation, whereas Calvin in his early works would continue to use the Vulgate. The congregation did not need to know that parts of the sermon were virtually lifted from Erasmus's *Paraclesis* and from Luther's *Kirchenpostillen* as translated into Latin by Bucer in 1530. It was for long wrongly thought that the sermon was inspired by Calvin, a theory based on the fragment of an extant copy in Calvin's hand, now recognized as having been made subsequent to delivery. The sermon's strongly evangelical tone caused the predictable furore during the course of which, taking with him the university seal, Cop disappeared from the college of Sainte-Barbe and from Paris, to appear again in Basle three months later.

Cop had understandably objected that the complaint against him to parlement usurped the rights of the university. During the weeks after the sermon Calvin, who had been staying at Sainte-Barbe, also fled Paris, as did the acting principal of Sainte-Barbe, Andrea de Gouvea, under whom the college had nurtured humanists while the titular principal, Andrea's uncle Diego de Gouvea, was acting on behalf of the king of Portugal as a peripatetic judge, attempting to extinguish Erasmian thinking from Portuguese domains. Andrea de Gouvea became principal of the Collège de Guyenne at Bordeaux. There were at least some dozens of arrests in Paris, including that of Roussel.

Calvin went to Noyon, back to Paris, where he found his rooms had been searched, to collect his belongings, and on to Poitiers and Angoulême, returning then to Orléans, where he composed the *Psychopannychia* on the immortality of the soul early in 1534. One of the leading anabaptists had been preaching the doctrine of sleep after death. It is quite possible that, if his conversion was as sudden as he was later to say it was, it had not yet occurred on the date of Cop's sermon. In the first autograph letter we possess, written to François Daniel at Orléans on 27 October 1533, Calvin gives the date as "the vigil of Saint Simon," a notation implying acceptance of the veneration of saints which he never used again. He also relates at length the events of the year, giving details of the skit at Navarre. For a period which is unlikely to have exceeded four or five months, Calvin stayed at Claix with a canon of Angoulême, Louis du Tillet. The first reflections leading to his own theological position appear to have been undertaken in relative independence of all but a general idea of Luther's thought, and to have been dominated by evangelical considerations. It seems likely that Calvin visited Lefèvre d'Etaples at Marguerite's court at Nérac in the spring of 1534, and travelled straight from there the 700 kilometres to Noyon, where he resigned his benefices, whether or not that had been the original purpose of his journey. He did not return to Noyon after 1534, but he might briefly have been there also in September.

There are two principal sources for any account of Calvin's conversion, his own preface to his commentary on the Psalms, and the three versions of Bèze's *Vita Calvini*, but the accounts do not entirely tally, and we are left uncertain about Calvin's movements and motivations during the period covering his break with Rome. It was, however, with Du Tillet, after the placards against the Mass had been posted up and down the country on the night of 17–18 October 1534, and royal policy had in consequence turned harshly against religious dissidence, that Calvin travelled via Strasbourg to Basle, where he arrived early in 1535, using the pseudonym of Martin Lucian. He was 25.

The reform of the town's religious life had been prepared by Christoph von Uttenheim, Wolfgang Capito, and Guillaume Farel, and carried through by Oecolampadius, who had died in 1531 after establishing an ecclesiastical discipline independent of the civil power. He had been succeeded by Oswald Myconius, Zwingli's biographer. At Basle were also Viret, Farel, Caroli and several of Calvin's future collaborators: Elie Couraud who was to go to Geneva; Claude de Feray to go to Strasbourg; and Pierre Toussaint at Montbéliard. That June, Erasmus was to return to Basle, to die on 12 July 1536. The dominant influence at Basle was probably still that of Zwingli, who had died in 1531, but Calvin appears now to have derived his principal inspiration from Luther.

Calvin's principal preoccupation at this date seems to have been the establishment of a method for the interpretation of scripture, on which he worked with Simon Grynaeus and which entailed the further study of both Greek and Hebrew. He also frequented Erasmus's disciple Capito, who had translated Erasmus's *De sarcienda ecclesiae concordia* and edited the psalms in Hebrew. Calvin submitted the *Psychopannychia* to him for comment. The first draft of the *Christianae religionis institutio* "totam fere pietatis summam et quicquid est in doctrina salutis cognitu necessarium complectens (containing the complete compendium of piety and the knowledge of whatever doctrine is necessary for salvation)," which cannot have been begun before the end of 1533, was ready by September 1535. The work appeared in March 1536.

Calvin had meanwhile written two prefaces to the Bible of his friend, also probably a relative, Robert Olivétan, in the first of which Calvin for the first time shows hostility to the Roman church. Writing in Latin, he not only defends, no longer at this date very daringly, the vernacular dissemination of scripture, but blames the pope for the substitution of fraudulent practices for scriptural teaching. Calvin still at this date implies the need for the authoritative interpretation of scripture. The second preface, to the New Testament, is in French. Limpid and touching, it uses a capital for the definite article before the word church, with a lower case initial: L'eglise. Calvin no doubt unwittingly claims for himself and the evangelical party continuity with the primitive church of the evangelists. Those who do not accept the gospel, or who refuse to follow it, will be cast out at the final judgement.

The *Institutio* of 1536 makes it possible to pinpoint Calvin's thought, and particularly its emphases and omissions, immediately after his break with Rome, but before he seriously thought in terms of a schismatic community, however authentic he believed its continuity with the primitive church and however far he thought the Roman church had diverged from its primitive character. At this date Calvin is indeed still preoccupied by the need for union. The only humanism he considered important for his evangelicalism concerns the need to know the learned languages in order to understand the self-revelation of Christ through them, and he still lacked any pastoral experience. The *Institutio* would grow from the small Latin handbook of 1535 through the successive Latin editions of 1543, 1550 and 1559, but also through the vernacular editions, translated by Calvin himself, of 1541, 1545, 1551, 1553, 1554, 1557, and 1560, as it took on an increasing catechetical role. Only the long prefatory 1536 letter to the king would be maintained unchanged through all the editions.

In late 1535, however, Calvin has come very near to a position in which he at least no longer finds it necessary to speak of any teaching authority interposed between the text of scripture made accessible to all, and each individual Christian. The need to create new visible forms, institutional, disciplinary, doctrinally authoritative, pastoral and liturgical, had not yet fully impinged on his mind, still concentrated on freeing from its trammels the full revelation of God in scripture.

Sometime before the end of March 1536, Calvin and Du Tillet had left Basle for the court of Renée de France, daughter of Louis XII and duchess of Ferrara, married to Hercule d'Este. They stayed only a fortnight or so before, on Good Friday 14 April, a French evangelical publicly walked out of the chapel immediately before the adoration of the cross. The revelation that the duchess was protecting dissident evangelicals forced Calvin, Du Tillet, and a number of others to quit Ferrara. Calvin left Du Tillet at Basle and, known as the author of the *Institutio*, profited from the edict of Coucy, which allowed the return of exiled schismatics intending to abjure, in order to fetch his brother Antoine from Paris, after giving power to Antoine and Charles to sell the remaining family holdings in Picardy. Calvin was returning with his brother, Antoine, and sister, Marie, to Strasbourg, but was diverted by military action from the direct road, and had to travel through Geneva, where he intended to spend a night.

Geneva's bishops had earlier in the century tried to maintain such authority as had not already been ceded to the Conseil général and the Petit Conseil of the city by seeking the protection of the dukes of Savoy. An anti-episcopal movement was therefore necessarily also part of a struggle for political independence. By 1536, the two councils were in fact exercising ecclesiastical as well as civil jurisdiction. Farel had been allowed by the civil authority to occupy churches, replace the Mass, break statues, and abolish the sacramental system in the interest of promoting an evangelical cult, while the presence at Geneva of allies from Berne assured him of both an army and a congregation. Recalcitrant priests faced prison. Farel begged Calvin to stay and help him to carry through the reorganization he envisaged in Geneva.

On 19 May the Petit Conseil had decided to convoke the Grand Conseil to ask whether each member wanted to live "selon la nouvelle reformation de la foy (according to the new reformation of the faith)." The word "reformation" was used of an evangelical movement which was more radical than that obtaining in the already schismatic Lutheran communions. The General Council abolished "Masses, images, idols and other papal abuses." On 24 July, a fortnight before Calvin's arrival, it had exiled a citizen who had been unwilling to accept the new dispensation. Calvin was later, in the 1564 *Discours d'adieu aux ministres*, to recollect that, on his arrival, there were no ecclesiastical structures:

> Il n'y avoit quasi rien. On preschoit et puis c'est tout. On cherchoit bien les idoles, et les brusloit-on, mais il n'y avoit aucune reformation. Tout estoit en tumulte

(There was almost nothing. There was preaching and that was all. Idols were being sought out and burnt, but there was no reformation. Everything was in tumult).

In that passage, Calvin clearly regarded the lack of institutionalized ecclesiastical structures as a defect which he had had later to remedy. He was also in 1564 using the word "reformation" to mean something like "forming again but differently." That is also the sense in which it is used in the phrases "serment de la Refformation (oath of the Reformation)" and "tielle [telle] Refformation jurer (to adhere by oath to that Reformation)" in the registers of the Genevan councils for 12 November 1537. It is the meaning the word has in all the titles of Calvin's publications.

It is essential to remember the word's real meaning, as used by Calvin, since the historical reality of his career and activity has been obscured ever since the 16th century by the adulteration of the significance of so many important words, forced to accommodate subsequent loadings of ideological freight. Only lexicographical precision in the narrative of events can reveal what actually took place, and what were its causes and consequences. The use of the term reformation, for instance, of any movement to put right late medieval ecclesiastical corruption or clerical abuse, has not only obscured what those responsible for such movements intended to achieve, did in fact achieve, and how they achieved it, but it has also simply removed the term's specific reference to a whole series of separate and distinct manifestations of religious behaviour and of reconstituted ecclesiastical structures dating from the mid-1530s, lumping them all together in a way which telescopes dates and distorts the social, moral, and religious realities.

Given the difference of date and nature between the various religious communities in Germany and Switzerland, and then all over northern Europe, it seems, for instance, clear that we should think in terms of a plurality of schisms. Of the communities which broke off from Rome some were structural re-formations of others, while by no means all were in communion with one another. Since it is now plainly impossible to exclude the Lutheran congregations from the umbrella of "The Reformation," but also plainly misleading to include them within what Calvin understood by it, the term has actually become useless as a historical category. The best word to describe the collectivity of all of the Christian communities which, for perceptibly different reasons, broke with Rome, may well be Protestant, but that word had not in 1536 yet been invented in French, and would today no doubt be repudiated by those communions whose doctrine has stayed nearest to Rome's.

Calvin agreed to stay in Geneva not as a minister or a preacher, but as a "sacrarum literarum doctor (teacher of sacred letters)." After a brief visit to Basle, he began to lecture on the Pauline epistles in Geneva in September 1536. Early in October his ability to quote from the Fathers won him a considerable victory in a series of discussions at Lausanne, and by the end of 1536 he had accepted appointment as a preacher. It was a civil promotion rather than a religious consecration, and led towards Calvin's collaboration in drawing up for the local community at Geneva a code of ecclesiastical discipline, a profession of faith, and a catechism. He also wrote two important epistles, the *De christiani hominis officio in sacerdotiis papalis ecclesiae vel administrandis vel abiiciendis* (*On the Christian's duty in administering or rejecting the priesthoods of the papal church*), probably with Gérard Roussel, now bishop of Oléron, in mind, and the *De fugiendis impiorum illicitis sacris, et puritate christianae religionis observanda* (*On fleeing the unlawful rites of the impious, and on observing the purity of the Christian religion*).

From now on Calvin's course was charted. The cult was to be organized round the celebration of the Lord's supper, for admission to which rigorous doctrinal orthodoxy was to be imposed, with provision for excommunication, although the institutional structures and the doctrinal orthodoxy were both to evolve before Calvin's death. After the difficulties created for the evangelicals in the wake of the placards of October 1534, Pierre Caroli had come to Switzerland and become principal pastor in Lausanne, where his importance soon eclipsed that of Viret. Calvin wrote to him reprehending him for recommending prayers for the dead, but Caroli replied in February 1537 accusing Calvin, Farel, and Viret of Arianism, that is of subordinating the second person of the Trinity to the Father. It was for his denial of the distinction of persons in God, symptomatic of a general drift towards deism which occurred at one extreme edge of the schismatic reform, that Calvin was eventually to have the Spanish doctor Michel Servet burnt. Servet's non-Trinitarian beliefs had already caused scandal when published in the 1531 *De Trinitatis erroribus* and the 1532 *Dialogues sur la Trinité* but, although Calvin was sensitive to accusations of unorthodoxy in Trinitarian theology, he refused to acknowledge the authoritative nature of the Athanasian Creed, in liturgical use for at least a millennium, although not attested in the first two or three centuries.

The dispute with Caroli was referred to Berne, where there was equal mistrust of both the Geneva and the Lausanne views, and some feeling that Calvin was arrogating too important a function to himself. Calvin moved towards the definition of evangelical doctrine by means of regional synods, but was not able to have accepted an ecclesiastical jurisdiction independent of the civil power. However, at a conference at Berne on 22–23 September 1537 Capito, Bucer, Myconius, Grynaeus, Farel, Viret, and Calvin agreed on both Eucharistic and Trinitarian theology, being nearer to Luther than to Zwingli on the Eucharist.

Calvin's brother Charles died on 1 October 1537. Parish priest of Roupy, he had been accused of heresy and excommunicated. He refused reconciliation with the Church on his deathbed, and was buried in unconsecrated ground. Du Tillet, himself an ordained priest, was shocked at the role Calvin had assumed of celebrant, pastor, and teacher, and left Calvin early in 1538 first for Bucer's Strasbourg and then for France, to be reconciled with the Catholic Church. The Genevan elections of 3 February 1538 gave power to those who were politically dependent on Berne and were hostile to Farel and Calvin. The council's syndics held an inquiry into one of Calvin's sermons, reprimanded him for interfering in their affairs, and imposed the Bernese ritual, with baptismal fonts, bread made without yeast, and observance of some traditional feasts. Calvin and Farel refused to accept the ritual, abstained from officiating at the Lord's Supper, were forbidden to preach, defied the prohibition on Easter Sunday 21 April 1538, and were exiled.

Calvin, whose letters at this date show some signs of uncertainty and a consciousness that he had made mistakes, went to Basle. He admitted to no more than error, but had at Geneva clearly been regarded both from Berne and by Geneva's own civil authorities as unacceptably brash and arrogant, however sincere. Du Tillet, by writing to suggest that Calvin abstain from further pastoral activity and by offering to support him financially, provoked a stubborn reaction in Calvin, who refused to have "his vocation" disputed. Bucer offered him pastoral responsibility for the French community at Strasbourg, and Calvin took up residence there in September 1538 for what proved to be two years, becoming also a theology lecturer at Sturm's school in January 1539, drawing a salary from the town from 1 May. In August 1540 Calvin married Idelette de Bure, the widow of an anabaptist whom he had converted. Their single child was born in 1542 but died in infancy, and Calvin's wife died in 1549. Farel returned to Neuchâtel on 23 July, remaining there until his death on 13 September 1565.

On 18 March 1539 Cardinal Jacopo Sadoleto, bishop of Carpentras, wrote to the Genevans to try to persuade them to return from their innovations to the Church of tradition. The Petit Conseil sent the letter to Berne, from where the authorities sent it on to Calvin for a reply. His answer of 1 September 1539 contains the ecclesiology which Sadoleto's letter had forced him to elaborate. On 30 January the Petit Conseil ordered it to be printed, and Calvin's enemies began to lose ground in Geneva. New syndics were elected. The three leaders who, with two others, had

ordered the banishment of Calvin and Farel were condemned to death on 5 June, and on 10 June the remaining leader of their party was executed.

In 1539 Calvin published a second Latin edition of the *Institutio* in August and in March 1540 he began his series of scripture commentaries with the *Commentarii in epistolam Pauli ad Romanos*, insisting on the doctrine of predestination. In 1540 he attended the colloquy at Hagenau (12 June to 16 July) and in 1541 the colloquies at Worms (28 October 1540–18 January 1541) and Ratisbon (now Regensburg, 27 April–22 May 1541), where he encouraged Melanchthon to refuse any compromise. Late in October 1540 the Genevan councils had begged Calvin to return. He eventually consented, entering Geneva on 13 September 1541, resolved on imposing the ecclesiastical discipline on which he had become determined. Ministers were appointed by the Grand Conseil from the ranks of the laity, to which they could be forced to return. They owed obedience to a consistory of six elected ministers and 12 laypeople elected by the council and the magistrates. The consistory claimed the right of excommunication, not at first formally conceded to it, and of denunciation to the councils, which could imprison. The consistory, however, was intended and inclined to usurp powers of civil jurisdiction to itself. Lip service at least was paid to scripture as an absolute norm, but with a leader as imperious as Calvin the result was virtually an attempt at a theocracy with a strong emphasis on the education of the population.

Calvin was authoritarian, believed himself endowed with a divine mission, and was not tactful with the older Swiss who retained a nostalgia for their Catholic observances and resented the power over them taken by the young Frenchman. There were also those who found Calvin's puritanism stifling. His position was sometimes threatened. Together with his theological works, Calvin wrote in 1543 against the cult of relics; in 1544 against the anabaptists and the Nicodemites who, having once tasted the gospel message, had turned back; in 1545 against the spiritual libertines; in 1549 against astrology; and in 1550 the *Des scandales*.

Calvin had Sébastien Castellio dismissed on 12 June 1544 as rector of the school for denying the canonicity of the *Song of Songs*. On 8 April 1546 a member of the Petit Conseil was made to do penance for insulting Calvin, and on 26 July 1547, Calvin had the free-thinker Jacques Gruet tried and beheaded. A month earlier he had placed on Calvin's pulpit a poster threatening him. Calvin's own credibility was threatened by the Erasmian Jérôme Hermès Bolsec, exiled on 23 December 1551. An influx of French exiles amounting to as many as 10% of the population of 13,000 strengthened Calvin's position, although the newcomers were denied citizenship. The party dependent on Bernese support was led by the captain-general Ami Perrin, whose wife had been imprisoned for dancing and for scolding. Perrin won a sweeping victory at the polls on 5 February 1553, but on 27 October that year, Calvin had Servet put to death, although he was against burning alive as the method of execution.

Open and terminal hostilities between Calvin and Servet had been continuing since 1531. The two had corresponded between 1539 and 1541 and again in 1546 and 1547, and Servet's 1553 *Christianismi Restitutio* had been a reply to Calvin's *Institutio*. Calvin denounced Servet to the inquisition at Vienne, on the Rhône, and Servet fled to what he had been led to believe would be the safety of Geneva, although it is possible that he knew what sort of battle was in store, and he may have expected to be victorious over Calvin. He was arrested on 13 August 1553 and burnt alive on 28 October. The Grand Conseil had been forced to allow the consistory to open proceedings for heresy. The churches of Zurich, Basle, and Strasbourg approved the condemnation, although Basle objected to the death penalty. The Grand Conseil established the mode of death. Calvin defended the right to execute heretics, and was controverted by Castellio, although supported by Théodore de Bèze, his successor, who had come to Geneva in 1548. Servet's execution left Calvin's position stronger.

For the last ten years of his life Calvin consolidated his position. In 1555 the formal right of excommunication was conceded to the consistory. The military victory of Saint-Quentin on 10 August 1557 united Berne and Geneva against Savoy, so depriving Perrin's followers of Bernese support, and from 4 February 1554 Calvin could count on the support at first of three and then of all four syndics. Calvin, and Perrin and his followers, strengthened their positions by banishments, executions, and enfranchisements. Between 1549 and 1559 over 5,000 new citizens were admitted. The university was founded in 1559 with Bèze as rector. By Calvin's death, there were 2,000 students. He gave a solemn farewell to his ministers on 28 April 1564, and died four weeks later, on 27 May.

WORKS

Calvin did not write in the imaginative genres and, while it is no doubt true that he helped to fashion the French language into a rhetorical tool for persuasion by argument, he also frequently employed other forms of rhetoric, notably by seeking to achieve pathos for the purposes of edification. His choice of language, Latin or French, is unpredictable, and sometimes surprising, although never quite arbitrary. In spite of what has so often been written about Calvin's French style, and his use of language for expository purposes, it is not at all clear that he did not write more effectively in Latin than in French. The polished cadences of his prose are more effortless and better balanced in his renaissance Latin than they are in an as yet less fully developed French.

However, for obvious reasons, attention here will be concentrated on his French writing. It is, however, also necessary first of all to state that in the present context it is the content of Calvin's thought rather than the style of its expression which established the cultural context in which later writers must be understood. Some idea must be given of what Calvin thought, and what were the often dangerous signs of sympathy for his positions, which might make later writers, and even readers of his works suspect to the authorities, and how, for instance, Calvinist or Huguenot sympathies differed from an openness to Lutheran, Erasmian humanist, or merely evangelical values. The modern reader needs to be alert to coded expressions of sympathy and hostility to Calvin's positions of which 16th-century readers were immediately aware, and needs therefore to know what those positions were.

Calvin's religious views are also important in the present context, in whatever language he expressed them, because for almost half a century they determined a whole range of poetic, dramatic, and polemical literary styles. "Calvinist" writing, not necessarily denoting doctrinal orthodoxy, strove for edifying effect, often echoed the rhetorical devices and prose rhythms of scripture, and sought by the intensification of emotion at depic-

tions of the steadfastness of saints, the courage of martyrs, or the merciful workings of providence to stimulate piety, to edify, and to encourage.

It leant heavily on pathos, but was simple, direct, and emotional, without decoration or obvious rhetorical ornamentation. It could lead both to a delicate awareness of metaphysical fragility, and to baroque distortion of imagery in the interest of intensifying emotional power. With such magnificent exceptions as d'Aubigné, the Calvinist literary aesthetic produced few masterpieces, mostly because a striving for intensity of edification conflicted with the interrogatory element on which works of the imagination must in the end rely. De la Taille's remarks on Bèze's merely edifying *Abraham sacrifiant*, devoid of conflict, make clear the reasons for the virtual impossibility of great literature which is also programmatically Calvinist, but no student of 16th-century French literature can afford to be unaware of the existence of a Calvinist literary aesthetic.

Calvin's early French style often seeks to register its emotional impact by accumulating words and asking rhetorical questions. In the second preface to Olivétan's Bible, intended to preface the New Testament, he answers Saint Paul's question, "Who will separate us from the love of Christ?":

Seront ce iniures, maledictions, opprobres, privations des honneurs mondains? Mais nous sçavons que.... Seront ce banissemens, proscriptions, privations de biens et richesses? Mais nous sçavons que.... Seront ce afflictions, prisons, tortures, tormentz? Mais nous cognoissons par l'exemple de Jesus Christ que c'est le chemin pour parvenir en gloire. Sera ce finalement la mort? Mais elle ne nous oste pas la vie qui est à souhaicter

(Will it be injuries, curses, insults, deprivations of worldly honours? But we know that.... Will it be banishments, proscriptions, privations of possessions and riches? But we know that....Will it be afflictions, prisons, tortures, and torments? But we know from the example of Jesus Christ that that is the route to arrive at glory. Is it finally death? But that does not take away the life which is to be desired).

Accumulations of words, rhetorical questions, crescendo, parallel, antithesis, and balance here produce an effective but uncomplicated emotional response, powerful because in 1535 even this modest level of rhetorical sophistication in French prose was new and forceful. Calvin's polemical prose was often vituperative, bitter with sarcasm and contempt, as in his Latin preface to the 1534 *Psychopannychia*. Here, in spite of the elegant, balanced Latin he had been brought up to write, the emotion sweeps Calvin into the sort of small lists of words and phrases he was using in French. There is an instance in the prefatory letter of the *Institutio* to François I where Calvin has six successive clauses starting "alii (some...others)." The styles appropriate to the two languages visibly contaminate one another.

The first edition of the *Christianae religionis institutio* of 1536 was a Latin primer of six chapters, with a preface addressed to François I. The 1539 edition was better ordered and almost three times as long. By 1559 it had four books divided into 80 chapters. Much of the thought it contained had been developed under the stimulus of particular constraints, notably the need to provide Geneva with what Calvin regarded as a satisfactory balance of civil and ecclesiastical authority, and this elaboration of doctrine in response to the haphazard incidence of practical problems to be resolved obscures any organic unity informing the reactions to individual stimuli. The probability is that, convinced only of the need to strip Christianity of all but its scriptural origins, and to reduce its values and norms to those of the New Testament, Calvin turned to Luther when faced with the need to elaborate theological principles, fastening on the grace alone, scripture alone, and Christ crucified alone of the earlier German theologian.

Calvin's scriptural commentaries, no longer capable of being informed by a living tradition of interpretation, are penetrated from the beginning by the theological principles Calvin brought to them, and read into them. There is only an appearance of exegetical rigour camouflaging a dogmatic tenacity which could only have been developed from the first generation of schismatic reformers. It notably concerned the corruption of human nature, the freedom of the Christian contrasted with the tyranny of the papacy, and the concept of the ministry not as a state but as an activity. Grace and faith are events, not states, in Calvin's first *Institution*, which is virtually without any properly elaborated notion of an institutionally structured community at all. It is a young man's book, sure only about what is wrong, and constructed round a handful of obsessive ideas which would later be blended together, and merged with others, and with the institutional realities. Much more than tyrannical popes, Calvin ended up attempting to legislate the citizens of Geneva into virtue. Puritanism, excessively severe penalties, cavalier attitudes to procedure, and profligate use of the death penalty have to be weighed against the university, the literacy level, and the level of care for the elderly and the sick in the Geneva of Calvin's last years.

The famous emphasis on the doctrine of predestination, apparently deduced with rigour in 1540 from the text of *Romans*, is now generally acknowledged to have come from Bucer, for whom Calvin was working at Strasbourg at the time. From Bucer, too, came the idea of structuring the community into pastors, teachers, elders, and deacons. The insistence on God's predestinatory decree illustrates, however, a further aspect of Calvin's spirituality. Like Luther, he needed to take the intolerable anxiety about salvation away from the individual Christian. One way in which this was done by both Luther and Calvin was through a shift in the emphasis from individual experience to a notion of the world, and everything that was or that occurred within it, as there solely as a manifestation of God's glory, not for the fulfilment of the human inhabitants of the earth. The universe is God-centred, and Christian spirituality theocentric, properly more concerned with the glory of God than, as in late medieval Catholicism, with the salvation of the soul.

Calvin's approach to scripture was in some respects critical. He affirmed against Castellio the canonicity of the *Song of Songs*, but doubted that of *II Peter, James*, and *Jude*. At least in principle he gave equal weight to both testaments, and saw Christ revealed in each, reversing Luther's tendency to emphasize the contrast between old and new laws. On the other hand, rather than elaborate a structured dogmatic theology, Calvin systematically confronts Christians with the fundamental antinomies, like immanence and transcendance, the need for a strong church combined with Christian liberty, the biblical text as the unique source of spiritual experience for the individual,

but also the need for ritual preaching even to those who could read for themselves.

The difficulty lies in what is read into the Bible, how, for instance, it was possible not to see the differences of ethic between the two testaments, and indeed between the documents in each. For Calvin, although no one can be certain of final perseverance, sinners could be converted and the just could fall away, there was an interior assurance dependent on a consciousness of a God-fearing life, a religious demeanour, and what is reducible to a feeling of faith in Christ and fellowship with him, sustained by the outer appurtenances of church-going. The theological antinomies preclude systematization but, if they make recourse to the Bible inevitable as the unique principle of Christian life, they also demanded the authenticating movement of the Holy Spirit. The combination of the Spirit and the word was ultimately the unique source mediating Christian experience. Calvin, frightened of anabaptist rationalism in thought, and spiritual exaltation, and also firmly moral in his outlook, did not regard mystical experience with any favour at all, preferring to trust the corporate moral judgement of the faithful for whose values he speedily became responsible.

Historically, Calvin's letters, as well as many administrative documents, are naturally important for an understanding of the work of what was probably the greatest exegete as well as the greatest dogmatic theologian of the schismatic communities. We have a very good idea of the personality, the manner of preaching, and the activity of the ecclesiastical administrator and politician, more flexible than has sometimes been allowed. For instance, Calvin was not wholly closed to the idea of an episcopacy. Our concern, however, once Calvin's theological position has been indicated, and its effect on Huguenot literary styles mentioned, must primarily be with Calvin as a literary author, and with the signposts which made "Calvinist" attitudes suspect.

The literary styles, even in French, blend into one another as Calvin is intimate, or systematic, or business-like, or sarcastic, or denunciatory. If, of the French works, the pedagogical writings, the forceful sermons, and formal scriptural commentaries are left on one side, we are left principally with the great French *Institution* and a handful of much shorter dogmatic treatises, a series of more intimate documents, including the correspondence, and the French treatises on relics, the "libertins spirituels" or free-thinkers, on the anabaptists, the Nicodemites, astrology, and benefices, and the *Des Scandales*. Calvin's style of polemical writing includes but is not exhausted by invective.

It is, for instance, quite clear that Calvin considers the use, exhibition, and veneration of relics as superstitious and worse. The method he chooses to attack the practice is mockery. The 1543 *Traité des reliques* is sub-titled

ou avertissement très utile du grand profit qui reviendrait à la Chrétienté s'il se faisait inventaire de tous les corps saints et reliques qui sont tant en Italie qu'en France, Allemagne, Espagne et autres royaumes et pays

(or most useful announcement of the great profit to be obtained by Christianity if an inventory were made of all the holy bodies and relics which there are, in Italy as in France, Germany, Spain, and other kingdoms and countries).

The straight-faced text still reads amusingly four and a half centuries later. Saint Augustine warned against forged saints' bones, but things in the world have got worse since then, and the situation in Calvin's day merited, he thought, looking into. There is a serious point:

> …le premier vice, et comme la racine du mal, a été, qu'au lieu de chercher Jésus-Christ en sa parole, en ses sacrements et en ses grâces spirituelles, le monde, selon sa coutume, s'est amusé à ses robes, chemises et drapeaux; et en ce faisant a laissé le principal pour suivre l'accessoire. Semblablement a-t-il fait des apôtres, martyrs et autres saints. Car au lieu de méditer leur vie, pour suivre leur exemple, il a mis toute son étude à contempler et tenir comme en trésor leurs os, chemises-ceintures, bonnets, et semblables fatras

> (the first vice, and the root, so to speak, of all the others, was that, instead of seeking Jesus Christ in his word, his sacraments, and his spiritual graces, the world, as is its custom, wasted its time on his robes, shirts, and sheets. In doing that it left aside the substance to follow what was accessory. It has done the same thing with the apostles, martyrs, and other saints. Instead of meditating on their lives in order to follow their example, it has devoted all its energy to contemplating and hoarding like treasure their bones, girdles, caps, and other bits and pieces).

After a few pages of discussion, Calvin announces that he is leaving behind theological principles to devote himself to the question of forgeries, about which he is very funny. If he had a list of relics, he claimed, he could demonstrate that each apostle had had at least four bodies, and each saint at least two or three; he goes on to give examples of legs which came not from saints but from stags. He would only need inventories from ten or a dozen towns. He ponders whether two slippers from the same apostle in different towns do not make a pair, how the Magdalen's head got to Marseilles, or Jesus's foreskin, removed at the circumcision mentioned in Luke's gospel, got to an abbey in the diocese of Poitiers. One wonders if Calvin had not been reading Erasmus. The table used at the Last Supper is at Rome, there is some of the left-over bread at San Salvador, and the knife used to cut the Paschal lamb is at Trier. The plate the lamb was on is in Rome, Genoa, and Arles, and the cloth with which Jesus dried the feet of the apostles after washing them is in Rome, Aix and elsewhere. Calvin's turn of phrase is undeniably witty.

The treatise against astrology of 1549 shares another attitude with Erasmus and Lefèvre d'Etaples, although for different reasons. They thought divination compromised free will, in which Calvin of course did not believe. Horoscopes are "amuse-fous (trivialities for fools)," though Calvin is conscious that they were taken seriously. For him, astrology is superstitious, and conflicts with true devotion. The true astrology is

> la connoissance de l'ordre naturel et disposition que Dieu a mise aux étoiles et planètes, pour juger de leur office, propriété et vertu, et réduire le tout à son usage

> (the knowledge of the natural order and disposition which God has given to the stars and planets, to judge their func-

tion, characteristics, and properties, and to accommodate them all to one's use).

There is, however, in this treatise a notable affirmation, whose most obvious parallel is to be found in Rabelais, with whom by this date Calvin was ready to exchange insults. Calvin declares that his own age has seen the "resurrection," and "restoration" of liberal arts as well as of theology. By 1549 the metaphor of rebirth had been used often enough, and Calvin's career had started as a humanist with the edition of Seneca. It is none the less important to notice his continued commitment to classical humanism implied in this passage of 1549:

> Quand Dieu ne nous auroit révélé de notre temps la pureté de son Evangile, toutefois, vu qu'il a ressuscité les sciences humaines, qui sont propres et utiles à la conduite de notre vie, et, en servant à notre utilité, peuvent aussi servir à sa gloire, encore auroit-il juste raison de punir l'ingratitude de ceux qui…appètent…de voltiger en l'air. Maintenant, puisqu'il nous a élargi tous les deux, c'est qu'il nous a remis les arts et les sciences en leur entier, et surtout nous a restitué la pure connoissance de sa doctrine céleste, pour nous mener jusqu'à lui…s'il advient qu'aucuns, au lieu d'en faire leur profit, aiment mieux de vaguer à travers champs que de se tenir entre les bornes, ne méritent-ils pas d'être châtiez au double?

> (Even if God had not revealed in our time the purity of his gospel, none the less, since he has resurrected the liberal arts, which are suited and useful to the conduct of our life and, by serving our purposes, can also serve his glory, he would have good cause to punish the ingratitude of those who…desire…to fly in the air. Now, since he has extended both, that is, he has given us back the arts and sciences in their fullness, and above all has restored the pure knowledge of his heavenly doctrine to lead us to him…if it should happen that some, instead of profiting from it, prefer to wander across fields rather than to keep to the pathways, do they not deserve to be doubly punished?).

The renaissance confidence is clear. Calvin links the commonplace that classical letters have been restored after an intervening period of decay with his own view that the Church has similarly decayed, and been restored through the exegetical work of his own era. All that is missing is a logical connection between the resurrected liberal arts and the restored theology which the evangelical humanists had felt for, and are still sometimes considered to have found.

The last French edition of the *Institution de la religion chrétienne* supervised by Calvin was published by Crespin at Geneva in 1560. The first French edition had been a translation of the 1539 Latin version and had been published in 1541 at Strasbourg. Although François I had died in 1547, the prefatory epistle to him is still there, dated 1535, the year prior to the first Latin edition, but now naturally in French. The lengthy text is followed by a summary in alphabetical order of subjects, giving references to the main text. What is most striking about the work is its low emotional key. Calvin argues with immense sophistication from a vast range of scriptural, patristic, and other authorities, and produces a masterpiece of technical theological writing. He appears to think that he has solved the notoriously difficult problems of free will, which he denies, and predestination, which he accepts, although, in spite of apparent thoroughness and rigour of argument, he comes nowhere near touching the heart of the problems he enunciates.

Book I, chapter xv is split into eight ample paragraphs devoted to man's creation in the image of God. Adam sinned because "la constance de perseverer ne luy estoit pas donnée (the constancy to persevere was not given to him)," but

de plaider precisement contre Dieu et le controller, comme s'il eust esté tenu de douer l'homme de telle vertu, cela est plus que desraisonnable, veu qu'il pouvoit lui donner tant peu qu'il lui eust pleu. Or quant à ce que Dieu ne l'a soutenu en la vertu de perseverance, cela est caché en son conseil estroit, et nostre devoir est de ne rien savoir qu'en sobriété

(to make a precise accusation against God and to examine him, as if he had been obliged to endow human beings with a particular virtue, is worse than unreasonable, since he could give human nature as little as he pleased. And as for the fact that God did not maintain Adam in the virtue of perseverance, that is hidden in his own secret counsel, and our duty is to know nothing except in a modest degree).

Calvin gives two references to Augustine, whose text he misuses, and must have thought that he had produced a solution to the big question about how evil could enter the universe, which he patently had not.

Chapter ii of Book II, "Que l'homme est maintenant despouillé de Franc-arbitre, et miserablement assujetty à tout mal (that the human race is now deprived of free will, and wretchedly subjected to all evil)," has 27 paragraphs and gives a brief philosophical conspectus, pointing out that the Greeks had no word for free choice, but picking on Origen's pinpointing the power to choose good or evil as the essence of free will. There follows a catena of references to Augustine, Bernard, Anselm, the Lombard, the scholastics, and Aquinas, followed by an analysis which does go beyond the standard manuals, but shows a mind much less acute, for instance, than that of Scotus. Calvin once more quotes Augustine who, here again, is being misused to support a view he did not hold, and Calvin returns to Saint Paul showing, to his own evident satisfaction, that a human aspiration to virtue, and freedom to choose, has to be a consequence of regeneration.

The principal treatment of predestination is in Book III, chapters xxi–xxiv. The heart of the matter comes in III, xxiii, 11.

Nous confessons l'offense estre universelle: mais nous disons que la misericorde de Dieu subvient à d'aucuns. Qu'elle subvienne donc à tous disent-ils. Mais nous repliquons, que c'est bien raison qu'il se monstre aussi juste Juge en punissant. Quand ils ne veulent endurer cela, ne s'efforcent-ils point d'oster à Dieu la faculté de faire misericorde: ou bien de luy permettre seulement à telle condition qu'il se demette de faire jugement?

(We admit that the offence is universal: but we say that God comes to the help of some with his mercy. Let mercy then, they say, be given to all. But, we reply, it is quite proper that he should show himself such a just judge by

punishing. When they will not accept that, are they not trying to deprive God of the power to be merciful, or allowing it to him only if he abdicates the power to judge?).

The only answer is that God's glory demands the condemnation to eternal torment of the majority of the human race.

More moving undoubtedly is Calvin's adieu to the pastors a month before his death.

Quant à ma doctrine, j'ay enseigné fidellement, et Dieu m'a faict la grâce d'escrire ce que j'ay faict le plus fidellement qu'il m'a esté possible, et n'ay pas corrompu un seul passage de l'Escriture, ne destourné à mon escient…Je n'ay escrit aucune chose par haine à l'encontre d'aucun, mais tousjours ay proposé fidellement ce que j'ay estimé estre pour la gloire de Dieu

(As for my doctrine, I have taught faithfully, and God has given me the grace to write what I have as faithfully as I could, and I have not altered a single passage of scripture, or misused one knowingly… I have written nothing out of hatred against anyone, but have always faithfully put forward what I thought was for the glory of God).

PUBLICATIONS

Collections

Opuscula omnia, 1552
Recueil des opuscules, 1566
Opera omnia, 9 vols., 1671
Johannis Calvini opera quae supersunt omnia (Corpus Reformatorum XXIX–LXXXVII), 59 vols., 1863–1900

Theological and moral works

Christianae religionis institutio, totam fere pietatis summam et quicquid est in doctrina salutis cognitu necessarium complectens, 1536
Instruction et confession de foi, 1537
Epistolae duae de rebus hoc saeculo cognitu apprime necessariis:
  De fugiendis impiorum illicitis sacris et puritate christianae religionis obervanda
  De christiani hominis officio in sacerdotiis papalis ecclesiae, 1537
Commentarii in epistolam Pauli ad Romanos, 1540; in French, 1550
De la Cène du Seigneur, 1541
Institution de la religion chrestienne, 1541
Psychopannychia, 1542
Traité des reliques, 1543
Defensio sanae et orthodoxae doctrinae de servitute et liberatione humani arbitrii adversus calumnias Alberti Pighii, 1543
Supplex exhortatio ad Carolum Quintum, 1543
Contre la secte fanatique et furieuse des libertins qui se nomment spirituels, 1544
Brieve instruction pour armer tous bons fideles contre les erreurs de la secte commune des anabaptistes, 1544
Excuse à Messieurs les Nicodemistes, 1544

Deux sermons faicts en la ville de Génève, 1546

Commentarii ad secundam Pauli epistolam ad Corinthios, 1548

L'excuse de noble seigneur Jacques de Bourgogne, 1548

Commentaire sur l'Epître aux Hébrieux, 1549

Admonitio adversus astrologiam quam iudiciariam vocant, 1549; in French, 1549

Des scandales, 1550; in Latin, 1550

Commentaire sur l'Epître à Tite, 1550

De praedestinatione et providentia Dei libellus, 1550; in French, 1560

De vitandis superstitionibus, 1550; in French, 1551

Commentaires sur les canoniques, 1551; augmented 1562

Commentarii in Isaiam prophetam, 1551

Quatre sermons, 1552

Vingt deux sermons auxquels est exposé le psaume cent dis-neufième, 1554

Commentaire sur le premier livre de Moyse, dit Genèse, 1554

Exposition continuelle et familiere sur les IIII Evangelistes, 1554

Harmonia ex tribus evangelistis composita Matthaeo, Marco et Luca, 1555; in French, 1555

Déclaration pour maintenir la vraie foi que tiennent tous chrestiens de la Trinité des personnes en un seul Dieu, contre les erreurs de Michel Servet; où il est aussi montré qu'il est licite de punir les hérétiques et qu'à bon droit ce méchant a été executé par justice, 1554; in Latin, 1554

Traité des bénéfices, 1554

Defensio sanae et orthodoxae doctrinae de sacramentis eorum-que natura, vi, fine, et fructu, 1555

Reformation pour imposer silence à un certain belitre nommé Antoine Catelan, jadis Cordelier d'Albigeois, 1556

Secunda defensio piae et orthodoxae de sacramentis fidei contra Ioachimi Westphali calumnias, 1556

In omnes Pauli apostoli epistolas, 1556; in French, 1561

In Hoseam prophetam, 1557

Ultima admonitio ad Ioch. Westphalium, 1557

Sermons sur les dix commandements de la loi, 1557

Plusieurs sermons touchant la divinité, humanité et nativité de nostre Seigneur Jesus-Christ, 1558

Le livre des psaumes exposé, 1558; in Latin, 1564

Praelectiones in duodecim prophetas, 1559

Deux traités touchant la reformation de l'Eglise chrestienne, 1559

Praelectiones in duodecim prophetas, 1559

Exhortation au martyre, 1560

Dix-huit sermons, 1560

Commentaires sur le second livre de Saint Luc, dit les Actes des Apostres, 1561; in Latin, 1564

Sermons sur le cantique que feit le bon roi Ezechias, 1562

Sermons sur l'épître S. Paul apostre aux Ephesiens, 1562

Soixante-cinq sermons, 1562

Sermons sur le V livre de Moyse, nommé Deuteronome, 1562

Treize sermons traitans de l'election gratuite de Dieu en Jacob et de la rejection en Esaü, 1562

Responsio ad Balduini convitia, 1562

Sermons sur l'episbre S. Paul apostre aux Galates, 1563

Mosis libri V cum commentariis, 1563

Quarante-sept sermons sur les huit derniers chapitres des propheties de Daniel, 1565

Sermons sur le livre de Job, 1569

Other

L. Annaei Senecae libri duo de clementia, 1532
Correspondance in vols. XI–XXI of the *Opera*

Biographical and critical studies

Lefranc, A., *La Jeunesse de Calvin*, 1888

Pannier, J., *Jean Calvin écrivain, sa place et son rôle dans l'histoire de la langue et de la littérature françaises*, 1930

————*Recherches sur la formation intellectuelle de Calvin*, 1931

Benoît, J.-D., *Calvin, directeur d'âmes*, 1947

Wendel, F., *Calvin, sources et évolution de sa pensée religieuse*, 1950; as *Calvin. Sources and evolution of his Religious Thought*

Boisset, J., *Calvin et la souveraineté de Dieu*, 1964

Ganoczy, Alexandre, *Calvin, théologien de l'Eglise et du ministère*, 1964

————*Le jeune Calvin. Génèse et évolution de sa vocation réformatrice*, 1966

Bibliographies

Tchmerzine, A., *J. Calvin. Bibliographie de ses oeuvres*, 1939
Niesel, W., *Calvin. Bibliographie 1901–1959*, 1961

CARTESIAN(ISM).

See Descartes.

The major questions concerning Cartesianism in a French and literary, rather than an international, philosophical, scientific, mathematical, or theological context, have to do with the relationship of Descartes's achievement to the moderate scepticism and neostoic reactions which flourished in the moralists during the religious wars; to the ethic of grandeur, heroism, and "gloire" which was being explored in fiction and drama by Descartes's own contemporaries; to the imaginative attempts being made to take an optimistic view of human nature and potential, whose essence was the union between virtue and happiness envisaged by Descartes; and to the later growth of religious scepticism in France. It is also important in a literary context to see that, while Descartes may well have been what we see as the inaugurator of modern philosophy, or at least its epistemology, he was also in fact summarizing, systematizing and rigorously re-thinking a whole body of neoplatonist renaissance thought erected to protect belief in the immortality of the soul. He made a clean sweep of Aristotelian premises in scholastic philosophy, but what he replaced was a debased, worn-out and no longer serviceable scholasticism on which in some ways he remained dependent, and which had itself once created in western Christendom the distinction between philosophy and theology which Descartes exploited to kill it off.

The question of Descartes's sources need not detain us, but is still open. His power of radical thought, his originality, and his fierce awareness of his own intellectual independence are not in doubt. The questions revolve round the actual extent of literary or philosophical indebtedness, even if Descartes had ceased to be aware of it. It is likely to have been substantial, but generalized, not narrowing to very significant verbal borrowings, except from perhaps Charron, certainly Du Vair, and probably Justus Lipsius. Less significantly, because textually at a greater remove, there was borrowing from Montaigne. It can scarcely be doubted that some of the apparently neoplatonist vocabulary, like the use of the term "amplitude" in the context of the nature of the will, derived from Gibieuf's *De libertate dei et creaturae*. Descartes signed an approbation to that work, although he differed fundamentally from the Oratorian in his own theory of liberty. For Descartes human freedom implied full moral autonomy in the individual. The Cartesian ethic indeed emphasized the importance of strength of soul in the attainment of happiness and virtue, and it is plainly related to the heroic moral attitudes being imaginatively probed by such contemporaries of Descartes as Pierre Corneille, and as d'Urfé, directly dependent on Ficino and Ebreo for the neoplatonist intellectualizing passages in *L'Astrée*.

Descartes's notion of a single universal normative reason common to all human beings, although not similarly well applied by all, is neostoic. The work of Justus Lipsius, in particular the *De constantia* and the *Manuductio ad stoicam philosophiam*, is shot through with it, as is Du Vair's *La philosophie morale des stoïques*, one of the few absolutely certain literary sources for Descartes. Both Justus Lipsius and Du Vair held that the wise man should assent to what was obviously true, reject what was obviously false, and suspend judgement in all matters where there was uncertainty. The origins of Descartes's methodic doubt lie in the sceptical suspension of judgement, or ἐποχὴς as transmitted by Justus Lipsius.

Even in antiquity there was a connection between scepticism and the stoic moral reaction to the human inability to know the real world taught by the sceptics. The 16th century became further confused because the doctrine of Pyrrho, the principal sceptic of antiquity, was transmitted by Cicero as stoic. Cicero always links Pyrrho's name with that of the well-known stoic Aristo of Chios, while Diogenes Laertius presents him as a sceptic whose principal doctrine was the suspension of judgement. Balzac wrote to Descartes on 30 March 1628 referring to the stoics as "les Cyniques mitigez (the modified sceptics)." There is therefore nothing surprising in the juxtaposition of neostoic moral adages, a stoic concept of reason, and the idea of a methodic doubt in the *Discours de la méthode*. The methodic doubt itself, far from being the sceptical tool for which some of the Dutch Calvinists took it, was an emphatic affirmation of confidence in reason's ability to construct a universal science.

The sheer audacity of the task Descartes set himself, or found himself inspired and encouraged to undertake, is an almost unbelievable manifestation of confidence in the powers of the human mind. It is true that for centuries philosophers had dreamed of a unified science, a universal tree of knowledge, a reorganization of the disciplines into a single "circle," and that the renaissance, inspired by Quintilian, had seriously dreamt of uniting the quadrivium and the trivium into an "encyclopedia" of the liberal arts, the εγχύχλιοσ παιδεία (circular doctrine), or "orbiculata series disciplinarum (circular series of the disci-plines)," mentioned by Martianus Capella in the late fourth-century *De nuptiis Philologiae et Mercurii* and taken up by Budé in the *Commentarii linguae graecae*.

Mario Nizolio, who had produced his famous Ciceronian lexicon in 1535, strongly advocated the renaissance union of philosophy and rhetoric allegorized by Capella in "tota ea facultas et professio, quam Graeci εγχύχλοπαίδειαν, Latini vero circulum omnium doctrinarum vocant (the whole programme and syllabus which the Greeks call the encyclopedia, and the Latins the circle of all the doctrines)." Lull's tree of knowledge had contributed the idea that the trees of science were more than mere classifications of knowledge, and in some way corresponded with the realities of the cosmos, a notion picked up in France by Pierre de la Ramée and Jacques Peletier du Mans, and which also lay behind the *Theologia naturalis* of Raimond Sebond, whom Montaigne purported to defend. Rabelais uses the term "encyclopedie" in *Pantagruel*. The idea of a unified corpus of science was therefore not new, and it is what may have attracted Descartes to the Rosicrucians, with whom the idea has also been associated. What was new was Descartes's conviction that the unified science had to proceed from one mind.

Descartes was too confident. By basing his system on what he thought was the self-evident truth that he, as a thinking subject, was necessarily a non-extended spiritual, and therefore immortal being, he had to invent the vortices in space to avoid clashing with what he took to be the revealed teaching behind the condemnation of Galileo's heliocentrism, and he had to invent the subtle matter at the top of Torricelli's upturned tube, since extension was predicable only of what was not spiritual. His system was bound to develop tensions with empirical science which would destroy its cosmological, physical, metaphysical, and physiological elements.

That the epistemology was neoplatonist in origin is in a literary context chiefly important for two apparently conflicting reasons. Firstly it reasserted the independence of the spiritual soul from a corruptible body with which, as Descartes admitted only from the sixth *Meditatio* onwards, it was nevertheless in a union he asserted against his disciple Henri le Roy (Regius) to be substantial. Body and soul made a single substance. None the less, Descartes abolished any vestigial theory of abstraction. All human ideas are innate, in the sense that they do not depend on sense perception. Natural, animal, and vital spirits are all material. To allow animals any power of gestating their own energy would be a step along the dreaded path which would make matter into mind. The reassertion of the soul's spirituality and immortality had been undertaken in a neoplatonist if often semi-mythological context in 15th-century Florence. If not inaugurated by, then it had at least been channelled through, and chiefly derived from, Marsilio Ficino's translations and commentaries, exceedingly important for writers of the French renaissance.

Ficinian optimism in uniting virtue and happiness, and in upgrading human nature so that ordinary human love, not exclusive of physical relationships between the sexes, served as a stepping stone to the beatifying love of God, lost its imaginative interest during the defensive moral stoicism of the religious wars. It regained its grip on the imaginations of a whole generation of writers during the first third of the 17th century (see d'Urfé). The defense of the soul's immortality, in the tradition stemming from Florentine neoplatonism of the 15th century, was strongly associated with the optimism about human nature and its potentiality to be found, in still recognizable form, in Descartes.

The second and apparently conflicting reason for the importance of the neoplatonist origins of Descartes's theory of knowledge, derives from its compatibility with, and possible derivation from, the teaching of Augustine, normally associated with Jansenism (q.v.) in the 17th century, although the exuberant spiritual optimism of François de Sales is also totally dependent on Augustine's teaching. The compatibility with Augustine is what allowed Descartes's thought to be nourished by the non-Aristotelian scholastic tradition in the middle ages, associated most notably with the Victorines, Bonaventure, Scotus and the Franciscan tradition generally, which not infrequently skirted illuminist accounts of the theory of knowledge. Descartes's epistemological doctrine, if not his ethical optimism about human nature, proved quite acceptable to the scientists of Port-Royal, who could agree with his account of animals as in the end, because not immortal and therefore without a spiritual soul, reducible to mechanical devices. It was Port-Royal's empirical scientists, like Pascal, who usually reacted most strongly against Descartes.

By the time Descartes came to write the ethical works, that is the letter-preface to the French *Principes*, the letters to Elizabeth, and *Les Passions de l'âme*, whose first draft dates from the winter of 1645–46, Marin Cureau de la Chambre had started to publish his vitalist work, *Les Caractères des passions*. It appeared in five volumes dated 1640, 1645, 1659, 1659, and 1662, and Descartes wrote to Mersenne on 18 January 1641, after he had seen the first volume, that he had looked through it, "sans y rien trouver que des paroles (without finding anything there except words)." Descartes's own thought is immeasurably more rigorous, but the work does at least anticipate Descartes in linking the passions to the physiological phenomena associated with each of them.

Whatever Descartes may have said about the primacy of ethics in any philosophical system, and whatever overriding importance *Les Passions de l'âme* might have in his complete corpus, particularly in a literary context, the friendship with Mersenne, whose *La Vérité des sciences* had appeared in 1625, and the encouragement of Bérulle to replace Aristotelian scholasticism with a suitable adaptation of Oratorian neoplatonism, suggest that Descartes's original inspiration was largely apologetic, the erection of a philosophical substructure to support belief in revelation and the immortality of the soul entailed by Christian belief. It is true that, after his death, the influence of the system forked, with its development by Spinoza in a semi-pantheistic generally deist direction, while Malebranche, the Oratorian, developed its potential in a way he thought compatible with Christian theology, emphasizing the distinction between body and soul rather than their union. But even during his lifetime it was the favour of Bérulle, Condren, and Gibieuf which assured the favourable view taken of Descartes's philosophy by Antoine Arnauld, later to have an important dispute with Malebranche, himself finally to become an ally of Bossuet against Fénelon.

Bossuet was himself, not surprisingly, in favour of the philosophy of Descartes, adopted by the pessimistic neoplatonist Oratorian tradition and supported by Arnauld. The team he recruited for the instruction of the dauphin was Cartesian and, when Huet left the fold, Bossuet did his best to dissuade him from turning against Descartes. None the less, in spite of Bossuet, Cartesianism came to be seen in France as the credo of a party of dissent. The Jansenists had adopted it. It acknowledged no authority but reason. It was embraced by those opposed to authority in intellectual matters, and that might spread to political independence of mind. Malebranche had captured its authority for the party of the "modernes" in the Querelle des anciens et des modernes (q.v.), and there were signs of the Aristotelian backlash still to come.

It was in the name of Cartesianism that the challenge to strict Calvinism inspired by Amyraut took place at Saumur, and the Dutch Calvinists who had challenged Calvin's strict predestinationism at Dort had started to adopt the philosophy of Descartes. Bossuet began to see trouble coming, although he still appointed Cartesians like Nicolas de Malézieu tutor to the duc du Maine. It was Bossuet who realized the dangerous implications for Christian belief of Huet's 1679 *Demonstratio evangelica*, written against Spinoza's 1670 *Tractatus theologico-politicus* but only appearing three years after the date of its achevé d'imprimer, and it was Bossuet who, initially worried by Malebranche's critical spirit, enlisted Fénelon's support against him.

While the Dutch were divided about Cartesianism, the university of Louvain was formally hostile. Vopiscus Fortunatus Plempius, the doctor, persuaded his colleagues to condemn Cartesianism as early as 1652, as hostile to orthodox Eucharistic doctrine. In 1662 Cartesianism was condemned by the theological faculty on orders from the nuncius at Brussels, Geronimo Vecchio, and Descartes was put on the Roman index of prohibited books in 1663. None the less, five Franciscans defended Cartesian theses at Louvain in 1667, dedicating them to the nuncius, and the teaching spread to the universities of first west then east Germany, often being developed in the direction of an even firmer separation of body and soul, as in Malebranche's occasionalism. In France the Jesuits had become hostile, although Fontenelle remained a Cartesian in physics, and as late as 1765 a eulogy of Descartes was the subject proposed by the Académie française for its rhetoric prize. Leibniz was to derive his inspiration from Descartes's system.

None the less, well before the philosophies of Newton and Locke replaced Cartesianism, Lallemand was forbidden on sudden orders from the court to give the panegyric on 24 June 1667 when the body of Descartes was returned to France in 1667, and Harlay forbade the teaching of Cartesianism in 1671. There were condemnations of Cartesianism at Angers in 1675 and at Caen in 1678. The Oratorians themselves to very little avail declared in 1678 that no one should "s'éloigner de la phisique ni des principes de phisique d'Aristote...pour s'attacher à la doctrine nouvelle de Monsieur Descartes (depart from the physics nor the principles of the physics of Aristotle...to adhere to the new teaching of M. Descartes)." In 1685 the teaching of Cartesian philosophy was forbidden by royal decree.

As early as 1652 the Oratorians had suspended the Marseilles professor André Martin from his teaching post for "Cartesianism," and the Oratorian General sent a letter to all teaching institutions of the congregation in 1654, desiring that they should limit themselves to teaching according to Aristotelian principles, a directive reiterated by their general assembly of the congregation in 1658. Cartesian theses were suppressed at Le Mans in 1661, and in Protestant Saumur three teachers were officially warned in 1672. The Oratorian General was summoned by Louis XIV, and one of the congregation's members, Bernard Lamy, was dismissed by lettre de cachet in 1670, while another Oratorian, Poisson, was rebuked for teaching Cartesian mechanics. Copies of his book were confiscated.

In the end it was not the non-empirical nature of the system which ensured its rejection, but its theological dangers, not just because it questioned authority in the name of reason, but essentially because it showed how it was possible to create a whole philosophical system, within the bounds of strict orthodoxy, and indeed apologetic in intention, without any explicit reference to revelation at all. Cartesianism marked one more step towards the emancipation from theological tutelage of secular thought in Europe.

CHALLE, Robert, 1659–c. 1720.

Novelist and traveller.

In spite of immense popularity in the half-century following their publication in 1713, and their undoubted literary historical importance, Challe's two anonymous volumes containing seven nouvelles entitled *Les Illustres Françoises* and purporting to be true stories, with first-person narrators, were almost completely forgotten for two hundred years. It is true that Champfleury devoted an enthusiastic passage to them in his 1857 *Le Réalisme*, and that the German literary historian M.F. von Waldberg gave 60 pages to the work in the different context of the rise of the sentimental novel, but further interest was aroused only when it was demonstrated in 1947 first that Prévost's *Manon Lescaut* had been influenced by an English translation of Challe, a suggestion first put forward in 1939, and then that Richardson, too, owed something to his work for both *Pamela* and *Clarissa Harlowe*, and that Marivaux drew on it in writing *La Vie de Marianne*. Interest has subsequently much increased, and in 1959 Frédéric Deloffre published a critical edition of *Les Illustres Françoises*, the first edition since the 18th century.

The author's name has been spelt in a variety of ways, notably Chasles and Challes, but the usage adopted here has since 1970 been regarded as the most correct. *Les Illustres Françoises* is Challe's only work of imaginative writing, but he is the author also of the *Journal de voyage*, a diary drawn up on a voyage to the Far East in 1690–91 and published in 1721, and of a series of memoirs published in 1931. Challes seems certain to have written a one-volume sequel to *Don Quixote*, published over someone else's name, and an unpublished work on the history of Catholicism, the "Tablettes chronologiques," of which the manuscript has not survived. A series of letters was exchanged between 1713 and 1718 with A. Prosper Marchand on behalf of the *Journal Littéraire de la Haye*. Marchand provided Challe's name and some details about his life for Rey's 1748 edition of *Les Illustres Françoises*. The *Journal* had published a long account of the novel on its appearance.

Challe was born in Paris on 17 August 1659. His father was a member of the garde du corps of Anne of Austria and died in 1681. His widow was still alive in 1690, and had had to sell furniture in order to pay for her husband's health care and funeral expenses. The various surviving documents suggest but do not conclusively prove that Challe was illegitimate, not the son of his father's widow. He was, however, sufficiently well provided for to be educated at the Collège de la Marche in the Place Maubert, where he made an enduring friend of the future marquis de Seignelay, Colbert's son and Challe's future protector. Challe tells us that on his travels he read Ovid, but also Saint Augustine, Saint Bernard, Thomas à Kempis, Petronius, Horace, and Juvenal as well as the 17th-century French dramatists.

Challe claims to have read Pascal's *Lettres Provinciales* a score of times, although in the *Journal de voyage* he declares himself against the doctrine of predestination and defends the views on free will of the Jesuits he disliked. *Les Illustres Françoises* quotes Rabelais, Montaigne, Brantôme, Cyrano, Scarron, and Sorel. Challe says he knew speeches from Corneille's *Polyeucte* by heart, and his memoirs tell us that he played a part in a Racine tragedy put on by young people for the marquise de Castelnau, but he refers slightingly to Gomberville's "ridiculous" adventure novel, *Polexandre*. Imaginative exuberance was something alien to him.

After his schooling Challe volunteered to take part in the Flanders campaign, and was present at the siege of Saint-Omer, fighting also at Mont-Cassel on 11 April 1677. After the Peace of Nijmegen he was briefly articled to a Paris lawyer, and appears to have studied canon law. It seems probable that it was on the death of his father that the family, perhaps wishing and now able to rid itself of an embarrassment, encouraged him, or through Seignelay, then Secretary for the navy, arranged for him to be attached as captain's secretary to an expedition of the "Pêche sédentaire de l'Acadie," a company organized to exploit the fishing resources of French Canada. Challe, who reported privately to Seignelay on French commercial activity in Canada, helped the leader of the expedition, Bergier, to buy a boat, and sailed in the summer of 1682 to what we know as Nova Scotia.

Dried and salted, the fish were brought back in winter for sale in La Rochelle, southwards along the Atlantic coast, and throughout the Mediterranean. Not all members of the expedition returned to France every year but, after visiting Lisbon and Cadiz, and witnessing an auto da fe, Challe certainly delivered his report to Seignelay very early in 1684, and received 3,000 livres. He was in Canada again in 1685 and 1687. He appears to have been doing well when on 23 June 1687 his settlement was attacked by the English. He was away with a detachment of men of whom he lost 17. Challe was himself wounded, arrested, and taken to Boston, then to England, where Saint-Evremond received him and gave him financial aid. His entire fortune had been in the form of furs which the English had taken.

Seignelay now arranged for Challe, his hopes of leading his own expedition and of enrichment by trading destroyed, to be taken on as the official legal supervisor or "écrivain" on a ship belonging to the Compagnie des Indes Orientales, of which Seignelay was president. Challe's duties were to keep a daily record of supplies, merchandise loaded and unloaded, the state of the vessel, and the number of people aboard, and to keep minutes of meetings of the ship's council. Challe's boat was diverted in 1688 to exercise surveillance over the English fleet for what turned out to be two years, but finally left for the east on 27 February 1690, in a squadron of six ships. The day-by-day account of the voyage is riveting in its meticulous attention to detail as well as in the atmosphere it conveys. There were quarrels, illnesses, disciplinary and other incidents, the captain's death, and a storm so bad that Challe loaded his pistols to shoot himself rather than drown. Unfortunately Seignelay, for whom Challe was writing private memoirs, died suddenly on 3 November 1690.

Challe embarked again on a different ship but with the same duties in 1692, and took part in the battle of the Hougue. An orthodox and even devout Catholic, he none the less disapproved of the chaplain's attempts to convince the crew that it was their sacred duty to exterminate the heretical English and Dutch, just as he had disapproved of the inquisition in Spain. Enough is clear from the *Journal de voyage* and the memoirs for us to know that Challe liked to drink, but did not smoke, that he did not take coffee, and that he was good company. He was also quite evidently quick-tempered and quarrelsome, rash and indiscreet, with a biting tongue, and there were three or four rows serious enough to have ended in drawn swords or to have demanded Seignelay's intervention, as well as quarrels at sea. Challe was later to have a dispute with the *Journal Littéraire*. However, we know little of the period from 1692 to 1713, except that Challe made a living in administrative posts connected with the navy.

The *Mémoires* were composed in 1716, but shed little light on the biography. Challe appears in 1702 to have written a sequel to *Don Quixote*, largely dealing with the position of women in society, but could not find a publisher for the *Tablettes chronologiques*, a manuscript of which the *Journal Littéraire* does not appear to have thought highly when Challe sought to enlist its help. It is probable that he did not change his mind after writing into the manuscript of the *Journal de voyage* a request to Seignelay not to publish the *Journal* while Challe was still alive, as he feared reprisals from the Jesuits, whom he had attacked. The avis de l'éditeur says that the author was dead, but Marchand maintains that that was a fiction. The *Journal* was published in three volumes in 1721 with a fictitious imprint, and the probability on balance is that Challe had recently died. However, in spite of what Abraham de Hondt, publisher of *Les Illustres Françoises* and the *Journal de voyage*, says, Challe plainly did not revise his fourth, 1722 edition of *Les Illustres Françoises*. 1720 is a reasonable conjecture for the date of death. It is impossible that it was earlier than 1719, and it cannot have been later than 1722. Marchand says that Challe died poor and in Chartres.

WORKS

Although the *Journal de voyage* was not published until 1721, probably after Challe's death, and although it is not professedly a work of the imagination, it contains qualities to which it is important to advert. The style is colloquial and unadorned, with a preference for direct statement and physical description. Among the lists of passengers and cargo are vividly realistic sketches of people, like the wretched Bouchetière, who owed his appointment as second-in-command to Mme de Maintenon, and who wanted to make himself captain when Hurtain, who had been the original captain, died at sea:

Il a trouvé le secret de se faire universellement haïr...Une taciturnité et une gravité inexprimable, une barbe en forme de garde de poignard, un orgueil et une morgue à faire peur aux vaches ou tout au plus aux petits enfans...

(He has managed to make everyone hate him...Inexpressibly taciturn and solemn, a beard shaped like the guard of a dagger, a pride and haughtiness to put fear into the cows, or at most into small children...).

The touches of colourful physical detail can be memorable, as in the description of the appearance of the governor of Saint-Yago, capital of the Cape Verde Islands, whose shirt looked as if he had been sweating ink, whose mouse-grey satin jacket had been delicately embroidered with silk flowers, now faded, and whose sword had a six-foot blade, making him "look like Mascarille in Molière's *Précieuses*."

Challe observes his world with detached objectivity, although he bandies about improbable accusations against the Jesuits and other missionaries, leads the organized taunting of his ship's chaplain, and quickly develops his own firm prejudices, impermeable to reason or evidence. His dislike of the English was understandably implacable, but the original editor in 1721 says of Challe, "good Catholic as he was," that he disliked the bullying involved in missionary activity, assuming that this attitude would commend Challe to his readers. Challe is also notably sensitive to the predicament of ordinary sailors—"Are they less human than other people?"—and in his memoirs relates with horror the death of a pregnant woman on the point of giving birth, caused by the rough treatment she suffered from bailiffs confiscating goods for unpaid tax.

The manuscript of the *Mémoires*, compiled mostly in 1716 and dealing with the period up to 1701, but including the private memoir about Canada drawn up for Seignelay, was lost, re-discovered and partially published in 1931. Its chief historical interest probably lies in its assessment of the state of France, for whose plight Challe principally blames the greed of the clergy, the depradations of the tax farmers, about which Challe is particularly virulent, the fiscal inequities, and the king's inability to get a true picture of the state of the kingdom because he is blinded by the court and his confessor. While this view doubtless does much credit to Challe's social sensitivities, it also shows how firmly he was affected by a particular set of liberal prejudices, determined to blame anyone but the king himself, who appears in the *Mémoires* as less well informed, less perceptive, and therefore less responsible for the state of France than he actually was. Not surprisingly, Challe emphasizes the importance to the French economy of overseas colonization.

The framework of *Les Illustres Françoises*, *histoires véritables* marks a considerable advance on any collection which had preceded it. By insisting that the seven nouvelles were true stories, Challe was only taking up the 17th-century tradition but, after a first-person preface in his own name, he uses a third-person narrator to introduce the characters who recount the true stories to one another. Each story is narrated to a group of friends awaiting their turn to tell their own stories, as in Marguerite d'Angoulême's *Heptameron*, but here each of the seven male narrators is telling a love story, in four out of seven cases his own, to a company purported to include participants in the events narrated in the story itself. What is new about the framework, whether or not it was consciously devised with this purpose in mind, is therefore that it allows Challe to exploit the advantages of the memoir novel, directly four times and indirectly twice, and only once using the third person, while appearing to guarantee the veracity of his narrators by the presence among their listeners of people in a position to corroborate or deny the historicity of the facts. In the one story which is not in personal memoir form, "L'Histoire de M. de Contamine et d'Angélique," Challe goes to elaborate lengths to ensure that the reader can trust the narrator, M. des Ronais, to be recounting a true story.

The seven nouvelles illustrate seven different moral platitudes listed in Challe's first-person preface. They can be paraphrased: the "Histoire de M. des Ronais et de Mlle Dupuis" shows that children should be brought up in the same enlightened manner as Mlle Dupuis was; the "Histoire de M. de Contamine et d'Angélique" shows how wisdom and virtue can overcome lowliness of station; the "Histoire de M. de Terny et de Mlle de Bernay" shows that fathers and mothers may be wise to prevent hot-headed marriages, but should not impose cold-hearted ones; the "Histoire de M. de Jussy et de Mlle Fenouil" shows that only fidelity can protect a woman against her fragility; the "Histoire de M. des Prez et de Mlle de l'Epine" shows the danger of passions and a woman's need to rely on her husband; the "Histoire de M. des Frans et de Silvie" that a woman of beauty and moral strength can become over-confident and be driven to excess by outraged love; and finally the "Histoire de M. Dupuis et de Mme de Londé" shows how a libertin retires from libertinage when he falls in love with a virtuous woman.

The correspondence between Challe and the *Journal Littéraire de La Haye* is of exceptional interest in assessing not only what cultivated contemporary taste found startling in the nouvelles, but also in elucidating from his replies what it was that Challes was trying to do. Briefly, the *Journal* thought Challe had sinned against "l'exactitude et la noble simplicité du style familier (the precision and noble simplicity of a colloquial style)," that occasionally the characters were untrue to their own natures, but above all that in almost all the nouvelles there are expressions or details which only false prudes will accept and that reasonable women will reject. The *Journal* thought the seventh nouvelle by far inferior to the others. Most of the other criticisms were on points of detail, some of which Challe ceded. According to Challe, his title was just three words. The rest of the original title was presumably added by the publishers: *Les Illustres Françoises, histoires véritables; où l'on trouve, dans des caracteres particuliers, et fort differens, un grand nombre d'exemples rares, et extraordinaires, des belles Manieres, de la Politesse, et de la Galanterie, des Personnes de l'un et l'autre sexe, de cette Nation.*

PUBLICATIONS

Les Illustres Françoises, 2 vols., 1713 [critical edition, 2 vols., 1959]; as *The Illustrious French Lovers*, 2 vols., 1727
Journal d'un voyage fait aux Indes Orientales, 3 vols., 1721
Un Colonial au temps de Colbert: Mémoires de Robert Challes Ecrivain du Roi, 1931
The sixth book of *Don Quixote*, claimed by Challe as his work, was published over the name of Filleau de Saint-Martin, 1713
The correspondence with the *Journal Littéraire de La Haye* was published in the *Annales Universitatis Saraviensis*, 1954, pp. 144–182

Biographical and critical studies

Forno, Lawrence J., *Robert Challe: Intimations of the Enlightenment*, 1972

CHAMFORT, Sébastien-Roch Nicolas de, known as, 1740–1794.

Moralist, epigrammatist and dramatist.

LIFE

There is a good deal of uncertainty about the details of Chamfort's life, starting with the identity of his parents and the date of his birth. One baptism certificate of 6 April 1740 proclaims him as the legitimate child of a grocer, François Nicolas, and his wife, Thérèse Croizet. The other is dated 22 June 1740 and gives the Christian names Sébastien Roch, says that the infant was born of parents unknown, and names as godparents a locksmith and a baker's wife. Chamfort was certainly born in Clermont, but there is also some archival support in the town-hall records for a date in 1741, and two solemn statements exist by Chamfort himself, one of which declares that he was born on 20 December 1742, and the other of which is contained in a police document stating that in September 1793 Chamfort said he was 51. The two baptism certificates give overwhelming support to 1740 as the year of birth. It is unlikely that Thérèse Croizet was his real mother, but it is not unlikely that his father was a canon (chanoine), probably of the Clermont cathedral chapter. That was a persistent rumour which may, however, derive from a confusion with the name of one of the godparents on one of the baptismal certificates, Catherine Chanoine. No real attempt has been made to solve the many outstanding problems of the biography.

The first of them is how Chamfort came to be taken up by a professor at the Collège de Navarre and sent with a bursary to the Collège des Grassins in Paris, apparently not much later that 1745. From various allusions and references we know that Chamfort was very strong, very good-looking, and much given to mordant witticisms and practical jokes. He was also very clever, carrying off all five first prizes in his penultimate class. He none the less either ran away or was expelled as the result of some practical joke that had gone too far, and made off intending to take ship for America with Pierre Letourneur, the future translator of Richardson and Ossian, and of Shakespeare, of whom his prose translation was to fill 20 volumes. They got as far as Cherbourg, and were indulgently taken back by the Collège. Chamfort later sent his Greek teacher a copy of his 1764 poem *Epître d'un père à son fils pour la naissance de son petit-fils*, for which he was awarded a prize by the Académie française, as an apology for his behaviour.

Around the time of graduation Chamfort assumed the name by which he is now known, adding the by now socially necessary "de" for good measure, and must also have accepted the tonsure. He was henceforward for some time referred to as the abbé de Chamfort and wore the petit collet, but had no intention of pursuing an ecclesiastical career: "C'est un costume et non point un état (It's a way of dressing, not a station in life)." Chamfort is reported to have said to the college principal,

Je ne serai jamais prêtre; j'aime trop le repos, la philosophie, les femmes, l'honneur, la vraie gloire; et trop peu les querelles, l'hypocrisie, les honneurs et l'argent

(I shall never be a priest. I like peace, philosophy, women, honour, and true glory too much, and quarrels, hypocrisy, honours, and money too little).

That slightly forced, slightly bitter wit was a characteristic of Chamfort's epigrams from the beginning.

On leaving the Collège des Grassins Chamfort appears initially to have found employment as a clerk, and then as a tutor in various families, where he is reputed to have proved too attractive to the mothers and sisters of his pupils to have been kept on for long. He needed to support his presumptive mother but, engaged by the comte van Eyck, in exile in Cologne, as tutor to his nephew, Chamfort quarrelled with his employer and by June 1761 was back in Paris. There he became Paris correspondent of Pierre Rousseau's *Journal encyclopédique*, a fortnightly journal of strongly encyclopédiste (q.v.) tendencies, devoted to reviewing new books and edited first from Liège and then from the small principality of Bouillon, now in Belgium, about three kilometres from the present French border near Sedan.

Chamfort stayed with the *Journal* for two years, enjoyed an active social life in Paris, got to know d'Alembert, Marmontel, and above all Duclos, presented to the academy of Amiens a discourse, which has been lost, on the utility of letters, was given a prize by the Académie française for his *Epître d'un père*, read before it by d'Alembert, and had his one-act verse comedy *La Jeune Indienne* played by the Comédie-Française on 30 April 1764. Critical reaction, notably from Grimm, Collé, and Fréron, was poor, although Voltaire wrote a letter of encouragement, and reception by the public was moderately good. The piece stayed on the bill for nine days, brought its author 524 livres, and remained in the repertoire until the Revolution. The king had it performed at Versailles in 1765.

During the next few years Chamfort had minor literary successes. In 1764 he had been ill, and had turned down an offer of 40,000 livres to accompany two young English nobles to Italy for two years. He won literary prizes for a poem *La Délivrance de Salerne et la fondation du Royaume des Deux-Siciles* at Rouen in 1765, an ode *Sur la grandeur de l'homme* at the Toulouse Jeux Floraux in 1766, a discourse *Combien le génie des grands écrivains influe sur l'esprit de leur siècle* in Marseilles in 1767. He ghosted two ballets for the duc de la Vallière and worked for Panckoucke's projected 30-volume "Grand Vocabulaire français." Most of Chamfort's essays appeared in the *Dictionnaire dramatique* of 1776. A *Discours philosophique en vers sur l'Homme de Lettres* failed to win a prize which went instead to La Harpe and, apart from some epigrams and his 1776 tragedy *Mustapha et Zéangir*, was Chamfort's last production in verse. Chamfort's real literary success came with his 1769 *L'Eloge de Molière*, awarded a prize by the Académie française. Voltaire wrote him a well-wishing letter, for the third time, on 27 September.

On 26 January 1770 the Comédie-Française played a new one-act prose comedy, *Le Marchand de Smyrne*, which had 13 performances in its initial run, making it a public success, although Grimm's review was pitiless, while Chamfort did not rise in the esteem of La Harpe, Fréron, or Collé. However, the abbé Galiani, former secretary of the Naples embassy and full-time frequenter of Parisian literary society, wrote to Mme d'Epinay to say how delightful he thought Chamfort's piece, later dismissed as a triviality by Chamfort himself, although later still used by him to testify to his revolutionary principles. In 1771 he contracted for the second time a sexually transmitted disease, chiefly affecting his skin, and was saved from destitution only when Guy de Chabanon, the dramatist and poet, passed over to him a pension of 1,200 livres from the *Mercure de France* (q.v.) which he did not need. Chamfort was able to take the waters at Contrexéville and retire to the country, where he worked for Panckoucke, for Pierre Rousseau's *Journal*, and on a compilation of anecdotes on the reign of Louis XIV and the regency for Delalain's *Bibliothèque de la Société*. He also appears to have assuaged some of the feelings of bitterness and frustration by which he was constantly attacked. The wit for which he was so much admired and on account of which his presence was sought had developed a sharp cutting edge.

Chamfort's work on Racine, mostly written in 1773, has been lost, but his 1774 *Eloge de La Fontaine* won the 2,000-livre prize offered by the academy of Marseilles, although the money had been put up by Necker as a discreet way of helping La Harpe, whom Chamfort defeated. This time even Grimm applauded, and there was praise from both sides of two eminent quarrels, Mme du Deffand and Julie de Lespinasse, and Fréron and Voltaire. Chamfort was now a celebrity. Taking the waters at Barèges, he became friendly with Choiseul's sister, Mme de Grammont. He lived modestly in Paris, worked hard at such mundane literary tasks as the *Dictionnaire dramatique*, which he and the abbé de la Porte were to publish in 1776, and then moved into an apartment at Auteuil furnished for him by Mme Helvétius. Her husband had died in 1771, and at various times she offered hospitality to a great range of liberal literary figures—Fontenelle, d'Alembert, Condillac, d'Holbach, Malesherbes, Diderot, Ducis, Garrick, and Franklin, who introduced Jefferson. Mme Helvétius herself said she disliked talking to Chamfort in the mornings, as it upset her for the day, so poisonous had his feelings become. To drag him from his depression she and her friends persuaded Chamfort to finish *Mustapha et Zéangir*, the verse tragedy which he had started a dozen years previously.

It was played triumphantly at Fontainebleau on 1 and 7 November 1776, moving Louis XVI and Marie-Antoinette to tears. Chamfort was awarded a pension of 1,200 livres. The tide of praise swelled, carrying Grimm with it, although La Harpe remained severe. When, two years later, it was published, Chamfort dedicated it to the queen. In Paris, however, the piece did less well. There were scarcely 15 performances, sparsely attended, but they brought Chamfort in 3,489 livres which, with the king's pension, and another 2,000 livres awarded by Condé the same evening, were enough to put Chamfort's financial situation in order. He was offered a position and lodging in Condé's household, but remained depressed at the scant public acclaim. He made difficulties about his appointment with Condé, needing above all freedom and isolation. Condé offered him the pension, the official title, and the accommodation without any functions at all. At this point Chamfort was plainly in paranoid need of absolute independence. After a year he left Condé's Palais-Bourbon and severed all connection with his benefactor. Although he joined Beaumarchais's league of dramatists and played chess with Talleyrand, he declined an attractive proposition from Panckoucke to write for the *Mercure*, which had just taken over *Le Journal de Politique et de Littérature*, *Le Journal français*, and *Le Journal des Dames*.

Chamfort's mood became blacker. His periods of illness began to weigh more heavily on him, and he began to live a more solitary existence, retiring to an apartment at Auteuil, now next door to Mme Helvétius, who continued to console and cosset him. He had been bitterly disappointed at the dismissal of Turgot in 1776, had begun to feel that little was worth the effort it cost, and started work on the sharply epigrammatic work for which he is remembered, the *Maximes et pensées*. Morellet left, after visiting him one evening, feeling as cheerful "as if he had just been to an execution." Chamfort found salvation in Boulogne, where from time to time he went to visit Mme Agasse, and where he finally fell in love with Marie-Anne Buffon, widow of one of the doctors of the comte d'Artois. They had met before at the house of Mme Panckoucke, but their liaison dates from Boulogne in 1781, when Mme Buffon was about 53.

In that year Chamfort was elected to the Académie française at his fifth attempt, after three in 1577 and one in 1580, plus another in which he retired to allow his friend Chabanon to be elected. Chamfort's election took place on 5 April 1781 and he was received on 19 July. He wrote a *Précis historique des révolutions de Naples et de Sicile* to preface a five-volume work by the abbé de Saint-Non published from 1781. In spring 1783 he retired to the small château of Vaudouleurs near Etampes with Mme Buffon, and for some months was happy, but she was taken suddenly ill and died on 28 August. A friend, the comte de Vaudreuil, immediately sent for Chamfort and took him to Holland, where his spirits remained very downcast. Only gradually, on his return to Paris, did he begin to take an interest again in the Académie, soon attending regularly, becoming its chancellor in 1786 and 1790, and its director in 1792. Vaudreuil offered him accommodation and found him a position as secretary to Mme Elisabeth, the king's sister, which he took up on 12 September 1784. Chamfort had been close to Mirabeau, at least since the preceding year, and had certainly had some part in Mirabeau's *Considérations sur l'ordre de Cincinnatus*, published in 1784.

As the Revolution approached, the divergence between Vaudreuil's views and Chamfort's became clearer but, as with Condé, Chamfort insisted on outspoken clarity so that no difference of viewpoint could mar the bond of affection between them. The Revolution fired Chamfort with a mixture of pent-up bitterness, idealism, and shrewd perceptivity. He realized that something could and would be done about the social mechanisms whose injustices he had observed and, from being sarcastic and lazy, found unknown reserves of energy. He had moved into an apartment in the Arcades du Palais-Royal early in 1789, had been at Versailles with Mirabeau for the opening of the Etats Généraux, and appears to have been among the crowd which stormed the Bastille. He also wrote for the *Mercure*, with a circulation of 10,000–12,000, filling the literary pages of what had been a staid periodical with republican views, particularly on social issues, and helped Claude Fauchet, not yet bishop of Calvados, to edit his *Tableaux de la Révolution*, seeming to have accepted the violence as possibly necessary and certainly justified.

In 1790 Chamfort was one of the 36 founding members of the "Société de 1789" with his friends Sieyès, La Fayette, Talleyrand, and Condorcet, although he was to leave it when it became too much of a forum for political intrigue. For Talleyrand, Chamfort wrote a famous speech known as the *Adresse au peuple français* delivered in February 1790, and he became noted for a number of famous slogans, including "guerre aux châteaux, paix aux chaumières (war to the châteaux; peace to the cottages)." From 1791 he was increasingly unwell, although still exceedingly active. For Mirabeau, he wrote the speech against the "tyrannies and crimes" of the former academies which was to underlie their replacement by the new Institut on 22 August 1795, although Mirabeau died on 2 April. In July 1791, when Danton and Desmoulins felt it too dangerous to stay in Paris after the republican manifestations on the Champ de Mars of 17 July calling for the dismissal of the king, Chamfort rallied to the radical Jacobin club, whose secretary he became. It is likely that he also helped Talleyrand with the report on national education which he read to the assembly in September 1791.

In August 1792 Chamfort was appointed joint administrator of the Bibliothèque Nationale when the directorship was converted from one post, paid at 12,000 livres a year, into two at 4,000 livres each. From 1793, however, the Terror was plainly approaching, and Chamfort was vigorously sarcastic at the infringements of liberty imposed in the name of a new fraternity. He refused to write against the freedom of the press and started openly to oppose Marat and Robespierre. He was twice delated to the Comité du salut public by one of his subordinates, Tobiesen-Duby, the second time on 21 July 1793 for having shown open sympathy, with others, for Charlotte Corday, who had been executed on 17 July for Marat's assassination on the 14th. Chamfort and a handful of others were arrested in August and imprisoned at the Madelonnettes, then released, but obliged to lodge and feed the warders who were put in charge of them. Chamfort counterattacked with a pamphlet against Tobiesen-Duby in which he boasted of the republican credentials he had shown as early as *Le Marchand de Smyrne*, but also did not withdraw his hostility to Marat.

On 9 September 1793, Chamfort resigned his post at the library. It was on 10 September that, as his friend Ginguené relates, the police came again. On the pretext of getting himself ready to leave he went into his study, locked himself in, and shot himself, but only broke the bridge of his nose and destroyed his right eye. He managed then to take hold of a razor, and tried to cut his throat, then to stab at his heart. On the point of fainting, he slashed the veins in his wrists. He was discovered when his housekeeper heard a cry, and, placed on his bed, Chamfort dictated a declaration that he had preferred to die free rather than be returned to prison as a slave. He was later to be ironic at his own expense when recounting his botched attempt to kill himself. Looked after by Cabanis, Sieyès, Mme Panckoucke and others, Chamfort recovered sufficiently to move into a different apartment. His imprisonment, the expense of maintaining his warder, and the cost of medical attention had impoverished him, but he discussed with Ginguené the possible foundation of a new journal, the *Décade philosophique*, and was able to get out, although he had little taste for any company except that of intimate friends. One of his wounds became infected, but the doctor did not realize the nature of the inflammation, and the necessary operation was performed too late. He died on 13 April 1794.

WORKS

According to Ginguené, his friend and first editor, Chamfort had left piled in boxes a large number of small pieces of paper on which he had written reflections "rédigés en maximes (presented as maxims)," anecdotes, facts useful "à l'histoire des moeurs (for social history)," witticisms, and reparties which he had heard or made. Ginguené says that on these pieces of paper he found written

Produits de la Civilisation Perfectionnée (Fruits of perfected culture)
1re Partie: Maximes et Pensées (Maxims and Reflections).
2e Partie. Caractères (Characteristics).
3e Partie. Anecdotes (Anecdotes).

Ginguené continues, "Reading that, I had no doubt that it was the title and divisions of a large work Chamfort had hinted at to very few people, and for which he had been collecting material for such a long time."

The works Chamfort published in his lifetime are not memorable, and are now no longer read. His extraordinary reputation as a misanthropic wit, revolutionary, and then defender of an ideal of social justice even against Robespierre and Marat would have ensured for him a footnote in biographies and in works of literary and Revolutionary history even without the reflections written on the pieces of paper in the boxes, but what makes him an important author is the collection of raw scraps, some or all of which he might, had he lived, have used for, or in, any of an infinite number of possible ways in one or more works. We can trust Ginguené that Chamfort had hinted from time to time that he was collecting material for a large work, and that the material he had collected was that discovered in the boxes. Three categories were mentioned: maxims and reflections, characteristics, and anecdotes. That is absolutely all we know. It is only a reasonable assumption that the general heading *Produits de la civilisation perfectionnée* is ironic. We do not know whether it was ever considered for use as a title. We have a few letters, the works Chamfort actually published, plays, journalism, pamphlets, literary hack work, and the contents of the boxes now conventionally presented as *Maximes, pensées, caractères et anecdotes*, 1,340 numbered reflections in eight chapters, with three appendixes and some dialogue fragments, the 73 *Petits dialogues philosophiques*.

If Ginguené was telling the literal truth—and there is no reason to suppose that he was not—in the "Notice" to the four-volume 1795 *Edition des Oeuvres de Chamfort recueillies et publiées par un de ses amis*, Chamfort did not indicate any order, chapter division, or subject division. We simply do not know what book he would have written. The contents suggest that it would have been some sort of ironic reflection on social issues containing sharply observed remarks and anecdotes illustrating forms of behaviour. The assemblage as it stands would have found a publisher as a collection of aphorisms and anecdotes, but could have been worked up into a series of chapters other than those as which it is now presented, and in sorting through what he had written Chamfort would at the very least have sharpened or blunted the tone of the collection, and organized its content.

There is much forced cleverness along with the real wit, and an almost touching total effort to grasp the mechanisms of society, to see straight through the distorting fog of convention and the interplay of individual interests. Chamfort is trying very hard to reduce what he knows to be complex issues into simple and pithy antitheses. It is noticeable that he fairly frequently uses the first person singular, and that there is a comparatively high proportion of anecdote to aphorism. There are snatches of conversation, exclamations, and questions. Some of the remarks are genuinely funny, and the formulations often brilliantly succinct, but the register varies from serious and not very remarkable observations about the need for or the utility of this or that to brilliantly honed expression of shrewdly observed truth. The remarks on the pieces of paper in the boxes are not at all homogeneous, and there is no reason that any individual one of them would have been incorporated into or used for the final work.

However, even when all of this is taken into account, there are some important conclusions that can be drawn about Chamfort's outlook on life as well as on his literary skills. He does believe that some individuals are more highly endowed than others. He is withering about the way in which education is conceived as training for conformity to the unjust values imposed in the name of sacred, public and legislative authority. He believes that society has deformed nature. Society is not nature's development, but its destruction, and we should have trusted natural instinct, not perverse reasoning:

L'homme, dans l'état actuel de la société, me paraît plus corrompu par sa raison que par ses passions. Ses passions (j'entends ici celles qui appartiennent à l'homme primitif) ont conservé, dans l'ordre social, le peu de nature qu'on y retrouve encore

(Humanity, in the present state of society, seems to me more corrupted by its reason than by its passions. Its passions (I mean here those which belong to primitive man) have conserved in the social order whatever little that is natural that can still be found there).

Is that too harsh on reason? Is it a second thought or a totally unrelated observation when Chamfort writes,

Pour parvenir à pardonner à la raison le mal qu'elle fait à la plupart des hommes, on a besoin de considérer ce que ce serait que l'homme sans raison. C'était un mal nécessaire

(To be able to pardon reason for the harm it has done to most of humanity, you have to consider what humanity without reason would be like. It was a necessary evil).

Or does he simply change his mind:

Notre raison nous rend quelquefois aussi malheureux que nos passions: et on peut dire de l'homme, quand il est dans ce cas, que c'est un malade empoisonné par son médecin

(Sometimes our reason makes us as unhappy as our passions, and it can be said that, when that is the case, we are invalids poisoned by our doctor).

Chamfort has passing remarks about great figures of the past, some of whom he genuinely admires. There are many anecdotes about literary figures. The vaunted pessimism is sometimes difficult to take seriously:

Vivre est une maladie dont le sommeil nous soulage toutes les 16 heures. C'est un palliatif. La mort est le remède

(Living is an illness to which sleep brings relief every 16 hours. That is a palliative. Death is the cure).

On love and marriage there is little more than cleverly turned worldly cynicism. Here, as elsewhere, there are brilliant encapsulations of half-truths, tantalizing hints of how great a work Chamfort might have achieved, and plain evidence of how skilfully he could write. Unhappily the unsynthesized insights and heterogeneity of register do not really allow of any adequate assessment of Chamfort's literary achievement. Much is lightweight, witty, amusing, almost all is fascinating, but the reflections as we have them represent too inchoate a state of a large work for it to be possible to make confident comments about the nature of the synthesis Chamfort might have produced, or the imaginative quality of the book he might have written.

PUBLICATIONS

Collections

Edition des Oeuvres de Chamfort recueillies et publiées par un de ses amis, 4 vols., 1795
Oeuvres complètes, 5 vols., 1824–25

Maxims

Maximes et pensées, caractères et anecdotes, 2 vols., 1953
Maximes et pensées, caractères et anecdotes, 1968

Plays

La jeune Indienne, comedy, one act in verse (1764), 1764
Le Marchand de Smyrne, comedy, one act in prose (1770), 1770
Mustapha et Zéangir, verse tragedy (1776), 1777

Other

Epître d'un père à son fils pour la naissance de son petit-fils, 1764
L'Homme de lettres, 1765
Grandeur de l'homme, ode, 1767
Combien le génie des grands écrivains influe sur l'esprit de leur siècle, 1768
L'Eloge de Molière, 1769
Sébastien Chamfort à ses concitoyens en reponse aux calomnies de Tobiesen Duby, 1793

Biographical and critical studies

Teppe, Julien, *Chamfort, sa vie, son oeuvre, sa pensée*, 1950
Richard, P.J., *Aspects de Chamfort*, 1959

CHAPELAIN, Jean, 1595–1674.

Man of letters, literary theorist, critic, and poet.

LIFE

Chapelain's father, Sébastien, was a lawyer with a lucrative practice. He had married Jehanne Corbière, daughter of a friend of Ronsard, in 1587. The marriage contract is dated 19 May. There were five children: a daughter, Marie, born on 23 July 1588, who married a lawyer who took over the legal practice; Chapelain himself, born in Paris on 4 December 1595; Jean II who died in infancy; Anne, born on 11 July 1600, who married a procureur au Grand Conseil; and Catherine, born on 22 April 1603, who married another procureur. Chapelain was marked by the family milieu all his life, frugal to the point of parsimony, trained to believe in the prudent counsels of the shrewd upper bourgeoisie, careful of dignity, reputation, and status, keen to remain economically secure, neither personally indulgent nor in any way inclined to whimsy, or even imagination.

Chapelain was taught early to read and write, and had a series of private tutors before being sent at the age of about 10 to the Collège de Lisieux, where he made little progress. After two years there he was sent to Frédéric Morel, the senior holder of a royal chair who took in pupils and was reputed to be the best tutor in Paris. Chapelain attended lectures in the university, finished his schooling back at the Collège de Lisieux, taught himself Italian and Spanish, and started to study medicine. On his father's death he was obliged to give up, and twice obtained employment in aristocratic households with the help of ecclesiastical protection. The bishop of Laon, Sourdeau, found him a place with the baron de Bec, and then L'Aubespine, bishop of Orléans, obtained for him a post with Sébastien le Hardy, seigneur de la Trousse, later Grand-Prévôt de France, whose secretary and steward he became, as well as tutor to the four children.

He stayed with the family for 17 years. He was given a titular post which, for a period, obliged him to wear a sword, a fact which 40 years later was to provoke ribald comments from Chapelle and Furetière. He was still secretary to La Trousse in 1631, but by 1633 had moved and was a sécretaire du roi. He remained, however, on the closest of terms with his former pupils, of whom the two older ones were killed in 1638 and 1648. He was especially fond of the fourth child, who became the marquise de Flamarens and might, but for Chapelain, have lost all her possessions when her son had to flee after fighting a duel.

Chapelain's first literary endeavour was undertaken in his capacity as a tutor. In 1619 and 1620 he published anonymously a translation of the two-part Spanish novel by Mateo Alemán which had started the vogue for the picaresque on its publication in 1599 and 1602, *Le Gueux; ou, La Vie de Guzman d'Alfarache, Image de la vie humaine*....Of Chapelain's near contemporaries, at least Marolles knew who the translator was; Chapelain's work seems to date from 1615 or soon thereafter. On assuming his post in the La Trousse household Chapelain, after a normal education we would regard as classical and some years of medical studies, had to develop a literary culture, but it is important that he appears to have had no inclination to write verse until he was perhaps 35. His poetry was to be a pondered undertaking, not the result of adolescent ardours. His uncertain grasp of history was to reflect the unsystematic nature of his wide reading.

Chapelain certainly read further in the authors of antiquity, as also in early French works, some of which he possessed in editions with Gothic type, and which he was to remember in his 1647 dialogue *La Lecture des vieux romans*. From the beginning, however, he had had no taste for the romances of chivalry. It is clear that he found Aristotle's *Poetics* impressive, as also J.-C. Scaliger's 1561 commentary on them and Heinsius's 1611 *De tragoediae constitutione liber*. Chapelain shared Malherbe's view of what he regarded as Ronsard's poetic effrontery, irregularity, and servility before his antique models, and also criticized Ronsard's inability to produce a sustained epic. Chapelain looked to Italy for advanced cultural values and practices, an important initial difference from Voiture, but quite soon adopted the constellation of pompously censorious attitudes which were to make him a figure of fun even when he was in the position of power to which he attained through his influence with Richelieu and François le Métel de Boisrobert, abbé de Châtillon, virtually Richelieu's secretary for literary affairs. Boileau notoriously scoffed at him, and Tallemant's *Historiette* of Chapelain is accurate, entertaining, and downright malicious.

Chapelain did achieve a real mastery of Italian and Spanish, helping Claude Lancelot produce his textbook on Spanish, although not apparently that on Italian. Like Ménage, he was made a member of the Florentine Accademia della Crusca, working on the purity of the Italian language, but Ménage, acting in concert with the habitués of the Saturday receptions of Madeleine de Scudéry, solemnly asked Chapelain to adjudicate between two madrigals, one of which, galant but in French, appeared to be based on the other, pastoral, and in Italian, which Ménage said was by Tasso, although he had written it himself. Sensitivity to poetic nuance was never Chapelain's strong suit in any language, and he was duly flattered, and duped. His judgement in a letter to Balzac of 11 July 1640 that Malherbe's gifts were more for elocution than for poetic inspiration was, however, undoubtedly correct. It shows not only that he was not a mere disciple of Malherbe, but also that he could see that Malherbe's verse was "de fort belle prose rimée (very fine rhymed prose)." His views were a lot wider than Malherbe's. In his late twenties, he also appears to have helped to get Toussaint de Bray to publish in 1622 Alessandro Tassoni's satirical and mock heroic *La secchia rapita*, which the author had not dared publish in Italy.

By 1620 Chapelain knew Vaugelas and Malherbe. The preface to the second part of *Guzman* had referred to a group of linguistic purists to which Chapelain did not belong, and whose rules, he said, he did not know. Chapelain must have meant the circle of Malherbe and his disciples, and he must have been invited to join them. The achevé d'imprimer of the second part of *Guzman* is 25 December 1619. When Malherbe and Vaugelas were consulted about his long narrative poem *Adone* by Giambattista Marino, invited to Paris by Marie de Medici in 1615 after three spells in Italian prisons, a probable murder, and a certain escape from assassination, they called in Chapelain, whose counsels Marino insisted on incorporating in the form of a letter-preface, written in 1620, when the work was published in Italian in Paris in 1623.

Chapelain's letter was translated into Italian for the Milan 1625 edition of Marino's work, and became better known than the poem it prefaced, for which Chapelain later said he had not much cared. The preface, intended to protect Marino from what the Italian academies would say, does contain Chapelain's fundamental principles, although it scarcely makes a convincing case for the poem. It was the only signed piece of literary criticism or theory which Chapelain ever published, but it did establish his reputation for holding articulate literary principles in accordance with the views of Malherbe and Vaugelas.

Chapelain's introduction to the Hôtel de Rambouillet (see: *Guirlande de Julie*), his friendship with Balzac, his acquaintance with the Arnauld family, and his first efforts at verse must all be dated from about 1627. It was presumably on La Trousse's death in 1632 that Chapelain left the household to move in with his younger sister, Catherine, married for two years to Louis Faroard. He was already almost a figure of fun. He was unkempt, small, dark, and notoriously mean. His personal mannerisms were unpleasant. He was not clean, his clothes were worn out, his handkerchiefs filthy, he spat a great deal, and he dribbled. The dirty wig, worn askew, was an object of ridicule years before the famous satire, the *Chapelain décoiffé*, probably written in 1664, although only published a year later.

It now seems clear that Chapelain quite deliberately set about acquiring a position of influence, systematically intriguing, buying support with favours of whose bestowal he had achieved control, while taking care to ingratiate himself with his most powerful critics. Tallemant writes

M. Chapelain est un des plus grands caballeurs du royaume: il a toujours une douzaine de cours à faire. Il court après un petit benefice de cent francs. Il en a quelques-uns…Assidu au *Samedy* chez Mlle de Scudéry, il neglige tous ceux qui ne caballent point ou qu'il ne craint pas

(M. Chapelain is one of the kingdom's great intriguers: he has always got a dozen fingers in the pie. He will chase after a little benefice worth 100 francs, and has collected a few… He is assiduous at the Saturdays of Mlle de Scudéry, but ignores all those who do not intrigue or whom he is not afraid of).

He certainly achieved status and wealth, and is said by contemporaries to have left 300,000 to 400,000 livres, of which 240,000 was in cash, along with the reputation of being self-important, touchy about his dignity, and insistent on his literary authority. In 1653 he lent 30,000 livres to the Marquise de Rambouillet, the Montauziers and Angélique-Clarisse d'Angennes. The apparent paradox in his position can be resolved because his judgements were in fact flexible, and his sympathies wide. He was astute enough to remain friendly with both sides in several major disputes, with Richelieu as well as the Arnauld family, with Condé as well as Mazarin. His philosophy was that of his friend Gassendi, an enlightened, undogmatic Epicureanism, scarcely differing in moral attitude from the widespread neostoicism of the magistracy.

He was a sincere if undevout Christian, more apt to suspend judgement than to look to religion for spiritual experience, as suspicious of baroque devotional practices as of the cult of the madrigal, although he wrote one, and he required the reassurance of properly asserted power structures, demanding conformity. He had close friends associated with Port-Royal (q.v.), and later sympathized with their cause. He was one of the few people in France, aristocrats, bourgeois, or simple populace, to approve of the execution of Montmorency, involved with the king's brother in armed rebellion, although really it was only a ridiculous last-ditch assertion of feudal privilege. The royal troops had ironically been forced on 1 September 1632 to take Montmorency prisoner on the battlefield at Castelnaudary, to save his life when his own side would not retrieve him as he lay, apparently dying. From all sides there were strong pleas for clemency, and even Richelieu at least seemed less disinclined to mercy than Louis XIII.

Chapelain objected not to scheming, but to flattery. What counted was the imposition of rational principles by a firm central power such as he found first in Richelieu, and subsequently in Mazarin and then Colbert. This did not, however, imply unlimited support for an hereditary monarchy, which was merely as convenient a way as any other to provide for the headship of state. Chapelain wrote to Balzac on 25 September 1632 that he thought politics, which contributed to society's well-being, more important than literature, which contributed only to its pleasure, an opinion he might not have been willing to reiterate 30 years later. On a number of occasions he did in fact turn down offers of political appointments, but he willingly enlisted artistic achievement in the service of political aims.

At the end of 1632 Chapelain was lent cardinal Bentivoglio's history of the war in Flanders, and circulated among friends an essay on the impartiality required in a historian's judgements. Boisrobert showed it to Richelieu, who disagreed, holding that it was the historian's duty to narrate without making any judgement at all. Chapelain wrote to Boisrobert defending his position, and matters might have stayed as they were, but Chapelain had now come to Richelieu's attention, and submitted to him the *Ode à Richelieu* which, after having been examined by the cardinal, was published, with the cardinal's own suggested improvements incorporated into the text, in 1633. On 5 August 1633 Chapelain was received by Richelieu. From then on, Chapelain was in the half-yearly pay of the cardinal until the payments became an annual pension in 1636.

Malherbe himself had frequented the Hôtel de Rambouillet. The marquise had become a devotee of his reform of the language, and welcomed Chapelain as Malherbe's continuator. Chapelain in turn brought Conrart, whom he must have known by 1627, to the chambre bleue (see: *Guirlande de Julie*). It was not before April 1638 that Chapelain also introduced Balzac who, true to the tradition of Malherbe, praised the reign of good sense over erudition and pedantry. Chapelain was in pursuit of a clientele to acknowledge him after Malherbe's death as the new leader of the new literary school, but in fact the Hôtel de Rambouillet was too joyously optimistic as well as too worldly and frivolous for Chapelain and his friends to use it as the platform they were seeking. The marquise became more hesitant, and Chapelain's alliance with Montauzier, whose later patronage of the "modernes" in the Querelle des anciens et des modernes (q.v.) was not based on any philosophical discernment of the implications of their position, became so strong that neither he nor Conrart, both with sensibilities attuned to the values of the "anciens," attended when Montauzier was not there. Almost open hostilities broke out with Voiture, who had dared to maintain that good sense took priority over literary rules, and with whom the imperious Julie d'Angennes's alliance must partly have been a way of manifesting her distaste for Montauzier, whom she did, however, finally agree to marry. On the whole the Marquise was on Voiture's side, with Pisani, her son, as well as Julie.

The first two cantos or "chants" of Chapelain's *La Pucelle* were read in the Hôtel de Rambouillet's chambre bleue in 1637. Arnauld d'Andilly, an habitué, had presented Chapelain to the duc de Longueville, and it was the opportunity the subject gave him to celebrate Longueville's ancestor Dunois which determined his choice of Jeanne d'Arc as the central figure of his projected epic. In 1632 Chapelain was still hard up and in February 1633 apparently keen on a likely appointment to Rome as secretary to the French ambassador, the comte de Noailles. He was not appointed, and may have been reluctant to have to go to Rome, or to undertake the duties proposed, or he may not have been offered the post, but it seems likely that the Arnauld family arranged instead for patronage from Longueville, to whom the first two chants of the poem were read, probably in March 1633. Le Maistre took Chapelain to call on Longueville. He left with 2,000 livres, soon to be converted into a regular pension. It is possible, and has been contended, that Chapelain's poetic inspiration might have developed differently and successfully had it not been for his deference to Arnauld d'Andilly's literary tutelage.

By 1637 there had been a revolt against Chapelain's ascendancy in the chambre bleue. Voiture, Mme de Rambouillet's son the marquis de Pisani, and his friends, the comte de Guiche and the comte de Vaillac, were defining their taste for sophisticated, witty, light-weight but elegant galanterie, of whose historical social function they might not even have been aware, against the more solemn attitudes of the Arnauld family, Chapelain, and Montauzier. Chapelain's prestige at the Hôtel no doubt increased his value to Richelieu, but his real sphere of influence became the small gatherings from 1629 at the house of the wealthy Valentin Conrart, a sécretaire du roi. These weekly gatherings became the nucleus of the future Académie française.

The group, one among several similar such circles, was mostly young, with the exception of the 59-year-old Gombauld, and its members were mostly well off. With Chapelain, Conrart, and Gombauld there were Malleville, secretary to the maréchal de Bassompierre, the lawyer Giry, Cerisay, intendant to the duc de la Rochefoucauld, Godeau, Philippe Habert, and his brother the abbé de Serisy, making nine in all. Conrart and Gombauld were Protestants. It was not a specifically literary group although, in the manner of such circles, poems, prefaces, or letters would be read out at the weekly gatherings. The occasions were informal, often ending in a walk or a meal. What united the group, apart from simple friendships, was a concern for purity of linguistic usage. Camus refers to the circle in 1629 as an "Académie de Puristes (academy of purists)." Faret got to hear of the meetings and told Boisrobert, who asked if he might attend. Boisrobert told Richelieu, who immediately saw how useful such a group could be to him.

Of its members, only Chapelain was not reluctant to accept official status for the group. Richelieu insisted on being its protector, and was annoyed with Boisrobert when he proposed Séguier for that position. The names of a director and a chancellor were picked out of a hat, and a secretary, Conrart, was elected. Desmarets, Boisrobert, and Séguier became members; statutes were drawn up; from 13 March 1634 a register was kept; and letters patent were signed by Louis XIII on 29 January 1635. The parlement de Paris, correctly sniffing a centralizing move from Richelieu and sharing with almost everyone else hostility to the new official body, took two and a half years to register the letters patent on 9 July 1637. Chapelain may have helped to still Balzac's initial distrust both on grounds of principle—"c'est une tyrannie qui va s'établir sur les esprits (it is a tyranny which will impose itself on people's minds)," and of implementation—"if those people belong to an academy, it is as its beadles"—but Chapelain himself noted that the cardinal wanted "à ne souffrir dans son assemblée que des gens qu'il connaisse ses serviteurs (to suffer in his assembly only those he knows to be willing to do his bidding)." The singing of the praises of the great, no novelty, was now being increasingly organized. Quite soon it would make servants out of flatterers. In 1635 the *Parnasse royal* celebrated Louis XIII, and the *Sacrifice des Muses* sang the glories of Richelieu. Both volumes were recueils or collections, had privilèges of 23 April 1633, and were published by Cramoisy.

Chapelain's interest in helping Richelieu was no doubt primarily literary. The new body was immediately given the task of drawing up a grammar and dictionary, so utilizing its interest in purity of linguistic usage, and these were to be followed by a rhetoric and a poetics. The new Académie was, however, also charged with theological and other censorship, and with finding polemicists like Jean Silhon and Jean Sirmond to defend Richelieu's policies. Chapelain was determined to make clear that the new body was not just the policy instrument that everyone feared. It would judge only texts freely submitted to it. Its principles were those of Malherbe, but its formalities rigorously kept it from being merely the literary extension of the administrative arm, as its behaviour was to demonstrate in the matter of Pierre Corneille's *Le Cid*.

Chapelain's attitude to literature became plain in what amounted to the dramatic manifesto of his *Lettre sur la règle des vingt-quatre heures* to Godeau of 29 November 1630. His attitude to literature is exactly the same as his attitude to medicine would have been, had he continued his medical studies. What are the rational norms by which the practice of the art should be guided? Intellectually, this is a "moderne" position. If Chapelain is not interested in genius, or the imaginative function of literature, he is not interested in authority either, unless it is supported by reasoning, as he thought Aristotle's views were. He did not, however, share the "moderne" sensibility, any more than his later opponent, Boileau.

Chapelain's views on the unity of time can be seen as half of a diptych, of which the *Adone* preface was the other part. He was still an employee of the La Trousse household, known only for *Guzman* and the preface. Boisrobert had not yet drawn Richelieu's attention to him. But the 24-hour rule was quickly asserted by Mairet in the preface to *Silvanire*, and began to win more general acceptance among the authors of pastorals, writing for audiences more cultivated than those for which the tragi-comédies were intended. It is only when the acting troupes wanted to move up-market that they forced the authors to observe the unities, not, as is sometimes supposed, the other way round. The acceptance of the unities by the classical French theatre was due more to Montdory than to anyone else. If Chapelain thought that reason validated antique custom, Montdory knew that the box office would be helped by catering for greater audience sophistication, which meant adopting the rules filtering down from the pastorals.

Chapelain may have discussed the unities with Richelieu, to whom he certainly spoke over the production of the *Comédie des Tuileries*, played before the queen on 4 March 1635. The play was by the "five authors" of Richelieu's society of drama-tists, Rotrou, L'Estoille, Corneille, Boisrobert, and Colletet, but Chapelain appears to have worked on a sketch of the play, which was probably by Richelieu himself. The two brief pieces *Discours de la poésie représentative*, clearly intended to become part of something else, may well have been elaborated for presentation to Richelieu after a discussion about the *Comédie des Tuileries*. On 6 August 1635 Chapelain read one of the 20 discourses presented to the academy. He chose as his subject "Contre l'amour (Against love)." At the Hôtel de Rambouillet he had played the galant of Angélique Paulet, born about 1591 and well into her forties, whose poetic "metamorphosis" into a lioness he had celebrated.

He had never thought highly of Pierre Corneille, and is certainly the substantial author of *Les Sentiments de l'Académie française* on *Le Cid*, dated 1638 but published in December 1637, although we cannot be quite sure of exactly what pressures on precisely which points Richelieu exercised on him. The indications are that he might have preferred not to have had to write the piece at all, but that it does reflect his opinions and judgements. Corneille's piece was testing the acceptability of new values, and Chapelain disliked disturbing the established order of society's attitudes, which he thought should be, and probably were, dictated by reason. He may, one suspects, have settled for political necessity. What he had originally praised had been Corneille's embellishments of detail. Richelieu dictated the document's severity of tone, even if the criticisms of the play's structure and intention were Chapelain's.

Chapelain continued to work at *La Pucelle*, while publishing a score or so of occasional grand odes and sonnets, including those on Richelieu's illness and death, for the duc d'Enghien in 1645, on the taking of Dunkirk in 1646, and to Mazarin in 1647. It was probably in 1647 that Chapelain wrote his unpublished dialogue *La Lecture des vieux romans*. From the early 1630s he had advised Richelieu and Séguier on writers worthy to receive royal liberalities, and he intervened in favour of Gombauld as well as Vaugelas. He succeeded in making himself the equivalent of official adviser on literary matters to a number of authors as well as to the administrations successively of Richelieu, of Mazarin, who asked Chapelain to stay in Paris when the rest of Longueville's household had to leave during the Fronde, and of Colbert. He ingratiated himself with several major aristocrats by sending them, with a brief personal note, an account of people and affairs, to keep them informed while they were at the front with the army. Originally prepared for Longueville, they were copied by secretaries and despatched once or twice a week.

The first part of *La Pucelle*, in 12 chants or cantos, was finally published by Courbé at the end of 1655, in a magnificent folio dated 1656. The ordinary edition cost 15 livres and the de luxe edition 25. Courbé produced a second, cheaper duodecimo edition in March. The duc de Longueville added a further 1,000 livres to Chapelain's pension, but the poem, of which the original first chant is now the seventh, sold well only to the curious. There were, however, six editions in two years, and there was a pamphlet war about the poem in which privilèges were withdrawn and violent and obscene language was used. There exist three notebooks full of corrections proposed to Chapelain by Arnauld d'Andilly as the poem was being written. In spite of everything, Chapelain undertook the projected second part, finally completed in 1670, but unpublished until 1882.

Chapelain's voluminous correspondence was from this point addressed to a wider range of recipients, but is more formal than it had been, semi-official instead of intimate. The great change in literary style inaugurated by Pascal's *Lettres provinciales* as one generation took over from another had passed Chapelain by. Then on 10 February 1659 Colletet died and Gilles Boileau was proposed as his replacement in the Académie française. Ménage was not a member of the Académie but, acting on Pellisson through Mlle de Scudéry, he succeeded in getting the election blocked. Pellisson had been absent for the first vote, but now got seven members to reverse their vote, and five who never attended to come and cast a black ball. He himself spoke for an hour and a half.

Chapelain directed the campaign in favour of Gilles Boileau, and in the end imposed a solution which involved his election, although Pellisson broke completely with Chapelain and Conrart, a matter not without its importance in view of the link between Pellisson and Foucquet, to be disgraced in 1661, and of the fact that Mazarin was to die in 1661 and that Chapelain was to work closely with his successor, Colbert, who had toppled Foucquet. Chapelain was not personally as vindictive as the ministers he worked for, and it should be remembered that Ménage was well treated, like Pellisson, on the list of "gens de lettres vivans en 1662 (men of letters living in 1662)" which Chapelain was invited to draw up for Colbert. The withdrawal of Ménage's pension from 1666 merely followed his refusal to write poetry for money, as he put it.

But Ménage had made his hostility to Chapelain perfectly clear, and the hostilities were prefigured between Foucquet's entourage—the nascent party of the "modernes" in the Querelle des anciens et des modernes, with Ménage, Mlle de Scudéry, and Pellisson—and that of Chapelain, with his fixed rules and the constant appeals to order, reason, and discipline to which the partisans of the "anciens" would rally. The groupings are not tidily congruent. Chapelain detested Boileau after the satire of 1664, and could work with Colbert to much the same ends as Perrault, the champion of the "modernes," while in Foucquet's entourage La Fontaine was not intellectually a partisan of the "modernes." But, when all due allowance is made for personal alliances and animosities, for financial inducements and political or religious necessities, the split in sensibility which was behind the confrontation of the Querelle was steadily opening up. It was to some extent disguised by the financial pressures exercised by Colbert.

In spite of the importance of the 1662 list, and its judgements, Chapelain's authority was dwindling before Mazarin died. The list itself is not a formal document drawn up for submission to a minister. It reads at best like hastily compiled notes, likely for several internal reasons to be minutes of one or more consultations, and the comments suggest that it was intended to indicate to Colbert on whom he should rely for various forms of royal homage—poets, historians, scholars, dramatists, panegyrists, and preachers—with the pressingly urgent aim of finding a royal historiographer. Chapelain may well have composed a formal document based on these notes, but, if he did, it has not survived. The gratifications followed only later, were not distributed in such a way as to relate them to Chapelain's comments, and were, to start with, quite strictly geared to services already rendered, or likely soon to be rendered, not to the general tenor of the abilities listed by Chapelain. Another list immediately follows that attributed to Chapelain on the same manuscript, which suggests that lists in addition to Chapelain's were solicited, drawn up, and submitted.

Chapelain had known Colbert well for some time before Mazarin's death, for which he sent Colbert his sympathies. Colbert had already some years previously asked Costar for a list of writers who might be persuaded to sing the glories of the monarch. It was reasonable that he should turn to Chapelain, who replied on 18 November 1662, no doubt following his letter with detailed suggestions for using men of letters and artists for the service of the king's grandeur. No time was being wasted. The notes attached to Ablancourt's name strongly suggest his suitability for appointment as historiographer, and imply that the need to make that appointment may have prompted Colbert's request for the *Mémoire* in the first place. Of the 90 writers, 18 are historians, or might have been thought of for the post of historiographer. Chapelain announced his provisional appointment to Ablancourt on 9 December. In the end the appointment fell through on religious grounds, and went to Mézeray instead, although Ablancourt was given a gratification of 1,500 livres.

The young man it was proposed to glorify was 24 and Colbert, the agent of the glorification, had just toppled from power those patrons and prospective patrons, the financiers, who had escaped the ruin which had befallen most of the remnants of the aristocracy before or during the Fronde. It has never been sufficiently emphasized that most of the great literature of 17th-century France not written for lucrative performance, whether strictly as drama or not, was, significantly, to a great extent published anonymously, and was either state-subsidized or written by authors whose means and dignity allowed or compelled them to avoid the professional status of writers. A whole class of prospective alternative patrons to the king, the landed aristocrats and recently enriched financiers, had either ceased to exist, or at least could not assume the function of patrons on the scale required.

Colbert's organization (see: Perrault) included control of all royal construction, painting, medals, history, and versification of all sorts, and was certainly thorough. The movement had begun even before the death of Mazarin. The technical arts were liberated from the old guilds, only to become subject to royal policy. Even the subjects of the tapestries were to be specified when Lebrun was put in charge at the Gobelins, and when in 1660 engraving was declared a liberal art, the price paid for properly professional status was effectively dependence on some form of state licensing. It was, however, from late in 1662 that the organization of literature was subjected to tighter control.

Chapelain's *Mémoire* comprises first 50 French authors not belonging to the Académie française, of whom 20 wrote in Latin. There follow the names of the 40 academicians. The list does not reflect known friendships and animosities, nor judgements of value, only of probable utility. Chapelain speaks highly of both Ménage and the disgraced Pellisson and, if he is erratic, it must be remembered that neither Pascal nor Boileau had published anything under their own name, and that at this date the omission of La Fontaine's name was not extraordinary. Chapelain includes academicians, like the archbishop of Paris, for whom he cannot have been seeking money. It seems unlikely that Chapelain knew just how influential his view would be in the distribution of largesse to those willing to play in Colbert's orchestra, and that the defects of his list derived not so much from prejudice as from a lack of taste and discernment, as well as an unwillingness to be harsh on writers with established reputations.

Chapelain was one of those invited by Colbert to attend the meeting with Perrault, Bourzeys, and Cassagne on 3 February

1663 leading to the establishment of the "petit conseil," which developed into the Académie des Inscriptions et Belles-Lettres. He was assiduous in gathering in and himself composing material for the ultimately abandoned *Recueil des Eloges du Roi*, intended to include his own notorious sonnet, comparing Louis XIV to Mars, Jupiter, and the sun, "Quel astre flamboyant sur nos provinces erre? (What fiery star traverses our country?)" Although he had no official post, Chapelain was clearly an indispensable cog in Colbert's vast machinery for establishing royal cultural hegemony in everything from poetry and history to science and medallions.

What was taking place was a quite extraordinary intensification and systematization of what had never been a totally disinterested patronage of the arts, although it had once been feudalized and princely rather than, as it had begun to become, centralized and royal. Richelieu had paid largely out of his private purse, but had effectively subjected many of the pensions he paid to annual revision. Mazarin had transferred the onus of payment to the state. Colbert was to tighten and institutionalize the whole system with internal public relations his chief aim. It was one of the conditions for peace and prosperity that the people should be made to believe in the king, his glory, and his administration, that what was left of the aristocracy should be kept under control, and even, if there was absolutely no way of avoiding it, that the king should be kept quiet by being given his new palace in the country and such other illusions of grandeur and tastes of power as he required.

It was Louvois who urged Louis XIV on to try to achieve international glory. He died before the bankruptcy to which his policies condemned France became unavoidable and obvious. Meanwhile the sums spent on the celebrated royal gratifications were small, only 77,500 livres in 1664. The peak year, 1669, saw a total of 108,350 livres, roughly the cost of Bernini's visit to Paris, or about two thirds of Mme de Montespan's annual allowance of 150,000 livres for the upkeep of the king's three illegitimate offspring. The idea of paying gratifications to foreigners was neither new nor wholly unconnected with the policy of satisfying domestic opinion.

From early in 1663 Chapelain was directly concerned with gratifications, and no longer with the position of historiographer. He instructed prospective French receivers of gratifications in ways of demonstrating their acceptability, and became easily Colbert's principal source of advice on the foreign list. By now Chapelain was plainly favouring his friends, especially Heinsius, from whom he also sought advice. He had correspondents in Madrid and Stockholm, and thought himself adequately informed about Italy. Unfortunately comprehensive information is available only from 1664. We are incompletely informed about dates, amounts, and foreign recipients of the 1663 emoluments. They included Heinsius, Gevaertius, Vossius, Huyghens, Boeclerus, Hevelius, Leo Allacius, and Graziani. Loret reported the distribution in the *Muse Historique* for 9 June 1663, lamenting in his usual doggerel his own omission. The announcements were also staggered, to encourage those with flatteries still to be composed. Some apparent gratifications were actually payments for other services rendered, like that to Priolo for spying. Chapelain attended assiduously to his obligations to get the right music from his choir; the whole chiaroscuro of greed, grasping, flattery, bribery, ruthlessness, sulking, and incense-burning looked almost as undignified and comic to Chapelain's more enlightened contemporaries as it does to us.

After 1664 Chapelain's advice was scarcely sought or heeded for the French list. The foreign list peaked at 14,800 livres in 1667, but declined steeply in 1674, the year of Chapelain's death, tardily reflecting the king's increasingly bellicose attitudes. As expenditure at Versailles mounted, so money for other cultural purpose also became tighter. By 1667 it is possible to be reasonably sure that there were few personal consultations between Colbert and Chapelain. The correspondence does not mention any; Colbert was too busy to be called on; and Chapelain was increasingly infirm and confined to home. From 1665, his influence diminished even more than over the preceding three years, and the younger generation could revenge itself with impunity on the slightly ridiculous, pompous, self-satisfied, and grubby old man.

The most pleasant features of Chapelain's activities are to be sought primarily in the letters, which were naturally not public. What was public was only the atrocious verse and the absurdly influential figure. The cabaret attacks (see: Boileau) became merciless, and Perrault largely took over Chapelain's functions as Colbert's literary adviser. The king's largesse became, probably on that account, less specifically directed towards thurification and took on a more disinterested appearance, honouring achievement as well as acknowledging compliments. Chapelain's correspondence shows clearly his awareness of diminishing credit, but he retained enough to have Boileau's privilège for a new edition of the *Satires* withdrawn in 1671.

On 15 November 1671 Julie d'Angennes died, and Chapelain wrote a moving letter to Montauzier, her husband, a protector of the "modernes," and in particular of Pradon against Racine, but joined with Chapelain in hostility to the sharp new satirical writing of Boileau, and in a friendship which went back to their opposition at the Hôtel de Rambouillet to Voiture and the frivolous poets of galanterie. Godeau died on 21 April 1672, and on 12 June that year, the young duc de Longueville. Chapelain himself had a stroke towards the end of November 1673 from which he never recovered. He died on 22 February 1674. He left a very detailed will, assigning money for a low Mass to be said for the salvation of his soul every day for a year, then an annual High Mass on the anniversary of his death, and giving punctilious instructions for the preservation of his library. They were not observed.

WORKS

It is quite clear from the preceding section that Chapelain's literary importance does not lie in what he wrote, except as a theorist and critic. His letters are of very great historical interest, and often afford skilful examples of an accomplished administrative style, with hinted threats and veiled promises, but they are overwhelmingly functional in intention and effect. No biographer, historian, or critic has a good word to say for *La Pucelle*. Even the most sympathetic have spoken only of its cold regularity, the absence of a single bold conception, original idea, or flicker of true emotion. Slow, digressive, monotonous, with a repetition of battles in the first twelve chants, and of celebrations in the second twelve, unpublished in Chapelain's lifetime, it is allegorical in form and moralizing in aim. Jeanne d'Arc is a figure of divine grace, Agnès Sorel of the human passions. The poem is empty of everything alive. People and feelings give way to abstractions, and the story simply meanders. Jeanne d'Arc disappears from the 12th to the 22nd chant, and again in the last.

Dunois, the figure of virtue, appears only in the second half.

The description of the building of the bonfire might have come from a badly rhymed instruction manual and is too bad to be believable. It could have been omitted. This, however, is what Chapelain makes of the contrast between Bedford's desire to find reason to spare Jeanne and her own desire for martyrdom:

> Mais la Sainte, en l'état où le sort l'a réduite,
> Tenoit pour son salut tout une autre conduite,
> Et son vray sentiment sur sa vie et sa mort
> N'estoit guères semblable à celuy de Bedford

> (But the saint, in the state to which fate had reduced her/
> Was going about her salvation in quite a different way,/
> And her true feelings about life and death/Were not at all
> like those of Bedford).

Chapelain seems almost to be writing a parody of himself, practically tempting the reader to wonder whether a caricature by Boileau could have done worse damage.

Chapelain contributed one of the opening madrigals, at what must have been Montauzier's invitation, to the *Guirlande de Julie* (q.v.). All the madrigals have names of flowers for titles, and Chapelain's single piece is one of several called "La couronne impériale (crown imperial)," a species of fritillary no doubt given pride of place on account of its name. It is as good a poem as Chapelain ever wrote, and at 26 lines one of the longest in the collection. The warrior-lover turns at death in battle into a flower called crown imperial. If the lover has no place in Julie's heart, may the crown find one on her brow. The heavy-handed, graceless madrigal ends with a fair example of Chapelain's wit.

> Au comble d'un succès qui les peuples étonne,
> Vainqueur des ennemis et vaincu du malheur,
> Je rencontray la mort dans le champ de Bellonne;
>   L'amour vid mon désastre, et, flattant ma douleur,
>   Me convertit en une illustre fleur,
>   Que DE L'EMPIRE il nomma la COURONNE.
> Ainsi je fus le prix que cherchoit ma valeur;
> Ainsi par mon trépas j'achevay ma conqueste;
> En cet état, Julie, accorde ma requeste:
>   Sois pitoyable à ma langueur,
>   Et si je n'ai place en ton coeur,
>   Que je l'aye au moins sur la teste

> (At the height of a success which calls forth the admiration
> of peoples,/Conqueror of enemies and conquered by
> unhappiness, I met death in the field of Bellona [goddess of
> war];/Love saw my disaster and, soothing my sorrow,/
> Turned me into an illustrious flower,/Which it named the
> CROWN of the EMPIRE.//So I became the prize sought
> by my valour;/So by my death I achieved my conquest;/In
> this state, Julie, grant my request:/Take pity on my
> languish,/And if I have no place in your heart,/May I at
> least have one on your head).

The translation of *Guzman d'Alfarache*, undertaken by Chapelain for his pupils in the La Trousse household, starts with disparaging comments about translations in general. It is in the "au

lecteur" of the second part that Chapelain defends his style against those whose passion or blindness takes away the proper use of their reason. He appeals to the few whose judgement he respects, mentioning the "puristes" belonging to "une vertueuse assemblée de gens doctes, faisant profession particulière d'examiner... les livres, pour le langage notamment (a virtuous gathering of learned people, whose particular intention is to examine books, particularly for their language)," and who wish "de le repurger de mille superfluités affectées lesquelles en offusquent la grâce et la beauté (to cleanse it again of a thousand superfluous affectations which obscure its grace and beauty)." The reference can only be to Malherbe's group of disciples, pledged to purging the language of gasconisms and Pléiade (q.v.) accretions, to whose judgement Chapelain therefore starts by totally deferring. He goes on to say that he follows the usage of "those two great lights of the century," du Vair and d'Urfé, which makes his deference merely ritual. He must be referring to d'Urfé's *Epistres morales*, and is simply seeking the protection of two great neostoic names, an impression confirmed when he goes on to compare the learned gathering he had just mentioned with the Florentine "Académie de la Crusca."

The letter-preface to Marino's *Adone* is a discourse about epic poetry, notably cautious about the poem it introduces. The text is full of the categories and sub-categories into which Chapelain compartmentalized everything. Marino is praised for having avoided obvious traps, like the mixture of sacred and profane and breaching the unity of action. Chapelain insists on a heroic, regular, properly proportioned, credible, and unified conception without, of course, defining these qualities. He does, however, introduce as early as 1623 the criterion of "vraisemblance (the fictionally or dramatically credible)" which he already pits against "la vérité (the historically true)," showing what will later make Pierre Corneille's theoretical justification of his dramatic practice unacceptable to Chapelain. True poetry, according to Chapelain, makes

> ...un insensible effort sur la fantaisie, en tant qu'elle ne lui
> apporte rien qui ne se juge pouvoir être facilement ainsi, ce
> que la vérité même ne fait pas, sinon autant qu'elle est
> vraisemblable

> (...only a slight demand on the imagination bringing it
> nothing which is not judged quite easily to be as it is repre-
> sented, which is not what the truth itself does, except in so
> far as it is probable).

The endless sub-divisions of Chapelain's preface do not really contain a code of practice, but more nearly provide a series of grids to be placed against a text, and it is not reducing it to a caricature to say that Chapelain's doctrine amounts to little more than the implicit assertion that imaginative texts can be treated in this way, measured against rationally structured grids to check on regularity, invention, novelty, credibility, authenticity, unity of action, and moral elevation. There are rational rules, outside which there cannot exist the full glory of the "poème." Chapelain's enemy, usurper, and successor, Boileau, would later call it the sublime.

The 1630 *Lettre sur la règle des vingt-quatre heures* shows that Chapelain did not at that date know of the existence of the unities as such. He returns to the question of poetic credibility, and the meaning of the criterion of "vraisemblance" becomes clearer. If poetic imitation of life is not exact, then the moral lesson will not be learnt, the passions will not be purged, and the poem's purpose therefore not be achieved.

> Je pose donc pour fondement que l'imitation en tous poèmes doit être si parfaite qu'il ne paraisse aucune différence entre la chose imitée et celle qui imite, car le principal effet de celle-ci consiste à proposer à l'esprit, pour le purger de ses passions déréglées, les objets comme vrais et comme présents; chose qui, régnant par tous les genres de la poésie, semble particulièrement encore regarder la scénique en laquelle on ne cache la personne du poète que pour mieux surprendre l'imagination du spectateur et pour le mieux conduire sans obstacle à la créance que l'on veut qu'il prenne en ce qui lui est représenté

> (I therefore take as the starting point that in all poems the imitation ought to be so perfect that no difference appears between what is imitated and what imitates, for the principal effect of the imitation consists in offering to the mind, in order to purge it of its disordered passions, objects as true and as present. That is something which holds true for all types of poetry, but seems particularly relevant to drama, in which the poet's personality is hidden only the better to capture the imagination of the audience, and the more easily to lead it without obstacle to the belief you want it to have in what is represented before it).

The audience has to believe in the reality of what is merely being enacted if the drama is to have its moral effect, so that truth to historical fact must yield to the suspension of disbelief. There is a sense in which Chapelain is obviously right. Tragedy, at least, depends on identification with a leading figure on the stage, and the argument from historical truth as Corneille was to deploy it was indeed factitious. It is difficult to hold that a play's effect depends on its truth to historical fact. For Chapelain what it depended on was partly the credibility of what was enacted. What was important for him, however, was the moral effect for which, for him, plausibility was at least a sine qua non.

Chapelain's two fragments on *Poésie représentative* are important for the relationship they postulate between the "vraisemblable" and the "merveilleux (marvellous)," which at first sight appear incompatible with one another. Again it is difficult to gainsay Chapelain when he holds that the dramatist's art consists in blending the ordinary with the extraordinary, in such a way as to make the extraordinary appear possible. He is now going as far as articulating the need for the dramatist to stretch the imagination of the audience. "Du judicieux mélange de la vraisemblance et de la merveille naît l'excellence des ouvrages de [la poésie dramatique] (From the judicious mixture of the probable and the marvellous is born the excellence of dramatic poetry)." Unfortunately Chapelain draws back from a discussion of this principle. It is difficult to see how he could have developed it without modifying the rest of his views on drama. The whole century was to see a continued discussion of the utility on stage of miraculous events that, not being psychologically motivated but only divinely caused, could not purge the passions by means of dramatic illusion. That, essentially, is Chapelain's objection to Desmarests de Saint-Sorlin's *Clovis* in a series of

scrappy notes jotted down in 1657 and not worked up into a piece of continuous prose.

Chapelain's original and milder text of *Les Sentiments de l'Académie française...sur la tragi-comédie du Cid* is still close to the final printed text, and is argued with such close reference to Corneille's 1637 text that it can only be read with a copy of that version of the play at hand. Chapelain misunderstands everything important about Corneille's text, but this does not mean he does not also make valid criticisms. The superfluity of the character of the Infanta to the action of the play is, for instance, at least arguable. The circumstances of the Academy's intervention are discussed in the entry on Corneille.

La Lecture des vieux romans is inconclusive. It is a brief dialogue with Ménage, hostile to the Arthurian romances, Sarasin, who praises them, and himself, in which Chapelain shows sympathy for the works he once admired, but whose irregularity he also deplores, and it does not lead to any very firm view. However, from the views expressed about galanterie, it is clear that Chapelain is by no means totally out of sympathy with what will become the "moderne" position. It is possible to extract some sort of corpus of critical writing from Chapelain's correspondence, but his views scarcely evolved, and their implementation was intertwined with other developments, notably in Chapelain's personal relationships and professional career, as is clear from the biography. Neither a great imaginative writer nor a great critic, nor even a lovable character, Chapelain yet had a kindly, sympathetic side to his nature, without which his enormous influence on the literary life of his times cannot really be understood.

PUBLICATIONS

Collection

Opuscules critiques, 1936

Prose

Le Gueux; ou La Vie de Guzman d'Alfarache, Image de la vie humaine, 2 vols., 1619–20 [some editions are entitled *Le Voleur; ou, La Vie de Guzman...*]
Lettre ou Discours...sur le poëme d'Adonis du chevalier Marino in *L'Adone Poëma del Cavalier Marino...*, 1623
Les Sentiments de l'Académie française sur la tragi-comédie du Cid, 1638
Lettres de Jean Chapelain, 2 vols., 1880–83
Dialogue de la Lecture des vieux romans, 1870; critical edition 1971

Verse

[*The collections in which generally single poems by Chapelain were originally published are not given*]
Ode à Mgr le Cardinal duc de Richelieu, 1633
Paraphrase du cinquantiesme psaume, 1637
Ode pour la naissance de Mgr le comte de Dunois, 1645
Ode pour Mgr le duc d'Anguien, 1646
Ode pour Mgr le Cardinal Mazarin, 1647
La Pucelle; ou, La France délivrée, 1656

Biographical and critical studies

Collas, Georges, *Jean Chapelain 1595–1674*, 1912

CHARRON, Pierre, 1541–1603.

Preacher, polemical religious writer, and moralist.

LIFE

Charron's biography goes some way towards explaining the disorder of his mind and the apparent volatility of his opinions. He was an important preacher, a close friend of Montaigne, an inept Catholic religious controversialist, and a hugely notorious popularizer, as he thought, of Montaigne. His most important work, the *De la sagesse*, was loudly denounced in the 17th century as naturalistic, "rationalist" and a seedbed of deism, but it was welcomed by Saint-Cyran and the moralists of Port-Royal (q.v.) as Augustinian. In view of its reception in 1601 it was widely reworked for the posthumous 1604 edition, It draws eclectically on a fashionable neostoicism, and the Bibliothèque Nationale has 39 editions from 1601 to 1672, of which 13 come between 1618 and 1634, although the work was put on the Roman index of prohibited books in 1606. There were at least five late 18th-century editions, although the work had not been published between 1672 and 1762. Montaigne's *Les Essais*, with which *De la sagesse* was connected in the public mind, was similarly unpublished in France between 1669 and 1724.

Modern commentators agree only that the early 17th century took *De la sagesse* very seriously but that Charron's work is devoid of strictly literary merit. Opinion remains divided about the extent of his naturalism or alternatively his Augustinianism. It has wrongly been suggested that he was guilty of duplicity, teaching one religion for the masses and another for the initiates, and with more justification that he simply did not know what he thought, and allowed his views not so much to oscillate as to remain incompatible with one another. It is, however, plain that he was not a deep thinker, but that his work, whatever its historical importance, was intended to convince by its arguments, to impress with its erudition, and to be religiously edifying, with morally uplifting considerations.

Charron's early biography is obscure, but he was born at Paris into a family of bookshop owners and was apparently one of 25 children of the same parents. The only contemporary account of Charron's life is the brief biography by his friend, G.M. La Rochemaillet, prefacing the 1604 edition of *De la sagesse*, which La Rochemaillet procured after Charron's death in the face of considerable difficulty and strong opposition from the Sorbonne. Charron is said to have had a good liberal arts education at the university of Paris, and certainly studied law at Montpellier, where he was imprisoned during the religious wars in 1567–68, graduated bachelier in 1568, and took his licentiate and doctorate in law in 1571. His name then appears on the list of advocates at the Paris bar, and he seems briefly to have practised law before abandoning it for theology and the priesthood. He was ordained in 1576, and taught theology and performed minor ecclesiastical functions in a number of dioceses in the south-west, especially in Gascony and Guyenne, by turns official preacher, teacher of theology, cantor, and administrator.

The most likely reconstruction of his life suggests that he continued to practise advocacy until his ordination, when he turned with immediate success to preaching. The bishop of Bazas, about 50 kilometres south-east of Bordeaux, invited him to preach, and he held temporary preaching appointments in the then customary fashion in the dioceses of Bazas, Dax, Lectoure, Cahors, and Condom, before becoming vicar general of Agen and then Bordeaux. His fame was probably assured by early success when he preached at the court of Nérac for Marguerite de Valois, the daughter of Henri II who had married Henri de Navarre in 1572, and for whom Montaigne had probably written the "Apologie de Raimond Sebond," the longest chapter in *Les Essais*. When Charron arrived at Angers in 1588, he was referred to as "Le plus grand prédicateur de France (France's greatest preacher)."

At the court of the Paris parlement, Charron must have mixed with Etienne Pasquier, Jean Bodin, and perhaps Michel de l'Hôpital. In and around Nérac and Bordeaux he met Brantôme, Pibrac, de Thou, and Scaliger, as well of course as Montaigne, of whose sister he became a close friend. The copy of Ochino's catechism which Montaigne gave to Charron is inscribed 1586, although their closer intimacy probably dates from rather later, when Charron established himself at Bordeaux in 1589. Charron was allowed by legal deed to bear the arms of Montaigne's sister and brother-in-law, in return for which Charron made them his heirs.

Early in 1589 Charron preached Lent at Angers. Earlier that year, carried by "un grand bouillon de colère et d'indignation (a great surge of anger and indignation)" on the swell of popular resentment at the murder by Henri III of the Guise brothers in December 1588, Charron had joined the League, on whose behalf he preached. During Lent, Angers was re-taken for the king, and on Easter Sunday Charron, having severed his connection with the League, preached a panegyric of the king, extolling him, as he said, to the third heaven. Later in 1589, Charron wrote his *Discours chrestien qu'il n'est permis…de se rebeller contre son Roy*, published only posthumously in 1606, in an attempt to justify himself. In a letter of April 1589, he wrote

> Recherchant pourquoi je m'étais égaré…j'ai trouvé que c'était la passion et la rage, et que, tant que j'avais été en quelque opinion de Ligue, j'étais toujours comme en colère, en fièvre et émotion continue, dont j'ai bien appris à mes dépens qu'il est impossible d'être ému et sage tout ensemble

> (Seeking why I had gone astray…I found that it was passion and anger and that, while I took the side of the League, I was always as it were enraged, in a continual fever and excitement, from which I learnt to my cost that it is impossible to be excited and wise at the same time).

The treatise on sagesse contains the fruit of a bitter experience.

Probably about 1593, Charron made two unsuccessful attempts to enter religious orders, first the Carthusians and then the Celestines. It may have been on account of his age, since he was already over 50, that he was turned down, although his temperament seems scarcely to have suited the contemplative life. "Théologal," or resident preacher at Condom from 1600, he lived with bourgeois ease in a double house with "Je ne sçay (I do not know)" inscribed on one of the door lintels, answering Montaigne's own motto, "Que sçay-je? (What do I know?)." He had the reputation of a bon viveur, perpetually laughing and cheerful, and was accused at Condom of having called his congregation from the pulpit "ignorant, brutish, without faith, and other unworthy things."

Charron's first published work, dedicated to Henri IV, was the anonymous 1593 *Les trois veritez contre les athees, idolatres, juifs, mahumetans, heretiques et schismatiques.* It was a rambling refutation of Duplessis-Mornay's 1578 *Traité de l'Eglise,* which had been dedicated to Henri IV when, as Henri de Navarre, he was still a Protestant. Charron undertakes to show that there is a God to be adored and served, that of all religions the Christian alone is true and, among Christian beliefs, only the "Catholique Romaine." The idea of an apologetic was inspired by Montaigne's "Apologie," and Charron's book led to discussions with the Protestants which lasted for several years. There was a Protestant reply in 1594, then an answer from Charron in 1595, and the dispute was still continuing in 1599.

Apart from the work of apologetic and *De la sagesse,* Charron published in his lifetime only a series of eight sermons, the two-volume *Octave du Saint-Sacrement* of 1600–01, heavily re-written, without excessive divisions or erudition, in a form suitable for meditative reading. The status of the two works called "Discours chrétiens" is obscure. The first, published posthumously in 1604, contains a series of sermons which appear never to have been preached, along with the *Octave,* and is entitled *Discours chrestiens de la divinité, création, rédemption et octaves du Saint-Sacrement.* The second volume was published only anonymously and only in 1606, entitled *Discours chrestien sur la benediction donnée par Isaac à Jacob son fils puisné, pensant la donner à Esaü son aisné.* It has been credibly dated not later than 1576, is said to have been repudiated by Charron, and contains an account of the election of Jacob, which is made reducible to an entirely arbitrary act of predestination on God's part, "Dieu a aimé l'un et haï l'autre…pour ce qu'il lui a plu (God loved one and hated the other…because it pleased him)."

However, even if this view was an early one, later repudiated, and even if the freedom of the human will is emphatically defended in the fourth discourse, "De la volonté de Dieu," of the *Discours de la divinité* as published in 1604, Charron can still reject as Pelagian in the 10th "discours" ("De la prédestination") of the *Discours de la divinité* the Molinist view that "Dieu prevoyant ceux qui bien appliqueroyent leur volonté, les a eleus, reprouvant aussi ceux qu'il a preveu devoir mal l'appliquer (God, foreseeing those who would apply their wills to good, elected them, reprobating at the same time those he foresaw would apply it to evil)."

The presumption has to be that Charron did in fact repudiate the early facile predestinationism of the *Bénédiction de Jacob,* but that he thereafter maintained simultaneously two orthodox solutions which he had not really thought through, and which were in fact irreconcilable, holding both that God did not force the human will, but left it free, and at the same time that it was heretical to suppose that God took into account what he foresaw about how individual human wills would act when he decreed predestination for some and reprobation for others. Whole pages of the discourses on divinity and on creation, largely composed in 1603, shortly before Charron's death, reproduce verbatim entire chapters from the 1601 version of *De la sagesse.*

In 1596 Charron attended the general assembly of the clergy in Paris and was elected its general secretary. He was obviously regarded as a person of some standing. He returned to Cahors and Bordeaux, moved to Condom in 1600 and, on a visit to Paris in 1603, died very suddenly of a heart attack in the street on 16 November.

WORKS

Les trois veritez is a revealingly unsatisfactory book, which opens the way to an understanding of the mixture of rumbustiousness, shallowness, and well-intentioned confusion which inhabited Charron's mind. In the first *Vérité* the existence of God is affirmed to be rationally demonstrable, and reason is the criterion which distinguishes man from beasts. Historically important is the reliance on an early form of the wager argument most commonly associated with Pascal, but in fact frequently, as here, used before him. Pascal was several times to mention Charron, and frequently remembers the text of *De la sagesse.* We do well to wager that God exists, because if we are right we have all to gain, and if we are wrong nothing to lose. If we wager that God does not exist and are wrong, there is a non-ending eternity of suffering to await us.

Charron also uses here a version of the famous ontological argument originating in Anselm but associated with, among others, Descartes:

> Concevant donc une chose, qui luy soit infinie par puissance et Dieu estant au dessus de toute conception, l'esprit est tenu de croire un Dieu actuellement infiny

> (Since therefore it can conceive something which is potentially infinite, and since God is greater than anything which can be conceived, the mind must believe in the existence of an actually infinite God).

Charron, however, offers a series of alternative arguments. His proofs run in parallel, not in series, and he does not long remain unequivocal on the possibility of a rational proof.

The second *Vérité* emphasizes the fall of man and the need for authority in matters of faith, against reason in what concerns knowledge adumbrating a distinction made more formally and more famously by Pascal in *L'Art de persuader.*

> Ce sont deux mains et deux moyens d'apprehender et recevoir une chose, la raison et l'authorité, ausquelles respondent la science et la foy: ceste là pour l'homme, ceste cy pour le Chrestien

> (There are two ways and two means of perceiving and grasping something, reason and authority, to which knowledge and faith correspond, knowledge for human beings, and faith for Christians).

The formulations of the third *Vérité* are openly fideist.

La creance et la doctrine Chrestienne…est contraire à toute Philosophie et discours de raison, comme il se void en tous les articles de la foy, qui ne peuvent estre comprins ny entendus par entendement humain, voire ils luy semblent impossibles et du tout estranges

(Christian belief and doctrine…is contrary to all philosophy and rational argument, as is seen in all the articles of faith, which cannot be understood or penetrated by the human mind, and even seem impossible, and totally alien).

Much of the material from *Les trois veritez* obviously lends itself to an Augustinian theology and spiritual outlook. *De la sagesse* itself was announced to La Rochemaillet in 1597, completed in 1599, and first published in 1601. There has been some dispute about the thrust of the revisions incorporated into the posthumous 1604 version, but it is now clear that when the important new preface and the motto "Je ne sçay" were added, the chapter order thoroughly revised, and the first book radically transformed, the changes that were introduced were intended to accentuate the fideism, mitigating reliance on nature at the expense of religion and on rational argument, for instance regarding immortality, at the expense of faith. The immortality of the soul becomes in 1604 "aucunement assez prouvée par plusieurs raisons naturelles et humaines, mais proprement et mieux establie par le ressort de la religion que par tout autre moyen (not at all adequately proved by many natural and human reasons, but more properly and better established by recourse to religion than by all other means)."

According to the admittedly unreliable *Naudeana* of 1701, Gabriel Naudé called *De la sagesse* the world's best book after the Bible, and Guy Patin includes it on the list of great books printed in his *Préceptes particuliers d'un médecin à son fils*. Gassendi had Charron's letters copied by Naudé for Peiresc, and Charron's reputation for naturalism spread very quickly. In 1604 the nuntius, Buffalo, wrote to Cardinal Aldobrandini that it was "un livre scandaleux, conforme à la doctrine impie de Machiavel (a scandalous book, in conformity with the impious doctrine of Machiavelli)," meaning that the validity of religious belief is made solely dependent on its social utility, which is only what Machiavelli was rumoured to have held, and not at all what he either said or thought. On the "raison d'état" Charron, remembering Montaigne, combats the notion that individuals may be unjustly treated if it is in the public interest. The Jesuit polemicist opponent of the libertines, François Garasse, attacked the book as "the breviary of the libertines," the Franciscan scientist Marin Mersenne for its naturalism in morals, while Scipion Dupleix referred to the follies of Charron's "sagesse libertine (free-thinking wisdom)," and the book was also castigated by Chanet, Sourdis, and Jean de Silhon.

It was defended not only by Sorel and Bayle, but also by the Port-Royal chaplain Saint-Cyran, perhaps not only on account of his quarrel with Garasse. The preface to the 1604 edition counters the allegations of naturalism by pointing out that Charron is concerned not with divine wisdom, but only with "sagesse humaine…l'excellence et la perfection de l'homme comme homme (human wisdom…the excellence and perfection of human beings as human). The wise man, free from passion, directs himself in all things "selon nature, c'est à dire la raison premiere, universelle loi et lumiere inspirée de Dieu (according to nature, that is to say, the first reason, universal law and light

inspired by God)." The terminology immediately relates the work, rather tardily, to the revival of stoicism. Charron borrows much, especially on the passions, from du Vair, whose text he acknowledges plundering. There are said to be 67 passages in the text of *De la sagesse* exactly copied from Montaigne's *Les Essais*.

There are three books, of which the first, almost unrecognizably transformed in the 1604 edition, deals with man, his nature, weakness, and faculties, his passions, and his social categories. The second book contains the "instructions et regles generales de Sagesse (the instructions and general rules governing wisdom)," and the third particular advice concerning the individual moral virtues and against the various passions. The first book opens with a chapter on self-knowledge, the foundation of wisdom:

regarde dedans toy, reconnois-toy, tiens-toy à toy; ton esprit et ta volonté, qui se consomme ailleurs, ramene-le à soy-mesme

(look within yourself, recognize yourself, contain yourself within yourself. Gather together your mind, and your will which is dissipating itself elsewhere).

The moral importance of self-knowledge and self-containment was a 16th-century commonplace, but Charron's opening is too exactly modelled on that of Sebond's *Theologia naturalis*, translated by Montaigne at his father's behest, for the implied allusion not to have been deliberate. Pascal has often enough been connected with both Montaigne and Charron, but the strong and fascinating possibility that the opening of Charron's *De la sagesse* might link Sebond himself to Pascal, whose purposes were so similar but whose religious outlook was so different from the Spanish theologian's, does not seem to have excited comment. Charron himself now reduces self-knowledge, as Pascal was to do, to a practical scheme for considering humanity under such headings as "vanity," "weakness," "inconstancy," "wretchedness," and "presumption." What follows is occasionally Pyrrhonist in tone, re-forging with du Vair and Justus Lipsius the antique link between stoicism and scepticism.

In the first of the *Trois veritez* Charron had attacked the sceptic Sextus Empiricus, whose views had stimulated wide discussion in France during the religious wars, after the text had been published in 1569 by Gentien Hervet, and it is certain that he did not himself doubt. But the 1604 preface's distinction between the "esprit fort" and the "esprit faible," punning on the strong/weak antithesis to suggest that the disbelievers had not strong minds but weak ones, and the differentiation between reason and authority as criteria of truth in different sorts of knowledge, suggest that Charron was forced back into a fideist position, as Montaigne had been, and both Pascal and Descartes were to be.

Some passages in the early part of *De la sagesse* emphasize the inability of the mind to reach truth, and Charron therefore praises the suspension of judgement, the sceptical ἐποχή (epokè) which he eclectically associates with Plato and Socrates and contrasts favourably with Aristotelian dogmatism. It was anyway a 16th-century commonplace that the cleverest were not the most credulous, and one of the first lessons of sagesse is to "retenir en surseance son jugement (maintain the judgement in suspense)," although here the divine truths of religion are expressly excepted, as they had been from the relativism of

Montaigne's "Apologie de Raimond Sebond," and would be from Descartes's methodic doubt and Pascal's quest for scientific evidence.

It is already clear how equivocal, because inconsistent, Charron's thought is. He could quite reasonably be attacked as naturalistic for some of the things he said or implied, and still legitimately be regarded on account of others as authentically Augustinian. He was as much a predecessor of Descartes as he was of Pascal. In 1601 he asserted the dependence of all human knowledge on sense perception, as the Aristotelian scholastics had done, and yet a score of pages later he is incompatibly relying on the innate ideas for which Descartes would become famous: "L'ame qui est la nature et la forme de tout animal, est de soy toute sçavante sans estre apprise (The soul which is the nature and form of every animal, knows by itself, without being taught)." In 1604 he simply deletes the first sentence about the dependence of knowledge on the senses and replaces it with its denial. The paragraph from chapter 12 which in 1601 had started with the principle, in the formulation taken from Montaigne, "Toute connoissance s'achemine en nous par les sens (All knowledge comes to us through the senses)" begins in 1604, when the chapter number has changed to 10, "Toute cognoissance s'achemine en nous par les sens, ce dit on en l'Eschole, mais n'est pas du tout vray (All knowledge comes to us through the senses, they say in the schools, but that is quite wrong)."

Charron treats the passions more systematically than du Vair, although he borrows from him, generally word for word, much of the physiology as well as the definition. However, he also changes the theory of the faculties in important ways without appearing to notice the implications of what he is doing. For du Vair the passions belonged to the sensitive appetite, which means that, for him, the good for which they strove was material and illusory, but du Vair does not refer them to the imagination. The scholastics had looked on the imagination as the faculty which evoked the passions. Montaigne had inherited this usage, and Charron here goes back beyond du Vair to Montaigne, while continuing, with important consequences, to regard the passions as opinions or errors of judgement. As a result he makes the imagination the source not only of error but also of delusion.

The whole tradition of renaissance scepticism can be shown to have justified itself philosophically by attributing belief in miracles to the imagination, in this matter following Pomponazzi's De incantationibus, which itself drew on a perfectly innocent, although no doubt philosophically vulnerable passage from Ficino's Theologia platonica. By referring the passions as false judgements to the imagination, Charron, following Montaigne, provided the sceptics with a physiological tool which, by exaggerating the power of the imagination, explained away belief in miracles. Charron has a chapter "On imagination and Opinion" in which he states that "la pluspart des choses que le vulgaire appelle miracles, visions, enchantemens (most of what the common people call miracles, visions, and the effects of magic)" derives from the imagination. Such beliefs are never subjected to the scrutiny of the understanding, which gives a "vray, entier et solide jugement des choses (true, whole, and solid judgement of things)," but only from the opinion, its

> ombre et image, mais vaine et fausse...mere de tous maux, confusion, desordres: d'elle viennent toutes les passions et les troubles; c'est le guide des fols, des sots, du vulgaire, comme la raison des Sages et habiles

(shadow and image, but vain and false...mother of all evils, confusion, disorders: from it derive all the passions and disturbances; it is the guide of the mad, the foolish, the common people, as reason of the wise and skilled).

From passages of this sort, it was not difficult for the libertine or sceptical tradition to build a rational substructure to support its doubts during the 17th century. Even Pascal has a fragment on the imagination which, had he used it, could have subverted the traditional apologetic based on miracles which he at one moment contemplated writing.

For Charron the eleven formal passions of the scholastic list need to be eradicated, a view which clearly presupposes that they are false judgements of the intellect rather than the physically based feelings, promptings of the ineradicable scholastic sensitive appetite for which, for instance, 15 years earlier the moralists of Henri III's Palace Academy, including Ronsard, Desportes, Jamyn, Pibrac, Du Perron, and Pontus de Tyard, had generally still taken them. "Sagesse" for Charron is a "maniement reglé de nostre ame, avec mesure et proportion (a properly regulated deployment of our soul, with moderation and harmony)," and it should be acquired not by bestial apathy, but by an again almost Cartesian "vive vertu, resolution et fermeté d'ame...c'est une forte, noble et glorieuse impassibilité, toute contraire à l'autre première (strong determination, resolution, and firmness of soul...it is a vigorous, noble, and glorious impassibility, quite contrary to the other one)."

When he comes to define his principal virtue, which Charron calls "preud'hommie," he uses exactly the same terms as had du Vair, when he was defining virtue,

> La preud'hommie est une droite et ferme disposition de la volonté, à suivre le conseil de la raison. Or cecy est en la puissance de l'homme, qui est maistre de sa volonté

> (Prudence [virtue] is a sound and firm disposition of the will to follow the judgement of the reason. And that is within human power, since we control our will).

"Preud'hommie," practically indistinguishable from what Descartes will call "générosité," is, like du Vair's virtue, defined in terms of a determination to follow extrinsic intellectual judgements of merit. In Charron, it is then directly linked to piety, which for du Vair's Epictetus is the first office of the upright man.

Because Charron, at least in places, regards rational and natural human virtue as distinct from the supernaturally infused virtue of grace, he can combine stoic assertions of the integrity of nature with the Augustinian accentuation of human weakness and the mind's capacity. He could be selectively exploited as a naturalistic, neostoic moralist, a sceptic, and as an Augustinian. He was not a very clear thinker, but he was not dishonest. He was much nearer to being a pragmatic popularizer of eclectically gathered moral platitudes, vigorously expounded in uplifting exhortation for the edification of all.

Since, however, the period immediately following the end of the half-century of religious wars saw the defensive culture of France catching up with the renaissance euphoria which had made continued progress in England, Spain, and Italy, Charron's very riot of confused justifications for, and inter-connections between the newly emerging moral and intellectual attitudes in

France opens up an important insight into the imaginative constraints bearing on less abstract writers as they explored the new views of human behaviour and the moral values and intellectual premisses on which they were being based. Almost because of his confusions, poured out with such energetically eclectic good will, Charron provides a sensitive indication of the cultural constraints at work among the pious and educated in France as the new century was being born.

PUBLICATIONS

Collection

Toutes les oeuvres, 1635

Moral and religious

Les trois veritez contre les athees, idolatres, juifs, mahumetans, heretiques et schismatiques, 1593
L'octave...du Saint-Sacrement, 2 vols., 1600–01
De la sagesse, 1601

Posthumous

De la sagesse, 1604; English version, 1670
Discours chrestiens de la divinité, création, rédemption et octave du Saint-Sacrement, 1604
Discours chrestien, qu'il n'est permis...de se Liguer...contre son Roy, 1606
Discours chrestien sur la benediction donnée par Isaac à Jacob, 1606

Biographical and critical studies

Strowski, F., *Pascal et son temps*, 3 vols., 1907
Sabrié, J.-P., *De l'humanisme au rationalisme. P. Charron, l'homme, l'oeuvre, l'influence*, 1913
Busson, Henri, *La Pensée religieuse française de Charron à Pascal*, 1933
Pintard, R., *Le Libertinage érudit dans la première moitié du XVIIe siècle*, 1943
Popkin, R.H., *The History of Scepticism from Erasmus to Descartes*, 1960
Charron, D.J., *The "Wisdom" of Pierre Charron*, 1961
Levi, A.H.T., *French Moralists; The Theory of the Passions, 1585–1649*, 1964

———————

CHASLES, Robert de: see **CHALLE, Robert**

———————

CHÉNIER, André-Marie, 1762–1794.

Poet.

LIFE

Although Chénier deserves his reputation as the greatest French lyric poet of the 18th century, he published only two poems in his lifetime. The true nature of his importance has emerged only in the 20th century, largely after World War II, although the Pléiade edition of his works dates from 1940. Chénier's execution by guillotine on 25 July 1794, two days before the fall of Robespierre, invited the generation of the 1820s to glorify him as the poet-martyr. His first editor, Henri de Latouche, editor of the early *Mercure de France* and of *Le Figaro*, saw in Chénier in 1819 a poet with the fresh sensibility which could not then have been known as pre-romantic and, although he did it with sureness of taste and excellent literary judgement, he retouched Chénier's poems. Sainte-Beuve, determined to make Chénier the precursor of his own friends, at first still including Hugo, wrote six essays on him between 1829 and 1864. Chénier was then idolized by the Parnassians for quite different but equally valid reasons. José-Maria de Heredia edited the *Bucoliques* in 1906, and Chénier was adopted as a model by the poets known as the "Ecole Romane," who were reacting against the symbolists. The history of his reputation shows how any balanced appreciation of Chénier's personality and poetic achievement was obscured for a century and a half.

Chénier was born at Galata, Constantinople, in 1762, and baptized on 30 October. His father, Louis, born in 1722, came from a middle-class Poitou family and went out to Constantinople in 1742 as agent for a French blanket company, of which he became a director before being elected representative of the French business community. His own father was in distressed financial circumstances, or Louis would no doubt have proceeded to further education, and probably written rather more than the *Recherches historiques sur les Maures* which he published in 1787. As things were, Chénier's father's career was advanced by the French ambassador, des Alleurs, who obtained for him the posts of consul and commercial attaché. Louis Chénier married Elisabeth Lomaca in 1754. She was probably Greek, probably the daughter of a prosperous goldsmith or jeweller, and probably had an entrée into the Turkish court. All three probabilities are disputed. She knew little French, spoke and sang in Greek, danced Greek dances, and died a member of the Greek Orthodox Church, although she was married as a Catholic. The two articles on Greek customs she published in French must have been dictated. Chénier himself became passionately attached to his supposed Hellenic origins, which played a determining part in his imaginative development.

Chénier's maternal aunt was the grandmother of Thiers, the prime minister and historian. Chénier himself had a sister, Hélène-Christine, born in 1758 and later to marry the impoverished comte Latour de Saint-Ygest, some of whose debts Chénier was called on to pay in 1788. He also had three brothers: Constantin, born in 1757, to become a lawyer, minor diplomat, and finally drunkard; Louis-Sauveur, who, born in 1761, joined the army, was at first a revolutionary and then a reactionary, and became a general under Napoleon; and Marie-Joseph (1764–1811), a poet and dramatist who helped to inspire the Revolution, wrote in 1694 the celebrated song "Le Chant du départ," which Méhul set to music, and had to defend himself in his 1797 *Epître sur la calomnie* against conniving at his brother's execution. He did in fact save other people from the guillotine.

The family returned to France in 1765. Chénier's father was posted to Morocco as consul general. He lived there in poverty until he retired in 1782, joined later by Constantin as his secretary, while Chénier's mother lived beyond her means in Paris, surrounded by scholars, artists, and writers, with her favourite, Marie-Joseph, and the other children. Her household included two uniformed men-servants and four maids. Chénier at the age of three appears to have been given into the care of his godfather André Béraud, a well-to-do draper in Carcassonne who may also have been his uncle. He spent some time in nearby Limoux, where his father had gone to school.

At 11 Chénier was sent to Paris to follow his two brothers to the Collège de Navarre, transformed by Napoleon into the Ecole Polytechnique in 1805. The syllabus stressed mathematics and the sciences, and the school passed for the best in Paris. Chénier stayed at least five years, and more probably eight, making friends in particular with the two brothers Louis Trudaine de Montigny and Charles-Michel Trudaine de la Sablière, sons of the Intendant des Finances, both to be beheaded the day after Chénier, and another pair of brothers from another very wealthy family, Louis and François de Pange. Louis de Pange was later to provide Chénier with financial support, and François became his closest friend.

Chénier was to stay with the parents of both pairs of brothers and appears to have fallen in love with one of François's cousins, who first married another cousin, who was guillotined, and then François himself, who died a year later. From his poetry it seems reasonable to assume that the wealthy milieu in which Chénier circulated during and after his schooldays, but from full integration into which he was excluded, wounded his self-confidence quite badly. At school Chénier won important national prizes and began to write verse, the often neoclassical *Bucoliques* with strikingly dislocated lines. From the beginning he asserted a notable independence of accepted models of regularity and literary decorum, declaring Malherbe with what was then daring iconoclasm to be simply "cold."

Among his mother's regular visitors were the painter Cazes, Pierre-Augustin Guys, a scholar and father of the painter, who helped with the articles on Greece, and the poet Ecouchard Le Brun, who was to inspire and guide Chénier in his first steps as a poet. Chénier, however, needed a career and from August 1782 for just over six months was a cadet, in the company of such richer and more rapidly promoted young men as did not buy their way round the cadetship altogether. Marie-Joseph had joined the army before Chénier, and he, too, stayed only a few months. Louis-Sauveur left the army after four years, but studied to become a military engineer, so opening the way to becoming a general in the ordnance. The proof of nobility required for Chénier seems, surprisingly, to have been obtainable, although there had been difficulty on that score in 1774, when either Chénier or one of his brothers wanted to train for a naval commission, and Chénier now called himself "de Saint-André." The military experience of all three brothers turned them against the social system in spite of their father's aspirations to nobility. He, too, was now Louis de Chénier.

Chénier suffered from nephritis and gallstones, and his health may have played a role in his being passed over for a commission. He appears now to have lived at home, writing intimate elegies as well as the *Bucoliques*. The love poetry patently springs from some personal experience. Chénier had naturally published nothing, but by 1782, before his enlistment, Le Brun had already written a poem to him, to be published in the 1792 *L'Almanach des Muses*. In 1784 Chénier was in Switzerland, almost certainly with the Trudaines, and in 1786 probably in Italy in the same company, each journey lasting two or three months. The year dates are uncertain and the financial arrangements obscure, but Chénier must largely have been the guest of the Trudaines, whose father had helped Chénier's in his Moroccan career. Both journeys were the fruitful source of poetic inspiration.

Chénier's Paris existence from 1783 to 1787 shows few signs of frugality. He was to be found in the company of his wealthy friends, whose extravagant behaviour was considered in some cases excessively dandified, and Chénier may have attended the wild banquets of Grimod de la Reynière, author of the *Almanach des Gourmands*. The *Elégies* refer to orgies, and we can only conjecture whether Chénier is likely to have attended any that took place. It would not be surprising, since the elegies undoubtedly show an unusual emotional vulnerability beneath their classical stereotypes, and sentimental attachments to women not prepared to take his affection seriously enough are the experience most likely to lie behind them. Admitting to a "jeunesse fougueuse (wild youth)," Chénier hoped that it did not "wither" his verse or his prose.

He was certainly writing serious verse by 1783, and there is evidence that two of his major poems, *Hermès* and *L'Amérique*, had been begun by this date. It is also likely that he had started to think about what he wanted to achieve through poetry, so that *L'Invention* was at least being considered. We know that Chénier was still working on it in London between 1787 and 1790. In the years following 1783 he was also studying, especially languages, including Greek, Latin, Italian, and Spanish, but also other subjects, like history and astronomy. He was to form a deep but frustrating platonic relationship with the beautiful, delicate, and wealthy Fanny Lecoulteux, to whom François de Pange introduced him in 1787, but in the meanwhile the "Camille" elegies seem certain to have been written for Michèle de Santuary, wife of the rich and elderly M. de Bonneuil, master of the household of Monsieur, the king's brother. Chénier shows himself in the poetry to have been frustrated and jealous of Mme de Bonneuil's past.

In the mid-1780s Chénier became the close friend of Louis David, then a young painter patronized principally by the Trudaine family, with whom he was to break some 10 years later when they became political enemies. David was to be appointed official painter to the Convention. At about this time Chénier also became friendly with Marie Cosway, the painter and wife of the English miniaturist Richard Cosway, whose house in Pall Mall Chénier was frequently to visit during his stay in London. He also got to know Mme Albany and her companion, the Italian poet Vittorio Alfieri. By 1787 Chénier's views were hardening towards the left. It was the year of his majority and it looks as if his father had been seriously ill. Chénier wrote *La Liberté*, giving its classical form a satirical purpose and a political edge, and the despairing *Hymne à la justice*, lyrically evoking France's lamentable social system. He had also begun the *Essai sur la décadence des lettres et des arts*, but he was short of money and still needed a career.

The Chevalier de la Luzerne, formerly ambassador to America and a friend of the Trudaines, had just been appointed to London and, thanks to his sister-in-law, Mme de Beaumont, Chénier became Luzerne's secretary and crossed the channel on 6 December 1787, five or six weeks before the ambassador. François de Pange had presented Chénier to her, and they were to become close friends, perhaps much more. Chénier submitted his verse to her for comment, and she later successfully introduced Chateaubriand to Chénier's poetry. In the embassy Chénier was underemployed, and London bored him. He studied Arabic and Spanish, learnt English, read Spenser, Milton, and Pope, and hesitated in his reaction to Shakespeare. He wrote "La jeune Tarentaine" and reflected about suicide in a poem first published by Chateaubriand in 1802, which means that Mme de Beaumont must have been sent a copy. Chénier appears, like so many of his generation in France and elsewhere, to have felt it important to cultivate and explore melancholy but proud feelings of rejection. He wrote of his depression certainly to his father and to Alfieri, although he did not elsewhere disguise the consolation he found with "pretty English girls," known only by their first names. We have several pages of bitter reflections about his solitude written from Hood's tavern in London in April 1879.

In 1789 he returned to France for some months and, with his father and brothers, welcomed the reforms which the Revolution seemed to promise, encouraged by the way he thought England was being governed, although by the end of 1789 he was alarmed at the lengths to which the radicals seemed willing to go. By 1790 Chénier had worked out a moderate constitutional position for himself, from which he did not subsequently depart. He was in Paris again by June 1790, and there is no evidence that he ever returned to London. He was able to help his father financially and pay off some of his brother-in-law's debts, and finally resigned his London post in January 1791.

Marie-Joseph's *Alzémire* had been booed off the stage in November 1786 in spite of the support of Palissot, a friend of his mother. Palissot supported Chénier as well as his brother, but Chénier was to have an argument with him in 1788, showing that he had by then largely absorbed the encyclopédiste philosophy of life (see: *Encyclopédie*). It was when Chénier returned from Italy in 1786 that he began the long, sharply satirical poem against literary punditry to be called *Les Cyclopes littéraires* or *La République des lettres*, and it is possible that his brother's setback, which inspired his poem, may have influenced him against any attempt to have his own verse published.

Outbursts of violence had begun to occur in France in 1787 and the almost political *Hymne à la justice* shows that it was partly disgust at France's social system which persuaded Chénier to take a job abroad. In 1788, while Chénier was in London, Necker replaced Brienne as finance minister. We do not know at what date in 1789 Chénier started his leave in Paris, but it may have been in time for the elder Trudaine's wedding on 13 June. He was to return to London in mid-November. The Bastille had fallen on 14 July, and in August Marie-Joseph's verse tragedy *Charles IX* was turned down by the censor, Suard, a friend of Chénier. Marie-Joseph, who was already in league with Fabre d'Eglantine, Danton, and Camille Desmoulins, arranged a salon reading, attacked the censorship in brochures and articles, enlisted help to interrupt a Molière play at the Théâtre-Français, and obtained a rehearing for himself. Talma played the lead when *Charles IX* was finally played at the Théâtre-Français on 4 November. It delighted audiences, who saw in the allusions to the renaissance king references to the political events of their own day. Louis-Sauveur had by this date sold all his possessions for 4,873 livres and was inciting the army to rebellion. Chénier stayed in London long enough to see the reception accorded to the first émigrés, ill adapted to London society.

From the beginning of 1790 Chénier's father's pension was halved to 3,000 livres, and Chénier himself was in debt. Money was urgently required, and Chénier borrowed 2,400 from Pange, enough to pay off his father's debt. That still left his mother's excessive expenditure, and a sum his father owed in tax, to meet which Chénier sold some possessions. In London, Chénier was already turning against Burke by March 1790. While still in England, on around 12 April 1790, he became a founding member of the "Société de 1789," which had 660 members, and a member of its inner circle of 89. This inner circle contained La Fayette, Mirabeau, Chamfort, Dupont de Nemours, and La Rochefoucauld, who, in 1792, was to direct one of the last plots to save the royal family, but both monarchists, like the Trudaines and the Panges, and Jacobins, like David and Collot d'Herbois, also joined. It was later to merge into the "Feuillant" party, with Chénier as its most powerful spokesman. He was to drive out its left wing, including Condorcet, Brissot de Warville, and Barère. Chénier was still in England on 5 May 1790, since Mme d'Albany wrote to him there on that date. She and Alfieri did not leave for England until the end of April 1791.

Immediately after his return to France, Chénier wrote for the August 1790 number of the *Journal de la Société de 1789*, edited by Condorcet, an article, also published as a pamphlet, *Avis au peuple français sur ses véritables ennemis*, advocating the restoration of the people's rights in accordance with the "Declaration of the Rights of Man" voted by the Assemblée constituante on the preceding 27 August, and thereafter a return to legitimate government. He respected property, discipline in the armed forces, and taxation, and warned against lynch law. The true enemies of France were foreign powers and those within responsible for the collapse of law, which hinted at Marat, Hébert, Desmoulins, Fréron, and those whom Chénier regarded as primarily interested in fostering a class struggle. Chénier was essentially turning a blind eye to the terrifying economic distress which fuelled the Revolution, and to the seriousness of a situation which he still considered insurrectionary rather than revolutionary. Still technically attached to the London embassy, and perhaps undecided about returning there, Chénier excised from his manuscript a passage about English maritime hegemony and the danger it posed to France. He then laid low, publishing only the long ode on the tennis-court oath, *Le Serment du Jeu de Paume*, in 1791 with the right-wing printer Bleuet, the first of the two poems he published.

The real aims of the constitutionalists had mostly been achieved by August 1789, with the abolition of feudalism, the adoption of the "Declaration of the Rights of Man," and the setting up of the Assemblée constituante. Since then the royal family had been brought back to virtual imprisonment at Versailles in October, church property had been confiscated in November, assignats had been issued in December, and pensions halved in January. Events had moved fast. Chénier felt moved again to defend the middle position, and on 3 March 1791 he finished a second article, *Réflexions sur l'esprit de parti*, which appeared in early April and was a direct attack on the Jacobins, tactlessly favourable to the émigrés, including the two royal aunts, Adélaïde and Victoire, who were a centre of intrigue in Rome. It was probably also in 1791 that Chénier wrote *Les Autels de la peur*, denouncing mob rule, which he did not and perhaps could not publish.

From July 1791, when the Feuillant party was formally founded, until 10 August 1792, when the monarchy fell and the freedom of the press came to an end, Chénier published 26 more articles, all arguing the Feuillant position, which was all the time being pushed further to the right. Some were printed in *Le Moniteur*, but 21 appeared in *Le Journal de Paris*, of which 11 were printed as "suppléments," and must be supposed to have been subsidized. The insertion of the supplements must have cost some 3,000 livres. By February 1792, Chénier had broken with Marie-Joseph and with David. Although he was now attacking all republican parties, Girondins as well as Jacobins, four of the 1792 articles were directed against the Jacobin attempt to treat the surviving mutineers of the Châteauvieux regiment in 1790 as martyrs, after their release from the galleys, a view supported in the first of the *Iambes*, the ironic *Hymne aux Suisses de Châteauvieux*, full of wit and fire, and the chief cause of the offence to the Jacobins which was to send Chénier to the guillotine. Of the Swiss mercenaries who had mutinied in the Châteauvieux regiment in August 1790, massacring a young officer, 23 were executed and 41 sent to the galleys. They were amnestied in December 1791 and freed in February 1792, when they marched drunkenly to Paris. Chénier's poem was published on 15 April 1792, the weekend of the Jacobin celebration of the event in which both Marie-Joseph and David played a part. The Swiss were understandably sensitive about the whole affair, given that France was to declare war on Austria on 20 April, and it became an important event in the rise of the Jacobin party.

Chénier made an attempt which came to nothing to get himself appointed ambassador to Switzerland. Le Brun had become a strong republican, in spite of his earlier royal pension, by the time he published his poem to Chénier, which may perhaps be seen as expressing a desire that their friendship should outlive their political differences. By May 1792 Chénier was replying to an article by Condorcet, showing outrage at the idea that local authorities, not national ones, should have power to investigate, accuse, and try those suspected of subversive activities, one of the proposals of the type that led to the Terror a few months later. Chénier's last article in the *Journal de Paris* was dated 27 July, and was a furious reply to Brissot, who had attacked him as a foreigner in *Le Patriote français*. He had been ill and went for a few days to Forges-les-Eaux to take the waters, writing there the "Fille du vieux pasteur" for the *Bucoliques*, but was back in Paris for 6 August. On 10 August the Tuileries were invaded, the king was dethroned, and 600 out of 900 guards were slaughtered after laying down their arms. Chénier's own name was put on the proscribed list. The premises of the *Journal de Paris* were sacked two days later, and several journalists were sought out and killed in various parts of Paris.

Chénier spent the rest of the summer in hiding. There were 3,000 people in prison by the end of August, special courts were set up, and the executions began. Chénier heard of the massacres of untried political prisoners in early September and wrote from Rouen on the 15th. He had been at Louveciennes with Mme Lecoulteux, and at Saint-Germain. He was to write an *Ode à Versailles* partly inspired by the massacres. Mme de Beaumont's father was murdered by a mob. Chénier passed through Paris,

spent a night at Forges, and went to Le Havre, which with Rouen was a rallying point against the Terror. It is also quite likely that he was with Mme de Beaumont, and in contact with friends of his brother Constantin at Le Havre. He used a pseudonym, must have had false papers, but found his post interfered with. He seems to have been trying hard to get someone away through Rouen, Le Havre, or Nantes, was in Rouen on 2 October, but back in Paris on the 28th. Royalty had been abolished on 21 September. It looks as if Chénier was trying to arrange either for the escape of the royal family or for the payment of a colossal bribe on their behalf, in which a banker relation of Fanny Lecoulteux was closely involved at Le Havre.

The defence of the king was eventually entrusted to Lamoignon de Malesherbes, himself to be decapitated in 1794 at the age of 73. He had come from Lausanne to help the king and seems certainly to have enlisted Chénier's help in preparing the defence. Chénier now published a number of anonymous articles, two of them in the *Mercure français* (q.v.) on 25 and 29 December. The king had been allowed to choose defence lawyers only on 11 December. Marie-Joseph, who had been elected a deputy for Seine-et-Oise in September, voted for the death sentence. In the Assembly, there was a very small majority in favour of the death penalty, duly carried out on 21 January 1793. Chénier obtained a medical certificate saying that he had to live in the country and retired to Versailles, where he stayed until his arrest, within a country walk of Mme Lecoulteux, for whom his affection now afforded him more happiness and became a principal subject of the *Odes*.

After the Loi des Suspects of September 1793, enforced in December, Chénier must have realized that his situation was becoming really dangerous. He was arrested on 7 March 1794, confused by the authorities with his elder brother, Louis-Sauveur, continued to study and write in the indescribable conditions of Saint-Lazare prison, and smuggled out his manuscripts. It is doubtful whether anything could have saved him, but his own scornful bearing and his father's intervention on his behalf were not tactically sound. He was one of a batch of 80 executed in three days after farcical trials. On 23 July, 25 prisoners were guillotined, and Chénier thought of suicide, but in his final *Iambe* he offered himself to execution so that history might vindicate justice and console the survivors. He was taken to the Conciergerie on 24 July, tried on the following day, and executed that afternoon, most of the evidence coming from his published journalism. The sustained attack on Marie-Joseph's reputation for conniving with his brother's executioners or failing to do what he reasonably could to save him has shown itself to be unjustified.

WORKS

What made Chénier's poetic reputation was "La jeune captive," written at Saint-Lazare, smuggled out, and published five months after his death in the *Décade philosophique* and then *L'Almanach des Muses*, then "La jeune Tarentaine," published first in the *Mercure* four years later under the title "Elégie dans le goût ancien," and the fragments quoted by Chateaubriand in *Le Génie du christianisme*. The manuscripts began to circulate, and Latouche published a substantial selection of the poems in 1819. The reception of the Latouche edition, criticizing Chénier's lack of dignity and discipline and his literary improprieties, makes clear how right Latouche had been to be cautious and selective, as well as enthusiastic. It also shows that, at that date, he was wise to cosmeticize the poetry as he did. Chénier's *Oeuvres complètes* was then revised and augmented in 1833, 1839, 1841, and 1847, but it is the sole authority for the text of most of what it contains, and it is known that poems were abridged, reconstituted, and modified.

The manuscripts were in the hands of Louis de Chénier until his death in 1795, when they passed to Chénier's brother, Constantin, who passed them to his mother when he became consul at Elbing in 1797, their custodian effectively becoming Marie-Joseph. It was he who published "La jeune Tarentaine" and showed the manuscripts to Chateaubriand and the poet Charles-Hubert Millevoye. Marie-Joseph died in 1811, and the manuscripts passed to Pierre-Claude-François Daunou, who was in charge of the Archives Nationales and, from 1816 until 1838, editor of the *Journal des Savants* (q.v.). Daunou was pressed by Charles-Julien de Chênedollé to publish them and had a portion of "Les Esclaves et les mendiants" from the *Bucoliques* published in an 1816 collection of *Mélanges littéraires* by M. Fayolle. The verse he passed on to Latouche. Although Gabriel de Chénier later disputed the account given by Latouche, it seems that there were two bundles, one containing material apparently considered sufficiently finished to warrant volume publication, and that alone was passed to Latouche, who was subsequently also given copies of some of the material in the second bundle. Anything Latouche published was considered his property. The rest he returned. His library, left to Pauline de Flaugergeues, who lived with him at La Vallée-aux-Loups, was either stolen or destroyed during the Franco-Prussian war in 1870–71.

The manuscripts returned by Latouche, together with the bundle never given to him, were left by Louis-Sauveur to his son Gabriel de Chénier in 1823. In 1839 Sainte-Beuve and in 1840 Paul Lacroix were allowed to publish fragments, but Becq de Fouquières, after a first brief visit, was not again allowed access to the papers. Gabriel de Chénier's widow left them to the Bibliothèque Nationale in 1892, with a seven-year embargo. Unfortunately the very faulty text published by D.C. Robert in a two-volume 1826 edition was taken up in the 1833 and subsequent revisions of the Latouche editions. However, Latouche published all the material he possessed but had not previously used in the *Revue de Paris* between December 1829 and March 1830. This, together with more material from the family, was also taken into the 1833 edition, while that of 1839 also incorporated material which Sainte-Beuve had published from manuscript in the *Revue des Deux Mondes* in February of that year. P.-L. Jacob published the prose in 1840.

The first attempt at a critical edition was that of Becq de Fouquières in 1862 and it was followed by that of Gabriel de Chénier, in three volumes, in 1874. Becq de Fouquières published no new material, but scrupulously worked over Latouche's text, identified the sources, and corrected the Latouche edition where he could. Gabriel de Chénier published much new material, but the grouping of the poems is arbitrary; different poems were run into one another to make single entities, and there are numerous simple mistakes. Each editor started from very different presuppositions and publicly disputed the demerits of the other's edition. The best edition of the *Bucoliques* is still that of Heredia in 1906, with illustrations by Fantin-Latour and a preface published in the *Revue des Deux Mondes* for 1 November 1805, but the definitive edition of the poetic works is that in three volumes by Paul Dimoff

(1908, 1910, 1912), based on a rediscovery of traces of a preparation for publication by Chénier himself, which included elements of a classification. Dimoff is the author also of a two-volume biography.

The essential difficulty derives partly from the state of the surviving manuscripts, and the disappearance of others, but also from the fact that Chénier published only two poems, leaving later editors the task of classifying the quite large corpus of poems, reconstituting fragments into poems, and imposing their own preferred punctuation, including exclamation marks and capital letters, which Chénier did not use. There are generally only very uncertain indications about dates of composition. It is however clear, and inevitable, that Chénier thought of his work in terms of genres, and it is now conventional to distinguish the *Bucoliques*, written over 15 years, from the *Poèmes*, the *Hymnes*, the *Elégies*, the *Epîtres*, the *Odes*, and the *Iambes*.

It is no accident that 18th-century France saw no flowering of lyric poetry before the death of Rousseau, and that only the pre-romantics revived that type of literature. It was uniquely suited to the cultivation, expression, and examination of the sorts of experience whose implications the pre-romantic generation of Chateaubriand, Constant, and Bernardin de Saint-Pierre needed to explore. Part of the difficulty in assessing Chénier's achievement, if also part of the fascination, lies in the way in which the reader is immediately aware of a new sensibility conscious that it is rediscovering the need to investigate the consequences of types of experience best examined in the lyrical genres.

We know enough about the dating of Chénier's work to realize that there was a discernible development in his poetic style as his verse emerged from formal poetic exercises erected on classical models. We can also now see him as a precursor of something towards which he obviously did not even know he was groping. It was he, for instance, who invented the short epic to be developed by Hugo, and then by Sully Prudhomme and Heredia. His poem *L'Invention* revivifies, as Chénier himself knew, the renaissance metaphor of the poet's divine afflatus, and points it, as Chénier could not know, in the direction of the romantic view of poetic inspiration. Chénier's lyric verse, like that of the renaissance poets, was learned, but his prosody, with the displaced caesura, the systematic enjambement, and the refusal to make line units coincide with sense units, was scarcely to be taken further before the symbolists.

Chénier left three long fragments of scarcely begun poems, *Hermès*, *L'Amérique*, and *Susanne*, of which we have the prose notes, collected over periods of up to 12 years, and which would have concerned, respectively, the history of man down to the invention of society and of the sciences, the history of explorations and religions, and a biblical subject inspired by Milton which was to have become a poem in honour of Fanny Lecoulteux. His most famous poem must still be "La jeune Tarentaine," normally considered the best of the marine idylls from the *Bucoliques*. It is the poem published by his brother, and it is one of a number describing funeral rites. It is also one of a number celebrating antique divinities and heroes. There are implied allusions to Manilius, Virgil, and Catullus; the poem consists of 30 alexandrines; the rhyme scheme is as simple as possible; and there is still striving for classical effect: the first two lines are a stiltedly rhetorical apostrophe:

Pleurez, doux alcyons, ô vous, oiseaux sacrés,
Oiseaux chers à Thétis, doux alcyons, pleurez

(Weep, sweet kingfishers, you, oh sacred birds,/Birds dear to the sea, sweet kingfishers, weep).

The incantatory repetition, the classical terminology, the elevated poetic language, and the self-conscious rhetoric scarcely distinguish the couplet from a competent exercise in translating the lines from book five of Manilius's *Astronomica*, whose Latin Chénier had just quoted, with a note to show where he thought a French translator had lost the grace of the original. Chénier now moves straight into narrative:

Elle a vécu, Myrto, la jeune Tarentaine.
Un vaisseau la portait aux bords de Camarine.
Là l'hymen, les chansons, les flûtes, lentement
Devaient la reconduire au seuil de son amant

(She has lived, Myrto, the young girl from Taranto./A boat was carrying her to the shores of Camarina./There, marriage, songs, flutes, slowly/Were supposed to bring her back to the portal of her lover).

According to Pausanias, part of the Aegean was called after Myrto, the girl addressed here. Chénier has established his credentials as a neoclassicist and continues to use elevated diction, but it may not be fanciful to see a link between Camarina, already renowned in antique literature, and the Taranto of 18th-century Sicily, which helps to bring the poem into the present. The effect striven for is now clearly not rhetorical but dramatic. Each of the three sentences effectively has a different tense. The narrative is tersely simple and the three nouns in the third line are carefully selected, but the striking effect of the enjambement at the end of the third line, presumably not consciously calculated, is to slow down the narrative pace. The initial past tense announces what is clearly going to be a sad story about a young girl destined to drown on the way to her lover, but the tragedy is not going to be brutal. That "lentement (slowly)" at the end of the line signifies in both sound and prosody that the poem is peaceful.

In fact the poem is elegiac. The elevated language continues, and ellipsis is still used, "cèdre (cedar)" for box, for instance, or "une clef vigilante (a vigilant key)" to close it. The poem, doubtless written to be recited, contains important soft assonances, "parés...parfums préparés (adorn...prepared scents)." After the six lines of introduction, there are four of description. Then come the six lines of story:

Mais seule sur la proue invoquant les étoiles,
Le vent impétueux qui soufflait dans les voiles
L'enveloppe. Etonnée, et loin des matelots,
Elle crie, elle tombe, elle est au sein des flots.
Elle est au sein des flots, la jeune Tarentine.
Son beau corps a roulé sous la vague marine

(But alone on the prow calling out to the stars,/the precipitate wind which was blowing into the sails/Takes hold of her. Startled, and far from the sailors,/She shouts, she falls, she is in the bosom of the waves./She is in the bosom of the waves, the young girl from Taranto./Her beautiful body has tumbled under the marine swell).

The sound values of the first line, both vowels and consonants,

are sibilant and soft, and the "s" is taken up in the second line, where the enjambement leads to a dramatic switch of tense, a sudden caesura, and a fourth "v." The drama peaks, and its sudden climax, "l'enveloppe," is again caressing. "Etonnée" begins an almost three-line cascade of "l" and "t" sounds, with three verbs in the dramatic present tense preceded by "elle." The fifth line now comes back like a refrain, insisting on the "l," "s," and "t" sounds again. Then comes the elimination in the sixth line of the harsh "t." Almost none of the sound magic can have been conscious, but it works with great lyrical intensity, joining 18th-century neoclassical poetic convention with quite daring prosody and intentionally dramatic prosody and syntax. The rest of the formally perfect poem is the story of the recovery of the body by the Nereides, and of their mourning with the nymphs.

We know that the ode "La jeune captive" was written in Saint-Lazare in 1794, days before the poet's death. It is about Aimée de Coigny, duchesse de Fleury, who was eventually released and married the man she had been arrested with, a gambler and a rake who devoured much of her fortune before they were divorced. Aimée de Coigny, who was 25 in 1794, went on notoriously to have a series of lovers, and died leaving her *Mémoires* in 1820 at the age of 51. Chénier's poem consists of nine six-line stanzas, of which the first seven are put into the woman's mouth. The third and sixth lines of each stanza are octosyllables and have feminine rhymes, so breaking the pattern of alexandrines with masculine rhymes. The poem is the affirmation of a desire to go on living. Why should she die so soon? She has so much still to enjoy. The poem is almost an idyll, but with ironic overtones. The woman is aware that life is not all roses. She uses a classical topos about honey and quotes La Fontaine:

L'épi naissant, mûrit de la faux respecté;
Sans crainte du pressoir, le pampre tout l'été
   Boit les doux présents de l'aurore;
Et moi, comme lui belle, et jeune comme lui,
Quoi que l'heure présente ait de trouble et d'ennui,
   Je ne veux point mourir encore

(The ear of corn being born ripens respected by the scythe;/Without fear of the press the vine-branch all summer/Drinks in the sweetnesses of the dawn;/And I, beautiful as the one, and young as the other,/Although the present moment brings worry and pain,/I don't want to die yet).

The poem was written in conditions of acute physical discomfort and indescribable anxiety, but its poignancy does not derive from our knowledge of the circumstances of its composition. The stanza does in fact have two weaknesses: the consciously antithetical rhetoric of the fourth line and the rather feeble fifth. What lifts it up is the emotion which informs it, the obviously calm evocation of what life might have been, if it were not going to be cut off before its bud had blossomed. After the poetically elevated language and carefully balanced syntax of the first tercet, the second brings us up suddenly against the brutal reality of the stanza's final line. That line comes again at the end of the final stanza in the woman's mouth, but all seven end as sharply. The poet then declares in the final two stanzas his desire to record the intensity of the woman's desire for life. His lines will survive, and someone will wonder who she was, and how those near her ended, too.

L'Invention is a didactic poem, and a formal set piece. The poetic theory cautiously welcomes audacity and innovativeness, while refusing to abandon the example of the antique or to "Blesser la vérité, le bon sens, la raison (Wound truth, good sense, reason)." Poetic distinction is not to be achieved through fevered, unregulated, fantasizing or delirious dreams, but through truth, harmony, clarity, and love. The poet's function is to take 20 aspects of "la nature mère (mother nature)," and he

Les fait renaître ensemble, et, par un art suprême,
Des traits de vingt beautés forme la beauté même

(Has them reborn together and, with supreme art,/From the features of twenty beauties forms beauty itself).

At his most slipshod Chénier often allows himself clumsy inversions, and in the didactic poetry there is sometimes a rhetorical bombast in the classical ornamentation. But *L'Invention* is resolutely modern in tone and welcomes the unified new learning of the *Encyclopédie*. Nature itself, "en nous la source et le modèle (in us the fountain and the model)," has changed, and by no means excludes the need for poetic inspiration, the "sainte folie (divine folly)," so often invoked in the renaissance. But the necessity of inspiration, as was also seen in the renaissance, by no means excludes the need for study, and Chénier three times enjoins on the young poet the injunction "travaille! (work!)." The ideal is to write now as Homer and Virgil would have written today:

Et sans suivre leurs pas imiter leur exemple;
Faire, en s'éloignant d'eux, avec un soin jaloux,
Ce qu'eux-mêmes ils feraient s'ils vivaient parmi nous!

(And without following in their footsteps, imitate their example;/Do, by moving away from them, with jealous care,/What they themselves would do if they were living among us!).

The unfinished prose *Essai sur les causes et les effets de la perfection et de la décadence des lettres et des arts* insists on the need for a free society if the arts are to flourish and the individual is to be free to create independently. It is on this view that Chénier founds his admiration for the Greeks, his hostility to academies, and his insistence on breaking away from mannered verse towards "une sensibilité vraie et une âme ouverte (truth of feeling and openness of heart)" and "la naïveté sublime (sublime simplicity)."

The *Elégies* are on the whole expressions of passion with sensibility and wit, drawing on a range of comic, tragic, ironic, and descriptive tones, remarkable for the freedom of their prosody, their range of mood, and their qualities of introspection. They do not compare with Chénier's most mature poems but do point towards much of what was to be developed by the romantic lyric poets. Chénier's own lyrical gifts reach their peak in some of the *Bucoliques*, which are directly related to the antique pastoral, but which show a freedom of poetic treatment, a sense of destiny and drama, and an obsession with the impermanence of beauty which once again link the renaissance directly to the romantics after the rise and fall of neoclassicism in the 17th and 18th centuries.

The *Bucoliques* contain extremes of emotion, tenderness, irony, humour, violence, sudden bursts of energy, some flawless lines, dense concentration, charm, and poetically effective restraint. Some of the poems are epigrams or short pieces in the grand manner, like "La mort d'Hercule," based on an engraving inspired by Ovid. The *Iambes*, like the odes, are political as well as personal. The "Ode à Versailles" is both, enlarging the love theme into a much wider context. The "Ode à Marie-Anne-Charlotte Corday," who was guillotined five days after assassinating Marat, is violent and impetuous, contrasting elevated and low styles, and combining both with irony and lyricism. Sometimes Chénier's restraint disappears, as when he allows himself to be engulfed in scarcely controlled disgust. *La Fête de l'Etre suprême* does, however, transform sarcasm into poetry. Chénier was deeply enthusiastic not only about the antique poets, but also about Pierre Corneille, Racine, La Fontaine, and Jean-Baptiste Rousseau. The probability is that he remains underestimated, largely due to the impossibility of producing an acceptably authentic edition of his texts.

The last of the *Iambes*, written in minute handwriting on scraps of wrapping paper, cannot have been written the night before Chénier died, because he was then no longer at Saint-Lazare, from where the work was smuggled out, and there are sufficient second thoughts in it for one to suppose that it was written, however quickly, with some care. Its blend of satire, gloom, fear, heroism, bitterness, melancholy, and resolution suggests that its content had been meditated, perhaps for days, and its tone determined, not necessarily consciously, before it was set down. It reads as if Chénier had wondered whether suicide would not be preferable to execution if execution became certain and had decided against it for the reasons he gives, and as if the poem was then articulated and set down on paper once execution was clearly ineluctable, probably the last night spent at Saint-Lazare, after the first tumbrils had left in the afternoon.

The poem is 88 lines long, alternating alexandrines with octosyllables, but cannot be read in four-line stanzas. It contains inversion, but comparatively little enjambement or irregularity in the alexandrine. The first lines announce the poem's blend of melancholy, hope, bitterness, and heroism as a basically satirical inspiration is elevated by a powerfully lyrical depth of feeling:

Comme un dernier rayon, comme un dernier zéphyre
    Anime la fin d'un beau jour,
Au pied de l'échafaud j'essaye encor ma lyre.
    Peut-être est-ce bientôt mon tour

(As a last ray, as a last breeze/Gives life to the end of a fine day,/At the foot of the scaffold I still sing my song./Perhaps it will soon be my turn).

The peaceful image of a twilight ending suddenly gives way, first to formal stylization in the words whose literal meaning is "I still make efforts with my lyre," and then to the hope defiantly and irrationally implicit in the "perhaps" uttered at the foot of the scaffold. The depiction of the arrival of the jailer with the final summons, "Le messager de mort, noir recruteur des ombres (The messenger of death, dark recruiter of/for the shadows)," with the announcement of the poet's name echoing in the long corridors, is vividly realistic. The vividness is heightened by the dramatic way the poem bursts into the poet's dialogue with himself as he momentarily decides to commit suicide. Then

…Non, non. Puissé-je vivre!
    Ma vie importe à la vertu

Car l'honnête homme enfin, victime de l'outrage,
    Dans les cachots, près du cercueil,
Relève plus altiers son front et son langage,
    Brillants d'un généreux orgueil.
S'il est écrit aux cieux que jamais une épée
    N'étincellera dans mes mains;

Dans l'encre et l'amertume une autre arme trempée
    Peut encor servir les humains

(…No, no. If only I could live!/My life matters to virtue/
Because the upright man, victim of outrage,/In the cells,
near the tomb,/Lifts up higher his forehead and his speech,/
Shimmering with a noble pride./If it is written in the heavens that no sword was ever/To shine in my hands,/Another
arm soaked in ink and bitterness/Will still be able to help
humanity).

By offering himself to execution, the poet will assure that the
outrage done to him is remembered, and that memory will help
future generations. The bitterest of satire breaks out again as the
poet thinks of France, yet "D'espérance un vaste torrente/Me
transporte (A vast torrent of hope/Carries me off)." Disgust, the
persecution of the good, the trampling of the law, impel him to
suicide, but then

Nul ne resterait donc pour attendrir l'histoire
    Sur tant de justes massacrés?
Pour consoler leurs fils, leurs veuves, leur mémoire

(Would there then be none left to move history/Over the
slaughter of so many just?/To console their children, their
widows, their memory).

The poet must use the triple whip, justice, truth, and virtue. The
poem ends:

Souffre, ô coeur gros de haine, affamé de justice.
    Toi, Vertu, pleure si je meurs

(Suffer, oh heart pregnant with hatred, starving for justice./
And you, Virtue, weep if I die).

PUBLICATIONS

Collections

Oeuvres complètes, edited by Henri de Latouche, 1819; revised
    and augmented edition, 1833, 1839, 1841, 1847
Oeuvres en prose, edited by P.-L. Jacob, 1840
Poésies, edited by Becq de Fouquières, 1862; revised and aug-
    mented edition, 1872
Oeuvres poétiques, edited by Gabriel de Chénier, 3 vols., 1874
Poésies, edited by P. Dimoff, 3 vols., 1908–12 (most authorita-
    tive edition)
Oeuvres complètes, Bibliothèque de la Pléiade, 1940

Verse

Bucoliques, edited by J.-M. de Heredia, 1906

Biographical and critical studies

Dimoff, Paul, *La Vie et l'oeuvre d'André Chénier jusqu'à la
    Révolution*, 1936
Fabre, J., *Chénier, l'homme et l'oeuvre*, 1955
Scarfe, Francis, *André Chénier, His Life and Work, 1762–1794*,
    1965

COMMEDIA DELL'ARTE.

*For individual French dramatists concerned with or drawing on
commedia dell'arte, see entries in General Index.*

The immense cultural importance in France of the Italian and
then italianate *commedia dell'arte* between the renaissance and
the Revolution derives partly from its interaction with indigenous French theatre and partly from the alternative theatrical
entertainment itself provided by the Italian troupes which
always or sometimes played it. It is so important, as a type of
theatre different from that dependent on dramatic dialogue in
French of whatever genre, that some account of its nature, and
its history in France, must be presented here.

From the arrival in Paris of the first troupe in 1571 until the
final amalgamation of the Italian company with the Opéra-
Comique in 1780, and with the interruptions of the periods from
1624 to 1644 and from 1697 to 1716, Italian theatre in France,
generally and sometimes exclusively offering *commedia
dell'arte*, presented a form of dramatic entertainment somewhere in between the least culturally demanding registers of the
legitimate French companies of the 17th and early 18th centuries and what was in general the bawdy vulgarity of the fairground farces, although certainly until 1697 there was overlap at
each edge. The stock-in-trade of the Italians invariably included
parody of the legitimate theatre and forceful satire. Although
commedia dell'arte itself was even in the 18th century held
down to mimed farce, normally by administrative regulations
reserving spoken dialogue to the official French companies, it
inspired in the Italian company increasingly sophisticated levels
of less and less light-weight comedy.

Commedia dell'arte is the only form of masked drama known
to renaissance Europe. Its legacies include pantomime, Harlequin, Pantaloon, Columbine, Punch and Judy, and the heavy
mask-like make-up of the modern circus clown. It seems originally to have developed from second century B.C. Latin theatre
in the town of Atella, now Aversa, in the Roman Campagna,
whose *Atellanae* were popular farces, parodies, and political satires. The roles were stereotyped, and characterized by a particular costume and mask, so that the audience knew immediately
the role, with its predictable pattern of behaviour and reaction,
from a character's appearance. At Atella, with its stone theatre,
and later at Rome, which at first still had only wooden ones, the

dialogue was improvised, with only the scenario or plot outline decided in advance. When verbal inventiveness failed there was always slapstick to fall back on, the stick that became Harlequin's bat or the Punch and Judy truncheon.

These features were retained in the renaissance, when Scaramuccia and Pantalone wore a phallus, the valets short tunics, with robes and capes reserved for the noble and the elderly. The renaissance also added an invariable all-purpose street decor on to which opened houses affording any number of entrances and exits, and from which the inhabitants emerged into the street to conduct their most intimate business, consult their doctors, quarrel with their husbands and wives, flirt, shop, fight, converse, and scandal-monger. The antique stock of characters already included the boastful soldier, often to be transformed into a burlesque Spanish conquistador, and Maccus, the white-clad ancestor of the sensuous Pulcinella. Again, the renaissance added its own crop of characters, including the senile lover, the university pedant, the knavish servant and the cowardly rascal. Until well into the 18th century only the young lovers were unmasked. They were direct descendants of the valets and maids of the renaissance *commedia*. Molière, Marivaux, and Beaumarchais are only three of the major authors of French comedy obviously to have drawn on traditional *commedia dell'arte* characters.

In the term *commedia dell'arte* the "dell'arte" means "of the profession," excluding nobles acting for relaxation, or peasants for purposes of pageantry or piety. It was originally one of several used to refer to farcical comedy played by professional troupes which made a living for their members by their performances. Other names referred specifically to the masks (*commedia dei maschere*), the improvisation (*all'improviso*), or the buffoonery (*dei zanni*). The *commedia dell'arte*, as it came generally to be known, contrasted with the literary *commedia erudita* performed by courtiers or members of academies. The improvisatory nature of the *commedia dell'arte* performances also specifically contrasted with the scripted *commedie sostenute* played by the regular companies not relying on clowning, acrobatics, and improvisation, and conduced to the development of "lazzi," the Lombard corruption of the Tuscan word for "knots," tricks to liven up flagging action or extempore inspiration, such as a piece of mime, like catching and munching a butterfly, an acrobatic display, a mock duel. Shakespeare used them, and the Elizabethans referred to them as "jigs," but we do not know of any 83-year-old French actor like the Scaramuccia who could effortlessly box another actor's ear with his foot, and there can have been few who could turn an audience from roars of laughter to tears of grief as ably as Tomasso Vicentini, "Thomassin," one of whose other feats as Trivelin was to turn a somersault without spilling a drop from a glass of water in his hand.

The overall effect on French theatre of the Italian troupes, both those that travelled and those that settled in Paris, cannot be reduced to what French writers derived from Italian plots and practice. It has to be seen much more in terms of the constant competition from clever, witty parodists, at their best marvellously inventive and brilliantly entertaining, with thrusting and sometimes bawdy satire and always mental agility at their disposal. The presence of the Italians, who prospered or perished by their ability to make an audience laugh and were unrepentant about their light-weight burlesque, may well have helped to shape the history of early French theatre, pushing it onto the high ground of tragedy, the serious imaginative use of pastoral,

and the almost affected parade of such pretentiously up-market paraphernalia as the 24-hour rule, the unities of time and action in tragi-comédie, the ritual decencies about female roles, monologues, on-stage reports of off-stage violence, and all the rest of what was for the most part fraudulently, or at least ignorantly, fostered on the learned respectability of Aristotle's authority.

The affectations of earnest moral purpose into which 17th-century French drama was forced as it emerged from the rhetorical exercises of the colleges, and the seriousness with which Aristotle's tragic catharsis or purgation of the passions was taken, its origin as a metaphor of a medical laxative conveniently left unregarded, have to be seen in counterpoint with the alternative attractions of the forthright, popular, and accessible Italian tradition, as attractive to the patrician youth of the 18th-century French regency as it had been to the young bloods of Atella, looking for theatrical amusement a little lighter than the comedies of Terence. There were naturally contaminations and take-overs. The Italians, for most of the time chiefly reliant on mime, were avid for spectacular, bizarre, and surprising effects, and certainly inspired the development of elaborate stage machinery in France, and the composition of the plays which relied on it. We know that Molière took *Dom Juan* from a current *commedia dell'arte* script, with its traditional speaking statue. *Commedia dell'arte* was extraordinarily demanding of both physical and mental skills, both of which had to be greater than those required of regular actors. It was less punishing for the actors when their effects could be achieved through machinery and without the intensity of concentration and physical agility needed for true pantomime.

The first travelling groups of Italian *commedia dell'arte* players we hear of date from the middle of the 16th century, and we know that the troupe of Alberto Naseli, known as Zan Ganassa, played in Paris in August 1571 when Charles IX and his young bride made their ceremonial entry into the city. Like most of the *commedia* troupes, they came to France by generally royal invitation, but stayed to give performances in public as well as at court. From 17 November 1548 the Confrérie de la Passion, which had become a commercial organization, was given a monopoly of most public entertainment rights in Paris. It owned the Hôtel de Bourgogne, and frequently enforced its interest through the parlement, which could refuse to register the letters patent by which Henri III sporadically tried to break the monopoly. At the Hôtel, the Confrérie was entitled to fix the entry prices, collect the receipts, vet the repertoire, and pay the troupes either a fee or a commission. Alternatively it rented out the hall, preserving perhaps the right to collect revenue from letting some or all of the 12 boxes. Any troupe which chose to perform elsewhere had to pay the Confrérie a flat fee. Henri IV renewed their privilège in April 1597.

In spite of protests from the parlement at the prices they were charging, on account of the lavishness of the costumes, masks and scenery four sols instead of the regular two, Ganassa's company carried on giving high-priced public performances. For this reason, and no doubt because it had refused to pay the required fee, the letters patent accorded to Ganassa's company were not registered, although the company was rewarded for its playing during the wedding celebrations of August 1572 for the marriage on 18 August of Marguerite de Valois, daughter of Catherine de Medici, to Henri, king of Navarre since the death of his mother, Jeanne d'Albret. Ganassa thereafter went to Spain, but there are traces of two other troupes in Paris during the 1570s, one Florentine and the other Venetian, giving comedies, acrobatic performances, and ballets at Blois and in Paris. The *commedia*, very popular in north Italy, spread into Bavaria and along the Danube basin, as well as into Spain, England, and France.

A fourth troupe, I Comici confidenti, was in France in 1571, and I Gelosi were invited from Venice by Henri III to play during the Blois Estates General which began on 15 November 1576. They had to be ransomed from Huguenot captivity, and began to play only in February 1577. They were highly successful in Paris that summer, paying the Confrérie its fee to waive the monopoly, although the company played in fact at the Petit-Bourbon, not at the Hôtel de Bourgogne. Their greatest success, *La Princesse qui a perdu l'esprit*, employed music and mechanical devices, and involved a huge naval combat onstage. In 1578 they returned to Italy, appearing in Paris again only briefly in 1588. In 1585 there had been a troupe in Paris directed by Battista Lazaro which, however, went bankrupt. I Confidenti also returned to Paris in 1584 and 1585, performing for the duc de Joyeuse. Like all the others, they had trouble with the Confrérie de la Passion, which eventually had them expelled.

I Gelosi were called back to Paris by Henri IV about the time of his marriage to Marie de Medici in 1600, and stayed there until 1604. The company's most celebrated member, Isabella Andreini, wrote on 7 December 1603 from Fontainebleau to her patron, the grand duke of Tuscany, that Henri IV was paying the company 600 livres a month, plus expenses. She was to die in childbirth at Lyons on her way back to Italy in 1604, and her son was to be the popular Lelio of I Fedeli at the court of Louis XIII. The sum mentioned appears to have been a standard royal subvention, even when approved Italian companies were playing to the public. The duke of Mantua's troupe led by Tristano Martinelli was with the French court in 1599 and in Lyons in 1600, but Marie de Medici had some difficulty in getting the duchess of Mantua to free them to return to France. There were Italian companies in Paris in 1607 and 1608, and Marie de Medici, as regent in 1613, herself arranged for the six-month rental of the Hôtel de Bourgogne for Martinelli's company, which she eventually had brought from Mantua. It played at Lyons on the way, and then at Fontainebleau. In Paris it also played for the court at the Louvre. Marie de Medici's letters to members of the troupe were intimately friendly.

When in 1621 Martinelli himself returned with the remnants of I Gelosi, now renamed I Fideli, Louis XIII attended 23 performances in January and February 1622 and insisted that the company stayed on through the carnival, following the court to Fontainebleau and back to Paris. The last sure indication of the presence of an Italian company in or around Paris before 1644 is a payment on 17 December 1624 of 2,400 livres to Martinelli's company, probably for expenses. The evidence of the increasing popularity of *commedia dell'arte* at the French court, especially with Henri IV, and then even more with Marie de Medici and Louis XIII personally, is obviously important in deciphering the development of French drama from the era of Montchrestien and the beginnings of Hardy to Théophile de Viau, Tristan l'Hermite, Racan, Rotrou, Mairet, and the early Pierre Corneille.

For whatever reasons of national pride or cultural interest French troupes were supported from royal or private patronage, the evidence suggests that, at least until about 1624, it was *commedia dell'arte* that commanded the attention of the court. The Italians had alternated with French troupes at court and at the Hôtel de Bourgogne for some time, and by that date the Italian company was also playing scripted material. It is noticeable that the culturally serious French drama of spoken dialogue scarcely began its spectacular 17th-century development before evidence of the playing of *commedia dell'arte* in France disappears, and it has been plausibly suggested that the ultimate reason for the absence of *commedia dell'arte* was the ascendancy of Richelieu, who had received the cardinal's hat from the hands of Louis XIII on 10 December 1622 and joined the king's Council in April 1624, becoming first minister in August 1624. Richelieu's interest in the theatre, traceable in the general index, was intense, but also nationalistic.

The Italians returned to Paris at the invitation of Mazarin and Anne of Austria to open on 13 June 1644, 18 months after Richelieu's death. Ironically, it seems probable that they were given the larger of the two theatres in Richelieu's old house, already renamed the Palais-Royal, to play in, moving in 1645 to the Palais-Bourbon, shortly to be demolished to make way for the Louvre's eastern colonnade. It was there that they gave *La Finta Pazza*, with singing, dancing, and machines. Improvisation had largely given way to pastorals, tragi-comédies, farces, and romances, terms that are more nearly interchangeable than they are mutually exclusive. The new company, almost certainly Giuseppe Bianchi's, probably already contained the famous Scaramuccia, Tiberio Fiorilli, and used mechanical devices, scripted texts and a great deal of music, giving plays interspersed with singing and dancing. The Italians' reliance on mechanical devices, music, dancing, singing, and stage effects remained substantial, and it was performances of this sort which were to be much developed in court entertainment under Louis XIV; eventually they were to turn into French opera and ballet, after Lulli had acquired his 1672 privilège establishing a quasi-monopoly over all dramatic entertainment in Paris which involved music.

The 1644 troupe remained probably until the Fronde in 1648, with some of the members of the company returning between 1653 and 1658, generally for short visits and by invitation. Under Louis XIV Italian troupes continued to attract royal support, but etiquette was more formal and relations stiffer than they had been between Marie de Medici and Louis XIII and their Italian companies. None the less, Louis XIV became godfather to the child of Domenico Biancolelli, "Dominique," the Harlequin of the established troupe, as he also became godfather to a child of Molière. When Molière returned to Paris in 1658 he started by having to share the large hall of the Petit-Bourbon, the extension to the Louvre about to be knocked down, with the Italians, who played on the "ordinary" days, Tuesday, Friday, and Sunday, avoiding the market days of Wednesday and Saturday, the departure day for coaches to the east and south, which was Monday, and the Thursday traditionally devoted to promenades and other social diversions incompatible with theatre-going.

The ultimate reason for the distinction between ordinary and extraordinary days must have been the light: the availability of audiences during daylight hours, and the cost of artificial lighting indoors. La Grange's register breaks down daily expenditure for the season 1661–62, showing a daily three livres for each of two porters, a daily 15 livres for a sergeant and 12 soldiers to keep order in the theatre and prevent the entry of gate-crashers, six livres to be divided between four musicians, but 11 livres for candles, more than two thirds of the cost of the sergeant with his

12 troopers. On 17 January 1671 the unbelievably spectacular production of *Psyché* cost more than a quarter of a million livres, of which 15,000 livres was for candles and oil alone. Henri IV had ordered that all performances be completed by 4.30 p.m. and, although times were later at court and under Louis XIV, in 1668 the abbé de Pure in his *Idée des spectacles anciens et nouveaux* was still recommending that performances should start at 3.30 p.m. in winter and 4.30 p.m. in summer. When Giacinto Bendinelli, the Italian troupe's jeune premier, died in 1668, he left a wife, two children, and debts: a quarter's rent, 1,500 livres for costumes, 60 livres for wine, and 58 livres for candles. Relatively, light was enormously expensive, so that play-going was an afternoon activity, and it mattered to the box office whether it was a market day, or a day of bustle for coaches to leave, and it therefore also mattered on which days performances were given. When the Italians returned in 1662 and shared the newly refurbished Palais-Royal hall with Molière, they were allocated the extraordinary days.

Loret tells us that on 31 May 1659, just over a month before the Italians left France, the two companies combined for a command performance at Vincennes, with the Italians contributing their Horazio, Scaramuccia, and Trivellino, the "masks" played by Romagnesi, married to Bianchi's daughter, Fiorilli, and Locatelli, and the French contributing Jodelet, Gros-René, and Docteur Gratian. The three Italians were named by their masks and the three French players by their stage-names. Gros-René was a white-faced clown, "enfariné" or made up with flour, in real life married to Thérèse de Gorla, soon to be famous by her stage-name, the marquise du Parc, as Racine's mistress. It is apparent from the membership of both French and Italian troupes how the Italian masks had given rise to French stage-names, and how members of the same family, parents and children, tended in both France and Italy to follow what became a family avocation in the same troupe. Thérèse du Parc and her husband, René Berthelot, had been taken on by Molière at Lyons in 1653, and he was the troupe's star dancer and acrobat. There is some evidence that during his days in the south Molière discovered from *commedia dell'arte* competition the need to offer acrobatics on stage.

Between 1644 and 1658, we are sure only of three plays in the Italian repertoire, alongside the traditional and probably still unscripted comedies, the parodies, and the elaborate tragi-comic pieces, often of Spanish derivation. All three were departures from the staple repertoire involving the standard masked characters in complex imbroglios. Giulio Strozzi's *La Finta Pazza* of December 1645, in Italy already virtually an opera, of which we have lost Francesco Sacrati's music, and *La Rosaura imperatrice di Constantinopoli* of 1658 were Italian machine plays, produced in the elaborate settings designed by Giacomo Torelli; and the 1658 *Il Convitato di pietra* was the first Don Juan play performed in Paris. *La Finta Pazza* had been created to open the Teatro Novissimo in Venice in 1641. In Paris, less of the libretto of *La Finta Pazza* was sung. It featured Torelli's perspective scenery which allowed a player to appear to walk down a street by taking four or five paces up-stage, and the garden alleys appear to go as far as it was possible to see. There were five sets in all: a garden; a city with a port; a palace with a vista of rooms; a city square with multiple vistas; and a royal garden.

There was machinery for flying chariots as well as flying players, and there was a water effect with moving ships, and a real fountain. The comic dance was choreographed by Giovanni

Battista Balbi, who had a series of engravings of his dances made, and brought with him from Florence and Venice the bears, apes, and ostriches required, although he pretended to have thought them up at court for the amusement of the six-year-old Louis XIV. The stage, wrote Torelli, was to light up gradually; gardens and flowers were to appear in the air, then five winged spirits, before Aurora's chariot is wafted up and the spirits return to fetch Flora. Elements of buffoonery remain, however, and the characters, who apparently still wore masks, seem closely related to the traditional characters of the *commedia*. The probability is that the Italian company's spectacular effects were emulated at the Marais, but forced the Hôtel de Bourgogne, too small to make the installation of stage machinery economically viable even if there had been space for it, to concentrate on the lofty declamation of elevated metaphorical rhetoric, carrying to the stage the essentially educated and refined expression of emotion in verse which was Racine's speciality. Actors of scripted prose drama were regarded by the inventive Italians as talking apes. The true professional could only improvise, sing, or declaim verse.

La Rosaura imperatrice di Constantinopoli, in spite of the ingenious use of machinery, was less ambitious in 1658 and closer to the old *commedia* tradition. Loret was there the night the court attended—Louis XIV and his mother, his brother with his bride-to-be, Henriette d'Angleterre, and the Grande Mademoiselle—and listed the attractions, which included a Turkish background to the plot and a female magician, four ballets, 12 decors, sea-monsters, dragons, demons, seas, mountains, forests, fire, lightning, thunder, and perspective vistas. Loret thought the best scene was one of several devoted to Scaramouche, valet to the male lead. The plot is pure fairy-tale, with magic, disguises, disappearances, armed combat, several breath-taking transformation scenes, a storm and ship-wreck, and a happy ending, and the play, except for verse songs, was probably not scripted. It has been conjectured that the 1645 *La Finta Pazza* was an attempt to fend off the importation into Paris of an Italian opera company, but by 1658 the Italian company was secure enough to revert to its own form of acting, and the Scaramouche scenes cannot have been scripted. There was a ballet after each act.

The Italians left Paris in 1659. Torelli was to design the sets for Molière's *Les Fâcheux* at Vaux-le-Vicomte in 1661, but when the Petit-Bourbon was pulled down to make way for the new east front of the Louvre the new stage designer, Carlo Vigarani, refused to allow Molière to instal Torelli's settings in the Tuileries opera theatre, and had the whole lot burnt. They had been kept behind at the Petit-Bourbon when the rest of the interior furnishings were transferred to the Palais-Royal after the surintendant des bâtiments, Ratabon, had started the demolition of the Petit-Bourbon without warning on 11 October 1660 and Molière had found himself without a theatre. Meanwhile the Italians returned, apparently playing at Fontainebleau in the second half of 1661 before opening in Paris on 8 January 1662. They were now "the king's Italian troupe" of ten players, with an annual subsidy of 15,000 livres, of which the first instalment, for the first quarter of 1663, was made in 1664 to the "Italian musicians" Domenico Locatelli and Domenico Biancolelli.

The relatively high subvention may reflect the number of court performances, and therefore of missed box office takings, but it looks as if the Italians at this date took less at public performances than the French companies, presumably because of the language barrier. At the Petit-Bourbon Molière's troupe had paid the Italians 1,500 livres in 1658 for the use of the hall on the extraordinary days. At the Palais-Royal Molière paid no rent, but the Italians paid him 2,000 livres, or half the cost of temporary repair and redecoration of the dilapidated hall, which it had cost Richelieu 300,000 livres to build, about a third going on the cost of stage machines installed for the inauguration with *Mirame* on 14 January 1641. It seems certain that *Mirame* was mostly by Richelieu, although attributed by him to Desmarets. It was noted for the magnificent lighting effects as well as the astonishingly impressive, if dramatically unnecessary use of stage machinery. Unfortunately the two-feet thick and two-feet wide oak beams were 63 feet long, and eventually deteriorated under the weight of what Richelieu later built on top of his theatre. When Molière had moved in, there had been a partly canvas roof.

A difficulty arises because the pattern of subsidies suggests that subventions were specifically calculated not to take away box-office incentives but to ensure that all actors with a full share in any approved troupe received a minimum income from about 1660 to after 1680 of around 3,000 livres a year, or pro rata if they did not play a full season. Stage carpenters might be paid by the troupe as little as one or as much as three livres a day. Such figures as have survived confirm what was antecedently to be expected, that patronage at royal or princely whim was being systematically replaced under Colbert by the provision of virtually salaried employment in exchange for tighter artistic control. There were also occasional special gifts from the privy purse, although the payment of both subventions and gifts was often intermittent. The Paris theatre was expensive, with the parterre now costing 15 sous, perhaps as much as three quarters of a labourer's daily wage as against a twelfth in England, and by 1662 the French and the Italians, who probably charged much the same, had virtually the same audience. Dorimond's 1662 *La Comédie de la comédie* makes clear that in the common view the French companies were safer havens for decent bourgeois family values and language. The Hôtel de Bourgogne at least was holding the high moral ground. The Italians offered more entertainment value, in spite of language difficulties.

The war of the Mantuan succession had shifted the centre of *commedia dell'arte* from Mantua to Modena, and the Parisian troupe of 1662 owed its first allegiance to the duke of Modena. After 1662 it so adapted to Parisian taste that its *commedia dell'arte* can be said to have been replaced by something that has been called "comédie italienne (Italian comedy)." In Italy, where the audience could understand the language, more emphasis had come to be laid on the intrigue involving the young lovers. In France the paradigm classifications for what did and what did not constitute pure *commedia dell'arte* are 18th-century pigeon-holes which do not do justice to the reality of the renaissance *commedia*, which was not, as the 18th century tended to assume, exclusively or primarily based on neo-Latin plots or even exclusively on nothing but the stereotyped set of masks, and the same companies often played scripted and unscripted comedy. In France, the language difficulty naturally promoted the unscripted comedy, and there are no real plot paradigms, just endlessly laid-out opportunities for improvisation, such as those afforded by the overcoming and replacing of obstacles preventing the union of young lovers, sometimes organized round set speeches, "lazzi," or other pieces of stage business, and pre-arranged effects. Much depended on mistaken

identities, surprise discoveries, or deceptions that often went wrong.

At the beginning of the 1668 season, however, there was a discontinuity in the development of the Italian comedy in France, no doubt connected with the membership of Marco Antonio Romagnesi and the departure of Tiberio Fiorilli, although the nature of the connections is obscure. Fiorilli may have disapproved of the measures to be taken to ensure survival. Specifically French dramaturgical elements and local colour as well as French language material were now combined with italianate intrigues. There were also elements of French social satire picked up, no doubt, from the tradition of which Molière is the most significant representative. The first play of the new type, *Le Régal des dames*, opened in May 1668 and received a 122-line eulogy in Robinet's *Gazette* (q.v.). The queen mother, who had brought the Italians back to Paris in 1644, had died in April 1667, and the new queen had her own Spanish troupe. That left the king, but Louis XIV was not so enthusiastic as his mother had been about his Italian players. When Molière died in 1673, and his troupe amalgamated with the Marais to form the Guénégaud company, Lulli took over the Palais-Royal.

The Italian company thereupon flirted heavily with the English court in London. When a settlement was negotiated whereby they shared the Guénégaud theatre, they were not permitted to use the machines, although a few of their plays in the 1670s did actually require machine effects. It seems quite likely that they arranged in the expected way for favourable publicity from the gazettes (see: *Mercure Galant*). The Guénégaud company is known to have paid Donneau de Visé 486 livres in September 1673 just as their new theatre was opening, and they gave 55 livres to Samuel Chappuzeau who had only pleasant things to say about it in his 1674 *Le Théâtre français*. Robinet's *Gazette* was particularly favourable to the Italians.

The final amalgamation of 1680 between the Guénégaud troupe and that of the Hôtel de Bourgogne, which created the Théâtre-Français or Comédie-Française, may well have been the result of the Italians' desire to use more machinery and spectacle, probably involving the cutting of trap-doors, and therefore to have their own house. On 14 December 1679 the Guénégaud company started negotiations with the players from the Hôtel de Bourgogne. The Guénégaud company was fresh from its triumph with the Donneau de Visé-Thomas Corneille *La Devineresse* (see: Donneau de Visé) which had depended on scenic effects like limbs flying together to form a body, and had started its prodigious success on 19 November 1679, during La Voisin's trial and just three months before her execution. There were several hearings and inspections before an agreement was imposed on 18 February, but the Italians took over the Hôtel de Bourgogne after the amalgamation in August. The king had dissolved the Confrérie de la Passion in 1667 and ownership of the Hôtel, renovated by the Confrérie in 1647, had passed to the Hôpital des Enfants-Trouvés, operated by Vincent de Paul's Sisters of Charity. The Marais, rebuilt after the 1644 fire, had been much the larger and better equipped theatre. A list of 53 pieces played by the French company at the Hôtel in the later years of its tenure shows that 43 used a single decor, and the other ten two decors simultaneously ready on stage, with one shuttered off, although machinery was installed in 1656 for *Le Grand Astyanax*.

The Italian repertory now turned increasingly to farce, comic business, and fantasy, while retaining its scatalogical elements, and play with nose-blowing, enemas, bladders, and chamber pots. There is, however, more reference to contemporary events, and recognizable parody. We have only skeleton sketches, and it it is difficult to tell, but the 1677 *Arlequin et Scaramouche errans de Babilonne* burlesques the account of Hippolyte's death in one or other of Racine's or Pradon's *Phèdre et Hippolyte* tragedies, both first played only weeks previously and both still in the repertoire. By *Arlequin Jason* of 1684 we know that the Italians were playing whole scenes in French and had begun again to rely on complex scenic effects and notable transformations, presumably dependent on freshly installed machinery capable, for instance, of producing water from 15 jets to cascade down three rows of eight basins which had cost 5,500 livres.

The Guénégaud, accommodating about 1,650 spectators, was bigger, but the Hôtel de Bourgogne cannot often have been filled to its capacity, at this date about 1,200. Average audiences may have been 400, but there are wisps of evidence pointing towards more fashionable audiences of greater sophistication, and probably education, for the French company. Only the parterre expressed displeasure by whistling. There may incidentally have been hissing, too, from about 1680, and the word "siffler" means both "whistle" and "hiss," but in 1687 Arlequin, saying he has just seen the Italians play *Le Banqueroutier*, recounts how he pulled what can only have been a real whistle out of his pocket. Boileau uses the word "siffler" of an audience reaction in the third chant of the 1674 *Art poétique*.

The organization of theatrical life in Paris, ultimately dictating what pieces were played and what scripts were written, while obviously remaining dependent on physical and economic circumstances, petty rivalries, serious jealousies, talent, flair, and failure, was also a personal concern of Colbert. Not only was the king paying subventions, still in 1680 15,000 livres a year to the Italians, but he had to provide for entertainment at court, even when in 1682 it moved permanently to Versailles. The king had earlier had his Italian and French companies playing alternately during the court's annual vacation at Fontainebleau, generally in October for the hunting, although the distance from Paris, some 65 kilometres, was such that the players had to be given money for food and lodging. Commuting to Versailles and Saint-Germain-en-Laye was just possible, but recompense had to be made for box-office takings missed in Paris. Through the amalgamations of 1673 and 1680 Colbert continued his rationalization of cultural life, establishing central control in return for subventions, by creating a French company large enough to play both at court and in town. Lulli's opera was primarily a court creation in the first place, although it played publicly in Paris, and the dauphin's wife, Marie-Anne-Victoire of Bavaria, was entrusted with drawing up new statutes for the Italian company soon after her wedding, early in 1680. Complex arrangements for remuneration, subsidy, and control were laid down.

At Versailles from 1682 there was an established pattern of entertainment for the court of some 10,000 persons, recorded by the *Mercure Galant* in January 1683. There was to be gambling on Mondays, Wednesdays, and Fridays, a dance and a play on Sundays, Tuesdays, and Thursdays, and an opera on Saturdays. That frequency was only approximately attained, and only in 1685. There was a remission in the summer, and October was reserved for Fontainebleau, but court interest in the Italian company, now no longer so distinctive in style or repertoire,

although still overwhelmingly playing in Italian, seems to have diminished. The king had not seen a play for a year when on 16 October 1684 he attended a performance by the Italian company at Fontainebleau. Dangeau says he found it very bad and was very bored.

The Italians lost money by playing at Versailles, where there was no permanently installed theatre. A provisional playing space was found on the ground floor in the 1680s, but there was no room for machines and so more onus placed on the costumes to impress. The court accounts go into great detail about the cost of light. The Versailles allocation per performance was 60 pounds of white candles, of which 844 were needed for the auditorium, 104 for the stage, along the side, at the back, and overhead; 35 pounds of yellow candles, for the dressing rooms and guards' room; and three pounds of tallow. Twelve torches were provided to lead the actors to their carriages at night.

The age of knockabout, ribald farce was over by 1680. Satire, fantasy, and spectacle were attracting increasingly bourgeois audiences, and Louis XIV, that is Colbert succeeded by Louvois, increased the size of the Italian company. The traditional Italian repertoire continued to be played alongside increasingly French and scripted material, and some new plays in Italian were given. There are two collections of material which, if used carefully enough, can give accurate pointers towards the sorts of material being played, but the conclusions to be drawn are not more than very general. Early in the 18th century Thomas-Simon Gueullette (1683–1766), then a young lawyer, joined with other young lawyers in playing, and then composing, pieces of street and fairground theatre. In 1756 he published anonymously the three-volume *Théâtre des Boulevards; ou, Recueil des parades* and his *Notes et souvenirs sur le théâtre italien du XVIIIe siècle* were published by J.-E. Guellette in 1938 from a manuscript in the Bibliothèque de l'Opéra, while Evaristo Gherardi, Harlequin of the troupe from 1689, published a one-volume 545-page collection of scenes and plays in French, *Le Théâtre italien*, to which both a *Suite* and a *Supplément* had been printed by 1697, and which was expanded into a six-volume collection in 1700.

Gueullette says he acquired from Domenico Biancolelli's son a note of the improvised scenes played by Biancolelli, who died in 1688, having been the troupe's Harlequin from 1662. But Gueullette changed some of the names and translated the Italian notes into French, and is therefore of limited help. Gherardi's first volume appeared with a privilège of 24 May 1694, but the company succeeded in having it suppressed on the grounds that the material it contained was corporately owned. The book was suppressed and Gherardi fined 200 livres on 17 September 1694, but on 30 October the company appealed for permission to sell the edition of 2,000 copies for collective benefit, only to be told that the edition had been burnt. It cannot have been, as too many copies have survived.

Gherardi claimed that the *Suite* was a Dutch counterfeit, probably of 1696, and the *Supplément* a Belgian pirated edition of 1697, containing material stolen from him. A comparison of all this material makes it clear that no reliable guide exists to what the Italian troupe actually did on stage, or even in what language. It is unlikely that Jean-François Regnard or Charles Dufresny gave away full-length plays to the company or, therefore, that Gherardi's six volumes of 1700 are an authentic guide to the company's practice, and we know that Gueullette's manuscript cannot be, although his translation seems to have been the more honest of the two undertakings. A reasonable conclusion from the Gherardi volumes is nevertheless the increasing reliance of the company on parody of what had already become classics of French theatre.

A month after the death of Domenico Biancolelli the company reopened on 1 September 1688. The costume and mask of Harlequin were used by Angelo Constantini, but he retained his own stage-name of Mezzetin. A great deal of money was spent on machinery. *Ulisse et Circé* on 20 October 1691 starts with Troy in flames behind the encampment of the Greeks. Then the scene shifts to an island with three swimming characters and a little wave-tossed boat with two more. There are four transformations and three chariots, which must have flown off, because chariots always did. In the 1692 carnival play *Arlequin Phaeton*, characters on clouds talk to characters on earth, and a chariot is upset in the air as Jupiter hits it with a thunderbolt. There is an engraving which makes the stunt look dangerous. The changes were successful, and the Italian company were comfortably outplaying the combined French troupes in the 1690s in Paris, although they had lost favour at court, where they performed at most four or five times in a year.

In the 1690s the Italians were performing Regnard, making savage allusions to their French rivals, playing to the parterre while the Comédie-Française had audiences down to 100. The Italians dealt better with the menace of whistling. In 1696 the secretary of state Pontchartrain wrote to the chief of police La Reynie that whistlers should be arrested. A butcher was sent to jail in August. He excused himself to the judge on grounds of over-excitement. He had used an instrument with which he woke his boys in the morning. He was clearly therefore not hissing, but using a whistle. The king intervened to have him released after three weeks. The practice of using whistles was over certainly by 1712, but already by 1688 the final danger for the Italians had started to grow. The company was told to remove the scatology. There were to be no more double entendres. The unpopularity at Versailles had something to do with the ascendancy of Mme de Maintenon and the new austerity.

Ironically, the Italians were more easily accorded access to the sacraments than French actors, subject to Gallican discipline. Biancolelli and Fiorilli were buried behind the altar at Saint-Eustache, the church which had refused burial in consecrated ground to Molière. But indecency was another matter, and from January 1696 there was a police spy at every performance of the Italian company to report any improvised obscenities. Annoyance was caused to the authorities as early as 1695 when a commissaire of the Châtelet complained of a burlesque commissaire in a French play put on by the Italians. Censorship was seriously considered but clearly found impracticable. The Italian troupe was banned on 14 May 1697.

No one quite knows why. It was only the *Gazette d'Amsterdam* that suggested that the king was suddenly saving 18,000 livres a year. In fact the subsidy was still nominally 15,000 livres. Neither the *Mercure Galant* nor the *Gazette de France* mentions the closure, but all the foreign gazettes gave it much space and it is in the diaries of Dangeau, Saint-Simon, and Elisabeth-Charlotte of Bavaria. Contemporary opinion felt that the camel's back had finally snapped under the cumulative weight of the straws. The suggestion that the company intended to stage a new play by Lenoble entitled *La Fausse Prude* which may have been going to have been hostile to Mme de Maintenon, whom it did not mention by name, first surfaced in the June *Mercure Historique et Politique* as one of three alternative conjectural possibilities. The author, however, plumped for the monetary saving as the real reason. Saint-Simon is certainly wrong when he says that the company was given a month's notice. The order was executed within 24 hours. He also says that *La Fausse Prude* was actually played with great success three or four times, but he was writing a long time after the event. Elisabeth-Charlotte of Bavaria in 1720 repeats the rumour of the intention to satirize Mme de Maintenon, saying that she herself warned the company in vain against doing it, heard it was very funny, but could then do nothing to help.

The most likely solution is that the Italian company had commissioned a translation of an Italian play *La Finta Matrigna* ("The False Mother-in-Law"), renamed "La Fausse Prude" to take advantage of a book of that title recently published in Amsterdam. The piece seems never to have been played, unless it was improvised and in Italian. No one has found the Amsterdam book, nor any text called "La Fausse Prude." The French company will have done nothing to save their rivals, and the decision to act in the general interests of propriety may have been partly due to some intrigue on behalf of the French troupe's interests; and it is not unlikely that the Bureau des menus plaisirs was nearly 100,000 livres in arrears with its payments of the subsidy.

The company recalled by the regent as soon as mourning for Louis XIV was over came from the Parma troupe of Antonio Farnese, and was led by Luigi Riccoboni, or "Lelio." His wife was a scholar as well as a player. The company contained a standard *commedia dell'arte* cast, two male lovers, Arlequin, Trivelin, Pantaloon, The Doctor, Scapin, Scaramouche, two female leads, a soubrette, and a singer. Further female roles were added, starting with Columbine in 1739. The opening was on 18 May 1716 in the Palais-Royal with *L'Inganno fortunato; ou, L'Heureuse Surprise*, from a three-act scenario in Italian much assisted by the "lazzi" of Thomassin. At first the success was enormous, in spite of the language. Then came complaints of vulgarity. The company did know hard times, but was saved by Jacques Autreau, writing in French but using traditional Italian characters in *Le Port à l'Anglais; ou, Les Nouvelles Débarqués*, with musical interludes by Joseph Mouret. Its real significance in the history of the literature of France was, however, to be the partnership developed with Marivaux.

The company moved back to the Hôtel de Bourgogne and its 15,000 livre subsidy was restored. It very quickly developed an italianate version of French comedy which, in combination with Marivaux, became imaginatively vigorous, but which was largely in verse and no longer improvised. *Commedia dell'arte*, which continued a fitful existence in Italy, underwent its own transformation as it became English in England, and French in France, where it laid more weight on singing and dancing, performed more original French plays and then turned to comic opera. As the Italian Comedy it amalgamated with what had once been the theatre of the Saint-Laurent fair to create the Opéra-Comique in 1762. By 1779, 16 years after he had masterminded Mozart's visit to Paris, Grimm reported that the company had replaced Italian plays with French ones from its old repertoire. Of the Italians only the Harlequin was left to play the Harlequin role in French pieces. In 1780 the company became the Théâtre des Italiens, although there were no longer any Italian members at all.

CONDORCET, Marie-Jean-Antoine-Nicolas Caritat, Marquis de, 1743–1794.

Philosophe, mathematician, social and political thinker.

LIFE

Condorcet's family, which traced its origins back to the middle ages, had become Huguenot in the 16th century, and owned a château at Nyons, about 40 km. east of the Rhône, halfway between Valence and Avignon. By the 18th century it had become impoverished, and its male members sought careers in the army or the church, although Condorcet's senior uncle, Jean-Laurent, who inherited the family property, was a lawyer at the Grenoble parlement. The family included Cardinal de Bernis and Yse de Saléon, bishop of Rodez, as well as Jacques-Marie, bishop of Gap, then of Auxerre and Lisieux.

Condorcet's father was a cavalry captain who, on garrison duty at Ribemont in Picardy, was thought to have contracted a mésalliance by marrying a devout bourgeois girl, Marie-Madeleine Gaudry. Condorcet's father died shortly after his birth. His mother dedicated him to the Blessed Virgin and dressed him in white until he was eight. It was the bishop of Gap who made arrangements for Condorcet's education, sending him at the age of 11 to the Jesuit college at Reims and then, when he was 15, to the Collège de Navarre in Paris, where he proved to be a precociously gifted mathematician, and defended a thesis before a jury which included d'Alembert. When in 1762, after finishing at Navarre and spending some months of reflection at home, he decided to become a professional mathematician, it was to his old teacher at Navarre, the abbé Giraud de Kéroudan, that he turned.

Living with Giraud de Kéroudan, Condorcet devoted himself not only to mathematics, but also to astronomy, physics, chemistry, history and literature. Although he was to publish an essay on the calculus of integrals in 1765, to win a prize for an essay on the trajectory of comets, and to publish distinguished work on resistance in fluids and further important work on calculus, infinite series, and particularly on the theory of probability, Condorcet's interests were to turn increasingly to economic and social, and then to political problems, and his concerns were to move from the theorizing of the 1770s to his more practical commitment in the 1780s to improving in a variety of ways the social conditions of the human community. He was to be a close friend of Turgot, whose life he was to write, whose religious scepticism he shared, and with whose views on free trade and reform through an enlightened monarchy he agreed until the Revolution broke out. Turgot, closely associated with Malesherbes and a contributor to the *Encyclopédie* (q.v.), had died in 1781.

By the time he left Navarre, Condorcet had undergone some moral turmoil, no doubt at the root of his later rejection of institutional Christianity, but already implicit in his rejection of a military career. By the time he left college, Condorcet was later to write to Turgot, he had noticed that our ideas on justice and virtue were founded on the need to avoid the pain experienced at seeing the suffering of other sentient creatures. Condorcet gave up shooting, of which he was fond, and even avoided harming insects "à moins qu'ils ne fassent beaucoup de mal (unless they are causing a great deal of pain)."

On 8 March 1769 he was elected to the Académie des Sciences, of which he was made perpetual secretary in 1777, and for which he wrote first the éloges of all its members who had died between 1666 and 1699, subsequently carrying on with those who had died before 1790. His election to the Académie française in 1782 was said by Grimm to be d'Alembert's greatest victory over Buffon. Condorcet's discourse on reception was devoted to the social advantages to be expected from unifying the physical and moral sciences. For both academies Condorcet composed and delivered a number of discourses and éloges. He was also made a member of the academies of Berlin, Turin, Bologna, Saint Petersburg, and Philadelphia. D'Alembert may have introduced Condorcet to the salon of Mme du Deffand, but he is above all associated with that of Julie de Lespinasse, who had broken with Mme du Deffand in 1764. It was in the salon of Julie de Lespinasse, which became a meeting place for the philosophes (q.v.), that Condorcet met Helvétius, Marmontel, Morellet, Condillac, Saint-Lambert, Bernardin de Saint-Pierre, and above all Turgot. D'Alembert also introduced Condorcet to Diderot and to Voltaire, with whom Condorcet sustained a long correspondence and stayed for a fortnight in September 1770.

In August 1774 Condorcet responded to the attacks on the philosophes in the *Trois siècles littéraires* of Sabatier de Castres with his violent but anonymous *Lettre à un théologien*, which was strong enough to worry Voltaire, to whom its authorship was inevitably imputed. At this early date Condorcet was insisting in private correspondence with Voltaire on the need to defend the proclaimed atheists, like Helvétius and Holbach, but was himself guarded in the expression of his intellectual commitment. He was sceptical, but above all empirically minded, probably inclined to accept a generally deist solution to the problem of the origins of the universe. In 1776 he edited the *Pensées* of Pascal, reinstating suppressed passages from the Port-Royal edition, but made cuts of his own where Pascal's fragments were too mystically inclined for Condorcet to follow them. His non-mathematical articles for the *Encyclopédie* dealing with political economy and philosophy were published over the pseudonym of Schwartz, and lean towards the physiocrat view that land is the only true source of wealth.

In August 1774, however, Turgot, the former intendant of the Limoges area, had come to power as comptroller-general of finances, and appointed Condorcet inspector-general of the Mint. Condorcet now lived at the Hôtel des Monnaies and energetically took part on Turgot's side in the pamphlet war against Necker, supporting free trade in corn after the disastrous harvest of 1774, in a way which would have given real bargaining power to the poor. Turgot lost the ideological battle, and was disgraced in 1776. Condorcet's *Vie de M. Turgot* appeared in 1786, the year before his 1787 *Vie de Voltaire*. By that time Condorcet had begun to press for the implementation of a whole series of social reforms. They included the emancipation of slaves, although Condorcet remained aware of the danger of replacing institutional by an even worse economic slavery; the need to increase the tolerance accorded to Protestants; the suppression of the corvée, or labour demanded of individuals by the state; the improvement of the rights of women; and the complete reorganization of the educational system. By the outbreak of the Revolution and in the light of the victorious American struggle for independence, Condorcet had become a convinced republican.

In December 1786 Condorcet married Sophie de Grouchy, born in 1764, sister of the future maréchal and Condillac's niece. She bore him a daughter, and held the last glittering salon for the philosophes before the Revolution. Among the habitués were Morellet, Chamfort, Beaumarchais, Grimm, Cabanis, and Mirabeau and among the important foreigners passing through Paris who called were Beccaria, Adam Smith, Alfieri, and Jefferson.

During the Revolution, Condorcet, who had a house at Mantes, first expressed his ideas to the liberal electoral assembly of the nobles there, then in 1790 became a member of the municipality of Paris and then in 1792, selecting the Aisne from the five districts which offered to nominate him, a representative at the Convention which succeeded the national assembly and which made him one of its secretaries. He had resigned from the Mint and now issued a series of pamphlets theoretically outlining much of what was later to be adopted, although too logical, abstract, and even-minded, and far too non-inflammatory, to make Condorcet a popular leader. He none the less went much further than the generality of liberal aristocrats and the moderate bourgeoisie, while giving the public impression of being on both sides at once—revolutionary and counter-revolutionary—by his insistence on fairness and justice in the application of liberal principles. By June 1791, Condorcet had been issuing warnings against the court, as well as against certain tendencies in the assembly. He spent the early months of 1792 working on his project of educational reform, founded on the ideas of human progress and perfectibility, which was to provide the basis for much of the organization of French education until well into the 20th century.

By mid-1792 Condorcet was plainly satisfying neither right nor left, and he was obviously worried when the populace started to by-pass the decisions of its own elected representatives. His attitude towards the king had pleased neither royalists nor republicans, proposing to leave the monarch virtually nothing except his title, but avoiding the abolition of the throne. The fundamental unifying basis for Condorcet's changing attitudes was his desire at all costs to preserve legality. Whatever was to happen must happen legally, and for the assembly to judge the king infringed the principle of separation of executive and juridical powers. In the end Condorcet abstained in the vote on the king's condemnation to death, although he approved of sending him to the galleys. He spent much time elaborating his draft constitution, felt the arrest of the 29 Girondin deputies and two ministers on 31 May and 2 June 1793 to be illegal, founded his *Journal d'instruction publique*, inserting into its prospectus sections bound to infuriate Robespierre, and anonymously, although his authorship was clear, issued his reply to the left-wing draft of a constitution, the *Aux citoyens français sur la nouvelle Constitution*.

Condorcet was now declared "hors la loi (outside the law)," and condemned to death on 2 October 1793, although encyclopedist friends enabled him to take refuge before he could be arrested. He wrote a number of brochures, some personal essays including the *Avis d'un proscrit à sa fille*, and the apparently long-meditated *Esquisse d'un tableau historique des progrès de l'esprit humain*, a monument to his unshakable idealism and an inspiration for the school of "idéologue" philosophers led by Cabanis, a doctor as well as philosopher whose work was largely concerned with ideas and the operations of the mind.

Early in January 1794 Condorcet's wife asked for a divorce to preserve for their four-year-old daughter Condorcet's possessions now juridically liable to confiscation. On 25 March, perhaps provoked by this request, Condorcet left his hiding place. While a friend went to try to obtain a passport for him, Con-

dorcet was denounced at an inn as suspect and on 28 March was taken to prison at Bourg-la-Reine. He died two days later, most probably from exposure and exhaustion, or a stroke, although self-administered poison was for a long time considered the probable cause of death. Condorcet's widow was left penniless. She translated some of Adam Smith's moral works, and had to support her sister Charlotte, who eventually married Cabanis, as well as her daughter, who in 1807 married General O'Connor. She herself helped to edit her husband's complete works, and died in 1822.

WORKS

The literary and philosophical importance of Condorcet rests chiefly on his *Esquisse d'un tableau historique des progrès de l'esprit humain*, of which the manuscript, dated according to the Revolution's calendar, is signed Friday, 4 October 1793. With the cleanly copied manuscript are sketches for further or alternative developments and preliminary drafts. The first printed edition, dated year V of the Revolution's calendar, contains passages not in the manuscript which for the most part further develop particular points, or provide examples. The general tenor of Condorcet's thought on the eve of his death is clear, and the manuscript must represent an early but formal literary presentation of a text we know to have been written in extreme circumstances, however Condorcet might subsequently have developed it, had he not left his hiding place, or if he had escaped arrest and survived. The *Esquisse* was written in the knowledge that it might well have to do service as a final testament.

Even at his most secularizing, Condorcet retained a certain respect for individual priests, even when disagreeing with their opinions or deploring their social role. Particularly in the éloge and the introduction to the edition of Pascal, he plainly thought that one day there might be discovered an explanation of the origins and functioning of the universe which did not postulate the need for a supernatural cause, though that moment had not yet in his view arrived.

> Avant de recourir à une cause surnaturelle, il faut non seulement avoir reconnu l'insuffisance des causes naturelles que l'on connaît, mais encore s'être assuré que l'esprit humain ne la pourra jamais découvrir
>
> (Before having recourse to a supernatural cause, we must not only have acknowledged the inadequacy of the natural causes we know, but also be certain that the human mind will never discover one).

Since advances in scientific knowledge were still to be anticipated, it seemed to Condorcet fruitless to conduct metaphysical speculations, especially since there existed recognizable social evils which we could devote our energies to remedying.

> Peu importe que tout soit bien, pourvu que nous fassions en sorte que tout soit mieux qu'il n'était avant nous
>
> (It matters little whether everything is well, providing we act so that everything becomes better than it was before us).

Condorcet's writings show that, however hesitant he might have been in practice during the Revolution, his theoretical idealism was boundlessly radical. He had no doubts that the corruption in moral values stemmed from the "inégalité des fortunes (uneven distribution of wealth)." While holding that all real wealth originates in the land, Condorcet, like Turgot, regarded industry as capable of enriching society. The people must acquire a power to counter-balance that of owners and merchants, which must come from the sale of their labour, which itself presupposed a liberal political and social regime. Increasingly Condorcet became impatient of manifest injustice, whether it lay in the exercise of feudal rights, the use of the corvée, the administration of the parliamentary courts, or the enslavement of blacks in North America.

The idealism comes through not only in the hopes placed in social engineering and political reform, but also in his belief in the physical as well as the moral perfectibility of human beings. The human mind "seems" to grow in its capacity to absorb knowledge. The discourse of reception to the Académie is a remarkable document in this respect. The human sciences have as their aim the increase of human happiness, and the rules by which happiness is acquired can be defined, Condorcet implies, as certainly as those established in the physical sciences. In 1781, writing on the influence of the American revolution he had stated that the only way to accelerate the progress of humanity was to work for the progress of the individual. In the 1782 discourse of reception he wrote:

Le projet de rendre tous les hommes vertueux est chimérique: mais pourquoi ne verrait-on pas un jour les lumières, jointes au génie, créer pour les générations plus heureuses une méthode d'éducation, un système de lois, qui rendraient presqu'inutiles le courage et la vertu. Dirigé par ces institutions salutaires, l'homme n'aurait besoin que d'écouter la voix de son coeur et celle de sa raison pour remplir, par un penchant naturel, les mêmes devoirs qui lui coûtent aujourd'hui des efforts et des souffrances

(The project of making all men virtuous is chimerical. But why one day should we not see insight joined to genius create for happier generations an educational method, a legal system, which would make courage and virtue almost superfluous. Directed by such well-conceived institutions, the individual would need to listen only to the voice of the heart and that of the reason to fulfil by a natural inclination the same duties which today require efforts and sufferings).

Constitutionally, all laws should proceed from reason alone. No minority should be sacrified to the happiness, still less the economic advantage, of others. Condorcet goes so far as to aim even at "la distribution plus égale des jouissances (the more equal distribution of pleasures)" as the aim of the quest for "le bonheur public (public happiness)." By the beginning of 1789 he saw that the Revolution was inevitable, although it would be much better if the aim could be achieved without crises, agitations, and the substitution of one set of abuses for another. In arguing the case for women's rights, Condorcet falls back on the argument that all human rights are founded on the capacity to feel, which is the foundation for all moral values and systems. Condorcet also argues strongly not only for everyone's right to education, but against the unpleasant social consequences of inequality of education within a society.

The *Esquisse* deals in succession with ten periods in the development of human society:

1. Les hommes sont réunis en peuplade (Men get together to form tribes)
2. Les peuples pasteurs. Passage de cet état à celui des peuples agriculteurs (Pastoral societies. Transition from this state to agricultural societies)
3. Progrès des peuples agriculteurs, jusqu'à l'invention de l'écriture alphabétique (Progress of agricultural societies up to the invention of alphabetical writing)
4. Progrès de l'esprit humain dans la Grèce, jusqu'au temps de la division des sciences, vers le siècle d'Alexandre (Progress of the human mind in Greece, up to the time when the sciences were divided, about the age of Alexander)
5. Progrès des sciences depuis leur division jusqu'à leur décadence (Progress of the sciences from their division to their decay)
6. Décadence des lumières, jusqu'à leur restauration, vers le temps des croisades (The decay of knowledge to its restoration, about the time of the crusades)
7. Depuis les premiers progrès des sciences, lors de leur restauration dans l'Occident, jusqu'à l'invention de l'imprimerie (From the early progress of the sciences at their restoration in the west, to the invention of printing)
8. Depuis l'invention de l'imprimerie jusqu'au temps où les sciences et la philosophie secouèrent le joug de l'autorité (From the invention of printing to the period when sciences and philosophy shook off the yoke of authority)
9. Depuis Descartes jusqu'à la formation de la République française (From Descartes to the formation of the French republic)
10. Des progrès futurs de l'esprit humain (Of the future progress of the human mind).

The most important things to be said about the content of the work are apparent from its table of contents. It contains a lyrical hymn to human perfectibility, it is a work of defiant confidence in human nature, and it contains a philosophy of history. Key points in the progress of the human mind are the invention of printing and the rebellion against authority in matters of knowledge. The work scarcely risks underestimating the French contribution to the march of human progress, although Locke, Newton, Huyghens, Leibniz and Copernicus are among the heroes of the ninth period, along with Condillac, d'Alembert, and the fighters for American independence. As history, Condorcet's work does not rank highly, but as a lyrical ode to the future of humanity it is a forceful piece of imaginative writing, however optimistic its implied relationship between knowledge, moral values, and increased happiness. Poignancy is naturally added from a knowledge of the date and circumstances of its composition.

PUBLICATIONS

Collections

Oeuvres complètes, 21 vols., 1801–4
Oeuvres de Condorcet, 12 vols., 1847–49
Eloges des académiciens de l'Académie Royale des Sciences morts depuis 1666 jusqu'en 1790, 5 vols., 1799

Politics and economics

Lettre sur le commerce des grains, 1774
Lettre d'un laboureur de Picardie à M. N[ecker], 1775
Réflexions sur le commerce des blés, 1776
Réflexions d'un citoyen catholique sur les lois…relatives aux protestants, 1778
Recueil des pièces sur l'état des protestants de France, 1781
Réflexions sur l'esclavage des nègres, par M. Schwartz, pasteur à Bienne, 1781
De l'influence de la révolution d'Amérique sur l'Europe, 1786
Essai sur la constitution, 2 vols., 1788
Réflexions sur la révolution de 1788, 1788
Recherches historiques et politiques, 4 vols., 1788
Bibliothèque de l'homme public, 28 vols., 1790–92
Aux Français, sur la constitution de 1793, 1793

Science and mathematics

Du calcul intégral, 1765
Du problème des trois corps, 1767
Essais d'analyse, 1768
Nouvelles expériences sur la résistance des fluides [with d'Alembert and Bossut], 1777
Dissertations sur la théorie des comètes, 1780
Essai sur l'application de l'analyse à la probabilité, 1785
Moyens d'apprendre à compter sûrement et avec facilité, 1799

Other

Lettre d'un théologien, 1774
Vie de M. Turgot, 1786
Vie de Voltaire, 1787
Esquisse d'un tableau historique des progrès de l'esprit humain, 1794; English translations 1955, 1957
Correspondance inédite de Turgot et de Condorcet, 1883
Avis d'un père proscrit à sa fille, 1812

Biographical and critical studies

Schapiro, J. Salwyn, *Condorcet and the Rise of Liberalism in France*, 1934
Bouissounousse, Janine, *Condorcet, le philosophe de la Révolution*, 1962
Hincker, Monique et François, Introduction to edition of the *Esquisse*, 1966

––––––––––

CORNEILLE, Pierre, 1606–1684.

Playwright: author of tragi-comedies, tragedies, and comedies; also of theoretical works; and poet.

LIFE

Corneille's thoroughly sharp, professional, money-making, and often unattractive approach to his theatrical career is at least partly explained by his birth into, and membership of, the newly emergent class of administrators and merchants. The divergence of this class from the old magistracy became increasingly clear in France with the end of the religious wars. Its members exercised none of the recognized professions or trades, but while neither peasants, nor labourers, nor land-owners, did not aspire to nobility, want clerical status, or have the entrepreneurial drive to become bankers or tax-farmers. Corneille must be the first really great French author never to have wanted to be anything other than a middle-class professional who had found a job he could make money from. Rather rigidly Catholic, he cared comparatively little for fame, not much for learning or virtue, and not at all for outward elegance. He ostentatiously retained a new sort of social respectability, but did not strive for refinement of behaviour, or even good manners.

We have contemporary comments from his nephew, Fontenelle, from Voltaire's father, from d'Aubignac, Méré, Villiers, Tallemant des Réaux, Charpentier, Segrais, and Vigneul-Marville to the effect that he dressed badly, had no conversation, behaved like a peasant, lacked any sort of personal distinction, was avaricious, ungracious, mercenary, brusque, and ill-tempered, but dreamt and lived his profession, which became writing plays for a living. He disdained the vulgarity of the world of the theatre which he exploited and could never have been, like Molière, an actor-manager or sought like him to achieve social preferment by becoming a court entertainer. He gave support to the Marais troupe of actors, because it was in his interest that the Hôtel de Bourgogne should not have a monopoly of the tragic stage. He was totally dedicated to the world he knew he could create on the stage and from which he lived. When he contemplated writing a play, he would go to bed, cover himself with blankets to induce a drenching sweat, and then get up and write.

Corneille prided himself on having got where he did by his own efforts: "Je ne dois qu'à moi seul toute ma Renommée (I owe to myself alone all my renown)." That alexandrine comes from the *Excuse à Ariste*, a remarkable document of just over 100 lines of verse in which Corneille, firing the first shot in his own defence in what was to become the famous Querelle des anciens et des modernes (q.v.) following the staging of *Le Cid* in 1637, sets out to explain why he could not write verse to be sung, is immediately side-tracked into vindicating his own literary independence, and apparently wanders off into an account of a schoolboy infatuation.

Charmé de deux beaux yeux, mon vers charma la Cour,
Et ce que j'ai de nom je le dois à l'amour.
J'adorai donc Philis, et la secrète estime
Que ce divin esprit faisait de notre rime
Me fit devenir Poète aussitôt qu'amoureux:
Elle eut mes premiers Vers, elle eut mes derniers feux,
Et bien que maintenant cette belle inhumaine
Traite mon souvenir avec un peu de haine,
Je me trouve toujours en état de l'aimer…

(Charmed myself by two beautiful eyes,/my verse charmed the court,/And what fame I have I owe to love./I adored Philis, then, and the private value/Which that divine spirit attached to our rhyming/Made me into a poet at the same time as a lover./She had my first poems and she had my last love./Although now that cruel beauty/Treats my memory with distaste,/I find myself still ready to love her…).

Corneille's youthful but enduring love is more important in the history of French literature than has generally been supposed. The *Excuse*, with its suggestion that some of Corneille's early verse may have been written jointly with "Philis," appeared immediately after he had explored in *Le Cid*, much more seriously than had the Spanish original, the daring possibility that innocent love, up-graded by being based on merit, might justify the flouting of all accepted social conventions, to the extent that Chimène, the heroine, might even marry Rodrigue, the hero who, in a duel he was in honour obliged to fight, had just killed her father. Corneille discovered, he tells us, that what he could do had become fashionable, and did not now blush to have profited from it. In fact it was not quite as easy as the *Excuse* makes it seem. Corneille is unlikely to have been trying to make his way up from comedy, through tragi-comedy, to tragedy, and was in 1637 still to live to discover that the heroic values he was interested in examining had lost their relevance in a society drawing sharply back, in what now looks like a moment of terrified moral reaction, from the exuberant, almost boisterous optimism of the generation whose attitudes, first treated with caution in the early 1620s, were still finding their canonical expression as late as the early 1640s.

Corneille's grandfather, Pierre, had bought two adjacent houses in Rouen, in one of which Corneille was to live until 1662. His father, also called Pierre, was an administrative official, master of rivers and forests, who married Marthe le Pesant, a lawyer's daughter, in 1602. Two years after his eldest son, whom he also called Pierre, was born on 1 June 1606, he bought a large farm and small house near Rouen. Corneille's five brothers and sisters included Thomas, the future ardent defender of the *modernes* in the Querelle, born only in 1625, and Marthe, who was to become the mother of Fontenelle. Corneille attended the Jesuit college at Rouen from 1615 to 1622, and Jesuit spirituality has been discerned behind some of his plays, notably in the forthright defence of free will by Thésée in *Oedipe*, Act III, scene 5, in 1659, at the height of the Jansenist (q.v.) controversy. The play was dedicated to Foucquet, the last great protector of a baroque style in art and life overflowing with radiant confidence.

Corneille won prizes for Latin in 1618 and 1620, and was both to write Latin poetry and to translate from it. His verse translation of the *De imitatione Christi* would begin to appear in 1651 and was published in its entirety in 1656, and *L'Office de la sainte Vierge* with other portions of the Roman breviary was to appear in verse in 1670. While still at school he fell in love with Catherine Hue, the Philis of the *Excuse*, later to become Mme du Pont, wife of a tax official, for and perhaps with whom he wrote his first poems and his first plays. He is said to have burnt the poems shortly before his death and to have acknowledged how much he profited from her criticism of the early plays. The *Excuse* makes it seem not only that his passion was a lasting one, but that it was she who turned away from him.

We do not know where he studied law, but he graduated on 18 June 1624 and enrolled at the bar of the parlement of Rouen. He must have found employment in routine jobs of an administrative kind, and continued to write verse, the best of which he was to publish as *Mélanges poétiques* with *Clitandre* in March 1632. In 1628 his father bought him two modest posts in the magistracy, paying 11,600 livres, or nearly twice the official cost, for administrative positions in the department of rivers and forests and in the admiralty, giving him responsibility for policing the Seine and the Normandy rivers and forests. In 1643–45 a surviving register shows us Corneille unexceptionably fulfilling his official duties. Very little more is known for certain, but strands of evidence strongly suggest that Corneille, in his early twenties cutting a certain dash among his often richer contemporaries in Rouen, affecting or indulging a certain raffishness, with a wandering eye or a pose of disinterest in women, made himself known to Montdory when he and Charles Lenoir brought their troupe to Rouen in the summer of 1629 and showed them what we now know as *Mélite; ou, Les Fausses Lettres*. It was this troupe which, after playing in three temporary locations, rented the jeu de paume, or tennis court, in the Marais from which the company took its name.

What we do not know is how Corneille happened to have a five-act verse comedy to hand, especially since as a genre comedy had virtually died out, dispersed into burlesque on the one hand and pastoral or tragi-comedy on the other. Montdory took Corneille's piece, and played it that winter in Paris, where he had rented the Berthault jeu de paume in the hope of establishing his company. From Corneille's published dedication to Liancourt it seems that the first three performances were indifferently attended, but that as soon as it was known that Liancourt had taken an interest in the play audiences improved, and it quickly turned into a success. A strong whiff of irony in the "Au lecteur" makes it clear that, unless Corneille was already preening himself, the professional dramatists were not overjoyed by the success of this provincial amateur. By going into print, said Corneille, "Je contenterai…deux sortes de personnes, mes amis, et mes envieux (I shall make two sorts of people happy, my friends and those who are envious of me)." It must be remembered that Liancourt's interest in the theatre was well known. He had been a close friend of Théophile de Viau and had been a patron of Hardy. He also knew Gomberville and Saint-Amant, and was a very early protector of Montdory, to whom no doubt Corneille owed the introduction. He was to become protected, with Baro, Mareschal, and du Ryer, by the Vendôme family and, more distantly, with Rotrou, by the Longuevilles.

Mélite's success was achieved at the expense of Mairet's *Silvanire*, which for the first time imposed the unities on a tragicomédie as distinct from a pastoral, and which was being played at the Hôtel de Bourgogne. *Mélite*'s success lasted, since the play was not printed until 12 February 1633, with a privilège of 31 January, which means that Montdory's company kept the copyright for an unusual four seasons. In 1634 the play was mentioned in Scudéry's *Comédie des comédiens* as part of a dramatic repertoire alongside plays by Mairet, Scudéry, and Rotrou. In 1644 Corneille suppressed 52 lines, the sub-title, and the "Au lecteur," and made 67 other changes in the text. The 1660 revision was even more radical, with the dedication to a Liancourt converted to Jansenism left out, 500 corrections made, and 170 more lines omitted. The language is refined to suit evolving canons of taste, the kissing is cut out, the overt threat of a duel between Eraste and Tircis is removed, and the crudity of the nurse's threat to avenge herself by ruining the wedding night is attenuated. There seems little doubt that Corneille's original plot remembers both an amorous episode in his life and the heavy weight of financial considerations in marriages as they were customarily agreed in his social circle, and as reflected in the "Dialogue" of the *Mélanges poétiques*. Catherine Hue's father's office was for instance worth three times, and that of Thomas du Pont, whom Catherine Hue married, five times those of Corneille.

Corneille seems now to have presented a play a season. The theatrical year ran from Easter until the following Lent's closure, with the companies stable during that time. Most premieres occurred between early December and late January and it was a simple accident of timing whether they fell before or after the start of the new calendar year. The tragi-comédie *Clitandre; ou, L'Innocence délivrée*, probably played by Montdory's troupe, probably in the 1630–31 season, published in March 1632 and dedicated to Longueville, was the first piece of Corneille's work to appear in print. Presumably in response to criticism of *Mélite*, he drew attention in the preface of *Clitandre* to the way in which the action was limited to one day, however crowded and, inspired by Saint-Amant, included a strong affirmation of "moderne" views: "Je me donne ici quelque sorte de liberté de choquer les Anciens (I allow myself here some freedom to shock the "Anciens")."

The sub-title disappeared in 1644, but in 1660 Corneille made some important changes, dropping the description "tragi-comédie," reducing the number of lines from 1872 to 1624, weakening the play in a number of important respects and, above all, declaring in the new "Examen" that the adherence to the twenty-four hour rule and the introduction of the numerous scenes of violence and melodrama were intended as a snub to the critics of *Mélite*:

Un voyage que je fis à Paris pour voir le succès de *Mélite* m'apprit qu'elle n'était pas dans les vingt et quatre heures. C'était l'unique Règle que l'on connût en ce temps-là. J'entendis que ceux du métier la blâmaient de peu d'effets et de ce que le style était trop familier. Pour la justifier contre cette censure par une espèce de bravade, et montrer que ce genre de pièces avait les vraies beautés du Théâtre, j'entrepris d'en faire une regulière (c'est-à-dire dans ces vingt et quatre heures), pleine d'incidents, et d'un style plus élevé, mais qui ne vaudrait rien du tout; en quoi je réussis parfaitement

(A journey I made to Paris to see how *Mélite* was doing taught me that it did not keep to 24 hours. That was the only rule they knew in those days. I heard that the professionals criticized the play for its paucity of dramatic effects and because the style was too everyday. To justify it against this criticism, and to show that that sort of play had real dramatic beauty, I undertook in a sort of bravado to write a regular play (that is, one within the 24-hour rule), which would be full of happenings, and in a higher style, but which would be worthless. I succeeded perfectly in my aim).

In 1660 Corneille was hitting at his critics of 1630, and perhaps defending himself against what was probably the failure of *Clitandre*. We do not need to take his statement quite at its face value, but it is true that *Clitandre* was played on a stage compartmentalized to represent a forest, with oak-tree and cave, a room in the royal palace, a prison, a square, and the room of the wounded Rosidor. Some of the compartments were covered up when not required, and the "happenings" included the tracking of a criminal by the blood he drips, and much play with disguises, attempted rape, faintings, swords, and daggers. In the original text Corneille was certainly making a point against the "anciens," who insisted on the use of messengers to give long accounts on stage of violent events reported from elsewhere, by allowing them to be enacted in front of the audience. It has been suggested, not implausibly but without proof, that he may also have intended an allusion to the conspiracy to encompass Richelieu's disgrace and dismissal on 11 November 1630, known as the "Journée des Dupes," for which Marillac was arrested on 21 November, interrogated in July 1631. He died in 1632. For her part in the plot Marie de Medici, the queen mother, was exiled to Compiègne, from where she escaped to Belgium, to die shortly afterwards.

In Corneille's third play he returned to comedy. *La Veuve; ou, Le Traître trahi*, probably played in 1631–32, was published in March 1634 with poems by Scudéry, Mairet, Rotrou, du Ryer, Boisrobert, and nearly a score of others. Corneille had been received as a colleague by the professionals. The "Au lecteur" is a forthright declaration of the author's intentions to write realistically, and deals in some detail with his attitude to all three unities. He has sought a middle way between the severity of the 24-hour rule and complete licence, but allows the rule of place to extend to a single town and observes the unity of action "à sa mode (in his own way)." The 86-line *Excusatio* in Latin verse was written in 1633 when the archbishop of Rouen had asked Corneille for complimentary verses for the king and Richelieu, before whom Montdory was performing a Corneille play. While none the less paying the required compliments, Corneille explains that his ability is restricted to writing for the stage. Inspired by Horace, he also declares that his art is to conceal artistry:

Ars artem fugasse mihi est.

Corneille's next three plays, all comedies, can be dated only conjecturally, *La Galerie du Palais* to 1632–33, and to 1633–34 both *La Suivante*, regarded as controversial even by Corneille's admirers, and *La Place Royale; ou, L'Amoureux extravagant*, on a subject on which Claveret later accused Corneille of knowing that he, Claveret, was already working. Claveret's comedy was played before Louis XIII in June 1633. As he would later show at the expense of both Molière and Racine, Corneille was quite willing to forge his own successes by attempting either to suppress his rivals or to usurp their subjects. In 1634 Mairet had inaugurated a vogue for historical tragedy with *Sophonisbe*, set in Rome, and Rotrou had brought renewed life to Seneca with *Hercule mourant*. Corneille followed in the season 1634–35 with a *Médée* modelled on Seneca in which Guez de Balzac tells us that Montdory excelled as Jason. By 1635 Paris had also seen tragedies by Scudéry, La Pinelière, and Bensserade. Corneille was bending to popular taste, but also trying to capture for himself mastery in all the dramatic genres.

By 1631, or soon after, Richelieu himself had decided to preside over the development of theatre in France. He started by taking under his wing Boisrobert, then Rotrou. For Desmarets he may even have provided sketches of plots, and he certainly established a team of five dramatists—Rotrou, l'Estoille, Corneille, Boisrobert, and Colletet, to be directed by Chapelain—to provide plays to order. The first fruits of this cooperation, *La Comédie des Tuileries*, was played before the queen on 4 March 1635. Its five acts were respectively by Rotrou, l'Estoille, Corneille, Boisrobert, and Colletet. The five authors were to produce two more plays, in both of which Richelieu himself had a hand: the lost *La Grande Pastorale* of January 1637 and *L'Aveu-*

gle de Smyrne, played privately for Richelieu by both Paris companies at the Palais Cardinal (the present Palais-Royal) on 22 February of the same year. In that year Richelieu was to commission the major hall in the Palais from the architect Mercier, who pitched the seating, broke with the jeu de paume rectangle to build a semicircular rear wall, and created a large dome. The new hall was to be inaugurated with a performance of *Mirame* on 14 January 1641, by which time Corneille had been excluded from membership of the group of five authors, probably before the composition of Baudouin's "Avis au lecteur" for *L'Aveugle*, dated 17 June 1638. The most likely reason for Corneille's exclusion was his distaste for subjects too ethereal for his preferred realism of treatment.

Richelieu instituted the Académie française, at first one among several informal groups of literary acquaintances, with letters patent in 1635. That winter Corneille returned to comedy with *L'Illusion comique*, played by the Marais company. The comedy was inspired by Gougenot's *Comédie des comédiens* and its immediate imitation in a play of the same title by Scudéry, but Corneille's piece is a defence of drama which suggests that he had had to defend himself for getting involved in the world of theatre in the first place, a possibility which would explain much about his attitude to his theatrical involvement as a lucrative side-line, when he was in fact by now thought to be the equal of the best-known dramatists in France.

Early in January 1637, probably on Friday 2nd or 9th, Montdory's Marais company played Corneille's new tragi-comédie, *Le Cid*, known as a tragedy only from the 1648 edition. Over a dozen new tragi-comédies had been performed in the preceding two years, plays swift in action, with melodramatic "coups de théâtre," bloody reversals of fortune, acts of vengeance, duels, heroic stanzas, amorous fealties, single combats with heroines for prizes, and happy endings. The sources were often Italian or Spanish. Corneille's choice of Guillén de Castro's *Mocedades del Cid* had nothing discernible to do with the outbreak or conduct of the war against Spain in May 1635, in which the Spaniards had been defeated towards the end of 1636.

The play's success was immediate and immense, attested by an enthusiastic letter written on 18 January by Montdory, who was playing Rodrigue, to Balzac, and another of 22 January from Chapelain to the same correspondent. The theatre was crowded out, and within a month the work had had three performances at the Louvre and two at the Palais Cardinal. Its success immediately became proverbial, setting a commonly accepted standard of all-conquering success in cultivated society, in which "beau comme *Le Cid* (as fine as *Le Cid*)" became a commonplace expression.

On 24 March Corneille's father was ennobled on Corneille's account. Corneille himself, already known to be mercenary, had used an intermediary to ask for a supplementary payment on account of the new play's success a fortnight after its opening. On being turned down he immediately, on 21 January, applied for a privilège to publish the text, thereby depriving the company from 23 March, the date of publication, of a conventional monopoly right which it might have expected to enjoy for up to a year or two. Then, about 20 February, Corneille circulated the *Excuse à Ariste*, regarded in the circumstances as a declaration of literary independence relevant to *Le Cid*. The play appeared in print on 23 March, dedicated to the widowed Mme de Combalet, Richelieu's niece, who was to be made duchesse d'Aiguillon the following year. The literary world reacted bitterly.

About the beginning of April two pamphlets appeared: Mairet's violent personal attack, *L'Auteur du vrai Cid espagnol*, and an important discussion of dramatic theory by Scudéry, *Observations sur Le Cid*. Corneille refused to reply on the level of theoretical debate, and published his *Lettre apologétique* addressed to Scudéry about the middle of May. The remarks he made about the mediocre abilities of his fellow-dramatist Claveret and about Mairet's poor origins were presumably intended to be hurtful, and certainly caused a resentment that was widespread as well as fierce. Scarron expressed his outrage in *La Suite du Cid en abrégé*. Early in June Scudéry, no doubt partly to flatter Richelieu, appealed to the nascent Académie for its view, but found that body, aware of the controversy attending its institution, reluctant to appear to be the Cardinal's tool. Richelieu for his part was delighted with the occasion to establish its authority.

Boisrobert, a Rouennais and apparently, but perhaps only apparently, a friend of Corneille, as well as Richelieu's principal intermediary with the world of letters, wrote to Corneille, trying to mediate. Acceptance of the Académie's role as arbitrator by authors was criticized before it was obligatory under the Académie's statutes, and Boisrobert drew from Corneille the coolest of consents to arbitration on 13 June. In July Chevreau staged his *La Suite et le Mariage du Cid*, and Desfontaines his *La Vraie Suite du Cid*. The Académie, meeting on 16 June, exceedingly careful to act within correct rules of procedure, appointed three "commissaires" (Bourzeys, Chapelain, and Desmarets) by secret ballot, only after Corneille's acceptance of the Académie's arbitration had been read out and they had been assured of Richelieu's approval. Much was in fact discussed before a decision was reached. The commission reported in both ordinary and extraordinary plenary sessions, individual lines complained about being in addition the subject of a report by Cerisy, Gombauld, Baro, and l'Estoille. A sheaf of reports was read to Richelieu, whose remarks were transcribed, and a report was drawn up. Richelieu read the proof and sent the report back to be prettified with "quelques poignées de fleurs (a few fistfuls of flowers)".

Another commission was then set up (Jacques de Cérisay, Germain Habert, Gombauld, and Sirmond), and there were more plenary sessions before the report was printed, but the Cardinal did not like the proofs, sent for the commissioners, held a meeting at which only Bautru and Boisrobert were otherwise present, and at which Cérisay did not turn up, and gave the job of re-writing the report to Sirmond. Again dissatisfied with the result, Richelieu had the report re-written once more, this time by Chapelain, who submitted one that was longer and more flowery, but substantially the same as the first. It was published about 20 December 1637, although dated the following year, as *Les Sentiments de l'Académie française sur la tragi-comédie du Cid*. Richelieu commanded a cessation of the pamphlet war when it became personally offensive, issuing to Mairet what Boisrobert in his letter of 5 October 1637 called an "order." Both sides were eventually disappointed by the report's dry academic tone. It was only with difficulty that Boisrobert had persuaded Corneille to undertake not to reply. He finally decided not to on 23 December out of consideration for Richelieu. Balzac alone, from outside Paris, had thoroughly supported Corneille in a letter to Scudéry replying to Chapelain's invitation to intervene. The letter was read to the Académie before 7 August.

The most important issues concerned were not the unities, or even versification, but the "bienséances," that is, what was and what was not suitable for the stage, and the quarrel about the "vrai (true)" and the "vraisemblable (probable)." Corneille was to return to the question at length in 1660. The Académie felt that, unlike the historian, the poet needed to present not what was true, but what was reasonably believable. It may have been true, Scudéry argues in the *Observations*, that Chimène married her father's murderer, but it was not reasonably believable, "d'autant qu'il choque la raison et les bonnes moeurs (because it offends reason and moral values)." The Académie held that the historical fact of the marriage should have been suppressed, or that the Count should in the end have been discovered not to have been the father of Chimène, or that he had not after all died of his wounds.

The point at issue was perfectly clear. Corneille in the 1647 "Au lecteur" to *Héraclius* goes as far as to say that the subject of a good tragedy should *not* be probable, making it clear that he means that it is tragedy's function precisely to call into question what are regarded as morally acceptable standards of behaviour or "bonnes moeurs." That text explains much about Corneille's career, and it is certainly one of the most powerful statements about literary theory to come out of 17th-century France. It sums up the whole of the "moderne" position in the Querelle. Corneille's insubmission and the Académie's reluctance to assume the role for which Richelieu had destined it, the jealousy of d'Aubignac, and Boisrobert's dislike of Corneille's protectors, the Liancourts, had opened a seam of distrust between the Cardinal and Corneille. It was to have perceptible repercussions in the politics of patronage under the successive ascendancies of Mazarin, Foucquet, and even Colbert.

There were two impressions of the first edition of *Le Cid* on 23 and 24 March 1637, three other editions in the same year, and further editions in 1639, 1644, 1645, and 1646. Richelieu had died in 1642 and, when Corneille came to prepare the collected edition of his works in 1648, he not only replaced the designation "tragi-comédie" with the now more fashionable title "tragédie" but, in his new "Avertissement," strongly defended his play by referring to the historicity of its plot, while in footnotes to the text he vindicated his independence by giving the original Spanish of Guillén de Castro he was supposed too slavishly to have imitated.

Then in the celebrated 1660 collected edition, he hesitated. The prefatory *Discours du poème dramatique* leaves no doubt at all that Corneille intended the audience should understand that the controversial marriage of Rodrigue and Chimène would indeed take place, if only when Rodrigue found it possible "après en avoir levé tous les empêchements, sans lui en faire déterminer le jour (after all the impediments have been removed, without making him [Rodrigue] decide on the date)." But in the "Examen" prefacing the play, Corneille now admitted wishing to give only a hint of a later marriage, "mais avec incertitude de l'effet (but with some uncertainty about it)", and he removed from the play the all-important couplet which made the marriage certain.

Sire, quelle apparence à ce triste Hyménée,
Qu'un même jour commence et finisse mon deuil...

(What appearance will this sad marriage have, when on the same day my mourning starts and finishes).

That couplet in 1637 necessarily entailed the future marriage. In 1660, by which date the exploration of an optimistic view of human instinct was yielding to strong reaction in the form as well as the content of cultural activity which used to be known as "classicism," the resolution was left open.

Chapelain reported on 15 January 1639 that Corneille, who had been staying with him for three days, seemed depressed, preoccupied with how Scudéry had affected the fate of *Le Cid*. A second office created at Rouen to bring money in to the royal treasury had diminished the value of Corneille's own, and on 12 February 1639 Corneille's father died, leaving him outright one of the Rouen houses and the responsibility of taking charge of his brothers and sisters. *Médée* and *L'Illusion comique* were published that March. Two other events also took place which were not entirely irrelevant to Corneille's literary career. A dauphin, the future Louis XIV, was born, removing Gaston d'Orléans, the king's brother, from the position of heir presumptive, thereby making his enemy, Richelieu, incomparably the more important patron of the theatre; and the appallingly antiquated financial administration of France provoked in 1639–40, among other rebellions against intolerable taxation, that of the "Va-nupieds" in Normandy, savagely repressed by the chancellor, Pierre Séguier, in spite of support in the region's capital from the Rouen parlement, which was dissolved.

Corneille was diffident about his new regular tragedy, *Horace*, written probably towards the end of 1639 and submitted by him to a panel over which Boisrobert presided, and which included Chapelain, Baro, Charpy, l'Estoille, and d'Aubignac. D'Aubignac wanted Camille to throw herself on Horace's sword rather than be killed by him, and Chapelain's opinion seems to have been much the same. Corneille hesitated again, but stuck to the historical truth. Exactly the same issues were at stake as had been in the Querelle du Cid. Corneille had almost gone out of his way to find an incident he could dramatize, for which there was historical evidence—on this occasion in Livy, although he also took much from Dionysius of Halicarnassus—but which questioned the received moral values, the "bienséances" of his audience.

The piece, played before 9 March 1640 for Richelieu, whose power Corneille was constrained to recognize and to whom the published text was finally dedicated, was performed regularly from 19 May, by which date it had been given three public performances, suggesting a premiere early in the month. It has been cogently argued that the play was a dramatized if generalized exploration of the justification for Richelieu's ruthless statecraft, and of the need for the raison d'état to rule supreme. It would not be surprising if what Corneille in 1660 referred to as the play's "chute (fall)" may have had something to do with a possible relationship between the plot of *Horace* and Richelieu's policies, and perhaps even in particular between the character Camille and Louis XIII's queen, Anne of Austria. It must have been in the first half of 1641 that Corneille married Marie de Lampérière, who bore him seven children of whom the eldest, Marie, was to be baptized on 10 January 1642.

Cinna; ou, La Clémence d'Auguste, whose relationship to the political plotting under Louis XIII, and to problems of absolute power and clemency, again remained on a fairly general level, was played early in the season 1642–43 and published in 1643. Based essentially on a passage from Seneca's *De Clementia* as transmitted by Montaigne, the play was created by the Marais company and came quickly to figure in the repertoire of the Hôtel de Bourgogne. *Polyeucte martyr*, published in October

1643 and dedicated to Anne of Austria, regent since the death on 14 May 1643 of Louis XIII, who had agreed to accept the dedication, must also have been played publicly in the 1642–43 season, more likely than not in January, although Richelieu, who died on 4 December 1642, appears to have known it. It may have been read in front of Richelieu and was criticized, at least by Voiture, shortly after a pre-premiere reading at the Hôtel de Rambouillet. The print in the play's first edition of October 1643 was retouched in 1660 to show the actors in slightly more austere apparel. Félix's gown becomes a tunic reaching only to the knees, which remain bare. More formal boots to halfway up the calf replace sandals.

In a sonnet no doubt known in manuscript but published in 1647, and in a quatrain published in 1653, Corneille himself had refused to sing the praises of the dead cardinal. A critical sonnet on the death of Louis XIII, stingingly harsh about the "tyrant" Richelieu whose "slave" the king had been, was not published until 1738. Both *Cinna* and *Polyeucte* fitted into an established tradition of dramatic pieces. *Cinna* broadly generalized the issues raised by contemporary politics. The tradition of religious plays to which *Polyeucte* belonged would lead to the disputes about the religious propriety of putting on the profane stage the "merveilleux chrétien," that is, events which also, because miraculous, removed the drama from the psychology of the characters. They therefore shifted the focus of the audience's attention from an examination of the workings of their experience. It was their refusal to divorce the theatre from real and evolving Christian values and their desire to substitute actual religious experience in a Christian society for the stereotyped cults of antiquity as subjects for tragedy that was on the whole to lead the "modernes" generally to advocate the importation of the miraculous into tragedy, although the possibility of supernatural intervention obviously also allowed more easily for optimistic views of life. It is clear that Corneille's intentions in writing *Polyeucte* were acceptable to the devout party, since it was the now converted maréchal de Schomberg, Liancourt's brother-in-law, who had arranged for Louis XIII to accept the dedication.

Richelieu's successor, Mazarin, while much less interested in patronage and the theatre, none the less made a "gratification" before the end of 1643 to Corneille, whose eldest son, another Pierre, was baptized on 7 September. Corneille made a vain attempt personally to retain the power to licence for performance the texts of *Cinna* and *Polyeucte* even after having them published. In addition to a share of each box office, he would have benefited twice from having a publisher's fee in addition to licencing rights. In spite of scant direct testimony, there is considerable circumstantial evidence that all Corneille's plays so far had been launched by the Marais company, but that the Hôtel de Bourgogne had been anxious to have at least some of them on its bill.

In the season 1643–44, Corneille's *La Mort de Pompée*, certainly remembering Richelieu's death in its outspoken lines about the encroachment of ministers on what ought to be royal power, and the comedy *Le Menteur* were both presented. *La Mort de Pompée* was dedicated to Mazarin on publication in February 1644, but *Le Menteur*'s dedication in October 1644 was fictitious. The Marais company's theatre had burnt down on 15 January, possibly during a performance of *Le Menteur*, in whose cast were both Floridor and Jodelet. The theatre was reopened in October, the company presumably having found temporary accommodation in a jeu de paume. In the meanwhile

Corneille had failed in August to be elected to the Académie. He was to succeed, replacing Mainard, in January 1647, after losing again in 1646 to du Ryer, who lived in Paris. To enable his election to proceed Corneille had had to undertake to spend part of each year in the capital, and Séguier's candidate, Ballesdens, had withdrawn in his favour.

The season 1644–45 saw the presentation of *La Suite du Menteur* published 1645, and *Rodogune*, published in January 1647, and the following season that of *Théodore*, published in October 1646, a failure, probably on account of the way in which a Christian saint is shown in a secular atmosphere surrounded by sinners. D'Aubignac in 1657 thought it Corneille's best play, but it may have had as few as five performances. In his 1654 *Poésies chrétiennes*, Antoine Godeau, the liberal humanist bishop of Grasse, was clearly uneasy about the union on the stage of sanctity and profanity:

…pour changer leurs moeurs et régler leur raison
Les chrétiens ont l'Eglise et non pas le théâtre

(…to change their moral attitudes and to regulate their reason/Christians have the Church and not the theatre).

On 18 May 1647 Corneille wrote to René Voyer d'Argenson II (1623–1700), who in 1651 was to succeed on his father's death to the Venice ambassadorship. His importance lies in his leadership of the Compagnie du Saint-Sacrement, which sought the enforcement by the civil administration of Christian moral values especially through the courts, through legislation, and in public entertainments with pretensions to appeal to cultivated taste. D'Argenson's religious commitment was behind his withdrawal from the Venice embassy in 1656. Corneille in the 1640s was moving nearer to devout Catholicism.

Corneille's second son was born in 1645 or 1646, and in the season 1646–47 Corneille returned to Roman historical tragedy, although this was admittedly still drawn from the *Annales ecclésiastiques* published in 12 folio volumes (1593–1607) by the ecclesiastical historian Baronius. *Héraclius* was published in June 1647 and dedicated to Séguier. At Easter 1647 Floridor had left the Marais company for the Hôtel de Bourgogne, and it seems certain that Corneille followed him. The speed with which the privilège for the play's publication was taken out on 17 April 1647 and printing was finished on 28 June, so removing the actors' copyright at the Marais, suggests that they might have taken the play with them, too. Corneille was to be godfather to Floridor's son in 1649.

In the summer of 1647 Mazarin commissioned a tragedy with music for the 1648 carnival. It was to use the same stage machinery as that required for the Italian *Orfeo*, which had been unpopular in the 1647 carnival, in the Palais-Royal, as Richelieu's Palais Cardinal had now been renamed. Mazarin was no doubt pleased to camouflage the Italian origins becoming so disadvantageous to his political standing. Corneille, paid 2,400 livres, composed *Andromède*, and the confused evidence suggests that the Marais company may have commissioned another piece of the same name. The queen, regent since the death of Louis XIII, occurring when her eldest son, to become Louis XIV, was still only five, had long had religious misgivings about her attendance at the theatre, and her feelings of guilt were at this time reinforced by the devout party, led in this instance by M. Vincent. The piece commissioned from Corneille was abandoned under pressure from the dévots even before the Fronde unrest of 1648 virtually abolished the theatre season of 1648–49. Parliamentary insurrection ended with the Declaration of Saint-Germain on 24 October 1648, although the princes—Condé, his brother, Conti, and his brother-in-law, Longueville—were still to be arrested on 19 January 1650. During the ensuing repression Corneille was made state procurator of Normandy on 15 February, in succession to a supporter of Longueville. In March he sold his office in the legal administration of Rouen.

In an extraordinary number of the *Gazette de France* for 18 February 1650, totally devoted to a court presentation of *Andromède* at the Petit-Bourbon, the vast hall to be occupied by Molière before it was knocked down to make way for the Louvre colonnade, Renaudot minutely analyses the performance in a way suggesting that the premiere had been held early that January, and that it had constituted a defeat for the party of the dévots. An "innocent diversion" for all categories of "ecclesiastics and seculars," it was intended as a celebration of the restoration of peace. Although published in August 1650, the first edition carried the date of 1651. During the season of 1649–50 Corneille also presented *Don Sanche d'Aragon*, dedicated on publication in May 1650 to the Dutch humanist Huygens. On 5 July Corneille's brother Thomas married his sister-in-law, Marguerite de Lampérière. The newly wed couple shared Corneille's Rouen house.

On 13 February 1651 Mazarin freed the princes and the former procurator of Normandy regained his post, leaving Corneille now with no official job. Mazarin on his return from his flight abroad did not compensate Corneille for the loss his loyalty had entailed. *Nicomède* seems to have been played towards the end of February, probably at the Hôtel de Bourgogne, with Floridor in the lead. It was published without dedication in November, a week after the appearance of Corneille's translation of the first 20 chapters of the *de Imitatione Christi* in verse. In England Charles I had been executed on 9 February 1649. Charles II, defeated at Worcester on 3 September 1651, arrived in Paris in October. His adventures and situation probably helped to inspire Corneille's *Pertharite*, played during the 1650–51 season but, in spite of a privilège dated 24 December 1651, not published until the end of April 1653.

The year 1652 saw the height of the Fronde, with "La Grande Mademoiselle," Anne-Marie-Louise de Montpensier, daughter of Gaston d'Orléans and niece of the dead Louis XIII, who had once hoped to marry her cousin, Louis XIV, now supporting the princes in their struggle against the king's party, which included Mazarin, and now Turenne, who until 1650 had been on the side of the rebels. For part of 1652 Condé, still loyal to the crown in 1649, had joined the rebels and occupied Paris, but he left on 13 October to join forces with the Spaniards. The king returned to Paris on 21 October 1652, Retz was imprisoned in December, Gaston d'Orléans and his daughter were exiled to Blois, and internal peace in France was re-established during 1653. Mazarin set about marrying his nieces into the most noble houses in France, and Corneille, whose published translation of the *De Imitatione* had reached the end of the sixth chapter by 31 October 1652 and whose fifth child was born about this time, announced that he would probably not return to the theatre. On 31 March 1656 his complete translation of the *De Imitatione* was published. It is said to have made more money for him than any of his plays.

By 4 July 1656 Corneille, who had thought of translating Scu-poli's *Le Combat spirituel*, was working on a tragedy commissioned by the marquis de Sourdéac which was eventually to become *La Toison d'or*, a tragedy "à machines," that is, depending on stage machinery like hoists and swings capable of mediating spectacular dramatic effects. It was much later given a new prologue to make it seem as if the piece had been written to celebrate peace with Spain and the king's marriage to Marie-Thérèse, daughter of Philip IV, in 1660. The first partial performance was given at the château de Sourdéac at Neubourg in November 1660, and the play was subsequently successful for a full year at the Marais.

In 1657, however, d'Aubignac had published his *Pratique du théâtre* which, while it praised Corneille, also made strong criticisms of him. D'Aubignac, much of whose work may have been written before Richelieu's death, preached above all the opening of a tragedy as near as possible to the dénouement, an action as simple as possible, and the moving of the emotions by the expression of the passions, so formalizing the tradition of declamatory rhetoric which had for educational reasons developed in the renaissance and was to continue until abolished by the generation whose work was first performed in the 1820s. Corneille's reply was to be contained in the three important treatises prefacing the three-volume octavo 1660 edition of his complete works, in which he revised them and substituted an "examen" of each play in turn for the former letters of dedication or prefaces "au lecteur."

In 1657 Corneille's brother, the priest Antoine, died and in 1658 Corneille, together with his brother Thomas, was fascinated by Thérèse du Parc when Molière's company played at Rouen. Early that year Corneille met Foucquet, through Pellison, who had assumed the function of designating writers and artists worthy of Foucquet's patronage, and by July Corneille had accepted a 2,000-livre commission to write *Oedipe*, choosing one of three subjects proposed by the Surintendant. Played at the Hôtel de Bourgogne on 25 January 1659, the tragedy attracted a warm notice by Loret, whose *Muse historique* continued to praise the piece on 8 and 11 February. The *Gazette* thought Corneille had surpassed himself, and the play was still on the bill on 6 December, having been published in March. In 1663 d'Aubignac, by then a personal enemy, detected traces of préciosité (q.v.) in the play, as Somaize already had done and noted in the 1661 *Grand dictionnaire des précieuses*.

Corneille continued to live at Rouen until his brother and he moved to Paris in 1662, perhaps finally decided by the success of *Sertorius*, played at the Marais on 25 February 1662, and published that July. Corneille himself was the guest of Henri II, duc de Guise, in whose Hôtel, containing a large number of separate apartments, Corneille was surrounded by a circle which included Tallemant, Donneau de Visé, Somaize, Mézeray, the abbé de Pure, and Boursault, a group which can be recognized as virtually constitutive of the party of the early "modernes" in the Querelle. For the composition of *Sertorius* we have actual evidence of what must have been generally true of Corneille's working methods. He wrote two acts, submitted them to the actors and to a friend, and completed the play to take into account their comments.

When it was played at the Marais, Loret was again flattering about the tragedy, and Molière's company was giving the piece ten days before publication, in the virtually certain absence of a licence, and therefore in defiance of the copyright convention. It was played also at the Hôtel de Bourgogne, presumably after publication and because Mlle des Oeillets, who had created the role of Viriate at the Marais, had moved to the Hôtel at Easter and taken *Sertorius* with her. Corneille was much pleased by her young successor Mlle Marotte (Marie Vallée), but the play itself, together with *Sophonisbe*, which was first performed probably on 12 January 1663 at the Hôtel and whose reception was enthusiastically described by Loret, was attacked by d'Aubignac in a pamphlet of some acerbity. Donneau de Visé replied in Corneille's defence.

Mazarin had died on 9 March 1661 and on 5 September Fouquet was arrested. A marriage contract for Corneille's eldest daughter was signed, and the second daughter, Marguerite, entered the Dominican convent at Rouen, no doubt before Corneille left for Paris. His most enthusiastic protectors were Montauzier, the patron of the "modernes," and the maréchal de Bellefonds. But the Marais company appears to have taken serious offence at the poaching of *Sertorius* by Molière on 23 June 1662. Molière did not play the piece again until 10 September, although he had featured *Rodogune* and *Héraclius* in the meanwhile. Molière's *L'Ecole des femmes*, played at the Palais-Royal on 26 December 1662 and published on 17 March 1663, did however hit back at the Corneille brothers, thereby doing nothing to decrease the tidal wave of polemic it generated. It included an injurious comment on Thomas Corneille, whose *Camma* of 1661 was probably the most successful French tragedy of the century, correctly referring to him as "M. de l'Isle" but mocking him for the pretentiousness of a claim to social status justified only by "un fossé bourbeux (a muddy ditch)." Molière may have been alluding to the Seine. He also mocked Corneille himself by borrowing for the end of Act two one of the more grandiloquent lines from *Sertorius*,

Je suis maître, je parle, allez, obéîssez

(I am master. I speak. Go. Obey).

Boileau was probably the first to attack *L'Ecole des femmes*, and d'Aubignac used Boileau's comments to insinuate that Corneille was jealous of Molière. Donneau de Visé joined in the attack on Molière, although he had not yet rallied to Corneille's defence against d'Aubignac, whose own hostility to Corneille had anyway abated by the end of July, leaving Corneille as the presumed inspiration of the continued campaign against Molière, the successful, and therefore threatening, and certainly cheeky, interloper from the provinces. Molière had indeed played with fire and been singed, although historians have shown some indignation at the vindictiveness of the Corneille brothers towards their young rival. A working relationship was later re-established in an alliance against Racine, but in 1663 Corneille's own position remained apparently still unassailable. He was on the first list of "gratifiés," or authors designated to receive royal benefactions, drawn up late in 1662, and he regularly received 2,000 livres, with whatever arrears, until 1674.

In 1664 the first of Corneille's grandchildren to survive infancy was born. An earlier grandchild, born in 1661, had not lived. In the following year Corneille's letters of nobility were confirmed. In August 1665 he also published his translation of the *Louanges de la sainte Vierge*, consisting in the original, traditionally attributed to Saint Bonaventure, of 83 verses of eight lines. He was later to publish his translation, into both prose and verse, of the *Officium parvum* or "Little Office" of the Blessed Virgin, officially intended largely for the use of the laity. The privilège is dated 1669 and the thick duodecimo itself appeared in 1670. We know that Corneille himself recited the breviary daily, and that Marian piety held a high place in his devotional life. It has been conjectured that his translations may have been intended to vie for popularity with those emanating from Port-Royal (q.v.).

In 1664 *Othon* was played on 31 July at Fontainebleau and then, from 5 November, at the Hôtel. When it was published in February 1665 Corneille said that his friends were pleased with it. Loret's note showed its by now characteristic warmth, but the piece's success has been doubted, and we can know little for certain, from the few remarks in the gazettes and some scattered allusions, about the reception of its successor, *Agésilas*. The haste with which it was published, with a privilège of 24 March following a premiere of 26 February 1666, suggests that Corneille may have hoped to gain an acclaim from the reading public denied him by his audiences. We do know that Corneille now sought to move from the Hôtel, probably on account of the actors' disappointment at what was probably the failure of *Agésilas*, and that *Attila, Roi des Huns* played on 4 March 1667 by Molière's troupe, who had paid 2,000 livres for the piece, saw diminishing receipts, falling on the sixth evening to 223 livres. From the eighth performance, support had to be provided by coupling the tragedy with one of Molière's own farces. Ominously, the play had been ready at least four months before it was performed. Corneille himself began to feel that he had written himself out, but used the "Au lecteur" on publication in November 1667 to make disdainful allusions to the attacks on the theatre, associated with the attitudes of Port-Royal, made by Varet and Conti in 1667, and Nicole in 1668.

Corneille wrote a number of celebratory official pieces, especially in connection with the Dutch campaign of 1667–68, in which his two sons were army officers. The younger was wounded, and in 1668 his son-in-law died fighting the Turks. It was in 1668 that Saint-Evremond's *Dissertation sur le Grand Alexandre*, published in the *Oeuvres meslées*, inaugurated the fashion for comparing Corneille with Racine which can scarcely be said ever to have died out. In the following year Corneille, freely translating a Latin poem by Jean-Baptiste Santeul, aligned himself light-heartedly on the side of using pagan mythology even in Christian verse. Racine's *Britannicus*, played on 13 December 1669, was published early in 1670, with a privilège of 7 January. The preface contained a harsh attack on Corneille, although it did not refer to him by name.

On 16 November 1670 Corneille read *Tite et Bérénice* to Monsieur, the king's brother. Its first night with Molière's troupe was on 28 November, exactly a week after the first night of Racine's *Bérénice* at the Hôtel de Bourgogne. Corneille was granted a privilège for publication on 31 December, together with a privilège for a translation of *La Thébaïde* of Statius. The translation, which would have been an attack by innuendo on Racine, whose career had started with his tragedy *La Thébaïde* in 1664, has been lost. That is extraordinary, since the type appears to have been set, and proof pulled. Did Corneille change his mind and try to soften what he knew would look like, and very possibly was intended as, a direct challenge to Racine which had miscarried? Molière had again paid 2,000 livres for Corneille's play, which was a failure, with the box-office takings falling catastrophically towards the end of its 21 performances. Even its title, "comédie héroïque," in alluding to the impropriety of calling a play a tragedy if there is no peril giving rise to pity or fear, is a subtle reproach to Racine, who called his play a "tragédie." The date of Racine's privilège is not known, but his achevé d'imprimer, as near as it is possible to come to today's "publication date," is 24 January, and that of Corneille 3 February. Racine's preface contains several implied but barbed allusions to Corneille.

On successive Fridays, Friday being the traditional evening for a premiere, two plays on the same subject had appeared in rival theatres, acted by rival companies, written by rival dramatists educated in traditions hostile to one another and representing different sides of the Querelle, and published by rival booksellers. The one thing which is relatively certain about those two events is that they did not clash by chance. It appears to be generally admitted that Racine was not issuing a direct challenge to Corneille when he chose his theme. It is inconceivable in the closed and interwoven worlds of court and theatre that both dramatists worked during the autumn of 1670 unaware that the other had chosen the same subject, and it is unlikely that Corneille started off by intending to challenge Racine's ascending star in order to demonstrate his supremacy. The only hypothesis which is at all probable, although it cannot possibly be proved, is that the two dramatists, whose rivalry with and hostility to one another were well known, were both manoeuvred by someone else into writing about a king who for reasons of state sent away a woman he loved.

It was, on the whole, at that court and at that date, entirely likely to have been thought entertaining to make mischief by separately approaching Racine and Corneille and, without making either aware of the approach being made to the other, to put them up to writing a play about a well-known antique subject which had an obvious, if generalized, relevance to the king's dalliance with Mazarin's niece, Marie Mancini, at a moment when the political interests of France, a concern for dynastic pride, and the views of the leader of the more severe "old court", Anne d'Autriche, about upholding the regal dignity of her late husband's family, all firmly required Louis XIV to marry the daughter of Philip IV. It was characteristically Racine rather than Corneille who put into the mouth of Bérénice words commonly associated with those used by Marie when accepting her dismissal. Corneille, from whose Roman historical terrain the subject came, and to whose dramatic talents its glorification of renunciation pandered, could well have found stimulating the challenge he may have been pitched into making.

Corneille's piece had not yet certainly failed when he took out his privilège for publication 33 days after the premiere. Racine's play had already become a theatrical success when it was printed. Racine knew before publication that he could afford the spiked smugness of his preface. Corneille may have withdrawn the verse translation of La Thébaïde when defeat became obvious in the course of January, although his supporters were ready once more to rally for Pulchérie. For this hypothesis to explain the relationship between the two plays, which has seemed recently to gain ground, there is, however, no hard evidence other than the sheer implausibility of all attempts to explain it in any other way.

All other hypotheses have had to have recourse either to plagiarism or to a fully deliberate challenge of one dramatist by the other. Neither explanation is at all likely, although there probably was at least an element of challenge, and it almost certainly came from Corneille. However, if, as seems likely, court conspiracy there was, its instigator must have been, or have been near to, the focal point of the "young" court with its more open frivolity—Henrietta of England, daughter to Charles I and first wife to Philippe d'Orléans, the brother of Louis XIV. Fontenelle openly declared in 1729, and Voltaire in 1751 and 1764, that the instigator of the coincidence of subject, and its choice, was the king's sister-in-law, while also, less plausibly, maintaining that the dramatists worked in total ignorance of each other's plans.

Corneille contributed only a fortnight's work to the collaborative tragédie-ballet Psyché for which he versified almost four acts. It appeared over Molière's name, and was performed by his troupe in the Tuileries before the king on 17 January 1671, to be played in public that July, and not again before November 1673. On 15 January 1672 Corneille gave at La Rochefoucauld's invitation one of what must have been several readings of his comédie héroïque, Pulchérie. It was also read before Retz, but Corneille appears to have had difficulty in getting a company to stage it, in spite of what amounted to a campaign in its favour by the Mercure galant (q.v.). It was finally put on by the declining Marais company in November and published in January 1673. The death of Molière the following month brought about the fusion of his troupe with that of the Marais to create the Guénégaud company.

Corneille's sister re-married in 1673. In 1674 his name was omitted from Boileau's brief history of tragedy in the Art poétique. His second son was killed during the evacuation of Holland, and late in 1674 his final tragedy, Suréna, Général des Parthes, was played at the Hôtel de Bourgogne. It was published early in 1675. Although several of his plays were still currently in the repertoire, and four tragedies were played before the court at Fontainebleau during the summer of 1675, and five at Versailles in 1676, Corneille's name was dropped from the annual list of "gratifiés" from 1674. An appeal to Colbert for its restoration in 1678 went unanswered, although final gratifications of 2,000 livres were granted for 1682 and 1683; one was paid in advance for 1684. Corneille had recently moved house within Paris when he died in his new house on 1 October.

WORKS

Corneille's biography shows how the dramatist only slowly established his personal style as the principal dramatic genres and their ranking with regard to one another themselves changed while he was in his twenties. It was only after the Querelle du Cid, and, twenty years later, after d'Aubignac's 1657 Pratique du théâtre, that Corneille produced a sustained reflection on his theory of dramatic art, in the three essays on tragedy prefacing the three books of the collected and revised works of 1660, with "examens" of each individual piece added in place of dedicatory epistles, which were removed. For their revelation of Corneille's mature consideration on the norms which he thought had governed, or should govern, the composition of the tragic poem, as it was called, these essays demand attention. In a letter to the abbé de Pure of 25 August 1660, announcing what the three Discours have attempted to do, Corneille declares that they refute the principles on which the Académie had based "la condamnation" of Le Cid.

The revision of the plays for the 1660 edition had shown a strong move towards keeping the proprieties. In all previous editions of La Suivante, for instance, Florame explains how the thought of Amarante pursues him. Even at night, in 1637, 1644, 1648, 1652, 1654, 1655, 1656, and 1657,

> Elle entre effrontément jusque dedans ma couche,
> Me redit ses propos, me présente sa bouche

(She goes as far as coming brazenly into bed with me,/ repeating what she has said, and offering me her mouth).

In 1660 that couplet is replaced by

> Le sommeil n'oserait me peindre une autre idée,
> J'en ai l'esprit rempli, j'en ai l'âme obsédée

(Sleep would not dare depict any other image,/ my mind is full of it, and my soul obsessed).

As has already been indicated, Corneille had become hesitant about the "patricidal" marriage of Chimène to Rodrigue. The move of his contemporaries towards regularity, even severity, and above all respect for the proprieties, had been gathering momentum in a backlash which was more than merely literary, and which looked for a moment shortly after the middle of the century as if it might reverse the incoming tide of trust in instinct. It was the relaxed adoption of the norms prompted by nature, suitably refined after their pre-classical extravagances of expression, rather than any imposed rules of art, which were to emerge all-conquering with the final acceptance of the cultural norms of the "modernes," clear before the end of the century. Corneille in the years immediately preceding 1660 was in fact responding to the increasing severity of public taste, which was also leading away from the great 10-volume novels of La Calprenède and Madeleine de Scudéry towards Segrais's shorter, more concise and more psychologically concentrated "nouvelle", away from opera and tragi-comédie towards tragedy, away in the visual arts from the effulgence of baroque radiance, and away from manifestations of exuberant cultural optimism everywhere, not least in matters of spirituality, where rigorism and anxiety momentarily threatened to displace confidence in God and peace of soul as spiritual ideals.

In spite of his radical revisions of 1660, Corneille could not keep pace with the movement of cultural reaction. No one so attuned as he to the attitudes and values which an earlier generation needed to explore could possibly have made the adaptations required to remain in the front rank of imaginative writers in 1660, and it is indeed a measure of his greatness that he had penetrated so deeply into the cultural roots of the decade or so following 1635 that he could in 1660 no longer altogether alter the focuses of his imagination. He was reduced to pruning and cosmeticizing, to choosing different subjects, and noticeably shifting his preoccupation from personal to public concerns. It is, however, difficult to think of any really major writer, whether in France or elsewhere, whose work has extended over a span of longer than a score of years and who also maintained for longer than that period an intensity of imaginative power and vision deeply relevant to the needs of the society in which it was written.

In France the cultural reaction which engulfed Corneille peaked in the decade following 1670. The *Discours* must be seen as Corneille's inadequate attempt in 1660 to justify norms which twenty years earlier had needed no justification. Recourse

in these circumstances to "rules," or to the authority of Aristotle, cannot therefore be taken as much more than token deference. Aristotle, said Corneille in the first *Discours,* wrote "obscurely enough to need interpreters." The form of the three *Discours,* and extended commentary on Aristotle's *Poetics,* conveniently split into three to preface each of three volumes, is in fact a not very serious blind. They are not an essay in exegesis at all, but were generally understood as an attempt to undermine the "ancien" monopoly of antique authority by using that authority to justify an aesthetic created in and by cultural conditions which in 1660 no longer existed.

The *Discours de l'utilité et des parties du poème dramatique* which prefaced the first volume concedes the need for rules, but harps on their ambiguity. At the very outset Corneille is explicit:

> …les grands sujets qui remuent fortement les passions, et en opposent l'impétuosité aux loix du devoir ou aux tendresses du sang, doivent toujours aller au-delà du vraisemblable, et ne trouveraient aucune croyance parmi les auditeurs, s'ils n'étaient soutenus, ou par l'autorité de l'histoire qui persuade avec empire, ou par la préoccupation de l'opinion commune qui nous donne ces mêmes auditeurs déjà tout persuadés. Il n'est pas vraisemblable que Médée tue ses enfants, que Clytemnestre assassine son mari, qu'Oreste poignarde sa mère; mais l'histoire le dit…

(…great subjects which move the passions strongly, and bring impetuousness into conflict with the laws of duty and the ties of blood, must always go beyond what is "probable," and would find no acceptance in the audience if they were not supported either by the authority of history, which imposes belief, or by the conviction of common opinion which delivers an audience already persuaded. It is not probable that Medea should kill her children, that Clytemnestra should assassinate her husband, that Orestes should stab his mother; but history says they did…).

It is apparent that the historicity of an event, or a developing consensus about the morality of an action depicted on the stage, can jolt the public into an awareness that moral attitudes need challenging, and Corneille implies 20 years later that that is what he had set out to do. It was certainly the reaction provoked by *Le Cid* which led him to an articulate recognition of the assumptions that had underlain his own dramatic activity and its function within French society. Although he did not clearly say so, he must have been conscious that moral attitudes can and do change, and that it is the poet's function in society to promote a perception of what they both are and might be. This, obviously, is the "moderne" position. It is not far from saying that the artist should seek to lead the evolution of moral values in society, being in advance of them, but not by so much as to be too unpersuasive to promote the perpetual need for reconsideration of social attitudes and personal moral standards.

Corneille's definition of the aim of drama as uniquely to "plaire (please)" does not, he wrote, exclude aiming at "utilité" for the audience. Horace had pointed out that what merely amused would eventually bore, and that therefore the useful was finally not to be separated from what gave pleasure. Since Corneille is intent on seeming to agree wherever possible with Aristotle, and if possible Horace too, he juggles with words like pleasure and profit and twists Aristotle's real meaning to the degree at which quotation without protracted commentary becomes pointless. None the less, he suggests, at a moment when drama in France was still seeking to establish itself as a serious artistic genre, that the "utilité" of a theatrical piece could be split into four categories: the elevation mediated by moral "sententiae," of the sort no doubt inherited from the commonplace books of renaissance schoolboys, who were taught rhetoric according to Aristotle's rules in order through dramatic declamation to learn to move the passions; the open depiction of virtues and vices on the stage, that is of good and evil moral attitudes; representation of the recompense of good actions and the punishment of evil ones; and finally the famous cathartic "purgation des passions par le moyen de la pitié et de la crainte (purgation of the passions by means of pity and terror)."

For Aristotle, according to Corneille, comedy required the presentation of the actions of persons of low condition, but even kings and queens who are merely in love are not thereby endowed with tragic status. Tragedy demands

> quelque grand intérêt d'Etat, ou quelque passion plus noble et plus mâle que l'amour, telles que sont l'ambition ou la vengeance, et veut donner à craindre des malheurs plus grands que la perte d'une maîtresse

> (some great interest of state, or some passion more noble and more virile than love, like ambition or vengeance, and it aims to arouse fear for misfortunes greater than the loss of a mistress).

Corneille claims that even in *Le Cid* family duty and ambition provide more important values than love, but he nevertheless incidentally points to a development central not only to French but to all western culture, from the middle ages to the present. The key to the cultural development of the west has to have a connection with its evolving treatment of love, never itself a truly tragic emotion even in Shakespeare, and its closely associated and equally changing view of the function of women in society. The first really great dramatist to treat love as itself habitually tragic was to be Racine, and even Racine generally reinforced the tragedies precipitated by love by recourse to political catastrophes which the satisfaction of love would have entailed.

It is in this first *Discours* that Corneille, now hesitant about the propriety of Rodrigue's marriage to Chimène, holds that a tragedy is resolved at the moment when threatened disaster is averted, before the action is resolved in a happy denouement, typically a marriage which might clash with the proprieties. He can therefore excuse himself from pushing his exploration of moral values beyond what the conventional norms admitted. If he had in fact refrained from pressing his challenge to socially accepted values, as the justification of 1660 now demanded that he should pretend to have refrained, his tragedies would have shrivelled in stature to a level much nearer pure entertainment. He himself points to another example of refusing directly to challenge the social convenances in *Rodogune* of 1644–45, where the love of Antiochus for Rodogune is left unresolved by marriage on account of considerations of seemliness after the suicide of his mother, Cléopâtre, and her attempt to murder him. Corneille's Cléopâtre comes close to symbolically exhausting the possibilities of evil, and Corneille is led to speculate about the propriety of putting her on the stage. He is brought to the insight, probably imported from Robortello, which becomes a

17th-century commonplace, to be found in Chapelain before its canonical formulation in La Rochefoucauld, that there is a form of moral grandeur which is ethically ambivalent:

> le caractère brillant et élevé d'une habitude vertueuse ou criminelle, selon qu'elle est propre et convenable à la personne qu'on introduit...

> (the brilliant and elevated nature of a virtuous or criminal way of behaving, according to what is appropriate to the character introduced).

Of Cléopâtre he wrote that

> tous ses crimes sont accompagnés d'une grandeur d'âme qui a quelque chose de si haut, qu'en même temps qu'on déteste ses actions, on admire la source dont elles partent

> (all her crimes are accompanied by a grandeur of soul so extraordinary that at the same moment as her actions are deplored the source from which they spring is admired).

The importance of this view is that it allows tragedy to be based not only on pity and fear, but also on the admiration of non-ethical moral qualities. Right does not need to be vindicated, so that tragedy's temptation to didacticism is removed. The addition of admiration to pity and fear as tragic emotions in the audience allows for heroic stature itself to be tragic, whatever the ethical value of the heroic activity, so that all tragedies with characters exhibiting behaviour, however wicked, which excites admiration, can end happily. The currents of cultural history make it clear why, at the moment of Racine's ascendancy, they did not, and why they again did for Voltaire and the 18th century in France, as also for Goethe, but not for the generation of French romantics.

Corneille's first discourse makes most of his important general points. The *Discours de la tragédie et des moyens de la traiter selon le vraisemblable ou le nécessaire*, prefacing the second volume of the 1660 *Oeuvres*, essentially deals with the problem Corneille realizes he has created for himself by implying that admiration as well as pity and fear could be a tragic emotion. By what psychological progress then does the tragic "catharsis," in Aristotle, in fact a medical metaphor for purgation, actually occur? Unlike the rest of the 17th century, Corneille could no longer really rely on the cathartic effect of pity and fear on the audience, as before him Robortello, Castelvetro, and Heinsius had done, but had like Beni to introduce a rational judgement:

> La pitié d'un malheur où nous voyons tomber nos semblables nous porte à la crainte d'un pareil pour nous

> (Pity for the misfortune into which we see someone like ourselves falling leads us to fear a similar misfortune for ourselves)

thereby leading us to modify our behaviour. In fact Corneille is almost inevitably led to doubt whether the purgation of the passions takes place in tragedy at all:

> Si la purgation des passions se fait dans la tragédie, je tiens qu'elle se doit faire de la manière que je l'explique; mais je doute si elle s'y fait jamais

(If the purgation of the passions takes place in tragedy, I hold that it must be in the way I explain it; but I doubt if it happens at all).

The "Examen" of *Nicomède*, having boasted of the play's independence of "la tendresse et les passions (tenderness and the passions)," relying alone on "la grandeur du courage (elevated courage)," goes on to discuss the purgation of passion by the admiration of virtue, even though Aristotle had not thought of it ("dont n'a point parlé Aristote"). Admiration for virtue drives us to hatred of vice. It naturally follows, as Corneille wrote in his *Discours*, following Aristotle, that a tragic hero cannot be wholly good, and therefore merely the unlucky victim of an arbitrary fate, or wholly bad, and therefore incapable of engaging the audience's sympathies. Corneille continues none the less in 1660 to turn his back on the "merveilleux chrétien," in spite of *Polyeucte*, no doubt because of the impossibility of building tragedies on heroes lacking a tragic flaw, and because of the interplay of duty and other interests on which the psychology of the tragic hero had normally to depend.

In the course of this second essay Corneille asserts that the 17th century has in fact found ways of improving on the categories and standards laid down by Aristotle, arguing at length for a reconsideration of Aristotle's hierarchy of sorts of tragedy, and for the existence of one category, admitting change of the hero's intent to destroy his enemy, and a wider spread among characters of effects of pity and fear, which "Aristotle would no doubt have preferred to the others, had he known it. To say this pays honour to our century without taking away from his authority…" A little later there is a quotation from Tacitus on the subject of the superiority of his age over previous ones. The unities are then made the subject of the final *Discours des trois unités d'action, de jour, et de lieu*, which is very largely an essay in definition, enlarging what the unities were commonly understood to mean, and detracting from the absolutely normative nature often thought to attach to their observance. Otherwise the third *Discours* is largely concerned with the techniques of dramatization rather than broader aesthetic matters.

The three *Discours* are, it must be remembered, an attempt to articulate the norms of Corneille's practice 20 years previously, partly discussed in the previous section of this entry, and at the same time to appear to defer to the authority of Aristotle. They undoubtedly show a spirit of subservience to the unities and the proprieties not always identical to that of the works themselves. The first comedy, *Mélite*, was written before Corneille knew of the newly important and already prescriptive unities, and the need for coups de théâtre. It was to be extensively modified in 1660, and was followed by the tragi-comédie *Clitandre*, itself even more extensively re-written in 1660, which was packed with action, kept the unities, and was, no doubt affectedly, despised by Corneille, partly on account of its probable failure. The re-written text of 1660 removes all the audaciousness of the original. Mairet's pastoral tragi-comédie *Silvanire*, played at the Hôtel, had already observed the unities, and Corneille's tragi-comédie not only uses them to concentrate the action, but almost avoids any truly comic element, insisting instead on a mixture of horror and galanterie in scenes like that in which Dorise, defending herself against rape, stabs Pymante in the eye with a hairpin. Pymante, the hairpin removed, reproaches Dorise with stabbing an eye which had reflected her beauty.

Corneille's third play was the comedy *La Veuve; ou, Le Traître trahi*, with small set pieces of realism, about women's conversation or the conflict of love and reason. The plot is complicated but entirely conventional. Of chief interest is the realistic language of the "gallanteries plus que bourgeoises (the worse than middle-class galanteries)" on which Claveret remarked, the "rhymed prose" which made possible the psychological finesse and amorous casuistry expected by a public largely brought up on the pastoral. The following play, *La Galerie du Palais; ou, L'Amie rivalle*, was another successful comedy. The sub-title was suppressed in 1644 and the title refers to a row of fashionable bookshops, grocers, and linen-merchants next to the Palais de Justice in the middle of Paris. As in *Clitandre* the decor consisted of a row of booths, each covered with a curtain to be drawn back as that scene was required, although the stage directions, an ironic feature of the 1632 *Clitandre* text, were first added to *La Galerie* in 1660, with a justification for allowing amorous conversation to take place across a street, the amendment perhaps suggesting that such matters could have been taken for granted earlier, during the period of the Italian company's greatest popularity. In *La Galerie* the character of "La Nourrice," traditionally played by a man, disappears, to be replaced by "Une suivante," a character who first appeared in du Ryer's *Lisandre et Caliste*, played at the Hôtel in 1630, and who was to provide the title for Corneille's next play. The plot of *La Galerie du Palais* is unremarkable, but the language has been seen as preparing the way for the full préciosité (q.v.) of the writers of the 1650s.

The following play, *La Suivante*, is a conventional comedy of intrigue, thwarted marriage projects, and misunderstandings. Although the date of its privilège is 21 January 1637, the same as that of *La Galerie du Palais, La Place Royale*, and *Le Cid*, it was not published until 9 September, shortly before the Académie's verdict on *Le Cid* was expected. Its prefatory "Epître" is therefore polemical, insisting on the play's observance of the unities, although the single decor must have been compartmentalized, and have used curtains, with the centre stage an extension of whichever booth was revealed behind it, so that a false unity of place was created by confirming changes to a switch between booths, each taking up less than a quarter of the background when uncovered. The intrigue balances the importance of wealth against that of lust in marital arrangements. Amarante, the pretty "suivante" of Daphnis, completes the transformation of the burlesque "La Nourrice" through the Florice of the *La Galerie du Palais* into an aristocratic if impoverished companion. Géraste, Daphnis's father, is the ageing lover, yearning for Florise, who is not a character in the play but is the sister of Florame, his daughter's "amant." In the end the love between Daphnis and Florame shines above the wealth which Géraste offers Florise, but the action is set in an ambience similar to that of the bourgeois marriage bargaining which will be satirized in Furetière's *Roman bourgeois* of 1666.

La Suivante provoked controversy among Corneille's admirers, although it followed smoothly enough on *La Galerie du Palais*, and Corneille changed direction for *La Place Royale; ou, L'Amoureux extravagant*, in which a tendency to portray the heroic obtrudes in Alidor, who cedes Angélique, whom he none the less loves, to Cléandre and then to Doraste, as if to explore the possibility that, even in comedy, heroism can demand the rejection of love. For Alidor, self-possession is a value of a higher order:

Je veux que l'on soit libre au milieu de ses fers…
Et toujours en état de disposer de moi,
Donner quand il me plaît, et retirer ma foi

(I look for freedom in the midst of bonds…/So that, always in a state in which I can control myself,/I can give my affection when I want and withdraw it at will).

Corneille's play appears to have been created to rival another of the same title, now lost, by Claveret. The problem it raises is that of the nature of Alidor's ideal. In seeking to free his own love from any sense of duty, he is unconcerned about the thraldom to love of Angélique, and may therefore be thought to be consumed not so much by heroic renunciation as by arrogance. The text draws attention to Corneille's obvious resolve to observe the unities and, as is usual in Corneille's early plays, there is a clear insistence on the physical realities,

Alidor, (quel amant!) n'ose me posséder

(Alidor—what a lover!—does not dare to possess me).

Médée, played by the Marais company in the 1634–35 season, probably early in 1635, was Corneille's first tragedy, performed in the wake of Rotrou's *Hercule mourant*, and was a new departure based on Seneca but strongly encouraged by Chapelain. Like that of La Pinelière's *Hippolyte*, Rotrou's subject was mythological, and his play had been presented during the preceding season, like Mairet's *Sophonisbe* which, however, was taken from Roman history, drawing on the Italian model of Trissino's *Sofonisba* of 1515. Tragedy, notionally acknowledged as the highest form of drama, was being re-born on the French stage, after pastoral and tragi-comédie had catered for a more refined taste during the era of effervescent baroque confidence.

In 1634 Mahelot's list of the 71 pieces in the repertoire of the Hôtel de Bourgogne included only two tragedies, but in 1635 Scudéry had presented *La Mort de César* and was already working on *Didon*, the Marais had performed Mairet's *Marc-Antoine*, and the Hôtel Bensserade's *Cléopâtre*. Corneille was uncertain about the suitability of his style for tragedy. Still inclined to insist on brutal physical realities and occasional effects of horror, he would not write another formal tragedy until the very different *Horace* six years later. For *Médée* he was quite closely inspired by Rotrou, with whom he shared a mythological subject and a model in Seneca, and from whom he took the exploitation of jealousy and poison. Corneille, however, suppressed the choruses and the long monologues in favour of more vigorous dramatic confrontations, promoted Jason's role to equal that of Médée, and diminished the stage effects dependent on machinery commonly called for by the mythological pieces.

L'Illusion comique is probably now the best known of the comedies. It was successful when first given at the Marais by Montdory in late 1635 or early 1636, although it does not seem to have been played again in its original form until the famous 1937 production by Louis Jouvet. Essentially the plot concerns a father, Pridamant, who, in search of his lost son Clindor, consults the magician Alcandre, who for the three central acts presents the adventures through which Clindor has passed. In the fifth act Clindor, an actor, himself acts in a play. The comedy ends with a conversation between Pridamant and Alcandre. The idea appears to have come from the Italian plays within plays on

which Gougenot had built for his 1633 *Comédie des comédiens*, and Corneille's piece must have drawn on Scudéry's own *Comédie des comédiens*, which was probably written towards the end of 1632, although its existence is not certainly attested until 28 November 1634, when it was performed at the Arsenal before the queen, and it was not published until 1635. By putting the magician on the stage, Corneille's play certainly involved making fun of the dramatic illusion ordinarily created by serious theatre, which demanded the acceptance by the audience that what was taking place on the stage was actually happening.

There are jokes in the published text about the splendour of the costumes, quite possibly the cast-off finery of an aristocratic patron. The magician presents Clindor's outfit as splendid, and Pridamant accepts it as such, although the text makes it probable that the audience may have been meant to see it as spurious, sharing Alcandre's joke at Pridamant's expense. Clindor's career is a parody of that of a picaresque adventurer, and he ends the first act as an ingenious valet, already prefiguring Beaumarchais's great invention, Figaro. Alcandre and Pridamant now turn themselves into spectators of the phantoms enacting the scenes from Clindor's life which fill the three middle acts, on which they comment in short scenes. Isabelle, straight from the jeune première role of a commedia dell'arte (q.v.) script, is destined by her father to marry a noble, is courted by the grotesque Matamore, but falls in love with his valet, Clindor. So does her maid, Lyse, who had Clindor and Isabelle surprised by Adraste, who is then killed in a duel by Clindor. Clindor is then arrested, but Lyse arranges for his release by seducing the jailer's brother.

Isabelle takes her father's money and flees with Lyse, Clindor and the jailer. The final act is tragic, although Clindor and Isabelle, clearly married, have risen socially, and Lyse has been promoted from "servante" to "suivante," from servant to companion. Isabelle catches Clindor out on the point of being unfaithful to her and hides when his would-be seductress, the princess Rosine, arrives in the garden by night. There is a scuffle when her husband's men come. Clindor and Rosine are both killed. In 1639, the ending may have been experienced by the audience as tragi-comic. Isabelle is carried off to Florilame, who has long desired her, but in the 1660 version the ending is tragic. Isabelle faints and dies over Clindor's body. However, from 1644 to 1660 the ending is comic. We are told that at this point Alcandre, offering to show Pridamant his son's funeral, has a curtain raised to show the actors counting the receipts. The last act, probably from the outset, and certainly from 1644, was a play in which Clindor, principal of a troupe of players, played the lead, making Corneille's piece a comedy.

The 1637 text of *Le Cid*, from 1648 described by Corneille as a "tragédie," was extensively modified in 1660, partly by suppressing the dialogue between the Comte and Elvire, originally the first scene of the play, to give the opening scenes more tragic dignity and also, of course, by the introduction of hesitancy about the marriage after the curtain falls at the end of the play. The "avertissement" of 1648, at which date the text retained the certainty of the marriage, relied heavily on the 1592 *Historiae de rebus Hispaniae* of the Jesuit historian Juan de Mariana to establish its historicity. In the original play of Guillén de Castro the marriage was more easily acceptable because the action lasted three years, but in the successive versions of Corneille's text the acceptability of the marriage changed as the nature of the duelling code in France evolved. In the Spanish original, Don Diègue, slapped by the Comte, found 500 men offering their support in armed combat. Corneille's source envisaged not so much a duel as a feudal battle, and Chimène's dedication to avenging her father had important military and political consequences for Castille, whose safety from the Moors depended on Rodrigue. As l'Infante says:

> Quoi? pour venger un père est-il jamais permis
> De livrer sa patrie aux mains des ennemis?

> (What? is it ever right in order to avenge a father/To deliver one's country into the hands of its enemies?).

Corneille, though strongly on Richelieu's side in his stance against personal combat as a way of settling questions of honour, in fact suppressed four lines which ridiculed duelling as early certainly as 12 May 1637. The play in 1637 celebrated not only the overriding rights of love based on merit, but also France's recent liberation from the real threat of Spanish domination.

As the play opens in Corneille's original version we learn from the conversation, later suppressed, between the Comte and Elvire that, of two possible husbands, either of whom Chimène would accept, her father, the Comte, has chosen Don Rodrigue for her. Overjoyed when Elvire informs her, Chimène awaits the end of the council meeting at which her father is to be made governor to the heir to the throne. L'Infante, who is without real dramatic function in Corneille's play, too, is in love with Rodrigue, but is sacrificing herself for Chimène. The council has meanwhile made Rodrigue's elderly and once heroic father, Don Diègue, the prince's governor, to the annoyance of the Comte, Castille's present leading warrior, who tells Diègue that his son should marry someone other than Chimène, and ends up slapping his face for his arrogance in accepting the governorship of the heir. There is a "rencontre," an unpremeditated altercation, and the two prepare to fight a duel on the spot. The Comte knocks Diègue's sword out of his hand, but refuses to kill him. In 1655 André Baron, playing Diègue, pricked his foot on the sword as it lay on the ground, and died of gangrene. Diègue rues his position, now devoid of honour, and charges Rodrigue with the task of avenging him, handing him the sword the Comte had knocked from his hand. Diègue tells his son that he must kill or die, issuing the formal challenge which is not a "rencontre," but an "appel." The altercation had contained a remarkable passage of one-line exchanges such as had been a set piece in earlier renaissance tragedies, and Rodrigue in the last scene of the first act has another set piece, six 10-line stanzas.

It is here that the clash of moral values is defined, with an alteration making it much sharper after the two impressions of the first of the (probably) four 1637 editions, of which the first had had two impressions on successive days. Rodrigue's first two stanzas make clear the conflict between the satisfaction of his love for Chimène and the fulfilment of his duty towards his father. He will have to lose Chimène to avenge his father, and must either betray his love or live "en infâme (without honour)." It is in the third stanza that Corneille, stumbling on the nature of the conflict he wanted to define, made the key change. With the exception of the stanza's second line, changed from 1644 to 1646 and then changed back, the first four lines read from after the initial edition

> Père, maîtresse, honneur, amour,
> Noble et dure contrainte, aimable tyrannie,

> Tous mes plaisirs sont morts ou ma gloire ternie:
> L'un me rend malheureux, l'autre indigne du jour

> (Father, beloved, honour, love,/Noble and harsh constraint, desirable tyranny,/All my pleasures are dead or my honour is tarnished:/One choice makes me wretched, the other unworthy to live).

The altered third line, changed to the form given only after the first edition, conceals Corneille's discovery. The conflict is not between love and honour, as the first-line contrast of father/honour and beloved/love suggests, but has been linguistically transposed into terms which change its nature, and thereby prejudge its necessary outcome. The conflict is now not between love and honour, but between pleasure/satisfaction and personal dignity or "gloire," which must in any heroic drama be victorious. To be "malheureux (wretched)" is a less dire fate than being "indigne du jour (unworthy to live)."

There is however, more. It is only by avenging his father, and therefore losing the possibility of happiness with Chimène, that Rodrigue merits her love. Whatever happens, he therefore loses her. She must either despise him for not avenging his father, and therefore cease to love him, or reject him for killing her own father. The relevant lines in 1637 read

> Je dois à ma maîtresse aussi bien qu'à mon père.
> Qui venge cet affront irrite sa colère,
> Et qui peut le souffrir, ne la mérite pas...

> (I owe a duty to my beloved as well as to my father./He who avenges this insult will rouse her anger,/But whoever can tolerate it is unworthy of her).

The last two lines are sharpened in 1660:

> J'attire en me vengeant sa haine et sa colère,
> J'attire ses mépris en ne me vengeant pas

> (By avenging myself I draw down her hatred and anger,/I draw down her contempt by not avenging myself).

Later in the play the situation is reversed. In the great Act 3, scene iv confrontation between Chimène and Rodrigue, when Rodrigue comes in with his sword dripping with her father's blood, Chimène says,

> Tu t'es, en m'offensant, montré digne de moi,
> Je me dois par ta mort montrer digne de toi

> (By offending me you have shown yourself worthy of me./I must, through your death, show myself worthy of you).

Corneille's increased hesitancy is however again made clear in 1660. He substituted for the daring interrogative "Dois-je à mon père avant qu'à ma maîtresse (Does my duty to my father takes precedence over that to my beloved?)" the timid affirmative "Je dois tout à mon père avant qu'à ma maîtresse (My duty to my father takes precedence over that to my beloved)."

The conflict is now between honour and pleasure; honour must therefore win; and the moral status of passion is strongly reinforced by basing it on merit, so that infamy destroys the possibility of love. The upgrading of instinctive emotion by associating it with the merit of its object is not new. It was already clear in the neostoic generation of Charron and du Vair, and became emphatic with d'Urfé. It can be found in François de Sales and was to be clear in Descartes. It is none the less very powerful in *Le Cid* and, since the assessment of merit implies an intellectual judgement, it is of historical importance that the immediate emotional response of love, like that of pity or fear in the tragic catharsis, is made for Corneille, as for Descartes, to depend on the implied interpolation of a rational judgement. The explanation and justification of emotional reactions in terms of rational judgements is a characteristic of the period during which the rehabilitation of instinctive behaviour was of central concern to French baroque culture.

The first scene of the second act, between the Comte and another nobleman, Don Arias, also betrays hesitancy. Don Arias argues the king of Castille's viewpoint, which was also Richelieu's, in prohibiting duels. Richelieu had in fact softened the legislation, but he enforced it, occasionally with the death penalty. Before the first printing, Corneille dropped at least four lines spoken by the Comte in defence of duelling, although they were spoken at the first performances. It is so obviously against the interests of the state that the Comte, its current military leader, and Rodrigue, his potential successor, should fight a duel, that the Comte is left appearing arrogantly and haughtily out of date in his conception of honour. Rodrigue tries to persuade the Comte not to force him to avenge his father, but the Comte, disdainfully certain of killing his opponent, admires Rodrigue's courage while certain he is about to kill him.

During the second act Chimène, lamenting the "impitoyable honneur, mortel à mes plaisirs (pitiless honour, fatal to my pleasures)," the Infante, and the king also comment on the situation as they see it. Chimène's alternative suitor Don Sanche vainly defends the Comte to the king, before news comes that the Moors are attacking, then that Rodrigue has killed Chimène's father. Chimène comes to the king to demand Rodrigue's death and dramatically splits six successive alexandrines equally with Don Diègue, who is pleading for mercy for Rodrigue. Chimène and Don Diègue then each make a formal plea to the king. In the third act Chimène disdains Don Sanche's offer to avenge her father by fighting Rodrigue, thereby avoiding the prospect of two young men fighting for the hand of the woman they both love. Rodrigue comes in with the dripping sword asking Chimène to kill him rather than let him die at the hand of the executioner. One alexandrine is split between four speeches, and the drama proceeds not only through a succession of dilemmas, whose resolution each time simply leads on to the next, but with a whole series of the most quotable lines of verse in the language:

Et pour leurs coups d'essai veulent des coups de maître

(And for their first attempts aspire to master-strokes).

Je le ferais encor si j'avais à le faire

(I would do it again if I had it to do).

Il y va de ma gloire, il faut que je me venge

(My honour is at stake; I must avenge myself).

L'amour n'est qu'un plaisir, et l'honneur un devoir

(Love is only a pleasure; honour is a duty).

Rodrigue elaborates the algebra of Corneille's new ethical equation: "Un homme sans honneur ne te méritait pas (A man without honour would not be worthy of you)," "Qui m'aima généreux ma haïrait infâme (She who loved me for my elevation of spirit would disdain me if I were without honour)." Chimène makes clear that she will do her utmost to have Rodrigue executed while hoping not to succeed. Rodrigue, spurning his father's gratitude, has, in a feudal manner, accepted the leadership of 500 "friends," gone off and conquered the Moors, and been acknowledged by their two kings, delivered by him into captivity, as their sovereign. The king pardons him; Chimène thinks him dead and faints but, when she recovers, announces she had been overcome by the thought that Rodrigue had been killed gloriously in battle and not, as her honour demanded, ignominiously executed to avenge her father.

The king consents to a duel between Rodrigue and a champion chosen by Chimène. In a further confrontation with Chimène Rodrigue says he will not defend himself. She urges him to fight in a duel "dont Chimène est le prix (in which Chimène is the prize)." Rodrigue disarms Don Sanche but refuses to kill him. Chimène thinks Rodrigue dead, confesses her love for him to the king and announces her determination to enter a convent. Rodrigue comes in, and in the 1637 version the final dilemma was resolved by the certainty of the marriage after a decent interval of anticipated military exploits. For concentrated imaginative power, the piece is scarcely equalled in French except by *Phèdre*.

The composition of *Horace*, delayed by the controversy following *Le Cid*, was finished by February 1640. We know from Chapelain's letters that the piece had been presented privately before Richelieu some time before 9 March, and there had been three public performances by 19 May. The privilège is dated 11 December and publication took place in January 1641. The delay in performance must have been occasioned by the objections raised by the friends Corneille consulted against *Horace*'s killing of Camille, but Corneille's sensitivity to the ethical values he was exploring is again reflected in his changes of mind about the ending.

The play pits the three champions of Rome, Horace and his two brothers, against those of Alba, Curiace and his brothers. However, Horace is married to Sabine, Curiace's sister and a character invented by Corneille, while Horace's sister, Camille, is in love with Curiace, to whom she is engaged. The play works by the same device as *Le Cid*, an evolving series of symmetrical dilemmas, although in this case asymmetrically resolved. At the opening, Sabine laments her dilemma, married to a Roman warrior but sister of three from Alba. Camille, who shares a confidante, Julie, with Sabine, is less torn. Her loyalty, she feels, lies with Curiace, whom she loves, rather than with her brother, but she can never be possessed by Curiace if he is to be "ou le vainqueur, ou l'esclave de Rome (either Rome's conqueror or its slave)." The three Alban champions to confront Horace and his brothers have not yet been chosen when Horace appears on stage for the first time at the beginning of the second act. The division of acts is used here dramatically, to separate the development of the action from the initial exposition in act one. A soldier brings Curiace the news of his selection by Alba while he is with

Horace. What Horace sees as a distinction and a chance to exhibit heroic qualities leaves Curiace more uncertain. He immediately reacts to Horace: "votre fermeté tient un peu du barbare (your resolution has something barbaric about it)."

Camille pleads with Curiace not to fight. He knows he must. "[Je] vivrai sans reproche, ou périrai sans honte (I will live without blame or die without shame)." The second act ends emotionally when the character, le vieil Horace, father of the brothers and Camille, encourages his sons to fight, to seek glory at the expense of love. Sabine leaves the stage in loud despair, Camille in silence. Horace's brothers are killed offstage, and his father, enraged to hear of Horace's own flight, swears to kill him himself. The flight, however, was a feint, and Horace has killed Curiace and both his brothers. Rome has conquered and he alone of the six has survived. In an encounter with the victor, Camille mourns Curiace and curses Rome, and Horace, furious, kills her. The final act had originally four scenes, not three. In the first le vieil Horace allows that, while his daughter deserved death, Horace should not have killed her. In the second the king enters and begins to pronounce judgement, as he says "en demi-Dieu (half God-like)." Valère, who also loved Camille, pleads for the punishment of Horace. Horace is told to speak in his own defence, but offers the king his life. In the third scene Sabine offers her own life in place of that of the husband who has killed her three brothers. Le vieil Horace addresses Sabine, Valère, the king, and his son. In the 1641 text the king forgives Horace. His crime is "great, wicked, inexcusable," but

Ta vertu met ta gloire au-dessus de ton crime.
Sa chaleur généreuse a produit ton forfait

(Your virtue puts your merit above your crime./Its valorous warmth is the source of your guilt).

In 1656 and 1657 "généreuse/valorous" is replaced by "dangereuse/dangerous," which completely alters the king's moral judgement. He is now forgiving on account not of valour, but of impetuosity. In 1660, Corneille put back "généreuse," but replaced the 12 final lines, in which Julie, the shared confidante, had commented in a final scene on the ironic way in which Camille's foreboding had been fulfilled, with 16 lines in which the king orders the burial of Curiace and Camille in the same grave.

The plot of *Cinna* is political, concerned generally with the exercise of power, but avoiding direct allusion to any of the numerous plots devised during the reign of Louis XIII. Its interest lies in the lengths to which Corneille takes magnanimity as a basis for heroic, and therefore tragic, elevation. The play opens with a soliloquy by Emilie, daughter of the tutor of the emperor Auguste, whom the emperor, when part of the triumvirate, was partly responsible for killing. She informs us that she is in love with Cinna, leader of a plot against Auguste which aims to restore the liberty of Rome, and she intends to encourage his plan, although she herself was brought up in the emperor's household. When her confidante, Fulvie, comes in, Emilie tells her that, although she loves Cinna, the murder of Auguste is the price of her hand. Cinna arrives, reporting on the prospects for the conspiracy and setting out the background in a speech of more than 100 lines. The exposition of the opening situation is complete when, at the end of act one, to the alarm of Emilie, Cinna and his co-conspirator, Maxime, are called before Auguste.

Auguste seeks only their advice on the principles of government, in a scene ironic both because he turns out to represent what they want to kill him to obtain, and also because he has called for guidance from two trusted counsellors who are in fact conspiring to kill him. Cinna emerges more resolute than Maxime that the conspiracy must continue. Cinna does not know that Maxime, too, is in love with Emilie. We are told this when Maxime confides in an ex-slave of his at the beginning of act three. Cinna feels the strain of being caught between Auguste's trust and Emilie's detestation of him, but Emilie is pitiless in spite of the emperor's benevolence, and her scorn forces Cinna forward.

In the fourth act Maxime's freed slave has betrayed the plot to Auguste, thrown into a turmoil expressed in a long speech of inner doubt. His wife, Livie, counsels clemency as the true sign of authority. Maxime tries in vain to persuade Emilie to flee with him. In the fifth act Auguste confronts Cinna with his treachery, and decides to punish him, when he is informed of Emilie's role in the conspiracy, and after listening to her defiant provocations, decides to destroy her with Cinna. Maxime now confesses that his instigation of the conspiracy's betrayal had been on account of his jealousy of Cinna, whom he wished to see destroyed because he stood between Emilie and himself. Auguste forgives them all:

Je suis maître de moi comme de l'Univers.
Je le suis, je veux l'être

(I am master of myself as of the universe./That is what I am and that is what I wish to be).

The interest of the tragedy *Polyeucte*, called by Corneille a Christian tragedy only from 1652, lies largely in Corneille's struggle with the problem of supernatural motivation. Was Polyeucte's vocation to martyrdom the miraculous work of grace, or the overweening result of heroic pride? The play starts with a reference to a dream presaging ill, like Camille's in *Horace*. The dreamer is Pauline, wife of Polyeucte, and consideration for her fears holds him back from becoming a Christian like his friend Néarque. Pauline confides in Stratonice that her dream concerned the vengeance to be wreaked on her husband of a fortnight, Polyeucte, by a Roman she had once loved, Sévère. In the last scene of act one Pauline's father, Félix, the governor of Armenia, tells her that Sévère is not dead, as had been thought, but is coming to Armenia.

Again the exposition is completed in the first act. Sévère appears at the beginning of the second and learns of Pauline's marriage. They meet, and Pauline, affirming that she loves Polyeucte, none the less tells him that she married him on account of her father's wishes. She and Sévère agree to separate and each wishes happiness to the other, but Pauline still has her premonition. The second act ends with Polyeucte's summons by Félix to attend the temple sacrifice. He intends, he tells Néarque, to overturn the altars, thanking God for the chance to prove his new faith. Néarque counsels caution, uncertain whether Polyeucte's inspiration comes from divine grace, bestowed in the baptism he has just received, or from human impetuosity; "Qui n'appréhende rien présume trop de soi (He who fears nothing trusts too much in himself)."

Pauline soliloquizes her anxiety about the unavoidable meeting between Polyeucte and Sévère at the sacrifice, and Stratonice brings her the news that Polyeucte had indeed proclaimed the omnipotence of the Christian God, denounced the idolatry of the temple rites, and with Néarque broken the sacred vessels and overturned the statues. Félix announces to his daughter that Polyeucte, whom he wishes to spare, will be given the chance to recant. He is made, offstage, to watch Néarque being put to death, but wants only martyrdom for himself. Félix cannot save him without himself being destroyed by the Roman emperor, to whom Sévère would report.

In the fourth act Polyeucte, alone, delivers a series of stanzas. Pauline comes to him and pleads in vain. Sévère hopes that Pauline, after Polyeucte's death, may consent to marry him, but is left by Pauline in no doubt that she will not. Sévère, moved, to the surprise of his servant goes to plead for Polyeucte with Félix. Act five opens with Félix overwhelmed. Sévère has threatened to ruin him with the emperor if he does *not* pardon Polyeucte. Félix tells Polyeucte that he himself wants to become a Christian, but then takes back his affirmation. At the end of a dramatic scene between Polyeucte, Félix, and Pauline, Polyeucte is taken to his death, Pauline becomes a Christian, and then Félix, too, declares himself a Christian. Sévère encourages Félix to serve both the Christian God and the Roman monarch.

Like its three immediate predecessors, *Polyeucte* is dramatically tense. It may well be that *Le Cid* remains essentially a suitably stripped down and concentrated tragi-comédie, whatever at different times it was called, but there is a progression in the series through *Horace*, *Cinna*, and *Polyeucte*. The Querelle after *Le Cid* turned on the audacious investigation of the possible elevation of instinctive love, about which Corneille himself became more hesitant. The more muted reaction to Horace's murder of his sister hinged on the reverse possibility that patriotic fervour might still outweigh the emotional sympathy roused in the audience or reader for Camille's love for Curiace, Rome's enemy. Corneille finally took refuge in historical truth, but by the end of the tragedy the heroic patriotism of Horace's father and of Horace himself has been roundly enough condemned for Corneille's negative reaction to the emotions he had put on the stage to have been confirmed. The 1660 ending underlines the ennobling nature of instinctive affection.

Corneille had by 1637 established on an imaginative register much more serious than that of the *Astrée* that physical passion was not only compatible with heroic moral elevation, but could even lead to it, as it did in *Le Cid*. He had also by 1642 established that a whole tragedy could be constructed round one single event occurring off the stage, as it was in *Le Cid*, *Horace*, and later *Polyeucte*, and that, compared to the potential elevation achievable through the medium of emotional love, even heroic patriotism had to yield. He was not ready to affirm that love itself could be a tragic emotion, but it appears as an exceedingly powerful motivating force in all four of these plays, even, in *Polyeucte*, reinforcing the action of grace on the personalities of Pauline and of Félix, whose attachment is to his daughter and son-in-law.

In all four plays the essential action takes place in the minds and emotions of the characters. The unities were more of a support than a constraint. In *Cinna* the dramatic crisis is the result of a betrayed conspiracy, not even of a violent event reported on the stage. It is the immense power of this concentration of dramatic interest around purely interior events, and the moral values which they reflect and which are articulated, contrasted, and debated, that makes it necessary to say quite simply that

Corneille created French classical tragedy. Racine borrowed from him many of his detailed dramatic techniques as well as the overall conception of emotional tragedy, although he developed what he borrowed in his own powerfully original way.

Of the other plays, *Rodogune* is normally regarded as the most important. With *Héraclius*, *Cinna*, *Le Cid*, and *La Mort de Pompée* it formed the repertoire from Corneille with which Molière unsuccessfully tried to establish himself in Paris, and it was instantly copied for the Hôtel de Bourgogne by Gabriel Gilbert's 1646 *Rhodogune*, which gave it a tragi-comic ending. *Rodogune's* interest lies largely in the heroic elevation of Cléopâtre's character and actions, themselves intrinsically evil, and it was a play for which Corneille himself had a special affection. Dramatically it has the same sort of symmetry as *Horace*, and it might, Corneille tells us, well have been called "Cléopâtre," had that not risked causing a confusion with the queen of Egypt.

As the play opens we learn that Cléopâtre, queen of Syria, is about to reveal which of her twin sons, recalled from the safety of Memphis, where they had been brought up, Séleucus or Antiochus, was born first and would inherit her kingdom. Cléopâtre's maid, Laonice, is conversing with her brother, Timagène, the twins' governor, and tells him that Cléopâtre's husband Nicanor had been believed dead, and Cléopâtre's people had forced her to remarry. She had therefore married Nicanor's brother, also called Antiochus. Before we learn more, Séleucus and Antiochus both reveal that they love Rodogune. They decide that whoever inherits the throne will marry Rodogune, too. Laonice then continues with her narration. Antiochus, Cléopâtre's second husband, had been defeated in battle and killed himself. Nicanor was still alive, but captive of the king of Parthia. Annoyed by Cléopâtre's marriage to his brother, he had decided to marry his captor's sister, the Rodogune with whom his sons were now in love, so both avenging himself and assuring union between Syria and Parthia through the children of the new marriage. Cléopâtre herself had taken part in an ambush she arranged, killed Nicanor herself, and taken Rodogune captive. Laonice alone contrived mild treatment for the hostage Rodogune. The Parthians were now friendly. The first act again ends the exposition. Rodogune has hinted to Laonice that she will marry whichever brother destroys Cléopâtre, his mother but Rodogune's enemy.

In the second act Cléopâtre reveals that she had threatened her second husband with the return of her sons, one of whom was the legitimate heir, if he did not do what she wanted. In that way she kept the power for herself. She would not even have worried about Nicanor's marriage to Rodogune if he had stayed away. Laonice does not understand that Cléopâtre is motivated uniquely by a lust for power.

N'apprendras-tu jamais, âme basse et grossière,
A voir par d'autres yeux que les yeux du vulgaire?...
Ne saurais-tu juger que si je nomme un Roi,
C'est pour le commander, et combattre pour moi?

(Will you never learn, coarse, base spirit,/To see through other eyes than those of the common people?.../Can't you understand that if I nominate a king,/It is to command him and make him fight for me?).

She will make king whichever son will destroy Rodogune. Corneille has loaded the dilemma by adding a possible desire for power to loyalty to their mother to one side of the equation, leaving sexual desire on the other. Cléopâtre confronts her sons, but neither shows any particular interest in power. She insists on the destruction of Rodogune:

Pour jouir de mon crime, il le faut achever

(To profit from my crime, you must complete it).

The second act ends after the brothers have talked together. Antiochus is less severe towards his mother than Séleucus.

The Parthian ambassador, Oronte, advises Rodogune to work on the affections of the twins to avoid destruction at their hands, an attitude she thinks beneath her dignity. She confronts the twins. She will marry whichever of them kills his mother. They confer. Antiochus hopes to reconcile Cléopâtre and Rodogune, Séleucus wants to rebel against them. In the fourth act Rodogune admits to Antiochus that it is he whom she loves, and she no longer insists on his murdering his mother. He tries to appease Cléopâtre, tells her that his brother and he would both die rather than kill Rodogune. Cléopâtre dissimulates, attempts to persuade Séleucus that he was born first, but still fails to wrest agreement from him. When the fifth act starts she has already killed Séleucus. She hands Antiochus a poisoned nuptial cup at the ceremony she has arranged, but Timagène arrives to announce that Séleucus's body has been found. Cléopâtre says it must have been suicide at losing Rodogune. Timagène repeats Séleucus's last words. His death had been caused by "a very dear hand." Rodogune's or Cléopâtre's? Antiochus begs whichever it was to kill him, too. He takes the poisoned cup. Rodogune prevents him from drinking, and asks for it to be tasted by a servant. Cléopâtre drinks it herself, curses Antiochus and Rodogune, and is helped from the stage to avoid dying at their feet.

Before the failure of *Pertharite* at the opening of the 1651–52 season, after which Corneille withdrew from the theatre for seven years, his successful political tragedy *Nicomède* was played while the release of Condé, Conti, and Longueville in February 1651 was still in the minds of the theatre-going public. The "Au lecteur" boasts of the play's independence from "la tendresse et les passions," and its importance is its reliance, even greater than *Cinna*'s, on admiration alone as the tragic emotion. Its contrasts are between important political attitudes, and the play depends entirely on Nicomède's ironic acceptance of the hostility which surrounds him when he returns to the court of his father Prusias. Prusias reigns in Bythinia under the influence of Arsinoé, Nicomède's step-mother, who dislikes him, and of Flaminius, the Roman ambassador responsible for the recent death of Hannibal. Nicomède's half-brother Attale is his rival in love for Laodice, the queen of Armenia. In the end he is helped by Attale to evade the plot to imprison him in Rome, and the play ends on a note of magnanimity and forgiveness. The relevance to the political situation in France is general, but it is difficult not to see some idealization of Condé in Nicomède, and in some of the play's situations an exploitation of the popular hostility to Mazarin.

PUBLICATIONS

Collections

Oeuvres de Corneille, 1644
Oeuvres de Corneille, 2 vols., 1648
Oeuvres de Corneille, 3 vols., 1652
Oeuvres de Corneille, 3 vols., 1654, 1655, 1656, 1657
Le Théâtre de P. Corneille, 3 vols., 1660
Le Théâtre de P. Corneille, 2 vols., 1663
Le Théâtre de P. Corneille, 4 vols., 1664
Le Théâtre de P. Corneille, 4 vols., 1668
Le Théâtre de P. Corneille, 4 vols., 1682
Oeuvres, 12 vols., 1862–8
Théâtre complet, 3 vols., Classiques Garnier, 1941
Oeuvres complètes, 3 vols., Bibliothèque de la Pléiade, 1980–87

Plays

[*The order of publication has been followed, since some of the preliminary material needs to be viewed in the light of contemporary controversy: dates in brackets refer to theatrical season of first production*]

Clitandre; ou, L'Innocence délivrée (1630–31), 1632
Mélite; ou, Les Fausses Lettres (1629–30), 1633; as *Melite*, 1776
La Veuve; ou, Le Traître trahi (1631–2), 1634
La Galerie du Palais; ou, L'Amie rivale (1632–33), 1637
La Place Royale; ou, L'Amoureux extravagant (1633–34), 1637
Le Cid (1636–37), 1637; as *The Cid*, 1637; 1975
La Suivante (1633–34), 1637
Médée (1634–35), 1639
L'Illusion comique (1635–36), 1639; as *The Theatrical Illusion*, 1975
Horace (1639–40), 1641; as *Horatius*, 1656
Cinna; ou, La Clémence d'Auguste (1642–43), 1643; as *Cinna*, 1975
Polyeucte martyr (1642–3), 1643; as *Polyeuctes*, 1655
La Mort de Pompée (1643–44), 1644; as *Pompey the Great*, 1664
Le Menteur (1643–44), 1644; as *The Mistaken Beauty; or, The Liar*, 1685; as *The Lying Lover*, 1717; as *The Liar*, 1980
La Suite du Menteur (1644–45), 1645
Rodogune, Princesse des Parthes (1644–45), 1647; as *Rodogune*, 1765
Théodore, vierge et martyre (1645–46), 1646
Héraclius, empereur d'Oreint (1646–47), 1647; as *Heraclius, Emperor of the East*, 1664
Andromède (1650), 1650
Don Sanche d'Aragon (1649–50), 1650
Nicomède (1650–51), 1651; as *Nicomede*, 1671
Pertharite, roi des Lombards (1651–52), 1653
Oedipe (1658–59), 1659
La Toison d'or (1660–61), 1661
Sertorius (1662–63), 1662
Sophonisbe (1662–63), 1663
Othon (1664–65), 1665
Agésilas (1665–66), 1666
Attila, Roi des Huns (1666–67), 1667
Tite et Bérénice (1670–71), 1671
Pulchérie (1671–72), 1673
Suréna, général des Parthes (1674–75), 1675 as *Surenas*, 1969.

Other

All Corneille's occasional writings, poems, and letters are

printed in the Bibliothèque de la Pléiade edition of the *Oeuvres complètes*

Trois discours sur le poème dramatique, 1963; as *Writings on the Theatre*, edited by H. T. Barnwell, 1965

Translations

Thomas à Kempis, *L'Imitation de Jésus-Christ*, 1651–56
L'Office de la sainte Vierge, 1670

Biographical and critical studies

Nadal, O., *Le Sentiment de l'amour dans l'oeuvre de P. Corneille*, 1948
Couton, Georges, *La Vieillesse de Corneille (1658–1684)*, 1949
    Corneille, 1958; 2nd edition, 1969
Dort, B., *Corneille dramaturge*, 1957; 2nd edition 1972
Yarrow, P.J., *Corneille* (in English), 1953
Benichou, P., *Morales du grand siècle*, 1958
Nelson, R.J., *Corneille. His Heroes and Their World*, 1963
Stegmann, A., *L'Héroïsme cornélien, genèse et signification*, 2 vols., 1968
Pocock, Gordon, *Corneille and Racine: Problems of Tragic Form*, 1973
Barnwell, H.T., *The Tragic Drama of Corneille and Racine*, 1982.

Bibliography

Picot, Emile, *Bibliographie cornélienne*, 1876
Le Verdier, P., and Pelay E., *Additions à la bibliographie cornélienne*, 1908
Cioranescu, A., *Bibliographie de la littérature du XVIIe siècle*, 1965
Klapp, O., *Bibliographie der französischen Literaturwissenschaft*, 1956ff.

CORNEILLE, Thomas, 1625–1709.

Dramatist and journalist.

LIFE

Corneille was 19 years younger than his more celebrated elder brother, to whom he was close, but from the direction of whose literary career his own in the end sharply diverged. The two brothers were brought up in the same way, educated at the Jesuit college in Rouen, were both called to the Rouen bar, settled together in Paris from 1662 to 1681, and in 1650 Corneille married Marguerite de Lampérière, the sister of his brother's wife and older than he was. The sister of the two brothers was Fontenelle's mother. The brothers and their families lived both in Rouen and Paris, says Ducis, "as a single household," sufficiently united, at least, for the Lampérière sisters not to have divided their inheritance between them, although there were periods when they did not share the same roof.

Corneille was born on 20 August 1625 and, since his father died when he was 14, he was effectively brought up by his elder brother. He was early introduced to the world of the theatre, in which his brother was already known by 1630, and he wrote his first tragedy at school. It was in Latin verse and has been lost. After becoming a barrister at the Normandy parlement in 1649, Corneille immediately turned to the stage, for which he wrote a series of comedies derived from Spanish models. Early in his career Corneille was protected by Foucquet, and by the duc de Guise, former archbishop of Reims, and according to Tallemant "one of the men in the world most inclined to love," a partisan of the précieux (q.v.), witty, generous, warm, and polite, although the duc de Chevreuse is reported to have said "C'est dommage qu'il est fou (It's a pity he's mad)."

Like his brother, Corneille received his patents of nobility in 1669, and he was henceforward known as M. Corneille de l'Isle, on which account Molière perhaps unjustly laughed at him in the first scene of *L'Ecole des femmes*. The title may have been assumed out of modesty in order to leave "M. de Corneille" unambiguously for Pierre. Corneille was to become a much more fashionable playwright than his elder brother and it is clear that, because he wrote some 40 comédies, tragi-comédies, tragédies, and lavish court entertainments, because he was strongly on the side of the partisans of the "modernes" in the Querelle des anciens et des modernes (q.v.), his most serious work has been under-valued. There is more imaginative vigour in Corneille's work than has normally been acknowledged. Voltaire put it immediately below that of Racine and Pierre Corneille.

By the time he was elected to the Académie française in succession to his brother, who died in 1684, Corneille's career was already mixing its ingredients in different proportions, and from 1680 he shared the direction of *Le Mercure Galant* (q.v.) with Donneau de Visé, with whom he signed an editorial contract in 1682, and with whom he also collaborated on a number of plays and court entertainments. Towards the end of his life, when his sight was already failing, he was to work on two dictionary-encyclopedias, intended to replace Furetière's dictionary, whose 1684 privilège the Académie had succeeded in having overthrown. Corneille published his *Notes* on Vaugelas's 1647 *Remarques sur la langue française* in 1687; in 1704 the Académie's *Observations* on Vaugelas's *Remarques*; in 1694 his *Dictionnaire des termes d'art et de science*; in 1697 a translation of Ovid; and in 1708 his *Dictionnaire universel géographique et historique*. In 1701 he became a member of the Académie des Inscriptions et Belles-lettres.

Corneille's first comedy, *Les Engagements du hasard*, adapted from two Calderon plays, was performed at the Hôtel de Bourgogne before 1650, almost certainly in 1649, but the dates traditionally assigned to this comedy and the other plays should be treated with caution. We often know for certain only the formal date carried by the printed first edition, which may itself not be entirely reliable, and it must anyway be remembered that for most purposes the theatrical season is more important than an accurate year date. The more important a new play was likely to be, the later before Christmas or the sooner in the new year it was likely to have its first performance, with due allowance made for the desire of one of the two French companies before 1658, or the three companies when Molière's had joined them, to be first with a play on a particular theme. Among the half-dozen early comedies, of which *Le Berger extravagant* is described as a "pastorale burlesque," *Le Geôlier de soy-mesme*, played in 1655, was a particular success.

Then in 1656 came the tragedy *Timocrate*, in box-office terms the most successful play of the century. Played at the Marais, probably from November 1656, it appears to have been given an unheard-of 80 consecutive performances and even, at one time, to have been put on by both companies at once, an astonishing tribute to its success. All Paris is said to have known the play by heart and, most unusually, the king was too impatient to wait for a court performance and went to the Marais with a large party on 12 December, seeing it again at his brother's residence in January 1657. Both Loret in *La Muse historique* for 16 December and the abbé de Pure in *La Précieuse* of 1657 give evidence of the play's popularity.

From just before 1650 and for the next 30 years, Corneille's life is simply the story of his existence in the theatre, although collaborators' names appear alongside or in place of his own, or are suppressed in favour of his own, from the mid-1670s. As the partnership with Donneau de Visé develops, it becomes impossible to know which of them is responsible for exactly what. *La Devineresse*, treated in this *Guide* under the name of Donneau de Visé, might well chiefly be the work of Corneille. It is difficult to be fastidious about authorship at a date and in situations in which collaboration was common, but it also matters less in those instances in which we know that the plays were not just scripts requiring interpretation and production just like any others, but that they also relied on the cooperation of a composer, as well as of singers, dancers, and musicians.

One at least of the reasons for the under-valuation of Corneille is the failure to realize that what we can read today is often no more than a script for the dramatic, and not necessarily the most important, part of an entertainment, with often spectacular stage effects as well as acting, singing, and dancing. The light-hearted improbabilities in the plots must often be explained by the theatrical necessity, perfectly understood by the audience, of finding excuses for the breath-taking swoops, descents, resurrections, assumptions, and ascents of characters, with the aid of the hoists, pulleys, cranes, ratchets, cogs and swings in which the Marais specialized.

By the late 1660s the insobriety of the sumptuous entertainments which disturbed Boileau, Chapelain, and d'Aubignac was already contrasting with the passionate, psychologically intense, declamatory drama of Racine, which needed the unities to support the detailed analysis of the characters' feelings. Corneille was still able to work in both the diverging traditions. *Ariane*, played at the Hôtel de Bourgogne in 1672, probably on 26 February after Racine's *Bajazet* in early January, contains elements which show that it was at least an attempt to rival Racine's *Bérénice* of 21 November 1670 at the Hôtel, which itself had been challenged a week after its first performance by Pierre Corneille's *Tite et Bérénice* in a battle which Racine had won. He was to win again when Corneille appeared unsuccessfully to challenge *Bajazet* with *Théodat* in November 1672. The structure of Corneille's plot seems obviously based on that of Racine as, late in December 1673, the plot structure of Corneille's *La Mort d'Achille* appears to be based on that underlying Racine's *Mithridate* of the previous February. Corneille's

borrowings from Racine, and Racine's from Corneille, are sufficiently complex to suggest that the full history of the relationship of Racine's dramatic writing to that of both Corneille brothers still needs writing, as does that of the relationship between the plays of the Corneille brothers themselves.

Corneille's straight dramatic tragedy continued with the three plays on subjects proposed by Foucquet to Pierre Corneille, who chose that of Oedipus and in two months wrote *Oedipe*, performed at the Hôtel de Bourgogne on 24 January 1659. The other two proposed subjects were treated by Corneille himself: *Camma*, played at the Hôtel on 28 January 1661, and *Stilicon*, nearly abandoned, like a "Stratonice" given up late in 1659 at the news that Quinault was preparing a tragedy on the same theme. The news of a double to *Stilicon*, as Corneille reported to the abbé de Pure in a letter of 1 December 1659, had turned out to be false, and Corneille's play was in fact staged by the Hôtel on 27 January 1660, marking Corneille's return there after an absence of seven years, during which his production had gone to the Marais.

Corneille had presented a tragedy each season for five years at the Hôtel de Bourgogne, including *Maximian* in February 1662, *Persée et Démétrius* in December 1662, and *Pyrrhus, roi d'Epire* during the 1663–64 season, after which he began to slow the rate of production down and, still at the Hôtel, turned to the tragi-comédie *Antiochus*, performed on 9 January 1666, followed by the tragédies *Laodice* at the beginning of February 1668, *La Mort d'Annibal* in November 1669, *Ariane* on 26 February 1672, and *Théodat* on 16 November of the same year. After *La Mort d'Achille* at the Guénégaud on 29 December 1673, after the fusion of the Marais company with Molière's troupe, Corneille returned to the Hôtel with the brilliantly successful *Le Comte d'Essex* on 7 January 1678. Most of these plays were successful, the exceptions being *Persée*, *Annibal*, and *Théodat*.

Not all even of Corneille's tragédies were Racinian in their degree of psychological concentration. *Timocrate* has too many surprises to be experienced as a tragedy, even though it is called one and keeps the unities. But there can be little doubt that Racine was thinking of Corneille's *Camma* when he wrote *Andromaque*, and of *Ariane* when he wrote *Phèdre*. It is possible, although unlikely, that Racine was simply demonstrating that he could present a similar subject better than Corneille. It is more probable that, even in his analysis of sentiment, Racine was sometimes indebted to Corneille, but that Corneille, when treating Racinian subjects, was challenging his junior rather than borrowing from him.

Where Corneille joins the other theatrical tradition relying more on stage effects or music, song, and dance than straight tragedy or tragi-comedy, even accompanied by music, is in such entertainments as *Circé*, "tragédie ornée de machines, de changemens de théâtre et de musique," inserted into his dramatic production in 1675 to rival the Quinault-Lulli partnership's work, or in his own cooperation with Lulli, during the 1677–80 eclipse of Quinault from favour, for *Psyché* at the Académie royale de Musique or the opera *Bellérophon* in 1678 and 1679. What here is of importance is that tragi-comédie, opera, ballet and drama dependent on spectacular effects are obviously more suitable vehicles for exploring an optimistic view of human nature than is tragedy, that Corneille turned away from tragedy towards the other genres shortly before devoting more of his energies to defending the "modernes" in the *Mer-*

cure Galant than to the stage, but that the "modernes" would not give up disputing the mastery of the tragic stage with Racine, putting up challenges to Racine's *Iphigénie* in 1674 and to his *Phèdre et Hippolyte* in 1677.

When Racine retired from the public theatre in 1677, Corneille, who had been writing comedies, including *L'Inconnu, comédie meslée d'ornemens* and *Le Triomphe des dames, comédie meslée d'ornemens, avec explication du combat à la barrière et de toutes les devises*, immediately stepped in with what turned out to be one of his successful straight tragedies, the 1678 *Le Comte d'Essex*, played significantly at the Hôtel de Bourgogne, the scene of Racine's great tragic successes, almost exactly a year after Racine's *Phèdre et Hippolyte*. What was at stake between Thomas Corneille and Racine, whose career as a dramatist intertwined with the younger Corneille's much more than it did with that of his elder brother Pierre, was much more than a battle between different genres for court and public attention. It concerned an underlying view of human nature which made elevated and dignified tragedy a less happy genre for Corneille than it was for a Racine fascinated by the destructive force of passion, and its accompanying guilt. The difficulty is to know whether to see *Le Comte d'Essex* as an opportunistic chance seized by Corneille to step into the vacancy of principal tragic dramatist; or as an attempt to create a type of tragic drama which would synthesize all that Corneille admired most in the work of his brother and in the work of Racine; or as yet another chance to capture the elevated tragic medium for a fundamentally "moderne" and optimistic exploration of the meaning of human experience.

Much that concerns Corneille's later journalistic activities is contained in the *Guide* entries on Donneau de Visé and on the *Mercure Galant*, particularly important for the Querelle des anciens et des modernes and the quarrel with La Bruyère which must be seen in its context. Accusations have been made against Corneille of mercenariness and mediocrity, of being the first writer to calculate and exploit the profitability of what was known to be tawdry work. Yet in the surprisingly unanimous judgement of his contemporaries he was industrious, warm-hearted, hard-working, and committed. Corneille's reception into the Académie française in January 1685, the year following the death of his brother, was the occasion for Racine's moving tribute to Pierre Corneille. Thereafter Corneille took seriously the lexicographic work of the Académie. His two *Dictionnaires* cost him immense amounts of labour, and he gradually went almost totally blind towards the end of his life. He also experienced considerable financial constraint. He died on 8 October 1709.

WORKS

Timocrate, the most commercially successful play staged in France during the 17th century, scarcely strikes us as a tragedy at all. It is, however, more than "an unbelievably complicated and absurd heroic melodrama," which is how it has been described. The source is the "Histoire d'Alcamène, roi des Scythes, et de la reine Ménalippe" from the eighth volume of La Calprenède's 1654 *Cléopâtre*, to which must be added details taken from Scudéry's 1635 tragi-comédie, *Le Prince déguisé*. The play was published with a long dedication to the duc de Guise, and an "au lecteur" defending it against accusations of

incredibility and of ending in such a way as to make the fifth act seem an unnecessary appendage, once "Cléomène" is revealed as Timocrate.

For four acts Timocrate, king of Crete, is disguised as Cléomène. The first scene, between Nicandre, a prince subject to the queen of Argos, and his confidant, makes clear how desirable a prize is Eriphile, the queen's daughter. Nicandre and two neighbouring kings, Cresphonte and Léontidas, are rivals for Eriphile's hand. "Cléomène," whose entry Corneille has carefully prepared for in the first scene, now enters to inquire after Timocrate who, as king of Crete, was the enemy of Argos, whose champion "Cléomène" was. He learns from Nicandre how Timocrate saved Crete from certain defeat by Argos, led by "Cléomène." The queen now enters and discusses with her daughter's three suitors, Nicandre, Cresphonte, and Léontidas, the offer of peace made by Timocrate in exchange for the hand of Eriphile. The scene in which the queen takes counsel from the three suitors, who advocate vengeance, and "Cléomène," who advocates acceptance, allows Corneille to put on the stage a searching discussion about the duties of sovereigns to their peoples and to their own dignity, about the relative claims of love and honour, and about the relative desirability of vengeance and peace. The queen, who has vowed to avenge her husband's death at the hands of the Cretans, offers the hand of Eriphile as a reward for the capture of Timocrate. "Cléomène," left alone with Nicandre, confesses to him his own love for Eriphile, to whose hand the aspirants at the end of the act are apparently Nicandre, Cresphonte, Léontidas, Timocrate, and "Cléomène."

Timocrate was written in 1656, the year in which Racine became 17, but already, as habitually in Racine's tragedies, the last major character enters at the beginning of the second act and, as in Racine, the secondary characters reflect the ordinary view of everyday reason rather than the elevated vision of the principal characters, in Racine generally distorted by passion. Why should Eriphile not marry Timocrate, asks her confidante, Cléone? Because, comes the answer from Eriphile, she loves Cléomène, whose advice it is that she should marry Timocrate. When in 1667 Racine staged *Andromaque* it is impossible not to suppose that he had at the back of his mind the century's most successful play. When Hermione said of Pyrrhus in *Andromaque*,

Ah! je l'ai trop aimé, pour ne le point haïr

(I [once] loved him too much not to hate him [now]).

it looks probable, given so much supporting evidence that he was drawing on Corneille, that he was remembering Eriphile's inability to rid herself of past love in spite of present hatred.

Je l'aimai, cet ingrat; oui, j'aimai Cléomène.
Mais qu'inutilement j'ose flatter ma peine,
Si malgré mon courroux par son crime enflammé
Je sens que j'aime encor, quand je dis que j'aimai!

(I loved him, that man without feeling; yes, I loved Cléomène./But how useless it is for me to try to assuage my suffering,/If in spite of my fury aroused by his offence/ I feel that I love him still when I say that I loved him once).

Corneille may only have been dramaturgically sowing the seed from which Racine, with a different background and in a generation with different imaginative needs, later reaped the corn, but it is Corneille who, building on his elder brother's exploration of the values of "gloire," begins again to explore love in terms of its destructive power. In those lines from *Timocrate* it has become a threat to the highest value of self-esteem based on personal merit, and not just one horn of the conventional tragicomic dilemma opposing love and duty. Corneille is reacting vigorously and immediately to the social world he inhabited. *Timocrate* is near enough to being exactly contemporaneous with the outbreak of préciosité (q.v.) as a social phenomenon, indicative not only of a desire to refine erotic relationships, but also of a fear of passion clear, for instance, in the 1654 Carte de Tendre from Madeleine de Scudéry's *Clélie*.

In the second scene of act II Eriphile dismisses Nicandre's aspirations to her hand on account, she says, of his insufficiently high rank, although, as Cléone points out in the next scene, she leaves him with some hope, having told him that her heart goes further towards him than towards Cresphonte and Léontidas. The act ends with a long scene between "Cléomène" and Eriphile, who reproaches him bitterly for his advice that her hand should be pledged to Argos's enemy, Timocrate, the king of Crete. He replies that he would expire in glory and despair if his advice were taken, and if she did marry Timocrate. Corneille contrives real suspense in an audience wondering how long the disguised Timocrate in love with Eriphile can possibly maintain his advice to her, in love with his disguised self as "Cléomène," that she should marry instead the king of her country's enemy. In view of the contemporary discussion of the need to justify rank by merit, Corneille is being courageously "moderne" in giving "Cléomène" the view that merit provides a claim to love superior to mere rank. Love itself is the supreme value, even if its satisfaction must be sacrificed. Unlike the love of the medieval courtly lover, the affection of "Cléomène" is clearly passionate.

> Renoncer pour l'amour au soin de sa fortune
> N'est que le foible effet d'une vertu commune,
> On a vu mille amants, dans ses moindres douceurs,
> Trouver la pente aisée au mépris des grandeurs,
> Et pour l'objet aimé, sans que rien les étonne,
> Quitter parents, amis, sceptre, trône, couronne;
> Mais il est inouï peut-être avant ce jour
> Qu'aucun ait immolé l'amour même à l'Amour.
> Pour consacrer mon nom au temple de Mémoire,
> C'est à moi que le Ciel en réservait la gloire

(To give up for love all care of fortune/Is nothing but the weak result of common virtue,/A thousand lovers have been seen, in love's lesser delights,/Finding easy the slope towards the contempt of honours,/And for the object of their love, without being deflected,/Leaving parents, friends, sceptre, throne, crown;/But it is unheard of perhaps before this day/For any to have sacrificed love itself to Love./To consecrate my name in the temple of memory,/It is for me that heaven has reserved the glory of that act).

The expression is hyperbolic, and only the irony of the situation prevents "Cléomène" from being ridiculous, but the intention of elevating passionate love into a life-enhancing force still shines forth in baroque splendour. In a way that is as metaphorically as it is literally true, Foucquet had not yet given way to Colbert. As for the rival princes,

> …ils n'ont rien en eux par-delà la naissance,
> Rien dont un grand courage ait lieu d'être jaloux,
> Hors l'illustre projet de soupirer pour vous

(…they have nothing in them beyond their birth,/Nothing of which great merit has reason to be jealous,/Except for the illustrious idea of sighing for you).

The political and social argument continues at a level which makes the play's success easy to understand. Is fame necessarily warranted? Are the exploits on which it is founded not sometimes evil? Corneille here is playing with the non-ethical forms of personal merit displayed by his brother's Cléopâtre in *Rodogune* of a dozen years earlier, and he is skilfully weaving together threads of political and social theory, concepts of merit, virtue, grandeur and rank, the ethical status of instinctive affection, and the ironic relationship of the two characters on the stage. The act ends on a further tightening of the irony as Eriphile leaves "Cléomène" to believe that he, too, might aspire to her hand if he were the conqueror of the enemy Timocrate.

The third act starts with a set of "stances" by Eriphile, probably inspired by those of the Infanta in *Le Cid*. Argos is winning the war, apparently on account of the valour of Nicandre, but then the queen enters to say that, just as victory was in sight, Timocrate had appeared and reversed the course of the war in favour of Crete. Cresphonte and Léontidas are dead. The queen has to enjoin Eriphile to keep her dignity and betray no emotion:

> …Gardez de rien faire paraître
> Qui démente le sang dont on vous a vu naître

(…Take care to reveal no emotion/Unworthy of the blood of which you were born).

Nicandre is a prisoner. "Cléomène" simply disappeared in the battle. Nicandre's confident, who is bringing the news, presumes "Cléomène" dead. At this point Nicandre enters, sent back by Timocrate. The queen, furious at Timocrate's act of generosity in releasing Nicandre, is surprised by the arrival of "Cléomène," whose safe return has already given cause for public rejoicing. He announces that he has captured Timocrate and claims his prize, the hand of Eriphile. Nicandre, believing he owes his rescue to "Cléomène," points out that he lacks the necessary princely rank. "Cléomène" replies that his very aspiring to the hand of Eriphile proves the nobility of his birth,

> Cette ambition même est un illustre signe
> Que ce que je suis né ne m'en rend pas indigne

(That ambition itself is an outstanding sign/That what I was born as does not make me unworthy of it).

To Nicandre's sarcasms "Cléomène" now retorts that it is easy enough to conquer by power of numbers, but that he owes his success to no one but himself. He appeals to the inviolability of the queen's promise, and asks for his rank to be taken on trust. The queen consents to the immediate betrothal. Act III ends with the assurance by Arcas, Nicandre's confident, that he still has a way of saving the situation for Nicandre, who reacts exactly as, 20 years later, Racine's Phèdre would more effectively react to Oenone's ruse in *Phèdre et Hippolyte*. Nicandre's words are

> Pressé trop vivement d'une atteinte mortelle,
> Sans rien examiner je laisse agir ton zèle

(Too badly upset by so mortal a blow,/Without looking into what you propose, I leave it all to you).

The fourth act tells us that Arcas has failed to get Timocrate to consent to be released from his imprisonment, but Nicandre, in spite of his desire to thwart the proposed marriage of Eriphile and "Cléomène," is appalled that Arcas has suggested to the queen that the imprisoned Timocrate is a false one, thereby impugning the honour of "Cléomène." Nicandre repudiates the ruse:

> Qu'à ce lâche dessein j'eusse abaissé mon âme!
> Non, Arcas, mon amour jaloux de son bonheur
> Peut attaquer son rang, mais non pas son honneur

(That I would have lowered myself to so base a purpose!/ No, Arcas, my love, jealous of his happiness/Can attack his rank, but not his honour).

It leaks out, however, that the prisoner cannot be Timocrate. Trasille, a prince subject to Crete and recently captured, does not recognize him. Nicandre learns it before "Cléomène," with whom he exchanges very effective stichomythia. Everything is to be left to Eriphile herself, who now enters. "Cléomène" refuses all pressure to reveal who he is, and Eriphile, who would be prepared to marry Timocrate if he were not king of Crete, leaves as her mother, the queen, enters. The queen will keep her word. Eriphile will marry "Cléomène," but only if he really is the conqueror of Timocrate.

Trasille is brought in. "Cléomène" tells him to speak. Does the queen have Timocrate "en son pouvoir (in her power)?" The words have of course two senses. No, Timocrate is not a prisoner in the fort, but yes, it is in the queen's power to grant Timocrate happiness in allowing Eriphile's marriage to "Cléomène," who now reveals his true identity. In the speech in which the queen expresses her confusion at finding "Timocrate haï dans Cléomène aimé (the hated Timocrate in the beloved Cléomène)," Corneille uses a half-line from his brother's *Cinna*. The final scene of act IV is brilliantly written. The queen is torn between her two vows, to avenge her husband through Timocrate's death, and to give the hand of Eriphile to the conqueror of Crete. Timocrate asks for and is granted permission to marry Eriphile before being executed.

When Eriphile hears what is to happen she immediately refuses her consent to be married. She asks Nicandre to save Timocrate. He refuses, alleging his duty to the state. Timocrate is now brought on stage, where he stays until the end. Eriphile reproaches him with the love which, as Cléomène, he had inspired in her. The queen joins them, intent on both marriage and execution, when news arrives that the town has been taken by the Cretans, led by Trasille, who enters and informs Timocrate that Argos is in his hands. The queen begs Timocrate to take her crown, so relieving her of the burden imposed on her

by her vow to seek his death. Nicandre had conspired to release Trasille, and is now invited by Timocrate to share his throne. The tragedy has a happy ending.

Historically, there can be no doubt about the importance of *Timocrate* in its relationship to the earlier work of Pierre Corneille, and the work of Racine still to begin, to préciosité, to the entourages of Guise and Foucquet, to the unities, which it keeps, to ways in which the baroque elements of disguise and reversals of fortune are combined with a determined imaginative effort to unite the twin forces of affection and admiration, and to new views about honour, non-ethical forms of moral grandeur, and the relationship between rank, authority, virtue, and merit. The social and political issues discussed certainly stretched the imaginations of 17th-century audiences, obviously willing to be convinced by the play's fundamentally optimistic resolution of the potential conflicts, especially between merit, authority, and affection.

Dramatically the piece is effective, and the professionalism of its construction can only in trivial ways be faulted. It is no doubt weakened by lacking depth of psychological penetration, and the happy dénouement is made possible only by an external event, Trasille's capture of Argos on behalf of Crete with the connivance of Nicandre, but the really important conflicts are powerfully examined, and the characters face real dilemmas. It is not at all clear that the court and the town were as wrong in making the play the greatest theatrical success of 17th-century Paris as subsequent critics have been in what must be regarded as their failure to discover why.

Stilicon marks the return of the now fashionable and profitable Corneille to the Hôtel de Bourgogne on 27 January 1660. *Timocrate* had been followed in 1657 by *Bérénice* and in 1658–59 by *Darius*. D'Aubignac's *Pratique du théâtre* of 1657 had forced Corneille's elder brother to rethink the principles of his dramaturgy in the first *Discours* of 1660. *Stilicon* may well have been influenced by the criticisms of Pierre Corneille by d'Aubignac, and by his elder brother's *Discours*. *Stilicon* certainly moves towards a greater emphasis on psychological verisimilitude than the earlier work. The play is dedicated to Mazarin.

Stilicon is the former tutor of Honorius, emperor of the west, and has two children with whom the play opens, his daughter Thermantie, the empress, and his son Eucherius, who loves Placidie, Honorius's sister. We are again immediately plunged into a tension between rank and merit. Placidie is too high-born for Eucherius but, as Thermantie points out,

> Elle a de la naissance, et vous de la vertu

(She has high birth, but you have merit).

Eucherius's love is involuntary:

> Un coeur n'est pas long-temps le maistre de ses voeux

(A heart is not for long master of its desires).

Thermantie and Eucherius are joined by Honorius and the captain of the guards, Marcellin. Honorius is upset at his sister's haughty insistence on the rights given her by birth, but Stilicon is sufficiently aggrieved to announce his intention to kill his ex-pupil and present son-in-law Honorius and put Eucherius in his place. The non-ethical nature of moral grandeur is canvassed in a couplet by Stilicon discussed by Clorante and Arimant in Donneau de Visé's 1663 *Nouvelles nouvelles*,

> Cet effort ne part point d'un courage abatu,
> Et pour faire un grand crime il faut de la vertu

(That effort proceeds from no mean courage,/And to commit a great crime strength of character is required).

In the second act we learn that Placidie does in fact love Eucherius, but that the aspirations to a throne with which her birth has endowed her have made her suppress her love.

> Eucherius me plaist; mais ce que je suis née
> Dans un si vaste orgueil pousse ma destinée,
> Qu'un Trône seul offert à mes brûlants desirs
> Me peut faire sans honte advoüer ses soupirs

(I love Eucherius; but what I was born/Urges me towards so vast a pride,/That only a throne offered to my burning ambitions/Could make me without shame allow his sighs).

There follows a long confrontation between Eucherius and Placidie, who urges Eucherius to be satisfied with loving her without reward, which he cannot be. Honorius has heard from Thermantie of the plot to kill him. Honorius asks Eucherius to find out more about the plot and confides in Stilicon, its author, who throws suspicion on Eucherius and then on Zenon, who was to carry out the attack for Stilicon. In the third act news is brought that Zenon has himself been murdered, and Honorius realizes that the author of the conspiracy against him must be either Stilicon or Eucherius. At the end of the act Stilicon still thinks he has the upper hand. The intrigue is kept alive by the use of surprising turns in events, as when Honorius is momentarily believed dead. He had been attacked, but we are no sooner told that Eucherius had saved his life than we hear that Eucherius himself was killed in the fighting. Placidie openly admits her love for him, and Stilicon his guilt, before he kills himself.

Ariane, of which a prose translation into English by Oscar Mandel appeared in 1982 and which has been thought to be Corneille's best play, is chiefly interesting because of the part it plays in Corneille's dialogue with Racine. Not all critics have liked it, and Mme de Sévigné thought it "fade (insipid)," although she considered La Champmeslé's entry as Ariane at the beginning of act II and her performance thereafter gave life to the piece. It was La Champmeslé who was to create Racine's Phèdre in *Phèdre et Hippolyte*, and Racine puts into that play verbal as well as other reminiscences of *Ariane*, inviting comparison, perhaps flattering Corneille by building on his success, or perhaps directly challenging Corneille by handling the Phaedra myth differently.

Ariane was probably performed for the first time at the Hôtel de Bourgogne, with La Champmeslé as the heroine, on 26 February 1672. There are numerous echoes of Racine, and the play appears to be a direct challenge to *Bérénice*. With *Le Comte d'Essex*, it is one of the two plays chosen by Voltaire for commentary after those of Pierre Corneille. The play starts when a conversation between Oenarus, king of Naxos, and his confident, Arcas, informs us that Oenarus is in love with Ariane, although Thésée is about to marry her, and that Thésée is waiting for the arrival of his friend Pirithoüs to share his happiness; Ariane returns Thésée's love. Oenarus, however, loves Ariane

and is jealous, while Thésée confides in Pirithoüs that he really loves not Ariane, but her sister, Phèdre. The first act ends with a scene between Thésée and Phèdre in which, in spite of their love for one another, Phèdre feels unable to forget her sister's love for Thésée and the debt of gratitude he has towards Ariane.

Ariane is aware both of Thésée's indifference and of Oenarus's passion, which Oenarus himself confirms to Thésée in act II scene 3. Much of the dramaturgy and the rhetoric is Racinian, especially the division of a single line into multiple speeches, and the broken syntax, with unfinished sentences to indicate emotion. Pirithoüs, aware of Thésée's passion, attempts to persuade Ariane to accept the wishes of her father, Minos, king of Crete, and marry Oenarus. The second act ends with a scene between Ariane and Phèdre, who agrees to plead with Thésée on Ariane's behalf although, as we already know, she returns Thésée's love for herself. The play consists largely in a series of emotional confrontations. Thésée persists in his rejection of Ariane, who in the fourth act accepts the homage of Oenarus, telling Phèdre this without knowing that it is for Phèdre that Thésée has deserted her.

There are differences between Corneille and Racine. Love may be uncontrollable for Corneille, but it is not unconcealable, as it generally is in Racine. It strikes for both once only. As Ariane says

> Les fortes passions ne touchent qu'une fois

(Strong passion moves us only once).

In both authors, the rejection of love can produce violently destructive jealousy. Corneille's Ariane seeks to destroy Thésée. His Phèdre thinks that her sister's jealousy is bound to result in her own death, and finally agrees to flee with Thésée to Athens. In the fifth act Ariane learns that it is Phèdre whom Thésée loves, and that Thésée has left by sea. It slowly becomes clear to Ariane that he has taken Phèdre with him. A note from Thésée to Pirithoüs is read to her. She throws herself on Pirithoüs's sword. The ending is ambiguous, but it is probable that Oenarus's first reaction is to revive Ariane from her swoon, probably modelled on that of Oreste in *Andromaque*, but that he finally lets her die.

> Elle semble pâmer. Qu'on la secoure. Vite!
> Sa douleur est un mal qu'un prompt remède irrite,
> Et c'en serait sans doute accroître les efforts
> Qu'opposer quelque obstacle à ses premiers transports

(She seems to be fainting. Help her. Quickly!/Her grief is an ill which a swift remedy makes worse,/And it would without doubt make its effects grow worse/If some obstacle were placed in the way of her first reactions).

PUBLICATIONS

[*Several of Corneille's plays were published only in the collected editions and are therefore not listed individually below.*]

Collections

Poèmes dramatiques de T. Corneille, 3, then 5 vols., 1661 (augmented 1666, 1669, 1682, 1692, 1706)
Théâtre complet de T. Corneille, 1881

Plays

Les Engagements du hasard, comédie (before 1650), 1657; English adaptations 1706 and 1707

Le Feint Astrologue, comédie, 1651; adapted by Dryden as *An Evening's Love,* 1671

D. Bertran de Cigarral, comédie (c. 1651), 1652

L'Amour à la mode (1651), 1653

Le Berger extravagant, pastorale burlesque; (1652), 1653; modern edition 1960

Le Geôlier de soi-même, comédie (1655), 1656

Timocrate, tragédie (1656), 1658; modern edition 1970; in Bibliothèque de la Pléiade *Théâtre du XVIIe siècle,* vol. 2, 1986

Darius, tragédie (1659), 1659

La Mort de l'empereur Commode, tragédie (1657), 1659

Les Illustres Ennemis, comédie (1655), 1657

Maximian, tragédie (1662), 1662

Stilicon, tragédie (1660), 1660

Antiochus, tragi-comédie (1666), 1666

Laodice, reyne de Cappadoce, tragédie (1668), 1668

Le baron d'Albikrac, comédie (1667), 1669

La Mort d'Annibal, tragédie (1669), 1670

La Comtesse d'Orgueil, comédie (1670), 1671

Ariane, tragédie (1672), 1672; re-created as *Ariadne,* 1982; in Bibliothèque de la Pléiade *Théâtre du XVIIe siècle,* vol. 2, 1986

Théodat, tragédie (1672), 1673

Circé, tragédie ornée de machines, de changements de théâtre et de musique, with Donneau de Visé, 1675

L'Inconnu, comédie mêlée d'ornements (1675), 1676 [music by Charpentier]

D. César d'Avalos, comédie (1674), 1676; adapted as *Tom Essence* (1676), 1677

Le Triomphe des dames, comédie mêlée d'ornements..., 1676

Le Comte d'Essex, tragédie (1678), 1678

Psyché, tragédie [libretto in collaboration, music by Lulli], 1678

Bellérophon, tragédie [opera libretto, music by Lulli], 1679

La Devineresse: see Donneau de Visé

La Pierre philosophale, comédie mêlée de spectacles, with Donneau de Visé, 1681

Camma, reine de Galatie (1661), 1690

Le Galand doublé, comédie (1660), 1690

La Mort d'Achille, tragédie (1673), 1690

Persée et Démétrius, tragédie (1662), 1690

Pyrrhus, roi d'Epire, tragédie (1663), 1665

Le Charme de la voix, comédie (1656), 1691

Médée, tragédie en musique, 1693 [music by Charpentier]

Bradamante, tragédie, 1696

Les Dames vengées, comédie, with Donneau de Visé (1695), 1696

Other

Pièces choisies d'Ovide traduites en vers françois, 1670

Notes on the *Remarques* of Vaugelas, 1687

Le Dictionnaire des arts et des sciences, 1694

Les Métamorphoses d'Ovide traduites en vers françois, 3 vols., 1697

Traduction des Fables d'Esope et de Philelphe, 1702

Observations de l'Académie française sur les Remarques de M. de Vaugelas, 1704

Dictionnaire universel géographique et historique, 1708.

Biographical and critical studies

Reynier, Gustave, *Thomas Corneille, sa vie et son théâtre,* 1892

Voxvrie, L. van Reninghe de, *Descendance de Thomas Corneille,* 1959

Collins, D.A., *Thomas Corneille, Protean Dramatist,* 1966

CRÉBILLON *fils,* **Claude-Prosper Jolyot de, 1707–1777.**

Novelist.

LIFE

On Crébillon's family background, see the next entry, devoted to his father. Crébillon, born on 14 February 1707, was the elder of two sons, and the only one to survive youth. His mother died in February 1711 when Crébillon was touching four years of age. His father was ruined in Law's bankruptcy. Crébillon's father, known as a writer of tragedies, was also a censor. Voltaire became obsessed by Crébillon's father as a rival dramatist, a hostile censor, and an enemy at court. Although Crébillon's father was short of money, Crébillon was sent to the socially smart Jesuit school in Paris, Louis-le-Grand, where, however there were no tuition fees and he was apparently encouraged to apply for admission to the Order.

In spite of a recent increase of interest and the work of a number of scholars, very little about Crébillon's life is known. A smattering of anecdotal gossip from his contemporaries is almost all we have. The picture which emerges is one of a tall, willowy, serious young man, with a cultivated dry wit. He was twice to be exiled, once probably more for satirical temerity than for licentiousness, and once on moral grounds, before in 1759 becoming through the mediation of Mme de Pompadour, as his father had been, himself one of the royal censors. As a young man Crébillon seems to have taken part in the composition of parodies which have not survived, and to have behaved more with dandified indolence than with real elegance, chic or moral deviance. He is known to have frequented the theatre and to have associated with the smart upper-class following of the Italian company, for whom the parodies were devised, but his behaviour was on the whole discreet.

"He knew women as much as it was possible to know them," wrote Sébastien Mercier in his anonymously published 1781 *Tableau de Paris,* and we know that Crébillon later helped with Charles Collé and Alexis Piron to found the "dîners du Caveau" held on the 1st and 16th of each month at the provisioner Landel's establishment at the Carrefour de Buci. These dinners were attended by Helvétius, Boucher, Rameau, and a number of light-hearted but witty authors and others connected with the arts. They read works to one another and sharpened their wits at one another's expense. A good epigram was rewarded with a glass of wine, and its victim was obliged to drink water. As a young man, Crébillon's relationship with his impoverished, ideologically conservative, but socially eccentric father was poor, although the son cared for his father during his final six months of illness in 1762.

Crébillon's first published works were the 1730 *Le Sylphe; ou, Songe de Mme de R***, écrit par elle-même à Mme de S**** and the 1732 *Lettres de la marquise de M*** au comte de R****, exploring before Richardson the possibilities of the letter form. In 1734 yielding to the fascination the oriental conte always held for him Crébillon published *L'Ecumoire; ou, Tanzaï et Néadarné, histoire japonaise*, for which he was imprisoned at Vincennes. The imprisonment, by lettre de cachet, was presumably due to satirical allusions to the anti-Jansenist (q.v.) constitution *Unigenitus*, references to Louis XV, a caricature of cardinal Dubois, who had died in 1723, and the use of the phrase "Le Grand Singe (the great monkey)" to refer to God. Whether or not, as has been both alleged and denied, *L'Ecumoire* was offensive to the ebullient duchesse du Maine, Crébillon was released after ten days on the intervention of the princesse de Conti, and thereafter taken up by the duchesse du Maine and her liberal intellectual coterie at Sceaux, which now opened to him the whole of salon society. He may have met his future wife in the salon of Mme de Sainte-Maure, and he frequented that of Mme de Margy, soon to become his mistress and to inspire the figure of Mme de Lursay in *Les Egarements*.

In 1736 Crébillon published the first part, in 1738 the second and third parts, of his best-known work, *Les Egarements du coeur et de l'esprit; ou, Mémoires de Monsieur de Meilcour*, an avowedly fictional memoir novel. In 1742 came the lubricious *Le Sopha couleur de rose, conte moral*, and another lettre de cachet; Crébillon was exiled 120 kilometres from Paris on 7 April 1742 at the demand of Mme de Pompadour. The terms of the exile were neither observed nor enforced, and on 22 July, protected by Marville, the lieutenant of police, Crébillon was given permission to return. He had argued that his text had been commissioned by Frederick of Prussia, and that the manuscript had mysteriously been leaked to the printers, a story which the authorities at least pretended to believe.

It was on reading his novels that Henrietta Maria Stafford made advances to him. She was the innocent, devout, gentle daughter of the chamberlain of James II, said by Charles Collé in his diary for January 1750 to have been poor and "shockingly ugly," and to have had a squint. She lived with Crébillon for four years before, aged 34, she married him on 23 April 1748. From 1749 Crébillon solicited the succession of his father's post as censor, to be granted only in 1759. Crébillon appears to have remained devoted to his wife until she died in 1756, and conscientiously to have exercised his office of censor. The only story on that subject is that one author, when requested by Crébillon to remove the word "boudoir" from his verses, replied by inquiring where, then, should he put Crébillon's sofa? Some time after 1756 Crébillon founded a club, the Pelletier, where he must have met Sterne, Garrick, and Wilkes. Mme de Pompadour had him paid a further 2,000 livres of pension from 1762, the year of his father's death.

Crébillon's later writing is often experimental, using, for instance, the dialogue as well as the memoir and letter forms, but he did not succeed in writing any single great work, and never aspired to a literary register beyond pleasant, graceful, and witty 18th-century suggestiveness. He contributed even late in life to collective volumes. Certain attributions to him are disputed, but he continued to publish work, some of which was written a score of years before it appeared, including *La Nuit et le moment; ou,*

Les Matinées de Cythère, dialogue, written in 1737 and published in 1755; *Le Hasard du coin du feu, dialogue moral*, written in 1737–1740 and published in 1763; *Ah, quel conte! conte politique et astronomique*, eight volumes published in 1754; and *Les Heureux Orphelins, histoire imitée de l'anglois*, four volumes published in 1754, part of which are translations. The other two works which are confidently attributed to Crébillon are the *Lettres de la duchesse de *** au duc de **** of 1769 and the *Lettres athéniennes, extraites du portefeuille d'Alcibiade* of 1771.

Crébillon was poor in later life, and died soon after he was 70, on 12 April 1777.

WORKS

Although Crébillon was a sometimes successful experimenter with innovatory literary techniques, his real interest lies in his graceful and epigrammatic exploration of the more superficial forms of emotional experience and amorous psychological warfare, and his examination of the new boundaries required by 18th-century society for the regulation of the manifestations of a refined and sophisticated sensuality. The cultivation and elegant exploitation of openly erotic but socially respectable relationships had necessarily to occur in a society which had by and large come to accept that natural impulses were neither plainly evil nor of their nature destructive. Crébillon's work must be seen in the context of the imaginative investigation required in the mid-18th century to establish new moral norms as well as new codes of social behaviour and restraint. The new confidence about nature's potential had led to new attitudes, admitting to polite social intercourse some expression of human nature's sensual needs.

Human nature's harmony with physical nature, even in its more awesome aspects, the other chief component of a freshly emerging sensibility in the mid-18th century, was to be a principal focus of concern for a slightly later generation of imaginative writers. Crébillon's fascination with the oriental, for instance in *L'Ecumoire* and *Le Sopha*, none the less already reflected the link being built between the new attitudes to sensuality asserting themselves in 18th-century society and the new rapport between human and physical nature which was the other half of the diptych.

Le Sylphe; ou, Songe de Mme de R***, écrit par elle-même à Mme de S*** is written in letter form. There is much grace, some wit, occasional elegance, but no great psychological profundity, only an amusing cynicism. There is no great pessimism, either. Instead there is a preoccupation with the problems to which Crébillon's age urgently needed new solutions, concerning how rules of behaviour, moral values, and the promptings of instinct are related to one another.

> Il est rare qu'une jolie femme soit prude, ou qu'une prude soit jolie femme, ce qui la condamne à se tenir justement à cette vertu que personne n'ose attaquer, et qui est sans cesse chagrine du repos dans lequel on la laisse languir. D'ailleurs, il n'y a point de femme qui n'ait quelque faible, et ce faible, quelque bien déguisé qu'il soit, n'échappe jamais à la recherche opiniâtre de l'amant. La voluptueuse se rend au plaisir des sens. La délicate, au charme de sentir son coeur occupé. La curieuse, au désir de s'instruire. Il en

coûterait trop à l'indolente pour refuser. La vaine perdrait trop, si ses appâts étaient ignorés; elle veut lire dans la fureur des désirs d'un amant l'impression qu'elle peut faire sur les hommes. L'avare cède au vil amour des présents. L'ambitieuse, aux conquêtes éclatantes; et la coquette, à l'habitude de se rendre

(It is rare for a pretty woman to be a prude, or for a prude to be a pretty woman, which condemns prudes to keeping precisely to that virtue which no one dares attack, but which ceaselessly frets at the peace in which it is left to languish. But there is no woman without a weak spot, and however well it is covered up, that weak spot never escapes the obstinate search of a lover. If she is voluptuous, she will yield to the pleasure of her senses; if sensitive, to the charm of feeling her heart involved; if curious, to the desire to find out. It would cost a lazy woman too much effort to refuse. A vain one would lose too much if her bait were not taken: she needs to read in the overwhelming desires of a lover the impression she can make on men. The miserly woman yields to the base desire for presents; the ambitious one to brilliant conquests; the flirt to the habit of giving in).

Crébillon has been accused of deep pessimism, of the cynical pulverization of love into pleasure, and praised for his lack of moral prejudice, but he is a manifest optimist, seeking a path between the socially attractive and the emotionally significant, and attempting to define the rules appropriate to quite new moral assumptions. He cannot here be regarded as taking any pessimistic view of human nature, or any attitude more negative than that of worldly salon cynicism. He is contributing not very seriously to something which was itself quite serious, the establishment of new social norms in the light of known natural impulses, patterns of behaviour, and new moral attitudes. The difficulty now is to see the seriousness without investing Crébillon with a solemnity he sought to avoid, and without condemning either his manifest fascination with techniques of seduction, or his general preference for keeping sensual gratifications free from emotional entanglements. The literary register is banter or persiflage, with an undertow of social seriousness.

Too rigid a code of "scrupuleuse délicatesse (punctilious restraint)," so ridiculous today, runs a passage in *Le Sopha*, was probably always more tedious than upright, but Crébillon is also aware of a nostalgia for a depth of emotional dedication and laments, again in *Le Sopha*,

Nous voulons satisfaire notre vanité, faire sans cesse parler de nous; passer de femme en femme; pour n'en pas manquer une, courir après les conquêtes, même les plus misérables; plus vains d'en avoir eu un certain nombre, que de n'en posséder qu'une digne de plaire; les chercher sans cesse et de ne les aimer jamais

(We want to satisfy our vanity, have ourselves spoken of the whole time; pass from woman to woman; in order not to miss one, to run after any conquest, even the most wretched; prouder to have had a certain number than to possess one worthy of pleasing; always looking for them and never loving them).

In the earlier works, in spite of snatches of gossip and satire and

a strong interest in seduction, the interest lies in the interplay of feelings and the manipulation of erotic prey by predators of either sex, and in shifts of tone and mood. The intricate stylization of the social rules of erotic behaviour which turn it into an elaborate game keeps vulgarity at bay, although it also prevents any real psychological profundity, and occasionally, as in *Le Sopha*, Crébillon allows the titillation to take over too absolutely from any seriousness of purpose. The story is narrated by a Hindu whose soul transmigrates into a sofa and recounts what is happening on it. Two virgins are making love.

Les Egarements du coeur et de l'esprit; ou, Memoires de M. de Meilcour was originally intended to be very much longer than it is. The first part of the novel as we have it was published in 1736 by Prault, and the second two parts by Gosse and Néaulme in 1738. There are five principal characters. The fictional first-person narrator, M. de Meilcour, writes of his life from the age of 17, essentially concentrating on his relationship with three women, the 40-year-old marquise de Mursay, the pretty and virtuous young Hortense de Théville, and the old coquette, Mme de Senanges, of whom Mme de Mursay is jealous. The fifth main character is the worldly-wise comte de Versac, introduced towards the end of the first part, whose function is to urge Meilcour knowingly in the accepted directions, so allowing him to portray himself as hesitant and undecided while moving the story on.

The novel starts with a dedication to Crébillon's father and a preface, in which Crébillon, not Meilcour, addresses the reader. After a brief but highly intelligent disquisition about the novel as such, Crébillon sets down his intentions:

On verra dans ces Mémoires un homme tel qu'ils sont presque tous dans une extrême jeunesse, simple d'abord et sans art, et ne connaissant pas le monde où il est obligé de vivre. La première et la seconde parties roulent sur cette ignorance et sur ses premiers amours. C'est, dans les suivantes, un homme plein de fausses idées, et pétri de ridicules, et qui est moins entraîné encore par lui-même, que par des personnes intéressées à lui corrompre le coeur, et l'esprit. On le verra enfin, dans les dernières, rendu à lui-même, devoir toutes ses vertus à une femme estimable; voilà quel est l'objet des *Egarements*...

(A man will be seen in these 'Mémoires' as most of them are in extreme youth, simple at first, artless, and ignorant of the world in which he has to live. The first and second parts turn on that ignorance and on his first loves. In the following parts he is full of wrong ideas, a ridiculous figure, still impelled less by himself than by those with an interest in corrupting his heart and his mind. Finally he will be seen in the last parts restored to himself, owing all his virtues to an estimable woman. That is the purpose of the *Egarements*...).

Crébillon plainly intended to write more than he did, a novel of initiation into adulthood and establishment, which is incidentally not at all a full-scale Bildungsroman, at this date still inconceivable.

There are weaknesses. The analysis of feeling tends to be abstract, the story diffuse, and the generalizations about social, and especially erotic relationships too pithy and clever to be true, let alone profound. But the novel brims over with intelligent observation and cultivated feeling, seeking gently for a resolution of the equation in which the moral norms, appropriate social restraints, and instinctive drives are unknowns to be given values which make the reconciliation possible. The novel was intended to explore possible avenues of reconciliation, and it makes its way forward with intelligence and skill.

Meilcour was high-born, and would be left money by his widowed mother. His education had been only modest, and at 17 he had entered the world seeking pleasure. Passionate, and with a lively imagination, Meilcour none the less sought satisfaction for his heart, and thought to find it in pleasure.

The style suggests that Crébillon was aware of the danger of expecting too long an attention span from his reader. Temptingly quotable epigrammatic wit is everywhere, mostly the cynical sort which might be discussed after dinner in an 18th-century gentleman's club in London as easily as in Paris. In a culture in which instinctive urges were beginning to be sentimentalized into the sources of beautiful and virtuous relationships, it cannot be regarded as more than light-weight urbanity to define love as an exchange "often without taste, in which convenience is preferred to sympathy, interest to pleasure, and vice to feeling." After a few pages of reflections of this level of profundity, Meilcour begins to tell us about Mme de Mursay.

That register of urbane cynicism continues, sardonic perhaps, and possibly, taken in the totality of Crébillon's oeuvre, indicative of real doubts about the perfectibility of nature and society, but certainly not itself intended at any very serious level, except possibly that of psychological perceptivity, at which it is no worse than graciously shallow. In fact the delicacy with which Meilcour recounts the way in which he allowed Mme de Mursay to initiate him sexually is almost exquisite. She does not "seduce" him; she plays a clever, elaborate, strictly regulated game to achieve her aim. The interplay of feelings, thoughts, reflected on years later by the Meilcour who is writing the memoirs, may well too easily be generalized in the text, but the care with which Crébillon recounts the effects striven for and achieved by Mme de Mursay is psychologically compelling.

Meilcour believes Hortense de Théville at first to be in love with the marquis de Germeuil, and it is Versac who nudges him in the direction of Mme de Senanges. The novel stops without ending, and it would have taken little ingenuity to spin its plot out indefinitely. It is a delicate small masterpiece, depicting the interplay of youthful ardour, social codes and moral proprieties. It teaches no lessons, presupposes no rules, and is historically important for its role in developing the fictional investigation of the arsenal of psychological weaponry that can be deployed in pursuit of erotic ambitions. Interest in Crébillon *fils* is increasing. It is to be hoped that his work will not be taken on a level of literary, psychological, or moral seriousness for which it was patently not intended.

PUBLICATIONS

Collections

Collection complète des oeuvres de M. de C. Fils, 14 vols., 1777
Oeuvres complètes, 5 vols., 1929–30

Fiction

Le Sylphe; ou, Songe de Mme de R***, écrit par elle-même à Mme de S***, 1730

Lettres de la marquise de M*** au comte de R***, 1733 (modern edition 1970); as *Letters from the Marchioness de M****, 1737
L'Ecumoire; ou, Tanzaï et Néadarné, histoire japonaise, 2 vols., 1734
Les Egarements du coeur et de l'esprit; ou, Mémoires de M. de Meilcour, 1736–38 (modern edition 1961); as *The Wanderings of the Heart and Mind; or, Memoirs of M. de Meilcour*, 1751
Le Sopha couleur de rose, conte moral, 2 vols., 1742; as *The Sopha*, 1742
Ah! quel conte! conte politique et astronomique, 8 vols., 1754
Les heureux orphelins, histoire imitée de l'anglois, 4 vols., 1754; as *The Happy Orphans*, 1770
La Nuit et le moment; ou, Les Matinées de Cythère, dialogue, 1755; as *The Opportunities of a Night*, 1925
Le Hasard du coin du feu, dialogue moral, 1763; as *Fortunes in the Fire*, 1927
Lettres de la duchesse de *** au duc de ***, 2 vols., 1769
Lettres athéniennes, extraites du portefeuille d'Alcibiade, 4 vols., 1771

Biographical and critical studies

Aby, Robert Peter, *The Problem of Crébillon fils*, 1955
Cherpack, Clifton, *An Essay on Crébillon fils*, 1962
Sturm, E., *Crébillon fils et le libertinage au dix-huitième siècle*, 1970

CRÉBILLON *père*, Prosper Jolyot, sieur de, 1674–1762.

Dramatist.

LIFE

Crébillon was born at Dijon on 13 January 1674, son of a royal notary, who on 14 January 1679 became maître clerc and in 1695 the sole greffier of the Dijon Chambre des Comptes, where his own father had been huissier. The family had been noble since the mid-15th century, and on 3 August 1686 Crébillon's father acquired the estate of Crais-Billon—the name had been corrupted into Crébillon—10 kilometres south of Dijon. Crébillon's mother, Henriette Gagnard, was the daughter of the lieutenant-general of Beaune and of Anne de Bretagne. Crébillon was the eldest of four children, three sons and a daughter. Like his predecessors, the Corneille brothers, and his future adversary, Voltaire, Crébillon was educated by the Jesuits. He attended their school at Dijon before registering as a barrister at the parlement de Paris, although probably with no intention of pleading. He had studied law almost certainly at Besançon, and in Paris worked in the offices of a procureur, Louis Prieur, at the Châtelet.

The Jesuits had noted that Crébillon, although very gifted,

"lived in the clouds." On his arrival in Paris he lived the life of a fashionable layabout, but impressed his superior by the constructive, if youthfully vivacious criticisms he made of the already great theatrical names of Pierre Corneille and Racine. Prieur encouraged his able but idle subordinate to try his own hand. The moment was propitious. Racine's retirement in 1677 had left as principal tragic authors the abbé Claude Boyer, who retired in 1682 for 13 years after the failure of *Artaxerxe*, and Jacques Pradon. The duchesse de Bouillon and the Vendômes sought to promote a younger generation, including the now forgotten Gaspard Abeille, Jean de la Chapelle, and du Boulay, but only Jean Galbert de Campistron, another Vendôme protégé, seemed for a moment able to dominate the stage. However, he turned away from the theatre, and neither Longepierre nor La Grange-Chancel fulfilled the hopes placed in them. Three or four authors tried their hands, but are now totally forgotten. By 1700 the supply of high-quality new tragedies had simply dried up.

There was a reason for this situation. Public taste had changed. The partisans of the "modernes" in the Querelle des anciens et des modernes (q.v.) were clearly victorious. People's awareness and attitudes were changing fast, as the flamboyance unleashed at court by the political ascendancy of Louvois gave way to a consciousness of military defeat, economic bankruptcy, and social deprivation, and as taste, metaphorically preparing itself for Marivaux, responded more to La Bruyère, Fénelon, and Fontenelle than to the generation of writers immediately preceding theirs. Tragedy could no longer depend on the sophisticated analysis of violent passion explored by the aristocratic literature of the 1670s. If tragedy was to survive as a dramatic genre into the 18th century, it was going to have to depend on a more optimistic underlying view of human nature, and therefore also for its tragic effects on such devices as chance, mistakes, recognitions, horrors, abductions, escapes, disguises, mistaken identities, and on-stage violence, and the generally more heartsearingly emotional devices on which first Crébillon and then Voltaire were to rely. Such devices were optimistic because they allowed the dramatist to avoid relating tragedy to guilt or other personal defects, so substituting misfortune for sin.

Legend recounts that Prieur heard Crébillon pacing up and down night after night in the upstairs room of his house near the Place Maubert, and confronted him with having taken his advice. Crébillon showed him "La Mort des enfants de Brute." It was turned down, but apparently the Comédie-Française, formed from the amalgamation of the three companies of Molière, the Marais, and the Hôtel de Bourgogne, and, since the expulsion of the Italians in 1697, enjoying monopoly rights to present the "straight" theatre of spoken dialogue in Paris, while rejecting Crébillon's play encouraged him to return. Crébillon never published his text and burnt it shortly before his death, but was apparently at the time exceedingly angry, denouncing the company and swearing he would never again expose himself to a humiliation of that sort.

He did none the less return with *Idoménée*, accepted on 10 September 1705 and played on 29 December, and given a decent 13 performances, although Crébillon had to re-work the final act within 24 hours after the first performance. The tragedy's success clearly depended on the strong element of terror in the plot, even more prominent as the mainspring of Crébillon's second successful tragedy, *Atrée et Thyeste*, played on 14 March 1707. Crébillon's father had just remarried after 20 years of widowhood, and Crébillon himself had got to know the daughter of the apothecary in the Place Maubert, Marie-Charlotte Péaget, 22 years old at the beginning of 1707, whose family also came from Burgundy. On Sunday 23 January the banns of marriage were called between Crébillon and Marie-Charlotte. A fee was paid in lieu of the prescribed calling of the banns on the two subsequent Sundays, and on Monday 31 January the wedding took place in a church just outside Paris. Marie-Charlotte bore him their first child, known to posterity as Crébillon *fils*, on 14 February, a fortnight after the wedding and a month before the first night of the new tragedy. The couple moved into the bride's parents' house, and Crébillon allowed it to be understood that the marriage had taken place some time previously. Crébillon's wife bore him another son on 9 November 1709, but he died young.

Crébillon's mother had died on 18 July 1686, having left everything to her husband except 1,000 livres for each of her three sons, Crébillon and his brothers, Melchior and Pierre, to be paid on their father's death. Crébillon's father did not attend Crébillon's wedding, and himself was to die on Christmas Eve 1707. Crébillon, who had been expecting to inherit enough money to be of independent means, went to Burgundy for the settlement of the estate, only to find that his father had never finished paying for his office, and that he had died consumed with debt. Law cases were still unresolved in 1720, and all Crébillon himself ever received was the original 1,000 livres, together with some 200 livres of accumulated interest.

He returned from Dijon, now Monsieur de Crébillon by right and not just by courtesy, with a third tragedy, *Electre*, successfully played on 14 December 1708. At this point in his career, Crébillon could reasonably expect election to the Académie française. There were seven vacancies between 1708 and 1711, but Crébillon was opposed by Houdar de la Motte, whom he had foolishly allowed himself to lampoon. La Motte was himself elected in 1710 and Crébillon was not elected until La Motte died in 1731. He was also opposed by J.-B. Rousseau on account of his association with the patrons of the café Laurent, on whom Rousseau blamed the failure of his plays. None the less *Rhadamiste et Zénobie*, presented on 23 January 1711 and generally considered Crébillon's best play, was sufficiently successful to run through two editions in eight days, and to continue its run after the Easter re-opening. Just over three weeks after the opening, Marie-Charlotte died of congestion of the lungs, leaving Crébillon with two young sons and very little to live on, although he was certainly receiving more than his office and his dramatic writing were bringing in. He did not return to the theatre until 7 February 1714, when *Xerxès* flopped and was taken off after two performances.

Help came from powerful but unidentified friends, through whom Crébillon was given the post of receiver of fines at the Cour des Aides on 2 August 1715. He also managed to speculate and enrich himself with Law's reform of the economic system until, like everyone else, he was ruined by it, receiving only 2,000 livres for one 57,000-livre bond. Although documents testify to the reality of the transactions, no one has been able to trace the source of Crébillon's original funds. As a result of the financial crash, Crébillon's post was also suppressed, leaving him with only what he had managed to save from the disaster. *Sémiramis*, played on 10 April 1717, had only seven performances, and Crébillon did not come back to the stage until 1726 with the more successful *Pyrrhus* of 29 April.

Crébillon had moved house on the death of his wife, and then again to a more modest residence when his post was suppressed.

His old dandified existence had been left behind, with its fine furniture and well-tailored clothes, and he took to perpetual pipe-smoking, even when visiting other people, and to living like a recluse, surrounded by stray dogs and cats, reading novels of galanterie, and composing plays which he did not bother to set down. On the death of the diplomat Leriget de la Faye in 1731 Crébillon was elected on 17 September to his place in the Académie. Voltaire, with whom he was not yet on bad terms, accompanied him on some of the formal visits to the other academicians which custom prescribed. Crébillon made his acceptance speech on 27 September in verse.

For a while Crébillon was attached to the Condé household at the Petit Luxembourg. In 1733 he was appointed royal censor, reading for approval books mostly in proof, but in 1735 he also became police censor, which gave him responsibility for the censorship of works for performance. It has been suggested, but is unlikely, that reservations Crébillon may have had about Voltaire's *Mahomet* were the cause of Voltaire's later antagonism.

Crébillon was perturbed when his son was exiled from Paris in 1742, but he was soon allowed to return, and in 1745 Crébillon himself received a pension through the good offices of Mme de Pompadour. He was also made a royal librarian, charged together with Danchet, the original censor of his *Sémiramis*, with buying books for the king's library. As elected director of the Académie for 1744–45, Crébillon had formally congratulated the king on the recovery of his health on 17 November 1744, and on various pretexts his emoluments as royal librarian were raised to 4,000 livres annually. *Catalina* had been one of the pieces read by Crébillon when Voltaire had accompanied him on the formal visits preceding election to the Académie. Crébillon now finished the play and read it at Choisy to Mme de Pompadour on 4 September 1748. The king paid for lavish costumes for the first performance on Friday 20 December 1748, attended by Mme de Pompadour. The king was personally concerned that Crébillon should have a success, asking Mme de Pompadour after the first night whether "we" had won. In fact the piece ran for 20 performances.

In 1748 Crébillon was 74. The quarrel with Voltaire had certainly broken out soon after Voltaire's *Sémiramis* had been played on 28 August. Crébillon had, to Voltaire's fury but fully in accordance with the ordinary norms, licensed the Italians to play a parody of it. The question is what, if anything, had Crébillon done to make Voltaire embark on a series of plays on subjects already treated by Crébillon, including *Sémiramis* which had been Crébillon's worst failure? Of the nine subjects used by Crébillon, five were re-worked by Voltaire, with *Sémiramis* in 1748, *Oreste* of 1750 using the subject from Crébillon's *Electre*, *Rome sauvée* of 1750 using *Catalina*, *Octave et le jeune Pompée* of 1764 using *Le Triumvirat; ou, La Mort de Cicéron* of 1754, and finally *Les Pélopides* of 1771 using Crébillon's *Atrée et Thyeste*. Voltaire pointed out in a letter of 10 November to d'Argental and in one of the 28th to Baculard d'Arnaud that Crébillon's own *Sémiramis* had not even been honoured by a parody. He tried to cap *Catalina* with his own 1752 *Rome sauvée* on the same subject. For a while Crébillon became a serious obsession for Voltaire.

Meanwhile, and no doubt partly to manifest his hostility to Voltaire, Louis XV paid for the magnificent Louvre quarto edition of Crébillon's works to be published in 1750, bringing Crébillon 6,000 livres. He was now earning that amount annually, but was still being pressed by creditors, who brought a case to distrain his literary rights but lost on the grounds that the products of the human mind were inalienable. *Le Triumvirat; ou, La Mort de Cicéron* was played on 29 December 1754 and ran for only ten performances. Although he was 80 that year, Crébillon started another play, but completed only three acts, which have been lost. During his last years he was attacked by some of those whose work he had censored, but remained unperturbed and in good health until 1 January 1762. His son then came to sleep in his room and care for him in his sickness. Crébillon died on 17 June.

WORKS

All we have from Crébillon's hand are nine five-act tragedies in alexandrines. No fragments, sketches, prose, comedy, or anything else at all except the prefaces, half a dozen letters, and the discours made on reception into the Académie. His early work undoubtedly found a wave of public demand and, whether he led public taste or was led by it, produced just what was required, formal five-act verse tragedy resting no more on the refined analysis of passions, but not yet cloyingly sentimental, no longer necessarily dependent on the great incidents of Greek myth and Roman history, but not yet systematically exploiting modern, and even geographically remote subjects on the tragic stage. By very early in the century it had become dangerous to allude even vaguely, in the guise of historical plots, to any current political situation or court scandal, or to draw attention to the plight of the people of France.

Crébillon hit on the only possible way in which the formal declamatory tradition of the French tragic stage could be continued in the second decade of the 18th century. He was challenged only when the regent lifted the prohibition on playing Racine's *Athalie*, whose first public performance on 3 March 1717 started a run of 14 performances leading up to the annual closure. The first new piece after the re-opening was the near-failure of Crébillon's *Sémiramis*, after which he presented nothing new for nine years. In 1718, as sentiment changed again, the most important new play was Voltaire's *Oedipe*, and by the end of the century's second decade neither Racine's sacred plays, riding on his reputation, nor even Crébillon's new mixture corresponded any longer to the imaginative needs of the public. Racine's *Esther*, reduced to three acts and stripped of its chorus, was given on 8 May 1722, but had only eight performances, and the next great success was La Motte's 1723 *Inès de Castro*.

As a result, it is as difficult to think of Crébillon succeeding with the Italian company, primarily devoted to mimed farce and light comedy, when it returned to Paris in 1716, as it is to think of Marivaux finding long-term success with the Comédie-Française, still dedicated to serious comedy and declamatory tragedy. It is generally agreed that Crébillon's fourth play, *Rhadamiste et Zénobie,* was his best. It was followed by two failures: a modest success nine years later, the 1748 *Catalina*, on the stocks for a score of years, finished virtually by royal command, paid for by the king, and championed by him against the talented but annoysome Voltaire 22 years after Crébillon's previous play; and then a final piece six years after that.

Since Crébillon could no longer depend on the analysis on the stage of the raw effects of passion, however motivated, he was forced to depend on complicated intrigues as well as on horror, and his new formula made it difficult to sustain tension, and therefore interest. Boileau naturally preferred the old order, and it was after seeing the first tragedies of Crébillon that he wrote

J'ai trop vécu; à quels Visigoths je laisse en proie la scène française! Les Boyers et les Pradons que nous avons tant bafoués, étaient des aigles auprès de ceux-ci

(I have lived too long: what Visigoths I'm leaving the French stage to! The Boyers and the Pradons we have so ridiculed were geniuses by comparison).

Idoménée is not so Visigothic as it might have been. The king of Crete is half mythical because, although he was a real human warrior who fought the Trojans, he is also the son of Deucalion, grandson of Minos and nephew of Phèdre, whose name in its Gallicized form preserves the Racinian associations. Idoménée had vowed to Neptune during a storm at sea to sacrifice the first human being he met on arrival back in Crete. Legend made it his son, but Crébillon draws back, and Idoménée's son, Idamante, kills himself at the end of the play. Crébillon's probable source for the legend is Fénelon's *Télémaque*.

Crébillon's dramatic difficulty is that Idoménée's vow to Neptune was made merely to save himself. He expounds the situation to his minister Sophronyme, referring to the curse attaching to his race through "Pasiphaé, Phèdre…Minos et Vénus." About to die in the storm, he tells Sophronyme, he made his "sacrilège voeu (sacrilegious vow)," which calmed the menacing sea:

Je tremblai, Sophronyme, et tremblai pour moi-même.
Pour apaiser les dieux, je priai… je promis…
Non, je ne promis rien: dieux cruels! j'en frémis…

(I trembled, Sophronyme, and trembled for myself,/To appease the gods, I begged…I promised…/No, I promised nothing, cruel gods! I shuddered…).

Idamante greets him on landing, cannot understand his father's reserve, and turns out to love Erixène, the daughter of the rebel Mérion whom he had killed. The first act ends after his profession of love and rejection by Erixène.

The second act starts with the revelation that she returns Idamante's passion:

Je respire un amour que ma raison abhorre

(I am filled with a love which my reason abhors).

In the second scene, Idoménée now reveals his own love for Erixène, and is rejected. Crébillon is perhaps remembering the love of Racine's Phèdre for the son of the father to whom she was married, as well as that of Mithridate and his two sons, all three in love with Monime. His plot relies on proven patterns of relationships, and his verse, although very fluent, does not quite successfully mimic Racine's exploitation of broken syntax to indicate the overwhelming force of irresistible passion. Idoménée thinks, as they prepare the sacrificial pyre, of abdicating in favour of Idamante, calculating that Neptune's revenge for reneging on the vow could then fall on him alone as a private person, when one of his officers, Egésippe, tells him that the gods have revealed to the priest that Idoménée himself is to be the sacrificial victim. Idoménée says that the king knows what the gods require. At this point, however, the audience does not. Idoménée's dilemma had been the classic conflict between reason and love, duty and desire. Dramatically the dilemma has

apparently been resolved by the need to sacrifice his own life. He tells Idamante that he is abdicating, but leaves him wondering what the reason could be.

In the third act Idoménée, believing it the only way to save Idamante, informs him that the fleet is getting ready to sail him into the storm. Idamante understands even less when Idoménée proposes that he should take Erixène with him, but is tricked into betraying his affection for her. Idoménée divulges to his son that they are rivals for Erixène's love, refusing to accept his plea of non-culpability for his feelings, and only just stops his son from killing himself, for offending his father by becoming his rival in love. The people meanwhile have been informed that Idamante is Idoménée's intended victim and are being incited by Erixène to rebellion. An abyss has opened in the earth and is poisoning people with the fumes it exhales.

In the fourth act Idamante comes to say goodbye to Erixène, is assured that she does not love his father, and pleads with her to become his father's queen. Idoménée, touched by the plight and feelings of his people, inflexibly and in spite of the pleas of Sophronyme resolves to sacrifice himself. He encourages Idamante not to believe the rumour he has heard that the gods require him to be the sacrificial victim, and goes to consult the gods. Sophronyme tells Idamante that the blood demanded by the gods is still his. In the fifth act Idamante resolves to die. Erixène admits to him her love for him, only to find Idamante pleading on behalf of his father. She is shamed by her own avowal, and feels that she herself must die. Idoménée confronts his son and refuses to order his death. Idamante refuses to be party to his father's death or flight and kills himself, leaving Idoménée to finish the play by saying that he himself looks forward to death.

The play for most of its length is a contest of rival heroic attitudes, father and son outdoing one another in renunciations, submissions, and self-sacrifice. Erixène simply extends the rivalry to the renunciation of love as well as of life. There is very little conflict, and in fact very little action. There is rivalry, mistake and confusion about the will of the gods, a mechanism for the generation of tragic inevitability, perhaps inspired by Racine's *Iphigénie*, and there are emotionally charged confrontations. Idoménée's opening position is so weak that the sole significant conflict takes place early in the play as he gears himself for the only alternative to cravenness, which is heroism. He alone has been subject to hesitation and change. But nothing is psychologically necessary, and changes in the positions of the protagonists are arbitrarily contrived. There is a reversion to Pierre Corneille's concept of heroism, with the significant innovation now that the sentiments of the populace contribute to the motivation of the principal characters. The existence of strong feelings is proclaimed, but otherwise shown only by the relatively simple device of broken syntax. Crébillon's poetic gifts scarcely rise above fluency, and the imaginative power of his first success does not approach that of Corneille or Racine at their peaks.

At what is generally thought to be his own best, *Rhadamiste et Zénobie*, Crébillon achieves scarcely more than a highly complex plot which strives to depict a moral heroism still based more on renunciation than on ferocity of passion, although there is an attempt to make them conflict. The difference between this play and Racine's great tragedies of renunciation, *Bérénice* and *Mithridate*, to which *Rhadamiste* obviously alludes by the very fact that Zénobie is Mithridate's daughter, lies in Racine's superior poetic and dramatic skills rather than the psychology. Racine's characters express their emotions more intensely, more convincingly, and with much greater poetry in plays much less dependent on the clutter of external events. Crébillon is still modelling himself on Racine but, by adapting to the change of taste and relying on situations to move his audiences, necessarily failing to achieve the same heights, even if we discount the over-fluent, rhetorically and poetically unimpressive alexandrines. Crébillon, too often unable to arouse emotion by the rhetoric of passions, relies on obliquely indicating to the audience what it is he intends them to be feeling, without however exploiting the sheer pathos of situations in the way Voltaire soon would.

Zénobie, daughter of Mithridate, king of Armenia, is married to and loved by her cousin Rhadamiste, the son of Pharasmane, her father's brother, but loved also by Pharasmane himself, and by another of Pharasmane's sons, Arsame. Since his father, Pharasmane, is jealously hostile to his marriage, Rhadamiste has carried Zénobie off and, when pursued, stabbed her and thrown her body into the river. When the play opens, Zénobie turns out to have survived and, under the name of Isménie, is an unrecognized prisoner at the court of Pharasmane. Her confidente, Phénice, not knowing that she is Zénobie, encourages her to respond to Pharasmane's advances. In the first scene Zénobie narrates the background to her present situation. When Mithridate had quarrelled with Pharasmane, Rhadamiste agreed to spare Mithridate only if Zénobie would marry him. She did, but Rhadamiste, perfidious, had killed Mithridate, and fled with Zénobie straight from the altar. He then in despair stabbed her and threw her, dying, into the Araxes. The first false supposition of the characters is therefore that Zénobie is dead.

The second, still narrated by Zénobie in the opening scene, is that Pharasmane, pretending to avenge his brother, but in fact jealous of his son, subsequently killed Rhadamiste. Zénobie therefore now believes herself free to marry again if she wishes. After ten years of wandering she had fallen in love, against the duty imposed on her since her father's murder by both her country and her lineage, with another son of Pharasmane, Rhadamiste's brother, Arsame. Her love is returned. Phénice counsels Zénobie to turn for help to the Roman ambassador. In the second scene Zénobie follows her duty against her inclination by rejecting the advances of the conquering Arsame. Pharasmane, not knowing of Arsame's return, but suspecting the reason for it when he discovers it, immediately sends him away again. Still ignorant of the identity of Zénobie/Isménie, Pharasmane pleads with her in vain. Zénobie resolves now to follow her inclination against her duty to her murdered father, and to yield to Arsame.

Crébillon is again following Racinian usage when he brings on the final main character at the beginning of the second act, and, once the initial situation is made clear, the intrigue proper can unfold. Rhadamiste, now king of Armenia, comes in and is greeted with surprise by the Armenian ambassador and Rhadamiste's confident, Hiéron. There are strong reminiscences of Phèdre's words when Rhadamiste describes his state of mind:

> …furieux, incertain,
> Criminel sans penchant, vertueux sans dessein,
> Jouet infortuné de ma douleur extrême,
> Dans l'état où je suis, me connais-je moi-même?…
> Dans ce cruel séjour sais-je ce qui m'entraîne,
> Si c'est le désespoir, ou l'amour, ou la haine?

(…mad, uncertain,/Criminal without evil, virtuous without intention,/Unhappy plaything of my extreme distress,/In the state I am in, can I even know myself?… /Do I know what draws me to this cruel place,/Whether it be despair, or love, or hate?).

Rhadamiste has had himself made ambassador of Rome, and Pharasmane rejects his mission from Néron.

In the third act Arsame seeks to meet Rhadamiste, but does not recognize him as his brother and enlists his aid in saving Isménie, whom Rhadamiste obviously does not suppose will turn out to be the wife he thought he had killed. He proposes to support Arsame against Pharasmane in the struggle for the hand of Isménie, said, Rhadamiste has heard, to have Roman blood. The confrontation between Rhadamiste and Zénobie takes place in the last scene of the third act. They recognize one another, and Zénobie offers to accompany Rhadamiste in spite of the fact that he had tried to murder her. In the fourth act we learn that she has agreed only out of duty, since Rhadamiste is her husband. She begs Arsame to flee and has, in a scene of great pathos, to reveal that Arsame's rival is at once his brother and her own husband.

There is a further confrontation between Arsame, Zénobie, and Rhadamiste. Zénobie explains the situation to Arsame, and affirms to them both that she is overcoming her inclination in order to follow her husband. Pharasmane has Arsame arrested. In the fifth act Pharasmane reaffirms his hatred of the Romans and suspects Rhadamiste of aiding Arsame to abduct Zénobie/Isménie. Arsame refuses to reveal the truth to his father, who reports to Arsame that he has killed Rhadamiste, caught trying to abduct Zénobie. Arsame knows he has therefore killed his own son and Zénobie's husband, but Rhadamiste turns out not yet to be dead. He is carried on stage, reveals his identity to Pharasmane and is reconciled to Arsame before he dies. Pharasmane renounces Zénobie who departs with Arsame to rule Armenia.

This is not melodrama, and is quite different from what the drama of pathos was to become a century later. It is, however, tragedy relying for its effects not on the psychological inevitability of personal catastrophe enacted on the stage, but on incidents, confrontations, disguises, recognitions, mistaken identities, confusions of meaning, and the engineering within the drama of situations calculated to produce a strong emotional reaction, not necessarily of pity, terror, or even admiration, in the audience. Crébillon's literary interest is primarily historical, it is true, but without some understanding of what was successful, and why, on the formal French stage in the first two decades of the 18th century, it becomes impossible to understand the achievements of later dramatists, especially Marivaux, but also Voltaire, the creation of the drame bourgeois, and the role played by the Italian and the fairground companies very soon after 1716.

PUBLICATIONS

Collections

Oeuvres, 1716 (privilège of 1711); augmented duodecimo editions appeared dated 1720, 1722, and 1749; the 2-vol. Louvre quarto edition appeared in 1850
Les Oeuvres complètes, 3 vols., 1785

Théâtre complet, 1885

Plays

Idoménée (1705), 1706
Atrée et Thyeste (1707), 1716
Electre (1708), 1709
Rhadamiste et Zénobie (1711), 1711
Xerxès (1714), 1749
Sémiramis (1717), 1717
Pyrrhus (1726), 1726
Catalina (1748), 1749
Le Triumvirat; ou, La Mort de Cicéron (1754), 1755

Biographical and critical studies

Vitu, Auguste, Introduction to the *Théâtre complet*, 1885
Dutrait, M., *Etude sur la vie et le théâtre de Crébillon*, 1895
Ciureanu, Petre, *Crébillon*, 1965

CYRANO DE BERGERAC, Savinien de, 1619–1655.

Playwright, author of philosophical fiction.

LIFE

Bergerac was the name of a pair of fiefs, Mauvières and Sous-Forêts in the Chevreuse valley, called Bergerac on account of the part played by a previous owner in the recapture of Bergerac at the end of the Hundred Years War. The fiefs were acquired by the well-off bourgeois Cyrano family from Paris late in the 16th century and sold in 1636 by Cyrano's father, Abel de Cyrano, a lawyer at the Paris parlement. It was only after that date that Savinien de Cyrano quite illegitimately arrogated to himself the appearance of nobility by adding the name of the estate to his own. Cyrano's grandfather had been a fish merchant who had bought a minor administrative legal post. Cyrano himself, one of seven children, was born in Paris, on or immediately before 6 March 1619 when he was baptized, in the rue Dussoubs, then rue des Deux-Portes. He spent a happy childhood at the château de Mauvières, on the banks of the Yvette, before being boarded with a priest who ran a rudimentary boarding school. Cyrano became the close life-long friend of another of the boys, his senior by one year, Henri Le Bret. When Cyrano was about 13 he was sent with Le Bret to the Collège de Beauvais, where he appears to have completed his studies. Its avaricious, severe, learned, and philandering principal, Jean Grangier, was to be the model for Granger in Cyrano's play, *Le Pédant joué*.

From 1637 Cyrano appears to have frequented the loose-living and free-thinking circles associated with Tristan l'Hermite and Saint-Amant, and it is at least plausibly conjectured that his life included regular gaming, womanizing, and excessive drinking, but we next hear of him for certain in 1638, when with Le Bret he enlisted into the largely Gascon 13th company of the regiment of gardes-nobles belonging to Carbon de Casteljaloux. He was twice seriously wounded, once by musket shot which went through his body at the siege of Mouzon in 1639, and once by a sword thrust in the throat at the siege of Arras in 1640. He was apparently sensitive about any reference to the parrot-beak shape of his nose. Le Bret, in his preface to Cyrano's posthumously published *Estats et empires de la lune*, explains that Cyrano abandoned his military career on account of the two severe wounds, the frequent duels he was involved in on account of his courage and his skill, seconding others more than 100 times, although never duelling on his own behalf, and the impossibility of finding a patron who would tolerate his inability to control his "génie tout libre (untrammelled spirit)." But above all the change of direction arose from his great love of reading. Le Bret's testimony always heavily tones down the extravagance of Cyrano's behaviour and beliefs.

Cyrano settled at the Collège de Lisieux, signed contracts in 1641 with dancing and fencing masters, and appears not only to have duelled excessively, but to have indulged in generally extravagant ways of living which have left in their trail a host of anecdotes, mostly about his fights and his travels to Toulouse, Italy, Poland, and England. In 1645 he was ill and obliged to stay with a surgeon-barber, which suggests that he was undergoing a cure for venereal disease, but he also took his intellectual life seriously, certainly mixing in the circle of the younger La Mothe le Vayer and his friends, and probably attending the lectures of Gassendi, tutor to Chapelle, the illegitimate son of the maître des requêtes, François Lhuillier.

He became closely associated with Chapelle and Tristan l'Hermite, and got to know well d'Assoucy, with whom he was later to have a celebrated quarrel. Undoubtedly inclined to religious and philosophical scepticism and to a widespread cynicism on other matters, he must already have begun to write before 1648, when he signed a preface to d'Assoucy's *Le Ravissement de Proserpine* "Hercule de Bergerac," but he also read widely. In the Gassendi milieu, whether or not Cyrano attended the lectures, he discussed, and probably met, Marolles, Campanella, Rohault. The comedy *Le Pédant joué* is unlikely to have been staged, but it contains a reference to the marriage of Marie de Gonzague on 6 November 1645 as to a recent event "the other day," so that it was probably written late in 1645 or in the first weeks of 1646, although not published until the *Oeuvres diverses* of 1654. Like many other works containing audacities of thought, *Le Pédant joué* circulated in manuscript, published without being printed, and was clearly well known by 1650, when its author's name was coupled with those of Sorel, Desmarets, and even Cervantes in the *Parasite Mormon, histoire comique* by the younger La Mothe le Vayer. The first known performance, in an abbreviated and expurgated version, which had to await the appearance of Rostand's 1897 play *Cyrano de Bergerac*, was at Harvard in 1899. The first known performance in France was given by the dramatic society of the French railway company, the Société nationale des chemins de fer français, in 1955. Molière borrowed from act II, scene iv and act III, scene ii for *Les Fourberies de Scapin*, act II, scene vii and act III, scene iii.

Cyrano's father died in 1648, by which time Cyrano had started to write his series of fictitious *Lettres*. At the outbreak of the Fronde Cyrano appears to have been the author of a series of "mazarinades," attacking Mazarin personally. The attribution to him of at least the 1649 *Le Ministre d'Etat flambé* is generally accepted. Thereafter Cyrano changed sides. Scarron, at first among Mazarin's supporters, had moved over to support the frondeurs, and in 1651 Cyrano strongly attacked him in his *Lettres contre les Frondeurs*, at much the same time breaking with d'Assoucy, although the celebrated story that the quarrel occurred when d'Assoucy tried to steal a cooked chicken from a famished Cyrano sounds suspiciously as if it was invented by d'Assoucy himself, whose account of the incident in the prose *Combat de Cyrano de Bergerac contre le singe de Brioché, au bout du Pont-Neuf* is a piece of burlesque in which d'Assoucy depicts himself as fleeing for his life to Turin.

Cyrano at this date was the probable author of a preface to the 1650 *Oeuvres poétiques* of Le Royer de Prade, defending the out-of-date "pointe" in poetry, generally a more or less witty conceit equivocating about beauty and ugliness, or otherwise exploiting double meanings and verbal surprises. Use of wild and witty metaphor was a characteristic of Cyrano's most extravagant style, but it was controlled and for the most part genuinely clever. Flamboyant conservatism of attitude and the overestimation of mere wit seem at least not uncharacteristic of the Cyrano of these years, during which *L'Autre Monde; ou, Les Estats et empires de la lune* and its sequel, *Les Estats et empires du soleil*, were being written. On the other hand, Cyrano's milieu ridiculed excessive tragic posing and declamatory pomposity, with a sureness of taste sometimes seen as being in advance of its time, heralding the need to ridicule all that was pretentious and affected which Molière was so strongly to feel.

In 1652 Cyrano was taken as secretary into the household and protection of the duc d'Arpajon, who paid for the publication of his first works, *La Mort d'Agrippine*, announced in the *Parasite Mormon, histoire comique*, and a volume of *Oeuvres diverses* containing the *Lettres* and *Le Pédant joué*. The *Parasite Mormon* is most likely to have been by the abbé La Mothe le Vayer and, although published only in 1650, it appears to have been written two or three years earlier. Cyrano's *La Mort d'Agrippine* was almost certainly staged at the Hôtel de Bourgogne in 1653 prior to publication. Contemporary echoes suggest that, probably on performance but, if not, on publication, it created for its author a reputation for real impiety. In a quarrel with the actor Montfleury, Cyrano is said to have forbidden him to act for a month. Both *Agrippine* and the *Oeuvres* were published by Charles de Sercy. Tallemant, who is disparaging about *Agrippine*, saying merely that it was the play in which "Sejanus disoit des choses horribles contre les dieux… un vray galimatias (Sejanus said terrible things against the gods…a real mess)," recounts that Sercy explained the success of the edition to an astonished Boisrobert, "Ah! but you see, there are beautiful impieties."

In 1654, in what is often said to have been an attack but seems to have been an accident, Cyrano received a bad head injury when a beam fell on his head as he left the Hôtel d'Arpajon, and he ceased to be protected by Arpajon, who may either have dismissed him or simply sent him to the country to recuperate. He became gravely ill in 1655, although we do not know whether it was as a consequence of the accident or from some other cause, like a relapse after the recovery of 1645 or a new infection. Le Bret, about to enter the priesthood, organized a pious plot to convert Cyrano, and was helped by Cyrano's aunt Catherine, prioress of the convent of the Daughters of the Cross, which took him in. He was, however, moved again, and cared for sufficiently well by Tanneguy Regnault des Bois-Clairs of the king's council to prompt hopes of recovery. But Cyrano felt the inevitability of approaching death, and finally went to stay with his cousin, Pierre de Cyrano, at Sannois, where he died on 28 July 1655, a few weeks before both Gassendi and Tristan. He was buried at the convent of the Daughters of the Cross.

Cyrano's death left a number of mysteries. The local priest signed a certificate testifying to his Christian end, although some scepticism has been expressed about its veracity and the wildest rumours about his atheism or madness circulated. One incomplete Cyrano manuscript, "L'Etincelle," was not published. Le Bret brought out *Les Estats et empires de la lune* in 1657, but the discovery of two manuscripts, one in Munich and one in Paris, suggests that Cyrano was working on his text up to his death and shows that Le Bret's edition had been heavily expurgated. The manuscript of *Les Estats et empires du soleil*, published in 1662, has never been recovered. The presumption has been made that the stored manuscript material was stolen by friends of Cyrano in order to safeguard his posthumous reputation, which explains why only the *Estats et empires de la lune*, which had not been stolen, but from which Le Bret had removed all the audacities, was initially published. No manuscript has survived to allow us to judge whether the text of the *Etats et empires du soleil* was toned down for publication in 1662, but it is generally considered likely that it was.

WORKS

Cyrano was obviously more than the burlesque and extravagant satirist for which he was for so long taken, although there was a nervous exaggeration as well as an audacity of radical thought in much of what he wrote. The most stylistically extravagant of Cyrano's works, depending on over-elaborate ingenuities and occasionally a too earnest desire to shock, are the *Lettres*. These include, for instance, those for and against witches, with their only semi-jocular rejection of superstition and of a good deal of authentic religion under the unexceptionable guise of a preference for rationality as a criterion over the authority of Aristotle—"plus savant que moi (more learned than me)"—Plato, or Socrates: "La raison seule est ma reine, à qui je donne volontairement les mains (reason alone is my queen, to whom I willingly give my aid)." Cyrano's *Lettres* may well be modelled on the 1642 *Lettres meslées* of Tristan l'Hermite and turn on the burlesque exploitation of hyperbole, metaphor, antithesis, and double meaning, with an underlying delicacy and an almost salon galanterie.

Since the second world war, Cyrano's reputation has undergone, not always for the same reasons, radical re-evaluation and Rostand's extravagant, touchy, witty, gallant, hot-tempered, and soft-hearted clown has given way to an author whose use of language and whose place in the history of ideas have both been considered of greater importance than may actually turn out to be warranted. Cyrano's pamphlets exaggerate the attitudinizing: "Je soustiens que le gouvernement populaire est le pire fléau dont Dieu afflige un Estat (I hold that a popular government is the worst scourge God inflicts on a state)." Like the rest of Cyrano's opinions, his political viewpoint is entirely empirical, without loyalties or patriotism, but generally expressed with burlesque self-parody.

The length more than the audacity of *Le Pédant joué* suggests that it cannot ever even have been intended to be staged. A five-act prose comedy, it must, for the reasons mentioned earlier, date from very late in 1645 or from early in the following year. It is clearly dependent on Rotrou's *La Soeur*, on a piece by Lope de Vega, and on the *commedia dell'arte* (q.v.), with characters denoted as "capitan," "paysan," and "fourbe (rogue) et valet;" and "pédant," a traditional Italian character, as well, here, as a satirical portrait of Jean Grangier, the principal of the Collège de Beauvais, who had died in 1643. What makes the text of more than routine interest is its sparkling language, coarse at the expense of the clergy, daring in its analogies between sacred history and antique mythology, irreverent about the sacred, and mocking about the desire for power, but cascading with energetic exuberance into puns, misunderstandings, misusages, double entendres, and overflowing with hyperboles, with ridiculous contrasts, metaphors, antitheses, and allusions. The manuscript ends with a breathtakingly audacious dialogue which Granger, by this point well out of character, says he has had with Death: irreverent, impertinent, unafraid, and cut from the printed text of 1654. No one who believed in an after-life conversed with death on the register of language, and in a play, with the degree of comic realism that Granger said he did, especially so shortly after the real Grangier's death.

The characters all speak in individually characteristic ways. Gareau, the peasant, is true to life in the way his patois is larded with Latinisms picked up in grand houses, but there is also a play on the impossibility of real communication, and a vivid demonstration that only a veneer of pretentious jargon and an ability to get away with misquoting learned texts really separates Granger the teacher from Gareau the peasant. It is now difficult to pick up the humour, which can depend on a knowledge of what were rules and what merely examples in "Despautère," the *Universa grammatica in commodiorem docendi et discendi usum redacta* by the Louvain professor van Pauteren (1460–1520), still in universal use in 17th-century France.

The grammar states, for instance, that "Hic dat or ('-or' gives 'hic')," meaning that Latin nouns ending in "-or" are normally masculine and therefore demand the correlative pronoun form of "hic" for "this." In the first scene, Granger, talking with absurd pretentiousness to Châteaufort, the "capitan" aspiring to the hand of his daughter, misunderstands the imposingly Latin-sounding phrase he remembers from his grammar book, regards it as a macaronic mixture of Latin and French, and takes "Hic dat" as the Latin for "he gives" and "or" as the French for "gold," splendidly displaying, almost in an aside, his characteristic blend of the charlatanism of pedants, the ignorance of the peasants and the avarice of the professional classes. It takes Cyrano less than half a line to sling in a stone which kills three birds at once.

Since the play is a send-up of a notorious, in fact genuinely learned but much-loathed recently deceased martinet with a reputation for avarice and a scandalous private life, written by an ex-member of his college in his mid-twenties, it not surprisingly uses the comedy of misunderstood text-books, mistaken allusions, and misquoted authorities. Much of Rabelais and some of Erasmus is written on a similar register. From the start the humour is chiefly in the language, and is mostly obvious. What is difficult to gauge is whether the burlesque tone is everywhere sufficient to carry the irreverence. Châteaufort ends his long first speech with a gleeful account of his command to the gods to sit astride their planets. "And what did you do with the other gods?"

asks Granger. "It was midday, so I had dinner." At this point Granger's valet interrupts. The printed text omits what is in square brackets.

Domine, ce fut assurément en ce temps-là, [et je m'en souviens bien,] que les oracles cessèrent

(*Lord*, that must have been just the time [and I remember it well] when the oracles stopped).

It was daring in 1645–46 to make a flippant reference in a comic vernacular text about the cessation of pagan oracles. There was a serious religious debate (see: Fontenelle) about whether or not the coming of Jesus caused the pagan oracles to cease. It is the deleted phrase, specifying that there was a particular date at which the oracles stopped prophesying, which might have been dangerous. Not many scholars or theologians disputed that they had stopped, only whether their cessation coincided with the mission of Jesus. But to flick in a reference to the cessation of the pagan oracles, and by inference a subversive allusion to Jesus's divine powers, in a discussion of the capitan's power to order the gods to sit astride the planets named after them is daring in inverse proportion to its jocularity. Any momentary suspension of the burlesque tone turns amusing irreverence into blasphemy.

There follows a speech by Granger with a poem of 73 octosyllabic lines all ending in "-if," confirming in its verbal virtuosity that Rabelais must be among Cyrano's comic paradigms. The play has a rudimentary plot. Granger and his son are rivals in love, and there are three aspirants for the hand of Granger's daughter, Manon, but the humour lies chiefly in Granger's ridiculously inflated language, in the contrast between Châteaufort's stream of bombastic verbiage and the peasant Gareau's patois, as well as in the allusions it is now necessary to dig out. The play was written for readers who might have known that the original Grangier was a deacon who obtained special permission to marry his housekeeper, by whom he had several children. Is an allusion to this behind Châteaufort's use of "Monsieur le curé" to Granger in the play's first scene? That has at least been suggested, and illustrates the difficulty of estimating with real precision what impression of comedy or daring this play might have given, circulating in manuscripts just before the Fronde. How bold was it to allow to Cupid in place of God the role of separating light from chaos? The allusion to *Genesis* is plain, and the best modern editor expresses surprise that the 1654 printer let it stand. The printer also allowed to pass what seems to be an allusion to the medieval bawdy joke that Saint Joseph was cuckolded.

The intrigue largely depends on perfunctory comic devices like mistaken identities and sexual imbroglios. Corbineli, the rogue valet of Granger's son, twice gets money out of his employer's father by trickery, and there are numerous stage directions about moving a ladder in act IV, scene i, consonant with a standard *commedia dell'arte* decor, which suggest that the reader is intended to suppose he is reading a script, however unplayable the dialect alone would make the play. With the help of a syllogism or two, Granger proves to Genevote, the sister of one of Manon's suitors, that he can incorporate her into the body of the university by incorporating her into his own body, to which she replies that sleeping one night with him would make her as learned as Hesiod, who slept on Parnassus. The humour does not oscillate: occasional scatology does nothing to alter its fundamental character of coarse comedy, against a backdrop of student life and clever language play.

The imaginativeness remains prodigious, and the extravagant verbal invention overflows as energetically as it does in Rabelais. The play, purged of its boisterousness, was a permanent quarry for Molière, not just for *Les Fourberies*. Its spiritual and almost certainly literary ancestor was Rabelais and, if it appears religiously daring in its irreverence about sacred matters, it must be remembered that what concerned the 1654 printer was not so much the burlesque, familiar, or dismissive tone towards the supernatural, as any specific reference to the text of scripture which might give offence. The substitution of Cupid for God was probably judged too light-hearted to be dangerous. What makes the piece a comic tour de force has not much to do with satire, but derives very largely from its enormous variety of language jokes.

La Mort d'Agrippine, however reminiscent its title of Tristan's 1644 *La Mort de Sénèque*, is a powerful Roman tragedy of love, vengeance, and jealousy which uses the extremes of passion to create an unusual intensity of emotional suspense. After the linguistic virtuosity of the satire and the extravagance of language it shares with the *Lettres*, the sparseness of the language in *Agrippine* comes as a surprise. The values once asserted by scoffing are now urged with tragic seriousness, as in the famous act II, scene iv, in which Sejanus, conspiring against Tiberius whose favourite he is, says to Terentius,

Encor qu'un toit de chaume eût couvert ma naissance,
Et qu'un Palais de marbre eût logé son enfance,
Qu'il fût né d'un grand Roi, moi d'un simple Pasteur,
Son sang auprès du mien est-il d'autre couleur?
Mon nom serait au rang des héros qu'on renomme,
Si mes prédécesseurs avaient saccagé Rome;
Mais je suis regardé comme un homme de rien,
Car mes prédécesseurs se nommoient gens de bien

(Although only a thatched roof covered me at birth,/And a marble palace was his childhood dwelling,/Even if he was born of a great king and I of a simple shepherd,/Is his blood a different colour from mine?/My name would be in the ranks of famous heroes,/If my ancestors had sacked Rome;/But I am looked on as a man of nothing,/Because my ancestors were known merely as decent folk).

That is as strong an assertion of the equal dignity of kings and commoners as the mid-17th century produced in France. Its extraordinary boldness in insinuating that the great are great because of the plundering and piracy of their ancestors, evidences a remarkable set of personal and social values for 1653. The passage also shows how Cyrano, partly by reining himself in from indulgent exuberance, gives his play great strength and dramatic intensity by bringing out the stark simplicity of the contrast in social status, but similarity in human dignity, between the peasant and the monarch. Cyrano may not have believed in popular government, but he could put passionate convictions about the equality of all into the mouth of a character on the formal stage. The date is important. Ten years later, with Colbert in power, views as radical as those could not have been declaimed without danger at the Hôtel de Bourgogne.

It is in the same scene with Terentius that Cyrano extends his views on equality to create in Sejanus a challenge to the gods themselves. Cyrano may have been counting on the register of tragic hyperbole to avoid accusations of impiety against himself personally, but we know from the reaction the play did actually cause that the implied dismissiveness of Christianity did create for him a personal reputation which the dramatic skill of the stage confrontation was not universally thought to excuse. Sejanus's first reply is almost flippant in tone:

Terentius: Respecte et crains des dieux l'effroyable tonnerre
(Respect and fear the fright-inspiring thunder of the Gods).

Sejanus: Il ne tombe jamais en hiver sur la terre,
J'ai six mois pour le moins à me moquer des dieux,
Ensuite je ferai ma paix avec les cieux
(It never strikes the earth in winter,/I have at least six months to laugh at the gods,/Then, afterwards, I'll make my peace with the heavens).

Terentius: Ces dieux renverseront tout ce que tu proposes
(The gods will overturn whatever you propose).

Sejanus: Un peu d'encens brûlé rajuste bien des choses
(Burning a little incense puts a lot of things right).

Terentius: Qui les craint ne craint rien.
(Who fears them has nothing to fear.)

Sejanus: Ces enfants de l'effroi,
Ces beaux riens qu'on adore, et sans savoir pourquoi,
Ces altérés du sang des bêtes qu'on assomme,
Ces dieux que l'homme a faits, et qui n'ont point fait l'homme
Des plus fermes Etats ce fantasque soutien,
Va, va, Terentius, qui les craint ne craint rien

(These children of fright,/These fine nothings whom we adore, and without knowing why,/Thirsting for the blood of the beasts we sacrifice,/These gods whom humans have made, and who have not made humans/This imaginary support of the securest states,/Go on with you, Terentius, who fears them has nothing to fear).

There is of course nothing unchristian about a Roman denouncing on a Paris stage Roman deities as a hoax perpetrated on the Roman people to keep them submissive, and there was a case for risking these lines in the interest of dramatic effect. How strong was the invitation to transpose them into a Christian or a French setting? It is important that there is now a consensus that the tragedy was actually played at the Hôtel de Bourgogne. Stage performance involved the whole company of the king's players in taking the risk that those lines would at the very least outweigh in box-office attractiveness anything they cost in public offence. The risk was no longer, as with the comedy, largely confined to a single author. No one was going to write off the

Hôtel de Bourgogne company more than 10 years after Richelieu's death as simple extravagant buffoons, as the Cyrano of *Le
Pédant* circulating in manuscript could, however wrongly, simply have been written off. It now seems certain that it was on
account of *Agrippine*'s reception that Arpajon withdrew his protection.

The other famous scene from *Agrippine* is act V, scene vi.
Sejanus is told by a raving Agrippine that, before himself being
executed, he will witness the execution of his son and the rape
of his daughter. He refuses to be moved. Is his defiance bravado?
Does his dismissiveness of such an end suggest that his thinking,
like his emotions, may be disturbed? How daring was it to put
an expression of disbelief in an after-life into the mouth of such
a character on the stage?

Sejanus: Etais-je malheureux lorsque je n'étais pas?
Une heure après la mort notre âme évanouie
Sera ce qu'elle a été une heure avant la vie...
J'ai beau plonger mon âme et mes regards
    funèbres
Dans ce vaste néant et ces longues ténèbres,
J'y rencontre partout un état sans douleur
Qui n'élève à mon front ni trouble ni terreur;
Car puisque l'on ne reste après ce grand passage
Que le songe léger d'une légère image,
Et que le coup fatal ne fait ni mal ni bien,
Vivant, parce qu'on est, mort, parce qu'on n'est
    rien,
Pourquoi perdre à regret la lumière reçue
Qu'on ne peut regretter après qu'elle est
    perdue?

(Was I miserable when I did not exist?/An hour
after death our soul without consciousness/Will
be what it was an hour before our birth.../In
vain I plunge my soul and my dying vision/Into
this vast nothingness and these long
darknesses,/I find everywhere there a state
without suffering/Which brings neither worry
nor terror to my brow;/For since after this long
journey we remain only the evanescent dream
of an evanescent life,/And since the fatal blow
does neither harm nor good,/Whether living
because we are, or dead because we are not,/
Why regret the loss of the light we have
received/That we are not able to regret after it
has been lost?).

Of the two novels we have the unexpurgated text of only one,
of which the expurgated version published in 1657 was entitled
Histoire comique... contenant les estats et empires de la lune.
L'Autre Monde is the title given in the published version of the
first novel, and then to the first critical edition of both novels
together. The inspiration for the comic techniques must again
derive from Rabelais. The normal is often simply turned upside
down so that, for instance, it is a sign of nobility on the moon to
wear not a sword but a phallus, since it is noble to give life, but
ignoble to take it away. The genre of imaginary journeys had
long been commonplace. Rabelais goes out of his way in the
journey in the *Quart livre* to acknowledge his dependence on
More's *Utopia*. Cyrano draws on a whole range of other sources

as well, notably Campanella's 1623 *Civitas solis*, itself deeply
indebted to More; John Wilkins's treatises translated into
French by Jean de la Montagne in 1655, the year of Cyrano's
death, as *Le Monde dans la lune, divisé en deux livres*; and Francis Godwin's novel drawing on Wilkins's ideas, *The Man in the
Moon; or, A Discourse of a Voyage*, translated into French by
Jean Baudouin in 1648.

The real interest of Cyrano's novels lies naturally in the philosophical perspectives which he opens up for discussion. These
are not only cosmological, but also concern personal, social, and
political philosophy, with a good seasoning of theology and
metaphysics. There is a first-person narrator, and the *Estats et
empires de la lune* begins when, returning home one evening, he
announces, in spite of his companions' more colourful speculations, his view that "la lune est un monde comme celui-ci, à qui
le nôtre sert de lune (the moon is a world like this one, for which
ours acts as a moon)." All-important is the literary register of the
discussions. Seriously to suggest other inhabited planets posed
immense problems for the theology of original sin and the
redemption (see: Fontenelle) and if, like stage burlesque, flippancy of narrative register was a well-tested mechanism for
avoiding suspicions of heresy, it could not be calibrated, and the
degrees of permitted innuendo anyway varied, not always predictably, or on account only of theological considerations.

It is generally true that the decade between the end of the
Fronde in 1653 and the death of Mazarin in 1661 with such consequent events as the assumption of power by Louis XIV, the
ruin of Foucquet and with him the whole old order of tax farmers, and the beginning of Colbert's ministry was, if not permis-
sive, at least artistically liberal, inclined to take a relaxed view
about the intellectual and moral implications of exuberant works
of the imagination. It was the decade of préciosité, the portrait,
and the analysis of sentiment, of the resumption of salon society,
of the century's most successful play, Thomas Corneille's
Timocrate, of Desmarets's *Clovis*, Chapelain's *La Pucelle*, and
Tallemant's unpublished *Les Historiettes*.

The narrator of *La Lune* says he referred to the views of
Pythagoras, Epicurus, and Democritus, "et, de notre âge, Coper-
nic et Képler (and, in our age, Copernicus and Kepler)," as if the
addition of the two controversial modern names did not introduce an altogether different order of insinuation. The difficulty
is to know how far the decade's artistic liberalism extended into
the realm of philosophy. It was also the decade of Pascal's
Lettres provinciales, the first shots in the counter-attack against
what might be called Jesuit baroque, in style as well as in values.
Cyrano's narrator drives home his point when, on arrival back in
his room, he finds a book by Cardano open on his table at a passage where Cardano recounts the visit of two old men who had
said they were from the moon. How had the book put itself on
his table and opened itself at that passage, he wonders. Cardano
was a doctor and a mathematician who died with a papal pension, but had written an *Ars magna* on algebra which made him
suspect of sorcery, and was the author of a famous autobiography.

We are entitled to wonder whether the fictional veil, with
fairy-tale magic which will take the narrator to the moon as well
as put open books on his table, is adequate covering for the boldness of the serious speculation mixed in with the fantasy. The
Estats is a fascinating work in the history of the popular dissemination of theologically disturbing scientific discovery. It is Cyrano's skill in achieving a balance between fantasy and innuendo

which makes it an important work of literature. There is in fact a passage in Cardano's autobiography alluded to by Cyrano's narrator, whose method of ascent and descent, through the action against gravity of phials of dew warmed by the sun, is very distantly related to the way an empty egg-shell with the hole blocked by wax can be made to bounce about when subjected to heat.

Cyrano's hero finds that the earth has turned underneath him while he was in the air, so that after a vertical ascent and descent he is not near Paris at midnight, but in Canada at midday. His first serious conversation is with the viceroy, essentially to do with the earth's motion about its axis, planetary orbits round the sun, and the size of the universe, infinite, like eternity. The viceroy has been reading Gassendi, at this date still much better known in France than Descartes. He reports one explanation he has been given of the earth's rotation: it could be caused by the damned, scrambling away from the heat towards the top of the vault of hell at the centre of the earth. Cyrano's hero and the viceroy laugh. But are not such childishly anthropomorphic explanations of the earth's rotation an invitation to the reader not just to ask questions about the physical location of hell, but to query the possibility of any satisfactory explanation at all of damnation, still taught as to including intolerable but unending physical pain? But without hell, could there even be personal survival after death?

For a page or two we go back to the children's story register, as the machine for space travel imagined by Cyrano twice falls back to earth. When the machine does take off successfully, there is a comic moment when the gravitational pulls of earth and moon exert equal but opposite forces. Cyrano has used little bits of 17th-century technology, which from at any rate 1634 included fused bombs, has drawn on Ariosto's *Orlando furioso*, and has amalgamated various accounts of the earthly paradise, where his hero lands, crashing on to the tree of life, before giving us a truly lyrical account of the wonders of the eternal spring. Only six people have ever been in the earthly paradise— Adam, Eve, Enoch, Saint John the evangelist, Cyrano's hero, and Elijah, whom he now meets. Adam had tried to avoid the wrath of God after his sin by fleeing to the moon, our earth, by the strength of his imagination, and Eve had been drawn after him by sympathy. The strength of the imagination, developed from Ficino by Pomponazzi in the *De incantationibus*, had been the subject of one of Montaigne's chapters, and was traditionally used in the sceptical tradition to discredit belief in miracles. Cyrano refers at some length in the *Estats et empires du soleil* to the tradition that the imagination of the mother affects the foetus, although he does not repeat the list of examples to which Montaigne refers. Cyrano's recourse to the magnetic power of sympathy could have come from a whole variety of neoplatonist sources.

Cyrano's erudition is less well coordinated than that of Rabelais had been but, like Rabelais, Cyrano peppers his texts with allusions the reader did not need to bother about. Cyrano is a good story-teller, and his narrator gets a fascinating account from Elijah of all sorts of things about which the Bible does not inform us, like the height of the Flood which made it possible to swim to the moon. The fantastic account of the Flood, however absurdly fairy-tale, keeps the theological rules. It allows the moon-dwellers to be descendants of Adam and Eve, so solving all the difficulties about a single original sin and a single incarnation. Adventures and misadventures follow each other swiftly,

and Cyrano intelligently, wittily, and inventively exploits the opportunity he has created to discuss anything that interests him, although much remains pure fantasy, without apparent imaginative effort, folk memory, or any of the other important ingredients of fairy-tales. Cyrano constantly rams home the relativity of experience. We could have been born to move about on all fours, to nourish ourselves on odour. Cyrano's hero is treated on the moon much as the inhabitants of the earth might have treated an intruder from the moon. The point is very clearly made that no one likes their patterns of experience disturbed. Or of belief?

Socrates's guiding spirit, known traditionally as his demon, proves helpful, and recounts to Cyrano's voyager how he knew Cardano, what he thought of the Rosicrucians, how he suggested to Campanella that he should write a *De sensu rerum*, and how he had frequented La Mothe le Vayer and Gassendi. He gives a eulogy of Tristan l'Hermite. He likes living on the moon, because people there cultivate the truth, hate pedants, and are persuaded by reason, not rank. They live for three or four thousand years, sleep on flowers, communicate with noises that are not languages but can be musically notated, and pay their bills with verses which are professionally assessed before being exchanged for money.

The inspiration does flag, and a great deal is fanciful without being tendentious. But Cyrano slips in important half-lines of text, such as the demon's views that nothing in nature is spiritual, only material, although exhibiting increasing degrees of subtleness. The traveller is made to defend his opinions, but he finds he cannot refute those of his hosts. He takes refuge in Aristotle.

Cet Aristote, dont vous vantez si fort la science, accommodait sans doute les principes à sa philosophie, au lieu d'accommoder sa philosophie aux principes, et encore devait-il les prouver au moins plus raisonnables que ceux des autres sectes, ce qu'il n'a pu faire

(This Aristotle, of course, whose learning you extol, suited principles to his philosophy, instead of suiting his philosophy to principles, and even then he needed to prove his principles to be at least more reasonable than those of the other sects, which he was not able to do).

The moon-dwellers' challenge to their visitor to justify his philosophy is recounted in such a way as to make it clear that Cyrano, only half in jest, is making the same challenge to mid-century France, where Aristotle's authority was more often used as a shield than his principles were examined for their empirical validity, in medicine, of course, even more than in literature. What Cyrano does semi-humorously in what pretends to be a fantasy story about a trip into space, Boileau was to do facetiously in the *Arrêt burlesque*, with respect to medicine, in 1671, just before a wave of reaction in favour of Aristotle in which successive universities were for a good half-century after Cyrano's text going to insist on Aristotle's authority against the new anti-authoritarianism of Descartes. Again, on the subject of peace the moon-dwellers' behaviour amounts to a sarcastic indictment of the earthly way of deciding matters by force and power. Erasmus had already made that plea in the name of the gospels.

When the narrator is tried back on earth for saying that he has come from the moon, he is eventually condemned to an "amende dishonorable (dishonourable recantation)," pointedly contrasting with the French "amende honorable." He is dressed up magnificently for his act of ignomy, and carried to the platform in a splendid carriage drawn by four princes. At each crossroads he has to recite

Peuple, je vous déclare que cette lune-ci n'est pas une lune, mais un monde; et que ce monde là-bas n'est pas un monde, mais une lune. Tel est ce que les prêtres trouvent bon que vous croyiez

(People, I declare to you that this moon is not a moon, but an earth; and that that earth out there is not an earth but a moon. That is what your priests think it fit you should believe).

To say that the earth is not an earth is buffoonery. To say that that is what your priests want you to believe, even if it is said by a character wrongly obliged to say it as a punishment for being right, comes quite near to being an open attack on Christianity, as do the lengthy demonstrations that all the arguments for the immortality of the human soul also prove that the animals, too, have immortal souls. It is tantalizing not to be able to judge what Cyrano would have left in his text had he lived to publish it. The abruptness of the narrator's return home is so peremptory that it has to be supposed that Cyrano, perhaps knowing he had little time left, finished in a hurry before his final move to Sannois. The traveller is clutching the legs of the Antéchrist, who is suddenly snatched off to hell, which is the centre of our earth. The voyager thinks he has landed back on the moon but finds himself in Italy.

The second imaginary journey, *Estats et empires du soleil*, is a longer text, and the version we have, that of 1662, not only is not certainly the text as left by Cyrano, but both internal and external evidence suggest that it is very unlikely not to have been expurgated and perhaps substantially altered, although there is certainly a text of Cyrano underlying the printed version. It is unfinished. Since the history of the manuscript, which has disappeared, makes it clear, too, that Cyrano is unlikely to have considered his text, in the unfinished state in which we possess it, as having been ready for dissemination, it is important not to regard it as more than uncompleted work.

It is often wrongly presented as the second part of a novel of which the *Lune* is considered the first, although there is no guarantee that Cyrano would have published it in that way when he had finished it, just as *Le Pédant joué* is often discussed as if it had been written for the stage, when it seems impossible that it should have been. Now that attention has come more and more to focus on the interest of Cyrano's expert use of language and skilful exploitation of literary registers, critical fastidiousness in such matters has become important, and quite enough can be gleaned from *La Lune* to make detailed analysis of the second piece unnecessary for any assessment of Cyrano's views or literary skills. He may not have redacted the final text of the *Soleil*. Descartes had been impatient in the 1637 *Dioptrique* with the "petites images corporelles qui voltigent en l'air (little corporeal images jumping through the air)," which he found in the scholastic handbook used when he was a student at La Flèche. A similar phrase from the last page of the *Soleil* can have come only from the *Dioptrique*, which it is unlikely that Cyrano had read.

Le Soleil contains less fantasy and adventure but more discus-sion than *La Lune*. However, it is more long-winded and less radical than its predecessor. Much of it is elaborate metaphor. The five streams of the senses are described, like the three rivers of memory, imagination, and judgement. There is a disquisition on the traditional sceptical theme of the world-soul. Both the role attributed to Campanella as a character in the text apparently in entire agreement with Descartes, and the explicit description of what goes on in "the noviceship of love" make it dangerous to suppose that someone else's pen was not at work after Cyrano's death. The toned-down exuberance, elaborate metaphorical descriptions, and the tamed imaginative zest make it likely that someone has taken an authentic Cyrano text of ten years earlier and tuned it to the taste of 1662.

PUBLICATIONS

Early and critical editions

Le Ministre d'Etat flambé, 1649
Lettre contre les frondeurs, 1651
La Mort d'Agrippine, 1654
Les Oeuvres diverses, 1654
Le Pédant joué, comédie, 1654; in *Théâtre du XVIIe siècle*, vol. 2, in Bibliothèque de la Pléiade edition, 1986
Histoire comique… contenant les états et empires de la lune, 1657; critical editions of Munich and Paris manuscripts, edited by Leo Jordan, 1910; edited by F. Lachèvre in *Les Oeuvres libertines de Cyrano de Bergerac*, 2 vols., 1921; as *Voyages of the Moon and the Sun*, translated by R. Aldington, 1922 (1st English translation, 1659)
Les Nouvelles Oeuvres…contenant l'Histoire comique des estats et empires du soleil, plusieurrs lettres et autres pièces divertissantes, 1662; as *Voyages of the Moon and the Sun*, 1922
Les Oeuvres diverses, 4 vols., 1663

Modern editions

Oeuvres diverses, edited by F. Lachèvre, 1933
L'Autre Monde; ou, Les États et empires de la lune et du soleil, edited by F. Lachèvre, 1933
Lettres, 1965

Biographical and critical studies

Lanius, E.W., *Cyrano de Bergerac and the universe of imagination*, 1965
Harth, E., *Cyrano de Bergerac and the polemics of modernity*, 1970
Mongrédien, G., *Cyrano de Bergerac*, 1964
Alcover, M., *La Pensée philosophique et scientifique de Cyrano de Bergerac*, 1970
Prévot, Jacques, *Cyrano de Bergerac romancier*, 1977
——*Cyrano de Bergerac, poète et dramaturge*, 1978

D

DANCOURT, Florent Carton, sieur d'Ancourt, known as, **1661–1725.**

Comic dramatist.

LIFE

Dancourt used to boast that he was born on the same day as the Dauphin, 1 November 1661. The family came from northern France, but it seems likely that Dancourt was born in Fontainebleau. His grandfather was a judge, and his father, who regarded himself as noble, was sénéchal of Saint-Quentin. In 1655 he married Louise de Londy, of whom Budé may have been an ancestor. Both families had been Protestant, although Dancourt himself was certainly brought up a Catholic. He may have had a younger brother, Benjamin. Dancourt certainly went to school at the Jesuit Collège de Clermont, where at the age of 13 he is credited with "a verse tragedy *Melchisédech.*" Niceron tells us that the Jesuits wanted him to join the Order, but that Dancourt later taunted one of his former teachers, the famous preacher Père de la Rue, with a remark to the effect that he would as soon be a comedian of the king as a comedian of the pope: "il n'y a pas tant de différence de votre état au mien (there is not that much difference between your calling and mine)." Dancourt had early established the reputation for being headstrong.

By the age of 17 he had finished school and is said to have taken legal examinations. Shortly thereafter he fell in love with Thérèse Le Noir de la Thorillière, born in 1663 and daughter of one of Molière's troupe who, at Easter 1673, immediately after Molière's death, had gone over to the Hôtel de Bourgogne with Baron and Beauval. Baron's nephew, Etienne, had married Thérèse's sister Charlotte in 1675. There is a tradition that Dancourt and Thérèse eloped, perhaps to force both families into agreement, but a contract of marriage between Dancourt and Thérèse was signed on 9 April 1680; for some reason Dancourt's father was imprisoned in the Châtelet, but his mother acted for him as well as for herself. Dancourt's parents would provide board and lodging, while Thérèse was to receive 500 livres a year. The wedding took place on 15 April, when Dancourt was 18½.

We do not know much about what happened between 1680 and 1685, except that Thérèse's father died on 28 July 1680. Thérèse may already have taken up an acting career, and Dancourt may have joined her, probably with Condé's troupe, the principal group of players touring northern and eastern France. We know that both Dancourt and his wife joined at Rouen on 2 October 1680, in principle for seven years, a troupe of players formed in 1677 from an amalgamation of Condé's troupe with that of the Dauphin. Dancourt had a whole part and Thérèse at first a probationary half-part. It was quite normal for actors to move on to writing plays, as Molière, Montfleury, Poisson, Brécourt, Champmeslé, Baron, and Hauteroche had done, but before Dancourt they had invariably stuck to comedy. Dancourt's first play was the 1683 verse tragedy *La Mort d'Hercule*, first played in Arras and Lille, and published in 1683 at Arras. It was revived for the Comédie-Française in 1704 under the title of *La Mort d'Alcide*, but did not go beyond half a dozen performances. In 1683 Dancourt played and published what was more a series of comic sketches than a play, *Les Nouvellistes de Lille*. This entertainment, in verse, was never given in Paris.

From Easter 1685 Dancourt and his wife each obtained half-parts in the Troupe française des Comédiens du Roi, the Comédie-Française. There were 29 members sharing 23 parts, and Dancourt's part rose by two steps to a full share in 1690. He was to stay with the company until 1718, its resident playwright and one of its principal actors, as well as fulfilling such other roles from time to time as financial administrator, orator, and, until his dismissal from the post in 1705, inspector. He was accused of distributing too many free tickets. During 30 years as a member of the company, Dancourt was only twice absent for more than a month. He was to put his name to 52 comedies, not all of which he actually wrote.

Dancourt's personal reputation was unpleasant. The *Nouveau Journal Universel* of Amsterdam announced in January 1690, the year in which his mistress, Mme Ulrich, purported to have written Dancourt's *La Folle Enchère*, that he had physically assaulted his wife off-stage at the theatre. He was slightly hurt by two sword strokes from another actor who came to her aid. There had been a separation of possessions as early as 1686, made into a complete separation in 1690, the root cause of the trouble having been the extra-marital sexual relationships of both spouses, but there was a reconciliation in 1693, although Thérèse continued to insist on controlling the disposal of her own income, and the list of her furnishings added to the notaried act suggests positive luxury rather than bourgeois ease. Thérèse owned Venetian mirrors and a harpsichord in marquetry, copper, and ebony. It has been plausibly suggested that as much as possible was put under Thérèse's name to keep it away from the bailiffs.

Both partners had high-ranking lovers at court. The duc d'Aumont and the marquis de Créqui seem to have supplied Thérèse with financial assistance, and by 1696 she had her own property in Auteuil. Dancourt's dedications show another likely source of income during years of notorious debt. There was gossip about his relationship with the dauphin's wife. Then in 1706 Dancourt was nearly killed by Etienne Baron, his brother-in-law. His touchiness also prompted him to take one of his colleagues to law. He cannot have been easy to live with.

The company had continuously to pay Dancourt's private debts, and these became so high that they could no longer just be overlooked, as for other members of the company they often were. Payments to Dancourt were withheld while matters were put in order. The police kept a file on his way of dealing with bailiffs. François Gacon's 1696 *Le poète sans fard*, lauding Regnard, openly accused Dancourt of plagiarism, while the song writer Maurepas publicly made fun of him for pimping. Dancourt defended the company's monopoly rights to the extent of having the fairground theatre of Dolet and Delaplace physically destroyed. When in 1697 the Italian company was banished from Paris, the fairground players regarded themselves as the legitimate inheritors of their traditions and privileges, and the official company was to be increasingly concerned under Dancourt with the preservation of its monopoly.

A complaint against him by a chamber-maid who claimed on 16 July 1692 that he had seduced her and left her pregnant in furnished rooms with unpaid rent was later published in Campardon's *Les Comédiens du roi de la troupe française*. The girl was certainly seduced, practically abducted, and Dancourt's role in the affair was discreditable even by the standards of his own society. But there may also have an attempt at blackmail. Dancourt was clearly easy to quarrel with, assertive and imperious, externally on the company's behalf as well as on his own within it, being as energetically committed to promoting the company's interests as he was to advancing his own.

It is quite important for an understanding of his theatre, which laughs so readily at social appearances, to keep in mind Dancourt's pretentions to social dignity, and indeed to aristocracy. Racine had climbed through his theatrical career to the ranks of the minor nobility, and Boileau, Lulli, Perrault, and even Molière can be regarded as having become at least courtiers. Offices admitting to noble rank could be openly purchased after a decree of 1696, and Dancourt, like his family before him, was sensitive to his social standing. From the beginning of his association with the Comédie-Française, Dancourt signed himself "officier du roi (officer of the king)" rather than "actor," and in 1697 he had his name entered on the register of arms-bearers. At Auteuil in 1710, neighbours of Boileau, the Dancourts bought a locked pew in their local parish church. In 1714, still in debt, the couple none the less bought the château at Courcelles, a few kilometres from the Loire, to which Dancourt withdrew on retirement to a life of somewhat ostentatious religious zeal. He had his tomb built, tried to write a religious tragedy, and ordered that his comedies should be burnt after his death. His wife is reported, no doubt apocryphally, to have burnt the psalm commentaries instead.

Dancourt's real début as a dramatist came in Paris with the three-act prose comedy *Le Notaire obligeant*, played on 6 June 1685. His career was to be distinguished, and his express ambition to be ranked second only to Molière, printed in the verse dedication to his 1712 *Sancho Pança gouverneur*, was not necessarily at that date absurd. He must have brought *Le Notaire* with him to the company. Its success was honourable. Although it was given with a longer, better-known piece, an actor's full share per performance depended on the new play. On 15 June *Le Notaire* with Racine's *Mithridate* was worth 20 livres per share, whereas on 16 June *Tartuffe* on its own brought in only one and a half livres per share. The piece was played 16 times that season, with box office receipts never falling below 300 livres, although never rising above 844. In 1684–85 and 1685–86 the company was distributing annually to the actors between 5,000 and 6,000 livres per share, plus the pension paid by the king.

Dancourt was more than a runner-up of social satire in whatever form seemed appropriate—one-act, three-act, or five-act,

brief satire for the town or court entertainment—although he was perfectly prepared to produce whatever the company needed for commercial success, especially one-act prose satires to stimulate custom in the summer doldrums, and including parodies of other people's work, re-utilized plots, and retouched versions of other people's texts. His own strength was to have prompted and followed the developing public taste for satire of the society which surrounded him. That society had emerged from Colbert's unsuccessful attempt to assert the admirable rewards to be achieved from plain bourgeois social climbing rather than those represented by the more flamboyant but also more adventurous tastes of the aristocracy, and from the canalization of power through the corridors of Versailles, Louis XIV's isolated new palace in the country, and the utimate seat of government. The distance between the court and the citizenry and legal machinery of the town had become geographical as well as metaphorical, and Dancourt was successful with both publics. *Le Notaire* laid down Dancourt's structural grid, from which he almost never departed, much as Molière only rarely moved from the scaffolding of a commedia dell'arte (q.v.) plot.

It gives some idea of social and theatrical life to notice that in the year Dancourt joined the company, 1685, there had been a successful Quinault-Lulli opera *Roland* played on 8 January at Versailles and on 8 February in Paris. Dancourt's *Le Notaire* was performed in June. His one-act light-hearted prose parody of *Roland*, *Angélique et Médor*, with 11 scenes was intensively rehearsed in July and played in Paris on 1 August, bringing in 963 livres at the first performance and 1,200 at the third. On 18 November it was commanded for a performance at Versailles. Since Quinault was busy with *Armide*, a text for *Le Ballet de la jeunesse* to be given at Versailles on 28 January 1686 was commissioned from Dancourt and set to music by Lalande. Dancourt was to parody *Armide* in its turn. The immensely successful opera was given in Paris on 15 February 1686, and Dancourt's parody, *Renaud et Armide* on 31 July. The difficulty, of course, was that the parody's success could not outlast public interest in the piece it was parodying.

In 1687 the company played 17 times at Versailles between 13 November and 30 December. Dancourt acted eight times, and Thérèse seven. He interrupted work on his five-act comedy *Le Chevalier à la mode*, his best-known play, to dash off a one-act satire, *La Désolation des joueuses*, to profit from the decree of 18 July 1687 tightening the anti-gaming laws. It was played on 23 August, and had 14 successive performances, interrupted only for a week while Thérèse was acting with part of the company for the dauphin at Anet. *La Désolation* was Dancourt's first real essay in social satire, and the social rank of the characters is high, mostly noble, although also running to a money-lender and a swindler, the Chevalier de Bellemonte. Its run was prematurely terminated by the traditional season of court command performances at Fontainebleau, but Dancourt was financially compensated by the company.

It was during the Fontainebleau season that *Le Chevalier à la mode* had its première in Paris on 24 October 1687, and was given 17 successive performances to 3 December. On 14 and 24 November it was put on at Versailles, but its revival in the new year was suddenly less successful. It was Dancourt's most ambitious play, the first of only seven in five acts, of which four were also to be in verse. It was written in collaboration with Sainctyon, who probably sketched the play's structure and drew out the plot to fill the five acts.

Dancourt's career was now following an established pattern as actor and playwright, although the first wave of ambitious comedy was checked, and there is an apparent renewal of creative energy, taking him back to the bigger genres, after 1707. His creative powers declined, and he was aware of it, although not perhaps prepared for the final comparative failure of one play, *La Métempsycose des amours*, performed on 17 December 1717, the rejection of *La Déroute du pharaon*, and the preference of the company for a similar play put on by the Italian company over his own *La Belle-Mère* on 21 April 1725.

Dancourt neither wrote tragedy, after the early *La Mort d'Hercule*, nor acted in it, except in minor roles. Records of the company show occasional marked indiscipline on his part, as in failing to turn up to act, or not bothering to come to meetings. He generally left discussion of proposed new plays to others. For two periods at least, from about 1690 to 1696 and from 1710 to 1718, Dancourt's financial troubles were pressing, and petty quarrels inside the company, debts, jealousies, arguments with other companies, the small change of theatrical life, filled the interstices of Dancourt's professional activity. From 1696 for over a decade the Dancourts seem to have reached a life of some financial ease. From 1701 they rented a large Paris house for 2,000 livres a year. Both daughters, Manon and Mimy, then 14½ and 13, had been admitted to the company in 1698.

Manon gave up the theatre on her marriage in 1702, while Mimy went from a quarter-share to a full share by four steps between 1701 and 1707. Several additional parcels of property were bought at Auteuil after the initial purchase by Thérèse alone in 1696. When Mimy married in 1711, she and her husband were lodged by the Dancourts, with a lackey and a chamber-maid, for three years. Courcelles was bought for 80,000 livres in the joint names of Dancourt and Thérèse on 9 June 1714, and the money was obviously difficult to find. It was, however, somehow found and Dancourt, who had slowly gone out of fashion during the decade before his retirement in 1718, retired to his assortment of feudal jurisdictions. Most of the debts, although not all, were settled by the company, leaving very little over by way of a final payment. There is some probability that there was an as yet undiscovered source of income. Fortunes were being made in property, and we know that Dancourt was interested in that.

It was on 22 April 1718 that Dancourt retired with his inalienable pension of 1,000 livres. Thérèse had ceased to act, but remained a member of the company until 1720. Her daughter Mimy, with a full part in the company from 1707, carried on until 1728. She was to become Dame de Courcelles. Thérèse died in the middle of 1725. Dancourt de Courcelles, as he had taken to signing himself, died on 5 or 6 December 1725.

WORKS

Dancourt's gifts were for short, incisive satirical comments on the foibles of contemporary society. His ambition was to write if not tragedies, then at least grand comedies—the seven in five acts, the eight in three. His mistake was to betray his real talent, and to allow his work to depend too exclusively on some immediate relevance to an event, a decree, a success to be parodied, a rival to be satirized. In 1699, for instance, it was 16 years since Dancourt had himself written a comedy in verse, the 1691 *Le Bon Soldat* having relied almost totally on Paul Poisson's verse.

It was seven years since Dancourt had attempted a five-act comedy even in prose. But in spite of a very modest success, the plot of *La Femme d'intrigues* played on 30 January 1692 was really too thin to sustain interest for five acts, while *Les Bourgeoises à la mode*, first given after the Fontainebleau season on 15 November and strongly dependent on Sainctyon for its intrigue, achieves its effect by the brilliance of its dialogue, and not at all by its plot. However, *Les Bourgeoises à la mode* had been a commercial success; an English adaptation had appeared in 1695. In 1699 it was time to make another attempt at the ambitious genre.

During the course of 1699 the dauphin commissioned a piece for Fontainebleau. Since Dancourt's daughters had just been admitted to full shares in the company he could scarcely refuse, but it interrupted work on the larger-scale piece he was engaged on. For the dauphin Dancourt wrote *Les Fées*, the title taken from Dufresny's 1697 *Les Fées; ou, Les Contes de ma mère l'oye*, a satire on the fairy-tale vogue. Each of the three acts in heavy prose is followed by an uninspired interlude. The idea could have become magically entertaining if the treatment had been as light as Marivaux might later have made it for the Italians, but Dancourt turns it into a glacial allegory, with satire that does not reach above the level of banality. The piece, however, was a success.

The five-act *La Famille à la mode* in verse, the piece on which work had been interrupted, was a clear attempt to rival Molière. The plot itself is practically borrowed from Molière, but Dancourt makes it too complicated, too moralistic, and too heavy-handed. The run was very short, six performances, although the takings were good. However, the play made clear that pastiche of Molière's language and dramatic structures could not serve the purposes Dancourt was best at achieving. He was best at the tiny satirical vignettes that kept some sort of audience coming during the hot days of the Paris summer, before the Fontainebleau season inaugurated the theatre's winter season proper.

In *L'Eté des coquettes*, for instance, a quite perfunctory intrigue has nothing to do with the piece's real merit, which depends on its evocation of the Paris summer of 1690, when all males of merit were away beating the imperial troops at Fleurus, leaving Paris empty apart from some dancing masters, a few lawyers, and some priests, together with the beautiful girls who were left with nothing to do but dream. Oddly, in spite of its concentrated allusiveness to a particular Paris summer, this was the Dancourt play that was revived for broadcasting in 1970, with *Le Chevalier à la mode* in 1978. *L'Eté* lived, because of its wistfulness and whimsicality, while the more ambitious plays did not.

Dancourt's best-known play is the five-act prose comedy *Le Chevalier à la mode*, first performed in 1687 on 24 October, when half the company was in Fontainebleau. In her magnificently equipped carriage Mme Patin, the rich bourgois widow of a financier, has had to give way to some marquise who pulled rank in an old carriage with a couple of blind horses. There are 45 scenes, which indicates a certain agitation onstage and already betrays Dancourt's weak ability to sustain interest through character alone. Mme Patin's men have been maltreated by those of the marquise. Her maid Lysette tells her to hasten to obtain rank for herself—"on achète facilement de la qualité avec de l'argent, mais la naissance ne donne pas toujours du bien (it is easy to buy nobility with money, but birth does not always confer wealth)." The satire therefore, it is clear, is aimed at the aristocratic ambitions of the rich bourgeois already, ostentatious, vulgar, and lacking in sensitivity, refinement, and dignity. Mme Patin is determined to marry the noble but destitute Chevalier de Villefontaine in order to achieve rank. Meanwhile her brother-in-law, Monsieur Serrefort ("Hold-tight") wants Mme Patin to marry a lawyer, M. Migaud, whose son will marry Serrefort's daughter, Lucile, so keeping the Patin wealth in the family.

Mme Patin is disconsolate. She knows she lacks "le bon air (the refined demeanour)," and would rather marry the most bankrupt marquis at court than remain the widow of the richest financier in France, but immediately shows us why she cannot ever attain quality. She disqualifies herself from true class by despising her own caste in her ambition to raise herself to another. The desire for refinement so expresses itself in Mme Patin as to show why she can never attain it. She objects to Lucile sitting next to her in a carriage as if she were her equal. The girl even dares to walk abreast with her. Worst of all, "elle attire les yeux de tout le monde, et ne laisse pas aller sur moy le moindre petit regard (she attracts everybody's attention without leaving the slightest glance for me)." Lysette, whose dramatic function is to provoke Mme Patin to even more vulgar displays of social ambition, now produces from her mistress an expression of contempt for the mere noblesse de robe. She wants "un nom de Cour, et de ceux qui emplissent le plus la bouche (a court name, and one of those that make the best mouthful)," and she does not care how poor the Chevalier is. There is even justice, she says, in restoring to the Norman nobility some of what her late husband not too scrupulously taxed from them.

The Chevalier uses several names, and keeps several women on the go at once, while trying to re-establish himself. Lucile is in love with him. The text is not light-hearted or witty, but there is an amusing irony when it is the avaricious and self-interested Serrefort who correctly, if for all the wrong motives, tells Mme Patin what a fool she is making of herself, while the way in which Lysette bends her views to fit in with her mistress's grotesquely vulgar social climbing, however heavy-handedly imitated from Molière, adds another ironic touch to the text. Quite quickly, the satirical aim established, the text changes to comic burlesque, with Villefontaine in particular freely using asides to make perfectly certain that the audience remembers what actually is the situation, as well as what each of the other characters thinks it is.

Lysette acts in concert with Migaud and Serrefort to prevent the marriage of Mme Patin with Villefontaine, who keeps having to extricate himself from absurd blunders and confusions. He dare not allow Mme Patin to see the carriage which he claims is his but has on it the arms of La Baronne, a woman who might turn out to be even richer than Mme Patin, but is equally ridiculous. He drops a list on which Mme Patin's name figures with that of a number of other women. He has addressed the same verses to Mme Patin, Lucile, and La Baronne. In the end Mme Patin does marry Migaud, and Lucile marries his son, who has not appeared on stage. Villefontaine goes off to look for better luck, turning to La Baronne for the time being. The characters are just complex enough to sustain interest, but the text gives the impression of being only artificially lengthened into five acts, the satirical point is made too early and too coarsely, and the whole over-complicated intrigue, with ten scenes more than a full Molière comedy, is treated too frivolously for its frothiness to combine well with the almost brutally cynical realism of the play's satirical raison d'être.

PUBLICATIONS

Collections

Les Oeuvres de M. Dancourt, 1693
Les Oeuvres de M. Dancourt, 5 vols., 1698
Les Oeuvres de M. Dancourt contenant les nouvelles pièces de théâtre…, vols. 1–6, 1706; vol. 7, 1716; vol. 8, 1717
Les Oeuvres de Monsieur Dancourt, 8 vols., 1742 [considered the definitive edition]
Les Oeuvres de M. Dancourt, 12 vols., 1760 [with music]

Plays [*Comedies unless otherwise stated, with dates of first production in round brackets. Plays whose texts have not survived are not listed*]

La Mort d'Hercule [5 acts, verse, tragedy] (1683), 1683
Les Nouvellistes de Lille [1 act, verse] (1683), 1683
Le Notaire obligeant [3 acts, prose], (1685), 1696
Angélique et Médor [1 act, prose] (1685), 1698
Le Ballet de la jeunesse [libretto] (1686), 1686
Renaud et Armide [1 act, verse] (1686), 1697
La Désolation des joueuses [1 act, prose] (1687), 1688
Le Chevalier à la mode [with Sainctyon, 5 acts, prose] (1687), 1688
La Maison de campagne [1 act, prose] (1688), 1691
La Folle Enchère [1 act, prose: attribution disputed] (1690), 1691
L'Eté des coquettes [1 act, prose] (1690), 1691
La Parisienne [1 act, prose] (1691), 1694
Le Bon Soldat [1 act, verse: adapted from Poisson] (1691), 1718
La Femme d'intrigues [5 acts, prose] (1692), 1694
La Gazette [1 act, prose] (1692), 1696
L'Opéra de village [1 act, prose] (1692), 1693
L'Impromptu de garnison [1 act, prose: retouched by Dancourt] (1692), 1693
Les Bourgeoises à la mode [with Sainctyon, 5 acts, prose] (1692), 1693
Les Vendanges [1 act, prose] (1694), 1694
Le Tuteur [1 act, prose] (1695), 1695
La Foire de Bezons [1 act, prose] (1695), 1695
Les Vendanges de Suresnes [1 act, prose] (1695), 1695
La Foire Saint-Germain [1 act, prose] (1696), 1696
Le Moulin de Javelle [1 act, prose: attribution disputed] (1696), 1696
Les Eaux de Bourbon [1 act, prose] (1696), 1696
Les Vacances [1 act, prose] (1696), 1697
La Loterie [1 act, prose] (1697), 1697
Le Charivari [1 act, prose] (1697), 1697
Le Retour des officiers [1 act, prose] (1697), 1698
Les Curieux de Compiègne [1 act, prose] (1698), 1698
Le Mari retrouvé [1 act, prose] (1698), 1698
Les Fées [Prologue and 3 acts, prose] (1699), 1699
La Famille à la mode [5 acts, verse] (1699); as *Les Enfants de Paris*, 1705
La Fête de village [3 acts, prose] (1700), 1700
Les Trois Cousines [Prologue and 3 acts, prose: attribution disputed] (1700), 1700
Colin-Maillard [1 act, prose] (1701), 1701
L'Opérateur Barry [Prologue and 1 act, prose] (1702), 1702
Le Galant Jardinier [1 act, prose] (1704), 1705

L'Impromptu de Livry [comédie-ballet] (1705), 1705
Divertissement de Sceaux [comédie-ballet] (1705)
Le Diable boiteux [Prologue and 1 act, prose] (1707), 1707
La Trahison punie [5 acts, verse: adapted from Boisrobert] (1707), 1708
Madame Artus [5 acts, verse] (1708), 1708
La Comédie des comédiens; ou, L'Amour charlatan [3 acts, prose] (1710), 1710
Les Agioteurs [3 acts, prose] (1710), 1710
Céphale et Procris [3 acts, verse] (1711), 1711
Sancho Pança Gouverneur [5 acts, verse: adapted from Guérin de Bouscal] (1712), 1713
L'Impromptu de Suresnes [verse prologue with 1 act, prose] (1713), 1713
Les Fêtes nocturnes du Cours [verse prologue with 1 act, prose], (1714), 1714
Le Vert-Galant [1 act, prose] (1714), 1714
Le Prix de l'arquebuse [1 act prose] (1717), 1717
La Métempsycose des amours [prologue and 3 acts, verse] (1717), 1718
La Déroute du pharaon [1 act, prose], 1718
L'Eclipse [1 act, prose: attribution disputed] (1724)

Biographical and critical studies

Attinger, Gustave, *L'Esprit de la Commedia dell' arte dans le théâtre français*, 1950
Blanc, André, *F.C. Dancourt (1661–1725)*, 1984

DESCARTES, René, 1596–1650.

Philosopher. See Cartesian(ism).

LIFE

Descartes was not a major author in the imaginative genres. He regarded himself primarily as a gentleman seriously dedicated to science and, more particularly, philosophy, but the implications for French culture generally of the task which Descartes set himself, and at least partly to his own satisfaction succeeded in completing, were immense, although no doubt more for scientific and religious thought than for attitudes towards the humanities.

In fact Descartes built on the way in which by the 17th century philosophy had become almost separable from theology, and attempted to sweep away that part of the antecedent philosophical tradition which had been dependent on specifically Aristotelian scholasticism, and replace it with what he felt to be a quite new philosophy unifying all the logically interconnected disciplines, almost by definition non-empirical, anchoring them in absolutely unchallengeable certainties, and creating a new

total philosophy of man, an ambition which has inspired French thinkers ever since, and is still reflected in their use of the term "philosophie" to cover the whole range of knowledge and speculation about the nature of human behaviour and human experience.

Descartes was born at the La Haye situated on the borders of Poitou and Touraine, on 31 March 1596, into an office-bearing family from the minor nobility, with écuyers on both sides. His father, an only child and the first lawyer from a family of doctors, bought the office of counsellor at the Brittany parlement on 14 February 1586. From his marriage on 15 January 1589 to Jeanne Brochard, born into the magistracy and daughter of the lieutenant-general of Poitiers, there were three surviving children, Pierre Descartes, sieur de la Bretaillière, also a counsellor at the Rennes parlement, a daughter who became Mme Rogier du Crévis, and René Descartes, called Descartes du Perron after a small fief in Poitou which he sold when he came of age. His mother died three days after giving birth to a fifth child on 13 May 1597.

Descartes was brought up by his widowed maternal grandmother, Jeanne Sain, and a nurse, to whom he later paid a pension. He was not strong as an infant and was to remain less than robust all his life. His father married again, had a further son and daughter, and settled at Rennes, leaving the three surviving children of his first marriage at La Haye. Descartes's earliest biographer, Adrien Baillet, who published in 1691, tells us that in 1604 Descartes was sent as a "chambriste," that is with the unusual privilege of a single room, to the Jesuit college at La Flèche, near Le Mans, but he cannot have been a "chambriste" until the buildings were completed in 1609, and probably did not start at La Flèche until at least 1606.

The Jesuits had been re-established in France by an edict of 2 January 1604 and immediately invited to take charge of La Flèche by Henri IV, who wanted to make it the premier college in Europe, and deliberately held the Jesuits back from re-establishing themselves in their Paris college, Clermont. Descartes was one of the 24 who carried the heart of Henri IV in procession to be buried at the college he had founded. Partly on account of his health, Descartes is said to have been allowed by the Jesuits to sleep late at school, and spent his early waking hours before rising thinking about mathematical and scientific problems. The habit of rising late certainly became an important feature of his adult life, and the need imposed on him by Christina of Sweden to break it was to be a contributory cause of his death.

Descartes himself comments on his programme of studies in the 1637 *Discours de la méthode*. Although he learned Latin and Greek, and probably Italian, enjoyed both poetry and fiction, and tells us that mathematics gave him particular pleasure on account of the certitude of its reasoning, in the *Discours* he relates his disappointment at not finding "une connaissance claire et assurée de tout ce qui est utile à la vie (a clear and certain knowledge of everything that is useful for life)." He became, he says, astonished that mechanics, built on such firm foundations, had not produced loftier results; disconcerted that philosophy had produced only disputed propositions, which were therefore open to doubt; and that the other disciplines, depending on philosophy, could not lead to conclusions which were more firmly founded. Theology did not teach the way to heaven, since that was open to the ignorant as well as the learned. The revealed truths which lead to salvation were beyond our understanding, and to examine them successfully required supernatural assistance.

At school Descartes must have been taught horsemanship, fencing, and dancing. He learned to enjoy and to write poetry. The considerations of the *Discours* on Descartes's education reflect a later repudiation of the erudition he wanted to replace by an exactly reasoned science, resting on self-evident foundations and leading to truths of complete certainty. In the meanwhile, after La Flèche, Descartes spent at least the academic year 1615–16 in Poitiers, and possibly the previous year as well. He graduated in law on 10 December 1616, and may also have followed a course in medicine. It seems probable that he spent some time in Paris, and he may also have travelled. There are suggestions that his life was ordinarily dissolute in accordance with his social rank, but the worst charge advanced is that he may have been addicted to gaming, and it seems to be at this time that he became friendly with Claude Mydorge, the important mathematician.

He signed two baptismal acts at Sucé in the diocese of Nantes on 22 October and 3 December 1617 and in 1617 may have been in Holland, where he spent over a year, starting sometime in 1618, finishing his education in a way common among the young aristocracy, with a period in one of the two French regiments in Holland. The war was over, and Descartes, equipped at his own expense, with a servant and without pay, served in the Breda garrison, about halfway between Utrecht and Antwerp, under the absent prince of Orange, Maurice of Nassau, stadtholder of the United Provinces of Holland, Zeeland, Utrecht, Overyssel, and Gelders. On his death on 23 April 1625, the prince was to be succeeded by his celebrated brother Frederick Henry, who brought the Netherlands to the height of its maritime and commercial power in Europe and in the east.

In the winter of 1618, Descartes got to know Isaac Beeckman, his senior by seven years, a doctor who had recently graduated at Caen and who had a special interest in physics. He had come to Breda on 16 October 1618 to help with the pig slaughter and look for a bride. He became successively assistant director of the Latin schools at Utrecht and Rotterdam, then in 1627 director of the school at Dordrecht, met Descartes at Breda on 10 November 1618, and quickly started to discuss mathematical and particularly geometrical problems with him. Descartes wrote to Beeckman in 1619 that Beeckman had re-kindled his interest in serious studies. Descartes had maintained contact with several Jesuits he had got to know at La Flèche and, according to Beeckman, was in contact with other French scientists and scholars. On 31 December 1618 Descartes dedicated to Beeckman his *Compendium musicae*, which he did not intend for publication. It was the fruit of a cooperation in applying mathematics to problems in the physics of sound-waves. With or for Beeckman, Descartes also wrote short treatises on such matters as water pressure, gravity, the summation of infinite mathematical series, and acceleration, while surprisingly studying painting, as well as military architecture and Dutch.

The letters to Beeckman, and especially the letter of farewell writen on 26 March 1619, show that Descartes was seriously given to mathematical reflections, and thought he saw new possibilities for developing the subject into a "science presque nouvelle (an almost new science)" permitting the resolution of problems concerning any order of continuous or discontinuous quantities. Maurice of Nassau, a strict Calvinist and himself a mathematician, had surrounded himself with mathematical

talent, and it is to be presumed that Descartes took some interest in the mathematics of architectural fortifications. His thinking was clearly already characterized by a quest for absolute certainty of the sort attainable in mathematics, and for a synthesis unifying at least the mathematical disciplines.

Descartes's departure from Breda after only around a year, but after having applied himself to learn Dutch, argues a change of plan. He appears from his letters to have been bored, perhaps discouraged in his solitary mathematical pursuits, and to have dreamt for a while of military glory. Beeckman had gone home. The intellectual ascendancy which came in the wake of Dutch mercantile prosperity was not yet fully established. Descartes was Catholic and French, and uninterested in the quarrels of the reformed churches about the softening of Calvin's doctrine of absolute predestination consequent on divine election or rejection without reference to Adam's sin. The country was split by the "remonstrant" Arminian liberals, suspicious of too tight a federal control of the provinces, and the "counter-remonstrant" strict Calvinists in favour of a strong central authority, with whom the military and Maurice of Nassau tended to side.

The matter was temporarily settled by the condemnation of the moderate doctrine of Arminius at the synod of Dort (Dordrecht) 1618–19, and by the subsequent execution of van Oldenbarnevelt at the age of 71, for religious as well as political reasons. Descartes may even have become disillusioned by the intolerant attitudes of Dutch Calvinism, as shown by the synod, which closed with a great celebration on 9 May. On 29 April 1619, Descartes had left for Denmark, intending to travel on overland to Bavaria, perhaps by way of Poland and Hungary. In Germany, he joined the Catholic army of Maximilian of Bavaria, opposed to the election of the Rhineland palatine to the kingship of Bohemia; from 20 July to 9 September he was at Frankfurt for the coronation of Ferdinand II.

Instead of returning to the army as he had originally intended, Descartes, his mind full of unsolved problems, hired a room, apparently near Ulm, in Germany, the famous "poêle (heated room)," and spent part of the winter in almost complete solitude, although he did find mathematicians with whom to discuss his work. The second chapter of the *Discours* gives some account of the reflections which led Descartes to undertake the intellectual experiment of attempting, on the supposition that nothing was true for which there was no rigorously certain evidence, to construct from first principles as much of a universal science as he was personally capable of doing.

It was on the evening of 10 November 1619 that Descartes underwent the experience of mental exaltation which resolved the intellectual tensions that had been building up within him. Unfortunately, a key text, the *Olympica* seen by Baillet and Leibniz, has been lost, and any statement about the precise nature of Descartes's intellectual illumination now partly depends on conjecture. For some months, as he tells us, having conceived of the possible unity of all mathematical knowledge, Descartes had been increasingly bewildered by the diversity of opinions among reasonable men, and even among great philosophers, and by the difference between cultures and periods, even in places he had been and during time he could remember.

The mental exhilaration of 10 November appears to have accompanied the realization that the mathematical method could be extended to universal knowledge, but that the principle unifying the sciences would have to be the work of an individual mind. The intellectual excitement either generated or was generated by some combination of the three distinct insights, that the mathematical sciences could be unified, that the principle of unification on a mathematical model was extensible to all non-empirical knowledge, and that the ground-plan for the unification of the sciences had to proceed from a single intelligence. It is not certain how instantaneous or intense the insights were, or in which order or over what period they were experienced. All we really know is that Descartes underwent a feverish intellectual stimulation, which had the impact of a revelation, on 10 November 1619. We really have only two clauses in renaissance Latin reported from the *Olympica* to go on, and their imperfect subjunctives imprecisely indicate the modality, tense, and anteriority of the two verbs: "X nov. 1619, cum plenus forem Enthusiasmo et mirabilis scientiae fundamenta reperirem (On 10 November 1619, when I was full of exhilaration and [had] discovered the foundations of the marvellous science)...."

That night, or just possibly the previous one, he also had three dreams whose content Baillet relates at length. Freud, asked about their meaning, said he would have to ask Descartes some questions before he could tell. The first two plainly have some anxiety content and the third might denote some resolution of psychological tension. It is obvious that, after having them, Descartes moved forward for the rest of his life in the general assurance that he knew what he was trying to do, and that he emerged from the crisis not only with calm certainty where there had for some months before been only nonplussed anxiety, but also with a clear sense of mission. The dream had answered a question of Ausonius it had recalled, "Quod vitae sectabor iter? (What route shall I follow in life?)."

Descartes, who took astrology seriously enough to want his date of birth kept secret, as knowledge of it could enable an astrologer to predict his death, himself interpreted especially the third dream as a sign of divine confirmation of the triple insight, particularly when the following day he met an Italian painter whom he recognized from a portrait he remembered seeing in the dream. There was apparently a third moment of intense intellectual excitement on 10 November (date in Descartes's *Cogitationes*) or 11 November (date in Baillet from the *Olympica*) 1620, about which we are less well informed. Descartes merely noted on that date, "coepi intelligere fundamentum Inventi mirabilis (I began to understand the foundation of the marvellous discovery)." What, if anything, was new in the product or cause of the 1620 experience is unclear, but has been much discussed.

Baillet says that following the experience of 1619 Descartes started work on a treatise to be finished by the following Easter, presumably on the structure of the unified discipline, but we know nothing for certain of Descartes's movements before he wrote to his brother from Rennes, where he was living with his family, on 3 April 1622. It is said that he tried to make contact with the Rosicrucians. It is likely that he had rejoined the army, possibly seeing action in Hungary, and that he further visited Silesia, Pomerania, and Poland. He may well have been present at Weisser Berg on 8 November 1620 when the territorial hopes of the elector were destroyed, and probably served under the comte de Buquoy in Hungary, leaving the army in the summer of July 1621 on Buquoy's death, after which Descartes probably travelled through Moravia, Pomerania, and Poland. In the winter of 1621–22 he appears to have been in Holland, and there is a generally accepted anecdote about an attempt to rob him on a boat on which he was sailing as the sole passenger, foiled because he understood the Dutch spoken by the sailors and on

account of his threat to use his sword. He had kept up his fencing, and was to write a treatise about the subject in 1628. It is reasonably conjectured that in Rennes he collected his inheritance from his mother, and that he spent some time in Paris, where his name seems wrongly to have been associated with the Rosicrucians, and visited Italy to settle the inheritance of his godmother.

From the summer of 1625 to the autumn of 1628, Descartes lived in Paris, making occasional journeys. He refused to tie himself down by marriage or an office, frequented scientific circles, but also indulged his enjoyment of literature, music, and poetry, writing to congratulate Balzac on the publication of his *Lettres*, and behaving like other young patricians, but with serious scientific and literary interests. He appears to have fought a duel over a woman, and to have gamed. His establishment in the faubourg Saint-Germain soon attracted too many people in search of scientific discussions, and he retreated to the household of friends, the Le Vasseur d'Etioles family, from which he also briefly disappeared in search of peace for study.

Scientifically Descartes was interested chiefly in his mathematical studies, and, with Mydorge, in the optics of refraction. He became expert in the fabrication of lenses, and in spite of his need for the freedom from constraint which allowed him time to think he built up a network of acquaintanceships among important scientists and thinkers—including some with reputations for scepticism—among the Oratorian theologians, and above all with the Minime Père Marin Mersenne, who had once been a pupil at La Flèche but, eight years older than Descartes, was already known for his resurrection, in the 1623 *Quaestiones celeberrimae in Genesim* and the 1625 *La Vérité des sciences contre les sceptiques ou pyrrhoniens*, of renaissance theories on the mathematical basis for music. Descartes came to rely heavily on his collaboration, and later used him to keep in touch with the learned world in France while he himself attempted to preserve his privacy in Holland.

It may well have been Bérulle whose encouragement led Descartes to devote his life exclusively to philosophy. Baillet tells us that it was in 1628 that the papal nuntius, archbishop, later cardinal, Giovanni-Francesco-Guido del Bagno, not to be confused with the marquis of the same name who commanded the papal troops in the Valtelline, held a discussion about new advances in philosophy at which a reticent Descartes was forced to reveal his brilliance to an astonished assembly. Bérulle was present, and invited Descartes to a series of private conversations at which, according to Baillet, Descartes outlined his project for extending his mathematical philosophical model, with its absolute certainties and rigorous deductions, to medicine and mechanics. Bérulle is said to have told Descartes that it was his duty to pursue his work, and to have been primarily responsible for forcing Descartes to commit himself to the elaboration, application, and dissemination of what we know as his method, a word which still in 1628 carried its renaissance resonance of "Guide" or "Pathway."

We cannot easily tell how honest Descartes was being with himself or with his readers when he wrote in the third part of the *Discours* that, having established the four rules of his method and the three maxims of what is normally called his "morale provisoire," he did not neglect his great enterprise, but spent nine years "travelling here and there in the world, trying to be a spectator rather than an actor in all the comedies being played there,"

Et ainsi, sans vivre d'autre façon en apparence que ceux qui, n'ayant aucun emploi qu'à passer une vie douce et innocente, s'étudient à séparer les plaisirs des vices, et qui, pour jouir de leur loisir sans s'ennuyer, usent de tous les divertissements qui sont honnêtes, je ne laissais pas de poursuivre mon dessein et de profiter en la connaissance de la vérité, peut-être plus que si je n'eusse fait que lire des livres ou fréquenter des gens de lettres

(And so, without apparently living in any way other than those who, having nothing to do except spend a life of innocence and tranquillity, try to separate pleasure from vice, and who, to enjoy their leisure without becoming bored, employ all decent distractions, I did not cease to persevere in my project and to progress in the knowledge of the truth perhaps more than I would have if I had done nothing but read books or mix with learned people).

Probably it is true that Descartes had never after November 1619 put from his mind his projected undertaking, and it is quite clear that he could never later have achieved the brilliance of penetration and breadth of scope he later showed without a long period of reflection, while the means and courage were mustered for so virtually inconceivable an undertaking as his, the creation of a unified science of nature and humanity which required rethinking the logical links between all that was knowable with certainty, including that part of it which was not yet known, within the bounds laid down by a theological orthodoxy accepted as revealed, normative, and unquestionable. It is not improbable that Bérulle failed to foresee the clash which he was promoting between an exceedingly powerful new philosophy and an unchangeable religious orthodoxy, or that Descartes was finally pushed by the religious considerations urged by Bérulle, the social pressures he himself mentions at the end of the third part of the *Discours*, and ultimately a sense both of ambition and of mission, into finally summoning up the necessary resolution to face the task he had set himself,

chercher les fondements d'aucune philosophie plus certaine que la vulgaire

(to look for the foundations of any philosophy more certain than the common one).

He went to Holland, choosing towns and country residences where he could live quietly, practising his Catholicism without molestation, and working with Beeckman again. He had sold the property he had inherited in Poitou and invested the proceeds to secure for himself an annual income estimated at between 6,000 and 7,000 livres. When he left France he had given charge of his financial affairs to the abbé Picot. Mersenne was acting as his correspondent with the learned world, although he was going to behave with more zeal than discretion.

The end of the third part of the *Discours*, accounting for Descartes's decision to live in Holland, certainly offers less than the whole explanation. He went in 1628, probably only settling definitively a year later. Beeckman notes that Descartes visited him on 8 October 1628. Unfortunately, the two friends were very soon to quarrel angrily. Beeckman had claimed in letters to Mersenne that Descartes's ideas on music, and much of the earlier work on mathematics, had been inspired by Beeckman's

own work. Mersenne sent the letters to Descartes, who exploded, writing a series of stingingly worded letters to Beeckman in September and October 1630. No doubt Beeckman badly exaggerated his role in Descartes's development, and Descartes had the right to vindicate his prized originality, but he need not have done so touchily, or in such oblivion of what he did truly owe to Beeckman. The quarrel was in Latin. There was a reconciliation, but the damage was done.

The importance of the matter lies in what it tells us about Descartes's consciousness of originality and daring. The originality in the conception of the project and the daring in its execution were both real, and without them it is doubtful whether Descartes could have penetrated with his method as far as he did, but neither the project nor the component elements of his final philosophy were as new as he needed to think they were. The touchiness merely indicates the intensity of personal commitment which Descartes's achievement required. His disposition was by nature inclined to indolence and instability, and he could not have done what he did had he not believed that he was much more independent of earlier traditions than in fact he was.

By the end of 1628 it seems certain that Descartes had written the *Regulae ad directionem ingenii*, more or less summing up the state of his studies when he called on Beeckman that October. By April 1629 Descartes was at Franeker, where he matriculated as a student on 26 April at the university founded only in 1585, and worked on projects centring on the newly invented telescope, trying to get his French lens-maker to join him, and trying to improve the instrument with the aid of hyperbola-shaped lenses. To Descartes's annoyance, Ferrier would not come. Descartes had been quite insistent to Ferrier that no one in France should know where he was.

After some months in Franeker, however, he based himself from 1629 to 1635 on Amsterdam, where he had a total of three addresses during that time, although from 27 June 1630 he was also a matriculated student at Leiden, where he also lived, and from May 1632 to November 1633 he was in Deventer. It was probably in Deventer that he had a liaison with Helen Jans, who kept house for him, and by whom he had a daughter, Francine. Her death at the age of five was, according to Baillet, the greatest sorrow of Descartes's life. In 1634 he also visited Denmark. In order to stay out of reach he kept on the move, and he is said to have lived altogether in 13 places in Holland, and at 24 addresses. Between 1639 and 1649 he visited France only three times: in 1644, to settle family affairs after the death of his father in 1640; in 1647 mostly on family and academic business, when he also received a pension of 3,000 livres from Mazarin; and in 1648, when he was summoned for new honours and an augmented pension, but immediately departed again on account of the Fronde.

By 1633 Descartes had produced a number of what in retrospect can be seen as sketches for the later works. On 15 April 1630 he had already written to Mersenne that he had found how metaphysical truths could be demonstrated even more conclusively than geometrical theorems. The *Regulae* are devoted to considerations of method, and by 1633 Descartes had his account of the physical doctrine of the universe in *Le Monde* ready to be transcribed for publication. He had earlier showed anxiety about the likely reception of his views on the infinity of the universe and the earth's rotation round the sun, and suppressed his own work, not even sending a copy to Mersenne when, in September 1633, he read a copy of the condemnation of Galileo. He wrote to Mersenne that he did not want to utter a single word which would meet with the Church's disapproval. Three cosmological and physiological treatises ready at this period were published only posthumously, by Clerselier in 1664.

It is important to understand that Descartes's scientific researches, which for a period took him almost daily to the Amsterdam abattoir, and which cover so astonishingly wide a variety of phenomena from the disciplines of what we call astronomy, botany, optics, sound, music, cosmology, anatomy, medicine, embryology, logic, geometry, algebra, arithmetic, and philosophy, were for him of interest, like the whole of his daily experience, because he wanted to discover the underlying laws of a universal science, which would link them all together. That is why his first published treatise was prefaced by a discourse on the history of his project for such a universal science. It is not surprising that he was interested even in a universal language, or that he could not see the point in the study of Latin and Greek. In spite of the early love of poetry, Descartes lacked an aesthetic sense, and, in spite of his early interest in painting, nothing he wrote contributed to an aesthetic or would even remind anyone that, not far away, Rembrandt painted *The Night Watch* in 1642, the year after the appearance of Descartes's *Meditationes*.

More important than the apparent diversity of subjects is the fact that theology is left severely alone, implicitly dependent not on reason but on authority, and that, while Descartes had clearly begun to think in terms of vast progress in medicine and mechanics, he had not yet undertaken serious work on ethics. He would not touch theology not because he was a doubter, but because he was a committed believer. The revealed truth could no more clash with his universal science than could the properly understood results of empirical scientific investigation. Descartes never realized how severe was the threat that would be created for religious belief by an explanation of human experience in terms of a metaphysic, a general physics, and in the end even an ethic, which did not depend on theological foundations, and were unconstrained by its dogmas.

Descartes is amusing about Holland, which he enjoyed, although he never really mastered the language. He could have his ten hours sleep a night and his famous breakfast omelette, for which he preferred eggs eight to ten days old. He wrote to Balzac that the Dutch, all merchants, were so interested in doing deals and making profits that he was left in perfect peace. He also, however, found much stimulation in Dutch intellectual circles, less inhibited by religious orthodoxies in scientific debate than the scientific community in France, and more open to Descartes's peculiar brand of radical, if never in Catholic terms heterodox, vision.

Much of the *Dioptrique* was written in Utrecht in 1635, where the finishing touches were probably made to the treatises on meteors and geometry. All three, prefaced by the *Discours de la méthode*, were printed in Leiden in the course of 1636. Descartes was by now on terms of close friendship with Constantin Huyghens, father of Christian, who helped with the plates and forwarded a set of proofs to Mersenne. The original title was to have been "Le Projet d'une science universelle qui puisse élever notre nature à son plus haut degré de perfection…(The project for a universal science able to elevate our nature to its highest degree of perfection)." In the event Descartes insisted against both Huyghens and Mersenne on the prefatory "Discours de" of the final title, since the work was a development of only some

points of the complete method. The print-run of 3,000 copies was ready on 8 June 1637. Descartes was 41. In December the work was on sale in Paris, with a privilège, but anonymous, and called *Discours de la Méthode pour bien conduire sa raison et chercher la vérité dans les sciences. Plus la Dioptrique, Les Metéores et la Géométrie. Qui sont des essais de cette méthode.*

Although the three treatises were purely scientific, they were presented as applications of a philosophical method. The use of French was almost a manifesto proclaiming the revolutionary content of a work which, however orthodox, swept away at a stroke the tradition of Aristotelian scholasticism, with an epistemology based on the abstraction by the intellect of essences from objects. Descartes distributed numerous presentation copies, and gave one to La Flèche. The anonymity was more an affectation than a precaution. Reaction was muted but on the whole critical, although the criticisms were of detail, chipping morsels off the three shorter treatises or the section of the *Discours* dealing with the physiology of the heart, rather than frontally attacking the whole method itself. Descartes did, however, show the touchiness which had already soured his relationship with Beeckman, when a new algebra written by a Dutch mathematician called Stampioen d'Jonghe appeared to challenge Descartes's work, and Descartes unnecessarily humiliated him.

Descartes lived for two or three years, including 1640, at Santpoort, then from the spring of 1641 to the spring of 1643 at Endegeest, where he had rented a small château. Picot spent a year with him there, and Samuel Sorbière paid him a visit. During 1640 Descartes elaborated the metaphysical considerations of the fourth part of the *Discours* into the six *Meditationes de prima philosophia*, building on an earlier treatise written in 1629 at Franeker, and now writing more formally, at greater depth, and in Latin. He had the manuscript approved by friends in Holland, and sent it via Huyghens to Mersenne in November 1640. Mersenne sent back six sets of comments, including those of Antoine Arnauld, Hobbes, and Gassendi, and printed *Objectiones*, to which Descartes duly replied, replying again later to instances made to his first replies.

The full title of the work is important: *Meditationes de prima philosophia, in qua Dei existentia et animae immortalitas demonstratur* ("Meditations on the first philosophy in which the existence of God and the immortality of the soul is demonstrated"). It had been a weakness of Aristotelian scholasticism that theories of knowledge based on abstraction had depended on corruptible bodily organs, so that it became difficult to explain the continuation of personal knowing after death, and hence the immortality of the soul. To demonstrate the soul's immortality, Descartes has to explain knowledge in such a way as not to make it depend on abstraction. The book, with its privilège, appeared in Paris in August 1641. In the second edition, an Elzevir of Amsterdam 1642, the title read…*in quibus Dei existentia et animae humanae a corpore distinctio, demonstrantur* ("in which the existence of God and the distinctness of the human soul from the body are demonstrated"). Descartes himself corrected the proofs of the Dutch edition, which he himself regarded as more authoritative. A French translation by the duc de Luynes appeared in 1647, with the objections and replies translated by Clerselier. The interest of Luynes helps to explain the Cartesianism of the Port-Royal solitaires.

The appearance of the *Meditationes* began to cause trouble for Descartes in Holland, particularly at the new but ultra-Aristotelian University of Utrecht, where public hostilities broke out between Descartes and a young professor of reformed theology, Gisbert Voët. Descartes again appeared ultra-sensitive, but could make no progress with the university authorities and retired to France for four months in 1644, staying in Paris with Picot and visiting Brittany to settle his father's estate, showing himself particularly anxious to gain the goodwill of the Jesuits. On his return to Holland on 15 November 1644, he established himself at Egmond op den Hoef with a small retinue of servants and a secretary. Almost a vegetarian, he drank very little wine, and worked hard, cultivating plants for botanical experiments, studying anatomy, and carrying on an acrimonious mathematical controversy with Roberval.

Four parts of the projected six of the general physics had appeared in the 1644 Amsterdam *Principia*, while Descartes was in Paris. He had again written in Latin, although he collaborated with Picot in his 1647 French translations. Although he clearly justified himself in an epistolary squabble with Voët, the university of Utrecht never revoked its hostility to Descartes or the ban it imposed on his works, and Descartes also slowly fell out with his principal remaining supporter, Henri le Roy, known as Regius. The Utrecht disputes had hardly died down before there was further trouble, this time at Leiden. Again the real fear was the religious consequences of a philosophy which started from doubt, and again the remedy was a ban, although now enforced less rigorously. The university's official teaching was to be based on Aristotle. Ultimately, although this was not how it was put, Thomist proofs of the existence of God based on causality seemed much safer than Cartesian reasoning on the nature of ideas.

As he approached 50 Descartes gave up practising his horsemanship, but it is while he was at Egmond that he established his friendship with Elizabeth, the eldest daughter of the ejected elector palatine, against whose father Descartes had once served in Bohemia, and whose mother maintained on credit the ostentatious luxury of a court at The Hague. It was in letters to Elizabeth that Descartes was first to elaborate the culminating point of his philosophy, the ethic. Elizabeth of Bohemia was the third of the 13 children of the elector palatine Frederick V and his wife, Elizabeth Stuart, daughter of James I of England. Frederick had been removed by the League under Maximilian I and had taken refuge in Holland in 1621 at the invitation of his uncles, Maurice and Frederick of Orange. Elizabeth and three other children of the family had been left behind in Brandenburg, and she joined her parents at The Hague only in 1628, when she was 10. She grew up educated, artistic, melancholy, and intellectually curious. Descartes, knowing her by reputation, tried to call on her, but she did not receive him. She did, however, inaugurate their long correspondence with a letter of 6 May 1643.

The letters are in French, at first even with a touch of galanterie, although from 1645 they are crucial in the elaboration of Descartes's philosophy. Descartes met the princess, and dedicated the *Principia* to her. The projected fifth part on plants and animals was never written, but the unwritten sixth part, on the all-important psycho-physics of the body-soul union in man, the central philosophical problem since Plato, was replaced by the first of the three parts of *Les Passions de l'âme*, offered by Descartes as a substitute and based on the reflections more or less forced out of him by Elizabeth's letters. He finally elaborated the link between physiology and ethics under the pressure of his desire to assist Elizabeth to overcome a feverish cough which Descartes believed had been brought on by the sadness of her

situation. She was an impoverished grandee whose family were living flamboyantly while humiliatingly in debt.

In 1647 Descartes returned to France. The letters to Elizabeth show him exasperated by the sniping at his philosophy emanating now principally from Leiden. He considered leaving Holland, but was recalled to France anyway and left Rotterdam on 8 June, travelling via Calais to Paris, where he stayed again with the abbé Picot, probably then writing the important preface to the French translation of the *Principia*. Pascal's father had just repeated Evangelista Torricelli's 1644 experiment which appeared to leave a vacuum at the top of a full tube of mercury when upturned in a bowl of the metal. Mersenne had met Torricelli in 1645 in Italy and had brought news of the experiment back to Paris. The *Principia* had maintained that there was no vacuum, and that wherever there was extension there had to be matter. Gassendi held that there could be extension without matter, but that the fact could not be experimentally demonstrated. Descartes found himself, less by chance than he imagined, on Aristotle's side but against the empirical scientists, including his old opponent Roberval, and Pascal. Père Noël took Descartes's side.

Later in June 1647 Descartes went to Rennes, where his elder brother still lived. He returned to Paris through Poitou and Touraine, arriving in September. Mersenne, to die a year later, was already terminally ill. On 23 September Descartes, accompanied by a small group of scientists, called on Pascal. Roberval, who was with Pascal, defended the existence of a vacuum. Descartes returned next day but Jacqueline Pascal, who reported to her sister on the first visit, was not present, and we do not know what was discussed, or how; but it is at least probable that Descartes suggested to Pascal that he should repeat Torricelli's experiment both at the top and at the bottom of a mountain. They agreed that the mercury level in Torricelli's upturned tube was caused by the pressure of air on the mercury in the bowl. The experiment at Puy-de-Dôme (see: Pascal) was to determine whether the air pressure changed with altitude. When later Pascal wrote the introduction to his account of the experiments he sent a copy to Descartes, which evoked a testy reaction.

It was in Paris that Descartes met Hobbes, and that he was reconciled with Gassendi, whose objections to the *Meditationes* had caused him irritation. Descartes was pleased at the pension bestowed on him, although it may never on account of the Fronde actually have been paid, and returned to Holland at the end of September 1647, bringing with him Picot, who stayed at Egmond until mid-January 1648. In May Descartes returned again to France, invited by the government, this time hiring through Picot an apartment in which he could entertain. Descartes complained of being put on display, and on the outbreak of the Fronde with the barricades of 26–27 August returned hurriedly to Holland, turning down private offers of a country house and annual sums for his living expenses and studies.

In 1645, Descartes's friend Pierre Chanut, Clerselier's brother-in-law, had been made French chargé d'affaires in Stockholm, at the court of Queen Christina, born in 1626, and as dedicated to study as she was to hunting and horsemanship. Chanut had stayed with Descartes at Amsterdam in 1645, had introduced Christina to Descartes's work, and was the intermediary in a relationship which started with requests for Descartes's opinions on various points of ethics, and with Descartes's replies. Direct correspondence started with a letter of 20 November 1647 from Descartes on the sovereign good. At the same time Descartes sent Chanut a manuscript copy of the as yet unpublished *Les Passions de l'âme*. Descartes received a letter of thanks from Christina dated 12 December 1648. Chanut had meanwhile read the *Principia* to Christina, who wanted to have the matters treated further explained.

Chanut's further efforts, and those of the German professor Freinsheim, later the royal librarian at Stockholm, led Christina to invite Descartes to Sweden, using Chanut as intermediary. The letter is dated 25 February 1649. An admiral would be despatched to bring him. Chanut had to send a second invitation on 6 March. Descartes would be expected to stay for some months and to teach Christina philosophy. Descartes was hesitant, not only on account of the uprooting, but because of the apparent capriciousness of the queen. He would only go if the tutorship was serious, and sent the admiral back empty-handed in the meanwhile, later protesting he had neither known he was an admiral, nor understood what he had come for. Chanut, returning to France, stopped off in Holland to reassure Descartes, who wondered about possible hostility in another Protestant culture. There was, said Chanut, no great hurry. Descartes made up his mind, took great care about his personal appearance and clothes, and left for what he called "the country of bears, between the mountains and the glaciers" on 31 August or 1 September 1649.

There was hostility in Stockholm. Descartes was not the only distinguished foreigner to be invited by the boyish, unkempt, small-statured Christina. The Amsterdam doctor Johan van Wullen was there, an old adversary who had tried to block Descartes's invitation, as were Isaac Vossius and Daniel Heinsius, not at all pleased to see Descartes monopolize Christina's intellectual interests. The queen welcomed Descartes, encouraged him to settle permanently, and then characteristically forgot about him for six weeks or so. For his part, he was contemptuous of her interest in Greek, which contributed nothing to the pursuit of truth. She none the less prevailed on him to write a verse ballet, *La Naissance de la paix*, to celebrate the peace of Munster, which had been signed on 30 January 1648. He also wrote a comedy, and drew up the constitutions for a scientific academy.

There is some reason to suppose that Descartes thought he was being seen as merely gracing the court as its resident philosopher. In a month he saw the queen only four or five times. Her energy was however inexhaustible; she managed on five hours sleep while Descartes needed ten; and on her return to Stockholm in mid-January, she bade Descartes to his teaching sessions with her at 5 a.m. at least three days a week. Later on, that regime ruined her health, but it was Descartes who immediately suffered, He fell ill and developed pneumonia. Christina had him looked after by van Wullen, whose medical views diverged sharply from his own. He insisted on taking an emetic, then on getting out of bed. The last sacraments could not be administered, but he was blessed by a priest while still conscious. He died at 4 a.m. on 11 February 1650.

WORKS

It is even more essential with a philosopher than with most other types of imaginative author to take account of what a writer decided to publish, in what form, and at what date. It is possible, and indeed customary, to take disparate evidence from heterogeneous sources in the attempt to reconstruct the development of Descartes's thought. In fact it is of the greatest importance to distinguish what works were published either by Descartes or with his approbation, and to take full account of the fact when manuscript drafts, simple sketches or possibly repudiated notes are being drawn on. In the case of letters, especially if they had a philosophical content, we need to know to whom they were written, under what circumstances, and whether they were intended only for the eyes of the recipient, before such material can be used in the reconstitution of Descartes's intellectual development.

Descartes was not a professional philosopher, and was active in a philosophical post for only the last few weeks of his life. He published only because he felt compelled to disseminate his views by a sense of mission or even duty. It is difficult to use even the word "publish" with precision. In his first printed work, the 1637 *Discours*, Descartes connived in what was only a semi-anonymous public dissemination of his vernacular reflections on a way to construct a universal science, with three attached examples of how that science might be applied to the physics of light, the cosmology of meteors, and the mathematics of geometry.

Thereafter he published only the *Meditationes*, allowing them to be translated and published with the *Objections* collected by Mersenne, his *Réponses* to the *Objections*, the instances of the objectors, and his own *Deuxième "Réponses;"* four out of the six projected books of the *Principia*, to whose translation he added two prefatory letters; and the posthumous treatise *Les Passions de l'âme*, which was in the course of publication when he died, but whose proofs he might yet have wished to correct, or whose text he might have wished to alter, as he altered the text of the *Meditationes* between the Paris and the Amsterdam editions.

Nothing else was formally published, although Descartes no doubt intended his polemic with the city of Utrecht, for instance, to be public knowledge, and much of what he wrote on mathematics was intended to be communicated to fellow-mathematicians. The task of reconstructing the ways in which Descartes's vision of a universal science changed depends on the accurate identification of the level of personal commitment behind any given statement, but it is more often than has been generally realized complicated by the need to disentangle what amount to degrees of publication from one another.

Some of Descartes's letters about personal or family matters contain unambiguous biographical testimony, but were not intended for any eyes other than those of the addressee, but there is nothing in the letters to Elizabeth on problems of psychology and ethics, in spite of a certain formal intimacy, which suggests that Descartes expected them to be entirely private. Not everything he wrote to Chanut was intended for Christina's eyes. Mersenne too readily communicated Descartes's comments to some of his critics. The real importance of distinguishing between correspondents, however, derives from the need to establish the degree of speculation or pure conjecture Descartes may have been permitting himself in any given text. Publication with a privilège entailed full commitment with no unstated element of the merely conjectural, whereas a letter to Elizabeth might well have included tentative solutions to which Descartes was not yet at all fully committed and which perhaps almost anticipated modifications in the light of objections.

Descartes's first published essay, the *Discours de la méthode*, is partly autobiographical, setting out his philosophical aims in 1637, how he had acquired them, and what he had done about achieving them. The first section starts as if Descartes were stating the obvious. "Bon sens," clearly meaning not "good sense" but "the power of reasoning," is defined as the ability to distinguish what is true from what is false. Descartes already makes huge assumptions in supposing that the power of reasoning is equal in all human beings, implicitly accepting the neostoic and Aristotelian view that all human beings share in a universal reason, a participation in the divine mind whose privileges the scholastics usurped when they bestowed the attributes of right reason on the human mental faculty. Since the individual mental capacities of human beings are clearly not the same, the difference between them must reside in more than the power of reasoning itself. It must lie in the ability and willingness to apply the equally distributed faculty of reason. Descartes digresses a little by throwing in the remark that

Les plus grandes âmes sont capables des plus grands vices aussi bien que des plus grandes vertus

(The greatest spirits are those which are capable of the greatest vices as well as the greatest virtues).

That view, implying the ethical ambivalence of moral grandeur is what most memorably Corneille was exploring in *Rodogune*, played during the 1644–45 season, but the problem it announces of the ethical ambiguity of heroic behaviour was to run right through the Augustinian moralists, whether Jansenist, like Pascal and Nicole, or writing, like La Rochefoucauld, in a secular context. In a writer so ostentatiously conscious of his own originality as Descartes, it is important to watch for the signs which inevitably tie him closely to his own cultural context.

He is modestly self-congratulatory. If there is a sure path to raising his mind to the highest point of its potential development, he dares to think he has found it. However, he could be mistaken, so he has not undertaken to lay down a method for others to follow, but merely wishes to give an account of his own intellectual history, so that they can judge. The intellectual biography follows immediately, with Descartes insisting on his desire from infancy to acquire "une connaissance claire et assurée de tout ce qui est utile à la vie (a clear and assured knowledge of everything that is useful in life)."

Descartes leant heavily on the side of modern culture against that of classical antiquity, partly because he hoped for technological advances in medicine which would contribute to human happiness, prolong life, and eliminate geriatric symptoms, and partly because he believed in the philosophical possibility of laying down an assured path to happiness. Progress was not to be achieved by studying or following the authors of antiquity, and for Descartes "notre siècle me semblait aussi fleurissant et aussi fertiles en bons esprits, qu'ait été aucun des précédents (our time seemed to me as flourishing and as fertile in brilliant minds as any which have preceded it)." He realized how good his schooling had been and knew that the knowledge he was seeking did not yet exist. He was still possessed by

un extrême désir d'apprendre à distinguer le vrai d'avec le faux, pour voir clair en mes actions et marcher avec assurance en cette vie

(an extreme desire to learn to distinguish what was true from what was false, in order to understand my actions and walk forward with assurance in this life).

The second part of the *Discours* is concerned with the experience of 10 November 1619 and its consequences. Descartes wants to adjust his mind to accept only those things he knows with absolute certainty to be true. The four rules of his method are

1. De ne recevoir jamais aucune chose pour vrai que je ne la connusse évidemment être telle; c'est-à-dire d'éviter soigneusement la précipitation et la prévention, et de ne comprendre rien de plus en mes jugements que ce qui se présenterait si clairement et si distinctement à mon esprit que je n'eusse aucune occasion de le mettre en doute.
2. De diviser chacune des difficultés que j'examinerais en autant de parcelles qu'il se pourrait et qu'il serait requis pour les mieux résoudre.
3. De conduire par ordre mes pensées, en commençant par les objets les plus simples et les plus aisés à connaître, pour monter peu à peu comme par degrés jusques à la connaissance des plus composés, et supposant même de l'ordre entre ceux qui ne se précèdent point naturellement les uns les autres.
4. De faire partout des dénombrements si entiers et des revues si générales, que je fusse assuré de ne rien omettre

(1. Not to accept as true anything that I did not know to be so on evidence; that is to say carefully to avoid haste and prejudice, and to include in my judgements no more than presented itself so clearly and distinctly to my mind that I had no possibility of doubting it.
2. To divide each of the difficulties that I examined into as many sections as possible and as was necessary for their more successful resolution.
3. To conduct my thoughts in order, beginning with the things which are simplest and easiest to know, to ascend little by little by steps to the knowledge of the most complex, presupposing order even between the things which do not precede one another naturally.
4. To establish everywhere enumerations full enough and reviews general enough to be certain to omit nothing).

Descartes has not yet quite decided to use "method" in a sense other than that denoting simple rules for guidance, virtually meaning handbook or notes for guidance, but he does slip in the implied criteria for truth of clarity and distinctness, and he assumes that there is a logical system connecting all that which is knowable. Having revealed his geometric model, he goes on to make the last assumption explicit, supposing that

toutes les choses qui peuvent tomber sous la connaissance des hommes s'entre-suivent en même façon... et il n'y en peut avoir de si éloignées auxquelles enfin on ne parvienne, ni de si cachées qu'on ne découvre

(all things humanly knowable are interconnected in the same way... and there cannot exist any so distant that they cannot in the end be reached nor so hidden that they cannot be discovered).

So optimistic an assertion of the unbridled power of human reason to reach truth is unmatchable. Most commentators assume that Descartes implies limitations he has not stated, but it is not impossible that Descartes wished to include even what we should regard as empirical knowledge. Descartes was certainly more interested in discovering by deduction under what conditions of humidity, temperature, altitude, and whatever other rules applied, it would be snowing, than he was in looking out of the window to see if it was, since empirical judgements of that sort could not be guaranteed by divine veracity.

Whatever the text of the *Discours* actually does imply, it is certain that Descartes was more interested in the establishment of rules for discovering truth than he was in measuring data, and that his confidence in human reason was huge. With Pierre Corneille and François de Sales he actually is exploring the potential of human nature with a measure of imaginative daring so optimistic that subsequent generations have rarely thought it possible that his text carries the implications which it clearly does.

Descartes congratulates himself on the successes he had by 1637 achieved with the method he had elaborated in 1619, and in the third section enumerates the four maxims of the moral code he had determined to live by until he had worked out through the method what the moral rules were which would lead infallibly to happiness. These rules, the "morale provisoire," were later, in a letter to Elizabeth of 4 August 1645, to be incorporated into Descartes's definitive ethic. They move from the moral order to that of rational truth, and are sufficient for "sagesse (wisdom)." Descartes enunciates them:

1. Obéir aux lois et aux coutumes de mon pays, retenant constamment la religion en laquelle Dieu m'a fait la grâce d'être instruit dès mon enfance, et me gouvernant en toute autre chose suivant les opinions les plus modérées et les plus éloignées de l'excès qui fussent communément reçues en pratique par les mieux sensés de ceux avec lesquels j'aurais à vivre.
2. Etre le plus ferme et le plus résolu en mes actions que je pourrais, et de ne suivre pas moins constamment les opinions les plus douteuses lorsque je m'y serais une fois déterminé qui si elles eussent été très-assurées.
3. Tâcher toujours plutôt à me vaincre que la fortune, et à changer mes désirs que l'ordre du monde, et généralement de m'accoutumer à croire qu'il n'y a rien qui soit entièrement en notre pouvoir que nos pensées.
[4. De faire une revue sur les diverses occupations qu'ont les hommes en cette vie, pour tâcher à faire choix de la meilleure]
(1. To obey the laws and customs of my country, constantly retaining the religion in which God gave me the grace to be instructed from my childhood, and directing myself in everything else according to the most moderate opinions, the furthest removed from excess, among those commonly accepted in practice by the most sensible people of those I should have to live among.
2. To be as firm and resolute in my actions as I could, and to follow the most doubtful opinions once I have decided on them no less constantly than if they had been most certain.
3. To try always rather to conquer myself than to conquer fortune, and to change my desires rather than the order of the world, and generally to accustom myself to believe that

there is nothing entirely in our power except our mental acts.
[4. To make a review of the different human occupations in this life, in order to try to choose the best]).

The first maxim is taken from Montaigne's practical advice in his chapter *De la vanité* in *Les Essais*, where Montaigne added Pibrac's famous quatrain CIX to the same effect. Pibrac's 126 quatrains, heavily tinged with the neostoicism of the religious wars, were published in 1574 as a guide to moral wisdom, and learned by heart for at least a quarter of a century by every grammar-school child. Descartes's second maxim draws attention to his refusal to remain inhibited in action while intellectually trying to resolve the notional doubts imposed on his by the method. The third maxim is simple neostoicism, of which Descartes's ethical thinking offers many examples. However, for Descartes, "pensées" includes acts of will, and in so optimistic a context it is not surprising to find this emphatic affirmation of free will, strongly upheld in its fullest sense by the Jesuits, of course, but also linking Descartes again to François de Sales and to Pierre Corneille. The fourth item is not really a maxim at all, but a declaration of intention.

Descartes carries on with an exceedingly important definition which, although paralleled in du Vair, Charron, François de Sales, d'Urfé, and Jean-Pierre Camus, is usually considered almost constitutive of Cartesian ethical rationalism. Descartes starts from the implicit assumption made in the first line of Epictetus's *Enchiridion*, that there are only two sorts of things, those which are in our power and those which are not, but our true good must be in our power. The faculty of the will, for the scholastics and Descartes, is different from the intellect, and cannot collaborate with it in the production of one act, a dilemma which lies behind Pascal's use of the term "coeur (heart)." Virtue lies in the will's firm resolution to follow the judgements about the good indicated to it by the intellect, and Descartes actually goes so far as to affirm that not only knowledge, but also virtue and happiness are in our power:

…pensant être assuré de toutes les connaissances dont je serais capable, je le pensais être par même moyen de celle de tous les vrais biens qui seraient jamais en mon pouvoir; d'autant que, ne se portant à suivre ni à fuir aucune chose que selon que notre entendement la lui représente bonne ou mauvaise, il suffit de bien juger pour bien faire, et de juger le mieux qu'on puisse pour faire aussi tout son mieux, c'est-à-dire pour acquérir toutes les vertus, et ensemble tous les autres biens qu'on puisse acquérir; et lorsqu'on est certain que cela est, on ne saurait manquer d'être content

(…thinking I was assured of all the knowledge of which I was capable, I considered that in the same way I would be assured of [the acquisition of] all the true goods which would ever be in my power; since, being led neither to follow nor to flee anything except in accordance with whether our judgement shows it to be good or evil, it is enough to judge correctly in order to act virtuously, and to judge as well as possible in order to behave as virtuously as possible, that is to say, to acquire all the virtues, and all the other goods which can be acquired; and when certainty is reached about that, it is impossible not to achieve happiness).

At this point Descartes, insisting once again that he is putting aside "les vérités de la foi (the truths of faith)," announces that he undertook his methodic doubt, constructing a make-believe world parallel to the real one, in which he would pretend that nothing at all was true except what he could actually show to be true. He let the nine years from 1619 to 1628 pass in observing before going to Holland and making serious progress. Without naming the thinkers to whom he alludes, he makes clear that he found inspiration in Bacon and Ramus, but that he regarded Telesio, Bruno, and Campanella as having gone astray. The elaboration of the mentally certain world inside which the universal science can be constructed takes up the fourth part of the *Discours*, and is then expounded at greater length in the six *Meditationes*.

Sense perception can obviously deceive, as Descartes's optical experiments demonstrated, or even the apparent angle in a straight stick plunged half into clear water. Descartes had brought with him to Holland a copy of Aquinas's *Summa Theologica*, but the scholastic handbook in use at La Flèche, Eustache de Saint-Paul's *Summa philosophiae quadripartita*, had contained a debased form of the epistemology of Suarez, which resolved the central difficulty of deriving a spiritual act, cognition, from a physical known object, by blurring the distinction between the corporeal and the spiritual. The abstracted species in the mind are said by Eustache to be material, but to preserve a "modus spiritualis in repraesentando (spiritual mode in representation)," evoking what Descartes in the *Dioptrique* referred to scathingly as the "images corporelles qui voltigent en l'air (corporeal images flying through the air)." Aquinas, whose central philosophical problem about the body-soul union had started in the context of a theory of knowledge and driven him to the apparently Aristotelian solutions involving the "intellectus agens (active/abstractive intellect)" of the Arab philosophers, had carefully preserved the distinction between the corporeal and the spiritual, but still left cognition too dependent on perception not to seem to have compromised the immortality of the soul.

Descartes sweeps away the Aristotelian scholasticism which bases knowledge on an abstractive process deriving from sense perception, but his discovery, or argument, "Je pense, donc je suis (I think, therefore I am)," has a long neoplatonist pedigree, and can be paralleled at least three times in different contexts in Augustine himself, and then not surprisingly in the 12th-century Victorine school in Paris, in Aquinas's principal critic and the most acute, if not the most daring of the scholastics, Scotus, and in the nominalist tradition starting with Ockham. It is quite likely that Descartes genuinely rediscovered a line of argument lodged in his head by Gibieuf's 1630 *De libertate dei et creaturae*, whose provenance from the entourage of Bérulle might have commended it to him. Unable to rely on sense perception, but sure of his own existence, Descartes now needed to establish the reality and knowability of the external world.

Descartes thought he had established not only his own existence, but his existence as a spiritual substance, whose nature it was to think:

dont toute l'essence ou la nature n'est que de penser, et qui, pour être, n'a besoin d'aucun lieu ni ne dépend d'aucune chose matérielle; en sorte que ce moi, c'est-à-dire l'âme, par laquelle je suis ce que je suis, est entièrement distincte du corps

(whose whole essence or nature is only to think, and which, in order to exist, does not need space or depend on any material thing; so that this "I," that is to say the soul, by which I am what I am, is entirely distinct from the body).

The spirituality, and therefore potential immortality of the soul is presupposed, and because the soul is a thinking substance, that is a self-contained independent entity, ὑπόστασις, it is incapable of extension, since where there is extension there must, as we have seen, be matter, as at the top of Torricelli's upturned tube. Further, if the soul is entirely distinct from the body, as Descartes thinks he has demonstrated, then an idea in the mind which is both clear and also separate or distinct from other ideas is unclouded by the effects of sensation, is caught in its pure spiritual state, is innate in the soul, and must correspond to an objective reality. Ideas cannot themselves be true, since truth is a quality not of concepts but of propositions, but it follows from the spirituality of the soul that clarity and distinctness of ideas are criteria of the external existence of a corresponding reality. Originally Descartes allowed three clear and distinct ideas, the soul, God, and the body, before adding a fourth, the body-soul union.

Perceiving that he is capable of doubting, Descartes argues that doubt is an imperfection: "je voyais clairement que c'était une plus grande perfection de connaître que de douter (I saw clearly that it was a greater perfection to know than to doubt)," and that the idea of a being of a greater perfection than his own entailed the existence of such a being, because of itself the human soul could not conceive of anything greater than itself. Descartes uses two avenues of proof. The first is by causality:

il restait que [l'idée d'un être plus parfait que le mien] eût été mise en moi par une nature qui fût véritablement plus parfaite que je n'étais, et même qui eût en soi toutes les perfections dont je pouvais avoir quelque idée, c'est-à-dire, pour m'expliquer en un mot, qui fût Dieu

(it remained that the idea of a being more perfect than mine had been put in me by a nature which was in reality more perfect than I was, and even which contained all the perfections of which I could have some idea, that is to say, to explain in a single word, who was God).

This proof is immediately repeated in a slightly different form. Only a page or so later does Descartes come to the "ontological" proof, dating from the 12th century. Whereas in any triangle the sum of the angles has to equal two right angles, but no triangle need ever exist, the idea of an "Etre parfait" includes existence as a perfection, a proposition made explicit in the fifth *Meditatio*, and a perfect being, God, must therefore exist.

With the existence of a perfect God the criteria of clarity and distinctness are more solidly established. What in our minds comes from the soul alone, that which is clear and distinct, comes from God and cannot of itself mislead us. Given God's veracity, without which he would not be perfect, our unconfused sense perception can be distinguished from dream, and our reason can be used to check on the truth of what we observe. In his replies to the objections to the second of the *Meditationes* Descartes goes so far as to maintain that although an atheist can know that the sum of the angles in any triangle equals two right angles, his knowledge is not scientific, since the atheist has no guarantee of certainty. In the fifth part of the *Discours*, Descartes outlines some further conclusions he has derived from the application of his method, largely taken from the suppressed *Traité du monde ou de la lumière*, the *Traité de l'homme*, and *De la formation du foetus*, and incidentally controverts Harvey's theory of the circulation of the blood, while the sixth part sums up what Descartes has achieved, and what he plans for the future, which includes a mechanist medicine, important because at this date it appeared to Descartes that the preservation of health led to both happiness and virtue:

> ...la conservation de la santé... est sans doute le premier bien et le fondement de tous les autres biens de cette vie; car même l'esprit dépend si fort du tempérament et de la disposition des organes du corps, que, s'il est possible de trouver quelque moyen qui rende communément les hommes plus sages et plus habiles qu'ils n'ont été jusqu'ici, je crois que c'est dans la médicine qu'on doit le chercher

> (...the preservation of health... is without doubt the foremost good and the foundation of all the other goods of this life; for even the mind depends so closely on the temperament and the disposition of the bodily organs that, if it is possible to find some means of making people generally wiser and more able than they have been in the past, it is in medicine that it must be looked for).

The *Meditationes* elaborate the metaphysics of the fourth part of the *Discours* and show an increasing preoccupation with the complexity of the union of body and soul, described from the sixth *Meditatio* as "substantial" union, that is forming a single substance, not a composition like that of a navigator and a ship, but in which the soul confers a philosophically conceived finality on the body. On the important matter of the relationship between the faculties, Descartes is forced back into a fideist position, in which faith is not an act of the intellect at all. The dilemma is clear. If the act of faith proceeds from the intellect, it is subject to rational norms and cannot be meritorious; if it proceeds from the will, it cannot be rational; it cannot by scholastic definition and subsequent tradition proceed from both at once. Descartes is for once obliged to discuss the action of grace in the soul, and he places faith firmly in the will, on which grace acts directly.

We can believe something either by the light of reason or by the power of grace. In the act of faith the formal reason on account of which we believe

> consiste en une certaine lumière intérieure, de laquelle Dieu nous ayant surnaturellement éclairés, nous avons une confiance certaine que les choses qui nous sont proposées à croire ont été révélées par lui, et qu'il est entièrement impossible qu'il soit menteur et qu'il nous trompe

> (consists in a certain interior light by which, God having supernaturally enlightened us, we have a sure and certain confidence that the things proposed for our belief haved been revealed by him, and that it is entirely impossible that he should lie or deceive us).

It follows therefore that Turks and other unbelievers do not sin for refusing to believe against their judgement, but because they either resist grace or have made themselves unworthy of it. An unbeliever who was converted without grace and believed on inadequate grounds drawn from reason would for Descartes sin "en ce qu'il ne se servirait pas comme il faut de sa raison (in not using his reason as he should)."

Descartes published the *Principia* in 1644. The four parts deal respectively with the principles of human knowledge, constituting with the *Meditationes* his metaphysics, the root of the tree of knowledge; with material things; with the visible world; and with the earth, constituting with the two preceding parts the general physics, or trunk of the tree of knowledge. The missing but projected fifth and sixth parts, continuing the general physics, would have been devoted respectively to the nature of animals and the nature of man. If the whole work were to constitute "un corps de philosophie tout entier (a complete philosophical corpus)," an exact treatment of medicine, ethics, and mechanics would have to be added. When the *Principes* were published in French in 1647, Descartes added an important prefatory letter to Picot. At that date a first draft of *Les Passions de l'âme* already existed. Its first part, elaborating the psychophysics of the union of body and soul, appears from a famous letter to Chanut of 15 June 1646 to have been offered as a substitute for the missing sixth part of the general physics. The mechanics and the medicine were never written. The letter-preface to the French edition of the *Principes*, *Les Passions de l'âme*, and the letters to Elizabeth must be taken together and constitute the fruit of the tree of knowledge, the ethic, a guide to both virtue and happiness, which Descartes regarded as the end-product of his whole enterprise.

He had changed his mind about the mechanist nature of the scientific ethics, and *Les Passions de l'âme* is not a completely polished text. About a third of it, although probably not just the third section, was added to the first draft, and the work is not based wholly on the mechanist medicine projected in the sixth part of the Discours. The change appears in the letters to Elizabeth of the summer of 1645, when Descartes shows how sadness can cause the heart to contract, slow the circulation of the blood, and therefore lead to physical indisposition. In the letter-preface the notion of "sagesse" is reintroduced. It is the goal towards which science should lead, and it unites happiness with virtue. Philosophy is the study of wisdom, and its final fruit, for Descartes as for Gassendi, was an ethic, which for Descartes, however, presupposed a complete knowledge of the other disciplines.

Ethically the passions for Descartes could be stimulated or calmed by association, and were therefore in our power. They were ethically neither good nor bad.

The first part of *Les Passions de l'âme* is subtitled "Des Passions en général. Et par occasion, de toute la nature de l'homme (On the Passions in general; and, at the same time, of the whole of human nature)." It treats of physiology, of the soul, and of the interaction of body and soul. It is the corruption of the bodily organs that causes the soul to leave the body at death, which is not caused by the departure of the soul as the body's source of motive power as in the "vitalist" view. Descartes conceives of the relationship in such a way that the soul, by its power, can conjure up associations which act through the imagination and the pineal gland to cause bodily changes, a conception leading towards his whole ethic of strength of will. The will is of its nature free; its acts are absolutely in its power; and its arms are "des jugements fermes et déterminés touchant la connaissance du bien et du mal (firm and determined judgements concerning the knowledge of good and evil)."

Traditionally there had been eleven passions only. The scholastics had distinguished the concupiscible from the irascible parts of the sensitive appetite. In the concupiscible there were six passions. The two general motions towards good and away from evil each had two subdivisions, giving six passions: generic love for a good; desire for a good not present; joy for a good that was present; generic hatred for an ill; flight from an ill not present; and sadness from a present ill. In the irascible appetite, concerned with the overcoming of difficulties, there were only five passions: hope and despair where a good was not yet present; fear and boldness where an ill was not yet present; and anger at a present ill. In this scholastic division, which had lasted with scarcely any modification from the 13th century to the late 16th, there could be no irascible passion for a present good; there could only be 11 passions; and love and hatred could not coexist in the same subject, at the same time, and with respect to the same object. The 17th-century French moralists were commonly to make the mixture of love and hatred characteristic of jealousy.

Descartes kept the incompatibility of love and hatred, but swept away the basis for the rest of the classification, giving a list of some 40 passions. The final ethic of Descartes rests naturally on the good usage of our free will. Descartes defines virtue in terms of what he calls "générosité,"

une ferme et constante résolution de bien user [de la libre disposition de nos volontés], c'est à dire de ne manquer jamais de volonté pour entreprendre et exécuter toutes les choses qu'il [un Homme] jugera être les meilleures. Ce qui est suivre parfaitement la vertu

(a firm and constant resolution to use well the free disposition of our wills, that is to say never to lack the will to undertake and execute all the things which are judged to be best. That is to follow virtue perfectly).

There is here the characteristic insistence on the strength and resolution of the will to follow judgements of value which are extrinsic to it and proposed by the intellect. The will is no longer, as for the scholastics, an appetite at all, but only an autonomous spiritual power. Descartes's summary of his ethic here could be paralleled two or three times in Les Passions de l'âme, and half a dozen more times from the correspondence with Christina and with Elizabeth, to whom Descartes wrote on 18 August 1645 and, following Du Vair, defined beatitude as "contentement de l'esprit (the mind's happiness)," adding that, for true happiness,

il est besoin de suivre la vertu, c'est à dire d'avoir une volonté ferme et constante d'executer tout ce que nous jugerons estre le meilleur, et d'employer toute la force de nostre entendement à en bien juger

(we must follow virtue, that is to say have a firm and constant will to execute everything we judge to be the best, and to employ the whole strength of our understanding to judge well).

It is sufficient however in the present context to show that Des-

cartes, starting from his basic metaphysics constructed on the methodic doubt, did in the end finally manage to produce the rigorously deductive ethic, the highest point of "sagesse," the fruit of the tree of philosophy, and the certain path to virtue and happiness, in a treatise he allowed to be printed before it was really finished, which he considerably augmented in draft, and which he did not live to see published.

Paradoxically its importance lies in its promotion of ethical values similar to those of relatively recent provenance in France at the time, and being contemporaneously explored by its novelists and dramatists, for whom it provides a counterpoint of apparently rigorous philosophical analysis. That does not mean that Descartes did not burn with a fierce and warranted sense of originality and independence, but it tells us a great deal about the nature of the values being examined in the imaginative literature of the first half of the 17th century in France.

PUBLICATIONS

Collections

Oeuvres de Descartes, 12 vols., 1897–1913
Correspondance, 6 vols., 1936–63
Descartes's Philosophical Writings, 1952
Philosophical Writings of Descartes, 1975ff

Philosophy

Discours de la méthode pour bien conduire sa raison et chercher la vérité dans les sciences, plus la Dioptrique, les Météores et la Géométrie qui sont des Essais de cette méthode, 1637; edited by E. Gilson, 1925; as *Discourse on the Method…*, 1952
Meditationes de prima philosophia in qua Dei existentia et animae immortalitas demonstratur, 1641; French translation 1647
Principia philosophiae, 1644; French translation 1647
Les Passions de l'âme, 1649; edited by G. Rodis-Lewis, 1955
Correspondance, 3 vols., 1656–67
Traité de l'homme et de la formation du foetus, 1664
Traité du monde ou de la lumière, 1664
Regulae ad directionem ingenii, 1701; edited by H. Gouhier, 1965

Biographical and critical studies

Baillet, Adrien, *La Vie de Monsieur Descartes*, 2 vols., 1691
Gilson, Etienne, *La Liberté chez Descartes et la théologie*, 1913
Chevalier, J., *Descartes*, 1921
Gouhier, Henri, *La Pensée religieuse de Descartes*, 1924
Sirven, J., *Les Années d'apprentissage de Descartes (1596–1628)*, 1928
Gilson, Etienne, *Etudes sur le rôle de la pensée médiévale dans la formation du système cartésien*, 1930
Roth, Léon, *Descartes's Discourse on Method*, 1937
Laporte, J., *Le Rationalisme de Descartes*, 1945
Serrurier, Cornelia, *Descartes, l'homme et le penseur*, 1951
Beck, L.J., *The Method of Descartes*, 1952
Rodis-Lewis, G., *La Morale de Descartes*, 1957

Guéroult, Maurice, *Descartes selon l'ordre des raisons*, 2 vols., 1953–56

Lefèvre, R., *La Vocation de Descartes*, 1956

——*L'Humanisme de Descartes*, 1957

Vrooman, Jack R., *René Descartes: A Biography*, 1970

Grene, Marjorie, *Descartes* (in English), 1985

Cottingham, J., *Descartes* (in English), 1986

DESMARETS, Jean, sieur de Saint-Sorlin, ?1600–1676.

Dramatist and poet.

LIFE

The most correct spelling of the name is probably Des Marests, but haphazard 17th-century practice knew perhaps a score of different ways of writing it, and the most recent practice has attempted to stabilize usage to that adopted here. Desmarets was not the author of any single literary masterpiece, but he was a prolific, popular, and original writer, sufficiently trusted by Richelieu, to whom he came to be very close, to be granted on 14 March 1639 an extraordinary privilège for all his books, written or to be written, for 20 years from first publication. His literary activities were joined to many others, diplomatic as well as cultural. His dedications to Louis XIII and Louis XIV, Anne of Austria and Marie-Thérèse, Richelieu and Mazarin, Gaston d'Orléans, Séguier, Foucquet, Colbert, Perrault, the duchesse de Longueville, and Mme du Vigean show him to have attracted the patronage of the highest members of the court.

But Desmarets was also an epic poet, a painter, an important administrator, and an architect; a provider of, and performer at, court entertainments; and a familiar companion and reliable cultural and political servant of Richelieu. He lost favour under Mazarin, and found himself culturally isolated for a score of years; he was an early associate of Conrart, and eventually became by lot the first chancellor of the new Académie; he was a supporter of the specifically Christian epic, and consequently of the "merveilleux chrétien (Christian marvellous)," and a strong protagonist of the "modernes" in the Querelle des anciens et des modernes (q.v.); a firm anti-Jansenist (q.v.); and a forceful opponent of quietism, although himself from the mid-1650s subject to fervent bouts of religious exaltation. His fanaticism became so extreme that before the end of his life he was said by his enemies, and considered sometimes even by his friends, to be more than slightly mad. In spite of all the evidence now adduced to demonstrate his sanity, Desmarets probably did undergo brief periods of mental semi-derangement during the period when he felt he had a divine mission to enforce Christian moral order on a world extensively infiltrated by Satan and his power.

Desmarets wrote the deposition which was the principal weapon used in the condemnation of the last person to be judicially burned in France, Simon Morin, executed in March 1663 for witchcraft and heresy; became himself a police agent before the post of lieutenant de police was established in 1667 and filled by La Reynie; and was responsible for the hunting down of Isaac Le Maître de Saci, incarcerated in the Bastille in 1666, together with other Jansenists then in hiding in Paris. It is disputed how much Desmarets's cultural attitudes, including his aesthetic, social, and spiritual values, actually changed, but his relationship to the mainstream of French cultural life certainly altered, and his biography has therefore tended to be over-compartmentalized into periods by all but the most recent critics. The most dramatic discontinuity came with Richelieu's death, when Desmarets ceased to write for the theatre, perhaps because he had done so only to please Richelieu, being himself more interested in his Christian epic, *Clovis*.

We know very little about his early life. The name was quite common, but Desmarets does not seem to have been closely related to any other known contemporary of the same name except his brother and sister. Desmarets's date of birth has recently been revised and is now put in 1600, on the basis only of a mutual gift of property between his presumptive parents on 29 July 1600. That is very slender evidence, especially since such a gift might have been expected to have been made on the birth, which an epitaph dates from 1593 or 1594, of an elder brother, Roland, later an important Latin stylist and a barrister at the Paris parlement, but it does accord with a statement from the 1674 poem *Le Triomphe de Louis et de son siècle, poëme lyrique* in which Desmarets's "Génie" notes that he was born at the first moment of the new century. A sister, Marguerite, was to marry Guillaume Dupré, a court doctor said by Gui Patin to have attended Condé, Conti, and Longueville during their 1650 imprisonment.

The family appear to have been well-to-do bourgeois merchants, but there were important relatives, and a cousin had married Jeanne-Isabelle, daughter of Nicolas Brûlart de Sillery, Chancellor and Garde des Sceaux, whose son Pierre Brûlart, Marquis de Puisieux, was the ambassador extraordinary sent to Spain to conclude the marriage arrangements between Louis XIII and Anne of Austria. Desmarets was also a first cousin once removed of Anne de Neubourg, baronne du Vigean, passionately attached to Richelieu's favourite niece, Mme de Combalet, from 1638 the duchesse d'Aiguillon. Mme du Vigean, born in 1600 and important in a number of literary contexts, had borne four children to her husband François Poussart, baron de Fors, marquis du Vigean: Louis in 1620; Anne and Marthe in 1622; and François in 1623; but gossip about her sexual ambivalence, as of that of the future duchesse d'Aiguillon, is very well attested. Tallemant is, as usual, well informed, although by no means the sole source. He either did not know that the prince de Guémené was Mme du Vigean's lover, too, or implied a denial of the popular view at court that he was.

Desmarets's second novel, the 1639 *Rosane*, was to be dedicated to her. She was a neighbour of Mme de Rambouillet just opposite the west wing of the Louvre and perhaps 200 metres from the river, was also known for the company she received, and was to play some part in Desmarets's life. He wrote a sonnet for her on the second capture in battle of her son, the marquis de Fors, and then another sonnet and an elegy when, at the age of 19, he was killed at the siege of Arras on 28 August 1640. It was her widowed daughter, Anne de Poussart de Pons, whose clandestine marriage Desmarets was to manage, in December 1649, to the duchesse d'Aiguillon's nephew, Armand-Jean du Plessis, born in 1629 and on his majority to become the second duc de Richelieu, in whose service Desmarets then was, and in whose house he was to die.

At the joint instance of the duchesse d'Aiguillon and Mme du Vigean, Desmarets was briefly to be imprisoned on 22 March 1650 for his part in the marriage, and he was still being held a week later for debts said to amount to 60,000 livres. The duchesse d'Aiguillon had her nephew himself detained until 27 June, after which he and his wife were exiled, but they escaped from the guards of their host, the comte de Saint-Mesme. At 15 the future second duc had in January 1643 succeeded his father as Général des galères, responsible for the navy, but also with jurisdiction along the coast, whereupon Desmarets was, at the instance of the duchesse d'Aiguillon, made secrétaire général de la Marine du Levant and steward of the late cardinal's household as a recompense for services rendered.

Desmarets was himself ennobled as secrétaire du roi sometime before 1639. He was not to become sieur de Saint-Sorlin until 1651, but in 1634 married Anne Fleury, daughter of a conseiller du roi who held various other high offices, and from whom Desmarets borrowed money to purchase the office of Surintendant des fortifications de France, which he had filled as a deputy as early as 1620. In August 1634 he also sold, for 5,000 livres, the minor offices of conseiller du roi and contrôleur de l'Extraordinaire des guerres, money received from the sale of offices and pensions, keeping, acquiring by purchase, or being promoted to the senior offices of conseiller du roi en ses conseils—one of only 38 before 1637, although the number rose to 122 in 1644—and contrôleur général de l'Extraordinaire des guerres, which must have given him an important role in the conseil d'état et des finances, and made him principal overseer of a department which was by 1660 spending an estimated 60,000,000 livres. There had been a huge escalation but, even in 1634, the extraordinaire des guerres may well have reached an eight-digit figure. Desmarets borrowed more from his father-in-law when, in anticipation of the birth of his son Armand-Jean, he and his wife moved from the Marais district to Saint-Germain-des-Prés early in 1635. There were also to be two other recorded children of the marriage, both daughters.

The first mention of what could possibly be, but may also more probably not be, the subject of this entry in any artistic or literary context dates from 28 February 1613, when Malherbe wrote that Desmarets had made the queen regent laugh when he appeared dressed as a shepherd with a man dressed as a dog, whom he pretended to make dance. It was apparently the only redeeming feature of *Le Ballet de la courtisane appellée La Ronde*, danced at the Louvre. The following year presumably the same Marets played the court fool in the *Ballet de la Blanque*, and must be identified with the Marais referred to by Tallemant as the "bouffon du roi (king's jester)," mentioned also by Saint-Amant, whom Tallemant reports as saying that there are two things in the royal trade he would not like, the need to eat in private and to excrete in public. Louis XIII was declared of age on 2 October 1614, and on the following 19 March, in anticipation of the king's marriage to Anne of Austria, presumably the same Marais sang in the *Ballet du triomphe de Minerve*.

There is constant reference in contemporary documents, in connection with the court and its entertainments, like *Le Ballet de la Délivrance de Renaud* of 19 January 1617, to the Marets who was court fool to Louis XIII, was known to Théophile and Saint-Amant, and may have been the one mentioned in Malher-

be's letter. It is almost certain that the Marets mentioned by Théophile in the deposition at his 1624 trial was the king's jester, and quite probable that he also was the Marets who danced the Grand Turk in *Le grand bal de la Douairière de Billebahaut* in February 1626, the year in which the future sieur de Saint-Sorlin is said first to have been presented by Bautru to Richelieu who, after taking the side of Marie de Medici, had lived in exile at Avignon, rejoined her at Angoulême in 1619, returned to court in 1620, progressively increasing his control over her affairs, and eventually, now a cardinal, joined her as a member of the king's small council in 1624.

The probability is that the Desmarets with whom this entry is concerned, who married and entered into Richelieu's direct service on 18 January 1634, is the one mentioned in connection with court entertainments only at the earliest from 1632, when a Marets danced the magician's role on Sunday 7 March in *Le Ballet du château de Bicêtre*, with verse by Pierre Corneille. Other performers included the ducs de Longueville and de Candale and the baron du Vigean, and the ballet was danced at the Arsenal and the Hôtel de Ville as well as the Louvre, where the *Gazette* (q.v.) says there were 4,000 spectators. Painted backdrops showed the château in the light of dawn, and then at night. Desmarets danced with Louis XIII in at least three ballets, *Le Ballet du roy: où la vieille Cour et les habitans des rives de la Seine viennent danser pour les triomphes de Sa Majesté* on 18 February 1635, a *Ballet de la reine* with which it made a single entertainment, and *Le Ballet de la Merlaizon*, danced on 15 March 1635 at Chantilly and two days later at Royaumont. The "merlaizon" was a species of thrush, an edible songbird; Louis XIII danced a female role; and a live horse also figured.

It has only recently been noticed how important in the history of the French stage, hitherto directed almost exclusively to bourgeois audiences, is the up-grading of scripted drama to a position in which it could vie with ballet, the extravagant court entertainment involving music, song, and dance, as well as scripted interludes, and often demanding ornate costumes, lavish and expensive settings, and machinery capable of creating spectacular effects. When Louis XIII danced *Le Ballet des Improvistes* on 12 February 1636 there were 26 entrées. On 19 February, a week later, Desmarets's *Aspasie*, followed by 12 entrées, was played for Richelieu at the Palais-Cardinal as part of an entertainment for the duke of Parma and Gaston d'Orléans which included a collation, music between the acts, a ballet, and a concert in the Cardinal's private apartment. Richelieu's patronage of scripted drama, although preceded by that of Belin and Montmorency, was both innovative and powerful. It changed the emphasis from spectacle to script, and from court entertainment to drama, and had a huge impact on the development of dramatic scripts as literature.

When on 28 November 1634 three of Richelieu's cousins married: Marguerite de Pontchâteau to Antoine de Lage, duc de Puylaurens; her elder sister, Marie de Pontchâteau, to the duc de la Valette, son of the duc d'Epernon; and Françoise-Marguerite du Plessis to Antoine de Grammont, still comte de Guiche, a whole festival of ballet was still held at the Arsenal, mixed with scripted drama by Corneille and Scudéry played by both the Paris companies. But when in March 1635 *La Comédie des Tuileries* was staged, Richelieu was emphasizing the importance he attached to scripted drama, although the authors chosen by Richelieu to collaborate on it—Boisrobert, Corneille, Rotrou, Colletet, and Lestoile—can only have been selected because of their success in connection with court entertainment. The reputations of Boisrobert, Colletet, and Lestoile were all solidly founded on ballets. Mairet and Scudéry, who were writers of scripted drama, were left out, while neither Colletet nor Lestoile was a dramatist at all.

Desmarets's first novel, *Ariane*, was published pseudonymously in 1632, signed "de Boisval," dedicated "Aux Dames (To Women)," with a privilège of 21 January and an achevé of 10 March 1632. It was the only novel which Desmarets succeeded in completing, and it follows a formula made familiar by Gomberville. Desmarets had read from it to Conrart's circle in 1631. It was quickly translated into English, German, Flemish, and Dutch, and had six French and six foreign editions by 1644. Authorship was acknowledged in the quarto edition of 1639. It was to be followed by the signed 1639 *Rosane, histoire tirée de celle des Romains et des Perses*, dedicated to the duchesse d'Aiguillon and translated in 1650 into Italian, and the signed two-volume 1648 *La Vérité des fables; ou, L'Histoire des dieux de l'antiquité*, dedicated to Anne of Austria.

From the early 1630s until the death of Richelieu, Desmarets was a very considerable literary figure, taken more seriously by Richelieu than Boisrobert, and used by Richelieu from the mid-1630s virtually to replace his five authors for the production of scripted drama for the small, and then the large, private theatre of the Palais-Cardinal. The inventory of Richelieu's possessions at death lists the quite luxurious furnishings of a room in the Palais-Cardinal next to the larger theatre "used by le sieur Desmarests." In fact the inventory, although published, has been quoted at second hand and misunderstood in the context of the lavishness of the equipment installed for *Mirame*, which it does not count at all. Henri Arnauld in 1640 said that the equipment was going to cost 100,000 livres, and nothing, at least in the inventory taken on Richelieu's decease and dated January 1643, suggests that he was wrong.

Before his close association with Richelieu, Desmarets appears to have moved in the literary circle loosely connected with the entourage of Gaston d'Orléans, and in particular with Nicolas Faret, who dedicated the celebrated 1630 *L'Honnête Homme; ou, L'Art de plaire à la cour* to Gaston d'Orléans, and to whose 1627 *Recueil de lettres* Desmarets had contributed. Some of the letters were flattering to Richelieu; their authors included Bautru, Boisrobert, Balzac, Malherbe, and Jean de Silhon. None of them was associated with Conrart's circle, which Richelieu was to erect into his Académie and which, according to Paul Pellisson, was constituted at least partly by Chapelain, Godeau, Gombauld, Giry, the Habert brothers Philippe and Germain, the abbé de Cérisy, Jacques de Sérisay, and Malleville.

Of the two groups, Conrart's looked much closer to Richelieu, but maréchal Bassompierre, a reliable general and once a close personal favourite of Louis XIII, had become involved with Marillac's conspiracy against Richelieu, and been sent to the Bastille on 25 February 1631. The conspiracy came to a head with the Journée des Dupes, which the most recent research puts on 11 November 1630 and not, as had previously been thought, on the day before. It was Bassompierre's secretary, Malleville, no doubt himself under suspicion on account of his association both with Bassompierre and with Gaston d'Orléans, who told Faret about the social gatherings with literary pretensions held by Conrart. Within weeks there was political trouble in which Gaston d'Orléans's entourage fell under suspicion. Gaston him-

self broke into open rebellion, and on 30 March his accomplices were charged with lèse-majesté. The parlement refused on 26 April to register the charge, and on Louis XIII held the "lit de justice" which forbade the parlement to consider matters of state. Marie de Medici fled in July.

If he had been informed by Boisrobert of the existence of Conrart's group before 1633, when Louis XIII recaptured Lorraine and his brother's marriage to the duke of Lorraine's sister had been effectively dissolved, it is quite likely that Richelieu would have suppressed Conrart's gatherings and regarded the group as potentially subversive rather than as a group to be exploited in the prosecution of cultural hegemony. Faret was admitted to it shortly after the appearance of *L'honnête homme*, and therefore probably before the end of 1630, within days of the Journée des Dupes. Through Faret, first Desmarets and then Boisrobert were invited to join the gatherings, and in 1633 Boisrobert published *Les Nouvelles Muses*, an anthology of poems including pieces by Chapelain, Desmarets, Godeau, Philippe Habert, and Malleville. Since the volume contained much in praise of Richelieu, the existence of Conrart's group was, by the time he heard about it, entirely acceptable to him. Other contributors to Boisrobert's collection had no connection with Conrart but much with court ballet, like Boisrobert himself, Baro, Lestoile, François Mainard, and Racan. In *Les Historiettes*, Tallemant makes it perfectly clear that Boisrobert, used to being Richelieu's licensed entertainer and literary factotum, was jealous of Desmarets and attempted to block his entry into Richelieu's service in 1634:

Il craignoit des Marestz, que Bautru introduisoit chez le Cardinal et qui, ayant un esprit universel et plein d'inventions, estoit assez bien ce qu'il luy falloit. Mais il n'estoit pas propre pour faire rire, et Boisrobert eust tousjours eu son veritable employ tout entier

(He was afraid of Desmarets, whom Bautru introduced to the entourage of the cardinal, and who, having a broadly based intelligence and being full of imagination, was indeed the person he needed. But he was not the one to make the cardinal laugh, so Boisrobert kept the whole of his real function).

Tallemant, who says that Boisrobert, reading to the cardinal lines in his praise, falsely said that they were by Pierre de Marbeuf when he knew that they were by Desmarets, goes on to recount another episode in which Boisrobert, "par une malice de vieux courtisan (using a typical old courtier's trick)," told the cardinal that his guards, not content with free admittance to the plays, used to take other people in. He then told the cardinal's servants that Desmarets had complained about them. Thereafter the guards on door duty made Desmarets's own servant pay even for the pieces Desmarets had written, until Desmarets himself complained to their lieutenant, and "On sceût que c'estoit une calomnie de Boisrobert (It was realized that it was Boisrobert making trouble)." Tallemant, who has shrewdly weighed up both Boisrobert and Desmarets, recounts the final disgrace of Boisrobert at great length, suggesting strongly that the command to him to retire to his abbey at Châtillon or his canonry at Rouen was made, or at least maintained, by order of the king.

Desmarets was taken into Richelieu's service, not to make him laugh, but to write plays for him. There are seven, performed between 19 February 1636 and 18 November 1642, just before the cardinal's death. The large theatre in the Palais-Cardinal, later restored by Molière's company when the building had become the Palais-Royal, was that inaugurated with Desmarets's *Mirame, tragicomédie* on 14 January 1641 and used for *Le Ballet de la Prospérité* of 1641, the year in which, by what cannot have been a coincidence, Louis XIII issued a decree on 24 April formally declaring the acting profession to be honorable. The occasion of Boisrobert's disgrace had been his admission against the cardinal's orders of two ostentatious and loosely behaved women to the inaugural performance of *Mirame*, and the exile lasted from 23 January 1641 until 16 November 1642, just days before Richelieu's death. The duchesse d'Aiguillon disliked Boisrobert, and Mazarin did not afford him the same protection as had Richelieu.

All seven of Desmarets's plays were performed at the Palais-Cardinal, some certainly, and most presumably, by one or other of the two established Paris companies. *Aspasie* of 1636 and *Les Visionnaires* of 1637 were described as comedies; *Scipion* (1638), *Roxane* (1639), *Mirame* (1641), and *Erigone* (1642) were tragicomedies; and *Europe* of 1642 was described as a heroic comedy. *Les Visionnaires* and *Scipion* were also played at the Marais, and a ballet, *Ballet de la Félicité sur le sujet de l'heureuse naissance de Monseigneur le Dauphin*, partly by Desmarets, was danced, according to the *Gazette* for 12 March 1639, at Saint-Germain, at the Palais-Cardinal, and at the Hôtel de Ville. Desmarets also contributed occasional verses for other ballets. Pellisson records the existence of a comedy which has been lost, and there were at least two unfinished scripts, apparently abandoned on the death of Richelieu.

A register of attendance at the inchoate Académie française, into which Conrart's group had been expanded and somewhat unwillingly institutionalized, with a note of business transacted, was kept from March 1634, when it was meeting at Desmarets's residence. Desmarets was himself responsible for revising the *Projet de l'Académie* which, like Desmarets's own 1633 *Discours de la poësie*, reiterated what was to be an incessant concern with eloquence. In the mock serious debates on love and friendship, Desmarets undertook to show on 13 August 1635 that love, providing it was spiritual, contained something divine, and the love of Lysis and Aspasie in Desmarets's comedy *Aspasie*, given with its attendant musical, gastronomic, and other entertainments on 19 February 1636, was to participate in the general upgrading of instinctive behaviour which was to constitute the main thrust of imaginative literature in France certainly until the brief interruption at the time of the Fronde. The view that even in its physical manifestations love was morally acceptable, defended by Pierre de Boissat, was the final contribution to the debate, made on 2 September 1635.

On 16 June 1637, after his own *Les Visionnaires*, first played between 15 February and 6 March 1637, and *L'Aveugle de Smyrne*, by Richelieu's five authors, Desmarets was appointed by the Académie, with Chapelain and Bourzeys, to undertake the report on Corneille's *Le Cid*, referred to the Académie at Scudéry's suggestion, probably in an attempt by Scudéry to curry favour with Richelieu, whose advocacy of the scripted drama in which Scudéry excelled was becoming quite clear. On 30 June Scudéry undertook to edit the observations on the versification of *Le Cid* compiled by Cerisy, Gombauld, Baro, and Lestoille. Desmarets himself, in the wake of Corneille's success, turned to tragicomedy with *Scipion*, first played with mediocre

success sometime in the winter of 1637–38. *Roxane* was given at an unknown date in 1639. On 5 March 1639 at Saint-Germain, on 8 March at the Palais-Cardinal, and on 17 March at the Hôtel de Ville, a ballet by Desmarets was danced, *Le Ballet de la Félicité sur l'heureuse naisssance de Monseigneur le Dauphin*. To the vast relief of the aristocracy loyal to Louis XIII, the queen had at last given birth to a male heir, the future Louis XIV, on 5 September 1638 at Saint-Germain-en-Laye, and the rejoicings were heroic.

The last ballet of which, according to Tallemant, Desmarets was the author, was *Le Ballet de la Prospérité des armes de la France*, danced on 7 and 14 February 1641 at the Palais-Cardinal for the marriage of the cardinal's niece, Clémence de Maillé-Brézé, to the duc d'Enghien, the future grand Condé, in the chapel of the Palais-Cardinal on 11 February. Like its predecessor it was more remarkable for its spectacular effects than for its literary ingenuity, although it does reflect an increasing politicization of Desmarets's vision, of which the final grandiose manifestation, rushed into performance on 17 or 18 November 1642, not three weeks before Richelieu's death, is reflected in *Europe*, Desmarets's heroic comedy looking forward to a Europe united under French leadership, as proposed by Richelieu as the end of the Thirty Years' War came into sight. Desmarets's allegorical heroic comedy must have been conceived in 1638, and the court ballet, no doubt subsequently attached to it as a prologue, was ready in 1639, when it was examined by the Académie. When *L'Europe* was finally performed Richelieu was terminally ill, and had just returned from Lyons after the trial and execution of Cinq-Mars and de Thou.

Desmarets was also a poet, who contributed to the *Guirlande de Julie* (q.v.), and published his own *Oeuvres poétiques*, the first edition of which contains his first four plays with an 80-page section of poems. The achevé is 20 November 1640, but the title page is dated 1641. Desmarets's first published poems date from 1630. Their survival has been haphazard. Some were anonymous, some printed in anthologies, and some certainly lost. The 1643 edition of the *Oeuvres poétiques* contained an added section, "Odes, poëmes et autres oeuvres." Further poems and extracts were printed with the 1670 *La Comparaison de la langue et de la poësie françoise, avec la grecque et la latine....* Desmarets's ambitious epic *Clovis* was begun about 1634, although not published until 1657. Desmarets was from quite early selectively hostile to the severe poetic reforms proposed by Malherbe, whose vision of the ordered society to emerge from the religious wars left no need for the poet as visionary, or for the language of poetic fancy.

Richelieu's death marked the end of a whole way of life for Desmarets, symbolized by the abrupt cessation of theatrical activity. Desmarets said in 1666 that he had undergone a conversion after his 1654 verse translations of what was known as Thomas à Kempis's *L'Imitation de Jésus-Christ* and of Scupoli's *Le Combat spirituel*, but in spite of modern biographical assertions, the psychological change seems to have come some time later than that, although it has been suggested that the death of Desmarets's brother, Roland, in 1653 may have had something to do with it. The "conversion" has traditionally been assigned dates as early as 1645, but Desmarets himself wrote that God used the two translations

> pour m'émouvoir à changer de vie. Puis je quittay toute
> volontaire production d'esprit, et je demeuray quatre ou

cinq ans ayant l'ame bien éloignée de penser de faire des livres

(to move me to change my life. Then I put aside all voluntary mental production, and remained four or five years with my mind far away from any intention to write books).

The only period which that statement approximately fits, unless it refers to some date before the publication of the translations, was between 1661, the year of Mazarin's death on 1 April and of the fall of Foucquet in September, and 1665, a spell during which Desmarets published nothing. *L'Imitation* and *Le Combat* had appeared in 1656 and in 1657, when *Clovis* was also finally published. The five volumes of *Les Delices de l'esprit* were published in 1658, and the *Lettres spirituelles*, although now generally accepted as attributable to Desmarets, appeared in six volumes, three in 1660, two in 1661, and one in 1663, collected by a priest from the diocese of Poitiers, Jean de Lessot. *La Vie et les oeuvres de sainte Catherine de Gênes* had been published in 1661, and then nothing appeared until 1665, when Desmarets published *Le Chemin de la paix* and launched into his controversy with Nicole.

In the meanwhile Desmarets worked, probably through the conseil de conscience, the small committee mostly of churchmen instituted by Louis XIII to advise on legal and political decisions in matters affecting religion, whose president from 1643 was Vincent de Paul, at the persecution of two secretaries in the Extraordinaire des guerres, Charpy de Sainte-Croix, whose 1657 *L'Ancienne Nouveauté de l'Ecriture sainte; ou, L'Eglise triomphante en terre* had been published without a permission, and Simon Morin, who was burnt alive in March 1663. Morin had previously been charged with heresy, released as insane, again imprisoned and released, and then imprisoned after publishing his *Pensées*; he abjured, was released, prophesied, was sent to an asylum, and had been released in 1656.

On the death of Richelieu, Desmarets had retired not only from theatrical life but apparently from Paris. He appears quite soon to have become steward to the young second duke, Richelieu's légataire universel, in Poitou. On her uncle's death the duke was removed by the duchesse d'Aiguillon, whose nephew he was, to Le Havre. He did not relish the idea of remaining in his aunt's charge until his majority in 1656, and on Christmas Day 1649 a marriage contract was signed at Trie in Normandy with Anne Poussart de Pons, Desmarets's cousin. The marriage was sponsored by Condé, who was married to another of Richelieu's nieces and hoped to gain power at Mazarin's expense, specifically by putting Le Havre into the hands of his brother-in-law, the duc de Longueville, and thereby making him all-powerful in Normandy. Various members of the Condé family signed the contract. In fact the power struggle was won by the duchesse, and the princes, Condé, Conti, and Longueville, were imprisoned on 18 January 1650. The duchesse d'Aiguillon tried to break the marriage, but Mazarin saw his political advantage in allowing it to stand.

Desmarets was briefly imprisoned on 22 March 1650 for his part in the marriage of the duc de Richelieu who, after his own detention, escaped to Brouage. In May 1651 the duke unsuccessfully attempted to take possession of the château de Richelieu. In the autumn he was in Saintonge, borrowed 600,000 livres, and raised troops for the princes. Desmarets was certainly at least from this point his steward, and was at Richelieu at least

from the summer of 1652. The duchesse d'Aiguillon rendered her account as guardian of both the duke and his brother on 19 December 1652, and shortly thereafter the duke, having come into his immense wealth, ordered the completion of the château at Richelieu. Desmarets's fiefdom of Saint-Sorlin, bestowed in 1651, was confirmed on 9 December 1653.

There is no real need to postulate any sudden conversion in Desmarets at all. In 1644 and 1645 appeared books of card games commissioned from him by Richelieu for the dauphin, part of an ambitious system of educational cards which was never completed. Thereafter the religious publications started with the 1645 *Office de la Vierge Marie*, dedicated to Anne of Austria, although that cannot indicate the "conversion," since Desmarets himself said that his conversion was marked by a suspension of publication. The third novel, *La Vérité des fables; ou, L'Histoire des dieux de l'antiquité*, was then published with an achevé of 16 November 1647 but a title page of 1648. Desmarets's next publication was the 1653 *Les Promenades de Richelieu; ou, Les Vertus chrestiennes*, the first of the important devotional prose works, antedating by a year his two devotional verse translations, the *Imitation* and the *Combat*.

Three years later came the 1657 *Clovis; ou, La France chrestienne. Poëme heroique*, part of an important attempt to create for France a national and Christian epic. The idea of a biblical epic was not restricted to France: the first edition of Milton's *Paradise Lost* dates from 1667. Pierre Le Moyne had in 1653 published *Saint Louys; ou, Le Héros chrestien*, and in the same year Saint-Amant his *Moyse sauvé, idyle heroïque*. In 1654 Georges de Scudéry had published *Alaric; ou, Rome vaincue*, and in 1656 Chapelain published *Pucelle; ou, La France délivrée*. Desmarets was to dedicate *Clovis* to Louis XIV in the 1673 edition, and to defend it in his last works. It deals essentially with the conversion of the first barbarian Christian king in western Europe.

In devotional prose, Desmarets's most ambitious work was the 1658 *Les Délices de l'esprit: dialogues dediez aux Beaux Esprits du Monde* with an achevé d'imprimer of 15 April 1658, and dedicated to Mazarin. The 1661 *La Vie et les oeuvres de sainte Catherine de Gênes* is almost certainly in essence a revision of one of the earlier studies of the saint, whose own vocabulary and imagery Desmarets may well himself have drawn on. Sometime in 1664 Desmarets wrote to Henry-Marie Boudon, archdeacon of Evreux, seeking support for what sounds rather like a new version of the suppressed Compagnie du Saint-Sacrement, to be called the "Société de Paris pour les intérêts de Dieu.", and it is in connection with the pursuit of the forcible imposition of orthodoxy, which had increasingly occupied Desmarets from rather earlier than 1660, that he produced the mystically exalted two volumes of *Le Chemin de la paix et celuy de l'inquiétude* in 1665 and 1666.

Between 1669 and 1671 Desmarets published two biblical poems, the 1669 *Marie-Madeleine; ou, Le Triomphe de la grâce* and four cantos of the pseudonymous 1670 *Esther*, dedicated to the king, with a verse preface *L'Excellence et les plaintes de la poësie héroïque*. *Esther* was modified, expanded to seven cantos, and dedicated to the duchesse de Richelieu in 1673, and that year Desmarets also published a short heroic poem *Regulus; ou; le vray genereux*, even further committing himself to biblical subjects, the Christian marvellous, and therefore, by affirming the superiority of Christian over pagan antiquity, to a "moderne" position in the Querelle des anciens et des modernes, to whose central issues, however, the question of the Christian marvellous remained largely peripheral.

The most important late work of Desmarets was the uncontrolled *Response à l'insolente Apologie [des religieuses] de Port-Royal* of which three parts were published in 1665, only the first containing the reference to the "religieuses," and one part appeared in 1668, with *Apologies* now in the plural. It was in this dispute that Desmarets developed the uncontrolled aggression against Nicole which led to suspicions that he had become mentally unstable. In its context Desmarets produced various other polemical works and prefaces, including the 1674 heroic poem *Le Triomphe de Louis et de son siècle*, and widened his aim into a general defence of the theatre, as well as of ecclesiastical orthodoxy and of the less disciplined forms of mysticism.

At the beginning of Desmarets's self-imposed task of publicly enforcing Christian dogmatic and moral norms, he had begun to feel strongly about Jansenism, as a manifestation of heterodoxy, disunity, and disloyalty rather than as a doctrine about grace and free will. He no doubt sympathized with the baroque optimism of the court of Louis XIII, as also did the Jesuits, whose rejoicing at the birth of the dauphin Louis in 1538 had outdone even his own. He may indeed have been brought up by the Jesuits at La Flèche, and Pascal momentarily suspected him in the fifteenth of the *Lettres provinciales*, dated 25 November 1656, of defending them. It was when Nicole attacked Desmarets in the first of the *Lettres visionnaires*, clandestinely published on 31 December 1665 and declaring him a poisoner not of the bodies but of the souls of the faithful, that Racine, exasperated, sharply attacked the party of those associated with Port-Royal (q.v.) who had adopted and educated him.

In 1665 Nicole had published, with Arnauld and Claude de Sainte-Marthe, a four-part *Apologie* on behalf of the Port-Royal nuns, and it was to this work that Desmarets was replying. Desmarets, in his 1664 letter to Henry-Marie Boudon pointing to the need for a new society to defend Christian teaching and morals, had boasted of his success, after the burning of Morin, in hounding down three "prêtres magiciens (priest magicians)," and two seculars who had indulged in satanism and witchcraft. Desmarets certainly at this point regarded himself as specially inspired by God, and appointed to further divine purposes on earth; no more clinically mad, no doubt, than the devil-worshippers he thought he was persecuting, but clearly not at this period fully possessed of balanced powers of judgement, and touched with the paranoia not uncommon among those who think they have a personal divine mission on earth.

Boileau was to attack Desmarets in the third "chant" of the *Art poétique*, as also in two epigrams. The whole thrust of Boileau's poem, as Desmarets accurately noticed, was to ruin the threat made by the Christian epic to the hegemony of the great epics of antiquity. Within five weeks of the appearance of Boileau's work Desmarets had published *La Deffense du poëme héroïque* on 18 August 1674, five days after the reception of Daniel Huet at the Académie française. Quinault, Perrault, and Desmarets all read poems at the session and, a few days later, Charpentier sent verses to Perrault on the superiority of contemporary culture. The victory of the moderne position was being ostentatiously established at the Académie française which, in 1674, for the first time proposed a biblical alongside a classical subject for its prize. The moderne ascendancy, established also at the Académie des Beaux-Arts, was a more deep-rooted phenomenon than has generally been realized. Desmarets's part in

the debate shows that it was not connected with the vogue for Descartes, as might logically have been supposed. That vogue had appeared quite compatible with the studies of the Port-Royal solitaires, against whom Desmarets ranged himself, while the salon of the duc de Richelieu was notoriously hostile to Cartesianism.

It was at the Hôtel de Richelieu that Desmarets died in 1676, protected by the duke, at whose instigation he appears to have undertaken both the *Imitation* and the *Combat* translations, both printed at Richelieu. Even more than Perrault, to whom he dedicated his last work, the 1675 *La Defense de la Poësie*, Desmarets, far from surviving as a left-over participant from the baroque exuberances of the court of Louis XIII under Richelieu, had come to stand for the glorification of France. Under Colbert, that meant the glorification of Louis XIV, an enterprise which, in spite of the pension of 1,200 livres granted to Desmarets in 1663, failed to inspire him with as much enthusiasm as Colbert might have wished, but one with which the success of the "moderne" party, while led by Perrault, came intimately to be associated.

WORKS

When in 1662 Chapelain was asked to comment on the suitability of possible candidates for the post of royal historiographer, which he wanted to go to Pellisson, he wrote of Desmarets,

> C'est un des esprits faciles de ce temps et qui, sans grand fonds, sait une plus grande quantité de choses et leur donne un meilleur jour. Son style de prose est pur mais sans élevation; en vers il est élevé ou abaissé selon qu'il le désire, et en l'un et l'autre genre il est inépuisable et rapide dans l'exécution, aimant mieux y laisser des taches et des négligences que de n'avoir bientôt fait. Son imagination est très fertile et souvent tient la place du jugement

> (He is one of the more light-weight minds of our time which, without much depth, knows a greater number of things and puts them in a better light. His prose style is pure but undistinguished; in verse he is uplifting or commonplace, as he wants, but inexhaustible in both styles, and he writes fast, preferring to leave blemishes and negligences rather than not to have done quickly. His imagination is very fertile, and often takes judgement's place).

Chapelain has recognized the unthinking ease with which Desmarets is capable of writing fluent pastiche of all sorts. A few more years would reveal the way in which passion and prejudice could sweep through what he wrote, turning polemic into invective and argument into denunciation. In a letter of 6 March 1666, Chapelain wrote

> Il y a long temps que Mr Conrart et moy nous estions apperçeus des égaremens du pauvre visionnaire dont vous me parlés, mais nous n'eussions jamais pensé qu'il deust aller si loin qu'il a fait

> (M. Conrart and I had noticed long ago the aberrations of the poor visionary of whom you speak, but we would never have thought he would go as far as he has).

Bremond, in the *Histoire littéraire du sentiment religieux en France*, seems surely to have been wrong to take the later outpourings of Desmarets's feverishly exalted mind for serious mystical writing, just as Bremond was over-critical of Nicole for his anti-mystical bias. Only one of Desmarets's three novels comes to an end, and it may well be that his scripted drama was written principally with no aim in mind higher than that of providing Richelieu with new pieces to stage. Some of the controversial writings of the last 15 years of Desmarets's life, preluding the major cultural clash of the Querelle des anciens et des modernes (q.v.), with its debates about a national and Christian epic, were undoubtedly important, but little of the poetry deserves to have survived, and *Clovis* does little more than demonstrate that the notion of a Christian epic in 17th-century France was self-contradictory. An epic, unlike a tragedy, requires a struggle that does not admit of divine intervention. It is the dilemmas he was caught up in rather than any successes he achieved that give Desmarets's writings their literary interest.

The 1632 novel *Ariane*, set in Nero's reign, borrows much from d'Urfé, although in structure it builds on what had been achieved by Gomberville and, like Boisrobert's 1629 *Histoire indienne d'Anaxandre et d'Orazie*, it derives a great deal from Heliodorus's novel, several times translated, in 1622 as *Les Amours de Theagene et Chariclée, histoire ethiopique*. It is not really a heroic novel at all, although there are accounts of theatrical entertainments, clearly drawn from Desmarets's experience but also emphasizing the dramatic gestures and posturizing associated with the portrayal of heroism in the baroque adventure novel. The language, too, is unsurprisingly hyperbolic in its free use of superlatives. Verse is used to emphasize emotional peaks.

There is a confident narrator, but many characters also tell their own stories within the main narration, creating flashbacks and episodic interest not themselves unusual in romanesque literature of this period. Despite the fluctuations of fortune, a providence is shown to have been at work throughout the novel, which centres on the love of Mélinte for Ariane, and the less committed affection of his friend, Palamède, for the apparent slave, Epicharis, Ariane's attendant. In reality, Epicharis turns out to be Mélinte's sister, and Palamède is Ariane's brother. The story is one of heroism, fulfilled prophecy, struggle, apparent deaths, including that of Mélinte, mistaken identities, recognitions, last-minute reprieves, constancy, and forgiveness. There is a chivalric emphasis on strength and valour, debased, though, because only one of Mélinte's opponents in combat is of his own moral rank, the pirate captain Eurymédon. He gets disarmed. The inferiors are slain, sometimes with massive feats of strength.

Ariane is crowned as a beauty queen long before her real coronation, and the novel's intrigue barely distinguishes it from many others of the same type. It does, however, lack d'Urfé's seriousness of imaginative purpose, and is more given to titillating histrionic extremes. There are more licentious episodes, and a consequent oscillation of tone, breaking the overall heroic mould, again fractured by the introduction of distinctly bourgeois characters and values, as when Epicharis adds on days of servitude to those already required of a boorish suitor. One episode is taken from a Boccaccio conte. At the climax of the novel in the last book, Desmarets's fundamental lack of imaginative vigour becomes again clear as he lapses into the stylized grotesque scene when Mélinte, thinking he is about to be sacrificed,

asks Ariane to take his heart and burn it, expressing his dying wish:

> c'est que ce coeur qui vous a tant aimée, apres avoir esté tiré de mon estomac, soit pris de vos belles mains, et porté par vous pour estre bruslé sur ce bûcher…et faites que n'ayant jamais bruslé que pour vous, il ne soit encore bruslé que par vous. Quelle joie pensez vous qu'il recevra, lors qu'apres vous avoir tant adorée sans vous connoistre que par le desir, il se sentira porté par ces mains si belles et si aimées? Ariane, promettez moy cette grace: n'ayez point d'horreur de toucher une chose qui vous a tant cherie

(it is that this heart which has so deeply loved you, having been plucked from my body, should be taken by your beautiful hands and carried by you to be burned on this pyre…so that, having burned only for you, it should be burned only by you. You can imagine how great its joy will be when, after having adored you without knowing you except by desire, it will feel itself carried by such beautiful and such beloved hands. Ariane, promise me this favour: do not draw back from touching something which has cherished you so dearly).

In the 1643 edition there is an engraving of the scene in which the executioner's knife is poised, set against a Palladian architectural setting with all the characters in careful poses; priest with knife and not even a mock-savage expression, Mélinte lying half naked and unbound on the block, his right hand clutching Ariane's left, as she turns her head away, ready to push a knife into her own side, and a whole crowd of barely indicated onlookers. Someone has painted a heart on Mélinte's skin to show the executioner where to cut. The theatricality of the bourgeois novel posing as heroic is here inadvertently made visually clear. There is no tension between hero and heroine, and the plot is propelled rather by the persecution of Marcelin, Nero's favourite and the Roman governor of Thessaly, and by that of Dicéarque, Ariane's uncle and guardian.

Chapelain, in a letter to Balzac of 4 December 1639, suggests that the unfinished 1639 *Rosane* was not only dedicated to but also contained a portrait of the duchesse d'Aiguillon, who must clearly have been flattered by her depiction as Uranie. Dionée has a close relationship with Uranie, and Dionée was a name given by Desmarets to Mme du Vigean in an elegy added late in 1640 to the *Oeuvres poëtiques*, but it would have been much too dangerous to allow lesbian innuendoes about Mme du Vigean, and by implication about Richelieu's niece, in a novel at this date. The preface moves towards justifying the use of allegory in the novel, which was in fact intended didactically, to be useful to the recently born dauphin. It was not reprinted, but it was translated into Italian and one of its principal episodes was turned into the tragicomédie *Erigone*. The third novel, the 1648 *La Vérité des fables*, was poorly received and remained unfinished. It is ingenious, although built on the usual recognitions, escapes, and mistaken identities, and sexual ambiguities of which much play is made, with Ganymede not revealed as a girl until near the end.

Les Visionnaires has always been considered the most important and has been the most successful, although not the most pretentious, of the plays. Desmarets insists in his preface that it was written for the educated, and there is some ostentation in the construction of the speeches, the learned allusions, the keeping of the 24-hour rule and the unity of place. The play concerns obsessions, the French words "visionnaire," "extravagant," and "fou," being used more or less interchangeably at this date. Each of the characters except the father of the family, Alcidon, has a different particular obsession, but is for the most part otherwise sane. The difficulty with the play is that Desmarets leaves his audience uncertain about his satirical intentions, about exactly what he regarded as insane in his characters.

Desmarets lists the obsessions of his characters in a long "Argument." Artabaze is a boastful but cowardly captain; the poet Amidor is a vehicle for satirizing any lingering admiration for Ronsard and, above all, Du Bartas, particularly for what Desmarets regards as their hyperbolic style and their use of mythology; Filidan sees artistic excellence where none exists, and admires what he does not understand; Phalante is rich only in his imagination—Desmarets says his folly appears only in the fifth act, no doubt because, before that, he has described the château de Richelieu, about which it would not have been prudent to make jokes, as the sort of place he would like to live in; Mélisse is in love with Alexander the Great; Hespérie thinks that everyone is in love with her; Sestiane is obsessed with the theatre whose rules she does not understand, although we are warned that some of the poets she quotes held correct views; Alcidon, the father of the three girls, is gullible and easy to please; and finally in the cast comes Lysandre, described by Desmarets as its only member to be "raisonnable (rational)."

The rest of the Argument constitutes an attack on the sorts of audience Desmarets despises, the unlettered, those who like gore in their tragedies, or comedies low enough to appeal to their sense of humour, the bizarre, grotesque, extravagant, and even the spectacular which depends on machines and stage effects. Among those to incur Desmarets's contempt are also those whose appreciation is reserved for witty verbal play, pompously inflated language, and complicated plots. There is no discernible hint that he was being ironic and, if he was not, he was being arrogant. He was looking for those who wanted only "les pures délicatesses de l'art… les nobles et véritables mouvements des passions dans les sujets sérieux (the purest delicacy of art… noble and authentic movements of the passions in serious subjects)" or "des railleries gentilles et honnêtes (respectful and decent mocking)" in comic subjects. Desmarets appears himself to have written the quatrain with which the Argument ends:

Ce n'est pas pour toi que j'écris,
Indocte et stupide vulgaire:
J'écris pour les nobles esprits,
Je serais marri de te plaire

(It is not for you that I am writing,/Unlearned and stupid common people:/I am writing for elevated minds,/I should be annoyed if I pleased you).

The plot is not memorable, and the verse does not improve in quality after the beginning, a 58-line tirade by Artabaze, which starts

Je suis l'amour du Ciel, et l'effroi de la terre,
L'ennemi de la paix, le foudre de la guerre,
Des dames le désir, des maris la terreur,
Et je traîne avec moi le carnage et l'horreur

(I am the love of heaven, and the dread of the earth,/The enemy of peace, the hero of war,/Of women the desire, of husbands the terror,/And I bring with me carnage and horror).

Artabaze bombastically, and Desmarets learnedly, include in the speech a list of four great warriors of antiquity, and eight conquered cities. The mocking intention is obvious, but it is the principal source of humour. Amidor enters, announcing his poetic delusion with the quatrain

Je sors des antres noirs du mont Parnassien,
Où le fils poil-doré du grand Saturnien
Dans l'esprit forge-vers plante le dithyrambe,
L'épode, l'antistrophe, et le tragique iambe

(I come out of the black caverns of the Parnassian mount,/Where the golden-haired son [Apollo] of the great Saturnian [Jupiter, son of Saturn]/Plants in the verse-forging mind the dithyramb,/the epode, the antistrophe, and the tragic iambus).

The Bibliothèque de la Pléiade edition of the play, which is sparing with its explanatory notes, has to explain nine allusions in Amidor's 30-line soliloquy which constitutes the third scene. Amidor's abuse of poetic procedures which French taste had long since left behind is not brought to life as satire, and as parody needs great acting as well as learning if it is to produce more than a flickering smile. In so far as there is a plot it has to do with the choice of a husband for one of the three girls, in which the trigger-happy Alcidon is wisely restrained by Lysandre. The girls themselves would not be out of place in burlesque. One of Amidor's dozen tragedies is rehearsed by the characters in the third act. Artabaze naturally plays Alexander the Great, his fantasy self, and Mélisse naturally takes the fantasy for the reality and falls in love with Artabaze. In the end Artabaze announces that he cannot do Alcidon the honour of marrying one of his daughters, since he is in love with no one but himself, and Lysandre sends everyone away content in their own delusions. They will be a thousand times happier than they would be without them.

In spite of its pretensions to the status of national and Christian epic, *Clovis* personally flatters Louis XIV, the memory of Louis XIII, and such other notables as the family of the duchesse de Richelieu's first husband, François-Alexandre d'Albret, sieur of Pons, a town near Cognac captured for Condé by Claude de la Trémoille. The poem is nearly an allegory, and concerns the life, baptism and activities of Clovis (A.D. 465–511), the first barbarian Christian king. The poem is not so much epic as romanesque. The whole weakness of the poem, and of Desmarets's literary aesthetic, lies in the fact that in a Christian poem divine intervention, the Christian marvellous, must be benevolent, while the epic demands a heroic struggle against forces that may not be. *Clovis* accordingly compromises with romanesque devices, flashbacks, storms, spells, apparitions, resurrections, and, an alarming sign of what was happening psychologically to Desmarets, allusions to current events seen in the light of Christian prophecy.

Desmarets is so much a figure of contradiction in the history of French literature that it requires more detailed attention than is here possible to see just why his reputation rode so high as a court entertainer, and then fell away so sharply through a succession of what posterity has judged to be failures, in the composition of a Christian epic, and then in his seeing the Christian epic and the Christian marvellous as the principal weapon in the powerful armoury of the modernes, whose real fire-power was much more potent. Desmarets becomes an almost sad figure as a religious versifier whose authentic sentiment seems adequately reproduced by the banality of his verse, as an imposer of orthodoxy, an exalted and possibly to some extent deranged pseudo-mystic, and as a polemicist against the sharper-minded Nicole. We may well feel that Desmarets was often enough on the right side, but his time passed him by. We might regard him as a much more important author if he had ceased to publish after the death of his patron, Richelieu.

PUBLICATIONS

Fiction

Ariane (signed "de Boisval"), 2 vols., 1632; as *Ariana*, 1636
Rosane, histoire tirée de celle des Romains et des Perses, 1639
La Vérité des fables; ou, L'Histoire des dieux de l'antiquité, 2 vols., 1648

Plays

Aspasie, comédie (1636), 1636
Les Visionnaires, comédie (1637), 1637; edited by H.G. Hall, 1963; in *Théâtre du XVIIe siècle*, vol. 2, Bibliothèque de la Pléiade, 1986
Scipion, tragicomédie (1638), 1639
Ballet de la Félicité sur le sujet de l'heureuse naissance de Monseigneur le Dauphin (1639), 1639
Roxane, tragicomédie (1639), 1640
Mirame, tragicomédie (1641), 1641
Ballet de la Prospérité des armes de la France (1641), 1641
Erigone, tragicomédie (1642), 1642
Europe, comédie héroïque (1642), 1643

Secular and heroic verse

Les Amours du Compas et de la Règle, et ceux du soleil et de l'ombre, 1637
Pour une Mascarade des Grâces et des Amours, 1640
Oeuvres poëtiques du Sieur Desmarets, with *Autres oeuvres poëtiques* and *Odes, poëmes et autres oeuvres*, 3 vols., 1641–43
Clovis; ou, La France chrestienne. Poëme héroïque, 1657; edited by F.R. Freudmann, 1972
Marie-Madeleine; ou, Le Triomphe de la grâce. Poëme, 1669
La Comparaison de la langue et de la poësie françoise, avec la grecque et la latine..., 1670
Esther. Poëme héroïque (signed "de Boisval"), 1670, augmented 1673
Regulus; ou, Le Vray Genereux. Poëme héroïque, 1671
Le Triomphe de Louis et de son siècle. Poëme lyrique, 1674

Religious verse

Office de la Vierge Marie, 1645

Prieres et oeuvres chrétiennes, 1669
Les quatre livres de l'Imitation de Jésus Christ, 1654
Le Combat spirituel; ou, De la perfection de la vie chrétienne, 1654

Other

Cartes des rois de France, 1644–45, augmented 1664
Les Promenades de Richelieu; ou, Les Vertus chrétiennes, 1653
Les Délices de l'esprit: dialogues dediés aux beaux esprits du monde, 5 vols., 1658
Examen du livre, intitulé, L'Ancienne Nouveauté de l'Ecriture sainte; ou, L'Eglise triomphante en terre, 1661
Lettres spirituelles, recueillies par un Ecclesiastique, 6 vols., 1660–3
La Vie et les oeuvres de sainte Catherine de Gênes (revision by Desmarets), 2 vols., 1661
Le Chemin de la paix et celui de l'inquiétude, 2 vols., 1665–66
Réponse à l'insolente Apologie [des religieuses] de Port-Royal, ...[aux insolentes Apologies de Port-Royal]...,4 vols., 1665–68
La Défense du poëme héroïque... (with Jacques Testu and the duc de Nevers), 1674
La Défense de la Poësie, et de la langue françoise, 1675

Biographical and critical studies

Stellwagen, J.H., *The Drama of Jean Desmarets de Saint-Sorlin*, 1944
Sayce, R.A., *The French Biblical Epic in the Seventeenth Century*, 1955
Maskell, D., *The Historical Epic in France 1500–1700*, 1973
Bannister, Mark, *Privileged Mortals. The French Heroic Novel, 1630–1660*, 1983
Hall, Hugh Gaston, *Richelieu's Desmarets and the Century of Louis XIV*, 1990

DESPORTES, Philippe, 1546–1606.

Poet.

LIFE

Desportes was born at Chartres in April or May 1546 into a family whose respectability may be judged by the number of échevins both sides of it had provided for the town council. His father was a cloth merchant who had bought a house in the town centre in 1538 and was himself to become a councillor in 1552. Desportes was the elder of two sons in a family of ten. The only account of his youth comes from Tallemant, but it seems likely that his parents had social aspirations for their elder son, and had him well educated. Tallemant fascinatingly wrote of Desportes that he was "of low birth, but well educated," and then substituted "good" for "low." Tallemant's hesitancy is revealing, but the final text is the nonsensical "of good birth, but well educated," and Tallemant jumps straight to Desportes's late adolescence and his love life. The younger brother's name was Thibault.

Dismissed by the lawyer who employed him but who, displeased with what was happening between Desportes and his wife, simply had Desportes's things bundled up and stuck at the door for collection, Desportes went to Avignon, "where the court may have been." That puts the journey in 1564, when the court arrived at Avignon on 24 September. On the celebrated bridge, where he had joined the servants waiting to be hired, Desportes heard that the bishop of Le Puy, Antoine de Senneterre, was in the town and needed a secretary. The bishop liked Desportes and gave him the job. Still according to Tallemant, Desportes fell promptly in love with one of the bishop's five nieces, the Cléonice of the poems, although a satire of 1581 says it was with their mother, the bishop's sister-in-law, Jeanne de Laval, married to his brother François. The satire's version is to be preferred to Tallemant's, since the daughters had in 1564 not yet been born. Mme de Senneterre was herself well known at court.

Desportes had probably been educated for the church. He learnt Greek as well as Latin, and there is strong circumstantial evidence that his later translation of the psalms involved a knowledge of Hebrew, of which he owned a dictionary. In 1562 he had received the tonsure. Tallemant's whole account of the Avignon episode has naturally been disputed, but Desportes went to Rome with a bishop, presumably Senneterre, certainly got to know the Italian poets, and was back in Paris at the latest towards the end of 1566. On 28 January 1567 Baïf's *Le Brave* was played before Charles IX and Catherine de Medici at the Hôtel de Guise. During the intervals verses were sung or recited. They were addressed by Ronsard to the king, by Baïf to Catherine de Medici, by Desportes to the duc d'Anjou, one day to be Henri III, by Nicolas Filleul to Anjou's younger brother, still the duc d'Alençon, and by Belleau to Madame Marguerite, sister of Henri II. Desportes was already in full possession of his talent, and he was to follow the future Henri III, whose praises he had sung, to the Polish court in 1573–74.

We do not know how the unknown Desportes suddenly, on his return from Rome, found himself in such exalted poetic company at the court command performance for which Baïf wrote his play. It has been conjectured that the Chouaine family, also from Chartres and probably already for some time in the service of Catherine, may have favoured Desportes's career by presenting him both at court and to Ronsard and his friends. There is no evidence about what happened, but some form of powerful patronage must have been involved. At the same time Desportes must at this period have acquired the doctorate in canon law twice attributed to him in 1582. However lax the academic requirements might at times and places have been, that degree always denoted at least some gesture towards what we would regard as tertiary education, and in Paris the requirements were serious.

Desportes wrote an elegy for the death of the Connétable Anne de Montmorency, leader of the Catholic troops, who was killed at Saint-Denis, dying on 11 November 1567, and by 1568 he had been awarded a payment by the king. There was some difficulty in the treasury about funding the royal largesse, and Desportes wrote a *Satire contre un juif*. He never published it,

and indeed progressively removed from his later *Oeuvres* any pieces which could give offence. The *Satire* did appear, but only well after his death, in the *Recueil de Sercy* of 1653.

In the years immediately following his return to Paris, Desportes somehow found himself put on the rungs of the ladder to an administrative career, probably by Claude de l'Aubespine, who succeeded his father as secretary of state in November 1567 but was to die suddenly on 13 September 1570, and whose sister, Madeleine, had since 1562 been married to Nicolas de Neufville, seigneur de Villeroy, who was to succeed his brother-in-law as secretary of state and later to be close to Mayenne. This entourage was anyway to be important for Desportes's later career, and he belonged to it certainly by 1573, when he was a secrétaire de la chambre du Roi. He had written a déploration for a collective but unpublished memorial tombeau on L'Aubespine's death, to which Ronsard, Baïf, Dorat, Passerat, Jamyn, and others had also contributed.

We know only from his verse and the manuscripts which can be dated that, during the winter of 1570–71, Desportes was ill for six months, subsequently leaving Paris for a period of convalescence. It must have been during these months that he wrote most of the verse in the manuscript collection he was to present to Charles IX at the end of 1571, containing pieces to be published in the *Premières oeuvres* of 1573. We know that the secrétaires formed a group of young men recruited from the lower aristocracy and upper bourgeoisie who were loosely attached to the court, and that their leisure pursuits, if cultivated, were frolicsome and sometimes bawdy; and there is every reason to assume that Desportes fitted in. Desportes's satirical verses about women, love, and marriage, particularly his "Stances du mariage," denote no more than participation in a fashionable pastime in the circle protected by Villeroy. Nothing leads us to suppose that Desportes did not enjoy the atmosphere of the group and take part in its activities, although he seems to have been left unsatisfied by it.

Altogether more cultivated was the other circle where the young Desportes was taken up, that of Claude-Catherine de Clermont-Dampierre, by her second marriage in 1565 maréchale de Retz. In this group the cult of female beauty demanded the refined Italianate semi-religious language of the Petrarchan tradition. It remained, however, at the level of an affectation, however serious an aspiration towards cultural refinement it reflected, rather than any resumption of the serious, if still tentative, imaginative upgrading of human instinctive affections brusquely interrupted by the more dour imaginative preoccupations imposed by the religious wars. It was this milieu which produced the collective volume of Ariosto adaptations with a substantial contribution by Desportes, the 1572 *Imitations de quelques chans de l'Arioste*, by a group of poets including, with Desportes, Saint-Gelais and Baïf. The imitations of Ariosto's *Roland furieux*, whose transformation through different versions has allowed the surviving manuscripts to be dated, and which had originally been dedicated to the Huguenot friend of Brantôme, Jérôme Lhuillier, seigneur de Maisonfleur, before losing its dedication altogether, appeared in this collection dedicated to Charles IX, who may have bestowed on Desportes a substantial financial reward. The report about that matter by Desportes's disciple, Claude Garnier, is confused.

The privilège for the first edition of *Les Premieres Oeuvres de Philippes Des Portes. Au roy de Pologne* is dated 28 July 1583 and signed by Villeroy. Garnier tells us that the future Henri III, victorious at Jarnac and Moncontour and about to become king of Poland, gave Desportes 30,000 livres for the printing. The volume, printed by Robert Estienne, is a sumptuous quarto, with 74 poems in the "Amours de Diane," 60 in the "Amours de Cléonice," 44 in the "Mélanges", 84 in the "Amours d'Hippolyte," 16 "Elégies," and five poems from the *Imitations*. At least 30 printings, many revised and augmented, are known from the next 20 years. Much was imitated from Ariosto, although now without acknowledgement, including Desportes's most famous poem, "O Nuit! jalouse Nuit," to remain a popular song for nearly a century. In addition to Ariosto, the earlier poems in the collection were heavily dependent on Petrarch and Pamphilo Sasso, to whom Desportes added Tebaldeo, and then Serafino, Cariteo, Bembo, and other less well-known poets whose work had been published in the collected volumes of Italian *Rime*.

It seems certain that the "Amours d'Hippolyte" were written by Desportes on behalf of Bussy d'Amboise to press his suit with Marguerite de Valois, about to marry Henri de Navarre. Ronsard and Jamyn had written the love poetry of Charles IX for him, and it seems quite probable that Desportes wrote love poetry on behalf of the future Henri III, and perhaps on behalf of others as well, although it is virtually impossible to attach any one poem to any particular lover or any particular woman, if indeed the identities were not intended from the beginning to be indistinct and indistinguishable. Circumstances have however made one "complainte" particularly memorable, that written by Desportes on behalf of the future king unenthusiastically preparing to leave Marie de Clèves, married in 1572 to Henri de Bourbon, in order to take up the Polish throne. He was sincerely in love with her but was never to see her again. She died in childbirth on 30 October 1574, after Henri had left Poland, but before his return to France.

Henri took Desportes with him to Poland as secretary to the chancelry. The retinue which left Paris on 4 November was large, and included two dukes—Mayenne and Nevers—the marquis d'Elbeuf, Retz, and Pompone de Bellièvre. Formal farewells were made at Vitry except by Catherine de Medici, who accompanied her son as far as Blamont. The French party reached Polish territory on 24 January 1574, but did not care for the discomfort, the cold, or the catering. They arrived in the capital, Cracow, on 18 February 1574. We know nothing at all of Desportes's stay, except that he must have felt the general cultural clash, with Henri and his mignons shocking the Polish court with their frivolity and licentiousness, and clearly failing to acclimatize themselves to their new cultural surroundings. Desportes's functions obliged him to stay, but he appears to have disliked Poland and to have succeeded in returning to Paris for a period, probably on leave, before the death of Charles IX on 31 May 1574. The Poles heard the news of the death via Vienna, before the French in Poland did, through their own diplomatic channels, on 14 June.

With the death of Charles IX Bellièvre's ambassadorship automatically ended, and he left Cracow on 17 June, in fact to set up the stages on the escape route for the king, who played for time before dodging what were effectively his guards on the night of 18 June and reaching Vienna on 24 June. Desportes was among those who covered his flight, reporting on the pursuit before rejoining Henri in Vienna and travelling with him through Italy, avoiding the hostile Palatinate in what is now south Germany. The party reached Lyons on 6 September. At some point Desportes may well have left it. The evidence is conflicting. As far as we know, his total poetic production in Poland had been limited to three satires.

Just as Ronsard had been particularly associated with Charles IX, so the accession of Henri III brought increased prominence and popularity to Desportes, who had been for some years what amounted to his household poet, as well as in his direct employ during the tenure of the Polish crown. Desportes wrote little for court entertainments, but was called on to compose laments for the deaths of his own friends, and friends of patrons. He wrote two pieces of lament for Le Guast, captain of the royal bodyguard, assassinated by the baron de Viteaux on 31 October 1575 while in bed with Françoise d'Estrées. Desportes lost another friend when Rémy Belleau died on 6 March 1577. Four days later Desportes carried his coffin, together with Ronsard, Baïf, and Jamyn.

On Sunday 27 April 1578 the "duel of the mignons" took place between Henri III's favourite, Jacques de Lévis, comte de Quélus, seconded by Maugiron and Livarot, and three followers of Guise, Charles de Balzac d'Entragues, seconded by Schomberg and de Ribérac. Schomberg, Maugiron, and de Ribérac were killed, Livarot was badly wounded, and Quélus, whose bedside Henri III assiduously attended, died of his 19 wounds on 29 May. Desportes wrote two pieces for each of the dead mignons, Quélus and Maugiron, and a long poem, *Cléophon*, incurring the accusation of condoning the homosexual relationships of the king, who had embraced Quélus's dead body, had locks cut from the blond hair, himself removed the ear-rings he had given him, erected two mausoleums, and commissioned verses from Ronsard, Passerat, and Jamyn as well as Desportes. Scarcely two months later, on 21 July, another mignon, Saint-Mégrin, was assassinated, probably on the orders of Guise, to whose wife he was paying too flagrant attention. The six-line stanza on all three mignons in the king's book of hours after the prayers for the dead bears Desportes's name.

The poetic activity, however, remained slender. Desportes was also a functionary, although the royal favours he received cannot yet primarily have been on that account. On 23 January 1577 his mother was exempted by the king from contributing to the cost of the fortifications at Chartres. On 7 February 1578 he bought a large house and garden adjoining the Seine, and the following year was given charge of the further instruction of the 24-year-old duc d'Epernon. It is usually presumed that it was about this time that Desportes entered the entourage of Anne, duc de Joyeuse, born in 1561, another favourite of Henri III and successor in that role to d'Epernon. It was the relationship to Joyeuse, to whom he was counsellor and secretary, but also an older person charged with acting as a moral, social, and political guide, which really established Desportes's career on a firm foundation and led to the preferment which made him independent of royal caprice. The bankrupt Henri III, who could not pay his army, nevertheless spent a fortune in 1581 on the wedding celebrations for Joyeuse's marriage to the queen's sister.

The most sought-after benefice was an abbacy. In an abbey the prior was only the second official, and Ronsard had to content himself with a priory. Abbacies were normally kept for members of the court. In 1579 Ronsard and Desportes very nearly obtained jointly the abbacy of Saint-Aubin-des-Bois near Brieuc, and finally in 1582 Desportes did receive two abbacies, the opulent abbacy of Tiron and that of Notre-Dame-de-Josaphat, smaller but none the less yielding between 3,500 and

4,500 livres a year; both were in the diocese of Chartres. In 1585 he received the abbacy of Saint-Géraud-d'Aurillac which he exchanged three years later for the abbey des-Vaux-de-Cernay, and in February 1592, while in Rouen and under siege, he received the abbey of Bonport in the diocese of Evreux. Tallemant says that his four abbacies brought him in 40,000 livres a year. From 1583 Desportes was also a prebend of the Chartres cathedral chapter, and of the Sainte–Chapelle. No doubt Desportes's personal reputation and unofficial position as court love poet helped, but the ecclesiastical offices were in fact rewards for administrative services undertaken first in the service of Joyeuse, but then as a member of the king's inner council to which Desportes was gradually admitted and in which the most important affairs of state were discussed, although no minutes were ever kept. Desportes acquired at court a reputation for liberal invitations to his excellent table, and for the magnificence of his library.

The editions of Desportes's works of 1575, 1576 and 1577 were all augmented. In 1578 there were only four new pieces, and thereafter Desportes renounced secular verse. Many of the 224 new pieces in the principal 1583 edition, which included the *Dernières amours*, later *Cléonice* and a book of 107 elegies, were actually ten years old. The chief difference in the newer poems is their derivation from the sonnets of Angelo di Costanzo, Bernardino Rota, Bernardo Tasso, Tansillo, and others collected in Ruscelli's *Fiori*, probably a consequence of the return from Poland by way of Italy in 1574.

Desportes had received minor orders on 3 September 1582, and probably later went on to the sub-diaconate, formally obliging to the recitation of the breviary and to celibacy. His abandonment of purely secular verse and his new ecclesiastical seriousness coincided perhaps more than haphazardly with the king's turn towards devotion, pilgrimages, pentitential exercises including flagellation, and confraternities, or so, at least, it was thought at the time. From the mid-1580s Desportes seems to have seen much more of his brother Thibault, whose administrative career he was favouring, and who may well have lived in the residence provided for Desportes as a canon of the Sainte-Chapelle. His own style of life, not quite ostentatious, allowed an ample measure of good living, and the possibility of extending much hospitality. He remained attached to Joyeuse, travelling in his suite, for instance, when Joyeuse made his entry into Caen as governor of Normandy in March 1583.

Ronsard's death on 28 December 1585 made clear Desportes's position as France's premier poet, although the title, awarded by the Jeux Floraux, was itself conferred on Baïf, and it was apparently Desportes who took charge of the details of the memorial ceremony at Boncourt, after the memorial lunch given by the Principal, Galland, and intended primarily for the court, at which Du Perron preached the panegyric. A more academic morning memorial service had already been held. Desportes did not however contribute to either of the collections of memorial verse.

The 1586 harvest had been poor and the winter of 1586–87 was particularly severe, although distress was alleviated by successful crops in 1587. There was famine, and the king's distracted state of mind did nothing to help his supporters deal with the threatening political situation. Joyeuse's sister-in-law died, and his widower brother became a Capucin. Desportes's correspondence shows that at this date he was virtually Joyeuse's agent in Paris. Then on 25 October news reached Paris of the murder of the captives at Coutras in revenge for that of the Protestant troops by the Catholics in June at Mothe-Saint-Héraye. Joyeuse and his young brother, Saint-Sauveur, had been killed, and most of the court had lost relatives. Desportes, deeply upset, went to stay with Baïf and took up again his own translation of the psalms, of which 60 would appear in 1591. It must have been known that he was working on a version, as there is an allusion to it in a pamphlet of 1587. He was to continue to protect Baïf's mistress, and Baïf's son by her, until his own death.

It was at least thought by contemporaries that Desportes ceased to serve Henri III before the king's assassination on 31 July 1589 and, with his brother, had before that date begun actively to support the League. Tallemant says that he filled for André de Brancas, seigneur de Villars and governor of Le Havre, the role he formerly filled for Joyeuse, while Palma Cayet recounts how he assisted Villars at the siege of Rouen. There is, however, a serious gap in biographical information for some years after the death of Joyeuse. Revenue from his abbeys was stopped when Desportes's support for the League became apparent. During the siege of Chartres, the key city for Paris's food supplies, Henri IV had made Desportes's abbey of Notre-Dame-de-Josaphat his headquarters. In July 1591 Desportes was almost certainly with Villars, negotiating with Mayenne for the governorship of Rouen, outside which he was camped, and the lieutenant-generalship of Normandy, without which Villars threatened to go over to Navarre. Mayenne effectively bestowed on Villars most elements of the position he required. On 27 July, a week later, Desportes was granted a privilège for the 60 psalms of David. They were printed in Rouen.

Meanwhile Rouen was making very serious preparations for being besieged, with Desportes as political counsellor to Villars. Although reduced to extreme distress and several times nearly lost, Rouen did not fall, and it appears that the counsels of Desportes were of some importance in the town's successful defence. We hear little of him, however, in the period immediately following the lifting of the siege on 20 April 1592. He seems to have remained with Villars during subsequent negotiations with Henri de Navarre prior to the king's anointing on 27 February 1594. Desportes's brother, Thibault, was the second ambassador sent by Mayenne to the Holy See to oppose any reconciliation between the pope and Henri de Navarre, and it was Thibault who finally treated with Henri IV to remove Mayenne's furniture and other belongings from Paris. Mayenne submitted in January 1596, and Thibault Desportes, by a secret provision in the treaty with Villars, was allowed to remained treasurer of Rouen.

Villars was killed fighting the Spaniards in July 1595, and Desportes continued to move between Rouen and Bonport, the abbey whose titular abbacy had been conferred on him during the siege of Rouen, and whose confirmation had been part of the price paid by the king for obtaining the obedience of Rouen. By 1598 Desportes was living in the residence placed at his disposal as a canon of the Sainte-Chapelle. During his last years Desportes spent time at Josaphat and Bonport, and in an establishment at Vanves, which he may either have bought or had built, which apparently had large gardens, and where Desportes entertained. His intimacy with Henri IV was never what it had been with Henri III, but after a period of coolness it is obvious that Desportes returned to favour when, for instance, the king took his advice about the custodianship of the royal library, appointing Isaac Casaubon sub-librarian very early in 1604, and making him librarian when the incumbent, Gosselin, died in November 1604.

It appears certain that Desportes had an illegitimate son by a Marie de Lastre, a well-known woman of low reputation, probably during or immediately after the siege of Rouen. Like Baïf's son Guillaume, Desportes's son Philippe was legitimized, and on 21 February 1598 Desportes assigned an annual income of 1,800 livres to the child. It seems very unlikely that he had a daughter by Louise de l'Hôpital-Vitry, married in 1586 to Jean de Simiers, and mistress to Villars during the siege, as Tallemant reports. In 1603 he finished the translation of the psalms. At Vanves the most welcome regular guest was Desportes's nephew, Mathurin Régnier, his sister Simone's son, who referred to the establishment in his satires rather as if it had been his own. It was presumably to Vanves that Régnier took Malherbe, newly arrived in Paris, for an occasion which was to become famous.

Malherbe, brought by Régnier to dine with Desportes either very late in 1605 or early in 1606, arrived late with him, after the "potage" had been served. Desportes rose and, greeting Malherbe, offered to get him from upstairs a copy of his psalms as a gift. Malherbe gruffly replied that he had already seen the psalms, that they were not worth the trouble of fetching, and not worth spoiling the potage for. There was a rudimentary system of courses on grand occasions, and "potage" could cover anything from consommé to stew. But whatever it was that he was late for, Malherbe was not being complimentary about the psalm translation. Desportes did not speak to him again during the course of the meal and, since he was to die within a few months, did not ever meet Malherbe again, although the incident probably accounts for Régnier's attack on Malherbe in his ninth satire.

On 16 March 1606 the marriage contract was signed between Thibault Desportes and Marguerite de Chantecler, daughter of one of the king's counsellors, and Desportes's own new standing with the king is confirmed by a project to nominate him as tutor to the young dauphin, later Louis XIII, born in 1601. Desportes's death prevented the fruition of the plan, and the replacement tutor nominated was Des Yveteaux. That spring, Desportes went as usual to collect his income from Vaux-de-Cernay, was obliged to arrange there for the repair of some walls, and moved on to his favourite summer residence at Bonport. He himself attributed his final illness to a lethargy which came from the excess of study to which he had resorted in the absence of visitors to distract him. L'Estoile maliciously says that his last words were a reference to the fact that his 30,000 livres a year were not going to prevent him from dying. Elsewhere we are told that he corrected a line of his psalm translation on the day of his death, which occurred, met with fortitude, on 5 October 1606.

WORKS

It is not totally unfair to point out that the chief interest of Desportes as a secular poet comes less from any authentic poetic feeling than from the examples he gives of fashionable and cultivated court poetry in the entourage of Henri III. As an administrator by career, the accidents of fortune took Desportes to Italy for virtually the whole of 1566. While there, he got to know the fashionable Italian poetry of the later Petrarchan tradition, with its attitudes, poses, mannerisms, stylizations, and affectations of language and sentiment. On his return to Paris it must have been the cultural polish acquired in Italy which promoted his success in the already Italianate circle of the maréchale de Retz, where the fastidiousness and refinement with which Malherbe later wanted to do away not only were cultivated, but provided for Desportes personally an attractive personal opportunity for developing a social life more exalted and less earthy than that of the more boisterous young administrators surrounding Villeroy. The apprenticeship for the powerful and lucrative administrative career contrasted with, and may even have been made tolerable by, the social atmosphere of a circle in which the culture which the young Desportes happened recently to have acquired was much admired.

Already lucky on those two scores, being carefully groomed for an established first-class administrative career and polished in the cultivated accomplishments of the most refined social strata in the country, Desportes was now also fortunate on a third score. The illness and convalescence for six or eight months, if not a little more, in 1570–71, enforced on him the leisure to write, and turned him into a ready, if never prolific, versifier. There followed the decade of closeness to Henri III, in a relationship cemented in Cracow, before that monarch turned his extravagant impulses to matters of devotion. Desportes became the established chief practitioner of Italianate court verse in French, singing the loves of grand gentlemen for great ladies, or possibly from time to time something a little more personal, but producing stylistically undifferentiated verses addressed by indistinguishable lovers to interchangeable women, with a fecundity and facility that was affected, superficial, clever, ornate, balanced, cultivated, skilful, and professionally designed to please. Desportes's secular poetry is chiefly memorable for what it tells us about the most refined taste in the French court at the apogee of the reign of Henri III, after Desportes had replenished his Italian sources of inspiration on the way back from Poland in 1574.

The two books of the Diane cycle appear to be a collection of most of the love verse written by Desportes up to 1571, often imitated from the Italian, written in pursuit of the courtships among others of Brantôme and of the future Henri III. The Hippolyte cycle is posterior, and is unified by the use of the Icarus theme, which comes from Ovid and is used by Desportes in the other cycles, too. The first Hippolyte sonnet is often considered to be one of Desportes's best poems. It is derived from Sannazaro's "Icaro cadde" in I Fiori,

Icare est cheut icy le jeune audacieux,
Qui pour voler au Ciel eut assez de courage:
Icy tomba son corps degarni de plumage,
Laissant tous braves coeurs de sa cheutte envieux.

O bien-heureux travail d'un esprit glorieux,
Qui tire un si grand gain d'un si petit dommage!
O bien-heureux malheur plein de tant d'avantage,
Qu'il rende le vaincu des ans victorieux!

Un chemin si nouveau n'estonna sa jeunesse,
Le pouvoir luy faillit mais non la hardiesse,
Il eut pour le brûler des astres le plus beau.

Il mourut poursuivant une haute avanture:
Le ciel fut son desir, la mer sa sepulture:
Est-il plus beau dessein ou plus riche tombeau?

(Icarus, the daring youth, fell here,/Who found the courage to fly up to the heavens:/Here came to earth his body stripped of its plumage,/Leaving all brave hearts envious of his fall. //O blessed achievement of a glorious spirit,/Which draws so great a profit from such slight damage!/O blessed the misfortune full of so great an advantage,/That it makes him who was vanquished the conqueror of the years!//So new a path did not dismay his youth,/Strength failed him, but not courage,/To burn him he had the finest of the heavenly bodies. //He died in pursuit of a high venture;/The sky was his aspiration, the sea his burial place:/Can there be a finer ideal or a richer tomb?).

The idea in the sonnet is more effective than its poetic execution, based almost exclusively on contrast, the syntactical parallels running in tension with the antitheses of meaning. The contrasts between flying and falling, sky and sea, victory and defeat, blessedness and misfortune, ambition and failure, are given poetic interest by the essential added ingredient that the magnificence of the aspiration more than compensates for the inevitability of failure. The language may seem to us clear, simple, and strong. The images, the syntax, and the cadences have been admired, like the sustaining of a single metaphor throughout the sonnet, but Malherbe underlined "coeurs de sa cheutte envieux" in disapproval, thought at line eight that the verb should be "rend," indicative and not subjunctive, that the first line of the last tercet was "unnecessary," and, on the last line, comments, "This last line speaks only of the aim, which was the sky, of the tomb, which was the sea; but it does not mention the murderer, who was the sun."

Desportes's most famous poem is little more than a cleverly amusing adaptation of an idea from Ariosto, whose terza rima of *Capitolo VII* is wittier. The lover needs darkness for his purposes, and Desportes's poem "Stances contre une nuit trop claire" contains 15 four-line stanzas in which the lover complains to the night that it is too bright,

O Nuit! jalouse Nuit, contre moi conjurée,
Qui renflamme le ciel de nouvelle clarté,
T'ai-je donc aujourd'hui tant de fois désirée,
Pour être si contraire à ma félicité?

Pauvre moi! je pensai qu'à ta brune rencontre
Les cieux d'un noir bandeau dussent être voilés;
Mais, comme un jour d'été, claire, tu fais ta montre,
Semant parmi le ciel mille feux étoilés

(O Night! jealous Night, conspiring against me,/Who rekindle the sky with a new daylight,/Have I today so often longed for you,/For you now to be so contrary to my happiness? //Poor me! I thought that at your dark arrival/The skies must wear a black blindfold;/But, like a summer day, bright, you show yourself,/scattering through the sky a thousand starry gleams).

What is not taken from the Italian tradition, using the familiar repertoire of poetic attitudes and devices, sometimes sinks to the level of versified prose and, although Desportes virtually never mentioned Ronsard in his verse, his own work repeatedly reverberates with phrases taken from that of his predecessor, just as it seems certain that Ronsard's "Comme on voit sur la branche au

mois de May la rose," first published in 1578, although drawing on a common-place from Ausonius, must none the less derive directly from a poem to Hélène de Surgères by Desportes, "Comme on voit au Printemps le bouton rougissant," which first appeared in 1573. The vast superiority of Ronsard's poem almost invites sympathy for Malherbe's ill-tempered and pedantic strictures on Desportes.

Any single example is too limited to generalize from, and is necessarily selected arbitrarily, but the following sonnet of Desportes, first published in 1573, gives a reasonable view of the sort of material he was at that date producing, and what it was in it that Malherbe objected to. To avoid too many different sorts of notes, it should first be remembered that Desportes assumes the reader knows that Zephir's husband is Flore, meaning "flower" or "foliage". Following the text are Malherbe's comments, translated into English. The poem derives from Navagero's "Et gelidus fons est, et nulla salubrior unda (The fountain is frozen, and no stream is more health-giving)," but Desportes takes it from an adaptation by Tansillo. The title is "D'une fontaine (Of a fountain)."

Cette fontaine est froide, et son eau doux-coulante
A la couleur d'argent[1], semble parler d'Amour:
Un herbage mollet reverdit tout autour,[2]
Et les aunes font ombre à la chaleur brulante.
Le feuillage obéyt à Zephir qui l'evante
Soupirant amoureux en ce plaisant sejour;[3]
Le Soleil clair de flame est au milieu du jour,
Et la terre se fend de l'ardeur violante.[3]
Passant par le travail du long chemin lassé,
Brulé de la chaleur, et de la soif pressé,
Arreste en ceste place où ton bon-heur te maine.[4]
L'agreable repos ton corps delassera,
L'ombrage et le vent frais ton ardeur chassera,
Et ta soif se perdra dans l'eau de la fontaine.

Malherbe's comments:

[1]'With the colour of silver' is a sort of adjective, but it does not fit well after 'sweet-flowing' unless he had wanted to put a third adjective, because he seems to be trying to say 'sweet-flowing, silver-coloured,' or even 'seems to speak of silver-coloured love'.

[2]'Tou, tau, tou.'

[3]This nonsense is without parallel. In the preceding lines he names the fountain's qualities; in these two he says that it is midday and that it is very hot. I wish he would say why he says it.

[4] It should be 'mène' and not 'maine.'

(This fountain is cold, and its sweet-flowing water/With the colour of silver seems to speak of love:/Soft grass spreads green all around, and the alders give shade from the burning heat. //The foliage obeys Zephyrus who fans it/Sighing amorously in this agreeable spot;/The Sun bright with fire is in the middle of the day,/And the earth is cracked open by the violent heat. //Passer-by, tired by the toil of the long journey,/Burnt with heat, and driven by thirst,/Stop in this place to which your good fortune leads you./The shade and the cool wind will drive away your fever,/And your thirst will be lost in the fountain's water).

Even in the later sixteenth century it was pretentious to base what is nothing but an elegant piece of whimsy on an Italian source, itself modelled on a neo-Latin one, and clumsily elephantine of Malherbe to make the objections he did. The use of the source was, however, part of the self-conscious game, an indication that this was stilted and stylized versification, not the poetry of cool spring water. Desportes had the reputation of being a great poet. The contrast with Ronsard, Desportes's dual position as poet and administrator, and his speedy abandonment of one role in favour of the other, his very different relationships with Henri III and with Henri IV, and the attack on his poetic style by the self-appointed monitor of language and usage, Malherbe, all come together to show that, even if he was not himself as great a poet as once was thought, Desportes was for a long time believed to have been a great poet, and a consideration of Desportes's work is central to any effort to understand what happened before and after him in the history of poetry in France.

Desportes's first spiritual verse appeared in 1575, a paraphrase of the "Libera me" and three spiritual sonnets. An ode and five more sonnets followed in 1576, with an additional seven pieces in the 1577 edition. Only six more poems were added when the religious verse was accorded its own section in the 1583 edition, but it seems therefore that Desportes was writing religious verse no later than his return from Poland. The first five psalm translations appeared in 1587. There were 60 psalms in the 1591 edition published in Rouen at the beginning of the siege, and 12 more psalms were added for a 1594 edition, which included the other religious verse and some prose prayers and meditations. The 1603 edition, with a privilège of 14 February, included the whole psalter. Desportes's translation is chiefly remarkable for its attractively ornate elegance.

Baïf's psalms had not even been printed. Desportes's psalter was a commercial success, although it attracted few favourable comments at the time and was forgotten until quite recently. It does, however, contain material of importance in any history of French prosody, and the metres are very varied. Desportes mostly follows the Vulgate, but he clearly knew Vatable's Hebrew version, the Aramaic, and the Septuagint, as well as most of the versions current in the 16th century.

PUBLICATIONS

Collection

Oeuvres de Philippe Desportes, 1858

Verse

Imitations de quelques chants de l'Arioste (with others), 1572
Les premières oeuvres de Philippes Des Portes, 1573; progressively augmented editions appeared in 1575, 1576 (two editions), 1577, 1578, 1579, 1580, 1582, 1583 (two editions), 1585, 1587, 1590, 1594, 1600 (two editions), 1602, and 1607, with one undated edition and many simple reprints.
Les Oeuvres de Philippe Des Portes, 1584, 1591, 1592, 1593, 1596, 1599, and 1606

Soixante psaumes de David, 1591; 1592
Paraphrase des Psaumes de David, 1593
Psaumes de David, 1594; 1595
Cent psaumes de David, 1597; augmented 1598, 1600, 1601
Les CL psaumes de David…,Prières et méditations chrétiennes…,Poésies chrétiennes, 1603 (three editions); 1604, 1605, 1607

Modern editions

Les Imitations de l'Arioste de Philippe Desportes, 1936
Cartels et mascarades, épitaphes, 1958
Le Amours de Diane, 2 vols., 1959
Les Amours d'Hippolyte, 1960
Elégies, 1961
Cléonice, dernières amours, 1962
Diverses amours et autres oeuvres mêlées, 1963

Biographical and critical studies

Vianey, J., *Le Pétrarquisme en France au XVIe siècle*, 1909
Lavaud, Jacques, *Philippe Desportes, Un poète de cour au temps des derniers Valois (1546–1606)*, 1936
Jeanneret, M., *Poésie et tradition biblique au XVIe siècle*, 1969
Cave, T.C., *Devotional Poetry in France*, 1969

DIDEROT, Denis, 1713–1784.

Editor of the "Encyclopédie"; philosopher, novelist, art critic, dramatist and journalist; author of philosophical dialogues.

LIFE

Diderot, born on 5 October 1713 the son of a surgical instrument maker and well-known craftsman at Langres 240 kilometres south-east of Paris, could trace his ancestors on both sides through generations of piously Catholic artisans, mostly tanners or cutlers, with large families. Diderot's father had been one of nine children and his mother one of eleven, but they lived sufficiently high up the social scale for education to have been the norm. Diderot's father owned property. Two of his mother's brothers were priests, one being a canon of Langres cathedral, and two of her uncles and two cousins had also been priests. One of his father's brothers was a Dominican. His mother, Angélique Vigneron, born on 12 October 1677, was the daughter of a merchant tanner. Late in 1711 or early in 1712, when she was already 34, she married Didier Diderot, born on 14 September 1685 and therefore eight years younger than she was.

There were seven children, of whom the first, a boy born on 5 November 1712, died in infancy. The eldest daughter, Denise, was born on 27 January 1715. Diderot himself had a marked affection and respect for both his parents, and admired Denise, who remained an austere spinster and developed a disfiguring cancer of the nose. Then came three other sisters, of whom one died in infancy and another as a child, and one, Angélique, who was also Diderot's goddaughter, became an Ursuline. Diderot's daughter, Mme de Vandeul, in the memoir written in the year of his death, tells us that Angélique became insane in the convent from overwork and died at 28; if that is true, it may help to explain much of the content of Diderot's novel, *La Religieuse*. The last child was a boy, Didier-Pierre, who was later a canon of Langres and came to deplore his brother's public image and proclaimed opinions.

Nothing much is known of Diderot's boyhood, although he is said by his daughter to have been deeply upset by the spectacle of a public execution when he was three. At 10 he was sent to the Jesuit school at Langres, attended by some 200 boys from all social classes. His accounts of the roughness of schoolboy games may be exaggerated, but Diderot is adamant that he learned to fence better than he learned to dance. His school record was excellent, and his later career shows how much he benefited from his classical education. He recalled with glee how he would use out-of-the-way Latin constructions and, when his masters had railed against the stylistic deficiencies, show them to have been used by Virgil, Cicero, or Tacitus. What is striking about Diderot's boyhood in the light of what happened later is the security of the family environment. There is a vivid contrast with Rousseau. Diderot grew up to establish normal ties, relationships, and patterns of domestic existence but, for all the vigour of his imagination and beliefs, he never produced a sustained literary or philosophical masterpiece. Rousseau's fierce defence of his independence from social ties cannot be unconnected with the circumstances of his youth, and may explain the more radical power of his imagination.

After apparently considering the possibility of becoming an instrument maker, Diderot accepted the tonsure on 22 August 1726, just over a year under the usual canonical age. This made him eligible to succeed to his uncle's canonry at Langres. The chapter objected and, when he was still 14, his uncle died before he had managed formally to register his renunciation of the benefice in favour of his nephew, it elected someone else. Diderot then underwent a not unusual adolescent crisis of intense religious fervour, involving self-inflicted physical penances, and contemplated entering the Jesuit order. In 1728 or 1729 he left for Paris, accompanied by his father, apparently to complete his schooling there.

What happened between 1729 and 1742 is almost totally unattested. Diderot graduated as a master of arts on 2 September 1732 and probably studied theology, but we do not know whether he completed his humanities with the Jesuits at Louis-le-Grand or the Jansenists at the Collège d'Harcourt. The accounts conflict, but Diderot certainly remained in Paris, probably working for a lawyer after abandoning any ambition to enter the priesthood. Mme de Vandeul tells us that he refused to settle down to the study of law or choose a profession, that his father then cut off his allowance, and that Diderot then spent ten years taking occasional employment, giving lessons, doing literary and academic chores, even writing sermons to order. He spent what time he could on languages, literature, and mathematics, and was occasionally helped out financially by his mother. It is not unlikely that he spent a period in advanced theological study.

In the end his father did settle his debts, complaining in 1750 that Diderot's Paris years had cost him 10,000 livres. Food, lodging, and tuition could be had at Louis-le-Grand for 400 livres a year, although independent theological study would have cost more. Diderot certainly borrowed, accepted payments in kind, did without, and interspersed periods of need and perhaps study with the indulgence of a passion he had conceived for the theatre, where he sporadically dreamt of making a living, and for which he learnt roles by heart. It was his interest in the theatre that led him to the Café Procope, opposite the Théâtre-Français and frequented by the theatrical and literary worlds. There he met Rousseau, whose closest intellectual companion he was to become. It seems not at all unlikely that Diderot was torn between the theatre and a career as priest and theologian when he met his future wife. The evidence is inconclusive, but would be consistent with his having early dropped the idea of a career in the law. There is a chance that he lived at Saint-Sulpice, the diocesan seminary founded in Paris by J.-J. Olier largely to provide an alternative sacerdotal spirituality to those of the various religious orders. Academically, Diderot's real love was mathematics, on which he had worked semi-professionally, drawing up arithmetical tables for publishers.

In personal appearance, Diderot was careless. He had a sturdy appearance and a bulky frame, and wore his own heavy, blond hair untidily. There is some circumstantial evidence that he was attractive to women, was quite careful about avoiding syphilis, and had a number of probably short-lived liaisons. It was about 1741 that he met Anne-Toinette Champion, born at La Ferté-Bernard on 22 February 1710 and therefore more than three years older than he was. She had been brought to Paris by her impoverished and widowed mother when she was three, and from the age of 16 had helped in the mother's lace and linen business. Diderot deliberately misled her to believe he was about to become a priest, a deception which he had previously used to extract money from the discalced Carmelites, and he only revealed that he was not when it was obvious that a true declaration of his intent was likely to be well received. The question of a legal career was again raised, and Diderot was sent back to Langres to obtain parental consent to his marriage. The family was much impressed when the galley proofs of Diderot's translation from the English of Temple Stanyan's 1739 *Grecian History* arrived.

Diderot had wanted his parents to commute his eventual inheritance into an annuity before he spoke of his intended marriage, but letters from Anne-Toinette received through the good offices of a cousin urged him to hurry, and he asked for his patrimony outright. There was a serious scene, recriminations, and reciprocal threats. Diderot went to stay with an aunt, and his father obtained lettres de cachet, imprisoning him in what must have been a monastery. He escaped through a window and lay low in Paris for a year. Anne-Toinette tried to break off with him, but heard that he was ill and took pity on him, and they were married on 6 November 1743, just 11 months after Diderot had left Paris for Langres and one month after he was 30, the age at which it became legally impossible to disinherit him. The marriage took advantage of arrangements available for quasi-clandestine ecclesiastical marriage ceremonies at the church of Saint-Pierre-aux-Boeufs in Paris, with virtually no public notice. Diderot's mother died in 1748, and his father did not hear of the marriage until 1749. Diderot had moved out of the centre of Paris, and Anne-Toinette was still using her maiden name.

Their first daughter, Angélique, was born on 13 August 1744 but died six weeks later. Anne-Toinette was making self-effacing sacrifices which entailed her subsequent exclusion from Diderot's social and intellectual life, and he was too jealous to allow her to carry on with the lace business, so that she could no longer assure her mother's comfort in old age. She lived in private parsimony so that Diderot could be reasonably provided for, taking his daily coffee at the Café de la Régence. He had first met Rousseau in August 1742 and they swiftly became close chess opponents in games which the impulsive Diderot invariably lost. Diderot must have been paid for anonymous reviews he wrote in the *Observations sur les Ecrits Modernes* of the abbé Desfontaines, who had founded this periodical in March 1735, and ran it virtually until he died in 1745. He had encouraged Diderot to turn to the theatre.

It was, however, as a translator from English that Diderot now scraped a living. The three volumes of Stanyan's *Histoire de Grèce*, for which Diderot received 300 livres from the publisher Briasson, appeared in 1743. In 1745 appeared Diderot's adaptation of Shaftesbury's *An Inquiry concerning Virtue and Merit* as *Principes de la philosophie morale; ou, Essai de M. S*** sur le mérite et la vertu, avec Réflexions*, purporting to have been published in Amsterdam, playing down in the "réflexions" Shaftesbury's optimism and theism, and rejecting his view that aesthetic norms were innate. The work, although cautiously anonymous, was teasingly dedicated "from a philosopher" to Diderot's young brother, then studying for the priesthood. From 1746 to 1748 Diderot's translation of Robert James's encyclopedic *Medical Dictionary* in three folio volumes was published by Briasson in six folio volumes as the *Dictionnaire universel de médecine*. Diderot was helped by François-Vincent Toussaint, author of *Les Moeurs*, a work on natural religion published and condemned in 1748, and Marc-Antoine Eidous, who made a living from translations.

In May 1746 a son was born, François-Jacques-Denis. Rousseau had returned to Paris from Venice in 1744, and by the time Diderot compiled his *Pensées philosophiques*, printed privately, published clandestinely by the bookseller Laurent Durand, and disseminated surreptitiously, he was dining weekly at the Hôtel du Panier Fleuri with Rousseau and Condillac, making a trio joined probably early in 1746 by d'Alembert. It was through Diderot that Durand, later to be associated with the publication of the *Encyclopédie* (q.v.), undertook the publication of Condillac's *Essai sur l'origine des connaissances humaines*.

The *Pensées philosophiques*, inspired by Diderot's work on Shaftesbury and condemned by the Paris parlement to be burnt on 7 July 1746, was probably written primarily to meet the increased expenditure Diderot had incurred by making Madeleine d'Arsant de Puisieux (1720–95) his mistress in 1745. It goes beyond anything that Condillac had suggested, but obviously builds on Diderot's discussions with him, as even more clearly does the 1749 *Lettre sur les aveugles à l'usage de ceux qui voient*, while Condillac's own *Traité des sensations*, of 1754, itself builds on Diderot's *Lettre*. We do not know why Diderot and Condillac drifted apart, or why Condillac did not contribute to the *Encyclopédie*, but it is likely that the reason had much more to do with the reluctance of Condillac, who had been ordained in 1740, to exacerbate ecclesiastical authority, than with his aristocratic status, or even lack of intellectual sympathy. In the meanwhile Diderot expanded on the *Pensées* in a short essay on natural religion, not published until 1770, *De la Suffisance de la religion naturelle*.

The liaison with Mme de Puisieux, wife of a translator from

English and non-practising lawyer, seems to have ended in bitterness and been over by 1751. Diderot had encouraged her to write and no doubt revised her early work, notably her first book, the 1749 *Conseils à une amie*. She is said to have been vain and presumptuous, and Diderot claimed to have written his conte *Les Bijoux indiscrets* in a fortnight at the end of 1747 to show how easy it was to write a novel. The conte was trivial and salacious in spite of the acuteness of its critical and speculative comments and the appositeness of its satirical allusions, and Diderot himself later said he regretted it. He did however at least 10 years later add two chapters, and Durand paid him 1,200 francs for the manuscript. Towards the end of 1747 Diderot had also written his *La Promenade du sceptique*, and in October 1747 also published in the *Mercure de France* a project for a new form of organ, a study characteristically combining an interest in applications of mathematics and physics with autobiographical information and an interest in music, while also hinting at the astonishing breadth of intellectual curiosity which is Diderot's outstanding mental quality.

Diderot's principal literary importance derives from his editorship of the *Encyclopédie*, of which the privilège was granted in 1746, for which the prospectus appeared in 1750, and of which 17 volumes of text and 11 volumes of plates were published between 1751 and 1772. Four additional volumes of text, one of plates, and two index volumes, in all of which Diderot had no hand, were published from 1776 to 1780. At its inception, the project had been to translate Ephraim Chambers's alphabetically arranged two-volume folio *Cyclopedia; or, Universal Dictionary of the Arts and Sciences* in four volumes of text and one of engravings. Similar projects conceived elsewhere had come to nothing, including one by André-François Le Breton to have the works of the German philosopher Christian Wolff translated. The prospective translator of Wolff, Godefroy Sellius, suggested to Le Breton in January 1745 the translation of Chambers, and with one John Mills signed the contract with Le Breton, who in February was granted a general licence for the project. A preliminary prospectus, not the now celebrated 1750 one, was issued, but Le Breton and Mills came to blows in August. Mills had misrepresented both his resources and his abilities. Le Breton had regarded himself as the printer, but found himself the entrepreneur. The chancellor, d'Aguesseau, charged with policing the book trade, intervened to prevent the various suits coming to court and cancelled the licence.

In October 1745 Le Breton joined forces with three other publishers—Briasson, the elder David, and Durand—to take up the project again. Le Breton had himself appointed printer, and a renewed licence was granted in December, by which date Diderot appears already to have been associated with the enterprise. He was known to all three publishers and may have been recruited by them, although probably in a capacity subordinate to that of the abbé Jean-Paul de Gua de Malves, to be appointed principal editor on 27 June 1746, and of d'Alembert, to whom an initial payment together with one to Gua de Malves is recorded in December 1745. The first payment to Diderot was some weeks later, but 1,200 livres was allocated to him, with another 1,200 to d'Alembert, from the 18,000 livres made available to the editor in June.

Gua was learned, may have conceived the expansion of the project, and may indeed have introduced Diderot and d'Alembert to one another. The circumstances in which he abandoned the editorship are not clear. Diderot alludes to him later only once, and then ungenerously, but his formal resignation is recorded on 3 August 1747, and on 16 October Diderot and d'Alembert signed a contract with the publishers as joint editors. Diderot's seniority in the arrangement was marked by an agreed payment of 1,200 livres on the publication of the first volume, in addition to 144 livres a month to make a total of 7,200 livres. D'Alembert was to receive 144 a month to a total of 2,400 livres only. The publishers spent 46 livres on a dinner for their two editors.

In fact Diderot worked on the project until 1772, thought he had been underpaid, and felt that his work on the *Encyclopédie* had kept him from a more substantial literary accomplishment. It is of course impossible to say whether this was true, especially since the need to produce so many articles on so wide a range of subjects forced Diderot to develop an aptitude for what has to be called academic journalism, but his thought was never as committed, deep, or imaginatively adventurous as Rousseau's, nor were his reflections on the human condition so radical; and neither his wit nor his intelligence was ever as incisively sharp as Voltaire's. It is true that Diderot had an interest in purely literary problems not shared by the other two men, and that his moral integrity gives his work its enormous power, but the whole manner of his life as husband, father, editor, and journeyman author does not suggest that the *Encyclopédie* was an unfitting monument to his talent. A new licence for the expanded project was granted on 30 April 1748, perhaps as the result of an interview of uncertain date granted to Diderot by d'Aguesseau, whose role in the enterprise may finally have amounted practically to choosing Diderot to be the editor rather than simply confirming him in that position.

Meanwhile Diderot undertook a translation of Joseph Bingham's *Antiquities of the Christian Church*, which he did not finish, and published his five papers devoted to music, mechanics, and geometry, with a re-print of the article on organ construction: the *Mémoires sur différents sujets de mathématiques*, issued in a de luxe edition by Durand in May 1748. At around this time he was also either ghost-writing or in some way popularizing Rameau's theory of harmony, although his relationship with Rameau was to cool when Rousseau attacked Rameau in the *Encyclopédie*. By December 1748 Diderot's mind had moved on. In his *Lettre au chirurgien Morand* he suggested the amalgamation of the superior order of physicians, once confined to clerics forbidden to let blood or earn their living with their hands, with the barber-surgeons. Diderot was to sustain his interest in medicine, to manifest it in *Le Rêve de d'Alembert* and his *Eléments de physiologie*, and to remain friendly with Europe's most famous doctor, Théodore Tronchin.

Reasonably amicable relations had been re-established between Diderot and his father, who still knew nothing of the marriage, but Diderot seems to have made no effort to go to Langres when his mother died in October 1748. He inherited some property, but we do not know how much, although a regular income and enhanced security must have lain behind his move to a larger apartment about this time. Only traces of what must have been massively demanding work on the *Encyclopédie* have survived. We know little of the calls made, the correspondence, the organizational work, and the traffic of proofs, and hear only of the notably rare permission to borrow from the royal library. The register noting the books borrowed is still extant.

Then in 1749, perhaps partly in order to demonstrate his credibility as editor of the now eagerly anticipated *Encyclopédie*, Diderot wrote his *Lettre sur les aveugles à l'usage de ceux qui voient*, purporting to be a disarmingly artless speculation about the ethical ideas of a person lacking one of the senses. Printed secretly, the anonymous text was ready for diffusion by Durand on 9 June 1749. It was at least partly a reaction to the unveiling of the eyes of a girl, said to have been born blind, on whom, under the auspices of Réaumur, a Prussian oculist called Hilmer had operated for cataract. Diderot, who is said by his daughter to have been present, is reported to have been sceptical, holding in any case that Réaumur had wanted the veil lifted in front only of *"eyes of no importance,"* alluding to Mme Dupré de Saint-Maur, a close friend of Marc-Pierre Voyer d'Argenson, secretary of state for war and since 1737 director of publications. The reason for Diderot's arrest six weeks later may have included an element of personal animosity on that account. Voltaire, to whom Diderot had sent a copy of the *Lettre*, was alarmed at the atheistic undertone and, although their relationships remained good, Voltaire was too subtle and too sensitive to danger to have wanted to keep up an intimate association with the forthright Diderot.

Early on the morning of 24 July 1749 Diderot was arrested at home by Joseph d'Hémery, the inspector of publications, and a commissioner called Rochebrune. The premises were searched for papers contrary to religion, the state, or morals, but so little was found that it is not unlikely that Diderot was expecting the visitation. He was confined at Vincennes and interrogated by the lieutenant-general of police, Nicolas-René Berryer, on 31 July, but denied the authorship of work already known to the police, on information from his publishers, to have been by him. His publishers saw the ruin of the *Encyclopédie* staring at them, and petitioned d'Argenson on the day itself of the arrest, but the police decided simply to wait. Diderot wrote on 10 August to both d'Argenson, to whom he offered the dedication of the *Encyclopédie*, and Berryer, then again on 13 August to Berryer, this time confessing. Within the next week he was allowed out of the keep, moved to more comfortable quarters, and given the freedom of the grounds. The governor, the marquis du Châtelet and a relative of Voltaire's mistress, did his best to make Diderot's life comfortable, and his wife was apparently allowed to come and stay with him. He received visitors, including Rousseau, who one day, on the way to Vincennes, conceived the idea of writing his first *Discours*.

Diderot's father sent money but no emotional support, and it seems as if an explicit undertaking about future publications was required of Diderot before his release on 3 November. Much, at least, of what he subsequently wrote remained unpublished during his lifetime. A second petition to d'Argenson from the publishers says in passing that without Diderot the mathematical material in the *Encyclopédie* could not be set up correctly, nor proof corrected, which suggests that d'Alembert's duties did not go as far as supervising the mathematical content, and it may well be that the importance of the *Encyclopédie* expedited Diderot's release. He naturally returned to a backlog of work. Much gossip about his relationship with Mme de Puisieux and its ending has survived, as have rumours of the public violence of Anne-Toinette. On 30 June 1750, Diderot's second child died, aged just four. The publisher Durand was godfather to a third, born a few months later, who did not survive to the end of the year. Marie-Angélique, the future Mme de Vandeul and the only child of Diderot's to survive to adulthood, was born on 2 September 1753 and had not therefore been conceived until her mother was 43.

It must have been in 1750 that Diderot met his future closest friend, Friedrich Melchior Grimm, introduced to him by Rousseau. The final prospectus for the *Encyclopédie*, circulated in November 1750, was issued with the express authority of d'Aguesseau and Berryer, and 8,000 copies were printed. It was controverted by the Jesuit Père Guillaume-François Berthier, editor of the generally moderate and highly respected Jesuit review, the *Journal de Trévoux*, on the ostensible grounds that the planned organization of knowledge too closely plagiarized Bacon. Diderot replied, and replied again to a subsequent article containing a dignified sneer at him, but the fierceness of his invective added nothing to the debate. The Jesuit Père Louis-Bertrand Castel attempted to mediate. The dispute died down, and both Diderot and d'Alembert were made members of the Prussian Academy.

Late in 1750 Diderot wrote his *Lettre sur les sourds et muets à l'usage de ceux qui entendent et qui parlent* for which, however, Malesherbes would not concede a privilège, confining himself to a recorded *"tacit permission,"* the chief consequence of which was an implied bargain. The authorities would connive at publication provided that the publishers would save them embarrassment by keeping the text anonymous or pseudonymous and the place of publication fictitious. In that way, merely semi-seditious literature might be published, but the authorities exercized control, disavowed responsibility, and kept the publishing industry in France flourishing. None the less Diderot's new letter, essentially a rebuttal of the abbé Charles Batteux's 1746 *Les Beaux-Arts réduits à un même principe*, was notably less audacious than its predecessor had been.

By July 1751 there were 1,431 subscribers to the *Encyclopédie*. On 28 June the first volume had been published. It was immediately clear that immense skill had been deployed in arranging for a publication which could be officially approved, was financially viable, and yet put forward a coherent view of human activity, even political and religious activity, at odds with a received orthodoxy from which it varied outside normally tolerated limits. Nothing offensive to Church or state could be said openly, so the text had to be coded, and at the same time a key to the code had to be provided. The chief means used to achieve this end was not, as has sometimes been supposed, deviousness, or even excessive insinuation, but a mixture of unstated inferences and open, quotable contradiction of what was obviously meant.

A pirate edition in English translation was immediately advertized, and had to be bought off. The subscription list grew, and Le Breton printed 2,075 copies in place of the 1,625 originally planned. The first criticisms, appearing in the September number of the *Journal des Savants*, warned against the possibly pernicious implications of Locke's view, embraced in d'Alembert's preliminary discourse, that all ideas are dependent on sensations. Then in October the *Journal de Trévoux* began a series of carping and generally accurate attacks on errors, typographical slips, and unacknowledged borrowings, while ostentatiously welcoming the work as a whole.

The real trouble, however, came with the scandal of the abbé Jean-Martin de Prades's thesis, successfully defended for the Sorbonne's licentiate of theology degree on 18 November 1751, after being duly approved, printed, and posted. It turned out not to have been read by the professor of theology, who lost his job, to attack the Mosaicity of the Pentateuch and the authenticity of some of the Gospel miracles, and to be a defence of natural reli-

gion modelled on d'Alembert's preliminary discourse to the *Encyclopédie's* first volume and on Diderot's early work on natural religion. The Sorbonne, alerted to what had been done in its name, held a protracted series of meetings and condemned parts of the thesis as heretical. Prades fled to Berlin, became reader to Frederick the Great, and finally made his peace with the Church, but the affair brought to public attention the real nature of Diderot's enterprise, and ecclesiastical hostility began to become voluble. It did not help that Prades was the author of the article on *"Certitude"* in the second volume, published on 22 January 1752. On 7 February 1752 the further publication and distribution of the *Encyclopédie* was forbidden by royal decree.

Diderot had to surrender all manscripts in hand for subsequent volumes, and the publishers all unsold copies of the first two volumes and the 25 sheets already printed for the third. They were fortunate in finding a friend in Malesherbes, director of the book trade, under his father as chancellor, since late in 1750, when he was only 29. He served until 1763. Later on, in 1775, he was a minister for a year, but was too eager for reform to have remained part of the administration for longer. He defended Louis XVI in the trial that preceded his execution, and was himself guillotined in 1794. Malesherbes's favoured solution in 1752 had been merely to substitute new passages in the two volumes for those that had offended. Since the court was more liberal than the parlement, he may, by assenting to a royal edict, have forestalled parliamentary action withdrawing the whole privilège, and he now offered the project's most hostile critic, the bishop of Mirepoix, Jean-François Boyer, the right to nominate a theologian as censor. In fact Boyer nominated three, and each article in all subsequent volumes was to be read by one or other of them. A decree authorizing resumption of the project was considered, but rejected in favour of a tacit lifting of the ban. Volume three, published in November 1753, had required a printing of 3,100 copies, and the edition was enlarged to 4,200 copies.

Prades was preparing his own two-part apologia when Diderot forestalled him with a *"third part"*, the rather self-righteously rhetorical *Suite de l'Apologie de M. l'abbé de Prades... Troisième partie*, which purported to have been printed in Berlin and was immediately pirated in Amsterdam. The piece is often proclaimed as a paragon of eloquence, but all available testimony suggests that Diderot was much more persuasive whenever he could put his case orally. Work on the *Encyclopédie* had resumed in the late spring of 1752, and Diderot's personal circumstances had begun to change. From 1751 to 1755 the publishers paid him 500 livres a quarter. In August 1752 Anne-Toinette made a successful visit to Langres, where she got on well with Diderot's father, and in 1753 Diderot, manoeuvring with much skill and energy to get Nicolas Caroillon, married to one of Diderot's earliest flames, the succession to the lucrative post of bonded tobacco warehouseman at Langres, entered into direct contact with Mme de Pompadour, the king's mistress.

Socially, Diderot grew close to the rich Paul Thiry, baron d'Holbach, who had settled in Paris, taken French citizenship in 1749, and contributed a number of articles to the second volume of the *Encyclopédie*. The two had much in common, enjoying exercise, over-eating, female company, and works of art. In religion and philosophy they were in sympathy, although Diderot's thought was more elusive and even subtle than d'Holbach's rather stolid atheism. As the relationship between Diderot and d'Holbach grew closer, that with Rousseau necessarily loosened, but Diderot, d'Holbach, and Grimm all took Rousseau's side in favouring the Italian operatic style, belonging to the "Queen's Corner" at the opera, near the box normally assigned to the queen, while the partisans of Lully, Rameau, and the French style congregated under Louis XV's box, in the "King's Corner." From 1 August 1752 to 7 March 1754 an Italian operatic company had sung curtain-raisers or postludes one or more times a week before or after a longer French piece given by the regular company.

The Italian repertory of 13 pieces was headed by Pergolesi's *La Serva padrona* and *Il Maestro di musica*, enthusiastically praised by Rousseau, in whose articles on music for the *Encyclopédie* an irritated Rameau, who had hoped to write the musical articles himself, began to reveal undoubted deficiencies. Diderot's annoyance with Rameau is revealed in *Le Neveu de Rameau*, which he did not destine for publication. But as a group the encyclopedists sensed danger. They seemed to feel that Rousseau, whose general attitude was no more in sympathy with their atheistically-orientated sensualism than was Voltaire's, might have taken them too far along a path dangerous to their enterprise. Rousseau also began to distance himself from them, not only in the preface to his comedy *Narcisse*, written late in 1752, but also in the not very amusing incident when, to the growing outrage of Rousseau, Diderot and d'Holbach teased the preposterous abbé Petit at d'Holbach's house on 3 February 1754. Petit had asked Diderot for his opinion on a madrigal of 700 lines, and had been told to go away and bring back a tragedy. He eventually brought it, with an absurd prefatory dissertation which no one could take seriously, and was strung along. Rousseau finally shouted at him, was insulted in return, and stormed out.

The group of philosophes round Diderot was changing its composition. Voltaire and now Rousseau were outside it. Condillac had drifted away and Diderot was coming to distrust d'Alembert. Grimm was very close to the centre and Diderot was about to rely extensively on the aristocratic Jaucourt. The changing composition of the group was, however inexactly, mirroring the gradual self-definition of Diderot's own direct but supple mind. The slow movement by which his vision of man and the world achieved focus can itself almost be calibrated. Little of what he wrote for the *Encyclopédie* was expositive of his own thought. Much that was remained unpublished during his lifetime, but there is enough evidence to show in what direction his mind was moving, under what constraints, and at what pace.

Voltaire had sensed the atheistic implications of the sensualism of the *Lettre sur les aveugles*. Diderot's subsequent imprisonment at Vincennes, together with his commitment to his family, his publishers, and his protectors, his temperamental inability to live the flight-ready life of a Voltaire, or anti-socially to dream utopian dreams like Rousseau, had made him cautious, and even the second edition of the *Lettre sur les sourds et muets*, published within weeks of the first, but containing replies to criticisms of it and introductory remarks dated 3 March 1751, had largely limited itself to the psychology of imaginative creativity. Then, late in 1753, appeared roughly at the same time as the third volume of the *Encyclopédie* the tacitly authorized but anonymously published *De l'Interprétation de la nature*, printed twice again in amplified form in 1754.

Concerned with the philosophy underlying scientific method,

Diderot's short essay, almost a handbook, was modelled in structure and method on Bacon, as Grimm noted at the time. It speculates extensively on zoological and biological problems and takes up from the *Lettre sur les aveugles* the need to study processes of change and diversification in living beings, as well as the relationship between electricity and magnetism, made clear in Benjamin Franklin's work published in 1751 and translated into French the following year. Diderot insisted on the close links required between experimentation, intuition, and deduction, although he continued to confine himself to speculations about structures, being in science a geographer, not an explorer. At his most daring Diderot sketched a possible model for a theory of the origin and transformation of species before falling back on Genesis. The reception of the *Interprétation* was cool. For obvious enough theological reasons the essay's arguments were not totally thought through, and the book was generally considered obscure. It was attacked in the leading article of the first number of what was to be Elie Fréron's immensely successful but conservative *Année littéraire* on 3 February 1754.

The third volume of the resumed *Encyclopédie* (CHA to CONS) had carried a new prefatory manifesto by d'Alembert and began to give more attention to the commercial world. Diderot devoted much space to chronological systems, thereby obviously throwing doubt on the revealed nature of the Old Testament while continuing to pay lip service to it, and he was tendentious in pieces such as those on Chaldeans, Chaos, and Christianity. The fourth volume appeared on 14 October 1754. Malesherbes had suppressed the article "Constitution" concerning the anti-Jansenist Bull *Unigenitus* of 8 September 1713, and the volume seemed less controversial than its predecessors in spite of straight-faced and ostensibly orthodox pieces such as those on hell (Enfer) and the flood (Déluge), provocative of irrepressible doubt. There was still much on machines, on economic and social improvement, and on scientific matters and technology, as well as on historical, cultural and more abstract and clearly religious themes. Voltaire was announced as a contributor to the fifth volume, which appeared in November 1755, but Diderot's quest for great names to be associated with his enterprise stopped short when the abbé Trublet passed on a piece on the Greek poets by Fontenelle, to die aged 100 in 1757, in which he said that Aeschylus was mad.

In the summer of 1754 Diderot visited Langres, probably for the first time since his marriage and for the last time before his father died on 3 June 1759. He went alone, and became godfather to the child of Nicolas Caroillon, one day to be his daughter's brother-in-law, and later wrote a dialogue depicting a family conversation during his visit, the *Entretien d'un père avec ses enfants; ou, Du danger de se mettre au-dessus des lois*. At Langres he discussed with a local lawyer his contract with his publishers, and on his return he negotiated with much difficulty new terms, allowing him 2,500 livres a volume, plus 20,000 when the last was published. In addition he was openly named as sole editor and allowed to keep the books hitherto procured for him for reference purposes. He was later to sell the library of which they formed the nucleus to Catherine II of Russia. He now moved house again, and Marmontel noted in his *Mémoires* the lack of cordiality between Diderot and d'Alembert.

As the group round Diderot coalesced into a coterie, meeting most frequently at the houses of d'Holbach or Helvétius, the great salons, especially those of Mme du Deffand, Mme Geoffrin, Mlle de Lespinasse, and Mme Necker were beginning to play a bigger role in the intellectual, political, and cultural lives of Paris. Mme Geoffrin, in particular, entertained artists to dinner on Mondays, and the less controversial men of letters on Wednesdays. Diderot, cordially received by Helvétius and d'Holbach, was treated generously with respect to money, but personally kept at arm's length by Mme Geoffrin. It was, however, around her that his collaborators gathered, and in her salon that respectability was conferred on them as a group. Fontenelle and Helvétius attended, and intellectuals would send her a dozen copies of their new books, which she would browbeat her habitués into buying.

Mme Geoffrin's dinner invitations were not extended to Diderot, on account of what she referred to as his "rashness and impetuosity." He showed both qualities in publishing a small brochure in 1755, *L'Histoire et le secret de la peinture en cire*, earlier intended as the article "Encaustic" for the fifth volume of the *Encyclopédie*, which appeared that November. In 1753 the comte de Caylus had published a paper in which he claimed to have deciphered the technique mentioned in the elder Pliny for painting in wax and fixing the colours by a heat process, but he kept the details secret. The withholding of scientific information irritated Diderot so considerably that he himself without permission published the mysterious technique subsequently discovered by an artist friend of his, leaving the *Encyclopédie* article to be written by someone else. The pamphlet was brilliant, rushed and, as Diderot admitted, very badly written. It was also immediately parodied by an "Art of Painting in Cheese..." in aid of "finding ways of painting worse than those at present in existence." Fréron thought the parody funny, but Grimm considered it to be in bad taste.

It was in 1755, too, that Diderot met and fell violently in love with Sophie Volland. The relationship lasted until her death, five months before Diderot's. Born on 27 November 1716, her real name was Louise-Henriette, and she was the daughter of a deceased and wealthy tax official, with two married sisters and a mother who tried to keep her away from Diderot. She destroyed all but 187 of the 550 letters Diderot wrote to her, and the first 134 are not extant. It is virtually certain that he and she were lovers, but we know nothing of the early phase of their relationship. It must have begun shortly after Diderot's 1755 chest illness, which involved sweating, coughing and chest pains, and reduced him to a diet of bread and milk. The fifth volume of the *Encyclopédie* was none the less delivered, with as usual more than 1,000 pages, taking the enterprise to "ESY." It included a resumption by Diderot of his concern with social organization, in the article on "Droit naturel (Natural right)." Rousseau wrote on "Economie", Jaucourt on "Egalité naturelle," and Voltaire on "Elégance," "Eloquence," and "Esprit." Diderot's own entry on "Eclecticism" is a valuable self-portrait, and his 34,000-word entry on "Encyclopedia" constitutes one of the key entries in the whole undertaking. Its pagination is peculiar, with 31 pages between those numbered 633 and 649. Did Diderot double the length after censorship, or had his illness made him late with his copy?

His naturalistic conception of the universe allowed Diderot, unlike Voltaire, to remain intellectually undisturbed by the Lisbon earthquake of 1 November, 1755. However many thousands of people died, Diderot no longer had a view of a beneficent deity which the catastrophe disturbed. He was also insensitive to the harm being done to France by the Seven Years' War against England and Prussia which started in 1756. In that year volume six of the *Encyclopédie* was published, probably late in April. There were 15 articles by Voltaire, with whom d'Alembert stayed that summer, and by whom he was inspired to write the famous article on Geneva for volume seven. Voltaire's closer association with the *Encyclopédie* had made him increasingly critical of it, and by 1756 the relationship between Rousseau and Diderot, too, was moving towards its unhappy rupture.

When in February 1757 Diderot's play *Le Fils naturel; ou, Les Epreuves de la vertu* appeared with the *Entretiens sur le Fils naturel*, Rousseau was living in the Hermitage, the cottage in the grounds of the estate of Grimm's mistress, Mme d'Epinay, at Montmorency, about 10 miles north of Paris. He had in December and January stayed with Diderot during the illness of Jean-Victor Capperonnier de Gauffecourt, at whose bedside Diderot incidentally met Mme d'Epinay for the first time. Diderot sent Rousseau a copy of his play when it was published in February, and Rousseau discovered Constance's line to Dorval, "Only the bad man is alone." Rousseau took the line personally and sent Diderot what he called a restrained protest. Diderot replied cheerfully with an invitation to Rousseau to come and stay. Rousseau's answer appears to have been angry, spelling out grievances, and a letter to Mme d'Epinay of 13 March 1757 is almost paranoid in its suspicion that Grimm and Diderot were in league against him. Diderot replied that he would walk out from Paris to visit Rousseau the following Saturday, whatever the weather. Rousseau wrote aggressively telling him not to bother, but Mme d'Epinay, to whom he had sent his letter, refused to have it delivered, and said instead to Diderot that Rousseau would come to Paris.

There was another exchange of letters and things quietened down, before the question arose whether Rousseau should accompany Mme d'Epinay to Geneva in October 1757. Diderot appeared to Rousseau to be bullying him into going as a duty, and Rousseau was certainly being abnormally touchy on the issue. He had not admitted to Diderot, or even to Grimm, or to Mme d'Epinay, his obvious feelings for Sophie d'Houdetot. Diderot had seen Rousseau in April, when a reconciliation took place, and again in July, when Rousseau stayed with him in Paris. Diderot probably came to the Hermitage in early September to offer Rousseau consolation and advice when he thought Saint-Lambert, her lover, had been told of Rousseau's passion for Sophie d'Houdetot, but there are contradictory accounts of their last meeting in December 1757, as there are of who refused to see whom when Rousseau was in Paris in 1765. Diderot was scarcely more than tactless and disorganized, but may have needled a little. He was also too ostentatiously long-suffering for the hyper-sensitive Rousseau, who wanted to re-forge their friendship after it was too late, but both were hurt by the final break. They did not actually ever meet again after 5 December 1757.

When Saint-Lambert, on his return from the war in March 1758, really did discover the strength of Rousseau's passion for his mistress, and Mme d'Houdetot broke off relations with Rousseau on 6 May, Rousseau thought that it was Diderot who had betrayed him, and gave public notice of the rupture of their friendship in a footnote referring to his "Aristarque" in the preface to the *Lettre à d'Alembert*. The quarrel was of more significance than a mere domestic incident among a circle of colleagues in which patterns of relationships were simply changing. The fundamental incompatibility between Diderot and Rousseau concerned Rousseau's belief that human nature could not be virtuous without being religious. Diderot had by now staked his whole life on believing that it could. The breaking of a friendship was, if not the first, at least one event in a perhaps protracted occurrence, which, taken as a whole, was of cataclysmic significance in the history of western culture.

There were four editions of *Le Fils naturel; ou, Les Epreuves de la vertu* in 1757, with its three attached dialogues discussing aspects of dramatic composition and acting. *Le Père de famille* with its *Discours sur la poésie dramatique* appeared in 1758. *Le Fils naturel* was published anonymously and with only tacit approval, although its authorship was an open secret. It was not played in Paris until 1771, but in 1757 a list of actors from the Comédie-Française was rather pitifully appended to the list of characters in the text, and it was twice acted, probably in a private theatre at St-Germain-en-Laye, in the year of its publication. There had been plays in prose about domestic middle-class characters before, but *Le Fils naturel* was regarded as a rallying call for an aesthetic connected with the essentially bourgeois cultural movement which had come to centre on the *Encyclopédie*.

Malesherbes, umpiring the dispute between the *Encyclopédie* and Fréron's *Année littéraire* as equitably as he could, was obliged to object to what the abbé Trublet as the appointed censor had let Fréron print about the *Encyclopédie*. The annexed works of theory, and the fact the *Le Père de famille*, played in Paris in 1761, was called a *"drame,"* make it clear that Diderot's aim was to move towards both a new realism and a bourgeois drama that was specifically tragic, as well as to make clear the utility of the stage for the mediation of new, and in fact bourgeois, values. A good deal was made by Fréron of Diderot's close dependence on Carlo Goldoni's *Il Vero Amico* for his initial inspiration and part of his text. Malesherbes would not let Fréron print a forged letter purporting to come from Goldoni himself objecting to "plagiarism," so Fréron simply printed synopses of the two plays in consecutive editions, using wherever possible the same terms to describe the action of the one and the other.

The hostilities between France and the Prussia which had honoured both Diderot and d'Alembert did not help the philosophe movement, hospitable to ideas from abroad. After Damiens had assaulted the king on 5 January 1757, France also underwent a cultural tremor, and anything at all that seemed potentially subversive became suspect. In October Jacob-Nicolas Moreau, otherwise obscure, invented for the *Mercure de France* the term "Cacouacs" to ridicule the philosophes. "Cacouacs" were savages with sacs of poison hidden under their tongues who mostly attacked from behind, unless their opponents were totally harmless. November 1757 was, however, the month when volume seven of the *Encyclopédie* appeared with d'Alembert's famous article attacking Geneva.

The eight-column article was longer than those normally devoted to sovereign states, and a whole column was taken up with the Genevan Calvinist inheritance which prohibited theatre. D'Alembert had at least made a start on the article while staying near Geneva in the summer of 1756 with Voltaire, who held strong views on the matter. Théodore Tronchin, the famous doctor who was the sponsor of inoculation against smallpox, headed a Genevan committee which tried to obtain a retraction of the d'Alembert article's insults to Calvinism, but succeeded only in getting Diderot to dissociate himself from his colleague.

It is not unlikely that renewed trouble for the *Encyclopédie* derived largely from the decision to print d'Alembert's article. It turned out that not since the fourth volume had all the articles been submitted to one of the three specifically theological censors who had been appointed. Feeling against the "Cacouacs" began again to rise, stirred up now by Charles Palissot, who had been hostile to d'Alembert since he had protested on Rousseau's behalf against Palissot's attack in the 1755 *Les Originaux, ou Le Cercle*, and who now in 1757 published the quite accurately aimed lampoon, *Les Petites Lettres sur les grands philosophes*, unsurprisingly well reviewed by Fréron. Moreau, too, returned quite wittily to the attack in the *Nouveau Mémoire pour servir à l'histoire des Cacouacs*. By January 1758 d'Alembert had announced his intention of retiring from the *Encyclopédie*, clearly assuming that the enterprise would therefore stop.

In spite of Voltaire's sudden feeling that the court was becoming hostile, and that it would be not only wise but also courageous for everyone now to withdraw, Diderot decided to stay in Paris and carry on, although with exactly what mixture of courage, honesty, obstinacy, inertia, and sense of obligation it is impossible to know. Rousseau wrote in February 1758 urging him to give up the *Encyclopédie* if d'Alembert did, and Diderot used the word "desertion" of d'Alembert's resignation. He was inevitably hurt, too, by the publication of Rousseau's *Lettre à d'Alembert*, on sale with a tacit approbation by 28 September 1758. It not only attacked the theatre a month before the appearance of *Le Père de famille*, but it also publicly advertized the breach between Diderot and Rousseau, commonly still regarded as belonging to the group of philosophes of the *Encyclopédie*.

To make things worse, Helvétius's *De l'Esprit* had been published with tacit permission on 27 July 1758. Early in the year Le Breton had issued a publisher's *Mémoire*, quoted at length in the April number of the *Mercure de France*, partly to explain the interruption of work on the *Encyclopédie* and partly to persuade d'Alembert to return to the undertaking. D'Alembert, hard up, was still vacillating. Diderot appears to have signed a new contract in the middle of 1758. Voltaire now changed his mind, and wrote asking if Diderot required any more articles from him. Diderot enthusiastically accepted the offer. Grimm was helping with the proofs of the eighth volume when Helvétius's book appeared. It attempted nothing that had not been done before, but it was still provocative in trying to erect an ethic on the basis of an analysis of behaviour, without recourse to the posthumous remuneration and vengeance of God on which Voltaire still thought social coherence made it necessary to rely.

De l'Esprit was new in emphasizing that the motivation of virtue was self-satisfaction. The style, especially of the footnotes, was inflammatory, and the vigorous reaction its marginalization of religion provoked was instantly connected by the public generally, and the Attorney General Omer Joly de Fleury in his speech to the Parlement de Paris on 23 January 1759 specifically, with Diderot and the movement associated with the *Encyclopédie*. The public perceived the contributors, most of whom did not even know one another, as conspirators, perhaps taking their cue from the announcement at the head of each volume that the writers were a "society" of men of letters. The censor who passed Helvétius's book was dismissed, and there were fulminations against it in both Paris and Rome. Helvétius was forced to retract.

In the preface to *Le Père de famille* Diderot makes clear that, although he does not share Rousseau's belief in man's primeval virtue, he does not think that the allure of sensual pleasure should be thought morally dangerous. In his speech of 23 January, the Attorney General, prompted by the *Préjugés légitimes contre l'Encyclopédie*, published in six volumes from October 1758 to January 1759 by Abraham de Chaumeix, mentioned four of Diderot's works by name. The Parlement de Paris, partly in furtherance of its perennial attempt to usurp the royal authority exercised through Malesherbes, suspended the sale and distribution of the *Encyclopédie*, and set up a commission of nine known Jansenists to examine the seven volumes already published while the eighth was at press. On 8 March the crown itself took back the initiative, and the *Encyclopédie's* privilège was revoked by royal decree. Almost everyone except Jaucourt now deserted the enterprise. Even Grimm went off to join Mme d'Epinay in early March. Diderot, however, continued to work on, although the circulation of a scurrilous pamphlet unfoundedly attributed to him made flight seem urgent. It is probably this year that the celebrated incident occurred in which Malesherbes, warning him that he was next day ordering his house to be searched, allowed Diderot to send him all his documents, which he would privately conceal.

On 3 June 1759, while he was travelling with d'Holbach, Diderot's father died. From 25 July to 16 August he was away from Paris, helping to settle his father's estate at Langres. Now it was clear that the *Encyclopédie*, by conveying ideas rather than mere information and, as it claimed itself, by "changing the general way of thinking", had upset the custodians of the realms of politics and religion, and they were willing to let the publishers go bankrupt. Malesherbes, however, circumvented an order that the 4,000 subscribers, because the publication had stopped at "G," should each be refunded what was in fact a rather mean 72 livres, by having the volumes of engravings licensed on 8 September and supplied against a credit for the 72 livres. Subscribers would have to pay 112 livres for the four volumes of plates, others 360 livres. No subscriptions were cancelled, but much trouble was caused by allegations that the drawings for the engravings were stolen. Diderot was also offered a contract including payments of one sixteenth of 15,000 livres for each of the remaining sixteen useful letters of the alphabet as the appropriate entries became ready. He was also to receive some 1,500 livres annually from his father's estate.

Diderot's wife had made jealous scenes over his relationship with Sophie Volland, who always herself took care not to disturb Diderot's marriage and whose first importance in Diderot's life, whatever the intimacy of the relationship, was always as an intellectual and emotional support. Diderot nevertheless managed to work, sketching a number of projects for new plays, and reporting on the Paris theatre for the *Correspondance littéraire*, the name given when they were collected to the fortnightly informal newsletters circulated in manuscript by Grimm, while Grimm spent the spring and summer of 1759 in Geneva. Diderot noted the improvement at the Comédie-Française since spectators had been cleared from the sides of the stage after the Easter vacation of 1759. It was also at Grimm's request that Diderot wrote for the *Correspondance littéraire* an anonymous report on the 1759 Salon, the biennial exhibition of paintings by members of the Academy of Painting and Sculpture established in 1748. Diderot's successive *Salons*, from 1759 to 1781, remained anonymous but established art criticism as a serious discipline in France. In important ways they linked Diderot's aesthetics to his ethics.

The salons had already attracted much public comment, but Diderot's substantial accounts were penetrating, sensitive, and absolutely frank, and they have come to be regarded as authoritative. He knew, of course, that Grimm's fortnightly letter was disseminated only in diplomatic bags and to less than a score of subscribers, all of them heads of state, who could not themselves visit the exhibition. He was therefore forced to describe the paintings in explicit detail, which reinforced his already developed interest in composition. He also wrote in the entertaining style, mixing sensitivity with realism and rhetorical devices, that gives his letters to Sophie Volland such literary interest. He developed an interest in the technique of painting in oils, and exhibited an astonishing visual memory. The 1759 *Salon* was written during a six-week stay with d'Holbach at his country house at Grandval, about 12 miles east of Paris, where he went on 3 September. D'Holbach's house was to become almost a rural headquarters for the philosophes, and Diderot wrote there many of his *Encyclopédie* entries on the history of philosophy. From 1759, apart from journalism and his *Encyclopédie* articles, he wrote only for posterity and himself. None of the major works of his maturity was published during his lifetime.

Diderot's novel *La Religieuse* (1796) notoriously grew out of a practical joke played on the witty and volatile marquis de Croismare (1694–1772), prized for his excellent company, who had gone off to live on his estate near Caen. The idea was to entice him back to Paris. He had tried during a much-publicized lawsuit from 1755 to 1758 to help a nun who wished to be released from her vows, but had had no success, had not met her, and did not even know her name. Early in 1760 Diderot, Grimm, and Mme d'Epinay wrote Croismare a letter purporting to come from this nun, saying she had got out of the convent, and asking for help in finding a job. Croismare invited her to Caen, and the conspirators had to make her ill to explain her non-appearance. After a considerable correspondence, they killed her off in May 1760. Croismare did not find out about the hoax until he returned to Paris in 1768 and discovered it by chance. Diderot, who had written all the nun's letters, and some in the name of a real Mme Madin, probably a friend of Mme d'Epinay, decided to turn the whole affair into a novel. He wrote it in fragments, then as a complete text in 1760, and then re-wrote it again in 1780, when he offered it to Grimm's successor, J.H. Meister, for publication in the *Correspondence littéraire*. The novel has been immensely popular. There were seven French editions between 1796 and 1800, and about 70 up to the beginning of World War II. Nineteen German translations have been counted, plus 10 Italian, six Spanish, seven English, and four Russian.

On 2 May 1760 Charles Palissot's *Les Philosophes* was played at the Comédie-Française and deeply wounded Diderot, who appealed to Voltaire. Voltaire's reply was an attack not on Palissot but, in his play *L'Ecossaise*, on Fréron, who had enthusiastically supported Palissot. By the end of May the philosophes had succeeded in having Palissot's play taken off, after 14 performances with an outstandingly large average attendance of 937 and an unheard-of first-night audience of 1,439; and Diderot had reached the end of the letter "M." *La Religieuse* was not yet finished, and Diderot was now also giving an account of new books to the readers of the *Correspondence littéraire*. He translated Edward Moore's *The Gamester*, presented by Garrick at Drury Lane in 1753, as *Le Jouer*, which was, however, turned down. *Le Père de famille*, having succeeded in Toulouse and Bordeaux (1759), Marseilles (1760), Hamburg and Lyons

(1762), was now played in Paris on 18 February 1761 by the Comédie-Française, with indifferent success. It lasted six performances against Palissot's 14, and its audience dwindled from 1,178 to 616. It was seen as a public test of the encyclopedists' vision of the world, and Diderot had hoped that its aesthetic would vindicate his whole outlook on life.

The result depressed him, and it is from that depression that the first draft (1761) of his dialogue *Le Neveu de Rameau*, focused partly on the nature of artistic failure, emerged. It was set in the Café de la Régence, which Diderot still regularly patronized; the text was frequently to be revised, notably in 1762, 1766, 1767, and 1775. In 1761 Diderot also produced his much developed second *Salon*, as well as the emotional 6,500-word *Eloge* of Richardson, whose death on 14 July it commemorated, not without a touch of mawkishness. It was, however, Diderot's most substantial attempt to date at literary criticism. Abundant letters to Sophie Volland have survived from 1759 to 1770. They show an exceedingly busy Diderot, pestering the friend to whose address Sophie's letters were sent, staying for periods at La Chevrette with Mme d'Epinay, of whom Grimm was beginning to tire, or at Grandval with d'Holbach, but often sensitive and introverted, shy, short of small talk, and affectionately willing to put himself out for his friends. Privately his marriage had broken down, although in public appearances were kept up.

Intellectually Diderot was moving between mathematical disputes about probability theory, on which Fréron had shown that d'Alembert had been wrong (article "Gageure"), but which Diderot could now put right (articles "Jouer" and "Probabilité"), to disputes about smallpox inoculation, of which Tronchin was the renowned protagonist and Diderot and Voltaire enthusiastic advocates, and the applicability of Newton's inverse square law to terrestrial as well as celestial forces of attraction, on which Diderot sent a piece anonymously to the *Journal de Trévoux*. There was a family dispute about money which resulted in the inclusion by Grimm of Diderot's *Encyclopédie* article on "Intolérance" in the *Correspondence littéraire* for 1 January 1761, in which it was specifically addressed to his brother, the canon, to whom it had been sent two days previously. Money difficulties must have resulted from the *Encyclopédie's* publishers' inability to continue to pay out large sums for work to some extent surreptitious. They did not, between 1759 and 1765, know that the remaining ten volumes of text would be so successfully published in 1765–66.

In the meanwhile Diderot turned down in 1762 an invitation, passed on by Voltaire from Catherine II, who had come to power on 6 July, to finish off his work in Russia. In 1765 he sold her his library, asking for 15,000 livres. She offered him the retention of the books during his lifetime and an annual pension of 1,000 livres as well. In 1762, however, following a financial scandal in Martinique, the Jesuits were suppressed in France. Since they ran 111 secondary schools, the repercussions for French society were considerable, and pressure on the encyclopedist group was much relieved. Diderot also probably met Sterne, who sent him a copy of the six volumes of *Tristram Shandy* which had so far appeared. Sophie Volland was away from Paris for four months, and we have an unusual run of 33 letters between 14 July and 25 November in which Diderot's mood soars and plummets, and subjects range from frivolities to serious reflections. There is much about his health, his wife's health, and the affection he felt for his daughter. Above all there is evidence of prodigious imag-

inative energy, and an underlying gentleness. His reputation for being golden-tongued had not diminished.

When peace returned in 1763 a number of important British visitors came to Paris, and Diderot met Edward Gibbon, John Wilkes, David Garrick, and David Hume. A little later Horace Walpole came over. In 1766 Cesare Beccaria visited Paris. His 1764 *Dei delitti e delle pene*, translated by Morellet in 1766, had been inspired by the encyclopedist movement and created a European sensation, and he was particularly well received by Diderot, d'Holbach, and d'Alembert. The Lieutenant-General of Police, Antoine de Sartine, had his powers extended to take over the directorship of the book trade, replacing Malesherbes in 1763, and Diderot was asked by Le Breton to argue the publishers' case in a memorandum, which was, however, considerably adjusted before its presentation. Diderot's *Salon* for 1763 restated his admiration for Chardin's realism, reiterated his liking for genre painting in general, admired Greuze's seriousness of moral purpose, disdained Boucher's painting as corrupting, and asked the fundamental questions about the nature of art and the role of imitation. It is often regarded as one of his best *Salons*, although the essays of 1765 and 1767 were both longer.

Diderot had himself to prepare an increasing number of the entries for the final volumes of the *Encyclopédie*. After 1759 Turgot and Marmontel ceased to contribute, d'Alembert's articles became sparser and more confined to technical pieces, and it was impossible to recruit new contributors to a suppressed work which was supposed not to be going to appear. Diderot ceased to use an asterisk to indicate his own authorship, and we do not know quite how much he himself wrote for the final volumes. Jaucourt wrote about a third of the text of the 10 volumes. Much risk attached to the proposal to publish all ten volumes of text together, since the project no longer officially existed and therefore no censors could be appointed. The authorities busily used their blind eye, but discovery in the final volumes of material dangerous enough to attract suppression would have meant bankruptcy for the publishers. On the other hand the global plan made for the avoidance of recurrent crises and for a uniformity of approach in what Charles Burney was shortly to call "an engine to subvert all established opinions."

In fact Le Breton, knowing that the danger of perquisition both required the destruction of all manuscript once type was set and prevented Diderot from retaining anything at home, took to the simple subterfuge of allowing everything to be set and then, only when Diderot had passed the last proof for press, removing with the help of his foreman anything they thought remotely dangerous. Diderot was furious when he discovered, but consented to finish off the nearly completed work. Subsequent discovery of at least part of the proof emended by Le Breton suggests that his emendations may have been limited to pieces by Jaucourt and Diderot, and on the whole confined simply to toning down their stridency.

From mid-1765 a number of new friends begin to appear in Diderot's entourage, headed by his somewhat unimaginatively atheistic disciple Jacques-André Naigeon, later to edit the 15-volume complete works of 1798 and also Diderot's philosophical entries to the *Encyclopédie*, known as the *Encyclopédie méthodique*. Diderot also made the acquaintance of Julie de Lespinasse, one or two other salon hostesses, and a number of painters. He attended the first night of Sedaine's *Le Philosophe sans le savoir*. When the final 4,000 sets of the final ten folio volumes of text of the *Encyclopédie* were ready for distribution, there was a hitch. In return for exemption from taxation it was the custom of the French clergy to make to the king every five years a "free gift," which in 1766 gave them much bargaining power. They wanted censorship of the book trade. The king wanted 12,000,000 livres. The problem was solved by allowing the distribution of sets of the *Encyclopédie* abroad and in the provinces, but not in Paris or at Versailles. There was a period during which subscribers were allowed to pick up their copies at a Paris warehouse, but that was then stopped, and Le Breton was taken briefly to the Bastille on 23 April to satisfy the clergy. The last sets of volumes were delivered to subscribers via country addresses.

In 1765 Diderot slid into a controversy with the sculptor Falconet, with whom he was to continue to sustain somewhat brittle friendship, and from whom on Diderot's recommendation Catherine II was to commission the famous St Petersburg statue of Peter the Great on horseback. Diderot regarded posthumous fame as the justification for his activity, while Falconet denied the importance to the artist of the judgements of posterity, and wanted to publish his correspondence with Diderot on the subject. When the letters did become available at various dates in the 19th century it became clear that Diderot was arguing for human perfectibility and a developing enhancement of values. Taste improves, is handed on enriched from one generation to the next towards a goal which is the perfection of the human spirit. Diderot's argument is the full statement at the level of pure aesthetics of the principles underlying the cultural movement which had been inaugurated at the renaissance and was culminating at the apex of the "enlightenment."

The fractious Falconet, with whom Diderot continued a lengthy correspondence, was a success in St Petersburg, and Catherine did not forget her debt to Diderot. When his pension was once in arrears, Catherine paid the next 50 years in advance. That would have taken him to the age of 103. Catherine also wanted to acquire Diderot's manuscripts, of which he made her a gift. Her generosity had cushioned him against a diminution of his income from the *Encyclopédie*, still 3,400 livres in 1764 and 3,548 in 1765, but then only 700 in 1766 and 350 in 1767, before stopping altogether with the completion of the engravings. Investments were bringing in 4,000 livres a year, but there was Angélique's dowry to think of. In the late 1760s, after Catherine's gift, Diderot's income was stable at about 6,500 livres, as against 255 for a labourer and over 11,000 for a full member of the Comédie-Française company.

Diderot visited the 1767 salon 12 times. By this time he had both read and meditated widely on the aesthetics specifically of the visual arts, and can be seen to have assimilated much from Leonardo and from Lebrun's 1702 *Méthode pour apprendre à deviner les passions*, as well as in particular from Jean-Baptiste de Bos's *Réflexions critiques sur la poésie et sur la peinture*. He disliked allegory, preferring broad historical or mythical subjects and of course genre painting, and he avidly viewed what paintings he could, assiduously studying engravings, especially admiring Poussin, chiefly for his grouping and composition and for his depiction of mood. His appreciation of Poussin's formal qualities, of the skill of his draperies and his use of gesture, shows an increased emphasis in his aesthetic towards control, but he never allowed his connoisseurship of technique to interfere with his fundamental judgement about the imaginative quality of a painting, and his criteria in painting became even more exclusively visual as the series of *Salons* progressed. In the

Essais sur la peinture (1795), which he completed in 1766, he insisted above all on draughtsmanship and observation, disliking the mannered and artificial work that comes from departing too far from natural models. It seems certain that Lessing's 1766 *Laokoon* on the difference between poetry and painting drew on Diderot's *Salons*, and that it was Diderot's development of de Bos's views that transformed the interpretation of Horace's well-known "Ut pictura poesis (poetry, like a picture...)" to define the distinction between the static plastic values of the visual arts, apprehended simultaneously, and those of poetry, which necessarily contain an element of succession.

On the "sublime," Diderot draws on Burke's *Philosophical Inquiry into the Origin of our Ideas of the Sublime and Beautiful* of 1757. The sublime is what provokes awe, terror, or wonder. Diderot therefore likes an element of mystery, even menace, associated with dark places, distant waterfalls, and overcast skies. Ruins, isolation, the sense of evanescence, the erosion of the human, bring Diderot even nearer to the full range of pre-romantic ways of seeing man and nature characteristic of the next generation, and particularly of Chateaubriand, although no doubt already also incipiently present in Rousseau. He likes what touches most readily the visual imagination, all that is melancholy, noble, and nostalgic, but also what is savage and raw. He dislikes the over-refinement of Watteau because, fundamentally, it lacks energy, and he ruminates at length about the evocative power of sketches, and their relationship to finished paintings. All in all, Diderot's habit of seeing the strength in incompatible principles, particularly those involving a conflict of natural energy and formal constraint, while it does not produce a coherent synthesis in aesthetics any more than he produced a coherent literary theory, leads him to make extraordinarily perceptive remarks. He noticed, for instance, the infinity of fragmented reflections of light that the impressionists were to build on, and even the immense number of different planes customarily used to depict depth, which the cubists were to develop.

Diderot wrote no major works during the late 1760s apart from the *Salons* of 1765 and 1767 and a dialogue of 1768, entitled *Mystification*, fictionalizing a spoof on which he was engaged on behalf of Dmitri Alexeevich Galitzin, the Russian ambassador replaced by a chargé d'affaires in 1767. Diderot suggested to Catherine II the purchase of pictures and books at the Gaignat sale in December 1768 and, as her agent, acquired for her a Jean-Baptiste van Loo, a Murillo, and three by Gerard Dou; but at this period his immense physical energy found no focus, and his stamina no challenge. An engineer called Guillaume Vialet humiliatingly turned down the prospect offered to him by Diderot of marriage to Angélique, and he had to put up with being shown off by Grimm to visiting grandees. Mme Geoffrin took to calling occasionally, and Diderot had his study redecorated, publishing in the *Correspondence littéraire* "Regrets sur ma vieille robe de chambre (Lament for my old dressing gown)". He almost certainly had something to do with d'Holbach's subversive *Le Christianisme dévoilé*, published in 1766. Unobtainable even at the 80 livres it fetched, anyone caught with a copy was in severe trouble. Diderot also got caught up in the "physiocrat" movement, whose principal tenet was the unfettered licence to export grain, much to the benefit of the producers, allowed by a decree of 19 July 1764. Food production, held the physiocrats, was the true source of the wealth of nations.

Diderot had edged towards this view by publishing in the *Encyclopédie* two entries by François Quesnay, "Fermiers" and "Grains," and seems by the mid-1760s to have become practically a convert. He may himself have written the entry "Laboureur," and was fascinated by *L'Ordre naturel et essentiel des sociétés politiques* by Pierre-Paul Le Mercier de la Rivière, the former Intendant of Martinique, whom he helped to recruit as an economist for Catherine II to assist in her famous compilation of a new code of laws. Diderot, like Ferdinando Galiani, came however to have doubts about the physiocrats' views in the light of the Naples famine of 1764. Galiani was recalled to Italy while writing his entertaining but persuasive *Dialogues sur le commerce des blés*, and Diderot was left to see his manuscript through the press in 1769, learning from it something of the value of historical precedent as evidence in economic argument. Galiani's master in that respect had been Vico; his doctrine split the encyclopédistes, being accepted by Diderot, Grimm, and d'Holbach but not by Turgot, Morellet, or Condorcet. Diderot himself defended Galiani against Morellet in his unpolished and posthumous *Apologie de l'abbé Galiani*.

In 1769 Diderot was in charge of what we know as the *Correspondance littéraire* while Grimm was in Germany, although no numbers were issued from 15 April to 1 October. He continued to work for Grimm under some protest in 1770 and 1771. He reviewed Saint-Lambert's poem *Les Saisons* and in the summer of 1769 wrote *Le Rêve de d'Alembert*, to be published only in 1831. *Le Rêve* is perhaps the most imaginatively powerful of all his works, and is also that which most successfully unites literature with philosophy. Diderot's friend, Etienne-Noël Damilaville, through whom he received Sophie Volland's letters, had died on 13 December 1768, and in 1769, in spite of Sophie, Diderot clearly fell in love with Damilaville's ex-mistress, Mme de Maux, 45-year-old daughter of the actor Quinault-Dufresne. She had married a lawyer at the age of 12. Diderot's affection for her gave rise in his mid-fifties to a series of stories and dialogues whose central concern was love or sexuality.

From 1769 Diderot began to spend part at least of his summers in a house borrowed from Belle, a jeweller friend at Sèvres, and that year his *Salon*, in the form of letters to Grimm which Grimm passed unedited on to his correspondents, was much briefer and more personal than its two immediate predecessors. The *Salon* and the letters of this period show that Diderot's mind, with all those contradictory principles apparently worthy of serious consideration, was still questing, almost uncommitted, certainly restless, regarding many fewer questions as closed than has often been thought to be the case. His attitudes and correspondence come near to suggesting that, although its principal dogmas could not be conceptually believed, Christianity might nonetheless be a necessary myth, that it was impossible to disregard events, and that everything that happened was equally important.

Diderot's published works and selections from the *Encyclopédie* were now being pirated, and the *Encyclopédie* itself was already selling at a premium. The publication price had been 980 livres, and by 1769 prices of between, 1,300 and 1,500 livres were being paid. A young publisher, Charles Panckoucke, invited Diderot to work on the reprint with the four supplementary volumes of text, but they quarrelled, and Diderot turned the offer down. Naigeon in 1770 edited a *Recueil philosophique*, publishing for the first time Diderot's *De la Suffisance de la reli-*

gion naturelle and his *Addition* to the *Pensées philosophiques*. At the same time d'Holbach's anonymous *Le Système de la nature* split the atheists from the deists among the Encyclopédistes. Diderot's reaction was formulated in the 1770 *Principes philosophiques sur la matière et le mouvement*, first published in 1792 in Naigeon's *Encyclopédie méthodique*, and depending much more on chemical explanations of natural phenomena than anything he had written before. Sartine asked Diderot's advice about licensing a play, *Le Satirique*, which Diderot did not know was by Palissot, but Diderot advised against a licence, and the play was not performed until 1782. Diderot's relationship with Le Breton also deteriorated further when, as leader of the Paris publishers, Le Breton was sued by Luneau de Boisjermain, whose de luxe edition of Racine the publishers had confiscated as infringing their copyright. Luneau de Boisjermain won his case, but Le Breton did not lightly forgive Diderot's intervention against him with Sartine to whom Diderot had written.

It was also in 1770 that 17 philosophes came together in the salon of Suzanne Necker (née Curchod), mother of the future Germaine de Staël, to inaugurate a fund to raise a statue to Voltaire. The company included d'Alembert, Diderot, Helvétius, Marmontel, Morellet, Raynal, and Saint-Lambert, and the eventual result was the nude figure by Jean-Baptiste Pigalle, also the sculptor of a fine bust of Diderot now in the Louvre. Diderot visited Langres to begin negotiations for Angélique's marriage to Caroillon de Vandeul, but failed to get his brother to overcome his religious objections to a reconciliation. It appears, however, to have been as a result of this visit that Diderot wrote the dialogue *L'Entretien d'un père avec ses enfants*, which first appeared in the *Correspondance littéraire* for 1 and 15 March 1771, preceded by a biographical note about Diderot's father by Grimm.

Diderot also wrote *Les Deux Amis de Bourbonne*, published in the *Correspondance littéraire* for 15 December 1770, its title alluding to Saint-Lambert's recent *Les Deux Amis, conte iroquois*. Diderot had timed his visit to Langres so as to meet Mme de Maux and her daughter, Mme de Prunevaux, who was staying 20 miles away at the hot springs of Bourbonne-les Bains, recovering from the birth of a child. He later found that Mme de Maux was encouraging the attentions of a young sciatica patient at Bourbonne and, although she and Diderot continued to see one another, their relationship was never again close. The result of the emotional upheaval includes the two contes *Ceci n'est pas un conte* and *Madame de la Carlière*, otherwise known by what was intended to be its subtitle, *Sur l'inconséquence du jugement public de nos actions particulières*. This conte leads directly to the *Supplément au Voyage de Bougainville*, whose first draft dates from 1772 and whose title alludes to Bougainville's account of sexual life on Tahiti in his 1771 *Voyage autour du monde*. Diderot is preoccupied with the moral qualities we attach to what perhaps should be regarded only as morally neutral, natural physical acts.

On 11 June 1773 Diderot left Paris for The Hague on his way to Russia. The preceding years had been as crammed as ever with incident, from the composition of occasional self-revelatory verses and of pieces of journalism, mostly for Grimm, or rewriting a text-book of musical dialogues by Anton Bemetzrieder, or acquiring for himself "a good, a very good pianoforte," or acting as the agent of Catherine II in the purchase of a number of important paintings, and buying on her behalf the whole Crozat-Thiers collection of 500 paintings for 460,000 livres early in 1772, to marrying his daughter to Vandeul on 9 September 1772 at the local parish church, which was Saint-Sulpice. The *Salon de 1771*, while not brief, remained unpolished, and leant heavily on a pamphlet by another hand. It was at that salon that Houdon exhibited his bust of Diderot, considered by its subject in his only recorded comment as *"a very good likeness."*

There was a further quarrel with Luneau de Boisjermain in which Diderot, now trying to defend the publishers of the *Encyclopédie* against further accusations, needlessly exposed himself to ridicule. Eventually Luneau de Boisjermain lost this case, but he had had to be allowed temporarily to have the last word. Diderot's reputation was meanwhile being consolidated. The first draft of *Jacques le fataliste* was written in 1771. Works were dedicated to Diderot, inauthentic pieces attributed to him, and in 1772–3 four editions of his collected works were published, all unauthorized and all outside France. Posthumously much harm was done to Diderot's reputation by the publication in the form of her authentic memoirs of a novel by Mme d'Epinay, *L'Histoire de Madame de Montbrillant*, with the names of Grimm, Charles Duclos, Diderot, and Rousseau substituted for characters who admittedly had been based on them, though they should not have been used as if they were biographical sources. We know, for instance, that when Mme d'Epinay and Diderot were working closely together during Grimm's absence in 1771, Diderot was making suggestions to turn the character of René, based on Rousseau, more cold and calculating than Rousseau ever actually was.

Diderot worked very hard at finding an administrative place for Vandeul which would keep his daughter in Paris. He was unsuccessful, but Vandeul did acquire mineral rights and leases of land which eventually made him a very wealthy ironmaster. The marriage badly upset both Anne-Toinette and Diderot himself, who had remained very close to Angélique. His brother would not come to the wedding or receive the couple, and Diderot's wife forbade him to invite any of his friends. Like the breakdown of the relationship with Mme de Maux, the marriage affected Diderot's imaginative preoccupations. In the late spring of 1772 he wrote his essay *Sur les femmes*, which first appeared in the *Correspondance littéraire* for 1 July 1772, and was partly inspired by the work of a friend, Antoine-Léonard Thomas, on women through the centuries.

Diderot saw the sea for the first time on the way to Russia, when he was very nearly 60. His wife remained with power of attorney in Paris. His own previous travels had been limited to the immediate neighbourhood of Paris and to less than half a dozen return trips between Langres and Paris, with one diversion to Bourbonne. He enjoyed Galitzin's hospitality at The Hague, where he stayed two months, read Helvétius's posthumous *De l'homme*, and began his own *Réfutation* of it, his *Satire première*, and his *Voyage en Hollande*. He also elaborated an earlier essay, the 1769 *Garrick; ou, Les Acteurs anglais*, into the *Paradoxe sur le comédien*. On 20 August Diderot left for St Petersburg with one of the chamberlains of Catherine II, Alexis Vassilievich Narishkin, born in 1742 and a friend of Beccaria. Diderot had known him in Paris. They had intended to visit Potsdam, but Diderot was ill with colic at Duisburg and, since Narishkin was in a hurry, they travelled by Leipzig and Dresden instead. Diderot stayed with Friedrich Jacobi at Pempelfort, saw what paintings he could, and wrote some occasional verse. They

arrived at St Petersburg, with Diderot ill again, on 8 October 1773. Diderot had expected to stay with Falconet, but there was no room. The Narishkins put him up in their town house for the whole of his stay.

Diderot was a sufficiently well-known personality for his pilgrimage to have helped Catherine's reputation, and he saw her daily. They discussed literature, but also political, economic, social and legal matters, with Diderot on most occasions presenting one of the 65 memoranda he would leave behind him. He made a strong and favourable impression, although he found the obsequiousness of courtly behaviour and its dissimulations trying. The vulgarity of his gesticulations, the heartiness of his appetite, his inadequacies as a listener, and his habit of dressing always in black were all remarked on, and he was found naively trusting. Grimm and Diderot were elected foreign members of the Russian Academy of Sciences. Diderot's correspondence reveals an on the whole affectionate relationship with his wife, to whom he was grateful for getting Pigalle to be godfather to Angélique's child, born in September 1773.

Diderot was certainly unwell in Russia, and his correspondence falls right off. He may have been depressed, and fear of the hostility of Frederick the Great stopped him from returning home with Grimm, who had to go to Berlin. Frederick the Great wanted Diderot at Potsdam, but Diderot had been alerted to danger by a sarcastically hostile review of the unauthorized Amsterdam 1773 edition of his works, inspired or written by the Prussian king. He left St Petersburg with the diplomat companion provided by Catherine on 5 March 1774, having apparently been the victim of various intrigues, and travelled to The Hague via Gdansk and Hamburg. By the time they arrived they were on to their fourth carriage, three having broken down on the way. Diderot stayed at The Hague for five months before returning to Paris on 21 October 1774.

He had turned down lavish presents in Russia, accepting from Catherine only small tokens and what amounted in addition to his travel to 12,600 livres in expenses. He himself gave presents to the value of 5,000 livres. It had for a moment seemed likely that he would return home rich with a commission from Catherine for a new encyclopedia, he did bring with him to The Hague detailed comments requested by François Hemsterhuis on his own *Lettre sur l'homme et ses rapports* which give a very good synopsis of Diderot's thought at this date. He also drew up a series of observations on Catherine's apparently liberal instructions to the committee charged with drawing up a new legal code, or *Nakaz*, for which Le Mercier de la Rivière had been enlisted. Diderot's *Observations sur le Nakaz* infuriated Catherine when she read them after Diderot's death. Since Diderot's relations with the Galitzins suddenly cooled, it looks as if, as was at the time alleged, Galitzin had been through Diderot's papers, and had on her instructions abstracted the original of his observations on Catherine's Nakaz.

Diderot had to tread carefully to avoid hurting the rivals Turgot and Necker, with both of whom he was friendly. Diderot's correspondence with the publisher Marc-Michel Rey, presumably about an edition of his complete works, was being intercepted by the police and, with the exception of Galiani, the philosophes were downcast when Necker replaced Turgot in July 1776. The last letter to Sophie Volland is dated 1774. The Volland estate had been sold, and Sophie, scarcely ever absent from Paris, did not need to be written to. A second grandchild was born on 27 June 1775, and Diderot again wrote a *Salon*. He also composed a series of *Pensées détachées sur la peinture, la sculpture, l'architecture et la poésie*, perhaps inspired by Christian von Hagedorn's *Réflexions sur la peinture* of 1775, and he subscribed to six sets of the Le Tourneur translation of Shakespeare.

During the winter of 1776–77 Diderot worked hard on the augmented third (1781) edition of the abbé Guillaume Raynal's *Histoire philosophique et politique des établissements et du commerce des Européens dans les deux Indes*, published in 1770 and, augmented, in 1774. Although Diderot had contributed to the two earlier editions, the work's emphasis on what we would regard as humanitarian and anti-colonial attitudes now intensified, and Diderot became passionately committed to its sense of moral obligation towards the world's exploited peoples. From the beginning Diderot had been interested in economic theory, but from his close relationship with the physiocrats his interests came to centre increasingly round what were actually for him moral issues, although they had strongly political implications. He had much resented the repressive policies on the administration of justice, censorship, and police powers of René-Nicolas Maupeou, chancellor from 1771. The visit to Russia strengthened and focused Diderot's detestation of despotism. The radicalization of his political views found its final expression in the re-working of the 1779 *Essai sur Sénèque* into the 1782 *Essai sur les règnes de Claude et de Néron*.

There must have been three identifiable stages of the play which was finally entitled *Est-il bon? Est-il méchant?* sketched in 1775, written in a weekend in 1777. He himself played in a private performance, perhaps for Mme de Maux, at whose house near Sèvres he still sometimes worked. The work on Seneca was undertaken as a favour, to supplement an edition being completed by Naigeon and d'Holbach, but it caused Diderot to change his views on social organization and attracted a hostile review spread over two numbers of the *Année littéraire*, even though Fréron was now dead. A remark made by Diderot and universally understood to refer to Rousseau, who had also died, betrays the extent to which Rousseau had become almost an obsession in Diderot's mind.

Diderot spent his last years working. There was a gift from Catherine II of 10,000 livres in 1779. His eyesight became too poor for him to work by candlelight. By 1780 he seems to have been working mostly at the *Eléments de physiologie*, intended itself to be an encyclopedic compilation, but also part of Diderot's continuing quest to discover man's real nature. To the end his materialism, of which atheism was only the consequence, was remarkably undogmatic. Personally and intellectually Diderot was now parting company with Grimm, who disliked the new edition of Raynal's *Histoire des deux Indes* and was becoming increasingly conservative in his attitudes. Raynal's third edition was in fact condemned on 25 May 1781, and Raynal, who had prudently left the country, was in his absence sentenced to imprisonment. Diderot's letter of remonstration to Grimm was one of his last completed pieces of work. The final piece was probably the *"Addition"* to the *Lettre sur les aveugles*.

In the summer of 1781 Diderot did not go to Sèvres, but wrote his customary *Salon* and was made an honorary member of the Scottish Society of Antiquaries. In 1781 and 1782 he was paying four professional copyists to prepare his works for a complete edition. The manuscripts went to Russia after his death, with his library. When the *Essai sur les règnes de Claude*

et de Néron appeared in 1782, it contained a strong attack on La Mettrie, not only on account of La Mettrie's own attack on Seneca, but because his ethics appeared to Diderot to have been far too individualistic, uninspired by Diderot's own strong sense of social obligation. Both authors associated virtue with happiness, but for Diderot happiness itself was a function of self-sacrifice and self-mastery rather than self-indulgence.

From early in 1783 Diderot was ill and, although he recovered a little during the summer, by September it was noted that the end was obviously not very far off. D'Alembert died on 29 October 1783. Rousseau and Voltaire had died in 1778, preceded in 1777 by Mme Geoffrin. Le Breton had died in 1779 and Jaucourt in 1780. Turgot and Tronchin died in 1781, and in April 1783 Mme d'Epinay died of cancer. Sophie Volland died in February 1784. Diderot's lungs and legs were giving out. He had emphysema and dropsy. He did manage to go to Sèvres in May 1784, and Catherine II, at Grimm's instigation, rented a ground-floor apartment for him in Paris. The ground-floor apartment helped with the health problems, and it also removed Diderot from the parish of Saint-Sulpice, which was unlikely to allow burial in consecrated ground, the alternative being the common grave, from consignment to which Voltaire's body had been rescued only by skill and deceit. D'Alembert's ecclesiastical burial came by virtue of his secretaryship of the Académie française and consequent royal intervention. Diderot himself died without immediate warning, sitting at table, at midday on 31 July 1784. He was buried in consecrated ground on 1 August 1784. M. de Vandeul apparently paid for the presence, at one livre a head, of 50 priests. Jacques-Henri Meister, who had taken over Grimm's newsletter in 1773 and who was, like Jaucourt, a Protestant encyclopedist, maliciously stated that the curé asked between 1,500 and 1,800 livres for the ceremony. Catherine sent Anne-Toinette 5,000 livres.

WORKS

Almost everything that Diderot wrote is an *"occasional"* piece, produced for a particular reason, often propagandist, constrained by the particular circumstances of its composition, and written in a not entirely straightforward style. The texts are often jocular, or anonymous, or not intended for publication, and very frequently carry a warning that whatever appears to be being affirmed, especially about the nature of man, is tentative, or purely speculative, or at any rate represents an uncommitted intellectual position. Comparatively little outside what Diderot produced for the *Encyclopédie* was simply written, published, and put on sale to the general public. It is in fact possible to trace a line of evolution in Diderot's mind, but only after a careful process of literary analysis. However unreconcilable the conflict between an ethical system and a view which denies human nature any spiritual autonomy, Diderot is never less than fully committed at any given moment to what he writes about personal, domestic, more broadly social, and finally political morality.

This does not of course mean that he cannot descend to mawkishness, or that he invariably refrains from sniggering about sex, but it does mean that there is much speculative toying with ideas about man, his nature, and his mind. There are contradictions. Much of what is set down is tentative, if not downright hypothetical, and the process of decoding any Diderot text must always start with a question about the literary register in which it is written. Is he saying the opposite of what he means or hinting at what he fears? How seriously are the imaginative works intended, and what are the rhetorical devices which are being used?

The failure of the Lisbon earthquake to find a resonance in Diderot's imagination argues that his atheism, unlike that of some of his contemporaries, has to have been more a corollary of his materialist analysis of what appeared to be human spiritual powers than the result of a metaphysical speculation about religion, God, or the mystery of how the universe came into being. The lack of interest in the Seven Years War suggests that any interest in social organization was prompted more by considerations about economic prosperity than by a preoccupation with political sovereignty. His impetuosity, mental energy, imaginative power, and intellectual curiosity can scarcely be denied, but was it doubts about human perfectibility or a fear of committing himself to belief in extinction at death which prevented him twice from allowing Falconet to publish their correspondence? As a constructive philosophical thinker of some originality it is for his work on aesthetics that Diderot is chiefly remembered.

His fierce invective demonstrates how easily Diderot could be outraged, but he went out of his way to do favours for friends, and was devoted to domestic arts, virtues, and values. His weakness for the little girls with broken pitchers or lame pets depicted by Greuze shows how sentimental his tenderness could be. How far did he really think it likely that he could liberalize the regime of a German princess whose protection alone allowed his Jesuit opponents to survive suppression in 1773, and who exercised absolute power from francophile St Petersburg over the vastnesses of Siberia? How far was it permissible merely to regard Catherine's patronage as acceptable support for a comfortable standard of living? The library for which she paid 15,000 livres had been valued at 13,185.

Entries in the *Encyclopédie* that masquerade as simply informative are sometimes intended to be ideologically subversive. Drama that Diderot obviously wanted to succeed as theatre nevertheless makes success dependent on the acceptability of particular moral, social, and aesthetic values. A great deal that Diderot supplied to Grimm from 1753 to 1773, and to Meister thereafter, for the fortnightly manuscript newsletter to a dozen or so European potentates, cannot be said to be have been "published" in something called the *Correspondance littéraire, philosophique et critique*. It was not a magazine. No one outside the circle of producers and recipients knew the letters existed until they were collected and given their title in 1812. The privacy of the medium must necessarily have affected the selection, presentation, and formalized intimacy of the content, and also immensely enhanced its propaganda value. Every enlightened European monarch was bombarded fortnightly by the liberal encyclopédiste view about everything cultural that happened in France. The stylized whimsicality underlying the text of *Jacques le fataliste* as we have it makes its meaning clear as soon as we know that it was serialized between November 1778 and June 1780 with two later supplementary instalments in a manuscript letter to less than a score of the crowned heads of Europe. When it was first drafted Diderot can at most have envisaged posthumous publication.

Since it is impossible to separate Diderot's works according to their imaginative category, or even with any real certainty according to the degree of intellectual or ideological commitment behind them, it is important to consider them as far as possible in strict chronological order, and in the light of the actual circumstances of their composition and, where appropriate, publication. Unhappily much that we are bound to rely on comes through the distorting prism of his correspondence and the well-intentioned but demonstrably unreliable memoirs of his daughter.

Diderot's first original work was the 60-page *Les Pensées philosophiques*, whose point of departure is an extended meditation on Shaftesbury into which Diderot blended philosophical reflections from clandestine pamphlets, mostly deist in tendency, and what, compared to Voltaire's, is a miniature anti-Pascal. The 72 entries go from the one-line aphorism to developments of a couple of pages, and take issue with some, mostly extreme, materialist positions. The form, epigrammatically concise but fragmented jottings, precludes any coherent account of man's nature, and there are almost as many question marks and clearly tentative affirmations as there are statements of belief; but there is a contribution to the systematic movement to rehabilitate the passions, understood as instinctive movements, which already had substantial momentum. Diderot is unhappy with the anthropomorphism of the notion of an angry God, dislikes Jansenism, believes with Shaftesbury in the union of virtue, instinct, and happiness, and recoils from what is overtly superstitious. Some of the insights are perceptive, if unportentous, like those attacking mere credulity. There is simply no recourse to revelation or to the need for it. Diderot is simply as good a Catholic as anyone else, and intends to remain one (LVIII). Much more dangerous material had long since been published. The difficulty for Diderot was the seriousness of his tone, and the fact that his booklet was both printed and popular. Decent clandestinity was being flouted.

La Promenade du sceptique, composed in 1747 although unpublished until 1830, is a somewhat self-conscious allegorical dialogue. In the preliminary discourse the putative author, Aristes, asks if it be better for an author to settle for mediocre dullness and live quietly at home, or should he bestir himself and flourish, even if it that means exile to the court of Frederick the Great? The allegory itself describes the path of thorns, Christianity, the path of chestnut trees, natural religion, and the path of flowers, sensual delights. As in the *Pensées Philosophiques* the path to orthodox Christianity involved extinguishing the candle, so here it involves a blindfold, and the white robe of innocence must be kept unspotted. None of the paths is without dangers. Once again there is a critical mind struggling with disbelief, but nothing that could be called an affirmation of disbelief. It is merely difficult to choose the right intellectual path, if there is one. Nearly the most interesting thing about this piece is its tendency to break into dialogue.

These works already make it clear that Diderot's literary forms lend themselves more easily to asking questions than to answering them. The licentious *Les Bijoux indiscrets*, written in 1747, printed anonymously by Durand, and on sale in 1748, was composed primarily to make money, although critics have inevitably, if forlornly, tried to read back into it signs of serious literary interest. Like many other highly intelligent and gifted authors who have resorted to imaginatively undemanding potboilers, Diderot borrowed his plot from a conte of uncertain authorship, *Nocrion, conte allobroge*, but he amused himself with a little anti-clerical satire and some fun about experimental science at the expense of metaphysicians. Only slightly less banal are remarks urging towards greater naturalism in the theatre, admitted by Lessing to have inspired part of the *Hamburgische Dramaturgie*, and others contrasting Lulli with Rameau.

None the less, Diderot did later add to the novel, at a time when he was preoccupied with problems of sexual psychology, probably again from a perfectly reasonable desire to increase his income. *Les Bijoux* ran through six editions in a few months and was translated once into English, twice into German, was republished in 1756, 1772, and 1786, and was included by Naigeon in the 1798 *Oeuvres complètes*. Its chief interest today is historical. It continues to show Diderot unable to confine himself to his chosen form, and included dialogue, theatre, and smaller fictional forms like allegory and dream, within the framework of a single novel. Raynal's account in the *Correspondance littéraire* immediately detected that Diderot was not very good at soft pornography, and Naigeon is probably to be believed when he said that Diderot regretted writing *Les Bijoux*.

Publication is an inadequate term to describe the dissemination of *Les Bijoux* and, for that matter, that of either the *Correspondance*, which was not printed, or the *Lettre sur les aveugles à l'usage de ceux qui voient*, clandestinely printed at Durand's expense and sold by him from June 1749. The question of how a blind man forms ethical and religious concepts, raised by William Molyneux, had been treated by Locke in his *Essay concerning Human Understanding* of 1690, translated by Pierre Coste in 1700. If a man born blind had been taught by touch to distinguish a cube from a sphere and then acquired sight, could he distinguish by vision between the two objects? Locke thought he would not be able to, as did Berkeley in 1709. In 1728 Cheselden, an oculist, was able to operate on a boy born blind, and said Locke was right. Voltaire, in the *Eléments de la philosophie de Newton*, agreed.

Condillac, drawing in the *Essai sur l'origine des connaissances humaines* on La Mettrie, thought Locke wrong and Cheselden prejudiced, holding that judgement did not occur at the level of simple perception. Like Diderot, Buffon took up the matter in 1749, but Diderot, provoked to thought by Hilmer's experiment undertaken under the aegis of Réaumur, focused his interest on the role of what the scholastics had called the "sensus communis" and what he calls the "sens interne," the power by which sense data are combined in the mind and allow judgements to be formed. In other words Diderot, in fact reflecting on the experience of Nicholas Saunderson, the blind Lucasian professor of mathematics at Cambridge, who specialized in optics and wrote an *Elements of Algebra*, moved away from the simple sensualism of Locke and the early Condillac, although later on Condillac further developed Diderot's ideas in the 1754 *Traité des sensations*.

The *Lettre* speculated on the formation of religious concepts in those deprived of one or more senses, but held it better to examine the experience of an educated and thoughtful blind person than to listen to the immediate reaction of a blind child given sight in an operation for cataract. Diderot put into Saunderson's mouth the words, "Si vous voulez que je croie en Dieu, il faut que vous me le fassiez toucher (If you want me to believe in God, then you must let me touch him)." In a few heated pages Diderot's anonymous letter-writer does no more than wonder how a blind man, deprived of the spectacle of nature, can possibly reason his way to the existence of God. What has an animal's mechanical system got to do with "un être souverainement intelligent (a being of sovereign intelligence)?" Do we need to have recourse to a God in order to explain everything that mystifies us? The letter-writer now, after publication in France of John Turbeville Needham's work, allows Saunderson to admit for a moment the possibility of spontaneous generation, but to wonder whether there really is order at the edge of the universe, and to suggest that we may be inventing myths, just as for the blind man the visible world is a "myth."

Saunderson on his death-bed says to the chaplain, "Le monde est éternel pour vous, comme vous êtes éternel pour l'être qui ne vit qu'un instant (the world is eternal for you, as you are eternal for the creature that lives only for a moment)." Diderot is neither arguing, nor even seriously questioning. He is alluding to the existence of problems, too readily dismissed, in the way beliefs and judgements are formed. Yet Saunderson, without the means of forging religious attitudes available to the sighted, had, writes the author of the letter, a "pureté de moeurs et une ingénuité de caractère (purity of behaviour and openness of character)," which the sighted often lack. They live as if they were blind. Saunderson died as if he had seen. He can hear nature's voice sufficiently with the organs he has. Diderot replied on 11 June 1749 to Voltaire's reproach of atheistic tendencies to say that he did not himself share Saunderson's view, any more than Voltaire did, but that none the less he believed in God. The *Lettre*, then, was another occasional piece, an imaginative foray into the territory opened up by the sensualism of Locke and Condillac, and by speculative interest about the formation of religious concepts in the blind.

Diderot's own contributions to the *Encyclopédie* were, at least before the interruption of 1759, distingushed by an asterisk. At first at any rate, the *Encyclopédie* was designed primarily to be theoretically informative, but also to bring out the principles and applications of all the arts and sciences. It is only later that it became the vehicle for attitudes and values as well as liberal ideas. The *Prospectus* was issued late in 1750. In February 1751 Diderot's *Lettre sur les sourds et muets à l'usage de ceux qui entendent et qui parlent*, although apparently uncontroversial, continued to explore the relationship between perceptions and mental processes, especially in relation to forms of communication and to aesthetic theory. Diderot touches, but does not delve deeply into, the relationship between gesture and language, poetry and painting, with poetry regarded as a tapestry of interwoven signs or emblems. The book went through three editions in its first year.

At the end of June 1751 the first volume of the *Encyclopédie* appeared. Diderot contributed pieces on up-to-date technology, but also a celebrated entry on political authority, with a ringing declaration of everyone's right to liberty and an affirmation that power acquired by violence is necessarily usurped. Legitimate power necessarily has limits, and the authority of the prince derives from the people. Very few of the other entries in the early volumes were anywhere near so outspoken. When Diderot wrote, on adoration, that the manner of adoring the true God ought never to deviate from reason, the tone and the place of the remark made it subversive of ecclesiastical authority, appearing to make the Church's teaching authority subject to rational criticism, but its content was actually the teaching of many of the 13th-century *Summae*. Again, under "Eagle," Diderot meandered off the ornithological track far enough to observe that the philosopher has only to follow reason "in order to arrive at our altars." Diderot's early contributions to the *Encyclopédie*, however occasional, do make clear his commitment to a religion which, even if also revealed, must be governed by the norms imprinted on nature and reason.

This is also the central message of Diderot's next work, the *Suite* to the *Apologie de M. l'abbé de Prades*. Diderot's third part of the *Apologie* was issued in July 1752, before the abbé's own first two parts, and again defended reason against "vague declamations against reason." Obviously the usage of the word reason attacked by the theologians was that which made it a weapon critical of the Church's magisterium, not the rationality which in human nature was a derivative of the divine reason for the scholastics, although Diderot sometimes defended the critical weapon as if the reason he was upholding was that underlying God's universal law. To rely on authority at the expense of common sense was, Diderot pointed out, to reduce humanity to the level of brute beasts. He was, not surprisingly, forced to re-import into his thought the age-old distinction between what was appropriate to faith and revelation on the one hand, and what was subject to scientific analysis and empirical deduction on the other. At the end of the *Suite* he clearly exaggerated the "atrocious calumnies" to which he imagined himself subject. Things were not yet as bad as that, and again the impetuosity of his imagination had taken Diderot beyond a cool statement of his considered position.

The second volume of the *Encyclopédie* had appeared at the beginning of 1752, with an apparently straight-faced use of Biblical chronology, as currently accepted, in a manner which made evident its contradictions, and therefore insinuated the absurdity of the claim of Mosaic authorship of the Pentateuch, long since challenged, but still a delicate point. The alternative would have been to surrender the inspiration which guaranteed Moses's inerrancy. There is also much insidious comparison of norms and customs considered absolute wherever they are in force, to the obvious detriment of the Church's claims to a monopoly of revealed truth. Diderot himself wrote the entries on "Bible," on the canon of books belonging to the Old Testament, on beauty, and on celibacy. Beauty, considered to be "the perception of relationships," was therefore not absolute, although not all real beauty is perceived.

The third volume came out in November 1753, after the suspension, and contained entries by Diderot on the crafts, on heat ("Chaleur"), "Comédiens," "Christianity," "the Chaldeans," "Chaos," and "Sacred Chronology." His later aesthetic theory is characteristically the product of an entry, "Composition in Painting," which had to be written in a hurry when the expected contributor let the editors down. Diderot had begun to write most of the entries on the history of philosophy which Naigeon was later to publish separately, and his entry "Encyclopédie" is of importance not only for its vast length, but for yet another restatement of the guiding principles of the whole undertaking.

Also in November 1753, but re-published in revised form in January 1754, appeared the anonymous but tacitly authorized *De l'Interprétation de la nature*, a short, dense, but uncoordinated book of 50 or so relatively brief articles, some headed "examples," with seven "conjectures" concerning obstetrics, electricity, elasticity, and the metallurgy of steel, ending with a series of "questions," about the constitution of matter, the unity of nature, transformism, and what gives life to matter. The book is typically disordered, stabbing out hypotheses, questions, and ideas about the origin of life and the development of species—more a guide to the state of current problems and suggested avenues of possible solution than a synthesis. Its real purpose must

have been to draw attention once again to the importance of the matters being discussed in the *Encyclopédie* by controverting Maupertuis in a way suggesting that the organizing principle of nature may have to be a "soul," understood as a "système infini de perceptions (an infinite system of perceptions)," and by pointing out what Buffon's work on animals, Euler's on vibrations in solids, Réaumur's on steel, and Nollet's and Franklin's on electricity were contributing to knowledge, discovery, and progress. However, the book starts off with a series of articles dismissive of d'Alembert and his purely mathematical preoccupations. The idea of world-soul identifiable with God is presented as simply one horn of a dilemma.

The *Entretien d'un père avec ses enfants; ou, Du danger de se mettre au-dessus des lois* is a conte in dialogue form, in which the characters include "Mon Père," "Ma Soeur," and "Mon Frère," with others. It is set round the hearth, and is devoted principally to a lengthy case of conscience raising the question whether, when it appears clearly preferable, natural justice should be allowed to take precedence over positive law, and who has the right to decide. It was included in the *Correspondance littéraire* for 1 and 15 March 1771 and published in 1772.

Diderot's five-act prose drama, *Le Fils naturel; ou, Les Epreuves de la vertu*, was published, together with the *Entretiens avec Dorval*, early in 1757, in which year there were also three further editions. It seems certain that it was offered to, but turned down by, the Comédie-Française. When it was produced 14 years later on 26 September 1771 with a first-night audience of 1,051, the performance several times came near to breaking down, and Diderot withdrew the play before it could be performed a second time. Success in print was, however, considerable. There were 25 French editions, four German, and three Russian before 1800, and the play was also published in Italian, Danish, Dutch, and English.

At the play's opening Dorval, the hero, is preparing to depart. He has fallen in love with Rosalie, the fiancée of his host, Clairville, whose widowed sister, Constance, is looking after her in Clairville's house, and has fallen in love with Dorval. Dorval, writing a farewell letter to Rosalie, is called to the assistance of Clairville, who is being attacked. Constance reads the unfinished letter, and mistakenly assumes that it is addressed to her. Dorval turns out to have saved Clairville's life. Clairville, Constance, and Rosalie all assume that Dorval is in love with Constance. Rosalie swoons, and tells Clairville that she hates him. News comes that her father had been captured, robbed, and imprisoned. He is now free, but impoverished. Dorval writes to his banker to restore Rosalie's fortune. He tells Constance that he is fleeing human society, at which point Constance makes the famous remark that "only the bad man lives alone," which Rousseau took so personally. Dorval reveals the secret, already hinted at, of his illegitimate birth. In the last act Rosalie's father arrives, and turns out also to be the father of Dorval. Rosalie marries Clairville and Constance marries Dorval, Rosalie's noble, honourable, and sensitive half-brother, recipient of two declarations of love on the same day, and the saviour of his friend.

The three *Entretiens*, which Lessing translated into German, advocate much greater realism in the theatre and greater emphasis on gesture than on declamation, which Diderot hoped would allow the development of domestic and bourgeois prose tragedy, with characters employed in middle-class occupations whose virtues he trusted the audience would admire and imitate. The text of the play itself has elaborate stage directions, and its broken sentences mimic everyday speech, although the "deus ex machina" ending was much criticized. The third *Entretien*, in particular, explains how easily comedy can degenerate into burlesque, and tragedy can lose its verisimilitude. In the middle is the "genre sérieux," a proper blend rather than, like tragicomedy, a mixture of two distinct genres in the same piece.

Between 1758 and 1800, 32 editions of Diderot's second prose drama, *Le Père de famille*, were published in French, together with ten in German, three each in English and Dutch, and editions in five other languages. The father of the family, for no apparent dramatic reason a widower, is M. d'Orbesson, and his son Saint-Albin comes home one night dressed as a workman, explaining that he has fallen in love with a girl, Sophie, virtuously attempting to earn enough money by spinning to be able to return home. She supposes that Saint-Albin is an artisan. D'Orbesson consents to see her and tries to buy her off by offering to provide for her if she will give up his son. After stormy scenes with his father and his father's brother-in-law, the Commander, Saint-Albin resolves to kidnap Sophie, but the Commander gets a lettre de cachet against her, although it is not used. In the end the Commander turns out to be Sophie's uncle, too, and she therefore is Saint-Albin's marriageable first cousin. The Commander alone remains unreconciled at the end. There are tableaux, as in a genre painting, and very detailed stage directions are given. Speech is disjointed, to show the effect of strong passion and to allow for the play of gesture Diderot demanded. D'Orbesson forbids his daughter Cécile to enter a convent and uselessly squander away her life. The absence of a wife for d'Orbesson and a mother for Saint-Albin in what is supposed to be a family drama has raised speculations about the role of Diderot's own subconscious in determining the focus of the world he needs to explore in his imagination.

The *Discours de la poésie dramatique* is a formal treatise, reviewed on the whole coolly by Marmontel in the *Mercure de France* and the abbé de la Porte in the *Observateur littéraire*. Even Grimm's enthusiasm was now more restrained, although Lessing's in his 1760 translation was not. The 22 short chapters are preceded by summaries. In the *Discours* Diderot is clearly writing in his own name, but it is self-analysis rather than autobiography. As we must have come to expect, the treatise is fuller of perceptive insights and firm principles than of reasoned arguments or sustained developments, and it is halfway between an apologetic for what Diderot has tried to accomplish and an outline sketch of how he wants to proceed. Rivetingly important for a historian of drama, the work still makes fascinating reading for any modern theatre-goer prepared to have thrown at him vast questions about the nature, purpose, and kinds of drama, particularly if he happens to be familiar with Terence as well as Corneille.

A similar darting profundity of understanding, with speculative intelligence in concentrated shafts, permeates the *Salons* of 1759, 1761, 1763, 1765, 1767, 1769, 1771, 1775, and 1782, written for the recipients of Grimm's letter who wanted to know what was going on in Paris. Again the *Salons* are essential reading for art historians, and fascinating for any habitual or occasional gallery visitor wishing to be made to consider the basic principles governing the plastic two-dimensional expression of imaginative vision. Diderot's insistence that only what is true and depicted realistically can move the emotions and incite to virtue, which marks his approach to the visual arts as well as to

the theatre, may now seem dated, but he himself came to think that his art criticism was his greatest literary achievement, and as a historian of fact and taste his importance is obvious and overwhelming.

As an art critic, his judgement has subsequently been questioned. As a writer on art, however, his enthusiasm, precision, and visual sensitivity, expressed in almost conversational style, and in an occasional amused pretence of dialogue with the painters, may well have found in the formal intimacy of the reports on the *Salons* the genre most perfectly suited to his literary talents. We do not have to agree with his judgements, or his aesthetic principles, to acknowledge the power and charm of his accounts of the exhibitions, and the brilliance with which he exploits the occasions afforded to him by Grimm. When in 1765 Diderot wrote on 10 November to Sophie Volland of that year's *Salon*, "C'est certainement la meilleure chose que j'ai faite depuis que je cultive les lettres (It is certainly the best thing I've done since I started to cultivate writing)," it may be unconventional, but it is not absurd to agree with him.

The writing is forceful. It is also scurrilous, torrential, witty, learned, scabrous, full of venom and charm, gleefully vituperative, with accurate visual accounts spiked by the acid-tipped pen of a straight-faced jester. Diderot knows that he has to bring the paintings to life for cultivated connoisseurs who are busy keeping an eye on their thrones, and that they enjoy being entertained with scandalous morsels about the painters' models, especially when they were known to have served the king's pleasures. There is Fragonard serving up "an omelette of children; there are hundreds of them, all caught up in one another, heads, thighs, legs, bodies, arms, in a carefully arranged way: but there is no strength, no colour, no depth, no distinction of planes." Or Boucher:

Imagine in the background a vase placed on its pedestal and crowned with a bunch of over-turned branches; underneath, a shepherd asleep on the knees of his shepherdess; scatter round about a crook, a little hat filled with roses, a dog, some sheep, a bit of landscape, and heaven knows how many other things piled on top of one another; paint the lot in your brightest colours and you've got Boucher's *Bergerie*.

What talent thrown away! what a waste of time! with less than half the effort you could have had more than half as much effect again. With so many details, each equally careful, the eye doesn't know where to stop; there's no air, no peace...

I don't know what to say about that man. The corruption of taste, colour, composition, characters, expression, draughtsmanship, has followed step by step the depravation of his morals. What do you want an artist like that to throw on to canvas? What he has in his imagination; and what can a man have in his imagination who spends his life with the lowest sort of tarts?

One of Boucher's favourite models, Louise Murphy, was also a mistress of Louis XV.

The letters forged by Diderot to Croismare in 1760 which formed the practical joke underlying *La Religieuse* were sent by Grimm in the 1770 *Correspondance littéraire* to his correspondents, including the dukes of Zweibrücken and Saxe-Gotha, the princes of Hesse-Darmstadt and Nassau-Sarrebruck, the queen of Sweden, the king of Poland, and the empress of Russia. The text we now have, the result of at least three revisions, was published in 1796. Suzanne Simonin is forced by her mother and the man she thinks is her father to enter a convent. She has no vocation for the life of a nun and refuses to take her final vows, but is eventually forced to enter another convent where she gets on well with the Mother Superior. When the Mother Superior dies, her successor and Suzanne get on very badly. Suzanne manages to contact a lawyer, fails to win her freedom, but is transferred to a different house at Arpajon, where the lesbian Mother Superior falls in love with her. Eventually, after paroxysms of fervour and guilt she, too, dies. Suzanne is then rather perfunctorily allowed by Diderot to escape to Paris, but hurts herself in an accident while getting away, and eventually dies.

The novel is often praised for its balanced depiction of female homosexuality within the cloister and of the results of sexual frustration on those subjected to enforced celibacy. It is true that some of the religious, male and female, are depicted as intelligent, devout, and humane, but that the author felt physical impulses should at any rate not automatically be frustrated as being in some way incompatible with moral fulfilment. Monastic celibacy seemed to Diderot to be socially wasteful, and he understood the ritual cruelty to which ecclesiastical discipline can lead. If the possibility of genuine vocations, saintly nuns, and discerning directors is respected in the book, there are also the clear and familiar warnings:

L'homme est né pour la société; séparez-le, isolez-le, ses idées se désuniront, son caractère se tournera, mille affections ridicules s'élèveront dans son coeur…

(Man is born for society. Segregate him, isolate him, and his ideas will become disintegrated, his character will be spoiled, a thousand ridiculous affections will rise in his heart).

From a literary point of view the most interesting thing about the novel is the way in which dialogue obtrudes, to the extent that parts of the text read as if they were written for the stage. The psychology is delicate, sometimes subtle, though the composition is hasty, but Diderot uses what is essentially a dramatic technique. He allows the reader psychological insight only into Suzanne, the supposed author of the first-person narrative, leaving us to make judgements about the other characters on the grounds alone of their externally observed behaviour, as recounted in the novel.

The reader is, however, aware throughout that the author has a point to make and, even if Diderot does seek to model himself on Richardson and to awake in the reader a natural aspiration to personal and social virtue more, as he said, by feeling than by demonstration, he does not always escape the danger of writing a fable to illustrate a moral. What the text as we have it shows is an almost astonishing mastery of rhetorical skills. However well calculated the original deception of Croismare, the novel as published could scarcely have been written by the Diderot of 1760. The writing is too practised, the psychology too subtle, and the dialogue too skilful. The propaganda is vigorous, the innocence of Suzanne cleverly exploited to avoid obscuring the message with an overlay of prurience, and a strong sense of the dramatic

does not interfere with verisimilitude; but the novel's imaginative vision and the exceptional qualities of its principal character may be thought scarcely adequate to make the novel a literary achievement at the highest level.

Yet another occasional piece, *Le Neveu de Rameau* as we have it, must have been begun by 1761, when Diderot was depressed by the relative failure of *Le Père de famille*, and cannot have been finished until 1776. It was probably re-worked also in 1762, 1766, 1767 and 1775. It was first published in Goethe's German translation in 1805, and first appeared in French re-translated out of German in 1821. Unauthentic texts were published in 1823, 1875 and 1884, but an autograph copy was finally discovered, and an authentic text printed in 1891. In form *Le Neveu*, called by Diderot a *"satire"*, probably in the antique sense of *"mixture,"* is a dialogue between *"Lui,"* an eccentric, parasitical genius without talent, who cannot accept conventional moral norms, identified as Rameau's nephew, and *"Moi,"* the satire's author, who defends the view that man must subordinate himself to society which, however, may be corrupt, and who is fictionally identified in the prefatory pages with Diderot himself.

In fact the dialogue is a confrontation between conflicting attitudes within Diderot himself. As author he can expound the two points of view and let one or other appear preferable. As a character, he pretends that one of the attitudes is his own. It is not at all sure that Diderot intends to resolve the clash of attitudes within the dialogue, which is also the clash of personal attitudes within himself. In the *Salon de 1765* he had gone so far as to write that he did not abhor great crimes, firstly because they made good paintings and good tragedies, but secondly because all great and sublime actions, good or bad, *"portent le même caractère d'énergie (have the same characteristic of energy)."*

Le Neveu is not a fiction, but an interior meditation set down in dialogue form with no necessary resolution of the problems raised, or even consistency of attitude within the characters. Technically what Diderot did must come near to having introduced himself as a character to take part in the sorts of conversation described by Sterne, without necessarily putting all or any of his own views into the mouth of *"Moi."* In any event, *Le Neveu* is a personal document, not intended for publication, or as a record. Its real purpose must have been to express feelings of frustration, depression, perhaps outrage. It fulfilled that function over at least 15 years, and there is no indication that Diderot ever intended or would have allowed anyone to read it.

There is no guarantee that Diderot in these circumstances wants or tries to be *"fair"* about those, like Fréron and Palissot, about whom he feels venomous. If he was simply writing his fury out on paper, why should he be fair? The fact that Rameau did have a nephew who was an unsuccessful musician, jailed for three weeks in 1748, to whom Grimm referred to as a lunatic in 1766, is simply a distraction. The text is not *"about"* him, and whether or not he existed is of no importance for the understanding of the dialogue. In so far as there is any subject other than various ways of looking at things which Diderot wanted to consider, it is the nature of happiness, the meaning of artistic creativity, the existence of genius, and the basis for morality. The self-defeating viewpoint of the impulsive *"Lui,"* the lying, avaricious cheat, is modified in the course of the text, but so is that of the moralistic, rather unthinking *"Moi."* The realism of the setting and the allusions are the devices used by Diderot to keep himself from the simple fantasizing which occasionally tempts him, but would not have resolved his tensions.

Jacques le fataliste is also printed in the form of a dialogue, principally between Jacques and Le Maître, his master, although there are episodes, a handful of other speakers, and quite long interludes of narration, like the perpetually interrupted story of Mme de la Pommeraye. The ending is again brusque, as if Diderot had simply decided to stop. Nothing is resolved. The inspiration comes from *Tristram Shandy*, in which the wounded ex-soldier, Corporal Trim, recounts in a few pages the story of his loves. Diderot uses the story of Jacques's loves as a central theme round which is woven an almost picaresque account of travels, with discussions at inns, episodes of psychological interest, like that of Mme de la Pommeraye, depictions of Paris life, like the love story of Le Maître, and bizarre characters, peasants, monks, and Jacques's captain, wandering in and out of the text as Jacques tries to get on with his story.

The theme is freedom and determinism, amusingly reflected in the constant intrusions of a narrator who pretends to be narrating, often in the historic present tense, something which has happened, and which therefore cannot now be changed, although as author he draws attention to the fact that what happens depends entirely on him. This is an obvious take-off of the novelist who, after all, can change what he gives out as the past. Indeed, if what happens was going to happen anyway, is there any point in talking about it? If matter, as Diderot was inclined to think, was simply the action and reaction occasioned by a universal sensibility, and events were conditioned by the resolution of opposing tendencies, then the world is determined by forces beyond our control, and the concepts of good and evil become emptied of meaning. The events depicted in the dialogue do not in fact depend on the actions of its characters, but seem to the characters to be the product of chance, although they are in fact determined by forces we do not know and whose interaction we do not understand. The dialogue does not consider whether God is the ultimate agent in the chain of causes and effects.

The fascination of the text is that the characters are simply unable to act in a way logically consequent on the determinist hypothesis. They are condemned to act as if they could influence events, and they think in terms of good and evil. Only rarely, as when they foresee what is going to happen, do they act in the knowledge that they cannot influence events. The text establishes its register from the beginning. This is the narrator's opening paragraph in its entirety:

Comment s'étaient-ils rencontrés? Par hasard, comme tout le monde. Comment s'appelaient-ils? Que vous importe? D'où venaient-ils? Du lieu le plus prochain. Où allaient-ils? Est-ce que l'on sait où l'on va? Que disaient-ils? Le maître ne disait rien; et Jacques disait que son capitaine disait que tout ce qui nous arrive de bien et de mal ici-bas était écrit là-haut

(How did they meet? By chance, like everyone else. What were they called? What's it to you? Where did they come from? From the nearest place. Where were they going? Does anyone know where they're going? What did they say? The master said nothing; and Jacques said his captain said that everything good and bad that happens to us down here was written up there).

The narrator, who is impertinent to the reader, is instantly distinguished from the author, and he immediately suggests that we cannot know very much and that it would not matter if we could. Is everything written in the stars? Not, obviously, Jacques's love story. That has already happened. The narrator plays with the reader, reminding him that he is also the author:

Vous voyez, lecteur, que je suis en beau chemin, et qu'il ne tiendrait qu'à moi de vous faire attendre un an, deux ans, trois ans, le récit des amours de Jacques...

(You can see, reader, that I'm well on my way, and that if I liked I could make you wait a year, two years, three years, for the account of Jacques's love story).

The narrator cuts into a discussion between Jacques, his master, and the marquis des Arcis:

Je vous entends, lecteur: vous me dites: Et les amours de Jacques?... Croyez-vous que je n'en sois pas aussi curieux que vous?... Tout ce que je vous débite là, lecteur, je le tiens de Jacques, je vous l'avoue, parce que je n'aime pas à me faire honneur de l'esprit d'autrui. Jacques ne connaissait ni le nom de vice, ni le nom de vertu; il prétendait qu'on était heureusement ou malheureusement né... Selon lui la récompense était l'encouragement des bons; le châtiment, l'effroi des méchants. Qu'est-ce autre chose, disait-il, s'il n'y a point de liberté, et que notre destinée soit écrite là-haut?... Quelle que soit la somme des éléments dont je suis composé, je suis un; or, une cause n'a qu'un effet; j'ai toujours été une cause une; je n'ai donc jamais eu qu'un effet à produire; ma durée n'est donc qu'une suite d'effets nécessaires. C'est ainsi que Jacques raisonnait d'après son capitaine. La distinction d'un monde physique et d'un monde moral lui semblait vide de sens...

D'après ce système, on pourrait imaginer que Jacques ne se réjouissait, ne s'affligeait de rien; cela n'était pourtant pas vrai. Il se conduisait à peu près comme vous et moi. Il remerciait son bienfaiteur, pour qu'il lui fît encore du bien. Il se mettait en colère contre l'homme injuste... Il tâchait à prévenir le mal; il était prudent avec le plus grand mépris pour la prudence

(I hear you, reader: you're saying to me, 'What about Jacques's love story?'... Don't you think I'm as curious as you are?... All that I've just been going on about, I had it from Jacques, I admit, because I don't like taking credit for someone else's intelligence. Jacques didn't know the word vice or the word virtue; he said you were born lucky or unlucky... According to him reward was encouragement for the good; punishment the deterrent for evil-doers. What else is there, he said, if there's no freedom, and if our destiny is written up there?... Whatever the sum of the elements I'm composed of, I'm one. But a single cause has only a single effect. I've always been a solitary cause; I've therefore only ever had one effect to produce... my whole life-span is therefore only a succession of necessary effects. And so Jacques reasoned, like his captain. The distinction between a physical world and a moral one seemed to him meaningless...

According to this system it could be thought that Jacques neither rejoiced nor grieved about anything; but that wasn't true. He behaved much the same as you and I do. He thanked his benefactor in order to receive more benefactions. He got angry with people who were unjust... He tried to forestall evil; he was prudent, while having the greatest contempt for prudence).

Diderot has spun a dense web. His narrator is sometimes author, sometimes unprejudiced observer recounting what happened, sometimes a character who can talk to Jacques, and sometimes as curious as the reader to know what comes next. Diderot leaves the reader to ask the questions in square brackets. If everything is pre-ordained, how can there be vice or virtue? [But didn't the Church teach that God fore-ordained everything?] What is the point of rewards and punishments [and isn't that why there has to be an after-life?]. If we are not free, then we have to be part of a sequential chain of causes and effects [but then we cannot be punished or rewarded or, if we are, then God is not being fair, reasonable, or lovable?] There are recognizable elements of parody and satire here, especially of Leibniz and Spinoza. The problem of the existence of evil is not solved by recourse to the distinction between moral and physical evil, sin and pain. But if Jacques thought as his captain taught him to argue, then he ought to live the life of a stoic, indifferent to what happens in an unknowable world. The real difficulty, of course, is that he cannot, any more than Diderot or Diderot's reader...

The light-hearted register was bound to provoke at least a chortle in a handful of liberal monarchs. The daring of the liberalism was only religious and philosophical, and the jokes were sophisticated. The narrator's identity problem neatly parodies any novelist's dilemma of needing to choose between being a puppeteer or a story-teller. There was no political difficulty or serious danger in slipping short bits of the text into the fortnightly newsletter. Nobody was going to suppose that *Jacques* was entirely serious; unlike *Le Neveu*, if it had been available for reading.

Insight into Diderot's mind can be derived from many other works, particularly from the unpublished *Réfutation* of Helvétius's 1772 *De l'Homme*, with which Diderot held a running dialogue from 1773 to 1778, using Helvétius's text as a springboard for his own urgent quest after a basis for human morality, to his mind too readily abandoned by Helvétius's identification of human and animal natures and his refusal to make any distinction between natural endowments. Two further works in Diderot's corpus do, however, require comment. He had long entertained the antique idea that "sensibilité," the capacity for feeling and reacting to perceived stimuli, was inert in all matter, but could be rendered active by, for instance, warmth. The "soul" then becomes the organic unity of a living and sentient being and its principle of growth.

Haller's eight volumes of *Elementa physiologiae corporis humani* had appeared from 1757–1766, and Diderot plundered them for the *Eléments de physiologie*. In the summer of 1769 he at last had leisure to return to physiology. Galiani was in Naples, d'Holbach at Grandval, Grimm in Germany, Sophie in Champagne, Mme de Maux in the Nivernais, and Anne-Toinette and Angélique were at Sèvres. In August Diderot wrote the three dialogues, known collectively under the title of the second: the *Entretien entre d'Alembert et Diderot*, *Le Rêve de d'Alembert*, and the *Suite de l'Entretien*. The characters in the *Rêve* are d'Alembert dreaming, Mlle de L'Espinasse, and the famous doctor, Théophile de Bordeu (1722–1776): "Cela est de la plus haute extravagance et tout à la fois de la philosophie la plus profonde (it is the highest degree of fantasy, and at the same time the deepest of philosophy)." The three dialogues, touched up during the autumn, were finally released to the recipients of the *Correspondance littéraire* 12 years later, from August to November 1782, well after the death of Julie de Lespinasse in May 1776. They were published in 1830.

The ideas are audacious enough, but the register is carefully tentative and, in the second dialogue, frankly poetic. Diderot's puts a thorough-going materialism into the mouth of a character with his own name, and d'Alembert repudiates the notion that only matter exists, endowed with a universal "sensibilité." The dialogue form, enhanced by its dialectical exploitation, precludes any very definite authorial affirmation. In addition much of the argument is inserted into existing debates, like the criticism of Spinoza, on the inertia of solids, of Toland, whose translation had recently been disseminated by d'Holbach, or Leibniz's of Descartes on the inherence of motion in matter. When d'Alembert concedes the inherence of sensibilité, but wants to attribute the cause of movement to God, he is taking up an argument from Maupertuis.

Diderot's metaphor of digestion comes from La Mettrie. Powdered marble is given sensibilité by being mixed with earth and then, from the humus formed, the peas are nourished which Diderot eats. Again, Diderot is being amusing, but covers himself by building one of many 18th-century processes which avoid discontuities in nature. It was merely provocative to chose marble and man, the sitter and his bust. He eliminates differences of kind between merely sentient beings and those endowed with memory. But if minerals, plants, animals, and men are the results of the different evolutionary organizations of a matter in which sensitivity and movement are inert, man has achieved a state in which his adaptation to social circumstances makes him capable of disinterest and even heroism, although he commonly binds himself in unreasonable conventions, like monogamy. Human endeavour should aim at "bienfaisance (benevolence)" and happiness, which in turn demands virtue. Man is not, in this view, free, but neither is he so absolutely conditioned by nature and environment as Helvétius unsubtly had it. He is determined by the sum total of his previous experience, and can accordingly be trained, develop natural aptitudes, and experience moral satisfactions. In no circumstances will Diderot abandon the union of virtue and happiness as the goal of human endeavour. The problem is to reconcile both with some form of advanced atomism.

For a while Diderot had thought of putting the central dialogue into the mouths of ancient philosophers, unconstricted by revelation, but then found the idea too philosophically constricting, and settled on Julie de Lespinasse, though she objected, Bordeu, and d'Alembert, who half-accepts the ideas of the Diderot of the *Entretien*, but only in a dream. Diderot is moving, about as tentatively as it is possible to move, towards the suggestion that, were it not for Genesis, it could be believed that the human race, with its perfectibility and its morality, might have evolved from primordial matter, its sensibilité necessarily present, but still inert. By 1769 the possibility of thinking matter, literally inconceivable in terms of Descartes's definition of matter, had been debated for almost a century. Diderot is speculatively playing with advanced materialistic ideas, with flashes of irony at the expense of his opponents. After all, as the Ash Wednesday liturgical formula says, they are made of dust, and unto dust they shall return.

Equally tentative is the *Supplément au Voyage de Bougainville; ou, Dialogue entre A. et B. sur l'inconvénient d'attacher des idées morales à certaines actions physiques qui n'en comportent pas*. Prefaced by a quotation from Diderot's beloved Horace, the dialogue, written in 1772 on the basis of an article of 1771 whose approval of sexual freedom, or perhaps its attitude to colonization, had been found too daring by Grimm, concerns the inappropriateness of shackling South Sea sexual habits with moral inhibitions imported from an alien culture. Bougainville's *Voyage autour du monde* had appeared in 1771. He had brought back with him the Tahitian Aotourou. All Paris took an interest as the islander was dressed in Parisian clothing, taken to the opera, paraded in the parks, and used to assuage the sometimes serious scientific curiosity of ethnographers, and indeed what we should today call social anthropologists of all sorts, including linguisticians and geographers.

Paris in 1771 was in fact waiting for the first edition of the abbé Raynal's *Histoire des deux Indes*. The principal interest of Diderot's dialogue was ethnographic, and the authentic vintage flavour of 18th-century speculation about such matters as the breaking up of the great land masses makes it difficult for today's reader to see exemplified in the *Supplément* just how far some of Diderot's work went in the insinuation of audacious conjecture into elegant works of scientific vulgarization. Diderot was not, however, the author of any serious philosophic study. His own opinions are not what is most interesting about him. There were more fervent atheists, sceptics, and materialists, but none pursuing Diderot's determined quest to combine the boldest of contemporary scientific speculation with a resolute effort to salvage a properly humanistic basis for justice, virtue, happiness, and a morality that, while compatible with natural religion, did not derive from a revelation which could not be given the status still claimed for it. Diderot was a vulgarizer of scientific and technological information on a very grand scale, with a restless intellectual energy. What has often been overlooked about this literary giant is just how tentative were the conclusions to which his powerful imagination was always reaching out.

PUBLICATIONS

[Note: *Many individual fragments, dialogues, pamphlets and entries to the "Encyclopédie" have never been published outside collected volumes*]

Collections

Collection complète des Oeuvres philosophiques, littéraires et dramatiques, 5 vols., 1773
Oeuvres (ed. Naigeon) 15 vols., 1798
Oeuvres complètes, 20 vols., 1875–77
Oeuvres, Bibliothèque de la Pléiade, 1951
Oeuvres complètes, 15 vols., 1969–73
Oeuvres complètes, 1975–
Oeuvres philosophiques, 1956
Oeuvres esthétiques, 1959
Oeuvres romanesques, 1962

Oeuvres politiques, 1962
Dialogues (in English), 1927
Contes, 1963

Fiction

Les Bijoux indiscrets, 1748; as *The Indiscreet Toys*, 1749
Contes moraux et nouvelles idylles, with Salomon Gessner, 1773
La Religieuse, 1796; as *The Nun*, 1797

Plays

Le Fils naturel; ou, Les Epreuves de la vertu, (produced 1771), 1757; as *Dorval; or, The Test of Virtue*, 1767
Le Père de famille, (produced 1761), 1758; as *The Father*, 1770
Est-il bon? est-il méchant? 1784
Le Joueur, after *The Gamester*, by Edward Moore, 1819

Aesthetic and philosophical

Pensées philosophiques, 1746; as *Philosophical Thoughts*, 1916
Mémoires sur différents sujets de mathématiques, 1748
Lettre sur les aveugles à l'usage de ceux qui voient, 1749; as *An Essay on Blindness*, 1750
Lettre sur les sourds et muets à l'usage de ceux qui entendent et qui parlent, 1751; as *Letter on the Deaf and Dumb*, 1916
Suite de l'Apologie de M. l'abbé de Prades, 1752
Arrêt rendu à l'amphithéâtre de l'Opéra, 1753
Au petit prophète de Boehmischbroda, 1753
Les Trois Chapitres; ou, La Vision de la nuit du mardi-gras au mercredi des cendres, 1753
De l'Interprétation de la nature, 1753
L'Histoire et le secret de la peinture en cire, 1755
Entretiens sur 'Le Fils naturel', 1757
Discours sur la poésie dramatique, 1758
Eloge de Richardson, 1762
De la Suffisance de la religion naturelle in *Recueil philosophique* (ed. Naigeon), 1770
Leçons de clavecin et principes d'harmonie, 1771
Essai sur Sénèque, 1779; as *Essais sur les règnes de Claude et de Néron*, 1782
Essais sur la peinture, 1795
Supplément au Voyage de Bougainville, 1796
Le Rêve de d'Alembert, 1951
Eléments de physiologie, 1964
Les Salons, 4 vols., 1957–67

Other

Jacques le fataliste et son maître, 1796; as *James the Fatalist and his Master*, 1797; as *Jacques the Fatalist and his Master*, 1962
Le Neveu de Rameau, 1821, as *Rameau's Nephew*, 1897
Correspondance, 16 vols., 1955–70
Mémoires pour Catherine II, 1899
Observations sur le Nakaz, 1920

Editor

Encyclopédie: ou, Dictionnaire raisonné des sciences, des arts, et des métiers, par une société des gens de lettres, 17 vols., plus 11 vols. of plates, 1751–1772

Translations

Stanyan, Temple, *Histoire de Grèce*, 3 vols., 1743
Shaftesbury, Anthony Ashley Cooper, earl of, *Principes de la Philosophie morale*, 1745
Les Oeuvres de Shaftesbury, 3 vols., 1769
James, Robert, *Dictionnaire universel de médecine*, 6 vols., 1746–48 (with Marc-Antoine Eidous and François-Vincent Toussaint)

Note: Many English translations of works not published separately or at all during Diderot's lifetime are available, often in composite volumes or selections.

Biographical and critical

Venturi, Franco, *Jeunesse de Diderot* (1713–1753), 1939
Diderot Studies, 1949–
Loy, J. Robert, *Diderot's Determined Fatalist*, 1950
Crocker, Lester G., *The Embattled philsopher: a Biography of Diderot*, 1954
    Diderot's Chaotic Order, 1974
Proust, Jacques, *Diderot et l'"Encyclopédie,"* 1962
Lough, John, *Essays on the "Encyclopédie" of Diderot and d'Alembert*, 1968
Wilson, Arthur M., *Diderot*, 1972
Blum, Carol, *Diderot: the Virtue of a Philosopher*, 1974
Fellows, Otis Edward, *Diderot*, 1977
France, Peter, *Diderot*, 1983
Furbank, P. N., *Diderot: A Critical Biography*, 1992

DONNEAU DE VISÉ, Jean, 1638–1710.

Dramatist, publicist, and editor.

Although Donneau de Visé was not the author of any single dramatic masterpiece, lacked both tact and taste as a critic, and was a shameless publicist as editor of France's first literary review, the *Mercure Galant* (q.v.), he was a figure of much more than merely historical importance. He certainly took part in, and in himself virtually encapsulated, the fundamental paradox of French culture in the period with which this *Guide* is concerned: that it was largely a series of frivolous, unconstrained and uncontrolled works, of no great imaginative concentration or literary merit, which provoked and reflected the confidence in human nature and perfectibility, both individual and social, struggling to emerge since the renaissance and finally victorious in the 18th-century enlightenment. The enigmas of the *Mercure Galant*, like the grosser excesses of the regency, were ultimately epiphenomena, almost spillage from a fermenting culture. An examination of the production of almost any writer between 1700 and 1720 shows why. Although Donneau de Visé belongs to the immediately preceding generation, he reveals even more clearly than those who wrote a score of years later how important were the underlying values ultimately at stake in his imaginative work.

Donneau de Visé was born in Paris early in December 1638. As so often, we are dependent for the date on Auguste Jal's transcription of archival material in his *Dictionnaire critique de biographie et d'histoire* (1864) since he was able to consult the Paris archives burnt in 1871. From other sources we know that Donneau de Visé came from a family of officers and major officials in the households of the very high-born. His father was maréchal des logis of the king's brother. He had several uncles of equivalent rank, a brother who was the queen's first valet de chambre, and a sister who was first lady-in-waiting to the duc d'Anjou. As a younger son he was destined for the church and endowed with several benefices, but preferred to try life in the world of letters.

Donneau de Visé's first publication was the anonymous three-volume *Nouvelles nouvelles*, published with an achevé d'imprimer of only 9 February 1663, although the privilège is dated a full year earlier, 28 February 1662. The collection has an amateur air, as if the pieces of which it consists had been assembled and published as a distraction rather than a serious literary endeavour. The first of the three volumes contains only two fairly conventional and rather insipid nouvelles, but the other two volumes are satirical, and show also that Donneau de Visé was very well informed about literary and theatrical life in Paris. The third part contains important criticism of Molière and Pierre Corneille plays, exploiting the disputes which had just broken out in 1662 in the wake of Molière's *L'Ecole des femmes*, on which Donneau de Visé's authorial character had made some biting criticisms while also praising Molière's talent, and includes the even more up-to-date dispute about Pierre Corneille's *Sophonisbe*, first played in January 1663, much praised by Loret in *La Muse historique* for 20th January, but attacked in the salons by d'Aubignac. D'Aubignac's resentment of Corneille's criticism of Mlle Desjardins's 1662 *Manlius*, about which Loret had also been enthusiastic, was well known to Donneau de Visé, who accused d'Aubignac of having provided the play's structure. The remarks in the *Nouvelles nouvelles* had strongly suggested that Donneau de Visé himself was, like his character, on the side of d'Aubignac and of Mlle Desjardins.

D'Aubignac's *Dissertation concernant le poème dramatique, en forme de Remarques sur la Tragédie de M. Corneille, intitulée Sophonisbe*, reproaching Pierre Corneille with having treated a subject already used by Mairet, was published in February 1663, a few days after Donneau de Visé's *Nouvelles nouvelles*, and was followed by three dissertations by d'Aubignac, against *Sertorius*, against *Oedipe*, and against the "calumnies" perpetrated by Corneille. Donneau de Visé, who gives the impression more of wanting to make himself known than of feeling any urgent compulsion to take sides, now issued two substantial essays in the course of 1663 in defence of Pierre Corneille's *Sophonisbe* and *Sertorius* respectively, starting the first essay with a violent assault on d'Aubignac. Donneau de Visé's defence of *Sophonisbe* is now as perceptive as his earlier attack had been. He acknowledges that the earlier criticisms had indeed been his own and not just his character's, but declares that he has now surrendered "à la raison," and to his own feelings, and that, having once found the defects he sought, he has now found also the "beautés" he was looking for. He knows of the coming attack by d'Aubignac on *Sertorius* and issues both a challenge and a warning to his senior. Both were intended to appear insolent. D'Aubignac's attack on *Sertorius* was virulent, and ended with an attack on Donneau de Visé. Donneau de Visé's defence of the Pierre Corneille play was dedicated flatteringly to the duc de Guise, and henceforward d'Aubignac's attacks on Corneille included in their target Donneau de Visé.

On 1 June 1663 Molière played the *Critique de l'Ecole des femmes*, of which Donneau de Visé had known before he finalized the text of the *Nouvelles nouvelles*. Molière's Lysidas was an answer to the character Straton used by Donneau de Visé to criticize the original *Ecole des femmes* in the *Nouvelles*, and Donneau de Visé attacked back again with *Zélinde; ou, La Véritable Critique de l'Ecole des Femmes et la Critique de la Critique*, for which he took out a privilège on 15 July and which he had published early in August. This work, unfair as criticism, amounted to little more than blatant self-publicizing. Although written in the form of a comedy, it was never likely to be played, and does not really belong to Donneau de Visé's dramatic oeuvre. It did not end the controversy. The Hôtel de Bourgogne urged the young Boursault to write his *Portrait du peintre; ou, La Contre-Critique de l'Ecole des Femmes*, a performance of which was attended by Molière before he wrote *L'Impromptu de Versailles*, played first at Versailles on 14 October and then in Paris on 4 November. Boursault, publishing his comedy, now added a preface hostile to Molière,

Molière had announced that he would not again reply, but Donneau de Visé renewed his attack with a short comedy performed at the Hôtel in late November, *Réponse à l'Impromptu de Versailles; ou, La Vengeance des Marquis*, published towards mid-December 1663 in *Les Diversités galantes* with a privilège of 14 September. The *Diversités* also included a "Lettre sur les affaires du théâtre," but was essentially a collection of two more nouvelles, "Les Soirées des Auberges" and "L'Apothicaire de qualité." Donneau de Visé simply used the same privilège to print the *Réponse à l'Impromptu* and the "Lettre" which again renewed the attack on Molière, at this point considered by Donneau de Visé a dramatist far inferior to Pierre Corneille. This was the end of Donneau de Visé's part in the dispute, on which the attack against Molière was continued by the dramatist A.-J. Montfleury, the gazetteer Robinet, and others. However when, in 1665, Donneau de Visé republished *Les Diversités galantes* with three more nouvelles, he none the less left in both the "Réponse" and the "Lettre" against Molière.

That same year, 1665, in which Donneau de Visé re-published the two works attacking Molière, his own comedy *La Mère coquette; ou, Les Amants brouillés* was, one would have thought amazingly, played on 23 October by Molière's company at the Palais-Royal, in the same month as a similar but superior play of the same title by Quinault was performed at the Hôtel de Bourgogne. It seems certain that Donneau de Visé had shown his piece, based on a comedy by the Spaniard Agustín Moreto y Cabaña, to the much better-known Quinault, who had improved on it and stolen it, without even bothering to change Donneau de Visé's title. Molière, in spite of the quarrel with Donneau de Visé, which had particularly turned on the question of his own originality, must have welcomed the chance to challenge with the original play the plagiarized version of the Hôtel de Bourgogne. The court, where Quinault enjoyed the favour of the duc

de Montauzier and his wife, the former Julie d'Angennes, had got to know of the prospective clash before the performances, and Quinault had necessarily put about the rumour that not he but his young rival was the plagiarist. Since in 1653 he had taken *Les Rivales* from Rotrou's *Les Deux Pucelles*, his position was weak.

Loret had died in 1665 and the function of his *Muse Historique* had been taken over by Charles Robinet de Saint-Jean's rhymed gazette. He had not hitherto been favourable to Molière, but Molière had now primed him and he came down heavily on the side of the originality of Donneau de Visé against Quinault in his gazette for 11 October 1665. Quinault's premier was five days later, on Friday 16 October. Molière's company was ready with Donneau de Visé's play a week after that, Friday 23 October. Robinet mentioned both works again on 25 October. They rivalled one another throughout November, with Donneau de Visé's running rather longer, for 14 performances in all. When they were taken off, it was so that the Hôtel de Bourgogne could revive Boyer's *Alexandre* to rival the piece of the same name written by the young Racine, to be played by Molière's troupe. Both Donneau de Visé and Quinault published their comedies early in 1666, with Donneau de Visé fiercely defending his own originality in his preface.

In 1666 Donneau de Visé married. His wife is said to have been rich, the daughter of a painter or sculptor favoured at court, although his family thought it a mésalliance. Molière became displeased with Donneau de Visé again when his publisher, Ribou, added to the published text of *Le Misanthrope*, which had been a failure on the stage in June 1666, a laudatory prefatory epistle, dated 24 December 1666, by Donneau de Visé, who had certainly not this time wished to offend. Molière had the edition as far as possible destroyed, although the preface contained some perceptive as well as flattering criticism, and although the personal relationships between the two do not seem to have in any real way again deteriorated. Whatever may have happened, it was with Donneau de Visé's one-act verse comedy *La Veuve à la mode* that on 15 May 1667 Molière tried to prop up the faltering fortunes of Pierre Corneille's *Attila*. Robinet was complimentary, but the box office was poor, successively 252, 83, 200, 200, 78 and 64 livres. The comedy's anonymous publication by Ribou, with an achevé d'imprimer of 15 December 1667, was noted by Robinet on 28 January 1668.

Later in 1667, on 28 October, Molière had presented at the Palais-Royal Donneau de Visé's pastorale *Délie*, published with an exceedingly fulsome dedicatory eulogy of the king. A command performance had already taken place on 7 November at Versailles, and Robinet was even more complimentary than usual. Donneau de Visé followed this success with a short one-act verse comedy, *L'Embarras de Godard; ou, L'Accouchée*, played on 9 November at court, and on 18 November. On 12 November Robinet was again congratulatory about the court performance. *Délie* and *L'Embarras* were published by Ribou on 10 and 24 January 1668. For Donneau de Visé, his in fact rather poor and occasionally simply gross comedies were a means ultimately to social success, probably even to achieving the esteem which would justify his reasonably elevated social rank. Dramatic authorship, if not the theatre itself, was slowly becoming acceptable as a diversion if not yet, in spite of Molière, quite as a calling.

Neither Pierre Corneille nor Racine, both of whom were touchy about the success of their plays, was quite committed to dramatic authorship as a profession. Donneau de Visé, having successfully striven to get himself known by his controversial stances and noticed at court, thereafter using his successes at Versailles to stimulate interest in Paris, now took advantage of the king's departure to support the victorious Condé in Franche-Comté and published through Mabre-Cramoisy a luxury 12-page quarto called *Dialogue sur le voyage du Roi en Franche-Comté*, an allegorical poem in dialogue form. He followed it with a slightly better four-page poem put out by the same publishers, and also in the formal quarto size, *La France au Roi sur le sujet de la Paix*.

There seems now to have been another quarrel with Molière. On 11 January 1668 Molière played Donneau de Visé's *Les Maux sans remèdes*. The box office takings were good at 528 livres, Robinet was enthusiastic on 12 January, and on 13 the second performance brought in 380 livres. There was no third performance, and Molière did not play another Donneau de Visé work, not even the successful ones in the repertoire, until *Les Maris infidèles* of 24 January 1673. Donneau de Visé did not publish it, and his plays were henceforward to be put on at the Marais. In the meanwhile Donneau de Visé turned back to the nouvelle, publishing with Gabriel Quinet early in February 1669 a series of three duodecimo volumes, *Les Nouvelles galantes, comiques et tragiques*. In November 1669 he published with Thomas Jolly a further series of 40 nouvelles in three volumes, *L'Amour échappé; ou, Les Diverses Manières d'aimer contenues en quarante histoires, avec Le Parlement d'amour*. It was a series of portraits with a key.

He returned to the theatre on 2 March 1670 with a five-act free verse tragedy with stage machinery at the Marais, *Les Amours de Vénus et d'Adonis*. Racine, whose *Britannicus* had been played the preceding December, had not yet established his own form of tragedy as normative, but Donneau de Visé's, in spite of a lengthy eulogy by Robinet, was setting sail in exactly the opposite direction. Far from the tight analysis of the dilemmas of passion, Donneau de Visé irreverently presents us with Mars and Adonis as rivals for the heart of Vénus, played by the notoriously beautiful Mme Champmeslé. Donneau de Visé was also no doubt helped to achieve his effect by the music of Charpentier.

The continued mythologization of passion is no doubt a way to suggest that it was not, after all, as threatening as Racine was beginning to suggest it might be, but it does not make for riveting tragedy, and at the precise date of 1670, a decade after the exaggerations of préciosité (q.v.) had been discarded, but still a decade before it would be possible to examine seriously whether the partisans of the "modernes" were exploring an important new set of attitudes and values, it was not well calculated to avoid the impression of triviality. Chryséis, who loves Adonis, ends up responsible for his death, but Donneau de Visé makes almost nothing of her interior conflict. Vénus is certainly either a goddess or a mere mortal, and therefore improbable as both. Barbin published the play in June 1670.

In August 1670 Donneau de Visé had the one-act verse comedy *Le Gentilhomme Guespin* put on at the Marais, perhaps to rival Montfleury's *Gentilhomme de Beauce* at the Hôtel de Bourgogne. He also had staged at the Marais on 17 August 1670 the three-act verse comedy *Les Intrigues de la loterie*, indicating the move towards social satire which would help to make the patronizing fashion pages of *Le Mercure Galant* so popular. However, he returned to the successful formula of a tragedy using stage machinery with the five-act mythological verse tragedy, *Les Amours du Soleil*, using Thomas Corneille's translation of Ovid and presented on 6 February 1671. Robinet, who had announced it on 31 January and again mentioned it on 28 February, was lost in admiration on 7 March for the expert use of complicated hoists and swings. The décor, specified by Donneau de Visé, was particularly magnificent, and was itself probably the major cause of the piece's protracted success.

It was followed by another spectacular, a three-act heroic comedy in free verse with music, *Le Mariage de Bacchus et d'Ariane*, presented on 7 January 1672. Again, as Robinet pointed out on 30 January, the success was chiefly due to the décor. Thomas Corneille used the same theme for his *Ariane* given on 4 March at the Hôtel de Bourgogne, to whose company Mme Champmeslé had now moved, and where it followed Racine's *Bajazet*. This was the year of the foundation of the *Mercure Galant*, to which Donneau de Visé was henceforward to devote most of his energies. Although the *Mercure* has its own entry in the *Guide*, it is important with regard to Donneau de Visé's personal career to note that the coolly sarcastic review of Racine's *Bajazet* "qui passa pour un ouvrage admirable (which was thought to be an admirable play)" first performed on 5 January 1672, was dated 9 January, although it refers to the play's preface—"à ce que l'auteur rapporte dans sa préface (according to what the author says in his preface)"—known only when the play was published on 20 February. Donneau de Visé evidently had an advanced manuscript of a preface written by a hostile rival. Meanwhile he of course agrees with his tongue in his cheek that Racine must belong somewhere between Sophocles and Euripides.

Donneau de Visé is complimentary about the rival *Ariane* by Thomas Corneille, and also about Molière's *Les Femmes savantes*, played on 11 March. Lulli's closeness to the king makes Donneau de Visé cautious about any denunciation of Lulli's graspingly egotistical behaviour in obtaining and exploiting his musical monopoly (see: Molière). In a piece of apparently impartial reporting that summer, Donneau de Visé makes quite clear his approbation of the work of both Corneille brothers, and of Molière, while writing with a touch of sarcastic disdain that no doubt Racine's *Mithridate* will be a success, because "les pièces de cet auteur ont toujours eu beaucoup d'amis (because that author's plays have always had many friends)."

Molière did put on Donneau de Visé's *Les Maris infidèles* on 24 January 1673, but it failed as soon as it became known that it was not by Molière. There were four performances, with box-office receipts successively of 893, 645, 599 and 179 livres. Meanwhile the Hôtel de Bourgogne had commissioned a *Mari infidèle* from the actor-dramatist known as Hauteroche, and Donneau de Visé had a difficult time in the *Mercure* explaining away the failures of Pierre Corneille's *Pulchérie*, about which Mme de Sévigné was blunt on 24 February 1673, and of Thomas Corneille's *Théodat*, and the success of Racine's *Mithridate*: "il ne lui est pas moins permis de changer la vérité des histoires anciennes pour faire un ouvrage agréable, qu'il lui a été d'habiller à la Turque nos amants et nos amantes (he is no less permitted to change the truth of antique history to make an agreeable work than he was to dress up our lovers and their ladies as Turks)."

Shortly after Molière's death, the Marais company merged on 9 July 1673 with Molière's to become the Guénégaud company, named after the road opposite which stood the building that had lodged the opera since 1669 and where there was already elaborate stage machinery. Thomas Corneille moved there from the Hôtel de Bourgogne for his *La Mort d'Achille*, played on 29 December 1673, and it is there that Thomas Corneille and Donneau de Visé collaborated on *Circé*. The expense of the projected production caused trouble in the newly amalgamated company, and it was only after quarrels and compromises that the first performance took place on 17 March 1674. Prices were doubled for the first nine performances, for which the box-office takings averaged 2,650 livres. After Easter a series of 13 performances brought in on average 1,100 livres, and the 54 further performances up to 15 October brought in an average of 500 to 700 livres.

Circé was immediately followed by another collaborative script by Donneau de Visé and Thomas Corneille, the five-act verse comedy *L'Inconnu*, with a prologue and songs in free verse and also with music by Charpentier, presented on 17 November at the theatre of the rue Guénégaud. Much less successful than *Circé*, *L'Inconnu* none the less averaged takings of 1,000 livres for its first run of 28 performances. The re-launching of the *Mercure* in 1677 absorbed much of Donneau de Visé's time, but in collaboration with Thomas Corneille he profited in the five-act prose comedy *Le Devineresse* from the current enormous public interest in fortune-telling and its darker associated practices: poisoning, black masses, abortion, and the sale of philtres and potions, mostly for sexual purposes.

The scandal was enormous: even Mme de Montespan was involved, and Louis XIV was clearly frightened by the list of names that at one time seemed likely to emerge if those arraigned before the special court set up on 10 April 1679 were pressed into confessing too freely. There were 210 sessions of the court up to 21 July 1682, 442 indictments, 218 condemnations, and 36 executions, although the highest and the not the least guilty were allowed to escape arrest. But on 12 March 1679 Catherine Deshayes, Mme Monvoisin, called "la Voisin," the most expensive and best known of all the fortune-tellers and suppliers of philtres and poisons, was arrested on leaving Mass. She was finally burnt on the Place de Grève on 22 February 1680. The first night of *La Devineresse* was in the middle of the trial, on 19 November 1679. Prices were doubled for the first 18 performances, and the takings for the first night were 1,276 livres and the average for the 46 performances to 10 March 1680 was around 1,000 livres. The play's authorization is mysterious. The risk of compromising people in high places was so great that no public allusion to the case was permitted, and no mention of it occurs in either the *Gazette* or the *Mercure*. It seems clear that the play, avoiding mention of poison, obtained official backing because it portrayed the fortune-teller, Mme Jobin, as a mere trickster. The interest is concentrated not on the characters or the intrigue, but on the trickery.

Surprisingly, the next collaborative attempt by Donneau de Visé and Thomas Corneille to provide the public with what it wanted, the five-act prose *La Pierre philosophale*, was a disastrous failure on 23 February 1681. The first performance brought in 1,794 livres, the second, 398, and there were no others. The play appears never to have been published. Late in 1681 and early in 1682 the formal contract was drawn up, agreed, and registered which made Donneau de Visé and Thomas Corneille jointly editors of the *Mercure*, and the two authors collaborated on a five-act comedy, *L'Usurier*, which was

successful on 13 February 1685, with box-office takings from 1,477 livres to 345 for the nine performances. It was apparently audacious enough on the subject of bankers to have been discreetly suppressed. It was never published.

The date at which Donneau de Visé was actually nominated royal historiographer is uncertain, although it cannot have been before 1698, but he was certainly granted accommodation in the Louvre, one of the normal perquisites of the post, and his eulogies of the king and his exploits accelerated from June 1684, usually in annexes to the *Mercure*. They are so extravagant that no one can have taken them seriously, and certainly not the king: flattery of the monarch had become a specialized art form, not of course confined to literature. Since the literary merit of these pieces is not often high, it is sufficient here to note that, especially on the king's recovery from his celebrated operation in 1687, the *Mercure* published a long *Relation de la réception de Louis XIV à Paris*, of which the king was given a luxuriously bound quarto presentation copy. The obsequiousness knew no bounds. Donneau de Visé could not even overlook the chance to praise the presentation of Racine's *Esther* when it was performed at Saint-Cyr in 1689. Its author, however much an enemy, was historiographer of the king and treasurer of France, and Donneau de Visé was too sharp to miss any chance to swing his thurible at the achievement of a king's favourite, even when the favourite was Racine. Indeed, when the following December Racine was made a gentilhomme ordinaire, the *Mercure* once more presented its genuflexion. By 1 February 1691 Donneau de Visé's liturgical homage to the king was bringing him in a pension of 12,000 livres a year.

In 1690 Donneau de Visé wrote a five-act comedy called *L'Illustre Aventurier; ou, Le Prince travesti*, which he had the greatest difficulty in getting the players to accept. After an exchange of increasingly acrimonious letters, in which Donneau showed an uncharacteristic willingness to climb down, the piece was eventually played, but not until 2 January 1696, and then it lasted for only a single performance. The reluctance of the company, and the outcome, make it look as if the matter is connected with the previous dramatic criticism of the *Mercure*, the sudden rise of hissing, and the power of the cabales. Whatever may have happened, the *Mercure* announced that from December 1694, it would limit its coverage of the theatre to announcements of what was going to be played. It was a promise kept only fleetingly, but as an expression of audience disapproval yawning had given way to hissing in 1685–86; spies had been appointed to detect and delate hissers; Donneau de Visé condemned the practice in the *Mercure* in 1694; by 1696, the police were being severe on hissers; and the practice had temporarily disappeared by 1700.

Donneau de Visé's next piece, *Les Dames vengées; ou, La Dupe de soi-même*, was announced in the *Mercure* for December 1694. It was in fact a reply to Boileau's satire—*Satire X*—against women written in 1688 but published only earlier in 1694, and was essentially still part of the Querelle des anciens et des modernes (q.v.). That its quality was higher than that of preceding plays by Donneau de Visé was noticed by the brothers Parfaict in the 1748 *Histoire du Théâtre français*, but its reception none the less disappointed Donneau de Visé when it was first played on 22 February 1695 and 15 times more before Easter. The reaction of the company and the public made clear that he could never, as he had hoped, become Molière's successor. He did however succeed in getting accepted *Le Vieillard couru; ou, Les Différents Caractères des femmes*, played on 24

March 1696, but only twice thereafter. It was never printed. The Guénégaud minuted in 1697 Donneau de Visé's undoubtedly involuntary retirement.

Boileau and Racine were royal historiographers, and it was no doubt Donneau de Visé's desire to share that title that drove him to compile, on the basis of what the *Mercure* had already published, the three large folio volumes of the *Mémoires pour servir à l'histoire de Louis le Grand* published on 3 December 1697. The last of the remaining seven volumes had all appeared by January 1703. In 1698 Donneau de Visé married again, the young daughter, Marie-Catherine, of the sculptor Le Hongre, and was both harshly and personally attacked by François Gacon, prior of Baillon. Donneau de Visé had him put in prison by lettre de cachet. He resented above all accusations of venality against the *Mercure*, but the imprisonment provoked a personal attack on what was alleged to be the questionable nobility of his origins, his wife's lowly social status, and his money-grabbing attitude to his professional activities. Donneau de Visé replied in the *Mercure* for February 1699.

By the end of the century the *Mercure* had practically become the journal of the court. Donneau de Visé's sight was declining, and by 1706 he was blind. Thomas Corneille, himself blind since 1704, had given up cooperation with the *Mercure* in the late 1890s. As late as 1706 the *Mercure* was still trying to shore up confidence in the king's catastrophic Dutch wars. Thomas Corneille died on 8 December 1709. Donneau de Visé himself died on 8 July 1710.

WORKS

A great deal of what Donneau de Visé wrote appeared in the *Mercure Galant* (q.v.). Much of it was critical or satirical, much more or less factual reporting, and a good deal either deferred to Donneau de Visé's desire to make a reputation for himself, particularly in the literary world, or constituted formal exercises in sycophancy in the interest of promoting his chances of preferment. None the less, Donneau de Visé's work as editor and journalist was immensely important in promoting the gestation of the radically new confidence in human nature which was to characterize the 18th century and which had ultimately been at stake in the Querelle des anciens et des modernes (q.v.). The paradox that the works themselves, including those by Donneau de Visé, which explored the new trust in instinct, were less imaginatively fraught in content and more flamboyant in literary register than those seeking refuge in severe, rigorous, and irreformable norms is easily resolved. The values and attitudes on the whole favourably examined by the partisans of the anciens demanded a formal constraint and an emotional intensity which would have clashed with the rococo style already visibly developing in the paintings of Mignard, Largillière, and Watteau, and most of the official architecture commissioned under Louvois.

Given the relaxed confidence in nature characteristic of the attitudes which interested him, it was essential for Donneau de Visé, as for so many others, to use theatrical forms favouring spectacle and display, splendour and ingenuity, over the declamatory rhetoric and emotional tautness of Racine. Aesthetically, the production of Donneau de Visé was bound to appear lacking in rigour and restraint, unelevated by the heights of passion. The real difficulty is to assess how far the serious imaginative need for flamboyance, for bewildering changes of scenery, for impressive flights up from and descents down to the stage, for the extravagant use of stage machinery and marvellous effects which, like setting fire to Wagner's Rhine in a later century, necessarily and no doubt happily took the theatre down market, may be thought to compensate for Donneau de Visé's vulgarity, occasional coarseness, and lack of either poetic or strictly dramatic talent.

The first performance of *Circé*, put on by the Marais company after Molière's death and the absorption at the Marais of the remainder of his company, took place on Sunday 17 March 1675. There can be little doubt that the cause of the successes of Donneau and his poetically more gifted colleague, Thomas Corneille, was not the entertainments' librettos, but the sumptuous costumes, the striking changes of scenery, the ballets, dancing, songs, and the brilliance of the effects. The Marais company's reputation at this date was largely founded on its ingenious use of swings and hoists, and stunts like mid-air duets and conversations on cloud-tops. Reliance on the staging must have been greater in the case of *Circé* because the only real interest of the text is the chance it gives for showing the effect of the magic spells cast by Circé on Glaucus, who is in love with Sylla, of whom Circé is jealous. Sylla herself is saved by Jupiter who makes her a nereid. The music was by Charpentier, but Lulli's monopoly was by now in force. Bayle in a letter to his brother of 24 June 1675 laments the effect of the limits imposed by the monopoly on the music and dancing. Without the monopoly, Bayle thought, this would have been the greatest opera yet seen, a view clearly shared by its part author, Donneau de Visé.

All we have to help us reconstruct Donneau de Visé's greatest artistic achievements are the bare scripts, and that would not be enough, even if we knew exactly what notes by Charpentier or Louis Mollier were played, on what instruments, what the décors actually looked like, and how many there were. We know, for instance, that there were in the 1671 *Les Amours du Soleil* 13 changes of décor and 24 flights. Vénus, disturbed in her intimacy with Mars by Apollon, decides to avenge herself, and inspires in Apollon a love for Leucothoé, for whom Apollon deserts Clitie, the daughter of Thétis and L'Océan. Leucothoé is denounced to her father who has her buried alive. Apollon cannot resurrect her and metamorphoses her into an incense-bearing tree. Clitie dies and is changed into a flower which opens itself to the sun and closes at night. The mythological plot is an almost impertinently confident affirmation of the power of love, an excuse for extravagance, spectacle, the exuberant expression of radiant joy. The script must have been the weakest part of the entertainment, of whose fifth act Donneau de Visé wrote,

> Tout le Théâtre se change en un théâtre de nues, et la porte d'argent du Palais de ce Dieu [Apollon] paraît comme Ovide la dépeint. La mer est gravée dessus, et les Tritons et le Zodiaque se voient tout autour…On aperçoit d'abord sur les amas de nuages les Heures, les Jours et les Mois, qui ont coutume d'accompagner le Soleil, et le Temps paraît au milieu, avec sa faux et son horloge. On voit de grandes clartés qui semblent se détacher… L'Amour s'envole en se précipitant; puis il va dans le cintre, en se relevant tout d'un coup, lorsqu'on croit qu'il va s'arrêter à terre. Ce vol est extraordinaire

> (The whole scene changes to a décor of clouds, and the silver gate of the palace of the god appears as Ovid depicts it. The sea is painted, and around it are seen the Tritons and

the Zodiac. First to be seen on the pile of clouds are the Hours, the Days, and the Months, who usually accompany the sun, and Time appears in the middle, with his scythe and his clock. Great shafts of light seem to come forth... Love swoops down in a rush, then suddenly shoots up into the flies, just when you think he is going to land. The flight is extraordinary).

Donneau de Visé was the master designer of a theatrical experience. At the date of *Les Amours du soleil*, Lulli had not yet fully established an unchallenged title to equality, let alone supremacy, for the composer over the author but, even if the company had not employed a composer and used musicians, it would clearly be unreasonable to look for the same passionate intensity in the spoken text written for such an entertainment as might be sought from the text of one of Racine's declamatory, emotional tragedies. Inevitably, historians of literature have paid too little attention to the Marais company's staging, and over-emphasized the superiority of the repertory of the Hôtel de Bourgogne, which more largely depended on the quality of the texts.

Le Veuve à la mode is a one-act verse comedy first played by Molière's troupe during the period of the reconciliation between Molière and Donneau de Visé, but after the short cooling of their relationship that followed the incident of the preface to Molière's *Le Misanthrope*. Molière used it as a programme-filler, but its drawing power at the box office was never great. After its anonymous publication, with an achevé d'imprimer of 15 December 1667, noticed by Robinet on 28 January 1668, there was a counterfeit edition. The comedy is notable for its realism, and for the touch of satire. How is death regarded in petit bourgeois Paris, and how does one set about everything connected with it? Cléon is dying. The valet Crispin is sent for a doctor, but he takes too long getting up and getting ready, and Cléon dies. What follows is a series of tableaux in which the young widow Miris is counselled by her sister Orphise and her servant Béatrix. Alcipe, a man of affairs, advises her to marry Cléon's nephew and heir, Clidamis. Miris affects intense mourning while her mind is on saving what she can of the inheritance. The undertaker's men call, then the commissaire sent to put the seals on all Cléon's possessions. Fortunately Clidamis loves Miris, so that the act of preserving the inheritance is identical with the act of surrendering to a lover's homage.

The interest is in the mockery of the affectations to which such situations oblige everyone, and the contrast of the macabre with the comic. There is skill in the stage writing: a single alexandrine is broken into five speeches parodying the tragic device to be used to such different effect by Racine; fun is made of the servant—"What! the poor deceased is now dead?"; the dead man's housekeeper uses patois forms—"Cent guièbles (a hundred devils)"; and above all there is the satire, apparent in the title, "The fashionable widow,"

On doit toujours pleurer quand on perd un époux

(You must always cry when you lose a husband).

PUBLICATIONS

Gazettes

Le Mercure Galant, 6 vols., 1672–74
Le Nouveau Mercure Galant, 10 vols., 1677

Mercure Galant, 417 volumes, 1678–1710
Extraordinaire du Mercure, 32 vols., 1678–85

Fiction

Nouvelles nouvelles, 1663
Les Diversités galantes, 1664; augmented 1665
Les Nouvelles galantes, comiques et tragiques, 3 vols., 1669
L'Amour échappé; ou, Les Diverses Manières d'aimer, 3 vols., 1669

Plays

Zélinde, comédie; ou, La Véritable Critique de "L'Ecole des femmes" et la Critique de "La Critique", (not staged) 1663
La Mère coquette; ou, Les Amants brouillés, comédie, (1665) 1666; critical edition 1940
Le Veuve à la mode, comédie, (1667) 1668; critical edition 1940; in *Théâtre du XVIIe siècle*, vol. 2, Bibliothèque de la Pléiade, 1986
Délie, pastorale, (1667) 1668
L'Embarras de Godard; ou, L'Accouchée, comédie, (1667) 1668
Les Amours de Vénus et d'Adonis, tragédie, (1670) 1670
Le Gentilhomme Guespin, comédie, (1670) 1670
Les Intrigues de la loterie, comédie, (1670) no date
Les Amours du Soleil, tragédie en machines, (1671), 1671
Le Mariage de Bacchus et d'Ariane, comédie héroïque, (1672) 1672
Circé, tragédie ornée de machines, (1674) 1675; critical edition, 1989
L'Inconnu, comédie mêlée d'ornements, (1674) 1675
La Devineresse; ou, Les Faux Enchantements, comédie, (1679), 1680
Argument de la pierre philosophale, comédie mêlée de spectacles, (1681) 1681
Les Dames vengés; ou, La Dupe de soi-même, (1695) 1695; critical edition 1940

Other

Défense de la Sophonisbe de M. de Corneille, 1663
Défense du Sertorius de M. de Corneille, 1663
Dialogue sur le voyage du roi dans la Franche-Comté, 1668
La France au roi sur le sujet de la paix, 1668
Eloge de Mgr le Dauphin, 1689
Mémoires pour servir à l'histoire de Louis le Grand, 10 vols., 1697–1703
Epître au roi de la Grande-Bretagne, 1703

Biographical and critical studies

Mélèse, Pierre, *Un homme de lettres au temps du grand roi, Donneau de Visé, fondateur du Mercure Galant*, 1936

DU BELLAY, Joachim, 1524–1560.

Poet.

LIFE

It is arguable that, given his largely elegiac poetic temperament, his grand family name, his early death, and the probability that the 1549 *Deffence et illustration de la langue françoyse* was a work of corporate inspiration, however personal its style, du Bellay's historical importance is greater than his poetic stature. He was certainly at the heart of the poetic revolution in renaissance France (see: Pléiade, La), and may at first have contributed more to it than did Ronsard, with whom his name is perpetually associated. Unhappily, comparatively little is known about du Bellay's life, although enough to make clear that it is unsafe to confuse the persona adopted by the poet with the real person.

Du Bellay's contemporaries may merely have been flattering him in acknowledging the early medieval origins to which his family pretended. It came into prominence in the 15th and, above all, the 16th century with a succession of army commanders, diplomats, and bishops. The name came from a small estate near Saumur. The younger branch, the seigneurs de Langey, produced the cardinal Jean du Bellay, who wrote Latin verse, his three brothers, Guillaume, the general and governor of Piedmont under François I, René, the bishop of Le Mans, and Martin. René and Martin both left memoirs. Du Bellay himself belonged to the senior branch, and was their cousin. His father, Jean, the third son of Eustache du Bellay and Catherine de Beaumont, sister of the bishop of Paris, studied at the Collège de Navarre, having been intended for the priesthood, but, instead of becoming a priest, on 12 October 1504 he married the 14-year-old orphan and heiress Renée Chabot.

They had a daughter, who married, and three sons, the spendthrift René, born in 1508, Jean, of whom nothing is known, and Joachim, who was born at the château de la Turmelière on the Loire. Not even the year date is quite certain. The traditional 1522 is perfectly possible, but less likely than 1524. Joachim was sickly at birth, and was never robust. His health deteriorated, probably from late in 1549, when he was ill for two years, apparently with a tubercular condition, on account of excessive study if Pierre de Paschal is to be believed. Both his parents died sometime before he was nine, and du Bellay later repeatedly complained that his eldest brother, recently married to Madeleine de Malestroit, neglected his instruction.

How du Bellay spent his youth can only be conjectured, although everything suggests that his upbringing was more suited to turning him into a country squire than anything else. The likelihood, given the family background, is that he was destined to some form of public career, probably administrative or diplomatic, built on an ecclesiastical or military foundation. It is certain, in view of his eligibility for benefices, that he received the tonsure and, even without ordination to the priesthood, there was a serious possibility, reported by Scévole de Sainte-Marthe, that his cousin Jean, a cardinal from 1535 and in 1555 a serious candidate for the papacy, might have arranged his appointment to the archbishopric of Bordeaux. Any idea of a military career was presumably abandoned well before du Bellay's health first gave way, when his cousin Guillaume, a diplomat as well as a general, died on 9 January 1543 attended by his doctor, who was Rabelais.

Du Bellay must have learnt Latin and, by the mid-1540s, he was studying law at Poitiers, whose university already had about 4,000 students and was an important centre for the study of civil law. Marc-Antoine Muret, later a regent at the Collège de Boncourt in Paris, joined him there a year or two later. Like Muret, du Bellay may well have devoted himself more to letters and the new learning than to the study of law. He must soon have begun to write verse, probably at first in Latin, and then in the style of the "grands rhétoriqueurs." We know from an epitaph that he admired Marot. He knew Salmon Macrin, and in 1546 he met Jacques Peletier du Mans, who was five years older than him. From 1540 to 1543 Peletier had been the secretary of René du Bellay, bishop of Le Mans, and it was he who persuaded Joachim to choose as poetic forms the sonnet and the ode. Peletier had recently published his translation of Horace's *Ars poetica*, with a dedication arguing in favour of the vernacular which contains in embryo the teaching of the 1549 *Deffence*.

The only authority for the chance meeting between Ronsard and du Bellay in an inn is Claude Binet. He mentions it only in the third 1597 text of his life of Ronsard, not in 1586 or 1587, and the date he gives is certainly wrong. But whenever and wherever the pair did meet, they were bound by a distant family relationship; a community of interest in poetry and especially the Latin odes; a number of mutual friends, since Ronsard had been in Italy with du Bellay's cousin Guillaume; and a shared friendship and admiration for Peletier. Du Bellay certainly joined Baïf and Ronsard at the Collège de Coqueret soon after they moved there, with Dorat as principal, for the academic year starting in 1547. It may well have been above all Peletier who attracted du Bellay to Paris. That year Peletier demitted the principalship of the Collège de Bayeux, which he owed to the patronage of René du Bellay and had held since 6 November 1543, delivered at Notre Dame the funeral oration of Henry VIII of England, and published *Les Oeuvres poëtiques de Jacques Peletier du Mans*, with a privilège dated 1 September and containing an epigram by du Bellay as well as an ode by Ronsard. He had already taken the most important positions, especially in relationship to the adornment and development of the vernacular, later to be adopted by du Bellay in the *Deffence*.

Du Bellay was to stay at Coqueret until 1553, absorbing a knowledge and love of Greek poetry as interpreted by Dorat, but also reading widely in often Petrarchan Italian verse, currently popular enough to be anthologized in the well-known collection of *Rime diverse* of Gabriel Giolito, published from 1545 to 1549. Du Bellay was less advanced in Greek than Baïf and Ronsard, and a more faithful disciple of Peletier, nourishing himself above all on the Latin tradition pre-eminently represented by Horace and on modern Italian verse, and taking the lead in the group's commitment to restoring the glories of the vernacular by imitating and rivalling the achievements of the poets of classical antiquity. The trio were inspired by Dorat's erudition and enthusiasm, although the unsureness of Dorat's own poetic tastes and talents made him as uncertain a guide to the fulfilment of the young group of poets' ambitions as he was sure of touch in providing them with encouragement.

Born with the name Dinemandi in 1508 in Limoges, and from early youth moving in humanist circles, Dorat had been made Jean-Antoine de Baïf's tutor in 1544, had moved to Coqueret in 1547 on the death of Lazare de Baïf, the poet's father, and had married Marguerite de Laval, who was to bear him two children, on 21 December 1548. Dorat was briefly to be tutor to the children of Henri II before becoming the royal professor of Greek in 1556, a position which was taken over by his son-in-law Nicolas Goulu in 1567. He was enumerated in Ronsard's list of six companions only in the final list transmitted after Ronsard's death by Binet. He replaced Peletier, who had died in 1582, having himself again become a private tutor and apparently experienced financial hardship. At 77 or 78 Dorat remarried. His bride was just 19 and bore him a son. He died in 1588.

Du Bellay, Baïf, and Ronsard had not yet formed a coherent group with their like-minded contemporaries from the Collège de Boncourt, Belleau, Jodelle, and La Péruse, when in the summer of 1548 an anonymous pamphlet appeared with a privilège of 25 June, the *Art poetique françois*, whose author was quickly identified as the lawyer Thomas Sebillet. Sebillet's tract not only emancipated poetry from its previous status as a "second rhetoric," subject only to a special set of rules, by insisting on its inspired and religious historical origins and on the priestly status of the poet as seer, prophet, and mediator of cosmic knowledge, but also advocated the study of the great poets of antiquity only as models alongside Marot, Scève, Salel, Saint-Gelais, and others from the rhétoriqueur tradition. In other words Sebillet prematurely enunciated the most important components of the programme being elaborated by the Coqueret group, while at the same time minimizing its revolutionary radicalism.

Du Bellay, certainly helped in particular by Ronsard, whose assistance he was fulsomely to acknowledge in the preface to the 1550 *L'Olive augmentée*, turned what had been intended as a simple epistle into a pamphlet and took out a privilège on 20 March 1549 for the *Deffence et illustration de la langue françoyse*, dedicated to his cousin the cardinal, together with another volume, published simultaneously on about 21 April, called *L'Olive et quelques autre oeuvres poeticques*, containing "Cinquante sonnetz á la louange de l'Olive," an invective poem, "L'Antérotique de la vieille et de la jeune amye," and a collection of "Vers lyriques," containing 13 odes. Both volumes were signed with the easily penetrable initials I.D.B.A. (Joachim du Bellay, Angevin). Together they moved powerfully towards the implementation of Peletier's programme.

Two months later, for Henri II's solemn entry into Paris on Sunday 16 June, du Bellay published *La Prosphonematique*, a song of welcome in 216 decasyllabic lines split into groups of six. By the end of 1549 du Bellay's health must have been beginning to break down, leading, in spite of an apparent cure celebrated by Ronsard in a poem, to a relapse late in 1550 and the speedy onset of deafness. In the meanwhile, however, in November 1549 du Bellay had published in the *Recueil de poésie* dedicated to the king's sister, Madame Marguerite, duchesse de Berry, the reprinted *La Prosphonematique*, a "Chant triumphal sur le voyage de Boulongne," a court piece prematurely celebrating the success of Henri II's failed effort to retake Boulogne from the English, and 16 new odes.

With a privilège of 3 October 1550 du Bellay published an expanded *L'Olive augmentée*, now containing an important polemical preface defending the *Deffence* against the attacks which had been made against it, what were now the 115 decasyllabic sonnets of the love cycle, together with *La Musagnoeomachie*, 43 12-line strophes in heptasyllables on the battle between the Muses and ignorance, followed by five new odes. *La Musagnoeomachie* is derived from the fourth-century parody of Homer known as the *Batrachomyomachia* and is intended to

restate the roll-call of poets favoured by the Muses, including Saint-Gelais, Héroët, Rabelais, Scève, Salel, Peletier, Jean Martin, Maclou de la Haye, Macrin, Tyard, and Pierre de Paschal, led by Lazare de Baïf and Dorat.

We know very little about any possible real-life "Olive," although there has been much speculation on the subject. The fifth sonnet, clearly modelled on Petrarch, with the tercets translated from Ariosto, announces that the poet was struck with love for his lady at midnight Mass one Christmas, no doubt an oblique allusion to Petrarch's meeting with Laura in the Avignon church at the Good Friday service on 6 April 1327. There probably was a girl who served as the stepping stone for du Bellay's idealization, but there is no evidence that she played any other part in his life. She may have been a cousin. During 1551 du Bellay published only one slight piece in the *Tombeau de Marguerite de Valois, royne de Navarre*. He was ill and much concerned by the guardianship of his nephew Claude, left an orphan at the age of 11 when du Bellay's brother René died on 15 June 1551, having already lost his mother in 1548. Du Bellay was to be involved until the end of his life in legal disputes about the family fiefdom of his late sister-in-law, confiscated from her brothers for counterfeiting, but returned, sold, and bought back by du Bellay's brother, although still claimed by his wife's family.

The *Deffence* had disparaged mere translations as a way of enriching the language, and in November 1549 Sebillet, who not surprisingly felt himself under attack from the group of which du Bellay was clearly the spokesman and Ronsard the leader, published a translation from Greek of Euripides' *Iphigénie* with a preface attacking the *Deffence*'s aristocratic conception of poetry and returning to the praise of Marot. In February or March 1550 Barthélemy Aneau, a fervent admirer and imitator of Marot and principal of the Lyons Collège de la Trinité, published his anonymous *Quintil Horatian*, directing against du Bellay even sharper personal attacks than he had himself been guilty of in the *Deffence*. Aneau saw that the doctrine of glorification of French through the imitation of antiquity was anomalous, but went as far as making any innovation seem impossible, was luke-warm about Petrarch, and contemptuously dismissive of the poetic tradition deriving from him.

In August 1550 the Lyonnais poet Guillaume des Autels, cousin of Pontus de Tyard and enumerated by Ronsard among his list of six chosen companions in the 1553 "Elegie à Jean de la Péruse," but dropped in favour of Peletier in the 1552 "Hymne de Henri II," reproached du Bellay with his contempt for the rhétoriqueurs and the medieval poetic forms in his *Replique aux furieuses defenses de Louis Meigret*, issued in the course of a polemic against Meigret's proposals for orthographic reform. The 20-year-old des Autels, who referred to those who thought they had conquered "l'empire de l'encyclopedie des Muses (the empire of the Muses' encyclopedia)," attacked du Bellay's core enthusiasm for imitation over translation in favour of an originality more complete than even imitation admitted of.

Du Bellay's replies to the predictable attacks on the *Deffence* which he had done nothing to avoid provoking came with the long and disdainful preface to *L'Olive augmentée* of late 1550. In his ode to Ronsard "Contre les envieux poëtes," du Bellay unfairly both concedes to Ronsard the honour of reinstating the ode and keeps for himself the glory of restoring the sonnet. As with the quarrel about the sole pre-eminence of Cicero, a cause notoriously espoused by Christophe de Longueil and Etienne Dolet, and the 16th-century Querelle des femmes, it is important not to overlook either the real warmth of feeling generated by the polemic or the stylized register of invective on which it was conducted. In 1552 du Bellay became sincerely reconciled with Sebillet, to whom he later dedicated a sonnet, and in 1553 with des Autels, whose views had come to accord with those of du Bellay, and who wrote two poems to him. Du Bellay does not on the other hand seem to have responded to a compliment from Aneau in the 1556 *Metamorphose d'Ovide*.

In February 1552 du Bellay published a translation of the fourth book of the *Aeneid* and the seventh of Ovid's *Heroides*, followed by a series of *Oeuvres de l'invention de l'auteur*, including 12 new odes, reflecting the experience of his illness in their touch of bitterness and disillusion. To publish a translation was in some sense both a betrayal and an admission of defeat. The letter-preface to Jean Morel d'Embrun, however, reaffirms du Bellay's faith in his poetic vocation and refuses to regret that part of his life spent in the service of "le non moins honneste que plaisant exercice poëtique (the not less noble than agreeable exercise of poetry)." However, in the March 1553 second edition of the *Recueil de poésie*, before the French vogue for Petrarchism had really touched its various peaks, whether abstract, sensuous, or even simpering, du Bellay includes the poem "A une Dame," later to be transformed into the "Contre les Pétrarquistes" of the *Divers jeux rustiques*, a witty and elegant satire of the spiritualizing of love of the whole Petrarchan tradition. It does not, of course, eschew self-parody.

By 1553 the young Boncourt and Coqueret groups had established their community of interests. Muret and Dorat were friends. The Coqueret poets attended the carnival production, no doubt in the Boncourt quadrangle, of Jodelle's *Cléopâtre captive*, with La Péruse and Belleau in the leading parts. The next day the famous excursion to Arcueil took place. Du Bellay did not attend. His frequently expressed ambitions for a diplomatic career sponsored by his cousin the cardinal had finally been heeded, and he was invited to become a member of the cardinal's suite when he left for Rome on a mission for Henri II to Julius III in April 1553. During a stopover in Lyons du Bellay met Scève, Pontus de Tyard, and des Autels. Crossing the Alps brought on a serious recurrence of his illness, but he recovered, reaching Rome in the course of June. It seems probable that du Bellay immediately wrote the 32 sonnets of what he published only in 1558 as the first book of *Les Antiquitez de Rome, contenant une generale description de sa grandeur et comme une deploration de sa ruine*, followed by "Un songe ou vision," 15 more sonnets on the same subject. No second book was ever published, no doubt because disillusion with Rome destroyed any impulse to continue in the same vein.

Du Bellay's preface to *L'Olive augmentée* of 1550, while regretting nothing, had none the less expressed his willingness to abandon his poetic commitment for what he no doubt envisaged as a more public career. He had already parodied his own Petrarchan enthusiasm. In Rome, surrounded by Italian humanists vying to excel at Latin verse, du Bellay was to abandon his earlier principles and write poetry in Latin. During these years Ronsard, with whom du Bellay must be presumed to have stayed in close contact, was firmly basing his most elaborate work on the neo-Latin hymns of Marullus. It was probably between 1554 and 1557 that du Bellay also composed in contrast to his earlier Petrarchan sonnets the fresher, less mannered, and less artificial French verse he was later to publish as the 38 pieces of the *Divers jeux rustiques*.

In 1555 du Bellay began to compose the collection which no doubt contains his best verse, *Les Regrets*, finished only after his return to France in 1557. Of the 191 sonnets, 127 were written in Italy, 10 on the way home, and the rest after du Bellay's return. The disillusion seems to have set in only after almost three years, to have been gradual, if deep, and to have been the result of du Bellay's duties, principally arranging for credit, staving off creditors, postponing the repayment of debt, taking responsibility for the running of a household of over 100 heads, arranging for receptions, banquets, and presents, and himself attending on the cardinal on all ceremonial occasions as part of his court. Not even the cardinal's huge income from benefices could finance the expenses of fulfilling his functions as grandly as he did.

There was an acute shortage of cash, but du Bellay stylized his protests at the life of lobbying, dealing, nepotism, intransigence, and intrigue which constituted the way in which counter-reformatory Rome conducted its affairs, with the pope living in indolent luxury outside the Vatican, hoping most that he would be left in peace. What du Bellay had hoped for was more humanism, archaeology, paintings, poetry, and courtly pursuits. What he was doing was fobbing off creditors and fulfilling purely ceremonial functions. Julius III died on 23 March 1555. His successor, the saintly, learned, austere, and impressive 55-year-old Marcellus II, lived to occupy the papal throne for 21 days. He was succeeded by the 79-year-old Paul IV, an austere, prickly, disciplinarian monk, notorious for advancing at least one notable family brigand, his nephew Carlo Carafa, who was absolved from all previous crimes and made a cardinal on 7 June 1555, and put in charge of the secular politics of the Holy See. Like his uncle, he was intensely hispanophobic and hoped, through a temporary alliance with France, to rid the peninsula of all imperial forces.

On 19 June 1555 du Bellay had himself been made a canon of Notre-Dame in Paris, a benefice which he resigned for unknown reasons on 12 June 1556. In France, the court case about the Malestroit fief was going wrong. Du Bellay had left it in the hands of a priest friend, Claude de Bize, and of his own sister Catherine and her husband, Christophe du Breil, but his opponents had ceded their claim to the powerful Connétable Montmorency. Meanwhile du Bellay disliked the bustle of Roman life and the cynical corruption of the city's morals, from its peculation on top to the flagrant sexual provocations of its street life. He had a severe and prolonged attack of home-sickness. Something very similar was happening to his close friend and fellow poet Olivier de Magny, secretary to Jean de Saint-Marcel, seigneur d'Avanson, whose *Gayetez* of 1554 were followed by the *Souspirs* of 1557.

Du Bellay, however, after three years in Rome fell in love in the spring of 1556 with a certain Faustina, referred to as his "dove," with whom a passionate liaison can be assumed. She must have been Italian, and du Bellay's poems are in Latin. She was married, but seems to have been separated and to have been living with her mother. None the less, her husband took her away and shut her up in a convent, leaving du Bellay to dream poetically of carrying her off by the sword. He got her back, presumably without recourse to armed attack, and wrote a delightful Latin poem in which he rejoices about it. His cousin, now dean of the sacred college, may well have had wind of the relationship, and certainly sent du Bellay home towards the end of August 1557. Faustina was later to absorb the attentions of

Brantôme. For safety's sake du Bellay travelled at least as far as Civita-Vecchia by water, out of the way of François de Guise's not yet repulsed troops, called in by the pope, who had bypassed the cardinal to call on French help in removing the Spaniards.

Du Bellay had come to Rome along the "grand chemin royal (great royal road)" via Fontainebleau, Nevers, Moulins, and Lyons, but the cardinal's party, which had set out with 200 horse, had then chosen to cross the alps not by the easier Chambéry–Mont Cenis route, but, no doubt on account of the risk from hostile troops, via Geneva, Como, Bologna, and Florence. Du Bellay now returned via Ferrara, Venice, Verona, the Bernina pass, Geneva, Lyons, Mâcon, Dijon, and Sens. He had never been privy to the cardinal's properly diplomatic activities, although he ran his personal affairs. He was now entrusted by the cardinal with the most delicate and intimate of personal missions.

The decrees of the Council of Trent obliged the cardinal to divest himself of four bishoprics, Paris, Limoges, Bordeaux, and Le Mans, as well as a large number of lesser benefices, but he needed as much of their income as he could keep, and also as much of the power as could be used to generate income. He needed to accept what amounted to fees for expediting business, or appointing to vacant prebends and benefices. The support of the dean of the sacred college was powerful, financially valuable, and more or less for sale. Du Bellay was its day-to-day administrator in France, necessarily involved in the administration of dioceses, and necessarily treading on the toes of those of whose lucrative power to bestow favours the cardinal wished to retain a share. The cardinal had handed over the bishopric of Paris to a cousin, a counsellor of the Paris parlement, Eustache du Bellay, who now objected to having prebends in his diocese allocated by du Bellay in his cousin's name during his own absences from the capital. Du Bellay and Eustache's brother, Jacques du Bellay, baron de Thouarcé, thoroughly disliked one another, and one dispute about who had the right to nominate to a benefice attracted Thouarcé's interference, and was for a moment bitter.

There are only spates of correspondence, so that for long periods we do not know exactly what happened between du Bellay, the cardinal, and the bishop of Paris. In 1559 relations were tense. The cardinal had written of his displeasure at reading *Les Regrets* to the bishop of Toulon, who had sent on to du Bellay his cousin's letters. Du Bellay wrote back to his cousin and protector a dignified, disingenuous, and clever letter, alleging that the manuscript of *Les Regrets* had been printed several times from unauthorized leaked copies which had effectively forced him to publish himself. Views critical of Rome and its way of life had been only playfully expressed, and no insinuations about the cardinal himself were intended. The letter cannot have had much effect, since du Bellay received no reply and had to follow it with a further one, while his French relations continued to stir up trouble between the cardinal and himself. Peace within the family was eventually restored, and although we have some letters clearly written in a state of serious annoyance by various interested parties, and enough evidence to see that du Bellay's actions were not always intended to be eirenic, we cannot quite reconstruct the rights and wrongs of the accusations and protestations that were exchanged. It emerges that du Bellay himself, even when his relationship with the cardinal was nearest to breaking, was always amply provided for.

On his return the only one of his close associates to publish any sign of welcome was Dorat. Whatever the complexities which involved the resignation of the benefice in 1556, du Bellay on his return had some 3,000 livres a year from benefices bestowed on him by the cardinal, as well as the purely honorific title of protonotary apostolic. More lucrative were an arch-deaconry at Château-du-Loir, a priorship near Bordeaux, at Bardenay, and a canonry at Le Mans which du Bellay resigned on 1 April 1559. A further benefice near Le Mans suggests that it was there du Bellay intended to reside, although he in fact stayed with his friend Claude de Bize, now a canon, who owned a small but enviable property in the Notre-Dame cloister in Paris. In the nearby establishment of Jean Morel d'Embrun, du Bellay met Charles Utenhove, tutor to his friend's daughters, and probably also Jacques de la Taille and Jacques Grévin. The court case was finally resolved on 9 August 1559 and the property given up for a sum judged equitable. Du Bellay's nephew, who was to die in 1562, was grateful and made over to du Bellay an annual pension of 600 livres.

Les Regrets and *Divers jeux rustiques* were both published early in 1558 with a privilège of 17 January, and *Les Antiquitez* and the four books of Latin *Poemata* very soon afterwards, each with a privilège of 3 March. In 1559 du Bellay published the satirical *Poëte courtisan* at Poitiers in a plaquette entitled *La nouvelle maniere de faire son profit des lettres: traduitte de Latin en François par I. Quintil du Tronssay en Poictou. Ensemble le Poëte courtisan*. The first work in the plaquette, which was to be reprinted in a posthumous anthology of du Bellay's work by Federic Morel in Paris in 1560, is a translation by du Bellay of an anonymously published satirical épître of 1559 by Turnèbe, written to his friend Léger du Chesne and satirizing Pierre de Paschal. Paschal was regarded by Ronsard's group and their friends as too indolent for his post as royal historiographer, in which he was paid 1,200 livres a year for a history he did not write, three times as much as Turnèbe was paid as the royal professor of Greek. Du Bellay had been close to him, had greatly missed him, less only than Ronsard and Morel, while in Rome, and was later again to be reconciled with him. Paschal was also to write a famous epitaph for du Bellay.

Du Bellay's health, in spite of one further period of recovery, quickly worsened in 1559. The deafness which had been in remission now returned, and du Bellay was in bed when he wished to be at the farewell for Madame Marguerite in the autumn of 1559 after her marriage to the duc de Savoie, for which he published an *Epithalame*. It was during the entertainments laid on to celebrate that marriage and that of the king's daughter, Elisabeth de Valois, born in 1545, to Phillip II, the widower of Mary Tudor, that Henri II died as a result of a wound inflicted during a tournament. François II, his successor, was 15 and already married to Mary Stuart when he was crowned at Reims on 18 September 1559.

Michel de l'Hôpital wrote to the cardinal de Guise of Lorraine a long Latin verse epistle, which was a treatise on the education of a prince, *De sacra Francisci II Galliarum regis initiatione, regnique ipsius administrandi providentia Sermo*, published by Federic Morel in 1560, and du Bellay translated it as the *Discours sur le sacre du treschrestien Roy Françoys II, avec la forme de bien regner accommodée aux moeurs de ce royaume. Faict premierement en vers latins par Michel de l'Hospital, et mis en vers françois par J. du B.* The translation, turning 363 hexameters into 426 alexandrines and posthumously published by Morel in 1560, was du Bellay's last important work, although it inspired him to compose a much longer verse treatise of his own which he left unfinished, but in which he placed first among the king's duties the preservation of peace and pleaded for proper care for the working population, particularly the producers of food, the reform of taxation, the retrenchment of royal expenditure, and ecclesiastical reform. It is not unlikely that Ronsard knew du Bellay's unfinished and unpublished *Ample discours au Roy* when he himself later wrote the *Institution pour l'adolescence du Roy Charles IX*.

Before du Bellay died, the bishop of Paris wrote to his cousin cardinal du Bellay that communication with the now completely deaf poet had to be on paper, implicitly asking for him to be replaced. Du Bellay's illness must have been intermittent, since there are at least three mentions, probably deriving from a single source, of a convivial evening on 1 January 1560. Although it was by then very late, du Bellay had sat down afterwards to write, when he suffered the attack of apoplexy, which sounds from its description very much like a stroke, that killed him.

WORKS

Du Bellay's biography makes clear that, although he wrote charming and occasionally passionate Latin verse, and was in his youth overwhelmed by the impact of Horace, he was not as serious a scholar as Ronsard. It is plain that his susceptibilities were readily aroused and that he found it easy to make points more forcibly than his contemporaries thought strictly necessary. His cousins, the cardinal, who survived him only briefly, and the bishop of Paris, were not necessarily wrong in showing some intolerance, and the *Deffence* is unnecessarily spiky. It is difficult not to regret that du Bellay's early death prevented the production of further examples of the piquant satirical verse of which there are outstanding examples among the sonnets of *Les Regrets* and which may, together with nostalgic lyricism, have been his best medium. His poetic reputation has no doubt suffered from the neglect of the Latin verse, the facile touch of the early Petrarchan pieces, the failure to achieve adequate depth either in the archaeological verse of ruins or in the delicate grace of the nature poetry, the often excessive reliance on rhetorical and syntactical devices like antithesis and repetition, the lack of passion in all except a few of the neglected Latin love poems, the exclusively elegiac register of his most intimately lyrical verse, and, perhaps most of all, his persistent deference to Ronsard, who in fact, and in spite of occasional deferences to du Bellay's originality and vigour of mind, actually owes more to du Bellay than he ever felt it necessary to acknowledge. Even today the extent of that debt is probably underestimated.

Ronsard always had a clearer view of what he wanted his poetry to achieve, and how it had to be formed in order to serve its purpose. Du Bellay's vision oscillated more, and, if the *Deffence* is written vigorously, it does not present more than a hasty personal reaction to Sebillet, its inner coherence threatened by the juxtaposition of ideas and feelings for which no logical connection had been worked out. It is not a group manifesto, although much of its inspiration derives from Ronsard in particular, but more a hasty and indeed irritated personal reaction, affirming the need to break with the acrostic tradition of verse writing cultivated by the rhétoriqueurs, and published before the underlying principles had been fully thought through. It was in a sense to be replaced by the preface to *L'Olive augmentée*, in

which volume the cycle of love poems was also turned into a proper "canzoniere," giving it a story from the birth of love through the awakening of jealousy to the death of the loved one and love's final religious apotheosis, and incidentally increasing the dependence on Petrarch. Nevertheless, du Bellay is the author of what remains historically the most important presentation of poetic theory of the northern renaissance and, if his verse is uneven in quality, it still shows a pronounced and individual poetic personality. At his peak du Bellay reached a pinnacle of achievement, especially in the lyrical and satirical registers, scarcely surpassed, although more often sustained, by Ronsard.

Of the 115 sonnets in the expanded *L'Olive* of 1550, at least 60 can be traced directly to an Italian source. No doubt du Bellay did not introduce the sonnet into France, but he is the first French author of a unified cycle of sonnets on the Petrarchan model, thereby definitively distancing the genre from the earlier French epigram. The fact is important because it explains the sense of urgency demonstrated by the initial 1549 publication of 50 poems with the *Antérotique* and *Vers lyriques*, together with the *Deffence*, as well as the vigour of the reaction to Sebillet. Du Bellay was vindicating what he felt was an important originality, although he kept to decasyllables and made only the most modest innovations, for the most part confined to the tercets, in the rhyme schemes of his Italian predecessors. It is the idealization of love that is Petrarchan, the object of love being the scarcely materialized reality of all beauty and all virtue.

It is exceedingly difficult for a modern reader to appreciate quite how powerful was the Petrarchan device which allowed the expression of passion to be directed towards a quasi-ethereal object which spiritualized and rendered virtuous, as well as life-enriching and emotionally pleasurable, what remained an overtly sexual drive, and how culturally important was its formal importation into France by du Bellay, five years after the erratic and tentative attempts made by Scève at Lyons, the first focal point of neoplatonist interest in the French renaissance, to introduce a new moral vision into the *Délie*. *L'Olive* is important, not seriously on account of any innovatory tinkering with Italian rhyme schemes, but because it is a not insignificant cog in the vast machine which engineered the cultural progression from a system of moral values which regarded physical sexual activity as degrading and bestial, or at best a necessary evil, to one in which it would eventually be regarded as capable of contributing to moral, and even religious, fulfilment.

It is possible to gain some inkling of the magnitude of the cultural change by reflecting that such male married saints as there were had always belonged to the category of "confessors" (with the accent on the second syllable). Even in the 20th century the ecclesiastical rubric to which the liturgical calendar found it appropriate to assign married women saints was still the sadly negative "nec virgo nec martyr (neither a virgin nor a martyr)." For much the same reason that it does not greatly matter who the "real" Olive was, once it is clear that the cycle was not underpinned by any emotional bond stronger than that which linked Ronsard to his Cassandre, the still persistent tendency to reduce the literary criticism of *L'Olive* to discussions about du Bellay's prosody, or to any primordiality in the introduction of the sonnet, is analogous to discussing the relationship of marriage to sanctity in terms of changes in liturgical categories, at best approximate calibrations of much more important underlying phenomena.

We know that a dozen sonnets of *L'Olive* are taken straight from Petrarch. Sometimes it is a rhetorical device that is used, sometimes a general idea. Two sonnets are simple translations. Sometimes a quatrain or a tercet alone is taken, and sometimes a single line. Ariosto's text is plundered as ruthlessly, and about 30 Italian poets contemporary with du Bellay, most still alive in 1549, have been identified as certain sources. The beauties of Olive's individual features are enumerated, but more important for an understanding of the structural elements of the neoplatonist myth are her learning, and her abilities to dance and to make music. The importance of these abilities is implicitly considered in this convention to be based on the fundamental mathematical ratios underlying all musical chords, all physical beauty, and the motion as well as the harmony of the spheres.

Du Bellay almost certainly derived his implied relationship between beauty, mathematical proportions, and musical harmony from Peletier, although the detailed structure of Peletier's powerful theory, involving the numerical structure of the memory, was not fully published until a mathematical *Oratio* of 1579, and a series of *Louanges* in 1581. It was, however, from Peletier that the 1550 preface tells us du Bellay also drew his decision to write in the sonnet and ode forms. The poet's love, also in this tradition conventionally, is instantaneous, irresistible, and unshakeable. It is also painful, because its physical and emotional ardours are, in the Petrarchan and courtly traditions, necessarily frustrated. They had remained frustrated, for instance, in Castiglione's 1528 *Il libro del Cortegiano*, which noticeably retreats from the much greater audacity of Ficino's radical *In Convivium Platonis de amore*, composed in the course of 1469, on which Castiglione partly draws. In Ficino, physical sexual congress is envisaged as a first possible step in the ascent to the beatifying and all-consuming love of God.

Poetically, du Bellay's *L'Olive* cycle is weak. The lack of emotional intensity forces the reader into too cerebral a reaction for this to be great poetry, however significant the cultural achievement. The *Deffence*, although ardent in its expression, suffers from the same sort of failure. Intellectual theorems are juxtaposed rather than amalgamated into a coherent body of doctrine. Du Bellay wanted to do for French what had already been done for Italian. Languages, he argued, owed their richness or poverty to the effort put into their cultivation. French was therefore as capable as Latin or Greek of attaining their richness of resources. A similar argument had been used by Charles de Bouelles in his 1533 *Liber de differentia vulgarium linguarum et Gallici sermonis varietate*, but in fact du Bellay took the whole of this part of his argument from Sperone Speroni's *Dialogo delle lingue* in the first volume of his *Dialogi* of 1542. Speroni, whose name du Bellay does not mention, was arguing the potentialities of Tuscan against confirmed Latinists, and du Bellay is embarrassed by wishing to show both that the achievements of France were in no way inferior to those of Italy and that his predecessors, including Marot, who none the less had himself used antique genres, had been playing merely rhetorical games. It was going to be necessary at least implicitly to admit that Tuscan had reached a degree of development superior to that attained by French.

Having established the bright hopes open for the progress of French, du Bellay switches in his third chapter to blaming its present weaknesses on "l'ignorance de nos majeurs (the ignorance of our predecessors)." In the fourth chapter, however, he is obviously again embarrassed when he points to the great progress already recently made under François I. He then goes on to attack translations as a possible way forwards. Translating does nothing to improve the orator's "elocution," according to Quintilian more difficult to master than the other four parts of oratory, invention, disposition, memory, and pronunciation. The attack on translation presumably has in its sights Etienne Dolet's *La maniere de bien traduire* of 1540. Dolet had been put to death in 1546, ostensibly for a subversive translation of the pseudo-Platonic *Axiochus*, and a whole constellation of attitudes accounts for the serious reservation felt about him by Dorat's disciples. Dolet, a Latinizing humanist, had made no secret of his reformed sympathies, was an avid Ciceronian, an opponent of Erasmus, and believed in translation, whereas the Coqueret group with Dorat was ardently Catholic, Erasmian, and for the most part preferred at this date Greek-orientated humanism.

The way in which the Romans enriched Latin was by "imitating" the best Greek authors:

> se transformant en eux, les devorant, et apres les avoir bien digerez, les convertissans en sang et nourriture, se proposant, chacun selon son naturel et l'argument qu'il vouloit elire, le meilleur aucteur, dont ilz observoint [*sic*] diligemment toutes les plus rares et exquises vertuz, et icelles comme grephes,… entoint et apliquoint à leur Langue

> (changing themselves into them, devouring them, and after having digested them properly, converting them into blood and nourishment, proposing to themselves, each according to personal temperament and the argument they wanted to choose, the best author, whose rarest and most refined virtues they diligently observed and grafted on to themselves,…splicing them and binding them to their Language). (I, vii)

This is the famous digestive metaphor, called by Faguet "innutrition," but it does not seriously help to distinguish translation from imitation, any more than do the attempts in the third chapter of book two:

> Avant toutes choses, faut qu'il ait ce jugement de cognoitre ses forces et tenter combien ses epaules peuvent porter: qu'il sonde diligemment son naturel, et se compose à l'imitation de celuy dont il se sentira approcher de plus pres. Autrement son immitation ressembleroit celle du singe

> (Above all they must have judgement sufficient to know their own strengths and how much their shoulders will carry. Let them work assiduously at understanding their own temperaments and write in imitation of those whom they feel they approach most nearly. Otherwise their imitation will be like a monkey's).

In the end du Bellay's criterion of the true poet is taken from Cicero's *de Oratore*:

> Celuy sera veritablement le poëte que je cherche en nostre Langue, qui me fera indigner, apayser, ejouyr, douloir, aymer, hayr, admirer, etonner, bref, qui tiendra la bride de mes affections, me tournant ça et la à son plaisir. Voyla la vraye pierre de touche, ou il fault que tu epreuves tous poëmes, et en toutes Langues

(The true poet I seek in our Language is the one who will make me indignant, will calm me, make me happy, make me sad, make me love, make me hate, make me admire, and make me wonder, in a word who will hold the bridle of my emotions, turning me here and there at his will. That is the true touchstone, against which you must test all poems, and in all Languages).

The criterion could have come from Aristotle's *Rhetoric*, but its point is that poetry should move the emotions, not remain the solution of an acrostic puzzle, as so often for the rhétoriqueurs. It remains, however, that du Bellay does not adequately distinguish between the imitation he advocates and the translation he proscribes, any more than he adequately reconciles the need for inspiration or imaginative vigour with the importance for the poet of studying models.

Other important features of the *Deffence* include the sparing from stricture of the two authors of the *Roman de la Rose*, Guillaume de Lorris and Jean de Meung, and of Jean Lemaire de Belges, the haughty disdain of uneducated opinion, the need for "doctrine et erudition" as well as "ardeur et allegresse d'esprit" ("learning and knowledge" as well as what amounts to "excitement and inspiration"), the importance given to the classical genres and, in particular, the idea that no language can really be rich that has not had an epic written in it, a view which was to dominate French poetic ambition from Ronsard to Voltaire and then Hugo, and the relatively large space given to technical matters of versification.

By 1553 du Bellay could amusingly renounce Petrarchism in his "A une Dame": "J'ay oublié l'art de petrarquizer./Je veulx d'amour franchement deviser (I've forgotten the art of Petrarchizing./I want to talk more openly about love)." He spends much time making lists of the Petrarchan conventions and making fun of their artificiality, culminating in the message of Horace, which Ronsard so insistently repeated, about the need to take advantage of the present moment:

N'attendez donq' que la grand' faulx du temps
Moissonne ainsi la fleur de voz printemps...

(Do not wait then until the great scythe of time/Harvests the flower of your springs like that...).

For examples of du Bellay's poetic achievement at its highest, most critics turn to *Les Regrets* or, increasingly, to the perhaps still relatively underestimated and learned *Les Antiquitez*, whose sonnets were originally unnumbered and were printed by Morel with a sonnet in alexandrines underneath one in decasyllables on each page. The poems generally contrast ancient with modern Rome, are full of often implied allusions and references to Latin poems, whether ancient or modern, and are more formal in style and grandiose in intention than the simple lyrical pieces. Inevitably some of the poems, particularly those in decasyllables, are close in theme and mood to those of *Les Regrets*. One of the best-known poems from *Les Antiquitez*, however, illustrates well du Bellay's attempt to achieve high-style poetic solemnity.

The poem, "Telle que dans son char...," is inspired by the prophecy of Rome's birth and greatness in the sixth book of the *Aeneid*. It elaborates the splendid image of Cybele in her chariot, the great mother goddess, also known as Demeter and Ceres, but here referred to only as "la Berecynthienne," from Mount Berecynthus, a principal centre of her cult, and "la Phrygienne," since her cult originated in Phrygia. The chariot is "couronnée de tours," from Virgil's "turrita," referring to the statues of the gods erected on Rome's walls, and in it Cybele, joyous at having given birth to so many gods, is an image of Rome to come, mother of even more children and holder of the world's power. There can never be seen "Pareille à sa grandeur, grandeur sinon la sienne (Like to her greatness, greatness which is not hers)."

Rome is mentioned by name only at the opening of the first tercet:

Rome seule pouvoit à Rome ressembler,
Rome seule pouvoit Rome faire trembler:
Aussi n'avoit permis l'ordonnance fatale

Qu'autre pouvoir humain, tant fust audacieux,
Se vantast d'égaler celle qui fit égale
Sa puissance à la terre et son courage aux cieux.

(Only Rome could be like Rome,/Only Rome could make Rome tremble:/For the decree of destiny did not permit// That any other human power, however brave,/Should boast of being equal to her who made equal/Her power to earth and her courage to the heavens).

In the first tercet du Bellay, still following Virgil, has slipped in a reference to Horace ("Suis et ipsa Roma viribus ruit," Ep. xvi, 2) about Rome alone trembling at her own power, drawn on a rhetorical conceit, setting resemblance and rivalry in parallel, from the collection of Latin poems published in Rome in 1553 by the Sicilian Janus Vitalis, whose patron was Leo X. It is not unlikely that he deliberately added two complex reminiscences of Lucan (I, 82–85), perhaps recalling the rivalry between Caesar and Pompey in that of Rome with itself, and in the content of the decree of what in Lucan was "Fortuna."

In one sonnet, "Qui voudra voir...," the traveller is summoned to see all that art and nature can contrive: "J'entens s'il peult ta grandeur concevoir/Par ce qui n'est que ta morte peinture (That is, if he can conceive of your grandeur/From what is your portrait after death)." "Rome n'est plus (Rome exists no longer)," and if the architecture allows some shadow of Rome to be seen still, it is as if a body were taken by night from its burial place. Rome's body has been reduced to ashes, and its soul has gone to join the great soul of the earth's sphere. Only Rome's writings, which time has snatched from the tomb, keep its image alive throughout the world. This poem contains reminiscences of Petrarch and the central contrast, used in a Latin epigram by Lazzaro Buonamici, was also exploited by du Bellay in a longer Latin poem.

Among the finest poems of *Les Regrets* is the sonnet in which "France, mère des arts (France, mother of the arts)," addressed as a shepherdess, is called on by the poet as a lamb calls on its mother, an image probably derived from a sonnet by Pamphilo Sasso. Only Echo answers the lamb's complaint, and the lamb is condemned to wander on the plain, a prey to the wolves. "But your other lambs don't lack for pasture/They don't fear the wolf, the wind, or the cold:/And yet, I'm not the worst of the flock." The best-known sonnet of the collection allows the poet's home-sickness to pierce the clear stylization with which the plaintiveness is expressed:

Heureux qui, comme Ulysse, a fait un beau voyage,
Ou comme cettui-là qui conquit la toison,
Et puis est retourné, plein d'usage et raison,
Vivre entre ses parents le reste de son âge!

Quand reverrai-je, Hélas, de mon petit village
Fumer la cheminée: et en quelle saison
Reverrai-je le clos de ma pauvre maison,
Qui m'est une province, et beaucoup davantage?

Plus me plaît le séjour qu'ont bâti mes aïeux,
Que des palais Romains le front audacieux:
Plus que le marbre dur me plaît l'ardoise fine,

Plus mon Loire Gaulois que le Tibre Latin,
Plus mon petit Lyré que le mont Palatin,
Et plus que l'air marin la douceur angevine

(Happy he who, like Ulysses, has completed a great journey,/Or like that other who conquered the fleece,/And then came back, full of experience and wisdom,/To live in the midst of his family the rest of his days!/When, Alas, shall I see in my little village/The chimney smoke; and at what season/Shall I see the enclosed garden of my poor house,/Which is a province to me, and more besides?/I am more happy with the home my forebears built/Than with the proud brows of the Roman palaces;/More than hard marble slender slates make me happy,/More my French Loire than the Latin Tiber,/More my little Liré than the mount Palatine,/And more than the sea air the mildness of Anjou).

The poetic technique is deliberately unpolished. "Hélas" scarcely does more than help the syllable count, while "et beaucoup davantage" adds nothing to the poetic value of the verse, and "cettui-là" is not a respectful way to refer to Jason. There is the stylized "petit" for village and du Bellay's natal parish, Liré, "pauvre" for "maison," and the topos of a smoking chimney from Homer and Ovid to represent home, safety, comfort, and freedom from worry. For his first quatrain du Bellay may have remembered Ronsard's "Ode au Pais de Vandomois." The images are sometimes recycled, with the Ulysses figure of the returning traveller recurring once more by name in quest of the smoking chimney and once by implication in the same volume. Loire, incidentally, was masculine in the 16th century. What makes the poem work is chiefly syntactical antithesis and verbal repetition, although some use is also made of sound values, with five "k" sounds in the first two lines, some play with "v" sounds, chiefly in the second quatrain, until they are replaced by the insistent "p" initial consonant in the tercets, and the internal rhyme "usage/âge."

The extreme simplicity of both technique and imagery reinforces the effect of sincere, refined sadness. The first quatrain lays down the stereotyped examplars in a single sentence. The second, with a rather weak inversion, "de mon petit village," is a simple rhetorical question addressed by the poet to himself. The references and allusions are intended not to be taxing. The tercets change the key, and the poetic effect is achieved syntactically. In the first tercet we have "Plus me plaît... que" in the first line, taken up again with the "que" of the second line, but simply and effectively reversed in the third, "Plus que... me plaît," and in each of the three lines of the second tercet "Plus... que," except that in the last line of all the subject of the comparison for the first time comes last, giving enormous emphasis to the key phrase denoting what the poem's expression of longing was for, "la douceur angevine."

The touchingly simple lyricism of the best poems of *Les Regrets* is challenged only by the fluent, witty irony of the *Poëte courtisan*. Here du Bellay, expertly exploiting what is nearer to sarcasm than what the French call "ironie," makes very effective use of repetitions which can grow into lists. The court poet trying to lengthen a line does not need to bite his nails, hit the table, dream, meditate, or confuse his mind to produce a wretched verse which will only bring him a long-drawn-out laugh wherever ignorance reigns supreme... Then the court poet must not allow himself to grow old looking at Greek and Latin texts. Such exercises do not help, making the poet only wheezing, sickly, feeble, lonely, touchy, silent, and dreamy... Put in ironic form, the message of the *Deffence* has in the decade of du Bellay's active poetic career become only stronger and sharper.

PUBLICATIONS

Collections

Les oeuvres françoises de I du B, 1569
Oeuvres poétiques, 6 vols., 1908–31; revised edition, 1982–

Verse

L'Olive... Cinquante sonnetz à la louange de l'Olive. L'Antérotique de la vieille et de la jeune amye. Vers lyriques, 1549
Vers lyriques, 1549
L'Olive augmentée... La Musagnoeomachie, et autres oeuvres poétiques, 1550; edited by E. Caldarini, 1974
Recueil de poésie, présenté à tresillustre princesse Ma Dame Marguerite, 1549
La Prosphonematique, 1549
Les Regrets et autres oeuvres poetiques, 1558; 2nd edition, edited by J. Jolliffe, 1974
Divers jeux rustiques et autres oeuvres poétiques, 1558; 2nd edition, edited by V.-L. Saulnier, 1965
Le premier livre des Antiquitez de Rome... Plus un songe ou vision, 1558; 2nd edition, edited by J. Jolliffe, 1974; as *Ruins of Rome*, translated by Edmund Spenser, 1591
Poemata, 4 books, 1558
La Courtisane romaine, 1558
Hymne au Roy sur la prinse de Callais, 1558
Discours au Roy sur la trefve de l'an MDLV, 1558
Epithalame sur le mariage de tresillustre prince Philibert Emanuel, duc de Savoye, et tresillustre princesse Marguerite de France, 1558
La nouvelle maniere de faire son profit des lettres, traduitte de latin [by Tunrèbe] par I. Quintil du Tronssay [du Bellay] en Poictou. Ensemble le Poëte courtisan, 1559
La Monomachie de David et de Goliath, 1560; edited by E. Caldarini, 1981
Discours sur le sacre du treschrestien Roy Françoys II, avec la forme de bien regner accommodée aux moeurs de ce royaume. Faict premierement en vers latins par Michel de l'Hospital, et mis en vers françois par J. du B., 1560

Ample discours au Roy sur le faict des quatre estats du royaume de France, 1567

I.B Xenia, 1569

Other

Deffence et illustration de la langue françoyse par I.D.B.A., 1549; edited by Chamard, 1961
Lettres, 1883
Translator, *Le quatriesme livre de l'Eneide de Virgile*, 1552

Bibliography

Wells, M.B., *Du Bellay: A Bibliography*, 1974

Biographical and critical studies

Chamard, Henri, *Joachim du Bellay (1522–1560)*, 1900 (du Bellay's date of birth has subsequently been challenged)
Saulnier, V.-L., *Du Bellay* (revised edition), 1951
Dickinson, Gladys, *Du Bellay in Rome*, 1960
Keating, Louis C., *Du Bellay*, 1971
Holyoake, S. John, *An Introduction to French Sixteenth-Century Poetic Theory*, 1972
Coleman, Dorothy G., *The Chaste Muse: A Study of du Bellay's Poetry*, 1980
Hall, K.M., and Wells, M.B., *Du Bellay: Poems*, 1985
Katz, R.A., *The Ordered Text: The Sonnet Sequences of du Bellay*, 1985
Cameron, K., *Concordance des oeuvres poétiques de Joachim du Bellay*, 1988
Tucker, George Hugo, *The Poet's Odyssey: Joachim du Bellay and the "Antiquitez de Rome,"* 1990

DUCLOS, Charles Pinot-, 1704–1772.

Moralist, historian, and novelist.

LIFE

Charles Pinot-Duclos, much esteemed in his own century but subsequently neglected, has recently been considered again a writer of some importance, notably since his 1741 novel *Les Confessions du comte de* *** was included by Etiemble in his two-volume 1965 selection of 18th-century novels in the Bibliothèque de la Pléiade. Although the novel has subsequently aroused critical interest, no consensus has emerged about whether its significance derives from the picture it gives of a certain level of Parisian society at a given date, or from its foreshadowing in some way something which had not yet taken place in the history of the 18th-century French novel, but which one or more of Rousseau, Sade, and Laclos are sometimes thought by

different critics later to have attempted; or whether its interest is intrinsic to its own achievement and, if so, in what that achievement lies. It is in the light of the strikingly various reasons given for the renewal of interest that Duclos needs to be considered.

Duclos was born into a comfortable bourgeois family at Dinan in Brittany on 12 February 1704. His father was a hatmaker and had a local monopoly in the sale of wrought iron. When he died in 1706 he left a considerable fortune. In 1713 Duclos was sent to school in Paris, at first to the pension Dangeau for five years, and then to the Collège d'Harcourt, where he proved exceptionally able and won all the major prizes. The family lost a great deal of money with the collapse of Law's system in 1720, and Duclos was recalled to Dinan to discuss his future. Wanting to return to Paris, Duclos agreed to study for the bar, although in fact he spent most of his time developing his social life, learning to fence, going to the theatre, and enjoying female company. In 1726, called to order by his mother, he renewed his registration as a student, but passed his time at the theatre, frequenting the café Procope with Fréret, Boindin, and the abbé Terrasson, forming a friendship with Caylus, and then moving on to join the literary clientele of the café Gradot.

Duclos did not entirely neglect study, however, and although he wrote an unsuccessful mock tragedy "La Mort de Mardi-Gras" in 1737 which he subsequently burnt, in 1739 he was made a member of the Académie des Inscriptions et Belles-Lettres, to which he read a series of memoirs, starting in November 1739. On 19 February 1740 Duclos, who never severed his connections with his Brittany homeland, presented a *Mémoire sur l'origine et les révolutions des langues celtique et française* and that December he published the light and successful historical novel, the *Histoire de Mme de Luz*. On 14 January 1741 he presented his second memoir on the two languages to the Académie. He was now commissioned to undertake the 1745 *Histoire de Louis XI*, began work in 1741 and, at the end of the year, published the hugely successful *Confessions du comte de* ***.

Frivolous and erudite occupations continued concurrently, with a learned memoir on *Les Jeux scéniques des Romains* presented to the Académie des Inscriptions on 13 November 1742, a three-act ballet libretto, *Les Caractères de la folie*, performed by the Académie royale de Musique on 20 August 1743, and the publication in 1744 of the conte *Acajou et Zirphile* written for a bet to use a series of woodcuts ordered from Boucher by the comte de Tessin. On 9 July 1744 Duclos was elected mayor of Dinan, a position he was to keep until 1749, and in the autumn of 1744 he was elected deputy for the Tiers Etat of Brittany, which he was to remain until 1754. The *Histoire de Louis XI* was published in January 1745, but put on the index of prohibited books in March, although trouble with the ecclesiastical authorities was later to be smoothed out. On 4 February 1746 Duclos returned to another Breton subject with his *Mémoire sur les Druides* at the Académie des Inscriptions. On 22 September 1746 he was elected to the Académie française, pronouncing his discourse of reception on 26 January 1747.

By this time Duclos, the local politician from Brittany, successful scholar, author, and man of the theatre, was at the pinnacle of social success. Mme de Pompadour obtained for him the sinecure of "arranging the French and Latin manuscripts" in the king's library, which was worth 1,000 livres a year, and on 20 September 1750 through her influence he was given the post of royal historiographer, from which Voltaire was virtually dismissed on his departure for Prussia. This post gave Duclos access to official papers which included, from 1760, the *Mémoires* of Saint-Simon, which Choiseul had impounded in the archives of the foreign ministry, and of which Duclos made good use for his posthumously published *Mémoires secrets sur les règnes de Louis XIV et de Louis XV.* This work was published in 1791, but written before any part of Saint-Simon's text had been leaked to a publisher. Like Saint-Simon's text the *Mémoires secrets* are more concerned with portraits of personalities than with narratives of historical events and, like Saint-Simon, they frequently refer to Law's economic management.

In February 1751 Duclos published the first edition of his *Considérations sur les moeurs,* and from May was granted official lodgings by the king. The *Mémoires pour servir à l'histoire des moeurs du XVIIIe siècle* appeared late in the autumn of 1751 and was not commercially successful, although Duclos himself remained a fashionable man of letters. The work was a fictional supplement to the *Considérations.* In 1754 Duclos published a series of *Remarques* on the Port-Royal (q.v.) *Grammaire,* and then on 15 November 1755 he was made perpetual secretary of the Académie française. From 1761 he worked on the Académie's projected dictionary. From April to June 1763 he was in England, where he was received by George III, and on 16 November 1766 he left for Italy where, in 1767, he was presented to the pope. The *Voyage en Italie* was published in 1791 with the *Mémoires secrets.* What had been taken from Saint-Simon was considered too scandalous to appear before the Revolution made publication possible.

Duclos was working on his autobiography when he died of pneumonia on 26 March 1772.

WORKS

On 19 January 1742 Voltaire wrote to d'Argental about the *Confessions du comte de **** that the work "had no title to be remembered by posterity; it is only a catalogue of conquests, a story of no consequence, a novel without a plot, a work which leaves nothing in the mind, and is forgotten as quickly as its hero forgets his mistresses." Modern critics admit that the work is "badly strung together," merely a list of sexual encounters satisfactory for its male narrator, with each partner representing a different aspect of female perfection. As late as 1969 one modern critic, writing in English, said of Duclos's two early novels that "they are now of little interest," while regarding the *Considérations* as a "polished and shrewd, if somewhat abstract, moral analysis of French society." Another English-language critic warned in 1959 that the *Confessions du comte de **** "throws light on the dissolute morals of contemporary society," but says of the novels, "the modern reader will find little to recommend these works."

Yet, in the 20 years before *La Nouvelle Héloïse* it was the most read and the most plagiarized book in France. There were 11 editions in Duclos's lifetime. At worst its importance stems from its overwhelming popularity among the French reading public in the middle of the 18th century. However there is more than that. There may be poor fictionalization, and little imaginative strength in the psychological analyses, but even so imaginatively crude a fiction as the *Confessions du comte de ***,* perhaps almost because of the stereotyped schematization of its

hierarchy of moral values, reveals almost with shrillness what it was about human sexual and emotional experience that the mid-18th century was interested in exploring, and how far down-market the need for that exploration was being made evident. "Le comte de ***" undertakes to tell why he has left the world. The novel is unpretentious and undemanding lightweight reading for the literate but only semi-educated classes, written in his thirties by a scholar and a local politician in his other guise, as a rather dandified aspiring amateur dramatist.

The libertinage is not serious, but neither is the remedy. Mme de Selve draws the comte away from his life of short-lived adventures with women, and marries him at the end of the novel's second part. She wants someone who will be both a lover and a friend. She says, correctly, having just surprised him in a wood with Mme Dorsigny in a situation coyly described as "without equivocation,"

Votre coeur est bon et fidèle; mais votre esprit est léger, et la dissipation fait le fond de votre caractère

(You heart is good and faithful, but your imagination is flighty, and dissipation is the foundation of your character).

Let others enjoy his ardours. Mme de Selve wants his trust. For two months he remains true to her, but without her favours. He starts his liaisons again, but without attempting to hide them. She discusses with him how he should go about them. Her indifference worries him. She chooses to keep his heart by her indulgence rather than lose it by severity. She, too, has a right to have intrigues since, after all, women have the same rights as men, but she is not inclined to, and obviously prefers the moral superiority of her position—"J'ai plus de plaisir à vous aimer que vous n'en trouvez dans votre inconstance (I obtain more pleasure from loving you than you do from your infidelities)."

Suddenly Mme de Selve agrees to marry him,

J'y consens aujourd'hui... Je ne crains plus de vous perdre; mais vous m'avouerez qu'il est bien singulier que, pour prendre un mari, j'aie été obligé d'attendre qu'il n'eût plus d'amour. C'est cependant ce qui me rend sûre de votre coeur. Ce n'est point mon amant que j'épouse; c'est un ami avec qui je m'unis, et dont la tendresse et l'estime me sont plus précieuses que les emportements d'un amour aveugle

(I agree today... I no longer fear losing you, but you will agree that it is very strange that, to take a husband, I have had to wait until he was no longer in love with me. That, however, is what makes me sure of your heart. It is not my lover that I am marrying, but a friend with whom I am uniting myself, and whose affection and esteem are more precious to me than the ardours of a blind love).

The point is very clear. The union of hearts takes precedence over the ardours of passion, and is the goal to be waited and striven for. What is less convincing is the psychology. We are less than a score or so of lines from the end of the novel, and the psychology is so weak that the moral ending is perfunctory. Life seldom imposes choices such as Duclos presents between fleeting but passionate encounters and undying emotional fulfilment. This is at best an attempt to suggest that the 18th century was ready in 1741, after a little titillation in the course of the novel, to seize on the idea that instinct might transcend the momentary physical satisfactions of a brief liaison and lead towards a permanent and satisfactory emotional fulfilment. Duclos's novel is nowhere near as powerful as Rousseau's, and its stammering articulacy comes nowhere near Laclos's brilliance of fictional organization. Sade's imaginative interests were altogether different. But, whatever its failings as a novel, Duclos's book and its popularity are pointers to the way in which public sensibility was shifting around 1741.

PUBLICATIONS

Collections

Oeuvres morales et galantes, 1797
Oeuvres complètes de Duclos, 10 vols., 1806
Oeuvres complètes, 9 vols., 1820–21

Fiction

Histoire de Mme de Luz, anecdote du règne de Henri IV, 2 vols., 1741
Les Confessions du comte de ***, écrites par lui-même à un ami, 1741; modern edition 1969
Acajou et Zirphile, conte, 1744
Mémoires pour servir à l'histoire des moeurs du XVIIIe siècle, 1751

Libretto

Les Caractères de la folie (1743), 1743

Other

Histoire de Louis XI, 4 vols., 1745–56
Considérations sur les moeurs de ce siècle, 1751; modern edition 1939
Grammaire générale et raisonnée de Port-Royal, containing *Remarques* by Duclos, 1754
Essai sur les ponts et les chaussées, la voirie et les corvées, 1759
Réflexions sur la corvée des chemins, 1762
Mémoires historiques de Duclos…, jusqu'à l'année 1777, 1790
Mémoires secrets sur le règne de Louis XIV, la Régence et le règne de Louis XV, 2 vols., 1791
Voyage en Italie, 1791
Correspondance, 1970

Biographical and critical studies

Meister, P., *Charles Duclos, 1704–1772*, 1956

DU VAIR, Guillaume, 1556–1621.

Moralist, statesman, bishop, and orator.

LIFE

Du Vair was born in Paris on 7 March 1556 into the noblesse de robe. His father, Jean, was a maître des requêtes in his native Auvergne, and procureur général to the duc d'Anjou and Catherine de Medici. He was still alive in 1600. Du Vair's younger brother, Pierre, was to be born in 1561 and in 1601 to be named to the see of Vence, where he became well known as a reforming bishop, and suggested to Louis XIII the name of his succesor, Antoine Godeau. A sister, Philippe, died in 1584. In 1572 du Vair's name is recorded at the Paris bar, which suggests that he had by that date already spent his two probationary years as a law student. He had also visited Italy. By 1577 he was a maître des requêtes and in the service of the duc d'Anjou, but he became either disillusioned or disgraced and returned to Paris in 1582. In 1584 he took the oath as a conseiller clerc of the Paris parlement. Among his acquaintances were Odet de Turnèbe and Jean Morel.

Du Vair was to become known principally as the author of Christian stoic moral treatises, of a translation of Epictetus—although he also translated other classical authors, including Aeschines, Demosthenes, and Cicero—and of a treatise on eloquence, but also as an orator and as a statesman. The significance of his moral treatises is plain from the fact that their texts can be shown to have been used by Pierre Corneille, Racine, La Fontaine, the later Montaigne, François de Sales, and Bossuet. Some of Pascal's most famous passages were inspired by him, Balzac paid testimony to his authority, Méré knew his work, and he is complimented by the *Satire Ménippée*. There are 15 editions of the *Oeuvres* from 1610 to 1641, and there is an English translation of 1636.

It is also plain that du Vair was active as a spokesman for the Paris parlement, but it is not entirely clear exactly how he changed his allegiance between political strategies during the difficult decade between the death of the duc d'Anjou in 1584, which left Henri de Navarre heir presumptive, and Henri's final abjuration of Protestantism and recognition as Henri IV in 1594. After the assassination of Henri III in 1589, du Vair certainly turned strongly against the League and in favour of the pacification of France under a converted Navarre, even risking his life in 1593 by open advocacy of his position, but there were understandable moments of hesitation, especially during the period between the Parisian insurrection with the barricades of 12 May 1588 and the assassination of the king, and thereafter at those moments when, as late in 1591, it seemed necessary to support Mayenne against the council of sixteen's attempt to have an alternative king imposed by Spain on France.

Du Vair's bibliography has proved almost as complex to work out as the correct interpretation of the biographical evidence and the political attitudes since, in addition to normal difficulties of dating, it had been a tactic in the political struggle to publish falsified accounts of past proceedings in support of present attitudes. Uncertainties have affected the interpretation even of the moral treatises. Until 1945 the accepted order and dates of their composition was seriously wrong, so that commentators have assumed that du Vair was both more of a stoic and less of a Christian than was, or on internal evidence could possibly have been the case.

It is to be presumed that du Vair received the tonsure early. At some period before 1617, when he became bishop of Lisieux, he must have taken major orders, perhaps before he turned down the see of Marseilles in 1603. The first privilège for a work by du Vair was taken out by the bookseller Abel l'Angelier on 22 February 1585 for *La Philosophie morale des Stoïques* and the translation into French of Epictetus' *Manuel* (the *Enchiridion*). If there was an actual edition of that date, it was anonymous, and there must in any case have been an earlier anonymous edition of the Epictetus translation. Three other works had been published anonymously before 1585: the *Méditation sur les Psaumes de la Pénitence de David*, probably not long after 1580; the important *La Sainte Philosophie*, drawing on an amalgam of renaissance traditions of moral writing, certainly including that deriving from Ficino's *De amore*, probably not long after the *Méditation* but probably ante-dating the Epictetus translation; and a second psalm meditation to accompany that on the penitential psalms, the *Méditation sur les sept Psaumes de la Consolation de David*.

The final moral treatise, *De la constance et consolation ès calamitéz publiques*, a series of four discourses dedicated to Henri de Bourbon, duc de Montpensier, linked by conversation between those in whose mouths they are put, was written during the siege of Paris of 1590 but not published until the second half of July 1594. The *De l'Eloquence françoise*, arguing against the excessive embellishment of contemporary rhetoric with classical references, must have been published before 1590, in which year there was a "new, revised, and augmented" edition, although no copy of any earlier edition appears to have survived.

The discourses pronounced between 1587 and 1596, covering the decade of changing political strategies before du Vair's formal recognition by Henri IV and the bestowal of high office, were mostly published for the first time in 1606. They offer the key to unravelling the biography of that difficult decade but, in the three texts of which earlier editions were published, the 1606 edition makes important changes, altering not only the tone, mostly by removing the violence, but also the political alignment of the original, while the speech attributed on 15 June 1586 to Achille de Harlay, premier président of the Paris parlement and an ardent supporter of the League, so distorts Harlay's own published text that on reading it in 1606 Harlay wrote a strong note of protest on his own manuscript, which survives and has been published.

Literary historians have sometimes overlooked the suddenness with which the political situation changed during the later phases of the French religious wars. The death in 1584 of the duc d'Anjou, the only surviving brother of Henri III, himself without issue, dramatically changed allegiances. It left the legitimate succession to a Protestant, in a country still riven by feudal factions which continued to exploit religious affiliations for political purposes. Most of France rallied to the League against what the parlements perceived to be a menace from the king to their own power. All the indications are that at this date du Vair was, with the majority of his colleagues in the magistracy, supporting the League.

On 18 February 1587 Mary Queen of Scots, widow in 1560 of François II, was finally executed on the orders of Elizabeth of England after 19 years' imprisonment. The reaction in France was particularly strong because Mary was a member of the house of Lorraine. She was the niece of François, duc de Guise, and of his brother Charles de Guise, cardinal de Lorraine, and

therefore cousin to François's three children, Henri, duc de Guise, leader of the League, Louis de Lorraine, cardinal de Guise, to be murdered with his brother Henri in 1588 at Blois on the orders of Henri III, and Charles de Lorraine, duc de Mayenne, subsequently leader of the League, who made his submission to Henri IV only in 1595 in the wake of the military defeats at Arques and Ivry. Henri III had tried in vain to save Mary, and now had a solemn service held at Notre-Dame in her honour at which Renauld de Beaune, the archbishop of Bourges, gave a funeral oration, which was not published. Du Vair delivered a discourse intended, as he himself said, to flatter the Guise family.

Du Vair's discourse was popular, with four known editions in 1588. It was omitted out of discretion from the 1606 collection, and only published over du Vair's name four years after his death, by a publisher's indiscretion, as an appendix to the 1625 *Oeuvres*. Du Vair's family was annoyed. The 1641 editors of the *Oeuvres* pretended that du Vair had meant his speech as a simple stylistic exercise and they excised the flattery of the Guise family on the patently spurious grounds that they were using an earlier manuscript than that from which the 1625 text had been printed. In fact they have been shown to have used the faulty 1588 Edinburgh edition, and reintroduced errors purged from it in 1625. In a section near the beginning, 50 of the 900 lines are devoted to a panegyric of the house of Lorraine.

In 1587 the royal army under Joyeuse, who was killed, had been defeated at Coutras by the superior generalship of Henri de Navarre, with a force half the size and in a little over an hour, but at Montargis and Auneau Henri de Guise defeated the Swiss and German troops which were trying to join up with Navarre. In February 1588, the League insultingly demanded from Henri III the dismissal of their enemies, the confiscation of Huguenot estates, and the promulgation of the decrees of the Council of Trent. Henri III promised nothing, but summoned reinforcements. The Parisians sent for Guise, who was told at Soissons that Henri III had forbidden him access to Paris. He defied the order, possibly with the connivance of Catherine de Medici, and the celebrated barricades were erected on 12 May, cutting communications between the groups of Swiss under the command of the elder Biron, brought in to keep order in the capital. On 13 May Henri III took a horse from his stables and, with a few followers, fled to Chartres, leaving Paris effectively in the power of "the sixteen," mostly lawyer representatives of the 16 sections of Paris whose council was controlled by the League.

Du Vair's speech "En Parlement, après les Barricades" purports as printed to have been delivered on 14 May in support of the parlement's decision to send a protestation of fidelity to the king. In fact it recalls to the king his promise, not attested before 22 May, to call together the Estates General, and repudiates the idea of a formal declaration of common cause between the parlement and the League which cannot have been made before the arrival of the Cardinal de Bourbon, archbishop of Rouen, on 16 May. It may be that du Vair spoke on 14 May in favour of a declaration of loyalty, and then, perhaps much later, on the need to reconcile the king and the League, for which du Vair, who always congratulated himself on his prescience, certainly saw the need. It seems that from May 1588 du Vair ceased to support the League, and advocated a reconciliation.

When the Estates met at Blois from 16 October 1588, the main speakers for each of the three estates supported the League. Henri III had Guise murdered on 23 December and his brother, the cardinal, on the following day. The Cardinal de Bourbon and other prominent supporters of the League were arrested and then, on 5 January 1589, Catherine de Medici died. Anti-royal hysteria had already broken out in Paris. The Sorbonne pronounced all citizens released from allegiance to Henri III. Except for the Loire valley towns, Caen, and Bordeaux, all the main towns in France came out for the League. When the Paris parlement would not rally to the king, its premier président, Achille de Harlay, and others were imprisoned, on 16 January, and du Vair's "Supplication au Roi" was an attempt to arrange an exchange of prisoners held by the king for those held by the League. It must have been delivered, spoken or not, late in January 1589. Mayenne entered Paris on 15 February, and Henri III was forced to seek an alliance with Navarre. Henri was preparing to attack Paris on 2 August, and had some hopes of success, when he was attacked by an assassin on 1 August, dying in the early hours of 2 August.

At this point du Vair, who had remained in Paris in spite of the king's summons to the courts to leave it, delivered on 5 August 1589 his discourse "Sur les assemblées illicites," signifying support for the quasi-legitimacy of Mayenne rather than for the revolutionary government of the sixteen. It was du Vair's attitude to the sixteen, to whom he was always opposed, which in the end dictated his changes of policy towards Mayenne. His speech was a plea to the parlement to rally against mob rule, and involved him in the defence of the rights of Mayenne. On 10 or 17 February 1590, when it had become urgent for Henri IV to consolidate the military victories of late 1589, du Vair spoke, however, in "Sur les garnisons de la Ligue," against voting for the town of Paris to support a League garrison, in spite of the likelihood of the siege which did in fact take place from May to September, and during which du Vair wrote the *De la constance et consolation.*

The "Exhortation à la paix," which contains some portions which must have been written before, and some which must have been written after the end of 1592, appreciates that the only hope of a resolution of France's difficulties is to combine the contriving of a willingness in Henri IV to make an abjuration of Protestantism with a willingness in the League to accept him as monarch if he does make such an abjuration. The long and important speech, aimed at preventing the secession of part of France under a new king, for which Spain was working, was written for delivery at the Estates General of the League at Paris in 1593, at which du Vair was a deputy for Paris.

On 20 June he walked out of a session in protest against a clergy proposal to nominate a French prince to marry the the Spanish infanta. This had been the proposal of the council of sixteen in 1591. Taking clever, if not cunning, refuge in a defence of the Salic law, du Vair argued at some personal danger on 28 June at a session of the general assembly against what was clearly a device to ensure the permanent Spanish domination of France, and in consequence the creation of a strong Catholic kernel for a western European union. Much of the rump of the Holy Roman Empire was politically fragmented and Protestant. The discussion had taken place without Mayenne's knowledge. Du Vair's "Suasion pour l'arrest de la manutention de la loy salique" was now turning away from any attempt to provide an alternative potential monarch to Henri IV, whether Mayenne or some other candidate, like the young duc de Guise, acceptable to the sixteen. Mayenne had in fact late in 1589 proposed the acceptance of the subsequently dead Cardinal de Bourbon as

Charles X. By 1593 du Vair had for some time been solidly in favour of a Catholic France united behind a French king and backed by traditional French laws and customs. He had become a strong supporter of Henri IV.

Henri IV's abjuration of Protestantism took place at Saint-Denis on 25 July 1593, but not all the supporters of the League rallied to his monarchical authority. Du Vair appears at one time to have contemplated marriage to Magdaleine Canaye, daughter of a famous Paris lawyer who had died on 2 February 1593. It was on leaving her house that du Vair was nearly assassinated on behalf of the League on 13 July 1593. One difficulty remaining in the path of pacification under Henri IV was the refusal of Pope Clement VIII to receive Henri IV's ambassador and to recognize the abjuration. The papal legate issued a Latin admonition to the League reminding them on 27 January 1594 of the position of the Holy See. On 10 February 1594, du Vair replied with his "Response d'un bourgeois de Paris," one of his most polished pieces of forensic oratory, forcefully and plainly making all the necessary points.

After the emergence of Henri IV in 1594 as undisputed king, du Vair was suitably rewarded. He was made maître des requêtes in 1594, and given the post of conseiller d'état. In 1596 he briefly accompanied Harlay de Sancy on an embassy to Elizabeth of England to try to negotiate a League against Spain. On his return, du Vair was made governor of Provence and charged with its pacification. He chose a number of lawyers from Aix to constitute a special court which he took with him to Marseilles, where its authority was registered by the parlement on 19 December 1596. The "Remonstrance aux habitans de Marseille" is headed with the note saying that it was given on 23 December, although the last digit may be a printer's error. The discourse was certainly delivered sometime towards the end of that month, and seeks eloquently to persuade the citizens of Marseilles to integrate their province into a unified France loyal to Henri IV.

Du Vair spent nearly 20 years in Provence. Premier président at the parlement of Aix from 21 July 1599, he read a harangue at the entry of Marie de Medici to the town on 17 November 1600. He was to turn down the bishopric of Marseilles in 1603, but got to know well those prominent in the world of letters in Provence, including both Malherbe and Peiresc. In 1605 he returned briefly to Paris with both of them in his suite, and was received by the king on 22 August.

We do not know whether it was by his own choice that he spent nearly two decades in quasi-exile in Provence. He was recalled in January 1616 by Villeroy to become Garde des Sceaux. Malherbe, who had just returned from court, and Peiresc were again members of his suite. Effectively, he replaced Nicolas Brûlart, marquis de Sillery, as chancellor. Since a chancellor could not be dismissed, the recognized procedure for removing him from power was to invest a Garde des Sceaux with his functions. Bernard de Nogaret, duc d'Epernon, representing the old military aristocracy against the noblesse de robe, attempted to quarrel with du Vair, who also exchanged insults with Sillery in open council in the presence of the king.

Du Vair's position was actually precarious. Leonora Galigaï, the wife of Concino Concini, maréchal d'Ancre, was Marie de Medici's foster-sister, and had accompanied her to France at the time of her marriage to Henri IV. Concini's immediate rise to power was universally regarded as scandalous, and its manner sufficiently flouted precedent to provoke intense resentment. Du

Vair's promotion in 1616 is said to have been initiated by Leonora Galigaï. He was, however, dismissed with Villeroy on 25 November when, after having Condé arrested on 1 September 1616, Marie de Medici got rid of all the ministers she knew to be unfavourable to Concini.

It was on 24 April 1616 that, spurred by Albert de Luynes, Louis XIII took power. Concini was shot while being arrested, his wife was tortured, and Marie de Medici retired to Blois. Villeroy and du Vair were immediately recalled, and Luynes took over the direction of affairs. It was only in 1619 that du Vair retired from political life and accepted the bishopric of Lisieux. He remained in favour with Louis XIII until he died at Tonneins, some 90 kilometres south-east of Bordeaux and 30 north-west of Agen, on 3 August 1621.

WORKS

The true interest of du Vair's work does not lie in his accomplished parliamentary eloquence, in the remarks on style which make him a precursor of Malherbe, or in what used to be considered his moral rationalism and intellectual scepticism, but in the imaginative power of his reaction to the miseries of the religious wars as shown in his three principal neostoic moral treatises. The most important of the three, the *Traité de la constance et de la consolation ès calamitez publiques*, was partly a disillusioned but resolute response to the illegitimate seizure of power in Paris by the council of sixteen on 16 January 1589, aggravated by the death of Henri III in August, which created a situation in which it seemed impossible not to choose between a Protestant king, an illegitimate government, or the barely legitimate claims dangerously and unpatriotically urged on behalf of the League. It was written under the acutely stressful conditions of war, famine, and plague during the siege of Paris in 1590.

Du Vair's reputation, high in his day, quickly sank. The 1641 edition of the *Oeuvres* is the last one, and appeared only because his nephew undertook the work of rejuvenating the text. Méré is ironic when he recounts of Pascal, a frequent borrower from du Vair, that "Il admirait l'esprit et l'éloquence de Monsieur du Vair (he admired the intelligence and the eloquence of Monsieur du Vair)." Balzac, indicating in his *Dissertations chrétiennes et morales* the immense authority which the principal neostoic moralists had been accorded, wrote that "Depuis la mort de Juste Lipse et de M. le Garde des Sceaux du Vair, il est permis de parler librement de Zénon et de Chrysippe (Since the death of Justus Lipsius and M. le Garde des Sceaux du Vair, we can speak freely of Zeno and Chrysippus)." Zeno and Chrysippus were the founders of antique stoicism, and Balzac was writing at the apogee of the cultural optimism of the first half of the 17th century in France. There was by then no longer any call for the Christian stoicism of the religious wars, which du Vair had helped to create.

De la sainte philosophie is the first of du Vair's works of moral philosophy and, according to the "Au lecteur" added by du Vair in 1600 to his text, it was antedated by the main works of piety. The prefatory letter "L'Auteur à Monsieur son Père," also added in 1600, was slightly altered in 1603, when Pythagoras alone was mentioned by name among the pagan philosophers whose "plus beaux traits (finest ideas)" du Vair says he wanted to "transférer à l'usage et instruction de notre religion (adapt to the use and teaching of our religion)." The text itself is not in any real sense neostoic, although critics before World War II, assuming a later date for its composition than is now known to have been possible, have normally overlooked the fact that it is scarcely more than a simple blend of standard platitudes from renaissance moral teaching.

Passions drive us away from the dictates of right reason, and they preclude the "contentement et plaisir d'esprit, auquel réside notre souveraine félicité (the happiness and pleasure of the mind in which our sovereign happiness lies)." Cicero, followed by Seneca, had used the Latin "sapientia" of the knowledge of first causes, but the French transliteration used by du Vair, "sapience," has the moral overtones of wisdom as well as the philosophical meaning of understanding, so that du Vair gives purely intellectual endeavour a moral and religious goal. He is now in a position to show how the pursuit of philosophy, starting from the delight of the senses in harmony and proportion, takes us beyond natural beauty to the soul's contemplation of itself until, forced above the contemplation of the world and of itself, all beauties and perfections are visible in their purity and at their origin.

Du Vair's source is plainly neoplatonist, a derivative of Ficino's *De amore*, with its ascent through self-knowledge to the source of the two perfections, goodness and beauty, so often linked in Plato that he created a new word for their conjunction (καλακαγαθοσ from καλοσ, beautiful, and ἀγαθοσ, good),

[Dieu] nous apprendra son art et sa science et nous fera tous parfaits et tous divins à son imitation… Nous verrons tous les rayons de cette divinité, répandus de tous côtés, se réunir à ce corps de lumière, auquel quand nous serons une fois conjoints de pensée, nous apercevrons tout d'un coup toutes les causes et les effets de la Sapience éternelle… Voilà donc le gîte de notre félicité. C'est à cette source inépuisable de beautés, à cette profonde mer de bontés, où il faut que les ruisseaux et les rivières du monde nous entraînent

([God] will teach us his art and knowledge and will make us all perfect and divine in his likeness… We shall see all the rays of that divinity, spread out on all sides, reunited in this body of light in which, when once we are joined to it by knowledge, we shall perceive together all the causes and effects of the eternal wisdom… That then is where our happiness lies. It is that inexhaustible source of beauty, that deep sea of goodness, to which all the streams and rivers of the world must lead us).

The conception of beatitude is uncompromisingly intellectualist, and du Vair goes on to mention Plotinus, from whom Ficino derived, as well as the famous metaphor in which the soul is compared to a mirror obscured by disordered passions, itself derived from Plato and Plotinus, probably via the Prooemium of Ficino's *Theologia platonica*.

Du Vair uses, about the evil wrought by passions, language no more strident than that of the Florentines, although the stoic, intellectualist component of Ficino's *De voluptate* appears in the identification of the source of our faults with "notre jugement perverti et corrompu (our perverted and corrupted judgement)." Du Vair quotes Plato's parable in the *Phaedrus* of the charioteer and his two horses, with its distinction between noble, obedient affections, and wild disobedient ones, regards the judgements of the intellect as extrinsic to the movements of the will they should govern, and defines virtue as the "disposition de notre esprit (the resolution of our mind)" to follow "right reason." He is a certain source for Descartes as well as for Pascal.

There is a long series of considerations on the virtues, and an exhortation to meditation and prayer. Du Vair is particularly harsh on the "sale concupiscence, qui nous attache à l'amour de la chair (filthy concupiscence, which attaches us to love of the flesh)." It does not lead, as it should, to the desire to produce servants of God to replace us, but rather to a "plaisir brutal et infâme volupté, qui aveuglent notre âme et enivrent nos esprits (brutal pleasure and wicked delight, which blind our soul and intoxicate our minds)."

Du Vair's translation of Epictetus' *Enchiridion* must have come between *De la sainte philosophie* and *La Philosophie morale des stoïques*. According to the "Au lecteur," it was no more than a rearrangement of Epictetus' work, intended to shame Christians by showing the ardour with which pagans have embraced virtue. The *Enchiridion* furnished an important component for the spirituality of François de Sales, and had earlier been well known from the 1561 translation by Hieronymus Wolff, normally printed with the neoplatonist commentary of Simplicius and the commentary ascribed to Arrian. Du Vair's Epictetan stoicism, which frequently refers to the will, again differs from the ordinary amalgam of earlier renaissance moral writing only by its frequent reference to Epictetus, and by the subtle but emphatic intellectualization of the ethical norms it contains.

Virtue, described in a complicated series of catchwords, "l'être et l'agir selon la nature (existing and acting in accordance with nature)" and "l'usage de la droite raison (the use of right reason)," is again defined in terms which are already Cartesian, "la ferme disposition de notre volonté à suivre ce qui est honnête et convenable (the firm resolution of our will to follow what is upright and good)." The intellect's judgement is something extrinsic to the determination of the will—a departure from scholastic faculty psychology which can well be regarded as constitutive of Cartesian rationalism, although it has nothing to do with "rationalism" in the sense of "scepticism" in which some critics have used it. For du Vair, as earlier for Epictetus and later for Descartes, all objects are themselves indifferent, but become good or bad according to the use made of them.

Much of the *Philosophie morale* is summed up in a single sentence:

Puisque l'heur de l'homme dépend de son bien, que son bien est de vivre selon sa nature, que vivre selon sa nature, c'est de n'être point troublé de passions et se comporter envers toutes choses qui se présentent selon la droite raison, il nous faut, pour être heureux, purger notre esprit des passions et apprendre comme nous nous devons affectionner envers ce qui se présente

(Since man's happiness depends on his good, and his good is to live according to his nature, that is, not to be disturbed by passions and to behave towards all things which we encounter according to right reason, we must, in order to be happy, cleanse our mind of its passions and learn how we should react towards what we encounter).

That sentence contains the familiar mingling of stoic adage with scholastic deductive method; it shows an almost ritual deference

both to nature and to right reason; and it clearly implies an intellectualist ethic in which virtue depends on knowing what attitude to adopt. In this work du Vair relies on a clearer distinction between body and soul than he had assumed in *De la sainte philosophie*, almost symbolically moving away from Ficinian perspectives towards those of Descartes. Unlike Descartes, du Vair does not, of course, have to explain the physics of the matter, but he holds that the body is the mere instrument of the soul, and that true happiness is simply happiness of the mind.

Although in the *Philosophie morale* the doctrine of the passions is largely scholastic, du Vair retains stoic overtones by linking passions to false judgements in the mind. Ethically, as Epictetus stated in the opening sentence of the *Enchiridion*, our true good must be in our power. Du Vair at least sometimes implies that its attainment must depend on the avoidance of passions, which are not so much caused as constituted by false judgements in the intellect about what constitutes our good. The classification of the passions is essentially based on the stoic doctrine that there are four, based on present or future good or evil, although du Vair tries to conflate the stoic doctrine with the eleven movements of the sensitive appetite which the scholastic classification makes possible. After the classification of the passions, the treatise becomes more practical, and the vocabulary more clearly anticipates Descartes. The transition from the consideration of the passions to the treatment of the "offices" which are in harmony with reason and follow the order of nature mimics a similar transition in Epictetus, and the treatise turns into an orthodox and eloquently Christian exhortation to virtue.

It is difficult to assign precise dates to the siege of Paris of 1590. Henri IV had routed the League forces at Ivry, sparing the lives of as many of the French as possible, but allowing the massacre of the foreign auxiliaries. He might have taken Paris by marching on it, but thought a siege likely to prove less cruel. Perhaps 100,000 citizens had fled, leaving about 200,000, augmented by an influx of peasants from the surrounding countryside. Famine was imminent at the end of May, and food convoys reached the city again on 1 September, although the Duke of Parma, sent expressly by the King of Spain at Mayenne's urgent request, did not reach Meaux until 30 August and was not able to re-victual the city by controlling the river until 6 September.

Du Vair's *Traité de la constance et consolation ès calamitez publiques* was written during the siege. It drew above all on Justus Lipsius's *De constantia* of 1583 and on a variety of classical sources, including Seneca and Plutarch. Du Vair had certainly also read the *Consolatio* attributed to Cicero and published in Venice in 1583, although there is no reason to suppose that he accepted its authenticity, already repudiated by Justus Lipsius.

There are four speakers in the dialogue, du Vair and three others. Musée is almost certainly modelled on Henri de Monantheuil, regent in the Paris medical faculty and holder of the royal chair of mathematics. He had been a pupil of Pierre de la Ramée and himself had taught Jacques-Auguste de Thou. A friend of Pierre Pithou, Jean Passerat, and Nicolas Goulu, he led the group which prepared the terms of the city's submission to Henri IV. Du Vair makes him the spokesman for constancy, a virtue which he never considered merely passive, but which Musée regards as an acceptance of the laws of nature which rule the world. He is given the first discourse.

Orphée is very probably modelled on Jacques Houllier, son of a famous doctor, a counsellor at the Cour des aides, a known friend of the other speakers, and of du Puy, de Thou, and Pithou, and certainly in Paris during the siege. He appears to have travelled widely, and such anecdotes as have survived point to his having been an amusing companion. He argues that the ills which afflict us are always salutary. Linus is modelled on Nicolas Le Fèvre, an ascetic scholar, made tutor to the duc de Condé by Henri IV in 1596, and by Marie de Medici tutor to Louis XIII in 1611. Le Fèvre was the author of a discourse on God's justice and mercy which probably antedates the *De la constance* and whose views on remuneration after death and joyous Christian resignation correspond exactly to those of Linus in the dialogue. Linus quotes at length a long speech said to have been made at the hour of his death by the président Christophe de Thou.

The dialogue opens with du Vair, writing in the first person, complaining to Musée about the inutility of philosophy when it comes to supporting real misfortunes, and discoursing on the evils that have befallen France. Musée hastens to the defence of philosophy, and the pair are joined by Orphée and Linus who, says Musée, will adjudicate between them. Musée takes up the challenge to show how useful philosophy can be in their present predicament. He produces an elaborate metaphor of man, with his understanding enthroned and served by a "estimative" power to evaluate whatever happens to him and to control his affections in the execution of his judgements. The senses record only the external form of things, not the inner realities, sending an opinion to take control of the imagination. The drift here is naturally Epictetan. Our true good cannot be affected by what is beyond our control.

The stoics, as transmitted by Amyot's translation of Plutarch's *De la vertu morale*, had held that there were three "eupathies" or rational affections corresponding to future and present good and future evil. Since present evil was only in the imagination, nothing which happened could be the source of rational grief in the wise man. There was no rational affection corresponding to pain. Musée gives a list of examples to show that there is no natural subject for grief. If we desire only what our nature requires "Nous trouverons toujours ce qu'il nous faut (we shall always find what we need)." Musée goes on to quote mostly well-known examples of people who for lesser causes than virtue have withstood extreme pain. Not even death is truly to be feared. Musée ends with hope for the future of France and the conversion of Henri IV.

The next day an alarm was given, and the dialogue's four participants rushed to arms. Du Vair recounts that they wondered if it would not be better simply to surrender the city. Orphée, much comforted by what Musée had said, devotes much of his discourse to the recent history of France. First, however, he sets out the consideration that God, through nature, governs creation by his providence. In spite of Orphée's arguments from nature and providence, there is a strong defence of human free will. Destiny takes free human choice into account when arranging the interaction of events,

> Car, combien que le destin ne change point le plus souvent rien en la nature des causes et qu'il laisse opérer les volontaires volontairement, les nécessaires nécessairement, les naturelles naturellement; si est-ce que, de la meslange et assemblage de toutes ensemble au point et à la forme qu'il les fait rencontrer, il fait sortir tels effets que bon lui semble; tirant bien souvent de mesmes causes de tout contraires effets

(For, although destiny most often changes nothing in the nature of the causes, which it permits to operate voluntary ones voluntarily, necessary ones necessarily, and natural ones naturally, none the less, from the mixture and coordination of all together at the place and in the manner in which it allows them to interact, it achieves whatever effects it likes, very often producing from similar causes opposite effects).

Orphée now continues with a recital of the miseries inflicted on France by recent history, adopting a royalist point of view, and not hesitating to blame the churchmen,

> les vices desquels ont autant qu'autre chose embrasé l'ire de Dieu sur nous et allumé cette guerre

(whose vices as much as anything else have kindled the anger of God against us and stirred up this war).

All the misfortunes are a disguised gift of God: "ce que nous appelons misères et calamitez, ce sont dons de Dieu très précieux et profitables (what we call miseries and calamities are most precious and profitable gifts of God)."

In the third book du Vair starts by asking why, if all that has been argued is true, we should not merely remain passive in the face of whatever life offers. Linus tries at length to answer this objection, concluding with a consolation drawn from the consideration of a future life and then the 25-page death speech of Christophe de Thou, the dialogue's high point and end, devoted to death as the beginning of true life.

PUBLICATIONS

[The dates of the original editions of many of du Vair's works are not known, and it is often uncertain whether a particular work was published at all outside the collected volumes. Editions of single speeches have been omitted. The first edition of any work over du Vair's name is dated 1594]

Collections

La Sainte Philosophie, La Philosophie morale des Stoïques, Le Manuel d'Epictète, Civile conversation et plusieurs autres traités de piété, 1600
Recueil des Harangues et Traités du Sr du Vair, 1606
Les Oeuvres du Sr du Vair, 1610
Les Oeuvres du Sr du Vair, 1625 (definitive edition); English translation, 1636
Les Oeuvres de G. du Vair, 1641

Early editions

Méditation sur les Psaumes de la Pénitence de David [before 1585]
La Sainte Philosophie [before 1585]
Méditation sur les sept Psaumes de la Consolation de David [before 1585]
Le "Manuel" d'Epictète (translation) [before 1585]
La Philosophie morale des Stoïques, (with translation of Epictetus) 1585; as *The Moral Philosophie of the Stoicks*, 1664

De l'Eloquence françoise, [before 1590]
De la constance et consolation ès calamités publiques, 1594; as
  A Buckler Against Adversitie, 1622

Modern editions

De l'Eloquence française, 1908
Actions et traités oratoires, 1911
Traité de la constance et consolation ès calamitez publiques,
  1915
Le Manuel d'Epictète… translaté… par G. du Vair, 1921
De la Sainte Philosophie; *Philosophie morale des Stoïques*,
  1946

Biographical and critical studies

Radouant, René, *G. du Vair, l'homme et l'orateur jusques à la
  fin des troubles de la Ligue (1556–1596)*, 1907

Zanta, Léontine, *La Renaissance du stoïcisme au XVIe siècle*,
  1914
Levi, A. H. T., *French Moralists*: *the Theory of the Passions*:
  1585–1649, 1964

DUVERGIER DE HAURANNE, Jean: see **SAINT-CYRAN,
abbé de**

E

ENCYCLOPÉDIE L'; Encyclopédiste.

See Alembert (d'), Diderot, and Philosophes.

A work of such overwhelming importance in the cultural history of Europe as the *Encyclopédie* has inevitably attracted its accretion of legend, and it is necessary to disentangle the historical realities from cocooning myths. The *Encyclopédie* was not only a vast publishing venture, smuggling ideological propaganda into a work ostensibly devoted merely to the systematization of up-to-date knowledge but, as time went on, it became increasingly the brainchild of one man, its general editor, Diderot. Much to do with the conception and publication of the *Encyclopédie* that concerns Diderot's biography is therefore considered in the entry devoted to him.

It must, however, be remembered that between June 1751 and December 1765, the dates of publication of the first and last volumes of the original edition, Diderot's personal thought developed; that there was no fixed table of entries established before work began, and subsequently adhered to; and that not only Diderot's personal thought but also the values of the whole of Europe were changing fast in the 1750s and 1760s, with a wave of reaction, quickly engulfed by the tide's onward sweep, striking France after the assassination attempt on Louis XV in January 1757. It was also not difficult to include reflections on any subject as large as Christianity or political sovereignty, for instance, at almost any point in a work whose successive volumes are devoted to covering sequential segments of the alphabet.

It is, however, precisely over its use as a propaganda vehicle, especially against Christian belief and Catholic ecclesiastical practice, but also in favour of a fundamentally new view of the sources, nature, and exercise of political power, that care must be taken. The time span of publication alone precludes the possibility of systematizing the doctrine of the *Encyclopédie*, but there are also such other difficulties impeding systematization as the cuts made in the final text by the printer, Le Breton, after Diderot had corrected the proofs, and the difficulty of distinguishing between the different stylistic registers employed by Diderot and his contributors, from straight exposition through the gentlest of irony to the harshest of sarcasm. The propaganda attack was more carefully aimed, and more skilfully controlled than the terminology still commonly used makes it possible to realize. The concept of the "enlightenment" in particular has become so battered as to be virtually useless, particularly since the Terror soon discredited the enlightened notion of the sovereignty of the people by showing what could be done in the people's name.

That there was a cultural movement in northern Europe during the second half of the 18th century involving a rejection of authority in most areas of speculative thought and an accelerated modification of personal and social values seems indisput-

able, but the difficulty is for us, as it was for Tocqueville's generation (see the Post-Revolution volume of the *Guide*), to discriminate between what in that which was rejected was genuinely superstitious and unreasonable, and what would still be rehabilitated in the 19th century after the often flailing hit-and-miss assaults on religion and absolute monarchy in the late 18th. The sovereignty of the people required to be exercised in practice in a way much closer to the American model than Robespierre's, and the Church not only survived the Revolution, but with what later came to be called triumphalism reaffirmed the integrity of its doctrines in the first Vatican council, adding on new definitions, as of papal infallibility and the Assumption of the Virgin, for what retrospectively seems almost to have been good measure. The use of the term "enlightenment" for whatever cultural movement took place in the second half of the 18th century in France is by now far too simplified and ideologically loaded to be warranted.

The *Encyclopédie* was a sufficiently big, important, and well-considered project to be regarded as a sort of rotating prism focusing certain types of thinking we can now regard as having been advanced, but there were "encyclopédistes" who were not "philosophes," like many of the priests who wrote on the history of philosophy, and there were philosophes, like Condillac, Buffon, Helvétius, and La Mettrie, who were not encyclopédistes.

To give an example of the difficulties confronting any attempt to define some central thrust in the movement focused by the *Encyclopédie* against what was identified both as a tyrannical political system and as the imposition of a religion whose foundations at least appeared to have been eroded by superstition, it would not be inappropriate to take two entries which differ both in date and in register. It was reasonable to allow an entry on adoration, "Adorer," published in the first volume in 1751, to contain reflections on forms of Christian religious worship gently insinuating that the cult of relics and images was no longer as careful to stay free from superstition as it had been in the early Church. The entry, anodyne enough, contained an editorial insertion by Diderot which provoked much offence.

La manière d'*adorer* le vrai Dieu ne doit jamais s'écarter de la raison parce que Dieu est l'auteur de la raison et qu'il a voulu qu'on s'en servît même dans les jugements de ce qu'il convient de faire ou de ne pas faire à son égard. On n'*honorait* peut-être les saints, ni on ne *révérait* peut-être pas leurs images et leurs reliques dans les premiers siècles de l'Eglise comme on a fait depuis

(The manner in which the true God is *adored* should never depart from reason because God is the author of reason and has desired that we should use our reason even in judgements concerning what we should or should not do with

272

respect to him. Saints were perhaps not *honoured* nor their images and relics *venerated* in the early centuries of the Church as they have been subsequently).

The irony here is gentle, and directed only at what Diderot pretends to regard as merely the possibility of superstition in more recent Christian worship.

But Diderot would not in 1751 have published the last entry in the *Encyclopédie* to contain a forthright attack on Christian dogma, "Ypaina" in the final volume, published in 1765 and almost certainly by d'Holbach (see: Philosophes), where an assault on belief in transsubstantiation is smuggled into an account of a Mexican religious festival in honour of the god Vitziliputzli. Two dedicated virgins make a paste of honey and flour which is formed into an idol to which a sacrifice is offered in the open air before it is brought back, adorned with rich ornaments, to its temple. The virgins make up more of the mixture into the shape of bones.

Les prêtres…bénissaient les morceaux de pâte que l'on distribuait au peuple; chacun les mangeait avec une dévotion merveilleuse, croyant se nourrir réellement de la chair du dieu. On en portait aux malades, et il n'était point permis de rien boire ou manger avant que de l'avoir consommé

(The priests would bless the pieces of pastry which were distributed to the people, each of whom would eat them with a marvellous devotion, believing that they were actually eating the flesh of the god. It was carried to the sick, and it was not permitted to eat or drink anything before consuming it).

The register has changed, and the caricature is grotesque. Diderot's subtlety has been replaced by d'Holbach's sharp nudge but, while it may be that Le Breton let that article through by oversight, there was too much money at stake for him to allow us lightly to make any such assumption. It is more likely that he knew, and that Diderot had known, that the blasphemy was removed by removing the association with flesh and blood, even glorified, because the god was made of clearly edible substances like flour and honey, and that a subject so recondite as "Ypaina" cloaking an attack on so coarse and also by that date so threadbare a cannibalistic distortion of eucharistic theology was unlikely to be taken seriously. The business of reading between the lines of the folio columns is not quite so straightforward as even modern historians have almost invariably supposed.

The pre-publication history of the *Encyclopédie* is sketched in the entry on Diderot. A delay between the appearance of volumes two and three was due to the suppression of the first two volumes in February 1752 occasioned by the affair of the thesis of the abbé de Prades, but publication was resumed in October 1773, and proceeded more or less on schedule until 1757, when the seventh volume, with d'Alembert's long entry "Genève," appeared in November, and triggered the events which led first to the delay in the publication of volume eight, and then, before it could appear, to the revocation of the privilège for the whole undertaking by royal decree on 8 March 1759. This took the matter out of the hands of a hostile Paris parlement, still allied with Jansenist (q.v.) Gallicanism and tinged therefore with Jansenist religious rigorism, and placed it firmly back in the area of royal jurisdiction, on which the parlement had undoubtedly trespassed.

Sentiment in France had changed with the penknife attack on Louis XV by Robert-François Damiens on 5 January 1757. There was only a small flesh wound, but Louis XV thought he was dying, called three times for the last sacraments, repented three times his adulterous relationship with Mme de Pompadour, and vainly sought to have her sent away. The fright was all over by 15 January but a royal edict was issued which decreed that

Tous ceux qui seront convaincus d'avoir composé, fait composer et imprimer des écrits tendant à attaquer la religion, à émouvoir les esprits, à donner atteinte à notre autorité, et à troubler l'ordre et la tranquillité de nos états, seront punis de mort

(All those convicted of having composed, or of having had composed and printed, writings tending to attack religion, to disturb minds, or to undermine our authority and disturb the order and peacefulness of our states, will be punished by death).

However unlikely that it would be invoked against Diderot, that decree obviously made the *Encyclopédie* a more perilous undertaking than it had hitherto been, and for some time it seemed as if the enterprise was finished. Another decree of 21 July fixed the compensation due to subscribers at 72 livres, but Malesherbes, official director of the book trade, kept the second decree out of the official press, and the publishers counted the 72 livres as part payment towards the volumes of engravings, for which a new privilège was taken out on 8 September 1759, and for which preparations continued uninterruptedly. It seems certain that the government, in order to prevent printing in Holland or Switzerland, connived at the preparation of the remaining volumes of text, at their printing, and at their simultaneous release in December 1765.

The original edition of the *Encyclopédie* therefore appeared as follows:

Vol.		
I	A to AZYMITES	June 1751
II	B to CEZIMBRA	January 1752 (1751 on title page)
III	CHA to CONSÉCRATION	October 1753
IV	CONSEIL to DIZIER, SAINT	October 1754
V	DO to ESMYNETE	November 1755
VI	ET to FNÉ	October 1756
VII	FOANG to GYTHIUM	November 1757
VIII	H to ITZEHOA	December 1765
IX	JU to MAMIRA	December 1765
X	MAMELLE to MYVA	December 1765
XI	N to PARKINSONE	December 1765
XII	PARLEMENT to POLYTRIC	December 1765
XIII	POMACIES to REGGIO	December 1765
XIV	REGGIO to SEMYDA	December 1765
XV	SEN to TCHUPRIKI	December 1765
XVI	TEANUM to VÉNÉRIE	December 1765
XVII	VÉNÉRIEN to ZZUÉNÉ	December 1765

The eleven volumes of plates were published in 1762, 1763 (two), 1765, 1767, 1768, 1769, 1771 (two) and 1772 (two). A supplement was issued with four volumes of text and one of plates, and a two-volume table of contents appeared; with none of which Diderot had anything to do,

Originally, the 1751 prospectus of the *Encyclopédie* had promised eight volumes of text and two of plates at a cost of 280 livres, for delivery by the end of 1754. Any additional volume would be sold at a reduction of 29%, but prospective subscribers were wrongly assured that the work had already been completed. In fact the last volumes were still being written well into the 1760s. The printer Le Breton was able to exercise his censorship because nothing needed to be or could be submitted for official approval, given that there was no privilège, and the authorities trusted Le Breton to exercise the necessary caution. It was he who stood to lose. He removed whole entries, as well as phrases, sentences, and paragraphs. Diderot wrote him a furious letter in November 1764, and never forgave him.

Distribution was carefully controlled by the government. Subscribers, of whom in the end there were 3,931 according to the publishers' books, had to provide a receipt to a bookseller, Samuel Fauche at Neuchâtel, for their payment of 200 livres for the initial sets of unbound sheets, and would then acquire the ten new unbound volumes of text. Subscribers abroad, perhaps about half of the total, and in the provinces received their copies quickly, but distribution in the Paris region was held up for two or three years, at first because the clergy assembly, a natural focus for complaints, was still in session. Subscribers had their sets sent to an address in the provinces, and Le Breton was imprisoned in the Bastille for a few days for prematurely distributing some sets at Versailles. A lawsuit was brought against the publishers by one subscriber, demanding all 28 volumes for the original 280 livres. In fact the cost in the end was 980 livres for the sheets, to which the cost of binding had to be added.

The original publishers sold the rights to Charles-Joseph Panckoucke who, after considerable difficulties with the French authorities and his Genevan partners, succeeded in bringing out a second folio edition with 17 volumes of texts and 11 of plates (1770–76), bringing the number of sets up to about 6,000. There had been an aborted attempt at a pirate edition in London and, as well as Panckoucke's edition, there were two Italian folio sets. Between them, the four folio editions, Paris, Geneva, Lucca, and Livorno, are estimated to have sold 10,000 sets. More important, however, were the two Swiss cheap and partly abridged editions, a quarto in 36 volumes of text with three of plates, printed three times by Pellet of Geneva between 1777 and 1779 with a six-volume table, and the Lausanne/Berne octavo edition in 36 volumes with three volumes of plates, published between 1778 and 1782. The Swiss editions accounted for some 60% of all the sets in existence at the Revolution, when over half the sets in France were Pellet's quartos, partly printed at Neuchâtel, with the entries from the *Supplément* entered into the text, and costing only 384 livres.

Much of the text of the *Encyclopédie* is hack work. The Chevalier de Jaucourt (1704–1780), a Swiss Protestant brought up in Geneva who had studied in Cambridge before taking up medicine under Boerhaave at Leiden, was an indefatigable compiler, relied on and looked down on by Diderot and his circle. Although he produced nothing for the first volume and only seven pieces for the second, he appears thereafter to have written nearly 18,000 articles out of a total of 71,818, or some 28% of the total, for very small reward, and indeed was paid so little that in order to pay his own secretarial staff he had to sell to Le Breton, who was paying him so badly, a Paris house he had inherited from his mother. He never contributed less than 25% to any of the final ten volumes, and appears himself to have written 45% of volume XVI. Among his other services he took over the geographical articles, writing proper geographical and historical descriptions instead of the derisorily scrappy geographical entries in the first two volumes. His 28% of the articles represents about 24% of the final text.

We know the names of about 130 contributors, but not always how much or even what they wrote. Diderot sometimes signed his own pieces with an editorial asterisk, and sometimes did not. A number of contributors were allocated letters of the alphabet for purposes of identification. We cannot however hope to know exactly who was on the final list of contributors, or to achieve complete attributions. The original seven volumes included articles by a good half-dozen priests, Guillaume Raynal, Edme Mallet, Jean-Martin de Prades—the author of the article on "Certitude," whose thesis was finally condemned by the Sorbonne—Claude Yvon, active on the first two volumes, but obliged to flee France with Prades, and an abbé Pestré about whom practically nothing is known. They were to be joined by the abbé Morellet, who contributed "Fatalité" and "Foi (faith)."

Among the famous names, Buffon actually contributed nothing. Both the articles signed by him are translations from Chambers's *Cyclopaedia*. Rousseau wrote the article on "Economie politique" and many of the pieces on music; La Condamine wrote many of the articles on American natural history and geography; Marmontel wrote a considerable number of literary ones; Voltaire finally wrote 43 articles, all between volumes V and VIII; Turgot wrote at least five articles for volumes VI and VII; Théodore Tronchin wrote on "Inoculation"; Falconet contributed "Sculpture"; parts of "Amitié" and "Amour" were taken from Vauvenargues; both Naigeon and Grimm signed only two articles; and there are the famous few lines by Montesquieu in the entry on "Goût (taste)." Otherwise Saint-Lambert, Dumarsais, Duclos, and Quesnay, founder of the physiocrat school of agricultural economists, together with d'Alembert and Diderot and the other contributors already mentioned, complete the list of generally known names.

From the outset the publishers wanted a luxurious up-to-date encyclopedia, a profitable business undertaking, and that is what Diderot intended to provide. The chief declarations of the editors' intentions are in the October 1750 *Prospectus* by Diderot, d'Alembert's *Discours préliminaire*, which included the 1750 *Prospectus*, d'Alembert's *Avertissement* to the third volume, and Diderot's article *Encyclopédie* in the fifth volume. The *Prospectus* merely underlined the intention to emphasize the logical interconnections between the disciplines, dividing them in the 16th-century way according to the faculty of the soul on which they depended, memory, reason, or imagination. Similar schemes were well known from the enthusiasm in the 16th century for the notion of a circular organization of the disciplines, Quintilian's ἐγχυχλοσ παιδεία, but Diderot may have been borrowing from Bacon. It is plain, however, that he wanted to produce a reference book. D'Alembert's gloss on the editors' intentions in the *Discours préliminaire* makes the utilitarian aim even clearer. The work will not only deal with logical connections but will also be a handbook or guide, a "dictionnaire raisonné" of the sciences, arts, and crafts. D'Alembert specifically disowns commitment to any belief in human perfectibility.

In the *Avertissement* to the third volume d'Alembert, defending the *Encyclopédie* against the accusations of anticlericalism and irreligion, admits that the distinguishing feature of the work is its "esprit philosophique," by which he comes close to meaning a rational and critical approach to mythology, history, philosophies, and religions. Philosophers are included because they formed opinions; Fathers of the Church are not because they merely passed on revealed doctrine; the genealogy of the sciences is there, but that of great families is not; the names of the great are included only in so far as they have promoted the advancement of knowledge.

Diderot's own article "Encyclopédie" for the fifth volume must have been put in at the last minute, because it interrupts the page numbering and is itself not numbered. It is lengthy, filling 27 double columns of folio, but it is not primarily a declaration of ideological intention, more a rather boastful justification of the undertaking despite its deficiencies of proportion, lack of style, and derivation from Chambers. Just occasionally the propaganda intention is allowed to appear:

Aujourd'hui que la philosophie s'avance à grands pas; qu'elle soumet à son empire tous les objets de son ressort; que son ton est le ton dominant; et qu'on commence à secouer le joug de l'autorité et de l'exemple pour s'en tenir aux lois de la raison....

Nous avons vu que l'*Encyclopédie* ne pouvait être que la tentative d'un siècle philosophe; que ce siècle était arrivée...

(Today, when philosophy is making such progress; when it is subjecting to its rule all the realms that belong to it; when its tone has become predominant; when the yoke of authority and example begins to be shaken off, and the laws of reason are being respected...

We have seen that the *Encyclopédie* could only be the effort of an age dominated by philosophical enquiry; that that age had arrived...).

Diderot did believe in the promotion of the union of virtue and happiness through knowledge, or at any rate the conquest of superstition, and his ideological aim clearly informed his editing of what remained, however, primarily a work of reference. The ideology was almost as fierce about tyranny as about superstition, but Diderot naturally expressed himself more freely in his letters than in material intended for publication. In September 1762 he wrote to Sophie Volland, "Nous aurons servi l'humanité (We shall have done service to humanity)," and three days later he explained to Voltaire why he would not accept Catherine the Great's invitation to finish the enterprise on Russian territory:

Notre devise est: Sans quartier pour les superstitieux, pour les fanatiques, pour les ignorants, pour les fous, pour les méchants et pour les tyrans: et j'espère que vous le recon-

naîtrez en plus d'un endroit. Est-ce qu'on s'appelle philosophe pour rien?

(Our motto is: No quarter for the superstitious, for fanatics, for the ignorant, for the mad, for the wicked, or for the tyrants: and I hope you will recognize that in more places than one. Do we call ourselves philosophers for nothing?).

Even more forthright is the pardonably exaggerated, because furious, letter to Le Breton of November 1764, when Diderot has found out about the cuts made after he had passed the proofs, and comes near to saying that the reference work was almost only an excuse for the ideological propaganda.

Vous avez oublié que ce n'est pas aux choses courantes, sensées et communes que vous deviez vos premiers succès; qu'il n'y a peut-être pas deux hommes dans le monde qui se soient donné la peine de lire une ligne d'histoire, de géographie, de mathématiques et même d'arts, et que ce qu'on y a recherché et ce qu'on y recherchera, c'est la philosophie ferme et hardie de quelques-uns de vos travailleurs. Vous l'avez châtrée, dépecée, mutilée, mise en lambeaux, sans jugement, sans ménagement et sans goût. Vous nous avez rendus insipides et plats. Vous avez banni de votre livre ce qui en a fait, ce qui en aurait fait encore l'attrait, le piquant, l'intéressant et la nouveauté

(You have forgotten that it is not to common, sensible, and ordinary matters that you owed your initial successes; that there can scarcely be two people in the world who have taken the trouble to read a line of the history, geography, mathematics, and even the arts, and that what people have looked for here, what they will still look for here, is the firm, bold philosophy of some of your contributors. You have emasculated it, cut it up, mutilated it, torn it into shreds, without judgement, moderation, or taste. You have made us insipid and flat. You have cut out of your book what was, what would still have been, its attraction, what was piquant, interesting, and new).

Not only does Diderot exaggerate, he understates the value of the work as a guide to arts and crafts. It is true that not all the technology was up to date, and that contemporaries heavily criticized such matters as the fourteen pages given to hats; that the engravings depicted out-of-date procedures; that the industrial revolution is nowhere in sight: and that the whole *Encyclopédie* took too little note that technology was moving as fast as values, but we know from contemporaries that Diderot underestimated the importance of the technical articles, in which he personally was so much less interested than in those touching on superstition and tyranny. Of the total cost of 980 livres, the eleven volumes of plates accounted for 654 livres, or two thirds, and in view of the economic success of the venture it looks as if the obsolescence of the technological information was not thought to impede the work's utility, nor the propaganda content much to affect it, either. Diderot's view that the set was being bought for its ideological focus appears to have been at best wishful thinking; the evidence suggests that it was certainly wrong.

For a knowledge of the reception and motives for purchase we have ourselves naturally to rely largely on the comments made by those ideologically opposed to Diderot's views and published by interested parties who had much greater freedom to promulgate their defence of traditional views and values than Diderot's circle had in their efforts to change them. The ideological content of the *Encyclopédie*, even discounting the caution in the first two volumes, the increased caution in the subsequent five, and Le Breton's cuts in the final ten, was in fact relatively muted. There was, as was only to have been expected, hostility from the Jansenist (q.v.) *Les Nouvelles ecclésiastiques*, and it emphasizes the flexibility of the planned content of the *Encyclopédie* that both d'Alembert, in "Ecclésiastique," and Diderot, in "Encyclopédie," could still react in volume five to attacks on volume two.

The ideology, as well as the means by which within the work it was expressed, clearly developed, and unfortunately the only volumes in which we might have pinned it down and defined it were the ten which were published simultaneously but doctored by Le Breton after the proofs had been corrected, and which therefore do not present us with the unadulterated editorial version. Even though it has now become possible, thanks to the single stray copy with Le Breton's cuts marked, to reconstitute what Diderot had decided to publish, it remains that his reconstituted text is not what was in fact printed. D'Alembert, as noted elsewhere, withdrew from all but the mathematical entries after "Infini," already written for volume eight when the interruption in publication occasioned by his "Genève" occurred. The pieces "Nature" and "Nature, Lois de la," also signed by d'Alembert, are merely translations from Chambers.

The *Encyclopédie* has often been trawled for its surreptitious innuendoes and snide insinuations, although it is possible that not enough attention has been paid to the time span from conception to execution, and it was only in 1947 that the re-established text of the last ten volumes as Diderot intended them was made public. However, there is yet another difficulty standing in the way of achieving a synthesis of its point of view: it was never consistent. There were at every stage, although more especially at the beginning of the enterprise and therefore the opening of the alphabet, impeccably orthodox statements of Christian doctrine with no comment to undermine them. Were they bluff or disguise? Did Diderot hope to encompass a developing ideological purpose by inserting merely here and there sometimes forceful insinuations that Christianity had lapsed into superstition and monarchy into absolutist tyranny?

It is more likely that the immensely intelligent, skilful, patient, and, at least in public, cautious Diderot held out against the brilliant but impetuous d'Alembert on grounds of prudence. When Voltaire wrote to d'Alembert complaining of the orthodoxy of some of the theology, d'Alembert replied,

Sans doute nous avons de mauvais articles de théologie et de métaphysique, mais, avec des censeurs théologiens et un privilège, je vous défie de les faire meilleurs. Il y a d'autres articles, moins au jour, où tout est réparé

(Doubtless we have some bad articles on theology and metaphysics but, with theologian censors and a privilege, I defy you to do better. There are other, less prominent articles, which make up for it).

It is also not impossible that it was the overwhelming amount of not on the whole religiously sensitive material contributed by Jaucourt, who appears never to have gone beyond a generally deist position, which persuaded Diderot to give freer rein to d'Holbach, still unknown to the general public, in the final ten

volumes. Since they were all to be published at once, it is conceivable that Diderot was permitting himself greater audacity than usual. He could always pretend that he had called on an outside specialist in good faith. Apart from "Ypaina," d'Holbach is known to have written the entry on priests, "Prêtres," in which the accusation goes beyond the encouragement of superstition and moves on to an obsession with power, enforced by cruelty. There is a whole series of entries and partial entries in the last ten volumes, including "Négus," "Chamans," "Théocratie," and "Ngombos," probably or certainly by d'Holbach, which together constitute what is apparently the strongest attack on Christianity in the whole work, but where anti-Christian sentiment is so strong, while imprecise, unsupported, and outwardly not heterodox, that it is reasonable to suppose that Le Breton calculated he could buy some shelter from Diderot's predictable outrage at the cuts by letting them through. They cannot just have been missed. There is naturally no evidence of Le Breton's thinking, but if that was in fact how he calculated, he was right.

Since a definition of the position or outlook of the *Encyclopédie* is, for the reasons indicated, simply unachievable, and since Diderot's own changing views are themselves discussed in the entry devoted to him, it may not be inappropriate to end by quoting Jaucourt on "Superstition," which he regards as "tout excès de la religion en général (any excess in religion generally)."

En effet, la *superstition* est un culte de religion faux, mal dirigé, plein de vaines terreurs, contraire à la raison et aux saines idées qu'on doit avoir de l'Etre suprême…

L'athéisme même (c'est tout dire) ne détruit point cependant les sentiments naturels, ne porte aucune atteinte aux lois, ni aux moeurs du peuple: mais la *superstition* est un tyran despotique qui fait tout céder à ses chimères. Ses préjugés sont supérieurs à tous les autres préjugés. Un athée est intéressé à la tranquillité publique par l'amour de son propre repos; mais la *superstition* fanatique, née du trouble de l'imagination, renverse les empires

(*Superstition* is in fact a false religious cult, wrongly directed, full of imaginary terrors, contrary to reason and to the healthy ideas we should entertain of the supreme Being…

However, not even atheism (which is going as far as is possible) destroys natural feelings or undermines the laws, or the morals of the people; but *superstition* is a despotic tyrant which makes everything yield to its delusions. Its prejudices are more powerful than other prejudices. An atheist has an interest in public order out of love of his own peace, but fanatical *superstition*, born of a disturbed imagination, overthrows empires).

That at least seems to target the real bull's eye at which the religious attack was aimed, an attack much more pronounced than those on the political and economic orders, sharper, and carried through with a more refined range of comparisons, contradictions and inconsistencies revealed, ironies, innuendoes, insinuations, and double meanings.

F

FÉNELON, François de Pons de Salignac de la Mothe-, 1651–1715.

Author of works of spirituality, mystical theology, and philosophy, also of literary works intended for educational use, of letters and of works of social, political, and pedagogical theory.

LIFE

Apart from his works of spiritual controversy, published to right a wrong and support a principle, the 1687 *Traité de l'éducation des filles*, written as a practical guide at the request of the duc de Beauvillier, husband of one of Colbert's daughters, and the slight 1688 work of anti-Protestant polemic, the *Traité du ministère des pasteurs*, Fénelon published nothing. The publisher Barbin's widow, or "The Widow Barbin," which was the name under which she traded, fraudulently passed off the manuscript of *Télémaque*, which, according to Bossuet's hierophant, the abbé Ledieu, was circulating in Paris late in 1698, as a continuation of the *Odyssey*, and on that account obtained a privilège. Fénelon disowned it and tried to have it suppressed, and the chancellor ordered its seizure, but it had sold 600 copies on its first day. The other three volumes were published surreptitiously, and only after nearly two centuries, in 1845 did *Télémaque* cease to be among the five best-selling books in France each year. From 1810 to 1845 alone, when it had been published for over a century, it sold 500,000 copies.

Only François de Sales could be adduced as a spiritual writer of comparable importance in post-renaissance France, and only Rousseau as an equally radical thinker over a comparable range of subjects. Fénelon was the foremost theologian of his age, at least an adequate metaphysician, an innovatory social and political philosopher, an educational theorist, an author of fables and dialogues, a literary scholar, a sensitive spiritual director whose letters on prayer and other intimate religious matters constitute an advanced treatise on the spiritual life, and an erudite historian of spirituality. Much of what he wrote, it is true, was the result of particular circumstances, composed with the education of the duc de Bourgogne in view, or in the course of sectarian, spiritual, theological, or philosophical polemic, or to formulate in letters his spiritual doctrine, or with particular social, political, and administrative reforms in mind. But his ideas were from the beginning original and radical. They became increasingly powerful.

It is only his less perceptive critics who still find the way in which Fénelon expressed himself excessively fastidious, too refined, cultivated, elegant, and delicate. It is true that he was impregnated with a sense of loyalty, to Madame Guyon, for instance, which he may have flaunted as a sign of caste, and in retrospect his aristocratic hauteur seems inevitably to have destined him to clash with the coarser-minded, scheming Bossuet, robustly dedicated to the pursuit of power and astute in acquiring and maintaining it. Court and the Académie were bound to bring Fénelon and Bossuet into close contact, but in every way the rigorous and ascetic aristocrat with grace and charm differed in style from the luxury-loving and generally time-serving court prelate, who none the less retained the sharpness of his peasant origins, and who needed to esteem the qualities of forthrightness of mind and deviousness of approach, which he abundantly possessed, more than the intellectual subtlety and disinterested sensitivity which he lacked. It did not help the furtherance of Fénelon's ideas or his influence that his abilities were subtler, more powerful, and of an altogether higher order of intellectual and literary ability than Bossuet's. Even after Bossuet's death, Fénelon's opposition to the flamboyant absolutism of the king prevented the possibility of any return to favour after the disgrace occasioned by Bossuet's accusations.

By the 1680s, Fénelon was close to Colbert's son, Seignelay, and his three daughters, who had married the ducs de Chevreuse, de Beauvillier, and de Mortemart. He himself remained faithful to the political attitudes of Colbert, who had died in 1683 in the virtual disgrace provoked by his rival and successor, Louvois. The difference in style as well as policy between Colbert and Louvois is crucial for an understanding of Fénelon's career. When Louvois himself died in 1691, he had already pushed Louis XIV into the revocation of the edict of Nantes, and had urged him firmly in the direction of his final disastrous wars.

Fénelon had early opposed the less refined methods with which Louvois promoted religious unity in France, and later on was to put forward a markedly moderate foreign policy, advocating for the nation's enrichment the strategy of advancing trade rather than conquering territory. He also favoured liberal constitutional developments to change the basis for monarchical sovereignty away from heredity and rule by divine right. His advanced views on these and other issues, like education and the role of the Académie française, may now seem unquestionably to have been vindicated, but the unifying principle of his thought has not been made adequately clear in critical discussion, with the result that the originality of his ideas, the power of his thought, and the delicacy of its expression have still not won him the position in the literary history of France which is his due.

Fénelon could trace his family back to the 13th century, and possibly, he thought, to the 10th. There were 33 portraits of illustrious ancestors in the gallery of the house where he was brought up. His paternal grandparents, however, had both been orphans when they married in 1599, produced at least 12 children, lost the considerable family fortune they had inherited and, when their affairs were separated in 1640, were between them over 50,000 livres in debt. They were ruined for the same reasons as the rest of the provincial aristocracy: the crippling cost of raising troops and satisfying other aristocratic obligations, the loss of administrative and judicial functions, the poor return from land, and the erosion of legacies by the divisions imposed by the number of their children. Fénelon's grandparents died in 1644 and 1658, and their eldest son, Pons, born in 1601 and destined to increase the indebtedness to the point at which it had finally to be written off, was to be Fénelon's father. Two of Pons's younger brothers were to become guardians to Fénelon: François, bishop of Sarlat and prior of Carennac, and the marquis Antoine, who had his own company in the army.

Pons de Fénelon married in 1629 after an honourable military career and when his first wife died, in 1647, he had eight living children. On 1 October 1647 he married Fénelon's mother, Louise de la Cropte de Saint-Abre, whose family can be traced back with certainty to the 13th century, and with some likelihood another century further still. She bore Pons de Fénelon at least five children, of whom Fénelon, baptized François-Armand, was the second. He was born at the very beginning of 1651, although not baptized until 6 August, almost certainly at the château de La Mothe-Fénelon, at Saint-Mondane, about 10 kilometres from Sarlat but in the diocese of Cahors. His father, who had stayed loyal to the court when, during the Fronde, Sarlat fell to rebel troops on 1 January 1653, died loaded down with debt on 7 March 1663, and his mother sometime after 1666, having, as was customary, moved after her husband's death out of the main family seat to their second château, Lamothe-Massaut, a couple of hours away on foot.

Without exception, all the accounts of Fénelon's youth and studies written before the appearance in 1972 of the first volume of Jean Orcibal's edition of the *Lettres*, and some published subsequently, have been shown to be conjectural; they are often erroneous and always unreliable. We know very little about Fénelon's early years. In February 1659 he joined, with the rest of his family, the pious association of "Pénitents bleus" at Sarlat. On his father's death, a local guardian was appointed, Charles Menissier, a farmer, and the presumption is that Fénelon's early education was partly in the hands of the family chaplain and parish priest of Saint-Mondane, Jean Pignol, largely overseen by his uncle and godfather, from 1659 the bishop of Sarlat, whose heir Fénelon was. The uncle, François II de Salignac, was a successful prelate who held court in the world of letters, the sixth successive member of his family to occupy the see, and a member of the Compagnie du Saint-Sacrement, part of whose team for implementing the Tridentine reforms in the south-west he became. Linked to Olier at Saint-Sulpice, the bishop was jealous of diocesan jurisdiction, disliked the exemption enjoyed by the religious orders, and was fiercely anti-Protestant. Fénelon may well have stayed with his uncle between 1663 and 1666.

More important in Fénelon's life was probably his other uncle and guardian, the marquis Antoine de Fénelon-Magnac, given by his family the captaincy of the regiment of his brother Claude, killed in 1638. Having married Catherine de Montberon in July 1647, he was left with a son, whose dissipated life at court his worried father discussed with the king, but who was to be wounded at his father's side at Candia and die on 10 June 1669, and an infant daughter, Marie-Thérèse-Françoise, who became the marquise de Laval.

Catherine de Montberon died within days of giving birth to her daughter in 1650. She was from a devout family associated with the old court and the entourage of Gaston d'Orléans, frequented also by her future husband, and she herself had at her death acquired a reputation for sanctity, attested by at least two

of Olier's letters. Her death may have brought about a change in her husband who, after 1650, devoted himself unsuccessfully to the establishment of a seminary at Magnac and, having himself been a notorious duellist, became a leader of the movement in the aristocracy to renounce duelling, while also urging the king to implement the full rigour of the anti-duelling edicts. He appears to have taken Olier, the agent of his conversion to a life of real devotion, as his director, and certainly became a prominent member of the Compagnie du Saint-Sacrement. Anne of Austria made the barony of Magnac into a marquisate in 1650, but it was partly the marquis's interference with the administration of justice to ensure severity against duellists that finally provoked Mazarin to suppress the Compagnie. The quip that Molière's Tartuffe should have been wearing not a soutane but a sword was aimed at Antoine de Fénelon-Magnac.

Antoine was incontestably the head of the family, and the rich uncle. He lived mostly in Paris, always in the parish of Saint-Sulpice, and brought Fénelon there, probably in 1669. His daughter, well-off, too, from her mother's inheritance in view of her brother's death, was to marry Pierre de Laval-Lezay, who could trace his ancestry back to the 13th-century Montmorency family, but was now yet another impoverished aristocrat. The list of signatories on the contract of 22 January 1681 was impressively headed by the king, the queen, the dauphin, Condé, his son, and the king's brother, Philippe d'Orléans. It was through Antoine's household that Fénelon first became acquainted with the court. While under the tutelage of the bishop of Sarlat, Fénelon had probably studied at the run-down university of Cahors, not the rival college run by the Jesuits. It is likely that it was in 1669 that Fénelon, after six years schooling at Cahors, graduated master of arts with good Greek and Latin, took the tonsure, and went to study from Antoine's residence under Charles Gobinet, the principal of the Collège du Plessis in Paris.

It is also clear that Fénelon's spiritual director during his time in Paris and the early part of his career was Louis Tronson, a close guide and counsellor, who had joined Saint-Sulpice in 1656 and from 1 July 1676 was the superior general of the congregation. What is not clear is Fénelon's institutional status at either the Collège du Plessis or the seminary, the parish, and the Congregation of Saint-Sulpice. The early biographers contradict one another, and their accounts do not square with documentary evidence now available, but the matter is of importance. Fénelon might have been sent to Gobinet because of his uncle's ultramontanism, in which case a later Gallicanism was a betrayal of family loyalties.

More importantly, the later attraction for him of the passive spirituality of Mme Guyon might have been the result of a spiritual formation such as that given by Tronson, sufficiently close to the ecclesiological side of Jansenism (q.v.) to make his penitents confront the inescapable and awesome implication of the Jansenist theology of grace, according to which they might not be predestined, and would therefore spend an eternity in hell. Even in its strictest "predestinationist" form, Calvinism had provided an implied criterion in the order of religious experience which could effectively still the anguish arising from that thought by imparting the empirical certainty of grace, but that Fénelon did feel the need to confront the possibility of damnation and to articulate its spiritual implications for the love of God is plain from two important letters he later wrote to Mme Guyon on 28 March and 11 August 1689.

In other words, Fénelon's "quietism" was closely linked to a spiritual need to combine the love of God with the possibility that an individual might have been born with no possibility of doing anything whatsoever to avoid damnation. The spiritual attitudes of François de Sales had been largely determined by his youthful conviction that he was among not the predestined, a term in Catholic theological usage strictly reserved for election, but the reprobate, those who, not necessarily on account of any autonomous moral act of their own, were going to be damned. That experience forced him into the Molinist position associated with the Jesuits, although not held in the same form by all of them, that human beings do have an autonomous power of moral self-determination respected by God. The Jansenists, like the reformers, considered that position to be "semi-Pelagian" and heretical. Unlike the reformers, and such early Port-Royal (q.v.) directors as Saint-Cyran himself, later Jansenists like Nicole came to regard the uncertainty about whether or not the soul was justified as necessary, and perhaps salutary.

Jansenist spirituality made it imperative to envisage the possibility that God would not, in any particular individual case, remit the eternal damnation which, on account of original sin, every member of the human race deserved. By attributing human demerit to Adam's sin, Pascal, in his *Ecrits sur la grâce*, like the *Pensées* of course unpublished, was at least mentally testing for himself the possibility of avoiding a concept of God, which he thought Calvin had not avoided, which attributed to him the creation of souls foreknown to be arbitrarily doomed to unending punishment. But Pascal was ruminating about theological explanations, not spiritual consequences. The spiritual reaction to the dilemma imposed on the individual by the possibility that he might be going to be damned and could do nothing at all about it was to determine the theological content of Fénelon's momentous dispute with Bossuet who, when it began, had read neither François de Sales nor the work of any of the major mystics. Spirituality came to interest Bossuet only when it threatened authority's ability to impose discipline.

The dispute, however, is central to the problem of combining an orthodox Christian theology with a religiously tolerable Christian spirituality, and that problem dominated the whole intellectual history of European culture from at any rate the early 16th century until the mid-18th. It caused schismatic Protestantism, and led to the weakened hold of Christian theologies, possibly as distinct from Christian spiritualities, on Europe's best minds in the 18th century. It is in that perspective that those seeking to understand the works of either Fénelon or Bossuet need to know whatever about the intellectual, theological, political, and spiritual constraints which formed the attitudes of each of them can with certainty be ascertained.

Fénelon was ordained priest probably in March 1677. On 26 March he took his baccalauréat and licentiate in theology at Cahors. He had long interviews with Tronson, sometimes with his uncle present, moved about with him, and preached for him at Saint-Sulpice, and at his instigation elsewhere, during the rest of the year. In the meanwhile he had in 1671 been given a canonry at Sarlat by his other uncle, the bishop, which he must have exchanged for a simple benefice with no residential requirement. A simple benefice could be held by a tonsured cleric for seven years with no obligation other than the recitation of the breviary, and that could be dispensed.

We know that Fénelon held the priory of Rauzel by 1675, when he was a diocesan delegate from Sarlat to the clergy assembly in Bordeaux. The following year he also held the priory of Douzains. A 1676 registry entry refers to Fénelon as still a deacon, and therefore not yet a priest, when he acquired a third priory at Sadillac, which later appears to have been exchanged for another at Saint-Front. He was to resign all three of these priory/abbacies in 1693. In 1681 his uncle resigned in his favour the family priory of Carennac, worth 3,000–4,000 livres a year, retaining something, however, for the building operations which were exercising a fascination for episcopal imaginations. Fénelon resigned the Carennac benefice on 10 March 1696 after he had been consecrated at Cambrai. He was elected to a fourth priory at Saint-Avit-Sénieur early in 1688. In 1678 and 1679 Tronson had twice mentioned Fénelon's name in connection with possible vacancies in the diocese of his cousin G. de Sève de Rochechouart, bishop of Arras, but it is unclear whether any approach was made.

In June 1679 Fénelon, probably living with his uncle at Saint-Germain-des-Prés, was made superior of the "Nouvelles Catholiques," a Paris house founded by the Company for the Propagation of the Faith and run by nuns for women who were thought to require religious assistance, normally to abjure heresy. There was a chaplain and a confessor on the staff, and preachers were brought in from outside. Women were consigned to or freed from the house by police warrant, normally signed by La Reynie, the lieutenant of police, or the procurator general, Achille de Harlay, and sufficient pressure was exercised to make it reasonable to describe the conversions as more or less compulsory. The house was a prison thinly disguised as a religious foundation. Acting in accordance with the constitutions, which have been preserved, the superior, who did not reside there, was responsible for the administration of the establishment and for the inspection of those whose abjurations had been obtained. The incarcerated women were normally put there by the authorities on a religious pretext, but the treatment they received was penal, and Fénelon must have been aware of what the institution was for, and how it achieved its aims. He remained titular superior, signing contracts, preaching, and otherwise exercising his supervisory duties, until he was appointed to the preceptorate in 1689.

Although from 1685 he took a Jesuit confessor, Père le Valois, and although there has never been a suggestion that he accepted the condemned Jansenist propositions, it looks as if in 1686 Fénelon was passed over for the bishopric of Poitiers because the archbishop of Paris, François de Harlay de Champvallon, had maintained that he leaned towards Jansenism. The same considerations may have been urged again, precluding nomination as coadjutor at La Rochelle in 1687. They must chiefly have been based on Fénelon's carelessness of the ecclesiastical niceties in his social relationships, notably with the rich, beautiful, and devout family friend Jeanne-Françoise de Garraud de Donneville, marquise d'Alègre. Much to the relief of Mme de Sévigné, who realized how extreme Mme d'Alègre was in all her behaviour, Mme de Lafayette had intervened with her son, Charles de Sévigné, in spite of her beauty and 300,000 livres of dowry, to stop him from marrying her, and it was imprudent of Fénelon to have mixed with her even casually. It was, however, also a sign of the generally high-handed disregard for what other people thought about him which was a principal reason for his later disgrace.

Fénelon's aristocratic hauteur was to keep him loyal to Mme Guyon, to whom he thought an injustice had been done, to keep him too blind for too long to Bossuet's no doubt vicious and contemptible but none the less successful tenacity in imposing the power structure he wanted, and to impel him to write a vitriolic letter to the king reproaching him with the wretchedness to which he had reduced the bulk of the population. At the date of his missions to the west of France, which ended in 1687, Fénelon also had other friends, less light-headed and extravagantly behaved than Mme d'Alègre, but thought in official circles to be too friendly with Jansenists. They included Mme de Brancas, associated with Tronson and the Oratorians, with whom for a period he frequently dined, and the bishops of La Rochelle and Luçon, but they were enough to serve as a pretext for the enemies he still had in common with Bossuet to throw suspicion on his doctrinal reliability. From 1699 Fénelon was in fact to be one of Jansenism's strongest opponents.

In fact Fénelon's spiritual austerity had nothing to do with Jansenist theology, or with his views on the disinterested love of God. It was not the theology of grace, but only the need to define the theological nature of the love of God, already the subject of a bitter dispute between Jean-Pierre Camus and the Jesuit Antoine Sirmond earlier in the century, which really made Fénelon confront the need to hold that the love of God must include the willingness to consent to being punished in a pain which would never end and never diminish. Like that of Rancé, the author of the fiendishly rigorous spirituality on which the reform of La Trappe was based and with whom Fénelon's relations were good, the spirituality which Fénelon developed even under Tronson's tutelage was independent of any strictly Jansenist theological inspiration.

Probably by 1679, and at latest by 1683, the year his uncle Antoine died, Fénelon had become known to Bossuet, whom he visited, perhaps for as much as weeks at a time, both at Meaux and at Bossuet's country retreat at Germigny. In 1684 Fénelon preached several short sets of sermons for Bossuet, and had by then become one of the small group of associates and disciples whom Bossuet had congregated around him. He was beginning also to be in demand as a preacher elsewhere when, in 1685, Colbert's son, Seignelay, who, born in 1651, had been given the reversion of three of his father's offices as early as 1669 and been made secretary of state in 1683, was given funds to send good preachers to unify the country's religion by bringing the south-west back to Catholicism. Seignelay knew Fénelon, and during the year preceding his death in 1690, before he was 40, he was to put himself under Fénelon's direction.

A series of letters in 1685 to the bishop of Saintes, G. de la Brunetière, shows Seignelay's admiration for Fénelon, to whom he wrote on 5 November, asking him to put together a team of good preachers, effectively giving him charge of the mission. The revocation of the edict of Nantes had been signed on 17 October 1685, and Seignelay was in a hurry. Fénelon had left Paris for Orléans, Saintes, and La Rochelle by about 5 December. The *Nouvelles Ecclesiastiques* announced on 1 December 1685 that Bossuet had given Fénelon and his companions their briefing. The missionaries were to implement the policies of Bossuet's liberal *Exposition de la foi catholique*, published in 1671, although written a little earlier. The handful of colleagues Fénelon had selected included Claude Fleury, the abbé de Cordemoy, and two future bishops, Bertier, bishop of Blois from 1693, and Milon, bishop of Condom from the same year.

On 28 December 1685 Fénelon fulfilled a promise to write to the duchesse de Beauvillier. Le Tellier, the chancellor and Lou-

vois's father, had died in October 1685 after signing the revocation of the edict, and the Colbert family had come back into favour. Fénelon mistakenly thought that Seignelay had already become a minister. In fact Seignelay had to wait until 1689, but his brother-in-law, Paul de Beauvillier, had just been made head of the Conseil des Finances and minister on 6 December 1685. Beauvillier was close to Tronson, whom he had taken as his director soon after their meeting in 1677. As gouverneur, a mixture of guardian, steward, and head of household to the duc de Bourgogne, he was to have Fénelon appointed to his preceptorate in 1689.

Fénelon wrote to Mme de Beauvillier again on 16 January 1686. The Jesuits at Marennes were too fierce in their preaching, "in this world, fines and prison; in the other, the devil and hell." On the other hand the diocesan clergy was not properly trained. What was required was more of the milder among the Jesuits. Fénelon may not have known that, when he wrote the letter, he had already been delated, probably by the four Jesuits, for omitting the customary "Ave Maria" before preaching, and had been accused, no doubt by Harlay de Champvallon, determined to pursue his vendetta against Bossuet through an attack on Fénelon, of saying that the veneration of images and the invocation of saints were useless practices. Fénelon went so far in this letter as to advocate the officially unthinkable, although not unknown, practice of saying Mass in French, a practice which was sufficiently anti-ultramontane to have on its own courted suspicions of Jansenism, although it did not touch the theology of grace.

Fénelon had sharp, scintillating eyes, but was frail. He was also a dreamer, and would walk by himself in the forest for relaxation. There is a story, even if it is true giving again only the slenderest basis for suspicion of Jansenist sympathies, that the Rochefort officers used to hide in the woods, calling out to Fénelon from behind trees, "M. Fénelon, you are going to be damned." Was it that experience which determined his later spiritual commitment to the disinterested love of God, as the experience of knowing he was to be damned had determined the spirituality of François de Sales? The possibility is both too slight to build on and too important to neglect, but it could provide a reason for the strength of Fénelon's later hostility to Jansenism, as it provided one for the Molinism of François de Sales before anything that could be called Jansenism had emerged in France.

For a moment, at least, it was possible that Fénelon would be recalled from the south-west in disgrace. It was clear that he was already attaching more importance to a common experience of evangelical religion than to a set of divisive confessional beliefs, an attitude held strongly against him in the later disputes, still today sometimes thought to relate him to pietistic or quietist religious tendencies, and against which Trent, with its meticulous elaboration of the propositional content of orthodoxy, had set itself. It is possible that the enthusiastic implementation of Fénelon's strategies, instead of their frustration, could have achieved the re-union of the Christian communities in late 17th-century France, as indeed an earlier acceptance of similar attitudes might have avoided schism in the first place.

The most striking inferences from the two letters to Mme de Beauvillier concern Fénelon's realistic appraisal of the religious situation, his acute analysis of the causes of Protestant pastoral success, and the religiously radical measures he was prepared to see used, including the establishment of mixed schools for boys and girls. In the letters, which are courteous but written in terms of personal friendship, Fénelon gives the impression that he is as much concerned for the unity of the kingdom as for the salvation of those whose conversion he was sent to obtain or confirm. In these respects his thought does not diverge from that of Bossuet. The political danger of bitterness in those whose conversions were merely formal was, Fénelon felt, a greater threat than France's lack of military preparedness.

To Seignelay, however, Fénelon wrote more formally on 28 January, defending himself against accusations of weakening the religious rules imposed by the Council of Trent, and reassuring him about the recitation of the Ave Maria, the litanies, and prayers to the saints. In fact, Fénelon was more punctilious in insisting on the acceptance of the full panoply of Tridentine Catholicism than most of his colleagues. What Fénelon did not know was that Mme de Beauvillier had let Seignelay see at least the second of his informal letters to her. Seignelay wrote to Fénelon on 4 February 1686 to say that he had shown Fénelon's letter to Mme de Beauvillier of 16 January to the king, who was disposed to accept Fénelon's analysis and take his advice with respect to getting milder Jesuits sent, but not in allowing Protestants to sing psalm paraphrases together with Catholics. Indeed the use of vernacular liturgical texts was taken at court as an indication of Jansenism, and the king's council had on 14 January 1686 ordered the suppression of Godeau's psalm paraphrases, which might powerfully have helped the missionaries in their religious task.

The king, now in what concerned religious unification turning back to the policy of Colbert from the more violent tactics advocated by Louvois, approved of the strategy with regard to the Protestants, "les ramener avec douceur (to bring them back gently)," as Seignelay wrote, but the Protestants and new converts had to be stopped from leaving France to accept the attractive offers being made by the Dutch. The real point of the mission from Seignelay's point of view was to prevent useful sailors who felt culturally alienated from France from being enticed away by the tax incentives on offer from Holland. The king and Seignelay, finally convinced of his orthodoxy, plainly wanted Fénelon and his companions to stay as missionaries in the west, but Fénelon privately wanted to come back to Paris. He was allowed to return in the summer, but was to be based again at La Rochelle from April to July 1687.

Fénelon's mission had been a relative failure. Unwilling to use force, and forbidden to mitigate the full rigours of Tridentine Catholicism by demoting the merely ritual and elevating the emphasis to the spiritual from the purely dogmatic, he had not achieved the results expected of him, and was passed over for the bishopric he could have expected. His credibility was not helped by the way in which he was distinguished from other Catholic writers in the avertissement to the immediate Amsterdam reprint of his 1687 Traité de l'éducation des filles, originally published in Paris. The work, strongly reliant on Fleury's Traité du choix de la méthode des études, which may have been circulating for nearly a decade prior to its publication in 1686, was probably written as early as 1685. At the date of its privilège, 21 February 1687, the duchesse de Beauvillier had seven daughters. There were to be two more before the first of her four sons was born on 10 January 1690.

The Huguenot editor points to Fénelon's lack of insistence on his Church's "thorny dogmas." He is not "extrêmement superstitieux (exceedingly superstitious)," had mixed in specifically papist doctrines "with regret," had not spoken of transsubstantiation, the adoration of the blessed sacrament, or purgatory, and had advocated teaching children neither "à se prosterner devant les images, ni à invoquer les saints, ni à prier pour les morts, ni à gagner les indulgences (to prostrate themselves before images, nor to invoke saints, nor to pray for the dead, nor to gain indulgences)." Bayle, too, put the accent on Fénelon's disregard of all rites and dogmas in a long review in his Nouvelles de la République des Lettres for October 1687. Well before the dispute with Bossuet, Fénelon had realized that the incidental by-product, as it were, of reliance on the all-important criterion of religious experience as a more important criterion of true Christianity than prescribed moral efforts and conceptual beliefs might be the reunification of Christendom.

It must have been during the winter of 1687–88 that Fénelon, no doubt at the pressing invitation of Bossuet, wrote the refutation of Malebranche's 1680 Traité de la Nature et de la Grâce called simply Réfutation du Traité de la Nature et de la Grâce. It is improbable that Malebranche ever learnt of its existence. The manuscript contains annotations in Bossuet's handwriting, and parts of the work were published in 1717 in Les Nouvelles Littéraires. Sainte-Beuve regarded the Réfutation as Fénelon's best philosophical work, although the fundamental considerations are in fact largely theological. In Port-Royal (VI, 5), he reported Victor Cousin's view that, without Bossuet, Fénelon was lost, "in the ninth heaven, it is true, but lost."

Fénelon particularly repudiated Malebranche's views about the necessity of God's creation, and of his creation of precisely this world, as also the way in which Malebranche seemed to Fénelon to compromise the freedom of the human will, removing the predestination of the elect from the will of God the Father to the will of the Word, somehow limited by its incarnation. There is little doubt, as Sainte-Beuve perceptively and maliciously points out, that Fénelon is echoing Bossuet's doctrine as it is to be found, for instance, in Bossuet's letter to a disciple of Malebranche of 21 May 1687, and Bossuet rightly perceived that Malebranche was generating a concept of God as constrained by his own being to only necessary acts. In different forms, the debate had been going on for centuries, but Bossuet correctly saw the danger. Malebranche was eluding the difficulties in ways too similar to those of Richard Simon in exegesis and Spinoza in metaphysics.

In 1688 Fénelon, inspired by a commentary of Bossuet, wrote a short explanation of the first verses of the ninth chapter of the Book of Revelation. On 1 May his remaining uncle, the bishop of Sarlat, died. On 11 June Fénelon obtained a privilège for his Traité du ministère des pasteurs, published in August and devoted to the view that the Protestant ministry has become invalid by breaking with apostolic succession and, in particular, allowing the election of pastors, and depriving priestly ordination of its sacramental character. Fénelon was again using Bossuet's arguments, as expressed particularly in the 1654 refutation of Ferry's catechism, although Fénelon's style is more lucid, elegant, and popular. During the remainder of 1688 he probably wrote his Mémoire concernant la cour de Rome in October, and the Ode sur la prise de Philippsbourg par le dauphin, celebrating the victory of 29 October, in the following month.

The Mémoire arose from Louis XIV's decision in 1673 to extend the régale, or right to the revenue from certain vacant sees, to all the sees in France. In reaction to the clergy's Décla-

ration du clergé gallican of 1682, Innocent XI, who had acceded to the papal throne in 1676 and who died on 12 August 1689, had withdrawn the right of what we know as diplomatic immunity from civil penalties hitherto afforded to the French and other embassies at Rome and, when Louis XIV refused to accept the withdrawal, had issued the bull *Cum alias* of 12 May 1687. He then excommunicated Louis's new ambassador, the marquis de Lavardin, and put an interdict on the French church in Rome. There was a real threat of a Gallican schism. Louis XIV sent troops into papal Avignon but, before deciding on any invasion of the Papal states, initiated a round of consultations by Achille de Harlay, the procureur général.

Seignelay asked Fénelon to draw up his *Mémoire* which, together with those written by three archbishops, went to Croissy de Colbert at the ministry of foreign affairs, as well as to Seignelay in charge of clergy affairs, to the chancellor, and to Pontchartrain, Beauvillier, and Louvois. It offers practical advice, and is moderate in tone, distrustful of the ancient religious orders, which were responsible only to Rome and exempt from French diocesan jurisdiction, dismissive about the personal infallibility of the pope, but critical of the parlement, and sensitive to the danger of a schism no one wanted. It obliged Fénelon to think out what he regarded as the correct relationship between church and state, in an age in which the debate about the principle of the papacy's temporal power had not yet begun, and when the erosion of the spiritual authority of national churches that was to reach its extreme during the 19th century had only just started.

On 1 January 1689 Fénelon preached at the Jesuit professed house at Paris, an occasion which sealed a more cordial relationship between Fénelon and the Jesuits than had hitherto existed, and one which was to assume increasing importance in France's religious life. Later that year, a gouverneur would be required for the duc de Bourgogne, the king's grandson and probably eventual successor to the throne, born on 6 August 1682. The name of Vardes had been mentioned, but he had died on 3 September 1688. There was considerable speculation that Montauzier wanted the appointment, or even Bossuet, who was naturally consulted. Beauvillier was appointed on 16 August 1689, and his choice for the preceptorate was Fénelon, whose nomination was announced on the 17th, and about whose suitability remaining doubts had been dispelled through consultations with Bossuet, Tronson, and Fénelon's Jesuit confessor, Le Valois. By early September Fénelon had resigned his position at Les Nouvelles Catholiques and taken up his new duties, extended in 1690 and 1691 to the tutorship of the duc de Bourgogne's brothers, the ducs d'Anjou and de Berry. Fleury was the assistant chosen by Fénelon, and his appointment was announced by the king on 14 September 1689.

In the meanwhile, at the beginning of October 1688, Fénelon, not yet acquainted with the writings of the mystics, had met Jeanne-Marie Bouvier de la Motte, Mme Guyon, at the château de Beynes, belonging to Marie Foucquet, duchesse de Charost, daughter of the now dead surintendant. Born in 1648, Mme Guyon had been unhappily married. Her husband had died in 1676, and from 1671 she had had a Barnabite director, Père La Combe. She appears to have carried on a homosexual relationship with a young girl, Catau Barbe, whom she took away with her, who slept in her bed, and whom she was finally forced to return to her family. In 1681 Mme Guyon had gone to Gex, to be near her director. She had journeyed to Turin, Genoa, and

Marseilles, giving conferences on prayer, had written the *Moyen court et très facile pour l'oraison* and *Le Cantique des Cantiques, interprété*, published with privilèges in 1685 and 1688, and was composing the *Torrents spirituels*. In 1686 she had returned to Paris, where she was put under police surveillance, probably at Harlay de Champvallon's instigation, imprisoned at the Visitation convent on 19 January 1688, and freed on 18 September. La Combe had also been imprisoned, probably suspected of political activity in the ultramontane interest. Mme de Maintenon, who strongly disliked Harlay, was won over to Mme Guyon's side, convinced by her spirituality, attracted by her charm, but dismayed at her vulgarity.

In the ensuing disputes Mme Guyon was accused of "quietism," a heresy condemned by Innocent XI in 1687 in the form of 68 propositions from the 1675 *Guida spirituale* of Miguel Molinos, although she took more from François de Sales and, above all, François Malaval, whose *Pratique facile pour élever l'âme à la contemplation* was published in 1664 and put on the Roman index of prohibited books on 24 May 1688. Fénelon's position cannot be understood unless a distinction is made between quietism, Mme Guyon's doctrine on passivity in prayer, and Fénelon's own defence of charity as implying the disinterested love of God. There is no necessary relationship between the three doctrinal positions implied, although Bossuet held that there was, and was against all three. The dispute is neither esoteric nor merely technical.

Fénelon was defending the gratuity of the supernatural order, that is, he was distinguishing between human nature itself, and a divine vocation that was not part of the "natural order," and Bossuet may genuinely have been mistaken about his doctrinal position, which was not in the end the issue between them. A confusion does run right through the religious disputes between Catholics in 17th-century France concerning the effects in the order of human psychological experience of the ontological status of human nature as affected by the fall and redemption of the human race as it was taught by the Christian revelation. Human beings might ontologically be justified or alternatively in a state of sin without being in any way psychologically affected. It was uncertain whether the love of God was simply a synonym for charity or sanctifying grace, essentially a supernaturally elevated state in the ontological order of being, which justified the soul and consequently allowed an eternity of bliss, but the love of God could also be understood as a psychological state of feeling subject to the ordinary laws of human motivation and self-deception, which could not provide reassurance about supernatural justification.

In a century in which belief in a personal and unending experience of ecstasy or torment after death was still at least very nearly universal, not only was the dispute not trivial, but the view held by any individual on such questions as whether the state of justification was discernible in the order of experience had to penetrate to the very core of the personality, and provide the ultimate determinant for the totality of personal attitudes. The difficulties were compounded for Fénelon by his inclination to believe that supernatural gifts were not so exclusively mediated by rational thought, moral effort, and institutional conformity as Bossuet insisted. The century's literature is not surprisingly saturated with explorations of the consequences of its central spiritual dilemma, although less attention has been paid to the need to define it among recent generations of critics.

The first letter of Fénelon to Mme Guyon which has been preserved is dated 2 December 1688, and presupposes previous correspondence, probably at least four letters from Mme Guyon, to whom Fénelon now offered the direct guidance she had obviously asked for. It was Mme Guyon who first interested Fénelon in mystical theology, and the correspondence suggests that it was he who, at first very tentatively, put himself under her direction. The early letters touch on receptivity to divine inspiration and the means of discerning it, abandonment to the divine will, and by 11 May the theme of pure love. By 30 April Fénelon can refer to John of the Cross, the Spanish mystic whose 16th-century *Ascent of Mount Carmel* had been translated into French in 1645. Mme de Maintenon had been won over, and Mme Guyon was invited to stay at her educational establishment at Saint-Cyr and to give conferences there. Fénelon himself began to write to Mme de Maintenon letters of spiritual advice which she treasured, had copied, and showed round. She invited her confessor, Godet des Marais, the bishop of Chartres, to comment on a very long letter from Fénelon of January 1690.

On 3 November 1690 Seignelay died, assisted on his deathbed by Fénelon. In February 1691 Fénelon was among the select few invited to attend a performance of Racine's *Athalie* at Saint-Cyr, and on 6 February 1693, he was sent with Bossuet and the king's confessor, Père de la Chaise, to Pellisson's deathbed. Pellisson agreed to confess and communicate on the following day, but died early in the morning. Fénelon was then elected to his place in the Académie française, where his reception took place on 31 March 1693. He had consented only with ill grace to submit his speech to the general secretary in advance. It was on eloquence and poetry and was re-worked into the posthumously published *Lettre à l'Académie*. The *Mercure Galant* said that "it was among the most eloquent ever to have been heard."

Later that year Fénelon wrote his devastating indictment of the king in a letter to him, reproaching him above all with the wretchedness to which he had reduced his people, but adding for good measure strong denunciations of his policies, his advisers, whose names he names and whose faults he catalogues, his injustice, his irreligion, his bellicose ambitions, his conceit, and his stupidity. Commentators have assumed that the document was not read by the king, or by Beauvillier, or by Mme de Maintenon, for whose eyes it was probably in fact chiefly intended. In fact, Louis XIV received a number of such letters, and read them without enjoyment but, if he respected their authors, without as much resentment as his reputation has led historians to expect. It is to this letter that Mme de Maintenon probably referred in her letters to Noailles of 21 and 27 December 1695 as "too harsh" but "well written." Luckily the 1694 harvest was to be a good one. Some of the starvation was to be alleviated.

Meanwhile, however, at Saint-Cyr some of the community had begun to behave almost as if the new doctrine had its own circle of adepts. They were denounced. Godet des Marais placed spies in the community and in 1693 confronted Mme de Maintenon with evidence of the disharmony being caused by Mme Guyon. Fénelon approved Mme de Maintenon's decision to ask Mme Guyon on 2 May 1693 not to return to Saint-Cyr. However, Harlay de Champvallon, still hostile to Mme de Maintenon, decided to exploit the situation and proposed to submit to the Sorbonne the "case of conscience" whether a Christian prince could allow his children to be brought up by a tutor suspected of quietism. Bossuet stopped its discussion, but by September 1693 Mme de Maintenon was intimidated, spoke to Bossuet, and asked for the opinion of others, in writing, on Mme

Guyon's doctrine. Mme Guyon, urged by Fénelon, had already, in Fénelon's presence, on 1 August at the house of the duc de Chevreuse, given her writings to Bossuet to examine. Bossuet spent the winter of 1693–94 studying them. Mme Guyon left Paris in September 1693 in order not to compromise anyone, and from then on Fénelon did not write to her or hear from her, except through intermediaries and very rarely. He did not himself know her whereabouts.

Probably on 7 May 1694, Fénelon wrote a severe letter to Mme de Maintenon, which she showed to Godet des Marais, who agreed with Fénelon's severity towards his penitent, but suggested, to avoid misunderstandings, a tactful prudence in the use of language. Then Mme Guyon, feeling trapped, asked in June 1694 for a commission to examine her behaviour, about which rumours were being spread. Instead, Bossuet, Noailles, and Tronson were appointed to examine her writings at what came to be known as the "conférences d'Issy," held from July 1694. Godet des Marais and Fénelon showered the commissioners with advice, with Fénelon in particular sending copious excerpts from François de Sales, Catherine of Genoa, and Surin.

So far only the archbishop, Harlay de Champvallon, described by Fénelon in his letter to the king as "corrompu, scandaleux, incorrigible, faux, malin, artificieux, ennemi de toute vertu, et qui fait gémir tous les gens de bien (corrupt, scandalous, incorrigible, treacherous, malicious, deceitful, enemy of all virtue, inspiring horror in all honest people)," was known to be pursuing Mme Guyon, but it gradually became clear that Bossuet had joined in, and was attacking not so much Mme Guyon as the whole spiritual tradition of interior prayer, and not so much her doubtful taste as her disdain for doctrine and her trust in nature. Unlike Fénelon, the theologian, she did not distinguish what in human experience was natural and what was dependent on grace.

Bossuet's friend Nicole had already in 1679 published anonymously his anti-mystical *Traité de l'oraison*, and in early 1694 Boileau's *Satire X* on women had sharply attacked "Molinosism." Later, in a private conversation recorded by Mathieu Marais, Boileau was to express his disagreement with Fénelon's position on disinterest, and Bossuet's own position sharpened to the point at which he would in 1697 declare Fénelon to have been accused at Issy, and to have capitulated. In fact in February 1695 the conferences were ending, and Bossuet drew up a list of 30 propositions. Fénelon had almost joined the commission and on 1 March produced another draft, adding articles 12, 13, 33, and 34, and changing 7, 17, 21, and 24. Bossuet later denied that there had ever been a draft without them, but a copy has subsequently been found, and Fénelon's redaction was signed on 10 March.

He was not in disgrace. In spite of his letter of December 1693, Louis XIV gave him in December 1694 the abbey of Saint-Valéry-sur-Somme, yielding an annual 14,000 livres, and then on 4 February 1695 the archbishopric of Cambrai, about 160 kilometres north of Paris, the richest in France, with a revenue of 100,000 livres, expressing the hope that Fénelon would continue his preceptorate. The promotion seemed double-edged. Fénelon might have hoped for Paris, but appearances were saved, and Bossuet consecrated Fénelon in the Saint-Cyr chapel on 10 July 1695, assisted by Noailles of Chalons—on Harlay's death on 6 August 1695 to succeed to the archbishopric of Paris, and soon to become a cardinal—and by Henri Feydeau de Brou, bishop of Amiens, in the presence of Mme de Maintenon.

Mme Guyon had agreed to retire to a monastery at Meaux, and both Bossuet and Fénelon had signed the articles. Bossuet intended to write a book about spiritual matters, and as late as December 1695 Fénelon thought he had been invited to collaborate. By February 1696 it was clear to him that Bossuet, assisted by Godet des Marais, intended to launch an attack both on Mme Guyon and on himself. Mme Guyon had been arrested and sent to Vincennes on 27 December 1695. Fénelon in haste wrote an "Explication des articles d'Issy," and, when asked, in June 1696 approved dom François Lamy's *Le nouvel athéisme renversé, ou, Réfutation du système de Spinoza*, but on 24 July refused to sign an approbation for Bossuet's *Instruction sur les états d'oraison*.

Before Bossuet heard on 5 August of his refusal, Fénelon had read on the 2nd to Noailles, Godet des Marais, Tronson and the ducs de Beauvillier and Chevreuse at Issy his *Mémoire pour motiver le refus d'approbation du livre de Monsieur de Meaux*, a copy of which reached Mme de Maintenon on 16 August. Urged on by Chevreuse, Fénelon now re-worked his "Explication" as the *Explication des maximes des saints sur la vie intérieure*, a reply to Bossuet's *Instruction*. The *Instruction*'s privilège is dated 21 October 1696. Fénelon's book was approved only by Pirot, the syndic of the theology faculty, but it was also shown to Tronson, Fleury, and Noailles, now archbishop of Paris, who warmly commended it. Bossuet, not consulted, was furious and, before he had seen it, denounced the book as subversive of all true religion. Fénelon had planned its publication for a month after Bossuet's *Instruction*, and his text was still being revised when Chevreuse, in charge of publication, heard that the impending issue of Fénelon's book had been leaked to Bossuet, and ordered immediate publication. The *Explication des maximes des saints sur la vie intérieure* was on sale on 29 January 1697. The first impression of Bossuet's *Instruction* was not completed until 25 February.

The explosion was considerable. Mme de Maintenon saw very well what was happening. A confrontation which challenged Bossuet's authority was the last way for Fénelon to win the argument, especially when, having refused his approbation to Bossuet's book, he got his own reply published before the *Instruction* had ever come out. Among the allies recruited by Bossuet was the archbishop of Reims, who had his own niece as his mistress. One historian notes with surprise that even Pontchartrain took time off from the scandalous accumulation of his fortune to support Bossuet, while Bossuet himself resorted to demeaning histrionics at court, begging the king's forgiveness on his knees for not having denounced Fénelon sooner. Noailles, the nuntius, and Godet des Marais all wanted a way out with dignity for both Fénelon, supported by half the clergy, and Bossuet, who finally got his censure signed. Fénelon received permission to write to Rome, but took care not to appeal over the head of the Gallican church. On 27 April 1697 he asked merely not to be condemned without a hearing. When the censure had been signed, he was ordered on 1 August to retire to his diocese. In the meanwhile it was Louis XIV who on 26 July appealed to Rome to decide the doctrinal issue. Bossuet, who confidently announced his expectation of a red hat, had drawn up the letter. Innocent XII assented to the king's request on 10 September. On 1 August the Paris Jesuits had defended the proposition that disinterested love of God is not only possible, but of obligation.

At Rome Fénelon was represented by one of Tronson's disciples, Gabriel de la Cropte, a distant relation of Fénelon's who was also his friend and vicar-general, Bossuet by his vicar-general, Phélipeaux, and his ordained nephew, twice in serious trouble on account of his love life, about to become his sister-in-law's lover at the episcopal palace at Meaux, and of whose scandalous behaviour Bossuet was certainly not ignorant. The pope appointed seven consultors, then added three more on Fénelon's side. The commission split five-five towards the end of 1698. A new commission of cardinals met 57 times from September 1698 to March 1699. The affair became politicized, and it looked as if the only way for Bossuet to get a condemnation was to prove a moral scandal involving Mme Guyon with Père La Combe and Fénelon. Mme Guyon had left the Meaux convent to the rage of Bossuet in July 1695 and hidden under assumed names in various places near Paris. After imprisonment at Vincennes from the end of December, she was kept in a convent again from 16 October 1696 to 4 June 1698, and then taken to the Bastille. Bossuet succeeded in getting her release postponed until 1703, when she retired to Touraine, and continued to write works of spirituality. She died in 1717. Père La Combe, in prison since 1687, was moved from Lourdes to Vincennes where he gradually became mad, and in 1712 was moved to the asylum at Charenton, where he died in 1715.

Bossuet's vindictive rage was glossed over by generations of French literary and church historians dedicated to the myth of a grand siècle, a roi soleil, and a classical literature, all of which he was long thought to represent. His reputation was still defended in the French literary press after a celebrated defence of an excellent thesis on his Gallicanism published in 1953. Thereafter the tide turned, and there is now virtual unanimity that Bossuet's behaviour was appalling, Fénelon's dignified, and that Fénelon's theology was better than Bossuet's, his intellect more subtle, and his spirituality and literary gifts of a quite different order. Meanwhile Bossuet fabricated the scandal which his nephew had told him was necessary, sexual innuendoes of which echoes are to be found in Bossuet's *Relation sur le quiétisme*. Although without any foundation, they were sufficient to cause the exile from court of Fénelon's more openly declared friends on 2 June 1698. His brother had to leave the army.

Meanwhile Fénelon himself behaved with at least apparent hauteur. A general letter "To a friend" of 3 August 1697 makes clear that Fénelon was taking his stand on the issue of disinterested love, and not on Molinos's contempt for dogma and rites, nor even on passivity in prayer; but it caused a furore on account of the hope it expressed of the pope, "qu'il ait la bonté de marquer précisément les endroits qu'il condamne, et les sens sur lesquels porte sa condamnation, afin que ma souscription soit sans restriction (that the pope would have the goodness to mark precisely what places he is condemning, and in what sense, so that my submission may be without reservation)." The full impertinence of that remark derives from an implied reference to the terms of various condemnations of Jansenist propositions. In a further letter, probably of 3 September, purporting to be to a different unnamed friend, Fénelon affected surprise at the comment caused by that remark from the earlier letter, which Beauvillier had had printed. Noailles had meanwhile made difficulties about signing the *Déclaration* against the *Explication*, in the first place. It was published only in September, and the rapidity with which the polemical tracts were published intensified.

Bossuet's *Relation sur le quiétisme* appeared on 26 June

1698. Louis XIV urged on by Bossuet ineffectually wrote to Rome in May and December pressing for the condemnation. Bossuet wrote to Louis XIV to warn him that it was his duty to frighten Rome into issuing the condemnation, but Rome was not in a hurry. In January 1699 Fénelon was stripped of his preceptorate and lost his Versailles apartment. Rome, not yet having received Louis XIV's ultimatum, did finally condemn 23 propositions from the *Explication des maximes des saints*, but the pope used a simple brief, *Cum alias*, not a bull, condemned the propositions globally and not individually, which had the effect of reducing the condemnation to an admonition, and used the mildest possible theological qualifications. In their obvious sense, and in their context, they were "dangerous," "at etiam respective erroneae (or respectively erroneous)." The insertion of the word "respective" makes the general reference to the 23 propositions, some consisting of several sentences, simply too doctrinally non-specific. The condemnatory statement could mean as little as that some of them could be, but not that they needed to be, understood as erroneous, and even then the brief did not say which.

As condemnations go, *Cum alias* was almost exculpatory. Since it did not say where the errors were, or what they were, it amounted to no more than a warning that the 23 propositions could lead to misunderstandings. Nothing was declared heretical, the only important theological note attached to condemnations, or even blasphemous, contumacious, impious, or hostile to religious truth or devotion, all terms generally used in the condemnation of error. The fundamental difficulty concealed in the scholastic concept of the will as a rational faculty was left untouched. Either the will had to be determined by some outside force, like desire, or Augustine's victorious delectation, understood as Jansen understood it, in which case disinterest was psychologically impossible, or it could be determined without seeking a satisfaction external to it, in which case the traditional definition of charity as the love of God for his own sake implied disinterest, as Catherine of Genoa, Theresa of Avila, John of the Cross, and François de Sales had all taught. Jansen, and Bossuet, now allied with Malebranche, chose the first horn of that dilemma, while Fénelon, supported by most of the authors in the spiritual tradition, recently and importantly including François Lamy, chose the other. There was not much Rome could do except prevent the use of the categories in such a way as to compromise traditional doctrines and practices, such as those involving the desire for eternal reward and the fear of everlasting punishment.

Rome's most enlightened theologians were almost solidly sympathetic to Fénelon, however dangerous they thought some of the formulations. Fénelon submitted to the brief before he knew the terms of the condemnation. Doctrinally they were in fact a vindication and, wherever it counted, the Latin was ambiguous, mixing references to states, like the "habitual state of the love of God, which is pure charity," with motives, like fear or desire, or qualities, like merit. That does no more than preserve the integrity of the theological virtue of hope, and is simply an averagely skilful example of Roman drafting, understandably warning spiritual authors against the use of the exaggerated language of self-immolation, while offering a veiled rebuke to the king of France dressed up as deference to his wishes, and scarcely concealing in the form of the condemnation its contempt for its instigator, who was now quite certain never to be offered elevation to the purple.

As far as Fénelon was concerned, however, the brief was made to look in France like a full-scale repudiation of his views, and he remained for the rest of his life in disgrace, and in exile. He preached, was devoted to his diocese, particularly when it was ravaged by the War of the Spanish Succession from 1701, and was an exemplary pastor who achieved a reputation for sanctity. He tried to find ways first of avoiding the war and then of ending it. The war did come to Cambrai, which had to care for the wounded after Malplaquet in September 1709. Fénelon turned his palace and seminary into hospitals, but the effects of the war were then aggravated by famine resulting from the severe winter of 1708. Cambrai had only ten parishes, and was mostly Flemish speaking. Fénelon's congregations were openly hostile to him to start with. His letters may exaggerate his dejection, but he was near to being disheartened. He was certainly shaken interiorly by what had happened.

His increasing dislike of Jansenism derived from his conviction that Jansen, if less crassly than Bossuet, allowed the love of God to be swamped in what Bossuet had not drawn back from referring to as the desire for pleasure. The Jesuits had been Fénelon's firm supporters, and he was now their ally. The Roman prelates favourable to him were rapidly receiving advancement and Fénelon, spied on in Cambrai, was none the less the author of a strategy in France for isolating Jansenists. He manoeuvred his opponents into impossible positions, and gradually achieved for himself overwhelming support. He came very near to running the affairs of the French church from Cambrai. His political, social, and literary doctrines came not in documents for publication, but in the letters and private memoranda which constitute the bulk of his works.

Only the hostility of Louis XIV, snubbed by Rome on Fénelon's account, prevented a recall to Versailles. Fénelon was twice allowed, if only in front of witnesses, to meet the duc de Bourgogne again, who remained faithful to his former teacher and, on his father's death on 14 April 1711, became his grandfather's heir presumptive. When the duc de Bourgogne himself died on 18 February 1712, the future Louis XV was still an infant, but the duc d'Orléans, nephew of Louis XIV and from 1715 to be regent, was favourable to Fénelon. In the end Louis XIV became convinced of the need to bring Fénelon back, if only to remove Noailles and the Jansenist influence. He was ready to call a national council, of which Fénelon would have been elected president, when Fénelon, in November 1714 a frail and tired 63, had an accident in his carriage, which hit a parapet while crossing a bridge. A horse was killed, and Fénelon was shaken. Weak with fever, he had to go to bed on 1 January 1715, and died on 7 January.

WORKS

The range, penetration and imaginative vigour of Fénelon's mind are beyond real question. Most of the works, however, other than those polemically concerned with the defence of pure love in the dispute with Bossuet, either are works of immediate circumstance, drawn from the need to react to particular situations and problems, or were intended for the instruction and education of young princes. The thought is as powerful and wide in compass as Rousseau's, and it is better organized, although it no doubt lacks Rousseau's passion as well as his refusal to be bound by the actual circumstances in which he wrote and thought. But because Fénelon wrote comparatively few sustained works of imaginative importance, because a chronological account of his numerous works is bound to look too like a list, and because he has so frequently been reproached with effeteness of style, a reasonable starting point for a consideration of his writings is the magnificently cadenced invective of the famous *Lettre à Louis XIV*, probably of December 1693.

Cast in audacious terms, it contains the elements of the social and political thought to be developed in *Les Aventures de Télémaque*, the *Examen de conscience sur les devoirs de la royauté*, and in the *Tables de Chaulnes*. Fénelon starts by stating that he has at heart only the communication of the truths "nécessaires à votre salut (necessary for your salvation)." Fénelon is sincere in acknowledging the king's natural uprightness:

Vous êtes né, Sire, avec un coeur droit et équitable; mais ceux qui vous ont élevé ne vous ont donné pour science de gouverner, que la défiance, la jalousie, l'éloignement de la vertu, la crainte de tout mérite éclatant, le goût des hommes souples et rampants, la hauteur, et l'attention à votre seul intérêt

(You were born, Sire, with an upright and honest disposition; but those who brought you up taught you an art of governing made up of nothing but mistrust, jealousy, distaste for virtue, fear of outstanding merit, a liking for men who were compliant and servile, aloofness, and concern only for your own interest).

Fénelon's estimate is not far out of line with discerning contemporary opinion. Behind his judgement is the peceptivity of an educator, even of a spiritual director. Louis XIV did sometimes go out of his way to get hold of the real truth which he knew was being concealed from him, and he was aware he was being flattered. His personal weakness was a liking for splendour, military glory, and physical prowess. Fénelon is in fact blaming Mazarin here, and even Richelieu, as he blamed them more light-heartedly for the instruction of the duc de Bourgogne in the 74th of the *Dialogues des morts* between Mazarin and Richelieu, written some time between 1692 and 1695. He continues:

Depuis environ trente ans, vos principaux ministres ont ébranlé et renversé toutes les anciennes maximes de l'Etat, pour faire monter jusqu'au comble votre autorité, qui était devenue la leur parce qu'elle était dans leurs mains. On n'a plus parlé de l'Etat ni des règles; on n'a parlé que du Roi et son bon plaisir. On a poussé vos revenus et vos dépenses à l'infini. On vous a élevé jusqu'au ciel… pour avoir appauvri la France entière, afin d'introduire à la cour un luxe monstrueux et incurable

(For about thirty years your chief ministers have weakened and overturned all the old principles of state in order to maximize your authority, which had become theirs because it was in their hands. There was no more talk of the state or of rules, only of the king and his good pleasure. Your revenues and expenditure have been extended to infinity. You have been praised to the skies… for having impoverished the whole of France in order to introduce at court a monstrous and incorrigible luxury).

This is not Savonarola thundering against profligate indulgence, nor the product of puritanical paranoia. The very rhythm of the prose shows that, while it may quiver with feeling, the *Lettre* is the product of reasoned considered reflection as well as being a passionate appeal. The logical structure of the letter suggests that it was indeed intended to have a practical effect, probably by persuading Mme de Maintenon to act on the king. The theme of extravagant expenditure, sometimes linked to the impoverishment of the people and the dependence of a whole class of office-bearers and courtiers on royal bounty, recurs in Saint-Simon, and in Fénelon's own works in different contexts and on different registers, particularly in *Télémaque*, the *Examen de conscience sur les devoirs de la royauté*, and the *Tables de Chaulnes*.

In the *Lettre*, Fénelon works his way round to the all-important topic of war and peace by way of the king's ministers, who have been "durs, hautains, injustes, violents, de mauvaise foi (harsh, haughty, unjust, violent, and double-dealing)." Then referring without naming him to Louvois, he moves on to "la vraie source de tous les maux que la France souffre (the real source of all the ills from which France is suffering)."

On a rendu votre nom odieux, et toute la nation française insupportable à tous nos voisins. On n'a conservé aucun ancien allié, parce qu'on n'a voulu que des esclaves. On a causé depuis plus de vingt ans des guerres sanglantes. Par exemple, Sire, on fit entreprendre à Votre Majesté, en 1672, la guerre de Hollande pour votre gloire, et pour punir les Hollandais, qui avaient fait quelque raillerie, dans le chagrin où on les avait mis en troublant les règles du commerce établies par le cardinal de Richelieu. Je cite en particulier cette guerre, parce qu'elle a été la source de toutes les autres. Elle n'a eu pour fondement qu'un motif de gloire et de vengeance, ce qui ne peut jamais rendre une guerre juste… une guerre injuste n'en est pas moins injuste pour être heureuse; d'où il s'ensuit que toutes les frontières que vous avez étendues par cette guerre sont injustement acquises dans l'origine…

En voilà assez, Sire, pour reconnaître que vous avez passé votre vie entière hors du chemin de la vérité et de la justice…Cependant vos peuples que vous devriez aimer comme vos enfants, et qui ont été jusqu'ici si passionnés pour vous, meurent de faim. La culture des terres est presque abandonnée, les villes et la campagne se dépeuplent; tous les métiers languissent et ne nourrissent plus les ouvriers. Tout commerce est anéanti. Par conséquent vous avez détruit la moitié des forces réelles du dedans de votre Etat, pour faire et pour défendre de vaines conquêtes au dehors

(They have made your name hated, and the whole French nation intolerable to all our neighbours. No former ally has been kept because only slaves were wanted. More than twenty years of bloody wars have been caused. For example, Sire, your majesty was persuaded in 1672 to undertake the Dutch war for your glory, and to punish the Dutch for an affront committed out of the annoyance caused them when the commercial arrangements established by cardinal Richelieu were disrupted. I quote that war in particular, because it has been the source of all the others. Its motive was only a matter of glory and vengeance, which can never make a war just… an unjust war is no less unjust for ending in victory; from which it follows that all the frontiers which you extended by that war were originally acquired unjustly…

That, Sire, is enough to show that you have passed your whole life outside the path of truth and justice…Meanwhile, your peoples whom you should love as your children, and who until now have committed themselves to you with such passion, are starving. The cultivation of the land has nearly been abandoned, the towns and the countryside are being depopulated; all the trades are in recession and no longer feed their work-forces. Trade has been ruined. So you have destroyed half the real strength within your state to make and defend worthless conquests outside it).

In the present context it is chiefly necessary, in order to estimate how audacious Fénelon may have been, to remember that Louis XIV was well aware of popular sentiment and literate feeling, that popular songs, minor uprisings, court gossip, and the comments of the gazettes like the *Nouvelles Ecclésiastiques* and the *Mercure Historique et Politique* made it impossible for him to be unaware of what was happening, and what was felt in his kingdom. He was 55, enjoyed power and pleasure, was no doubt attuned to social values and attitudes which literary historians can see to have been obsolescent, and was willing not to think too much about the consequences not of his whims so much as of his desires and rages. But he was neither stupid, nor ignorant, nor entirely insensitive to at least the political need to have a conscience he could hear.

Fénelon, his reputation cleansed of its light wash of suspected Jansenism, tutor to Louis XIV's grandson, a court ecclesiastic no doubt destined for a prelacy, a friend of Mme de Maintenon and a representative of aristocratic but seriously devout opinion, was part of the licensed and paid corporate conscience employed by the king. He will have been listened to, partly as a necessary counter-balance to more established ecclesiastics, and partly because he was obviously right in so many of his judgements, as in the terrible strictures in his letter on Harlay de Champvallon, already quoted, and on the mediocrity of the king's powerful Jesuit confessor, Père de la Chaise: "son esprit est court et grossier… Les Jésuites mêmes le méprisent… il ne se connaît point en hommes, non plus qu'en autre chose (his mind is small and coarse…The Jesuits themseves despise him… he is not discerning about people any more than about anything else)." Indeed, it has been argued that, after Bossuet had conspired to fabricate the calumny that would discredit Fénelon in the *Relation sur le quiétisme* in 1698, thereby for the second time breaking the seal of the confessional, it was Louis XIV himself who, in spite of his public attitude, deliberately leaked to Beauvillier the detailed and curiously up-to-date information about the procedures of both Mme de Maintenon and Bossuet which Fénelon continued to receive.

That is not to say that there are no moments in Fénelon's letter in which he ran risks, but it is difficult to know which they were. The best modern Fénelon scholars have selected different audacities to point to. What is quite clear is that Fénelon, like La Bruyère, is sensitive to the need for a change, towards liberalism, in social and personal attitudes. Fénelon is intransigent about the injustice of war fought for personal aggrandizement,

about its cruelty and injustice, and about a sovereign's duty to his people. The passages quoted already give some idea of the nervous vigour of the letter's style, and the thrust towards new determining considerations in both foreign and domestic policies. What is perhaps personally daring is the risk Fénelon took in appearing to share not a theology but a spirituality with Protestants and Jansenists. Mme Guyon's inspiration is clear.

Dieu saura bien enfin lever le voile qui vous couvre les yeux, et vous montrer ce que vous évitez de voir. Il y a longtemps qu'il tient son bras levé sur vous, mais il est lent à vous frapper, parce qu'il a pitié d'un prince qui a été toute sa vie obsédé de flatteurs, et parce que, d'ailleurs, vos ennemis sont aussi les siens. Mais il saura bien séparer sa cause juste, d'avec la vôtre qui ne l'est pas, et vous humilier pour vous convertir; car vous ne serez chrétien que dans l'humiliation. Vous n'aimez point Dieu; vous ne le craignez même que d'une crainte d'esclave; c'est l'enfer, et non point Dieu, que vous craignez. Votre religion ne consiste qu'en superstitions, en petites pratiques superficielles…Vous êtes scrupuleux sur des bagatelles, et endurci sur des maux terribles. Vous n'aimez que votre gloire et votre commodité…Vous ne connaissez point Dieu, vous ne l'aimez point, vous ne le priez point du coeur, et vous ne faites rien pour le connaître

(God will eventually remove the veil from before your eyes, and show you what you avoid seeing. For a long time now he has held his arm raised above you, but he is slow to strike you because he has pity on a prince who has been pestered all his life by flatterers and because, anyway, your enemies are also his. But he will be able to separate his just cause from yours which is not just, and humiliate you to convert you, because you will only ever be a Christian if you are humiliated. You do not love God; you do not even fear him except with the fear of a slave. What you are afraid of is not God, but hell. Your religion consists only of superstitions, of little superficial practices… you have scruples about trifles and are hardened to terrible evils. You love only your own glory and your own comfort…You do not know God, you do not love him, you do not pray to him with your heart, and you make no effort to know him).

The God poised ready to strike is Calvinist and Jansenist. The idea that Louis was hostile to the enemies of God, presumably heretics, was current in Mme de Maintenon's circle, and can be found in Racine's *Esther*. The most interesting aspect of this passage, apart from its undoubted audacity, concerns the delicacy of the balance. Is the idea that human love of God might require humiliation, rather than just humility, for its purification an expression of devotional ardour that can be matched from a thousand reputable sources, or does it betray a hint of psychological abnormality, the beginnings of a dangerous self-loathing which can be the prelude to derangement? The compatibility of scrupulous observance with major miscreancy, care for the way a habit is worn, for instance, coupled with unconcern about betrayal of all monastic vows, is a commonplace in spiritual literature.

Fénelon's three *Dialogues sur l'éloquence en général et sur celle de la chaire en particulier* date from relatively early, between 1677 and 1681, and may derive much from an unpublished dialogue of 1664 by Fleury, "Si on doit citer dans les plaidoyers." They reflect an early interest in styles of oratory, and use the dialogue form which Fénelon took from the Plato of the *Gorgias* and especially from Cicero's *De oratore*. Fénelon designates his three speakers only by the letters A, B, and C. B is the preacher who wants to learn, and whose old-fashioned ideas Fénelon wants to correct. A replies to the questions and puts forward the newer views, while C is the advocate of an extreme evangelical simplicity which A finds excessive, but which Fénelon here flies as a kite, without committing himself. The dialogues are not otherwise particularly original in their analysis of the rules of oratory. They start from the consideration of how oratory should move, instruct, and please, and merely confirm the contemporary deference to all that is rational, useful and moral, moving away with a number of other writers associated with the Hôtel Lamoignon from the arid use of figures and examples.

The short essay *De l'éducation des filles* is not intrinsically important, but Fénelon published it himself and it must have been seen as qualifying him for the preceptorate, in spite of its relative lack of success in Paris, where the bookseller Pierre Emery provided unsold copies of the first 1687 edition with a new title page for the 1699 "edition," in the hope of unloading surplus stock on the back of the success of *Télémaque*. There was a 1696 Paris edition, and Amsterdam editions of 1687, 1697, 1702, and 1708. The immediate Huguenot Amsterdam 1687 reprint and its preface showed how little in Fénelon's treatise was specifically Catholic, and the simultaneous appearance of Pierre Coustel's 2-volume *Les Régles de l'éducation des enfants*, originating in the "petites écoles" of Port-Royal (q.v.), shared so many of Fénelon's ideas that both works must be considered to have been drawing on a sensibility which was becoming widespread and which, even at Port-Royal, drew on a new trust in nature and instinct. Apart from several works by Fleury, Fénelon's actual sources were on the whole antique, and his views traditional, with concessions made to the practical utility which he thought should shape female education.

Neither the *Traité du ministère des pasteurs* nor the *Réfutation du Traité de la Nature et de la Grâce* is a work of the imagination, and sufficient has been said in the previous section to indicate the general tenor of each. Neither is particularly original, although both are gracefully written, the product of a clear, well-organized, perceptive mind, with a slightly wry elegance of style. The interest of each is primarily specialist, in the context of Catholic-Protestant polemic and of the Catholic reaction to the rationalist divine principle of Spinoza and eventually of Cartesianism (q.v.).

It has become customary to consider together the disparate works of uncertain date written not so much for the education of the duc de Bourgogne as in its context. Fénelon encouraged his young pupil to write imaginary dialogues of his own between adults he knew, and some of Fénelon's own dialogues may merely be virtually the product of lessons. The *Fables* and the *Dialogues des morts* are plainly adapted to the changing needs principally of the duc de Bourgogne, one day likely to become king of France, at different ages and stages in his development, and must be read in the context of the educational process, itself based on stimulating the imagination of the young prince. La Fontaine, for instance, was translated to Latin, and we know that the antique texts used included Cornelius Nepos, then Tacitus, Ovid, Virgil, Horace, and Terence. Fénelon's own compositions

include fairy stories, imaginary journeys, adaptations of antique authors, oriental tales, and mythological fables.

Fontenelle's *Nouvelles Dialogues des morts* had been published in 1683, and were not written for children, but during the 1690s the fairy story emerged from its status as a surreptitious amusement for adults (see: Perrault) into a fashionable literary genre, which demanded the adaptation of the old and often horrific folk tales for the amusement of children. At the same time La Fontaine's success in elevating the children's fable to the status of parable for adults had stimulated widespread competition. In so far as fables, fairy stories, and imaginary dialogues remained educational instruments, whether for the edification of the young or to stir them to emulation, they were chiefly exploited, as by Fénelon himself, to give children "une idée agréable du bien et une idée affreuse du mal (an attractive notion of goodness and a hideous notion of evil)." Fénelon's desire to shape and inform the natural dispositions and temperament of his pupils symptomizes a new trust in natural instinct which was not only also discernible in the approaches to education of his contemporaries, but was naturally also extended to Fénelon's own thinking in other realms—spirituality, theology, philosophy, and social and political reflection. The duc de Bourgogne, Fénelon's young pupil, himself suggested subjects for fables to La Fontaine, who dedicated the 12th book to him: "il y a des sujets dont je vous suis redevable (there are subjects I owe to you)." They included "Le vieux chat et la jeune souris" and "Le loup et le renard" from that book.

The whole collection of Fénelon's fables and imaginary dialogues is naturally graceful, witty, and amusing, but the important elements of social and political thought are better brought out in other works. The lessons of the pedagogical pieces are all straightforward. Pleasure can be the enemy of happiness, passion and whim can lead to disaster, excess can lead to catastrophe, money cannot alleviate senility, flatterers make poor counsellors. In this age-old wisdom, elegantly presented, and incidentally in prose, it is only the moral attitudes already indicated that, because they change from generation to generation and are socially and culturally conditioned, require comment. Of the fables and fairy stories only "Aristonoüs et Sophronime" was published, as an appendix to the pirated *Télémaque* of which it might well at one time have been intended to become an episode, during Fénelon's lifetime, and it exists in two versions, both authentic. In the *Dialogues* Fénelon takes some knowledge of antique myth and modern history for granted, and concentrates on the moral and political lessons to be learned.

Like his antique and modern predecessors, Lucian and Fontenelle, Fénelon uses the form to ridicule the pretentions of the living, as well as the mythical stature of dead heroes. The dead, too, reveal the vanity of ambition and of worldly glory. Many of the dead, especially those who died young—Néron, Alcibiade, Alexandre, Pompée—betrayed the hopes put in them by others, and were led astray by flattery, passion, or presumptuousness. On the whole the underlying morality is monitory, concentrating on the corruption induced by power. Virtue, peace, government according to law, and moderation are held up as examples. The accent on patience in adversity and the attractions of solitary retirement have made some commentators wonder whether Fénelon was anticipating or preparing for a storm to come. It may be so.

For all its apparent vigour, Fénelon's defence against Bossuet after the *Relation sur le quiétisme* was not as fiercely self-vindicatory as it might have been if he had set up a robust counter-attack. Everyone in Rome knew that Bossuet's moral position and intellectual apparatus were appallingly weak. Fénelon, by and large, was to content himself with a defence, and the disgrace came not from Rome, but from Versailles.

Some of the *Dialogues des morts* circulated in manuscript. A few were anonymously published, with a first unattributed substantial collection in 1711, but dated 1712. A review in the *Journal des Savants* of 8 February 1712 did not mention Fénelon's name, first indicated in the 1713 Brussels edition, *Dialogues des grands hommes aux Champs Elisées, appliqués aux Moeurs de ce siècle. Par l'Auteur de Télémaque.*

Télémaque, originally without sub-divisions but now normally presented in 18 books, is also a practical exercise for the instruction of a prince. It probably dates from about 1694, and can only be understood as a witty, amusing, and elegant instrument for imparting moral and political wisdom to a 12-year-old prince, destined one day to become king of France. There is a sophisticated touch of irony in the narrative, but not the personal attack which Louis XIV read into the text when, after the disgrace, the widow Barbin published it without Fénelon's consent in 1699. Louis XIV apparently sent his grandson to fetch the copy which the boy kept locked in a drawer and, on reading it, thought he had been depicted as Pygmalion, "en proie à la défiance, à l'amour et à l'avarice (in thraldom to mistrust, lust, and greed)," who trusted no one and was himself trusted by no one. Mme de Maintenon thought herself portrayed as the perfidious Astarbé, the lover of an unfaithful Joazar and the murderess of her mistrustful husband Pygmalion, who when she is finally discovered kills herself. It is not reasonable to complain that Fénelon uses the perfunctory "craven and treacherous" of an unfaithful woman who murders her husband in a story written to retain the interest of a young adolescent. *Télémaque's* need for stereotyped villains and heroes, and its relationship to the fable and the fairy story should not be totally overlooked.

Both Louis XIV and Mme de Maintenon, who had long since abandoned Fénelon, were furious. In fact the moral and political teaching in *Télémaque* goes no further, even in its opposition to wars of conquest, than that of many other writers associated with the Hôtel Lamoignon, Cordemoy, Boileau, Fleury, Lefèvre d'Ormesson, and Bossuet himself. The views held up as models to the young prince were those of Mme de Maintenon, and were overtly hostile to scarcely anyone more moderate than Louvois, depicted as Protésilas. Like François Hébert, the future bishop of Agen, in his *Mémoires*, who strongly criticized the lavish expenditure on Versailles, Fénelon is critical of the prodigal expenditure of rulers at the expense of their people. But Versailles was reputed to have cost 300 million livres, and it was always going to be possible to see allusions to the behaviour of Louis XIV in any attempt to establish norms of private decency even in a book destined for the education of his grandchild.

Hostility to Fénelon's moral, social, and political doctrine was on the whole restricted to the Jansenists, who disliked the assumption of a natural predisposition to virtue, and to circles friendly to Bossuet, or his memory, unwilling to welcome anything from Fénelon's pen as well as inimical to Fénelon's view of nature's potential as a guide to virtue. The text was controversial because it was made by the Jansenist faction to seem insufficiently repressive of corrupt nature, while to the faction of the partisans of the "anciens" in the Querelle des anciens et des modernes (q.v.) it was unsatisfactory because of its failure to meet its reactionary canons of adult literary taste. *Télémaque* then began its amazingly sustained ascent to popularity, coming to be regarded even among adults as a masterpiece of new-style literature. There was an edition a year on average for the next 150 years, with a translation every two years during the same period. The work places strong emphasis on naturalness, of appearance, of behaviour, and of dress. In Calypso's grotto natural beauty is the consequence of the absence of art and artifice. Montesquieu and Houdar de la Motte were both enchanted by the book. Critics have reasonably complained of the negligence of its style, the banality of the descriptions, and the lack of narrative vigour, but the text, it must be remembered, was written to amuse and instruct a boy who was probably about 12.

Fénelon playfully invents a continuation of the *Odyssey*. The story is simple. The nymph Calypso, sorrowing over the departure of Ulysse and now distressed by her own immortality, welcomes to her island two survivors of the shipwreck, Minerve disguised as Mentor and the young man Télémaque, whose guide he is. Calypso falls in love with Télémaque, offers him immortality, and asks him to recount his adventures, which are much what any inventive devotee of antique culture might have made up for the instruction and edification of a young adolescent he was grooming for real power. The tale takes Télémaque through situations obviously designed to show different ways in which power is exercised, and different attitudes to pleasure and virtue.

There are, of course, adventurous imprisonments, escapes, glorious moments and dangerous ones to be recounted. Télémaque's story ends with the fifth book but, as if Fénelon were being inspired or pressed to go on with his lesson in story form, a narrator takes over. Mentor takes Télémaque away from Calypso's island. Mentor and Télémaque undertake more journeys and visit further countries, from the eighth to the eleventh book establishing for Idoménée, king of Salente, a just, peaceful, and prosperous rule after his disastrous reliance on Protésilas. Mentor is shown to be an exemplary tutor in making Télémaque feel not only the need for justice, but also the advantages of considerate government, a prosperous commercial life, a restriction of profligate expenditure, the virtues of frugality, and the cultivation of the useful arts. Both the manner and the content of the education given by Mentor to Télémaque, and by Fénelon to the duc de Bourgogne, are advanced and liberal, still conscious of the social and personal catastrophes consequent upon thoughtless or tyrannical government, but also hopeful of what may be achieved by enlightened social engineering on the basis of all that is best in human instinct. The text, a series of fables more than a novel, naturally ends happily.

Almost certainly later than *Télémaque* is the *Examen de conscience sur les devoirs de la royauté*, which is in fact exactly what it says, an examination of conscience. There are 38 questions. They insist on a constitutional approach to the exercise of monarchical duties, a concern for the welfare of the people, a knowledge of their affairs and of the country's economy, and the need for the monarch's private life to be an example, as well as for the court to be simple, for taxation to be minimized, for care to be taken in the appointment of office-bearers, and for grievances to be heard. The penal regime and recruitment to the army should be the prince's concern, although the overriding necessity is to avoid war, and that depends on making peace settlements that are neither unreasonable nor too onerous:

Toute compensation exactement faite, il n'y a presque point de guerre, même heureusement terminée, qui ne fasse beaucoup plus de mal que de bien à un Etat

(When everything has been taken exactly into account, there is practically no war, not even a victorious one, that does not do more harm than good to a state).

It is impressive not only that Fénelon takes his radical liberal values seriously, but that he is realistic about the difficulties in the way of their implementation. He is apprehensive about the play of power, but intends the guidance he gives to be practical. We are no longer in the land of dreams, but have descended to the realm of vigorous and entirely serious political thinking.

The weakness in Fénelon's political thought derives from the fact that while, like Voltaire, he sees in detail what is wrong, he attempts, like Rousseau, to erect an ideal political system on general principles, but allows them, unlike Rousseau, however muddled, to be too strongly influenced by his perception of present evils. He had before him wars of aggression and aggrandizement, vast and frivolous expenditure juxtaposed with starvation, corruption, and exploitation. His positive thought was based too firmly on the need to right wrongs. As it began to seem likely that he might be recalled to power, his thought became more immediately practical.

The *Mémoire sur la situation déplorable de la France en 1710*, the *Lettre à Chevreuse* of 4 August 1710, and the *Tables de Chaulnes*, drawn up during the period when the duc de Bourgogne, after his father's death, was the heir presumptive to Louis XIV and after Fénelon's conversations with the duc de Chevreuse in November 1711, are all practical documents containing concrete proposals rather than theoretical considerations. Fénelon urgently wanted an end to the war of the Spanish Succession, even if it meant sacrificing Arras and Cambrai. On the return of peace, the army should be reduced in size. Fénelon envisaged a reform of taxation, a decentralized and simplified administration and judiciary, the foundations of what we now call the separation of church and state, and a revamped function for the aristocracy which would deprive them of power, but not of a useful role in the country's affairs. Its members would be allowed to hold offices in the magistracy and take part in commercial activity.

The *Explication des maximes des saints* of early 1697 is a magnificently clear-headed exposition of Fénelon's spirituality drawn up to demonstrate its conformity with Christian tradition and to show its divergence from any form of spiritual heterodoxy. It starts by distinguishing five types of love of God, of which the highest is "une charité pure, et sans aucun mélange du motif de l'intérêt propre (a pure charity with no mixture of any motive of self-interest)." The work is technical and, like most of the spiritual discussion of the 17th century, moves unobtrusively from the discussion of theological states, which may not be empirically discernible, to that of psychological motivations, which generally are. The fundamental ambiguity on the nature and function of the will which became apparent in the 13th century made it perfectly possible to draw heterodox inferences from orthodox statements, and to maintain the necessity of positions contrary to the Church's spiritual tradition. Traditionally the love of God was disinterested. Philosophically, the determination of the will's act had to depend on an appetite or desire.

Fénelon considers his doctrine in 45 articles, in each of which he distinguishes a true and a false sense. The real difficulty in Fénelon's position, abstracting from Bossuet's extra-theological animosity, is put by Malebranche in his 1697 *Traité de l'amour de Dieu*:

Il ne peut donc y avoir d'amour désintéressé dans le sens qui accommode les Quiétistes, si on ne veut soutenir cette hérésie des Pélagiens qu'on peut sans grâce, sans délectation, aimer Dieu de la manière la plus parfaite

(There can therefore be no disinterested love in the sense which accommodates the quietists, without upholding the Pelagian heresy that God can be loved in the most perfect manner without grace and without delectation).

That view follows from Malebranche's metaphysical concept of the will, which must either be dependent on some external force to determine its individual acts, or must be able to determine itself, in which case the will is not dependent on grace in the production of virtuous acts, a position which is Pelagian, or more technically, semi-Pelagian. But Fénelon and the orthodox authorities he quotes were not using a metaphysical concept of the will. They were considering the determination of the will's acts in terms of empirically experienced psychological motivations.

In the actual dispute, obscured by Bossuet's attempts to obtain a condemnation for other than purely doctrinal reasons, both sides were right most of the time. The ambiguity, which was clear in Descartes, is ultimately the legacy of the 13th-century attempt to systematize Augustine's teaching, which introduced the faculty of the "voluntas (will)" into western thought, into neatly defined scholastic categories, which distinguished human acts in terms of their objects, and faculties in terms of their acts. Once the will and the intellect were considered to be separate faculties, however interdependent in operation, difficulties similar to those with which Fénelon was concerned were certain to arise. They are to be found in Descartes and Pascal, who were among the earliest French writers to discuss such matters as faculty psychology in the vernacular.

The volume of polemic in the pure love dispute is so huge that no blow-by-blow analysis is here possible. The power relationships which determined the course of the dispute have been touched on in the first section of this entry. In the present context it is probably sufficient to indicate that the dispute not only recalled that about pure love between Camus and Sirmond, but it also inherited Ockham's desire to ward off what he regarded as the dangers of Aquinas's naturalism by insisting that God's law was entirely and totally arbitrary, and that whatever was morally good became good only by virtue of God's law, and was not good independently of it.

To illustrate his point Ockham, followed by the whole nominalist tradition of late medieval scholasticism, had held that it was in God's power to decree that it was virtuous to hate him. That is the famous impossible supposition which naturally called into question the whole nature and purpose of human life. All assumptions about human purpose and destiny were subverted by any view that nature was not necessarily directed towards a good which was independent of God's whim. But that is what the nominalists held. To quote Holcot, one of the nominalist theologians, "…potest deus precipere alicui, quod odiat deum (God can order someone to hate God)." It is is possible to see how a need to be emphatic about God's transcendance might have led a late medieval theologian to write that, although it reduces Christian teaching to absurdity. Fénelon is much more careful. What he said in his letter to Mme Guyon of 28 March 1689 was

Le chrétien, qui s'abandonne sans réserve, peut bien consentir à être éternellement puni et malheureux... mais il me semble qu'il ne peut jamais consentir à haïr Dieu dans l'enfer

(The Christian who abandons himself without reserve can indeed consent to be eternally punished and deprived of happiness... but it seems to me that the Christian can never consent to hate God in hell).

Holcot and Fénelon when they talk about hating and loving God are using the psychological plane, but Malebranche was using a metaphysical, not a psychological concept of the will. That is the kernel of the dispute. Bossuet apparently defended the same position as Malebranche, but his language suggests that the plane was not, like that of Malebranche, metaphysical, but psychological, in which case by denying psychological disinterest he was writing against the whole spiritual tradition, which he had anyway at no point given any sign of understanding.

Fénelon's literary doctrine was articulated only relatively late. His discourse of reception into the Académie française of 31 March 1693 was dominated by the need to vindicate the reputation of the converted Pellisson, whose death without the sacraments had provoked comment from the Protestant *Gazette de Rotterdam* of 16 February and the Jansenist *Nouvelles Ecclésiastiques*. However, when the academy called for projects for its future activity from all its members, Fénelon's, read out on 26 May 1714, caused particular delight. When it was proposed to print it, Fénelon asked for the manuscript back and returned it, revised, on 25 October. It was published only more than a year after his death. Perhaps unsurprisingly, it refuses to take clear sides in the Querelle des anciens et des modernes.

Fénelon was devoted to the major authors of antiquity, disliked fussy ornamentation and was inclined to the severity, even austerity, of the greatest classical authors. On the other hand his enemies were all partisans of the anciens, and his friends partisans of the modernes. In so far as what was at stake was a new sensibility, Fénelon belonged on the moderne side. Like Perrault he was linked in all non-aesthetic matters to the values of Colbert, and like Perrault he had written fairy stories. But like Perrault his aesthetic sensibility belonged to a later, more confidently optimistic generation.

After the anti-Jansenist Constitution *Unigenitus* had been issued on 8 May 1713 Fénelon, whose relationship with the Jansenist Oratorian Pasquier Quesnel had sharply deteriorated from 1710, issued his 1714 *Instruction pastorale en forme de dialogues sur le système de Jansénius*. As a work of literature it suffers from inevitable comparison with Pascal's *Lettres provinciales*. The introduction and 24 letters are witty and entertaining but, although they clearly show how Jansenist thought had distorted the theology of Augustine himself, the work is more lightweight than Pascal's.

Fénelon's real gift was shown to best effect in his serious spiritual writings, above all the letters of direction. He had a refined, delicate, but exceedingly penetrating mind which enabled him to produce easily the most radical thought of his generation over a huge range of human experience, and to write with vigour as well as accuracy. It was partly his wryness, his aristocratic disdain, which kept him away from the grand synthesis. All his works were occasional, generally produced to fulfil a specific purpose, and they were very often technical.

Fénelon is still undervalued as a thinker. He modelled himself on François de Sales whom in so many ways he resembled and with whom he totally agreed. The masterpieces of both are the mountains of spiritual letters they wrote. There was, however, a difference. François de Sales was robust and, after the initial crisis in Paris, purposeful and confident. Fénelon was more obviously ascetic, frail, aristocratic, and withdrawn. The question-mark that remains concerns the life before it concerns the works. How far was Fénelon's public disgrace provoked by his own inner uncertainties? It looks as if he saw it coming, could have prevented it, allowed things to happen which his intelligence told him would bring about his public ruin, and spent almost a decade practically daring it to befall him, as by writing the *Lettre à Louis XIV*. If he did yield to an interior uncertainty, then the disenchanted note of the *Fables* and so much of the political writing, in particular, demands more attention. Fénelon was certainly well in advance of his time in the liberal optimism of his view of human nature and human potential. He may not have been so optimistic about the future of human society about which he cared so much, and for which he worked so hard.

PUBLICATIONS

[*Very few of Fénelon's works were published in his lifetime, and some even of those were published without his consent. Works listed below without dates have not been published separately*]

Collections

Oeuvres de M. François de Salignac de la Mothe Fénelon, 9 vols., 1787–92
Oeuvres complètes de Fénelon, 35 vols., 1820–30
Oeuvres de Fénelon, 3 vols., 1835 [the first collected edition to contain the *Explication des maximes des saints*]
Oeuvres complètes, 10 vols., 1850–52
Oeuvres, Bibliothèque de la Pléiade, 2 vols., 1983

Selections

Oeuvres choisies, edited by A. Cherel, 2nd ed. 1930
Oeuvres spirituelles, edited by François Varillon, 1954
Ecrits et lettres politiques, edited C. Urbain, 1920

Single works

[*Works published separately are listed according to date of publication: those available only in collections are listed according to estimated order of composition*]

Dialogues sur l'éloquence; as *Dialogues concerning Eloquence*, 1722

De l'Education des filles, 1687; as *Instruction for the Education of a Daughter*, 1707

Réfutation du système du Père Malebranche

Commentaire de quelques versets de l'Apocalypse

Traité du ministère des pasteurs, 1688

Mémoire concernant la cour de Rome

Ode sur la prise de Philippsbourg par le dauphin

De la véritable et solide piété, 1690

Lettre à Louis XIV, 1961

Fables; in English, 1729; in *Fables and Dialogues of the Dead*, 1723

Mémoire sur l'état passif, 1956

Le Gnostique de saint Clément d'Alexandrie, 1930

Explication des articles d'Issy, 1915

Mémoire pour motiver le refus d'approbation du livre de Monsieur de Meaux

Explication des maximes des saints sur la vie intérieure, 1697; critical edition 1911; as *The Maxims of the Saints Explained*, 1698

Vingt questions proposées à Monsieur de Paris, 1697

Mémoire à Mgr l'archevêque de Paris, 1697

Première réponse aux difficultés de Mgr l'évêque de Chartres, 1697

Vingt questions proposées à Monsieur de Meaux, 1697

Réponse à quatre questions de Monsieur de Meaux and Quatre nouvelles questions, 1697

Réponse aux difficultés proposées par M. l'archevêque de Paris, 1697

Lettre à un de ses amis, 1697 [not published by Fénelon]

Réponse aux observations de Mgr l'évêque de Chartres, 1697

Second lettre à un de ses amis, 1697 [not published by Fénelon]

Instruction pastorale...sur le livres intitulé Explication des maximes des saints, 1697

Réponse à la déclaration de Mgr l'archevêque de Paris, de M. l'évêque de Meaux et de M. l'évêque de Chartres and Réponse à l'ouvrage de M. de Meaux intitulé Summa doctrinae, 1697

Lettres...à Mgr l'archevêque de Paris sur son Instruction pastorale du 27e jour d'octobre 1697, 1698

Lettres...à Mgr l'évêque de Meaux, 1698

Responsio ad epistolam illustrissimi D. Parisiensis archiepiscopi, 1698

Première réponse à la Relation sur le quiétisme, 1901

Réponse à l'écrit de Mgr l'évêque de Meaux intitulé Relation sur le quiétisme, 1698

Lettres pour servir de réponse à celle de Mgr l'évêque de Meaux, 1698

Première lettre pour servir de réponse à la lettre pastorale de Mgr l'évêque de Chartres, 1698

Lettre à Mgr l'évêque de Meaux pour répondre à son traité latin intitulé Mystici in tuto sur l'oraison passive, 1698

Réponse...aux remarques...sur la Réponse à la Relation sur le quiétisme, 1698

Réponse à l'écrit de Mgr l'évêque de Meaux intitulé Quaestiuncula, 1698

Les principales propositions du livre des maximes des saints justifiées, 1698

Préjugés décisifs...contre Mgr l'évêque de Meaux, 1698

Lettre à Mgr l'évêque de Meaux sur la charité, 1699

Lettres à Mgr l'évêque de Meaux sur les douze propositions..., 1699

Lettre sur la réponse de Mgr de Meaux à l'ouvrage intitulé Préjugés décisifs, 1699

Lettres à Mgr de Meaux en réponse à l'écrit intitulé Les Passages éclaircis, 1699

Lettres à Mgr l'évêque de Chartres en réponse à la lettre d'un théologien, 1699

Aventures de Télémaque, 1699 [not published by Fénelon]; as *The Adventures of Telemachus*, 1742

Aventures d'Aristonoüs, 1699 [not published by Fénelon]

Examen de conscience sur les devoirs de la royauté, 1961; as *Proper Heads of Self-examination for a King*, 1747

Dialogues divers, 1700

Lettre à Louville

Mémoire sur les moyens de prévenir la guerre de la succession d'Espagne, 1787

Mémoire de la campagne de 1702

Epistola ad Cardinalem Gabrielli

Mémoire sur l'état de diocèse de Cambrai par rapport au jansénisme...

Lettre à un évêque sur l'ordonnance...

Ordonnance et instruction pastorale portant condamnation d'un imprimé intitulé: Cas de conscience...

Dissertatio de summi Pontificis auctoritate

Memoriale de decreto contra casum conscientiae

Sentiments de Pénitence et de piété, 1713

Seconde instruction pastorale...pour éclaircir les difficultés... proposées contre [la] première instruction pastorale du 10 février 1704, 1705

Troisième instruction pastorale...contenant les preuves de la tradition sur l'infaillibilité de l'Eglise, 1705

Quatrième instruction pastorale..., 1705

Ordonnance et instruction pastorale...pour la publication de la constitution..., 1706

Réflexions saintes pour tous les jours du mois

Discours pour le sacre de l'Electeur de Cologne

Instruction pastorale sur le livre intitulé: Justification sur le silence respectueux, 1708

Mémoire sur la situation déplorable de la France en 1710, 1787

Mémoire sur les raisons qui semblent obliger Philippe V à abdiquer la couronne d'Espagne

Lettre à Chevreuse, 1961

Ordonnance et instruction pastorale... portant condamnation d'un livre intitulé Theologia dogmatica et moralis

Dialogues des morts, 1712; as *Fables and Dialogues of the Dead*, 1723

Plans de gouvernement [Tables de Chaulnes]

Mémoire sur la campagne de 1712

Mémoires sur les précautiomns et mesures à prendre après la mort du duc de Bourgogne

Démonstration de l'existence de Dieu, 1712; as *A Demonstration of the Wisdom and Omnipotence of God*, 1713

Mémoire sur la paix

Mémoire sur la souveraineté de Cambrai

Dissertatio de physica premotione

Lettres sur divers sujets de métaphysique et de religion, 1718; augmented 1791

Dissertatio de nova quadam fidei professione

Instruction pastorale...en forme de dialogues sur le système de Jansénius, 1714; as *The Archbishop of Cambrai's Pastoral*

Letter concerning the love of God, 1715

Lettre à l'Académie, 1716; critical edition 1970; as *Letter to the French Academy*, 1750

Correspondence

Correspondance, 11 vols., 1827–29

Correspondance de Fénelon, 1972ff. [15 vols. to 1992]

Biographical and critical studies

Bremond, Henri, *Apologie pour Fénelon*, 1910

Cherel, A., *Fénelon; ou, La religion du pur amour*, 1934

May, J. Lewis, *Fénelon, a study*, 1938

Joppin, G., *Fénelon et la mystique du pur amour*, 1938

Carcassonne,   Ely, *Etat présent des travaux sur Fénelon*, 1939

———————— *Fénelon, l'homme et l'oeuvre*, 1946

Montcheuil, Yves de, *Malebranche et le quiétisme*, 1946

Little, Katherine Day, *François de Fénelon* (in English), 1951

Schmittlein, Raymond, *L'Aspect politique du différend Bossuet-Fénelon*, 1954

Bedoyère, Michael de la, *The Archbishop and the Lady*, 1956

Varillon, François, *Fénelon et le pur amour*, 1957

Goré, J.-L., *L'Itinéraire de Fénelon. Humanisme et spiritualité*, 1957

————————*La Notion d'indifférence chez Fénelon et ses sources*, 1956

Gorce, A. de la, *Le vrai visage de Fénelon*, 1958

Cognet, Louis, *Crépuscule des mystiques*, 1958

Gallouédec-Genuys, F., *Le Prince selon Fénelon*, 1963

Hillenaar, Henk, *Fénelon et les Jésuites*, 1967

Raymond, Marcel, *Fénelon*, 1967

Haillant, M., *Fénelon et la prédication*, 1969

Gouhier, Henri, *Fénelon philosophe*, 1977

Bibliography

Centre National de Bibliographie Mundaneum, *Bibliographie: Fénelon*, 1965

————————————

FONTENELLE, Bernard le Bovier, sieur de, 1657–1757.

Man of letters, publicist, author of fiction, drama, and satirical dialogues.

LIFE

Although Fontenelle, born at Rouen on 11 February 1657, lived to be 99 years and 11 months old, he had ceased to write works of literary or philosophical importance by the date of his admission to the Académie française on 5 May 1691 and his immediately subsequent move from Rouen to Paris. His activity as a scientist, his series of 69 panegyrics on members of the Académie des Sciences deceased after he became perpetual sec-

retary in 1697, his salon presence, his friendship with Houdar de la Motte, and his partisanship of the "modernes" in the Querelle des anciens et des modernes (q.v.) continued to make him a figure of literary and philosophical interest, but his last publication of real literary significance was his renewed intervention in the Querelle published in the 1688 *Poésies pastorales* with the *Discours sur l'églogue*, and the *Digression sur les anciens et les modernes*, when he was 31. His first intervention had been with the *Nouveaux dialogues des morts* of 1683.

Fontenelle's father, François, was an écuyer and a barrister at the Rouen parlement. His mother was Marthe Corneille, sister of Pierre and Thomas. The family was not rich, athough Fontenelle surprised his contemporaries by acquiring more wealth than was usual for a man of letters. At his death, he is said to have had an annual income of 21,000 livres and about 80,000 livres in cash, with a house, furniture which fetched 73,000 livres, and a library of 1,500 books. His health as an infant was fragile, and he was not at first expected to survive. He studied from 1664 to 1672 at the famous Jesuit college at Rouen, winning four prizes for Latin and French verse given by the Rouen academy in 1670 and 1671.

Fontenelle may have intended to study for the priesthood, but on the death of his elder brother was obliged to envisage succeeding to his father's post. His friend and first biographer, the prolix and gossip-prone abbé Trublet, on whom we still for the most part have to rely, tells us that Fontenelle then studied law from 1672 to 1677, became a barrister, pleaded one case which he lost, and then renounced the bar for literature and philosophy. He may have spent up to two years in Paris, staying with his Corneille uncles in 1674–75 and again occasionally before he himself moved there. He was protected chiefly by Thomas Corneille, the elder brother, Pierre, the author of *Le Cid*, having died in 1684.

Fontenelle won "accessits" for verse from the Académie française in 1675 and 1677, and in May 1677 Thomas Corneille presented his nephew's poem "L'amour noyé" in hyperbolically eulogistic terms in the *Mercure Galant* (q.v.), saying that it was "murder" to waste such talent at Rouen. The *Mercure* continued to print occasional items by Fontenelle in prose or verse. Meanwhile he collaborated with Thomas Corneille in the operas for which Lulli wrote the music, *Psyché* of 1678 and *Bellérophon* of 1679, and published a comedy, *La Comète*, in 1681, played on 29 January of that year and five times subsequently, under the name of his friend, and his uncle's collaborator on the *Mercure*, Donneau de Visé. The title alluded to the famous and much talked-of comet of 1680 which we now know as Halley's. On 7 December 1680 Fontenelle's tragedy *Aspar* had failed. Racine wrote a sneering epigram, and Fontenelle destroyed the text.

His literary activity during the next decade was unremitting. The *Mercure*, founded in 1672, had been interrupted in 1674 and restarted in April 1677. The equal partnership of Thomas Corneille and Donneau de Visé as its owners and directors, which we know to have been profitable, dates from January 1682, and the *Mercure* began to be accorded quasi-official status when Donneau de Visé was awarded an annual pension of 6,000 livres. Fontenelle wrote an article for it on *La Princesse de Clèves* in May 1678, and two short stories, the *Histoire de mon coeur* published in January 1681 and, in the following month, the *Histoire de mes conquêtes*. He did not give up the theatre, but in 1690 composed in collaboration with his relation from the Rouen Protestant community, Catherine Bernard, the tragedy

Brutus, later to inspire Voltaire's piece of the same name. Fontenelle may have helped Catherine Bernard with her three novels, and certainly wrote very favourably of the first, *Eléonire d'Yrée*, in the *Mercure* for September 1687. He also turned out two opera libretti, the 1689 *Thétis et Pélée* and the 1690 *Enée et Lavinie*, and much later a series of seven comedies which were never staged, although he published a preface, a tragedy, and ten comedies in 1752. *Endymion, pastorale héroïque* was performed by the academy of music on 17 May 1731.

In the period immediately following 1680 Fontenelle was frequently in Paris, mixing in literary company, especially that still devoted to light-weight galanterie to be met in the drawing-room of Madame Deshoulières, but also in more serious scientific circles. He was close to Mme de la Mésangère, the second daughter of Mme de la Sablière, and wife of a conseiller at the parlement of Rouen; she was, according to Trublet, the "marquise" of Fontenelle's *Entretiens sur la pluralité des mondes*. She belonged to the milieu of the Protestant magistracy of Rouen, and it was for her mother, Mme de la Sablière, that Bernier had written his 1678 *Abrégé de la philosophie de Gassendi*, which had first brought the thought of that philosopher to popular attention. Mme de la Mésangère was widowed in 1682, married again a M. de Nocé, and died without having had children in 1714; she was also close to Perrault. It would be wrong, in spite of Thomas Corneille's recommendation of his nephew, to regard Rouen at this time as a provincial backwater. Its intellectual life was intense, and Fontenelle spent most of his time there until later in the 1680s.

It must, however, have been in Paris, mostly in the small establishment of the abbé de Saint-Pierre in the Faubourg Saint-Jacques, that he formed friendships with the mathematicians Varignon—Newton's disciple—de la Hire, and Auzout; the historian Vertot; the important Protestant chemist from Rouen, Lémery, converted to Catholicism in 1686, the year after the revocation of the edict of Nantes; the anatomist Duverney, du Hamel, and Bernier; the disciples of Descartes, Rohault, author of the 1671 *Traité de physique*, and Régis, author of the 1690 *Système de philosophie*; and the doctor, Tournefort, who in 1683 returned from a long journey to the East. The key figure in this society had been Henri Justel, conseiller and sécrétaire of the king, but a Protestant who left France for England in 1681, and in whose well-stocked library until then a series of weekly conferences had been held. He had corresponded with the secretary of the Royal Society in London, received Locke, and had been at the centre of a group which on the whole preferred Gassendi, publicly perceived as more empirically inclined, to Descartes, and wanted to discuss the implications of Richard Simon's 1678 *Histoire critique du Vieux Testament* and Spinoza's *Tractatus*. On Justel's departure, the Perrault brothers sought to keep alive the spirit of sceptical inquiry, and it was, for instance, through Perrault that Huyghens in January 1683 forwarded to the abbé Gallois, the director of the *Journal des Savants* (q.v.), the 1678 *Oeuvres posthumes* of Spinoza.

Fontenelle, as Voltaire noticed in the article on oracles in his *Dictionnaire philosophique*, knew how to speak Norman, that is to insinuate what he meant without even ironically stating it. That is unfair, but Fontenelle's early works reverberate with innuendos, suggestions, implications, queries, and questions without actually stating very much. The pieces are occasional, the genres oblique, and the registers elegant, tentative, and often apparently trivial. Fontenelle was genuinely feeling his way.

Unfortunately the dating of his early texts is disputed. For most of the 20th century, it was supposed that the treatise *De l'origine des fables*, in reality a treatise on the origin of religions, first published in 1724, was the re-working of a text *Sur l'histoire* which was thought possibly to have been written before 1680. It now seems much more likely that it was written between 1686 and 1690, perhaps suggested by an article by Le Clerc in the *Bibliothèque Universelle* for March 1686 calling for a historical explanation of ancient fable.

Fontenelle seems to have known this text, judging from what seems likely to be an allusion to it in the sixth of the *Entretiens* added to the text in 1687. But if the original *Sur l'histoire* dates from after 1686, there is no particular reason to doubt Trublet's statement that *De l'origine des fables* dates from between 1691 and 1699. The matter is important because, after 1690, it is reasonable to suppose that Fontenelle may have been wondering whether fables were not early attempts at a scientific explanation of the universe, no doubt superseded by the Christian revelation, but with the implication that the explanation of the creation in *Genesis* might also have been adapted to a particular stage in the evolution of our understanding of the origins and destiny of the human race. The concept of history was changing fast, and it would not be reasonable to find that assumption in a text written by Fontenelle before 1680, so the meaning and the daring of the treatise alters according to the date assigned to its composition. Trublet's dating demands that Fontenelle be considered a fully constituted enlightment historian, insinuating awkard questions about the developing attempts of the human race to comprehend its religious experience, rather than the mere archaeologist of myth the earlier dating would make him.

The *Nouveaux dialogues des morts*, consisting of two sets of 18 dialogues, were published anonymously in 1683, with a 1684 postlude, the *Jugement de Pluton sur les deux parties des Nouveaux Dialogues des morts*. They were inspired by Pierre d'Ablancourt's loose translation of Lucian's dialogues in 1654–55. Fontenelle enjoys bringing together the most improbable interlocutors, and those who permit the most pointed exchanges. The underlying moral tone is of sophisticated epicureanism. Then in 1686 came the explosive work of astronomical education and vulgarization, largely derived from Pierre Borel's 1657 *Discours nouveau prouvant la pluralité des mondes* and the 1656 French translation of John Wilkins's 1638–40 *Discovery of a New World*, the *Entretiens sur la pluralité des mondes*, published anonymously, and no doubt exploiting the vogue for speculation inaugurated by the comet of 1680. Its daring did not consist uniquely, or even principally, in embracing the respectable basis in Cartesian (q.v.) physics for Copernican astronomy, or even in offering scope for satirizing human society by reference to possible extra-terrestrial forms of civilization but, as Fontenelle makes clear, in making the dogmas of Christ's redemption and original sin appear to be compromised by the existence of human life on another planet. Fontenelle also discusses human progress, and makes his interlocutor a woman, thereby simultaneously both nailing his flag to the mast and lightening the tone of his discourse, which is, as the title implies, in the uncommitted form of dialogues.

It is uncertain whether the attribution to Fontenelle of *L'Histoire des Ajaoiens*, posthumously published in 1768 as Fontenelle's work, is justified or not. On the other hand the *Relation de l'île de Bornéo*, sent by Fontenelle to his friend Basnage at Rotterdam, was published in Bayle's *Nouvelles de la Répub-*

lique des Lettres for January 1686 by Bayle over Fontenelle's name. Bayle, who may never have met Fontenelle, had virtually put his review at Fontenelle's service from its foundation in March 1684, publishing Fontenelle's *Eloge de Pierre Corneille* in January 1685 and treatise *Sur le numéro 9* from September to November 1685, and printing a number of other pieces designed to please Fontenelle before publishing the *Relation*, with a eulogy of its author. It was immediately after the revocation of the edict of Nantes, which cost Rouen some 20,000 Protestant departures, including those of the brothers Basnage, sons of a Rouen barrister: Jacques, from 1676 Protestant pastor of Rouen, and Henri Basnage de Beauval, himself also a barrister, who was later to continue Bayle's review. Bayle says that he did not understand the implications of Fontenelle's Borneo text, and that neither did Jurieu. Voltaire, who was mostly irritated by Fontenelle, thought that he had risked the Bastille by publishing it. In fact it deals with a conflict between three queens, Mliséo (Solime, or Jerusalem), Eénegu (Geneva), and Mréo (Rome), and was a brief satire on religious disputes.

Whether or not it was in order to avoid trouble, Fontenelle immediately published in 1687 *Le Triomphe de la religion sous Louis le grand*. In the same year he brought out a *Discours sur la patience*, on the pre-eminence of Christian philosophy over all others, while also publishing an adaptation of van Dale's 1683 *De oraculis ethnicorum*, the 1687 *Histoire des oracles*, whose purpose was to destroy a commonly used proof of Christ's divinity, that the pagan oracles which had been thought to foretell his coming were silent after his birth. Pascal, Bossuet, and Huet had all used it. Van Dale had proposed to attack not only the superstition and idolatry which made Christianity open to atheist assaults, but also, within Christianity, Catholicism, assimilated to paganism. Bayle in his 1682 *Pensées sur la comète* had already declared the pagan oracles to be fraudulent. Fontenelle's adaptation of van Dale removed the identification of Catholicism with superstition, but re-opened the whole question of the changing historical forms taken by the quest to understand the nature and implications of human experience. Oracles were not the work of demons, and did not stop with the coming of Christ.

Early in 1686 Fontenelle, who had kept away from metaphysics in the *Entretiens*, anonymously published his *Doutes sur le système physique des causes occasionnelles*, criticizing not only Malebranche's metaphysics, but also the need established by Malebranche in the wake of Descartes to preserve the credibility of the immortality of the soul by making human knowledge in the end independent of perception by bodily organs. A second edition of the *Doutes* revealed Fontenelle's authorship later in 1686, and Bayle edited a *Retour des pièces choisies; ou, Bigarrures curieuses* containing a reply by Malebranche, a reply by Fontenelle to Bayle's objections, and Bayle's own *Réflexions sur la lettre de l'auteur des Doutes*.

Fontenelle shows that he remains strongly deist, in spite of the apparently mechanistic leanings of the *Entretiens* but, however light his tone and apparently insubstantial his literary registers, by 1686 he had sketched important positions on virtually all the major cultural questions to be more seriously, radically, and committedly discussed by the major enlightenment authors, from the nature of the cosmos to the evolution of human belief, from the triviality of religious disputes to the metaphysics of knowledge. The 1688 *Digression sur les anciens et les modernes*, typically also an occasional piece, rounded off the inter-

ventions into what had already emerged as the spectrum of major religious, philosophical, and cultural issues confronting his generation which the death of Colbert in 1683 and the revocation of the edict in 1685 had almost suddenly precipitated into prominence. Fontenelle, needless to say, intervened heavily on the side of Perrault and the partisans of the "modernes" in the Querelle des anciens et des modernes (q.v.).

In 1683 Fontenelle had published the lighter salon pieces of the *Lettres diverses de M. le chevalier d'Her****, imaginary love letters also known in later augmented editions as the *Lettres galantes*, and in 1688 came the *Poésies pastorales*, important not only because it included the *Digression*, but also on account of the work's nostalgia for a carefree, unambitious, innocent country life, undisturbed by the violence of the passions, but in which love would lead to happiness; the combination explains the blend of very radical reflection and lightness of touch which has so often perplexed his contemporaries as well as subsequent commentators. He appeared to be a sceptical dilettante. In 1694 La Bruyère could add to the eighth edition of his *Caractères* the cruelly supercilious portrait of Fontenelle as Cydias, the affected, self-promoting know-all. In fact Fontenelle's elegance and clarity were combined with a piercing intelligence and a capacity for very radical vision. His style is firm and his mode of expression precise. What he lacked was any taste for serious polemic.

Only on his fifth attempt, in 1691, was Fontenelle admitted to the Académie française. He had been too closely identified with the "modernes." Then in 1697 he was made perpetual secretary of the Académie des Sciences and in 1701 was elected to the Académie des Inscriptions et des Belles-Lettres, which he was scarcely ever to attend. He also became a member of the Arcadian Academy of Rome, of the Royal Society of London, of the Academies of Berlin and Nancy, and of that of his native Rouen. He became immensely well known. The *Entretiens* were published at least 28 times during Fontenelle's lifetime; there were three English translations before the end of the 17th century. By the time of his death there were at least ten editions of four different English translations, and there were translations into Italian and Russian.

Fontenelle's subsequent career is mostly bound up with his scientific preoccupations. The first half of the 18th century saw a revolution in astronomy as the modern science was being founded. By Colbert's death the major centres of private scientific activity in Paris had been organized into the Académie des Sciences, with a proper constitution and state patronage. By the mid-1680s Louvois was insisting on practical applications of scientific discoveries to help the royal wars. Both Huyghens and Cassini spent much time in Paris, and the Académie des Sciences was at the centre of Europe's scientific activity. Fontenelle had to read all the memoirs submitted to it and assess their importance, and he wrote the history of the Académie for the years 1666–79 and 1699–1740. In the light of his work for the Académie Fontenelle naturally made changes to the various successive editions of the *Entretiens*, always, however, preserving their relaxed popularizing and light-hearted informative style.

The important exception was Newton's gravitational theory, which built on Kepler's discovery that the cubes of the distances of the planets from the sun was proportional to the square of their periodical times of revolution, and destroyed the notion of Cartesian vortices, invented because, for Descartes, in order to distinguish and separate the spiritual substance from the material one, wherever there was extension there had to be matter. Newton was elected to the Académie des Sciences in 1699, but his influence in France was not at first great, and Fontenelle's summary of a 1700 paper by Varignon dismisses its reliance on the Newtonian gravitational or centripetal "central" forces of the universe to emphasize instead the centrifugal force which was the principle of the Cartesian vortices or "tourbillons." Fontenelle was trying to force Newtonian physics into agreement with Cartesian postulates, and was later less than assiduous in publishing Varignon's posthumous papers which had been entrusted to him.

Fontenelle was especially pleased when, in 1701, Philippe Villemot's *Système nouveau; ou, Nouvelle Explication du mouvement des planètes* gave a Cartesian explanation of the "central forces," centrifugal and centripetal, which were the basis for disagreement. Together with Malebranche's restatement of his position on tourbillons in the 1712 sixth and last edition of the *Recherche de la vérité*, Newtonian physics was being driven back. Personal relationships between Fontenelle and Newton remained good, Fontenelle thanked Newton effusively for the gift of the second edition of the *Principia*, and his éloge of Newton in 1727 contains a brilliant comparison of Newton and Descartes, more penetrating if less polemical than that of Voltaire in the 14th of the 1734 *Lettres philosophiques*. The real acceptance of Newton's theory of gravity had to await Voltaire's *Eléments de la philosophie de Newton* and Maupertuis's 1732 *Discours sur les différentes figures des astres*. Fontenelle thought he was opposing not scientific advance but obscurantist regression when, in 1752, he returned to the attack with his *Théories des tourbillons cartésiens*. In spite of attempts both to imitate Fontenelle and to be polite to him, Voltaire's fundamental dislike of the older man is apparent, notably in the satire of him in *Micromégas* as secretary of the academy of Saturn, and in a whole collection of dismissive asides which clearly refer to him.

After the turn of the century Fontenelle frequented the duchesse du Maine at the château de Sceaux, and the salons of Mme du Tencin, whose vows as a canoness at Montfleury near Grenoble he helped to have lifted in 1715, while also assisting in the career of her brother the cardinal, of Mme de Lambert, and then of Mme Geoffrin, his executor. From the beginning of the century until 1730 Fontenelle was lodged at the Palais-Royal by the duc d'Orléans. Having in the *Entretiens* preceded by four years Locke's forthright declaration of the empirical principle in science, Fontenelle occupied himself after the turn of the century with almost entirely scientific activities. Much of what he wrote that was not scientific, like the *Histoire du théâtre français*, the *Vie de Corneille*, and the *Réflexions sur la poétique* of 1742, appeared first in collected editions. The scientific material often appeared in the volumes devoted to the history of the Académie des Sciences. In 1727 he published separately his *Eléments de la géométrie de l'infini* and, long after it was written, the *Théorie des tourbillons cartésiens, avec des réflexions sur l'attraction* was published in 1752.

It has been remarked on that the impression made by Fontenelle on women was rarely favourable. Like the later encyclopédistes, they appear generally to have found him too cultivated and self-centred, too conscious of the effect he was trying to achieve, to behave naturally, openly, or forthrightly. Scientific popularizer no doubt, Fontenelle none the less invented a new role for the writer in the serious discussion of important ideas, whether in science, history, philosophy, or religion. When he died in Paris on 9 January 1757 there had already appeared five collected editions of his works, including the three-volume folio of *Oeuvres diverses* of 1728–29 and the six-volume duodecimo *Oeuvres* of 1742.

WORKS

The *Nouveaux dialogues des morts* are witty, ironic, and irreverent, divided into dialogues among the ancient dead, the modern dead, and one dead member of each group. They presuppose a culture which in 1683–84 was more than superficial, even if not more than could be derived from a good Jesuit education. A modern commentator would need, for instance, to point out that the purpose of confronting Dido and Stratonice was the creation of a dialogue between the epitome of marital fidelity and the exemplar of adulterous attraction. Aristotle, the pompous philosopher, takes himself too seriously when confronted with Anacreon, the poet of wine, roses, and love. Aesop teases Homer, who is anxious to deny having put any serious moral content into his poetry. Homer has to explain to Aesop, but leaves a lingering taste of having said something too true for comfort.

> Vous vous imaginez que l'esprit humain ne cherche que le vrai; détrompez-vous. L'esprit humain et le faux sympathisent extrêmement. Si vous avez la vérité à dire, vous ferez fort bien de l'envelopper dans les fables, elle en plaira beaucoup plus. Si vous voulez dire des fables, elles pourront bien plaire sans contenir aucune vérité. Ainsi le vrai a besoin d'emprunter la figure du faux pour être agréablement reçu dans l'esprit humain; mais le faux y entre bien sous sa propre figure, car c'est le lieu de sa naissance et de sa demeure ordinaire

> (You think the human mind seeks only the truth; learn better. There is an extraordinary sympathy between the human mind and what is false. If you have the truth to tell, you will do well to wrap it up in fables. It will be enjoyed much more. If you want to tell fables they may well be enjoyed without containing any truth. So the true needs to borrow the shape of the false to be welcomed into the human mind, but the false can go in its own shape, since that is its place of birth and its natural habitat).

That is characteristic early Fontenelle. The second sentence is an aphorism, and the speech might better have stopped after it. But there is a chance to poke fun at the solemn determination of the "anciens" to justify antique literature with reference to the allegorical moral message it was supposed according to the pedagogical heritage of the renaissance to contain. Voltaire's vision would not have been more focused, but his language might have been more lapidary. It takes a moment's reflection to realize how subversive Homer is being: the human mind believes what it wants, and there is no criterion by which it can distinguish the true from the false. Petrarch's Laura agrees with Sappho that the point of female resistance to the male is not really to win the combat, and Socrates explains to Montaigne how inevitable it is that moderns shall wrongly think that the ancients had a superior culture.

The *Relation de l'île de Bornéo* tells how, when Mréo (Rome) first succeeded Mliséo (Solime, or Jerusalem), all her subjects were content. Then she began to introduce novelties, insisting for instance that all her ministers should be eunuchs, although the mutilation was not such as to stop husbands from complaining. There is a light-heartedly blasphemous allusion to transsubstantiation and the paid magicians who made bread disappear by their words, another to purgatory, the newly constructed prisons from which release could be achieved by payment, and a third to the veneration of corpses, that is the cult of saints and relics. At this point a new claimant to the throne appeared, the princess Eénegu (Geneva), who started by abolishing all Mréo's novelties. She looked much more like Mliséo whose daughter she said she was. There are further involved allusions, as to the Catholic dislike of translations of scripture which undercut the authority of the Vulgate. It looked, at the time of writing, as if the oath of allegiance extracted from much of Eénegu's army meant that Mréo was going to win the struggle, a clear allusion to the revocation of the edict of Nantes.

The *Entretiens sur la pluralité des mondes* were intended to be instructive. From 1698 they were no longer anonymous, and they had appeared with a privilège in spite of their systematic exploitation of what their editor calls "veiled allusion and parenthetic hint." The technique is apparent from the preface:

Quand on vous dit que la lune est habitée, vous vous y représentez aussitôt des hommes faits comme nous; et puis, si vous êtes un peu théologien, vous voilà plein de difficultés. La postérité d'Adam n'a pas pu s'étendre jusque dans la lune, ni envoyer des colonies en ce pays-là. Les hommes qui sont dans la lune ne sont donc pas fils d'Adam …Il n'est pas besoin d'en dire davantage; toutes les difficultés imaginables se réduisent à cela, et les termes qu'il faudrait employer dans une plus longue explication sont trop dignes de respect, pour être mis dans un livre aussi peu grave que celui-ci. L'objection roule donc tout entière sur les hommes de la lune;…Moi, je n'y en mets point; j'y mets des habitants qui ne sont point du tout des hommes

(When you are told that the moon is inhabited, you immediately imagine men like us there: and then if you are a bit of a theologian you are faced with a lot of difficulties. Adam's descendants could not have spread as far as the moon nor sent people to set up colonies in the countries up there. So the men who are on the moon are not the sons of Adam…There is no need to say any more. All imaginable difficulties reduce to that one, and the terms we would need to use for a longer explanation are too worthy of respect to be put into so unserious a book as this. The objection centres entirely on the men in the moon… Myself, I say there aren't any; I say there are inhabitants who are not men at all).

Both Campanella and Wilkins had mentioned the difficulty about original sin, on which Fontenelle at least insinuates doubts. Fontenelle here merely eludes the question. Do the inhabitants of the moon have immortal souls? If not, how could they differ from animals? Was there original sin on the moon? Could there have been a second incarnation and redemption? The conundrums thrown up by traditional scholastic theology are endless. Fontenelle is also indulging his sense of paradox:

Toute la philosophie… n'est fondée que sur deux choses, sur ce qu'on a l'esprit curieux et les yeux mauvais… on veut savoir plus qu'on ne voit, c'est là la difficulté

(The whole of philosophy… is founded on only two things, the facts that we have curious minds and poor eyesight… we want to know more than we can see, that's the difficulty).

Elegant paradox? Yes, but with the innuendo that all true knowing is based on seeing, that all true knowledge is therefore empirical. What makes that statement interesting is the fact that Fontenelle genuinely thought the Cartesian explanation of the orbits of the planets in terms of outward pressure from the sun more empirical than the Newtonian explanation of the inward pull of the gravitational field. As late as 1686 Cartesian physics, ultimately an elaborate scaffolding for belief in the plenum on which the credibility of the soul's immortality for Descartes in the end rested, was considered to provide the basis for an advanced scientific understanding of the cosmos.

The apparent adaptation of van Dale's 1683 Latin text which we know as Fontenelle's *Histoire des oracles*, published anonymously but with privilège in late 1686 but whose derivation was revealed only in the 1687 second edition, purports to defend the orthodox apologetic argument which held that pagan oracles foretelling the coming of the messiah were not due to demons, and did not cease with the coming of Christ. Both these assertions had commonly been made by Christian historians for apologetic purposes. Debate had re-opened in 1649 with the publication of the *Sibylles célèbres* by the Protestant professor and pastor David Blondel, seeking to show that the pagan predictions traditionally taken to foretell the coming of Christianity were pious deceptions.

Van Dale, a doctor, merchant, and anabaptist preacher, was a Protestant rationalist who wished to remove from Christianity the elements of superstition which could stimulate the scoffing that led to atheism, in particular attacking the "idolatry" he attributed to Catholicism, reinforcing that attack in his 1700 edition. Even inside Catholicism apologists like Père Thomassin in his 1681 *Méthode d'étudier et d'enseigner chrétiennement et solidement les lettres humaines* were by now regarding most pagan prophecies of the coming of Christ as post-Christian impostures, and their silence after the birth of Christ was now attributed to the availability from that time of the Christian gospel.

Fontenelle, even while pretending to address only a specific historical question, naturally did not allow himself to go beyond the general scepticism about credulity and superstition which he felt. He removed van Dale's association of Catholicism and paganism and inverted his logic. Van Dale showed first that the oracles had not ceased with the coming of Christ, while Fontenelle showed first why and how Christians were led to believe in the demonic origin of oracles, thereby, of course, incidentally reducing the credibility of miracles in general. He was building on a whole renaissance tradition about the strength of the imagination going back to Ficino, Pomponazzi and, in France, filtering through to Montaigne and even to Pascal. There was a psychological reason for erroneous belief as well as deliberate deceit and then, because the pagan oracles had nothing to do with demons, they did not suddenly fall silent. Fontenelle was edging towards a rational criticism of sacred history well before Montesquieu, who inherited so much of his style and method. Fontenelle excluded from his scepticism the possibility of magic but, again, there was no need to have recourse to magic to explain effects which had already been given a natural explanation.

When in 1707 the Jesuit Père Baltus replied to Fontenelle, he singled out for attack a not untypical passage (*Histoire des oracles*, I, xi), also criticized by the Jesuit *Journal de Trévoux* for August 1707:

Donnez-moi une demy douzaine de personnes, à qui je puisse persuader que ce n'est pas le Soleil qui fait le jour, je ne desespereray pas que des Nations entieres n'embrassent cette opinion. Quelque ridicule que soit une pensée, il ne faut que trouver moyen de la maintenir pendant quelque temps, la voilà qui devient ancienne, et elle est suffisamment prouvée

(Give me half a dozen people whom I can persuade that daylight does not come from the sun, and I shall not despair of whole nations coming to believe it. However ridiculous an opinion is, some means has only to be found to uphold it for a time and it has become ancient, and is sufficiently proved).

Fontenelle undertakes first to show that oracles were not the work of demons. Voltaire was to recall the phraseology of Fontenelle's opening when writing on the immortality of the soul, and the slightly flippant approach naturally constitutes a cloak for the obvious cynicism. Fontenelle not only states that reason teaches what it clearly does not teach, but he also talks about demonic oracles being rendered by statues, when what was really at stake was whether oracles rendered by pagan priests and idols were demonically inspired (Introduction to Première dissertation):

Il est constant qu'il y a des Demons, des Genies malfaisans, et condamnez à des tourmens éternels. La religion nous l'aprend, la raison nous apprend ensuite que ces Demons ont pû animer des Statuës, et rendre des Oracles, si Dieu le leur a permis; il n'est question que de sçavoir s'ils ont receu de Dieu cette permission

(It is certain that there are demons, evil spirits condemned to eternal torments. Religion teaches us this, and reason subsequently teaches that such demons may have animated statues, and rendered oracles, if God permitted them to. The only question is whether God did give them that permission).

Fontenelle continues in much the same tone. Revelation contains nothing about demonically inspired oracles, so we can make up our own minds. But people have always believed in them, so they are true:

On a cru dans les premiers Siecles du Christianisme, que les Oracles étaient rendus par des Demons, il ne nous en faut pas davantage pour le croire aujourd'huy

(In the first centuries of Christianity it was believed that oracles were rendered by demons, and that is enough for us to believe it today).

Fontenelle now develops the devastating technique to which Voltaire owes so much. In a bantering salon style intended to amuse readers Fontenelle discusses matters about which he knows judgements can properly be made only by scholars familiar with the Greek and Latin classics, the history of religions, the Church Fathers, and theology. It is the technique of Pascal's first three *Lettres provinciales*, which deal with properly theological issues. The tone is smiling, the message obvious, the material well beyond the depth of the readership the presentation is meant to attract.

De l'origine des fables goes even further in its progress towards a critical examination of the history of human beliefs. The emphasis is taken away from history as a source in which to study the unchanging nature of humanity or in which to find moral lessons and examples. Switching to fables as attempts by primitive humanity to explain natural but incomprehensible phenomena, like the origin of rivers, into which gods may have been thought constantly to have poured water, or thunder and lightning, which arose when the gods sent arrows of fire, Fontenelle adds to *Sur l'histoire* a passage about religious belief. The primitive gods always depended on the idea, he says, of power.

De cette philosophie grossière, qui régna nécessairement dans les premiers siècles, sont nés les dieux et les déesses. Il est assez curieux de voir comment l'imagination humaine a enfanté les fausses divinités. Les hommes voyaient bien des choses qu'ils n'eussent pas pu faire: lancer les foudres, exciter les vents, agiter les flots de la mer; tout cela était beaucoup au-dessus de leur pouvoir. Ils imaginèrent des êtres plus puissants qu'eux, et capables de produire ces grands effets

(From that coarse philosophy, which necessarily reigned in the first centuries, gods and goddesses were born. It is quite interesting to see how the human imagination gave birth to false divinities. Men saw many things which they could not have done: releasing thunderbolts, raising winds, whipping up the waves of the sea. All that was far beyond their power. They invented beings more powerful than themselves, capable of producing these great effects).

In the *Digression sur les anciens et les modernes* Fontenelle has recourse to the same essential device of reducing a serious and complex issue to a trivial and simple one: the whole question is whether the trees were taller in ancient times. If not, the moderns can equal the ancients, and nature has not exhausted itself. Fontenelle then changes his metaphor. The human race has grown towards maturity from its ancient childhood. The best modern works, including one by each of Fontenelle's Corneille uncles, *Cinna* by Pierre and *Ariane* by Thomas, are not only better than anything produced by antiquity, but are themselves unlikely to be surpassed. Fontenelle does not name, but alludes to, Quinault, La Fontaine, and himself among recent authors of unsurpassable works.

Rien n'arrête tant le progrès des choses, rien ne borne tant les esprits, que l'admiration excessive des anciens

(Nothing so much inhibits the progress of things, nothing so limits minds as the excessive admiration of the authors of antiquity).

Partly because of the frequently protective flippancy of his style, the strength of Fontenelle's imagination has often been underestimated and he has been taken to be of lesser historical and literary significance than his work warrants. He believed in the possibility, but not the necessity, of progress, he saw the fundamental unity of science and therefore the impossibility of predicting when and where it would yield practically and immediately useful results, and he saw that scientific progress, on which any improvement in social conditions must ultimately depend, demanded the existence of an educated élite of practitioners. In his *Eloge* of Peter the Great, Fontenelle showed the importance the czar had rightly attached to opening up his despotic states to the knowledge and ideas of western scientists, administrators, doctors, and artisans, and how difficult the czar found it to convince his citizens that happiness was attainable through enlightenment.

The 1702 preface to the history of the Académie des Sciences contains some remarkable passages. We have, says Fontenelle, one moon to illuminate our nights. What does it matter to us that Jupiter has four? He is thinking of the four discovered by Galileo in 1610. The fifth of the 12 we now know was not discovered until 1892, and in fact Galileo's discovery gave rise to the idea that, however fast, light travelled at a finite speed. In fact Fontenelle could point to the immediate utility of the discovery of the four moons for navigational purposes and marine cartography. Only geometers working privately have made it possible, Fontenelle points out, to change the course of rivers and construct canals, although that practical application was not originally foreseen when they worked away at their theorems.

Navigation needs astronomy, astronomy needs telescopes, telescopes must have lenses, only opticians can make lenses, and the manufacture of lenses depends on the geometers, who themselves need algebra. Fontenelle quotes a number of instances of apparently useless theorems in some branch of pure mathematics whose practical importance has subsequently turned out to be significant. But, even if it had not, all knowledge is unified:

Toutes les vérités deviennent plus lumineuses les unes par les autres

(all truths are made more luminous by one another).

It should not be forgotten that Fontenelle was an early but true writer in the French philosophe tradition, especially in his dislike of what was clearly superstitious, obviously retrogressive, or opposed to the advancement of knowledge, and that he was committed to the application of scientific method in all areas of human activity, including religious and cultural history.

PUBLICATIONS

[*Note: Many of Fontenelle's works have never been published in individual volumes and are therefore not listed here*]

Collections

Oeuvres diverses, 2 vols., 1707
Oeuvres diverses, 8 vols., 1715
Oeuvres diverses, 3 vols. [folio], 1728–29

Oeuvres, 6 vols., 1742
Oeuvres, 10 vols., 1758
Oeuvres, 11 vols., 1761
Oeuvres, 12 vols., 1764
Eloges des académiciens, 2 vols., 1766

Scientific Works

Histoire de l'Académie royale des Sciences, 1733 [1666 to 1679 by Fontenelle]
Histoire et Mémoires de l'Académie royale des Sciences, 42 vols., 1699–1740 [The *Histoire* is by Fontenelle]
Doutes sur le système physique des causes occasionnelles, 1686
Eléments de la géométrie de l'infini, 1727
Théorie des tourbillons cartésiens, 1752

Plays

Psyché, 1678
Bellérophon, 1679
Thétis et Pélée, tragédie, 1689 [5 acts, verse]
Enée et Lavinie, 1690
Brutus, 1691
Endymion, 1731

Other

Nouveaux dialogues des morts, 2 vols., 1683–84; as *New Dialogues of the Dead*, 2 vols., 1683–84
Entretiens sur la pluralité des mondes, 1686 [critical edition 1955]; as *A Discovery of New Worlds*, 1688
Histoire des oracles, 1687 [critical edition 1908]; as *The History of Oracles and the Cheats of the Pagan Priests*, 1688
Lettres diverses de M. le chevalier d'Her***, 1683–87; critical edition 1961; as *Letters of Wit...*, 1701; translated, same title, in *The Works of G. Russel*, 1769
Poésies pastorales, 1688
Relation de l'île de Bornéo, 1807 (for original publication, see text)
De l'origine des fables, 1932

Biographical and critical studies

Trublet, abbé N.C.J., *Mémoires pour servir à l'histoire de la vie et des ouvrages de M. de Fontenelle* [in *Oeuvres*, 1764]
Maigron, L., *Fontenelle, l'homme, l'oeuvre, l'influence*, 1906
Carré, J.-R., *La Philosophie de Fontenelle; ou, Le Sourire de la raison*, 1932
Grégoire, F., *Fontenelle: une philosophie désabusée*, 1947
Consentini, J.W., *Fontenelle's Art of Dialogue*, 1952
Erde, J. van, "Le théâtre de Fontenelle" in *Studi francesi*, May–August, 1962
Roelens, Maurice, *Fontenelle, textes choisis et commentés*, 1966

FRANÇOIS DE SALES: see **SALES, François de**

FRÉRON, Elie-Catherine, 1718–1776

Critic and editor.

LIFE

Fréron's father, Daniel, was a Quimper goldsmith who married three times. At the age of 25 he married his employer's widow, by whom he had three children, of whom two survived. His wife died four years later, in October 1701, and within three months, having his former employer's children to look after as well as his own, he had married a young orphan. She bore him nine children before she, too, died in 1715. Within three months Daniel then married the 20-year-old Marie-Anne Campion (1695–1754), Fréron's mother, who was distantly related to Malherbe. Probably as few as three of the 12 children of his earlier marriages had survived, and one of those was to die in 1716, leaving one girl from each marriage, Louise, nearly 16, and Thérèse-Jacquette, who was eight. A girl was born towards the end of 1716, and Fréron himself on 20 January 1718. His names were those of his godparents, a merchant and a merchant's wife, Elie Maryas and Catherine Le Roy, and he was brought up speaking Breton. A younger brother, born in 1722, died young, leaving Fréron his father's only male descendant.

We know from the tax roll of 1750 that the family was not well off, although Fréron's father claimed noble status. He lived until 1756, when he was 84, and had worked on until his wife died in 1754. Fréron himself was sent to the Jesuit college at Quimper. The Jesuits appear to have taken charge of his education, and to have sent him in 1734 to finish his schooling at Louis-le-Grand in Paris, where he was taught by Père Porée, much esteemed by another of his pupils, Voltaire. Fréron, a co-pupil of the later foreign minister, the duc de Choiseul, became a Jesuit novice in 1735, and appears to have undergone his final year's schooling while already a first-year novice. By 1736 he had charge of a junior class at Caen, where he published a Latin ode before returning to Louis-le-Grand on the teaching staff. He was there for two years and published a second Latin ode. Early in 1739, however, he was seen at the theatre, forbidden to clerics, in borrowed lay clothes, and sent as a punishment to Alençon, where on 10 April, by mutual agreement, he left the Jesuit order before his properly clerical studies had started.

Already sure he wanted a career in letters, Fréron, who retained his clerical status as abbé, was helped by a distant relation, the ex-Jesuit abbé de Boismorand, who had abandoned a notoriously debauched way of life and was now eking out a living as a literary hack in Paris. When Fréron once returned proud of having won money gaming, Boismorand made him promise never again to gamble. He also introduced him to Pierre-François Guyot-Desfontaines, an acerbic journalist who had worked for the *Journal des Savants* and in 1730 had founded *Le Nouvelliste du Parnasse; ou, Réflexions sur les ouvrages nouveaux*, intended to review mostly light fiction in a tone of some tartness. It was banned on 15 March 1532 after 52 numbers but, with François Granet, Desfontaines refounded it in 1735 as *Observations sur les écrits modernes*, again in duodecimo format, but now leading a vituperative polemic against Voltaire, whose associate Desfontaines had once been, whose private affairs and reputation for mercenariness were publicly reviewed in offensive detail in his *Voltairomanie*, but whose vitriolic replies to Desfontaines abandoned all restraint and included accusations of sodomy against him. A remark of Desfontaines, however, finally annoyed the Académie, and he was to lose the privilège for his review in the summer of 1743. In the meanwhile Fréron became his associate.

Boismorand died on 20 July 1740, leaving Fréron with no mentor other than the irritable Desfontaines, and Granet died on 2 April 1741, leaving him to inherit his role as Desfontaines's principal collaborator, and to supplement his income with such other literary jobs as he could find. Fréron revised Marsy's *Histoire de Marie Stuart* and appears to have written most of a history of Germany, which appeared only in 1771 in eight duodecimo volumes. He had little to do with Desfontaines's next venture, the pseudonymous *Jugements sur quelques ouvrages nouveaux*, which lasted until his death in 1746, and was itself a riposte to the marquis d'Argens's *Mémoires secrets de la République des lettres*. Fréron later attributed his life-long antipathy to the philosophes, against whom he led an important wing of the reaction, to Voltaire's intemperance about Desfontaines, who had warned him against the perils of becoming Voltaire's sycophant. Voltaire referred to Fréron as "un insecte sorti du cadavre de l'abbé Desfontaines (an insect emerging from the corpse of the abbé Desfontaines)." Grimm, reporting Voltaire, still felt in 1749 that most of what Fréron said was right, if irritating. Fréron was to give him cause to change his mind.

Before turning definitively to criticism Fréron, who had by now abandoned his clerical state, published several occasional pieces and wrote three odes in 1744 and 1745, of which two celebrated royal victories, and some burlesque verses, including Voltaire among the objects of his quips. He finally opted for journalism when, on 1 September 1745, he founded the *Lettres de Mme la comtesse de *** sur quelques écrits modernes*, in which he was also sarcastic at the expense of Voltaire's opera given at Versailles on 27 November 1745, *Le Temple de la Gloire*. Among Fréron's targets were Fontenelle and Piron, but the 19th issue on 12 January 1746 was disrespectful to Mme de Pompadour, who had too blatantly advanced the literary career of one of her young protégés, comte Bernis de Brioude. Her displeasure earned Fréron two months in prison at Vincennes, from 17 January to 12 March 1746, followed by exile. He succeeded Desfontaines, who had died in December 1745, to the academy of Montauban, and was allowed to return to Paris on 26 June, where he undertook various journalistic commissions, collaborating for instance with Colbert d'Estouteville, and assisting with an edition of La Fontaine's *Contes*.

The *Lettres* had been suppressed in January 1746, although on 1 January 1749 Fréron, helped by La Porte, refounded them as the *Lettres sur quelques écrits de ce temps*, immediately attacking on publication the successfully staged tragedy by Voltaire's protégé, Marmontel, *Denys le tyran*. This was followed by an equally severe analysis of the same author's 1749 *Aristomène* on 15 and 29 December, alluding to a not very serious sword fight between Marmontel and Fréron after an exchange of insults on 5 November. In the meanwhile, on 4 August 1749, a serious and very sharp attack on Voltaire had appeared. He was suspected of being the author of a brochure in praise of himself which bore a London imprint. Voltaire replied with an appendix to the published edition of *Sémiramis* attacking Desfontaines, which provoked from Fréron a stingingly sarcastic article in counter-attack on 15 January 1750, and a little later an amusing, mocking, but rather lengthy French epigram about Voltaire's niece, said to have gone weeping to Malesherbes, which made the rounds in Paris.

On 12 January 1750 Voltaire's *Oreste* had fallen victim in Paris to Crébillon's cabal in spite of the care Voltaire had taken with his own, which had succeeded so well with *Sémiramis*. Since Fréron's *Lettres* were appearing with only a tacit, and therefore revocable, permission, Voltaire complained to the lieutenant of police, Berryer, about them in two letters of March 1750, finally exercising pressure on the chancellor d'Aguesseau when Berryer did nothing. The *Lettres* were suppressed and did not reappear until October. Presumably foreseeing that he was likely to lose his livelihood, Fréron signed a contract on 16 February with Cailleau and Duchesne, two publisher-booksellers, giving them perpetual rights to the *Lettres* in exchange for 170 livres per 72 pages, so that he was at least able to live. When the renewal of publication was permitted, authorization was accorded at Quimper on 28 October 1750 for the marriage at Saint-Sulpice on 21 January 1751 of Fréron, just 33, to his 20-year-old niece Thérèse Jacquette Guyomarat, daughter of his father's daughter by his first marriage. She had been living with Fréron for over a year and was to bear him eight children before herself dying on 17 June 1762.

After his arrival in Berlin on 24 July 1750, Voltaire was constantly to needle Fréron, and by then Voltaire had with some effort succeeded in imposing his own candidate, the abbé Raynal, on Frederick the Great in place of Fréron as his literary correspondent in succession to d'Arnaud de Baculard. Baculard was a former acolyte of Voltaire who had gone to Berlin in March, and whose favour with Frederick then caused Voltaire to break with him. Frederick was later to hold Voltaire's intervention in the appointment of literary correspondent against him. Meanwhile, from the beginning of 1750, Malesherbes had succeeded d'Argenson in charge of the book trade, and it was with his tacit approval that the *Lettres* had been allowed to appear again in October.

Although the quarrel with Voltaire spluttered on, Fréron was restrained until an old letter of Voltaire's to Thiriot of November 1750 was leaked to him. Fréron now published an anonymous, sharp, but easily recognizable portrait of Voltaire in the *Lettres* on 25 March 1752, accusing him of striving to become the sovereign of Parnassus. Malesherbes, who, though not favourable to Voltaire, was annoyed by periodical polemic and unwilling to be seen to align officialdom with the reactionary pressures against the encyclopédistes, again suppressed the *Lettres*. Publication was not allowed to resume until September 1752. There was another brief suspension after Fréron published a scathing review of a translation of Bolingbroke's *Lettres sur l'histoire* on 30 October and 18 November 1752. By now, however, Fréron had powerful conservative protection, including that of the ex-king of Poland, Stanislaus Leszczynski, Louis XV's father-in-law, and things began to look brighter for him. Late in 1752 he was able to improve his contract, which was now with Duchesne alone, since Cailleau had died, to 240 livres per sheet of 72 pages. The four volumes which appeared in 1753 must therefore have brought in about 5,000 livres. The attempted assassination of Louis XV by Robert-François Damiens on 5 January 1757 was also to move opinion in Fréron's direction by irritating the country against all movements seen as subversive, including that of the philosophes.

In 1754 Fréron broke with Duchesne, changed over to the bookseller Lambert, left the 13th volume of the *Lettres* incomplete, and on 3 February published the first number of his famous *Année littéraire*, of which he directed and largely wrote 174 volumes from 1754 to 1775. La Harpe pointed out that the periodical filled a gap between the uncritical *Mercure de France* and the specialized and learned *Journal des Savants*. It offered greater variety than the *Journal de Trévoux* and, after the disappearance of the *Gazette littéraire de l'Europe* in 1766, it devoted more coverage to foreign works. Each number consisted of 72 pages, making a total of eight volumes a year, each of 360 pages, entirely devoted to the review of recent publications. Again according to La Harpe, the review produced for Fréron the large income of over 20,000 livres a year, although Fréron's real income in 1754 seems more probably to have been about 10,000 livres from the *Année littéraire*, to which was briefly to be added in 1755 the 8,000 livres from the editorship of the *Journal étranger*. The *Année littéraire* was to dwindle before suppression on 10 March 1776, an event which was directly responsible for Fréron's death, although he had been ill for some time. The review was revived by his son, who did not however take any editorial part in it. In 36 years, from 1754 to 1790, it reviewed some 12,000 books.

The battle with Voltaire had become central to Fréron's activity. His position as leader of a conservative opposition to Voltaire's subversive influence, to his aesthetic views, and to his abilities as a playwright was confirmed by the only occasionally playful vindictiveness of Voltaire's constant personal harassment, in which he exercised his superior political skills with malicious glee, moderated only infrequently, grudgingly, and from tactical considerations. However, Fréron, who had once been invited to collaborate on the *Encyclopédie* (q.v.), was resolutely opposed to the spirit which animated Diderot's great undertaking well before Voltaire was associated with it. The first number of the *Année littéraire* had nailed Fréron's flag to his mast with a mocking account of Diderot's 1753 *Pensées sur l'interprétation de la nature* and attacks on Raynal's *Anecdotes historiques* and Duclos's *Grammaire raisonnée*.

In 1753 Fréron, already from 13 December 1752 an associate member of the academy of Angers, was made a member of the academy founded by the exiled Polish king Stanislaus Leszczynski at Nancy, where he held a small court, a principal centre of opposition to the encyclopédistes. Fréron, also shortly to be made a member of the academies of Caen, Marseilles, and the Arcades de Rome, found on his return to Paris that an anonymous publisher, in fact Duchesne, printing "Amsterdam 1753" on the title page, had issued his collected works in three volumes, the *Opuscules de M. F****, some of which he would not himself have wished to reissue, although Palissot, by then hostile to Fréron, notes as late as 1777 how favourable an impression the volume made.

Malesherbes received a constant trickle of complaints about the *Année littéraire*. He not infrequently refused to act, but there were short suspensions: once after Grimm had defended *Les Heureux Orphelins* of Crébillon *fils* on 1 July 1754 in his newsletter, the *Correspondance littéraire, philosophique et critique*, against Fréron's hostile notice of 19 June; again after a complaint by the economist Forbonnais in August 1756, when the censor, Trublet, intervened to have the suspension immediately lifted; and again in September for a fortnight, when the suspension was lifted only after the intervention of the Polish ex-king and the duc de Luynes. An article was banned in December. What finally brought about renewed suspension was an account of d'Alembert's *Discours* on his reception by the Académie française on 19 December 1754, printed by Lambert, who was unaware that the censor, Morand, a surgeon at the Invalides and d'Alembert's colleague at the Académie des Sciences, had delayed consent by submitting the article to Malesherbes, who had kept it overnight, and had not informed Lambert of its unacceptability until three hours after it had been printed, at nine a.m. the next day, 28 December. Morand thereupon informed Malesherbes of the publication and resigned as censor. A good deal of powerful patronage had to be exercised before publication could be resumed on 10 February 1755.

In September 1755, against strong opposition from the philosophes and with the approbation of Malesherbes, Fréron also succeeded the abbé Prévost, who for six months had been the director of the *Journal étranger*, a monthly review of foreign publications founded in 1754. The abbé Trublet, archdeacon of Saint-Malo, had succeeded Morand as censor, and had had to defend Fréron against d'Alembert's instances with Malesherbes, but resigned shortly after the Forbonnais affair. Alexandre Deleyre, author of the 1755 *Analyse de la philosophie de Bacon* and Fréron's rival, sponsored by the encyclopédistes for the editorship of the *Journal étranger*, published an anonymous pamphlet against him in 1756, *La Revue des feuilles de M. Fréron*, as a result of which he succeeded in replacing Fréron as the *Journal*'s editor in September 1756. He was himself replaced six months later, having lost a third of the 1,500 subscribers. Meanwhile, however, the *Année littéraire* had again been suppressed, and the tacit permission again been restored on the intervention of Leszczynski, but in November an annotated extract from Coste's *Lettres sur le voyage d'Espagne* allowed Fréron's enemies to stir the Spanish ambassador to complain to the ministry of foreign affairs, and Fréron was imprisoned in the Bastille on 25 January 1757, with instructions from Berryer that he should be given a fire, books, paper, ink, and be allowed to exercise and hear Mass. Coste was imprisoned, too, but Fréron, released on 15 February, immediately renewed his attack on the *Encyclopédie*.

Malesherbes himself tried to bring about a reconciliation between Diderot and Fréron, who interrupted the typesetting of the article revealing the derivation from Goldoni of Diderot's *Le Fils naturel* early in 1757, and on 21 March wrote an important letter to Malesherbes. The article appeared only on 30 June and did not mention Goldoni. Malesherbes vetoed the publication of a letter purporting to be from Goldoni congratulating Diderot on his "translation," and Fréron was allowed only to print extracts from Goldoni's play later in the year, although as early as 1756 the wavering Malesherbes appeared to have responded to public sentiment in allowing more astringent criticism of the encyclopédistes than hitherto. Trublet had not been replaced as the periodical's censor and only in November 1757 did Coqueley de Chaussepierre consent to appointment, provided that he was not publicly named. In the meanwhile the attempted assassination of Louis XV on 5 January 1757 had opened up a vista of potential anarchy and rallied support for the defenders of traditional values, above all Fréron, who wittily and forcefully pressed home the attack, especially on d'Alembert. D'Alembert was already under pressure from both Geneva and Rousseau for his article "Genève" in the *Encyclopédie*, now joined in their attack, if from a different standpoint, by Palissot and Nicolas Moreau,

author of the 1757 *Nouveau mémoire pour servir à l'histoire des Cacouacs*.

By the end of 1757 Fréron, whose wife had born him Anne-Françoise-Thérèse in 1753, Stanislaus in 1754, Françoise-Charles, baptized on 1 January 1756, and Louise-Philippine in 1757, and who lived well and entertained copiously, was considerably in debt to Lambert, his publisher. Fréron claimed that Lambert had reduced the sum allowed on the 1754 contract of 500 livres per 72 pages to 340 livres because Lambert was losing money, but that the review had subsequently become profitable. Lambert claimed that Fréron had received advances of over 7,000 livres and, when threatened by Fréron with the loss of the contract for the *Année littéraire*, allied himself with Fréron's associate and former rival, the ex-Jesuit Joseph de la Porte, founder in 1749 of the *Observations sur la littérature moderne*, collaborator on the *Année littéraire* to 1754, and, after the quarrel with Fréron, an ally of the encyclopédistes and editor of the monthly *Observateur littéraire* from 1758 to 1761. Voltaire, in his *Anecdotes sur Fréron*, accused Fréron of cheating La Porte and, while Voltaire seems certainly to have misrepresented the facts, arbitration upheld Lambert's financial claim, Malesherbes refused Fréron a privilège and the right to move to another publisher without settling his debt, La Porte broke definitively with Fréron, and somehow the rupture with Lambert was healed, presumably with the help of a semi-official subsidy, perhaps from Choiseul, minister of foreign affairs from August 1758. Lambert went on publishing the *Année littéraire*.

From April 1758, the year in which the reaction to the *De l'esprit* of Helvétius had led to the suppression of the *Encyclopédie*, Marmontel had taken over the editorship of the *Mercure de France*, published monthly with occasional supplementary numbers, a post in the gift of the government. Raynal had edited the *Mercure* from 1750 to 1754, and Louis de Boissy from 1755 to 1758. With Marmontel's appointment, Voltaire hoped that the review could be used to rival Fréron's. Marmontel's modernized adaptation of Rotrou's *Wenceslas*, about which even the actors had doubts, was mercilessly dismissed by Fréron in 1759 and, when Marmontel tried subterfuges, deceits, and démarches with Malesherbes, Fréron published later in the year a hurtful piece of personal invective directed against Marmontel, shortly to be dismissed and sent to the Bastille for a parody of *Cinna* satirizing the duc d'Aumont. The attack on Voltaire was energetically resumed with a coruscating account of *La Femme qui a raison*. Then on 2 May 1760 Palissot, whose light comedy *Les Originaux; ou, Le Cercle* had satirized Rousseau as Balise-Nicodème le Philosophe before the king at Nancy on 26 November 1755, presented the highly successful *Les Philosophes*. It ran for 14 successive performances, making fun of Diderot ("Dortidius"), Rousseau ("Crispin"), Duclos ("Théophraste"), Helvétius ("Valère"), Grimm, Mme Geoffrin, and Mlle Clairon, the actress friend of Marmontel who had tried to organize the troupe against Fréron. Fréron's notice was characteristic of his best criticism. Despite a clear victory for his side, his review was unenthusiastic, indicating several reservations about the play.

The philosophes counted on Voltaire for a reply, which, for reasons of prudence, was slow in coming. In the end Voltaire's *L'Ecossaise* was directed more against Fréron ("Frélon") than against Palissot, as was his polemical poem *Le Pauvre Diable*, which was obscene at Fréron's expense. On 26 July 1760 Fréron and his wife courageously attended the first night of *L'Ecossaise*, packed out with supporters of the philosophes. It ran for

16 performances, and the first-night box office was 3,760 livres, against 4,379 for Palissot's first night 11 weeks earlier. Fréron's censored first article on the play has none the less been regarded as a masterpiece of waspishness. He attended the second night and wrote four articles in all. Voltaire's scurrilous *Anecdotes sur Fréron* appeared anonymously in the summer of 1760, to be revised and augumented in 1770 and again in 1777. Fréron's reply was a satirical portrait of Voltaire presented as the pseudo-biography of the Persian poet Sadi.

The literary quarrel continued. The *Année littéraire* carried a respectful obituary of Crébillon in 1762, while Voltaire anonymously published his acrimonious *Eloge de Crébillon*, subsequently attacked by Fréron, who also published an article throwing discredit on Voltaire four days before the marriage of Corneille's grand-niece, whose dowry was largely to come as a gift from Voltaire as the recent editor of Corneille's works. But by 1765 Fréron was clearly losing his battle. Palissot moved into the orbit of Voltaire, and on 24 December 1762 Fréron published a strongly hostile review of his failed *Les Méprises; ou, Le Rival par ressemblance*, presented the preceding 7 June and recently published. The realignment of positions is clear from the way in which Palissot's play attacked Fréron, Diderot, Marmontel, and Duclos, while his satirical *La Dunciade; ou, La Guerre des sots* of 1764 spared Voltaire, d'Alembert, and Le Brun. Lefranc de Pompignon, whose discourse to the Académie on 10 March 1760 had aroused intense feeling against the encyclopédistes, had been reduced to silence, and Choiseul, who was about to suppress the Jesuits in France, had become more sympathetic to the philosophes. Fréron was even imprisoned by Choiseul at For-l'Evêque for five days in December 1763, apparently as the result of a misreading and at the instigation of Antoine-Léonard Thomas, the derivation of whose *Eloge de Sully* from Forbonnais Fréron had revealed.

In the summer of 1764 Fréron spent three months at the court of Mannheim, where he was an honoured guest. Later that year Lambert's successor, Panckoucke, who was also Voltaire's publisher, tried to bring the critic and the philosophe together, but succeeded only in allowing Voltaire one of the literary victories he cherished, achieved by leaking allegedly authentic letters to places where their predicted publication did the most mischief possible. Panckoucke ceased to publish the *Année littéraire* in February 1766. It was taken over by La Combe until the end of 1769, when Delalain took it over. An attack on Mlle Clairon, Voltaire's favourite actress, would have sent Fréron back to For-l'Evêque if an attack of gout had not given time for the queen to intervene on his behalf, and an accurate enough but deflating analysis of Voltaire's motives in the Calas affair, written from the standpoint of a Protestant philosophe, made clearer than ever how strongly the tide was flowing against Fréron.

When his 32-year-old wife died on 17 June 1762, Fréron had at least three surviving children. Although La Harpe must have overestimated his income, by 1760 he was well off. He bought a three-storey country house at Montrouge, just south of Paris, where he lived from 1765, and had a carriage. In that year, aged 48, he went to Brittany with the express intention of finding a second wife to act as mother to his children, and returned to Pont-l'Abbé near Quimper to marry his 19-year-old bride, Annetic Pennanrun, one of 13 children of the local procurator fiscal, on 4 September 1766. Her brother, Thomas, was already Fréron's assistant at the *Année littéraire*. The first number of the *Année littéraire* of 1766 had carried what amounted to his literary manifesto.

In Paris Fréron was clearly attached to defending the old order, out of religious even more than political loyalty, but his critical writing came for a period more obviously than before to observe a self-imposed refusal to controvert values, techniques, and characteristics that did not have plainly literary implications. The attack was now directed at Diderot's obscurities, d'Alembert's taste, Marmontel's verbosity, and the inadequacy of Voltaire's sense of the dramatic, at the moral values and the motivation of the encyclopédistes, and at the implications of their increasingly open materialism. If dislike of Fréron had long been a dangerous obsession with Voltaire, however occasionally playful, and if success in outwitting or discountenancing Fréron had long brought him disproportionate joy, it was largely because Fréron's speciality lay in deflating self-esteem, Voltaire's weakest spot, and in his gadfly ability to twist his dagger in the wound by laying bare for public comment plagiarisms, solecisms, ineptitudes and structural, dialectical, or stylistic failings.

A number of attempts to supplant the *Année littéraire* failed, mostly because they lacked Fréron's irritatingly reactionary outlook. Joseph de la Porte's *Observateur littéraire*, aimed at Fréron after their rupture, closed after 1761. Two reviews edited by Le Brun lasted no more than weeks, and the *Journal étranger* finally ceased publication in 1763, to be revived as the *Gazette littéraire de l'Europe*, which itself appeared fortnightly only from March 1764 until February 1766. In that year Fréron's took Rousseau's side in the quarrel with Hume, making on the mischief-making letter of Horace Walpole, purporting to be from the king of Prussia, a tactless comment which offended Mme du Deffand.

Voltaire and the philosophes made as much trouble for Fréron as they could, whenever the opportunity for an intrigue presented itself: an academy election, the appointment of a censor, a forged letter, a calumny put about in someone's interest, or an epigram. Occasionally even Voltaire was overcome with scruples at the pure inventions about Fréron which arrived accompanying hard luck stories from the senders. Fréron cannot have been surprised when the subscription committee refused his contribution to the fund to raise Pigalle's statue of Voltaire, but thought a committee might accept a contribution from him to a statue of gout. It is difficult to know how publicly damaged or privately upset he was by the battery of false accusations and other hostile emanations. He must have known that the cynicism of his contemporaries extended beyond matters of religion. All Paris was amused by the epigram about Voltaire, probably by Alexis Piron, printed by Fréron, and ending: "S'il n'avait point écrit, il eût assassiné (If he had not become a writer he would have been an assassin)." It was shocked by the history of Voltaire's animosities anonymously assembled in the 1771 *Tableau philosophique de l'esprit de M. de Voltaire* by Antoine Sabatier, who returned to the attack a year later with *Trois siècles de la littérature*. It enjoyed the affray between Voltaire and Fréron.

In the early 1770s a number of young writers rallied to Fréron against the now massively dominating forces of the philosophes. His last years were none the less difficult. His eldest brother-in-law had written an atrocious libel to whose dissemination Voltaire had seen, and the *Anecdotes* must have taken their toll, but the fall in the circulation of the *Année littéraire* may also have been due to the diminishing importance of its gadfly role to what was happening in France. The philosophes had systematically conquered control of the Académie française, respect for which was demanded by law, and had thereby taken over the literary establishment, while Fréron's health had begun to give way. Expenses had begun to exceed income, and when the second Pennanrun son, Jacques, aged 23, married Fréron's daughter Louise-Philippine, aged 17, in 1773, the dowry had still not been fully paid four months after it was due.

The attacks on his enemies from Fréron's pen none the less blended humour, wit, and irony into new levels of invective skill. His satirical account from "Stockholm" of the 1773–74 winter spent at the court of Catherine II by Diderot and Grimm hit its targets with elegantly aimed malice. Fréron, who during most of his career had camouflaged aggressive distaste as impartial analysis and confined himself to what was at worst mordant sarcasm, was at the end no longer purporting to be any fairer than Voltaire. The *Année littéraire* was suspended for another three months. The final blow came when Fréron was at Montrouge, suffering from gout. His last article, on Justus Lipsius, which attacked Voltaire, had appeared on 24 November 1775. His enemies finally succeeded in having the privilège which Fréron had obtained in 1770 withdrawn by Miromesnil. The *Année littéraire* was finally suppressed on 10 March 1776. Fréron's wife immediately left for Versailles and obtained the promise of Louis XVI that it would be restored. When she arrived back at Montrouge, Fréron was dead.

WORKS

Fréron's literary reputation deserves to be higher than it is. He was a perceptive critic, capable of detailed, sensitive, and impartial analysis, and of judgements based on a fine perception of tone, register, structure, and balance. If the taste on which his judgements were based can be broken down into a series of moral attitudes, it must be remembered that it has never been either possible or desirable to insulate literary analysis from a discernment of the social tensions reflected in literary texts, and that literary criticism, particularly in France, grew out of a preoccupation with social and personal values. Saint-Evremond, more even than Boileau and La Bruyère and the 17th-century predecessors of all of them, had allowed his literary judgements to be determined by his moral attitudes. Fréron, the first great French writer whose important literary output is entirely critical, obviously derives from the tradition of critical comment established in the 17th century, and is as bound to the moral qualities of a text as was the art criticism of his contemporary and opponent Diderot to the moral qualities of the painters of the canvases on which he reported.

Like Diderot, and above all Grimm, Fréron was reporting on works whose content had to be described for those wanting to be informed about cultural activity which they were unwilling or unable themselves directly to experience. A century later Sainte-Beuve's criticism would grow out of historical and social analysis. In 18th-century France the need was to give an account of what was happening abroad, to comment on what was happening in Paris, and to project a moral light as far as possible on all cultural activity in western Europe. The major literary works of 18th-century France were at first merely subversive of the intellectual, political, and social norms whose destruction they were partly to effect as well as necessarily to reflect, and it was not only in France that strongly republican values were being forged. Historically Fréron is important for recording in detail the developing strengths and weaknesses of the major literary works and figures of French liberal thought.

How hurtful or merely ritual were the exchanges of insults, how subtle the ironies, and how bitterly resented the sarcasms? Exactly how widely and easily identifiable were the allusions? What was the relationship between public attitudes, private reactions, and unspoken understandings? Any attempt to understand Fréron's biography or his texts is liable at any instant to get caught up in a whole play of apparently ritually prescribed choices in which the participants understood, as we do not, the potential resolutions of a given situation and the probable consequences of making or refusing to make a move into which one was being forced or nudged. It is clear that umpires emerged, that cultivated society imposed the observance of a graduated series of norms, that rules were enforced as well as broken, and that both penal and pecuniary administrative measures could be used to reconcile the imposition of respect for authority with an acknowledgement of the right to defy it. It was known in elegant society where influence lay, and how strongly or often it was exercised, to whom an elegantly turned compliment had to be addressed for the granting of a favour, the restoration of a privilège, the public righting of a privately felt grievance.

The literary skills, audacities, and misjudgements of Fréron can only be gauged with real accuracy against an intimate knowledge of the relatively closed society in which he lived, in which power was exercised in the most fastidiously restrained as well as in the most brutally physical of ways, and in which allegiances and opinions could never entirely be counted on. When Fréron started his *Lettres de Mme la Comtesse de *** sur quelques écrits modernes* on 1 September 1745 he was clearly being careful, although the conditions of his tacit permission required the pretence of anonymity, a fictitious place of publication, and the risk that, if he gave offence, the police would be allowed, encouraged, or obliged to enforce the law against surreptitiously sold printed matter. Fréron's *Lettres*, printed by Prault, appeared under the imprint of the "Frères Philbert," Geneva, signed by "La Comtesse de ***," and, in order not to rival Desfontaines, disclaiming any form of erudition.

The tone was no more than dangerously supercilious. The abbé Le Blanc, secretary of the duchesse du Maine at Sceaux, became a repeated target. When he published the three-volume *Lettres d'un Français*, the countess wrote that she had "derived as much pleasure from them as she would have done from a good book." Le Blanc is condescendingly defended. He has, after all, done no worse than impose on the public "de méchants vers et de mauvaise prose (wretched verse and bad prose)," and are his letters really all that "pitoyables (pitiful)"?

The first serious mistake came from a misjudgement. The abbé Bernis, a protégé of the marquise de Pompadour, had become a member of the Académie on 29 December 1744 at the age of 29. The marquise got him a pension. Fréron's countess wrote with apparent ingenuousness to her correspondent of her great joy. Interest in who is elected to fill the dead men's shoes at the Académie will be gratifyingly reawakened. Isn't it nice that their new young abbé, "illustre par sa naissance et par deux petites odes (illustrious by his birth and by two little odes)," has been given not just a benefice, like all the other "ecclésiastiques" (the sense here is "tonsured worldlings"), but a pension? "Just after leaving school he's been lifted to the highest literary dignity," and Fréron throws in a gratuitous reference to the rare dignity, which he presumes his readership will know about, recently bestowed on Mme de Noailles, who had become a female member of the Order of Malta.

Perhaps the countess and her correspondent can hope to become female academicians? The countess is herself not interested in money, but it will be useful to the abbé. Parnassus, whatever Desfontaines says, does open the way to fortune as well as fame, and there is no Parnassus outside the Académie. "Why, by the way, isn't the modern Quinault [Voltaire] a member?" Voltaire's failures to be elected to the Académie were well known, and he was not actually to succeed until 25 April 1746. The letter appeared on 12 January 1746. Mme de Pompadour, a marquise since the preceding September, was furious. Marville, the lieutenant of police, found the piece excessive. By 17 January Fréron was in jail.

An amusing piece of doggerel sent to the director of the book trade, offering even to praise the abbé Le Blanc, failed to secure Fréron's release, finally accorded on 12 March at the not very powerful request of the president of the tax court of Montpellier. In some capricious but not entirely arbitrary way, justice was deemed to have been done, guilt purged, order restored, a scolding administered, a lesson at any rate taught, all at the discretion of the authorities. The difficulty in reading Fréron, as in all pre-Revolutionary satirical literature, lies in knowing how to decipher the tortuosities of the complicated forms of private communication and public or semi-public warnings. The probability is that any author who used mockery, with whatever satirical skill, had no sure means of knowing when he would be thought to have gone too far, even if his work had previously been passed by the censor. Voltaire solved the problem by having residences within a few miles of one another subject to different jurisdictions. Fréron's repeated sarcasms were pointed, elegant, amusing, witty, and effective, and he performed a serious literary function in pricking the pomposities, castigating the vanities, and continually evaluating the pretensions of the encyclopé-distes, measuring their literary and in the end philosophical claims against their actual achievements. But his weapon was dangerous, his enemies were powerful, and he was on the losing side against the roller-coasting philosophes.

At the outset Fréron announced to his poet friend Roy that he wanted to eschew "tout trait dur, toute raillerie piquante, toute allusion personnelle (all harsh thrusts, all stinging repartee, all personal allusion)," and merely to ridicule those works which deserved it. His attack was to be "contre les présomptu-eux (against the presumptuous)." The danger, naturally, was that he would end up scoffing at the social and political attitudes which informed the works whose literary status he was then prompted to challenge, and that his public would enjoy his boutades, encourage his insistent examination of the works reflecting the shift in social and religious attitudes, and rejoice at the jousting, without accepting the classical, unchanging, and out-of-date literary norms on which Fréron's sneers were based. His own technical literary skills were linked to a sureness of perception when it came to the discernment of literary preening: "Les faiseurs de vers ressemblent aux dévots: un rien allume leur courroux: *genus irritabile vatum*. Mais qu'y faire?...Tous les hommes sont sujets à la mort: tous les auteurs à la critique (Writers of verse are like the devout: the tiniest thing arouses their fury: *the poet belongs to an excitable species*. But what can be done?...All men are subject to death: all authors to criticism)."

The difficulty is that few plots cannot be reduced to ridiculous schemata and that it was disingenuous of Fréron to hold, for instance, against Marmontel, that an analysis of *Aristomène*

could be entirely independent of implications about Marmontel the author and the man. Marmontel was the protégé of Voltaire, whose maltreatment of Desfontaines first alerted Fréron to Voltaire's weaknesses and the potent menace he represented to established religious and social orders. Marmontel had presented *Denys le tyran* in 1748. In 1749, after Fréron and he had come to sword blows on meeting in the theatre foyer, Fréron wrote with what was intended to appear to be ostentatious restraint two pieces examining first the structure and then the execution of *Aristomène*. The second article ended:

Je puis vous assurer, sans craindre que l'on me soupçonne de partialité, que toute la pièce est écrite d'un style rude, bas, ampoulé, plein d'ambiguités, d'inversions vicieuses et de fautes de langage. Je ne vous parle pas des vers imités, pour ne rien dire de plus, de tous les poètes que nous connaissons. Il y en a quantité raisonnable. Il m'eût été fort aisé de vous indiquer les sources où un génie aussi fécond a daigné puiser... Il n'y a donc dans ce tableau ni ordonnance, ni dessin, ni traits neufs, ni coloris, ni correction, ni chaleur; c'est une peinture bizarre, sèche et morte...

(I can assure you, without fear of being suspected of prejudice, that the whole play is written in a rough, low, rhetorical style, full of ambiguities, faulty inversions, and errors of language. I will not tell you about the imitated lines, not to call them more, from all the poets we know. There are quite a lot of them, and it would have been very easy for me to show you the wells from which so prolific a genius has deigned to draw... There is therefore in this picture neither ordering, nor structure, nor new conceptions, nor colour, nor correctness, nor warmth; it is a strange painting, dry and dead...).

Bolingbroke had died in 1751. When Fréron wrote in October and November 1752 of the translation of his *Lettres sur l'Histoire* that the work lacked structure, contained long, tedious passages, and was shot through with prejudice against Catholicism and ingratitude towards his benefactors Louis XIV and Louis XV, he had not reckoned on the power of the French allies of the partisans of a Stuart restoration, and on Matignon's loyalty to the translator, Dubourg, who had been tutor to his son. Malesherbes yielded to the pressures and suspended the *Lettres sur quelques écrits de ce temps*. Had Fréron broken the rules, and should he have known better? D'Hémery, inspector of the book trade, wrote: "Fréron's magazine has been suppressed again on account of the last article on Bolingbroke. Don't you find that ridiculous?" The point of interest in any assessment of just how daring Fréron's forthright outspokenness could be is not only d'Hémery's reaction, but that of cultivated society acting virtually in concert. The lifting of the suspension appears to have been organized in the salon of Mme de Graffigny by way of the comte de Tressan, governor of Toul, later an ally of Voltaire and opponent of Fréron and the Polish court.

Already, however, Fréron's comments were not limited to literary criticism. In 1752 he had contemptuously drawn attention to the "apostles of humanity." He naturally defended French music against the cultural avant-grade, which, with Rousseau, preferred Italian melodic grace to Rameau's harmonic inventions, but his preference is plainly based on nationalistic rather than aesthetic criteria. On the other hand, in 1754 he took over from La Condamine the leadership of the campaign to introduce into France the British practice of inoculating against smallpox, advocated earlier but to little effect by Voltaire. On the questions of Catholicism and the monarchy, Fréron was a convinced conservative, but in social matters his views were almost surprisingly egalitarian and advanced. He disliked the way Voltaire made capital out of the Calas affair, but he also strongly disapproved of the legal system which produced the original injustice in the first place.

On the question of sovereignty Fréron believed in enlightened despotism, a position very like that of Voltaire, and nowhere near as radical as that of Rousseau. On fiscal policy, too, Fréron was an opponent of the taxation system and the way in which it exempted the nobility and threw the principal burden on the poor. He objected also to the exploitation of agricultural labour, the "corvée," for public works which should be properly paid for, to the exemptions from military service enjoyed by the servants of the aristocracy, and advocated the abolition of internal tariffs and tolls, and universal access to primary education. On penal, educational, fiscal, and social reform, Fréron was often in the vanguard even when his encyclopédiste opponents were not.

On aesthetic matters, however, Fréron was a stalwart partisan of the "anciens," believing in the unchangeable norms of taste, defended with superciliousness, invective, jibes, and sometimes cheap quips rather than by reasoned argument. The contemptuous deployment of disdain, sometimes polemically sharpened into controlled invective, was his strongest weapon. Cantwell, the doctor who opposed inoculation, was the friend and doctor of Desfontaines. Desfontaines is dead. What a friend! What a doctor! And Fréron has him as an enemy. He puts into the mind of Mailhol, whose comedy *La Nouvelle du jour* he reviewed in 1754, the insulting reflection "What masterpiece shall I produce today? Shall I make a tragedy, a comedy, write history or a novel? My tragedy didn't do badly; my comedy ought to succeed; my history is being printed; let's amuse ourselves with a novel…" Of Mailhol's comedy *Les Lacédémoniennes*, Fréron wrote that it had been picked up in the pit of the Italian theatre by a bookseller who, out of pity, had found it a corner on a shelf. Of Raynal's *Anecdotes historiques, militaires et politiques de l'Europe*, he could only echo Tacitus: the book "was good enough until Raynal wrote it." Tacitus wrote of Galba that he would have been capable of governing if he had not tried to govern.

Much of Fréron's published work consists of reports on what was happening in the cultural world, and is therefore of historical interest only, but he had a powerful memory, and a favourite device of his analytical criticism was to show the line-by-line antecedents of a speech or a scene from a play he disliked. He would sometimes print the original after the copy, and demonstrated the derivation of two of the chapters of Voltaire's *Zadig*. With d'Holbach's *Système de la nature* of 1770, he proved himself an able controversialist, laying bare the assumptions of his opponent:

Effacez dans tout son livre le mot *nature* et substituez-y la *matière*, les *combinaisons et les mouvements que nous voyons dans l'univers*, et vous verrez que tout l'ouvrage ne sera qu'un non-sens perpétuel… En niant l'existence de Dieu, [l'auteur] divinise la nature, il lui attribue des intentions, de la bonté, de l'impartialité… Il lui adresse même de ferventes prières

(Strike out in the whole book the word "nature" and substitute for it "matter," the "combinations and movements which we see in the universe," and you will see that the whole work is only continuous nonsense… In denying the existence of God, the author divinizes nature, attributes to it intentions, goodness, impartiality… He even addresses fervent prayers to it).

In the first number of the *Année littéraire* of 1766, after his second marriage had been decided but before it took place, Fréron wrote his manifesto. A well-written and at times moving piece when read in its entirety, it also lays down the principles to which Fréron believed, on the whole rightly, that he had adhered, and by which he intended to continue to be guided. The aesthetic norms derive from the moral ones. He attacks above all the vanity of the encyclopédistes:

Ils ignorent que le premier mérite de l'homme en société, quels que soient ses titres, ses talents et ses emplois, est de ne les afficher jamais, et d'être simple, modeste, sensible… La critique la plus ménagée les irrite; à plus forte raison, une critique vive, comme celles que je me suis permises quelquefois, moins par envie de nuire, par humeur ou par ressentiment que par un amour extrême pour la vérité, par une sorte d'enthousiasme en faveur du goût, par une révolte involontaire de mon esprit contre la médiocrité à prétentions, à cabales et à succès

(They do not understand that the first merit of man in society, whatever his qualifications, his talents, and his tasks, is never to parade them, and to be simple, modest, sensitive… The most restrained criticism irritates them, and naturally, even more, biting criticisms, like those I have sometimes allowed myself, less from any desire to hurt, from temper or annoyance than from an extreme love of truth, a sort of intoxication in favour of taste, and an involuntary revolt of my mind against a pretentious mediocrity which depends on cabals and on successes).

Fréron goes on to recount how one of the publishers of the *Encyclopédie* had invited him to participate in the venture, and how easy that would have made his life, how many letters full of compliments he would have received from Voltaire, how Voltaire would have hailed the *Année littéraire* as the foremost of the journals because it would exaggeratedly have praised him each month, and what literary honours would have been heaped on Fréron: "Mais ce protocole de louanges répugne à mon caractère autant qu'il ennuie le public (But this protocol of praise is as repugnant to my character as it is boring to the public)." At least he has never changed his views with changes in the literary tide:

Ainsi… je suis bien résolu de dire [la vérité] tant que je vivrai, au risque de me faire encore des ennemis, que je ne puis même soupçonner; car, en critiquant tel auteur, j'offense sans le savoir tel protecteur, telle protectrice que je connais pas. La littérature est parmi nous une affaire d'intrigue et de coterie. Pour moi je ne tiens à aucune cabale, à aucun bureau de bel-esprit, à aucun parti, si ce n'est à celui de la religion, des moeurs et de l'honnêteté: et malheureusement c'en est un aujourd'hui.

(Therefore… I am thoroughly determined to tell [the truth] as long as I live, at the risk of making myself more enemies, whom I do not even suspect; because, in criticizing such and such an author, I offend without knowing it some protector, male or female, whom I do not know. Literature amongst us is a matter of intrigue and clans. For myself, I belong to no cabal, to no association of wits, to no party, except for that of religion, morality, and good behaviour. Unhappily that today is all the same thing).

PUBLICATIONS

Collections

Observations sur les écrits modernes, with others, 33 vols., 1735–43
Jugements sur quelques ouvrages nouveaux, with others, 11 vols., 1744–46
Lettres sur quelques écrits de ce temps, 13 vols., 1749–54
Lettres de Mme la comtesse de *** sur quelques écrits modernes, 19 numbers, 1746
Opuscules de M. F***, 3 vols., 1753
Année littéraire, 174 vols., 1754–75
Journal étranger, 7 vols., 1755–56

Verse

Les Conquestes du roy (ode), 1744
La Renommée (ode), 1744
La Journée de Fontenoy, 1745
Ode sur la mort de Mgr le Dauphin, 1766
Ad Famam, in divum Joan. Fr. Regisium sanctorum numero solemniter adscriptum, n.d.

Pamphlets and occasional pieces

Histoire de Marie Stuart, reine d'Ecosse et de France, 2 vols., 1742
Lettre de l'auteur de l'ode sur "Les Conquestes du roy," 1744
Lettre à M. l'abbé Guyot-Desfontaines, 1744
Les Vrais Plaisirs; ou, Les Amours de Vénus et d'Adonis, with Colbert d'Estouteville, 1748
Réponse de l'amateur à la première "Lettre sur la peinture," 1750
Réponse du public à l'auteur d'"Acajou," 1751
La Critique désintéressée sur les satyres du temps, no date
Histoire de l'empire d'Allemagne et principalement de ses révolutions, 8 vols., 1771
Lettre sur les derniers discours prononcés à l'Académie française, no date
Lettre sur l'oraison funèbre du cardinal Fleury, no date

Biographical and critical studies

Cornu, François, *Elie Fréron (1718–1776): trente années de luttes contre Voltaire et les philosophes du XVIIIe siècle*, 1922

FURETIÈRE, Antoine, 1619–1688.

Novelist, satirist, man of letters, and lexicographer.

LIFE

Very little is known for certain about Furetière before he was nearly 30. He was born on 28 December 1619, the eldest of five sons and four daughters, and became a lawyer, like two of his brothers. The other two brothers became priests. The family belonged to the office-bearing old Paris bourgeoisie, and Furetière's father was a secrétaire de la chambre du roi. Sometime before 1652 Furetière acquired the office of fiscal procurator of the baillage of Saint-Germain-des-Prés, one of the 25 private jurisdictions inherited from the middle ages by the 17th century. In a pamphlet entitled *Dialogue de M. D[espréaux] de l'Académie françoyse, et de M. L[e] M[aistre], Avocat en parlement*, written against Furetière by Charpentier during the literary battle following Furetière's exclusion from the Académie, Furetière is accused of having tricked his mother, Marie Sauvage, out of the 6,000 livres the baillage cost him, by pretending that his youngest sister needed the money as a dowry. The charade was carefully planned and executed over some months, with enquiries made by his mother in distant regions, and spurious letters organized from different parts of France. Its success, regarded by Charpentier as criminal, much amused the sister involved.

In office, Furetière was accused of peculation, but all we know with certainty comes from a pamphlet produced on his behalf. He appears to have had a complacent and ignorant superior, to have been caught taking bribes, and to have been excluded from any judicial function. It is at least clear that Furetière ceased to be fiscal procurator, became an abbé, and, no doubt with the help of the duc de Verneuil, illegitimate son of Henri IV and holder of the abbacy of Saint-Germain-des-Prés, he obtained two priories, Saint-Laurent-sur-Saône and Saint-Pierre-de-Gigny, on whose revenues he lived in a house with a small garden near the western boundary of the city, spending much of his time playing bowls. He exchanged the priories by an act of 22 August 1662 for the abbacy of Chalivoy, which he kept until his death. It was also in 1662 that on 15 May Furetière was elected to the Académie française.

We know of Furetière's childhood only the famous anecdote related by Tallemant, in which Furetière asked his father for money to buy a book. "But do you know," he was asked, "everything in the one you bought the other day?" The book "bought the other day" was, Tallemant scornfully relates, a dictionary. Furetière is first mentioned in any literary context soon after 1645 at the Table Ronde, in the entourage of Patru, with the ageing Mainard, Perrot d'Ablancourt, and with a young group which included Pellisson, Charpentier, Maucroix, Tallemant, and La Fontaine. The company was cheerful, amusing, irreverent, and given to satirical wit although, like the company at the Hôtel de Rambouillet (see: *Guirlande de Julie*), it was to be fractured into two groups which recognizably developed into partisans of the "anciens" and those of the "modernes" in the Querelle des anciens et des modernes (q.v.).

Furetière's first publication, a product of his association with this companionable group, was an anonymous burlesque translation of the fourth book of the *Aeneid*, entitled *L'Aenéide travestie*, which appeared in 1648 but was dated 1649. It was followed by the 1653 *Le Voyage de Mercure*, also anonymous and in verse, for which a privilège had been taken out in 1651, and which makes fun of pedants, lawyers, court poets, and financiers. In 1655 Furetière published his signed *Poésies diverses* containing often amusing satirical verse about merchants and poets, and a caricature of the doctor, Guy Patin. In a letter of 28 January 1651, Pellisson refers to Furetière as an "intimate friend," and about this time Furetière was also on terms of close personal friendship with Madeleine de Scudéry, one of her "très humbles et très obéissans amans," as he wrote to her. It was with Charpentier, Madeleine de Scudéry, Pellisson, the modernes, that Furetière was to break.

When the split came in the mid-1650s, Furetière who, unlike the others, had never benefited from Foucquet's patronage, broke with Ménage and Pellisson to side with d'Aubignac and Gilles Boileau. By 1654 the cult of salon refinement in social relationships had driven elegant and cultivated galanterie to the point at which a group of fastidious patrician ladies acknowledged the appellation "précieuses" (q.v.), and at which the exaggerated and affected idealization of women, rooted in the respect demanded for them in the whole pre-Fronde romanesque tradition, began to provoke amusing and often satirical comment. After Richelieu's death in 1642 the literary influence of Chapelain and Conrart had begun to diminish, while that of the abbé d'Aubignac augmented. D'Aubignac's 1657 *Pratique du théatre* was an attempt to provide dramatic theory with a rational and immutable basis, but, in this unlike Cartesianism (q.v.), it respected ancient models, is said to have been commissioned by Richelieu and begun while he was still alive. From 1663 d'Aubignac was officially authorized to hold literary gatherings, but they were certainly taking place by 1659, when Sorel referred to them as the "académie allégorique." Among d'Aubignac's closest associates in the late 1650s were Gilles Boileau and Furetière.

D'Aubignac promoted the cult of allegory, but with satirical intent. While incidentally disbelieving that "Homer" was a single poet, he thought that both the *Iliad* and the *Odyssey* were allegories. His own 1655 satirical allegory *Nouvelle Histoire du temps; ou, Relation véritable du Royaume de Coquetterie* contained remarks intended to wound Madeleine de Scudéry. In 1656 Boileau, virtually his disciple, who disdained Chapelain's *La Pucelle* while also feigning an admiration for it, attacked Ménage, at whose Wednesday receptions he was until 1655 none the less assiduous, in his *Avis à M. Ménage sur son églogue intitulée Christine*. The same duplicity that he showed towards Chapelain and Ménage is obvious in Boileau's view of Balzac, which changed according to whom he was addressing, while what can only be regarded as an inflated view of his own status and abilities as a critic made enemies also in due course of Costar and Scarron.

Furetière, more talented and open, none the less in 1658 placed himself firmly in the d'Aubignac camp with Gilles Boileau by publishing his satirical allegory in prose, *Nouvelle allégorique; ou, Histoire des derniers troubles arrivez au Royaume d'éloquence*. The allegorical hostilities it evokes between "Bon sens (good sense)" and "Galimatias" do not appear even to the satire's 1967 editor to correspond to any literary or ideological line-up, and it certainly confused Furetière's contemporaries. The piece may well have been chiefly a successful bid for election to the Académie française.

Sorel who, with Costar and Madeleine de Scudéry, was among the satire's targets, replied in his 1659 *La Relation véritable de ce qui s'est passé au Royaume de Sophie depuis les troubles excitez par la rhétorique et l'éloquence. Avec un Discours sur la Nouvelle Allégorique*, saying that the work's intentions were obscure, "whether to criticize certain people, or to bestow praise; to support some doctrine, or to attack one." Tallemant reports that, on the belated appearance of Saint-Amant's poem *Moyse sauvé* (*Moses saved*), which catered for the taste formed during the vogue in France for the works of the Italian poet Marino in the late 1630s but was long neglected and published only in 1653, Furetière referred to it as "Moyse noyé (Moses drowned)," and Furetière, if not so unpleasantly as Gilles Boileau, also gained a reputation for being clever at other people's expense. The changes he made in the second edition of the *Nouvelle allégorique* suggest that he was aware of this, and wanted to live it down.

D'Aubignac's circle, while conservative in taste, and opposed to the insipidities of the madrigalists, liked to think of itself as entitled to be satirically critical on the grounds of its rational good sense, and was therefore opposed to merely traditionalist values, as well as to all forms of pedantry, and even erudition, because of the implied reliance on authority. This attitude was quite compatible with respect for those antique authors who were thought to have reached the highest possible peaks of imaginative creativity. D'Aubignac himself continued, in his 1660 *Portraits égarez* to attack female salon pretentiousness, and did so again in the 1665 *Conseils d'Ariste à Célimène*, so that a substantial part of his output at this date was devoted to his opposition to the literary manifestations of galanterie. His 1663 allegorical novel *Macarise* contains a strong warning against allowing behaviour to be controlled by custom and authority: "il y a de l'abus et du péril à prendre l'exemple d'autruy pour règle de notre vie (there is error and danger in taking the example of others as a rule of life)." The rather more formal gatherings centred on d'Aubignac were attended by a group which blended into another more informal circle round the abbé de Marolles, of whom it can be said that he received, while d'Aubignac presided.

The literary company kept by Furetière considerably assists students of 17th-century French literature to see how the literary alignments were sometimes reflected in personal relationships, but sometimes obscured by them. By 1662, the year of Furetière's election to the Académie française, he was to be found with François Payot de Lignières and Gilles Boileau closely linked to Marolles, whose literary importance derives entirely from his status as a protégé since 1644 of the Estrées family. The maréchal, François-Annibal, born in 1573, had three sons by his first marriage, of whom the eldest was given the same forename as his father, and the third, César, became the cardinal. The maréchal, himself a widower, had after his first wife's death married the widowed Anne Habert de Montmort on 8 April 1634. In 1660 her brother, Habert de Montmort, at the centre of a learned group favourable to Cartesianism, was still an immensely rich maître des requêtes with 100,000 livres a year, although he was later to be ruined; and the protection of the influential Estrées family, whose members the evidence available to us does not allow us entirely to avoid confusing, was much prized in the world of letters. Germain and Philippe Habert were also considered in the 1630s to be among the finest poets of their generation. It was from the Marolles circle and the

Estrées household that came the sharpest attacks on the new conception of love floated by Madeleine de Scudéry in the final book of *Le Grand Cyrus* and in *Clélie*. Associated with the circle were Lignières, Cotin, Maulévrier, Mme Deshoulières, Sorel and the third Boileau brother, the abbé Jacques, as well as Furetière.

The circle, generally hostile to Madeleine de Scudéry, Ménage, and Pellisson, paid surface deference to Chapelain, and Habert de Montmort used the power of the Estrées name to contrive in 1659 the election to the Académie française of Gilles Boileau in succession to Colletet. Chapelain acquiesced, not knowing that Habert de Montmort had written a pointed Latin epigram against his *La Pucelle*. Furetière and Gilles Boileau helped Lignières to write against the unsuspecting Chapelain. Maulévrier and César d'Estrées were responsible for a famous chanson aimed at Mlle de Vandy, an enemy of Henri-Louis Habert's wife, Marie-Henriette de Frontenac, which identified Mlle de Vandy as a member of the small group who jokingly admitted to being précieuses. The Marolles circle was merely polite to Ménage, whom d'Aubignac strongly disliked.

Furetière was to play a relatively low-key part in literary political life between the mid-1660s and the mid-1680s, but it is important for an understanding of the major issues to be debated towards the end of the century to see where Furetière's allegiances lay, and how the development of personal relationships could obscure the alignments dictated by literary ideologies. Furetière was notably less strident after the death in 1669 of Gilles Boileau. Apart from slight occasional works, the 1671 *Fables morales et nouvelles*, and the 1672 verse translations of the gospel parables, Furetière published nothing between 1666 and 1684.

Among Ménage's genuine friends were Costar, La Ménardière, Martin de Pinchesne, who was Voiture's nephew and editor of his letters, and Charpentier. Gilles Boileau had been a sincere admirer of Ménage. Even the 1655 *Avis à M. Ménage sur son églogue intitulée Christine* was not a serious act of hostility, and Gilles Boileau merely circulated it in manuscript while continuing to attend Ménage's Wednesday receptions known as his "mercuriales." When Ménage discovered Gilles Boileau's authorship of the *Avis* on his eclogue, sometime in the summer of 1655, Chapelain smoothed matters over, and Ménage bought in all the copies he could find of a reply to Boileau by Henri Le Bret, a friend of Cyrano de Bergerac.

Harsh things he had said about Gilles Boileau were, however, reported back, and Costar published in support of Ménage a *Suite de la Défense*. Boileau, regarding himself as provoked, took out a privilège for the *Avis* on 20 December 1655, and the literary world was split. Furetière, with Chapelain—*La Pucelle* still unpublished—and Conrart, feeling that Ménage deserved to be punished for supporting Costar's criticisms of Balzac in three works between 1653 and 1655, supported Boileau. Pellisson not only supported Ménage but broke personally with Boileau, his former friend. Patru tried to mediate, but Ménage would not call on Boileau, an essential part of the peace treaty. Chapelain's support for Boileau, whose most flagrant perfidy had not yet taken place, is to be explained partly because he quickly discovered that the *Lettre du Sr du Rivage* of January 1656, criticizing *La Pucelle*, was by La Mesnardière, a friend of Ménage, Costar, and Pinchesne.

There was real animosity, considerable duplicity, and a certain amount of good humour. Lignières wrote epigrams against everybody, Chapelain, Conrart, Gombauld, and Boisrobert, but also against Costar, Ménage, and Pellisson. That had the effect of uniting the opposing parties against Lignières. Chapelain continued to come to Ménage's mercuriales, in spite of La Mesnardière's attack, and when Charpentier permitted himself satirical allusions to Chapelain in the 1658 *Voyage héroïque*, Costar persuaded him to drop them. The peace was however ruptured by the canvassing over the election of Gilles Boileau to the Académie française. Hostilities became personal and bitter, and the alignment can be seen in retrospect clearly to prefigure that of the Querelle des anciens et des modernes, with Chapelain, Conrart, Despréaux, Cotin, Habert de Montmort, the Estrées household and the rapidly rising Colbert ranged against the pro-moderne group, Ménage, Charpentier, Costar, La Ménardière, and the friends of Pellisson and Foucquet, Madeleine de Scudéry, and Scarron.

Furetière's position was almost certainly determined by his antagonism towards Sorel. Both had frequented Marolles and are associated as subjects of dedications of poems by Marolles's cousin Mme de Montbel. But if Furetière's attitude to Marolles was ambiguous in the 1658 *Nouvelle allégorique*, his closeness to the Marolles circle was remarked on in 1662. As early as 1655 Furetière had made a satirical allusion to Sorel in his third *Epître* as also in the preface to the *Poésies diverses*. Sorel was sufficiently badly treated in the *Nouvelle allégorique* to have replied in the 1659 *Relation véritable*. The *Voyage de Mercure* had taken as one its principal targets Guy Patin, close to Sorel, and Furetière was a friend of Renaudot, whom Patin thoroughly disliked. In the 1666 *Le Roman bourgeois* Furetière was to mount a full-scale satirical attack on Sorel, who in 1659 had been ironic about d'Aubignac's gatherings, attended by Furetière.

Furetière was not at all prominent in the disputes involving his close friend Gilles Boileau, but there can be little doubt of the sincerity of the admiration expressed for Conrart in the *Nouvelle allégorique*, in which work it is, however, also difficult to miss the irony at the expense of Chapelain and Marolles. The probability is that Furetière was forced into virtual silence by his desire neither to side with Sorel nor to side against Gilles Boileau. Personal relationships and literary line-ups may have clashed, but the most likely explanation of Furetière's remarks, allusions, and silences is that he had a personal quarrel with Sorel for reasons which are unrecorded but appear to have been deep, and that he was not profoundly attached to either of the available literary ideologies. His differences with both sides, Patru's and Charpentier's, in the Académie's later quarrel over the dictionary confirm his relative independence of ideological as distinct from personal commitments.

His reactions were simply based on his personal friendships and the reciprocated antagonism with Sorel. Even there, Furetière appears to have gone some way towards toning down the references to Sorel and Madeleine de Scudéry in the second 1658 edition of the *Nouvelle allégorique*. The first edition of 1658 was reprinted in 1658 and 1659, but it must be distinguished from the second 1658 edition also reprinted in 1659. When on 15 May 1662 Furetière was himself elected to the Académie française, it was not on any literary platform at all, but as a grammarian with Patru, Richelet, and Mézeray. Either there was some unrecorded reason for the hostility between Furetière and Sorel strong enough to account for Furetière's silence in the clash of literary ideologies, or it may be, as has been suggested, that Furetière was defending the Cartesianism of Habert de Montmort's salon, against Sorel's preference for Méré and the philosophy of Gassendi.

There is not sufficient evidence about Furetière's literary relationships to be completely sure about the vision behind his satirical comments or even his literary motivation. After the close relationship with Marolles and election to the Académie of 1662, it is certain that Furetière was deeply concerned with, and probably part author of the satirical sketch *Chapelain décoiffé* of the second half of 1664, in which Despréaux and Chapelle certainly, and Racine possibly were all concerned. Then late in 1666 Furetière published *Le Roman bourgeois*, essentially a parody of the heroic novel, but deliberately attached to the tradition of the comic novel as defined in Sorel's *Bibliothèque françoyse* of 1664. The literary affiliation is with the Despréaux of the early satirical works, the sixth and third satires known as the *Embarras de Paris* and the *Repas ridicule*, both written in 1665, and the 1666 *Dialogue des héros des romans*. There are also precise coincidences of detail with Racine's single comedy, the 1668 *Les Plaideurs*. When in 1668 Edme Boursault published his one-act comedy *La Satyre des satyres*, he was regrouping the enemies of Despréaux as well as of Molière, reforming Costar's circle, and was on friendly terms with Quinault, Boyer, Charpentier, and Colletet. Furetière was clearly still associated at this date with Despréaux, and he was to remain loyal to him after Gilles's death.

It was in 1672 that the Académie was given a privilège for its dictionary that was intended to be a virtual monopoly. Vaugelas had died in 1650, and none of the members of the Académie had shown any haste in taking over his work on the dictionary. Finally Mézeray offered to take it on for 4,000 livres a year. He had been undertaking the work of perpetual secretary during Conrart's incapacity and, on Conrart's death in 1675, Mézeray inherited the title as well as the task. When the dictionary project was formally proposed for detailed discussion, he found dissent. The victorious party was that of Charpentier, Perrault, Bensserade, Quinault, and Huet, who wanted the dictionary faithfully to reflect the state of perfection attained by the everyday French language during the preceding half-century. Patru and Richelet wanted essentially to record the literary language of authors acknowledged to be authoritative, while Furetière wanted a more descriptive, encyclopedic compilation, recording historical usage and recondite terms.

The Académie's dictionary was printed over 14 years, from 1678 to 1692, but the first printing of 500 copies revealed the implementation of the mandate to have been so badly executed that the work was suppressed, revised, and reissued in 1694. It has been continuously revised ever since, starting in 1718, and has always been intended to be mandatory for educational usage. In 1694 the individual words were arranged in families and not simply in alphabetical order, so that, although the definitions were concise and accurate, the work itself was useless for its purpose. Its compilation was also negligent. As originally published, it was the least good of the three dictionaries.

Patru, born in 1604 and a member of the Académie from 1640, was a lawyer who mingled in the literary world with Boileau, Maucroix, Tallemant, Richelet, and Cassandre. He fell into a state of poverty before his death, but earned something from work on Richelet's dictionary, and was helped financially first by Montauzier and then by a royal gift on 19 May 1679 of two abbacies, which he immediately surrendered for 4,500 livres a year. It was he who organized Richelet's dictionary, enlisting with Richelet a team which included Maucroix and the Jesuits Rapin and Bouhours.

Richelet had been friendly with Perrot d'Ablancourt and initially with d'Aubignac, with whom he later quarrelled. On account of the Académie's monopoly Richelet's dictionary was printed by Witerhold in Geneva, first in 1680, but with reprints in 1685, 1689, and 1690. It considered as authoritative the usage of Nicolas Perrot d'Ablancourt, the celebrated translator who had died in 1664 and whose work was regarded with disdain by Huet, Charpentier, Bensserade, and Marolles. The earliest copies of Richelet's dictionary to come into France got no further than Lyons and were confiscated as contravening the Académie's monopoly.

Furetière obtained a privilège on 24 August 1684 for his three-volume folio dictionary of the whole language, the 1690 *Dictionnaire universel, contenant tous les mots françois, tant vieux que modernes, et les termes de toutes les sciences et des arts*. The chancellor had refused a privilège unless Furetière presented the authorization of Charpentier as custodian of the Académie's privilège. Charpentier relates that he was entertained by Furetière, shown a number of plans and, thinking the work was going to be an encyclopedia of the arts, trades, and sciences which did not infringe the Académie's monopoly, signed a paper with which Furetière obtained a privilège for a more general dictionary. Although the definitions are long-winded and descriptive, it is much fuller than the other two dictionaries, less disordered and much fuller than Richelet, and utilizable as the Académie's dictionary was not. Basnage was to emend it in 1701, and the Jesuits virtually reprinted it at Trévoux. Known as the *Dictionnaire de Trévoux*, it was developed by the Jesuits in the 18th century into a compilation which they hoped would counter the influence of the *Encyclopédie*; they revised it for the 1704 first edition under the new name, and subsequently for editions in 1720, 1752, and 1771. It was deservedly the most successful of the three dictionaries.

In 1684 Furetière published a prospectus for his dictionary, with specimen entries, the *Essai d'un Dictionnaire universel contenant généralement tous les mots Français tant vieux que modernes, et les Termes de toutes les sciences et des arts*. Furetière's colleagues in the Académie tried to persuade him to renounce his privilège, but he would not. They therefore voted quasi-unanimously to exclude him from the Académie on 22 January 1685, petitioned the king on 30 January, and had Furetière's privilège annulled on 9 March. Racine voted against the exclusion, but La Fontaine voted in favour, with Charpentier, Paul and François Tallemant and, among others, Le Clerc, Boyer, Quinault, Perrault, Bensserade, Huet, Lavau, Thomas Corneille, and Pellisson.

Furetière issued a series of half a dozen satirical pamphlets against the Académie, its proceedings, and its dictionary in 1687 and 1688 and won the battle for public opinion. He attacked La Fontaine, some of whose friends, like Mme de Sévigné, judged Furetière's behaviour severely. Personal allegiances again played their role. La Fontaine's old association with Foucquet's entourage may explain his siding with the *modernes*, even against the almost neutral Furetière, but it carried weight with Mme de Sévigné and Furetière was hurt by it. However, the king refused to have Furetière's vacant seat at the Académie filled until after his death, which took place on 14 March 1688, two years before his dictionary was printed in Holland, at The Hague by Arnout and in Rotterdam by Reinier Leers.

WORKS

Furetière owes his reputation to his position in the literary world of 17th-century France, to his friendships with Gilles Boileau and his brother, to his literary connection with Molière and Racine, his attitude in the Querelle des anciens et des modernes (q.v.) and his hostility towards the précieuses (q.v.), to the quarrel with the Académie française, and to the great *Dictionnaire*. His satirical works—the *Nouvelle allégorique*, *Le Roman bourgeois* and the later lampoons directed against his former colleagues—are witty, amusing and light weight. It is the role he played in literary life which makes it impossible to overlook him.

The *Nouvelle allégorique; ou, Histoire des derniers troubles arrivés au royaume d'éloquence* first appeared in 1658, and was revised the same year, although the unrevised version was reprinted in both 1658 and 1659. It clearly, although perhaps not deliberately, attempts to blend together two genres which in fact can mix only with difficulty. The allegories of the 1650s, often geographies of love, were to give way to the satire of the 1660s, as notably practised by Despréaux. The polemical invective, light-hearted or not, of such pieces as Cotin's *Ménagerie* and Gilles Boileau's *Avis à M. Ménage* belonged to a different genre altogether. Furetière's difficulty was to write an allegorical description of a battle between the forces of sound rhetoric and those of babble, in which both sides had to be capable of being clearly related by the reader to whatever or whomsoever they represented, and at the same time a satire, which traditionally dealt with types rather than named individuals. The combination of satire and allegory defeated him. The tradition of using only types, known by their characteristics, had been eroded, but had none the less been observed in Furetière's early satires, devoted to individuals only in so far as they typified a group, "merchants," "poets," and "the pedantic doctor," in whom we nevertheless recognize Guy Patin.

In the *Nouvelle allégorique*, Galimatias, not clearly identified with any person, doctrine, or literary alignment, but recently banished from the kingdom of eloquence, decides to declare war on princess Rhetoric. The word "galimatias" by this date means any sort of disordered discourse, and here the character, Galimatias, occupies various provinces, "Dicae," "Homiliaire," "Epistolaire," and "Romanie," roughly equivalent to rules, homilies, letters, and novels, but cannot penetrate "Alcôves (alcoves; that is, small conversation areas giving on to a large reception room)." The princess asks for assistance from 40 barons and from her sister, Poésie. The princess's forces, representing rhetoric, are more disciplined, but those of Galimatias more numerous and powerful. Whole battalions of figures and authorities are wiped out. Poetry was having to deal with a rebellion by Aristotle. Galimatias is reinforced by the creatures of Aristotle, arguments. In the end Poésie's man of business, Intrigue, agrees a compromise. The allegorical peace treaty corresponds to the literary reality as Furetière wishes it to be established, or thinks perhaps that it has been. The best works will be dominated by eloquence, but Galimatias prevails in the majority of books.

The lack of clear correlations between the allegorical characters and events and those of the literary realities makes the *Nouvelle allégorique* little more than a declaration of party membership, committing its unnamed but scarcely anonymous author to a general handclap in favour of common sense rather than to anything specific, except in its repudiation of Aristotle and of total irregularity in ambitious literary writing, and in its unflattering allusions to Sorel and Madeleine de Scudéry. There are also references to the disputes about Pierre Corneille's *Le Cid*, and to those between La Mothe le Vayer and Vaugelas about his 1647 *Remarques sur la langue française*, between Ménage and his opponents, and between La Mesnardière and Chapelain. Furetière gives his allegory a top dressing of contemporary allusion, and it remains therefore of historical interest, although it does little to boost the contextual understanding of more important texts.

The modern editor of *Le Roman bourgeois* doubts whether it would still be remembered if it were not for Furetière's distinguished friends and the *Dictionnaire*. Its purpose may well have been the cruel caricature of Sorel as Charrosselles, but the real originality is the use at centre stage of what Furetière refers to as "de bonnes gens de médiocre condition (good folk of modest condition)." The work describes in realistic detail the life, dwellings, furniture, speech habits, and such things as the meals of the lower Paris bourgeoisie, but is a parody of the adventure novel, implicitly questioning all its conventions and, given the social status of the characters and the date, the novel is of course comic. Furetière shows little sympathy for the milieu he depicts, merely contrasting town dwellers with old-fashioned peasant mentalities, like his characters Bedout and Vollichon, with the socially ascending lawyer like Nicodème or with the coquette Lucrèce.

There are no heroes or heroines. The narrator can tell the reader nothing that could not be seen or heard, like what passed between Lucrèce and the marquis: "On ne sait rien de tout cela, parce que la chose se passa en secret (We don't know anything about that, because it took place in private)." Furetière is not a natural novelist. He has invented a way of writing a fiction to demonstrate the absurdity of the romanesque conventions, and he pedantically sticks to the rules he has invented. His narrative shows the sort of respect for disordered reality as his attitude to Galimatias did for the reality of disorder in language.

Furetière quite certainly had definite people in mind at various points in the novel, and they will have been identified by those likely to have been present at the salon readings. Among the few certainties are the fact that Furetière had in front of him, as he wrote, at least part of the text of Tallemant's *Les Historiettes*, from which he borrows, and that Racine drew on Furetière's novel for *Les Plaideurs*. The conformity of spirit and detail is so close that there must have been some form of collaboration with Despréaux, drafts of whose texts Furetière may well have seen. It is not impossible that there was some borrowing of material, as narrow as a particular situation or as broad as a relish for certain types of comic effect, between Furetière and Molière. They shared a milieu, and an audience, although the *Roman bourgeois*, which Richelet tells us was a failure, was not in fact ever reprinted in the 17th century. The attempt to demonstrate the ridicule particularly of the novels of galanterie misfired. The attempt at realism is short in focus, narrow in vision, and tedious in telling. Madeleine de Scudéry's imagination was a great deal more powerful, and the light she threw on the meaning of human experience much more penetrating.

At best the *Roman bourgeois* is informative about lower middle class life, and there are sporadically amusing episodes, and witty pages. The only obviously identifiable allusion is to Sorel in the character Charrosselles, an indefatigable compiler of burlesque lists and catalogues. Most other attempted identifications remain unsupported by evidence and have met with critical scepticism. It is naturally in accordance with Furetière's aims that the events should be ridiculous or scandalous, the characters foolish or scurrilous, the language vulgar, and most of the jokes vapid. The trouble is that the caricature is so drearily heavy-handed and so often unfunny: "I shall leave it to the binder to look after the book's order."

The novel is sub-titled "ouvrage comique (comic work)," and there is an avertissement from the bookseller to the reader about the author's intention to be instructive as well as diverting. The heaviness of the laboured humour is quite clear from the opening dozen lines; explanatory notes have been added in square brackets in the translation.

Je chante les amours et les advantures de plusieurs bourgeois de Paris, de l'un et de l'autre sexe; et ce qui est de plus merveilleux, c'est que je les chante, et si je ne sçay pas la musique. Mais puisque un roman n'est rien qu'une poésie en prose, je croirais mal débuter si je ne suivois l'exemple de mes maistres, et si je faisois un autre exorde: car, depuis que feu Virgile a chanté Aenée et ses armes, et que le Tasse, de poëtique memoire, a distingué son ouvrage par chants, leurs successeurs, qui n'estoient pas meilleurs musiciens que moy, ont tous repeté la mesme chanson, et ont commencé d'entonner sur la mesme notte...

(I sing the loves and adventures of some Parisian bourgeois of both sexes [the *Aeneid* starts "Arma virumque cano {I sing of arms and the man}." Furetière parodies Virgil with the opening announcement of his intention to sing of low life]; and what is even more extraordinary, I sing them without knowing any music. But since a novel is only a poem in prose [allusion to Tasso's *Discorsi del poema eroico* arguing that the novel is a prose epic], I'd think I had started badly if I didn't follow the example of my masters, and if I began differently: for, since the late Virgil sang of Aeneas and his arms, and Tasso, of poetic memory, divided his work into cantos, their successors, who were no better musicians than I, have all repeated the same song, and have begun by sounding the same note...).

The narrator tells us that his stories have neither heroes nor heroines, just characters who neither bear arms nor overturn kingdoms, but are good folk of modest condition, some handsome, some ugly; some wise, some—and that is most of them—foolish. There follows a long paragraph on what another author might have done about describing the Carmelite church where the story starts. The point is to make fun of technical architectural terms.

The church was full: some people had come out of devotion, others to listen to the music, others to hear the preacher, and Furetière is at his best in the famous opening description of the collection at the service. All the men gave according to how pretty they thought the girl taking the collection, and the prettiest girl was the one who collected the most money. It was through the collection that Nicodème met Javotte, Vollichon's daughter. Within half a dozen pages Nicodème is asking Vollichon if he can marry Javotte. Vollichon finds him altogether too well washed and well dressed, but agrees. The narrator then teases the reader for two paragraphs about his concluding so quickly with a wedding, ending with a paragraph Diderot must have remembered for *Jacques le fataliste*,

Il ne tiendroit qu'à moi de faire icy une heroïne qu'on enleveroit autant de fois que je ne voudrois faire de volumes...

(If I cared to I could create here a heroine who would be abducted as many times as I wanted to make volumes...).

The narrator resolves his dilemma by telling us that there was an objection to the banns, and that a girl called Lucrèce maintained she had a promise of marriage from Nicodème, "ce qui le perdit de reputation chez les parens de Javotte (which cost him his reputation with Javotte's parents)." At this point Furetière interpolates the "Histoire de Lucrèce la bourgeoise (Story of the bourgeois girl Lucrèce)." When Furetière does decide to stop he ends with a conundrum which again suggests that the novel fascinated Diderot. What happens in fairyland when a hound who has the gift of always catching his prey chases a hare who has the gift of never getting caught? Whose victory "estoit écrit dans la destinée de chacun (was written in the destiny of each)?" The answer, of course, is that they, and his characters, are still running, and the book ends

il en est de mesme des procès de Collantine et de Charroselle: ils ont tousjours plaidé et plaident encore, et plaideront tant qu'il plaira à Dieu de les laisser vivre

(it is the same with the court cases of Collantine and Charroselle: they have always had cases in court; they still have; and they will go on having them as long as it pleases God for them to live).

The novel quickly breaks down into a series of episodes. Lucrèce had no money, but great ambitions. She lived by her charms but pretended to have 45,000 livres. Unhappily they were secured by "the fogs on the River Loire." The much quoted burlesque marriage tariff has so often been taken as a serious guide to mid-17th-century matrimonial economics that it should be reproduced as a tail-piece. The functions associated with legal and administrative posts are noted in the glossary; some of those offices are grandiloquently made up by Furetière:

A girl should expect with a dowry of
1. 2,000–6,000 livres: Un marchand du Palais, ou un petit commis, sergent ou solliciteur de procez
   (a shopkeeper at the Palais-Royal, a junior clerk or legal agent)
2. 6,000–12,000 livres: Un marchand de soye, drappier, mouleur de bois, procureur du Chastelet, maistre d'hostel et secretaire de grand seigneur
   (a silk or cloth merchant, controller of weights and measures, counsel at the Paris district court, steward and manager of a lord)
3. 12,000–20,000 livres: Un Procureur en Parlement, huissier, notaire ou greffier
   (a high court solicitor, court officer, notary, or registrar)
4. 20,000–30,000 livres: Un advocat, conseiller du Tresor ou des Eaüës et Forests, substitut du Parquet et general des Monnoyes
   (a barrister, treasury inspector, inspector of rivers and forests, assistant prosecutor, and inspector of the mint)
5. 30,000–45,000 livres: Un auditeur des Comptes, tresorier de France ou payeur de rentes
   (an auditor, tax commissioner or treasurer of bonds)

6. 45,000–75,000 livres: Un Conseiller de la Cour des Aydes, ou conseiller du Grand Conseil

   (a tax judge or member of the king's council)

7. 75,000–150,000 livres: Un Conseiller au Parlement ou un maistre des Comptes

   (a member of the parliamentary court or a treasury secretary)

8. 150,000–300,000 livres: Un maistre des Requestes, intendant des Finances, greffier et secretaire du Conseil, president aux Enquêtes

   (a high court judge, Treasury inspector, secretary to the privy council, law lord)

9. 300,000–600,000 livres: Un president au mortier, vray marquis, sur-intendant, duc et pair

   (a Lord of Appeal, a real marquis, treasury lord, duke and peer)

If you are male, have no post, but live on interest, you have no right to look for a marriage partner. Perhaps you should content yourself with celibacy, the church and a benefice? A girl who must marry a man living on interest should calculate "au denier six," that is estimating the notional capital at six times the actual interest. Furetière's narrator is being generous, estimating the capital on a 16.66% yield when interest rates were actually 5%.

PUBLICATIONS

Verse

L'Aenéide travestie, Livre quatriesme, 1649
Le Voyage de Mercure, satyre, 1653
Poesies diverses, 1655; edition annotated in English 1908
Fables morales et nouvelles, 1671
Les Paraboles de l'Evangile, 1672

Fiction, allegory and satire

Nouvelle allégorique; ou, Histoire des derniers troubles arrivés au Royaume d'Eloquence, 1658; modern edition 1967

Le Roman bourgeois, ouvrage comique, 1666; in *Romanciers du XVIIe siècle* in the Bibliothèque de la Pléiade, 1958

Polemic and *Dictionnaire*

Essais de lettres familières, 1684
Essai d'un dictionnaire universel, contenant généralement tous les mots françois, tant vieux que modernes, 1684
Factum pour messire Antoine de Furetière…contre quelques-uns de l'Académie française, 1685
Second Factum, 1686
Troisième Factum, 1688
Preuves par escrit des faits contenus dans les précédents factums de M. l'abbé Furetière, ?1686
Recueil des pièces du sieur Furetière et de Messieurs de l'Académie française, 1686
Plan et dessein du poème allégorique et tragico-burlesque intitulé Les couches de l'Académie, 1687
Recueil de plusieurs vers, épigrammes et autres pièces, 4 vols., 1687
Lettre de M. Furetière à M. Doujat, doyen de l'Académie française, 1688
Dictionnaire universel, contenant tous les mots français, tant vieux que modernes, et les termes de toutes les sciences et des arts, 3 vols., 1690
Recueil des Factums d'Antoine Furetière, 2 vols., 1858–59

The biographical and critical literature is confined to introductions, specialist articles, and treatments in general works. The only book-length biographies are in German.

Leuscher, K., *Antoine Furetière und sein Streit mit der französischen Akademie*, 1915
Fisher, H., *Antoine Furetière. Versuch eines Beitrages zur Wesenskunde des französischen Menschen*, 1937

G

GARNIER, Robert, c.1545–1590.

Dramatist and poet.

LIFE

Although Garnier has for a long time been regarded from a literary point of view as the most important writer of vernacular tragedy in 16th-century France, the reasons given for this pre-eminence have disconcertingly oscillated, suggesting an uncertainty among critics about what constitutes literary quality in French renaissance drama. What Garnier's contemporaries thought is relatively clear. Ronsard's perfunctory preliminary sonnet for Garnier's 1574 *Cornélie, épouse de Pompée* selects the style for faint praise, and Belleau's ode, printed alongside it, comments chiefly on the bloodiness of the action. Other of his contemporaries praised in Garnier the use of forces not under human or rational control, the emotional intensity of the scripts, or their dignity and grandeur.

Garnier was later inevitably judged in the unhelpful light of norms adopted by dramatists a century later, or until very recently for minor technical aspects of the rhetorical style, like the imagery, the evocations of physical cruelty, or the structure of the dramas, or their lyrical inspiration. The most recent criticism has concentrated on the tragedies, and on the political aspects of the intrigues. The actual focuses of imaginative interest in the complete oeuvre can most easily be uncovered against the background of the biography.

Garnier was born in La Ferté-Bernard which, in the 16th century, rivalled nearby Le Mans in size and importance. His family had been settled there for rather less than a century. His father, Louis Garnier, came from a line of merchants, aspiring to cross the line into the minor aristocracy, but of no substantial means. It was probably in 1542 that he married Garnier's mother, Anne Guillois, who was of higher rank and to whom the family house belonged, and it is certain that Garnier had at least two sisters. His parents married young, but both appear to have died within a year or two of 1553. In 1574 Garnier would himself claim aristocratic status, but the grounds are uncertain. The date of birth, which is generally computed by subtracting the age at death given by one source from the date of death given by another, must have been 1544 or 1545, very probably 1545 new style, that is before Easter. It is reasonable to assume that by the time his age reached double figures, Garnier was an orphan, and that he was brought up by his father's younger brother, Nicolas, whose own third child was not born until 1565.

There was a local school which Garnier must have attended, but thereafter we know only that he was at Toulouse in May 1564. By that date he had studied his humanities, absolved the first two years of the course in law, although probably not at Toulouse, where the course, the best in France, was notoriously expensive, got to know Ronsard and Baïf, written his first verse, and made contact with the Le Mans poets of the generation before his own, Denisot, Peletier du Mans, and Jacques Tahureau. Garnier probably studied his humanities at one of the colleges in Le Mans, the Collège de la Couture being the most likely, but is unlikely to have gone straight on to Toulouse, which was sought after and distant, as well as expensive.

In 1552 Henri II had created a new series of civil courts, the présidiaux, with intermediate jurisdictions between those of the baillages and those of the parlements. The parlements were naturally hostile, and the legislation was to be frequently amended, but the creation of 500 new low-grade legal offices for sale to those whose resources did not stretch to a parliamentary office offered an opportunity to families like the Garniers, whose members had hitherto gone to universities only to make possible an ecclesiastical career. The 1552 decree probably explains Garnier's legal studies.

They must have begun in 1561. The five and a half years for baccalauréat and licence could be reduced if the first semester of law was also the last of arts, and again if the student taught elementary classes. Garnier spent the academic year 1563–64 in Toulouse, probably having completed the baccalauréat at Angers. The university had just returned to normal after the strong wave of anti-Protestant sentiment which followed the start of the religious wars in 1562, the ending of the council of Trent early in 1563, and an outbreak of plague in the spring of that year.

The celebrated Jeux Floraux of Toulouse have from time to time changed their form. In 1564 there was a prescribed genre, the metrically complex chant royal, and Garnier won the first prize, the violet, for an openly political poem on the troubles of France in which he took the tolerant view which the president of the judges, Guy du Faur de Pibrac, shared with the chancellor, Michel de l'Hôpital, whom he knew well. Immediately famous, Garnier may have composed *Porcie* that summer, probably while staying with Etienne Potier de la Terrasse, a friend's father, who owned the château de Castelnouvel a dozen kilometres west of Toulouse and to whom the play was dedicated when it appeared in 1568. The privilège was dated June 1567.

It seems probable that a play was simply commissioned from the winner of the Jeux, to be played at the king's triumphal entry to the city in February 1565. Garnier, no doubt fortunate to have won the first prize in the year preceding the royal entry, was certainly given municipal commissions to write triumphal inscriptions and declamatory verse, published in a volume of which no copy is at present known, but which the conditions of the 1564 prize obliged Garnier to present to the Jeux in 1565, the *Plaintes amoureuses de R. Garnier Manceau, contenant élégies, Sonetz, Epitres, Chansons. Plus deux églogues*....The affection of the title alludes to a married woman known in the poems as Agnette.

Garnier, as the preceding year's winner, was debarred from

competing in 1565, but he won the eglantine or third prize on 5 May at the 1566 Jeux, and by that June was in Paris. Usage, to be codified in the ordinance of Blois in 1576, demanded that a conseiller at a présidial should have practised as a barrister for three years and be 25 years old, conditions just fulfilled when Garnier bought his position as conseiller at the Le Mans présidial in May, and was installed on 26 September 1569. In spite of the general prohibition still in force against it, the teaching of civil law in Paris was officially permitted between 1563 and 1573, and Garnier, who later described himself as qualified "in both laws (canon and civil)," seems to have graduated in Paris in canon law in order to be able to qualify as civil lawyer and practise as an advocate for the stipulated three years.

Garnier's period in Paris coincided with the resumption of the civil wars which had begun in 1562 and in which the death of Montmorency at Saint-Denis on 12 November 1567, and the dismissal as chancellor of Michel de l'Hôpital in 1568, ended the hopes of the moderates in favour of religious toleration. In 1567 he published his moderate *Hymne de la monarchye*, dedicated to Pibrac and perhaps intended as a personal political manifesto. When *Porcie* was published in 1568, there were preliminary poems contributed by Ronsard, Belleau, and Baïf. Dorat appears to have held himself aloof until he addressed lines to Garnier in 1585 largely, it seems, to give Robert Estienne the opportunity to translate them into Latin and Greek. Ronsard would use his preliminary sonnet to Garnier's *Cornélie* deliberately to humiliate Jodelle.

Garnier was to continue to return at intervals from Le Mans to the capital where, as a practising lawyer, his political formation had been completed. We have to trace the pattern of his movements largely from such evidence as the appearance of his name as godfather on baptismal registers, and the rhythm and place of the publication of his works, but he seems to have tried to visit Paris annually, both while he was a conseiller at the Le Mans présidial, that is until 14 April 1574, and thereafter, when he was lieutenant criminel at Le Mans, until 2 August 1586. The role he was to play in the political life of Le Mans needs to be taken into account in any assessment of the thrust of his literary activity and the political intention of his plays.

After his break with the Agnette of the Toulouse verse, Garnier claims to have been free of emotional ties until he got to know Françoise Hubert from Nogent-le-Rotrou, a stage on the route from Le Mans to Paris, whom he met probably in 1570 and married in 1575, and to whom he appears to have remained faithful until her death on 5 August 1588. No marriage contract has been discovered, but there would have been no need for one, since Garnier, orphaned, had received his inheritance on reaching his majority, and any dowry given to his wife would have removed her right to her share of her parents' succession. She must have been born within a year of 1548, was the youngest of five children of a family from the minor but ancient nobility, was herself a poet, and bore her husband two daughters, Diane and Françoise. If there were any other children, they did not survive infancy. Garnier and his wife were not rich but could with care live up to their social rank in the provincial squirearchy.

Garnier produced five tragedies between 1573 and 1580: *Hippolyte* in 1573; *Cornelie* in 1574; *Marc-Antoine* in 1578; *La Troade* in 1579; and *Antigone; ou, La Piété* in 1580. They were certainly concerned with political issues in that their focus of interest was the deployment of political power and, from the death of Charles IX on 31 May 1574, Garnier began to write

occasional verse constituting political propaganda in the narrow sense. The question of the succession to the throne of France had been obscured by the acceptance by Catherine de Medici's third son of the Polish throne.

Catherine de Medici and Henri had four sons, but it is unfortunately confusing to refer to them by the name they bore at their deaths, since the heir apparent was generally given the duchy-peerage of Orléans, if it happened to be free, which made him duc d'Orléans, while his next younger living brother generally became the duc d'Anjou, and the next after that the duc d'Alençon, a system which ensured that many male princes "of the blood," that is kings' sons of legitimate birth, changed their names, most importantly from Alençon to Anjou, or from Anjou to Orléans, on a monarch's death. New dukedoms could be created only by erecting territories, even small estates, into duchy-peerages.

Of the four sons of Henri II and Catherine, François II presents no difficulty. Born in 1544, he acceded in 1559 and died the following year. He was succeeded by his brother Charles IX, born in 1550, who acceded in 1560 and died in 1574. The next brother, Henri, had been the duc d'Anjou when he had in 1573 accepted the Polish throne. When he became Henri III in 1574, the fourth brother, hitherto Alençon, became Anjou, and heir presumptive until Henri III should produce legitimate male issue, which he never did. When Anjou, Catherine's fourth son and Henri III's younger brother, died in 1584, Henri III still had no issue, and Henri de Navarre was considered to have a better hereditary claim to the throne than anyone else, and was therefore regarded as heir presumptive.

Catherine's eldest son, François II, had died without issue. Her second son, Charles IX, confirmed his next brother, the current duc d'Anjou, as his successor by letters patent in May 1573. But if the acceptance of the Polish throne really did constitute an abdication by Catherine's third son, then the crown would pass to the duc d'Alençon, who was in fact to become duc d'Anjou on his brother's accession and who was the leader of the "Politiques," the recently formed group of moderates which included Michel de l'Hôpital, all three marshals of France, Montmorency, Damville, and Cossé, as well as La Noue, Turenne, and Condé.

By the end of 1572, after the massacre of Saint Bartholomew's Day, 24 August, Henri de Navarre had abjured and was kept under surveillance at court. The ensuing hostilities of 1573 had come to an end in July with the edict of La Rochelle, after the election of Catherine's third son to the Polish throne. Charles IX had fallen terminally ill before the end of 1573, and a general uprising by the Protestants and moderates was planned for early 1574 to prevent the recall of Henri III from Poland and the continued ascendancy of Catherine de Medici. The uprising failed, and Catherine's three armies, in the west, the south-east, and Normandy, were quickly organized against the threatened coup. Charles IX had gone to Vincennes about 8 March 1574. On the Thursday before Easter, 8 April, a plot to allow the escape from court of Alençon and Navarre was betrayed, and on 9 April the lesser conspirators, La Môle and Coconnato, were arrested. On that day Garnier resigned his post as conseiller to the présidial before a court notary.

La Môle and Coconnato were tortured, tried, and executed on 30 April. Alençon and Navarre were interrogated, and on 4 May Montmorency and Cossé were sent to the Bastille. On 25 May Montgomery, the Protestant leader, was to be defeated in Normandy. Catherine de Medici, no doubt rancorous on account of the tournament at which Montgomery had accidentally killed her husband, Henri II, was to insist on his execution. On 31 May, Charles IX died, two days after reaffirming the king of Poland as his successor, and his mother as regent until his return. Lucid, and aware that he was dying, he constrained Alençon and Navarre to appear before him and to accept the succession of the king of Poland. Charles's confessor, Arnaud Sorbin, had had to go and preach at Vespers because it was Pentecost Sunday, but his old tutor, Jacques Amyot, had been with him.

On 14 April 1574, five days after the arrest of the Vincennes conspirators and his own resignation as conseiller, Garnier was at court, where he took the oath as lieutenant-criminel, to which post he had been appointed 24 hours earlier, on the day when Alençon had been interrogated. He was at court again on 10 July. He had therefore been a close witness of the final conspiracy, the king's death, and the immediate consequences of both. He wrote a sonnet which appeared in the *Vray discours des derniers propos mémorables et trépas de feu roy de très bonne mémoire Charles neufiesme*, with a privilège of 16 June and, accompanied by a second sonnet, in Ronsard's *Tombeau de feu roy très chrestien Charles neufiesme*, to which only Jamyn, Ronsard, and himself contributed.

Catherine's purposes were best served by a policy of appeasement towards her opponents, best achieved by delaying the arrival back in France of Henri III. A strong case has been made out for supposing that Catherine dictated the line to be taken by Garnier in the *Vray discours* and in the *Tombeau*; that much care was taken in both documents to emphasize the legitimacy of the succession of Henri III; that Catherine wanted it to be supposed that the death of Charles IX had been sudden; and that it was Garnier who transmitted her wishes to Ronsard and Jamyn. The narrator of the *Vray discours* is at pains to underline Alençon's acceptance of his brother's last wishes, giving the reader no idea of the La Môle conspiracy.

Henri III had heard of his brother's death on 14 June; had been forced by Protestant troops to return by Venice and Savoy; and did not enter French territory until 5 September. In the meanwhile Arnaud Sorbin, the king's confessor, had published his *Histoire contenant un abrégé de la vie, moeurs, et vertus du roy très chrestien Charles IX*, with an achevé d'imprimer of 16 July 1574, but utilizing a privilège of 1564, and taking a strongly anti-Protestant line. Sorbin exults in the Bartholomew Day massacre, insinuates that Charles IX was poisoned, though he insists on a history of bad health which undermines the unexpectedness of the death, blames the Protestants for the La Môle conspiracy although La Môle and Coconnato had both died Catholics, attacks Protestants and moderates alike, and goes out of his way to refute the *Vray discours* on points of detail.

Garnier's fullest and most recent biographer argues from Sorbin's attack that the *Vray discours* must have been written by Amyot. Ronsard, who had quarrelled with Amyot, had contributed a piece to Sorbin's work in spite of the poet's identification with the *Tombeau*, but not to the *Vray discours*. In exchange for his political propaganda supporting the smoothness of the succession from Charles IX to Henri III and the need for a truce until Henri III, favoured by God in succeeding on Whit Sunday, could be brought back and crowned, Garnier, although his role was less publicly prominent than Ronsard's, was made lieutenant-criminel by Catherine de Medici. In the years 1576 to 1578 Ronsard, Dorat, and Baïf were receiving 1,200 livres pension, and Jamyn 400 livres, but Garnier was not on the list at all.

In 1580 the first collected edition of Garnier's works contained no dedication, but in 1582 there were two dedications to Henri III, one in verse and one in prose. As early as 1582 opinion was being stirred up about the succession to Henri III. He was 32 and had been married for seven years, but had produced no heir. The heir presumptive, Henri's brother, now the duc d'Anjou, was 30 years old. The initial 1580 publication of the seven-volume genealogy *Stemmatum Lotharingiae ac Barri ducum Tomi septem* by François de Rosières, arrested only in 1583, had begun to prepare the public for the legitimacy of the Guise claim to descendance from Charlemagne. Garnier's 1582 dedications play down the urgency of any discussion about the succession.

In Paris, there had been flickering centres of literary life in the houses of important patrons, and in such salons as those of Jean de Morel, blind and in English exile from 1572, and the maréchale de Retz, which finished in 1573 with her husband's disgrace. Some writers, such as Baïf and Desportes, received, and there was the Académie du Palais, where the best-known poets and scholars were invited to read papers and Garnier himself gave a discourse on "Crainte (fear)." Garnier knew most of the surviving friends of Ronsard, the prominent literary members of the magistracy, and the circle of Desportes. His own literary work was written chiefly before 1574, when he was made lieutenant-criminel in charge of the region's criminal justice, and for a few years between 1580 and 1583, during which time he retouched his earlier pieces. After the collected volume of 1585 nothing further by him was published in his lifetime.

On 12 October 1587 Garnier was made a member of the grand conseil, technically a division of the royal council which exercised royal jurisdiction in the king's name and made administrative arrangements in the king's interest. As the parlements had evolved from simple courts into quasi-legislative bodies by arrogating to themselves the power of veto over legislation and the power to initiate some forms of legislation, and by the creative administration of the law, so the grand conseil had been increasingly used by the royal court as a judicial and administrative body intended to be more pliant to royal policy. Subject to royal discretion, cases were taken out of the hands of all lower courts, including the parlements, whose sentences the grand conseil could overturn. Its decisions were attributed to "the king acting in council," and it sat where it liked, mostly outside Paris, where the parlement was too powerful for it. Between July 1586 and October 1587 Henri III and the grand conseil were in dispute about appointments which would have increased its size and altered its political colouring away from the League, the relationship having been critical for three months in the summer of 1586.

Garnier had become a conseiller of the grand conseil in June 1586, but is sometimes thought quite shortly after his entry as a member to have inclined towards the League. Before 1580 Garnier's allegiance had been with Michel de l'Hôpital, Pibrac, and Bodin. All his protectors had been loyal to Henri III or even, like Pibrac, leaned towards the Protestant party. From about 1580 Garnier's dedications to Brisson of *Antigone*, to Cheverny of *Bradamante*, and to Joyeuse of *Les Juifves* are equivocal. Apparent allusions to political situations have been seen in the last two plays which, if intentional, would not be incompatible with a commitment to the League's political views, although they do not on the other hand necessarily entail acceptance of them. After Garnier's death his name was invoked by League supporters.

From 1583 Garnier was seeking a change of post. That summer in Paris his servants had tried to poison the family with a view to robbery, and Garnier's wife was taken briefly ill. The perpetrators were apparently caught and punished. Garnier's wife was not to die until August 1588. The nomination to the grand conseil came from the king, but Garnier had difficulty in raising the 3,600 livres in cash which was required to purchase the office, especially when the purchaser of his own post as lieutenant-criminel had difficulty in paying him. He was largely helped by a family loan made from political motives. Garnier was expected for family reasons to support the personal policies of Henri III.

It became the treasonable crime of lèse-majesté to support the League only after 24 December 1588, and Garnier's formal commitment to the League does not seem to have been earlier than the end of April 1589 when Vendôme, where the grand conseil had been moved to, fell to the League. It was therefore made only later than the last of his published works, under apparent duress, and was short-lived. Garnier was certainly at Vendôme by 25 March 1589. The town fell to the League a day or two before 28 April. Many of its members were forced to sign documents adhering to the League, and it seems likely that Garnier was among them. Most were pardoned shortly after Garnier had died. Garnier was in any event treated favourably by the League in Vendôme that spring. From mid-May to mid-September 1589 Garnier was at La Ferté-Bernard, after which the biographer is left with an absence of signatures on documents which Garnier might normally have signed. On 19 March 1590 we know that he was confined to Le Mans, at that date only slightly more important a town than Garnier's native La Ferté-Bernard. Mayenne had entered Le Mans and taken over the town on behalf of the League on 17 May 1589. A taxation list drawn up on that date shows that at Le Mans Garnier, who must have bought his freedom by joining the League at Vendôme a fortnight previously, was still considered as loyal to Henri III. Le Mans returned to Henri IV's allegiance on 2 December 1589. On 19 March 1590 we know that Garnier was confined to Le Mans. He was by then chronically and probably terminally ill.

Garnier's motivations at the end of his life are obscure. His royalism seems not to have been popular at Le Mans. Like Paris and Toulouse, the town went over to the League, and it became treasonable voluntarily to live there on 22 April 1589. Garnier's fortune and reputation had been publicly committed by his successful attempt to gain nomination to the grand conseil, and the fortune of his family, too, was used to back his plainly royalist enterprise in support of Henri III. However, at least technically, he ended by committing treason.

Contemporaries like de Thou and Colletet were indulgent in their judgements about him, as they were not indulgent to some others. Relatives and close friends risked serious political compromise to comfort Garnier's last months. His financial troubles were such that his furniture had to be sold a week after his death. From 1586 to his death in 1590, he had passed from a situation in which his circumstances were still comfortable to one in which he could no longer meet interest payments, or even buy seed for his fields. Part of the disaster may have come from a ransom paid to the League after the taking of Vendôme. His brief association with the League does not seem to have been a matter of personal conviction, and still less of a momentary moral scruple that France might be going to have a Protestant king, as has been argued. Henri III was only 37 when he died,

assassinated, on 2 August 1589, and three months earlier it was almost as likely that he would still produce an heir as that he would be murdered so soon. Like the sudden deterioration in Garnier's financial circumstances, the brief adhesion to the League remains unexplained, but it seems almost certain that Garnier was under some form of constraint. It would not be surprising if the adhesion to the League and the financial situation were in some way connected, and blackmail has been conjectured, but there is no evidence. Garnier died on 20 September 1590.

WORKS

There was often a long gap between the composition and the publication of Garnier's tragedies, although exactly how long can be established only conjecturally, and often on slender and controverted evidence. The real difficulty is that we do not know whether the plays were performed. Some 16th-century tragedies, classical and biblical, were performed as rhetorical exercises in moving an audience in the highest humanities classes of the colleges, especially the Jesuit colleges. Others were performed in the course of grand entertainments, a regal entry or a court festivity. Garnier is known to have been disappointed that his tragedies were not played at court, and there is no clear evidence, after *Porcie*, that they were ever played at all.

However, there is also no evidence that they were not, and firm conclusions would be dangerous, since it is merely because of haphazard circumstance that we have come, for instance, to hear of two performances of Montchrestien in 1596 and 1601. It may be, although it is unlikely, that public performances at Le Mans were too commonplace to have been remarked on. There may have been private performances; or it may be that Garnier went on writing in the hope that there would be; or perhaps, however disappointed, he went on writing in declamatory tragic form, not expecting his plays to be performed at all. All modern commentators have supposed that Garnier wrote with performance in mind, whether private or public, but none of them has justified the supposition, which is not really at all probable. The criteria used in assessing the literary merit of what were published chiefly as tragedies must take account of the fact that it is unlikely that Garnier had more than at most occasional or semi-private performance in mind. Dramatic progression then becomes irrelevant, discussion of any intrigue unnecessary, and dramatic tension can be positively distracting. The scripts have to be considered almost as if they were dramatic eclogues, and the stylized attitudes and static but poetic expressions of emotion rhetorically and repetitiously put into the mouths of different characters become entirely understandable.

Garnier's plays were not performed regularly before paying audiences, and the criteria which governed their composition were not what we should call dramatic norms. It follows that what is of interest, apart from the poetry, is not the plot, even in so far as there is one, but attitudes and emotions which confront one another, without any necessary resolution. There is no need for anything we would recognize as characterization or even emotional subtlety. *Porcie*, for instance, contains much that is naive, like the chorus's view in the third act that foreign wars are preferable to civil ones, and much that is banal, like Porcie's view that dying for one's country does not necessarily do much good:

Nourrice: Qui meurt pour le païs vit éternellement.
Porcie: Qui meurt pour des ingrats meurt inutilement

(Nurse: Those who die for their country live for ever.
Porcie: Those who die for the ungrateful die uselessly).

There is only a restricted sense in which most modern readers would find poetry, drama, or moral edification in such rhetorical exchanges of commonplace aphorisms. The play, probably first written in 1564, was described when published in 1568 as

representant la cruelle et sanglante saison des guerres civiles de Rome. Propre et convenable pour y voir depeincte la calamité de ce temps

(representing the cruel and bloody period of Rome's civil wars. Appropriate and suitable for the visible depiction of the calamity of the present time).

Garnier is saying therefore that he intended to present a situation in Roman history, analogous to that in France in 1564, from which it might be possible to draw some relevant moral inference for the conduct of affairs. He is undoubtedly more poetically effective when he fights free of his Senecan model, whose Latin verse-forms had a built-in concentration which French alexandrines did not. When he follows Seneca, Garnier tones down the not infrequently gruesome details of Seneca's verse. His heightened feeling is transmitted by an insistence on realistic detail and a complicated but unified cross-pattern of metre, vowel-sound and consonantal reiteration, so that it matters where in the line the sounds are repeated or varied.

L'un a les bras tronquez, ou la cuisse avalée,
L'autre une autre partie en son corps mutilée;
Vous n'oyez que souspirs des blessez qui mouroyent,
Que menaces et cris de ceux qui demeuroyent:
Vous n'aviez sous les pieds que chevaus et gensdarmes,
Que picques et pavois, que divers outils d'armes,
Qui gisoyent sur le champ, demy noyez du sang,
Qui flottoit par la plaine ainsi qu'en un estang

(One has his arms cut off, or his thigh cut off,/Another a part of his body mutilated;/You heard only the sighs of the wounded who were dying,/And the threats and shouts of those who remained alive:/Under your feet you had only horses and soldiers,/Pikes and shields, different sorts of arms,/Lying on the field, half submerged in the blood,/Which flooded as in a pool over the plain).

The 1567 *Hymne de la monarchye* is not a great poem, but it does unequivocally state the poet's preference for a monarchy over a republic, and it confirms what we know about Garnier's commitment at that date to Charles IX. It was followed by *Hippolyte*, written before the Saint Bartholomew's Day massacre, probably in 1569 or 1570, but published only afterwards, in 1573. Parts of it are loose translations from Seneca and, although it may not be a matter for congratulation, Garnier "fills out Seneca's over-epigrammatic style." It may have nothing to do with any desire of Garnier's to be staged, but most readers would regard Garnier's text as an improvement for leaving out Seneca's description of Theseus's attempts to put back together

the fragments of Hippolytus's body. *Hippolyte* is not a political play, and shows signs of having been reworked, but there is no evidence to support any conjecture about the removal of contemporary political allusion.

Cornélie, published in 1574, appears to have been written in the period 1571 to 1572, before the death of Charles IX. The king's ambiguous instructions to provincial governors have subsequently been considered to have made him at least unwittingly responsible for some of the atrocities outside Paris which followed the Saint Bartholomew's Day massacre in the capital. The play, again taking a woman as the protagonist, contains some of Garnier's most vividly bloody descriptions and is, therefore, a denunciation of the horror of war as well as a plea for political liberty. What detracts from its interpretation as a piece of 16th-century political propaganda is Cornélie's simple assumption that the gods could punish her remarriage after the death of her husband by civil discord among the people of Rome. The political values allocating such importance to the private guilt of rulers and treating the sufferings of peoples so trivially derive from a stilted convention and are obviously not those of renaissance France. Any transposition of the comment by the characters on what they affect to regard as the Roman situation to that of the political position in 16th-century France cannot be univocal. In fact the play appears to invite interpretation primarily in general terms about human experience and the workings of political power.

Marc-Antoine was probably written in 1573, although it was not published until 1578. In essence the script contrasts the destructive thraldom of love, freely chosen and never regretted, with the exercise of power. Garnier's focus of imaginative interest is by now apparent. His pieces deal with the balanced interplay of personal emotions and political forces, with or without possible advertence to the situation existing in France as he wrote. It is very difficult to suppose that Garnier's intention is other than poetic. It is even quite difficult to detect from the text what his viewpoint was, if indeed he had one. Freely embraced love destroys both Marc-Antoine and Cléopâtre and costs each of them everything, even one another. Garnier goes out of his way to make each claim responsibility for their emotions. The play ends with the extinction in foreseen death of the hopes of the lovers, but it would be grotesque to read the play as showing the preferability of the alternative set of values, shown in Octave's power-grabbing avarice for political authority, barely tempered by decent regret when he first hears of Marc-Antoine's death.

Garnier's next two plays, *La Troade*, probably begun in 1574 although not published until 1579, and *Antigone*, written between 1574 and 1576 and published in 1580, turn to Greek themes. There is unanimity among critics that *La Troade* is not a political play, in the sense of a piece precisely relevant to the political situation in 1579 or the five years immediately preceding it, during which the play was probably being written or retouched. It is almost a dramatic threnody on the inutility of war, political only in the sense that its principal theme is the imbalance between human suffering and military victory. The Trojans fought and lost a just war on their own territory. The Greeks won, but lost as many heroes as the Trojans, and had only treachery and death to look forward to when they returned home.

Antigone; ou, La Piété is a long piece, getting on for double the standard length of a play realistically designed for public stage performance. The confrontation is not dissimilar to that in *Marc-Antoine* between private conscience and publicly exercised political power, but Antigone, the protagonist, is presented in contrast first to her father, Edipe, and then to her brother, Polynice, before being condemned to death by the king, Creon. Although a messenger brings news which changes the situations and attitudes of the characters, and although the action is slowed and commented on by a chorus of old men and a chorus of young girls, Garnier does extract much emotional intensity from the whole of the Oedipus legend, drawing, he tells us, on Aeschylus, Sophocles, Euripides, Seneca, and Statius.

The play starts at the point in the myth when Edipe, having married Iocaste, widow of the king of Thebes, and having discovered that he had killed his father and that Iocaste was his mother, has put out his own eyes and is doing penance in isolation, attended by his daughter Antigone, who insists on her father's innocence, since he had not known either who his father was when he killed him, or that Iocaste was his mother when he married her. From the beginning Antigone stands for the values of a personal integrity which can be in tension with the judgements of the gods, less mocked by Garnier than they had been in some of the Greek treatments of the myth:

Personne n'est mechant qu'avecques volonté

(No one is evil except by their own will).

The whole of the first act is taken up with Antigone's assertion of the primacy of personal responsibility over ineluctable guilt, in a long scene with her father, followed by a chorus. In the second act Antigone pleads with her mother, Iocaste, to intervene to stop the murderous warfare between her brothers, Edipe and Iocaste's sons, Polynice and Eteocle, each of whom wants to rule Thebes. Iocaste fails and in act three, informed by the Messenger that Polynice and Eteocle have killed each other in single combat, she kills herself. The act continues when Hemon, son of Iocaste's brother Creon, suddenly speaks. He had been listed as a character in the act at the beginning and, had the play been acted in accordance with the indications on paper, would suddenly have had to come to life as he stepped forward to comfort Antigone in apparent ignorance of all that had been said in his presence. The act ends with the usual chorus.

The fourth act is shared between Antigone and her sister, Ismene. Creon, who intends to take over the kingship of Thebes, has had Eteocle buried, but forbidden the burial of Polynice, who had sought Greek allies to fight against his native city. Antigone insists on burying her second brother. Creon enters halfway through the act and formally forbids her to bury Polynice, but Antigone disobeys in the name of a higher authority, her conscience, God. There are half a dozen pages of stichomythia. The old men observe of Antigone,

Pour sa condition elle a le coeur trop haut

(For her station she has too high a courage).

She is condemned to starve to death in a cave, goes in, bidding farewell to the world, and strangles herself. Hemon enters after her, finds her dead, and kills himself. The fifth act adds only the news that, on hearing what has happened, Eurydice, Creon's wife and Hemon's mother, has killed herself.

The script is virtually unstageable as a dramatic entertainment, demanding suspension of disbelief for the whole length of time it would take to play, although parts could be read out and, especially if the act divisions were changed from those indicated, the script could be presented as a series of impressive tableaux. The various stages of the tragic vortex which suck a whole family to destruction are very movingly arranged, the emotional reactions stark and gripping, the progressive extension of the grasp of guilt and death terrifying. There is not so much a plot as a growing momentum in the horror, and there is a genuine blind inevitability which depends entirely on the poetry and the unfolding situation and not, as it does in Racine, on the skills of professional actors. And Garnier's poetry, if patchy, is at its best both skilful and affecting. There are too many lines like the chorus's "Mais las! c'est grande pitié (Alas! how piteous)," but few 16th-century dramatic poems contain passages of much higher quality than Antigone's farewell:

> Adieu, luisant Soleil, adieu rayons ardans,
> Adieu pour tout jamais! car dans ce pleureuz antre,
> Mon supreme manoir, jamais ta clairté n'entre.
> Adieu, mon cher Hemon, vous ne me verrez plus,
> Je m'en vay confiner en cet antre reclus:
> Souvenez-vous de moy, que la mort on me donne,
> Qu'on me livre à la mort pour avoir esté bonne

(Farewell, shining sun, farewell burning rays,/Farewell for evermore! for into this mournful cave,/My final domain, your brightness never penetrates./Farewell, my dear Hemon, you will not see me again,/I am going to shut myself up in this lonely cave:/Remember me, that I have been put to death,/That I have been handed over to death for having been virtuous)"

The consonantal rhyme of the last couplet skilfully achieves the effect of finality, and thereby emphasizes Antigone's offence: virtue.

It is the remaining two plays which are Garnier's most famous. *Bradamante* was published in 1582 as a "tragecomedie," a new word used perhaps because the subject was modern, the ending happy, or perhaps simply because it was necessary to find a new name for a piece which did not have the chorus obligatory in a tragedy. It may originally have been written as much as a decade before publication. *Les Juifves* was a biblical tragedy published in 1583. *Antigone* had been dedicated to Brisson at a moment when there was not even a remote connection between Brisson and the League. *Bradamante* was dedicated to Cheverny, whose *Mémoires*, begun in 1586, do show some sympathy with the League, but who was Garnier's immediate hierarchical superior in the civil administration, and about to become chancellor. Cheverny was equivocal in his attitude to the League from the summer of 1588, and was momentarily disgraced by Henri III on 13 September 1588 as a precaution before the meeting of the Etats, but by September 1590 he had rallied to the cause of Henri IV, and no reasonable conclusion about a warming of Garnier to the League can be made on the basis of the dedication.

Bradamante is freely developed from the last three books of Ariosto's *Orlando furioso*. It is the first of Garnier's plays to be divided into scenes, and some adaptation of it was certainly given on 3 August 1611 at a private court performance, an account of which Malherbe wrote to Peiresc the next day. Charlemagne, who has a long monologue in the first act, is a good king, and the play is notable for the concept of kingship on which it insists. For Garnier the contract between a prince and his subjects was inviolable. Cléopâtre had betrayed her contract with her people in the interests of her passion for Marc-Antoine, and Polynice had betrayed the Thebans by rejecting their choice of Eteocle for king. One of the difficulties in a republic is that there is no prince to whom subjects owe allegiance, and the political body can therefore disintegrate. In *Bradamante*, Charlemagne is encouraged by Nymes, the duke of Bavaria, to observe the princely duties to his subjects. He wants to give Roger as a reward for his services the hand of Bradamante, whose parents, Aymon and Béatrix, would rather give her to Léon, son of the emperor of Bavaria and heir to the Byzantine throne.

Bradamante loves Roger, and threatens to enter a convent if she cannot have him. The king has ordered a combat between Roger and Léon, but Aymon is firm that his daughter will marry Léon. In the third act Léon talks to Roger, whose life he once saved but whose real identity he does not know. Roger is trapped between his gratitude to Léon and his love for Bradamante, who comes on stage to expound her affections for Roger. Charlemagne reaffirms his decision that Bradamante will marry only the winner of the combat. It is Bradamante in the end who fights Roger, thinking he is Léon; it is Léon who magnanimously cedes Bradamante to Roger; and Roger who promises to be a good king to the Bulgarians, who come and ask him to take their throne. Roger's invitation to be king of the Bulgarians is too similar to Henri III's to be king of the Poles, when he was still duc d'Anjou, for the similarity not to have been deliberate. It implies very little more than a compliment to the king, and no doubt an expression of Garnier's belief that a prince has a duty to be just and kind to his people.

Les Juifves was dedicated to Joyeuse, a favourite mignon of no very obvious gifts who married the queen's sister, had his lands made into a duché and pairie, had bought the office of admiral on 1 June 1582, and on 24 February 1583 became governor of Normandy. His career was little more than a succession of failures, and he joined the League at the end of 1586 or early in the following year. He died at Coutras on 20 October 1587. Almost certainly, the dedication of *Les Juifves* was inspired by Henri III, who wanted a semi-official disclaimer that Joyeuse was in disgrace, while warning Joyeuse that he would not be spared the punishment any rebellious act would attract.

The play is sometimes regarded as the first neoclassical religious drama "of stature" and Garnier's best. It is a biblical tragedy without scenes, and with a prophet, a chorus of queens, wives of Sédécie, king of Jerusalem, and a chorus of Jewish women, essentially therefore again a series of tableaux rather than "a masterpiece with structural defects." It is a political tragedy because Sédécie rebels against his legitimate political overlord, Nabuchodonosor, who may be cruel and tyrannical, but who has the right to put down rebellion. In so far as Garnier is writing a political tragedy, he is exploring a system of political rather than of moral rights and obligations.

In fact *Les Juifves*, by its length, its lyricism of tone, and the disproportion between the lengths of the "acts," can only be called a biblical poem. The piece would read equally well as three dramatic poems, with a prologue and an epilogue both dominated by the character Le Prophète. The first known theatrical performance was given in 1922. The alternatives left to the Jews, to plead and to suffer, allow the exploitation of strong seams of lyrical inspiration within the absolute constraints of rights and obligations. It does not occur to Garnier, not even in *Antigone*, to explore the possibility that personal emotions, suffering, or the need for the individual's moral integrity might outweigh what he would no doubt have argued were the divinely imposed rights and duties of political association. The strength of *Les Juifves* lies accordingly in its lyricism, with grandeur added by the way in which even the cruel and unpardonable Nabuchodonosor is seen to be an instrument of divine providence in the punishment of the Jews, whose dreadful suffering he enjoys inflicting.

In the immensely powerful fourth act king Sédécie and the high pontiff Sarrée wait in prison for death. Sarrée, who is executed, prays beforehand for the Jews, misled by Sédécie and himself. Their only duty and only sin had been to obey. Nabuchodonosor relishes inflicting his hideous punishment and monstrously exults in his own cruelty. Sédécie achieves a moving dignity in the inevitable stichomythia and his acceptance of Nabuchodonosor's vengeance as God's punishment. In the fifth act Le Prophète gives the appalling description of the murders carried out in front of Sédécie, and of Sédécie's own blinding as his eyes are put out, and the lament comes to an end with the glimmer of hope in the Messiah to come.

PUBLICATIONS

Collections

Les tragédies de Robert Garnier, 1580, reprint 1582
Les tragédies de Robert Garnier, 1585
Les tragédies de Robert Garnier augmentées, 1592
Oeuvres complètes, 3 vols., 1923–52

Works in dramatic form

Porcie, tragédie française, représentant la cruelle et sanglante saison des guerres civiles de Rome. Propre et convenable pour y voir dépeinte la calamité de ce temps, 1568
Hippolyte, tragédie, 1573
Cornélie, tragédie, 1574
Marc-Antoine, tragédie, 1578
La Troade, tragédie, 1579
Antigone; ou, La Piété, 1580
Bradamante, tragecomedie, 1582
Les Juives, tragédie, 1583

Other

Plaintes amoureuses de Robert Garnier Manceau, contenant élégies, sonnets, epîtres, chansons. Plus deux églogues, 1565
Hymne de la monarchie, 1567

Biographical and critical studies

Mouflard, Marie-Madeleine, *Robert Garnier (1545–1590)*, 3 vols., 1961–64
Gras, Maurice, *Robert Garnier. Son art et sa méthode*, 1965
Jondorf, Gillian, *Robert Garnier and the Themes of Political Tragedy in the Sixteenth Century*, 1969
Street, J.S., *French Sacred Drama from Bèze to Corneille*, 1983

GASSENDI, Pierre, 1592–1655.

Philosopher.

LIFE

Although Gassendi wrote neither in French nor in the imaginative genres, his importance as a philosopher for the writers of 17th- and 18th-century France threatened for a period to eclipse that of Descartes. Not only must some knowledge of his teaching be presupposed in the context of the work of a host of later writers, but the nature and dates of his availability in French, as well as his rivalry to Descartes and their apparently different sorts of compatibility with orthodox Christian teaching, require at least to be mentioned. Descartes thought the immortality of the individual soul could be defended only on the basis of the absolute distinction between spirit and matter. Gassendi thought a belief in immortality compatible with a corpuscular theory of the universe, and at least provided a basis from which Descartes's distinction could be eroded. When general acceptance of a corpuscular theory emerged with Boyle and Newton, and when Locke envisaged the possibility of thinking matter, it was not Descartes but Gassendi who provided the Christian apologists with their intellectual lines of defence.

Gassendi was among those who, at Mersenne's invitation, wrote criticisms, which he called *Dubitationes*, of Descartes's *Meditationes de prima philosophia*. He then wrote his *Instantiae* to Descartes's replies. Both philosophers agreed, although for different reasons, that Aristotelian philosophy had been worn out, and that the point of all philosophical endeavour was the production of an ethic. At roughly the same date they offered alternative possible metaphysical views. Descartes's philosophy seemed at first to provide the stronger bulwark against unbelief. The dangers of Cartesianism (q.v.) were, however, beginning to be perceived just when the philosophy of Gassendi was being made available in the vernacular by François Bernier in his 1674 *Abrégé de la philosophie de Gassendi*. After the work especially of Locke, it was the philosophy of Gassendi which appeared to provide the better philosophical substructure needed by Christianity in the 18th century.

Gassendi was born at the hamlet of La Grange at Champtercier, near Digne, on 22 January 1592. His father, Antoine Gassend, farmed his own land, and Gassendi was brought up at first by his mother's brother, the local curé, Thomas Fabry, and then for a year by a priest in neighbouring Riez. Highly gifted, he was admitted at the age of seven to the collège de Digne, where his name was latinized to Gassendi. He appears to have been genuinely precocious and is known to have impressed the bishop of Digne with a Latin oration he delivered in the local church at Champtercier when he was 11. He composed schoolboy farces for performance by his companions, staying at school at Digne until 1606.

He received the tonsure very young and, after two years at home he was sent to study philosophy and then theology at the university of Aix. Briefly made principal of the collège de Digne in 1612 at the age of 20, Gassendi was ordained sub-deacon in 1614, and in that year received his doctorate in theology from Avignon and was made a canon of Digne; he became théologal, or preacher, at Forcalquier on 1 September the same year. He was also made théologal at Digne, but the bishop had nominated another candidate and Gassendi had to defend his title to the benefice before the conseil du roi in Paris, where he spent from April to November 1615. He was successful, and was ordained priest at Digne in 1616. That year he competed for the chairs of philosophy and theology at Aix, was offered both, and chose philosophy, occupying the position for six years.

By this time Gassendi's own philosophical dissatisfaction not only with scholasticism but with all other systems had become clear. He believed only in the Pyrrhonist or sceptical suspension of judgement, the ἀκαταλεξψα (akatalepsia) of Sextus Empiricus or the ἐποχὴ (epoké) advocated by Pyrrho and many of Gassendi's immediate neostoic predecessors, most notably by Justus Lipsius and Guillaume du Vair, who certainly inspired Descartes in matters of psychology and ethics, and from whom Descartes may possibly have derived the idea for his methodic doubt. It was out of the Aix lectures that grew Gassendi's first work, the 1624 *Exercitationes paradoxicae adversus Aristoteleos*. While at Aix, Gassendi stayed with Joseph Gautier, sieur de la Valette, who stimulated his interest in astronomy and with him observed the 1618 comet, a lunar eclipse in 1620, and a solar eclipse in 1621.

In April that year, with a postscript dated 10 June, Gassendi wrote to Henri du Faur de Pibrac, second son of the author of the *Quatrains* and later to be first president at the parlement de Provence, to thank him for sending him Charron's religious treatises. Gassendi incidentally mentions some of his favourite reading, Charron, Montaigne, Lipsius, Seneca, and Cicero. Sometimes, Gassendi says, he lays them aside for the poets, Lucretius, Horace, or Juvenal, or for Lucian or Erasmus. Commentators have read rather too much into that list. It was the rather conservative reading list of any educated, humanistically inclined person around 1620, and may have been drawn up in deference to the known tastes of Gassendi's correspondent, to whom the letter is excessively reverential. The postscript relates details of the solar eclipse, with time and angle; announces that the Jesuits are to take over the university at Aix; says that Gassendi wants to visit all of Italy, and to call on the great men of Germany if there is peace; and announces that he is putting the *Exercitationes* in order.

Soon after his return to Digne in 1622, Gassendi was sent by his chapter to the Grenoble parlement in connection with a disputed priory. While there he put the finishing touches to the first book of the projected seven of the *Exercitationes* and published it at Grenoble in 1624. The only other book of the planned work to be completed, on dialectic, was not published until the 1658 *Omnia Opera*. A certain understandable caution is observable in Gassendi's journeys to Paris to defend his theological orthodoxy in learned company. The book he had published had strongly attacked the possibility of finding on any fundamental topic the sort of consensus that certainty would have led to, an attitude which, not extended to dogmatic truths, was a legacy from the humanist relativism which had enabled the moderates in the magistracy to bring about the reconciliations which had ended the religious wars.

Montaigne had assumed, while Charron, du Vair, and Justus Lipsius had argued, that there was much room for legitimate doubt in most areas of human opinion. But their willingness to suspend judgement, leading to a neostoic ethic in which the passions were simply false judgements, and indifference the only possible attitude in the face of an unknowable reality, had given way to renewed certainties during the reign of Louis XIII. In August 1624 there had been condemnations in Paris for attacks on Aristotle. In the middle of October that year Gassendi was in Paris, where he stayed until April 1625. Gassendi's first visit to Paris may have been disappointing. It was later that he became associated with La Mothe le Vayer and Naudé. He was soon to meet Elie Diodati on a visit to Grenoble in 1625, and to be converted by him to the views of his close friend Galileo, with whom Gassendi was to exchange letters. Meanwhile in Paris he discussed mathematics with Claude Mydorge, the Treasurer of France, and became part of Marin Mersenne's network of learned correspondents.

Gassendi was to become associated with the whole group of orthodox but urbane Catholic humanists, open-minded, intellectually curious, not adverse to radical thinking, and subversive only of a refusal to adjust orthodox thinking to the demands of evidence, but it is not clear how much of a beginning he made during the winter of 1624–25. In 1625 Gassendi was back in Grenoble by June, and in Provence by the autumn, having complained that in Paris there was more interest in astrology than in astronomy, and very little in experimental science. From the autumn of 1625 Gassendi spent two years at Aix and Digne. On 25 April 1626 a letter informs Peiresc of Gassendi's new interest in Epicurus, about whom he was to publish only in 1647 the *De vita et moribus Epicuri*. The rehabilitation of Epicurus can in many ways be considered Gassendi's life-work.

In 1626 it was still daring to think that Epicurus must have been misrepresented, and could be rehabilitated to accord with Christian dogma. He was normally considered to have denied the immortality of the soul, to be an atomist, hedonist, and materialist. The chief channel of transmission of his thought was the proselytizing and openly anti-religious Lucretius, whose *De rerum natura* was normally thought quite incompatible with a Christian view of the universe. However, a letter of 24 March 1628 demonstrates that Gassendi had been studying Seneca's account of Epicurus, very different from that of Lucretius, which reduces Epicurean "voluptas (pleasure)" to identity with the stoic "virtus (virtue)." Ficino had already identified Epicurus's voluptas with tranquillity of mind, and Montaigne himself is aware of the strict and virtuous form of Epicurean "volupté."

Gassendi returned to Paris by way of Grenoble and Lyons in April 1628, carrying with him letters of introduction to François Luillier, who was to put a house at his disposal, and from Peiresc to the Dupuy brothers, at the centre of the liberal group of scholars and thinkers which met in the library of the celebrated historian, Jacques-Auguste de Thou, who had died in 1617. Most of the group surrounding the Dupuy brothers came from families in the magistracy and had emerged from the moderates whose generally neostoic views had flourished during the wars. They were now in touch, like Mersenne, with most of Europe's learned men, especially the scientists. Gassendi found their company congenial and in December 1628 set out on a tour of Holland with Luillier, just a year before Descartes settled there to work out the problems of his new philosophy. Gassendi extended his network of international relations, met and was welcomed by Heinsius and Vossius, and attracted in Paris a number of younger followers. He was in no hurry to return to Digne, where there was plague.

Like Descartes, Gassendi met and was impressed by Beeckmann, who persuaded him to enlarge the scope of his work on Epicurus. Gassendi at this moment intended to include a single volume on Epicurus in the *Exercitationes*. It was sometime between March 1629 and April 1630, no doubt in the light of his

discussions of atomism with Beeckmann, that Gassendi decided to widen the scope of his work on Epicurus, and move towards the full-scale exploitation of Epicureanism as he now understood it as a possible replacement in the schools for the Aristotelianism which had held sway for centuries. The similarities with Descartes's quite independent philosophical undertaking are remarkable, even if the inspiration, method, and results were at least at first antithetically opposed.

Gassendi had written from Holland on 8 August 1629 asking Peiresc to forward his notes on Epicurus to Paris from Aix. By 28 August he and his notes were reunited in Paris. The decreasingly tolerant intellectual climate seemed too unfavourable to publish any more of the *Exercitationes*, and on Epicurus work trailed. Gassendi considered going to Constantinople with the French ambassador there, and Naudé tried hard to dissuade him in order that he should proceed with the work on Epicurus. The trip did not take place, and by April 1631 work on Epicurus had made progress. The book was half written. Naudé kept up his encouragement from Rome, but Gassendi left Paris for Provence in October 1632 without much further progress. Work had been delayed by the correspondence and the composition of some minor pieces, the 1630 *Epistolica exercitatio in qua principia philosophiae Roberti Fludd reteguntur*, a refutation of the English Rosicrucian Robert Fludd undertaken for Mersenne, whose 1623 *Quaestiones celeberrimae in Genesim* Fludd had attacked in 1630; a book on sun-spots, the *Parhelia*, which also appeared in 1630, and a pamphlet confirming Kepler's prediction of 1629 that Mercury would pass across the sun in 1630, *Mercurius in sole visus et Venus invisa*, published in 1632.

Late in 1632 Gassendi returned to Provence and decided to begin the Epicurus commentary from the beginning again. In March 1633 he went to stay with Peiresc and for some years was busy with ecclesiastical duties, astronomical and optical observations, and a reply undertaken at the request of Mersenne, Peiresc, and Diodati to the *De veritate* of Lord Edward Herbert of Cherbury, who had been British ambassador to France from 1619 to 1624. It was while staying with Peiresc at Aix from the autumn of 1636 until the spring of 1637, when he returned to Digne, that Gassendi took up work again on what he referred to as his "grand dessein (great project)." He had nearly finished when, on 24 June 1637, Peiresc died. Gassendi interrupted work on Epicurus for four years, from the first two of which only one of the letters he must have written survives. He travelled round Provence, and accompanied the governor, Louis de Valois, comte d'Alais, on an official tour.

Gassendi was installed on 24 December 1634 as prévôt of the diocese of Digne, an office which carried with it the lucrative seigneurie of Notre-Dame du Bourg from which it derived its revenues. He was now sheltered from financial worries. In 1639 he was elected to the general assembly of the clergy, with the support of Alais and of Louis XIII, and set out for Paris and then Nantes, where the assembly was to meet. The bishop of Embrun wanted, however, to nominate his nephew. Gassendi was financially rewarded for resigning, although he was neither greedy nor ambitious. He was a vegetarian, did not drink alcohol, and a little later allowed himself to be displaced as commendatory prior of Roumoules, an office left to him by Conti.

The post of professor of mathematics at the Collège Royal in Paris, for which Gassendi was proposed by Louis-Alphonse de Richelieu, the archbishop of Lyons, and which he accepted in 1644, was only parsimoniously remunerated. Gassendi gave his inaugural lecture on 23 November 1645, and lectured chiefly on astronomy. He had published the *De apparente magnitudine solis humilis et sublimis* in 1642, and between 1640 and 1643 he wrote the three letters about the earth's movement which constitute the *De motu impresso a motore translato*. Two years before Descartes, although for different reasons, Gassendi happened on the first principle of inertia. Two of the letters were addressed to Pierre Dupuy and the third, to Joseph Gautier, was a reply to Gassendi's former friend Jean-Baptiste Morin, who had attacked in his *Alae telluris fractae* the first two letters, written in 1640 and published together in 1642. Gassendi had very carefully limited himself to demonstrating, on the basis of experiments undertaken with Alais, the truth of Galileo's claim that the question of the earth's rotation, as proclaimed by Copernicus, cannot be resolved by experiments with projectiles or falling bodies. Gassendi replied also to objections other than those proposed by Morin, notably in three letters published in 1646 as the *De proportione*.

Gassendi published further works of cosmology, including a letter written to Naudé concerning the nine satellites of Jupiter rather than the four propounded by Galileo's 1610 *Nuncius sidereus*. The principal parts of the course of lectures at the Collège Royal were published in the 1647 *Institutio astronomica juxta hypotheseis tam veterum quam Copernici et Tychonis*. Gassendi, although known in his lifetime much more for work as an experimental astronomer and a cosmologist than as a speculative philosopher, had been invited by Mersenne to comment on Descartes's *Meditationes* in 1641, shortly after he had arrived in Paris. His objections irritated Descartes, and Gassendi was himself irritated by Descartes's replies.

Descartes had asked Mersenne to publish his replies to Gassendi's *Dubitationes* but, when Diodati pressed Gassendi to reply again, he refused. Both Descartes and Gassendi were convinced that their arguments would win the day when published together with the *Meditationes* on 21 August 1641, but Gassendi did draw up his *Instantiae*, which were eventually published in 1644. Descartes replied again in a cursory letter to Clerselier, published in the first French edition of the *Meditationes*, the *Méditations*, in 1647. There was a real rift between Descartes and Gassendi, but a cordial reconciliation was effected on 5 November 1647 at a banquet given by César d'Estrées at which Descartes, Roberval, and Mersenne were present. They all called afterwards on Gassendi, who had not attended because he was confined to bed. Gassendi had resigned his chair in favour of Roberval in 1647, when he returned to Provence, going back to Digne only in 1648 after six months as the guest of Alais.

Up to 1636, all the evidence about the progress of Gassendi's philosophical studies comes from letters, but there are manuscript drafts of what was written at Aix in the winter of 1636–37 and in Paris from 1641 to 1645. In 1636 Gassendi, like Descartes, was seeking to know whether there was any criterion of truth, and just beginning to concede that, in certain areas, there might be. His method was different, and he went about his task by interrogating all the ancient philosophical systems rather than his own experience and reason. Unlike Descartes, Gassendi did not find a criterion of truth, and merely went on to reconstitute and expound the thought of Epicurus as fully, although not perhaps as fairly, as he could.

He had stayed with Luillier on his return to Paris in 1641, and in September of that year published his life of Peiresc. A series of letters to Alais provides an intelligent layman's guide to the progress of Gassendi's work on Epicurus. Some of the physics of Epicurus is rejected as incompatible with Christian belief in the workings of an unknowable providence, although Gassendi agrees with Epicurus that it is the function of philosophy to mediate as deep an understanding as possible of the laws governing the universe. He continued to hold that both the divinity and the human soul had to be incorporeal. He accepted a spatially unlimited universe, but, since God alone is infinite, not an infinity of atoms, and he would never accept an eternal uncreated universe, although in fact such a view, taught for centuries in the name of Aristotle, was not incompatible with Christian dogma.

From June 1642 Sorbière had been pressing Gassendi to publish what was ready of his work on Epicurus. Gassendi resisted the urging of Sorbière on at least three occasions, and allowed nothing to be published until 1647, and then only the *Apologia*, which had been ready since 1634. On 9 September 1647, Joseph Gautier died, leaving Gassendi much moved at the loss of his friend of 30 years. Then on 1 September 1648 Mersenne died. Later that month Gassendi yielded to the plea of Louis de Valois that he should return south, and he left Paris in October, visiting Lyons and Tarascon on his way to Aix. The *De vita et moribus Epicuri libri octo* had been published without his approval. The translation of the life of Epicurus from the tenth book of Diogenes Laertius's *De clarorum philosophorum vitis* had been finished in 1629. Encouraged by Gilles Ménage, Gassendi now released it, together with assorted notes and commentaries. The printer of the *De Vita* reorganized the whole and published it as the 1649 three-volume *Animadversiones in decimum librum Diogenis Laertii*. The second appendix to this work, entitled *Philosophiae Epicuri syntagma*, marks the points at which Gassendi has corrected Epicurus to accord with Christian doctrine. Gassendi had thought of dedicating the work to Pierre Séguier, the chancellor, but considered its publication premature.

Gassendi moved to Digne in April 1649, but his lungs, which had earlier given him sporadic trouble, now made him seriously ill, at times preventing him even from holding a pen. In December he left for Toulon accompanied by his secretary, La Poterie, and Luillier, who left for Italy in April 1651 and died at Pisa in the following year. By February 1650 Gassendi was well enough to climb the highest cliff in Toulon to conduct an experiment with mercury. He left Toulon for Digne in April 1651, and spent two years there before leaving for the last time for Paris in April 1653. Gassendi's life in Provence had been leisurely. In Paris he stayed now with Habert de Monmort, but his health again deteriorated. Naudé died on 29 July 1653, and Gassendi was again much moved, as he was to be by news of Alais's death on 14 November. In Paris in 1654 Gassendi published a volume containing the biographies of Tycho Brahé, Copernicus, Puerbach, and Regiomontanus, together with a number of pamphlets on coinage, music, and the history of the diocese of Digne.

Chiefly, however, Gassendi was preparing a more satisfactory version, the third, of his commentary on Epicurus, the *Syntagma philosophicum* which he did not live to complete. From August to October 1654 he was at Montmort's country residence, but was then kept to his bed with fever from 17 November until 6 January 1655. On 22 February he was again taken ill. Guy Patin carried out a phlebotomy which relieved the symptoms, but on 23 August 1655 Gassendi fell ill with another violent fever which lasted 63 days. He was repeatedly bled but continued to decline. He received the last sacraments, and died on 24 October.

He left an ardent supporter and disciple, François Bernier, destined to make Gassendi's philosophy known to a wide French public. Bernier, born in 1620, orphaned at four, had been brought up by an uncle. Destined for the Church, he was a friend of Claude Chapelle, the illegitimate son of François Luillier by Marie Chanut, and the later associate of Boileau, La Fontaine, and the frequenters of the tavern of La Croix-Blanche. Chapelle presented Bernier to Gassendi, whose student he became and who eventually took him on as an amanuensis. Bernier left Paris in 1648 for Poland, Holland, Gdansk, south Germany, and Italy, to join Gassendi again at Toulon, where he helped with the experiments. He wrote against Gassendi's opponents, became a doctor of medicine at Montpellier in 1652, and was taken by Gassendi to Paris in 1653, living with him until Gassendi died.

Thereafter Bernier travelled in the east, in Palestine, Syria, and Egypt, and in India, where he was active as a doctor, went further to Bengal and Tibet, wrote a *Mémoire sur l'établissement du commerce dans l'Inde* which attracted Colbert's attention, and travelled on to Persia. After writing various works on the east, he returned to Paris in 1669, mixed with a group of writers which included Boileau, and spent seven or eight years with Mme de la Sablière, in whose household he became close to La Fontaine. Before he died, Bernier had visited Saint-Evremond in England and Bayle in Holland. His *Abrégé de la philosophie de Gassendi* appeared first in 1674, but in much augmented form with an important preface in 1678, and then again in the seven volumes of 1684.

WORKS

Gassendi was an astronomer and mathematician who wrote for publication exclusively in Latin. Although he was involved in philosophical controversy, notably with Descartes, and his views on cosmology were sufficiently innovative to make prudence important, Gassendi lived and died a devout Catholic prelate, and never actually completed the great philosophical work he had contemplated, the full-scale exposition and rehabilitation of the philosophy of Epicurus. Since that philosopher was popularly associated, for instance by Racan, above all with the denial of individual survival after death, Gassendi's undertaking appears to us to have been dangerous, but the preceding generation had seen Christian rehabilitations of stoics and sceptics in the work of Du Vair and Justus Lipsius, and Gassendi was correct in very early detecting inconsistencies in the transmission of Epicurus's doctrine which rightly suggested to him that the sources need a thorough reinvestigation.

What makes him an important author in a literary context is the group of admirers he attracted, and the mixture of imaginative authors, scientists, philosophers, and scholars who frequented particularly the meetings of the Dupuy group, which included such men of letters as Chapelain, La Mothe le Vayer, d'Ablancourt, and Ménage. To all but quite recent historians Gassendi has seemed to have been, if not a covert sceptic, then at least an inspiration to scepticism. In fact, none of his friends doubted his committed Christianity. Although Gassendi was on intimate terms with Naudé, La Mothe le Vayer, and Diodati, often, but too readily, considered religious doubters, as also with many others associated with them, including Bernier, Chapelle, Patin, and Sorbière, and although ecclesiastical authority was suspicious of any empirical scientific investigation, particularly

if it involved cosmological calculations implying the earth's rotation round the sun, or on its own axis, which risked producing results incompatible with the Church's interpretation of *Genesis*, it is in fact grotesque to regard any of the circles in which Gassendi was even one of the most prominent figures as sceptical in the sense of being subversive of orthodox Christian belief.

They were interested in science and travel, tended to be hostile towards Louis XIII and Richelieu, and were open to serious scholarship as well as to new ideas. There was undoubtedly some private disbelief, but little more than stray crystals precipitated from a pool of doubts. Atheism in the modern sense is too strong a word to describe the attitude of more perhaps than one or two, possibly, but only possibly, of such marginal members of the group as Jean-Jacques Bouchard and François Guyet. Detachment from dogmatic belief is a nearer description. In important ways the Dupuy circle was inheriting the humanist tradition of the relativist moderates of the religious wars, just as Gassendi, writing in Latin, was undertaking in the rehabilitation of Epicurus a task not unlike those undertaken by Du Vair and Justus Lipsius, while Descartes, no doubt synthesizing a whole renaissance neoplatonist tradition, was attempting to sweep all previous philosophy away in his new rationally constructed doubt-proof philosophical edifice. It is not fortuitous that Descartes was an abstract thinker, a mathematician and a geometer, whose physics was deductive. Gassendi was an observer and measurer, a scholar as well as an empirical scientist, who depended for his mathematics largely on a friend, Fermat, and thought his readers would be as interested in the ideas of Democritus as they would be in his own, if not more so.

However, since Gassendi's best known work prior to Bernier's *Abrégé* was his *Dubitationes* to Descartes's *Meditationes*, together with his *Instantiae* to Descartes's replies, it is not totally surprising that his reputation should have made him suspect of scepticism, and it is easy to sympathize with his reluctance to publish speculative as distinct from empirically verifiable conclusions. From the early 1624 *Exercitationes paradoxicae*, he would allege against the Aristotelian scholastics and against Fludd, Cherbury, and Descartes the empirical fact of human disagreement against all arguments leading to certain knowledge. In the 1630s his works begin to admit some forms of certainty in human knowledge, and the early quasi-universal scepticism is eroded by concessions. Human minds can be certain of knowledge that is pragmatic, on which predictions can with certainty be made. Mathematical and geometrical proofs can be certain, like revelation. In the end Gassendi comes close to attempting merely to define what it is that the human mind may never know, and in what realms it may move towards certainty beyond mere appearances.

Gassendi's later works claw back the consequences of what he had earlier maintained, and it is essential to remember that he never finished his great work, and that what he did publish of it he later thought too hastily conceived. His later works and letters disconcertingly rely on arguments from universal consent, whose existence he had previously enjoyed denying. He forces Epicureanism in the direction of allowing presuppositions leading to probabilities, unlike Cartesian innate ideas which led to certainties. His importance lies not as some focus for intellectual doubts, but as the architect of the fall-back position adopted by Catholic apologists when the absolute Cartesian distinction between mind and matter grew to be untenable.

PUBLICATIONS

Collections

Opera omnia, 6 vols., 1658

Abrégé de la philosophie de Gassendi (Bernier), 1674, augmented, 8 vols., 1678

The Selected Works of Pierre Gassendi, 1972

Philosophy

Exercitationes paradoxicae adversus Aristoteleos, 1624; modern edition (French), 1959

Disquisitio metaphysica, seu dubitationes et instantiae adversus Renati Cartesii metaphysica et responsa, 1644; modern edition (French) 1959

De vita et moribus Epicuri libri octo, 1647

Animadversiones in decimum librum Diogenis Laertii, 3 vols., 1649

Syntagma philosophicum, in *Opera omnia*, 1658

Institutio logica (in English), 1981

Science

Epistolica exercitatio in qua principia philosophiae Roberti Fludd reteguntur, 1630

Parhelia sive soles quatuor spurii qui circa verum apparuerunt Romae die 20 Martii anno 1629, 1629

Mercurius in sole visus e Venus invisa, 1632

De apparente magnitudine solis humilis et sublimis, 1642

De motu impresso a motore translato, 1643

De proportione, 1646

Proportio Gnomonis ad solstitialem umbram, 1643

Novem stellae circa Iovem visae, 1643

De proportione, 1646

Institutio astronomica, 1647

Other

Tychonis Brahei, Equitis Dani, Astronomorum Coryphoi... Nicolai Copernici, Georgii Puerbachi, et Johannis Regiomontani, astronomorum celebrium, vita, 1654

Lettres familières à François Luillier pendant l'hiver 1632–33, 1944

Biographical and critical studies

Pintard, R., *Le Libertinage érudit dans la première moitié du XVIIe siècle*, 2 vols., 1943

Rochot, B., *Les Travaux de Gassendi sur Epicure et sur l'atomisme 1619–1658*, 1944

Pierre Gassendi, 1592–1655, sa vie et son oeuvre, 1955

Bloch, O.R., *La Philosophie de Gassendi*, 1971

Jones, Howard, *Pierre Gassendi, 1592–1655. An Intellectual Biography*, 1981

GAZETTE (La), later known as GAZETTE DE FRANCE (La)

The history of the periodical press during the period covered by this volume of the *Guide* is important primarily for two reasons. Firstly, as the date advances toward the Revolution of 1789, the press not only played an increasingly important part in the dissemination of news and the formation of opinion, but it also began to provide a forum for the publication and dissemination of works of literature, and an income for editors and authors. The fact that a piece of writing was originally intended for publication in a periodical meant that it might well have been written for dissemination at a specific time and place, often with a predictable political alignment. Rivarol's descriptions of Revolutionary behaviour, whether in the streets or in the National Assembly, were published in the *Journal National Politique* with the aim of disgusting his readership and persuading it to accept his interpretation of the events he recounted, and it had earlier been from press accounts of social events in Paris that he had made a living. The press therefore provided not only information, but also both a forum for authors and the possibility of a livelihood.

Secondly, the periodical press, by providing a forum for the discussion of cultural events, new books, new plays, other entertainments, literary disputes, prizes, and elections to cultural bodies, obviously reflected and guided public taste. Technical faults and errors in scientific works were pointed out and often ridiculed, positions were attacked, and the implications of works of science and of the imagination were publicly dissected. Even when the journalism did not aspire to or reach any elevated literary status, it necessarily affected the content of works which did, and the manner of their presentation. It was also largely the development of the periodical press which drove monarchs and then their ministers and administrations to an awareness of the power of the printed text and therefore to use both patronage and the imposition or relaxation of controls over publication to exploit, manipulate, and curb the expression of public opinion, seriously affecting what it was possible at different moments to publish in France or to import from outside its borders. Regulations controlling the periodical press both affected and were affected by regulations concerning printed books, so that the periodical press exercised a general influence on censorship as well as inaugurating critical discussion of newly published works.

It is conventional to date the birth of the periodical press in France from the foundation of *La Gazette* by Théophraste Renaudot in 1631. Born at Loudun of a Burgundian family in 1586, a year after Richelieu, Renaudot came from a Protestant family, studied medicine at Montpellier, travelled, studied surgery in Paris, and while abroad discovered printed bulletins with war news, lists of prices, and other desirable information in Florence, Strasburg, and Amsterdam. At Loudun, among his patients was François le Clerc du Tremblay, "Père Joseph," the original "Grey eminence" on whom Richelieu so much relied. It was Père Joseph in 1612 who first called Renaudot to Paris, where he was given a monopoly right to open an office where he might display the sources and prices at which various commodities could be acquired. The idea had been thrown off by Montaigne (*Les Essais*, Book I, ch. xxxv: opening paragraph), and Renaudot, called again in 1625 to Paris, this time by Richelieu, in 1628 became a Catholic and opened his bureau for announcements, essentially attempting to match supply and demand of virtually anything.

Renaudot's enterprise was partly charitable. He issued an "inventory" of rooms to let, loans to be had, sources for the acquisition of medicines, situations vacant and offers of labour, apprenticeships, property for sale and rent, and much else, in an *Inventaire des adresses du Bureau de rencontre où chacun peut donner et recevoir avis de toutes les nécessitéz et commoditéz de la vie*. On 1 September 1633 there were on offer land, opportunities for investments against annuities, a new scarlet cloak, a Flanders tapestry of dyed material, an amethyst rosary of six decades, a dromedary, and a place as a travelling companion to Italy. There was no intrinsic connection between the regularly updated inventory and the *Gazette*, but it immediately created trouble with the printers' guild, and the *Gazette* inherited its hostility. The printers were still dependent on the university, which had Renaudot's printing font seized in 1631. Louis XIII had to intervene to get it back, and to have Renaudot's privilège respected.

The printers returned to court, accusing Renaudot of merely copying what he got from abroad, and of much else. On 18 November 1631 judgement was given for Renaudot, and the printer Vendosme's news-sheet, the *Nouvelles ordinaires de divers endroits,* became the title of a column in Renaudot's *Gazette*. On 28 November 1631 Renaudot increased the size of the *Gazette*, and at the end of the year combined all the numbers into a *Recueil*. Opposition continued, but officialdom supported Renaudot; the king's council declared in his favour on 11 March 1633; Renaudot was awarded a pension of 800 livres; and in February 1635 he obtained letters patent. The bureau took up pawn-broking, offering 33⅓% of valuation at 3% interest, and in 1637 obtained a licence to sell off unredeemed goods. The *Mercure Français* (q.v.) printed a piece by Renaudot on the usefulness of the services he offered. From 1639 a police regulation forced the out-of-work to register with Renaudot who, in turn, put the *Gazette* at the disposal of Richelieu and the king. Virtually from the beginning, it was used to filter to the public what the administration wanted it to know. A special number explained why the king went to war with Spain in June 1635. In 1640 the *Gazette* announced the queen's pregnancy.

The privilège is dated 30 May 1631. At that date, and for another 200 years, until 1811 in England and 1823 in France, presses could print between 200 and 350 sheets an hour. With the contents printed on two sheets and folded, that produced not quite 150 copies an hour of a four-page journal. There was a network of official communications, which included important news items, but in the early 17th century private people still had to use the postal service controlled by the universities for letters and small parcels. Provincial booksellers handled the distribution of periodicals, often selling to hawkers. Two-wheeled carriages without springs or relays of horses regularly conveyed official communications, parcels, and periodicals on fixed days. Times from Paris were 62 hours for Brest, 72 for Toulouse, and 47 hours for Bordeaux and Lyons. They were not improved until 1820, when better suspension cut a third of the time 30 years before the arrival of railways, although carrier pigeons were in regular official use from 1794. Before the end of the period covered by this volume the *Gazette* was appearing in 12 pages twice a week with a print run of 12,000. Its nearest rival, the *Mercure de France*, was at that time appearing every ten days and printing only 2,600 copies. There were no dailies in France until 1777, a century and a quarter after the first dailies appeared in Germany.

The *Gazette*'s first number, undated but appearing on or close to 30 May 1631, consisted of four small quarto pages, and cost a tenth of a livre. The news carried datelines: Constantinople 2 April; Rome 26 April; Upper Germany 30 April; Silesia 1 May; Venice 2 May; Stettin 4 May; Prague 5 May; Frankfurt 14 May; Amsterdam 17 May; and Antwerp 24 May. On 31 December 1633, the 121st number carried news from Rome, Venice, Schaffhausen, The Hague, Brussels, Reims, Rouen, Saint-Germain, and Paris. There were reports on charitable activities, of the war, and of the health of the duchesse de Longueville. News from France had appeared only from the sixth number, of 4 July 1631, and was printed last. That issue reported a drought. The court was drinking mineral water at Saint-Germain. In Paris the Bible was being printed in eight languages.

The *Gazette* came out weekly, at first on Fridays, then on Saturdays. There were special numbers, "extraordinaires," giving details of battles, publishing official documents, or devoted to particular events. Renaudot recruited a team in which were Mézeray, Voiture, and La Calprenède, and on whose composition Tallemant des Réaux reported. Then on Mondays a series of conferences was started for the discussion of mathematics, astronomy, physics, and moral philosophy. The proceedings were published, forerunners of the *Journal des Savants* (q.v.). Several parodies appeared.

Renaudot had been made commissaire général in charge of works of charity on behalf of the poor, but in 1640 Guy Patin initiated a court action against him, in fact on behalf of the Paris medical faculty, which believed in therapeutic bleeding against the new medicine, represented by Renaudot's Montpellier, which preferred other remedies, in particular the use of antimony. The debate became bitter. The association with Loudun, where Grandier had been burnt in 1634 after the hysterical manifestations of diabolic possession by the Ursuline nuns, caused Renaudot to be accused even of witchcraft. There was a pamphlet battle in which trouble was caused on account of a piece inserted into the *Gazette* at Richelieu's request. Renaudot, used to printing documents, news, and explanations at official request, was made royal historiographer, with an official lodging, but Patin and the faculty had him forbidden to practise medicine in Paris. Louis XIII regarded the *Gazette* as a mouthpiece.

After Richelieu's death and that of Louis XIII, Renaudot became a protégé of Mazarin and when, during the Fronde, the court retired to Saint-Germain, Renaudot was put in charge of the printing works. From 8 January 1649 the *Gazette* was printed at Saint-Germain, and the parlement sought an alternative favourable to its point of view. Renaudot's two sons, Isaac and Eusèbe, accordingly founded the rival *Courrier Français*, successful enough to be parodied, counterfeited, and even put into verse. The hawkers paid deposits in advance to have early copies each week. At the time of his return to Paris in April, Renaudot found a whole range of journals and broad-sheets with "Mercure" or "Courrier" in the title, which purported to carry news, as well as counterfeited and plagiarized versions of the *Gazette*, and had the greatest difficulty in re-establishing his privilège. The support for Mazarin and the opposition of Patin had cost him much success. His wife had died in 1640, and in 1651 he remarried, a young, pretty girl, much to the derision of Loret in his rhymed *Muse Historique* for 31 December 1651 and again on 8 September 1652. When Renaudot died in 1653, Patin says improbably that he was ruined.

The *Gazette* itself prospered as Louis XIV clamped down on clandestine publications. Renaudot left it to his sons. Isaac died without an heir in 1688, but Eusèbe passed on the privilège by letters patent in 1679 to his son, the abbé Eusèbe Renaudot, a scholar, orientalist, diplomat, a friend of Port-Royal (q.v.) and Boileau, and welcome at court, who controlled the *Gazette* nearly until his death in 1720. The number of 27 October 1685 contained 16 pages, still with pagination continuous throughout the year. An editorial team was concerned with style as well as accuracy. Bayle and La Bruyère both went out of their way to compliment the organ, and provincial printers were licensed to publish it. Eusèbe Renaudot said that the *Gazette* brought him 12,000 livres a year, and in 1748 the abbé Amilhon bought the privilège for 97,000 livres from a M. de Verneuil, who had held it for 37 years. However, the official character of the *Gazette* had become increasingly emphasized. The full text of official documents was printed with scrupulous accuracy, and the publication was losing money. Amilhon disposed of it at a loss, but the new proprietor of the privilège, the chevalier de Meslé, who had been given it as a reward for the Bohemian campaign he had fought under Belle-Isle, refused to honour the contracts with the provincial printers who had already paid for the right to publish.

The *Gazette* had lost its real influence well before the middle of the 18th century, and in 1761 the de facto situation was regularized when the journal was taken over by the ministry of foreign affairs under Choiseul. A new editor was appointed who wanted to take the *Gazette* in a more literary direction but was prevented by Malesherbes, who did not wish to infringe the rights of the *Journal des Savants*; there were further editorial and organizational re-shuffles, in which for ten years two editors farmed the periodical, in the sense of collecting what they could against their payment to the ministry for the monopoly rights; the periodical appeared in four pages of two columns each Monday and Friday, and its subscription price was reduced from 18 to 12 livres; newsvendors were allowed a 15% mark-up; and the royal arms were printed on each issue. From 1762 the periodical became officially the *Gazette de France*.

The farmer–editors were dismissed in 1771, and François Marin took over. The *Gazette* had been reduced to little more than a ministerial bulletin board. It none the less sold 12,000 subscriptions in 1780, now at 15 livres, and paid pensions to Chamfort, Raynal, Delille, and d'Alembert. The government, however, sold so many new privilèges for periodicals that the *Gazette* itself began to founder. By 1785 the number of subscriptions was down to 6,793, and the government was glad to get rid of the *Gazette* to Panckoucke in 1787. One of the farmer-editors had been Jean-Baptiste Suard, introduced into Mme Geoffrin's salon by Marmontel, and husband of Panckoucke's sister. The *Gazette* remained an official paper until it ceased publication after the execution of Louis XVI. It came to life again as a daily and a royalist paper under Napoleon, and stayed sympathetic to the royalist cause throughout the 19th century.

GOMBERVILLE, Marin Le Roy, sieur de, 1599–1674.

Novelist, historian, and poet.

LIFE

Very little is known of Gomberville's early life. The ubiquitously and confidently reiterated date of 1600 for Gomberville's birth is probably a year out. It is based on a 1643 portrait made when the sitter was 43, or just possibly in his 43rd year. But Gomberville later maintained that the 110 quatrains and eight sonnets, the *Tableau du bonheur de la vieillesse opposé au malheur de la jeunesse* of 1614, had been published when he was 15. Tallemant devoted a historiette to him, saying that his family was noble, although the generally less reliable *Menagiana* implies that it was not. However, there is certainly a misreading where the text of the *Menagiana* has Gomberville's father as "buvetier (innkeeper)" instead of "boursier (retainer in a household)," and Gomberville's later career suggests that his social standing was compatible with that of the lower nobility.

Gomberville's father is described as a bourgeois in a document of 1628, although there are several indications that Gomberville himself was regarded as noble from as early as 1621. His mother was Marie de Vallençon. In a document of 22 June 1632 Gomberville was given by his parents a library of some 3,000 volumes, four houses in different quarters of Paris, fiefs, estates at Gomberville near Châteauneuf in the Vallée de Chevreuse as well as the seigneurie, and a nearby estate with a farm at Magny-les-Hameaux. Tallemant remarks how rich Gomberville was for an author, mentioning an annual income of 15,000 livres, attributed by Tallemant, who clearly disliked him, chiefly to Gomberville's meanness, "car c'est un homme qui n'a jamais donné un verre d'eau à personne (since he's a man who never gave anyone a glass of water)". The tax archives show Gomberville's income constantly increasing. At the marriage of his youngest child on 8 May 1664, he is estimated to have been worth 100,000 livres. On 24 December 1635, and probably on other unrecorded occasions after Richelieu's new Académie had ceased to be merely an informal gathering which met in Conrart's house, but before it had its own meeting place, Gomberville held its session at his own house.

No one knows where Gomberville was born, Paris, Etampes, or Chevreuse, but his secondary education was with the Jesuits at the Paris Collège de la Marche, which he attended at much the same time as Michel de Marolles and Pierre Chanut. He must have left, according to Marolles's testimony, in 1616. He had not only published his quatrains, but had written pseudonymous Latin verse, signed Thassalius-Basilides. In 1618 he published his *Ode sur l'heureux succès des actions du Roy*, and in 1619 a collection of *Vers du Sieur Le Roy*. His social standing, whatever it was, allowed him to become a conseiller-secrétaire on 23 December 1619 but, according to Tallemant, he was obliged to resign on 9 September 1621. His disgrace may have been due to a slighting attitude towards royalty shown in pieces he had published in the 1620 *Discours des vertus et des vices de l'Histoire*, or to poems published in *Le Second Livre des Delices de la Poesie françoise* of the same year, showing the same irreverent attitude as Théophile towards established values.

As early as 1619 Gomberville published his first novel *L'Exil de Polexandre et d'Ericlée* under the pseudonym of Orile, an anagram of Le Roy. He was to take the work up again and progressively augment its size. Meanwhile in 1621 he published the 735-page *Carithée*. In that year he also married Barbe Fauveau, the daughter of one of the 12 suppliers of wine to the king, who was to bear him at least nine children, Claude-François, born on 7 September 1622, Philippe-Frédéric, Marin II, Marc-Antoine, Bonaventure, Philippe-François, Louis, Aymable, and Marie.

At the age of 21 or 22 Gomberville was therefore married, had been forced to resign a post assuring him of an administrator's income, was a poet and a novelist, and was at least considering the possibility of writing history. In 1622 Gomberville published *Remarques sur la vie du Roy et sur celle d'Alexandre Severe*. He preened himself in imitation of Théophile on the disorder of his imagination and the brevity of his concentration:

Un grand dessin ne me desplaist pas, pour ce qu'il est bientost imaginé: mais l'exécution m'en est insupportable, pour ce qu'il y faut beaucoup de temps, beaucoup d'attention, beaucoup de servitude et beaucoup d'ordre…L'irrégularité de mon esprit ne peut souffrir ces importunes et perpétuelles justesses. Il se plaist au désordre. Il aime les déreiglements

(I like a great project, because it doesn't take long to devise; but I find carrying it out intolerable, because that needs much time, much concentration, much hard work, and method…. The erratic nature of my mind cannot abide these importunate and constant demands for accuracy. It enjoys disorder. It likes to be unbridled).

Given his age and position, it is not surprising that Gomberville appears not yet to have been certain of his vocation. He may, however, never have been fully sure of himself, and was at least to continue to disconcert those who knew him, as by his later conversion to Jansenism (q.v.), although that was no doubt prepared by his earlier friendship with the duc de Liancourt. As late as 1639 Chapelain could write of the difficulty he had in reconciling the two sides of Gomberville, and there is in fact some evidence that at least until his mid-twenties he was inclined to follow two paths leading in quite different directions.

Gomberville was a firm admirer of Malherbe from at the latest 1620, and when, in 1637, Gomberville proscribed the usage of the conjunction "car (because, for)," he was seen, at least, as representing the tradition of Malherbe, to whom he several times paid fulsome tribute in writing, notably in the three-volume 1671 collection *Le Recueil de poésies chrétiennes et diverses*. The debate was not as serious as the participants amused themselves by pretending, but Chapelain and Balzac corresponded about the word, and Julie d'Angennes wrote to Voiture to ask him what he thought. Ménage composed some satirical verses about the fate of the "Gothic" word which was the subject of the dispute, and everybody laughed at Gomberville. Tallemant maliciously tells us that the valet of Bassompierre, in the Bastille, read the five volumes which *Polexandre* had reached, and found numerous usages of "car." In 1639 La Mothe le Vayer enraged Gomberville by accusing him of outrageous purism.

On the other hand, in late adolescence, Gomberville was certainly attracted by the poetry of Théophile de Viau, at that date a quasi-official court poet. Gomberville made identifiable borrowings from him, and adopted some of his poetic themes and historical and aesthetic theories. It has recently been argued that

Gomberville may, however, have turned away early from Théophile's example, as shown by his insertion of an "avis" into the 1625 *Somme théologique* of Théophile's opponent, Père Garasse, and his disavowal of excessive deference to the court in the introduction to *La Carithée*.

Gomberville appears to have gone on living in Paris after his resignation, and from 1620 was certainly on friendly terms with Henri-Auguste de Loménie, comte de Brienne, the secretary of state for foreign affairs from 1643, to whom he had dedicated his edition of the poems of Jean Bertaut, preferred by Malherbe to "toute la volée (the whole brood)" of Ronsard, Desportes, Régnier, and d'Aubigné. From the birth of his first child in 1622 nothing more is heard of Gomberville until 1625, when there is a letter of 10 February which makes clear that Achille de Harlay, marquis de Bréval, had recommended Gomberville to the duc de Chevreuse, and when the insertion into Garasse's *Somme* testifies to the fact that Gomberville had reconciled Garasse and Balzac. By 1628 Gomberville was part of the household of Henri de Lorraine, comte d'Harcourt, possibly introduced by Faret, who belonged to a group of literary figures from the south-east which Gomberville frequented in Paris. It was the duchesse Nicole de Lorraine who persuaded Gomberville not to write the history of the civil wars, but to take up *Polexandre* again.

Gomberville's connection with the Liancourt family probably dates from the mid-1620s or a little later, and Rapin, who tells us about Gomberville's literary fame from the mid-1630s, tells us also that it was Gomberville who introduced the abbé de Bourzeys to the hôtel de Liancourt, where he must also have met Pierre Corneille. Gomberville was, with Camus, Saint-Amant, Robert Arnauld d'Andilly and the actor Montdory, one of the prominent literary figures cultivated by the Liancourts, and through them met Mme de Liancourt's brother, Henri de Schomberg, from 1619 to 1623 Surintendant des finances, who intervened in vain on Gomberville's behalf in a matter of taxation. From the beginning Gomberville was a member of the Académie française, and with Gombauld worked on the statutes and the protocol for producing the Académie's grammar and dictionary. His protectors, however, were generally hostile to Richelieu, and Gomberville himself had some difficulty in keeping the cardinal's goodwill. During the Fronde Gomberville's sympathies were to lie with Retz, as were those of a whole group of writers, including Chapelain, Ménage, Saint-Amant, and Sarrazin. Gomberville and Chapelain dined with Retz on 26 August 1648, the first day of barricades in Paris.

The first part of the re-worked *Polexandre* appeared in 1629, and again re-worked, but now with its second part, in 1632. From this date onwards, Gomberville was famous, as well as rich from his parents' gift. In 1632 *Polexandre* was dedicated to Louis XIII and to Saint-Simon, father of the memorialist. It then appeared in four parts in 1637, with a *Suitte de la Quatriesme et derniere partie de Polexandre* of the same year, addressed to Louis XIII, Richelieu, and Séguier, but also to Liancourt and Schomberg. According to Brienne, immediately after the death of Richelieu and Louis XIII Gomberville wrote a quatrain against Richelieu, Louis XIII, Olivarès, the favourite of Philip IV of Spain, and Philip IV himself. There is some doubt about the publication history of *La Cythérée*, dedicated to the duchesse de Lorraine. The privilège was for 10 May 1639, and we know from Chapelain's letters that the first two parts, with an achevé d'imprimer of 10 October, were available by 4 December. The achevé of the third part is 10 February 1641, and the fourth part was probably published first with the other three in 1642.

Towards 1641, Gomberville fell seriously ill. Mainard expressed his anxiety, and it is to be assumed that Gomberville began to spend longer periods on his estates, not far away from Port-Royal-des-Champs (q.v.), where he was in contact with the solitaires. He encouraged Mainard to publish his *Oeuvres*, for which Gomberville wrote a preface mentioning his new Port-Royal friends. The *Oeuvres*, and Gomberville's book for children, *La Doctrine des moeurs*, both appeared in 1646. By that date Gomberville had established close links with Port-Royal and had become churchwarden at the church of Saint-Louis-de-Paris, where Tallement says he infuriated everyone with the austerity of his views: "Il pensa faire enrager les gens avec ses austeritez, car il est jansseniste (He nearly drove everyone crazy with his austerities; for he is a Jansenist)." Ten years later he was even suspected of writing the first *Lettres provinciales*.

None the less, in 1651 the first part of *La jeune Alcidiane* was published. Tallemant said it was a Jansenist novel, full of sermons and prayers, but it has been strongly defended against that provocative accusation. The novel remained unfinished. The publisher claimed that he had been holding the text for nearly five years, waiting for the writer's authorization to publish. He also tells us that Gomberville was ill. The privilège is dated 26 July 1649. From 1656 onwards Gomberville seems to have led a generally solitary life, dedicated to work. He went back to history and in 1665 published the two folios *Les Mémoires de M. le duc de Nevers, prince de Mantoue, pair de France*. However, in 1664 the witnesses to his youngest daughter's marriage to Claude de Nossey, seigneur de Fontenay and tutor of the comte de Saint-Paul, were from the highest social ranks: the princesse de Conti, Condé, the princesse de Nemours, and the duchesse de Longueville.

Guy Patin tells us that Gomberville, together with Bourzeys, Chapelain and Denis de Sallo, founded the *Journal des Savants* (q.v.), and at the same time he was translating the Jesuit Christophle d'Acuña's *Relation de la rivière des Amazones*. The translation appeared in 1682. He also actively helped Arnauld, Brienne, La Fontaine, and Racine in putting together the 1671 *Recueil de poésies chrétiennes et diverses*, containing some 60 of his pieces. Brienne found him "le plus mordant de tous les critiques (the most biting of all critics)" and was amused to hear him say that he did not think he could bring Bussy's *Amours des Gaules* to a greater peak of perfection than it had already achieved. Whatever the intensity of his final devotion, Gomberville did not repudiate the novels of his youth. He died on 14 June 1674.

WORKS

The immense popularity of Gomberville in his day is scarcely controverted. Balzac thought *Polexandre* "un ouvrage parfait en son espèce (a work perfect in its kind);" Sorel said of it that "les inventions sont hautes et magnifiques… le langage est fort, et l'on remarque par tout du sçavoir et de l'art (its inventiveness is high and magnificent… the language powerful, and everywhere knowledge and art are to be found);" and La Fontaine read the novel repeatedly. It was put on the same level as the novels of Desmarets, La Calprenède, and Scudéry. The difficulty is that this might have been for the wrong reasons.

There are four questions of concern to modern commentators. Does the real power of *Polexandre* reside in its presentation of a universe entirely dominated by forces outside human control? Does Gomberville's originality lie in a pessimism which his contemporaries, when they applauded him, simply did not notice? Does Gomberville anticipate a Jansenist world of uncontrollable destinies even as early as 1637? Does the heroine of *Polexandre* pre-figure a later préciosité (q.v.)? All four questions were answered in 1972 affirmatively in France and in 1983 negatively in England. Whatever the ultimate solution to the questions, the debate itself clearly has a moral.

The early 17th-century novel was a forum for the serious exploration of the values by which human beings might be destined, or might choose, or might in vain wish, to live. The view universally held until the beginning of the second half of the 20th century, still commonly held as recently as a score of years ago, and perhaps lingering even in the 1990s, that nothing of the highest literary value, except one or two plays by Pierre Corneille, was written in the first half of the 17th century in France has finally been successfully challenged. The most exciting investigations in the literary culture of 17th-century France were conducted before the advent of Colbert to power, and the administrative revolution represented by the overthrow of Foucquet in 1661.

Sorel is uncomplimentary about the construction of *La Carithée*, in which he saw only the episode of Pan's death from Plutarch, the loves of Germanicus and Agrippine, "et au reste quelques amours des bergers de l'Isle heureuse (and, for the rest, some shepherds' loves from the Isles of the Blessed)." In fact there are also anagrams, disguising Charles IX as Cérinthe and Louis XIII as prince Sivol, with the name of his squire, Sunile, an anagram of Luynes. There is a sense in which Gomberville's first novel performs the transfer from the pastoral decor, with its presumption of the innocence of whatever is natural, to the court setting, where the conventional values are heroic.

Perhaps as importantly, the intrigue is put in motion by the sudden incursion of unexpected and irresistible love. Cérinthe is an adolescent totally devoted to hunting. For a long time he has known Cidarie, the friend of his sister Mérissée. One day, while out hunting, his hounds put up a hare which dashes into a clearing where Cidarie and Mérissée are walking and jumps for protection into Cidarie's arms. Cérinthe suddenly sees Cidarie in a new light.

> Comme si en ceste action l'Amour m'eust osté le bandeau que j'avois devant les yeux, pour y mettre celuy qu'il porte devant les siens, je demeuray tout ravy de voir ceste jeune merveille, à laquelle je ne m'estois jamais arresté, encore que je l'eusse desja veuë plus de vingt fois

> (As if in that action Love had removed the bandage which I had in front of my eyes to replace it with that which Love wears in front of its own, I stood in ecstasy before this marvellous young creature, to whom I had never paid attention, although I had seen her more than a score of times).

A number of points need to be made about that incident. Firstly, Gomberville's attitude to realism in the narrative intrigue is less even than perfunctory. It is of no concern to him that in order to escape from pursuing hounds, hares do not actually jump into the arms of pretty girls. They do in fairy-land, so to speak, and in a quite instinctive, no doubt uncalculated way, Gomberville is indicating a fairy-tale suspension of the ordinary laws of behaviour. For his imaginative purposes, he needs an extraordinary world in which the common rules of psychology are in abeyance, in which love strikes and elevates unpredictably, instantaneously, and irresistibly, in which it makes the ultra-human heroic achievable, and in which instinct can be trusted, the hare's as well as Cérinthe's. Cérinthe continues

> Pleust aux Dieux que tout ce qui se rendra, ou qui s'est desja rendu entre vos bras plus volontairement et plus judicieusement que n'a pas fait ce lievre, peut avoir d'esperance de son salut que ceste beste en doit avoir de sa vie

> (Would to Heaven that any being which throws itself or which has already thrown itself into your arms with more deliberation and consideration than this hare can hope for salvation [as surely] as this beast must hope for its life).

The rough adolescent is instantly transformed into an expert at galanterie, and the irresistibility of love is not disturbing when instinctive affection is examined for only its ennobling effects. Racine will ask in *Phèdre* what happens when it is not.

Unlike d'Urfé's Céladon in *L'Astrée*, Cérinthe is not faithful to a single love. *La Carithée* is also an adventure story which works on an adolescent level. But Cérinthe does finally fall in love with Carithée before he has ever seen even a picture of her: "J'aymay sans l'avoir veuë... avec autant d'ardeur et de fidelité, que je l'ayme à cet'heure (I loved without having seen her... with as much ardour and faithfulness as I love her now)." She is the ideal, and the life-enhancing qualities of Cérinthe's affection are emphasized by the down-grading of physical passion. He has not seen her, travels to the Isles of the blessed in search of her, and when he finds her, the narrator's emphasis is on her moral rather than on her physical qualities. Carithée herself has a premonition that the lover of her life is about to appear, and we are told that what attracted Cérinthe in Carithée was

> une si grande innocence en ses paroles, une si rare modestie en ses actions, une grâce si charmante sur son visage, une si saine vivacité en son esprit, et une force si surnaturelle en son jugement

> (so great an innocence in her words, so rare a modesty in her actions, such a charming grace on her countenance, such a glowing liveliness in her mind, and such a superhuman strength in her judgement).

The imaginative pattern of ennobling love occasioned by a simple report of outstanding moral stature recurs so often in Gomberville that there can be little doubt that it responds to a core imaginative need. His fiction was too unsophisticatedly written, on a register at which it could divert and relax its readers, to be imaginatively demanding enough to rank as high art, but it was popular enough to show that Gomberville's imaginative concerns were indeed those of his generation, and powerful enough to make patently clear the way in which his generation needed to understand human potential. *La Carithée* presents us with what is virtually a limiting case in the way it combines puerility of fantasy with earnestness of imaginative endeavour.

A shepherd in love carves his woes on to the bark of a tree, and they take nine printed pages to reproduce. Gomberville's novel can also in fact be criticized for its erudition. Instead of sticking to the exploration of the ennobling potential of human instinct and to contributing to the great cultural movement upgrading the potential of human nature, it offers also erudite references to Ronsard's celebration of two of the loves of Charles IX, "Astrée" and "Calirée," and some real learning about ancient Egypt. It would none the less be foolhardy to write off the novel's literary importance.

L'Exil de Polexandre et d'Ericlée had been published in 1619, two years before *La Carithée*, but was taken up again to be rewritten, first as *L'Exil de Polexandre* in 1629, and then simply as *Polexandre* in 1637, after an intervening stage in 1632. The year 1637 saw in January the particularly radical imaginative investigation of the ennobling power of heroic emotional force, carefully justified by the merit of its object, when Pierre Corneille's *Le Cid* was staged with its original ending. Gomberville's amorous casuistry had by 1637 much advanced, and its successive refinements as Polexandre comes to play an increasingly central part in the intrigue can be followed through its various stages, but it was much more tentative than that proposed in Corneille's tragi-comédie. Chronologically, however, the 1637 *Polexandre* is usually regarded as the first of the major heroic novels in the literature of France.

The first version, *L'Exil de Polexandre et d'Ericlée*, is an only loosely connected succession of adventure stories, set in a real world of characters with recognizable trades, callings, and emotions. Without any knowledge of the circumstances of its composition, most modern readers would be likely to put the author's probable age at a little younger than the 18 Gomberville must have been. Polexandre himself is 16 when he wins a treasured portrait of Alcidiane in a tournament. The picture is stolen from him while he is asleep on a beach by Almanzor, in whom it awakens a dark passion, and who returns it only after fighting a duel for it with Polexandre. In the fifth and last chapter the characters read a book called "L'Exil de Polexandre et d'Ericlée," which tells how Polexandre came to the court of Henri II as a boy, fell in love with Ericlée, was exiled for fighting and killing a rival, met a hermit who was in fact his mother, and himself became a hermit. The court of Henri II, who had died at a tournament in 1559 on the eve of the religious wars, was to provide the chivalrous setting Mme de Lafayette required for *La Princesse de Clèves*, in which the theft of a portrait also assumes central importance. The court of Henri II was clearly already regarded as a nostalgic paradigm of chivalry as soon as the religious wars were over.

Earlier than *La Carithée* love was ennobling, but only when, as in the courtly tradition, it was frustrated of its physical fulfilment. For the troubadors, their ladies were the untouchable hypostasizations of moral aspirations, never present or future spouses. The affected love of a troubador was in fact a moral aspiration, in that culture absolutely incompatible with physical sexual contact. Even as recent an author as Montaigne had assumed that sexual pleasure had no place in love-making between husband and wife, which took place with the absolute minimum of physical contact. For the Church love-making within marriage was a duty. Outside marriage, it was a sin. Gomberville is writing when it was still daring to assume in France, what Ficino had almost coyly suggested in the *De amore* in late 15th-century Italy, and Marguerite d'Angoulême allows her Parlamente to be laughed at for suggesting in the mid-16th-century *Heptameron*, that physical sex might be compatible with, or even a step in the direction of, the beatifying love of God.

In the 1629 *L'Exil de Polexandre*, Polexandre falls in love with Olimpe at the court of Henri II. The central interest of the love of Aligénor and Eolinde of 1619 disappears with the character of Eolinde. Polexandre heads a procession of allegorical figures, as in the 1619 version, fights against the Huguenots in the religious wars, is banished for a year, and goes to Denmark to fight Phélismond, whose attentions have offended Olimpe. Polexandre is emerging only gradually as the central character, appearing only late in the novel. The centre of interest is not single combat, but naval battles and military actions. Gomberville himself said that he wanted to make the Polexandre of 1629 "aussi haut que mon imagination pouvoit aller (as high as my imagination could go)," with more "mérite" than in 1619. Although Polexandre captains a boat for the pirate chief Bajazet and there are descriptions of drunken revelry, the principal characters are all linked by superiority of caste. The pirate Bajazet, the Inca Zelmatide, and the young French courtier are concerned about the qualities of behaviour, especially the "mérite," "gloire," and "générosité" by which heroic behaviour is measured.

Olimpe had ordered Polexandre to challenge Phélismond, but their shared quality draws them together and their combat is chiefly a competition in moral grandeur. In 1632 the tone was further elevated by the omission of the more coarsely realistic episodes, and the emphasis was changed to individual feats of heroism not so much tempered as enhanced by galanterie. In the combat between Polexandre and Phélismond, each now offers to die for the other. The novel even in 1637 is still too eager to introduce the reader to Mexico, Senegal, the Congo, and Denmark, with flavours of authenticity. By 1637 Polexandre has become king of the Canary islands, and is described in hyperbolic terms and moral superlatives which put him far above the rest of humanity. Even events must conspire to confirm his superhuman status. Alcippe tells him

Vous ne seriez pas ce que vous estes, si les choses ne vous arrivoient autrement qu'au reste des hommes

(You would not be the person you are if things did not happen to you differently from the way they happen to the rest of humanity).

His life is the pursuit of Alcidiane, and union with her the summit of ecstasy, requiring the epitome of all possible forms of moral heroism, including even the risk of being chosen as the human sacrifice on the Ile du Soleil in order to reach Alcidiane. Should he perish,

Je souhaitterois de perir en lieu où vos beaux yeux fussent tesmoins de ma perte, afin que rien ne vous peust empescher de croire que je meurs pour vous seulement

(I should like to die where your beautiful eyes could witness my death, so that nothing could prevent you from believing that I was dying only for you).

Some characters are possessed by passion and often come to grief. Ordinary heroes, like Zelmatide the Inca prince with Iza-

tide, and Bajazet with Cydarie, have the ordinary cultivated relationships involving a declaration, acceptance for a probationary period, a declaration by the woman, and marriage. But the love of Alcidiane cannot be earned by the acquired merits of gold-chained subservience; it requires her acknowledgement of quality in the suitor. The difficulty, as with Cydarie, is the element of submission involved in acceptance by the female of the male. Alcidiane can give way to her feelings only when she believes Polexandre dead. The problem is never really resolved, although the narrator disguises the marriage in an apotheosis of reciprocal grandeur. When in the marriage ceremony Polexandre appears on the same balcony and at the same level as Alcidiane, the narrator can only call off the conflict:

Contentons nous de sçavoir que Polexandre et Alcidiane sont ensemble; et puisque nous les avons si long temps possedez, ayons assez de justice pour trouver bon qu'ils se possedent eux mesmes

(Let us be satisfied to know that Polexandre and Alcidiane are together; and since we have had them for so long, let us be fair enough to accept that they now have one another).

The literary registers of *Polexandre* are confusing, reaching from realism to a cornucopia of utopian ingredients. Alcidiane's almost inaccessible island has two harvests a year, plus constant fruit, and abounds in gold, silver, and diamonds. At the age of 80 its inhabitants are vigorous and seem young. But Alcidiane can issue orders which affect the inhabitants of real places, like Denmark and Morocco. None of the inconsistencies seriously disturbed contemporary readers. It strikes modern commentators as important to know whether or not Alcidiane is so idealized that Polexandre's striving for her is its own reward, like stoic virtue, or whether, as appears to be suggested, the physical consummation of his love would destroy him. Historically, of course, the neostoic values of the late 16th century can be shown to have led to the heroic values explored in the literature of the first half of the 17th century. But the point to be made here is that Gomberville's ambiguities tentatively probe the compatibility, and even the coincidence, of the virtue which lies in the aspiration towards unattainable perfection with the happiness attendant on its achievement. On the highest possible level imaginable, can the moral fulfilment of striving for perfection coexist with the physical satisfaction of instinctive desire?

That is the question examined by Gomberville. Neostoic reason imposes limitations on human potential, and does not represent the highest form of virtue. *Polexandre* ends in the marriage and happiness of Polexandre and Alcidiane, with all that that implies. But that happiness, reposing on the satisfaction of instinctive desire, is compatible with Polexandre's much-displayed and certainly unsurpassable virtue:

Il faut que j'obeïsse à mes destinées, et que sans craindre l'orage, ny esperer le calme, j'acheve le voyage qu'elles m'ont fait entreprendre. Je sçay que cette timidité qu'on appelle raison voudroit bien par ses considerations specieuses me faire perdre l'envie, apres m'avoir osté l'esperance. Mais ses conseils sont trop lasches pour estre escoutez, et la grande Alcidiane ne seroit pas ce qu'elle est, si la raison ou la fortune se pouvoient opposer à ce qu'elle a resolu

(I must obey my destinies, and without fearing the storm or hoping for calm, I must finish the journey they made me undertake. I know that that timidity which people call reason would like, by its specious arguments, to make me lose desire after having removed hope. But its promptings are too cowardly to be listened to, and the great Alcidiane would not be who she is, if reason or fortune could stand in the way of what she has decreed).

PUBLICATIONS

Fiction

L'Exil de Polexandre et d'Ericlée, 1619
La Carithée, 1621
L'Exil de Polexandre. Première partie, 1629
La première partie de Polexandre, 1632
La seconde partie de Polexandre, 1632
La première partie de Polexandre, revue, changée et augmentée, 1637
La seconde partie de Polexandre, revue, changée et augmentée, 1637
La troisième partie de Polexandre, 1637
La quatrième et dernière partie de Polexandre, 1637
Suite de la quatrième et dernière partie de Polexandre, 1637
Cythérée. I partie, 1642
Cythérée. Seconde partie, 1642
Cythérée. Troisième partie, 1642
La quatrième et dernière partie de Cythérée, 1647
La jeune Alcidiane, 1651

Other

Tableau du bonheur de la vieillesse opposé au malheur de la jeunesse, 1614
Ode sur les heureux succès des actions du roi, 1618
Vers du Sieur le Roy, 1619
Discours des vertus et des vices de l'Histoire, 1620
Remarques sur la vie du roi et sur celle d'Alexandre Severe, 1622
La Doctrine des moeurs tirée de la philosophie des stoïques… pour l'instruction de la jeunesse, 1646
Les Mémoires de Monsieur le duc de Nevers, 2 vols., 1665

Translation

Acuña, P. Christophle d', *Relation de la rivière des Amazones*, 4 vols., 1682

Biographical and critical studies

Kerviler, R., *Marin le Roy de Gomberville*, 1876
Wadsworth, P.A., *The Novels of Gomberville. A Critical Study of "Polexandre" and "Cythérée"*, 1942
Kévorkian, S., *Le thème de l'amour dans l'oeuvre romanesque de Gomberville*, 1972
Turk, Edward B., *Baroque Fiction-making: a study of Gomberville's "Polexandre"*, 1978
Bannister, Mark, *Privileged Mortals. The French Heroic Novel 1630–1660*, 1983

GRIMM, Friedrich Melchior, Baron von, 1723–1807.

Critic and editor.

LIFE

Apart from a tragedy when he was 19, and a pair of pamphlets produced in the context of the mid-18th-century dispute about the respective merits of French and Italian operatic styles, Grimm wrote almost nothing for publication except ephemeral journalism. He edited, largely himself wrote, and had copied in longhand a fortnightly newsletter of which copies, no two exactly identical in content, were sent to less than a score of European rulers anxious to know what was happening in liberal Paris. The addressees paid to receive their letters, but Grimm enjoined on them the strictest prohibition on having them copied, let alone printed. The existence of the cultural content of the letters was for more than half a century one of Europe's better-kept secrets. From the number of extant runs we know that copies must have been made, but it was generally thought by those who knew about it that Grimm's correspondence with the European courts was confined to diplomatic matters. He became after all a baron of the Holy Roman Empire, chevalier grand-croix (second class) of the Imperial Order of Saint Vladimir, and a Counsellor of State of Her Majesty, the Empress of all the Russias. He was also the organizer of a brilliantly successful propagandist enterprise for the dissemination of encyclopédiste (q.v.) ideas, and the author of some of the most influential literary and art criticism to have been written in 18th-century France.

It was only after Grimm's death that the nature of the correspondence was discovered, that runs were found in the private libraries of European monarchs, and that, for its publication in 1812–13, it was given the name *Correspondance littéraire, philosophique et critique*. It was not a periodical in which authors like Diderot "published" art criticism or fiction and it did not have an "editor" or "subscribers" in any conventional sense. The letters were manuscript, private, secret, witty, well informed, carefully written, with often perspicacious judgements on all important new books, as well as on exhibitions and dramatic and musical performances. There was also a good deal of cultural gossip and information about comings and goings.

Grimm had weaknesses as well as strengths, but in the light of the way historians have sometimes written about it, it is important from the outset to realize that the *Correspondance littéraire* was a series of intensely confidential private letters, often subversive of official French thinking, for which the recipients paid, but none of the contents of which was ever intended for publication. As Grimm wrote to Frederick the Great,

la liberté et la sûreté de cette correspondance exigent un secret inviolable,… les amis même de l'auteur ne sauraient être exceptés de cette règle

(the freedom and security of this correspondence demand inviolable secrecy,… not even the author's friends can be excepted from that rule).

Grimm was born at Ratisbon, now Regensburg, on 26 December 1723. He father was a high-ranking German pastor and the family socially respected but not moneyed. At the local high school, where he developed a taste for the moralists, for French, and for Gottsched, Grimm was already known as "the critic," and at the age of 17, on 19 April 1741, he wrote to Johann Christoph Gottsched, sending him an ode and a satire and enthusiastically professing discipleship. Gottsched, although professor of logic and metaphysics at Leipzig, was devoting himself chiefly to assimilating German literature to French stylistic models, especially in epic and drama, and had in 1730 published a German poetics, the *Versuch einer critischen Dichtkunst*. Grimm's elder brother had given him the first volume of Gottsched's collection of German plays, *Die deutsche Schaubühne*, and the correspondence with Gottsched developed. In 1742 the already Francophile Grimm went to Leipzig to follow Gottsched's courses, and re-wrote his tragedy *Banise* in accordance with Gottched's advice, five acts and in alexandrines. It was successfully played in Frankfurt and Strasburg and published in the fourth volume of Gottsched's collection in 1743.

At Leipzig Grimm also got to know the Hellenist J.A. Ernesti, who gradually came to replace Gottsched as his model and from whom Grimm derived his taste for Greek and Latin literature. A letter to Gottsched of 10 April 1746 tells us that Grimm was turning away from poetry and drama towards criticism and discussion, and he was later frequently to quote Ernesti, eight of whose works were in his library. Grimm left Leipzig in 1745 and was employed by the Graf von Schönberg, ambassador of Saxony at the imperial diet of Regensburg, as tutor to his son, Adolph-Heinrich, whom Grimm accompanied in 1749 to Paris, where he looked for another position. We do not know whether it had earlier been agreed that he would leave his post as soon as he got his pupil to Paris.

While still at Regensburg Grimm had published in 1746 or 1747 a critical article in the Regensburg *Gazette* on the poems of Johann Ulrich von König, printed posthumously in 1745, and Grimm also published in 1747 a Latin dissertation on imperial law under Maximilian I. He wrote to Gottsched of a project to translate some Voltaire into German, which came to nothing. Probably through the good offices of his previous employer, Grimm found a temporary post in Paris in the Saxe-Gotha household as reader to the young Prince Frederick, to whom he gave lessons in Latin and German. Rousseau commented that Grimm appeared in urgent need of a position, but he had certainly found one a few months later, when he was secretary to the count von Friesen, a nephew of the Graf von Schönberg, with whom he stayed until von Friesen died on 29 March 1755, although for the last two years Grimm was his companion rather than his secretary.

Through the Saxe-Gothas and the Friesens, Grimm met the Parisian literary world, becoming through their joint interest in music quickly drawn to Rousseau, who in August 1749 visited the château of Fontenay-sous-Pois at the invitation of the prince's governor, the Baron von Thun. When Grimm moved to the Friesen household, he met Rousseau almost daily. Together they enjoyed Italian music but not the Italian theatre, for which Rousseau had a free pass. He was obliged to pay for his ticket to accompany Grimm to the Comédie-Française, which Grimm preferred. There was a boisterous evening which involved the successive retirement of both Grimm and Rousseau to the bedroom of the mistress of Christophe Klüpfel, a colleague of Grimm's with the Saxe-Gothas. According to Rousseau, Grimm swore that he did not touch her. He got to know Diderot and Mme Dupin, dined on Thursdays with Holbach, met Saint-Lam-

bert, Marmontel, Jaucourt, Raynal, Duclos, La Condamine, and the abbé Morellet, and in 1750 Mme d'Epinay.

Grimm weekly entertained Rousseau, Diderot, Helvétius, and Marmontel, and he often dined with Rousseau and sometimes Klüpfel. D'Alembert soon joined the group. Grimm now made several apparently unsuccessful efforts to interest the French in German literature, starting with a six-page letter surveying German literature, dated 4 August 1750 and published in the October 1750 *Mercure de France* (q.v.), followed by a second letter, dated 20 November 1751 and published the following February, devoted to the achievements of Gottsched. Then in 1752 Grimm published a piece on the German theatre in the *Almanach historique et chronologique de tous les spectacles*.

For that summer a new visit to Paris by Eustachio Bambini's Italian opera buffa company had been announced, with its repertoire of Pergolesi and Scarlatti. It was to open with the celebrated *La serva padrona*. Early in the year, on the occasion of Destouches's lyrical tragedy *Omphale*, Grimm had published on 14 January his *Lettre de M. Grimm sur Omphale*, seeking to assert the superiority of foreign, and especially Italian, music over French, although the pamphlet remained moderate in tone, and praised Rameau. Replies inevitably appeared, and on 2 April Grimm answered them with his *Lettre à l'abbé Raynal* published in the *Mercure de France* for May 1752. In April a more virulent *Lettre à M. Grimm au sujet des remarques ajoutées à sa lettre sur Omphale* had appeared in support of Grimm. It attacked Rameau and seems certain to have been the work of Rousseau. The battle between the parisans of Italian and those of French music sparked off a pamphlet war, and on 25 January 1753 Grimm produced *Le petit prophète de Boemischbroda*, a satirical pamphlet mordantly attacking the French musical tradition, which ran through three editions in a month and provoked 25 more pamphlets in nine months. Diderot entered the fray posing as neutral, but in fact coming down on the Italian side. The Italians were none the less sent home.

Grimm was now famous, and was a member of the newly emerging group of thinkers soon to be known as the philosophes (q.v.), whose principal organ of expression was to be the *Encyclopédie* (q.v.). There was a connection between a preference for Italian opera and liberal anti-clerical thought on social and philosophical issues, since the French musical tradition also stood for authority, inflexibility, and academic values. Grimm himself was offered the editorship of the monthly *Journal étranger* founded in April 1754, but resigned after the first number, having written only the prefatory manifesto indicating the interest of foreign literature tactlessly enough to provoke a blistering response from Raynal, who thought Rousseau had written it, in his *Nouvelles littéraires*. Toussaint took over the direction of the *Journal étranger*, but Prévost was in charge before the end of the year. Grimm himself made a resumé of his views on Italian music in the article "Poème lyrique" for the *Encyclopédie* but, apart from that piece, published nothing else.

He devoted himself entirely to his letters to the princes of the European courts. He could write to Gottsched on 23 June 1753 that he was earning himself a little revenue "from a literary occupation" which can only have been the letters. Many of the minor European courts had for some time had semi-official correspondents in Paris to keep them informed, a tradition perhaps started by Thiériot, who from December 1736 had been the Paris literary correspondent of Frederick, then crown prince of Prussia. It was on Voltaire's recommendation that Thiériot's place was taken from June 1748 by Baculard d'Arnaud, who was replaced in 1750 by Pierre Morand and may also have been the correspondent of the prince of Württemburg. La Harpe fulfilled the same function for the grand duke Paolo of Russia and the empress's chamberlain, Showalow, from 1774 to 1789, and we have quite precise details about at least half a dozen more comparable relationships between courts and their correspondents in the Paris literary world. Bachaumont tells us that Fréron received 1,000 livres for corresponding with Piedmont. Voltaire offered an arrangement to Mouhi involving 200 livres a year for two secret letters a week.

Before ever coming to France, Grimm had read some copies of the *Nouvelles littéraires* which Raynal sent more or less fortnightly to the duchess of Saxe-Gotha from 29 July 1747 to 27 December 1751 and from 1 April 1754 to 15 February 1755. Copies for the intervening period have probably merely been lost. Raynal reviewed all books of interest, two or three a month in considerable detail and the others in shorter notices. Although his *Nouvelles littéraires* and Grimm's letters may have been the product of some collaboration, they ran alongside one another for ten months in 1754 and 1755. Grimm's letters appear to have started in May 1753, and to have been sent by diplomatic courier twice a month. Magazine items began to infiltrate the reviews and critical discussions, and letters, anecdotes, verse, and unpublished fragments began to enliven the critical pages and review articles, themselves broadened to include scientific works, and books dealing with politics, history, trade, and economics as well as plays, poetry and fiction.

Individual correspondents would have their tastes catered for in their individual copies of Grimm's letters. Sweden got more details about the theatre than Saxe-Gotha. Recipients had to be princes or princesses of European royal houses. "For a long time now," Grimm wrote to the landgrave of Hesse on 15 July 1766, "I have made it a rule to send these letters only to princes, and several good reasons make me keep to it. I sometimes get offers of 2,000 or 1,200 livres a year to send them to individuals of importance in England, but I have never wanted to." There is no accurate list of recipients at any date. The best guess includes Catherine of Russia, the queen of Sweden, the king of Poland, the duchess of Saxe-Gotha, the duke of Zweibrücken, the princess of Hesse-Darmstadt, Prince Georg of Hesse-Darmstadt, and the princess of Nassau-Saarbrück.

Grimm's secretary and successor, the Swiss Jacques-Henri Meister, estimates that the letters went out to 15 or 16 courts. That is probably about the maximum of simultaneous addressees. Some must have dropped out, and new ones came in. From various references, manuscript collections, and allusions, it seems clear that the queen of Sweden started to receive the letters in 1760, and that different princes rewarded Grimm with different sums. Pressure was put by Grimm on Frederick II to receive the letters through the queen of Sweden, Frederick's sister, and the duchess of Saxe-Gotha. Frederick did allow himself to become an addressee from July 1763, but he did not think highly of Grimm and appears never to have paid, as he had earlier never paid Thiériot. Grimm decided to stop sending his letters to Frederick on 1 June 1766.

Catherine of Russia started to receive the letters in January 1764, Georg of Hesse-Darmstadt in 1765. The mediation of Mme Geoffrin secured the king of Poland in 1767, and for the first time something like an informal bill accompanied the first despatch. It was for 400 livres a year. In 1768 the margrave of Ansbach and the grand-duke of Tuscany joined the list. Grimm was showing concern for his circulation, and spoke regretfully of the reluctance of the Mediterranean courts to take the letters. Odd letters at odd dates permit only rough estimates of where the letters might have been going at any given date. Grimm had some difficulty in getting paid. He estimated actual annual receipts at about 9,000 livres, not including money owing, and costs at about 3,000 livres. Material for the letters was supplied not only by himself, but also by a series of collaborators, especially Diderot, Mme d'Epinay, and Grimm's successor, Meister.

When Grimm was absent from Paris, as from April to September 1757 when he was with the duc d'Estrées as his secretary during the Westphalian campaign, and when he went to Geneva in the summer of 1758, it was his close friend Diderot who organized the enterprise, although Diderot then did not himself supply much of the material, and Grimm continued to control the content of the letters. Diderot's role became more important when Grimm was in Geneva with Mme d'Epinay from March to October 1759, and Diderot himself was told to write what he liked. He devoted most of his space to the theatre. Diderot found Grimm a very difficult taskmaster to please, especially with the art criticism, but provided increasing amounts of material, including all his *Salons* and, after Grimm had handed over to Meister in 1773, he sent to Meister, for the letters, *Jacques le fataliste*, written at irregular intervals and sent out on and off to fill space from November 1778 to June 1780, with additions in July 1780 and April 1786.

Grimm was absent in Westphalia for three months from September 1762, going on to Gotha and Frankfurt, leaving his letters to Mme d'Epinay and Diderot. From January 1763 he stayed in Paris until 1769, when he warned his addresses that he would be visiting Vienna and Berlin, and that the letters from Paris would be sent by Diderot. In fact nothing appears to have been sent from May to October that year. Grimm did not entirely trust Diderot, whose judgement he found excellent for worthwhile material, but whose attention, Grimm thought, wandered too easily when he had to write about anything which bored him. Diderot was then inclined to become too inventive. Grimm also made stylistic emendations to Diderot's material where he thought them appropriate.

It was to Diderot that Grimm handed over again when he went to England for the winter of 1771–72. When, less than a year later, he went to Russia, and was absent from Paris from March 1773 until September 1774, he handed over responsibility for the newsletters, henceforward despatched only monthly, to Meister. Mme d'Epinay supplied a certain amount of the material. On returning from Russia, where he had been with Diderot, Grimm went to Berlin, too dangerous for Diderot, and then to Karlsbad. Grimm resumed his letters only briefly, before setting off for Italy. His Russian visit, in the suite of Wilhelmina von Hesse-Darmstadt on her marriage to the czarevitch, had allowed him to get to know Catherine of Russia well, and from his return in 1774 he corresponded with her personally, but on his return from Italy he handed the newsletter enterprise "avec ses charges et ses bénéfices (with its costs and profits)" permanently over to Meister. Meister carried it on until 1813, doing Grimm's job less brilliantly but more reliably until 1793, when he went to Zurich and the interest of the letters declined.

Grimm's relationship with Rousseau had begun to cool soon after they had taken the same side in the opera war. Grimm probably had been infatuated with the Italian company's leading lady, although Rousseau's later account of the matter cannot be trusted. References to Rousseau in Grimm's letters almost calibrate the drop in the temperature of a friendship which in 1757 turned to hostility. In December 1753 the reference to Rousseau is complimentary, but by February 1754 Rousseau's defence of his first *Discours* is given only lukewarm commendation, and there are critical remarks about other things Rousseau had written. By the summer of 1756 Rousseau no longer cared for Grimm, who had already while with the count von Friesen fought a duel to defend the honour of Mme d'Epinay. Mme d'Epinay had been accused, when sorting through the papers of her dead sister, of destroying those which proved that she herself owed money to her sister's heirs. Grimm and his opponent had both been slightly wounded, but Grimm had taken on for Mme d'Epinay a glamour which led to his becoming her lover, and he was installed at her house, La Chevrette, when Rousseau came in April 1756 to live at the Hermitage on Mme d'Epinay's estate.

Rousseau had come to disapprove of Grimm's social climbing, dandified attitudes, and careful personal grooming, on which Mme d'Epinay's son also remarked. Black suits gave way to embroidered coats, white silk stockings, court shoes, powder, scent, and a sword. Rousseau also resented the way in which his housekeeper, mistress, servant, and future wife Thérèse, usurping his control of his own affairs, was in contact through her own mother and by way of Grimm with Mme d'Epinay. From April 1757 Grimm was with d'Estrées in Westphalia, and Mme d'Epinay saw much more of Rousseau. It was the year of *Le Fils naturel*, of Rousseau's break with Diderot, and of the question whether he should accompany Mme d'Epinay to Geneva. Rousseau did not want to have to leave Sophie d'Houdetot, nor to make it seem that he might be the father of any child Mme d'Epinay might be carrying. He suspected her of being pregnant by Grimm, to whom he wrote a long letter on 26 October, virtually suggesting that it was Grimm's duty to go to Geneva with his mistress. Grimm sent a provisional reply, and then a short but angry definitive letter. Their friendship was over by the end of the month, and any mention of Grimm thereafter intensely annoyed Rousseau, who could not subsequently bring himself to pronounce Grimm's name, particularly because of Grimm's generosity towards Thérèse's mother.

In 1759 Grimm became minister of the town of Frankfurt at Versailles, although he was deprived of that office for criticizing the comte de Broglie in a despatch intercepted by Louis XV. The barony of the Holy Roman Empire was acquired through a German mistress, who paid for it, in 1772. In 1776 Grimm became minister plenipotentiary of Saxe-Gotha at the court of France, but in 1777 left again to spend nearly a year in Russia, seeing Catherine daily. He was appointed a Russian counsellor of state and on his return he was involved in buying paintings and executing confidential commissions for Catherine, taking over what had previously been Diderot's functions. Mme d'Epinay died in 1783, and then, in 1784, Diderot. When the Revolution broke out, Grimm left Paris, stopping at Brussels on his way to Saint Petersburg. Catherine made him Russian minister in Hamburg, where so many of the aristocratic émigrés were settling. On her death he was cared for by Mme d'Epinay's granddaughter, whose dowry Grimm had previously procured from the empress. Grimm finally settled to die, impoverished and bitter, at Gotha at the age of 84, on 19 December 1807.

WORKS

Grimm was much more a man of letters than an author, and he wrote nothing significant for publication. Much that is contained in his newsletters was not originally written by him. He was an endearing, if in some ways slightly comic, highly intelligent observer and recorder of the whole French cultural scene, as viewed from Paris by a German who knew it intimately, was on intimate terms with its liberal reformers, but also was a dashing social climber, luxuriating in such titles, honours, dignities, and confidences as anyone would bestow on him, always careful, often lacking in finesse, but generous as well as shrewd. He was always true to his early vocation, of interpreting the French culture he loved for the peoples of eastern and northern Europe to whose cultures he really belonged. He lacked, but admired, French elegance and delicacy, was happiest with French writing at its most serious, philosophical, and earnest, and never quite penetrated to the aristocratic heights of the French social pyramid. He was not a success at Versailles, and was most at ease in brilliant bourgeois company—Rousseau until the quarrel, Diderot, Mme d'Epinay, and the encyclopédistes (q.v.)—where the glitter even of Helvétius and Holbach was restrained.

His *Petit prophète de Boehmischbroda* is a clever parable, about a Bohemian boy who reports on the lamentable state of French opera, which not even Rameau has been able to restore. Providence sends one last saviour for it to accept, Pergolesi. Grimm was not a stylist, although he was a punctiliously exact writer. The *Petit prophète* is a work of circumstance, but it demonstrates Grimm's real importance, his ability to create a forum in which the phenomena of French cultural, and not just literary or artistic life could be demystified and presented in a way which made issues and attitudes easily intelligible to the non-French. There were other private newsletters, but none had Grimm's skill, standing, and effrontery. It may not be entirely fortuitous that the Mediteranean courts did not feel the need of Grimm's help or information. The English did, although Grimm would not send them his letters.

Grimm was at his best when writing about the philosophes (q.v.), though his personal views and relationships always affect his judgement and it would be unfair, for instance, to take him to task for what he wrote about Rousseau privately—but none the less as the paid purveyor of comment that his addressees might have expected to be reasonably impartial. However, even at the very beginning of his enterprise, and before there was any serious clash with Rousseau about Mme d'Epinay or anything else, Grimm revealingly wrote that Rousseau had spoiled his triumph in the opera debate by the "préface outrée (immoderate preface)" to his "mauvaise comédie (bad comedy)," *Narcisse*. It seems likely that, in that preface, it was the passage about philosophy that irked Grimm:

> Le goût de la philosophie, écrit Rousseau, relâche tous les liens d'estime et de bienveillance qui attachent les hommes à la société... A force de réfléchir sur l'humanité, à force d'observer les hommes, le philosophe apprend à les apprécier selon leur valeur; et il est difficile d'avoir bien de l'affection pour ce qu'on méprise... son mépris pour les autres tourne au profit de son orgueil; son amour-propre augmente en même proportion que son indifférence pour le reste de l'univers. La famille, la patrie, deviennent pour lui des mots vides de sens: il n'est ni parent, ni citoyen, ni homme; il est philosophe

(The taste for philosophy, writes Rousseau, slackens all the bonds of esteem and good will which link human beings to society... By dint of reflecting on humanity, and by dint of observing people, the philosopher learns to appreciate them at their true value; and it is difficult to have affection for what you despise. The philosopher's contempt for others turns to the profit of his own pride; his self-love increases in the same proportion as his contempt for the rest of the world. Family, fatherland become words empty of meaning. The philosopher is neither parent, nor citizen, nor human person: simply a philosopher).

The passage is harsh, but it is well written, clear, and shrewd even if exaggerated into near-caricature. Its rhetoric is effective, and it shows why Grimm and Rousseau could never have been intellectually compatible, even if there had been no Mme d'Epinay and no quarrel. Rousseau could only achieve his immensely radical vision of the human condition by isolating himself from social constraints. Grimm, in spite of the social climbing, the pomposity, and the touch of self-importance, was not going to surrender the individual thinker's participation in the society he might want to reform.

As a cultural observer sympathetic to the encyclopédistes (q.v.) Grimm was naturally also a propagandist as well as an interpreter. He saw in Diderot's dramatic theory an originality whose fecundity was to turn out short of his expectations, and it is difficult not to think that, even in the atmosphere of 1758, he was not exaggerating the importance of Diderot's *Le Père de famille*, whatever its effect in Paris. We know, from the way Grimm later wrote that Diderot would be standing in for him during his absence, that Grimm did not necessarily expect his addressees really to know who Diderot may have been, and we can write off something of the earlier praise in the interests of Grimm's friendship for Diderot and his desire to foster Diderot's aesthetic.

The question must however be asked, even of so radically thoughtful a critic as Grimm, whether or not he had the taste to sustain a properly critical function. Grimm had inaugurated, or at least developed and institutionalized, his own forum in which, on account of its privacy and restricted availability, approximately total honesty and freedom uninhibitedly to convey what he thought were at least possible. The fact that Grimm farmed out to Diderot virtually the whole of the criticism of painting is also important since, for Grimm, reporting about books depended much less on taste than did the selection and judgement of paintings to be described.

The paintings could be described, but the addressees of the letters could not see them. Diderot was eloquent about the moral feelings which did inspire, or which he thought should have inspired, the paintings, but his word had to be taken largely on trust. The addressees could, however, read the books whose ideas were expounded and criticized by Grimm. Since the paintings might in fact be purchased or others from the same painters commissioned by recipients of the letters, the art criticism in the letters filled a radically different function from the literary criticism. Grimm's correspondents wanted to know what new books had been published, and what was thought about them, but they could acquire copies of any books they wanted in their own courts. About the paintings of Greuze, for instance, they wanted a reaction essentially dependent on the aesthetic and moral sensibility of their informant. They could not themselves see the canvases. Grimm certainly had a developed critical ability in the realm of ideas, where his ability could be put to the test, but he did not write about pictures, or much about poetry. Did he also have taste?

That question is normally answered negatively, even before we import the distinction of function between the art criticism of works which could not be seen and the criticism of the written word in books which could be read. Grimm is accused of not bothering about style or form, of lacking finesse, delicacy, and nuance. In fact, Grimm did not really believe in the existence of taste, saying about even Diderot,

Il se fait un modèle idéal composé du beau épars dans la nature, dont il réunit les parties et forme un ensemble auquel il rapporte ensuite ses jugements sur les ouvrages de goût...Cette méthode n'est peut-être la bonne que parce que nous n'avons pas les yeux assez fins pour en saisir l'absurdité. Si nous pouvions aiguiser nos organes à un certain point, nous verrions sans doute que les différentes belles parties dont le statuaire académique a composé sa figure ne pouvaient former un ensemble sans blesser toutes les lois de la nécessité, c'est-à-dire de la beauté, car la nécessité s'appelle tantôt beauté, tantôt laideur, tantôt vice et tantôt vertu

(He creates an ideal model composed of the beautiful scattered throughout nature whose parts he brings together to form a unity, against which he then measures the judgements he makes on works of taste...This is the right method perhaps only because our vision is not sensitive enough for us to grasp its absurdity. If we could sharpen our organs of sight sufficiently, we would doubtless see that the different beautiful parts from which the academic sculptor has fashioned his figure could not form a unity without breaking all the rules of necessity, that is of beauty, because the name of necessity is sometimes beauty, sometimes ugliness, sometimes vice, and sometimes virtue).

Taste is simply the consensus of the more discerning, says Grimm tautologically. There is no fixed ideal or norm of beauty against which things can be judged. Grimm seems scarcely to draw back from the obvious conclusion that there can be no objective basis for taste other than the consensus of the people who can persuade other people that they have it. Groping for firmer ground Grimm revealingly, if inadmissibly, moves away from judgement towards feeling,

Voilà une règle qu'il faut étendre sur tous les grands hommes dont les ouvrages ont obtenu les honneurs de l'immortalité. Si un sentiment intérieur vous en découvre les beautés, si vous êtes vraiment et sincèrement affecté, vous avez le droit de vous associer au petit nombre de ceux dont le suffrage doit fixer le jugement de la postérité

(That is a rule which must be extended to cover all the great creators whose works have achieved the honours of immortality. If an interior feeling reveals its beauties to you, if you are truly and sincerely moved, you have the right to regard yourself as belonging to the small number of those whose approbation ought to determine the judgement of posterity).

Grimm's criterion of taste is no less helpful than most: taste is something you know you have if you are really moved by art which has survived the critical judgements of successive generations. It is a criterion which validates the taste which Grimm had acquired from Ernesti in Leipzig, because it is biased against instant discernment and superficial judgement in favour of the solid good sense which survives time's test.

It is finally as a chronicler and analyst of new thinking that Grimm's philosophically sharp mind interacts most fruitfully with the insights and values of his encyclopédiste friends, whose expression might glitter with surface brilliance but might lack real depth. Grimm was the sympathetic outsider whose criticism they needed, not the hostile defender of established interests. He was also a publicist of genius. What Grimm chiefly did with great brilliance was to purvey intellectual propaganda dressed up as critical analysis as if it were inside information, and to flatter German princelings into the belief that they had direct access to Europe's most advanced cultural centre.

PUBLICATIONS

De historia Imperatoris Maximiliani I, 1747
Lettre sur Omphale, 1752
Petit prophète de Boehmischbroda, 1753
Correspondance littéraire, philosophique et critique adressée à un souverain d'Allemagne, depuis 1770 jusqu'en 1782, 5 vols., 1812
Correspondance littéraire, philosophique et critique adressée à un souverain d'Allemagne, depuis 1753 jusqu'en 1769, 6 vols., 1813
Correspondance littéraire, philosophique et critique adressée à un souverain d'Allemagne, pendant une partie des années 1775–1776 et pendant les années 1782 à 1790 inclusivement, 5 vols., 1813
Supplément à la Correspondance littéraire, 1814
Correspondance littéraire, philosophique et critique par Grimm, Diderot, Raynal, Meister, etc., 16 vols., 1877–82

Biographical and critical studies

Cazes, André, *Grimm et les encyclopédistes*, 1933
Monty, Jeanne R., *La Critique littéraire de Melchior Grimm*, 1961

GUILLERAGUES, Gabriel-Joseph de Lavergne, vicomte de, 1628–1685.

Novelist.

LIFE

Guilleragues was long considered to be the translator, and then suspected of being the author, of the *Lettres portugaises*. His authorship has been generally conceded since the work's appearance in 1962 in the Classiques Garnier series, although the evidence is not absolutely conclusive. What is incontrovertible is only the existence of an entry in the register of privilèges dated 17 November 1668 stating that a privilège had been granted on 28 October 1668 for a book called *Les Valentins lettres portugaises, Epigrammes et Madrigaux* by Guilleraques. Both the *Lettres portugaises traduites en françois* and the *Valantins, questions d'Amour; & autres Pieces Galantes* were published anonymously by Claude Barbin, with achevés d'imprimer respectively of 4 January and 20 August 1669. There is some internal evidence that the two volumes were by the same author, although it is not strong.

The baptismal register of the Bordeaux parish of Saint-André tells us that Guilleragues was born on Saturday, 18 November 1628. His family had owned the estate and seigneurie of Guilleragues since 1528, and after it had been held by four generations of magistrates the estate of Guilleragues was registered as a viscounty. Guilleragues's father, Jacques, inherited his father's post as conseiller at the Bordeaux parlement, and in 1625 married Olive de Mullet, also from a family of Bordeaux magistrates belonging to the minor nobility. Guilleragues was their eldest son. His father died late in 1630 of an infectious disease, no doubt plague, and Guilleragues's mother, who already had a daughter, was left pregnant with Guilleragues's younger brother, of whom we know only that in due course he had a son who carried on the name and title. There was a rented family house in Bordeaux, with a 2,000-volume library whose catalogue has survived, as well as the estate of Guilleragues, near La Réole, about 50 kilometres from Bordeaux on the Toulouse road, where the family had restored the 12th-century château.

Guilleragues was sent to Paris to study at the Collège de Navarre, and must then have read law. By 1650 he was a barrister in Bordeaux. In 1651 the family sold two small houses in Bordeaux. After the release by Mazarin of Condé, Conti, and their sister's husband Longueville, from their imprisonment at Le Havre, they had come to Bordeaux. When Condé went to take command of his troops in Saintonge, Conti was left in charge of Bordeaux, and Guilleragues, recommended by Daniel de Cosnac, future bishop of Valence, became increasingly prominent in his entourage. Both Cosnac's *Mémoires* and Tallemant's *Historiettes* suggest that Guilleragues's life was at this date dissipated, duel- and debt-ridden, and we know that he ran up a bill of 1,232 livres tournois for provisions, a sum so big that it had to be certified before a notary on the afternoon of 1 July 1653.

Saint-Simon tells us that Guilleragues was a gourmand, and Tallemant that he boasted too often about his family. When after Condé's defeat at the Porte Saint-Antoine in May 1652, Conti was declared guilty of lèse-majesté on 13 November 1652 and saw Bordeaux threatened by defeat in the spring of 1653, it was Guilleragues who was charged with the mission to make peace with Mazarin, although he was not granted the necessary passport to leave Bordeaux. At that juncture Gourville arrived, acting for Mazarin. Gourville later declared in his *Mémoires* that Guilleragues, Cosnac, and Sarrazin had advised Conti to have him thrown into the river. It was with Gourville that Conti negotiated the peace of Bordeaux signed on 31 July 1653. Guilleragues and Gourville thereafter formed a friendship which lasted even during Gourville's period of disgrace and exile, before he returned to enter the service of the Condé family.

Guilleragues was not charged with negotiating the marriage between Conti and Mazarin's niece, Anne-Marie Martinozzi, but he was entrusted with making arrangements for Conti's mistress, Mme de Calvimont, and he may have mediated Conti's patronage of the young Molière, with whom Guilleragues later became friendly. Guilleragues and Cosnac did negotiate with Mazarin on Conti's behalf and, after the wedding on 21 February 1654, Guilleragues's political position increased in importance as Conti assumed successively the presidency of the Estates of Languedoc, the government of Guyenne, which he resigned in favour of the duc d'Epernon on 7 November 1659, and finally on 26 February 1660 the government of Languedoc, when Gaston d'Orléans died. Guilleragues was, however, only sporadically close to Conti until Sarrazin's death on 10 December 1654. Whatever his titular position, and the sources do not make it clear, Guilleragues was acting as a steward to Conti by early in 1656, and he had been with him during the campaign of late 1655. He gradually came to oust Cosnac as Conti's principal adviser, as Cosnac was increasingly taken up with his diocese, and with his duties as chaplain to Monsieur.

The Estates had opened at Montpellier on 7 December 1654, to close only on 12 May 1655. They re-opened at Pézenas on 4 November 1655, and Guilleragues was in charge of arranging Conti's amusements. It was the winter of Conti's conversion, when he turned against the theatre, and the Estates lasted until 22 February 1656. Conti spent most of the year in Paris, while Molière's company was waiting for instructions in Bordeaux. Guilleragues was no doubt in Paris with Conti, who rejoined the Italian army of which he had been given charge in succession to Mercoeur on 5 May 1657. On his way through Lyons, after his conversion, Conti withdrew the patronage he had accorded in 1653 to Molière's troupe. Guilleragues was with him and, after the failure of the Italian campaign with the siege of Alexandria, played an important role in Conti's official entry into Bordeaux on 2 June 1658. Conti made his entry by water, and was to bestow various signs of marked favour on Guilleragues, calling on him at his house.

On 19 July 1658 Guilleragues married Marie-Anne de Pontac, daughter of the sieur de Monplaisir, a gentilhomme ordinaire of the king. The dowry was 45,000 livres, and it seems to have been used to buy for Guilleragues the charge of premier président at the Bordeaux Cour des Aides, which brought in about 4,000 livres annually, and will therefore have cost about 80,000 livres. It was to be sold in 1667. Guilleragues's mother gave him two Paris houses, worth about 30,500 livres, and also 2,500 livres annually. The protection of Conti was written into the contract, as part of Guilleragues's contribution to the settlement. In 1659–60 Guilleragues had exchanged two Paris houses which were getting in the way of the king's kitchen extension at the Louvre for the seigneurie of Monségur, probably worth a little less than the houses. Conti was now governor of Languedoc, with Guilleragues now formally charged with dispensing charity on his behalf, as well as arranging for appropriate votes in the Estates of which he kept Colbert apprised and in return for which Colbert allowed him to make navigable the Drot, a tributary of the Garonne useful for irrigating his lands and transporting his wines.

Conti died on 21 February 1666, having left Guilleragues increasingly to stand in for him at the Estates, which were still in session. Guilleragues followed the princess back to Paris and wrote to ask Colbert for a job. It is presumably in connection with his predicament after Conti's death that Guilleragues sold the charge at Bordeaux. In Paris he appears to have been linked with the circle surrounding Mme de Sablé. The Barbin privilège was dated 28 October 1668. During 1669 the *Lettres* and the *Valantins* were published. At the end of that year Guilleragues bought the charge of secrétaire ordinaire de la chambre et du cabinet de Sa Majesté for which the king gave him a brévet d'assurance, ensuring that the value of the office would not drop below 150,000 livres and guaranteeing its value in the eyes of potential lenders of the purchase money.

Guilleragues's mother was to die in 1672. His wife and daughter were living in Bordeaux, and he brought them to visit him in Paris in 1674. Guilleragues was finding it difficult to exercise his land-owning rights in Bordeaux, but does not seem to have done very much about asserting them, and was plainly well established in Paris society, known for his wit, and associating with Mme Scarron, Mme de Lafayette, and Mme de Sévigné. Boileau was to dedicate to him the *Epître V* of 1674, and Guilleragues had been at a reading of *L'Art poétique* in 1673. He had become a channel of royal patronage and if, after 1669, he put behind him his brief literary career, he became a quasi-official correspondent for *La Gazette de France* (q.v.) for which he not only reported from 1675, and perhaps earlier, in a half literary, half political capacity, but whose quasi-official censor he became. Richelieu had already had the *Gazette* overseen by such writers as Bautru, Mézeray, Voiture and La Calprenède, and Mazarin had the unofficial censorship continued. When Eusèbe Renaudot succeeded his grandfather and then his uncle as director on 6 August 1672, Guilleragues was one of two designated "revisors" for both style and content. He continued his work there until the appointment to Constantinople.

There are unmistakable echoes in contemporary gossip of Guilleragues's prodigal expenditure and expensive habits. When in 1675 he sold his office to Louis de Verjus, comte de Crécy, Saint-Simon tells us that it was because he had overspent and needed the money. A letter to Colbert of 24 April 1675 asks for help because the tobacco tax farmers were refusing to honour his "billets" made out in favour of his creditors, documents which then fulfilled much the same function as post-dated cheques do now. Colbert's intervention was required to secure the cash payments necessary to meet the bills as they fell due. Guilleragues had over-extended his credit and his bills were not being honoured. On 22 August 1679, after he had set out for Constantinople, he was obliged to write to Seignelay to protect himself from rumours that he had spent the money given him for ambassadorial purposes in order to liquidate private debts.

It is difficult to tell exactly how much surviving gossip was well founded. It is true that the duc de Nevers was friendly with Conti, but Guilleragues has been persistently associated both with Racine, to whom a letter of 9 June 1684 suggests Guilleragues may have supplied some form of advice relevant to the tragedies, and with the famous sonnet accusing Nevers of morally infamous conduct, written in reply to one originally thought to have been directed against Racine by Nevers after the first night of *Phèdre et Hippolyte* on 1 January 1677. The sonnet attacking Nevers, originally attributed to Racine and Boileau, is now generally supposed to have been written by a group led by Nantouillet, but probably including all or any of Fiesque, Effiat, Manicamp, and Guilleragues. According to Mme de Sévigné, writing to Mme de Grignan on 16 July 1677, Guilleragues certainly did write a satirical parody of a lightweight poem by the pompous, dignified, but not very gifted maître des requêtes Coulanges, set to a tune from Lulli's *Alceste* which Coulanges himself had used, a riposte of the same type as the anti-Nevers sonnet, using elements of an original in the composition of a satirical response. It was apparently at least the second time Guilleragues had been damagingly satirical at Coulanges's expense. La Fontaine also used Guilleragues's name in his support in the course of a satirical verse written during his quarrel with Furetière.

According to Saint-Simon, it was thanks to Mme de Maintenon that in December 1677 Guilleragues was named ambassador at Constantinople. But Scarron's widow's property at Maintenon was not made into a marquisate until 1678, and in 1677 the future Mme de Maintenon was still "la veuve Scarron." According to Guilleragues's somewhat malevolent successor in Constantinople, Bonnac, the post was obtained for him by his two influential friends Seignelay and Bonrepaus, to enable him to pay debts of 36,000 livres and to live at Constantinople on the 16,000 livres provided annually by the Marseilles chamber of commerce. His predecessor, Nointel, had ended up disgraced and reduced to destitution by wildly excessive expenditure which France refused to meet, and by consequent measures taken by Nointel which had strained relationships between Constantinople and Marseilles. Guilleragues, who had the confidence of the king, appeared admirably suited to repair the damage. The Turkish ambassadorship was for commercial reasons an exceedingly important as well as a highly sensitive post, and the Palais de France at Constantinople, residence of the ambassador, is an imposing building.

Guilleragues's departure was delayed, probably as a matter of French diplomatic policy, and in fact he was not paid any considerable sum until the end of May 1679. He left Paris on 19 July 1679, but did not sail from Toulon until 12 September, taking with him his wife, daughter, two Jesuits, and Antoine Galland, future translator of the *Arabian Nights*, on his second mission to buy manuscripts and medals. He arrived early in November, lived almost frugally, paid off Nointel's debts, and discharged his duties in an exemplary fashion, although he had the captain of a galley beaten, as it turned out to death, for speaking ill of the king. He successfully conducted a delicate negotiation over compensation when the French navy bombarded Chios, which was protecting pirate vessels, a number of which the French captain Duquesne had sunk, damaging property on land in the process, including a number of mosques. Guilleragues and his daughter took Greek lessons from Galland, through whom Guilleragues also bought manuscripts and medals for Colbert and then Seignelay. On 28 October 1684 he achieved the honour on which he had been instructed to insist, that he should be granted the "sofa," that is received by the grand vizir on the same level as that on which the vizir was himself seated. Guilleragues did not, however, enjoy the perfumed coffee or the odour of amber. On 26 November he was solemnly received by the sultan.

On 27 February 1685, at Constantinople, Guilleragues had a stroke, of which he died on 4 March, having concluded a number of important and often delicate diplomatic arrangements, including one which is at the origin of the practice of diplomatic bags. Galland dedicated the translation of the *Arabian Nights* to Guilleragues's daughter.

WORKS

The five *Lettres portugaises* anonymously published by Barbin in 1669 purported to have been by a Portuguese nun to a French officer. An unauthorized edition, also of 1669 but printed in Cologne, named the officer as Noël Bouton, chevalier de Chamilly, who had in fact fought in Portugal between 1663 or 1664 and 1668. It also named the translator as Guilleragues. In 1810 it was known that on one old copy the nun had been named in a manuscript addition as Mariana Alcaforada, of the monastery of Beja. There was such a nun, and she had become abbess. Since she had died in 1723 at the age of 87, she was born in 1636, the same year as Chamilly. At the date of the letters they were both about 30. However, even if there was a real Portuguese nun who fell in love around 1665 with a real French officer, and we have both names right, the letters as they stand cannot be authentic. Not only was Maria Alcofarado's mother, spoken of as living, dead before 1665, but the monastery's balcony from which the town of Mertola is supposed to be visible is 55 kilometres away.

Probably more important is the nature of the passion revealed in the letters. It is too vividly similar to the overwhelming and contradictory force which sweeps through Racine's Hermione and threatens the Princesse de Clèves, its depiction far too close to what quite suddenly was being analysed in fiction and tragedy in Paris, for it to have been composed anywhere else, or at any time except during the late 1660s, certainly after the *Questions d'amour* of about 1661 by Marie Linage, and before the first known writings of Mme de Lafayette. The overwhelming probability is that the text of the *Lettres* was composed at about the same time as the *Questions d'amour* of Charlotte Saumaize de Chazan, comtesse de Brégy, and the marquis de Sourdis, possibly in the same milieu, that is in the entourage of Mme de Sablé. On internal evidence Rousseau correctly detected that, whatever the original story out of which the fictional letters were fabricated, they had to have been written by a man, just as the treatment of passion in Racine's tragedies means that they had to have been, and the *Princesse de Clèves*, as a recent editor has pointed out, could not have been. In particular the *Lettres* give all the strength of passion to the woman, who combines complete abandon with intense modesty, and pride with total abjection.

The letters start with the denouement. The writer is in despair at having been abandoned by the love on which she had fastened such hopes. The interest is to be the analysis of passion, not any fictional suspense, and it is immediately concentrated on the apparently incompatible feelings of which the writer is aware. She will never again see the eyes in which such intensity of love was apparent. Her own, deprived now of all light, serve only for weeping at the absence which will soon make her die.

Cependant il me semble que j'ai quelque attachement pour des malheurs dont vous êtes la seule cause: je vous ai destiné ma vie aussitôt que je vous ai vu, et je sens quelque plaisir en vous la sacrifiant

(Yet I seem to cherish some attachment for unhappinesses of which you alone are the cause. I dedicated my life to you the moment I saw you, and I feel some pleasure in sacrificing it to you).

The writer refers to herself as Mariane, addresses herself and her passion in the intimate singular but the lover who has abandoned her with the formal "vous," and uses the familiar vocabulary of destiny and fate, although she avoids the great Racinian abstracts like "flame" and "fire." The interest is in the sheer psychological penetration into the intensity of passion as Mariane tries to understand what is going on inside her. The text is very short, perhaps only eight to nine thousand words, under 30 pages of normal print, and there are pages with half a dozen each of question marks and exclamation marks, although the sentences are generally built up of very carefully constructed periods with complex punctuation and occasional parentheses.

There are commonplaces. Why, the writer wonders, are memories of past happiness now so painful? The best-known expression of that feeling is probably Dante's. The best understanding of the nature of the text is mediated by quoting not its emotional climaxes or exclamations of pain, but the long, carefully built up reproduction of the efforts to understand, like this single sentence from the first letter, in which Mariane speaks of her heart:

> Hélas! votre dernière lettre le réduisit en un étrange état: il eut des mouvements si sensibles qu'il fit, ce semble, des efforts pour se séparer de moi, et pour vous aller trouver; je fus si accablée de toutes ces émotions violentes, que je demeurai plus de trois heures abandonnée de tous mes sens: je me défendis de revenir à une vie que je dois perdre pour vous, puisque je ne puis la conserver pour vous; je revis enfin, malgré moi, la lumière, je me flattais de sentir que je mourais d'amour; et d'ailleurs j'étais bien aise de n'être plus exposé à voir mon coeur déchiré par la douleur de votre absence

> (Alas! your last letter reduced it to a strange state: it reacted with movements so palpable that it made, it seems, efforts to separate itself from me, and go to you; I was so overcome by all these violent emotions that I remained more than three hours bereft of all my senses: I stopped myself from coming back to a life which I must lose for you, since I cannot keep it for you; finally, in spite of myself, I saw the light again, and was glad to feel that I was dying of love; and happy too to be exposed no longer to seeing my heart torn by the pain of your absence).

The author is no doubt exploring how far love's distraughtness can credibly be pushed, as also when, later in the first letter, Mariane cannot understand the need she feels for an increase of her suffering, even discovering a dismay at moments of relief from it; but there is here no mythological force, or reinforcing imagery, as for instance in *Phèdre*, only an intensification of that perceptive psychological analysis of violent emotion which satisfied an imaginative need in the closed and intimate aristocratic society for which the *Lettres* were produced. It is not entirely fortuitous that so many of the writers of this period treated in these pages knew one another, wrote about the same narrow range of experiences, and were anonymously published by Barbin.

The first four of the five letters are not paragraphed, but the emotional pace varies, and is reflected in the syntax.

> Je vous conjure de me dire pourquoi vous vous êtes attaché à m'enchanter comme vous avez fait, puisque vous saviez bien que vous deviez m'abandonner? Et pourquoi avez-vous été si acharné à me rendre malheureuse? que ne me laissiez-vous en repos dans mon cloître? vous avais-je fait quelque injure? Mais je vous demande pardon: je ne vous impute rien; je ne suis pas en état de penser à ma vengeance, et j'accuse seulement la rigueur de mon destin

> (I beg you to tell me why you set out to entrance me as you did, since you knew very well you would abandon me? And why were you so determined to make me unhappy? Why didn't you leave me in peace in my cloister? Had I done you an injury? But I ask your pardon. I blame you for nothing. I am not in any state to think of my vengeance, and I protest only at the harshness of my destiny).

Mariane runs through the whole spectrum of reactions to her predicament, but always with dignity, even in the utter degradation to which her need has reduced her. She protests, despises, challenges, pleads, but never hopes, and can only cherish the pain brought to her by the memories she would not be without. She becomes increasingly aware of the contradictions:

> Je vous ai trahi, je vous en demande pardon. Mais ne me l'accordez pas! Traitez-moi sévèrement

> (I have betrayed you. I ask pardon for it. Don't give it. Treat me severely).

However extraordinary its gestation may yet turn out to have been, as a brief exploration of the psychology of intense passion, the *Lettres portugaises* is the equal of almost any other fictional work produced in 17th-century France.

Les Valentins is a mere game, an organization of salon galanteries already out of date in 1669. The idea is to draw haphazardly the names of an equal number of men and women and double the number of love epigrams, and derive amusement from who is found saying what to whom. It is quite plainly the game of a closed society. This collection breaks its own rules, or the order became disturbed in printing because, of the 64 epigrams, the second of those given to men is clearly to be attributed to a woman, and the 63rd is similarly misplaced the other way round. There is nothing very remarkable about the ironically flirtatious tone of the verse, except a possiby strained praise of the monarch.

PUBLICATIONS

Lettres portugaises, 1669
Valantins, questions d'Amour; & autres Pièces Galantes, 1669
Modern edition, with full introduction and supporting material
Lettres portugaises, edited by F. Deloffre and J. Rougeot, 1962

GUIRLANDE DE JULIE (La).

See Balzac, Bensserade, Chapelain, Malherbe, Voiture, and Préciosité.

In the history of French literature, the content of the *Guirlande de Julie*, a collection of 30 flower paintings and over 60 poems, mostly madrigals and all bearing the names of flowers, is much less significant than the circumstances of its composition. A corporate work, the poetic bouquet was presented to Julie d'Angennes, eldest daughter of the marquise de Rambouillet, on her name day on 22 May 1641, an exquisite volume, bound in red morocco leather with calligraphy by Nicolas Jarry and flower paintings on vellum by Nicolas Robert. Three copies were made, and the poems it contains were subsequently published in the second volume of the *Recueil de Sercy* of 1653. Undistinguished as a collection of poems, it was always much more than that, and has come to epitomize the artistic production associated with the inner circle of those received in the Hôtel de Rambouillet, where interest was always greater in language than in literature.

However, for the quarter of a century preceding the Fronde, the "chambre bleue" of the marquise de Rambouillet was the nursery which can in retrospect be seen to have fostered the principal stems of France's secular literary culture for the middle 50 years of the century, although the Hôtel itself never recovered its active role after the Fronde, and had begun to decline in influence and interest before it. It had been the seedbed of the literature of galanterie, which reflected the refinement of manners, the sophistication of behaviour, and the elegance of wit which the Hôtel promoted, and which was itself to flower into the literature dealing with the analysis of affective states, as well as that concerned with portraits, aphorisms, maxims, or caractères. The chambre bleue nourished the severe neo-classicism deriving from Balzac and Chapelain, as well as the portraits associated with Madeleine de Scudéry, the novels of psychological analysis by Mme de Lafayette, the *Maximes* discussed by La Rochefoucauld in the salon of Mme de Sablé, and the elegance of Foucquet's circle which encouraged the lyrical talents of La Fontaine.

Catherine de Vivonne, not strictly marquise de Rambouillet until 1611, was born in Rome about 1588, the only child of an aristocratic Italian mother, Giulia Savelli—descended from the Strozzis and the Medicis of Florence and a member of one of the four great Roman families, with the Orsinis, the Colonnas, and the Contis—and her second husband, Jean de Vivonne, marquis de Pisani, French ambassador in Rome, whom she had married in Rome on 8 November 1587. The mother, whose first husband, Ludovici Orsini, had been executed in a Venice prison on 27 December 1585 for having Virginia Accoramboni killed six days before, was sent by Henri IV in 1600 to welcome Marie de Medici at Marseilles. That year the contract of marriage had been signed on 27 January between Catherine, who had become a French citizen in 1594 and had 30,000 livres a year, but was not yet 12, and the Vidame du Mans, marquis de Pisani and, from 1611, marquis de Rambouillet.

Much of the information we have about her comes from the letters of Chapelain and Voiture, but most from Tallemant des Réaux, a privileged informant, although not necessarily an entirely impartial one. Although his mother's name was Rambouillet and he married the daughter of a Rambouillet cousin in 1646, he was from a quite different family from that of the marquise, and was probably introduced to the chambre bleue after his return with Retz from Rome at the very end of 1638 by his new friend, Voiture, whom he had met in Rome. Tallemant tells us that the marquise, of whom he became an intimate friend, confided in him how happy her marriage had been but that, if she had not been married before she was 20, she would not have married at all.

The meaning of his "historiette" is disputed, but it appears that the marquise withdrew from court functions at the Louvre during the first decade of the 17th century not, as once was thought, on account of their boisterousness, or, as has also been maintained, on account of her confinements, but because the public nature of the entertainments bored her. It is not unlikely that she found their sycophantic decorum little to her taste. Of her seven children, five girls and two boys, three among the girls became religious. Julie-Lucine, the oldest child and the recipient of the Guirlande, was baptized on 15 June 1607; Claire-Diane, the future abbess of Yerres, was baptized on 3 June 1611 at the age of 16 months; Léon-Pompée, marquis de Pisani, was born in 1615; the Vidame du Mans died of the plague in 1631, aged eight; there were two other daughters who became nuns, Louise-Isabelle, who became titular abbess of Saint-Etienne-de-Reims, and Catherine-Charlotte, who succeeded her elder sister at Yerres; the seventh child and fifth daughter, Angélique-Clarisse, married François-Adhémar de Monteil, comte de Grignan, on 27 April 1658.

Tallemant notes that the marquise "always liked beautiful things," and was about to learn Latin so that she could read Virgil without a translation when she fell ill and thereafter contented herself with Spanish. Her mother tongue was Italian. In 1599 the family acquired on her behalf the old Hôtel du Halde in the Rue Saint-Thomas-du-Louvre, to be demolished in 1604 after a series of law cases had definitively settled the ownership, and replaced by the Hôtel de Rambouillet, where the future marquise de Rambouillet and her husband were installed by 1607. The site is just to the west of the old Louvre, near today's Ministère des Finances, and on the north side of the Cour du Carrousel, next door to the Hôtel de Chevreuse, between the Palais-Royal and the river. The new Hôtel was built according to sketches by the future marquise herself, who was fascinated by the design of buildings, and seems suddenly to have stumbled on the design for her dream house, saying "Quickly, bring me some paper. I've discovered how to do what I want to."

Her solution became common practice in the more palatial buildings of 17th-century Paris. She removed the principal staircase to the side of the structure, so allowing the large rooms to open on to one another in series, through antechambers, doing away with corridors, and permitting very high ceilings with windows opposite one another on facing walls, so that the maximum of light could penetrate into the succession of rooms on to which the staircase gave access through one another on each floor. Instead of the ordinary colouring of red and brown, Mme de Rambouillet changed the dominating colour of the principal room to blue with gold. Louis XIII was to give her husband eight Flemish tapestries, coloured blue on a gold background. The decoration was completed with exquisite furniture.

The Italian-born marquise liked to keep herself warm, but her skin became progressively more sensitive to direct exposure to any source of heat as well as to cold, so she imported from Spain the system of alcoves, to become widely adopted in other salons and famous in the literature of galanterie. They provided shelter from the sun's heat, intensified in summer by the large windows, and from the direct heat of stoves. After fainting one day at Saint-Cloud, she had to give up going out whenever it was hot or cold, and was practically, to her frustration, confined to the house. Her own large and decorative bed with walnut pillars, from which she received, was in an alcove giving on to the antechamber which opened on to the chambre bleue.

The marquise's skin became so sensitive that, in cold weather, she had to keep warm on her bed, with her legs in a bear-skin rug and so many head-coverings that she said she became deaf in the autumn and recovered her hearing at Easter. Her guests had to keep warm in the antechamber. As the marquise grew older the sensitivity of her skin got worse. She suffered greatly from the stove she had to use during an extreme frost, probably in the early weeks of 1658, although she had herself screened from it, as also from the heat of the following summer, though her house was very cool.

The marquis de Rambouillet's distinguished military and court careers and his friendship with Marie de Medici and Concini were crowned in 1614, when Marie de Medici, about to marry Louis XIII to the Spanish infanta, entrusted him with the delicate mission of reconciling France's relationships with Savoy and with Spain. He succeeded in achieving some agreement over Montferrat between the Duke of Savoy and the Spanish governor of Milan, but his relations with Richelieu were never good, although Richelieu sent him to Spain in 1626 to negotiate over the Valtelline, and they became warmer when Rambouillet rallied to Richelieu's support after the "Journée des dupes," 11 November 1630. Rambouillet was thought to have wanted Richelieu's position.

Tallemant says he was obstinate and insisted on administering his own affairs instead of employing competent help, with the result that he ended up spending 30,000 crowns for what should have cost 2,000. He spent much more money than he had, and was eventually obliged to sell his court offices one after the other. He was finally to go blind, and died early in 1652. The beginning of the diminution in the cultural significance of the Hôtel de Rambouillet had already taken place before that. Julie had married Charles de Saint-Maur, marquis de Montauzier, then governor of Saintonge, on 4 July 1645. The marquis de Pisani, her only surviving brother, was killed at Nördlingen on 23 August 1645. Among the verses of condolence which survive are those from Chapelain, Gombauld, Tristan, La Mesnardière, Scudéry, Colletet, and Heinsius. Voiture died in 1648, Angélique Paulet in 1650, and the marquis de Rambouillet himself, aged 75, on 26 February 1652. Although the marquise herself survived until 27 December 1665, the Hôtel's importance as a centre of diplomatic and literary life declined sharply after 1645.

The marquise, bursting with mental energy, curious, lively, pretty, vivacious, intelligent, was always in search of amusement more refined, and company more hand-picked for its intelligence and imagination, than was to be had at the Louvre, literally across the road. She had quite deliberately and by an ample margin created what was physically the smartest drawing room in Paris, in its most elegant new house, on the best site in the town. She set out to attract the witty more than the learned, the aristocracy more than the diplomats, the amusing more than the pedantic. Admission was by right of birth for the higher aristocracy, discerning invitation, or presentation by an existing habitué. There was elaborate, expensive, and cultivated gaiety, but no shadow of misbehaviour. Most striking now are the exceedingly expensive surprises arranged to please people, like the cascade of waterfalls at Rambouillet which workmen toiled at through the night to have ready on the right day, or the loggia later known, after the *Amadis de Gaule*, as "la loge de Zirfée," built secretly behind one of the tapestries in the chambre bleue, sumptuously lit and decorated, "almost as big as a room," and casually revealed one evening when there was a noise behind the tapestry and a superbly dressed Julie was found in the new annexe.

At first, too, there were outings and picnics, sometimes to the large family château at Rambouillet. Several have become famous, like that in 1627 on which the marquise and Cospeau, walking in fields to a favourite spot in which there was a series of boulders, came across a tableau of young nymphs, led by Julie dressed as Diana, with a bow and arrow. The marquise at first pretended to Cospeau, in order to bemuse him, not to see what he was looking at. At a reception in 1630 arranged by Mme du Vigean at the château de la Barre for Charlotte-Marguerite de Montmorency, the princesse de Condé, the party, accompanied by 24 violinists, was walking in the woods when they suddenly came across her daughter, the 11-year-old Anne-Geneviève, later to become Mme de Longueville, waiting for them dressed again as Diana. The evening ended in a ball.

Tallemant has a whole list of the sometimes mildly malicious and often cleverly unkind practical jokes in which the marquise and especially the younger members of her intimate circle indulged (see: Voiture). The comte de Guiche was forced by Mlle Paulet on behalf of the marquise to allow himself to be served a whole series of dishes he was well known to dislike, before being given a sumptuous meal. On another occasion his clothes were taken in so that he thought he was dying from a swelling caused by eating too many mushrooms, until someone remembered that there was an antidote for his ailment, and produced the prescription, a pair of scissors.

It was in this atmosphere of elegance, flair, and malice that foreign diplomats were entertained, that Chapelain's courtship of the marquise was allowed to go no further than the invention of the anagram "Arthénice," that the marquise took sides with Malherbe and, later, Balzac, on such linguistic issues as whether Gomberville's avoidance of the word "car (because)" in *Polexandre* in favour of "pour ce que" was to be applauded or, as Voiture thought, laughed at, that a performance of Théophile de Viau's *Les Amours tragiques de Pyrame et Thisbé* was organized in 1627, and one of Mairet's *Sophonisbe* in 1630, that Chapelain read the first canto of *La Pucelle* in 1637, that Pierre Corneille read *Polyeucte* in 1640, and that Voiture became the supreme entertainer.

There were fads for rondeaux, around 1638 for Cotin's enigmas, or riddles in verse, about 1640 for metamorphoses, as of Julie into a rose by the jealousy of Venus, and for madrigals. The totally frivolous assumption by the habitués of the galant names bestowed them has been misinterpreted as an absurd affectation rather than one of the no doubt silly games through which closed societies invariably indicate membership of the group. In fact, it was rather more than that, suggesting rather an engaging touch of self-parody in a group conscious of the privileged position it had created for itself, and the pretentious cultural ambitions it had conceived. Both socially and culturally the marquise de Rambouillet, for all her sense of fun, could reasonably feel superior to the court, the cardinal, and Richelieu's academy, with those in her circle priding themselves on their own preference for sophistication of wit over pedantry.

Conrart was never especially liked by the marquise, although he was made welcome, and for a moment Cotin seemed likely to eclipse Voiture. The Arnauld family were frequent visitors. Arnauld d'Andilly, in spite of sharing his family's association with Jansenism (q.v.), took it in good part when two or three of the male habitués dressed up as billeting officers and tried to make d'Andilly lodge a number of soldiers. While he expostulated, a trumpet rang out, and Godeau attacked him with a straw lance, while the rest of the party arrived on horseback or in coaches. There were what amounted at first to merely domestic disputes, with the marquise's family, especially her son Pisani, and Guiche, Voiture and the younger habitués signalling the later rise of the partisans of the "modernes" in the Querelle des anciens et des modernes (q.v.).

There was, however, a serious side. To start with the differences were over trivia, with Chapelain and Balzac defending the spelling "muscardin" against "muscadin (fop)" and admiring Ariosto's *Suppositi*, criticized on grounds of taste by Voiture, Julie, and Pisani. Tallemant himself was assiduous at the Hôtel, and among others of literary importance who frequented it were Madeleine and Georges de Scudéry, Sarrazin, Godeau, the marquise de Sablé—still with liaisons in store and not yet dedicated to the piety and hypochondria which took her later to live at Port-Royal (q.v.)—Gombauld, Segrais, Saint-Amant, Malleville, and Vaugelas. Ménage paid an annual visit on Shrove Tuesday. Of less literary importance, although of high entertainment value, was Angélique Paulet, the singer known as the lioness for her red mane, her roar, and no doubt her redoubtably fierce reputation. Soon after 1638 there was also a close association with the Condés.

Although the marquise de Rambouillet quite passionately disliked Louis XIII, and although her husband had been compromised by his earlier fidelity to Marie de Medici, bridges to Richelieu were kept open through Mme du Vigean, whose great passions were first Mme de Puisieux, and then the cardinal's favourite niece, Mme de Combalet duchesse d'Aiguillon. "Madame la Princesse," the mistress of cardinal de la Valette, the mother of Condé and of the future Mme de Longueville, was a frequent visitor to the Hôtel de Rambouillet and the best friend of the marquise, so that by the mid-1640s there was a close social relationship between the Bourbon-Condés and the Rambouillets, with the great ladies of each family friendly with Richelieu's niece and heir. What was left of the once united company which had frequented the Hôtel was split into factions by the Fronde. Montauzier and Julie were firmly opposed to the Condé party, although Julie and Mme de Longueville, 12 years younger, had once been close friends.

Julie does appear to have been likeable as well as beautiful when young, although Tallemant tries hard not to give that impression, and her later reputation was of a grasping, imperious, malevolent creature, devoted to intrigue, for whom no one had a good word. Voiture made her the object of his galanteries, and once went too far by kissing her arm. Montauzier, Voiture, and one of the Arnaulds, probably the maître de camp, sang her praises. It is possible that Chavaroche and Chaudebonne were in love with her. In fact Jul 's destined husband was Hector Montauzier, killed in the Valtelline campaign on 19 July 1635. His younger brother, still called the marquis de Salles, had been one of the first to call to offer condolences on the death of Julie's youngest brother, the Vidame du Mans, in 1631, and on his own brother's death had inherited his title and his position as Julie's expected future husband. It is certain that the courtship was conducted without much romantic involvement, indeed none at all on the part of the bride, who is often said finally to have married Montauzier merely to please her mother and prolong her active social life. Balzac in a letter to Chapelain seemed quite surprised at the news of the marriage.

We first hear of the *Guirlande* in a letter by Chapelain of 9 September 1633. His own contribution was modelled on one of those in a similar Italian collection of 1595, the *Ghirlanda della contessa Angela-Bianca Beccaria*. Those contributed by Scudéry were published by him in 1635. The probability is that the *Guirlande* was gathered together as a present from Montauzier to Julie for 1 January 1634, while his brother was still alive, but was then magnificently calligraphed on superb paper, with the illustrations on vellum, perhaps in an augmented version, for Julie's name day in 1641. The authors of the poems, each bearing the name of a flower, included her future husband with 16 pieces, Scudéry, Chapelain, Malleville, d'Andilly, Cerisy, Godeau, Colletet, Desmarets, and Gombauld.

Since a quarter of the madrigals were written by Montauzier, it is not surprising that the average poetic quality of the *Guirlande* entries is weak. The attributions are not all certain, but there is a "hyacinth" quatrain of disconcerting flatness, normally thought to have been written by Conrart, who ought to have been capable of better. Philippe Habert, one of five brothers, all well known in galant society, was in the artillery and was killed in an explosion in 1637. His 1633 *Temple de la Mort* was much admired and put forward in the Querelle des anciens et des modernes as better than anything Virgil ever wrote. Here is his marigold quatrain from the *Guirlande*, with its "pour ceux que," a probable allusion to the "pour ce que" dispute:

Ne pouvant vous donner ni sceptre ni couronne,
Ni ce qui peut flatter les coeurs ambitieux,
Recevez ce SOUCY, qu'aujourd'hui je vous donne,
Pour ceux que tous les jours me donnent vos beaux yeux

(Not being able to give you sceptre or crown,/Or what could satisfy ambitious desires,/Receive this MARIGOLD [in French, also "care"] which I give you today,/In exchange for those which your beautiful eyes daily give me).

After her marriage Julie devoted herself to court intrigue. The barony of Montauzier became a marquisate in 1644, and it was on account of Julie's political services that in August 1644 Louis erected it into a dukedom, which conferred on her the privilege of the tabouret, allowing her to remain seated before the queen. Her husband retained considerable political importance as governor of Normandy, but also as strong protector of the "modernes" in the Querelle, although, perhaps stung by Voiture's jealousy at his role as Julie's husband designate, he had, before his marriage, always sided with the conservative "anticorps" led by Chapelain among the literary figures at the Hôtel de Rambouillet (see: Voiture).

It is arguable that the informal group round Conrart, turned by Richelieu into the Académie française, was a less effective instrument for introducing even Malherbe's linguistic reforms than was the Hôtel de Rambouillet, whose civilizing influence on French cultural life was immeasurable, and whose influence on the development of the peculiarly aristocratic mainstream literature of 17th-century France was, at least until the 1680s, much more significant than that of the Académie. It was however merely a private forum whose cultural power was necessarily ephemeral, and whose effectiveness was exercised through its ability to create and impose fashions in behaviour as well as in linguistic usage. France needed and produced cultural institutions, but the contribution of the amateur enthusiasms of the Hôtel de Rambouillet to the creation in France of a lively literary tradition should not be under-estimated. The cultural refinement it inspired was the result of the judicious mingling of those members of the aristocracy who came because they found the atmosphere congenial, with writers who were mostly welcomed because they cared about either linguistic usage or literary style.

Underneath the froth, the fun, and the exclusiveness, there was a consciousness of a serious cultural mission deliberately fostered by the marquise, and effectively pursued under her direction. She never wrote a word for publication in any form, but she is one of the outstanding figures in the linguistic, literary, and above all cultural life of 17th-century France. The *Guirlande* itself, although often treated by literary historians as a collection of poems, is much more than that. It was a genuine tribute from Montauzier, a notoriously prickly grand seigneur who wrote almost a quarter of the poems, to his future wife; it was a work of craftsmanship whose calligraphy, illustrations, and binding were more impressive than its literary content; and it epitomized in all its aspects, including the social circumstances in which it was produced by the habitués of the Hôtel, the aspiration towards a refinement in taste, attitudes, and values in which it already constitutes a peak.

PUBLICATION

Recueil de Sercy, vol. 2, 1653; modern edition (A. van Bever) 1907.
Livet, Charles, *Précieux et Précieuses*, 1865

H

HARDY, Alexandre, ?1572–1632.

Dramatist.

Life

Hardy might reasonably be called France's first professional playwright. He was the author of some 600 plays, and easily the most historically important dramatist whose career spanned the period lasting from the retirement from the stage of Montchrestien to the generation of Racan and Théophile and of Malherbe's reform. His active life as a dramatist took French theatre to the moment at which tragedies, no doubt more for their own imaginative purposes than on account of any external pressures, adopted the observance of the dramatic unities as normative practice.

For the literary and associated social history of the French theatre Hardy is therefore of outstanding importance, although the literary quality of his work has not on the whole been highly regarded. However, apart from a late 19th-century German edition (5 volumes, 1883–84), none of the plays was reprinted between 1628 and the 1957 edition of the anonymously published comedy *Les Ramoneurs* and the 1975 publication of two verse tragedies and a verse tragi-comedy in the first volume of the *Théâtre du XVIIe siècle* in the Bibliothèque de la Pléiade. It seems certain that renewed critical discussion will lead to a re-evaluation.

Hardy signed himself "Parisien." In the dedication of the 1623 edition of *Théagène et Cariclée*, presumably written before the privilège, which is dated 8 October 1622, Hardy said that he had been writing for 30 years. It is therefore generally admitted as likely that he started to write plays when he was about 20 in about 1592, and that he was born in Paris. He certainly knew Latin and had a wide humanist culture, showing familiarity among the Latins with Virgil, Tibullus, Ovid, Seneca, Martial, Quintus Curtius, and Claudian, and among the Greeks, all available in Latin translation, with Euripides, Xenophon, Pausanias, Josephus, Plutarch, Lucian, and Heliodorus. Hardy knew also the work of Montemayor, Boccaccio, and Ronsard. Stanzas in Latin and Greek were addressed to him. The probability therefore is that his background was educated and affluent. In his 1628 *La Berne des deux rimeurs de l'Hostel de Bourgogne*, Hardy defends himself against the imputation of lowly social origins, claiming at least equality of birth with his two bourgeois opponents, "ces avortons des Muses (those miserable runts of the Muses)." He may well have come from a family of lettered courtiers or from the magistracy. It was not uncommon for members of such families to take some interest in theatre, or even before 1600 to write rhetorical declamatory tragedy for humanist pedagogical purposes.

Hardy, probably not quite ten years Shakespeare's junior, is likely to have been the first Frenchman with a humanist education to dedicate himself totally to a professional career among plays and players. He must early have discovered in himself a gift for fluent versification, but he must also have been an actor. There is a notaried act of 1611 signed by him in his capacity as "comédien ordinaire du roi (royal actor by appointment)" and another of 29 August 1626 in which, signing himself "poète ordinaire du roi (royal poet by appointment)," Hardy had the document emended to have his name placed above that of the troupe's principal actor.

The Confrérie de la Passion continued to exercise its monopoly rights in Paris until 28 November 1598, when the parlement prohibited the performance of all mysteries, in spite of a royal authorization of the preceding year and although from 17 November 1548 the Confrérie had already been restricted to "mistères profanes, honnêtes et licites (secular, decent, and legitimate mysteries)." There was only one public theatre in Paris, the Hôtel de Bourgogne, a long narrow room with rising tiers of benches at one end and boxes along the sides, with the pit running only half the length of the room. It was occasionally leased out by the Confrérie, mostly to provincial companies and to visiting Italian troupes, chiefly concerned to entertain the court, but there is no sign that it was used at all from 1588 to 1596. Tragedy was being developed as a pedagogical exercise in the colleges. From 1595 visiting companies were also allowed to play at the winter and summer fairs of Saint-Germain and Saint-Laurent, but offered either biblical tragedy, morality and mystery plays, or pantomime, farce, satire, and parody, perhaps stretching now and then to comedy.

One fairground company, managed by Agnan Sarat and led by Valleran le Conte, profited from the 1595 edict but immediately moved on from the spring fair to the Hôtel d'Argent where, on payment of a levy to the Confrérie, it was allowed to remain. In the preceding years the troupe has been traced in Bordeaux, Rouen, Frankfurt, Strasbourg, Langres, and Metz, and it seems to have played a biblical repertoire of Garnier, Desmasures, and Bèze. Seasons were sporadic, but the leading lady of this company is the first French actress to be known by name, Marie Venier, and it is the first troupe to have had a resident playwright, Hardy. The company settled briefly in the Hôtel de Bourgogne as the "Comédiens du roi." A rival company under Charles Lenoir competed in other Paris locations, but provincial centres were of equal importance, and Rouen was at least as interesting as Paris for dramatic performances. Twice as many dramatic texts were published there as were published in Paris. The Corneille brothers came from Rouen, and Molière's troupe was to play there while looking for a home in Paris.

It was outside Paris that tragedy, tragi-comedy, pastoral, and comedy began to oust the medieval genres, the farces, epics, moralities and mysteries. There was no absolute distinction of genres, but irregular tragedy began to grow up alongside the regular tragedy of the colleges, and to replace biblical theatre and medieval mysteries. During the period 1580–1600, of 34 known performances, 23 were of "tragedies", three of "tragi-comedies", seven of "comedies" and one of a "pastoral". By the end of the 16th century there were semi-professional and then professional players in France, of whom Hardy must have been one, joining from a bourgeois background the players who had risen from the fairground like Bruscambille, Jean Farine, and the trio Turlupin, Gaultier-Garguille, and Gros-Guillaume.

In 1592, when there was no permanent live theatre in Paris, Hardy must have left the capital to start on his theatrical career. It is no more than an educated guess, or perhaps a reasonable conjecture from the tone and content of *La Berne*, that Hardy broke with his family to follow a troupe of itinerant players. Tallemant is withering about the reputations of such companies for moral laxity. We know of three or four, and there are clear if slender indications that Hardy started not with Valleran Le Conte or with Charles Chautron but with Adrien Talmy. What is quite clear, apart from the insecurity and poverty of his beginnings, was the boldness with which he embraced the new genres—irregular tragedy, pastoral, tragi-comedy, and probably comedy—when, with a reputation for writing in the newly popular genres already established, he became a salaried writer, perhaps around 1598, and probably for the Valleran Le Conte company, which amalgamated with the troupe of Adrien Talmy on 16 March 1598.

The joint company is known to have played in Paris, but not at the Hôtel de Bourgogne, from 1598, before Adrien Talmy's troupe split off again. Valleran Le Conte formed an association with the troupe of Benoist Petit, which was virtually bankrupt, taking the Hôtel de Bourgogne from January 1599. The Le Conte company had been in Bordeaux for part of the preceding year, but was to stay in Paris, playing Hardy, for 13 months from January 1599. On 25 February 1600 Le Conte, exceedingly short of money, formed a new association with a visiting Italian company which had seriously pushed down his own box office takings. The new amalgamation did not last. By 17 May 1600 Le Conte, who had dropped Hardy, was hiring another hall, but not for Hardy's material. The conservative Paris public preferred farce and commedia dell'arte. The Hôtel de Bourgogne was empty.

At this point there was a further re-organization. Valleran Le Conte and Hardy left again together for the provinces and seem unlikely to have been in Paris between 1601 and December 1605, by which time the team existed in the form not of a troupe to share the takings, but as a company run by a manager with a small handful of hired professional actors, an apprentice or two, and Hardy as playwright. Bankruptcy was never far away. Costumes and instruments had to be sold; wages, rent, and bills went unpaid; and the company had again to leave Paris for a year.

They were back by May 1607, at Bordeaux in June and July, and Hardy appears to have called at Fontenay-le-Comte on Nicolas Rapin, for whom he wrote an elegy. From this date we know in some detail who were members of the company. After performances elsewhere in Paris during September, the company was back at the Hôtel de Bourgogne in October 1607. Again, however, Paris showed no appetite for Hardy's pastorals and tragedies. Valleran Le Conte remained steadfast and, when some of the troupe's best actors gave notice, he founded a new company to play Hardy's material, engaging himself for a year from Lent 1608. Receipts fell off, however, and Le Conte with

Hardy disappeared from Paris. The Hôtel de Bourgogne was let occasionally to other troupes during 1608. When Valleran Le Conte reappeared in 1609 he established what has been referred to as France's first school of drama. There were at least five apprentices, three of them female, with properly witnessed contracts. Hardy represented a branch of theatre in which acting could be regarded as a respectable professional activity. Hardy's role was to provide the material for a new, loftier concept of drama, conducted in an ambiance quite different from that of the troupes of strolling players.

In April 1609 Valleran Le Conte needed a guarantor for the new lease of the Hôtel, to run from that September until Lent 1610. In August the theatre was let to another company, which moved out in September and became rivals of the Le Conte troupe before amalgamating with it in January 1610 to play Hardy's tragedies, tragi-comedies, and pastorals at the Hôtel de Bourgogne until Passion Sunday. Financial constraints forced the amalgamated company to slim down, and it played in a different Paris location briefly in April–May 1610, and then from 19 July to the end of the 1611 carnival. The summer of 1610 was probably spent at Senlis and Orléans. Meanwhile the financial situation remained desperate, with bills for food and accommodation unpaid, theatrical costumes sold and seized, and patrons persuaded to help out. When Valleran's sister, Marguerite, died, a patron had to be found to pay for the funeral.

Three of the company gave up, and bought themselves out of the troupe, but Le Conte continued to struggle, still supporting Hardy's elevated concept of theatre, and from 21 February 1611 the Hôtel de Bourgogne was again taken for a disastrous few weeks. One of Le Conte's main lenders insisted on a formal legal admission of liability for a debt of 1,266 livres tournois. Other actors left, and the troupe dissolved. Another company was formed, with ten members, to play at the Hôtel for the season 1611–12. The right to sell the boxes was sold off, with the company guaranteeing to play three times a week, and the lessee to charge for seated places at least twice the price of tickets for the parterre. The expedient of selling space en bloc was born of financial despair. Hardy himself, to help out, took again to acting as well as writing for the company.

The public still stayed away. To make matters worse, a visiting Italian troupe under Jehan Paul Alfieri came to Paris early in 1612. Valleran Le Conte agreed to share the stage with them, with each company giving a play at each performance. There was brief success, but then more poor houses. The Italians left Paris, and in 1612 Valleran Le Conte's company dissolved again, this time to be reconstituted uniquely with young players, including two women trained by Le Conte, and Guillaume des Gilberts, later to be known as Montdory. He also was a former pupil, in 1612 allocated a half-share in the Le Conte company. The troupe left Paris and became a touring company. It is known to have been at Leiden and The Hague in 1613, and appears to have played virtually nothing except Hardy. The two women left, probably to marry. Some of company joined other troupes. Montdory returned to Paris with the players of the Prince of Orange. Antoine Cossart founded his own troupe. Le Conte seems to have died, and the management of the company was taken over by Pierre le Messier, "Bellerose," as he became known, one of Le Conte's early pupils and associated with his company in early 1610. He re-engaged Hardy, signing a contract with him in Marseilles in 1620.

Hardy's contract stipulated a simple sale of the copyright. He lost all right to publish his own material, whereas soon now authors would regain the right to publish, generally at the end of the first run of a play. From about 1620 Hardy seems to have been having much greater success, but the company returned to Paris in 1622 too late to profit from the intervening vogue for material of the type Hardy had been supplying and which the provinces had enthusiastically welcomed. The centre of activity had moved from Rouen to Paris. The major Paris troupe had changed a great deal from 1612 to 1622 while Hardy had been in the provinces, and in 1622 there was an immediate desire for amalgamation, each company wanting Hardy's material. The troupes were united and played at the Hôtel de Bourgogne, although the Hôtel was also hired out to others.

Each of the four troupes in Paris in 1624, the Comédiens du roi with whom Le Messier and Hardy had amalgamated, the troupe under Charles Husson with Montdory, that under Estienne de Ruffin, and the Comédiens du Prince d'Orange, managed by Charles Lenoir, also toured the provinces. Some of the principal actors had two stage names: Robert Guérin was Gros-Guillaume for farce and La Fleur for tragedy, Hugues Guéru was Gaultier-Garguille and Fléchelles, Henri le Grand was Turlupin and Belleville. Hardy himself had become eager for publication, but Bellerose did not want to let go of the copyright. Publication would put the Hardy plays in the public domain, and they had become too valuable.

Manuscript copies had circulated, and unauthorized performances had been given. Booksellers had been passing off as Hardy's the work of others, and had even published lightly altered versions of Hardy's own text. Perhaps as a result of the 1620 Marseilles contract, of which we have no copy, Hardy did get some understanding about the right at a later date to publish some of his own work. Quesnel at any rate printed in 1623, with a privilège of 8 October 1622, *Théagène et Cariclée*, in which Hardy had turned Heliodorus's novel into eight "days" or five-act tragi-comedies. Quesnel also printed three volumes of the five-volume 1624–28 edition of the *Oeuvres*. We know only that most of the contents of the first three volumes were not less than a decade old when they were published, and that Hardy had written 300 plays before *Théagène*, which probably dates from 1612. Although Hardy appears badly to have needed the income from the company which his plays brought him, the titular sum for each, if he received it, has been calculated as a very reasonable 100 livres tournois a play. Over half a century later, when writing for the theatre was much more highly rewarded, Quinault was accepting 150 livres for a play.

From some period before 1620 Hardy was no longer without a reasonable middle-class income, comparable to more than twice that of a leading actor. We know that he married only because, after his death, his widow was active in pursuing copyright fees, but we do not know when he married, whom, or if they had any children. The history of the publication of Hardy's plays has had to be reconstructed conjecturally, but it is clear that from 1620 he increasingly felt that he should be allowed to profit from the publication of the plays he had sold to the company, that he from time to time exacted concessions from Bellerose which did allow him to publish specified pieces, and that in the end the issue soured relationships with Bellerose to the point that Hardy left the company. It is clear from documents which still exist that Hardy's copyright had become valuable, that the performance of his material by rival companies was damaging Bellerose's commercial prospects, but that the whole system was changing, and other authors were beginning to sell monopoly rights to their material for only limited periods.

The first volume of Hardy's *Théâtre* appeared in 1624 with a privilège of 16 March, the second in 1625, with a privilège of 28 May 1625 and the third volume, using the same privilège, was at press before the end of 1625. Quesnel paid Hardy 180 livres tournois for the 12 plays of the second and third volumes together. In 1626, with the third volume, the first volume was also reprinted, but Hardy gave the fourth volume to David du Petit Val "imprimeur du Roy à Rouen" with a privilège of 26 June 1626. An "au lecteur" attacks Quesnel, whose workmanship "had made him blush." In the meanwhile there had been other difficulties. Bellerose and his troupe were in 1625 playing in the Hôtel de Bourgogne and wanted to renew their lease there, but the Confrérie gave the lease to the Prince of Orange's troupe under Lenoir. Bellerose's company played in the street immediately outside, and the resulting riot forced the lieutenant civil on 14 August 1625 to forbid them to continue to play in the street. Lenoir started to entice players away from Bellerose, who had already lost some of his best to Estienne de Ruffin. Bellerose took out his fury on Hardy, who sought permission to publish yet more of his material, thereby putting it at the disposition of the rival companies, both of which were now daily playing Hardy's material.

In the autumn of 1626 Hardy left Bellerose and the Comédiens du roi for a company formed for two years on 10 April 1624 under Husson and Montdory. In the summer of 1626 their players, back in Paris, formed a new company, the Vieux comédiens du roi, under one of their number, Claude Deschamps, sieur de Villiers. Hardy gave them a first play on 15 November 1626 and a second on 5 January 1627, signing a formal agreement in which he retained the title "poète du roi" which he is first known to have used in 1622. He promised six plays annually for six years and not to supply any material elsewhere, in exchange not for a fixed sum but for a share in the box office takings, an arrangement previously thought to have dated only from 1653. Hardy's share was to be delivered to his house, the official address of the leaders of the troupe. He did not need to attend performances or to go on tour. He probably stayed in Paris when the company left to tour in February 1627. His rights were protected in the case of any further amalgamation, and no change was to be allowed in his text, a stipulation which suggests that there had been friction with Bellerose about unauthorized modifications. Reconstituted, the new company would later in the century become the Théâtre du Marais.

Hardy had in fact made his income much more erratic, as well as smaller, and he had moved away from the Comédiens du roi, now almost permanently settled at the Hôtel de Bourgogne, who were establishing themselves at the centre of the capital's theatrical life. They ceased to play Hardy and found replacement suppliers of tragedies, pastorals, and tragi-comedies. The number and importance of the authors publishing congratulatory material at the head of Hardy's works dwindled dramatically, from over a dozen in his first two volumes to reach zero, and by the end of the decade Hardy's own productive fluency seems to have been diminishing. He was becoming bitter.

The "au lecteur" of the fifth volume, which appeared not in Rouen but in Paris, contains a diatribe against two young lawyers, Pierre du Ryer and Auvray, who were successfully replacing him, alongside the more committed professionals. The ensuing controversy makes clear that a whole group of young dramatists was now turning against his style of dramatic writing and adopting the linguistic purism of Malherbe. Unfortunately, Du Ryer and Auvray have more to say in the *Lettres à Poliarque et Damon sur les médisances de l'auteur du Théâtre* about Hardy's prickly personality, his traits, and his background, than about their own dramatic philosophy. Hardy replied in *La Berne des deux rimeurs de l'Hostel de Bourgogne* of 1628, but he was himself now clearly out of date. A younger generation was rejecting his models, Seneca, Ovid, Martial, Tibullus, Ronsard, and Garnier.

Nothing is known of Hardy's last years, and no play subsequent to 1628 has survived. There is one report that he died of the plague. His death must certainly have taken place in 1632, although we do not know where, or on what date. His widow continued in vain to try to get back the copyright of the plays in Bellerose's archives.

Works

The evidence we have suggests it is reasonable to assume that Hardy wrote about 600 plays, perhaps a dozen or so more. He boasted of one pastoral that it took him a fortnight, so his plays presumably needed on average longer to write, but it is generally assumed that, to fit in with the known figures, he must have turned out around 20 plays a year for well over 30 years. Only the 34 published during his lifetime, including *Théagène* as one, have survived, and we know the titles of 13 more. Fourteen can be roughly dated. Of the 34, twelve are called tragedies, 14 tragi-comedies, three "poèmes dramatiques," and five pastorals.

However, there are eight notarized contracts in which "comedies" appear with other named dramatic genres in connection with Le Conte's company, and it is virtually certain that, especially at the beginning of his career, from which period nothing at all has survived, Hardy was writing comedies, if not occasional farces, referred to as "autres jeux (other plays)." The notarized documents are punctiliously precise, and *Le Jalloux* of 1625 was referred to as "une comedie" in a receipt of 19 September 1625. Exactly a week later, in exchange for permission to publish certain named plays, Hardy agreed to deliver to Le Messier (Bellerose) a *Meliandre; ou, Le Ravissement volontaire*. A play about a voluntary abduction seems likely to have been a comedy.

Each of the five volumes in the *Théâtre* contains not more than eight and not fewer than six five-act plays, ends with a pastoral, and contains no comedies. Much remains in the early renaissance style, with tragedies modelled on Garnier, violent action, including rape, on the stage, and with no worries about the unities. Sometimes the action takes place within 24 hours and sometimes it lasts a month or more. Among the traditional features of renaissance tragedy, Hardy, still relatively conservative, keeps the five-act division, messengers, ghosts, dreams, and choruses, singing sometimes in lyrical metres and sometimes in alexandrines. Choruses are not always used. The subjects draw on Hardy's wide reading, but above all on Plutarch, the antique historians, and historical compilations. In some plays the setting is important. Hardy is often referred to as a poor poet but an excellent playwright, and his texts must have been demanding to deliver from the stage. As printed, the complexity of their syntax makes it time-consuming to decipher the meaning of many of the sentences.

What is new is the dramatic note. The characters interact and struggle with their fates rather than use a series of tirades to lament, despair, or rebel. In tragedy the clash is transferred to the struggle between human personalities, not between a character and fate, as formerly, and not yet between conflicting emotions within the same character. Attention is concentrated on actions rather than emotions, but the feelings which inspire the characters do notably include love as well as honour, patriotism, vengeance, and admiration. The tragi-comedies, whose proportion in the total output appears to increase with time, share the imaginative effort of the period to upgrade the moral status of instinctive human behaviour, as in the early sentimental novels, the *Astrée*, and in tragi-comedy generally, while having recourse to monstrously improbable plots. In a plot borrowed from Montemayor for *Félismène*, a girl in travesty follows her unfaithful lover to Germany, becomes his page, and re-conquers his love.

The first volume of the Bibliothèque de la Pléiade *Théâtre du XVIIe siècle* prints three Hardy plays. The first, *Scédase; ou, L'Hospitalité violée,* is a tragedy from the first volume of the *Théâtre*, probably written before 1610. The source is a few lines from Plutarch about the struggle between Thebes and Sparta, but with the accent taken by Hardy away from the political towards the purely human emotions. The play is in alexandrines, except for the single chorus in octosyllables. The simple country-dwelling Boeotian Scédase has two beautiful daughters who, to help their father, receive two Spartans who fall in love, rape, and murder them, throwing their bodies into a well. Their father returns, complains, fails to get justice in Sparta, returns, and immolates himself on his daughters' tombs. The first act starts with a monologue by the king of Sparta, lamenting a little sententiously the decline in the city's moral standards and therefore also in its political influence.

Charilas and Euribiade, young Spartans, come on to the stage with the old man Iphicrate, who has a foreboding about the ardours the youths express for Scédase's daughters. The second act opens with Scédase and his daughters, Evexipe and Théane. Scédase, also portentously reflecting on the order of the cosmos, announces his imminent departure for three days and admonishes his daughters to virtue. When he goes off, Charilas, Euribiade, and Iphicrate come in. The language is not only high-style, but the mode of speech, particularly of Iphicrate, presupposes at least an educated knowledge of antique mythology as well as renaissance rhetoric, with its peculiar use of such inverted paradoxes as a lion fleeing a hare in fear, for which the editor rightly supposes that a modern reader is likely to need notes. The Sirens, for instance, become periphrastically the "daughters of Achellois." Iphicrate comments to the audience on the psychology of the embarrassment caused to Evexipe and Théane by the compliments of Euribiade and Charilas.

The first two acts had had two scenes each. The third has one. Iphicrate is on stage with the two women and the young men, but the dialogue presupposes that Charilas and Euribiade can plot together unheard by the others, who presumably step forward when it is their turn to speak, with those supposed to be hearing what is said remaining in the light. Iphicrate is clearly presumed absent after his brief intervention and, after more discussion, Charilas propositions the women. Marriage is half-promised, although the social differences as well as the circumstances make the offer unrealistic.

The women resist, refuse, are raped, cry out, and are killed, all on stage, although presumably on a darkened part of it, so that the audience can hear the text but not see the action. It is possible that Hardy was already using different booths whose interiors were opened and closed by curtains to reveal different settings as the action moved its geographical location, but the characters in play at any given moment occupied the centre of the stage. In the fourth act Scédase returns with three neighbours, but cannot get his daughters to answer the door, and various fears about their fate are expressed. Ponocrate, one of the neighbours, remembers that Euribiade had been detained at Scédase's house by illness, that there had been a message for Scédase which had delayed the departure of Euribiade and Charilas that the two women had seemed shocked at something that had been said, that the old man had gone off, that his own horses had whinnied. Then Ponocrate finds the two bodies in a well. There is stylized lamentation, and Ponocrate needs help to get the bodies out.

In act V, Agésilas, another king of Sparta, refuses to send after the two murderers who may, after all be innocent. Three Spartan judges, Androclide, Léonide, and Xantippe, explain to Scédase that he must find the criminals and prove their guilt before the authorities can act, and the slightest false accusation is of course punishable by death. Scédase's other two neighbours, Evandre and Phorbante, give evidence. The Spartan judges have Scédase thrown out. The chorus laments and moralizes as Scédase kills himself on his daughters' tomb, reproaching Evandre with not preventing him. The last two dozen lines of the play are Evandre's reply, starting

> Simples, ne présumez que ce ne fût un crime
> De vouloir s'opposer à ce coup magnanime;
> Veuf, sans aucun soulas, en l'arrière-saison,
> L'âme n'a que bien fait de rompre sa prison.
> Depuis que le malheur étouffe l'espérance,
> L'homme doit courageux se tirer de souffrance;…

(Simple folk, do not suppose that it would not have been a crime to want to oppose this noble act. Widowed, with no consolation, in the autumn of life, his soul only acted well in breaking out of its prison. When grief has smothered hope, we must bravely put an end to our suffering…).

The on-stage violence may well have been a function of the lighting arrangements and the indication of décor, indicating more the desire to intensify the audience's emotional reaction than to breach any rules of taste. But there are two young Spartans, two daughters, two kings of Sparta, three judges and three neighbours, when one of each would have been adequate for the plot. Presumably the audience wanted something less minimalist. In time the action must have covered weeks, but it concentrates on the preparation for one deed, its execution, and its aftermath. It is an emotional tragedy based on the interplay of perfectly plausible, if histrionically intensified, human emotions.

La Force du sang, later than 1615, is a tragi-comédie based on Cervantes, chosen for the Bibliothèque de la Pléiade volume as exemplifying another way in which Hardy treats the dual themes of rape and social inequality. In *La Force du sang*, the guilt of the rape is resolved by a subsequent marriage which overcomes the social gulf, as if to show that the ravages caused by instinctive love can not only be put right, but can lead to the conquest of social disparities. It is difficult to imagine how this tragi-

comedy can have been played without conventions admitting instantaneous changes of time and location in mid-act, with no one scene taking up all the playing space. Action which the audience was to see must have taken place in centre stage, with a token indication of place revealed, perhaps, by the uncovering of a booth. Act III takes place with scenes separated by some hundreds of kilometres and about ten years.

In the first scene the principal woman, Léocadie, is out walking with her parents, Pizare and Estéfanie, who quarrel as Pizare speaks disrespectfully of women and wants to narrate a dream, which tells us in effect that the play's ending will be happy. The scene switches to Alphonse, son of a Spanish noble, who enlists the aid of two friends, Rodéric and Fernande, to engineer a daylight abduction of Léocadie in the street. All six characters appear together in the third scene, when Léocadie speaks for the first time to say she is afraid, having just spied a mouse. The three youths jostle Léocadie's parents, but Alphonse fails to seize her. They return to the attack, snatching Léocadie at knife- and sword-point. The parents' lines, as printed, seem more likely to make a reader laugh than weep, but it is possible to see how, within a declamatory convention, and properly delivered, they might have been moving. The danger is that they are over-fluently written and could sound like ineffectively conventional sentiments merely trotted out:

> ô vieillard déplorable! ô père malheureux,
> ô siècle perverti! ô destins rigoureux!

(O lamentable old man! O sorrowing father, O perverted times! O harsh fates!).

The second act starts with Alphonse's passion satisfied as Léocadie recovers from her faint. She notices the rich trappings of the room and threatens Alphonse with nails, fists, and teeth unless she is taken out into the street and left. If Alphonse is frightened he can blindfold her. He is and he does. She finds her way to her parents and is now genuinely touching in shame and guilt. She remembers the furnishings of the room, and has brought away with her a miniature recognizable as a Hercules. In the third scene of Act II Alphonse's father, Dom Inigue, sends him to Italy to finish off his education and come back cultivated. His father's exalted birth will then ensure that he can have his pick of the brides of Toledo.

In the third act Léocadie is pregnant in the first scene, which takes place in her father's house. In the second scene, which takes place in his own house, Dom Inigue is called off to a tournament, as Hardy again insists heavily on his social elevation. In the third scene we are with Alphonse in Italy, and in the fourth Léocadie's son by Alphonse, Ludovic, has a speaking role, having been slightly hurt at the tournament and attracted the attention of Dom Inigue who, learning that Ludovic has no father and impressed by his looks, guesses who he must be, offers to take his father's place, and asks Ludovic to bring his mother to him. There is of course a recognition, sealed by Léocadie's memory of the room and the Hercules miniature, and Alphonse marries Léocadie. Alphonse's mother has no reason to suppose, when correctly she does suppose, that the villain of Léocadie's story is her own son. The implausibility is deliberately provocative. It challenges the audience to forget about dramatic credibility and concentrate on the central question, which is whether and how nature can put right the effects of the instincts with which human beings have been naturally endowed.

Such critical comment as is available on Hardy certainly underestimates the intrinsic value of his achievement, seeing it as foreshadowing something that was not yet necessary and had not yet happened. It is neither difficult nor interesting to see how Hardy's dramatic techniques adumbrate those of Pierre Corneille or Racine. It is more important to see how he shifts the focus of imaginative interest towards an altogether more optimistic view of human experience than that of his predecessors from the religious wars, especially in his tragi-comedies, in spite of his dependence on Garnier and the moralistic dramatization of medieval forms of theatre. What Hardy does help us to understand is the later resistance to the unities and the criterion of vraisemblance, as simply irrelevant to the imaginative exploration of moral attitudes that French society still required in the first third or more of the 17th century.

PUBLICATIONS

Collection

Le Théâtre, 5 vols., 1624–28; reprinted 1883–84

Plays

Les chastes et loyalles amours de Théagène et Cariclée…en huict poèmes dramatiques, 1623
Les Ramoneurs, comédie, 1957

Other

La Berne des deux rimeurs de l'Hôtel de Bourgogne, 1628

Biographical and critical studies

Rigal, Eugène, *Alexandre Hardy et le théâtre français*, 1889
Sirich, E.H., *A Study in the Syntax of Alexandre Hardy*, 1915
Deierkauf-Holsboer, S. Wilma, *Vie d'Alexandre Hardy, poète du Roi in Proceedings of the American Philosophical Society*, 1947
——————————————*La Succession d'Alexandre Hardy in XVIIe siècle*, 1954
Scherer, Jacques, Introduction and notes to *Théâtre du XVIIe siècle*, Bibliothèque de la Pléiade, vol. 1, 1975

———————

HÉROËT, Antoine, 1492–1568.

Poet.

LIFE

Although, for a 16th-century poet, Héroët revealed in the prefatory material at the front of his publications unusually few biographical facts about himself, he was a bishop whose life and works have been thought to link the Church with the reform, and the rhétoriqueurs both with the neoplatonism of the circle of Marguerite d'Angoulême and with the Pléiade (q.v.) poets, who admired him. In addition, his role in the "Querelle des amyes" makes him a key figure in any effort to understand the changes in cultural and social standards into which his verse offers a clear window and which made essential contributions to the renaissance in France.

Héroët is generally thought to have been born in 1492, although no evidence attesting that date survives. The family were administrators attached to the royal court, and Héroët's father, Jehan, was made royal treasurer when in 1498 the duc d'Orléans, in whose service he was, became Louis XII. Héroët's mother, Marie Malingre, was the daughter of a lawyer at the parlement de Paris. On widowhood, she married some time after 1527 le chevalier de la Balue, steward of François I and of the queen of Navarre, as Marguerite d'Angoulême was called from that date. Since Héroët inherited the title "de la Maison Neuve," he was almost certainly the eldest son.

He had at least two brothers—Nicolas, who renounced a benefice in Héroët's favour in 1543, and Georges, listed as one of the secretaries, virtually ministers, of François I, at 400 livres a year—and a sister, whose tombstone informs us that she was a lady-in-waiting to the queen. Another sister was made abbess of Giy near Montargis by the king, and Marguerite chose Héroët's mother's close relation, François Olivier, probably in 1528, to be chancellor of her duchy of Alençon. Héroët was born and must have studied in Paris, but is first heard of in 1524, still in Paris, when he received a pension of 200 livres from Marguerite, at that date duchesse d'Alençon.

From 1529 to 1539 Héroët was receiving a pension from Marguerite de Navarre and her mother, Louise de Savoie. A lease still exists by which on 25 July 1532 he rented a house in Paris, where he was a poet attached to the court. Louise de Savoie died on 22 September, and within 25 days G. Tory had published a collection of poems in her praise, *In Lodoicae Regis matris mortem…*, among which two epitaphs in French were by Héroët, both signed simply "L[a] M[aison] N[euve]." Some time later Héroët contributed ten eight-line stanzas, no doubt on commission, to a poem which must date from about or before 1540, describing a set of tapestries on Cupid and Psyché, to which Claude Chappuys and Mellin de Saint-Gelais also contributed sets of stanzas.

We know that Héroët's *L'Androgyne*, an adaptation with commentary of Ficino's Latin translation of Plato's *Symposium*, rather than the straight translation suggested in its sub-title, was presented to François I in the early days of 1537 in reply to the king's reproach that Héroët was not making his verse available. It is clear that Héroët was already more concerned with polishing his poetic production than with augmenting its volume. His minor work is both more careful and more powerful than that of his literary contemporaries, many of whom he must inevitably have known. Charles de Sainte-Marthe, a steward in Marguerite's household, tells us in a poem that, among the "Poètes divins," Héroët was "une personne unie (one single person)" with Charles Fontaine. A Latin poem in a publication of 1537 was addressed to Héroët by Salmon Macrin, and several of Marot's poems indicate a close connection between himself and Héroët, whom he called "Thony." More significant historically are the facts that Ronsard in the preface to the 1550 *Odes* placed Héroët among the few predecessors he esteemed and that du

Bellay singled him out for praise in the preface to the first edition of *L'Olive* as well as in the *Deffence et illustration*. Du Bellay also included a poem to Héroët in his 1549 *Recueil*, and mentioned him in the *Musagnoeomachie*. Peletier du Mans included an enthusiastic eulogy of Héroët in the first book of the 1555 *Art poétique*.

Héroët's "Blason de l'oeil" was written probably in 1535 as part of a poetic competition organized in response to a challenge which Marot had sent from Ferrara in the form of his "Blason du beau tetin (In Praise of the Beautiful Nipple)." Most contemporary poets of note then wrote mainly short pieces describing in detail some part of the female body, or sometimes, like Héroët's blason of the eye, or Scève's piece on the eyebrow, some part of the body which was not gender-specific. The formality of the competition has been disputed, but the results were judged by Renée de France, duchess of Ferrara and daughter of Louis XII, who awarded first place to the unknown Scève, and some at least of the "blasons" were published in the corporate collection, *Blasons anatomiques des parties du corps féminin* of 1536, whose 1543 augmented version was re-printed at least three times. In 1539 Marot was to choose Héroët to arbitrate in a pastoral poetic contest between himself and Mellin de Saint-Gelais. It is probable that, through Marot, Héroët met both Dolet, who was to publish him, and Rabelais. Dolet's publishing activity had suddenly shot up in 1542 and was showing strongly reformist sympathies. Almost half of his production of 34 books in one six-month period during 1542 was religious, and all 14 religious books were condemned.

Like *L'Androgyne*, Héroët's principal work, *La parfaicte amye*, owes a good deal to Ficino's translation of Plato's *Symposium* and to his celebrated fiction containing seven speeches purporting to have been given at the Platonic banquet held at Careggi on 7 November 1468, elaborating on the ideas put forward by the characters in Plato's original dialogue. Early 16th-century French literature was still overwhelmingly anti-feminist, reducing love to physical pleasure and women to seducers, and affirming the superiority of the warrior male in social and sexual relationships. It was a characteristic of the Platonism of the circle of Marguerite de Navarre in the 1540s, and of humanist literature generally in 16th-century France, to seek to promote the social position of women and to insist on the morally enriching nature of love. The movement is most often seen as starting with Petrarch. Ficino's real but often unrecognized originality was to make the love which is morally and spiritually perfective compatible with and even dependent on that which entails ordinary physical sexual relationships. Much play is made of Ficino's view in, for instance, Marguerite de Navarre's *Heptaméron* and, for that matter, in Rabelais's *Tiers livre*, and there are early works of irony and parody making fun of the new feminism, like Agrippa of Nettesheim's *De nobilitate et praecellentia Foeminei sexus*.

In 1528, Baldassare Castiglione published his dialogue *Il libro del Cortegiano* (The book of the Courtier). The work had been undertaken at the instigation of François I, as its author, in a manuscript passage dropped for political reasons before the first edition, himself acknowledged. Essentially it was a code of polite Italian courtly behaviour written as a manual of guidance for the French. The first translation, made by Jacques Colin d'Auxerre, a member of the king's household, and revised by Mellin de Saint-Gelais, was published in 1537 by Jehan Longis and Vincent Sartenas, reprinted by Denys de Harsy at Lyons,

and printed again at Lyons in 1538 by Etienne Dolet. Castiglione puts into Bembo's mouth at the end of the fourth dialogue and the book, set in Urbino in 1507, a theory of love to an astonishing degree more timid than Ficino's and noticeably distrustful of the distractions of sense, excusing its indulgence only in the young, and only allowing the physical kiss, not to stir the courtier "to any dishonest desire, but because he feeleth that that bond is an opening of the entry to the souls."

Bertrand de la Borderie's *L'Amie de Court*, for which Corrozet acquired a privilège on 9 March 1542, put into verse some of the attitudes of courtly hauteur presented in Castiglione's third book as examples of what women have to endure, but now justified by La Borderie. The courtly lady's merit lies in loving no one, but being loved by all; she accepts gifts but rejects advances; she does not yield to sentiment, but calculates to advantage. The poem was immediately re-published by Dolet who, in an introductory epistle to the reader dated 15 May 1542, announced a reply in Héroët's *La parfaicte amye* a month later. Since already the poets were assumed to be the praisers of women, untouchable objects no doubt of courtly adoration, devotion to whom led to the performance of heroic male deeds, and the denigration of women was chiefly associated with the realistic medieval contes of lechery and debauch, La Borderie's poetic cynicism about courtly female attitudes immediately attracted attention.

Charles Fontaine wrote a 1,282-line *Contr'Amye de Court* defending love, and attacking the courtly attitudes described by Castiglione and justified by La Borderie. The three books of Héroët's 1,662-line *La parfaicte amye* were obviously written quite quickly, but are intended as a full, formal refutation of *L'Amie de Court*, as the title, changed from "Perfection d'amour," was intended to make clear. Héroët, in his glorification of love, goes back on his more conventional "Douleur et volupté," which must pre-date *La parfaicte amye*, although it was not published until it appeared anonymously in a 1544 *Recueil de vraye Poesie Françoyse*. For a long time wrongly attributed to Marot, the poem occurs in a manuscript of no later than 1540. Although *La parfaicte amye* is not uniformly as explicit as Ficino had been, Héroët has at least understood the point of the *De amore*, and in his poem the relationship between physical attraction and the perfective love of God to which it should ascend is at least very close. It certainly progresses beyond the Platonism dismissive of physical relationships to be found both in Caviceo's *Dialogue...intitulé le Peregrin*, translated from the Italian for Marguerite de Navarre by Françoys Dassy in 1527, which had had 10 editions by 1540, and in Gilles Corrozet's 1546 *Conte du Rossignol*.

Héroët was supported in his defence of love against La Borderie's debasement of love into galanterie by Mellin de Saint-Gelais and Guillaume Des Autels. A general, non-specific, and less interesting series of poems in love's defence, merely skirting the surface of its psychology, quickly became fashionable among authors like Almanque Papillon, Charles de Sainte-Marthe, and Marot himself, all connected with Marguerite de Navarre. A defence by Paul Angier of the *Amye de Court* appeared in 1545, but it may have been written by La Borderie himself. The controversy between La Borderie, Fontaine, and Héroët, known as the "Querelle des amyes," widened into the much better-known "Querelle des femmes" which culminated in the 1550s, until the religious wars put a quite sudden stop to imaginative explorations of culturally advanced values, such as those based on a neoplatonist mythology and demanding for women a more elevated social status. With the outbreak of the wars the neoplatonism of the mid-century was transmuted into one of two major forms of neostoicism, both linked with Pyrrhonist scepticism, one deriving primarily from Epictetus and the other through Cicero and Seneca from Zeno and Chrysippus.

Héroët, whose total poetic production outside *L'Androgyne* and *La parfaicte amye* does not amount to 2,000 lines, stopped publishing verse after *La parfaicte amye* of 1542, apart from a short epitaph for Marguerite de Navarre. On 28 March 1543 his brother Nicolas made over to him the abbacy of Notre-Dame de Cercanceaux. On 18 May 1545 François Olivier was made chancellor of France; he seems to have patronized men of letters, certainly Bonaventure des Périers, Adrien Turnèbe, and Louis le Roy, who was also among those who recorded his enthusiastic praise for Héroët. In 1552 Héroët succeeded a brother of François Olivier as bishop of Digne, and conscientiously fulfilled his episcopal functions until his death in 1568.

WORKS

There are 16 known editions of Héroët's *L'Androgyne* from 1542 to 1568. Their interest does not lie simply in the versification of Plato's myth, but in the resulting psychology of love. Love is essentially the "Recouvrement de perdue moytié (Rediscovery of the lost half)," but we sometimes make mistakes, even when there is physical attraction. The resulting "disloyalty" should be blamed on nature, since it is nature itself which then forces us apart, not just the whim of our will. When the discovery of our true partner is made, all else is forgotten:

Deux cueurs en ung s'arrestent pour leur vie

(Two hearts come together in one for their lifetime).

In an age of dynastic alliances and consequent pre-pubertal marriages, Héroët's realistic psychology simply changes the register here from the ethereal beauty of Platonist myth to a much more powerful attempt actually to use the myth in an effort to understand human emotional experience. Many humans do not have second halves and are left with no alternative "Que consommer les biens qui sont sus terre (Than to use up the goods which are on earth)." Love is capable of waking the heart and shedding light. Then the lyricism intensifies as Héroët describes the discovery by the adolescent of his semi-obscurity and semi-completeness. Héroët's psychological insight now forces him to extend the myth beyond Plato and Ficino, and takes him into a poetic disquisition on the two forms of light needed to understand experience,

Dont l'une estoit infuse par laquelle
Cognoissoit tout estant au dessus d'elle,
Et l'aultre moyndre, acquise de nature,
Pour voir les corps et choses d'adventure

(Of which one was innate, by which/It knew everything higher than itself,/And the other, less, acquired from nature/To see bodies and contingent things).

The temptation is naturally to forget the higher light, the higher love. The soul must seek completeness in the quest for goodness alone.

In spite of psychological interest and occasional lyrical intensity, *L'Androgyne* remains anchored in the poetic technique of its age, especially in its exploitation of complicated poetic conceits. Much the same must be said of the "Aultre invention," an 88-line poem adapted from Mario Equicola's 1525 *Libro di natura d'amore*, which also derives from Ficino. *La parfaicte amye* is different. Like *L'Amye de Court*, the poem is put into a woman's mouth, and it, too, is preceded in Dolet's edition by a letter to the reader extolling the virtues of translation.

The first book announces the work's title "Parfection d'amour," and goes on to renounce invocations to Muses. It will appeal only to "le mien ami (the man I love)."

Je l'ay aymé, je l'ayme et l'aymeray

(I did love him, I do love him, and I will go on loving him).

However, the woman speaker goes on to say that she cannot, much as it would be to her honour if she could, claim that her love is based on an appreciation of his virtues. Too young to appreciate "Les biens que son esprit offroit (The merits offered by his mind)," she did not found her love on his "beauté, fondement non durable (beauty, a transient basis)," since her love has increased with his age. The speaker goes on to ask what it was about her lover that cost her her liberty. Not, she says, his articulateness, not merely pity, because "j'aimay devant que le congoistre,/Et vis l'amour, en le congnoissant, croystre (I loved him before I knew him,/And saw my love increase with knowledge)." Héroët is here, not very seriously, using the poles of an extremely important debate in scholastic psychology for which either the will was determined by preceding knowledge of the good, and was itself no longer free, or the will was a blind appetite, desiring before knowing, in which case the rationality of choice could not be explained. The dilemma was still to be important for both Descartes and Pascal, and is one of the principal points of difference between Scotus and the Franciscan tradition and Aquinas's Aristotelianism. But whether or not knowledge preceded love had become a well-worn debating topic.

The speaker now declares that the riches and honours of her lover were so many impediments. In the *Symposium* the mother of love had been the goddess of poverty. All Héroët's speaker loved was her lover himself. The foundation of her love was simply the divine will, the "voulunté divine." Héroët cannot resist the captious end to which his logic takes him:

Or semble amour, à qui vouldra, peché;...
...si divin fut son commencement,
Entretenu je l'ay divinement

(But let love seem sin to whomsoever wishes,.../...if its beginning was divine,/I have divinely maintained it).

Stylization in the religious imagery should not mislead us. The actual application of the categories deriving from the fusion of Christianity and Platonism, as recently transmitted through Ficino, to the psychology of female love by the poem's speaker takes this poem into a powerful imaginative leap. How far will the neoplatonist myth and the realistic psychological account of loving need to be modified before they satisfactorily interlock? To that question, *La parfaicte amye* sets out to find the answer.

Firstly, says the speaker, her love has been nourished imaginatively "d'une pensée pure (by a purely mental process)," enough, she says, you would have thought, to tire her mind. She lived more in the object of her love than in herself. There follow a number of Petrarchan topoi about exchanging hearts, dying and living again in the object of love—"O beau mourir, pour en celluy revivre (O lovely death, to live again in him)"—and the poet, protected by her love from all fear, even rejoices to see the object of her "terrestre Dieu (earthly God)" attract others. Who will believe what she says about her love? She is never jealous:

Touts les plaisirs de mon amy je tiens
Non aultrement, que si les sentois miens

(I regard all my lover's pleasures/Not otherwise than if I felt them myself).

Most of this part of the poem is a direct attack on the attitudes of the woman speaker in the *Amie de Court*. The female speaker in *La parfaicte amye* is incapable of infidelity:

Mais j'ayme tant, que je n'ay le pouvoir
N'y voulunté d'autre amy recepvoir

(But I love so much that I do not have the power/Or desire to receive any other lover).

A woman should be able to attract someone who truly loves her, while turning away anyone who is merely importunate. The speaker realizes that she enjoys a privileged social position. She prefers to keep her love private:

Quant est à moy, je ne veulx publier
Le neud qui sceut ma voulonté lyer.
Et me plaist bien, couvert et incongneu

(As for me, I do not want to make public/The knot which succeeded in binding my will./And it pleases me, covered up and unknown [as it is]).

But it would not worry the speaker if it did become known. The "vulgaire et sotte multitude/N'a jugement, scavoir, ny certitude (The common and stupid mob/Has no judgement, knowledge or certainty)." Contempt for the multitude, not so much by the aristocracy as by the refined courtly class, most of whom could at least pay for the services of the literate, diminished only slowly during the 16th century. It can be watched happening as even Montaigne, who had himself been humanistically educated, modified the text of *Les Essais* over the 20 years he spent writing the book, and by the era of La Rochefoucauld, it was obtrusively out of date. The social arrangements of medieval Europe, however, were such that, until the slow emergence of secular administrators, bankers, and merchants, only in the courts could the possibilities of refined relationships between the sexes emerge, the arts be cultivated, and aesthetic sensibilities be developed. All three required the help of an education until the 16th century exclusively mediated by ecclesiastics, the monopolistic and professedly celibate custodians of academically based culture. It is difficult to see how the contempt of "la parfaicte amie" for those enslaved by birth to peasanthood could altogether have been avoided.

It is towards the end of the first book that Héroët, very possibly for the first time in France, and preceding by two years the much more tentative Scève, stumbles on the solution which dovetails the realistic psychology of the emotions into the neoplatonist calculus of morally perfective love. He puts into the mouth of his speaker these astonishing lines:

Dames, croyez qu'il n'ayme pas, qui veult.
Plusieurs ont dict leurs amoureux desirs
Qui oncq amour n'eurent ny ses plaisirs.
Je les ay touts; et si n'en diray qu'ung,
Qui est bien rare et vous semble commun.
Quand deux esprits au ciel devant liés,
Puis recongneus en terre, et r'alliés,
Trouvent les corps propices, et les sens
Touts attentifz, serfz, et obéissants,
De mutuelle et telle affection,
L'ung a de l'aultre une fruition,
Ung aise grand', certain contentement,
Qui n'est congneu que de l'entendement.
De quel plaisir ces deux là sont munys,
En se voyant en divers corps unis?

(Ladies, believe me, not everyone who wishes can love. / Many have affirmed their desire to love/Who have never experienced love or its pleasures./I have them all; and I shall recount to you only one/Which indeed is rare, even if it seems to you to be commonplace./When two spirits, linked before in heaven,/Then recognized by one another on earth and bound together again,/Find their bodies ready, and their senses/all alert, biddable, and obedient,/With reciprocal and great affection,/The one has of the other an enjoyment,/A great satisfaction and assured happiness,/ Known only to the mind./With what pleasure are those two fortified,/Seeing themselves in different bodies united?).

The pleasure of the senses here mediates spiritual fulfilment. There had to come a moment, and everything in French culture was conspiring to make it the early 1540s, when that discovery would become articulate, and it had to entail bringing together a proper understanding of Ficino's *De amore* with a convincing analysis of the psychology of emotional love. Héroët is visibly stung into making that discovery in an immediate reaction to La Borderie's effort to downgrade cultivated relationships between courtiers and their ladies into teasing torture by women who were haughty and inviolate.

The second book of the poem draws more fully on the neoplatonist structural elements of the *De amore*. External beauty is a manifestation of interior goodness, a spark of the divine beauty reflected in a material element. Earthly beauty should not distract the soul from the divine perfection of which it is only the derivative. The soul

Use d'amour et de beaultés humaines,
Pour ung degré propre à plus haulte attente

(Exploits love and human beauty,/As a step towards a higher aim).

The poet speculates on the state of the soul between individual death and the general resurrection, a real problem in a Christian society for which creation, fall, redemption, death, and the general resurrection including the resurrection of the body were still necessarily arranged with chronological sequentiality, so that, for instance, God's foreknowledge was almost impossible to reconcile with the individual's power of self-determination. Various passages of Plato are drawn on to conjure up visions of the blessed isles to the invention of whose possible delights so many 16th-century writers devoted strenuous imaginative effort. How would the earthly paradise be constituted, where individual contentment, social harmony, and climatic perfection all come together? The poet knows that this is all fable, but whoever first thought up the blessed isles "Nous a voulu dire une vérité (Wanted to teach us a truth)" about a state of eternal bliss.

The third book opens with the praise of love's "volupté (pleasure)," a word associated with Epicurus, but generally as he was interpreted by Seneca in the *De beata vita*. That work makes the Epicurean end of man more or less coincide with stoic virtue, although there is a distinction, in Montaigne, for instance, between sensual and spiritual "volupté." Love, in this book of *La Parfaicte amie*, banishes ignorance, having earlier been said to penetrate the secrets of the heavens. Ignorance, for the stoics and for many of the moralists of the renaissance, was quite technically the source of passion, not just because emotions were inflamed by what was not properly understood, but because passion, being irrational, had to have its source in a false judgement about good and evil by the practical intellect.

Love also binds the world together as in Ficino, a function which in 1546, in the *Tiers Livre*, Rabelais will satirically transfer to debt. And since external beauty is the sign of inner goodness, that which is ugly cannot be loved. Love therefore heals ugliness, athough Héroët's poet is here confused about whether love removes the ugliness in its subject or in its object. We have left the realms of credible psychological realism by this point. "Amour peult plus en beaulté que nature (Love can achieve more in beauty than nature can)." We are safe in the realms of fantasy again, however much the poet uses the language of realism. Don't look for ointments and lotions to maintain the beauty of your complexions. Love...

> Qui n'ayme point, ne scauroit estre belle;
> Qui ayme bien, pour le moins devient telle
> Qu'on ne la peult tenir pour ignorante,
> Et du peché de laydeur est exempte

(She who does not love could not be beautiful;/She who truly loves at the least becomes/Such that she cannot be thought ignorant,/And is free of the sin of ugliness).

With what is now tongue-in-cheek realism the poet holds that those in love cannot even suffer from fever. The planes of fantasy and reality have parted company again, which relaxes the imaginative strain, makes the poem less audacious than it would have been if it had stopped after its first book, and explains why its real daring has so often been missed by historians. Scattered clues remain, as they will in the Pléiade, that stylized Petrarchan images are no longer adequately realistic for poetry's task:

> Touts les escripts et larmoyants autheurs,
> Tout le Petrarcque et ses imitateurs,
> Qui de souspirs et de froydes querelles

> Remplissent l'air en parlant aux estoilles,
> Ne facent point soupsonner qu'à aymer
> Entre le doux il y ayt de l'amer.

(All the writings and tear-ridden authors,/All of Petrarch and his imitators,/Who with sighs and cold quarrels/Fill the air while talking to the stars/Never lead one to suspect that in loving/Intermingled with the sweet there is also the bitter)."

To few people is it given to love. There are imitations, but they do not satisfy, and they result in desertion, affliction, quarrels. There are good passions, and love is a passion, but it does not disturb the judgement. It excludes all the other passions.

Agreement about Héroët's stature necessarily awaits acceptance of a consensus not yet generally achieved about the exploitation of neoplatonism in 16th-century France. If the historical perspectives are as suggested here, Héroët is a much more powerful poet than has usually been thought, even if his achievement was mostly concentrated into one moment of supreme imaginative concentration, hurriedly produced at the stimulus of the work by La Borderie which had been particularly dangerous because sophisticated and cynical in its reactionary implications. On any reading of the literary culture of 16th-century France, however, Héroët's poetic achievement, as Ronsard and du Bellay well saw, must rank as high as that of any other pre-Pléiade poet of the French renaissance.

PUBLICATIONS

Collection

Oeuvres poétiques, 1909

Verse

La Parfaicte Amye. Nouvellement composée par Antoine Héroët, dict la Maison neufve, 1542
Opuscules d'amour, par Héroët, la Borderie, et autres divins poëtes, 1547
Le Mespris de la court (Recueil), 1549

Biographical and critical studies

Gohin, Ferdinand, edition of Héroët's *Oeuvres poëtiques*, 1909 (2nd edition 1943)

HOUDAR DE LA MOTTE, Antoine-Charles de, 1672–1731.

Dramatist, librettist, fabulist, poet, and critic.

LIFE

Houdar de la Motte owes his place in the catalogue of great French writers to his immensely successful 1723 play *Inès de Castro*, and it is usually conceded that much of his other work, particularly the poetry, shows limited talent. What is not at all clear is whether his other provocative, almost nonchalantly light-weight literary activities, and his almost teasingly expressed views that poetry was merely an ornate form of prose and that the conventions of French tragedy required abolition in the name of common sense should not have been taken by subsequent critics more seriously than they have been. There is a certain possibly blinkered logic in his position on the matter, for instance, of Homer in the early 18th century which uncovers some fundamental questions about the nature of literary values and the importance of the evolution of taste, however extreme Houdar de la Motte's own position.

He was born on 14 January 1672, the son of a Parisian hatter, Antoine Houdar de la Motte, with a shop on the Pont Saint-Michel, and of his wife, Marguerite Ruau. Houdar de la Motte was sent to the Jesuits to school and subsequently studied law, but instead of registering as a barrister he turned to the theatre. From 1680, after the amalgamation of the Comédiens du roi with the Guénégaud company, which had already integrated the remnants of Molière's troupe with the Marais company in 1673, there were only two companies in Paris concerned with straight drama, with the Académie royale de Musique playing an increasingly important part in the development of musical entertainments more heavily dependent on singing and dancing. What we now know as the Comédie-Française troupe moved in 1689 to premises in the Fossés-Saint-Germain-des-Prés, while the Italian company played from 1680 at the Hôtel de Bourgogne until it was banished from Paris in May 1697. This occurred after Mme de Maintenon had been offended by the Italian stage adaptation, *La Finta Matrigna*, of the anonymous French novel published in Holland and thought likely to lampoon Mme de Maintenon, *La Fausse Prude* (see: *Commedia dell'arte*).

The history of the re-establishment of Italian theatre in Paris from 1716 (see: Marivaux) is of cultural importance as, at least at first, the company was obliged by the poverty of its command of French to rely more on mime than on speech; it was more accessible than the legitimate theatre, which stimulated the emotions of the audience through the deployment of declamatory rhetoric along the rules laid down by Aristotle; was favoured by the partisans of the "modernes" in the Querelle des anciens et des modernes (q.v.); and it notoriously attracted the patronage of the less culturally earnest young aristocrats. Marivaux's successful dramatic writing was almost wholly for the Italians, for whom he developed his gossamer dramatic explorations of the reliability of instinctive emotional relations as a guide to happiness and virtue. Houdar de la Motte's first play, *Les Originaux; ou, L'Italien*, a farce of mixed verse and prose with music by Masse, was unsuccessfully performed by the Italian company on 13 August 1693. During the period when there was no Italian company in Paris, Houdar de la Motte was to write libretti for the Académie royale de Musique and straight comedy for the Comédie-Française, although he also gave one comedy, *L'Amante difficile*, to the new Italian company in October 1716, almost immediately after its début in Paris on the preceding 18 May. The play marked his own return to the non-musical theatre, and preluded a series of tragedies played by the Comédie-Française.

When his first farce failed in 1693, Houdar de la Motte joined the Trappist order at Soligny, but Rancé sent him away after only two months and he returned to the stage with a series of operas and ballets, developing three distinct genres of musical entertainment, the ballet, the pastorale, and the comédie-ballet, while also writing comedies and tragedies for the straight theatre. The pieces performed at the Académie royale de Musique were invariably nearer to what we would regard as ballet or opera than to straight drama. When, later on, Houdar de la Motte attacked the constrictions imposed on tragedy by the unities, thereby demonstrating a joyous, optimistic way of looking at human nature which did not require any Racinian examination of emotional intensity, he did not hide his desire to follow the British example of "ces actions frappantes qui demandent de l'appareil et du spectacle (those striking intrigues which depend on mechanical effects and spectacle)."

After the Trappist venture, Houdar de la Motte had successively put on his "ballet en musique," or opera, *L'Europe galante*, at the Académie royale de Musique on 24 October 1697 with music by Campra; his "pastorale héroïque en musique" *Issé*, with music by Destouches, performed at the Trianon before the king on 17 December 1697; *Amadis de Grèce*, described as a tragédie, with music by Destouches, played before the king at Fontainebleau in October, and then at the Académie on 29 November 1699; the "ballet" *Le Triomphe des arts* with music by La Barre, performed at the Académie on 16 May 1700; the tragédie *Canente* with music by Colasse, performed at the Académie on 4 November 1700; the tragédie *Omphale* with music by Destouches, performed at the Académie on 10 December 1701; *Le Carnaval et la folie*, described as a comédie-ballet, performed with music by Destouches at the Académie on 10 November 1701; the ballet *La Vénitienne* with music by La Barre, performed at the Académie on 26 May 1705; *Alcione*, a tragédie with music by Marais, performed at the Académie on 18 February 1706; and *Sémélé*, a tragédie with music by Marais, performed at the Académie on 9 January 1709. During the same period the Théâtre-Français played three of Houdar de la Motte's comedies, *Les Trois Gascons* on 4 June 1701, *La Matrone d'Ephèse* on 23 September 1702, and *Le Port de mer* on 29 May 1704.

It was as a poet, frequently successful at the Toulouse Jeux Floraux, that Houdar de la Motte was elected to the Académie française in succession to Thomas Corneille in 1709, in spite of opposition from Jean-Baptiste Rousseau, jealous of his dramatic successes, among the victims of whose epigrams he ranked high. He was received on 8 February 1710, and on 19 December 1715 it was he who pronounced the panegyric of Louis XIV. Houdar de la Motte's verse *Odes* had appeared in 1707, with augmented editions in 1709 and 1711, and he also wrote odes in prose. He has not unjustly been related to a whole series of writers who disdained first rhyme, like Pascal and Fénelon, and then verse forms altogether, like Montesquieu, Vauvenargues, Houdar de la Motte's friend Fontenelle, and Buffon. The abbé de Pons thought poetry frivolous, and Duclos, like Buffon, thought prose a finer instrument of expression.

Critics have sometimes linked to Descartes this distrust of verse, in which the demands of metre and rhyme can lead to the neglect of conciseness and syntactical precision. They were apparently thinking of the diminished importance accorded by verse to clarity in its attempts to achieve sublimity and elevation. But the failure of the 17th century from Malherbe to Boileau to prize lyrical intensity above lucidity of expression had much less to do with Descartes's reliance on rational proof than with the need to refine the nuances of the literary register while avoiding the ornamentation and the clumsiness obvious in so much 17th-century French verse. Much of this verse, as in the *Guirlande de Julie* (q.v.), Loret's *Muse historique*, or Boileau's *L'Art poétique*, is rhyming prose with an occasional touch of elegance, while the intensity and conflict of the emotions of Racine's characters, dependent on an astonishingly small vocabulary, allows for very little subtlety in gradations of sentiment.

Houdar de la Motte preferred the natural and the elegant to the artificial and the affected: "le but du discours n'étant que de se faire entendre, il ne paraît pas raisonnable de s'imposer une contrainte qui nuit souvent à ce dessein (the aim of discourse being only to make oneself understood, it does not seem reasonable to impose on oneself a constraint which often makes this more difficult)." He thought that poetry did not depend on metre, or indeed any form of versification, but that it consisted solely in "la hardiesse des pensées, la vivacité des images et l'énergie de l'expression (the boldness of the ideas, the brilliance of the images and the energy of the expression)." The analysis of feeling which, for cultural and social reasons, played so prominent a role in the literature of France under Colbert needed the precision of prose. Lyric poetry virtually took refuge in the fable. When Houdar de la Motte in the 1707 *Discours sur la poésie en général et sur l'ode en particulier* prefacing the 1707 *Odes* that "L'art poétique a ses axiomes, ses théorèmes, ses corollaires et ses démonstrations (The art of poetry has its axioms, its theorems, its corollaries, and its demonstrations)," he was talking not about logic, like Descartes, but about rhetoric, at best tangential to Descartes's preoccupations.

From the date of his reception into the Académie, Houdar de la Motte's career took a somewhat different direction. A person of considerable charm, who bore increasing ill-health with fortitude even when he went blind soon after he was 43, Houdar de la Motte was as well known in the salons of Mme de Lambert and the duchesse du Maine as at the café Procope. Everything about his taste and imagination led to an optimism about human experience which differed only in the exuberance of its expression from those of Fénelon, with whom Houdar de la Motte corresponded about literary matters and with whom he was in greater agreement than was immediately clear, and of Fontenelle, to whom he was personally close. He almost riotously indulged his confident conviction that nature, life, and instinct should be the subjects of celebration rather than of fear or of awe. It was his sensibility more than his taste or judgement that were "moderne," and which precipitated the clash with Mme Dacier. It is because Voltaire, who, when young, had been irritated by Pascal's gloomily Jansenistic (q.v.) views about the corruption of human nature, was not himself able to sustain his own early optimism, that he allowed himself among his plentiful and often unfair sneers the well-known quip about Houdar de la Motte, "Il prouva que dans l'art d'écrire on peut être encore quelque chose au second rang (He proved that in the art of writing something can be achieved even by the second rate)."

Anne Le Fèvre, Mme Dacier, daughter of the Protestant humanist professor at the academy of Saumur, Tanneguy Le Fèvre, had married on 4 December 1783 her fellow pupil at the academy, André Dacier, already publishing his translation of Horace. Both became Catholics and were given the usual pension on the revocation of the edict of Nantes in 1685, and both became well-known scholars, each of them editing and translating Greek and Latin classics. Mme Dacier became renowned throughout Europe for her considerable learning and academic ability. Her achievement was crowned by the translations of

Homer into French prose: the 4-volume *Illiade* with "remarques" aimed at Perrault of 1699, better known from the 1711 edition, and the Amsterdam 1708 *Odessey*, better known from the Paris 1716 edition. She did in fact make concessions to the modern bienséances, as at *Illiade* V, ll. 65–8 and *Odessey* XXII, ll. 465–73, and both before and after their quarrel was friendly with Houdar de la Motte. But in 1714 he published a verse adaptation of the *Illiade* to suit modern taste, halving the number of cantos from 24 to 12, adding embellishments, changing Achilles's shield, and altering Hector's death. The work, dedicated to the king, was prefaced by a *Discours sur Homère* stridently criticizing Homer and proclaiming the superior virtues of modern poets.

Mme Dacier replied with a virulent pamphlet of over 600 pages, the *Traité des causes de la corruption du goût*, refuting Houdar de la Motte point for point. Houdar de la Motte's reply, the 1715 *Réflexions sur la critique*, which included letters by Fénelon, was the more courteous, its refinement in comparison to the tone of attack on him establishing him in public esteem on the higher aesthetic ground. In the meanwhile Fénelon, in response to the request of the Académie française to all its members, had written a *Lettre sur les occupations de l'Académie*, read out on 26 May 1714. Fénelon reworked his text for publication by the Académie, returning it on 25 October. It took care to come down on neither side, blaming antiquity for its barbarism but praising its poets for their sublimity in spite of it. Like Houdar de la Motte Fénelon preferred everything that was natural, true, uncontaminated by précieux (q.v.) affectation, while yet sharing Houdar de la Motte's appreciation of the grace and elegance admired by the partisans of the "modernes" but despised by those of the "anciens."

Houdar de la Motte had been supported by the abbé de Pons in his 1714 *Lettre sur l'Illiade de La Motte*, and his position was in 1715 again affirmed by the abbé Terrasson's *Dissertation critique sur l'Illiade*, although Mme Dacier did not cease to defend Homer's text in its integrity against its detractors, and even against one admirer, Père Hardouin, who had treated Homer's poem as an allegory. She was however reconciled with Houdar de la Motte at a dinner organized by Valincourt and Etienne Fourmont on Palm Sunday, 5 April 1716, at the instigation of Mme de Lambert, when they all drank to Homer's health. The dinner took place shortly before the appearance of the 1716 edition of Mme Dacier's *Odessey*, which does not mention Houdar de la Motte. He had himself cut short his own *Réflexions sur la critique* to avoid giving further provocation.

This whole continuation of the Querelle des anciens et des modernes (q.v.) had its farcical side. The simple and sincere Mme Dacier did not know English, and deeply offended Pope by attacking him as an enemy of Homer. Houdar de la Motte's "translation" of the *Iliad* was hindered by his total ignorance of Greek. What was at stake remained, however, what had been at stake between Boileau and Perrault. Were literary values in the end merely aesthetic, and therefore immutable, possibly having reached a peak in antiquity, as Boileau and Bossuet thought? Or was literature a means by which society reflected, examined, affirmed, and encouraged refinements in behaviour, manners, and values, as Perrault, Fénelon, Fontenelle and Houdar de la Motte thought? Fénelon was of course by 1714 committed to his admiration for Homer, but his enemies, led by Bossuet, were aligned supporters of the "anciens," and his religious, aesthetic and social sensibilities were thoroughly "moderne."

It was only on 6 March 1721 that Houdar de la Motte had his first tragedy performed, *Les Macchabées*. At that date tragedy in Paris was allowed to be given only by the French company, to which Houdar de la Motte accordingly returned. This first tragedy—in the sense of tragic non-musical drama—was followed on 8 January 1722 by *Romulus*, a tragedy of which Alexis Piron made fun in his *Arlequin-Deucalion*, played on 25 February at the fairground theatre. In 1718 the French company had succeeded in having the full rigour of its monopoly rights over spoken dialogue enforced, so that Piron's play had to be a monologue. It is said to have been written by its indigent author in 24 hours, to save the fairground theatre manager Francisque from financial disaster, and it evaded the prohibition of dialogue by putting the whole story of the re-creation of mankind after the flood into the mouth of Deucalion. He is the only character with formal lines, although he sums up what other characters on stage are thinking or dreaming.

At least two couplets and one prose passage in the torrent of Piron's "monologue" parodied passages from Houdar de la Motte's *Romulus*, which had had its first performance only seven weeks previously, and a flute tune of André-Cardinal Destouches from Houdar de la Motte's *Issé* was also played. Piron also parodied Crébillon, Marivaux, and Voltaire, as well as some of Jean-Baptiste Rousseau's defamatory couplets aimed at Houdar de la Motte which had led to the noisily expressed bitterness between them, and eventually also to Rousseau's exile by a decree of the Châtelet in April 1712.

Houdar de la Motte's third tragedy was the highly successful *Inès de Castro* of 6 April 1723. Its first night clashed with the Italian company's première of Marivaux's *La double inconstance*. The fourth, *Oedipe*, of 18 March 1726, on a subject whose successful treatment by Voltaire Houdar de la Motte, acting as official censor, had much admired, failed when performed in verse. Houdar de la Motte rewrote it in prose, publishing it with four *Discours sur la tragédie* in the 1730 *Oeuvres*. It was in this volume that he took to extremes his theoretical and critical ideas about both poetry and drama. He had himself written rhymed verse, and *Inès* observes the unities. Only at this late moment in his life did Houdar de la Motte think that tragedy in verse was no longer possible. He still believed in the beauty rhyme and metre could add to prose, although as early as 1707 an ode to Fontenelle *Sur l'émulation* had contained the couplet

Dépouillons ces respects serviles
Que l'on rend aux siècles passés

(Let us rid ourselves of our servility to past centuries).

Houdar de la Motte's views on the ode, which by no means excluded versification, had probably been formed in reaction against the lyrical ideas of Claude Fleury, for whom the function of odes was to sing the heroic deeds of gods and heroes. Besides his odes in prose, Houdar de la Motte did provocatively write odes to algebra and geometry and it was his dislike of lyricism which provoked his harshest comments on Jean-Baptiste Rousseau. The attack in the 1730 *Discours* against the unities as antagonistic to dramatic illusion, against monologues, moral "sentences," and even the use of verse does not represent what had been in any sense his own committed practice, and was largely intended as a speculative goad. Above all, Houdar de la Motte felt that the stage was there for spectacle, and that emotional warmth was more important than moral lessons. Voltaire ungratefully made himself the defender of traditional dramaturgy against Houdar de la Motte in the preface to the 1730 edition of his *Oedipe*.

Houdar de la Motte's final stage piece was the comedy *Les Magnifiques; ou, L'Italie galante*, played on 11 May 1731. He had been completely blind since 1718, and suffered increasingly from a number of infirmities, including at the end paralysis. He died on 26 December 1731.

WORKS

Historically, Inès de Castro, the illegitimate mistress of the heir to the Portuguese throne, by whom he had three children and with whom he lived openly after his wife's death, was beheaded. Since the marriage contract expressly stipulated that the heir should have no concubine, his father finally had Inès executed during his son's absence. When in 1357 after a civil war the prince succeeded to the throne, the counsellors responsible for the execution were tortured and put to death. Houdar de la Motte softens the ending of the story. In his version Dom Pèdre, son of Alphonse, king of Portugal, marries Inès, and she dies of self-administered poison in Dom Pèdre's arms after the king has repented of his sentence. There is no civil war or vengeance. The emphasis has moved from what might have been a stark political tragedy with a central pair of young lovers in a relationship incompatible with the needs of the state, to a personal play in which the dramatist attempts to move the audience through the presentation of domestic affections and political constraints, with selflessness valued more highly than combative heroism, and violence reduced to a death by poison, allowing for characters to deliver speeches after the process of dying has begun.

This version of events establishes Houdar de la Motte's principal source, the 1722 novel *Inès de Castro; ou, Histoire de Pierre de Portugal* by the abbé Desfontaines, although Houdar de la Motte also drew on Camoëns and on the 1652 *Reinar después de morir* of Luis Velez de Guevara. Houdar de la Motte, without of course knowing it, was moving in the direction of the drame bourgeois when he wrote that conjugal love and paternal affection were the twin springs on which the dramatic effect depended. The introduction of Inès's children onto the stage to add pathos to the emotional effect as their mother dies was also audacious. It is true that children had appeared in *Athalie*, but Racine's play had not been intended for public performance and was written to be played by adolescents.

Houdar de la Motte, who points out how carefully each act constitutes a dramatic tableau, wrote of his play in the 1730 *Discours*

La convenance est ici le pathétique, puisque l'amour conjugal et l'amour paternel sont l'âme de toute la pièce. Ce n'est ni le sublime de la religion, ni l'héroïque de l'ambition. La matière n'est que touchante et demande qu'on s'y propose toujours d'aller au coeur

(What moves the emotions here is propriety, since conjugal love and paternal love are the soul of the whole play, not the sublime in religion or the heroism of ambition. The content is simply moving and demands that the aim should be to go straight to the heart).

Houdar de la Motte congratulated himself on the tears he drew even from his critics. There are undoubtedly reminiscences of Corneille in the characterization, but they are not so strong as the apparent desire to manage the characterization more powerfully than a Racine, but in a way opposed to Racine's. Constance, betrothed to Dom Pèdre, refuses to be jealous of Inès. Alphonse explains to his son that there are more important considerations than love in the marriage unions of sovereigns. The two counsellors, one of whom owes his life to Dom Pèdre and the other of whom is his rival in love, demand verdicts for and against the death of Inès entirely contradictory to their natural instincts. Inès herself would rather face her own death than acquiesce in Dom Pèdre's rebellion, and insists on Alphonse's duty to his family. Houdar de la Motte has distorted the historical sources to deliver a moral and sentimental dramatic depiction of domestic virtue, based on paternal and conjugal affection. The play's success was immense, comparable to that of Voltaire's *Oedipe* and even, if we are to take Houdar de la Motte literally, to that of *Le Cid*. He preens himself in the published preface on having been parodied, "the same honour done by Scarron to Virgil."

Apart from Alphonse king of Portugal and the queen of Castille, and the triangle of Dom Pèdre, the king's son, with his betrothed, Constance, daughter of the queen, and his mistress, Inès, there are two other principal characters, the counsellors Dom Rodrigue and Dom Henrique. In the first act the royal marriage, long mooted, is finally arranged after the military victory of Dom Pèdre over the Africans has shown him worthy of the hand of Constance, who is in love with him. The preface had drawn attention to a similarity with Corneille's heroes' sentiments, but what had seemed imaginatively audacious in 1637 had by 1723 acquired a jaded ring. It was no longer stirring that the hero's father should want the hero to show himself worthy of the heroine. The queen expresses her worry at Dom Pèdre's lack of interest, accuses Inès, her lady-in-waiting, of being Dom Pèdre's mistress, and threatens violent vengeance on whoever it may be that has captured Dom Pèdre's affection. The act ends with a scene between Inès and Dom Pèdre, with his servant on the lookout in case they are interrupted. Should the queen discover the secret marriage of Dom Pèdre and Inès only Inès's death is going to enable her to fulfil her ambition of marrying her daughter to Dom Pèdre. Inès had agreed to her own marriage, legally an act of rebellion, only to avert Dom Pèdre's threatened suicide if she did not. She begs him not to start a civil war, and prevails on him with notably feeble reasoning not to make her flee with him.

The second act starts with the appearance of the only principal character not yet introduced, Constance, who asks Alphonse to wait until his son really wants to marry her before hastening the marriage which the audience already knows to be impossible. Alphonse is implacable. His son will obey and, anyway, "à tant de traits ne peut être insensible (cannot be insensitive to so many attractive features)," as those possessed by Constance. Alphonse now argues with Dom Pèdre the primacy of the interests of the state, demonstrating a series of values that had been important to the generation of Mairet, Rotrou, and even the Corneille brothers, but that must have sounded gratingly obsolete to an audience of 1723 on the side of the young lovers, against which interests of state no longer weighed as heavily as they had nearly a century before. Alphonse becomes a potential villain when he says to Dom Pèdre

Mais vous figurez-vous que ces grands hymenées
Qui des enfants des rois règlent les destinées
Attendent le concert des vulgaires ardeurs,
Et, pour être achevés, veuillent l'aveu des coeurs?...
Nous sommes affranchis de la commune loi;
L'intérêt des Etats donne seul notre foi.
Laissons à nos sujets cet égard populaire,
De n'approuver d'hymen que celui qui sait plaire,
D'y chercher le rapport des coeurs et des esprits;
Mais ce bonheur pour nous n'est pas d'assez haut prix:
Il nous est glorieux qu'un hymen politique
Assure à nos dépens la fortune publique

(But do you really think that the great marriages/Which determine the destinies of the families of kings/Wait on the harmony of common passions,/And, for their completion, require the consent of the heart?.../We are liberated from the law of common people;/What commands our commitment is alone the interest of states./Let us leave to our subjects the view of the crowd/That assents to a marriage only where there is love,/Looking for a relationship of hearts and minds;/But this happiness is too cheap for us;/It is a source of pride to us that a political marriage/Should secure at our expense public well-being).

Houdar de la Motte is testing public tolerance to the utmost in the Alphonse of the early part of the play, and it is significant in any attempt to understand the play's imaginative purposes that he should find it expedient to soften Alphonse's attitude in the direction of augmented paternal solicitude before the end of the play. In Alphonse's speech in reply to Dom Pèdre's answer to the lines just quoted, the clash in Alphonse between his high principles of kingship and his domestic fondness for his son already clearly clash. Houdar de la Motte quotes a verse from *Le Cid* which makes no concessions to family bonds, and which he said was his own before he was aware that it had been used before:

Vous parlez en soldat, je dois agir en roi

(You speak as a soldier, I must act as a king).

Still in act II, the queen reveals to Alphonse that Inès is the object of Dom Pèdre's devotion. Neither of them denies it, and Inès is entrusted to the safe-keeping of her bitterest enemy, the queen, who seems about to threaten her with vengeance against Dom Pèdre when Constance comes in. Informed of the situation by the queen, Constance asks her not to avenge her repudiation by Dom Pèdre in favour of Inès. It will not assuage her grief.

In the third act Alphonse sends for Inès, sees that she is irrevocably in love with Dom Pèdre, and threatens her with death should she ever dare to marry him secretly. The queen announces the rebellion of Dom Pèdre. Inès, alone with the queen, heroically says how sad she must herself be whatever the outcome. As for Alphonse, she will weep for his life if he is defeated, and for his virtue if, victorious, he opposes the love which binds her to Dom Pèdre, and kills either or both of them. Alone with Dom Pèdre, Inès reproaches him with his rebellion. When he says he has left the decision to the populace, she urges him to go to the defence of his father. He is outraged when he still refuses to let him take her to a place of shelter. Constance enters and, in spite of the rejection she has suffered, urges Dom Pèdre in the presence of Inès to save himself. Alphonse comes in and tells Dom Pèdre to choose. He must hand over his sword and be killed or himself kill his father. He hands over the sword, pleading for the life at least of Inès.

The whole play has so far centred on the clash between attitudes taken up for reasons of politics or pride and those dictated by love, with the three younger characters, Dom Pèdre, Inès, and Constance, all making renunciations of heroic generosity as well. Inès has been the defender of Dom Pèdre's duty to his father, and Constance's concern for the man who has rejected her has been heroic. The fourth act starts with a monologue spoken by Alphonse. He supposes that his counsellors will demand the execution of his son, but when Dom Pèdre comes in gives him a last chance to save himself by marrying Constance. Act IV, scene 3 is the great council scene. Rodrigue loves Inès, but demands clemency for Dom Pèdre. Henrique owes his life to Dom Pèdre, but thinks he should be executed. If he is, he will kill himself. Alphonse decides on the death penalty. Constance cannot believe it. Alphonse thinks the queen only pretends to regret it. Constance informs Inès and offers her rival any help she can still give to avert the catastrophe.

In the fifth act the queen, hearing that her daughter still loves Dom Pèdre, is intent not only on his death but also on that of her daughter's rival, Inès. She tells Alphonse that she regards Inès as the more blameworthy of the two. Constance pleads for Inès. Inès sends for what is in fact the poison which will kill her. She explains to Alphonse that his son, still not known to be her husband, is not responsible for the rebellion, and then reveals to Alphonse that she is married to Dom Pèdre, insisting that she alone is guilty. Inès's two children are now brought in by their governess and Inès challenges Alphonse to kill them, too, with her husband and herself, then offers herself as the only victim required by the law. Alphonse forgives Dom Pèdre and is prepared to bless his union with Inès: touched by the sight of his grand-children he now puts family sentiment before oaths and laws. Dom Pèdre comes in, but it is too late. Inès has taken the poison and dies in the arms of her husband and his father. The law is avenged, but true love and domestic values have proved stronger than the interests of politics and pride.

If the emotional reactions and dilemmas of the characters had been portrayed as less affected or exaggerated, Houdar de la Motte might have written a very strong play, but he has tried too hard to assert domestic, sentimental values. He wanted to move his audience with emotional dilemmas which strike modern readers and would strike modern audiences as inauthentic and sometimes artificial. The contemporary success of the tragedy is not surprising, but its imaginative interest, once strong, is now chiefly historical. It is not astonishing that Houdar de la Motte's reputation today rests finally on his jovially speculative, blinkered, but in the end probing questions about the nature of literature as essentially "moderne."

PUBLICATIONS

[*A number of individual works can be found only in the collected editions, and their titles are therefore not individually listed below. Dates of performance of all important works are given in the text*]

Collections

Oeuvres de M. Houdar de la Motte, 9 vols., 1754
Les Oeuvres de théâtre de M. de la Motte avec plusieurs discours sur la tragédie, 2 vols., 1730 [contains the four *Discours*]

Plays and libretti

L'Europe galante, ballet en musique (1697), 1697
Issé, pastorale héroïque en musique (1697), 1697
Amadis de Grèce, tragédie (1699), 1699
Marthésie, première reine des Amazones, tragédie, 1699
Canente, tragédie (1700), 1700
Les Originaux; ou, L'Italien, comédie (1693), in *Théâtre italien*, 1700, vol. 4
Le Triomphe des arts, ballet (1700), 1700
La Matrone d'Ephèse, comédie (1702), 1702
Les Trois Gascons, comédie (1701), 1702
Le Carnaval et la folie, comédie-ballet (1701), 1703
Le Port de mer, comédie (1704), 1704
La Vénitienne, ballet (1705), 1705
Alcione, tragédie (1706), 1706
Sémélé, tragédie (1709), 1709
Omphale, tragédie (1701), 1721
Les Macchabées, tragédie (1721), 1722
Romulus, tragédie (1722), 1722
Inès de Castro, tragédie (1723), 1723; modern edition in the Bibliothèque de la Pléiade *Théâtre du XVIIIe siècle*, vol. 1, 1972

Verse

Le premier livre de l'Illiade, 1701
L'Illiade, poème, avec un discours sur Homère, 1714
Odes... avec un Discours sur la poésie en général et sur l'ode en particulier, 1707
Fables nouvelles, 1719

Other

Réflexions sur la critique...avec plusieurs lettres de M. l'archevêque de Cambrai et de l'auteur, 3 vols., 1715
Suite des réflexions sur la tragédie, 1730

Biographical and critical studies

Dupont, Paul, *Un poète philosophe au commencement du XVIIIe siècle. Houdar de la Motte (1672–1731)*, 1898
Finch, R., *The Sixth Sense*, 1966

HUET, Pierre-Daniel, 1630–1721.

Bishop, scholar, and man of letters.

LIFE

Although Huet did write in the imaginative genres, his real importance lies in his role from 1674 at the Académie française, which had been reorganized and given a much greater role in literary affairs in 1672–73. On the occasion of his election Huet had been little more than a pawn in the struggle between conflicting parties, but he came to mediate as a moderate between the opposing sides in the Querelle des anciens et des modernes (q.v.). He was also an habitué of the Hôtel de Rambouillet, visited the court of Christina of Sweden, cooperated closely with Mme de Lafayette in the preparation of *Zaïde*, became assistant to Bossuet as tutor to the dauphin, turned against Cartesianism, and became bishop successively of Soissons (1685) and Avranches (1689).

He was also a translator, critic, classical scholar, and theologian of note. He lived to be 91, publishing almost to the end, so that his adult career, neatly spanning the whole of the second half of the 17th century and the first years of the 18th, is of extraordinary literary interest. There is still a considerable amount of unedited material by and about him, but he himself wrote an account of his life, the *Commentarius de rebus ad eum pertinentibus* of 1718, translated into English in 1810 and by Nisard into French in 1853 as *Mémoires*. Huet's younger friend, the abbé Pierre-Joseph d'Olivet (1682–1768), who continued Pellisson's *Histoire de l'Académie française*, published the fragmentary *Huetiana* in 1722, and in 1723 an *Eloge historique de M. Huet* as a preface to Huet's own *Traité philosophique de la faiblesse de l'esprit humain*.

Huet was born in Caen on 8 February 1630. His father, a Catholic convert from Calvinism and a churchwarden of the parish in which Huet was baptized, was a senior government official who earned a substantial income and may have belonged to the minor nobility. He had received a classical education and was interested in music and the technical aspects of ballet. He died when Huet was three. Huet's much younger mother, Isabelle Pillon de Bertouville, died when he was just six. Huet was looked after by his uncle, Gilles Macé, himself a mathematician, and then by his widow. Macé's son, Daniel, became Huet's official guardian. Daniel Macé gave Huet his father's mathematical books and astronomical instruments, which Huet used to observe the 1664 comet and in connection with his founding of the Académie des sciences at Caen.

Huet was sent to a convent at Rouen where he had aunts in the community and then, when he was eight, to the Jesuit college at Caen. Among his teachers was Père Mambrun, who, in the preface to his 1658 poem *Constantius*, already vaunted the superiority of contemporary French culture over that of Greece and Rome. Huet went on to study law, and became an early disciple of Descartes, although he was to turn against Cartesianism, with the circle surrounding Montauzier, probably under the influence of Chapelain. Mme de Sévigné wrote to her daughter on 15 June 1689 that Huet had turned anti-Cartesian simply to please Montauzier. As early as 1650 Huet marked disagreements in his copy of Descartes's *Les Passions de l'âme*, and in 1667 he annotated his edition of Descartes's letters with views contrary to those expressed in the text. Huet disliked Descartes's independence from antique authority. He had himself learnt Greek and Hebrew, and had also begun to study Arabic and Syriac. At the age of 18 he translated Longus's pastoral romance *Daphnis and Chloé* from Greeek into Latin, possibly with the help of Amyot's earlier French translation, and read his sisters passages from d'Urfé's *L'Astrée*.

By 1652 Huet, regarding himself above all as a scholar, was in contact with many of the most eminent figures of the learned world, the elderly Père Sirmond, Peteau, and Gassendi. He was introduced to the court of Christina of Sweden by the Calvinist pastor Samuel Bochart and went with him to Stockholm, where he found the manuscript of Origen's commentary on Matthew. He was to publish a translation of it in 1668. He appears to have quarrelled with Bochart in Stockholm, with the result that Bochart leaked a poem of Huet's which was disobliging towards the learning of the Swedish court. After her abdication, however, Christina was to invite Huet to join her in Rome in 1659 and to recommend him as tutor to Charles-Gustav XI, although he declined both invitations. On his return to Caen from Sweden in 1652, he stopped at Leiden (to see Heinsius), Utrecht, Amsterdam (to see Vossius, who had recommended him to Christina), and Louvain. At Amsterdam conversations with Rabbi Mannassé-ben-Israël led eventually to Huet's *Demonstratio evangelica* of 1679. As a result of the war between England and the Netherlands Huet's luggage, including the copy he had made of the Origen manuscript, was detained at the border for two years. Bochart first saw the work in 1654 and attacked the transcription of one line as faulty.

Huet already knew Ménage and Segrais, and was elected to the Académie de Caen before or immediately after his return from Sweden. He may well sometimes have attended Ménage's Wednesday "Mercuriales," in the Cloître Notre-Dame in Paris, as well as Madeleine de Scudéry's Saturday receptions, the famous "samedis." While establishing himself as a scholar, and working on the translation of Origen, Huet also found time to write a novel inspired by d'Urfé, *Diane de Castro; ou, Le Faux Inca*. It was published only posthumously, in 1728, but, the manuscript circulated and helped his reputation in salon society. Huet visited Paris briefly and infrequently but later became an habitué of the Hôtel de Rambouillet in its declining years, and also received the protection of Montauzier. About this time he must have taken to dining regularly with half a dozen "libertin" friends, forming what he refers to in a letter to a nephew of 1711 as an "académie burlesque," at which were produced satirical "ouvrages burlesques mais ingénieux (burlesque but witty piece" In 1656 Huet took minor orders, remaining on terms of emotionally intimate but chaste friendship with Marie-Eléonore de Rohan, daughter of Mme de Montbazon and abbess of the convent of the Trinity at Caen. He came to the notice of Chapelain, whose *La Pucelle* he was later to defend. Chapelain described him in 1660 as "a new Horace" and said of him in the 1662 *Mémoires de quelques gens de lettres* that he wrote "galamment (gallantly)" in Latin verse and prose.

Chapelain's recommendation ensured Huet an income for life. The first list of "gratifications" in 1663, granted by Colbert on behalf of the king and partly on the recommendation of Chapelain, included 4,000 livres for the king's historiographer, Mézeray, reduced to 2,000 from 1671, 3,000 each for Chapelain, "the greatest poet there had ever been," and Bourzeis until their deaths, 2,000 livres for Pierre Corneille until 1674, and 1,500 livres apiece for Huet, (for translating Origen), Bensserade, Conrart, Perrot d'Ablancourt, Perrault, Charpentier, and Cassagne, all for life. Thereafter, 1,200 livres apiece were allocated to Desmarets de Saint-Sorlin, Gombauld, and Cotin, 1,000 to Molière, Thomas Corneille, La Mothe le Vayer, and the abbé de Pure, 800 to Quinault, Boyer, and Fléchier, and 600 to Racine, generally for life. The only changes not mentioned were increases for Racine, Quinault, and Perrault. Boileau was paid a pension from the privy purse from 1674, and 2,000 livres a year on the general list from 1676.

The later partisans of the "modernes" in the Querelle des anciens et des modernes were still standing high in official favour two years after Fouquet's disgrace in 1661, although it is important for Huet's later career to appreciate that the camps were not quite so clearly divided as the list of "gratifiés" of 1663, from which Boileau was pointedly excluded, has subsequently been thought to suggest. The incipient split between the two parties was, however, observed by La Mesnardière as early as 1656, by which date Ménage had taken the side of Voiture and, in spite of differences of opinion and quarrels between them, could be seen to share a delight in salon literature with Costar, Pellisson, Sarrazin, and Chapelain. It came out into the open when Gilles Boileau, who had attacked Chapelain, was excluded at first from the Académie, and avenged by Cotin in *La Ménagerie*. Huet already had reservations about the system, and on 17 August 1663 wrote to Ménage: "Il y a quelque sorte de honte de faire des vers pour de l'argent, comme vous le dites avec raison (There is a sort of shame in writing verse for money, as you rightly say)."

Meanwhile, in 1661, Huet, who never lost his liking for antique authors, had published a treatise on translation in the form of a dialogue, the *De interpretatione*, by implication castigating the freedom of translation widespread in the first half of the century and typified in the approach to translation of Perrot d'Ablancourt. In 1662 Huet created the Académie des sciences at Caen, attracting an official subsidy from Colbert. He was already known at court, since he had helped Segrais gather together the 59 *Divers portraits*, including one of himself and one by himself, published early in 1659 by the Grande Mademoiselle, duchesse de Montpensier, whose service Segrais had entered in 1648. It was in 1659 that Huet was presented by Ménage to Mme de Lafayette, who came to rely on him for advice, and for whom he corrected the sketches and drafts of *Zaïde* at least twice. As early as 1656 Segrais, purporting merely to collect the six stories of *Les Nouvelles françaises; ou, Les Divertissements de la Princesse Aurélie*, reported Aurélie's distinction between the imagination of the adventure novelists, drawing on fantasy, and that of the authors of "nouvelles," sticking to historical authenticity and psychological realism. On this point, there was widespread agreement. Poetic enthusiasm was important for Marolles, Charpentier, and even Cotin, but poetry, for Charpentier and the précieux (q.v.) Louis le Laboureur in 1664, was essentially the imitation of nature. Huet, too, opposed natural and "artificial" beauties.

By 1670 Huet's playfully intimate relationship with Mme de Montespan had developed. After her abandonment by Louis XIV, by whom she had the first of two children in 1670, she retired to Fontevrault, where her sister was abbess, and where Huet came from time to time to stay until, in the end, she dismissed him. In that year Montauzier failed to obtain for him the post of tutor to the dauphin, and he had to be content with becoming Bossuet's assistant in the post. In 1671 Fléchier, whom Huet must have known from the Hôtel de Rambouillet and who was just about to start his career as a successful preacher, joined Huet as lecteur to the dauphin. Huet himself now organized the team he employed to turn out the 60 volumes of annotated and commentated classical texts "ad usum delphini," known in France as "dauphins." Bossuet encouraged Huet to undertake the anti-Cartesian *Demonstratio evangelica*, finished in 1676, partly to refute Spinoza's *Tractatus theologico-politicus* of 1670. In spite of difficulties, about which Mon-

tauzier wrote to him in 1677, Bossuet and three other bishops had signed the *Demonstratio's* approbation, although Bossuet soon discovered that the work, published in 1679, was a poor defence against Spinoza. Huet had argued from universal consent, which weakened the work's apologetic utility, and further incurred Bossuet's displeasure by applying general principles of historical criticism to the Bible. A remark in the *Demonstratio* that the "Fiat lux" of Genesis did not belong to the sublime also aggravated Boileau, who was still writing about it in a *Dissertation* of 1710 and three *Remarques* which appeared in 1713.

Huet's *Lettre de l'origine des romans*, printed separately a year or two previously, had appeared as the preface to *Zaïde* in 1669. The dauphin was not a rewarding pupil. His reading was largely confined to the "Births" and "Deaths" announcements in the *Gazette*, and he spent whole days in bed with a stick, hitting his shoes, reducing Bossuet to despair. Huet had himself been ordained priest by Claude Avry, bishop of Coutances, in 1676. On account of the delay since his minor orders he needed a special dispensation, and in 1678 was made abbot of Aulnai near Caen. His relationship with Bossuet had cooled, and in 1680 he was dispensed from his duties with the dauphin and took up residence in his abbey. In the meanwhile, on 13 August 1674, he had been elected a member of the Académie française in succession to Le Roy de Gomberville.

Boileau's *Art poétique* had appeared with an "achevé d'imprimer" of 10 July 1674, although there had been salon readings since at least March 1672. It was partly directed against Desmarets de Saint-Sorlin, who, in the preface to his *Esther* of 1670, had defended the modern heroic poem, with Christian miracle ("le merveilleux chrétien") instead of pagan figures, and partly against the powerful Charles Perrault. In 1673 Desmarets had returned to the attack with a new edition of *Clovis*, and five weeks after the appearance of the *Art poétique* and five days after Huet's reception, Desmarets published the *Défense du poème héroïque*. Huet was received by Fléchier, but Quinault recited a *Relation nouvelle du Parnasse*, and Perrault replied with a forthright expression of views associated with the "modernes." Desmarests himself read a poem, and a few days later Charpentier sent Perrault a poem expressing the same views. Poems were also recited at Huet's reception by Cotin and by Furetière, later to become a close friend.

Huet was a moderate supporter of the "anciens" who remained on friendly terms with Perrault, and to whom La Fontaine, friendly with both and anxious to see an alliance between both sides in the Querelle, wrote a famous verse epistle in 1674, distancing himself from the extreme views of Boileau. It was published only in 1687. Huet's position was not so much moderate as with a foot in both camps. He sided with the "modernes" in the Académie in the matter of the *Dictionnaire*. The various academies had all been more or less reduced to instruments of royal policy by 1672, in which year, on 28 January, Séguier, the protector of the Académie française, died. The constitution was changed. Reception ceremonies became public, but the court was able to impose its own candidates, and was indeed used by Colbert partly as a private fiefdom. It was the court which imposed, alongside Bossuet, the elections of Valincour, Fleury, La Bruyère, and Boileau, and which held up the election of La Fontaine in an attempt to break the power of the "modernes," Perrault, Bensserade, Quinault, and Charpentier.

Although Huet agreed with the "anciens," including Patru, Furetière, Richelet, and Mézeray, that the French language had degenerated into elegant but ignorant salon usage, he none the less supported the "modernes," whose position derived essentially from the view that the language had reached its point of perfection, and that the *Dictionnaire* ought anyway to reflect current usage, not a usage in conformity with arbitrary and unchangeable norms. He also tried to restrain Boileau's protest at the Académie during the reading by Perrault of his *Siècle de Louis le Grand*. Huet published a *Censura* of the philosophy of Descartes in 1689 and in 1690 the *Alnetanae quaestiones*, on the relation between faith and reason, against Descartes. He was to live long enough to welcome to the Académie, when he was 90, the Czar Peter the Great.

In 1699 Huet fell ill. Owing to a dispute between the Holy See and the king, he never took proper possession of the bishopric of Soissons, to which he was appointed in 1685. The necessary papal bulls did not arrive. He did not enjoy his period as bishop of Avranches from 1689 to 1699, when he retired. The king made Huet abbot of Fontenay, near Caen, but the court cases concerning the abbey's property were too much for him, and he retired again in 1701, this time to spend the rest of his life with the Jesuits. He had always believed in vigorous exercise, enjoyed hill-walking when he was 60, insisted on a sunny south-facing room, lived at the top of 80 stairs, and from time to time complained. From the age of 40 he had avoided all stews, ate well at midday, drank almost no alcohol, and took no more than a bowl of clear soup in the evening. Until his death in 1704, Bourdaloue visited him daily. Between 1681 and 1712, Huet compiled his notes on the Vulgate. He is said during this period to have spent two or three hours daily on the Hebrew text. He published further anti-Cartesian essays, works on Solomon's journeys, the history of Caen, and the trade of the ancients, and, in 1709, his own *Carmina*. In 1712, when he was 82, he had to spend six months in bed, possibly suffering from a cerebral haemorrhage, and it was on his recovery that he wrote his memoirs. He regularly saw Pierre-Joseph d'Olivet (1682–1768), who published his posthumous works, and was close to Mabillon before he died in 1707.

Huet left his books to the Jesuits, and a vast correspondence with many of Europe's more important thinkers. There had been over 8,000 bound volumes and 200 manuscripts, but much was destroyed when Huet's Normandy house fell in during the winter of 1693. When the Jesuits were expelled from France in 1763, the collection reverted to Huet's nephew. Catherine the Great made an offer for it, but it was sold to the Bibliothèque Royale, now the Bibliothèque Nationale.

WORKS

Huet correctly regarded himself as a serious scholar, and Sainte-Beuve said of him that he had "la plume la plus savante d'Europe (the most knowledgeable pen in Europe)." His attitude to the salon literature composed by himself and others can be judged by two lines from his *Dialogue de Climène et de Tirsis*:

L'amour en prose est dangereux
En vers il est sans conséquence

(Love discussed in prose is dangerous / In verse it is of no consequence).

The *Huetiana* publishes his view:

Notre nation, notre goût, sont ennemis des grands ouvrages. Tout ce qui demande de l'application nous rebute. Une ode nous ennuie par sa longueur. A peine peut on souffrir un sonnet. Notre génie se borne à l'étendue du madrigal. Nous sommes au siècle des colifichets. Toute notre industrie ne va qu'à faire de fort grandes petites choses…[Chapelain] n'a pas connu le génie de notre nation et de notre siècle…brusque, ardent, impatient et incapable de la longue et constante attention que demande l'élévation et l'étendue du poème épique

(Our nation, our taste, are hostile to great works. Everything that demands mental effort repels us. An ode annoys us by its length. We can scarcely put up with a sonnet. Our response limits us to the demands of a madrigal. We are in a century of knick-knacks. All our effort goes into making very big little things… [Chapelain] did not understand the characteristic of our nation and our time… quick, burning, impatient and incapable of the long and sustained attention which the elevation and the length of the epic poem requires).

Even the *Lettre de l'origine des romans*, an essay in comparative literary history, intended to provide the basis for a theory of the novel, is approached as a work of scholarship. Its real importance is the connection it suggests between the contemporary French novel and the advanced attitudes of cultivated French salon life towards the role of women in society, and towards personally enriching instinctive affection, or love. According to Huet, the dialogue was written in 1666. The first known edition is its publication as a preface to the first volume of Mme de Lafayette's *Zaïde* in 1669, but it is at least likely that it was published in brochure form before that date. It was written at the convent of Malnoue, in the midst of the platonic intrigue between Huet and the abbess Eléonore de Rohan, and Huet starts with the novel's definition, on the constituent parts of which he then comments. What today are properly called novels, he writes, are

des histoires feintes amoureuses, écrites en prose avec art, pour le plaisir et l'instruction des lecteurs

(fictitious stories about love, written according to artistic norms in prose for the pleasure and the instruction of readers).

The story must be fictitious; love should be the principal subject; and the present time demands the use of prose. The "artistic norms" refer to rules, without which literary material cannot achieve order or beauty.

The principal aim is instruction. Virtue must be rewarded and wrongdoing punished. The diversion, amusement, or pleasure given to readers is no more than bait, enabling the principal end to be achieved, "l'instruction de l'esprit et la correction des moeurs (the enlightenment of the mind and the correction of behaviour)." "Vraisemblance," or probability, is essential. In the context of 17th-century literary discussion, that meant that verisimilitude, or retention of the intrigue within currently accepted norms of behaviour, was essential, a view which deprived the novel of any role in imaginatively exploring attitudes which would subvert those currently regarded as normative. Huet is here taking the conservative view against that which allows the novel, like those of Mme de Lafayette herself, to investigate new and startling interpretations of experience.

None the less Huet does come quite near a modern understanding of the cultural role of narrative fiction when he affirms that it derives from the author's desire to "learn and communicate what he has learned." He finds the origins of the novel in the Orient, including what we would refer to as the near and middle east, and in antiquity, and follows the well-established tradition which saw the origin of fiction in the allegorization of a theological truth revealed in its purity only to the initiated. Although the Greeks are acknowledged to have inherited the allegorical theology of the Egyptians, Huet does not repeat the legend of an Egyptian transmission to Plato of God's revelation to Moses, although he does note that "L'Ecriture sainte est toute mystique, toute allégorique, toute énigmatique (Holy Scripture is mystical, allegorical, and mysterious)."

Huet goes on to trace the development of the novel in Greece and Italy, indulging himself in various esoteric polemics against some antique authors, mostly on account of their scatological content, and against some inauthentic texts. France, having yielded to other countries the prizes in epic poetry and history, has easily achieved the first place in the novel, no doubt, thinks Huet, on account of "la politesse de notre galanterie (the cultivation in our social behaviour)," and especially of the way women are treated in French society. In spite of its occasional licentiousness, Huet likes *L'Astrée*:

M. d'Urfé fut le premier qui tira nos romans de la barbarie et les assujettit aux règles dans son incomparable *Astrée*, l'ouvrage le plus ingénieux et le plus poli qui eût jamais paru en ce genre…

(M. d'Urfé was the first to draw our novels from barbarism and subject them to the rules in his incomparable *Astrée*,

the most inventive and elevated work which had ever appeared in this genre…).

PUBLICATIONS

Literary works in French

Traité de l'origine des romans, 1670; as *Lettre de M.H. à M. de Segrais, de l'origine des romans*, 1978
Diane de Castro; ou, Le Faux Inca, 1728

Literary works in Latin

De interpretatione libri duo, 1661
P.D.H. commentarius de rebus ad eum pertinentibus, 1718; as *Memoir of the Life of P.D.H., bishop of Avranches*, 1810; as *Mémoires de D.H.*, 1853
P.D.H. poemata latina et graeca, 1694; revised edition, 1700
Carmina, 1709

Other

Originis in sacras Scripturas commentarii, 2 vols., 1668
Demonstratio evangelica, 1679
Censura philosophiae Cartesianae, 1689
Alnetanae quaestiones de concordia rationis et fidei, 1690
Traité de la situation du Paradis terrestre, 1691
Les Origines de la ville de Caen et des lieux circonvoisins, 1702
Le Grand Trésor historique et politique du florissant commerce des Hollandais dans tous les états et empires du monde, 1712
Histoire du commerce et de la navigation des anciens, 1716
Traité philosophique de la faiblesse de l'esprit humain, 1723

J

JANSENISM (JANSEN, Cornelius; JANSENIST).

See Pascal, Port-Royal, Saint-Cyran, and General Index.

In so far as the term Jansenism is used with precision, and not just as a synonym for Catholic religious rigorism in France, it has come to denote two different things. Firstly, and more correctly, Jansenism is the name given to a position in the theology of grace associated with the Dutch theologian from Louvain, Cornelius Jansen (1585–1638), and set out in his large 1,640-folio volume, the *Augustinus*, purporting to refute various recent and especially Jesuit views in the light of what Jansen took to be the authentic teaching of the Church as originally set forth in the later occasional works of Augustine (A.D. 354–430), written against the heresy of Pelagius between A.D. 426 and A.D. 429, of which the most important is the *De correptione et gratia*.

In abstract theological terms the problem concerned the way the relationship should be envisaged between divine grace and human free will within the general parameters defined by original sin, the Incarnation, Redemption, and the reciprocally exclusive, but eternal and unchangeable alternatives of salvation or damnation for each human being at the moment of death. What was in fact at stake was, as so often before, the existence or absence of any power in human beings on earth who had the "use of reason," that is, who were adult and sane, to influence their eternal fates by choosing to act in such a way as to accept, merit or reject justifying grace. To allow the existence of any such power without the compulsion of grace was considered by Jansen to be heretical, but by his Jesuit opponents, in particular, to be fundamental to any proper understanding of the Christian revelation.

The term Jansenism is also much more loosely used for any Catholic spirituality in 17th- or 18th-century France consonant with Jansen's theological position that not all human beings are offered any chance of avoiding damnation. Such spiritualities deeply marked the religious life and literary investigations of the 17th century especially, and are associated with Saint-Cyran, the Arnauld family, and such supporters of Jansen as the congregation of nuns at the monastery of Port-Royal (q.v.) and their lay admirers, including Pascal and Nicole. The monastery had two houses, one in the faubourg Saint-Jacques, known as Port-Royal-de-Paris, and the other in the Chevreuse valley, at the abbey known as Port-Royal-des-Champs. For the history of Jansenist spirituality, and of the events which involved the abbey, users of the *Guide* are referred particularly to the entries on Port-Royal, Saint-Cyran, and Nicole, and to the General Index.

There are several reasons why Augustine is of peculiar importance in the Jansenist debates. It was Augustine who had formed, almost single-handedly, the first great synthesis of western Christian thought by combining the Christological and Trinitarian definitions of the early councils, defining that Jesus was one person with both divine and human natures, and that the Trinity was one God with one nature and three persons, with the neoplatonism he inherited from Plotinus and Porphyry, seeing God as primarily one, immanent in the various layers of multiplicity in the cosmos. Augustine also introduced the will as an operative faculty of the soul distinct from the intellect. Most significantly, his teaching on grace in particular, although always subjected to different interpretations, had been accepted as authoritative by the western Church since his death, notably determining the teaching imposed by Pope Zosimus in 418, while Augustine was still alive, and that of the council of Ephesus in 431, the year after his death.

The high medieval dispute about "universal" ideas, whether or not a tree was an individual modification of some abstract "treeness," was in fact a dispute about how human mental processes might be envisaged in such a way as to respect theological orthodoxy and to allow for cognition after death, that is the immortality of the soul. If a tree was an individual modification of "treeness," then knowledge depended on a process of abstraction which in turn depended on corruptible bodily organs. There could then apparently be no cognition after death, and therefore no personal immortality.

If each tree existed only in its own right, and there was no abstraction, then it seemed that the logical consequence was either an unthinkable tritheism, turning the three persons of the Trinity into three distinct entities, or an equally intolerable triple incarnation of all three persons of the one God. It was for a solution to such epistemological concerns that Aquinas in the 13th century turned to Aristotle, as transmitted with the Islamic glosses of the Arab theologians and philosophers. Aquinas, building on Aristotle, attempted to define what, in actual human experience, was "supernatural," and what attributable to "nature," and how the intellect's judgements of preference were integrated into the actual act of choice, which emanated from the will.

The psychology of the act of choice created huge difficulties for the scholastics, best illustrated by an example. If you buy a pair of shoes you will have performed various acts proceeding from the intellect. Will they suit their intended purpose? Is the colour right? Are they properly priced? What about the quality? Do they fit? You may have tried on and compared several pairs but, since you bought them, there will have been an act of decision which proceeded from the will, which is free. The problem derives from the difficulty in explaining how intellectual acts enter into the determination of the act of the will in the exercise of preference or choice. The colour and cost of the shoes must have some effect, but the will must remain free. Scholastic psychology, in spite of intricate arguments about rationality, appetites, acts, and faculties, never really succeeded in explaining how an intellectual act of judgement, which could not be free because constrained by reason, could enter into the determination of an act of will, which had to be.

Aquinas's solutions were immediately controverted, on the dual grounds of intellectual determinism in his explanation of the act of choice, and of naturalism. If God's law proceeded from reason, then why did it need revealing? If it did not proceed from reason, and whatever was good was good merely because it was decreed by God, did not God necessarily become arbitrary and capricious? Aquinas, like Augustine, was both ambiguous and on any understanding certainly misinterpreted, but in his theology, and in the reaction to it led first by Bonaventure and Scotus, and then by Ockham and the nominalists, lay the roots of all the principal controversies and religious tensions of the late middle ages and the 16th-century schisms. Common to all Catholic parties was an acceptance of the doctrine of predestination; of salvation by grace alone; and of some at least notional acceptance of the existence—dismissed altogether by all the reformers who went into schism—of "free will," not necessarily in the sense of any autonomous power of moral self-determination.

The questions of predestination and free will could be resolved in different ways. For Aquinas and the 16th-century Dominicans, there was a tendency chronologically as well as logically to postpone the will's "free" act of choice until after the determination of the will by grace or by the intellect. At least one 16th-century Dominican, Medina, whose doctrine was repudiated inside his own order, made the act of the intellect the actual cause of the will's determination. In the 13th century Scotus had regarded the will as absolutely free to determine itself, but had also held that God predetermined the salvation of individual souls and thereby, in order to avoid a doctrine involving nature's own cooperation in human salvation, created a quasi-chronology of divine acts.

Augustine himself, needless to say, had always allowed human cooperation in salvation, but that was before Aquinas had attempted to distinguish what in actual human experience was purely natural, what were the capabilities of fallen nature, and what, in our present experience, was supernatural. The idea that nature itself was redeemed and therefore by virtue of the redemption capable of cooperating with proffered grace, was impossible by the 13th century, because it would have meant allowing grace to the pagans. By 1302 it was defined dogma that outside the Church there was no salvation, although it had been taught long before that date, notably by Augustine's disciple, Fulgentius. A decree of 1690 made it clear that grace, after all, was available to non-believers.

The chronological concept of divine activity was not surprisingly rejected out of hand by the nominalists who, in consequence, had therefore to accept the absolute predestination of the elect, without any "prior" divine knowledge about their acts of will. It was the nominalist theologians who finally created the late medieval religion against which the 16th-century evangelical humanists and the reformers in different ways rebelled. God predetermined whether an individual was saved or damned, but Christians were offered the shoulder-shrugging crumb of comfort that those would be saved "who did whatever lay within them," a recipe for superstitious practices as well as for a religion of moral tension. Not only the reformers, but also that section of the counter-reformatory Catholic church which included the Jansenists, took as their starting point the rejection of any such religious position.

The dilemmas were atrocious. It seemed religiously intolerable to suppose that God, infusing into each foetus some time after conception, at a moment which the canonists thought differed according to gender, a newly created soul carrying the guilt of original sin, could be the author of sin, or that he could create creatures he knew he was inescapably going to damn. On the other hand it was clearly heretical to suppose that human beings could in any way contribute to their own supernatural salvations, consisting in a "vision of God" which demanded the communication of some form of participation in the divine essence, "uncreated grace," by their natural powers alone, even before the fall of Adam and even by the acceptance of proffered grace. That left the other possibility, that human beings were damned on account of their freely chosen sins, but saved because God had from the beginning decreed their salvation. But that is a logical impossibility.

It was naturally possible to attempt simply to by-pass these scholastic dilemmas, as did most writers of the Italian renaissance, the northern reformers, and the evangelical humanists, together with the late medieval mystics, the Brethren of the Common Life, and some important counter-reformers. The Jansenist debate arose from an attempt not to by-pass, but to confront them. Luther, Calvin, Zwingli, and even Ignatius of Loyola had turned their backs on the scholastic disputes, and even the council of Trent had resolutely refused to have anything to do with attempts to reconcile merit, freedom, and the gratuity of grace. Molina, however, attempted to resolve them. A Jesuit, he attempted in his remarkable 1588 *Concordia liberi arbitrii cum gratiae donis, divina praescientia, providentia, praedestinatione et reprobatione ad nonnullos primae partis divi Thomae articulos* to refute the Dominican Bañez's views about efficacious grace, which God simply decides to give or to withhold.

For Molina the will is free, but God foresees what an individual would have decided to do if the choice had been in that person's power, before deciding whether or not to bestow on that individual irresistibly efficacious grace in accordance with that knowledge. The solution may be intricate, but it ingeniously keeps the will free, divine foreknowledge infallible, and salvation the work totally of God. It does, however, again establish a quasi-chronology between divine acts, as well as allowing divine knowledge of future contingents, that is of things which would happen if certain circumstances were to be realized which in fact never come to pass. The idea of attributing that form of knowledge to God seems to have been Molina's own. Molina also edges very near the position, to which his fellow-Jesuit Leonard Lessius finally committed himself, that there is no real difference between efficacious and inefficacious grace, except that one has been accepted but the other has not. The difference is entirely extrinsic to the grace itself. Jansen referred to the doctrine he set out to attack as "Molinism."

As early as 1542 the newly founded Jesuits had opened their own theology faculty in Louvain alongside the august university in that town. In the 1560s a Louvain theologian, Michel du Bay (Baius), had attempted to restate the Church's teaching on grace in purely Augustinian terms, without reference to Aquinas's attempts to distinguish pure human nature from the elevated nature of Adam before the fall, from fallen human nature after it, from fallen but justified human nature, and from what in human nature was there on account of a gratuitous supernatural destiny. For Aquinas, the state of pure nature had never existed. From the beginning a supernatural element added to Adam's nature had destined him for the vision of God. For Du Bay, Adam's desire for the vision of God was part of his nature. There was no need to discuss a pure nature which no one thought had ever existed, and after the fall human beings needed supernatural grace even to regain the nature that had been Adam's.

The difficulty is that this theology, by requiring supernatural grace after the fall for the soul to return to its original nature, ruins Augustine's teaching on divine justice, and allows that only some human beings are elected to a destiny that belongs properly to all. Du Bay thinks in terms of merits, rights, and rewards. Since pagans are denied the rights bestowed by grace, all their works, even the apparently virtuous ones, are sinful. Du Bay was condemned, at first in 1560 by the Sorbonne for exaggerating the effects of Adam's sin on human liberty. He did not obey an injunction to be silent in 1561, and the king of Spain sent him as a theologian to the council of Trent. He continued to publish his brief works, and in 1567 Pius V condemned 79 propositions without naming their author. Du Bay did not acknowledge them as his own, and there was a famous dispute about a comma.

The condemnation reads as if the 79 propositions, even if some can be acceptably interpreted, none the less, "in rigour, and in the proper sense of the words intended by those who put them forward," were "heretical, erroneous, suspect, temerarious, scandalous and the cause of offence to pious ears." It was argued by Jansen and others that the comma had been misplaced, and that the original punctuation extended the "acceptable interpretation" of the condemned propositions to their understanding "in rigour and in the proper sense of the words intended by those who put them forward." It is unlikely that the comma was misplaced, but it was certainly meant to be unclear exactly who held what propositions, in what sense, and whether all or some were heretical, and whether singly or only together. This meticulously coded expression of disapproval contrasts stridently with the harsh and clear later condemnation of Jansen's propositions. Du Bay was notified personally of a further condemnation in 1580, but submitted, and died peacefully and obscurely in 1589. Jansen's original intention was to defend at least parts of the Baianist doctrine.

It was in the 1580s that the disputes broke out known as *De auxiliis* (on grace), the word "auxilium (help)" having replaced "gratia (grace)" in the second edition of the Jesuit teaching programme, the *Ratio studiorum*. There had been a quarrel at Valladolid about the freedom of Jesus in 1582. Did freedom necessarily imply choice? Jansen would hold that any act of will was "voluntary" and therefore "free." The argument moved to Salamanca, where in 1584 Bañez published his course. Molina published an extract of his. The publication of Molina's *Concordia* at Lisbon set light to the whole controversy, but in Louvain rather than Spain. The second edition of the *Concordia* was published in 1695 in Antwerp.

It is a long, not totally consistent or clear, but very clever book of considerable subtlety. The principal confusion comes from the desire to distinguish between the realm of experience and that of theological analysis, which would be, and in a sense had to be, characteristic of the whole Jansenist debate. Molina needed to distinguish between the continuous act of creation by which God keeps the universe in being and the supernatural grace which permits certain empirically identifiable forms of behaviour or experience and is therefore susceptible to psychological analysis, just as Jansen in the *Augustinus* moves continuously to and fro in an interpretation of Augustine's "victorious delectation" as something which is felt and as something which

is a metaphysical postulate not directly experienced in the order of sensation or constraint.

The contents of Molina's *Concordia* were instantly seized on, vulgarized, and simplified by Lessius, who imported into his exposition the concept of grace "post praevisa merita (after the prevision of merits)." Molina's merely sufficient grace becomes efficacious for Lessius through human cooperation, but only after God has foreseen and predetermined human actions in the light of his knowledge of future contingents. Notes taken by Lessius's students were made the basis of 34 propositions censured by the hostile university faculty, and what was virtually its subsidiary at Douai, between 1586 and 1588. Lessius was felt even by the two leading Jesuit theologians, Suarez and Bellarmine, to have gone too far in exalting natural powers. Both insisted on predestination before the prevision of merits.

It is a measure of the constraints on theological thinking imposed by the boundary posts of condemnations that both Suarez and Bellarmine compromise with theories of "congruous" grace. Having seen what Peter would do if he had had the power to choose meritorious activity, God gives him a grace which, while it does no physical violence to Peter's will, is calculated by God, knowing Peter's temperament, to be guaranteed to attract him sufficiently for its efficaciousness to be certain. With grace efficacious in itself, Bañez had in fact destroyed freedom. Lessius had allowed human nature to choose whether or not to accept grace. In Suarez and Bellarmine, freedom is reconciled with predeterminism in what seems, until one realizes what was at stake in the daily lives of human beings, like an abstract game of recondite skills played according to arcane rules.

The scholastic controversy between Jesuits and Dominicans had actually died down. Molina was to die in 1600, Bañez in 1604. But the Louvain theologians had wanted to call a provincial council of bishops to condemn Lessius as early as 1588. Sixtus V felt obliged to forbid it, but in face of the virtual certainty that the *Concordia* was going to be condemned, Clement VIII decided to settle the matter at Rome, and it was principally between Jesuits and Dominicans that for nine years from 2 January 1598 the *De auxiliis* congregations dragged on at Rome, mostly in the presence of the pope. Clement VIII died on 3 March 1605, and on 28 August 1607 Paul V held the last congregation and sent everyone home. No decree was published, but on 1 December 1611 the Holy Office formally but ineffectually forbade any theologian to publish material concerning grace, a prohibition, renewed under Urban VIII on 22 March 1625, under whose terms the Jesuits attempted to prevent the publication of the *Augustinus*.

Lessius, however, defended his position in a 1610 dissertation on efficacious grace and predestination, *De gratia efficaci, decretis divinis, libertate arbitrii et praescientia Dei conditionata*, but this time it was the frightened Jesuit general, Aquaviva, who enjoined silence. It is today clear that part of the reason for the inconclusiveness of the argument is that the same words were being used with quite different meanings, that grace could be an ontological state or a juridical right, that motion could be used of either moral or physical forces, that "before" and "after" could have either chronological or logical meanings, and that the same vocabulary could be applied to real states, like justification and sinfulness, as well as to psychological motives, without even the participants in the debate noticing the switches of register.

Jansen's undertaking can be understood in the light only of what du Bay had attempted, and the subsequent scholastic debates. He was made bishop of Ypres in 1634, and was much more of a scholastic than is often allowed, but his original inspiration was a defence of du Bay and those who, like his own master Jacques Jansson, had aimed to defend du Bay's views. Theologically, Jansen's thought starts from a distinction between the grace given to Adam before the fall which endowed him with a supernatural destiny he was free to choose or reject, and the irresistible grace given to selected fallen human beings on account of the redemption operated by Christ. This was the doctrine which Jansen thought he had discovered in Augustine and which excited Saint-Cyran and himself in the late summer of 1621. It has long been clear that Jansen had virtually mesmerized himself into anachronistically reading into Augustine's writings on grace propositions where there were only metaphors, and into applying Augustine's principles in a way which the refinements of medieval thought had made simply impossible. Jansen's view of grace depends, for instance, on discrediting the concept of pure nature, which it had been necessary for the medieval theologians to invent in order to explain such matters as the Church's sacramental dispensation and the meaning of the freedom of the will.

Jansen was a hard-working professor of scripture who shared with Saint-Cyran the dream of renewing the Church to accord with the values and theology of the 5th-century Church, making salvation more dependent on interior commitment and less on external works. After the 1621 discovery of the theological importance of the description of Adam's pre-lapsarian state, there was in 1623 a change of plan. Henceforward, the scheme would be to promote reform not through politically effective activity, but through a vast statement of primitive Christian theology, undertaken in the humanistic way characteristic of post-reformation Louvain, where the faculty favoured theological activity which was scriptural, "positive" as opposed to scholastic, and "humanist" in that the return to the Fathers and to scripture normally demanded mastery of Greek and Hebrew. Jansen would work at a meticulously thorough restatement of Augustine's theological anthropology, concentrating on the nature of the dispensation of grace by which human beings profited from the redemption.

In 1624 Jansen was sent by his colleagues at Louvain to defend their position in Spain against the Jesuits. The actual composition of the *Augustinus* was started in 1628. Jansen sent Saint-Cyran a résumé of the first volume in March 1630, and wrote to him that the second was finished in April 1634. From 1635 war stopped the exchange of letters between Flanders and Paris. By the date of Jansen's consecration as bishop of Ypres on 23 October 1636, his book was nearly finished. He had begun arrangements for its printing when he died of the plague on 6 May 1638. The Jesuits tried to stop publication by appealing to the decrees of 1611 and 1625, whose authority the Louvain faculty refused to recognize. The book finally appeared in September 1640, but without its dedication to Urban VIII, no doubt omitted in deference to the 1625 decree.

The work is one enormous folio, 1,300 double-column pages, divided into three "volumes," the first consisting of eight books on the nature and history of Pelagianism; the second of a *Liber prooemalis*, a methodological manifesto, followed by three treatises, on the state of primitive innocence, the state of fallen nature (four books), and the state of pure nature (three books);

and a third volume containing ten books on the grace of Christ the Saviour. Although the work parades its intention of writing historically, it is shot through with scholastic argument. Molina is identified as the chief opponent by the eighth chapter of the first volume, and Jansen's intentions can only be understood with reference to the scholastic categories he so disliked.

Everything depends on Jansen's concepts of nature. Pure human nature could not have aspired to supernatural fulfilment, so that, for Jansen, Adam could not have been created in a state of pure nature. Most Jesuits thought that Adam could have been created in a state of pure nature, aspiring to a fulfilment limited to the natural order, and they also thought, on the basis of Cajetan's great commentary on Aquinas, that Aquinas had thought so, too. By denying the possibility, Jansen could hold that Adam did not merely lose additional privileges at the fall, but that his nature itself, with divinization the term of its built-in aspiration, was fractured, and that it was therefore ruined by the fall in such a way that it could not even reach out towards the end for which it was created. The fallen human soul could achieve nothing at all to further individual salvation.

Jansen therefore rejected salvation in the light of the prevision of merits. The decree of election had to be absolute, and it followed, although he did not want to say so, that it had to be arbitrary. To hold that individuals might accomplish anything to achieve justification was Pelagian and heretical. To hold that they could merit or cooperate with any initial impulse towards behaviour which could earn salvation was semi-Pelagian. The grace of final perseverance for the justified was also purely gratuitous, decreed without any prevision of behaviour. The very concept of sufficient grace entailed heresy, since it meant that justification depended on cooperation. Jansen had already left Augustine a long way behind, and rigidified his doctrine beyond recognition. There is no possible doubt that Augustine taught that the individual had to cooperate with divine grace. It is also, on the technical level, clear that Augustine's distinction in the *De correptione et gratia* between the "adiutorium quo (grace by which)," pertaining to the justified sinner who perseveres, and the "adiutorium sine quo non (grace without which not)," needed by fallen man, cannot possibly be identified with what the 17th century meant by "grâce efficace (efficacious grace)" and "grâce suffisante (sufficient grace)."

Did Jansen hold that the individual could resist divine election? Here again Jansen turned Augustine's "victorious delectation" into an external force which determined the will. The Aristotelian scholastics, at least, had regarded the will as a rational appetite, in spite of the difficulties which that position entailed in explaining how the intellect influenced the determination of the will in the act of choice. For Jansen, the will was not a rational but a natural appetite. What pertained to the will was, in Jansen's technical sense, voluntary, and what was voluntary was free. Unlike the Dominicans, he did not get bogged down in discussions about the anteriority of grace or choice. The human will was inherently free although, in the fallen and unjustified state, it was incapable on its own of escaping from the domination of concupiscence. The will's freedom did not for even the Dominicans imply the power of choice, but it retained a physical capacity of which it was only morally deprived for choosing the good. For Jansen the fallen human will had no power either moral or even physical of choosing the good until moved by grace. All acts of fallen and unjustified human beings were always necessarily sinful.

Spiritually Jansen, who was a bishop and believed in a hierarchical Church and a sacramental dispensation, not at all clearly reliant on personal religious experience, was worlds apart from Calvin, whose interests, like those of Saint-Cyran, were more spiritual and religious than theological and scholarly, although Calvin was a scholar. But even theologically, Jansen's interests diverged very widely from Calvin's. For Jansen everything hinged on the fall, without which human individuals could without further assistance themselves have chosen the path to supernatural reward. Calvin's spirituality was not in the final analysis theologically dependent on original sin at all. None the less, for Jansen, children dying without baptism were simply damned, with the vast majority of the human race, including all pagans, the Jews who lived before Christ, most sinners, and those even of the just whose perseverance had not been decreed before the beginning of time. Only Christ's efficacious grace can restore to fallen human individuals the power to achieve their supernatural destiny, but Christ did not die for all human beings.

The furore aroused by the publication of the *Augustinus* was predictably enormous. By the end of 1640 six Parisian doctors had given their approval for a second edition in Paris in 1641, and a third was to appear at Rouen in 1643. Saint-Cyran's eyesight was too feeble for him to read the volume, but he is said to have been disappointed when he was guided through its content. He had hoped for something less dry and technical, with more spiritual unction. However, the religious consequences of even so dry and formidable a technical theological folio were so audacious that condemnation could never be in doubt.

Theological argument in the 17th century was still of course conducted with scriptural passages ripped out of context and without any real sense of how historical circumstances had conditioned theological pronouncements, but it was apparent even in 1640 that Augustine could not properly be read as Jansen read him, heedless of the precision introduced by the great scholastics, however damaging the dilemmas revealed by their definitions. It was also, and much more importantly, clear that Jansen's theology subverted any Christian religion based on a loving God. Whatever can be said about the intricacies of Jesuit attempts to elude over-reliance on nature, they were not destroying Christianity. The real difference between the two approaches is that Jesuit theology started off from pastoral and religious considerations, while both du Bay and Jansen were more interested in abstract theological matrices which emphasized the dependence of salvation on grace.

Controversy was immediate and bitter. What had happened to the universality of the divine salvific will of I Timothy ii, 4? Jansen had formally denied it. There was a hail-storm of pamphlets. Another attempt to impose silence was made by the Holy Office on 1 August 1641, but the decree was rejected by the Louvain faculty. The bull *In eminenti* of 6 March 1642 repeated the condemnations against Baianism, the injunctions to silence of 1611 and 1625, and the decree of 1641, while also proscribing the *Augustinus* by name. The bull was not promulgated until 19 June 1643 and had certainly been changed since it was signed, so that time was gained while the bull's authenticity was disputed. There was some approval for the *Augustinus* in France, particularly from the Oratorians, but Richelieu had not forgotten Jansen's 1635 *Mars gallicus*, attacking his alliance with the Protestant Germans and his policy towards the Low Countries, and shortly before his death on 4 December had charged the théologal of Notre-Dame, Isaac Habert, to preach against the *Augustinus*. Meanwhile Antoine Arnauld, "Le grand Arnauld," who had abandoned law for theology in 1632, had defended strongly Jansenizing theses under the aegis of Saint-Cyran for his bachelor's degree on 14 November 1635, and under his spiritual, moral and intellectual guidance, had proceeded to take the doctorate of which he would later be stripped (see: Pascal) on 19 December 1641.

Habert duly preached against the *Augustinus* on the first and last Sundays of Advent 1642, and on Septuagesima Sunday 1643, but Richelieu was now dead, and on 4 March François de Gondi, archbishop of Paris, forbade further sermons on grace. Among the works of controversy which now appeared was Arnauld's *Apologie pour Jansénius*, written in 1643 but, on account of a court judgement by Molé, not published until 1644. Saint-Cyran was dead, and a new leader of what can now be called the Jansenist faction had emerged. Habert brought out a *Défense de la foi de l'Eglise*, to which Arnauld replied with a *Seconde apologie* in 1645. He also published an *Apologie pour M. de Saint-Cyran*, partly written in 1639 but not published then on account of the imprisonment of its subject at Vincennes. The last two parts of it were written by Le Maître de Saci. On the whole, the defenders of Jansen contented themselves with affirming the conformity of his doctrine with that of Augustine, while his opponents tried to identify his view with Calvin's. By about 1645 the dogmatic controversy had for the moment died down in France.

What in fact had happened is that it had changed ground. In the summer of 1643 Arnauld had published his *De la fréquente communion* purporting to reply to an occasional work by the Jesuit Père de Sesmaisons and warning against the easy-going and flamboyant eucharistic piety of the baroque era. In June 1648 a letter of Vincent de Paul blamed Arnauld's book for cutting the number of Easter communicants at Saint-Sulpice by 3,000. Mme de Sablé had expressed to Mme de Guéméné the opinion that it was legitimate to communicate in the morning and to go to a ball in the evening, and Mme de Guéméné had given to Mme de Sablé a rule of life given her by her own confessor, which Mme de Sablé passed on to Père de Sesmaisons, who with two colleagues undertook to refute it. It was that refutation which provoked from Arnauld what was in fact a defence of the rigorism of Saint-Cyran's spirituality.

The preface, by Saint-Cyran's nephew Barcos, dangerously put Saint Paul on the same level as Saint Peter not as an apostle, which would in tradition have been acceptable, especially in a France where the church had long sought to assert the equality of its vaunted if erroneous Pauline apostolic descent with that of the Roman church, descended from Saint Peter, but in such a way as to compromise the jurisdictional and teaching primacy of the Roman see. Barcos defended himself in two works which were condemned by the Holy Office on 25 January 1647, but *De la fréquente communion* itself escaped censure, and indeed provoked an influx of "solitaires" to Port-Royal. At the same time as the focus of dispute shifted from the dogmatic to the publicly affiliated and culturally related spiritual terrain, battle was engaged on a third front, that of moral theology, whose literary consequences culminated in Pascal's *Lettres provinciales*.

The dogmatic controversy was, however, not yet over, and the first three of the *Lettres provinciales* are devoted to the dogmatic issue over which Arnauld was finally stripped of his doctorate in February 1656. It is at that point, beginning with the fourth letter, that Pascal turns his attack against the Jesuits. They had much earlier been among the leading "casuists," so-called after the books of cases of conscience used for training priests in such a manner as to ensure uniformity of practice in dispensing sacramental absolution. In fact, of course, the application of any abstract constitutional or legal principle to a set of real circumstances allows for a decision which must in the end depend on some form of invariably evolving public consensus. The process is behind all constitutional development. But Pascal's letter-writer was to take the view, in the fifth letter, that Jesuit moral teaching was the cause of their doctrine on grace. This view is in fact untenable, but it explains why Pascal turned at that point to the specifically Jesuit exploitation of casuist devices.

The casuistry by which the moral judgements of guilt on which sacramental absolution depended were made was common to all orders, although the Jesuits, whose chief concerns had always been pastoral, were certainly among those who most effectively used the devices which enabled them to relax the conditions under which absolution could be granted. These devices, like the "direction of intention," and the right to follow any genuinely probable opinion of the legitimacy of an act, even if a more rigorous view were more probable, were themselves perfectly legitimate. It was really Pascal's very likely affected and in any case false assumption that the minimum conditions under which Jesuit confessors would grant absolution represented Jesuit moral teaching itself that tarred them with the brush of laxism.

Jesuit moral teaching had, however, overstepped all prudent boundaries with the defence by Mariana of regicide. His *De rege et regis institutione* was condemned in Paris after the assassination of Henri IV in 1610. The casuist handbook chiefly to be castigated by Pascal was that of Antonio de Escobar y Mendoza, first published in Spanish about 1630, but quickly translated into Latin and published notably at Lyons in 1644. The Brussels 1651 edition used by Pascal says that there had been more than 40 earlier ones. In October 1640 Père Etienne Bauny's *Somme des péchés qui se commettent en tous états* had been put on the Roman index of prohibited books with two others of his works. Bauny had helped Sesmaisons with the book that provoked the *De la fréquente communion*.

The French supporters of Saint-Cyran and of Jansen were united under the leadership of Antoine Arnauld at least very soon after the death of Richelieu, and were from the beginning of 1643 much freer to carry on hostilities. The situation invited a three-pronged battle, on the dogmatic, spiritual, and moral theological fronts, which is what now occurred. Positions on all three fronts are commonly referred to as Jansenist or, even less accurately, as "Augustinian." It is necessary to follow the principal events on all of the three fronts, especially on account of the relationship between Jesuit moral and dogmatic theology endorsed by Pascal's letter-writer.

In 1643 a short collaborative volume, finally compiled by Arnauld, was anonymously published as the *Théologie morale des jésuites extraite fidèlement de leurs livres*. In 1644 Nicolas Caussin, the confessor of Louis XIII dismissed by Richelieu for being spiritually too exigent, replied with an *Apologie*, and the battle on the moral theology front spluttered on until fanned into flames in the *Lettres provinciales*. Meanwhile on 1 July 1649 the Paris theology faculty was asked by Nicolas Cornet, its chairman, to condemn a list of seven propositions which he said he had found in theses to be defended in the faculty. In fact they were very near to being verbally taken from the *Augustinus*, as everybody present knew. A commission was appointed and an

intense pamphlet war ensued, with a great deal of behind-the-scenes pressure.

In the spring of 1650 Habert, by now bishop of Vabres, wrote a letter signed by 85 bishops to Innocent X, asking for the condemnation of Cornet's first five propositions, omitting only the assertion that all pagan actions are sinful and an obscure statement to the effect that the primitive church had not accepted the private absolution of hidden sins. The predictable lobbying in Rome by both sides generated much written material but no literary masterpiece, and on 31 May 1653 the bull *Cum occasione* was issued. Brief, imperious, and unequivocal, it simply condemned as heretical each of five propositions, attributing them to Jansen by name. The propositions are

1. Aliqua Dei praecepta hominibus iustis volentibus et conantibus, secundum praesentes, quas habent vires, sunt impossibilia: deest quoque illis gratia, qua possibilia fiant

   (There are some commandments of God which, even for those in a state of grace who have the will and make the effort, are impossible with their present forces. They lack the grace which would make observance possible).

2. Interiori gratiae in statu naturae lapsae nunquam resistitur

   (In the state of fallen nature, interior grace can never be resisted).

3. Ad merendum et demerendum in statu naturae lapsae non requiritur in homine libertas a necessitate, sed sufficit libertas a coactione

   (In the state of fallen nature, in order to merit, and incur guilt, it is not necessary to be free from all interior necessity, but it is sufficient to be free from external constraint).

4. Semipelagiani admittebant praevenientis gratiae interioris necessitatem ad singulos actus, etiam ad initium fidei; et in hoc erant haeretici, quod vellent eam gratiam talem esse, cui posset humana voluntas resistere et obtemperare

   (The Semi-Pelagians admitted the necessity of foregoing interior grace for each act, even for the beginning of faith; they were heretical in that they wanted that grace to be such that the human will could either resist it or yield to it).

5. Semipelagianum est dicere, Christum pro omnibus omnino hominibus mortuum esse aut sanguinem fudisse

   (It is semi-Pelagian to say that Christ died or shed his blood generally for all human beings).

A number of things require to be noted, particularly since the formal documents of the Roman curia are always meticulously precise in their meaning, but carefully coded in their communication. Unlike the deliberately ambiguous censure of Du Bay, which actually communicated strong disapproval and flashed warning lights without in fact condemning anything or anyone, this bull is brief and sharply clear. Each of the five propositions is individually condemned as heretical except the last, which is "declared and condemned as false, temerarious, scandalous, and, if understood in the sense that Christ died for the salvation of only the predestined, impious, blasphemous, contumacious, detracting from religious piety, and heretical."

The first proposition is textually in the *Augustinus*, as is the fifth in the sense noted as heretical. The other three are not verbally in the text, although they are each implied by it and were certainly held by Jansen. Unlike modern commentators unfamiliar with papal documents, no one who understood the codes ever supposed that the five propositions were an attempt to sum up the teaching of the *Augustinus*. They were selected for the ease with which on the one hand they could be connected to Jansen's thought and, on the other, the ease with which they could be censured. Fighting for a condemnation of the two propositions which were dropped might have endangered the whole operation. As it was, the required note of "heretical" was appended to one of the propositions only in such a way as to suggest that it might also have been capable of an acceptable sense. However, Rome had now defined, in the technical sense, that Jesus died for all men; that the justified, if not yet everybody, always received the grace necessary to keep the commandments; that grace could be resisted; that true freedom of the will requires freedom in the will from internal determining forces; and that Jansen had wrongly identified the heresy in semi-Pelagianism.

It would still be judged necessary on 16 October 1656 to issue a further constitution that the five propositions had been condemned in Jansen's own sense, because the Jansenist party, while submitting to the condemnation of the five propositions, had refused to admit that Jansen had ever held them. But if, on the dogmatic front, the battle was nearly but not quite over, the spiritual link between the Jansenists and the monastery of Port-Royal, of which Saint-Cyran had been the director, was very strong. Arnauld's eldest living brother, Robert Arnauld d'Andilly, had had eight children who survived into adolescence. The five daughters were or had been nuns of Port-Royal, and one son was a "solitaire." One was a priest and the other became a minister of Louis XIV. Of Arnauld's sisters, Catherine, who died in 1651, had had five sons, all solitaires at Port-Royal. Catherine herself as a widow had taken the veil at Port-Royal. Two other of Arnauld's sisters survived, and both were nuns at Port-Royal, where another had died as a nun. Port-Royal was therefore linked to the Jansenist party through Saint-Cyran, its former director and close friend of Jansen; through its close connections with the Arnauld family, including Arnauld's sisters, nephews, and nieces, of whom at least nine in 1655 were or had been nuns and six solitaires at Port-Royal; and through Pascal, whose sister Jacqueline had become a nun there and whose niece was about to become the subject there of an apparently miraculous cure.

Pascal was already on the friendliest of terms with Port-Royal when the war of the *Lettres provinciales* broke out, which brought him into the centre of the moral theology debate and into the closest contact with the dogmatic issues, as his *Ecrits sur la grâce* testify. They may well have been begun in 1655. On 1 February that year a well-known sympathizer with Port-Royal, Roger du Plessis, marquis de Liancourt, was refused absolution at Saint-Sulpice by the abbé Picoté, acting under the instruction of Jean-Jacques Olier, unless he ceased to retain the Jansenist abbé de Bourzeys as a member of his household and broke off all contact with the monastery, where his grand-daughter, the future princesse de Marcillac, was a pupil.

Arnauld intervened, writing a public *Lettre d'un Docteur de Sorbonne à une personne de condition* dated 24 February 1655 and provoking a storm of replies. To those he replied on 10 July 1655 in a *Second lettre à un duc et pair*, in fact a quarto manifesto of the Jansenist position in 250 pages addressed to the duc de Luynes, a close friend of both Port-Royal and Liancourt. A commission was set up by the Sorbonne, to examine the second letter on 4 November 1655. It reported on 1 and 2 December, finding five propositions worthy of censure, of which the essential two were one affirming that the condemned propositions were not in the *Augustinus* and the second affirming that Saint Peter, when he denied Christ, sinned because he was denied the grace to do otherwise:

> Un juste en la personne de saint Pierre, à qui la grâce sans laquelle on ne peut rien a manqué dans une occasion où on ne peut pas dire qu'il n'ait point péché…

> (A justified human being in the person of Saint Peter, to whom the grace without which nothing can be achieved was lacking on an occasion when it cannot be said that he did not sin…).

That proposition flatly asserts what was condemned in the first incriminated proposition from the *Augustinus*. Arnauld fled to Port-Royal-des-Champs where he wrote a defence on account of each proposition. On the proposition concerning the matter of fact, that is whether or not the believer is obliged to find propositions in a book if it is defined that they are there, Arnauld was condemned on 14 January 1656. There were irregularities of procedure, protests, and a walk-out by Arnauld's sympathizers. Arnauld himself protested in a formal document at the invalidity of the proceedings. He was none the less censured on 29 January. The condemnation was drawn up on 31 January excluding Arnauld from the Sorbonne if he did not retract before 15 February. For the non-theological aspects of Jansenism, users of the *Guide* are referred to the entries on Saint-Cyran and Port-Royal.

The dogmatic battle dragged on until the early 18th century. Quesnel intransigently restated Jansen's doctrine and was in turn condemned. The final end of Jansenism as a theology of grace must be taken to be the constitution *Unigenitus* of 8 September 1713. Gradually confidence in the powers of human nature re-established itself, in religion as in all other branches of cultural activity.

JODELLE, Étienne, seigneur de Limodin, 1532–1573.

Poet and dramatist.

LIFE

It is no doubt on account of his youthful activity as a dramatist that Ronsard included Jodelle's name in all the lists of six other poets who, with himself, would constitute a new "Pléiade (q.v.)." Ronsard's original list was selected from the "brigade" of early companions mentioned twice in the poem about the Arcueil picnic of July 1549. Jodelle was the only Parisian by birth. The property of which he was seigneur scarcely extended to 50 hectares on the town's outskirts, a diminutive farm with a tumbledown small house which Jodelle inherited from his father, also called Etienne, who died sometime between 1532 and 1535. Jodelle's mother, Marie Drouet, was a lawyer's daughter from a well-off bourgeois family. Although the Drouets were a merchant family, Marie's mother was a Passavant, and her family owned an impressive collection of books and manuscripts. Marie's grandfather knew Greek. Jodelle had a sister who married Jean Habert, a tax official, and whose son, a lawyer, became Jodelle's heir.

It is not clear how Jodelle came to the Collège de Boncourt, or how, in a 1546 edition of Marot's *Oeuvres* printed by Jean de Tournes at Lyons, he came to sign a prefatory epitaph at the presumed age of 14. The accepted date of birth is 1532, but it should perhaps be queried. Jodelle's posthumous editor, Charles de la Mothe, said in the preface to his 1574 volume, *Les Oeuvres et Meslanges Poëtiques d'Estienne Jodelle*, that Jodelle, "noble Parisien (a Parisian nobleman)" was the first after Ronsard to write in the new way against "l'ignorance et rudesse (the ignorance and roughness)," of a whole list of predecessors, including Marot, and that as early as 1549 Jodelle had published several "sonnets, odes et charontides," followed in 1552 by the first classical tragedy and comedy in French. Jodelle published no collection of verse in his life, nor have we any manuscripts in his hand. His verse was exclusively published as prefatory material for the volumes of other poets, or as contributions to collective "recueils," very often "tombeaux" or memorial volumes. There has been some speculation about what a "charontide" might have been, and Jodelle's first tragedy was in fact not written and performed until 1553.

The farm at Limodin was leased out in 1549. By the end of 1551 Jodelle had written a sonnet to celebrate the psalm translations of Bèze and an epigram grieving for the illness of Bèze, who had caught the plague in June. Late in 1552 Guillaume Guéroult wrote in Lyons a long poem deploring Jodelle's silence, and two further sonnets, written for Jodelle's departure from Lyons, although not published until 1558, may also have been written at about the same time. Since they mention Jodelle's fame only as a lyric poet, they were presumably written before the two performances of *Cléopâtre captive* early in 1553. Muret, to whom Jodelle owes his humanist education, was a regent teacher at Boncourt from 1551 to 1553, but Jodelle appears to have spent some time at Lyons during that period. In the second half of 1552 Jodelle wrote two short Latin pieces for Muret's *Juvenilia*, in which Muret's *Julius Caesar* was first published—Montaigne had played the leading role in the play at the Collège de Guyenne when he was 12. Muret replied in the collection with a long flattering piece thanking Jodelle and, in the prefatory dedication to Brinon, Muret associates Jodelle with his other friends, including Denisot and Jean-Antoine de Baïf.

It was probably in September 1552 that Jodelle's *L'Eugène*, the first regular comedy written in French, was performed, again probably in a Parisian college. At this date Jodelle seems not to have known Ronsard and the Coqueret group at all. He is associated in prefaces, dedications, and allusions with a group surrounding Muret, patronized by Jean Brinon, seigneur de Médan, and consisting of Claude Colet, Hugues Salel, Rémy Belleau, Olivier de Magny, and Nicolas Denisot. Although Jodelle did not know du Bellay and his friends, and was indeed devoted to Marot's memory, it may well have been in response to the challenge issued in du Bellay's 1549 *Deffence et illustration de la langue françoise* that Jodelle undertook to restore comedies and tragedies to their former dignity. Their places had been taken by farces and morality plays. In his prologue Jodelle strongly attacks the medieval farces and moralities, although there has been discussion about how much he none the less derived from them.

Early in 1553 Jodelle wrote a sonnet congratulating Henri II on the relief of Metz by François de Guise. There were celebrations for his return on 9 February, as for the marriage of Diane d'Angoulême, the king's illegitimate daughter, to Horatio Farnese on 14 February, and, no doubt through the mediation of Muret, the king attended a performance of Jodelle's *Cléopâtre captive* at the Hôtel de Reims, the residence in Paris of the cardinal of Lorraine, Charles de Guise, brother of the hero of Metz. Rémy Belleau and Jean de la Péruse played the leading parts. The cardinal presented Jodelle to the king, who rewarded him, as Brantôme tells us, with 1,500 livres. Charles de la Mothe noted that Jodelle always composed quickly, "sans estude et sans labeur (without study or exertion)."

In April Ronsard published in the *Livret des folastries* his "Dithyrambes chantés au bouc de E. Jodelle, poète tragicq," the famous account of the celebratory excursion on which Ronsard, riding into the chosen tavern on the garlanded goat, presented it to Jodelle, the new Sophocles, before turning it loose into the field again. The incident became famous when the local curé found what he regarded as a pagan rite offensive, and Ronsard later had irately to defend himself against attacks on account of irreligion based on the episode.

In May Jodelle wrote a sonnet for Ronsard, printed in the second edition of Ronsard's *Les Amours*. Dorat at Coqueret had contributed an epigram to Muret's *Juvenilia*. Contact had been made and friendship established between the Boncourt and Coqueret groups, with the interest in drama at the Collège de Boncourt no doubt now strengthened by the arrival early in 1533 from Guyenne of Buchanan, author of two translations of Euripides and two biblical tragedies. Jodelle's success had created a sensation. Ronsard included his name in the poem for Muret, "Les Iles fortunées," and Tahureau published an enthusiastic poem to Jodelle on his return to Poitiers. From the positioning of the preliminary verses in Magny's *Les Amours*, probably of early 1553, Jodelle appears at least momentarily to have been considered as leader of the group of young humanist poets, before Ronsard. A poem by des Autelz alludes to *L'Eugène* but not *Cléopâtre*, and is ironic about the praise that may be going to Jodelle's head. Later in 1553 Jodelle wrote an ode for the *Monophile* of Etienne Pasquier, who had been present at the Boncourt performance of *Cléopâtre*. Pasquier was to drop the homage from the 1566 and 1567 editions.

Jodelle's reputation, alliances, and coolnesses, and the slight signs of setbacks, can be charted in great detail from the appearance and positioning of his work in the prefatory material of volumes by others, in dedications of verses to him, and in allusions to his achievements during the two years following *Cléopâtre*. But in 1555 he was borrowing money secured on five named properties, and two more notaried documents exist for loans to Jodelle in March and May 1556, and on 1 December 1557. He appears to have written only one long poem in 1554, and then nothing of consequence until 1556. It seems clear that, having tasted the enthusiasm provoked by *Cléopâtre*, Jodelle had began to behave haughtily and to feel unappreciated.

Then on 8 February 1558 Henri II, returning from Guise's victory at Calais, said that he would dine with the prévôt and the échevins of Paris, and Jodelle presented himself to ask for a commission to prepare a comedy for the celebratory banquet of 17 February. It was, according to the registers of the city council, an expensive disaster, with unprepared actors and mal-functioning machinery. Jodelle himself wrote a memoir, the only single volume publication of his during his lifetime, saying that the initiative had been not his own, but the city's. He had tried hastily to organize a sumptuous entertainment and needed to explain what had gone wrong. Among other things, where he had asked for "rochers (rocks)," what had been provided was "clochers (bell-towers)." That was not the only disaster. The crown was not ready for Virtue to place on the head of Diane de Poitiers, now the duchesse de Valentinois. Jodelle was ill for days thereafter.

He left the court, probably for the protection of Philippe de Boulainvilliers. A poem of Guillaume des Autelz of 1559 informs us that Jodelle abandoned poetry to take up arms, and in December 1560 Ronsard published a very warm sonnet about Jodelle, apparently written during the period of his disgrace following the episode at the Hôtel de Ville in 1558. In 1561 Jodelle and his sister formally divided the inheritance left by their mother. Jodelle had been borrowing further sums, and borrowed again on this occasion. Most of his verse at this period had a semi-official character, congratulating the great on their achievements or marriages, or sympathizing with them in their griefs. In February 1564 he moved into a new house recently built in Paris by Philippe de Boulainvilliers, for whom he wrote a series of Latin verses.

For some reason we do not know Jodelle had been condemned to death and to the confiscation of his goods, probably around the beginning of 1564. The fact is referred to in a document of 10 October 1566, when a Paris lawyer, Médard Tusan, sought the payment of interest two and a half years in arrears, the debt having been constituted before the condemnation. Comparatively little is known of Jodelle's life, but he appears not to have circulated much, and to have written seldom except to solicit the protection of the great. In 1567 he was writing anti-Protestant poems, blaming the Huguenots for the wars and accusing them of rebellion and treason. In the first part of 1568 he wrote both a satire in French and a Latin poem, against the chancellor, Michel de l'Hôpital, whom he had earlier praised. The chancellor was dismissed on 24 March. At the same time Jodelle expressed the anxieties felt by Catholics at the terms of the peace of Longjumeau. Later that year Jodelle's verse was again to express extreme Catholic sentiment. He also wrote five sonnets to Catherine de Medici at the death on 3 October 1568 of her eldest daughter, Elisabeth de Valois, wife of Philip II and queen of Spain.

The pattern of publication of occasional verse suggests that Jodelle was probably away from Paris in the first half of 1569, although the preparations for battle and the victories of the duc d'Anjou at Jarnac on 13 March 1569 and at Moncontour on 3 October both inspired poems, as did the peace of Saint-Germain on 8 August 1570, the marriage of Charles IX to Elizabeth of Austria on 26 November, and the birth of the first child of that union on 27 October 1572. Two days later Charles IX made Jodelle a gift of 500 livres tournois, "in addition to what he has already had." On 30 July 1572 an injunction had been served on Jodelle to pay a debt on pain of confiscation of goods. Jodelle wrote three sonnets approving of the St Bartholomew's Day massacre on 24 August.

On 4 July 1573 the Limodin property was in fact seized. On 23 July Jodelle made his will. He died a few days later the same month, still occupying the two rooms into which he had moved in February 1564. Charles de la Mothe, who was to collect his works, was his executor. A list of creditors was opened up before the sale of Limodin by auction. It was bought by Jodelle's cousin Jean Drouet for 1,700 livres tournois. The first and in fact only volume of the *Oeuvres et meslanges poetiques d'Estienne de Jodelle, sieur de Lymodin* was published by La Mothe with a privilège of 24 September and an achevé of 6 November 1574. One contemporary text mentions that Jodelle was briefly at Geneva, and briefly a Calvinist. At his death he was blamed for selling his pen to the royal Catholic cause for money, and the Huguenots, with the notable exception of d'Aubigné, wrote against him. Ronsard had not mentioned him since 1561, but now said that his reputation would improve if his poetry were burnt. In a famous paragraph Pierre de l'Estoile said that Jodelle had died an atheist. Very little is certain, except that after his early successes, Jodelle acquired the reputation of being haughty and arrogant. He was pretentious, he overspent, and he disdained the status the publication of a volume of his own verse would have brought him. Both he and his work became widely unpopular, although he did retain a nucleus of admirers. He prided himself on his speed of improvisation, and Ronsard has not been alone in pointing out that his verse suffered as a result.

WORKS

We know very little of the circumstances in which Jodelle's love poetry was written. The 1574 volume opened with a collection of 47 sonnets, 11 chansons, and a handful of other pieces, certainly written for different women and at widely different dates. It is possible, although not necessarily rewarding, to reconstitute with some probability the likely chronological order of the love poetry. His style at first resembled that of Marot, avoiding neo-platonist and Petrarchan usages in language and imagery, and keeping clear of the pagan mythology used by Ronsard and his friends. As he grew older, Jodelle increasingly drew from this common stock of poetic source material, but none of his lyrical verse is particularly sensitive, original, or imaginatively forceful. No attempt is made, for instance, to use the neoplatonist matrixes in such as a way as to explore the morally uplifting potential of human instinct, even in the years before the outbreak of the religious wars brought such forms of cultural optimism in France to an abrupt halt.

At best the love poetry has been seen as historically interesting, providing another link between the rhétoriqueurs, Marot, and the Pléiade, but the case for holding that Jodelle attempted or achieved any such ambition is weak. There is a certain search for technical variety, and although Jodelle moved slowly towards a general reliance on alexandrines, it is true that the love poetry does draw on an unusually large repertoire of metres, experimenting particularly with terza rima. The impression, however, is one more of uncertainty of style than of technical skill, and it is striking that the verse modern critics have found most pleasing was clearly written a decade or so later than that which impressed Jodelle's own contemporaries. He is praised, for instance, for the "Contr'amours," anti-love poems which are simply witty inversions of what seemed to Jodelle little more than a conventional verse form.

It is not surprising, in view of the weakness of his lyrical inspiration, that it is as a satirist that Jodelle shows more polished poetic expertise, although here again what distinguished his verse is invective vigour rather than imaginative inspiration. The reader is crushed rather than touched by the coruscatingly energetic denunciation of homosexuality in the unfinished "Contre la Riere-Venus," a poem which may help to explain something of d'Aubigné's sympathy for Jodelle. The effect is cumulative and achieved largely by repetition and the frequent reliance on words like "ordure (filth)" and "puanteur (stench)." Jodelle does not really give true poetic form to what remains merely the expression of extreme strength of moral indignation.

The verse celebrating the Saint Bartholomew's Day massacre contains too much denunciatory outrage to be taken merely as flattery of royal policy. Coligny's murder is defended, but the last of the three sonnets is scarcely notable for anything except the violence of its imagery, exulting in the Huguenots' "charognes puantes (stinking carcasses)" floating down the river, serving only "d'amorse aux poissons et de gorge aux corbeaux (as bait for the fish and carrion for the crows)."

Of the four plays whose titles were mentioned by Jodelle's contemporaries, we have lost *La Rencontre*. Jodelle himself said he had several more, some unfinished, when he was invited to prepare the celebrated entertainment of 17 February 1558, and Charles de la Mothe claims to have had enough material for "five or six" volumes in addition to the one he published. We have probably lost a good deal of drama as well as much verse. Of the three plays we have, we do not know if *Didon se sacrifiant* was ever performed, and there is only one reference to it, in a sonnet of Baïf, in the whole of contemporary literature. The primary source is Virgil himself, in the fourth book of the *Aeneid*, although Jodelle also drew on the seventh of Ovid's *Heroïdes*. Its steady use of alexandrines suggests composition after 1555, and it may possibly have been performed at Dol in Brittany, where Jodelle's friend, the bishop Charles d'Espinay, is said by Charles de la Mothe to have put on some of the plays.

Didon se sacrifiant is not really a drama at all. It is a series of intensifying elegiac tableaux consisting of long orations, designed to move the emotions of the audience by the transposition of Virgil's succinct narrative into rhetorical declamations. There are stichomythia, one-line speeches, as in the score exchanged between Enée and the chorus at the end of the second act, but they come nearer to being exchanges of moral aphorisms than true dialogue, and the characters do not influence one another's attitudes. Two groups of characters confront one another, Enée and his companions, and Didon, with her nurse, Barce, and her sister, Anne. At the beginning Enée, having heard that Jupiter has ordered the departure of the Trojans from Carthage, has given the order to prepare to leave. Achate wonders whether Enée's departure will not entail the death of Didon, but Enée enters and explains how duty must conquer love. He must go.

In the second act Didon, in front of Anne, tries in vain to detain Enée, and in the third Anne tries, also in vain, to persuade Enée at least to postpone his journey. Here Jodelle makes a concession to drama by allowing Enée to feel a troubled conscience, which does not appear in Virgil. In the fourth act Didon, without revealing her intention, asks Anne to have the large pyre prepared, and in the fifth, after her speeches of farewell, she mounts

it and sets fire to it. The chorus not only comments on the moral lesson, but expresses the emotions which the audience is expected to feel. In fact, the rhetoric is not moving. It is too involved, prolix, and repetitive. There are not more than a couple of score of lines in the whole play in which the oratory is touching enough to be poetic.

Jodelle boasted of the speed with which he had written *L'Eugène*, in four sessions, probably to be played in September 1552. It has more characters than a farce, is longer, and is divided into acts and scenes, but the tone is farcical. The background is the war with Charles V which led to the relief of Metz. Eugène is a worldly young priest who confides in his chaplain, Messire Jean, his love for Alix, whose absent husband, Guillaume, for whom Eugène had arranged and performed the marriage ceremony, is a fool. Jean has nothing but contempt for Eugène and Alix, and reveals that Alix was for a long time the mistress of Florimond, who had vainly been in love with Eugène's sister, Hélène. Florimond is away fighting with the king, and Guillaume returns, pursued by creditors. In the second act Florimond returns, celebrating the glories of war against the emperor, and seeking to restore himself as Alix's lover. Allusions to Charles V's intended crossing of the Rhine, which took place on 14 September 1552, locate the action in September 1552. Hélène knows that Florimond has returned and decides to tell Eugène.

In the third act, Florimond is told that Alix is married to Guillaume and is the mistress of Eugène. Florimond goes to take away the furnishings he had given Alix, and finds her at table with Guillaume and Jean, who laments the loss of the benefice entailed by his failure to protect Eugène's interests. Eugène calls on Alix, then retires to reflect. Florimond comes in again and starts to beat Alix, Guillaume runs away, and Alix is left alone. In Act IV Matthieu, Guillaume's creditor, seeks to protect his interest in the furniture, and amidst general confusion, Florimond threatens to kill Eugène the next day. In the final act a plan conceived by Eugène works. Hélène abandons herself to Florimond after all, Eugène finds a benefice for Matthieu, promises to get Jean a wife, and obtains Guillaume's consent to an arrangement allowing him to keep Alix as his mistress.

This is still in fact a farce rather than a neo-classical comedy, although the action is now contained with 24 hours. Comparatively little derives from Terence, apart from the polemic and apologetic function of the prologue, which also identifies the characters. Dramatically, the action is unfolded, conducted, and resolved more or less efficiently, although the motivations of entries and exits, which scarcely matter in farce, are not strong. That the ending is simply dismissive of conventional morality has been found deplorable, but scarcely affects the merits of the piece as farce.

It is not easy to understand the triumphant success of *Cléopâtre captive* except in terms of its programmatic attempt to restore rhetorical declamation to the classical stage. Jodelle makes tentative progress from the more complicated fixed verse forms of earlier poets towards the fluidity of the alexandrine, used only for the first act, with all feminine endings. Only later does he turn more enthusiastically to the alexandrine, and his later verse makes technically interesting use of enjambement and unusual breaks in the line. In *Cléopâtre* the alexandrine's break occurs almost invariably after six syllables.

The narrative source is Plutarch. There is an eminent victim of destiny deploring the inevitable awaiting fate. This was the first example in French of an original tragedy on a classical theme, intended as an exercise for teaching college pupils how to move an audience by rhetorical devices, of which the easiest were the lamentations which touched off feelings of pity and terror. The intention was not to create drama, but to move feelings by declamation, and the text is full of the rhetorical devices prescribed by Quintilian and Cicero: periphrasis, metaphor, hesitation, antithesis, alliteration, apostrophe, a dream and an onstage narration of events of whose occurrence the audience had to know but whose depiction before them would have disturbed the rhetorical control of their reactions.

As the play opens Antoine is dead and Cléopâtre, who loved him and blames his death on his love for her, dreads being forced to contribute by her presence to the glory of the triumphal chariot ride of Antoine's conqueror, Octavien, through Rome. In the first act the shade of Antoine recites the exposition. Cléopâtre enters, reproaching herself for Antoine's death, dreams that he asks her to join him, and decides to die. The appearance of the shade is borrowed from Seneca, and the dream probably from Muret. In the second act Octavien suspects that Cléopâtre will commit suicide to prevent his triumph, and the chorus moralizes about human pride; in the third there is a confrontation between Octavien and Cléopâtre, after which comes a grating incident when Cléopâtre attacks Séleuque, one of Octavien's servants who accuses her of cheating his master, to whom Cléopâtre had offered all her possessions. In the fourth act Cléopâtre reveals that she had wanted only to save the lives of her children. The reactions to her between-the-acts suicide are the subject of the fifth act. Historically the play was of great importance, but it can scarcely be admired as either poetry or drama. It was rapturously received in 1553 primarily because it helped to fulfil the programme of renewing the language and literature of France, and its intrinsic value has subsequently brought about perhaps too firm a devaluation of its author's achievement.

PUBLICATIONS

[*During Jodelle's lifetime the texts of the three surviving plays remained unpublished, and no volume devoted wholly or chiefly to Jodelle's verse appeared. Much has certainly been lost. The numerous original collections in which Jodelle's verse was published during his lifetime are listed in the Balmas edition of the Oeuvres complètes*]

Collections

Oeuvres et mélanges poétiques d'Etienne Jodelle, 1574
Les Oeuvres et mélanges poétiques, 2 vols., 1868–70
Etienne Jodelle: Oeuvres complètes, edited by Enea Balmas, 2 vols., 1965–68

Plays

L'Eugène, 1987; in *Four French Renaissance Plays*, 1978
Cléopâtre captive, 1979
Didon se sacrifiant in Balmas, *Oeuvres complètes*

Other

Le Recueil des inscriptions, figures, devises, et masquarades,

ordonnées en l'Hôtel de Ville à Paris, le jeudi 17 de février 1558, 1558

Biographical and critical studies

Chamard, H., *Histoire de la Pléiade*, 4 vols., 1939–40
Balmas, E., *Un Poeta del Rinascimento francese, Etienne Jodelle*, 1962
Jeffrey, Brian, *French Renaissance Comedy, 1552–1630*, 1969
Lazard, Madeleine, *Le Théâtre en France au XVIe siècle*, 1980

Bibliography

Horváth, K.A., *Etienne Jodelle*, 1932

JOURNAL DES SAVANTS (Le).

See also Chapelain and Voltaire.

The enormous correspondence of the Franciscan Marin Mersenne, in touch with most of Europe's leading scientists in the early 17th century, as well as the correspondences of the individual scientists themselves, showed quite early the need for an organ for the discussion and dissemination of scientific opinion, such as slowly came to exist for literary matters. The first authorization to publish notices of all new discoveries in the sciences and the arts, but expressly prohibiting comments relevant to religion, politics, or morals, was given in 1663 by Louis XIV to the royal historiographer, Eudes de Mézeray.

The project was realized in 1665 by Denis de Sallo, sieur de la Coudraye, a magistrate from a Poitou family with a military background, who in 1652, at the age of 26, had entered the parlement de Paris. His father had been a magistrate, and he was himself known more for his devotion to books than for his application to administrative and legal work. Among the notes he left are 2,000 pages of annotated extracts copied from works in Greek, Latin, Italian, French, Spanish, and German. It was Chapelain who in January 1663 wrote to Colbert about him, shortly after the establishment of the "petite académie," the small committee set up in that year for the supervision of the cultural life of the country. In 1664 Sallo was given a 20-year privilège to comment regularly on new works of mathematics, science, history, literature, and theology, and on 5 January 1665 the first number of the *Journal des Savants* appeared.

The *Journal*, comprising 12 quarto pages, appeared on Mondays. It was announced that it would contain a list of important new publications, with notes about their contents, as well as obituaries, accounts of scientific experiments, and notices of legal decisions and condemnations by the Sorbonne and other institutions. In other words, the whole fields of science, technology, literature, and the arts were to be covered. There was at first a good deal of uncertainty about how technical and how specifically scientific the new organ should be. Sallo took the pseud-onym of Hédouville, after his valet's birthplace, and formed a team which included Amable Bourzeis, Le Roy de Gomberville, Chapelain, and the abbé Gallois, a list of names which links the journal from its inception with Colbert's ambitions to focus cultural activity in France, but at first there is no strongly scientific emphasis. Works by Pierre Corneille and La Fontaine are announced, with Bassompierre's *Mémoires*. Mme de Sablé is invited to contribute a note on La Rochefoucauld's *Maximes*.

Almost immediately the *Journal* provoked opposition, notably from Ménage, whose *Aegidii Menagii iuris civilis amaenitates* it savaged, from the Lyons engraver Grégoire Huret, and from Charles Patin, whose father, the famous doctor Guy Patin, warned him that Colbert would act if necessary to protect the editors of the *Journal*. Sallo was Gallican, anti-Jesuit, and ready to take the side of the parlement and the Sorbonne against all manifestations of Roman power. By 30 March 1665 publication of the *Journal* was suspended following complaints from Rome. Sallo resigned as editor and Colbert ensured that the succession passed to the abbé Gallois, former tutor to his children. In his first number, dated 4 January 1666, Gallois undertook to concern himself more with reporting the contents of new works than with criticizing them.

Under Gallois from 1666 to 1675 the *Journal* turned firmly towards natural science. In 1668 Gallois became perpetual secretary of the Académie des Sciences, reporting privately to Colbert and publicly in the *Journal* on the fruits of royal patronage of the sciences. The journal's pages were also opened to individuals wishing to expound or defend particular views, and on the whole Gallois did not comment on what he reported, sometimes even omitting the names of authors of papers, and restricting his subject matter to the natural sciences and theology. He soon tired, and the rhythm of publication quickly diminished, from 42 numbers in 1666 to 16 in 1667, 13 in 1668, four in 1669, one in 1670, three in 1671, and eight in 1672. There was no publication in 1673, the year of Gallois's election to the Académie française. Fontenelle suggests that Gallois was being otherwise employed by Colbert, without saying how. The non-appearance of the *Journal* provoked the publication at irregular dates of supplements devoted to physics and medicine, edited by the king's physician Jean-Baptist Denys, until, in 1674, the chancellor gave the editorship of the *Journal* to the abbé Jean-Paul de la Roque.

La Roque's industrious editorship from 1675 to 1686 produced 342 numbers, averaging more than one a fortnight. A new privilège was granted in 1679, still obviously envisaging a review which, if it did not exclude literature, meant by "arts" the mechanical arts, and was primarily devoted to the natural sciences and decrees deciding on the orthodoxy of theological opinions. The critical function abrogated by the *Journal* was inevitably taken over, particularly by Bayle's *Nouvelles de la République des Lettres* from 1684, and then also by Le Clerc's *Bibliothèque universelle et historique* from 1686. Bayle, himself aiming at profitability, wrote to Le Clerc on 18 June 1684 that the *Journal des Savants* behaved too stiffly and narrowly. Under attack for blinkered vision, La Roque resigned, asking for a pension equivalent to a bishopric, and for ten months the review did not appear.

In November 1687, the editorship of the *Journal des Savants* was undertaken by Louis Cousin, a judge, scholar, and translator. He would select interesting books, print extracts or résumés,

and bestow neither praise nor blame. Under his direction the review appeared weekly, except in summer, from 1687 to 1701, now more obviously addressed to the specialist. Livelier rivals began sporadically to appear outside France, particularly in Holland, but the reputation of the *Journal des Savants* remained high. On Cousin's retirement in 1701, the chancellor, Pontchartrain, gave the editorship to his nephew, the abbé Jean-Paul Bignon, who was a friend of Fontenelle and became a member of the Académie des Sciences and the Académie française. He formed a team of reviewers recruited from the royal censors which included Ellies du Pin and Fontenelle. The review appeared each Monday, and there was a weekly editorial conference, with each of the half-dozen reviewers drawing 400 livres a year. Publishers were put under an obligation to notify the review of any new books. There were complaints that the review did not indicate the number of pages, and omitted to mention the year of publication, so concealing the delay in publishing notices of books.

Bignon gave up the editorship from 1714 until, after an interruption of seven months in publication, he took it back in 1723. In the meanwhile d'Aguesseau had twice been editor, and both d'Argenson brothers had held the post. For a period the review was devoted almost exclusively to medical topics. Bignon's return saved it from extinction, and he called in the abbé Desfontaines, former Jesuit and future target for Voltaire's most concentrated venom. Desfontaines left to found in 1730 his own *Le Nouvelliste du Parnasse*, which lasted for a year, and then, in 1735, the *Observations sur les écrits modernes*. When that was suppressed, Desfontaines followed it with the *Jugements sur quelques ouvrages nouveaux*, each time clearly infringing the *Journal*'s monopoly.

The *Journal des Savants* itself became a monthly from 1724, and the 1729 privilège gave it a monopoly right for 15 years to comment not only on works of science and on works on painting and sculpture, but also to report the sessions of the parlement, university decisions, and all news of the arts and sciences from foreign periodicals. A contract was signed with the bookseller Chaubert, and the editor undertook to pay each of the six specialists 400 livres a year, reduced to 300 in 1736. A breakdown for the period from 1715 to 1719 has shown that the works analysed were 18% theology, 9% law, 23% history, more than 25% sciences and arts, with 20% works of literature.

Bignon resigned again in 1739, and the appointment of future editors was confided to royal censors nominated by the director of the book trade. The editors were responsible to the chancellor or the Garde des Sceaux. However, not only the Desfontaines titles, but also Prévost's 1733 *Le Pour et Contre*, the 1734 *Le Glaneur Français*, and the 1736 *Réflexions sur les ouvrages de littérature*, together with several periodicals masquerading as single-volume collections of fictitious correspondence, had in fact made a huge breach in the monopoly of the *Journal des Savants*. It was no longer possible to compete with lofty impartiality against spicier rival publications, although Malesherbes tried several devices to defend the *Journal des Savants*, including the offer of licensing other reviews if they allowed themselves to be put under the same editorship as the *Journal*, by which they would of course then have been swallowed up. Tacit permissions were also accorded against payment of a fee to the *Journal des Savants*. A tariff of payments was established, but the monopoly was protected. On 13 July 1745 the censor of the *Mercure de France* was sharply reminded by the chancellor d'Aguesseau that the privilège of the *Journal* meant that the *Mercure* had to devote itself exclusively to light literature. Malesherbes defended the *Journal*'s privilège with utter determination, but with the ultimate result only of making it a quasi-official publication.

The *Journal des Savants*, while always careful not to commit itself to any form of overt anti-clericalism, gradually warmed towards the encyclopédistes (q.v.). In a literary context its overwhelming importance was to serve during the 18th century as the forum for the vulgarizing of the scientific knowledge on which materialism and deism would be erected. It was in the *Journal des Savants*, for instance, that Voltaire published in 1738 his two memoirs on the *Eléments de la philosophie de Newton mis à la portée de tout le monde*. In 1779 Buffon's ideas were welcomed in it, even if Lalande congratulated him on "his respect for Scripture." The *Journal de Savants* published both Malebranche and Leibniz. In the end its semi-official status put the *Journal* in the position of giving advance warning about the acceptability of new and often daring ideas. It was an important cog in the cultural machinery which made the publication of the *Encyclopédie* possible, and allowed the ideas to gestate on which the proclamation of the individual's personal and social perfectibility was to be based. *The Journal* was to continue to be important in the post-Revolution period.

L

LA BOÉTIE, Étienne de, 1530–1563.

Translator, poet, and political writer.

LIFE

La Boétie, gifted young humanist and magistrate that he was, political writer, translator, poet, and active controversialist, is chiefly known to us on account of his intimate friendship with Montaigne. The devotion he inspired in Montaigne led directly to one of the most famous chapters in *Les Essais*, to other memorable passages in that work and, no doubt indirectly, to the initial conception of Montaigne's whole book, which can be seen as the quest for an intellectual and emotional intimacy once shared with La Boétie, just over two years Montaigne's senior. Its writing was at any rate dominated by the memory of La Boétie. They got to know one another only on an official occasion, probably in 1559, although they were in some sense colleagues from 1557, when the former members of the suppressed Cour des Aides at Périgueux were resentfully accepted in to the parlement at Bordeaux, into which their full social incorporation scarcely dates from earlier than 1561. The extremely close relationship between the virtuous, married, hard-working, and determined legal officer, La Boétie, and the more imaginatively gifted, but more easy-going and less ambitious country squire, Montaigne, poses perhaps three intractable problems.

Montaigne, to whom La Boétie bequeathed his books, was present at La Boétie's deathbed, wrote a long and detailed account of the death to his own father, and thereafter spent some years, after two of which he married, dedicating himself to the publication of La Boétie's works. However, he did not publish *Le Discours de la servitude volontaire*, which he had read before meeting La Boétie, and whose circulation in manuscript Montaigne himself apparently himself helped to boost. About a fifth of it was first published in the Huguenot interest spliced into the second, 1574 edition of the *Reveille-Matin*, before the whole text appeared in the three volumes of Simon Goulart's 1576 *Mémoires*. Perhaps on account of the Huguenot hijacking of the text, Montaigne is dismissive about it, calling it an exercise of La Boétie's early youth (*Les Essais*, I, 28). Either the text as published was modified after La Boétie's death to include an apparent reference to Ronsard's *La Franciade*, first published in 1572 or, more likely, that reference is a simple interpolation. The point, however, is not so much that the text as circulated in manuscript after 1563, and as subsequently printed, is not as La Boétie had allowed it to circulate it before his death, as that it poses the question why Montaigne did not himself publish it, when he published so much else of La Boétie's literary inheritance.

The second difficulty is similar. Montaigne must have known that La Boétie had left a not particularly moderate manuscript *Mémoire sur l'édit de janvier 1562*, which Montaigne suppressed. It was found and published by La Boétie's modern editor, Paul Bonnefon, only a score of years after his edition of La Boétie's other works. One wonders how strongly Montaigne disagreed with the content of the text discovered in 1917 at Aix-Méjanes.

Finally, describing La Boétie's death in the letter to his father published only at the end of 1570, but written probably at the end of August 1563, within days of his friend's death on the 19th, Montaigne reports that La Boétie, at first in what could have been delirium, but then more composedly, asked several times to be reassured by Montaigne that he had a "place." He dismissed his wife from the room, perhaps not wishing to cause her the distress of seeing him suffer, saying he wanted to rest, asked Montaigne to stay near him, then struggled violently to turn in bed, giving some hope that he might in fact be recovering strength, "Then, among other things, he began to beg me and beg me again with an extreme affection to give him 'une place.'"

Montaigne was reporting, and therefore also glossing what was said. He thought La Boétie was delirious, but La Boétie would not be reasoned with, and cried even more strongly, "My brother, my brother, are you going to refuse me 'une place,' then?" Montaigne says that he replied that La Boétie had a body, and therefore also "son lieu." That, had said La Boétie at the point of death, is not what he had meant. Montaigne says that he said that God would soon give him a better "lieu." La Boétie's last reported words are, "My brother, I wish I were there already. For three days I have been straining to leave." He sought reassurance that Montaigne was still with him, started to rest peacefully, called out for Montaigne once or twice, and died an hour or two after Montaigne, talking to La Boétie's wife, had left the room.

Montaigne clearly wanted his father to believe that La Boétie had died having waited three days to be separated from his body and to be with God. La Boétie felt he no longer any "estre," he demanded in delirium reassurance that he would still have a "place," and Montaigne had told him he still had a body and therefore a "lieu." All three words can mean much the same in this sort of context, and we do not anyway know how accurate Montaigne was being. It is possible that Montaigne thought that La Boétie was seeking certainty that he would remain at the centre of Montaigne's affections, "My brother, my brother, are you going to refuse me a place, then?" It is possible that La Boétie was simply delirious, or thinking of his body, as Montaigne pretends, or of his posthumous reputation, or of his grave, or of heaven. But the resolution of the three problems is of central importance for the understanding of La Boétie's life and works. To what, at the instant of death, in his last lucid moments, did he really attach importance? If we knew the answer, it might also contribute much to our understanding of Montaigne.

La Boétie was born at Sarlat on 1 November 1530. His father

was a lawyer and lieutenant of the sénéchal of Périgord and could trace his ancestry back to the 14th century. One of six children, he died soon after 1540, leaving La Boétie in the hands of his uncle and godfather, Etienne, curé of Bouilhonnas. There were two other children, both daughters and both younger than La Boétie. Etienne's mother, Philippe de Calvimont, also came from a family of magistrates. After his early studies at home, La Boétie trained as a lawyer at the famous faculty of Orléans, where he graduated in September 1553. He had already begun to write some of the Latin verse which Montaigne would publish in 1570. On 17 May 1554 La Boétie was admitted as a conseiller at the Bordeaux bar, although he was still 18 months short of the statutory age of 25 and required a royal dispensation. One of his uncles was already a judge at the parlement, and at some date before his admission La Boétie had himself married a widow with two daughters, Marguerite de Carle, sister of the bishop of Riez, and of one of the Bordeaux présidents. The couple were not themselves to have children, and we do not know by how long Marguerite de Carle survived La Boétie. She made a will in 1580.

La Boétie's professional career was efficiently conducted, and by the later 1550s he was certainly regarded as distinguished, if still with unfulfilled promise. Even if allusions to Ronsard and his associates were interpolated into the text of the *Discours de la servitude volontaire*, it is clear from dedications to and by La Boétie, and from references in his poems, and in those of others, that he knew and was esteemed by Jean-Antoine de Baïf and Dorat. A number of mutual friends and relatives linked La Boétie to Ronsard, who was a friend of La Boétie's brother-in-law, Lancelot de Carle, and of his uncle, Jean Amelin, the translator of Livy. Later on La Boétie's close friend Jean Belot was to become another of Ronsard's friends. A Bordeaux lawyer, trained at Orléans, La Boétie was loosely associated with a whole nascent world of Catholic humanists who cultivated Greek studies, either knew one another or had close mutual friends, often had in common patrons, like cardinal Charles de Lorraine at Meudon, or models, like J.-C. Scaliger, to whom La Boétie dedicated a poem, gave one another introductions, and dedicated verse to one another. This loose and loosely related network had one mid-century nucleus in the entourage of Dorat, and then Ronsard, geographically located in Paris and the Loire valley. It had another towards the south-west, centred on Orléans and Bordeaux.

In 1559 La Boétie rented a large house in Bordeaux near the Collège de Guyenne, whose principal was then Andrea de Gouvea, who had left Sainte-Barbe in Paris, of which in the absence of Diego, his uncle, he had been in charge, at the same time as Calvin and Cop, after Cop's famous sermon on 1 November 1533. The humanist education at the Collège de Guyenne had become renowned throughout France, and the humanist educational method of using drama pedagogically for the teaching of rhetoric in the Aristotelian sense, that is, of the art of moving the passions, had largely been pioneered at Guyenne before being taken up notably at the Collège de Boncourt in Paris, and then systematically in the Jesuit colleges as they were founded. The dramas were sometimes classical and sometimes, like those by Muret and Buchanan, composed for the pupils, but still, at least at Guyenne, normally in Latin.

At Bordeaux in the 1550s the plays had become too pointedly allusive about the disputed questions of religious practice, and there had been sufficient public disorder for the parlement to demand prior censorship of all texts intended for performance. The first major task outside the ordinary court duties entrusted to La Boétie by the parlement was that of censoring the texts submitted in 1560, one of which was in French. Then at the end of 1560 the parlement sent La Boétie and a colleague to Paris to secure from the king some more assured way of getting their parliamentary salaries paid on time. François II died on 5 December 1560, and La Boétie and his colleague were joined in Paris by another deputation sent from the parlement to pay hommage to Charles IX, born only ten years previously. La Boétie returned in March 1561, having got to know Michel de l'Hôpital, chancellor from March 1560. Bordeaux was to show itself reluctant to accept the chancellor's policy of moderation, which was also that of Catherine de Medici, and in 1560 the parlement had refused to register the edict of Romorantin on tolerance, now to be confirmed and widened by that of Orléans. La Boétie was charged by L'Hôpital with the task of explaining official policy in Bordeaux and then, by the Bordeaux parlement, with implementing it.

Trouble had broken out in particular at Agen, a stronghold of the Reform, early in 1561, and the Bordeaux parlement had called on the new regent, Catherine de Medici, for strong repressive measures. Catherine de Medici and L'Hôpital preferred more temperate counsels. The king's lieutenant in Bordeaux, Burie, also a moderate, went to Agen and succeeded in restoring order, although immediately he left there was more rioting. On 4 September 1561 detailed instructions were issued for Burie to go back to punish not religious dissidence, but only public disorder. Burie, acting in the name of the king, asked for La Boétie to be authorized to accompany him on the parlement's behalf. The king would pay, and La Boétie's mission was subsequently extended in length. His task clearly was to reconcile the moderate policy of Paris with the rather more embattled anti-Huguenot stance taken by the parlement at Bordeaux. At Agen, where the task was at its most difficult, a community of monks was given back its pillaged houses, but second churches, where they existed, were given to Huguenots, and where there was only one church, it was to be used for both Catholic and Huguenot services. The policy proved too liberal. In the face of further disorders a disarmament was to be imposed, but no agreement could be reached on the composition of the committee to oversee it and the region slowly slid towards war.

The colloque of Poissy had failed in September 1561. The regent wanted to try pacification through the courts, and the eight parlements sent delegates to Saint-Germain for a meeting of the private council which opened on 3 January 1562. L'Hôpital addressed the assembly, and the edict of January was signed on 17 January 1562, the most liberal legislation before the edict of Nantes. Paris, under Guise influence, refused to register the edict, but it was accepted at Bordeaux and promulgated on 6 February. The reason Montaigne was to give in 1570 for not publishing either La Boétie's *Mémoire* or the *Contr'Un*, as the *Discours de la servitude volontaire* was eventually called, was that they were written in "une façon trop délicate et trop mignarde pour les abandonner au grossier et pesant air d'une si malplaisante saison (too delicate and gentle a manner to be released in the coarse and heavy atmosphere of so intemperate a season)." Montaigne presumably thought that La Boétie had gone too far in the direction of Bordeaux's hard line to make the posthumous publication of the *Mémoire* appropriate in the changed circumstances of 1570, after the outbreak of the wars, while the argument of the *Discours*, as was soon to be shown, had become decidedly two-edged. Paul Bonnefon had originally conjectured that the *Mémoire*'s content would be more moderate than, when he found it, it turned out to be.

During the summer of 1562, the religious and political tensions grew worse. On 10 December the town of Bordeaux decided to raise 12 companies of 100 soldiers each. La Boétie was one of the 12 councillors put in charge of a company. The Huguenots under Armand de Clermont had already taken Bergerac. The following year La Boétie went to Agen. There was a severe outbreak of plague throughout Périgord in the summer of 1563, and the town of Sarlat is reported to have emptied itself except for a consul and some doctors, which presumably means that those citizens left who had somewhere to go to in the country. It is probably of plague that La Boétie died, although his illness started as a stomach chill after a game of tennis and developed into violent dysentery.

Montaigne, on his way back from the parlement on Monday 9 August 1563 had sent word to La Boétie to dine at his house, but La Boétie replied that he felt unwell and was going to the country, where his wife had property, next day, and asked Montaigne to come round for an hour after dinner. Montaigne found him lying down but fully dressed, and thought he would be better for a ride next day, but should keep it short, and on 10 August La Boétie with his wife and uncle set off for Germignan, only a few kilometres away, where the party presumably stayed with Richard de Lestonnac, a parliamentary colleague and Montaigne's brother-in-law. La Boétie's wife sent for Montaigne early on 11 August, and kept him overnight when he arrived in the evening. Montaigne left La Boétie on the Thursday, returned that evening, left again on the Friday, but returned to see La Boétie on the Saturday, finding him much weakened. Knowing that his illness was contagious, La Boétie asked Montaigne to stay with him for only short periods, but as often as he could.

By Sunday he knew he was dying and accepted Montaigne's tactful invitation to put his affairs in order. He called only for his wife and his uncle, conscious of the gap his death would cause in Montaigne's life, and in theirs. It was La Boétie who was aware of the need to console them, and Montaigne reports his friend's address to each, as later that to his niece and stepdaughter, Jacquette d'Arsac, shortly to marry Montaigne's Protestant brother. To Montaigne's brother, Thomas de Beauregard, La Boétie said that he thought the cause of the religious dissension largely to be the corruption within the Church, and the need for reform, but begged him to avoid violence. Lawyer and priest were called. La Boétie made his confession, heard Mass, received another councillor friend, and was then left alone with Montaigne for the final hours before Montaigne left him asleep an hour or two before his death early in the morning of Wednesday, 18 August 1563. He was not yet 33, and had died less than 18 months after the Wassy incident signalling the outbreak of the religious wars.

The details of Montaigne's account ring authentically true, although there is a degree of stylization in the whole account of the edifying Christian humanist death, with its appropriate speeches and sentiments. That Montaigne recounted exactly what happened can scarcely be doubted in view of the amount of realistic detail, but he made it fit into an almost stereotyped narrative account of a good death, intended to edify colleagues and posterity as well as to inform, and no doubt to release his own emotional tension by recounting the scene in such detail. It

is virtually certain that the letter was actually sent by Montaigne to his father very much as it was published by Montaigne in his 1570 edition of La Boétie's *Oeuvres*.

WORKS

La Boétie was a more accomplished humanist than Montaigne, his first editor, seems to have realized. The original rough Greek text of Plutarch published in March 1509 by Aldus had been overtaken by Froben's 1542 text of the *Moralia*, some of which had already appeared the previous year in Latin. La Boétie was using the Froben text, as was his friend and colleague in the Bordeaux parlement, Arnaud de Ferron, who translated other Plutarch treatises which were published at Lyons in 1555, 1556, and 1557 by Jean de Tournes. The third volume acknowledged La Boétie's assistance with points of philological erudition. La Boétie himself translated Plutarch's *Lettre de consolation* to his wife on the death of their child, and the *Règles de mariage*, the sixth French translation since 1535, with Amyot's translation of the *Oeuvres morales* still to follow in 1572. Amyot's *Vies* had appeared in 1559 and while there can be no doubt about Amyot's superior style, grace, and elegance, the translation of the two short pieces by La Boétie are more accurate in their fidelity to Plutarch's precise meaning.

The piece translated by La Boétie from Xenophon's *Oeconomicus*, entitled *Le Mesnagerie de Xenophon*, reflects the extraordinary interest in Xenophon that existed in 16th-century France. There were no fewer than eight editions of the Greek text of the complete works between 1516 and 1561, in addition to three partial editions of the *Oeconomicus*. La Boétie was the first French translator from the Greek, and he stumbles over the technical terms and some of the syntax which the French language was not yet sufficiently developed to provide. Horace had the city-dweller's nostalgia for relaxed Epicurean enjoyment of the countryside, and Virgil as a poet of nature cultivated its melancholy. French could manage both attitudes, but not yet with ease the down-to-earth precision of Xenophon.

The achevé d'imprimer of the translations and Latin verses is dated 24 November 1570. Montaigne had intended to include the French verse with the Latin, but finally published the 25 sonnets written for La Boétie's future wife and two longer poems, one loosely taken from Ariosto's *Orlando furioso*, separately in 1571, with a prefatory letter dated 1 September 1570. Six different versions of what were essentially the same poems must have been given to Baïf before La Boétie had ever met Montaigne. Presumably reminded of them by Montaigne's publication, Baïf included them in the second book of his *Diverses amours* in 1571, published in the *Euvres en rime* of 1572. The presumption resulting from a comparison of styles is that Baïf considerably improved on the texts of the poems he printed, and that La Boétie's own strength lay in faithful prose translation, and in writing in his own vigorous and clear prose idiom. Montaigne wrote of the 25 sonnets that they smacked already of "je ne sçay quelle froideur maritale (a certain marital coolness) (I, 29)."

Montaigne had originally intended to print the *Discours de la servitude volontaire* next to his chapter "De l'amitié" and make of them both the centrepiece of the first volume of *Les Essais*. In fact, at I, 29, he printed the 29 sonnets of La Boétie passed to him by a Seigneur de Poyferré, referred to, by name only, in the 1580 edition of *Les Essais*. They were written, Montaigne says, when La Boétie was "en sa plus verte jeunesse, et eschaufé d'une belle et noble ardeur (in his most verdant youth, and inflamed by a fine and noble ardour)." Montaigne, who dedicated the later 25 sonnets to Paul de Foix, comte de Carmain, an ambassador and archbishop, and the Latin poems to L'Hôpital, dedicated the 29 sonnets he printed in *Les Essais* to Diane d'Andoins, comtesse de Guiche et de Gramont, later one of the mistresses of Henri de Navarre, who was addressed in the dedication as "Corisande," the name of a character from the *Amadis* stories. The poems lack any real inspiration, or even poetic talent.

The *Mémoire sur l'édit de janvier 1562* needs to be understood not as the expression of a private opinion so much as the hammered-out solution to the dilemma of finding a working policy which suited La Boétie's own temperament, but also compromised between the conciliatory attitude of Catherine de Medici and her chancellor on the one hand and the more embattled posture adopted in the threatened capital of the south-west on the other. The *Mémoire* does forthrightly condemn the effort to use force against intellectual dissidence, regarding it as both wrong and useless to try "par le couteau extirper les opinions (to use the knife to extirpate opinions)," but he does not see any possibility of the equal co-existence of two religions, and expects it would be only "une manifeste ruine de voir en ce royaume deux religions ordonnées et établies (an obvious disaster to see two religions ordered and established in this kingdom)." La Boétie had nearly been forced to concede such an arrangement by Burie at Agen. On his deathbed he was to say to Beauregard that "les seuls vices de noz prelats, et quelques imperfections que le cours du temps a apporté en nostre Eglise (only the vices of our prelates and some imperfections which the course of time has brought to our Church)" had been responsible for the schism. La Boétie was also to tell Beauregard that he wanted to persuade no one to act against his conscience, and plead with him to avoid violence, whereas in the *Mémoire* his emphasis is perceptibly harder: there can be only one official religion, and it must be Catholicism.

It is in the context of the *Discourse de la servitude volontaire* which he does not print that, at the end of I, 28, Montaigne says of La Boétie that a maxim he had "sovereignly imprinted on his soul" was "d'obeyr et de se soubmettre très-religieusement aux loix sous lesquelles il estoit nay (to obey and with utmost religious deference to submit to the laws under which he was born)," a common enough 16th-century rule of thumb, and one which Montaigne elsewhere quotes from Pibrac's *Quatrains*, although it is at odds with his own disapproval in the "Apologie de Raymond Sebond" (II, 12) of Christians who believe only because of their cultural background. Montaigne himself was simply more flexible and more pragmatic than La Boétie. They were both conservatives. Neither wished to violate consciences. But the opening pages of Montaigne's "De l'utile et de l'honnête" (III, 1) make it clear that Montaigne is prepared to leave the maintenance of public order to someone else. La Boétie saw that that position was not really tenable, and was more concerned with the difficult task of working out what the norms for the imposition of social harmony should be. In the end, according to the end of I, 28, Montaigne did not print the *Discours* because of the use made of it by the Huguenots.

We have no real idea when La Boétie wrote the *Discours*. De Thou connects it with the Guyenne revolt against the gabelle or salt tax in 1548. Paul Bonnefon thinks a date as early as 1549

most unlikely. At the end of "De l'amitié," when he has decided not to print it, Montaigne says that it was written by La Boétie "in his childhood," "as an exercise," and "comme subject vulgaire et tracassé en mille endroits des livres (as a common subject thrashed out in a thousand places in books)," and earlier in the same chapter he had said that he knew the text, written "par maniere d'essay (as a sort of trial)," a long time before he ever seen La Boétie, which means before 1557. But we know that Montaigne by the date of "De l'amitié," as it was published in 1580, wanted to disparage La Boétie's treatise against tyranny because of the use made of it both in the *Reveille-matin* and in Goulart's *Mémoires*, and we know that he dismissed it as something which La Boétie never revised after it first left his hands. However, Montaigne also wrote in I, 28 that La Boétie had written it when he was 18. Sometime after 1588 Montaigne changed that figure to 16. He may have wanted to excuse its forthrightness of tone and the unrestrained vigour of the argument now being used by the Hugeunots, by ascribing the whole tract to extreme youth, treating it as a scholastic exercise, a commonplace written by a mere child.

Perhaps Montaigne protests too much, but there could only be the mildest presumption in favour of a very early date, perhaps 1549 if de Thou is right and La Boétie was deploying his youthful ardour in writing an aggrieved pamphlet against the savage repression of the Bordeaux revolt as well as in the 29 love sonnets. There is no allusion in the text we have to the events of 1548. Were any ever there, perhaps removed as by 1574 irrelevant to the purposes for which the pamphlet was published? There almost certainly was some text of the *Discours* which Montaigne had read when he first "saw" La Boétie, which was presumably in 1557. Since one-fifth of the text we actually have was first published in 1574 and four-fifths in 1576, and we know that parts of what we have were added or changed, we are dealing with a particularly elusive document. Its date is uncertain, and its text has been tampered with, but we are uncertain who did the tampering, when, or in what interest, and we do not know what the original literary register was, whether of schoolboy exercise, which was Sainte-Beuve's final verdict, or of violently polemical and courageous pamphlet, as some more recent critics have contended.

What is left is a virtually unattributable document. Its argument logically entails the legitimacy of tyrannicide and points to the willingness of peoples to invite tyrants to rule over them. Its author is fascinated by the willing acquiescence of peoples in their own servitude and in the abrogation of their own rights. In the text as printed, the analysis of how a tyranny works is no more than any competent student of Livy or Machiavelli might be expected to produce. The remedy of non-violent resistance proposed does not really take account of the political realities as outlined in the text, and the logical conclusion of legitimate tyrannicide could not have been hedged by enough qualifications to make it other than seditious until well after 1574. The text, its style, ideas, purpose, and register have all been tampered with far too much to make it possible to use it as a basis for concluding anything at all about La Boétie's literary status. It can be evaluated only in the light of the use to which it was put and for which it was modified in 1574. Even if Montaigne had had in his possession a text which La Boétie would still not have wished to emend in 1563, and even if it had been a considered work of political theory which had not been tampered with, nor used as in fact it had been used in 1574 and 1576, Montaigne would have done La Boétie no service by publishing a tract written before 1557, before the outbreak of the wars, in the changed circumstances of 1580.

PUBLICATIONS

Oeuvres complètes, 1892

Prose

Discours sur la servitude volontaire, in S. Goulart, *Mémoires sur l'état de France sous Charles neufiesme*, 3 vols., 1577; as *Anti-Dictator*, 1942
Mémoire touchant l'édit de janvier 1562, 1922
La Mesnagerie de Xenophon…,1571

Verse

Vers françois, 1571
Vingt-neuf sonnets, in Montaigne, *Les Essais*, 1580

Biographical and critical studies

Bonnefon, Paul, Introduction to *Oeuvres complètes*, 1892

LA BRUYÈRE, Jean de, 1645–1696.

Social satirist and religious controversialist.

LIFE

La Bruyère's personal timidity not unnaturally overflowed into both the content and the mode of presentation of *Les Caractères*, which is certainly not just the witty and graceful social comment masquerading as an anonymous prolongation of Theophrastus which it has been taken for, and certainly not just a stylistic exercise tacked on to a court literature already, in 1688, conscious of its own cohesion and grandeur. La Bruyère was being not intentionally paradoxical but shy when, after the "Discours sur Théophraste," the translation of Theophrastus's 28 portraits in larger type than the rest of the volume, and a short preface, he started the "Caractères ou moeurs de ce siècle" with the statement that "Tout est dit, et l'on vient trop tard depuis plus de sept mille ans qu'il y a des hommes et qui pensent (Everything has been said, and we come too late, when for more than seven thousand years there have been men, and men able to think)." Similarly, he was being not provocative, but only shy, when one day in the autumn of 1687 he tossed his unsigned manuscript to the book-seller Etienne Michallet, whose shop he visited almost daily, drily suggesting that he might like to publish it and that, if he made

any money out of it, it would provide a dowry for Michallet's daughter and assistant, with whom La Bruyère had become quite friendly. The anecdote comes from Formey, the permanent secretary of the Prussian academy, who had it from Maupertuis, an acquaintance in later life of Michallet's daughter, whom the legacy had made rich.

In both the content and the presentation of his anonymous work, La Bruyère's diffidence had driven him to camouflage what he had done, much as Montaigne had camouflaged, with the declared intention to portray himself, the intimacy with his reader on which he came increasingly to presume. La Bruyère not only shared the desire of so many contemporary authors to avoid the plebeian vulgarity of the writer's craft, but he also felt the need to shelter under the twin umbrellas of anonymity and scholarship, pretending as well that nothing new was being said by the unnamed translator.

The appendix on "Les Caractères ou les moeurs de ce siècle" yielded pride of place and typographical distinction to the translation of an antique author. Although its text started with the declaration that there was nothing new to say, what was said was indeed new. It demonstrated an unprecedented social awareness, and a sensitivity which already announced the century to come and would demand the repudiation of the values of the society in which La Bruyère himself had been nurtured, and to which he remained attached. He felt that what he actually did want to say was important, invited comments on the text, polished it, and took only apparently nonchalant measures to see that it was published, although he sought neither material reward from it nor public recognition of his authorship. However elegant, the social satire, intentionally untidy in both organization and expression, was already mordant. It was never quite to overcome the timidity of its conception and attain the cohesion of values and the focus of view whose lack has puzzled so many generations of readers.

Although the name is attested in Paris from the high middle ages, we know only that La Bruyère himself is descended from a great-grandfather prominent in the late 16th century, an apothecary whose tax payment of 160 livres on his town house indicates substantial wealth. It was backed up by estates and feudal rights in the Loire valley. A direct ancestor La Bruyère had helped to found the League in 1576 and was elected to the Seize, the insurrectionary anti-royalist council which took over the government of Paris in 1588. He had continued to play a prominent role among the city's dignitaries thereafter. His son, La Bruyère's great-grandfather Mathias, acquired the office of king's counsel at the Cour des Aides, became deputy-governor of Paris, and made a wealthy marriage. Both he and his father were implicated in the hanging on 16 November 1591 of Barnabé Brisson, president of the Paris parlement, with two others, for suspected opposition to the invitation to the king of Spain to appoint a new French sovereign, and both were in danger when Mayenne returned and hanged four of the Seize to restore order. When both La Bruyères refused to take the oath of loyalty to Henri IV, their possessions were confiscated, and they fled to the Netherlands. La Bruyère himself was certainly conscious in *Les Caractères* of the part played by his ancestors in the League.

La Bruyère's grandfather, Guillaume, came back from the Netherlands to France, succeeded in having returned to him property that had once belonged to his mother, acquired a post of secretary to the king, and had two sons and a daughter. The younger son followed his father as secretary to the king, and the elder, La Bruyère's father Louis, a contrôleur général of finance, married Elisabeth Hamonyn, daughter of a Procureur at the Châtelet. La Bruyère, the eldest of eight children of whom three died young, was baptized on 17 August 1645, having been born into the upper bourgeoisie of Paris, with fading memories of ancestral grandeur. We know nothing of his upbringing. He may have been tonsured, and he studied law, perhaps at home. He took the trouble to defend his theses in person at Orléans on 3 June 1665 and was inscribed on the roll of advocates at the Paris parlement, but we do not know if he practised.

La Bruyère's father died in 1666, leaving very little money. However, his unmarried uncle died at 54 in 1671, apparently providing an income for his nieces and a substantial sum for his three nephews. With his share La Bruyère bought the office of king's counsellor and trésorier général at Caen, worth a little under 18,000 livres and producing annual emoluments of about 2,350 livres, with a title to nobility. We do not know how much he paid for the post, but it may have been more than he could afford. We know at least that he borrowed 3,352 livres from his mother on 14 January 1678, and that he reimbursed his family after her death in 1685. La Bruyère's letters patent were dated 29 March 1674. He took the oath at Rouen on 19 September, was installed at Caen on the 22nd, and never went back there. Since residence, or a dispensation from it, was normally required, some form of connivance must have been involved, but La Bruyère seems to have felt bitter when he sold his office in 1686, and it looks also as if something in connection with his arrangements for absence also went wrong.

From 1674 La Bruyère was tutor to his sister's daughters. He lived at first with his mother, brothers, and sisters, all sharing the household expenses. He paid 900 livres for board and lodging for himself and his servants, whose number he was soon to reduce to one, plus half the cost of the stables. The family moved twice, reducing its circumstances each time. Finally a brother and one of his two sisters went off to live together, while La Bruyère shared accommodation with his brother Louis, even after Louis's marriage. He was also robbed of seven bags containing 2,490 livres which he could certainly not afford to lose, by a servant he had borrowed from one of his brothers. By 1670 we are told by contemporaries that he had begun the observations later to be enshrined in *Les Caractères*. He is said by his friend and admirer, the lawyer Brillon, to have spent 10 years after their completion before deciding to publish them. That would imply ten years taken to write and ten more to think about them. Both sets of ten years are certainly exaggerated, but La Bruyère obviously took his time. He also plainly spent much time reading, particularly works of philosophy, showing a particular interest in Descartes.

The signs are that he lived most of his life under financial constraint, a matter of significance in view of the way in which he gave away the rights to *Les Caractères*. Although he could not have known it at the time, they were to make Michallet's daughter rich. She received between 200,000 and 300,000 livres, and was able to marry the already wealthy tax farmer Rémy du July. La Bruyère when he died left only a little over 2,000 livres in cash, with not many possessions. For a man of his status, he had lived almost frugally. He continued to use Louis's Paris address, although he owned nothing in the house, shared another in the country with his brother and sister, and lived comfortably but not luxuriously in a two-room apartment in the Hôtel de Condé in the Rue de Vaugirard in Paris, where from 1684 he was a member of the household. At his death his books were valued at 278 livres. In his similar apartment at the Condé hôtel at Versailles there was a good deal of fine linen, a collection of 145 books, and a picture of Bossuet, as well as the guitar which le grand Condé had made him play and dance to, apparently amused at the shy La Bruyère's ungainliness, which Condé mockingly applauded.

It seems likely that it was for financial reasons that in August 1684 he accepted a post as one of the tutors of the 16-year-old duc de Bourbon, grandson of le grand Condé, although he did not take up the position until October, and then had to wait a year for his first annual salary payment of 1,500 livres, generally paid, but always with arrears. For his first year, La Bruyère borrowed another 2,000 livres. In 1686 he renounced his share in the inheritance he was expecting to divide with his brothers and sisters, a gesture prompted much more probably by generosity towards them, now that he had decided to become permanently established in the Condé household, than by any prior cash settlement with them which he might have needed. In 1686 he sold his treasury office in Caen but kept the title to nobility it had brought with it. In 1695, although a member of the Académie, he was also to offer his unremunerated services as tutor to his brother Louis's children.

The young duc de Bourbon had for six years attended the Jesuit collège de Clermont, soon to have its name changed to Louis-le-Grand, with two Jesuits and one lay tutor assigned to him, and a special miniature throne to sit on. What the rector, the Jesuits, and the lay tutor said and failed to say about him requires skilful interpretation. Even the Jesuits thought their august pupil malicious, violent, a bully, scornfully arrogant, and incapable of concentration, but they were more tolerant of him than the layman, who gave up, in apparent despair at the youth's vicious character. Saint-Evremond was to note how successfully Bourbon had overcome the remnants of a good education. His grandfather, le grand Condé, now known as "Monsieur le Prince," had been disappointed by his son Henri-Jules, known until le grand Condé's death as "Monsieur le duc." Henri-Jules was universally regarded as intolerably unpleasant; his malice, despotic whims, and dislikable personality prevented anyone from having a good word to say about him. Henri-Jules's mother had gone mad at the age of 43. After the recorded cruelties to his wife, Anne of Bavaria, Henri-Jules was in turn to lose his sanity. His son Bourbon was both epileptic and, according to Saint-Simon, physically ugly to the point of being partially deformed.

M. le Prince, however, took a close interest in his grandson, Louis III, even when he had returned from schooling in Paris to live with his tutors at Versailles. Bourbon was at least more literate and a little less unmanageably wilful than his father. It was when the young duke was on holiday at Chantilly, staying with his grandfather, that the lay tutor resigned, and La Bruyère, together with the mathematician Sauveur, later to be a professor at the Collège Royal, was brought in, wrongly thinking that he would be in complete charge of finishing the youth's education. Two Jesuits who had taught Bourbon at school were retained in the household to report to M. le Prince on what was going on, and to supervise his grandson's moral and religious education.

La Bruyère had waited in Paris to assist Cordemoy, the academician whom Bossuet had recruited to help with the education of the dauphin, in his final illness, and did not join the Condé household until Cordemoy's death in October 1684, following his pupil thereafter round the Condé residences, in Paris near the Luxembourg, out at Versailles, accompanying him also to Fontainebleau, Chantilly, and Chambord as occasion demanded. It was Fontenelle who first pointed out that Bossuet had made a speciality of provisioning young princelings with learned tutors, and found them for Louis XIV's illegitimate sons by Mme de Montespan as well as for the dauphin. Since it was Bossuet who had recommended Cordemoy for the dauphin, Fleury for the duc de Vermandois, and Malézieu for the duc du Maine at the court of Sceaux, it is more than probable that it was Bossuet who recommended La Bruyère, known to him as a philosophically inclined Christian, to the Condés for Bourbon. On 20 February 1685 Bossuet himself listened in on one of La Bruyère's lessons on Descartes's *Principes* and said how pleased he was with the pedagogy. La Bruyère, very close to Bossuet's brother Antoine, was always to remain loyal to Bossuet himself, even when Bossuet was being tetchily self-important, as he was in the controversy with Fénelon in which La Bruyère supported him.

The duc de Bourbon married the legitimized daughter of Louis XIV and Mme de Montespan, Louise-Françoise de Nantes, on 24 July 1685, although they continued to live apart until the marriage was consummated on 23 April 1686. She, too, became La Bruyère's pupil although, on instructions from le grand Condé, who occasionally himself attended his grandson's lessons, she was taught at different times from her husband. La Bruyère's took his tutorial position very seriously, and the surviving 17 letters written before Condé's death on 11 December 1686 show a determined but disappointed tutor unable to obtain from his pupil the attention which La Bruyère thought study deserved. In view of the many court diversions currently available, and the other pursuits making demands on his charge's attention, it is difficult to be surprised. On the death of le grand Condé, Henri-Jules happily discontinued his son's lessons, dismissing Sauveur and the two Jesuits but keeping on La Bruyère as a gentleman of the household, making him librarian, with undefined and unonerous duties but at double the salary.

La Bruyère's decision to sell the Caen post must have been linked with his decision to move up from the position of co-tutor of the former duc de Bourbon to the sinecured position of Condé household courtier. Years later Valincour was to recollect that the Condés laughed at the social timidities and comparative gaucheness of their lettered retainer, and there are muted indications in *Les Caractères* to suggest that La Bruyère was kept conscious of the unelevated social rank and limited comforts to which his services entitled him, but the Condé steward, Gourville, always referred to him respectfully as "Monsieur de La Bruyère," and he had kept his entitlement to nobility. It is unlikely that La Bruyère was as humiliatingly treated as similarly placed tutors, librarians, or secretaries were in some other grand households, or as others, like the canon and poet Jean-Baptiste Santeul, were treated in the Condé household itself: Bouhier informs us that he was slapped by Bourbon's sister, the duchesse du Maine, who then threw a glass of water over his face to cool it off.

It would obviously be helpful, in the context of any attempt to evaluate the social criticism which was the powerful novelty of *Les Caractères*, to know with certainty more than we do about the actual social experience on which it was based. Whatever unpleasantnesses La Bruyère's situation subjected him to, the manners tolerated, indulged, and admired among the aristocracy of whose entourage he formed part fascinated him. The hint of

revenge which endows *Les Caractères* with some of its piquancy suggests that he enjoyed his vantage point, and compensated for its discomforts by formulating his observations and portraits. It is perfectly possible that *Les Caractères* contains echoes picked up from members of the court being ironic at their own expense.

By the beginning of 1687, La Bruyère knew that he wanted to publish a collection of the satirical remarks and pen sketches, of which he had been putting together a portfolio. By this date the moral maxim was an accepted literary genre, associated with La Rochefoucauld above all, but also with Mme de Sablé and, for instance, Arnauld d'Andilly. Madeleine de Scudéry had made the word-portrait fashionable, multiplying examples in the later volumes of *Clélie*; Mme de Lafayette, writing to Ménage from Auvergne on 24 September 1658, complained that she had not been able to recognize most of the subjects. Early in 1659 Anne-Marie d'Orléans, duchesse de Montpensier, helped by Segrais and Huet, issued at Caen somewhere between 30 and 60 luxuriously bound copies of the 59 *Divers Portraits*, of which she had composed 16. Barbin and Sercy, the most fashionable bookseller-publishers in Paris, immediately issued a collection of 500, entitled *Recueil de portraits et éloges en vers et en prose*, with an achevé d'imprimer of 25 January 1659.

La Bruyère's book was to be composed of maxims, portraits, and what, since the first edition of La Rochefoucauld, were also known as *Réflexions ou Sentences*. We do not know when he decided to publish what, to use a neutral term, can be called his remarks as a sort of appendix to Theophrastus, although we do know from the *Préface* to his *Discours à l'Académie* that he had been diffident about publishing at all, hesitating, he claimed, "entre le désir d'être utile à sa patrie par ses écrits et la crainte de fournir à quelques-uns de quoi exercer leur malignité (between the desire to be useful to his country through his writings and the fear of affording certain people the opportunity of exercising their malevolence)." That statement can more easily be believed because we know that La Bruyère was anxious to collect opinions before he finally, if with apparent unconcern, committed his manuscript to a Michallet whose first reaction was hesitancy rather than gratitude for so dubious, and potentially expensive, a "dowry" for his daughter. He sought, for instance, the judgement of Bussy.

When Boileau wrote to Racine on 19 May 1687: "Maximilien m'est venu voir à Auteuil et m'a lu quelque chose de son Théophraste (Maximilian came to see me and read me something from his Theophrastus)," it is not immediately clear whether what Maximilian read from was the translation or some of the remarks, maxims, reflections, or most probably portraits. La Bruyère had presumably already decided to use the cloak of Theophrastus, and to publish his own remarks as an appendage to a translation. "Maximilien" could well be an unremarkable coinage for someone who had called to read maxims, and Boileau went on, "C'est un fort bon homme et à qui il ne manquerait rien, si la nature l'avait fait aussi agréable qu'il a envie de l'être (He's a very nice man, who would have everything if nature had made him as pleasant as he would like to be)." That makes it seem not unlikely that what La Bruyère read from included portraits, some of which were too sharp to be "pleasant."

The subterfuge involved in presenting his remarks in the guise of an appendix to a translation of Theophrastus's short portraits of people with a predominating moral characteristic, like verbosity or avarice, was exactly what La Bruyère at first required.

His timidity dictated some disguise, however perfunctory. His first edition contained a dozen portraits, half of which, like those of Zoïle, Philémon, Dorinne, Cléante, and Oronte, are scarcely finished sketches at all. Forty more were to be added for the first revised edition, which was the fourth, published in 1689. Only that of the king in the original volume seems rounded. Did La Bruyère add the portraits to fit the disguise of an appendage to the translation and, if he did, was it before he called on Boileau in May 1687? The answer to both questions is probably yes.

The remarks other than portraits must have been compiled first. Then came the idea of hiding his own work behind the authority of Theophrastus in the guise of an appendage to his text, of which the translation was then prepared and probably prefaced, before the portraits were drawn up to add verisimilitude to the pretence. Only part of the portfolio of remarks can have been published, since 351 remarks were added in 1689 to the original 440. Theophrastus had called his work *Characters* (χαραχτηρεσ), and the word had already been used to denote the physical and physiological characteristics of the individual passions in *Les Caractères des Passions*, by Marin Cureau de la Chambre, doctor of the chancellor Séguier, published in five volumes from 1640 to 1662; so that the portraits, at least, could plausibly be put forward as a continuation of a Greek work whose title transliterated as *Les Caractères* and already had a quasi-moral significance. Apart from the well-known title of Cureau de la Chambre, the word had appeared in titles of other works, notably by Joseph Hall, whose *Caractères* were twice translated from English and had a total of 15 French editions between 1610 and 1667, and by Pierre Lemoyne, who in 1640 published his *Peintures morales où les passions sont représentées par tableaux, par caractères et par questions nouvelles et curieuses*.

Theophrastus, the second-ranking fourth-century B.C. disciple and successor of Aristotle at Athens, was not well known in 17th-century France, and La Bruyère's Greek was actually very weak. Although he clearly consulted and used the Greek text, what he translated into French was the Latin translation of Theophrastus published by Casaubon in 1592, with occasional reference, if only near the beginning, to Furlanus and Poliziano. Michallet took out a privilège on 8 October 1687 for ten years, registered a week later, and the work's achevé d'imprimer is dated at the beginning of January 1688. La Bruyère showed signs of hesitancy up to the last moment, making corrections and insertions while the work was at press, and having unbound copies which could still be emended sent out for approval before the book was released. Bussy-Rabutin had received his copy through the marquis de Termes on 26 January and, knowing the name of the author, wrote of La Bruyère to Termes on 10 March

Il est entré plus avant que lui [Théophraste] dans le coeur de l'homme. Il y est même entré plus délicatement et par des expériences plus fines. Ce ne sont point des portraits de fantaisie qu'il nous a donnés; il a travaillé d'après nature, et il n'y a pas une décision sur laquelle il n'ait eu quelqu'un en vue...il y a un beau sens enveloppé sous des tours fins

(He has penetrated further than Theophrastus into the human heart. He has even penetrated it more delicately and with more sensitive probes. What he has given us are not fantasy portraits. He has worked from nature, and has made

no judgements without having someone in mind...there is good sense wrapped up in discerning turns of phrase).

La Bruyère could scarcely resist such acclamation, and the book was released for sale. The character of the work completely altered in the course of the nine editions to 1696, the year of La Bruyère's death. The ninth edition, although posthumous, was prepared by La Bruyère and was the first, not to acknowledge authorship, but to be openly signed on the title page. It constitutes the authoritative, definitive text, but needs to be understood in the light of its genesis, which means using a scholarly edition which indicates how, when, and what La Bruyère, reacting to controversy and to changing situations, progressively added to the original text.

The successive editions, all duodecimos, changed in more than bulk. In the first edition, the "Discours sur Théophraste" and the translation of the 28 portraits are printed in much bigger type than La Bruyère's own preface—which comprised only the first two and last three sentences of the definitive version—and than the 16 chapters of remarks, most of them brief general characterizations of human behaviour as La Bruyère observed it, but about a tenth of them, mostly longer, devoted to particular people or forms of behaviour, with a dozen portraits. The positioning of the first chapter, "Des ouvrages de l'esprit," contained a deliberate allusion to Pascal, whose *Pensées*, as first published by Port-Royal in 1670, had been prefaced by his reflections on the art of writing. The book itself was an immediate runaway success.

The second and third editions, both still of 1688, changed comparatively little, but the fourth, of 1689, practically doubled the length of La Bruyère's remarks and is altogether more confident in tone. The change is almost summed up in the use of the word caractères in La Bruyère's *Préface*, in which previously he had disclaimed any intention to write maxims, or to prescribe moral laws, and referred to his entries more modestly as remarques. The fifth edition of 1690 added another 154 new caractères, showing in the new material a diminished proportion of maxims, and in the sixth, of 1691, the preface shows an awareness that the character of the whole book is changing. There are 103 new caractères, La Bruyère's material is now in larger characters than the translation of Theophrastus, and some clearly polemical material is introduced for the first time.

The seventh and eighth editions of 1692 and 1694, adding respectively 77 and 42 new caractères, were separated by the controversy occasioned by La Bruyère's reception into the Académie française, and the eighth edition includes La Bruyère's *Discours à l'Académie* and its vengeful *Préface*. At the same time the *Préface* to *Les Caractères ou moeurs de ce siècle* replies to Charpentier's loaded speech of welcome to the Académie, which had accused La Bruyère of moving on from Theophrastus's generalized statements about vices to particular portraits, sometimes of recognized individuals. La Bruyère's work had successfully infuriated the partisans of the "modernes" in the famous Querelle des anciens et des modernes (q.v.), while displeasing neither the king nor the Condé household. The posthumous ninth edition of 1696 made only minor alterations. The number of "caractères" had grown from 418 in 1688 to 1,120 in 1696, with additions made to a further 45.

Les Caractères soon began to be talked about, and it may well have been for reasons of other than literary quality that it sold so well in 1688. Henri Basnage de Beauval, whose *Histoire des ouvrages des Savants* had taken over its function from Bayle's *Nouvelles de la République des Lettres*, abandoned in 1687 to Jacques Bernard, had announced La Bruyère's volume in March, and in May published an account of it, emphasizing the element of exaggeration and the identifiability of the recently ennobled or otherwise elevated targets, including worldly prelates. "Il montre comme au doigt…il ne s'embarrasse point de désigner…Une liberté si vigoureuse est bien rare aujourd'hui (He almost points a finger…he is not afraid to name…so trenchant a liberty is today very rare)."

Within weeks *Les Caractères* had therefore been taken to be a series of malicious comments about the behaviour of identifiable individuals and been vested with all the entertaining interest of a gossip column, made socially exclusive by light washes of pseudonymity or anonymity. It was not long before manuscript "keys" circulated. The Arsenal library has three of 17th-century confection, and a key to the ninth edition was published within a year of its appearance. One late 17th-century manuscript by Simon de Troyes brilliantly describes La Bruyère under the name of "Ménippe" at work, "not just a painter but an anatomist." If he finds only reasonable people, he groans and thinks the day lost. Fools are flattered by his attention until they see the result in print.

In March 1690, the fifth edition had claimed openly the author's descent from a 12th-century "Geoffroy D…," replaced in the sixth edition, published in June 1691, by "Geoffroy Delabruyère." La Bruyère had got his ancestor's date wrong by a century, but he had brought his own name out into the open. It has been not improbably conjectured that the abandonment of anonymity was connected with a growing aspiration to be elected to the Académie.

The story of his election was to become an episode in the Querelle des anciens et des modernes. Perrault and Boileau had already clashed publicly at the Académie, Fontenelle had published his *Digression sur les anciens et les modernes* in January 1688, and in that year Perrault had published the first volume of his *Parallèle des anciens et des modernes*. An election was held in April 1691 to replace Villayer, who had once invented a prototype lift, installed at the Condé house at Versailles at the request of the wife of La Bruyère's ex-pupil, the former duc de Bourbon, who had been stuck in it for three hours during a breakdown. There is no firm evidence that La Bruyère's name had been put forward but, had he succeeded Villayer, he would have had to pronounce his panegyric. In fact he put a satirical portrait of "Hermippe," parodying Villayer, into the fifth edition of *Les Caractères*, together with "Théobalde," plainly based on the ageing Bensserade, the proposer of the "moderne" Fontenelle, the successful candidate.

In November 1691 an election had to be held to replace Bensserade himself. La Bruyère's name was proposed by seven members, of whom we know that Bussy-Rabutin was one, but there followed a deadlock with a candidate whose name is not preserved, and Pavillon was elected as a compromise. The other six names, to judge by La Bruyère's *Discours* when he had been elected, may well have been Bossuet, Racine, Boileau, the permanent secretary Régnier-Desmarais, La Fontaine, and Segrais. In January 1692 Jacques de Tourreil, tutor to the son of the naval minister Louis Phélypeaux de Pontchartrain, was elected to replace Leclerc, and in March 1693 Pellisson was replaced by Bossuet's protégé Fénelon, in whose favour La Bruyère probably stood down. Then in April 1693 Pontchartrain wanted two vacan-

cies caused by the deaths of Bussy-Rabutin and Pierre Cureau de la Chambre, son of Marin, to go one to his nephew, the abbé Bignon, and the other to another family tutor, La Loubère, who stood aside for La Bruyère, so in fact assuring his own election to replace Tallemant later in the year. Bignon and La Bruyère were elected, although the "modernes," in the ascendancy, resented the ministerial pressure from Pontchartrain for both candidates and, unusually, Fontenelle and Thomas Corneille voted against La Bruyère even after the king had confirmed the election.

These were the circumstances in which La Bruyère decided to reinstitute the tradition originally inaugurated by Patru in 1640, of using his "discours de réception" on 15 June as the occasion for a grand literary proclamation. The welcome should have been pronounced by Boileau, but he had to call that day on a treasury official with Racine's wife to ensure the payment of Racine's pension, so François Charpentier presided in his place. Bignon spoke first, perfunctorily and to acclaim, repeating his discourse when Harlay, the archbishop of Paris, arrived late. La Bruyère's discourse irritated even his supporters by breaking with the established formalities, such as expressions of gratitude, modesty, and astonishment at his success.

After lauding Richelieu and his foundation, La Bruyère praised his seven earlier supporters by name, substituting Fénelon for the dead Bussy-Rabutin, and, going out of his way to denigrate the achievements of Pierre Corneille, who had died in 1684, praised the rest of his new colleagues with no more than ritual deference. He paid his predecessor a double-edged compliment, saying that his virtue was such as to make his literary skills "the least of his qualities." His silences were eloquent, relegating Harlay to the praiseworthy group of "diserts orateurs (fluent orators)" in the gathering. After a eulogy of Louis XIV, he congratulated the members of the Académie for electing him "avec un consentement si unanime (with such unanimous consent)" on account only of his work, unconstrained "by any post, or influence, or wealth, or titles, or authority, or favour."

Charpentier's discourse of welcome was an immediate put-down, comparing La Bruyère unfavourably with Theophrastus, whose moral comment had abstracted from individual behaviour. In fact Charpentier was making a quite trenchant criticism. *Les Caractères*, like the work of Marin Cureau de la Chambre, did concentrate on external manifestations of sometimes idiosyncratic behaviour rather than focusing on inner and general moral qualities as, for instance, La Rochefoucauld had done. La Bruyère's discours had been favourably received by the king at Marly, and at Chantilly, but the cry was quickly taken up by a harsh 25-page admirably well-targeted attack in the *Mercure Galant* (q.v.) for June 1693, inspired by Fontenelle but written by Thomas Corneille and Donneau de Visé. They spoiled their effect chiefly by exaggerating the gossipy scandal produced by the portraits of the first edition, which had actually contained so few. The rush to buy, suggested the *Mercure*, had been caused by the fear that the bookseller would be ordered to cut out most of the portraits. The demand had been created, it was suggested, by the satirical content, "by which authors are often dazzled, attributing to the skill of their works what is due only to the ill they speak about people."

What stung most was the insinuation that La Bruyère was, as he himself had seemed in the *Discours sur Théophraste* to admit, unable to produce sustained discourse. *Les Caractères* was a book only because it had a cover and, like other books, was bound.

Ce n'est qu'un amas de pièces détachées qui ne peut faire connaître si celui qui les a faites avait assez de génie et de lumières pour bien conduire un ouvrage qui serait suivi. Rien n'est plus aisé que de faire trois ou quatre pages d'un portrait qui ne demande point d'ordre, et il n'y a pas de génie si borné qui ne soit capable de coudre ensemble quelques médisances de son prochain

(It is only a heap of separate pieces from which one cannot tell whether the author had enough talent and intelligence to compose a coherent work. Nothing is easier than to write three or four pages of a portrait which does not require any order, and there is no talent so limited that its owner cannot stitch together a few slanders about his neighbour).

Fontenelle and Thomas Corneille tried to stop La Bruyère's discours from being officially published, and then to have the mention of Corneille suppressed. Bossuet and Racine both railed, but the only effect was a rule that future speeches of acceptance should be vetted before they were pronounced. Both Bayle and on 10 August 1693 the *Journal des Savants* (q.v.) admired La Bruyère's speech, but La Bruyère, furious, introduced the cruel and recognizable portrait of Fontenelle as Cydias into the eighth edition of *Les Caractères*. He also printed in that edition not only his *Discours*, but also a bitter preface to it, fiercely ridiculing Fontenelle in the camp of his adversaries, but referring also, although not by name, to Pavillon, Pellisson, Thomas Corneille, Quinault, and Perrault.

La Bruyère did not attend the Académie frequently. In the last three years of his life he wrote only the unfinished *Dialogues sur le Quiétisme*, seven of the nine which were completed and no doubt reworked by the abbé Ellies du Pin for publication in 1698. Ellies du Pin was a Jansenist (q.v.), hostile to Fénelon; he was suspected himself of Protestant inclinations, and his *Bibliothèque des auteurs ecclésiastiques* was itself condemned in Paris and Rome. His editorship and completion of the dialogues was allowed to remain anonymous. La Bruyère must have begun his dialogues in 1694. He was not a theologian, and understood nothing of the deeper forms of spiritual commitment. He had died before what was really at stake, whether theologically or personally, between Bossuet and Fénelon became discernible, and his anti-quietist views must have been formulated simply from the vantage point of the moralist wanting to expose fraud and casuistry.

The chapter "Des femmes" of *Les Caractères* makes clear that La Bruyère had observed patent abuses in the role of male spiritual directors towards women. He appears, not unreasonably, to have thought devotional passivity a modish cover-up for inauthentically religious emotions and potentially disruptive of moral effort. He was also loyal to Bossuet and the values he stood for, which did not include any theological subtlety likely to disturb hierarchical authority, stern spiritual endeavour, and moral effort. La Bruyère was on the other hand a brilliant sniffer out of false appearances and psychological fraud. He had no doubt come across fraudulent exploitations of Mme Guyon's adaptation of Molinos's quietist spiritual teaching.

La Bruyère himself never published his *Dialogues sur le quiétisme*, and we have absolutely no means of knowing what they would have contained if he had, particularly if he had lived on through the crucial years of the controversy, in which the weight of argument was on Fénelon's side. The dialogues as we have them are very closely modelled on Pascal's *Lettres provinciales*, and although they do not use Pascal's lay spokesman, they see the spiritual confrontation from the lay point of view. The text we have of the first seven dialogues is not necessarily or wholly the product of La Bruyère's pen. *Les Caractères* does not avoid religious matters, and the dialogues may unjustly have damaged his reputation. The bishop's brother, Antoine Bossuet, wrote with relish to his son, who had been sent to Rome by his uncle to seek Fénelon's condemnation, about what La Bruyère had read to him from them two days before he died.

On Monday 7 May 1696 La Bruyère, surrounded by other people, suddenly went deaf, but without any pain. On 8 May at Versailles he dined with Antoine Bossuet, read from his dialogues, and drank to the health of Antoine Bossuet's son, the bishop's nephew, to whom the dialogues were going to be sent. It was only on the evening of Thursday 10 May that he felt ill after dinner, vomited, and could not speak. He died at about 2 a.m. He was universally regarded as shy, upright, ungainly, not handsome, and not much sought-after for the charm of his company or conversation.

WORKS

La Bruyère's counter-attack on his critics in the *Discours de réception à l'Académie française* reproached them bitterly:

N'ont-ils pas observé que de seize chapitres qui le composent, il y en a quinze qui, s'attachant à découvrir le faux et le ridicule qui se rencontrent dans les objets des passions et des attachements humains, ne tendent qu'à ruiner tous les obstacles qui affaiblissent d'abord, et qui éteignent ensuite dans tous les hommes la connaissance de Dieu qu'ainsi ils ne sont que des préparations au seizième et dernier chapitre, où l'athéisme est attaqué, et peut-être confondu

(Have they not noticed that of the sixteen chapters of which it is made up there are fifteen which, seeking to uncover what is to be found that is false and absurd in the objects of human passions and attachments, strive only to destroy all the obstacles which first weaken and then extinguish in everyone the knowledge of God, and that they are therefore only preparations for the sixteenth and last chapter in which atheism is attacked and perhaps confuted).

This, naturally, is special pleading in reply to an attack. La Bruyère, having started as Pascal's *Pensées* as presented in 1670 had started, was seeking to travel in the slipstream: with an aim analogous to Pascal's too, he had been building psychological comments on human behaviour into an apologetic for the existence of God. Sainte-Beuve commented that the first five chapters did not seem to be connected together so as to lead in any particular direction, but that the four which followed dealt with the behaviour of particular classes of society, leading up to "Du souverain ou de la république," before descending suddenly to "De l'homme," and mentally criss-crossing for three further chapters before the two final ones on religion, "De la chaire" and "Des esprits forts." It seems reasonable to stay with Sainte-Beuve, who was looking for an order. There scarcely is one, at most a classification by social groups mixed with classifications based on characteristics of behaviour and types of experience, but ending with the two chapters on religion. A virtue can be found in the variety of subject matter, and also of the perspective from which it is viewed and classified.

What is clear in La Bruyère's mind in the eighth and ninth editions is what he is against. His enemies, against whom he is counter-attacking in the *Discours*, are the poets,

mais quels poètes?…des faiseurs de stances et d'élégies amoureuses, de ces beaux esprits qui tournent un sonnet sur une absence ou sur un retour, qui font une épigramme sur une belle gorge, et un madrigal sur une jouissance

(but what poets?…concoctors of stanzas and amorous elegies, wits who turn a sonnet on an absence or a return, who compose an epigram on a pretty bosom, and a madrigal on a pleasure).

Those are the elegant froth of salon-dwellers, the frivolous products of the 17th century's serious tendency to rehabilitate the moral status of behaviour that is in accordance with natural impulse, the too-easy targets whose exaggerated, over-refined, and merely silly versifying came near to discrediting the immensely important imaginative movement exploring the shift to new and altogether more humane moral attitudes. La Bruyère's self-imposed task was to listen to the false notes and bring them, not without elegance, wit and perceptivity, to our attention, to point out what was sham, pretentious, and almost above all, what was ridiculous, disproportionate, or unfair.

Enough has been said in the previous section to give some idea how the text evolved from the early remarks to the final set of maxims, social observations, psychological generalizations, penetrating remarks about motivation, vignettes, and portraits of forms of social behaviour. As it stood at La Bruyère's death, the *Discours sur Théophraste* and the translation of the 28 portraits from the Athens of the fourth century B.C. are important only as debris left by the gestation of La Bruyère's own later text. The *Discours sur Théophraste* does however establish the permanently important distinction between the court and the town, and La Bruyère's intention not merely to define, or to link the characteristics of inner movements to their external manifestations, like Marin Cureau de la Chambre, but to improve behaviour, applying the analysis of motivation, "ce qu'il y de vain, de faible et de ridicule…de bon, de sain et de louable (what is vain, weak and ridiculous…good, healthy, and praiseworthy)" to the manners of the time in order to correct the behaviour of men. We need only to note that Theophrastus mixed portraits of people dominated by some characteristic or other with analyses of particular moral qualities themselves, like vanity and avarice.

The first of La Bruyère's 16 chapters is entitled "Des ouvrages de l'esprit." Between the first and ninth editions it increased only from 35 to 49 caractères and, although the chapter can be read as a kind of extra preface, gathering together thoughts on writing, it also opens up to the reader a number of perspectives which become important in the other chapters; the most important is probably that of the writer's relationship to his age. We know that La Bruyère was on the side of the partisans of the "anciens" in the Querelle (q.v.). He shared with his senior contemporaries not only the view expressed in his *Préface* that the writer should write only for the moral improvement of his readership—"On ne doit parler, on ne doit écrire que pour l'in-

struction (One should speak, one should write only to instruct)"—but also that writing required craftsmanship, a view he expresses almost brutally: "C'est un métier de faire un livre, comme de faire une pendule (Making a book, like making a clock, requires craftsmanship)" ("Des ouvrages," 3).

Yet even in this preliminary chapter La Bruyère is plainly straining to be released from the leash of the restrictions imposed by classical norms. He is in very important respects both post-classical in chafing at stylistic constraints, and pre-enlightenment in seeking such new forms of expression as those involving the use of accumulated rhetorical questions, or relying on the intrusive "je" of the author expressing a personal view about the world and also playing a part in his own dialogues. The opening consciousness of the first caractère of having come "too late" is matched by what we can now see as that of having anticipated not only a style of writing, but also a fresh series of values and attitudes newly emerging in French society. By 1688, one can see already the inevitability of the victory of the partisans of the "modernes," with whom La Bruyère, in fact, and in spite of his attested admiration for Mme Dacier, has so much in common.

He frequently draws attention to a consciousness of his own audacity, repeatedly prefacing or concluding a caractère with "si j'ose dire… (if I may say so…)," conveying an equal blend of aggression and deference. He sees with indignation much of what is wrong with society, yet perceives no likelihood of improvement outside the reform of the human heart, and not yet the possibility of an adjustment of society's political or economic balance. He moves more easily between reason and faith, the criteria appropriate respectively to worldly and to religious behaviour, than Descartes, Pascal, or any major moralist since François de Sales, and strives towards the unity between belief and sensibility which the 18th century would seek to restore. La Bruyère escapes from the abstract vocabulary to which Racine, Boileau, and La Rochefoucauld had largely confined themselves, and concentrates on external details as a manifestation of moral stature, the "caractère" rather than the maxim. His moral reactions are presented as more personal and less universal than those of his predecessors. If he has more developed feelings of indignation at social inequity than they, he is also a great deal more optimistic.

Even when, in his preliminary chapter, La Bruyère admires the post-baroque style of his immediate predecessors, his vocabulary almost dangerously suggests he also has feelings of confinement and restraint, and he ends up virtually excusing himself for moving beyond established norms of reaction, as he had already earlier excused himself in number 57 of "Des ouvrages de l'esprit." This is the whole of number 60:

L'on écrit regulièrement depuis vingt années; l'on est esclave de la construction; l'on a enrichi la langue de nouveaux mots, secoué le joug du latinisme, et réduit le style à la phrase purement française; l'on a presque retrouvé le nombre que Malherbe et Balzac avaient les premiers rencontré, et que tant d'auteurs depuis eux ont laissé perdre; l'on a mis enfin dans le discours tout l'ordre et toute la netteté dont il est capable: cela conduit insensiblement à y mettre de l'esprit

(For twenty years we have written within the rules. We are slaves of sentence construction. We have enriched the language with new words, shaken off the yoke of Latinity and reduced our style to the purely French sentence. We have almost rediscovered the rhythms that Malherbe and Balzac were the first to find and which so many authors since them have allowed to be lost. We have finally put into our prose all the order and clarity of which it is capable. That leads us imperceptibly to add wit).

In caractère 67 La Bruyère shows himself perfectly aware that a writer must take risks by going beyond the norms of his own time:

il faut toujours tendre à la perfection, et alors cette justice qui nous est quelquefois refusée par nos contemporains, la postérité sait nous la rendre

(we must always strive towards perfection, and then the justice sometimes refused to us by our contemporaries will be granted by posterity).

The boundaries drawn by reason and nature define the ideal, but a difficult one. "Combien d'art pour rentrer dans la nature! (How much skill it takes to return to nature!)" ("Des Jugements," 34). La Bruyère is, in a different way and for different reasons, as concerned to emphasize the personal character of his reactions as was Montaigne. It is because he is so changeable that he so often wants to change what he has written or the manner of its expression ("Des ouvrages," 17) and that, like others, he is constantly seeing the same things in different lights, and therefore judging them differently: "Je me contredis, il est vrai (I contradict myself, it is true)" ("Des jugements," 93).

It is the passages which show impatience with classical constraints acting on moral norms and literary style which set the dominant tone of the book, and which must be balanced against the preference for Marot and then Malherbe and Racan, over the poets of the Pléiade, against the declaration of objective foundations for taste of "Des ouvrages," 10, and the tidy classifications, such as that of "Des jugements," 47, where the tidiness is echoed in the style when the key words, "vice" and "défaut," are neatly repeated, and their overlapping meanings are exploited:

Les vices partent d'une dépravation du coeur; les défauts, d'un vice de tempérament; le ridicule, d'un défaut d'esprit

(Vices derive from a depravation of heart; defects, from a vice of temperament; the ridiculous, from a defect of intelligence).

In number 15 of that same first chapter, the original single sentence in the first edition, elevating the taste of antiquity into a model based on "le simple et le naturel (the simple and the natural)," is modified first in the fourth edition, with additions suggesting that antiquity is no longer always exemplary, and then, in the fifth, with an addition allowing that the achievements of antiquity can be surpassed, on the foundation of imitation. In "Des ouvrages," 31, La Bruyère is explicit about the ultimate criterion he accepts:

Quand une lecture vous élève l'esprit, et qu'elle vous inspire des sentiments nobles et courageux, ne cherchez pas une autre règle pour juger l'ouvrage; il est bon, et fait de main d'ouvrier

(If something you read elevates your mind and inspires you with noble and courageous feelings, do not look for any other rule to judge the work by; it is good, and well crafted).

The fourth edition added to the first chapter considerations on opera, and the sixth a caractère contrasting tragedy favourably with galanterie, excessive delicacy, and cultivated sentiment. The first edition already contained the long and nuanced comparison between Pierre Corneille and Racine in what has become number 54.

The next five chapters, "Du mérite personnel," "Des femmes," "Du coeur," "De la société et de la conversation," and "Des biens de fortune," take us to the heart of the book, contain some of its best portraits, economical, ferocious, and penetrating, and concentrate what is clearly now a satirical attack on all variants of the fake, the fraudulent, the pretentious, and the sham. One of La Bruyère's most perceptive interpreters has pointed out that the easiest way to approach the mass of caractères as they stand is to regard them as a private diary in which La Bruyère recorded points or features of behaviour, motivation, or anomalies concerning the tension between external appearances and inner realities, in order to point out the reaction they occasioned in him, and often to try to understand them, sometimes to generalize from them. That probably was the psychological genesis of the caractères, and one that might confidently have been predicted of a shy but intelligent observer of the social scene living at the humbler outer edges of French court circles in the later 17th century, aspiring to recognition by these circles but contemptuous of their diversions, standards, and attitudes, and conscious both of humiliations sustained and of intellectual if not also moral superiority over those who inflicted them.

One result of this constant concern to understand, coupled with the desire to cultivate sharp economy of expression, was the mannerism of the rhetorical question.

S'il est ordinaire d'être vivement touché des choses rares, pourquoi le sommes-nous si peu de la vertu?

(We are ordinarily much moved by what is unusual, why then so little by virtue?) ("Du mérite personnel," 20).

Even so brief a caractère immediately gives rise to three considerations. The first is the exploitation of French syntax. The sentence is made up of two clauses in French, the conditional clause with its antithesis ordinary-unusual, and the main interrogative clause. Both have finite verbs, but to put a finite verb into the English interrogative clause would ruin the epigrammatic effect, which La Bruyère often cultivates. In "De l'homme," 102, for instance, La Bruyère coined an aphorism for the first edition, in which he changed the word "première" to "meilleure" only in the ninth edition:

La plupart des hommes emploient la meilleure [première] partie de leur vie à rendre l'autre misérable

(Most of humanity spends the best [first] part of life making the rest of it wretched).

In the French of "Du mérite personnel," 20, there is also another antithesis, that between "ordinaire" and "rare," and La Bruyère ironically insinuates the rarity of virtue without actually stating it. Secondly, the rhetorical question prompts us to ask who is it that is puzzled. The "I" of the author has become intrusive, as it does in all the little snatches of dialogue. La Bruyère is using the intrusive "I" as a literary device to increase immediacy of impact. He is also ironically insinuating a whole range of possible answers to his "rhetorical" question. And thirdly, there is the whole matter of being moved.

The mechanics of emotional reaction fascinated La Bruyère, and he is perfectly capable of esteeming emotional sensitivity above the satisfaction afforded even by intellectual superiority. In this as in so much else he was announcing the arrival of the 18th century:

Le plaisir de la critique nous ôte celui d'être vivement touchés de très belles choses

(The pleasure of criticizing deprives us of that of being deeply touched by beautiful things) ("Des ouvrages de l'esprit," 20).

Three of the features just mentioned, accumulated rhetorical and substantive questions, the consequential intrusion of the writer's "I," and readiness to be moved taken as a sign of personal cultivation, can be found together with others in the rather long number 50 of "Des ouvrages de l'esprit."

"Du mérite personnel" contains the reflection on Egésippe, relying on indigence as his entitlement to employment when he should have passed the time he wasted, "corrompu par la paresse ou par le plaisir (corrupted by laziness or pleasure)," in being trained for something (10). True merit requires personal modesty (14, and see 42). There are those who have merit to an extraordinary extent who apparently acquire it from nowhere and leave it to no one (22). La Bruyère hesitates noticeably between a concept of "gloire" which demands public recognition, and one in which, born of virtue, and therefore as for the neostoic moralists of an earlier generation its own reward, "gloire" can be an interior quality, like merit (Du mérite personnel, 42). La Bruyère perceptively blames the sycophants for the arrogance of the high born (27); this is one of the ideas underlying the brilliant and pithy, but lengthy, double portrait of Giton and Phédon, the rich man and the poor man, added to the sixth edition and etched in rapid, clipped clauses in the present tense in a balanced, cadenced prose clearly inspired by Pascal, and constructed largely out of a series of chiasmuses following one another, or even erected inside one another ("Des biens de fortune," 83).

Chronologically later, from the seventh edition, but inserted earlier in the book, in "Du mérite personnel," is the fiercely cruel portrait of Ménippe, in his borrowed conversational plumage. This was generally understood to be an accurate caricature of the maréchal de Villeroy, able to sustain a social role for the quarter of an hour which his memory lasted before he appeared threadbare. A well-executed caractère from the fourth edition ("Du mérite personnel," 41) is of interest partly because it must have been written before 1683, the date at which Louis XIV took his court away from the Louvre to Versailles, but chiefly because of the emphasis on motivation as the source of the moral quality of actions, and on disinterest, which was to be the point defended by Fénelon but attacked by Bossuet:

Le motif seul fait le mérite des actions des hommes, et le désintéressement y met la perfection

(Motive alone constitutes the merit of human actions, and disinterest is its perfection).

La Bruyère is a writer capable of and fascinated by the finest nuances of feeling and language. He distinguishes, for instance, between the qualities of coquetterie and galanterie as applicable to men and to women (See "Des femmes," 20–22, 41, and 44). He plays on the ambiguity of the French "aimer," meaning both to like and to love, sometimes distinguishing the meanings ("Du coeur," 25–27), and sometimes leaving the ambiguity ("Du coeur," 23). In "Des femmes," 55, the first sentence demands that "aimer" in the second should mean "like":

Les femmes vont plus loin en amour que la plupart des hommes; mais les hommes l'emportent sur elles en amitié.

Les hommes sont cause que les femmes ne s'aiment point

(Women go further in love than most men; but men are superior to them in friendship.//Men are the reason why women do not like one another).

The delicate dissection of refinements of feeling reduced to epigram sometimes depends on a literary device which provokes a reaction of shock, but La Bruyère never so compresses his material, even at his most subtle, as to be obscure. The analysis in "De la société," 16, is extraordinarily nuanced, depends on ambiguous use of the word "esprit," meaning "spirit" as well as "wit," and is plainly a generalization deriving from a particular experience, perhaps tested over a period, but admitted to the first edition:

L'esprit de la conversation consiste bien moins à en montrer beaucoup qu'à en faire trouver aux autres: celui qui sort de votre entretien content de soi et de son esprit, l'est de vous parfaitement. Les hommes n'aiment point à vous admirer, ils veulent plaire; ils cherchent moins à être instruits, et même réjouis, qu'à être goûtés et applaudis; et le plaisir le plus délicat est de faire celui d'autrui

(The spirit ["esprit"] of conversation consists much less in showing a lot of wit ["esprit"] than in allowing others to discover their own. Anyone who leaves your company pleased with himself and his wit [esprit] is also perfectly [pleased] with you. People don't want to admire you, they want to be liked; they seek less to be instructed, or even amused, than to be appreciated and applauded; and the most delicate of pleasures is to be the cause of another's).

The ambiguity of the word "esprit," which made almost impossible the translation of a reflection expressed so concisely as that just quoted, recurs.

In the fourth edition ("Des jugements," 102) La Bruyère talks of not despising "human creatures of God" who have "une âme qui est esprit (a soul which is an intelligence)" even if they only saw up marble all day. Some people do nothing at all. In the following caractère (103) from the fifth edition, the word "âme (soul)" has overtones of immortality, judgement, and eternity not carried by "esprit":

La plupart des hommes oublient si fort qu'ils ont une âme, et se répandent en tant d'actions et d'exercices où il semble qu'elle est inutile, que l'on croit parler avantageusement de quelqu'un en disant qu'il pense; cet éloge même est devenu vulgaire, qui pourtant ne met cet homme qu'au-dessus du chien ou du cheval

(Most people forget so completely that they have a soul [mind?], and spend their time performing so many actions and exercises for which a soul [mind?] seems superfluous, that you believe you are paying someone a compliment if you say that they think. This has even become a common form of praise, although it puts that person only above dogs and horses).

The systematic, perhaps deliberately ironic, exploitation of that particular ambiguity then recurs in the sixth edition, but earlier in the book ("De l'homme," 143, following on from 142, already in the fifth edition),

Le sot ne meurt point; ou si cela lui arrive selon notre manière de parler, il est vrai de dire qu'il gagne à mourir, et que dans ce moment où les autres meurent, il commence à vivre. Son âme alors pense, raisonne, infère, conclut, juge, prévoit, fait précisément tout ce qu'elle ne faisait point

(The foolish man does not die; or if it happens that he does according to our way of speaking, it is true to say that he gains by dying, and that at the moment when others die, he starts to live. At that moment his soul [mind?] thinks, reasons, infers, concludes, judges, foresees and does precisely what it used not to do).

The organization of La Bruyère's language is so tight that it is difficult to think he was not intentionally exploiting the ambiguity âme/esprit, but merely blurring the distinction. He was an exceedingly careful, conscious, and deliberate linguistic craftsman, intensely sensitive to nuances of meaning as well as of feeling.

Mixed in with the observations and the reflections are the portraits, dialogues, impulsive self-questionings, and the occasional short stories, such as "Des femmes," 81, from the fourth edition. The analyses of "Du coeur" are naturally among the most psychologically subtle and perceptive. Pure friendship requires elevated natural endowments, but can exist between members of different sexes, although it excludes love, which can be sudden and irresistible but is weakened by time, which strengthens friendship. The first forty caractères in this chapter are aphorisms about love and friendship, some of them different only in subtlety, complexity, and above all psychological realism from those in the more serious collections from the era of preciosity (q.v.), like Marie Linage's *Questions d'amour* of 1661. La Bruyère remembers La Rochefoucauld and Nicole on the ways in which vice can appear as counterfeit virtue. Sometimes he is rueful ("Du coeur," 20, 35, 62, 85); and sometimes the moraliste not only observes, but in the English sense, moralizes.

The underlying optimism is clear from La Bruyère's commitment to belief in the possibility of human grandeur, heroic stature, and authentic virtue, stated or implied in many of the caractères and linked also with the twin notes of socially conscious indignation and compassion new at this date. Nature, even in ordinary people, can be trusted.

Il y a de certains grands sentiments, de certaines actions nobles et élevées, que nous devons moins à la force de notre esprit qu'à la bonté de notre naturel

(There are certain exalted feelings, certain noble and elevated actions, which we owe less to the strength of our mind than to the goodness of our instincts ("Du coeur," 79).

With adequate natural endowment, cultivated instinct leads us to compassion; La Bruyère adds a touch of irony:

Il semble qu'aux âmes bien nées les fêtes, les spectacles, la symphonie rapprochent et font mieux sentir l'infortune de nos proches ou de nos amis.

Une grande âme est au-dessus de l'injure, de l'injustice, de la douleur, de la moquerie; et elle serait invulnérable si elle ne souffrait par la compassion

(It seems that to naturally well-endowed temperaments feasts, spectacles, music bring us nearer to the misfortune of our neighbours or our friends and help us to feel it more.

A great soul is above injury, injustice, suffering, mockery; it would be invulnerable if it did not suffer through compassion.) ("De l'homme," 80, 81).

"Du mérite personnel," 44, even talks about laying down life itself for other people, a clear allusion to scripture, but here envisaged as a possibility outside any religious context.

Perhaps the major part of the content is devoted to often brilliant exposures of the workings of affectation, ostentation, flattery, status-seeking, and social climbing. Some of the portraits, whether or not their models were recognizable, are withering, remorseless, and devastatingly clever. La Bruyère can use sarcasm to annihilating effect, enhancing it by starting with the external details before delving into the interior motivation. He was very annoyed indeed at Fontenelle's reaction to his *Discours de réception à l'Académie*. His dislike of the *Mercure Galant* had already been made clear in the first edition ("Des ouvrages de l'esprit," 46). His revenge on Fontenelle was now the long portrait of Cydias ("De la société," 75), added, like the *Discours*, to the eighth edition. Cydias's workshop will run you off an elegy, an idyll, a few stanzas, a letter of consolation, whatever you will, in prose or verse.

Cydias, après avoir toussé, relevé sa manchette, étendu la main et ouvert les doigts, débite gravement ses pensées quintessenciées et ses raisonnements sophistiqués…C'est en un mot un composé du pédant et du précieux, fait pour être admiré de la bourgeoisie et de la province, en qui néanmoins on n'aperçoit rien de grand que l'opinion qu'il a de lui-même

(Cydias, after coughing, turning back his cuff, stretching out his hand, and spreading his fingers, gravely gives out his quintessentialized thoughts and his elaborate reasonings…In a word he is a mixture of pedant and précieux, fit to be wondered at by the bourgeois and the provincials, but in whom nothing great can be perceived other than the opinion he has of himself).

The mixture of social satire with deep indignation and compassion, the uncertainty about the meaning of forms of behaviour obviously without any proper foundation in personal qualities or merit, the delicate analyses of nuances of behaviour, the meditations about the fundamental verities, and the blend of humour, wit, and sarcasm directed at the surface follies of a decadent court make it impossible to do justice in a small compass to La Bruyère's range of subject matter and style. Occasionally, as in "De l'homme," 128, he sets out to pull up his readership with a start by describing the state of the peasants starving during the Fronde, or to shock it by writing with whipping irony about the administrator who, soporific after a good dinner and too much wine, can no doubt be excused for signing a document condemning a whole province to starvation ("Des biens de fortune," 18). He jolts one by using phrases like "âmes sales, pétries de boue et d'ordure (unclean souls, steeped in mud and filth)" ("Des biens de fortune," 58) of the rich, avaricious, and mercenary. Mostly, however, the register is lighter, the underlying sour taste smothered by the wit, elegance, and genuine bewilderment of the reflections, and by the tension between La Bruyère's fascination with and his distaste for what he disapproves of, or at least sees through.

The abiding importance of *Les Caractères* remains the extremely sensitive indication of a change in sensibility communicated by its extraordinary precision of language and hesitance of view. On a vast range of topics discussed in religious, court, and other social contexts, La Bruyère shows how faith and reason are coming together again, social awareness is being born on the fringes of court society, trust in human instinct is developing, and sham, pretence, and ritual deference, where merit is absent, are beginning to be seriously questioned. La Bruyère's sensibility was no doubt advanced for his date and milieu. The sales success was no doubt partly attributable to the gossipy portraits. But there can be little doubt that *Les Caractères* announced a whole new range of moral attitudes and personal reactions emerging in the ranks even of the partisans of the "anciens."

PUBLICATIONS

Collections

Oeuvres de La Bruyère, 3 vols. and 1 album, 1865–82
Oeuvres complètes de La Bruyère, Bibliothèque de la Pléiade, 1935

Les Caractères and associated texts

Les Caractères de Théophraste traduits du grec, avec les Caractères ou moeurs de ce siècle, 1688 (three editions)
Substantially augmented editions appeared in 1689 (fourth edition), 1690 (fifth edition), 1691 (sixth edition), 1692 (seventh edition), 1694 (eighth edition, containing the *Discours de Réception à l'Académie françoise* and its *Préface*), 1696 (ninth edition); as *The Characters, or the Manners of the Age*, 1699

Other

Discours prononcé dans l'Académie française par M. de La Bruyère, 1693

Dialogues posthumes sur le Quiétisme, 1698

Biographical and critical studies

Michaut, G., *La Bruyère*, 1936
Richard, Pierre, *La Bruyère et ses "Caractères"*, 1965
Delft, Louis van, *La Bruyère moraliste*, 1971
Jasinski, René, *Deux Accès à La Bruyère*, 1971
Mourgues, Odette de, *Two French Moralists: La Rochefoucauld and La Bruyère*, 1978

LA CALPRENÈDE, Gautier de Costes, sieur de, ?1610–1663.

Dramatist and novelist.

LIFE

La Calprenède's plays and novels in many ways represented the logical culmination of a literature reasonably referred to as baroque and certainly confident, exulting in a potential synthesis of virtue, happiness, and instinctive human activity. It explored the full power of moral liberty, the nature of heroic endeavour, and the whole spectrum of refined social behaviour and elevated spiritual values. That literature which, reaching a peak only after the Fronde and the aristocratic lionization of Condé in the 1650s, quickly subsided with the death of Mazarin, the rise of Colbert, and the disgrace of Foucquet in 1661–62, gave way to what for generations was thought of as a particularly resplendent period for the literature of France, foreshadowed or inaugurated by the early masterpiece of Pascal's *Lettres provinciales*, of 1656–57.

Inevitably that view of the literary history of France, elevating what came after 1660 at the expense of what had gone before it, and based on a series of misunderstandings about the social function of literature and on the neglect of considerations about the nature, function, provenance, and destination of imaginative literary works, resulted in the undervaluation of the flamboyantly confident plays and novels of La Calprenède. It is important that, after nine tragedies and tragi-comedies, destined by definition to be scripts for theatrical entertainments and therefore accessible to the illiterate, he should have needed, in order to continue his imaginative exploration of the potentialities of human heroism, to turn to prose fiction, dependent on a literate, and in fact overwhelmingly aristocratic, readership. The legendary length of the novels makes it obvious that only the smallest fragments could have been the subject of salon readings. La Calprenède was obliged to turn from writing in condensed dramatic form for a public that was not necessarily literate, to a different public, more widely dispersed, which had to be.

La Calprenède was the eldest of ten children, born probably in 1610 in the château de Toulgoud, near Sarlat, of a family of

Gascon country squires. The will of his father, Pierre de Costes, dated 27 April 1635, still exists, naming seven children then surviving, of whom one had entered religion. Destined for the magistracy, La Calprenède studied in Toulouse before coming to Paris probably in 1632 or 1633. He appears not to have known for certain what he wanted to do, but to have assisted Gomberville with the revision of his novel *Polexandre*, which was to be published in 1637. His own first play, *La Mort de Mithridate*, was played during the season 1635–36. Tallemant, who devotes one of *Les Historiettes* to La Calprenède, notes that it was a success, "but that there were not so many good plays then as there are now."

The known facts about La Calprenède's career do not fit in well with one another. He was certainly a cadet and probably an officer in the royal guard regiment. He enjoyed the company of Anne of Austria's ladies-in-waiting. He was sent to Germany where he suffered from famine and was then taken under the protection of Anne de Rohan, princesse de Guémené and duchesse de Montbazon, to whom he dedicated the 1637 *Le Comte d'Essex*, published in 1639, and of the queen, Anne of Austria, to whom the 1635 *La Mort de Mithridate*, published in 1637 with a privilège of September 1636, must already have been dedicated. He wrote, in the dedication of *Le Comte d'Essex* to the princess, "You had the kindness to support the beginnings of a young cadet leaving the Guards, still stumbling and weak after his famine in Germany…" The achevé d'imprimer is dated 30 May 1639. By that date La Calprenède had clearly left the army.

The difficulty is in integrating the military career with that of the dramatist, but some of the plays must have been written while La Calprenède was attached to his regiment, since the publisher of the 1638 tragedy *Jeanne, reyne d'Angleterre* wrongly informed readers of the author's death, a slip likely only if he was at the front. The original series of nine plays, with known or presumed dates of performance, consists of *La Mort de Mithridate, tragédie*, 1635; *Bradamante, tragi-comédie*, 1637; *Clarionte; ou, Le Sacrifice sanglant, tragi-comédie*, 1637; *Jeanne, reyne d'Angleterre, tragédie*, 1638; *Le Comte d'Essex, tragédie*, 1637; *La Mort des enfants d'Hérode; ou, La Suite de Marianne, tragédie*, 1639; *Edouard, tragi-comédie*, 1640; *Phalante, tragédie*, 1641; and *Herménigilde, tragédie*, 1643. Some of these plays were taken into the repertoire of the Hôtel de Bourgogne, and the company may have put on the first performances. Much later, in 1659, La Calprenède returned to the theatre with a lost *Bellissaire* which appears never to have been published, and in March 1663 Molière paid him 800 livres for a play which an accident of the same month, and then death, prevented him from completing.

There is a good deal of self-deprecating affectation in the "au lecteur" to *La Mort de Mithridate*, which may however also be ironic. La Calprenède excuses his lack of polish, asking what can be expected of a Gascon with barely enough French to read the *Amadis de Gaule* stories. In fact Gascons had a reputation for boastfulness, and La Calprenède would have needed the knowledge of proper French he said he lacked to read the novels. Tallemant makes much fun of La Calprenède's Gascon accent, which he tries to reproduce in writing. When La Calprenède tells us in the "au lecteur" that he wrote his play only a fortnight after leaving Périgord, he was discounting three years in Toulouse.

Tallemant tells us that "although" La Calprenède was well born, when he came to Paris he was a "buttress" of the bureau d'adresses, and never missed a conference there. Renaudot (see: *Gazette*) had founded his bureau in 1636, and it advertised items for sale and jobs vacant, as well as serving as a centre for lectures and an incipient centre for the collection and dissemination of news. That "although" of Tallemant's can mean many things, and it has been conjectured that Renaudot, or at least his bureau, may have played some part in La Calprenède's literary initiation. It appears that his father opposed La Calprenède's literary ambitions.

Tallemant has a small collection of anecdotes about La Calprenède's Gasconisms and regional quirks, including an attempt to have a colour named "Mithridate," just as Céladon, the name of d'Urfé's hero in *L'Astrée*, had notoriously been used as a colour shade. Tallemant explains La Calprenède's decision to write *Cassandre* in terms of his rejected love for Mlle Hamon, who was being kept by the father of the maréchal d'Hocquincourt. Tallemant says that he offered her his sword a hundred times for her to kill him and "played a lover from a novel so much that he finally wrote one, where most of the heroines are widows, because his mistress was one."

Tallemant also recounts that Magdeleine de Lyée had written into her marriage contract of 6 December 1648 with La Calprenède the guarantee that he would finish his new novel, *Cléopâtre*, begun in 1647 and apparently offered to the booksellers in sections, two or four volumes at a time. The earlier *Cassandre*, his first novel, had appeared in ten volumes from 1642 to 1645, with a total of 5,483 pages. He is said to have wanted to stretch *Cléopâtre* to thirty volumes, but in fact finished the novel in 1656 after twelve volumes of 24 books and 4,153 pages, dedicating it to Condé. *Cassandre* had been a publishing success. We know that in 1646 La Calprenède received 3,000 livres from Sommaville for parts two and three of *Cléopâtre*, each part to consist of four books of 40 or 50 feuillets (printer's sheets). The achevé d'imprimer of part one is dated 17 April 1646, although the novel was not put on sale until 1647. All the main booksellers in the fashionable shopping arcade on the west side of the Palais-Royal were involved at some point in the novel's gestation.

The marriage contract has been destroyed, but it was seen by Auguste Jal, who mentions it in the 1864 *Dictionnaire critique de biographie et d'histoire*. Magdeleine de Lyée was born between about 1618 and 1620, dame de Saint-Jean de Livet, du Coudray, and de Vatimesnil, with other estates in Normandy, the only daughter of a rich land-owner and widower who sent Magdeleine to his sister to be brought up. The sister was having a liaison with someone called La Lande, and put the young Magdeleine through a form of marriage with him, blessed by a lackey dressed as a priest, which legitimized La Lande's constant attendance on herself. In due course Magdeleine was properly married to Jean de Vieux-Pont, seigneur de Compans, by whom she had a male child. Her husband died, and the child, who had inherited from his father, was claimed by La Lande as his own on account of the inheritance. La Lande lost his case and Magdeleine de Lyée remarried on 3 August 1643 an army captain Arnoul de Braque, sieur de Château-Vert, with whom she lived in the fashionable Marais district of Paris. He was apparently killed in a duel early in 1645, although Tallemant alleges that he was shot by La Lande.

Magdeleine de Lyée was herself to publish her 1658 *Oeuvres diverses d'Octavie*, and there was a quarrel between the brother of her recently deceased husband and La Calprenède about the dowry. La Calprenède won, and in 1650 acquired the office of gentilhomme ordinaire de la chambre du roi. His wife bore him a daughter, but his marriage was unhappy and there was a formal separation in 1659. On 20 May 1658 La Calprenède had taken out a privilège for his third novel *Faramond*, of which the first three volumes appeared on 25 September 1661. Seven volumes had been written when he died, and the novel was finished in five more by Pierre d'Ortigue, sieur de Vaumorière.

On 31 March 1663 Loret announced in *La Muse historique* that the illustrious La Calprenède had wounded himself when a gun had gone off between his hands. Seven months later he announced La Calprenède's death on 20 October as the result of a fall from a horse. His wife died in furnished accommodation in the Faubourg Saint-Germain and was buried on 14 March 1668.

Works

La Calprenède was later to deplore the fact that his fictions were called "romans" rather than "histoires." His first play, *La Mort de Mithridate*, dedicated to the queen, freely adapts antique sources, as explained in the "au lecteur," to make a regular tragedy, which keeps the 24-hour rule, and starts as near the dénouement as possible, allowing the intrigue to consist only in drawing explicit consequences from an existing situation. Its geographical location is in two warring camps, besiegers and besieged, necessarily close to one another. La Calprenède's play clearly derives structurally from Mairet's *La Sophonisbe* in its use of Roman power as a source of a tragically inevitable event and in its exploitation of a Roman overseer set to supervise the ruler of a conquered kingdom. There is also the same failed breakout, the conquest of the town, the surrender of the populace before the palace, and suicides among the conquered.

The stage directions make clear that La Calprenède envisaged a conventional but diminished system of booths covered by a curtain so that a scene could be changed by covering one booth and uncovering another at the back of the acting space. It was also possible to use a single backdrop behind more than one booth, so, for instance, utilizing two rooms in the same house, unified by the same garden behind them. Earlier in the 17th century there had usually been five booths, perhaps with a sixth space for the curtain to go when one of the painted booths was uncovered. In *La Mort de Mithridate* La Calprenède uses only two scenes, but he changes scenes within acts, and he does not motivate changes of the character playing on centre stage.

The play opens with a scene between Pharnace, roi du Pont (king of Pontus), and his Roman overseer Pompée. To keep the protection of the Romans, and therefore his crown, Pharnace must be disloyal to his family, destroy the autonomy of its rule, and act in accordance with the interests of Rome. La Calprenède sets out from the beginning to balance the pressure on Pharnace of Rome's political power and military might against that of the human laws which bind him to his father, formerly king Mithridate, his wife, Bérénice, his stepmother, Hypsicratée, and her daughters, Mithridatie and Nise. The second scene is between his father and his stepmother, with her daughters present, and they are joined in the third by Pharnace's wife, Bérénice, so visually emphasizing the importance of the family bond. Mithridate is pleased to be supported by Hypsicratée and Bérénice against Pharnace and Rome, which wants Pharnace as puppet ruler under the Roman thumb. Ménandre, his chief cavalry officer, announces that the Romans are ready to attack.

Hypsicratée has never known fear and will fight alongside her husband. Much is made of her "générosité (greatness of spirit)." Mithridate does not fear death. Bérénice, knowing that Pharnace loves her but has betrayed his family, offers herself to Mithridate's daughters as a victim in place of Pharnace if they wish to avenge themselves against him. They applaud such nobility of heart. When Pharnace, left in charge of the Roman forces by Pompée, meets Emile, the Roman captain, he is not yet totally determined to fight against his family, and is afraid for Bérénice, the wife who has taken his family's side, but whom he still loves. Emile gives him firmly if unimaginatively neostoic advice. His generalized moral aphorisms are almost banal: those who are "généreux" need never be unhappy.

By the third act Mithridate's forces have been totally defeated. The town has surrendered, and Mithridate is shut with his family within the walls of the palace. He would kill himself if that course would not condemn his wife to a slave's place in the triumphal chariot. Hypsicratée would kill herself rather than be submitted to that indignity. Pharnace is persuading the citizens to accept his rule when a message to him is flung from the battlements. Bérénice asks for an interview with her husband. It takes place in act III, scene iii, and ends with disagreement. In act four Mithridate sees that neither love nor duty will cause Pharnace to change his mind, but is persuaded himself to seek to move his son. Pharnace is hesitant, and the confrontation between Pharnace and his father takes place, against Emile's advice, in act IV, scene iii, but Pharnace does not yield to his father any more than to his wife or, in scene iv, to Hypsicratée, Mithridatie and Nise.

In the fifth act Mithridate, Hypsicratée, Mithridatie, and Nise in turn swallow from a poisoned cup. Then Bérénice comes in and she, too, drinks from the cup. Mithridatie and Nise die first, then Hypsicratée, then Bérénice. Mithridate, who has not died from the poison, kills himself. When Pharnace comes in they are revealed, the bodies of Mithridate and Hypsicratée on thrones, Bérénice, Mithridatie and Nise on their knees in front of them. Pharnace is overwhelmed with guilt and, as the play ends, feels he should kill himself. This is not a play about any sort of conflict, except that which makes Pharnace momentarily hesitate. It is an exploration of the heroic motivation moving to a choice of death rather than indignity, its meaning revealed in the final throne scene. Mithridate and Hypsicratée appear in regal pose, even if dead. With the two children and Bérénice at their feet, they are still a family group, spiritually more powerful than the military might of Rome.

Whereas we know the season, 1635–36, of the first performance of *La Mort de Mithridate*, for *Le Comte d'Essex* we know only the calendar year, 1637. The piece was played at the end of one season or at the beginning of the next, and is one of three of the series of nine plays between 1635 and 1642 which take English history as their subject. Essex was executed by Elizabeth in 1601, so the history is recent. The unities are rather forced, demanding most of London as a localized geographical unit, and cramming the events immediately leading to Essex's arrest, his trial, execution and its consequences, into 24 hours. As in *La Mort de Mithridate*, what interests La Calprenède is not the intrigue but the attitudes of his characters. The consequences of an existing situation are unfolded and the reactions of the character to the revelation of the implications of the original situation are examined.

The play starts with a scene in which Elisabeth reproaches Essex with treachery with the comte de Tirron, Hugh O'Neill, count of Tyrone, who had risen against the English and been defeated by Essex, but whom Essex had subsequently met, giving grounds for the allegation of treason. Elisabeth also orders Essex's friend Soubtantonne (Southampton) to be imprisoned, and in act I, scene v, Essex and Soubtantonne meet. Again in this play, power, now represented by Elisabeth, is absolute.

La puissance des Rois ne peut être bornée,
Leur caprice à leur gré fait notre destinée

(The power of monarchs cannot be limited,/Their caprice, as they wish it to be, decides our fate).

Essex thinks he has tokens of the queen's friendship which will save him, but Soubtantonne warns him that her love will turn to hatred. As they converse the guards come to arrest them both.

In the second act, Elisabeth meets Cécile and Salisbury. Cécile urges rigour, Salisbury merely caution. Elisabeth delivers herself of a long and passionate harangue against Essex in the presence of Mme Cécile, who is not allowed to interrupt. She then leaves, and Mme Cécile tells us of her own love for Essex, who deserted her for the queen. The rhetorical organisation, normally weak, does have heightened moments. Mme Cécile, unable to believe that Essex really prefers Elisabeth, laments in her monologue,

Tout ce qu'une âme double eut jamais d'éloquence,
Ce traître l'employa pour vaincre ma constance.
Amour en fut vainqueur, amour fut obéi;
Amour gagna ce coeur, et ce coeur fut trahi

(All the eloquence which a duplicitous soul ever had,/That traitor used it to overcome my resistance./Love was the victor, love was obeyed;/Love conquered this heart, and this heart was betrayed).

Raleig visits Essex in prison, and then, in act II, scene v, Mme Cécile visits Essex and tells him to beg the king's pardon. He is, of course, far too proud, and she warns him

Votre obstination visiblement vous traîne
Dans le chemin certain d'une perte certaine

(Your obstinacy visibly draws you/In the certain path of certain destruction).

The third act consists uniquely of the trial scene, in which Essex behaves with breath-taking haughtiness towards the judges, who once took orders from him, openly despising them, accepting the verdict he knows they will reach, and doing nothing to avert it. This time it is the sheer consciousness of personal merit rather than family unity which is flaunted in the face of irresistible power. Essex accuses Cécile of jealousy on account of Mme Cécile's affection for him, more even than of his treason with Spain, while Soubtantonne in his turn accuses the judges themselves of treason. In the fourth act Elisabeth hesitates, wants to delay the executions, and is given an excuse to differentiate between the case of Essex and that of Soubtantonne, who is pardoned, and supplicates vainly on Essex's behalf. There is

another meeting between Essex and Mme Cécile, who professes herself ready to die with him. Essex gives her, to take to the queen, the ring Elisabeth had given him to serve as a guarantee of his personal safety, even if it cost her her crown. He makes clear that, in sending the ring, it is shame he fears, not death.

The spurned Mme Cécile now has Essex's fate in her hands. Should she take the ring to the queen? The act closes as she talks to her husband. In the fifth act Essex is marched defiantly away to execution. From the scaffold he sends a message to Mme Cécile that he is sorry to have put her to useless trouble. News of his death reaches Elisabeth just as she might have been going to weaken:

Oui, toujours plein d'orgueil, et toujours invincible,
Il a du coup mortel en se plaignant de vous
Vomi sur l'échafaud son sang et son courroux

(Yes, still full of pride and still invincible,/At the blow of death cursing you, he/Disgorged on the scaffold his blood and his fury).

Mme Cécile calls for Elisabeth in order to confess to her that she loved Essex, and did not deliver the ring she was waiting for. Mme Cécile is taken away dying and Elisabeth asks her maid to put her to bed for the last time.

Once again the play has followed the move away from neo-stoic passivity towards the ethics of "gloire" or personal merit, whose rehabilitation after pejorative use by Justus Lipsius and Du Vair had already begun in Charron. What is explored in *Le Comte d'Essex* is the extent to which the individual may go in order to affirm personal elevation of spirit, whether Essex was too haughty, too easily touched by shame or love, and whether Elisabeth was motivated by base jealousy or a righteous need to affirm her queenly dignity. The vacillation of Mme Cécile finally precipitates the disaster, and she alone momentarily suffered psychological uncertainty. Racine was going to remember that in *Bajazet*. Essex and Elisabeth knew how they had to act, under what circumstances. These two plays could scarcely constitute a stronger dramatic affirmation of personal heroism in the face of impending disaster. Essex, like Mithridate, chooses to die, because that is how his personal integrity can most emphatically be affirmed.

The novels are obviously more diffuse than the plays, but were the only escape from simple repetition which allowed further and deeper penetration into the implications and potential practicality of an elevated system of heroic values. If we find the novels tedious or trivial, it is because we are no longer interested in the values they explore. The possible reaffirmation of some such values in real life obsessed the dispossessed aristocracy just before and after the Fronde, but the will to interrogate them further crumbled with the double movement summed up in the rise of Colbert and the fall of Foucquet, characteristically wandering off into regions of the pure escapist fantasy of the adventure novels just before the collapse. Historically, the literary critic can only register the existence of the more widespread phenomenon of the collapse of cultural confidence. But the reason why the attitudes imaginatively paraded in La Calprenède's novels were rejected in the later 1650s must have something, if perhaps not very much, to do with their masculine chauvinism, partly hidden in the emphasis they put on physical strength, and with the increased licentiousness of, for instance,

Desmarets's 1632 *Ariane* compared with *L'Astrée*. Préciosité (q.v.), whose emergence as a recognizable phenomenon dates unambiguously to 1654, was the product of a feminist reaction to the excessive masculinity of the cultural values of the preceding score of years.

In *Cassandre* there is a change of tone from the fifth volume on. The author tells us that he is moving away at that point from the style of Plutarch, Curtius, and Justinus and adopting the manner of Homer, Virgil, and Tasso, effectively protesting that even fictionalized history in acceptable form imposes too many constraints on his imaginative purposes, and that he needs something more epic in form. Perrault will later reproach the Homeric epic with its glorification of male physical prowess, and in 1632 Desmarets's Mélinte, in *Ariane*, had knocked heads from shoulders, split helmets and heads with a single blow, cut off Pisistrate's head with one stroke, and was taken on the battlefield by the Scythians for Mars himself, so many heads did he break and chests smash in. From volume V of *Cassandre* there is incidentally but perceptibly greater emphasis on the characters' physical strength, with instances of soldiers being cut in half at a single stroke.

The setting is Babylon in the time of Alexander the Great, whose conquests are depicted as a search by individuals for chances to test and prove their merit. They explore the extreme circumstances in which they can prove themselves true to themselves, and they therefore recognize and admire one another irrespective of political objectives, of national interests, that means of whose side they are fighting on. Oroondate, son of the Scythian king, aspires to values at levels that are not within the range of normal experience. He leads his father's army against the Persians, rescues the royal Persian women from the threat of capture by his own soldiers, falls in love with their princess, Statira, and, true to himself if not to his military, family, and national duty, he abandons his army to stay on in disguise at the Persian court. He rescues from a group of Scythian soldiers a knight with whom he feels an instant affinity, and discovers him to be Ataxerxe, Statira's brother. In the second battle from the first volume, between the Scythians and the Persians, Oroondate takes the Persian side:

> Je n'apprehenderay point d'estre fils desnaturé pour estre loyal Amant et amy irreprochable, ny ne feray conscience de combattre contre un Pere qui vient renverser la fortune que mon amy m'a establie

> (I shall not fear being an unnatural son because I am a loyal lover and a faultless friend, and shall not scruple to fight against a father who wants to overturn the fortune in which my companion has established me).

When he does return home, the narrator manifestly expects the reader to share his sense of outrage that his father should have had him thrown into prison for fighting on the other side.

> Mon Prince se leva de devant luy, et croyant avoir satisfaict à ce qu'il devoit à son Père, il luy sçeut si mauvais gré d'un accueil si inhumain apres une absence si longue, qu'il ne daigna luy dire une seule parole pour sa justification

> (My Prince rose from in front of him, and believing that he had fulfilled the duty he owed to his father, he was suffi-

ciently annoyed at so cruel a welcome after so long an absence, that he did not deign to address to him a single word of justification).

Two years later Oroondate agrees for the sake of his own greater glory to lead a Scythian army against Zopirion, one of Alexandre's lieutenants. He defeats Zopirion, himself becomes king of Persia and, at the beginning of a moral squabble which was to absorb Arnauld d'Andilly and the entourage of Mme de Sablé later in the century, unequivocally puts the duties of friendship and loyalty before those imposed by family and birth. Not even physical slavery can break personal integrity, as Lisimachus says to his friends:

> C'est aux ames lasches à craindre en esclaves, je suis né libre et Prince, et je ne feray jamais de lascheté qui vous fasse rougir pour moy, ny qui me rende indigne de la gloire de mes Ancestres

> (Only cowardly spirits fear like slaves. I was born free and royal, and I shall never commit a cowardly act which will make you blush for me, or which makes me unworthy of the glory of my ancestors).

In the ethic explored by La Calprenède both mercy and its opposite, vengeance, are exercised in the pursuit of personal integrity, to sustain self-admiration and the approval of other similarly elevated spirits. "Générosité" is always self-centred, never altruistic. Self-esteem based on extraordinary merit is explored as the criterion of supreme personal value. Those who benefit from the générosité of others are necessarily thereby put on a lower moral plane. Oroondate, released by Alexandre, recalls "le déplaisir qu'il receut de se voir vaincu en generosité (the chagrin he experienced at being outdone in générosité)." When Oroondate rescues his rival, Alexandre, from drowning, he places him at the feet of Statira and disappears unrecognized. He explains to Araxe that, although Alexandre could not have complained if Oroondate had left him to drown, his own self-esteem could not have allowed it.

> Si Alexandre n'avoit point subjet de se plaindre de moy, j'en avois beaucoup moy-mesme, et comme ma satisfaction m'est plus chere que la sienne, le reproche que je me pouvois faire (pour avoir manqué à faire une bonne action; ou par quelque crainte de peril, ou par quelque consideration d'interest) m'eust esté bien plus sensible que celuy que je pourrois recevoir de luy, de qui je pretends, ny de recompenses, ny de remercimens

> (If Alexander had no reason to complain about me, I had myself much reason to do so, and since my own satisfaction is more important to me than his, the reproach I could have made to myself (of having failed to do a good action, whether out of some fear of danger, or from some consideration of personal interest) would have pained me much more than any I might have received from him, from whom I expect neither rewards nor thanks).

Love, too, necessarily becomes a struggle between two self-assertive lovers as, of course, it had in Pierre Corneille's *Le Cid*, but it is assumed that battles of self-assertion will be won by the male. Once the female has signified acceptance of a lover, however passively, the male cannot concede defeat to rivals and must destroy them. Female moral integrity is measured by the care with which acceptance is signified strictly in accordance with the male's perceived merit. Parisatis does finally signify her acceptance of Lisimachus's service, but it is almost calibrated:

J'ai une bienveillance pour vous qui va au delà de l'estime, mais je n'ay pas une si forte affection pour vous qu'elle me fasse oublier ce que je me dois à moy mesme et me porte à faire des fautes qui blesseroient ma reputation et offenceroient mortellement le sang illustre d'où je suis sortie

(I have a fondness for you which goes beyond esteem, but my affection for you is not so strong as to make me forget what I owe to myself and let me commit faults which would wound my reputation and mortally offend the illustrious blood of which I come).

It cannot sufficiently be emphasized that what La Calprenède's heroic novels offered was not a firm system of values, but a number of situations which imposed a choice between different possible moral reactions, between which his contemporaries were interested in choosing. He was exploring, not expounding. That fact is important not only because it means that La Calprenède's novels had a relevance to the serious exploration of real, potentially viable values at a given date and in that part of a given society which had leisure, taste, education, and money enough to read them, but also because the exploration of what was implied by the acceptance of various moral assumptions is a universal function of literature. Literary value must in the end be quantifiable in accordance with the power of literary texts to fulfil whatever function they are agreed to have, and the exploration of the implications of sets of moral values was certainly one such function. It is on that consideration that the literary status of La Calprenède must finally rest.

There is an interesting example which makes particularly clear what La Calprenède was trying to achieve in *Cassandre*. Oroondate has a sister Bérénice. Her father has ordered her to marry Arsacome, but she loves Arsace. She will kill herself if she is forced to marry Arsacome. Arsace descends and carries her off. Is Bérénice right to reproach him? La Calprenède seems unsure. Arsace is sure that he acted as a male lover should: "J'ay fait ce que vous deviez attendre de mon amour; et je vous ay retirée des bras de cét indigne mari qu'on vous destinoit (I did what you should have expected of my love; I took you from the arms of that unworthy husband who had been chosen for you)." But, said Bérénice, "vous m'avez arrachée de ceux de mon père (you have taken me from those of my father)," and she asks for her freedom back.

Je vous ay promis que j'espouserois la mort plustost qu'Arsacome; mais je ne vous ay fait esperer, ny par mes discours, ny par mes actions, que je fuyrois des bras de mon pere pour vous suivre, et que je me licencierois en vostre faveur à des actions honteuses et indignes d'une Princesse

(I promised you that I would marry death rather than Arsacome; but I did not lead you, by either my words or my actions, to expect that I would flee from the arms of my father to follow you, and that I should permit myself in your favour shameful actions unworthy of a Princess).

It is not at all clear whether the readership for whom La Calprenède was actually writing would feel with Bérénice that Arsace has trespassed on her integrity, whether they would have agreed with her that the best solution was her suicide, or whether her loyalty to her father would have appeared to them to have been exaggerated. La Calprenède, by writing imaginative literature, and for the reasons indicated above doing it here in the form of a prose fiction, was inviting them not so much to think about it as to examine their sympathies.

Much else follows from what La Calprenède was trying to achieve. The characters, while reacting within restricted parameters, do react differently to the same or very similar dilemmas. Alexandre had been responsible for the death of Statira's father, and she had not loved him when, to spite Oroondate, she had married him, but after his death she cherishes his memory, and rejects Oroondate. There is genuine exploration, if always within a few degrees of a precise compass bearing, and much narrower than the alternatives proposed for discussion in the *Heptameron* of Marguerite de Navarre, or in d'Urfé's *L'Astrée*, but modern critics, determined to find a ready-made ethic, have condemned as inconsistent the inclusion of the inadequately masculine Démétrius, the impulsive, passionate, and involuntary cause of the death of Hermione, whom he loves, when La Calprenède appears seriously to be asking whether courage in battle can go with hypersensitivity in love. When Démétrius recovers from his solitary sorrow he falls in love again, and eventually marries Déidamie, but is clearly introspective and melancholic.

For that matter can the Amazonian features of the character Talestris be accommodated within the structures of femininity? The characters had to be elevated, freed from mundane constraints, and suited to a world in which moral dilemmas might occur, and on a suitably huge scale. They had therefore to be royal. Bérénice is puzzled that she can be so affected by the noble qualities of Arsace—"pleust aux Dieux qu'il fût né prince (would to Heaven that he had been born a prince)." His merit will make up for any deficiency in empires to run, or will put him on a path to conquer them. But there is still the obsolescent identification of birth and merit in Bérénice's mind.

Tallemant was amusing, unfair, and in the end wrong about *Cassandre*, but he gives a good idea of what a moderately malicious contemporary reader might have found to say about the novel:

la matière en est belle et riche, car c'est l'histoire d'Alexandre: il y a mesme de l'oechonomie; mais les heros se ressemblent comme deux gouttes d'eau, parlent tous Phoebus, et sont des gens cent lieües au-dessus des autres hommes. Les dames y sont un peu sujettes à donner des rendez-vous du vivant de leurs marys, et cela, au goust de l'auteur, est fort dans la bienséance

(the content is fine and rich, because it's the story of Alexander: there is even a well-ordered plot; but the heroes are as alike as two drops of water, all talk pretentious nonsense, and are a hundred leagues above ordinary men. The ladies are rather apt to make assignations while their husbands are still alive, but in the author's eyes, that does not shock the proprieties).

Cléopâtre took a lot longer to write than *Cassandre*. Mme de Sévigné took a bet that she would finish reading it. On 15 July 1671 she reports progress to her daughter.

Nous lisons toujours Le Tasse avec plaisir…Cette *Morale* de Nicole est admirable, et *Cléopâtre* va son train, sans empressement toutefois; c'est aux heures perdues. C'est ordinairement sur cette lecture que je m'endors; le caractère m'en plaît beaucoup plus que le style. Pour les sentiments, j'avoue qu'ils me plaisent aussi et qu'ils sont d'une perfection qui remplit mon idée sur les belles âmes. Vous savez aussi que je ne hais pas les grands coups d'épée, tellement que voilà qui va bien, pourvu qu'on m'en garde le secret.

(We are still enjoying reading Tasso…Nicole's *Morale* [vol. 1 of the *Essais de morales* had just appeared] is admirable and *Cléopâtre* goes on, although in a leisurely fashion, in odd moments. That is generally what I read before I go to sleep; I like the characters much more than the style. As to the feelings, I must admit to liking them, too. They have the perfection which seems to me appropriate to noble souls. You know, too, that I quite like great sword fights, so this is just the thing for me—so long as you don't tell anyone).

There is much of interest in those few words, Mme de Sévigné in Brittany in July, the reading aloud, the choice of Tasso, La Calprenède, and the severe Nicole. Mme de Sévigné enjoys trembling for her salvation, but is still deeply attached to Retz, and to the values of the Fronde he was to represent between the years when La Calprenède started the novel and those during which he had finished it.

In fact the "au lecteur" of the 1648 fourth volume suggests that *Cléopâtre* was not so successful as *Cassandre* had been. The novel starts off much as *Cassandre* does, with the three central male heroes Coriolan, Césarion, and Artaban, all capable of feats of great physical strength and heroic courage. Démétrius, in *Cassandre*, either provoked some sort of reader acclaim or especially pleased La Calprenède, because his strain of reflectiveness is considerably expanded in the episode from the first volume of *Cléopâtre* between Tyridate and the woman he loves, Mariamne, news of whose execution causes Tyridate first to faint and then to waste away and die. But by 1648 vaudevilles had appeared, parodying the Tyridate episode. The new privilège of 21 February 1648 suggests that parts four and five, published later that year, were to conclude the novel, but the end of part five is not a conclusion, and volume VI followed in 1649.

The Fronde may have caused the break before volumes VII and VIII in 1653—although Madeleine de Scudéry had continued to publish *Le Grand Cyrus*—and no more of *Cléopâtre* was published before the final four volumes in 1657. The novel is not conceived as a whole, as *Cassandre* clearly had been, and there are too many sub-plots. From volume V, of 1648, the main plot rather ebbs away, and there are no more set-piece battles. Since even *Le Grand Cyrus* totally changes its perspectives in the tenth book, of 1653, it seems quite likely that the Fronde, its preceding tensions, and its immediate consequences may have been both the product and the cause of a deeper cultural change which also affected the conduct of La Calprenède's novel. Experience firmly teaches that taste seldom markedly or permanently changes without some profound cultural reasons.

From the beginning of *Cléopâtre* interest centres more on love than on battle, and the external trappings of grandeur, thrones, diadems, empires, and armies, are now less desirable than an enduring partnership in love. The male dominance has flowed away, except perhaps in the single instance of the episode between Alcamène and Ménalippe in volume VIII. Elsewhere, the ideal has become the refined and elegant court or salon notion of service, which no longer regards reward as a right. Love has already ceased to be an act of will asserting moral integrity, but is already being examined as an irresistible passion, and therefore a sign of weakness. Its justification in terms of the merit of its object is being questioned. The heroic values erected on the baroque confidence in human self-determination was beginning to undergo the correction from which it would again emerge only after Colbert's death in 1683. Love's gradations are noticeably more subtle and refined in the female characters, while Adallas is simply condemned by forces beyond his control to love his sister incestuously. None of the women quite loses control.

La Calprenède is not a careful writer, and his prose style is almost insultingly negligent. He was also over-concerned to react against the successes of Madeleine de Scudéry. He did however sensitively, radically, and powerfully respond to the need felt by his contemporaries to examine imaginatively the nature and limits of fundamental moral values, first in the theatre, and then in the heroic novel. The period he understood, and to whose needs he best responded, was that of the dozen years preceding the Fronde, and the different preoccupations that period imposed after the final defeat of the old military aristocracy in the Fronde. It is difficult not to wish he had been a better craftsman, but his negligence did not prevent him from being a great writer.

PUBLICATIONS

Plays

La Mort de Mithridate, tragédie (1635), 1637 [achevé d'imprimer 16 November 1636]
La Bradamante, tragi-comédie (1637), 1637
La Clarionte; ou, Le Sacrifice sanglant, tragi-comédie (1637), 1637
Jeanne, reine d'Angleterre, tragédie (1638), 1638
Le Comte d'Essex, tragédie (1637), 1639
La Mort des enfants d'Hérode; ou, La Suite de Mariane, tragédie (1639), 1639
Edouard, tragi-comédie (1640), 1640
Phalante, tragédie (1641), 1642
Herménigilde, tragédie (1643), 1643

Fiction

Cassandre, 10 vols., 1642–45
Cléopâtre, 12 vols., 1646–57
Faramond; ou, L'Histoire de France, finished by Pierre d'Ortigue de Vaumorière, 12 vols., 1661–1670

Biographical and critical studies

Seillière, Ernest, *Le Romancier du Grand Condé, Gautier de Coste, sieur de la Calprenède*, 1921
Bannister, Mark, *Privileged Mortals, The French Heroic Novel 1630–1660*, 1983

LA CHAUSSÉE, Pierre-Claude NIVELLE DE: see
NIVELLE DE LA CHAUSSÉE, Pierre-Claude

LACLOS, Pierre-Ambroise-François, Choderlos de, 1741–1803.

Novelist.

LIFE

Born at Amiens into a family of administrative officials, Laclos was without high protection and felt throughout his adult life a seething frustration at the slow advancement of his military career, from 1760, when he entered the Ecole d'Artillerie at La Fère, through a long round of service in provincial garrisons. He took to making short cuts, seeking prominence through literature, in the entourage of Philippe d'Orléans—a focus in the years before the Revolution for liberal opposition to the regime—then in politics, and finally again, when almost 59, in Napoleon's army, believing perhaps rightly that his merit was never sufficiently recognized or rewarded.

His father had done well as secretary to the Governor of Picardy, who himself had successfully helped to turn Amiens, which had lost 1,600 Huguenots at the revocation of the Edict of Nantes, into a thriving textile town, by 1746 known to be the most important exporting centre in France. Laclos had himself written the libretti of two unsuccessful comic operas and some light verse when, apparently out of frustration at his failure to gain promotion above the rank of captain in the aristocratic commissioned ranks of the peacetime French army, he determined to write a book which would be remembered. He asked for leave in 1781, and published his famous epistolary novel, the most tightly constructed fictional work of the century.

Laclos was born on 18 October 1741 into a family which had penetrated to the ranks of the minor nobility. His grandfather, Thomas, a financial administrator in the ministry of war, had in 1725 bought an ennobling office of secrétaire du roi and, first in his branch of the family, added "de Laclos" to his name. No-one knows of any property of that name connected with the family. Thomas had earlier improved his social status by marrying Marie de Gau de Fréjeville, who was already ennobled and whose family became from 1722 entitled to use the title of marquis. The couple had one daughter and three sons, of whom the eldest, Laclos's father Jean-Ambroise, was born in 1704.

In 1718, at the age of 14, Jean-Ambroise was taken to Amiens away from his family, which appears to have been ambitious for him in all ways. The new governor of Picardy, Bernard Chauvelin, became, at least informally, his guardian. Laclos's father inherited his own father's charge and title in 1729, two years after Bernard Chauvelin had been replaced by his son, Jacques-Bernard, whose principal administrative officer Jean-Ambroise became. On 17 December 1737, already 33, Laclos's father married Catherine Gallois, daughter of the wealthy bourgeois steward of the king's estates in Picardy, at a ceremony over which the bishop presided. A first son, Jean-Charles-Marie, Laclos's elder brother by almost exactly three years, was born on 16 November 1738. The date of birth of a sister who died in 1754 is unknown.

Of the two brothers of Jean-Ambroise, Laclos's uncles, one became a canon. The other, Philippe-Jean-Baptiste, a captain in the artillery, was the only known family link with the military. Jacques-Bernard Chauvelin was promoted to Paris in 1751 and took with him Jean-Ambroise and his family. Laclos was 10 when they moved to the still fashionable Marais district in Paris. As regards Laclos's schooling we have only conjectures to go on, mostly erected on later scraps of verse alluding to adolescent loves. We know that by the beginning of 1759, during the Seven Years War against England, Laclos's family was contemplating a military career for him. He was sent to a mathematics tutor with whom he worked until October, when he was interviewed at the Ecole d'Artillerie. He was officially confirmed as an "aspirant" on 1 December, and as a cadet on 23 January 1760. The precise dates were later to become important.

The regulations limiting commissions to aristocrats had been tightened in 1718 and 1727, although the rigour with which they were applied differed between the three army corps, with the line regiments stricter than the provincial militia, and the troops of the royal household the most exigent of all. For entry into the Ecole Militaire, created essentially for the younger sons of the aristocracy who were not going to inherit entailed estates, four generations of nobility had to be proved on the father's side, and Laclos had only three. The criteria were eased in time of war, and account was taken of engineering skills. The artillery regiment, created in 1693, had grown to 6,400 members by 1748, at the end of the War of the Austrian Succession, and entry was eased for those who promised technical competence, were closely related to officers, and whose fathers exercised honourable professions.

Laclos was a younger son from a well-placed family with three generations of nobility and had an uncle who had retired as an artillery captain after a career which, given his rank, cannot have been distinguished. The artillery corps had just been created, dating from December 1755. Entry was through the Ecole Militaire at La Fère, 130 kilometres from Paris, which had been created in 1716 but whose re-organization dated only from 8 April 1756. Passes in examinations in arithmetic, geometry, and mechanics were required, with a further examination at the end of the first year. Napoleon was later to turn the Ecole Militaire into the Ecole Polytechnique, but in the 18th century it was considered to offer an ideal career for an intelligent younger son from the minor nobility. Laclos became an under-lieutenant on 8 March 1761 and, at the end of his two-year course, on 15 January 1762, a sub-lieutenant. The salary of 840 livres a year, unless supplemented from home, meant skimping. There were no messing facilities. Officers ate in inns, and the minister of war noted in 1763 that many of them could afford only one meal a day.

Laclos was posted to La Rochelle which, until the Seven Years War, had prospered from its role as France's premier Atlantic port, from which flotillas of up to 40 ships at a time would leave for the new world. However, if the war brought commercial disaster, with 43 ships lost to the enemy in 1757 and 39 in 1758, and with bankruptcies already alarmingly common, it also promised military opportunities for young officers. Laclos had sought his posting, hoping to see military action, but was to find promotion blocked by 30 years of peace. In 1763 he was sent to Toul, 25 miles west of Nancy, near the Lorraine border. He appears to have led an uneventful military existence, no doubt with a junior officer's entitlement to one winter off every two years, while the army was re-organized and its equipment modernized. At the end of August 1765 Laclos's regiment was moved to Strasbourg, and six weeks later, on 15 October 1765, he was made a first lieutenant. He also became a freemason, which may have had something to do with his staff appointment on 31 July 1767.

In *L'Almanach des Muses* for that year Laclos published the first of his poems, "A Mademoiselle de Saint-S…, en lui envoyant des mirabelles de Metz." It is not a distinguished piece, but it must have been thought good enough to have been sent to and accepted by *L'Almanach*, and it gives a rough idea of Laclos's modest literary culture and aspirations. We know only, in addition, that he read Richardson in Prévost's translations and that he admired Rousseau. He was clearly interested in the responses to natural phenomena and emotional relationships being explored in the most advanced European literature of his day. In 1769 he was posted to Grenoble, on the border with Savoy, and was there for the abolition of the Grenoble parlement by Maupeou's reform of November 1771, which replaced it by a simple court with 30 magistrates. Louis XVI was to re-establish the parlement in 1775.

Grenoble afforded Laclos his first adult experience of elegant, cultivated, and decadent French society. It must have been there that he observed the prototypes of the social relationships to be fictionalized in his novel. There are a number of improbable keys to *Les Liaisons dangereuses* relating the characters in the novel to real people in Grenoble whom Laclos is said to have known. It was there, too, that Laclos wrote the "Epître à Margot," a slight satirical skit on "Margot," the name commonly used to designate a prostitute who successfully exploits her charms to attain the highest social rank. The verses circulated in manuscript in Paris in 1770 as part of a *Recueil* entitled *L'Occasion et le moment*. The comtesse du Barry, mistress of Louis XV from 1768, appears to have taken the satire personally and to have been annoyed, although not until 1774; surprisingly in the circumstances, since this was one among scores circulating about her. What is of interest about the lines is the sympathy they show for the prostitute who cannot read. The education of women was among Laclos's major concerns. He was to write a treatise on it.

In 1773 *L'Almanach des Muses* printed "Les souvenirs," a poem in which real feeling appears. In 1775 he was moved with his regiment to Besançon. We have a series of brief notes from his personal file, made mostly at the annual inspections. He fulfilled his functions impeccably, although there are also signs on his part of impatience at the lack of promotion. He had been made a captain on 23 January 1771 but felt that he was being overtaken. He was in fact to remain a captain for 18 years, although he was promoted within that grade on 1 January 1777 and was entrusted with making the necessary arrangements at Valence to transfer the artillery school there. Louis XV had died in 1774, and in 1777 "L'Epître à Margot" was published by *L'Almanach des Muses* over Laclos's own name.

The preceding year he had made what he himself came to see as an unsuccessful attempt to write a poem, the "Epître à la mort," on a more noble register. It was on 19 July 1777 that the Italian company in Paris gave the single performance of Laclos's opéra-comique *Ernestine*, adapted from a novel by Jeanne Laboras de Mézières, Mme Riccoboni, wife of Lélio II, the son of the Lélio who had brought the company back to Paris in 1716. The play was re-written by Desfontaines and set to music by Saint-Georges. The audience, which included Marie-Antoinette and her two sisters-in-law, apparently booed throughout, finding the verse even worse than the music. Grimm's newsletter, later known as the *Correspondance littéraire,* noted that it would be difficult to find a better subject, or treat it worse. The text has been lost. We may owe *Les Liaisons dangereuses* to Laclos's painful discovery that he was no better at dramatic writing than he was at poetry.

For a moment in 1778 it looked as if Laclos might at last see active service in America, but it was the other half of his regiment which was sent to Le Havre. On 30 April 1779 he was put at the disposition of the marquis de Montalembert to fortify the île d'Aix against the English, presumably to direct the troops constructing the fortifications, whose design would not have been given to an artillery officer. In fact Laclos usurped the place of his rivals in Montalembert's confidence, and carried the day against the traditionalists and fortifications specialists, risking his whole career for more speedy advancement. The viability of his fortress was never really tested, and it was soon taken down. He achieved a token promotion, without apparently doing much more than increase the official but unrecorded distrust which was now plainly beginning to hold him up. But it seems likely that, before he left for the west, he had been inspired by Rousseau's *Julie; ou, La Nouvelle Héloïse* to write an epistolary novel, for which he had drawn up a plan, and at least a sketch of the first 70 letters. The final version of the novel contains 175. *L'Almanach des Muses* for 1779 published another poem, "Le bon choix." It may well have been in 1780 that Laclos wrote the "Epître à Mme de Montalembert" which, for obvious reasons, he did not publish. Laclos was 39, Montalembert 66, and Marie de Commarieu, whom the marquis had married in 1770, was only 30.

The remaining letters of *Les Liaisons dangereuses* were probably composed in 1781. On 4 September Laclos applied for six months' special leave, and in October for tacit permission to publish his novel. Both were accorded in mid-December 1781, and Laclos spent the first ten weeks of his leave correcting and copying the work known at first as "Du danger des liaisons." The contract with the bookseller-publisher Durand *neveu* stipulated a printing of 2,000 copies, 1,200 of which Durand would sell on his own account at 30 livres for the 4-volume set. Laclos would receive two thirds of the price of the remaining 800 copies, making 16,000 livres, six months in arrears.

Published between 7 and 10 April 1782, the book was called *Les Liaisons dangereuses; ou, Lettres recueillies dans une société particulière et publiées pour l'instruction de quelques autres,* signed only "M. C…de L…," and using a fictional place of publication, Amsterdam, while giving the real name of the Paris publisher, Durand. The first printing was sold out in a fortnight, and a contract similar to the first for a second printing of 2,000 copies was signed on 21 April. By and large the irony was missed and the reactions were severe. They either defended society against its depiction by Laclos or treated his novel as itself an invitation to corruption. For their part, his army superiors sent him a tart note ordering him back from the île d'Aix to his regiment at Brest, eventually reversing their decision, rather to Laclos's regret, on Montalembert's appeal, and clearly surprised at the alacrity with which Laclos had accepted their first ruling. For the first time a claim by Laclos for expenses was cut back. Only 800 livres was accorded on a claim for 1,220 supported by Montalembert. Disfavour was being signalled.

From the autumn of 1782, with the war nearing its end, the administration had no relish for spending more money on Montalembert's fort, and Laclos was moved to La Rochelle. The town was still in decline. No fewer than 31 commercial houses had had to suspend payments in 1763. In 1770 one of the biggest ships' provisioners failed, and Rochefort was providing important rivalry as a port. The La Rochelle ships began their triangular run to Africa with goods, then sailed to the new world with slaves, returning to France with cocoa, indigo, precious wood, cotton, sugar, and rum. In La Rochelle Laclos got to know the family of Jean-Augustin Duperré, an administrator who, like the Laclos family, had penetrated into the lowest rank of nobility. Duperré, whose wife had borne him 22 children, had died in 1775. In 1783 Laclos, aged 41, formed a liaison with the 18-year-old Marie-Soulange Duperré, who became pregnant by him. Her mother had serious misgivings about the idea of a marriage, although Laclos was in fact to prove a devoted husband. In the meanwhile he lived next door to Marie-Soulange, the houses apparently linked by an underground passage.

Early in 1783 Laclos had also drafted an essay on the education of women for a prize offered by the academy of Châlons. It was to be published only in 1903 and was never finished, but Laclos did publish a review of Fanny Burney's 1782 *Cecilia*, which had appeared in French in London in 1783 as *Cecilia; ou, Les Malheurs d'une héritière*. The review was spread over three numbers of the *Mercure de France* (q.v.) for 17 and 24 April and 15 May 1784. His son, Etienne-Fargeau, was born on 1 May 1784 and put out to nurse. On 17 August, Laclos's father died and his mother then moved to a convent. Laclos at La Rochelle now decided to write another essay, this time for a prize offered by the Académie française. Vauban had been the great 17th-century military engineer and architect, whose *Eloge* by Lazare Carnot had been awarded first prize in the 1784 essay competition organized by the Dijon academy. Carnot had had to publish his essay at his own expense. Montalembert's work, and that of Laclos, had been dedicated to undermining the principles which had governed Vauban's constructions, and Laclos's essay was an attack not only on Carnot, who never wholly forgave the author of the *Lettre sur l'éloge de Vauban*, but also on the whole military establishment, more formidable opponents than the decadent aristocracy lampooned in *Les Liaisons dangereuses*.

Laclos had finished his *Lettre* by the end of January 1786. It was dated 21 March and published at his own expense early in April. On 11 April Laclos's application for permission to marry was forwarded to his superiors, accompanied by the required letter from his mother giving her permission, although Laclos was now 44. There was also a request for special leave for one month from 1 May. Both permissions were accorded by the minister Ségur, to whom Laclos had despatched a copy of his *Lettre* only on 12 April. On 29 April the marriage contract was signed and on 3 May the wedding took place. The next day Laclos and his wife left for Paris.

Ségur was annoyed that Laclos had not sought permission to publish the *Lettre*, but incensed at the attack on Vauban, whose theories on fortification had become military dogma. The projected punishment was to order Laclos to return to his regiment, by now at Metz. Laclos received the letter in Paris on 16 May

and left for Metz on the 21st, alone. Determined to keep his profile high, he applied in September for the croix de Saint-Louis, an honour to which, with his rank, he had a right only after 28 years of service. He was in effect asking for his preparatory year studying mathematics to be counted, partly perhaps to achieve a public rehabilitation, but perhaps partly too on account of the 800 livres pension attaching to it. His immediate superiors supported his application, which was, however, inevitably turned down.

In October 1786 the regiment was sent to La Fère, where Marie-Soulange and Etienne joined Laclos. Early in 1787 Laclos published a four-volume set of works, including correspondence with Mme Riccoboni, some hitherto unpublished verse, and a declaration that *Les Liaisons dangereuses* was meant to be understood as a satire. That year a book and an article appeared defending Vauban, so that Laclos's *Lettre* was not forgotten. Although Ségur had now been replaced by the first minister's brother, Athanase de Brienne, an application by Laclos to be transferred to the Turkish artillery in Constantinople was turned down. Louis XVI had created 1,322 generals in 18 years, and promotion at home was getting more difficult as the army became overloaded with senior officers. Laclos did, however, receive his croix de Saint-Louis on 2 December 1787.

He and his wife had returned on a visit during the year to La Rochelle, where the eldest Duperré son had gone bankrupt. On his subsequent disappearance, the Laclos's house had also been sealed and, in spite of Laclos's efforts, he was not able to succeed in claiming that much even of the contents belonged not to his brother-in-law but to himself. He had to go to law to salvage clothes and linen, and was made to pay costs. Laclos's mother-in-law returned to her native Versailles. His own daughter was born there on 4 December 1787. His wife stayed at Versailles, while he spent what time he had to with his regiment.

Towards the end of 1788 Laclos obtained leave and was put in touch with Philippe (Philippe-Egalité), duc d'Orléans since the death of his father three years previously, and father of Louis-Philippe, to become head of state in 1830. The introduction may have been made by Ségur's wayward son, but the evidence is uncertain. It is, however, clear that by January 1789, by which date the size of the Tiers Etat had already been doubled to make it equal to the nobility and clergy together, Laclos was in league with the Orléans camp. He was working for them at Versailles, according to Talleyrand in the first place as a pamphleteer in the wake of the lifting of restrictions on political writing of 5 July 1788, and was on the way to becoming a trusted political adviser and agent to the cunning, irresolute, conspiratorial, flighty, but timid Orléans himself. That winter was the hardest of the century. There were 80,000 unemployed in Paris, and the Seine was frozen from Paris to Le Havre. Orléans was doing his best to make himself popular by works of charity, but also working through his masonic friends along more or less reformatory lines.

Laclos was presented by Armand Biron, the duc de Lauzun, at the club des Constitutionnels, and was also introduced into the highly aristocratic club des Valois. His function was the redaction of political demands and their dissemination in the enormous areas controlled by Orléans, elected in April, to represent the nobility, for Villers-Cotterets and Crépy-en-Valois. On 17 June the Tiers Etat declared itself the Assemblée Nationale, and on the 20th the Tennis Court Oath was sworn. Forty-seven nobles headed by Orléans joined the revolution on the

24th, and on 3 July Orléans was elected to the presidency of the Assemblée, which he declined. Laclos, not without difficulty, managed to get his leave prolonged by eight months from 1 October 1789.

Like Orléans, Laclos was thought to have been behind the insurrectionary crowd which killed two guards at Versailles and brought the royal family back to Paris on 6 October. It seems to have been on 7 October that Laclos with his wife and children moved from Versailles into the Orléans enclosure near the Palais-Royal in Paris. Laclos, clear-headed and obstinate, was now a principal adviser to the indecisive Orléans, and with Clarke, Agnès de Buffon, and his German doctor André Seiffert, was taken by Orléans to England on 14 October. At Boulogne the crowd thought Orléans was being exiled and refused to let him go. He had to wait three days while Clarke got papers from Paris to prove that his mission was official, but instantly thereby forfeited his popularity in the capital.

Laclos was in England for nine months, returning to Paris on 10 July 1790. His mission was officially recognized by the army, but his remuneration was reduced to 4,000 livres, perhaps because he was being given bed and board. Essentially Orléans was in London because Louis XVI wanted him out of Paris. He was expected to discover what role was being played and what policy followed by the English, and was sometimes better informed than the ambassador. Laclos, however, was more interested in producing a grand scheme for France's foreign policy which would finally bring him the importance he had so long been looking for, but which might also have saved France from the Terror and the Napoleonic wars. Back in Paris, he obtained approval for himself as editor of the *Journal des Amis de la Constitution* for which he proposed a vastly over-ambitious programme. The first number appeared on 30 November 1790, 48 pages of small octavo.

Laclos's leave was due to run out on 1 December, and his mission in London with Orléans had not advanced his promised military promotion, which looked decreasingly likely. No new leave was at first forthcoming, and he was still six months short of entitlement to retirement. Finally he was given unpaid leave, and then his pay, too, was restored. He was immensely busy, but appears to have contributed to the *Galerie des dames françaises* which appeared at the end of 1790, and was perhaps the author of the portraits of Mme du Barry and of his arch-enemy, the governess of the Orléans children, Mme de Genlis. In April 1791, when Orléans and his wife split up, Orléans was plainly bankrupt. Laclos was playing a more active role among the Jacobins, whose club he had joined on 21 November 1790. On the flight of the king during the night of 20 June 1791, Orléans could easily have claimed the succession. He hesitated and decided to do nothing, but was at the Tuileries when the royal family was brought back on the 25th.

For a moment Laclos, furious at the royal family, turned wholeheartedly towards the Revolution, at least in its political rather than its social aspects. But he either remained at or quickly returned to a legitimist position. By 17 July he was caught between the monarchists and the republicans in middle ground which both sides had made untenable. He remained in the service of Orléans, and was technically in the army at least until his final leave expired on 1 June 1792. On 10 August the monarchy came to an end. Laclos was elected that day to the Paris committee of administration, but his relationship with Orléans caused the election to be disputed. War with Austria had broken out in April, and in July the fatherland had been declared in danger. Laclos was re-elected but resigned the following day, 31 August, to re-join the army, and is immediately referred to as a colonel and, only days later, as a maréchal du camp. He was employed as a chief of staff by the minister of war, and then put in charge of communications, with a staff of five and the salary of a maréchal du camp, plus an additional campaign allowance, a living allowance proportional to his rank, and 4,000 livres paid in advance.

From 6 September Laclos was stationed at Châlons and then, after a brief return to Paris, he was made chief of staff of the new army of the Pyrenees, in fact a few ill-equipped and neglected companies around Toulouse. He left Paris for his new post during the second fortnight of October 1792 and was this time allowed to take his wife. His mother died on 25 November and he received a modest inheritance. He was recalled to Paris at his own request, for consultations, and on 1 December appointed governor-general of the French establishments in the East Indies. He and his wife were back in their Paris quarters before Christmas, ready to organize the necessary 15,000 men and 15 ships. Orléans, with whom Laclos can now have had little contact, voted for the king's execution, which took place on 21 January 1793. Then, on the 25th, Laclos explained to the defence committee that it would be necessary to declare war on England before his expedition could leave. The committee postponed the expedition indefinitely. On 1 February war against England was declared. A further disappointment was in store when Laclos failed to be made lieutenant-general of India for the moment when, as the French hoped, it was going to be taken back from the English. His salary was also three months in arrears.

He now shared the disgrace of the entourage of Orléans, and on 2 April 1793, together with Orléans's two sons, Mme de Genlis, and her husband, the marquis de Sillery, Laclos was arrested. He was released two days later. He must have been protected, most probably by Danton, whose earlier connection with Orléans Laclos knew well: the spells of arrest, of house arrest, and of mere suspicion under which he had to pass the period until December 1794 constituted gentle treatment. He remained in the army, conducting experiments with the hollowed-out cannon balls he had invented, capable of being charged with gun-powder, and, being lighter than normal cannon balls, of going further and being aimed more accurately. There was a sudden and unexpected arrest on 5 November, the day before the execution of Orléans. Prison was naturally a very dangerous place to be, but conditions at La Force, where Laclos was at first held, were extraordinarily mild, with private visits allowed, food sent in, and all the newspapers. On 20 December he was transferred to Picpus, a privately run establishment which undertook detention services for the state and could be used to protect suspects from anything worse that might otherwise happen to them. Only at the very end of the Terror, in June and July 1794, were the conditions of Laclos's incarceration at Picpus particularly harsh. They were bad again when in October he was transferred to the Luxembourg.

He was released on 30 November. We do not know how he managed financially. After the Terror, price controls were abolished, resulting in increases by factors of between 100 and 200 that reduced to starvation anyone on a fixed income. The quantity of flour that had cost 2 livres in 1790 sold for 225 in 1795; a pound of candles went from 18 sols to 41 livres; haricot beans increased by a factor of only 30. Rationing was introduced, and the average factor by which prices increased between 1789 and 1795 seems to have been about 100. In addition the winter of 1794–95 was again harsh, with temperatures in Paris of –18°. Laclos's children were aged ten and seven, but his wife was again pregnant. A son, Charles, conceived in prison, was born on 4 June 1795. In December 1795 Laclos was appointed secretary-general of the loans service. Life slowly resumed normality. Servants re-appeared in the household of the most modest functionaries.

Laclos wrote, but did not publish, an account of the notes of La Pérouse on his last voyage of 1785–88, and wrote again on the education of women. He may also have written a short moral tale, the *Histoire de Pauline*, and he considered associating himself with others in a financial enterprise which came to nothing. The detail of how he came to be associated with Bonaparte is not known, and it is clear that there was opposition to him in Bonaparte's entourage, but on 16 January 1800 he was made a general in the artillery, with retrospective effect to 22 September 1792, the date at which he had been made maréchal de camp. It may be, as with Danton, that Laclos had too intimate an acquaintanceship with Bonaparte's past political record for him to be ignored. Official correspondence must have passed between them when Bonaparte was secretary of the Valence Jacobins, and it is always possible that Laclos had been part of the conspiracy leading to Napoleon's coup d'état of 9 November 1799.

For the first time Laclos now saw action. He asked for a quick decision about his posting, and lunched with Bonaparte before departing for the Rhine army. There are 142 affectionate letters to his wife surviving from the campaigns of 12 April 1800 to 12 May 1801, and from 3 May to 27 August 1803. Laclos's last campaign, in Italy, was the result of his final attempt to become general of a division, the army's highest rank. He ran into serious financial difficulties when he had himself to find money that should have come from the king of Naples. In July 1803, he fell ill with dysentery at the siege of Taranto. There were moments of hope, but he was clearly sinking. Ambition was at last on the brink of fulfilment in the military career to which he was clearly more suited than to the worlds of politics, letters, or business. But he was now nearly 62, and success had been too long in coming. On the day of his death he dictated a letter to Bonaparte: "I am afflicted by the sad situation of my wife and three children, whom I am leaving absolutely without resources. My hope that you will help them makes me die more peacefully."

Laclos died of dysentery on 5 September 1803.

Works

Even though commonly supposed to be a novel of amorous intrigue, *Les Liaisons dangereuses* required a mind of military precision and tactical expertise for its execution. The satirical intention is quite clear, and the society satirized clearly late 18th-century French provincial. What makes the work a masterpiece, apart from the tightness of its organization, is the closeness with which the workings of a decadent society are observed, and the way the fundamentally depraved power struggle between Valmont and Mme de Merteuil is tactically deployed for the systematic corruption of Cécile and Danceny. It is perfectly clear, from the lowness of key with which the debauched intentions of the two principal characters is set out,

that the work was intended to shock by the lucid brutality with which the attack on innocence is marshalled. An ironic comment on Laclos's views on the education of women, it shows how easily it is possible to corrupt them.

That the text is a long ironic comment on *Julie; ou, La Nouvelle Héloïse* is made clear on the title page: *Les Liaisons dangereuses; ou, Lettres recueillies dans une société, et publiées pour l'instruction de quelques autres*, followed by the dry quotation from Rousseau: "J'ai vu les moeurs de ce siècle et j'ai publié ces lettres (I have seen the moral values of this society, and I have published these letters)." The task was to contrive a novel which could be guaranteed to attract attention by shocking, but itself be written from an impeccably uncorrupted point of view. The solution had to be irony, to which the military organization of the campaign to deprave itself contributed. The wickedness of the intention to corrupt is underlined by the unsentimentality of its execution much more than by the conventionally retributive ending. In fact Laclos miscalculated. Too many of his readers missed the irony.

Yet the warning signs are not only on the fly-leaf. That is followed by an "avertissement de l'éditeur" so heavily ironic as almost to labour what should already be quite clear. The book is not only to be a probably amusing but certainly cynical parody of *Julie*, but it is also, Laclos tells us, obviously a novel, and not the collection of letters it purports to be, because the deliberate verisimilitude has involved depicting characters who have

de si mauvaises moeurs, qu'il est impossible de supposer qu'ils aient vécu dans notre siècle: dans ce siècle de philosophie, où les lumières, répandues de toutes parts, ont rendu, comme chacun sait, tous les hommes si honnêtes et toutes les femmes si modestes et si réservées

(such evil moral standards that it is impossible to suppose that they have lived in our century, in this century of philosophy in which enlightenment, spreading everywhere, has, as everyone knows, made all men so upright and all women so modest and reserved).

In the last paragraph of the "avertissement" the irony is even more savage. You don't see a young woman with an annual income of 60,000 livres becoming a nun these days, or a young and pretty présidente dying of grief, do you? Such things, Laclos sarcastically assumes, happen only in corrupt societies...

The irony continues, less clearly, in the "Préface du rédacteur." The "editor" of the letters has eliminated everything not rigorously necessary "soit à l'intelligence des événements, soit au développement des caractères (either to the understanding of events or to the development of the characters)." The full irony comes when the editor tells his readers that he was not allowed to correct the style, thereby drawing attention to the care with which the author of what we have already been told is a novel has taken to adapt the language and manner of the letters to the characters of their writers. The first letter from Cécile Volanges to her friend Sophie Carnay almost overdoes the schoolgirl style. The editor draws attention again to the way in which "almost all" the sentiments expressed by the writers of the letters are "feints ou dissimulés (feigned or concealed)." On the other hand, the editor's announced intention to uncover the ways in which those with evil moral standards corrupt those with good ones sounds too like a conventional disclaimer to be ironic.

Indeed the editor is plainly giving the author's view when stating that the letters show that a woman who admits a man with low standards of moral behaviour to her company will inevitably become his victim, and that mothers are imprudent if they allow anyone but themselves to win the confidence of their daughters.

The editor is not being ironic at all, although perhaps a little naive, in declaring that the depraved will not welcome a work which demonstrates how corruption can be set about and successfully achieved. There are very occasional blemishes in the novel's structure, as when letters are interrupted, so breaking with verisimilitude for the sake of the plot, or letters are written that need not have been, or are printed in the wrong order for the sake of an orderly development of the intrigue. But the technical faults are infrequent and unimportant. On the whole Laclos uses the letter form brilliantly to show the same events credibly seen from different points of view, and to add suspense to the story while concentrating on what interests him, which is the characterization.

The opening letter from Cécile to her friend Sophie, dated 3 August, relates that her mother is taking her away from the convent where she is at school, presumably with a marriage in view. She is innocent, naive, and excited. The second letter, written the next day, 4 August, from the marquise de Merteuil in Paris to the vicomte de Valmont at a château, obviously nearby but in the country, is an immediate contrast. Valmont is being summoned by his ex-mistress for a project worthy of him, combining love and vengeance, another "*rouerie* (debauchery [and in italics in the text])" to add to his memoirs. The letter does at least bend the convention in that it is conversational rather than epistolary, anticipating reactions and assuming interruptions from Valmont, its addressee. Paris, also, was already too large and cosmopolitan for the plot credibly to be placed there, although the action, even if inspired by Grenoble, is vaguely placed in and around Paris.

The "editor" adds a note. Cécile's mother has destined her for the comte de Gercourt, another ex-lover of Mme de Merteuil, who jettisoned her for someone else and on whom she wants revenge. Gercourt has sworn never to marry a girl who is not blonde and does not come straight from her convent. Valmont is to seduce Cécile and, by making a fool of Gercourt, who will become the laughing stock of Paris, avenge Mme de Merteuil. Since the mistress for whom Gercourt had abandoned Mme de Merteuil had herself abandoned Valmont for him, Valmont, too, has a motive for revenge. The liaison between Valmont and Mme de Merteuil dates from their respective and simultaneous rejections by Gercourt and his new mistress. It is at least not surprising that the author of the book had been trained to plan artillery campaigns.

We learn that Cécile is 15, a rose bud, gauche as they come, with "un certain regard langoureux qui promet beaucoup en vérité (a certain languorous look which indeed promises much)." Mme de Merteuil is not wrong. Cécile is a disconcertingly apt pupil for Valmont's art. From her first letter, however, it is clear that Mme de Merteuil has put herself in charge of operations: "vous n'avez plus qu'à me remercier et m'obéir (you only have to thank me and obey me)." He is to come at seven o'clock the next evening, and not even her present lover, who could not be trusted to manage an affair like this, will be received before eight. Valmont is then to come back at 10 to dine. Cécile and her mother will be there.

On 4 August, the day after her last letter, Cécile writes again to her friend. She had dined at home the previous evening. Mme de Merteuil had been there and had said something about her being pretty but gauche. A man had said, "We must let that one ripen; we'll see this winter." Was that the one she was going to be married to? On 5 August Valmont replies with courteous irony to Mme de Merteuil. What is the interest in taking a young girl with no defences, sure to be intoxicated at the first compliment, and likely to give herself as much out of curiosity as out of desire? The marquise could find twenty other men who would succeed as well as he. Anyway, he is too busy with a more difficult project, promising "autant de gloire que de plaisir (as much glory as pleasure),"—the conquest of the présidente de Tourvel, devout, austere, and devoted to a husband at present away dealing with a court case in Burgundy. Daily Mass, visits to the poor, morning and evening prayers, lonely walks, pious conversations with Valmont's aunt, and an occasional hand at whist are her only diversions. Valmont is getting more effective ones ready for her. He thought he had to make a tedious 24-hour visit to his aunt. Now nothing will drag him away. Happily he is needed to make a fourth at whist. Solitude has added strength to his desire, which totally obsesses him. The tone is refined, elegant, witty, and debauched.

Mme de Merteuil is not pleased on the 7th.

Savez-vous, vicomte, que votre lettre est d'une insolence rare, et qu'il n'a tenu qu'à moi de m'en fâcher?...Vous, avoir la présidente de Tourvel! mais quel ridicule caprice! Je reconnais bien là votre mauvaise tête, qui ne sait désirer que ce qu'elle croit ne pas pouvoir obtenir. Qu'est-ce donc que cette femme? des traits réguliers si vous voulez, mais nulle expression: passablement faite, mais sans grâce: toujours mise à faire rire! avec ces paquets de fichus sur la gorge, et son corps qui remonte au menton!...Quelle honte si vous échouez! sans que le succès puisse vous faire le moindre honneur. Je dis plus; n'en espérez aucun plaisir. En est-il avec les prudes? j'entends celles de bonne foi: réservées au sein même du plaisir, elles ne vous offrent que des demis-jouissances. Cet entier abandon de soi-même, ce délire de la volupté où le plaisir s'épure par son excès, ces biens de l'amour, ne sont pas connus d'elles

(Do you know, vicomte, that your letter is extremely insolent, and that I might well have been annoyed? You, have the présidente de Tourvel! what an idiotic whim! I recognize your awkward character, wanting only what it thinks it can't have. What sort of a woman is she? Regular features, granted, but completely inexpressive; not a bad figure, but no style; always ludicrously dressed, with bundles of fichus round her neck, and the bodice of her dress going right up to her chin...What shame if you fail, while success won't do you any honour at all. I'll say more: don't expect any pleasure. Is there any to be got out of prudes? I mean real prudes: reserved even at the height of rapture, they offer you only half-enjoyments. That complete abandon, that delirious ecstasy in which pleasure is purified by its own excess—they know nothing of those joys of love).

The ruthlessness of the description of the présidente is savage and the lucid analysis of sexual pleasure intended to be shocking. Yet the irony drives away any suggestion of erotic titillation. The passage is wittily and amusingly forthright, mostly because the conventional reticences are devastatingly stripped away, and it is important because of the ironic way in which even the most intimate relationships are seen in terms of power struggles. Love, in an age of sentiment of which Laclos is clearly a product, is caricatured as a battle, in which victory is achieved, defeat suffered, and honour gained or lost. Mme de Merteuil is also asserting a power supremacy over Valmont, ridiculing him as well as reasoning with him, and insinuating that she is prepared to be annoyed with him if he does not do as she says.

In this fifth letter Mme de Merteuil mentions that "young Danceny" has fallen for Cécile, but he's only a child and will get nowhere. Certainly the whole thing will be less fun than Valmont could have made it ("beaucoup moins plaisant que vous n'auriez pu le rendre"). She is feeling angry, and might throw out her current chevalier. He'd be in despair, and she'd enjoy that. After being called cruel, having herself called faithless is a woman's sweetest pleasure, and it's easier to get. It's all Valmont's fault anyway, if she has a row with her lover. She lays it on his conscience.

The book now continues on the register that the reader has been taught to expect. The strategies are expertly deployed, the emotions clinically dissected, the parodic caricature of Rousseau superbly sustained, and only the bantering irony ebbs and flows in sympathy with the intrigue. In the sixth letter Valmont gives a clear parody of a "portrait." He and Mme de Merteuil are irredeemably cynical. The book is not. Cécile falls in love with Danceny (letter 7 of 7 August to Sophie); the présidente writes to Cécile's mother, reserved about Gercourt, wishing Cécile all the happiness she herself has had, and saying that she is staying in the country with Valmont's aunt, and likes Valmont more than she thought she would.

The 9th letter, of 11 August, from Cécile's mother to the présidente, is important for its sarcasm about Valmont. "Vous me parlez de sa *rare candeur*? Oh! oui, la candeur de Valmont doit être en effet très rare (You tell me of his 'rare candour.' Oh, yes, Valmont's candour must indeed be rare)." "Il sait calculer tout ce qu'un homme peut se permettre d'horreurs sans se compromettre (He can calculate exactly how many outrages a man can commit without compromising himself)," and has chosen women for victims. Only Mme de Merteuil has been able to resist him and subdue the evil in him. Gercourt has to go to Corsica and won't be free now to get married until the winter.

By letter 10, of 12 August, Mme de Merteuil realizes that Valmont is actually in love with his présidente, teases him with the recollection of the sofa on which they sealed their own "éternelle rupture (eternal break)," and recounts in bantering detail exactly how she has toyed with her chevalier. On 13 August a letter from the présidente to Cécile's mother tells the reader that Valmont's tactics are working, and an exchange of notes between Cécile and Mme de Merteuil reveals that Mme de Merteuil is taking charge of the Cécile–Danceny relationship. A letter of 15 August to Mme de Merteuil from Valmont suggests that he is not totally happy about having his position with her usurped by her new chevalier. The reader is promptly recalled to the nature of the fiction by a note from the rédacteur to say that a letter must have gone missing, but we are still informed of everything we need to know. Danceny has slipped Cécile a note, and she tells Sophie on 19 August that she is thinking of asking Mme de Merteuil what to do.

And so the knot tightens. The next letter is Danceny's note of 18 August, the day before the preceding letter. Then we are given a letter from Cécile to Sophie of 21 August. Her friend has written that Cécile should not reply to Danceny, but "je ne crois pas que personne se soit jamais trouvé dans le cas où je suis (I don't think anyone has ever been in this situation before)," and she feels guiltless at having let him hold her hand. The reply from Cécile to Danceny follows, dated 21 August, before we are given one from the marquise to Valmont dated 19 August, which the rédacteur tells us must have crossed that of the 15th to her from Valmont, followed by another from Valmont, of the 18th and therefore crossing again. Saying that he was going shooting, Valmont has successfully lured his présidente to watch him make a charitable visit to the local poor. The présidente writes triumphantly to Cécile's mother, also on the 18th, to say that her high view of Valmont has been confirmed.

Valmont's account of his declaration of love to the présidente is written to Mme de Merteuil on 19 August at 3 a.m. and is followed by his subsequent note to the présidente, also dated the 19th, asking her to help him to restrain the passion he feels for her. Valmont's letter to Mme de Merteuil recounting his visit, in the presence of his aunt, to the présidente, who is feigning sickness in bed, is dated 20 August, and the présidente's dignified reply to Valmont, betraying just enough self-analysis to show a dent in her armour, is dated the 19th. In the following letters Mme de Merteuil takes over the management of Cécile's emotional life, obviously exploiting her naivety as Cécile yields to Danceny's request that she should speak of her "amour" for him rather than simple "amitié," love rather than friendship. On 22 August Mme de Merteuil writes an extremely shrewd commentary to Valmont on the présidente's letter to him.

Not the least brilliant feature of the text is the appalling inexorability with which everything happens, at least until the very end. There is a quite remorseless progress in the intrigue, and a wicked brilliance in Mme de Merteuil's mind. By 27 August she can write about Cécile with sharp perceptiveness:

> Cela n'a ni caractère ni principes…Je ne crois pas qu'elle brille jamais par le sentiment; mais tout annonce en elle les sensations les plus vives. Sans esprit et sans finesse, elle a pourtant une certaine fausseté naturelle…qui réussira d'autant mieux, que sa figure offre l'image de la candeur et de l'ingenuité

> (The child hasn't got either character or principles…I don't think she will ever be noted for fine feelings, but everything suggests she has a lively sensuality. Without wit and without subtlety, she has none the less a certain natural duplicity…which will succeed the better because her face is the very picture of candour and ingenuousness).

Laclos does not, however, hide the perverse cruelty with which, for instance, in pursuit of her own amusing enough ends, Mme de Merteuil sacrifices Cécile's chances of happiness with Gercourt. There is on the contrary a chilling lucidity. An exchange of letters between Valmont and the présidente of 25 August interrupts a letter from Valmont to Mme de Merteuil of 26 August. Laclos makes the surrender of the présidente, from shame at which she dies, sufficiently difficult both to preserve probability and to show the obstinate determination of which Valmont is capable in the pursuit of his ends.

Above all, however, the strength of the novel lies in its parody of Rousseau. Can sexual relationships be reduced to power struggles? Valmont on 11 September insists that the présidente, still only 22, should be conscious that she has surrendered, almost in the military sense:

> Mon projet…est qu'elle sente, qu'elle sente bien la valeur et l'étendue de chacun des sacrifices qu'elle me fera; de ne pas la conduire si vite, que les remords ne puisse la suivre; de faire expirer sa vertu dans une lente agonie; de la fixer sans cesse sur ce désolant spectacle; et de ne lui accorder le bonheur de m'avoir dans ses bras, qu'après l'avoir forcée à n'en plus dissimuler le désir

> (My plan…is that she should feel, that she should really feel the value and extent of each of the sacrifices she will make to me; not to take her so fast that remorse cannot follow; to make her virtue die in a slow agony; to concentrate her mind ceaselessly on that sad spectacle; and to grant her the happiness of having me in her arms only after I have forced her no longer to hide her desire to do so).

Valmont, however, is here defending himself against an accusation of emotional weakness. On 29 October he writes to Mme de Merteuil, "La voilà donc vaincue! (She is conquered!)," but the seduction of Cécile is not described in the same terms at all. Valmont does have redeeming features denied in the novel to Mme de Merteuil, who wins her power struggle over him. She correctly sees that Valmont, in spite of what he says in protest, does indeed feel a strong emotional attraction for the présidente, whereas for herself sexual relationships involve only pleasure and power, but never emotion. She seduces Danceny, but is not in love with him. Valmont's weakness loses him the power contest, but wins him the reader's sympathy. In no way does Laclos wish us to take his parody so seriously that we believe he was really conniving with the cynicism of his principal character.

When Valmont and Mme de Merteuil begin to quarrel seriously, it is because she wishes to exercise power over him, as over everyone else with whom she comes into contact:

> Savez-vous, Vicomte, pourquoi je ne me suis jamais remariée? Ce n'est assurément pas faute d'avoir trouvé assez de partis avantageux; c'est uniquement pour que personne n'ait le droit de trouver à redire à mes actions

> (Do you know, vicomte, why I never re-married? It was certainly not for want of finding suitable partners. It was solely so that no-one would have the right to criticize my actions).

When Valmont presses her to resume their liaison, writing on 4 December, "de ce jour même je serai votre amant, ou votre ennemi (from this day forth I shall be your lover or your enemy)," she writes at the bottom of his letter "Hé bien! la guerre (All right then! war)." She shows Danceny Valmont's letters, and Danceny, knowing that Valmont has seduced Cécile, kills him in a duel on 7 December. Mme de Merteuil loses a court case and catches smallpox, losing her money, reputation, and looks all at once. Cécile becomes a nun, and Danceny goes off to Malta to take the vows of the order.

The breath-taking audacity of the character of Mme de Merteuil, her perfect lucidity, and extraordinary perceptivity have led too many historians and critics to misread the novel. Its meaning is perfectly clear, even if Laclos too easily assumed that the elements of irony and parody would not be missed, and that the character he created would not actually appear less unattractive than he intended her to be and any analysis reveals her to be. He miscalculated the public reaction of his own day. He can scarcely be blamed for what subsequent generations have made of his work. But he has been misunderstood, and the misunderstanding detracts from his achievement, which is an extremely powerful, if still amusing analysis of exactly how damaging it is to remove sentiment, emotion, and affection from sexual relationships.

PUBLICATIONS

Collections

Oeuvres complètes, Bibliothèque de la Pléiade, 1944

Fiction

Les Liaisons dangereuses; ou, Lettres recueillies dans une société et publiées pour l'instruction de quelques autres, 4 vols., 1782; in English, 1961

Other

Epître à MM de l'Académie française sur l'Eloge de M. Le maréchal de Vauban, 1786
De l'Education des femmes, 1903

Editor

Journal des Amis de la Constitution, 41 numbers, 1790–91

Biographical and critical studies

Dard, E., *Le Général Choderlos de Laclos*, 1936
Seylaz, J.-L., *Les Liaisons dangereuses et la création romanesque chez Laclos*, 1958
Delmas, A. and Y., *A la recherche des Liaisons dangereuses*, 1964
Belaval, Yvon, *Choderlos de Laclos*, 1972
Poisson, Georges, *Choderlos de Laclos; ou, L'Obstination*, 1985

LAFAYETTE, Marie-Madeleine Pioche de la Vergne, comtesse de, 1634–1693.

Novelist and memorialist.

LIFE

From its first anonymous publication in March 1678, attention has been focused on Marie-Madeleine de Lafayette's great fictional récit, *La Princesse de Clèves*, for a whole series of wrong reasons, making difficult a proper understanding of a remarkable text. Even to call it a novel is to prejudice its interpretation, since it is presented as a historical mémoire with a third-person narrator, and none of the obvious pigeon-holes, "roman," "conte," or "nouvelle," is neutral enough to avoid possibly unwarranted assumptions about its literary register. The interpretation has been controverted ever since Donneau de Visé, in the discussion that he immediately inaugurated in the *Mercure galant* (q.v.) for April 1678 and whose conclusions he summed up in the special quarterly number for October of the same year, first concentrated attention on the prudence rather than the propriety of the heroine's celebrated confession to her husband of the adulterous attraction she felt towards the duc de Nemours, who had been pursuing her and to whose advances she was afraid of yielding.

Donneau de Visé's publicity campaign in the *Mercure* stood him in good stead, but public discussion had actually ranged far more widely than might be supposed from the results of the *Mercure*'s inquiry, as we know from Jean-Baptiste-Henri du Trousset de Valincour's critical *Lettres à Madame la Marquise *** sur le sujet de "La Princesse de Clèves,"* published by Sebastien Marbre-Cramoisy in September 1678, and J.-A. de Charnes's defence of the work in the *Conversations sur la critique de "La Princesse de Clèves,"* brought out by Lafayette's own publisher, Claude Barbin, in February 1679. None the less Donneau de Visé was sufficiently good a journalist to realize how central to the interest of his cultivated salon readership was the social desirability of the confession or "aveu," and how a discussion of that issue could stimulate his circulation. Indeed, in his attempt to re-launch the flagging *Mercure*, he had printed in January a short story, "La Vertu malheureuse," containing a similar "aveu," and there had been an earlier example in Mme de Villedieu's *Les Désordres de l'amour* of 1675, which Charnes says Lafayette could not have known when she wrote her book.

Unfortunately, not enough is known about "Ménie" de Lafayette's youthful experience to make it possible to use biographical evidence to reinforce the results of purely literary analysis in establishing how far the book's central concerns actually extend, and therefore whether the ethical and psychological problems to which Lafayette explores morally and socially acceptable solutions are the focuses of its imaginative interest rather, for instance, than questions of social propriety, precious casuistry, idealized galanterie, or historical reconstitution. The text leaves so many major questions unresolved, not only those of amorous casuistry, that it is more than usually important to approach the biographical details bearing in mind both the later fictional writing itself and, since social constraints on behaviour play so obviously important a part in it, the exact social circumstances in which it was composed. In any case, Marie-Madeleine's illness in 1654, its attendant circumstances, and the psychological breakdown which may have caused or been occasioned by it, but which certainly accompanied it, marked her for life, and determined the tensions which lay behind her stoical acceptance of whatever role was thrust upon her. They explain her continuous ill health and the limits she set to her ambitions and activities, and contain the key to an understanding of her works.

Much of the mystery with which Lafayette took care to surround her writing, and which the texts themselves deliberately generated, must be explained as simple camouflage. She may have felt the need to keep any possible autobiographical inspiration for her imaginative works carefully disguised and, in doing so, she may well have chosen an anyway not unusual anonymity

and a painstakingly accurate historical setting to give the coincidences of the narrative intrigues she needed an appearance of authenticity, hoping perhaps to make up through apparent historicity what her plots lacked in inherent probability. The top dressing of renaissance court entertainment used as local colour in *La Princesse de Clèves*, some refined flirtatiousness, a sprinkling of the sort of préciosité (q.v.) which, by 1678, had been out of date for over fifteen years, and a series of digressions inherited from the great adventure novels complete the disguise. Camouflage in place, Lafayette could take to their extreme points the series of emotional problems which interested her, subjecting them, with minute precision and what turned out to be exquisite sensitivity, to psychological analysis.

The text of *La Princesse de Clèves* does not attempt to suggest any convincing resolution of the major emotional problems with which it deals. They arose, in the acute form in which they are analysed in the book, only from the clash between uncontrollable emotion and received norms of acceptable behaviour as both were experienced in cultivated French society between at the earliest 1660 and at the latest 1680, roughly during the ascendancy of Colbert, or between La Rochefoucauld's *Maximes* and Racine's *Phèdre* or Boileau's later *Epîtres*, so that the use of the renaissance setting already presupposes some element of anachronistic disguise. It looks likely that the text contains elements intended to deflect attention from speculation about the not altogether anonymous author's personal experience, that much critical comment has in consequence allowed itself to be sidetracked, and that Lafayette did not wish it to be known that her imaginative concerns 20 years later could be directly related to the build-up to her illness and breakdown in the late summer of 1654 and her subsequent marriage. Her refusal to acknowledge authorship marked a care not only for her social dignity, but also a wish not to be connected with the sense of emotional defeat which inspired her heroine's retirement from any ambition for social acclaim.

Marie-Madeleine Pioche de la Vergne was born in Paris and baptized in the church of Saint-Sulpice on 18 March 1634. Her godfather was the governor of Saumur, Urbain de Maillé-Brézé, Richelieu's brother-in-law, and her godmother Marie-Madeleine de Vignerot, Mme de Combalet, Richelieu's favourite niece, to be made duchesse d'Aiguillon in 1638. The father, Marc Pioche, sieur de la Vergne, was a mathematician and architect, first married in 1619, who in 1622 had been promoted captain in the Picardy regiment but sold his post in February 1630 to become tutor to Armand de Maillé-Brézé, the 11-year-old son of Richelieu's deceased sister, Nicole, now looked after by Mme de Combalet. A childless widower, on 5 February 1633 Marc Pioche married Isabelle Péna, lady-in-waiting to Richelieu's niece and therefore a member of the same household, at Saint-Sulpice.

Isabelle Péna was the daughter of one court doctor and the niece of another. We know of her only that she was still under 25 when she married and had high-born friends: Marguerite de Montmorency, princesse de Condé; her daughter, Anne-Geneviève de Bourbon, the future Mme de Longueville; and Julie d'Angennes, daughter of Catherine de Vivonne, marquise de Rambouillet. Two thirds of the dowry of 15,000 livres was provided by Mme de Combalet, no doubt as payment for Isabelle Péna's services as lady-in-waiting. Both bride and groom had been residing with her at the Petit Luxembourg, given to Richelieu by Marie de Médicis in 1626, and passed on by him to his niece.

They were a cultivated couple, who lived their married life in superbly elegant surroundings and had strongly intellectual interests. Marc Pioche, who left a sizeable library, undertook building works at Fontainebleau and made his fortune building houses in the Rue de Vaugirard and the Rue Férou near the Petit Luxembourg. With his wife he paid 7,000 livres on 13 April 1634 for a large piece of ground on which he built the house in which the future Mme de Lafayette grew up. She was to sell it for 45,000 livres in 1661. In 1640, her mother paid 16,500 livres for a piece of ground adjoining that which she and her husband already owned, and three times the size. Three houses were built as a speculation, and Marie-Madeleine's parents moved into one of them, together with various close relatives, mostly of her mother, who came to regard it as the family home. Mme de Lafayette was to die there.

Two sisters were born in 1635 and 1636, and the family continued to live in the shadow and under the protection of the Richelieus. When Armand de Maillé-Brézé was 17, Richelieu formed a regiment for him, putting his former tutor in charge. Marc Pioche was at Pontoise, expecting a Spanish attack, in August 1636, and sporadically saw action thereafter, from March 1639 at sea. From tutor he became adviser, perhaps part steward, to Armand, who was killed on 14 June 1646 at Orbitello at the age of 27. Meanwhile Mme Combalet entrusted Marc Pioche with the education of her own nephew, Armand-Jean de Vignerot, born in 1629 and later to become duc de Richelieu. With him, too, Marc Pioche went to sea in 1645 and, since his new charge was still a minor, exercised on his behalf the function of lieutenant-governor of Le Havre, bestowed on the boy by Richelieu before he died in 1642. Marc Pioche was at Le Havre from 1647. In September 1648 Anne of Austria left Paris for Rueil with the king and Mazarin on account of the violence in Paris announcing the outbreak of the Fronde, and in October Isabelle Péna also left Paris, presumably for either Rueil or Le Havre. Marc Pioche was promoted maréchal on 15 March 1649, shortly before he re-took Harfleur for the court against the princes. Peace was signed and the court returned to Paris. Marc Pioche stayed at Le Havre and died there in December. He was buried at Saint-Sulpice on 20 December. His eldest daughter was fifteen and a half.

On 21 December 1650, at the church of her parents' wedding, her own baptism, and her father's funeral, her mother married the cultivated 43-year-old Renaud-René de Sévigné, for 28 years a knight of Malta and therefore celibate, and an ex-officer with a distinguished military career behind him in the service of Louis XIII's sister, the regent of Savoy, Christine de France, "Madame Royale." The bride's contract was signed by the duchesse d'Aiguillon and a dozen friends from the higher aristocracy. René-Renaud's family was ancient, and Jean-François-Paul de Gondi, coadjutor bishop of Paris and the future cardinal de Retz, signed on his behalf. The groom's niece by marriage, the Mme de Sévigné who wrote the famous letters, was to boast of her husband's noble ancestry, traced for 350 years through 14 generations, and his wife was to usurp the title of marquise, actually due only to the wives of his elder brother, Charles, who in 1621 had married Marguerite de Vassé, daughter of Françoise de Gondi, and of the son of that union, Henri, whose marriage in 1644 to Marie de Rabutin-Chantal had been arranged by the future cardinal.

René-Renaud's own marriage deprived his nephew, Henri, of an inheritance on which he had come to rely. No doubt, like

Loret, who had publicly announced in his Gazette (q.v.) his expectation that René-Renaud would marry Marc Pioche's eldest daughter, Henri de Sévigné had imagined that his uncle had frequented the Rue de Vaugirard on account of Marie-Madeleine herself, not her mother. Loret, whose speculations about René-Renaud's intentions had spiced his gazette's accounts of Gondi's hopes for a cardinal's hat and the imprisonment by Mazarin of Condé and Conti at Le Havre, made the wedding his principal news item on 1 January 1651, and did not hide the daughter's sense of outrage at her new step-father's preference for her mother. In fact Marie-Madeleine's mother made over outright to her new husband, meagrely provided for by his own family, the maximum permitted amount of her wealth, should he survive her. The evidence suggests that the preference for the mother, who was perhaps 40, over the smarting 16-year-old daughter must have been connected with the financial security it entailed.

It seems to have been Marie-Madeleine's mother who decided to send her two younger daughters to become nuns in order to increase the dowry, and the chances of a brilliant marriage, for Marie-Madeleine. This probability is particularly important in view of the way in which enforced celibacy in the country, such as that imposed on her sisters in admittedly more understanding religious surroundings, has been alleged as the reason for Marie-Madeleine's illness and breakdown in 1654. The duchesse d'Aiguillon obtained for her an appointment as lady-in-waiting to Anne of Austria, the queen regent, and the wealth jointly owned by Marie-Madeleine's late father and her mother was divided on 29 March 1651 into two equal parts, of which one went to her mother and the other was to be shared between her and her two sisters, both of whom were to cede their rights to her on their religious professions, which took place later, but on dates before Marie-Madeleine's marriage on 15 February 1655. During the years between 1648 and 1655 René-Renaud wrote 97 letters, supplemented by three from his wife, reporting to Madame Royale on events in the French capital. Lafayette herself was similarly to keep informed a later regent duchess of Savoy, her friend Jeanne-Baptiste de Nemours, when her husband, Charles-Emmanuel II, died in 1675. Meanwhile, after her public embarrassment, Marie-Madeleine developed her streak of headstrong independence.

Tallemant recounts a trick played on Mlle de Chevreuse, who occasionally substituted for Gondi's regular mistress, Mme de Pommereuil, in January 1651, when Henri de Sévigné borrowed from her a pair of spectacular ear-rings, mentioned by Retz in his *Mémoires*, on the pretext that Marie-Madeleine wanted to wear them. In fact Marie-Madeleine knew nothing about it. "Lolo," the notoriously loose Mme de Gondran, with whom Henri was in love, was seen wearing them, and the fact naturally got reported back to Mlle de Chevreuse. Marie-Madeleine went along with her new cousin Henri's prank, calling on Mlle de Chevreuse to thank her for the loan. Unfortunately, Henri de Sévigné was killed by his close friend the Chevalier d'Albret in a duel concerning Mme de Gondran fought on 4 February. He died on the 6th, the day after his wife's 25th birthday. When, in June 1652, Rohan and Tonquedec were about to fight a duel over Henri's widow, Loret's *Muse historique* plainly insinuated on the 23rd that René-Renaud was in love with her.

It was in these circumstances that the 18-year-old Marie-Madeleine got to know Mme de Sévigné, called "the widow" to distinguish her from René-Renaud's wife. Banished by Henri to

Brittany, she had not had a Paris address and had stayed at the Hôtel de Retz after her husband's death, renting lodgings in Paris from November. She became a frequent visitor at the Rue de Vaugirard, came to look on Marie-Madeleine as a young sister, and was later her closest friend. It looks as though Marie-Madeleine may at this period have courted comment on her behaviour. The 39-year-old Gondi used the house to attempt in vain to break down the defences of Marie-Madeleine's friend and neighbour, to whom she had a communicating door, the 18-year-old Catherine-Henriette d'Angennes de la Louppe, whose conduct after her marriage to Louis de la Trémoille, comte d'Olonne, was later to become notorious. Guy Joly, the later intimate friend and confidant of Retz, recounts in his *Mémoires* the dalliances of the duc de Brissac, and of Retz himself, a cardinal from 1652, with Marie-Madeleine and her friend. Bussy-Rabutin's *Carte du Pays de Braquerie* makes more than insinuations in 1654 about Marie-Madeleine and Brissac, while the frequency with which her name appears in the *Gazette* suggests that Marie-Madeleine's social activities were regarded as a matter of legitimate comment in salon society.

Her mother herself received regularly, her salon being one among many which took over the less culturally demanding functions of the Hôtel de Rambouillet after the marriage of Julie d'Angennes to Montauzier in 1645 and the death of Voiture in 1648. Around December 1651 Scarron used the word "précieuse" (q.v.) of Marie-Madeleine, and on 3 April 1654 René-Renaud had explained to Christine de France who the précieuses were. It was the first time the term's usage in its semi-technical sense had been recorded. Maulévrier, a friend of Marie-Madeleine, then described the "Carte du Royaume des Précieuses," and at the end of August, the famous *Carte de Tendre* was to be printed at the front of the first volume of Madeleine de Scudéry's *Clélie*. In 1654 the word "précieuse", which had originally been used in the dignified sense of worthy of attention, endowed with developed taste and intelligence, cultivated and worthy of cultivation in the context of female emancipation from a status of total subordination to the male, was just beginning to take on its pejorative overtones denoting affected language and behaviour.

Gilles Ménage, coming like René-Renaud from Anjou and the Hôtel de Retz, had got to know Marie-Madeleine soon after her mother's re-marriage. Born in 1613, a tonsured cleric, and a poet, bridging the gap from the generation of late renaissance scholars to the "galants" of 17th-century salon society, he lived well from benefices but was never ordained. In 1650 he had published his *Dictionnaire étymologique; ou, Les Origines de la Langue française*, and continued to be well regarded and consulted by the authorities, although he had published a satire against the Académie. His poetic *Miscellanea* in Latin, Greek, and French appeared on 27 August 1652, while Marie-Madeleine—the "Amaranthe" and the "Doris" of the collection—and Mme de Sévigné were disputing his favours. Later, when Marie-Madeleine was living in the country and needed intellectual stimulation, Ménage added Italian verse addressed to her to his 1656 revised and augmented volume. Emboldened by her success with Ménage, Marie-Madeleine took the initiative in writing to Pierre Costar, the 49-year-old archdeacon of Le Mans where, after being Ménage's secretary, he had been appointed in 1652. He was a friend of Voiture although never an habitué of the Hôtel de Rambouillet.

In 1649, while Marc Pioche was leading troops for the queen regent, who fled Paris in the face of the violence of the Fronde, René-Renaud had stayed behind and remained loyal to Gondi, who gave him the command of the regiment of Corinth, named after the foreign see titularly attributed to the coadjutor, following the device ordinarily used to give bishoprics territories as a basis for their jurisdictional powers. René-Renaud was defeated and was among the 22 amnestied by name after the Peace of Rueil, and he was given a payment of 22,000 livres in January 1650. After the imprisonment of Condé, together with Condé's brother, Conti, and their brother-in-law, Longueville, in January 1650, René-Renaud was promoted in July, but Gondi's cardinalate was too long in coming, and in December 1651 Gondi sought to ally himself with the princes against Mazarin, but, having had them liberated and obtained Mazarin's flight, he then broke with them.

There was a grand moment of reconciliation on 22 August 1651 when Condé at the head of a procession crossed Gondi's path in Paris, got out of his carriage, and knelt to receive the coadjutor bishop's blessing. Gondi became the cardinal de Retz only on 19 February 1652, and in that year Condé was victorious against the king's troops in April but failed to stir the citizens of Paris to rebellion in July. On 21 October 1652 the king returned, to be followed by Mazarin in February. In the meanwhile he heard Retz preach on 1 November. Seven weeks later, on 19 December, the queen regent sent Retz to prison at Vincennes, and René-Renaud was himself exiled a few days later to his property at Champiré in Anjou. The duchesse d'Aiguillon prevented the exiling of Marie-Madeleine and her mother, but René-Renaud insisted that his wife should join him. She gave power of attorney to a friend, appointed a steward for six years to look after her affairs in Paris for 50 livres a year, and took her daughter to Anjou. Just as she was about to be 19 and might have expected to make a brilliant marriage, Marie-Madeleine found herself in bucolic exile. The presumption is that, in spite of the duchesse d'Aiguillon's protection, Marie-Madeleine's step-father's association with the disgraced Retz had for the moment ruined all prospects of the prominent social career for which she had been groomed.

The history of the Fronde and the leading personalities connected with it is in its way comic as well as complicated, although the reality was serious enough. Lives were lost, mobs were incited to riot, there were deaths from hunger, and property was pillaged. Retz braved a menacingly hostile crowd to cross the road from the Luxembourg to call on the Sévignés. For Marie-Madeleine, however, by now acquainted with the more cultivated wing of galant society, the struggle was an initiation into the realities of political life and divided loyalties. Her father had been on the side of the court. Her step-father was ineluctably associated with Retz. Condé, whose entourage was notorious for its easy-going amorous liaisons, was building a palace where the Odéon theatre now is, a short walk away from the Sévigné house, and in 1641 had married the sister of her father's first pupil, Richelieu's other niece, daughter of his sister Nicole and of Urbain de Maillé-Brézé and cousin to the duchesse d'Aiguillon. The wilful, flirtatious, and self-confident heiress had had a chance to develop intellectual self-esteem, a cultivated taste, and a precocious if still largely vicarious experience of the worlds of military expertise, amorous intrigue, and political power-broking.

Ménage had come into his inheritance and, deciding to leave Retz, moved into spacious lodgings near Notre-Dame where he was to stay until two months before his death in 1692. Meanwhile he had family business in his native Anjou, near Angers, and travelled there in February 1653 with Marie-Madeleine and her mother. Marie-Madeleine and he both retained fond memories of that journey years later. En route they stopped at Le Mans and met Costar. René-Renaud's château turned out to be thirty kilometres from Chateaubriant, on a small and badly kept estate, scarcely ever visited by its owners and officially described in 1697 as uninhabitable and not worth restoring; in 1687 it had fetched only 40,000 livres. It can scarcely have been elegant in 1653. Ménage sent Marie-Madeleine books, and she was anxious to get hold of the final volume of Madeleine de Scudéry's *Le Grand Cyrus*, with its new precious conception of love as spiritual harmony, the "tendresse" which exorcized the physical and turbulent emotional aspects of "amour." He was never a tutor to her, but he wrote to her in Italian, reported to her a quarrel with Chapelain about the meaning of a line in Petrarch, and attempted to keep her mind active. He dedicated poems to her, as well as the 1669 *Le origini della lingua italiana*.

The enforced exile threw Marie-Madeleine back on reading, French as well as Italian, and writing to her friends became her principal activity. It was on 18 September 1653, when she was 19, that she wrote to Ménage the famous sentence, "Je suis si persuadée que l'amour est une chose incommode que j'ai de la joie que mes amis et moi en soient exempts (I am so convinced that love is unpleasant that I'm glad that my friends and I are free of it)." Is that an early, impeccably précieux affectation, a glimmering perception that the turmoil of violent affection is not necessarily preferable to emotional tranquillity or, more probably, a determination to come to terms with an existence far from the interest, excitement, and civilized stimulus of the court, an early defence against the perceived inevitability of defeat? Marie-Madeleine appears to have adapted well enough to her first year of exile. Ménage came to stay in the late spring of 1653 and discussed literature with her, including Tasso's *Aminta* on which he was to publish *Observations* dedicated to Marie-Madeleine in 1655.

Retz's uncle, the archbishop of Paris, to whom Retz was coadjutor with right of succession, died on 21 March 1654. From Vincennes, in spite of royal efforts, he managed to assert his claim to the archbishopric, but he was forced by the president of the Paris parlement to trade a promise not to exercise archiepiscopal authority for financial benefits. While waiting for papal consent to the arrangement, Retz was moved in April to much easier conditions of imprisonment at Nantes where, he tells us, Marie-Madeleine failed to respond to his no doubt playful advances. René-Renaud, who lived not far away, contrived with Brissac to manoeuvre Retz's escape on 8 August, and got him to Belle-Ile, off the Atlantic coast, in spite of a fall from his horse. Retz left for a long exile in Spain on 9 September, but her step-father's role in the escape had indefinitely postponed any prospect that Marie-Madeleine might return to Paris, although neither she nor her mother were proscribed there. Ménage proposed to sound out official opinion. Marie-Madeleine thought it wiser for her to lie low for a while, in case she became officially proscribed. Her mother, dashing to Nantes in the hope of getting a passport to Belle-Ile, left her daughter first at the château de Brissac, then at Angers, ten miles to the north.

For the first time in her life Marie-Madeleine fell ill, returning home with a "fièvre tierce" and a pain in her side. The fever at first got better before turning into the longer-term "fièvre quarte." "Tierce" and "quarte" refer to peaks of high tempera-ture at 48- or 72-hour intervals, and came generally to indicate a malarial infection. It is uncertain what French country doctors might have inferred from the incidence of the troughs and peaks of fever in the mid-17th century, but the received wisdom connected the shorter cycle with impurities in the blood and the longer cycle with melancholy. The switch from one to the other indicated that an apparent infection had settled into some sort of longer-term psychological or nervous breakdown. The pain in the side was probably interpreted as deriving from the liver. Works of medicine had naturally worked out a theory of the humours by which the wasting sicknesses of young girls could be explained by the noxious retention of fluids released in married life. Three months later Marie-Madeleine was married and cured, but by the beginning of December her mother had taken her to Paris where, according to a letter of 29 November 1654, "help could be hoped for."

The physical symptoms recorded of her indisposition are such that they are unlikely even in that society to have been thought curable only by marriage. They certainly disappeared shortly after it. And not even in the mid-17th century, not even in circles much less sophisticated than those in which Marie-Madeleine de la Vergne moved, could it possibly have been supposed that the cure for the accompanying breakdown, ostensibly caused by the sudden withdrawal of all hope of return to Paris and a brilliant social life, was marriage to an elderly and ruinously indebted aristocratic widower who was totally devoted to life on his country estates. The likeliest hypothesis to explain the circumstances attending Marie-Madeleine's marriage is that she was pregnant, but this suggestion, naturally enough widespread among her contemporaries, although with what degree of scurrilously dismissive flippancy it is difficult to guess, has only recently been revived, and there is unlikely ever to be more than circumstantial evidence. There is little even of that, but perhaps enough for cautious probability.

The real problem is to know why so rich and fashionable an heiress as Marc Pioche de la Vergne's daughter was so hurriedly married off to quite so indebted a provincial aristocrat, of impeccably ancient lineage but with nothing except a name to offer. There are two real possibilities. Either it was thought that only the physical realities of marriage could cure her sudden illness and breakdown occurring when, after a gilded adolescence in the highest Parisian society, she seemed suddenly for ever condemned to exile in the country. Or, as looks suspiciously likely, she was already pregnant by someone else, so that only a hasty marriage would avoid her exclusion from the levels of society in which she could hope to move.

The letter of 29 November 1654 foresaw a departure from Champiré in about three weeks. Since the elaborate marriage contract was signed on 14 February 1655, the day before the marriage, either the five- or six-day journey to Paris was brought forward, for Marie-Madeleine and her mother to arrive during the first week of December, or the negotiations for the marriage to an as yet unchosen groom were pushed through in days. René-Renaud signed a document in Paris on 20 January, and may well have been in hiding there on the date of the wedding. The groom, François de Lafayette, was, it is true, the brother of an abbess at Rennes, and the nephew of the bishop of Limoges, who, according to Tallemant, arranged everything, but as far as we know neither Marie-Madeleine nor her mother was anywhere nearer than two days' journey from either Rennes or Limoges at any time in 1654.

François de Motier, comte de Lafayette, was born on 18 September 1616. The family, whose ancestry was traced back to the crusades, had incurred the distrust of Richelieu. Another uncle had written to the bishop of Limoges in 1638 that François was cold, reserved, and unsociable, and spoke of "the little good he has in him." In 1641 he had married an earlier lady-in-waiting to the queen regent, Sibylle d'Amalvy, and in 1644, shortly after her death, he sold his army commission and retired to the vast family estates in Auvergne and Bourbonnais, to which he inherited a threatened title on his father's death in December 1651, with the three largest estates under imminent threat of seizure for debt. Three sisters were nuns, one was married, a brother was dead, another was preparing for a military career as a knight of Malta, and the last was studying for the priesthood.

A series of extremely complex legal battles had come to a head in July 1654, by which date François badly needed to find a rich heiress, and his uncle, the bishop of Limoges, set about accomplishing the task. Marie-Madeleine, worth some 150,000 livres immediately, with almost 200,000 more to come on the death of her mother, which in fact took place at Angers on 3 February 1656, less than a year after the wedding, was suggested either by François's aunt, the reverend mother at Rennes, or by his sister, a reverend mother in Paris. Marie-Madeleine's mother wanted urgently to conclude negotiations, and Marie-Madeleine's own feelings are not recorded, although she cannot have relished a mere change of exile from Anjou to an even less exciting Auvergne. She could also eventually expect another 100,000 livres from her mother's brother. The marriage resulted in a loan of over 250,000 livres from Lafayette to her husband to free his family estates from debt, but there was no proper dowry.

The couple cannot have met before December 1654. The contract was scantily witnessed, by only one relation of the groom in person, plus a representative of the bishop of Limoges and, for the bride, the duchesse d'Aiguillon, the marquise Marie de Sévigné, an uncle and an aunt. It stipulated ratification by René-Renaud, and an inventory of the wealth of the bride before the wedding. Those documents are dated 21 and 17 February, by which dates the wedding had in fact taken place on the 15th. It must have been brought forward. The speed with which events had moved from early November is, at that date and that social level, simply stupefying. Only the belief, at least, of her mother that Marie-Madeleine was pregnant makes it credible.

When, on 27 August 1655, Lafayette wrote to Ménage from her husband's château at Espinasse, actually little more than a farmhouse with a tower, near Vichy, she joked that he would not have told Mme de Sévigné about her "couches." The ordinary way of talking about a miscarriage was to use the euphemism "se blesser (to hurt yourself)," but "couches" could mean any of miscarriage, still birth, or live birth. We know from Bussy that Paris gossiped for a long time about a liaison with Brissac, but we do not know exactly when Marie-Madeleine stayed at his château, or when he returned from Belle-Ile. By 29 November of the preceding year Marie-Madeleine was feeling seriously unwell, but she still talked about the return to Paris, which must actually have started within a day or two, as if it was still three weeks or so off.

When Mme de Sévigné wrote to her daughter in June 1671 about a similarly hurried marriage in which the groom had to pass off a healthy baby as a miscarriage, she ended that the lady was lucky: "L'enfant mourut, heureusement (The child died, luckily)." Tallemant relates in the *Historiettes* how, when Scarron told the story of a hurried marriage in which the husband could say (with Caesar) "veni, vidi, vici (I came, I saw, I conquered)," he had added that he did not know if the victory had been a bloody one. Scarron in fact published that story on 16 February 1655, the day after Marie-Madeleine's marriage, and Tallemant says it was immediately taken to allude to the Lafayette wedding. The denial a week later failed to say who the joke actually was about, if not Lafayette. When on 20 February Loret in the *Muse historique* made a joke about "La Vergne" having finished her abstinence at the beginning of Lent, he was plainly inviting his readers to believe something else.

Lafayette's mother and René-Renaud left Paris a week after the wedding. In March Lafayette and her husband set off for Auvergne. At the end of 1657 she came back to Paris to decide where to live, and though there were some months in Auvergne in 1658, from 1659 she never again lived anywhere else. Her husband, however, did come to Paris from time to time, sometimes for a month or so.

The only letters surviving from the first months of the marriage are those to Ménage. There was the confinement, or at the very least the miscarriage, and Lafayette clearly pined for a more active social life. After her mother died in February 1656 without returning to Paris, Lafayette returned to Paris with François to draw up the inventory in March. Of the two possibilities open to her, Lafayette preferred to allow her step-father the revenue from the whole of her mother's estate rather than divide the capital with him. François returned to Auvergne early in May, to be followed by his wife in mid-summer. She did not come to Paris again before the very end of 1657 or perhaps the beginning of 1658. She was bored by the provincial round of visits made and received, and took refuge again in intellectual pursuits, in the life of her imagination, in agreeable solitude, and in letter-writing. She enjoyed running her household, appears to have got on well with a husband she esteemed and who was just old enough to have been her father, and did not spend too much time dwelling on what might have been.

She did, however, languish. She had headaches, took the waters at Vichy in August 1656, drinking 14 large glassfuls every morning, and got better, on account of either the waters or the company she found at Vichy, but her health was never again robust. Ménage kept her in touch with Paris, where préciosité and galanterie were now replacing works of more polished style and learning, and sent her books, including *Clélie*, the models for whose characters she recognized, and on whose style she began to form her own. She announced the full Querelle des anciens et des modernes (q.v.) in preferring the "tendresse" and galanterie of *Clélie* to Ménage's admired Roman culture. Lafayette, and Ménage, too, began to look back with nostalgia on the journey to Anjou, the time of their greatest emotional intimacy. She avidly read Costar defending Voiture, noting none the less that his work was becoming too technical for her. Voiture had led the way in adapting erudite discussion to public understanding. Ménage, Costar, and then Pascal with *Les Lettres provinciales* were to follow suit.

Ménage's fulsome public tributes to Lafayette, as well as his private correspondence with her, reflected the closeness of their relationship and began to attract comment. Ménage began obviously to pay Lafayette more attention than he did Mme de Sévigné, and Gilles Boileau wrote a satirical poem *Avis à M. Ménage sur son églogue intitulée "Christine"* which circulated at first in manuscript and mentioned by name "Doris," recognized by everybody as Lafayette. It appeared in a signed edition only on 20 January 1656, after Ménage had attacked Boileau in the 1655 *Suite de la Défense de Voiture*, and its accusations of borrowing gave rise to a series of cultured literary games. Who could tell an original from its imitation? When did the legitimate use of standard themes lapse into plagiarism? Lafayette began indeed to see her own experience in terms of the Scudéry novels. Ménage, she complained, could not love her as he used to if he also had a mistress, as he may have had. She suspected him of turning his affection for her into a literary pose. She must have begun to learn Latin, because Ménage published Latin verse dedicated to her at the end of 1657.

René-Renaud returned to Paris from exile in December 1656, now converted to a life of piety, although he did not yet exclude re-marriage. In a new will he left what he could to the poor, and in 1659, in correspondence with Angélique Arnauld, he sought to place himself under the spiritual direction of Singlin. Lafayette's mother's brother, Gabriel Péna de Saint-Pons, twice a widower, re-married again. His new wife was twice a widow, too, with two young children. He was to die in 1659, leaving Lafayette 100,000 livres. Business affairs, including endless lawsuits, began to take up more of François de Lafayette's time, and Lafayette's own inheritance, partly in property which was let, needed administering. Her headaches got worse again, and a second cure at Vichy in the spring of 1657 did not bring as much alleviation as had the first one. When she returned to Paris she first stayed with her uncle Gabriel and then rented from her stepfather the house which would revert to her when he died, in which Mme de la Louppe had previously been her neighbour.

On 7 March 1658, her son Louis was baptized. He was left in Paris when the Lafayettes returned to Auvergne that August. A new cure at Vichy proved painful and ineffective. Then all track has been lost of Lafayette between November 1658 and March 1659, when she was in Paris, and again pregnant. Her son René-Armand was to be born there on 17 September. Meanwhile, early in the year, helped by Segrais and Huet, la grande Mademoiselle, Anne-Marie d'Orléans, duchesse de Montpensier, daughter of Gaston d'Orléans, Louis XIII's brother, and cousin of Louis XIV, had had published at Caen in a luxury edition of fewer than 60 copies, at a date when the print run might have been expected to be 500 or so, the 59 *Divers portraits* of which she herself had written 16. They were inspired by those contained in the final volumes of *Clélie*, and contained the portrait of Mme de Sévigné by Lafayette, the only published work she ever signed. There was a touch of spite in the invitation to contribute a portrait of the friend who was also the rival she had by now eclipsed in Ménage's published works. Barbin and Sercy, the Paris booksellers, riposted with a collection of as many portraits as they could get together, printing more than 500 in their *Recueil de portraits et éloges en vers et en prose*, including 21 from the *Divers portraits*.

In Paris, where Lafayette made it clear that she had come for reasons to do with the administration of her inheritance and her husband's law cases, she was, as a woman who wanted to write, virtually bound to incline towards both the side of the "modernes" in the Querelle (q.v.) and the minor literary genres, letters, portraits or, at the outside, light fiction. Even *Clélie*, although written almost wholly by Madeleine de Scudéry, was published over her brother's name. Lafayette, after Molière's *Les Précieuses ridicules* of 1659, was anxious not to show literary ambitions in public, and declined to allow Ménage to pub-

lish their correspondence. At least until the end of 1661 François was never away for long at a time, and a dispute over the succession of Gabriel Roussel, who had acted as her mother's Paris agent, added yet another lawsuit to Lafayette's business load.

1659 was the year of Lafayette's legal majority, as well as that of the death of her uncle Gabriel Péna de Saint-Pons. Within days of her birthday, receipts were signed showing the discharge of some of François's family debts. Like so many of the aristocracy with entailed estates to be passed on intact to the principal heir, François had needed to marry a wealthy heiress for ready cash. Since she was a minor, they had begun by gaining time. In the end they won some cases and lost others. François did not achieve significantly more than he required, which was time to put himself in a position to free his estates from the charges on them. In April 1661 Lafayette sold the first of the houses built by her father. The year before, René-Renaud, who was to die in 1676, had become a "solitaire" at Port-Royal de Paris (q.v.), building himself a house with Mère Agnès's permission within the precincts of the monastery, which he engaged himself to bequeath to it. With the expulsion of the community, he was to leave with them for Port-Royal-des-Champs. Lafayette moved to the house he had himself occupied, the other of those which would revert to her on his death, and where she had spent most of her youth. She did not visit Auvergne again. François left to see to his business there in September 1661, not to return until 1663, and then only for the summer. Thereafter Lafayette and her husband, dynastic provision having been made, lived virtually separate lives. Lafayette's literary coterie still largely depended on Ménage, but it soon also included both Segrais and Huet.

In 1659 the Treaty of the Pyrenees had put a final end to the Fronde as well as to the war with Spain, and in 1660 Louis XIV married the infanta Marie-Thérèse. On 31 March 1661 Louis's brother, Philippe d'Orléans, married Henriette d'Angleterre, granddaughter of Henri IV and Marie de Médicis, daughter of Henriette de France and Charles I, and sister of Charles II. Lafayette was to write the *Histoire de Madame Henriette d'Angleterre*. Henriette had been brought up by her impoverished mother, widowed by her husband's execution, at the Visitandine convent of Chaillot, founded in 1651 as a retreat for her and under the charge of François's sister, Louise-Angélique, a former platonic favourite of Louis XIII, and vice-superior before becoming reverend mother in 1655. In 1660 Henriette's fortune changed when her brother became Charles II of England. Her wedding gave her friend Lafayette an entrée to the highest circles of court and government in addition to her circle of poets and scholars. She was 27 in 1661, but Henriette was only 17, Henriette's new husband 21, and the king himself not 23 until September 1661. Mazarin had died three weeks before Henriette's wedding, and Louis XIV had decided to rule without nominating a new chief minister. The court was dominated by the distractions of youth. Lafayette accompanied the princess to Vaux on 17 August 1661 for the famous celebration given by Foucquet three weeks before his arrest. She appears not to have been invited to the dinner, perhaps on account of the hostility of Mlle de la Vallière, the favourite of Louis XIV later to become a Carmelite, but in compensation to have had a lunch arranged for her by Monsieur, Henriette's husband, a fortnight later.

Her life in Paris was dominated chiefly by her energetic social activities and her sporadically poor health, aggravated by her resigned refusal to fight it. The acceptance of defeat, or at least diminished exuberance, was the enduring result of the exile to Champiré, and the breakdown at the prospect of its indefinite prolongation after Retz's escape, which had led to her marriage. Ménage wrote news of Paris to Auvergne, and François's steward and secretary, the abbé Bayard, himself now integrated into Lafayette's Paris circle, wrote back. The close intimacy with Ménage became again intense, in a relationship that could not have survived the intrusion of the sensuality of either of them. Occasionally they read Ovid together, and Ménage tried to persuade Lafayette, recovering from a bout of dysentery, to learn Greek. Writing to Huet and Segrais in 1663, Lafayette laughed at Aeneas, so timid and devout that he should have been sent to bed, not to war, a view which was a harbinger of the 17th-century confidence in the superiority of its own refinement over the culture of Greece and Rome.

Costar died in 1660. Foucquet was disgraced in September 1661, and Pellisson, the close friend of Madeleine de Scudéry, was arrested with him, to be released only in 1666. Préciosité had become an object of satire, and by 1664 Boileau had begun to write his satires. Lafayette began to frequent the Hôtel de Nevers, the magnificent house of the financier, Henri du Plessis-Guénégaud, and his wife, Elisabeth de Choiseul-Praslin, bought in 1641 and re-designed for them by Mansart. Their salon, of which their château at Fresnes was a metaphorical extension, took over from the Hôtel de Rambouillet the onus of providing in Paris a meeting place for the aristocratic and artistic worlds. Politically discreet, it became an extremely distinguished forum for dissent, inclined against Mazarin and the court and towards the Jansenists (q.v.), rather from a spirit of independence than from spiritual conviction, although Foucquet's pro-Jesuit friends and the early defenders of the "modernes" in the Querelle were also welcome. As at the Hôtel de Rambouillet, the tone at the Hôtel de Nevers and at Fresnes could be light-hearted.

On 27 July 1662 Ménage's publisher, Thomas Billaine, took out a privilège for *La Princesse de Montpensier*, immediately selling it on to Thomas Jolly and Louis Billaine, who cut in Charles Sercy, so justifiably confident of success were the three book-sellers. The work appeared on 20 August. Its author, for whom anonymity was socially essential, was 28. A copy had been stolen before publication and shown to a score of people. It was perhaps that incident which led to publication in the first place. Lafayette immediately alerted Ménage to see to it that any rumour about her authorship was scotched, thereby acknowledging it in a letter we know about, and she was annoyed with Huet for allowing his sister to learn she had written it, as if she had been "un auteur de profession (a professional writer)." Literary esteem was in fact beginning to be more highly prized, although not yet seriously at the expense of birth or of social rank acquired through marriage. No great French authors before Malherbe had regarded themselves as professional literary figures in the imaginative genres, any more than Erasmus had. Lafayette owed her social acceptability to her marriage, and she was not going to compromise it, although by the mid-17th century interest in the literary world was perceptibly increasing outside it. Lafayette was proud of her book, but as a literary exercise. Manuscript copies have survived. Lafayette had the text heavily rectified by Ménage.

It was probably the close collaboration on the text of *La Princesse de Montpensier*, causing Ménage to press too strongly against the rules imposed by Lafayette, as she sharply recalled

to him, rather than her jealous need to monopolize his public attentions, which was at the root of their rupture, not complete until 1666, and never culminating in much more than an affected sulk as Ménage withdrew to his learned work and Lafayette abandoned her own further education, speaking ceaselessly of her natural "paresse (laziness)." Lafayette had by then used of him the word "serviteur," twisting its meaning to signify not the male role in a stylized intimacy, but employee, which Ménage never was. He was, at the end, increasingly jealous of La Rochefoucauld's growing ascendancy over Lafayette.

She had appeared in Somaize's 1661 *Grand Dictionnaire des Précieuses*, and from 1662 to 1666 became closer still to Mme de Sévigné, who was then dividing her time between Paris and Livry. Lafayette also spent time both at Fresnes, where she was jestingly known as Amalthée and even referred to as the nymph of the Allier, the river which flows through the Auvergne, and with Henriette d'Angleterre. She got to know Mme de Maintenon, Gourville, Langlade, the abbé Testu and, later, Bossuet. She was a member of the party of Monsieur and Madame when they were entertained by Condé at Villers-Cotterets in 1663, and accompanied Henriette to Versailles for the first big celebration held there in May 1664. She continued to write, sometimes showing what she had done to Ménage, sometimes having copies made to be handed round, which was as far as many of those writing for salon audiences ever went, and in the end having a few texts published. It must be remembered that it was only the hazard of a leaked copy of La Rochefoucauld's *Maximes* which led to that work's publication.

To some extent Huet replaced Ménage as Lafayette's intellectual mentor. Segrais came back to Paris after Mademoiselle's exile to Saint-Fargeau from October 1662 to spring 1664 for having refused to marry the king of Portugal. Lafayette may well have met La Rochefoucauld before Champiré and almost certainly did so in 1656. Their friendship, however, dates from not much earlier than 1661, by which date they must have been meeting one another at the Hôtel de Nevers. Lafayette was one of those asked to comment on the manuscript of the *Maximes* circulated in 1663, which she discussed with Mme Du Plessis-Guénégaud at Fresnes. She wrote with feigned shock in reply to Mme de Sablé's request, "Ha, Madame! quelle corruption il faut avoir dans l'esprit et dans le coeur pour être capable d'imaginer tout cela (Oh! Madame, what a corrupted heart and mind you have to have to be capable of thinking up all that)." Mme de Sablé may well have felt that Lafayette was making too great demands on La Rochefoucauld's time.

After Foucquet's fall Henri de Guénégaud's brother Claude was imprisoned, in April 1663. He was finally pardoned, at the instigation of Turenne and in spite of Colbert, in 1667, but Henri was also fined 600,000 livres, and in 1669 had to resign as secretary of state and sell both the château at Fresnes and the Hôtel de Nevers. Lafayette lost the ordinary forum for her meetings with La Rochefoucauld. None the less, it was through him that drafts and sketches for *Zaïde* were passed round for comment. Mme de Sablé was consulted, and Huet commented well before there was a finished draft to correct. First, the plot was invented, intrigue and sentiments, then the form discussed, and several versions produced before a final draft was passed for correction and revision. Huet's *Traité de l'origine des romans*, dedicated to Segrais, prefaced the first volume of *Zaïde, histoire espagnole, par Monsieur de Segrais* on its publication by Claude Barbin in November 1669, with the printed date of 1670. Segrais does in fact seem chiefly to have been responsible for the plan, the order of events, and the stages of the intrigue.

In 1670 Lafayette was with Henriette d'Angleterre when, just back from a diplomatic mission to her brother, Charles II, she suddenly became ill and died on 29 June. Lafayette had been with her the preceding night at Saint-Cloud and subsequently spent the day talking to her. It was a third blow. She had broken with Ménage, the Hôtel de Nevers had closed, and now Henriette was dead. Lafayette now had only her friendship with La Rochefoucauld to rely on. He was 56 and her relationship with him was quite different from that with Ménage, although it was also, like Mme de Sévigné's for her daughter, an outlet for affectivity that did not involve physical passion. It was based on trust and confidence, more a working partnership resting on an intellectual community of ideas, interests, and tastes than had been the "tendresse" of the earlier relationship.

The second part of *Zaïde*, showing obvious signs of carelessness, appeared at the beginning of January 1671. Segrais, dismissed by Mademoiselle for interfering with her arrangements to receive Lauzun, whom she finally succeeded in marrying, crossed the road, staying in Lafayette's household until he returned home to a rich marriage to a Norman cousin in 1676. Lafayette was not only repaying the man of letters who had signed *Zaïde*, but also establishing her position in the face of Mademoiselle's protection of Cotin, whose *Ménagerie* had attacked her old friend. Furthermore, it was in Segrais's favour that he had lost his position by attempting to further the interest of Longueville, the illegitimate son of La Rochefoucauld. He lived to be nearly 77, calling on Lafayette whenever he came to Paris. Lafayette was now regularly receiving La Rochefoucauld with a small select band of other friends: Mme de Sévigné, to whom she was very close, Mme de Schomberg, Mme de Brissac, since 1663 the wife of the Brissac at whose château in Anjou the young Marie-Madeleine had stayed, and Condé's son, the duc d'Enghien. Lafayette returned the visits of the Condés, and went to Chantilly to stay with them. She did not belong to the court, preferring to receive chosen friends at home, but was invited to Versailles and shown round the gardens with other ladies by Louis XIV.

The duc de Longueville and another son of La Rochefoucauld were both killed, and a third wounded, in June 1672. The news was brought to him at the house of Lafayette, whose health was deteriorating again. It was in this atmosphere of ill health and sadness that the *Princesse de Clèves* was conceived. Barbin had registered on 4 January 1672 a collective privilège of 18 December 1671 for *Le Prince de Clèves*, *Béralde* and *Les Nouvelles Oeuvres du sieur Le Pays*. An anonymous *Béralde, prince de Savoie* did in fact appear in 1672. Barbin was hoping to get a new novel from Lafayette. It took him six years, and the secret was well kept, except by Mme de Sévigné who tossed off a remark in a letter to her daughter of 16 March 1672 about "that hound Barbin's" lack of assiduity in fulfilling her orders because she does not write him "des *Princesses de Clèves* et *de Montpensier*." The manuscript of the letter has not survived, and we do not know how the Prince of the privilège became the Princess of the letter, but what had happened is clear. Barbin had extracted by December 1671 some sort of promise from Lafayette to write a *Prince(sse) de Clèves*. A chance remark of Mme de Sévigné two and a half months later, using the phrase "derrière une palissade (behind a palissade)," may just possibly have referred to a key scene in the book. Lafayette began to spend

some of her time at Saint-Maur in a small country house belonging to the Condés but at the disposal of Jean Hérault de Gourville, now their financial manager, where there was always a room for La Rochefoucauld, whose family Gourville had earlier served before sharing Foucquet's disgrace.

Lafayette moved between town and country, fatigued by business but unable to put up with more than short periods of solitude. She liked to have her children with her, needed friends who would support her and keep her in touch but not tire her out, and she would have liked more influence than she had. She had access to the court through Mme de Thianges, who was close to Mme de Sévigné, and Mme de Thianges's sister Mme de Montespan, mother of seven of Louis XIV's children, and she acquired for her elder son one of the benefices resigned by the ailing bishop of Limoges, her husband's uncle. Louis de Lafayette had two benefices before he was 18. Louis XIV was always courteous to the mother, who came to thank him. In the same year, 1675, Charles-Emmanuel de Savoie died, and Lafayette began her correspondence with her friend, Madame Royale, his widow and now regent of Savoy. She began to show an interest in and an aptitude for intrigue, engineering the suppression of a printed attack on Madame Royale, *Les Amours de Madame Royale*, in spite of her friend's habit of taking and then discarding young lovers.

Lafayette passed on information about Versailles, pressed Madame Royale's policies with Louvois, furthered France's alliance with Savoy against the Netherlands and Spain, in spite of the new duke's desire to reverse his mother's policy, and later admitted to Ménage that political intrigue interested her more than literary composition. Throughout the winter of 1675–76 Lafayette was again in poor health. In 1676 both René-Renaud and Henri du Plessis-Guénégaud died, on 16 March, and then, on 3 May, at the age of 86, the bishop of Limoges. Lafayette now had full possession of what her mother had left, but she had no-one whose function it was to help her write.

Huet was busy as assistant tutor to the dauphin. Even before 1676 Segrais, in spite of the help he had given with *Zaïde*, did little to encourage Lafayette, unwell, busy, and preoccupied with her personal problems, to settle down to work on her current novel and, once he was gone, La Rochefoucauld's interests can have encouraged her only to reflect on portraits and insights about motivation. Segrais is unlikely to have done more than help Lafayette with the setting, perhaps directing her reading on the court of Henri II. Unlike that of Segrais and Huet, La Rochefoucauld's culture was not classical but modern, and he was neither a scholar nor a professional writer, but at home only in the witty and intimate atmosphere of the salon. He did not help in the process of composition. Lafayette's own inspiration for the *Maximes* does not date from the earlier editions, but only from those of 1671, 1675, and 1678, that is from the period when La Rochefoucauld was seeing her daily.

By the beginning of December 1677 the existence of the *Princesse de Clèves* was being talked about, and publication excitedly awaited. Copies had certainly been circulating. The book was a success before it was ever published. On 16 January 1678 Barbin, who had published Mme de Villedieu's *Les Désordres de l'amour* in the meanwhile, probably in 1675, took out a new privilège with the new name to prevent a pirate edition. It was probably to increase public anticipation that he waited until 17 March to put the book anonymously on sale. That July Barbin took out a privilège for a new edition of the *Maximes*, which went on sale the same month. By then Lafayette was again unwell. Mme du Plessis-Guénégaud died on 9 August, and François's companion, Bayard, on 26 September in the Rue de Vaugirard, while Lafayette was at Saint-Maur. After 1677 that retreat was closed to her by Gourville, who formalized the arrangement with the Condés by which he had exclusive rights to it. Mme de Maintenon and others were beginning to find her friendship too exigent, and friends remarked on a certain pretentiousness. The work for Savoy may have been productive of income.

Lafayette now spent time and energy acting on behalf of the regent of Savoy. At the end of August 1679 Retz died. Lafayette's second son was rapidly promoted in the army and, with the help of Louvois, got his own regiment at the age of 23. He was to die at Landau in 1694, just before his 35th birthday. Lafayette's relations with Louvois, the minister in charge of the army, seem to have been particularly close. Meanwhile, in 1679, her elder son, Louis, received his third benefice, although he had not taken orders nor finished his studies. La Rochefoucauld's health was now weakening, and he died on 16 March 1680, with Bossuet in attendance. Mme de Sévigné thought that Lafayette would herself never recover. She underestimated her friend's resilience. Lafayette had previously been reduced to a diet of nothing but milk, and survived. She grieved for La Rochefoucauld, and she never again experienced the support he had given her, but she recovered, and went on accommodating herself, if with an intensified feeling of defeat, to whatever life had to offer.

Her husband died in 1683. He had continued from time to time to come to Paris, but the marriage had for 21 years been conducted as a business relationship carried on in an entirely friendly manner. Lafayette's interest in music and painting developed. She admired Lulli, disliked Quinault's verse, was in relations with Piere Mignard, and had an unusual appreciation of landscape, her favourite being that of Chantilly. She continued to act somewhat obtrusively as an intermediary between Savoy and the French court. In November 1686 she wrote the first of a number of letters to Armand-Jean le Bouthillier de Rancé, whose fierce spirituality had dictated the reform at La Trappe, fashionable but extremely austere, and for those not robust in body and unusually stable in mind frankly dangerous. Rancé tempered the tone and rigour of his spiritual advice according to the addressees of his correspondence, correctly regarding Lafayette as, in the strict sense, unconverted, still turned towards worldly interests, but unfulfilled by their satisfaction. He discerned her unassuaged quest for the "repos (peace)" he had not himself found in the world, but also the need Lafayette shared with her own Princesse de Clèves for compromise, the need for a "repos" that fell short of true conversion.

Rancé was not a theologian, but even his spirituality was based on premises quite different from those of the Jansenists, and indeed incompatible with them. Rancé required great efforts of will from his monks, his penitents, and his correspondents, which would have been pointless for those who adopted all but the most attenuated forms of Jansenist spirituality. It is only barely possible to reconcile Rancé's spiritual teaching with that even of Nicole, and it is not obvious that his advice inspired any noticeable change of attitude in Lafayette. She was naturally also well acquainted with Port-Royal, where René-Renaud had retired, and with its spirituality, which attracted Mme de Sévigné and others with whom Lafayette was or had been friendly, like Mme de Sablé. She admired the *Pensées* of Pascal.

Lafayette's health occasionally weakened sufficiently to arouse fears for her survival, and periods of relative good health became diminishingly frequent. On 10 December 1689 her second son, René-Armand, married into one of the highest families of the magistrature, the "noblesse de robe." Anne-Madeleine de Marillac brought him a dowry of 200,000 livres. René-Armand, belonging to the socially more highly esteemed military nobility, the "noblesse d'épée," would inherit all his mother's wealth, his elder brother, the abbé, having ceded to him his share in the patrimony. Lafayette had held back a small capital sum to dispose of in her will as she chose. One of her sisters, an Ursuline at Valençay, was still alive, and 60 livres a year was left so that if necessary she could be cared for. Lafayette's self-imposed tasks, the restoration of her husband's lands and the settling of her two sons, were completed by 1689.

In July 1691 Louvois, who had continued to protect her faithfully, died suddenly. That September a granddaughter was born. On 2 February 1692 Lafayette added to her will a codicil mentioning by name her six domestic staff. Relations with Ménage had been resumed in 1684 after he had had a fall, and were again to grow familiar before his death on 23 July 1692. Towards the end he enabled her to take a new interest in life. On 30 March 1693 René-Armand was made a brigadier. She saw him for the last time in May. Her elder son was accompanying cardinal de Janson to Rome on a diplomatic mission. On 21 May, with her health no worse than usual, she confessed, communicated, and made the devotions she usually kept for Pentecost. The next day she fell into a coma, and on 25 May she died. A post mortem showed that her ailments had been real and protracted. She was buried at Saint-Sulpice on 27 May 1693.

WORKS

In 1656 Jean Regnault de Segrais, in the service of Mlle de Montpensier since 1648, anonymously published a volume containing six short stories, *Les Nouvelles françaises; ou, Les Divertissements de la princesse Aurélie*. Segrais affected to be only the corporate secretary of the six ladies, Mademoiselle and five others, who, assembled at the château de Six-Tours (Saint-Fargeau), had recounted the stories. It was he who was to lend his name to *Zaïde* and he was to be elected to the Académie française in 1662. The narrative style of his collection was conversational and he put into the mouth of Aurélie the definition of the difference between the "roman [qui] écrit les choses comme la bienséance le veut et à la manière du poète (novel [which] describes things as propriety demands and in the manner of a poet)" and the "nouvelle [qui] doit un peu davantage tenir de l'histoire et s'attacher plutôt à donner les images des choses comme d'ordinaire nous les voyons arriver que comme notre imagination se les figure (short story [which] should be rather more like history and strive to present things as we ordinarily see them happen rather than as our imagination pictures them)."

The age of the long novels of adventure and chivalry, as practised by Madeleine and Georges de Scudéry and La Calprenède, was over, but it would be mistaken to see in Segrais's fictional character's words a new "theory," first put into practice by Lafayette. Like so many of the great writers of classical French literature, however interesting their work—her friends Mme de Sévigné and La Rochefoucauld, for instance, and even to some extent Racine—she was an amateur. What literary theory there was derived not from theoretical assumptions, but from practical criticism, public comment, the increasing expertise of the gazettes, and private discussions. Lafayette, forced back on her imagination by life at Champiré, and encouraged by Ménage to read modern poetry and novels, the modern Italians and, with less success, the classics, enjoyed writing letters and gradually turned her hand from stylized or disguised accounts of real events to a more consistent fictionalization of real experience.

The essential change in French narrative prose writing came in the last volume of *Le Grand Cyrus*, when the emphasis moved away from the adventure story towards the analysis of cultivated, refined sentiment. The baroque exuberance represented by François de Sales in spirituality, Descartes in philosophical ambition, and Pierre Corneille in the glorification of instinctive love justified by the merit of its object needed, by the middle of the century, to be replaced by an increasingly realistic type of imaginative investigation. Among the avenues in which satisfaction for that need was sought were the tragedies of Racine, the literary canons of Boileau, the balanced prose of Pascal, and the prose fictions of Lafayette. There were four of them.

La Princesse de Montpensier, written under the guidance of Ménage and published through his mediation, appeared in 1662, after Segrais's *Nouvelles françaises*, but before any other important 17th-century work bearing on the history or criticism of narrative fiction, excepting only Georges de Scudéry's preface to *Ibrahim* of 1641 concerning the adventure novel, and Chapelain's dialogue *La Lecture des vieux romans* of 1647, limited to a discussion of the genre in the middle ages. Lafayette's text presents the narrative as history, in a renaissance setting with real characters, even if it places an amorous intrigue during the reign of Charles IX at the centre of the wars of religion. Sorel, in *La Bibliothèque française* of 1664, immediately suspected that the setting camouflaged a contemporary episode, although he did not name the characters alluded to. No convincing identification has been found, although Lafayette's contemporaries were not wrong to find the emotional intrigue of more relevance to their own society than to that of the renaissance wars.

Mlle de Mézières, the historical daughter of Nicolas d'Anjou, born in 1550 and aged 16 when the narrative begins, was a rich heiress, showing "les commencements d'une grande beauté (the beginnings of great beauty)," who had been promised to the duc du Maine, the 12-year-old younger brother of the duc de Guise who, seeing her frequently, "en devint amoureux et en fut aimé (fell in love with her and was loved in return)." However, for political reasons, she was married in 1566 to François de Bourbon, who became duc de Montpensier in 1582, on the eve of the second civil war, consenting, according to the narrator, partly because she feared being married to the younger brother of someone she loved and who loved her. A hatred sprang up between Guise and Montpensier "which ended only with their lives." The text suggests resignation in the face of inevitability:

Ils cachèrent leur amour avec beaucoup de soin. Le duc de Guise...souhaitait ardemment de l'épouser; mais la crainte du cardinal de Lorraine, qui lui tenait lieu de père, l'empêchait de se déclarer...Mlle de Mézières, tourmentée par ses parents d'épouser ce prince [de Montpensier], voyant d'ailleurs qu'elle ne pouvait épouser le duc de Guise et connaissant par sa vertu qu'il était dangereux d'avoir pour beau-frère un homme qu'elle eût souhaité pour mari, se résolut enfin de suivre le sentiment de ses proches et conjura M. de Guise de ne plus apporter d'obstacle à son mariage

(They hid their love with great care. The duc de Guise ardently wanted to marry her, but his fear of the cardinal de Lorraine, who took the place of a father for him, prevented him from declaring himself...Mlle de Mézières, harried by her parents to marry this prince [de Montpensier], seeing, too, that she could not marry the duc de Guise, and knowing by her virtue that it was dangerous to have for a brother-in-law someone she would rather have had for a husband, finally resolved to follow the wishes of her family, and begged M. de Guise to put no further obstacle in the way of her marriage).

She therefore marries in resignation and without love, but is determined to make as much of a success of it as she can. To escape Paris, threatened by Huguenot armies, Montpensier takes her to the family château at Champigny, where she is looked after by a much older friend of his "d'un mérite extraordinaire (of extraordinary merit)," an invented character called Chabanes.

The Princesse confides in Chabanes who, from admiring her sincerity, "devint passionnément amoureux de cette princesse (fell passionately in love with the princess)." Nobody, however, suspects, and he successfully hides his passion for a full year before declaring it, expecting "to incur the storms with which the pride of the princess threatened him." She is not even angry, points to the differences in their rank and age, recalls that he knows about both her virtue and her love for Guise, and reminds him of all he owes to the friendship and trust of her husband, who protected him from arrest as an ex-ally of Condé whose conversion Catherine de Médicis had thought suspect. Chabanes is resigned but desolate. The Princesse tries to console him, "assuring him that she would never remember what he had just said, that she would never convince herself of anything so damaging to him, and that she would never look on him except as her best friend." "Il sentit le mépris des paroles de la princesse dans toute leur étendue (He felt the contempt of the princess's words in all its depth)."

Montpensier returns from the wars covered with glory, finds his wife's beauty in full blossom and, "par le sentiment d'une jalousie qui lui était naturelle, il en eut quelque chagrin, prévoyant bien qu'il ne serait pas seul à la trouver belle (with a feeling of jealousy natural to him, he felt some pain, foreseeing that he would not be the only one to find her beautiful)." When war breaks out again, Chabanes accompanies Montpensier. In what reads almost like a throwback to the pastoral, except that the realism of the psychological analysis is much sharper, subtler, and more nuanced than anything in *L'Astrée*, the king's brother, the duke of Anjou, leads a party including Guise to inspect fortifications, gets lost, finds the Princesse de Montpensier and others in a boat, and gets given a lift with Guise across the river. Montpensier is not pleased to see his wife bring Anjou and Guise to Champigny and neither, naturally, is Chabanes.

Anjou looks on the Princesse as a potential conquest, but comes very near falling in love with her and, after the departure of Anjou and Guise, Montpensier feels most uneasy about what had happened. The scene of the fighting has moved, and it now seems expedient to Montpensier to bring his wife to Paris. Anjou remains strongly attracted to her, and Guise finds an occasion to declare his passion, only to be interrupted by Montpensier, who forbids his wife ever again to speak to Guise. At court a mistake at a masked dance reveals to Anjou Guise's secret passion, and leads Guise to demonstrate his passion for the Princesse by abandoning a projected marriage to Marguerite de Valois, daughter of Henri II and Catherine de Médicis, and future wife of Henri de Navarre, later to become Henri IV. Chabanes, in spite of the inner outrage he feels, allows letters from Guise to the Princesse to be sent through him. She does not even show "reconnaissance (gratitude)" towards him, treating him roughly when he does ask for considerateness, and reading to him Guise's letters to her.

In the end Guise sends an urgent note via Chabanes to Champigny, and Chabanes arranges for him to be admitted secretly to the Princesse's room at midnight. Montpensier hears a noise, is suspicious, and is told that the drawbridge is down. Chabanes, who has been waiting nearby while the Princesse received Guise, realizing that Montpensier would certainly kill Guise and possibly the Princesse, too, "se résolut, par une générosité sans exemple, de s'exposer pour sauver une maîtresse ingrate et un rival aimé (resolved, with unparalleled magnanimity, to endanger himself to save a woman he was spurned by and the rival she loved)." When Montpensier breaks in, he finds an anguished but enigmatic Chabanes and a half-fainting wife. Chabanes offers Montpensier his life, Montpensier tells him to take it himself or explain, the Princesse faints, Chabanes escapes to Paris, and is killed by mistake two days later in the St Bartholomew's Day massacre of 24 August 1572. Guise forgets about the Princesse and falls in love with the marquise de Noirmoutier. The Princesse dies of sorrow at losing "l'estime de son mari, le coeur de son amant et le plus parfait ami qui fut jamais (the respect of her husband, the heart of her lover, and the most perfect friend who ever lived)." There is a moral. She was

> une des plus belles princesses du monde, et...aurait été sans doute la plus heureuse, si la vertu et la prudence eussent conduit toutes ses actions
>
> (one of the most beautiful princesses in the world, and would doubtless have been the happiest, if virtue and prudence had guided all her actions).

The interest of the text does not lie in a plot so improbable that the jealous Montpensier can simply forget that he was told the drawbridge was down, or in the reconstitution of an amorous intrigue during the wars of religion, but in the refined subtlety of its psychology, and incidentally in the aptness of the vocabulary used to communicate the meticulously precise analysis of emotion. If the Princesse and Guise recognize one another before the other members of their respective parties when they meet in the middle of the river, or if Montpensier is so sensitive to the effect his wife has on Guise, it can only be because love, whether or not reciprocated, sharpens perceptive powers. The date of 1662, five years before Racine's *Andromaque*, is very early indeed to find such acute observation in a French text, although by this time properly précieux (q.v.) forms of communication and deportment had passed their peak as a serious subject of cultural discussion.

The realistic, often apparently cynical, analysis of human behaviour was taking its place in cultivated and intelligent, if still determinedly amateur, circles of debate. However, it is not important that Lafayette may well have come first in isolated feats of psychological acuity. What is important is that their innovativeness and profusion demonstrate an impressive imaginative power which is locked into Lafayette's texts, even when the psychology itself looks out-dated or commonplace, or the social norms productive of the dilemmas have changed. Lafayette's imaginative strength, concentrated in the meticulous psychological analysis of emotions which the intrigues merely precipitate, can perhaps be calibrated in terms of their originality, but is constituted not by mere novelty, which can be overtaken, but by an intellectual vigour of which her best work cannot be deprived by any subsequent event.

By 1662 some of the key terms were familiar. The justification of instinctive affection by reference to the merit of their object had been commonplace since du Vair and d'Urfé. Instinctive affection, love, based on esteem and gratitude, had featured in the Carte de Tendre from *Clélie*'s first volume. By 1662 the need for polite dissimulation, "hypocrisy," and the dangers of sincerity, leading to "médisance (back-biting)," and jealousy, were being quite widely examined, not least by Molière. Disinterested love had taken on a new significance in the context of discussions about the nature of charity much earlier in the century. The word "tendre" was itself largely discredited by 1662. But these were the words, together with such others as "amour," "amitié," "repos," heart, passion, merit, virtue, prudence, empire, which Lafayette had at her disposal. To achieve her penetration into the psychology of passion, she is forced to enrich her analysis by establishing, for instance, the physiological effects of different sorts of strong emotional experience, or the parallel destruction wreaked by war and love, established in the opening sentence, "While civil war was tearing France apart in the reign of Charles IX, love did not fail to find its place among so many disorders and to cause many in its own realm."

There is, for instance, throughout the *Princesse de Montpensier* a powerful moral comment implicit in the adverse effect of various emotional states on physical health. The princesse dies of "douleur (sorrow)." The repression of emotion is more damaging to the female than to the male characters. Chabanes survives an emotional torment that would, in Lafayette's world, have killed the Princesse. Female sensitivity is beginning to reflect spiritual superiority over the merely physical strength which scarcely elevates the male without emotional refinement and intellectual cultivation above the animal kingdom. No doubt there are too many adverbs. "Extremely," "extraordinarily," "violently," "ardently," "unbelievably," "passionately," go hand in hand with a whole catalogue of adverbial phrases of intensity, but the fine analysis of emotional reactions is nevertheless the heart of the text, and the source of an astonishingly powerful imaginative innovativeness. The *Princesse de Montpensier* has no digressions. It is a unified short masterpiece of analytic psychological fiction. Its tone, however, while still strongly affirming the ennobling effects of instinctive, natural affection, is defeatist. Love can be instantaneous, irresistible, and unconcealable. Its pressure on behaviour can be overwhelmingly strong. There is no remedy for a virtuous woman who loves outside her marriage. The *Princesse de Clèves* will go on to question whether there is any prospect of happiness even if love occurs within marriage. Lafayette's investigations into the mechanics of emotional happiness within prescribed social norms are not encouraging.

Zaïde, histoire espagnole, par Monsieur de Segrais owes its general conception and outline more to Segrais than to anyone else. "Il est vrai que j'y ai eu quelque part, mais seulement pour la disposition du roman, où les règles de l'art sont observées avec grande exactitude (It is true that I had some hand in it, but only for the plan of the novel, in which the rules of the art are observed with the greatest fidelity)." By the use of long, interpolated first-person accounts of what has happened in the past, the events of the novel itself are in fact successfully crammed into a relatively short time. Huet planned the content of the individual scenes and revised the final text at least twice. La Rochefoucauld contributed occasional pages, and submitted sketches and drafts to Mme de Sablé and her friends for their opinions. D'Aubignac had published his *Macarise* and the *Conjectures académiques* in 1664, demanding greater realism than in the adventure novels, and turning away from the purely historical. In the same year Sorel had published his *Bibliothèque française*, and Boileau's *Dialogue des Héros de roman* was circulating in manuscript. Everything was moving the novel in the direction of greater probability and psychological realism.

Lafayette was responsible for the novel's original conception, and she wrote the text. It is, however, a compromise. Huet and Segrais had quarrelled about the interpretation of a passage of Virgil, and their relationship had become embittered by 1669, but Lafayette did not wish to dispense with Huet's erudition or Segrais's more fashionable literary abilities. The *Traité sur l'origine des romans* by Huet, a supporter of the "anciens" in the famous "Querelle," in fact defends the old style of adventure novel, and had been published separately some time between 1666 and its appearance as a preface to the first volume of *Zaïde* in 1669. The text itself is a mixture of analysis of sentiment and novel of adventure, with mistaken identities, storms, shipwrecks, duels, disguises, and intercepted letters.

The scene is set in ninth-century Spain, of which Lafayette will have learnt from Mariana's history of Spain, translated into French before the end of the previous century, and from Marmol's *L'Afrique*, published in a posthumous translation by Nicolas Perrot d'Ablancourt in 1667. The novel opens with a purely historical paragraph and then, in the second, introduces among authentically historic counts of Castille the central character, Consalve, whose mind and bearing are so remarkable that "il semblait que le ciel l'eût formé d'une manière différente du reste des hommes (it seemed as if heaven had made him in a different way from the rest of humanity)." "Des raisons importantes (important considerations)" have made him leave Castille. He wants to seek solitude on a Greek island, gets lost, finds a port in Catalonia, discovers that all the boats are away fishing until the next day, and meets a recluse of whom we only later learn that his name is Alphonse Ximénès of Navarre. They immediately recognize in each other a nobility of deportment, and instantly perceive each other's sadness. Consalve stays with the recluse.

The paragraphs are shorter than those of *La Princesse de Montpensier*, but by the seventh Consalve and Alphonse are engaged in a long discussion about whether it is worse to know that you are to blame for your own misfortune or to have had it inflicted by the treachery of someone you loved. By the end of the twelfth paragraph, the scene has been set. "Voilà donc Consalve établi dans cette solitude avec la résolution de n'en sortir jamais; le voilà abandonné à la réflexion de ses malheurs… (There then is Consalve settled in that solitude with the determi-

nation never to leave it; there he is, given over to meditation upon his misfortunes)." We are ready for the first episode.

Late in autumn there is a storm, a shipwreck, wreckage on the shore, and there, lying on the sand, Consalve sees "une femme magnifiquement habillée (a magnificently clad woman)" of "la plus grande beauté qu'il eût jamais vue (the greatest beauty he had ever seen)." She turns out to be Zaïde, and an equally well clad and beautiful woman, Félime, is discovered further along the beach by some fishermen. Consalve falls instantaneously in love with Zaïde and, on finding her in tears, is jealous of the lover for whom he supposes she is weeping, without ever having known that he was in love: "la jalousie seule m'a fait sentir que j'étais amoureuse (only the feeling of jealously made me aware that I was in love)." Consalve's reserve is now easily enough broken down by Alphonse, and he tells the story of his disillusion and his thwarted love for Nugna Bella, who let him down out of ambition. Alphonse's view of his merit and virtue has been increased. Consalve had tried to communicate with Zaïde in Arabic, Spanish, and Italian without success. The point is made that love transcends linguistic forms of communication, and that Consalve's view that love must be based on knowledge and esteem was wrong. Don Garcie, son of the king of Leon, has held against Consalve that love must strike immediately:

si je ne suis surpris d'abord, je ne puis être touché. Je crois que les inclinations naturelles se font sentir dans leurs premiers moments; et les passions, qui ne viennent que par le temps, ne se peuvent appeler de véritables passions

(if I am not immediately struck, I cannot be touched. I believe that natural inclinations are felt in their first moments, and that passions which develop only with time cannot be called true passions).

The text contains various interpolated "histoires," narratives of the adventures of Consalve, but also of Alphonse and Bélasire, turning on the dangers of jealousy, of Don Garcie and Hermenesilde, of Zaïde and Félime, and of Alamir, prince of Tharsis, who, no doubt as a concession to Huet, addressed Zaïde and Félime in their own language, Greek, 'avec toute la politesse de l'ancienne Grèce (with all the courtesy of ancient Greece)." The lack of refinement in the manners of the ancient Greeks was to be one of the focuses of the arguments of the "modernes" in favour of the superior elevation of their own sophisticated values, particularly in the way women were treated.

Alamir offers yet another lesson in love. He can love only when his love is unrequited, "Je n'ai pu aimer toutes celles qui m'ont aimé: Zaïde me méprise et je l'adore (I have never been able to love all those who loved me. Zaïde spurns me, and I adore her)." Alamir dies from wounds, having been spared after defeat by Consalve when he returned to Leon. Félime dies of unfulfilled love for Alamir. Zaïde turns out to be a Christian, Consalve to be the subject of the portrait Zaïde's father has sworn that she will wed, and the main story, the love of Consalve and Zaïde, ends happily with their marriage. *Zaïde* therefore is a composite work, with adventure narratives bunched together like a collection of loosely inter-connected short stories with a central love interest, some penetrating psychological observation, and meticulously precise descriptions of emotional states, their causes, effects, and the unhappiness they can cause. As a literary text it suffers chiefly because too much depends on coincidence and chance, and because the incidents are too often and obviously pretexts for the analysis of sentiment, but it does not lack historical interest, or fascinating opportunities of catching some of the major themes and uncertainties of *La Princesse de Clèves* at an inchoate stage in their development.

From quite soon after the end of the religious wars, writers of fiction had looked back nostalgically on the court of Henri II for the dominance of values of the courtly chivalry and romance. Gomberville found the stable and stylized values a necessary foundation for this type of heroism his generation needed soon after 1630 to explore. Although *La Princesse de Clèves* is meticulously given an authentic renaissance setting, not only the psychology of the emotions, but also the general tenor of the plot dates it to the decade starting in 1670.

Lafayette had considered calling her text "Mémoires." It reflects the tone of the "young court" of Henriette d'Angleterre, given more to the enjoyment of life than the direction of affairs, rather than the "old court" of Anne of Austria, associated now with more serious preoccupations. Stripped to its outline structure, the story concerns a virtuous and beautiful girl, Mlle de Chartres, whose position makes desirable a marriage to M. de Clèves, who loves her but whom she does not love. The marriage takes place, the duc de Nemours falls in love with Mme de Clèves and pursues her. She tries to give him no sign that she is emotionally moved by him, although he finds out when he overhears her despairingly confess to her husband her love for someone else, in the context of a plea to be dispensed from attendance at court, where she cannot help meeting the object of her affection.

Her mother had warned her that happiness could come only from loving her husband, and rightly, as the narrator tells us, admired her daughter's sincerity, of which much is made. Her husband had encouraged the princesse to tell him if she ever did fall in love with anyone else. He becomes jealous, bullies out of her the name of his rival, and dies of grief. Mme de Clèves, now free to marry Nemours, whose love she continues to return, does not marry him, partly out of propriety, but mostly because she prefers "repos" to the tortures of jealousy she is sure Nemours would inflict on her. She retires to a convent and dies young.

How should a virtuous woman behave when an irresistible emotion, to which she does not voluntarily abandon herself, clashes with a strong social ethic? Should she have dissimulated? How strong was the ethic which prevented the concealment of an illicit liaison by apparently impeccable public behaviour? It is clear that the imaginative strength of the text depends on the acceptance of defeat. The text would have become trivialized if Mme de Clèves had merely pursued a possibly illusory happiness in marriage to Nemours after the death from jealousy of her husband. The narrative gains its power from Lafayette's imaginative examination of the possible need to accept defeat in the pursuit of happiness. On the way, it offers delicate investigations into the most finely balanced of moral dilemmas and the most subtly poised emotional states, into the virtues of sincerity, the ravages of jealousy, the possibility of merit and esteem as a basis for love, the consequences of the irresistibility and the instantaneity of passion, and the unlikelihood that passionate love, even when reciprocated, might provide the foundation for happiness in marriage.

The text is now built up with much concern for credibility, and the psychological states are drawn from the intrigue, whose events are no longer so obviously selected for the opportunities they give for analysis. The first of the three main characters to whom we are introduced is Nemours, "un chef-d'oeuvre de la nature…l'homme du monde le mieux fait et le plus beau…une valeur incomparable…un air dans toute sa personne qui faisait qu'on ne pouvait regarder que lui dans tous les lieux où il paraissait (a masterpiece of nature,…the best built and handsomest man in the world…an incomparable worth…an air in everything about him which focused attention only on him wherever he appeared)." The importance of the introduction of Nemours as a paragon of all the elegances and all the perfections, indeed of all the virtues except the moral ones, is that the self-esteem which allows him so ruthlessly to pursue Mme de Clèves might to some extent be excused. Lafayette's public were not ready for a virtuous young heroine to love a villain and, since Nemours's pursuit is certainly worse than inconsiderate, she must retain some esteem for him in the minds of her readers.

Mlle de Chartres's mother is a widow who has dedicated herself to her daughter's upbringing: "elle ne travailla pas seulement à cultiver son esprit et sa beauté; elle songea aussi à lui donner de la vertu et à la lui rendre aimable (she not only worked to cultivate her mind and her beauty, but tried also to inspire her with virtue and a love of virtue)." Her mother

> faisait souvent à sa fille des peintures de l'amour; elle lui montrait ce qu'il a d'agréable pour la persuader plus aisément sur ce qu'elle lui apprenoit de dangereux; elle lui contait le peu de sincérité des hommes, leurs tromperies et leur infidelité, les malheurs domestiques où plongent les engagemens; et elle lui faisait voir, d'un autre côté, quelle tranquillité suivait la vie d'une honnête femme, et combien la vertu donnait d'éclat et d'élévation à une personne qui avait de la beauté et de la naissance; mais elle lui faisait voir aussi combien il était difficile de conserver cette vertu que par une extrême défiance de soi-même, et par un grand soin de s'attacher à ce qui seul peut faire le bonheur d'une femme, qui est d'aimer son mari et d'en être aimée

(often gave her daughter descriptions of love. She pointed out its pleasures in order to persuade her more easily of the dangerous lessons it taught. She told her of men's lack of sincerity, their deceits and their infidelity, the family unhappiness entailed by emotional involvements. She made her see, on the other hand, what peace attached to the life of a good woman, and how much lustre and elevation virtue gave to the life of someone who had both birth and beauty; but she also made her see how difficult it was to keep that virtue except by an extreme distrust of oneself and by taking great care to concentrate on the only thing which can bring a woman happiness, loving her husband and being loved by him).

M. de Clèves first sees Mlle de Chartres in a jeweller's shop. His astonishment at her beauty made her blush and it seemed to him that that was why she hurried out of the shop. He instantly conceived for her "une passion et une estime extraordinaires (an extraordinary passion and esteem)." Both M. de Clèves and the chevalier de Guise fall in love with Mlle de Chartres, and the passion of each allows him to perceive that of the other. The choice of husband runs into social complications, but in the end Mlle de Chartres marries M. de Clèves "avec moins de répugnance qu'un autre (with less unwillingness than any other)," but with no special "inclination." M. de Clèves was disappointed that her feelings "ne passaient pas ceux de l'estime et la reconnaissance (did not go beyond those of esteem and gratitude)," the two sorts of love providing alternatives to passion in the Carte de Tendre. She is modest, blushes easily, and does not understand the refinements of feeling about which M. de Clèves is talking when he says he would rather she blushed from a movement of her heart than from modesty.

It is at this point that the narrator steps in and tells the reader that Mme de Chartres admired the sincerity of her daughter "avec raison (rightly)." The wedding takes place, and M. de Clèves is not entirely happy. While he was her husband, he was still her lover because ("parce que" in the French text) there was something he wanted beyond simple possession. His joy was disturbed by a "passion violente et inquiète (a violent and anxious passion)" for his wife in which, the narrator assures us, jealousy had no part. On the eve of the wedding of Charles II of Lorraine and the 11-year-old Claude de France, daughter of Henri II and Catherine de Médicis, which actually took place in 1558, Mme de Clèves attends the court ball and is bidden by the king to dance with Nemours. Murmurs of admiration break out. The dauphin's wife notices that Mme de Clèves has indeed experienced a movement of inclination, as Guise, too, has noticed, "soit qu'en effet il eût paru quelque trouble sur son visage, ou que la jalousie fît voir au chevalier de Guise au delà de la vérité (whether in fact some embarrassment had appeared in her countenance, or whether jealousy made the chevalier de Guise see beyond the truth)."

Mme de Clèves has necessarily frequently to be in the company of Nemours, and he naturally behaves in order to please her. Mme de Clèves does not dare confide in her mother who, however, observes what is taking place. There is a precious discussion about whether a lover should or should not rejoice at seeing his lady at a ball, where she must dance with others, the opinion of Nemours in the discussion being dictated by his feelings for Mme de Clèves. She finally perceives that her feelings for Nemours are those her husband had wanted for himself, and is ashamed. Her mother falls ill, and there is a last interview two days before she dies. She has been afraid to talk to her daughter about her feelings for Nemours:

Je ne vous en ai pas voulu parler d'abord, de peur de vous en faire apercevoir vous-même. Vous ne le connaissez que trop présentement; vous êtes sur le bord du précipice: il faut de grands efforts et de grandes violences pour vous retenir...

(At the beginning I didn't want to speak to you about it, for fear of making you aware of it yourself. Now you know it only too well. You are on the edge of the abyss. You need to make great efforts and to do your feelings great violence if you are not to go over the edge).

The second of the four parts of the narrative starts with what is in fact the second of the four digressions in the text. The first, concerning Diane de Poitiers, duchesse de Valentinois, is only slenderly linked to the main themes and appears to be there chiefly to help establish historical authenticity. The second is about Sancerre's discovery of Mme de Tournon's infidelity after her death, plays on the sound values Sancerre/sincère, and is related by M. de Clèves to his wife. M. de Clèves recounts the advice he gave to Sancerre:

La sincérité me touche d'une telle sorte, que je crois que, si ma maîtresse, et même ma femme, m'avouaient que quelqu'un lui plût, j'en serais affligé sans être aigri; je quitterais le personnage d'amant ou de mari, pour la conseiller et pour la plaindre

(Sincerity touches me so much that I believe if my mistress or even my wife were to tell me she loved someone else, I would be hurt without being embittered. I should lay down the role of lover or husband to give her advice and to pity her).

Nemours, meanwhile, is so in love with Mme de Clèves that he neglects a possible marriage with Elizabeth of England. Both he and Mme de Clèves try to withdraw from company, he to dream, she to avoid the pain of seeing him. Nemours makes several covert declarations, mostly speaking in a way which has a particular significance for her. Then comes the third digression, the reine dauphine's account of Anne Boleyn. Nemours then manages to take from a dressing table a portrait of Mme de Clèves. She sees him.

La raison voulait qu'elle demandât son portrait; mais en le demandant publiquement, c'était apprendre à tout le monde les sentiments que ce prince avait pour elle, et, en le lui demandant en particulier, c'était quasi l'engager à lui parler de sa passion: enfin, elle jugea qu'il valait mieux le lui laisser, et elle fut bien aise de lui accorder une faveur qu'elle lui pouvait faire, sans qu'il sût même qu'elle la lui faisait

(Reason required her to ask for her portrait back but, by asking for it publicly, she would be telling the whole world of the feelings the prince had for her while, if she asked for it in private, she would practically be inviting him to speak to her of his passion. In the end she thought it better to let him keep it, and she was very glad to be able to grant him a favour that she could do without his knowing that she was doing him one).

The subtlety of that analysis of feeling suggests the mind of La Rochefoucauld. The convoluted syntax is indeed Lafayette's.

Mme de Clèves remembers all her mother said on her death bed, and what M. de Clèves said about sincerity. Nemours is slightly hurt at a tournament, and Guise notices the signs of alarm shown by Mme de Clèves. A love letter falls from Nemours's pocket and Mme de Clèves, thinking that it had been written to him by a woman, feels intense jealousy. Her worst pain, however, comes from having let Nemours see that she loves him. The letter turns out not to have been written to Nemours at all, but it serves its purpose in the text by making Mme de Clèves aware of the extent of her passion, and by allowing the reine dauphine to say to her, further preparing us for the confession, "Il n'y que vous de femme au monde qui fasse confidence à son mari de toutes les choses qu'elle sait (You are the only woman in the world to confide to her husband everything she knows)." Mme de Clèves goes to Coulommiers in the country on a pretext of ill health which her husband does not believe. She does not know that Nemours is listening from the garden when, on her knees, she confesses to her husband that she loves someone else, and asks his help to stay away from that person, insisting that she has never betrayed her affection for him.

We are immediately given a long, subtle, and complex analysis by M. de Clèves of the contradictory feelings he experiences. Both Nemours in the garden and her husband in the room are anxious to hear from her the vital name. The rest of the narrative is very largely devoted to analyses of sentiment, extremely precise, sensitive, and psychologically penetrating. Passion is irresistible, jealousy inevitable and exceedingly painful. M. de Clèves does discover the name, by trickery. He also exhibits the mixture of love and hate traditionally, and as late as Descartes in 1649, considered incapable of co-existing in the same person with respect to the same object, but used to describe jealousy in both La Rochefoucauld and Racine:

> Je ne me trouve plus digne de vous; vous ne paraissez plus digne de moi. Je vous adore, je vous hais; je vous offense, je vous demande pardon; je vous admire, j'ai honte de vous admirer

> (I no longer feel worthy of you; you no longer seem worthy of me. I adore you; I hate you. I offend you; I ask your pardon. I admire you; I'm ashamed of admiring you).

M. de Clèves dies. Nemours and Mme de Clèves are brought together to talk alone for the first time. In case the reader has had any doubts, the narrator steps in again. "Madame de Clèves céda pour la première fois au penchant qu'elle avait avait pour M. de Nemours (Madame de Clèves yielded for the first time to the inclination she had for M. de Nemours)." She feels that her husband was perhaps the only man in the world capable of keeping alive his love inside marriage. Twice in the last few pages we are told why Mme de Clèves cannot marry Nemours. The narrator's version accords with her own:

> Les raisons qu'elle avait de ne point épouser M. de Nemours lui paraissaient fortes du côté de son devoir, et insurmontables du côté de son repos. Le fin de l'amour de ce prince et les maux de la jalousie qu'elle croyait infaillibles dans un mariage lui montraient un malheur certain où elle s'allait jeter…Elle jugea que l'absence seule, et l'éloignement, pouvait lui donner quelque force

> (The reasons she had for not marrying M. de Nemours seemed to her strong from the point of view of her duty, and insurmountable from the point of view of her peace of mind. The end of the prince's love for her, and the pains of jealousy which she thought inevitable in marriage showed her the certain unhappiness into which she was about to throw herself…She considered that only absence and distance could give her any strength).

Nemours eventually recovered. Mme de Clèves spent half her year in a convent and the other half in pious occupations at home. "Sa vie, qui fut assez courte, laissa des exemples de vertu inimitables (Her life, which was quite short, left examples of virtue that cannot be imitated)."

What Lafayette has explored, with all the force deriving from those meticulously precise analyses of sentiment, is whether the overwhelming strength of a love which is not in our power must inevitably lead to jealousy, and can be countered only by withdrawal and the admission of defeat in the pursuit of happiness. Donneau de Visé's inquiry trivializes the text, concentrating on the confession and tabulating the results, advantages and disadvantages firstly of saying nothing, and then of making the confession. According to his readers, as reported in the quarterly special number of the *Mercure galant* for October 1678, the disadvantages of silence were the risk to virtue and peace of mind, the risk of nourishing the illegitimate passion, and the risk that the passion would anyway burst out. The advantages of silence are listed as promoting harmony with one's husband, keeping intact a virtuous reputation, giving in to a sweetly pleasing inclination, and not exposing oneself to the judgement of others. The disadvantages of confessing were to upset one's husband, to lose his esteem for your virtue, and to expose your lover to your husband's jealousy, while the advantages in confessing were to safeguard a virtue under pressure, to forestall the consequences of a liaison, and to give your husband a rare proof of trust.

La Comtesse de Tende is very short, again set in the renaissance, and sub-titled "Nouvelle historique." We know from the beginning that the Comte de Tende, rich, powerful, and selfish, is adored by his much younger wife, the former Clarisse Strozzi, to whom he is also unfaithful. She abets her friend, the princesse de Neufchâtel, in a galant relationship with the chevalier de Navarre, who abruptly declares that his real passion is for the comtesse herself. Her amour-propre is flattered, and she falls violently in love with him. However, when she thinks of her friend:

> Cette trahison lui fit horreur. La honte et les malheurs d'une galanterie se présentèrent à son esprit; elle vit l'abîme où elle se précipitait et elle résolut de l'éviter

> (This betrayal filled her with horror. The shame and unhappinesses of a love affair presented themselves to her mind. She saw the abyss into which she was throwing herself and resolved to avoid it).

But her resolution does not last. When she thinks she has cause to doubt the passion she has inspired, she instantly becomes jealous. The chevalier wants to abandon his proposed marriage to the princesse, and the princesse confides to the comtesse that she knows her projected husband loves someone else. The marriage, however, goes ahead. One day the Comte de Tende finds the chevalier on his knees at the foot of the comtesse's bed. He says he was imploring her to lie on his behalf because he had been unfaithful to his wife, and only if the Comtesse Tende gave him an alibi could he save his dignity and honour.

The Comte de Tende agrees to help, but asks in vain who the chevalier's mistress actually is. The comtesse, still in love with the chevalier, becomes jealous, and meanwhile the Comte de Tende "devint aussi amoureux d'elle que si elle n'eût point été sa femme (fell as deeply in love with her as if she had not been his wife)." When she resists him, the count leaves haughtily. She then finds that she is pregnant by the chevalier de Navarre. He is killed in the wars. Distraught, she has no further interest in her "repos," her reputation, or her life. The Comte de Tende, recounting to his wife the death of Navarre, begins to understand what must have happened, "mais il lui restait néanmoins ce doute que l'amour-propre nous laisse toujours pour les choses qui coûtent trop cher à croire (none the less there still remained to him that doubt that self-interest always leaves us for things that are too painful to believe)."

The comtesse writes her husband a letter confessing her pregnancy and offering him her life. He sends back a note to say that she should allow her pregnancy to appear, and he will consider what to do. The comtesse prepares for her death without losing her reputation. "La honte est la plus violente de toutes les passions (Shame is the greatest of all the passions)." She gives birth to a child at six months. Neither she nor the child survives. This is the harshest of all Lafayette's fictions, envisaging the possibility of a defeat by life's inevitabilities much more damaging than anything in the earlier texts. It was first published in 1724 and has been thought to be a first sketch for *La Princesse de Clèves*. Of the suggested possible dates of composition, the internal evidence points to a much later one. 1690 is not impossible.

PUBLICATIONS

Collections

Oeuvres, 3 vols., 1925–30

Fiction

La Princesse de Montpensier, 1662; as *The Princess Montpensier*, 1805; tr. T.C. Cave, 1992
Zayde, histoire espagnole, par Monsieur de Segrais, 1670–71; as *A Spanish History*, 1678
La Princesse de Clèves, 1678; as *The Princess of Clèves*, 1679; tr. T.C. Cave, 1992
La Comtesse de Tende, 1724; tr. T.C. Cave, 1992

Other

Histoire de Madame Henriette d'Angleterre, 1720
Mémoires de la Cour de France pour les années 1688 et 1689, 1731
Correspondance, 2 vols., 1942

Biographical and critical studies

Magne, Emile, *Madame de Lafayette en ménage*, 1926
——*Le Coeur et l'esprit de Mme de Lafayette*, 1927
Haig, Stirling, *Madame de Lafayette* (in English), 1970
Duchêne, Roger, *Madame de Lafayette*, 1988

Bibliography

Scott, James W., *Madame de Lafayette: A Selected Critical Bibliography*, 1974

LA FONTAINE, Jean de, 1621–1695.

Poet.

LIFE

La Fontaine, baptized on 8 July 1621, was the son of a king's counsellor, master of rivers and forests at Château-Thierry and steward of the hunt in the same duchy, who usurped the title "écuyer," thereby arrogating to himself membership of the minor aristocracy. His date of birth is unknown, but in 1617 he married Françoise Pidoux, a 35-year-old widow, whose first husband had been a rich merchant from Coulommiers, whose father had been the doctor of Henri IV, and whose brother became mayor of Poitiers. Little else is known of La Fontaine's background, except that a younger brother, Claude, was born in 1623.

La Fontaine appears to have started school at Château-Thierry but to have finished in Paris. On 27 April 1641, followed shortly by his brother, he entered the Congregation of the Oratory with the idea of becoming a priest. His superiors soon became anxious at his lack of religious enthusiasm and sent him from their house in the Rue Saint-Honoré to that in the Rue d'Enfer, where he was pressed to get down to his theological studies. He appears to have spent about 18 months in all with the Oratory and to have developed a cynical view of the religious observances to which he was expected to commit himself. On leaving in the autumn of 1642, he may well have begun to study law, and certainly, to his father's pleasure, started writing verse. A close relative, Pierre Pinterel de l'Etang, seems to have encouraged him to read Horace, Virgil, and Terence.

He early adopted the pose of ironic, uncommitted indolence which he was to affect all his life, and towards 1647 became connected with a circle of free-thinking and like-minded young men loosely associated together as a small academy called after the Arthurian "Table ronde (Round Table)." They met on Thursdays, declaimed their work, took it in turn to preside, and included Paul Pellisson, François Charpentier, Gédéon Tallement des Réaux, Antoine Furetière, and Madame de la Sablière's future husband, Antoine Rambouillet de la Sablière. The group cultivated a senior literary circle to which it looked up and whose members included François Mainard, Valentin Conrart, Nicolas Perrot d'Ablancourt, Jean Ogier de Gombauld, Jean Chapelain, and Olivier Patru. There was also La Fontaine's life-long intimate friend, François Maucroix, a lawyer who, having been violently in love with the aristocratic Henriette de Joyeuse de Maupas, aspiring to marry her both before she married and during her widowhood, finally joined the Church and in 1647 became a canon of Reims. La Fontaine always showed him his work before finishing it. However, where Maucroix's own work is characterized by its light-hearted gracefulness, La Fontaine's was always dreamier and more melancholy.

He was himself distinguished for his detestation of war and everything to do with it, and for his distaste for Mazarin. He gamed, was renowned for indolence, and after the Fronde was at the centre of a small group of precious (q.v.) men of letters surrounding Patru who admired Malherbe and were devoted to Roman and Greek literature, but gave one another poetic names and cultivated an altogether more refined "galanterie." La Fontaine read widely, enjoying Plato, Horace, Rabelais, Montaigne, Marot, and Voiture. We know that he was devoted to the novels of antiquity, to the pastoral, and in particular to *L'Astrée*, from which late in life he was to extract an opera libretto, to Cervantes, and to the novels of Gomberville and La Calprenède; that he enjoyed the luxury of his idleness; and that he divided his time between Paris, Reims, and Château-Thierry, and continued a series of amorous liaisons before and after his marriage to the 14-year-old Marie Héricart in 1647. She was educated, came from a distinguished bourgeois family, brought to the marriage 30,000 livres, and was to bear La Fontaine a son, Charles, baptized on 30 October 1653 and apparently brought up by Maucroix. Little is known of him, except that he obtained a modest official appointment, had four children, and died in 1723. He played no part in his father's life.

La Fontaine spent much of his time with his wife at Château-Thierry, and she sometimes accompanied him to Paris, where they stayed with Marie's uncle, Jacques Jannart, an important Parisian lawyer, Foucquet's substitute procurator at the Paris parlement, and his wife, who together treated La Fontaine as a son. When, in 1659, La Fontaine and his wife legally separated their possessions, it was little more than a way of eluding creditors, but the actual separation of the couple became complete before 1671, after which La Fontaine does not seem to have stayed with the Jannarts or seen his wife again. He regarded himself as "volage en vers comme en amours (flighty in verse as in love)," "inquiet et fécond en nouvelles amours (restless and always embarking on new loves)," and a "butterfly of Parnassus."

In 1652 La Fontaine bought a three-year office as master of rivers and forests, for a sum certainly in excess of 12,500 livres, from the husband of his half-sister, his mother's daughter by an earlier marriage, while waiting to acquire the two offices to be inherited from his father, but he had to sell a farm, no doubt inherited from his mother, in 1653. The post involved serious administrative and some quasi-judicial responsibilities, which La Fontaine appears to have fulfilled with no less than average assiduity.

In 1654 appeared his first published work, a five-act verse adaptation of Terence's play L'Eunuque. By the time his father died in April 1658, leaving only debts, including 18,000 livres to Maucroix and 12,000 to La Fontaine himself, La Fontaine had been introduced to Foucquet by Pellisson. That June, he presented Foucquet with a copy of his heroic idyll Adonis, first published after much revision only with Psyché in 1669: it was no doubt Foucquet who had the famous copy calligraphed by Nicolas Jarry. In the first half of 1659 La Fontaine undertook to pay Foucquet a "pension" in the form of madrigals, ballads, sonnets, and other light verse. Mostly in the style of Marot or Voiture, about a score have survived.

La Fontaine had plainly entered Foucquet's service, joining Pellisson and Maucroix, although he still exercised his official functions at Château-Thierry, where he put on his ballet Les Rieurs du Beau-Richard, probably for the 1660 carnival, and he was often seen in Paris. It was he who was chosen to celebrate the great building and gardening operation at Vaux, although Le Songe de Vaux was never finished. Some of the fragments are still in prose. La Fontaine published four of them, "Les Amours de Mars et de Vénus," in the 1665 Contes, and three others in the 1671 Fables nouvelles. Five further fragments were posthumously published in the 1729 Oeuvres diverses.

La Fontaine attended the great celebration to inaugurate the splendours of Foucquet's mansion at Vaux on 17 August 1661, when Molière's Les Fâcheux was given after a prologue by Pellisson. On the arrest of Foucquet on 5 September, when Pellisson also was imprisoned, La Fontaine courted official disgrace with the Elégie pour M.F., "aux nymphes de Vaux," asking them to implore the king's mercy for his patron, whom he calls "Oronte," and with his Ode au Roi. He was, however, never completely identified with the Vaux group and, as later on in the Querelle des anciens et des modernes (q.v.), he remained on friendly terms with members of generally hostile groups, like

Chapelain and Conrart, who disliked the Vaux circle. Like Chapelain, Boileau himself conspicuously omits La Fontaine from the catalogues of poets from whom at this date he withholds approval. Meanwhile it was at Vaux that La Fontaine got to know Molière, Charles Perrault, Saint-Evremond, and Madeleine de Scudéry. It was in that heady atmosphere that he met Mme de Sévigné, Mme de Lafayette, and La Rochefoucauld, and became committed to a literary vocation.

In August 1661 La Fontaine's inherited offices were valued at 14,000 livres, and the triennial one at 12,667 livres. He had taken on his father's debts, and his brother, who had renounced his inheritance in exchange for a pension, now demanded a further 8,000 livres. La Fontaine had to borrow from Pinterel, from Jannart, and from his wife. The duc de Bouillon, Godefroy Maurice de la Tour, grand chamberlain of France, having on 16 September 1657, in accordance with an agreement of 10 March 1651, taken over Château-Thierry in exchange for Sedan, which henceforward belonged to the crown, was in principle obliged to redeem all the offices of the duchy, although they remained with their holders until they were reimbursed in full, which did not occur in the department of rivers and forests until the necessary trees had been harvested and sold. This for La Fontaine meant 1671. The office-holders had the right to buy back their positions, but La Fontaine had no money and on 21 September 1671 he resigned his rights.

It has been remarked that his style towards this period became less meditatively concerned with woods and springs, more mocking and ironic, moving towards the later pessimism of the Fables. Although the later love poetry became almost completely stylized, La Fontaine was all his life to remain open to the sensual stimulus provided by nature and by love, and to be ready to follow the moment's whim. By 1662, when he was in trouble for following his father in appropriating the title of "écuyer," to which he had no right, we find him seeking help from the duc de Bouillon and his wife. Marie-Anne Mancini, Mazarin's niece, had married Bouillon on 22 April 1662, when she was still only 15. She was to become La Fontaine's protector, baptized by him "Olympe". He came obviously to be very close to the frivolous and witty young duchess, who may have encouraged him to write the Contes.

In 1663, perhaps also under official constraint, La Fontaine accompanied Jacques Jannart into exile at Limoges, writing to his wife a series of not unaffectionate letters in a mixture of verse and prose, of which six have survived and were posthumously published as the Relation d'un voyage de Paris en Limousin. On his return in 1664 La Fontaine entered the service of Marguerite de Lorraine, the pious widow of Gaston d'Orléans, brother of Louis XIII, thereby earning his "brevet" of nobility, and perhaps conceiving the ambition to improve on the literary work of the late duke's late steward, Bouillon—no relation of the Mazarin's niece's husband's family—whose Oeuvres posthumes had appeared in 1663. One of nine officers who took turns to direct the service at table, La Fontaine was given 200 livres a year and board, but not lodging, in the gloomily pious atmosphere cultivated in Madame's wing of the Luxembourg, although he continued to exercise his functions at Château-Thierry.

La Fontaine's amalgamated offices were now valued together at the reduced figure of 17,367 livres on account of "abuse of position," a term signifying little more than a pretext for a general tightening up of norms of administrative licence in the wake of the practices allowed and indulged by Foucquet, and a way also of diminishing the sums which Bouillon had to repay to redeem the duchy's offices. Colbert wrote dryly in 1666 demanding that La Fontaine should institute an investigation into similar abuses practised by other officials in the administration of forests, but in fact this was Colbert's normal attitude to a protégé of Foucquet, and La Fontaine seems to have exercised perfectly reasonable vigilance in policing the fishing, hunting, and cutting and selling of wood in the rivers and forests for which he was responsible. Still in 1666 he wrote on behalf of his colleagues seeking permission for them to harvest their annual crop of trees. The exercise of his office stimulated his interest, incidentally, in the trees, birds, and beasts which were to inhabit the *Fables*. The knowledge of natural history they show may not be the most remarkable quality of the *Fables*, but La Fontaine learnt to love the unique attractivenesses of a forest at night.

On 14 January 1664, Barbin took out a privilège for La Fontaine's translation of Ariosto's *Joconde*, probably intended to challenge an octosyllabic version by Bouillon, who had died in 1662. In spite of the likely popularity of yet another treatment of female infidelity, the volume did not appear, but bets were taken on whether La Fontaine's adaptation would be thought better than Bouillon's, and the debate ranged as far as Italy. A jury with Brienne as president and Molière as scrutineer was duly constituted; a compromise was reached, and Bouillon's backer got his stake back, but had to pay for the jury's lunch. The *Journal des Savants* (q.v.) gave an account of the discussions in January 1665. It is very likely, but not quite certain, that Boileau was the author of the *Dissertation sur "Joconde"* which was printed in a Dutch edition of La Fontaine's *Contes* in 1668.

Barbin did publish the *Nouvelles en vers tirée* [sic] *de Boccace et de l'Arioste*, dated 1665, but with an "achevé d'imprimer" of 10 December 1664. The "s" which puts "nouvelles" into the plural seems to have been added, which would explain the negligently uncorrected grammatical singular of the adjective "tirée." The volume contains the adaptation of *Joconde; ou, L'infidélité des femmes* and *Le Cocu battu et content*. It was followed a month later by *Contes et nouvelles en vers*, with an "achevé d'imprimer" of 10 January 1665, containing the two earlier pieces, one new nouvelle, *Richard Minutolo*, adapted from Boccaccio, seven contes in the style of Marot, of which six were new and one, of only 10 lines, was among several reduced almost to epigrams, plus a fragment of the *Songe de Vaux* included, no doubt, as a discreet compliment to Foucquet, an *Arrêt galant*, and a *Ballade*. Surviving manuscripts suggest that the contes were probably written before 1665. La Fontaine and Barbin were obviously trying to profit from public interest in La Fontaine by putting together as a volume whatever he could find at the bottom of his drawer. La Fontaine admits as much in his preface: "To increase its size I have taken from my papers some kind of 'Imitation des arrêtes d'amours'" but, even stretched as it was and including the preface, the first part of the *Contes et nouvelles en vers* scarcely ran to a hundred pages.

The second part of the *Contes et nouvelles en vers* was published in January 1666. Three contes appeared in a collective *Recueil* of 1667 and a third collection of *Contes*, including *Le Faucon* and *La Courtisane amoureuse*, came out in 1671. The fourth volume, published without privilège or permission, and with a false place-name, was overtly obscene and suppressed on 5 April 1675; it carries the date 1674, although it probably did not appear before the new year. There were no more contes until

1782. During the same decade from 1664 to 1674 La Fontaine also published a novel, half the *Fables*, a comedy, translations from Latin, elegies, and, at the same time, a series of religiously inspired works, often related to a Jansenist (q.v.) spirituality. He also helped with the translation of the first volume of Augustine's *De civitate dei*, published under Jansenist inspiration by the abbé Pierre le Petit. La Fontaine is responsible for the translation of the verse quotations in the text. He was to die seriously committed to an austerely penitential spirituality.

The double series of works is the outward manifestation of a character both unusually withdrawn and amorphously undecided. The overwhelming impression La Fontaine makes at this period is of wanting to be left in peace, of needing freedom from any pressure to achieve decisiveness or strict personal definition. He wrote contemporaneously the sometimes licentious *Contes*, the religious pieces in the *Recueil de poésies chrétiennes et diverses*, dedicated to Conti and compiled with the help of Racine and Henri Loménie de Brienne under the direction of Arnauld d'Andilly and Gomberville in 1671 (achevé d'imprimer 20 December 1670), and, without privilège, the devout, if poetically unsuccessful, *La Captivité de Saint Malc* of 1673.

The cultivated melancholy discernible behind the *Fables* and the constant refusal to align with any of the literary factions which solicited his support must be accounted for. An apparently carefree cynicism and luxuriation in indolence, a deep feeling of boredom, and an acute awareness of political and social realities were all combined. La Fontaine in his later years had little to say, coming to life conversationally only when serious issues were to be discussed. Even in his fifties he appeared heavy, almost witless, and neglected his personal appearance, dress, and manners, although he had once been charming, elegant and witty. The key is in his relationships, often teasingly affectionate, but emotionally never more than shallow. He enjoyed acting so well the role he had to assume, needed and found patronage, and paid for it with flattery, but his expressions of affection became increasingly stylized, and neither within nor outside his own family was he ever emotionally close to anyone, certainly not to his father, mother, wife, son, or brother. His relationships, like the *Fables*, were all dominated by a protective playfulness. Mme de la Sablière once penetratingly said of him that "La Fontaine does not lie in prose." She meant that he could be taken literally only when he was writing with a directness he preferred to avoid.

On 3 February 1672 the duchesse d'Orléans died, leaving La Fontaine with no post at all until, probably early in 1673, the educated, relaxed, and artistically gifted Marguerite Hessein, Mme de la Sablière, 32 years old, married in 1654, separated in 1668 from the husband whom La Fontaine had known from the Table ronde, and poetically addressed by La Fontaine as "Iris," offered him a roof, board, and enlightened patronage. On the separation from her husband Mme de la Sablière had recovered her dowry, and she lived with her three children. She had a meagre income of 1,000 livres a year from her husband. Like him, she had come from a rich Protestant banking family, although her father had died crippled with debt in 1661. She now received members of the social and learned worlds in her salon in the Rue Neuve-des-Petits-Champs, did not exclude Ninon de Lenclos, was a close friend of Charles Perrault, her "master," and was interested in the exact sciences. She discussed mathematics with Roberval, was the niece of Menjot, Mme de Sablé's doctor, and was a close friend of the Orientalist popularizer of

Gassendi, François Bernier, whom La Fontaine, too, got to know well. He was also protected by Mme de Montespan, her sister Mme de Thianges, and therefore by the small Condé court at Chantilly. From 1670, when Brienne, the great admirer of Pellisson, left Paris, only La Rochefoucauld remained of the Vaux circle. La Fontaine was friendly with him, as with Mme de Lafayette and Mme de Sévigné.

The first volume of *Fables*, with a privilège of 6 June 1667 and containing six books, was published by Barbin with an achevé d'imprimer of 31 March 1668. Nine of them appear together in an extant manuscript with a tenth in which the squirrel (Foucquet) will be pardoned and the fox (Colbert) driven off. The tenth fable was not in the 1668 collection, and the manuscript with all ten seems likely to date from before the journey to Limoges of 1663, although it is possible that the fable hoping for Foucquet's rehabilitation and Colbert's fall may have been written as late as 1667, that therefore the other nine do not predate 1667, and that only the tenth fable was too dangerous to publish in 1668.

Aesop had in fact been fashionable around 1660, when Isaac-Nicolas Névelet's collection, *Mythologia aesopica*, printing the texts in Latin as well as Greek and probably used by La Fontaine, was reprinted with the Latin verse fables of Phaedrus. In 1659 Patru had held up Aesop as an example in his *Lettres à Olinde*, concentrating on the moral message, and the reprinted *Fables d'Esope phrygien traduites et moralisées*, also of 1659, had equally concentrated on the moral discourse attached to each. Another collection of fables with morals, by Audin, prior of Termes, and the engraver La Fage, was reprinted in 1660. In view of the apparent ease with which La Fontaine moved between the religiously austere and the frivolously scabrous, and of his dependence on Phaedrus for the overwhelming majority of the fables of the first four books, it is important to recall his use of the 1646 Port-Royal (q.v.) school edition of Phaedrus in Latin and French by Le Maître de Sacy, about to reach its eighth edition in 1668. In spite of the disclaimer in his 1668 preface, "le corps est la fable; l'âme, la moralité (the body is the fable, the soul the moral)," La Fontaine's first originality is to have transformed the moral tale into lyric poetry.

Denys Thierry had associated himself with Barbin in the publication of the original quarto volume, containing 126 poems, including dedication and epilogue, arranged in six books, with vignettes by the fashionable François Chauveau, possibly inspired by those in the Névelet volume, on which La Fontaine seems to have drawn increasingly for the more episodic fables of the fifth and sixth books. Success was immediate. Barbin published two two-volume duodecimo editions in 1668 and three new editions in 1669. The first collection, dedicated to the seven-year-old dauphin, had an extraordinary 40 known editions during La Fontaine's lifetime. The *Fables* remained more popular than any other work of literature in France until at least the middle of the 19th century, with estimated sales of 600,000 copies from 1810 to 1850. Barbin instantly exploited his commercial advantage by publishing in 1670 the anonymous *Oeuvres* of Pierre de Saint-Glas, abbot of Saint-Ussans, "contenant plusieurs fables d'Esope mises en vers (containing several of Aesop's fables put into verse)" and Mme de Villedieu's *Fables et histoires allégoriques*, and in 1671 the *Fables morales et nouvelles* of Furetière, still friendly with La Fontaine, to whom he pays a prefatory compliment.

The second part of the *Contes* was reprinted in an augmented edition in 1669, and on 31 January of that year Barbin published, two years before the first performance of the celebrated Molière-Quinault-Corneille *Psyché*, La Fontaine's *Amours de Psyché et de Cupidon*, derived from Apuleius and dedicated to the duchesse de Bouillon, together with the first printed edition of *Adonis*. The *Amours de Psyché et de Cupidon*, a mixture of verse and prose, attempted to treat heroic characters according to the conventions of galanterie, allying the two literary registers as in *Adonis* and the *Songe de Vaux*. The piece concerns four poets, Acante, Polyphile, Ariste, and Gélaste, who spend the day at Versailles, in 1668 still under construction, where Polyphile reads his poem to the other three. There has been much speculation about the "real" identities of the poets, almost certainly all composite portraits with each taking various characteristics from different real people. The text, obviously a counter-weight to *Le Songe de Vaux* as Versailles itself was a riposte to Foucquet's mansion, was a failure. There was a counterfeit edition in 1669, but La Fontaine never re-published his text.

The three-volume *Recueil de poésies chrétiennes*, whose achevé d'imprimer is 20 December 1670, appeared under Jansenist auspices. La Fontaine wrote the dedicatory verses to the elder of the two princes de Conti, published a signed verse paraphrase of a psalm among the religious poems of the first volume, and in the third followed two pieces by Maucroix with his own already published *Elégie* and *Ode* written after Foucquet's arrest, 16 of the published fables, and four fragments of *Psyché*. He included a poem expressing loyal regret for the orange trees, removed with other exotic trees from Vaux by Le Nôtre, once employed by Foucquet and now by Louis XIV acting through Colbert. Colbert disliked Le Vau, the principal architect of both Vaux and Versailles, and his general hostility to the move to Versailles was impelling him to accelerate work on the rebuilding of the Louvre.

Colbert controlled enough patronage to gain eventually for himself, provided only that he kept the king happy, virtual monopoly powers over all branches of the cultural establishment, but in 1670 La Fontaine could still in public join sympathy for Foucquet to an alignment with Port-Royal, two anti-Colbert attitudes whose social acceptability was no doubt precisely calculated by La Fontaine. They exactly represented the stance of the Hôtel de Nevers, closed on the disgrace of Henri Du Plessis-Guénégaud in 1669, where Colbert had been regarded as a social climber, and where pro-Foucquet, pro-Jesuit, and pro-"moderne" sentiment was reconciled with sympathy for the apparently conflicting values which reigned at Port-Royal, in the interests of opposing the prudish but powerful upstart who was hostile to the well-being of an aristocracy busy marrying its daughters to the tax-farmers.

On 27 January 1671 La Fontaine published the third part of the *Contes et nouvelles en vers*, containing the text of *Clymène*, a comedy in dramatic form but not intended to be played, and on 12 March a new collection of *Fables* dedicated to the son-in-law of the dowager duchesse of Orléans, the duc de Guise, who was to die four months later. This volume contained eight new fables, four elegies, and some occasional verse written during the Vaux period, or for the Bouillons. The fables, read at La Rochefoucauld's, aroused great excitement in Mme de Sévigné, who tried to persuade Mme de Grignan, her cynical daughter, in letters of 29 April and of 6 May, of the merit of what were regarded by her correspondent merely as childish amusements.

Mme de Sévigné revealingly said that she would like to write a fable which would convince La Fontaine that he should stick to what he was good at. She realized that his personality was not firm enough, and that his judgement was too easily swayed by what he thought would prove most acceptable to most people. Often, in spite of his attachment to the era of madrigals inaugurated by Voiture, La Fontaine adjusted his output to a changing public taste he perfectly judged. *Les Amours de Psyché et de Cupidon* had been a miscalculation. In 1673 came another, the *Poème de la captivité de Saint Malc*, without privilège, a heroic idyll, like Saint-Amant's *Moïse sauvé* of 1653 and his own *Adonis*. It was a Christian poem of nearly 600 lines, placed under the protection of the Virgin Mary, and with a compliment to Arnauld d'Andilly neatly balanced by a dedication to the cardinal de Bouillon, a celebrated friend of the Jesuits. La Fontaine had still not made up his mind whether to adhere to the rigorist aesthetic and spiritual norms of Port-Royal, or to remain free, uncommitted, and cynically frivolous underneath the artistry and penetration of the *Fables*. It was a decision he finally brought himself to make only on the spiritual plane, and when death seemed imminent.

La Fontaine published two fables as individual plaquettes in 1672, the year of Madame's death. One was a political allegory relevant to the outbreak of the Dutch war. Never more than a close friend, La Fontaine now stayed with Mme de la Sablière, relegated to a freezing attic. He remained with her until her death early in 1693. She was in fact in 1676 to endure a strong passion for the marquis de la Fare, superficial in character and a gambler, who left her after four years, by which time her husband had died and her daughters were married. She was converted to Catholicism by the Jesuit Père Rapin and devoted herself to the care of the sick, in 1687 becoming a penitent of Rancé. It was while she was working at the Incurables that she moved to the Rue Saint-Honoré, putting La Fontaine up in a small neighbouring house. In the meanwhile, in 1674, he had written his letter to Huet, not to be published until 1687, admitting his liking for the taste of the "modernes," but defending the norms of the "anciens" with reasoned argument. This, 1674, was the year of Racine's *Iphigénie*, partly a riposte to Quinault's *Alceste; ou, Le triomphe d'Alcide* with music by Lulli which had failed earlier in the year at the Palais-Royal, and of Boileau's *Art poétique*, attacking Desmarests de Saint Sorlin. In 1675 La Fontaine figured among a set of toy wax effigies arranged in the "Chambre du sublime," given by Mme de Thianges to the duc du Maine; among others, including La Rochefoucauld, Bossuet, and Mme de Lafayette, next to Racine, was Boileau sweeping away seven or eight bad poets. He was beckoning to La Fontaine who, characteristically, was in the background.

La Fontaine had been close to Racine in his youth, and again when preparing the 1671 *Recueil* for Port-Royal. Like Racine and Boileau, he was protected by Mme de Montespan and Mme de Thianges. It was perhaps they who tried to persuade Lulli to commission a libretto from La Fontaine after the failure of the Quinault *Alceste* in 1674. La Fontaine appears to have been helped by Racine and Boileau with his work on *Daphné*, while Lulli covertly commissioned another libretto, *Thésée*, from Quinault, persuading the king that La Fontaine had written only a routine pastoral. *Daphné* was never played, and La Fontaine may have avenged himself by taking part in drawing up a satire against Lulli, *Le Florentin*, for which the lost *Epître à Mme de Thianges* half atoned. It was probably at the very beginning of 1675, although it may have been still in 1674, that the *Nouveaux contes* appeared.

In 1676 La Fontaine had sold the house at Château-Thierry, together with his church pew there. On 29 July 1677 he was granted a privilège for a four-volume duodecimo edition of his *Fables choisies mises en vers* which he sold to Barbin and Thierry. The first two volumes reprint the six books of 1668. The third volume shares with the first two an achevé d'imprimer of 3 May 1678, and contains what we have come to call books seven and eight. The fourth volume has an achevé d'imprimer of 15 June 1679 and contains books nine to eleven. The eight new fables of 1671 are scattered through books seven, eight, and nine, and the two new volumes are dedicated to Mme de Montespan. The fables no longer even purport to be written for children.

La Fontaine was, however, still short of money, and tells us twice that he gambled. With conscious cynicism he exploited his literary success to sing the praises and win the favours of the great. In 1680, the year of Foucquet's death in prison at Pignerol, La Fontaine courted patronage from Condé, sending him verses and the translation of a dialogue of Plato, and seems regularly to have received money from the Contis. He was certainly ready to provide apparently demeaning social services for wealthy acquaintances like the playwright Mme Ulrich or the comte de Clermont-Tonnerre, who replaced Racine as La Champmesle's lover, and he aspired to join the comparatively large number of friends he had at the Académie. He enjoyed the company of François Girardon, the friend of Lebrun and sculptor at the Louvre and Versailles, and Pierre Mignard, the painter who replaced Lebrun in royal favour on the death of Colbert in 1683.

La Fontaine even occasionally called on Boileau at Autueil, although they were by now almost invariably in different camps, with La Fontaine and the entourages of the duchesse de Bouillon and of Mme de la Sablière inimical to that of Boileau. Open hostility broke out slowly, indicated at first only by gestures, silences, and the observations of third parties. When La Fontaine's enemy Colbert died on 6 September 1683 there was a vacant place in the Académie, and La Fontaine was elected on 15 November by 13 votes out of 23. Most of his enemies voted for Boileau, and the election was not ratified by the king until 20 April 1684, after La Fontaine had published a discreet ballad to the king in the *Mercure galant* (q.v.) renewing his promise to abandon the contes and Boileau himself had been elected on 17 April. A sitting on 24 April confirmed both elections. When La Fontaine took his seat on 2 May, at a ceremony reported in detail in the *Mercure*, he read out the self-analytical poem on his own inner uncertainties, the *Discours à Madame de la Sablière* ("Désormais que ma Muse…," not the poem of the same title in the ninth book of fables, "Iris, je vous louerais…").

La Fontaine also read a poem at Boileau's reception on 1 July. He attended the Académie assiduously, sometimes slept, and bitterly and successfully fought against the election of his former friend, Furetière, on 22 January 1685. In spite of his public repentance for the *Contes*, La Fontaine published five more in the first volume of the *Ouvrages de prose et de poésie des sieurs de Maucroix et de La Fontaine*, issued by Barbin with an achevé d'imprimer of 28 July 1685. The first volume was filled with La Fontaine's work, some of it dating back 20 years, but also including 11 new fables, to re-appear in the 12th book.

In 1681 La Fontaine had published a revision of Pinterel's translation of Seneca's letters, and 24 January 1682 was the date of the achevé d'imprimer of the *Poème du quinquina et autres ouvrages en vers*. This "poème," dedicated to the duchesse de Bouillon, comprises two parts of some 300 lines each, and is generally considered a failed attempt to enliven scientific verse with a whole repertoire of poetical conceits. From 6 to 11 May 1683 the Comédie-Française played La Fontaine's lost *Le Rendez-vous*, four times in all, and always after a tragedy. By the date of his election La Fontaine was becoming so withdrawn into personal melancholy that his company was regarded as tedious and his presentation of himself negligent. La Bruyère was struck by the contrast typified in La Fontaine:

Un homme paraît grossier, lourd, stupide; il ne sait pas parler, ni raconter ce qu'il vient de voir: s'il se met à écrire, c'est le modèle des bons contes; il fait parler les animaux, les arbres, les pierres, tout ce qui ne parle point: ce n'est que légèreté, qu'élégance, que beau naturel, et que délicatesse dans ses ouvrages

(A man appears coarse, heavy, stupid. He can neither talk nor recount what he has just seen. But if he starts to write, he produces the model for good stories. He makes animals speak—trees, stones, everything that does not speak, and all is lightness, elegance, charm, and delicacy in his works).

It was on 27 January 1687 that Charles Perrault read in the Académie his pro-"moderne" poem *Le Siècle de Louis le Grand*. Boileau rose to interrupt and had to be restrained by Huet. On 5 February La Fontaine obtained permission to publish the pro-"ancien" *Epître à Huet* written in 1674. In the late 1680s La Fontaine knew that he would soon have to choose between dreamy scepticism and religious commitment, although the attitude of the doubters semed to him as distasteful as that of the dévots, and a letter of 1687 to M. de Bonrepaus shows that he was in no hurry. He may at this time have collaborated with Champmeslé in a number of stage pieces: *Ragotin, Le Florentin, La Coupe enchantée, Je vous prends sans vert*, and *Le Veau perdu*. In 1688 François-Louis, prince de Conti, the duchesse de Bouillon's son, married Marie-Thérèse de Bourbon. La Fontaine wrote a congratulatory poem and dedicated a fable to him. He dedicated another to the duc de Bourgogne in the December 1690 number of the *Mercure galant*, and published two further fables there in each of the following two years. He also wrote a libretto for an opera by Colasse, *L'Astrée*, which was first performed before the dauphin and the princesse de Conti on 28 November 1691, but failed after its sixth performance.

In 1692 La Fontaine was seriously ill. Fénelon wanted more fables for his young pupil, the duc be Bourgogne, and, like Maucroix, Mme de la Sablière, and the 26-year-old priest who came to comfort him, wanted La Fontaine to die piously. On 12 February 1693 La Fontaine, who had already burnt a new comedy on the insistence of his young confessor, formally repudiated his contes, renounced any income the new Dutch edition might produce, bitterly regretted having written them, and declared his intention henceforward to write only works of piety. A letter from the confessor to the abbé Olivet sets out in detail all La Fontaine said in the presence of a deputation from the Académie. The 10-year-old duc de Bourgogne sent him what remained of his pocket money for the month, which was 50 louis, wishing it were more. During his remaining two years of life La Fontaine did in fact compose some hymns, which have been lost. Mme de la Sablière had died on 6 January 1693, and La Fontaine was taken in by his friends the d'Hervarts. He was to die in their house in the Rue Plâtrière, where there was a ceiling by his friend, Mignard, depicting the apotheosis of Psyché.

Two new fables were published in a *Recueil de vers choisis* of 1 June edited by Père Dominique Bouhours, La Fontaine's paraphrase of the "Dies Irae" was read to the Académie on 15 June, and a new edition of the *Fables*, dated 1694 and adding the 12th book, was published by Barbin on 1 September 1693. What we regard as the 12th book, comprising the late fables written for the duc de Bourgogne, was in 1694 called the seventh, which suggests that La Fontaine wanted the fables for the duc de Bourgogne, essentially book seven, to follow those written for the dauphin, books one to six, and to precede the more philosophical, social and political fables written for Mme de Montespan in the remaining five books, now seven to eleven. On 1 October La Fontaine was chosen by lottery as the new chancellor of the Académie. On 2 October 1694 he became its director.

On 10 February 1695 he wrote to Maucroix that he suffered "un malaise (an attack)" on returning from the Académie. He died on 13 April, having taken to a life of penance, with hair shirt and scourge.

WORKS

Although La Fontaine needed every penny his pen could earn him, he was not what we would today regard as a professional writer, writing for as wide a group of readers as he might find for his work. He was grateful for whatever sums he could derive directly from publishers, but the money his pen made came to him chiefly in indirect ways, as patronage sometimes gratuitously bestowed, but often in return for services rendered, for flattery that was necessarily stylized. *Les Amours de Psyché et de Cupidon* might have celebrated Versailles as *Le Songe de Vaux* might have celebrated Vaux. As the biographical details make clear, the poet's pen was frankly for sale, the need for money usually pressing, and patronage actively solicited. La Fontaine was still unusual in his generation in his chosen way of life. He was not of the Church, but none the less exploited his minor aristocracy, with its social acceptability, in order to gain a living from his pen. He needed a material reward for virtually every madrigal. The resulting flattery of the rich, their friends, lovers, mistresses, children, houses, ambitions, and self-aggrandizement demanded a cultivated amateurism which called for a pretence of sincerity not intended to deceive, but whose presence decorum demanded.

Much of La Fontaine's poetry, often skilful, intelligent, and witty, occasionally amusing, and generally elegant, was none the less routine, not so much insincere as on any level unfelt. The tone of the 1693 recantation in which the profits of the new Dutch edition of the contes were renounced, and La Fontaine's sobbing reaction to the arrival of the duc de Bourgogne's pocket money in compensation, makes clear how much those profits mattered to him. The preface to the skimpy first part of the *Contes et nouvelles en vers* is an outrageously honest statement of pure venality. Much of La Fontaine's published work is of no great literary interest, but his amateur pose was professional enough for it to matter to him that we should know he knew it. Critics have too often sought for shoots of sprouting genius in pieces which were no more than perfunctory, or in which La

Fontaine had lost his way. He is an author to whom no service is paid by an assiduous and continuing reappraisal of material in which his true literary power is not readily perceivable. Probably only the contes need proper reassessment.

The key indicator to the nature of La Fontaine's poetic achievement is biographical. He showed a perpetual inner uncertainty—his "âme inquiète (fretful soul)"—from the moment when, as an elder son with expectations and aristocratic pretentions, he surprisingly entered the Oratorians, only to find that he had made a mistake, through the oscillations of register between the cynical licentiousness of the contes and a rigid piety, to the histrionics of the 1693 renunciation, which might after the recent serious illness have been sincere, but which was certainly stage-managed. From the first association of knights of the round table, through the quasi-official appointment as Foucquet's poet, La Fontaine carefully refused to align himself with any group, as he refused to align himself in the dispute between "anciens" and "modernes" either in 1674 or in 1687.

The pattern continues through the vicissitudinous relationships with Racine, Boileau, and Furetière, whose formal literary norms La Fontaine understood and admired, but to whom La Fontaine refused to commit himself in an alliance against Pellisson, Charpentier, and Perrault, with whom he had the greater spiritual affinity, and whose sensibility he more nearly shared. He balanced his affiliations with friends of Port-Royal against homage paid to friends of the Jesuits, his links with friends of Foucquet against dealings with sycophants of Louis XIV, Colbert, and the court. It requires no great psychological acumen to realize that the literary achievement must lie in a tension between realistic awareness of the motivations of human behaviour at all levels of power and the personal need to avoid commitment to any system of values or attitudes.

La Fontaine required, for the deepest expression of his poetic needs, genres calling for wit, elegance, concision, and insight, but which could also remain playful, teasing, apparently superficial, supported by formal structures that were rigorous and complicated. What he found to hand was the fable, which he turned into a formidable poetic genre, while exploiting its unique ability to purport to be something it was not. La Fontaine's fables were never really aimed at the moral formation of children. Slowly and tentatively the fables of books seven to eleven in our modern numbering begin to drop the pretence, almost gratefully reverted to when Fénelon's post from 1689 as tutor to the duc de Bourgogne offered La Fontaine the opportunity to put the mask back on. Both Fénelon and La Fontaine understood the rules of the game La Fontaine was being asked to resume playing.

When La Fontaine presented his *Adonis* to Foucquet in June 1658, he was already looking for a form which would combine respect for the poetic norms of antiquity with the new sensibility of cultured refinement which, purified of excessive exuberance, would be distilled into the aesthetic principles directing the partisans of the "moderne" position in the Querelle. Just as Madeleine de Scudéry was abandoning the adventure novel for the analyses of a new attitude to love in *Clélie*, La Fontaine in *Adonis* was virtually inventing the heroic idyll of which the unfinished *Le Songe de Vaux* might have been a further example, together with *Les Amours de Psyché et de Cupidon*.

La Fontaine's introductory poem renounces any ambition to follow Homer and Virgil. The model for *Adonis* is in fact Ovid's *Metamorphoses*, but the element of stylized pretence is already

there. La Fontaine's verse, as Mme de la Sablière was to insinuate, generally contains affectation:

> Je n'ai jamais chanté que l'ombrage des bois,
> Flore, Echo, les Zéphirs et leurs molles haleines

(I have only ever sung of the shade of the woods, of Flora, Echo, the Zephyrs and their sweet breaths).

The inspiration of *Adonis* was eventually to lead towards the fables, that of *L'Eunuque* to the contes. La Fontaine risked affronting propriety by keeping Terence's title, but he seems never to have intended his comedy to be staged, adapts Terence's intrigue, which hinges on a rape, to the refinements of 17th-century taste in a culture still trying to rid itself of an obsession with physical feats and, after following his original almost scene by scene, leaves it behind between the middle of the third act and the ending. The courtisan Thaïs has become a well-brought-up young widow, and the whole play is toned down when Cherée, travestied as a eunuch in order to be in a position to court Pamphile, loses his rough vigour, Phédrie and Thaïs marry, and Thrason loses his real function. *Les Rieurs du Beau-Richard*, written about 1659, is a racy ballet, appropriate to carnival performance and inspired by the 15th-century *La Farce de Maistre Pierre Pathelin*. It was written only for, and played only by, friends of La Fontaine at Château-Thierry.

Le Songe de Vaux was commissioned in 1659 to describe the magnificence of Foucquet's mansion, its gardens, and its landscape. It was never finished, and the best of the published fragments are generally thought to be the five published only in the 1729 *Oeuvres diverses*, although the description of the tapestry *Les Amours de Mars et de Vénus* was published in the 1665 *Contes*, and three more fragments appeared in the 1671 *Fables nouvelles*. Construction work at Vaux had begun early in 1657, and the final effect of the newly planted gardens had still to be imagined. La Fontaine thought he had plenty of time, and seems at first to have thought of describing a fictitious celebration, given by Oronte to mark a contest between the fairies of architecture, painting, gardens, and poetry. Which has contributed most to the glories of Vaux? The fairies plead on their own behalf, but the result is left undecided, and La Fontaine may have thought of writing in the form of an account of a dream, set at night in the grounds. The result is confused by the description of Lebrun's ceiling of Night, naturally seen by day.

In spite of what must be presumed to be Boileau's *Dissertation sur "Joconde"*, although never published or acknowledged and probably regretted by him, Boileau described La Fontaine's Joconde in the 1694 *Satire X* as a "conte odieux (a detestable conte)." La Fontaine calls it a "nouvelle." Well before Ariosto the story was considered a classic of the satirical literature of female infidelity, and La Fontaine's adaptation of it to 17th-century taste in metres much more complex than Bouillon's shows him well on the way to the technical mastery of rhetorical devices which were to be developed in the *Fables*.

The variable and irregular metres of *Joconde* contrast with the dominating decasyllables of most of the contes, including those in the 1665 *Contes et nouvelles en vers* and in *Le Cocu battu et content* with which alone *Joconde* was first published, demanding a much stricter versification and rhyme scheme. We know there was real hesitation between the forms as well as the poetic registers of the contes and the fables from letters and advice proffered, notably by Turenne, as well as from the celebrated wager on the outcome of the popularity test between Bouillon's version of *Joconde* and La Fontaine's. The contes are generally licentious to some degree, in the manner of Boccaccio, although La Fontaine is less boisterously comic and the technique comes from Marot and Voiture rather than the Italian renaissance. Boileau and Chapelain praised the contes without remarking on the fundamental coarseness of the humour. La Fontaine himself felt the need to excuse himself in his preface, disclaiming the contes as simply a game of no consequence, in which neither the true nor the probable plays any part. The interest is concentrated not on the stories, but on "la manière de les conter (the way in which they are told)."

The collection of *Fables* published in 1668, whenever the earliest of them was written, makes clear in its preface the stylization inherent in the form. The letter to the dauphin, which no seven-year-old child could understand, pays a deference which is clearly ritual to Aesop, from whom the majority of the fables did not derive, to Socrates, mentioned by Le Maître de Sacy in his edition of Phaedrus, from whom they did derive, to the stoic "semina virtutum (seeds of virtue)," to Horace's mixture of the pleasant with the useful, and to the learned tradition that important moral truths had always needed to be wrapped in fable. The preface affirms the legitimacy of La Fontaine's enterprise against Patru, accepts the challenge of keeping the fables short, and re-asserts the renaissance link between poetry and music to justify putting Aesop's prose into French verse. After expounding his intention, La Fontaine talks of the execution:

On ne trouvera pas ici l'élégance ni l'extrême brèveté qui rendent Phèdre recommandable; ce sont qualités au-dessus de ma portée. Comme il m'était impossible de l'imiter en cela, j'ai cru qu'il fallait en récompense égayer l'ouvrage plus qu'il n'a fait

(Neither the elegance nor the extreme brevity which make Phaedrus so estimable will be found here. Those are qualities beyond my grasp. Since I could not imitate him in those respects, it seemed to me necessary to compensate by making the work more lively than he did).

The key word is "égayer (brighten/cheer up/make more lively)," which opposed La Fontaine to Patru, who did not like fables in verse, and Boileau, who admitted verse but insisted above all on brevity and was in practice and precept against "égaiement (enlivening)" in La Fontaine's sense, which meant adding colour.

La Fontaine had composed the rather dry "La Mort et le Malheureux" (I, xv), a brief but vividly rhetorical dialogue between the unhappy man who calls on death and death herself. Death obliges by coming when called: "Elle frappe à sa porte, elle entre, elle se montre (She knocks at the door, she comes in, she shows herself)." The unhappy man cries out to have death taken away, before himself addressing her and telling her never to come back. It was probably Patru who reproached La Fontaine for departing too far from Aesop's "The old Man and Death," and sacrificing the quip at the end, when the suddenly frightened woodcutter simply asks death to help him load up. The young Boileau thought he could do better, and produced "Le Bûcheron et la Mort," first published in 1701, with the quip, and all but the last of the nine lines alexandrines, ending

La Mort vint à la fin. "Que veux-tu?" cria-t-elle.
"Qui moi?" dit-il alors, prompt à se corriger,
"Que tu m'aides à me charger"

(In the end death came. "What do you want?" she exclaimed./"Who, me?" he said, quick to put right his mistake,/"I want you to help me to load up").

La Fontaine, who presumably had not seen Boileau's version, was stung into re-writing his own fable in a version closer to Aesop now normally but incorrectly distinguished from the first one by the title "La Mort et le Bûcheron." He now takes 12 lines for a brilliantly colourful description of the woodcutter's plight, using alliteration, assonance, a more complex rhyme scheme, and onomatopoeia, then four lines for the story, now including the quip, and four for the moral. Now that the point is clearly not the uninspired moral didacticism, he can afford to rhyme the conventionally aphoristic moral at the end. When in 1668 Boileau published the fable "L'Huître et les Plaideurs," in alexandrines, at the end of his first *Epître*, from where he subsequently removed it to the second *Epître*, La Fontaine riposted with his own fable of the same title (IX, ix), a brilliant little satirical comedy of 25 lines.

In his preface La Fontaine returns to the point:

C'est ce qu'on demande aujourd'hui. On veut de la nouveauté et de la gaieté. Je n'appelle pas gaieté ce qui excite le rire; mais un certain charme, un air agréable, qu'on peut donner à toutes sortes de sujets, même les plus sérieux

(It is what is asked for today. People want novelty and liveliness. What I call liveliness is not what makes people laugh, but a certain charm, a pleasantness that can be given to all sorts of subjects, even the most serious ones).

He goes on to argue the usefulness of fables for the teaching of children, but his argument depends more on the vividness of the brief story than on the superiority of fables over history as the source of moral wisdom. When his justification runs to what his fables teach children about natural history, one wonders where he saw cats crunching weasels. More to the point is the single human trait typified by each of the individual inhabitants of the animal world. When Prometheus made man, he took, says La Fontaine, the dominant qualities of each animal. La Fontaine also justifies the inclusion in his fables of humans and vegetable life.

La Fontaine was widely read in classical literature, most of it by then available in Latin or French. His moral lessons are almost all reducible to peasant canniness and street wisdom. He was not devoid of joy in life. The only remarkable thing is the absence of any prominent stoic tinge. It is also no doubt true that his imaginative inventiveness was not fictional. He was too much of a moralist and a realist to have been capable of writing well in the novel form, and the common reproach that he lacked inventiveness should be replaced by the acknowledgement that his imaginative purposes would not have been served by being fanciful. He was at home with the miniature, revealing his personal vulnerability only in the repeated defensiveness of the morals, and the preference for brilliantly vivid description, characterization, and conversation over straight narrative.

Metres, rhythms, and rhyme schemes are varied, the verse is

fluid, the language often quite deliberately poetic, the economy magisterial. The poetic techniques are rich from the beginning, although they are deployed later with greater assurance and at greater length. The spectrum is wide, ranging from simple assonance, alliteration, and onomatopoeia to the construction of a comic scene in direct speech, often with beautifully calculated incongruities, as when the grasshopper offers to repay "interest and principal, on my faith as an animal," or when a moral is reduced to a memorable epigram. Most of the early fables concentrate on a single human characteristic considered typical of a particular animal—the lion's power, the fox's cunning, the lamb's unsuspecting docility, the cat's hypocrisy, or the wolf's bullying—but the imaginative strength lies in the vigour of the evocation.

There are about 250 poems in the *Fables*, all but a handful of them fables published by La Fontaine during his lifetime. Almost always it is the poetic achievement rather than the intellectual or moral content which demands comment. Even the simplest fables hide technical skills. One of the simplest and best known, for instance, is "Le Corbeau et le Renard (The Crow and the Fox)" (I, ii). By references to the crow and the fox as "Maître Corbeau" and "Maître Renard," we are immediately removed from the real world which La Fontaine so dislikes into the world of make-believe, although it is not the make-believe of children. We do not in the real world talk about crows and foxes as if they were people, and children would miss the irony. There are 18 lines. The first four insist again on the stylization of the imaginative register. Foxes in the real world are not attracted by the smell of cheese held in the beak of a crow perched on a tree. We ourselves are not on the other hand above being tempted to take advantage of a fool's vanity for our profit.

The fox, "Maître" Renard, addresses the crow as "Monsieur *du* Corbeau." "How pretty you are!" "Monsieur," unlike "maître," was a title denoting respect and rank, while "du," "de la," etc., before a place-name, indicated aristocratic status, but is here, in the interests of flattery, used ungrammatically. The fox says to the crow, in preposterously inflated language, if your voice matches your plumage, "You are the phoenix among the residents of these woods." The crow, immediately rattled into showing off its voice, lets go of the cheese, and "Le Renard s'en saisit (The fox snatches it)." The extremely brisk narration, over in half a line, is characteristic of La Fontaine's style, as is the sharply ironic comment on human behaviour he implies. The comic effect is swiftly and expertly contrived, leaving the reader sorry for the silly, ugly, and raucous crow's susceptibility to blarney, and ashamed at admiring the wickedly clever fox's neat little trick. The layers of irony are already too complex for children.

The second collection contains more elaborate, complex feats of poetic skill, like "Le Chat, la Belette, et le petit Lapin (The Cat, the Weasel, and the little Rabbit)" (VII, xv). There are 47 lines, of which 18 are octosyllabic, the rest alexandrines. The last two are devoted to the moral. The rhymes are very weak, and the scheme complex to the point of convolution. The story is simple. A weasel goes and occupies the burrow of an absent rabbit. On his return they argue, then agree to go to a learned cat for arbitration. He grabs them simultaneously, one with each of his forepaws, and crunches them to death. So much for the natural history. The moral is different. Petty sovereigns should avoid asking great kings to settle their disputes.

The poetry is different again. This is the first book dedicated to Mme de Montespan, but the first line of the fable again sets up the land of make-believe that, as in the previous example, is not for children:

Du palais d'un jeune Lapin
Dame Belette un beau matin
S'empara; c'est une rusée

(Madame Weasel one fine morning took possession of the palace of a young rabbit: she is crafty).

One main verb, and the action has happened, also as in the previous example. And once again, the inflated poetic language is at once lyrical and ironic. The burrow is a palace, and is referred to as "souterrains séjours (subterranean dwellings)," then as the "paternel logis (paternal residence)."

The weasel's possessions are her "pénates (belongings)," a word used only in the legal Latin term "lares et penates," but by this time the reader has, for the sake of the pretend land of enchantment, suspended his awareness that weasels do not have legal ownership of anything. The fable uses a whole scattering of legal terms like "octroi (bestowal)," and "la coutume et l'usage (custom and usage)." The poet laughs at his rabbit, using the affectionate diminutive "Janot," when recounting his return after "going to pay his court to the dawn" (the poetic "Aurore" rather than the prosaic "aube") "parmi le thym et la rosée (amid the thyme and the dew)."

The excitement of the dawn and the dew is marvellously communicated in a succession of "t" sounds and very short vowels: "Après qu'il eut brouté, trotté, fait tous ses tours (After he had nibbled, trotted, been through all his paces)." La Fontaine was adept at manipulating long and short vowels, and consonantal sounds, to suit the pace of the action described. In "Le Torrent et la Rivière" (VIII, xxiii), the shallow torrent made a lot of noise but was harmless—"Un torrent tombait des montagnes (A torrent tumbled down from the mountains)"—while the dangerous river followed a slower course—"Image d'un sommeil doux, paisible et tranquille (The image of a sweet, peaceful, quiet sleep)." The sounds convey the same message as the meaning of the words.

The legal wrangle between the rabbit and the weasel is a clever little skit, comic, and quite complicated. The laws of inheritance are intricate, and the weasel will have none of them. The name of the cat, Raminagrobis, comes from Rabelais and Voiture:

C'était un chat vivant comme un dévot ermite,
    Un chat faisant la chattemite,
Un saint homme de chat, bien fourré, gros et gras,
    Arbitre expert sur tous les cas

(He was a cat living like a devout hermit,/A cat pretending to be a humble creature,/A holy man of a cat, with thick fur, glossy and plump,/An expert judge on every sort of case).

The end naturally comes very swiftly. The cat "mit les plaideurs d'accord en croquant l'un et l'autre (brought the opposing parties together by gobbling them both up)."

Not all the fables have quite the same gloomy warnings. The two pigeons love one another tenderly (IX, ii), but the extended moral points out that happiness is far too fragile to be risked.

Then the gloom returns. Love is the greatest happiness of all but, asks the poet, "Ai-je passé le temps d'aimer? (Have I passed the time for love?)." There is little direct contemporary allusion. The lion is not Louis XIV: he is the generalized figure of power, against whom we would do well to defend what we have with the suspicious tenacity of Aesop's Attic peasants. The fox is not generally Colbert. He is the sly, crafty creature of guile, not the dangerous barking wolf, whom no one could admire.

There are, naturally, semi-private allusions, as to literary disputes, which are of no great account. It is not essential to know that the half-line "Il faut que je me venge" of "Le Loup et l'Agneau" (I, x) must ironically refer to a famous line of Chimène in Le Cid, and that 17th-century French readers will have recognized it, although modern editors do not. There is not much social satire, but there is a great deal of sharp observation relevant to human society and to social relationships, not all of it derived from the antique. Above all there is the gentle cynicism which lends an ironic edge to the lyrical impulse it might have blunted, and there are the extraordinary miniaturist skills of the accomplished poetic craftsman.

Neither Les Amours de Psyché et de Cupidon, interesting today primarily on account of the conversation between the four characters and the Versailles setting, nor the theatrical works, nor the occasional verse are today thought to be of other than historical importance. It is quite rightly for the Fables that La Fontaine is remembered. To understand them it is essential to remember that their make-believe is a protective covering, and not at all what it purports to be. It is make-believe make-believe.

PUBLICATIONS

Collections

Oeuvres de M. de L.F., 3 vols., 1728
Oeuvres complètes, 8 vols., 1820–21
Oeuvres, 6 vols., 1827
Oeuvres complètes, 11 vols., 1883–92
Oeuvres complètes, Bibliothèque de la Pléiade, 2 vols., 1954 and 1968
Oeuvres complètes, Bibliothèque de la Pléiade, 2 vols., 1991

Verse

Adonis (1658 manuscript), 1825
Elégie aux Nymphes de Vaux, 1661
Nouvelles en vers tirée [sic] de Boccace et de l'Arioste, 1665
Contes et nouvelles en vers, 1665
Contes et nouvelles en vers, 2nd part, 1666
Contes et nouvelles en vers, 3rd part, 1671
Contes et nouvelles en vers, 4th part, 1674
Fables choisies, mises en vers, 1668
Recueil de poésies chrétiennes et diverses, 3 vols., 1671
Poème de la captivité de saint Malc, 1673
Fables choisies, mises en vers...revues, corrigées et augmentées, 5 vols., 1678–94
Ode pour la paix, 1679
Poème du quinquina et autres ouvrages en vers, 1682
Ouvrages de prose et de poésie des Srs de Maucroix et de L.F., 2 vols., 1685
A Mgr l'Evêque de Soissons, en lui donnant un Quintilien de la

traduction d'Oratio Toscanella (the Epître à Huet), 1687

The Fables were translated into English in 1804. Further translations have been published by Edward Marsh (1931), Marianne Moore (1954), and Reginald Jarman (1962)

Plays

L'Eunuque, comédie, 1654
Astrée, tragédie, 1691
Le Florentin, comédie, 1699

Other

Les Amours de Psyché et de Cupidon, 1669

Biographical and critical studies

Clarac, P., La Fontaine, l'homme et l'oeuvre, 1947
Wadsworth, P., Young La Fontaine, 1952
Sutherland, M., La Fontaine (in English), 1953
Couton, Georges, La Poétique de La Fontaine, 1957
——La Politique de La Fontaine, 1959
Mourgues, Odette de, La Fontaine: Fables (in English), 1960
Guiton, Margaret O., La Fontaine, Poet and Counterpoet, 1961
Biard, Jean-Dominique, The Style of La Fontaine's Fables, 1966
Jasinski, René, La Fontaine et le premier recueil des "Fables", 2 vols., 1966
Lapp, John C., The Aesthetics of Negligence: La Fontaine's "Contes", 1971
MacKay, Agnes Ethel, La Fontaine and his Friends: A Biography, 1972
Richard, Noël, La Fontaine et les "Fables" du deuxième recueil, 1972
Bornecque, Pierre, La Fontaine fabuliste, 1973

LA MOTTE: see **HOUDAR DE LA MOTTE**

LA ROCHEFOUCAULD, François VI, duc de, 1613–1680.

Moralist and memorialist.

LIFE

La Rochefoucauld's family can be traced back to the 11th century but became prominent only in the 15th. In the 16th century its head, François III, went over to the Reform and was a victim of the St Bartholomew Day massacre. François IV, supporting the king, was killed by the League, and François V, a Catholic, congratulated by Louis XIII for the vigour with which he suppressed the Reform, was made a duke and peer in 1622. The eldest sons in the family were known as the princes de Marcillac, after a property near the Gironde which had belonged to the family since the 14th century, and La Rochefoucauld was called Marcillac until his father died in 1650. His mother was Gabrielle du Plessis-Liancourt. Destined to arms, chivalresque and more than just fashionably melancholic in disposition, he shared with only moderate enthusiasm the political attitudes of his caste, and there is universal agreement among those who knew him that he was not so much a man of action as a dreamer, always detached from the causes he espoused. To La Rochefoucauld itself, 16 miles to the east of Angoulême, the family preferred the château de Verteuil, overlooking the Charente, about 25 miles north of the town. In spite of its vast estates, the family was short of money.

A professional soldier, too idealist to make a successful conspirator, La Rochefoucauld, born on 15 September 1613, was married at the age of 14½ to Andrée de Vivonne, by whom he had eight children and to whom he remained permanently attached. In 1629 he was maître de camp of a regiment at the age of 15½, fighting in Italy in the army led by Richelieu and Louis XIII. The French campaign was aimed at imposing the duc de Nevers, against Spanish opposition, on the duchy of Mantua, which he had inherited. La Rochefoucauld was to serve in the Netherlands in 1635–36 and was to be present both at Rocroi in 1643 and at the siege of Gravelines in 1644. Towards the end of his life he served again, in Louis XIV's Dutch campaign of 1667–68, during which he took part in the siege of Lille.

In 1630 La Rochefoucauld appeared at court, where he became the gallantly devoted servant of the famous court beauty, Marie de Hautefort, the object of Louis XIII's platonic affection, to whom he was himself also seriously attached. She was a lady-in-waiting to the queen, Anne of Austria, to whom Richelieu had become increasingly hostile. Richelieu's hostility to the queen mother, Marie de Medici, had led in 1630 to her alliance with Anne of Austria against him and, when in the autumn of that year the king fell gravely ill, Richelieu was nearly removed from his position as principal minister. The conspiracy failed. On Monday 11 November 1630, the "day of dupes," Louis XIII finally defied his mother and reaffirmed his confidence in Richelieu. Michel de Marillac, the elderly keeper of the seals, was dismissed, to die two years later in prison, while his brother, the maréchal Louis de Marillac, leading the army in Italy, was brought back, treated mercilessly by the king, handed to a special court which narrowly voted for the death penalty, and on 10 May 1632 beheaded on the Place de Grève.

Marie de Medici would not go to Moulins, of which she was governor, and was therefore made to stay in Compiègne, where she had accompanied Louis XIII and Anne of Austria, until, in the summer of 1631, she fled to Belgium, finally to die in Cologne in 1641. In 1637 the heir apparent was still Gaston d'Orléans, officially reconciled to his brother, the king, from 1634, but in fact, with the queen, still a focus of discontent for those, like most of the remnants of the grand feudal aristocracy—the Vendômes, the Retz, and the Nevers—opposed to Richelieu and the house of Condé, which supported him, as they were to go on being opposed to his successor, Mazarin, continuing the same policies.

It is against this background that in 1637 the young La Roche-

foucauld, his imagination inflamed, agreed to arrange the abduction of the queen and Marie de Hautefort from the court to Brussels. The conspiracy was abandoned but, without La Rochefoucauld's knowledge, his horses were taken by the duchesse de Chevreuse in order to flee to Spain. She had been born Marie de Rohan-Montbazon, was the wife then widow of the Constable of France, Albert de Luynes, and had subsequently married Claude de Lorraine, duc de Chevreuse. She was the mistress of Charles d'Aubespine, marquis de Châteauneuf. An intimate of Anne of Austria, she had been exiled to Lorraine when her protégé, Chalais, was executed for complicity in the opposition to the marriage between the king's brother, then the duc d'Anjou but later to become the duc d'Orléans, and the princesse de Montpensier. Retz was the lover of her daughter, and her political intrigues, not entirely without historical significance, cannot be neglected; they are important in the life, thought, and literature of her century.

La Rochefoucauld was imprisoned by Richelieu in the Bastille for eight days, and then banished for two years to Verteuil. It is difficult to take the 1637 episode with total seriousness. It was clearly amateur, undertaken in a spirit of dashing youthful bravado. The merely token penalty suggests that Richelieu did not regard it as much more than a silly prank. When, shortly before his own death on 4 December 1642, Richelieu found his political plans the object of an inchoate plot mounted by only marginally more competent conspirators, he had Cinq-Mars and de Thou executed. La Rochefoucauld, like most of the grander aristocracy, sent a note of sympathy to de Thou's brother to mark disapproval of the dying Richelieu's behaviour.

When, soon after Richelieu's death, Louis XIII himself died on 14 May 1643, the parlement overturned his final wishes and appointed as regent not his brother but his widow. She immediately re-appointed Mazarin her chief minister, and La Rochefoucauld was out-manoeuvred as she came increasingly to rely on the minister. On his return from the victory of Enghien, the future Condé, at Rocroi in May 1643, and only days after the king's death, La Rochefoucauld negotiated with the nobility opposed to Mazarin, who thought that La Rochefoucauld, like the regent herself, had betrayed them. La Rochefoucauld also worked for the return to France of the duchesse de Chevreuse, but he did not succeed in advancing his own cause politically. He was then badly injured at the battle of Mardick in August 1646, the year in which he bought the governorship of Poitou where, in 1648, he repressed on behalf of the crown the first troubles resulting from Mazarin's quarrel with the Paris parlement.

He was again disappointed by the lack of recognition, especially the failure to place him on a list of new peerages and so to confer on him a peerage in his own right, before he inherited his father's. He attached much importance to obtaining for his wife the privilege of the "tabouret (stool)," allowing her to remain seated in the presence of the king and queen. From 1648 he felt sufficiently bitter to work with the party of the "princes," which at first did not include Condé or the king's brother, but Beaufort, Bouillon, Retz, Conti, and Conti's sister, Mme de Longueville, who were to make common cause with the Paris parlement against Mazarin. When once the Thirty Years War had ended with the Treaty of Westphalia in 1648, Condé himself, brother of Conti and Mme de Longueville, blockaded Paris on behalf of the king early in 1649. In January 1649 Mme de Longueville, who for three years had been his mistress, bore La Rochefoucauld an illegitimate child, the comte de Saint-Paul. In February 1649 La Rochefoucauld, fighting against the crown near Lagny, was badly wounded for the second time. Longueville himself, raising Normandy for the princes, was contained by Harcourt, and Turenne, also on the side of the rebels, had to take refuge in the Netherlands.

The parliamentary Fronde of 1648, which had resulted in the regent's flight to Saint-Germain, had led to an uneasy and unenforceable agreement at Rueil in March 1649, achieved partly on the advice of Condé. La Rochefoucauld was given the "honneurs du Louvre," chiefly to drive his carriage in, and the "tabouret" privilege for his wife, but these distinctions were withdrawn when other members of the nobility protested at them. Condé's own personal demands now made clear that his ambition was too great to be compatible with Mazarin's authority, and Mazarin's determination to curb Condé's power made the second Fronde inevitable. Mme de Longueville brought about the reconciliation between Condé, her brother, and La Rochefoucauld, her lover, and Condé joined the princes, while Retz momentarily allied himself with Mazarin.

A series of mostly trivial incidents in the second part of 1649 led to the arrest of Longueville, Condé, and Conti, and their imprisonment in Vincennes. La Rochefoucauld managed to take Mme de Longueville to safety, and organized the resistance to Mazarin, who was for the moment supported by Orléans and the Vendôme family. Royal troops pillaged and destroyed Verteuil before peace was made. Retz now allied himself with Orléans in an attempt to sweep Mazarin from power; La Rochefoucauld negotiated the release of Longueville, Condé, and Conti, who had twice had to be moved out of the way of advancing rebel troops and were freed on 13 February 1651; and Mazarin was obliged to flee. La Rochefoucauld, who had inherited the title on his father's death, which had taken place on 18 February 1650, remained attached to Condé. On 21 August, jammed in a doorway with Retz at a meeting of the parlement, he briefly thought of assassinating him, but was dissuaded (see: Retz). In September he left Paris with the princes, and the war started again. The princes signed a treaty with Spain in November and, sometime during the autumn, Mme de Longueville left La Rochefoucauld to become the mistress of the duc de Nemours.

In January 1652 Mazarin was recalled, and in February Turenne and Bouillon came to reinforce the royal army, which steadily advanced. Condé came from the south, took command on the Loire, and routed the royal army at Bléneau, only to be defeated by Turenne at Gien. Condé now dallied in Paris, which gave Turenne the opportunity to reorganize. With 12,000 men at Saint-Denis he was a threat to Condé, with 6,000 at Saint-Cloud. Condé, refused permission to cross Paris to Charenton, went round by the south, and on 2 July was forced by Turenne to engage in the Faubourg Saint-Antoine, where La Rochefoucauld was wounded in the face. This was the celebrated occasion on which Mlle de Montpensier, daughter of Gaston d'Orléans, opened the gates of Paris to allow the cannon of the Bastille to fire towards the royal troops and to permit what remained of Condé's army to take refuge in Paris. A provisional government with Orléans, Condé, and Beaufort was established, but could not impose its authority. Beaufort killed Nemours in a duel; the parlement transferred to Pontoise; Mazarin withdrew from France in August to make agreement easier; an amnesty was offered; Turenne held a Spanish army, raised to support Condé,

in check; and on 21 October the king returned to Paris, leaving Gaston d'Orléans to retire to Blois. La Rochefoucauld's head was covered in bandages and he was wearing glasses. Retz, who had opened negotiations for the return of the court, was arrested on 19 December.

La Rochefoucauld's sight was threatened by his wound and only an operation saved it. He was ruined, ill, and under threat of arrest. Loyal to Condé, he refused an amnesty but was given a passport to Luxembourg. He was allowed to return to France, where he lived in the ruins of Verteuil, in 1653, and then in 1656 was allowed back to Paris. He may have intrigued a little with Foucquet, from whom he received 10,000 livres, perhaps through the good offices of Gourville, and he was given a pension by the young king, Louis XIV, but he was never to gain his confidence, and in August 1671 ceded his dukedom and peerage to his eldest son, who showed him little gratitude. It was during his exile at Verteuil and his subsequent stay in Paris that La Rochefoucauld meditated on the wars and on his life, and read the Latin historians and moralists, especially Seneca, Tacitus, and Sallust, and Montaigne. He was unlettered in any formal sense and had only inadequate Latin, but he acquired a lucid insight into the history of the political struggles in which he had taken part.

From 1656 La Rochefoucauld lived in Paris in the house of his uncle, his mother's brother the duc de Liancourt, whose granddaughter and only heir was to marry La Rochefoucauld's eldest son. His mother did not herself die until 1672. He himself frequented précieux (q.v.) society, and was mixed up in such galant social pastimes as the confection of portraits, proverbs, aphorisms, pseudo-geographical maps of types of relationship, and "questions d'amour (questionnaires about love)," such as that of 1661 by Marie Linage, published only in 1972, or the Questions d'amour of Mme de Brégy, published in the Lettres et poésies of 1666. The Maximes were an only slightly more demanding development of this type of activity, which clearly related the sophisticated fastidiousness about the physical aspects of love characteristic of the précieux, called by Ninon de Lenclos "the Jansenists (q.v.) of love," to its austerely pious renunciation, although of course the dévots also rejected the galanterie as frivolous, and even pernicious.

La Rochefoucauld's Maximes were largely elaborated in the company of Mme de Sablé, his senior by 14 years, who had always taken the same political view as he and who had been a well-known précieuse, close to Mlle de Hautefort. She had been led towards the severe piety of Port-Royal (q.v.) by the princesse de Guéménée and, on being forced to sell her marquisat to Abel Servien in 1654, she moved into a lodging she had had built as an annexe to the monastery in 1656. La Rochefoucauld's letters about maxims, mostly to Mme de Sablé, indicate that the habit of fabricating sentences "is catching, like a cold," and ask for certain favourite dishes to be served—stews and chicken with plums, large helpings of jams—and for the recipe for a carrot soup mentioned twice.

Among the friends received by Mme de Sablé were the duchesse de Longueville, the duchesse de Liancourt, the princesse de Guéménée, the duchesse de Schomberg, formerly Mlle de Hautefort, Mme de Montauzier, and Mme de Lafayette, but we know that Pascal was an occasional visitor, and that matters of theology, philosophy, and especially medicine were also discussed, with Jesuits, Jansenists, and natural scientists also present. It is obvious that the company frequented by La Rochefoucauld, at least until he began to be a daily visitor of Mme de Lafayette, was Jansenistically inclined, although his presence was also still much appreciated in galant society, and the discussion of psychological maxims was the characteristic pastime at Mme de Sablé's residence.

In a letter of 1662 he asked Mme de Sablé about the current feelings for him of Mme de Longueville, who had become converted to a penitential piety some time before 1658. He also visited the. Hôtel de Nevers. Through Mme de Lafayette, with whom his close association must date from about 1664, he met Mme de Sévigné and became reconciled with his old enemy, Retz. In 1672 the comte de Saint-Paul, who the year before had become duc de Longueville in succession to his brother, who had been ordained in 1669, was killed at the crossing of the Rhine with one of La Rochefoucauld's legitimate sons, another of whom was injured. In 1674 La Rochefoucauld inherited the Hôtel de Liancourt from his uncle. From 1669 he was ill, sometimes practically paralysed by gout. That year he took a cure at Barèges, but without beneficial results. In 1670 his wife died.

He was shy, a dreamer, and, in spite of his personal loyalty, always ideologically detached, although it is difficult to find any but the most restrained cynicism in the *Maximes*, which were, of course, not written for publication. They were circulated by Mme de Sablé among a few friends from 1661, with requests for comments, but a copy, probably of 1663, was leaked and published anonymously in Holland, as *Sentences et maximes de morale*. They owe much to the Jansenist moralist Jacques Esprit, himself the author of a two-volume *De la fausseté des vertus humaines* of which the first volume is dated 1678 and the second 1677. The privilège is dated 1 June 1674 and the achevé d'imprimer for both volumes 12 October 1677. Esprit died in 1678, and his book is a laborious compilation demonstrating how apparent virtues are vitiated by their motivation on the psychological level when they are not informed by grace in the real supernatural order. Mme de Sablé was herself the author of the *Maximes* in the *Maximes et pensées diverses* published in 1678—the year in which she died on 16 January—by the abbé d'Ailly, tutor to the children of Mme de Longueville.

La Rochefoucauld's first work was the passionate *Apologie de M. le Prince de Marcillac* of 1649, written in anger and in disdain for Mazarin. The earliest books of the *Mémoires*, III to VI, may have been written before 1656. Book II appears to have followed, with the first book much later. They not intended for immediate publication and circulated only within a small circle, before a leaked copy was published in Brussels by Foppens in July 1662, though the false title page attributed publication to van Dyck at Cologne. The French authorities were incensed by the book and thought it had come from Amsterdam. Copies were on sale in Paris, where it was denounced to Séguier on 5 August. The following year we know of administrative measures taken in Rouen to ban the work, and three Caen booksellers were arrested in connection with it. Condé and Mme de Longueville were offended, and Liancourt was obliged to intervene to calm matters, but more than half the published text was not by La Rochefoucauld, who complained that it was two thirds by other hands and that the remaining third had been changed beyond recognition. However, he resisted Ménage's recommendation to publish an authentic text, and none was printed until the 19th century.

La Rochefoucauld did publish a subtle self-portrait written in 1658 and included in the *Galerie des portraits* of Mlle de Mont-

pensier. The achevé d'imprimer was 25 January 1659, the year from which dates the first known mention of La Rochefoucauld's "Sentences," in a letter to Mme de Sablé, and in which, on 10 November, La Rochefoucauld's eldest son married Mlle de Liancourt. The *Réflexions et Sentences ou Maximes morales* themselves may have been distilled from material analogous to La Rochefoucauld's posthumously published *Réflexions morales*. We know from his letters that by 1662 La Rochefoucauld was interested in the story of the lackey who danced on the scaffold before he was put to death.

By 1659 a joint volume of maxims by Mme de Sablé, Jacques Esprit, and La Rochefoucauld was plainly envisaged, and there is a series of letters showing the closeness of the relationship between Mme de Sablé, Esprit, and La Rochefoucauld normally printed with the *Maximes*, and including the replies to Mme de Sablé's enquiries of 1663. Towards the end of 1660 La Rochefoucauld, at Verteuil, copied out a text of his maxims, and after that date there is no further reference to the composite volume. This does not mean that La Rochefoucauld then envisaged publication on his own. In view of his social position, that is unlikely. After 1660 La Rochefoucauld may have visited Mme de Sablé less frequently, although they went on corresponding, and her enthusiasm for his maxims continued.

The reflection on amour-propre was originally published anonymously in 1660, in the third part of the *Recueil de pièces en prose, les plus agréables de ce temps, composées par divers auteurs* put out by the publisher, Charles de Sercy, with an achevé d'imprimer of 13 December 1659. It was probably in the Jansenist interest that a copy of the manuscript of the *Maximes* was leaked, possibly by Thomas Esprit, brother of Jacques. The 1663 manuscript had misleadingly appeared to lend itself to a Jansenist interpretation.

The pirated Dutch edition is dated 1664 but was certainly known to La Rochefoucauld on 6 February of that year and was probably printed in 1663. La Rochefoucauld's own privilège is dated 14 January 1664, which suggests that he knew by then about the perhaps not yet published pirate edition. The achevé d'imprimer of the anonymous first authentic edition, published by Barbin, is 27 October 1664, but the volume carries the date 1665. It was only after some hesitation that La Rochefoucauld decided to put the long reflection on amour-propre at the head of the volume. Its length and position made it seem as if the rest of the volume was an elaboration of what it contained, and it was simply removed from later editions. In the first edition, it was preceded by a frontispiece in which "L'Amour de la vérité (The Love of truth)" unmasks Seneca.

There were three more pirated editions in 1665, one openly announcing La Rochefoucauld's authorship, and in that year Mme de Sablé published an article on the *Maximes* in the *Journal des Savants* (q.v.). La Rochefoucauld himself published revised editions in 1666, 1671, 1675, and 1678, making additions and deletions which change the nature of the book. The definitive edition is that of 1678, although the posthumous 1693 edition contains, in addition to the supplementary maxims published in the fourth edition, another 25 which are undoubtedly authentic. We do not know why they were not published during the author's lifetime. An edition of seven *Réflexions morales* was published in 1713. The remaining 12 were published in 1863 from a manuscript no longer available.

Letters from La Rochefoucauld show that he sent Mme de Sablé further maxims in 1667 and 1675, and that he composed others between 1671 and 1674 which he sent to Marie-Eléonore de Rohan, abbess of Malnoue, a convent a few miles to the east of Paris, for comment, before including them in the 1675 edition, actually printed in December 1674. Towards the end of 1673 Christina of Sweden annotated a copy of the third edition, maxim by maxim. The document is of capital importance not only on account of the queen's extraordinary background but also for its intrinsic interest. Descartes had died fulfilling his duties as her philosophy tutor in Stockholm, and after her abdication, conversion to Catholicism, and visit to Paris in 1656–57, she spent her remaining years in Rome, where she was to die in 1689.

On 19 June 1675 Mme de Sévigné sent her daughter a pen-sketch of Retz by La Rochefoucauld, with whom he was now reconciled. Mme de Sévigné wrote on 3 July that Retz had been pleased with it, which suggests that the copy she showed him is not the one she sent, which was printed by Perrin in his 1754 editions of her *Lettres*. The sketch was not meant to be shown to Retz, and what Mme de Sévigné did show him may have been the text published in 1717 in the *Nouveau Mercure* (see: *Mercure*). Both texts are published in the 1967 Truchet edition of the *Maximes*, as are the comments of Christina of Sweden.

The *Maximes* have an edge of personal disappointment rather than bitterness. Their author was sharply perceptive, intelligent enough to work out how best to develop tactics but not truly interested in grand strategies, and idealist enough to feel let down by the ambition and ingratitude of those around him. He enjoyed subtlety more than success, and combined great charm with caustic wit, and a desire to please with a perfect understanding of the vanities it was necessary to flatter. Mme de Sévigné more than once remarked on his desire to be obliging, his delight, for example, in the company of children. He was incapable of being mercenary or calculating, and too lucid to find any cause worth the devotion he was prepared to bestow. Scheming in the manner of Retz bored him, and he did not lead, but followed, Mme de Longueville into the Fronde. He did not become a member of the Académie because he was too shy to speak in public.

His illness caused him much agony, and reduced him to crying out for the release of death. He was tended on his death-bed by Bossuet, from whom he received the last sacraments. Mme de Sévigné sent a graphic account of his last hours to her daughter on 17 March. He had died "at midnight" the night before.

WORKS

La Rochefoucauld's self-portrait, which first appeared in the *Recueil des Portraits et Eloges en vers et en prose dédié à son Altesse Royale Mademoiselle*, published simultaneously in duodecimo and octavo by Sercy and Barbin early in 1659, may well have been written as early as 1655 or 1656. It gives a physical description and insists that physiologically his "humeur" is chiefly "mélancolique," technical terms denoting that La Rochefoucauld saw himself as introverted, not easily amused, irresolute, unambitious, perhaps inclined to indolence, but also perceptive and penetrating. He likes conversing with "des honnêtes gens (cultivated people)," especially about issues which touch on moral attitudes, enjoys reading, and feels that he might have gifts as a writer "si j'étais sensible à la gloire qui vient de ce côté-là (if I were susceptible to the fame that comes from that

sort of activity)." He regards his literary judgement as good. He is sensitive to matters affecting his honour, but is honest and trustworthy, and has given up trivial compliments, although he thinks the capacity for dedicated love ("les belles passions") a sign of greatness of soul ("grandeur d'âme").

Retz's portrait of La Rochefoucauld harps on the irresolution, says that La Rochefoucauld was never a warrior although very much a soldier, and that he never succeeded as a courtier, or committed himself totally to a cause. La Rochefoucauld, for Retz, was shy, and in his maxims lacked faith in the reality of virtue. On Retz, assuming the genuine text is the less harsh one of the *Nouveau Mercure*, La Rochefoucauld is perceptive and a little sardonic. He remarks on Retz's wit and courage, his extraordinary memory, the way he spoke with more vigour than courtesy ("plus de force que de politesse") and was pious without being devout ("peu de piété et beaucoup de religion"), vain more than ambitious, but determined. During his imprisonment and exile he was supported as much by indolence as by strength. In both texts of La Rochefoucauld's portrait of Retz the French words "paresse (laziness)" and "oisiveté (indolence)" are used interchangeably, a usage which abolishes the important overtones of "paresse" which, in the *Maximes*, had been the chief vice and hinted at the quasi-theological meaning which Pascal had given to the work. Equally the word "repos" is used neutrally for "rest," not in the sense of freedom from passion with which Racine and Mme de Lafayette invested it. The *Mercure* text is sceptical about Retz's motivation for his final monastic retirement. The text of the portrait printed by Perrin in 1754 and in subsequent editions of the Sévigné letters simply calls the retirement hypocritical. Perrin's text is unlikely to be genuine.

The *Mémoires*, constantly revised, were not intended for publication or, in spite of the provocation of the inauthentic text and the advice of Ménage, ever published by La Rochefoucauld. They pose a recurrent problem. What right have we to read them? Whatever answer we might be disposed to give, the decoding of an abandoned text, neither completed nor destroyed, obviously demands care. La Rochefoucauld was writing to overcome his own sense of frustration, not to present a case, and needed to confront his own failure, not to give an account of his conscience to posterity. The *Mémoires* deal frankly with the history of the civil wars, concentrating on the motives, hypocrisies, ingratitude, unreliability, and political constraints to which the central characters were subjected. The liaison with Mme de Longueville is inaccurately presented as a simple political manoeuvre to acquire influence over her brothers.

Books I and II use a narratorial "Je," suggesting an increase of literary confidence after the books which were certainly written earlier, and they renounce any further self-depiction. It is clear that the six books were never completed, and we do not know why not. Most striking today is probably the laconic mode of narrating, with no obvious awareness of the fragile nature of the values instilled by the pedigree of the "noblesse d'épée."

Richelieu had lost an elder brother in a duel, disapproved of duelling as a statesman and a churchman, and disliked the caste system represented by the duelling ethic. Since the late 16th century, seconds had been expected to fight as well. The anti-duelling edict of 1626 was the first actually to be enforced. It prescribed the death sentence for killing in the course of a duel or for any second challenge to fight. When François de Montmorency, comte de Bouteville, close friend of Celse-Bénigne de Sévigné, fought his 22nd duel at midday in the Place Royale on

12 May 1627 against Beuvron, a Harcourt, he and his second were arrested, and were beheaded on 21 June. Five years later two others were hanged upside down.

La Rochefoucauld gives an account of the famous duel between the duc de Guise and the comte de Coligny, the last to be fought in the Place Royale. Guise, who ended by disarming Coligny and inflicting on him a humiliating tap with the side of his sword, had started by saying, "Nous allons décider des anciennes querelles de nos deux maisons, et on verra quelle différence on doit mettre entre le sang de Guise et celui de Coligny (We are going to settle the ancient disputes between our two houses, and we shall see what the difference is between the blood of the Guises and that of the Colignys)." La Rochefoucauld, who boasted that he read *L'Astrée* annually, was as cynical about the duelling ethic as Richelieu, but he was brought up to believe in the values it represented, and does not comment.

The *Réflexions ou Sentences et Maximes morales* in their definitive 1678 form present a whole array of quite different problems, of which the first is the title. The 504 maxims, prefixed with Arabic numbers, are headed "Réflexions morales," although modern usage has kept "Réflexions" for the 19 *Réflexions diverses*, of which seven were published in 1731 and 12 in 1863, all appearing together in the "Grands Ecrivains" edition in 1868. There has been some dispute about whether the maxims, as they are now generally called, were distilled out of earlier "réflexions," but that view has not recently found adherents. The work is normally referred to as *Maximes*, but the aphorisms it contains are neither wholly prescriptive nor wholly either particularized or generalized observations about human conduct. It contains all three sorts, but the meaning of the 1678 edition is not clear without reference to the genesis of the printed text. It powerfully helps our understanding, for instance of their literary register, to draw on the unpublished evidence of the surviving letters. It is clear that La Rochefoucauld sought to change the effect of his immensely popular book by changing its presentation.

The evidence suggests that La Rochefoucauld exploited the Jansenist interpretation of what he feared might be taken as over-cynical comments on human behaviour if they did not shelter behind a spiritual doctrine, found that he was being mis-read, and more or less systematically laicized the aphorisms, blunting their sharpness, adding modifying adverbs like "sometimes" or "usually," removing all those maxims of direct religious relevance, then secularizing, generalizing, and qualifying those that remained or were added. Unfortunately two apparently autograph manuscripts have disappeared from public availability, and a third has been stolen, which makes the reconstitution of the work's genesis and the consequent elucidation of its meaning considerably more conjectural. It seems likely however that, at least on textual matters, the 1967 edition of Jacques Truchet is likely to remain authoritative. It prints all important manuscripts and editions or, where that is unnecessary, gives notes on them.

The key document, of which a facsimile was obtained before it was stolen, and published in 1931, is the Liancourt manuscript, partly in La Rochefoucauld's hand, noting the maxims as they were fabricated between about 1659 and 1664. This manuscript was added to, even after it had been used as the basis for the series of copies made in 1663 and submitted for comment among Mme de Sablé's circle of friends. One of those copies was used for the unauthorized Dutch edition dated 1664. The Liancourt manuscript has no obvious structural order, whereas the first authorized edition, re-ordering the maxims from the earlier manuscript, does have a structure. The Dutch edition presents the maxims as a pointed attack on human virtue but does not seek to make a religious point. The Augustinian moral theology of the first authorized edition was put there quite deliberately, probably to disguise the sharpness of the social observation by focusing attention on the central concept of "amour-propre."

What was at stake is actually quite simple. Augustine, or at least his disciple Fulgentius, had taught that the effects of original sin were such that the nature of all human beings was so corrupt that they could not even accept unaided the divine "sanctifying" grace which alone could make it possible for them to be saved. To hold otherwise became at least semi-Pelagian, and therefore heretical. It followed that the only true virtue was supernatural. The papal bull *Unam sanctam* of 1302, confirmed by the decree of the Council of Florence for the Jacobites in 1441, was at any rate generally taken to define that only believing Catholics could be saved and, by implication, that the bestowal of sanctifying grace was confined to them. This is the dilemma on which Pascal, for instance, was impaled. When, by the renaissance, it was known that there were peoples who had never had an opportunity to hear the Gospel, the doctrine was blunted, and the whole question of pagan virtue became acute. When, in the face of a rising wave of Augustinianism in 17th-century France, La Mothe le Vayer argued the authenticity of pagan virtue in his 1642 *De la vertu des païens*, he was being deliberately provocative. For the Augustinians, for Saint-Cyran, Arnauld, Pascal, Nicole, and a host of others, there could be no authentic pagan virtue.

In his *De civitate dei* (XIV, 28) Augustine had founded the city of God on the love of God taken as far as the contempt of self, and the earthly city on the love of self ("amor sui") taken as far as the contempt of God. That doctrine is taken up by Jansen in the 1640 *Augustinus* (De statu naturae lapsae, 25), where the love of God is identified with efficacious grace, and the love of self is made incompatible with it. The associations which Jansen created for "amor sui" came to be adopted in religious moral writing in Augustinian circles, and were, for instance, transferred to the French "amour-propre" as early as 1641 in J.F. Senault's *De l'Usage des passions*, a work well known to Pascal and La Rochefoucauld, and pillaged by both of them. Pascal uses the term "amour-propre," notably in his fragments on grace and in a letter to his sister on the death of their father, as absolutely opposed to charity, sanctifying grace, and the love of God.

From 1641 until at least Nicole's *Essais de morale* in the 1670s the word "amour-propre" in French was frequently used in a way which made it incompatible with charity, sanctifying grace, and true virtue. The word was therefore ambiguous. For Jansenists and the more generally Augustinian dévots, "amour-propre" meant sin and therefore the absence of grace in the soul. Those who died in the state of amour-propre were quite simply damned for all eternity. But the word also retained its earlier and more ordinary usage to indicate a psychological motivation, in which sense it meant merely self-interest, and had no serious implications in the religious order, at least outside the "pure love" and quietist controversies. The key to an understanding of the *Maximes* is the realization that La Rochefoucauld played on the ambiguity of the word "amour-propre."

Of the replies received to her enquiries about the 1663 manuscripts of the *Maximes* at least two, both anonymous, congratulate the author on demonstrating the inauthenticity of any virtue not based on supernatural grace, a doctrine not at all salient in the 1663 copies, where the development on amour-propre occurs at maxim 96, although much clearer in the original Liancourt manuscript. In both, as in the first authentic edition, La Rochefoucauld leaves no doubt that he is using the word in its theological sense, because its definition is a parody of the catechism definition of charity. Charity was always defined as the love of God for his own sake, and of all things for God's sake. The first maxim of the first edition starts, "L'amour-propre est l'amour de soi-même, et de toutes choses pour soi (Self-love is the love of oneself, and of all things for oneself)." There is a similar definition in Pascal.

In case the point was missed, the first edition was prefaced by a "Discours" by Henri de la Chapelle-Bessé, a councillor in the parlement of Metz, in which it is important to note how the meaning of the word oscillates between its theological and its purely psychological significances. La Chapelle-Bessé says that the Fathers and the saints taught that "l'amour-propre et l'orgueil étaient l'âme des plus belles actions des païens (self-love and pride were the soul of the finest actions of the pagans)." Pride ("orgueil"), too, was incompatible with grace for Pascal. The first edition of the *Maximes*, prefaced by the discours of La Chapelle-Bessé and prefixed by the long development on amour-propre as a parodic inversion of charity, was, however, simply disguising itself as an attack on pagan virtue. In fact La Rochefoucauld is perfectly clear that self-interest is quite compatible with authentic virtue. However, whenever he admits that compatibility, he invariably uses for self-interest the French word "intérêt," which can in the context only refer to the psychological motivation, and almost never the word "amour-propre," which he has defined as incompatible with virtue.

That self-interest and authentic virtue are compatible is clear from a number of the maxims: "L'intérêt met en oeuvre toutes sortes de vertus et de vices (Self-interest motivates all sorts of virtues and vices)" (1678 edition: 253); "L'intérêt que l'on accuse de tous nos crimes mérite souvent d'être loué de nos bonnes actions (Self-interest, which we accuse of all our crimes, should often be praised for our good actions)" (maxim 305); and "Le nom de la vertu sert à l'intérêt aussi utilement que les vices (The name of virtue covers a self-interested motive as well as vices do)" (maxim 187). In a maxim virtually borrowed from Senault, La Rochefoucauld expresses the common idea that what we call vice is itself not incompatible with what we call virtue: "Les vices entrent dans la composition des vertus comme les poisons entrent dans la composition des remèdes…(Vices enter into the composition of virtues as poisons enter into the composition of their antidotes…)" (maxim 182). Virtues can simply disappear into the flood of self-interest, as rivers into the sea (maxim 171), and even the noble virtue of friendship depends on self-interest:

Nous ne pouvons rien aimer que par rapport à nous, et nous ne faisons que suivre notre goùt et notre plaisir quand nous préférons nos amis à nous-mêmes; c'est néanmoins par cette préférence seule que l'amitié peut être vraie et parfaite

(We cannot love anything except with respect to ourselves, and we are only following our taste and our pleasure when we prefer our friends to ourselves. Nevertheless it is only

by that preference that friendship can be true and perfect) (maxim 81).

In one or two maxims "amour-propre" is quite plainly used in its ordinary sense as denoting a psychological motivation without Jansen's or Pascal's theological overtones. One of the posthumous maxims (Truchet edition, 26) starts, "L'intérêt est l'âme de l'amour-propre (Self-interest is the soul of amour-propre)," and one of the more famous maxims runs

Ce que les hommes ont nommé amitié n'est qu'une société, qu'un ménagement réciproque d'intérêts, et qu'un échange de bons offices; ce n'est enfin qu'un commerce où l'amour-propre se propose toujours quelque chose à gagner

(What we have called friendship is only an alliance, a mutual assuaging of self-interest and an exchange of services; it is in the end only a trade in which our amour-propre always seeks some gain) (maxim 83).

The word "amour-propre" was still used in France without theological associations, it was soon to have a full-scale rehabilitation in the work of Mandeville, Pope, and Voltaire. Louis de Sacy wrote in his *Traité de l'amitié* of 1703 that amour-propre was "the first and perhaps sole motive force of man," but that it "led men to virtue itself." La Rochefoucauld is therefore commenting, in what for his society was a slightly shocking way, that our behaviour is dominated by the motivation of self-interest but, in doing so, he is quite deliberately secularizing the religious moral teaching deriving from Jansen and the strong Augustinian tradition of moral writing subsequent to 1640 in France. La Rochefoucauld deliberately set out to be understood as saying that self-interested actions, based on self-love, were not only incompatible with virtue, but also positively sinful. That, however, is also something he was very careful never to say, and in his later editions he toned down his provocation to the reader to assume that he had said it.

La Rochefoucauld's own connection with Augustinianism is scant. La Chapelle-Bessé's Jansenizing preliminary discourse was dropped from the second edition of the *Maximes*, as was La Rochefoucauld's own Augustinian Avant-propos with the long maxim on "amour-propre." Mme de Sablé's Jansenism was never doctrinally committed, or even as spiritually committed as that of her friend Mme de Longueville, who had taken Singlin as her confessor, and La Rochefoucauld himself scarcely goes further than to make a humorous remark about the dangers of a Molinist (that is, Jesuit) confessor in a letter to his niece. He did, naturally, know Port-Royal well, and many of those associated with the monastery.

He not only believes in the possibility of true virtue, but he takes up the ordinary spiritual criterion for it, humility:

L'humilité est la véritable preuve des vertus chrétiennes: sans elle nous conservons tous nos défauts, et ils sont seulement couverts par l'orgueil qui les cache aux autres, et souvent à nous-mêmes

(Humility is the true criterion of Christian virtues. Without it we retain all our faults, and they are merely covered up by the pride which conceals them from others, and often from ourselves) (maxim 358).

What he has done by exploiting the theological associations of the word "amour-propre" is largely to cover up the assumption, characteristic of the era in which Pierre Corneille's great plays explored the nature of greatness, that there are forms of moral energy and personal elevation which are not ethically based. Corneille had made explicit the idea that there could be "glorious crimes" in the analysis of our admiration for Cléopâtre in his *Rodogune*. La Rochefoucauld, no doubt following Jacques Esprit, to whose judgement the letters clearly show him to have deferred, notoriously held that "Il y a des héros en mal comme en bien (There are heroes of evil as well as of good)" (maxim 185), betraying a form of moral superiority which has no ethical basis, Christian or otherwise, although it can be shown to be implicit in the ethical assumptions of the code of behaviour of his caste.

In spite of what he said about wanting to reveal the falsity of apparent virtue, La Rochefoucauld in fact comes quite near to justifying systematically not so much the moral value of self-interest as a code of behaviour which does without any system of ethical values, and is based not on concepts of good and evil but simply on those of personal honour, vigour, and "honnêteté," perhaps best translated as "cultivation." "Il y a du mérite sans élévation, mais il n'y a point d'élévation sans quelque mérite (There is merit without elevation, but no elevation without some merit)." "L'élévation est au mérite ce que la parure est aux belles personnes (Elevation is to merit as ornamentation to beautiful women)" (maxims 400 and 401), and

> Il y a une élévation qui ne dépend point de la fortune: c'est un certain air qui nous distingue et qui semble nous destiner aux grandes choses: c'est un prix que nous nous donnons imperceptiblement à nous-mêmes; c'est par cette qualité que nous usurpons les déférences des autres hommes, et c'est elle d'ordinaire qui nous met plus au-dessus d'eux que la naissance, les dignités, et le mérite même

(There is an elevation which does not depend on wealth. It is a certain air which distinguishes us and seems to mark us out for great achievements. It is a value which we give ourselves without noticing. It is by that trait that we commandeer the respect of others and it is normally the trait which raises us higher above them than birth, honours, and even merit) (maxim 399).

In the long final development on the falsity of contempt for death, La Rochefoucauld talks of the lackey who danced on the scaffold before he was broken on the wheel. In great men the contempt for death springs from "l'amour de la gloire (the sense of honour/dignity)," whereas in "les gens du commun (common people)," it is their "peu de lumière (scant intelligence/imagination)" (maxim 504). The virtue he does unreservedly praise, alongside the qualities of elevation and the Christian criterion of humility, is what he calls magnanimity, which he refers to in its etymological meaning, "greatness of soul" (maxim 285), and of which he says "La magnanimité méprise tout pour avoir tout (Magnanimity despises everything, because it possesses everything)" (maxim 248). Most of the overtly theological maxims were systematically removed after the first edition and are now known as the suppressed maxims, to distinguish them from the posthumous ones, sent to the abbess of Malnoue for comment and incorporated into the first posthumous edition of 1693.

For La Rochefoucauld, as before him for Senault, the worst vice is "paresse," normally meaning laziness. He dislikes the languishing, lackadaisical vices which denote weakness. But "paresse," too, had acquired theological overtones to make it sound worse than mere indolence. Pascal had contrasted the "paresse" of those who do not even try to keep the divine law with the contrasting "orgueil (pride/sin/concupiscence)" or "charité (grace)" of those who keep the law, but might be inspired by mere sinful amour-propre. La Rochefoucauld, too, contrasts "paresse," signifying mere indolence, with "orgueil," in such a way as to draw down opprobrium acquired by the word in a theological context on a vice he despises. "La promptitude à croire le mal sans l'avoir assez examiné est un effet de l'orgueil et de la paresse (Readiness to believe ill without having looked closely enough at it comes from pride and sloth)" (maxim 267).

The *Réflexions diverses* appear to be more extended observations on human behaviour than the *Maximes*. The themes are mostly very similar. La Rochefoucauld writes on the true, on society, on the need to keep to the bearing and behaviour warranted by our true qualities, and not to pretend to be what we are not. We can improve, learn, follow examples, but any note of falsity in our behaviour will be noticed and held against us. There is a réflexion on conversation, and another on confidence which raises Mme de Lafayette's problem, and Molière's, of sincerity. Example can lead us astray as well as towards virtue. Jealousy is importantly, as for Racine and Mme de Lafayette, a mixture of two passions—love and hatred—which Descartes in 1649 had still in the traditional way made rigorously incompatible with one another. The development is important in the new need to explore irresistible affection for its destructive power rather than study the life-enhancing qualities of instinctive affection which an earlier generation had needed to examine:

> On veut haïr et on veut aimer, mais on aime encore quand on hait, et on hait encore quand on aime

(You want to hate and you want to love, but you still love when you hate, and hate when you love) (De l'incertitude de la jalousie).

La Rochefoucauld goes on to treat of taste, love and life, falseness, and similar moral topics, but not as trenchantly as in the *Maximes*. Not all his remarks about human behaviour, either in the *Maximes* or in the *Réflexions*, are compatible with one another. He suggests, for instance, in maxim 44, that strength and weakness of mind are physiologically determined by "la bonne ou la mauvaise disposition des organes du corps (the good or bad disposition of the body's organs)," a remark which does not fit in with the implications of most of the rest of the maxims. There is no system. The strength of the *Maximes* does not even lie in their psychological penetration or audacity, but rather in the ethical and non-ethical assumptions La Rochefoucauld makes about social behaviour and personal distinction.

PUBLICATIONS

Collections

Oeuvres, 1818
Oeuvres complètes, 1825

Oeuvres inédites, 1863
Oeuvres complètes, 4 vols., 1868–83
Oeuvres complètes, Bibliothèque de la Pléiade, 1935, revised 1957, 1964

Maxims

Sentences et maximes de morale, The Hague, 1664 (pirate edition)
Réflexions ou Sentences et Maximes morales, 1665 (first edition)
    (second edition), 1666
    (third edition), 1671
    (fourth edition), 1675
    (fifth and definitive edition), 1678; translated by L.W. Tancock, 1959
    (posthumous edition, augmented with 1678 supplement: *Nouvelles réflexions ou sentences et maximes morales*), 1693
Maximes, edited by J. Truchet (Classiques Garnier), 1967 (includes all early editions and *Réflexions diverses*)

Other

Mémoires de M.D.L.R., 1662 (pirate edition)
Mémoires du duc de L.R., 1817

Biographical and critical studies

Magne, Emile, *Le vrai visage de La Rochefoucauld*, 1923
Bishop, M., *The Life and Adventures of La Rochefoucauld*, 1951
Zeller, Mary F., *New Aspects of Style in the Maxims of La Rochefoucauld*, 1954
Butrick, M.W., *The Concept of Love in the Maxims of La Rochefoucauld*, 1959
Ansmann, Liane, *Die "Maximen" von La Rochefoucauld*, 1972
Mourgues, Odette de, *Two French Moralists: La Rochefoucauld and La Bruyère*, 1978
Images de La Rochefoucauld: Actes du tricentenaire, 1680–1980, 1984

Bibliography

Mora, Edith, *François de la Rochefoucauld*, 1965

LA TAILLE, Jean de, ?1533–after 1607.

Dramatist.

LIFE

Very little is known of the details of La Taille's life. In addition to his own two biblical tragedies, *Saül le furieux* with its prefatory *De l'art de la tragédie*, and *La Famine; ou, Les Gabéonites*, La Taille left two comedies, *Les Corrivaus*, heavily dependent on Boccaccio and perhaps on Parabosco's 1547 *Viluppo*, and *Le Negromant*, presented as a translation of Ariosto, but using the faulty 1535 version of Ariosto's *Il Negromante* rather than the original 1520 text. In 1573 he also published most of his poems, and in the same year the two tragedies of his young brother, Jacques, *Daïre* and *La Mort d'Alexandre*. Jacques, born in 1542, had died of the plague in 1562 when he was not yet 21, and also left a treatise on quantitative verse—*L'Art de faire des vers en françois, comme en grec et en latin*—poems, and inscriptions.

La Taille was born at Bondaroy close to the Loir into a family of the minor nobility which was not wealthy and which was to become Calvinist. His parents were Louis de la Taille and Jacqueline de l'Estendart de Heurteloup. By his own account, La Taille was sent for six years to study at Paris, where he heard Marc-Antoine Muret, regent at the collège de Boncourt from 1551–53. La Taille said in the avis au lecteur of *Saül le furieux* that it was his father's lack of education which caused him to send his sons to Paris to study the liberal arts, not so as to prepare them for the Church or the law, but because "le sçavoir est le seul parement d'un Gentilhomme pour le faire hardy à parler seurement à un chascun (learning is the only adornment of a noble which gives him the confidence to talk to every kind of person."

Muret's course commented on the comedies of Terence, and in 1553 he published his own Latin tragedy *Julius Caesar*. La Taille was in Paris for the famous first performance of Jodelle's *Cléopâtre*, and must have known Buchanan among the teachers at Boncourt, and among the students Jodelle, La Péruse, and Jacques Grévin. La Taille had strangely little contact with the young poets surrounding Dorat at Coqueret, or with the students interested in humanistic drama clustered at Boncourt; perhaps, as has been conjectured, on account of having some private establishment in Paris, working with his own tutor and therefore sharing little in the communal life of Boncourt. It is much more likely that the reason was religious. The group around Ronsard was to develop into a vanguard of Catholic reaction, and La Taille was a Protestant. Even the solitary sonnet by Du Bellay prefacing Jacques's *La Mort d'Alexandre*, the only clear written evidence of a personal link between either La Taille brother and the groups of either Coqueret or Boncourt, may have been written more to publicize its author's own return from Italy than to boost esteem for the play.

La Taille went on from Paris to Orléans to study civil law, teaching of which was still banned in Paris, and then returned to Paris, where he turned to writing, inspired, he says, by the examples of Marc-Antoine Muret, Ronsard, and Du Bellay. When Jacques came to Paris, La Taille recommended to his brother the courses of Dorat and the verse of Ronsard and Du Bellay. Towards 1558 both brothers seem to have begun writing in dramatic forms, "selon le vray art et à la façon antique (according to true literary norms and in the manner of antiquity)." By 1562, the year of Jacques's death, La Taille seems to have held an office at court, and had probably written his four plays. Jacques had written a sonnet on *Les Corrivaus* before he died. La Taille stated in 1562, in the preface to his *Remonstrance pour le Roy à tous ses subjects qui ont pris les armes*, that he had written *Saül le furieux* and a comedy. In spite of his reformed convictions, La Taille fought in the royal forces during the religious wars, writing love verse during the intermissions. He was probably with the royal forces at Dreux for the costly victory of December 1562. The lowest estimate of dead is 6,000.

By 1568 La Taille had changed sides and was fighting with the Huguenot armies. He was present at the battles lost by the Huguenots in 1569, Jarnac and Moncontour, and on 25 June 1570 was wounded in the face at Arnay-le-Duc by a blow from a lance, embraced on the field by Henri de Navarre, and shortly thereafter robbed by bandits. He never returned to the battlefield, and his disgust at the soldier's life is strongly expressed in his sonnets. He was also to illustrate his reactions to the ravaging of France by war from his own experience in a standard dispraise of the courtier's lot, *Le Courtisan retiré*, and to leave behind him a verse treatise on government, unpublished until 1882, *Le Prince nécessaire*.

La Taille's father, who had felt betrayed by his sons' literary ambitions and may indeed have thwarted them, died in 1571. La Taille had taken out a privilège for *Saül* dated 18 October 1570, although he did not publish it until 1572, after his father's death, and *De l'Art de la tragédie*, printed as a preface to the play, almost certainly presupposes a knowledge of Castelvetro's *La Poetica d'Aristotele*, published in 1570 in Vienna. When *Saül le furieux* appeared, it was also accompanied by Jacques de la Taille's *Recueil des inscriptions*, and was followed in 1573 by four other volumes of La Taille's works, or those of his brother published by him. The first contained La Taille's *La Famine, Les Corrivaus, Le Negromant*, and the poems; the second Jacques's *Daïre*; the third Jacques's *La Mort d'Alexandre*; and the fourth Jacques's *L'Art de faire des vers en françois, comme en grec et en latin*. La Taille's comedies were not reprinted until the late 19th century.

There were reissues of the two tragedies in 1601 and 1602 in a series of reprints, but otherwise there are only instances of the re-utilization of the original sheets for fresh editions by later publishers who had bought up unsold stock. La Taille's only other works, apart from occasional verse like *Le Combat de Fortune et de Pauvreté*, were the prose abridgement of a guide to fortune-telling by the Genoese soldier Cattaneo, the 1574 *La Geomance abrégée*; the 1574 *Le Blason des pierres precieuses, contenant leurs vertus et proprietez*, dedicated to Marie de Clèves and Marguerite de Navarre and two years earlier than the 1576 *Les Amours des pierres precieuses* of Belleau, often regarded by his contemporaries as that poet's best work; and the 1607 *Discours notable des duels, de leur origine en France et du malheur qui en arrive tous les jours*. The attribution to La Taille of a satirical pamphlet, the 1595 *Histoire abrégée des singeries de la Ligue...*, rests on too little evidence.

From 1574 La Taille gave up writing for publication. In 1575 he married Charlotte Dumoulin de Rouville and retired with her to Bondaroy. In 1607 his son killed his daughter's fiancé in a duel, an incident which occasioned the work on duelling of the same year. He was probably 74 that year. No account has been left of the date or circumstances of his death. He is known to have been dead in 1617.

WORKS

By 1572, when *Saül le furieux* was published, Latin tragedies had for some years been played in the colleges at the end of the humanities class, both in the original and in translation, in the course of teaching rhetoric, understood primarily as the art of moving an audience. Neolatin tragedies had also been written by humanist teachers, as had original vernacular tragedies, on clas-

sical or biblical subjects, which observed generally Senecan norms. Tragedies with antique classical subjects, but often with contemporary allusions, were also occasionally incorporated into court entertainments, royal entries into cities, and a few other highly formal occasions.

For more popular dramatic entertainments, there were still the huge mystères, sometimes requiring casts of 100, and still occasionally played outside Paris after the decree of the parlement de Paris prohibiting them there dated 17 November 1548. There were also the doctrinal dramas written to be played in church, the pieces written for purposes of sectarian propaganda or simply satirizing ecclesiastical abuse, and neoclassical comedies, generally modelled on Terence, for use mostly on less solemn occasions than the tragedies. The medieval moralités were adapted to polemical ends, but the farces and "soties" had given way, by soon after the mid-16th century, to the whole spectrum of popular entertainment ranging from serious and often neoclassical comedy, through translations and imitations of modern Italian comedy, to commedia dell'arte (q.v.), which could have an acrobatic content and coarseness of register such that it merged with circus and other forms of fairground entertainment.

La Taille's two tragedies both belonged to a biblical tradition which by 1572 was well established. Bèze's *Abraham sacrifiant* had been both played and published in 1550 and Louis Desmasures had published his *David* trilogy in 1563. A careful chronology of the vernacular French sacred theatre published in 1983 lists a score of published texts to 1572 and some three score of performances, including known representations of passions and mystères and college performances. Lazare de Baïf had published a *Diffinition de la tragedie* to preface his 1537 French translation of Sophocles's *Electra*. In a brief reference in the 1549 *Deffence et illustration de la langue françoyse* (II, 4), Du Bellay had hoped that the usurpation of comedies and tragedies by "farces et moralités," would soon be ended, clearly implying that the moralités were fulfilling a function better suited to vernacular neoclassical tragedies, and in 1555 Jacques Peletier du Mans had devoted a chapter (II, 7) of his *L'Art poëtique* to comedy and tragedy. He summed up the ordinary doctrine such as was to be found in the *Praenotamenta* to Josse Bade's 1504 edition of Terence: tragedy should have only distinguished characters of high social rank, with an ending "tousjours luctueuse e lamantablǫ, ou horriblǫ a voǫr (always disastrous and cause for lament, or horrible to see)," a chorus expressing the author's point of view, and a style which is "sublimǫ." The models for Peletier are Euripides, Sophocles, and Seneca.

Jacques Grévin had published a *Bref discours pour l'intelligence de ce théâtre* with his tragedy *César* in 1561, and it was in the same year that Jules-César Scaliger published the *Poetices libri septem* introducing to France the doctrine of Aristotle's *Poetics*, as transmitted by the Italian tradition, but insisting for the first time in France on the importance of dramatic action, the didactic function of tragedy, and the need for credibility, on which later writers would base the need for the unities of time and place. The most important inspiration for La Taille, as for all the renaissance theorists, is still, however, the series of commentaries of the fourth-century rhetorician on the comedies of Terence, whose texts, celebrated for the purity of their style, were heavily used in the renaissance to teach colloquial Latin. It is from Donatus that the French renaissance absorbed or confirmed the generally held views that tragedy should have noble characters, a catastrophic ending, an atmosphere of fear and terror, real historical subjects, and only noble passions. Comedy was distinguished by everyday characters, a happy ending, emotions which were not crushing, and invented subjects. The five-act convention came from Donatus, supported by the authority of Horace.

Many classical conventions which had simply been pragmatically adopted in antiquity were taken up as dogmatic prescriptions in the renaissance. The four choruses separating five acts in Greek tragedy were regarded in the renaissance as an essential element of the form of antique tragedy. Donatus had divided Terence's comedies into acts and scenes, and the limitation of scenes to three characters, which had been adopted for pragmatic reasons in antiquity and noted as normative by Donatus, was in the renaissance regarded as prescriptive. Peletier had been the first to use the word "bienséance," which for him translated the Latin "decorum." The "bienséances" derive from Horace rather than from Aristotle, and included the separation of the comic from the tragic into different dramas, the need to represent on the comic stage recognizable types rather than individuals, and the need in tragedy to sustain, but in comedy to avoid, a register which was noble, poetic, and sublime. The resulting dramatic theory was purely formal. The renaissance humanists, entranced by the simplicity and clarity of the antique forms, replaced with prescriptions features that had been simply noted down as practices and that were often due to circumstances, political systems, and values which by the renaissance had been unrecoverable for a millennium.

La Taille had written his four plays before the outbreak of the religious wars, in which at first he was loyal to the royal cause, although no doubt a Protestant. When, between 1570 and 1572, he wrote his *De l'art de la tragédie*, he had fought several campaigns in the Huguenot interest. The treatise is in the form of a prefatory letter to Henriette de Clèves, duchesse de Nevers, a Bourbon cousin of Henri de Navarre and niece of the prince de Condé, who had died at the siege of Rouen. After expounding the views taken from Aristotle through Castelvetro, La Taille states his preference for Sophocles, Euripides, and Seneca over the farces and moralités written for the ignorant and the unworthy, "ameres espiceries qui gastent le goust de nostre langue (bitter spices which spoil the taste of our language)," a phrase repeated verbally in Le Prologue's address in *Les Corrivaus*.

La Taille's contemporaries should rather cultivate and naturalize true tragedy and comedy. They should cater not for scholars and pedants, but for the relaxation of persons of rank, after hunting or falconry. La Taille protests that he does not share the contempt common among fighting men for men of letters,

comme si la science et la vertu, qui ne gist qu'en l'esprit, affoiblissoit le corps, le coeur et le bras, et que Noblesse fust deshonorée d'une autre Noblesse qui est la Science

(as if learning and virtue, which lie only in the mind, enfeebled the body, the heart and the arm, and as if nobility were dishonoured by that other nobility, which is learning).

The names of philosopher and poet are not as derogatory as courtiers think, who have perhaps seen tragedies and comedies which only have the names, without the subject or the structure,

and only so many rhymes without art or learning, composed by the ignorant, and too easily published. The "fureur divine (divine inspiration)" necessary to dramatic art is the product only of hard work and ability: "There are many rhymers but few poets."

La Taille's freshness and spontaneity make up for a certain lack of order in his preface. He is writing with direct reference to Aristotle, about the restoration of antique tragedy in present circumstances, and not, like Scaliger, codifying antique usage into prescriptive norms. The essential aim of tragedy, like that of poetry in Du Bellay's *Deffence*, is to move.

La Tragedie donc est une espece et un genre de Poësie non vulgaire, mais autant elegant, beau et excellent qu'il est possible. Son vray subject ne traicte que de piteuses ruines des grands Seigneurs, que des inconstances de Fortune, que banissements, guerres, pestes, famines, captivitez, execrables cruautez des Tyrans; et bref que larmes et miseres extremes, et non point de choses qui arrivent tous les jours naturellement et par raison commune, comme d'un qui mourroit de sa propre mort, d'un qui seroit tué de son ennemy, ou d'un qui seroit condamné à mourir par les loix, et pour ses demerites: car tout cela n'esmouveroit pas aisément, et à peine m'arracheroit il une larme de l'oeil, veu que la vraye et seule intention d'une tragedie est d'esmouvoir et de poindre merveilleusement les affections d'un chascun

(Tragedy therefore is a kind and genre of poetry which is not ordinary, but as elegant, fine, and elevated as is possible. Its true subject treats only of the pitiable ruining of great lords, of Fortune's inconstancy, of banishments, wars, plagues, famines, captivities, and the detestable cruelties of tyrants; in short, of tears and extreme misfortunes, and not of things which happen normally every day and for ordinary reasons, like someone dying a natural death, or being killed by an enemy, or being condemned to die by law, and for his own faults. That would not easily move, and would scarcely draw a tear from my eye. The true and unique aim of tragedy is to move and skilfully control everyone's emotions).

The protagonists cannot be either all wicked, simply meriting the punishment they receive, nor totally admirable, of a virtuous and holy life, like a Socrates, even if he was wrongly poisoned. For this reason, La Taille thinks Bèze's *Abraham sacrifiant* and Desmasures's *David* trilogy unsuitable subjects for tragic treatment. It is at this point that La Taille announces

Il fault tousjours representer l'histoire ou le jeu en un mesme jour, en un mesme temps, et en un mesme lieu; aussi se garder de ne faire chose sur la scene qui ne s'y puisse commodément et honnestement faire

(The history or fiction must always be played on one day [i.e. not on a succession of days], within one span of time, and in one place; and also only those things should take place on the stage which can conveniently and decently be done there).

La Taille appears to be following Castelvetro. "On the same

day" means that, unlike what had happened with the mystères, a single performance should not be spread over several days. The unity of time in Aristotle and Scaliger regarded a duration of 12 or 24 hours for the action depicted as normative, but the unity of place had hitherto seemed vague. La Taille appears to suggest that the time covered by the intrigue should not exceed the time required for its representation, and that the geographical location of the action should be restricted to the physical space available on a stage. The reference to what can "conveniently and decently" be done is intended to exclude stage artifices representing unstageable events, like executions.

La Taille now appears again to follow Castelvetro in opposing the idea that comedy must start with a sad situation and end with a happy one, and that tragedy should always have a joyous start. That depends on the nature of the particular intrigue. La Taille then reasserts his central criterion:

C'est le principal poinct d'une Tragedie de la sçavoir bien disposer, bien bastir, et de la deduire de sorte qu'elle change, transforme, manie, et tourne l'esprit des escoutans de ça, de là, et faire qu'ils voyent maintenant une joye tournée tout soudain en tristesse, en maintenant au rebours, à l'exemple des choses humaines

(It is the principal point in a tragedy to know how to arrange it, construct it, and direct the action so that it changes, transforms, manipulates, and turns the mind of the listeners hither and thither, making them see now a joy turned suddenly into distress, and now the other way round, as in human affairs).

There should be nothing to distract from the central intrigue, nothing useless and, in a biblical tragedy, not too much theology, more suitable for a sermon. La Taille now dismisses the allegorical characters, like Death, Truth, Avarice, and The World, of the moralités. There should be five acts, each complete within itself, and when the stage is empty, an act should be over. The intrigue should start as near the climax of the action as possible. La Taille finally writes a relatively long passage defending, with a quotation from the *De occulta philosophia* of the early renaissance humanist Cornelius Agrippa of Nettesheim, his use of Samuël's ghost.

We do not know the conditions under which *Saül le furieux* was played at Amiens in 1584 and in the Jesuit college at Pont-à-Mousson in 1599. La Taille himself recounts from I Samuel 15ff in a preliminary argument the situation of Saül, ordered on behalf of God by the prophet Samuël to raze the town of Amalec and to destroy all living creatures within it. Saül, however, had kept the best of the herds and spared the king, Agag, on account of which God had sent him spasmodically mad and raised against him a powerful enemy, Achis, king of the Philistines. In the first act the raving Saül, thinking his children Jonathe, Abinade, and Melchis to be his enemies, wants to kill them. Jonathe wants to lead the Israelites against the Philistines, whom David has refused to support. Grévin's *César* had given the chorus an identity within the drama by making it into a group of soldiers, and La Taille makes his chorus into Levites. They appear at the end of each of the first four acts.

In the second act Saül's écuyer laments his master's madness when Saül himself emerges from the tent where he had been sleeping. His opening speech is the product of his madness:

Voyla le jour venu, ja l'aurore vermeille
A bigarré les cieux: ça ça qu'on m'appareille
Mon arc, que je decoche à ces monstres cornus
Qui dans ces nues là se combattent tous nus…
Je veux monter au ciel, que mon char on attelle,
Et comme les Géants entassent monts sur monts
Je ferai trébucher les Anges et Démons,
Et serai Roi des cieux, puisque j'ai mis en fuite
Mes ennemis, dont j'ai la semence détruite

(Day is here, already rosy dawn/Has streaked the heavens. Come, come, prepare me/My bow, so that I can shoot at those horned monsters/Who are fighting with one another naked in the clouds there…/I want to climb to heaven. Have my chariot harnessed,/And as the giants pile mountain on mountain,/I shall make angels and demons fall,/And shall be king of the heavens, since I have put to flight/My enemies, whose seed I have destroyed).

As soon as Saül has come to himself, his écuyer recalls to him the approaching confrontation with the Philistines, and his sin in drawing down the anger of God. Saül in despair has resolved to have recourse to a sorcerer, and one is found. In the third act the spirit of Samuël is conjured up. He predicts the death of Saül and his replacement by David. In the fourth act Saül hears that his sons have been killed in battle. In the final act we learn of Saül's furious fighting, before his suicide over the dead body of Jonathe is confirmed. He dies stoically, but is insubmissive. His crime is the clear arrogation to himself of the authority, power, and position due to God alone. His écuyer has also killed himself. The play ends with an 83-line lament by David for Saül, his father-in-law. La Taille skilfully balances Saül's guilt against our sympathy for his predicament, by allowing the possibility that sparing Agag was an act of mercy.

La Taille is chiefly exploring Saül's human guilt, but there are episodes, like that of the condemnation by David of Saül's écuyer, who had said that he himself assisted Saül's suicide by making the final thrust of the sword, which simply confuse the play's moral vision. The religious meaning of the play is compromised by La Taille's need to exonerate God from merciless severity by permitting ambiguity about whether or not what happened was the action of divine retributive justice or the working out of fate. The condemnation of the écuyer is ambiguous. He could have died as the result of his own miscalculation that he would ingratiate himself with David by falsely claiming he had assisted Saül to die, or as an indication that David, like Saül, was capable of injustice, or simply because the incident is in the Bible.

La Famine; ou, Les Gabéonites is based on II Kings 21, and on the account in Josephus. There is no single protagonist. There has been a great famine and David has prayed to God to know what should be done. God demanded revenge for the Gabéonites slaughtered by Saül. The famine would be lifted when the Gabéonites were allowed their revenge. They asked for seven members of Saül's family to hang, and took them away to die. It then rained, and the ground again became fertile. Much opportunity is provided by a whole range of reactions to this desperate situation. La Taille is working on the emotions of his readers or audience, as would be recommended in *De l'art de la tragédie*, inciting a rapid change between different emotions. Saül's widow Resefe resists the Gabeonite demand, but his daughter

Merobe submits, passively enduring God's decree. David's constable, Joabe, carries out his duties compassionately, while the children submit heroically. The strong pathos of the destruction of the children replaces all considerations about submission to the will of God, and no explanation is offered about how God's justice operates.

Les Corrivaus is La Taille's sole original comedy, *Le Negromant* being a translation of Ariosto. Both are in prose. Although *Les Corrivaus* must have been written by 1562, the text was updated before publication, so that the action seems to take place in 1570. It is a well-conceived, clear comedy with a relatively uncluttered plot, and is certainly written to be performed. "Le Prologue" addresses an audience and is therefore an actor:

> Il semble, Messieurs, à vous voir ainsi assemblez en ce lieu, que vous y soyez venus pour ouir une Comedie: vrayment vous ne serez point deceus de vostre intention. Une Comedie pour certain vous y verrez, non point une farce ny une moralité: car nous ne nous amusons point en chose ne si basse, ne si sotte, et qui ne monstre qu'une pure ignorance de nos vieus François. Vous y verrez jouer une Comedie faite au patron, à la mode et au pourtrait des anciens Grecs, Latins et quelques nouveaux Italiens, qui premiers que nous ont enrichi le magnifique et ample cabinet de leur langue de ce beau joyau

> (It seems, gentlemen, seeing you assembled here, that you have come to hear a comedy: in that, you will not be disappointed. A comedy is certainly what you will see, not a farce or a moralité, because we don't waste our time on anything so vulgar or stupid, showing only the complete ignorance of our French forebears. You will see a comedy made from a proper model, in the style and after the manner of the ancient Greeks, Romans, and some recent Italians, who have forestalled us in enriching the magnificent and extensive treasury of their language with this fine jewel).

The French incidentally uses the adjective "premiers" adverbially, which suggests that La Taille's language is influenced by Greek usage. La Taille continues his attack on the medieval forms, before explaining his title, which means "the rivals," and expounding his argument. He draws attention to the way in which his characters are typical of people belonging to various states of life.

The setting is a street scene between two houses, those of Fremin and of dame Jacqueline. At the start of the play dame Jacqueline's daughter Restitue confesses to her nurse that she has been seduced by Filadelphe, who has now left her for Fremin's daughter, Fleurdelys. Restitue and the nurse presumably go off stage and Filadelfe has a soliloquy, and then, in the third and fourth scenes, plots first with Fremin's servant Claude and then with his own valet Gillet to gain access to Fleurdelys. He knows he has a rival. The second act opens with the rival, Euverture, talking to his servant, Felippes. Euverture's father's avarice has prevented a proper match, so Euverture decides to abduct Fleurdelys with the help of her maid, Alizon, who will get rid of Claude. Fremin goes out.

In the third act dame Jacqueline hears of her daughter's pregnancy. There is a scene full of asides for part of which Alizon does not know that Claude can hear her talking to herself. Restitue's nurse has a scene with Alizon. The nurse wants to tell Filadelfe that he has made Restitue pregnant. In the end Filadelfe and Euverture have both gained access to Fleurdelys, but their fight made so much noise that the guard was called and they were taken off to prison. Felippes and Gillet go off to the tavern. In the fourth act Filadelfe's father, Benard, from whom he has been estranged, is assailed successively by dame Jacqueline, Fremin, and Alizon on account of Filadelfe's behaviour. He learns that Fleurdelys, adopted by Fremin, is in fact his own daughter. The fifth act is now pre-ordained. Filadelfe cannot marry his sister, so marries the girl he has made pregnant, Restitue, while Fleurdelys is now going to be rich enough to satisfy Euverture's father, Gerard. For good measure, Benard marries dame Jacqueline. Filadelfe and Euverture are brought to the street in chains, and duly sentenced to be married.

PUBLICATIONS

Collections

Oeuvres poétiques de Jean et Jacques de la Taille, 4 vols., 1598
Oeuvres, 4 vols., 1878–82
Dramatic Works (English edition of French text), 1972
Saül le furieux; La Famine; ou, Les Gabéonites, 1968

Plays

Saül le furieux. Tragédie prise de la Bible. Faicte selon l'art et à la mode des vieux auteurs tragiques...avec autres oeuvres, 1572
La Famine; ou, Les Gabéonites. Tragedie prise de la Bible...Ensemble plusieurs autres oeuvres poétiques, 1573

Other

Remonstrance pour le roi à tous ses subjects qui ont pris les armes, 1562
Le Blason des pierres precieuses, contenant leurs vertus et propriétés, 1574
La Géomance abrégée...pour savoir les choses passées, presentes et futures, 1574
Le Combat de fortune et de pauvreté, 1601
Discours notable des duels, de leur origine en France et du malheur qui en arrive tous les jours, 1607
De l'art de la tragédie, 1939

Biographical and critical studies

Daley, Tatham A., *Jean de la Taille (1533–1608), étude historique et littéraire*, 1934
Jeffery, Brian, *French Renaissance Comedy, 1552–1630*, 1969
Street, J.S., *French Sacred Drama from Bèze to Corneille*, 1983

LEFÈVRE D'ÉTAPLES, Jacques, c.1460–1536.

Theologian, philosopher, and translator.

LIFE

Lefèvre d'Etaples's works and editions, of which there were over 350 printings between 1492 and 1550, are of primordial importance in any attempt to understand the growth of evangelicalism in France during the first third of the 16th century, but they are not homogeneous. Lefèvre knew Greek, was much inspired by three visits to Italy, and realized the need to apply humanist methods of linguistic and textual criticism to the Bible. But the focuses of his interlocking interests gradually moved: from Aristotle's text to Ramón Lull, astrology, and the mystical understanding of numbers; to the neoplatonist mysticism of the pseudo-Denis, the *Corpus Hermeticum*, and Nicolas of Cusa; then to practical reform of religious practice; and finally to the interpretation and then the widespread vernacular dissemination of the scriptures.

Luther was inspired by Lefèvre, who died in the same year as Erasmus, his junior by less than a decade. Lefèvre read Erasmus and Luther, but was not greatly inspired by either. Although their interests overlapped and their careers ran in important respects parallel to one another, Lefèvre on the whole distrusted Erasmus, and he both debated and quarrelled with him. Both firmly chose to remain Catholics but, while Lefèvre contributed more than Erasmus to the promotion of a popular evangelical piety, the less cosmopolitan Lefèvre lacked Erasmus's clarity of mind and sharply critical acumen.

Lefèvre said in December 1501 that his pupil Charles de Bouelles, to whose *Introductio in artem oppositorum* he was writing an introduction, was then 20, and that he himself was double that age. An Augustinian monk, Jerome of Pavia, writing to Symphorien Champier in 1511, referred to Lefèvre as "senex," which does not need to mean much more than 50, and there is a record in 1479 of the graduation of a Jacobus Faber, who may or may not have been the Lefèvre with whom we are concerned. It is now however assumed that Lefèvre was born in Etaples in Picardy about 1460, and that he matriculated at Paris in 1474 or 1475, graduated B.A. in 1479, and took his licentiate and M.A. probably in 1480. Nothing at all is known about the next ten years of his life, although an anonymous author mentioned in 1512 that Lefèvre had owned property at Etaples but had given it away to devote himself to scholarship.

Lefèvre probably studied at the Collège Cardinal Lemoine, in principle reserved for Picards, where he certainly later taught. The fact that by 1490 Lefèvre had written a textbook introduction to Aristotle's metaphysics, the *Introductio in metaphysicorum libros Aristotelis*, published only in February 1494 (new style), and that during the winter of 1491–92 he went to Italy especially to meet Ermalao Barbaro and Pico della Mirandola, suggests that he spent the decade following graduation in Paris, possibly beginning to teach and taking an interest in the less overtly pagan facets of the new Italian humanism starting to infiltrate Paris. Pico's famous letter to Barbaro defending in perfect humanist style the rough Latin of the Parisian scholastics was written in 1485, and Pico was to spend nine months in Paris from July 1485 to March 1486, no doubt frequenting the inchoate humanist circle which had been inaugurated by Guillaume Fichet, the Sorbonne librarian who introduced printing to Paris,

and the Trinitarian Robert Gaguin, canon lawyer, diplomat, and historian.

From the Greeks attending the Council of Florence a tiny and interrupted trickle of Greek teaching sporadically reached Paris, as did reverberations of the immensely important but relatively under-studied debates of the defenders of Aristotle, who were suspected in Italy of affirming an inert deity whose metaphysical function was to support an eternally existing "creation," and the protagonists of Plato, accused of making God the centre of a pantheistic universe in which the immortal survival of the individual soul was ensured only because all creation partook in some degree of the divine nature. Although important for Lefèvre, these disputes, humanist printing, and the teaching of Greek remained tangential to the concerns of the university, still chiefly centred on the establishment of Ockham's theology against that of Scotus. For those dissatisfied with late medieval religion and nominalist theology, there was a vogue for the monastic life, which Lefèvre, fresh from reading Lull, later tells us that he came close to joining in 1491, and the spiritualities of the northern mystics, Harphius, Eckhart, and Ruysbroeck, whom Lefèvre was to edit. Three or four of Lefèvre's colleagues became monks at about this time. He was himself retained in the world, he says, by business, the dissuasion of friends, and unfinished studies.

Fichet had been to Italy for a period during 1469 and 1470, and left permanently for Rome in 1472. The first wave of interest in antique literature passed quickly. The Sorbonne press had swiftly abandoned printing humanist titles, in favour of liturgical, devotional, and Ockhamist works. Louis XI had tried to prohibit the teaching of a nominalist theory of knowledge in a decree of March 1473, but he was forced to surrender on 30 April 1481. In the decade after Lefèvre's graduation, decadent scholasticism had turned to the anti-Aristotelianism of the nominalists, which increased the element of moral strain in religious observance by making the divine law arbitrary. The Aristotelian teachers of a realist theory of knowledge had also necessarily had to hold that divine law could, at least in principle, be known by human reason. This view seemed too naturalist to the late medieval theologians, who turned to nominalism in an effort to defend God's absolute transcendence. God did not need to offer anyone salvation but he established a dispensation in which those would be saved "who did all that lay within them" in the order of salvation which God had in fact established. The older and, in important senses, more humane scholastics, Scotus, Aquinas, and Albertus Magnus, were chiefly printed outside Paris, at Cologne, Strasbourg, Basle, Venice, or Rome. Paris was scarcely touched by any new invigoration of interest in antique literature.

Theology teaching in Paris depended more on the 12th-century *Sententiae* of Peter the Lombard than on the great 13th-century *Summae*. The non-scriptural doctrine of the Immaculate Conception of the mother of Jesus was accepted, and the full integrity of the sacramental system upheld against occasional later adherents of the more spiritual traditions of Wyclef and Hus. The 15th-century French humanist theologians like Gerson and Pierre d'Ailly were published almost only away from Paris, and the Sorbonne press printed the Bible only after it had appeared at Mainz, Bamberg, Strasbourg, Cologne, Basle, Rome, Piacenza, Nuremberg, Venice and Vienna.

Italian humanists other than Pico also started to arrive in Paris in the crucial decade during which Lefèvre began work on Aristotle and made up his mind to go to Italy. Paolo Emilio came in 1483, Girolamo Balbi, quarrelsome, critical, and soon to disgrace himself, in 1484, Cornelio Vitelli and Fausto Andrelini in 1488. Vitelli soon left, while Andrelini and Balbi quarrelled. Andrelini was driven from Paris for some months, while Balbi put about the rumour that he had been burnt. He returned, and Balbi had to flee in January 1491, accused of sodomy. The early humanist milieu in the 1480s was therefore turbulent. Balbi's fame had reached Erasmus, then a young monk at Steyn, while Andrelini's commentaries and poems, some of them obscene, finally gained for him an important humanist following, and it was under his tutelage that the serious study of classical texts began to be undertaken in Paris—Aristotle and Plato as well as Cicero, Virgil, and Terence. Gaguin had been in Italy in 1471, 1483, and 1486. The French repaid the importance Pico had attached to Paris by interceding successfully for his release early in 1488 after his condemnation by Innocent VIII. By the end of the decade Giles of Delft had begun publishing translations of Aristotle in Paris.

Lefèvre must certainly have been a member of the humanist circle in Paris, still favourable to the monastic ideal and not yet hostile to the scholastics, although inclined to be opposed to the nominalists, but interested in Greek, in textual work, in antique literature, and in alternatives to the prevailing Ockhamist orthodoxy in philosophy and the multiplied practices of late medieval spirituality. He later said that at this date he had already been suspicious of the pagan poets, Tibullus, Catullus, Terence, and Ovid. Symphorien Champier tells us that Lefèvre went to Italy to meet not only Pico and Ermalao, but also Ficino and Poliziano. He travelled with a student secretary. He missed Barbaro in Venice, for though now eminent he was exiled from Venice to Rome; and Lefèvre may not himself have gone to Venice before 1500, when he was to stay with Aldus Manutius.

Lefèvre did go to Florence, where Ficino's Plotinianism was enthusiastically regarded, and he was thereafter inclined to use in a more optimistic way the neoplatonist matrix of a spirituality he would still express in terms taken from the pseudo-Denis. It may well be that it is from this first Italian journey that dates a diminishing reliance on Aristotle, at least for the foundations of a spirituality. At best Lefèvre was following Ermolao, who had held that the Paduan commentators, more or less doubting the immortality of the soul, had been in error, and who had produced a religious and almost Christian version of Aristotle, not a great deal different from Ficino's Plotinian theology. Transitory events, Lefèvre was to write, were also divine mysteries, and the material world opened a path to that which was divine and intelligible. Lefèvre also heard Savonarola preach; met Pico, who was occupied with the synthesis of Plato and Aristotle and who lent him a translation from Aristotle by Bessarion to copy; and went to Rome, where he must finally have found Ermalao.

On his return to Paris in 1492 Lefèvre resumed his philosophy teaching at Cardinal Lemoine, and in the same year published his *Totius Aristotelis philosophiae naturalis paraphrases*, at the expense of the printer, Johann Higman, who is thanked in the volume. This was the first to be published of a series of commentaries to cover virtually the whole Aristotelian corpus. Although Lefèvre's prefaces and paraphrases do differ from other commentaries in their helpfulness and concision, the work is essentially a set of class-notes, adorned with quotations from the ancient poets, and augmented with brief prefatory para-

graphs explaining the essential concepts of Aristotle's physics. The final two dialogues give in catechism form a systematic exposition of Aristotle's meaning. There were also two prefaces, both accompanied by commentaries by Lefèvre's intimate friend and collaborator, Josse Clichtove, strongly hostile to Erasmus from 1512.

The prefatory letter to Ambroise de Cambrai, the chancellor of the university from 13 September 1482, whose death on 19 April 1496 was to provoke strikingly few expressions of grief, opens with a reminiscence of Ficino's dedication to Lorenzo de Medici of the 1489 *De triplici vita* close enough to be called an allusion. Lefèvre wishes his undertaking to be likened to Ficino's. It was Ficino's Plotinian third book "De vita coelitus," concerned with the astral influences, presumed before the modern developments in the physical sciences to be a principal determining force on physical and mental health, which inspired Lefèvre's work on natural magic. The Arabian philosophers had elaborated astrology, of which there was a chair at Pavia, into a precise doctrine complementing magic, and horoscopes were almost universally feared or trusted. Ermolao, Poliziano, and Ficino believed in the possibility of foretelling the future and, although Pico, Erasmus, and Rabelais rejected divination in favour of emphasizing the freedom of the will, the French and Italian courts relied on occult knowledge, and even Descartes was to be frightened of his horoscope.

Lefèvre wrote a treatise on natural magic early in 1493 for Germain de Ganay, the brother of the chancellor of France and himself an important ecclesiastic and patron, eventually imposed as bishop on the diocese of Cahors in opposition to Guy de Châteauneuf, elected by the chapter, and from 10 August 1514 until his death on 8 March 1520 bishop of Orléans.

However, Simon de Pharès, son of Charles VIII's astrologer of the same name, had been foretelling the future at Lyons since 1488, and had 200 books on the occult. In the spring of 1493, 40 of them were seized by the archbishop of Lyons and submitted for examination by the Paris theology faculty. In 1494, after 10 months, the faculty condemned the art of foretelling the future, and all but two of the 40 books. Lefèvre did not publish his text, part of whose manuscript subsequently perished.

As Lefèvre proceeded to edit and introduce the Aristotelian corpus, with students of the single undergraduate faculty, arts, in mind, and increasingly furnished with commentaries by Clichtove, something about his life and standing as well as his intellectual and spiritual biographies is revealed by his dedications. When the *Introductio in metaphysicorum libros Aristotelis* was published in February 1494 with a dedication to Germain de Ganay, Lefèvre had already dedicated the editio princeps of the *Arithmetica* of Jordanus Nemorarius, the 13th-century mathematician and physicist, to his brother, Jean de Ganay, the chancellor. During the final decade of the century Lefèvre's opinion of the scholastic method declined; metaphysics was more clearly regarded by him as a theology; Aristotelians taught a doctrine wholly compatible with Christianity; and the fourth and last of the dialogues following the 1494 *Introduction* is openly neoplatonist. On 10 June 1494 Lefèvre published the *Ars moralis*, with a prefatory letter to Germain de Ganay introducing the *Nicomachean Ethics* and making of that work a late 15th-century humanist compendium of instruction on the theory and practice of civic and personal virtues. Aristotle, the most subtle of reasoners in logic, a physicist who understood the real world, in politics a master of jurisprudence, is now "sacerdos atque theologus (a priest and a theologian)," although the quotations from Plato have multiplied.

On 3 July 1494 Lefèvre published with Wolfgang Hopyl the complete *Corpus Hermeticum* in the 1471 edition dedicated by Ficino to Cosimo de Medici, fourteen discourses and dialogues attributed to Hermes Trismegistus and thought to contain God's original revelation on the creation of the world, although in fact a late fourth-century neoplatonist document subsequent to Plotinus. The attribution of a neoplatonist text to an original divine inspiration responded to the unperceived constraint to harmonize the neoplatonism of Plotinus, Porphyry, and the *Corpus* with God's revelation to Moses, as Pico della Mirandola had attempted to do, just as also did the identification of Denis, Saint Paul's first convert in the Athens Areopagus, with the pseudo-Denis, author of the *Corpus Dionysiacum*, and with Denis, the first martyr of France.

The *Corpus Dionysiacum* probably arose in early sixth-century Syria. The identification of the author with Saint Paul's convert and with Denis, the first martyr of France in about 250 A.D., mentioned by Gregory of Tours, was due to Hilduin, the abbot of Saint-Denis in the ninth century, had already been attacked by Valla, and was to become increasingly controverted, notably by Erasmus and Luther. The utility for the authority of the French church of apostolic succession from Saint Paul was obvious, but the upgrading of the neoplatonism of the pseudo-Denis to the status of a derivative of Saint Paul's teaching was also of great importance for late medieval spirituality. It offered a theological foundation for interiorized Christian piety in reaction to the excessive emphasis generally placed on religious practices in the popular piety of the late middle ages, and provided a metaphysical base on which to erect an understanding of human immortality.

Meanwhile Lefèvre was proceeding with the difficult, daring, but more mundane task of providing class notes on a proper text of Aristotle for students of the arts syllabus. A remark of Hermonymus inspired Lefèvre to devote a year to mathematics, and he duly produced a commentary on the arts textbook, John of Sacrobosco's *De Sphaera*, on 12 February 1495. It was dedicated to Charles Bourré, who was about to become treasurer of France, having plunged himself into debt for the purchase of two parchment books of hours. Lefèvre dedicated further mathematical and musical works to Nicole de Hacqueville, a président des enquêtes in the Paris parlement and important for installing in France the Windesheim reformers associated with the devotio moderna, and to Gianstefano Ferrero, bishop designate of Vercelli, and later archbishop of Bologna and cardinal. The *Decem librorum Moralium Aristotelis, tres conversiones* was dedicated to Jean de Rély, a prominent ecclesiastic, royal candidate for the see of Paris in 1492, and an enthusiastic supporter of the reforms of Standonck, the principal of the Collège de Montaigu, who was himself also a product of the devotio moderna and associated with the attempt to bring the devotio moderna with the Windesheim congregation to Paris. Rély was also a supporter of Jean Raulin, the reforming principal of the Collège de Navarre, which accepted only graduates to study theology. The volume of Aristotle's ethics was preceded also by a dedicatory epistle to Budé.

About 6 February 1499, Lefèvre published Ambrogio Traversari's translation of the pseudo-Denis, finished in 1436 and already printed in 1480. He included the entire *Corpus Dionysiacum*, now holding that Plotinus and the other neoplatonists had developed their doctrine from the apostolic tradition of the *Corpus* in the light of the teaching of the Fathers. The *Corpus* in April 1499 was followed by Lefèvre's edition of four unpublished works by Ramón Lull. In 1500 Lefèvre paid a second visit to Italy, during which he went to Rome for the jubilee and stayed with Aldus Manutius, who had just produced the five volumes of the editio princeps of Aristotle, from 1495 to 1498.

Soon after his return the focus of Lefèvre's interests changed, although he did not give up his teaching at Cardinal Lemoine, or the publishing of Aristotle in translation. The *Organon* or *Libri logicorum ad archetypos recogniti* appeared in parts, published by Wolfgang Hopyl at first alone and then with Henri Estienne, from 26 October 1501 until its completion on 17 October 1503 in a single volume with consecutive pagination. The title was intended to be programmatic, and the volume's three parts included the *Isagoge* of Porphyry, the *Categories*, and the *De interpretatione*, the *Prior* and *Posterior Analytics*, and the *Topics* and the *Sophistici Elenchi*. Lefèvre was to publish the political and apocryphal economic works with Henri Estienne in 1506, and finally on 20 October 1515, also with Henri Estienne, Aristotle's *Opus metaphysicum*.

Lefèvre now also turned his attention towards the early mystics and hermits, on 13 July 1504 publishing a selection of other anchorite works, including the *Paradysus Heraclidius*, a shortened version of the *Historia Lausiaca* of the early fifth-century Palladius. He was by now leading a group of commentators, editors, proof-readers, and collaborators, mostly colleagues and pupils from Lemoine, although support also came from other Parisian reformers and humanists. Students, like Basile and Bruno Amerbach, were now coming to him from all over Europe, and regarded him with awe. Closely associated with Lefèvre, along with Clichtove, were Beatus Rhenanus, and, in particular, the exalted and at times semi-deranged devotee of Nicolas of Cusa, Charles de Bouelles. Symphorien Champier collaborated closely with Lefèvre only later. For all of them, even Beatus, who bought Erasmus's translations of Lucian and Euripides, Erasmus's attitude to sacred matters seemed too light-hearted in its cynicism.

In 1506, the year in which he graduated both master and doctor, Clichtove published the works of Hugo of Saint-Victor—dedicated to Jacques d'Amboise, abbot of Cluny, who had paid Clichtove's examination fee for the doctorate, and to whose two nephews Clichtove had just been made tutor—in the hope that the 12th-century Victorine spirituality would nourish reformed monastic piety. Lefèvre, possibly dejected, left Paris in late 1506 to accompany his new patron, Guillaume Briçonnet, to Bourges, where Lefèvre was admitted into the court of Louis XII. He translated from Greek the theological compendium of John Damascene, *De fide orthodoxa*, and published in April 1507 the Latin editio princeps, dedicating it to Giles of Delft, most of whose life was spent in Holland and Germany.

The first work Lefèvre prefaced with a dedicatory letter to Guillaume Briçonnet, his greatest patron, was the second edition of the *Corpus Hermeticum*. It was written in 1505 when Briçonnet was vicar-general of Reims, and about to become abbot of Saint-Germain-des-Prés on 1 October 1507. Aristotle's *Politicorum libri octo* had also by then been dedicated to Briçonnet. In 1507 Lefèvre accompanied the entourage of Louis XII to Genoa, triumphantly entered on 29 April, and followed the ambassadors to Milan. He found Charles de Bouelles again at Rome, met Giles of Viterbo, and copied a Cusa manuscript. He must have been back in Paris by the late summer. His group was beginning to break up. Bruno Amerbach and Beatus Rhenanus both left Paris. Lefèvre decided to publish George of Trebizond's Aristotelian *Dialectica*, but his dedicatory letter to Robert Fortuné at the Collège du Plessis suggests a moment of discouragement.

At this date Lefèvre was already making plans for his great edition of Nicolas of Cusa, finally to appear in three folio volumes in 1514, dedicated to Denis Briçonnet, brother of Lefèvre's patron and bishop-designate of Toulon from 1497 at the age of 18. The Briçonnets were an important family. Robert, the uncle of Lefèvre's patron, was chancellor of France after being president of the chambre des enquêtes. He was also a canon of Orléans and then archbishop of Reims from 1493. When he died on 26 June 1497, his brother, Guillaume Briçonnet, who had been married and had had two sons, Lefèvre's patron Guillaume and his brother Denis, aspired to the see of Reims, which by nepotism, bribery, and corruption he acquired. He was helped by his son Guillaume, and strongly opposed by the reforming party led by Standonck, who fought an important legal action against him.

After his wife's death Guillaume Briçonnet senior was made bishop of Saint-Malo in October 1493, became a close adviser of Charles VIII, and was made a cardinal in January 1495 by Alexander VI. He became bishop of Nîmes on buying off Jacques Faucon, elected by the chapter, and in spite of the opposition succeeded his brother to the archiepiscopal see of Reims, also becoming, in 1504, commendatory abbot of Saint-Germain-des-Prés, to be ceded, under pressure from the reformatory party and against compensation, to his son Guillaume, Lefèvre's patron, in 1507, when Guillaume senior also resigned Reims and accepted the see of Narbonne and the governorship of Languedoc. At Saint-Germain-des-Prés a reforming group demanded the right of election, and it was not until after force had been used and the matter tested in the courts that Briçonnet was left uncontested as abbot on 9 June 1508. Late in 1511, with his sons Guillaume and Denis, he organized on behalf of Louis XII the Council of Pisa, an alternative to the Lateran Council and aimed against Julius II, who excommunicated and degraded Guillaume senior and Denis, although they were reinstated by Leo X in 1514. Before he died on 13 December 1514, Guillaume senior resigned Saint-Malo to his son Denis, and Nîmes to his nephew, Michel. Denis became bishop of Lodève on the transfer of Guillaume junior, his brother, to Meaux in 1516.

Lefèvre's patron, Guillaume Briçonnet junior, born in 1472, was made bishop of Lodève in April 1489 at the age of just 17. Commendatory abbot of Saint-Germain-des-Prés, Briçonnet invited Lefèvre to reside there from 1508, but did not attempt a reform until, at least not improbably inspired by Lefèvre, in 1513 he imposed the primitive Benedictine rule already adopted between 1480 and 1491 by the abbey of Chezal-Benoît, where several of Lefèvre's contemporaries had become monks. With his brother Denis, Briçonnet was sent by François I in 1517 to Rome to negotiate matters concerned with the concordat. He stayed two years and on his return in 1519 inaugurated at Meaux France's first attempt at a full-scale diocesan reform on evangelical principles, which he hoped would be a model for reformatory measures throughout France. His brother Denis was to attempt a reform in Saint-Malo, publishing in April 1518 Gerson's *L'instruction des curez pour instruire le simple peuple*. For some years he was the intimate adviser and spiritual director of

the king's sister, Marguerite d'Angoulême. He was to bring Lefèvre to Meaux putting him in charge of the hospital in the spring of 1521, and in his wake the Greek scholar, Gérard Roussel, with Martial Masurier, Pierre Caroli, Guillaume Farel, Michel d'Arande, and the Hebraist François Vatable. The spirituality behind the Meaux reform and the letters of direction to Marguerite was recognizably that of Lefèvre.

On his removal at Briçonnet's invitation to Saint-Germain-des-Prés in 1508, Lefèvre gave up teaching and, again at Briçonnet's suggestion, turned his attention to the text of scripture itself. He had learned Greek with difficulty in the 1480s, and could now manage to decipher Hebrew. Leaving Beatus and Clichtove to edit Ficino's *De religione christiana* and to correct George of Trebizond's translation of Cyril of Alexandria on the fourth gospel, Lefèvre established four different texts of the psalms: the primitive version used by the early Christian communities; its first revision by Jerome in 383 known as the "Roman" version; Jerome's second revision from the Septuagint, which was finished in 392 after the composition of Origen's *Hexapla* and had entered the Vulgate Bible; and the version which depended on Jerome's knowledge of Hebrew and was finished in 405. To these Lefèvre added a new fifth version of his own which tried to reconcile the other four, and a commentary. The method derives from that Lefèvre had used for Aristotle, modified by Valla's critical annotations on the New Testament as published by Erasmus in 1505, but all the psalms are interpreted with reference either to Jesus in person, or to the Christian life.

The *Quincuplex psalterium. Gallicum. Romanum. Hebraicum. Vetus. Conciliatum* appeared on 31 July 1509, dedicated to Cardinal Briçonnet, with a manifesto at its head. It was an immediate success. Since the avaricious, ambitious, and learned Aleander had started teaching Greek in Paris, François Tissard had moved over to Hebrew, and on 19 January 1509 had produced France's first Hebrew grammar. In April Aleander decided to make his Greek courses public, and Gourmont published three small treatises of Plutarch edited by Aleander. Beatus wrote eulogistically about the psalter, and on 16 November Ximenes wrote to Charles de Bouelles from Alcala, where he was founding a university to produce the Complutensian critical edition of the Bible, asking him to congratulate and thank Lefèvre. In the light of the nature of Lefèvre's textual work, humanist because based on a knowledge of Greek and Hebrew, but not based on properly critical principles, it is important that he should on 27 November 1509 have published new editions of two anti-Muslim works dedicated to Guillaume Petit, the king's confessor. Lefèvre was one of the few highly placed people in Europe who believed that the real object of the new crusade was Constantinople rather than Venice.

Manuscripts for the great edition of Cusa were gradually being gathered together. On 19 December 1509 Petit published a new edition of Sebond's *Theologia naturalis*, according with the spirit of Lull, and fitting closely into the mind of Lefèvre, emphasizing the harmony of reason and faith, natural and revealed truth, while still holding that, in fact, revelation was necessary on account of reason's weakness. Bouelles was particularly sympathetic to Sebond. Lefèvre also discovered the works of another 12th-century Victorine, Richard of Saint-Victor, whose mixture of rational and mystical theology linked the thought of the pseudo-Denis to that of Lull and Cusa and had inspired the mystical spirituality of Ruysbroeck, whom Lefèvre was to edit in 1512, as well as that of Pierre d'Ailly and Gerson.

Lefèvre edited the *De bello judaico* of the pseudo-Hegesippus in June 1510, a month before the *De superdivina Trinitate* of Richard of Saint-Victor. Early in June he had gone to Aix-la-Chapelle, hoping to meet Beatus there, and in July he was the guest of the Brethren of the Common Life at Cologne. He read the German mystics, Ruysbroeck and Hildegarde, whose *Scivias* [*Sci vias Domini*] he was to edit in 1513 in a volume devoted to half a dozen Rhine mystics. Bade had just reprinted John Mombaer's *Rosetum*, which contained a set of spiritual exercises derived from the tradition of the devotio moderna, and Lefèvre's practical concerns became clear when, with perfect intellectual consistency, he edited in defence of the sacraments, rites and ceremonies of the Church Berno's *De officio Missae*, seeking to promote an understanding of the inner meaning of the external ceremonies. He was also active in promoting the publication of the works of controversy and spirituality by Saint Hilary and the letters of Pope Saint Leo the Great.

In December 1512 Lefèvre edited his own Latin translation of Saint Paul alongside the Vulgate, but in smaller characters. He wrote a long commentary on the Vulgate text which, because it was clearly faulty, seemed to Lefèvre not possibly to have been the work of Jerome. The volume, dedicated to the younger Guillaume Briçonnet, contains negligently incomplete work and includes all the Pauline apocrypha, even the correspondence with Seneca, of which it is the editio princeps. Lefèvre's work, while clearly pitted against the theological methods of the Paris scholastics, led by Tateret and Mair, was not at first felt to be disturbing.

It was the Reuchlin affair which caused trouble. The converted Jew, Johannes Pfefferkorn, a friend of the Cologne Dominicans, had argued the need, for the conversion of the Jews, to suppress the Talmud—a commentary on the law codified in the second century, with further commentaries from the two groups of schools, Palestinian and Babylonian, in the fourth and fifth centuries—and the cabala, a secret doctrine of philosophical speculations on the origins of the universe, the infinity of substances, the hierarchy of spirits, and metempsychosis, developed in the 13th century and attaching, for instance, mystical significance to the characters of the Hebrew alphabet. Johannes Reuchlin, who had attended the lectures in Paris of Fichet, Gaguin, and Tardif, and learnt Greek from Hermonymus, following Heynlin to Tübingen and Basle, had taught Greek in Stuttgart and Heidelberg and in 1496 published his commentary on the cabala, *De Verbo mirifico*—quoted by Lefèvre in the preface to the psalter—after his Hebrew textbook, the *Rudimenta linguae hebraicae*. Protected by the archbishop of Mainz, Reuchlin managed to have the suppression of the sacred Hebrew texts halted in 1509 until there had been a consultation which had, finally, to take place in writing when it was clear that the consultors could not be brought together. The result was the incident which for the first time put the humanists at loggerheads with the scholastics in central Europe. The document on which the dispute was to centre was Reuchlin's 1511 pamphlet *Augenspiegel*.

Reuchlin's interests largely overlapped those of Lefèvre, and he had sent Lefèvre a Cusa manuscript. At one point Reuchlin was condemned, but then there was a complex series of appeals and counter-appeals. Juridically Reuchlin was clearly winning when the Cologne Dominicans appealed on the doctrinal issue

to the theological faculty, which had the *Augenspiegel* burnt and, towards the end of April 1514 sought support from Erfurt, Louvain, and Paris. The Paris faculty set up a commission slightly weighted towards the scholastic and against the new philological methods in theology. The final judgement at Paris, unpardonably rushed to avoid an anticipated Roman intervention in Reuchlin's favour, gave the *Augenspiegel* a doctrinal note no worse than "suspect of heresy." Lefèvre had been thoroughly committed on Reuchlin's side and was now himself clearly regarded as theologically dangerous, although Rome had not yet pronounced any disciplinary decision in the Reuchlin case, which it protracted until it had virtually ebbed away, and Reuchlin could resume teaching for the final years of his life.

Lefèvre's edition of Saint Paul came under attack, from Marteen van Dorp among others, who was to react strongly in 1514 to Erasmus's *Moriae encomium*, although the three-volume folio Cusa edition appeared without difficulty, dedicated to Denis Briçonnet and signed by the printer Josse Bade on 23 August 1514. Erasmus had left England, been welcomed at Mainz by Reuchlin, at Strasbourg by Wimpfeling, Brant, and Geyler von Kayserberg, and arrived at Basle, where Froben was to print the editio princeps of the Greek New Testament. Erasmus wrote to encourage Lefèvre, who wrote back a long letter of homage. A variety of circumstances now ensured the victory of Lefèvre's supporters against those firmly opposed to anything which detracted from the impression that the Vulgate itself was inspired. Lefèvre's cause was helped not least by the accession of François I, the unpopularity of Lefèvre's Dominican opponents with the Gallican faculty, the high positions of many of those like Petit, who, although a Dominican, leaned to the Lefèvre camp, and the clear favour of Rome. The result, none the less, was a split in the university. The learned world was obliged to choose between the attitudes of Montaigu, with Tateret, Raulin, and Beda, or Lemoine, with Lefèvre and his followers.

In October 1515 Lefèvre edited for Henri Estienne Aristotle's *Metaphysica* in Bessarion's translation, dedicated to Robert Fortuné. He had for years been overworking, and during much of 1516 was gravely ill, to the point at which he could not even dictate a letter. His incapacity lasted about two years. His interests were, however, changing again, this time in a more textual direction. Erasmus criticized Lefèvre's reading of Hebrews ii, 7, where the Hebrew and the Vulgate read "You have made us a little lower than the angels" and Lefèvre had read "a little lower than God." The dispute became acrimonious with the second edition of Lefèvre's *Epistolae Pauli* in 1515, Erasmus's *Apologia ad Jacobum Fabrum Stapulensem* of 5 August 1517 to which Lefèvre did not reply, and a series of letters between Erasmus and his friends. What was at stake was Lefèvre's refusal to acknowledge as clearly as Erasmus the reality of Jesus's suffering and death. Erasmus had had a similar debate with Colet in 1499, although without acrimony, and appreciated more than his opponents that the orthodox economy of the redemption depended on the actual reality of the human experience of Jesus, whose person was divine.

François I acceded in 1515. His mother, Louise de Savoie, had a great devotion to Mary Magdalen and in January 1516 had made a pilgrimage to La Baume, where Mary Magdalen was supposed to have come after Jesus's death. On her return Louise asked François du Moulin de Rochefort, who had been the new king's tutor and was soon to become his grand almoner, to write the Magdalen's life. Rochefort turned to his old tutor, Lefèvre, explaining to Louise who Lefèvre was, and thereby introducing him to the household of the new king, and no doubt in time to the king's sister, Marguerite d'Angoulême, who would absorb Lefèvre's piety through Briçonnet's letters to her. Lefèvre must have written at least preliminary drafts of portions of the letters. Lefèvre turned his back on the Latin tradition deriving from Gregory the Great, which was not finally proved until 1987 to be apocryphal, and thereby destroyed one of the most popular medieval saints, an amalgam of three women always distinguished in the Greek tradition: the prostitute of Luke vii, 36–50 who washed Jesus's feet at the Pharisee's house, the Mary Magdalen of Luke viii, 2 from whom Jesus cast out seven devils, allegorized by the pseudo-Gregory as the seven deadly sins, and who was the first to see the risen Jesus (John xx, 11–18), and Mary the sister of Martha and Lazarus (John xi, 19), who also anointed Jesus (John xii, 1–18).

Du Moulin wrote his *Vie de sainct Madeleine* between February 1517 and February 1518, and Lefèvre, when questioned about the legend connecting the Magdalen with Marseilles, also wrote his *De Maria Magdalena et triduo Christi disceptatio*, published by Henri Estienne in the spring of 1518. Lefèvre published a second edition some months later, adding a new treatise *De una ex tribus Maria* arguing against the accepted tradition that Saint Anne, the mother of Mary, did not have three husbands. The first attack came in September from Marc de Grandval, prior of Athis, near Versailles, a champion of monastic reform, who had recently helped to join the abbey of Saint-Victor, just outside Paris, to the new congregation of Livry, part of the Windesheim reform based on the devotio moderna and recently introduced by Standonck from Holland. The second attack was from John Fisher, bishop of Rochester and chancellor of the University of Cambridge.

Lefèvre wrote a second *Disceptatio*, published by Henri Estienne in 1519. Agrippa of Nettesheim, an ally in the battle for Reuchlin's innocence, was allowed to write on Lefèvre's behalf, as were Clichtove and Symphorien Champier. Fisher answered Clichtove with an *Eversio* and Lefèvre with a *Confutatio*. Erasmus stayed on the sidelines, but Grandval issued an *Anchora* and Noel Beda rallied to the scholastic side with the *Scholastica declaratio*. Pirckheimer wrote on Lefèvre's behalf. The flurry of pamphlets died down, but Lefèvre's views were officially censured by the Paris theology faculty on 9 November 1521, after Martial Masurier had preached at Meaux on the feast of Saint Mary Magdalen reviving all Lefèvre's theories. François prevented the charge from proceeding to the parlement, where it would have been treated as civil crime. Clichtove maintained that Lefèvre and he had changed their views, and it is clear that by 1521 Clichtove was beginning to veer strongly into a reactionary position with regard to anything which was redolent of Lutheran innovation in doctrine or practice. A series of works made him a fierce opponent of Erasmus in his quest for monastic reform and then reform of diocesan clergy, starting with the 1513 *De laude monasticae religionis* and the 1516 *Elucidatorium ecclesiasticum*.

Briçonnet called Lefèvre to Meaux in 1521 to be in charge of the hospital, making him vicar general "in spiritualibus (in spiritual matters)" in 1523. His real job was to orchestrate the evangelical reform, possibly inspired by the work of Giberti in Verona, and the fruit of Briçonnet's two years in Italy. Briçonnet had returned to find "scarcely fourteen" priests capable of preaching and administering the sacraments. In some parishes no sermon had been preached for ten years. Briçonnet made regular visitations, imposed the obligation of residence on parish priests, and sent preachers to each of the 32 stations into which he divided the diocese. The first synodal decree against absentees was promulgated in 1519. There were further synods in January and October 1520. That August, feast-day dances were forbidden. Briçonnet began to reorganize the hospital and to assemble his largely humanist reforming team. By October 1523 he had taken fright, and had begun to pass decrees against Lutheran publications. The Franciscans strongly resented the suppression of their lucrative preaching monopoly, and finally achieved the break-up of the reform during the absence from France of Marguerite d'Angoulême, who had gone to attempt to redeem the captive François I after the defeat at Pavia in 1525. Briçonnet was himself made to appear before the Paris parlement in October and December 1525, but was cleared of all heresy.

There had been minor liturgical irregularities at Meaux, changes in the liturgy of the Mass for the dead, omission of the customary Ave Maria before sermons, simplification of the liturgy elsewhere, a strong distaste for relics, and vernacular scriptural texts were disseminated. Michel d'Arande was almost permanently court preacher to Marguerite d'Angoulême. Farel (see: Calvin) left Meaux in 1523 to join the reform in Switzerland, publishing in Basle in 1525 a famous *Sommaire et briefve declaration*, and Caroli, a canon of Sens who later became a Calvinist for a while, although he insisted on praying for the dead, may at Meaux have been verging on heresy. Masurier, like Caroli a member of the theology faculty, had to spend some time in the Conciergerie before his orthodoxy was vindicated. The coincidence of date between Briçonnet's attempted reform of the diocese of Meaux and Luther's protest and excommunication is fortuitous, although both stem from the same underlying cause, a religious conception which makes religious perfection something extrinsic to moral stature, not uniquely dependent on interior conversion, and allows the soul's fate after death to be affected by something other than its moral state at the moment of death. It is not surprising that the upholders of the official Sorbonne spirituality of sacraments, works, and ritual observance should have become hyper-sensitive to any innovations redolent of "Lutheranism," which they consistently and often successfully reduced to terms of propositional heterodoxy.

From his arrival at Meaux, Lefèvre's principal activity for the rest of his life was the translation and dissemination of the scriptures in the vernacular. In June 1522 he published his *Commentarii initiatorii* on the four gospels and then, on 8 June 1523, a French translation of them, with the rest of the New Testament in French later in the year. The epistles and gospels for the 52 Sundays and the main feasts of the year were published in 1525, with a vernacular commentary, and the "Catholic" Epistles appeared later in the same year.

The theological faculty of the university of Paris began an official examination into Lefèvre's *Commentarii initiatorii* on 16 June 1523. The chancellor, Antoine Duprat, together with Briçonnet and the bishops of Langres and Senlis, summoned the dean on the 18th to inform him of the king's displeasure and instruct him to submit any of Lefèvre's propositions suspect of heterodoxy to the chancellor before the faculty acted. In the end the faculty produced a list of eleven "errors," of which the first read, "The primitive Church which dedicated so many martyrs to Christ knew no rule except the gospel." It was not until the matter had passed into the secular realm of the parlement's jurisdiction, and Lefèvre had been summoned to appear before that body that, in the late summer of 1525, he and Roussel fled to Strasbourg.

François, returned from captivity in Madrid, brought Lefèvre back to France, and made him custodian of his books at Blois and tutor of his third son, Charles, duc d'Angoulême, for whose use, and that of his sister Madeleine, Lefèvre wrote three schoolbooks. Lefèvre spent his last years translating the rest of the Bible, and published the whole work in a single volume at Antwerp in 1530. He probably had help, but certainly did not retire to the entourage of Marguerite, the king's sister, at Nérac, until the autumn of 1531, and must therefore have finished the translation while still at Blois. He may have had a meeting with Erasmus at Basle in 1526 on his way back from Strasbourg. Erasmus thereafter at any rate spoke well of him and made efforts to keep in touch with him, although Lefèvre did not respond.

Lefèvre died in 1536. His spirituality remained essentially mystical, although its evangelical basis became more pronounced. He was certainly not ever heretical, since heresy, the ecclesiastical "crimen" of which blasphemy was the corresponding civil crime, is the public dissemination of theological heterodoxy, of which he was never guilty. His private thoughts, devotions, and beliefs, as far as we can determine them, were never theologically heterodox when measured against any standards not themselves regarded by educated moderates as superstitious. Although much has been written to the contrary, there is no reason to suppose that Lefèvre ever had even serious misgivings about any dogma of the Roman church, and it is most unlikely that he did, as even Aleander acknowledged. He had never tried as radically as Erasmus to synthesize evangelicalism with classical humanism and, like Budé, found it easier than Erasmus, when forced, to make the choice in favour of ecclesiastical orthodoxy.

WORKS

Although Lefèvre published a vernacular translation of the whole of the Bible after publishing much of it in sections, he himself wrote almost uniquely in Latin, the only notable exception being the commentaries on the epistles and gospels for Sundays and feast days. He did not write in the imaginative genres but, in the context of the *Guide*, he is of importance because his activities offer the key to an understanding of much of French literary culture in the first third of the 16th century. Lefèvre's career and publications also provide us with important indications of how a knowledge of the learned languages, although scarcely of antique imaginative literature, was demanded for religious purposes to subvert the late medieval nominalist stranglehold on the interpretation of the Bible, even when it was manipulated by those late scholastics in favour of sometimes ruthlessly ascetic reform, like Raulin and Standonck.

Lefèvre's interests changed, but their development can be understood only if their relationship to unlearned piety, to evangelicalism, to the religious utility of Greek and Hebrew, to Wyclef, Hus, and to the reformatory movements of Luther and the Swiss reformers is properly evaluated. The relationship between Lefèvre's piety, the reformatory, non-classical human-

ism of Gerson and d'Ailly, the learned ignorance of Cusa's theology, the rationalism of Lull and Sebond, and the Windesheim reform imported into the decaying Paris abbey of Saint-Victor by the Brethren of the Common Life and based on the devotio moderna, has never been properly analysed.

The most common errors have to do with the incorrect suppositions that the Meaux reform was inspired by Luther's teaching, and that the members of the Paris theological faculty most relentlessly insistent on absolute conformity to traditional norms of belief and practice were corrupt, and not also capable of favouring the most rigorous measures of religious reform. The accusations they could scarcely be defended against are those of pastoral neglect, inadequate supervision of the theological activities of some of the mendicants, and insufficient vigilance against flagrant superstition. There was widespread corruption and superstition in the French church, but these were by no means automatically exempt from vigorous opposition on the part of the Paris scholastics, whether belonging to the old schools deriving from Aquinas or Scotus, or to the late medieval nominalist school deriving from Ockham and the terminists.

It is reasonable to see, if not a discontinuity, then at least a change of direction in Lefèvre's religious thought, marked by his long illness just after the middle of the second decade of the 16th century. He had already started work on the text of scripture, and his most important theological statements are probably to be found in the commentaries and ancillary material of the 1509 *Quincuplex psalterium* and the 1512 *Epistolae Pauli*, but after his recovery he devoted himself entirely to the spreading of religious devotion based on vernacular versions of scripture.

Although he was still to publish the 1515 Aristotle *Metaphysica* and other texts belonging to the series inaugurated during his teaching years, Lefèvre's preoccupations during the decade before his illness centred, alongside the scripture on which his patron, Guillaume Briçonnet, had invited him to work, on a whole series of writings not only mystical but generally at the same time inclined to rationalism. Cusa may have praised learned ignorance and seen in it the only possible knowledge of God, but with the spiritualities of the pseudo-Denis, Lull, the *Corpus Hermeticum*, the Rhine mystics chosen by Lefèvre, and the Victorines, Cusa has in common a natural theology based on rational assumptions and arguments about the nature of the cosmos. Lefèvre's self-imposed task came in that first decade at Saint-Germain-des-Prés to define itself as the integration of a rational and an evangelical theology. Greek was a tool acquired in the course of a projected career in teaching, and antique literature never seriously occupied Lefèvre's attention more than momentarily.

Lefèvre lists his first masters for us in the prefatory letter to the 1505 *Contemplationes Remondi* (Lull) addressed to a Carthusian novice at the order's Paris house at Vauvert known simply as Gabriel. He cultivated those who "elevated their minds to God," naming four well-known monastic reformers, all ascetics and firm defenders of scholastic orthodoxy: Jean Raulin, the reformer of the Collège de Navarre who abandoned everything to become a novice at Cluny, Philippe Bourgoing, the Cluny monk, John Mombaer, who led the Windesheim mission invited by Standonck to the abbeys of Château-Landon and Saint-Victor, and Jean Standonck, the famous reformer of the Collège de Montaigu.

It is true that Lefèvre goes out of his way in his introductions to the Aristotelian corpus to quote the moral sayings of the antique poets, but the function of the quotations and allusions is decorative, and the content always moral or religious. By the 1515 *Epistolae Pauli* he forthrightly at I Cor. xv, 33–34 repudiates not only Tibullus, Catullus, Terence and Ovid, but also the sceptical tradition of interpreters of Aristotle associated with Padua, against whom Ficino had written in the Prooemium to the commentary on Plotinus, the Alexandrians who did not believe in immortality and the Averroists who believed that the individual soul would be merged into the world soul. If Erasmus was a monk who wanted to achieve the synthesis of classical humanism and evangelical piety, Lefèvre was a scholastic who believed in going back to Aristotle's text and nearly gave up his erudite activity to become a monk.

Since Lefèvre's own opinions are expressed overwhelmingly only in prefaces and commentaries, it seems reasonable to consider them in three groups, roughly those preceding the move to Saint-Germain-des-Prés, those of the decade he spent there, and those subsequent to the moves to Meaux and Blois. Before the turn of the century, or at least until the pseudo-Denis edition of 6 February 1499, we are concerned entirely with the sets of class-notes on the texts of Aristotle, the other works of mathematics and music, the suppressed manuscript on natural magic, whose composition and suppression need none the less to be noted, the four short treatises in the first Lull volume, and with the Ficino translation of the *Corpus Hermeticum* edited by Lefèvre and published on 31 July 1494, the *Mercurii Trismegisti Liber de Potestate et Sapientia Dei: per Marsilium Ficinum traductus: ad Cosmum Medicem*. In the pseudo-Denis volume are also 11 epistles of Ignatius of Antioch. To the seven genuine letters a fifth-century heretic added long interpolations and six forgeries. Minus one letter which was to Ignatius rather than from him, this collection, translated into Latin in the sixth or seventh century, is that printed by Lefèvre, less one letter that he dropped or forgot, to Mary of Cassobola. The volume is signed 6 February 1499 and its title lists the Pseudo-Denis's treatises: *Theologia vivificans. Cibus solidus. Dionysii Celestis hierarchia. Ecclesiastica hierarchia. Divina nomina. Mystica theologia. Undecim epistole. Ignatii Undecim epistole*[sic]. *Polycarpi Epistola una.*

Lefèvre's professional but not spiritual model was Ermalao Barbaro, Pico's opponent, whom Lefèvre had missed at Venice but caught at Rome in 1491–92. On his return to Paris Lefèvre attacked the scholastic commentators on Aristotle in his 1492 *Totius Aristotelis philosophiae naturalis paraphrases* for their useless distinctions, subdivisions, and categories which they put in the way of the quest "for the beautiful and the contemplation of beautiful things." Lefèvre states that each subject requires its own method, foreshadowing the unease he will later display at having to allow the four traditional medieval levels of meaning in scripture: allegorical, tropological or metaphorical, anagogical or moral, and literal. In the *Paraphrases* he is brief, the professional pedagogue, and explains in seven paragraphs the seven principal concepts of Aristotle's physics: nature, cause, movement, the infinite, space, vacuum, and time. The paraphrases presuppose the availability of a text, such as Bricot had recently published. The commentary succinctly deals with the difficult parts of the text, but still uses decorative classical allusions and quotations from Ovid and Virgil. Lefèvre ends with two helpfully expository dialogues, borrowing the form from Plato, having in his preface attacked the syncategoremata of medieval logic.

The preface had made clear the pre-eminent position of Aristotle among the philosophers, noted the "analogia secreta (hidden analogy)" which pervaded his text, and stated

cum de caducis ad horamque transitoriis agat, pariter divina tractare. Immo vero hanc totam sensibilis naturae philosophicam lectionem ad divina tendere et ex sensibilibus intelligibilis mundi parare introitum

(When he treats of petty and transitory things, he treats at the same time equally of divine mysteries. Indeed this whole study of the philosophy of sensible nature tends to that which is divine, and from that which is sensible we are prepared for introduction to that which is divine).

In the February 1494 *Introductio in metaphysicorum libros Aristotelis* Lefèvre wrote to Germain de Ganay, using the term theology for metaphysics

Tibi vero theologicum opus tamquam sacerdoti divina mysteria potissimum curanti dico offeroque

(I offer you indeed this work of theology as divine mysteries to a priest to whose custody they are entrusted).

Lefèvre clearly had in mind the religious nature of his philosophical activity from the beginning, just as he would later bear in mind the rational foundations for his spirituality.

More apparently provocative than to regard Aristotle's metaphysics as a concealed discussion of the sacred truths was Lefèvre's assault on medieval logic itself, the foundation of the dialectic in which scholastic arguments were conducted. The essential medieval textbook, Peter of Spain's *Summulae logicales*, which identified dialectic with logic and brought into popular academic use such terms as "supposition," which has to do with the range of predicates, and "terminist," applied originally to those nominalists who dealt with universal ideas from the point of view of specialists in dialectic, had just been republished in 1494 and 1496, and is known to have been printed 160 times before 1530. The author, who has been called the greatest of the scholastics and who was certainly the most influential of their pure logicians, later became Pope John XXI.

Pierre Tateret had in 1495 attacked Lefèvre's commentary on the metaphysics, and on 7 June 1496 had reprinted his defence of Peter of Spain, while Thomas Bricot and Georges de Bruxelles had opposed their scholastic Aristotle to the spiritual, Italianized version of Lefèvre, who replied in the preface to his edition of Aristotle's *Introductiones logicales. In suppositiones. In praedicabilia. In divisiones. In praedicamenta. In librum de enunciatione. In primum priorum. In secundum priorum. In libros posteriorum. In locos dialecticos. In fallacias. In obligationes. In insolubilia*. It is here that Lefèvre is at his nearest to Erasmus, sharing with him, and for the same reasons, a dislike of the barbaric Latin used by Peter of Spain to refine endless categories such that, if all the spiritual meaning went out of texts passed through his logical grid, the dialectical tool was honed to a surgical cutting edge. The precision instrument was too sharp to be used for the delineation of the limits of Christian orthodoxy. It was almost impossible to classify spiritual truths and aspirations in the precise Latin categories which Peter of Spain's logic was fashioned to create, and which were unique to the

Christianity of western Europe. Lefèvre, like Erasmus, is indignant:

> A gotica enim illa dudum Latinorum litteris illata plaga, bonae litterae omnes nescio quid goticum passae sunt

> (Latin letters have been swept up by a Gothic trap, and all good learning has suffered from Gothic destruction).

Lefèvre does not of course state that it is the precision of the categories which has made theology a branch of dialectic rather than of spirituality or religion, but that is what is at issue in the prefatory dedication of October 1496 to Thibault Petit and Gilles de Lille. It brings us very near to the core conflict which determined the pattern of the French reformation.

Lefèvre's defence of the authenticity of the pseudo-Denis not only signifies a move away from the neoplatonist syncretism of the *Corpus Hermeticum*, but it is also an early indication of the extent to which he allowed devotional impulse to swamp a truly critical faculty. In spite of what we should regard as the strident differences of style and content between the Pauline epistles and the pseudo-Denis's corpus which Lefèvre supposed to have been derived from them, Lefèvre insisted that it must have been the neoplatonists who borrowed from Paul's convert, not a pseudo-Denis who was developing the doctrine of the neoplatonists, as was in fact the case.

> Secundum est: Hunc sacratissimum divinae reserationis sapientiae neque auctorem neque Platonicum, Aristotelicum, Stoicum aut Epicureum, sed Iesu vitae auctoris et spiritus sancti sub divinissimis Paulo et Hierotheo praeceptoribus esse philosophum

> (Secondly: The most sacred philosopher of this revelation of divine wisdom can be neither Plato, Aristotle, stoic, or Epicurean, but only Jesus the author of life, and the Holy Spirit acting through his divine teachers, Paul and Hierotheus).

Hierotheus was said by the pseudo-Denis to be his master, alongside the apostle Paul, but does not correspond to any real historical figure. Lefèvre goes on to quote Ficino on the way in which the list of neoplatonist authors quoted by Ficino in the *De religione christiana* had used the insights of the Christian revelation to interpret Plato. Lefèvre recalls that, according to Basil and Augustine, the neoplatonists had "usurped" from John's gospel whatever they said about the divine mind, the angels, and theology. Lefèvre would be willing, were it not fitting to be more restrained, to say they stole it. He himself found a whole theology, and even more a whole spirituality, in the component treatises of the pseudo-Denis's corpus. He insists heavily on the threefold division of the spiritual life into purgative, illuminative, and unitive or perfective ways, which is used in almost incantatory fashion in the commentary on the *Celestis hierarchia*, and obtrudes also in Briçonnet's letters to Marguerite d'Angoulême.

There are other instances in Lefèvre which show how critical acumen is submerged in pious sentiment. He defends the Pauline authorship of *Hebrews* as well as of the correspondence with Seneca and suggests, with the ordinary anti-feminism of medieval Christianity that, if Saint Paul was married, he had a vow of chastity with his wife; also that he could not really have disputed with Peter "to the face." If the Vulgate was faulty, it could not be the work of Jerome, a Father of the Church. It is only after his illness that, while still reluctant to allow that the divine person, Jesus, actually felt pain during his passion, he attacked the medieval traditions identifying the three Marys and giving Saint Anne three husbands.

In 1501 Lefèvre, writing his prefatory letter to Germain de Ganay for the 1503 edition of the *Organon*, had not yet given up the struggle to save scholastic dialectic for the defence of a spiritual theology and a proper reinvigoration of the humanities. He blames on the decay of dialectic the decline both of the humanities and, what he says is worse, of theology itself, preceding his letter with an invocation ending,

> Si autem dialecticam artem cum modestia suscipitis: consequens est ut bone discipline redeant omnes. bonas autem disciplinas morum probitas et vite decor concomitatur omnis, omnisque virtus, quod summopere studiis et optamus et imprecamur

> (If you take up with modesty the art of dialectic, humane learning will return in all the disciplines; all uprightness of behaviour and honesty of life will accompany human learning, and all virtue, for which we earnestly long, work, and pray).

The decay of dialectic into sophistry can be reversed by a return to Aristotle, and Lefèvre restored the different treatises into a series of chapters for the *Organon*, dropping the various accretions for which there was no antique authority from the text. When he publishes in 1509 the *Quincuplex psalterium* and in 1512 the *Epistolae Pauli*, he leaves his readers in no doubt that by having recourse to the authentic text of scripture he hopes to mediate an interior religious experience.

The prefatory letter to the psalter, addressed to Cardinal Briçonnet, is an important manifesto. For a long time, Lefèvre writes, he has been studying the humanities, but they now appear to him to be mere darkness when compared to the light with which the study of the sacred text has filled him. Neglect of the scriptures has caused the ruin of the monasteries, devotion has perished, and religion has been extinguished, the spiritual has been exchanged for the material, and heaven for earth. Yet it is not the literal sense alone that satisfies the spirit. The apostles, evangelists, and prophets have opened the gate to him,

> et videor mihi alium videre sensum, qui scilicet est intentionis prophetae et spiritus sancti in eo loquentis, et hunc litteralem appello, sed qui cum spiritu coincidit

> (and I think I can see another sense, which is intended by the prophet and the Holy Spirit speaking through it, which I also call literal, but which coincides with the spiritual).

Lefèvre goes on explicitly not to reject the other three traditional senses of scripture in the middle ages, allegorical, tropological, and anagogical, and ends up with two literal senses, one which blinds and is understood only in a carnal human sense, as by the adherents of the rabbinic tradition, the other of which enlightens, illuminates, and is infused with the divine spirit. It has been referred to as Lefèvre's mystical sense. Lefèvre has to explain how the rabbis are not converted by the scripture which gives him his spiritual experience, and needs therefore to emphasize the prayerful effort required to open the soul to the spiritual experience mediated by the word of God. He gives a series of five examples of psalm verses which might have been taken from the celebrated *Postillae* of Nicolas of Lyra, and which can be understood both with reference to events in David's life and with reference to the coming of the Messiah. Lefèvre understands all the psalms with reference either to the coming of Jesus or to the Christian life.

The essential difference between the two literal senses is that the sense which blinds is that in which the text is regarded "passibiliter (passively)," whereas in the mystical experience the text acts on the individual, infusing the mind with the divine spirit. In the mystical sense, it is the individual who is passive and God, through the scriptural text, who is active, which is why the reading of scripture requires to be prepared by a life of prayer and the practice of virtue. Lefèvre has succeeded in combining objective textual study with mystical illumination, integrating the two sides of his mind, and finding the convergence he had been seeking.

The integration of the rational, philosophical stream of Lefèvre's mental activities represented by his work on Aristotle with the mystical and religious satisfactions towards which his work on predominantly neoplatonist authors had led, becomes clearer during the period at Saint-Germain-des-Prés, particular in the commentary on the Pauline epistles. There Lefèvre can combine a strongly mystical with a quasi-rationalist religion. Immediately before publishing the commentary on Paul, Lefèvre published on 3 August 1512 Ruysbroeck's *De ornatu spiritualium nuptiarum libri tres*. In his preface, addressed to a Carthusian novice known simply as Raemundus, Lefèvre explains how the individual spiritualities of the monastic orders all mediate the sweetness of the experience of union with God, but that what alone is necessary in all is adhesion to the One. Only the dead can live the spiritual life perfectly, but it can be lived even on earth by divine gift. The regeneration which gives spiritual validity to earthly virtue is necessary for the life of the spirit. To act in accordance with the law of reason, or even with the decalogue, itself only an expression of natural law, is only a preparation.

Lefèvre is in the end prepared to concede authentic virtue to the pagans. Writing in 1512, the year in which Jacques Merlin published his famous apologia for Origen at the head of the four-volume editio princeps of Origen in Latin, with its notoriously rationalistic neoplatonist spirituality, Lefèvre could with apparent spontaneity take much the same position:

Ut enim a sole illuminatio, sic a deo justificatio immortalitas et christiformitas. Et ut revelatio pupillae non est solis illuminatio, sed solum quaedam praeparatio ad illuminationem et ad quandam oculi soliformitatem, ita bonorum operatio non est justificatio, sed praeparatio ad divinam justificationem et diviniformitatem

(Just as illumination comes from the sun, so from God comes justification, immortality and Christiformity. And just as the opening of the pupil in the eye is not the sun's brightness, but only a preparation for the illumination and the conformity of the eye to the sun, so the operation of good works is not justification, but a preparation for divine justification and conformity to the divine).

But, for Lefèvre, the salvation of the inhabitants of those parts of the world which the gospel has not reached is neither "divina pietate (cujus misericordia plena est terra) indignum (unworthy of the divine piety, of whose mercy the earth is full)," nor against the view of the apostle Paul, providing that natural virtue is observed, and that the inhabitants, regretting their faults and believing in the author of providence,

naturali lege deum diligant ex operum magnificentia jam cognitum et proximum ut suos consimiles, parentes officiose colant, injusticias quas sibi fieri nolint ad alios vitent, et caetera, quae lex divina (excepto cerimoniarum ritu) mandat, faciant

(by the natural law love God, known from the magnificence of his works, look after their neighbours and families, do not inflict on others injustices which they would themselves like to avoid, and do everything else which the divine law commands, with the exception of the ritual ceremonies).

Natural law and reason take us therefore to the verge of justification and revealed truth. Lefèvre does not spurn the utility of traditional works or ascetic practices, but he diminishes their importance in favour of mystical rather than moral fervour. The goal of life is the perfect union with Christ, Lefèvre writes explicitly in the commentary on I Cor. vi, and at I Tim. vi, 20 Lefèvre reiterates the contrast between the Catholic and the neoplatonist view, at best a halfway house. Understandably Lefèvre, writing his letter-prefaces over quarter of a century, is repetitive. Succinct expressions of his view are scattered throughout the prefaces and commentaries. But more than in any other single work, it is the edition of Paul's epistles which sums up his doctrine, with its strong mystical insistence on the union of the individual soul with Christ's body, the Church in heaven and on earth. Theology for Lefèvre is not a rational construct so much as an intellectual penetration into spiritual truth which, in its higher stages, demands a divine initiative.

Lefèvre simply refuses to choose between free will and predetermination, justification by faith and justification by works, each time seeing the force of each position, and their irreconcilability, but refusing to allow them to clash as sharply as they were clearly destined to, and elsewhere in fact very soon did. Lefèvre is tolerant of even clearly superstitious practices if he can find a spiritual significance which legitimizes them. He allows the cult of Mary, the veneration of relics, pilgrimages, and ascetic practices as signs of penitence, holding only that forgiveness comes not from self-inflicted punishment, but from God. Baptism is a sign of justification in God and the Mass is a "memoria ac recordatio (remembrance and memory)" of the passion of Jesus, a phrase which neither denies nor affirms its representational function, but takes the weight of discussion away from the controversial point, which was how the Mass could be a re-enactment of the sacrifice of Calvary without being a repetition of it. On both practical and intellectual matters Lefèvre showed a pronounced timidity, dominated above all by the horror of schism he expressed most clearly at Eph. iv, 10:

Servanda est unitas spiritus in vinculo pacis, unitas corporis Christi quae est una sancta Ecclesia catholica, unitas spei eternorum bonorum, unitas domini, unitas fidei, unitas

baptismatis; ex his unitatibus servatis ad eam quae est con-
summatio omnium solo Deo in ipso et sua infinibili unitate
illam tribuente pervenitur unitatem

(The unity of spirit must be kept in the bond of peace, the
unity of the body of Christ which is the one, holy Catholic
Church, the unity of the hope of eternal gifts, the unity of
the Lord, the unity of faith, the unity of baptism; from the
preservation of these unities can be reached with God's
help the unity which is the consummation of all in God
alone in himself and in his boundless unity).

The *Commentarii initiatorii* are still in Latin, but the preface
explains that this is not intended to be a learned work. Faith must
precede understanding, which is transcended by true knowledge. There is a passage in Matthew vii where Lefèvre produces
a theological compromise between allowing and refusing validity to meritorious human endeavour in the acquisition of justifying grace that might conceivably have had some part in the
gestation of the "duplex iustitia (twofold justification)" compromise which Seripando offered the Council of Trent, but Lefèvre
was far more interested in the spiritual than in the doctrinal
implications of his views, and clearly concerned to avoid being
pinned down to explanations of the mechanics of the operation
of grace and free will.

The *Commentarii* are almost disappointingly brief, which
does not mean they are not also long-winded. Lefèvre's point is
now not textual but spiritual, and again almost incantatory:

Et hoc sit cunctis unicum studium, solatium, desiderium,
scire evangelium, sequi evangelium, ubique promovere
evangelium

(And for all let this be the sole study, solace, desire, to
know the gospel, to follow the gospel, everywhere to
preach the gospel).

The gospel is to be believed, not understood, but Lefèvre reaffirms his commitment to the necessary learned languages for the
uncovering of its text. God is unknowable in this life, but faith is
the path to vision.

Clichtove had moved in a different direction from Lefèvre
during the second decade of the century, becoming increasingly
concerned with practical reform, and with monastic and sacerdotal regulations. He was accused of defending simonaical practices, and became increasingly hostile to the views of Erasmus,
which appeared to him to reduce religion to morality. There is
no sign that Lefèvre himself ever allowed his own evangelicalism and his orthodoxy to come near clashing with one another,
and it would be difficult to regard him as a major theologian or
religious writer if it were not for the historical interest of his
position alongside those of Budé, Luther, and Erasmus, for his
indefatigable editing, and his immense achievements in spreading the vernacular text of scripture.

It was too late for a purely scriptural piety to put to rest the
anxieties about salvation generated by late medieval Christianity, and it was perhaps as early as 1510 that the questions would
inevitably be pointedly asked which led to the Lutheran and
Swiss schisms. The questions about predestination and free will,
faith and works, and whether religious perfection was extrinsic
or intrinsic to moral stature, had understandably become objects
of obsessive worry, and the sharp confrontations which in fact
resulted in schism could no longer be avoided, although the

schisms themselves might well still have been. It is possible that,
in spite of Lefèvre's sporadic ineptitude as a textual critic, and
the blind eye he turned to so many real problems, he may yet be
seen as having represented an option to the northern renaissance
which, on looking back, Europe might feel it would have been
wiser to take.

PUBLICATIONS

[*All Lefèvre's works were editions, translations, or commentaries*]

Totius Aristotelis philosophiae naturalis paraphrases, 1492
In Aristotelis metaphysica introductio, 1494
*Mercurii Trismegisti Liber de Potestate et Sapientia Dei: per
    Marsilium Ficinum traductus*, 1494
In Aristotelis ethica Nichomachea introductio, 1494
Textus de Sphaera Ioannis de Sacrobosco, 1495
Opuscula mathematica, 1496
Introductiones logicales, 1496
S. Dionysii Areopagitae opera omnia, 1499
Raymundi Lulii opera quaedam, 1499
In Arithmetica Boetii epitome, 1500
Libri de anima Aristotelis, 1500
Ars suppositionum, 1500
Aristotelis libri logicorum, 1503
Palladii historia Lausiaca…Paradisus Heraclidius, 1504
Primum volumen contemplationum Remundi [Lulii], 1505
Aristotelis politica et oeconomica, 1506
Ioannis Damasceni de orthodoxa fide, 1507
Georgii Trapezontii dialectica, 1508
Quincuplex psalterium, 1509
Hegesippi de bello judaico, 1510
Ricardi de superdivina Trinitate, 1510
Bernonis de officio Missae, 1510
*Ioannis Rusberi [Ruysbroeck] de ornatu spiritualium nup-
    tiarum*, 1512
Meteorologiae Aristotelis paraphrasis, 1512
Epistolae Pauli, 1512
Opuscula mystica, 1513
Nicolae Cusae opera omnia, 3 vols., 1514
Aristotelis metaphysica, 1515
Raymundi Lulii proverbia, 1516
De Maria Magdalena et triduo Christi disceptatio, 1518
De tribus et unica Magdalena disceptatio secunda, 1519
Commentarii initiatorii in quatuor evangelia, 1522
Les quatre évangiles, 1523
Le Nouveau Testament, Partie II, 1523
Le Psautier de David, 1524
*Epîtres et évangiles pour les cinquante et deux sepmaines de
    l'an*, 1525
Commentarii in epistolas catholicas, 1527
L'Ancien Testament, 1528
La Sainte Bible, 1530

Biographical and critical studies

Renaudet, A., *Préréforme et humanisme à Paris pendant les
    premières guerres d'Italie (1494–1517)*, 1953
Rice, Eugene F., jr., *The Prefatory Epistles of Jacques Lefèvre
    d'Etaples*, 1972

LESAGE, Alain-René, 1668–1747.

Dramatist and novelist.

LIFE

Lesage was born at Sarzeau, near Vannes in Brittany, on 8 May 1668. His father was a lawyer, and both parents came from legal families. Lesage, too, was to become a lawyer, changing his career only comparatively late to make an industrious living as a full-time writer. It has been remarked that his life was unadventurous, with his sharp sense of fantasy diverted exclusively into nourishing his plays and novels; the law-abiding citizen was fascinated by the crooks, confidence tricksters, and swindlers who inhabited his works. In fact he was an early member of a class of professional writers independent of government patronage, which had almost disappeared under Colbert and which began to emerge again only with the country's financial ruin and the consequent freeing of literary, and especially dramatic activity from royal subsidy and therefore effective control.

It is actually not at all a paradox that Lesage's best-known play, *Turcaret*, should have as its background an economic crisis, which allowed a new generation of independent dramatists, of which Lesage was in the vanguard, to re-assert themselves and sometimes to prosper. It is also not strange that Lesage's non-literary career, like that of numbers of the new generation of French writers, should have left little mark and, unlike that of the well-known and generally aristocratic court writers of the preceding generation, should be difficult to reconstruct for biographical purposes. Unlike most of his predecessors during the preceding half-century, Lesage was a professional writer, and most of his time was spent living quietly, pursuing his career in the hope of making enough money out of it to be able to live.

Lesage's father, Claude, was a greffier, occupying a position roughly corresponding to that of recorder, or minor judge, at the royal court of Rhuys, while his mother, Jeanne Brenugat, was the daughter of the procureur of Redon. Lesage's mother died on 11 September 1677, and his father on 24 December 1682. Lesage was an orphan at 14, left to be brought up by his guardians, his father's brother, Gabriel, and his mother's, Blaise Brenugat, who sent him to board at the Jesuit school at Vannes in about 1686, after which Lesage's career started to follow its pre-ordained course. He followed family tradition and trained for the bar in Paris, graduating in 1692. His uncle had meanwhile lost Lesage's fortune and, although he had been brought up in comfortable bourgeois surroundings, had been well educated, and appears to have circulated in reasonably elegant social circles in Paris, Lesage by 1692 urgently needed to earn a living. He became clerk first to a notary, and then probably to a tax-farmer, possibly at Vitré.

Lesage had met the poet and librettist Danchet and the dramatist Dancourt. He also frequented the liberal society of the Temple under Philippe de Vendôme, grand prior of the order of Malta, and the salon of the duchesse de Bouillon. There is said to have been a liaison with someone socially prominent whose name has not been leaked, but on 28 September 1694 he married at Saint-Sulpice the 22-year-old Marie-Elisabeth Huyard, daughter of a Parisian bourgeois said to have been a carpenter, and of Marie Carlos, through whom must have developed what was to become an all-important connection with Spain. The marriage was happy. The couple had three sons and a daughter, and Lesage died in his wife's arms fifty years later.

Much against the wishes of Lesage, who developed a strong dislike of the acting profession, two of his sons became actors, and the eldest, René-André, known as Montménil, had a successful career before dying in a hunting accident in 1743, after which Lesage retired and took his wife and daughter to spend his last years living with the second son, Julien-François, a canon at Boulogne. Lesage had become reconciled to René-André only when he was successful and had finally played the lead in his own *Turcaret*. The stage career of the third son, Pitténec, was unsuccessful, and history lost track of him in the course of what Paris-based historians refer to as provincial tours, although we know he returned to Paris, where he put on *Le Testament de la Foire* and *Le Miroir véridique*, adaptations of his father's work, during the winter fair. He was eventually reconciled with his father. Marie Carlos died five years after Lesage, and her daughter, Marie-Elisabeth, in 1779.

In 1695 Lesage, still working in a legal office, was persuaded by Danchet to publish at Chartres a translation, probably made from a Latin translation, of the late Greek writer Aristaenetus— the *Lettres galantes d'Aristénète*. The book was not a commercial success but, although it brought him no money, it may well have sharpened Lesage's appetite for a literary as an alternative to a legal career. By 1698 he was back in Paris, and began to receive through Jules de Lyonne, son of the ambassador to Spain, an annual pension of 600 livres, which was to last until his protector's death in 1715, and on which he managed to live until literary earnings began to arrive. Lyonne suggested that Lesage turn his attention to the literature of the Spanish golden age. Lesage began on Lyonne's advice to learn Spanish, and in 1700 published under the title *Théâtre espagnol* two five-act comedies freely translated from Spanish, *Le Traître puni* by Francisco de Rojas, and *Don Feliz de Mendoce* by Lope de Vega. In 1702, by which time his fourth child had been born, the Théâtre-Français presented Lesage's *Le Point d'honneur*, an adaptation of a three-act skit on duelling which failed after two performances.

In 1704 Lesage published a free translation of the 1614 two-volume continuation of *Don Quixote*, Alonso Fernández de Avellaneda's *Nouvelles Aventures de l'admirable don Quichotte de la Manche*. It was Lesage's translation which was translated into English in 1705, and again in 1784. Then on 15 March 1707 the Théâtre-Français presented as a double bill the one-act curtain-raiser *Crispin rival de son maître* adapted from Hurtado de Mendoza's *Los Empeños del mentir*, originally written sometime after 1634 and now grafted by Lesage on to the French burlesque tradition, and the five-act adaptation of Calderón's *Don César des Ursins*. The boxes liked the Calderón, but the success of the evening was the rapturous reception in the parterre of *Crispin*, recognizably halfway between Molière and Marivaux, as the date suggests.

It was also in 1707 that Lesage published *Le Diable boiteux*, a novel drawing on the Saragossa 1671 edition of Luis Vélez de Guevara's 1641 *El Diablo cojuelo*, in a Spanish framework, but in fact a satire on Parisian society and some of its better-known figures, like Ninon de Lenclos and Mme de Lambert. The transposition into a Parisian setting transforms the character of Asmodée, and the work draws also on La Bruyère. Success was instantaneous, with two counterfeit editions in the year of publication, 35 editions in 18th-century France, including simple reprints with new title pages, and about 60 in the 19th century; there were 25 editions in English before 1900.

By the date of *Le Diable boiteux* Lesage was going deaf and had to use an ear-trumpet. The family had moved to the Faubourg Saint-Jacques, but the financial situation was still tight. France's own background of military ambition and economic catastrophe is discernible in Lesage's next play, the one-act *La Tontine*, received by the Théâtre-Français on 27 February 1708, but then turned down by them, probably for political reasons, although the mainspring of the plot was a satire on doctors. The "tontine" was a public loan which purchased an annuity that ingeniously increased in amount as other subscribers in the original age group died off; tontines had been raised in 1689 and 1696. The whole principle of public fund-raising was being widely discussed in 1708, and the presumption is that any reference to general economic policy was considered too dangerous for the Paris stage.

Lesage then offered the company another one-act comedy, *Les Etrennes*, which was also turned down on account of political pressure in 1708. Lesage reworked it into the five-act *Turcaret; ou, Les Etrennes*, but it too was turned down under pressure—allegedly exercised through the actresses of the company—from the financiers, themselves the butt of increasingly acid satirical attack ever since Colbert had re-organized the system of tax collection, in effect ceding to a company of 40 tax farmers, for a capital sum, the right to collect taxes of different sorts. The farmers themselves were financiers, who paid the state its annual capital sum and then appointed paid officials to collect the taxes for them. Rights to collect particular taxes, or to collect in particular regions, for specified periods of time, were then sold off, so that a whole minor society of tax officials, themselves all tax-exempt and mostly hoping for titles of nobility, came into being.

A series of wounding comedies and embittered pamphlets, of which some, like the 1707 *Nouvelle École des finances; ou, L'Art de voler sans ailes*, simply descended to coarse invective, had shown that the issue of taxation was close to the centre of public attention. Lesage read his reworked comedy in the salons to arouse interest, much assisted by the rumour going the rounds that he was being offered 10,000 francs to keep it off the stage. Monsieur appears to have intervened on 13 October 1708, and the French company put on *Turcaret* on 14 February 1709, but withdrew it after only seven performances. The box-office receipt for the final performance was just over 653 livres, well above the acknowledged figure at which a play "failed," 500 livres in winter and 300 in summer.

Lesage understood the message, but still needed to earn a livelihood. The Italian company had been banished from Paris after audiences had taken *La Finta Matrigna* of 1697 to allude to Mme de Maintenon. Only in 1716 was an Italian company under "Lelio" (Luigi Riccoboni) invited back to the Palais-Royal, to open on 18 May, before moving to the refurbished Hôtel de Bourgogne in June. Before its exile, the Italian company under "Dominique" (Giuseppe-Domenico Biancolelli) who, before his death in 1688, had won the personal favour of Louis XIV, had been allowed to perform in French, and such dramatists as Dufresny, briefly Donneau de Visé's successor as editor of the *Mercure Galant* (q.v.), Fatouville, Palaprat, and even Regnard had not hesitated to exploit the lucrative popular market for stage entertainments which the Italians had opened up. On their expulsion, their popular function had increasingly been taken

over by strolling players, visiting companies, and mountebanks, acrobats, circus performers, tightrope walkers, and others, operating at the winter fair of Saint-Germain from 3 February to Palm Sunday and at the summer fair of Saint-Laurent each July, with the season extended to run from late June to early October.

The jealously enforced privileges of the established Théâtre-Français drove the fair performers to every sort of ingenious and wildly popular expedient to circumvent the prohibitions. Forbidden to give regular plays, they resorted to monologues, pantomimes, and comic ballads, gave several parts to one actor in the same scene, used a speaker who would comically intone what actors dressed for their characters would pretend to write on the palms of their hands, or made each actor enter and exit alone for a single speech or line. Inevitably, heavy-handed official proceduralism produced mockingly brilliant forms of popular subversion, and also, at the more organized end of the comic scale, more formal elements of satire and parody. Lesage rewrote *La Tontine* as *Arlequin colonel* for the fairground, and turned to the alternative fairground market for his living, producing over 100 plays, often in collaboration, not all published, perhaps not all scripted, and certainly not all original. Lesage himself was responsible for scarcely more than the outlines. Most of the scripts for not more than one speaking actor were the work of Alexis Piron. *Arlequin colonel* was finally played by the Théâtre-Français in 1732.

There is a formal canon of 88 plays, none of more than three acts, printed in the ten-volume 1737 *Théâtre de la foire*, of which 29 are attributed to Lesage alone and virtually all the rest to Lesage in collaboration with d'Orneval, with or without Fuzelier as well. Collections were published in 1721, 1724, 1731, and 1734. Their historical importance is immense. Not only are they an obvious link to modern pantomime, circus acts, Punch and Judy, and the high culture forms of Harlequinade, but the prohibition of dialogue and singing on all stages other than those of the Théâtre-Français and the Opéra, which was developing the tragédie lyrique and the opéra-ballet, was leading Lesage and others towards the creation of comic opera. Lesage specialized in comédies-vaudevilles.

In addition to the enormous output of fairground material, fascinatingly interesting for the social historian but not, in the modern sense of the term, literature, Lesage produced a great deal of fiction. His most important novel is undoubtedly the *Histoire de Gil Blas de Santillane* of which books 1 to 6 appeared in two volumes in 1715, books 7 to 9 in 1724, and books 10 to 12 in 1735, making four volumes in all. The novel draws on a whole series of Spanish and Italian originals, and is a realist study of manners presented in picaresque form with often quasi-theatrical episodes. The single volumes of 1724 and 1735 are in fact added-on continuations, and Lesage carried on updating and adding to his earlier work, in particular multiplying the allusions as he did in *Le Diable boiteux*, and making the comedy more lively. There are about 30 known 18th-century French editions of *Gil Blas*, but a sudden acceleration of interest took place, and 342 full 19th-century editions of the text have been counted, in addition to abridgements, adaptations for children, and translations, especially into English.

As well as the works already noted, Lesage published a two-volume verse adaptation of the *Roland amoureux*; a novel in verse by Boïardo (1717–21); a romance, the 1732 *Les Aventures de M. Robert, chevalier, dit de Beauchêne, capitaine des flibustiers dans la Nouvelle-France*; and three further picaresque novels: the *Histoire de don Guzman d'Alfarache*, based on the work which originally popularized the picaresque novel, Aléman's two-volume *Guzmán de Alfarache* (1599–1602); the four-volume *Estevanille Gonzalez, surnommé le garçon de bonne humeur* (?1734–41); and *Le Bachelier de Salamanque; ou, Les Mémoires de D. Chérubin de la Ronda*. There was also some minor fiction, *Une journée des Parques* of 1735 and *La Valise trouvée* of 1740, and Lesage had some hand in one of the many parodies of *The Arabian Nights*, translated by Antoine Galland (1704–17).

By the time Lesage, accompanied by his wife and daughter, retired to Boulogne to live with his son the canon, he was very deaf, and he spent his last years clearly senescent. The military commander of the region called on him and, much later, reported that in 1745 he had found Lesage devoid of means and supported almost entirely from his son's modest income. He died on 17 November 1747.

WORKS

Crispin rival de son maître is often considered to be among the best-constructed one-act comedies ever to have been written in French, but its stature as a fast-moving comedy of intrigue has often been overshadowed by its historical importance in the development of the comic servant or valet character, from earlier antique, then Italian and Spanish models, via Molière and popular French fair theatre, towards the very different creations first of Marivaux and then of Beaumarchais. Lesage's leaning towards realism, as well as the changed imaginative needs of the first decade of the 18th century in France, partly account for the way the new relationship between master and servant is reflected in their different speech patterns.

By the first decade of the 18th century, a new social consciousness was subjecting that relationship to closer imaginative scrutiny, as a new economic awareness among the taxed bourgeoisie was bringing money into the focus of imaginative interest. The servant, who in the Spanish and Italian traditions had always been more concerned about money than interested in promoting an employer's interests, is transformed by Lesage into a creature whose unique interest is in money, and whose willingness to usurp the employer's position corresponds to an imaginative exploration of the possibility that social differences had come to depend not on class but on money. Nobility could increasingly be bought. Did only language remain to indicate the class barrier?

In *Crispin* the characters' names still reflect their social status. Indeed, except for Crispin and Damis's valet, La Branche, the names actually had all been used by Molière. Crispin correctly describes La Branche as being, like himself, a "fripon honoraire (honorary villain)." The bourgeois Monsieur and Madame Oronte have a daughter, Angélique, promised to Damis, the son of M. Orgon. Angélique, however, is loved by Valère, of whom Crispin is the valet and, as it turns out, the rival, even if all he really wants is the dowry. The play opens with a scene between Valère and Crispin:

Valère: Ah! te voilà, bourreau! (Oh! There you are, you rogue!)

Crispin: Parlons sans emportement. (Don't let's lose our tempers.)

Valère: Coquin! (Scoundrel!)

Crispin: Laissons là, je vous prie, nos qualités…De quoi vous plaignez-vous? (Let's leave our quality out of it, if you please…What are you complaining about?)

Valère: De quoi je me plains, traître! Tu m'avais demandé congé pour huit jours, et il y a plus d'un mois que je ne t'ai vu. Est-ce ainsi qu'un valet doit servir? (What am I complaining about, traitor! You asked me if you could go away for a week, and it's more than a month since I've seen you. Is that the way a valet should do service?)

Crispin: Parbleu! monsieur, je vous sers comme vous me payez. Il me semble que l'un n'a pas plus de sujet de se plaindre que l'autre. (Well, sure, monsieur, I serve you as I am paid. It seems to me that neither of us has any more to complain of than the other.)

Valère: Je voudrais bien savoir d'où tu peux venir. (I should like to know where you've been to.)

Crispin: Je viens de travailler à ma fortune. J'ai été en Touraine, avec un chevalier de mes amis, faire une petite expédition. (I've been working at my fortune, I've been in Touraine with a nobleman of my acquaintance, making a little expedition.)

Valère: Quelle expédition? (What expedition?)

Crispin: Lever un droit qu'il s'est acquis sur les gens de province par sa manière de jouer. (Getting himself paid a debt which he got some provincials to owe him by the way he played cards.)

Valère: Tu viens donc fort à propos; car je n'ai pas d'argent, et tu dois être en état de m'en prêter. (Then you've come at the right time, because I haven't got any money, and you should be able to lend me some.)

Crispin: Non, monsieur. Nous n'avons pas fait une heureuse pêche. Le poisson a vu l'hameçon; il n'a point voulu mordre à l'appât. (No, monsieur, we didn't have a catch; the fish saw the hook and didn't take the bait.)

That is the opening of the play. It establishes in less than a minute that the master is haughtily conscious of his status. He calls Crispin a rogue, reprimands him, addresses him with the familiar "tu," but tries to borrow money from him, thereby pointing instantly, in an attitude reflected in the language he uses, to the non-alignment of social status and wealth. Crispin, his servant, is impertinent, wealthier, has smarter friends, even if they have become rich and bought a title by card-sharping, but calls his master "monsieur," and uses the formal "vous" even when insolently asserting his equality. What already betrays his class is the vulgarity of his final snub, which lacks a dignity retained by Valère even while he tries to borrow money from his valet. Lesage allows the crudity of Crispin's greed for Angélique's dowry, as well as the impudence of his disrespect for the social proprieties, to impinge on the audience sufficiently for his imposture to be judged unworthy of success.

Crispin despises his master, laughs at him to his face, dresses in his rival's clothes, absurdly flatters his prospective parents-in-law, and nearly gets away with the dowry. The skill, wit, and unrepentant impertinence were new and daring, nearer to Beaumarchais and his Spanish models than to Molière and his Italian ones. The dramatic economy and rapidity of movement announce the best work of Marivaux, although Lesage does not attempt his delicacy of language and control of nuance. Crispin excels Harlequin in sheer effrontery, and for the first time the comic valet regards money as more desirable than social status.

Turcaret rather bitterly reflects the France of military decline, with a fading aristocracy and the ascendancy of unattractive bourgeois arrivistes. Lesage exploits the resentment against the tax farmers felt both by the aristocracy, whose social role they were in many ways replacing, and by the populace, on whom the weight of their extortions fell. The action, which contains some discontinuities, centres on the possibility of the marriage of M. Turcaret, the rich tax farmer, to the young widow, the Baronne. In fact Turcaret is already married, but has not been paying his wife the pension he had promised her to stay quietly away from Paris. The plot is wound up by the intervention of external agencies, the appearance of Mme Turcaret and the declaration at the instance of his creditors of her husband's insolvency, rather than by any development within the action itself, so that the comedy is more important for its general display of the coarseness, ruthlessness, and odious complacency of the financier than as a dramatic artefact moving ineluctably to a comic climax, although parts of the action are skilfully handled, and swiftly conducted.

In the first act the chevalier, to whom the Baronne is attracted, sets her up to ruin Turcaret, himself the cause of the ruin of many others. The chevalier's valet, Frontin, is to be placed in Turcaret's service. Frontin's last speech in the first act sums up the plot:

J'admire le train de la vie humaine! Nous plumons une coquette; la coquette mange un homme d'affaires; l'homme d'affaires en pille d'autres: cela fait un ricochet de fourberies le plus plaisant du monde

(I find the pattern of human affairs quite admirable! We fleece a coquette; the coquette devours a man of business; the man of business robs a lot of others: that makes a most amusing chain of dirty tricks).

In the second act Turcaret, jealous of the chevalier, reveals himself as a bad-tempered bully. In a rage, he breaks a cabinet and the porcelain it contains. The Baronne makes him feel his social inferiority and the way she demeans herself by considering him as a possible partner. He falls to his knees and asks forgiveness. Frontin obtains a place in the Baronne's household for his protégée, Lisette. In the third act, as Frontin is preparing a banquet on Turcaret's behalf, a marquis appears and informs the Baronne what sort of usurer Turcaret actually is. The act ends with Lisette telling the audience that she is in love with Frontin, and that she thinks they will do well together.

In the fourth act a forged demand for 10,000 livres is presented to the Baronne, which Turcaret promises to pay, but Turcaret's sister reveals to the Baronne that Turcaret is married. Lisette encourages her not to break with him until she has ruined him, and in the fifth act a series of mistaken identities makes the imbroglio exceedingly swift and complex. The chevalier is revealed as a swindler, Turcaret is ruined, and the Baronne has lost a lot of money. Only Frontin is richer by 40,000 francs. He ends the play by announcing that with Lisette he will found an honourable dynasty: "Voilà le règne de M. Turcaret fini; le mien va commencer (That is M. Turcaret's reign over: mine is about to begin)."

Le Diable boiteux was sufficiently popular for a story at least to have gone the rounds that swords were drawn in Barbin's bookshop between two potential purchasers of the last copy of the second edition. Novels about blind, lame, talkative, and avaricious devils proliferated. Boileau found his servant reading *Le Diable Boiteux* and threatened to dismiss him if he found the book under his roof. As indicated in the preceding section, the novel was a runaway success. It was also continuously reworked. By 1726 it was longer by a third, with four new long stories inserted, a hundred new anecdotes added, and thirty-nine taken out, with about 1,300 corrections of detail. The writing is made more effective, more precise and concise, with smoother transitions, more sudden endings, and greater liveliness. Success had originally been due largely to the satirical account of contemporary French society, the inspiration of La Bruyère, and the figures alluded to in their fictional guise—Dufresny, Dancourt, Houdar de la Motte, and many others.

There is no particular reason for the narrative ever to end. It starts straight-facedly one October night in Madrid, when the streets had already been left free for lovers to serenade ladies on balconies and the sounds of guitars were causing alarm to fathers and jealousy to husbands. Don Cleofas Leandro Perez Zambullo, "écolier d'Alcala (student at Alcala)," climbs hurriedly out of a window through which "le fils indiscret de la déesse de Cythère l'avait fait entrer (the indiscreet son of the goddess of Cythera [Cupid] had made him enter)." By the end of this first sentence we know the narrative is comic. Don Cleofas has to escape from "three or four" assailants who want to kill him or make him marry the woman with whom they found him. She turns out to be doña Thomasa, and to have hidden the men to force don Cleofas to marry her. He, however, escapes into a garret where he finds a devil corked into a phial by a magician, and tries to guess which devil he is, and what devilry he is in charge of. He is Asmodée, the "Diable boiteux (limping devil)."

Je fais des mariages ridicules; j'unis des barbons avec des mineures, des maîtres avec leurs servantes, des filles mal dotées avec de tendres amants qui n'ont point de fortune. C'est moi qui ai introduit dans le monde le luxe, la débauche, les jeux de hasard et la chimie. Je suis l'inventeur des carrousels, de la danse, de la musique, de la comédie et de toutes les modes nouvelles de France

(I make absurd marriages; I unite grey-beards with young girls, masters with serving-maids, ill-dowered girls with impoverished swains. It is I who introduced into the world luxury, debauchery, games of chance, and chemistry. I invented carrousels, dancing, music, comedy, and all the new fashions in France).

The relationship between don Cleofas and Asmodée is instantly symbiotic. They make a pact, and don Cleofas releases Asmodée from the phial. Asmodée has crutches, and we are given details of his unattractive physical appearance before he starts to explain to don Cleofas what everyone they see is doing and thinking, and from what motives. The satirical structure is now set up. Eventually the magician recalls Asmodée, who hopes to do the magician a service, win his liberty, and rejoin don Cleofas, who marries the beautiful girl Asmodée has saved for him from a fire which would have destroyed her. The 21st and last chapter tells us "de quelle façon l'auteur de cet ouvrage a jugé à propos de le finir (how the author of this work thought it appropriate to end it)."

The *Histoire de Gil Blas de Santillane* is more unified by its characters. It is a long comedy of manners in the form of an adventure novel narrated in the first person with unashamedly derivative elements which shocked, of all people, Voltaire, who himself plundered Lesage's text, borrowed his style, and took over his narrative method. The narrative is much advantaged by the skills which Lesage had acquired as a dramatist and, like that of *Le Diable boiteux*, the structure allowed the content to be indefinitely extended, although the episodes are now more nearly in the form of tableaux. Sentences are generally short, which adds pace, and the consistent use of the past tense keeps the illusion of continuous narrative. It remains true that the order of episodes does not seem dictated by any particular necessity, and that characters appear and disappear somewhat arbitrarily as inspiration ebbs and flows.

The central thread is provided by the principal character, Gil Blas, and the cast includes a vast and rich array of personalities. Gil Blas, 17 at the outset, is full of ambitions, naive, anxious for success and happiness, in pursuit of which he makes his way through life, not guided by any moral principles other than those imposed by the goal of his own advancement. The character matures during the 20 years Lesage was working on the four books, and in the third volume, published in 1724, Gil Blas undergoes corruption at court. Lesage is at pains to give him a richer variety of experience as time goes on. Gil Blas is memorable for his wit and almost above all for the aphoristic skills which were already seen in the early comedies. The strength of the book lies in the way Lesage exploits the first-person narrative of the naive fortune-seeker not only to give an incisive picture of his life and times, but above all to imply a wholly non-explicit moral comment on the way people behave.

PUBLICATIONS

[*Many of the fairground pieces have never been published at all and exist only in manuscript. Those available in print were originally published uniquely in the* Théâtre de la foire]

Collections

Oeuvres complètes, 12 vols., 1821
Le Théâtre de la foire, 10 vols., 1721–37
Oeuvres de Le Sage, 1877
Théâtre, Classiques Garnier, 1948
Il Teatro della foire, 1965

Plays

Théâtre espagnol, 1700
Le Point d'honneur, 1702

Crispin rival de son maître, 1707; as *Crispin, Rival of his Master*, 1915 [edited by T. Lawrenson, 1961]
La Tontine, 1739
Turcaret, 1709; as *Turcaret* (in English), 1923 [edited by Spaziani, 1965]

Fiction

Lettres galantes d'Aristénète, 1695
Nouvelles Aventures de l'admirable don Quichotte de la Manche, 1704; as *The New Adventures of don Quixote*, 1705
Le Diable boiteux, 1707; anonymous translation 1708; as *Asmodeus*, 1924 [edited by Etiemble, Bibliothèque de la Pléiade, *Romanciers du XVIIIe siècle*, vol. 1, 1960; also edited by R. Laufer, 1970]
Les Mille et un jours, contes persans [satire of the *Arabian Nights*], 5 vols., 1710–12; translated 1714
Histoire de Gil Blas de Santillane, vols. 1–2, 1715; vol. 3, 1724; vol. 4, 1735; translated by Smollett as *The Adventures of Gil Blas of Santillane*, 1749; [edited by Etiemble, Bibliothèque de la Pléiade, *Romanciers du XVIIIe siècle*, vol. 1, 1960]
Nouvelle Traduction de Roland l'Amoureux (Boïardo), 2 vols., 1717
Histoire de don Guzman d'Alfarache, 2 vols., 1732; translated 2 vols., 1783
Les Aventures de M. Robert, chevalier, capitaine des flibustiers dans la Nouvelle-France, 2 vols., 1732; translated 2 vols., 1745; [edited by H. Kurz, 1926]
Histoire d'Estevanille Gonzalez, surnommé le garçon de bonne humeur, 4 vols., ?1734–41; translated 1735, 1737, 1816
Une Journée des Parques, 1735; translated 1745
Le Bachelier de Salamanque; ou, Les Mémoires de D. Chérubin de la Ronda, 2 vols., 1736–38; translated 1737–39
La Valise trouvée, 1740

Biographical and critical studies

Barbaret, V., *Lesage et le théâtre de la foire*, 1887
Lintilhac, E., *Lesage*, 1893
Dédéyan, C., *Lesage et Gil Blas*, 1965

Bibliography

Cordier, H., *Essai bibliographique sur les oeuvres d'Alain-René Lesage*, 1910

L'HERMITE, Tristan: see **TRISTAN**

M

MAIRET, Jean de, 1604–1686.

Dramatist and poet.

LIFE

Mairet, French by culture but not by nationality, was born in the free imperial city of Besançon, where he was baptized on 10 May 1604, son of a well-to-do bourgeois mother from Troyes and of a father from a German Catholic family which left Germany at the Reformation. We know little of his youth. He was still young when his parents died, but provision had been made for his education and he underwent schooling first at Besançon and then at the Paris collège des Grassins. Details of Mairet's biography come chiefly from the prefatory *Epître dédicatoire, comique et familière* to his 1636 *Galanteries du duc d'Ossonne*. Little other certain information is available before 1625 when, according to the preface of the 1628 *La Sylvie*, with a privilège of 17 September 1527, Mairet joined the service of the duc de Montmorency, then governor of Languedoc. Mairet was poor, had come to Paris in the wake of his countryman and friend Antoine Brun, from about 1620 a member of the group of satirical poets surrounding Colletet, and may have spent no more than the single academic year 1624–25 at Grassins.

Montmorency had been recalled to the court at Fontainebleau to raise an army against the Huguenots under Soubise, who had annexed to La Rochelle the Ile de Ré and the Ile de l'Oléron. It must have been in June or July 1625 that Mairet entered his service, no doubt both as a "gentilhomme volontaire," and as an official chronicler and propagandist, temporarily replacing in Montmorency's service Théophile de Viau, who had entered Montmorency's household probably in 1621, but was in prison from 28 September 1623 until 1 September 1625. Montmorency needed to get his force together in a hurry, and Mairet was almost certainly in urgent need of a job. The campaign was a success. Montmorency, still admiral of France, took the Ile de Ré after a sea and a land battle on 15–17 September 1625. Soubise scuttled his fleet, and a fortnight afterwards Oléron was taken. An ode he was to write later suggests that Mairet saw action and was either wounded or ill and also that he sided against the Sorbonne in favour of the new medicine based not on bleeding and the theory of the humours but on the use of drugs and the chemicals extracted from them.

Montmorency, not privy to the peace negotiations leading to the treaty of 6 February 1626, was not allowed to attack La Rochelle as he wished, but forced to maintain a semi-siege. It was during this inactive period that Mairet wrote some at least of his early verse, the "Ode à Monseigneur de Montmorency," and the "Prosopopée d'Alcide après son combat naval de l'Isle de Ré," neither of them entirely serious, as well as some pure propaganda, like the "Sonnet aux Rochelois." In November

1625 Montmorency returned briefly to Paris and took back into his service Théophile, who was to die on 25 September 1626 and from whom Mairet appears to have borrowed money. In spite of their intimacy, and the strong inspiration demonstrably drawn from Théophile by Mairet, it is difficult to suppose that they met before Montmorency's brief visit to Paris in November 1625, or that they got to know one another well before Mairet was established as a member of Montmorency's household and Théophile was again able in the spring of 1626 to visit Montmorency's château at Chantilly, where tolerance of his morally and religiously audacious work had set the tone. Théophile was to die in 1626 in Montmorency's town house in the rue de Bracque, and only the intervention of his patron secured a religious burial.

In November 1625 Montmorency stopped at Bourges on his way back to the Atlantic to call on his brother-in-law, the prince de Condé, who would not receive Théophile. Montmorency was unwell for most of the winter, and it seems not improbable that Mairet spent from late November until April with Théophile at Selles, with the young Hippolyte, comte de Béthune, just back from Rome, where he may well have known Théophile. That not unlikely hypothesis would account for their apparently close collaboration. Montmorency probably collected both Théophile and Mairet in April, and probably took Mairet to Bourges, where Montmorency held the future Grand Condé at his baptism on 6 May 1626. Montmorency then returned to Chantilly, where Théophile at least had probably been since April.

The chronology has been debated, but it is not improbable that Mairet's first play, the tragi-comédie *Chryséide et Arimand*, had been written during the winter. Its characters and ideas both seem to derive from Théophile, and it has been suggested that Théophile had some part in its composition or may even have taken over an existing version which had possibly been rejected. Théophile himself wrote nothing of consequence under his own name that winter, translating only an ode of Horace, and might reasonably have felt at that juncture in his affairs that it was safer to get Mairet to publish what was virtually a joint *Chryséide*.

Three times Mairet was to say that he had written *Chryséide* at the age of 16—in the "avertissement au lecteur" prefacing the third edition of *La Sylvie* in 1630, in the *Epître comique et familière*, and in the 1637 *Epître familière* to Corneille—but it was not published until printed without Mairet's permission in Rouen in 1630, and was then disowned by him in the 1630 "avertissement," possibly on account of its irregularity, inopportune just as he was about to publish *La Silvanire*, observing and, in its preface, vindicating the rules in a pastoral tragi-comédie. By 1637, when Mairet was still writing it off as a schoolboy frivolity, *Chryséide* had become a staple success in the repertoire of the Marais troupe, but we do not know when or where it was first played, or exactly what function Mairet filled in Montmorency's household from the spring of 1626. The pension of

1,500 livres may have been accorded only after Théophile's death.

The household at Chantilly was notably liberal in religion and philosophy. Its head, Henri II de Montmorency, born in 1595, was never made Connétable as his father had been, but, although previously cautious, was probably persuaded by his wife, the beautiful and fearless Marie-Félicie Orsini (des Ursins), the queen mother's niece hostile to Richelieu, to conspire with Gaston d'Orléans against Richelieu shortly after the execution of Marillac on 10 May 1632. In the event of the insurrection's failure, Montmorency was willing even to offer his services to Gustavus Adolphus, the Protestant king of Sweden, a recourse so extreme that his conspiracy must be interpreted largely as a despairing attempt to assert fading feudal rights.

The king's brother behaved with predictable impetuosity, failed to carry Dijon with him, accepted the king's terms for surrender and abandoned Montmorency, for whom only a few towns in Languedoc had declared: Albi, Lodève, Uzès, and Saint-Pons. Armoured and helmeted like a knight, Montmorency was defeated by the much smaller royal army at Castelnaudary on 1 September, and was dying on the field when the royal officers, finding that his own troops would not retrieve him, took him prisoner. In spite of universal pleas to Louis XIII for clemency, he was beheaded on 31 October 1632.

Mairet's real patron at Chantilly had already increasingly become the duchesse, after her husband's death to become a Visitandine at the Moulins convent which she had founded. On her behalf Mairet had pleaded increasingly with Montmorency to abandon the quest for military glory in favour of domestic happiness. Her father, Virginio Orsini, had supported Guarini against Tasso, and she was herself more interested in poetry than in the theatre. Under her inspiration Mairet's poetry concentrates on the idealization of female beauty, while he also sympathizes with the attitudes of the noblesse d'épée when, in the "Prosopopée de la Nymphe de Ré" he appears to be pleading for the life of the comte de Bouteville, to be executed for provocative duelling on 21 June 1627, but for whom much sympathy was felt by the old aristocracy. Montmorency had himself fought a duel with the duc de Retz, elder brother of the future cardinal, in July 1615.

At Chantilly in 1626 Mairet wrote, or more probably finished, La Sylvie. There are signs that sections were added to a preexisting pastoral written along the lines of Théophile's Pyrame et Thisbé. Théophile's play had been published in 1623 although first performed perhaps two years previously. Mairet's original draft pastoral may not have contained what is now the dialogue of Act I, scene 3. There had been an implied allusion to the three-year imprisonment by Marie de Medici of Henri II de Bourbon, Montmorency's brother-in-law and father of the Grand Condé, in a 1616 Dialogue de Damon et de Silvie published in the Mercure Français (q.v.). The dialogue which Mairet added to his 1626 play and which alluded to the dialogue published in 1616, was itself published in 1627, a year before the play as a whole. What Mairet added in the early summer of 1626 was an obviously hostile allusion to the proposed marriage of the king's brother Gaston on whom the title of Orléans was about to be conferred, to Marie de Bourbon-Montpensier, daughter of the duchess de Guise, on 6 August 1626, clear in the fourth act, and in the perfunctory dénouement with the spectacular and no doubt hastily contrived effects of the fifth act. Orléans's bride was to die the next year giving birth to their child, later the Grande Mademoiselle.

Gaston d'Orléans's marriage was of great importance to all those near to the throne. The queen was still childless, although relations with her husband had been normal since Luynes, in January 1619 had grabbed hold of Louis XIII, forced him to his wife's bed, and virtually obliged him to consummate the marriage. It looked as if any heir of the king's brother would eventually succeed to the throne. Richelieu had decided on the appropriateness of the marriage of Gaston d'Orléans, but those already close to the succession, or for other reasons hostile, were organizing vocal opposition. "The party adverse to the marriage," as it was called, included Soissons, who wanted the bride's massive inheritance for himself, all the Condé family, since Condé would lose the reversion of the crown if the king died childless but his brother had a son, and Mme de Chevreuse and Anne of Austria, who disliked Richelieu.

Mairet, through Montmorency, inherited Théophile's papers, two volumes bound in white vellum with pink ribbons, and it is not unlikely that his 1634 Sophonisbe also derives partly from Théophile. La Sylvie, clearly a play with a strong political resonance, was played privately at Chantilly, and was both successful and influential when played in Paris. There were 14 editions between the first in 1628, dedicated to Montmorency, and 1635, and there were eight further 17th-century editions. After its hasty completion Mairet does not seem to have written much for a year or so, except for encomiastic verses seeking the patronage of the great. His reputation was now established, and he made contact with the Schomberg and Liancourt families as well as the cardinal de la Valette who, with the comte de Cramail, persuaded Mairet to adopt into French pastoral the regularity of the Italians. Cramail was himself an author, whose works were edited by Cotin. He commissioned the 1609 Question royale from Duvergier de Hauranne, later abbé de Saint-Cyran, was exiled for his liaisons with Mme du Fargis, and was then sent to the Bastille in 1635 for hostility to Richelieu.

Mairet addressed a sonnet in 1627 to La Valette, who left Paris for the siege of La Rochelle in the autumn of that year, finally managing to resign from the see of Toulouse in 1628. He was in Paris again, and in possible contact with Mairet, from May 1628 until the 28 December 1629, when he left to fight in Italy. Although a friend of Richelieu, whose reconciliation with Louis XIII he helped to achieve on 11 November 1630, La Valette was also a friend of Montmorency, adding his plea for mercy to that of the rest of the feudal aristocracy and remaining on close terms with Montmorency's sister, the princesse de Condé, his mistress, after the execution. He was a patron to Godeau, Voiture, Balzac, and Costar, and an assiduous frequenter of the Hôtel de Rambouillet (see: Guirlande de Julie), to which he introduced Mairet. Mairet's 1633 La Virginie was played there in the presence of La Valette and the comte de Belin, Mairet's later protector. Mairet did not, however, depend in the same way on the Hôtel as Voiture did, and when, from the late 1620s, published collections of verse reflect Richelieu's tightening hold on the world of letters, Mairet's name never appears alongside those of Faret, Malherbe, Boisrobert, Balzac, Silhon, and Desmarets.

Mairet returned to his homeland at least once at this period and went to Beaucaire with the duchesse de Montmorency in 1628. She stayed for a year before going to Pézenas in March 1629, at which date Mairet was in Paris supporting Orléans in his project of marrying Louise-Marie de Gonzague, daughter of the duc de Nevers and later queen of Poland. To prevent the marriage, Marie de Medici had imprisoned her at Vincennes, releasing her only on her promise to go back immediately to Italy. The Montmorencys returned to the proximity of Paris after three years in 1629. Mairet was with them for the last three months of that year, and no doubt undertook for suitable recompense the composition of *La Silvanire; ou, La Morte-vive. Tragi-comédie pastorale*, privately performed for the Montmorencys before being taken to the Hôtel de Bourgogne. It was virtually an adaptation of d'Urfé's play drawing on *L'Astrée*. It was published in March 1631, dedicated to the duchesse de Montmorency, with a prefatory manifesto addressed to Cramail.

The piece was not a great success at the Hôtel, although Montdory's company subsequently put it on the bill at the Marais, perhaps at Belin's instigation. This makes clear, however, that the taste for which Mairet was catering was that not of the public but of his patrons. He seems to have been with the duchesse at Lyons during part of 1630 but to have returned to Chantilly before his employers. Montmorency was made a maréchal on 19 December 1630 and, a few days later, Richelieu and the duchess were godparents to the second son of Condé and Charlotte de Montmorency, the prince de Conti. Mairet took out a privilège for his second collection of lyrical verse, the *Autres oeuvres lyriques*, at the same time as that for *La Silvanire* on 3 February. That summer Montmorency and Chevreuse had to be stopped from fighting a duel. Their seconds were sent to the Bastille. It was this incident, together with the exile of Marie de Medici, his wife's aunt, which caused to germinate in Montmorency the desire to reassert the old position of the noblesse d'épée against the king that led to his eventual beheading. When Montmorency left Chantilly and Paris in October 1630, he was never to return.

There are suggestions of an emotional attachment to someone above his social rank in Mairet's poetry of the late 1620s. By this time, the vogue for pastorals based, like *La Silvanire*, on *L'Astrée*, was touching its peak, and the move towards regularity on the Italian model in pastorals was also gaining much ground. Corneille's 1632 *Clitandre* is the first regular tragi-comédie. Already at the end of 1630 Mareschal's preface to *La Généreuse Allemande*, with a privilège of 1 October and an achevé d'imprimer of 8 November, defended romanesque tragi-comédie and attacked the need for regularity, taking a view opposite to that of Chapelain in his letter to Godeau of 29 November 1630, which argued from universal reason the need for the three dramatic unities of place, time, and action. The stream of supporters of the three unities broadened, but it is noticeable that at first all the supporters of the position of Mairet and Chapelain either were attached to great households or belonged to circles of erudition, while the attainment by Mairet of all his social and professional ambitions by 1631 had resulted in five years in which his work was becoming steadily less personal, and more dominated by the need to satisfy his patrons.

Montmorency, who had definitively committed himself to the cause of revolt by late July 1632, was stripped of his rank and deprived of all possessions, including Chantilly, by royal decree of 23 August. Mairet cannot have stayed at Chantilly much after the news of the Castelnaudary defeat had arrived. By the date of Montmorency's execution in the main square of Toulouse on 31 October, Mairet was already with the comte de Belin, with whom he would remain for six years. He was to find future patrons less generous than Montmorency had been, and financial need accelerated his output accordingly. He was never in fact employed or regularly paid by Belin, although he had freedom to come and go between the three residences in Maine—the house in Le Mans, the château d'Averton, and the château du Plessis—and the Paris house near the Marais theatre. From 1636 to 1638 we know from his correspondence that he was continually with Belin in Maine.

Almost immediately, and apparently to achieve swift economic success, Mairet produced his bawdy and irreverent comedy of romanesque realism, *Les Galanteries du duc d'Ossonne, vice-roy de Naples*, completed no later than the 1633 carnival, although not published until 1636, when it was preceded by the dedicatory *Epître comique* to Antoine Brun, by now procureur général of the Dôle parlement. The probability is that the first three acts may have been written at Chantilly, with some traits of the central character resembling those of Montmorency, while the last two acts, which do not easily fit the first three, were written after the move to Belin's household, probably to start with in Paris. Belin himself was quite closely linked to the Marais troupe. Tallemant tells us that he was emotionally attached to Lenoir's wife, who with three other principal members of the Marais company was ordered by the king to move to the Hôtel de Bourgogne in 1634. Belin was sufficiently interested in the Marais company to become involved in its day-to-day business, and from late in 1632 Mairet's name is attached to preliminary verses in the traditional collections printed in front of dramatic works, suggesting a loose association with the other poets represented, many of whom were or had been connected with the group of playwrights which had formed round Du Ryer. Other authors with whose verses those of Mairet appeared, not in collected volumes, but frequently, until about 1635, at the head of the works of other authors, include Corneille, Scudéry, Rotrou, Du Ryer, Claveret, and Boisrobert.

Belin, the immensely rich son of the governor of Paris during the League who had finally gone over to Henri IV, had been under a shadow since he refused in 1620 to declare either for Louis XIII or for the queen-mother, so displeasing both and condemning himself to an only minor political role as bailli of Alençon. He had had eight children by his wife, who had died in 1626, and his interest in gastronomy, hospitality, and the theatre inspired the character of Orsé in Scarron's *Roman comique*. Scarron's host, Charles de Beaumanoir-Lavardin, bishop of Le Mans, was Belin's closest friend, and through Belin Mairet met Scarron, who supported him in the dispute following Corneille's *Le Cid*. It was partly through the mediation of Rotrou, another protégé of Belin, that Mairet, although not before the Querelle du *Cid*, came closer to Richelieu's orbit. Mairet was needy, but Richelieu was in no hurry to be helpful, and there are signs that Boisrobert, Rotrou, and Chapelain all had to speak on his behalf before Mairet was accorded a gratification of 600 livres at the end of 1637.

The French theatre saw much experimentation with different understandings of the unities and their applications in different degrees, for different types of audience and to different genres, themselves not yet clearly distinguished into tragedy, tragi-comédie, and comedy, of which certainly the last two could be, but did not need also to be, pastorals. If it was not yet possible to distinguish clearly between the court and the town, there was a distinction to be drawn between the sophisticated audiences invited to performances in grand houses, like Belin's Averton, often with aristocratic enthusiasts as actors, such as Mairet catered for, and the predominantly bourgeois audiences of the two French troupes in Paris, for whom Rotrou wrote. It is with respect to their way of combining the variables: regularity, genres with only blurred distinctions between them, and projected audience, that plays of the period 1630–35 need to be evaluated.

Underneath, there is generally the question of how best to persuade an audience to envisage the ethical up-grading of instinctive human behaviour. Mairet's *La Virginie* is called a tragi-comédie, advertises its regularity, and is intended for a more or less aristocratic audience with some pretensions to refinement, which at least knew about Faret's 1630 *L'honneste homme; ou, L'Art de plaire à la cour*. *La Virginie* is not a work of great imaginative power, and it does not invite its intended audience to question the ethical values on which its behaviour strove to be based, but it does concentrate the whole emphasis on moral portraiture rather than plot or motivation, and inevitably raises the question of the need to be satisfied with codes of polite behaviour where once moral righteousness might have reigned.

Between the beginning of 1634 and the end of 1635 Mairet wrote three more plays, all tragedies: *La Sophonisbe*, dedicated to the chancellor, Pierre Séguier, and first played at the Marais in September or October 1634, *Le Marc-Antoine; ou, La Cléopâtre*, played at the Marais in May 1635, and *Le Grand et Dernier Solyman; ou, La Mort de Mustapha*, written during the second half of 1635 but played only late in 1637 at the Hôtel de Bourgogne. Montdory's troupe had opened at the Marais on 1 April 1634, and *La Sophonisbe* had been its first great success, making Mairet indisputably France's leading dramatist. His return to what he formally termed tragedy as a genre had no doubt been inspired by Belin. The first example to be played of the new wave of tragedies had been Rotrou's *Hercule mourant* at the Hôtel de Bourgogne for the end of the carnival in 1634.

After Mairet's *La Sophonisbe* Scudéry's *La Mort de César* followed early in 1635. Even at the very beginning of 1637, the date of *Le Cid*, there was some doubt about what exactly constituted the difference between tragédie and tragi-comédie, whether both needed to observe the three unities, whether the presence or absence of regularity did not itself define the distinction between the genres, or whether the title tragi-comédie should be reserved for pastorals, and whether the designation tragédie rather than tragi-comédie was a sufficient sign of seriousness of moral purpose to risk lowering likely box-office receipts. In view of the terminology to be used in the Querelle du *Cid* in 1637, it is important to remember that Scudéry, writing in 1637 of his two tragedies, could announce that, having satisfied the learned with regularity in *La Mort de César*, "il faut parfois contenter le peuple, par la diversité des spectacles et par les differentes faces du Theatre (it is sometimes necessary to make the people happy by variety of spectacle and differences of dramatic effect)," referring to the much more tragi-comic *Didon*, still however published as a tragedy. Corneille's own *Médée*, although not published until 1639, was played early in 1635 as a tragedy.

Mairet had sent his dramatist colleagues back to Senecan models, and himself powerfully inspired them to write tragedies, but historians have much confused matters by failing to distinguish between tragedy as a genre, and plays exploiting a modish seriousness of moral purpose which moved an audience with refined sensibilities more deeply than did the perfunctory peripeteia of tragi-comic intrigues. Mairet congratulated himself in his épître to Séguier that *La Sophonisbe* "se peut vanter

d'avoir tiré des soupirs des plus grands coeurs et des larmes des plus beaux yeux de France (can boast of having drawn sighs from the greatest hearts and tears from the most beautiful eyes in France)." Saint-Evremond was to see that Mairet's tragedy had above all succeeded "pour avoir rencontré le goût des Dames, et le vrai esprit des gens de la Cour (by meeting female taste, and the true imagination of the members of court)." *La Sophonisbe* itself was played on 18 December 1634 privately for the duc de Puylaurens, favourite and companion in the recently terminated exile of Gaston d'Orléans, who was himself present. On 1 November 1636 it was played at the château de Rambouillet, with Julie d'Angennes sharing the leading role with Mlle de Clermont.

It was immediately after *La Sophonisbe*'s success that on 15 December 1634 Louis XIII had four of the company's leading actors transferred to his own royal players at the Hôtel de Bourgogne. The privilège for *Les Galanteries*, *La Virginie*, and *La Sophonisbe*, granted on 5 February 1635, was conceded to Pierre Ricolet, although all Mairet's earlier plays except *Chryséide* had been published by François Targa. This fact suggests that Mairet's position now allowed him to barter terms with publisher-booksellers, but also that he now needed to take pains to secure an income from the sale of the scripts of his plays. The achevés for *La Virginie* and *La Sophonisbe* were 22 May 1635, that for *Les Galanteries* only 7 January 1636.

The change of publisher, and the dedication of *La Sophonisbe* to Séguier, of whom Ricolet was a protégé, was an apparently successful strategy in pursuit of financial reward, and denoted at the same time Mairet's obvious desire to gain access to the circle protected by Richelieu. Most of the poets to whom Séguier was a patron—Colletet, Conrart, Habert, and both the Cureau de la Chambre brothers—belonged to Boisrobert's circle. However, in spite of the strength of Mairet's position and legitimate hopes in 1635, it has become usual to date from that year an accelerating decline in his literary fortunes. Bensserade was doubling up the subject of Mairet's *Cléopâtre*, which Mairet had himself announced, for the Hôtel, probably at the instigation of Bellerose, the director of the royal troupe, with parts for some of the actors who had created the successful Mairet roles at the Marais. Bellerose may have been revenging himself for Mairet's desertion to the Marais on accepting Belin's patronage on Montmorency's execution.

The success of Bensserade's play, one of the very early instances of competition between playwrights—and finally even painters, when Mignard challenged Lebrun's famous masterpiece, "The Tent of Darius," by treating the same subject—was to be used by Corneille as a weapon in his quarrel with Mairet. Bensserade's play was dedicated to Richelieu, Mairet's to Belin, and the real pain inflicted on Mairet came from Bensserade's instantaneous success with Richelieu, the consequent 3,000-livre pension, and Bensserade's subsequent career as a court librettist. Mairet may have been surprised at the challenge arising from his announcement that he was going to write a play on the Cléopâtre theme, but he repeated the over-confidence by saying in the "au lecteur" to *La Sophonisbe* that he hoped one day to adapt Prosper Bonarelli's *Solyman* into French. Vion d'Alibray then worked on an adaptation of the Bonarelli during the same months as Mairet in the autumn of 1635.

It is difficult to know exactly what then happened. Neither piece was put on immediately. Montdory's company did eventually play d'Alibray's tragi-comédie at the Marais, probably in the first half of 1637, perhaps immediately after *Le Cid*. It appeared with an achevé of 30 June 1637, while Mairet's tragédie was played at the Hôtel only some months later, two years after it had been finished. It was not published until June 1639. The "au lecteur" of d'Alibray's 1636 *Torrismon* is complimentary about Mairet, whose *La Sophonisbe* is regarded as "cette merveille (that marvel)," and Mairet's "au lecteur" to *Solyman* mentions that d'Alibray is "plus honnest-homme et plus advancé dans le Parnasse (more personally polished and further advanced on the road to Parnassus)" than Mairet.

It is not easy to know whether Mairet was complimenting d'Alibray or allowing himself a muted sneer at d'Alibray's social and economic success. D'Alibray says that his piece, which appeared first, had been held back for Mairet's to be the first to appear. It is debated whether, apart from the well-known rivalry between the two troupes, there was any split in the world of dramatic authorship along the lines to be revealed by the Querelle du *Cid* before the performance of Corneille's play (see: Georges de Scudéry) very early in 1637 and the publication of the *Excuse à Ariste* shortly thereafter. It has been argued that there was a cabal against Corneille in 1635, and alternatively that there was animosity towards Mairet. It would not be strange if Corneille's aloofness had excited antagonism before *Le Cid*, or if Mairet's over-confidence had appeared arrogant and had started to attract hostility, but the evidence for both hypotheses is wholly conjectural.

In 1636 Mairet published nothing. Not too much needs to be made of his silence. He was in Maine; he was certainly looking for patronage from Richelieu; the *Solyman* affair was dragging on, perhaps revealing cool relationships with both companies; but his absence from Paris might explain the failure to receive an invitation to be a member of the new Académie and to be invited to join Richelieu's five authors (see: Pierre Corneille), Rotrou, L'Estoille, Corneille, Boisrobert, and Colletet. After recognition from the cardinal did come, at the end of 1637, Mairet wrote only four more perfunctory romanesque tragi-comédies, as if performing an official duty: *L'Illustre corsaire*, *Le Roland furieux*, *La Sidonie*, and *L'Athénaïs*, important for its early introduction onto the stage of a Christian subject.

In the meanwhile, however, something had snapped. Perhaps threatened by a deteriorating relationship with the Paris companies or by the threat of a younger generation spear-headed by Bensserade, or gnawed by poverty and missing the light-hearted approach to life at Chantilly, and no doubt fuelled by a touch of arrogance as well as infuriated by Corneille's *Excuse à Ariste* (see: Georges de Scudéry), Mairet unleashed a short violent poem more against Corneille than against his play, early in April 1637, *L'Autheur du vray Cid espagnol à son traducteur français sur une lettre en vers qu'il a faict, intitulée "Excuse à Ariste"*.

Mairet's poem occupies two sheets, and its title announces that it is concerned not with *Le Cid*, but with the *Excuse*. It was written in Maine, and was certainly not the product of any agreement to concert an attack on Corneille. Corneille replied, personally and injuriously, taunting Mairet with low birth and present poverty, although their relationship had hitherto been amicable. Mairet then issued in the course of 1637 his series of pamphlets against *Le Cid*. It was eventually Boisrobert who, at Richelieu's insistence, commanded him on 5 October 1637 to desist from further polemic. The prestige from the great trio of works, *La Sylvie*, *La Sylvanire*, and *La Sophonisbe* had carried Mairet to a peak of celebrity and importance in 1634, but by the

end of 1637 he had dissipated his credit. Belin died on 29 September 1637, leaving Mairet his horse. It was doubtless in 1637 that Mairet wrote his last play, *Sidonie*, published finally in 1643 with an "au lecteur" affecting contempt both for the actors and for their audiences.

Mairet was made the diplomatic representative of Franche-Comté at the court of France, actively negotiating and implementing the peace of Westphalia from 1647 to about 1651. He had married in 1647, but his wife died childless in 1658. In 1654 he was banished to Besançon, where he stayed for five years before returning to Paris. He finally retired again to Besançon, dying there on 31 January 1686.

WORKS

Mairet's constant repudiation of *Chryséide et Arimand*, his insistence that it was an adolescent piece, and its unauthorized publication, as well as the clear inspiration of Théophile, make it unlikely that Mairet himself can be considered its sole or even its final author. The presumption must be that Mairet was dropped off with Théophile at Selles by Montmorency on his return from Paris to the Atlantic coast in November 1625, and that *Chryséide* was at least retouched, and probably re-written, by Théophile in the last weeks of 1625 or early in the new year.

Mairet took the intrigue from *L'Astrée*, developing the character of the king Gondebaut, whose defiance of the gods goes much further in *Chryséide* than the attitude of Le Roi in Théophile's *Les Amours tragiques de Pyrame et Thisbé*, probably first played in 1621. The text contains audacious passages in which Arimand insubmissively defies the gods to do what they can, affirms the primacy he attaches to his own affections over divinely established moral order, and bitterly reproaches the gods with the physical powerlessness in which they have left him and the deprivation of moral freedom they seek to impose. *Chryséide* regards the gods as indifferent, uncaring, unable, and unwilling to help. Only love can save human dignity.

Like much of what Théophile wrote, this play feels its way not towards the ethical and religious acceptability of instinctive behaviour, but towards a revolt against the whole moral order. In the end, and in spite of advice from his friend Bellaris, Arimand simply refuses to extinguish his frustrated love. Mairet replaces what throughout Théophile's work was a clear social egalitarianism with a more conventional attack on the arrogance of the great, and probably wished Montmorency to recognize himself in the dramatically useless but noble and right-thinking character of Bellimard. Gondebaut's final release of Chryséide into the arms of Arimand is presented as an act of moral heroism necessary for the achievement of his own fulfilment as well, obviously, of allowing Mairet the happy ending he wanted.

La Sylvie is a pastoral tragi-comédie. Florestan, prince de Candie, goes in search of Méliphile with whom he had fallen in love on account of a portrait he has seen. In the first scene Thyrsis, a "chevalier errant (knight errant)," shows Florestan the portrait, revealing "un grand combat de l'Art avecque la Nature (a great combat between art and nature)," and reassuring him that Méliphile is the only daughter of the king of Sicily, "aimable et fortuné séjour (pleasant and prosperous place)", with whom he may therefore safely fall in love. Everything warns us that Mairet has his tongue in his cheek. This is a prelude in fairyland, and what happens after this scene is not to be taken as more than an attempt to be entertaining.

Méliphile's brother, Thélame, dresses as a shepherd in order to be closer to the shepherdess Sylvie, to the despair of Philène, who enlists Sylvie's father, Damon, in a ruse to make Sylvie think Thélame unfaithful with another shepherdess, Dorise, who does, however, love Philène. The father of Méliphile and Thélame, Agatoclès, king of Sicily, decides to marry Thélame to the infanta of Cyprus. When Thélame resists, his father first wants to kill him and Sylvie, and then decides instead to use magic. Florestan, ship-wrecked, learns what has happened; the king has repented and promised Méliphile to whoever will undo his spell; Florestan chases away the demons, and breaks the crystal that holds the power of the magic spell. The piece ends with the triple marriage, Florestan-Méliphile, Thélame-Sylvie, and Philène-Dorise.

Sylvie was the poetic name of the duchesse de Montmorency. The play is clearly inspired by Théophile and Racan, and the concessions to a pastoral setting are minimal, but the trappings of pastoral were already on the way out in 1626. There is relatively little magic for a tragi-comédie, and the romanesque is diminished in favour of the political and the study of sentiment and codes of behaviour. The intrigue is skilfully handled, although Méliphile is only there to motivate the arrival of Florestan, the adventurer-hero. Bonds of strong affection are allowed to clash with social constraints, parental and royal, but are victorious. Nothing is allowed to go so far as to weigh the play down by moral considerations, neither the comic realism of the second act, nor the spice of political allusion in the third scene of the first act and in act four, nor Philène's ruse in making Dorise pretend she has a fly in her eye, so that Thélame shall be caught by Sylvie in the intimacies of fly-removal. To prevent jealousy even of *Astrée*-like intensity, Philène carefully reassures Sylvie himself, by telling her of his ruse before the end of the act—the third—in which it is used.

The jealousy of the heroine at the beginning of *L'Astrée* clearly established a register of fantasy. In *La Sylvie* Mairet, not only in the third act, but particularly in the second-act dialogue between Damon and Macée, Sylvie's parents, injects doses of true comic realism, however unsustained. He cannot have known quite where the path he had taken would lead, but in retrospect his refusal to allow magic and miracle before the fourth act, his treatment of Damon and Macée, his merely perfunctory acknowledgement of the pastoral convention, and his refusal to allow artificially contrived jealousy to make any emotional impact can be seen to lead towards the comedy of manners. The upgrading of instinctive affection to overcome social barriers and lead to moral fulfilment is carried by an atmosphere of freshness, grace, and charm, less dramatically gripping but in the end imaginatively more effective than the style of moral and religious revolt explored by Théophile's characters.

The verse is competent and fluid, if a little over-laden with what might be ironically over-predictable adjectives: "implacable" for "colère (anger)," "innocents" for "desseins (plans)," and "sains (healthy)" for "sentiments," although in each case the consonantal repetition is euphonious. The 1616 dialogue, in which Damon was the imprisoned Henri II de Bourbon-Condé and Silvie the regent, Marie de Medici, had turned on the ambiguity between real political and metaphorical amorous imprisonment. It had started

| Damon: | Dois-je perdre tout mon âge |
| | Sans repos ni liberté? |

Silvie:	Berger, vous étiez volage,
	Mais vous êtes arrêté.
Damon:	Au moins, qu'on me fasse entendre
	Pourquoi je suis détenu.
Silvie:	Berger, vous me vouliez prendre,
	Mais je vous ai prévenu.
Damon:	Pour vous, en cette contrainte,
	Je meurs la nuit et le jour.
Silvie:	C'est de regret ou de crainte;
	Vous ne mourez pas d'amour

(Damon: Must I lose all my life/Without rest or freedom?
Silvie: Shepherd, you were inconstant,/But you have been stopped.
Damon: At least, let me know/Why I am detained.
Silvie: Shepherd, you wanted to capture me,/but I forestalled you.
Damon: For you, under this duress,/I die night and day.
Silvie: From regret or from fear;/You are not dying from love).

The dialogue of act I, scene 3 of *La Sylvie* starts

Philène:	Beau sujet de mes feux et de mes infortunes,
	Ce jour te soit plus doux et plus heureux qu'à moi.
Sylvie:	Injurieux berger qui toujours m'importunes,
	Je te rends tout souhait, et ne veux rien de toi.
Philène:	Comme avecque le temps toute chose se change,
	De même ta rigueur un jour s'adoucira.
Sylvie:	Ce sera donc alors que d'une course étrange
	Ce ruisseau révolté contre sa source ira.
Philène:	Ce sera bien plutôt lorsque ta conscience
	T'accusera d'un crime en m'oyant soupirer.
Sylvie:	Tes discours ont besoin de trop de patience,
	Adieu, le temps me presse, il me faut retirer

(Philène: Beautiful object of my desires and my misfortunes,/May this day be sweeter and happier to you than to me.
Sylvie: Insolent shepherd always pestering me,/I return all your good wishes, and want nothing from you.
Philène: As all things change with time,/So one day your rigour will soften.
Sylvie: That will be on the day when, following some strange route,/This stream in rebellion returns to its source.
Philène: No, rather it will be when your conscience,/As you hear me sigh, will accuse you of your crime.
Sylvie: Listening to your talk demands too much patience,/Goodbye, time presses, I must go).

There is in the Mairet passage the same sustained metaphor of love as enslavement as in the 1616 one, and the dialogue couplets are a neat artifice, perfectly in place in the rather stilted register of attitudes and language expected in a pastoral, especially since the shepherds are quite likely to include princes in token disguise, and therefore to be assiduous courters of harsh mistresses. But if this dialogue, no doubt circulated in manuscript before Gaston d'Orléans's wedding, is read with sustained reference to the coming marriage, building on the similarities and dissimilarities with the political situation in 1616, two things follow.

Firstly, Mairet is writing initially, in the dialogue, for a readership and then, in the play, for an audience with predictable political sympathies, that is the party "adverse to the marriage," and of high literary, political, and social sophistication. Secondly, the treatment in *La Sylvie* as a whole of the pastoral convention, the cavalier attitude towards verisimilitude, the diminution of the tragi-comic elements, and the gestures towards the unities, all belong to that same level of cultural sophistication, establishing what might even be called the language of the play's discourse. The use of a highly allusive text, exclusively comprehensible to a tight social group and on an imaginative level of immense cultural urbanity, itself both constitutes and confirms the nonchalantly optimistic assumption of the text, that a trust in the guidance of instinct will lead to personal fulfilment.

At the highest pinnacle of French pastoral tragi-comedy Mairet can therefore write a dramatically effective play, be constantly ironic at the expense at any given moment of well over half his readership or audience, be genuinely and idyllically touching, exhibit movingly the effects of amorous and other passions, laugh at the pastoral convention, toss in a flamboyant ending for fun, and write a comedy of manners with maliciously clever political satire. Political sympathy for the imprisoned Condé of 1616 is matched by political hostility to the Orléans of 1626 in a dialogue which depends on a semi-private literary allusion, and can be read as favouring either the male, if read with the 1616 situation in mind, or the female partner, to encourage an attitude to her suitor which Marie de Bourbon-Montpensier was in fact in 1626 in no position to take.

In case any one is worried about the unities, Le Roi explicitly draws attention in act IV, scene 1, to the fact that the shepherd's flocks are scarcely three arrow-flights from his palace. If we forget the prefatory first scene in Candia, we therefore have unity of place. Mairet deliberately makes the time-scales incompatible. Bright dawns, midday heat and evening shadows suggest that days pass by, but if Florestan's journey lasted three days, then the effect of the magic spell cannot have lasted its apparent eight days. And no doubt the spectacular final act and the triple marriage will make the audience indulgent towards any apparent fractures in the unity of action. Mairet uses quite flagrantly inadequate reasons for producing characters as and when they are required to keep his drama happily running along. There is more to *Sylvie* than most critics have thought, and no one has yet subjected it to the thorough-going critical analysis it deserves.

The register of *La Silvanire* is quite different. It is a real pastoral. It takes the unities seriously. It avoids politics, realism, coarseness, and strong language, but not strong sensuality. It is introduced by a long, careful dedicatory letter to the duchesse de Montmorency, and an unsatisfactorily meandering prefatory "discours poétique," with neither consistency of tone, nor rigour of argument. A prologue is spoken by L'Amour honnête, and there is a chorus. Ménandre and Lérice are among the richest shepherds and shepherdesses of Forez and want to marry their beautiful and virtuous daughter, Silvanire, to the rich, stupid, and ugly Théante. Silvanire, however, who confides in Fossinde, loves and is loved by Aglante, who is poor, but, knowing her love is hopeless, she has hidden it from him. Hylas, whose character is much softer than it was in *L'Astrée*, tries to act on Silvanire in the interests of Aglante.

A third suitor, Tirinte, wants to kill himself when he hears Silvanire is to marry Théante, but his friend Alciron dissuades him, providing him with an enchanted mirror to give to Silvanire which will ensure that she returns Tirinte's love. Tirinte hears that Silvanire has died staring at the mirror, pursues Alciron, finds him in a boat on the Lignon, makes his peace with him, and they go together to Silvanire's tomb and wake her from apparent death. Tirinte, left alone with her, wants to remove her to another cave. Other shepherds arrive, led by Aglante. Fossinde, in love with Tirinte, saves him from the death to which he had been sentenced for attempting to force himself on Silvanire. He marries her, and Ménandre allows Aglante and Silvanire to marry, having already once given and then rescinded permission. The intrigue is taken from *L'Astrée*.

The importation in general of regularity into French pastoral tragi-comédie derives neither from Aristotle nor from the Italian theoreticians, but from the practice of Tasso's *Aminta* and Guarini's *Il Pastor fido*. Instead of romanesque fantasy, with ever more picaresque and improbable adventures, the exploitation of the unities concentrated the audience's attention on a psychological crisis in the emotions of the characters. In so far as there is a clear assumption about moral values in *La Silvanire* it lies in the presumption that Tirinte's desire to capture Silvanire by force is intolerable, but also that Aglante's persistent virtue is worthy of reward. Mairet appears to have understood d'Urfé; the perfection of love is not contained in unrequited service, but is rewarded in a mutual, monogamous, but not at all spiritualized marital relationship.

Instinctive affection is allowed to transgress the boundaries, if not in *La Silvanire* of rank, at least of wealth. Critics who have persisted in seeing in the play the implied message that sensual impulses must be suppressed for the sake of social boundaries, or that the introduction of the unities has to do with the re-imposition of strict moral proprieties in the Montmorency entourage, have missed the point of the play, however imaginatively undemanding it is. The last French tragi-comedies were again to trample on the very idea of the unities, and were to revert to all the old tragi-comic ingredients: spells, oracles, dreams, discoveries, recognitions, and adventures.

In the meanwhile the twelfth and final strophe of the prologue of *La Silvanire* puts these words into the mouth of L'Honnête Amour:

Depuis quatre ou cinq ans Aglante et Silvanire
Echauffent mes autels de soupirs amoureux;
Enfin j'ai résolu de finir leur martyre
Par un coup de ma main qui s'apprête pour eux;
    Je fais la récompense
    Lorsque moins on y pense,
Et peu certes encor m'ont servi quelque temps
    Qui n'aient été contents

(For four or five years Aglante and Silvanire/Have warmed my altars with amorous sighs;/I have finally resolved to put an end to their suffering/By a plan I have set in motion for them;/I give the reward/When it is least expected,/And there are certainly few who have served me for any time/Who have not been made happy).

The next two plays were the comedy *Les Galanteries du duc d'Ossonne*, finished, at least, after the execution of Montmorency on 31 October 1632 and in the theatrically very different entourage of Belin, and the tragi-comédie *La Virginie*. Then came *La Sophonisbe*, Mairet's first tragedy, written in the first half of 1634 and first played in September or October that year. It was drawn from Livy, with alterations. Mairet was well aware of the emotional concentration which the genre of tragedy forced on him. *La Virginie* had been a tragi-comédie and, comparing it in 1635 with *La Sophonisbe* in the preface to both pieces, Mairet had praised the "variété de ses effets (variety of its effects)," and written of it,

Ce n'a pas été sans peine et sans bonheur que j'ai pu restreindre tant de matière en si peu de vers, sans confusion et sans sortir des règles fondamentales de la scène… Sophonisbe a ses passions plus étendues, mais Virginie la surpasse de beaucoup en la diversité de sa peinture et de ses incidents

(It was not without difficulty and satisfaction that I was able to restrict so much material to so few lines, without confusing the audience or departing from the basic rules of stagecraft… *Sophonisbe* has deeper passions, but *Virginie* far surpasses her in range of character and incident).

Sophonisbe, wife of Syphax, king of Numidie, is loved by her husband's enemy, Massinisse. The play opens with Syphax's reproach to Sophonisbe, for whom, he says in the second scene to his general Philon, he still has affection instead of what she deserves, "mépris" and "haine," a coupling of emotions quite unremarkable, except that Corneille was to make it famous in 1637, and any reason to suspect Corneille of deriving material from Mairet would, if confirmed, help to explain the bitterness of Mairet's criticisms of *Le Cid* after the initial irascible reaction not to the play, but to the *Excuse à Ariste*. Syphax has acquired a letter from Sophonisbe to Massinisse, whose forces are drawn up against his own. Syphax and Philon, together in scene two, are replaced in scene three by Sophonisbe and her two confidentes, the scene change in mid-act confirming that Mairet was now writing with the professional theatre in mind, with scene changes indicated by dropping or lifting a curtain in front of one of several booths at the back of the stage, an arrangement presumably not generally available in private houses.

The first act ends with an emphatic declaration by Sophonisbe of the irresistibility of her love:

Encore à ce matin je pleurais en rêvant
Au malheur inconnu qui me va poursuivant;
Faisant réflexion sur mon erreur extrême,
Je ne pouvais treuver que je fusse moi-même
Et que dans la rigueur d'un temps si malheureux,
Je pusse concevoir des pensers amoureux.
Hélas, il paraît bien que l'Amour pour mes crimes
M'alluma dans le coeur ces feux illégitimes

(Again this morning I wept as I dreamed/Of the unknown destiny which pursues me;/Reflecting on my extreme lapse,/I could not believe that I was myself/And that in the rigours of so unhappy a situation/I could conceive thoughts of love./Alas, it does indeed seem that for my crimes Love/Kindled in my heart these illicit flames).

Irresistible love was not seriously threatening in French literature so long as baroque optimism required the examination of instinctive behaviour as life-enriching. Irresistible affection leading to guilt was to become prominent with the spread of Jansenist (q.v.) spirituality soon after the middle of the century, but it was not seriously to be examined as tragic again in French literature much before Racine, and never in Pierre Corneille's great plays, in which, as he said, a passion was required "plus mâle que l'amour (more manly than love)," and in which, in fact, the heroic characters were normally in control of their own destiny.

The second act of *La Sophonisbe* is devoted entirely to the heroine, who receives news of the defeat of Cirta, the Numidian town in which the play is set, and calls on her attendants to agree to kill her. Since the battle is virtually within earshot, the unity of place is maintained, this time clearly without any ironic intent. The other two unities are observed only if the insertion of Massinisse's meeting with Sophonisbe and marriage to her are fitted into the same day as the battle for Cirta and the results of the Roman consul Scipion's decision that the public interest requires the marriage be cancelled. The unity of action depends on accepting the play as a succession of not very well linked tableaux of Sophonisbe in a succession of different emotional situations.

The third act switches to Massinisse. Mairet has altered Livy's account, in which Syphax was merely taken prisoner. In the play Massinisse informs us at the beginning of the third act that Syphax has been killed in battle. The annulment of the marriage between Massinisse and Sophonisbe therefore depends entirely on the Roman view of the interests of the Roman state. The scene switches to Sophonisbe in the palace, where she asks her attendants to kill her. They reply that she should seek to charm Massinisse with her beauty. The confrontation between Massinisse and Sophonisbe occurs in the fourth and last scene of act three. After Massinisse's first four lines, we are given a "Harangue de Massinisse" followed by the "Réponse de Sophonisbe." During the course of the scene, Massinisse's sentiments for Sophonisbe change from pity to passion, and they agree to marry.

In the fourth act Sophonisbe reveals that she had been destined to be the bride of Massinisse, but her father had broken off the engagement. A Roman soldier interrupts, and calls Massinisse to see Scipion, who declares that the marriage without Roman approbation is null, a view that Massinisse does not challenge. Scipion is driven to refuse Roman permission, because his decision is based on what is "Nécessaire au salut de la chose publique (Necessary for the good of the state)." It is an obvious weakness in the structure of the play that the inevitability of a tragic ending is not psychologically apparent. There was no need for Sophonisbe to contemplate suicide, and no need for the irruption of the Roman consul to block a happy ending halfway through the fourth act. We are merely presented with a succession of peripeteia which could be regarded as a tightened form of tragi-comedy.

In the fifth act Scipion's lieutenant, Lélie, repeats that Massinisse must leave Sophonisbe "Comme chose au public utile et nécessaire (as something useful and necessary to the public)," and asks whether he has decided to do so. He inquires into the fate reserved for Sophonisbe and is told that she will be spared enslavement by being put to death. A message arrives from Sophonisbe, asking Massinisse for poison. He is not allowed to deliver the poison personally, but it is delivered and Sophonisbe kills herself. The news is brought to Massinisse. The room containing the dead Sophonisbe is revealed (the stage direction says "La chambre paraît [the room appears]"), and Massinisse begins a powerful speech with words again to be echoed in only slightly changed form by Corneille,

O vue! ô désespoir… (Oh sight, oh despair…).

What is a strong attack on the tyrannous barbarity of Roman laws, customs, and behaviour continues, and Massinisse kills himself with a knife he has concealed, although Scipion had only left him because he was sure he had neither a blade nor poison. Massinisse uncovers his dagger, and the play ends with these six lines before he kills himself,

Sophonisbe en ceci t'a voulu prévenir;
Et puisque tes efforts n'ont pu la retenir,
Donne-toi pour le moins le plaisir de la suivre,
Et cesse de mourir en achevant de vivre.
Montre que les rigueurs du Romain sans pitié
Peuvent tout sur l'amant, et rien sur l'amitié

(In this Sophonisbe wanted to precede you;/And since your efforts could not prevent her,/Allow yourself at least the pleasure of following her,/And cease to die by not continuing to live./Show that the harshness of the pitiless Roman/Can do everything to the lover, but nothing to his love).

Mairet's dramatic achievement cannot easily be summed up, but the need for careful re-assessment in the light of the political, social, and economic circumstances is clear. A critical evaluation must depend on the emergence of a consensus about the possibility of irony in his work and about the exact registers of communication with which he was patently experimenting. Historically, Mairet's importance is incontrovertible. A strong case can be made out for regarding both *La Sylvie* and *La Silvanire* as important imaginative achievements in their own right as well as landmarks in the history of French drama.

PUBLICATIONS

Plays and verse

[*The Bibliothèque de la Pléiade* Théâtre du XVIIe siècle, *vol. 1, 1975, contains* La Sylvie, La Silvanire, Les Galanteries du duc d'Ossonne, vice-roi de Naples, *and* La Sophonisbe]

La Sylvie… tragi-comédie pastorale, (?1626), with *Autres oeuvres poétiques,* 1628; modern edition 1905; adapted as *The Shepherd's Holiday,* 1631
Chriséide et Arimand…tragi-comédie (?1626), 1630; modern edition 1925
La Silvanire; ou, La Morte-vive…tragi-comédie pastorale, (1630), with *Autres oeuvres lyriques,* 1631; modern edition 1890; adapted as *The Shepherd's Holiday,* 1631
La Sophonisbe… tragédie, (1634) 1635; modern edition 1945
La Virginie… tragi-comédie, 1635
Les Galanteries du duc d'Ossonne, vice-roi de Naples, comédie, (1632) 1636

Le Marc-Antoine; ou, La Cléopâtre, tragédie, (1635) 1637
Le Grand et Dernier Solyman; ou, La mort de Mustapha… tragédie, (1637) 1639
L'Illustre corsaire, tragi-comédie, 1640
Le Roland furieux, tragi-comédie, 1640
La Sidonie, tragi-comédie héroïque, 1643
L'Athénaïs, tragi-comédie, 1642

Other

L'Auteur du vrai Cid espagnol à son traducteur françois sur une lettre en vers qu'il a faict, intitulée "Excuse à Ariste", 1637
Epître familière… au sieur Corneille sur la tragi-comédie du "Cid", 1637
Apologie… contre les calomnies du S. Corneille, 1637
Discours à Cliton sur les Observations du Cid, avec un traité de la disposition du poème dramatique et de la prétendue règle de 24 heures, 1637

Biographical and critical studies

Bizos, G., *Etude sur la vie et les moeurs de Jean de Mairet,* 1877
Marsan, J., *La Pastrale dramatique,* 1905
Kay, W.B., *The Theatre of Jean Mairet: the Metamorphosis of Sensuality,* 1965
Tomlinson, Philip, *Jean Mairet et ses protecteurs. Une oeuvre dans son milieu,* 1983

MALEBRANCHE, Nicolas, 1638–1715.

Philosopher and theologian.

LIFE

Although Malebranche is not primarily associated with the imaginative genres, it is impossible to understand many of the great imaginative works of the literature of the late 17th century in France without some knowledge of the controversies in which Malebranche played an important part, like the Jansenist (q.v.) disputes in theology, the quietist and other controversies in spirituality, the conflict between Cartesianism (q.v.) and the philosophy of Gassendi, and the reaction which Malebranche's development of Cartesianism provoked in the 18th-century philosophes (q.v.). Since Malebranche's views in these different realms are linked by a unified set of principles, it is necessary, in order to understand his contributions to the development of what was the new commonly accepted view of human nature and its potential, to unite them in a single account of his thought.

At a general level, his great originality as a thinker was to attempt to reunite the philosophical thought by which Descartes had sought to defend the immortality of the soul, with the revealed religion from which Descartes had kept his philosophy separate. Malebranche was fighting a rearguard action to defend the immateriality of the soul, because he thought that only an immaterial soul, entirely different from matter, could be immortal. That assumption was to be questioned, rendering any defence of immateriality less religiously fraught. On the literary level, Malebranche has been admired for the simplicity and lucidity of his prose style, finely balanced and clearly cadenced. He has been called "one of the best prose writers of the 17th century," and Brunetière went so far as to write "Il n'y a pas en français de style comparable à celui de Malebranche (There is in French no style comparable to that of Malebranche)."

Malebranche was the child of another Nicolas, one of Louis XIII's royal secretaries, and of Catherine de Lauzon, whose brother was viceroy of Canada, from a similar family of high-ranking office holders. Malebranche was born in Paris, sickly and slightly deformed, on 5 August 1638, the 10th or 13th, but at any rate the last, of his parents' children. He was educated by a private tutor until he was 16, when he started to attend the Collège de La Marche in Paris for the two-year philosophy course. We do not know what textbooks were used, but the Aristotelian scholasticism on which the course was erected is unlikely to have come from any source less debased than the manual of Eustache de Saint-Paul in use at La Flèche when Descartes was a pupil there and the Jesuits were making the school into a showpiece. Malebranche was to receive ample encouragement, notably from his subsequent Oratorian professors, in his violent intellectual reaction to the philosophy he was taught at La Marche, but the nature of the teaching Malebranche received is important on account of the extent to which anti-Aristotelianism has been seen to be the starting point and unifying force of all his later thinking.

When at 18 Malebranche left the Collège de La Marche as a master of arts, he went on to the Sorbonne to study theology. Both his parents died within days of one another when he was 20, and Malebranche, who would have become a Trappist monk if his poor health had not prevented him, turned down the offer of a canonry at Notre-Dame. He left the Sorbonne without any further examinations or qualifications and on 8 January 1660 at the age of 21 entered the congregation of the Oratory, a community of priests whose rule did not include a vow of poverty, and which in 1660 was still closely linked to the neoplatonist spirituality of its founder, Bérulle, his spiritual leader, Condren, and Gibieuf, in which the spirituality of Saint-Cyran had established its roots. There was at this date still a close link between Jansenist theology, the philosophy of Descartes, and Oratorian spirituality.

After his noviceship, Malebranche completed his regulation study of theology at Notre-Dame des Ardilliers from April 1661, although he was back in Paris by October that year. On 22 March 1662 Malebranche was ordained sub-deacon, in September 1663 deacon, and on 20 September 1664 he was ordained priest at the congregation's mother house in Paris, in the rue Saint-Honoré, where he was to stay until he died at the age of 77. The superior, Père Amelote, was closely associated with Bérulle's disciple, assistant, and successor, Père Bourgoing, who had died in 1662, in disseminating Bérulle's spirituality and directing the young congregation. He had written in his 1643 *Vie du Père Charles de Condren* that the Oratorians did not follow Aristotle, but rather "le grand saint Denys," the strongly neoplatonist pseudo-Denis, author of the *Celestial Hierarchies* on which Bérulle's spirituality was founded, and still in France in the 17th century generally identified with Saint Paul's first convert at the Areopagus in Athens.

The Oratorians had tried at first to make an ecclesiastical historian of Malebranche but, although he studied assiduously, he showed no aptitude, and Richard Simon, who had entered the Oratory provisionally in 1659 but definitively in 1662, with the same date of birth as Malebranche, tried to teach him Hebrew and a critical attitude to the biblical text, but with no greater success. It was in the year of his ordination, 1664, that Malebranche happened in a bookshop on a copy of Descartes's work on the development of the human foetus, posthumously published in 1662 and translated into French in 1664 as the *L'Homme de René Descartes et son traité de la formation du foetus*. It is to Fontenelle's *Eloge* at the Académie des Sciences, of which Malebranche was made a member during the reorganization of 1699, that we owe the original account of the legendary impact of this work on Malebranche:

Il se mit à feuilleter le livre, et fut frappé comme d'une lumière qui en sortit toute nouvelle à ses yeux…Il acheta le livre, le lut avec empressement, et…avec un tel transport, qu'il lui en prenait des battements de coeur qui l'obligeaient quelquefois d'interrompre sa lecture

(He began to leaf through the book and was struck as by a light coming from it quite new to his eyes.…He bought the book, read it eagerly and…with such emotion that it brought on palpitations which forced him to interrupt his reading from time to time).

Fontenelle wrongly concluded that from that moment Malebranche dedicated himself wholly to the study of the philosophy of Descartes. It would be more accurate to say that Descartes's book instantly revealed to Malebranche the way to pursue his vocation as a Christian apologist. It is at least possible that the last pages of Descartes's book, which might well have attracted Malebranche's attention when he was flicking through it in the bookshop, indicated to him the way out of the explanation of the animation of the foetus by an Aristotelian substantial form, an account patently impossible to reconcile with immortality, but taught to Descartes at La Flèche and no doubt to Malebranche at La Marche. At the end of his treatise, Descartes had written

Je désire que vous considériez que ces fonctions suivent toutes naturellement, en cette machine [le foetus], de la seule disposition de ses organes, ni plus ni moins que font les mouvements d'une horloge…en sorte qu'il ne faut point à leur occasion concevoir en elle aucune autre Ame végétative, ni sensitive, ni aucun autre principe de mouvement et de vie, que son sang et ses esprits, agités par la chaleur du feu qui brûle continuellement dans son coeur

(I want you to believe that these functions follow quite naturally in this machine [the foetus], from the disposition of its organs alone, neither more nor less than do the movements of a clock…so that there is no reason to conceive on their account any other vegetative or sensitive soul within it, or any other principle of movement and of life, than its blood and spirits, moved by the warmth of the fire which burns continually in its heart…).

Malebranche was never either purely a philosopher, or purely a theologian, and certainly not ever purely a Cartesian, however enthusiastically he admired Descartes. He did not enjoy polemic, but was drawn into it largely in defence of his view, in effect, that Descartes's work needed to be crowned by drawing together a sound metaphysical foundation, in which, as apparently in Descartes but not in the animist Aristotelianism of the scholastics, mind and matter could not interact, and an ethic compatible with a theology of grace which escaped the twofold danger of depriving the human will of its autonomous power of moral self-determination on the one hand, and leaving human salvation totally the work of God on the other.

Malebranche's first decade of study after the discovery of Descartes's book produced the *De la Recherche de la vérité où l'on traite de la nature de l'esprit de l'homme et de l'usage qu'il en doit faire pour éviter l'erreur dans les sciences*, of which the first three books were published in one volume in 1674 and the second three books in a second volume of 1675. The format was the unpretentious duodecimo. The first volume was instantly attacked by Simon Foucher's 1675 *Critique de la recherche de la vérité* for the "occasionalism" by which God was considered the only real cause in the universe, reducing human causes to simple occasions. Foucher returned to the attack in 1676, and again in 1679.

Foucher was a canon and a member of the Académie française, but also a sceptic who certainly confused Descartes's distinction between the sensible and intelligible qualities of material things, regarding them all as sensible, but important for having drawn from Leibniz his theory of "monads" as an alternative to Cartesian innate ideas, and from Malebranche a distinction between mental ideas and material objects which does away with the notion of resemblance between ideas and what they represent. Foucher thereby forced Malebranche into making one of the decisive leaps in the history of philosophy, ultimately more philosophically important, if less religiously fraught with consequences for belief in personal immortality, than Locke's thinking matter. Mainstream philosophical thinking since Malebranche has increasingly abandoned the requirement of resemblance in the mental image for representation. With Malebranche the mental event became purely epistemological, and abstraction had in serious philosophical thinking been banished for good.

Foucher was clearly right to press home his question about what, if not mental modifications or properties, ideas actually were. Malebranche just held back from being pushed into answering that they were a series of miraculous epistemological events perpetually produced in human minds by God, but did not answer the question. For Malebranche, sensations are modifications or properties of the mind, but ideas are not, although ideas were to continue to be actual modifications of the mind, if not for Leibniz, then at least for Locke. For Malebranche, and for the whole empirical tradition in philosophy, ideas are not in our mind as modifications or properties of the mind. The question of what ideas actually are is still in the late 20th century unresolved but, for Malebranche, they had to be "in God," where, too, they could not be properties. Malebranche was still able to rely heavily, in his attempt to define knowledge in its limiting conditions of pure spirituality, on the nature of angelic knowledge, which could clearly not depend on perception through bodily organs, and on the great scholastic treatises on angels, particularly that by the Jesuit Suarez.

In 1675 Malebranche also published the *Conversations chrétiennes*, explicitly connecting the epistemology with Christian belief, and thereby forging the apologetic. The first five books of *De la recherche* had been devoted to an attack on the roots of human error, and only the sixth, generally endorsing Descartes, to the positive means of achieving truth. The *Conversations* were not so much the mere application of what was in essence a philosophical method, as a harmonization of divine revelation with its philosophical substructure. Malebranche followed that work with the more popularly intended 1677 *Méditations pour se disposer à l'humilité et à la pénitence avec quelques considerations de piété pour tous les jours de la semaine*.

The following year, 1678, appeared a series of 16 *Eclaircissements* by Malebranche, explaining his central positions. As in all the great philosopher-theologians of the central European tradition since the 12th century, Malebranche had started out from the problem of the apparent interaction of what were conceived of as spirit and matter. Descartes had been determined at all costs to defend their incommensurability and total distinctness so that the survival of the mind after death should make personal immortality explicable and credible. In following him, Malebranche had refined the theory of knowledge and, confronted by Foucher, had had to concede that external objects did not in any strict sense cause ideas. They "occasioned" them. For Malebranche no finite creature exercised true causality.

In what sense, therefore, did the human will remain capable of the free and autonomous moral self-determination of the individual? It was to answer this question that Malebranche now advanced into the theology of grace with the 1680 *Traité de la nature et de la grâce*. The intention was obviously religious more than, in the narrow sense, theological. Bossuet had heard enough about the manuscript by late 1679 or early 1680 to want to have the book stopped on the grounds simply that Malebranche's reconciliation of grace and free will was new, and presumably, therefore, likely to be tiresome. Bossuet remained at first unruffled, but was irritated when Malebranche responded to criticisms by a 1681 second edition, with an *Eclaircissement*. There was an interview, perhaps of late 1681 or early 1682, at which, when Bossuet threatened to write against Malebranche, Malebranche declared that he would be honoured. Bossuet did write, but suppressed his manuscript when he was shown by the marquis d'Allemans, who served as a go-between, that he had not understood what Malebranche was saying. Unfortunately many of d'Allemans's letters were lost in a fire at the château de Montardy in 1871, and we do not know the precise details of the dispute.

The *Traité de la nature et de la grâce* was also controverted by Arnauld who, ironically in view of his own position, went as far as accusing Malebranche of destroying human liberty. The Port-Royal (q.v.) faction had been used to regarding the Oratorian Cartesians as theological allies, and Arnauld saw Malebranche's *Traité* virtually as a betrayal. Arnauld's attack is based on the epistemology, and it has been cogently argued that only resentment at Malebranche's assault on the Jansenist view that concupiscence can determine the will to sinful self-determination can explain Arnauld's lack of any coherent philosophical position from which to argue. Malebranche's position on God's desire to save all men was always to be based on the view that God did indeed have such a will, that the human will could cause nothing, and that the fact of the damnation of the majority of the human race had to be ascribed to God's simplicity.

God, by definition the essence of all perfections, simply could not act other than in accordance with his own nature, which in turn entailed that God should not force human beings to act. God alone is the true cause of all that happens, and Malebranche in the end fails to harmonize that fact with the accountability of human beings for their own volitions. The best that the human will can autonomously achieve is to consent to, or to suspend consent to, the motives which arise within it. Malebranche is caught between the need to make the will the cause of acts for which it is responsible, thereby ruining his occasionalism but salvaging the foundation of guilt, and the alternative need to make the human will an illusion because, as Spinoza had argued, human beings were unfree modes of the divine substance.

The *Méditations chrestiennes et métaphysiques* followed in 1683, and the *Traité de morale* was published in 1684. Bossuet's funeral oration for Queen Marie-Thérèse on 1 September 1683 had spoken contemptuously of those who made God merely the author of an

> ordre général d'où le reste se développe comme il peut! Comme s'il avait à notre manière des vues générales et confuses, et comme si la souveraine intelligence pouvait ne pas comprendre dans ses desseins les choses particulières qui seules subsistent véritablement

> (general order from which the rest derives as best it can! As if he had as we do general and confused ideas, and as if the sovereign intelligence could not comprehend in its designs the individual things which alone really exist).

Much circumstantial evidence makes it likely that the reference was to Malebranche and was intended to be picked up, an episcopal condemnation on a solemn occasion rather than a theological confrontation. In 1683 Arnauld had issued his first attack on Malebranche's epistemology, *Des vrayes et des fausses idées*. Malebranche published a *Réponse de l'auteur de la Recherche de la Vérité, au livre de M. Arnauld, des vrayes et des fausses idées* in 1684, and in that year Arnauld replied again with a *Défense*. In 1685 Arnauld replied again, but this time on the tangential subject of Malebranche's recourse to miracles worked through angels. Malebranche replied in July 1685 with a *Réponse* defending and explaining the original 1680 *Traité*. By 1686, however, Bossuet, who may in the interim have been brought nearer to agreement with Malebranche by d'Allemans, was regarding Malebranche as no less than heretical.

In a letter to Nicole of 28 August 1686 Arnauld even reports the suggestion that he might be allowed back into France from the Low Countries, where he had been in exile since 1679, in order to refute Malebranche. It was on 21 May 1687 that Bossuet wrote his very harsh judgement, including this famous passage which, it is sometimes forgotten, was aimed not at Descartes, but at Malebranche:

> Je vois non seulement en ce point de la nature et de la grâce, mais encore sur beaucoup d'autres articles très importants de la religion, un grand combat se préparer contre l'Eglise, sous le nom de philosophie cartésienne. Je vois naître de son sein et de ses principes, à mon avis mal entendus, plus d'une hérésie, et je prévois que les conséquences qu'on en tire contre les dogmes que nos Pères ont tenus, la vont rendre odieuse, et feront perdre à l'Eglise tout le fruit qu'elle en pouvait espérer pur établir dans l'esprit des philosophes la Divinité et l'immortalité de l'âme

> (I see not only on this matter of nature and grace, but also on many other most important points of religion a great struggle being prepared against the Church in the name of Cartesian philosophy. I see being born from its self and from its principles, in my view wrongly understood, more than one heresy, and I foresee that the consequences that are drawn from these contrary to the dogmas held by our Fathers will make it hateful, and will cost the Church all the help it could hope for from it in establishing in the minds of philosophers the divinity and the immortality of the soul).

Bossuet's letter is so important that it has been disputed that it was ever actually sent to d'Allemans. It was published only from the draft or copy in Bossuet's papers. In fact it seems certain that d'Allemans received it. Bossuet acknowledged that Malebranche repudiated both Molinism and Thomism, but saw also that he put nothing in their place. The heresy is neither Molinism nor Jansenism, but Bossuet does not of course see that without the concept of a redeemed nature which would heretically allow even to pagans supernatural aspirations, implied acts of faith, and justification, the problem was quite simply incapable of resolution. Matters between Bossuet and Malebranche got worse before they got better, and in the course of 1687 Malebranche refused a personal confrontation with Bossuet, and Bossuet a written debate with Malebranche. There is some doubt about when and how the reconciliation took place. There was one, and it is overwhelmingly probable that the occasion was Bossuet's dispute with Fénelon on the spiritual doctrine of pure love.

In the meanwhile several of Malebranche's works had been put on the Roman index of prohibited works. The *Traité de la nature et de la grâce* was condemned with three minor polemical works on a date noted at Rome as 21 November 1689, although different dates are suggested by other documents, and the *Recherche de la vérité* was condemned on 17 January 1707, followed at different dates the same year by the *Entretiens sur la métaphysique et sur la religion* (17 January) and the *Traité de morale* (19 September). The condemnations were not particularly serious, scarcely affirming more than inappositeness, and Malebranche continued to publish the proscribed works in France where, he maintained with some plausibility, the juridical act had no force.

Bossuet had urged Fénelon to write his *Réfutation du système du P. Malebranche sur la grâce* towards the end of 1687, but may have been appeased by the 1688 *Entretiens sur la métaphysique et sur la religion*, a recapitulation of all Malebranche's major thinking, shown to him in draft by Père François Lamy towards the beginning of January 1688, when Malebranche incorrectly supposed that the *Entretiens* was in the course of being printed. Fénelon appears to have written his refutation of Malebranche at Bossuet's behest before seeing Malebranche's 1684 *Traité de morale*, but that was not an important work, and it clearly did not affect Bossuet's view of Malebranche's doctrine. However, the draft of the *Entretiens* apparently persuaded Bossuet that a public conflict, at least, ought to be avoided, particularly because two of his close associates, d'Allemans and Lamy, took Malebranche's side. It was probably not until, by then obsessed by the need to repudiate Fénelon, he had read Malebranche's slim 1697 *Traité de l'amour de Dieu* that Bossuet realized how useful Malebranche would be to him in the dispute with Fénelon, and that a full reconciliation took place.

When once Fénelon had published his sweeping and not very penetrating refutation of Malebranche he did not read anything else Malebranche published on the subject of nature and grace. But it is improbable that Malebranche ever knew of Fénelon's *Réfutation of the De la recherche* and it has been suggested that there was a personal friendship between Malebranche and Fénelon more cordial than the clash of intellectual positions in the pure love dispute would suggest. There is, however, no evidence of any friendship between them. On the other hand, there is considerable evidence that their intellectual positions on the question of disinterested love of God were nearer than had generally been believed. Malebranche repudiated only the concept of pure love underlying what was to be called the "impossible supposition" of the 33rd article of Issy that perfect love of God would entail consent even to the unjust condemnation to the eternal pains of hell of those who were just and in a state of grace. He rejected the condemned quietism of Molinos, based on the impossible supposition of an unjust God, but not the disinterest which, for Fénelon, characterized the highest forms of love of God.

Malebranche's writings on the subject included, as well as the *Traité de l'amour de Dieu*, the three *Lettres au Père Lamy* and the *Réponse générale*. Malebranche was grievously ill in 1694, after which, in 1696, he added *Trois entretiens sur la mort* to the earlier *Entretiens*. Unfortunately the list of his published works gives an inadequate indication of the growth of Malebranche's fame, and the spread of his interests. It is for instance possible to regard the philosophies of Leibniz and of Malebranche as epitomizing the two potential ways in which the philosophical ideas of Descartes could be developed, but all we have of the discussions between Leibniz and Malebranche is an exchange on the laws of the communication of movement. In 1692 Malebranche published the *Traité de la communication des mouvements*. He was also a theoretical physicist and a mathematician. Towards the end of his life he was visited by and had lively discussions with Berkeley. The completeness of their disagreement derived from Malebranche's willingness to seek a solution to the non-representational nature of ideas through however vague a knowledge in God, which did not involve a modification in the mind, while Berkeley's refusal to seek a non-representational form of knowledge left him with no guarantee at all that what was known was the real.

In 1708, when he reached the age of 70, Malebranche published his *Entretien d'un philosophe chrétien et d'un philosophe chinois sur la nature et l'existence de Dieu*, and in 1715 his last work, returning to the theology of grace, the *Réflexions sur la prémotion physique*. His life ended in four months of painful illness, although he retained perfect lucidity of mind. He was courteous and sensitive; tall, gaunt, hollow-cheeked, and naturally drawn to asceticism. He died in the rue Saint-Honoré, surrounded by his Oratory colleagues, on 13 October 1715.

WORKS

Malebranche's brilliant, flexible, and penetratingly lucid mind could, of course, not resolve the irresolvable metaphysical, theo-

logical, and religious dilemmas with which it was faced. In order to elude the dilemmas within the bounds of Christian orthodoxy, Malebranche risked relying on a relationship between humanity and God which skirted Spinozan pantheism but also brushed closely against too continuous a recourse to the miraculous intervention of God into individual lives. His works, all part of an internally consistent and vast apologetic for a Christian understanding of the universe, papered over the cracks appearing between what might already have been perceived as the only two seriously credible alternatives allowed by contemporary trends, of which neither in the end solved all the problems anyway. The view was opening up of the universe as a series of modalities of a single spiritual being. The alternative view appeared to be that of a world in which individual consciousness and freedom, dependent on material organs, did not permit of personal immortality. All Malebranche's writings were aimed at avoiding the need to choose between those unacceptable and unsatisfactory alternatives.

Although bound together by unified principles, Malebranche's writings can be roughly separated into three major groups, the purely philosophical writings, which came first; the theological works of the controversy with Arnauld, centred more on the nature of ideas than on the clash between the operation of grace in the soul and the soul's responsibility for its own volitions; and the writings against quietism in the condemned sense, and against the concept of pure or disinterested love of God which appeared to lie behind the 33rd article signed by Bossuet and Fénelon at Issy in 1695. There remain the papers on mathematics and mechanics.

The *De la recherche de la vérité* takes up Descartes's unfinished business. Having in the 1637 *Discours de la méthode* established the absolute difference between the extended substance, matter, and the thinking substance, mind, Descartes goes on in the 1641 *Principia philosophiae* to deal with the general physics. However he wrote only four of the six projected books of physics and, for the projected psychophysics of the body-soul union which should have been the sixth book of the *Principia*, Descartes offered the first of the three parts of *Les Passions de l'âme*, in which soul and body interact through the pineal gland. In his replies to Gassendi's objections to the sixth of the *Meditationes*, Descartes makes his fatal admission.

Gassendi asks how the soul, being immaterial, can move the body, and how it could receive from the body "les espèces des objets corporels (the species [representations] of corporeal objects)?" Descartes replied that the supposition was untrue that, because the soul and the body were two substances of different natures, they were prevented from acting on one another. He wrote to Gassendi in his *Remarques sur les Ves objections*,

Je vous dirai à vous, que toute la difficulté ne procède que d'une supposition qui est fausse...à savoir que, si l'âme et le corps sont deux substances de diverses natures, cela les empêche de pouvoir agir l'une contre l'autre

(I will tell you, just for yourself, that the whole difficulty proceeds only from a supposition which is false...that is to say, if the soul and the body are two substances of different natures, that prevents them from acting on one another).

Malebranche did not believe that that supposition was untrue. For him a material object could not modify a spiritual substance, nor a spiritual substance like the soul move a material object like the body. Descartes had, with the reluctance apparent in the postponement of the compilation of the psychophysics from the *Principia* to *Les Passions de l'âme*, allowed the interaction of mind and matter through the pineal gland. Malebranche was more rigorous. For him the only possible solution had to involve the mind's knowledge of all things, even of itself and of intelligible ideas, through God. And only God could be a true cause. Malebranche sums up his view, which of course confirms a deep Christian religious commitment:

Ainsi nos âmes dépendent de Dieu en toutes façons. Car de même que c'est lui qui leur fait sentir la douleur, le plaisir, et toutes les autres sensations, par l'union naturelle qu'il a mise entre elles et nos corps qui n'est autre que son décret et sa volonté générale: ainsi c'est lui qui par l'union naturelle qu'il a mise aussi entre la volonté de l'homme, et la représentation des idées que renferme l'immensité de l'être divin, leur fait connaître tout ce qu'elles connaissent, et cette union naturelle n'est aussi que sa volonté générale. De sorte qu'il n'y a que lui qui nous puisse éclairer, en nous représentant toutes choses; de même qu'il n'y a que lui qui nous puisse rendre heureux, en nous faisant goûter toutes sortes de plaisirs

(Our souls therefore depend in all ways on God. Just as it is he who makes them feel pain, pleasure, and all the other sensations, by the natural union which he has established between them and our bodies, which is nothing other than his decree and general will, so it is he who, by the natural union which he has also put between the human will and the representation of the ideas which are encompassed within the the immensity of the divine being, makes them know everything they know, and this natural union is also nothing other than merely his general will. So that he alone can enlighten us, by representing everything [we know] to us; just as he alone can make us happy, by making us taste all kinds of pleasures).

The notion of occasional cause becomes clear in the communication of momentum between a moving solid and another, whether at rest or already in motion. The sense of constraint is clear in Malebranche's deployment of his searching mental flexibility. His embarrassment is almost palpable when he speaks as if a contingent event could determine the divine will. When a moving ball strikes another, it cannot be the cause of setting the second ball in motion, but only the "natural" or occasional cause. Malebranche goes as far as to say the event determines the divine will:

Une cause naturelle n'est donc point une cause réelle et véritable, mais seulement une cause occasionnelle, et qui détermine l'auteur de la nature à agir de telle et telle manière, en telle et telle rencontre

(A natural cause is therefore not a real and true cause, but only an occasional cause, which determines the author of nature to act in such and such a manner in such and such circumstances).

"Natural" laws, as of the communication of momentum, are divinely ordained, and that is why they work as they do, although that leaves unexplained how all intra-mundane events avoid being miraculous.

Il n'y a donc point de forces, de puissances, de causes véritables dans le monde matériel et sensible

(There are therefore no real forces, powers, or causes in the material, sensible world).

To Leibniz's objection that Malebranche required a stream of miracles from God to account for each idea and each sensation in each human being all of the time, Arnauld pointed out that most ideas and sensations were covered by the rules established by God's general will, into which are subsumed the ordinary rules of mechanics. The concept of God's general will, not to be confused with the use Rousseau makes of the same term, consequently assumes major importance in Malebranche's philosophy.

In ethics, Malebranche has to construct a moral system within the constraint that only God can cause anything. If we hurt ourselves, or become angry, there can be external occasions, but only God is the real cause, through the laws established by his general will, of what happens within us, of our feeling the pain occasioned by the pin-prick. What Descartes regarded as actions of the body which were transformed into passions of the soul become for Malebranche the results of direct divine action:

Les passions de l'âme sont des impressions de l'auteur de la nature, lesquelles nous inclinent à aimer notre corps et tout ce qui peut être utile à sa conservation…

(The passions of the soul are the impressions put there by the author of nature which incline us to love our body and everything which can be useful to its preservation).

Ethical obligation, for Malebranche, is founded on divine simplicity. The general divine will had established the rule that people injure or kill themselves if they jump from a high window. In one of the many defences of the treatise on nature and grace, the *Réponse au livre de M. Arnauld…*, Malebranche holds that the sin in jumping, rather than taking the trouble to walk downstairs, is that it would tempt God by obliging him to disturb the simplicity of his nature, and the order he has established, in order to avoid the destruction of his work, which includes the individual who jumps.

A human act is good or evil according to whether the individual gives or withholds consent to the motive God, through the operation of his general will, causes to arise within him. Since God knows that more human beings will be damned than will be saved, his decision to create them, the inefficacity of his will to save them, and his failure to resolve the apparent conflict between justice, mercy, and love by acting in such a way that all human beings would be saved, must for Malebranche all be explained in terms of the divine nature itself, and its simplicity, in accordance with which God must act. Not surprisingly the Jesuits felt that Malebranche did not in fact allow for any autonomous power of self-determination, while the Jansenists felt that the ethics of consenting or withholding consent to motives allowed too much to the order of nature and too little to the order of grace. The Jesuit Rudolfe du Tertre's three-volume 1715

Réfutation d'un nouveau système de métaphysique proposé par le P. Malebranche accuses Malebranche of holding only that God would will that all human beings would be saved if that were possible, although it is not possible, because there is no other way for God to act which is as worthy of his attributes as that in which he does act, with the result that the majority of the human race will be damned.

Malebranche in different works and at different dates reworks the same material, but he also gradually changes and extends his view, so that a full account of his evolving thought would demand recourse to whole sets of correspondences, sometimes between third parties. It is, however, not unreasonable to suggest that the original statement of the occasionalist position in the sixth book of the *De la recherche* was subsequently extended, first to an ethic, and then to a theology proper. The model remained that derived from mechanics, in which God could most clearly and least controversially be shown to have established fixed laws which, for reasons to do with safeguarding the immortality of the soul, had to be regarded as depending on God's general will, and therefore to rely on physical occasions rather than proper causes. Malebranche finally extended his theory to theology in the *Traité de la nature et de la grâce* by making the human soul of Jesus the occasional cause of the distribution of grace to particular individuals.

Malebranche retained a clear distinction between philosophy and theology, even when he linked them by the same principles. He pointed out in the *Conversations chrétiennes* that the moral content of Jesus's teaching surpasses what can be known philosophically. The *Traité de l'amour de Dieu* is not, as has often been supposed, an attack on disinterested love of God as the highest form of charity, which is a commonplace of mystical theology. The *Traité* is an attack on the "impossible supposition" that God could impose eternal damnation on a human soul in a state of grace. God would be contradicting himself. To conform in those circumstances to God's will would not be virtuous:

> Si pour être juste, il faut toujours vouloir ce que Dieu veut, c'est uniquement et précisément parce que Dieu veut toujours selon l'Ordre immuable de ses perfections et qu'Il ne peut jamais se démentir. C'est à quoi il faut bien prendre garde. Car lorsqu'on attribue à Dieu des volontés purement arbitraires ou indépendantes de cette loi et qu'on s'imagine que c'est vertu de s'y soumettre, on tombe dans l'erreur et le dérèglement. On fait Dieu l'injuste, c'est là l'erreur; et le dérèglement consiste dans la conformité de sa volonté avec celle d'un Dieu imaginaire

> (If, in order to belong to the just, it is necessary always to will what God wills, it is uniquely and precisely because God always wills according to the immutable order of his perfections and because he can never be untrue to himself. It is this we must realize. For when we attribute to God acts of will that are purely arbitrary or independent of that law, and when we imagine that it is virtuous to submit to them, we fall into error and evil. We make God unjust, that is the error; and the evil consists in conforming our will with that of an imaginary God).

It is inappropriate to use the categories of right and wrong of a world vision as toweringly powerful as that of Malebranche.

The power comes from the compression, density, ingenuity, and even the inconsistencies with which it is contained inside the cultural constraints imposed on it by its aims, essentially to develop the Cartesian defence of immortality into an apologetic. Malebranche's aim naturally required an ethic and a theology consistent with a basic epistemology and metaphysic. It was eventually also to require a mystical theology, when Bossuet's dispute with Fénelon threatened to submerge Malebranche's fundamental principles.

The teaching of the history of philosophy has demanded a more accentuated set of differences between Malebranche and Descartes or Spinoza before him, or Locke, Bayle, Fénelon, and Leibniz who were more or less contemporaries, than the intellectual facts really warrant. All of them believed in God and immortality, and the important divergences had not yet shown themselves for what they were. The problem remained essentially the same once the polarization of the issues had been made clear by the clash between Jansenists and Jesuits. The proposed solutions edged forward, diverging in direction, but sharing a parallel audacity. Without some account of Malebranche, it would be difficult to see what large-scale metaphysical issues were raised by the Jesuit-Jansenist clash, and without an account of the solutions Malebranche proposed, it would be difficult to understand the development of literature and philosophy in 18th-century France.

PUBLICATIONS

Collections

Oeuvres complètes, 20 vols., 1958–67

Philosophy and theology

De la recherche de la vérité où l'on traite de la nature de l'esprit de l'homme, et de l'usage qu'on en doit faire pour éviter l'erreur des sciences, 6 books in 2 vols., 1674–75; with *Eclaircissements*, 1678; first English translations 1694; as *The Search after Truth*, 1980
Conversations chrétiennes, 1675; as *Christian Conferences*, 1695
Méditations pour se disposer à l'humilité et à la pénitence avec quelques considérations de piété pour tous les jours de la semaine, 1677; in *Christian Conferences*, 1695
Traité de la nature et de la grâce, 1680; with *Eclaircissement*, 1681; English translation, 1695; as *Treatise of Nature and Grace*, 1991
Défense de l'auteur de la Recherche de la vérité contre l'accusation de M. de la Ville, 1682
Traité de morale, 1684; English translation 1699
Méditations chrétiennes, 1683; as *Christian Conferences*, 1695
Réponse de l'auteur de la Recherche de la vérité au livre de M. Arnauld des vraies et des fausses idées, 1684
Réponse à une dissertation de M. Arnauld contre un Eclaircissement du Traité de la nature et de la grâce. Dans laquelle on établit les principes nécessaires à l'intelligence de ce même traité, 1685
Trois Lettres...touchant la Défense de Mr. Arnauld Contre la réponse au livre des vraies et fausses idées, 1685
Lettres du Père Malebranche à un de ses amis. Dans lesquelles

il répond aux Réflexions philosophiques et théologiques de Mr Arnauld sur le traité de la nature et de la grâce, 1686

Deux Lettres du Père Malebranche…touchant le II et le III volume des Réflexions philosophiques et théologiques de Mr Arnauld, 1687

Lettres du Pere Malebranche touchant celles de Mr Arnauld, 1687

Entretiens sur la métaphysique et sur la religion, 1688; augmented, 1696; as *Dialogues on Metaphysics and Religion*, 1923

Des Lois de la communication des mouvements, 1692

Réponse du P. Malebranche… à M. Regis, 1693

Réflexions sur la lumière et les couleurs et la génération du feu, 1699

Réponse à la troisième lettre de M. Arnauld docteur de Sorbonne touchant les idées et les plaisirs, 1704

Traité de l'amour de Dieu, en quel sens il doit être désintéressé. Trois Lettres au R. P. Lamy, et une quatrième ou réponse générale à celle de ce même Père, 2 vols., 1707

Entretien d'un philosophe chrétien et d'un philosophe chinois, 1708; as *Dialogue between a Christian Philosopher and a Chinese Philosopher on the Existence and Nature of God*, 1980

Réflexions sur la prémotion physique, 1715

Biographical and critical studies

Gouhier, Henri, *La Vocation de Malebranche*, 1923

————————*La Philosophie de Malebranche et son expérience religieuse*, 1926

Montcheuil, Yves de, *Malebranche et le quiétisme*, 1946

Watson, Richard A., *The Downfall of Cartesianism, 1673–1712*, 1966

————————*The Breakdown of Cartesian Metaphysics*, 1987

Riley, Patrick, *The General Will before Rousseau: The Transformation of the Divine into the Civic*, 1986

Nadler, Stephen M., *Arnauld and the Cartesian Philosophy of Ideas*, 1989

Jolley, Nicholas, *The Light of the Soul: Theories of Ideas of Leibniz, Malebranche, and Descartes*, 1990

Nicolas Malebranche: His Philosophical Critics and Successors, edited by Stuart Brown, 1991

MALEBRANCHE, François de, 1555–1628.

Poet and literary theorist.

LIFE

Malherbe's poetic oeuvre is slim, but his position at the court of Marie de Medici, his concept of poetry as stylized and minutely regulated versification to be put by the courtier at the service of aristocratic patrons, whose achievements were to be celebrated with skill and whose sentiments expressed with grace, his codification of the strict rules of rhyme, metre, and the other technicalities of versification, his baroque images, and the success with which he imposed his views, have combined to make him an important figure. He was professionally dedicated to the development of a purer French grammar and vocabulary, and to a disciplined view of the poet's social role serving the interests and flattering the achievements of wealthy patrons.

He endured poverty and subservience, took himself very seriously, early cultivated a school of disciples most of whose names, apart from those of Racan and Mainard, have long been forgotten, and was more of a theoretician than a poet. He in fact achieved comparatively little either in advancing the changes of which he approved or to halt those, eventually leading to préciosité (q.v.), of which he did not, but he was a perfectionist, now seen not so much to have led a reaction against Ronsard and Desportes as to have carried on their work. If he reacted against Ronsard's metaphorical sacralization of the poet's function in society, he laid down norms which mark an identifiable stage in the development of French poetry towards limpid and straightforward Racinian simplicity.

Malherbe was born in Caen, the eldest son of a Protestant counsellor of the présidial of Caen, who was also seigneur d'Igny, and of Louise le Valloys. He was boarded at Caen with the family of the university booksellers, spent a year boarding in Paris with a cousin, and returned to board again at Caen. He was next put in the charge of one private tutor for a year, and then, for six months or so, another, who accompanied him in 1571 to Germany, where he stayed two years. His name was entered on the student roll at Basle in 1571 and at Heidelberg in 1573. Among those mixing with the group of humanists at Caen in the 1570s was Geneviève Rouxel, a famous lawyer's cultivated and apparently beautiful niece, who flaunted her unwillingness to marry and died suddenly at 24 in 1575. Malherbe's translation of one of the epitaphs written on that occasion is the first piece of his verse which has survived. He never published it.

In 1576 Malherbe left Caen for Paris and a life as neither a Protestant nor a lawyer. In the following year he joined the household of Henri d'Angoulême, illegitimate son of Henri II and Grand Prieur of France, as secretary. He accompanied his employer to Marseilles when he was made general of the galleys in March 1578, and then to Aix when he became governor and lieutenant-general of Provence in 1579. On 1 October 1581 Malherbe signed his marriage contract with Madeleine de Carriolis, the widowed daughter of a judge by whom he had four children, three of whom died young. Malherbe's first surviving letter is a moving document written from Caen to his wife in Provence to tell her of the death on 23 June 1599 of their daughter Jourdaine, born on 22 September 1591. The letter is important because it shows a tenderness never obvious in such of the love verse as was written for his own mistress, the vicomtesse d'Auchy, whom he addressed as "Caliste," and an affection which, in view of Malherbe's notoriously unashamed womanizing, might not otherwise have been suspected. Known as "Le Père Luxure" after the ecclesiastical term for sins of sexual indulgence, Malherbe had to be treated on several occasions for venereal disease, and was once obliged to go as far as Nantes to be cured.

His eldest son, Henri, was born on 21 July 1585. Few of any poems Malherbe wrote at this time have survived. There was a small Provençal humanist circle, open to Spanish and Italian influences, which amused itself by writing amorous and religious verse. It relied little on the antique, or on mythology, and when Malherbe left Provence in April 1586 to return briefly to Caen, where his wife had joined him by the 22nd, he must already have had with him "Les Larmes de Saint Pierre," a 396-line poem in 66 six-line strophes, imitated from a text by Luigi Tansillo which had been published in 1560 in Venice and dedicated to Henri III. Malherbe was later to repudiate his adaptation as over-emphatic in its exaggerations of imagery and sentiment, but it had considerable success when published in 1587, and attracted from Henri III a gratification of 500 écus. Malherbe's employer, the duc d'Angoulême, had been assassinated at Aix on 2 June 1586. Malherbe was in Paris, no doubt hoping for a benefice, and now he found himself without a job.

From 1586 until 1595 Malherbe's permanent base was Caen, where he was supported by his family. He was later to translate Seneca's *De naturalibus quaestionibus*, and is known during this period at Caen to have been interested in Seneca. The poem known as the "Consolation à Cléophon" (more properly, "Consolation funèbre à un de ses amis sur la mort de sa fille"), is clearly neostoic in inspiration, and important especially because the later and more famous "Consolation à Monsieur Du Périer" is based on it and shows how Malherbe's techniques became stricter and his tone purer between the two poems. We do not know who Cléophon was, but the daughter, Rosette, appears to have been an adolescent at the time of her death. The earlier poem was probably written between 1589 and 1595. François du Périer, who was a lawyer at the parlement of Aix, lost his daughter, baptized on 2 February 1593, when she was five, and Malherbe's later poem must date from the earlier part of 1598, before his return to Normandy that July.

Malherbe's standing at Caen was high enough for him to be elected gouverneur-échevin of the town on 23 February 1594. His wife had returned to Provence in 1593 and Malherbe followed her in May 1595. Peace had not yet been re-established in the south, and Marseilles was still in the hands of the League, of which its first consul, Charles Casaulx, was a devoted adherent. Henri IV surrounded the town with an army led by the young duc de Guise, son of the League leader assassinated on the orders of Henri III, and on the night of 16–17 February 1596 Casaulx was killed by two brothers, Pierre and Barthélemy de Libertat, who opened the town gates to the royal troops. Malherbe wrote the first of his solemn odes for great occasions, "Au Roi Henri le Grand, sur la prise de Marseille." He may not have finished it, and he did not himself publish it.

It first appeared, with a second fragment of the same title and clearly of the same date, in the posthumous 1630 edition of the 1627 (privilège 2 June 1626) *Recueil des plus beaux vers de MM. de Malherbe, Racan, Monfuron, Maynard, Boisrobert, L'Estoille, Lingendes, Touvant, Motin, Mareschal. Et autres des plus fameux esprits de la cour*. The volume, published by Toussaint Du Bray, contained 62 poems by Malherbe in 1627, of which 13 were new. The "Avis aux lecteurs" described the poems it contained as "sorties de M. de Malherbe et de ceux qu'il avoue pour ses écoliers (written by M. de Malherbe and those whom he recognizes as his students)."

It was late in 1596 that Guillaume du Vair was appointed président of the special court at Marseilles and must have got to know Malherbe as a humanist contemporary also attracted to Christian stoicism. It was du Vair's prescriptions in the *De l'Eloquence* which were to guide Malherbe's reformatory ideas on linguistic usage. Malherbe's son Henri had died on 28 October 1587, and a second son François late in 1589. His daughter Jourdaine had stayed at Caen with his parents while he had been in Provence from 1595 to 1598, and was being brought up with his sister's child, Madeleine. Malherbe returned to Caen from Provence in August 1598 to stay for a little over a year. Both his daughter Jourdaine and her cousin Madeleine were to die of plague within a week of one another in June 1599. It was at this period that Malherbe got to know Antoine de Montchrestien. He was certainly behind some of the revisions Montchrestien made to the text of his play *Sophonisbe* between 1596 and 1601, when he got rid of archaisms, neologisms, and repetitions, striving to achieve greater clarity and much stricter prosody.

That December, Malherbe returned to Provence and when, on 17 November 1600, Marie de Medici made her solemn entry into Aix on her way from Florence to marry Henri IV, Malherbe read his formal ode of welcome after du Vair's harangue and M. de la Ceppède's distillation of "la rosée et le nectar de ses paroles (the dew and the nectar of his words)." It seems certain that the ode as it was published as a plaquette in 1601 is at best an augmented and perhaps a totally re-written version of what Malherbe declaimed at Aix, but it was on account of Malherbe's success on this occasion that du Perron recommended him to Henri IV at Lyons a month later as the best poet in France. That December, too, Malherbe's fourth child Marc-Antoine was born.

Legal proceedings kept Malherbe in Provence from 1601 until 1605. He was protected by du Vair, and worked on translations of Seneca. His formal ode "Pour les pairs de France, assaillants au combat de barrière" appears to have been commissioned by the four aristocratic "assaillants" who took up the tournament challenge of the four "tenants" to a joust on Sunday 27 February 1605, the only such "combat à la barrière" to be held in the reign. Malherbe's piece, however, was not printed in the *Recueil des cartels* put together for the occasion. Single poems of Malherbe had now been sporadically published, "Victoire de la constance" in a Rouen collection of 1597, *Diverses poésies nouvelles*, and "Les Larmes de Saint Pierre" in the 1598 *Recueil de plusieurs diverses poésies*. Both appeared also elsewhere, and two new poems were published in the *Seconde partie des Muses françaises ralliées* of 1600. Four more new poems appeared in the 1603 version of the original *Les Muses françaises ralliées*.

Then in August 1605 du Vair was briefly recalled to Paris. Malherbe and Nicolas-Claude Fabri de Peiresc travelled in his suite. Malherbe was touching 50. He had been separated from his wife and family, and was to see his wife again only twice in the remaining 23 years he had to live, although he cared for her well-being and was concerned about her happiness. After suffering from a lack of material resources he now had none. He had published scarcely a dozen poems, although he had had the recommendation of du Perron. du Vair was received by the king, to whom Malherbe also was presented. The king, about to go off that month to suppress the uprising in favour of the Protestant duc de Bouillon near Limoges, was persuaded to commission a poem from Malherbe. The uprising was put down without difficulty, although there were executions, and on the king's return to Paris on 20 November Malherbe presented his ode, "Prière pour le Roi allant en Limousin." The king found it admirable and affected Malherbe to the service of M. de Bellegarde, the Grand Ecuyer, with a salary of 1,000 livres, board, lodging, a horse, and a servant.

The post involved much discomfort whenever the court moved to Fontainebleau, but Malherbe was in no position to complain. He had been without a situation. Henri IV was not interested in artistic patronage, and Malherbe adjusted himself perfectly to the formal celebratory odes which were expected of him on all royal occasions, births, marriages, and deaths, and to collaboration in court entertainments in return for his position of chief royal poet, in however unceremonious a light his post was at first viewed. His own opinion is recorded that "un bon poëte n'est pas plus utile à l'état qu'un bon joueur de quilles (a good poet is of no more use to his country than a good skittle-player)." He obediently versified Henri IV's passionate feelings for Charlotte de Montmorency, and was at least made a gentilhomme ordinaire de la chambre. Since his arrival in Paris he had become friendly with Desportes's nephew, Mathurin Régnier, whom he is said by Racan to have ranked with the Latin poets, but he early conceived the ambition of ousting Desportes from his unofficial position as France's premier poet.

Racan has left an often-repeated account of the occasion, which must have been very late in 1605 or very early in 1606, when Malherbe was taken by Régnier to dine with Desportes. When Desportes made to go upstairs to fetch for his guest a copy of his versified *Psaumes*, Malherbe told him not to bother, saying that his soup was better than his *Psaumes*. Malherbe and Desportes did not speak to one another during the meal and did not meet again before Desportes's death on 5 October 1606. The antipathy was founded on more than differences of literary principles and practice, and may indeed have helped give rise to their expression. Malherbe cannot have avoided some touch of envy at Desportes's beneficed ease, established on the foundations of a facile prosody, of which Malherbe came increasingly to disapprove. In fact Malherbe severely annotated a copy of Desportes's *Poésies* in 1606, and for a time intended to publish it. Desportes, however, died, and it is not unlikely that Malherbe was overcome by the habitual lethargy which also largely accounts for his scant production.

A tournament at the Louvre on 25 February 1606 involved four teams, "water," "earth," "air," and "fire," of which the first was led by Bellegarde, who commissioned Malherbe's appropriately named "Aux Dames pour les demi-dieuz marins, conduits par Neptune." Malherbe, a slow worker, had only five days to write the piece, of which he was afterwards proud. It reads today simply like a skilled apprentice exercise in poetic composition. Malherbe's slowness had become proverbial. Pierre Berthelot said it took him six months to write an ode, and the joke ran that his "Consolation à Monsieur le premier président sur la mort de Madame sa femme" took him so long to write that its addressee, Nicolas de Verdun, was already remarried when he received it.

During the Lent of 1606, threatened again by an insurrectionary movement in favour of Bouillon, Henri IV set out to take Sedan, fortified against him, and commissioned a poem. Events moved too fast and Malherbe gave up work on his piece, but the king recalled his duties to him on several occasions, and six months after the commission Malherbe was "working seriously" at his task. The "Ode au feu Roi sur l'heureux succès du voyage de Sedan" was finished only by mid-December, when Malherbe presented it to the king. He subsequently thought it one of his most successful poems.

In the summer his father had died and he had returned to Caen to arrange the consequent legal matters. It is probably

while he was there that he first wrote to the vicomtesse d'Auchy, the mistress whom he was later notoriously to slap in public. By the 1 August he had returned to Paris, and in September 1606 he went with the court to Fontainebleau, where he was again by the end of May 1607. He presented two sonnets to the king there in June and returned to Paris with the court in July, managing to avoid the October return to the discomfort of Fontainebleau.

In 1608 Malherbe visited Burgundy with Bellegarde for the Estates. It was on 31 January 1609, at the end of the performance of a ballet at the Arsenal for which Malherbe had written "Pleine de langues et de voix," that Henri IV told Malherbe of his love for Charlotte de Montmorency. Her engagement contract to Henri de Bourbon, prince de Condé, was signed at the Louvre on 2 March, and the marriage took place at Chantilly on 17 May. A month later, on 17 June, Condé, worried by the king's attitude to his wife, took her to Vallery, returning to the court only for the marriage of the duc de Vendôme on 7 July. Malherbe, who spent all year in Paris apart from a few days at Fontainebleau in July, must have missed the wedding. Condé moved his wife to Muret in September, appeared alone in Paris for the queen's confinement in November, and immediately after the birth of the queen's daughter took his wife to Spanish territory in the Netherlands. In December the Connétable de Montmorency wrote to Brussels to demand his daughter back, and by the end of March 1610 Malherbe was writing love verse for the king to Charlotte, "attending on the king," wrote the Spanish ambassador, "at most extraordinary times." The queen was crowned at Saint-Denis on 13 May, and on 14 May Henri IV was assassinated.

Happily for Malherbe, Bellegarde's friendship with the princess de Conti, who was close to Marie de Medici, ensured Malherbe's continued protection. He was given 30,000 livres and from April 1611 allocated a pension of 1,200 livres, raised to 1,500 in June 1612, although payment was often difficult to obtain and always late. Socially Malherbe's career was now reaching its apogee. He may have been admitted daily to Marie de Medici's company, and he frequented the princesse de Condé. He privately wrote satirical verse against both Concini and then Luynes during the periods of their respective ascendancies, and in 1617 rejoiced at the death of Concini, to whom he had referred as "L'Esprit sacré (The sacred spirit)" in 1612. He got to know Guise and Bassompierre, and dined in 1613 with Mme de Longueville, having, in 1611, travelled in the princesse de Conti's carriage to Lyons in the suite of Marie de Medici. His letters to Peiresc show that he did not disdain a certain affectation now that at least externally he was accepted by the court as one of its members.

From the late summer of 1615, Malherbe's situation declined. Bellegarde did not hide his hostility to Concini, with whom he quarrelled fiercely in January 1611 and, when Louis XIII, abetted by Albert de Luynes, took power personally in 1617 and Concini was killed, Marie de Medici was forced to live in exile at Blois and could no longer assist Malherbe. He was still without a benefice, in spite of the reiterated assurances of Henri IV that he would be provided with one, and may again have known poverty. It took him four months of wrangling in 1613 to have his pension paid.

By that date Condé had clearly become the focus of potential opposition to Louis XIII. Of the new king's two brothers, Philippe, duc d'Orléans, had died in 1611 at the age of four. Gaston, duc d'Anjou and from 17 November 1611 his brother's successor as duc d'Orléans, had been born only in 1608. After him, Condé was the king's nearest male relative, and next in line to the throne. By the spring of 1614 he was in open rebellion until virtually bought off that May by the treaty of Sainte-Menehould. The solemn proclamation of the king's majority on 2 October 1614 changed nothing, and Marie de Medici, forced to summon the Estates-General, was in effect compelled to give to the nation an account of her regency. During this turbulent year Malherbe composed his paraphrase of Psalm 128. In March 1615 he wrote the "Récit d'un berger" for the exceptional festivities in honour of the marriage of Madame Elisabeth, the king's sister, to the king of Spain.

In 1615 Malherbe had obtained royal authorization to build two houses at Toulon where, however, the Cour des comptes resisted registration of his letters patent until April 1618, after his third attempt, and he still had to take the Toulon consuls to law in 1619. He had himself gone to Toulon in January 1616 in a vain attempt to hasten matters. In April he returned to Paris in the suite of du Vair, brought back from Provence as Garde des Sceaux by Villeroy to take over the functions of Sillery, the chancellor. Malherbe remained on intimate terms with du Vair. In 1616 he published 16 chapters of Livy's 33rd book. The complete translation of Book 33 in a rotund, rhetorical style appeared in February 1621, and deliberately broke away from what Malherbe regarded as a "grotesque" literal fidelity to the original text. He came to regard his translation as a model of French prose writing, as he regarded his poetry as a model of French versification.

He had been in Caen late in 1619, and returned there in 1621 to sell his house. The deed is dated 13 September 1621. Against a down payment in cash of 6,000 livres the transaction was left for completion in the hands of Malherbe's sister-in-law. Meanwhile on 15 December 1621, Luynes died. In 1622 Malherbe went to Aix, where he was commissioned to compose the inscriptions for three triumphal arches for the solemn entry of Louis XIII. Two days after his arrival, his son, Marc-Antoine, was put under house arrest in the wake of a quarrel which may have been going to end in a duel. Malherbe succeeded in having the matter taken out of the jurisdiction of the Aix authorities, who favoured his son's adversaries, although he could not get him released to come to Paris in March 1623.

Malherbe received 1,500 livres from the king in February 1624 for "Muses, je suis confus," but in June Marc-Antoine fought another duel, with an apparently unconnected opponent whom he killed. He was condemned to be beheaded but escaped to Normandy. Malherbe meanwhile continued to have difficulty in getting his pension paid. He relied now on hopes of being advanced by Richelieu, and was in fact in 1626 accorded a newly created post of treasurer of France. Marc-Antoine was pardoned. His pardon was confirmed on 13 February 1627, but on 13 July he was killed near Aix in a new duel with his former enemies. His opponents were condemned to death on 14 August, and Malherbe wrested from Louis XIII the promise that they would never be pardoned. A final sonnet calls down divine vengeance on those who killed his son, and does not recoil from pointing out that, as Jews, they were descended from the executioners of Jesus.

Two volumes appeared collecting together his works with those of his disciples, the *Recueil des plus beaux vers* and the *Recueil de lettres nouvelles*, and on 15 December 1627 Malherbe received 2,000 livres in pension and gratifications for the year. In 1628 he sent to the king and to Richelieu verses composed in the context of the siege of La Rochelle, and wrote to the archbishop of Aix, asking him to withdraw support for the opponents who had killed Marc-Antoine. In July he went after Louis XIII to La Rochelle, but learnt on 24 September that his son's opponents had received a remission and that the whole matter, as they had wished, had gone before the parlement of Toulouse. Malherbe, at 73, even thought of himself challenging his son's principal opponent.

He returned ill to Paris, and died on Friday 6 October 1628.

WORKS

In spite of the exasperating serenity of his formal and frigid consolations, Malherbe was an author of deep feelings. They were, however, suppressed in the interests of producing the sort of official verse on which he founded the career which he hoped would satisfy his social pretensions and literary ambitions. He could be harsh and brutal as well as sensitive, but rarely expressed any genuine feeling in verse. His ambition was to obtain advancement by becoming the kingdom's principal professional versifier and, partly on that account, he developed to an extraordinary extent singularly exigent norms of linguistic purity and prosodic craftsmanship. He liked order first, and then clarity, did not particularly admire the antique, showed little taste and no imagination, and believed in keeping the external proprieties, social and religious, with as little personal inconvenience as possible.

He had not enjoyed arriving in Paris at 50 with little but a reputation based on an output which remained exiguous and with no money, but succeeded in imposing his social respectability and his literary authority and in codifying the linguistic purification which he also advanced. Mainard had begun to look on Malherbe as his master as early as 1607. Then Racan, who lived in the Bellegarde household, set no boundary to his admiration, and he was quite soon joined by lesser names, more after 1615 and more still after 1620. Mainard and, after 1621, Racan were no longer in Paris, but their places were taken by Chapelain, then Balzac, Faret, and Vaugelas. Malherbe wished to be revered. He received daily in his small apartment in the Rue des Petits-Champs the disciples who submitted their work for critical dissection, and simply closed the door when the last chair was taken. The class was assembled.

Malherbe often complained of his own laziness, but as his own rules of prosody became stricter and versification consequently more difficult, he had increasingly taken to writing in prose, and particularly to translating, although most of his projects were abandoned. He frequented the Chambre bleue of Mme de Rambouillet, for whom he is credited with creating the anagram "Arthénice" from her Christian name, Catherine, and remained intimate with Racan and the more scholarly Peiresc. During the regency of Marie de Medici, when he was celebrating the submission of the princes in 1614 and the Spanish marriages in 1615, Malherbe also began writing religious verse, the "Stances spirituelles" and psalm paraphrases. The only verse addressed to women was to the great, and the only collection in which Malherbe allowed his verse to appear during the regency, the 1615 *Délices de la poésie française*, was dedicated to the princesse de Conti.

Malherbe's doctrine no doubt accelerated, and in any case did not reverse, tendencies already observable before he came to Paris. The revisions made to their work by Ronsard and then Desportes had moved towards the elimination of neologisms, archaisms and regionalisms. Desportes plainly, but even the later Ronsard, had begun to dismantle the vatic ambitions of the early Pléiade (q.v.), and to see the poet more as a graceful stylist, even entertainer. There is a sense in which Malherbe, by lowering the poet's status to that of professionally employed courtier, also augmented the dignity of poetry. He gave it the ceremonial ode in its most elevated form, and largely limited its serious subject matter to affairs of state, victories in battle, royal encomia, and the loves of princes, although he never freed the court poet from the obligation to contribute to lighter court festivities. Malherbe regarded it as the function of the poet to write the sort of political verse which Ronsard had undertaken only with reluctance just before the outbreak of the religious wars.

In language Malherbe demanded simple, pure French. In metre he came more and more to eliminate irregularities. He disapproved of adjectives used adverbially as advocated by du Bellay in the *Deffence et illustration de la langue françoyse*, and in prosody insisted on the division of the alexandrine into two sets of six syllables. He proscribed inversion and the omission of articles and pronouns, insisted on a natural word order, and excluded mythological erudition; he demanded a noble, purified style; he developed strict norms for the syntax of the strophe, demanding that in elegies the sense should be complete in each group of four lines, that six-line stanzas should be split into two groups of three, that there should be stops after the fourth and seventh lines of ten-line stanzas; and above all he tightened the rules for permissible rhymes. Desportes, by imitating the graceful stylization of the Italians had already started on the path away from the re-creation in French of Homer and Pindar. Malherbe wanted also to remove the influence of the Italians.

Only very slowly did he reduce his reliance on the forced and exaggerated imagery of baroque. When Marie de Medici's second son died in 1611 and the other two were still alive, Malherbe wrote a consolatory sonnet, first published posthumously in 1630:

Consolez-vous Madame, apaisez votre plainte;
La France, à qui vos yeux tiennent lieu de soleil,
Ne dormira jamais d'un paisible sommeil
Tant que sur votre front la douleur sera peinte.

Rendez-vous à vous-même, assurez votre crainte,
Et de votre vertu recevez ce conseil,
Que souffrir sans murmure est le seul appareil
Qui peut guérir l'ennui dont vous êtes atteinte.

Le ciel, en qui votre âme a borné ses amours,
Etait bien obligé de vous donner des jours
Qui fussent sans orage, et qui n'eussent point d'ombre.

Mais ayant de vos fils les grands coeurs découverts,
N'a-t-il pas moins failli d'en ôter un du nombre,
Que d'en partager trois en un seul univers?

(Console yourself, Madame, give peace to your complaint;/France, for whom your eyes take the place of the sun,/Will never sleep with a peaceful rest/As long as on your forehead sorrow is depicted.//Return yourself to

yourself, calm your fears,/And from your virtue receive this advice,/That to suffer without protest is the only remedy/Which can cure the malady with which you are afflicted.//Heaven, to which your soul has limited its loves/Was indeed obliged to give you a life/Without storm, and without shadow.//But, having uncovered the great hearts of your sons,/Did it not do better to remove one of their number,/Rather than have three of them to a single world?).

It should be admitted that Malherbe's poetic gifts show at their best in odes longer than it is possible to analyse in the present context. This sonnet may not necessarily be considered his best, but it revealingly catches Malherbe at a point at which both the earlier and the later constraints on his style are apparent, and neither set is fully resolved.

The construction of the sonnet is very nearly perfect. The rhyme scheme is precisely correct; each half-alexandrine has two perceptible accents; the sense is complete at the end of each quatrain and tercet; there is a natural pause at the end of each line; the language is simple, clear, and unfigured; the final line reveals the high-point to which the whole sonnet works up; and the worst that can be said about the technique is that, given the desirability of ending with the question mark, there is some slight strain on natural prose word order in lines four and twelve. Other skills are apparent, too. The "l" sounds with the soft "p" and "m" consonants of the first quatrain themselves mimic the peace the poet wishes to bring, while three "v" sounds in each of the first two lines of the second quatrain reinforce the imperiousness of the content.

None the less, as a consolation this sonnet is frostily cold for any age. From its tone, the poem could be the perfunctory acquittal of a formal obligation inspired by no feeling at all. Although we do in fact know from the biographical evidence that it was more than that, the sonnet does not itself reveal any strong emotion. The advice is neostoic and commonplace, suggesting without a hint of irony that the mother who has just lost a four-year-old son should pull herself together without complaining. Malherbe is still in 1611 indoctrinated with du Vair's neostoic recipe for moral uplift. And if the vocabulary, syntax, rhyme scheme, and prosody are now practically as tightly wrought as he can make them, the imagery is still baroque. That Marie de Medici's eyes fulfil for France the role of the sun is exaggerated enough, but the final consideration is simply grotesque in its distortion of ordinary psychology. The three sons have hearts so great that each should have the world to himself. Then comes the point of the compliment. Was it not fitting, asks Malherbe by way of consolation, and without irony, that at least one should be taken away to give the others larger shares and so that the world should not be overwhelmed with greatness?

Maherbe's most famous poem, the earlier and even more neostoic 1598 "Consolation à Du Périer," actually borrows its form from Ronsard's "Epitaphe de Jan de la Peruse," published in the 1555 *Odes*. It marks a poetic development beyond its prototype, the "Consolation à Cléophon," but still contains mythological references to and reminiscences of Statius—Malherbe's favourite Latin poet—Horace, and even Guarini. Even in the solemn and elevated psalm paraphrases Malherbe seldom aspires to much more than adequate felicity in his choice of language. He is not, however, pompous, bombastic or grandiose. Quite late in his poetic career he continues to use strings of metaphors in the baroque fashion rather than straight descriptions, although gradually a sense of grandeur, of the noble and the sublime, comes to dominate his odes, which are also not totally devoid of grace, or even humour, as in this stanza addressing the nymphs, partly remembered from Tibullus, from "Pour la reine mère du roi pendant sa régence," probably of 1613:

> Quand le sang bouillant en mes veines
> Me donnait de jeunes désirs,
> Tantôt vous soupiriez mes peines,
> Tantôt vous chantiez mes plaisirs;
> Mais aujourd'hui que mes années
> Vers leur fin s'en vont terminées,
> Siérait-il bien à mes écrits
> D'ennuyer les races futures
> Des ridicules aventures
> D'un amoureux en cheveux gris?

(When the hot blood in my veins/Gave me young desires,/ Sometimes you sighed for my sufferings,/Sometimes you sang my pleasures;/But today, now that my years/Are over and go towards their end,/Would it be appropriate for my writings/To bore future generations/With the ridiculous adventures/Of a lover with grey hair?).

Malherbe never finished the long poem from which that stanza is taken. Much of what was finally published was either still unfinished, or contained pieces stitched in or tacked on to other poems, not always seamlessly. Among several pieces wrongly attributed to Malherbe, there is a handful of authentic obscene poems to be found in the satirical collections of 1618 and 1620. Perhaps because it has matured for so long since its prototype, the "Consolation à Du Périer" will no doubt continue to be regarded as containing the epitome of his poetic achievement. Its final couplet rings solemnly, but frigidly:

> Vouloir ce que Dieu veut est la seule science,
>   Qui nous met en repos.

(To want what God wants is the only knowledge/Which puts us at peace).

PUBLICATIONS

[*Malherbe published no volume containing merely his own poems during his lifetime. The list below notes the poems that were published on their own, and the collections in which new poems by Malherbe appeared during his lifetime, as well as modern collections.*]

Modern collections

Oeuvres de Malherbe, 5 vols., 1862–69
Les Poésies de Malherbe, 1926
Les Poésies de M. de Malherbe, 1936
Oeuvres, Bibliothèque de la Pléiade, 1971

Single poems

Les Larmes de saint Pierre, imitées du Tansille, 1587

Ode du sieur de Malherbe à la Reine. Pour sa bienvenue en France, 1601
Ode sur l'attentat commis en la personne de Sa Majesté, le 19 décembre 1605 [no date]
Vers du sieur de Malherbe. A la reine, 1611
Récit d'un berger au ballet de Madame [1615]
Récit d'un berger sur les alliances de France et d'Espagne, [1615]
Pour le marquis de La Vieuville, superintendant des Finances [no date]
Au roy. Sonnet [no date]
Amphion au Roi [no date]
A Monseigneur le cardinal de Richelieu. Sonnet [no date]
Pour Monseigneur. Sonnet [no date]
A Monsieur de Verdun [no date]
Pour le Roi allant châtier la rébellion des Rochelois… Ode [no date]

Collections in which previously unpublished poems of Malherbe appeared, to 1630

Diverses poésies nouvelles, 1597
Seconde partie des Muses françaises ralliées, 1600
Les Muses françaises ralliées (second edition), 1603
Le Parnasse des plus excellents poètes de ce temps, 2 vols., 1607
Nouveau recueil des plus beaux vers de ce temps, 1609
Le Temple d'Apollon, 2 vols., 1611
Les Délices de la poésie française, 1615; corrected versions, 1618
Le Cabinet satirique, 1618
Les Délices satiriques, 1620
Le second livre des Délices de la poésie française, 1620
Dernier recueil des plus beaux vers de ce temps, 1620 or 1621
Recueil des plus beaux vers de MM. de Malherbe, Racan, Monfuron, Maynard, Boisrobert, L'Estoille, Lingendes, Touvant, Motin, Mareschal. Et autres des plus fameux esprits de la cour, 1627
Les Oeuvres de M. François de Malherbe, 1630

Biographical and critical studies

Brunot, Ferdinand, *La Doctrine de Malherbe*, 1891
Counson, Albert, *Malherbe et ses sources*, 1904
Fromilhague, René, *La Vie de Malherbe. Apprentissage et luttes (1555–1610)*, 1954
——————————*Malherbe. Technique et création poétique*, 1954
Perceau, Louis, *François de Malherbe et ses escholiers*, 1932
Celles, Jean de, *Malherbe, sa vie, son caractère, sa doctrine*, 1937
Winegarten, Renée, *French Lyric Poetry in the Age of Malherbe*, 1954
Lebègue, Raymond, *Malherbe et Du Perrier…suivis d'une étude sur Malherbe et l'éloquence d'apparat*, 1956
Ponge, Francis, *Pour un Malherbe*, 1965

MARGUERITE D'ANGOULÊME, duchesse d'Alençon, reine de Navarre, 1492–1549.

Author of contes, plays, and verse.

LIFE

Politically, the fifteenth century had seen the consolidation of royal power in France. By 1481 Louis XI, who had acceded to the throne in 1461, had largely overcome the great feudal overlords and absorbed their lands into a unified France. When he was succeeded in 1483 by his son, the 13-year-old invalid Charles VIII, whose sister Anne de Beaujeu he had nominated to be regent, some of the feudal aristocracy, including the duc de Bretagne and Louis d'Orléans, went into open revolt. They were defeated, and in July 1488 Louis d'Orléans was taken prisoner at Saint-Aubin-du-Cormier, to be released only in 1491. In 1488 Anne de Beaujeu put pressure on Charles, comte d'Angoulême, cousin and a potentially dangerous political rival to her young brother Charles VIII, to marry the niece she had had to bring up, Louise, the obscure and moneyless daughter of the younger branch of the house of Savoy, whose own mother had died when she was five. It was Louis XI who had first wanted to force Angoulême to marry her.

Charles d'Angoulême, who had already had a daughter by Jeanne de Polignac, one of his mother's ladies-in-waiting, fomented an insurrection, lost, and duly married Louise in February 1488, after which he went with her to live politically inactive on his estates. The duc de Bretagne signed a peace treaty at Sablé, but died in 1491. He left an only daughter Anne, married by proxy to Maximilian of Austria in December 1490, but that marriage was repudiated before it was consummated, and in December 1491 Charles VIII married Anne de Bretagne, who committed herself, should she outlive him, to marry his successor, so opening the way for the incorporation of Brittany into France, formally agreed by the Brittany estates only in 1532 and implemented in 1547.

In the meanwhile the Angoulêmes's eldest child, Marguerite, was born at the château of Angoulême, apparently at 2 a.m. on 11 April 1492. Such precision is, of course, suspect. Brantôme puts the birth four hours earlier, so changing the date—presumably, since he also tells us to the minute the time of her conception, which was incidentally before lunch, to get the right astrological prediction. In spite of Charles d'Angoulême's nearness to the throne, the frivolity of Marguerite's paternal grandfather had left no money with which to maintain a display of rank. Marguerite's baptism was quiet, without a public celebration that could not be afforded. Her mother was just 17, and was to give birth to a son, François, in 1494.

Charles VIII had had a son in 1492, but the child died in December 1495. That made Angoulême's cousin, the duc d'Orléans, married by Louis XI to his saintly but sterile second daughter, and head of the Orléans branch of the Valois family, heir presumptive again. Louis XI had cynically calculated that the marriage of his daughter to the duc d'Orléans would ensure the extinction of the line. No doubt to discuss the new situation, Angoulême went to visit his cousin, Orléans. Angoulême, although he had once hoped to recoup his social situation through military distinction, was not robust, and a cold caught on the way turned into a fever from which he died at Châteauneuf on 1 January 1496. His will made it clear that his widow,

Marguerite's mother, should be appointed her guardian. Angoulême usage allowed such an arrangement when the guardian was 14, although French law stipulated 25. Louise de Savoie was 18, and Orléans wanted the education of his currently presumptive successor, the young François, to be in his own hands. Charles VIII tried to help Louise de Savoie, but there were other legal wrangles over vast estates in Périgord to worry the young widow, and the sudden change in dynastic circumstance was radically to change Marguerite's future when Charles VIII died on 8 April 1498.

The duc d'Orléans, once the prisoner of Saint-Aubin-du-Cormier, duly succeeded as Louis XII, and was now in a position to impose his will on the family of his late cousin. Louise and her children were brought to Chinon, given the maréchal de Gié to look after them, and sent to live at Blois before being moved to Amboise. François was made duc de Valois. In 1499, however, Louis XII repudiated his marriage to the daughter of Louis XI, in order to conserve Brittany by marrying on 8 January 1499 the ambitious and independent widow of Charles VIII, Anne de Bretagne. This complicated life for Louise de Savoie, as she could now hope to put her son François on the throne only if Louis XII and Anne de Bretagne had no heir. Both Anne de Bretagne's sons by Charles VIII were dead, and the child to whom she had given birth at the end of 1499 was a daughter, Claude. It was Gié who worked for the solution which was eventually imposed, much against the will of Anne de Bretagne, whereby her and Louis XII's daughter Claude would be married to the heir presumptive, the young François, comte d'Angoulême, the son of his late cousin. The chief difficulty was Anne, Louis's wife and queen, who disliked both Louise de Savoie and Gié. Louise also disliked Gié, regarding him primarily as her jailer, and was largely instrumental in his disgrace in 1504.

Gié had planned that François would marry the king's daughter, Claude, primarily because he saw the arrangement as a way of keeping Brittany within France. The queen wanted Claude to have the chance to take Brittany back again for herself. In fact Anne de Bretagne was to die in February 1514, François would marry Claude in May, and Louis XII, having married Henry VIII's sister, Mary Tudor, as his third wife, was still to have no son before he died during the night of 31 December. On 1 January 1515 the king of France would be François d'Orléans, comte d'Angoulême, duc de Valois, henceforward François I. He was 20. Since 2 December 1509, when she was 17, his elder sister had been married to Charles, duc d'Alençon.

Marguerite's upbringing had been insecure. With no father, and her mother jealously watched by security forces charged as much with guarding as with protecting her, she was from early childhood a pawn in a series of political games, two of which concerned marriage to one or other of the sons of Henry VII. The Spaniards were alarmed enough to seek to get in first with a suitable princess. Then in 1505 the English proposed two marriages, between Henry VII and Louise de Savoie, and between prince Henry and Marguerite. There was even serious discussion of a marriage between Henry VII and Marguerite. The most important obstacle may have been Marguerite's refusal. That summer Louise de Savoie and her children came quite close again to Louis XII, while Anne can only be said to have sulked in Brittany. Another project involved the son of the King of Naples, whom Marguerite failed to please. Either her future was going to be that of sister to the king, in which case she could hope for a brilliant marriage, or, should Louis and Anne have an heir, she would be not much of a match for anyone at all and, like any other impoverished aristocrat, would be condemned to keeping up appearances in the distant provinces. A whole list of marriage projects foundered on the uncertainty.

At the little Angoulême court at Cognac there had been books and music. Octovien de Saint-Gelais had been made bishop of Angoulême by Marguerite's father in 1494, and his brother, Jean de Saint-Gelais, was her mother's close companion, often rumoured also to have been her lover. He and his other brother Nicolas, who was to become François I's steward, followed her to Chinon. Louise de Savoie, pretty, cultivated, ambitious for her children, devoted her widowhood to their education and guidance, although her principal concern was always to be François. Marguerite, no doubt brought up in the company of her father's illegitimate children, including the daughter of Jeanne de Polignac, now lady-in-waiting to her mother, developed a bent for reading and reflective meditation. She had a brief and light attack of smallpox. Her mother's culture was Italianate, relaxed, informal, literary, and musical. Louise was rich, with a household pay roll of well over 100, and surrounded herself by the cultivated aristocracy and its often erudite army of dependent scholars and devotees of the arts, many of them ecclesiastics. The first decade of the 16th century meanwhile saw the early wave of importation into France of many manifestations of Italian renaissance culture, by no means limited merely to architecture and the decorative arts.

Marguerite's education formed her not only for the intoxication of her late twenties with the mysticism of the pseudo-Denis which she was to absorb through Briçonnet, and which led to the serious interest in some of the ideas of the team of ecclesiastical reformers Briçonnet was to recruit and whom Marguerite was later to protect at Nérac, but also for the coarseness of parts of the *Heptaméron*. The way was opened to the speculative mystical poetry of the *Prisons* as well as to the farces and comedies she was to write as entertainments. She learned some Latin, Italian and Spanish, although not enough to make her a "humanist," and was given a solid religious education. Her governesses and tutors were carefully chosen from the best available talent but, in spite of her brother's later patronage of the serious scholarship of the French renaissance, with its real interest in Greek, it is not surprising that Marguerite's later circle should have been chiefly restricted to authors in the vernacular, and to translators. To have replied to the two letters Erasmus was to write to her on 28 September 1525 and 13 August 1527 would have required a cultural range wider than that which her limited upbringing had already imposed on her by the date of her brother's accession.

François was taken away from his mother by the king on 3 August 1508, and it was the king who arranged the marriage on 2 December 1509 of Marguerite, still aged 17, with Charles d'Alençon, a soldier, born in 1489, of conservative tastes and with no interest in the new renaissance culture. The purpose of the match was to put an end to a feud between the houses of Angoulême and Alençon about the succession of Armagnac. The château at Alençon was vast, austere and Gothic. Alençon's pious mother had paid off the debts of his father, but Italian influence had not yet penetrated to Alençon, and Marguerite missed the airy lightness of the Loire valley's renaissance culture. Her relationship with her husband was perhaps less chilly than once was thought, but her future remained uncertain. She

returned to court at Amboise from time to time, received her mother's visits at Alençon, and must have speculated on the sex of the babies being carried by the queen in 1510 and 1511. Both were daughters. François remained heir.

Marguerite, having heard advent preached at Amboise in 1513, went with her husband to stay with her mother at Cognac, where they were joined by François, who made a solemn entry there on 4 January 1514. On 10 January they heard of the queen's death at the age of 38. Neither Louise de Savoie nor François hid their satisfaction. With Alençon and Marguerite they attended the funeral at Blois, and on 18 May Marguerite and her mother naturally attended the wedding at Saint-Germain–en–Laye of François and Claude. Their future seemed bright until the marriage was announced between the 53-year-old Louis XII and the 17-year-old Mary Tudor, sister of Henry VIII. Alençon and François were sent to meet the bride at Abbeville, and the wedding took place on 9 October. Marguerite also attended the coronation of the new queen at Saint-Denis in November, no doubt sharing the surprise of the court at the way her brother risked openly flirting with his father-in-law's new bride. Louis XII ardently wanted a son. Marguerite and her mother retired to Romorantin. On the night of 31 December the exhausted Louis XII died peacefully, and François I was king.

He immediately made Alençon lieutenant general of Armagnac, Normandy, and Brittany and second ranking person in France, a title that was actually lucrative rather than honorific. It allowed Marguerite or her husband to create a master of each trade in each town, posts which could be sold. François's coronation took place on 25 January 1515, having been held up for the three weeks necessary for Mary to declare that she was not pregnant, and there was a solemn entry into Paris on 15 February, followed by a succession of further gifts and privileges from the king to his elder sister and her husband. Marguerite, for whom the early years of marriage had been tinged with the gloom of life at Alençon and the anxieties about her brother's probable succession, now entered a period during which life was more obviously enjoyable, full of courtly festivities and entertainments rather than less formal frivolities, but also more serious in that she was able and called on to play a useful role in the development of state strategy during the early years of her brother's reign. It did not go unremarked by the chroniclers that Marguerite was fulfilling the role that might have been taken by a more energetic queen than Claude. It was Marguerite who presided in 1520 at the Field of the Cloth of Gold.

The spirit of the courts of Europe, with Charles I in Spain, Henry VIII in England and François I in France, was youthful. Military expertise and skills were prized and practised at court festivities as much as dancing, music-making, and versifying, in France first at Blois, Amboise, and Romorantin, then from 1519 at Saint-Germain-en-Laye, from 1526 at Chenonceaux and Chambord, and then from 1528 at Fontainebleau. In 1515 Marguerite, her mother, and the queen had all travelled together via Arles to Marseilles to meet François, returning victorious from Marignan, near Milan. Splendidly apparelled, as evidently she often was, Marguerite held Claude's train when she was anointed queen at Saint-Denis on 9 May 1517. She never, even at this period of her life, forgot the administration of her newly acquired wealth, and of the estates she had acquired. In the face of some opposition from Lizet and the Paris parlement, the king bestowed on her the duchy of Berry as a thankyou present for three weeks of entertainment in Normandy in the autumn of

1517, possibly with the further intention of allowing her independence from her husband, should she ever need it. Marguerite also began to interest herself in religious questions, even during the first five years of her brother's reign.

On 28 February 1519 the queen gave birth to a son, and Marguerite became godmother to the future Henri II. The godfather was the pope. This was a year of feasting, balls, jousts and exceedingly lavish entertainments, many lasting several days, especially those connected either with births and marriages, or with the visits to the French provincial towns on which Marguerite accompanied François, successfully promoting in France the consciousness that it was a single realm. The royal party was at Cognac for the Lent of 1520, welcomed on arrival by pagan gods, mock battles, the re-enactment of mythological scenes, fireworks, a dinner, and a night's dancing in a decor of tapestries representing Petrarch's *Trionfi*. Although the festivities continued for days, with canons, trumpets, tournaments, jousting, masked balls, and heavy feasting, Lent was not forgotten. François I daily attended Mass and vespers and heard a sermon preached. When Marguerite and her husband returned to Normandy to see to the proper running of their by now complex affairs, Marguerite's mother-in-law renounced all her possessions, partly in Marguerite's favour, and ended her days as a nun. The gaiety of court life in 1520 was, however, halted by an outbreak of plague.

But from 1521 Marguerite's life changed again. Especially in view of her social position, the realization that, for whatever reason, she was unable to bear her husband a child must have had a psychological effect, although we cannot date it, and above all nothing allows us to regard Marguerite's metaphysical interest in speculative mysticism and her committed religious devotion as phenomena merely of compensation, or even sublimation. She was in fact to have children by her second marriage, a son who died and Jeanne d'Albret, herself to become the mother of Henri de Navarre, later Henri IV. Meanwhile, however, the Italian campaigns became more serious once Charles I, king of Spain, had become the emperor Charles V, and France was increasingly isolated in Europe. Marguerite's first surviving letter to Briçonnet, the bishop of Meaux, pleads with him to intercede with God to protect her husband, charged with safeguarding the northeast region of France. From at the latest 1519 Marguerite had shown a real interest in having properly pastoral bishops appointed. In spite of the strong disapproval to be shown in the *Heptaméron* at the lechery and avarice of the clergy, monks, nuns, and mendicants, she founded a monastery at Essai in the winter of 1519–1520, seeking to assure her own salvation, and did not herself cease to frequent monasteries and convents for occasional purposes of pious retreat.

Marguerite must have known Guillaume Briçonnet from soon after her brother's accession. Born about 1470, Briçonnet, whose father was to take orders after the death of his wife and also rise to become a bishop and a cardinal, was appointed bishop of Lodève in 1489. He early became interested in the reform of the clergy and, while still at Lodève, formed an esteem for Josse Clichtove, who may well have introduced to Briçonnet Jacques Lefèvre d'Etaples, whose collaborator he was. Among the monasteries reformed by Briçonnet was that of Saint-Germain-des-Prés, of which his father made him abbot in October 1507, and where he brought Lefèvre to continue his work on the "commentaries" on Aristotle, often little more than classroom notes, his editions of the mystics and mystical theologians—the pseudo-

Denis, the *Corpus hermeticum*, Rámon Lull, Nicolas of Cusa, and others—and his scriptural translations and editions, first of five versions of the Psalter in the 1509 *Psalterium quincuplex*, and then of the epistles of St Paul. When Briçonnet was made bishop of Meaux in 1516 he went to Rome, from where, probably inspired by Gian Matteo Giberti, the future bishop of Verona, he returned to undertake the reform of his diocese. He intended to use Marguerite's influence to have its arrangements adopted as the paradigm for a systematic reform of the French church.

There was trouble with the Sorbonne, and Briçonnet, supported by Clichtove, who had come out strongly against Erasmus, ended up having to pass anti-Lutheran decrees. In the meanwhile, however, he had succeeded in persuading Lefèvre to move from Saint-Germain-des-Prés to Meaux, first as administrator of the Hôpital in April 1521, then as vicar-general "in spiritualibus" from 1523, to lead a reforming team mostly of translators, including Michel d'Arande, Pierre Caroli, Gérard Roussel, Guillaume Farel, François Vatable, and Martial Masurier. Some eventually joined the schism and what was left of the team split up in 1525. Thereafter Marguerite was to protect or employ a number of them at Nérac. Lefèvre, titularly Marguerite's librarian, finally issued a complete translation of the Bible into French. He had tacitly and grudgingly conceded victory to Erasmus in a dispute about scriptural interpretation towards the end of the second decade of the century. It was Lefèvre's mystical spirituality with which Briçonnet, in furtherance of his ambition to use Marguerite in the interests of advancing practical reform in the French church, filled the long letters he wrote to Marguerite between 1521 and 1524. These sometimes verge on being letters of spiritual direction.

Luther had undertaken to defend his theses against the sale of indulgences on 1 November 1517. By the following year his writings were clearly heretical. The bull of excommunication, which did not mention heresy, was dated 15 June 1520. Neither Luther's original reformatory endeavours, nor Briçonnet's attempts at reform in France, and not even the life-long activity of Lefèvre d'Etaples, were essentially humanist in any sense other than that they depended on the translation of scripture from the original languages. The Sorbonne wished above all to defend the traditional Vulgate Latin text as a touchstone of ecclesiastical authority in interpreting revelation, in ordering the Church's moral teaching and in ordaining the liturgical rites in which dogmatic commitment was reflected. The principal thrust of the reforming forces, apart from the vernacular dissemination of the sources of revelation, was towards a renewed emphasis on interior religious experience as against exteriorly prescribed practices, not themselves necessarily experienced as morally or spiritually fulfilling.

In attempting to understand Marguerite's position, it is essential to distinguish between reform which Marguerite believed in and wanted to protect; heresy, which eventually entailed schism and with which she would have nothing to do; and humanism, which never really engaged her interest, except marginally, in so far as translation was necessary for the prosecution of reform. Furthermore, her emphasis on the intensity of religious experience was largely speculative rather than devotional. This emphasis was quite compatible with a belief in the efficacy of traditional rites and practices, and with an acceptance of the Church's teaching authority in faith and morals going well beyond mere deference on political grounds; it was consistent with the whole spectrum of coarse medieval values. Marguerite could combine within her personal reactions not only the fear of hell that was responsible for toppling so much genuine medieval religious devotion over the border into superstition, but also a tolerance of the rougher, physical exercises which accompanied court entertainments, and the openness of some contes of the *Heptaméron* about sexual behaviour, particularly among those who should have been celibate. She also herself had an unusually strong affectivity and an organizational ability which enormously boosted her contribution to the running of her brother's kingdom.

It is clear that the outward circumstances of Marguerite's life changed radically many times: on the accession of Louis XII, on her marriage, on the accession of her brother, on the developments in Europe's political and religious conflicts about 1520, again after the defeat of François I at Pavia in 1525 and his incarceration in Madrid, on the death of her husband and her second marriage, again when she lost influence at court in 1542, and finally when her brother died in March 1547. However, the development of her interior, spiritual life shows waves of personal disquiet rather than intellectual or moral discontinuities. None of her writing on different registers was incompatible with anything else she wrote at a different date. In particular, her religious preoccupations clearly began during the years of triumph at court, just as her political and domestic activities continued during the period of the correspondence with Briçonnet and the composition of the most intense of the spiritual verse. What is striking about the dates is the way in which they suggest that any internal dissatisfaction in her life, to whose assuaging the spiritual relationship with Briçonnet may have led, seems to have crystallized within her not as the result of a disillusion with her marriage, or even because of her infertility, but on the realisation of the hollowness of the court success for which she once pined and which was from 1515 offered to the point of satiety.

The poet Clément Marot must have entered Marguerite's service in 1519. He was certainly a member of her household by 1520, and in 1521 he wrote back reassuringly from Champagne, where he was in her husband's camp as secretary. Marguerite's husband did not himself either mention her in his letters or write to her, and the copy which Marguerite had made of her letters to and from Briçonnet from 12 June 1521, presupposing previous acquaintance, suggests that Marguerite's relationship with the bishop of Meaux was reaching the point at which it seemed appropriate to keep a formal copy of the correspondence, if only for her own consultation. In 1521 her young aunt and close friend Philiberte de Savoie, duchesse de Nemours, had returned to Savoy, and Marguerite showed some anxiety, probably about her husband's chances of safety and success in Champagne. She asked Briçonnet to send her "maître Michel," probably Michel d'Arande, which would imply some knowledge of what Briçonnet was doing at Meaux. D'Arande did not come, but it was apparently he who wrote two letters of spiritual advice, which Marguerite wrote about to Philiberte de Savoie, with whom she shared her enthusiasm for the contorted spiritual metaphors with which Briçonnet filled his letters.

Marguerite now declared herself the spiritual daughter of Briçonnet, who declared in a style innocent of any effort at renaissance elegance that she was the daughter and spouse of God alone. Marguerite was none the less kept busy by her own affairs, particularly the contested gift of the Berry income, and by her political role. She was now being increasingly sought out by foreign rulers and domestic princes as a channel of communication with the sources of power, for which she was also called on to speak. In September she took her mother to Meaux. They were Briçonnet's guests, but Marguerite was more obviously worried about temporal than about spiritual affairs.

Her letters to Briçonnet are still affected and stylized in ways that the early spiritual verse only suggests. Briçonnet's rendition of Lefèvre's mystical doctrine so wraps up comparatively simple spiritual teaching in Gothically complex images and verbal games as to make it impenetrably stilted and precious. His letters of spiritual direction, a genre in which the literature of France is extraordinarily rich, lack discernment, sensitivity, and often even simple intelligence. Briçonnet's projected reform was vastly over-ambitious and unnecessarily aggressive, but might well have succeeded if it had limited its aims to the elimination of what was obviously superstitious, and insisted, like the *devotio moderna*, simply on the primacy of interior religious experience over the performance of formal rites. Unhappily, a certain lack of imagination, coupled with administrative ineptitude, simply caused conservative reaction to reform, even humanist reform, to crystallize into a fear of what was covertly schismatic, Lutheran, and heretical.

If it is not always easy to understand exactly what Briçonnet is trying to say in his letters to Marguerite, it is quite clear how liable from the beginning he was to miscalculate his activity in the way he did. The difficulty is to penetrate beneath the stylization which Marguerite considered appropriate in her letters to him to know what spiritual benefit she actually derived from the advice and instruction she constantly asked for. Her alms-giving increased, but so did her use of metaphorical cliché playing on death to the world, on burning with the love of God, on contempt for worldly knowledge, and on the whole repertoire of commonplaces concerning lambs, wolves, sowing, harvesting, crumbs, and spiritual hunger from the late medieval vocabulary of religious intensity.

Marguerite was humble, devout, and aware of her lack of a serious education. She was deeply concerned for her own spiritual welfare, and she wanted to spread throughout France the cultivation of an interior religious spirit which would inform a devotional practice that had often become empty. She probably sensed that a properly executed implementation of Briçonnet's reformatory principles over the whole country was not only religiously desirable, but also politically necessary to save France from possible schism and certain civil disaster. Though no theologian, she could still see that the Sorbonne's reactionary attitudes were unreasonable and dangerous. She obviously needed from Briçonnet the encouragement with which he was willing so remorselessly to ply her. No one, of course, could yet have foreseen the magnitude of the catastrophe which was to take the form of the religious wars, whose outbreak a successful reform of the diocese of Meaux in the early 1520s might well have made unnecessary.

Marguerite's mother-in-law, now a professed nun, died on 2 November 1521. She is remembered in a strongly stylized 74-line account of her death interpolated into Marguerite's *Les Prisons*. By the beginning of 1522 France's political situation looked exceedingly vulnerable. The emperor controlled Spain and Germany, was winning in Italy, and was allied with the pope and the English. Weightier preoccupations began to take over from court festivities. Late in 1521 Marguerite was in Lyons with her brother, and early in 1522 in Alençon with her husband, reforming the financial administration. That summer there was a break in the correspondence with Briçonnet, re-started at Marguerite's request during the autumn. For an instant she thought she might be pregnant. Briçonnet saw the grave illness of Louise de Savoie as God's punishment on account of the king's inadequate gratitude for the divine protection accorded to him. D'Arande was now spending protracted periods with Marguerite and her mother. The Sorbonne was becoming worried, suspecting d'Arande of Lutheran tendencies, and Marguerite of listening too readily. D'Arande, an Augustinian, was denounced in November 1522 by the king's confessor, Guillaume Petit, for sermons preached at court. When the king's displeasure was made clear, Petit said he had been misrepresented, and the Sorbonne backed down.

Early in 1523 Marguerite was mixing her courtly activities with an attempt to encourage wherever she could a deeper interior piety, but was also much taken up with domestic concerns and with politics. She did, however, intervene when Berquin's house was perquisitioned on 13 May 1523. That occasion involved a series of misunderstandings and changes of mind, and Berquin's books were burnt against the king's wishes, although Berquin was himself released by royal guards from what was technically legal custody. Marguerite was now sometimes acting almost as if she were sovereign in her own right. The Connétable Charles de Bourbon had gone over to the imperial side, and the whole eastern border of France was now being challenged, as well as the south-west from across the Pyrenees.

In the summer of 1523 Marguerite felt in urgent need of Briçonnet's consoling presence, but he would not come, perhaps still afraid, as in late 1522, that her ardour might be compromising his reform. "Cover up the fire," he had written, "for the wood you want to burn is too green." He wanted more to have pressure put on the king in his episcopal appointments than to inflame the perhaps dangerous fervour of Marguerite's religious enthusiasms. In 1524 he tried to restrain her fury when the archbishop of Bourges successfully ignored her formal orders and stopped d'Arande after his first sermon from preaching Lent in the cathedral. It is possible, if unsafe, to guess from a long letter of Briçonnet of 14 June 1524 that Marguerite was worried about the state of her marriage. She was never explicit about such matters.

Early in 1524 the queen and Marguerite's mother were both ill. François went to join his army in July, accompanied as far as Bourges by his sister and their mother, recovered but enfeebled, leaving his sick wife at Blois. They arrived on 24 July, and the ladies learnt of Claude's death on 26 July before they had arrived back at Blois. Marguerite had been much affected only weeks earlier by receiving news of the death of Philiberte de Savoie. Her mother became ill again. Marguerite was frightened of the effect on the king of his wife's death; their eight-year-old daughter, Marguerite's niece Charlotte, was already grievously ill with the measles which would cause her death early in September. Marguerite herself would now be responsible for the upbringing of at least the two remaining royal princesses. Her position at court had been due partly at any rate to the queen's constant pregnancies. Claude had borne François I three sons and four daughters, in order Louise (1515), Charlotte (1516), François (1517), Henri (1519), Madeleine (1520), Charles (1522), and Marguerite (1523). Only Henri and the princess Marguerite survived their father.

The duchesse Marguerite went with her mother to Lyons, where the military situation had improved. François I held

Marseilles against imperial troops led by Bourbon, and followed the retreating army to Milan, which he took. Marguerite wrote a rough account of the situation and received in reply the letter to her from Briçonnet, dated 18 November 1524, the last we have. It is unlikely to have been the last he wrote, but after the interruption of Pavia, Spain, and the situation occasioned by her remarriage, Marguerite's need for the spiritual support afforded by Briçonnet presumably diminished. All we can know with certainty is that Briçonnet had helped Marguerite through a period of private anxiety whose occasion can be a matter only of conjecture.

François, having taken Milan, sent part of his forces to attack Naples, leaving himself vulnerable to the terrible defeat inflicted on him at Pavia on 24 February 1525, with the biggest slaughter of the French nobility since Agincourt. The only important nobleman to escape death or capture was Alençon, Marguerite's husband, whose death on Tuesday 11 April, after his return home, must have been partly caused by shock. François's strategy seems to have been faulty. He had not counted on the damage that could be done by the hidden Spanish arquebusiers. He himself had gone on fighting after his horse had fallen, before surrendering to the Viceroy of Naples. Thanks to his armour he was unhurt. He was taken to Pavia and served a meal by Bourbon and the Viceroy, and wrote to his mother the same day to reassure her. The emperor heard of François's capture only on 10 March. He ordered him to be well treated, and had him moved to Pizzighettone, west of Cremona, for three months, then to Genoa, and finally, at his own request, to Spain rather than Naples. His mother received his letter on 1 March. Marguerite sent him the epistles of Saint Paul. In Spain he was lavishly treated, entertained, given presents, and taken to the Alcazar in Madrid, where he was kept from 11 August 1525 until February 1526.

Louise de Savoie was regent until her son's return on 17 March 1526, in exchange for his two eldest sons, who were to be kept hostages in Spain. They were François the dauphin and Henri, duc d'Orléans, dauphin after his brother's death in 1536, and later Henri II. Louise remained throughout her son's captivity at Saint-Just, just outside Lyons, and Marguerite did not have much time to mourn her husband. Talk about marrying her to Bourbon started in Europe's chancelleries before Alençon was buried. As soon as it could be arranged, Marguerite left for Spain, partly to share her brother's sorrows, partly to arrange for his release, and partly to negotiate a peace treaty. She travelled in great haste, redoubled when she learnt that her brother was ill. Without waiting for the receptions laid on for her arrival, she pressed ahead on horseback, leaving her suite to keep up with her if they could. On the evening of 19 September she was in Madrid. François was too ill to recognize her, and for three days, until he lost consciousness, the fever got worse.

Diplomatically, Marguerite achieved little. François recovered, and she was involved in a plot for his escape which was betrayed. The ultimate resolution of the situation was chiefly engineered by her mother, well assisted by professional negotiators. Marguerite left Madrid on 27 November, deeply depressed, arriving at Narbonne on 23 December. Further progress towards meeting her mother was delayed by a fall from her horse, and by her mother's gout. Though dejected, she was now a heroine. She had probably helped to make possible her brother's re-marriage to Eleanor, the emperor's sister and queen of Portugal. During her absence the parlement de Paris had taken action against Berquin again, but Marguerite was able to obtain his release through the king's intervention, and the king himself had intervened from Madrid on 12 November, ordering the parlement de Paris to suspend proceedings against Lefèvre, Caroli, and Roussel, all of whom took refuge in Strasburg. Briçonnet had issued his anti-Lutheran decrees in 1525. Farel had joined the reform in Switzerland, and Masurier was forced to recant. The Meaux reform had failed, but François protected the principal members of Briçonnet's team. Lefèvre took charge of the royal library at Blois, Roussel became Marguerite's almoner, and Caroli was allowed to resume preaching in Paris.

Marguerite spent the summer of 1526 with the court on the Loire; it ended with the formal funeral of the late queen. The king spent some time visiting Bordeaux, Cognac, Angoulême, and Amboise, broke his arm in a riding accident on 9 June, and took up with a new mistress, Anne d'Heilly, an 18-year-old lady-in-waiting to his mother. An earlier mistress, the shadowy Françoise de Foix, comtesse de Châteaubriant, had been cast off before Pavia. After the death of his mother in September 1531, François was to make Anne governess of his daughters before marrying her off to Jean be Brosse, seigneur de Penthièvre, making him first comte then duc d'Etampes.

Endless rumours circulated about a possible re-marriage for Marguerite, but quite suddenly she married Henri d'Albret, king of the tiny kingdom of Navarre, still in Spanish hands. He was a national hero after escaping from captivity in the castle of Pavia. The wedding took place on 30 January 1527 and was followed by eight days of festivities and tournaments at Saint-Germain. At the end of the year the couple paid a brief visit to Navarre. On 16 November 1528, after a difficult delivery during which her life was in danger, Marguerite gave birth to her first child, Jeanne d'Albret, the mother of Henri IV. She vowed that she would make a pilgrimage to Notre-Dame de Cléry if she recovered, and acquitted her obligation in the following March.

She had again intervened successfully with the Sorbonne on behalf of Pierre Caroli, now one of her private chaplains, but on 17 April 1529 she was unable, in the king's absence, to save Berquin from the consequences of an imprudent appeal to the parlement, and he was strangled before being burnt immediately after condemnation and sentence. By this date both François and the emperor were anxious for a peace treaty. Margaret of Savoy, regent of the Netherlands, although initially cautious, agreed to mediate. She was the sister-in-law of Louise de Savoie and the emperor's aunt. She met Louise de Savoie with Marguerite at Cambrai. Talks began on 5 July and lasted nearly a month. The treaty was finally signed on 3 August 1529, and celebrated on 5 August in the cathedral in the king's presence. Essentially it was a re-working of the ad hoc treaty of Madrid under which François had been released, but meant that France, against an enormous indemnity, would after all be allowed to keep Burgundy, and that the princes would be returned. Marguerite's situation was difficult, as she was in no position to insist on the return to France of Navarre.

Early in 1530 Marguerite was again pregnant. She was obviously beginning to be known for her patronage not of the new learning but of the old generation of poets. Her praises were sung by Macrin and Nicolas Bourbon. At 3 a.m. on 15 July, she gave birth to a son, Jean, who was to die that year on Christmas day. In the meanwhile Marguerite showed signs of boredom. She now missed some of the court distractions of the early years of the reign. When her son died, she at least seemed in public to find within herself the spiritual resources to thank God for this manifestation of his will. Almost immediately afterwards she and her doctor both thought for a brief period that she was again pregnant. By the end of February it was clear that she was not.

Joining the king at Chambord, she went with the court to Paris for the coronation of the new queen Eleanor. There were entertainments and tournaments before the coronation at Saint-Denis on 5 March 1531 and the solemn entry into Paris on 16 March. That Lent she attended the sermons of Gérard Roussel, and she seems to have spent most of the summer at Saint-Germain. She inquired into the infant mortality rate at the Paris Hôtel-Dieu, whose reform she was to initiate, and at the end of August accompanied her mother to Fontainebleau, from which the plague drove them to Romorantin. They had got no further than Grèz-en-Gâtinais when Louise de Savoie's health gave way. She died piously on 22 September. Héroët, Macault, Saint-Gelais, Macrin, Marot, and Alemanni wrote tributes. Marguerite's own emotion appears to have been deeper than on previously recorded similar occasions.

In 1532 Marguerite was with the queen, following her brother, and largely occupied arranging the marriages of her husband's sisters and establishing the dauphin as governor of Normandy. Most of the year she was in the west of France. For some time now Marguerite had been writing verse, although nothing was published until *Le Miroir de l'ame pecheresse, ouquel elle recongnoist ses faultes et pechez, aussi ses grâces et benefices à elle faicts par Jesuchrist son espoux* appeared at Alençon, published anonymously by Simon Dubois and dated 1531, which may well mean early in 1532 according to our new style of dating. In the first three months of 1533, new style, there were three further printings, now including Marot's translation of the sixth psalm and "L'instruction et Foy d'ung chrestien." Two of the printings identified the author: *Le Miroir de treschrestienne princesse M. de France, auquel elle voit et son neant et son tout.*

Marguerite spent the carnival days attending the festivities and talking earnestly with ambassadors. When the king left for Picardy, she had Lent preached at the Louvre by Roussel and two Augustinians, Bertault and Courault. Four of the newly appointed royal "lecteurs" are said to have attended, suggesting that the links between evangelicalism and philological humanism, still associated in France at this date chiefly with Budé, were becoming publicly clear. Sermons were held daily. They were popular and evangelical, and aroused the reactionary fury of the theological faculty, led by Noël Beda, determined to impose the Sorbonne's power to define and impose the limits of orthodoxy of belief, and its derivative, religious practice, which, for complex misguided but not fundamentally dishonourable reasons had simply come adrift from the personal religious experience of the faithful.

In 1533, Easter was on 13 April. On 7 May the Sorbonne, headquarters of the theology faculty, ordered a list of suspect propositions from Roussel's sermons to be drawn up, and approved it on 12 May. There followed a pamphlet war and attempts to stir up popular unrest, particularly against Marguerite and her husband. On 18 May the king exiled Beda, had Roussel put under house arrest, and asked the chancellor to hold an enquiry. Eventually François left for the south of France. When her husband set off to join the king, Marguerite was again pregnant. Early in October, a student skit at the Collège de Navarre, one of four solely devoted to theology, portrayed Marguerite preaching heresy at the instigation of "Mégère,"—the name of one of the furies—representing Roussel (M[aître] Gér[ard Roussel]). Marguerite had the college searched by archers, and two of its senior members were arrested.

The faculty now had a list drawn up of books containing suspect doctrines, and included the second edition of the *Miroir*. When the king wrote to ask for an explanation, the rector, Nicolas Cop, called a meeting of all four faculties: theology, canon law, medicine, and arts, civil law having long been exiled to Poitiers, Orléans, and Toulouse. Cop came from the humanist college of Sainte-Barbe with its strong Iberian connections. Its titular principal, Diego de Gouvea, was an ally of Beda, but he was invariably absent as a peripatetic judge acting on behalf of the King of Portugal, and the college was in fact in the hands of his humanist and evangelical nephew Andrea de Gouvea. The theologians denied that the *Miroir* was on the list for any reason other than that it had no printed imprimatur, and took it off, the probability being that it had actually been put on because the new edition included the Marot psalm translation, and therefore contributed to popularizing dissemination of vernacular scripture, which was undermining the theological authority of the Vulgate. No less than 58 masters of theology signed a document to say that they had no knowledge of the content of the *Miroir* at all, and that the faculty as such had neither approved nor disapproved of it.

It was on the feast of All Saints, 1 November 1533, that the rector delivered the customary sermon to open the academic year. He gave an exhortation on the gospel of the day, itself a provocative gesture not alleviated by the fact that the appointed text was that on the eight beatitudes, with prominence given to "Blessed be those who suffer persecution…" After the sermon, although in no great hurry, Calvin, who had spent the summer in Paris at Sainte-Barbe, Cop himself, and Andrea de Gouvea all found it expedient to leave Paris. Beda was obliged to make an amende honorable before being confined at Mont Saint-Michel, and strenuous efforts were made to integrate evangelical and humanistic elements into what was briefly envisaged almost as a reformed Gallican church on the early Anglican model, although without the schism occasioned in England by the king's divorce. The death-knell of those efforts was sounded on the publication in Basle, dated 1536, of the first Latin edition of Calvin's *Christianae religionis institutio*.

On the night of the 17 to 18 October 1534 the famous fly-sheets known as the "placards," violently denouncing the Mass, were posted throughout France, in several places in Paris, at Orléans, Blois, Tours, and Rouen, and at Amboise, where one was found in the royal apartments. Written by Antoine Marcourt, the first pastor of Neuchâtel, and printed in that town, the placards' text denied the sacrificial nature of the Mass, the doctrine of transsubstantiation, and the real presence. A fourth paragraph maintained that the Mass was a memorial service, not a miracle. Doctrinally the text went well beyond Luther and represented the militant sacramentarian position which had been taken by Zwingli.

It created a hysterical public reaction, and official policy, which had never protected anything that clearly led to schism, or anyone other than a few humanist scholars and evangelical preachers, all at least arguably orthodox, immediately became repressive at the aggressive challenge of heterodoxy and the clear threat of schism. The persecution was initiated not by the king, although he subsequently ratified it, but by the parlement,

and there was a six-month wave of expiatory processions, denunciations, arrests, and burnings. On 13 January 1535 there was further outrage when copies of Marcourt's *Petit traité… de la sainte eucharistie* were left in the streets of Paris. The publication of all new books was banned until further notice, and a huge procession of the Blessed Sacrament was ordered for 21 January.

Marguerite left the court. She was henceforward to spend more time in Béarn, and in November and December 1535 toured Navarre. It was probably at Nérac that Marguerite received, sheltered, and sometimes employed refugees like Marot, whom she recommended to the court of Ferrara. It is possible that Calvin, still a young humanist whose only published work was a commentary on Seneca, was received at Nérac. Marguerite's relationship with François remained intimate, and that with the new pope, Paul III, was cordial. She remained in the south, however, apparently picking up the old task of confirming the unity of France by visiting its provinces. She met François at Dijon late in 1535, and was with the court at Lyons early in 1536, as François prepared to invade Savoy. She took Bonaventure des Périers into her service, and threw herself with enthusiasm into preparations for the campaign. The French army took Piedmont before having to retreat in front of the imperial troops advancing into Provence. On 10 August François's eldest son died suddenly at Tournus, almost certainly from natural causes, although Sebastiano de Montecuculli, one of his squires, was accused of poisoning him and executed with great cruelty, and apparently to the disgust of Marguerite, at Lyons on 7 October.

Marguerite's occupations now became more peaceable. She arranged for Marot's pardon and return, probably met Dolet and Héroët, interested herself in the project for a university at Nîmes. Having promoted heavily the marriage of the king's daughter Madeleine to James V of Scotland, Marguerite attended the wedding, on 1 January 1537, with its attendant festivities. She took a fuller part than hitherto in the organisation of public assistance for the poor. For the second time she reorganized the Hôpital at Alençon. There are signs that she was much hurt by the notorious infidelities of her husband, but that she was working in concert with him to reach an agreement with the emperor Charles V about the Spanish portion of the kingdom of Navarre, which François wanted to take by force.

Although relations between them continued to be as cordial as ever throughout 1537 and 1538, Marguerite and her brother were drifting apart politically, even if the evidence also strongly suggests that in the interests of recovering that part of Navarre in Spanish hands her husband Henri de Navarre was pursuing initiatives with the emperor to which Marguerite was not herself privy. François's refusal to include any reference to the Navarre territory in the original Madrid treaty was now being interpreted by Henri de Navarre, with some justification, as an invitation to look after the recovery of his kingdom himself, but François did not want the matter dragged in to clog up more complicated bargaining. From 1538 François, fearing that his sister would arrange a marriage for her daughter which would suit her interests and her husband's, but not his, had the young Jeanne d'Albret kept at Plessis-lez-Tours.

It was in 1538 that François's foreign policy changed to one of friendship towards the emperor, although its aim remained the same, the recovery of Milan. The minister responsible for the change was the Connétable Anne de Montmorency, who controlled foreign policy from 1538 until 1540, but the real impulse for change came from the pope, who urgently needed lasting peace between France and Spain both for the general council, finally moved to Trent, and for a crusade against the infidel. In 1539 the emperor travelled through France, with lavish entertainments and displays laid on everywhere he passed. Nothing had changed, however, and hostilities between Charles and François were bound to break out again. Meanwhile between 15 May and 20 June 1538 the emperor, the pope, and, reluctantly, François, had met at Nice, although never all together. Marguerite was naturally there.

It must have been very soon after this that Marguerite composed parts at least of her most important poems and, although the dates are not quite certain, it seems to have been in the winter of 1539–40 that Marguerite's daughter was grievously ill at Plessis. Marguerite immediately left the triumphal entertainments laid on in Paris for the emperor's visit and plainly travelled taut with anxiety. At Bourg-la-Reine she had to stop, and spent an hour praying feverishly in church for the recovery of her daughter's health. Yet she seemed composed to accept God's will should Jeanne die. It is a measure of the intensity of her anxiety that she forced herself to anticipate receiving the chilling news that she was dead, although, when news came, it was good. The fever had subsided.

François was resolutely opposed to any marriage between Jeanne d'Albret and the emperor's son. The fragile understanding between François and the emperor was collapsing, and with it Montmorency's policy and power. The duchesse d'Etampes saw the chance to topple him. In October 1540 the emperor invested his own son with the duchy of Milan. Earlier that year François had simply accepted a request for the hand of the 12-year-old Jeanne d'Albret from William, duke of Cleves, who was 24, offering to placate her father, his brother-in-law, with an army to re-take Navarre. Cleves, in league with his brother-in-law, the elector of Saxony, was a small German prince, but he had now definitively cut himself free from the emperor, and the marriage allowed François to keep alive his relationship with the German princes.

Jeanne d'Albret had finally consented to marry Cleves, but had changed her mind. Marguerite had dreamed of a much grander match, and her husband had nearly persuaded the emperor to ask outright for Jeanne's hand for his son. Jeanne was threatened by the king with imprisonment if she refused consent. Eventually both Marguerite and her daughter gave way, and the wedding took place at Châtellerault on 14 June 1541. Jeanne's refusal on the eve of the wedding had been so absolute that her mother had had her whipped. Montmorency was actually forced physically to carry the bride, fastened tightly into her wedding dress, to the altar. The next day he left court, not to return during François's reign.

Not only were appearances saved for François by the wedding, but they were simultaneously betrayed by the realities. The marriage was not consummated, and Jeanne returned after it to Plessis. The pope was eventually to annul the marriage in April 1545 after Cleves had surrendered to the emperor at Venloo and become a Catholic again. Marguerite would be present at her daughter's second marriage, to Antoine de Bourbon, in October 1548, just over a year before she herself died.

Marguerite lost some of her old intimacy with her brother, although not the external manifestations of esteem. She also gained in political power until September 1542. Once again she was encouraged to behave as if she had been the real queen of France. What she really thought is by no means clear, since the evidence, partly hearsay and partly smothered in the language of diplomatic protocol, is by no means univocal.

It looks unlikely that Marguerite was now enthusiastic about friendship with the emperor, although she might have been content to let her husband try that way of winning back Navarre. It seems she may have been less enthusiastic about friendship with the pope than her correspondence would lead one to suppose if the letters had not formed part of a diplomatic exchange. She appears to have remained a sincere supporter of her brother's policy, even of friendship with England and the German princes, but certainly of hostility against Spain. What is absolutely clear is the fact that the face value of what Marguerite is known to have written does not accord with the calculated results of her political activity and with ostensibly accurate accounts of her conversation.

That, in her position, Marguerite should have learnt the art of successful dissimulation is not surprising. That she practised it in the prosecution of national, marital, and personal diplomacy successfully enough to take in those she intended to deceive is only to be expected. She was astute, and the formulating, coding, and decoding of political intentions had by now even in northern Europe become a huge industry, employing substantial numbers of high-born diplomats and armies of secretaries in the chancelleries of every state. François may have spent a great deal of his time hunting stags, but, like his sister, he had available a great deal of often professional advice, sifted, sorted, and backed before presentation with different types of advocacy. What is revealing is the extent to which Marguerite's political activities were still determined by her intense affectivity, now, however, also seeking a new outlet in literary composition.

When war with Spain broke out again in July 1542, François had been unwilling to allow himself to be restrained from leading his troops. He was with them when they had to raise camp in September, having failed to take Narbonne. Marguerite returned to Navarre. Like the duchesse d'Etampes, she suddenly lost influence with the king. François followed her to visit her in Navarre on his way to La Rochelle. She became pregnant again, but again lost her child. Marguerite had little to do with the conduct of the war against the emperor, the alliance with the Turks, and the attempt to enlist Scottish support against England during the period from 1542 to 1544. She was disappointed that the final peace treaty, signed at Crépy-en-Laonnais on 18 September 1544, and the consequential arrangements, did not involve Navarre, and she reacted firmly by getting from her daughter at Plessis, on Easter Sunday 1545, the formal documentation on which the annulment of the Cleves marriage would be based.

It is of some importance for the evaluation of Marguerite's religious views that she had welcomed to her court at a date which has not been determined, but which was in or before 1543, two Flemish purveyors of a mystical illuminism which had sufficiently aggravated Calvin to provoke the 1544 pamphlet *Contre la secte fanatique et furieuse des libertins qui se nomment spirituels*. Called Pocque and Quintin, they allowed performance of the rites of the Church, but called for a passive spirituality which depended on an identification between God and the individual close enough to place human activity totally under divine control, so that the human being became analogous to a divine instrument, with the risk inherent in all such spiritualities that the human will would not in the end be considered responsible for its own attitudes and actions. Calvin went so far as to write to Marguerite, warning her of the spiritual peril in which she was putting herself.

In September 1545 the king's second son, Charles, duc d'Orléans, died suddenly, leaving the succession to Henri, married since 28 October 1533, when he was 15, to the 12-year-old Catherine de Medici. Their first son, ensuring the further succession, had just been born in 1544. Marguerite was encouraged in her hopes that the emperor's son would now marry Jeanne. François had other plans, however, and she left court at the end of 1545 as the king was convalescing after a serious illness, her husband furious at the frustration of his hopes of incorporating into France the totality of his kingdom, and herself disappointed. In 1546 she did not intervene, as once she might have done, when Dolet was condemned and executed, but spent her time seeing to the administration of her husband's estates. A storm at Cauterets in September gave her the idea for the setting of the *Heptaméron*, but she was now often tired. It would not be surprising if the lavish dispensation of nervous energy for half a century had not exhausted even her robust constitution. Increasingly she spent days at a nearby convent, and the pope authorized the abbess, always to be accompanied, to visit Marguerite at her château 12 times a year.

In December François asked her to come to him at court, but she was too tired to face the journey in the winter weather. She had sent him a doublet she had made for Christmas, and would come when the weather improved. In March 1547 she made a retreat at the monastery at Tusson and heard that her brother had been saddened at the death of Henry VIII, for so long his friend and opponent, on 28 January. François spent his last weeks incessantly travelling. At Rambouillet he fell fatally ill. Marguerite seems to have thought only of her brother. At Tusson they did not dare tell her when he died on Thursday 31 March 1547. She stayed on at the monastery for four months after she did wrest the news from an elderly nun, experiencing some relief in prayer, and meditating on death. She wrote most of the *Chansons*, the *Comédie sur le trépas du Roy*, the *Navire*, and the last book of the *Prisons*.

The projected marriage between Jeanne and Antoine de Bourbon-Vendôme had been the work of the cardinal de Tournon, now stripped of any influence by Henri II, who was himself against the marriage. Marguerite was unsure of her relationship with the new king, worried about the continuance of her pension, and not allowed any part in determining her daughter's fate. Henri II finally decided for the marriage with Bourbon, although for a moment François de Lorraine, comte d'Aumale, a Guise, seemed to offer an alternative choice. When the papal nuntius left his successor a note of those in France, starting with the king and queen, whose confidence he should try to win, Marguerite's name was 11th and her husband's was not there at all. Diane de Poitiers had become an all-important figure. Marguerite did not attend the coronation of Henri II, tried to postpone consent to the projected marriage, took the waters briefly at Cauterets, and found pretexts not to go to court, where consent to the marriage would have been extracted from her. She turned down an invitation to become godmother to the king's daughter, born in October 1547, and Henri II had to send emissaries to Navarre on two occasions.

Marguerite slowly resigned herself to the marriage. On Ash Wednesday she had had played at Mont-Saint-Marsan a comédie she had written expressing her religious convictions. She had largely lost interest in the affairs of this world since her brother's death. We know little about her life in 1548. She left Navarre in July and was at Lyons in August, where she was present at the solemn entry of Henri II, who was having her correspondence with her husband monitored. The marriage of Jeanne took place on 20 October and the bride, at least, was happy. Marguerite was still working on the *Heptaméron*, and wrote *L'art et usage du souverain mirouer du chrestien*, a product more of devotion than of literature after her return to Pau early in 1549. She was to spend some time alone with Jeanne, to come to like her husband, and to be overcome again by waves of affection as Jeanne left her in early summer for what proved to be the last time. In September Marguerite went to Odos, a château she had had repaired in 1542. Her husband left for Paris in December.

Her final illness was brief, lasting less than three weeks. Finally she lost her voice. She died three days later, in the early hours of Saturday, 21 December 1549.

WORKS

Marguerite d'Angoulême was always referred to as Madame la Duchesse (d'Alençon) until her second marriage in 1527, after which she always called herself the queen of Navarre. It is only relatively recently that interest in her writings has grown sufficiently to ensure that the considerable difficulties involved in making proper texts available were overcome, opening the way to more than rudimentary critical and historical analysis which, however inspired, had to be based on inadequate textual and historical presentation. There remain at least three major areas of difficulty in understanding the works. Firstly, if the letters are for the most part exactly dated, and intelligent guesses have been made about the date of composition of the two major sections of the *Heptaméron*, the apparent impossibility of dating precisely most of the considerable corpus of the poetry poses insoluble problems in its interpretation. Were there changes of emphasis, or changes of mind? The other areas of difficulty are more complex.

Marguerite did not write for publication. She must, it is true, have allowed Dubois to publish the *Miroir* in both its versions, 1531 and 1533, but the overwhelming probability is that she will have written with the intention of showing some at least of what she wrote to members of her entourage, of the court, and of her family. If so, she must have operated a first selection in deciding what to have copied for private circulation and, in the case of the *Miroir* alone, have further authorized its printing. The number of manuscripts of her work which has survived suggests that only very few copies can ever have been made. The result of this method of production for intimate private circulation, or merely for personal satisfaction and subsequent private reference, is that we have no means of knowing what part of her work Marguerite herself would have wished outsiders to see, or how far she wished to entertain, to instruct, to explore, or to move.

We have no alternative but to start by taking together everything which has survived and which we know her to have written, and ourselves deciding whether the interest is more than archival. We need in particular to settle several questions: first, the poetic value of the writings which, often partly reflective or even speculative, were prompted by such traumatic emotional experiences as the deaths which so obviously affected her; second, the nature of the spiritual satisfaction, or alternatively malnutrition, expressed in Marguerite's replies to Briçonnet's sometimes treatise-length epistles, however fascinating her letters may also be for historians of spirituality; and third, to what extent the literary value of the *Heptaméron* is enhanced, constituted, or left untouched by the intervening dialogue of the ten "devisants."

The fourth and greatest difficulty lies in transcending sectarian disputes about Marguerite's religious affiliations. There is still no real consensus about the proper use of terms like humanism, evangelicalism, and Lutheranism, or about the boundaries between orthodoxy, heterodoxy, and reaction in the first half of the sixteenth century. There are still too few specialist historians of late medieval theology, and almost no professional historians of spirituality, so that religious views, attitudes, and reactions are still evaluated not so much in terms of spiritual content as of regimental alignment. Whatever interior spiritual experience Marguerite strove for or achieved, it was clearly in her mind compatible with reliance on the sacramental rites of the Catholic Church, which, at least when supplemented by prayer, reflection, and charitable works, appeared to her capable of mediating that experience. She was more given to being provocative than to being hypocritical.

For those seeking to understand and evaluate Marguerite's texts, it is important in particular to take a view about the nature of the bond which linked Marguerite to Briçonnet during the period of their correspondence. Briçonnet came from a line of financial and ecclesiastical administrators. He was the nephew of Jacques de Beaune, baron de Semblançay, the banker and ex-minister of finance (général des finances), disgracefully hanged at Montfaucon, aged about 80, on 11 August 1527, chiefly because François I, who owed him money, wanted an example made. No malpractice was ever proved or is likely. Briçonnet, made bishop of Lodève when he was 17, and his brother Denis, made bishop of Toulon when he was 18, had bribed and intrigued to get their widowed father, bishop of Saint-Malo, appointed to their dead uncle's archbishopric of Reims, which he finally exchanged for Narbonne. He died a cardinal.

Briçonnet's wish to reform first Saint-Germain-des-Prés while he was apparently himself still excommunicated, and then the diocese of Meaux, may well, after his stays in Rome, have been genuinely founded on a desire to restore the primacy of the religious values laid down in scripture. This primacy had currently been usurped by the calculus of salvation upheld by the Sorbonne and the mendicants and based on the onerous practices called for by the Ockhamist spirituality of the late 15th century. But Briçonnet was essentially a rich administrator, to whom François I entrusted two missions to Rome in 1516 and in 1517, immediately after signature of the Concordat of 18 August 1516, who had technically been deprived of his benefices as well as excommunicated soon after François's accession, and who was admirably adapted to the foundation of a truly Gallican church. He was no doubt politically adept, but as out of his depth in theological arguments about "Lutheranism" as he was in the contorted spiritual dissertations from which his elevated disciple sought so hard to extract nourishment. They elaborate in metaphors obscure enough to approach allegory what are in essence the neoplatonist doctrines of the *Corpus hermeticum*, especially the *Poimandres*, of the Pseudo-Denis; and of Nicolas of Cusa, all of which had been edited by Lefèvre.

Literary evaluation of at least the more intense religious verse of Marguerite ultimately requires a critical evaluation of the underlying spiritual experience, as well as an assessment of the originality or derivativeness of its expression. It has too often been made subject to a simple calibration of attitudes and beliefs in terms of an orthodoxy which was nowhere defined until its limits were transgressed, and whose touchstones certainly included over-sensitive reactions to gestures of provocation which may have been justifiable, unconsidered, or simply miscalculated. Outside the Creeds and the documents of the councils of the early Church, the strict limits of orthodoxy were laid down chiefly by condemnations whose authority, like that of such positive statements as had been made, was often unclear. Marguerite, the king's sister, was disinclined to have her conduct regulated either by the parlement or by the faculty of theology.

She hungered for an internal experience. What she required could not be mediated by intellectual satisfaction, or even moral commitment. It was more emotional than mystical, and was most stimulated and best expressed by what defeated logical articulation—the reiteration of what were spiritual commonplaces, even if often they were scripturally based. What she obtained were the Cusan paradoxes of learned ignorance spun out into long disquisitions, antitheses playing on what was all and nothing at the same time, phrases like "I am who am," and "I am who is," ideas like the circle whose centre is everywhere and whose circumference nowhere, and names like "Jesus" invested by Marguerite, as for Ignatius of Loyola, with intense emotional significance. The religious verse is occasionally incantatory, often culminating in lists of metaphors, intensely felt, but not poeticized. It gains comparatively little in concentration between 1524 and 1547.

It is also difficult to read into the published texts quite the spiritual evolution detected in Marguerite by Wolfgang Capito (Köpfel), one of Bucer's Strasbourg assistants, according to the introductory epistle addressed to her in the March 1528 *In Hoseam prophetam… Commentarius*. Capito implies a first disillusion in Marguerite with external works of piety and observance, which would have to have taken place in 1520 or 1521, and a second disillusion with Briçonnet's speculative mysticism, of about 1524–25, leading to the discovery of a spirituality based on the crucified Jesus. The writings which can with some precision be dated preclude any such precise periodization of Marguerite's spirituality either before or after 1528. The three strands, Catholic ritual and observance, speculative mysticism, and the Jesus-centred piety of the crucified saviour co-existed in Marguerite's texts almost from the beginning, and certainly until the end.

It seems almost certain that it was in November 1524 that, after the death on 8 September of the king's eldest daughter, the 8-year-old Charlotte, Marguerite wrote the *Dialogue en forme de vision nocturne*, 1,292 lines starting with three sonnets and carrying on in triplets using Dante's terza rima. Once it gets under way, almost all the poem is given to Charlotte to speak, the poet interjecting mostly with only one or two triplets at a time. The spirituality is entirely traditional, the terminology Pauline, the metaphysics Platonist, and the verse discursive. If the body is corruptible, the soul lives on unchanged after death, which is not painful. Many of the metaphors are liturgical, contrasting Adam with Christ, disobedience with obedience, although the thornier theological points are avoided. Charlotte teaches her aunt, for instance, that the soul's free will is destroyed by sin but restored by grace, a statement which is theologically meaningless unless it is reduced to an affirmation of the dependence of merit on grace, which on the Roman side of the schism no one at all disputed. The difficulties here avoided concern man's possible right to grace in the present dispensation, which included the fall and the redemption, even after he had sinned.

Marguerite even goes so far at this date as emphatically and unnecessarily to demonstrate complete orthodoxy by denying the possibility of pagan virtue, holding the strictest medieval view that Christian belief was absolutely necessary to salvation, although Lefèvre had already in 1512 tentatively abandoned it. Poetically the passage is reasonably typical of Marguerite's verse expositions of religious intensity:

Ung Turc, ayant lettres et cognoissance
Naturelle, sera bien vertueux,
Combien qu'en Dieu il ne croit ni ne pense;
De ses vices sera victorieux
Et de vertuz sera sy fort remply,
Qu'ung chrestien ne sçaurroit faire mieulx.
Mais sy est il cloz en son premier ply,
En son Adam, chair, terre, mort, péché,
Et ce qu'il faict c'est nul bien accomply

(A Turk with education and natural knowledge/Can act virtuously/Even though he neither believes in God nor thinks about him;/He can be victorious over his vices/And so filled with virtues/That no Christian could behave better./But he is still enclosed in his original nature,/In his Adam, flesh, earth, death, sin,/And whatever he does can accomplish nothing in the order of good).

Only when he is converted do things change.

Lhors son oeuvre est faicte bonne et digne,
L'homme est à Dieu plaisant et aggreable,
Soit qu'il dorme, veille, souppe ou disne

(Then his work is made good and worthy,/The man becomes acceptable and agreeable to God,/Whether he is asleep, awake, supping or dining).

Marguerite does in fact come back from this position in the third book of Les Prisons, certainly written after the death of her brother in 1547, by which time the need for a theology acknowledging the possibility of salvation for the unevangelized, a notorious subject of Erasmus's concern, was becoming widely recognized. Having recounted the disillusion following the failed quest for human knowledge, the poet puts into verse Socrates's death speech from Plato's Phaedo,

Clarté de Dieu, c'est l'esprit veritable.
Ceste lumiere a Socrates receue
Quant doulcement accepta la cigüe,
Croyant si bien que l'ame est immortelle
Que pour avoir ceste vie eternelle
La mort receut comme en alant aux nopces

(The brightness of God is true intelligence./That is the light that Socrates received/When he quietly drank the hemlock,/So firmly believing that the soul was immortal/

That in order to have this eternal life/He accepted death as if he were going to his wedding).

We do not know why Marguerite did not release the Dialogue for the first edition of the Miroir and can only surmise that she may have felt it too intimate. The 1531 volume chiefly contained the Miroir itself, a 1,434-line poem, versifying in prosaic language a somewhat trite medieval piety, and relying on such familiar topoi as those about motherhood and childhood. The poem again goes out of its way unnecessarily to affirm conservative orthodoxy on points of belief which were already experienced as difficulties. The virgin birth of Christ had been dogmatically defined in the early Church, but the middle phrase of the famous formula used of Mary's virginity, "ante partum scilicet, in partu et perpetuo post partum (before birth, at birth, and perpetually after birth)" was first imposed in those words, making precisely clear the nature of the defined physical integrity, by Paul IV's anti-Socinian constitution of 1555, Cum quorundam. In the Miroir the poet addresses Mary thus: "Et mere et vierge estes parfaitement,/Avant, apres, et en l'enfantement (And you are perfectly mother and virgin,/before, after and during the giving of birth)."

The volume also contained an 1,800-line "Oraison de l'âme fidèle," a 542-line "Petit oeuvre dévot," an almost literal translation from Luther of a commentary on the Lord's Prayer in dialogue form and, among other shorter pieces, a verse "Oraison à Notre-Seigneur Jésus-Christ." One of the prose prayers is a transposition of the Compline hymn "Salve Regina" (known as 'Hail, Holy Queen') into a prayer to Jesus which avoids any mention of Mary. Such a transposition, like the borrowing from Luther, while orthodox, was certainly provocative, insinuating that contemporary piety had added the mediatorship of Mary to that of her son, whether in series or in parallel. It was not, however, new. The "Salve," too, had already appeared transposed into a hymn to Jesus Christ in a 1525 Latin work by Sebaldus Heyden, Unum Christum mediatorem esse, the basis for a French translation by an ex-priest called Dumolin published in 1527 in his Notable et utile Traité du zèle et grand désir que doibt avoir ung vray chrestien, pour garder à Jésus-Christ son honneur entier. The preface is dated Wittemberg 1526. Marguerite was willing and occasionally anxious to be provocative. She would never at any point have entertained heterodoxy.

A further volume of Marguerite's verse was published by her secretary, J. de la Haye, in 1547, the Marguerites de la Marguerite des princesses, tres illustre Royne de Navarre—presumably, and especially in view of the title which puns on the meaning of "marguerite" as "pearl," again with no more than Marguerite's authorization. By this date Marguerite, living more or less retired in Navarre, had encouraged, or indeed commissioned, a whole series of translations of Plato, which appeared in her entourage. The final book of the Prisons and "Le Navire" were still to come. Meanwhile the poem "Discord estant en l'homme par la contrarieté de l'esprit et de la chair, et paix par vie spirituelle" sings the praises of faith "en Christ regnateur (in Christ reigning)," and is built on the war between flesh/sin and spirit/grace. The piety is basic, and its expression quite without even rudimentary spiritual sophistication. The jauntier, more popular Chansons spirituelles, lyrical and frequently dependent on syntactical parallels or repetitions, still have fundamentally religious themes.

It is unlikely that more than a fraction of the dramatic texts has survived, but what we have can clearly be divided into sacred plays, almost tableaux, carrying on the tradition of the medieval mystère, and the profane comedies, mostly allegorical derivatives of the moralités in a pastoral setting. Very uncertain in date, they are still linked by the basic theme of divine love. It is unlikely that they were written for publication, and quite likely that they were actually played. In the context of Marguerite's total oeuvre the plays are less historically interesting than the correspondence. As in the *Heptaméron*, a serious undertone appears almost stealthily to engulf what purports to be an entertainment.

Le Mallade, for instance, is a farce with four characters. The invalid looking for a cure is advised by his wife to have recourse to popular remedies. This allegorizes the individual's quest for spiritual fulfilment and salvation, and the possible solution in a fundamentally superstitious religious practice. The invalid sends his wife for the doctor, representing theological assistance, and is meanwhile advised by the servant ("chambrière") to rely on faith. The doctor is surprised on his arrival to find the invalid cured. Outside the historical context of author, place, and period, the farce would be considered unremarkable. Not much more can be said for the Nativity tetralogy, which starts more directly than most similar nativity plays with the departure of the holy family from Nazareth, and omits some of the traditional non-scriptural elements, as well as the Annunciation story from Luke's gospel. There is some advance—in scriptural authenticity, and, a little, in dramatic concentration on the humility of incarnation—over contemporary versions. After "La Nativité" itself, the cycle contains three more plays, "Les trois Roys," "Les Innocents," and "Le Desert," of which only the last departs far from tradition, relying for its theme on the sparse scriptural details of the flight into Egypt.

The *Comédie jouée au Mont de Marsan: le jour de Caresme prenant 1547* is dated old style. It was written early in 1548, after François's death. Its importance again lies in the stylized characters, La Mondaine, given over to earthly satisfactions, La Superstitieuse, relying once more on onerous pious observances, with devout remedies guaranteed to protect her from all ills, La Sage, representing reasoned wisdom, and La Reine de l'amour de Dieu, also appearing in the text as La Bergère, who clearly represents the love of God which transcends the merely rational conciliation of opposing theological positions. La Sage had carefully pointed out by rational argument to La Mondaine and to La Superstitieuse the error of their ways, but the limits of her attitude are made clear by the simple shepherdess:

> Voila l'estat de bergerie/Qui suivant d'Amour la banniere/
> D'autre chose ne se soucye

(That is the true state of the shepherd/Who, following the banner of Love,/Has no care for anything else).

The message is the same in what must be Marguerite's best poem, *Le Navire*, written no doubt in an effort to master her feelings at the death of her brother. It is love that will draw her to join him:

> De toute moy morte en est la moictié;
> L'autre moictié en dueil et en tristesse
> Ne doibt avoir de sa vie pitié.
> Raison ne fut oncques d'amour maistresse;
> Amour vaincq tout...

(Of all that I am half is dead;/The other half in mourning and grief/Should have no pity for its life./Reason was never the victor over love;/Love conquers all...).

It is reasonably safe to assume a good deal about *L'Heptaméron* that cannot strictly be proved. It was certainly intended to be a collection of entertaining stories, roughly modelled on Boccaccio's *Decameron*, which Marguerite, certainly by 1541 or 1542 and perhaps much earlier, was encouraging Antoine le Maçon to translate; the translation appeared in 1545. Marguerite's prologue and the discussion of religious and moral issues after each conte, which actually lend the collection its chief interest, purport to be subsidiary to the compilation of contes itself, introducing them and drawing attention to what is going on within them. There are 72 extant contes out of the 100 no doubt projected. The fiction is that ten ladies and gentlemen, the "devisants" or story-tellers, trapped by floods at the abbey of Notre-Dame de Serrance, each undertook to tell a true story on each of the ten following days, thereby carrying out a project of the king, his sister, and their immediate family. The stories we have, some of them actually true, are arranged into ten "days," and are likely really to have been collected by Marguerite from friends. Each of the devisants has identifiable characteristics, mostly representing easily distinguishable attitudes.

As we have the text, the contes are normally preceded by brief and perfectly accurate summaries added in a 1553 manuscript. There was clearly an interruption in the composition, and there are strong indications that it was broken after a first section of between forty and fifty contes had been completed, and that the cause of the interruption was Marguerite's reception at Tusson in April 1547 of the news of the death of François I. Until that point each day was started by a different character. Long, serious contes alternated with short, gay ones, and the contes were related alternately by men and women, with each devisant telling one conte each day, and nominating who was to come next. One incident narrated in the 66th conte took place in late 1548, so it is certain that some at least of the text was posterior to that date. The assumption is that Marguerite resumed work on the *Heptaméron* after her daughter's second marriage, a year before her own death.

The prologue is itself clearly a fiction, but gives the story-telling a superficially realistic background, mentioning real people, real places, and real events. It is quite likely that the readership at the French or the Navarre court for which the collection was intended would have been able to put names to any real people, presumably those from whom the contes were collected, of whom the devisants may be fictionalizations. A fictionalized version of Marguerite herself certainly appears as Parlamente, and of her husband as Hircan. There is a strong argument for holding that the other devisants were all prominent members of Marguerite's household in Navarre, and that the discussions reflect a real and changing series of attitudes among actual people who knew one another in Marguerite's household in the later 1540s. Marguerite herself is quite often referred to by name by one or other of the devisants, although never by Parlamente. There is a narratorial "I," appearing rarely enough to suggest that Marguerite occasionally forgot that she was writing a fiction with an assumed third-person narrator. There is some reason to suppose that the religious frame-work of specified scripture readings was only retrospectively introduced after the resumption of work, probably in late 1548, and that work on the final section, from the sixth day onwards, was hurried.

The contes are not arbitrarily allocated, but fit the characters of the devisants as brought out in the opinions they express when discussing the moral reaction appropriate to each conte. Oisille is elderly, wise, much deferred to, practical, and evangelical. After the 23rd conte she comes out in favour of burning alive for some crimes against religion, and her harshness is even more pronounced after the 31st. The prologue puts a long speech into her mouth in praise of reading scripture.

en laquelle se trouve la vraie et parfaicte joie de l'esprit, dont procede le repos et la santé du corps... ceste saincte parolle et bonne nouvelle, par laquelle il permect remission de tous pechez, satisfaction de toutes debtes par le don qu'il nous faict de son amour, passion et merites... Et ce contentement là que je en ay me faict tant de bien que tous les maulx qui le jour me peuvent advenir me semblent estre benedictions, veu que j'ay en mon cueur par foy Celluy qui les a portez pour moy...

(in which can be found the true and perfect joy of the spirit, from which the relaxation and health of the body proceed... that holy word and good news by which he [Christ] allows the remission of all sins and the satisfaction of all debts by the gift which he makes us of his love, passion, and merits...And that happiness which I derive from it does me so much good that all the ills the day can bring seem blessings to me, since I have in my heart by faith Him who bore them for me...).

If, as is to be supposed, this passage dates from after the death of François I and the second marriage of Marguerite's daughter, it is possible to glimpse through it the attraction which an almost quietist spirituality of abandonment to providence held for Marguerite, practically forced on her as it was by the need to bear the anguish to which the calamities of her life made her so susceptible.

Parlamente is depicted as a wife attached to the ideal of conjugal fidelity, but scorned by her husband, Hircan. She is capable of a rather surprising breadth of view, agrees with and defers to Oisille, but can also be prudish. She is not tempted by Simontault's advances. Of the other women, Nomerfide is the youngest, flightiest, and crudest. She tells the short, disgusting 11th conte, could be encouraged to flirt with Hircan, and is the least predictable of the devisants. Longarine is a youthful widow with spiritual depth, no longer interested is the joys of sense, but intelligent and with a clear judgement. Ennasuite tends to uphold the chivalrous, courtly ethic, although she does not defend hypocrisy or coquetterie. She wrongly believes that Saffredent has a special feeling for her, and shows a readiness to respond.

Hircan is the hedonistic male warrior, who does not understand the virtues of fidelity, although he is not stupid and can, indeed, be subtle. He is neither virtuous nor sensitive, and is the only devisant to have a good word for the Franciscans, whom he defends after the 41st conte. He has a strong sense of honour, despises women, reduces love to pleasure, and is a cynic. Simontault plays Parlamente's martyred lover, but is exasperated after the 56th conte by the frustrations imposed by the courtly conventions. He is proud of his sentimental vulnerability and rather likes to shock. The 45th conte shows him capable of irony, and the sharpness of his tongue is brought out in the con-

versation after the 32nd conte. Geburon, the oldest of the male devisants, is tender and indulgent, apt to be satisfied with sighing, while Dagoucin, more or less sharing the same attitude to love, is more melancholy and reserved.

In the narrative technique of the contes, which is not where the real interest resides, the *Heptaméron* does mark substantial progress over earlier French collections. Marguerite makes a clear effort at realism, referring to actual people, historical events, and precise places, and giving details of dress and customs. She is obviously better at understanding and describing people of her own class. She deliberately varies the pace and tone of the contes, mixing in the slapstick of the 28th conte with the crudeness of the 52nd, and on several occasions is wryly ironic.

As in the plays, Marguerite starts straight into the action as near to its climax as possible, "in medias res," sometimes excessively. The 36th and 71st contes might have benefited from longer introductions, but Marguerite is obviously striving for maximum rapidity to illustrate the moral point to be discussed after each narrative. There is some lack of ingenuity in the plots, many of which feature the dreary procession of debauched monks, cuckolded husbands, and neglected wives of popular medieval culture. The style is almost conversational and certainly relaxed. Marguerite seems to realise that she is not good at description, and avoids it. On the other hand she makes her narrative more vivid by the skilful use of dialogue.

After each conte the devisants, most often light-heartedly, tease one another, discuss the morality of what they have just listened to, and occasionally lapse into serious debate. The text is liberally laced with evangelical piety and comments on such matters as clerical behaviour, as after the 22nd conte. The attention given to incest in the 30th and 33rd contes is worthy of notice, but the most important ethical questions, evangelical religion apart, concern on the one hand scandal and hypocrisy, and on the other, love. On hypocrisy, for instance, Longarine after the 10th conte could not bear to be thought well of if she knew she was evil. Oisille is not so sure. Is not scandal worse than sin, she asks after the 25th conte? The discussion on honour and hypocrisy after the 42nd conte is particularly important.

Dagoucin is the advocate of the old courtly view of love, in which the woman is idealized into an object not to be desired but to be worshipped. Even to reveal such love is to profane it. After the eighth conte there is an unusually important discussion in which Dagoucin uses a Platonist scaffolding for his argument that love is uncontrollable, since its object must be the other half of the lover, and the lover therefore loves himself in loving the object of his love outside himself. Simontault objects, but Dagoucin is clear:

Je veux dire que, si nostre amour est fondée sur la beauté, bonne grace, amour et faveur d'une femme, et nostre fin soit plaisir, honneur ou proffict, l'amour ne peult longuement durer; car, si la chose sur quoy nous la fondons default, nostre amour s'envolle hors de nous. Mais je suis ferme à mon oppinion, que celluy qui ayme, n'ayant autre fin ne desir que bien aymer, laissera plus tost son ame par la mort que ceste forte amour saille de son cueur... J'ay aymé, j'ayme encores, et aymeray tant que vivray. Mais j'ai si grand paour que la demonstration face tort à la perfection de mon amour, que je crainctz que celle de qui je debvrois desirer l'amityé semblable, l'entende; et mesmes je n'ose penser ma pensée, de paour que mes oielz en revelent quelque chose; car, tant plus je tiens ce feu couvert, et plus en moy croist le plaisir de sçavoir que j'ayme parfaictement…

(I want to say that, if our love is founded on the beauty, fine bearing, love, and favour of a woman, and our aim is pleasure, honour, or profit, love cannot last long. If that on which it is based comes to lack, our love flies out of us. But I hold strongly to the view that he who loves, and has no other aim or desire than to love properly, would sooner let his soul leave him by death than let that strong love leave his heart… I have loved, I still love, and I will love as long as I live, but I am so frightened that its manifestation would damage the perfection of my love that I fear lest she whose like affection I ought to desire should hear it, and I do not even dare think my thoughts, for fear that my eyes might reveal something of them; for the more I keep that fire covered, the more there grows in me the pleasure of knowing that I love perfectly…).

That is the strongest affirmation of Dagoucin's view. After the 12th conte there is another long discussion of the courtly convention. Dagoucin repeats his opinion. Hircan says that he had never loved any woman other than his wife without being tempted to offend God truly and properly. Simontault agrees, but Geburon now introduces the criterion of esteem. He would rather die than allow his lady to do for him something that would make him esteem her less:

Car mon amour estoit fondée en ses vertuz, tant que, pour quelque bien que je en eusse sceu avoir, je n'y eusse voulu veoir une tache

(For my love was based on her virtues so that, for whatever pleasure I might have had from her, I would not have wished to see her blemished).

Saffredent laughs. It is much better to love a woman as a woman than to idolize several, like an image. The women all take Geburon's side.

In all this light-hearted amorous casuistry there is a very serious undercurrent, as almost always in the literature of the renaissance, as of baroque and again of the enlightenment, to do with the up-grading of normal sexual relationships between men and women. Their avoidance, in the interests of moral enhancement, through medieval forms of sublimation and processes of idolization, is beginning to be laughed at. Basing passion of the merit of its object is one step in the direction of its ethical rehabilitation. After the 19th conte Parlamente draws directly on Ficino's gloss on Plato, answering an objection from Saffredent:

Encores ay-je une opinion, dist Parlamente, que jamais homme n'aymera parfaictement Dieu, qu'il n'ayt parfaictement aymé quelque creature en ce monde. Qu'appelezvous parfaictement aymer? dit Saffredent: estimez-vous parfaictz amans ceulx qui sont transiz et qui adorent les dames de loing, sans oser monstrer leur volunté?—J'appelle parfaictz amans, luy respondit Parlamente, ceulx qui cerchent, en ce qu'ilz aiment, quelque parfection, soit beaulté, bonté ou bonne grace; tousjours tendans à la vertu,

et qui ont le cueur si hault et si honneste qu'ilz ne veullent, pour mourir, mectre leur fin aux choses basses que l'honneur et la conscience repreuvent; car l'ame, qui n'est creée que pour retourner en son souverain bien, ne faict, tant qu'elle est dedans ce corps, que desirer d'y parvenir. Mais à cause que les sens, par lesquelz elle en peut avoir nouvelles, sont obscurs et charnelz par le peché du premier pere, ne luy peuvent monstrer que les choses visibles plus approchantes de la parfection, après quoy l'ame court, cuydans trouver, en une beaulté exterieure, en une grace visible et aux vertuz morales, la souveraine beaulté, grace et vertu. Mais, quant elle les a cerchez et experimentez, et elle n'y treuve poinct Celluy qu'elle ayme, elle passe oultre

('I still believe,' said Parlamente, 'that no one will ever love God perfectly who has not perfectly loved some creature in this world.' 'What do you mean by loving perfectly?' said Saffredent. 'Do you think that those are perfect lovers who are bashful and adore women from afar without daring to show their will?' 'I call perfect lovers,' Parlamente replied to him, 'those who seek in what they love some perfection, whether beauty, goodness or fine bearing, who always strive after virtue and who have a heart so noble and upright that they would rather die than seek for their end base things that honour and conscience condemn. For the soul, which is created only to return to its sovereign good, does nothing while it is in the body except desire to achieve this. But because the senses, by which it can perceive it, have become dark and carnal through the sin of our first father, they can show it only those visible things which most approach perfection, after which the soul runs, hoping to find in an external beauty, in a visible grace, and in moral virtues sovereign beauty, grace and virtue. But when it has sought and tested them without finding Him whom it loves, it passes on).

This passage establishes, with an evangelical gloss, the whole Ficinian ascent of love, seen from the point of view of the male. For Parlamente it is sin, not merely imprisonment in the body, which makes the soul dependent on a physical beauty, itself an outward sign of moral virtue, in its quest to seek the sovereign beauty/good which in this life is only partial. The soul, in its quest for reunification and the union with God which is its sovereign good, must start by loving earthly creatures, before passing beyond to the love of God. When the same Ficinian ascent of love is appealed to in d'Urfé's L'Astrée, the objection is made that it demands that every man must love the most beautiful woman, a view partly countered in the Heptaméron by the doctrine that, to achieve reunification, which in the Ficinian commentary on love is identical to beatification and union with God, the soul must seek not perfect beauty, but its own other half, who need not be the most beautiful woman on earth.

After the 36th conte Saffredent makes fun of Parlamente's view. No man can sin through love "except venially." God will surely not punish those who love, "veu que c'est ung degré pour monter à l'amour parfaicte de luy, où jamais nul ne monta, qu'il n'ait passé par l'eschelle de l'amour de ce monde (given that it is a step to ascend to the perfect love of [God], to which no one ever ascended without climbing the ladder of earthly love)." Of course the amorous casuistry gets amusingly caught up in its own intricacies, but that does not make its imaginative purposes trivial. The *Heptaméron* marks an important step in the progress from the chivalrous medieval notion of perfective love as exclusive of physical contact towards the ethical rehabilitation of what we regard as normal physical relationships capable of mediating moral enrichment. Oisille is more realistic than Parlamente, holding after the 50th conte that no one ever died from love although, after the 70th conte, she looks to Saint Paul to support her view that even within marriage physical relationships are to be avoided:

> Et vous voiez que sanct Pol, encores aux gens mariez ne veult qu'ilz aient ceste grande amour ensemble

> (and you see that Saint Paul does not wish that even married people should have that great love together).

In spite of a lack of formal training, and even, sometimes, reactionary tastes, Marguerite's imagination was highly developed. Properly understood, behind the bantering discussions after the tales of the *Heptaméron*, a very powerful cultural engine is at work propelling the forces of both religion and love from their medieval anchorages into the full expanse of renaissance optimism about human nature and reliance on personal religious experience.

PUBLICATIONS

Prose

L'Heptaméron, 1943
L'Heptaméron in *Conteurs français du XVIe siècle*, Bibliothèque de la Pléiade, 1956
Nouvelles, (*L'Heptaméron*), 1967
Lettres de Marguerite d'Angoulême, 2 vols., 1841–42
Lettres de Marguerite de Valois-Angoulême, 1927
Correspondance, (*1521–1524*), 2 vols., 1975 and 1979

Plays

Oeuvres de Marguerite de Navarre, Comédies, 1924
Comédie de la nativité de Jésus-Christ, 1939
Théâtre profane, 1946

Verse

Le Miroir de l'ame pecheresse, 1531; as *Le Miroir de treschrestienne princesse M. de France*, 1533
Marguerite de la Marguerite des princesses, 1547; 4 vols., 1873
Dernières poésies, 1896
Dialogue en forme de vision nocturne, 1533; 1926
Petit oeuvre devot et contemplatif, 1960
Chansons spirituelles, 1971
La Coche, 1971
La Navire; ou, Consolation du Roy François I à sa soeur Marguerite, 1956
Les Prisons, 1978

Biographical and critical studies

La Ferrière, H. de, *Marguerite d'Angoulême, soeur de François*

I. Son livre de dépenses (1540–1549). Etudes sur ses dernières années, 1862
Jourda, Pierre, *Marguerite d'Angoulême, duchesse d'Alençon, reine de Navarre (1492–1549)*, 2 vols., 1930
Telle, Emile V., *L'Oeuvre de Marguerite d'Angoulême, reine de Navarre*, 1937
Febvre, Lucien, *Amour sacré, amour profane. Autour de l'Heptaméron*, 1944
Ritter, Raymond, *Les Solitudes de la Reine de Navarre*, 1953
Krailsheimer, A.J., *The "Heptaméron" Reconsidered*, in *The French Renaissance and its Heritage*, edited by D. R. Haggis, 1968, pp. 75–92
Sage, Pierre, *Le Platonisme de Marguerite de Navarre*, 1969
Tetel, Marcel, *Marguerite de Navarre's "Heptaméron": Themes, Language, and Structure*, 1973
Toussaint du Waast, Nicole, *Marguerite de Navarre. La perle des Valois*, 1976

Bibliography

Jourda, Pierre, *Repertoire analytique et chronologique de la Correspondance de Marguerite d'Angoulême*, 1930

MARGUERITE DE NAVARRE: see **MARGUERITE D'ANGOULÊME**

MARIVAUX, Pierre Carlet de Chamblain de, 1688–1763.

Dramatist and novelist.

LIFE

Marivaux was born in Paris on 4 February 1688, the only child of a Le Havre port official, Nicolas Carlet, who in 1682 had married Marie-Anne Bullet, daughter of a deceased court artist and sister of a court architect. In 1698 Marivaux's father was appointed director of the mint at Riom, the administrative capital of Auvergne. He was re-instated in June 1704 after the mint had been shut down for four years. After his death on 14 April 1719, he was succeeded by Marivaux's mother. She died shortly afterwards. The post carried with it a modest income and an apartment.

Nothing certain is known of Marivaux before his career as an unenthusiastic student of law in Paris from 1710 to 1713. He registered as Pierre de Carlet, but did not graduate. He appears to have frequented the salon of Mme de Lambert and to have mixed in literary, particularly theatrical circles, aligning himself with the party of Houdar de la Motte against the Daciers in the Querelle des anciens et des modernes. He was at any rate writing a great deal, and his only verse play, *Le Père prudent et équitable; ou, Crispin l'heureux fourbe*, a one-act comedy derived from Regnard and said to have been written in a week for a bet, was approved on 22 March 1712. It was published later that year in Limoges, and was also on sale in Paris. The dedication of the piece to a Limoges official was signed M***. It seems to have been played in that town by an amateur company during the winter of 1711–12, and its author was probably already using the name Marivaux, first fully attested in the dedication of the *Illiade travestie*, published 1716 but probably written a year or two earlier.

Marivaux, while still supposed by his family to be studying law, was clearly seeking a personal style as a writer. In July 1712 he obtained a privilège, signed by Fontenelle, for the first three volumes of an adventure novel, *Les Effets surprenants de la sympathie; ou, Les Aventures de ***. Two volumes were published by Prault early in 1713 and were noticed favourably by the *Journal des Savants*, no doubt prompted by Fontenelle, on 3 April. The remaining three volumes, also approved by Fontenelle, were published unsigned by Prault in 1714. Meanwhile on 22 October 1713, Fontenelle had additionally approved the short novel *La Voiture embourbée*, to be published by Prault as "from the same pen" as the first two volumes of *Les Effets* early in 1714, and *Pharsamon; ou, Les Nouvelles Folies romanesques*, inspired by Cervantes and Sorel, but to be disavowed by Marivaux on its publication, still by Prault, in 1737. The probable reason for the delay in the appearance of *Pharsamon* is a failure of *La Voiture embourbée*. Early in 1714 Prault also published, unsigned, *Le Triomphe du Bilboquet* by Marivaux, forgotten until a copy was discovered in 1938.

Le Télémaque travesti, approved by the censor on 24 June 1714, remained unpublished until the Dutch edition of the first part in 1736, probably because Marivaux could not agree a fee for putting the prose version which had been approved into the verse which, since Scarron, had conventionally been required for a burlesque travesty. Marivaux effectively blocked circulation of the other three parts, republished only in 1956. The signed *Homère travesti; ou, L'Iliade en vers burlesques*, intended to take La Motte's side in the quarrel with Anne Dacier, came out only at the very end of 1716, eight months after the public reconciliation of the two protagonists. Approved by Fontenelle, the piece marked a sort of public debut. A launch had clearly been arranged and, although sporadically obscene and generally considered dreary, its 12 cantos were none the less given a 13-page notice in *Le Nouveau Mercure* and three pages in the new periodical *Les Nouvelles Littéraires*, of which 12 volumes were edited in The Hague by Henri du Sauzet from 1715 to 1720.

Marivaux now became a regular contributor to *Le Nouveau Mercure*, the pro-"moderne" review edited by the abbé Buchet from 1716 to his death in 1721. It published his *Lettres sur les habitants de Paris*, inspired by La Bruyère and, more obviously, Dufresny, from August 1717 to August 1718. Also in 1717, Marivaux married Colombe Bologne of Sens, five years his senior and at 34 unusually old for a bride. She was the daughter of a lawyer and brought a dowry of 40,000 livres. The contract was signed on 7 July and Marivaux, whose parents had con-

sented but were not present, had the elder Crébillon as a witness. Marivaux's daughter Colombe-Prospère, who was to become a nun in 1746, was born probably in 1719, the year in which Marivaux's father died just after he himself had published in the *Mercure* in March his *Pensées sur la clarté du discours* followed by the *Pensées sur le sublime*. From November 1719 until April 1720 the *Mercure* printed his unfinished conte *Lettres contenant une aventure*.

Up to this point in his life Marivaux's means had allowed him to write at leisure prose fiction, journalism, and parody. In July 1720 he lost his fortune when the Banque Royale suspended payments on the collapse of John Law's financial system. Presumably some portion of his wife's dowry was lost as well, although Marivaux does not at first seem to have lived by his pen. From then on he did, however, need to earn a living. The theatre was to provide it, and circumstances, in the form of Luigi Riccoboni's Italian troupe, were to force Marivaux to find the unique personal style in which his greatest work was composed. The company had played in Paris with outstanding success since 18 May 1716. Marivaux swiftly became an enthusiastic follower. He was already a "moderne," and an admirer of *Le Théâtre italien* (1694) of Evaristo Gherardi, the famous Harlequin, and was soon to become the recognized inheritor of the tradition of Dufresny and Regnard.

The company did not play its first piece in French until April 1718, but we know that Marivaux had received as early as 29 May 1717 an authorization signed by Houdar de la Motte for *La Surprise de l'amour*, presumably a three-act comedy which served as a draft for that played by the Italian company 13 times from 3 May 1722 and often revived, but apparently based on Moreto's *Desdén con el desdén*, not first played until 23 June 1717. The apparently irreconcilable dates suggest a close informal collaboration between Marivaux and "Lélio" Riccoboni from quite soon after the arrival of the Italian troupe, although the first production of a Marivaux play by the Italian company, *L'Amour et la vérité*, written jointly with Rustaing de Saint-Jory, failed after one performance on 3 March 1720. Saint-Jory, closely associated with *Le Nouveau Mercure*, had translated several of the Italians' scripts into French. Only the prologue of the play has survived, a dialogue between Love and Truth published in the *Mercure* in the same March.

On 17 October 1720 Marivaux had his first success with *Arlequin poli par l'amour*, written specifically for the Italian company at the Hôtel de Bourgogne. There was an initial run of 12 performances, and thereafter there were frequent revivals. Marivaux, still hesitant, had also submitted a five-act tragedy, *Annibal*, to the Théâtre-Français. It was finally produced on 16 December 1720, but failed after three performances. Although *Annibal* was successful when revived in 1747, Marivaux wrote no further tragedies. He must be assumed to have realized that he had found his own style not in the stiff conventions of French tragic drama, but in the comedies he was to write chiefly for the Italians, closely derived from the commedia dell'arte (q.v.) tradition, and specifically adapted to the talents of the actors: Luigi Riccoboni himself (c. 1675–1753); his wife, Elena Balleti, who played Flaminia; his brother-in-law, Antonio Balleti, called "Mario"; the harlequin Tomasso Antonio Vicentini, "Thomassin," who died in 1739; and the wife of Antonio Balleti, Zanetta Rosa Benozzi, "Silvia," with whom Marivaux was to develop a close professional relationship.

Unhappily, however, the Italian company ran into financial

difficulties, and had to abandon the Hôtel de Bourgogne in July 1721 for the more popular productions of works by Lesage and his team at the Foire Saint-Laurent. In July 1721 Marivaux issued the first number of his *Le Spectateur Français*, imitated from *The Spectator* of Addison and Steele. Its second number was published only after a six-month delay, and the periodical was then to run in principle fortnightly but in fact sporadically for 25 numbers until October 1724. It was followed by another periodical, *L'Indigent Philosophe*, most of which Marivaux seems to have written in 1726 and of which there were seven issues dated from March to July 1727, now known only from their volume publication by Prault in the 1728 edition, and by *Le Cabinet du Philosophe* in 1734, which produced 11 numbers.

In the meanwhile *La Surprise de l'amour*, staged by the Italians on 3 May 1722, was regarded by the *Mercure* as successful, although the first run of 16 performances produced only modest receipts. These were more than doubled when the play was revived in September for five performances, and the following February and March, when it ran for 15. Its relationship to the text approved in 1717 can only be conjectured, but it was certainly rewritten to suit the actors, and it promoted Silvia over her rival Flaminia in the company. Riccoboni played Lélio and Thomassin his valet, Arlequin. Most of Marivaux's female lead roles in plays for the company were henceforward to be written for Silvia. Future candidates for the position of male lead in the company were tried out in the role of Lélio.

Marivaux's wife appears to have died towards the end of 1723. On 6 April that year Marivaux had had another success with *La Double Inconstance* for the Italian company. Its first run was 15 performances. It was revived and played at court but, although it was followed by 15 more comedies for the Italians, it established Marivaux's reputation for what the *Mercure* regarded as too complex a "métaphysique du coeur (metaphysics of the emotions)." The single official company in Paris was the Théâtre-Français, and the Italians, still playing the traditional commedia dell'arte repertoire in masks alongside their scripted plays in French, often parodied the formal conventions of their rivals. Although Marivaux wrote about a third of his comedies for the French company, he was clearly more at ease manipulating the traditional Italian figures, the old man, the pedant, the boaster, the maids, coachmen, and gardeners, the young lovers with their brothers, sisters, and in-laws, the harlequin figure, whom he turned from a clumsy country clown into a sensitive, witty, mischievous and subtle creation of grace and agility, the beautiful and disturbing young ingénue, and the director of the troupe, Trivelin, himself put on the stage as ringmaster of his puppets.

These characters allowed Marivaux to bring out sophistication of manners and emotional relationships, with love affairs among masters reflected in coarser ones among servants. Obstinacies, misunderstandings, hesitancies, concealments, imaginary social barriers, self-absorption, and false presuppositions are discovered, tested, and surmounted in plots of extreme subtlety and language of exquisite refinement, capable of conveying hints, suspicions, inchoate feelings, and possibilities of desire, all distinguished from simple "galanterie." Underneath the badinage, fantasy, frivolity, and romance, underneath the poetry, radiance, dreams, and hopes, there lies a serious dramatic technique, which generally sweeps up towards an unsuspected but longed-for moment of revelation, itself brought out in the varied gestures, rhythms, tempi, intonations, and mimes of the Italian histrionic tradition. The psychology is tender and lucid, exploiting to the full the potentiality of a pout, a doubt, the more serious implication of a mood or a tiff, but these tensions are always controlled, and swept away at the moment of rapture.

It is escapist drama, but only because real life is portrayed in the sheltered economic security of the salon, and the drama is cut off at the moment of culminating happiness before the dream dissolves. D'Alembert, whose éloge of his predecessor in the Académie française is a perceptive source for our knowledge of Marivaux's career, relates that he wanted his comedies played so that the actors "ne paraissent jamais sentir la valeur de ce qu'ils disent (appear never to understand the implications of what they are saying)." Marivaux had to contend with some hostility from less nostalgic arbiters of taste, from Voltaire, Grimm, Crébillon, Lesage, Marmontel, and such leading critics as Destouches, Desfontaines, and La Harpe. He also conspicuously failed to align himself with the "philosophes," who disapproved of the theatre as pure entertainment.

Marivaux's next play, *Le Prince travesti; ou, L'Illustre Aventurier* was in fact played on 5 February 1724 without being billed, in order to forestall the critics. The first night was none the less a failure, although the public warmed quite soon to the play, whose first run consisted of 18 performances. Critical comment, when it did come, showed that prejudice had built up against Marivaux's subtleties of sentiment. In July *La Fausse Suivante; ou, Le Fourbe puni*, developing the role of Trivelin, was also successfully played by the Italians, with an initial run of 13 performances.

Between 1724 and the period of the great masterpieces starting in 1730, however, Marivaux wrote more for the official Théâtre-Français, starting with the relatively unsuccessful one-act *Le Dénouement imprévu* on 2 December 1724. He changed his style even in the pieces put on by the Italians. Silvia for a while was ill, and Marivaux was clearly attempting to adapt to more formal French taste, possibly feeling as he reached middle age that light-hearted irreverence was becoming increasingly out of place. Almost ironically his next piece for the Italian company, *L'Ile des esclaves*, although the most serious of all his plays in intent, won him the greatest immediate success of his theatrical career, and played 21 times consecutively to full houses. The Italians also gave the one-act *L'Héritier de village*, although there are signs that it was not written for their company. Played on 19 August 1725 with no prior announcement, it was anonymous, satirical, light-weight, and a relative failure, with only nine performances and no revivals, although to be admired by Lessing.

Most of 1726 was presumably taken up with the new periodical, *L'Indigent Philosophe*, and of the two plays of 1727, both produced at the Théâtre-Français, *L'Ile de la raison*, played on 11 September, was an immediate failure, largely because the advance publicity had led the public to expect a staged reminiscence of *Gulliver's Travels*, currently popular in the translation of Desfontaines published in the preceding May. Within a fortnight the Italians had staged a successful skit on it. The second play, the second *La Surprise de l'amour*, played only on 31 December, after nearly a year's delay, was modestly successful, and remained in the repertoire after its initial run of 14 performances. Although Adrienne Lecouvreur played the lead, Marivaux was unhappy with both the staging and the acting, presumably because he had become used to the more natural style of the Italians.

In 1728 the Italians performed the anonymous *Le Triomphe de Plutus*, another only modest success, with an initial run of 12 performances, and subsequent revivals. Marivaux continued to follow his satirical inspiration, trying to exploit popular themes, with the three-act *La Nouvelle Colonie; ou, La Ligue des femmes*, given by the Italian company on 18 June 1729, withdrawn after its only performance, and now known only from a synopsis and an abridged version, both printed in the *Mercure de France* (q.v.) (June 1729 and December 1750), founded by Dufresny, La Roque, and Fuselier in 1724 after the disappearance of *Le Nouveau Mercure* in 1721.

Only on 23 January 1730 did Marivaux return to his brilliant Italian style with *Le Jeu de l'amour et du hasard*, given by the Italians, at first with only modest financial success, average box-office receipts being 1,200 livres. But the first run of 14 performances led to two performances at court and one for the duchesse du Maine, and a long review three months later in the *Mercure*. The play was to become Marivaux's first established classic, but by the time it was written he had begun work on his novel *La Vie de Marianne*, of which the first of the 11 existing parts was approved on 28 April 1728 and the last published in 1742. It is not entirely coincidental that Marivaux was working on the first parts of *La Vie de Marianne* while he was producing his acknowledged theatrical masterpieces from 1729 to 1733.

In *Le Jeu de l'amour et du hasard* Silvia and Mario had played under their own names, with Lélio as Dorante and Thomassin as Arlequin, and the play shows Marivaux at his technically most skilful. On 9 March 1731, however, *Les Serments indiscrets* was accepted by the Théâtre-Français. It was Marivaux's supreme bid for acceptance on the legitimate French stage. The company kept him waiting 15 months before putting the piece on, and on 8 June 1732, to Marivaux's bitter disappointment, it failed. Marivaux denied in his published "Avertissement" that there had been a cabal, and the probability is that the play's intrigue was too slight to support its adaptation to the French five-act convention. It was taken off after nine performances. In the meanwhile, on 5 November 1731, the French company played Marivaux's "official" parade, *La Réunion des amours*, a one-act allegorical showpiece, with a conventional dosage of didactic intent, in honour of the Dauphin. It was not intended to have any dramatic interest, but was reasonably well received and given 10 performances.

On 12 March 1732 Marivaux had another disappointment. Frustrated by the delay imposed on *Les Serments indiscrets* by the French company, he had turned to the Italians with what he had intended to be his masterpiece in the Italian style. Riccoboni had retired, and Marivaux wrote for Silvia, now the mainstay of the troupe, the part of Léonide, princesse de Sparte, to be played in male dress under the name of Phocion in the three-act comedy *Le Triomphe de l'amour*. The play, Marivaux complains in his "Avertissement," was neither a failure nor a success. It simply did not please, played to poor houses, and was taken off after six performances, the main criticism having concerned what was considered to be the unbecoming behaviour of the princess, who disguised herself and had recourse to deceit to pursue a young man of whose love she was not assured.

On 25 July 1732, a few weeks after the failure of *Les Serment indiscrets*, the Italian company successfully played Marivaux's one-act *L'Ecole des mères*, inspired by Molière and again admired by Lessing, but in fact carried by what was apparently an outstanding performance by Silvia. The Italians succeeded again with 18 performances of the unpretentious *L'Heureux Stratagème* on 6 June 1733, although the subsequent *La Méprise*, given by the Italians on 16 August 1734, ran for only three performances. The first part of *La Vie de Marianne* had been published in May 1731, three years after its approval, and the second part, approved on 15 January 1734, was published in the same month, at much the same time as the first of the 11 issues of *Le Cabinet du Philosophe*, almost all of which was ready by the end of the preceding autumn.

In May, June, August, and October 1734 appeared the first four parts of Marivaux's novel *Le Paysan parvenu*, published, like all the parts of *La Vie de Marianne* up to the eighth, by Prault *père* and *fils*. The fifth and last authentic part appeared in April 1735, with Prault *père* retaining the rights to only the first two parts of each novel. In the meanwhile Marivaux's *Le Petit-maître corrigé*, written in 1732 and approved on 4 February 1733 for publication, failed on 6 November 1734 when presented by the French company for whom it was written. It was taken off after two performances and was not in fact published until 1739. The shouting down appears to have been a concerted intensification of what had greeted *Les Serments indiscrets*, and must have been due to a cabal, perhaps inspired by the younger Crébillon, who had parodied Marivaux in his *Tanzaï et Néadarné* earlier in 1734, and had received a stern riposte in the fourth part of *Le Paysan parvenu* in October. There is in the play something of a comedy of manners. The arrogant condescension and dandified pretensions, the "façons," of Rosimond, were a recognizable caricature of a "petit-maître."

The period from 1733 to 1735, during which Marivaux's creative activity is generally regarded as having reached its peak, is characteristically littered with unfinished work. Neither of the novels was concluded by Marivaux, and there is also at least one play, "L'Auberge provinciale," scheduled for performance in December 1735, which seems never to have been completed. Although *Le Cabinet du Philosophe* was issued in 11 numbers, it is in fact little more than a collection of often unfinished fragments and reflections of various sorts, published rather as if Marivaux had been afraid of losing whatever could be extracted from anything at all he had jotted down on paper. The most extended piece is a philosophical conte such as Voltaire was to write, although possibly inspired by Fontenelle, "Le Voyageur dans le Nouveau Monde," which by the end was clearly growing into another unfinished novel. These years of Marivaux's most intense creative activity ended with the successful presentation by the Italians of the three-act comedy *La Mère confidente* on 9 May 1735. With 19 performances, it had the longest initial run of any full-length Marivaux play.

Before Marivaux's pace slackened, he produced in March, September, and December 1736 the fourth, fifth, and sixth parts, and in February 1737 the seventh part of *La Vie de Marianne*, having in the intervening period had *Le Legs* given with modest success on 11 June 1736 by the French company. There had been no advance publicity in order to avoid attracting the cabal, and the *Mercure* respected an anonymity which had instantly become transparent. *Le Legs* was to become in a somewhat truncated version one of Marivaux's greatest successes. On 16 March 1737 the Italians presented *Les Fausses Confidences*, which, after a slow start, was to be one of Marivaux's best-known plays, and is now generally acknowledged to be among his finest pieces. On 7 July 1738 it was joined on the Italians' bill by *La Joie imprévue*, a slight one-act comedy which had little success. In January of that year the eighth part of *La Vie de Marianne* had appeared in Holland, printed by Néaulme, who had already reprinted the seventh part in France in May 1737. Néaulme was to complete the publication from The Hague, although there is a Prault printing of all 11 parts in 1742.

On 13 January 1739 the Italian company gave the one-act *Les Sincères*. The records are missing, but the *Mercure* reported in February that the first-night success was not repeated at subsequent performances, and blamed the excessive ratio of dialogue to action. The probability is that the hissing started as soon as the name of the author became known. *L'Epreuve*, played by the Italians on 19 November 1740, was on the other hand an instant and enduring success. In spite of her age Silvia apparently gave a remarkable performance as Marianne, the character whose name was subsequently changed to Angélique. Mlle Chantilly was to make her debut in the role, and Silvia's daughter Manon finally took it over.

In March 1742 the final three parts of *La Vie de Marianne* appeared in Holland, and in December Marivaux was unanimously elected to the Académie française, an event which changed his whole way of life. He had not attained theatrical eminence, which required success with the French company in one of the noble genres, and in verse, but had written prose texts for the intellectually and artistically down-market Italian entertainers who also relied on masks, mime, clowning, parodies, dance, song, and fireworks to top up the box-office receipts. Attempts to take Marivaux seriously had been torpedoed with quips about the metaphysics of the emotions, the contortions of the syntax, the garrulousness of the dialogue, and the stereotyped intrigues to which the commedia dell'arte characters sometimes too alluringly beckoned him. Marivaux was liked, esteemed, and found amusing, but he was not, during his lifetime, ever taken seriously as a literary figure. Montesquieu, Diderot, Rousseau, and Voltaire were all dismissive in so far as they took any notice at all, and not even the Italians themselves knew what Marivaux had done for them. They esteemed Nivelle de la Chaussée and Crébillon *père* more highly.

It had taken Mme de Tencin ten years of intrigue to get Marivaux into the Académie française. The speech of welcome was so insulting that, according to d'Alembert, Marivaux contemplated public protest. He became an assiduous attender, which is unlikely to have been on account of the payment made for each registered attendance. On 1 October 1750 Marivaux became Chancellor of the academy, virtually its public orator, and on 1 October 1759 a draw designated him its Director. A number of the papers he delivered were subsequently reprinted in the *Mercure*. Mme de Tencin had died on 4 December 1749, and Marivaux took to frequenting the salons of Mme du Deffand, who received the highest aristocracy, some politicians, and a few favoured authors, and of Mme Geoffrin, who took over from Mme de Tencin the task of receiving the artistic community, painters on Mondays and men of letters on Wednesdays. Trublet depicts him there as forgotten and touchy.

The last plays included the one-act *La Dispute*, which was presented by the French company but failed on its first night on 19 October 1744, and *Le Préjugé vaincu*, modestly successful when presented anonymously by the same company on 6 August 1746. With break-even at 500 livres, the first-night receipts of *Le Préjugé vaincu* were a gratifying 1,493 livres, and during the short first run of seven commercial performances the takings only ever once dipped below 500 livres. There was also a command performance at court, which resulted in the increase of the pensions of the two female leads from 1,000 to 1,500 livres. Marivaux was now 58. After 1746 he presented only one more comedy, *La Femme fidèle*, played privately in 1755, although he went on to publish *Félicie* in the *Mercure*. The French company had shown no interest, and they actually lost the text of *L'Amante frivole*, which Marivaux read to them on 5 May 1757 and for which, together with *Les Acteurs de bonne foi*, published in *Le Conservateur* in November 1757, the publisher Duchesne paid him 500 livres.

We do not know how short of money Marivaux was during the last 20 years of his life. It looks as if he had made philanthropy a vice, but there is little documentary evidence. Most of what we have to go on is wisps of reported conversation, elliptical allusions in memoirs, and occasional references in published gazettes, prefaces, or discourses. On 6 April 1745 Marivaux's daughter entered the Cistercian novitiate at the Abbaye de Thrésor and on her religious profession a year later she was provided with an endowment of 110 francs annually by the duc d'Orléans. The presumption is that she had failed to find a husband, but that she knew what she was doing, having read her father's strictures on false vocations in *La Vie de Marianne*. We know that Marivaux lived from about 1744 with a Mlle Angélique Gabrielle Anquetin de la Chapelle de Saint-Jean, that d'Alembert is ostentatiously discreet about the nature of the relationship, but that it was a very close companionship.

It seems certain that Marivaux received money from the wealthy Helvétius, and that some of it was passed on to an otherwise unknown Jean Michaut, "bourgeois de Paris." On 7 July 1753 Marivaux acknowledged in a properly drawn-up legal document a debt of 20,900 francs to Mlle de Saint-Jean in arrears of rent, board, and loans, and the pair took out a joint annuity for 2,800 francs on 10 October 1757, for which the money must have come from the contract with Duchesne for the five-volume edition of the dramatic works. It appeared in 1758 with an approval by Crébillon dated 1 November 1757. Marivaux left everything to Mlle de Saint-Jean, but paid her nothing after the settlement of 1757 until his death from "pleurisy" on 12 February 1763, an event which went publicly unnoticed.

WORKS

Marivaux is today chiefly associated with the delicate analysis of sentiment, light-hearted, sophisticated, and charming, but not shallow. The subtleties of the emotional experiences portrayed, and the brilliance of the terse dialogue used to express them, gave rise to the term "marivaudage," first used by Diderot in 1760 to denote what he regarded as an excessive refinement of feeling. The term is now often used without its original overtones of disparagement, since the wit and sensitivity of the dialogue and the psychological penetration have come to command more general admiration. Marivaux's star has steadily ascended in the 20th century. He is now seen to be probably the most civilized representative of his generation, although Grimm thought his taste "bien mauvais (quite dreadful)," and reported Voltaire's quip about weighing nothing on scales of spiders' webs.

Marivaux's achievement, like that of many other subjects of the entries in these pages, was dependent partly on a happy confluence of circumstances. He was himself witty, and naturally fastidious and elegant, in dress, appearance, taste, and behaviour. For its adequate dramatic expression, Marivaux's genius needed a troupe of actors which, because it was foreign and had difficulty with the oratorical declamation of French, had no choice but to achieve its effects by acting, using whatever help its actors could get from masks, mime, athletic agility, and gesture, as well as nimbleness of movement and of wit. Marivaux was also at least powerfully aided by the ready-made cast of characters whose roles the Italian company's actors were used to improvising round skeleton plots and in front of an unvarying backdrop.

Marivaux of course transformed the basic commedia characters, but they provided him with a built-in invitation to create impertinent valets, cheeky maids, canny gardeners, and the equivalents of rude chauffeurs and imperious cooks. They invited him to make the relationships of masters and those of servants parody one another, so allowing quite sharp social comment on such matters as privilege, birth, refinement, greed, depth of feeling, and social distinctions. His plots, because they were always protected by the conventions of salon politeness and the need for a happy ending, could go quite far in exposing the agonies and the cruelties inflicted in the name of what never actually needs to be depicted as unrestrained passion. The whole art was never to allow the interplay of emotions, the exposition of social injustices, the snobberies and the demonstrations of exploitation of the weak to weigh heavily enough to break the filigree of a spider's web.

Marivaux's dramatic talent was finally given the boost it needed by the fortuitous availability of the extraordinarily gifted Silvia, whose great talent was to act out on the surface what the dialogue indicated that she should be feeling, while actually communicating to the audience, but not to the other characters, a quite different spectrum of sentiment, so that the tiniest hesitancy, movement, or gesture could with fastidious delicacy convey the deep emotional tension between what she was supposed to be feeling, was trying to feel, and was saying she felt, and what she pretended was really going on inside her. It may well be in the manipulation of that double register that great comic acting consists, but it would certainly be wrong to see Silvia's technique in terms merely of a naturalistic flouting of dramatic convention. It depended on the communication of intense emotion through the complicated conventions of stilted understatement. Marivaux's critics pin-pointed the technique accurately enough. What they missed, or occasionally objected to, was the power Marivaux achieved through it.

The Italians had been expelled from France in 1697 for ridiculing Mme de Maintenon in *La Finta Matrigna*, and Marivaux's success depended partly on the fact that the Riccoboni troupe, recalled by the Regent in May 1716, could not at first use French dialogue at all, but depended solely on their acting skills. Their productions also naturally attracted the adherence of the "moderne" faction, more open in its tastes and its social attitudes than the still powerful cultural coterie of "anciens," and it was under the protection of the "modernes" that Marivaux made his debut. His dramatic output always centred on the "moderne" belief in the innate goodness of man. Virtue can be inculcated, man is educable, society in the end is perfectible, and social wrongs can be righted with goodwill and clever engineering. The highest and most refined instincts can be trusted as a guide to virtue and happiness. Marianne's prompt tears betray nobility of birth as well as aristocracy of temperament.

It has often escaped notice how surprisingly advanced Marivaux's social values actually are. Birth never triumphs over merit. Love does not seek to avoid commitment, but aspires to a rapture inside marriage which the legitimate theatre, and indeed serious literature generally, was able only very much later to explore on a more serious register: for this the literate public of the ancien régime was too deeply permeated with the idea that marriage was a dynastic, or at any rate a financial arrangement. Marivaux's utopian vision could be presented only on the most light-hearted of registers. Even much later the advanced social values examined in the Beaumarchais trilogy could be effectively conveyed only in the light-hearted commedia dell'arte world of *Le Barbier de Séville*. When they were more seriously examined, it had to be in the drearier bourgeois environment of *La Mère coupable*.

Arlequin poli par l'amour is of interest partly because it shows Marivaux interacting with the Riccoboni troupe. *L'Amour et la vérité*, written with Saint-Jory, had failed in March 1720. Law's bankruptcy occurred in July. *Arlequin* was performed on 17 October, a cross between the French "féerie," developed from the "comédie-ballet," and the commedia dell'arte. It contains in germ one of Marivaux's principal dramatic mechanisms, calling for the transformation by Silvia, the shepherdess from the pastoral tradition, of the harlequin of the same tradition, from the bergamesque lout in search of more sleep and more food into the resourceful and witty swain capable of the delicacies of love. The ultimate source is obviously the Daphnis and Chloë legend. Riccoboni, in search of French scripts to suit his company, had turned to his friend Autreau. Marivaux took up the development of the Daphnis legend in Autreau's *Les Amants ignorants* given by the Italians six months earlier, in April, and, by transforming the pastoral into a "féerie," universalized the significance of the plot.

La Fée, hitherto in love with the great magician Merlin, who does not appear, has used her supernatural powers in pursuit of an entirely natural desire for the country clot whom she sees with a supernatural vision. She sins by confusing the artificial and supernatural fairy-magician realm with the pastoral setting in which rustics make love to shepherdesses who are able to refine them. La Fée emerges enraged at the transformation wrought in Arlequin by the natural love Silvia awakens in him. Right is done, happiness is achieved, and nature is vindicated. La Fée should never have abused her tyrannical powers by transporting Arlequin into captivity. As a play *Arlequin poli par l'amour* is on one level a wittily absurd fable, but it leaves a lurking aftertaste. Is there just possibly an undertow of seriousness in this gracious frivolity? Is it just because the actors are Italian that Arlequin does not speak in patois? Is there not some significance in the way in which the scene keeps switching from the artificiality of the interior of La Fée's palace to the open meadows and pastoral vision outside it, some hint at a serious upgrading of what is simultaneously natural and instinctive, a possible return to the pre-classical perspectives of d'Urfé?

Might the audience at the end still remember the words of Trivelin, La Fée's servant, at the beginning, "Vous soupirez, Madame; et, malheureusement pour vous, vous risquez de soupirer longtemps, si votre raison n'y met ordre (You are sighing, Madame; and unhappily for you, you may have to go on sighing for a long time, unless your reason takes over)." Marivaux was to make a habit of saying at the outset of each play what it was going to be about. He cannot have known it, but *Arlequin* was a sketch for what he was going to build out of salon life, the Italian company, commedia dell'arte characters, and an imagination capable of bringing the lightest of possible touches to the deepest of serious issues.

If the 1722 text of *La Surprise de l'amour* was based on a rewriting of something approved early in 1717, drawing on the initial Italian mimed repertoire, and re-worked perhaps in the light of Arteau's *L'Amante romanesque; ou, La Capricieuse* of December 1718, then it shows the process by which Marivaux completed his apprenticeship. Direct liftings from the commedia dell'arte repertoire probably include

1. Lélio's soliloquy of love and hate
2. The dialogue of disdain between Lélio and La Comtesse
3. The dialogue of tiff and reconciliation between Arlequin and Columbine
4. The dialogue of reproach and scorn between Lélio and La Comtesse

The likelihood that Marivaux's coaching of the Italian actors slowly improved the box-office receipts needs to be kept in mind.

The essential importance of the play lies in the way in which its intrigue is stripped down to the barest essentials. Instinctive love overcomes prejudice and will vindicate its rights in virtuous consummation. The whole interest lies in the skirmishing while the prejudices are being undermined. When they have gone, the moment of rapture arrives, and the play is over. Nobody bothers to mention that the resolution will be sealed by the eternal union of the principals in marriage. No other resolution is conceivable.

Lélio starts by hating women because of one woman's infidelity. La Comtesse despises men. Both are surprised when they fall in love with each other. Pierre, La Comtesse's gardener, and Jacqueline, Lélio's servant, now speak in patois. Incapable of refined emotions, Jacqueline simply wants Pierre as a husband. Their relationship brings together Lélio and La Comtesse. Lélio's friend Le Baron is the catalyst who starts off the intrigue which centres on them. Arlequin and Columbine mirror the relationship of the principals and comment on it. They too will get married. A touch of deceit hastens what is not so much an action as a dénouement with reflections and commentary. The whole interest is focused on the way love comes unbidden and initiates a skirmish that unravels prejudices blocking off the fulfilment instinct requires. Comic, light-weight, comfortably traditional on the Italian pattern, the play in all its structural simplicity reveals the profundity of its real subject, the strength and nobility of refined instinct, even if it also shows us something of a dramatist mastering his skills.

Marivaux's first play to attain formal recognition as a classic was *Le Jeu de l'amour et du hasard*. Its first run of 14 performances brought in an average of 1,200 livres a night, but there were also two court performances and one for the duchesse du Maine before the *Mercure* devoted a long article to it. In about 1740 it replaced *La Surprise de l'amour* as the play in which aspiring leads were tested by the Italian company. The intrigue, in spite of its quadruple disguise, is entirely simple. Dorante and Silvia, chosen for one another by their families, change places with their servants, Silvia with Lisette and Dorante with Arlequin, so that each hopes to spy on the other while posing as a servant. Silvia's father, M. Orgon, and her brother, Mario, let into

her secret, also know that Dorante has changed places with Arlequin. Silvia, of course, does not. Lisette and Arlequin, taking one another for Dorante and Silvia, try to make apparently advantageous marriages for themselves. When each discovers who the other really is, it does not bother them. When Silvia talks to Lisette about her quandary in choosing a husband, Lisette replies simply: "Un mari? c'est un mari; vous ne deviez pas finir par ce mot-là; il me raccommode avec tout le reste (A husband? It's a husband. You shouldn't end with that word. It allows me to put up with everything else)." A husband is a husband, and any will do.

Silvia and Dorante have much more difficulty in overcoming the social difficulty that arises from thinking themselves in love with a servant. Dorante declares his true identity first, taking the weight off Silvia's mind. He is reduced to saying he will never marry. He cannot marry the girl who is Silvia's maid, so he won't marry at all. Silvia has, for her own dignity, to extract from Dorante a willingness to marry her even if she is a maid, before she reveals that she is not. She succeeds because Dorante has recognized her true inner nobility, and Dorante is delighted that he has passed his test, as he had been to know that he was loved for his own and not just his family's sake. If Silvia had revealed herself in response to Dorante's own revelation of his true identity an act earlier, the play would have become trivialized. Silvia owed it to herself to wring proper recognition of her dignity out of Dorante, and she could do that only by making him say he would marry her even as the servant he believed her to be. Instinct has won, prejudice has been overcome, and the moment of rapture brings down the curtain on the happiness of both couples. Silvia reveals her true identity on the last half-page of the text. The important line is Dorante's, "Il n'est ni rang, ni naissance, ni fortune qui ne disparaisse devant une âme comme la tienne (Rank, and birth, and fortune all count for nothing, beside a soul like yours)."

Les Fausses Confidences is often considered Marivaux's greatest play. As usual Marivaux tells us what his play is about at the beginning. Both Araminte and Dorante belong to roughly the same social class, upper bourgeois opera-goers, although the mother of the rich widow Araminte is a social climber, and we never learn anything at all about the family of the poor but well brought-up Dorante, whose nobility of heart is, however, quickly brought to the audience's attention. The barrier in this play is not money alone, although that is at its heart. It is also constituted by aspirations to restored or improved social status, but this does not matter much as far as the comedy is concerned. Marivaux, the Italians, and the audience were not as interested in class as has often been suggested. Money would do well enough as the obstacle to be overcome, as Dubois says, by "l'amour et moi (love and me)." Dorante's former valet and present friend is charged with arranging for Dorante first to meet and then to marry Araminte. It is important that Marivaux holds the audience firmly to the convention that merit can be discerned from afar and from appearance alone. The comic expectations are to be observed, however interesting the psychology is allowed to become.

The character of Dubois is so complex that Jean-Louis Barrault kept it for himself in his company's famous 20th-century production, and thereby disturbed the play's balance. The comedy loses its force if Dubois's part is not kept secondary to that of Dorante, even if Dubois, the ex-valet, is now a fascinating character in his own right, vicariously in love with the object of

Dorante's passion, and symbiotically related to Dorante himself. The alienated second identity of the comic hero, representing his comic delusion, is traditional, and had already notoriously been made into a separate character, for instance, in Molière's *Dom Juan*. The relationship between Don Juan and Sganarelle is recalled by that between Dorante and Dubois. In *Les Fausses Confidences* Dubois consistently regards Dorante's passion as if it were his own, playing as it were the wily and cunning half of the character whose diffident, passionate side is represented by Dorante. The false confidence of the title is made when Dubois pretends that it is to protect Araminte from Dorante's love that he tells Araminte about it, when in fact his intention is to stimulate her interest in Dorante.

Dubois has got Dorante taken on as Araminte's business manager or "Intendant." Araminte's mother wants her to marry "Le Comte" Dorimont with whom Araminte is having a legal wrangle. He is extremely rich and could complete the process of Mme Argante's climb up the social ladder if her daughter, now a wealthy widow, would marry him. Again, the whole intrigue lies in building down the constraints preventing Araminte from marrying Dorante, to whom she is instantly attracted. Dramatically the complications are quite funny, and the Dorante-Dubois relationship has an interesting psychological complexity, but the essence of the play lies in Araminte's need to follow her own instincts, and to make her own choices, irrespective of all constraints imposed from whatever quarter. The other interests in conflict with her own, notably that of her companion Marton, are or will be resolved, and again the dénouement scarcely occupies a page of the text. The comedy is denser than most of the others, with more fully developed and older characters in play, but the central thrust is the same as in *Le Jeu de l'amour et du hasard*. Only Araminte's mother is left to atone for the unpleasantness of her character. All that has really changed is that Marivaux has lowered his register. In the seven years since *Le Jeu* Marivaux has gained the confidence to leave his serious concerns less obviously covered by frivolity, although he still writes within stilted comic conventions. He continues to use disguise, misunderstandings, tricks. The mistakes about the delivery and object of Dorante's portrait of Araminte, the pompous parody of Arlequin's attempt at ingratiation in the service of Araminte, and the embarrassments suffered by the characters are often very funny; but the underlying comedy no longer even pretends to be merely flippant.

If Marivaux's plays end almost perfunctorily, his two novels do not even achieve that amount of resolution. Both are written in memoir form, derive from earlier works, and fit like the plays into accepted traditions which they none the less transform. *La Vie de Marianne; ou, Les Aventures de Madame la comtesse de ****, whose first part was approved in 1728, was published between 1731 and 1741. After the eighth part had been published in Holland in 1738, an apocryphal ninth part appeared in 1739, and Marivaux himself published the three final parts, virtually a new novel and not devoted to the principal theme of the main work, in 1741. Twelfth parts, not by Marivaux, were published in 1745 and 1761. An apocryphal three-part ending to *Le Paysan parvenu* was published in 1770, seven years after Marivaux's death.

La Vie de Marianne concerns the adventures of a young girl who escapes from an accident in which her parents are killed, is taken in by the sister of a curé, becomes a "lingère," meets the unfaithful Comte de Valville, is protected by various grand ladies, and is sent to a convent. The novel tails off into the memoirs of a nun, Mlle de Tervire. Some episodes were included with an eye to possible illustrations, the narrative is written as if it were spoken, and the style was much criticized. The point was that the device of confessional letter-writing allowed Marivaux to exploit variations of style to reflect, and by implication criticize, social distinctions. Marianne knows that she is of noble birth: "J'avais de la douceur et de la gaieté, le geste fin, l'esprit vif,... j'avais le coeur plus fin et plus avancé que l'esprit (I was gentle and joyful; my gestures were refined, my wit lively,... my heart was more refined and developed than my mind)."

As always in Marivaux when human instinct and nature are being examined for their reliability as guides to behaviour, happiness and virtue go together: "la vertu est si douce, si consolante dans le coeur de ceux qui en ont (virtue is so sweet, so consoling in the heart of those who possess it)." This view was commonplace in the salon of Mme Lambert. Its proclamation was almost constitutive of the victory of the "moderne" view of human activity and ethics. The deep distrust of human instinct which had permeated the "classical" authors of the late 17th century had finally been dissipated. Destiny and instinct together rule Marianne's fate, but the instinct is sure, virtuous, and bound to lead to fulfilment. "Où est-ce que j'avais pris mes délicatesses? Etaient-elles dans mon sang? Cela se pourrait bien (Where did I get my refinement? Was it in my blood? It could well have been)."

Marianne's lucidity gives her the power to perceive nobility of soul, and her innocent awareness of different social strata, sensitively reflected in the use of language, occasions both social satire and emotional adventures. The extended portraits, as of Mme Lambert as Mme de Miran and Mme de Tencin as Mme Dorsin, provide the opportunity for moral elevation, and while the analysis of sentiment is subtle, delicate, and powerful, there is enough suspense to keep the reader interested in the plot. Marivaux's contemporaries, however, although more than anxious to see "sensibilité" as a sign of nobility, were more resistant to the relentless psychological analysis to which Marianne's lucidity carries her. "Elle conte bien, mais elle moralise trop (She narrates well, but moralizes too much)," says Desfontaines in his *Nouvelliste du Parnasse*. He misses the point, which lies not so much in the low density of events—although around 1740 the reaction against the straight adventure novel has a literary-historical importance—as in the chance Marivaux exploits to present the events with both Marianne's immediate reactions to them, as they took place from about 1640 onwards, and her mature reflections as she wrote about them, which, according to her fictional "editor," was about 1690. The growing but still daring interest in refined and penetrating analysis of feeling was what, of course, created its perfect vehicle, the memoir novel, clearly developed from simple historical fiction. Subsequent critics have regretted that Marivaux gave in to Desfontaines. The novel becomes noticeably more episodic as it progresses and, for the modern reader, its interest diminishes as the analytic intensity dwindles.

In fact *La Vie de Marianne* contains its fair share of deplorable behaviour. Not all persons, even of high birth, are virtuous or happy, and neither merit nor its opposite is always given its due. The womanizing M. de Climal gets away with much more than he should, and Marianne should not have had to undergo all she did. She is sharply aware that the organization of society, which appears designed to exclude her in spite of her merit, is far from perfect. That indeed, obliquely, is the point Marivaux wishes to make, in the novels as in the plays. In *La Vie de Marianne* even God, and all the paraphernalia of the Church and its institutions, seems to be on the side of a society organized for the protection of the rich. The chief spokesman for Marivaux's challenge to society's vested interests is the "ministre," modelled on Fleury. The climax of the novel is Marianne's willingness to renounce Valville in the seventh part, in spite of the readiness of Mme de Miran, who has virtually adopted her, to accept her as a daughter-in-law. Marianne rejects the solutions to her predicament which, by finding a dowry and a convent for her, or arranging a marriage less flagrantly in breach of the "convenances," would connive at safeguarding the mechanisms by which society sought to exclude her from participation at the level which was her due. Valville loses interest. Another marriage for Marianne is proposed, but we are not told of her decision.

La Paysan parvenu was produced more quickly, between parts two and three of *La Vie de Marianne*, that is, just after Marivaux had written with apparent relish the low-life description of the quarrel between the coachman and the shopkeeper. The hero of *Le Paysan parvenu*, Jacob, is the rustic, uneducated, cynical, but good-looking and healthy farmer's son who, like Marianne, is looking for his rightful place in society, although he starts from the opposite end. He comes to Paris as a wine-carter with a load for the nouveau riche landowner who owns the ground his father works. The novel opens suspiciously like the parody of an adventure novel, and that is what Marivaux might well have started by intending it to be. Jacob in Paris is an instant success with the financier's wife who retains him as a servant for her nephew, and also with one of the maids, Geneviève, from whom he accepts money to give her lessons. The money comes from the financier, who looks to Jacob to marry Geneviève, whom he intends to set up for his own convenience. Jacob, poor but honest, demurs when the arrangement is proposed to him, and the financier dies of apoplexy during the 24 hours Jacob is given to think things over.

Adventure follows adventure. Jacob comes to the help of a pious 30-year-old who collapses, fainting, on the Pont Neuf and becomes first her servant and then her husband. He has affairs with the high-born, discovers in himself a disinterestedness that makes him almost interesting, and moves through a series of impromptu responses to extraordinary coincidences which give him the chance to prove himself to have been from the beginning worthy of high social status. A traffic jam gives him the opportunity to use a sword his wife has just bought him as a symbol of status. A man whose life he instinctively saves turns out to be rich. He uses his charm and his intelligence to his own advantage. It is his sincerity which is constantly underlined, and he finds no virtue in hiding his origins. Marivaux drops him when he has risen to the level of social elegance and when the novel could only have continued by describing the life of Paris society.

Jacob is full of insights about his own behaviour. Unlike Marianne, he expresses them aphoristically. He has no qualms about infidelities, eavesdropping, social climbing generally, and in particular the use of his considerable sexual powers in pursuit of that goal, but he is more than an engaging rogue. He has genuine merit, and the novel is the improbable story of its recognition, recounted with subversively cynical humour and some psychological penetration. Its use of improbability does make it incidentally into a parody of the picaresque adventure story, but it is

also much more than that, beautifully balancing a whole series of sources of interest: plot, social rise, portraits, engaging sincerity, unrepentant infidelity, psychological analysis, and social criticism.

Marivaux may have left no one entirely satisfying masterpiece, but it is not surprising that his literary stature continues to grow as the audacity of his vision is increasingly appreciated.

PUBLICATIONS

Collections

Oeuvres complètes, 12 vols., 1781
Romans, 1949
Théâtre complet, edited by Frédéric Deloffre, 2 vols., 1968
Journaux et oeuvres diverses, edited by Frédéric Deloffre and Michel Gilot, 1969
Oeuvres de jeunesse, edited by Frédéric Deloffre and Claude Rigault, 1972

Plays (The starred items were written for the Italian company)

Le Père prudent et équitable; ou, Crispin l'heureux fourbe, 1712
L'Amour et la vérité, with Chevalier Rustaing de Saint-Jory (produced 1720); in *Théâtre complet*, 1968
Arlequin poli par l'amour (produced 1720); 1723; as *Robin, Bachelor of Love*, in *Seven Comedies*, 1968
*Annibal (produced 1720), 1727
La Surprise de l'amour (produced 1722), 1723
La Double Inconstance (produced 1723), 1724; as *Double Infidelity*, in *Seven Comedies*, 1968; as *Infidelities*, 1980
Le Prince travesti; ou, L'Illustre Aventurier (produced 1724), 1727
La Fausse Suivante; ou, Le Fourbe puni (produced 1724), 1729
*Le Dénouement imprévu (produced 1724), 1727
L'Ile des esclaves (produced 1725), 1725
L'Héritier du village (produced 1725), 1729
*L'Ile de la raison; ou, Les Petits Hommes (produced 1727), 1727
*La (Seconde) Surprise de l'amour (produced 1727), 1728
Le Triomphe de Plutus (produced 1728), 1739; as *Money Makes the World Go Round*, in *Seven Comedies*, 1968
La Colonie (as *La Nouvelle Colonie*, produced 1729; revised version, produced 1750); in *Théâtre complet*, 1968
Le Jeu de l'amour et du hasard (produced 1730), 1730; as *Love in Livery*, 1907; as *The Game of Love and Chance*, in *French Comedies of the 18th Century*, 1923, and in *Seven Comedies*, 1968
*La Réunion des amours (produced 1731), 1732
Le Triomphe de l'amour (produced 1732), 1732
*Les Serments indiscrets (produced 1732), 1732
L'École des mères (produced 1732), 1732
L'Heureux Strategème (produced 1733), 1733; as *The Agreeable Surprise*, 1766; as *The Wiles of Love*, in *Seven Comedies*, 1968
Le Méprise (produced 1734), 1739
*Le Petit-maître corrigé (produced 1734), 1739
La Mère confidente (produced 1735), 1735
*Le Legs (produced 1736), 1736; as *The Legacy*, 1915

Les Fausses Confidences (produced 1737), 1738; as *The False Confessions*, in *The Classic Theatre 4*, edited by Eric Bentley, 1961; as *Sylvia Hears a Secret*, in *Seven Comedies*, 1968

La Joie imprévue (produced 1738), 1738

Les Sincères (produced 1739), 1739

L'Épreuve (produced 1740), 1740; as *The Test*, in *Seven Comedies*, 1968

La Commère (produced 1741); in *Théâtre complet*, 1968

*La Dispute (produced 1744), 1747

*Le Préjugé vaincu (produced 1746), 1747

La Femme fidèle (produced 1755); in *Théâtre complet*, 1968

Les Acteurs de bonne foi; in *Théâtre complet*, 1968

Félicie; in *Théâtre complet*, 1968

Seven Comedies, edited and translated by Oscar Mandel, 1968

Fiction

Les Aventures de ***; ou, Les Effets surprenants de la sympathie, 5 vols., 1713–14

La Voiture embourbée, 1714

La Vie de Marianne; ou, Les Aventures de Mme. la comtesse de ***. 11 vols., 1731–41, edited by Frédéric Deloffre, 1957; as *The Life of Marianne*, 1736–42; as *The Virtuous Orphan*. 1743; as *The Life and Adventures of Indiana*, 1746; as *The Hand of Destiny*, 1889

Le Paysan parvenu; ou, Les Mémoires de M.***, 5 vols., 1734–35; edited by Frédéric Deloffre, 1959; as *The Fortunate Villager*, 1765; as *The Upstart Peasant*, 1974

Le Télémaque travesti, 1736

Pharsamon; ou, Les nouvelles folies romanesques, 1737; translated as *Pharsamond*, 1950

Verse

Homère travesti; ou, L'Iliade en vers burlesques, 2 vols., 1716

Other

Le Spectateur Français, 2 vols., 1721–24; augmented edition, 1725

L'Indigent Philosophe; ou, L'Homme sans souci, 1728

Le Cabinet du philosophe, 1734

Le Miroir, 1755; edited by Mario Matucci, 1958

Journal et oeuvres diverses, edited by Frédéric Deloffre and Michel Gilot, 1969

Oeuvres de jeunesse, edited by Frédéric Deloffre and Claude Rigault, 1972

Biographical and critical studies

Deloffre, Frédéric, *Une Préciosité nouvelle: Marivaux et le marivaudage*, revised edition, 1955

McKee, Kenneth N., *The Theatre of Marivaux*, 1958

Greene, E. J. H., *Marivaux*, 1965

Brooks, Peter P., *The Novel of Worldliness: Crébillon, Marivaux, Laclos and Stendhal*, 1969

Brady, Valenti Papadopoulou, *Love in the Theatre of Marivaux*, 1970

Haac, Oscar A., *Marivaux*. 1973

Coulet, Henri and Gilot, Michel, *Marivaux: Un Humanisme expérimental*, 1973

Rosbottom, Ronald C., *Marivaux' Novels*, 1974

MAROT, Clément, 1496–1544.

Poet.

LIFE

Whatever an author's literary achievement, it is axiomatic that it cannot have been merely to be the precursor of someone or something else. The assessment of Marot's work has been more than usually affected, its importance having been at different recent dates both exaggerated and unduly diminished by the fact that it has seemed to provide a historical link between the tradition of court poetry in the late middle ages and one or more of the poetic traditions which had developed by the middle of the sixteenth century. No one doubts Marot's fluency, his capacity for elegance and wit, and his independence of spirit. But his actual achievement is still debated among those chiefly interested in his historical relationship to the renaissance, to humanism, to evangelicalism, to the schismatic communities, to translation, and to the adoption of classical rather than medieval verse forms. Partly because his independence of mind repeatedly got him into trouble, with the result that he falsified or exaggerated accounts of his circumstances, we know comparatively little about him. There remain doubts about dates and attributions, and a number of hypotheses about his career and attitudes still look unsafe.

We know nothing about Marot's mother, his wife, and his children. It is at least likely that Marot's father, Jean, was born in 1463 in a village near Caen which he left for Cahors, where Marot was born. Of his father's career thereafter we know only what can reliably be reconstructed from Marot's own verse, but the father, who sold hats, plainly left Cahors and in 1506 became in some capacity attached to the court of Anne de Bretagne, where he wrote propagandist poetry in favour of the Italian campaigns of Louis XII in 1507 and 1509. Jean Marot's most important poems appeared only in a collection of 1533 and have never been considered of literary interest. If his son always regarded him with affection, it is no doubt partly on account of the opportunities afforded Clément by his father's emergence from provincial obscurity and his introduction to the court.

Marot must have been just or very nearly 10 when he came with his father from Cahors. He tells us he spent his childhood on the Loire, so must have remained with his father at court, and a mention of "regents" or schoolmasters suggests some formal schooling somewhere. Marot was never a scholar and never learnt Greek, but picked up enough Latin for the propriety of making him a character in a dialogue about the Latin language to have been disputed later between Jean de Boyssoné and Jacques de Lect. He also started his poetic career by translating

Virgil's first *Eclogue* and later translated Ovid. Since he had met and discussed his verse with Jean Lemaire de Belges, who entered the service of Anne de Bretagne in 1511, Marot must then still have been at court at least from time to time.

At an unknown date, but quite probably at the normal age of 14, in or soon after 1510, Marot became a page of a royal secretary, Nicolas de Neufville, seigneur de Villeroy, lieutenant-general of the Ile-de-France and prévôt of the merchants of Paris. Marot's poem "Le Temple de Cupido," dedicated to François I, was written in response to some sort of invitation, command, or commission from Neufville, and was probably published before 1520. Since Marot entered the service of Marguerite d'Angoulême as secretary in 1519, he may well have spent the whole period from 1510 to 1519 in the Neufville household, appearing at least now and again with his father at court, at least until Anne de Bretagne's death in 1514, and first undergoing whatever schooling he had, before working in the Paris chancelry under Antoine Duprat, to whom he addressed a congratulatory epistle, referring to his time there, when Duprat was made a cardinal. His father may have been hoping for an administrative post for him.

Marot's father appears to have remained in court service, and became at some period valet-de-chambre to François I. After his father's death in 1526 Marot was to ask the king for his post. In the meanwhile François recommended Marot to his sister, Marguerite d'Alençon as she then was, who appointed him to her household in 1519 at an annual salary of 95 livres. She was to continue to protect him after he left her employment in 1526. Marot accompanied Marguerite to the Field of the Cloth of Gold in 1520, and in 1521 acted as her husband's secretary during the Hainaut campaign, when Alençon was defending France in the north-east from his camp at Attigny. It was Marot who wrote to Marguerite on her husband's behalf. By the end of 1521 he had returned to Paris, where he now had a permanent residence. He probably did not travel incessantly, as the court did, but was with it at least once at Orléans and once at Lyons.

Apart from the fact that Marot must by 1526 have written the rest of the poems published in 1532 as *L'Adolescence clementine*, and whatever can be deduced from that volume's contents, we know nothing at all of his activities from late in 1521 until the spring of 1526. His verse was still in the tradition of the rhétoriqueurs, of whose allegories and personifications he nonetheless occasionally makes fun, but he shows traces of the direct inspiration of Petrarch as well as of such Italian Petrarchists as Bembo and Serafino. Some of the Petrarchan poems were later re-published as epigrams, and some were intended to be suitable for musical accompaniment. Such inspiration as can be traced to Anacreon or the Greek anthology was at this date derived from the Italian poets. At Ferrara in 1535, Marot was merely following Italian fashion in turning against the preciosity of the Italian Petrarchan poets, but at this early period he was already also moving away from the medieval French traditions, although he was still drawing inspiration from them even while writing his early "épîtres." The verse written later for Anne d'Alençon, daughter of the duc d'Alençon's illegitimate brother, who was to marry Nicolas de Bernay in 1540 and whom Marot probably got to know while he was in the service of Marguerite, is stylized if delicate love poetry, and probably corresponds to no intimate personal emotion, still less to any serious relationship.

In the spring of 1526 Marot was imprisoned at the Châtelet in Paris. As a result of that experience he wrote *L'Enfer*, first published at Antwerp in 1539 but almost certainly written towards the end of 1526. All we actually know of the circumstances of Marot's imprisonment has to be inferred from the strongly satirical *L'Enfer* and five other poems in which Marot refers to it, not always in a tone which suggests that he is attempting to narrate the historical truth, and from conjecture based on known incidents and procedures. The five poems were all published in the final section, entitled "certaines oeuvres qu'il feit en prison," of the 1534 volume containing the translation of the first book of Ovid's *Metamorphoses*, and were: the rondeau "A ses Amys ausquelz on rapporta qu'il estoit prisonnier"; an épître, "A son amy Lyon Jamet"; the ballade, "Contre celle qui fut s'amye"; a second rondeau, "De l'inconstance de Ysabeau"; and the "Rondeau parfaict A ses Amys apres sa delivrance." The reconstitution of the crime, arrest, trial, imprisonment, and liberation has attracted much controversy, because it seems virtually certain that Marot made a provocative gesture of open contempt for anti-Lutheran legislation and policy.

Traditionally Marot is supposed to have eaten bacon during the Lenten abstinence from meat, to have been denounced by an ex-mistress whose infidelity to him he had himself made the subject of a poem, and to have written two "épîtres," of which the first, "A Monsieur Bouchart," does not actually refer to what happened, and of which the second, to Jamet, resulted in his transfer to an inn at Chartres, from which he was soon freed. Two of the titles of the five poems were changed for republication in 1538, when the name "Ysabeau" first appears, so that Marot may well have been laying a false scent. He often made alterations to his texts, especially if they were in any degree dangerous and perhaps, as has been suggested, he here attempted to make a potentially damaging matter, possibly involving the capital offence of "blasphemy," look as if what had happened had been only a jealous squabble. It seems improbable that "eating bacon in Lent" was more than a proverbial expression to indicate provocation of the civil authorities executing anti-Lutheran policy in France, and unlikely that a woman was involved in Marot's offence, or that the satirical *L'Enfer*, reasonably well known in France from manuscript copies even before its first French publication by Dolet in 1542, without Marot's consent, provides any hard historical information at all. Marot was certainly imprisoned, probably for about six months, and whatever he had said or done made him suspect of a Lutheranism which the French authorities were concerned to suppress.

In 1527 Marot was nonetheless appointed to his recently deceased father's post of valet-de-chambre at the court of François I. His published verse includes pieces written in a plainly successful attempt to get paid, and there are extant documents from both the king and his sister written to ensure that Marot was not overlooked when the list of holders of household posts was drawn up. On 11 August 1527 Semblançay, the elderly former général des finances, was hanged amid much public sympathy, and after being kept waiting for six hours at the foot of the scaffold. Semblançay had been a harsh creditor, but no malpractice had been proved, and Marot wrote two poems on the execution, a "complainte," published the same year, and an epigram, published in 1533.

In October 1527 Marot was again arrested and imprisoned, this time in the Conciergerie, from where he wrote, presumably with the connivance of the authorities, a verse épître to the King "pour sa delivrance." On 1 November the king wrote to the Cour des aides of the parlement, and Marot's release was ordered on

5 November. All we know of the circumstances is that Marot had been involved in the escape of "certains prisonniers" from arrest or custody. The procedure used suggests that there must have been at least a scuffle, and the outcome that there cannot have been much more. On 29 November Florimond Robertet, seigneur d'Alluye, died in Paris. He was treasurer of France, and Marot wrote a "déploration," which may only have been a court piece, although Robertet may also have been a protector of the poet, since he probably attended the funeral at Blois, where that winter he certainly heard Thomas Malingre, the Dominican, preach on Saint Paul. The "déploration" is Marot's most overtly religious poem.

Fifteen years later, when Malingre was pastor of Yverdon and Marot had just arrived at Geneva, Malingre wrote him a letter of welcome, referring to his Blois preaching of 1527 as having denounced the Mass, which Malingre had come to regard as an attempt to repeat or replace the sacrifice of Calvary which alone had forgiven sins. While the "déploration," based on an acceptably neoplatonist spirituality which Marot shared, for instance, with the king's sister, Marguerite d'Angoulême, at this date, does not actually say anything very daring, the satire of ecclesiastical wealth and papal aggressivity and the references to Paul and Augustine, to Christ as the unique source of grace, and to his unique sacrifice as the source of remission of sins, were calculated to show sympathy for those, like Luther, who had gone on to deny the propriety of the whole sacramental system.

Marot puts into the mouth of death the finely tuned statement that man cannot live on earth without sin. As a psychological statement or an exhortation to a life of repentant humility, that is quite unremarkable. To a paranoid churchman anxious to know whether that statement was intended to mean that God's forgiveness on earth implied not the extinction of guilt, with the retention merely of the remaining "temporal debt," which was Catholic teaching, but merely its juridical non-imputation, which was Luther's doctrine, it smelt strongly of the faggot.

It is difficult to date any deepened commitment of Marot to reformist ideas precisely to the winter of 1527, partly because he still seems content with carefully calculated negative insinuation, and partly because he had nevertheless gone beyond the point at which, were he a theologian, Luther's doctrine would have assuaged his distaste for rites and practices or appeased his need for a doctrine permitting reliance on personal and direct religious experience. He was not yet uncomfortable enough to give up going through the motions necessary to signify a commitment to orthodoxy, and was too theologically unsophisticated to pick up the doctrinal nuances of the Swiss reformers. We know from the manuscripts that he toned down the theological and spiritual implications of such religious verse as he had written, chiefly the "déploration," for publication in the 1532 *Adolescence*.

On the other hand 1527 does mark a poetic watershed. From now on Marot almost completely abandoned such medieval poetic forms as the rondeau, ballade, and chant royal. Of his 66 rondeaux he had already written 58, and of the 19 ballades 14 were already composed. Marot was to infuse a new spirit into the poetic genres he did retain. The famous "badinage" of Boileau's description of Marot's production as "badinage élégant," the light-hearted wit, takes over the épîtres, examples of which develop into Marot's own invention, the "coq-à-l'âne" parodies of confused, chatty verse letters, but the new tone, whether it leads or follows, remains in harmony with court taste. Marot still

naturally continued to write court verse for a living, the épithalame, for instance, for the wedding in 1528 of Ercole II d'Este, from 1534 duke of Ferrara, to Renée de France, although he did not on that occasion meet the future duchess.

In 1529 Marot was with the court at Cambrai for the signing of the peace treaty with the imperial forces, and in 1530 he was with the king on 2 July when his two sons, the dauphin François and Henri, released from Spanish captivity, and the king's new bride, Eleanor of Portugal, made their entry into Bayonne. Marot duly wrote verse for both occasions, as for the entry of the king and his new queen into Bordeaux a few days after their wedding at Beyries on 7 July. On Louise de Savoie's death from the plague on 22 September 1531, Marot wrote not a complaint but the first original poem in French to be entitled "eclogue." It drew on the original Greek models of Theocritus and Moschos.

From July 1530 to the summer of 1534 Marot's presence is attested only in Paris. He may have been married, but as a mere court poet his wife may never have been received in a royal residence, and he never mentioned her in his writings, any more than his father had mentioned Marot's mother. Twice in 1536 Marot refers to his children in the plural. In 1529 he was suspected, it is generally thought wrongly, of being the author of a scandalous satirical poem aimed at six bourgeois women, which appeared in the unauthorized 12 July 1533 Lyons edition, by François Juste, of the *Adolescence*, with two authentic Marot poems repudiating the authorship. In 1531 Marot was attacked by the plague, and on 1 January 1532 he presented to the king his épître "Au Roy, pour avoir esté desrobé," quite light-heartedly recounting the theft by his valet of all his most precious possessions, including the better of his two horses. The king reimbursed the stolen 300 livres on 13 February.

On 18 March Marot was again arrested, but he was saved from prison by the intervention of Marguerite, now queen of Navarre. There appears to have been a conflation of this episode with that of 1527, and only recently has it become clear that in 1532 the real victim of the authorities was always intended to be Laurent Meigret, the wealthy banker, who lost his possessions, had to make an amende honorable, and apparently spent two years in prison. There was certainly an accusation involving some public crime against religion, but the charge seems to have been trumped up, although Meigret took refuge in Geneva from 1534 and became committed to the radical wing of the reform. Marot will have been associated in the accusation on account of his reputation after the 1527 imprisonment. There seems little doubt that Anne de Montmorency in particular had his eye on the wealth of the bankers disgraced in the wake of Semblançay's execution, and that Louise de Savoie's role in the downfall of Semblançay himself, who owed her less money than he was himself owed by her son, was influenced by mercenary considerations and was scarcely creditable. Montmorency ended up as the owner of the hôtel which had belonged to Lambert Meigret, Laurent's brother, also disgraced, imprisoned, and exiled. In 1532 Marot was momentarily and unnecessarily caught up in a crown attempt to re-organize the financial system and to lay hands on the rich pickings to be had from the take-over of the wealth of the bankers.

The *Adolescence clementine*, carefully printed at Paris by the humanist printer Geoffroy Tory for Pierre Roffet and issued on 12 August 1532, was Marot's response to the appearance as *Opuscules* at Lyons of a volume of his previously published plaquettes, issued without authorization by Olivier Arnoullet either very late in 1531 or early in 1532 and also containing three non-authentic poems, and to another unauthorized collection known as the *Petit traicté*, comprising the content of the *Les Opuscules* and two unpublished pieces. It is clear that Marot's poems were circulating in manuscript and that he sometimes himself diffused them for limited circulation in that way. The *Adolescence* innovates by printing the poems grouped according to their genre, including in a supplement all the poems from *Les Opuscules* and the *Petit Traicté* written since 1527, and everything published as plaquettes. There are also important early poems not published in the *Adolescence*, of which Roffet published further Paris editions in November 1532 and February and June 1533, and Juste published Lyons editions in February and July 1533. From the end of July 1538, when the *Oeuvres* were published, copies from 22 editions of the *Adolescence* have survived.

In September 1533, Marot published the poems of Villon, always an important source of inspiration for him, and occasionally drawn on by him when he was inventing details of his own autobiography. Towards the end of 1533 Pierre Roffet's widow published *La Suite de l'Adolescence Clementine*, of which she brought out two further editions in 1534. By the end of that year the text of editions of his works had become corrupt, and he had fled in the wake of the affair of the "placards" against the Mass distributed in half a dozen major towns during the night of the 17–18 October. In the meanwhile Estienne Roffet, brother of Pierre, had published, probably in the first half of 1534, the Ovid translation, *Le Premier Livre de la Métamorphose*, which also contained the pieces connected with the 1526 imprisonment. On 16 August 1534 the niece of Marguerite de Navarre, Ysabeau d'Albret, had married René, the vicomte de Rohan. Marot, a guest at the wedding, had a quarrel with another poet, François Sagon, a not totally unsuccessful rhétoriqueur who had won the poet's crown at Le Puy de Rouen and whose account of the dispute maintains that Marot, who had reproached him with his Catholicism, had turned violent towards him.

Sagon's poetic narrative is stylized, with Marot's dagger poised and Sagon's buckling on the grace of God for his defence. There must have been a quarrel to account for the subsequent hostility. There may well have been a clash of devotional attitudes. There is no evidence in support of the most likely hypothesis, which is that Marot was goaded into one of his too readily available waves of intellectual aggressiveness such as had caused the trouble in 1526, and realized, perhaps to his surprise, quite how far his inner attitudes had become incompatible with the sacramental trappings of orthodox religion. On the night of the placards Marot was at Blois, where no placards were distributed. The king was at Amboise, where a copy of the fly-sheet was introduced into the royal apartments. Marot immediately took flight. It is not at all likely that he was implicated, but he may well have felt that, in view of the obvious gravity of the situation, he either could not or did not wish to rely on royal protection. Steps subsequently taken against him may well have been precipitated by his flight. They included the searching of his Paris house and the confiscation of his books and papers, some of which were probably prohibited.

In the context of Marot criticism it is important to remember that the authorities in France, even after the placards, were still concerned with the distinction between private belief which, whatever the Sorbonne said, was never itself criminal, and associated behaviour, including the public dissemination of heterodox views, which could be. Criminal offences were dealt with by the parlements or other courts, never by the Sorbonne, which could not directly impose even ecclesiastical penalties. Discussion about whether or not Marot was a "Lutheran" is otiose, since the term had no meaning outside membership of a community which worshipped according to Lutheran norms.

The placards contained open and downright blasphemy. They caused such waves of shock because they departed from the system of coded signals via which sympathy with the new distaste for anything smacking of superstition was a great deal more widespread than "Lutheran" doctrines. Such sympathy had hitherto normally been communicated most often by a minor liturgical modification, but more often merely by an allusion here or an omission there. Marot now seems rightly to have foreseen what would be a hysterical reaction which, in view of his reputation, would suddenly make his situation dangerous. In fact he was arrested at Bordeaux and interrogated by authority of the parlement. His own burlesque account of the incident in the third coq-à-l'âne differs so widely from the official record that it would be as imprudent to believe that he escaped at all as that he was arrested by "twenty or forty beadles," or that he was followed "by people on horseback and people on foot." For whatever reason, they let him go.

Nothing very sinister needs to be read into the fact that Marot's name was seventh on the list of 73 "luthériens" who, having fled Paris, were summoned by proclamation on Monday 25 January 1535 to return there. It could surprise no one if the authorities were interested in interviewing anyone with Marot's reputation who had disappeared from Blois the day after the placards had been distributed round the country. Those of the 73 who did not return were banished. Their goods were confiscated, and they were condemned to be burnt, not for heresy but for contumacy. Whatever the realities of the situation, the wording even of the savage decree of 29 January respects the distinction between private beliefs and heresy, of which public manifestation was a constitutive element. For public authority to move towards "l'extirpation et extermination de la secte Lutherienne et autres heresies (the extirpation and extermination of the Lutheran sect and other heresies)" may be considered to have been oppressive and obnoxious, but it was not the persecution of a merely private offence, and it was not considered to be outside the competence of the civil power.

In fact Marguerite advised Marot to leave Navarre, perhaps concerned that she could not protect him, perhaps herself unwilling to compromise her relationship with her brother by shielding so prominent and recalcitrant a fugitive, and perhaps because Marot, with no theological expertise, came too near to being a mere rebel. Marot had been interrogated at Bordeaux on 27 November. He left Navarre, probably in early spring 1535, with a recommendation from Marguerite to her distant cousin and friend, Renée de France, now duchess of Ferrara. He was to continue to enjoy the protection of both the queen and the duchess, and immediately entered the household of the duchess. As soon as he arrived he sent François I a long verse épître recounting his adventures, and attacking the parlement, which had taken offence at his *L'Enfer*, the Sorbonne, for its opposition to humanist learning, and his own accusers, for calling him a Lutheran. He correctly pointed out that he belonged to no sect, and protested against the seizure of his books.

Although the épître was not published until 1536 in an Antwerp edition of the *Adolescence*, it circulated widely and three answers were composed. These were Sagon's major attack on Marot, *Le Coup d'essay*, the much more perceptive but anonymous *Epistre du general Chambor*, and an anonymous *Epistre à Clement Marot*. All seem to have been written in 1535 and were published in 1536. In 1535 Marot sent to France his "Blason du beau tetin" which was probably meant and certainly accepted as a challenge to rival poets. From exile in Ferrara, Marot was testing his continued acceptance as leader of poetic activity in France. The "blason" was any sort of descriptive poem, long, short, encomiastic, or satirical, and dozens appear to have been written in response to Marot's challenge. He received ten, all devoted to parts of the body, and Renée de France awarded the first place to the unknown young Maurice Scève. Two volumes were published, the *Blasons anatomiques des parties du corps féminin*, brought out by François Juste at Lyons in 1536 or 1537, and a further volume of 1543, including "contreblasons."

This was the period when Marot abandoned his earlier Petrarchan inspiration, now out of fashion in Italy, where Bembo was replacing as a model Tebaldeo, Serafino, Olimpo, and, perhaps of greatest importance for Marot, Cariteo. Trouble, however, was now being made at the Ferrara court. For political reasons Ercole d'Este resented the French domination of his wife's entourage, but he was also under pressure to cease harbouring French religious dissidents. One of the Frenchmen on the proscribed list in Paris, Jehannet de Bouchefort, was apprehended for leaving the Good Friday service on 14 April 1536 before the adoration of the cross, and was apparently tortured on Easter Monday. He, however, was employed by the duke of Ferrara, and it was therefore easier to arrest him than it was to arrest members of the duchess's household, who appear effectively to have been protected from examination.

Marot's reputation for heterodoxy was well known but, although he was still technically in France a condemned criminal, he was not molested. In the edict of Coucy of 16 July 1535 François I had ordered proceedings against suspected heretics to be halted and allowed refugees to return to France within six months, providing they lived "as good and true Catholic Christians should" and abjured their errors. Excepted from the pardon were those implicated in the affair of the placards, and those who "spoke ill" about the Blessed Sacrament. It is, however, clear that official restraint was not always implemented by over-zealous parlements. François I intervened through his ambassador in Venice when he heard that the Ferrara inquisitor was demanding to interrogate French subjects, and it is possible that Marot's probable presence at Venice roughly from June to November 1536, known only from allusions in verse he did not himself publish, indicates that, once again, he had chosen to avoid possible danger by flight. Among the poems written in Venice are four épîtres—to the king, to Marguerite, to Renée de France, and to the dauphin—the third and fourth coq-à-l'âne, and a "cantique."

On 31 May 1536 François renewed his amnesty in absolute terms, expressly mentioning the category of those condemned for contumacy. For whatever reason, Marot persisted in asking for a personal guarantee of safety, and seems to have obtained one. In December 1536 he returned to Lyons, probably via Geneva, and made his abjuration before the governor, the Cardinal de Tournon. There is no evidence at all that he acted otherwise than in good faith, or that his religious beliefs or outward behaviour had ever changed. His triple flight, from Blois, Navarre, and Ferrara, shows that he had learned prudence, and

he may gradually have become less impulsive. We have no record of his beliefs, or of where he thought acceptable Catholic practice may have toppled over into superstition. All we know is that he did something in 1526 which could be indicated by the phrase "eating bacon in Lent," that he had an imprudent quarrel with Sagon, that such poems as come near touching on religion show an evangelical preference for a piety based on personal religious experience, and that he was constantly suspected of a heterodoxy for which we have no evidence at all. It is probable that it was Marot's behaviour rather than his beliefs which caused antagonism, and that official anxiety about him derived from his reputation as France's premier poet and his position in the king's household.

At the end of February 1537 Marot attended the meal celebrating Dolet's pardon after the killing the painter Compaing. Budé, Rabelais, and Bérault were also present, but Marot's firm friendship with Dolet does not date from earlier than this meeting. On 8 March Marot returned to the court, which was at Compiègne, and he was taken back into the royal household in the same capacity as previously. After some difficulty, his arrears of wages were paid. He wrote a poem for the marriage of the king's daughter, Madeleine, to James V of Scotland, which had been celebrated on 1 January 1537. In the spring Marot met Sagon again, at a celebration held by Marguerite at Saint-Cloud. Sagon had continued to pour out attacks against Marot during his exile, and after the Saint-Cloud meeting Marot replied with the vigorous invective of the satirical "Epître de Frippelippes," whose first title had been "Le Valet de Marot contre Sagon." Sagon replied with a long poem "Rabais du caquet de Frippelippes," followed by a series of pamphlets to which various of Marot's friends replied.

Marot appears to have spent the summer of 1537 with Marguerite at Fontainebleau where the queen was ill. Marguerite's daughter was also ill, but at Blois, and Marot accompanied Marguerite there at the end of October, staying with her when she took her daughter down river to Tours by boat, and on her subsequent visit to Brittany, return to Tours, and journey to Alençon, Limoges, and the south, including Cahors. The party was at Toulouse in January of 1538, during which year Marot spent some time at Lyons. On the 10 February 1538 Anne de Montmorency became Connétable. Proverbially greedy and brutally cruel, he had invented the scorched earth policy, hounded the financiers for their wealth, and built the château at Chantilly. A staunch defender of traditional Catholicism, he had also been a protector of Marot since 1527. In March 1538 Marot presented him with a magnificently executed manuscript selection of his officially unpublished works, with passages omitted and lines changed wherever Marot thought that Montmorency's ultra-Catholic but unrefined susceptibilities might be irritated. There is a poem catering for the taste to which the nipple blason had pandered.

During his exile, Marot may have written the first French poem to be known as a sonnet. From the end of 1536, perhaps deriving it from Dolet, he was also using the term epigram, sometimes for poems previously referred to as "huitains" or "dizains," according to the number of lines they contained. Always self-consciously aware of his lack of education, Marot was exceedingly sensitive to whatever might gain him greater consideration in the world of humanism, and it is largely for this reason that the relationship with Dolet, one of France's best Latinists, is particularly important. On 6 March 1538 François I gave Dolet a blanket privilege to publish any books he had written, translated, revised, or annotated.

Marot intended to use Dolet's privilege in 1538 for the only complete edition of such of his works as he wanted to see published, and in fact the Lyons 1538 *Les Oeuvres de C.M.* is the second work to be issued by Dolet's press, after the *Cato christianus*. It contained a fulsome prefatory letter from Marot to his "cher Amy Dolet (dear friend Dolet)." Much the same letter, however, also appeared without mention of Dolet's name or privilège in an edition of Marot's works by Sébastien Gryphius which appeared a few days after Dolet's, and we have a special privilège accorded to Marot himself by François I. Dolet had in fact worked as a corrector for Gryphius, and it is on Gryphius's presses that the Dolet edition of Marot was printed. Although Marot supervised the printing, and made a substantial number of changes, it is plain that the actual printing was not closely enough supervised to prevent errors in the text. It is also clear that Dolet quarrelled with both Marot and Gryphius, although we do not know whether the quarrels were simultaneous or, if not, in what order they came.

The supplementary prison poems of the *Adolescence* were dropped from the 1538 *Oeuvres*, in which the "complaintes" had already been classified from 1533–34 as elegies. In 1538 the short poems, blasons, and envoys are all re-classified as epigrams, a term used for the first time in the Chantilly manuscript. Together with the *Suite de l'adolescence* and the first book of the *Métamorphoses*, the collection contained only the two books of "epigrams." The edition is important because it is the last authorized by Marot. Seventeen other editions were made from it before the Lyons 1544 "Constantin" edition, which was not authorized. Between 1538 and his death Marot himself published only a handful of works, including *Les Cantiques de la paix*, dated 1539, the *Etrennes aux Dames de la Cour* of 1541, and the two Roffet editions of the *Psaumes* of 1541 and 1543. Marot seems to have spent most of 1538 and 1539 working on his psalm translations, perhaps returning to a task taken up before his exile and resumed, in place of epigrams written in imitation of Martial, after the quarrel with Dolet. In 1539 François I gave Marot a house in Paris, in gratitude for which he wrote his third eclogue, the "Eglogue soubz les noms de Pan et Robin," largely imitated from Battista Spagnuoli.

The first edition of Marot psalm translations was in a Strasburg 1539 collection, *Aulcuns pseaulmes et cantiques mys en chant*, with musical settings. Marot's psalms were i, ii, iii, xv, xxxii, li, ciii, cxiv, cxv, cxxx, cxxxvii, and cxliii. In 1541 another collection dropped one psalm by Marot but added 18 more, and towards the end of the year Marot himself published a collection of 30 psalms with Estienne Roffet, and with a royal privilège. The psalms were those already published, but the text was now appreciably changed. That trouble was taken to obtain the privilège makes it clear that the translation was not intended as an act of pro-reformatory polemic. In 1543 came from Estienne Roffet another collection with 19 new psalms and the "Nunc dimittis," but with an incorrect title, starting *Trente-deux Pseaulmes de David…*, and in the same year there was another complete edition of 50 psalms. It is impossible to say what texts Marot used to translate from, but his translations, in fact better described as adaptations, all in verse, were outstandingly successful, with more than 500 16th-century editions, in addition to the psalm collections reprinted in the *Oeuvres*.

As court poet Marot celebrated the arrival in Paris on 1 January 1540 of the emperor, crossing France on his way to put down the revolution at Ghent. He presented Charles V with a copy of his psalms, which suggests that the translation was not intended to have the religious significance with which it was later invested. He also attended the marriage of Marguerite's daughter Jeanne d'Albret to the duke of Cleves at Châtellerault. Between 1538 and 1542 Marot also did translations: six Petrarch sonnets; Museus's *Histoire de Leander et de Hero* from a Latin translation, Marot's own being pirated three times in 1541 before the authorized edition of that October; the second book of Ovid's *Metamorphoses*, published only in Dolet's 1543 edition of Marot's *Oeuvres*; and three colloquies of Erasmus. We know very little of Marot's activities in 1541 and 1542, and even his publications are almost entirely reprints, with his *Oeuvres* issued by at least half a dozen printers. In 1542 Dolet published *L'Enfer*, first printed in 1539 at Antwerp, although well enough known to have been read by Marot before the king shortly after its composition towards the end of 1526. The matter is complicated by false and doubtful attributions like the "Sermon" or "Bergerie du bon pasteur ou du mauvais," more likely to have been by Almanque Papillon than by Marot.

At the end of 1542, for reasons that we do not know but that may have to do with the official reaction to the Dolet publication of *L'Enfer*, Marot left France for the last time. Three editions of the psalms were to be condemned by the Sorbonne in the first months of 1543. A letter from Calvin to Viret, probably of 8 December 1542, tells us that Marot, already in Geneva, had heard of a summons for his arrest. Malingre's long verse welcome is dated from Yverdon on 2 December 1542. Calvin tried on 15 October 1543 to get financial support for Marot to finish his psalm translations, but failed. Marot was authorized to publish various works, presumably because he needed an income. It does not appear to have occurred to him that printing the Angelus could not possibly have been allowed in Geneva, and the town council had it removed before authorizing one of his publications. Marot left the town towards the end of 1543 and spent some time at Longefan, just south of Annecy, staying with a friend's sister-in-law, before moving to the château de Bellegarde, near Chambéry, to stay with an important member of the same family, François Noël, seigneur de Bellegarde and maître d'hôtel of the duc de Savoie.

An eclogue on the birth of the future François II to Catherine de Medici suggests that Marot may still have hoped to return to France. During the summer of 1544 he was in Piedmont, perhaps trying to return to France with the triumphant French army. He died quite suddenly in Turin, probably in September.

WORKS

The historical importance of Marot is immense. Whatever he may have been the precursor of, he changed the whole framework of the genres and metres of French poetry, reflecting not only the new interest in classical forms but also modern Italian fashions. He demonstrated as well a huge variety of tones and moods, and used verse forms ranging from the simplest to the most complicated, from the condensed and pithy to the long and formally constructed, from the merely elegant to the deeply felt, the frivolous to the devotional, the coarse to the refined, the reflective to the chatty, and from the serious court piece to the teasing or flattering poetic triviality. He could be satirical or witty, write simple invective or light-hearted parody. It is probable that too much of what critical discussion has not been devoted to the impossible task of distilling his opinions or his biography out of his poetry has centred on his innovations of genre or his range of registers rather than on the poetic quality of what he wrote.

Marot's language seldom rises very far above the density or consistency of prose, the emotion is seldom intense, and the imagery is not often striking. Nonetheless, his innovations are not merely factitious attempts to create, lead, follow, or adapt a fashion, but do respond to an inner poetic requirement. His poetic development was clearly set off by the need he felt to simplify the poetic tradition of complicated metres, allegories, and intricate verbal games which he had inherited from the rhétoriqueurs of his father's generation, and on which he tested his skills in the excessively derivative and not very entertaining *Le Temple de Cupido*, which passes as poetry only on account of the blending of prose, rhythm, rhyme, and metrical variety. The very early verse reads like uninspired if correct exercise in the complex late medieval forms, composed according to a series of rhetorical rules.

By 1526 Marot obviously found his earlier poetic solemnity a constraint. He entered the period for which Boileau's allusion to his verse as "badinage élégant" is most appropriate. In what must have been highly unpleasant circumstances, Marot cultivated the art of light-hearted elegance, achieving a certain graceful charm in the prison poem "A son amy Lyon" of 1526, not only punning on Lyon Jamet's name, but insinuating into the narrative of the lion and the rat a good deal of the story of his own predicament. The poem still, however, depends on its verbal ingenuity, its assonance, puns, and neologisms, although the characterization of the two animals is both witty and amusing.

Poetically, *L'Enfer* is almost a step backwards:

Comme douleurs de nouvel amassées
Font souvenir des lyesses passées,
Ainsi plaisir de nouvel amassé
Faict souvenir du mal qui est passé

(As sorrows once more piled up/Stir the memory of past joys,/So pleasure once more piled up/Stirs the memory of the ill that is past).

The interest of the poem lies in the satire, not the poetry. The colloquial narrative style is scarcely elevated by rhyme and rhythm, but there is variety in the rhetorical devices employed, like the denunciation of the court in which nine out of ten successive lines start with "Là (there)," and eight of them are independent statements.

Là les plus grands les plus petitz destruisent,
Là les petitz peu ou poinct aux grands nuisent,
Là trouve l'on façon de prolonger
Ce qui se doibt et se peult abreger

(There the greatest destroy the smallest,/There the small harm the great little or not at all,/There a way is found of dragging out/What should and could be cut short).

The epigram which Voltaire thought the best "epigramme héroïque" in the French language and which appears in all the anthologies was originally known simply as a "huitain," "Du Lieutenant Criminel de Paris et de Semblançay." It must have been written within a day or two of Semblançay's hanging, on 12 August 1527, at Montfaucon. Maillart, the "lieutenant criminel" had been depicted as Rhadamante in *L'Enfer*, as yet unpublished, and Marot's first line alludes to his appearance there.

Lors que Maillart, Juge d'enfer, menoit
A Montfaulcon Semblançay, l'ame rendre,
A vostre advis lequel des deux tenoit
Meilleur maintien? pour le vous faire entendre:
Mailard sembloit homme qui mort va prendre;
Et Samblançay fut si ferme vieillart
Que l'on cuidoit (pour vray) qu'il menast pendre
A Montfaulcon le Lieutenant Maillart

(When Maillart, judge from hell, led/To Montfaucon Semblançay, to give up his soul,/In your view, which of the two cut/A better figure? So that you shall understand:/ Maillard seemed to be the man going to his death;/And Semblançay was an old man so self-possessed/That you would have thought (truly) that he was leading to be hanged/At Montfaucon Lieutenant Maillart).

Purely as a poem, without reference to Semblançay's age, innocence, and steadfastness, or to popular sentiment about his execution, the epigram lacks concision and concentration. The rhyme scheme is complicated and for that reason, with the syntax, holds the piece together. There is some play with the "m" sound, and perhaps the liquid "l." But the first-line allusion somehow weakens the poem by detracting from its purely internal integrity, and the penultimate line only clumsily sets up the syntax which allows the last line to contrast with the second.

Into the "Déploration de Florimond Robertet" Marot weaves a satirical attack on the Church, and blends in so great a dependence on Petrarch's *Trionfi* in the description of death's cortege as almost to constitute an implicit allusion. There is still much reliance on alliteration and assonance, lists and repetitions. The description of death in her chariot watching the procession pass by contains satirical references to the Church's wealth, belligerence, and intolerance. The passage ends with a quatrain, here reproduced as originally printed. The alternative first line, here in brackets, represents a toning down for publication in *L'Adolescence* of 1532.

Ceste grant dame est l'eglise Romaine
[Ceste grand Dame est nommée Rommaine]
Qui ce corps mort jusques au tombeau meine,
La croix davant, en grant ceremonie
Chantant mottetz de pyteuse armonye

(That great lady is the Roman church [That great lady is called Romane]/Who leads this dead body to the tomb,/The cross in front, with great ceremony/Singing motets in a harmony moving to pity).

The prolixity of the coq-à-l'âne poems and the begging epistles has much criticized, for instance as "garrulous, waggish, shapeless solicitations." What gives them interest is their variety of pace, and Marot's light-hearted ability to see himself from the outside and laugh at his own misfortunes. There is real skill in the amusing and amused burlesque of the rapid narration of his robbery by his "drunken, lying, swearing, thieving" valet,

Au demeurant, le meilleur filz du monde

(For all that, the best fellow in the world).

The valet, having taken the poet's purse, would not go away with so little, so he nicked tunic and hat, breeches, doublet and cape, "so you would have taken him for his master".

Finablement, de ma Chambre il s'en va
Droit à l'Estable, où deux Chevaulx trouva;
Laisse le pire, et sur le meilleur monte,
Picque et s'en va. Pour abreger le compte,
Soiez certain q'au partir dudict lieu
N'oublia rien, fors à me dire Adieu

(Finally, from my room he goes off/Straight to the stable, where he found two horses;/Leaves the poorer and mounts the better,/Spurs, and off he goes. To shorten the story,/Be assured that on leaving the aforesaid place/He forgot nothing, except to say Goodbye).

Marot is better at this mocking humour than at the light-weight Petrarchan imitations of love poetry, composed with skill but without feeling, or the occasional and never sustained reflections on serious issues, but it should be noticed that the pace of the six lines just quoted is only kept going because Marot suddenly slips a past tense into the second line in order to find a quick rhyme. The rather breathless narrative scarcely transcends witty rhymed prose in poetic concentration, but it is graceful.

His poetry is at its best not on the solemn court occasions, or when he needs something, or has worked up indignation, but when he is at his most relaxed, brisk, and mocking, jumbling together words, ideas, exclamations, in verse letters to friends. The third coq-à-l'âne reads as a gossipy letter containing personal news and a little comment, reducing verse-writing to a game, which Marot played best when he took it least seriously. Even the psalm translations are in fact paraphrases, reducing the delicate rhythms of the Hebrew poems into words for popular hymns. Marot's achievement was to test the medieval verse-making moulds, find them wanting, break them, and leave the whole field of serious poetry open to subsequent development.

The 15 "Anne" poems are light-hearted pieces in the Italian style and depend on Italian models. They make good anthology pieces but are too light of touch and too derivative to contribute much to Marot's poetic stature. Gestures, words, wit, and feeling are all ritualized in the short love epigrams, but there is a winsome charm in the rather laboured word-play with which Marot begs for a new horse from a patron, when one he owned had just died.

…Or en suis démonté;
La mort l'a pris, la mort l'a surmonté;
Mais c'est tout un: votre bonté naïve
Morte n'est pas, ainsi est si très vive,
Qu'elle pourrait non le resusciter,
Mais d'un pareil bien me faire hériter

(But I am unmounted;/Death has taken him, death has surmounted him;/But it is all the same: your natural goodness/Is not dead, but alive enough,/Not to be able to bring him back to life,/But to allow me to inherit an equal one).

It is worth noticing that to mediate the antitheses démonté/surmonté and what death has done and what it has not, Marot has had to stick in a half-line just to fill up, "Mais c'est tout un."

He did have a sure if again light-weight touch with popular rhythms. Two shepherds sing this Christmas song:

Te souvient-il plus du prophète,
Qui nous dit cas de si haut fait,
Que d'une pucelle parfaite
Naïtrait un enfant tout parfait?
    L'effet
    Est fait:
    La belle
    Pucelle
A un fils du Ciel avoué.
Chantons Noé, Noé, Noé!

(Do you still remember the prophet,/Who told us about the great event,/That of a perfect virgin/A perfect child would be born?/That happening/Took place:/The beautiful/Virgin/Has a son acknowledged by heaven./ Sing Noël, Noël, Noël!).

It is the popular rhythms, too, which made Marot's psalms so successful:

Mon Dieu me paît sous sa puissance haute,
C'est mon berger, de rien je n'aurai faute.
En toi bien sûr, joignant les beaux herbages,
Coucher me fait, me mène aux clairs rivages…

(My God gives me pasture under his high protection,/He is my shepherd and I shall want for nothing./Safe in thee, close to the fine pastures,/He gives me rest, and leads me to the clear waters…).

PUBLICATIONS

[All Marot's works are in verse. Many poems circulated before publication, were changed, given different titles, and included in different collections. Several volumes were published in one or more unauthorized versions before the generally authorized publications noted below]

Collections

Les Oeuvres de Clément Marot, 4 vols., 1538
Les Oeuvres, 1542
Oeuvres complètes, 5 vols., 1875–1931
Oeuvres complètes, 6 vols., 1958–72

Verse

Le Temple de Cupido, c. 1515

Deploration sur la mort de…Florimond Robertet, 1534

Eglogue sur le Trespas de ma Dame Loyse de Savoye, 1531

Les Opuscules et petitz Traictez de Clement Marot, (1531 or 1532)

L' Adolescence clementine, 1532; revised 1534

La Suite de l'Adolescence clementine, 1534

Le Dieu gard de Clement Marot, 1537

Le Valet de Marot contre Sagon, 1537

L' Eglogue de Marot au Roy, soubz les noms de Pan et Robin, 1539

Les Cantiques de la Paix, 1539

L' Enfer, 1542

Eglogue sur la naissance du fils de Monseigneur le Daulphin, 1544

Translations

Ovid, *Le Premier Livre de la Métamorphose*, 1534; augmented 1536

——*Les trois premiers livres de la Métamorphose d'Ovid*, 1556

Musaeus, *L'Histoire de Leander et de Hero*, 1541

Petrarch, *Six sonnets*, (1539)

Biographical and critical studies

Mayer, C.A., *La Religion de Marot*, 1960

—————*Clément Marot*, 1972

Bibliography

Mayer, C.A., *Bibliographie des Oeuvres de Clement Marot*, 2 vols., 1954

MERCURE (Le), short title used successively for

MERCURE FRANÇAIS (Le)

MERCURE GALANT (Le), and

MERCURE DE FRANCE (Le)

See also Donneau de Visé, La Bruyère, Lafayette, and Querelle des anciens et des modernes.

The name of the winged messenger of the gods had been borrowed in Germany for the Frankfurt *Mercurius gallo-belgicus* before it came to France, where the first volume of a *Mercure Français* was published in 1611 by Jean Richer. A résumé of the work of the royal chronologer, Pierre-Victor Palma-Cayet, during the period from 1605–10, it narrates the principal events in France and elsewhere for those years and was followed by a series of annual volumes by Etienne Richer and then Olivier de Varennes, putting out the royal point of view on major political occurrences, and incorporating appropriate official brochures. Special issues would be devoted to particular events, like natural disasters, sometimes with comments, as on the causes of comets, or even to serious discussions. It was Richelieu who realized the potential offered by an annual presentation of news, and who charged Père Joseph, the Capucin "grey eminence" on whom he so much relied, to edit the *Mercure* from 1624 to 1638.

In 1638, on the death of Père Joseph, Théophraste Renaudot took over the *Mercure Français*, making it a sort of annex to his *Gazette* (q.v.). When, in 1644, he dropped it, he had inchoately established the distinction between gazettes, regularly carrying news and the forerunners of modern newspapers, and "mercures," the forerunners of modern magazines, with more reflective pieces. Renaudot stated the policy of the *Mercure*:

Ce ne sera pas une histoire accomplie dans toutes les conditions requises à la perfection, mais de l'étoffe pour la faire

(It will not be history written in the full conditions required for its perfection, but the raw material for it).

Regularity of publication, which distinguished the periodical press from the brochures, pamphlets, and leaflets commemorating definite events, was to start with very rough. Just as the earliest books had been viewed as surrogate manuscripts, and made to look as much like copied manuscripts as was compatible with the economic exploitation of the new printing technology allowed by movable type, so the early gazettes and mercures resembled as closely as possible miniature books. In particular their pagination was generally continuous through the year in which they appeared with whatever regularity could be achieved.

Le Mercure Galant, founded by the gazetteer and dramatist Jean Donneau de Visé in association with the bookseller-publishers Claude Barbin and Théodore Girard, took only the "Mercure" from the title discontinued in 1644, suitably embellishing it as "galant," although some allusion to the aims of the *Le Mercure Français* was certainly thought, for instance by Bayle, to have been intentional. There was an unsatisfied market for something modish, even smart, to fill the gap between the dry official style of the *Gazette*, the book reviews and necrologies of the *Journal des Savants*, the scant Paris coverage of the *Gazette d'Amsterdam*, and Robinet's socially over-enthusiastic *Lettres en vers*. Some pecuniary inducement is thought to have helped with the privilège, and Donneau de Visé engaged himself to produce a fictitious weekly letter from 1 January 1672, although the privilège is dated only 27 February.

In May 1672 a first volume of the epistolary reports was published, a 340-page duodecimo volume entitled *Le Mercure Galant*, claiming to contain several true stories and to cover everything that had happened in Paris from 1 January 1672 to the king's departure to join his troops at Charleroi on 5 May for the Dutch campaign. Donneau de Visé's introduction to the first volume promised his readers novels, news of persons "de naissance ou de mérite (of birth or merit)," information about the provinces and foreign courts, and book reviews restricted to love stories and books about the merit of persons of intelligence. The letters were to contain both true stories and fiction, and his use of the French word "histoire," which can refer to either, sometimes makes Donneau de Visé's intentions unclear. The first letter repeated an invitation to readers to send in their own galanteries for Donneau de Visé to print. He would report on social matters, marriages and deaths, military actions, law suits, fashion news, and news from the most cultivated drawing rooms, and he would print "sonnets, madrigaux et autres ouvrages semblables et des aventures nouvelles en forme d'histoire (sonnets, madrigals, and other similar works, and new adventures in the form of history/fiction)."

The ambiguity of "histoire," meaning either "history," or simply "story," is tantalizing, since it was in 1672 that Barbin took out a privilège for what might have been a novel by Mme de Lafayette (q.v.). The *Princesse de Clèves*, when it appeared in 1678, had a historical setting which was patently no more than cosmetic, and it plainly marked the move away from the historical adventure novel it still half pretended to be towards the novel of psychological analysis it actually was. The debate about the novel which the *Mercure* stimulated left doubtful to what extent Donneau de Visé and his readers took the fiction to be wholly true, wholly fictional, part historical and part fictional or, most probably, understood it precisely to be fiction purporting to be history. The summary of the results of the questionnaire the *Mercure* published was altogether in the spirit of Donneau de Visé's aims as stated in May 1672. After repeating in his first letter his request in the prospectus for readers' material to print, he promised to review new comedies and works of galanterie. In the first volume, after a short story of his own, came a variety of assorted news items.

The *Mercure Galant* was in principle to appear in three-monthly collections of fictitious weekly letters with supplementary volumes dictated by significant events, or with extraordinary numbers devoted to a particular topic, like that later on devoted to Mme de Lafayette's novel. The initial contract with Barbin and Girard was for six volumes over three years, but volumes two and three, dedicated to the Garde des Sceaux, appeared together in December in 1672. The fourth volume was promised for the end of January 1673 but appeared only in June, when the form of fictitious letters was dropped. The fifth volume appeared only with the sixth and with a new publisher, Henry Loyson, in the first half of December 1673. It is clear from the imaginary conversations featuring in the *Mercure* that some of the public wanted more smartness and more fictional analysis of sentiment, while others were more interested in the military news, and these two categories of material now squeezed out everything except dramatic criticism. For reasons about which we can only conjecture, publication was now suspended for two years. Donneau de Visé may have been ill. There had certainly been opposition, and commercial success seems to have been mediocre.

Then in April 1677 there was a re-launch with the bookseller-publisher Blagaert. *Le Nouveau Mercure Galant* in its first number covered the three months from January to March 1677, promising regular publication on the first of each month, and items of interest to everyone. There would be news of war, love, deaths, marriages, abbacies, and bishoprics, together with fiction and reviews. Fashion news from the capital would be available for provincial readers. The review was again in the form of a fictitious letter, and the first number covered the conflict between the partisans of Racine's and those of Pradon's *Phèdre*

et Hippolyte, first performed on 1 and 3 January 1677 respectively. Single numbers were offered calf-bound at one livre, bound in cardboard at three-quarters of a livre, and unbound at half a livre, and subscriptions were invited for three, six, and twelve months. The second number was on time in the early part of May, and on 31 December 1677 Donneau de Visé obtained a new privilège, ceded to Blageart. From 1678 to April 1714 there were 511 volumes of 300–400 pages, with a 500-page "extraordinaire" devoted to galanteries every three months from 1678 to 1685.

Each number generally contained fiction and verse, perhaps an obituary or a panegyric, imaginary conversations, military news, reports about the wounded, official documents, social items, with perhaps a description of the Versailles fountains or an account of an academy reception, something about fashion, lists of promotions, discussions of not very demanding works about words or grammar, and reviews of theatrical performances and new fiction. There were engravings and dedications, puzzles, and lists of those who sent in correct solutions. This was a magazine for the socially smart, written on the credible assumption that most of its readers knew one another, or at any rate about one another. For the merely aspiring, there were practical hints.

The fashion rubric included furnishings. "People of quality" were abandoning carpets, which collected dust, in favour of coloured parquet floors, but in fashion people of quality could never keep pace with the truly grands seigneurs, who changed a fashion as soon as others caught up with it. They were warned that painted and printed silks were now cheap and therefore everywhere to be seen. The implication was that the truly distinguished should no longer be seen in Chinese silk, which the cheap imitations had deprived of its rarity and therefore fashion value. It has been unkindly though not implausibly suggested that the mention of purveyors' names, especially in the fashion rubric, may have been lucrative, but the *Mercure*'s readership was certainly being extended, and the review itself was plagiarized and counterfeited.

The re-launch turned the *Mercure Galant* into a literary review. Donneau de Visé must have got some knowledge of the manuscript versions of the still anonymous *Princesse de Clèves* which was circulating at the end of 1677, and he could not have been unaware that the author was Mme de Lafayette, whom he had probably offended with a portrait in his three-volume *L'Amour échappé*, also known as *Les Nouvelles galantes*, of 1669. In January 1678 he had included in the *Mercure* a short story, *La Vertu malheureuse*, anticipating the famous "aveu (confession)" scene from *La Princesse de Clèves*, in an episode which gives no more than a foretaste but which strongly suggests some knowledge of, or about, Mme de Lafayette's text, now shortly to appear. In the extraordinaire of January 1678 the *Mercure* asked whether a lover would prefer to be abandoned or deceived, promising to publish the best answers in the April extraordinaire.

La Princesse de Clèves appeared in March, duly announced in the ordinaire for that month. In April Donneau de Visé organized the enquiry about readers' reactions to the Princesse de Clèves's confession to her husband of her love for someone else. The responses were published and tabulated in the October extraordinaire, with interim letters in July. The novel is mentioned, always with praise, in five numbers of the *Mercure*. The *Mercure Galant* had found its public, its vocation, and its sense of humour. The July extraordinaire carried eleven letters on the confession, signed as diversely as "Insensible" from Beauvais, and "Le Berger des rives de la Juïne (The shepherd from the banks of the Juïne)." Two fiancés from Bassigny had broken off their engagement as a result of the incompatibilities revealed by a discussion of the question.

The extraordinaires were attracting between 500 and 600 letters a month. By 1679 the *Mercure*'s price had gone up and was 1½ livres per calf-bound number. The contents still followed one another without order—the appointment of an ambassador, a reception at the Académie, a piece on whether love is blind, the confinement of the comtesse de Matignon, the art of silence, war news, a map. In 1680 Thomas Corneille was brought in as co-editor and given a share in the profits of the enterprise, which interestingly included "gifts which might be made to us," no doubt from merchants and nobles alluded to in its pages, of "money, furnishings, jewels and pensions." It is not impossible that interested parties contributed something to ensure good reviews, or a mention of new books or plays. The formal contract with Thomas Corneille was signed on 15 December 1681 and registered on 18 January 1682, and that August a whole number was devoted to the birth of the duc de Bourgogne. The king did not immediately respond to the specially bound copy, the letters, and the pressure exercised on Donneau de Visé's behalf.

In the light of the Querelle des anciens et des modernes (q.v.) it is important that the *Mercure*, which was to be heavily in favour of the partisans of the modernes, was on good terms with the Italian company, which at least twice parodied the review, in 1681 and 1683, with *Arlequin Mercure Galant* and *Arlequin avocat*, with Arlequin played by Dominique Biancocelli. Donneau de Visé did, however, go to court to force Boursault in February 1683 to change the title of the five-act verse comedy for the French company from "Le Mercure Galant" to *La Comédie sans titre*. The piece was played successfully on 5 March and, although consisting of little more than a satirical parade of the review's readers, it ran for 18 performances. From 28 February 1684 Donneau de Visé received a pension of 6,000 livres from the king, rising by stages to 15,000 livres by 1697.

In March 1688 the *Mercure* was harshly attacked by La Bruyère in his anonymous *Les Caractères*:

Le H*** G*** est immédiatement au-dessous de rien. Il y a bien d'autres ouvrages qui lui ressemblent. Il y a autant d'invention de s'enrichir par un sot livre qu'il y a de sottise à l'acheter: c'est ignorer le goût du peuple que de ne pas hasarder quelquefois de grandes fadaises

(The H*** G*** rates just below nothing. There are a lot of other works like it. There is as much ingenuity in getting rich through a stupid book as there is stupidity in buying it: you have to be ignorant of the people's taste not sometimes to take a chance with complete nonsense).

"H** G**" stands for "Hermès Galant," Hermes being another winged messenger of the gods, and the initials were in fact replaced by "M.G." in later editions of La Bruyère. The scandal of Perrault's *Siècle de Louis le Grand*, making modern poets and dramatists equal or superior to those of antiquity, had broken out at the Académie in 1687, and Fontenelle's collaboration with the *Mercure* as well as his sympathy with the advocates of the mod-

ernes were both well known before the end of 1687. The presumption must be that the strength of La Bruyère's hostility to the *Mercure* derived specifically from the review's attitude in the Querelle, rather than from the generally modish, superficial, and intellectually undemanding worldliness which clearly clashed with La Bruyère's own more serious vision of life and deeply-ingrained values.

It is characteristic of the attacks on the *Mercure* that, as in La Bruyère's remark, a strong odour of moral disapprobation is mingled with criticism on grounds of taste, and it is paradoxical that the lighter-weight skirmishers of the *Mercure* and the Italian company when it returned to Paris in 1716 should, for all their triviality, have in the end proved right against the heavy battalions of learning and austerity represented by the neo-classical school of literature and the spirituality of Port-Royal (q.v.). But what the *Mercure* fundamentally stood for underneath the quest for profit, the glitter, and the frivolity was the refinement of natural, instinctively based behaviour, in the conviction that human nature did not require suppression or excessive abnegation for its perfecting, but that, properly civilized, it could itself lead to virtue. The difficulty is that, however fundamentally right on the serious moral issues, the *Mercure* was often judged to have been even grossly tasteless, for instance in its excessive grovelling to the monarch, or in some of its less successful pieces, like Donneau de Visé's pastiche of a funeral oration on the death of Molière, published in his fourth volume.

Controversy surrounding the review spluttered on, fired partly by moral indignation, partly by a defence of different aesthetic values, and partly by envy. Donneau de Visé had at first acted with restraint in face of the attack by La Bruyère, although opportunities arose when he might reasonably have riposted, as when Thomas Corneille received his nephew, Fontenelle, into the Académie in May 1691. Donneau de Visé did, however, reply in kind when reporting La Bruyère's own discourse on his reception into the Académie on 15 June 1693. La Bruyère had delivered his discourse in the presence of Pierre Corneille's brother, Thomas, and nephew, Fontenelle, praising the antique, Boileau, and Racine at the expense of Pierre Corneille. Donneau de Visé wrote a very angry reply in the *Mercure* to which La Bruyère replied in the preface to the published version of his discourse of reception, and in the notorious portrait of Fontenelle as Cydias in the eighth edition of *Les Caractères* in 1694. Donneau de Visé did not reply again, and the *Mercure* even found amiable things to say about Boileau after the 1700 reconciliation with Perrault.

When Donneau de Visé died in 1710, a year after Thomas Corneille, the *Mercure Galant* passed to Charles Rivière Dufresny—said to be the great-grandson of Henri IV—who tried to give it an air of not very serious piety, but passed on the privilège in 1713 to Le Fèvre de Fontenay, reserving a pension for himself. Le Fèvre directed the review from May 1714 until October 1716, when it was suspended for libel. After two months the privilège passed to the abbé Pierre-François Buchet, who published the review as *Le Nouveau Mercure* from January 1717 until his death in May 1721, when Rivière Dufresny took it back, now in conjunction with the abbé Jean-Paul de La Roque and Louis Fuselier, and revived it under the favourable eye of the regent. Its platform was neutrality and impartiality. Then in 1724 the administration of the review was reorganized, and Louis XV allowed it to change its title to the *Mercure de France*. It still contained dramatic criticism, accounts of new books, reports of entertainments, a social chronicle, news of marriages and deaths, small news items, occasional more reflective pieces, and a recital of royal doings.

From 1724 the *Mercure de France* added satire and fiction to its recent staple content of reviews, and its directorship became a government appointment. In some months more than one volume was published, so there were 53 volumes from 1744 to 1748, while 64 were edited by the abbé Raynal from 1750 to 1754. Louis de Boissy was director from 1755 to 1758. The review was successful. Raynal received 1,200 livres annually until the publication and suppression in 1772 of his *Histoire philosophique et politique des éstablissements et du commerce de Européens dans les deux Indes*, while Mme de Pompadour appears to have been responsible for arranging for the *Mercure* to pay pensions to writers whom she protected, the cost of which rose in 1762 to 28,000 livres out of a total budget of 60,000. Between 1762 and 1764 there were 1,600 subscribers, of which only 660 were from Paris, 40 from abroad, and the remaining 900 from the provinces. By 1778 the review appeared every ten days in duodecimo format, with a print run of 2,600. The review had become more serious, with occasional articles devoted to such subjects as the collapse of Law's system, the philosophy of Pierre Bayle, Montesquieu's *Lettres persanes*, and political science.

In 1758 Mme de Pompadour procured the editorship for Marmontel, who wrote his *Contes moraux* for the review. The wide range of contents dismayed him, particularly when he realized that the review's profitability was chiefly assured by publishing puzzles, epigrams, and madrigals sent in from the provinces. He himself kept the journal as serious as in the circumstances he could, publishing important essays, some of them on scientific subjects like inoculation and Halley's comet. From 1762 to 1764 the privilège was held by Pierre-Antoine de la Place but, like the *Gazette* a little earlier, in 1764 it was taken over by the government under Choiseul. In 1754 the review had been making about 22,000 livres a year, and La Place was compensated with a pension of 5,000 livres. The editorship was given to Jacques Lacombe. He was succeeded by the abbé Philippe Bridard de Lagarde and then by the author of contes, Nicolas Bricaire de la Dixmerie.

The various columnists specialized in law, chemistry, natural history, politics, and metaphysics. Others supplied fiction. Some were very distinguished: d'Alembert, Condorcet, Chamfort, Ginguené, La Harpe, and Naigeon. Voltaire himself condescended to send something from time to time. An analysis of the content has shown for 1750 and 1751 a total of 11 political articles and 26 on science, with analyses of over 60 poems and 20 plays. By about 1750 the *Mercure* was showing considerable sympathy for the encyclopédistes (q.v.). It was expensive, with a subscription of 24 livres in Paris and 32 outside. Its readership distribution was surprising. A quarter of the subscribers were officers, and less than a tenth ecclesiastics or lawyers. A third either were nobles or used the aristocratic "de."

In 1778 the privilège was acquired by Charles-Joseph Panckoucke, who amalgamated the review with the *Journal de Bruxelles* and had acquired monopoly rights to journals devoted to political comment. There would be two pages of political comment in a supplement every ten days, to be called *Journal de politique*, and this portion of the review would be subject to scrutiny by two specially appointed censors. La Harpe was briefly editor, but tried to take the journal in a direction which

proved unacceptable and resigned, although he remained literary critic and drama critic. Under Panckoucke's ownership, the *Mercure* swallowed up nine other titles, and the circulation shot up. From the 2,600 copies every 10 days of 1778, the review became a weekly, apparently with 15,000 subscribers by 1786.

In spite of a clear sympathy for the new ideas of the encyclopédistes, the *Mercure* always avoided the danger of being thought subversive, and kept clear of any implied commitment to materialist or deist views. There were only subdued expressions of fashionably liberal views, works of piety were reviewed, and the journal emanated an atmosphere of responsible unwillingness to cause controversy. The death of Voltaire was suitably commemorated with a dozen pieces, and the deaths of Rousseau, Helvétius and Diderot were treated with respect. Right up to the Revolution the *Mercure* published the traditional amalgam of verse, reviews, notes on inventions, and reports on the academies. The *Mercure* was briefly revived after the Revolution, but the title was dormant for most of the 19th century.

The review's literary importance was chiefly concentrated in the period of the editorship of Donneau de Visé from 1672 to 1710, when its judgement on literary works and its stance in literary battles were focal points in the major cultural battle in France, on which its views, favouring the partisans of the "modernes" and of trust in nature and instinct, were ultimately to be victorious.

MOLIÈRE, Jean-Baptiste POQUELIN, known as, 1622–1673.

Actor-manager and playwright.

LIFE

Both Molière's grandfathers were "tapissiers," and his great-grandmother was the widow of a "tapissier." His mother, Marie Cresé, aged 20 when Molière was born, was the daughter of a "tapissier," and his father, Jean Pouguelin (1597–1669), then 25, was a successful merchant, who in 1632 bought the minor offices of "tapissier ordinaire" and "valet de chambre" in the royal household. "Tapissier" means much more than upholsterer. The use of fabrics in interior decoration, as testified by the magnificent tapestries produced for the French court in the late 16th century for hanging on walls, was luxurious, and upholstered chairs were still sufficiently valuable for the materials and designs used to have been noted, for instance, on the inventory of his possessions taken at Richelieu's death in 1642. Molière's family was from the upper bourgeoisie, which could legitimately have aspired to join the minor nobility.

Molière, born on 13 or 14 January 1622, was the oldest of three boys and three girls. The inventory taken on his mother's death on 11 May 1632 shows a prosperous business and a lifestyle of decent comfort. Molière's father, now spelling his name "Poquelin", remarried on 11 April 1633. His step-mother was under 25, daughter of a carriage maker, and she kept the shop. She was to have three daughters, one of whom became a nun, and one of whom died at birth, but she herself died on 12 November 1636, three and a half years after her marriage, leaving Molière's father with five surviving children. The inheritance of his father's offices in the royal household was arranged for Molière on 14 December 1637.

The earliest life of Molière, Grimarest's *La Vie de M. de Molière* (1705), is so frequently at variance with verifiable facts that its value as historical evidence can seldom be rated much higher than "not impossible." Much more reliable, but only on the period after he joined Molière's company at Easter 1659, is La Grange, who played mostly jeune premier roles until the arrival of Michel Baron in 1670. La Grange became the company's secretary and business manager, and from 1664 its orateur, whose function was to make announcements to the audience. He was keeper of the company's *Registre*, a mixture of account book and diary, from 1659 to 1685 (2 vols., 1967). He co-edited Molière's *Oeuvres* in 1682. In fact we know very little for certain about Molière's life before 1643, although it seems quite probable that he attended the Jesuit Collège de Clermont (later the Lycée Louis-le-Grand), and possible that he knew François Bernier and Chapelle, both disciples of Gassendi. He appears to have studied law at Orléans, to have graduated in 1642, and for a few months to have practised at the Paris bar.

It is uncertain how he first came into contact with actors, although one or other of his grandparents may have taken him to the theatre, and he may have had something to do with a troupe of players hired by a pharmacist to draw public attention to his products. The evidence is very scant, but it does point to a period of virtual destitution, and some sort of quasi-fairground activity does not seem improbable. Molière does not seem quite to have broken with his family, but may well have become obsessed by Madeleine Béjart, four years his senior, mother of at least one child by Esprit de Rémond de Mormoiron, the count of Modena, who was a friend of Monsieur, Gaston d'Orléans, the king's brother, and employed by the comte de Guise. Madeleine was the eldest of at least ten children of Marie Hervé.

Her father regarded himself as belonging to the minor nobility. It is not improbable that Molière, already living with Madeleine Béjart, was sent by his father to take his place in fulfilling official duties at Narbonne in 1642 in the suite of Louis XIII, perhaps in the hope of breaking his relationship with the actress, who had her own house near the Béjart family home. Molière must have lived with her there, and there is documentary evidence that he was virtually adopted into her family, although we know only that in January 1643 he received a modest sum left by his mother, to which his father added something, and that he renounced the succession to the household offices in favour of his brother, Jean. When Jean died on 6 April 1660, his father arranged for Molière again to become their inheritor.

On 30 June 1643, in association with several others, including three members of the Béjart family, Jean-Baptiste Poquelin founded "L'Illustre Théâtre," which took a three-year lease on a "jeu de paume (tennis court)" in the Faubourg Saint-Germain, for 1,900 livres, had it prepared for use as a theatre, hired four musicians on 31 October, and went to Rouen for the autumn fair. When in 1644 the troupe hired a dancer, the first signature on the contract was "Molière," although Madeleine Béjart was from

the beginning the dominant figure, and the only one with the right to choose all her own parts. There was nothing sinister about Poquelin's choice of a stage name. Jodelet, Montdory, and Floridor were all stage names, such as were adopted by virtually all important actors. But that Molière adopted his remains, however slight, a form of commitment; he may have been the chief figure of the troupe; and the failure of his grandmother's will to name him suggests that his relationship with his family had at least considerably cooled.

The company, intending to rival the Comédiens du Roi at the Hôtel de Bourgogne and the Marais company which, having been founded by Montdory, who had retired in 1637, was now led by Floridor, opened in Paris on 1 January 1644, drawing its repertoire largely from dramatists who wrote specially for it, like du Ryer and Tristan l'Hermite, a friend of the Béjart family. Although the Théâtre du Marais burned down on 15 January, so reducing the competition, and the Illustre Théâtre received some help from the duc de Guise, who donated at least part of their wardrobe, possibly on account of Modena's connection with Madeleine Béjart, the new venture was in financial difficulties within six months. The actors had to renounce their rights to money due to them from the company, which borrowed again twice later in the year, although it had found a nominal protector in the young king Louis XIV's uncle, Gaston d'Orléans, whose name it used but who is unlikely to have paid anything.

There is no evidence for the view that it was on account of opposition from Jean-Jacques Olier, the curé of Saint-Sulpice and founder of what is usually known as the French school of spirituality, rather than for purely commercial reasons of location and economy, that the Illustre Théâtre was forced to move to the right bank, near the fashionable Place Royale, the present Place des Vosges, built in the first decade of the seventeenth century. Molière, signing himself Poquelin, was now plainly responsible for the troupe's finances. The company leased a new "jeu de paume" for 2,400 livres, but paid less than on the previous occasion to have it got ready. The opening was in January 1645. Failure had become certain by the late spring.

Molière was twice imprisoned for a few days for debt, being freed on 2 August 1645, then imprisoned and released again on 4 August, probably against his father's guarantee. Debts amounting to at least 5,248 livres were repaid only slowly over the following 20 years. Molière apparently left Paris almost immediately, before the costumes pledged by the company against a loan were sold off by Anthoinette Simony in June 1546, but his whereabouts were attested again with certainty only at Nantes on 11 June 1648, and the probability is that he had joined the company of Charles Dufresne, son of Claude Dufresne, the painter, which was protected by the duc d'Epernon, the governor of Languedoc. Molière was soon joined by Madeleine Béjart and her family, and the rest of the troupe of the Illustre Théâtre appears to have dispersed. The Dufresne company, based in Bordeaux, toured the south-west, with Molière at its head probably from the successful season it enjoyed during the Languedoc Estates which were held in December 1650 and January 1651. For some years it played regularly during the Estates General at Carcassonne, Montpellier, and Pézenas.

The evidence is confusing, but the centre of operations later became Lyons, seat of the prince de Conti, whose conversion to austere moral views, however, turned him against the theatre in 1656, and whose patronage may have been unenthusiastically sporadic. In February 1653 one of the actors, du Parc, married at

Lyons Marquise-Thérèse de Gorle, who joined the company and later, known as La du Parc, notoriously became Racine's mistress. The troupe was, or became, something nearer to an established touring company than to a band of habitually strolling players. D'Assoucy, the author of the *Aventures burlesques*, gives an attractive account of his life with the company, whose guest he was for a winter, probably that of 1656–57. In 1657, however, with Conti's protection withdrawn, Molière met La Grange, and also the 47-year-old painter Pierre Mignard, back from Italy and later to be a close friend and supporter, and no doubt contemplated the move to Paris.

Molière's own first five-act play, *L'Etourdi*, a comedy in verse based on Barbieri's *Inavvertito* (1629), with borrowings from other Italian models, was staged probably late in 1654. Like the one-act prose farces Molière had earlier played, some of which were at least partially unscripted, it was heavily dependent on the commedia dell'arte (q.v.). Like its successor, *Le Dépit amoureux*, also five acts and in verse, partly based on Secchi's *Interesse* (1581), and played on 16 December 1656 at Béziers, it was published only in 1663. Molière was already finding it easier to earn a living at comedy than as the tragic actor he dreamt of becoming. By the mid-1650s Molière's players show signs of having been comfortably off.

By May 1658 the company, now financially successful, had moved north, first to Rouen and then to Paris. It included Catherine de Brie and her husband, the Du Parc pair, and four members of the Béjart family—Joseph (1616–59), who died shortly after the move north, Madeleine (1618–72), Molière's constant companion and for a long time his mistress, Geneviève (1624–75), who normally played only minor roles but worked back-stage, and the limping Louis (1630–78), who retired in 1670. Armande Béjart (1643–1700) was to join the company after her marriage to Molière on 20 February 1662 and to run it after his death. It seems certain, as Grimarest said and everyone believed, that Armande was Madeleine's second daughter. The father might or might not have been Modena.

Neither of the alternative possibilities, that Armande was Madeleine's half-sister, and therefore born of a 53-year-old widow, or that she was Madeleine's daughter by Molière himself, seems likely. The difficulty is that Grimarest is unreliable, had every reason to whitewash, and was anyway relying on Baron, who appears to have joined the company in 1666, leaving it after a quarrel with Armande, but who certainly returned in 1670, and was later Armande's lover. There is historical evidence enough to cast doubt on Grimarest's account of Armande's parentage, but so much more doubt attaches to the evidence for any other view that we must assume that Molière's wife was the daughter, probably by Modena, of an ex-mistress with whom he was still closely associated by a friendly relationship and professional ties.

In May 1658 the company, having been at Grenoble for the carnival, moved to Rouen, where they played until October and where both Corneille brothers were emotionally drawn to Thérèse de Parc. In July Madeleine Béjart obtained a sub-lease of the Marais troupe's hall for 18 months from September, to play there alternately with the resident company, no doubt partly because it was in serious financial trouble. From Rouen, however, Molière succeeded in attracting the patronage of the 18-year-old Monsieur, who was to promise but, as La Grange notes, not to pay, 300 livres a year for each member of the company. However, on 24 October 1658 the company played Pierre Cor-

neille's *Nicomède* at the Louvre, before the young Louis XIV and his court, including the queen mother, Mazarin, and Monsieur. The style was less histrionic than that of Montfleury, the notoriously obese tragic actor from the Hôtel de Bourgogne who was to be hostile, as well as a rival, to Molière. The performance of *Nicomède* was not a notable success, although the lost one-act farce by Molière which followed it, *Le Docteur amoureux*, was instantly acclaimed.

As a result, the king ordered that the Petit-Bourbon stage should be made available to Molière's troupe on the "extraordinary" days (Mondays, Wednesdays, Thursdays, and Saturdays). Molière shared the hall with the Italian company, contributed 1,500 livres towards the costs, and had to adapt his plays to Tiberio Fiorilli's fixed commedia dell'arte scenery of houses round a square. Fiorilli had already dropped the traditional commedia dell'arte mask he had worn as "Scaramouche," while much of his technique inspired Molière's acting, which also drew on Domenico Locatelli, who played the commedia character Trivelin, valet and adventurer, and sometimes wore Harlequin's mask. Until the mid-1660s Molière was often to dress in a way which led the audience to expect the character he was playing to resemble some elaboration of the Italian Scaramouche.

The lease on the Marais theatre was renounced, and on 2 November 1658 Molière's company began playing at the Petit-Bourbon to Parisian audiences. The pamphlet in the form of a verse play, *Elomire hypochondre; ou, Les Médecins vengés*, published in 1670 by Le Boulanger de Chalussay and bitterly hostile to Molière, of whose name "Elomire" is an anagram, suggests that the troupe's attempts to play Pierre Corneille's older tragedies had met with disaster. Molière was gradually forced to renounce tragedy both as an actor and as a playwright, leaving the Hôtel de Bourgogne for the moment with a monopoly of tragedy. In desperation he resorted to the farces with which he had done so well in the provinces, and which also proved immediately successful in Paris.

At Easter 1659, the beginning of the theatrical year, Charles Dufresne retired, and the du Parc pair left for the Marais company. They regretted it, and that autumn signed a contract to work with Molière's troupe from Easter 1660 for four years. In the meanwhile Jodelet, who was to die in 1660, and his brother L'Espy came to the company from the Marais, and La Grange, du Croisy, and his wife joined the troupe. In July 1659 the Italian troupe returned to Italy, and Molière played on the "ordinary days," on which there were also performances in the Marais and at the Hôtel de Bourgogne. He was also freed from his dependence on Italian scenery, and therefore from commedia dell'arte type plots. The final breakthrough came with Molière's one-act prose comedy *Les Précieuses ridicules*, played after Pierre Corneille's *Cinna* on 18 November 1659. The play was essentially built on a degree of caricature which made it into farce, but it introduced the type of satire with a strongly contemporary relevance for which Molière was to become celebrated, which is the enduring basis of his achievement, and for which his contemporaries were not easily to forgive him.

There were allusions to recognizable figures in Paris society, and the play did not altogether break with burlesque Italian models. It was acted partly in masks, with characters—La Grange and du Croisy, Jodelet and Mascarille, played by Molière—bearing names denoting well-known stock commedia dell'arte characters. The text was pirated before it was officially published in 1660 in what was probably a toned-down version, without the allusions to Paris society, and aimed against only provincials aping Parisian manners and at "false" preciosity. Préciosité (q.v.) had earlier in the century emerged as part of a vast civilizing movement in French society towards refinement and fastidiousness. It had, however, sunk into stereotypes by 1659, although Molière's caricature was to leave him with enemies, like Somaize and, for a period, Donneau de Visé, who were on the side of the advance towards sophisticated and liberal social attitudes which was to become strongly associated with the sometimes euphoric views of personal and social experience almost exclusively explored by the "moderne" faction in the Querelle des anciens et des modernes (q.v.). Molière underlined his anxiety not to offend by staging Gabriel Gilbert's lost *La vraie ou la fausse Précieuse* in May 1660, but from December 1659 had been able to double the entry price for his own play, although its erratic appearance on his bill suggests that pressure of some sort must have been organized against it.

On 28 May 1660 Molière's short one-act verse comedy, *Sganarelle; ou, Le Cocu imaginaire* was another success, with 34 performances in its first 3-month run. Molière played the lead, and the piece, performed during the celebrations for the marriage of Louis XIV and Marie-Thérèse, was staged more often than any other of his plays during his own lifetime. The valet of the commedia began to lose his satirical relevance and to be deepened into a character capable of conveying pathos, starting his slow transformation into the modern circus clown, the pantomime dame, and the Punch, derived more directly from the figure of Pulcinella, of "Punch and Judy" fame. Molière began to publish his plays, taking out a privilège on 31 May 1660 for *L'Etourdi*, *Le Dépit amoureux*, *Le Cocu imaginaire*, and *Dom Garcie de Navarre*.

On 11 October 1660 the destruction of the Petit-Bourbon, whose demolition was scheduled and had been discussed in Jean Loret's rhymed gazette *La Muse Historique* for 5 July 1659, was begun without warning, on the authority of the superintendant of works, M. de Ratabon. He was certainly acting with the collusion of the other two companies, who immediately made favourable offers to Molière's actors. They stayed faithful to him, however, and the king offered them the only other hall in Paris suitable for theatrical performance, the large theatre in the Palais-Royal which Richelieu had had built for himself. It took three months to get even provisionally ready, and it was not thoroughly re-equipped until 1671. In the meanwhile, seating was brought over from the comparative magnificence of the Palais-Bourbon, and Molière played in a small theatre under a makeshift canvas roof.

During the time they lacked anywhere at all to play, Molière's troupe was invited to perform in various grand houses—four times for the king in the Louvre, twice for Mazarin, and also for Foucquet and half a dozen others. When the Palais-Royal hall was inaugurated by the company on 20 January 1661 with *Le Dépit amoureux*, Molière's was the only Paris company not paying rent for its hall, although the Marais company, again fashionable, was attracting substantial support from the king and was from 1665 to become the "troupe du roi." From January 1662 the Italian company returned to Paris and again shared Molière's stage. This time they were led by their melancholy Harlequin, Giuseppe-Domenico Biancolelli, "Dominique."

Molière's first new play at the Palais-Royal, created on 4 February 1661, was the five-act "comédie héroïque" in verse *Dom Garcie de Navarre*. It was based on an Italian model, had been written some time previously, was in spite of its privilège published only in the posthumous 1682 *Oeuvres*, and was perhaps, by adopting its conventions, intended to appease "galant" society. It was a relative failure, with the box office takings tailing off sharply from 600 livres to a mere 70 at the seventh performance. Portions of it were used for later plays. During the Easter closure Molière, now undisputed head of the company, was granted a double share in the takings, hitherto split equally among its members, but his share was to stay double even if he married, so that his marriage to Armande Béjart appears already to have been predicted. The three-act verse comedy *L'Ecole des maris* was created in Paris on 24 June 1661, a farce to be performed after a tragedy, perhaps adapted from a Spanish original, but directly challenging a play put on by Montfleury three months earlier, *L'Ecole des cocus*. Molière took the part of Sganarelle, now depicted as seriously deluded in the rigour of his moral principles. The play shows Molière in fundamental sympathy with advanced feelings among his contemporaries on the need to liberate women from marital and other tyrannies, and it was much applauded in the entourage of Foucquet.

On 17 August 1661 *Les Fâcheux*, a comedy-ballet of three acts and in verse, essentially a series of ten satirical sketches with mime and ballet, was created for Foucquet at Vaux-le-Vicomte, with help from Pellisson, a décor by Lebrun, and music by Lulli, during the famous evening of festivities which started with Vatel's celebrated supper (see: Mme de Sévigné), and ended with the firework display described by La Fontaine, just three weeks before Foucquet's arrest for embezzlement. He had earlier been a patron of Molière, during the October of the troupe's enforced unemployment, and then on 12 and 13 July 1661. After it opened in Paris on 4 November 1661, *Les Fâcheux* was given 39 successive performances. During their course Molière married on 20 February 1662. He and his wife were to have three children, born in 1664, 1665 and 1672, although only one, Esprit-Madeleine (1665–1723) survived infancy and outlived her father. Armande's extra-marital liaisons were the subject of much gossip, and there seems to have been an estrangement and a reconciliation. Armande was at Molière's deathbed on 17 February 1673.

From the Easter break of 1662, there were 15 shares in the company. We also have then the first clear evidence that Molière had translated Lucretius into prose and verse. By this time Molière was enjoying protection at court, without which his company would probably not have survived. Louis XIV had given him 3,000 livres when the company played for Mazarin after the destruction of the Petit-Bourbon, and in 1661 Molière received 1,500 livres for himself and the same amount for his troupe. In March 1663 he received a first annual "gratification" of 1,000 livres and in October of that year another 2,000 livres for a performance of *L'Impromptu de Versailles*. In addition, in spite of the submission to the king by Montfleury of a memoir alleging Molière's possibly incestuous marriage, Louis XIV went out of his way to show his esteem for Molière by becoming godfather by proxy to Molière's first child in 1664. The godmother was Henriette d'Angleterre, wife of Monsieur and the king's sister-in-law.

From August 1665 the company ceased to bear the name of Monsieur, and became "la troupe du Roi," paid an annual 6,000 livres. At that date the Hôtel de Bourgogne was receiving an annual 12,000 livres from the king, the Marais nothing at all, and the Italians 16,000 livres, in addition to personal annual pensions for their principal players. Molière's troupe was the favourite to amuse the king at the celebrations at Versailles, Saint-Germain, and Chambord. Only in the last year of his life did Molière lose his position as royal favourite to Lulli, who was granted a patent for all musical performances, thereby preventing Molière from independently staging at court his own comedy-ballets. As a result *Le Malade imaginaire*, written for the court, was to be confined to the Palais-Royal, and played with much diminished splendour. In 1662, however, Molière's troupe stayed at court from 8 to 14 May.

Later that year the premiere of *L'Ecole des femmes* was to be given at the Palais-Royal on 26 December. Partly challenging Scarron's *La Précaution inutile*, recently staged at the Hôtel de Bourgogne by Montfleury, it was a five-act comedy in verse which also drew on a conte by Straparole from his *Facétieuses nuits*, translated partly in 1560 and partly in 1573. Probably Molière's greatest public success, and clearly aligning him with the précieuses in their desire for emancipation, *L'Ecole des femmes* also deepened the Sganarelle figure into that of the deluded guardian, retaining a daring element of social satire, implying a criticism of rigorous religious morality, and lifting pure farce to what were considered to be dangerous levels of comic seriousness. The first ten performances brought in 11,000 livres, half as much again as Molière's previous greatest successes. There were 31 performances before Easter and 32 after the re-opening, in addition to specially arranged occasions for private patrons. On 13 January 1663 Loret gave his account of a performance before the king.

Foucquet's successor, Colbert, to whom Molière owed his place on the list of gratifiés, also invited Molière to perform his new piece. It is, however, unlikely that Molière, patronized by Foucquet, and at court by Henriette d'Angleterre, and temperamentally averse to Colbert's artistic policies and sympathy with the anciens (see: Querelle), did not align himself with the opposition to the king's new minister. Although Colbert was to employ the team assembled by Foucquet at Vaux to finish the construction of Versailles in its original severe classical grandeur, he wanted the king to stay in Paris, and disapproved of the spirit of frivolous modernity in which the king was to keep the court subservient to him at Versailles.

L'Ecole des femmes was the occasion of considerable public controversy. On his return to Paris from the provinces, Molière had been associated with a group, including Patru, the abbé d'Aubignac, Cotin, Marie-Catherine Desjardins, Gilles Boileau, and others who frequented the comtesse de la Suze. A little later Molière is to be found more often in the company of the mildly sceptical and licentious group who frequented the inn "La Croix Blanche," including La Mothe le Vayer's brother, des Barreaux, Chapelle, and even Boileau. Opposition to the piece, for which the plentiful theatrical jealousy alone does not account, was waiting for the premiere of *L'Ecole des femmes*, partly because of the reputation for intellectual scepticism of the company Molière kept, but mostly on account of his purely farcical presentation of properly comic material, sustained by pathos, with a sharp satirical cutting edge. At the core of the attack was a hostility which Molière had created in some parts of fashionable Paris, to which was quickly added the jealousy of rivals in the theatrical world and the spite of literary journalists against the combination of serious innovation and popular success.

An acid, if apparently moderate attack, by Donneau de Visé,
later to become an ally but perhaps still remembering *Les Précieuses ridicules*, appeared in his *Nouvelles nouvelles*. D'Aubignac defended the piece against Pierre Corneille, also later to ally with Molière and to provide him with material to stage, and Boileau, who did not yet know Molière, wrote his *Stances* in defence of Molière, who himself had taken out a privilège within five weeks of the premiere. *L'Ecole des femmes* was published on 17 March 1663 with a dedication to Henriette d'Angleterre and a preface by the author threatening to defend his play with what turned out to be the one-act prose comedy *La Critique de l'Ecole des femmes*, put on at the end of a performance on 1 June. The box office jumped from 100 livres for the preceding performance to 1,375 for the first night of *La Critique*.

Donneau de Visé replied with *Zélinde; ou, La Véritable Critique de l'Ecole des femmes* and then with *La Critique de la Critique*; these may not have been played but their texts were on sale in August. Early in October a protégé of Pierre Corneille, Boursault, renewed the attack on Molière with his *Portrait du peintre*, played at the Hôtel de Bourgogne with a song in it by Donneau de Visé, suppressed in the published version, which bawdily repeated the accusation of incest. Molière, who had been to see the Boursault play, replied, encouraged by the king, with the one-act prose comedy *L'Impromptu de Versailles*, a direct satirical attack on the players of the Hôtel de Bourgogne, given before the king in mid-October 1663, with the actors of the company, including Molière, playing themselves. It sharply warned Molière's critics not to attack his private life. *L'Impromptu* was put on in Paris on 4 November.

The king had given gratifications of 4,000 livres to the company and 1,000 livres to Molière personally for *La Critique de l'Ecole des femmes*, but there were further polemical comedies by Robinet, Donneau de Visé and Montfleury's son. In 1664 the father had formally submitted his memoir to the king accusing Molière of incest. Donneau de Visé, at this time a young man anxious to make an impression, was to write again against Molière in his *Lettre sur les affaires du théâtre* before becoming a close friend. The essence of the objection levelled against *L'Ecole des femmes* was expressed in terms of its vulgarity. Fault was also found in the construction, and blasphemous innuendoes were projected into the text. Molière had hit hard at prudes and the social climbers who affected aristocratic status, and *La Critique* was intended to exacerbate the injuries inflicted on those whose pretensions he had ridiculed. His attackers were of course not wholly wrong. Some of the lines in the original play do lend themselves to being understood as salacious; the humour does not always avoid a mild coarseness; and the ten maxims on marriage may not quite unreasonably have been thought in poor religious taste.

The controversy of *L'Ecole des femmes* had occupied most of 1663. Molière's increasing importance is indicated by the two-volume publication of his previously printed plays as *Oeuvres* in that year. On 29 January 1664 he presented a three-act prose comedy-ballet, *Le Mariage forcé*, in which the king, dressed as a gipsy, danced a ballet. It was played from 15 February at the Palais-Royal, where it did not win public favour, and it had to be dropped before Easter. In its printed version of 1668 it is reduced to a single act. For a six-day fête at Versailles from 7 to 12 May 1664 in honour of the king's new mistress, Mme de la Vallière, Molière produced a five-act comedy-ballet, *La Princesse d'Elide*, derived from a Spanish comedy by Moreto, which attracted a gratification of 2,000 livres. Only one and a half acts are in verse. The piece was played in Paris in November. The Versailles performance was on 8 May. On 12 May Molière presented to the court the first three acts of *Tartuffe*. Molière's known intention to write a satire with a religious basis had caused opposition to coalesce some weeks earlier and, although the king did what he could to protect Molière's interests, pressure, organized notably by the Compagnie du Saint-Sacrement, obliged him to ban the play. On 17 May the *Gazette* announced that it would not be played again. Molière enlisted the support of the Papal legate but was unable to have the ban lifted. On 12 June he put on Racine's *La Thébaïde*.

Parts of *Tartuffe* were read in private houses, and the three acts were performed for Monsieur on 25 September 1664. By 29 November a full five-act version appears to have been played for Condé, although Molière is also said still to have been under pressure to finish a fourth act a year later. The presumption is that by 1664 Molière had developed his originally burlesque style into serious social comedy, capable of pathos, but satirizing with a diminishingly grotesque element of caricature recognizable tendencies—idiocies of behaviour, fatuities of attitude, hypocrisies, stupidities, and exaggerations—in the behaviour of his contemporaries. Only on this assumption can the actual history of the public and official receptions given to his plays be cogently explained. They plainly ran through the whole spectrum, from injured hostility on the part of sectional interests and those who felt themselves possible models for the lampoons, through amused tolerance from the king, the streetwise and the frivolous, to the almost ribald enjoyment by well-off bourgeois society of the discomfiture of the pretentious and the affected.

It was in 1664 that Armande's infidelities first caused gossip. On 15 February 1665 the five-act prose comedy *Dom Juan; ou, Le Festin de Pierre* was played at the Palais-Royal. There were 15 performances of which the last was on 20 March but, in spite of takings which reached 2,108 livres at the sixth performance and totalled 16,243 livres for the first 10, the piece did not reappear on the bill after Easter. The privilège for the text, dated 11 March, was not used, and a ferocious attack, pseudonymous but Jansenist (q.v.), appeared under the title *Observations*. Two pamphlets defending Molière against the *Observations* were also published in the weeks following the premiere. There are signs that the play itself was turned out in a hurry, that Molière was simply putting together a piece on a well-known theme, recently treated three times (by Dorimond, Villiers, and Dominique), which it would have been possible to clothe with some innocuous satire. The various authors had drawn on other legendary heroes, too, and Dominique's version was actually being played by the Italian company at the Palais-Royal as recently, we know, as 1664. Molière, however, had returned in *Dom Juan* to the subject of the banned *Tartuffe*, hypocrisy.

He suppressed part of act 3, scene 2, at the second performance; later revivals stitched together only inoffensive parts of the text; the Dutch published Dorimond's text over Molière's name in 1674; Thomas Corneille versified Molière's text for performance in 1677, and received an enthusiastic notice from Donneau de Visé, his friend and collaborator at *Le Mercure Galant* (q.v.). The text published in Molière's posthumous *Oeuvres* was bowdlerized, and then, after printing, again cut in places with scissors, although three copies escaped. Finally in 1683 a text was printed in Amsterdam which may just possibly have been one of the original actors' copies of 1665. What is perfectly clear is that Molière's treatment of religious issues,

whether considered as farce or as satire, provoked strong feelings of hostility, and the play must be regarded as having been suppressed at Easter in 1665, even if no formal prohibition was issued. The king did not see the play.

On 4 August 1665 Molière's daughter Esprit-Madeleine was baptized. It seems probable that the god-parents, Modena and Madeleine Béjart, were chosen and agreed to act as a public demonstration that they were the maternal grandparents. On 14 September what had just become "la troupe du Roi" gave the first performance of *L'Amour médecin* at Versailles, followed by its premiere in Paris on the 22nd. A light-hearted comedy-ballet in three acts, played after something more serious, it was a financial success with a long run, but the doctors it makes fun of were recognizable by the masks they wore. They included the king's doctor, Henri-Louis Daquin, who was also Molière's landlord and with whom Molière had just quarrelled when his rent went up. Lulli had composed the music, but performances at the Palais-Royal took place without the expensive ballets of the Versailles production. It was at the end of this year that Racine moved his *Alexandre* to the Hôtel de Bourgogne. Molière fell gravely ill, and the troupe gave no performances between 29 December 1665 and 21 February 1666. Molière may have continued to be ill, as the Easter closure lasted longer than usual, from 11 April to 9 May.

On 4 June Molière presented *Le Misanthrope*, often considered his greatest play, in which he no doubt mocks his own personal depression. His health was poor—as the result of a chest infection late in 1665 he was allowed only milk to drink—and his marriage was in trouble, but the main cause of his depression appears to have been literary. *Tartuffe* remained suppressed and there had been the difficulties with *Dom Juan*, but the fact that Alceste in *Le Misanthrope* turns out unnecessarily to be a writer whose enemies have promoted the rumour that he was the author of a "livre abominable" suggests that Molière was gently laughing at himself, not without a touch of bitterness. *Le Livre abominable*, a pamphlet of five dialogues in verse attacking Colbert, Mazarin, Anne of Austria, and above all the "dévots," had been circulating in Paris since about 1663 and, although Molière was not the author, he was associated with the circle in which it was produced. Financially *Le Misanthrope* was a failure, with the box-office receipts falling heavily on the third performance to 886 livres, and then to 212 livres by the tenth. In all the first ten performances brought in 8,444 livres.

The three-act prose comedy *Le Médecin malgré lui* was presented on 6 August 1666. It was based on a medieval fabliau and had undergone various transformations ("Le Fagotier" of 1661, "Le Médecin par force" of 1664). In the context of Molière's production it is important for the development in the role of the valet figure. Given after something more substantial, the piece eventually helped to increase the receipts from *Le Misanthrope*. During the next 18 months Molière produced only slight pieces for court entertainments: *Mélicerte*, a contribution to *Le Ballet des Muses* staged at Saint-Germain in December 1666 and later replaced by *La Pastorale comique*, and the one-act prose comedy *Le Sicilien; ou, L'Amour peintre*, played at Saint-Germain in February 1667 and on 10 June at the Palais-Royal.

By the middle of 1666 the question of the morality of the theatre had been raised by the dispute between Nicole and Racine. Late in August d'Aubignac's *Dissertation sur la condamnation des théâtres* clearly alluded to Molière's corruptive influence. The *Dissertation* was followed by Conti's posthumous *Traité de la comédie*, published in December, which obviously attacked Molière. Molière appears to have been sporadically ill in 1667 and 1668, the years during which Louis XIV fought his successful Flanders campaign, starting with the invasion of the Spanish Low Countries on 24 May 1667 and ending with the peace of Aix-la-Chapelle on 2 May 1668. Before Louis XIV left Paris, Molière believed that he had been authorized to play *Tartuffe*. Accordingly a toned-down version of the piece, now called *Panulphe; ou, L'Imposteur*, was staged on 5 August 1667. Panulphe, the hypocrite, was no longer a cleric. The play, however, was forbidden the next day by Lamoignon, the premier président of the parlement and chief administrative officer left in Paris, and until its dissolution in 1666 a member of the Compagnie du Saint-Sacrement. A week later the archbishop, Hardouin de Péréfixe, banned all performance or reading of the work, or attendance at a reading. Molière once again tried hard to have the ban removed, even sending emissaries to Louis XIV at his camp, but succeeding only in having the ecclesiastical ban virtually rescinded. The troupe remained seven weeks without playing. Only on 5 February 1669 was performance authorized. The play was staged that night, with box-office takings of 2,860 livres, and remained on the bill beyond the Easter break, with 44 consecutive performances. Molière obtained a privilège on 15 March and published the text almost immediately, on 23 March. His father had died on 27 February. The office of tapissier and valet de chambre was to bring Molière 4,400 livres a year thereafter.

Meanwhile *Amphitryon*, a three-act verse comedy in a mixture of alexandrines and octosyllables, created at the Palais-Royal on 13 January 1668, clearly alludes to the king, represented by a metaphorical god sending emissaries back from Flanders to earth to see what is going on at Versailles. It is also a poeticized satire on court intrigue. The play was popular and had 29 performances. That summer, after Condé's victories in Franche-Comté and the peace of Aix-la-Chapelle, there was much to celebrate, and there were the gardens at Versailles to inaugurate. Probably on 18 July 1668 Molière staged the three-act prose comedy *George Dandin* at Versailles as his contribution to "Le grand divertissement royal." When it was given in Paris on 9 November the piece virtually failed. It was obviously light-weight and hastily written, but it did inaugurate a series of comedies in which the humour is almost bitter.

Before *Dandin*'s Paris premiere, however, Molière presented one of his most elaborate plays, the prose five-act *L'Avare*, played for the first time at the Palais-Royal on 9 September 1668. Its failure disappointed him and has never been convincingly explained, although it may have had to do with the choice of prose for so ambitious a comedy. Molière wrote no more five-act comedies for three years, collaborating with Lulli, Pierre Corneille and Quinault on *Psyché* (performed at the Tuileries, January 1671), which was already practically an opera, and presenting only a tragedy-ballet, *Les Amants magnifiques* (at Saint-Germain, February 1670), in which Louis XIV played Neptune, and two comedy-ballets, *Monsieur de Pourceaugnac* (at Chambord, 6 October 1669) and *Le Bourgeois gentilhomme* (also at Chambord, October 1670), which must have seemed to allude to Colbert's humble origins, and was a considerable financial success. Colbert was known to have enjoyed and defended the attack on Molière and Mignard in the satirical *La Coupe du Val de Grâce* in 1669, and Molière could feel safe in avenging himself in what, after all, was only a comedy-ballet.

The Tuileries, where the elaborate and expensive *Psyché* was first performed, was an immense hall capable of accommodating 7,000 spectators. When *Psyché* was moved to the Palais-Royal it provided the final incentive for rebuilding the theatre, which now had to accommodate the complicated stage machinery. The refurbishment cost 4,359 livres, an expense partly borne by the Italian company, and the entertainment, which had 38 consecutive performances, was itself costly to mount, although it was nevertheless a financial success. Lulli was now providing Molière with all the music he required.

On 24 May 1671 Molière staged the three-act prose comedy *Les Fourberies de Scapin*, which did not succeed, perhaps because it lacked any obvious satirical relevance to contemporary society. In December Molière presented at Saint-Germain a one-act comedy in prose, *La Comtesse d'Escarbagnas*, not transferred to the Palais-Royal until July 1672. Molière marked his break with Lulli by asking Charpentier for the music. Lulli was gaining the ascendancy, and French opera was about to emerge from the comedy-ballets for which Lulli had hitherto provided Bensserade and Molière with music. Mazarin's attempts to import Venetian opera had failed, notably with the rejection of the work of Monteverdi and Cavalli by Parisian audiences around 1660. During the following decade Bensserade and Lulli presented a comedy-ballet at court virtually every year. Tragedies dependent on complicated stage hoists, musical scores, and mythological subjects became popular. Molière himself had given music an increasing importance in his comedy-ballets, with *Monsieur de Pourceaugnac* not far from opera buffa.

In 1659 Pierre Perrin, a literary adventurer, social climber, and minor poet who had sided with the précieuses against Molière and spent several spells in prison, probably for debt, had staged the apparently successful *La Pastorale d'Issi*. It consisted of 14 linked songs with orchestral accompaniment. In 1653, when he must have been about 30, he had married a widow of 62; he had his marriage judicially dissolved in 1666 and died in 1675. On 28 June 1669 he obtained a privilège for an Académie d'opéras, and worked together with the marquis de Sourdéac and Bersac de Champeron, employing Cambert as composer. They took a jeu de paume, equipped it superbly, and inaugurated it on 3 March 1671 with *Pomone*, by Perrin and Cambert, heavily dependent on stage machinery. *Pomone* started a fashion, with at least four musical and dramatic entertainments in the winter of 1671–72: at Versailles; at Saint-Germain, with Gilbert and Cambert's *Les Peines et les plaisirs de l'amour*, published with a dedication praising the modernes for again associating music and drama; at the Académie d'opéras; and, with Donneau de Visé's *Le Mariage de Bacchus et d'Ariane*, with music by Mollier, at the Marais. Cambert appears now to have been driven out without having been paid, to die in London, murdered, in 1677. Perrin quarrelled with Sourdéac and went back to prison.

Lulli, from 1661 royal composer, and not yet the common subject of scandalous gossip, obtained Colbert's backing to get Perrin out of prison early in 1672 in exchange for the Académie's privilège. On 13 March Lulli was granted letters patent to which Molière's company objected on 29 March. Lulli's letters from the king forbade anyone else, including the "officiers de notre maison (our household officials)," a phrase designed to include Molière as valet de chambre, from having any verse sung in any language without Lulli's permission. Colbert was hesitant, and the king gave Molière oral permission for six singers and a dozen instrumentalists, but on 1 April 1672 the hall used by Sourdéac and Champeron was definitively closed, although they went on paying rent until it became the Théâtre Guénégaud, to whose company they sub-let it, and with which they later became more closely associated as profit-sharers. On 22 April, after the Easter recess, Lulli had Molière's concession reduced to two singers, half a dozen instrumentalists, and no dancers. On 20 September Lulli's monopoly was extended to the printing of any of the words which Lulli had set to music. He thereby became the legal owner of any Molière text for which he had composed music. Lulli's own efforts to obtain the use of the great hall in the Louvre were thwarted, but he was able to inaugurate another jeu de paume on 15 November 1672.

Madeleine Béjart had died on 17 December 1671, having renounced the profession of actress. She was accordingly buried in sanctified ground. On 11 March 1672 Molière had presented a new five-act verse comedy Les Femmes savantes, satirically aimed at the enemy he had in common with Boileau, Charles Cotin, presumed author of the pamphlet La Critique désintéressée sur les Satyres du temps, probably of 1664. The play has been severely criticized, but Molière thought highly of it and it was at first a box-office success, with the first seven performances bringing in over 1,000 livres each. It had 20 consecutive performances, although its drawing power fell away badly after the recess, when receipts went down to 268 and then 258 livres.

Molière's last comedy-ballet, Le Malade imaginaire, although intended for Versailles, had to be staged at the Palais-Royal on 10 February 1673. In prose, it is also one of Molière's most brilliant satirical comedies, its aims associated with those of Boileau's Arrêt burlesque. It attacked not only the medical faculty but also the Cartesianism of the Augustinians owing allegiance to Port-Royal (q.v.). The music was by Charpentier. The box-office receipts averaged nearly 2,000 livres for the first three performances. On the day of the fourth performance, 17 February, Molière felt unusually tired, but with Condé coming to see the play, he was concerned about letting down the company and those who depended on it. Part of the audience noticed a momentary malaise during the final ballet, but Molière finished the performance, rested in Baron's box, and had himself taken home. Baron was with him when, in bed, he began to cough up blood. Armande was fetched, but Molière had died before a priest could be found who would come. Louis XIV had personally to intervene to obtain ecclesiastical burial by night.

On 27 April Lulli and Quinault presented before the king Cadmus et Hermione, commonly thought of as the first French opera. The following day, Lulli was given the Palais-Royal for musical performances, and his monopoly was extended, with all other companies being reduced to two singers and six violins. Four members of Molière's company—La Thorillière, who had joined in 1662, Baron, Mlle Beauval, and her husband, all of whom had joined in 1670—moved to the Hôtel de Bourgogne. Armande, who was to marry again, and the other seven amalgamated with the Marais company, took over the jeu de paume from Sourdéac and Champeron, moved in with the furniture from the Palais-Royal, and on 9 July opened there the Théâtre Guénégaud, which was to specialize in plays requiring stage machinery. The income per player at first fell to 2,586 livres, before climbing higher than it had ever been in Molière's day, to 6,585 livres, although the company had lost royal financial support and scarcely ever again played before the king. On 21 Octo-

ber 1680 the two companies, the new "troupe du Roi" of the Rue Guénégaud and the "Grands comédiens" of the Hôtel de Bourgogne, fused into the Comédie-Française. Between 1680 and 1700 the new company played Tartuffe 172 times, Le Misanthrope 165 times, L'Avare 155 times, Amphitryon 144 times, George Dandin 135 times, and Le Médecin malgré lui 131 times. Of the 95 plays put on by Molière during his 15 years in Paris, he was the author of 31. It was as author rather than as director of the troupe that he was allocated a double share of the income, otherwise equally divided into "parts," normally one to a player.

As an actor, Molière's gift, the public forced him to realize, was for farce, although as an author his best plays are undoubtedly those containing pointed social satire of contemporary relevance, directed often at identifiable target personnages, and always at people in the upper reaches of bourgeois society who could laugh at caricatures of their own pretensions and follies and on whom Molière primarily relied for his audiences. His acting technique was inspired by the Italians. He grimaced, rolled his eyes, and mimed. From 1665 he exploited his illness in the roles of Harpagon, Pourceaugnac, Jourdain, and Argan, and intended those characters to be portrayed as underweight, physically crushed by their obsessions.

Molière died rich. During the last 14 years of his life he probably earned 130,000 livres, with his wife bringing in perhaps 46,000 more. His actors earned more than just respectable bourgeois livings—between 3,000 and 4,000 livres a year, rarely less and sometimes a good deal more. Lunch for a dozen actors rehearsing cost one livre, a day's wage for an unskilled workman. A skilled stage hand would receive two livres a day, three times a week. With 20 sols to the livre, a standing place cost 15 sols. The best boxes, with eight places, cost five livres 12 sols. Ribou paid Molière 200 livres for the text of Tartuffe. He was a bookseller who started by pirating Molière's texts and printing his enemies' pamphlets, but ended up befriended by him. Molière gave him texts to publish, lent him money, and saved him from being hanged when he lampooned the king in 1670. Armande got 1,500 livres for the seven unpublished plays after Molière's death. The Oeuvres de Monsieur de Molière, revues, corrigées et augmentées were published in eight volumes in 1682, volumes one to six in June and the two volumes of Oeuvres posthumes in October.

WORKS

The Italian company whose stage Molière shared, whose scenery he had to use, and whose acting he both admired and imitated, used partly unscripted texts, with only a few main incidents sketched out. Molière, too, although decreasingly, relied on the improvisations of his actors, and on the effect of their masks and apparel, so that, even when the words alluded to particular individuals or a particular class of persons, the masks themselves showed the stereotypes as which they were being caricatured. The total effect often depended on mime, often even on the grimaces derived from dumbshow, as well as on musical interludes, and on the singing and dancing of the court entertainments provided by Molière and others, which at Versailles, as with Les Fâcheux at Vaux, almost always started life as comedy-ballets.

Verse, especially the tragic verse solemnly declaimed by Molière's contemporaries at the Hôtel de Bourgogne, was normally printed as it had been spoken, giving the dramatic script a literary value higher in proportion to the total theatrical creation than was ever possible in comedy, where the words contributed proportionately less to the total effect. Molière's early prose farces not only were not, but could not have been, scripted in words alone. Even the comedies in verse, which did not allow for verbal improvisation, depended for their effects on reminiscences of commedia dell'arte stereotypes recalled by Molière's enduringly Italianate acting style, itself no doubt originally derived from provincial commedia dell'arte troupes seen by Molière well before his return to Paris.

The Italian tradition, however firmly derived from subjection to the monopoly rights of others to stage dialogue, and from sheer linguistic incapacity, incidentally allied Molière, despite much personal sadness and the sharpness of his satirical attacks, to those of his contemporaries who preferred to examine the range of exuberant and optimistic attitudes to human life. His artistic affinity was with the "modernes," to whose inchoate grouping, however, he avoided ideological commitment. In any discussion of Molière's work it must also be remembered that the "Comédie italienne," as it later and somewhat pretentiously came to be know, did not exclude satire. Whatever the Italian company intended in *La Finta Matrigna* of 1697, it was expelled from France because the butt of its attack was understood as being Mme de Maintenon. Molière's satire, indeed, developed quite smoothly from his Italianate burlesque.

Live farce consisted in something much more than the recitation of lines. In addition, since Molière took sometimes wrongly calculated risks in combining farce with sharp social satire, he found it prudent to tone down the text of some of his plays between performances, and certainly before publication. The printed text of *Les Précieuses ridicules* may not explain the dramatic experience it mediated on 18 November 1659 in the Petit-Bourbon. Scarron had already made fun of préciosité in *L'Héritier ridicule*. The four parts of the abbé de Pure's novel *La Prétieuse; ou, Le Mystère des ruelles* had appeared from 1656 to 1658, suggesting that the original movement refining taste and social behaviour had opened itself to affectation, and that its exaggerations were now ripe for observers to ridicule, without mocking the seriousness of the cause of female emancipation. Somaize, who was to defend the précieux movement against Molière, records that Pure's lost comedy of 1656, which was played in Italian and probably never scripted, was given at the Petit-Bourbon itself by the Italian company. Somaize says that Molière took the device of two disguised valets from it, although Pure's sketch of his own plot suggests that Molière, while he must have derived from Pure, did not borrow his plot, which satirizes an unidentified contemporary writer and in which a girl is converted both to a précieux distrust of passion and to a précieux antipathy to the subjugation implied by early marriage.

Molière did not expect his farce to be the success it was. He neither doubled his prices when it was given its premiere as an after-piece to Pierre Corneille's *Cinna* on that 18 November, nor played it after the new tragedy his troupe was currently performing. It did not re-appear on the bill until needed on 2 December to prop up a revival of du Ryer's 1640 *Alcyonée*, when the prices were doubled and the box-office amounted to 1,400 livres. The 44 performances it received in its first season represent a successful run, and the subject of précieux affectation suddenly, if briefly, became fashionable, with a spate of short satirical outbursts of literary venom or pastiche.

The play is difficult to interpret because we do not know how far, or with real certainty even whether, the text was toned down for publication; whether the play's run was interrupted by outside intervention, as, apparently with Molière's connivance, reported by Marie-Catherine Desjardins; whether the objects of satirical attack were personally identifiable, or merely associated with the circle probably of Madeleine de Scudéry, or whether they were limited, as *L'Ecole des femmes* would suggest, to exaggerations of language. It is difficult to think that Molière was ridiculing the literary pretensions of women, disliked by d'Aubignac and Patru. He certainly caricatured. No-one ever actually called a mirror "le conseiller des grâces (the adviser on beauty)" or asked anyone to bring chairs in terms as stilted as those used by Magdelon—"Voiturez-nous ici les commodités de la conversation (Activate for us forthwith the presence here of the conveniences of conversation)"—even if "chaise de commodité" was used for a type of lean-back chair.

La Grange and du Croisy, using their own names, are the rejected suitors of Magdelon and Cathos, the daughter and niece of the bourgeois Gorgibus, probably played by Madeleine Béjart and Catherine de Brie. The young women farcically affect an exaggeratedly fastidious personal style. The suitors, to avenge themselves, send their valets, Mascarille, Molière's own stage name, and Jodelet, to pay court in the guise of a marquis and a viscount. The valets used masks, so stereotyping the intrigue as to inhibit any sympathy in the audience for Magdelon and Cathos. The deception works. The real suitors come in and have their finery taken off the backs of the valets, and Gorgibus tells the women it all serves them right. The text demands that the valets should be stripped "down to the smallest item." The musicians who have played during the performance demand to be paid off by Gorgibus, in an ending which underlines that the play was farce by shattering any vestige of dramatic illusion, a device Molière was later to use to prevent too much sympathy from being generated for Harpagon in *L'Avare*.

Sganarelle; ou, Le Cocu imaginaire is another short farce, to be played as an after-piece, on the theme of false appearances, borrowed from countless sources, including an Italian commedia dell'arte sketch. Molière creates here for the second time the role of Sganarelle which he has already played in *Le Médecin volant*. This time, however, the farce is in verse. Although its box-office drawing power was not great, Molière played it in all 122 times, including the occasion on 20 January 1661 when the Palais-Royal was inaugurated in the king's presence. The intrigue, turning on the husband's fear that his wife is deceiving him, is trivial and traditional, but Molière significantly deepened the buffoon role of Sganarelle by making the mime and the spoken lines innovatively dependent on one another. The stage "business" flows naturally from the sentiments expressed, and leads back towards them, gradually nudging farce towards a much more serious form of comedy.

Although *Dom Garcie de Navarre; ou, Le Prince jaloux*, with five acts in verse, is called a "comédie héroïque," it aspires to tragic status, giving its eponymous lead a self-doubt which deepens that of Sganarelle, and anticipates the misanthropy of Alceste. Molière played the title role himself, and then stepped down from it in case it was his acting techniques which were holding off success, as Donneau de Visé was to suggest in the 1663 *Nouvelles nouvelles*. None the less, the public did not take to the play, and Molière did not publish it, although he did re-use pieces of it for later comedies.

L'Ecole des maris, although in verse, is linked by its three-act form to the improvised commedia dell'arte rather than the more formal five-act commedia sostenuta of the Italian tradition. Taken from an adaptation of Mendoza's *El marido hace mujer* by Scarron, and with its title borrowed from Montfleury's recent *L'Ecole des cocus*, it was played as a farce after one or other of a number of weightier pieces. It concerns Sganarelle, played by Molière, who comes to grief believing that women are by nature vicious and require to be subjected to the severity of male authority. Sganarelle is rejected by Isabelle, while her sister Lénor loves and marries Ariste, Sganarelle's liberal sexagenarian brother, whose belief in the responsibility and autonomy of women links Molière to the central précieux advocacy of female autonomy.

The plot of *L'Ecole des femmes* is derived from Scarron's *La Précaution inutile*. Arnolphe, played by Molière, brings up his ward Agnès, played by Catherine de Brie, in a state of total ignorance, naivety, and innocence, with the intention of marrying her. The fear of being cuckolded has become an almost obsessive focus of Molière's comic imagination. Agnès nevertheless falls in love with Horace. The cause of young love is furthered by the unexpected return of Agnès's father, who had long ago destined his daughter to marry the man with whom she is now in love. It is a five-act verse comedy, with a romanesque happy ending in the tradition of the commedia sostenuta, although there are also clear reminiscences of the comedia dell'arte: in the name of Horace, for instance, the Gallicized form of the name of the young male lead in the Italian troupe which until recently had shared Molière's stage; in the notary scene; and in the parodic repetition at the end of act two of a famous line from Pierre Corneille's recent *Sertorius* of 25 February 1662,

…C'est assez.
Je suis maître, je parle, allez, obéissez

(That is enough/I am master, I have spoken. Go. Obey).

Arnolphe, again a derivative of Sganarelle and an anticipation of Alceste, is the first of many Molière characters to wish to sacrifice young love to protect his own comic delusion. Arnolphe is to be scoffed at, but the audience also sympathizes with him. He is, after all, genuinely fond of Agnès. The famous reference in Act I, scene 1 to "une tarte à la crème (a cream tart)" contains in its context not only a punning obscenity about sexual intercourse, but also an allusion to Agnès's extreme simplicity which draws attention to it. The game of "corbillon" in punning assonance with "corbeille" (literally: "basket") to which Arnolphe refers is a child's game in which players have to reply to a set question with a word ending, as "crème" does not, with a rhyme in "-on." The accusation of vulgarity centres on another example of Agnès's simplicity when, also in Act I, scene 1, Arnolphe tells his friend Chrysalde that she wondered whether children were born from their mother's ear. In Rabelais's book, Gargantua was born through his mother's left ear.

The text of *Le Tartuffe; ou, L'Imposteur* as we have it is plainly the result of a modification of Molière's original intention, in which most probably the comic delusion about Tartuffe's piety to which Orgon sacrificed the well-being of his family would not even at the end have been shattered. Orgon's mother, Mme Pernelle, still at the end believes that Tartuffe, led away to be locked up, is a saint. In the play's first scene, with seven characters on the stage, she cuffs the ear of her servant Flipote, the only character who has not said a word. The play's relationship with farce is, however, most memorably embedded in the line spoken about Orgon while he is hiding under the table between Tartuffe and Orgon's wife, Elmire, who is trying to persuade her husband how dishonourable Tartuffe's attentions really are. Tartuffe says to her what is true in a physical sense in which he did not know it was,

C'est un homme, entre nous, à mener par le nez

(He's a man, between ourselves, to be led by the nose) (Act IV, scene 5).

Together with the sharpness of the satire for which the play is famous, there are still grotesque elements of knockabout farce, especially in the depiction of Orgon's obsessive belief in Tartuffe's piety. Farce and satire are now combined in a formal five-act verse play, and Molière introduces a character, Orgon's brother-in-law Cléante, whose reasonableness allows the audience to gauge the comic distortions of the others. There is a serious background to the comedy in its consciousness of the clash between the need for civil dissimulation, here caricatured as hypocrisy, and the aggressive honesty we shall see in Alceste caricatured into arrogance, which in *Tartuffe* and elsewhere is toned down into "médisance," or backbiting, necessarily entailed by saying in the interests of sincerity what you really think about other people.

To some extent social norms always demand a compromise between those two extremes, but the nature of the compromise was clearly a matter which needed serious and repeated examination in an age which had only just emerged from the rough brutality of the court of Henri IV into the elegant frivolities at the periphery of the court societies of Vaux and Versailles and, ultimately more important, the social norms of the emerging upper bourgeoisie in Paris. After the traditional burlesque subject of cuckoldry inherited from the Italian commedia, the delicate relationship between hypocrisy and médisance, a more concentrated form of the perennial comic preoccupation with the tension between appearance and reality, is at the recurring centre of Molière's imaginative concerns.

In the final text, at least, Tartuffe is not a priest, although the model appears quite likely to have been the preacher Gabriel de Roquette. According to Molière, Tartuffe's dress indicated in 1664 that he was probably, like Racine, a tonsured cleric, eligible for benefices but not bound by a vow of chastity. By 1667 he had long hair, wore lace, and carried a sword. He was clearly a layman and was called Panulphe. It also seems unlikely that the first 1664 version delayed Tartuffe's entrance until Act three, as in the final text, so that we may reasonably assume that at least the second act, in the final text dramatically weak, was rewritten between 1664 and 1667. After 1667, apart from reverting to the name Tartuffe and to ecclesiastical non-sacerdotal status for his central character, Molière appears to have made no really important changes to his final five-act verse text. Tartuffe, played by du Croisy, is no doubt a rogue, but a stout, red-faced, thrusting one, lustful and avaricious. not at all as thin and calculating as he is so often depicted. It needed the daring of Molière's comic inventiveness to elevate the comedy by making Tartuffe actually fall in love with Elmire, so reducing his greed for Orgon's money to the status of a device for ending the play. The purely perfunctory intervention of the prince at the play's end, to undo Orgon's gift to Tartuffe, merely tidies up the intrigue. It does not seriously weaken the comedy.

The play itself tells us very little about Molière's beliefs, beyond suggesting a dislike of cant, and a willingness to satirize pretentiousness and hypocrisy, particularly in ecclesiastical life, where economic and social opportunities made it particularly rife. The credulity and even superstition of the public opened the way for rogues to extend hypocrisy, seeking respect, into fraud, seeking reward. It is not difficult to understand why a satire on the really possible fraudulent exploitation of a pious demeanour disquieted the ecclesiastical authorities, to whatever farcical imprudence love had driven Tartuffe, the satire's vulgar butt. The psychology is too penetrating, the decor too domestically intimate, to prevent the amusement of the audience from including elements of personal involvement which mere farce would have kept at bay.

Orgon, played by Molière, impressed by the apparent intensity of Tartuffe's piety, and plainly blind to obvious humbug, allows Tartuffe to come into his household, and eventually to dominate it in spite of the efforts of most of its members to disillusion Orgon, who makes a gift of all his wealth to Tartuffe, is prepared to give him his daughter as a wife, and strongly resists believing his wife when she protests that Tartuffe has been making approaches to her. Presumably as a concession to the authorities, Tartuffe is unmasked when Orgon is persuaded to hide under the table while Tartuffe makes his advances to her, and Tartuffe then behaves villainously, attempting to use tyranically the powers over the family legally conferred on him by Orgon.

Until very recently it was customary for reasons which now appear pedantic to spell the title of the principal character in *Dom Juan; ou, Le Festin de Pierre* as "Don," so distinguishing between the title of the play and the name of the character. In the 17th-century editions both were spelt "Dom" and, since Molière did not publish his text during his lifetime, there is no real authority for reverting to the Spanish form used by later editors. There is a textual problem, because the Amsterdam 1683 text may quite probably have been based on an actor's copy, used in February 1665 and therefore nearer to what was actually said on stage than even the uncut but toned-down 1682 text of which three copies have survived. Part of Act III, scene 2 was suppressed after the first performance, and part of scene 1 was removed from the text printed in 1682. The play itself was taken off after a brief but successful run and what is certain to have been strong official pressure. Molière employs a standard plot, seems to have written in a hurry, and uses his framework to make satirical boutades aimed at what might almost be described as a job-lot of targets for his animosity, recognizably taking revenge for the prohibition of *Tartuffe*. The play starts with a finely calculated mock encomium of tobacco by Sganarelle, played by Molière. It was the Compagnie du Saint-Sacrement, with its desire to impose Christian moral standards by civil administrative measures, which constituted the anti-tobacco lobby.

Molière's comic inventiveness prevented him from leaving even such banal material as the Dom Juan story without serious theatrical interest. He turns what had become tragi-comic material back into farce, thereby flaunting disrespect for religious awe, and he creates a relationship of mutual dependence between Dom Juan and his servant Sganarelle which gives him

an extraordinary control of satirical nuance. Mostly Sganarelle and Dom Juan agree, but Sganarelle is the cravenly superstitious believer in everything supernatural, in whose mouth Molière with straight-faced irony puts the defence of religion. Dom Juan on the contrary is the fearlessly mocking atheist perfunctorily damned when he shakes hands with the statue and is pulled down into hell. Molière is careful to retain Dom Juan's womanizing and the structure of the traditional plot, and Loret's gazette, *La Muse historique*, was to report a few days before Loret's death early in April that Molière's changes of decor, of which he had six for five acts, and his use of stage machinery had been a success with his audiences, but, having moved away from the physically agile acrobatics of the Italians, Molière now simplified the miraculous elements of the tragi-comic plot, turning his piece into something not far from a send-up of a morality play.

Dom Juan has left his wife, Done Elvire, and lectures Sganarelle on the idiocies of fidelity. The play opens with a scene between Sganarelle and Gusman, Done Elvire's groom. Dom Juan, says Sganarelle, is

le plus grand scélérat que la terre ait jamais porté, un enragé, un chien, un Diable, un Turc, un Hérétique, qui ne croit ni Ciel, [ni saint, ni Dieu (*1683 text*)], ni loup-garou, qui passe cette vie en véritable bête brute, en pourceau d'Epicure...

(the greatest rascal who has ever walked the earth, a madman, a dog, a devil, a Turk, a heretic, who believes neither in heaven, [nor in saints, nor in God (*1683 text*)], nor in werewolves, who passes this life like a veritable brute beast, a swine from Epicurus' herd).

Dom Juan is "un grand seigneur méchant homme (a great lord and an evil man)," according to Sganarelle, who protests that fear alone binds him to his master while showing by his tone that there is affection, too. Admitting that Dom Juan may have his reasons for disbelief, Sganarelle goes on to deride the "petits impertinents... qui sont libertins sans savoir pourquoi, qui font les esprits forts, parce qu'ils croient que cela leur sied bien (impertinent young pups... who are freethinkers without knowing why, who affect disbelief because they think it suits them)."

Confronted by Done Elvire, Dom Juan justifies his desertion by invoking his repentance at stealing her from a convent. He behaves quite outrageously towards her while preserving all the external signs of politeness. The second act, partly in patois, is largely a harlequinade between the peasant lovers Charlotte and Pierrot. In the third, Done Elvire's brothers, Dom Carlos and Dom Alonse, intent on revenge, catch up with Dom Juan. Sganarelle watches as his master tries to make a saintly but starving beggar swear by offering him money. This is the passage that was cut for the second performance. Sganarelle flees in the face of the likely assault on his master by the two brothers, who leave Dom Juan to a fate that will be worse than death, although for the moment its nature remains unrevealed. Sganarelle and Dom Juan enter the mausoleum of Le Commandeur, whom Dom Juan had killed, and Sganarelle is forced by Dom Juan to convey to the statue an invitation to supper. The statue nods acceptance.

In Act IV Dom Juan overwhelms a merchant with affabilities, thereby preventing him from even mentioning the money he is owed. Dom Juan's father comes to upbraid him, his wife, veiled, to warn him, and after a lot of stage business in which a hungry Sganarelle gets nothing to eat, the statue comes to supper, and Sganarelle loses interest in food. Dom Juan makes a long speech in praise of hypocrisy. The final warnings come from one of Done Elvire's brothers and a veiled spectre who is transformed into a figure of Time with a scythe. Dom Juan pursues the spectre with a sword. It flees, Sganarelle begs his master in vain not to go to supper with the statue, and shouts for his wages as the statue drags Dom Juan into hell. The ending, "mes gages, mes gages (my wages, my wages)," which emphasizes the farcical nature of the action, was played in 1665, but is absent from the uncut version of the 1682 edition. The play achieves a semblance of unity and makes its dramatic impact by the total dependence on each other of Dom Juan and Sganarelle as contrasting caricatures.

Le Misanthrope, five acts in verse, further develops Molière's treatment of the problem of hypocrisy. Alceste is not only agressively, but also arrogantly and morosely honest. He believes in sincerity, and though in love with the flighty Célimène has come to dislike human society with the flattery, hypocrisy and politenesses on which it depends. Very often, he visibly speaks for Molière. The first scene of Act I between himself and his friend Philinte, whose reasonableness measures Alceste's own comic distortion, makes clear the exaggeration of sincerity into arrogance,

Je refuse d'un coeur la vaste complaisance
Qui ne fait de mérite aucune différence;
Je veux qu'on me distingue; et pour le trancher net,
L'ami du genre humain n'est point du tout mon fait

(I scorn the indiscriminate goodwill of a heart/that takes no account of merit;/I want to be singled out, and to speak plainly,/the friend of everybody is not the friend for me).

Psychologically, Alceste is Molière's sad clown taken by way of Arnolphe towards his furthest point, the crowning misfit destined by temperament and choice to be miserable, but never forfeiting the audience's sympathy. On the contrary, Molière uses Alceste to denounce exaggerated forms of social politeness, and the socially acceptable coquetterie and backbiting—médisance—of Célimène.

Alceste's judgement of Oronte's sonnet as inferior to a couplet from a popular song is obviously intended to appear correct, and Alceste is meant to appear in the right even in his contempt for those who accept, as well as those who deliver, undeserved flattery. From the text itself it is clear that the character of Alceste, with his exaggerated bitterness at the world around him, must contain a self-parody by the author. The central character is too often disastrously right in too many different circumstances for the character not to contain wry self-mockery, although the play is aimed not so much at Alceste's brooding antipathy to the shallow frivolities and the philistinism which surrounded him as at the social conventions themselves, together with the behaviour and attitudes they breed. Alceste loses a court case in which he knows he is in the right. Any Paris audience in 1665 will have seen the similarity between Alceste's position and that of Molière, who played him.

Alceste expounds his philosophy to Philinte in the play's first scene:

…je hais tous les hommes:
Les uns, parce qu'ils sont méchants et malfaisants,
Et les autres, pour être aux méchants complaisants

(I hate all men:/some because they are evil and wrongdoers,/and the others for pandering to them).

Sincerity is the principal virtue, but Alceste loves Célimène, whose coquetterie makes her a quite unsuitable partner for Alceste, but whose backbiting ironically reflects on Alceste's insistence on speaking the truth. After the play's second scene, in which Alceste mercilessly points out the vapidities in Oronte's sonnet, he is again alone with Philinte. Three consecutive twelve-syllable lines are amusingly split between three, then four, then six different speeches, a device already used notably in *L'Ecole des femmes*. The first entry of Célimène is at the beginning of the second act. Racine had moved his *Alexandre* away from Molière's company six months before the premiere of *Le Misanthrope*. His technique was always to draw on such dramatic devices of Molière as the heavily split alexandrine and the proper dramatic exploitation of the first act for purposes of exposition, before the start of the intrigue.

In *Le Misanthrope* there is very little plot. Oronte loves Célimène, and Eliante, Célimène's cousin, would be a more suitable partner for Alceste. The irony touches a peak when, in the middle scene of the play, Act III, scene 4, Célimène and the trouble-making, vindictive Arsinoé say to one another exactly what they think of each other, with devastating consequences for their friendship. Oronte and Alceste force Célimène to choose between them, and Célimène seeks advice from Eliante. In the end Célimène's friends turn against her, but Alceste remains and offers to marry her, if she will come and live with him in the "désert," by which he means the country, in retirement from Paris society. She would marry him, but she cannot give up her socializing. Alceste leaves alone.

Amphitryon, although in verse, has only three acts, and although created at the Palais-Royal is plainly a poeticization of court intrigue involving the king, mythologized into Jupiter. In addition, it requires the use of stage machinery and the support of musicians, and it ends in a ballet. Its real interest is therefore historical. Taken out of its contemporary setting and looked on merely as a dramatic text, away from its stage machinery, its music, song, and dance, and all immediate reference to the court of Louis XIV, *Amphitryon*'s interest has seemed to be concentrated on the incidental skill of its versification in a mixture of octosyllabic lines and alexandrines. Yet even as straight comic drama, remote from its source of inspiration at Versailles, the text repays examination. The story is the well-worn one, most notably treated by Plautus and, in 1636, by Rotrou. Jupiter, who wants a liaison with Amphitryon's wife, Alcmène, takes on the appearance of Amphitryon while Mercury, his servant, impersonates Amphitryon's servant, Sosie, married to Cléanthis. Their respective liaisons are interrupted by the inopportunely premature return of the real Amphitryon and the real Sosie. Everyone's honour is saved, and Alcmène's son, Hercules, will be passed off as Amphitryon's when he is born.

The literary importance of the bare text as it stands derives partly from the reflection of the Jupiter/Amphitryon-Alcmène relationship in that of Mercure/Sosie-Cléanthis, but more from the manner in which Molière's habitual comic play on double identities is here twice split into sets of two outwardly identical characters. The comic delusions of Molière's central characters, who often sacrifice particularly the young and marriageable members of their families to their phobias, and are in tension with their own saner selves, often also represented by perfectly normal friends known as Molière's "raisonneur" characters, are in *Amphitryon* represented by two quite separate characters instead of single deluded ones. In spite of what Molière garnered from Plautus and Rotrou, the text alone of this play attests to his extraordinary comic inventiveness, even without the allusions to court life and by implication also to the Dutch campaign of Louis XIV, and without the music and the ballets.

In the total context of Molière's comic output *George Dandin*, although essentially a court entertainment of three acts in prose, is not without interest. It is one of the few plays in which the comic delusion of the central character is punctured, in this case from the beginning of the play, when Dandin is already disillusioned, and the play on double identities is adroitly underlined by Dandin's use of the formal "vous" form of the second person when addressing his former deluded self. He keeps the intimate "tu" for his present disillusioned identity. He says to himself, referring to his treatment by his wife and her family, "Vous l'avez voulu, vous l'avez voulu, George Dandin, vous l'avez voulu... vous avez justement ce que vous méritez (You asked for it, you asked for it, George Dandin, you brought it on yourself... you've got just what you deserve)." For several complete scenes, including the opening one, Dandin soliloquizes in this way. He is a rich peasant who has married Angélique de Sotenville in order to have aristocratic children. The Sotenvilles are portrayed as pompously puffed up, and also stupid, but Dandin is unable to gain the upper hand over his wife on the three occasions when she deceives him. The plot is perfunctory commedia dell' arte material, and the moral values of the Sotenvilles would have been unacceptable had the play's tone not been so light. Both the court and the bourgeois Paris audiences were confidently invited to laugh both at the practically retarded rustic provincial nobility and at their poverty. The play is slight, but the quality of the laughter begins to show a new touch of bitterness.

In *L'Avare*, five acts in prose, Molière pushes his comic daring to its extreme point, taking the miser's comic delusion well beyond the limits of credibility, but leaving him still a miser and deluded at the end, so avoiding any risk that tragedy might intrude. The dénouement, with the arrival from nowhere of the father of the lovers of the miser's son and daughter, is derisively dismissive of credibility, but serves quite adequately to tie up the intrigue once the real comedy, which concerns the presentation of Harpagon's comic delusion, has been taken momentarily just beyond the outer limits of sanity.

There is a great deal of verbal wit, as in Act V, scene 3, whose idea Molière borrows from Plautus. Harpagon is talking about what he takes to be Valère's theft of his money, and Valère is talking about what he takes Harpagon to be describing as the theft of his daughter. There is much comic stage business, as when Maître Jacques changes his uniform from coachman to cook. There are exceedingly comic situations, for example when the usurer from whom Harpagon's son, Cléante, wishes to borrow turns out to be Harpagon himself, and there are seriously comic devices which lift the play from pure farce into a vehicle for pathos, like Harpagon's love for the young Mariane, who is in love with and is loved by Cléante, tricked by his father into admitting his love. This may well be the play in which Molière most daringly generates comic tension in the audience, by com-

bining the farcical antics of Harpagon's miserliness at which it laughs, with the serious personality distortion of the senile miser in love with a pretty young girl but even more obsessed by his money, at which Molière probably did not wish it merely to scoff. The greatness of Molière's comic achievement lies in this tension he can create between the audience's identification with his characters, which is never allowed to become acutely enough involved in their downfall to be tragic, and its hilarity at their buffoonery, which is seldom, and never in the great five-act plays, permitted to stay simply at the level of burlesque.

The lengths to which Molière takes his comic tension are particularly clear in the famous monologue of act IV, scene 7. Most of the essential devices used here are already in Plautus, even the equation of robbery and murder. To steal from Harpagon is indeed to destroy the distorted character he has become. But Plautus does not so go far as Molière in his play on the miser's deluded personality. Harpagon breaks dramatic convention by accusing the audience of the theft. He is of course right, because the audience knows where the money is. Then he accuses himself, as if to confirm the split between a comic and a sane identity, and grabs at his own arm as if it were that of the thief:

Au voleur! Au voleur! à l'assassin! Au meurtrier! Justice, juste Ciel! je suis perdu, je suis assassiné, on m'a coupé la gorge, on m'a dérobé mon argent. Qui peut-ce être? Qu'est-il devenu? Où est-il? Où se cache-t-il? Que ferai-je pour le trouver? Où courir? Où ne pas courir? N'est-il point là? N'est-il point ici? Qui est-ce? Arrête. Rends-moi mon argent, coquin...[*Il se prend lui-même le bras*]. Ah! c'est moi. Mon esprit est troublé, et j'ignore où je suis, qui je suis, et ce que je fais. Hélas, mon pauvre argent, mon pauvre argent, mon cher ami! on m'a privé de toi...sans toi il m'est impossible de vivre. C'en est fait, je n'en puis plus; je me meurs, je suis mort, je suis enterré. N'y a-t-il personne qui veuille me ressusciter, en me rendant mon cher argent, ou en m'apprenant qui l'a pris?....Sortons. Je veux aller querir la justice, et faire donner la question à toute la maison: à servantes, à valets, à fils, à fille, et à moi aussi. Que de gens assemblés...ils me regardent tous, et se mettent à rire...

(Thief! Thief! Assassin! Murderer! Justice, great heavens! I'm lost, I'm killed, my throat has been cut, my money has been stolen. Who can it be? What has happened to him? Where is he? Where is he hiding? What shall I do to find him? Where shall I go? Where not? Isn't he there? Isn't he here? Who is he? Stop. Wretch, give me back my money...[*He grasps his own arm...*]. Oh! it's me. My mind is wandering. I don't know where I am, who I am, or what I'm doing. Alas, my poor money, my poor money, my dear friend! You've been taken away from me...I can't live without you. That's it, I can't go on. I'm dying, I'm dead, I'm buried. Won't anyone bring me back to life by giving me back my dear money or telling me who has taken it?...Let's go. I'm going to call in the law and have the whole household tortured, maidservants, menservants, son, daughter, and myself, too. What a crowd of people there are here...they're all looking at me and beginning to laugh...).

As well as from Plautus, Molière borrowed from modern

sources: Boisrobert's *La Belle Plaideuse*, Donneau de Visé's *La Mère coquette*, and Chappuzeau's *La Dame d'intrigue*, from which Molière took the idea of Froisine, a sane character who flatters the comic delusion of the central character for her own purposes, a device Molière uses again in *Le Malade imaginaire*. Little details come from half a dozen other plays, and the comedy in many ways merely unifies, mostly in the scenes figuring the lovers, a series of comic episodes based on the stage tricks of the Italians. Like *Tartuffe* it puts a bourgeois domestic interior on the stage, although Harpagon, played by Molière, is old, ill, crushed in spite of his amorous obsession by the cumulative burdens of a lifetime's struggle. There is a harshness in the humour. The moral is the acceptance of the rules imposed by life's circumstances. It is difficult to know why the play failed so resoundingly, and particularly why its premiere attracted such comparatively slight interest, bringing in 1,069 livres as against 1,518 for *L'Ecole des femmes*, 1,830 for *Dom Juan*, an easily explainable 2,860 for *Tartuffe*, 1,447 for *Le Misanthrope*, and 1,668 for *Amphitryon*. Could it have been because it was known not to be in verse?

L'Avare was followed by a number of comédies-ballets, including *Le bourgeois gentilhomme*, which is scarcely more than the mocking portrait of a bourgeois, depicted with all sorts of verbal, visual and choreographic aid, again unsuccessfully attempting to climb into the ranks of the aristocracy. There is no intrigue, merely a farcical fantasy with music. M. Jourdain has himself taught music, dancing, fencing, and philosophy. He wants to marry his daughter Lucile into the aristocracy, but she loves Cléonte, who passes himself off as the son of the Grand Turk, and is allowed to marry Lucile after Jourdain in a burlesque ceremony is dubbed Mamamouchi, a buffoonish Turkish-sounding title dreamed up by Molière.

The last formal five-act comedy was in verse, *Les Femmes savantes*, and directed against an enemy of Boileau and Molière, the abbé Cotin, author of *La Critique désintéressée*. Boileau hit back at Cotin in 1667, and Molière makes him his butt in the character of Trissotin. The play was probably begun in 1668. Vadius, treated much more gently by Molière, represented Ménage. Although at first a box-office success, *Les Femmes savantes* is now regarded as much inferior to the earlier full-scale comedies. Chrysale is an unpretentious bourgeois, supported in his attitudes by his younger daughter, Henriette. However, his wife, Philaminte, his sister, Bélise, and his elder daughter, Armande, attempt to parade their learning. As usual, the happiness of a young person is at stake. Philaminte wants Henriette to marry Trissotin, a third-rate poet, instead of the acceptable, sensible Clitandre, who loves her. A false rumour of the family's ruin reveals that Trissotin's motives were mercenary.

Philaminte retains her comic delusion of intellectual grandeur. There is much farce, and an amusing quarrel between Trissotin and Vadius. The play's comic weakness derives essentially from the encroaching bitterness which allowed Molière for the first time to present a young person as the subject of a seriously distorting comic delusion. The Sganarelle figures had been comic, attractive, and wrong. Transformed into Arnolphe, Orgon and Harpagon, they had wanted to sacrifice the young and attractive to their delusions. Here for the first time Molière presents us with an attractive young person, Armande, herself the subject of the same comic delusion as her mother. The comic structure will not stand up to the weight now imposed on it.

Le Malade imaginaire is a comedy-ballet which moves from comedy into fantasy. Argan's personality distortion is hypochondria. He wants his daughter Angélique to marry his doctor's son, Thomas Diafoirus, although she loves and is loved by Cléante. Argan's second wife, Béline, married him only for his money and is waiting for him to die. Argan pretends to, and everyone's true feelings are revealed. Wrongs are righted, and Argan himself becomes a doctor in a ludicrous ceremony which is almost a pantomime transformation scene and once again makes clear Molière's views on the medical profession. Unhappily, what might have been a brilliant entertainment, with elaborate ballets, was prevented by Lulli's monopoly from ever being played at Versailles, which is what it was designed for, and Molière died just after finishing his fourth performance as Argan. There are scenes of magnificent burlesque. Gide thought this play Molière's finest work.

PUBLICATIONS

Collections

Oeuvres de M. Molière, 2 vols., 1663; 2 vols., 1664
Oeuvres de M. Molière, 2 vols., 1666
Oeuvres de M. Molière, 7 vols., 1673
Les Oeuvres de M. de Molière, 8 vols., (of which vols. VII and VIII *Oeuvres posthumes*), edited by La Grange and Vinet, 1682
Oeuvres de Molière, 6 vols., 1734
Oeuvres complètes, edited by E. Despois and P. Mesnard, 14 vols., 1873–1900
Oeuvres complètes, Bibliothèque de la Pléiade, 2 vols., 1933, 1959, 1971
Oeuvres complètes, 2 vols., 1962
Works, tr. A.R. Waller, 8 vols., 1926
Comedies, 2 vols., 1929

Plays

La Jalousie du barbouillé; le Médecin volant (attributed to Molière; produced on tour before 1655), 1819
L'Etourdi; ou, Les Contre-temps (produced 1654?) 1663; as *The Blunderers*, 1762
Le Dépit amoureux (produced 1656). 1663; as *The Amorous Quarrel*, 1762
Les Précieuses ridicules (produced 1659), 1660; as *The Conceited Young Ladies*, 1762
Sganarelle; ou, Le Cocu imaginaire (produced 1660), 1660; as *The Picture*, 1745
Dom Garcie de Navarre; ou, Le Prince jaloux (produced 1661), in *Oeuvres posthumes*, 1682
L'École des maris (produced 1661), 1661
Les Fâcheux (produced 1661), 1662; as *The Impertinents*, 1732
L'École des femmes (produced 1662), 1663; as *The School for Wives*, 1971
La Critique de L'École des femmes (produced 1663), 1663
L'Impromptu de Versailles (produced 1663); in *Oeuvres posthumes*, 1684
Le Mariage forcé (produced 1664), 1668; as *The Forced Marriage*, 1762
La Princesse d'Élide (produced 1664), 1674

Tartuffe; ou, L'Imposteur (produced 1664; revised version produced 1667) 1669; translated as *Tartuffe*, 1670

Les Plaisirs de l'île enchantée (produced 1664), 1664

Dom Juan; ou, Le Festin de Pierre (produced 1665), 1682

L'Amour médecin (produced 1665), 1666; as *The Quacks*, 1705; as *Doctor Love*, 1915

Le Misanthrope (produced 1666), 1667; as *The Misanthrope*, 1762; as *The Man-Hater*, 1770

Le Médecin malgré lui (produced 1666), 1667; as *The Dumb Lady*, 1672; as *Love's Contrivance*, 1703; as *The Mock Doctor*, 1732; as *The Doctor in Spite of Himself*, 1914

Mélicerte (produced 1666), in *Oeuvres posthumes*, 1684

La Pastorale comique, music by Lulli (produced 1666), in *Théâtre*, 1888–93

Le Sicilien; ou, L'Amour peintre (produced 1667), 1668; as *The Sicilian*, 1732

Amphitryon (produced 1668), 1668; translated as *Amphitryon*, 1690

George Dandin; ou, Le Mari confondu (produced 1668), 1669; as *George Dandin; or, The Husband Defeated*, 1732

L'Avare (produced 1668), 1669; as *The Miser*, 1672

Monsieur de Pourceaugnac (produced 1669), 1670; as *The Cornish Squire*, 1734

Les Amants magnifiques (produced 1670), in *Oeuvres posthumes*, 1684

Le Bourgeois gentilhomme (produced 1670), 1670; as *The Citizen Turned Gentleman*, 1672

Psyché, with Pierre Corneille and Philippe Quinault, music by Lulli (produced 1671), 1671

Les Fourberies de Scapin (produced 1671), 1671; as *The Cheats of Scapin*, 1677

La Comtesse d'Escarbagnas (produced 1671), in *Oeuvres posthumes*, 1684

Les Femmes savantes (produced 1672), 1673; as *The Female Virtuosos*, 1693; as *Blue-stockings*, 1884

La Malade imaginaire (produced 1673), 1673–74; as *Doctor Last in His Chariot*, 1769; as *The Imaginary Invalid*, 1925

Biographical and critical studies

Grimarest, Jean-Léonor Le Gallois, sieur de, *Vie de M. de Molière*, 1705; 1930.

Moore, W. G., *Molière: a new criticism*, 1949

Hubert Judd, *Molière and the Comedy of Intellect*, 1962

Gossman, Lionel, *Men and Masks: a study of Molière*, 1963

Jurgens, Madeleine and Maxfield-Miller, Elisabeth, *Cent ans de recherches sur Molière*, 1963

Mongrédien, G., *Recueil des textes et des documents du XVIIe siècle relatifs à Molière*, 2 vols., 1965

La Grange (Varlet, Charles, sieur de, known as), *Registre*, 1876; 1947; edited by E. and G. Young, 2 vols., 1967

Lawrence, F.L., *Molière: The Comedy of Unreason*, 1968

Howarth, W.D. and Thomas, M., editors, *Molière: Stage and Study*, 1973

Howarth, W.D., *Molière: A Playwright and his Audience*, 1982

Bibliography

Guibert, *Bibliographie des Oeuvres de Molière imprimées au XVIIe siècle*, 2 vols., 1961; supplement, 1965

Lacroix, P., *Bibliographie moliéresque*, 2nd ed., 1875

Saintonge, Paul and Wilson Christ, Robert, *Fifty Years of Molière Studies. A Bibliography, 1892–1941*, 1942

MONTAIGNE, Michel Eyquem de, 1533–1592.

Humanist, author of "Les Essais".

LIFE

Montaigne was born into the bourgeois aristocracy of Bordeaux at the Château de Montaigne, 30 miles to the east of the town, on 28 February 1533. He was the third but eldest to survive of the ten children of Pierre Eyquem de Montaigne (1495–1568) and Antoinette de Louppes (Lopez). They had married in 1529 and lost two earlier children in infancy. Montaigne was born only after an 11-month pregnancy. His mother's date of birth is unknown, but on her marriage she was "of age," which means over 12, although she must still have been very young, since her last child was born in 1560. She came from a family of rich Jewish marranos, convert refugees from persecution in late 15th-century Spain, where some of her ancestors had been burned at the stake. She was to die only in 1601. Montaigne refers to her only twice, although he frequently mentions his father, whom he admired and whose family had lived in Bordeaux for generations. The estate had been bought in 1477 by Montaigne's great-grandfather, a merchant of Bordeaux who had become rich trading in wines, pastel—the main ingredient of black and dark blue dyes until the introduction of indigo—and salted fish. Montaigne's grandfather, who had become his father's sole heir, successfully carried on the business and became first a deputy mayor (jurat) of Bordeaux and then a royal judge (prévôt).

He died intestate, and his sons had to appeal to the pope to secure their rights and those of their sisters. His eldest son, Montaigne's father, the first of the family to be born at Montaigne and to adopt the noble profession of arms, fought under Lautrec during the Italian wars before returning home to marry, and in his turn to become a deputy mayor and a judge. He served several terms in various high local offices and in 1554 was elected mayor for two difficult years, during which he had to plead with Henri II for the restoration of the privileges of which the city had been deprived after the 1548 uprising against the salt tax. Vicious repression had followed the mob lynching of the king's lieutenant.

Montaigne's father's Latin was apparently mediocre, but his Italian and Spanish were said by Montaigne to have been good. He much increased his holdings of land, wryly and wrongly predicting that Montaigne would ruin the estate. Montaigne did not, but he did not much enjoy or enlarge it, either. He was to maintain it, probably with considerable help from his wife, but apparently could not himself be much bothered with business matters. Since the main source of our impression of his character is his own extended self-portrait in *Les Essais*, it is sometimes difficult to know the degree of affectation in the attitudes he assigns to himself. Montaigne's three uncles were all lawyers, and two of them also ecclesiastics, while both aunts married into the magistracy. It was one of Montaigne's uncles who in 1554 bought the position in the tax court (Cour des Aides) of Périgueux which was transferred to Montaigne sometime during the following three years.

At his christening Montaigne was held at the font by representatives of the local poor and, unusually, sent out to a poor family to nurse. In 1535 he was entrusted to a German tutor, Horstanus, who did not know French, spoke Latin to his charge, and was subsequently to teach at the famous humanist Collège de Guyenne at Bordeaux. Montaigne was later to criticize his father for the awe in which he held the new humanists and their learning. His father was able, vigorous, physically very strong, and never ill until at 66 he suffered from a stone in his bladder. He had brought back from Italy views about education, and the language of Montaigne's early upbringing was Latin. Both his mother and his father mastered Latin sufficiently well for Montaigne to hear no other language at home. Even the servants had to learn enough to manage with.

The young Montaigne was treated gently, wakened with music, and "taught to enjoy knowledge and duty by his own free will and desire." From the age of six he attended the Collège de Guyenne, whose principal, Andrea de Gouvea, had been forced in 1533, on account of his humanist theological leanings, to leave the Paris Collège de Sainte-Barbe, where he had been acting principal, when Cop preached the famous sermon on 1 November which signalled the beginning of the Reformation in France. School was a disappointment. Montaigne started from too advanced a level of competence and had to have special tuition. But he was allowed to develop a love of books: Ovid, whose *Metamorphoses* he read for pleasure in preference to romances such as the *Amadis* stories when he was "seven or eight," Virgil, Terence, Plautus, then Italian comedies. His father tried to master Greek with him by turning it all into a game. Montaigne never confessed to achieving mastery of Greek, but *Les Essais* shows that he was not totally ignorant of it, whatever use of translations he may have made. He congratulates the master who, pretending not to notice, connived at his reading when he should have been attending to his lessons. Having disliked the discipline and the reliance on memorizing, Montaigne left school at 13. He had finished the 12-year course in seven years. The theory had been liberal, as Montaigne's own educational views were to be, although in practice Montaigne was lucky not to have suffered worse than he did from being out of step with fellow-pupils from less enlightened backgrounds.

Looking back, he felt that he might have learned more if his disposition had not been so sluggish, slothful, and drowsy ("si poisant, mal et endormi") that he could not be roused from torpor even to play. His mind was like his character: "Le danger n'estoit pas que je fisse mal, mais que je ne fisse rien. Nul ne prognostiquoit que je deusse devenir mauvais, mais inutile (The danger was not that I would do wrong, but that I would do nothing. No one predicted that I was going to be villainous, only useless)." Despite the apparent self-satisfaction with which it is made, this statement, from the key chapter on education, "De l'institution des enfans" (I, xxvi), is important because it was chiefly to achieve intellectual focus for his disorganized imagination that Montaigne started to write his single book, and it was in grappling with his intellectual slovenliness that he slowly became aware that he was creating a masterpiece.

We know little of Montaigne's life from 1546, when he left school, until 1557, when he became a counsellor at the Bordeaux parlement. The presumption is that from 1549 he was sent to read law in Toulouse, the home of his mother's family. Civil law had been banned in Paris during the middle ages because it took many students away from theology, and Parisians who wanted to study law went to Orléans, like Calvin, or to Poitiers. Toulouse was the most humanistically advanced faculty in the country, counting among its teachers Coras, Turnèbe—much praised by Montaigne in the chapter "Du pédantisme" (I, xxv)—Cujas, and Bunel, who stayed at Montaigne and gave Montaigne's father the copy of Raymond Sebond's *Theologia naturalis, sive liber creaturarum* which he later asked his son to translate. Montaigne was to sign the translation's dedication in Paris on 18 June 1568, the day his father died.

In 1554 Montaigne's father became mayor of Bordeaux, and had the château enlarged and fortified. He must, judging from a stray remark, have taken Montaigne with him to Paris to plead with Henri II, bringing with him 20 casks of Bordeaux wine with which to acquire good will. Montaigne was quite frequently to visit Paris between 1559 and 1570, at least partly on official missions, as well as on private business like the publication of his translation. He tells us he was clumsy but active, unable to keep either his mind or his body still, although entirely without ability in any athletic or graceful pursuit, in this quite unlike his father. His reactions could be vehement. His love life was something he appears simply to have taken for granted. It is however clear that he was unusually given to observing himself, and even experimenting on himself, varying his exploitation of such physical functions as sleep, diet, and sex. There were two slight touches of venereal disease.

The post of counsellor at the new Périgueux Cour des Aides was transferred to him quite probably at the court's inception in 1554. When in 1557 the court was suppressed, Montaigne's post was incorporated into the Bordeaux parlement, joint third in importance with that of Grenoble after those of Paris and Toulouse, and in front of the other four, Dijon, Rouen, Aix, and Rennes. Bordeaux was overtly reluctant to admit the newcomers, and subjected them to much petty harasment, but it was there that Montaigne met La Boétie, over two years his senior, who became the object of the most intense affection he ever bestowed. La Boétie was accomplished, well known, married, respected, and sure of himself. He had been early orphaned, and his requirements seem to have complemented those of Montaigne, whose unrestrained upbringing must have created in him the need for someone to play the role of elder brother in his life. Their friendship was clearly very close, although what we know of it emerges largely through the stylization of La Boétie's verse tributes to Montaigne, and Montaigne's posthumous and possibly idealized reminiscences of their friendship.

They met only in 1559, and from the beginning La Boétie was the senior partner, in the sense that Montaigne sought his advice. Their intimacy developed speedily. In August 1563 La Boétie was invited by Montaigne to dine, but had stomach pains and asked Montaigne to call on him instead. Montaigne persuaded his friend to move out of Bordeaux, with its danger of plague, and to stay with Montaigne's sister Jeanne, now married to Richard de Lestonnac and living just outside the city. On the following day, Tuesday, 10 August 1563, La Boétie's wife sent for Montaigne, who spent that night and Thursday night in the house. By Saturday La Boétie was clearly dying. A priest was sent for and a will was made, the books being left to Montaigne, who at the end stayed at the bedside after La Boétie had sent his wife to rest. La Boétie died early on the morning of Wednesday, 18 August; he was not yet 33. Montaigne was to cherish and even idealize the memory of their friendship for the rest of his life. He was to recall it 18 years later in his Italian diary, not intended for publication, and Les Essais often reads as if the ideal reader for whom Montaigne was writing was his dead friend. He himself said he would rather have written Les Essais in letter form. He devoted himself to publishing his friend's works, and put his chapter on friendship at the centre of the first book of Les Essais.

When Montaigne married on 23 September 1565, he already esteemed marriage below friendship. His bride was Françoise de la Chassaigne, born on 13 December 1544 into a loyal Catholic family from the upper magistracy. She brought a dowry of 7,000 livres tournois, and Montaigne's father gave him a quarter of the revenue from the estate excluding the buildings. They had six children from 1570 to 1583, all girls, of whom only one, Léonor (1571–1616), survived infancy. Lénor married at 18, was widowed, and remarried at 37, having one daughter by each marriage. Montaigne's wife survived until 7 March 1627, leaving 19 letters to her spiritual director dated from August 1617 to about 1625. In old age she was short of money. Montaigne himself saw no particular reason to be a faithful husband, and it is not unlikely that his wife took her revenge by having a liaison with his brother. Montaigne approved of dynastic marriages arranged by families, but none the less himself looked for, and worked at, a form of companionship in his own marriage which, if less than ideal friendship, he was surprised to find as satisfying as he claims to have done. He was, however, articulate later about the different roles to be expected of wife and mistress and disapproved of passionate ardours inside marriage.

On her marriage to Montaigne's father, Montaigne's mother had brought the considerable dowry of 4,000 livres tournois, and the terms of his father's first will, drawn up in February 1561, suggest that his father trusted his wife's managerial abilities more than his eldest son's, although his confidence in Montaigne had increased by September 1567, when he made a second will just nine months before he died. The complex provisions suggest that he correctly foresaw a struggle for domestic authority between Montaigne and his mother, and allowed for the possible need for accommodation for his widow to be provided elsewhere. The family quarrels are difficult to disentangle, but it looks as if Montaigne's brother, Arnaud de Saint-Martin (1541–69), before dying at 27 after being hit by a tennis ball, had had a liaison with Montaigne's wife, to whom he had given a gold chain. Montaigne's mother claimed the necklace for her own, presumably to spite him and shield her daughter-in-law. The chain was formally restored to her in front of witnesses, and there is a notaried document to prove it.

On her husband's death in 1568, Montaigne's mother, who was to survive Montaigne by nine years, seems to have resented the usurpation by her eldest son of her dominion over what for 40 years had been her house even though Montaigne was 35 by then, and had been married for three years. She also seems not to have lived at Montaigne from the late 1580s, and her will, drawn up on 19 April 1597, is complimentary neither about Montaigne, who had died nearly five years earlier, nor about his father. Affection is reserved for her two surviving sons, Montaigne's daughter Lénor, and especially Lénor's 15-year-old

daughter. She resented the way in which Montaigne's father had failed either to invest her dowry for her as stipulated in her marriage contract, or to recognize the part she had played in managing the household and estates. She seems to have been strong-minded, cautious, hard-working, competent, and bitter.

Montaigne himself did not relish his role as householder, resenting trivial domestic annoyances. He liked travel, which he seldom felt able to afford, and he enjoyed fresh air, but his father had ambitions for him beyond what he seemed likely to achieve in his professional career in the magistracy. The charge to translate Sebond's work on natural theology, which set out to establish by reason the principal truths of Christianity, must have seemed to Montaigne's father a reasonable way of extracting from his heir something suited to his bookish talents and at the same time something useful to the Catholic cause, which would do him no harm professionally. Montaigne certainly knew Jean Martin's French version, first published in 1551, of the Latin abridgement by Pierre Dorland, which Martin hoped would bring doubters straying towards Lutheranism back to the Catholic fold. He must also have shared Martin's hopes about rounding up doubters, since he expanded Sebond's text to strengthen the argument. The translation incidentally makes clear that, at least when he was constrained by another author's text, Montaigne was able to write coordinated prose free from the "unruliness" which in Les Essais he finds difficulty in controlling.

Sebond had died in Toulouse in 1436. His book, when eventually published in 1484, had been a great success. It belonged to the well-known tradition inaugurated by Ramon Llull but had in fact been put on the Index of prohibited books of 1558–9, that is, well after Montaigne's father was given it, but before he asked Montaigne to translate it. The text was removed from the Index in 1564, but not the prologue, which made extravagant claims Montaigne was to tone down. Montaigne probably worked on the translation during 1567 and in 1568, the year of the dedication and of his father's death. The privilège was granted in October 1568, printing finished on 30 December, and publication took place early in 1569. Montaigne published a revised version in 1581. In a passage from Les Essais printed in 1580 he deplored the number of errors "left in it by the printer." That remark was omitted from the text printed in 1582.

The complicated arrangements for the inheritance of Montaigne's father's estate were apparently felt to be generally fair, the only difficulty being the other agreement, made on 31 August 1568, between Montaigne and his mother, specifying her rights in the household. After the summer of 1569, Montaigne did seek promotion to one of the higher courts of the Bordeaux parlement, but was declared ineligible because his father-in-law sat in one and his brother-in-law in another. Rather than request a dispensation from the king, Montaigne sold his office to Florimond de Raemond on 10 April 1570, and retired, at first devoting himself to the publication of La Boétie's works, the Latin poems being dedicated to Michel de l'Hôpital and a translation of Plutarch to Henri de Mesmes. He celebrated his 38th birthday and his retirement by having painted on the wall of the small room next to his study a Latin inscription dedicating the rest of his life to "freedom, tranquillity, and leisure."

Sometime in 1569 or 1570 he had a serious accident when his horse and he were knocked over in a narrow lane by a much heavier horse galloping past. He was thought to be dead, and afterwards wrote a fascinating account of what he remembered of his feelings as he gradually recovered consciousness. The incident reminds us that even when he was writing *Les Essais*, and had given up ambitions in the magistracy, he was mindful of his position as a country landowner, only just ennobled, with an entitlement still only in its third generation, and was anxious to tend his estates and not to be disdained by less lettered colleagues totally devoted to the pursuit of arms, duties at court, and the management of their estates. The accident also radically diminished Montaigne's fear of death, although not yet of pain. His first real experience of intense pain came with that caused from 1578 by a kidney stone blocking the urinary tract. At least once he seriously considered suicide, but he learned instead to live with pain, an experience which, as *Les Essais* shows, changed his early stoic views on endurance into a more relaxed pursuit of pleasure. There was, it came to seem, no experience so bad it made life not worth living.

The wars of religion, particularly in the Bordeaux region, were not quite so clearly divided into discrete episodes as the history books often suggest. There had been executions for Lutheranism in Bordeaux in 1544, and by the late 1550s frankly vigilante squadrons, of which many of Montaigne's friends were members, were being formed to keep Protestant insurgents at bay. The crown and parlement at this date were still supporting the moderates, but there was resentment among hard-line Catholics in 1562 at the January edict allowing limited freedom of worship to Protestants, and the "war" of 1562–63 was more nearly a series of engagements between vigilantes and guerillas in the south-west. In 1562 Montaigne had made his Catholic profession of faith in Paris and followed the royal army to Rouen, where he incidentally met the Brazilians mentioned in *Les Essais*. In 1572 he joined Montpensier's Catholic army and was sent by its leader on an important mission to the Bordeaux parlement. He was a Catholic loyalist opposed to Lutheranism, on account of the way it invited a personal interpretation of the Christian message, as well as by instinctive social conservatism.

One of his brothers was at least for a time a Protestant, and his sister Jeanne was a convinced Protestant who, although married to the Catholic Richard de Lestonnac, tried to bring up her six children as Calvinists. Her daughter Jeanne (1556–1640) resisted, and wanted to enter a convent, but was dissuaded and in 1573 married instead. Montaigne signed his niece's marriage contract. Her Catholic husband died, and she left her children in 1605 to go and found a teaching order of nuns affiliated to the Benedictines. She was canonized in 1949. Montaigne's immediate colleagues, and what may be described during his period in the magistracy as his peer group, were all Catholic, and some militantly anti-Protestant. His own stance was less repressive than that of La Boétie, while his piety and belief cannot any longer be doubted. He was however tolerant, intensely disliked persecution, and found superstition distasteful. He genuinely believed in the validity of Sebond's arguments and the utility of a rational demonstration of the truth of Catholic belief, although one of his personal discoveries was the unwisdom of thinking that rationality generally or ever governed human behaviour.

The first edition of *Les Essais* was published in Bordeaux, the preface having been signed on 1 March 1580. From 22 June 1580 to 30 November 1581 Montaigne travelled. The journey would have lasted longer, had he not been called back to France. The purpose of his travels was partly to visit mineral baths which sometimes relieved his pain for weeks or months, and partly cultural. He wanted to spend some time away from home and was disillusioned at the state of France. He distrusted doc-

tors, and kept a detailed account of how he experimented with his own treatment, noting how much mineral water he drank, how much he passed in urine, how often, and what size of stone he passed. He was aware at the same time of the humorous aspect of compiling so detailed an account of his intestinal functions. He dictated his diary to a secretary whom he dismissed in Rome, after which he wrote the diary himself, in Italian, for the last six months of his stay there. Rome in particular enchanted him, and Venice impressed him. His curiosity was unassuageable, and his secretary remarks how much further afield he would have liked to go. It was the rest of his party, less impelled by omnivorous inquisitiveness, who reined him in. Montaigne himself wanted to talk to everyone. "There was not a lackey," he said, "who could not tell them news of Florence or Ferrara."

Montaigne had started his journey by taking part in the siege of La Fère, for which he had set off from home on 22 June 1580, having left the administration of his affairs in the hands of his wife. The siege began on 7 July, and on 2 August Montaigne witnessed the mortal wounding of Philibert de Gramont, one of Henri's "mignons," the handsome young men of his bodyguard, famous for their duelling exploits and for their effeminacy. The siege ended successfully on 12 September, but by that time Montaigne had already left. Two missing pages at the front of his diary mean that we cannot tell exactly how the trip began, but on 5 September the group was just north of Paris where Charles d'Estissac joined it with a friend. The party also included one of Montaigne's brothers, and the widower of his recently dead sister, Marie. None of Montaigne's companions was yet 20. There were about a dozen servants.

The route took them east along the Marne, through the Vosges to Basel, then via Schaffhausen to Augsburg, Munich, and then Innsbruck, across the Brenner to Padua and Venice, then to Bologna and across the Apennines to Florence and Rome. They returned via Milan and the Mont Cenis to Chambéry, Lyons, Clermont-Ferrand, and Limoges. Montaigne was in Rome from 30 November 1580 until 19 April 1581, and spent the summer months visiting Florence, Lucca and Siena before spending the first fortnight of October in Rome again. In all, he visited Florence, to which he only grudgingly conceded admiration, three times. The diary is full of descriptions of interiors, furnishings, urine measurements, prices, inns, incidents, and gadgets. There are accounts of the water supply arrangements at Neufchâteau, Constance, and Augsburg. An interest is shown in all manifestations of human ingenuity, and a less surprising pleasure in views and peaceful natural settings.

Montaigne carefully adapted his behaviour to the customs and practices of wherever he was, commenting on what he found commendable and what caused him irritation, like the size of table-napkins in Switzerland. Spoons and forks were at this time new, and Montaigne was reluctant to use them. If you ate with your fingers, napkins were important. In Germany, deferring to local custom, Montaigne did not water his wine. Most important, however, is his fascination with religious behaviour. He attended Jewish and Protestant services, was present at a circumcision, discussed Calvinist theology with a Lutheran, and was duly disedified by the casual Italian attitude to liturgical ceremony. With the Jesuit Maldonado, said by one observer to have been his spiritual director, Montaigne discussed the danger that Lutheranism would lead to atheism, a term which in the late sixteenth century meant any sort of insubmission to what was considered divinely constituted authority, disbelief being diagnosed by analogy more than by implication. He appears to have accepted miracles at their face value and is more perplexed by flagellant practices than by the translation to Loreto of the house where Jesus was born.

Montaigne's books were taken from him by the customs on entry into Rome, as was in fact normal. Some books had been censured for mentioning the heresies they were refuting, but Montaigne had no dangerous material with him. *Les Essais* was returned four months later, having been read for the Master of the Sacred Palace, soon to become the Dominican General, who did not understand French. It was left to Montaigne to put right such "errors of taste" as the use of the word "fortune," his excusing of the apostate Julian, the naming of heretical poets, his criticism of torture, and his objection to the view that those at prayer should at the time necessarily be free of evil impulses. The Master argued for Montaigne against an appointed censor, and the interview was conducted courteously, obviously with nothing but the mildest of suggestions for improvement. A second interview, when Montaigne called to say good-bye, was even more dismissive of the censor's criticisms. Montaigne did add two sentences to the text, explaining his practice, but otherwise made no changes.

He was at the baths of La Villa, near Lucca, where he had been in great pain before passing a huge stone when, on 7 September 1581, he received news that he had been elected mayor of Bordeaux. His agony had made him reflect on the need to accept death uncomplainingly ("sans peine") when it comes,

Car enfin la raison nous recommande de recevoir joyeusement le bien qu'il plaît à Dieu de nous envoyer. Or le seul remède, la seule règle et l'unique science, pour éviter tous les maux qui assiègent l'homme de toutes parts et à toute heure, quels qu'ils soient, c'est de se résoudre à les souffrir humainement, ou à les terminer courageusement et promptement

(For finally reason tells us to accept with joy whatever good it pleases God to send us. The only remedy, the only rule, and the sole method for avoiding the ills, whatever they may be, which assault man from all sides and at every moment, is to resolve to suffer them as we can or to end them courageously and promptly).

Montaigne's diary continues without reference to the Bordeaux invitation. He went alone on horseback up a mountain and talked to some local people. An old man told him they never used the waters of La Villa, and that the baths had been ruined by doctors who made people take so much medicine with the waters that more died than were cured. Montaigne took his time about getting to Rome, where he arrived on Sunday 1 October, but by 20 September he was having things packed in Lucca for the return to France, noting that wine-making had begun and that he could not get a decent haircut in Italy. He scarcely dallied over his return, however, when once he had left Rome, and was back at Montaigne by 30 November. He had probably thought of turning down the mayoralty, sought advice in Rome, heard that Henri III virtually commanded him to accept, and made up his mind. The king wrote on 25 November, not knowing that Montaigne was already nearly home.

In fact Montaigne was by far the most suitable choice. He was loyal to Henri III, and known to the king's mother, Catherine de'

Medici, and his brother, the duc d'Anjou, the heir apparent, but also to Henri's sister, Marguerite de Valois, married to the Protestant leader, Henri de Navarre. It was for Marguerite that Montaigne had written the "Apologie de Raymond Sebond," the longest of his chapters (II, 12). Navarre had distrusted his brother-in-law, the king, and Catherine, ever since his enforced abjuration after the St Bartholomew Day massacre of 1572, shortly after his marriage. Virtually held captive at court, Navarre escaped in 1576, and became a Protestant again. His wife only rejoined him at Nérac two years later. On Anjou's death from consumption on 10 June 1584 Navarre became the legitimate heir to the throne, and by the time Henri III was assassinated in July 1589, shortly after his mother's death, Navarre, finally to emerge victorious as Henri IV in 1594, had been in alliance with the king against the forces of the League, headed by Henri de Guise until his assassination in 1588. It was with Guise that his wife had actually once been in love.

Guise, nominally the king's chief general, cared as little for religion as did Navarre, nominally the king's chief administrator, as well, after 1584, as heir apparent, with whom Guise had once vainly sought an alliance. Guise found political support in the pro-Spanish Catholic party, and had disliked Protestants since his father, responsible for the massacre of Protestants at Wassy in 1562 which had started off the religious wars, had been assassinated by one in 1563. Owing to the king's unpopular vices and political indecisiveness, Guise was for long, in spite of his pro-Spanish stance, virtually the national leader of overwhelmingly Catholic France. Navarre reconverted to Catholicism, and peace was finally sealed by the Edict of Nantes of 13 April 1598, which allowed a measure of toleration for Protestantism. In 1588, four years after Anjou's death, and a year before the assassination of Henri III, Montaigne was to play an important part in effecting the reconciliation between Henri III and Navarre.

Bordeaux was a loyalist stronghold in the largely Protestant southwest. The key figures in keeping peace were the king's lieutenant and the mayor. Arnaud de Gontaut, baron de Biron had filled both posts, but had incurred such hostility from Marguerite that he was replaced, as lieutenant by Matignon and as mayor by Montaigne. By convention the mayor was from the noblesse d'épée. Montaigne made clear to the Bordeaux parlement that they could expect from him neither military leadership nor the exhausting devotion which had so tired his physically much stronger father. On 26 January 1582, at the first official appearance we know of, Montaigne had met distinguished figures who would be connected with the "politiques" or moderate party, Pierre Pithou, Antoine Loisel, Claude Dupuy, and Jacques-Auguste de Thou, and on 8 February 1582 he called on Marguerite de Valois, now queen of Navarre, who had been godmother to the daughter of Louis de Gurson and Diane de Foix-Candale, at whose wedding Montaigne had represented the groom's parents, and for whose unborn daughter, of gender therefore still unknown, he had written "De l'institution des enfans." He travelled to Paris on mayoral business in August, and in 1583 was elected for a second term, although his re-election was opposed. His brother-in-law, Richard de Lestonnac, was on the side of the opposing candidate.

During his second term Montaigne had to mediate between Matignon and Navarre, and engaged in a complicated correspondence with the Protestant Philippe Duplessis-Mornay, who kept him informed of Navarre's position and tried to win Montaigne's support. In December 1584 Navarre paid a two-day visit to Montaigne, with a retinue of about 45 in addition to valets, pages, and soldiers, with as many again sleeping in the locality. The visit ended with a two-day stag hunt. A little later League forces threatened to take over Bordeaux, but Montaigne was among the leaders whose wariness managed to avert serious disturbances. On 12 June 1585 Matignon and Navarre finally met. That summer brought a heatwave, and the warm air from the marshes started an epidemic of the plague. Between June and December more than 14,000 people died, about a third of the normal population, or half of those who had remained. Only a skeleton administration stayed, and outsiders were not allowed to enter the city. Montaigne demitted office on 31 July without re-entering the city. He was not an officious mayor, but he was effective in keeping a potentially explosive situation under control, did everything that was required of him, and served the city well.

In July 1585 Henri III had signed the treaty of Nemours, making common cause with Guise, and that December Matignon's troops were joined by a large League army under Mayenne. Some small Protestant towns were captured, and Castillon, about five miles southwest of Montaigne, was put under siege. Montaigne himself was suspect on account of his friendship with Navarre, and his tenants and estate suffered from the besieging army of somewhere between 15,000 and 25,000 men. Then the plague swept through both the besieging force and Castillon itself, which fell on 1 September. From September 1586 to March 1587 Montaigne, who had by now virtually finished the third book of Les Essais, took his family away from danger, although possible infectiousness made it difficult for him to find hospitality. He had been touched by the simple way in which the surrounding peasants, who had no means of escape and no classical authorities to teach them to prepare for death by philosophizing about it, died calmly and without fright, led by nature itself.

The 1588 edition of Les Essais, including the whole of the third book, was published in June. It is nearly twice as long as the 1580 text. There are between 500 and 600 additions to the text of the first two books, and virtually all the new material dates from the period from the end of the mayoralty to the siege of Castillon (August 1585–June 1586) and from the return after the plague to the departure for Paris (April 1587–January 1588). The tone has changed with the experience of proximity to death, pain, and ageing, and the interest focuses more confidently on human nature and conduct, as seen in the light of Montaigne's personal and social experience. The thematic connections are now a lot clearer than they were, and that makes the chapters a lot longer, with only 13 in the third book out of the total 107.

It seems likely that Catherine de' Medici summoned Montaigne to help in her discussions with Navarre at the château de Saint-Brice near Cognac between December 1586 and March 1587. The pressure was great. It looked as if France might be going to have to choose between Catholicism but with Spanish domination, or a legitimate but Protestant succession. When, late in 1587, there were two Protestant armies, the German and Swiss in Lorraine being contained by Guise, and Navarre's being pursued southwards from La Rochelle by Joyeuse, it may well have been Montaigne who advised Matignon against committing his forces with those of Joyeuse to a pitched confrontation with Navarre. The confrontation took place at Coutras, leaving Joyeuse dead and Navarre victorious.

Three days after the battle, Navarre spent the night at Montaigne, after which he adopted the tactic of consolidating his position as heir to the throne rather than that of leading a rebel army against Henri III, which he was expected to do, and which would have lost him the throne that eventually became his. Montaigne seems certainly to have been Navarre's mediator with Henri III after Coutras, when the likely course of open rebellion was in fact averted. In January 1588 Montaigne travelled to Paris after conferring again with Navarre and Matignon. His party was set upon and robbed in what was probably a retaliatory raid by a Protestant band, but they were allowed by Condé, Navarre's lieutenant, to proceed, although without money or possessions. Montaigne's secret mission, presumably to unite Navarre and the king against the League, was reported by the Spanish and English ambassadors to their respective governments. The Paris Protestants were afraid that Navarre might abjure again, as indeed he eventually did, and that his failure to follow up the victory of Coutras had simply been due to dalliance with his mistress, a friend of Montaigne's, Diane "Corisande" d'Andoins, with whom Navarre, although by now tired of her, did in fact spend a month.

Montaigne was ill on his journey, and he suffered more than he said on account of his concern for public affairs. He was later to be molested by the League and, like the mayoralty, his mediation was a charge he would no doubt have preferred not to assume. It was, however, important to France, and Montaigne felt it his duty to accept it. He remained in the north for almost all of 1588, following the king to Chartres after the Day of the Barricades on 12 May. He may have been at Blois when Guise was assassinated. It was soon after he arrived in Paris that he received a note from Marie Jars de Gournay, fervent in her admiration for Les Essais, which she had read before she was 20. She was staying with her mother in Paris, and Montaigne called the next day. According to her account, the only one we have, the sympathy between them was immediate and intense.

She was intelligent, had instantly fastened on Les Essais as fully the equal of any book written in antiquity, and aspired to the place left vacant by La Boétie. Her enthusiasm was so hyperbolic that it was not until it was confirmed by the known opinion of Justus Lipsius, the Dutch moralist and scholar whom Montaigne had himself much praised, that anyone took her view of Montaigne seriously. She was to become not only Montaigne's literary executor, working tirelessly at the editing and diffusion of Les Essais, but also his defender, as well as Ronsard's, against the strictures of Malherbe. Montaigne readily assented to making her his unofficially adopted daughter, his "fille d'alliance," spent several months at her home, and even dictated passages of Les Essais to her. After his death she spent a year and a half with his wife and daughter.

Montaigne had just returned from Rouen to Paris and was in bed with gout when adherents of the League came and took him away on his horse to the Bastille in a reprisal for the king's arrest of a League member in Rouen. Guise had him released at the instigation of Catherine de' Medici, who had heard within five hours of what had taken place. Montaigne was still clearly a marked man. It was very probably soon after this incident that he became seriously ill, "hoping only for death," as his friend Pierre de Brach wrote to Justus Lipsius. Montaigne seems to have spent some time convalescing with the Gournays and then to have gone on to the Etats Généraux at Blois on 23 November

1588, before Henri III in desperation had the Guises murdered. On Montaigne's return to the south he cooperated closely with Matignon, who was having difficulty in restraining the support for the League from breaking out into open revolt. After the death of Henri III, Navarre, not yet ready to make the second abjuration which resolved matters, was being hard pressed in the field, and in fact losing to Mayenne until his victory at Arques on 21 September 1589. Montaigne did not see Navarre after he had become *de iure* Henri IV, but there is an exchange of cordial letters, and Montaigne renewed his pledge of unswerving loyalty.

The last additions to *Les Essais* in the Bordeaux copy add engagingly to Montaigne's obscenity. He adds copiously to the already outspoken "Sur des vers de Vergile," which is largely about sex—sexual organs and sexual pleasure not excluded—and it is here that he is forthright, if prudish, about the role of sex in marriage. To introduce sexual pleasure into marriage is, according to him, to profane something much more valuable. The criticism of Protestantism becomes stronger, and the moral idealism more relaxed.

For the last two years of his life Montaigne was increasingly confined to his château. He received visitors, expecially Pierre Charron and Marie de Gournay. On 27 May 1590 his only surviving child, Léonor, was married at 18 to the 30-year-old François de la Tour, who would die in 1594. They spent about four weeks at Montaigne before leaving for Léonor's new home at Saintonge. The first child was born at La Tour on 31 March 1591. She was to marry and die in childbirth. The line was carried on by Léonor's daughter by her second marriage. Montaigne himself died of quinsy on 13 September 1592. His death was apparently devout. Before he died he himself distributed to the domestic staff the legacies indicated in his will, so that no trouble would be made about paying them out after his death.

WORKS

The peculiar importance of Montaigne's biography in the context of an attempt to understand the various versions of his book, *Les Essais*, derives from the fact that we need to know why he wrote it, and for whom, before we can begin to penetrate behind what were apparently affected if engaging ramblings about himself and various other topics, generally philosophical, moral, or historical, which he spent 20 years writing and adding to. In a mixture of two languages Montaigne wrote a travel diary which he did not publish. We have also from his pen some scrappy notes, three dozen letters, and his published works consisting of the translation of a work of natural theology, two brief prefaces to editions of works by La Boétie, the friend of his youth, and nothing else at all except one large book, which was patiently and frequently reworked from before he was 40 until his death at 59. *Les Essais* was published in 1580, with additions in 1582. There were two more unchanged editions, of one of which no copy has survived, before the vastly augmented edition of 1588, which also contained the new third book. It was mostly in the margins of the sheets for a copy of that edition, known as the "Bordeaux Copy," that Montaigne added about another third to his text, without however increasing the number of chapters or books.

The set of annotated sheets, with further additional hand-written leaves where necessary, was copied as Montaigne had left it

at his death. Two copies, at least nearly identical, were made, of which one was left in the library of the Feuillants of Bordeaux and eventually transferred to the Bordeaux Municipal Library. The other copy, incorporating all the notes, corrections, modifications, deletions, and additions which Montaigne had made since 1588, was the basis for the 1595 edition procured by his covenanted daughter and literary executor, Marie de Gournay, and has subsequently been lost. She dropped her 1595 preface from the 1598 edition, but re-wrote it for her last edition, the handsome 1635 folio dedicated to Richelieu, which made Montaigne's book universally known to educated France in the mid-17th century. There is no reason to suppose that Montaigne would not have gone on making additions and corrections if he had lived. He mostly added to his text, occasionally modified it, and only very rarely deleted from it, except for stylistic reasons. Some of the luxuriant verbiage he trimmed back. Some of his additions changed the sense, or the focus, or the perspective of what had been there before. Montaigne at least twice remarks that he had himself been unable to pin down his original meaning: once prior to 1588 in the "Apologie de Raymond Sebond" (II, 12) and once later, in a passage added on to "Du parler prompt ou tardif" (I, 10).

It was strange that anyone in Montaigne's position should write a book at all, particularly a book, like his, without any obvious historical subject, political purpose, or moral aim, and *Les Essais* clearly created a new type of book. Its title had never been used before. Plutarch's *Moralia*, on which it drew, had not been called essays until Montaigne had used the word. The essay did not exist as a genre, and in Montaigne it refers to a method of writing, not its product: something like "self-examinations," or "samplings," which could be in any genre. Montaigne himself never really defined what "essai" meant, but the dominant sense of the word as it is used in his text suggests experimenting or testing. The book puzzled people, although some liked the moral aphorisms which Montaigne almost haphazardly flicked into his text, and others liked or disliked what Montaigne's 1580 "Au lecteur" misleadingly enticed the prospective reader into believing would be a pen-portrait of himself: "Je suis moy-mesmes la matiere de mon livre (I am myself the subject of my book)." That statement must be taken as a sign of tentativeness, a form of precautionary disguise. For autobiographical writing there were at least respectable precedents. Montaigne's preoccupation with his own reactions to his reading and experience was, however, interpreted in about 1602 by Etienne Pasquier, who listed his favourite aphorisms from *Les Essais*, as a sign of premature senility.

The book clearly started almost as a common-place book, the scrapbook which the few renaissance children lucky enough to receive a humanist education were taught to keep, with odds and ends of information they picked up from reading, or even from their own observation, although almost always with a moral or historical axis. Some of Montaigne's early chapters are short groups of anecdotes with a moral, or brief meditations on human frailty and inconsistency. Montaigne's mind was inquisitive, clearly fascinated by differences of opinion, background, and experience, as the *Journal de Voyage*, finally to be published in 1774, was to confirm. The exotic fascinated him, as did any instance of diversity of customs or beliefs, but, as he continued to write, he reflected on his reasons for putting pen to paper, as well as on what he was writing about, which is something that occasionally slips his mind altogether. As he writes, his mind reverberates with associations and reminiscences of something read or remembered. The process by which *Les Essais* developed really only starts when Montaigne, in what he struggles to prevent becoming free association, reads what he has written, assimilates it to a new set of mental resonances, and then reshapes it, a process he carried out almost continuously. He expected the reader's own experience to make him generate within himself, as he read, ideas, associations, and even feelings, which were not Montaigne's own.

There are not, as on the basis of the modern convention of indicating only the readings of the 1580, 1588, and 1595 edition has sometimes been supposed, just three states of the text. The process of re-reading, assimilating, and re-writing was continuous, and there was an indefinite number of states of much of the text. More importantly, what Montaigne wrote was a book with chapters, each with some focus of attention, although he did not always say what that was. It is sometimes, as he admitted, not even clear on a casual reading what the contents of a chapter has to do with its title. He sometimes put in the experience, observation, or quotation he had originally had in mind only later on, perhaps even only after a chapter's first publication. *Les Essais* is not just a collection of sometimes dialectically organized and sometimes simply rambling and disorganized treatments of topics. It is a collection of its author's reflections on the process of generating often disconnected conjectures and assertions of which something has put him in mind, which on re-reading have put him in mind of something else, and which he expects will put his reader, necessarily drawing on a different context of experience, in mind of something different again.

It is essential to make this point about the nature of the book before discussing its content, on account of the interest of modern critics and theoreticians in what the reader's own experience contributes to the understanding of literary texts, and consequently in the possibility that, in the absence of any single "correct" meaning assignable to a text even by its author, literary texts are merely open-ended, non-decodable organized systems of language rather than communicative statements. Montaigne has therefore been found particularly fascinating by modern critics who, like their baroque predecessors, have too exclusively examined his work in the light of their preoccupations rather than his. The signs are that he slowly came round to the realization that his method of writing may have been too self-indulgent, and too taxing even for the ideal reader with whom he converses, sometimes very informally and always frankly, on terms of some intimacy. *Les Essais* is ultimately the instrument used by Montaigne to enforce some discipline on the rogue excesses of his imagination. That is what explains the book's enormous power, and why its fascination for readers is well into its fifth century. Its individual chapters are "essais" in that each probes, articulately observes, assimilates, enriches and reshapes the expression of the mental process by which the text is being produced. Montaigne is also therefore analysing for the reader the experience which reading him entails.

Quite early, soon after he started toying with his commonplace book, probably about 1571, and certainly well before 1580, Montaigne felt a need to write, although he almost certainly was not consciously aware of what or why. He started with short groups of anecdotes with a brief moral, and went on to treat of human frailty or inconsistency. Within a year or two, between 1572 and 1574, Montaigne began to feel that what he was doing might be of interest to a small group of people who would share his enthusiasm for analysing the process he observed going on inside himself while he wrote, and reflected on what he had written, and brought a new experience to understanding it before he watched himself re-shaping it.

Only after 1580, when he knew that *Les Essais* was a success, did he envisage being read by a wider public, for whom his interior world needed clearer lighting and his thought processes better sign-posting. Even so, he knew he was not writing either for scholars or for those uninterested in meditating on the lessons to be drawn from their own experience. He tells us in a passage subsequent to 1588 that he was writing, not for the learned in search of "doctrine," who required properly presented erudition, "de l'erudition et de l'art," and would not read on if they found you confusing the two Scipios, nor for "les ames communes et populaires (those with dull, unsophisticated minds)," who could not see the force and strength of elevated but unconnected reflections. He was probably wasting his time, but he was writing for very rare "ames reglées et fortes d'elles-mesmes (minds which are themselves well-ordered and strong)" (II, 17, "De la praesumption"). Montaigne was looking for those sufficiently attracted by the prospect of admission to the intimacy of his raw mental processes to make the effort to follow his dense and dishevelled thought processes as they tumbled out in their layered complexity.

Montaigne's style did become less demanding as he developed away from the early attraction of Epictetan stoicism towards a more forthright pursuit of pleasure as an end in life. His preoccupations with pain and death lose their astringency. Life becomes worth living for itself, and in spite of its hardships. As he relaxed his views and his manner, he did not so much become more garrulous, or self-revelatory, as paradoxically more disciplined. Montaigne stumbled in Book I chapter 20 on the way to do what turned out to be what he wanted to do. The patterns of association and the logical connections between reflections are clearer both before he wrote that chapter and later, in what he added after 1580. The later additions to his existing text, while sometimes altering the focus of what had previously been written, generally moved towards longer passages of connected thought, so that Montaigne became less taxing to read. When he lapsed, he reflected about why. In "De la vanité," (III, 9), first published in 1588, he caught himself out making a "farcisseure (embellishment)" but added

> Cette farcisseure est un peu hors de mon theme. Je m'esgare, mais plustost par licence que par mesgarde. Mes fantasies se suyvent, mais par fois c'est de loing, et se regardent, mais d'une veuë oblique.

> /[*Post-1588 example*]/Les noms de mes chapitres n'en embrassent pas toujours la matiere; souvent ils la denotent seulement par quelque marque... J'ayme l'alleure poetique, à sauts et à gambades./[*Post-1588*]... Il est des ouvrages en Plutarque où il oublie son theme, où le propos de son argument ne se trouve que par incident, tout estouffé en matiere estrangere: voyez ses alleures au *Daemon de Socrates*. O Dieu, que ces gaillardes escapades, que cette variation a de beauté, et plus lors que plus elle retire au nonchalant et fortuite! C'est l'indiligent lecteur qui pert mon subject, non pas moy; il s'en trouvera tousjours en un coing quelque mot qui ne laisse pas d'estre bastant, quoy qu'il soit serré./[*Pre-1588*] Je vais au change, indiscrette-

ment et tumultuairement./[*Post-1588*] Mon stile et mon esprit vont vagabondant de mesmes./[*Pre-1588*] Il faut avoir un peu de foliee, qui ne veut avoit plus de sottise,/ [*Post-1588*] disent et les preceptes de nos maistres et encores plus leurs exemples

(This embellishment takes me a little away from my subject. I'm wandering, but more because I let it happen than because I don't notice. My reflections are connected, but sometimes in a roundabout way, and they're linked to one another, but not directly.

/[*Post-1588 example*]/The titles of my chapters don't always say what they're about; often they indicate it only by a sign...I like the poetic style, jumping and skipping about./[*Post-1588*]...There are parts of Plutarch where he forgets what he is writing about, where the thread of the argument comes in only incidentally, buried among other material. Look at how he tackles *The Demon of Socrates* [in the *Io*]. O God, how splendid those inspired digressions are, that diversity, the more so the more carefree and haphazard it becomes! It's the superficial reader who loses my subject, not I. There'll always be a word about it tucked away somewhere which is quite enough, however brief./ [*Pre-1588*] I change tack recklessly, at a rush./[*Post-1588*] My style and my mind go wandering off together./[*Pre-1588*] A little foolishness is necessary to avoid a lot of stupidity,/[*Post-1588*] say the precepts of our masters, and even more their examples).

Montaigne now goes bounding off again to hold that the best qualities of prose are the inspired, poetic ones. The whole passage is ironic, the implied literary theory at best semi-serious. The author invites his reader to congratulate him on his skill at defending a position which Montaigne cannot have thought really defensible. It was not possible in the 16th century to tell your readers to do your work for you because you could not be bothered to do it for them, even if, like Montaigne, you were concerned to protect your amateur status. However, the passage quoted makes the layering technique quite clear. There is a subject, "De la vanité," but Montaigne had digressed from his treatment of it, and wrote about the fact that he had digressed, and more or less justified the practice of digressing, anyway, before going on to do it again, and more formally, on the subject of poetic qualities in prose.

In one of the sentences omitted from the passage, Montaigne actually gave the amused and friendly reader whose intimacy and comprehension he could take for granted examples of how titles are used, as if he, the writer, were one of the pedants he despises, quoting "authorities," although he was in fact having fun at the expense of the stodgy seriousness of the pedants' prose expositions. In fact he was of course not really digressing at all, except from the subject of vanity, with which for the moment, he virtually indicates, he had got bored, and which anyway was never more than a pretext for him to discuss his thoughts, and the problem of disciplining his mind sufficiently to write them down.

He was conducting a sophisticated conversation with the reader about his boredom with his apparent subject, while fascinatingly discussing his real one in the form of an ironic defence of an untenable position. It is, however, exceedingly difficult for a modern reader to pick up the stylistic register of a 16th-century text even when, as here, the light layers of ironic varnish are still clearly discernible. The end of the passage praises folly, which gives the irony away even to the modern reader not necessarily familiar with the popularity of the mock encomium as a genre in the 16th century, let alone with the solemnity of stoic reflections about vanity, with Montaigne's views on schoolmasters and, by 1588, spoilsports, or with what in Montaigne's view was the nonsense talked about Plato's theories of poetic inspiration as expounded in the *Io*, which Montaigne's friendly reader could scarcely not have known.

The frequently alleged falsification of the self-portrait is only superficial, and to do with playing down social status and political importance. If Montaigne catches himself out lying, for instance, about his attitude to money, he does not change what he had written, but writes some more to confess that he had lied, although his boast, "J'adjouste, mais je ne corrige pas (I add, but I do not correct)" is excessive (III, 9, "De la vanité"). He not only changes his view in the course of writing *Les Essais*, on pain and death for instance, but is clearly pleased to discover that his writing had been sufficiently honest to pin him down as once he was. In a quite moving passage of "De la vanité" added after 1588, Montaigne reflects that in twenty years he has got older, but not wiser, "Moy à cette heure et moy tantost, sommes bien deux; mais quand meilleur? (I am a different man now from the one I was then; but which is better?)." The real self-portrait, the revelation of the workings of Montaigne's mind, is never distorted in a way which Montaigne thought might deceive his readers.

The chapters of *Les Essais* were not written in the order in which Montaigne arranged them for publication. We know that, even if most of Book I was written before most of Book II, the first six chapters of the second book were written before the first two of Book I, and that in Book I two important chapters were written late: "De l'institution des enfans," sketching out a humanist educational system and "Des cannibales," in which it is observed that primitive peoples might be considered barbaric in relation to the norms of reason, but not in regard to us, "qui les surpassons en toute sorte de barbarie (who surpass them in every sort of barbarism)."

We also know that Montaigne had originally intended to publish La Boétie's *Discours de la servitude volontaire*, which he says was written as early as 1548, but which after the outbreak of the wars of religion was usurped by the Protestant faction for propaganda purposes. It is largely a rhetorical exercise on the problem of tyranny, and was first published only partially in the expanded *Reveille-Matin* in 1574, and then, in its entirety, in Goulart's *Mémoires* of 1576–7. Montaigne then substituted La Boétie's 29 sonnets, which he erased sometime between 1588 and 1592 following their separate publication. His testimony to La Boétie, "De l'amitié," was placed in the middle of the 57 chapters of the first book.

The publication of the first and second editions of *Les Essais* at Bordeaux by Simon Millanges is a sign of diffidence. Not until 1587 did Montaigne move to Paris with the Jean Richer edition, and the much more elaborately presented 1588 quarto Paris edition by Abel l'Angelier announces Montaigne's growing confidence as much by its physical appearance and choice of publisher as by its content. It was l'Angelier, too, who was charged with the 1595 folio edition by Marie de Gournay, although she moved to Camusat for her luxuriously presented definitive folio of 1635.

The first score of chapters, with the exception of that which Montaigne placed first, were all written early in his retirement, at the latest by 1574. As published in modern editions, which necessarily obscure the skeletal structure of the chapters in their first published form, even when indicating what was added after 1580, it is difficult to see immediately just how short and schematic the chapters were. In almost all of the very early chapters more than half their length was added after original publication, including nearly all the reflective portions. Some are very brief anecdotes, often, although not invariably, classical in origin, with exceedingly simple morals.

Any reader approaching the second chapter, "De la tristesse," today, for instance, and reading only that part of the text published in 1580, will find simply an anecdote taken from Herodotus, one about the Guise family, and two taken from one or other of the popular humanist compilations of examples with almost no comment at all. Montaigne, by his additions in the course of time, turned a curiosity about oddities of behaviour into a moral comment about "sadness," the affective state most strongly denounced by the stoics, although, in the absence of suitable texts, the reader wishing to analyse the process has to select from the chapter first what was printed in 1580, then what was printed in 1588, and finally what was printed posthumously. An identifiable shift can be discerned in Montaigne's viewpoint, as well as in his style. Much the same progress can be observed in Montaigne's treatment of constancy, the stoics' favourite virtue, in the 12th chapter. In 1580 he was merely curious about forms of behaviour. The moral attitudes of stoics and Aristotelians are discussed only in a post-1588 passage.

The rather longer 14th chapter firmly draws the reader's attention to Montaigne's original centre of interest, the variety and inconsistency of human behaviour, although the later insertions much expand the reflections on the role of the imagination, which makes us fear pain more than death, and include a reflection on the history of Montaigne's financial circumstances. It is, however, not until the 20th chapter that later insertions simply disrupt the original intention. Agreeing with Cicero that the point of philosophy is to prepare us for death, Montaigne puts in a whole development arguing that the end of life is pleasure, although not merely transient physical enjoyment, which is more arduous and less satisfying than the other kinds. It is here that in 1580 the self-portrait really began. Montaigne recounts the date and time of his birth, specifying that he is using the "new style" of the 1564 edict, starting the year on 1 January, and no longer, as had previously been the convention, at Easter. He then goes on to speculate about the uncertain length of life and the equally unpredictable manner of its ending.

The chapter "De l'imagination" (I, 21) is important on account of the renaissance tradition attributing both physiological effects and belief in miracles to the power of the imagination. It is now accepted that Montaigne was a devout Catholic not exempt from beliefs today regarded as superstitious, like the "translation" of the house where Jesus lived to Loreto, but this chapter used frequently to be adduced as evidence of his scepticism. Montaigne reproduces parts of the usual renaissance list of events and beliefs which can be ascribed to the power of the imagination, including Laban's ewes, whose lambs' colouring had been affected by the striped posts Jacob had forced them to see, in Genesis XXX, xxxvii, 59, quoted by Augustine, and in the renaissance by authors like Paré and Cornelius Agrippa of Nettesheim. The doctrine of the power of the imagination is

developed from the neoplatonism of Marsilio Ficino in the first chapter of the 13th book of the *De theologia platonica* of 1482, from which Pietro Pomponazzi had extensively quoted in the *De incantationibus*. It would have been surprising if Montaigne's interest in the extraordinary had not led him to make use of this tradition as well as of the list which accompanied it, irrespective of the extent of his own scepticism,

Il est vray semblable que le principal credit des miracles, des visions, des enchantements et de tels effects extraordinaires, vienne de la puissance de l'imagination agissant principalement contre les ames du vulgaire, plus molles. On leur a si fort saisi la creance qu'ils pensent voir ce qu'ils ne voyent pas

(It is probable that faith in miracles, visions, spells, and similar extraordinary phenomena comes mainly from the power of the imagination principally acting on the souls of ordinary people, more readily impressed. Their powers of belief have been so strongly affected that they think they see what they do not see).

It was probably not until about 1575, which is likely to have been after those lines had been written, that Montaigne had most of the 57 sometimes sceptical aphorisms painted on the rafters of his library ceiling. Two thirds of them are quoted in "L'Apologie de Raymond Sebond." A score come from Scripture, and about half as many from the sceptical *Hypotyposes* of Sextus Empiricus, published in 1562 and again in 1569 by Gentien Hervet. It was in 1576 that Montaigne had had struck the medal with his arms on one side and on the other a pair of scales in balance with the motto from Sextus's Ἐπέχω (I suspend judgement).

On a number of occasions in the 1580 edition of *Les Essais* chapters are paired out of considerations to do with their content. In the first book the later "De l'institution des enfans" (II, 26), an important source of autobiographical material which must have been written late in 1579, is put next to the earlier "Du pédantisme" (II, 25), since both treat of education. In the earlier essay Montaigne was not setting out to write a theory of education, and even in the later one, solicited by Diane de Foix who was expecting her first child, he merely lets his mind range, showing in the more relaxed linking of his reflections a growing confidence in his self-portraiture. Montaigne's attitude to education is a useful guide to his thought. Education is an important concern in an age of humanist reform and it is a separable philosophical topic which invites both moral reflection and personal reminiscence. Naturally enough, his theme provokes Montaigne into displaying his intolerance of theoretical strait jackets, and shows at their most powerful his empirical approach to his subjects and his fascination with complexity, diversity, and common sense.

Brought up to admire learning, Montaigne recalls how, when young, he wished to defend it against the stereotyped pedants portrayed in the commedia dell'arte, but has had to confront the paradox that the people who know the most are not the most mentally or morally elevated. It is not that the nourishment is too rich to be assimilated. In times past great statesmen and leaders were among the most learned, and philosophers who stood apart from human affairs were laughed at, for obvious reasons emphasized in a post-1580 addition. The point is engagingly and aphoristically elaborated. We should ask "qui est mieux sçavant, non qui est plus sçavant (who knows best, not who knows most)." Again, "Nous ne travaillons qu'à remplir la memoire, et laissons l'entendement et la conscience vuide (we work only at filling the memory, leaving the understanding and the moral sense empty)." At this point there is an important post-1588 addition as Montaigne catches himself out. "But aren't I doing the same, as I write this?" He has switched from talking about education to talking familiarly about the way he is doing it, gathering books full of fine sentences. Then we return to the early text. What is the point of knowing what Cicero said, how Plato behaved, what Aristotle's words were? The point is what do we say, how do we judge, in what manner do we act? Otherwise we might as well be parrots.

The tone is earthy, almost vulgar, and it gets worse after 1588. Montaigne knows someone who needs a book to show you what he knows, and wouldn't dare say he had an itchy bottom without going to look up "itchy" in the dictionary, and then "bottom." The argument here, far from being digressive, is kept from being weighed down by repetitiveness only by the irreverence of its tone, and the neatness of its turns of phrase. As elsewhere, elevated neoplatonist considerations on love are scoffed at, so here there is an anecdote, anti-feminist even by the bluff barrack-room standards of the uneducated soldier-nobility of the 16th century, before Montaigne meanders off onto serious, although not solemn, reflections about how little can be done where there is no natural endowment. The metaphors are strong and always down to earth. Knowledge cannot give sight to the blind, but it can train the sight of those who have vision. Everything in the end depends on nature: "Nature peut tout et fait tout (nature can and does do everything)." The finest science is that of obeying and commanding. Examples are scattered through the chapter, which ends with a whole list of examples of how learning saps the cultivation of a military spirit and military skills.

"De l'institution des enfans" is much more personal, with the post-1588 insertions more outspoken than the text of 1580. Montaigne makes an inventory of his school learning. With regard to the "facultez naturelles qui sont en moy, dequoy c'est ici l'essay (my natural abilities, which I'm putting to the test here)", they are too weak to withstand the weight. Montaigne digresses a little to talk about collecting epigrams, where he finds his own greatest weaknesses, and the impossibility of teaching what is worth learning.

Car aussi ce sont icy mes humeurs et opinions; je les donne pour ce qui est en ma creance, non pour ce qui est à croire. Je ne vise icy qu'à découvrir moy mesmes, qui seray par adventure autre demain, si nouveau apprentissage me change. Je n'ay point l'authorité d'estre creu, ny ne le desire, me sentant trop mal instruit pour instruire autruy

(For these are my views and feelings. I set them out as what I believe, not as what ought to be believed. I'm trying only to discover myself, and perhaps tomorrow I'll find I'm different, if some new experience changes me. I have no authority to be believed, and don't want to be, feeling too ill instructed to instruct anyone else).

Montaigne says he is assuming Diane de Foix's child will be male, which in fact it was not. The difficulty, he points out, is not in having a child. It is in bringing it up. There follows a whole

series of sensible, practical principles. The authority of those who teach is an obstacle in the way of those who learn. A child must be taught how to make up its own mind. Confronted with the great diversity of views, let it decide if it can, and if not remain in doubt. Only fools are sure and clear. The attack on the accumulation of knowledge about what other people think is vigorous. "Le guain de nostre estude, c'est en estre devenu meilleur et plus sage (Our profit from our study is to have become better and wiser)." Physical exercise is important.

Just as too much has been made of Montaigne's caution about intellectual commitment, once considered to have been a systematic scepticism, so also too much has been made of his educational theory, which in fact represents little more than sensible and sensitive reactions to the best renaissance practice, in Montaigne's view still a little too reliant on book-learning and not keeping steadily enough in mind as the end of education the practical assimilation of right values, for Montaigne still half military. Loyalty to the prince is important, and devotion to the public welfare, but the real difficulty is to get outside our own narrow worlds, to see something of the diversity of customs and behaviour in the world, to learn the commerce of men. Montaigne is not averse to giving a few practical hints. He believes in gentleness, especially for the "nature bien née," using the term "well-born," like Erasmus and Rabelais, here and elsewhere to mean well-endowed. He goes on to speak at length about his own upbringing. There is no point in bringing up an ass loaded with books, and whipping it to keep a pocket full of learning. To succeed it is necessary not only to have learning at hand. You must marry it.

On education, therefore, the advice is sensible and practical, the discussion wide-ranging, the metaphors striking, and the point clear. The layered structures of communication, with Montaigne's self-awareness brought to bear even on the activity of self-analysis are of literary importance, and the ironic earthiness is engaging. However, the real power lies in the self-portrait, and in the derivation of practical norms from a deep and clearly focused self-analysis. It is the same focused self-analysis which provides the power in "De l'amitié," a memorial certainly to Montaigne's friendship with La Boétie, but also, in its wry way, a challenge to the great authors of antiquity on their own ground. Like constancy, in particular, friendship had been since Plato one of the great classical subjects, with treatises from Cicero and Ambrose imitated and challenged by those written in the middle ages.

There is a sense in which Montaigne's lack of pretentiousness was a sign not so much of modesty as of strength. The self-analysis, perhaps originally developed as a means of self-affirmation or even self-protection in the shadow of a flamboyantly confident but also idiosyncratic father and a domineering and energetically competent mother, seems to have provided Montaigne with the only shelter strong enough to allow him to develop without needing to pretend he was other than he was. The way Les Essais developed certainly suggests the slow emergence from extreme diffidence of a personality driven by the need for self-discovery and the desire to acquire the self-confidence and self-control which Montaigne had not had when first intervening in public life at Bordeaux, after his post had been transferred from Périgueux. The friendship with La Boétie meant so much to him partly because it eased him away from what must have been crushing parental tutelage.

Among the other chapters of particular interest in the first book is the late "Des cannibales," probably written after 1578, which continues to testify to Montaigne's inquisitiveness and his interest in sorts of beliefs and values other than those current in his own circle, of whose narrowness he was becoming conscious. It is also notable as the source from which Rousseau was to derive the solution for a particularly important problem in his social thinking. "Des prières," chapter 56, is of importance for the evidence it contains of Montaigne's real piety. It relates how impressed Marguerite de Navarre, sister of François I, had been at her brother's devotions when his amorous enterprises caused him to pass through a church in their pursuit. Montaigne contemptuously concludes "that women scarcely had the gifts necessary to write about matters of theology."

Not very far short of half the second book is taken up with a single chapter, "L'Apologie de Raymond Sebond" (II, 12). The book starts with a chapter on the inconsistencies in human behaviour, the strength within us of different motives, and our indecisiveness, and it is followed by one on drunkenness. "Le pire estat de l'homme, c'est quand il pert la connoissance et gouvernement de soy (The worst state of man is when he loses knowledge and control of himself)." Montaigne is clearly fighting his vagabond temperament, lamenting the difficulty of achieving single-mindedness, before going on to compare different attitudes to alcohol, different capacities for drink, and its different effects on the libido. It is here that Montaigne slips in a long paragraph on his father's physical prowess. "Revenons à nos bouteilles (Let's get back to our bottles)," he writes, pretending to have digressed, with the wry allusion to Rabelais, whose narrator, for much of the time ostensibly writing about drink, was for ever suggesting in the proverbial way, "Let's get back to our sheep."

The third chapter, "Coustume de l'Isle de Cea," comes out strongly against suicide. There are further reflections about what Montaigne discovers himself doing. In relating the trivia of his existence he is in fact succeeding in something which is clearly of importance to himself—the self-analysis—and of potential interest to anyone concerned with the diversity of human behaviour, and its basis. "Ce ne sont mes gestes que j'écris, c'est moy, c'est mon essence (I'm not writing about what I do, but about me, who I am)." This statement is only apparently in contradiction with the assertion that he is depicting the transient moment: "Je ne peints pas l'estre. Je peints le passage (I am not painting the essence. I am painting the transient moment)." which refers at the beginning of "Du repentir" (III, 2) to his refusal to rewrite the past.

From the seventh chapter onwards the text printed in 1580 dates only from the two years immediately preceding publication, and this is reflected in the growing confidence of the self-portrait, especially, for instance, in chapter 10, "Des livres," where we learn that even in entertainment Montaigne's taste led him to Rabelais and Boccaccio rather than the romances. He dislikes the *Axiochus*, whose ascription to Plato had been correctly doubted by Henri Estienne in 1578. Montaigne likes Virgil, Lucretius, Catullus, and Horace, but prefers the *Georgics* to the *Aeneid*, of which he thinks the best book is the fifth. For his moral edification he likes Plutarch, especially in Amyot's translation, Seneca, and Cicero, whose lack of refinement he deplores.

The "Apologie de Raymond Sebond" purports to be a defence of the *Theologia naturalis sive liber creaturarum* which Montaigne had translated at his father's request in 1569, re-publishing his translation in 1581. There had been a French translation in 1519, a French translation of the Latin abridgement by P. Dorland known as the *Viola animae*, published in Latin in 1544, 1550, 1558, and 1568, and a new French translation, by Jean Martin, of the unabridged version, published in 1551, 1555 and 1566. Sebond's book had been put on the Index of prohibited books of 1558–9, but the Index issued by the Council of Trent in 1564 had restricted the censure to the prologue, which was dropped from subsequent Latin editions and much attenuated in Montaigne's translation. A Spanish translation of the *Viola* was banned in 1559 in Spain. The trouble had presumably been Sebond's too exclusive reliance on reason and experience of the natural world. Montaigne introduced modifying adverbs. The book of nature, necessary for Sebond, is "useful" in Montaigne's translation, which inserts into the prologue an "as much as possible" and an "almost." Whatever caution Montaigne may have shown in the "Apologie," which he compiled for Marguerite de Valois, whose Memoirs show how much satisfaction she had found in reading Montaigne's translation in 1576, it must be remembered that Montaigne republished his translation in 1581, while he was making the Italian journey during which he left at Loreto silver figures of his wife, his daughter and himself, arranged in a shrine on the analogy of the Holy Family. The "Apologie" appears to incorporate pre-existing material composed in 1573 and 1576—an essay comparing human and animal behaviour and another on the weakness of human reason. Montaigne clearly distances himself from Sebond in the introduction. He is unnecessarily impolite about Sebond's Latin. He lies about the date of his father's request to make the translation of the *Theologia naturalis*; this could not have been "a few days before his death," since the dedication was signed by Montaigne in Paris on the day itself of his father's death, and the translation must have taken months. He wrongly dismisses Sebond as a "Spaniard practising medicine at Toulouse." Sebond was also a theologian, and by 1576 well enough known, as the abridgement and the translations attest.

Montaigne sets out to defend Sebond against two objections. The first objection is against Sebond's use of any "raisons humaines" at all to defend religious truth. No doubt faith is more important, but reason is a "rayon de la divinité (a ray of divinity)"—an old stoic doctrine—and even Christians ought to use it. Sometimes it enables pagans to behave better than Christians. To give grace to reason is like giving form to matter. Those who put forward the second objection, that Sebond's reasoning is worthless, must be more roughly refuted. They are attacking religion with "armes pures humaines (purely human weapons)." In other words, their objection proceeded from fallen nature and a nature not elevated by grace. Montaigne simply assumes that Sebond's opponents, being by supposition either pagans or heretics, cannot have been illuminated or strengthened by grace. Such was indeed defined doctrine, as implied by the Bull *Unam sanctam* in 1302 and explicitly laid down in 1441 by the Council of Florence. The development which now starts takes up the last 100 pages of the 110-page chapter.

Considerons donq pour cette heure l'homme seul, sans secours estranger, armé seulement des ses armes, et despourveu de la grace et cognoissance divine, qui est tout son honneur, sa force et fondement de son estre

(Let us then for the moment consider man alone, without outside help, armed only with his own arms, and deprived of divine grace and knowledge, which is all his honour and strength, and the foundation of his being).

The long discourse on human weakness and ineptitude which follows is all governed by this supposition, at which the Vatican censors made no remark at all. The trust in faith, rather than in a human reason by supposition deprived of grace and weakened by sin, was perfectly normal doctrine, only later to be used as a basis for philosophical scepticism, and as a reason for regarding Montaigne himself as a sceptic, which in 1580 he quite clearly was not.

Of the remaining chapters of Book II, the most important, and the longest, is II, 17 "De la praesumption," paired with "De la gloire," of which it starts like a continuation, devoting long passages to self-analysis.

Book III is written with much greater confidence than its predecessors. There are only 13 chapters, which makes the book longer than the first but shorter than the second, but the developments are now much longer and better connected. Montaigne is now quite confident about what he is doing. Book III was written from summer 1585 to summer 1586 and during 1587. The publisher of the 1588 edition, which included it, was one of the best in France.

The first chapter, "De l'utile et de l'honneste," is concerned with questions of public morality. It returns to a favourite theme, that nothing in nature is useless, not even our vices, a notion to become important for a whole tradition of thought in late 17th-century France. Montaigne even anticipates La Rochefoucauld in his reference to the "aigre-douce poincte de volupté maligne à voir souffrir autruy (the bitter-sweet malicious pleasure of seeing other people suffer)," but, when it comes to the need to betray in the public interest, Montaigne refuses to have any part in it: "resignons cette commission à gens plus obeissans et plus souples (let us leave that to those more disciplined and flexible)," adding after 1588 to "betray" the words "and lie, and kill."

"Du repentir," the second chapter, opens with a forthright statement about the self-portrait. It counter-attacks against those who had criticized the self-portrait of the 1580 edition, as announced in its "Au lecteur," and shrugs off the earlier stoic preoccupations with constancy as the principal virtue. "La constance mesme n'est autre chose qu'un branle plus languissant (Even constancy is only a slower movement)." The chapter is largely a denunciation of repentance, so easily counterfeited, and so often due to the enfeeblement of passion with age. True repentance must be effected by God. The chapter contains the famous plea to recognize natural temperaments and gifts:

il n'est personne, s'il s'escoute, qui ne descouvre en soy une forme sienne, une forme maistresse, qui luicte contre l'institution, et contre la tempeste des passions qui luy sont contraires

(there is no one, if he listens to himself, who does not discover within himself a personal disposition, a dominant disposition, which fights against training, and against the wind of passions which oppose it).

Montaigne's writing gets more aphoristic, his tone earthier and occasionally even bawdy. The sixth chapter, "Sur des vers de Virgile," contains Montaigne's chief consideration of sexual matters. The trouble now, in his old age, is excessive temperance. Erotic playfulness and pleasure have no place in marriage, as Montaigne seems to remember having already said somewhere, referring not without affectation to "De la moderation" (I, 30). Here he regards erotic play in marriage as "une espece d'inceste (a sort of incest)." A husband should not seek to give sexual pleasure to his wife and should make love only at decent intervals. Too much ardour lessens the chances of conception. "Ung bon mariage, s'il en est, refuse la compaignie et conditions de l'amour. Il tache a representer celles de l'amitié (A good marriage, if there is such a thing, turns away from the affections and circumstances of love, and tries to adopt those of friendship)." Any woman who has tasted the mutual favours and obligations of marriage much prefers the position of wife to that of mistress. As for himself, Montaigne has been surprised by the pleasantness of being married. He has even been more faithful than he had promised or hoped. He is however impatient with the idealization and poetization of love in the Italian neoplatonist tradition of Ficino, and regards sexual congress as a purely physical act, wrong only if immoderate or indiscreet. He has come to look on men and women as different chiefly on account of training and custom.

"Des coches" is an indictment of European behaviour in the new world, while "De l'art de conferer" and "De la vanité" are both important, relaxed chapters in which Montaigne talks familiarly, sometimes on great moral or public issues. His essential conservatism is brought out in his quotation of one of Pibrac's famous quatrains. Whether you are born in a monarchy, an aristocracy or a democracy, you should submit to the rules of the society in which God has put you. There is a good deal about public life, and a wary caution takes over from anything which could be referred to as scepticism in the philosophical sense (III, 11, "Des Boyteux"). The final chapter, "De l'experience," the counterpart to the earlier "De la vanité," is a long meditation on life's diversity and an affirmation of self-confidence and the need to rely on experience. The aphorisms come fast as Montaigne moves through the different sorts of experience he is reviewing, and *Les Essais* ends on a note not far from triumph, although Montaigne remains aware of the paradoxes of the human situation. Man, as he makes the Delphic oracle announce at the end of "De la vanité," is the observer without knowledge, the magistrate without jurisdiction, and after all the director of life's farce.

PUBLICATIONS

Collections

Oeuvres complètes, 12 vols., 1924–41
Oeuvres complètes, Bibliothèque de la Pléiade, 1962 [1965 printing much to be preferred]
Complete Works, translated and edited by Donald M. Frame, 1957
The Complete Essays, translated by M.A. Screech, 1991

Principal early editions

Les Essais, 1580

Les Essais, 1582
Les Essais, 1587
Les Essais, 1588 [500–600 passages and third book added]
Les Essais, 1595 [incorporating Montaigne's final emendations and additions]
Les Essais, 1635 [definitive edition by Marie de Gournay]
Journal de voyage en Italie, 1774

Reference editions

Les Essais, edited by R. Dezeimeris and H. Barckhausen, 2 vols., 1870–3 [Edition of 1580 version, with variants of 1582 and 1587]
Les Essais, edited by F. Strowski and others, 5 vols., 1906–33 [Edition Municipale, Bordeaux: standard edition, with variants from all principal early editions]
Les Essais, edited by F. Strowski, 3 vols., 1912 [Phototype reproduction of Bordeaux Copy]
Les Essais, edited by E. Courbet and others, 3 vols., 1906–31 [Typographic reproduction of Bordeaux copy]
Les Essais, edited by M. Françon, 1969 [Photographic reproduction of 1582 edition]
Les Essais, edited by D. Martin, 2 vols., 1976 [Photographic reproduction of 1580 edition]

Other editions of *Les Essais*

edited by Maurice Rat, Classiques Garnier, 3 vols., (no indication of strata) 1952
edited by Pierre Villey, re-edited V.-L. Saulnier, 1965
edited by A. Micha, Garnier Flammarion, 3 vols., 1969

Editor

Etienne de la Boétie, *La Mesnagerie de Xenophon, Les 'Règles de mariage' de Plutarque, Lettre de consolation de Plutarque à sa femme...*, 1571
Etienne de la Boétie, *Vers françois*, 1571

Biographical and critical studies

Villey, Pierre, *Les Sources et l'évolution des Essais de Montaigne*, 2 vols., Paris 1908
Coppin, Joseph, *Montaigne, Traducteur de Raymond Sebond*, 1925
Boase, A.M., *The Fortunes of Montaigne*, 1935
Dreano, M., *La Pensée religieuse de Montaigne*, 1937
Frame, D.M., *Montaigne's Discovery of Man: The Humanization of a Humanist*, 1955
——————*Montaigne: A Biography*, 1965
——————*Montaigne's 'Essais'. A Study*, 1969
Gray, Floyd, *Le Style de Montaigne*, 1958
Brown, Frieda S., *Religious and Political Conservatism in the 'Essais' of Montaigne*, 1963
Bowman, F.P., *Montaigne: Essais*, 1965 (in English)
Brush, Craig B., *Montaigne and Bayle. Variations on the Theme of Skepticism*, 1966
La Charité, R.C., *The Concept of Judgment in Montaigne*, 1968
Baraz, M., *L'Etre et la connaissance selon Montaigne*, 1968
Friedrich, Hugo, *Montaigne*, 1968 (French)
Joukovsky, F., *Montaigne et le problème du temps*, 1972

Norton, Glyn P., *Montaigne and the Introspective Mind*, 1975
Regosin Richard L., *The Matter of my Book, Montaigne's 'Essays' as the Book of the Self*, 1977
Sayce, Richard, *The Essays of Montaigne: a critical exploration*, 1972
Screech, M.A., *Montaigne and Melancholy*, 1983
Starobinski, Jean, *Montaigne en mouvement*, 1982; as *Montaigne in Motion*, 1985
Supple, James, *Arms versus Letters. The Military and Literary Ideals in the 'Essais' of Montaigne*, 1984

MONTCHRESTIEN, Antoine de, 1575 or 1576–1621.

Dramatist.

LIFE

What we know about Montchrestien's biography derives largely from the hostile comments in the *Mercure Français* (q.v.) for 1621, which regarded him primarily as avaricious, unscrupulous, and mercenary, and only secondarily as a rebel and a convinced, if not over-zealous, Protestant. Malherbe was slightly acquainted with Montchrestien, although he clearly played down the extent of the acquaintanceship after the rebellious activities in Normandy which resulted in Montchrestien's death. However, the linguistic emendations and stylistic changes made subsequently to the original publication of Montchrestien's plays, the date of which is usually given as 1601, and incorporated into the 1604 text, were certainly not due to any corrections by Malherbe, in spite of the tenacity with which that conjecture was defended for almost half a century after first being put forward in 1934.

Malherbe's acquaintanceship with Montchrestien is known from two letters. Writing to his cousin, M. de Bouillon, on 2 August 1618, Malherbe refers to "un nommé M. de Montchrestien (someone called M. de Montchrestien)," from whom he had heard some unspecified information "not once but a dozen times." Then, in a letter to Peiresc of 14 October 1621, Malherbe recounts the circumstances of Montchrestien's death and what Malherbe knew about his life. At the time he wrote his tragedies Montchrestien was probably a more or less detached Catholic and, although he exercised many functions, he was essentially an adventurer and an opportunist, with an ambition to occupy a position of social esteem and to become wealthy.

The date of Montchrestien's birth has to be arrived at by subtracting his age at the date of his portrait prefacing the first edition of the tragedies, given as 25, from the presumed date of publication, 1601, although we cannot be sure that publication did take place in 1601, since the 1603 version of *L'Escossaise* was still exploiting the 1601 privilège, or that the portrait was not made before 1601. It is, however, reasonably certain that Montchrestien must have been born in 1575 or 1576. Both sources, Malherbe and the *Mercure*, say that his name was Mauchrestien, and he was the son of an apothecary, a prescriber and dispenser of drugs probably still rather higher in the professional hierarchy than a surgeon-barber. One of Montchrestien's cousins was a sieur des Ventes, so there was probably an aristocratic family connection.

Montchrestien was born in Falaise, Normandy, and was orphaned while young. The courts put him in the custody of a neighbour, "le sieur de sainct André Bernier," no one having volunteered. The *Mercure* suggests that he was sufficiently destitute for it not to have been necessary to make an inventory of his belongings but, on reaching his majority, which in Normandy was at the age of 20, Montchrestien took his guardian to court, queried the accounts which were rendered, and was awarded 1,000 livres. That means that he was born into a reasonably well-to-do, trading but quasi-professional bourgeois family, with a network of relations, neighbours, and acquaintances which stretched from the middle bourgeoisie to the minor office holders and small land owners. It is not surprising that he should in later life have aspired to both wealth and status.

In fact, Montchrestien quite early found a place as page-companion to Jacques and François, the two sons of François Thésart, baron de Tournebu et des Essarts, whom he followed to university, waiting on them, but being taught with them not only his humanities but also horsemanship and all that went with sword-bearing. The brothers may well have had not only Montchrestien but a private chaplain and tutor, as well as an establishment of ordinary servants, with them at university. The Thésart brothers must have been about the same age as Montchrestien. Their father had married Jeanne de Mondy in 1572 or 1573, and was to die in 1582. Their mother married again, a Paul de Briqueville. Montchrestien was to marry their sister, Suzanne, on 31 January 1618, after her widowhood. She was the youngest child, born about 1577, and around 1598 married Léonard Hamon, sieur de l'Isle, described by the *Mercure* as a "gentilhomme riche, mais imbécile de corps et d'esprit (rich nobleman, but feeble in body and mind)." The Thésart family was strongly Protestant, and Montchrestien may have become a Protestant on his marriage, but he never showed any strong sign of religious commitment, believed in toleration, and was almost certainly conventionally Catholic, without being devout, during most of his life.

He was to grow up litigious and quarrelsome. By the time he was 20 he had clashed with a certain baron de Gouville who, with a brother-in-law and a soldier, attacked him. Montchrestien used his sword, was left for dead, recovered, sued the baron and the baron's brother-in-law, and set himself up with the 12,000 livres he received in damages. We do not know what the quarrel was about, but Montchrestien, as the *Mercure* did not fail to notice, had clearly seen in the courts a useful source of income. Apart from that 12,000 livres, there was the award at about the same time of 1,000 livres from his former guardian, the dishonest Sainct-André Bernier, and in 1611, when François Thésart was already dead, Montchrestien was bringing a court case against the elder brother, Jacques, who had inherited the title. On 4 April 1616 there is another reference to a dispute over 600 livres with Jacques Thésart which had reached the courts at Rouen on the preceding 16 July. Later on, Montchrestien acted for Suzanne Thésart in a lawsuit against her husband. Suzanne made over to Montchrestien everything she could when they married in 1618, but died within a year or two, and Jacques Thésart successfully challenged the marriage settlement, so that Montchrestien did not succeed in keeping any of his wife's fortune.

Since the preliminary verses to his first play are chiefly by teachers at the Normandy university of Caen, it is to be presumed that that is where Montchrestien and the Thésart brothers studied. Even the *Mercure* acknowledges the thoroughness of his training: "il estudie, il s'adonne à la Poësie Françoise, fait bien des vers (he studies, devotes himself to French poetry and writes verse well)." In 1596 Montchrestien published his first play *Sophonisbe*, known in subsequent editions as *La Cartaginoise; ou, La Liberté*. Two of the preliminary pieces refer to the poem *Susane ou la Chasteté*, published in 1601 with a respectful dedication to Suzanne Thésart, extended in 1604. Montchrestien's first poem to her therefore dates from no later than 1596. It is likely that *Sophonisbe* was written for performance in the context of the university, but it was dedicated to the wife of the governor of Caen, Mme de la Vérune, in whose presence it had been played before its publication. Since it was published at Caen, while Montchrestien's later publications appeared at Rouen, starting with the 1599 slim volume of poetry *Les Derniers Propos, avec le Tombeau de feu noble dame Barbe Guiffart*, it is also probable that Montchrestien finished his university studies between 1596 and 1599, and moved to Rouen.

The small volume was signed "A. M. Sr. D. V.," the first indication that Montchrestien had acquired the noble title of "de Vatteville." The *Mercure* pointed out that "he had himself called Vatteville, but there is no property or fief of Vatteville, and no feudal title of that name." There is however a notaried act of 13 September 1612 referring to contracts concerning property purchases in the parish of "Anbleville" in the vicomté of Falaise in 1603 and 1604. Montchrestien's friends in Rouen were mostly associated with the Normandy parlement. The 1601 edition of the tragedies was dedicated to Henri II de Bourbon, born in 1588, future father of the Grand Condé, to fight against Montchrestien on the king's side when in 1621 Montchrestien was leading a Huguenot band. The 1601 volume included five, but not all, of the poems printed in 1599. Until Henri IV's divorce in 1599 from Marguerite de Valois, remarriage to Marie de Medici in 1600, and the birth of the future Louis XIII in 1601, Henri de Bourbon, prince de Condé, had been the heir presumptive to the French throne. The 1601 edition of Montchrestien's tragedies also included *Susane; ou, La Chasteté*, several short pieces in verse and prose, some sonnets, a *Bergerie* and five tragedies: *L'Escossaise; ou, Le Desastre*; *La Cartaginoise; ou, La Liberté*; *Les Lacènes; ou, La Constance*; *David; ou, L'Adultère*; and *Aman; ou, La Vanité*.

We know that *L'Escossaise*, about Mary, queen of Scots, who was the niece of the duc de Guise and, as wife of François II, briefly queen of France, was performed in public during the Lent of 1601, because on 17 March Sir Ralph Woodward wrote to Cecil about it, and complained to Villeroy, the minister, who banned it. According to a letter of 21 June 1603 from the lieutenant général, M. de Beauharnais, to the chancellor Pompone de Bellièvre, the play was also performed by a travelling company at Orléans, and then again in Paris, apparently only once, in February 1604. Parry, the English ambassador, wrote to Cecil that the players had been imprisoned the day afterwards, and that the author and printer were being searched for. There were, however, new editions of the plays in 1603 and 1604. In 1604 *L'Escossaise* became *La Reine d'Escosse*, *Hector* was added, and most lines of the other plays were changed, no doubt in the general direction of Malherbe's proposed linguistic reforms, and probably already on account of the personal influence of

Malherbe in Normandy. Between 1596 and 1601, of the 2,237 lines of *Sophonisbe*, 2,127 had already been changed. In 1604 the *Bergerie* and the other smaller pieces except *Susane* had been dropped, and there was a new privilège of 10 April 1604. The apparent rigour shown in suppressing *L'Escossaise* had merely been a smoke-screen to keep the English happy.

In 1605 Montchrestien went to England. Both the *Mercure* in 1621 and Montchrestien's own poem to the king, asking for pardon and printed in 1607, suggest that his journey was to avoid the scaffold, and the *Mercure* says that he had killed the son of the sieur de Grichy-Moinnes in a duel. He had finished writing tragedies, and his dedication to Condé of the 1604 edition had said he did not want them printed again subsequently. He was looking for a subject more worthy of Condé and more suited to his present interests. The *Mercure* says he was thinking of a verse translation of the psalms and a history of Normandy. In fact, although Montchrestien continued to write occasional verse, the only other work he ever published was to be the 1615 *Traicté de l'oeconomie politique*.

Montchrestien seems probably to have been in England by 8 March 1605 and to have lived there, although he visited Holland. We know only that he was back in France by 23 July 1611, on which date he is described in a legal document as a noble, living at Ousonne-sur-Loire. He had set up a steel workshop there to make cutlery and no doubt surgical instruments. The *Mercure* says he was suspected of counterfeiting the coinage. His enterprise failed, and no doubt prompted the gestation of the ideas to be found in the treatise on political economy. The stray survival of legal documents allows us to know that in September 1612 he was merely lodging at Ousonne, and in the process of selling Anbleville. By April 1616 he was again living in Rouen.

Between 1617 and 1619 Montchrestien had been concerned with an enterprise involving shipping. On 11 February and 22 September 1617 he borrowed money to pay off crews from a ship called "Le Régent." The *Mercure* tells us that in 1619 there was another law suit about the control of a ship, and that Montchrestien wished to "faire un embarquement suivant ses inconstances ordinaires (load a vessel according to his usual capriciousness)." When he married Suzanne Thésart on 31 January 1618, it was in Paris, and Montchrestien had three witnesses, all noble, two connected with the admiralty, and the other one a Protestant. He was, as ever, highly connected, and it was no doubt due to high connections that he was made governor of Châtillon-sur-Loire, where his servant, Pierre Paris, describes him as "vivant de son bien est revenu, faisant profession de la religion prétendue Réformée (living from his wealth and income, and professing the Protestant religion)." "Religion prétendue réformée (religion affecting to be reformed)" was so commonplace a derogatory term for Protestantism that it was often reduced to its acronym "RPR." However, by 1621 Montchrestien appears, according to the *Mercure*, to have been reduced to difficult financial circumstances again, no doubt after losing his wife's legacy to Jacques Thésart.

Montchrestien may of course have been a Protestant for some time. The Thésart family was Protestant, and Montchrestien's choice of words indicates that he used a Protestant bible, almost certainly Olivétan, for his tragedies. But there is strong circumstantial evidence that he was a Catholic at Caen, and most of his Rouen friends were distinguished Catholics. It seems certain that in 1605 he contributed one or, more probably, two poems to a very Catholic posthumous collection by a Dominican nun who

had died in 1588. The 1615 *Oeconomie politique* also reads as though it was written by a Catholic, although it deplored the uselessness of monks to the community and, for the sake of the country's economy, advocated toleration. It is therefore on the whole likely that Montchrestien was a Catholic for most of his life, but that he may have become at least a surface Protestant either to marry Suzanne Thésart, or shortly after his marriage, or because it fitted in with the political or financial ambitions which inspired his participation in the 1621 uprising. The *Mercure* tells us that Montchrestien was only lukewarm as a Protestant.

The Protestant rebellion had been announcing its approach for some time. It was inevitably in part a rebellion of a particular section of the feudal aristocracy which felt disadvantaged partly on account of its religion. Condé had not only lost his position as heir presumptive on the birth of the future Louis XIII, but he slipped further away from the succession when Louis's two brothers were born, Philippe, who had died in 1611, and Gaston, at first d'Anjou and then d'Orléans, who was born in 1608. Mayenne had died in 1611 and Soissons at the end of 1612, but that left Condé, Conti, Bouillon, Longueville, Nevers, and Vendôme, each of whom intrigued against the crown.

Of the five children of Henri IV and Marie de Medici surviving after 1611, three were daughters: Elisabeth, who married Philip IV of Spain; Christine, who married Victor Amadeus I, duc de Savoie; and Henriette, who was to marry Charles I of England. Gaston, born in 1608, remained next in line to the throne from the time of his brother Philippe's death in 1611 until the birth of the future Louis XIV to Louis XIII and Anne of Austria in 1638, and next in line after Gaston during that time was Condé, pushed forward as the focus of discontent. In 1614 peace had been signed between Marie de Medici, the regent, on the one hand, and on the other Condé and Nevers, at Sainte-Menehould. The Estates were called together to meet in the winter of 1614–15. Marie de Medici managed to break the community of interest between the parlements and the princes, and it was the Protestants under Rohan who roused the south-west and tried to impede the Spanish marriages, Louis XIII to Anne of Austria and his sister Elisabeth to the future Philip IV.

Condé's popularity in Paris in 1616 led Marie de Medici to send him to the Bastille. Nevers revived the princes' party and, in 1618, Louis XIII dangerously decided to re-establish Catholicism in Protestant Béarn, where his authority was unhampered by the edict of Nantes, which had never applied there. For perfectly understandable reasons the alignment and even the religious affiliations of important leaders in the struggles involving Marie de Medici, Louis XIII, Protestants and Catholics, Normandy, the west, the Bordeaux region, the south-west and the Cévennes was continually changing. Condé was restored to favour in 1619, and Rohan led forces against the crown. As Louis XIII, guided by Luynes, determined to restore the Huguenot provinces of Poitou, Guyenne, Saintonge, and Languedoc to obedience, the Protestants rallied at La Rochelle. In 1620 Marie de Medici, in alliance now with Epernon, Mayenne, Longueville, Soissons, the two Vendômes, Nemours, Retz, La Trémoille, Roannes, and Rohan, appeared much more powerful than she was.

A small army bearing Marie de Medici's colours under Vendôme and Retz was dispersed by the king's troops at Ponts-de-Cé on 8 August 1620 but, in spite of the peace settlement on 10 August, Louis XIII, pious, and now abetted by Bérulle and advice from a sometimes hysterical wing of the Catholic revival, became even more determined to uproot Protestantism from Béarn. He successfully led his army to Poitiers, Bordeaux, and then Pau, where he arrived on 14 October. On his return to Paris, all seemed well. Epernon's son, La Valette, had received a cardinal's hat; Richelieu's favourite niece was to marry Luynes's nephew, the marquis de Combalet; and Marie de Medici had handsomely endowed the bride. The Protestants, however, were assembling at La Rochelle and, although the rebellion now, more clearly than previous unrest, had religious roots it is difficult not to suppose that it was ambition rather than religious conviction which ultimately persuaded Montchrestien to join the Protestant forces. The Protestants under Rohan demanded the reversal of all that the king had done in Béarn. A number of Protestants, including Bouillon and Lesdiguières, did not take part. Condé, Mayenne, and Epernon were now fighting for the king.

The royal forces took to the field in April 1621. Montchrestien set out from Châtillon in May to relieve Jargeau, which had capitulated before he arrived. Montchrestien with 200 men entered the town by river on 23 May but, unable to stir the inhabitants, left again with a band now numbering some 400 to take over the town of Sancerre. On 28 May Condé arrived outside the town with 4,500 men. On the next day Montchrestien capitulated to Condé, and was given a month to find somewhere safe to live. The *Mercure* says Condé gave Montchrestien 6,000 livres to leave the city. Pierre Paris put the sum rather lower, at 3,000 livres.

Montchrestien, apparently enriched, went on fighting. He took the town of Sully, was besieged by the comte de Saint-Paul and by Vitry, but surrendered only when Condé arrived on 19 July. He was again set free, went to Paris, and then to La Rochelle, where he stayed only 15 days, but was given a commission and money to raise troops in Maine and Normandy. Montchrestien was successful enough to raise fears for Caen which Malherbe expressed in a letter. The forces were to rendezvous on 11 October, and success might have had serious consequences for the history of the French monarchy. But on the night of 7 October Montchrestien, with a few companions, was in an inn at Les Tourailles, a small village near Athis. The innkeeper warned the local seigneur and former minister, Claude Turgot des Tourailles, who arrived with a score of musketeers. Montchrestien, who had probably been recognized by the innkeeper, was identified in spite of giving a false name and came out of the inn with his men firing their guns. In the resulting scuffle he was killed. With the exception of Pierre Paris, the others fled. Paris was eventually compelled to give the evidence on which this account is based.

Montchrestien, dead, was tried on 12 October, and his body was broken and then burned. The parlement of Rouen also wanted to mutilate the corpse, but made its wishes known too late. Montchrestien's death was sufficiently important to put an end to the rebellion in Normandy. Even the *Mercure* regarded Montchrestien in 1621 as one of the good tragic poets of his day although, after the edition of 1627, Montchrestien's works shared the general disfavour during Colbert's artistic reign of the works of the French renaissance.

WORKS

The gap of 20 years between the first publication of Montchrestien's last tragedy and the publication of anything at all by Hardy, France's first professional dramatist, is more than fortuitous. In almost all ways Montchrestien's tragedies constitute the apogee of the learned theatre of the French renaissance. They come at the end of a whole tradition, which had scarcely evolved in half a century, and which then broke off. Hardy came at the start of a new tradition, which grew organically from the dramatic entertainments of travelling players and circus performers through the great pastorals and tragicomedies of French baroque, to fan out into dramatic entertainments which absorbed all sorts of outside influences, like the commedia dell'arte (q.v.), and included the bravura tragedy of Racine, as well as tragicomedy—a term at first denoting merely a play without a chorus—farce, burlesque, social satire, ballet, opera, and a mixture of two or more of these genres.

The essential difference between what Montchrestien and his renaissance predecessors were trying to do, and what was undertaken later by Hardy, Théophile de Viau, Racan, Mairet, Pierre Corneille, Scudéry, and La Calprenède, revolves round the question of audiences. The neoclassical tragedies of the renaissance, whether French translations of antique classics, or antique classics played in Latin, or new pieces modelled on the antique, written and played in Latin or French, grew essentially out of educational exercises in rhetoric, and were played in colleges, by students at the peak of their education in the humanities. The performances were amateur, occasional, and intended to be educative, but could be part of such festivities as were occasioned by a royal visit, although they were also a learned substitute in the colleges for the coarser carnival diversions to whose attractions students were not necessarily immune. Such tragedies were also played at court, often with nobles taking parts, in a few of the grander houses in the country, and in public on such great occasions as a royal entry, and possibly on the occasion of other, lesser celebrations.

It was in the *Rhetoric*, and not the ethical writings, that Aristotle had treated of the passions. He was interested in how to move an audience, not necessarily for purposes of entertainment or even as training in forensic oratory. At least in the Jesuit colleges, the final class of the humanities course was called rhetoric, and it succeeded the classes of grammar and poetry. Rhetoric was the art of persuasion, best taught to students finishing their humanities by analysing the great forensic speeches of Cicero, or the expressions of emotion in antique drama, and by reproducing exemplary reactions to great calamities. Freshly composed tragedies did not need any dramatic interaction, and the action at best worked its way through a series of tableaux, in each of which opportunity was afforded for characters to lament or display other emotions appropriate to the changed situation, ranging from dangerous defiance to miserable despair.

There was no need for an intrigue. The situations of the characters could be changed by a messenger's announcement of some catastrophe or victory. The interventions of a chorus to indicate to the audience the acceptable or normal reaction to what was portrayed was at first obligatory. The tragedies quickly moved to political subjects, then biblical ones, and came to include topical allusions, even semi-official warnings, as from Henri III to Joyeuse in Garnier's *Les Juifves*. Only the alexandrine appeared to offer the required metrical versatility. Tragedies were obviously the more intense, the less intrigue that needed to be included between the beginning and the denouement. The educational effect was also increased by the sublimity and universality of the subject, as offered in the incomparable myths of Homer, Virgil, Aeschylus, Sophocles, and Euripides, or the great truths of the Judeo-Christian revelation.

Montchrestien's decision to take so modern and politically sensitive a topic as the history of Mary, queen of Scots, as a subject was although not unprecedented, still bold. Mary was the daughter of James V of Scotland and his wife Marie de Guise-Lorraine, married in 1538. James V had died only a week after the birth of his daughter and successor, who was originally destined to marry the future Edward VI but was in fact betrothed at the age of five to the dauphin, son of Henri II, who became François II. When Elizabeth acceded to the English crown, Mary had some real claim to it. Military success and astute diplomacy obtained recognition from the Scots for the legitimacy of Elizabeth's reign, and Mary's crossing from France to land at Leith on 19 August 1561 was followed by a series of incidents which discredited her. In 1567 she abdicated the Scottish crown in favour of her son, who in 1603 was to become James I of England. She was kept in prison by Elizabeth for 16 years, and on 8 February 1587 she was beheaded. Montchrestien's principal source for the story was Pierre Matthieu's 1587 *Histoire des derniers troubles de France*.

It was not so much French feelings in favour of Mary, who was a Catholic, that made the subject dangerous but also fascinating, as the French horror at the action of Elizabeth, head of the Church of England. Montchrestien was no doubt correctly counting on this when choosing so modern and politically sensitive a subject, but he did not treat its rich seams of political and religious conflict in the way any dramatist would surely have done whose principal interest lay in the interplay of motives and dramatic actions. Jean de la Taille, today considered the principal theoretician of French renaissance drama, had proscribed the use of contemporary subjects. Montchrestien, although no doubt not on that account, treated his subject apolitically, extracting from its tragic ending the maximum emotional intensity of which it was capable, stressing the added poignancy given it by its chronological recentness and its tragic ending, and by the political and religious conflicts which ensured that the subject would keep its emotional charge. The English forms of their names are used here to avoid constant repetition of what the play calls the principal characters: The Queen of Scotland and The Queen of England. Montchrestien emphasizes the exemplary Christian stoicism of Mary's death, and goes out of his way to present both sides of the political picture. It is not a modern drama dependent on dramatic tension, and Montchrestien makes Elizabeth the centre of action for two acts, and Mary for the last three. There are no scenes, but two choruses. Most of the play is in alexandrines, but octosyllables are frequently used for the chorus, and there are other metrical variations.

The play opens with a presentation of Elizabeth's case for allowing Mary's execution. Mary was a focus of political danger, a rallying point for Catholic dissent and French ambition. Elizabeth is in danger "Du poison domestique et du glaive estranger (From poison at home and attack from abroad)." The first act is totally taken up by a scene between Elizabeth and a "conseiller (advisor)," doubtless modelled on Cecil, followed by a chorus. Elizabeth starts with a 100-line monologue expanding on her feelings. In spite of the wonder of nations at her achievements,

J'estime quant à moy malheureux mon bon-heur,
Qui prend pour les seduire un vain masque d'honneur.

Le glaive de Damocle appendu sur ma teste,
Menace de la cheute, et moins que rien l'arreste:...

(For my own part I think my success a misfortune,/which, to make itself the envy [of nations], puts on an empty mask of honour./The sword of Damocles suspended over my head,/Threatens to fall, and less than nothing holds it up).

Allusions are made in a way vague enough to make it clear that Montchrestien presupposes in his readers, whom he will rightly have expected to be much more numerous than his audiences, a reasonably detailed knowledge of the threats faced by Elizabeth since the death in 1558 of Mary Tudor. As in so much late renaissance French verse, there is a certain lingering on horrific detail, here apparent when Elizabeth conjures up the possible consequences of a civil war. The chorus contents itself with sententious commonplaces.

The second act takes place between Elizabeth and the parliamentary delegation, reduced to a chorus.

Il n'est temps qu'au pardon ta bonté se hazarde,
Garde ta Majesté afin qu'elle nous garde

(This is no time for your goodness to risk making you grant a pardon,/Keep your Majesty safe, so that it may in turn keep us safe).

By the end of the second act there has been only the most stilted of conversational interchanges, but there have been long expositions of the attitudes and feelings of Elizabeth, her counsellor, and the parliamentary delegation.

The third act confronts Mary with Davison, Elizabeth's secretary, and the chorus of her maids. Her own monologue is 157 lines long, recounting her history in dignified periphrastic terms and lamenting her fate. Her maids have a long chorus—very nearly 100 lines—of consolation and encouragement in the face of death. The fourth act is given wholly over to a monologue by Mary, followed by a chorus from her maids, written in alexandrines. In the fifth act a lament by Mary's steward leads to the entry of a Messenger announcing, and then describing, her death. The tragedy, while non-dramatic in any modern sense, is none the less not just a series of disconnected elegiac poems, since there is some logical progression through the tableaux, and a strong sense of irony in the way the two principal characters, who never meet, quite misunderstand one another, each in the play wrongly attributing to the other unwarranted motives, feelings, and characteristics.

Montchrestien in this play is not otherwise interested in dramatic development, nor in the projection of any political, religious, or simply moral viewpoint. He does write primarily as a poet, and his verse is most noteworthy not for intensity of emotional power, but for its handling of both language and imagery. Parts of Mary's splendid farewell to life in the fourth act are addressed to France, its king, its Louvre, Mary's own suite of ladies-in-waiting, and even to herself. Most of it, however, is a prayer, and among the most successful of Montchrestien's lines are the 32 starting "Tu nous a relevez (You have lifted us up...)" which together constitute a syntactical expansion of the best collects in the Roman liturgy, normally cast in the form "O God who...; we pray thee that..." They contain a single neatly sustained image:

Comme quant au matin l'air est chargé de nuës
Le Soleil décochant ses oeillades menuës
Fait soudain disparoir les broüillats espandus
Entre le terre et luy comme un voile tendus;
Tu dissipes ainsi clair Soleil de Justice
Quand tu leves sur nous l'amas de nostre vice,
Qui sans les doux regards qui partent de tes yeux,
Feroit comme un obstacle entre nous et le Cieux

(As, when in the morning the air is loaded with clouds,/The sun, unleashing his tiny glances,/Quickly dispels the drifting mists/Between itself and the earth stretched out like a veil;/So you, O bright sun of justice,/When you rise clear away the mass of our sins,/Which, without the kindly looks which come from your eyes,/Would act like an obstacle between us and heaven).

Aman; ou, La Vanité was very considerably changed between 1601 and 1604. It is modelled on Claude Roillet's 1556 play of the same name, as *La Cartaginoise* had been modelled on Trissino's *Sofonisba*, although there was also a 1566 *Aman* by Rivaudeau and a 1559 *Sophonisbe* by Saint-Gelais. In *Aman* the advantage of the Roillet paradigm was that it offered Montchrestien ample scope for his set pieces of exultation, persecution, supplication, and victory. Aman, in accordance with what is recounted in the biblical *Book of Esther*, seeks to wipe out the Jews because of the refusal of one of them, Mardochée, to submit to him. The king, Assuérus, has doubts, but permits Aman to execute his plan. Mardochée pleads with God to look after his chosen people, and the queen, Esther, Mardochée's adopted daughter, agrees to intercede. The ends of the acts are devoted as usual to choruses. Esther's plea is successful, Assuérus discovers the true, personal, motive of Aman, and he is hanged. Esther and the Jews render thanks for their deliverance.

There is no single dominating character in *Aman*, but a number of scenes which allow a quite large number of characters lengthy monologues, sometimes briefly interrupted, to give expression to their feelings as their fortunes change. Most of these expressions and analyses of their feelings by the characters are dramatically gratuitous, although they are the point of the play. Esther risks much by inviting Assuérus to the banquet she is giving, but she spends very much longer explaining the danger she is running, and her reasons for incurring the risks, than she does in actually delivering the invitation. But linking together Montchrestien's tirades, monologues, stichomythia, conversations, and choruses there is generally a theme, in *Aman* God's punishment of human pride, and the chorus is there to remind us of what it is. All the characters in *Aman* are measured against their willingness to challenge, defy, or submit to the Jewish God, although not all the reactions are consistent. Aman may well deserve his fate when he is hanged, but Assuérus might have been made to seem less inconsistent if his sentencing of Aman had been better prepared earlier in the piece.

Hector, first added in the 1604 edition of the tragedies, is presumably the last of the plays to be written. It is notable for the interest it shows in the tactics of warfare, for being the most regular of the plays, and for the very extensive use made of stichomythia, in which one character takes up, generally in a single line, an argument used by another character expressing a different view. Stichomythia in the renaissance began to extend beyond one-line replies, and could consist in the confrontation of mutually contradictory aphorisms. *Hector* opens with a long monologue by Cassandre, followed by an exchange between Cassandre and the chorus, and then by a long exchange between Andromache and her husband, Hector. Readers and any audience are expected to know that Hector is the Trojan hero from the house of Priam who is killed in battle with the Greeks. Cassandre foretells his death in the opening monologue, after which Andromache pleads with him not to fight. Hector will not be deflected from his warrior's role, and Andromache brings him their son.

Hector's address to the gods on behalf of his son is filled with elevated pleas that his son should be filled with lofty ambitions and merciful sentiments. Both he and Andromache know that his death is inevitable, and the poetry reaches a summit of emotional intensity as Andromache laments to Hector her inability to move him. In the second act Andromache and Hector are joined by Priam and the child's nurse. There are no stage directions about place, but the speeches suggest that in any stage performance Andromache is appearing at the beginning of act II before Hector's father, Priam, who, like the nurse, encourages Andromache to overcome her panic at what he, too, regards as Hector's certain death. The effect of the whole act is much enhanced by the switches made between lamenting, pleading, and exchanges in stichomythia between Hector and his father, increasing the element of wit and momentarily relaxing the emotional intensity. Priam attempts to calm Hector's enthusiasm for battle, important not only because it increases the emotion felt after his death and the humiliation and mutilation of his corpse, but also because it invests Hector with the taint of overconfidence, not moral guilt but tragic pride, or hubris. Even Priam, moved by the pleas of Hecube and Andromache, attempts to recall Hector from the field of battle, but it is too late.

In the third act the stichomythia are exchanged between Hector and the chorus before the Messenger arrives to announce that the Greeks are calling Hector a coward. The act finishes after a chorus and an unexpected lamentation by Heleine, speaking for the first time, but omitted from the list of characters appearing in the play and then from that at the head of the act.

O miserable Heleine! ô Dame infortunée!
Tu pleures à bon droit, puis que tu ne fus née
Que pour causer la mort de tant d'hommes vaillans
Au front des murs Troyens à l'envi bataillans.
Ceste fleur de beauté qui tombe en peu d'années,
Ces Lys soudain passez, ces roses tost fanées,
Cet oeil en moins de rien couvert d'obscurité
Devoit-il estre ô Dieux à tel pris acheté?

(O wretched Helen! O unfortunate lady!/You are right to weep because you were born only/To cause the death of so many brave men/Fighting furiously before the walls of Troy./This flower of beauty which withers in so few years,/These lilies so quickly over, these roses so soon faded,/This eye covered with darkness in less time than none,/Should it, O gods, have been bought at so great a price?).

In the fourth act Andromache's mood turns to outrage at Hector's departure from her. Cassandre tells her to reconcile herself to fate, and there is a long exchange with the chorus. Priam and Hecube, his wife and Hector's mother, clearly come on stage, and there is a long interim report of the battle between Achille and Hector which still leaves room for hope at the end of the act. In the fifth act the Messager reports the death, humiliation, and mutilation of Hector, and we are given a single couplet from Priam, who declares himself unable to speak, before the laments of Hecube and Andromache. The text finishes with a chorus.

Hector's interest is increased not only by the intensity of the characters' emotions, but by the extent of their variety, and by the way in which the monologues are varied by passages of dialogue and stichomythia between different pairs. It is easy to understand why it stands at the end of a tradition. The changes of situation have become sufficiently numerous and rapid to prompt the change to a dramatic form in which the characters themselves would move the drama forward, and in which their roles would not largely be confined to expressing, however poetically, reactions to narrated or reported events, and to the swift exchanges which reiterate arguments and state aphorisms. Montchrestien is renowned for his masterly use of language, but his properly poetic inspiration requires acknowledgement, as does his incipient feeling for the creation of stage drama based on intrigue.

PUBLICATIONS

Collections

Les Tragedies de Ant. de Montchrestien, sieur de Vasteville, plus une Bergerie et un poème de Susan, 1601
Les Tragedies d'Antoine de Montchrestien, sieur de Vasteville… Edition nouvelle augmentée par l'auteur, 1604

Plays

Sophonisbe, Tragédie, 1596
L'Escossaise; ou, Le Désastre, tragedie. Seconde édition, 1603
Aman, 1939
Les Lacènes, 1943
David, 1963
Hector. La Reine d'Escosse, 1972
Hector in *Théâtre du XVIIe siècle*, Bibliothèque de la Pléiade, vol. 1, 1975

Other

Les Derniers Propos, avec le Tombeau de feu noble dame Barbe Guiffart…, 1599
Bergerie, ?1600
Au Roy, ?1607
L'Economie politique patronale, traicté de l'oeconomie politique, 1615

Biographical and critical studies

Griffiths, Richard, *The Dramatic Technique of Antoine de Montchrestien*, 1970
Street, J.S., *French Sacred Drama from Bèze to Corneille*, 1983

MONTESQUIEU, Charles-Louis de Secondat, Baron de, 1689–1755.

Social and political philosopher. Satirist and historian.

LIFE

Charles-Louis de Secondat de Montesquieu was born into a family of minor "noblesse d'épée," originally Protestant on his father's side, lords of Montesquieu, in Guyenne, since 1561, and promoted barons by Henry IV in 1606 with the courtesy title of marquis, never used. There was Plantagenet blood in the family, which had become Catholic. Montesquieu's paternal grandfather was a lawyer who had 10 children, of whom three were to be ecclesiastics and three nuns. The third son, Jacques, was Montesquieu's father. He was a soldier with not much money, who in 1686 married Marie-Françoise de Pesnel, an heiress of partly English ancestry but also descended from Saint-Louis. She was exceedingly pious, affectionate, ascetic, and devoted to the poor. It was she who brought the 15th-century wine-producing château of La Brède into the family. There, 10 miles southeast of Bordeaux, Montesquieu was born on 18 January 1689. He was baptized on the same day, his godfather being a beggar from the village, chosen to remind the child later of his obligations towards the poor. An elder and a younger sister both became nuns, and a younger brother, Joseph, went into the Church. Another brother and sister died in infancy, and it was in 1696, at her sixth confinement, when Montesquieu was seven, that his mother died. He inherited her wealth, and became Baron de la Brède.

He had been sent out to nurse at the local flourmill, and never lost the rustic accent he acquired there. Until he was 11, Montesquieu was educated at home. He was taught to write by the local schoolmaster. In 1700 his father sent him to the famous Oratorian Collège de Juilly in the diocese of Meaux, where Bossuet was still bishop. The journey to Juilly cost 60 livres, but a number of boys from the south-west, some related to Montesquieu, were sent to school there, now that the once celebrated Collège de Guyenne at Bordeaux had declined. Montesquieu and two cousins travelled on horseback, accompanied by a servant. The fees were 342 livres a year. In 1702 Montesquieu's younger brother came to join him. From 1704, for a further payment of 50 livres a year, the boys were allowed wine with their meals. Montesquieu stayed for exactly five years in all and then, from 1705 to 1708, studied law at Bordeaux. He did not learn much. The dean was 98, his son an absentee, and the instruction was from a blind 80-year-old whose lectures were read out by a student. The first professor, recently appointed, sent a deputy who did not speak French. Montesquieu, however, graduated, and then went on from 1709 to 1713 to further study of law in Paris, where we know little of his life.

He seems to have been looked after in Paris by a brilliant young Oratorian, Père Nicolas Desmolets, from, or at least through whom he acquired an elementary scientific and literary education. He made notes from a scrapbook the Oratorian lent him, added to them, and in this way constituted his *Spicilège*, published in 1944, the self-compiled commonplace book which had since the Renaissance been one of the staple instruments of education. We know from the *Spicilège* that while in Paris Montesquieu was acquainted with the proceedings of the academies of science and of inscriptions. He also acquired his enduring interest in the East, even vainly attempting to learn Chinese. He early became aware of the boldest currents of thought then circulating. He certainly knew of Boulainvilliers's heterodox, even atheistic thinking before the relevant books were published.

On 15 November 1713, while Montesquieu was still in Paris, his father died. Montesquieu, as he began to call himself, was now a feudal proprietor, a bachelor of almost 25. He chose as a bride Jeanne (de) Lartigue, a wealthy neighbour from a recently ennobled Huguenot family with two houses in the close vicinity of La Brède. The bride made over a dowry of 100,000 livres and the marriage took place in Bordeaux on 30 April 1715. A son, Jean-Baptiste, was born on 10 February 1716, and two daughters, Marie-Catherine and Marie-Josèphe Denise, in 1717 and 1727. On 24 April 1716 Montesquieu's uncle died childless, leaving him his estates, the barony of Montesquieu, and the office of "président à mortier" at the parlement of Bordeaux, where since 24 February 1714 Montesquieu had already been a counsellor, a charge which he now sold.

The parlement's function, originally legal, had become increasingly political. Montesquieu's uncle had played a distinguished role in the often rebellious magistracy as Louis XIV assumed absolute monarchical powers, and the power of the parlements had considerably increased since Louis's death in 1715. Although the "premier Président" was appointed from Paris, the offices of "président à mortier," like those of the counsellors who assisted them, were hereditary and marketable. They brought their holders a moderate income of 1,425 livres a year net of 450 livres deducted in tax, an opportunity to earn fees, some pecuniary perquisites, the "épices" paid by litigants, and much prestige. Montesquieu, already holding a dispensation required on account of his relationship to his uncle, was dispensed from the age limit of 40 and took the oath in July 1716 but, in spite of a serious interest, to which the *Spicilège* attests, in complex legal matters involving, in addition to French and Roman law, several customary systems, he took little part in the parlement's proceedings. His position did, however, allow him to form a friendship with the military governor of Bordeaux, the Duke of Berwick, illegitimate son of James II of England, an English and a Spanish general, and a duke in the peerages of both England and France.

Montesquieu's mixed religious background, together with the influence of Paris and of his uncle at Bordeaux, had predisposed him to liberal attitudes. In 1711 he had written, probably under the influence of Bayle, a paper, now lost, on the possible salvation of the pagans. In it he praised Cicero for his resistance to tyranny and his attack on superstition. In 1715, the year before John Law arrived in France, Montesquieu wrote a mémoire for the Regent containing an ingenious system for reducing the national debt. He proposed a mixture of capital levy, graded to penalize those unwilling to hold government stock, and simple repudiation, in this way avoiding the need for any increase in taxation. In 1716 he was elected to the newly established Académie de Bordeaux, at which he read a paper on Roman religion, indicating his interest in religion as above all a social phenomenon; he established an anatomy prize, performed various official functions, and in 1721 presented a paper on natural history. He had carried out a number of experiments himself on plants and animals, not avoiding the vivisection of a frog under a microscope, and now insisted with Malebranche, whose doctrine had been in favour at Juilly, on the mechanist structure of the vegetable world.

In or soon after 1717 Montesquieu began work on the *Lettres persanes*, a satirical novel in letter form purporting to give an account of France as seen from the correspondence of two Moslem visitors, and intended to destroy prejudice, and attack absolutist claims in both politics and religion. Interest in the Orient had been stimulated by Galland's translation (1704–17) of *The Arabian Nights*, and Addison's 1711 satire on English life, purporting to have been written by an Iroquois, had been published in a 1714 French translation. In 1715 the shah of Persia sent his ambassador to Paris. The Koran was known in Europe principally from the 1647 du Ryer translation until the English version by George Sale appeared in 1734. Montesquieu possessed a copy of the du Ryer, as of the accounts of their travels by two merchants, Jean Chardin, whose three-volume *Voyage en Perse et aux Indes orientales* was published in Amsterdam in 1711, and Jean-Baptiste Tavernier, who published *Les six voyages de Jean-Baptiste Tavernier* in 1676. Montesquieu drew heavily on all three works, but acquired the Chardin, from which his plot derives, only in 1720. He took as a model Giovanni Paolo Marana's *L'Esploratore turco* (1684) of which he possessed the 1717 translation, the six-volume *L'Espion dans les cours*, a widely read collection of letters purporting to have been written from France by a Turkish spy.

In 1720 or 1721 Montesquieu took his manuscript to Paris, was told by Desmolets that the work would sell like bread and, rightly supposing that it would be regarded in France as subversive, sent his secretary to find a publisher in Holland. The book appeared in the first half of 1721, published in Amsterdam by a French Protestant whose family had left France after the revocation of the Edict of Nantes in 1685. It was pseudonymous. A false place and the name of a non-existent publisher were printed on the title page. It was an immense success, with at least 10 editions in its first year. It not only established Montesquieu as an important thinker on moral and social issues, particularly as they interacted with political and religious systems as both their cause and their consequence, but it also brought these and other matters of historical causation and dogmatic relativism into the forum of popular discussion. Different pseudonyms had been used for Amsterdam and Cologne editions. Originally there had been 150 letters, but Montesquieu added three and suppressed 13, then put them back, adding eight more. There were 161 letters and a supplementary note in the last edition revised by Montesquieu, that of 1754.

From 1721 Montesquieu began to visit Paris more frequently, spending up to six months at a time there, sometimes representing the interest of the Bordeaux parlement or the academy, but mostly enjoying metropolitan intellectual and social life. He was certainly in Paris for part of every year from 1720 to 1728, when he set off on the long journey that kept him away from La Brède until 1731. Having left his wife at La Brède, he went gaming, once winning 275 livres in a single all-night session, and must have shared the more or less dissolute amusements of the court, although he was closest to the not particularly debauched circle of the Duke of Berwick. Through Berwick Montesquieu got to know some of the military aristocracy, notably the Matignons. His relationship with Mme de Graves, daughter of the elderly Maréchal de Matignon, made her husband jealous, and Montesquieu was not far from the most scandalous centres of upper-class licentiousness, although his behaviour appears from surviving documentary evidence to have been no worse than that of the average rake of his age in that society. He was, however, associated with the circle at Bellébat, near Fontainebleau, of Agnès de Prie, the notorious daughter of a particularly squalid financier and a well-known courtesan. Montesquieu addressed two quatrains to Mme de Prie, who was the wife of the French ambassador to Turin and whose lovers included Law and the duc de Bourbon himself, whose recognized mistress she became.

In 1725 Montesquieu published *Le Temple de Gnide*, anonymously but in Paris and with a "privilège." It purported to be the translation from the Greek of an account of the passions of a son of a priest of Venus. Only 600 copies out of the printing of 2,000 were sold, although the book, which is more elegant than obscene, did occasion a good deal of curiosity. The text had first appeared in the 1724 *Bibliothèque Française*. It may have been teasingly inspired by Mlle de Clermont, the duc de Bourbon's sister, and granddaughter of Condé. Until the replacement of Bourbon by Fleury as prime minister in 1726, the Bourbon court at Chantilly was still politically influential, and it offered Montesquieu the only contact with governmental circles which he ever had, although he was shortly to become France's greatest political philosopher. From this period date Montesquieu's early minor political writings, of which the most important is the *Lettres de Xénocrate à Phérès*, an allegory, unpublished until 1892, in praise of the duc d'Orléans, the recently deceased regent.

Montesquieu also got to know Viscount Bolingbroke, who did not return to live permanently in England after his exile until 1725, and was later to provide a principal inspiration for much of Montesquieu's political thought. Montesquieu also frequented the salon of Mme de Lambert, which was primarily "moderne" (see: Querelle des anciens et des modernes) in intellectual tone, although Mme Dacier was also to be seen there. It was noted for its debates on moral topics. Tuesdays were mostly for the nobility, and Wednesdays for the literary world. To be admitted at all was a privilege. Gambling was not allowed, the scandalously behaved were excluded, and membership of the Académie française was not infrequently arranged. Montesquieu attended on Tuesdays. His *Pensées* records ideas, particularly about happiness, certainly intended originally for discussion in Mme de Lambert's salon. Mme de Lambert herself initiated a discussion on taste. In 1726 Montesquieu replied to a paper criticizing a theory of taste expounded in an essay which he wrote in part before 1728, and which became the basis for his *Essai sur le goût*, finally revised for posthumous publication in the *Encyclopédie* (q.v.).

Montesquieu was also present at the more practical discussions of the Club de l'Entresol, one of the important nurseries of early Enlightenment thought. The informal gatherings were held in the rooms of the abbé Alary, and discussions, attended by important members of the aristocracy of sword as well as robe, were devoted to controversial historical, social, and political problems. Suspecting it of breeding intrigue as well as of dangerous ideas, Fleury had it dissolved after seven years, in 1731. Montesquieu had almost certainly been a member, and he appears to have read there a dialogue on Roman despotism published in 1745 in the *Mercure de France* (q.v.), the *Dialogue de Sylla et d'Eucrate*, which was not highly thought of, and has indeed subsequently been regarded as trivial. In the meantime he was also active in the Bordeaux academy. He seems to have read there a paper on movement as essential to matter, an idea generally felt to be atheistic since, if movement was essential to

matter, there was no need for Aristotle's prime mover to set matter in motion. Of that paper we have only reports, but it looks as if the materialistic tendencies of the *Lettres persanes* were making further inroads into Montequieu's thought.

In 1725 Montesquieu presented to the Bordeaux academy a discourse, *De la considération et de la réputation*, which was in fact published in the collected works of Mme de Lambert in 1748, having been in her possession when she died. On 1 May that year Montesquieu read a lost *Traité des devoirs* which attacked Spinozan fatalism, argued the existence of a benevolent God, extolled the stoics, and was generally inspired by Samuel Pufendorf, the disciple of Grotius from whom Montesquieu derived much material for *De l'Esprit des lois* and whose *De officio hominis* he possessed in Barbeyrac's translation. The *Traité* was the sketch for a first completely serious book and the first sign of a systematic interest in political philosophy. The attacks on Spinoza and Hobbes suggest that Montesquieu's mind, like his personality, was not yet fully formed. The *Pensées* show that at this period he was contemplating a large variety of different projects, of which many fragments still exist. There is clearly intensifying focus on political philosophy, and on the organizing principle that in any political association necessarily emerges as a "union d'esprit (union of spirit)," and a common character. This "universal soul" is the name for the corporate agreement which must emerge and predominate in any society.

Montesquieu already had trouble with his eyesight, and lived in terror of going blind. We know that he was affable, generous, and absent-minded. He appears not to have enjoyed his wife's company, although he had full confidence in her ability to run the affairs of his estate. By the end of 1725 he was short of ready money. His son was at the Jesuit college of Louis-le-Grand in Paris, or may already have transferred to the Collège d'Harcourt, more open to Jansenist influence. Montesquieu's brother now possessed lucrative benefices, and he himself sold his Bordeaux house, staying with Joseph whenever business called him to Bordeaux. His sisters, both nuns, received from him an endowment of 150 livres a year. At the end of 1725 his accounts none the less show debts of 31,000 livres to his banker, 13,000 livres to friends, and 2,500 more of small personal obligations. His mother-in-law owed him 12,000 livres, but his realizable assets were otherwise only corn to the value of 2,000 livres, some farm equipment, a credit of 3,500 livres in Sweden, and 125 casks of wine, with duty still to be paid on 85 of them.

Montesquieu still of course owned his four main properties, La Brède, Martillac, Baron, and Montesquieu, and sought to increase his holdings of land. The legal office of "président à mortier" at Bordeaux kept him from Paris, and his stipend was usually in arrears. In 1726 Montesquieu sold a life interest in it for 5,200 livres a year, increasing his income by about 3,000 livres a year without having to do any actual legal work, with the residence it would entail, and rather ineffectively hoping that his son, who was interested in natural science, would eventually take up a legal career. Montesquieu himself lost the dignity of being "Le Président," although the title continued to be used as a courtesy. Early in 1728 he travelled to Paris, leaving his wife in charge of his affairs at La Brède, where he returned only in 1731. On 24 January 1728, after some difficulty, perhaps on account of lack of residence in Paris, but chiefly because the *Lettres persanes* had described the king and the pope as magicians, Montesquieu was received into the Académie française. He had still not openly acknowledged authorship of the *Lettres*.

On 5 April he left Paris with the Duke of Berwick's nephew, Earl Waldgrave, who was on his way to become George II's ambassador to Vienna.

Montesquieu left unrevised notes for a formal account of his travels which he never wrote. He visited copper mines in Hungary and went nearly as far as Cracow before going south through Graz to Venice, from where he moved on to Milan, Turin, Genoa, Florence, Rome, and Naples, returning through Bologna and the Brenner. He had introductions everywhere, but his impressions of people and places still show him hesitating between credulity and disbelief, with his interest increasingly concentrated on problems of social and political organization. It was probably in Naples that Montesquieu became aware of the work of Gian Vincenzo Gravina, who had died in 1718 after relating the study of Roman law to the study of politics and the history of institutions, thus establishing in Montesquieu's mind the link between the conventional history of Roman law and the development of institutions that was to lie at the heart of *De l'esprit des lois*.

In 1729 Montesquieu travelled to Munich and Augsburg and through the Rhineland to Hanover, and then to Utrecht, Amsterdam, and England, reaching London on 3 November. Unfortunately the notes on his stay in England were destroyed, although it is certain that he drew inspiration from English political thinking, notably in his statement of the doctrine of the separation of powers in an unpublished description of the English constitution finished by 1734, but published only as the sixth chapter of Book XI of *De l'Esprit des lois*. In 1732 he returned to La Brède, where he wrote the *Réflexions sur la monarchie universelle*, printed in 1734, but immediately withdrawn, probably on account of a passage about Louis XIV. The work contends that the ideal of a universal monarchy has become even more difficult during recent history, but contains a classification of nations according to climate, distinguishing in particular between northern nations and southern ones and between constitutional and tyrannical governments, and insisting that wealth must be based on productivity rather than the possession of bullion. It also comes out in praise of liberty and develops the idea that the nature of appropriate government depends on the size of the territory to be governed.

Montesquieu spent from June 1731 until the spring of 1733 at La Brède working on the *Considérations sur les causes de la grandeur des Romains et de leur décadence*, elaborating a theory of historical causation which reconciles chance and choice with general physical and moral forms of historical determinism. Caution was clearly required, and Montesquieu sides sporadically with Bossuet against Bodin by allowing a role in history for divine providence. The hostile government reaction to Voltaire's *Lettres philosophiques* in fact broke out while Montesquieu's book was actually being printed. Montesquieu had used the good offices of the Dutch ambassador in Paris to find a Dutch publisher, but now decided to cover himself, firstly by submitting the book for approval to a Jesuit in Paris, and secondly by publishing a Paris edition with "privilège," in which stratagem Mme de Tencin helped him. The book, whose Dutch edition was published in June, appeared in Paris in July 1734, and received a lukewarm reception. Subsequent critics have regarded it as poor history. Montesquieu's ambition was clearly to avoid controversy, to escape from the reputation for frivolity he had acquired more than a decade previously, and to be taken seriously as an academician.

From 1733 to 1748 Montesquieu spent more time in Paris than at La Brède, travelling in each direction at least seven times. He regularly attended the Académie, becoming its director for a quarter in 1739, and necessarily meeting the whole of the literary world. Another interest, acquired in London, was freemasonry. He also frequented salon society, was close to Mme de Tencin, knew Mme du Deffand, Mme Geoffrin, and the Brancas household well, and mixed with Helvétius, Jaucourt, and Réaumur. At La Brède he talked patois to the peasants, with whom he was perfectly comfortable, maintained a correct relationship with his irascible, competent, and Protestant wife, and enjoyed his position as a proprietor of wine-producing country estates. His elder daughter married a local landowner taking with her a modest dowry of 10,000 livres. His son was made director of the Bordeaux academy, and duly became an advocate. In 1736 Montesquieu bought him a counsellorship at the Bordeaux parlement and in 1740 he married at Bordeaux. Both sets of parents bound themselves eventually to settle 300,000 livres on the couple, with Montesquieu also meanwhile providing an annual 6,000 livres and the bride's father a home, food, servants, and an annual 2,000 livres.

The son's marriage proved sterile for some years, until in 1749 a son was born who died in 1824 without issue. Montesquieu arranged for his second daughter to marry his third cousin to ensure the lineage. His brother, who had performed the other two ceremonies, again officiated, and the wedding took place on 25 March 1745. The bride, Denise, had a settlement of a house, 40,000 livres on the deaths of her parents, and 500 livres a year. The bridegroom was to endow his bride with 5,000 livres. Montesquieu was punctilious in the management of his estates, buying, exchanging, and selling land, litigating for often very small sums or over trivial issues, regarding it as a duty to enforce the smallest of his rights but also to assist debtors in times of distress.

Montesquieu had a well-deserved reputation for parsimony, distraining for debts of under one penny, but, although he held very extensive estates and kept large households, he was dependent on the sale of wine for ready cash. Like all the Bordeaux wine growers, he was badly hit by the war of Austrian Succession (1740–48) which cut off the English market. He was obliged to stay at La Brède for three years from 1743 to 1746 and to borrow 7,000 livres. Meanwhile, the life interest in the presidency sold in 1726 reverted to him, and it was sold for 300,000 livres, payable over eight years. Montesquieu's son no longer wanted the counsellorship, so that, too, was sold for 40,000 livres. Montesquieu owned property worth about 500,000 livres, with an income from it of about 20,000 or 25,000 livres a year, about £800 to £1,000 at the then rate of exchange. His most modest wines sold for about 90 livres a cask, and his best for 200 livres. His income increased, and by the end of his life it may have touched 60,000 livres. One biographer points out that this was 50 times Diderot's stipend as editor of the *Encyclopédie*, but that several landowners in France had incomes of 500,000 livres or more, and that Voltaire's income at death was not less that 200,000 livres. Agricultural land yielded on average about four per cent annually.

Montesquieu continued to write fragments of important but subsequently abandoned work, as well as ephemeral salon trivia, passed round in manuscript. He was not a witty conversationalist. He was a provincial landowner, unknown except for the *Lettres persanes*, an amateur scholar who had found the duties of the magistracy too onerous, who had in spite of every opportunity failed to make any serious impact in any sphere of national life, and who had as yet given no sign of the ability to gestate intellectually, or physically to produce, what is generally, and no doubt rightly, considered to be the greatest work of political economy ever to be written in French. By the end of 1734 he had decided to collect his scattered fragments of serious reflection into a single life work. He was now nearly 46. He had the leisure and the means to dedicate himself to producing a synthesis of his ideas, and he resolved to start with an open mind about all matters of legal, political, and social organization.

He had a good deal of help from amanuenses, and 19 different hands have been identified in his papers. Differences in the types of paper used and in Montesquieu's handwriting as his eyesight failed have helped to allow careful chronological reconstruction of the composition of *De l'Esprit des lois*. We know that the final text was the result of painstaking polishing and revision. Portions of the work were moved around in an attempt to increase the mind-catching effects of epigram and paradox. Links between ideas were suppressed as consequences were consciously placed before conclusions. By late in 1741 Montesquieu was labouring eight hours a day at his masterpiece, and early the following year he had completed 18 out of the then 24 projected Books or sections, starting with the present Book 3. He worked better at La Brède than among the distractions of Paris. He undertook a second revision of the whole text in 1745. By 1746 the book was ready for final transcription. It was finished by June 1747.

Since the censorship made publication in France inappropriate and French relations with Holland were poor, Montesquieu used Pierre Mussard, a Swiss diplomat in Paris, to find a Swiss publisher. This turned out to be Barrillot of Geneva, who had just published Burlamaqui's *Principes du droit naturel*. Montesquieu's close friend the abbé Ottaviano di Guasco immediately started on an Italian translation. The Calvinist minister Jacob Vernet, engaged by Montesquieu to see *De l'Esprit des lois* through the press, persuaded him to add three more books, including those on feudal laws, which arrived in Geneva in September 1748. After some passages had been slightly toned down in proof, the work was finally published in late October. It was the most important treatise on constitutional theory to be written anywhere in the 18th century. More concerned with the mode of the operation of power than with its location, it was situated firmly in the liberal tradition. It was empirical in its observation, relativist in its counsels and in its concept of law. From it was to be derived the American "Declaration of Independence" of 1776, as also *The Rights of Man* (2 vols., 1791 and 1792), in which Thomas Paine would defend the French Revolution and the Assemblée Nationale's "Declaration of the Rights of Man and of the Citizen," passed in 1789 and adopted as the preface to the French Constitution of 1791, against Edmund Burke's attack in *Reflections on the Revolution in France*. *De l'Esprit des lois* marked a considerable step forward, taken during his stay in England, from Montesquieu's own previous view of the importance of constitutional liberty, and incorporated as chapter six of Book XI the unpublished treatise on the English constitution.

The reception of the work was uneven. Mme de Tencin's partly read copy had been snatched from her by Fontenelle by 14 November 1748. There was much praise from Montesquieu's friends, especially Helvétius, Mme Geoffrin, Cerati, and Horace

Walpole, but the Jesuits, with some of whom Montesquieu was on intimate terms, were mildly hostile in their *Mémoires de Trévoux* in April 1749, although they strangely failed to criticize the implied relativism of the religious views expressed by Montesquieu. A crude attack appeared in volume form later in 1749. Although anonymous, it was in fact written, probably with Jesuit support, by Claude Dupin, the tax farmer whose wife, in spite of her illegitimacy, had established in Paris a salon of real intellectual distinction which Montesquieu had earlier attended. Dupin's book had been copied out by Jean-Jacques Rousseau, his wife's secretary, but only eight copies were ever printed and only one survives. The reason for the work's withdrawal has occasioned much speculation, but is uncertain. A later elaboration in three volumes much attentuates the original strictures. The chief attack on *De l'Esprit des lois* came on 9 and 16 October 1749 from the Jansenist *Nouvelles Ecclésiastiques*, and was written by the editor, the abbé de la Roche. Another, weaker attack, by the abbé de la Porte, appeared early in 1750. In February Montesquieu published the *Défense de l'Esprit des lois* under the false imprint of Barrillot. It was largely devoted to the social influence of Christianity, but included no element of apology or withdrawal.

Jesuit criticism softened, but the Jansenist attack hardened, with two further articles of 24 April and 1 May in the *Nouvelles Ecclésiastiques* now adding elements of polemical invective. That stung Voltaire, not a close friend or normally a strong ally, into writing in Montesquieu's defence the strongly ironic pamphlet *Remerciement sincère à un homme charitable*. Elie-Catherine Fréron, the leader of the opposition to the "philosophes", had used his *Lettres sur quelques écrits de ce temps* to attack Voltaire's *Remerciement* on 9 November 1749, but then switched to Montesquieu's defence in the issue of 19 December. The controversy widened, with hostile comments slightly more numerous in 1751, but with Montesquieu victorious in France from 1752. The chancellor, d'Aguesseau, had at first forbidden the book, but allowed it to be printed in Paris in 1749, providing that a foreign town appeared on the title page. The Paris edition of Huart and Moreau *fils* duly proclaimed its origin as "Geneva, 1749." In Italy, in spite of a great deal of lobbying, the book was placed on the Index on 29 November 1751. To the puzzlement only of modern commentators, the reasons given were trivial and the condemnation was treated more jocularly in Rome than in France.

Short-sighted, unusually kind towards intellectual neophytes, and exaggeratedly absent-minded, Montesquieu passed the remainder of his life as a celebrity. He frequented the salon of Mme du Deffand and was sought out in particular by Englishmen on the Grand Tour. When in Paris, Montesquieu attended the Académie, of which he became director on 2 April 1753. He prepared new editions of the *Lettres persanes* and the *Esprit des lois*, took up old materials to write the *Essai sur le goût* and the *Mémoire sur la Constitution*, to be published posthumously with *Arsace et Isménie*, written in 1742 for Mlle de Charolais, sister of the Duc de Bourbon, and published a slight prose narrative, *Lysimaque*, for the Polish court. No great friend of either Diderot or Voltaire, Montesquieu had none the less anticipated most of the ideas of the philosophes, the majority of whom he knew well before they formed a coherent group in the 1760s.

From July to December 1754 he was at La Brède, where he decided to spend the rest of his life. His brother died in August. Montesquieu went to Paris to wind up his affairs there, and had terminated his lease and given notice to his housekeeper when he fell victim to fever epidemic early in 1755. He became ill on 29 January, was excessively bled, and discussed with some solemnity the choice of a confessor before sending for his old friend and later critic the Jesuit Père Louis-Bertrand Castel, who presented himself at the dying man's bedside with an Irish Jesuit, Bernard Routh, whom Montesquieu already knew, before himself withdrawing. Routh obtained Montesquieu's permission to publish his final statements, which were of the humblest submission and repentance, before sending for the curé of Saint-Sulpice who, unlike Routh, was not left alone with Montesquieu, from whom he exacted another submission before giving him the viaticum and the last sacrament. Routh appears to have gone too far in trying to obtain a literary testament in the form of emendations to the *Lettres persanes*, and Montesquieu preferred to give it to others present at his deathbed. He died on 10 February 1755. Diderot, alone of the philosophes, attended the funeral at Saint-Sulpice the next day.

WORKS

There is nothing very remarkable about the use of the letter form for what purported to be an unprejudiced account of an event, a place, a person, or a dispute, but was in fact a satire. When the *Lettres persanes* appeared, it had been well established in France as a literary convention by Pascal, still during the 18th century known chiefly as the author of the "petites lettres," as Mme de Sévigné called the *Lettres provinciales*. Montesquieu was no doubt drawing, too, on the fictional if non-satirical form of the *Lettres d'une religieuse portugaise* of 1669, still thought to have been merely translated by Guilleragues. For his content he probably imitated the satirical portrayals of customs and people in La Bruyère's *Les Caractères*. Montesquieu was also inspired by Addison's piece in *The Spectator* for 27 April 1711, translated into French as early as 1714, satirizing English political life and purporting to be a letter written by one of the three Iroquois kings who had accompanied their emperor Te Yee Neen Ho Ga Prow to Europe in 1710. The growing public interest in the East was mentioned in the previous section. The ground had also been prepared by some remarks of Bayle in the *Dictionnaire* (see: Bayle), by Malebranche's *Entretien d'un philosophe chrétien et d'un philosophe chinois* of 1708, by a *Lettre italienne écrite par un Sicilien à un de ses amis* of 1700, by J.-F. Bernard's *Réflexions morales, satiriques et comiques* (1715), Charles Dufresny's *Amusements sérieux et comiques*, and by Joseph Bonnet's *Lettre écrite à Musala*, for which the author went to prison, and which probably served Montesquieu as a direct source.

The *Lettres persanes* pays careful attention to local colour but, while the generally entertaining book is carefully accurate on such matters as topography, the dating system, and the religious, social, and political backgrounds, the satire often goes little deeper than would readily be found amusing in the better-informed salons. Montesquieu's treatment of the Persians' letters to and from home also allows him to weave in an erotic interest generated by the three dozen-odd letters concerning the harem which provide the framework of a plot. The two wealthy Persians, Usbek and Rica, set off from Ispahan for France in search of wisdom. They arrive in Paris in 1711 and stay until 1720. They write back home, to one another, and to a third trav-

eller, Rhedi, with ostensibly naive comments on the social customs, religion, political insitutions, and moral values they find. The Persians comment naturally on whatever takes Montesquieu's fancy, from Law's financial system to sectarian religious disputes, cafés, duelling, science, the legal system, the university, the Académie française, card playing, social and political organization, medicine, confessors, and the necessity of virtue.

Montesquieu, no doubt in an attempt to destroy prejudice in all realms of personal and social behaviour, imports a strongly relativistic perspective into his travellers' comments. Paris "is as big as Ispahan," its houses are taller, the rhythm of its life much more hurried. Rica writes to Smyrna about getting jostled in the Paris street and splashed with mud: "j'enrage quelquefois comme un chrétien (sometimes I get as furious as a Christian)." The Persians speak of the French with amazement, and write with an entertaining affectation of simplicity. The king of France is the most powerful in Europe although he has not got the gold mines of the king of Spain. He is richer, however, on account of the vanity of his subjects. "On lui a vu entreprendre ou soutenir de grandes guerres, n'ayant d'autres fonds que des titres d'honneur à vendre (He has been known to undertake or support large-scale wars, with no resources except from the sale of aristocratic titles)."

The king can double the value of money, or even substitute pieces of paper for it. But there is an even greater magician, the pope. He can make people believe that three and one are the same, that the bread that people eat is not bread, the wine they drink not wine, "et mille autres choses de cette espèce (and a thousand other things like that)." What Rica here wrote about religion was considered less offensive than what he had just said about the king, and it is important to note the lightness of the literary register. Had Montesquieu been less obviously flippant when condemning or comparing Islamic and Christian beliefs and practices, he might not have been allowed so much licence, and while much that the *Esprit des lois* contains about tolerance, sovereignty and the relativism of political, legal, social, and religious systems appropriate to different societies can be read back into the *Lettres persanes*, it is important not to overlook the earlier work's light-hearted tone.

Coffee, writes Usbek to Rhedi, who was in Venice, is much used in Paris, and there are lots of houses open to the public where it is dispensed. In some, people tell one another the news, in others they play chess. There is one where the coffee is prepared "de telle manière qu'il donne de l'esprit à ceux qui en prennent (in such a way that it gives wit to those who drink it)." At least, nobody leaving fails to think himself four times as clever as when he went in. Montesquieu's readers were naturally expected to recognize the Procope, established opposite the then home of the Comédie-Française well before 1700 by the Sicilian Francesco Procopio di Coltelli, and for a period the foremost literary and political coffee-house in Paris. It was later frequented by Voltaire, Diderot, d'Alembert, Buffon, Crébillon, Marmontel, and Rousseau. Before the Revolution it became the Café Zoppi, and was used by Robespierre, Marat, Fabre d'Eglantine, Danton, and Hébert.

Some of the psychological portraits painted by the Persians in the manner of La Bruyère, although not especially profound, are still amusingly accurate depictions of well-known social types, such as are to be found, for instance, in Erasmus's *Praise of Folly*. There are allusions to the political events of the second decade of the 18th century, to the tsar of Russia and the king of

Sweden, and in letter 37 there is a sharp portrait of Louis XIV. Montesquieu's deepest criticism, however, is veiled by the skill with which he uses his form. By allowing his Persians to judge French things, persons and institutions, however amusingly, from the point of view of natives of Ispahan, Montesquieu implies that other ways of organizing social and political life are at least thinkable, and that the norms assumed to be absolute in France could be challenged. By allowing his Persians to look at them from their own standpoints, Montesquieu implies that such matters not only could, but also should, be subjected to rational reassessment, although again the register is kept quite light, and leavened by the intrigue of passion and jealousy in the harem. As Usbek says in letter 59.

Il me semble que nous ne jugeons jamais des choses que par un retour secret que nous faisons sur nous-mêmes. Je ne suis pas surpris que les Nègres peignent le diable d'une blancheur éblouissante et leurs dieux noirs comme du charbon…On a dit fort bien que, si les triangles faisaient un dieu, ils lui donneraient trois côtés

(It seems to me that we judge things only by a secret reference to ourselves. I'm not surprised that Negroes depict the devil as dazzling white and their gods as black as coal…It's been well said that if triangles gave themselves a god, they would give it three sides).

The Persians accept fixed standards of rationality, but of little else. Various forms of government other than that which prevails in France actually exist, and their relative advantages and dangers are discussed. There are other forms of religion. The best form of government for Usbek is that which empirically achieves its aim "à moins de frais (at the lesser cost)." In letters 11 to 14 there is a long parable about the Troglodytes who, acting out Hobbes's beliefs about man, founded their society on the rights of the strongest. They all perished except for two righteous families who saw that "l'intérêt des particuliers se trouve toujours dans l'intérêt commun (the interest of individuals always lies in the common good)," and founded a happy society with a natural religion based on mutual cooperation and defence. They had, however, to choose a king and, while man is naturally inclined to virtue, as Shaftesbury thought, law is no substitute for virtue, and man still needs educating.

Arguments about divine prescience, predestination, and free will appear nugatory to the Persians. It is best to be able to say to God, with Montaigne, that you intend to "vivre en bon citoyen dans la société où vous m'avez fait naître (to live as a good citizen in the society in which you had me born)." Montesquieu shows some resentment against the papal imposition of the anti-Jansenist (q.v.) Bull *Unigenitus*, but no sympathy for the Jansenist cause. He remains jocular in his treatment of dogma, superstition, and religious practices, and clearly believes in a close connection between happiness, virtue, and the body's physical wellbeing. Only on the subjects of toleration, historical causation, and the demographic effects of divorce, monogamy, polygamy, slavery, chastity, and the laws of inheritance does he exercise real speculative ingenuity. Voltaire was to mock him for his pains in the *Essai sur les moeurs*.

Montesquieu's interest in the causes of political growth and decay is developed in the *Considérations sur les causes de la grandeur des Romains et de leur décadence*, which is intended to be not history, but historiography. In history Montesquieu chooses arbitrary authorities whom he uses uncritically— Dionysius of Halicarnassus but not Livy for the first chapter, only Vegetius and Frontinus for the second, and then usually only Appian or Polybius, rather than Sallust or Florus, for the next 10 chapters with Greek authors read in Latin. Historiographically Montesquieu adheres to the tradition of separating sacred from secular history inaugurated by Bodin's *Methodus ad facilem historiarum cognitionem* (1566), but then followed for different reasons by Bossuet in the *Discours sur l'histoire universelle* (1681) and Lenain de Tillemont in the six-volume *Histoire des empereurs et des autres princes qui ont regné pendant les six premiers siècles de l'Eglise* (1690–1738) and the 16-volume *Mémoires pour servir à l'histoire ecclésiastique des six premiers siècles* (1693–1712).

However, whereas Bossuet and Tillemont had wanted to preserve sacred history from investigation by critical methods, Montesquieu's successors, starting with Voltaire and, of course, including Gibbon, were to extend critical historical investigation to sacred history as well. Montesquieu himself, anxious to prove his orthodoxy as well as his seriousness, and perhaps still hoping for a diplomatic appointment, sought Jesuit censorship of the *Considérations*, made consequent changes, had lengthy extracts printed in the Jesuit *Mémoires de Trévoux*, and published the book in Paris with approbation and privilège. He almost ostentatiously says nothing about the rise of Christianity in the context of the decline of imperial Rome, a reticence for which the abbé Raynal, for instance, was to reprove him in the *Histoire philosophique et politique des deux Indes* of 1776, and which marks a step back from the place accorded to Christianity in the development of societies in the *Lettres persanes*. Montesquieu's occasionally explicit acceptance of the separation of secular history from sacred history, in which he allowed the operation of divine Providence, was in fact due to caution.

Montesquieu's central distinction in the *Considérations* between the occasion of historical events and their causes, which are outside human control, occurs in Vico's *Scienza nuova prima* of 1725, but is borrowed by Montesquieu directly from *La Vita civile* of Vico's friend Paolo Mattia Doria (1710). It is linked to the concept of the "esprit général," the social and political culture common to any given society at any given moment, developed in some detail in the 19th book of the *Esprit des lois*, where it is of primordial importance, and where it is defined as a variable mixture of forces proceeding from "le climat, la religion, les lois, les maximes du gouvernement, les exemples des choses passées, les moeurs, les manières (climate, religion, laws, principles of government, examples from the past, customs, and habits)" (Book XIX, 4).

In spite both of its success and its importance, *De l'esprit des lois; ou, Du rapport que les lois doivent avoir avec la constitution de chaque gouvernement, les moeurs, le climat, la religion, le commerce etc.* is a rambling, loosely arranged work. The word "constitution" in the title is an anglicism. There were 20 editions of the work inside two years, and it was translated into most European languages. The two opening books, as Hume pointed out, dealing respectively with general laws, including the principles of natural and positive law, and with laws deriving from forms of government, sit somewhat awkwardly as an abstract theoretical preface to the work proper, which rests largely on sociological considerations. They do however open the way to the later relativism as Montesquieu proceeds in

Books III to VIII to consider principles, education, positive laws, criminal codes, social conventions, and the causes of decay in the various forms of government.

The second and third parts (Books IX to XIII and XIV to XIX) deal with the principles of military force, constitutional liberties, climate, and customs relative to the different sorts of government, and contain the heart and chief originality of the whole work. Forms of government, and therefore a population's appropriate way of life, are held to depend on the geographical climate in which the state is situated, although in more sophisticated states legislation can to some extent counteract climatic influence. Legislation must, if it is not to provoke revolution, respect the "esprit général" of a nation. The fourth and fifth parts (Books XX to XXIII and XXIV to XXVI) deal with the commerce, currency, demography, religion, and scope of legislation appropriate to the state, and the sixth part (Books XXVII to XXXI) is chiefly historical, treating of Roman, French, and feudal law.

The incorporation of pre-existing material accounts for the somewhat episodic nature of parts of the treatise, which is at times even anecdotal. Its real importance for posterity, however, lies in its application of Montesquieu's theories of historical causation and comparative studies to the theory of government, and to the different principles underlying various forms of government: virtue in a republic, honour in a monarchy, and fear in a despotism, which Montesquieu regards as wholly bad. Democracy, however admirable, was for a better and simpler age. The important factors in monarchy advocated by Montesquieu were the power of the Church, nobility, and parlements to counterbalance the power of the monarch, so preventing decline into despotism, and separation of the executive, legislative, and judicial functions on what Montesquieu took to be the English model.

Throughout the treatise Montesquieu pursues a balance between climatic determinism and the role of the legislator, between the conservatism which resists the imposition of ideal forms of government where conditions are unsuitable for it and the recognition of the ideal in theory, between the claims of religion and its political practicality and utility. Tyranny and intolerance were everywhere deplorable. Successive revisions attenuated criticisms of the monarchy and religious institutions, but what made the work so influential was Montesquieu's moderate criticism of the established order, his patient, constructive, and conservative advocacy of change, his condemnations of torture, war, poverty, and slavery, and his liberal concept of political freedom guaranteed by a balance of powers within the state.

The work, however, was more subversive than it appeared. If laws must respect national characteristics, which in turn depend on such determining causes as the climate, then no sovereign can reasonably exercise authority without the consent implied by legislation in accordance with the "esprit général,"

S'il est vrai que le caractère de l'esprit et les passions du coeur soient extrêmement différents dans les divers climats, les lois doivent être relatives et à la différence de ces passions, et à la différence de ces caractères

(If it is true that mental characteristics and the passions of the heart are extremely different in different climates, laws must reflect the difference both between these passions and between these characteristics) (Book XIV, chapter 1).

Montesquieu in fact follows Burlamaqui's pedestrian handbook, the 1747 *Principes du droit naturel*, which codified the natural law theory of Grotius's follower, Samuel von Pufendorf, in allowing a sovereignty divided into legislative, executive, and judicial powers, which is the foundation of the French liberal tradition of political thought in the 18th century. Rousseau was to prefer the doctrine of the inalienability of the sovereignty of the people, which he took from Althusius's *Politica* of 1603 and which, although it sounded liberal, in fact led necessarily to the delegation of sovereignty which produced the Terror. Montesquieu's relativistic views made the actual location of sovereignty unimportant. What mattered was the mode of its exercise. For this reason Montesquieu diverged from the traditional Aristotelian categorization of governments into monarchies, aristocracies, and democracies, according to the location of power. He preferred an empirically more realistic division according to the modes of exercising power: monarchical, despotic, and republican—the last could be either democratic or aristocratic. His political theory therefore shifts the balance from an abstract analysis of the nature of sovereignty to the ways in which sovereignty can actually be exercised,

Le gouvernement républicain est celui où le peuple en corps, ou seulement une partie du peuple, a la souveraine puissance; le monarchique, celui où un seul gouverne, mais par des lois fixes et établies; au lieu que, dans le despotique, un seul, sans loi et sans règles, entraîne tout par sa volonté et par ses caprices

(Republican [later sub-divided into democratic and aristocratic] government is that in which the people as a body, or only a part of the people, has sovereign power; monarchical, that in which one only reigns, but with fixed and established laws; whereas in despotic government, one alone, without law or rule, prescribes everything according to his will and whims) (Book II, chapter 1).

Not only government but also religion is regarded empirically. What actually interests Montesquieu is the extent to which false religions "sont conformes au bien de la société… Je n'examinerai donc les diverses religions du monde, que par rapport au bien que l'on en tire dans l'état civil (are in conformity with the good of society…I shall therefore examine the different religions in the world only with respect to their social utility)." (Book XXIV, chapter 1). Such an approach, as Montesquieu very well knew, was bound to erode the Church's claim to the universal validity of its teaching, and to belief in that teaching as the unique path to salvation after death.

More innocent-seeming, although potentially even more devastating, was the natural law definition of law as a necessary relationship between things. Aquinas had regarded law as a promulgation of the divine reason, of which human reason was the reflected derivative. That position, based on the 13th-century attempt to find a philosophical substructure for Christian belief, had seemed to the Franciscan tradition to be too naturalistic and to pare away God's transcendance of his own creation, and Scotus immediately reacted, returning to the concept of law as a promulgation of the divine will, whose potential arbitrariness later scholastics were to emphasize. Grotius had further developed Aquinas's view in his own unpublished *De iure praedae* of 1604, which had led on to the total theory of human rights, duties, and responsibilities elaborated independently of reference to the divine will in his 1625 *De iure belli ac pacis*. Montesquieu's work opens with a rallying call, a ringing declaration that law is not based on any divine command, however rational, but derives simply from the necessary relationships between things:

> Les lois, dans la signification la plus étendue, sont les rapports nécessaires qui dérivent de la nature des choses: et, dans ce sens, tous les êtres ont leurs lois; la Divinité a ses lois; le monde matériel a ses lois; les intelligences supérieures à l'homme ont leurs lois; les bêtes ont leurs lois; l'homme a ses lois

> (Laws in the widest sense are the necessary relationships which derive from the nature of things and, in this sense, all beings have their laws. The Divinity has its laws, the physical world has its laws, the intelligences above man have their laws; animals have their laws; man has his laws)
> (Book I, chapter 1).

The fact that Montesquieu throws in as a note a perfunctory reference to Plutarch on law, and that he is using the established tradition of five orders of being—God, angels, man, animals, inert matter—which puts man at the centre, scarcely detracts from the radical nature of this opening declaration. Montesquieu believed in God, and could not conceive of the world without a rational creator, but he did not think that man needed God to prescribe for him the laws of behaviour, which he could work out for himself, and which were not universal, absolute, or, by implication, the subject of revelation. It would be disingenuous to suppose that, because laws were essentially relationships, they were not sufficiently prescriptive to entail rewards and sanctions in the conduct of life on earth.

It is, however, important to remember that even the *Esprit des lois* is anecdotal. Montesquieu, we know, earnestly believed that the different physiologies caused by different climatic conditions produced different temperaments, and that laws should take these differences into account. The same operas, even with the same actors, were capable of producing widely differing effects in England and in Italy. Montesquieu's own experiments had confirmed that nerves responded differently to stimuli at different temperatures. The effect of alcohol differs in north and south, so that Mahomet had to legislate against the consumption of wine. The number of dervishes increases with the heat of the climate. Some races, notably in warmer climates, are slower than others to change their ways. Laws must take these facts, affecting the "esprit général," into account.

Montesquieu must have known that this mixture of scientific fact, personal impression, hunch, and anecdote did not produce a rigorously organized political theory. Historians ought surely to have taken more account of the fact that Montesquieu must deliberately have retained an amateur quality in his exposition. Had he not done so, the result could have been personally dangerous and socially explosive. Of the three major works, the *Lettres persanes* could be radical because they were flippant. The perfunctory historical content of the *Considérations* must surely have been intentional, but only partly because the book's real subject is not history but historical causation. Its gravity of tone entailed a lessening of the audacity hidden in the views of the Persians in the *Lettres persanes*, the increased caution appearing particularly in the failure properly to deal with the role of Christianity in the decline of imperial Rome, and in the reservation of a place in sacred history for providential causation by God. If the *Esprit des lois* rambles, it is difficult not to suppose that, even if not quite deliberately, Montesquieu found it necessary to edge towards his very radical liberalism by employing registers that would invite speculative interest rather than revolutionary sentiment.

PUBLICATIONS

Collections

Oeuvres complètes, Bibliothèque de la Pléiade, 2 vols., 1951.
Oeuvres complètes, 3 vols., edited by A. Masson, 1950–55

Works

Lettres persanes, 1721; as *The Persian Letters*, 1961
Le Temple de Gnide, 1725
Considérations sur les causes de la grandeur des Romains et de leur décadence, 1734; as *The Greatness of the Romans and Their Decline*, 1965
De l'Esprit des lois, 1748; as *The Spirit of the Laws*, 1750; same title, 1989
Défense de l'Esprit des lois, 1750
Essai sur le goût 1756

Biographical and critical studies

Shackleton, R., *Montesquieu: A Critical Biography*, 1961
Pangle, T.L., *Montesquieu's Philosophy of Liberalism: A Commentary on 'The Spirit of the Laws,'* 1973
Shklar, Judith N., *Montesquieu* (in English), 1987

Bibliography

Cabeen, D.C., *Montesquieu: A Bibliography*, 1947
Shackleton, R., in *Montesquieu. A Critical Biography*, 1961
Desgraves, Louis, *Montesquieu*, 1986

N

NAVARRE, Marguerite de: see **MARGUERITE D'ANGOULÊME**

NICOLE, Pierre, 1625–1695.

Moralist and controversialist.

LIFE

It is difficult to know how willing a recruit Nicole was to the theological campaigns of Antoine Arnauld "le grand." Nicole is best remembered for his cooperation with Pascal in the *Lettres provinciales*, which he also translated into Latin. In philosophy he was, with reservations, like Arnauld a Cartesian, although his mind and his manners were both more refined than Arnauld's and, unlike Arnauld, he was a penetrating moralist. As a moralist, he shared categories and points of view with both Pascal and La Rochefoucauld; as a spiritual author, he was led to seek to modify Jansenist (q.v.) theology; as a theologian he attacked Calvinism, quietism (see: Fénelon), and illuminism; he is remembered for his brush with Racine, who later came to admire him; and he was above all one of the two or three principal controversialists and pedagogues associated with Port-Royal (q.v.). Both his personality and his reputation contain unresolved contradictions.

Nicole's writings were combative, but his physical timidity was notorious. His prodigiously wide reading was disordered and his style is prolix, so that, while he was looked up to by Bossuet, Rancé, Racine, Boileau, and particularly by Mme de Sévigné, even such admirers as Sainte-Beuve admit that he can be boring, and most modern critics are inclined to accept the judgement not of Mme de Sévigné, who appreciated the subtlety of his psychological analyses, but of her son Charles, who found the treatise *De la connoissance de soi-même* "tedious practically from one end to the other," and thought Nicole's style "distillé, sophistiqué (elaborate, complicated)." It is often argued that he did not write well, but sometimes overlooked that what he wrote was often important, that he appears not to have enjoyed composing the works of controversy which made him famous, and that as a moralist his insights impressed some of the most refined and sensitive minds of his generation.

Nicole was born at Chartres on 13 October 1625, son of Louise Constant and of Jean Nicole, a lawyer friend of Chapelain who had translated a work attributed to Quintilian and published verse sufficiently licentious for Nicole later to have sought to buy in as much of the edition as he could. Of his three sisters, the two older ones became nuns, the younger of these, Charlotte, being educated at Port-Royal-des-Champs, where Nicole had two aunts in the community, Madeleine Prisque de l'Ascension and Marie des Anges. The third sister, Louise, married, and died in November 1665. After being taught at home, Nicole was sent to Paris in 1642 to complete the philosophy part of the course at the Collège d'Harcourt. He studied theology under the later supporter of Jansen, Jacques de Sainte-Beuve, and defended his bachelor's theses on beatitude, the Trinity, and grace, dedicated to Jacques Lescot, the bishop of Chartres, on 17 June 1649. He was never particularly attracted to the reputation of Saint-Cyran and had read with distaste the 1645 *La Grandeur de l'Eglise romaine* of Saint-Cyran's nephew, Martin Barcos, published by Barcos in defence of his unfortunate phrase making equal the authority of Saints Peter and Paul slipped by him into the preface to Arnauld's *De la fréquente communion.* Nicole found Barcos's book slipshod and wrote a critique of it, which he circulated in manuscript. He tried to learn Hebrew but in the end gave up on account of his poor eyesight.

Certainly by 1650, and probably earlier, he was teaching at the "petites écoles" of Port-Royal, which had grown out of the lessons organized by Saint-Cyran for his nephews and the two Bignon boys, tutored by Le Maître de Saci, Lancelot, and Singlin from 1637. The term "petites écoles" means "junior classes," teaching little more than primary education, reading, writing, arithmetic, and grammar. With Saint-Cyran imprisoned from 1638, Lancelot left Paris for the abbaye de Saint-Cyran in October 1639, and the handful of boys from the "petites écoles," all sons of persons closely associated with the monastery, accompanied him. By 1642 they were back at Port-Royal-des-Champs, joined by two more, and then in 1643 by the three sons of Gentien Thomas. At the end of that year the boys were sent to Chesnay, belonging to a Pelletier des Touches, a former penitent of Saint-Cyran.

Nicole appears to have been involved from the beginning of the rudimentary organization of the classes in Paris in the autumn of 1646. The boys had not found life in the country sufficiently conducive to study. Accommodation was obtained near the Paris monastery; Wallon de Beaupuis was put in charge; and there were four groups of half a dozen boys. Nicole was in charge of the top class, that of philosophy and rhetoric, with Lancelot teaching Greek and mathematics, Thomas Guyot teaching Latin, and a M. Coustel, known only for a later work on pedagogy, also helping. There appears to have been a certain formality: a uniform, a chapel, and vespers, with Singlin's sermon at Port-Royal on Sundays. The celebrated *Logique de Port-Royal*, written for the boys, almost certainly owes more to Nicole than to Arnauld, although both, being Cartesians, wanted to sweep away the old pedagogy and start again.

Nicole, possibly in an effort to stay free of the trap into which Arnauld was to fall, turned away from the idea of a doctorate and even an ecclesiastical career, never taking more than the tonsure. Singlin, more pliable than Saci, became his director. Nicole wrote fluent, elegant Latin, was not easily moved by the large amount of imaginative literature that he read, and had a developed critical mind, as much at home with the scholastics as with the Fathers. From 1654 Arnauld enlisted him as his lieutenant in theological controversy(see: Jansenism and Port-Royal). The original bull of 1653, condemning the five propositions purportedly from the *Augustinus*, and known from its opening words as *Cum occasione*, had condemned the five propositions only "on the occasion" of the publication of the *Augustinus*. It was the further decree of 23 April 1654 which declared, if only by inference, that the doctrine condemned had been Jansen's.

Nicole now shared with Arnauld the hospitality of Jean Hamelin—in charge of "ponts et chaussées (bridges and highways)"—in the faubourg Saint-Jacques, accompanying Arnauld to new quarters, changing aliases when necessary, during the campaign of Pascal's *Lettres provinciales*, for which he disinterred ammunition from casuists and scholastics. From 1654 he also started to publish polemical pamphlets in French and Latin, at first jointly with Arnauld and then over his own name. It was Nicole who was most ready to abandon the condemned propositions in order to save Port-Royal, and who relied most heavily on the distinction between the substance of the doctrine condemned and its presence in Jansen's book. To the dismay of others of the Port-Royal party, Nicole went so far as to defend the idea of a general grace which seemed to them to be indistinguishable from sufficient grace, which of its nature allows for human cooperation in salvific activity. In 1658–59 Nicole journeyed to Holland and the Rhine where, under the name of Wendrock, he translated the *Lettres provinciales*, to be published in Cologne in 1658.

From this point on Nicole appears to have held a conciliatory theory of grace which he did not publish during his life, but which is contained in the unpublished *Ecrit sur la grâce* of 1674, and the posthumous *Traité de la grâce générale*. For Nicole maintained accurately that Jansen had postulated in fallen man both a natural impotence to do good which Adam had had, and a wilful impotence, deriving from the dominion of concupiscence over the will, but that Jansen had then neglected the natural impotence. According to Nicole, therefore, Jansen did not deny to fallen man the physical power to do good, but only the moral power of which concupiscence deprived him. Nicole certainly pointed to flaws in the arguments of the *Augustinus* and probably had a more acute mind than any of the other theological disputants of his generation, but he did not, like Arnauld, feel compelled by the spirituality of Saint-Cyran, which had become the real motive power behind the position of the other Port-Royal theologians.

Not surprisingly, Nicole was also the most moderate of the Port-Royal party when it came to the politics of condemnations and counter-attacks. Not only was Nicole in favour of signing the formulary with appropriate restrictions in 1661, but he played a leading part in the effort at reconciling the positions on grace led by Gilbert de Choiseul, the bishop of Comminges, in 1663. He was suspect to a number of the more committed Jansenists, but none the less continued to serve as Arnauld's lieutenant, hiding with him under a variety of names in the house of Mme Angran. They moved about, spent some time at Châtillon, and even went to ground at the Hôtel de Longueville in the rue Saint-Thomas-du-Louvre, where they insisted on paying for their board and lodging.

Nicole had not much heart for the fight, and considered retiring to the country. He was easily upset by opposition or hostility and his distaste for controversy augmented with time. His timidity is legendary. He would not cross a river in a rowing boat without wearing a life-belt; he said to a parish priest who had just taken him up a new tower that he would have a parish full of good Christians if their resolution not to sin was as strong as his never to go up that tower again; at Troyes he would not go out in a wind in case he was hit by a falling tile; and while writing the *Essais de morale* at the abbey of Saint-Martin-ez-Aires at Troyes, he had a trapdoor put into a ground floor room in a nearby country house where he worked, so that his writing table and everything on it could be made to disappear at the touch of his foot. He had developed a persecution complex.

It was not enough to stop him from being an entertaining talker. He yielded easily in conversation, covering his views with authorities he liked to quote, but had a fluent style, and was much sharper with his pen than with his tongue, at least in sustained discourse. In conversation in 1687 he went so far as to refer slightingly to Pascal, dead for quarter of a century but immensely venerated, as a "ramasseur de coquilles (collector of shells)." That remark takes on some interest in the light not only of Nicole's obvious dependence on Pascal for his moral writings but also of the possibility that some of Pascal's fragments, perhaps among those published by Port-Royal in 1670, might originally have been Nicole's, noted down among Pascal's miscellaneous jottings during the period of their close collaboration.

Nicole's life-style was frugal, sober, but without gratuitous austerities. He was likeable, learned, naive, and incapable either of shaving himself or of putting his wig on straight. A great deal of his time was consumed in writing but, in the midst of the apologias for this and that, the factums, the indignation, the sharply pointed analyses, he kept a sense of humour and a gentle irony which allowed him to send up the whole debate about the presence or absence of the five propositions in Jansen's book, notably in the first of his letters on *L'hérésie imaginaire*, dated 24 January 1664. The ten *Imaginaires* were followed by eight *Visionnaires*, directed chiefly against Desmarets de Saint-Sorlin, once a protégé of Richelieu, author of the 1637 comedy *Les Visionnaires*, declared enemy of Port-Royal, whose solitaires in hiding he was dedicated to spying out, but also himself the victim of a mystical exaltation which brought discredit on the whole mystical tradition and resulted in the burning alive of the disturbed Simon Morin in 1663. It was in referring to the semi-deranged Desmarets that Nicole called novelists and playwrights "empoisonneurs publics non des corps, mais des âmes des fidèles (public poisoners not of the bodies, but of the souls of the faithful)," the remark to which Racine took such exception.

In 1659 Nicole had written a preface to an *Office du Saint-Sacrement* by Le Maître which the duc de Luynes had translated into French. Nicole's preface, judged too polemical, was not printed, but it did circulate in manuscript and was read by the pastor Jean Claude, who wrote a refutation which also circulated in manuscript. Thereupon Nicole decided to print his original piece with a refutation of Claude's reply. The 1664 pseudonymous volume, signed "sieur Barthélémy," was called *La Perpétuité de la foi de l'église catholique touchant l'Eucharistie* and later known as the "petite *Perpétuité*." Claude then published the reply which Nicole had already refuted, and a further answer. Nicole then set to work on the "grande *Perpétuité*," publishing the first volume in 1669 with the approbations of 27 prelates, more than a score of doctors, and Bossuet, still a simple priest. There was a Latin dedication by Arnauld to Clement IX. A second volume appeared in 1672 and a third in 1674. Three other works of Nicole belong to the same anti-Calvinist controversy, the 1671 *Préjugés légitimes contre les Calvinistes*, the 1684 *Les Prétendus Réformés convaincus de schisme*, and the 1687 *L'Unité de l'église*. The techniques used by Nicole, appealing not to snippets of scripture but to the historical belief of the Church, virtually changed the rules of theological controversy.

Unlike the controversial writings, the *Essais de morale* were the result of Nicole's natural inspiration. Later editors have made it exceedingly difficult to know what was written when, chapters of reasonable length having been substituted for the original short numbered paragraphs. Other works were incorporated, including some not by Nicole, and posthumous volumes were printed as if they had been part of the original collection. The first three volumes, dated 1671, 1671, and 1675, were published pseudonymously, the first volume under the name of Mombrigny and the other two under the name of Chanteresne. The fourth volume, published in 1678, carried no author's name, but Nicole's authorship was by now public knowledge.

With the Paix de l'église, the resolution of the conflict with Port-Royal from 1668 to 1679, Nicole felt the need to get away from the intense atmosphere of secrecy, hiding, and intrigue in which he had been living. Retz found him a lodging at the abbaye Saint-Denis to which he could withdraw when he wanted to. He also had a lodging in Paris at the Ecuries of Mme de Longueville, who now had residences in the courtyard of the Carmelite convent in Paris as well as at Port-Royal-des-Champs. Nicole took to spending the winter in Paris and the summer at Troyes, Chartres, or Beauvais. He remained very close to Arnauld and went to Angers with him in the autumn of 1671. He was under pressure to resume an ecclesiastical career, which would have meant taking orders, and went to Aleth in 1676 to talk the matter over with the bishop, travelling by Lyons, Avignon and Nîmes and returning through Grenoble. He saw Retz at Chambéry, and passed through Annecy.

Soon after his return two bishops asked him in 1677 to compose a letter to the pope complaining again about relaxed confessional practice. Although Nicole at first refused, he was persuaded by Mme de Longueville. His authorship was soon known to the king, who saw the fragile peace shattered and had his displeasure communicated to Nicole through d'Andilly's son, Pomponne, now a minister. Nicole was frightened, and left Paris for Chartres, Troyes, and then Beauvais, where he had a small benefice, and where he was when Mme de Longueville died in 1679, and the persecution of Port-Royal began again. That year he not only lost his Paris lodging with Mme de Longueville's death, but the deaths of Retz and Buzanval deprived him of his other two places of refuge, at the abbey of Saint-Denis and at Saint-Nicolas at Beauvais. He decided to go to Brussels to avoid any possibility of imprisonment in France, and Arnauld joined him there. It was there that they parted. Nicole was 54, ill, and wanted to negotiate a peaceful retirement in France rather than endure the permanent exile in Holland chosen by Arnauld.

Many of the Port-Royal supporters did not forgive him for the letter he wrote to the archbishop of Paris, Harlay de Champvallon, seeking his return to grace. He went to Liège, then up the Meuse to Sedan, and in the winter of 1679–80 had 16 known addresses. Arnauld continued to act in his interests, and Nicole never blamed Arnauld for the unfair and numerous reproaches flung at him. In the end he was allowed to retire to Chartres where once again he lived under a false name from 1681 to 1683. In May 1683 he was allowed back to Paris. His heart was scarcely in his last controversies against quietism. His view was much consulted, especially by Bossuet. Racine had come to admire him and elicit from him information for the history of Port-Royal. On 11 November 1695 he had a stroke. Five days later, on 16 November 1695, he was killed by a second one at the age of 70. The friend whom he had asked to have his heart buried next to Arnauld's at Port-Royal heard only too late about his death.

WORKS

Although the works of Nicole normally considered to be of literary interest are limited to the *Essais de morale*, the literary and spiritual works are intimately linked to Nicole's theological writings about grace. For the whole of the period from the reformation to the Revolution it is possible to divide the Christian moralists, whether teachers, observers, or explorers of moral behaviour and the values which do or should inspire it, into two categories, those who believed or hoped that human beings could, by their behaviour while briefly on earth, influence the state of extreme happiness or unimaginably intense deprivation which they would enter after death, and which could then never either change or cease, and those who did not.

The concept of redeemed nature would have allowed the human being to choose to accept proffered supernatural grace, and therefore salvation, without heretical implications for the theology of grace. But the ineluctable consequence of holding that fallen nature was itself from the moment of the fall also redeemed would have meant allowing the possibility of salvation outside the church understood, as it then was, as the communion of orthodox believers. Hence the importance of the disputes about "pagan virtue." But without the concept of a redeemed human nature, it seemed to many Christian moralists and theologians that it was heretical, at best semi-Pelagian, to hold that moral and spiritual self-determination, even if it involved no more than the acceptance of proffered grace, was within the autonomous power of human beings.

The connection between the theology of grace and moral writing is not difficult to understand. If the autonomous power of self-determination to good, that is to merit or at least to accept the justifying grace leading to salvation, was within the power of the human being, the moralists were bound, whatever the difficulties for the theology of grace, to emphasize the need for moral effort, good works, and behaviour compatible with the acceptance of salvation. If the theology of grace made it impossible to maintain any effective power of autonomous spiritual self-determination in man, the moralist was faced with the urgent need of any Christian believer for reassurance about being among the number of the predestined.

The 16th-century moralists were, from the period of Colet, More, and Erasmus, and on both sides of the schism, inclined to have recourse to criteria in the order of direct religious experience. Most of the specifically religious moralists, certainly before the onset of neostoicism in France during the religious wars, were inclined to explore the possibility that, even if the Christian could not always and instantly feel acceptability in the sight of God, reassurance could none the less be obtained in the order of behaviour or at least in some empirically detectable way. French moralists of the 17th century, after the religious wars had ended, were more doubtful. They were writing after the council of Trent which, while not deciding the issue whether or not there really was any really autonomous human power to accept or earn justifying grace, had at least defined some of the boundaries within which any solution had to be contained.

For the individual believer, the question of salvation or damnation was the only important one. Its overwhelming weight on even the emotionally balanced members of that section of the population not wholly preoccupied with the daily struggle to survive, and educated enough to reflect on their situation, accounts for much that the social historian meets in the way of superstition even among the literate. For the moralist, the pressure to accept autonomous self-determination and explore an ethic of meritorious behaviour was huge. If the theology made that impossible, as at Port-Royal, where was the urgently demanded reassurance to come from? It is possible that Nicole alone tried to do without it, and that that was the reason which forced him into demonstrating inconsistencies in Jansen's theology of the fall and producing his own theory of "general grace" which, he hoped, might have proved the basis for a compromise solution.

Jansen's own concerns had not been pastoral. His effort was directed towards reaffirming what he took to be the Church's traditional teaching on the ways in which individuals were saved, and he did not seriously concern himself with how, in the light of his theology, even justified Christians should live their lives, let alone sinners, heretics, pagans, Jews, and those who lived before Jesus. It is probable that Saint-Cyran's spiritual exaltation drove him to emphasize the glorification of divine justice at the expense of those who were not currently justified Christians destined to persevere. He probably did think that the presence of justifying grace in the soul was palpable, but his refusal to concern himself with the predicament of the majority of the human race diminished his spiritual, personal, and in the end also literary stature.

It seems almost certain that Pascal, perhaps even drawing on Nicole, considered the possibility that nobody could know whether they were keeping the law out of self-love, and therefore in a state of sin, or whether they were inspired by efficacious grace, but Pascal's consciousness of the pastoral consequences of that dilemma may, like the purposelessness of writing an apologetic when belief alone could achieve nothing in the order of salvation, for which grace-inspired faith was required, have contributed to his withdrawal from the debate at the end of 1661 after refusing to sign the second mandement (see: Port-Royal), and to his failure to complete the great project in view of which so many of much we know as the *Pensées* had been assembled.

Nicole's positions cannot be dated precisely. We know that in 1656–57 he was committed to the fight against what he believed to be the moral values upheld by the Jesuits, but thereafter he showed a marked distaste for the disputes on grace, refusing in the end to specify whether or not the general grace, which he thought Jansen ought to have admitted in fallen nature, was or was not really sufficient, whether human salvation in the present order of individual human beings did or did not depend on God's arbitrary caprice. By 1660 Nicole was looking for an accommodation with the Molinists. In that year he held discussions with Claude Girard, who had not taken the doctorate "to save himself 500 livres and the mortal sin of signing Arnauld's degradation."

In 1661 Nicole had observed the agonized terror with which Mère Angélique had faced the death which came to her on 6 August, "waiting," she wrote, "like a criminal at the foot of the gallows for the execution of her judge's sentence."

During the attempts of Gilbert de Choiseul, bishop of Comminges, to mediate late in 1662 and in 1663, there are different accounts of Nicole's role. Choiseul was informed by the court that Père Jean Ferrier, the Jesuit who was to succeed Père Annat as the king's confessor, was authorized to conduct negotiations. The bishop arrived in Paris on 31 December 1662 and obtained permission for Arnauld, Singlin, Barcos, and a docteur Taignier to appear openly in Paris. Arnauld would not attend any discussions personally but sent Lalane and Girard. A dignified reconciliation would have been possible, but Arnauld was by now too entrenched not to be determined never to appear to yield. Nicole, who by this time certainly wanted nothing more than agreement on the theology of grace, is said to have supported Arnauld's refusal to sign any document starting "subjicimus (we submit)," however purely external the submission. Nicole is said with Roannez and Saci to have supported Arnauld's intransigence, with Pomponne, Lamoignon, and docteur Sainte-Beuve urging acceptance. But in 1663 Choiseul turned directly to the pope, sending him five articles with a document drawn up by Nicole and Girard. It is alleged that Annat, acting through a Roman agent and François Albizzi, an assessor of the Holy Office, had a meeting of cardinals called on 21 July 1663, after which the Vatican, supported by a letter from 15 French bishops, refused to reply to Choiseul.

Much later a letter from Nicole to Quesnel was published as the preface to the second volume of the posthumous *Traité de la grâce générale*, pointing out that the five articles of 1663 had been only

une réduction de toutes les opinions que l'on tenoit sur les cinq Propositions à la doctrine commune des Thomistes

(a reduction of all the opinions held [by the Jansenists] to the common teaching of the Thomists).

In other words, within four or five years of the first *Lettres provinciales* Nicole had not only grasped at the possible life-line of a "grâce générale," but was adopting his final position, applying the method most importantly deployed in the *Perpétuité de la foi*, which had nothing to do either with Augustine or with the scholastic argument, but rested entirely on the fact that any view taught openly, clearly, widely, and freely in the Church for half a millennium could not be inconsistent with the faith of the Church, and that since Jansenism was such a view, it had to be, if not right, then at least orthodox. The last letters between Nicole and Quesnel relapse on both sides simply into gentle teasing.

It is necessary to understand the constraints impinging on Nicole's moral and spiritual writings from the theology of grace, and indeed the reciprocal influence of the spiritual, moral, and pastoral concerns on the dogmatic theology itself, but the standard Desprez editions of Nicole from the first half of the 18th century understandably omit the ephemeral works of polemic.

Since we do not more than vaguely know the order of composition of what Desprez printed as treatises in the first six volumes of his uniform 13-volume editions of Nicole, and since the Desprez editions are the sole source for all but a few anthologized texts, it is to them we must turn, and by and large their order we must follow in any consideration of Nicole's literary interest. A 14th volume was added in 1732 containing the abbé Goujet's biography of Nicole, still the most important source of information about his life, copiously plundered by everyone who has written about Port-Royal.

The moral writings are clearly related to those of both Pascal and La Rochefoucauld, and at least historically show how Augustine's identification at the beginning of the *De civitate dei*, xiv, 28 of "amor sui (amour-propre/self-love)" with sin, and of "amor dei (love of God/grace-inspired charity)," to be found in Pascal, was secularized for La Rochefoucauld and even Saint-Evremond, for neither of whom the word "amour-propre" could be used of a virtuous movement of the soul. The incompatibility with virtue was attached to the word, even outside the theological context in which it implied the absence of grace, not to the psychological reality of self-love or "intérêt," which could for La Rochefoucauld be the basis for authentically virtuous activity. For Nicole, the impossibility of knowing whether apparently virtuous activity masked authentically grace-inspired behaviour or its sinful counterfeit was to give a sharp edge to his perception of the human moral dilemma.

Goujet has a long-winded paragraph about the title *Essais de morale*:

Ce titre modeste… ne doit pas faire croire… qu'on n'a prétendu y proposer que des vûës incertaines et confuses, ou de légeres idées de la perfection Chrétienne….M. Nicole a mieux aimé essayer de traiter la Morale Chrétienne par parties… en se contentant sur chaque matiere de proposer diverses verités, selon qu'elles sont venuës dans son esprit, sans se mettre en peine de les disposer dans un ordre méthodique, quoique l'on y trouve beaucoup de méthode. C'est ce qu'il a voulu marquer par ce mot d'*Essais*

(This modest title…should not lead us to believe…that what has been attempted is only to put forward uncertain and confused views or superficial ideas about Christian perfection….M. Nicole has preferred to treat of Christian moral teaching in sections…contenting himself on each topic to put forward different truths as they came into his mind, without going to the trouble of putting them methodically into order, although there is much method to be found in them. That is what he meant to denote by this word *Essays*).

The first volume starts with what, by the time Goujet wrote, was already a "treatise" *De la foiblesse de l'homme*. Nicole has so often been adversely compared to Pascal, who never actually wrote a moral treatise, that it is important to emphasize from the beginning that we are in the presence of a strong new note in 17th-century Christian moral writing, not so much because of the initial definition of pride as somehow "a puffing up of the heart by which human beings extend and enlarge themselves and elevate their image of themselves by the ideas of strength, greatness, and excellence," as because of the acute observation of characteristics. We are already arrived at a date later than the peak of the fashion for analysing motivation and for creating recognizable individual portraits, and moving towards the depiction of "caractères" as La Bruyère understood the word. There is also a new and refreshing scepticism about reliance on social or military rank:

Un General d'armée se represente toujours à lui-même au milieu de tous ses soldats. Ainsi chacun tâche d'occuper le plus de place qu'il peut dans son imagination, et l'on ne se pousse et ne s'agrandit dans le monde que pour augmenter l'idée que chacun se forme de soi-même…Si l'on demande pourquoi le Grand Seigneur a fait depuis peu perir cent mille hommes devant Candie, on peut répondre sûrement, que ce n'est que pour attacher encore à cette image interieure qu'il a de lui-même, le titre de Conquerant

(An army general always thinks of himself surrounded by his soldiers. Everyone tries to take the biggest possible place in their own imagination, and no one pursues or achieves success in the world except to increase the idea they have of themselves…If it is asked why the Grand Seigneur recently caused 100,000 men to die before Candia, you can be sure of being right if you reply that it is only to add to the interior image he has of himself the title of Conqueror).

Candia had surrendered to the Turks after a 20-year siege in 1669. It is not surprising that, just after the Flanders campaign of 1667–68, Louis XIV should find subversive such sentiments as those expressed in this passage. What would be more surprising would be the failure of critics to have drawn more attention to such sharp comment, if Nicole did not go on to repeat himself and allow his impact to become blunted by verbosity.

Goujet is right in pointing to the disjointed nature of Nicole's comments, full of resonances and reminiscences. There is traditional spiritual caution, a reliance on Descartes as well as virtual folk wisdom concerning the vanity of worldly power, an insistence on human weakness and ignorance. The strong, forceful writing comes almost in nuggets, independent concentrations of sometimes great density and vigour. In the observations grouped together in *De la civilité chrétienne*, Nicole is fascinatingly uncertain, in what is printed as a first chapter "Comment l'amour-propre produit la civilité," whether "amour-propre" denotes not only a state of sin but also a form of behaviour. In chapter 11 of *De la charité et de l'amour-propre* it is quite clear that the same external behaviour can be a manifestation of grace or a counterfeit. There is no way of telling whether the appearances of grace are fraudulent.

Pour rendre les hommes heureux dès cette vie même, il ne faudroit au défaut de la charité, que leur donner à tous un amour propre éclairé, qui sût discerner ses vrais interêts, et y tendre par les voies que la droite raison lui découvriroit. Quelque corrompue que cette societé fût au-dedans et aux yeux de Dieu, il n'y auroit rien au-dehors de mieux reglé, de plus civil, de plus juste, de plus pacifique, de plus honnête, de plus genereux; et ce qui seroit de plus admirable, c'est qu'en n'étant animée et remuée que par l'amour propre, l'amour propre n'y paroîtroit point, et qu'étant entierement vuide de charité, on ne verroit par tout que la forme et les caractères de la charité

(To make people already happy in this life, in the absence of charity all that would be needed would be to give them all an enlightened amour-propre, able to distinguish their true interests and to strive to reach them along the paths which right reason would reveal to them. However corrupt that society might be within, and in the eyes of God, there would be nothing externally better regulated, more polite, more just, more peace-loving, more upright, more open-hearted. What would be even more remarkable is that, being given life and movement only by amour-propre, amour-propre would not appear, and everything while entirely devoid of charity, would exhibit the appearance and characteristics of charity).

The ambiguity is systematic:

Quoiqu'il n'y ait rien de si opposé à la charité qui rapporte tout à Dieu, que l'amour propre qui rapporte tout à soi, il n'y a rien néanmoins de si semblable aux effets de la charité que ceux de l'amour propre; car il marche tellement par les mêmes voies, qu'on ne sauroit presque mieux marquer celles où la charité nous doit porter, qu'en découvrant celles que prend un amour propre éclairé, qui fait connoître ses vrais interêts, et qui tend par raison à la fin qu'il se propose

(Although there is nothing so opposed to the charity which refers everything to God as the amour-propre which refers everything to the self, there is nevertheless nothing so similar to the effects of charity as those of amour-propre; for it moves so exactly along the same paths that you could scarcely mark out better those where charity should lead us than by uncovering those taken by an enlightened amour-propre, which makes known its true interests and tends by reason to the goal it sets itself).

Grace therefore does demand forms of virtuous behaviour, but the behaviour itself is no sign of grace. It can, as for Pascal, derive from sin, and is ethically ambiguous.

Nicole comes quite near identifying dryness in prayer with the absence of grace, a doctrine which goes of course against the traditional teaching of mystical theology, but which again hankers after the empirically ascertainable certainty of the presence of grace in the soul.

The ambiguity of behaviour fascinates Nicole:

Que voyent, par exemple, les gens du monde dans un bal? Une assemblée de personnes agréables, qui ne pensent qu'à se divertir, à prendre part, et à contribuer au plaisir commun… Mais qu'est-ce que la lumiere de la foi découvre dans ces assemblées profanes à ceux qu'elle éclaire, et à qui il fait voir tout le spectacle… un massacre horrible d'âmes qui s'entretuent les unes les autres; elle leur découvre des femmes en qui le démon habite, qui font à de misérables hommes mille plaies mortelles; et des hommes qui percent le coeur de ces femmes par leurs criminelles idolateries

(What for example do people of the world see at a ball? A gathering of attractive people intent only on amusing themselves, on taking part in and contributing to the general enjoyment… But what does the light of faith reveal in these profane gatherings to those whom it illumines and to whom it shows the complete vision… a horrible massacre of souls killing each other. It shows them women in whom the devil lives, who inflict on wretched men a thousand deathly wounds, and men who pierce the heart of those women by their criminal worship).

On the subject of the theatre, Nicole's objection is that the display on stage of violent passion could not move us without exciting in us some complicity, and that Christian virtues are of their nature incapable of making good theatre. Since the only psychologically plausible explanations of the Aristotelian "catharsis" depended on the use of small doses of the poison for purposes of inoculation, Nicole can be said to have done no more than draw a perfectly logical conclusion from current dramatic theory. The only alternative justification for serious theatrical entertainment involved the implausible interpolation of an intellectual judgement in the audience.

Those who commit the crimes committed on stage will meet tragic fates, as the dramas suggest. Those who justified the theatre in this way as an efficient warning may well not have been conscious that they were merely rationalizing, providing what gave them pleasure with what they hoped might be the learned protection of Aristotelian authority. Serious drama in the French renaissance had originated in the rhetorical declamations by which adolescents were taught, in accordance with the rules of Aristotle's *Rhetoric*, to move the passions of the audience. Theoretical discussion was still dominated by those origins and by Aristotelian authority, now diluted by that of other antique authors, who did imply some complicity in the audience with the passions depicted on the stage. But Nicole, who had read all the popular modern fiction, had certainly detected the general tendency to upgrade human instinctive activity in a way which was bound to arouse Port-Royal's antagonism. On the premises of 17th-century dramatic theory, Nicole's remarks on the theatre are perceptive. At bottom, he was irked by dishonesty and adept at tearing away blindfolds and blinkers, in the matter of the theatre as in every other realm.

Nicole's moral perception, like the theology on which it depends, may not have achieved total consistency, or even coherence, but it has very powerful moments. His mind was less sharp than Pascal's, his style less pointed, and his personality less intense, but his problem was identical. It is not the banal contrast between appearance and reality, but the agonizing choice involved in seeing human beings either as the victims of divine caprice or as the agents of their own salvation.

PUBLICATIONS

[The standard edition(s) of Nicole are those published by Desprez, best regarded as a single edition which grew from 10 volumes to 26 between 1705ff and 1768, with each volume reprinted as required. The first three pseudonymous volumes of the Essais de morale *of 1671, 1671, and 1675 were rearranged into chapters before 1679. The fourth volume of 1678 was anonymous. Brief pamphlets of controversy or justification in Latin and French are omitted, as of too specialized interest. It is also necessary to avoid making an unwarranted distinction between the nature of printed material and what circulated in manuscript. Works published but not printed are not listed]*

Collections

Essais de morale, 10 vols. (5 of treatises, 5 of homilies), 1705ff

—— 13 vols. (6 of treatises, 2 of letters, 5 of homilies), 1715

—— *Vie de Nicole*, added 1732, 1 or 2 vols. (printed in Luxemburg)

—— *Instruction sur l'oraison dominicale*, added 1740

—— *Instructions sur le symbole*, 2 vols., added 1740

—— *Instructions sur les sacrements*, 2 vols., added 1741

—— *Instructions sur le Décalogue*, 2 vols., added 1741

—— *Lettres*, 2 vols., 1743 (printed in Holland)

—— *L'Esprit de Nicole*, 1765

—— *Traité de la prière*, 1768

Theological and controversial, non-posthumous

De la foy humaine, 1664

Lettres sur l'hérésie imaginaire and *Les Visionnaires*, 18 parts, 1664–66

Traité de la comédie, 1667 (reprinted in *Essais de morale*, vol. 3, 1675)

La ("petite") Perpétuité de la foi catholique, 1664

La ("grande") Perpétuité de la foi catholique, 3 vols., 1669–74 (perhaps with, or by, Arnauld)

De l'éducation d'un prince, 1670 (reprinted in vol. 2 of Desprez editions)

Préjugés légitimes contre les Calvinistes, 1671

Traité de l'oraison, 1679 (as *Traité de la prière*, 2 vols., 1694)

Les Prétendus Réformés convaincus de schisme, 1684

De l'unité de l'Eglise, 1687

Other non-posthumous

La Logique; ou, L'Art de penser [*Logique de Port-Royal*], anonymous, with Arnauld, 1662

Posthumous

Traité de la grâce générale, 2 vols., 1715

Biographical and critical studies

Sainte-Beuve, C.-A., *Port-Royal*, Bibliothèque de la Pléiade edition, 3 vols., 1954–61

Bremond, Henri, *Histoire littéraire du sentiment religieux en France*, 12 vols., 1916–33

Thouverez, E., *Pierre Nicole*, 1926

Le Breton-Grandmaison, P., *Nicole; ou, La Civilité chrétienne*

James, E.D., *Pierre Nicole, Jansenist and Humanist. A Study of his Thought*, 1972

NIVELLE DE LA CHAUSSÉE, Pierre-Claude, 1691 or 1692–1754.

Dramatist.

LIFE

Nivelle de la Chaussée was a Parisian socialite from an established bourgeois family of tax farmers, who toyed briefly with a career in business, whose family lost three quarters of its fortune in the economic collapse following the failure of Law's system in 1720, but who could still towards the end of his life lose 4,000 livres in a coal-mining enterprise, and still live stylishly with one house in Paris and a second one in a nearby village, and who did not start writing seriously for publication or performance until he was over 40. He played the theatrical market with skill, writing in a spectrum of styles, and living at odds with the attitudes he knew would move his public in the "comédie larmoyantes (tearful comedies)" which he invented and for which he is chiefly remembered.

If we are to believe the burial document, the date of Nivelle de la Chaussée's birth must have fallen within the 12 months preceding 14 March 1692, since at that date in 1754 he was said to be 62. His father and mother lived until he was well into middle age, dying respectively in 1737 and 1740. He apparently had an excellent education, first, according to near-contemporary chroniclers, at the Jesuit college of Louis-le-Grand, and then at the Collège du Plessis. He was small and ugly. His early life was rich and uninhibited. He relished the charming, titillating, and sexually relaxed social life of the regency salons, flirting casually, enjoying women's favours, and surviving their rejections without apparently ever being in love. He had a good time, was serious, teasing, and sarcastic in turns, clowning and drinking, obscene, cultivated, and what we would regard as simply coarse.

His first publication was the anonymous and witty criticism of Houdar de la Motte's 1719 *Fables*, the *Lettres de Madame la marquise de l*** à une de ses amies sur les Fables nouvelles*. Nivelle de la Chaussée's authorship remained unsuspected. In 1720 he was in Amsterdam on business which clearly bored him. A set of 14 letters, straining for licentious effect, testify not only to boredom in Holland, but also to a nostalgia for the cultural life of Paris and to a desire to write. His social circle in Paris was drawn from the educated upper bourgeoisie, minor office-holders, lawyers, and financiers, but also from a higher stratum of the richer and grander, like Mme de Maupeou, said to have the best table in Paris, and known for receiving and entertaining. He was also enthusiastic about making music in small groups.

Between 1720 and 1730 Nivelle de la Chaussée wrote a series of contes. He and such friends as the chevalier d'Orléans, his own later editor Charles Sablier, M. de Maurepas, Maurepas's secretary, and the comtes d'Argenson and de Caylus, attracted to the performances of the Italian company, used to dress down to mingle with the crowd at the parades put on at the Paris fairs to attract paying customers into the performances being put on inside the booths. These parades were also developed, or simply adopted, as country-house entertainments. A number of minor authors, Fagan, Piron, Gueulette, Collé, and Sallé adapted what was basically fairground material for polite, if often still coarse entertainment in grand residences, where some of the most socially elevated members of society themselves not infrequently took part, as if, it has been suggested, to take refuge in schoolboy smut and in patois from the constricting etiquette which more refined society was beginning to demand.

Nivelle de la Chaussée's first dramatic efforts seem to have been contributions to parades. Some of those in which he must have had some hand have survived, and we know that things got out of hand when, as late as 1737, a piece to which he had contributed was due to be played on Good Friday by a cast of marquises, counts, and dukes at Champs, the country house of the duc de Vaujours, about to become duc de la Vallière. Fleury got to hear about it and had the entertainment stopped to avoid sacrilegious blasphemy of the day. The cast simply went off to have supper with some Parisian girls at the "petite maison" of the duc d'Aumont, acquired for just such evenings, when young aristocrats wanted discreet sexual fun. A similar group to which Nivelle de la Chaussée also belonged and where Voltaire, too, could indulge his passion for acting, congregated round the comte de Livry, and it was to the château at Livry that Nivelle de la Chaussée was sometimes to go when he wanted to work in peace. It was there that in 1735 he wrote *L'Ecole des amis*.

It was in the Livry circle that he found Mlle Quinault, an actress from the Comédie–Française company with whom Nivelle de la Chaussée formed a close liaison. She retired in 1741, received at the highest social level as well as in the world of the theatre and, alternating with Caylus, gave dinners for a company including the chevalier d'Orléans, d'Argenson, Maurepas, Voltaire, Destouches, Fagan, Collé, Duclos, Voisenon, and Crébillon *fils*. It was Mlle Quinault who suggested to Nivelle de la Chaussée the subject of *Le Préjugé à la mode*, and among her guests that originated the obscene *Recueil de ces Messieurs* and *Les Etrennes de la Saint-Jean* to which Nivelle de la Chaussée contributed. He attended other salons, too, less coarse in tone and taste, like that of Mme Duché-Lemarchant, author of some *Nouveaux contes de fées allégoriques* in 1736, and a friend of Coypel. Towards the end of his life Nivelle de la Chaussée's protector was the comte de Clermont.

Nivelle de la Chaussée was elected to the Académie française, where he was received on 2 June 1736, but his preferred company was always more aristocratic than intellectual or even, in any true sense, literary. He was exceedingly sensitive to criticism, but a whole series of his own mordant comments about the works of his contemporaries has come down to us. He clearly had an acid if also sometimes witty tongue. Although he was accepted at court, and even made welcome there by Louis XV, Nivelle de la Chaussée's taste did not accord well with such constraints of outward decorum as court life imposed. None the less Mme de Pompadour had his *Le Préjugé à la mode* played several times, and commissioned *L'Homme de fortune* from him. Letters that have been preserved show how coldly exploitative of women he was, concentratedly egotistical and cavalier with those of his substantial number of female admirers whose social rank did not demand greater respect than he normally showed. He took favours for granted, looked for subservience, missed rendez-vous, and generally behaved with inconsiderate high-handedness.

The first work published over his name was a defence in verse of poetry directed against Houdar de la Motte, *L'Epître de Clio à M. de B.[ercy] au sujet des opinions répandues depuis peu contre la poésie*, published shortly after Houdar de la Motte's death in 1731, but written, and read to small groups, much earlier. Its success was remarkable. Voltaire claimed to be impressed by it. However, it scarcely announced the 40 or so

plays which were to follow, and especially not the comédies larmoyantes, starting with the highly successful *La Fausse Antipathie*, first performed on 2 October 1733, and its sentimentally moralizing tone, at first sight surprising, although perhaps not unconnected with those manifestations of official attitudes which moved the authorities, three days later, to seize Prévost's *Manon Lescaut*. It is difficult to resist the impression that Nivelle de la Chaussée's dramatically innovative successes, for all their historical importance, were as little the result of any genuine feeling as his amorous liaisons, although certainly calculated with greater care.

The published text was dedicated to the Académie française, to membership of which Nivelle de là Chaussée immediately aspired. Successful at his second attempt, partly because Voltaire, whose *Lettres philosophiques* had been burnt in 1734, did not dare to allow his name to go forward, Nivelle de la Chaussée was assiduous in attendance and was often designated by the Académie to represent it on formal court occasions. The speech of the archbishop of Sens, Languet de Gergy, in reply to Nivelle de la Chaussée's discourse of reception, encouraged him to continue to foster the moral standards of the young but caused a reaction amongst the Jansenists (q.v.), who thought all theatre immoral of sufficient intensity to ensure that, seven years later, the archbishop's address was a great deal more aloof when he received Marivaux into the Académie. Nivelle de la Chaussée's best play is normally considered to have been *Mélanide*, created by the Comédie-Française on 12 May 1741.

WORKS

Nivelle de la Chaussée's production is today often considered of insufficient artistic merit to warrant consideration in any presentation of French literature based on an alphabetically organized list of great authors. There are two principal reasons why his achievement should not in the present context be entirely overlooked. Firstly, his work is historically important from both a technical literary and a wider cultural point of view. The verse may be relatively facile, but he could continue to use the five-act alexandrine form associated with formal tragedy in combination with the domestic interiors and events more usually associated with comedy. He was perceived by his contemporaries as breaking both the tragic mould of Racine and the pattern of Molière's comic intrigues by combining elements of both in a new type of sentimental comedy linking the earlier separate genres to Diderot's bourgeois drama. Its immense popularity makes the new comédie larmoyante important not only in the context of dramatic history, but also in a general cultural context; it demonstrates how radically moral and aesthetic sensibilities were changing and converging in the theatre-going public who frequented the more formal French company's productions in the Paris of the middle years of Louis XV's reign.

The second reason why some consideration of Nivelle de la Chaussée's work is required is that the popular acclamation and the literary reputation it brought its author appears to a degree unknown before him to have been the result of a coolly calculated series of successfully achieved sentimental effects which did not proceed from any moral reaction, intellectual conviction, or aesthetic response in its author. To a quite new degree Nivelle de la Chaussée consistently and deeply moved audiences to emotions he never felt, or which at least did not produce in himself the same type of reaction which he elicited from his audiences. He must therefore have been among the earlier authors to separate purely professional dramatic creativity from any personal emotion, as well as among the earliest to import some tragic dignity into characters not in socially elevated and isolated positions, an innovation echoing socio-historical developments of huge proportions in the evolution of western European culture generally.

There is however with Nivelle de la Chaussée one important difficulty. Virtually all critical discussion of him derives directly from the brilliant doctoral thesis of Gustave Lanson presented as long ago as 1887, and necessarily incorporating critical stances, particularly in its moral judgements about the regency and the earlier years of the personal reign of Louis XV, which can no longer be sustained. The point is of particular consequence because the imaginative explorations of the meaning of human experience in the early 18th century are based on norms of family, social, and particularly sexual morality very different from those obtaining in the 19th century and, in other ways, from those obtaining now. It is, for instance, especially necessary to be more punctilious than Lanson was in using only contemporary 18th-century standards when employing words like "coarse" or "licentious" to describe early 18th-century ways of speaking or behaving, even if we have subsequently become more censorious in our views than the mid-18th century was.

From the very beginning, the parade Le Repatriage parodies the high tragic style still in vogue, with its invocations of massively significant words like "Love," "God," "Nature," and "Duty," and the stage convention which allows certain parts of characters' speeches to be heard by the audience but not by other characters on stage. Very early it became plain that Nivelle de la Chaussée was never going to be able to write either high tragedy or comedy of intrigue. He felt that such earnestness required parodying. The 1719 attack on the Fables of La Motte again uses the criterion of commonsense to attack exaggerations of language. None of this was, of itself, new, but from the beginnings of Nivelle de la Chaussée's career the necessary conditions, not the causes, of comédie larmoyante were coming together. The attack is pressed home in the verse Epître à Clio. La Motte, holding that a passage of Racine lost nothing of its poetry even if transposed out of rhyme and metre, was an easy target, but Nivelle de la Chaussée had also Fontenelle, Terrasson, and Trublet in his sights. In defending verse he was taking up where Voltaire had left off in the preface of the 1718 Oedipe.

It was Lanson who first used the term "comédie larmoyante":

La comédie larmoyante est un genre intermédiaire entre la comédie et la tragédie, qui introduit des personnages de condition privée, vertueux ou tout près de l'être, dans une action sérieuse, grave, parfois pathétique et qui nous excite à la vertu en nous attendrissant sur ses infortunes et en nous faisant applaudir à son triomphe

(Tearful comedy is an intermediate genre between comedy and tragedy which puts on the stage private persons, either virtuous or very nearly so, in a serious, solemn, sometimes moving plot, which incites us to virtue by making us feel for virtue's misfortunes and applaud its triumph).

Lanson held that there was no essential difference between what he called comédie larmoyante and the drame bourgeois associated with Diderot, of which he regarded comédie larmoyante as merely the first form and Nivelle de la Chaussée as the inventor. There was considerable discussion in the 18th century about whether or not Nivelle de la Chaussée's new type of comedy qualified as a new genre or not.

The first of the new plays, and Nivelle de la Chaussée's first piece of professional dramatic writing, was La Fausse antipathie, performed on 2 October 1733 with Dufresne in the lead and Mlle Quinault in the cast. It was an instant success, although also criticized in a number of epigrams, notably by Piron, and Nivelle de la Chaussée added a Critique de la Fausse Antipathie, played after the original comedy at performances after 11 March 1734. The source was Regnard's Démocrite, whose light and charming piece Nivelle de la Chaussée turns into sentimental drama. Silvie and Sainflore were forced by their families to marry against their wishes. Immediately after the wedding Sainflore had killed a despairing rival and had had to flee while Silvie entered a convent. Twelve years later, having changed their names to Léonore and Damon, they meet at the house of Géronte, an uncle of Silvie, do not recognize one another, but immediately fall in love. In the end, after much heart-rending, everything is sorted out:

O sort trop fortuné! c'est mon époux que j'aime

(Oh more than happy destiny, it is my husband I am in love with).

However imaginatively light-weight drama of this sort may be, instinct does at least lead both lovers in the right direction, and the success of the play, whatever it says about the evolution of taste, must reflect the increasingly middle-class audience serious theatre in Paris was attracting, with probably also an increased proportion of female theatre-goers. The play's great achievement was to create a demand for more of the same.

Nivelle de la Chausée duly provided Le Préjugé à la mode. The idea came through Mlle Quinault, who had seen a farce by Voltaire, Monsieur du Cap-Vert, contrasting a young man who thought it socially ridiculous to be seen to be in love with his wife, and his wife, who was determined to make him show his love in public. According to Voltaire, writing with a touch of contempt in the Dictionnaire philosophique, and perhaps with annoyance that he had not himself sensed what the public wanted, Mlle Quinault had asked him to treat the plot in a regular drama, in noble style, but he refused, although he gave her permission to give the subject to Nivelle de la Chaussée. Le Préjugé was played on 3 February 1735, and was given 20 performances in its first run. Dufresne again took the lead, and again Mlle Quinault was in the cast. The play was revived a dozen times before 1752, and at least nine performances were given at court, where the play was a favourite of Mme de Pompadour.

In Voltaire's original the principal role is given to the son of a rich Bordeaux merchant, whose wife gives herself airs, comes to Paris, and marries her son to a well-born woman. A model of virtue, the bride loves her husband, anonymously pays his debts and sends him presents, while he despises her. His father finally puts matters right. Nivelle de la Chaussée introduces the fear of ridicule as the husband's principal motivation, and it is overcome only by his jealousy. Nivelle de la Chaussée gets round his own lack of inventive ingenuity by borrowing heavily from Campistron's 1709 La Jalousie désabusée. In Le Préjugé,

Durval, the husband, loves Constance and anonymously sends her splendid presents which she refuses, believing them to come from other admirers. Various misunderstandings and pretexts for jealousies arise, but Durval finally admits his love at a masked ball when dancing with his wife, who did not at first recognize him. All is then well, and Durval's friend and adviser Damon marries Constance's cousin, Sophie, as well. With the triumph of Constance and the humiliation of Durval, Nivelle de la Chaussée was playing to the female section of his audience. He had seized on the feminist implications of the newly emerging sensibility.

At this point he was elected to the Académie. On 25 February 1737 *L'Ecole des amis* was successfully performed in Paris, with two performances commanded for Versailles. The future Frederick the Great wrote to Voltaire with presumed sarcasm that he liked the title, but that the verses were "ordinaires, faibles, monotones et ennuyeux (mediocre, weak, monotonous, and boring)." A young officer, Monrose, inherits from an uncle the guardianship of Hortense, who loves him and whom he loves. False friends conspire to ruin his reputation in the court and in the town. Hortense thinks he has been unfaithful, but sells her diamonds to pay off his debts. He sells his estates because he thinks his uncle ruined Hortense. Then a real friend, Ariste, appears, pays the debts, puts everything right and Monrose marries Hortense after all.

Nivelle de la Chaussée's next play was the tragedy *Maximien*, cautiously presented without revealing the author's name until the second performance, in case a failure should compromise the success of the comedies. There were 20 performances, a splendid box office, on eight occasions in excess of 2,000 livres, and two parodies. However neither contemporary critics nor posterity has seen merit in the piece, and Nivelle de la Chaussée must have realized that comédie larmoyante was more suited to his abilities. Whether or not he recognized it, he was unable successfully to venture beyond the emotional shallows.

Mélanide, of which the premiere was 12 May 1741, is generally considered to be Nivelle de la Chaussée's best play. The initial run was 16 performances, but it was never left long off the bill and met with extraordinary acclaim. Even the abbé Desfontaines, hitherto one of his principal critics, was won over, and finally admitted that Nivelle de la Chaussée had created a new genre, which Desfontaines was inclined to refer to as "drame romanesque." The title of the new play was pretentious. A single name, preferably recognizable as a historical character, was acceptable only for tragedies, and *Mélanide, pièce nouvelle en cinq actes* used a name that was not only unqualified by any adjective but neutral, indicating neither hero nor villain, king nor slave, suggesting merely modern and female. It implicitly gave to understand that there was no source, while pretending to five-act dignity without naming a genre.

The valets and maidservants had gradually had their roles reduced in the comedies, and by *Mélanide* they have been altogether eliminated. The inspiration for the intrigue came from Gueulette's 1738 fiction *Mémoires de mademoiselle Bontemps*, itself based on a true stroy, in which the confrontation between father and son which resolves the action in Nivelle de la Chaussée's penultimate scene is already fully sketched. The list of "acteurs" heading the play now indicates their emotional and family relationships to one another. Mélanide comes to Paris to live with the widow Dorisée who seeks a good marriage for her daughter, Rosalie. The marquis d'Orvigny is an acceptable

suitor, but Rosalie prefers a younger man, an officer called D'Arviane, who happens to be Mélanide's nephew. The only other speaking character is Théodon, Dorisée's brother-in-law.

Mélanide tries to send d'Arviane back to the army to further the plans of her friend Dorisée. Rosalie says she has no option but to follow her mother's wishes. The first act ends with the agreement of the lovers to a temporary separation. In the second Théodon agrees to speak to Mélanide on behalf of d'Orvigny. Mélanide had once had a lover, the comte d'Ormancé, by whom she had a son, on account of which she was disinherited. Théodon thinks d'Ormancé and d'Orvigny must be the same person. A meeting is arranged, the lovers recognize one another, and Mélanide faints. D'Orvigny, however, is no longer interested. He loves Rosalie. Mélanide eventually reveals to d'Arviane that he is illegitimate and hints that she is his mother. In the fifth act d'Arviane confronts d'Orvigny, who recognizes him as his son, although the formal revelation of his parentage is made to d'Arviane by Mélanide. D'Orvigny's passion for Mélanide is reawakened, and d'Arviane can marry Rosalie. Once again, however coincidentally, and after whatever emotional suspense, instinctive love turns out to have been virtuous and to have led to happiness. The emotion may spuriously derive from excessive reliance on mistakes, recognitions, and coincidences, and its articulation scarcely lifts the verse into the realm of poetry, but the reassurance that tenderness could lead to happiness, and that by the machinations of whatever good fairy, love might lead against outward appearances to virtuous fulfilment was exactly calculated to satisfy what was beginning to be recognizably middle-class taste in 18th-century Paris.

The complete failure of *Paméla*, hissed off the stage on 6 December 1743, seems to have been anticipated by the company, which had organized in the parterre a measure of support which turned out to be inadequate. An adaptation of Richardson's novel had already been a failure with the Italian company, who had gone on to make fun of themselves with *La Déroute des Paméla*. The French company, judged in retrospect, was certainly being foolhardy. On the other hand *L'Ecole des mères*, played on 27 April 1744, with 13 performances in the first run, and *La Gouvernante, comédie nouvelle en cinq actes en vers*, played on 18 January 1747, with 17 performances in the first run, were both given enthusiastic public welcomes. There were further plays, of which one originally entitled "Le Retour sur soi-même," which Collé amusingly announced as "un sermon du révérend Père de la Chaussée," "for which all seats had already been booked," and another, *L'Homme de fortune*, had been commissioned by Mme de Pompadour. Neither was successful.

Critics, in the wake of Lanson, have been harsh to Nivelle de la Chaussée. It is true that he had no sense of the comic and no power of invention, that he had neither a sufficiently developed sense of the ridiculous to write comedy, nor sufficient imaginative vigour to explore any major aspect of the human situation and to create tragedy. What he could do was accurately calculate the new tastes, attitudes, and values of his own generation, and cater for them further down the scale of literacy and sophistication than had previously been attempted. In doing that, he invented a new dramatic genre involving potentially tragic emotions in ordinary domestic situations in the lives of middle-class characters. He added pathos to the stiff neoclassical tragedy of the French company, and kept his pieces far more emotionally charged than suited the lightness of touch admitted by the Italians, to whom from time to time he did threaten to take his work, and who did create *L'Amour castillan*.

PUBLICATIONS

Collections

Oeuvres de théâtre, 8 parts, 1741–47
Oeuvres de M. N. de la C., 6 vols., 1762
Oeuvres de N. de la C., 6 parts, 1777–78

Plays

La Fausse Antipathie, comédie avec un prologue et la critique de cette pièce, par M. N. de la C., (1733), 1734
Le Préjugé à la mode, comédie en vers et en cinq actes, (1735) 1735
L'Ecole des amis, comédie en vers et en cinq actes, (1737) 1737
Maximien, tragédie, (1738) 1738
Mélanide, pièce nouvelle en cinq actes en vers, (1741) 1741
Amour pour amour, comédie en trois actes en vers, (1742) 1742

L'Ecole des mères, comédie nouvelle en cinq actes, (1744) 1745
Le Rival de lui-même, comédie nouvelle en un acte en vers, (1746) 1746
L'Amour castillan, (1747) 1747
La Gouvernante, comédie, (1747) 1747

Other

*Lettres de Mme la marquise de *** sur les "Fables nouvelles," avec la réponse servant d'apologie*, 1719
Epître à Clio, 1732
Contes et poésies de La C, 1880

Biographical and critical studies

Lanson, Gustave, *Nivelle de la Chaussée et la comédie larmoyante*, 1903

P

PALISSOT DE MONTENOY, Charles, 1730–1814.

Dramatist and poet.

LIFE

Palissot de Montenoy is not normally considered an important dramatist or poet in his own right. However, he came from a reactionary background and, while still little more than an ambitious tyro with one modest Paris success, he rightly calculated that he could achieve public acclaim by defying the modish new movement of intellectual liberalism coming to centre round the group to be known as the philosophes (q.v.). What gives his work importance is neither its intrinsic merits, in spite of the brilliance of the comic writing in the satirical comedy *Les Philosophes*, nor its significance in the history of literature, but the public reception it received, the use to which it was put, and the crystallisation of literary, social, and intellectual camps it brought about.

Palissot was born at Nancy on 3 January 1730, the son of a well-known Nancy lawyer and counsellor of the exiled king of Poland, Stanislas Leszczynski, Louis XV's father-in-law. Stanislas had been made sovereign duke of Bar and Lorraine by the treaty of Vienna in 1738, after failing to regain the throne of Poland in the war of Polish succession from 1733 to 1735, during which he had been backed by France. It was at Nancy, the capital of Lorraine, that he held his court. It was to become a centre of strong Catholic, aristocratic, and conservative reaction to the strongly emerging views and attitudes of the encyclopédiste (q.v.) movement.

The young Palissot was destined for the priesthood, and had begun his theological studies in preparation for joining the Congregation of the Oratory, but was not attracted by an ecclesiastical career and by the age of 19 had already composed two tragedies, *Zarès* and *Ninus II*. Both failed, and Palissot turned his hand to comedy with the two-act verse piece, *Les Tuteurs*, which was successful in 1754 at the Comédie-Française, and a short farce, *Le Barbier de Bagdad*. In the meanwhile, on the strength of a small pamphlet praising Montesquieu, Voltaire, and England, Palissot had in 1753 been admitted to the Société Royale des Sciences et Belles-Lettres founded by Stanislas Lesczcynski.

In September 1751 the *Mercure de France* (q.v.) had published a serious and lengthy critique of Rousseau's first *Discours*, at least partly by Stanislas himself. The *Discours*, published in 1750, was heavily pushed by the new editor of the *Mercure de France*, the abbé Raynal, to whom Grimm had introduced Rousseau, and who printed a letter and some verse of Rousseau in his September 1750 issue, an article praising the *Discours* in November, and excerpts from the *Discours* in January 1751. Raynal continued to draw attention to it thereafter, and in June printed some observations critical of it, together with Rousseau's reply. Three other pieces critical of Rousseau, in addition to that at least partly by the exiled king, were also published.

Palissot was also protected by the Choiseul family from Lunéville, 25 kilometres from Nancy, whose head, Louis XV's foreign minister from 1758 to 1770, was in 1754 not yet at all friendly towards Voltaire and the philosophes, although he was later to support them. With his 1753 brochure, Palissot could, however, quite unusually count on the support both of the party favourable to the encyclopédiste movement, with which Rousseau was still associated, and of that of the Nancy court, and of such other enemies of Voltaire as Fréron. The 1754 comedy was a success, and for the inauguration of a statue of Louis XV at Lunéville a play was commissioned from Palissot.

Palissot miscalculated. He based himself on Molière's paradigms, *Tartuffe* for the dynamics of comedy and for the structure *Les Fâcheux*, which had been written in a fortnight for Foucquet at Vaux in such a way that the dancers for the accompanying ballet had had time to change during the acts. Molière's play at Vaux had therefore been little more than a procession or portrait gallery of comic dramatic interludes. Palissot's play, originally called "Les Originaux" but then renamed *Le Cercle*, was essentially a procession of burlesquely caricatured philosophes, including a lampoon of Rousseau. Palissot thought his dismissive treatment of the philosophe, by now on account also of the second *Discours* popularly associated with the advocacy of a return to nature, would commend itself to Stanislas, who was present. In fact the ex-king's grand marshal, the comte de Tressan, and d'Alembert, who had not yet broken with either Rousseau or the *Encyclopédie*, both protested, and Stanislas, annoyed and embarrassed, gave instructions to remove Palissot from the membership of his academy, rescinding them only when Rousseau pleaded on Palissot's behalf.

Palissot, who was never himself to fall out with Voltaire, now penned a grovelling apology to Stanislas, drafted but did not send a sarcastic one to Rousseau—"Your behaviour shows the true philosopher that I do not always see in your writings"—and wrote to Rousseau's Protestant friend, Jacob Vernes, that he thought it wily of Rousseau to have "rectified an imaginary offence by demanding pardon for the accused." Rousseau wrote to Vernes rightly "doubting if M. Palissot will forgive the good turn I have done him," and Palissot, feeling that he cast his die and could now only hope to succeed by advancing further along his chosen path, published in 1757 the *Petites Lettres sur de grands philosophes*, astutely attacking more the arrogant assumptions of righteousness among the encyclopédistes than their actual opinions, but making a central thrust against Diderot's *Le Fils naturel*, going straight for the flagship of the movement. He had in the meanwhile been granted the lucrative monopoly of tobacco sales at Avignon in 1756, whose profits allowed him to buy the house at Argenteuil to which he eventually retired.

By 1760 Choiseul was foreign minister, and the *Encyclopédie* was apparently foundering. D'Alembert had withdrawn from everything except the mathematical entries; Voltaire was suggesting that it was time to abandon the enterprise altogether; the *Encyclopédie*'s privilège had been revoked; Rome had condemned it; in November 1759 Diderot had been accused of fraudulently using Réaumur's plates, and legal proceedings were pending. This was the moment which Palissot sensibly chose for what might have been a coup de grâce, his celebrated comedy *Les Philosophes*. Its acceptance by the company of the Comédie-Française on 22 March 1760 may well have been due to official pressure, since it was backed by Choiseul and the dauphin. Some members of the company, including Mlle Clairon, were unhappy that the company had agreed to play it at all. The first performance on 2 May was noisy but successful, largely because the actor Préville, playing Crispin, the caricature of Rousseau, whose break with the encyclopédistes was naturally public knowledge, came in for one of his entrances on all fours, as laid down by Palissot. The first run of 14 performances made the play honourably successful, although the critical reception, even by those hostile to the philosophes, like Fréron and Collé, was not good.

There was no very great sensation. The list of certainly or probably recognizable caricatures or allusions excluded Voltaire, but included Rousseau, Duclos, Diderot, Grimm, and perhaps Mme d'Epinay. Rousseau, against whom the attack had been indulgent, later said that he had returned a copy of the play to the publisher, Duchesne, who had sent it to him, remarking that he was friendly with someone whom it had calumniated. Diderot, at whom the attack was chiefly aimed, remained silent, although he did confide his anger to *Le Neveu de Rameau*, which he did not intend anyone but himself ever to read. Voltaire replied in *Le Café; ou, L'Ecossaise*, first performed on 26 July, although written in January and published at much the same time as the opening run of *Les Philosophes*. However, Voltaire's play, written before he had seen Palissot's text, attacked not Palissot so much as Fréron. An anonymous preface to Palissot's play, attacking it, was published after the play was already on sale. The author, Morellet, was uncovered and sent to the Bastille for two months, after which he was released through the mediation of the maréchal de Luxembourg at the instigation of Rousseau. Palissot published an authentic preface pressing home his original attack. The Comédie-Française played both Voltaire's *Le Café; ou, L'Ecossaise* and Diderot's *Le Père de famille*, a gesture of reparation which ran for no more than seven performances. It was only the revival in a toned-down version of 1769 which established Diderot's play as a theatrical success.

After 1760 Palissot achieved no further literary fame. In 1764 he published the satirical poem modelled on Pope against the encyclopédistes, *La Dunciade; ou, La Guerre des sots*, in three cantos, to which would be added a further seven for the three-volume London 1771 edition. Diderot and Duclos were attacked, but also Fréron, with whom Palissot had apparently quarrelled. Official policy, recognizing the strength of the new ideas, had come to protect the philosophes and, at their request, a new play by Palissot, *L'Homme dangereux*, was banned in 1770. The Comédie–Française played four of Palissot's plays together in 1782, including a new *Les Courtisanes*. Rousseau had died in 1778, and the text of *Les Philosophes* was toned down. In the revival Crispin no longer came on walking on all fours, after the first performance, at which he was interrupted by

a cabale when he did. The name of the character caricaturing Diderot was changed from Dortidius to Marphurius, the sceptical doctor from Molière's *Le Mariage forcé*.

At the Revolution Palissot turned wholly to the republican spirit, became the idol of M.-J. Chénier, undertook an edition of Voltaire's works, attended the club des Jacobins, and delivered a diatribe against religion whose violence alarmed even Robespierre. The convention voted him a pension in 1795, and he was quick to attach himself to the rising star of Bonaparte. He was made administrator of the Mazarine library but Naigeon prevented his appointment to the Institut, except as a corresponding member. The notes he left show that Palissot's opposition to the philosophes did not diminish. He became a member of the Conseil des Anciens for Seine-et-Oise in 1798–99 and, after joining an esoteric religious sect, became a Catholic again, and died in retirement in June 1814.

WORKS

Much ill has been spoken of *Les Philosophes*, which is a workmanlike polemical 18th-century piece, visibly inspired by Molière, whose matrix from *Les Femmes savantes* it uses, as the audience will instantly have recognized. The play's ephemeral success derived from the precision and sharpness of its pointed satire in the particular situation whose boldness in the circumstances of the spring of 1760 it is now virtually impossible for any non-specialist to gauge. The question has unfortunately obscured proper critical discussion of the not so ephemeral skill of the brilliant, if superficial, comic writing. Palissot seems to have estimated correctly just what would succeed in public, producing vigorous shafts of satire which did little permanent damage, but were accurately calculated to fit into the mechanism by which shifting public attitudes and opinions restrained progress from moving too fast, and prevented reaction from refusing to cede ground the theatre-going public was ready to yield.

Palissot combines a general attack on encyclopédiste attitudes with quite specific allusions to individuals and their writings. He avoids any direct reference to Voltaire or d'Alembert, both of whom had more or less dissociated themselves from the *Encyclopédie*, concentrates the attack on Diderot, its editor, caricatured as Dortidius, and is quite restrained about Rousseau, "Au fond plein de droiture et de sincérité (In reality, filled with uprightness and sincerity)" (Act II, sc,vi), and no longer associated with Diderot and Grimm. The philosophers are depicted as the aggressors, a set of pantomime villains attacking the traditional attitudes to behaviour, religion, the family and the country.

Palissot's authentic preface, replying to the satirical pseudo-preface by Morellet, is strong, tarring the *Encyclopédie* with the brush of Hobbes and Spinoza, underlining the strong points of Palissot's attack:

Une secte impérieuse, formée à l'ombre d'un ouvrage dont l'exécution pouvait illustrer le siècle, exerçait un despotisme rigoureux sur les sciences, les lettres, les arts et les moeurs. Armée du flambeau de la philosophie, elle avait porté l'incendie dans les esprits, au lieu d'y répandre la lumière; elle attaquait la religion, les lois et la morale; elle prêchait le pyrrhonisme, l'indépendance; et, dans le temps où elle détruisait toute autorité, elle usurpait une tyrannie universelle

(An imperious sect, formed in the shadow of a work whose execution might have added glory to the century, exercised a rigorous despotism over the sciences, letters, technology, and moral values. Armed with the torch of philosophy, it had set minds on fire instead of flooding them with light; it attacked religion, law, and morality; it preached scepticism and independence; and at the same time as it destroyed all authority, it arrogated to itself a universal tyranny).

The play is set "in Paris" and only one of the ten characters, "M. Propice the hawker" is listed by more than a bare name. There are three acts, in alexandrines. It reads today like a light-weight satirical comedy, and deliberately adopts the sort of tone assumed by Molière when attacking a fashionable fad in *Les Précieuses ridicules*, but there are obvious direct allusions which have not been identified. It is quite likely that the characters in the play are composite, caricaturing simultaneously a number of different originals.

The play opens when Damis, an officer in love with, and loved by, Rosalie, is told by Marton, employed as a companion by Cydalise, Rosalie's mother, how things have changed. For Rosalie to marry an officer would be a mésalliance, they need a philosopher. Perhaps in another three months everything will have changed again. Damis should come back and see. Marton gives a portrait of Cydalise which may to allude to some individual figure whom the audience was expected to recognize:

Toute femme est, monsieur, un animal changeant.
On pourrait calculer les jours de Cydalise
Par les différents goûts dont son âme est éprise:
Quelquefois étourdie, enjouée à l'excès,
D'autres fois sérieuse et boudant par accès;
Coquette, s'il en fut, même jusqu'au scandale;
Prude à nous étourdir de son aigre morale;
Courant le bal la nuit, et le jour les sermons,
Tantôt les directeurs et tantôt les bouffons.
C'était là le bon temps. Mais aujourd'hui que l'âge
Fait place à d'autres moeurs, et veut un ton plus sage,
Madame a depuis peu réformé sa maison.
Nous n'extravaguons plus qu'à force de raison.
D'abord on a banni cette gaîté grossière,
Délices des traitants, aliment du vulgaire;
A nos soupers décents tout au plus on sourit.
Si l'on s'ennuie, au moins c'est avec de l'esprit

(Every woman, Monsieur, is a changeable animal./You could measure the age of Cydalise/By the different tastes which have possessed her:/Sometimes scatter-brained, playful to excess,/At other times serious with sulky fits;/A coquette if ever there was one, even to the point of scandal;/Then a prude deafening us with her sour moralising;/Going dancing by night and to sermons by day,/Sometimes it was spiritual directors and sometimes buffoons./Those were the good old days. But now that age/Has substituted different behavior, demanding a more sedate tone,/Madame has recently reformed her household./Our only excesses now are those of reason./To start with that vulgar cheerfulness has been banished,/Delight of financiers, food for the mob;/At our respectable suppers the very most we do is smile./If we are bored, at least we do it with wit).

Since some amusement is necessary, there is serious music, reasoned debate, political discussion, "Enfin tout disparut sous la métaphysique (Finally everything was engulfed in metaphysics)."

On its own register that passage is good theatre, light-hearted satire on excess, with neatly pointed antitheses and a touch of wit. It is an obvious little set piece in an opening scene, more than averagely entertaining. Is he talking about Mme d'Epinay, insiders in the audience might have wondered? It does not really matter. Damis insists, "What about Rosalie?" "The same as everyone else, Monsieur; she is bored." We learn at least that she is not interested in Damis's rival, and Marton tells Damis that his chances depend on the mother, whose heart Damis had once touched. She is now, Marton lets drop, around 50, but there is, she says, worse to come. Madame has written a book, a proper quarto. Damis wonders whether one of her new friends could not tell her that she is making a fool of herself. No, says Marton. They laugh at her: "Ils ont tous conspiré de gâter sa cervelle,/ Surtout votre rival (They have all connived to ruin her brain/ Especially your rival)."

The intrigue is Molière's, but instead of one Tartuffe there is a whole group of philosophers to exploit the rich, foolish, and illusioned Cydalise. Marton suspects one of the people they have got Cydalise to employ, M. Carondas, of being placed in the household by Damis's rival, about whom we still know nothing. As the first scene ends, Damis mentions his friend Crispin, and we gather Marton is attached to him. Rosalie professes her love for Damis, but her mother plans to marry her to the philosophe Valère who will guide, instruct, and educate Rosalie, and teach her to think. When Rosalie adduces the wishes of her dead father, Cydalise gives another long portrait of this "Défenseur ennuyeux des préjugés gothiques (Boring defender of medieval prejudices)" of much the same standard as that of Cydalise given by Marton. Any modern audience which can laugh at Molière could not help being amused at the advantages Cydalise depicts to Rosalie as ensuing from the marriage to Valère planned for that evening.

Act II starts when Valère addresses the planted scholar, "Tout hérissé de grec et de termes d'école (All bristling with Greek and the terminology of the schools)," by his real name of Frontin, as if a philosopher could have so ordinary a name. The contempt of Valère and M. Carondas for the public baffled by the learning and authority of the philosophers is boundless. Valère's contempt for Cydalise is cruel. His defence of acting in no-one's interest but his own is wicked, but very funny. The plan to plant half a dozen scandalous statements in Cydalise's book to ensure its success is maliciously ingenious and wittily defended. Valère has a whole quiver-full of darted aphorisms at his disposal—"La franchise est la vertu d'un sot (sincerity is a fool's virtue)"; "Il s'agit d'être heureux, il n'importe comment (What is important is being happy. It does not matter how),"—but is of course furious when he catches M. Carondas attempting to pick his pocket, taking full advantage of the right conferred on him by "L'intérêt personnel (self-interest)."

Palissot sustains this level of comedy. It often touches farce, and the verse never rises to poetry but, played fast enough, the piece would still be very entertaining. It is more important to be able to quote Diderot than to know who Thales or Anaxagoras were. The polemical intent, the ridiculing of Diderot, viciously unmasked by Damis and absurdly defended by Cydalise, and the relevance to a particular ideological dispute have unfortunately made *Les Philosophes* the preserve of scholars, although for comic verve it ranks with Beaumarchais.

Crispin, who shares with Rousseau his trade of copying, comes to Damis's aid. They will simply abduct Rosalie. They do not have to as Crispin, on all fours, comes in to give Cydalise a note deriding her, written by Valère. She is disillusioned and, after the deployment of various comic devices, particularly very brief interrupted speeches, the hawker offering works of the encyclopédistes for sale, the organization of a defence by the philosophers against some comic dramatist who wanted to make fun of them, Cydalise's disillusion allows Marton to marry Crispin and Rosalie to marry Damis. To Rosalie's relief, Cydalise is restored to her senses.

PUBLICATIONS

Collections

Théâtre et oeuvres diverses, 3 vols., 1763
Oeuvres, 6 vols., 1777
Oeuvres complètes, 4 vols., 1788; 6 vols., 1809

Plays

Zarès, tragédie, 1751
Le Cercle, (1755) 1755
Les Tuteurs, comédie en deux actes (1754), 1755
Les Philosophes, (1760), 1760; in *Théâtre du XVIIIe siècle*, Bibliothèque de la Pleiade edition, 1974
Le Rival par ressemblance, comédie en cinq actes et en vers, 1762
L'Homme dangereux, 1770
Les Courtisanes; ou, L'École des moeurs, comédie en trois actes et en vers, (1775) 1775
Le Triomphe de Sophocle, (1782) 1782
Le Satirique, (1782) 1782

Other

Apollon menteur; ou, Le Télémaque moderne, 1748
Epître au roi sur ses victoires et sur la paix 1749
Zelinga, histoire chinoise, 1749
Histoire raisonnée des premiers siècles de Rome, 2 vols., 1756
Petites Lettres sur de grands philosophes, 1757
Préface de la comédie des philosophes, 1760
La Dunciade; ou, La Guerre des sots, poème, 3 cantos 1764; 10 cantos, 1771
Mémoires pour servir à l'histoire de notre littérature, 2 vols., 1771
La Mort de Voltaire, ode, 1780
Questions importantes sur quelques opinions religieuses, 1791

Biographical and critical studies

Delafarge, D., *La Vie et l'oeuvre de Palissot*, 1912,

PASCAL, Blaise, 1623–1662.

Religious writer and scientist.

LIFE

Pascal, although he is often correctly thought to have been the first great writer of classical French prose, never wrote a book. He was a scientist, who left a number of mathematical and scientific papers, some of which are of outstanding interest, but he is remembered for his moral and spiritual writings, especially the series of fly-sheets known as *Les Lettres provinciales* written in 1656–57, and a series of fragments, some at least of which were noted down in view of Pascal's intention to compose a Christian apologetic, which were published in 1670, under the somewhat misleading title of *Pensées* and in heavily cosmeticized form, by Pascal's Jansenist (q.v.) associates connected with the monastery of Port-Royal (q.v.). The *Pensées* contain a very powerful analysis of some aspects of human spiritual experience in the light of Pascal's understanding of the Christian revelation, but are not homogeneous, and vary from relatively long fragments of polished prose about man's nature and destiny to short *aide-mémoires*, some of which are too elliptical to be comprehensible.

Pascal was born on 19 June 1623 at Clermont, a small provincial town near the administrative centres of Montferrand and Riom, where his grandfather had headed the financial administration of Auvergne. Pascal's father, Etienne (1588–1651), was one of at least seven children and the eldest son. After Etienne had studied law in Paris the post of tax assessor (conseiller élu) was bought for him in 1610, and then, in 1626, the year Pascal's mother died, that of second judge (Président) in the tax court (Cour des Aides) of Montferrand, for 31,000 livres. He thereby became a member of the minor nobility. In 1616 or 1617 he had married Antoinette Begon (1596–1626), daughter of a wealthy merchant, by whom he had three children who survived infancy, a first daughter, born in December 1617, having lived only a few days. The eldest surviving child was Gilberte (1620–87), who was in 1641 to marry Florin Périer, a rich lawyer from Clermont, and later to write her brother's life. Then came Pascal himself, and lastly Jacqueline, to become Soeur Sainte-Euphémie at Port-Royal. Pascal, whose later poor health is often, but perhaps incorrectly, thought to have prevented the completion of the apologetic, was seriously ill for a year during his infancy, of which we know very little. In 1631 Etienne took his three children to live in Paris, returning each year for a few months to Clermont, where he sold in 1633 his house and in 1634 his legal post to his brother.

The children were cared for by a governess, Louise Delfault, who remained with the family for 20 years. Etienne rather surprisingly did not remarry, and himself taught his children according to his own plan, which involved starting Latin and Greek later than in the Jesuit schools, for instance, and leaving mathematics until last, when Pascal was 14 or 15. At all stages he used teaching material which excited the imagination of his children, and which they could master. Etienne was an enthusiastic amateur scientist and mathematician, and a person of some social standing. His children were quickly introduced into leading social and intellectual groups in Paris, particularly into the circle of Mme Saintot, the former mistress of Voiture, sister of the poet Vion-d'Alibray, and friend of Bensserade and Saint-

Amant, but also of the learned group mostly of scientists and mathematicians which formed from 1635 round Père Mersenne of the Minim branch of the Franciscan order. Etienne, and apparently his friends, treated his children from very early on as young adults.

In 1635 Etienne was appointed to a commission formed to examine a new method of determining longitude. With Roberval he was to be sceptical about the non-empirical theories of Descartes. Pascal was to inherit many of his father's views, particularly on scientific and mathematical method, preferring Fermat to Descartes, and geometry to algebra. He appears to have shown a real precociousness in the elaboration of geometrical theorems and, having written an essay on sounds by 1634, while he was still 16, had the first sketch printed of a much longer treatise on conic sections which has subsequently been lost. Etienne, while observing the religious decencies, was not devout, and the family did not then feel drawn to a life of committed piety. Jacqueline, according to her sister, at this date even regarded religious life with some abhorrence. In 1636 Etienne, leaving Jacqueline with Mme Saintot and her children, went with Gilberte and Blaise to Auvergne, whence they returned in 1637.

There had been a financial crisis. Within weeks of arriving in Paris in November 1631 Etienne was paying a rent of 440 livres a year for a residence near the fashionable Marais, where the Place Royale, now the Place des Vosges, had just been built. In 1633 the Clermont house had been sold in March, and Pascal's father had borrowed 3,500 livres in May. The family moved to a grander establishment at a rent of 600 livres in April 1634, and that November Etienne sold his post at the Cour des Aides. In 1635, however, he moved again, to the neighbourhood of the Hôtel de Roannez, where Pascal established his firm friendship with the young duc de Roannez. The apartment was to be kept until 1648, even while the family was living in Rouen, and the rent was 225 livres. We know that Pascal's father had invested his money in state bonds, but by 1638 the interest payments were in arrears. Gilberte in 1679 was able to redeem what was left for no more than a sixth of their nominal value. In 1638, Etienne took part in a protest by bond-holders to the Chancellor, Séguier. Richelieu had the chief protesters put in the Bastille. Etienne went into hiding and, after nursing Jacqueline through smallpox, took refuge in Auvergne.

His rehabilitation was arranged early in 1639. Jacqueline, whose precocious poetic talent was well known at court, was invited by Richelieu's niece, the duchesse d'Aiguillon, and his resident poet, Boisrobert, to play Cassandre in a private performance of Scudéry's *Amour tyannique* before Richelieu. Gilberte had made some difficulty, but Jacqueline was received by the Cardinal and was taken on his knee. Her father was then received with his children by the Cardinal at Rueil, and soon given the post of tax collector in Normandy. Etienne arrived in Rouen on 2 January 1640 in Séguier's entourage, charged with getting the tax for which it was assessed out of an impoverished Normandy population almost in open rebellion. Pascal was sufficiently aware of what was going on to conceive his horror of popular uprisings.

When Gilberte married on 13 June 1641, with a dowry worth about 21,000 livres, Etienne had her husband posted to Normandy. In 1642 the young couple had the first of their six children, Etienne, whom they left with his grandfather when in 1643 they returned to Clermont. Etienne Pascal at this time got to know Pierre Corneille, who took an interest in Jacqueline's attempts at writing verse. Pascal himself was now being sent on errands to Paris and Clermont on behalf of his father, whose mathematical calculations inspired Pascal to invent his manual calculating machine. It was not really ready until 1644. Six versions of it exist. A dedicatory letter to Séguier was published in 1645 in return for a privilège which amounted to a patent. Although, when it was sold commercially, it was considered expensive at 100 livres, it did make Pascal's name.

In January 1646 Etienne Pascal fell on the ice and dislocated his thigh. He was cared for by the two Deschamps brothers, members of a small group from the minor aristocracy who, under the direction of Jean Guillebert, a former penitent of Saint-Cyran's, were devoting themselves to caring for the sick. They stayed in the Pascal house for three months and succeeded in converting first Pascal, then Jacqueline, and then through them their father, to an austerely intense devotional life, also adopted by the Périers when they came to stay later in the year. Pascal, however did not abandon his scientific pursuits. The Périers continued to climb socially, although Gilberte took away from her children the ribbons with which they had enjoyed playing, and Jacqueline gave up the idea of marriage. When, however, two years later she finally decided to become a nun, her father strongly opposed her.

As a child Pascal had clearly been nervous and intense. He is said by Gilberte's daughter, Marguerite, presumably relying on family gossip, to have been unable as an infant to endure the sight of running water, or of his parents embracing. As a baby he had been given up for lost. At 18 he had been seriously ill, paralyzed to the waist, and from 1641 on his health was never good, although we have no reliable record of the dates of the various symptoms. In the spring of 1647 he now suffered from severe headaches and became able to take only very warm liquid nourishment administered drop by drop. He returned with Jacqueline to Paris, where his doctors, presumably in an attempt to relax the damaging nervous intensity which had gained him a reputation for irascibility and impatience, encouraged him to cultivate wider interests.

Late in 1646 Pierre Petit, the "intendant" in charge of ports and fortifications, called to see Etienne Pascal on his way to Dieppe to inspect a diving bell. They discussed Torricelli's experiments in which a tube of mercury, turned upside down into a bowl of the metal, exhibited a gap at the top. Petit and the Pascals successfully repeated the experiment, and an account was sent to Pierre Chanut, the French ambassador in Sweden, who was also a friend of Descartes. Descartes, like the scholastics, held that there could not be a vacuum at the top of the tube. Pascal invented a number of experiments employing different sized tubes and different liquids, in one case using two 40-foot tubes tied to a ship's mast. Descartes called on him in Paris on 23 and 24 September 1647, and in October Pascal published a paper on the Rouen experiments, the *Expériences nouvelles touchant le vide*. His experiments became increasingly rigorous, ingenious, and elaborate. They depended partly on the skill of the Rouen glass-blowers.

Pascal appears never to have acknowledged that it was Descartes who suggested repeating the same experiment at the top and at the bottom of a mountain, but on 15 November 1647 wrote to his brother-in-law, asking him to carry out such an experiment. Mersenne's circle had resisted Torricelli's conclusions about atmospheric pressure, but they had already been experimentally proved in June by Adrien Auzout, a friend of Mersenne and Pascal, when Périer confirmed the results on 19 September 1648, making the necessary measurements at the Puy-de-Dôme, just 18 days after Mersenne's death. Pascal published the *Récit de la grande expérience de l'équilibre des liqueurs* in October, confirming both the action of atmospheric pressure and Galileo's hypothesis on the existence of a vacuum. Pascal was later to exaggerate the originality of his own ideas, and to behave with some superciliousness towards the Père Noël, rector of the Jesuit Collège de Clermont in Paris, an Aristotelian and a former teacher of Descartes, who had written to Pascal in defence of the semi-Cartesian hypothesis that the top of the tube was filled with "purified" air. Pascal was also to be prickly when he published a letter in reply to a casual remark about the possibility that he might have claimed the credit for Torricelli's originality.

Early in 1647 Pascal, together with Auzout, had launched himself with some zeal into an attack on a former Capucin, Père Saint-Ange, author of a 3-volume work on the alliance of faith and reason, who was hoping for a benefice at Rouen. Saint-Ange had already caused some trouble with his strange religious opinions, although his belief that the doctrine of the Trinity could be rationally proved was one which Sebond had maintained in the famous *Theologia naturalis* defended by Montaigne. Pascal brought the matter to Jean-Pierre Camus, the coadjutor bishop, who took no action. Pascal and his friends then took things further, to the retired archbishop, and forced Saint-Ange to make humiliating retractions, although he obtained his benefice. Not much more can be inferred from this episode than Pascal's aggressive righteousness, and his desire to keep rational speculation to its own domain, which was that neither of faith nor of empirical science.

From late in 1647 Pascal and Jacqueline had started to go to Port-Royal, where Guillebert had taken them to hear Antoine Singlin preach. Pascal was soon keener to take Port-Royal's side in the religious disputes than Port-Royal was to have his support. The touch of arrogance in his partisanship did not now or in the future go unremarked by the more spiritually discerning of the religious figures associated with the monastery, especially not by Singlin and, later on, Saci. Etienne Pascal's post in Normandy had been discontinued and, on 1 October 1648, he had taken up residence again in Paris, this time paying a rent of 700 livres. By this date Jacqueline knew that she wished to become a nun at Port-Royal, and Pascal took her side against their father. Meanwhile, she lived a withdrawn life at home, as she also did at Clermont, where Etienne took Pascal and his sister from May 1649 to November 1650 to escape the Fronde. Etienne Pascal died on 24 September 1651, within a year of returning to Paris. Pascal's letter to Gilberte on that occasion is considered the most important of the handful of his spiritual letters which have survived.

On his father's death Pascal moved into a smaller apartment and asked Jacqueline at least to postpone her entry to the convent. Gilberte had come to Paris in December 1651 in connection with her father's estate, and arranged for Jacqueline to slip away before dawn on 4 January 1652. She was to take the veil in May. Etienne's succession was complicated. There were debts to be paid, provisions to be made, and Gilberte's dowry to be taken into account, and it seems certain that Pascal resented the amount of money which Jacqueline wanted given to the monastery, which finally offered to profess her without a dowry.

From October 1652 until May 1653 Pascal was at Clermont, still settling the inheritance, having sent one of his arithmetic machines to Queen Christina of Sweden. In the end he allowed the convent to have more than Jacqueline had asked for, and he attended her profession on 5 June 1653. He was however himself short of money, unable to afford to live in the style called for by his position.

It looks as if Pascal's own religious enthusiasm may have waned, and there are uncertain indications of a female presence in his life. There is some evidence that he was thinking of marrying. He spent some time in the company of Méré and the financier Mitton, who frequented his old friend, the duc de Roannez, now governor of Poitou. He had probably written the important *Préface. Sur le traité du vide* in 1651 and, perhaps stimulated by Méré's gambling interests, he concerned himself with the mathematical calculation of probabilities, corresponded about it with Fermat, and wrote his *Traité du triangle arithmétique*. In the autumn of 1653 Pascal was in Poitou staying with Roannez and with Méré. During the summer of 1654 his intellectual life was at its most intense, although Jacqueline tells us that he was already depressed by the shallowness of his existence. Religious devotion however did not yet offer an attractive alternative. He moved his lodgings on 1 October. Then on the 23 November he underwent the famous spiritual experience recorded in the *Mémorial* which for the rest of his life he kept on his person. The event no doubt released a spiritual tension which had been building up within him for months. By early December, Jacqueline announced on the 8th, Pascal had given himself into the hands of his spiritual director, Singlin.

Pascal confided in Roannez before leaving on 7 January 1655 to make a retreat at Port-Royal-des-Champs. He stayed a fortnight, partly at the Granges, where the "solitaires" gathered, and where he had the conversation recorded as the *Entretien avec M de Saci* by Fontaine, Saci's secretary, to whom Pascal must have given written notes. What Pascal is recorded as having said is clearly also not the result of a sudden inspiration, but the elegant expression of a mature reflection. Pascal spent some days at the Paris Port-Royal monastery before returning home. His housekeeper, the sister of Louise Delfault, lived in the house with her husband and two daughters, and there was also a man-servant and a cook. Jacqueline found her brother a little too pleased with himself for a true penitent. In the spring he stayed with Roannez and was successful in converting him. Roannez, short of money although a duke and peer, abandoned the idea of a marriage that would have restored the family fortunes, and there may well have been a family conspiracy to have Pascal assassinated. He is said to have escaped by getting up and going out earlier than expected on the appointed day. During the course of the year Arnauld wrote the two letters which resulted in the campaign to have him stripped of his doctorate. The case came before the Sorbonne in January. Pascal made another retreat at Port-Royal-des-Champs, where Arnauld was in semi-hiding, and Pascal was asked to "do something." The first of the *Lettres provinciales* was dated 23 January 1656.

Arnauld was in fact condemned, the solitaires were to be dispersed and the Port-Royal schools closed (see: Port-Royal). Pascal continued with the *Lettres*, changing subject matter, tone, and eventually addressee. The letters at first tried to demonstrate that Arnauld's position did not go any further than Augustine's, then turned to the moral law, to casuistry, Jesuit confessional practice and its relationship to Jesuit doctrine on grace, and then to defending Pascal's own position against attack. The documentation was provided by Arnauld, Nicole, and a small team of sympathizers with the Port-Royal cause. There are 18 full letters, of which the last is dated 24 March 1657. A 19th was scarcely begun. The Port-Royal party was greatly encouraged by what they took to be divine intervention in their favour when, on 24 March 1656, after the fifth letter, Gilberte's 12-year-old daughter, Pascal's niece Marguerite, a boarder at Port-Royal suffering from an ulcer, or perhaps a tumour in the lachrymal duct, was cured within days after the application to her eye of a borrowed relic of the Crown of Thorns. She had been medically examined eight weeks before the incident, and medical evidence is available again seven days after it. Port-Royal knew many such cures, one earlier and many later, but the miraculous nature of this one was declared on 22 October by the diocesan authorities.

The *Lettres provinciales* were published anonymously and disseminated by a small group headed by Nicolas Vitart, Racine's cousin and the intendant of the duc de Luynes, a friend of Port-Royal with whom Pascal had stayed for a few days before making his first retreat at Port-Royal-des-Champs in January 1655. It was to Luynes that Arnauld had written the *Seconde lettre à un duc et pair*, accepting, at least theoretically, that the five propositions condemned by the bull *Cum occasione* of 1653 were erroneous (the question of "droit" or right), but denying that they were in the 1640 *Augustinus* of Jansen (see: Jansenism) (the question of "fait" or fact). It was this letter that caused the authorities to seek to strip Arnauld of his doctorate, and which therefore started the train of events leading to the "petites lettres." They were published in volume form and pseudonymously ascribed to "Louis de Montalte" in 1657 and put on the Index of forbidden books in late October, ostensibly because, being in the vernacular, they brought what should have remained theological dispute into the public domain. They were translated into Latin by Nicole, under the name of Guillaume Wendrock, in 1658.

While he was writing them Pascal lived an almost fugitive life, although in fact the Chancellor Séguier's police caught only printers, some of whom were briefly imprisoned. Pascal himself spent some time at an inn, stayed with Roannez, who came back from Poitou in May 1656, and was occasionally at Port-Royal-des-Champs. An *Apologie pour les casuistes* by Georges Pirot, a Jesuit theology professor from the Collège de Clermont, appeared in December 1657. It was later to be put on the Roman Index of prohibited books, was inept, and was immediately attacked by a series of *Ecrits des curés de Paris* in the first two of which Pascal certainly had some hand, and the fifth of which he is said to have regarded as the best thing he had written. Meanwhile, after the cure of Marguerite Périer, Pascal began to think of writing an apologetic. It would have been of the traditional type, based on the probative power of miracles and the realization of prophecies. Later in 1657 he was to abandon this idea in favour of a much wider apologetic project, based on an analysis of the human situation in the world, the significance bestowed on human life only in the light of the Christian revelation, and the certainty of death. This was the project on which Pascal gave a conference at Port-Royal probably in May 1658, although it may have been in October of that year, and in view of which during the course of 1658 he partially completed the classification of his fragmentary notes, to which, in the light of what he now intended to write, he must also at this period have added.

Probably towards the end of 1655, although it may have been later, Pascal had written *De l'esprit géométrique*, including *De l'art de persuader*, and at least revised the *Ecrits sur la grâce*, which may have been drafted earlier. He had written what amounted virtually to letters of austere spiritual direction to Roannez's younger sister who, in spite of the opposition of her mother, became a nun at Port-Royal in 1657. She was later to leave the monastery, but to keep her vow of chastity until relieved of it in 1667 to marry the duc de la Feuillade. On 1 June 1657 Pascal collaborated in the *Lettre d'un Avocat au Parlement* drawn up by Antoine le Maistre, which succeeded in persuading the parlement not, in any very serious way, to implement the Bull *Ad sacram* of 16 October 1656. The Bull assumed that the five propositions were in fact in the *Augustinus* and had been accepted by Louis XIV. The parlement, however, was strongly attached to the liberties of the Gallican church and did not welcome Rome's interference in its affairs. It registered the Bull without imposing a formulary to be signed, so that for the time being peace was established. Pascal's own moral fervour was still undiminished when, in 1659, the Périers were envisaging a rich marriage for their daughter Jacqueline, not apparently herself consulted and still at 15 a boarder at Port-Royal. The nuns were strongly opposed and Pascal wrote a very strong denunciation of marriage as "the most dangerous and lowest of Christian conditions."

In the meanwhile, however, Pascal, who had already invented a proof of the binomial theorem, had in 1658 been working on the properties of the cycloid. He had been writing textbooks of grammar and geometry for the Port-Royal schools, and on his return to serious mathematical investigation had made discoveries that were to lead to modern integral calculus, although he was far too much of a geometrician to draw the algebraical conclusions. In the interests of establishing that rigorous intellectual procedures were not incompatible with the Port-Royal position, Roannez offered a prize in 1658 to any mathematician who could solve six problems to which Pascal had already found solutions. In the end Pascal discovered that Roberval had already solved four of them, and there were only two contenders for the prize. The whole affair collapsed among bitternesses and recriminations.

From February 1659 until June 1660 Pascal was again ill. The accurate assessment of his state of health from 1658 until his death is of crucial importance for the interpretation of the fragments for which he is best remembered, the *Pensées*. Gilberte, often reliable in the two versions of her account of her brother's life, is also often verifiably inaccurate. In particular she plays down the extent of his scientific activities and the importance he attached to them, and tries always to present his life with an edifying gloss. She tells us a good deal about his last years which we know to be untrue, and it cannot be the case that he was, as she says, during the last four years of his life, that is from the summer of 1658, so "pitiably" suffering from nervous exhaustion ("langueur") that "il ne put rien faire (he could do nothing)." There are internal indications in the fragments that the apologetic task Pascal had set himself was impossible, and that he came to know that to be so. The generally held view, not vigorously challenged until 1982, that Pascal was too ill to finish his apologetic, relies almost totally on Gilberte Périer's declaration, and is certainly wrong. Did Gilberte exaggerate her brother's illness in order to protect his reputation, giving out after his death, and perhaps believing, that only illness had prevented him from extracting from the disordered and mutually incompatible fragments the eagerly awaited apologetic?

Pascal was indeed ill from February 1659, when Carcavi mentioned it in a letter to Huyghens, until May 1660, when he left Paris to stay with the Périers and to take the waters at Clermont. On 28 July 1660 Saint-Gilles wrote to Huyghens to say that Pascal was very much better than he had been. The year of illness is well attested. The symptoms were above all an inability to concentrate, although Pascal did manage to write works of piety. By early in 1660 he appears to have been recovering. In August he wrote to Fermat from Clermont that he needed a stick for walking and could not ride. He still found reading and writing difficult, and was uncertain about a projected visit to Poitou until Christmas, travelling by river, but this does not suggest enduring intellectual incapacity. By October he was back in Paris and in November he wrote the three *Discours sur la condition des grands* for the duc de Chevreuse, Luynes's son and Lancelot's pupil. In the following month he wrote to Mme de Sablé about the content of a book she had sent him, written by her Protestant doctor, Menjot.

In 1661 the attack on Port-Royal and Jansenism was renewed. On 13 April a civil decree demanded the signature of a formulary by all teachers, ecclesiastics, and religious. The Port-Royal schools were closed, Port-Royal was forbidden to accept further novices, and the solitaires living a quasi-hermit existence at Port-Royal-des-Champs were dispersed, but the formulary, which Pascal may have helped to draw up, still allowed the mental reservation of distinguishing between the erroneous propositions and their existence in Jansen's book. Jacqueline Pascal did not want to sign, but Pascal persuaded her, and she signed with the rest of the nuns on 22 June. Partly overcome by remorse at her own submission, she died on 4 October.

On 31 October a new formulary was imposed, this time apparently not allowing of any distinction between "droit" and "fait." Pascal, perhaps influenced by Jacqueline's death, and with the support of Domat and Roannez, found it impossible to sign, showing what has generally been regarded as unnecessary intransigence. Arnauld and Nicole felt able to sign, holding that the Jansen whom they were condemning was a figment of the pope's imagination, and that it was possible to sign "quant à la foi (as far as faith goes)." Pascal wrote an *Ecrit sur la signature* of which we have only an abbreviated version, and withdrew from further controversy. His doctrinal position had hardened, perhaps unreasonably, and the last months of his life were informed by an impressive spirituality. There is no question of a diminution of religious fervour, but the apologetic remained unwritten. In the light of all the attempts that continue to be made to interpret Pascal's thought, it is essential to remember that he never wrote what was obviously intended to be the realization of his greatest project. Geometry was "le plus haut exercice de l'esprit...le plus beau métier du monde (the mind's loftiest activity... the finest occupation on earth)," but, after all, "ce n'est qu'un métier (it's only an occupation)." We cannot say what an unwritten book would have contained, especially since there are indications that its author knew it to be unwritable.

On 18 March 1662 Pascal and Roannez inaugurated the first regular omnibus service in Paris. The first line went from the Porte Saint-Antoine to the Luxembourg, and other lines soon followed. Pascal intended to raise money for the poor from this service, and did in fact leave half of his income from the "carosses à cinq sols (the five-sols omnibuses)" to the poor,

whom he also visited personally. The Périers had been living in Paris since late in 1661, and when Pascal fell ill in the spring Gilberte called regularly to look after him. He had sold his horses and his furniture and had begun to live with great simplicity. However the daughter of the couple who cared for him at home caught smallpox, and Gilberte was afraid of carrying the infection to her own children. Pascal therefore had himself moved to the Périers' on 29 June. After a few days he had to go to bed, suffering from violent headaches and stomach pains, although no one thought him in danger. He received visitors, including Arnauld, who was supposed to be in hiding but was still allowed to visit Louis XIV, and Nicole, and he confessed frequently. He seems to have thought he was dying and on 3 August made his will. On 17 August he received the last sacraments, and on 19 August, at 1 a.m., he died.

WORKS

It is at least arguable that Pascal was one of the half-dozen greatest imaginative authors ever to have written in French, but his thought was always both technical and dense even in theology, a field in which he was untrained and in which his dabbling has generally been considered by professional theologians to have been naive. Apart from the dated pieces of polemic, some letters, and the mathematical and scientific papers, Pascal's most important work, especially the fragmentary *Pensées*, the *Ecrits sur la grâce*, the *De l'esprit géométrique*, and even the *Préface*. *Sur le traité du vide* can also be only roughly dated. The uncertainty about dates of composition has therefore further complicated a situation in which there have been countless invariably controversial attempts to penetrate to the heart of his thinking, all trying to interpret heterogeneous and contradictory fragments, and to "reconstruct" a book that was never written, and of which nothing that has been shown to be a definitive plan has ever existed.

The evidence for what form the proposed apologetic would have taken is scrappy, and its interpretation has never been the subject of a consensus. A great deal of reliance has been placed on what Pascal is said by others either to have said, or at some time to have intended to say, but the status of the principal documents has contributed much more to controversy than to consensus. The three major surviving manuscripts, the other relevant papers, the classification of about a third of the fragments, the titles of the classified bundles, and the first edition of 2 January 1670, *Pensées de M. Pascal sur la religion et sur quelques autres sujets, qui ont été trouvées après sa mort parmi ses papiers*, especially when compared with the internal evidence provided by the fragments themselves, have provoked often acrimonious discussions about the nature of Pascal's insights into human existence and destiny. Particular attention needs therefore to be paid to the distinction between the little that is certain, much that is generally but perhaps not rightly assumed, and what must still be regarded as frankly conjectural, however passionately the advocates of some particular point of view may be convinced of its absolute immunity from attack.

It is also essential to distinguish between matters of spirituality—the religious attitudes with which Pascal and many of those associated with Port-Royal were impregnated—and the theology of grace to which they had intellectual recourse. It is perfectly possible to base a wholly admirable spirituality on an inadequate theology and, even if themselves unexceptionable, a given series of theological propositions may well not actually provide the necessary or sufficient foundation for the religious attitudes they are drawn up to support. In the case of Jansenism, the spirituality we call by that name existed before the theology of the 1640 *Augustinus* and, in spite of Arnauld's efforts to combine the two, never depended on it. There is no conclusive evidence that Pascal ever read the *Augustinus* in its entirety, although he is almost certain to have known the prooemial book of the second volume, which may have been based on a sketch by Saint-Cyran and differs in character from the rest of the work.

Pascal's religious attitude hardened after the death of his sister Jacqueline, but the cooling of his relationship with Port-Royal was still due to a difference about whether the signing of the second formulary involved admitting the pope's right to declare that the condemned propositions were "in" the text. Nothing suggests that he had felt more than distaste for his former readiness, on which he never formally went back, to assent to the condemnation of the propositions themselves. Pascal's final spiritual attitude has nothing at all to do with the acceptance or rejection of five condemned propositions, but with a quite independent moral principle concerning the authority of papal rulings on matters of fact. Furthermore, while theological propositions can be condemned and declared heretical, that is, incompatible with the belief of the Church, the set of interior attitudes which make up a spirituality can be condemned only if it leads to heretical utterances, which in Pascal's case it did not. Partly because of the disputed relationship between Jansenist theology, which was condemned, and Jansenist spirituality, which was not, but also on account of the generally technical nature of the subject matter, its importance for so many 17th-century French authors, and its integration into the principal reactionary stream in the great flow of French cultural history from the Renaissance to the Revolution, the user of the *Guide* is referred to the formal treatment of the theology under "Jansenism" and of the spirituality as well as the history of the convent under "Port-Royal."

The *Préface. Sur le traité du vide* must date from 1651, although it was not published until 1779. In his letter of 12 July 1651 to Ribeyre, Pascal announced that he was finishing his treatise on the vacuum. It was apparently never finished. The *Préface* is itself only a project, often with only paragraph openings to indicate developments, and the text comes from a manuscript given in 1715 by Pascal's niece Marguerite to a Clermont Oratorian, Père Pierre Guerrier, whose heir gave it in 1779 to what became the Bibliothèque Nationale.

Its importance derives from the polarity which Pascal establishes between authority and reason, acknowledging the supremacy of authority in all disciplines depending on memory, like history, geography, jurisprudence and, above all, theology. Pascal almost rejoices in the inadequacy of reason in theology, in which we can know the truth only by authority, "de sorte que pour donner la certitude entière des matières les plus incompréhensibles à la raison, il suffit de les faire voir dans les livres sacrés (so that to give entire certainty to matters incomprehensible to reason, it is enough to show them in the sacred books)." The principles of theology are "above nature and reason" and can be reached by man only with the assistance of an all-powerful and supernatural force. On the other hand authority is useless in those subjects which fall under the senses or the intellect, and Pascal lists geometry, arithmetic, music, physics, medicine,

architecture, "et toutes les sciences qui sont soumises à l'expérience et au raisonnement (and all the sciences which are subject to experiment and reasoning)." In the empirical disciplines, progress is possible and necessary, and it is as damaging to use authority as a principle in experimental physics as it is to use reasoning alone in theology "instead of the authority of Scripture and the Fathers." It is none the less by reason that man differs from the animals, whose instinct does not admit of progress, "Les ruches des abeilles étaient aussi bien mesurées il y a mille ans qu'aujourd'hui (beehives were as perfectly constructed a thousand years ago as they are today)."

Pascal's *Mémorial* contains an important single-page text noted down by him during, or immediately after, an intense experience he underwent on the night of 23 November 1654. He kept the paper sewn into the lining of his jacket, a not unusual custom. The language is strongly religious. The central portion, in handwriting that shows the influence of strong emotion, indicates under the heading "Fire" the discovery of the God of Abraham, Isaac, and Jacob, "non des Philosophes et des savants (not of the philosophers and the learned)." The deeply spiritual experience includes the note of "Joie, Joie, Joie, pleurs de joie (Joy, Joy, Joy, tears of joy)" and there is a liturgical resonance in the two Latin phrases in the body of the text. The first six lines, giving the date and the time of the experience, from 10.30 p.m. to 12.30 a.m., were added later. The handwriting is calmer, and the date is given formally in liturgical style, except that Pascal makes a mistake. The 23 November was the feast of St Clement, whom he mentions as being in the martyrology, but the Roman martyrology read at Prime on one day always refers to the next day's saints. The reference in the last three lines to submission to a director suggests that those lines, too, were written later, a hypothesis for which the manuscript tradition offers supporting evidence. Whatever psychological status is accorded to Pascal's experience, and in whatever sense it may have constituted, or have been at the apex of, a "conversion," its effect was to take him early in the new year first to stay with Luynes at Vaumurier and then, still in January, to make his retreat at Port-Royal-des-Champs. He was clearly not yet really familiar with liturgical usage.

The text of the *Entretien avec M. de Saci*, first published in 1728, must have derived from one or more conversations which took place on the occasion in question, and appears to be a conflation of at least two separate accounts of possibly more than one discussion. Fontaine wrote it up from notes of which some must have been supplied by Pascal, and included it in the *Mémoires pour servir à l'histoire de Port-Royal* of 1736. Pascal, whose consciousness of his intellectual gifts pierces through the narrator's slightly amused style, talks of the opposing strengths and weaknesses of Epictetus and Montaigne. Epictetus was deeply aware of human obligations, but presumptuously ignorant of human weakness, while Montaigne, conscious of human weakness, remained proudly unperturbed about the need to seek divine aid. Epictetus establishes human certainty and greatness, Montaigne human doubt and weakness. The two attitudes destroy one another and can neither exist in isolation nor combine. Only the Gospel can reconcile the contradictions of human experience. The stylized polarities are skilfully developed, and present a particularly fine example of the device used frequently by Pascal in the *Ecrits sur la grâce*, the *Lettres provinciales*, and the *Pensées*, by which his own view is shown to steer a middle course between two extremes, combining the advantages of both and explaining human grandeur and weakness in terms of the Gospel message and a Jansenist spirituality.

In the *Entretien* Pascal uses one of his key words in a special way. "Paresse" normally means laziness, but it has a particular meaning in an Augustinian context, in which it tends to refer to a refusal to bother about spiritual matters. Its use had been striking in Senault and would again be so in La Rochefoucauld. Pascal uses it in the ninth *Lettre* to translate the technical sin, acedia, to which the desert fathers succumbed if they gave up the rigours of their life, but he also uses it in both the *Entretien* and the *Pensées* (ed. Sellier 240) to denote the guilt attributable to those who do not do bother to keep the law. It is true that, even if they do keep the law, they cannot know whether they do so out of self-love/pride or out of grace, but those not in grace act out of one of two underlying sources of guilt which renders their actions sinful: "paresse" or pride. The *Entretien* faithfully gives Pascal's sense, and probably his language, when suggesting that a preoccupation with human grandeur leads to pride, while a preoccupation with human weakness leads to the abandonment of effort:

> ainsi ces deux états…conduisent nécessairement à l'un de ces deux vices, d'orgueil et de paresse, où sont infailliblement tous les hommes avant la grâce, puisque s'ils ne demeurent dans leurs désordres par lâcheté, ils en sortent par vanité

> (so these two states…lead necessarily to one of these two vices, pride and lack of effort, in which all human beings are before grace since, if they do not continue in their sinful ways through unconcern, they abandon them through vanity).

In the *Pensées* the two states are called "paresse" and "orgueil," ordinarily meaning laziness and pride.

Les Réflexions sur la géométrie en général: de l'esprit géométrique et de l'art de persuader appears to date from late in 1655, although it has also been allocated to the years 1657–58. It is contained in the manuscript which belonged to Pascal's nephew, Louis Périer, was partially published in 1728, and was fortunately copied in about 1740 before being lost. Most of the text was published in 1779, but it did not appear in its entirety until 1844. It is a disquisition on scientific method and the nature of geometrical proof, and on rhetorical persuasion, "persuasion" being a concept essential for any understanding of the *Pensées*. It introduces the celebrated notion of a double infinity, the infinitely large and the infinitely small, illustrated by a fraction which can always be made smaller if multiplied by a tenth. However, the text's real importance is to introduce Pascal's notion of the heart, clearly central to any understanding at all of the *Pensées* on account of no. 142 (ed. Sellier), referring to the heart's intuitive knowledge.

Classical psychology, from the 13th century onwards, had failed to explain adequately the distinction in the human mind between cognitive and volitive functions, which it assigned to different faculties, the intellect and the will. By the 17th century the problem had reached epic proportions, as the way Descartes had to wrestle with it made clear. Quite apart from the psychology itself, any distinction of faculties, as they were then understood, made religious commitment, necessarily entailing belief, either cognitive but not volitive, in which case it was a rational judgement and could not be meritorious, or volitive but not cognitive, in which case it derived from an act of will that was not fully rational. There was no adequate explanation available, once there was a distinction of faculties, of how cognitive and volitive functions could combine in a single act. Scripture, however, and especially the Psalms, had made the heart the seat of religious activity. It seemed, although it only seemed, to solve the dilemma, and Pascal clutched at the possibility of by-passing the distinction of faculties by combining the functions of both in the heart.

Pascal discusses the art of persuasion, which is not the same thing as proof. There are, he says, two ways by which truth enters the soul: through the intellect ("entendement") and through the will ("volonté"). The more natural is the intellect, whose assent depends on proof, but the more normal is the will, since most people believe what they believe because they want to. That way of believing is "basse, indigne et étrangère (low, unworthy and alien)," but not, of course where divine truths are concerned. God desires "qu'elles entrent du coeur dans l'esprit, et non pas de l'esprit dans le coeur, pour humilier cette superbe puissance du raisonnement (that they should enter from the heart into the mind, and not from the mind into the heart, to humiliate that proud power of reasoning…). It is important to notice the stealth with which, in half a dozen lines, Pascal has switched from "volonté" to "coeur" as the organ which accepts religious truth, and to see how that allows him to attack rationally based religious scepticism. Elsewhere he shows extreme reluctance to abandon rationality as the foundation of human dignity as in the fragment "Infini-rien" (*Pensées*, ed. Sellier, no. 680). Having written on all four sides of a sheet of paper, folded once, an argument leading to the need for simple self-abasement and humiliation as the only sure way to religious belief, he writes up the left-hand margin,

> C'est le coeur qui sent Dieu, et non la raison: voilà ce que c'est que la foi. Dieu sensible au coeur, non à la raison

> (It is the heart which feels God and not the reason. That is what faith is, God felt in the heart, not in the reason).

In a despairing attempt to safeguard the criterion of rationality, Pascal then writes, upside down at the top of the page, the famous but in its context meaningless statement,

> Le coeur a ses raisons, que la raison ne connaît point

> (The heart has its reasons of which the reason knows nothing).

It is the same problem which leads Pascal himself in the *Pensées* to discover the inutility of proving the Christian religion. It does not help. He begins (ed. Sellier, no. 142),

> Nous connaissons la vérité non seulement par la raison, mais encore par le coeur

> (We know the truth not only through the reason, but also through the heart).

The heart is the source of the knowledge of first principles: that there is an infinity of numbers, or that there are three dimensions in space. Principles are felt, and after that propositions are proved. Then, in one of his most scathing attacks on reason, Pascal can only regret that we cannot know even more by feeling and instinct, "to humiliate reason, which wants to be the judge of everything." Unhappily, however, for the most part we must rely on reason, but those to whom God has given religion by "sentiment du coeur (feeling in the heart)" are fortunate ("bien heureux") and quite legitimately persuaded. To those who have not been given religion in this way we can only give it by reason,

> en attendant que Dieu la leur donne par sentiment du coeur. Sans quoi la foi n'est qu'humaine et inutile pour le salut

> (while waiting for God to give it to them by feeling through the heart. Without which faith is only human, and useless for salvation).

If Pascal really believed that, there was no point in writing an apologetic, or proving the truths of faith. Only God could give the faith which saved, and we know from Pascal's whole theology that he was bitterly opposed to the idea that man's salvation could ever depend on his own unaided human intiative. "La foi est un don de Dieu, ne croyez pas que nous disions que c'est un don de raisonnement (Faith is a gift of God. Do not think we say it is a gift of reason)."

Recent criticism has tended to push back the probable date at which the *Ecrits sur la grâce* were first sketched out, but the end of 1655 or the beginning of 1656 seems most likely, at least for their revision. Publication has been piecemeal since 1779, but the text published in 1954 in the Bibliothèque de la Pléiade is still generally used, although the relevant third (1991) volume in Pascal's *Oeuvres Complètes* edited by Jean Mesnard now contains a much superior text, and what are known as the *Ecrits sur la grâce* must now be regarded as drafts and notes for three related documents, a *Lettre*, a *Discours* and a *Traité*. The exact status of the fragments is conjectural, and Pascal never drew up a formal statement of his position for publication. However, the thrust of his argument is reasonably clear.

The problem considered is how exactly both God and the human being combine in achieving the salvation of those who are saved and the damnation of those who are not.

Does God decide whom he will save and whom he will damn, and then bestow grace irresistibly or withhold it, as Pascal says the Calvinists think? Or does God merely foresee how human beings would use their free wills if they were free to accept or reject grace, and "submitting the use of his grace to the freedom of the human will," accordingly give irresistible grace or withhold it, as Pascal claims the Molinists held? There is, given the terms in which the question is posed, naturally a third way, that of "the disciples of Saint Augustine." What Pascal regards as the Calvinist view would make God the author of sin, and what he regards as the Molinist one would involve distinguishing between different acts in a God whose activity cannot be split into segregated acts or, as he himself points out, making a divine decision contingent on a human one. The problem is an old, scholastic one, bitterly disputed since the 13th century. In spite of Pascal's dislike of scholastic argument and his preference for "positive" theology based on Scripture or the Fathers, Pascal's solution is indistinguishable from that of Gregory of Rimini, who died in 1358.

The question, of course, could only arise in traditions, like those of Islam or of western Christianity, which sought a philosophical foundation for the theological propositions which supported spiritual attitudes. For Pascal the disciples of Augustine differ from the Calvinists by holding that the reprobation of the damned is due to original sin, and is not therefore the direct consequence of an arbitrary divine act. They differ from the Molinists by holding that God alone infallibly determines who are those who will persevere in grace. In this life no one can know to whom God will choose to give grace at the end of their lives, and consequently to save, and from whom he will withhold the grace of perseverance. The spiritual consequence of Pascal's view was to have reverberations well into the 18th century, notably in the quietist reaction associated with Fénelon. The solution is weak, because it does not explain the existence of original sin, the culpability of the individual for the weakness of the nature with which he was born, and it allows no one themselves by an autonomous act of moral self-determination to affect their own eternal destiny. Spiritually Pascal's teaching is bleaker for the individual Christian than that of the medieval nominalists. The Christian can do nothing whatever about his own salvation, except live in a "créance mêlée de crainte (a belief mixed with fear)."

Pascal's position is capable of being reconciled with a concept of free will adequate in the 17th century to keep Pascal within the bounds of orthodoxy. He was not in the theological sense a Jansenist, and not a heretic. He did not hold in an unqualified form any of the five condemned propositions. Most of his argument comes from the authority of Augustine, some also comes from the stricter Fulgentius, and Pascal relies on works whose authenticity has subsequently been discredited. He also demonstrates his compatibility with the Council of Trent, which absolutely refused to decide the question. It condemned the "Pelagian" (more strictly "semi-Pelagian") doctrine that man could contribute to his own salvation, maintained that he had free will and was to blame for his own sin, and made no attempt to reconcile the two positions, regarding its business as merely to lay down the boundaries of orthodoxy.

The first of the *Lettres provinciales*, an eight-page fly-sheet, is based on an argument supplied by Nicole, and attempts to show the factitious nature of the alliance against Arnauld, dependent as it was on agreement to use the concept of the "proximate power to avoid sin," to which, argues Pascal, the Dominicans ranged in the anti-Arnauld alliance gave an interpretation which did not differ from Arnauld's. Arnauld had already been condemned on 14 January on the question of "fact," and the question of "right" was due to be discussed in the following days. Arnauld had held in his *Seconde lettre* of 10 July 1655 that, when he sinfully denied Christ, Saint Peter had been "un juste...à qui la grâce, sans laquelle on ne peut rien, a manqué (a just man who lacked the grace without which nothing can be achieved)." Since there was no agreement about the precise implications of the word "proximate," not used, as Pascal's letter-writer finds out, by Scripture, Fathers, Councils, Popes, or Saint Thomas, Pascal can satirically reduce the whole dispute to a semantic quarrel. "S'il appelle ce pouvoir *pouvoir prochain*, il sera Thomiste, et partant catholique; sinon, il sera Janséniste, et partant hérétique (If he calls that power a *proximate power*, he'll be a Thomist, and therefore a Catholic; otherwise he'll be a Jansenist, and therefore a heretic)," "il n'y plus que le mot de *prochain* sans aucun sens qui court risque (it's only the word *proximate* without any meaning which runs runs a risk)." The pose of naivety is struck in the dry, well-calculated irony of the opening sentences:

> Nous étions bien abusés. Je ne suis détrompé que d'hier. Jusque-là j'ai pensé que le sujet des disputes de Sorbonne était bien important, et d'une extrême conséquence pour la religion

> (We were quite wrong. I only found out yesterday. Until then I thought that the subject of Sorbonne debates was indeed important and entailed serious consequences for religion).

On 25 January Arnauld's friends walked out of the debate, for which the voting laws had been rigged to ensure the passing of the motion of censure. Arnauld contested the legitimacy of the assembly, which debated the matter on 29 January, definitively censuring Arnauld two days later. The second *Provinciale* is dated 29 January. It contains further little comic scenes with direct speech, as the letter-writer takes his friend in search of enlightenment from learned theologians about the issues at stake, this time made to turn on the insufficiency of "sufficient," but still "inefficacious" grace. The letter was not printed until 1 February and not disseminated until 5 February. It still tries to rally the support of the Dominicans, who have ended up with a grace which is "suffisante sans l'être (sufficient, only not)," thus agreeing with the Jesuits on the use of the word, but with Arnauld on its absence of content.

In the second letter Pascal uses the word "extravagant" referring to that which exceeds the bounds of common sense. Its importance derives from the way in which, later, Pascal will reproach the Jesuits with their "extravagance" almost as much as with their "morale relâchée (lax moral doctrine)." The clash of religious values is reflected in the much wider contrast between the austere Pascal, Jansenist in the spiritual sense, with his classical taste, Augustinian style, and beautifully balanced, antithetical, chiasmic syntactical patterns, and the flamboyant, over-confident, baroque optimism of the mannered Jesuit style, reflected in their self-congratulatory centenary *Imago primi saeculi*, its frontispiece a woodcut by their favourite painter, Rubens. Pascal made much fun of the *Imago*, notably in the fifth and tenth letters, and reacted instinctively against a whole series of baroque attitudes of which at least traces were noticeable in Jesuit "bizarreries," "railleries," and "disproportion." His spirituality enabled him to sense what most subsequent historians of literature have missed, that behind everything to do with préciosité (q.v.) and galanterie, there was an incipient and tentative movement not only towards a refinement of manners, as is generally accepted, but also towards a rehabilitation of instinct as a guide to virtue.

In his fifth letter, in a passage too rarely remarked on, Pascal says that he is attacking the Jesuits' moral teaching because it is the cause of their theology of grace. His letter-writer refers patronizingly to "ces bons pères".

> Je m'assure que vous remarquerez aisément, dans le relâchement de leur morale, la cause de leur doctrine touchant la grâce

> (I'm sure that you'll easily see in the laxness of their moral teaching the cause of their doctrine on grace).

The disputes about grace, Augustinian theology, spirituality, style in prose, and moral principles were reflected across the whole spectrum of contemporary cultural activity, with writers and painters like Boileau, Bossuet, Pascal, Racine, Philippe de Champagne, Lebrun and even Poussin not only aligned against their baroque predecessors, the habitués of the Chambre bleue, François de Sales, tragi-comédie, the writers of madrigals, like Voiture and Bensserade, worldly but harmless Jesuits like Pierre Le Moyne, novelists like La Calprenède and the Scudérys, but also opposed by a later generation whose members gained influence after the death of Colbert and the disappearance of his style of dispensing royal patronage: Perrault, Fénelon, Fontenelle, Mignard, and Mansart, the authors of novels, the colourists in painting, Quinault and Lulli in music, everyone who preferred opera to tragedy, and the whole of rococo.

Louvois's political influence was catastrophic, both in foreign policy and in the flamboyant over-confidence which led to the anti-Huguenot revocation of the Edict of Nantes in 1685, but the artistic patronage reflected a movement forward in social values and moral attitudes, whatever may be felt about the aesthetic merits of Mignard's *Tent of Darius* commissioned in 1689 to rival Lebrun's acknowledged masterpiece of the same title in 1661, or of Hardouin-Mansart's destruction of Le Vau's Ionic simplicity at Versailles. The *Lettres provinciales* are an early and clear announcement of what will ultimately be at stake in the Querelle des anciens et des modernes (q.v.), which narrowly focused in a few isolated skirmishes what was in fact a sweepingly all-embracing cultural phenomenon by which the renaissance in the end imposed itself victoriously on the enlightenment, successfully overcoming the 17th-century French classical reaction and its ally, Augustinian spirituality, by rehabilitating human instinct as a guide to virtue.

For the third letter the writer gets an apparently neutral theologian to explain how what was wanted was Arnauld's blood, and that his opinions were not really at stake: "ce qui est catholique dans les Pères devient hérétique dans M. Arnauld... ce qui était hérétique, dans les semi-pélagiens devient orthodoxe dans les écrits des Jésuites (what is Catholic in the Fathers becomes heretical in M. Arnauld... what is heretical in the semi-Pelagians becomes orthodox in the writings of the Jesuits)." Angélique Arnauld thought the letters should have stopped there, but with the fourth, of 25 February, Pascal broadened the issue: "Il n'y a rien tel que les Jésuites (There's nothing like the Jesuits)." He starts his attack on Jesuit moral teaching, opposing the view that the law is one, immutable, arbitrary, universal, revealed, and not necessarily correlative to human moral aspirations, to the Jesuit view: that the application of the law must change with changes in the underlying social organization. On this assumption, there was no point in enforcing the ban on the charging of interest, "usury," once a feudal system had given way to a mercantile economic organization, in which entrepreneurs could reasonably be expected to pay for the capital they borrowed. However elevated the Christian moral ideal might be, the Jesuits felt that it was appropriate to be lenient in the imposition of a sacramental discipline, so as not to withold the means of salvation. But for Pascal ignorance of God's law does not excuse guilt in transgressing it. There can be no implied acts of faith or charity, and intention is not to be taken into account. There is no room for natural virtue or for a distinction between crime and sin.

The art of applying apparently immutable norms to changing

circumstances is known as casuistry. As social attitudes change it is still practised in all legal systems, by having recourse sometimes to norms of equity, sometimes to what is assumed to have been in the mind of the law-giver, just as a changing political situation was once allowed by Bartolo di Sassaferrato in the 14th century to vindicate the sovereignty claimed by the Italian city states. The immutable edict of Roman law giving sovereignty to the emperor applied, said Bartolo casuistically, to the empire as a whole, and not to any of its constituent individual parts. "Casuistry" was taught in handbooks of "cases of conscience" for the training of confessors, and was not intended to incorporate moral norms, merely to standardize practice in giving absolution and imposing penances. However, some of the devices used to justify absolution had, in the exuberance of baroque practices not at all confined to Jesuit confessors, become puerile, particularly the use of "probable" opinions in the penitent's favour, and the "direction of intention" by which a valet, helping his employer to sin by holding a ladder while he climbed to a lady's room, could be excused from cooperating in a sinful act on the grounds that it was his intention merely to keep his job. Pascal ridicules the puerilities, the chicanery, the self-congratulatory tone, the extensive recourse to intention to excuse guilt, the foreign names of the casuists, and the incongruous legalism which meticulously respected the letter of the law while travestying its spirit.

Sometimes the social premises underlying casuist practice make us sharply aware of social assumptions which more purely imaginative and less analytical authors were still largely taking for granted. The onus of restoring stolen goods or of giving to the poor was, for instance, to be urged only after sufficient was retained to maintain a "state of life" to which a penitent might be entitled. Honour could be more precious than life, so that the taking of life in defence of honour could be justified. Pascal is almost prudish about sexual morality, generally leaving the authorities he indicts in Latin for purposes of decency. Does it augment or diminish his guilt if an ecclesiastic removes his habit in order to visit a brothel? Pascal cannot however resist some of the more obvious targets presented by the corporate prurience of celibate imaginations. Filliutius, discussing whether an immoral contract, as with a prostitute, creates a valid moral obligation, surely goes too far in discussing how the values differ for sexual services rendered by different categories of women, including common prostitutes, nuns, virgins, and married women. This is the first passage in which Pascal returns to the accusation of "extravagance," and claims to be shocked ("choqué") at the aberrations ("égarements") of his adversaries. By the seventh and eight letters, the printings had reached 6,000.

The ninth is an attack on what is known as "la dévotion aisée (devotion made easy)" which was a characteristic of baroque religiosity, and produced books such as that entitled *Le Paradis ouvert à Philagie, par cent dévotions à la Mère de Dieu, aisées à pratiquer*, modelled in many places on François de Sales's *Introduction à la vie dévote*, the implication being, although not in the work of François de Sales, that there were ways to salvation which by-passed the need for real moral conversion, engendering, says Pascal, "la fausse paix que cette confiance téméraire apporte (the false peace which that presumptuous confidence brings)." From the 11th onwards, the letters are directed to the Jesuits corporately until the last two, addressed personally to Père Annat. Pascal is now defending himself, and his beautifully balanced prose becomes almost incandescent with rage. He is savage about the "Mohatra" contract which resolves the illegitimate loan at interest into a present sale and future contract to repurchase for a higher sum, which merely legitimizes the transaction. The 14th letter returns to Pascal's insistence on the arbitrary nature of divine choice. In the last two letters the irony finally drops, and the polemic becomes more direct and sharper.

Enough has been said about the *Pensées* to indicate something of the difficulty occasioned by the text of the fragments. Victor Cousin pointed out in 1842 that the original 1670 Port-Royal edition was only an embellished selection, and it is incorrect to refer to the content of that or any other edition as "pensées," as if the text contained a homogeneous collection of reflections. *Pensées* is simply the title the Port-Royal editors gave to a book of jottings selected from those left by Pascal. It is quite clear that some of the fragments contain the germs of an exceedingly powerful vision of humanity, and that any apologetic movement would have had to go from an analysis of some aspect of actual human experience, emphasizing its frailness and contingency, to a consideration of human destiny, either heaven or hell after death, with neither of them ever ending. Conclusions would have had to be drawn about how human life should be lived on earth. It is not clear how Pascal would have built up his argument, which of his texts he would have incorporated, which of the structures for the intended apologetic he would have used, which potential lines of argument he would have developed, or how he would have resolved the polarities in which intellectually he revelled. We do not know whether he would have written a straight exposition, or used letter form or dialogue form, and whether he never wrote the book because illness prevented him, or for some other reason.

There are many indications in the fragments, including some already quoted, to the effect that even if the truths of Christianity could be proved, that would not confer a belief which did more than encourage behaviour in accordance with the law. Disregard for the law, like disbelief, could preclude the possibility of salvation, but belief could itself accomplish nothing at all in the order of grace, or in any way contribute to salvation. What then was the point of an apologetic? Many of the fragments turn on the difference between proof, which is merely intellectual, and persuasion, which requires moral commitment, an attempt to conquer sinful habits and inclinations, to break the hold over the individual of passions and vices. Nothing, however, except an arbitrary divine decree, could turn moral commitment or ascetic behaviour into virtue.

Erasmus, More, Luther, Calvin, Zwingli and, for that matter, Ignatius Loyola had turned from the uncertainties of late medieval religion, with its transcendent but arbitrary God, towards a renaissance reliance on the reassurance of direct religious experience, with all the difficulties and controversies about discernment, authority, and authenticity that that entailed. Pascal could substitute nothing for the uncertainty in which, in his spirituality, the Christian was condemned to live, which Nicole was later to systematize, and from which Fénelon was to draw the conclusion. Unlike the late medieval nominalists he could not promise that God would not deny grace to those who did all that lay within their power. After the experience which gave rise to the *Mémorial*, Pascal himself could feel the encouragement of direct religious experience. Could anything he wrote mediate it to anyone else? Would apologetic have turned into exhortation?

Unhappily there is simply insufficient evidence, in spite of so many ingenious attempts, each in turn severely criticized, to know what book Pascal would have written, if he had written one at all. There is not even enough evidence to know exactly what book Pascal intended to write at any given moment after the end of 1657, by which time he had abandoned the idea of a merely traditional apologetic. We do not know the date of the Port-Royal conference at which Pascal expounded his intentions, and it is still just possible that the conference was a rhetorical fiction. According to Filleau de la Chaise in 1668, in a proposed preface for the 1670 edition rejected by the editorial committee, and to Etienne Périer in 1669, who closely follows Filleau de la Chaise, the conference lasted two or three hours, but was neither prepared nor written up.

Filleau de la Chaise gives an account of the conference based on that of someone who, he says, was there. It is more likely to have taken place in May than in October 1658, but there is nothing to connect it with the fragments classified "A. P. R.," nor any reason to suppose that the classification of the fragments into bundles came specifically before or after the conference. The account given by Filleau de la Chaise and followed by Etienne Périer, whose preface the committee did accept, has been heavily criticized as not squaring with the actual fragments as Pascal subsequently left them. Editions of the *Pensées* based on his account have become discredited for that reason, as well as for the unreliability of his testimony and the question of principle about the propriety of reconstructing a book from a series of jottings and no indication at any point of a plan.

There are three main manuscripts. On Pascal's death the slips of paper, some of them classified into 27 bundles, although there are 28 titles, were meticulously copied, once exactly as they had been left, in the "seconde copie," and once in a series of exercise books which were subsequently separated, corrected by the hands of Arnauld and Nicole, and brought together again. That is the "première copie," the basis for the Port-Royal edition and, like the second, no doubt deriving from a lost original copy. It omits three fragments. The classified fragments had been attached with a thread in the top lefthand corner, and we know that the classification into bundles was taken as far as Pascal wished to take it, because he closed the bundles, although some non-classified fragments are gathered under titles, and some titles of non-classified fragments appear to have been lost.

The Port-Royal editors found no order within each of the bundles, although Pascal's markings and interspersed blank slips suggest that there was one, and that he knew what it was. Louis Périer, after the copies had been made, had the bundles undone and all the fragments stuck into an album, cutting holes in the album leaves where that was necessary to show what had been written on the reverse side of the slips on which the fragments had been jotted down. The album was subsequently bound, and constitutes the *Recueil original*. The best indication we have of how Pascal left the fragments on his death is the "seconde copie," the basis of the text quoted in this entry (ed. Philippe Sellier 1976). Since 1976 there have been further editions, one of the first "copie" and a further attempt to reconstruct the unwritten apologetic.

The "seconde copie," unlike the first, starts with an untitled bundle which reads as if it were a table of contents as one might have been drawn up sometime in 1658, although no one can prove that Pascal intended at that date to write his book according to that plan. The next bundle, "Ordre (Order)," contains incompatible suggestions for possible structures for the apologetic and shows awareness of the problem posed by the useful-

ness of proofs. Pascal suggests that proof might be the instrument of true faith, but he does not explain how. "*Justus ex fide vivit.* C'est de cette foi que Dieu lui-même met dans le coeur dont la preuve est souvent l'instrument... (The just man lives by faith. By that faith which God himself puts into the heart, of which proof is often the instrument...)." There follows the bundle on vanity, in which Pascal regards the imagination as a "maîtresse d'erreur et de fausseté (mistress of error and falseness)," taking up the sceptical tradition which used the power of the imagination to discredit belief in miracles; then a series of bundles on human misery, boredom, the need to find causes for observable phenomena, and human greatness, which includes a fragment already referred to (142), the only one to use the heart as the seat of non-religious intuitive cognition.

Throughout runs the heavily polarized exposition of human experience, and Pascal's sense of the paradoxes in the human situation, that human greatness, for example, should consist in the fact that human beings can know their own misery. Reason is treated mercilessly in a long fragment on scepticism. "Connaissez donc, superbe, quel paradoxe vous êtes à vous-même! Humiliez-vous, raison impuissante! Taisez-vous, nature imbécile! Apprenez que l'homme passe infiniment l'homme (Know then, proud man, what a paradox you are to yourself! Powerless reason, humble yourself! Imbecile nature, be silent! Learn that man infinitely transcends man...)." This passage immediately precedes an important development on original sin:

Car il est sans doute qu'il n'y a rien qui choque plus notre raison que de dire que le péché du premier homme ait rendu coupables ceux qui, étant si éloignés de cette source, semblent incapables d'y participer. Cet écoulement ne nous paraît pas seulement impossible, il nous semble même très injuste. Car qu'y a-t-il de plus contraire aux règles de notre misérable justice que de damner éternellement un enfant incapable de volonté pour un péché où il paraît avoir si peu de part qu'il est commis six mille ans avant qu'il fût en être. Certainement rien ne nous heurte plus rudement que cette doctrine. Et cependant, sans ce mystère le plus incompréhensible de tous nous sommes incompréhensibles à nous-mêmes

(For truly there is nothing which offends our reason more than saying that the sin of the first man made guilty those who, coming so long after that source of guilt, seem incapable of sharing in it. This contamination seems to us not only impossible, but also very unjust. For what is more contrary to the rules of our miserable justice than the eternal damnation of a child incapable of willing, for a sin in which it seems he can have no part, for it was committed six thousand years before he existed. Certainly nothing shocks us more acutely than this doctrine. And yet, without this least understandable of all mysteries, we cannot understand ourselves).

The movement of Pascal's thought from an analysis of human experience to its unique possible explanation in the light of the Christian revelation is quite clear. The human situation is like that of a man condemned to death who, says Pascal, knowing he was to die in an hour and that he could effectively devote that hour to preventing his execution, spends it playing cards.

Among the fragments there are constant brief attempts to

safeguard the honour of reason, and to show the need to find God through Christ, the need for a spirituality based more on fear than on love. The difficulty, as the fragments were left, is to see if any resolution of the different strands of imaginative investigation indicated in them was ever likely to prove possible. Pascal liked to emphasize the contradictions in human experience. Without polarizing his thought too far, it must be said that the fragments as we have them contain sharp and often brilliantly formulated remarks about the human situation, but that it is very difficult to see how even the most penetrating of them could be combined. Any apologetic would have run into the difficulty that proof, and even persuasion, can achieve nothing in the only important order, which is that of salvation. The most fascinating possibility is that Pascal could have built on his own religious experience a deeply persuasive exhortation to a Christian mode of living based on a spirituality which, whatever theological parameters contained it, would have vindicated itself as pointing towards the way to conduct life on earth.

APPENDIX

Because of the frequent and justifiable claims that Pascal was the first great master of classical French prose, one of his more elaborately constructed paragraphs is appended. It is taken from the 11th of the *Lettres provinciales*.

Car, mes Pères, puisque vous m'obligez d'entrer en ce discours, je vous prie de considérer que, comme les vérités chrétiennes sont dignes d'amour et de respect, les erreurs qui leur sont contraires sont dignes de mépris et de haine; parce qu'il y a deux choses dans les vérités de notre religion: une beauté divine qui les rend aimables, et une sainte majesté qui les rend vénérables; et qu'il y a aussi deux choses dans les erreurs: l'impiété qui les rend horribles, et l'impertinence qui les rend ridicules. Et c'est pourquoi, comme les saints ont toujours pour la vérité ces deux sentiments d'amour et de crainte, et que leur sagesse est toute comprise entre la crainte qui en est le principe, et l'amour qui en est la fin, les saints ont aussi pour l'erreur ces deux sentiments de haine et de mépris, et leur zèle s'emploie également à repousser avec force la malice des impies, et à confondre avec risée leur égarement et leur folie

(For, Fathers, since you force me to raise the matter, I beg you to consider that, just as Christian truths are worthy of love and respect, the errors which contradict them are worthy of contempt and hatred; because there are two things in the truths of our religion: a divine beauty which makes them attractive, and a sacred majesty which makes them venerable; and there are also two things in the errors: the impiety which makes them horrifying, and the absurdity which makes them ridiculous. And that is why, just as the saints always have for the truth the two feelings of love and fear, and all their wisdom is encompassed by the fear which is its beginning, and the love which is its end, the saints also have for error the two feelings of hatred and contempt, and their zeal is employed both to repudiate strongly the evil intent of the impious, and to confound with derision their aberration and their folly).

PUBLICATIONS

Collections
Oeuvres complètes, edited by Bossut, 5 vols., 1779
Oeuvres complètes, edited by Brunschvicg, Boutroux, Gazier, 14 vols., 1904–14
Oeuvres complètes, edited by Strowski, 4 vols., 1923–31
Oeuvres complètes, edited by Chevalier, Bibliothèque de la Pléiade, 1954
Oeuvres complètes, edited by Lafuma, 1963
Oeuvres complètes, edited by Mesnard, 5 vols (3 appeared), 1964–

During his lifetime Pascal published no book under his own name. The two important first editions are:

Les Provinciales ou les Lettres escrites par Louis de Montalte à un Provincial de ses amis et aux RR. PP. Jésuites sur le sujet de la morale et de la politique de ces Pères, 1657 [The place of publication is falsely given as Cologne]
Pensées de M. Pascal sur la religion et sur quelques autres sujets, qui ont été trouvées après sa mort parmi ses papiers, 1670

Pascal's works are grouped in the 1963 "Intégrale" edition of the *Oeuvres complètes* as follows
Traité des coniques
Le Règle des partis
Traité du triangle arithmétique
Les Carrés magiques
Adresse à l'Académie parisienne
La Roulette
Dimensions des lignes courbes
La Machine d'arithmétique
Le Vide, l'équilibre des liqueurs et la pesanteur de l'air
Lettres
Sur la conversion du pécheur
Entretien avec M. de Saci
Abrégé de la vie de Jésus-Christ
Ecrits sur la grâce
De l'esprit géométrique et de l'art de persuader
Comparaison des chrétiens des premiers temps avec ceux d'aujourd'hui
Prière pour demander à Dieu le bon usage des maladies
Trois discours sur la condition des Grands
Ecrit sur la signature du Formulaire
Les Lettres provinciales
Les Ecrits des curés de Paris
Pensées

From the three manuscripts of Pascal's writings (the *Recueil Original*, the *Première Copie* and the *Seconde Copie*), different arrangements were chosen by different editors. The different editions are listed below

Port-Royal, 1670 and 1678
Condorcet, 1776
Condorcet-Voltaire, 1778
Bossut, 1779
Ducreux, 1785
Frontin, 1835
Faugère, 1844

Havet, 1852
Louandre, 1854
Astié, 1857
Rocher, 1873
Molinier, 1877
Drioux, 1881
Jeannin, 1883
Vialard, 1895
Guthlin, 1896
Didiot, 1897
Brunschvicg, 1897 and 1904
Gazier, 1907
Margival, 1911
Chevalier, 1925, 1936, 1949, and 1954
Massis, 1929
Strowski, 1931
Souriau, 1933
Dedieu, 1937
Stewart, 1950
Guersant, 1954
Kaplan, 1982
Recueil original
Michaut, 1896
Première copie
Tourneur, 1938 and 1942
Tourneur-Anzieu, 1960
Lafuma, 1947 and 1952
Edition du Luxembourg, 1951
Club du meilleur livre, 1958
Le Guern, 1977
Seconde copie
Sellier, 1976
Les Lettres provinciales, ed. Cognet, 1965

Translations

Pensées (Lafuma arrangement) 1962 (première copie), (in English) 1966
The Provincial Letters, 1967
The Physical Treatises, 1937
The Provincial Letters, Pensées and Scientific Treatises, 1952

Bibliography

A. Maire, *Bibliographie générale des oeuvres de Blaise Pascal*, 5 vols., Paris 1925–7

Biographies in English

Bishop, Morris, *Pascal, The Life of a Genius*, 1936
Mesnard, Jean, *Pascal, His Life and Works*, 1952
Mortimer, Ernest, *Blaise Pascal: The Life and Work of a Realist*, 1959
Cailliet, Emile, *Pascal: The Emergence of Genius*, 1961
Steinmann, Jean, *Pascal*, 1965

Critical works

Brunet, Georges, *Le Pari de Pascal*, 1956
Goldmann, Lucien, *Le Dieu caché*, 1959
Broome, J.H., *Pascal*, 1965

Sellier, Philippe, *Pascal et Saint Augustin*, 1970
Miel, Jan, *Pascal and Theology*, 1969
Mesnard, Jean, *Pascal*, 1967
————————*Les Pensées de Pascal*, 1976
Rex, W., *Pascal's Provincial Letters: An Introduction*, 1977
Nelson, Robert J., *Pascal, Adversary and Advance*, 1981
Duchêne, Roger, *L'Imposture littéraire dans les Provinciales de Pascal*, 2nd edition, 1985
Coleman, Francis X.J., *The Life and Works of Blaise Pascal: Neither Angel nor Beast*, 1986
Parish, Richard, *Pascal's 'Lettres provinciales'*, 1989

PELETIER DU MANS, Jacques, 1517–1582.

Poet, doctor, mathematician, grammarian, jurist, and scholar.

LIFE

Not only does Peletier appear from the list of headings above to have engaged in too many activities to have excelled at any of them, but he also seems to have lived in too many places—successively Paris, Le Mans, Paris, Bordeaux, Languedoc, Poitiers, Piedmont, Lyons, Basle, Savoy, Bordeaux, and again Paris—to have made his mark in any of them, and for that matter to have had too many jobs to have done any of them well. Yet, if it was Dorat who read the Greek and Latin poets with Ronsard, Baïf, and du Bellay at the Collège de Coqueret, it was Peletier who encouraged Ronsard's inchoate enthusiasm for Horace, who proposed to du Bellay that he should turn to the ode and sonnet forms, and who first fired the poets later to be compared to a Pléiade (q.v.) with the desire to make their vernacular illustrious by imitating in it the achievements of the poets of antiquity.

Peletier's lack of success as a head of the colleges first of Bayeux in Paris, and then, much later, of Guyenne at Bordeaux, the rejection of the reform of French orthography which he advocated, the admitted but perhaps only apparent dissipation of his talents, added to our failure until recently to appreciate the interest of his attempt to create a universal science on a mathematical model, have all contributed to what appears to be an unwarranted lack of esteem from critics perhaps exaggeratedly unimpressed by the aesthetic qualities of Peletier's imaginative output. Yet in 1555 Ronsard named Peletier in place of des Autels among the members of the changing list of six contemporary poets with whom he most wished to be associated, a group which, according to his biographer, Claude Binet, Ronsard referred to as a Pléiade. Peletier was not replaced in the list until after his death, in Binet's third edition of the Ronsard biography.

Peletier, born at Le Mans on 25 July 1517, was the ninth child of a family of 15. His father, Pierre, was a lawyer who had married Jeanne le Royer in 1499. Three of his brothers became ecclesiastics and two became lawyers. Peletier appears to have been about 12 when he was sent to Paris to study at the Collège de Navarre under his brother Jean who, nine years older and about to become a prominent theologian, was teaching the undergraduate arts course. Another brother, Julien, who studied at Navarre, might also have been there at the same time, and it is at least possible that Peletier went on after graduation in arts briefly to study theology. He says that, now guided by his brother Victor, a lawyer, he spent five years studying law, and claims to have taught himself mathematics. The legal studies are most likely to have taken place at Poitiers. Peletier certainly acquired an advanced humanist interest in the poets of antiquity, and at some date learned enough Greek to publish in 1547 his verse translation of the first two books of the *Odyssey* and to understand Euclid, but the dates, locations, and order of his preoccupations are uncertain from his arrival at Navarre about 1529 until 1540, when he entered the service of René du Bellay, bishop of Le Mans, as his secretary.

By 5 March 1543, the date of the funeral of Guillaume du Bellay and therefore the day before that on which Ronsard received the tonsure from the bishop of Le Mans, Peletier was working on the verse translation of Horace's *Ars poetica*, which he is thought by La Croix du Maine to have published the following year, although the earliest surviving copy, which states that it is a re-impression, dates from 1545. Its preface is a sketch of the principal ideas to be developed by Joachim du Bellay in the 1549 *Deffence et illustration de la langue françoyse*. It was René du Bellay, who had long disagreed with Peletier about the spelling reform he projected who, with the connivance of his co-patron the bishop of Angers, obtained for Peletier the post of Principal of the Paris Collège de Bayeux to which he was appointed from 6 November 1543.

The appointment involved a breach of the 1308 statutes, and the king must himself have abrogated them in favour of Peletier, since the appeal to the parlement by the deposed Stéphane Allard against the appointment was dismissed in 1551 in virtue of a royal directive of 1544. It is not improbable that Peletier's resignation on 18 March 1547 had something to do with the king's health a fortnight before his death on 31 March, although Peletier later ascribed it to his desire to travel and to the humble status of a university teacher: "ce n'ét le moyen de garder sa dinitè que d'anseigner (teaching is no way of maintaining one's dignity)."

In Paris Peletier renewed contact with Ronsard, who returned there after his father's death in 1544 and to whom Peletier sent two poems, one of which was to thank him for his reply to the first. All three were to be published in Peletier's *Oeuvres poetiques* of 1547. By the end of 1546, whether at Paris or not is disputed, Peletier had met du Bellay, who was to contribute the epilogue to Peletier's 1547 collection, to pick up echoes of the poems Peletier published in it for his own early verse, and to use the preface to the Horace translation as well as Peletier's practice in the 1547 volume for the *Deffence et illustration de la langue françoyse*. In February Peletier had been entrusted with pronouncing at Notre-Dame a solemn panegyric of Henry VIII, of which only fragments have been published. The decision to resign scarcely a month later seems, in spite of what Peletier later said, to have been sudden. In Paris Peletier's friends included the scholars from the Collège de Coqueret, Ronsard and du Bellay, as well as Jean Martin and Théodore de Bèze, and he was well known at court, especially after the prominence accorded to him following the panegyric.

He left Paris in September 1548, a year after the publication of the *Oeuvres*. In addition to his verse collection and translation of Horace, he published, at Poitiers in February 1549, his four books of *L'Aritmétique*, dedicated to Théodore de Bèze, then prior of Longjumeau, and obtained a privilège for the *Dialogue de l'ortografe* to appear, also at Poitiers, in 1550. The *Dialogue* was partly intended to defend Louis Meigret against Guillaume des Autels, but so modified Meigret's proposals as to attract from him a vigorous rejoinder. The arithmetic textbook was unusual in being in the vernacular, and four reprints are known. Peletier had perfected his Italian, started to learn Spanish and, during the year following his resignation, begun to study medicine. On leaving Paris he had hoped to teach mathematics at the famous Collège de Guyenne at Bordeaux, but the principal from 1547, Jean Gelida, had preferred to employ Elie Vinet, who took up his appointment at the end of 1549, and Peletier went to Poitiers, where he stayed for four years to continue his medical studies, and also taught mathematics.

He left Poitiers at the end of 1552, stayed at Bordeaux, and travelled in Languedoc. Towards the end of 1553 he was teaching mathematics in Lyons. He left for Piedmont in the train of the maréchal de Cossé-Brissac, to whose 10-year-old son, for whom he wrote a lost educational work, he was probably tutor. On his return to Lyons after a few months, Peletier stayed there from 1554 to 1557, forming friendships with both Maurice Scève and Pontus de Tyard, both of whom shared his interest in what must be regarded as the much more than casual fusion of poetry and mathematics, although in the preface to *L'Art poëtique* Peletier was explicitly to state that he looked on poetic composition as a relaxation from mathematics, an addictive but "bien dousse folie (very enjoyable madness)." Since he also held that a well-endowed person ("un homme bien né") should have several occupations, there could here be more than a touch of affectation, as well as self-justification.

There is evidence that he frequented the notorious salon in the Rue Confort of Louise Labé, "la Belle Cordière." He taught mathematics to the son of the printer Jean de Tournes, who had a special font cast to reproduce the characters necessary for Peletier's orthography and was henceforward his publisher. In 1554 Tournes issued the two books of Peletier's *L'Algèbre*. Peletier also met Guillaume des Autels, who had just published the 1553 *L'amoureux repos*, and Charles Fontaine. At the beginning of 1555 Peletier published his Petrarchan sonnets *L'Amour des amours*. From the account he gives, *L'Art poétique* of May 1555 is an assemblage of odd notes, written at different times and places on "petiz coins de papier (little scraps of paper)." Even if that detail was literally true, putting it in the preface was an act of affectation.

The preface goes on to establish rather laboriously that Peletier is indeed being affected, a fact which could turn out to demonstrate the need for a total reassessment of his achievement. Peletier recounts that, while preparing for a move ("an remuant ménage"), he found in the "chaos" of his writings, "certeins preceptes de Poësie (certain rules of poetry)," which he thought would give pleasure to lovers of poetry. He therefore set himself to put them in order, which gave him much more work than he had expected. If he now added, as in fact he did, a few, in fact 18, perhaps previously rejected examples ("opuscules") of his own, it was to show that he taught better than he performed ("pour me fere estimer meilheur anseigneur que bon feseur"). What he was actually doing in the preface was revising the ideas developed by du Bellay from Peletier's own preface to the Horace translation, but subsequently more or less dropped by du Bellay, while Ronsard had undergone an equally startling evolution away from the early Coqueret enthusiasm for imitating the poets of antiquity. The work has rightly been regarded as a mellower Pléiade manifesto than du Bellay's original *Deffence*, but it also signals an important change of direction in Peletier.

During these years at Lyons, Peletier had maintained, or reestablished, close links with Ronsard, and had himself now noticeably come under the influence of the Lyons poets, particularly Scève and Pontus de Tyard. Du Bellay, who returned from Rome through Lyons, may have seen him there in September 1557, and anyway included a sonnet dedicated to him in *Les Regrets*. In 1554, at the end of his *Algèbre*, Peletier threatened those who opposed him, chiefly in the matter of the spelling reform, that he would go back to writing in Latin. In 1557 he issued the six books of his *In Euclidis elementa geometrica* in Latin, with a privilège dating back to 1555 and an appendix containing a series of important letters to poets, to his brother Jean, and to various learned persons, including Cardano. In a letter to Tyard, Peletier, discouraged, abandons hope of getting the French to take their language seriously and promises himself a better destiny in Latin.

By the end of 1557 Peletier had returned to Paris, having occupied himself with the posthumous publication of *Les nouvelles recréations et joyeux devis* of Bonaventure des Périers. To his brother Jean his Latin letter had expressed poetic defeat. Henceforward he would devote himself only to mathematics. He now lived for the study that used merely to delight him. Back in Paris, he immediately published a Latin poem, composed in Lyons, the *Exhortatio pacificatoria*, and in 1560 published a Latin translation of his *Algèbre*. This volume included a letter of 4 November 1559 affirming his intention henceforward to devote himself again to medicine, and we know that he attended the courses of the medical faculty in Paris in 1558, became a bachelor of medicine that year, defended his theses in 1559, and took his licentiate in 1560, in which year he also issued a work reconciling apparently contradictory passages in Galen. It was apparently as a doctor that Peletier henceforward earned his living.

In 1563 he was in Basle. On his way there on 5 March he was robbed, and feared he was going to be killed when his money and clothes were taken. In Basle Jean Oporin published a folio of three works by Peletier, two short mathematical treatises and one on horoscopes. Oporin also brought out a short treatise by Peletier on the plague, for which Peletier thought he had found a remedy. In 1567 Peletier published his *Disquisitiones geometricae* in Lyons, and was therefore probably again on a visit to that city. Only in 1569, however, does he seem to have left Paris for as long as the two years he then spent in Savoy, at the Annecy court of Marguerite de France, duchess of Savoy and daughter of François I, where he could meet Jacques Grévin and Bartolomeo Delbene. He was seeking escape from the religious wars, and was inspired by his stay to return to French poetry with his long decasyllabic poem, *La Savoye*, largely geographical in content, published at Annecy in 1572 and drawing much from Virgil's *Georgics*.

Peletier returned to Paris during the summer of 1572. He signed his *De usu geometriae* that year "medicus et mathematicus (doctor and mathematician)," and had prepared a French version when he was offered the post of Principal at the Collège de Guyenne. Vinet had become Principal in 1562 but resigned in 1570, remaining merely to teach, and was succeeded by Raymond Lorteau. However, the institution's prestige had fallen. The Jesuits had founded a rival college. There were financial stringencies in both the college and the town, and Lorteau felt unable to continue. Peletier accepted the post, went to Bordeaux, returned to Paris to recruit teachers, and was back in Bordeaux in April 1573. He taught Latin, leaving Greek and mathematics to Vinet. Trouble soon broke out, first with the teaching staff and then with city officials. Peletier appealed to the Bordeaux parlement but seems to have lost. He wrote an unpublished defence of himself, which was attached to an unpublished treatise on reading Cicero doubtless also dating from his activities at Guyenne.

The main source for the events surrounding Peletier's dismissal in 1573 is a Latin oration given by him at Poitiers in 1579, an autobiographical inaugural lecture delivered in connection with his teaching of mathematics during part of the academic year 1578–79. It seems to have been the St Bartholomew's Day massacre of 1572 which had kept him from returning to Paris, and he remained at Bordeaux until near the end of 1578, publishing only, in 1573, a Latin translation with the Greek text of the 15 books of Euclid's *Elementa*. Peletier's lecture informs us that he continued to work on geometry, algebra, and arithmetic, studied the first ten numbers and their mystical properties, and wrote against the new sceptics. He also addressed himself to the study of comets and the movement of land and sea masses, to Galen and the Latin classics. At the date of his oration, Peletier intended to polish and publish his Bordeaux writings, but they were not published and have not survived. Twice mentioned by Montaigne in *Les Essais*, Peletier stayed in the château de Montaigne in the company of du Bartas and Pierre de Brach. In Bordeaux he also knew Florimond de Raemond.

Back in Paris in October 1579 Peletier replied, in a work prefaced by a dedication to Pontus de Tyard, to a criticism of his geometry by a Roman Jesuit, Père Christophe Clavier. At the same time the holder of la Ramée's chair of mathematics at the Collège Royal had to submit his post again to a triennial competition, as its rules prescribed. Peletier probably hoped to replace the holder, Maurice Bressieu, who now wrote against Peletier, drawing down on himself a harsh attack, the 1580 *In Mauricium Bressium*. Bressieu none the less managed to hold his chair, and in 1580 Peletier was made Principal of the Collège du Mans, quite close to Coqueret.

We know very little about Peletier's last three years. In 1581 appeared his miscellany of five pieces of scientific and mathematical verse in French, *Les Louanges*, with an appendix comprising short poems on Jupiter and Saturn, and fragments of translation from the *Aeneid*. Peletier died during July 1582.

WORKS

If it seemed clear to his contemporaries that Peletier's geographical restlessness reflected a dissipation of mental energies, it is because too few of them understood the significance for Peletier of the fertile period he spent at Lyons, in the sporadic company of Scève and Pontus de Tyard, from 1554 to 1557. During that period, undoubtedly discouraged by the hostility occasioned by his defence of his projected reform of French orthography, Peletier can be shown not only to have relaxed his obsessional desire to enrich the French language by imitating in it the poets of antiquity and of modern Italy, but also to have come to conceive the poet's function as the understanding and reconstituting of the universe according to its spiritual form. That form, the structure of the cosmos, is based on simple mathematical ratios, innate in the mind, so that the harmony of the spheres is dependent on the same ratios as those which determine that the note given out by a plucked string rises by an octave if the length of the string is halved.

Since the structure of the human mind, like that of music, poetry, and the universe, is based on simple underlying mathematical ratios, there is a connection between music, poetry, human moral and religious harmony with the creation and its creator, the structure of the divine mind and of the human mind, the physical study of the world, medicine, mathematics, the study of the mystical properties of numbers, the poetic description of physical objects, particularly if they are endowed like small animals and precious stones with hermetic qualities, and the poetic description of astronomical and geographical phenomena.

Some variant of some part of this basically neoplatonist theory was explored by the neoplatonist poets of 16th-century Lyons, Peletier, Scève, and Pontus de Tyard, and underlay the poetic practice of each of them. Clearly the theory is immensely powerful. It can, for instance, be used to unify all that is knowable, all the disciplines, on a mathematical model. Without such a theory there could have been no Descartes, no Cartesian (q.v.) recourse to innate ideas in an effort to unify metaphysics, physics, mechanics, medicine, and ethics into a single deductively unified body of knowledge encompassing all that is non-empirically knowable and based on a single metaphysical certainty.

The notion of a universe constructed on simple mathematical ratios innate in the human mind was used to explain music and poetry, and not only the way each reinforced the effect of the other, but also the morally elevating properties of both, each capable of restoring the soul's harmony with its creator. It was used to justify and unite the efforts of poets, scientists, and mathematicians to penetrate the mysteries of the cosmos and re-create its inner form. It defined the purpose of poetry in an astonishingly modern way. Claudel comes near it in his theory of the poet's co-creation with God, and it has a close affinity with Rilke's concept of the poetic "Auftrag (task)" in the Duino elegies, which is to give names to things, thereby seizing on their essence and giving them intelligible form, already a sacred function in the Old Testament. Modern attempts to provide unified accounts of human experience still invoke debates about such things as the innateness of syntactical structures.

In the 16th century, other poets used other forms of the renaissance neoplatonist myth in other ways, to explore, for instance, the morally enriching potentialities of even physical sexual relationships. It was a very potent myth indeed. For Peletier it explained the unity between such only apparently diverse activities of his as medicine, mathematics, and writing poetry. It could have become the basis for an understanding of virtually the whole of human activity as well as the potential basis for a humanist educational programme, and a foundation for the correlative "cycle of the sciences" of whose elaboration the humanists of the French renaissance dreamt, as their Greek predecessors had done. By the sixteenth century there had arisen a clear demand to add other disciplines to the seven liberal arts of the quadrivium and the trivium, which themselves had originally been techniques, but by the renaissance had been transformed into defined areas of subject matter. The renaissance humanists needed in consequence a new unifying principle in the organization of the syllabus. Quintilian had used the image

of circularity, translating the Greek ἐγκύκλιος παιδεία into Latin as "orbis doctrinae (the circle of learning)." The transliteration of the Greek as "encyclopedia" for what the sixteenth-century humanists also called the "disciplinae cyclicae (circular disciplines)" from the late fourth-century Martianus Capella's De nuptiis Philologiae et Mercurii was, of course, quickly to become naturalized. For Peletier, circularity is also an important image, often developed from Nicolas of Cusa and applied to God.

In fact Peletier was, from his early encouragement of Ronsard to the final Louanges, always more distinguished as a theoretician of French renaissance humanism than as one of its leading poetic practitioners. It is probably correct to look on him as being as much a pedagogue or a psychologist as a speculative mathematician. It is, however, his final attempt to solve the great renaissance problem of producing a unified theory of human experience that lends such extraordinary interest and power to his published verse, and even to his mathematical works, as well as to his self-discovery at Lyons, fully articulated only in the inaugural lecture of 1579 at Poitiers but already obscurely perceptible through the affectedly negligent Art poëtique. Although he used classical models and revived classical forms, Peletier's own poetic technique was, like that of the rhétoriqueurs, too reliant on obviously rhetorical devices.

Peletier's first published work, the verse translation of Horace's Ars poetica, is prefaced by an epistle which protests stridently at the contempt in which the vernacular is held, left behind in the pursuit of Latin and Greek to which, however, we owe "toute la congnoissance des disciplines (our knowledge of all the subjects)" and our knowledge of history. We need to know both ancient languages in order to use the vernacular correctly, but we should remember that the Romans did not abandon Latin for Greek, or the Italians Tuscan for Latin, a point Peletier was still to emphasize in his own more moderate Art poëtique of 1555. The difficulty about using ancient languages, argues Peletier, is that they condemn us to remain inferior to our models. The French language is capable of surpassing Italian and Spanish "d'autant que les François en religion et bonne meurs surpassent les autres nations (just as in religion and in manners the French surpass other nations)."

The poems of the 1547 Oeuvres poëtiques were written when Marot, on whom Peletier is plainly modelling himself, had begun to adopt classical verse forms. Peletier's verse, however, is considerably more prolix and laboured than Marot's, lacking his verbal elegance and powers of imaginative invention. Peletier's collection has understandably been criticized for containing over-cerebral versified prose, but it also shows a receptive freshness, and an openness to nature and pastoral scenes which amounts almost to an allusion to the beginning of Homer's Odyssey and of Virgil's Georgics. There are poems on each of the four seasons. Just over half the volume is devoted to translations, including the first parts of the Odyssey and the Georgics, three odes of Horace, an epigram of Martial, and a dozen sonnets of Petrarch.

Although it is very unlikely that another 25 years that Peletier could have been articulate about the justification he was to find for it, the fascination with the description of the earth and natural phenomena is already at least perceptible. There is, for instance, an ode "A ceulx qui blament les Mathematiques," in which the imaginative examination of "La facture et grande merveille/De la ronde machine (the constitution and great wonder/of the spherical mechanism)" leads to a knowledge of "L'immense Deité (the immense divinity)." Peletier can reasonably be seen in this collection to be developing the descriptive "blason" in the direction of scientific, if also mock-scientific, verse, and as introducing into French poetry the ode as a genre, a Horatian epicureanism, and a sincere lyrical emotion, and as bringing a new realistic precision to descriptive verse.

It is important in the present context that Peletier chose to publish the 1549 *Aritmetique* in French. In 1550 came the *Dialogue de l'Ortografe e Prononciation francoęse departi, an deus liures*, which provoked so much hostility. While no doubt on an abstract level it advocated an arguably desirable reform attempting to bring spelling into line with pronunciation, it was altogether too complicated, radical, and learned to have any hope of acceptance. The mere publication of the project betrays an aggressive over-confidence already discernible in the already radical, but more acceptable, earlier advocacy of the vernacular and the Horatian ode. The work was prefaced by the *Apologie a Louis Meigręt Lionnoęs*, less radical than Meigret's own proposals, but with an argument of blinkered logic which itself stirred up much hostility. Peletier wanted the suppression of unpronounced letters, and orthographical distinctions to be made between the three different "e" sounds in French, with "ę" to denote the Latin diphthong æ and *ɇ* to denote Sébillet's "e couppé," or simple feminine ending. Peletier would have liked to see "bataille" spelt "batailhe," "entends" spelt "antans," and "toutefois" spelt "toutɇffoęs". He also required new letters like *ſ*. The dialogue is between Théodore de Bèze, defending the traditional usage, as Bèze in fact actually did, and Peletier under the name of Daubron, in the presence of Jean Martin and Denys Sauvage.

By the time Peletier's *L'Art poëtique* appeared, Ronsard and du Bellay had already gone a long way towards accomplishing their poetic revolution, and du Bellay had published the *Deffence et illustration de la langue françoyse*. Peletier, as noted in the previous section, purported to be publishing merely odd scraps of paper he had found when tidying up. His verse collection *L'Amour des amours—vęrs liriquɇs* had been printed by Jean de Tournes early in the year. The title has no radical ring, but the 1579 Poitiers inaugural lecture puts the poems on a more serious level than those published in 1547. They were now not light-hearted love poems, but written "in imitation of Plato," and the prefatory letter of *L'Art Poëtique* makes clear that in the 1555 collection Peletier moved from consideration of a simple affection to that of a "general and universal" love entailing "profit and importance," and involving the application of "natural sciences, cosmography [and] astrology." Starting therefore from the 96 generally Petrarchan sonnets in decasyllabic verse celebrating a single woman which, with a preliminary sonnet to fame and two lyrical "chants," comprise the first part, Peletier moves on to the 16 odes and the seven "vers liriquɇs" of the second part.

The collection is important not so much for purely poetic qualities as for its use of scientific imagery. Love is the creator of the universe. If the language and expression remain prosaic, the imagery does not. Love emerges as the principle of order, so that the understanding of the cosmos can become the propaedeutic to the knowledge of God:

Dirè je pas bien sans erreur,
Que par l'amoureuse antreprise

De ce Caos la vague horreur
Sa belle corporance a prise?

(Can I not say without error,/That by this loving undertaking/From this chaos, shapeless horror/Has assumed its beautiful form?).

The final poems of the collection, devoted to planets and other astral bodies, by transforming love into a cosmic force, create a matrix inside which scientific verse, the astronomical understanding of the workings of the cosmos, and the religious elevation of the individual become necessarily linked.

L'Art poëtique was published in May, which can only have been weeks after *L'Amour des amours*, and is a much more moderate statement of the position taken up by Ronsard and du Bellay after Peletier's preface to the translation of the *Ars poetica* had inspired the somewhat ill-argued and unequal *Deffence et illustration de la langue françoyse*. In a way similar to du Bellay, Peletier devotes the first section of his work to general principles and the second to matters of sometimes technical detail. He starts, like Sebillet, by holding that poetry is a gift of God, but he also relates all speech to numerical proportions. Nature's capacity for generating novelty is unlimited, and its first gift to humanity was the "mesure et nombre de parler (the measure and number of speech)." The psychology relating syntactical expression to the fundamental numerical ratios is not here elaborated, but is also clear in Pontus de Tyard, whose inspiration is already obvious in *L'Amour des amours*, and will underlie Baïf's lifetime preoccupation with the "measured" verse of his psalm translations.

Peletier digresses so much that his argument defies simple restatement and allows only an indication of its more important implications, but he takes up the enhanced status of poets, "mętres e reformateurs dɇ la vie… intęrpretɇs des Dieus, quand iz sont an leur seinte fureur (masters and reformers of life… interpreters of the gods, when they are in their holy rapture)," rather from Sebillet and the more recent Ronsard of the hymns than from the *Deffence*, and progresses in what purports to be a jumble of odd jottings to a full-scale theory. Poets "conçoęuɇt les sɇcręz celestɇs, diuins, naturęz e mondeins: pour les manifester aus hommɇs (penetrate the heavenly mysteries, divine, natural, and earthly, to reveal them to men)." In his second chapter, closely following Horace, Peletier attempts the reconciliation of the need for inspiration with that for study, a matter on which earlier Pléiade theory had been notoriously vague, partly because Ronsard certainly, and others very probably, had missed the irony in Plato's *Io*. With great prolixity and some playing with words, Peletier comes clearly to the conclusion that poetry requires both inspiration and the skill to whose teaching his work is directed. Peletier pays compliments here to Ronsard, the "sublime" restorer of antique poetry to France, to du Bellay, Scève, Pontus de Tyard, des Masures, Baïf, and Jodelle, before going out of his way to single out Héroët and Marot.

Peletier now distinguishes between the subjects appropriate to poetry, which requires ornamentation and is for the educated, and plainer oratory, designed for "le peuple." He counsels poetic audacity. French poets are still too near the "langage vulgaire (everyday language)," and what is needed is the "Euurɇ Heroïque (heroic work)" that amounts to an epic. He then deals separately with invention, disposition, and elocution, from the traditional parts of rhetoric, before considering imitation, and its "truest species," translation, adjusting the balance which du Bellay had lost in his earlier polemic. The seventh chapter of the first book is still an advocacy of the vernacular. Peletier's contemporaries can no longer hope to "anrichir la Latinite (enrich the Latin language)," but both limbs of du Bellay's programme to enrich the vernacular by imitation have now disappeared. Chapters follow on neologisms, ornamentation, and poetic vices (chapter 10), of which the first is obscurity.

The second book opens with chapters on rhyme and metre before coming to the genres. The sonnet appears merely as a superior and Italianate form of the epigram. Part of the chapter on the ode is devoted to the invention of books and to deploring that of artillery, before Peletier, here following du Bellay, vaunts the superiority of the ode over the medieval forms, ballades, rondeaux, lays, virelays and triolays. Peletier thinks that Marot's psalms can be called odes and, inspired by Horace and agreeing more or less with du Bellay and Ronsard, regards the ode as a poem in praise of gods, demi-gods, princes, or of loves, banquets, festive games, and similar entertainments. No real distinction is made between the epistle and the elegy, and Marot's "coq-à-l'âne" poems are regarded as true satires. In his chapter on comedy and tragedy Peletier is of note chiefly for his re-importation of classical definitions. Comedies have, in particular, happy endings, and deal with ordinary people, while tragedies require kings, princes, or great nobles, and end sadly. Peletier laments the death of Lazare de Baïf, attributing to him, as did everyone else, the translation of Euripides's *Hecuba*, and he lauds Jodelle's success in Paris, which he can have heard about only through letters. He ends with a renewed call for a French epic, which should vie with those of Homer and Virgil.

We have lost both the 1558 *Exhortatio pacificatoria* and its translation, published separately in the same year. If the translation was by Peletier, it is the only new French work he published between 1555 and 1572. There were only works of mathematics in Latin, and reprints, particularly of the French *Aritmetique*. In 1567 appeared an Italian translation of the 1545 Latin *Arithmeticae practicae methodus*, but the next new French work was the 1572 decasyllabic *La Savoye* in three "chants." The poem is largely devoted not so much to penetrating into the mysterious scientific laws governing the operations of the earth's crust as to simple intellectual curiosity about them. It may well be that the intoxicating theory of the unifying ratios which underlie the workings of the cosmos and whose understanding can lead man to God, although it must have been in Peletier's mind by 1555, did not consciously govern his activity until much later, if indeed at all. It may well primarily have been articulated in Poitiers in 1579 to justify and make corporately meaningful the study and writing to which intellectual curiosity and interests in mathematics, geography, geology, and astronomy had anyway impelled him.

La Savoye deals with more technical aspects of water flow, the functioning of the system of mountains, lakes, and France's great rivers, and their roles in the civil wars, rather than their visual, threatening, or aesthetic, impact on human life. The second "chant" goes from a description of gardens to lists of animals which can be hunted, to trees, towns in Savoy and their famous inhabitants, and the third is chiefly concerned with astrologically predicted disasters, the return of the prince to Annecy, and the medicinal properties of the Savoy flora. From time to time there is a flickering interest in the idyll of rustic life and labour.

It was not until 1581 that the *Euvrés poëtiques intituleéz Louangés* appeared. There are five "louanges (praises)", devoted to the ant—remaking Ronsard's poem on the theme—honour, the three Graces, speech, and science. Critics and historians have understandably found little poetic merit in these poems. Their interest lies elsewhere, and is confined to the last two, although that devoted to speech, the "Louange de la Parole," does not spare the reader the physiology of the speech organs put in verse. The poem meanders, making remarks about eloquence, neologisms, Cicero, printing, and other subjects associated in Peletier's mind. The neoplatonism appears in the "Louange de la Sciance," which takes up Cusa's notion of God as circular, with a centre everywhere but no circumference, "Infini en efet, fini en aparence (Infinite in effect, finite in appearance)." There is Cusa, too, behind Peletier's assertion of God's unknowability, although that was itself a more ancient neoplatonist theme. The thirst for knowledge reaches an intensity which identifies it with the quest for God.

Creation's perfection depends on the poetic reconstitution of its spiritual form:

> Nature se délecte à se faire chercher
> Par tant d'Esprits humains…

(Nature delights in having itself sought/By so many human minds).

Only the external appearance of the world is instantly accessible to the mind. The inner reality must be sought out by the scientist or the poet, but can never be totally possessed because, as Peletier repeatedly insists, knowledge feeds on its own need to penetrate ever deeper. Peletier is not primarily interested in religion. He does not mention Christ, and God, for him, is the infinity, or the point, from which everything originates, and towards which everything tends. That, however, does not deprive human striving of a moral or even religious dimension.

> L'Homme, qui en vivant toujours désire entendre,
> Et qui trouve sans fin où ses désirs étendre,
> Puisque ses pensements n'ont terme défini,
> Où peut-il s'arrêter, qu'à un Dieu infini?

Man, who, in living, perpetually desires to know,/And who endlessly finds further goals for these desires,/Since his thoughts have no defined limits,/Where can he stop except in an infinite God?).

Man's mind is limited to the external manifestations of the divinity, which is what confers such significance on their investigation by the empirical sciences, and the mathematical reconstitution of their inner form. The memory is not only a box "Où se met le trésor, ainsi qu'en une armoire,/De précieux joyaux… (Where the treasure is put, as in a cupboard/Of precious jewels), but it is determined by points spaced equally, and "déduite/De l'ordre Arithmétique et Géométrien,/Où gît le vrai savoir, Céleste et Terrien (deduced/From arithmetical and geometric order/In which is found all true knowledge, heavenly and earthly)." In the Poitiers oration Peletier had referred to the faculty of enumerating and measuring as that in which all judgement and reasoning consists. In the "Louange de la Sciance," he writes of arithmetic and geometry,

...Ces deux ensemble apprennent
Aux Esprits d'ordonner tous les faits qu'ils comprennent

(These two together teach/Minds to order all the facts which they take in).

Nothing, Peletier had held in the inaugural lecture, can be known truly and certainly "extra Mathematicarum notionem (unless through mathematical concepts)." The whole face of nature is known, as in a clear mirror, through the order and ratio of numbers and figures ("Numerorum et Figurarum ordine et collocatione"). Only the mathematical concepts of number and proportion, Peletier said, allow us to order our lives, administer our affairs, or achieve our enjoyment. Everything needs to be subjected to mathematical concepts. By numbers man penetrates to a knowledge of God, who himself created with the aid of numbers. God is in all created things as the number one is in all integers, yet subsists infinitely outside them. Like the circle, unity is the nearest metaphor to God we can achieve, and the understanding of ratios is the way in which we approach knowledge of him.

Des choses de ce Monde, et de leurs portions,
L'Homme ne cherche rien que les Proportions:
Car c'est le haut savoir, qui Nature conserve,
Que Dieu à lui tout seul, en elle se réserve

(Of the things of this world and their parts,/The human mind seeks only the proportions,/For that is the high science which preserves the natural order,/And which, in Nature, God keeps to himself alone).

As Peletier had said in his inaugural lecture,

No human deeds, no affairs, no actions, no associations are conducted which are not contained in their numbers and ratios ("suis numeris, suisque proportionibus"). We count by number all things external and internal which we use, and we distinguish them by measurement and ratio. Ratio is what has to be considered in the whole conduct of our lives.

PUBLICATIONS

Verse, verse translations, and literary theory

Horace, *L'Art Poëtique*, 1544 (presumed date of first edition); 2nd edition 1545
Les Oeuvres poëtiques, 1547
Dialogue de l'Ortografe e Prononciation francoȩse, 1550
L'Amour des amours—Vȩrs liriquȩs, 1555
L'Art poëtique, 1555
La Savoye, 1572
Euvrȩs poëtiquȩs intituleȩz Louanges avȩc quelquȩs autrȩs ecriz, 1581

Other

Arithmeticae practicae methodus: annotationes, 1545
L'Aritmetique, 1549

L'Algebrȩ, 1554
In Euclidis elementa…, 1557
De occulta parte numerorum quam Algebram vocant, 1560
De conciliatione locorum Galeni, 1560
De contactu linearum with *De constitutione Horoscopi*, 1563
De peste compendium, 1563?
Disquisitiones geometricae, 1567
De usu Geometriae, 1572
De l'usage de Geometrie, 1573
Euclidis Elementorum libri XV. Graece et latine, 1573
In Christophorum Clavium de Contactu linearum Apologia, 1579
In Mauricium Bressium Apologia, 1580

Biographical and critical studies

Jugé, Clément, *Jacques Peletier du Mans (1517–1582)*, 1907
Chamard, Henri, *Histoire de la Pléiade*, 4 vols., 1930
Boulanger, André, *L'Art poëtique de Jacques Peletier du Mans (1555)*, 1930
Staub, Hans, *Le curieux désir*, 1967
Holyoake, S. John, *An Introduction to French Sixteenth-Century Poetic Theory*, 1972.

PERRAULT, Charles, 1628–1703.

Poet, fairy-tale writer, and literary polemicist.

LIFE

Charles Perrault is known above all not as a poet but as the reorganiser of the Académie française and other French cultural activities under Colbert, as the author of traditional popular fairy stories which he adapted for children, and for his role in leading the party of the modernes in the Querelle des anciens et des modernes (q.v.). Born on 12 January 1628, he was the youngest of the six children of his parents who survived infancy. His twin brother, François, born a few hours earlier, died at six months. The other five children were Marie, who died at 13, and four brothers: Jean, a little-known lawyer who died at Bordeaux in 1669; Pierre, who was to become the Receveur général des Finances but was disgraced under Colbert, sold his office, took up natural science, translated Tassoni, and wrote criticism; Claude, a doctor and then an architect; and Nicolas, a professor of theology and doctor of the Sorbonne, eventually excluded from that body for Jansenism (q.v.) demonstrated in his defence of Antoine Arnauld.

Claude Perrault published a translation of Vitruvius's ten books on architecture in 1673, was an engineer as well as an anatomist, and was enlisted by his brother when Charles was Colbert's chief assistant at the Surintendance des Bâtiments, although the final sketches for the Louvre's eastern colonnade, drawn up after Bernini's plans had been abandoned and long attributed to Claude Perrault, appear to have originated entirely within the Le Vau circle. Claude Perrault was, however, with Le Vau and Lebrun, a member of the committee charged in 1667 with completing the Louvre, and he designed the Observatory (1667), made a model in 1669 for the triumphal arch at the Porte Saint-Antoine which was begun but never completed, and in 1673 or 1674 designed the château de Sceaux for Colbert. He opposed Descartes on animals' souls, was an animist in physiology, a founding member of the Académie des Sciences, and did become a distinguished architect. Boileau, whom he had treated medically, thought him a poor doctor and avenged himself in the fourth chant of the *Art poétique*. Claude Perrault, charged by Colbert with the reception of exotic animals at the royal zoo at Versailles, dissected an elephant there in 1681, and died from an infection caught while dissecting a diseased camel.

Charles Perrault's biography has been complicated by his self-justificatory *Mémoires de ma vie*, written in 1702 when he was nearly 75 but while the animosity of Boileau was not yet totally appeased. The full text, intended for his family, was left in manuscript until 1909. Not surprisingly, it departs from historical accuracy when recounting the family history, as also naturally does the sometimes vituperative published polemical literature, unreliable as a source of historical fact, thrown up by his own and his family's involvement with Jansenism, Colbert's ministry and patronage, and the Querelle des anciens et des modernes. Finally the interpretation of his career has been strained by the efforts of historians to link particular 17th-century attitudes, demonstrated in such matters as the view taken of Jansenism, of the Jesuits, of the administration of justice, of the taxation system, or of what was popularly supposed to be witchcraft, with particular social classes.

The family came from Touraine, and had doubtless made the ascent from the mercantile into the administrative and professional strata of society while the class chasm opened and the peasants slipped further into poverty. Perrault's father, Pierre, was a lawyer at the bar of the Paris parlement, a believer in humanist education and in strictly evangelical Catholicism. His mother, Paquette Leclerc, had brought to her marriage a house at Viry-sur-Orge, which Perrault and his brother Pierre were to enlarge, and which was to be sold for 15,000 livres in 1684. Since it was Pierre Perrault's share in the family inheritance, and there were at least four other heirs, the family was well off, but there are indications that money was used carefully to establish Perrault and his brothers solidly among the professional administrative classes. The family had been unwilling to find the money for the pointless and expensive defence of Perrault's legal theses after two years' study, and when the receivership was bought for Pierre in 1654, after his father's death in 1652 but before his own marriage in 1666, his mother's dowry must have been involved, and Pierre then offered Perrault himself an undemanding post in his office, allowing Perrault to devote himself to literature, as if Pierre had been acquitting a family debt.

Perrault's experience of education is unclear. He attended the collège de Beauvais in Paris from 1636 to 1644, and appears to have had to repeat some classes, to have had some difficulty in learning to read and write, but to have been regarded nonetheless as an excellent pupil. The curriculum was traditional and Latin-based, although the Jansenists and Oratorians were soon to experiment with more vernacular elements in the syllabus. The *Mémoires* lead us to believe that Perrault walked out of his class, followed by a friend called Beaurain, and that the two of them then continued their studies together without assistance. The

probability is that Perrault had taken part in a public academic debate and conceivably defended a point of view which may already have been suspect, whether or not it was identifiably Augustinian. The teacher mentioned in the *Mémoires* may have felt compromised by being publicly associated with views he had actually taught, and what was described as a walk-out may well have been the result of an agreement.

By 1644 Perrault's schooling in the arts faculty was in any case practically finished, and it was normal for aspiring lawyers in Paris to study alone or with only private tuition before taking their civil law degrees at Poitiers, Orléans, or Toulouse, as the Paris law faculty, forbidden to teach Roman and civil law since the middle ages, remained restricted by royal decree to canon law until 1679. At any rate, on leaving school Perrault appears to have indulged in a period of wide reading no longer constricted, as it had been at school, by meticulous attention to grammatical detail. After his humanist training at school, Perrault read a great variety of sometimes religious texts, no longer in excerpts selected for their pedagogical utility, but in integral versions. His reading, allied to the family atmosphere of austerity in matters of religion, may well have taken Perrault some way towards his deep commitment to Colbert's pursuit of cultural absolutism.

Any rejection by Perrault during the years of collaboration with Colbert of the last flowering of the baroque spirit which Foucquet had continued to uphold was, however, only temporary. Colbert wanted to orchestrate the praise of the king and his reign, and was therefore a moderne in strategy, although not in taste. Perrault was fundamentally a moderne on grounds of taste and of his feeling for the cultural realities. Colbert's strategy and Perrault's need to chant the glories of the present coincided, but in all realms of cultural activity Colbert's reactionary tastes were swiftly to be abandoned under Louvois. Aesthetically, Louvois took over where Foucquet had been interrupted, and Perrault was on his side.

Perrault was to rally to the literary groups protected by Foucquet well before the financier's arrest in 1661. By that date his optimistic view of human nature and its emotional and spiritual activities, to be reinforced by his genuine dedication to the forms of cultural advance he was to help Colbert to organize for the glorification of Louis XIV, already destined him to take the side of the modernes, when the Querelle broke out.

Sometime between 1644 and 1648, the date at which Nicolas Perrault took his doctorate in theology, Perrault and Beaurain, whose laughter over their task attracted first the attention and then the assistance of Nicolas, turned the sixth book of Virgil's *Aeneid* into burlesque verse. Scarron's burlesque poem *Typhon; ou, La Gigantomachie* had appeared in 1644, and the first seven books of his *Virgile travesti* were to be published in 1648, establishing a vogue. Between 1649 and 1652 parodies of Virgil appeared by Furetière, Jaulnay, Dufresnoy, Brébeuf, and Claude Petit Jehan, and there were several of Ovid. Some of these parodies were disguised attacks on Mazarin. Perrault and Beaurain did not publish, and their 3,000 lines of verse first appeared in 1901, a light-hearted frolic, drenched in the scatology of late adolescence, whose chief literary device is anachronism, but whose irreverence towards the greatest of the Latin poets was a harbinger of more serious attitudes to come. The brothers continued their collaboration and produced *Les Murs de Troie; ou, L'Origine du burlesque*, published in 1653 but chiefly, it seems the work of Claude.

Perrault took the prescribed oral examination to obtain his licenciate in law at Orléans in 1651, at the age of 23. He claimed in the *Mémoires* that he had had to get the examining professors out of bed. It is difficult to know just how perfunctory the examination was but, although what counted for the board of three examiners was the fee, the content of the examination cannot have been entirely nugatory, and the probability is that candidates had at least to be able to talk intelligibly about Roman law in Latin, which presupposed something on top of the standard Paris arts curriculum, itself guaranteeing no such ability. Perrault's father died in 1652, and it is not impossible that Perrault himself desultorily practised law. From the purchase of the receivership in 1654 for Pierre, Perrault himself had gained a post whose exigences he himself later described as derisory. The Perrault family was acting after the Fronde according to the carefully calculated interests of its caste, and heavily backing the stability that for a moment had seemed threatened. Their mother was to die in 1657, and the redeployment of her dowry included the enlargement of the Viry house. Perrault spent much time among the books purchased by his brother from the heirs of Germain Habert, the author of the 1638 poem *La Métamorphose des yeux de Philis en astres*, published in 1639.

There are obvious connections between préciosité (q.v.) and such similar literary phenomena as the cultivation of the madrigal and other fixed-form light poetic genres used for turning facile compliments, presenting gifts or greetings, and playing elegant word games, for which the vogue can be traced back to Voiture and the Hôtel de Rambouillet. Préciosité itself came later than Germain Habert and the principal flowering of the coterie of the Chambre bleue, but its apogee had already passed by the end of the 1550s. The bourgeois salons, such as that of Madeleine de Scudéry, had taken over from the Hôtel de Rambouillet; honnêteté had taken over from galanterie; Pascal had made the severe spirituality associated more with Port-Royal than with Jansen's *Augustinus* seem more authentically Christian than Jesuit confessional practice; and the word–portrait had taken over from the madrigal.

The vogue for portraits took off with the later volumes of Madeleine de Scudéry's *Clélie*, whose sixth volume, of March 1657, had been followed by the seventh and eighth, which appeared on 1 August 1658. It culminated in the exquisite limited edition of Mlle de Montpensier's collection of 59 *Divers portraits*, published at Caen at the very beginning of 1659 and immediately followed by the *Recueil de portraits et éloges en vers et en prose*, published in Paris by the booksellers Barbin and Sercy, whose achevé d'imprimer was 25 January 1659. The *Divers portraits* contained Perrault's poems "Portrait d'Iris" and "Portrait de la voix d'Iris." Both must have been circulating for some months. The first was much admired and frequently recited by Quinault, who is known on one occasion not to have disowned its authorship. The second is to be found in a manuscript of 1658.

It is at this date that Perrault can be found in contact with Foucquet's circle. The surintendant, who had works of literature which particularly pleased him copied on vellum and bound with gilt edging, accorded this honour to Perrault's *Dialogue de l'Amour et de l'Amitié*, somewhat surprisingly dedicated to d'Aubignac and published by Sercy in 1660. Perrault had become friendly with Quinault, whose inspiration can be discerned behind his next work, the prose *Le Miroir; ou, La Métamorphose d'Orante* of 1661, which Boileau was to attack in the ninth *Epître* of 1685. Comparing it in the first volume of the *Parallèles des anciens et des modernes* to Gilles Boileau's 1653 translation of the *Tableau de Cébès*, Perrault's Abbé was to call *Le Miroir d'Oronte* an allegory, taking up the quarrel in which, roughly during the decade between 1655 and 1665, the partisans of allegory, d'Aubignac, Furetière, Cotin, and Gilles Boileau, had confronted those they referred to as pedants, like Ménage and Huet, as well as those concerned with the refined analysis of sentiment, like Madeleine de Scudéry, Scarron, Pellisson, and the précieux.

The connection with Foucquet's entourage was established through the circle round Etienne Martin de Pinchesne, the nephew of Mme de Rambouillet's principal poet, Voiture, and editor of his letters. Since 1656 Pinchesne had regularly received a group of poets and jovially Epicurean libertins at partly gastronomic gatherings, supplied from Le Mans with guinea-fowl and capons by the archdeacon and canon, Pierre Costar, the author of the 1653 *Défense des ouvrages de M. de Voiture* and its follow-ups, *Les Entretiens de M. Voiture et de M. Costar* and the 1655 *Suite de la Défense*. With the gourmets Jacques Vallée, sieur Des Barreaux, and Alexandre d'Elbène, the group notably included both Hippolyte Jules Pilet de La Mesnardière, who was doctor to Richelieu, the duc d'Orléans, and Mme de Sablé, and the author of an unfinished *Poétique* of 1639 warning against the salon trivialization of poetry, and François Charpentier, a resolute supporter of the modernes, enemy of Boileau-Despréaux, and made secretary by Colbert of the small private council, inaugurated in 1663, which was later to become the Académie des Inscriptions when it was publicly institutionalized.

Guillaume Colletet, Tallement des Réaux, and François Payot de Lignières were also associated with this group. It was friendly towards Ménage, Scarron, Pellisson, and Madeleine de Scudéry, but generally hostile to Chapelain, Gilles Boileau, d'Aubignac, Furetière, referred to by them as "the young crows," and also to the dwindling authority of Conrart and Balzac. In fact it was the kernel of what would later become the party of the modernes, joined in this way to the still baroque sensibility favoured and fostered by Foucquet. It was a trivial incident which finally separated the parties. Gilles Boileau had been flattering Ménage, seeking advice from him and attending his Wednesday gatherings, while at the same time committing himself to Ménage's implacable enemy, d'Aubignac. He was later to flatter Colbert at the same time as lampooning him, but at this point he circulated a satirical attack on Ménage, the *Avis à M. Ménage sur son églogue intitulée Christine*, and his authorship was leaked. Ménage, urged by Chapelain, tried to keep the peace, buying back all available copies of a defence of himself by Le Bret against Gilles Boileau, but Gilles Boileau thought that Costar's *Suite de la Défense* had broken the truce and on 20 December 1655 took out a privilège for his injurious *Avis à M. Ménage* which was published, with an attack on Costar tacked on, early in 1656.

Essentially the effect of this petty squabble, ostensibly about a worthless eclogue, was to unite the worldly group around Costar with the more erudite but also precious circle surrounding Ménage. What finally threw Gilles Boileau and Chapelain together was the courteous but wounding 60-page attack on Chapelain's *La Pucelle*, appearing in the same month, January 1656, and pseudonymously entitled *Lettre du Sr du Rivage contenant quelques observations sur le poème épique et sur le poème de la Pucelle*. Everyone knew it was by La Mesnardière, at this time a friend of Pinchesne, Costar, and Ménage. What had occurred was a taking of sides and almost a preliminary round in the match which was to become the Querelle. Chapelain replied with a *Lettre du sieur de la Montagne au sieur du Rivage*.

Ironically, the division was almost healed by a series of perfidious epigrams aimed at members of both parties by Lignières, from 1674 to be more or less permanently an alcoholic attached to the Condé household at Chantilly. Directed against Chapelain, Conrart, Boisrobert, and Gombauld, as well as against Costar, Ménage, and Pellisson, they incensed and almost reconciled both opposing sides, but the rupture became definitive when Chapelain, perhaps because of Colbert's insistence, proposed Gilles Boileau as Colletet's successor at the Académie in 1659. Ménage was not a member, but successfully organized Boileau's defeat. Pellisson spoke for an hour against Boileau, and five members who never came were persuaded to attend the session and vote against him.

By the end of the year Cotin had circulated his *Ménagerie*. Foucquet backed Scarron and Ménage's party. The cultural hostility between Ménage and Chapelain mimicked the political enmity and growing personal rivalry between Foucquet and Colbert, and the aesthetic tastes of each in turn. In 1661 Perrault also wrote *La Chambre de justice d'amour*, not to be published until the 1675 *Recueil de divers ouvrages en prose et en vers*. On 9 March 1661 Mazarin died, incidentally leaving a fortune that can only have been amassed with the help of Foucquet, and only after the Fronde, but which was administered for him by Colbert, whose warning in 1659 on the death of Servien, nominally Foucquet's equal, about Foucquet's administrative financial practices Mazarin ignored.

Political events between 1660 and 1662 were to change Perrault's career. At this date about a third of the 23,000 convicts in France's prisons were there for failure to pay tax, and much of the country was reduced to near starvation by the pillaging of unpaid troops, piracy in the Mediterranean, and the poor harvests of 1658 and 1660. Gaston d'Orléans died in 1660, the year of the marriage of Louis XIV to the daughter of Philip IV of Spain, and the king's brother, the new duc d'Orléans, married Henriette d'Angleterre in the month of Mazarin's death. Louis XIV was 23 when he proclaimed to the amusement and incredulity of the court his decision henceforward to rule without a chief minister. In fact the king's personal rule resulted in a huge increase of political power for his principal administrative officials, in the first instance for Colbert.

The king now ruled through the three advisory councils over whose meetings he presided. The three were concerned respectively with all matters of state (the Conseil d'Etat), with interior administration (the Conseil des Dépêches), and with finances (the Conseil des Finances); the king was careful to keep the feudal aristocracy and the great ecclesiastics out of all of them. The Conseil privé consisted of maîtres de requêtes and represented the king's supreme judicial authority. It met at the Louvre but not, like the others, in the king's apartments.

The person on whom Louis XIV chiefly relied was Colbert, who had been destined for commerce, but had entered the service of Le Tellier and graduated to that of Mazarin. In 1661 he successfully negotiated the fall of Foucquet, arrested that September and finally imprisoned for life, and himself took control of the small council in charge of financial administration,

assuming from 1667 the title of contrôleur-général. Under him, the administration of affairs was in the hands of secretaries of state. The last vestiges of a governmental function had been removed from the landed aristocracy, and France was run from the summit of a steep pyramid of professional administrators at whose peak was Colbert. On 1 January 1664 Colbert became surintendant des bâtiments, and gradually acquired even more titles, offices, and power. In bringing to its highest point royal absolutism, he counted heavily on concerting the arts to depict, celebrate, and further the glories of the monarch, and attempted accordingly the successful organization of cultural pursuits, concentrating especially on buildings, painting, and literature.

He turned to Chapelain, author of what was intended to be the great French epic, *La Pucelle*. Chapelain's letter of 9 December 1661 to Heinsius showed what Colbert must have known, that Chapelain hated Foucquet, as well as the aesthetic values he promoted and enjoyed, and appeared to relish the prospect of his execution. After Boisrobert, Chapelain had already been the chief intermediary between Richelieu and the literary world, and Colbert had known Chapelain well during the ascendancy of Mazarin. When he needed support from a dominating literary figure opposed to Foucquet's friends and unsympathetic to the popular support which Foucquet enjoyed, the choice was obvious. By 18 December 1662 Chapelain was replying to a letter of Colbert's approving his proposals for cultural re-organization, which embraced medals, poetry, history, panegyrics, "pyramids, columns, equestrian statues, colossuses, triumphal arches, busts of marble and bronze," and much else. By 1663 Colbert had refounded the Académie de Peinture et de Sculpture, and by 1668 founded the Académie des Sciences and the Académie de France à Rome, which in 1676 became dependent on the Paris Académie de Peinture et de Sculpture. The Académie de l'Architecture was founded in 1671, the Académie de la Musique in 1672. Late in November or early in December 1662 Chapelain had drawn up for Colbert his celebrated *Mémoire sur quelques gens de lettres vivans en 1662 dressé par ordre de M. Colbert*, a list of 90 names, adding to an initial enumeration of 50 names those of all 40 members of the Académie.

In 1660 Perrault had taken care to write his "Ode sur le mariage du roi," and an "Ode sur la paix." In 1661 came the "Ode au roi sur la naissance de Mgr le Dauphin." Colbert had appointed two literary abbés, Bourzeys and Cassagnes, to help Chapelain in his reorganization of the arts, and it was Chapelain who turned to Perrault. He may have been aware that Colbert and Pierre Perrault had known one another, and probably collaborated closely, when they had both still been working in the finance department charged with the creation and sale of offices. Colbert, Chapelain, Bourzeys, Cassagnes, and Perrault met for the first time at Colbert's residence on 3 February 1663, and decided to meet henceforward privately on Tuesdays and Fridays. They were soon to be joined by Charpentier, and the informal council, the petit conseil, was to grow into the Académie des Inscriptions et Belles-Lettres charged, as the name suggests, with organizing the cultural glorification of the king, but constituting more a strategic weapon designed by Colbert to be used in promoting the wealth and power of France than a committee to institutionalize celebrations of achievement or orgies of flattery.

France bought Dunkirk from England for 2,500,000 livres, and it was handed over on 27 October 1662. Perrault wrote his "Discours sur l'acquisition de Dunkerque par le roi" in 1663. It may almost have been a task set as a test of Perrault's ability to defend publicly Colbert's political strategy before he was fully entrusted with the organization of the royal thurifers. The regime of "gratifications," pensions of from 800 to 3,000 livres awarded annually to writers, started in 1663, with the first distribution decided in March or April. The first list proposed had contained 15 names of non-nationals. The total cost was supposed to be 100,000 livres, but in 1663 only 80,000 livres were allocated. The sum rose to 110,000 livres in 1669, but sank again with the Dutch war, to 86,000 livres in 1672, 62,000 in 1674, and 49,000 in 1676. Corneille's name was struck off, payments were delayed, and Perrault remarked that the year had begun to have 15 or 16 months, although his own gratification was always paid on time.

Perrault devoted himself whole-heartedly to Colbert's plan for the extolling of the king and the control of the arts, not forgetting as he went, any more than did Colbert, the promotion of his own interests and those of his family. For 20 years he wrote practically nothing, but if he later sought in the *Mémoires* to convey the impression that he had disinterestedly given himself to the good of the kingdom, and especially of its more desperately poor inhabitants, it is important to remember that he was writing the interpretation of his life he wanted his surviving child to have. He white-washes the behaviour of his elder brother Pierre, ruined in 1664 when, dismissed by Colbert, he was obliged to sell his office at a loss and the Viry house had eventually to be auctioned.

In the wake of the Fronde, the king had started to curry the favour of the populace by restoring to them the perquisites hitherto thought to be legitimately enjoyed by the receveurs des finances. It was the office-buying classes of the bourgeoisie which had backed the dissident aristocracy against the court in the Fronde, using the threat of popular insurrection as a weapon. Those classes now needed to have order restored, but were to have their wings clipped in the process. It was now the king who could count on popular support in threatening the tax-farming classes, together with the whole of the office-buying magistracy, whose income and opportunities he squeezed.

Colbert restored order, but he increased the pressure on the tax farmers, a policy whose inauguration had been signalled with the toppling of Foucquet and no less than 4,000 others, fined by the same tribunal as had confiscated Foucquet's possessions. Perrault's *Mémoires* strongly insinuate Pierre Perrault's connivance with Colbert during the 1650s in what amounts to setting Foucquet up as the scapegoat for malpractices which in the end also damaged the interests only of his subordinate tax collectors. Perrault complains of the king's liberality in restoring to the people everything due to them from the taxation of the last ten years,

> libéralité admirable si elle n'eût point été faite aux dépens des receveurs généraux, à qui ces restes appartenaient et qui ont presque tous péri, faute d'en avoir fait le recouvrement

> (an admirable generosity if it had not been made at the expense of the tax collectors, to whom these left-overs belonged, and who have almost all gone under, because they have been unable to recover them).

Investments in official posts were being made to yield less, and their number was also being reduced. Pierre had helped himself

to what certainly by custom, virtually by right, but not by Colbert's new rule-book, belonged to him. Even when most active in promoting the interests of Perrault himself, who pleaded strongly for his brother, Colbert was unmoved by the plight of his old accomplice, Pierre. Perrault's career was as independent of Pierre's as his views were independent of the Jansenism of his brother Nicolas, however closely the family cooperated in furthering one another's careers.

Perrault, who by 1664 had held his sinecure in Pierre's office for 10 years, fared better than his brother. It is to be presumed that he impressed Colbert, who quickly extended his reliance on Perrault beyond the small but immensely influential council of reorganization. Perrault was lodged in an official residence and given land at Versailles to build on, and gradually he took on parts of the role for which Chapelain had been cast. It was nonetheless in spite of Chapelain's opposition that, at the death of the chancellor Pierre Séguier on 28 January 1672, when the king became protector and Colbert vice-protector of the Académie française, Perrault arranged for the re-structuring of the Académie. He had himself been received as a member on 23 November 1671, and was in 1672 and again, exceptionally, in 1673, elected its chancellor to deputize for the director, Harlay de Champvallon, the generally absent archbishop of Paris. Perrault was himself to become director in 1681.

In 1672 he immediately proposed a series of reforms not, it can be supposed, designed to displease Colbert, who wanted his academies to work hard at furthering his political aims by implementing his cultural strategy. Sessions at which new members were received were made public, starting with that of 13 January 1673. The *Discours de réception* were to be published. Sessions were also to be held more frequently, to start more promptly, and to last exactly two hours; members were paid a small allowance if they were there on time for the start. Those who were received a redeemable "jeton," and some fun was had at the expense of the "jetonniers," who turned up for the money. La Fontaine was the most famous. The celebrated "fauteuils" were installed at the Louvre itself in place of the old chairs, and work was started on the dictionary. Patru gave up coming when debate got stuck at determining the gender of the letter "A," the first entry.

In the meanwhile Perrault had been employed by Colbert on a variety of projects, from the supplying of water to the organization of court festivities and the expansion of France's commercial activities. He tells us in the *Mémoires* that he retained for Parisians the right of access to the Tuileries, and vetoed Riquet's expensive project to divert part of the Loire through Versailles, but in neither case does he tell us that he also had a private political end in view although, thinking that he is writing for his family alone, he has given us enough information to work it out. He drew up a memoir, for instance, for building a royal palace, with water supply, near Viry, where he may well at the time have had property of his own, in addition to the house owned by Pierre. He controlled the development of the Gobelins, which he changed for Colbert from a workshop weaving tapestries to the "Manufacture royale des meubles de la Couronne", producing everything necessary to furnish royal palaces. Lebrun was appointed director in 1663, and allowed to employ some 250 craftsmen. Above all Perrault was in charge of what has been described as "the department of the king's glorification," overseeing the industry of dedications, prefaces, and epigrams, and the whole personality cult of the king, including provision for the writing of the history of the reign, and the composition of inscriptions for medals, arches, tapestries, monuments, statues, and pediments.

Everything was made to contribute to the central political strategy, which was to build France into a strong and unified nation. The strategy was still based on the view that there was a limited amount of wealth in the world, and that it was in France's interests to acquire as much of it as possible, a process which depended on commerce, territorial aggrandizement, political power, and commercial endeavour. Mining, agriculture, forestry, and fishing could be expanded, but the wealth they produced was finite, measurable, and no substitute for taxation which, even if more predictable and flexible, depended on the acquisition of territory. To acquire territory on favourable terms France needed to be perceived as mighty, led by a strong, determined, and preferably invincible monarch.

None the less, Perrault did not neglect the need to compete more effectively in the east with England and the Low Countries. The home country had to be rallied in support of building up the king's image, however, and the propaganda of which Perrault was put in charge became for the first time obviously important. It was nationalistic considerations of this sort, based on archaic economic concepts more than chivalric ideals of personal merit and public esteem, which account for everything that was done to project the image of the sun king. Perrault himself was officially appointed in 1668 to the Surintendance des Bâtiments, where he was to become contrôleur in 1672 and, in virtue of authority delegated directly by Colbert, practically fulfilled the functions of a minister for the arts, sciences, and urban development. For instance, he also supervised the installation of a chemistry laboratory in the Bibliothèque Royale and advised Colbert against mining for minerals in France. His powers of patronage became considerable.

Perrault collaborated in enforcing the increased vigilance that was exercised over publishing permissions, over the importation of unlicensed material, and over the operation of the book trade. Colbert set out to reduce the number of printers in Paris, which stood at 84. From December 1666 new printers could be licensed only by the king. As at the Gobelins, the power of the old guilds was systematically broken. The removal of the unrestricted right to admit to membership was simply symbolic. Craftsmen were given a superb basic training, at the Gobelins always beginning with drawing; and they improved their social position, but lost their right to individual inventiveness. The emphasis on draughtsmanship rather than colour at the Gobelins under Lebrun echoes the defence of the anciens favoured by Colbert over the modernes, preferred by his successor, Louvois. The formal stringency of Lebrun, who held up Poussin's draughtsmanship as a model against Rubens and the colourists, was analogous to Boileau's preference in literature for Malherbe and strict metrical proprieties over the more flamboyant works of Ronsard and the loosely structured fiction and light-weight madrigals of the baroque. Perrault's personal taste was for the colourists, as his intellectual commitment was to the modernes, a commitment perhaps strengthened by, but not essentially founded on, his cultural activity under Colbert. What was at stake in the Querelle, however, was more than literature. When Louvois commissioned Mignard's Tent of Darius of 1689, it was a direct challenge to the artist to rival Lebrun's acknowledged greatest achievement of 1661, depicting the same scene, and it was under Louvois that Jules Hardouin-Mansart replaced Le Vau's Orangery at Versailles between 1681 and 1686, and his

Trianon in 1687. With the coming of rococo, Perrault's modernes were to win in painting as well as in literature.

Perrault must have known that what he was assisting Colbert to achieve was not in accordance with his own artistic preferences, however much it might have accorded with his economic interests. The later clash had inevitably to occur as Perrault's intellectual commitment came to diverge more openly from Colbert's political aims, whose sinister aspect emerged when it became clear how the various academies, most notoriously the academy of music, had become monopolies, and therefore effective tools for the implementation of royal policy in their respective domains. Literature was different, in that demand for writers' products came from the town, which often favoured the modernes, as well as from the court where—in view of the glorification procedures, paradoxically—the party of the anciens remained strong.

However, even in literature the gratifications counted, as did membership of the Académie, and Perrault's reform had delivered to the king a stranglehold on membership, which he was later to exploit, for instance in the matter of La Fontaine's election. The rules put forward by Perrault and adopted prescribed that, whenever there was a vacancy, candidates were proposed and spoken for, and a secret vote was taken. A single name was later reported to the members by the presiding official, chancellor or director, and a simple vote was taken for or against the candidate. If there was a majority in favour, the agreement of the Académie's protector was sought, a euphemistic way of saying that the king's permission was needed, and only when it had been obtained could the members proceed to the election proper. This third vote was invariably in favour, and generally unanimous, with the exception of Mézeray's black ball, a personal manifestation in defence of the academy's freedom, which quickly became accepted as a ritual.

Perrault also took a position on the sensitive question of superstition and witchcraft, a matter of some importance in view of the attitude to popular legend shown by the fairy stories, and the hostility to superstition often associated with Jansenism. Officially, there was no softening of official attitudes before 1682, although Louis XIV commuted the 12 sentences of burning confirmed by the parlement de Rouen in 1669. The Bordeaux parlement had condemned 120 witches to be burnt in 1630; there were 17 condemnations in the Orléannais between 1615 and 1616; the bailli of Loudiniers hanged eight shepherds in 1618; 15 people were hanged in Neuchâtel in 1638; it was only when the Jesuit Surin took over from Père Tranquille at Loudun after the burning of Grandier in 1634 that the diabolic possessions among the nuns were shown to be hysterical. There had been doubters from Montaigne's time onwards. Malebranche did not think he was wrecking belief in the miraculous by doubting the existence of any witchcraft at all. Perrault simply equivocates, and seems readier to admit the reality of witchcraft than at least the more enlightened of his contemporaries. That readiness also appears to increase as he began to write the Contes.

Perrault's financial affairs remain obscure. They are naturally not discussed in detail in Mémoires drawn up for family consumption. From 1672, the year of his marriage, he was receiving an official income of 7,625 livres, of which 2,000 was his gratification, 1,500 came from his post in the Surintendance des Bâtiments, increased to 2,000 in 1675, and 4,125 was his salary as its contrôleur. From 1674 the chancelry also paid him 800 livres a year, taking his official income to 8,925 from 1675. Neither his earnings nor his patrimony explains the inventory taken on the eve of his marriage of the furnishings in the magnificent house put at his disposal, "the prettiest in Paris" according to the marquis de Sourches, overlooking the gardens of the Palais-Royal. His wife's dowry of 70,000 livres included two houses valued respectively at 18,000 and 21,500 livres, but he already had three Paris houses, one in the Rue des Vieux-Augustins, one in the Rue de Thorigny, and one in the Rue des Petits-Champs, in which his study had its ceiling decorated with the eleven paintings described in his 1690 *Le Cabinet des Beaux Arts*, all by painters employed by Jules Hardouin-Mansart. In 1685 Perrault was to have two more houses built, one for himself and one for his brother Claude, having lost from his annual income the 2,000 livres from the office in the Surintendance in 1680, the 2,000 livres of gratification in 1681, and the 4,125 livres as contrôleur in 1683. He must have speculated in property. He bought and sold at Viry, associating himself with a Vincent Hotman in one 180,000-livre contract for a hôtel that had belonged to Foucquet.

Perrault's brothers were not doing as well as he was. Pierre is said in the *Mémoires* to have been without a servant after 1664. Jean, the eldest, had no clients. Claude, having graduated on 19 December 1641, must still have been earning a living as a doctor. From 1666, Claude was paid as an "academician" physician. Together with such other habitués of the salon held by Louis-Henri Habert de Montmort under the patronage of César d'Estrées as the mathematicians Roberval and Carcavy, Claude Perrault was in 1668 to become a founder member of the Académie des Sciences, whose members received an annual payment of 2,000 livres. Habert de Montmort's circle was devoted to experimental science and included distinguished physicists, but it also fostered a spin-off group round the abbé de Villeloin, Michel de Marolles. The Marolles circle itself, like that of d'Aubignac, encompassed the Boileau brothers, Furetière, the marquis de Maulévrier, and La Mesnardière, and by the mid-1660s was hostile to Chapelain as well as to préciosité, Ménage, and the literary group to which Perrault belonged.

Perrault recruited his brothers Jean and Claude in connection with the administrative reorganization and urban development of Bordeaux. There were at least five members in the team, constituted in Paris, and the exact functions of the Perrault brothers are unclear, except that Claude's was basically architectural. Jean was to die in Bordeaux on 30 October 1699, but Claude was to gain favour with Colbert, who was impressed by the Vitruvius translation, which he had commissioned, when it appeared, dedicated to him, in 1673. Long before that, Claude Perrault had been given important architectural tasks, including in 1667 the design for the Observatory. He was also made part of the three-man committee with Le Vau and Lebrun for the completion of the Louvre. This project was close to the heart of Colbert, who urgently wanted to keep Louis XIV in Paris, although the monarch wanted the firmer control he would have of his court in the country at Versailles, which had the additional advantage, seldom adverted to, of making the security problems much easier in an entourage in which assassination had not been extinct for long enough.

It seems that after the fiasco of Bernini's vaunted journey to Paris in 1665, which left in the end only the single great bust of Louis XIV, when Colbert had decided on a French solution to the problem of the eastern colonnade of the Louvre, and Bernini's design had been abandoned after the foundation stone had been laid, that the design adopted was essentially that produced by Le Vau's workshop, probably by François d'Orbay, his son-in-law. François Mansart had died in 1666, and Colbert did not share the king's confidence in his only serious rival, Louis Le Vau. Claude Perrault's own designs for the colonnade perished in the Louvre fire of 1871. What seems almost certain to have been a Le Vau-d'Orbay design was unhappily executed without the bridge that would have linked the Louvre to the Collège des Quatre Nations, now the Institut, designed by Le Vau for Mazarin's executors, built on the same axis as the square court of the Louvre, finished by d'Orbay, and intended to become part of the same ensemble. What crosses the river there now is a rather feeble substitute we know as the Pont des Arts.

As the Querelle drew nearer, culminating in the almost entirely symbolic clash between Perrault and Boileau, and even after 1694, the literary line-up did not always correspond to the alliances and enmities dictated by ordinary social relationships. La Mesnardière had changed sides, but Lignières and Gilles Boileau had both satirically attacked members of groups to which they had affected to belong. Perrault himself, understandably, in view of the association with Quinault, supported Quinault's collaborator, Lulli, in obtaining for him his exclusive privileges and the use of the Palais-Royal theatre, but he also procured a pension for Gilles Boileau, and the reasons he alleged to Colbert for giving the theatre in the Palais-Royal to Lulli were cynical. The people, for whom Perrault's feeling, unless there was a political gain to be glimpsed, scarcely rose above indulgent contempt, would enjoy being admitted to the palace of princes. That, as has been remarked, is only a variant of buying popularity with "bread and circuses." In the 1660s, having abandoned the pursuit of literature for administration, Perrault had become a courtier. Racine, a decade later, was to follow much the same route.

Perrault's literary activity from 1661 had consisted entirely of descriptions of festivals, short encomiastic pieces, or editions of *Recueils* such as the *Eloges du Cardinal Mazarin* of 1666. He wrote a celebration of Louis XIV's winter campaign in 1667–68, *Le Parnasse poussé à bout*, with a mythological stylization of the monarch's portrait in verse and prose and, also in 1668, a long poem praising the painters employed by the king, in which he was notably enthusiastic about Lebrun. In 1670 he published a description of the festivities held for Mlle de la Vallière in 1662, *Courses de têtes faites par le roi…*, and in 1675 his occasional poems and speeches, in the *Recueil de divers ouvrages en prose et en vers*, including a description of the Versailles gardens, with a poem appended to the detailed accounts of each fountain, mimicking La Fontaine, perhaps thinking of his brother Pierre's 1674 *De l'origine des fontaines*, and clearly prefiguring the *Contes*.

He also included in the *Recueil* the famous defence of the Quinault-Lulli *Alceste* by his brother Pierre, the *Critique de l'opéra; ou, Examen de la tragédie intitulée Alceste ou le Triomphe d'Alcide*, to which Racine was to take such exception in the preface to *Iphigénie*. Perrault had not succeeded in getting Boileau's gratification rescinded after the attack on his brother in the *Art poétique*, and by 1674 his relationship with Colbert was anyway showing signs of strain. There is a reply to Racine entitled *Lettre à M. Charpentier de l'Académie française* in the 1676 edition of the *Recueil*, but that edition, according to information written on the fly-leaf of the copy belonging to the Paris

Bibliothèque Nationale, was suppressed, which suggests that the reply was by Perrault, not Pierre, and that Colbert did not want to see a public conflict between his official and Racine, protégé of the hated but powerful Mme de Montespan.

In 1672, at the age of 44, Perrault married the 19-year-old Marie Guichon, as the result of a deliberate decision to settle down and have children to inherit his name. He had met his future wife only once before the engagement, but seems genuinely to have fallen in love with her after marriage. Her health was weak, and her pregnancies succeeded one another swiftly, but she appears to have borne Perrault a daughter early in 1673, and there was certainly a miscarriage late that summer, before the three sons were born: Charles-Samuel on 25 May 1675, Charles, the only one to survive his father and to have been alive while the *Mémoires* were being written, on 28 October 1676, and Pierre, whose name was used to sign the dedication of the 1697 *Histoires ou contes du temps passé avec des moralités*, born on 21 March 1678, three months before his mother died of smallpox.

Perrault continued to work for Colbert until a final quarrel in 1682, when the court moved to Versailles. In 1683 Colbert died, and his long-time rival, the flamboyant, incautious, arrogant Louvois, Le Tellier's son, replaced him. Perrault complained that he was dismissed from the royal service, and given only 22,000 livres for his post, which he valued at 75,000 livres, the rest being shared between Le Nôtre, the designer of the gardens at Vaux and Versailles, and Lebrun. Louvois may have dismissed him from the private council and taken his name off the list of gratifications, but Perrault's enthusiasm for non-literary activity clearly diminished very shortly after his wife's death, well before the final clash with Colbert, and it is difficult to know to what extent he was in the process of resigning, and under what pressures, when he left. He would have liked his family to believe that he wanted to dedicate his remaining years to the education of his children, but his own account in the *Mémoires* was written 20 years after he demitted office and, although intended for his family, may also have responded to a personal need to see his own motivations throughout a long life in a particular way.

Perrault returned to literature with the 1682 *Le Banquet des dieux pour la naissance de Mgr le duc de Bourgogne*, and then an épître in verse "La Pénitence" and an "Ode aux nouveaux convertis" for the fund to promote conversions to Catholicism administered by Pellisson, an intimate friend of Madeleine de Scudéry. Pellisson, once a Protestant, employed by Foucquet to manage his private affairs, on Foucquet's downfall imprisoned without paper and ink for over four years, was royal historiographer from 1668, a convert to Catholicism that October, and provided with benefices worth 20,000 livres a year. Perrault also started his Christian epic in six cantos dedicated to Bossuet, *Saint Paulin évêque de Nole*, published with the two religious poems in 1686, and the result of much discussion with Huet and Bossuet, and of much reflection about the necessary superiority of a Christian over a pagan epic in spite of the literary problems involved by the introduction of the supernatural and the miraculous.

It was Perrault's view that literature should contain a moral lesson, but it should operate indirectly, by suggestion, not teaching it didactically. While he was elaborating his views on literature, Perrault was also devoting much attention to the education of his children, precisely between the ages at which fairy stories

have to be invented. In the theatre, antique myth must be brought into harmony with taste both modern and feminine, but Perrault thought the epic should remain faithful to history, even when it concerned a married bishop. Perrault's argument is not logically consistent, but the fundamental need to up-date, modernize, and adapt to a new series of social attitudes and personal reactions is victorious in the debate in which, already a decade previously, Perrault had supported Quinault against Racine.

On 27 January 1687 the Académie held a full session to celebrate the recovery of Louis XIV from his operation for an anal fistula. Perrault had written what sounded as if it would be a celebratory ode, a fitting poem for a public occasion entitled *Le Siècle de Louis le Grand*. Declaimed by the abbé de Lavau, it was a full-scale declaration in just over 530 lines of the superiority of modern culture over the antique, about as provocative on a controversial topic as it was possible to be, not only covering the arts individually, and glorifying the king's military prowess, but insisting on the superiority of nature, man, and reason in contemporary France over the personal, social, artistic, and intellectual achievements of antiquity. Decently nationalistic as the situation demanded, but not at all Christian, as prudence might have dictated, it implied an attack on the renaissance ideal of a restoration of antique values and style, but in fact was the proclamation of a peak of the cultural movement inaugurated by the renaissance in northern Europe. It is Perrault who tells us that Boileau interrupted in protest:

> Après avoir grondé longtemps tout bas, M. Despréaux s'éleva dans l'Académie et dit que c'était une honte qu'on fît une telle lecture qui blâmait les plus grands hommes de l'antiquité

> (After muttering for a long time under his breath, M. Despréaux rose in the Academy and said that it was shameful that a reading like that should be given, denigrating the greatest men of antiquity).

In fact, after Huet had tried to restrain him, Boileau left the room and slammed the door. Perrault, whose poem had listed by name a dozen 17th-century authors, including Molière and Corneille, but had not mentioned among the great men of the century three of those present in his audience, Boileau, Racine, and La Fontaine, returned to the attack with the reading in the Academy of his *Epistre au Roy* on 25 August. Boileau had lost his voice and was taking the waters at a spa. La Fontaine published the conciliatory *A Monseigneur l'Evêque de Soissons (Epître à Huet)* in 1687, and on 12 July 1688, at the reception of La Chapelle, Perrault attacked again in the Académie with *Le Génie (Epistre à M. de Fontenelle)*, a poem dedicated to Corneille's nephew, whose pro-"moderne" *Digression sur les anciens et les modernes* had appeared in January 1688.

By the end of 1688 Perrault had started his four-volume *Parallèle des anciens et des modernes en ce qui regardent les arts et les sciences. Dialogues*, published in 1688, 1690, 1692, and in 1697, after the formal reconciliation in the Académie with Boileau on 30 August 1694. The work is the fullest-scale and most fully orchestrated statement of the doctrine of the personal and social perfectibility of human nature of which 17th-century France proved itself capable. It summarized the tentative aspirations of the northern European renaissance, quietened in France by the religious wars, vigorously articulated again in the earlier part of the century, and now emerging successful from the blurred alignments of loosely knit groups clustered round representatives of "Augustinian" spirituality and what used to be called "classicism" in literature.

The actual events of the Querelle were largely dictated by clashes and friendships between persons in the world of letters, and the mixture of aesthetic, philosophical, philological, scientific, literary, and religious considerations played its part, but the occurrences were caused by the collision and confluence of different surface currents on top of a much deeper cultural movement. There were disputes about the viability and necessity of a Christian epic, the potential of the French language, and the superior refinement of 17th-century French sensitivity of manners and feelings, but these created merely superficial disturbances swirling above the fundamental reassessment of the nature of human fulfilment which was being carried out in European society.

Imaginative literature pointed to the principal particular points at issue. Provocative behaviour and bad manners in the conduct of the affairs of the Académie française helped to indicate what was going on, but the implications of Perrault's attitudes have not been examined in depth, perhaps because his own literary achievement has seemed to centre on the *Contes*, whose interest is only peripherally concerned with the values his century lived by. Critics of 18th-century literature have been more abruptly confronted with the need felt by enlightenment authors to reconsider the major issues at stake in the onward surge of optimism before France was forced by the Revolution to reconsider the nature and driving forces of cultural advance.

Perrault himself reverted to official poetry, publishing the succession of celebratory pieces starting in 1688 with *A Mgr le Dauphin sur la prise de Philisbourg, Ode*. He sent Boileau the third volume of the *Parallèle* with an amiable *Lettre à M. Despréaux en lui envoyant le présent livre* of 25 November 1692, to which Boileau replied with asperity in the Avis au lecteur of his *Ode sur la prise de Namur* of 1693. The ode, in the manner of Pindar, contains a slighting reference to *Saint Paulin*. Perrault, still in 1693, replied with his own *Ode au Roi*, read to the Académie on Saint Louis's day, 25 August. With it he published a preface directed against Boileau and a *Lettre à M. de D*** touchant la préface de son Ode sur Namur*, reminding Despréaux that he had once obtained for his brother, Gilles Boileau, the post of contrôleur de l'argenterie. Then in 1694 Boileau published his satire against women, *Satire X*, first sketched twenty years previously, then re-worked again in 1676–77, but left unpublished. Perrault was genuinely shocked, and replied in the *Préface* to his *Apologie des Femmes* of 1694. Pradon, Pierre Bellocq, Regnard, and others also replied. Boileau had weighed in with a piece essentially aimed against préciosité a lot too late in the day, but he also attacked the whole Perrault family in the nine *Réflexions sur Longin* of 1694. To the *Réflexions* Perrault replied with his *Réponse aux Réflexions critiques de Mr. D*** sur Longin* and his 1694 *Apologie des Femmes*, of which he sent a copy to the exiled Arnauld.

Port-Royal (q.v.), where the strongly "Augustinian" spirituality had long rubbed shoulders with Cartesianism (q.v.) in science, had on the whole been rather surprisingly behind Perrault in the Querelle, but Arnauld was firmly in favour of Boileau in the dispute about women in his letter to Perrault of 5 May 1694. Bossuet was agreed as arbitrator and declared Boileau's poem unchristian. The formal reconciliation between Perrault and

Boileau took place that August; the fourth volume of the *Parallèle* was a great deal more restrained than the other three had been; and in 1700 Boileau published a conciliatory *Lettre à Perrault*. The surface ripples had for the moment died away, and both Perrault and Boileau were dead when the affair broke out again in the dispute between Houdar de la Motte and Mme Dacier over Houdar de la Motte's 1713 *Iliad* in French verse.

Perrault had meanwhile published two poems in 1692, *La Chasse* and *La Création du monde*, the first "chant" of *Adam*, to be published in 1697. There were more minor pieces, mostly republished in the 1694 *Recueil de pièces curieuses et nouvelles* published by Adrian Moetjens at The Hague, and the two volumes of *Les Hommes illustres qui ont paru en France pendant ce siècle, avec leurs portraits au naturel* appeared in 1696 and 1700. It was from 1691 to 1697 that the children's tales were published. Three are in verse: *La Marquise de Salusses; ou, La Patience de Griselidis. Nouvelle*, read first at the Académie française by the abbé de Lavau on the feast of Saint Louis, 1691; *Peau d'âne*, published in 1694 and, in Perrault's mind, an admirable example of the legitimate reliance in modern literature on supernatural forces; and *Les Souhaits ridicules*, first published in the *Mercure Galant* (q.v.) for November 1693.

Of the prose contes, a first version of *La Belle au bois dormant* appeared anonymously in the *Mercure Galant* for February 1696. Boileau had scoffed loudly in an epigram at *Peau d'âne* in verse. Perrault did not wish to be seen yet to go further by putting magic into prose. There is a manuscript of the prose contes, apparently of 1695, but some reservations have been expressed about the dating, and in any case the first authorized publication of the other seven prose tales, "Le Petit Chaperon rouge," "La Barbe–bleue," "Le Maître Chat; ou, Le Chat botté," "Les Fées," "Cendrillon; ou, La Petite Pantoufle de verre," "Riquet à la houppe," and "Le Petit Poucet" was in the Barbin 1697 *Histoires ou contes du temps passé*, reprinted in the same year. All seven appeared in a Moetjens *Recueil* of the same year, and there was a Dutch counterfeit, also of 1697, reprinted in 1698, 1700, and 1708. The privilège was taken out on 28 October 1696 in the name of "sieur P[errault] Darmancour," Perrault's 18-year-old son, and ceded to Claude Barbin. Perrault's last publication was a verse translation of Faerno's *Fables* in 1699.

The dates of publication are important, because the fairy-tales are part of the Querelle, whose incidents their publication punctuates. They deal with the marvellous and the magic, and they do it in prose, so rallying in two ways to the standard of the modernes. There was a vogue for fables, for popular stories, and for children's stories, all of which constitute at least minor, and sometimes more than minor, literary genres at the end of the 17th century. Perrault, however, was consciously defying what he regarded as outdated literary norms, and in particular using the power of fairy-stories, like opera, to charm, in this way vindicating psychological implausibility, the absence of vraisemblance. It is not improbable that Perrault's close collaboration with his niece and supporter, Marie-Jeanne L'Héritier de Villandon, resulted in some blurring of authorship in the attribution to her of the contes she published in her 1695 *Oeuvres mêlées*. It is certain that Perrault's niece was close to Donneau de Visé and the *Mercure Galant*, and publications and rectifications in the *Mercure* make it clear that the publication of Perrault's material in the *Mercure* was coordinated with the material published elsewhere, notably by Jean-Baptiste Coignard, in the context of the Querelle.

Pierre Perrault Darmancour, the son born in 1678 to whom the privilège for the *Contes* was granted, died in March 1700. He had been involved in killing someone in November 1697, probably by accident, but probably with a sword. Perrault had to pay the mother of the young man killed 2,079 livres by sentence of the Châtelet of 15 April 1698. The surviving papers tells us only that she was a widow, and that she had remarried by the time she signed the receipt. A 22-page obituary notice of Perrault in the *Mercure Galant* goes out of its way to comment on the happiness of his marriage, and tells us in May 1703 that he left only one living child. Perrault died in the night of 15 to 16 May, 1703. His son Charles, his brother-in-law, and Boileau attended his funeral. We do not know if he had been ill, or of what he died. He had attended the Académie on 11 April.

Works

It is Perrault himself who tells us in the *Mémoires de ma vie* that the *Dialogue de l'Amour et de l'Amitié* was accorded by Foucquet the honour of calligraphy on vellum, illustration, and gilt binding. It was published in 1660; Perrault assures us that it had "beaucoup de vogue (was very popular)." Its interest in the present context derives primarily from the link it establishes between Perrault and Foucquet's circle and its taste, which shows how different his overall style and taste were from those of Colbert, whom he was to serve, but with whom relationships were from the beginning bound to become strained. Perrault's association with Foucquet contains the germ of his later break with Boileau and of his position in the Querelle des anciens et des modernes.

The *Dialogue*'s dedicatory letter to d'Aubignac, who was already moving away from the circles of Ménage and Madeleine de Scudéry where Perrault felt at ease, refers to the dialogue as a "galanterie." Ingeniously appealing to Plato's *Symposium*, no doubt as known through Ficino's *De amore*, Perrault demonstrates that, if love is called by Plato the desire of beauty, it is because it is the daughter of both Desire and Beauty, just as Friendship is the daughter of Desire and Goodness. The point of such dialectical pirouettes is to establish the association between desire and both goodness and beauty, and thereby to upgrade the moral status of instinctively based affection, with the additional convenience that it makes love and friendship half-brother and half-sister. In a clever hour or so with pen and paper Perrault sketches a little conte, respecting the gender of the words and capitalizing qualities and emotions into people. Male Desire marries female Beauty and begets male Love, and then marries female Goodness and begets female Friendship.

The dialogue of half-brother and half-sister carries on with the same graceful, rather dry wit. Amour complains at the things they say he does, and Amitié complains that people pretend to talk about her when they are really talking about him. There is much sending up of exaggeratedly precious language, and allusion to the vogue for word-portraits when they both sketch their own. Amour thinks Amitié should have said something about her distinterested generosity, and they discuss their different habits, abilities, and ways of going about their business. Amitié is bothered by having to ward off her enemy Intérêt. The whole effect is graceful and charming. The reader ends up amused, but wondering whether the dialogue was substantial enough to have been worth the trouble.

What is clear about Perrault in 1660 is that there is no way in which he can share an aesthetic with Boileau, whose attitudes both to women and to frivolity were openly contemptuous and who preferred satire to sophisticated salon repartee, or with Racine, although 1660 was the year when Perrault admired the young Racine's ode *La Nymphe de la Seine*. Racine had not yet developed his later awe at the intensity of female passion. It does not even take hindsight to see the clash of sensibilities looming, although the actual point of dispute was not yet predictable as a quarrel about the relative superiority of the antique and the modern.

Apart from a very few formal pieces of encomiastic verse, Perrault now wrote nothing of literary interest until after he demitted office in 1682. Even then the only real importance of the religious verse which he started to write is that he treats a saint's life, with its accessibility to supernatural forces, with the same realism as was used in pre-Christian epics and as he himself was to use in the fairy-tales. We have the *Mémoires* from 1702, begun at the earliest only a year or two before, and plenty of other evidence, but no published literary text of any importance to announce exactly what Perrault felt, or how strongly, until that gesture of calculated belligerence on 27 January 1687 when, on what was expected to be a purely formal occasion, he launched the enormously powerful if not altogether poetically successful missile, *Le Siècle de Louis le Grand*.

Perrault rushed straight into the attack. The poem starts

La belle Antiquité fut toujours venerable,
Mais je ne crus jamais qu'elle fust adorable.
Je voy les Anciens, sans plier les genoux,
Ils sont grands, il est vray, mais hommes comme nous:
Et l'on peut comparer sans craindre d'estre injuste,
Le Siecle de LOUIS au beau Siecle d'Auguste

(Antiquity with its splendours was always to be venerated,/ But I never thought it needed to be adored./I see the authors of Antiquity without bending my knee,/They are great, it is true, but mortals like us:/And without fear of being unjust you can compare/The century of Louis with that of Augustus).

Were the anciens more victorious as warriors? We must remove the "voile spécieux (specious veil)" of prejudice, and we shall find at least that we now know more than they did. In an attack on Plato's translator, François de Maucroix, whose name is given in a note, Perrault says that, if Plato used to be "divine," he is now sometimes boring, and no-one can read a whole dialogue through. Nobody reads Aristotle, and why should they? He is a worse guide to physics than Herodotus to history. The most knowledgeable of humans, he nonetheless saw only "phantosmes vains (vain shadows)." After all, we now have telescopes and microscopes, and know more about the functioning of the body. As for their orators, would you trust Cicero or Demosthenes to plead a case of disputed ownership in our courts?

In a long passage respectfully addressed to "inimitable" Homer, Perrault criticizes his lack of realism. Do warriors, their lances poised, really discourse lengthily about their ancestry? In this 17th century would those heroes, those demi-gods, have been "moins brutaux, moins cruels et moins capricieux (less brutal, less cruel, less capricious)," and would not Homer have cut out some of the endless descriptions, digressions, and allegories? Perrault now twists the sword in the wound. Horace, Menander, Virgil, and Ovid all deserve praise, but Martial tells us that they went unappreciated by their own century. Their fame has grown only with age, like a tiny stream swelling into a great river as time has passed. Will the same not happen to authors like Régnier, Mainard, Gombauld, Malherbe, Godeau, Racan? What about Sarrazin, Voiture, Molière, Rotrou, Tristan, especially Pierre Corneille (who gets eight lines),

> Du Theatre françois l'honneur et la merveille,
> Qui scût si bien mêler aux grands évenemens,
> L'héroïque beauté des noble sentimens?

> (The honour and glory of the French theatre,/Who could mingle so well with great events,/The heroic beauty of elevated feelings?).

It is of course the names missing from that list which are important.

Sometimes Perrault throws in an allusion, a justification, a reference which his audience will have picked up, as to the exotic fruit trees once removed from Vaux to Versailles on the authority of Colbert. Perrault reviews the other arts, painting, decoration, architecture, garden lay-out, and music, giving here the emotional characteristics associated with the principal Greek modes. Greek music was after all powerful enough to have kept Clytemnestra safe from seduction for five years until the flautist was driven off. A pity the Greeks did not know about harmony and counterpoint. The argument, swinging to technology, parries the possible riposte that nature has now exhausted her resources.

> La Nature en tout temps fait les mesmes efforts,
> Son estre est immuable, et cette force aisée
> Dont elle produit tout, ne s'est point épuisée

> (In all ages nature makes the same efforts,/Its being is unchangeable, and that easy strength/With which it produces everything, is not spent).

The poem ends with a short panegyric of Louis XIV and his achievements. Although the epistle presented in August 1687 merely summarizes the argument again, mentioning some of the same modern names, including Lebrun, it had an important subtitle, suggesting that there really was popular interest in the king's recovery. In full the title runs *Epistre au Roy, à l'occasion du poeme precedent. Et sur l'excez de joye que Paris tesmoigna de la convalescence de Sa Majesté. Le Génie.* The *Epistre à Monsieur de Fontenelle* is shorter, 150 lines, and is devoted to the need not merely for craftsmanship, but for warmth, charm, and above all an ability in the poet to stir the emotions. The poem is largely a eulogy of Fontenelle's uncle, Corneille, and its language is full of discreet references, as to the "sainte fureur (divine fury)" of inspiration in the renaissance neoplatonist tradition, important because Perrault admired the high seriousness of Ronsard's poetic aspirations as much as he deplored his imitation of the poets of antiquity.

The four volumes of dialogues constituting the *Parallèle des anciens et des modernes* differ in tone and subject matter, but not in form. In the first volume there are two dialogues making five in all, with three interlocutors. An author, who writes the prefaces in the first person, briefly intervenes to introduce and conclude, adds examples of ancient and modern oratory on his own authority, and tells us in the preface to the second volume that "en ce qui concerne l'éloquence (on the subject of oratory)" "je ne me rends responsable que des choses que dit l'Abbé (I take responsibility for the opinions of only the Abbé)." The Abbé argues the moderne position. The Chevalier, the preface continues, "sometimes exaggerates," and has been introduced to put forward "des propositions un peu hardies (views which are rather daring)." The author gives examples of places where he thinks the Chevalier, professedly neutral, but in fact a young uncomplicated aristocrat, naturally disposed to exaggeration on the moderne side, may have gone too far, as in referring to Plato and Socrates as charlatans, in holding that Mézeray, the royal historiographer, wrote more clearly than Thucydides, and that Quintilian was not in good faith when he preferred older orators to those of his own day. The third speaker in the dialogues is "Le Président," an admirer of the anciens, but open-minded.

The scene is set in the gardens at Versailles, itself an ultra-modern blend of the best that could be found in all the arts, and the participants are given names indicating not individuals but membership of social groups, the ecclesiastic, the young noble, and the intelligent bourgeois professional, whose attitudes, however, they only partly represent. The four volumes of the *Parallèle* constitute a manifesto rather than a debate, with the semi-dramatic form, a genre particularly associated with the modernes, exploited chiefly to announce the popular form in which the content is cast. The work is not important for the quality of its writing, the force of its argument, or any way in which it may be thought to have changed opinion, but as a symbolic, if imperfectly enunciated, declaration of belief in human progress. The argument is sometimes banal: there is obviously a sense in which technological progress is cumulative, and the moderns can do, make, and know things which the ancients could not. Indeed, Perrault sometimes defeats the advancement of the acceptance of his most important insight, that modern social and personal values are higher than those which prevailed in antiquity. He clearly senses the importance of the refinement of manners, the more considerate attitude to women and their accomplishments, and the diminished recourse generally to violence, but he too often relies for his case on technological advance, which is easier to demonstrate but in the end less important that the elevation of standards of moral behaviour.

The preface to the first volume points out how easy it is to overvalue what is antique on account of its antiquity alone. The point had frequently been made since renaissance scholars, wrongly blaming the medieval separation of religious stature from moral achievement on a scholastic Latin which was very precise but unpolished, had taken to absurdity the elevation of Cicero as a stylistic model. It was none the less still true that the upholders of immutable aesthetic and even moral norms could reasonably claim that Socrates offered a moral example, and Homer an aesthetic one, which had not been equalled since the renaissance, and could even perversely delight in that view. That, of course, was one reason for the alliance of the "moderne" aesthetic with its advocacy of specifically Christian literature, since antiquity in this context was by definition pagan.

Perrault presents his dialogues in this first preface as a defence against the attacks provoked by *Le Siècle de Louis le Grand*. Even the preface itself quickly gets tied down in detailed refutations of points of geographical detail. Perrault had got himself into trouble for referring to the river Meander, known for repeatedly turning back on itself, as a Greek river, and now gives too much space to justifying himself against the reproach of ignorance. The river spent most of its course in Asia Minor, a fact, as Perrault testily points out, which changes nothing in the appositeness of his metaphor.

After attacking pedantic admiration for antiquity, Perrault sets forth his own aim, which is to

> examiner en détail tous les beaux Arts et toutes les sciences, de voir à quel degré de perfection ils sont parvenus dans les plus beaux jours de l'antiquité, et de remarquer en mesme temps ce que le raisonnement et l'experience y ont depuis ajousté, et particulierement dans le Siècle où nous sommes

> (to examine in detail all the fine arts and all the sciences, to see what degree of perfection they attained in the finest days of antiquity, and at the same time to observe what reasoning and experience have subsequently added, especially in the century we are in).

The sights have been lowered from the modern elevation of moral standards asserted in the Académie poem, and the argument can now be conducted on the level of improvements in knowledge due to the invention of telescopes and microscopes. Only at the end of the preface does Perrault climb back to moral high ground by ridiculing a passage from a recently translated eclogue of Theocritus in which a woman is reduced to tears when she is slapped twice by a young host from whose advances she wants to withdraw.

> On dira que c'estoient les moeurs de ce temps-là. Voilà de vilaines moeurs, et par consequent un vilain siecle bien different du nostre

> (You will say that such were the customs in those days. Ugly customs, and consequently an ugly century, very different from ours).

In fact, during the course of the first dialogue, Perrault's Abbé is careful to point out that the advance in civilized rhetorical style was comparatively recent, and had taken place since the time of the humanists of the mid-16th century, who were right to prefer the products of the antique to those of their own generation. Perrault is ambiguous in his attitude towards renaissance culture, sometimes, as here, regarding it through the eyes of Malherbe, but also, and more disastrously, giving the no doubt correct impression that he has not thought his argument through. The *Parallèle* might be right-minded and forceful, but the dialogues put forward a controversial attitude which is not here given the articulate support it needs.

The first dialogue is happier on matters of knowledge and technology than on style and behaviour. The second, still in the first volume, is devoted to architecture, sculpture, and painting, and its argument is spoiled by over-reliance on the technicalities of artistic creation, anatomy, composition, and geometry. There is too much of the technical knowledge Perrault picked up at the Surintendance des Bâtiments, on the function of pillars, the differences between the different sorts of column, gradations of light and colour, and the proportions of the human body. The

dialogue is important, however, because it launches criticism of the plastic arts in France in a way which shows an understanding of techniques. The values discussed between the three characters are not purely formal.

The second volume concerns oratory, and prints examples of both spoken and written eloquence, funeral orations by Bossuet and letters of Balzac and Voiture. Perrault is sensitive to what the "belles infidèles," the elegant but inaccurate versions of ancient texts that non-literal translators like d'Ablancourt, were trying to achieve. D'Ablancourt allows those without Greek to judge Greek authors, but not to judge the Greek of those authors he translates. The heart of the *Parallèle* is in this dialogue. Just as modern anatomy has revealed more about the workings of the human body, so also, the Abbé tells us,

> la Morale y a trouvé des inclinations, des aversions, des desirs et des dégousts, que les mesmes Anciens n'ont jamais connus: Je pourrais vous faire voir ce que j'avance en examinant toutes les passions l'une aprés l'autre, et vous convaincre qu'il y mille sentimens delicats sur chacune d'elles dans le Ouvrages de nos Auteurs, dans leurs Traitez de Morale, dans leurs Tragedies, dans leurs Romans, et dans leurs pieces d'eloquence, qui ne se rencontrent point chez les Anciens. Dans les seules Tragedies de Corneille il y plus de pensées fines et delicates sur l'Ambition, sur la Vengeance, sur la Jalousie, qu'il n'y en a dans tous les livres de l'antiquité

> (the study of morals has found attractions, aversions, desires and distastes of which those antique authors never knew. I could show you what I mean by examining all the passions one after the other, and convince you that there are a thousand delicate thoughts on each of them in the works of our authors, in their treatises on morals, in their tragedies, in their novels, and in their pieces of oratory, which cannot be found in the writers of antiquity. In the tragedies of Corneille alone there are more subtle and delicate ideas on ambition, on vengeance, and on jealousy than there are in all the books of antiquity).

Perrault has brought us back to the kernel of the argument again. The example of Corneille is provocative, but the argument holds. There is a finer, more sensitive, and more delicate examination of human feelings in Corneille than there is in any antique author, and that is the nub of Perrault's contention. The Chevalier had put it even more forcefully:

> rien ne marque davantage le peu de politesse des siecles d'Alexandre et d'Auguste que la maniere brutale dont ils traittoient l'amour. Toutes les delicatesses qu'on y a trouvées depuis leur estoient inconnuës, vous ne trouverez peut-estre pas un seul Amant dans tous les livres des Anciens qui dise n'avoir osé declarer sa passion par respect, et de peur d'offenser ce qu'il aime. Un Amant sortoit le soir avec une bonne hache pour enfoncer la porte de sa maistresse si elle ne la luy ouvroit pas assez promptement, c'estoit la mode, et mesme une hache estoit une piece de l'equipage d'un Amant plus essentielle qu'une Lyre

> (nothing shows up better the scant refinement of manners of the ages of Alexander and Augustus than the brutal way

in which they treated love. All the delicateness that has subsequently been developed was unknown to them, and you probably won't find a single lover in all the books of antiquity who says that he did not dare declare his passion out of respect, and for fear of offending the woman he loved. A lover went out at night with a good axe to break down his mistress's door if she didn't open it quickly enough; it was the fashion; in fact an axe was a more essential piece of equipment for a lover than a lyre).

The Président talks of this outburst as "galanterie outrée (exaggerated galanterie)", "mollesse (softness)," and the Abbé has to agree that love is too dangerous an emotion to be allowed to be presented as merely charming, but the point has been made.

The second volume contains a praise of intellectual "method," unknown to the ancients. It is referred to by Perrault primarily in connection with the *Logique* of Port-Royal, and used by him not in its fashionable renaissance or even strictly Cartesian (q.v.) contexts, but to mean simply combining propositions, and the arguments which are constructed from them, into properly structured discourse. Perrault is concerned more with persuasion and rhetoric than he is with intellectual conviction and proof.

Aware that a devotion to Plato, although derived from antiquity, had always gone hand in hand with an advanced and obviously moderne position on the role of women in society, Perrault is clearly embarrassed. His Abbé suggests that the women of Athens, said to have been so charmed by Plato that one even disguised herself as a man to become a pupil of his, might have found charms in Plato other than those of philosophy. The Président writes that off as gossip, and the Chevalier says that, since his own century was said to be so corrupt, it did honour to Plato not to please it. Perrault has taken refuge in shoulder-shrugging, but returns to the centre of his argument again when the Abbé holds up as an example the learned reader who had found not only "more inventiveness and imagination," but also a better observance of "les moeurs et les bienséances (standards of behaviour and decorum)" in modern novelists than in Homer. Even the Président admits to an admiration for Voiture's verse.

The dialogues contain a great deal of criticism of the roughness of the manners of antiquity. They are perhaps intentionally episodic. Their structure as well as their content reminds us that Perrault, having created his explosion in the sacred precincts of the Académie, was now appealing above literary opinion directly to as wide a public as he could reach. He wanted a large audience, and especially a female one, and knew that the dialogues were more likely to be read aloud in selection than to be privately scrutinized for the validity of their arguments. The likely audience explains not only the form of the dialogues, but the way even serious arguments are broken down. Perrault obviously welcomes much in Descartes's way of looking at the world, but needs to distance himself from the Cartesian view that animals, not having immortal souls, must be simple machines. The argument is popularized, but its real philosophical basis is ignored, and in its dialogue form it is presented gracefully and amusingly.

The third volume, on poetry, distinguishes that modern verse which is merely a jeu d'esprit from more serious poetry. Chapelain may not have been very amusing, but his use of the miraculous was fully justified. Later on it becomes clear that the Abbé thinks much of the criticism of Chapelain has been occasioned by his "3,000 livres de pension" and the 4,000 livres which he

tells us that Longueville added. The advent of Christianity has naturally changed the way supernatural intervention in the affairs of men is depicted. The animosity met with against Homer must, the Abbé believes, be partly a reaction against the moralized versions current in the French renaissance, propagated for instance by Dorat, as part of the general humanist movement to depict the moral ideals of the major classical authors as higher than those required by the social attitudes of late 15th-century religion.

It is the moral attitudes of Homer's characters which are under constant attack, together with their lack of refinement and the implied view that women are less important than men in human affairs. Some of the ideas thrown out in this dialogue are more important than they are made to seem. Is verse essential to poetry? Why is Virgil superior as an epic poet to Homer and, if neither has a challenger amongst the modern poets as a writer of epics, what about satire? In lyric poetry it is Ronsard's absurd imitation of antique models which appears to be at the root of the Chevalier's hostility to Pindar. Almost all the judgements on a host of ancient and modern poets are put forward provocatively, as the paradoxes they often are. There remains a real admiration for Ovid, Horace, and Martial, as among the modernes for Quinault, Saint-Amant, Molière, and La Fontaine.

The preface to the eirenic fourth volume containing the fifth dialogue becomes self-congratulatory. Perrault recalls his promise to give "un examen exact des plus beaux endroits des Poëtes Anciens et des Modernes, et de les comparer ensemble (an exact examination of the finest passages in the poets of antiquity and those of today, and to compare them with one another)." He had, he says, already started the fifth dialogue containing the contentious comparison, when the love of peace "m'a fait abandonner cet ouvrage (made me abandon that work)," although his cause was invincible, and the public preferred the spectacle of war to that of peace. It is in the interests of peace that he has changed to examine the other arts and sciences, to show how far the modern society has here surpassed the antique. The abrupt change of subject actually occurs when the three interlocutors nearly have a real quarrel just over a dozen pages from the start of the final dialogue, a very large part of which is devoted to Descartes, although among others Huygens, the personal friend of the Perrault family, is chosen for particular praise. In the end, therefore, Perrault bows gracefully out, content with claiming converts to his cause and victory in his dispute.

The *Contes* are altogether different. Though they were published in his son's name, opinion is now practically solid in attributing them to Perrault himself, just possibly stimulated or helped by his eldest son. It is much more likely that they were conceived as part of the Querelle than that they were merely the spin-off from Perrault's story-telling when, as a widower, he took charge of the education of his children, of whom the youngest was already 13 when the first verse story was published. It is for the *Contes* that Perrault is principally remembered, and interest in them has grown with interest in the oral tradition of culture. The importance of the *Contes* has been increasingly perceived in the context of the cultural forces at work in the transformation of frightening popular superstitious legend into fairy-tales, which so often still abundantly give away their derivation, even when we do not any longer have innumerable earlier written narrations of the same tales.

In the late 17th century the fairy story for adults had been an accepted salon genre for some time. Mme de Sévigné, writing on 30 October 1656 to Mlle de Montpensier, daughter of Gaston d'Orléans and his first wife, Marie de Bourbon, had already put an eight-line poem into her letter, saying it was not quite "un conte de ma mère l'oye (a Mother Goose tale)," but very like one. A letter from Mme de Sévigné to her daughter on 6 August 1677 tells of a visit during which Mme de Coulanges told some of the stories "avec quoi l'on amuse les dames de Versailles (with which they amuse the ladies of Versailles)" about fairies, a beautiful princess, and, naturally, a prince. La Fontaine mentions "Peau-d'âne" in the fourth fable of Book VIII, "Le Pouvoir des fables;" Louis XIV as a child needed to be told a fairy story to send him to sleep; Colbert liked to be told fairy stories during the day even when he was no longer a child; and the same stories seem to have been repeated in the salons of Mme de Lambert, Mlle de la Force, and the duchesse d'Epernon. Mme Le Camus de Melsons told them at Versailles, and Fénelon made up similar ones for the duc de Bourgogne. In 1690 Mme d'Aulnoy published one in prose, slipped cautiously into a novel, *Histoire d'Hypolite, comte de Duglas*. After the first appearance of Mlle l'Héritier's *Oeuvres mêlées* at the end of 1695, with four fairy stories, "L'Avare puni," "Marmoisan," "Les Enchantements de l'eloquence," and "L'Adroite Princesse," fairy stories appeared in torrents. Some of those of Mlle L'Héritier were in prose, and the vogue culminated, after Perrault's death, in the first volume of Galland's translation of the *Mille et Une Nuits, contes arabes*, published in 1704 by Barbin's widow.

Perrault's model was La Fontaine. The use of his son's name was part of an initial and tentative, but systematic, campaign of disguise. The fairy-tale genre was provocatively a product of the moderne aesthetic and philosophy, and it was considered even more audacious to narrate it in prose than to ritualize it in verse. The 1694 reconciliation with Boileau was still fragile, and Boileau had been withering about "Peau d'âne." "La Belle au bois dormant" was published anonymously in the *Mercure Galant* (q.v.), attributed there by Donneau de Visé first to someone whose work had published a year previously and then, as if in a correction, to a "fils de maître (a craftmaster's son)," presumably when the decision had been taken to use Pierre's name, in which that October the privilège to be ceded to Barbin for the *Histoires ou Contes du temps passé* was then taken out. The use of Pierre's name to sign the dedication to Mademoiselle, the king's great-niece, Elisabeth-Charlotte d'Orléans, may also not have been disinterested. All the authors of prose fairy-tales were to use pseudonyms, as if in deference to the traditional nature of the material. Perrault's collection was on sale in January 1697. Even the coarseness of the vignettes helped to disguise the authorship.

Some of the sources, at least by the time they reached Perrault, were literary. "Riquet à la houppe" comes from Catherine Bernard's 1696 *Inès de Cordoue, nouvelle espagnole*, "Le Chat botté" as we have it owes much to Giovan Francesco Straparola, and both "Les Fées" and "La Belle au bois dormant" depend on "Sole, Luna e Talia" from *Lo Cunto de li cunti*, or the *Pentamerone*, as the collection of Basile (Gian Alesio Abbattutis) was known from 1674. Among the systematic procedures used by Perrault are the transformations of magic, supernatural creatures into benevolent human beings—fairies into godmothers—and there is clearly an element of parody and private allusion in the depiction, for instance, of self-satisfaction in the grander characters, or of luxurious surroundings and fawning behaviour.

The name Griselidis was substituted for Griselde in the second edition of Perrault's traditional story about female patience. It starts in a mythical past of long ago. Petrarch had translated Boccaccio's version of the story into Latin, and Chaucer had taken it from Petrarch. Petrarch intended to take the side of women in the quarrel about their place in society which had been episodic since the early French renaissance. "Peau d'âne" was already a generic term for a fairy story. Perrault's version follows many others in its essential feature, which is disguise in an animal skin. It starts with the age-old formula "Il était une fois (Once upon a time)," exactly as Apuleius had started the story of Psyche in his *Metamorphoses*, but in spite of the realism of the narrative style, introduces a strong element of magic and is obviously set in fairy-land. It incidentally uses the word ogre, which appeared in no 17th-century dictionary, but was used by Perrault also in the *Parallèle*. There must be a private allusion to Versailles and Louis XIV in the description of the king and the royal palace, and a sense of parody in the ass to be found in the magnificent stables. Like La Fontaine, Perrault uses dialogue, but he is much longer, less epigrammatic, and more reliant on the suggestion of narrative suspense appropriate to the bedtime story his nouvelle pretends to be. There is a moral after the happy ending. He writes, as in his other poems, not great poetry, but serviceable verse.

The first prose conte, "La Belle au bois dormant," tells the familiar story of the Sleeping Beauty, starting again "Il était une fois." The traditional ingredients are humanized. The princess is given the seven fairies for godmothers, and each brings her a gift "as was the habit of fairies in those days." The fairies were entertained to a meal before they gave their presents, but it was discovered that one had been forgotten. She had been thought dead or perhaps lived on under a spell. Putting fairies under a spell must humanize them, even though convention allows them to retain magic properties and powers. After the marvellous gifts of the others, the wicked fairy predicted the princess's death, but the youngest fairy of all had hidden, came last, and had enough power to turn the spell into a century's sleep, after which the princess would be awakened by her prince. The "Moralité" at the end is in verse, and expresses Perrault's doubts about the ultimate significance of the tale. "Le Petit Chaperon rouge," only two pages long, is semi-dramatic in style, with a "Moralité" in verse quite near in tenor to the Attic distrust attached by Aesop to his fables.

All the other contes in prose end with verse "Moralités," sometimes more than one, although they are not even the apparent point of the preceding fairy-tales. In spite of their enormous interest from all sorts of points of view, the fairy stories do not represent Perrault's greatest contribution to France's literary culture, which was his hesitant, almost stammering articulation in *Le Siecle de Louis le Grand* and the *Parallèle* of the underlying issues in the Querelle.

PUBLICATIONS

Collections

Recueil de divers ouvrages en prose et en vers, 1675
Oeuvres complètes de Charles Perrault, 3 vols., 1969–70

Contes

Histoires ou contes du temps passé avec des moralités, 1697; as
    Histories or Tales of Past Times, 1729; as *Fairy Tales*, 1957;

as *Perrault's Fairy Tales*, 1967 [there have been about a dozen translations into English in all]
Contes de Perrault, edited by Gilbert Rouger, 1967

Other

Les Murs de Troie; ou, L'Origine du burlesque, 1653
Carrousel; ou, Courses de tête et de bague, 1670
Banquet des dieux pour la naissance du duc de Bourgogne, 1682
Saint Paulin, évêque de Nole, 1686
Parallèle des anciens et des modernes, 4 vols., 1688, 1690, 1692, and 1697
A Mgr le Dauphin sur la prise de Philisbourg, 1688
A l'Académie française. Ode, 1690
Le Cabinet des Beaux-Arts, 1690
A M. le Président Rose, 1691
Au Roi, sur la prise de Mons, 1691
La Chasse, 1692
Ode au Roi. Lettre à M. D*** touchant la préface de son Ode sur la prise de Namur, 1692
Le Triomphe de Sainte Geneviève, 1694
Réponse aux Réflexions critiques de M. D*** sur Longin, 1694
L'Apologie des Femmes, 1694; as *The Vindication of Wives*, 1694
Les Hommes illustres qui ont paru en France pendant ce siècle, 2 vols. 1697, 1700
Adam; ou, La Création de l'homme, sa chute et sa réparation, 1697
Portrait de Messire Benigne Bossuet, 1698
Pour le roi de Suède, 1702
L'Oublieux, comedy, 1868
Mémoires de ma vie, edited by P. Bonnefon, 1909

Translation

Fables de Faërne, 1699

Biographical and critical studies

Hallays, André, *Les Perrault*, 1926
Barchilon, Jacques, *Perrault's Tales of Mother Goose*, 1956
Soriano, Marc, *Les Contes de Perrault: Culture savante et traditions populaires*, 1968
——————— *Le Dossier Perrault*, 1972
Barchilon, Jacques, and Flinders, Peter, *Charles Perrault* (in English), 1981

PHILOSOPHES   (Les).

See Alembert (d'), Condorcet, Diderot, Duclos, "Encyclopédie," Grimm, Rousseau, and Voltaire

The term "philosophe" is now generally used of any 18th-century French writer or experimental scientist whose speculative beliefs or whose views on matters of personal, social, political, or religious morality were in the mid-18th century or a little later considered rationalistically advanced. It is applied to all those whose work is thought to have shown some confidence in humanity's autonomous ability to make material, technical, or moral progress, or some tendency towards deism, or rationalism, or towards the rejection of authority in religious, philosophical, scientific, or even literary contexts. The philosophes did not all know one another; they did not all write for the *Encyclopédie* (q.v.); they did not all agree with one another on any central issue; and they would not all have acknowledged that they were philosophes in the sense in which the word is now used of them.

The term philosophe had already become charged with ideological significance in the 18th century, and it was commonly used more to denote approbation or disapproval than in any neutrally descriptive sense certainly by 1760, the date of Palissot's satirical comedy *Les Philosophes* and of Poinsinet's parody of it, *Le Petit Philosophe*. At that date the word could, however, still retain its neutral popular meaning, which implied wisdom, common sense, and a touch of resignation, as in the title of Sedaine's prose comedy of 1765, *Le Philosophe sans le savoir*.

In cultural history generally it is still common to find categories being used which either have become so all-embracing as to be virtually useless, or have been shown to have been misconceived in the first place, generally because their ideological loading has now been rejected. The "renaissance" was not simply a literary phenomenon, but the historiography shows that it was once considered to be the period at which classical studies, neglected for a millennium, were reborn. When that view proved untenable, as the "dark ages" were finally reduced bit by bit to a decade or so in the 14th century, attempts were made to move the dates commonly assigned to the beginning and end of the renaissance, or to alter the nature of whatever it was that underwent rebirth.

Like the renaissance, the enlightenment, generally thought of as brought about by the work of the philosophes, is a non-literary category with built-in ideological significance. To use the word is to imply the emergence from superstition. The history of the concept shows how, in the 20th century, the date of the beginning of the enlightenment, generalized to include the birth of a scientific understanding, independent of revelation, of the physical norms governing the conduct of the universe and of the moral norms which should govern the conduct of society, has been extended backwards by historians. The work of intellectual historians like Brunetière, Lanson, Hazard, Busson, Lenoble, and Pintard has steadily moved the start of the cultural movement still referred to as the enlightenment from about 1750 to as far back certainly as the late 15th century.

There has been a reaction, and both categories, renaissance and enlightenment, their ideological implications more or less jettisoned, are now increasingly used to cover the totality of cultural phenomena which occurred within quite tightly defined periods, and in geographically delimited areas. The French enlightenment can no longer be defined as Kant, in a famous pamphlet of 1784, defined the equivalent German concept, "Aufklärung," while the event was still taking place, in terms of the casting off by humanity of its self-imposed immaturity, or even as Ernst Cassirer defined it in 1932, in terms of humanity's substitution of human reason for divine revelation as the basis for our understanding of the world. The word "enlightenment" has today in the present context to be used of the totality of cultural currents interacting in France between about 1750 and the

Revolution. That period roughly coincides with the decades during which the *Encyclopédie* was conceived and published.

The 18th century itself was quite conscious of the special meaning given to the term "philosophe." Quite early in the century a deterministic essay *Le Philosophe*, certainly earlier than 1728 and probably composed by a later contributor to the *Encyclopédie*, the grammarian César du Marsais, circulated in manuscript. Du Marsais probably also wrote *La Religion chrétienne analysée*, showing up inconsistencies in the Bible, attacking the doctrines of the Trinity and of original sin, and promoting the substitution of natural reason and social morality for revealed doctrines and norms. *Le Philosophe*, of which a modern edition appeared in 1948, was printed in a volume entitled *Nouvelles libertés de penser* in 1743, and was certainly known to Voltaire, for whom the philosophe was characterized by logical rigour, a power of observation, and a willingness to suspend judgement. Reason, said Voltaire, borrowing from the *Encyclopédie*, should be for the philosophe what, in the system of Saint Augustine, grace was to the Christian; a rhetorical declaration which declared an ideological position, but said very little.

It is Diderot himself in the *Encyclopédie* (q.v.) article "Philosophe," published in 1765, who, alongside entries treating of philosophy itself and the philosopher's stone, draws on *Le Philosophe* attributed to Du Marsais. It is not difficult, he says, to acquire the reputation of being a philosopher. Living quietly, showing some outward signs of common sense, and having read a little are enough for people to pass as philosophers without deserving to. Then comes the biting second paragraph, repudiating any identification of philosophes with free-thinkers:

D'autres en qui la liberté de penser tient lieu de raisonnement, se regardent comme les seuls véritables *philosophes*, parce qu'ils ont osé renverser les bornes sacrées posées par la religion, et qu'ils ont brisé les entraves où la foi mettait leur raison. Fiers de s'être défaits des préjugées de l'éducation, en matière de religion, ils regardent avec mépris les autres comme des ames foibles, des génies serviles, des esprits pusillanimes qui se laissent effrayer par les conséquences où conduit l'irreligion, et qui n'osant sortir un instant du cercle des vérités établies, ni marcher dans des routes nouvelles, s'endorment sous le joug de la superstition

(Others, in whom freedom of thought takes the place of reasoning, look on themselves as the only true *philosophes*, because they have dared to overturn the sacred boundary posts placed by religion and have broken the hobbles by which faith constrained their reason. Proud of having got rid of the prejudices of their education concerning religion, they look on others with contempt as weak spirits, subservient minds, timid intellects who allow themselves to be frightened by the consequences to which irreligion leads and who, not daring for a moment to leave the circle of established truths or to tread new paths, fall asleep under the yoke of superstition).

It cannot very easily be argued that in 1765 Diderot, the presumptive author of the unsigned entry, was merely being cautious. The censorship did not call on him to put in so gratuitous an attack on unbelief, even if it is understandable that, in the wake of Palissot's play, he should have wished to preserve for the philosophes a sober and responsible image. The articles on philosophers in the earlier volumes of the *Encyclopédie* had caused trouble, and Diderot was noticeably more careful in the final ten volumes. He was genuinely irritated by the group who were endangering his serious work by brashly throwing religious belief overboard and, without real mental effort, proclaiming themselves the only true philosophes, with the right to look down on everyone else. In 1765, in any case, the *Encyclopédie* contemptuously dismissed the boastful free-thinkers who regarded themselves as philosophes, as Diderot took the opportunity to publish, continuing the same entry, his own definition of the philosophe, no doubt in the hope of giving the word back a respectable gloss. Bayle, in his *Dictionnaire historique et critique*, had had no entry under philosophe or any related word. Since Diderot's definition takes three folio columns, it is possible to quote only snippets from what he described as the characteristics of the true philosophe:

Les autres hommes sont déterminés à agir sans sentir, ni connoître les causes qui les font mouvoir, sans même songer qu'il y en ait. Le *philosophe* au contraire demêle les causes autant qu'il est en lui, et souvent même les prévient, et se livre à elles avec connoissance. La raison est à l'égard du *philosophe*, ce que la grace est à l'égard du chrétien. La grace détermine le chrétien à agir; la raison détermine le *philosophe*...

Le *philosophe* dans ses passions mêmes, n'agit qu'après la réflexion; il marche la nuit, mais il est précédé d'un flambeau...

Le *philosophe* croit que l'esprit consiste à bien juger: il est plus content de lui-même quand il a suspendu la faculté de se déterminer que s'il s'étoit déterminé avant d'avoir senti le motif propre à la décision. Ainsi il juge et parle moins, mais il juge plus surement et parle mieux

(Other men act without feeling or knowing the causes which make them move, without even imagining that there are any. The *philosophe* on the other hand works out the causes as far as he can, and often anticipates them, and yields to them with full cognizance. Reason is to the *philosophe* what grace is to the Christian. Grace determines the Christian to act; reason determines the *philosophe*...

The *philosophe* even in his passions, acts only after reflection; he walks at night, but he is preceded by a torch...

The *philosophe* believes that intelligence consists in judging well; he is better satisfied with himself when he has suspended his power to determine his action than if he had determined himself to act before having discovered the proper motive for action. He therefore judges and speaks less, but he judges more certainly, and speaks better).

From this point the entry expands into the social virtues required of the *philosophe*, and it becomes clear that the *philosophe* not only is not a stoic sage, but that his model is taken from the old manuals for the education of princes. The perfect philosopher makes the perfect sovereign:

Le *philosophe* est donc un honnête homme qui agit en tout par raison, et qui joint à un esprit de réflexion et de justesse les moeurs et les qualités sociables

(The *philosophe* is therefore an upright person who in everything acts by reason, and who joins to a spirit of reflection and justice properly social qualities and behaviour).

It is therefore clear that an attempt was made to recapture the usage of the word philosophe and invest it with ideal moral and intellectual qualities after proprietary rights in it had been pre-empted for anti-Christian free thinkers in the years before Palissot's 1760 play. Voltaire's *Dictionnaire philosophique portatif* appeared in 1764, but his entry "Philosophe" was added only in 1765, giving as modern examples of philosophes Montaigne, Bayle, Descartes and Gassendi. When the entry was more than doubled in length in 1771, Voltaire counter-attacked the scholastics and the Jesuits, and threw in the information that for the first three centuries all the Fathers of the Church thought the soul was made of "matière légère (light matter)," but was none the less immortal. A further small addition was made in 1774. The *Encyclopédie* entry was published in 1765.

Most subsequent commentators have not declared precisely in whose sense they were using the term philosophe, and the imprecision made the word useless in any serious attempt to describe a single corpus of opinions or attitudes in the third quarter of the 18th century. The early articles of the *Encyclopédie* on philosophers, in spite of the trouble they caused, had largely been written by priests, and they had overwhelmingly drawn on Jakob Brucker's five-volume *Historia critica philosophiae* published between 1742 and 1744. They were mild in their criticisms of contemporary Catholicism. It has been suggested, on the basis of what d'Alembert added to a pedestrian entry by the abbé Pestré on "Cartésianisme" (q.v.), that the philosophes regarded themselves as in some sense the heirs to Descartes. There is no consensus on what degree of scepticism about which ingredients of contemporary religious life at what date any body of philosophes actually felt. We are left with some agreement only on who are regarded as being the principal philosophes.

Most of the principal names wrote enough imaginative literature to have entries under their own names in the *Guide*, and they are listed at the head of this entry. Some writers connected with the *Encyclopédie* are mentioned in the entry on that work. Of the rest, some were scientists whose work had philosophical or religious implications, others started from a sense of outrage at the behaviour of Church or state, while the principal interests of yet others were merely tangential to those of the main body of philosophes, as for example mechanics, algebra, or geometry. In the literary context which concerns us, consideration needs to be given primarily to the philosophical and religious consequences of the discussions in which the philosophes were involved who did not themselves write major works in the imaginative genres.

The philosophical background was still dominated by the need to explain the relationship between human spiritual and corporeal functions in such a way as to preserve the possibility of continued personal experience after death. The discussions of Descartes and Gassendi had given way to those between Malebranche and Leibniz after Spinoza's death. Whatever their very considerable real differences it was possible even for so acute an observer as Bayle, in the remarks on the entry "Rorarius" in his *Dictionnaire*, to fail to see any very important differences between Malebranche's occasionalism and Leibniz's pre-established harmony. Both enabled the phenomenon of perception to be explained without compromising the soul's spirituality and therefore immortality.

In his 1697 treatise *De la connaissance de Dieu et de soi-même*, provoked by Malebranche's *Traité de l'amour de Dieu* earlier in the same year, the Benedictine Dom François Lamy had admittedly pointed out how Malebranche's doctrine might be thought to compromise the dogma of original sin, while Leibniz's view made it difficult to account for free will, but the real danger, as Voltaire was to show, was Locke's inference in the 1690 *Essay concerning Human Understanding*, quite incidental to his explanation of the nature of knowledge, that we cannot be certain whether the substance that thinks within us is material or immaterial. Locke's view had been disseminated in France as early as 1688, when a synopsis of the *Essay* appeared in Jean Leclerc's *Bibliothèque universelle*. Pierre Coste's authoritative translation, undertaken under Locke's own supervision, appeared in 1700, and again in 1729 with the addition of a discussion between Locke and Bishop Stillingfleet about thinking matter.

Locke, having repudiated in the first book of the *Essay* the notion that ideas were innate, had gone on to show that ideas arose from the combination of sense impressions and reflections on them, implying the mind's active power of synthesis, and then to deal with the relationship between ideas and language. In his fourth book he distinguishes the fields in which certainty can be acquired from those in which we must be content with probability. It was while discussing the limitations of human knowledge that Locke had suggested it was impossible to know if it was within God's power to create thinking matter. Gassendi had already come near to suggesting that God could create thinking matter, but of course thinking matter seemed to breach the dam protecting the soul's immortality, although attempts, however unconvincingly, were later to be made to maintain that immortality did not after all depend on immateriality.

Locke was much of the time in surprisingly close agreement with Descartes, as indeed Leibniz was with Malebranche. But Locke had also read Arnauld's refutation of Malebranche, the 1683 *Des vraies et fausses idées et ce qu'enseigne l'auteur de la Recherche de la Vérité*. Descartes's essential distinction between the thinking substance and the extended substance had been almost casually questioned in Locke's complex and technical arguments about perception and knowledge. The possibility of a material substratum for the thinking substance in Locke opened up the way for the 18th-century erosion of belief in the immortality of the soul.

However, the perceived danger was still from Spinoza, and the necessary existence of the universe. The apparent focus of philosophical dispute was God's relationship with the cosmos. In fact, disputes about atheism, whether the cosmos was the term of a free creative act or a necessary emanation of God, were not the true centre of the debate. Perhaps because it was known that, in spite of the Septuagint Greek and the Vulgate Latin, the celebrated first Hebrew word in *Genesis* does not actually mean "In the beginning" in any literal sense, the doctrine that the universe had existed eternally had never been condemned, and the way by which the world had come into existence mattered little to the individual Christian. Indeed it is difficult to know precisely what atheism could at this date mean.

In the 16th century the term had meant any deviation from the law of God, divine, natural, or ecclesiastical, since disregard for the law implied disbelief in the God of rewards and punishments. In 1765 belief in some form of creation was virtually universal, in spite of detectable tendencies towards a Manichaean belief in the eternity of evil or towards a Spinozan pantheism, with the world as a necessary emanation from God. Atheism still meant primarily extinction at death, or the merging of the individual into Averroes's world soul. What did matter was personal survival after death, and the argument concerning the possible existence of atheist societies, held together with no idea of recompense and punishment beyond the grave, was much more important than any metaphysical disputes about pantheism or deism. The philosophical breeding ground for the rejection of ecclesiastical authority is to be found rooted in the breakdown of the impossible alternative, the Cartesian dualism of mind and matter.

It was Leibniz who notoriously pointed out the materialist implications of Newtonian mechanics, as set out in the 1687 *Principia mathematica* seized upon gleefully by Voltaire. Just how Newton came to his repudiation of Descartes is still a matter of dispute, but whether or not Newton's starting point was an acceptance of the arguments in Descartes's 1637 *Dioptrique*, he came to oppose his empirical findings to Descartes's assumptions about the "tourbillons (vortices)," whose existence it was necessary to postulate if extension without matter was to be avoided and the dualism of matter and spirit consequently preserved. It is also true that Newtonian gravity could explain observable phenomena about the speed and shape of astral orbits which Cartesian vortices could not, although the editor of the 1713 second edition of the *Principia* seemed to Huyghens and Bernouilli to make gravitational "attraction" a quasi-medieval occult property of matter, which kept Fontenelle a Cartesian in astronomy and impeded the acceptance of Newton's views in France.

When Newton's empirical findings and Locke's rejection of the absolute necessity of an immaterial substance for thought became popularly known in France in their vulgarization by Voltaire in the 1730s, the ground was prepared for the growth of the attitudes associated with the philosophes of the 1740s. Locke and Newton had both been good Christians. It was Voltaire who, having been in England when Newton's state funeral took place in 1727, having read Pemberton's 1728 *A View of Sir Isaac Newton's Philosophy*, and having heard about Newton from Samuel Clarke, his guide to English philosophy and theology, seized on the subversive potential of the thought of Newton and Locke, although he may have written about Newton before reading him. His instructor was Pierre-Louis Moreau de Maupertuis.

Maupertuis was a cavalry officer from Saint-Malo who studied in Paris at the collège de la Marche and gave up the army for a scientific career. Born in 1698, he became interested in geometry and in Paris mixed with Marivaux and, especially, Houdar de la Motte. In 1723 he became an adjoint, in 1725 an associé and in 1731 a full member of the Académie des Sciences. In 1728 he was in London at the same time as Voltaire, and was convinced by Newtonianism. He was the first Frenchman to be made a member of the Royal Society of London. In 1732 he read a paper *Sur les lois de l'attraction* at the Académie des Sciences and the same year published a comparison between Descartes and Newton entitled *Discours sur les différentes figures des astres où l'on essaye d'expliquer les principaux phénomènes du ciel.* It was Maupertuis who explained to French scientists that for Newton attraction was a mathematical equation, not a physical property nor the cause of weight. Attraction was actually a wrong name given to what, for Newton, was an empirically verifiable mathematical relationship. It was Maupertuis, too, who convinced the brilliant young algebraist Clairault that gravity was a mathematical relationship rather than a physical or occult force. Clairault was to be Mme du Châtelet's mathematical adviser at Cirey while she translated and wrote her commentary on Newton's *Principia*.

In 1736, soon after La Condamine had been sent to Ecuador on a similar mission, Maupertuis was sent to Lapland by Maurepas to measure the angle of the earth's meridian, and if possible to verify Newton's theory about the flattening of the earth towards the pole. He was warmly welcomed back in Paris with figures which purported to substantiate Newton's prediction, and was invited to Potsdam in 1740 by Frederick II. As a member of the Académie française from 27 June 1743, his arrogance made him unpopular, and his discourse on reception, maintaining that the same principles ruled literature as ruled geometry, did not help his reputation.

He was happy in 1744 to accept Frederick's invitation to reorganize and direct the Berlin academy of Sciences, turned to philosophy, published the 1751 *Essai de philosophie morale*, quarrelled with the mathematician König and then, soon after Voltaire's arrival in Berlin in 1752, with Voltaire, too. He never recovered credibility after Voltaire's satires against him, *Micromégas* and the *Histoire du docteur Akakia et du natif de Saint-Malo* of 1753. He was to die in Basle in 1759. It is as a philosopher, not a scientist, that his stature has subsequently grown, particularly for his attempt to cross the all-important divide between spirit and matter by turning Leibniz's spiritual unit, the monad, into a material molecule.

Condillac, whose full name was Etienne Bonnot de Condillac, abbé de Mureaux, was a devotee of Locke who acted as a channel of transmission for his ideas, much as Maupertuis had for those of Newton. Born at Grenoble in 1715 of a family of lawyers at the parlement, Condillac suffered from ill health which delayed the start of his schooling, at first private, under the direction of a priest, and then probably at the Jesuit college at Lyons. His oldest brother became the provost of Lyons who employed Rousseau for a year, but Condillac accompanied another older brother, the abbé de Mably, to Paris, where he studied theology, philosophy, and the natural sciences, receiving priestly orders in 1740.

His life was simple and austere. Supported by private means, he devoted himself to philosophy, frequented the salons first of Mme du Deffand and then of Julie de Lespinasse, was a friend of Diderot and Helvétius, joined the company of Diderot and Rousseau in their discussions at the Panier Fleuri, and in 1758 was appointed tutor to don Ferdinando, son of the duchess of Parma and grandson of Marie Leczinska. He wrote for his pupil a *Cours d'étude* to fill 13 volumes between 1679 and 1773, and then returned to Paris in 1767 and was elected to the Académie française in 1768. In 1773 he went to live with his niece, Antoinette de Mably, at the château de Flux, near Beaugency, interrupting his retirement only for brief stays in Paris. He died at Flux on the night of 2 August 1780.

Condillac shares with the other philosophes chiefly an interest in empirical science. He started as a student of Descartes, with whose distinction between body and soul he always agreed, from whose rigorous philosophical method he never departed, and whose aim to derive all knowledge by a logical process from assured foundations he shared. He moved quickly on from Descartes's premises, however, to Newton and Locke, whose thinking he wished to combine by finding a single psychological principle to explain the formation of ideas and the operations of the soul. His first work was the 1746 *Essai sur l'origine des connaissances humaines*, in which he criticized the power of synthesizing sense data which Locke had postulated in human mental processes, and most of the rest of his work defends or extends what is already contained in the *Essai*.

In the *Essai* Condillac defines, as his objective, knowledge not of the nature of the mind, but of its operations.

Ce n'est que par la voie des observations que nous pouvons faire ces recherches avec succès et nous ne devons aspirer qu'à découvrir une première expérience que personne ne puisse revoquer en doute et qui suffise pour expliquer toutes les autres

(It is only by the path of observation that we can successfully undertake these researches, and we should not aim at discovering more than a first experience which no one can doubt, and which is sufficient to explain all the others).

Unlike Descartes, but like Locke, Condillac therefore sets out from sensation. He goes on to identify all intellective operations as combinations of perceptions, which are in fact sensations, and replaces the active power of synthesizing ideas by a mechanistic operation relying on language, itself always a system of mostly artificial signs, produced, however, on the basis of simple sensations. Condillac thought he had succeeded in his aim of explaining all intellective operations, however complex, on the basis of simple sensation by the intermediary of language.

Condillac went on to compose his 1749 two-volume *Traité des systèmes*, attacking systematic metaphysics and discussing in particular the systems of Malebranche, Leibniz, and Spinoza, and sometimes considered to be his best work, although adding little positive new thought to the *Essai*. In 1754 Condillac published his *Traité des sensations*, in which he elaborated his claim that perception, that is sensory experience, must be the basis for all knowledge, and employed his famous metaphor of human beings as marble statues on which five senses have been bestowed, responding to the challenge issued by Diderot's 1749 *Lettre sur les aveugles à l'usage de ceux qui voient*, which claimed that, in Condillac's system, all knowledge, being based on sensation, had to be subjective, with the resulting system necessarily some form of idealism.

Condillac, then, supposes that human beings are marble statues, with no way of exercising the five senses. By opening up the sense of smell, he shows how it is possible, on the basis of the sensations of smells alone, which must be simple modes of thinking, to accomplish all the functions of knowing, such as attention, memory, judgement, and imagination, and of willing. He also accounts for the passions. But so far, he is still shut into Berkeley's idealism. In the second book of the *Traité des sensations*, Condillac privileges the sense of touch, by which we know the reality of the outside world. Although the sensations themselves can only be modifications of consciousness, sensations of touch are always accompanied by an awareness of the existence of the object touched, through which we know the existence of external space. In his third book Condillac associates the other four senses with those of touch, so that the existence of what they perceive can be assured.

The 1755 *Traité des animaux* is essentially an attack on Buffon, who had taken to extremes the Cartesian view that animals were automata. For Condillac, animals feel, remember, compare, and desire, but they do not have language or the power of abstract thought. Condillac here also incidentally repudiates Diderot's materialism. Condillac was to return to his fundamental philosophical insight especially in the 1780 *Art de penser* in which he finally states that the self is the sum of sensations, and that our idea of God is material, based on unending numbers. Ethics, too, became a matter of conforming our actions to social habits. Condillac can within his system explain free will as the power to act or not to act, virtue as action in pursuit of the desire for goodness, and aesthetic pleasure as the satisfaction of the desire for beauty.

Given the nature of his philosophy as well as his post of tutor, it was inevitable that Condillac should also take a real interest in education. He wrote, in addition to the *Cours*, a *Logique*, an *Art de raisonner*, an *Art d'écrire*, and a *Langue des calculs* as well, in 1776, as *Le Commerce et le gouvernement considérés relativement l'un à l'autre*, extending his psychological theories even into economics.

Julien-Jean Offray de la Mettrie has been taken much too seriously as an atheist. He was at heart a practising doctor with an impish sense of humour and a gift for satire with a waspish sting. "Altogether too cavalier," was Voltaire's verdict, "a thousand darts of flame and not a sensible half-page." In 1747 you could not both take yourself with entire seriousness and publish *L'Homme machine*. La Mettrie's 1745 *Histoire naturelle de l'âme* may have been over-systematized, exaggerated, and deliberately irritating, but it contained a serious hypothesis and deserved proper consideration. Burning it merely forced mischievously presented insight into an irremediable resolve to provoke.

La Mettrie was born at Saint-Malo in 1709, son of a wealthy textile merchant. He was sent to school at Coutances and Caen, and then to the collège du Plessis in Paris to become at least a tonsured cleric, leaving open the possibility of a future clerical, and beneficed, career. In 1725 he moved to study medicine at the collège d'Harcourt, taking his degree at Reims, where it was cheaper, on 2 March 1733. He became a doctor on 29 May. From 1733 to 1735 he spent two years working with the famous doctor Boerhaave at Leiden, before returning to practise at Saint-Malo and start disseminating in French the work of Boerhaave: *Système de M. Boerhaave sur les maladies vénériennes* in 1735; *Aphorismes sur la connaissance et la cure des maladies* in 1738; *Traité de la matière médicale* in 1739; *Les Institutions de Médecine* in 1739–40; and the *Abrégé de théorie chimique* of 1751. La Mettrie married a widow, Marie-Louise Droneau, on 14 November 1739; a daughter was born in 1741, and in 1745 a son died in infancy. La Mettrie also published two original works, the 1737 *Traité du Vertige* and a not entirely solemn *Nouveau traité des maladies vénériennes* of 1739. He was a responsible and intellectually curious medical practitioner with an unhappy marriage, a sense of mission, and an inability to take himself quite seriously.

La Mettrie left Saint-Malo in the last fortnight of 1742, and was soon personal physician to the duc de Grammont and medical officer to his regiment of guards. During the war of the Austrian Succession, La Mettrie was at Dettingen on 27 June 1743, at the siege of Freiburg in the autumn of 1744, and at Fontenoy, where Grammont was killed, on 11 May 1745, spending time in Paris in between campaigns. He seems to have been in Paris from the autumn of 1743 to the spring of 1744, and for the early months of 1745. He must have met Fontenelle's future biographer, the abbé Trublet, probably met Fontenelle himself, and certainly made the acquaintance of Maupertuis, also from Saint-Malo, and through him of Mme du Châtelet, one of whose lovers he must have been. She was probably the subject of the dedication of the 1745 *La Volupté*, and she was the named addressee of the "Lettre critique" prefacing the 1747 edition of the 1745 *Histoire naturelle de l'âme*.

The experience of war had given La Mettrie an enduring love of peace and a great deal of opportunity to view the medical consequences of blood-shedding. At Freiburg he had had fever, and realized how much mental faculties depended on the proper functioning of bodily organs, the subject of the *Histoire naturelle de l'âme*. The theological implications of that work cost him his post as medical officer, and it was ordered to be burnt on 9 July 1746, but La Mettrie himself appears to have been promoted as medical inspector of the military hospitals of Lille, Ghent, Brussels, Antwerp, and Worms. He had, however, been stung into publishing his attack on the Paris medical establishment of 1746, the burlesque *Politique du médecin de Machiavel*, purporting to be a translation from the Chinese, and thought it prudent to leave for Holland.

During 1747 he wrote the satirical comedy *La Faculté vengée* and *L'Homme machine*, written in obvious haste and in a surge of feeling, and published, with an apparent hope of preserving true anonymity, by a young French Protestant in Leiden, Elie Luzac, towards the end of the same year. The Walloon Consistory of the Calvinist church which had, of course, no civil powers, made Luzac surrender all copies of the book in his possession and apologize for printing it, but he would not or, quite probably, could not reveal the author's name. Luzac did actually release enough copies to satisfy demand, and then went abroad himself for a period. Meanwhile La Mettrie's anonymity was pierced and he had to leave Holland. He arrived in Berlin on 7 February 1748, invited by Frederick II through the good offices of Maupertuis. The escape route appears to have been secured some time previously.

La Mettrie delighted Frederick, was elected to the Berlin academy of sciences and made reader and doctor to the king. He also made enemies, quarrelled, acquired a possibly ill-deserved reputation for debauchery, and felt homesick. He published *L'Homme plante* in 1748; *Discours sur le bonheur* in 1748; *Les Animaux plus que les machines* in 1750; *Le Système d'Epicure* in 1750; a *Traité sur la dysenterie* and a *Traité de l'asthme* in 1750; and also wrote a long satire of French medicine, *L'Ouvrage de Pénélope; ou, Machiavel en médecine*, in 1748–50. La Mettrie fell suddenly ill after eating a large amount of pheasant pâté with the French ambassador, and died on 11 November 1751. It was variously and unverifiably said that he had died from gluttony, from food poisoning, from peritonitis, and that he was struck down by the wrath of God.

L'Homme machine is presented as no more than a hasty and over-assertive working hypothesis to annoy the theologians, but it goes a long way towards showing that human beings might reasonably be treated as mechanical entities in which organic causes generate mental events. Hidden behind the obvious delight in provocation, there is sufficient in the way of real argument to suggest that La Mettrie more or less expected that something quite serious could be worked out along the lines he was indicating. He correctly guessed that his book would raise the anger of the Christian establishment, but he might have underestimated how seriously he would be taken. He would have been pleasantly surprised at how much annoyance he caused.

Claude-Adrien Helvétius, born in 1715, came from a family of doctors originally called Schweitzer, but the name was Latinized as Helvétius when in the middle of the 17th century they were Catholic refugees in Holland from the Palatinate. Helvétius's father was medically consulted during the last illness of Louis XIV and successfully bled the foot of the five-year-old Louis XV, a service on account of which he was appointed in 1720 the king's physician in ordinary, and in 1728 principal physician to the queen, Marie Leszczynska. Helvétius, an only son, profited from his father's favour with the queen and, after assisting the tax-farming enterprise of a maternal uncle, became in 1738 a farmer general himself, a post which generated for him 300,000 livres a year. In 1748 he could retire with immense wealth, and was bought by his father the post of master of the queen's household. At least until his father's death in 1755 he was to keep the queen's favour. He later lost it on account of the clash between the views expressed in *De l'esprit* and the queen's piety.

Helvétius married in 1751 Anne-Catherine de Ligneville d'Autricourt, one of the family of 21 children of an impoverished but highly born and well-connected Lorraine family whom Helvétius met at the salon of her aunt, Mme de Graffigny. After Helvétius's death in 1771, his wife kept her own salon, in which she notably received Condillac, d'Holbach, Franklin, Turgot, Jefferson, Chamfort and Morellet. To Cabanis she gave her house at Auteuil. Other names mentioned in connection with this group include Condorcet, d'Alembert, Marmontel, and Duclos. Helvétius himself was kindly and generous, and was personally liked both by Rousseau and by Voltaire, with whom, however, Helvétius quarrelled, breaking off communication from 1741 to 1759, as well certainly as by Montesquieu, Turgot, and Buffon. He knew Grimm, Diderot, and Galiani and became probably the most important point of contact between those philosophes who were also encyclopédistes and those who were not.

His wife's salon, that of d'Holbach, the entourage of Diderot, and the salons first of Mme de Tencin and the marquise de Lambert, then of Mme Geoffrin, the marquise du Deffand, and Julie de Lespinasse represented so many nodal points for meetings of advanced thinkers and others, with differences of tone, elegance, intellectual seriousness, social glamour, clientele, standards and forms of behaviour and catering, which need to be kept in mind. Some of those now commonly referred to as philosophes belonged to more than one of the slightly different groups who frequented the various hosts and hostesses. Most were received somewhere, or knew some of the others through the Académie française, the Académie des Sciences, Helvétius or d'Holbach. Diderot was not welcome at the grander salons, but Helvétius's association with him must date from the early 1750s, and must have originated at a salon meeting. Helvétius's own work is not the most intellectually distinguished of his generation, but it was unkind of Mme de Graffigny to refer to it as "des balayures de mon appartement (sweepings from my apartment)."

Helvétius's initial intellectual ambitions had leant towards mathematics and poetry, at neither of which did he have success, although his abridgement of his *De l'esprit* into the six-canto poem *Le Bonheur* was to be published posthumously in 1772. It had been begun before the break with Voltaire in 1741, when Helvétius insisted that Mme du Châtelet should honour the bill of exchange she had signed when he had lent her money to pay off her gaming debts, and Voltaire thought he was being mean. With Voltaire's guidance Helvétius had by that date completed a number of verse *Epîtres*. He worked hard to satisfy his intellectual ambitions, which turned towards philosophy, and slowly produced *De l'esprit* in 1757. It contains four discours, of which the first, short, deals with the epistemological foundations of the system, the second with ethics, the third with education and the fourth with aesthetics. Beneath a surface fideism was a synthesis of unoriginal ideas, dangerous in combination, destructive by implication both of free will and of belief in immortality. Helvétius proposed a system in which volition was a mechanical response to external stimuli, and in which behaviour was to be controlled only by sanctions on earth.

Condillac's sensationalism was tolerated, but he was a priest and had not said anything which went obviously beyond the bounds of orthodoxy. The erosion of Cartesian dualism to allow sensitivity to purely material beings was also tolerated, but the Church was not in 1758 going to go so far as to allow that sensitivity was both the sole prequisite of thought and also a potential quality of all matter, and so to open the doors wide to thinking matter. Indeed, La Mettrie's *L'Homme machine* had made the ecclesiastical teaching authority more sensitive than it had previously been. Condillac had been very careful to remain within the boundaries of orthodoxy. Inevitably, however, the unsatisfactory features of his system would be resolved as Helvétius rather blithely resolved them, undermining all possibility of religious belief without apparently realising quite what he was doing. There were still ten years to go before d'Holbach started to publish, and he made no attempt to publish in France with a privilège.

Helvétius's system threw the whole onus of creating a social morality on to education, which alone for him could explain differences in character and intelligence. He lengthily dismissed both physical make-up and environmental constraint as determinants. Any one who was "communément bien organisé (normally well constituted)" could be turned into a genius if properly educated. The mind merely measured the pleasures and pains resulting from sensations, so that the quest for material pleasure alone motivated human activity. Since, according to the calculus of pleasure and pain, the quest for the satisfaction of desire, self-love, had to be the sole motivation, moral behaviour, or any other behaviour deemed to be admirable, like the promotion of the greatest good of the greatest number, had to be achieved by an artificial system of rewards and punishments. Hitherto that system, according to Helvétius, had been manipulated by the clergy and the aristocracy for their own ends.

A good deal of chicanery was needed to get *De l'esprit* its approbation and privilège, and a second censor was appointed halfway through the printing, undertaken by Laurent Durand, Diderot's usual publisher, who died in 1763. The book was ostensibly anonymous. Importantly, patristic references from which the material nature of the soul could be inferred, or where it was actually stated, had to be removed. The importance derives from the fact that the earliest Fathers of the Church were writing in the wake of antique stoicism, with its presupposition of a material soul, and well before the sharp scholastic distinctions of the high middle ages had been elaborated. The materiality of the soul would have been considered absolutely incompatible with personal immortality by any Christian theologian from at least the 12th century to the 17th, and almost certainly since Augustine in the early fifth century, although it could be argued that Ambrose's fourth-century exemption only of God from "material composition" was still ambiguous.

Helvétius, under pressure from his mother, a close friend of the queen, and from the queen herself, was forced to make three retractations, but his book was universally condemned by the Paris parlement, the theology faculty, the Church, and the court, and was burnt on 10 February 1759 with seven other works condemned on 3 February, including Voltaire's *La Pucelle d'Orléans*, Rousseau's *Discours sur l'inégalité*, Condillac's *Traité des sensations*, and three works by Diderot. The burning, provoked more by the attack on despotism than by the heterodox implications of the thought, amounted to scarcely more than a ritual gesture which increased the dangers, but also the rewards, of future dissemination of the incinerated books. Helvétius had to resign as master of the queen's household but was saved from further ignominy by Malesherbes, from 1750–63 director of the book trade, Choiseul, who was Mme Helvétius's cousin, ambassador in Vienna, and minister for foreign affairs from 2 December 1758, and Mme de Pompadour, much loathed by the queen as her husband's mistress, who prevailed on the king to intervene privately.

Helvétius had, in the accurate view of Voltaire, Diderot, and Grimm, acted inappositely and, like La Mettrie, endangered what was regarded by them as a corporate undertaking. In the views particularly of Rousseau and Diderot, he was also wrong in all the essential elements of his philosophy. Rousseau's major works contain assaults on Helvétius's most important positions, to which Helvétius replied in his posthumously published *De l'Homme, de ses facultés intellectuelles et de son éducation* of 1772. To that work, which he had read in manuscript, Diderot replied in a *Réfutation* unpublished in his lifetime. Helvétius travelled for two years in England and Prussia, and spent his retirement on the country estate he had bought at Voré. He died on 26 December 1771.

Paul-Henri Thiry, baron d'Holbach (1723–1789), whose surname usually carries the "particule" "d'," like d'Alembert's, by custom but against the rules even when used without the title, was born at Hildesheim in Baden in 1723 but settled in Paris in 1749. He was rich and kindly, much famed for his hospitality, and lived at the centre of a circle of publicly successful men of letters, philosophers, and scientists. He died on 21 January 1789. However advanced the positions of himself and his friends had been, those who survived him were generally appalled at the destruction of the privileged society in which their liberal sentiments had been nurtured. D'Holbach wrote over 450 articles for the *Encyclopédie*, starting with translations from German, then treating of the natural sciences, before moving on in other works to the subject of religion. He violently attacked the Church, and his 1770 *Le Système de la nature; ou, Des lois du monde physique et moral* reduced human beings to merely physical entities, and denied the immortality of the soul, the freedom of the will, and the existence of a moral order. The work was attributed to a dead author, Mirabaud, and horrified both Frederick II and Voltaire.

Much assisted by Jacques-André Naigeon, about whom very little is known apart from his work with d'Holbach and Diderot, d'Holbach's enormous output started with his articles for the *Encyclopédie* and went on to a whole series of militantly atheistic, materialistic, and deterministic works: *Le Christianisme dévolié; ou, Examen des principes et des effets de la religion chrétienne*, in dictionary form, published over the name of Boulanger in 1766; *Le Christianisme primitif vengé des entreprises et des excès de nos prêtres modernes* and *De l'imposture sacerdotale; ou, Recueil de pièces sur le clergé* both also of 1766; *La Contagion sacrée; ou, Histoire naturelle de la superstition* of 1768; the *Essai sur les préjugés* and *Le Système de la nature* of 1770; *Le bon sens; ou, Idées naturelles opposées aux idées surnaturelles* of 1772, nicknamed the Bible of atheism and reprinted in 1791; the *Système social; ou, Principes naturels de la morale et de la politique* of 1773; *Ethocratie; ou, Le gouvernement fondé sur la morale*; and the more moderate 1790 *Les Eléments de la morale universelle; ou, Les Devoirs de l'homme fondés sur la nature*. There were also further collaborative works with Naigeon, and translations from the English, without exception devoted to attacks on Catholicism as superstitious, or to questions of politics or ethical systems. D'Holbach's publisher was Marc-Michel Rey of Amsterdam, and part of Naigeon's function was to see the stream of works through the press.

D'Holbach's philosophical originality was to be found not so much in his anti-religious feelings as in his social and political views. The human soul is not distinct from the body, and the human being is integrated into the complicated network of causes and effects which is nature. All our judgements derive from a quest for satisfaction, and we consist of matter so organized as to have feeling and to think. What chiefly interested d'Holbach was his quest for a social morality and a political system, the object of which must be to limit the abuse of power. Society originates in a pact, and the law is the sum of all the individual wills. It must be shown to derive from a necessity, like all morality. There is very little rigorous thought in d'Holbach, but a strong effort to make clear that the best interests of each are served by promoting the interests of the community, which means the interests of others.

The two parts of the *Système de la nature* establish first that human beings are purely material, that there is no God, only matter and movement, and then that society is formed by a bond of material need. The second part undertakes to show that God is a projection of the human mind objectifying our need to be delivered from evil. But all evil is ignorance, and as ignorance is dispelled, so will the need for divine activity to explain the world's workings diminish. Legislation and morality should reinforce one another. D'Holbach's philosophy is a fascinating hotch-potch of inherited elements, bound together with a utopian vision of a humanity whose experience can be explained in terms of the experimental sciences, and whose morality and social organization does not require the hypotheses of a divinity or any immortal spiritual principle at all. But, however important it once seemed, d'Holbach's vision lacked power, the fantasy component well out-weighing the properly imaginative one. D'Holbach did however loudly encourage the further demolition of crumbling political and ecclesiastical institutions.

In many ways more interesting than his actual thought was the company d'Holbach received, what Rousseau sneeringly referred to as his "coterie," which, for the Rousseau of the *Con-*

fessions, composed in the late 1760s, included Diderot and Grimm. In fact for 35 years d'Holbach received not only thinkers, but also diplomats, scientists, political figures, opponents as well as allies, mostly to dinner at his establishment in the rue Royale, purchased in 1759, and mostly on Thursdays and Sundays, although he also received people at his family estate at Grandval near Paris, sometimes for weeks on end during the summer. At Grandval there were often family friends as well as coterie members, but obviously coterie dinners were also held there during the summer. Regular coterie guests in Paris or in the country came to regard themselves almost as members of a club. On 10 December 1765 Diderot wrote to Sophie Volland that the formal dinners at the rue Royale had ceased, "The baron finally became tired of having 27 to 28 people, when he was expecting only 20." Grimm referred to the rue Royale apartment as if it were a place of worship, and sneeringly called it the Great Synagogue.

The inner circle of participants for most of the period from 1750 to 1780 included Diderot, Grimm, Charles-Georges Le Roy, Jean-François Marmontel, Guillaume-Thomas-François Raynal, Augustin Roux, Jean-François de Saint-Lambert, and Jean-Baptiste-Antoine Suard. Among those who joined that group for most of the period 1760–80 were François-Jean de Chastellux, André Morellet, and Jacques-André Naigeon. The abbé Galiani took part while he was in Paris, from 1759 to 1769 with the exception of an 18-month return to Naples, and Helvétius came during the four months of the year he did not spend at Voré.

But there were, especially in the early days, scientists of all sorts. In the course of the 1750s Rousseau, d'Alembert, and Buffon dropped out, and Duclos left the coterie in 1762. The dinners gradually attained a less and less worldly and increasingly philosophical conversational level. Among the guests of literary interest, Marmontel should be singled out. He was a poet, published two well-known novels, the 1767 *Bélisaire* and the 1772 *Les Incas*, and the enormously successful *Contes moraux* throughout the 1750s and 1760s, managed the *Mercure* (q.v.) in 1758–59, worked with Grétry and wrote Piccini's libretti. He also left the valuable posthumously published six-volume *Mémoires d'un père*, and was perpetual secretary of the Académie française from 1783, and royal historiographer from 1771.

The fame of Raynal in his day equalled that of Voltaire and Rousseau. Essentially a historian, he published his *Histoire philosophique et politique des établissements du commerce des Européens dans les deux Indes* in 1770. Among d'Holbach's other guests, Raynal was on especially close terms with Diderot and Grimm. Saint-Lambert (1716–1803) is of interest partly on account of Rousseau's jealousies. He was Sophie d'Houdetot's lover and companion for nearly 50 years, and it was he who arranged, while on military business at Nancy, for the publication of d'Holbach's *Le Christianisme dévoilé* of 1756. He was to become the dominating personality of the salon of Mme Necker, the redoubtable mother of Germaine de Staël.

The abbé André Morellet, whose niece Marmontel married, is best known for his posthumously published *Mémoires*. He lived with his sister; he frequented Mme Geoffrin's salon, and was left a bequest by her. His defence of unbelieving friends cost him two months in the Bastille. The repudiation of Palissot's *La Vision de Charles Palissot* had implied an attack on the princesse de Robecq. Morellet was released only on the initiative of

Rousseau, through the mediation of the maréchale de Luxembourg. He was in England in 1772 and received a royal pension for his services there. Professionally he was an economist, and he translated Beccaria's *Dei Delitti et delle Pene*.

Ferdinando Galiani (1728–1787), a priest, diplomat, and economic theoretician, wrote against free trade, and particularly against the free circulation of grain in his 1770 *Dialogues sur le commerce des blés*. In Paris he was secretary of the ambassador of the king of Naples, Ferdinand IV. An indiscreet remark about the loyalty of one of Ferdinand's ministers made to the Danish ambassador got back to the ears of Choiseul, who disliked Galiani, and had him recalled in 1769 to Naples, where he was marginally demoted. He also frequented Mme Geoffrin's salon. It is important to realize that even d'Holbach's intimate coterie, dominated no doubt by those who shared his atheist views, had its scattering of enlightened priests.

It would be difficult to maintain that the category philosophe is improperly used of Maupertuis, Condillac, La Mettrie, Helvétius, d'Holbach, or any of the members of d'Holbach's coterie named above, or of any of the writers named at the head of this entry, d'Alembert, Condorcet, Diderot, Duclos, Grimm, Rousseau, and Voltaire. Yet all that they have in common is a reliance on progress in the natural sciences, and that was shared by many who are not normally considered philosophes. The term was first used in its new sense of anti-religious well before 1760, after which an attempt to recapture it for use as a respectable cloak for smuggled anti-clerical innuendoes is clear in Voltaire and the *Encyclopédie*. Modern usage has taken Diderot's bait. The word is now considered to have anti-clerical, anti-Christian, anti-Catholic, or atheist connotations, but sounds respectably associated with the earnestly academic pursuit of truth. It is important only to be aware of the tension between meaning and usage. To use the term philosophe of any 18th-century French thinker tells us absolutely nothing about the content of the thought.

PLÉIADE, La.

See also Baïf, Belleau, Du Bellay, Jodelle, Peletier du Mans, Ronsard, Tyard.

The *Pléiade* is essentially a list of seven French poets, active mostly in the third quarter of the 16th century. The list changed, but it was first drawn up by Ronsard, who remembered in the 1563 "Epistre au lecteur" to the *Trois livres du Recueil des nouvelles poësies* that "autrefois (formerly)" he had compared himself and six other poets of his own age to the seven stars of the Pleiad, as once seven Greek poets flourishing at the court of Ptolemy Philadelphus had been compared to them. Ronsard's definitive list of names keeps the number up to seven. It dates in fact from 1555, after the replacement in that year by Jacques Peletier du Mans of Guillaume des Autels, author of the 1553 *Amoureux repos*, but whose *Repliques aux furieuses defenses de*

Louis Meigret, printed at Lyons in August 1550, had contained an attack on du Bellay's 1549 *Deffense et illustration de la langue françoise*, generally considered a manifesto embodying the poetic and linguistic principles of Ronsard's reform, and the replacement of La Péruse, who had died, with Belleau, whose translation of Anacreon was about to appear.

The term *Pléiade* had not been used of the seven poets when in the 1553 "Elegie à J. de la Péruse" the list had first been drawn up. It consisted of poets with whose names Ronsard wanted his own to be associated in the poetic reform, although at no time did the poets on it constitute a coherent group differing in poetic stance or stature from other contemporary poets. At no time, either, did all the poets on the list all know one another, live in the same place, write in the same genres, accept the same aesthetic criteria, adopt the same literary programme, or share a common attitude to language, poetry, drama, or the poets of antiquity. The assumption that they all did any of those things, and that the *Pléiade* can in any sense be regarded as a single identifiable group of French poets, has held back the critical and historical appreciation of the work both of the poets whose names were at some time listed among the seven, and who have therefore been judged in the light of a programme to which they did not necessarily at all subscribe, and of those whose names were not, thought to have been judged inferior on account of their exclusion.

The list was changed again, when the name of Dorat was substituted for that of Peletier du Mans, who died in 1582, although there is no document to testify that the definitive list which has gained currency is the result of any emendation by Ronsard subsequent to 1556, rather than by his biographer after his death in 1585. Critical tradition has now therefore consecrated a definitive list of seven names of poets who are referred to as the *Pléiade*, although that list was publicly made known only after Ronsard had been dead for a dozen years, and it is anyway doubtful whether he ever intended his list of seven names drawn up in 1553 and twice modified before late 1555 to be changed again, or indeed to be treated with the critical solemnity which has subsequently been accorded to it.

The definitive seven names are mentioned together and in isolation for the first time only by Claude Binet, Ronsard's executor and biographer, and only in the third edition of his *Vie de Ronsard*, dated 1597, as the poets whom Binet reported as having been loved and esteemed above all by Ronsard "tant pour la grande doctrine, et pour avoir le mieux escrit, que pour l'amitié à laquelle l'excellence de son sçavoir les avoit obligez (as much for their great knowledge, and for having written best, as for the friendship towards him to which the excellence of his learning had compelled them)." Binet now mentions five names, Baïf, du Bellay, Tyard, Jodelle, and Belleau. Du Bellay had died in 1560, and Ronsard had become contemptuous of Jodelle, whom he does not mention after 1563 except to say that Jodelle's reputation would have been improved if his poems had been burnt. The only date at which it can possibly have been true that Ronsard singled out those five poets for special esteem, and at which there can have been any special bond of affection between him and each of them, is around 1554, after Belleau had started work on Anacreon and before Jodelle's reputation had sharply waned. It was ruined in February 1558. Between 1553 and 1555 Tyard, like his cousin des Autels, and Peletier du Mans, was in Lyons.

Binet's 1597 list must have been a conjectural reconstruction of Ronsard's state of mind sometime during the years 1553–55, and not the definitive statement for which it has been taken. Binet continues that the five, with Ronsard himself and Dorat, were referred to by Ronsard as the *Pléiade*, "à l'imitation des sept excellens poëtes grecs qui florissoient presque d'un mesme temps (after the seven excellent Greek poets who flourished almost simultaneously)." Dorat, who had been private tutor to Baïf and Ronsard, had become principal of the Collège de Coqueret before being appointed in 1555 tutor to the children of Henri II. The list of the seven Greek poets comprising the third century B.C. Alexandrian "Pleiad," so-called after the seven daughters of Atlas and Pleïone, who were transformed into the stars of the Pleiad constellation, is disputed, but Ronsard was almost certainly thinking of the list given by the 12th-century Byzantine scholar, Johannes Tzetzes, in the scholia on Lycophron which we know Ronsard, du Bellay, and Baïf were given by Dorat to study.

Binet goes on to give a further reason why the five named poets, with Ronsard and Dorat, were referred to by Ronsard as the *Pléiade*, which always implies seven names. They were "les premiers et plus excellens, par la diligence desquels la Poësie Françoise estoit montée au comble de tout honneur (the first and most excellent, through whose industry French poetry had risen to the peak of all dignity)." That statement confirms that Binet was thinking back from 1597 to the period of the revolutionary ardour of the young poets under Dorat, and that he was conflating the names of the original group at the Collège de Coqueret studying the antique poets under Dorat, that is Ronsard, Baïf and du Bellay, with the group under Muret from the Collège de Boncourt, including Jodelle, La Péruse, and Belleau, and with Tyard, whose neoplatonist *Solitaire premier* had appeared in Lyons in 1552, whose 1555 *Erreurs amoureuses* and *Vers liriques* shows some influence of Ronsard, and who was one of the Lyons poets adopted by Ronsard into the loose confederation of young innovators.

Ronsard had very early assumed leadership of the group at Coqueret which was attempting a radical renewal of the language and literary culture of France. At first he had thought of his like-minded companions as a "Brigade," probably taking the word from a piece in the first book of Pontano's *Hendecasyllabi*, "Sodales invitat ad Martinalia," and using it twice in his account of the 1549 Arcueil excursion, added to the 1552 fifth book of *Odes*, "Les Bacchanales ou le folastrissime voyage d'Hercueil pres Paris, dedié a la joyeuse troupe de ses compagnons. Fait l'an 1549." Ronsard talks again of the "brigade" in the similar context of a festive romp in the "Dithyrambes à la pompe du bouc de Jodelle, poëte tragicq" from the 1553 *Livret des folastries*. In the edition of *Les Amours* of the same year Ronsard includes a poem to Muret, "Les isles fortunées," in which he mentions many more than seven poets inside a dozen lines: Baïf, Denisot, Tahureau, Mesme, du Parc (Denys Sauvage), du Bellay, Dorat, Jodelle, Maclou de la Haye, Castaigne, Paschal, Maumont, Belleau, Fremiot, des Autels, Tyard, La Fare, Claude Colet, Claude Gruget, Navières, Péruse, and Tagaut.

The selection of seven names is first operated in the "Elegie à J. de la Péruse" from the fifth book of *Odes* of 1553, where those named are himself, du Bellay, Tyard, Baïf, des Autelz, Jodelle, and La Péruse. In 1554 La Péruse died, and the 1556 "Elegie" to Belleau, reprinted in the 1556 *Les Hymnes* as the "Elegie à Chretophle de Choiseul," contains the invitation to Belleau to replace La Péruse, "viens en la brigade/Des bons, pour acomplir la septiesme Pliade (come into the brigade/Of the good, to

become the seventh in the *Pléiade*)." In the earlier 1555 "Hymne de Henri II," Belleau had already figured on the list, and Peletier had replaced des Autelz, and, with Ronsard, we have "un Belay, un Jodelle/Un Baïf, Pelletier, un Belleau et Tiard." That statement of the list is the final one we have from Ronsard's pen, although Ronsard did use the term *Pléiade* again in the 1563 "Epistre au lecteur" at the head of the *Trois livres du Recueil des nouvelles Poësies*, if only of the seven stars in the constellation, when he recalled the comparison he had made in 1553. In the 1563 "Responce aux injures," when Ronsard recalls the old triumphs, incidentally alluding to the success of Jodelle's *Cléopâtre captive* and to the garlanded goat of the 1553 excursion, he again reverts to the term "brigade."

The list of seven names was therefore neither unchangeable nor unchanged, and constituted a selection from a much larger number of like-minded poets sporadically referred to as the "brigade". By 1566 the term *Pléiade* was being used in his *Apologie pour Hérodote* by Henri Estienne, who twice mentions the poets of the *Pléiade* without specifying who he thought they were, and even coins the verb "pleïadizer (to Pleiadize)." There is a touch of indulgent irony in the neologism, but the collective noun *Pléiade* denoting the seven poets is again used twice in Estienne's 1578 *Dialogues du nouveau langage françois italianizé*. In the same year a poem by Gérard-Marie Imbert from his *Sonnets exoteriques* implies that the *Pléiade* is some inner group, known as the *Pléiade*, selected from Dorat's learned "brigade," to which Imbert regretfully acknowledges that he does not belong.

The term *Pléiade* has undoubtedly been abused. It never denoted a closed group in spite of the invariable number of seven names on the list. Ronsard used the term as a metaphor, remembering the seven tragic poets mentioned in the Lycophron scholia and, more or less jokingly, naming six companions with whose achievements he wanted to associate himself. For a year or two he kept the list of seven up to date, but there was never a group, and above all never a common purpose or a common programme. Entries in the present work on the individual poets show how divergent were their aims and interests, and Binet's view that Dorat's name was included by Ronsard among the seven "whom he called the Pléiade" seems almost certainly to have been incorrect, for however closely the original Coqueret trio depended on Dorat's inspiration, he scarcely wrote in French.

Not all the greatest poets or those who contributed most to the renovation of French poetry among Ronsard's French contemporaries are enumerated by him as belonging even to the "brigade." There are, however, two poets who at one moment figured on the list of seven, Jean de la Péruse and Guillaume des Autels, who should briefly be mentioned.

Jean Baslier de la Péruse (1529–54), born in the Loire valley, is first heard of at the Collège de Boncourt, where he played with Belleau a leading part in Jodelle's *Cléopâtre captive*. Thereafter he continued his studies in Poitiers where he was joined by Tahureau and Baïf early in 1554. Poitiers's university and its celebrated legal faculty had made the town a cultural centre. La Péruse had himself found there Jean Vauquelin de la Fresnaye and Scévole de Sainte-Marthe. During 1553 he composed his own tragedy *Medée*, to be published only in 1556 after his death of the plague late in 1554. He wrote three alexandrine sonnets in 1553, also a sonnet to congratulate Muret on his *Juvenilia*, and appears to have been amongst the most active in cementing the friendship between the Boncourt and Coqueret groups. Ronsard, who had written an elegy to him, wrote an epitaph for his death.

Guillaume des Autels (1529–81) was a cousin of Pontus de Tyard and, like him, came from the south-east. His first publication, *Le Mois de May*, may have appeared as early as 1544. In 1548 he attacked Louis Meigret's proposed reform of French orthography in the 1548 *Traité touchant l'ancien orthographe françois, contre l'orthographe des Meygretistes*, which was followed by a 1551 *Replique* to Meigret's reply. There was a vigorous three-cornered controversy, also involving Jacques Peletier du Mans. It was in the 1550 *Replique aux furieuses defenses de Louis Meigret* that des Autels criticized the attitude taken to their predecessors by Ronsard and his group, "ceux qui pensent avoir conquesté l'empire de l'encyclopedie des Muses (those who think they have conquered the realm of the encyclopedia of the Muses)." Fundamentally his view was that there was no real difference between the imitation which du Bellay advocated and the translation which he proscribed, and that the restoration of the French poetic tradition required greater originality than du Bellay had allowed, and full independence from Greek, Latin and Italian predecessors.

Des Autels also defends the rhétoriqueurs' production against du Bellay's description of it as "episseries (groceries)." He champions the Toulouse "Jeux floraux," a poetic competition in which craftsmanship counted for everything, and of which du Bellay had been contemptuous, and he stands up for the ballade as a genre, while welcoming both what Ronsard had done for the ode, and Marot's grace and fluency. Du Bellay was to react by refining as well as re-defining what he meant by imitation in the preface to the second edition of the *Olive* late in 1550, published with a privilège of 3 October. Du Bellay was to meet des Autels when passing through Lyons in May 1553, and to write a sonnet jointly to Tyard and to des Autels, who then addressed two poems to du Bellay, with whom he had also come to agree. Des Autels's three principal volumes of verse are the 1550 *Repos de plus grand travail*, the 1551 *Suite de repos*, and the 1553 *Amoureux repos*, with the poems to du Bellay. He later published writings in the Catholic and royalist interest, and court and ceremonial verse.

PORT-ROYAL.

See Jansenism, Nicole, Pascal, and Saint-Cyran.

The intricate way in which the history of the abbey of Port-Royal threads its way in and out of the important occurrences in the literary, religious, social, and even political history of 17th-century France separates it sufficiently from the mass of religious institutions which underwent reform at roughly the same time to make its treatment in isolation not only useful but virtually necessary. Since Sainte-Beuve wove a whole tapestry of 17th-century French literary history round the monastery when he entitled his famous Lausanne lectures of 1837–38, subsequently worked up into the five volumes of 1840–59, simply *Port-Royal*, this focus has also become traditional.

Sainte-Beuve found that the history of the monastery, with its immense literary, religious, and social interest, could be used as a central narrative thread to hold together a substantial portion of the literary history of the 17th century. Literary critics and historians, following in the wake of Henri Bremond's 12-volume *Histoire littéraire du sentiment religieux en France depuis la fin des guerres de religion jusqu'à nos jours*, published between 1921 and 1936, have subsequently only begun to discover the riches buried in the religious literature of 17th-century France, particularly in the great sets of spiritual letters and the letters of direction by often neglected writers like the Jesuits Lallemant, Surin, and Caussade, and in what has been transmitted to us of the period's pulpit oratory.

In the 17th century the history of Port-Royal is inextricably connected with the history of the Arnauld family. Tallemant, writing no later than 1659, devotes a long chapter of *Les Historiettes* to the Arnaulds. The first member of the family of interest in the present context was the eldest son of the second marriage of an Antoine Arnauld, seigneur de la Mothe, near Riom, reconverted to Catholicism after the 1572 Saint Bartholomew's Day massacre and finally becoming Marie de Médici's procureur général. Rich, elegantly housed in Paris with a garden of 5,000 square metres, and also seigneur de Corbeville, he died in 1585, having had 11 known children by his second wife, of whom the eldest (1560–1619), a lawyer, was known as Antoine Arnauld l'avocat. L'avocat was passionately anti-League and anti-Jesuit, and in 1590 published his *Anti-Espagnol*, a reply to the duc du Maine. He had to flee Paris disguised as a building worker. In 1593 he published his anti-Spanish *La Fleur de Lys*, but is best remembered for his court harangue of 12 and 13 July 1594 on behalf of the university against the Jesuits, which preceded their exile, subsequently enforced over a fairly long period in different parts of France. In 1603 Arnauld l'avocat published a *Franc et véritable discours au Roy* against their readmission. The *Discours* displeased Henri IV and was condemned at Rome.

Antoine l'avocat's youngest son was Antoine "le grand" Arnauld, the celebrated leader of the Jansenist faction after the death of his director, Saint-Cyran, in 1643, and close friend of Port-Royal, where his widowed mother and four of his sisters were or had been nuns. Arnauld l'avocat's eldest surviving son, Robert Arnauld d'Andilly (1588–1674), had five daughters who survived childhood; all became nuns at Port-Royal. His eldest daughter Catherine (1590–1651) married Isaac Le Maître, a maître des requêtes, in 1605, but the marriage broke up in 1615 and on 17 July 1619 Catherine made a vow of chastity received by François de Sales. When the Port-Royal community came to Paris she became a professed nun in it, and all five of her children were male "solitaires," loosely attached to the monastery. Catherine, as the eldest daughter, had married. All l'avocat's other daughters entered the cloister, three of the five certainly at Port-Royal. Among them were Mère Angélique (1591–1661) and Mère Agnès (1593–1671). Their maternal grandfather, Henri IV's advocate general, was keen to have them provided with suitable convents before he died.

The monastery itself was situated in a hollow swamp in the Chevreuse valley to the south-west of Paris, and dated its foundation to 1204 during the fourth crusade. The first nuns were reformed Benedictines, and at some unknown date the obedience passed to Cîteaux. In the late 15th century the monastery acquired land, Les Granges, on one of the surrounding hills. In the 16th century ineffective attempts to introduce more religious seriousness were made by abbots of Cîteaux, and in 1599 the abbess, Jeanne de Boulehart, at the instance of the then abbot of Cîteaux, a friend of the advocate general, took as her coadjutor abbess the seven-and-a-half-year-old Jacqueline-Marie Arnauld, later Mère Angélique. The younger sister, Jeanne, later Mère Agnès, was provided with the Benedictine abbey of Saint-Cyr, although the abbess's functions were to be exercised by someone else until she was 20. The Arnauld family had to lie about the girls', ages to obtain the necessary bulls from Rome. Jacqueline's clothing ceremony was in Paris itself on 1 September 1599, Jeanne's eight months later at Saint-Cyr.

They spent the intervening period together, until Jacqueline was sent to Maubuisson, under the abbess Angélique d'Estrées, sister of Gabrielle, the mistress of Henri IV. The abbess took Jacqueline to another monastery, Bertaucourt, near Amiens, of which also she was abbess, where Jacqueline was confirmed, taking the name of Angélique, by which she has become known to history, as a compliment to the Maubuisson abbess and as a means of deceiving Rome by changing the identity of the abbess to whom, on account of excessive youth, bulls had been refused. Jacqueline was professed on 29 October 1600, after her year's noviceship was over, in a ceremony whose validity could easily have been overturned. She was nine, and stayed on at Maubuisson until 5 July 1602 when, Jeanne de Boulehart having died, she took possession of the monastery of which she was coadjutor abbess. New bulls had been postulated in the name of Angélique, declared as being 17. Rome found that still too young, and was not well disposed towards her father, the enemy of the Jesuits and the Spaniards. It needed all the persuasion that cardinal d'Ossat could bring to bear in Rome before the bulls were granted.

The monastery was lax without being scandalous. The confessor was ignorant, read nothing but his breviary, and enjoyed nothing so much as hunting. Sermons had been preached, but only at professions, seven or eight in 30 years. The nuns communicated monthly and on feast days, but not at the Purification, in February, which was generally during the carnival, when the nuns, the male servants, and the chaplain put on mascarades. Revenues were not high; the nuns were robbed by the servants; there was about 6,000 livres a year to keep the 13 professed religious, of whom the oldest was 33. Mère Angélique was made full abbess when she was 11, on the day of her first communion.

Since a canonization process was envisaged while she was still alive, a dossier was built up about Mère Angélique behind her back. Even her outgoing letters were intercepted and copied, and Antoine Singlin, her director, later compelled her to write down the details of her early life. We are therefore remarkably well informed about her doings, as indeed we are about those of many of the solitaires, of whom Le Maître became the semi-professional biographer. It was to be a characteristic of the monastery during the Jansenist troubles that there was a self-consciousness about everything, as if the least gesture needed to be performed with its chronicler in mind and demanded an awareness of what posterity might think. The chroniclers and memorialists suggest more than a little attitudinizing.

Apart from getting up for matins at 4 a.m. in the unhealthy abbey in the marshes, Angélique, as she now was, grew up with relative normality, going for walks when it was fine, reading novels and Roman history when it was wet. A visitation of 1604 found everything in order, but suggested increasing the size of the community from 12 to 16. Angélique, however, while developing a strong distaste for an abbess's life, was too proud to admit it. Even if her life was as profane as she could decently make it, she had been brain-washed into feeling a demanding consciousness that her social privilege had to be accompanied by religious obligation. Her mother, before she herself became a nun, reproached her with the social calls she made and received. Angélique was trapped above all by the social proprieties and caste code, backed by genuine affection for her family, which allowed her no escape. She read Plutarch's *Lives* fantasizing about her own heroism, but at 15 seriously considered escape without informing her parents. She thought she might want to marry. Her Protestant aunts might look after her at La Rochelle. The late abbess had left a carriage in which Angélique had her sister Jeanne fetched from Saint-Cyr. Jeanne's outlook was quite different: cheerful, vainglorious; but she was well-behaved, devout though romanesque. She wondered why God had not had her born to higher rank.

Angélique was ill in 1607, and, taken home, visited and cared for by rich relations, wanted more than ever to return to a life of worldly ease. But she was of an age to commit herself of her own will, and her father made her sign a paper she was not given time to read, reaffirming her religious vows. In the Lent of 1608 the nun placed by her mother to watch over her gave her some Capucin meditations to read. One evening a Capucin, Père Basile, arrived late and asked to preach. Angélique enjoyed the distraction of passing preachers and, although she first thought the hour too late, called the community together to listen to the sermon, which was on the self-abasement of the Son of God. During it, Angélique was overwhelmed by a sensation of contentment at her religious state. She could later write, in a prose style as strong, lucid, and apparently simple as anything produced in her century, although it is difficult to miss the aristocratic hauteur of the first sentence and the histrionic undertow of the second,

> Je vis aussitôt la nécessité de la vraie obéissance, du mépris de la chair et de tous les plaisirs sensuels et le mérite de la vraie pauvreté et Dieu me donna tant d'affection pour ces vertus que je ne respirais que de trouver les moyens de les pouvoir pratiquer. Mais ma misère, ma légèreté, le peu de vraie assistance que j'avais eue pour correspondre à cette première grâce, quoique ma volonté soit demeurée ferme au fond de mon coeur pour chercher les moyens de la suivre, m'ont fait commettre de très grandes fautes et infidelités

> (I immediately saw the necessity of true obedience, of contempt for the flesh and all sensual pleasures, and the merit of true poverty, and God gave me such affection for these virtues that I lived only to find the means to be able to practise them. But my wretchedness, my frivolousness, the little real help I had had to correspond with this first grace, although my will remained firm at the bottom of my heart to seek the means to follow it, made me commit great faults and infidelities).

Mère Angélique spent a tortured 18 months moving from one extreme to another, wanting to lay down the dignity of being abbess, and alternatively to reform her abbey. A young Capucin,

Père Bernard, urged her towards the excesses to which her temperament anyway carried her, although his advice was tempered by a wiser and older colleague, Père Pacifique. She deprived herself of sleep, inflicted painful bodily austerities on herself, slept on hard surfaces, wore garments of coarse cloth, did not undress, and allowed herself to become flea-ridden. The self-infliction of various forms of physical filthiness and the cultivation of bodily vermin was considered unusual, but was not altogether unknown as an ascetic practice.

Mère Angélique's asceticism was, as far as can be judged, scarcely more than thorough-going. Père Bernard's reformatory activities met with opposition chiefly from those members of the community whose behaviour least needed reforming, and when he protested to the Cistercian superiors, they immediately consulted Angélique's father. L'avocat insisted on a visit from his daughter at Andilly during the grape-picking season of 1608, found her depressed, accused the Capucins of wanting to turn Port-Royal into a profitable dependent farm, and declared himself against the reform. His daughter's health got worse, but she returned to her convent on 18 October.

On 1 November 1608 Mère Angélique underwent another intense spiritual experience after a sermon, this time on the eighth beatitude by a young Cistercian. It appears to have been the abbess's increasing depression which finally determined the community of which she was abbess to cede to her wishes rather than see her health further decline. During Lent 1609 everything they possessed was put in common, the most difficult sacrifice being the key to her private garden finally surrendered by the oldest member of the community. Jeanne came to join the community from Saint-Cyr, and full monastic enclosure was enforced. Mère Angélique became increasingly apprehensive as the parliamentary vacation approached, when she would inevitably be visited by her father, to whom she was going to have to deny access to the enclosed parts of the monastery. The visit of l'avocat and the family was announced for the morning of 25 September 1609. He came with his wife, Angélique's mother, with Catherine, now married, d'Andilly, the eldest son, and a young sister, Anne, of about 15.

This was the famous Journée du Guichet (day of the grille), and everyone had a part which they now formally acted out. It is not even certain that l'avocat had not previously been informed what was going to happen, so that he knew what would be expected of him. Everything went according to plan. All the keys to the monastery had been collected, and Mère Angélique advanced from the church to the cloister gate to open the grille. L'avocat demanded admittance, Angélique asked him into the parlour for visitors. He predictably shouted, thundered, and banged. Mère Angélique's mother called her ungrateful; the 20-year-old d'Andilly called her a monster and a patricide; dissent broke out in the community, some taking the abbess's side, some the family's; l'avocat demanded at least the return of the 16-year-old Jeanne and the 9-year-old Marie-Claire, later to be professed; Angélique, afraid her father would get his foot inside the door and force an entrance, had the girls surreptitiously released through a side door; Jeanne quoted the ordinances of the council of Trent concerning religious enclosure at her father; and l'avocat ordered the horses reharnessed. At Angélique's pleas he relented sufficiently to speak to her through the grille, was tender, sad, said he would never see her again, and enjoined her not to ruin her health with austerities. Angélique fainted.

Thereafter a compromise was reached. L'avocat stayed; matters were discussed over several days; the enclosure of the cloister would be respected but l'avocat was allowed by the abbot of Cîteaux into other parts of the monastery to give instructions to gardeners and workmen. After l'avocat's death in 1619, Mère Angélique's mother herself became a religious in her daughter's abbey, making her profession at the age of 56 on 4 February 1629. Towards the end of the second and during the third decade of the century, Port-Royal became a centre of monastic reform, despatching religious at the request of other convents, including Maubuisson, to guide the reform of other communities. Maubuisson was particularly dramatic. When all milder measures proved fruitless, Louis XIII authorized the abbot to break in with armed soldiers and remove the abbess, still Angélique d'Estrées, to a convent for penitents. After consultation with l'avocat, the abbot of Cîteaux sent Mère Angélique to take her place. She found the religious in the habit of dancing with local monks, inviting guests to meals in their private gardens, acting plays for visitors, and not knowing how to go about confession. Mère Angélique, finding the old nuns irreformable, introduced some 30 new ones.

In September 1619 Angélique d'Estrées escaped, returned, and demanded her abbey back, even having Mère Angélique threatened in church by patricians with drawn swords. One went so far as to discharge a pistol. They removed Mère Angélique by physical force and would have driven away with her, but other religious clung to the carriage and horses. The incident ended with Mère Angélique marching at the head of a column of 30 nuns to Pontoise, where she demanded and obtained a house for her community. In the absence from Paris of her father, one of her brothers, Henry, the future bishop of Angers, obtained a warrant for the removal of Angélique d'Estrées from Maubuisson and the restoration to her abbacy there of Mère Angélique. She and her nuns were escorted back from Pontoise by 150 archers as soon as they arrived, although it was night. It was while she was at Maubuisson that Mère Angélique got to know François de Sales, who wrote to her regularly, continually counselling prudence and trying to moderate all those components of her psychological make-up which made her imperious, intransigent, and proud. He came to Maubuisson several times at her invitation, and then to Port-Royal. There were by now few prelates who long resisted her summons, and François de Sales was soon cultivated by the whole Arnauld family.

The new abbess of Maubuisson was named as Mme de Soissons, the illegitimate daughter of Charles de Bourbon, comte de Soissons, and half-sister of the future duchesse de Longueville, but Mère Angélique stayed on for 13 months while the bulls arrived. There was trouble, because her 30 new religious were inadequately endowed for Maubuisson, which had an annual income of 30,000 livres. Mère Angélique arranged for them to be accepted by Port-Royal, which had still only 6,000 livres, and she had ceased to accept l'avocat's help well before his death in 1619. Their arrival on 3 March 1623 was inevitably again due to be chronicled, and doubtless therefore dramatized. Mère Angélique had enjoined on them complete silence until she herself arrived. They had their names attached to their sleeves, and had to say the psalm verse "Place, O Lord, a sentinel on my lips" as soon as they saw the Port-Royal steeple top from the nearby hill.

It was in July 1623 that Saint-Cyran first wrote to Mère Angélique, congratulating Port-Royal on its acceptance of the 30 Maubuisson nuns. He was visiting the Arnauld family, having got to know d'Andilly in 1620 at Poitiers, where d'Andilly had arrived in the suite of M. de Schomberg, and having just returned from Péronne, where he had spent two months with Jansen. It had become clear that the monastery of Port-Royal was too small to house its 80 nuns. The marsh was unhealthy, and 15 nuns had died in two years. Madame Arnauld wanted to prolong her stays with the community but also wanted it to move to Paris. A house was acquired at the edge of the faubourg Saint-Jacques, practically still in the country, and by the beginning of 1626 the whole community was housed there.

Mère Angélique still had at least velleities of laying down her abbacy, and had indeed taken real steps to join the Visitation when François de Sales died. On the other hand she attracted the interest of Bérulle, always keen to gather the movement of Catholic reform under his influence, and of Condren, his lieutenant, whose spirituality of self-annihilation, although the antithesis of that of François de Sales in its attitude to human nature, was bound to attract Mère Angélique. At the same time, difficulties arose with the new abbot of Cîteaux, who was distrustful of Mère Angélique's austerity of observance, while Sébastien Zamet, the bishop of Langres, former chaplain of Marie de Medici, was seeking to establish a new congregation in honour of the Blessed Sacrament. He had moved the Cistercian community from Tard to Dijon, where he had had it placed under his own jurisdiction.

Once in Paris, Mère Angélique succeeded in obtaining a brief from Urban VIII transferring Port-Royal to the jurisdiction of the archbishop, who for the time being was Gondi, and then through Marie de Medici obtained the authorization for the community triennially to elect their own abbess. The convent had been given 24,000 livres by Mme de Pontcarré, a penitent of Zamet's who lived with the community, but had had to borrow 36,000 livres to finish its new buildings. The time was ripe for Zamet to unite the Tard and the Port-Royal communities. Port-Royal sent to Dijon Mère Agnès and Mère Geneviève Le Tardif. Mère Geneviève soon returned, was elected abbess of Port-Royal in succession to Mère Angélique in 1630, and changed the regime in ways of which Mère Angélique disapproved. She insisted, for instance, that all the religious should learn to write. Mère Angélique had been inclined to think that that skill went with a series of other accomplishments which we would no doubt consider socially conditioned. Too much time now seemed to Mère Angélique to be spent in the parlours with a stream of Oratorian directors, and the intake of young girls to be educated became plainly more aristocratic. Zamet's insistence on sumptuous ceremonies, with flowers, incense, and a church filled with perfume, contrasted with his advocacy of private fasting, terrifying physical austerities, and grotesque humiliations. Everything seemed to have become exaggerated into a great game.

Zamet finally succeeded in setting up his new foundation in the rue Coquillière. Gondi, unhappy at having to share authority with Bellegarde, the archbishop of Sens, and Zamet, insisted on having Mère Angélique as superior, but Zamet introduced a spy. Sainte-Beuve is indignant:

Ce n'étaient plus que des dévotions petites, chimériques, continuelles idées d'illumination, des emportements austères mêlés à des élégances profanes, longs manteaux traînants, scapulaires d'écarlate, disciplines presque sanglantes au milieu des parfums: tout le faux enfin de l'imagination mystique qui se mettait à délirer

(There was now nothing but cranky little cults, constant notions of illumination, frenzies of austerity mixed with worldly elegance, long trailing cloaks, scarlet scapulars, scourges practically bleeding in the midst of perfumes: all the falsity of the mystical imagination beginning to lose control).

It was in this atmosphere that in 1633 the *Chapelet secret* (see: Saint-Cyran), composed years before for her own use by Mère Agnès and approved by Zamet, was passed by Bellegarde, who had previously approved it, to the Sorbonne for censure. Using the *Chapelet* simply as a weapon against Zamet, Bellegarde tried to get it condemned also at Rome, but it was merely suppressed. It was at this point that in desperation Zamet turned to Saint-Cyran, who considered the matter and then had the booklet approved by Jansen and others. Zamet then allowed Saint-Cyran free rein, the nuns regarded him as their saviour, and his ascendancy became total. Port-Royal's role as the institutional nucleus of Jansenist spirituality and, for a time, as a refuge for doctrinal Jansenists, was now virtually inescapable.

It took Saint-Cyran almost a year to impose his own spirituality, which shared with Zamet's a tendency to childishness and exaltation, allied to a hollow affectation of the sublime and a combativeness which he put at the service of Bérulle and directed generally against traditional monastic and modern Jesuit spiritualities. It was Saint-Cyran who introduced the rather ineffective Singlin and the learned Lancelot to Port-Royal. Mère Angélique successfully sought with Gondi's help to return to Port-Royal in February 1636. Gondi also sent the Tard nuns back to Dijon and brought back to Paris Mère Agnès, who had twice been elected abbess at Tard for three-year terms and was now in 1636 elected abbess of Port-Royal in place of Mère Geneviève Le Tardif, who had herself been re-elected in 1633 for a second three-year term.

Although Séguier, the chancellor, and his brother, the bishop of Meaux, had a niece at Zamet's Institut du Saint-Sacrement whom they interrogated, they found nothing out of order there. However, the Institut was closed and all the nuns were sent back to Port-Royal by Gondi on 16 May 1638, two days after Saint-Cyran's imprisonment. The nuns from the Institut used the Port-Royal habit but, with trivial adjustments, retained their Benedictine rule. From October 1647, largely on account of a forgotten trunk discovered at Port-Royal containing scapulars once intended for the Institut, the Port-Royal habit became the famous white scapular with the scarlet cross, used to such startling visual effect in the Jansenistically simple portraits by Philippe de Champaigne. The Institut's endowment was legally transferred to Port-Royal and used to build the church, whose foundation stone was placed by the daughter of Mme de Longueville, the future duchesse de Nemours, in April 1646.

It was late in 1637 that Antoine le Maître, having decided not to become a Carthusian, resolved to live his life as a solitaire. His mother was living at Port-Royal and immediately had a small dwelling constructed outside but up against the monastery. The walls were still damp when, in January 1638, first Le Maître and then his brother, Séricourt, moved in. They were soon joined by Claude Lancelot, and the three, with Gaudon and Singlin, made up the first band of solitaires. Between 1637 and 1660 the list extends to some 70 known names, with a large influx between 1643, when there were four, and 1646, when there were

12. The first small band would assemble in Singlin's room for matins at 1 a.m.

After Saint-Cyran's imprisonment in 1638 the first solitaires, made by the archbishop to leave Port-Royal on orders from the court, went first to Port-Royal-des-Champs, overgrown and in ruins after 12 years of neglect since the move to town in 1626. On 5 July the commissaire Laubardemont came to interrogate them. On 14 July they returned to Paris, near but not at Port-Royal. The third son of Catherine Arnauld, Le Maître de Saci, went to live with Saint-Cyran's nephews in Saint-Cyran's house, of which Barcos, one of the nephews, was in charge. Lancelot, Singlin, Le Maître, and Séricourt went to the Vitart household at La Ferté-Milon (see: Racine), leaving the house only to hear Mass. The following summer, 1639, they took the air in the evening, as they had at Port-Royal-des-Champs. Le Maître and Séricourt, now together with M. Vitart, returned to the Chevreuse house at the end of 1639. Vitart died in August 1642, and the others took to cultivating the land. Among those who joined them, first in 1644, and then from late in 1645 or early the following year until the 1656 dispersal, was d'Andilly. Lancelot had joined them briefly but was recalled to Port-Royal in the faubourg Saint-Jacques to attend to the education of the two children of Jérôme Bignon. On his release from Vincennes, Saint-Cyran was formally received at Port-Royal with a solemn Mass of thanksgiving, and he also visited the solitaires at Port-Royal-des-Champs.

With Saint-Cyran's death in 1643, Antoine le grand Arnauld's defence of the *Augustinus*, and his 1643 *De la fréquente communion* (see: Jansen), made him the natural leader of the Jansenist faction, and the close adhesion of the whole family, acting as if it regarded itself more as a dynasty bound by loyalty than as a group constituted by conviction, inevitably ensured Port-Royal's close association with Jansen's position as defended by Arnauld. Yet, in spite of the fact that Arnauld himself had the mind not of a theologian but of a lawyer, that Saint-Cyran was dead, and that Jansen had no spiritual teaching to offer beyond submission to the hierarchical Church, it was the spirituality rather than the theology which proved so potent a force in French cultural life immediately before the Fronde. Women could join the Port-Royal religious community or, if they were wealthy enough, live near or within the convent. A number did live within the precincts, notably Mme de Guéméné and Mme de Sablé. It was in theory naturally possible to shut down a monastery, but it was exceedingly difficult and required action from Rome. The nuns themselves were anyway never more than an irritation to the authorities, on account of the focus they provided for the doctrinal sympathizers. It is doubtful whether more than two or three of them ever understood the arguments about nature and grace.

The solitaires may have been an organized ecclesiastical group, but they neither strictly belonged to Port-Royal nor had any canonical institution to fall back on. As a group they disposed of more theological expertise and greater scholarship, although few took to writing; they were, however, both more dangerous and more easily suppressed. However technically separate, it is customary to consider them as part of "Port-Royal." When their numbers began to augment quite speedily after 1643, the first recruit was Victor Pallu, doctor of the comte de Soissons, killed in 1641 at La Marfée near Sedan. In October Pallu joined Le Maître, Séricourt, M. de Bascle—a comparatively young man who had come to Paris after a disastrous marriage in search of a tutorship and had met Saint-Cyran—and Luzanci, one of d'Andilly's sons. Saci was still in Paris with Barcos.

The conversion of the Thomas du Fossé family, which shocked Rouen, brought to be educated at Port-Royal three girls, two of whom took the veil, and to Les Granges three boys, to be instructed by Bascle. Among those who came to Port-Royal-des-Champs was Monsieur Manguelen, who undertook the direction of the solitaires but died of a fever on 24 September 1646. Singlin took over from him again until Saci was ordained. It was d'Andilly who set about the draining and general embellishment of the site, introducing flowers as well as fruit trees. D'Andilly, whose son, Arnauld de Pomponne, was to become prominent as a minister of Louis XIV, remained a go-between for the monastery and the court, especially during Mazarin's lifetime. The solitaires retained their private interests and idiosyncrasies and, to some extent, adopted different styles of life, putting the emphasis more or less on study, manual labour, in particular gardening, or formal prayer. Some were priests or even prelates, but most were from the upper bourgeoisie or the magistracy.

At the same time, patrician women were moving to Port-Royal de Paris. The marquise d'Aumont came to live there in 1646 and, although she was not allowed to take the veil, she was buried in 1658 with the title "Sister." Mère Angélique, who had succeeded Mère Agnès as abbess again in October 1642 and was to be re-elected for three-year periods again in 1645, 1648, and 1651, visited the deserted Port-Royal-des-Champs in 1646 and obtained permission to take a section of the community back there. Repairs were carried out during 1647, and on 13 May 1648 she led a group of seven choir nuns and two lay sisters back to Port-Royal-des-Champs. The coadjutor bishop, not yet cardinal de Retz, not displeased to be in alliance with so powerful a faction, came to bless the nuns due to leave Paris. There was now not enough room at Port-Royal-des-Champs. Le Maître, Séricourt, and several others lived at Les Granges on the hill. D'Andilly had his own small house. For a period a house near the Paris monastery was rented for some of the others while further buildings were erected on the hill.

During the Fronde Port-Royal-des-Champs offered refuge not only to the local nobility but also to the peasantry, and food supplies, escorted by the solitaires, were regularly sent to Port-Royal in Paris until the community of about 30 was moved temporarily into the centre of the town by its protectors on 12 January 1649, leaving a skeletal team of religious under Mère Marie des Anges, recently returned from Maubuisson. Singlin spent most of his time in the faubourg, although he also looked after the Chevreuse and the town houses until the faubourg became safer again in March. Singlin was put momentarily under interdict for a sermon at the Paris house on 28 August 1649, preached before five bishops, Père de Gondi of the Oratory, the maréchal de Schomberg, and the duc de Liancourt.

Séricourt died on 4 October 1650, and his mother, Soeur Sainte-Catherine de Saint-Jean, on 22 January 1651. In 1652 the second Fronde made Port-Royal-des-Champs too dangerous, and the community returned to Paris, where the house over a few months took in some 400 nuns from other communities. Some stayed. Mère Angélique wrote to Le Maître that a dozen Benedictine nuns had joined the community. The revenue was 10,000 livres, but Port-Royal could now depend on benefactions. The duc de Luynes had just built his château at Vaumurier, which was scarcely a place, more the name of the corner of a farm a matter of metres away from the monastery in the Chevreuse valley and on land belonging to it. Luynes had the nuns' quarters rebuilt from 1651, and received the remaining solitaires at the château during the second Fronde war. The 72 cells built for the nuns seemed excessive, but there would be almost exactly 72 members in the community when the Paris nuns were finally forced to come to Port-Royal-des-Champs in 1665. During the war up to 100 persons ate together with Luynes in silence at the château, while someone read from a pious book.

When the Port-Royal community returned to the valley under Mère Angélique on 15 January 1653, Luynes had also had the church floor raised nearly three metres to avoid the damp. There was even a plan to build 12 hermitages, each with access to a communal chapel. When the solitaires returned, a number of them would continue to visit the château at Vaumurier to discuss Descartes with Luynes and Antoine Arnauld. The vogue for Descartes at Port-Royal importantly indicates how little the anthropological consequences of Jansen's theology had yet been understood, even by Arnauld, at this date daringly advocating what he regarded as the two autonomous views contained in Jansenist theology and Cartesian philosophy. They are in fact incompatible with one another, alike only in being sweepingly innovative. Sainte-Beuve saw this and, choosing to admire the Jansenism, regarded Arnauld's Cartesianism as an aberration. Brunetière was misleadingly to go to the other extreme, and chose to envisage the whole of the history of ideas in 17th-century France in terms of the conflict between Jansenism and Cartesianism.

The intensely pious duchesse de Luynes, Louise de Séguier, cousin of the chancellor, deeply concerned about the poverty and suffering she saw everywhere, had died at 27 giving birth to a fifth child on 13 September 1651. Luynes himself, born in 1620, was the son of the Connétable and the future duchesse de Chevreuse. He returned to the world and in 1661 married the beautiful but unintelligent Anne de Rohan, born in 1640, his mother's half-sister and daughter of his grandfather, Hercule de Rohan. Luynes, in other words, married his aunt, and his mother's half-sister became also her daughter-in-law. Fontaine, who was born in 1625 and had been taken in at Port-Royal-des-Champs in 1644, where he served Le Maître as secretary, remembered while composing his precious *Mémoires* from about 1696 to 1700, how strongly Singlin and Mme de Longueville had disapproved of Luynes's second marriage, although the Port-Royal reaction to Luynes's return to the world cannot totally be gauged by what Mme de Longueville thought. It is impossible to get very far into the history of 17th-century France without stumbling over the Condé-Longueville hostility to the houses of Rohan and Chevreuse. When Anne de Rohan died in 1684, Luynes was to marry a third time. It was Mère Angélique de Saint-Jean who had the deserted château at Vaumurier pulled down when the dauphin, noticing it empty when out hunting, asked the king if he could have it, intending to instal one of his mistresses. Louis XIV was delighted with the abbess's action.

The bull condemning the five propositions, *Cum occasione* (see: Jansen), was signed in Rome on 31 May 1653 and published on 9 June. The propositions were condemned in themselves, "on the occasion" of the appearance of Jansen's book. It was the further decree of 23 April 1654 which implied that Jansen had actually held them. Mazarin suspected some complicity between Port-Royal, now firmly regarded as the headquarters of the Jansenist party, and Retz. He wanted Rome's acquiescence in Retz's resignation from the see of Paris, which he was going to inherit in fact on 21 March 1654, and so was certainly not going to oppose the formal reception of the bull in France. Letters patent accepting the bull were signed on 4 July 1653 and a mandement was drawn up, slipping in the words "extracted from Jansen's book," which Rome had carefully avoided putting into the bull. The first formulary was drawn up in 1655 and decreed by the general assembly of the clergy in 1656. But on 16 October 1656 Alexander VII confirmed Innocent X's *Cum occasione* with *Ad sacram beati Petri sedem*, and a reference to the new Roman document now had to be added to the formulary. The assembly passed the revision in 1657. The parlement de Paris refused at first to register it; Mazarin thought the whole matter was taking up too much time; and the formulary and signature, both voted, were left on the shelf until 1660, probably because of the impact of Pascal's *Lettres provinciales*. Arnauld seems in 1654 even to have proposed to Mazarin a truce of silence.

While the Sorbonne was considering the two propositions from Arnauld's *Seconde lettre à un duc et pair* in December 1655 and the following January (see: Jansenism and Pascal), Arnauld took refuge at Port-Royal-des-Champs. The "Sorbonne" in this context means the faculty of theology, to which however also belonged at this date teaching members of the Collège de Navarre, the Collège des Cholets, and a few others. Deliberations of the faculty took place on the premises of the Sorbonne, and the voting procedures are not entirely clear. Each of the four older mendicant orders, Dominicans (also known as "Jacobins"), Carmelites, Franciscans of all sorts ("Cordeliers"), and Augustinians, was allowed two votes, but since many more of them were teaching members of the faculty, and their orders were exempt from episcopal jurisdiction and therefore on the whole anti-Gallican, and since the limitation of their voting powers was of doubtful legitimacy anyway, ultramontane measures could often be pressed through by closing a blind eye to the number of exempt religious who voted. Sainte-Beuve says he found in "le plumitif" that as many as 40 regulars were allowed to vote. From 20 December the chancellor himself, Pierre Séguier, was ordered by the king to be present at all sessions, naturally with ushers, bailiffs, and other officials, not to preside over but to "supervise" the proceedings.

The actual count of the votes is uncertain, but that most favourable to Arnauld gives a condemnation on the question of fact, declaring that Jansen himself was not orthodox, by 124 votes to 71 on 14 January 1656. Subsequent proceedings concerned with the heterodoxy of Arnauld's own assertion that Saint Peter denied Jesus because he did not have the grace to act otherwise were too disturbed for any counting of votes to be meaningful, and public opinion was from early 1656 anyway largely determined in Arnauld's favour by what turned out later to have been the collaboration of Arnauld and Nicole with Pascal in the redaction of the *Lettres provinciales*. For some years, until 1648, Arnauld had lain low after the publication of *De la fréquente communion*. From 1648 he spent much of his time openly with the solitaires at Port-Royal-des-Champs. From 1656 to 1668 he was again in hiding, although he would never have been really difficult to find, and from 1679 until his death in 1694 he was abroad, permanently hidden, underground, "like a mole" as Mme de Sévigné put it on 31 May 1680.

Arnauld was allowed the first fortnight of February 1656 to recant, but did not. Thereafter all the doctors of the faculty were obliged to sign his condemnation, as were all those on whom degrees were later conferred. The royal professor of theology, M. de Sainte-Beuve, was dismissed and replaced for refusing to sign. During the six weeks following the censure of 31 January d'Andilly was writing to Mazarin through third parties and receiving signals back; intrigues of all manner were being conducted at court; and the highest clergy were placed under intense pressures. It became clear, however, that the solitaires would be made to disperse, and that the teaching would have to stop, at least for a token period. Most of the solitaires left on 20 March. Some of the 15 children being taught were sent home, others looked after in various grand houses. Jansenist messengers rode to Port-Royal-des-Champs alongside the law officer charged to ensure that the court's orders had been obeyed, the lieutenant-civil Daubray. There was a touch of menace and a great deal of farce: priests pretending to be gardeners, deliberate misunderstandings. Daubray wanted to see the printing presses. What he was shown by a solitaire speaking patois were the wine presses. The exchange with Mère Angélique was equally good-humoured, points for wit being shared with the lieutenant about equally.

On Friday 24 March 1656 Marguerite Périer, Pascal's niece, was the subject of what was subsequently adjudged to have been a miraculous cure of an ulcer of the lachrymal duct when touched by a relic of the crown of thorns at Port-Royal in the faubourg Saint-Jacques. The effect on morale at Port-Royal was not so electrifying as has been stated, and there is a fascinating letter of Mère Angélique, who had disapproved of the *Lettres provinciales* after the dogmatic dispute had ended with the third, quite undramatically narrating how calmly the cure was perceived at Port-Royal. Whether it was the miracle, or whether Pascal's *Lettres* had rallied opinion, pressure on Port-Royal let up for a few years. By the time pressure was reapplied in April 1661, Pascal's sister, Soeur de Sainte-Euphémie, had become sub-prior and mistress of novices at Port-Royal-des-Champs.

It was in December 1660, before the death of Mazarin on 9 March 1661 and the subsequent assumption of power by the 23-year-old Louis XIV, that the king, no doubt reacting to strong pressure to keep France's relationship with Rome under central control and to purge a doctrinal dissidence capable of rallying disaffected sections of the aristocracy, intervened personally in the Jansenist dispute. What is not clear is why the king should have made his initial move at the time and in the manner he chose. Whatever may be the reason, the king called the presiding council of the assembly of the clergy to the Louvre on Monday, 13 December 1660. He told them that Mazarin had not been well enough to come to them.

The members were astonished that the king turned out to have meant it when he had told them to come early, and that they were then left alone with Mazarin and Louis XIV. It was the king who said that he had decided to eliminate all traces of Jansenism, and Mazarin who subsequently spoke for an hour and a quarter to make the matter clear. On 1 February 1661 the assembly of the clergy decided to impose the formulary passed by the assembly in 1657, and its signature. The Conseil d'Etat ratified the measure on 13 April, and on 23 April Daubray, accompanied this time by an officer of the Châtelet, visited Port-Royal de Paris, giving three days notice that the boarders should be sent home. Seven were given the veils of novices during the next two days.

On 24 April the order to send away boarders was given at Port-Royal-des-Champs and on 4 May the order was extended to postulants and novices in Paris, and the day after at Port-Royal-des-Champs. The court had not liked the precipitate clothings. On 25 July Daubray called early at the Paris house, had Mme de Sablé awakened and removed, later having her door locked, and also that of M. de Sévigné. Mme de Guéméné was absent, but others with lodgings in the courtyard were told to go away. Daubray had specific orders from the king to wall up Mme de Sablé's celebrated grille opening on to the choir of the church which allowed her to hear Mass without being infected by germs from the congregation, and which she claimed to have opened only occasionally for la Grande Mademoiselle and Mme de Longueville.

Mère Angélique came from the Chevreuse house to help Mère Agnès, who was abbess, but this time police action was to be serious. On 8 May Singlin had to go into hiding to avoid a lettre de cachet exiling him to Quimper, signed that day. The solitaires had to disperse and the children were again sent away. The order to sign the formulary, dated 8 June 1661, was couched in such a way as to obscure the question of fact. It was quite probably drawn up by Pascal himself, and Arnauld thought the adhesion to the truths of faith which the formulary demanded was acceptable, writing a pamphlet on the subject in June, *De la signature du Formulaire*. There was opposition to the signature amongst the religious, particularly Jacqueline Pascal and Angélique de Saint-Jean, but on 22 and 23 June they all signed, at both houses. There was firmer opposition at Port-Royal-des-Champs, and Jacqueline Pascal herself died on 4 October partly, it is supposed, from moral anguish. Mère Angélique Arnauld died on 6 August.

However, the first mandement was attacked by the Jesuits and others as inadequate, suppressed by the council of state on 14 July, and condemned at Rome on 1 August. A second mandement was prepared and signed by the grand vicars of Paris on 31 October, making impossible any reservation about the presence in the *Augustinus* of the condemned propositions. At this point Pascal, supported by the lawyer Domat and by his own friend Roannez, differed from Arnauld and Nicole, who thought that a submission stating that it was explicitly "quant à la foi (in what concerns faith)," was still allowable. The reservation restricted assent to what the Church could impose by virtue of its teaching rather than of its legislative authority. Pascal's biographer and the editor of the critical edition of his works thinks that Pascal's position at this point became incoherent. A short work, *Ecrit sur la signature*, is unsatisfactory, and a longer one has been lost. Pascal himself from 1661 retired from all theological controversy.

A new superior, M. Bail, was imposed at Port-Royal. He examined in detail both communities and both houses from 12 July to 2 September 1661. The next few months were filled chiefly with harassments. Neither Retz nor the Port-Royal communities were disposed to cooperate with the court, and the king would have been prepared to concede a truce, but by this time Arnauld felt that matters had gone too far, and conciliatory moves mediated by Gilbert de Choiseul, bishop of Comminges, came to nothing. When Retz finally resigned the archbishopric on 14 February 1662, his successor was Marca, the author of the original formulary. Marca's bulls arrived from Rome only three days before his death on 29 June 1662. Port-Royal was relieved at the respite.

Marca was succeeded by the king's former tutor, Hardouin de Beaumont de Péréfixe, bishop of Rodez, but this was the moment when on 20 August 1662, the day after Pascal's death, the pope's Corsican guards fired on the carriage of the French ambassador, the maréchal de Créqui, on the steps of his residence, the Farnese palace. Créqui was known for his coarseness and had been tactless, but the incident strained Franco-Vatican relations almost to breaking point. Louis XIV exacted heavy reparations at a moment when the supporters of Gallican theses in the theology faculty were irritating the Jesuits and Rome. Franco-papal relations were at a low point and Péréfixe had to wait nearly two years for the confirmation of his appointment with the arrival of his bulls on 10 April 1664. On 19 April Louis XIV made signature of the formulary mandatory for anyone in university or ecclesiastical life, or holding a benefice. Singlin died in the spring. Lancelot called on the archbishop, to present the compliments of the Port-Royal communities, but ended by presenting the archbishop with a virtual ultimatum.

Péréfixe was unpredictable, jovial and violent by turns; endowed neither with learning nor with subtlety, he foresaw no difficulty in imposing his will on the nuns. His mandement of 8 June 1664 seemed to offer hope. The degree of commitment required in the matter of the presence of the propositions in the *Augustinus* was specified as of "human" rather than "divine" faith, like the teaching itself. Nicole devoted the fourth of his *Lettres sur l'hérésie imaginaire* of 19 June to the distinction, as also his *Traité de la foi humaine* of August 1664. The olive branch could have been accepted and no one needed to lose face. Péréfixe had visited Port-Royal de Paris from 9 to 14 June and finally given the nuns three weeks to think about the consequences of what he regarded as a rebellion against authority and the superior wisdom of those who were recommending signature. During the three weeks, filled with intensive lobbying and incessant discussions, the archbishop fell ill, and the nuns organized a novena of prayer for his recovery.

On 21 August, the day the novena ended, Péréfixe came to the monastery and told the nuns he was now ordering them to sign the mandement. They had gathered in Mère Agnès's room, and she had opened a New Testament haphazardly, only to find a verse encouraging resistance to the powers of darkness. The nuns were confirmed in their feelings, and unanimously refused to sign. Péréfixe addressed them, ranting about obstinacy, rebellion, disobedience, and pride. They were forbidden access to the sacraments. As he swept out he saw too many great ladies, in particular the princesse de Guémené, in the courtyard, and returned to the parlour where the nuns still were. There he lost his archiepiscopal temper and descended to the coarsest invective. Mère de Ligny, the abbess, was called obstinate, ignorant, proud, stupid, and "pimbêche (stuck-up)," a little fool—everyone could see that from her face.

Every word, of course, had been taken down. The archbishop's movements and intentions, too, were reported back to Port-Royal. When on 26 August he arrived back again with half an army of soldiers, policemen, ecclesiastics, and court officers, the nuns as usual knew their lines. D'Andilly threw himself on his knees, the archbishop read out the names of 12 nuns he intended to place in other convents; Mère Angélique de Saint-Jean demanded authorization in writing to leave the cloister; the archbishop dispensed her from the requirement. It is tempting to suppose that each side had already had previous knowledge of the other's script, but that the nuns had had a better script-writer.

The archbishop left behind a new superior from the Visitation and five new nuns. A complete transcript of the day's proceedings, ending with the archbishop's blessing, was available the next day, signed by all the Port-Royal community, immediately printed, and sent to the parlement. The council of state inevitably prevented a humiliating declaration by the parlement of abuse of procedure by the archbishop, but the move had considerable publicity value. The archbishop, by now a laughingstock, kept on arriving with mandement, pen and ink; he took away more nuns on 29 November and 19 December; he changed carriages to avoid being laughed at in the street; but the war continued. Things were conducted more calmly at Port-Royal-des-Champs, where the archbishop spent from 15 to 17 November 1664. The prioress was Mère du Fargis, and the archbishop, losing his temper again, excommunicated her and her community. On 30 November a lettre de cachet removed all confessors, solitaires, and male servants. In the end all the Port-Royal religious who had not signed, whether they were from Paris, among those dispersed to other convents, or already in the valley, were united at Port-Royal-des-Champs, under guard, without sacraments, for three and a half years, from July 1665 to February 1669.

Jansen himself, who was almost certainly an ultramontane, would have signed at least the first and probably the second mandement. There had been no real argument on a matter of theological substance since January 1656, when Arnauld was condemned for his assertion that Saint Peter denied Christ because he was not given the efficacious grace which would have forced him to act otherwise. What had been, with Saint-Cyran's spirituality and Jansen's theology, a major argument about the nature of Christian religious activity had been made by a skilful and courageous, if obstinate and insensitive lawyer to centre on the absurd question of whether or not Jansen had held five propositions. Arnauld's cleverness lay in making that question appear to be the real issue. His insensitivity lay in refusing to allow it to be resolved, as it easily could have been, and to posture as a persecuted martyr by allowing a convent-full of patrician nuns and their male, female, lay and ecclesiastical supporters, almost all of whom had seriously developed spiritual lives, to undergo major harassment as sacrificial victims in a battle in which he left almost all of them bemused into thinking that they were defending truths essential to the Christian religion. It is difficult to suppose that at bottom what he was fighting for was anything other than family honour.

About a dozen Paris nuns had signed the formulary, using as their external publicist Desmarets, to be attacked by Nicole in the *Visionnaires*. Early in 1665 Arnauld and Nicole published their successful *Apologie pour les religieuses de Port-Royal*. Louis XIV, who had imposed the signature by virtue only of his own Gallican authority, was finally obliged to write to the pope, who congratulated the king on this piety, supplied a new formulary, and simply indicated that he would henceforward use his own authority. The brief was dated 16 December 1664. Louis XIV needed more than a brief, and was made to ask formally for a bull. He wrote on 25 January 1665 and Alexander VII recognized his capitulation by issuing the bull *Regiminis apostolici* on 25 February 1665.

Many of the clergy found ways of eluding the direct and unmodified signature, but four bishops in particular, Nicolas Pavillon of Alet, François de Caulet of Pamiers, Henry Arnauld of Angers, and Nicolas Choart de Buzanval of Beauvais, issued pastoral guidance in the form of instructions reserving the matter of "fait (fact)," while conceding that of substance, or "droit." The pope reserved to himself a right to intervene which the Gallican church was not prepared to concede. Louis XIV was violently angry, but the pope won. The four bishops' instructions were condemned by the Holy Office in January 1667, and a commission of nine bishops was nominated by the pope on 22 April to bring the four into line or be prepared to face degradation. Then on 22 May Alexander VII died, and Clement IX sought a peace for which Louis XIV, too, pressed by the prospect of expensive military campaigns, was also ready. An accommodation was reached in 1668 in which the pope tacitly conceded the principle of fact. Signatures which did actually allow the question of whether Jansen had held the five propositions or not to remain open were now acceptable. Peace was made official by a decree of the council of state in France of 23 October 1668. On the next day the king received Arnauld, and the brief of Clement IX to the four bishops was signed on 19 January 1669. On 13 February 1669 the nuns submitted in a form considered acceptable. Arnauld and Nicole were present. Five days later the interdict or corporate excommunication was lifted.

Louis XIV split the two monasteries by a decree of the council of state dated 13 May 1669. The Paris Port-Royal house, whose community had accepted the formulary, consisted of seven nuns and three lay-sisters, and was given 10,000 livres a year. Port-Royal-des-Champs contained 69 professed nuns and between 25 and 30 lay-sisters. It was allocated 19,500 livres, plus its estates. The schools were not reopened, but the community was allowed to receive novices again and to accept boarders. Mme de Longueville built a small lodging which she used occasionally from 1671, and Mlle de Vertus permanently occupied hers. Saci, caught in hiding and kept in the Bastille from 13 May 1666 until 13 October 1668, was not the nominal but the effective superior. Arnauld and Nicole went on to controvert the Calvinist view of the Eucharist, and the first volume of *La Perpétuité de la foi* was to appear in 1669. Arnauld's final great controversy was against Malebranche. The interest of Quesnel is entirely theological. The central religious and literary importance of Port-Royal was now over.

The activity which led to the final dissolution of the monastery started in 1679 and was essentially political. Many of the visitors who streamed to Port-Royal-des-Champs came from the great French families in which opposition to Louis XIV's absolutism still lingered. From 1675 Arnauld took the pope's side in the quarrel with the king about the "régale," or right to the income from vacant benefices. The king simply decided to eliminate what had been a seedbed of dissidence for too long. Arnauld, warned in time, joined Nicole in exile in Brussels on his way to Holland, leaving Paris on 18 June 1679. It is possible that Innocent XI might well have made Arnauld a cardinal had he chosen a Roman exile, and probable that his disappearance was less embarrassing for Louis XIV than his continued presence and consequent imprisonment would have been. The end of Port-Royal-des-Champs came slowly. More signatures to further protestations of orthodoxy were exacted. Barcos's posthumous *Exposition de la foi* was condemned in 1696. The monastery was forbidden to elect an abbess in 1706. Its possessions were transferred to Port-Royal in Paris on 9 February 1707; the community was excommunicated in November 1707; and on 29 October 1709 the community was dispersed. In June 1710 the buildings were razed.

The literary importance of Port-Royal is two-fold. This is partly because the history of the monastery, together with the histories of Jansenist spirituality and Jansenist theology in France, dovetails so tightly into the whole evolution of French culture, and especially of its moral and spiritual values, as to make it an obvious guide to the understanding of the development of the century's literature. From the baroque effervescence of Zamet and the confident neoplatonism of Bérulle, through the suggestion of reaction in Condren and the severe mystical exaltation of the still charming Saint-Cyran to the conscious theological argument of Arnauld that some human beings were born to be damned, and the final victory of a contrary and optimistic view of human nature, the century's spiritual development reflects a much wider cultural evolution explored, canvassed, and then imaginatively tested in its literature. Port-Royal's history offers the literary historian the advantage of a massively documented parallel phenomenon, incidentally necessary to any real understanding of a whole range of major authors, notably Pascal and Racine, but, if less obviously, also La Rochefoucauld, Retz, La Bruyère, Bossuet, and Fénelon.

Secondly, however, historians of Port-Royal have drawn attention to a number of works and writers of literary importance. It remains a matter for regret that the letter of direction is not yet normally considered as powerful an imaginative genre as it undoubtedly sometimes was. The spiritual correspondence of the 17th century is more moving, more probing, and more fundamentally serious in its imaginative purposes than much that is ordinarily considered of literary importance, and it is often as well written.

Much that emanated from Port-Royal admittedly is pedagogy, like the *Logique de Port-Royal*. Much, like the endless factums and apologetics is ephemerally polemical, or consists of chronicles and memoirs more of historical than of literary interest. Regrettably, there is no very strong case for including in a guide to French literature any detailed consideration of the Port-Royal memorialists, pedagogues, and chroniclers, Claude Lancelot, Nicolas Fontaine, Pierre Thomas du Fossé, or even of such great controversialists as Antoine Arnauld himself, or Martin Barcos, less important as a writer than for the historical role he played. From the literary point of view, the charming d'Andilly is of greatest interest as a translator, but his cultural contribution to the life of his century is such that to treat him as a merely literary figure, another of the madrigalists of the chambre bleue (see: *Guirlande de Julie*) would somehow demean him.

The greatest literary loss is undoubtedly the letters. Those of Jansen, Saint-Cyran and, less adequately, Louis-Isaac Le Maître de Saci, are available in modern editions, but there is very little that can easily be read written by Mère Angélique, Mère Agnès, Mère Angélique de Saint-Jean, and Jacqueline Pascal. Furthermore, such interest as their letters have attracted has largely been due to the Port-Royal connection. Intrinsically the letters of Jeanne-Françoise de Chantal, Olier, Surin, and Rancé are of greater literary, if not necessarily spiritual importance than those emanating from Port-Royal and those associated with it. In the present context it has not seemed possible to do more than is attempted by the present entry, together with those entries on Saint-Cyran for the early spirituality associated with the monastery, on Jansen for the theology, although the various works of Arnauld arguing Jansen's position are as important as the *Augustinus* itself in the history of the French church, and on

Pierre Nicole, the most prominent religious moralist other than Pascal associated with Port-Royal.

The work of Henri Bremond requires now to be undertaken again. Even so brief a consideration of Port-Royal as the present one reveals an urgent need for a new literary map of the spiritual works of 17th-century France.

PRADON, Jacques, 1644–1698.

Dramatist.

LIFE

The dramatic career of Jacques Pradon instantly raises in their acutest form the most fundamental issues of literary history. Pradon's *Phèdre et Hippolyte* was played at the Hôtel de Guénégaud on 3 January 1677, two days after the *Phèdre et Hippolyte*, as it was then called, of Racine, played at the Hôtel de Bourgogne. The relative merits of the two tragedies were seriously debated. The plays undoubtedly differ in poetic intensity and, in a different although related way, in the imaginative daring of their moral vision. The difficulty is to know which criterion should be considered the more important, particularly since the 17th-century quality of "le sublime" referred indiscriminately to both. The contemporaries of Racine and Pradon were more interested in moral vision than they were in either imaginative daring or in poetic intensity.

This was not simply one of the large number of instances in 17th-century Paris when rival professional playwrights challenged one another by "doubling," or simultaneously treating the same subject. Pradon had certainly seen Racine's text and, while keeping Racine's major innovation, the new character of Aricie, and most of his version of the legend, significantly altered Racine's plot in sometimes quite small, but exceedingly important respects. Pradon was also being supported by a very powerful group of patrons. He was a big dramatic success, not just the small-time playwright he has sometimes been made to appear, insolently daring to take on his peer and being made to look a fool for his pains.

Racine personally tried to have Pradon's play banned, and he apparently succeeded in getting two female leads of the Guénégaud company in turn to decline to play Pradon's heroine, although the historical sources do not agree on the pair of names. The older tradition says that the part was turned down by Mlle de Brie, and then Mlle Molière, finally to be taken by Mlle du Pin. More recently it has been maintained that the part was turned down first by Mlle Molière, then by Mlle du Pin, and was finally accepted by Mlle Guyon. Pradon maintained that an attempt was also made to stop his publisher from publishing the play.

The group which supported Pradon had tried and failed to worst Racine three years earlier by putting on Le Clerc and Coras's *Iphigénie* to rival Racine's play of the same name. On that occasion Racine had succeeded in getting the rival play suppressed for at least a season. The opposing group was now returning to the attack with Pradon as its new champion. It certainly included Montauzier, and may well have been able to enlist sympathy from everyone connected with the powerful Hôtel de Soissons, the ducs de Nevers and d'Aumont, Mme de Bouillon and the Vendôme entourage, the Mazarin family connections as well as Mme Deshoulières, Des Marets de Saint-Sorlin, Armand-Jean Vignerot de Richelieu—the cardinal's great-nephew, an open leader of the opposition to Racine—Madeleine de Scudéry, and everyone associated with the Corneille brothers and Donneau de Visé's *Mercure Galant* (q.v.).

But why the energy packed into the animosity? Pradon at first felt strong resentment against Boileau, and then included Racine among the targets for his hostility. He may have had genuine justification for resenting Racine's behaviour towards him. The Guénégaud troupe certainly had reason to feel antagonism towards the company at the Hôtel de Bourgogne. But neither these feelings, nor any personal reactions to Racine's character, nor any preference for opera over tragedy such as had aroused Racine's indignation over the Quinault/Lulli *Alceste*, nor any purely aesthetic dispute, whether about modern and antique authors or about anything else, can explain the intensity of the acrimony.

In a sense the actual dispute over the two *Phèdres* was trivial. A group of people surrounding Mme Deshoulières, or perhaps more probably she herself, wrote a harmlessly disobliging anti-Racine sonnet after his first night. The rumour went round that it was by Nevers. Immediately another sonnet was fitted to the same rhymes attacking Nevers with atrocious insinuations of incest, sodomy, and libertinage, the more hurtful for being probably true. Eventually it became clear that neither Nevers, nor Racine, nor Boileau had written either sonnet, but that the second one had been the work of a group of bright young things, probably Nantouillet, Guilleragues, Effiat and Manicamp, intent on stirring up trouble for sheer amusement, and peace was restored. Racine stopped writing tragedies; Boileau stopped writing "satirically"; both became royal historiographers, and there was no more trouble.

That was not the point. Why had so many people gone to so much trouble to get Pradon's alternative *Phèdre et Hippolyte* on to the stage? The answer to that question cannot be unconnected to the century's central spiritual dilemma, besides which aesthetic considerations concerning poetic ability are of little consequence. No doubt there were those who, after a little prompting, began to see the superior poetic skills of Racine, the concentrated destructive force of female passion as he depicted it, its instantaneity, unconcealability, unavoidability, and guilt. Racine's theatre vigorously investigated the possibility that guilt, in *Phèdre et Hippolyte* from incest, adultery, and jealousy, was unavoidable. Racine's plays were exploring the possibility that the human will could not control human moral stature, with the plain result, however dressed up in mythological terms, that the human soul was perhaps simply unable to do anything at all to avoid a torment after death which simply never ended.

Pradon's Phèdre is not guilty of incest or adultery. Pradon follows an older tradition which makes her merely betrothed, not married to Thésée. She kills herself when, at Thésée's jealous request, Neptune sends the monster responsible for frightening Hippolyte's horses and so, indirectly, for his death. Pradon is less of a poet than Racine, but he is not exactly a plagiarist. On the basis of Racine's text, he wrote a brilliant tragedy which went out of its way to avoid examining the central, terrifying threat of human moral powerlessness, entailing a final reward or punishment which no autonomous human choice could alter.

The centrality of that dilemma runs right through the century, and inevitably dominates its imaginative literature. It is at the heart of the Jesuit-Jansenist debate; it determined the two greatest spiritualities of the century, those of François de Sales and of Fénelon; it is the reason why Pascal never wrote his apologetic; it is behind the moral reflections of Nicole; it is secularised in La Rochefoucauld, and it lies behind the dilemmas of Mme de Lafayette's heroines. It is what the Querelle des anciens et des modernes (q.v.) is finally about, from the appearance of the first tensions at the Hôtel de Rambouillet (see entries on Voiture and Chapelain) to its temporary resolution in the reconciliation of Boileau and Perrault.

Jacques Pradon was born early in 1644 and baptized on 21 January, the fourth child of a family of five, with three elder sisters and a younger brother who became a priest. His parents were from the magistracy, from families of lawyers, minor office bearers. Pradon's father was a lawyer at the Rouen parlement from 1631, and Pradon himself studied law. His mother, Marguerite Delastre, was the heir of her father, whose verse had several times won prizes at the Rouen Académie des Palinods. Both Pradon and his brother also won prizes for pious verses from the same Académie. It was probably in 1668 that Pradon came to Paris, where he sought, if he had not already been promised, the protection of Montauzier, governor of Normandy. This was Charles de Sainte-Maure, marquis de Salles, who had become marquis de Montauzier on the death of his elder brother, had frequented the Hôtel de Rambouillet, had married Julie d'Angennes (see: Guirlande de Julie) in 1645, was governor of Normandy from 1663 to 1668, and had been made duc de Montauzier in 1664. A friend of Chapelain's from the days when Chapelain was vainly trying to impose his authority as Ménage's successor at the Hôtel de Rambouillet, Montauzier was automatically an enemy of the young satirist, Boileau-Despréaux, about whom Montauzier is reliably reported to have used unusually virulent invective. Boileau had defended himself against Montauzier, although not by name, in both the ninth Satire and the Discours sur la satire with which it had been published in 1668.

Pradon's first tragedy, Pirame et Thisbé, played with great success at the Hôtel de Bourgogne during the 1673–74 season, was dedicated to Montauzier. It was to be revived by the Guénégaud troupe for the season 1679–80, and we know of 49 performances by the Comédie–Française, newly formed from the amalgamated troupes of the Rue de Guénégaud and the Hôtel de Bourgogne, between 1680 and 1711. Pradon disingenuously denied in his preface the use of modern sources, but he did in fact draw on Théophile de Viau's Les Amours tragiques de Pirame et Thisbé. Pradon's Paris debut therefore already aligned him with the "modernes" in the anti-Boileau camp. It is necessary, as so often, to remember that the ideological line-ups are always disturbed by personal friendships, allegiances, and distastes. Boileau, for instance, was with reserves an admirer of Pierre Corneille from 1664. The ninth Satire defended Corneille's Attila, played by Molière's troupe on 4 March 1667. We know, however, from a leaked letter from Huet to Boileau of 26 March 1683, never sent, but replying to a paragraph against a point made by Huet's 1679 Demonstratio evangelica inserted by

Boileau into his 1683 Oeuvres, that Montauzier's dislike for Boileau continued without abatement. Of the Rouen group protected by Montauzier, generally "moderne" in taste, Pierre Corneille's was the only one whose hostility had been assuaged at the date of Pradon's debut.

Pradon's second tragedy, Tamerlan; ou, La Mort de Bajazet was performed at the Hôtel de Bourgogne, in the season 1675–76, probably in the new year. Although Segrais had drawn on the moving story of the murder of Bayezid in 1635 for his short story Bajazet in 1656, and Racine certainly knew the Segrais, as well as what he had been told by François Duprat, chevalier de Nantouillet, who had been a child slave on the Bosphorus at the time, there had been a spate of interest in Turkey going back to Mairet's 1639 Grand et dernier Solyman and Georges de Scudéry's 1641 Ibrahim; ou, L'Illustre Bassa and to later plays like Tristan's Osman in 1645–46 and Magnon's 1647 Le Grand Tamerlan et Bajazet, or entertainments like Lulli's 1660 Le Récit turquesque. However, there had been a real resurgence of Ottoman power in the 1660s. Vienna had been threatened, Venice lost Crete, the Turkish hold on Hungary was firm, and Polish resistance to Turkey looked fragile.

A Turkish ambassador to Louis XIV with a suite of 20 had disembarked at Toulon on 4 August 1669; Molière had exploited the Turkish theme, with costumes and decor to match, in Le Bourgeois Gentilhomme at Chambord in October 1670; and Racine's play was given at the Hôtel de Bourgogne at the beginning of January 1672. Corneille had already challenged Racine's Bérénice with his own Tite et Bérénice in November 1670. Pradon's Tamerlan, drawing on Magnon, must have been a direct provocation to Racine, a trial run, as it was to turn out, for Phèdre et Hippolyte. Pradon's Tamerlan may have been too successful. He at any rate thought that its success had been deliberately wrecked, and blamed Racine. The claim cannot be substantiated, but should not lightly be dismissed. It fits in too well with the known stage squabbles, rivalries, and animosities, as well as with the characters of both the intense and touchy Racine and the mean and cheerless Pradon. Indeed, for ruthless, ambitious, and aggressive thrusting at the expense of established reputations, it would be quite difficult to know how to award the prize between Boileau, Racine, and Pradon.

What Pradon wrote in the printed preface to Tamerlan in 1676, the year after Paris had been shocked by Racine's successful scheming to get the rival Iphigénie delayed, was that, if Thisbé had not been so successful,

peut-être qu'on eût laissé un libre cours à Tamerlan et qu'on ne l'eût pas étouffé, comme on l'a fait, dans le plus fort de son succès. C'est le jugement que tous les gens désintéressés, et qui n'agissent point par les ressorts de la cabale, ont fait de cette injustice, qui m'a été plus glorieuse dans le monde qu'un plus ample succès

(perhaps Tamerlan would have been allowed a free run, and would not have been stifled, as it was at the height of its success. That is the judgement made by all those who have no personal interest, and who are not motivated by a spirit of cabal, concerning this injustice, and it has brought me more glory in the world than greater success would have done).

It would have been too risky to publish that if there had not been some plausibility in it, but was it aimed at Racine, whom the preface does not mention? If it was, why did Boileau hold his riposte until after the double *Phèdre et Hippolyte* of 1 and 3 January the following year?

What confirms with some certainty that Racine was aimed at, and that everyone was intended to know it, was Pradon's further statement that those whose "malice et chagrin (malice and annoyance)" lay behind the accusations against him of plagiarism, had themselves availed themselves "of the beauties in Tristan, in Mairet, and in Rotrou," as well as those in "Homer, Sophocles, and Euripides." That is a direct reply to Racine's attack on the Quinault-Lulli *Alceste* in the 1675 preface to *Iphigénie*, in which Racine boasts justifiably but ungraciously of his superior understanding of the Greek text. The *Thébaïde*, in particular, had relied on Rotrou, *Britannicus* on Tristan, and *Bajazet* on Mairet.

Racine must have known how low his reputation had dropped after letting Molière down, after his apparent ingratitude to Port-Royal (q.v.), after the rumours circulating on the death of Thérèse du Parc, and after the intriguing to suppress the rival *Iphigénie*. He must have known that the protection of Mme de Montespan did not make him popular. Pradon had not quite named him. He did not need to reply, and was plainly wise to ignore Pradon's preface, even if everyone supposed that it was directed at him. Baillet thought it was, as later did the author of the *Dissertation sur les tragédies de Phèdre et Hippolyte*, almost certainly Subligny, who did not know whether the failure of *Tamerlan* was the fault of the play or of the "brigues indignes (unworthy intrigues)" of Racine, whom he names. Pradon certainly thought that Racine had mounted a cabal against him. *Tamerlan* was being performed at the Hôtel de Bourgogne, and it would have been easy for Racine to have had Pradon's play simply taken off. Boileau advised him to postpone his *Phèdre et Hippolyte* play until after Pradon's, but la Champmeslé had already learnt her part, and Racine decided to go ahead.

Contemporary comment, particularly in the *Gazette d'Amsterdam*, shows that Pradon's *Phèdre et Hippolyte* at least threatened to win the public vote against Racine's play during the six weeks before Lent (see: Racine), but it is difficult to evaluate that information. Performances were held three times a week, and Pradon's play was given 16 successive performances starting on 3 January, then three more later in February, and six following the re-opening after Easter, a total of 25 which made it a considerable success. The first-night takings were a recent record: 1,375 livres. The play was published on 13 March 1677.

First principles suggest that, whatever subsequent apologists and polemicists may have said, Racine's putting on the stage for the first time a woman guilty of an adulterous and incestuous affection was not calculated to keep the audiences away. Adultery of course was commonplace, and incest not at all rare in 17th-century court circles, as also lower down the social scale, and there is nowhere in Racine's play any suggestion that Phèdre might be guilty of any actual immoral deed. The nearest she comes to doing anything wrong is to acquiesce in Oenone's idea that Hippolyte should be blamed for a love in which not he, but she herself, was guilty, and then to say in jealous rage that Aricie must be destroyed, making her just culpable enough for the audience to be able to accept her guilt-inspired suicide. Pradon's Phèdre kills herself out of frustrated love after Hippolyte's death.

Pradon's initial superior popular success was not due to the "bienséances," his greater decorum, if only for the same reasons that popular success seldom is. It was also not due to superior fidelity to any modern or antique original version of the much-used legend, or to any superior poetic skill. The roughest of 17th-century audiences was discriminating enough to realize that Racine's characters found a language more or less adequate to express their emotions, in spite of the unwanted titter on his first night, whereas Pradon was using language in such a way as to hope to indicate the existence of emotions that the characters were unable actually to express. Racine's moral vision may momentarily have been felt by a section of the public to have been superior to Pradon's, but his ultimate victory was due to his much greater imaginative daring.

After *Phèdre et Hippolyte* Racine retired from the stage, perhaps converted to devotion or at least to more highly regarded diversions than play-writing, perhaps preferring to settle down to his lucrative career as courtier and royal historiographer, bought off by the king, perhaps simply wanting a more respectable life of marriage and fatherhood. His wife never went to any of his plays. There are signs that Racine may have been disdaining the theatre as too undignified an activity to be compatible with his newly acquired grandeur since perhaps 1674. He had earlier still resumed amicable relations with Port-Royal and, however factitious, the preface to *Phèdre et Hippolyte* indicated how the terrifying psychological possibility of unavoidable guilt fitted in with the truly unimaginable horrors of Jansenist theology, with its arbitrarily inflicted eternity of punishment for those not at God's arbitrary whim predestined to glory.

Pradon went on to a successful dramatic career. Through the former précieuse (q.v.), Antoinette du Ligier de la Garde, Mme Deshoulières, a firm supporter of the "modernes," he was introduced into the entourage of Marie-Anne Mancini, duchesse de Bouillon, the youngest of Mazarin's seven nieces and of the five sisters of the duc de Nevers. He was a natural ally of the victims of Boileau's biting saracasms. As a dramatist, Pradon, helped by the publicity of the original quarrel and its continuing reverberations, presented seven more tragedies, *Electre* of 1677, which was not published, *La Troade* of 1679, *Statire* of 1680, *Tarquin*, unpublished, of 1682, *Regulus* of 1688, *Germanicus*, unpublished, of 1694, and *Scipion l'Africain* of 1697. They are on the whole perfectly adequate late 17th-century tragic entertainments, well-made, not aspiring to be great poetry, unpretentious, but not searching enough in their imaginative explorations into the meaning of human experience to be great literature.

Pradon, however, also found himself, as much by inclination as by necessity, forced to become a literary polemicist, and what he had to say in response to Boileau's goads is not unworthy of attention. When in 1677 it looked for a moment as if Racine was facing his first stage defeat since the sweeping success of *Andromaque* in 1667, Boileau wrote to him the consolatory seventh *Epître*. It was not generous towards Pradon, but fairly routine 17th-century invective, written in the doggerel to which connoisseurs of what Pradon referred to, with Racine, as the poet of the sublime have long become accustomed. However, the *Epître* ends with an implied allusion to Horace (Satires I, x), and it works its way round to end on the name of Pradon, incidentally throwing in a reference to the involuntary nature of the iniquity of Racine's Phèdre—"Phèdre malgré soy perfide, incestueuse (Phèdre in spite of herself traitrous and incestuous)."

Oddly, this is a compliment. Boileau compares Pradon's characters to marionettes, little more than an unexceptional way of saying that they lack the passions of Racine's characters, but he takes Pradon a great deal more seriously than all except the most modern critics. He makes a stock joke about Pradon's ignorance, about which Pradon himself could be witty, and he drops a lot of names, encouraging the disconsolate Racine to think highly of his dramatic ancestry, and to despise the "pasles Envieux (pale enviers)" and the "flot de vains Auteurs (flood of would-be authors)," that is, Pradon and his friends. He does not, however, criticize Pradon's play. All Boileau actually does is express global dislike and condemnation. In 1694, Pradon is substituted for Boursault in the seventh *Satire* and for Maurois in the ninth.

Boileau is keeping hostilities going, but he is writing little more than cliquish pieces, setting forth the authorized list of objects of disapprobation agreed by his diminishing clientele, "…Perrin, Bardin, Pradon, Haynaut, Colletet, Pelletier, Titreville, Quinaut." Such lists are not exactly the stuff of which great satirical verse is fabricated. There was a contemporary joke in which Pradon was said to have mixed up chronology and geography. Like Perrault, Pradon had criticized Boileau's use of metonymy. So the tenth *Epître* laughs back that Pradon presumably thinks metonymy is a term from chemistry. It is important to emphasize the weakness of the jokes in order to demonstrate the register on which this particular literary controversy came to be conducted. It came in the end to be the light-hearted banter of literary insider-groups ritually baring teeth at each other.

The tenth *Satire* mentions the hissing Pradon received from the parterre. That is probably an allusion to the story that Pradon one day went himself into the parterre and duly joined in the hissing at his own play, only to be challenged by another member of the audience to be quiet, "The play is good: the author is no fool." Pradon defended his right to hiss, and was set upon. The story cannot reasonably be thought to be true, but it indicates that subsequent critics, believing themselves to have been elevating the defender of the sublime against vulgarizers and modernizers may have been taking Parnassus's legislator, as Boileau was called, a little too seriously. The references to Pradon in the correspondence between Racine and Boileau are simply jokes of the sort which shared literary campaigns still generate.

Pradon's own polemical writings, which are largely in prose, show a much firmer tendency to come to grips with the underlying issues. There are three of them, *Le Triomphe de Pradon sur les Satires du Sieur D**** of 1684 and 1686, the 1685 *Nouvelles Remarques sur tous les ouvrages du Sieur D****, and the 1694 *Réponse à la Satire X du Sieur S****. Pradon's greatest dramatic success was with *Regulus*, with 37 performances in 1688. Pradon died from a stroke while playing cards, about the 14 January 1698. The *Mercure Galant* (q.v.), organ of the "modernes," noted only that he came from Rouen, and was the author of several plays, including *Pirame et Thisbé* and *Regulus*.

WORKS

The apparently pleasing style of Pradon's first play, *Pirame et Thisbé* depended on the sorts of dramatic devices and inadequately motivated feelings that we do not today expect to find in any genre more realistic than grand opera. What we now regard as great tragedy performed in 17th-century France has been selected with hindsight. It is characterized by a relatively ferocious psychological tautness, with tight moral dilemmas, exag-

gerated but plausible reactions, and plots depending more on the resolution of great moral conflicts than on trapdoors and secret passages.

To write as the Corneilles or Racine did, it was necessary to be single-mindedly innovatory, psychologically intense, thrusting, and aggressive. Pradon did not lack aggression, but he was less innovatory. Thisbé's couplet has been singled out for obloquy:

Qu'entends-je? Ah, Dieux! que vois-je? Où suis-je? je frissonne;
Je tremble! Que d'horreurs! Pirame m'abandonne!

(What do I hear? Oh gods! what do I see? where am I? I shudder; / I tremble! what horrors! Pirame is abandoning me!).

The whole weight of the feeling is taken off the notes and put on the dynamics. Thisbé has to tell us that she is bewildered, and why. In the bare text only her syntax indicates her emotion. The mechanism of the emotional reaction is not revealed to be commensurate with the effect, so that the actress's poses become simply melodramatic. However, 17th-century audiences were on the whole more interested in a moral vision than a credible plot, and Pradon was acceptably workmanlike in both respects.

That there was some intervention to halt the decent success of *Tamerlan* seems not at all improbable and, if there was, it would be quite likely that Racine was personally behind it. Racine may even have fallen into a trap perhaps unwittingly laid by Pradon when he chose the same Turkish subject that Racine had so recently treated. Racine may well have reacted in the way in which Pradon, in the light of Racine's reaction to the Le Clerc and Coras *Iphigénie*, had supposed that he might, winning for himself further public disapproval. By the last three months of 1676 Pradon had at any rate put himself in a position where he seemed to have a grievance that warranted his public and avowed challenge to Racine. His *Phèdre et Hippolyte* depends on a quite detailed knowledge of Racine's text.

Pradon leaves out the traditional nurse, Racine's Oenone, more than doubles the number of lines given to Aricie and the number of scenes in which she appears, but deliberately diminishes the emotional intensity of the play, notably by allowing Phèdre and Aricie to come together, and by quite deliberately toning down the forceful passions demonstrated in Racine when Hippolyte irresistibly blurts out to Aricie his love for her, and Phèdre hers to Hippolyte. When Pradon's play begins, Hippolyte already suspects Phèdre's love. In Racine, Hippolyte intends to leave Trézène ostensibly to seek his father, but primarily because of his forbidden love for his father's enemy, Aricie, to which he is afraid of yielding. In Pradon, he makes clear that the quest for his father is only a pretext. He leaves on account of Phèdre, who is betrothed to his father. He is impelled partly by an intimation that she may be the instrument of divine punishment, and partly by the feeling that she is too fond of him.

Je crains qu'elle ne soit le fatal instrument
De la haine des Dieux et de leur châtiment…
Ce trop d'égars, de soins, qui fait mon embarras,
Sa trop tendre amitié me pese et m'importune

(I fear she may be the fatal instrument/Of the gods' hate

and punishment…/This excess of attentions and sollici-
tude which gives me concern,/Her over-emotional friendship weighs on me and disturbs me).

Pradon comes very near to stealing some of Racine's lines,
and much too much ill has been said of Pradon's versifying. It is
a great deal better than most of what filled the tragic stage, and
not far short of average Pierre Corneille. What Pradon has done
to earn himself so bad a name concerns his moral vision. When,
forty years on from *Le Cid*, Racine was exploring the inexorable
destructive force of irrestistible passion, Pradon was still re-
modelling Corneille's equation by which the merit of love's
object could be used to upgrade the moral status of instinct. The
real motive for Hippolyte's departure in Pradon is to demonstrate by the very act of leaving her that he merits Aricie's love.

Ah! Madame, faut-il que par un sort bizarre,
Quand l'Amour nous unit, la Gloire nous separe?
Puis qu'enfin de Thesée Hippolyte jaloux
Veut en suivant son Pere estre digne de vous

(Ah! Madame, why by some bizarre fate,/When love
unites us, must glory separate us?/Because Hippolyte, jealous of Thésée, [i.e. his reputation for valour],/Wants by
following his father to be worthy of you).

Pradon keeps very largely to Racine's plot, so that the
changed focus of tragic interest, from destructive passion to
moral heroism, considerably weakens the play. Hippolyte's reasons for leaving Trézène are already confused by the end of Pradon's second scene. He is fleeing Phèdre's love, frightened that
she might be an instrument of the gods' wrath, of which he is
also independently afraid, looking for his father, and trying to
make himself worthy of Aricie's love. In the third scene, Phèdre
tells Aricie of her plan to spread the rumour of Thésée's death.
She will then inherit the throne, Hippolyte will have to marry her
to reign, and her brother Deucalion will come to court Aricie,
with an army to make sure that everything goes according to
plan. If she loses Hippolyte, she will kill herself. The first act
ends with an 18-line monologue by Aricie. She wonders at her
own failure to perceive Hippolyte's love, is frightened by Phèdre's rivalry, and by Phèdre's power to destroy Hippolyte, whom
Phèdre does not know that Aricie loves, and by whom she does
not know that Aricie is loved.

Aricie, despite her love, determines to encourage Hippolyte
to flee. The verse is no more perfunctory than might be expected
to announce the end of the first-act exposition and the beginning
of the action's development. Like Racine, Pradon makes his first
act a dramatic unit, with a defined function. At its end, we know
what the situation is, and how the main characters want it unravelled. Aricie finishes, addressing the absent prince,

Cher Hippolyte helas! tu voyois ce danger?
Elle peut tout, du moins elle peut se vanger;
Fuis de ces tristes Lieux; va, si tu m'en veux croire,
Mettre en depost ton coeur dans le sein de la Gloire,
Et malgré mon amour qui veut me démentir,
Je cours en soûpirant t'ordonner de partir

(Alas, dear Hippolyte, did you see that danger?/She
[Phèdre] can do anything, and she can certainly avenge

herself;/Flee this ill-omened place; go, I urge you,/Entrust
your heart to glory,/And, in spite of my love, which wants
to say the opposite,/I hasten sighing to tell you to depart).

The moral vision, by which Hippolyte earns his title to Aricie's love by deserting her, and she hers to his by encouraging
him to depart, clearly comes from *Le Cid*. But it is Racine's language that Pradon clearly echoes, together with his syntax and
such dramatic devices as Aricie's interruption of a confession
speech by Phèdre to repeat the single word "Hippolyte," which
Racine's Phèdre had been unable to utter. Pradon also takes,
although not from his *Phèdre et Hippolyte*, Racine's intensity in
the depiction of female passion. Pradon's Phèdre is prepared, as
once Racine's Bérénice had been, to take her own life if she
could not possess the object of her love. Pradon has departed
from Corneille and rejoined Racine to treat love as itself capable
of sustaining the weight of tragedy as here, in the end, it does.
Pradon's Phèdre does not kill herself from guilt but, as the
legend demanded, after the destruction of Hippolyte as a consequence of the appearance of Neptune's sea-monster. Aricie has
to be restrained by Thésée from suicide.

In the Pradon play, therefore, love bears the full weight of the
tragedy, and is sufficiently intense to lead to suicide. From Corneille comes its relationship to merit and gloire. But Pradon also
uses Corneille's type of dramatic structure. In Racine, it is
Aricie who enters at the beginning of act two, the last major
character to appear on stage apart from Thésée, who is absent at
first and may even be dead. In Pradon, as generally in Corneille,
act one ends with a definite task to be performed, and its performance leads to the final scene of reward and retribution, in
Pradon, but not in Racine, in spite of the nugatory political element. In act two Pradon's Phèdre reads into Hippolyte a struggle
between his gloire, requiring him to depart, and his love, which
urges him to stay because, as she at that point still thinks, he
returns her love after all. When Thésée returns, Phèdre has not
revealed her love to her betrothed's son, and Pradon does not
need the nurse to blame for the stratagem to which Racine's
exhausted Phèdre consents.

When in act three Thésée announces his intention to marry
Phèdre immediately, he already suspects Hippolyte of loving
her, and entrusts Phèdre with arranging a second marriage, that
of Hippolyte and Aricie as well as her own to Thésée. The use
of the Delos oracle by Pradon to predict the love of Hippolyte
and Phèdre, speaking rather openly for an oracle, takes the
weight off the strength of the characters' passions as the cause
of the disaster in a way Racine does not. It also reinforces Hippolyte's initial apprehensiveness of imminent disaster. For
Racine, Phèdre's tainted ancestry and the vengeance of Venus
work through her passion. For Pradon the sighing characters
seem to a greater extent merely to be acting out roles predicted
and supernaturally determined by the oracle in the words spoken
to Thésée:

Tu seras à ton retour
Malheureux Amant et Pere,
Puisqu'une main qui t'est chere
T'enlevera l'objet de ton amour

(You will on your return be/An unhappy lover and father,/
Since a hand dear to you/Will take away from you the
object of your love).

Importantly, this oracle is not ambiguous, as that of Agamemnon had been in Racine's *Iphigénie*. Its purpose in Pradon can only be to remind the audience of the story, often used by 17th-century dramatists but not necessarily remembered by their audiences, and to alleviate the weight put on the characters' passions by Racine, by transferring responsibility to supernatural fate. Pradon retreats from Racine's examination of passion to what had once been Corneille's bold exploration of cultural advance but was now actually a retreat into an earlier optimism, which was to be re-examined in a new way by the survivors from Foucquet's generation after the death of Colbert in 1683, Perrault, Saint-Evremond, Fontenelle, and the advocates of the "modernes." Pradon takes his depiction of passion from Racine and his moral vision from Corneille. But he protects himself with a now accepted moral vision which no longer demonstrates imaginative daring.

When, in the great confrontation scene of act three, Pradon's Phèdre, like Racine's, switches from "vous" to "tu" as she blurts out her love for Hippolyte, whom she has tricked into revealing his for Aricie, the language rises to Racinian heights. The mixture of love and hatred as a reaction to spurned passion is here a reminiscence of Hermione's outburst in Racine's *Andromaque*, and Pradon takes the unconcealability of love from the same play. He even takes from Racine the faltering weakness of the male characters, as in this scene Hippolyte. This is Pradon's Phèdre:

Je t'aimois, il est vray, Barbare, et je te hais…
Je t'aimois cependant, et tu l'as dû connoître,
Mille fois dans mes yeux ma flamme a dû paroître,
Infidelle à Thesée, et toute entiere à toy,
Tu luy volois mon coeur, mes sermens, et ma foy […]
Pour toy seul j'immolé [immolai] ma gloire et mon repos,
Ton amour me força d'oublier ce Héros

(I loved you, it is true, cruel wretch, and now I hate you…/ But I loved you, and you must have known it,/My ardour must have appeared a thousand times in my eyes,/ Unfaithful to Thésée, wholly and utterly yours,/You stole my heart from him, my vows, and my pledged faith…/For you alone I sacrificed my honour and my peace,/Loving you forced me to forget that hero).

The use of the word "repos (peace)" should be remarked in a text antedating by a year the prominence given to it when *La Princesse de Clèves* was actually published. Was Pradon anticipating Mme de Lafayette's examination of resignation to defeat as possibly the best resolution of the problems of love? Was that possibility being seriously talked about? Did Pradon feel compelled, as Mme de Lafayette did, to explore the price of renunciation as the cost of moral innocence? Pradon's play is undoubtedly good theatre. It has its moments of poetic splendour. Its passions are less intense, less concentrated, and of themselves less destructive than those in Racine's play, but above all Pradon fails to achieve the feats of imaginative daring that Corneille had once reached, forty years previously, and which both Racine and Mme de Lafayette were currently reaching on the subject of love.

In his prose works Pradon defends Madeleine de Scudéry against Boileau's sneers in *Le Lutrin* which, unlike his *Dialogue des héros de roman* had been published with his consent during Madeleine de Scudery's lifetime. Pradon is not afraid to point to the plainly apparent fact that Boileau's satirical verse succeeds not in being poetic, but only in being hurtful. Unlike classical satire, it was invariably directed at individuals, and it is difficult not to sympathize with Pradon when he writes in a good take-off of Boileau's own style,

Il est temps de montrer d'un Rimeur insolent
Le Mérite imposteur et le petit talent

(It is time to show openly of an insolent rhymester/That the merit is a pretence and the talent small).

More important than the arguments, however, are still the positions taken, especially in favour of Corneille, and the refusal to accept Boileau's valuations of the work of his contemporaries. It must have afforded Pradon in all the circumstances considerable pleasure to be able to point to the fact that Racine had put as much "sugar and honey" into his *Alexandre* as Quinault had into his operas. Pradon's parodies of Boileau now used against Boileau are often amusing. He is particularly malicious in pointing to the delay in the appearance of any works of historiography. The historiographical duties included accompanying the king on his campaigns, and Pradon has an amusing verse portrait of "Les Messieurs du Sublime," by which he means Racine and Boileau, able apparently to write only receipts for money received but not, apparently, earned, going off on their mounts to frighten the Dutch with their pens. Their sublimity amounted to blaming the innocent horse when one of them fell off into the mud.

PUBLICATIONS

Collections

Les Oeuvres de Mr Pradon, 1679, augmented 1688

Plays

Pirame et Thisbé (produced 1673–74), 1674
Tamerlan; ou, La Mort de Bajazet, (produced 1675–76), 1676
Phèdre et Hippolyte (produced 1677), 1677; critical edition 1987
La Troade, 1679
Statire, 1680
Regulus, 1688
Scipion l'Africain, 1697

Literary polemic

Le Triomphe de Pradon sur les Satires du Sieur D***, 1684
Nouvelles remarques sur tous les ouvrages du Sieur D***, 1685
Réponse à la Satire X du Sieur D***, 1694

Biographical and critical studies

Beaurepaire, Charles de, *Notice sur le Poète Pradon*, 1899
Bussom, Thomas W., *The Life and Works of Pradon*, 1922

PRÉCIOSITÉ   (PRÉCIEUX, PRÉCIEUSES).

*See General Index and entries on Balzac, Bensserade,
Chapelain, (La) Guirlande de Julie, Malherbe, Madeleine de
Scudéry, and Voiture.*

Préciosité was a short-lived social phenomenon of great literary
and linguistic significance which loses all intelligibility and
interest if, on the one hand, it is not separated from its probable
origins in a group of half a dozen young women who were first
collectively referred to as *précieuses* in 1654 or if, on the other,
it is confused with the more general European cult of galanterie.
The word *préciosité* and its cognates are currently used in
French as in English with ordinary dictionary meanings, but in
a French literary historical context the word can properly be
used only in the quite technical sense in which it denotes a
restricted phenomenon that lasted for less then a decade in the
mid-17th century, often with overtones of more or less affectionate disparagement.

The *précieuses*, significantly the group of young women, not
the abstract *préciosité*, were the subject of much often satirical
literary concern during the clearly defined period from 1654,
when *préciosité* can first be identified, to 1663, or a little earlier,
by which date the group had dispersed and the phenomenon
itself was no longer anywhere near the centre of literary interest.
After 1663 there are scarcely even vestiges of *préciosité* of any
social or linguistic importance to be found, and their intensity
had already diminished sharply from about 1660. What was left
was a serious discussion about the role of women in society carried on as part of the Querelle des anciens et des modernes (q.v.).

Essentially *préciosité* is a specifically post-Fronde social phenomenon of exaggeration originating in a more or less identifiable group at a known date, spun off by the general movement
towards the refinement of manners, speech habits, and social
behaviour led by the most cultivated sections of Parisian society
in the mid-17th century. Authors who satirized it generally
regarded the *précieuses*, invariably female, as affected, but
sometimes took too much at face value the exaggerated feminism of their expressed views and an exaggerated purism in their
cult of linguistic refinement. The principal literary importance
of *préciosité* as it widened out into a general social phenomenon
derives not from its status as a butt for satirists, including
Molière and Boileau, or from its linguistic or other effects on literary composition, but from the attention it drew, for instance in
the last volume of Madeleine de Scudéry's *Le Grand Cyrus*, to
the culturally vital developments which underlay it, and which
included a strong movement towards female social emancipation.

In both its social and linguistic aspects, the most helpful and
in serious works of literary history still the most usual introduction to the phenomenon of *préciosité* is a detailed examination
of the discussions and diversions associated with Mme de Rambouillet's chambre bleue, largely discussed in the *Guide* entry
"(La) Guirlande de Julie." There can be little doubt that the mixture of aristocratic and literary figures received by the marquise
promoted a code of social behaviour regarded as civilized,
together with a refinement of taste, a cultivation of elegance, and
an interest in linguistic propriety which prepared the ground for
the phenomenon of *préciosité*. There were, however, also ways
in which *préciosité*, starting at least very near the company of
the chambre bleue as a private joke, came to denote a reaction

against everything which the chambre bleue represented.

Whereas, in terms of the values of later historians, the chambre bleue represented a movement forward in elegance, cultivation, and, above all, taste, it had been only with some struggle
that wit and delicacy had imposed themselves over the pedantry
and earnestness of which the "anticorps," Chapelain, Balzac,
and the admirers of Malherbe, possibly even including the marquise herself, would have liked to make the chambre bleue the
nucleus. The phenomenon of *préciosité* itself got submerged in
a pedantic sea of minute distinctions and an earnest bourgeois
discussion of affective states which quickly lost flair, sensitivity,
and penetration, removing it to registers of complex triviality
and simple fantasy quite alien to the spirit of the social gatherings at the Hôtel de Rambouillet.

The Fronde marked a considerable discontinuity in inchoate
salon life. The Hôtel de Rambouillet had, even before the
Fronde and the ascendancy established over the chambre bleue
by the Condé family and their friends, lost the will to maintain
the prestige it had once successfully set out to acquire. Julie
d'Angennes, the animated centrepiece of the salon's madrigals,
games, and practical jokes, had finally married Montauzier on 4
July 1645, and Pisani, the marquise's heir and only surviving
son, had been killed at Nördlingen seven weeks later on 23
August. Shortly after the Fronde the marquis himself died on 26
February 1652, and the not entirely serious aristocratic attitudinizing of the young group was vulgarized into the social phenomenon which we have come to call *préciosité* without being
able to define in what precisely it consisted. The phenomenon,
like the salons in which it was based, became bourgeois, prone
to inhibitions, more seriously taken affectations, even gauche-
ries, and without the self-confident whimsy and nonchalant
sureness of touch no doubt promoted by the great wealth still
possessed by some of the marquise's aristocratic guests.

Further, the old noblesse d'épée had by the outbreak of the
Fronde lost the final battle to have its social assumptions
respected. Not even extreme personal merit could, after 1650,
publicly justify the old privileges of rank, once based on military
exploits but transmitted through the acquisition of landed estates
erected into marquisates, comtés, or even duchies, which conferred the associated titles on their proprietors. The wider social
manifestation of *préciosité* was nourished by the surrender,
which Colbert did nothing to hinder, of the cultural high ground
and the custodianship of the cultural advance to the noblesse de
robe and the upper bourgeois strata of society. This was the terrain on which the fundamental battle between "anciens" and
"modernes" in the famous Querelle des anciens et des modernes
would also be fought, with aristocratic salon society, if not necessarily the court, on the whole energetic supporters of the
"modernes," while a new and intensely aristocratic literature of
self-justificatory memoirs, portraits, epigrams, and epistolary
exchanges was being gestated, although generally not for publication, by the often impoverished or disgraced members of the
noblesse d'épée.

There was also naturally a continuity linking pre-Fronde to
post-Fronde society. It would be generally agreed that, however
préciosité might be defined, the years just after 1654 did see the
flourishing of an exaggerated if not necessarily affected disdain
for the common and the ordinary in such young women as the
marquise de Rambouillet's youngest daughter, Angélique-
Clarisse d'Angennes, who was married on 27 April 1658 to
François-Adhémar de Monteil, comte de Grignan; in Suzanne

d'Aumale, who later married Frédéric-Armand de Schomberg, maréchal de France in 1676; in her sister Jeanne d'Hautcourt, rich and beautiful, who was once engaged to a cousin but died unmarried; even in Mme d'Olonne, once Mlle de la Louppe, rather anachronistically described much later by Retz as a "précieuse" before her marriage in 1652. In any discussion of *préciosité*, and the possible existence of real models for the parodists and the satirists, the often haphazard survival of evidence makes this quartet of particular significance.

Conrart's *Mémoires*, published only in 1826, recount an anecdote about Angélique-Clarisse d'Angennes and Suzanne d'Aumale, whose intimate friendship dated back to 1652. The pair of them were well known by the date at which Conrart was writing, both for the ease with which they expressed disgust, and for their prudishness, two characteristics which, when taken together, are essential to, and may well be constitutive of, the *préciosité* affected by the original group of *précieuses*, whose bourgeois successors, certainly, not only combined an excessive fastidiousness with an expressed desire to free women from male tyranny, often in marriages arranged for them, but also drew back from physical sexual relationships altogether, envisaging as an ideal relationship that dreamt of by Sapho in the tenth book of *Le Grand Cyrus* (see: Madeleine de Scudéry), published in 1653, just before the word *précieuse* acquired the special meaning with which we are concerned.

In the seventh book of *Le Grand Cyrus*, Madeleine de Scudéry had depicted Angélique-Clarisse d'Angennes as "Anacrise."

Il y a si peu de choses qui la satisfacent; si peu de personnes qui luy plaisent; un si petit nombre de plaisirs qui touchent son inclination qu'il n'est pas possible que les choses s'ajustent si parfaitement qu'elle puisse passer un jour tout à fait heureux en toute une année; tant elle a l'imagination délicate, le goût exquis et particulier, et l'humeur difficile à contenter...Ses chagrins mesmes sont divertissans, car lorsqu'on luy entend exagérer la longueur d'une journée passée à la campagne, ou celle d'une après-disnée en mauvaise compagnie, elle le fait si agréablement et d'une manière si charmante qu'il n'est pas possible de ne l'admirer point

(There are so few things which satisfy her; so few people who please her; so few pleasures which take her fancy, that it is not possible for things to combine so that she can spend a single completely happy day in a whole year, so fastidious is her imagination, so cultivated and idiosyncratic her taste and so difficult to please her mood...Even her annoyance is amusing, because when she goes on about the tedium of a day spent in the country, or an after-dinner time in company she does not like, she does it so pleasantly and with such charm that it is impossible not to admire her).

That flattering portrait indulgently emphasizes but refuses to take seriously Angélique-Clarisse's fastidiousness and charm when she was probably still 17 or 18. Conrart's anecdote connecting her to Suzanne d'Aumale almost certainly refers to a later date. Tallemant tells us that Angélique-Clarisse's face was ravaged by smallpox, but that she had wit and an unkind tongue, and was less civil than her sister Julie, whose later arrogance and taste for intrigue is well attested. Writing between 1657 and 1659, Tallemant said that he intended to write a *historiette* not, it should be noted, about *préciosité*, but about "Les Précieuses," but he did not. However, he certainly regarded them as an identifiable group, and the connection between Angélique-Clarisse d'Angennes and Suzanne d'Aumale mentioned by Conrart occurs with the word *précieuses* in a 1655 volume, *Fine galerie du temps*:

Précieuses, vos maximes
Tyrannisent nos désirs.
Vous faites passer pour crimes
Les plus innocens plaisirs.
Rambouillet, et vous, Daumale,
Quoy, ne verrons-nous jamais
L'Amour et vostre caballe
Faire un bon traité de paix?

(Précieuses, your maxims/Impose themselves on our desires./You make appear as crimes/The most innocent pleasures./Rambouillet, and you, d'Aumale,/Shall we never see/Love and your cabal/Make a good peace treaty together?).

The lines, which also occur in the *Ballet de la déroute des précieuses*, were first published as an anonymous and perfunctory scurrility, but they are important. They use the term "précieuses" in 1655, emphasize not fastidiousness but prudishness, mention the maxims which are a quick vulgarization of the *précieux* view, and to which we shall return, and suggest that the *précieuses* are already a cabal.

Meanwhile the text by which Tallemant's *Les Historiettes* can be dated (see: Tallemant des Réaux), itself written after the others and between February 1659 and February 1661, concerns a scandal about which all Paris was laughing: René de Cordouan, marquis de Langey, having called for a formal "congrès" to settle the matter, failed to demonstrate that he was not impotent and that he had consummated his marriage. Since she was a Huguenot the examination of his wife was not ecclesiastically conducted but was undertaken by the lieutenant civil in the presence of twelve assistants. Mme de Sévigné and her great friend, Mme de Lavardin, were in a coach outside and could be heard laughing. Tallemant could not resist making the event into a "historiette," and crammed it in at the end of his table of contents. It contains a mildly scatological passage which is of importance because it shows that, at the date at which Tallemant wrote and, if he is telling the truth, a little earlier, the essence of *préciosité* was repugnance at sexual intercourse. It also formally states that Molière's "models" for the "précieuses" of *Les Précieuses ridicules* were Angélique-Clarisse d'Angennes and Suzanne d'Aumale. Brief notes of identification are given in square brackets in the translation.

Il n'y a pas long-temps que le bruit courut qu'il espousoit Mlle d'Aumalle, puis on le dit bien davantage de Mlle d'Hautcourt, sa soeur, et on faisait dire à ce fat: "Au moins, sage et dévote comme elle est, quand elle aura des enfans, on ne dira pas que ce sera d'un autre que de moy." Voicy d'où est venû ce bruit-là: quand M. de Lillebonne espousa feu Mlle d'Estrées, qui estoit precieuse, on dit de luy comme de Grignan, quand il espousa Mlle de Rambouillet, un des originaux des *Précieuses*, qu'il avoit fait de grands exploits la nuict de leurs nopces; Mme de Montauzier écrivit à sa soeur, en Provence: "On fait des medisances de Mme de Lillebonne comme de vous." Mme de Grignan respondit que, pour remettre les Precieuses en reputation, elle ne sçavoit plus qu'un moyen, c'estoit que Mlle d'Aumale espousast Langey

(There was a rumour going round not long ago that he [Langey] would marry Mlle d'Aumale, then it was much stronger about Mlle d'Hautcourt, her sister [the third of three sisters, tall, handsome, very rich, often called a *précieuse*, unmarried, mentioned in the *Journal* of the Villiers brothers on 1 November 1657], and the idiot [Langey] is supposed to have remarked, "At least, she is well-behaved and religious, so when she has children people won't say they aren't mine." Here is how that rumour came about: when M. de Lillebonne [François-Marie de Lorraine-Elbeuf, brother of the comte d'Harcourt] married the late Mlle d'Estrées [Christine, daughter of the maréchal, who married Lillebonne on 3 September 1658 and died on 18 December], who was a "précieuse," it was said of him as of Grignan [husband of Angélique-Clarisse] when he married Mlle de Rambouillet, one of the originals for the *Précieuses* [*ridicules*] [the Molière play] that he had achieved great feats on the night of their wedding; Mme de Montauzier (Julie d'Angennes) wrote to her sister in Provence: "People are calumniating Mme de Lillebonne, as they do you." Mme de Grignan replied that she could think of only one way to reestablish the reputation of the "précieuses," which was for Mlle d'Aumale to marry Langey.

Angélique-Clarisse's perky reply to her sister implicitly acknowledges that the whole group, including herself, her sister Julie, Suzanne d'Aumale, and Suzanne's sister, Jeanne d'Hautcourt, were "précieuses." Proposing the marriage of an impotent man to her supposedly frigid friend, whose aversion to the institution of marriage was almost certainly an affectation and who, unlike her sister Jeanne, actually did marry, makes aristocratic fun of the whole affair, but it does show that the popular perception of *précieux* fastidiousness hinged more on a repugnance to physical relationships than on anything else. It is in fact remarkable that the early texts do not speak of *précieux*. When a masculine equivalent for *précieuse* is needed, what is used is invariably the much broader "galant." *Préciosité* is a phenomenon which at first derived from semi-jocular attitudes affected by a group of cultivated young women.

We first find the term *précieuses* in the specific sense which concerns us in a letter written by the chevalier de Sévigné to Christine de France, duchesse de Savoie, on 3 April 1654:

Il y une nature de filles et de femmes à Paris que l'on nomme *Précieuses*, qui ont un jargon et des mines, avec un démanchement merveilleux: L'on a fait depuis peu une carte pour naviguer en leur pays

(There is a new sort of girl and woman in Paris called *Précieuses*. They have their own very fussy jargon and ways of behaving. A little while ago a map was drawn up for navigating their country).

We have now moved down the social scale. The atmosphere of

Madeleine de Scudéry's *samedis* was overwhelmingly bourgeois, and her preference for the sort of intimate emotional union sketched by Sapho in the tenth book of *Le Grand Cyrus*, and discussed, for instance, in Sorel's *Discours pour et contre l'amitié tendre hors le mariage* may, in view of her relationship with Pellisson, have been real enough. Nevertheless, she does not hide her astonishment at the attitudes of Angélique-Clarisse d'Angennes when she draws her portrait in the seventh book of the novel. The vogue for portraits which she largely inaugurated in *Le Grand Cyrus* and on which *Clélie* almost totally rests, not very closely bound to *préciosité* as a phenomenon, peaked in 1659 and sharply declined thereafter.

The final parts of *Clélie* appeared on 1 March 1660, but by late in 1658 the famous 59 *Divers portraits* collected by Segrais, helped by Huet, had been published at Caen in an edition of 30 copies by La Grande Mademoiselle, Anne-Marie d'Orléans, duchesse de Montpensier, and daughter of Gaston d'Orléans, who had herself composed 16 of them. The booksellers Barbin and Sercy were to cash in on the fashion with their *Recueil de portraits et éloges en vers et en prose* containing 105 items collected from wherever they could be found. Like *préciosité* itself, the fashion for portraits on that scale was quickly over. Although the inspiration lingered on much longer, what it gave birth to when it was resurrected were "caractères" of the sort contained in La Bruyère's collection and expanded by his imitators, more concerned with values and typical forms of behaviour than with often embellished depictions of individuals. Tallemant's great collection of portraits was virtually complete by 1659.

A manifestation of *préciosité* more ephemeral than the portraits, but occurring very little later than the final parts of *Le Grand Cyrus*, was the fashion for cartographic indications of the paths of love. Madeleine de Scudéry regretted her own Carte de Tendre, sketched in February 1654 and inserted into the first volume of *Clélie*, on account of the accusations of pedantry to which it gave rise. It was, however, immediately followed by a cascade of imitations, many of them published by Sercy, and many still in manuscript. Among the more important cartographers of galanterie were Furetière, Maulévrier, Tristan l'Hermite, the abbé Tallemant, Sorel, and Somaize. After 1659, of course, the whole private joke of the original group of "précieuses" was lost sight of and misunderstood, being known to the wide bourgeois public in Paris almost exclusively through Molière's caricature in *Les Précieuses ridicules*, first played at the Palais-Bourbon on 18 November.

The date of 1654 for the identifiable emergence in Parisian society of a group of *précieuses* who were indicated and isolated by that term does not depend on the chevalier de Sévigné's letter of 3 April alone, but was quickly confirmed by the production early in 1654 of Maulévrier's *Carte du Royaume des précieuses*, printed in the first of the five volumes of Sercy's 1658–63 *Recueil de pièces en prose*, not to be confused with the other five-volume verse collection of *Poésies choisies* known as the *Recueil Sercy*, which appeared from 1653 to 1660. The marquis de Maulévrier was a member of the household of Gaston d'Orléans, before whom was also danced the ballet *La Déroute des Précieuses*, which contained the verses *La fine galanterie du temps* already quoted, naming Angélique-Clarisse d'Angennes and Mlle d'Aumale in connection with the "cabal" hostile to love, and was republished in 1661. The word, therefore, appears first to have been used with a derogatory sense in 1654 before being jocularly accepted by the group to which it was applied.

The pejorative meaning emerged in the entourage of Gaston d'Orléans, whose daughter, La Grande Mademoiselle, the composer and collector of the *Divers portraits*, makes clear in her own *Mémoires* what we also know from elsewhere, that she detested Suzanne d'Aumale on account of her liking for intrigue and her ostentatious parade of virtue.

No doubt Mademoiselle was hostile to the group of affectedly prudish women to whom the word was applied, but their attitudes may therefore have from the beginning been caricatured. The group included Mlle de Vandy, against whom Maulévrier also wrote a lampoon, although Mademoiselle's relationships with Mlle de Vandy were friendly. Mlle de Vandy was, however, the sworn enemy of Mme de Frontenac, Mademoiselle's lady-in-waiting. The group also included Mme d'Olonne, the close friend of the future Mme de Lafayette. Her behaviour, soon to become scandalous, was in 1654 still publicly impeccable. If we are to believe Bussy-Rabutin's 1654 *Carte du pays de Braquerie*, through which flowed the Précieuse "river of great reputation," the inhabitants of Prudomagne included Julie d'Angennes and Marie de Lorraine, daughter of the duc de Guise.

The word *précieuse* may well have been used in conscious contrast with "coquette." At least originally in 1654, the term *précieuse* was used of a particular circle of aristocratic young women, although we cannot now identify it with any given salon or intrigue. By 1659 the meaning had widened to refer no longer to a group of identifiable people but to a form of behaviour and speech no longer confined to the young or the highest aristocracy. The behaviour associated with "les précieuses" was generalized into a general opposition to the codes of galanterie, to coquetterie and flirtatiousness, but it was not altogether prudish. The term was applied to Madeleine de Scudéry, no doubt on account of the views on love expressed by her Sapho.

Among the high aristocracy who did not belong to the original group but who may have been important in developing its attitudes, it seems clear that Mme de Sablé's name should not be overlooked. Born Madeleine de Souvray in 1599, she was unhappily married against her will on 9 January 1614. Since she was only 14, she can scarcely have been consulted. Her husband, to whom she bore nine children, was notorious for his liaisons and, after four or five years, she lived for a period mostly on the estates in Maine, made into a marquisate in 1602, which her husband had given her. She herself subsequently had numerous liaisons. Her husband died in 1640, and Madeleine de Scudéry wrote an approving portrait of her in the sixth book of *Le Grand Cyrus*. The marquise, whose cuisine was celebrated and who, to everyone's amusement, was morbidly afraid of ill health, retired to Port-Royal (q.v.) where she had a house built in 1656, and became the centre of a circle specializing in the discussion of moral aphorisms. Julie d'Angennes, married and in Normandy, started a letter to her by reminding her to be sure it was read to her from down-wind, in case the note-paper carried marsh organisms which could infect her. Mme de Sablé's own maxims were published in 1678, the year of her death, but there had earlier been question of a joint publication with La Rochefoucauld and Jacques Esprit.

By 1656 Mme de Sablé, in spite of the association with Port-Royal never quite a Jansenist (q.v.), was devout, austere, resentful about the early arranged marriage, and still influential. Her sympathies added weight to the attitudes of the original group of *précieuses* castigated in the entourage of Mademoiselle, and her association with it may be the reason why "les précieuses" came

to be taken so seriously. It is in the sense of their moral austerity, not their half-frivolous views on matrimony, that Ninon de Lenclos spoke in 1656 of the *précieuses* as "Les Jansénistes de l'amour (the Jansenists of love)," and Saint-Evremond used the term in *La Prude et la Précieuse*, once again in the feminine. A *précieuse* also came to mean any woman opposed to what was regarded as male sexual tyranny. The feminist element remained attached to the word *précieuse* long after it had ceased to denote fastidious prudishness, when it was perfectly possible to regard *précieuse* behaviour, and the minute calculus of emotive states associated with it, as coquettish.

The waters of *préciosité* have been muddied for historians subsequently seeking to understand the phenomenon not only by Molière's famous satirical comedy, but also by the often hostile or ironical accounts of a number of other authors, of which the principal are the abbé Michel de Pure, whose novel *La Prétieuse; ou, Le Mystère des ruelles* was published, with a privilège of December 1655, from 1656 to 1658. Pure had a comedy, *Les Précieuses*, now lost, but alleged to have been drawn on by Molière, played by the Italian company in 1656. Baptized at Lyons on 19 November 1620, Pure became a doctor of theology in 1647 at Paris, returned to Lyons during the Fronde, and in 1653 wrote a Latin biography of Richelieu's elder brother, cardinal archbishop of Lyons after surrendering the family see of Luçon to his brother in order to become a Carthusian. Pure then wrote the biography of Richelieu himself in 1656. He was made a chaplain to the king, and then royal historiographer with a remuneration of 2,000 livres. He translated from Italian and Latin, had a tragedy *Ostorius* performed at the Hôtel de Bourgogne in 1659, edited a gazette, and became the contemporary social historian of galanterie in Paris salon society. His unsuccessful 1668 *Idée des spectacles anciens et nouveaux* contained advice to the king which cost him the pension that his translation of Quintilian had earned him. He was a friend of d'Aubignac, the author not only of *La Pratique du théâtre* but of a *Relation véritable du Royaume de coquetterie*.

Pure's novel is difficult to interpret, or to use as a historical guide, because its attitude to *préciosité* oscillated between satirical parody and frank admiration. The characters are drawn from the whole spectrum of salon life, from the exaggeratedly galant to the absurdly philistine. Pure suggests unseriously that the species "Prétieuse" appeared suddenly, as a natural mutation, and he is as sarcastic about the collectivity as he is guardedly indulgent towards individuals among its members. Since he uses poetic names, and no key has been discovered, we are left with his inconsistent narratorial viewpoint, and cannot therefore pinpoint the ironies as accurately as if we knew the names underneath the characters portrayed. Much nevertheless can be gleaned from Pure's novel. It makes it clear, for instance, that the *précieuses* sought to substitute taste for learning. His generation was becoming more confident. And there must be social development behind Pure's need for his narrator to explain that each hostess opens her doors on a particular day, so that anyone can meet anyone else merely by consulting their diary, the "Calendrier de Ruelle (salon calendar)." There is a mock series of dictionary definitions of terms including "Prude," "Coquette," "Esprit fort," and "Précieuse." "Gename," an anagram of Ménage, is made to maintain that the "Précieuses" were not brought to France by Vanité and Coquetterie, but says

La Précieuse n'est point la fille de son père ni de sa mère;

elle n'a ni l'un ni l'autre…Elle n'est pas non plus l'ouvrage de la nature sensible et matérielle; elle est un extrait de l'esprit, un précis de raison. Cet esprit, et cette raison, est le germe qui les produit, mais, comme la perle vient de l'Orient et se forme dans des coquilles…ainsi la Précieuse se forme dans la Ruelle par la culture de dons suprêmes que le ciel a versés dans son âme

(The Précieuse is not the daughter of her father or mother; she has neither…Nor is she the product of the nature of senses and matter; she is an extract of mind, an essence of reason. This mind, this reason, is the germ which produces them but, as the pearl comes from the Orient and is formed in shells, so the Précieuse is formed in the salon by the culture of those supreme gifts which heaven has poured into her soul).

Among the characters allusive names and probable quasi-anagrams refer for example to Chapelain (Parthénoïde) and Sarrazin (Niassare), and Gename makes much play of all sorts of distinctions, divisions and sub-divisions, and further sub-categories of beauties. He makes apparent the *précieux* quest for "bons mots (correctly used words)" and "expressions extraordinaires (extraordinary expressions)," and speaks of their vows, which include subtlety of thought, purity of style, and undying war against pedants and provincials. Pure gives himself the name of Gelasire for the purposes of narration. The novel contains a long explanation of love along the lines of those more succinctly expounded by Madeleine de Scudéry's Sapho, of whom Pure is no doubt thinking. The lover's interests must be totally subordinated to those of the loved one, to the extent of the complete deprivation of the lover's liberty. Where once there has been love, there can never be hate, a view in direct contradiction with the experience notably of Racine's Hermione in *Andromaque*. Marriage is opposed to spinsterhood as *esclavage* to *liberté*, with the words in italics in the text. A dutiful wife cannot even avail herself of the dispensations which the coquette enjoys. Even if a wife loves her husband, marriage imposes "un poids insupportable et un joug accablant (an intolerable burden and a crushing yoke)."

Pure's novel is not itself of literary interest. The endless subdivisions and discourses about affective states are, however, of considerable significance for what they tell us about the underlying social and literary phenomena of Parisian cultural life as the capital recovered from the Fronde. As at the end of the religious wars there was predictably a sudden spurt in the long-term movement to rehabilitate instinctive affection which had at some point to bring with it a revolt against female servitude. As in the resumption of essentially the same long-term movement after the religious wars, there was a spin-off of exaggeration, but the speed with which it was recognized accounts for the fact that we know of *préciosité* chiefly from those administering the exaggeration's correction.

The second author of importance in this connection is Antoine Baudeau de Somaize. Little is known of him except that he became secretary to Mazarin's niece, Marie Mancini, and followed her to Italy. He successfully extracted from the fashionable interest in *préciosité* every last scrap of literary profit, inventing what he could not discover and thereby, as has now been acknowledged, leading generations of gullible historians up blind alleys. It is much more difficult to use Somaize's works

than it is even to use Pure's novel as a guide to what actually constituted *préciosité* as distinct from what could be lampooned under its guise.

Somaize first became known through a pamphlet attack in 1658 on Boisrobert's *Théodore*. He appears to have been in league with Jean Ribou, who obtained without Molière's authority a privilège to print *Les Précieuses ridicules*. Molière had the privilège cancelled, and Ribou then published Somaize's *Les Veritables Précieuses*, which sold well as a book in January 1660 but does not ever seem to have been performed. The preface accuses Molière of plagiarizing Pure's *Les Précieuses*, and Somaize also put Molière's play into verse. At the same time he published his *Grand Dictionnaire des prétieuses*. Molière's company had riposted in May 1660 with Gabriel Gilbert's *La Vraie et la Fausse prétieuse*, but the profitable parody of what had started off as a small aristocratic group, and continued as a serious bourgeois reflection about the nature of affective bonds and the need to emancipate women from male marital domination, was not yet exhausted.

Having both repudiated and built on Molière's successful satire, and published his own comedy, his verse version of Molière's comedy, and his April 1660 *Grand Dictionnaire des précieuses; ou, La Clef de la langue des ruelles*, with perhaps 200 alphabetically arranged key words and their definitions, Somaize proceeded to publish three more works, the July 1660 *Le Procès des Précieuses en vers burlesques, Le Dialogue de deux précieuses sur les affaires de leur communauté*, and a second dictionary, the June 1661 *Le Grand Dictionnaire des précieuses, historique, poétique, géographique, cosmographique, chronologique, et armoirique*, not at all a guide to *précieux* usage, but a satirical gallery caricaturing the fashion for salon names and adding fake portraits.

At best, Somaize is useful as a guide at two removes to *préciosité*. He shows what could still be accepted as a lampoon of what was at best the public perception of *préciosité*. Important in the first *Dictionnaire* are the absurd circumlocutions which draw attention to the personal fastidiousness which preferred not to name objects directly, even if no one ever actually called chairs "les commodités de la conversation (the conveniences of conversation)." Some of Somaize's inventions do not lack wit and many draw on a strong fantasy. The portraits are too unsafe to rely on and they must now be taken to be simply skilful pastiche. The pastiche, if that is what it is, is good enough to have taken in some centuries of critics and historians.

Most important of all in Somaize are the maxims, with their insistence on freedom from the social constraints of marriage, and from all physical relationships. Since it was unthinkable for marital obligations to be openly attacked in France in the early 1660s, the maxims, advocating the refusal of visible expressions of love, are less than fully serious, like Pure's notion that *précieuses* are composed of purely spiritual or rational essences. Again, however, the maxims indicate the underlying thrust towards the emancipation of women and the drive towards love as a reciprocated emotional commitment rather than a relationship of predation and surrender. La Calprenède (q.v.) had already examined the transition. Préciosité, too, once the word was used of a general attitude rather than of a small group of in principle identifiable persons, had its place in the great European-wide movement towards a quite new way of looking at instinctive behaviour.

The endless casuistry of emotional propriety, seeking to classify and codify affective states, laying down rules for dealing with them and answering questions about the meaning of affective states such as can be discovered in the *Cinq Questions d'amour* of Charlotte de Brégy or the *Questions d'amour* of Marie Linage first published by Liane Ansmann as recently as 1972, are scarcely more than frivolities, sometimes with a varnish of rational psychology or physiology, games less serious than the Carte de Tendre. The feminist element was not a protest against the legitimate outlet for instinctive drives offered by marriage, but simply a revolt against the confining of marital relationships within an institution where in practice they were determined by male desire, although in fact also carefully regulated by moral theology and canon law.

Préciosité itself produced no literature, only satire, caricature, and lampoon aimed against rather than for it. It was an excrescence, an aristocratic and affected epiphenomenon of social protest which none the less clearly indicates the underlying significance, so often missed, of the explorations of behaviour and attitudes being conducted in the literature of France in the decade following the end of the Fronde.

PRÉVOST, Antoine-François, abbé (later known as **PRÉVOST D'EXILES**), 1697–1763.

Novelist and journalist.

LIFE

Prévost was born on 1 April 1697, the second child of a well-off bourgeois family at Hesdin, due north of Paris, about 35 kilometres inland from Etaples and 50 from Boulogne. His grandfather, a rich brewer, had been town treasurer. An uncle was dean of a group of local parishes. Prévost's father, who belonged to the local administration and was a conseiller du roi, married Marie Duclaie, who came from a background of rich farmers as well-to-do as, but less socially elevated than, his own. She was to bear him at least nine children, of whom five were boys. The eldest, Liévin-Norbert, became a Jesuit, but left the Society in 1725, soon after ordination, and finally became a canon of Cambrai. The youngest, Bernard-Joseph, became a Premonstratensian and a professor of theology. Two others acquired appointments in the magistracy. Jérôme-Pierre became lieutenant civil, and like Louis-Eustache, who was an officer for a time before becoming maître des eaux et forêts, was a conseiller du roi. There was a surviving sister, Thérèse-Claire, born in 1698, to whom Prévost was very close, and who died in 1711, the same year as Prévost's mother, who died on 28 August, leaving the bereaved 14-year-old suffering from the double loss of the two women he was closest to, his mother and his sister.

We know of Prévost's adolescence only that he was at the Jesuit college at Hesdin for a period, almost certainly from 1711 until 1713. He may have boarded at the Jesuit junior seminary while at Hesdin, attending classes at the college, and appears to have been in the army briefly before the peace of Utrecht in April 1713. He was 16 at the beginning of that month. At the start of the academic year in 1713, he was at the Collège d'Harcourt in Paris, repeating his year of "rhetoric." On 11 March 1717 Prévost entered the Jesuit novitiate in Paris, and after a six-month noviceship was sent to their famous college at La Flèche for his philosophy, starting his first year that October. It is not known whether he returned to Paris before leaving the Jesuits, who, unusually, readmitted him, probably in 1719, after he had spent a further period in the army. He left again, and this may have been the period at which various biographers allege that he went to Holland. The dates from 1718 are uncertain, and the biography for two years thereafter consists of merely conjectural attempts to reconcile wisps of conflicting evidence. Prévost certainly oscillated to an extent which caused public comment between a religious vocation and a military one, either of which could have fitted in with family ambitions for him. The unhappy adolescent love affair to which Prévost later alluded has the status of no more than a reasonable probability.

There seem at any rate to have been two periods in the army and two training as a Jesuit after school, and it is certain that Prévost was professed as a Benedictine at Jumièges on 9 November 1721, which means entry into the noviceship certainly no later and probably no earlier than early October 1720. Prévost's own early career increases the likelihood that there is some fictionalized autobiography blended into *Manon Lescaut*, but there is no evidence that it concerns Prévost's relationship with any prototype of Manon. Even if we do not know what happened between 1718 and 1720, it is of that period that Prévost must have been thinking when he later wrote:

Quelques années se passèrent. Vif et sensible au plaisir, j'avouerai…que la sagesse demande bien des précautions qui m'échappèrent…La malheureuse fin d'un engagement trop tendre me conduisit au *tombeau*: c'est le nom que je donne à l'ordre respectable où j'allai m'ensevelir

(Some years passed. Lively and sensitive to pleasure, I will admit that wisdom demanded from me many precautions I did not take…The unhappy end of too tender a bond led me to the *tomb*: that's the name I give to the respectable order in which I went to bury myself).

Prévost's father was present at his religious profession and swore that if his son did not keep his vows he would search for him and blow his brains out.

The biography resumes reasonably firm ground when Prévost was sent on profession as a Benedictine to the abbey of Saint-Ouen at Rouen, where he had a dispute with a Jesuit. He then went for his theology to the abbey of Bec, where he must have met Louis de Brancas, the duc de Villars, who had retired there from the world to repent. Sainte-Beuve thought that the duke inspired Prévost with the idea of an "Homme de qualité retiré du monde," whose "Mémoires et aventures" made up the title of his famous novel, and it is at least likely that Prévost either wrote, or helped to write, the satirical *Les Aventures de Pomponius, chevalier romain; ou, L'Histoire de notre temps,* published in 1724, but apparently written in 1722. The work shows a detailed grasp of recent history as well as of gossip.

In 1725 or 1726 Prévost was at the abbey of Fécamp, from where he sent to Holland for publication by Jean le Clerc in

1726 Dom le Cerf de la Viéville's *Bibliothèque historique et critique de la Congrégation de Saint Maur*, which its author had been forbidden to publish on account of the Benedictines it criticized. It was probably at the abbey of Saint-Germer, where he was teaching, and probably in 1726, that Prévost was ordained priest. He preached successfully at Evreux, and spent some time at the abbey of Saint-Martin, near Sées, not far from Alençon, where he worked on a translation of de Thou's *Historia sui temporis*, published in 1733–34 as *Histoire de mon temps*.

Prévost then moved to Paris, first to the monastery of Blancs-Manteaux, and then in late 1727 or early 1728 to Saint-Germain-des-Prés. He may have preached, but he certainly worked with two other Benedictines on the fifth volume of the *Gallia Christiana*, for which he was paid 600 livres a year. He had narrowly missed the Académie of Marseilles' first prize for an *Ode à la gloire de Saint François Xavier*, published in a 1726 *Recueil* there. It was now republished by the *Mercure* in May 1728. On 15 February, meanwhile, Prévost had submitted for a privilège a manuscript entitled *Les Aventures d'un Homme de qualité qui s'est retiré du monde*. The privilège was granted on 16 April and the work, the first part of a novel, and an apologia for love, appeared in two volumes early in July. It was favourably reviewed in the *Journal de Verdun* in September. An indiscreet passage about the duke of Tuscany had later to be removed from the text, but by then Prévost was already working on the next two volumes, approved on 29 November 1728. The third volume contained a satirical pen portrait of some eminent Benedictines. There is ample evidence to show that the Benedictines did not know how best to accommodate Prévost to the contemplative life strongly emphasized by the Saint-Maur congregation of the Order and did not really trust him, and that he himself felt irked by that lack of trust, as well as restless because of the constant moving.

Much has been made of anything which, in Prévost's life, could turn him into the prototype of his hero, des Grieux, but his departure from the rigorous congregation of Saint-Maur seems to have been the result of the collusion, and perhaps active encouragement, of his superiors. What Prévost apparently did wrong was to move out of his monastery and change out of his habit into the soutane of a diocesan priest on 18 October 1728 in the Luxembourg gardens before the necessary rescript from Rome had been received, so technically rendering himself liable to prosecution. It is perfectly possible that matters in Rome were handled through Mme de Tencin, sister of the bishop of Embrun. However, on 30 October 1728, 12 days after his disappearance, the superiors of the Saint-Maur congregation did demand Prévost's arrest, and Hérault, the lieutenant of police, gave instructions accordingly on 6 November.

Prévost, presumably furnished with an advance by the publishers of his novel, of which the third and fourth volumes were awaiting only their privilège, set off for England, leaving a poste restante address at Amiens, having either genuinely become or pretended to become a Protestant convert, more probably after than before leaving his monastery. The chaplain of the Dutch embassy in Paris, a Pastor Dumont, wrote on 30 November 1728 to Jean Alphonse Turrettini of Geneva that Prévost's books, destined for the archbishop of Canterbury, had been entrusted to him on 22 November. Most likely, especially in view of Prévost's later life, the change of allegiance was a matter of convenience rather than doctrinal conviction. There are hints throughout the work that Prévost believed that Christianity demanded essentially only a belief in the major mysteries and acceptance of a moral code, so that sectarian divisions may not have had for him a significance any greater than what split Jesuits from Jansenists (q.v.) inside the Roman communion.

In England, Prévost became tutor to Francis Eyles, son of the former governor of the Bank of England, Lord Mayor of London in 1726–27, member of parliament for Chippenham (1713–27) and then for the City of London (1727–34), and assistant director of the South Sea Company. He travelled throughout south England with his charge, learnt English, met a number of important authors, went frequently to the theatre, and translated, among others, Dryden and Richardson. The success of a July 1730 edition of the four published volumes of the *Homme de qualité* by the Compagnie des Libraires d'Amsterdam may have led to Prévost's Dutch journey, or at any rate to a negotiation for the sale of volumes five, six, and seven. It seems clear that he was dismissed by the Eyles family after an emotional entanglement with his charge's sister, Mary, who was swiftly married on 22 February 1731 at the Eyles country house at Romford to William Bumstead, the future sheriff of Warwickshire. Prévost had left for Holland in October 1730 with a companion, known apparently only under the pseudonym of the "chevalier de Ravanne," for whose treatment Prévost had paid after being introduced by Ravanne's doctor, and who then became his copyist.

After two days at the Hague, both went on to Amsterdam, where a fair copy of the first four volumes of *Le Philosophe anglais; ou, Histoire de Monsieur Cleveland, fils naturel de Cromwell* was produced in three weeks. The intention was to produce three more books, but Etienne Néaulme of Utrecht bought the first four in December 1730 in the hope of ensuring delivery of the rest for the following 1 February. The first two parts were in fact available in July 1731, a manuscript having been sent to the French censorship on 2 April. An English edition of the first two books had appeared in March. The Dutch edition of books three and four appeared only in October. Prévost meanwhile, once he had money available, turned to the de Thou translation, which he promised to two bookseller-publishers at the Hague, P. Gosse and J. Néaulme, Etienne's brother, who announced in the *Gazette d'Amsterdam* for 23 January 1731 a volume every six months. They finally forced Prévost to live in the Hague, probably from February or March 1731, where they could keep a watchful eye on him. The dates are important, because both the date of publication of *Manon Lescaut*, now generally admitted to have been April 1731, and the possible influence on the novel of Prévost's liaison with Lenki Eckhardt, which cannot have started before April 1731, have been disputed.

Manon Lescaut, the seventh volume of the *Mémoires et aventures d'un homme de qualité*, had appeared with volumes five and six by 18 April 1731. It is impossible that the manuscript of the printed volume, which appeared with copper engravings, was not submitted by the end of February 1731. Prévost had not met Lenki before he had finished *Manon Lescaut*. We are left to suppose that, having failed to exorcize by literary composition his dangerous frame of mind, he was compelled to live through the adventures to which it led him. His life with Lenki has been described by Ravanne, who disliked her, and whose own three-volume largely fictionalized *Mémoires* were published in 1752. Lenki was well known, and had exhausted a number of previous lovers, including a Swiss officer by whom she appears to have had several children. Prévost was totally obsessed, unable to work, using all his charm and cunning to get hold of the very large sums of money she required for her support, and quite unable to break with her, even when he realized that he was ruining himself in more than merely financial ways. When, in January 1733, he fled with Lenki to England, he left in Holland unpaid debts of 10,000 francs, having had at least nearly double that amount in publishers' advances. In Holland, his possessions were immediately sold on 17 January. On 19 January appeared a first satirical attack on him in the *Glaneur historique, moral, littéraire et galant*. Others were later to follow.

1732 had been a dramatic year. Augmented delays in delivering material had set in early on. On 3 January, Prévost promised to finish *Cleveland* in three months, and received 100 florins, something over 1,000 livres. By 19 March only a quarter of the promised sheets were ready, and none was to be forthcoming during the rest of the year. On 7 June and 31 July, the need to finish the de Thou translation was offered as an excuse. By the end of October Prévost had a debt maturing which he could not meet. He tried in vain to break with Lenki, knowing what all his friends thought about her. With affected nonchalance he proposed to repay all publishers' advances, and to start again with new publishers. When the crash came in January 1733, Prévost owed about 900 florins, which might have been covered by what he had just received for the de Thou *Histoire*. In fact he seems to have taken about 1,500 florins with him to England, enough, he must have hoped, to start him off again.

Prévost found a new position in England as a tutor and, to augment his income, started a review, modelled on Addison's *The Spectator* and called *Le Pour et Contre*. The approbation was signed on 24 March 1733, and the first number appeared at the beginning of June. On 17 June Didot obtained a privilège to publish in Paris. The review ran until 1740, giving news of English affairs, first fortnightly and then weekly, introducing the French to much admired English scientific and literary cultures, the major English literary figures, discussing scientific matters, and giving much information about Prévost himself. Then, pressed again for money, Prévost forged a letter of exchange for £50 over the genuine signature of Francis Eyles, writing out the bill in the space between "your humble servant" and the signature of a genuine letter, and then cutting off everything down to and including "your humble servant." The penalty could have been death, but Eyles did not prosecute, although Prévost was jailed for five days on 13 December.

He now sought to return to Paris. *Manon* had been condemned there, mostly as licentious, at the end of 1733, but a pro-Jansenist bias had been detected in des Grieux, as also in *Cleveland* and even the notes for the de Thou *Histoire*, while Etienne Néaulme had finally hired a hack writer to finish off *Cleveland* in a way plainly offensive to the Jesuits. Tension between Prévost and the Jesuits carried on through the 1735 preface to *Le Doyen de Killerine: histoire morale composée sur les mémoires d'une illustre famille d'Irlande*, the August 1735 issue of *Le Pour et Contre*, and the November 1735 issue of the Jesuit *Journal de Trévoux*, before peace was restored with a final letter from Prévost.

He may have spent most of 1734 in England, or near Calais, and it is not improbable that he made a clandestine trip to Paris, after which Mme de Tencin set matters in motion at Rome. We know that Prévost was in Paris by October 1734, that Cardinal de Bissy, titular abbot of Saint-Germain-des-Prés, and the prince de Conti supported Prévost's application, and that on 5 June

1734 a papal indult allowed him to transfer to a less strict Benedictine congregation. That month he had been attacked in the *Bibliothèque des Romans* by a journalist, Lenglet-Dufresnoy, who signed himself Gordon de Percel, was well informed, and had an obvious grievance against Prévost. The attack drew from Prévost the only autobiographical sketch we have, published in number 47 of *Le Pour et Contre*, probably of December 1734. It contains much special pleading, but is clearly an important source for the biography. The same number contains a repudiation of the fifth inauthentic volume of *Cleveland*.

In fact the 61st number of *Le Pour et Contre* had already made public Prévost's intention to return to Paris. On 3 February 1735 he was assigned to the abbey of la Grenetière, near Nantes, where he was to undertake another year of noviceship, but he had it transferred to the abbey of Croix-Saint-Leufroy, near Evreux. A letter of 10 September suggests that Prévost was not short of social engagements and elegant company. He was allowed back to Paris after his noviceship ended on 10 December 1735, and it may have been then that he turned down the offer of an appointment from Cardinal de Bissy. He accepted one much less conducive to preferment by becoming chaplain to the prince de Conti in January 1736 and, although he was lodged and dispensed from residence in his monastery, he would have to earn his living with his pen. Voltaire made overtures through Thiériot, his factotum, inviting Prévost to Cirey, and there were public exchanges of flattery before they finally met, almost by chance, in Holland in 1736–37. As Voltaire had hoped, Prévost allowed him the use of *Le Pour et Contre* from time to time to conduct his propagandist activities.

Lenki had almost certainly rejoined Prévost in Paris before the start of the new noviceship, which must have marked a break. After it, Prévost was in financial difficulties again. However, the final books of *Cleveland* were published by Néaulme, books eight to 10 in 1738, and 11 to 15 in 1739. Volumes two and three of *Le Doyen de Killerine* were published in 1739 and volumes four to six in 1740, but as early as 8 October 1738 Prévost hoped to find employment with the Cardinal de Rohan. Then, from the spring of 1739, he interrupted *Le Pour et Contre* for a year, although it provided his basic income. In 1740 he was trying to borrow money for Voltaire, offering to hire his pen in Voltaire's defence, and was reduced to virtually begging from a Benedictine friend. The poverty now is puzzling, because Prévost's own tastes were not excessive, his income appears to have been adequate, and among his creditors are listed tailors and upholsterers. The puzzle is scarcely unravelled by the arrest of a hack writer at the end of 1740 who named Prévost as a collaborator. Prévost claimed to have helped him financially, but was himself under threat of arrest. The prince de Conti sent Prévost to Belgium with money and recommendations, and Prévost went on with the maréchal de Belle-Isle to Frankfurt. An important letter of 9 November 1741 to Bachaumont suggests that Prévost wanted then to retire to his family, who were comfortably off as the result of a legacy, and enquires after someone who has apparently recently remarried. Could Lenki have been in Paris again in or after 1736? At any rate the sheer bulk and speed of Prévost's literary production, and the urgency and size of his unexplained need for money, make that explanation the most likely one.

At least five volumes of fictionalized history by Prévost appeared between 1740 and 1742. After his return to his family, life became slower and more studious. He translated the *Histoire de Cicéron* by Conyers Middleton in 1743, followed by the correspondence with Brutus (1744) and the *Lettres familières* (1745–47). The 15 volumes of the *Histoire générale des voyages* commissioned by the chancellor d'Aguesseau were published between 1745 and 1770. Prévost turned down a lucrative offer which would have allowed him to keep the 100,000 livres profit from the volumes in order to be faithful to Didot, his habitual publisher. He was now well enough off to rent himself his own residence at Chaillot, with a small household staff. *Manon* was officially revised and republished in 1753, and on 20 July 1754 Prévost was given a priory as a benefice by Benedict XIV. Prévost's father had died in 1739, his elder brother in 1742, and Louis-Eustache in 1759. His brother Jérôme-Pierre died in 1763. He himself died at Courteuil after dining with the Benedictines at the priory of Saint-Nicolas-d'Acy on 25 November 1763. They paid for the right to bury him themselves, and it was a Benedictine who wrote his first biography the following year.

WORKS

It would be a mistake to underestimate the importance for French culture generally of the works of Prévost's maturity, even those written during the final hectic months before Cissy sent him to Belgium, but especially those written after his return from Frankfurt. During the first half of the 18th century England, as was widely acknowledged even in France, was producing Europe's most powerful literature and its most exciting ideas. Prévost's two years in the household of one of the most prominent members of its business community, his mastery of the language, and his understanding of the culture did much to diffuse in France new English ways of reacting and feeling. The *Histoire générale des voyages*, adapted from the English and issued at first in weekly parts, improved on the English original with better maps and engravings, preparing the way for the *Encyclopédie* not only by satisfying intellectual curiosity about the world, but also by taking the technology of scientific vulgarization a step forward. Prévost helped to pave the way for a whole new sensibility in France, to be developed into preromanticism by Rousseau and Diderot, for the technical and scientific achievements of Buffon, and for the standards of typographical excellence in the *Encyclopédie*.

Whether or not Prévost was inspired by the duc de Villars to write the first two volumes of the *Mémoires et aventures d'un homme de qualité qui s'est retiré du monde*, published in 1728, that work, like *Les Aventures de Pomponius*, in which he had certainly had a hand, belonged to the increasingly popular genre of wholly or partly fictionalized memoirs purporting to be autobiography. The genre developed from the fiction in a historical setting typified by *La Princesse de Clèves* into what is now recognized as the memoir novel, the most characteristic fictional form of the first half of the 18th century in France, and it is often almost impossible to know what is historical fact, what hearsay, what a fictional elaboration or recreation, and what frankly imaginative. It seems for instance necessary to recognize that Prévost in *Manon Lescaut* was drawing on his own indecision between an effort to dominate his strongly passionate nature and the abandonment of any struggle against it, dramatized in the oscillation between military and religious careers. On the other hand, it is clear that Prévost did not draw for his novel on his experience with Lenki, but rather that that experience involved

the living out of the adventure his imagination had already warned him about or enticed him with, or perhaps both.

The most cautious hypothesis is that the *Histoire du chevalier des Grieux et de Manon Lescaut* was written in England before October 1730, but it deals with passion in a way which suggests that it was conceived after the books of *Cleveland* written immediately on arrival in Holland. Its composition would better fit Prévost's known state of mind in January and February 1731, and its speedy completion during the first six weeks of the year is not quite impossible to envisage if it is assumed, as would not be unreasonable, that the fifth and sixth volumes of the *Mémoires* had been completed before the departure from England. It is therefore on the whole more likely that *Cleveland* was broken off after the signature of the contract in December 1730, and that Prévost then wrote *Manon* before returning to de Thou and the third and fourth books of *Cleveland*. When it was tacked on to the end of the *Mémoires d'un homme de qualité* as the seventh volume of that work, Prévost put into the mouth of the Homme de Qualité, whose name is Renoncour, an "Avis de l'auteur des Mémoires d'un Homme de Qualité," which explains that it has scant connection with what has gone before:

> Quoique j'eusse pu faire entrer dans mes Mémoires les aventures du chevalier des Grieux, il m'a semblé que n'y ayant point un rapport nécessaire, le lecteur trouverait plus de satisfaction à les voir séparément. Un récit de cette longueur aurait interrompu trop longtemps le fil de ma propre histoire
>
> (Although I could have inserted the adventures of the chevalier des Grieux into my Mémoires, it seemed to me that, since there was no necessary connection, the reader would be more satisfied to see them separately. A narrative of this length would have interrupted the thread of my own story for too long).

It is quite impossible that Manon was modelled on Lenki, but it is quite likely that Prévost, in Paris in 1728, had heard about a certain Marie-Madeleine Aydou, known as Manon, born on 3 September 1707, daughter of one Antoinette Levieux and a prisoner who had escaped from the galleys. Taken from the age of five into the care of her grandfather, Manon was abducted at 12 by her mother, no doubt for exploitative purposes. Her first lover, then aged 21, was Louis-Antoine de Viantaix, an ex-soldier. He behaved with her in such a manner that her grandfather, if with some difficulty, obtained a lettre de cachet, and Manon was imprisoned in the Salpêtrière on 9 December 1721 at the age of 14. Viantaix wanted to marry her, but was not allowed to, and retired to Besançon. Manon was not freed either in 1724, after her grandfather's death, or three years later, owing to the opposition of the superior, Mlle Bailly, on the grounds of her "corruption." It required the intervention of the duc de Bourbon's capitaine des chasses, the former first minister Sarrobert, to obtain her release in 1731. Prévost cannot have known her, but her story may have been known in Paris, and perhaps remembered by Prévost in England. In spite of much speculation, no connection between Prévost and Manon Aydou has been proved, or has even been shown to have been at all likely.

Manon Lescaut, an immediate success in Holland, Germany, and England, was not published in France until June 1733, when it appeared anonymously as an independent volume entitled either *Les Avantures du chevalier des Grieux et de Manon Lescaut* or *Suite des Mémoires et aventures d'un homme de qualité qui s'est retiré du monde*. The more or less private and manuscript *Journal de la Cour et de Paris* notes the book's appearance and, in October, its seizure. It was formally "suppressed" only on 18 July 1735. Desfontaines gave it a detailed notice in *Le Pour et Contre* in 1734, while he was running the review during Prévost's absence, after a less favourable account of *Cleveland*. It was, however, for the longer novels, the *Mémoires*, *Cleveland*, and *Killerine*, rather than *Manon* that Prévost was chiefly known. Neither Rousseau nor Diderot ever mentions *Manon*, although both admired *Cleveland*, which obviously exploits the English connection.

It seems at least likely that Prévost modelled *Manon* on the collection of seven stories contained in *Les Illustres Françaises* by Robert Challes, of which there are eight known editions between 1713 and 1731, and which Prévost most probably read in its two-volume English translation of 1727 by Mrs Aubin, *The Illustrious French Lovers, being the history of the Amours of several French Persons of Quality...* The heroine of the first story is called Manon, and there are in Prévost apparent verbal reminiscences of Challes which could be based only on the English version. Elements of the plot of *Manon* are too improbably close to Challes's *L'Histoire de M. des Prez et de Mlle de l'Epine* for us to avoid the assumption of direct borrowing, and it is clear that Prévost's general conception owes much also to the conte which follows in Challes's collection, *L'Histoire de M. des Frans et de Silvie*. More generally, however, Prévost follows Challes in pointing carefully, if disingenuously, to his moral.

The "Avis au lecteur" warns the reader that the novel, really only a long conte, presents an "exemple terrible de la force des passions (a terrifying example of the strength of passion)," as if this were something which had crystallized in Prévost's imagination as a result of writing the six books of the *Mémoires* and the first two books of *Cleveland*. Des Grieux is "a mixture of virtues and vices," "un contraste perpétuel de bons sentiments et d'actions mauvaises (a perpetual contrast between good feelings and evil actions)." When the Homme de Qualité tells us that the conte is only "un traité de morale, réduit agréablement en exercice (a moral treatise entertainingly shown in practice)," Prévost is drawing attention to what the conte makes obvious enough, that the intrigue is not intended to be the centre of interest, but merely a pretext to consider moral problems and psychological reaction. Prévost was aware that, even if his intention was to bring the novel back to life after its long displacement by pseudo-historical narratives or pseudo-autobiographical memoirs, he had taken the intrigue well beyond the bounds of credibility. Abstracted from its psychological and moral anchors, it is almost a caricature of the picaresque. Essentially, *Manon* sharply raises the problems of personal moral responsibility for outrageous actions performed under strong psychological constraint, and the psychological possibility of dominating headstrong passion.

In 1753 the book's ostensible centre of interest is shown in the vignette depicting, almost certainly at Prévost's own suggestion, des Grieux as Fénelon's Télémaque being led by Mentor in the guise of Pallas towards a calvary and away from Charybdis, standing for Calypso's nymph Eucharis, represented in the novel by Manon. Tiberge, calling des Grieux towards the virtuous life in which grace determines the soul to virtue, clearly fulfils in *Manon* the role of Mentor in *Télémaque*; des Grieux/Télémaque

has to be led away from the temptations of unregenerate passion. Underneath is a couplet from Horace (*Odes* I, xxvii) "quanta laborabas Charybdi,/digne puer meliore flamma (what torments did you endure in Charybdis,/young man worthy of a higher love)." Charybdis, originally a whirlpool, came allegorically to stand for the mistress who sucked from the lover gold and blood, and hence for passionate love, whereas Pallas, leading to a higher love, displayed on calvary, stands for divine grace.

The allegory opposing divine love to passionate love, grace to sin, refers deliberately to Fénelon's *Télémaque*, and obliquely to Ulysses and Calypso. But whereas the medieval allegories of Charybdis, the female seducer, and Calypso's nymph Eucharis in Fénelon represent temptation to be avoided, des Grieux's passion for Manon, as des Grieux relates it to the Homme de Qualité in Prévost's novel, is quite emphatically not condemned. Prévost takes a giant stride forwards in the 18th-century rehabilitation of instinctive affection when the Homme de Qualité recounts des Grieux's belief that his passion in itself is innocent, and when he himself accepts in the first volume of the *Mémoires* that "la grandeur de l'âme suppose de grandes passions; l'importance est de les tourner à la vertu (greatness of soul presupposes great passions; the important thing is to turn them to good)."

Manon starts with the account by the Homme de Qualité of his meeting with des Grieux. After the first half-dozen pages, the rest of the novel is given over to des Grieux's own account of his adventures, as reported by the Homme de Qualité. The reader has therefore to remember that des Grieux may be, perhaps inadvertently, putting a moral or psychological gloss on his behaviour as he recounts it, or an interpretation on events; that the Homme de Qualité has already predisposed the reader to accept his own favourable impression of des Grieux before we know anything about him at all; and that Prévost's "avant-propos" may be at variance with what is implied by the tone of the subsequent narration, a mere insurance policy against the accusation of immorality which it did not succeed in warding off. In fact it becomes almost a stylistic trick to manipulate the reader's judgement by suggesting the interpretation to be put on actions before the actions themselves are narrated.

The Homme de Qualité, the marquis de Renoncour, notionally inserts the action between the narratives of books five and six of the *Mémoires*. At Pacy, about 16 kilometres east of Evreux, he had met two carts drawn up outside the hostelry. They were taking a dozen prostitutes to deportation from Havre-de-Grâce to America. The convoys were popularly regarded as a disgraceful brutality, and the Homme de Qualité notes that the girls were chained together. We are immediately told that one girl had an "air et figure... si peu conformes à sa condition, qu'en tout autre état je l'eusse prise pour une personne du premier rang (air and demeanour... so little in accordance with her condition that in any other state I would have taken her for someone of the highest social rank)." We are told how distinguished and distinctive Manon's appearance was before we know anything at all about her, and we are also led to suppose that rank is discernible from appearance. In this passage the Homme de Qualité is still addressing the reader in his own words.

In spite of the girl's sadness and filthy clothes, she remained free from ugliness, and inspired "respect et pitié (respect and pity)." The chief guard, too, had noticed this girl's distinguished air and draws the attention of the Homme de Qualité to a young man who has followed her weeping from Paris. He was in a corner "enseveli dans une rêverie profonde (buried in a deep dream)." The reader is therefore made to feel sympathy for him, too, without knowing, any more than the guard, whether he is the girl's brother or lover. We are also told, not as a personal impression, but off-handedly as a matter of fact, that "on distingue, au premier coup d'oeil, un homme qui a de la naissance et de l'éducation (you can see at first glance a man who has birth and education)." The Homme de Qualité then reports his first conversation with des Grieux, who, having failed to get Manon liberated from prison, had tried to capture her by force, been let down by four men he had paid to intercept the convoy with him, and been forced to pay the guards every time he wished to speak to the girl, had no money left, was now obliged to sell his horse, and intended to go to America with her.

The Homme de Qualité gave the young man money, bribed the guards to let him talk to Manon, himself greeted Manon, and, interestingly in view of what is to come, for the second time in two brief comments on her appearance, remarks on her modesty. Two years later he met the young man again, immediately recognizing him by the distinction of his appearance. The rest of the novel is des Grieux's narrative, starting when he was 17. We are only occasionally and implicitly reminded that des Grieux is imposing his own view on what he recounts, and that his narrative is necessarily selectively remembered by the Homme de Qualité, who is supposed to be passing it on to the reader. Des Grieux tells us that he was well born, studious, and inclined to virtue. Although his parents wanted him to become a knight of Malta, effectively combining a military career with a quasi-ecclesiastical one, the bishop wanted him to become a priest. We learn from him that he is the chevalier des Grieux, and that something might have been saved from the shipwreck of his fortune and reputation if he had profited from the reproaches of his close friend Tiberge "dans le précipice où mes passions m'ont entraîné (in the abyss into which my passions dragged me)." In the context of early 18th-century French fictional writing, the pathos of the self-inculpation is not meant to be overdramatized, and the vocabulary used by des Grieux in fact implicitly exculpates him from any personal choice in wrongdoing. He was "dragged" by his passions, a metaphor most famously used by Plato.

Des Grieux relates his first glimpse of Manon. It was the day before he left school at Amiens, and she stood out from the crowd by her demeanour. From what we learn later she must have been 15 or 16, and we are told of her merely that she appeared "charmante." Des Grieux was "enflammé tout d'un coup jusqu'au transport (suddenly inflamed and taken out of myself)." Prévost, while staying close to the instantaneity of irresistible love explored by Racine and Mme de Lafayette, differs from them in the theological explanation of helplessness he will later provide. He shares with Mme de Lafayette the notion that love sharpens perception: "l'amour me rendait déjà si éclairé (love already so enlightened my mind)." Manon had said that she was being sent "malgré elle (against her will)" to a convent to become a nun, no doubt to "arrêter... son penchant au plaisir (arrest... her passion for pleasure)." The vocabulary is all-important. "Arrêter" here suggests the forcible domination of an inner impulse without necessarily quite entailing it, and "penchant" could signify a mild inclination as well as the irresistible compulsion it turns out subsequently to have indicated here. The ground for a theological interpretation of the psychological

event is reinforced when des Grieux, still reporting the first meeting, at which he had simply gone to speak to a pretty stranger, tells us:

La douceur de ses regards, un air charmant de tristesse en prononçant ces paroles, ou plutôt, l'ascendant de ma destinée qui m'entraînait à ma perte, ne me permirent pas de balancer un moment sur ma réponse. Je l'assurai que... j'emploierais ma vie pour la délivrer de la tyrannie de ses parents, et pour la rendre heureuse

(The gentleness of her appearance, a charming air of sadness in uttering those words, or, rather, the inevitability of my destiny, which dragged me to my loss, did not allow me to hesitate for a moment over my reply...I would devote my life to delivering her from the tyranny of her parents, and to making her happy).

There remain unanswered two important questions. Does des Grieux use the language of grace and sin, as he uses the vocabulary of astrology or the Greek pantheon in his references to fate and destiny, in a literal or a merely metaphorical sense? Are fate and destiny mere euphemisms for grace and its absence, or not? Are they just metaphors of strong desire? And, if des Grieux really does think that he is the victim of a conflict between grace and corruption, is he deceiving himself? Part of his narrative concerns a progressive awareness of self-deception about Manon's behaviour. Since on any account this is a powerful but above all imaginative investigation into the psychology and ethics of passion, it seems a priori probable that Prévost is asking these questions and, instinctively rather than with calculation, leaving the answers open. Whatever the avant-propos takes cover in asserting, the form in which *Manon* is cast makes it impossible to regard it as a moral treatise.

Psychologically speaking, Prévost's own literary activity is likely to have obliged him, after writing the third two volumes of the *Mémoires* and the first two of *Cleveland*, articulately to confront a problem to which he could offer only a range of imaginatively possible avenues of solution, rather than any firm view. His own attempts at seeking a refuge from the storms of passion in monastic renunciation, and then at confronting the problems of irresistibility, and of what, if passion were really to be so incapable of domination, it might lead to, or even excuse, patently did not offer him personally any firm and viable structure within which to control or perhaps even understand his own experience.

Meanwhile, at the end of the first meeting with des Grieux, Manon shows a ready aptitude for subterfuge, telling the guardian appointed to look after her that the man she was talking to was her cousin, and that she would defer entry to the convent for 24 hours in order to dine with him. Going over the meeting in his mind, des Grieux tells us the girl's name, Manon, and is overcome by another "transport," which he says left him voiceless. Manon "parut fort satisfaite de cet effet de ses charmes (appeared very pleased with that effect of her charms)." No doubt again instinctively Prévost has recourse to an important literary device. Since this is an account by des Grieux as the Homme de Qualité purports to have heard it, we have no omniscient narrator to tell us what Manon did feel, but we can be told only what the Homme de Qualité said that she seemed to des Grieux to have felt. That becomes very important later on, since des Grieux naturally twists everything round to see it in the light most favourable to her. Montesquieu notoriously wrote in 1734 that des Grieux was a fraud ("fripon") and Manon a tart ("catin"). Was he being cynical? Posterity has on the whole judged so, but Prévost, perhaps not entirely out of caution, leaves open the possibility of self-determining moral guilt in each character, however much he may load our sympathies on their behalf.

Prévost's daring is considerable. Just how far can he take the sympathy of his readers? Just what would a reader in 1731 have made of the fact that, being "point de qualité, quoique d'assez bonne naissance (not of quality, although of fairly good birth)," or in 1753, when the phrase was sharpened to "étant d'une naissance commune (being of common birth)," Manon felt flattered at having "fait la conquête d'un amant tel que moi (conquered a lover like me)"? Marivaux explores the possibility that adequately refined looks and demeanour may reflect uncertified breeding and therefore rank, but Prévost implicitly wonders whether they may even excuse their absence, increasing his egalitarian inclinations between 1731 and 1753.

About to abduct Manon as soon as the Amiens town gates opened at five a.m., des Grieux had run into the objections of his friend Tiberge, three years his senior. Tiberge, however close a friend, foresaw such disaster that, if he could not dissuade des Grieux from the project, he would denounce it. Des Grieux, "l'amour m'ayant ouvert extrêmement l'esprit (love having made me extremely perceptive)," succeeded in deceiving Tiberge, and got Manon to Saint-Denis the following day, a journey just possible on a summer day by "chaise," but normally requiring nearly two days by "post chaise," or three by coach. Des Grieux rode alongside. Of that night he says: "Nous fraudâmes les droits de l'Eglise (We cheated the Church of its rights)." The narrative is interspersed with reflections metaphorically starting "if only…," but the first three weeks passed happily in a furnished room. The expressions of regret at what it all led to do not sound as if they had been wrung from the heart, but the flat narrative register makes it impossible to tell.

Des Grieux, whose funds no longer seemed inexhaustible, anticipated a reconciliation with his father, from whom he hoped to get permission to marry Manon, a project she looked on "froidement (frostily)." In Challes, des Prez does find a Norman priest who accepts a heavy bribe to marry him under age, but such a marriage without parental permission entailed disinheritance, and was a criminal offence on the priest's part if the couple had not resided within his jurisdiction for six months. Des Grieux explains Manon's coolness in terms of her fear at losing him, should his father not consent. She could, she said, get money from relations, and she sweetened her refusal with "des caresses si tendres et passionnées (such tender and passionate kisses)" that he did not doubt her heart. She must have got hold of money, as she was catering for them beyond his means. Trouble started when the maid kept des Grieux waiting at his own door and, when pressed, said that she had instructions not to let him in until a local tax farmer, M. de B…, had been let out down the back stairs. Des Grieux went away, having forbidden the maid to tell her mistress that he now knew about M. de B…, and shedding tears, "sans savoir encore de quel sentiment elles partaient (without yet knowing from what feeling they derived)."

Des Grieux, by his own account, deceived himself into thinking that M. de B… was simply delivering money on behalf of friends or relatives of Manon. At dinner that evening Manon's demeanour surprised him, but "je ne pouvais démêler si c'était de l'amour ou de la compassion, quoiqu'il me parût que c'était un sentiment doux et languissant (but I could not work out whether it was love or compassion, although it appeared to me to be a sweet and tender feeling)." Des Grieux recounts that Manon began to cry, and interjects: "perfides larmes (perfidious tears)." There was a knock at the door; Manon disappeared into the sleeping chamber; des Grieux opened the door and was seized by three of his father's servants. His brother was waiting in a carriage. "Monsieur B…," as des Grieux's father, being himself of rank, had the right to call him, but Manon's servant did not, had written to des Grieux's father, whom he did not know, 11 days previously. Des Grieux's father was contemptuous of M. de B…, but then scoffed at his son for having been unable to keep his conquest to himself for more than 12 days. Des Grieux fainted, and on coming to, opened his eyes, he says, to weep, and his mouth to wail.

Des Grieux was kept under house arrest, guarded by two servants, and Prévost has come so far from 17th-century attempts to justify emotional love on the grounds of the merit of its object, still clear in Mme de Lafayette, that he puts into des Grieux's mouth the words

Il est certain que je ne l'estimais plus; comment aurais-je estimé la plus volage et la plus perfide de toutes les créatures? Mais son image, ses traits charmants que je portais au fond du coeur, subsistaient toujours

(It is certain that I no longer esteemed her. How could I have esteemed the flightiest and most perfidious of creatures? But her image, the impression of her charm which I carried at the bottom of my heart, remained with me).

Des Grieux continued to love when he had ceased to esteem. Love was infatuation, no longer based on the interpolated intellectual judgement of merit we find in L'Astrée or Descartes, but Prévost still feels some need to go into the psychology of the situation. Des Grieux says that it is not, as his father supposes, that he just likes pretty girls. His father switches from the intimate "tu" to the more formal "vous" to denote his annoyance. Des Grieux does not intentionally irritate his father: "C'était un mouvement involontaire qui me faisait prendre ainsi le parti de mon infidèle (It was an involuntary movement which made me take the side of my unfaithful [mistress] in this way)." The "involuntary" is naturally just dropped in, no doubt self-exculpatorily, but not consciously.

Like Prévost in the monastery, des Grieux took refuge and pleasure in study while under house arrest, his heart filled alternately with love and hatred for Manon. Tiberge called. "J'avais autant de penchant que vous vers la volupté," he said, "mais le Ciel m'avait donné, en même temps, du goût pour la vertu (I had as strong a leaning towards pleasure as you, but Heaven at the same time had given me a taste for virtue)." He was convinced now of the "poison du plaisir (pleasure's poison)," and it was only on account of des Grieux that he had not fled to solitude. He had followed des Grieux from Amiens to Paris, looked for him there, seen Manon dressed in finery at the theatre, followed her carriage home, and heard about Monsieur B… He had then called on Manon, but found she would not talk of des Grieux, and left her. His visit rekindled in des Grieux the desire to lead a religious life. His heart would desire only what it esteemed, and his imagination leapt immediately to the cottage, wood, stream, library, the few virtuous friends, and the good but frugal table. On thinking it through, des Grieux discovered that it would still need Manon for him to be happy in such a life, but he none the less decided to start his theology at Saint-Sulpice. No longer the chevalier, but now the abbé des Grieux, "j'avais de la ferveur pour tous les exercices (I approached all the exercises with fervour)" and tasted ("goûtais") "la joie intérieure (inner joy)" in putting into effect these resolutions.

It is at this point that des Grieux asks himself one of the most important questions in the book. How could he so easily have broken all his pious resolutions?

S'il est vrai que les secours célestes sont à tous moments d'une force égale à celle des passions, qu'on m'explique donc par quel funeste ascendant on se trouve emporté tout d'un coup loin de son devoir, sans se trouver capable de la moindre résistance, et sans ressentir le moindre remords

(If it is true that heavenly grace always has a force equal to that of the passions, I would like to know by what fatal destiny we can suddenly be taken far from our duty without finding ourselves capable of the least resistance, and without feeling the least remorse)

After nearly a year in Paris, des Grieux had to hold a public defence of various propositions, an ordinary part of the course, but one to which the student ordinarily invited friends. Manon appeared with some other women, unbidden, whether out of curiosity or out of shame at her betrayal des Grieux says he does not know. On his return to Saint-Sulpice with the customary congratulations, des Grieux was told that a woman wanted to see him. When he went to the parlour, he found that it was Manon.

From this point on the pace of the narrative quickens into a caricature of a novel. The most dramatic events crowd one another out, scarcely generating suspense. The ethical and psychological framework is in place; the questions have been asked; the rest of the novel shows what any answers would have to imply, and Prévost virtually challenges his readers to see how far he can stretch their sympathies. Manon, says des Grieux, maintained she could not live without his heart. He said she had never ceased to have it and "elle se leva avec transport pour venir m'embrasser. Elle m'accabla de mille caresses passionnées (she rose to embrace me without knowing what she was doing. She overwhelmed me with a thousand passionate kisses)." He used a "mélange profane d'expressions amoureuses et théologiques (profane mixture of amorous and theological expressions)," and felt his heart overcome by a "délectation victorieuse (victorious delectation)," a technical expression in Augustinian theology to denote the non-resistibility of efficacious grace loaded, as Jansen's (q.v.) followers had loaded it, with the implication that the delectation was felt, and could therefore more easily be seen as the equal but opposite not only of a state of sin, which could not be felt, but also of love, which was a sentiment.

In the parlour at Saint-Sulpice Des Grieux was instantly aware that he was going to lose his fortune and reputation for Manon. He read his "destiny" in her eyes, left the seminary without going back to his room, joined her carriage round the corner, bought second-hand or ready-made officers' clothes paid for by Manon, and decided to live near enough to Paris for Manon, but far enough away to hope that he would not be rec-

ognized. The compromise was Chaillot. It took an hour for Manon and her maid to pack jewels and clothes. The couple spent a night at the inn, and next day found somewhere to live. If they stayed at Chaillot, had a carriage, went to the opera twice a week, and limited losses at gaming to 20 livres, Manon had enough money to last them 10 years. In fact they stuck to the budget for only a month, since "Manon était passionnée pour le plaisir; je l'étais pour elle (Manon had a passion for pleasure, and I one for her)."

They took in addition a furnished room in town, met Manon's coarse and unprincipled brother ("brutal et sans principes d'honneur"), who speedily took over their carriage, their house, and their whole lives, inviting guests, dressing at Manon's expense, taking money from her, and getting her to pay his debts. Then there was a fire at the Chaillot house, and the chest containing the money disappeared. By now des Grieux knew his Manon: "Il ne fallait pas compter sur elle dans la misère. Elle aimait trop l'abondance et les plaisirs pour me les sacrifier (She was not to be counted on in poverty. She was too fond of plenty and pleasure to sacrifice them for me)." Des Grieux persuaded himself that someone as intelligent as he could, indeed had a right to, make a living from rich fools. Manon's brother suggested that Manon sell her favours and, when des Grieux was incensed, advised him to sell his own. The best solution seemed an association which systematically defrauded gamblers at cards.

Des Grieux held a long conversation with Tiberge, was brought momentarily to the brink of repentance, but borrowed money from him. After the account of their meeting, he inserts into his narrative a long character analysis of Manon; though unattached to money, she was totally devoted to the pleasure for which it can be indispensable. She needed to be amused, entertained, and diverted, and had no other interest in life. She required not riches, but enjoyment. In order to keep her, Des Grieux resolved to sacrifice even the things he most needed himself, so as not to deprive her even of what was superfluous. By a necessity, which in 1753 became "cruel," he decided to join the association of card sharpers. Speedily developing the necessary skills, he quickly amassed a great deal of money. He disappointed Tiberge by repaying the loan and doubling his expenditure. The money was obviously not honestly come by, and des Grieux was genuinely troubled in conscience, although not enough voluntarily to give up the delights of life with a Manon he could amuse to her satisfaction.

The next disaster was a theft by a male and female servant of all that des Grieux and Manon possessed. This time it could not be kept from Manon, and while des Grieux went fruitlessly to the police, Manon's brother persuaded her to exploit her charms with the rich and debauched M. de G...M... She left des Grieux a note saying: "c'est une sotte vertu que la fidelité... (fidelity is a stupid virtue...)." Des Grieux's ensuing reflection takes up again the question of responsibility. Does misfortune which is not your own fault excuse misbehaviour, which may be culpable?

Par quelle fatalité, disais-je, suis-je devenu si criminel? L'amour est une passion innocente; comment s'est-il changé, pour moi, en une source de misères et de désordres? Qui m'empêchait de vivre tranquille et vertueux avec Manon? Pourquoi ne l'épousais-je point?

(By what destiny, I said, have I become so criminal? Love

is an innocent passion. How has it changed for me into a source of miseries and disorders? Who prevented me from living in peace and virtue with Manon? Why didn't I marry her?).

The style suggests that Prévost does not expect the reader to lose sympathy with des Grieux by answering the questions. He started calling on Manon, now with M. de G...M..., and she was delighted to see him. She wanted to be kissed. He was full of sighs and reproaches. She started to cry and used "tu," while he addressed her with the formal "vous." She promised to return to him, and a supper was arranged for M. de G...M..., Manon, her brother, and des Grieux. Des Grieux, clearly pleased with the way he had played his part, thought he had made M. de G...M... look a fool, and recounts the escape in the waiting carriage. M. de G...M..., however, quickly found out about Manon and des Grieux's past and had them arrested in bed. We are not yet told what happened to Manon, and the word "Hôpital," involving incarceration, used in 1731 is replaced by the vaguer "retraite" in 1753 to increase not suspense, but curiosity. Des Grieux was imprisoned in Saint-Lazare.

The superior there was kind, and des Grieux suffered above all from shame. Unlike ordinary men, subject only to love, hate, pleasure, pain, hope, and fear, those of des Grieux's refinement, he assures us, suffer more from shame and humiliation. He did, however, again according to what he himself says, hypocritically exploit what the superior called his "Naturel si doux et si aimable (his naturally sweet and pleasant disposition)," and twice in one paragraph he refers to "destiny." M. de G...M... came to visit him, this time appearing not at all a fool, but when des Grieux learnt from him that Manon was at the Hôpital, of which the Salpêtrière was the principal part, he attacked him physically. Explaining subsequently to the superior what had happened, des Grieux spoke of his "insurmountable passion" for Manon, and reflected on the "inexpressible torture" of thinking of the conditions of her confinement. The superior, deeply sympathetic, allowed Tiberge to be informed of des Grieux's whereabouts, and another conversation ensued about celestial and earthly rewards. Des Grieux maintained that the more certain earthly rewards are as much worth suffering for as the remoter heavenly ones, and Tiberge was shocked.

Des Grieux, taking up a perennial theme, probably from Montaigne's treatment of "volupté (pleasure)," now holds that human nature, as it is, tends inexorably towards pleasure: "il est certain que notre félicité consiste dans le plaisir (it is certain that our happiness consists in pleasure)." Of all the pleasures, the greatest are those afforded by love. With hearts such as they have, "les délices de l'amour sont ici-bas nos plus parfaites félicités (the delights of love are our greatest happiness here on earth)." Tiberge actually reproaches des Grieux with Jansenism when he says: "Hélas! oui, c'est mon devoir d'agir comme je raisonne! mais l'action est-elle en mon pouvoir? (Alas! yes, it's my duty to act according to my reason, but is my activity in my power?)." From the theological point of view, Tiberge is right. The Jansenists held that virtuous activity was not in our power.

Manon's brother, having received a note through Tiberge, called, and agreed to get des Grieux a pistol, which, des Grieux said, did not even have to be loaded: "Je l'assurais que j'avais si peu dessein de tuer qu'il n'était pas même nécessaire que le pistolet fût chargé (I assured him that I had so little intention to kill that it wasn't even necessary for the pistol to be loaded)." It was

to be brought the next day, and Manon's brother was to be outside the prison at 11 pm with two or three friends. The narrative is casual. The gun was brought. At the appropriate moment, the superior was awakened and threatened with the gun. He was saddened at the recalcitrance of his favourite prisoner, who remained cool and courteous, but opened the gate. However, a servant was alarmed and came to the superior's rescue. The servant threw himself at des Grieux, holding a candle in one hand and a gun in the other:

Je ne le marchandai point; je lui lâchai le coup au milieu de la poitrine. Voilà de quoi vous êtes cause, mon Père, dis-je assez fièrement à mon guide. Mais que cela ne vous empêche pas d'achever, ajoutai-je en le poussant vers la dernière porte. Il n'osa refuser de l'ouvrir

(I didn't spare him. I let him have the shot in the middle of his chest. That's what you're the cause of, Father, I said quite proudly to my guide. But don't let that stop you finishing, I added, pushing him towards the last gate. He didn't dare refuse to open it).

As the Homme de Qualité relates the narrative, it is clear that des Grieux knew that the pistol was loaded, although Prévost had earlier established that the intention was simply to threaten. Prévost does not completely resolve the question of what des Grieux was guilty of, although the account of the shooting makes it sound like unpremeditated murder. However, when he got outside, Manon's brother was surprised at having heard what he thought was a pistol shot:

C'est votre faute, lui dis-je; pourquoi me l'apportiez-vous chargé? Cependant je le remerciai d'avoir eu cette précaution, sans laquelle j'étais sans doute à Saint-Lazare pour longtemps

(It's your fault, I told him. Why did you bring it to me loaded? However, I thanked him for taking that precaution, without which I would doubtless have been at Saint-Lazare for a long time).

Prévost has gone too far. That des Grieux should have asked for an unloaded pistol is credible, and it is understandable that Prévost should want us to know this. That, after several mentions of searched pockets, Manon's brother should have been able to hand a loaded gun over to a prisoner at Saint-Lazare is dismissive of any care for probability. Des Grieux's account implies that he knew that the pistol was loaded, and it is anyway not conceivable that he should coolly have pulled the trigger of a pistol he believed to be unloaded with the intention of removing the servant's threat to his escape. He assumed, of course, that the pistol had been loaded as a "precaution." Lescaut's surprise at hearing the shot may have derived from the fact that des Grieux had actually used the pistol as a weapon rather than merely as a threat, as he had intended, but he cannot possibly merely have wondered whether it was a pistol shot he had heard. Prévost, trying to blur des Grieux's guiltiness of murder in the furtherance of his escape, has here become simply careless of consistency as well as of credibility. But the carelessness about the story makes his dilemma, and his intention, clearer. How deep is the guilt that love can redeem? To what actions can love impel us? Could we avoid them?

Prévost's points are now made, and if he was himself, as seems likely, stealing the time he had already twice sold, once for *Cleveland*'s second two parts, and once for the de Thou translation, and if, finally, he wanted *Manon* printed with volumes five and six of the *Mémoires*, he was by this point in a hurry to finish. The risks taken by des Grieux, now presumably wanted for murder, in attempting to liberate Manon from the Salpêtrière take the novel into the realm of fantasy, as does the ease with which des Grieux there visits his known associate, enlisting the help of M. de T..., the son of one of the prison governors, bribes one of the jailers to unlock Manon's room, and slips her a set of men's clothing. Little deferences towards realism become almost risible. Only the psychology is important.

Des Grieux and Manon went to her brother's apartment and called him down to pay the coachman. He would not pay what des Grieux had promised, and all three walked away in case the coachman has gone off to get the police. Within five or six minutes Manon's brother was recognized in the street and shot dead. "Je pressai Manon de fuir, car nos secours étaient inutiles à un cadavre, et je craignais d'être arrêté par le guet (I pressed Manon to flee, since our help was of no avail to a corpse, and I was afraid of being arrested by the watch)." Des Grieux and Manon bargained with another coachman, and got to Chaillot by 11 pm.

The superior at Saint-Lazare had hushed up the servant's death, and Tiberge lent money again. Des Grieux says he hoped now to obtain some more from his family, to whom he wrote. The Salpêtrière had merely found it strange that Manon should apparently have run away with a valet, and it was well known that Manon's brother's death was due to a gaming dispute earlier in the evening. Prévost is strikingly high-handed in getting rid of a character who is no longer more than an encumbrance to the story, but his plot is now perfunctorily tidied up in a page or two, and he lets the Homme de Qualité give des Grieux a rest from telling him his story. The first part of the book is over, its derisory attitude to its own plot again emphasizing how the point of the book lies in its exploration of the psychology and ethics of guilt redeemed by amorous devotion, and not at all in anything in the story that happens after Manon has renounced M. de G...M...

The much shorter second part adds comparatively little except a rider to the moral reflection. Des Grieux and Manon live happily, and des Grieux is now lucky enough at the card table no longer to need to resort to swindling. An Italian prince falls in love with Manon, but is toughly told to compare his reflection in a mirror with the appearance of des Grieux, as if Prévost had wanted to write another M. de G...M... episode but thought better of it, or ran out of time. Still careless of motivation, he arranges a new disaster to provoke the moral and psychological reactions he is examining. Des Grieux now has for Manon nothing "qui ne fût de l'estime et de l'amour (except esteem and love)," but at the request of the son of the governor of the Salpêtrière, M. de T..., who is dining with them, has become a firm friend, and is constantly to supply money when trouble demands it, they admit the son of M. de G...M..., who is strongly attracted to Manon and quickly plans to remove her from des Grieux.

He offers her lavish riches and arranges a rendezvous. She is to take what she can get on a first encounter, and meet des Grieux at the theatre. What he receives is a note delivered by "one of the prettiest girls in Paris," whom Manon places at his disposal. This time des Grieux feels a "jalousie mortelle (mortal jealousy)," and a "transport terrible de fureur (overwhelming

sense of outrage)," which quickly turns to tears, to a "profonde douleur (deep sorrow)," and a conflict between the emotions undergone by Pierre Corneille's Cid, rage and despair. Des Grieux wants to murder Manon and the young G...M..., then to kill himself.

There is a cursory repetition of earlier events. Des Grieux calls, and Manon is merely pleased to see him. He reproaches her with calculated perfidy but, as he now told the Homme de Qualité, was wrong. Manon, as des Grieux now presents her, acts almost innocently. Prévost, having alluded to Corneille, slips in a famous phrase from Rabelais about "ifs and buts." Manon and des Grieux conspire with foolhardiness to have G...M... arrested by some army friends of her brother, plan to dine at his house and to spend the night together in his bed, and are disconcerted when M. de G...M...senior, alerted about his son's arrest, works out what has happened, and arrives to have them both arrested, saying he will have des Grieux hanged if he does not disclose the whereabouts of his son. Des Grieux points out by implication that, if it came to executions, M. de G...M... would be hanged as a commoner while he, des Grieux, would have the right to decapitation as a nobleman.

Manon and des Grieux are taken to prison, where des Grieux is again treated well. His father calls on him, and he is finally to be set free, but Manon will be locked up for life, or deported to America. On learning this, Des Grieux faints, and it is notable that he always reports extreme reactions in himself whenever Manon's welfare is concerned. These naturally contribute to the reader's impression of the emotional violence he undergoes and help at least partially to excuse his behaviour, as the police lieutenants and prison governors do. The violence of the emotions remains allied to a delicacy of feeling, also calculated by Prévost to attract our sympathy for a central figure already warranted for by the Homme de Qualité, passing the story on to us. Having abandoned thoughts of assassination, des Grieux is now touched to tears when he is given money by M. de T... His father remains inflexible, although des Grieux wants him to put an end to his sorrows by killing him. They part quarrelling. Des Grieux had planned to attack the convoy taking Manon to deportation, is deserted by the band he has recruited, has ingratiated himself with the escort he had wanted to assault, and, after his meeting with the Homme de Qualité at Amiens, has gone with Manon to America.

Des Grieux profits from the free passage offered to those going to colonize Louisiana and again exploits his refined demeanour to win favourable treatment for Manon and himself on the boat. The other girls are distributed on arrival to young colonizers wanting wives. Manon and des Grieux, again on account of their appearance, are welcomed by the governor of New Orleans and taken to their "miserable single-floor cabin" and, after a touching protestation of her devotion by Manon, have advanced within 10 months to a social rank in the town second only to that of the governor. They acquire servants, and des Grieux assures the Homme de Qualité

Manon n'avait jamais été une fille impie. Je n'étais pas non plus de ces libertins outrés, qui font gloire d'ajouter l'irréligion à la dépravation des moeurs

(Manon had never been irreligious. And I myself did not belong to those exaggerated free-thinkers who pride themselves on adding disbelief to depravity of behaviour).

They decide to marry. This involves the governor's chaplain and therefore his permission. They are consequently obliged to reveal that they are not already married, which means that Manon is free to be married off by the governor to his nephew, Synnelet, who has fallen in love with her. Des Grieux fights a duel with Synnelet, wounds and disarms him and, when he will still not renounce Manon, contemplates killing him, but, as he tells the Homme de Qualité, "un sang généreux ne se dément jamais (highly bred blood aways reveals itself)," and he gives Synnelet back his sword. He is wounded, but thinks he has killed Synnelet: "L'amour conduisit mon épée (Love led my blade)."

Manon faints at the news, but insists on fleeing with des Grieux the certain vengeance of the governor. Synnelet needs to die if Manon's heroic flight is to be adequately motivated. But Des Grieux's ultimate recuperation from the deserts demands that Synnelet is not killed. Prévost can more easily contrive the moral rehabilitation of his hero if Synnelet is not dead, and he is now decidedly finishing his novel in a hurry. The duel is fought at a hundred paces from New Orleans, and the couple rush to flee because "le corps de Synnelet peut avoir été trouvé par hasard (Synnelet's body might have been found by chance)." Manon dies of exhaustion. Des Grieux stays with the body, and finally buries it. Synnelet turns out not to have been killed, or even seriously hurt, and praises des Grieux to his uncle. A search is made, and des Grieux is brought back. He is ill for three months. Six weeks after his recovery Tiberge comes to get him. Back in France, where his father has died he now intends to live virtuously. He tells Tiberge that the "semences de vertu (seeds of virtue)", imported from the stoics into the whole tradition of French moral writing since the renaissance, which Tiberge had once strewn in his heart, are now going to bear fruit.

The point of the work's second part is simply to demonstrate Manon's fundamental devotion and des Grieux's uprightness when not driven by passion to crime. Prévost almost goes out of his way to avoid here, although not in the fifth book of Cleveland, any evocation of colonial America and he plainly needs Manon's fatal self-sacrifice to keep the moral problem at worst unresolved. In the second part Manon and des Grieux move perceptibly nearer to the idealized figures of a Rousseau or a Goethe. Whatever gloss des Grieux may have put on Manon's behaviour, we are not entitled to doubt his account of the fact that she chose to follow him in flight, and died as a result. More curious is the moral implication of the discovery that Synnelet, left as a corpse, turns out to be unharmed, almost as if Prévost, frightened he had left too inescapable an assumption of guilt in the reader's mind after the servant's murder at the gate of Saint-Lazare, had wanted to redress the balance.

Only in Manon does Prévost persistently raise important moral issues to which, in what is the most perfunctory of plots, he perpetually returns. The narrative comes to the reader through the whole series of screens imposed first by des Grieux's memory, and then by any distortion of his story, deliberate or otherwise, under the pressure of recollected emotion, by the Homme de Qualité's reproduction of the story, written down by him and transmitted when we are already aware of his personal reaction to des Grieux, and by Prévost's own comment in the "Avis au lecteur." There is no impartial narrator. Prévost does not in the first part move firmly towards any resolution of the psychological and ethical problems to which he keeps returning. The indications in the text oscillate. What Prévost is discussing is not so much moral ambiguity as the repeated and straightfor-

ward statement of the problems of responsibility and behaviour, as complicated by the intervention of passion and its possible irresistibility. Prévost leaves it to the reader to decide whether passion can be irresistible and whether, if it is, it can excuse, and whether fate or grace are metaphors or explanations.

Manon Lescaut, properly understood, is undoubtedly a masterpiece, but it can only be understood if it is read as a hasty fiction designed to point sharply to the most fundamental ethical problems. It was almost certainly written in a hurry; it must have embodied Prévost's own reflections on the forces pulling him towards religious peace on the one hand and the ardours of passion on the other, but cannot reflect any particular liaison; and it must have been nourished by the problems buried in the early volumes of the Mémoires and quite clear in Challes. The internal evidence points strongly to composition after the author's arrival in Holland late in 1730, and after the first two volumes of Cleveland, although Prévost certainly had a copy of the English translation of Challes available during his work on Manon.

The other works do not bring the reader sharply up against the ethical and psychological problems of passion in the way Manon does. Cleveland is Cromwell's illegitimate son, and the story of his adventures in the new world is certainly inspired by known accounts of explorers, colonizers, and travellers. Cleveland's education has been resolutely modern, including English, French, science, history, but no Latin, and a moral code based on nature. Prévost is here transposing English deism into French, and holding up bluff English honesty in contrast with refined and elegant French sophistication. Mme Lallin falls in love with Cleveland, and when he will not marry her follows him to the wilder parts of north America in pursuit of his beloved Fanny Axminster, whom he marries in a jungle ceremony, tethered to her by a symbolic rope. Religion for the Abaqui tribe, of which Cleveland is elected chief, consists in "the obligation of recognizing an omnipotent God, creator and absolute master of all, to be adored without reservation or hope of rewards." Cleveland refuses to build temples, regarding the universe as God's own temple, created by God himself. Reason, however, proves inadequate, and he nearly commits suicide. He is eventually converted from deism to revealed Christianity by a Jesuit, although his hesitations required the suppression of the account of visits by an Oratorian, a Jesuit, and a Protestant in 1732.

The novel is already tinged with the dreamy melancholy of the forthcoming pre-romantic generation. Nature is explored in its friendly aspects, and natural morality for precepts sounder than those which society was living by, but not yet with any confidence. Axminster is taken prisoner by the cannibals and eventually dies in the presence of Fanny and Cleveland, sold into Spanish slavery. The Abaquis are taken prisoner by the Rouintons. Prisoners are burnt alive, and it appears that Cleveland's daughter is among them. In fact she escapes death, and her father unwittingly falls in love with her, some years and books later. Cleveland confuses Cécile with the memory of Fanny, and Cécile dies on discovering that she is in love with her father. Nature cannot appease the sufferings inflicted on the human heart.

It has been suggested that the part of Cleveland published in July 1731 in two volumes comprised three books. In the end there were to be 15, distributed in eight volumes. The four-volume edition of 1731 contains seven books, while books eight to 10 first appeared in the six-volume edition of 1738, with books 11 to 15 in a seventh volume which appeared in 1739.

Only the first three books, written immediately on arrival in Holland, were certainly written before the meeting with Lenki. Only after that meeting does Cleveland find that he cannot concentrate on study in the presence of Fanny. The sixth book is the most emotional of all. Technically *Le Philosophe anglais; ou, Histoire de Monsieur Cleveland, fils naturel de Cromwell* is doubtless too badly constructed to have won the position the power of its imaginative investigation actually demands, but its literary interest is more than purely historical, and it has been underestimated.

PUBLICATIONS

Collections

Oeuvres choisies, 39 vols., 1783–85
Oeuvres, 8 vols., 1978–84.

Fiction

(*Manon Lescaut*: the best modern edition is that by F. Deloffre and R. Picard, Classiques Garnier, 1965)

Les Aventures de Pomponius, chevalier romain; ou, L'Histoire de notre temps 1724
Mémoires et aventures d'un homme de qualité qui s'est retiré du monde, vols. 1–2, 1728; vols. 3–4, 1729; vols. 5–7, 1731 (volume 7 contains *Manon Lescaut*, published as *Les Avantures du chevalier des Grieux et de Manon Lescaut*, 1733; revised edition, 1735; as *Manon Lescaut* (in English), 1738; same title, 1949); all French editions were originally anonymous
Le Philosophe anglais; ou, Histoire de Monsieur Cleveland, fils naturel de Cromwell, 7 vols., 1731–39; as *The Life and Adventures of Mr Cleveland*, 1734
Le Doyen de Killerine: histoire morale composée sur les mémoires d'une illustre famille d'Irlande, 6 vols., 1735–40; as *The Dean of Coleraine*, 1742
Histoire d'une Grecque moderne, 2 vols., 1740; as *The History of a Fair Greek*, 1755
Voyages du capitaine Robert Lade, 2 vols., 1744
Mémoires d'un honnête homme, 4 vols., 1745
Le Monde moral; ou, Mémoires pour servir à l'histoire du coeur humain, 2 vols., 1760

Other

Histoire de Marguerite d'Anjou, reine d'Angleterre, 1740; as *The History of Margaret of Anjou, Queen of England*, 1755
Campagnes philosophiques; ou, Mémoires de M. de Monteal, contenant l'histoire de la guerre d'Irlande, 4 vols., 1741
Mémoires pour servir à l'histoire de Malte, 2 vols., 1741
Histoire de Guillaume le Conquérant, duc de Normandie, 2 vols., 1742
Histoire générale des voyages, 15 vols., 1745–70 (continued by others: 80 vols., 1749–89)
Manuel lexique; ou, Dictionnaire portatif, 2 vols., 1750

Editor

Le Pour et Contre, 20 vols., 1733–40

Translator

Histoire universelle, by J.-A. de Thou, 16 vols., 1734
Tout pour l'amour; ou, Le Monde bien perdu, by Dryden, 1735
Histoire de Cicéron, by Conyers Middleton, 4 vols., 1743
Lettres à Brutus, by Cicero, 1744
Lettres familières, by Cicero, 5 vols., 1745–47
Paméla; ou, La Vertu récompensée, by S. Richardson, 4 vols., 1742
Lettres anglaises; ou, Histoire de Miss Clarissa Harlove, by S. Richardson, 12 vols., 1751–52
Nouvelles lettres anglaises; ou, Histoire du chevalier de Grandisson, 6 vols., 1755
Histoire de la maison de Stuart sur le trône d'Angleterre, by D. Hume, 3 vols., 1760
Almoran et Hamet, anecdote oriental, by J. Hawkesworth, 1763

Biographical and critical studies

Harrisse, Henry, *L'Abbé Prévost: histoire de sa vie et de ses oeuvres*, 1896
Roddier, Henri, *L'Abbé Prévost, l'homme et l'oeuvre*, 1955
Sgard, Jean, *Prévost romancier*, 1968
Mylne, Vivienne, *Prévost: Manon Lescaut*, 1972

Q

QUERELLE DES ANCIENS ET DES MODERNES (La).

See General Index; also especially Boileau, Chapelain, Thomas Corneille, Descartes, Desmarets de Saint-Sorlin, Donneau de Visé, Fontenelle, Houdar de la Motte, Huet, La Bruyère, Perrault, Pradon, Préciosité, and Racine.

In its widest sense France's Querelle des anciens et des modernes concerns the nature and possibility, or even the inevitability, of human progress, in private behaviour, personal values, and social organization. In a less broad sense, it culminated in a series of literary confrontations between attitudes which assumed characteristic and recognizable forms from soon after the mid-17th century until the end of the second decade of the 18th.

In its narrowest sense the *Querelle* was concentrated into debates about the superiority of contemporary social and cultural phenomena, and especially modern literary artefacts, over those of antiquity; about the introduction of the "Christian marvellous" in the efforts notably by Chapelain, Saint-Amant, Le Moyne, Georges de Scudéry, and Desmarets to produce a Christian and national epic; over the relative merits of French and Latin debated by Le Laboureur and Desmarets de Saint-Sorlin between 1667 and the 1673 edition of Desmarets's *Clovis*; over the language to be used for the inscription of Louis XIV's triumphal arch at the Porte Saint-Antoine in 1670; it emerged in the quarrels surrounding Racine's *Iphigénie* and *Phèdre*; the disputes closely following the death of Colbert in 1683 which culminated in those of the Académie française in 1687 and 1688; and the altercation about translating Homer, centring on Mme Dacier and Houdar de la Motte at the start of the second decade of the 18th century.

The literary skirmishes should be regarded as small eruptions disturbing the smooth progress of the renaissance attempt to view what was natural and instinctive in human experience as something which could also be morally enriching and spiritually fulfilling. That is one of the principal reasons why the *Querelle* is intimately bound up with disputes about love, about marriage, about the intellectual capacities of women, and about their role in society. It is the name now given to some or all of the literary clashes referred to, episodes in the battle, inaugurated in the renaissance and won in the 18th century, to gain recognition for human instinct as a guide to virtue, to affirm human perfectibility, and to envisage the inevitability of perpetual moral and social progress, after late medieval religion, and the theology which had accompanied it, had urged Christians to the intense moral effort of doing "everything which lay within them" while remaining totally dependent for salvation on an apparently arbitrary divine decree.

The medieval view, in which human religious perfection was regarded as something extrinsic to moral achievement, had also been connected with views heavily suspicious of manifestations of human sexuality, and with attitudes envisaging women as socially and intellectually inferior to men, even as either temptresses or chattels. The literature of the period with which we are concerned, from 1500 to 1789, explored at least the inception of what we now regard as having been an urgently necessary adjustment. The morally enriching potential of human emotional and physical love had been vehicled by the widely adopted semi-mythological neoplatonism of Ficino, taken over in the northern renaissance from 15th-century Florence (see: Rabelais, Scève, Marguerite de Navarre), in which love for an earthly creature was the first step on the ladder of ascent to the love of God. For this reason Ficinian neoplatonism, sometimes joined with a justification of instinctive human love in terms of the merit of its object (see: Pierre Corneille, d'Urfé, du Vair), always appears on the side of the "modernes," although a priori it might have been expected that the unchanging nature of the Platonic ideas would have provided a plank to support the contention of the "anciens" that there were immutable and unchanging norms to which antique authors had approached as nearly as was possible, and that both perfectibility and unending progress were chimera.

Although the *Querelle* is normally regarded primarily as a series of literary disputes about aesthetic and moral norms, it was connected with phenomena in both philosophy and experimental science generally linked with the rejection of authority. Authority, the weapon of the supporters of the anciens, was attacked in philosophy in the name of rational argument, as in Descartes, and even in theology, although later and more dangerously, by Richard Simon, who applied critical norms to the text of scripture. In the experimental sciences authority was eroded by empirical investigation, even in astronomy, where the results appearing throughout the 17th century following on the discovery of the telescope, developed by Galileo from 1609 to 1612, increasingly appeared to be at variance with the revelation of the creation in *Genesis*, still considered to have been written by Moses. Galileo was made the subject of an ecclesiastical disciplinary decree in 1616, which allowed him to hold his views only hypothetically, but he was in further trouble in 1633 for flagrant breach of the conditions imposed in 1616, and spent 18 days in April imprisoned in the most comfortable quarters of the palace of the Inquisition. On 22 June, after interrogation, he made a formal submission, but from 1616 onwards the Church was aware of the potential challenge from experimental science to the authority of *Genesis*.

The earlier part of the 17th century had established in France a climate of unrestrained optimism, only partly explained by the need for cultural confidence to catch up with the continuing progress of renaissance cultural buoyancy in England, Spain, and Italy and east of the Rhine. The development of d'Urfé's writing from the *Epîtres morales* through the various parts of

L'Astrée shows how he turned away from the neostoicism of the religious wars to the Ficinian neoplatonist scaffolding supporting new cultural values. The baroque adventure novel was sometimes puerile in its exuberance. François de Sales, subsequently both canonized for his personal sanctity and made a doctor of the Church in recognition of the integrity of his teaching, not only had allowed the legitimacy of dancing and cosmetics but had erected the whole of his spirituality, an exigent one however flowery his style, on what he calls the natural desire to love God. Descartes had swept all previous philosophy aside in an attempt to unify the body of the sciences, founding a new, universal science on absolutely certain metaphysical foundations, and was at least in 1637 confident that, by improvements in medicine, he could also produce a doctrine of behaviour which would infallibly lead not only to virtue, but actually even to happiness. Pierre Corneille in *Le Cid* had explored the possibility that human love, based on sufficient merit, could be sufficiently enriching to permit the marriage of Rodrigue to Chimène, whose father he had just killed.

It is true that the optimism was being undermined by the Oratorian form of neoplatonism behind the spirituality of Bérulle and particularly Condren's view that spiritual progress consisted of nature's annihilation and replacement by a life of grace; that Gibieuf was producing the matching theology, only the terminology of which was to be repudiated by Jansen (q.v.) and in the 1630s Saint-Cyran's spirituality was reversing the confident spiritual attitudes of Zamet (see: Port-Royal); that the Fronde was soon going to impose severe suffering on parts of France; that Jansenism would gain ground in Paris; and that the hesitations about passion shown in Madeleine de Scudéry's 1654 Carte de tendre and the *préciosité* (q.v.) of 1657 and the years immediately following would foreshadow the questioning of the confidence in the present shown during the various episodes of the *Querelle*. But it was not until the establishment of the ascendancy of Colbert, paradoxically the principal architect of the glorification of the ruling monarch as a strategy in French cultural policy, and the fall of the financiers with Foucquet in 1661, which Colbert accomplished, that the repeated skirmishes suggested any serious wave of reactionary doubts about the propriety of replacing authorities with reason or experiment, and that the tentative upgrading of properly controlled instinctive behaviour came seriously to be questioned.

Paradoxically, too, it had been Ronsard and his associates who had turned to the major, and sometimes the minor, authors of antiquity in the great outbreak of renaissance confidence in human nature which had been the predominant feature of the French renaissance around 1550. Malherbe had attempted to prune back what he regarded as the neoclassical and other excesses of the Pléiade, especially in language and prosody, but he had not attacked the authority of Aristotle, to which even Pierre Corneille's theoretical writings of 1660 pay deference. The first really substantial attack on the Aristotelian hegemony came in philosophy in 1637, with Descartes's announcement of his intentions in the *Discours de la méthode*, and in theology in 1640 with Jansen's (q.v.) *Augustinus*. In spite of Boileau's 1671 *Arrêt burlesque* and Bossuet's early protection of upholders of the new philosophy, the links—which were never more than loose and were rooted in antagonism to specifically anti-Aristotelian authority—to be found in a Boileau or a Bossuet, between support for a Jansenist Augustinianism in theology and antique authority in literature, were to be expected, like the alliance between philosophical Cartesianism and theological Jansenism among the solitaires at Port-Royal (q.v.)

The first important victories of Cartesianism outside professional philosophical and theological circles are connected with the circle of Habert de Montmort, maître des requêtes, cousin of Philippe and Germain Habert and, like them, an early member of the new Académie française, the abbé de Marolles, a well-connected parasite of the world of letters but also a famous collector of engravings, and the brilliant young lawyer and later companion of Bossuet, Claude Fleury. It was from this circle that emanated the first signs of conflict. The list of national and Christian epics owing more in mid-17th-century France to Tasso than to Homer or Virgil, and replacing fate, destiny, and the hostile gods of antiquity with the miracles, demons, angels, and magicians of Christian and romanesque mythologies, is normally held to include Pierre Le Moyne's 1653 *Saint Louys; ou, Le Héros chrestien*, Antoine Godeau's 1654 *Saint Paul, poème chrestien*, Georges de Scudéry's 1654 *Alaric; ou, Rome vaincue*, Chapelain's 1656 *La Pucelle; ou, La France délivrée*, and Desmarets's 1657 *Clovis; ou, La France chrestienne*. A little later came Louis le Laboureur's 1664 *Charlemagne, poëme héroïque* and Carel de Saint-Garde's epic on Charles Martel, the 1667 *Les Sarrazins chassez de France*, and there were further poems on biblical subjects: Jacques de Coras's 1663 *Jonas* and 1665 *David*, and Desmarets de Saint-Sorlin's 1669 *Marie-Madeleine* and 1670 *Esther*. This list, often repeated, is in fact not exhaustive.

It was in 1662 that the abbé Michel de Marolles, protected by César d'Estrées, although always hostile to that which was merely galant and had threatened to oust Malherbe, Maynard, Gombauld, Chapelain, and Cotin, dedicated to Habert de Montmort his *Traité du poème épique*, defending the Cartesian criterion of "bon sens (common sense)," much as Sorel had used it to attack Furetière's assault on antique authority disguised as "Galimatias" in the 1659 *Nouvelle allégorique; ou, Histoire des derniers troubles arrivez au Royaume d'Eloquence*. Marolles and Habert de Montmort, representing what might be termed literary Cartesianism, were implacably opposed to all the literary values which Pellisson and Madeleine de Scudéry stood for. The alliance between the Cartesians, in favour of a modern epic, and the salon amateurs of galanteries, more interested in madrigals, both eventually to join forces in the camp of the modernes, had not yet been formed, but although Marolles did not like Chapelain's *Pucelle* he none the less advocated the adaptation of the modern epic to contemporary taste and Christian belief. Two years later, in 1664, Louis Le Laboureur preceded his *Charlemagne*, in which an angel expounds the philosophy of Descartes, with an important essay defending the epic, declaring the Christian and patriotic intention "de paroistre également bon Chrestien et bon François (to appear equally a good Christian and a good Frenchman)," which Colbert was seeking to promote.

Claude Fleury's unpublished but highly important 1665 *Lettre sur Homère* could still idealize mankind's primitive state. He refused to accept that the coarseness of manners and roughness of behaviour of Homer's day, later to be castigated by Perrault, precluded genuine nobility. "Peut-être," he wrote, "y avoit-il plus de finesse, d'art et de véritable politesse dans le monde du temps d'Homère que du nôtre (Perhaps there was more delicacy, more subtlety, and more courtesy in the world in Homer's time than there is in ours)." In 1667 Le Laboureur not only attacked neo-Latin poetry in *Les Avantages de la langue françoise sur la langue latine*, dedicated to Habert de Montmort and reissued in 1669, but went so far as to hold the superiority over anything written in antiquity of Philippe and Germain Habert's 1637 *Temple de la mort*, an elegy on the death of Marie Ruzé d'Effiat, the first wife of the maréchal de la Meilleraye, and their *La Métamorphose des yeux de Philis en astres*, holding that a living language, like French, must be superior to a dead one, like Latin. Together with the early Pléiade's excited, if still patchy, enthusiasm about the potential of human experience, Le Laboureur inherited their advocacy of the cultivation of the vernacular, but it was precisely the two Habert pieces he mentioned that Rapin chose to attack in his treatise *Du grand ou du sublime dans les moeurs*, written in 1674–5. Opposing attitudes were becoming discernible in different cultivated circles in Paris, but their expression was for the most part restrained to the level of intelligent debate.

The *Querelle* is normally assumed to have started a few years later, although Descartes had long separated off divine truths from the truths belonging to the universal science to be founded on reason alone, and Pascal had clearly distinguished between the sciences which depended on memory, and therefore authority, and those which depended on reasoning, like the empirical sciences. Each philosopher, in fact for theological reasons, was driving a wedge between what should be regarded as deriving from reason and what should depend on authority. La Mothe le Vayer's 1669 *Mémorial de quelques conférences* introduced a clearly Cartesian advocate of the superiority of the culture of the *modernes* into his group of characters.

At this point Desmarets, preparing the new edition of *Clovis*, weighed in heavily on the side of the modernes with his characteristic lack of restraint. His *La Comparaison de la langue et de la poësie Françoise, avec la Grecque et la Latine, Et des Poëtes Grecs, Latins et Françoys* maintained that the question should be judged not by academics but by persons of taste, by which he meant women. He praised a number of near-contemporary poets and novelists but, while undoubtedly lowering the intellectual tone of the discussion and increasing its stridency, he forged the alliance of the party of galanteries with that of the modern epic. The new 1673 edition of *Clovis* appeared with a provocative *Traité pour juger des Poëtes Grecs, Latins et François*, attacking the "Faux doctes (pseudo-erudite)," who defended the authority of the antique. Marolles replied with a defence of Virgil and *Observations sur le poème de Clovis*. In July 1674 appeared the long-awaited *L'Art poétique* of Boileau.

The young Boileau was witty as a satirist but intellectually never more than shallow, and although he was neither gifted as a poet nor in any real sense learned, he became increasingly pompous as he grew older. For *L'Art poétique* he depended heavily on Claude Fleury, whom he knew through the important salon of the premier président of the Paris parlement, Guillaume de Lamoignon, the doctrine of whose *Lettre sur Homère* Boileau's poem reduces to maxims spiced with personal invective. Lamoignon, a member of the Compagnie du Saint-Sacrement until its suppression, and totally hostile to Colbert's centralizing intiatives, also received often learned supporters of the modernes, like the Jesuit Père René Rapin.

After a period in which there were irregular private meetings, Lamoignon held a series of weekly conferences on Mondays from 5 to 7 p.m. for the discussion of previously announced subjects, attended by some major members of the magistracy, by Lamoignon's close friend Guy Patin, by Pellisson, by Géraud de Cordemoy, author of the 1666 *Discernement du corps et de l'âme*, occasionally by such staunch Cartesians as Jacques Rohault and Claude Clerselier, and a little later by Huet, Bossuet, and La Bruyère. Politically inclined to pacifism and with an openness favourable to Cartesianism, the salon none the less allowed room for open intellectual discussion, and it was on the basis of what he heard there that Rapin published his defence of scholastic philosophy and of Aristotle in the 1676 *Réflexions sur la philosophie ancienne et moderne et sur l'usage qu'on en doit faire pour la religion* and, at the request of Lamoignon himself, his 1678 *La Comparaison de Platon et d'Aristote avec les sentiments des Pères sur leur doctrine*.

On literary topics, we know that on 11 July 1667 Pellisson gave a conference on Tasso's life and spoke on 2 August about Homer and Virgil. At Lamoignon's request Rapin defended Virgil against Homer on 18 November, and the opposite viewpoint was taken in a discourse improvised by Guy Patin's son, Charles. On 16 January 1668 Fleury addressed the assembly on Herodotus and in 1670 he spoke about Plato. Later that year Bossuet spoke on biblical poetry and, on 5 January 1671, Pellisson on the problems of writing history. The literary tone is given by the titles of Rapin's compilatory accounts of comparisons of Homer and Virgil, Demosthenes and Cicero, Plato and Aristotle, Thucydides and Livy, with *Réflexions* on poetry, history, philosophy, and eloquence. Discussions on these and no doubt similar topics carried on until Lamoignon's death in 1677.

The Lamoignon salon, generally hostile to Colbert, was perhaps on that account not unfavourable to Foucquet, balancing an openness to Cartesianism with a bias towards conservatism and, according to Rapin, a preference for nobility and simplicity over both erudition and a galanterie associated with female salon taste, a style in which women could do as well as men, and the "ignorance universelle des gens de qualité (the universal ignorance of the nobility." The debate between the Cartesian, moderne approach to philosophy and the authority of Aristotle, together with a literary discussion about the stature of Homer, was not, at the Hôtel de Lamoignon, accompanied by any enthusiasm for the vogue for love poetry, or even, apparently, for the nationalistic epic.

It is in the works above all of Claude Fleury that the primitive virtues and attitudes of Homer's day, and the qualities of his poetry, are linked with the early days of Israel. After the *Lettre sur Homère*, of primordial importance in the discussion, came the 1670 *Discours sur Platon*, showing the conformity of practice between the ancient biblical patriarchs and the citizens of Plato's ideal state; then in 1673 the *Histoire de la poésie antique*, indicating the similarity of inspiration between antique Greek and ancient Hebrew religious poetry; and then the 1681 *Moeurs des Israélites où l'on voit le modèle d'une politique simple et sincère pour le gouvernement des Etats et la réforme des moeurs*, demonstrating the similarity between the habits of the primitive Greeks, Jews, Orientals, and Romans. The Jews, as the chosen people, were merely the best example of a natural community until the true norms were laid down with the coming of Jesus. The early Greeks, Romans, people of the east, and Jews would have made better Christians than modern lawyers, financiers, and doctors, and we have got the balance wrong between the peasants, who produce food, and the cumbersome superstructure of courtiers, lawyers, and financiers, who live well, contribute nothing to the common good, and impose so many constraints on the freedom of the rest of the population.

Les moeurs sont si différentes des nôtres, que d'abord elles nous choquent. Nous ne voyons chez les Israélites ni ces titres de noblesse, ni cette multitude d'offices, ni cette diversité des conditions qui se trouvent parmi nous; ce ne sont que des laboureurs et des bergers, tous travaillent de leurs mains... il y a une noble simplicité meilleure que tous les raffinements...On apprend alors à distinguer, [en] ce que leurs moeurs ont de choquant pour nous, ce qui est effectivement blamable; ce qui vient de la seule distance des temps et des lieux étant de soi indifférent; et ce qui étant de bonne foi ne nous déplaît que par la corruption de nos moeurs

(The customs are so different from ours that at first they shock us. We do not see in the Jews either those titles of nobility, or that multiplicity of offices, or that difference in social standing which we ourselves have; they are only ploughmen and shepherds, all working with their hands... there is a noble simplicity better than all our refinements... Then we learn to distinguish in what shocks us about their customs what is really to be blamed, what, itself indifferent, simply comes from the differences of time and place, and what if we were honest we would admit displeases us only on account of the corruption of our morals).

Fleury has skilfully defended the primitive for its nobility and simplicity, implicitly condemned his own generation for its division by social distinctions, admitted that his view of society is dominated by his view of it as corrupt, and connected a Jansenistically tinged spirituality with an inchoate defence of the anciens. Most of the social criticism of La Bruyère and Fénelon is already in Fleury at the latest in 1681, and he is particularly strong on the need for the prince not to put himself above the law. Princes like David and Ulysses are described as richer in lands, herds, and possessions than others, but they have no powers over other people, and there is no instance of the royal promulgation in Israel of any new law.

It was in the Hôtel de Lamoignon, inclined to oppose moderne positions except in philosophy, that the more serious issues presented by the *Querelle* in the 1670s were intelligently argued out, although it is naturally the public polemics and temperamental rivalries which have caught the attention of historians. The Hôtel was generally hostile to Perrault on account of what he had been doing, before he fell from favour during the early 1670s, to help Colbert to glorify the monarch and to control cultural policy through the granting or withholding of gratifications, and Boileau disliked Desmarets de Saint-Sorlin strongly enough for his feelings to account for his opposition to the whole idea of a Christian epic, against which the case he presents is embarrassingly trivial. The Hôtel's social criticism of the government's handling of the nation's wealth, although only broadly relevant to the various individual literary episodes of the *Querelle*, is ultimately of greater significance than the literary aesthetics, but the literary importance of the Hôtel de Lamoignon can be gauged from the way Boileau's *L'Art poétique*, the great manifesto of the partisans of the anciens, can be seen to be little more than the dressing up of Fleury's strong literary aesthetic in banal aphorisms.

It seems in fact likely that Boileau was less than totally committed to his own doctrine. His behaviour has been cogently presented as opportunistic and successful social climbing in the years previous to 1674. He had had himself invited to read his material before Scarron's widow, later Mme de Maintenon, Mme de Lafayette and Mme de Sévigné, Ninon de Lenclos and La Rochefoucauld, and he became acceptable in the Condé household, for which he had cause to be grateful after the incidents following the first night of Racine's *Phèdre*, while still attracting the protection of Mme de Montespan and her sister, Mme de Thiange. He even managed to read the Jansenizing eighth *Satire* of 1668, expressly approved by Antoine Arnauld and ironically dedicated to the anti-Jansenist Claude Morel, in the salon of Mme Colbert, no doubt because, for the first time clearly showing his derivation from the Hôtel de Lamoignon, he took Colbert's side against Louvois in advocating a peaceful foreign policy.

Mme de Sévigné, who did not like Racine's *Bajazet*, said that Boileau thought even worse of it than she did, and Bussy mentions Boileau's reference to writing in alexandrines as "psalmody." Boileau had used that word in the first canto of *L'Art poétique*, but had not there been alluding to everything written in 12–syllable rhyming lines. By 1674 he was cautious about what he said in public. That he did not understand the real strength of the ancien position is confirmed by his views that the antique myths are simply ornamentation, as in his view also was the Christian marvellous. Fleury's arguments from primitive dignity and nobility are much stronger, and to see what was really at stake in the *Querelle* it is necessary to consider the contextualization of the epic by Fleury in its historical period and setting, rather than the clashing of conventions to which Boileau reduced Fleury's critical analysis of the aesthetic and moral confrontation.

After the polemics of Le Laboureur and Desmarets between 1667 and 1673, the publication of *L'Art poétique* marked the serious opening of literary hostilities. In 1670 a dispute had already begun about the language to be used for the inscription on the foundation stone of a triumphal arch it was proposed to build in honour of Louis XIV near the Porte Saint-Antoine in the Place du Trône. The stone was laid on 6 August 1670. The arch was never finished, and there was never an inscription, but for some years it had been hotly disputed whether the inscription should be in Latin or French, with the Jesuits and the university, for once on the same side, advocating Latin, while the majority at the Académie was for French.

Desmarets published his 1670 *Comparaison*, with one of his remarkable appeals to female taste:

Même les femmes...à proportion qu'elles ont connu des hommes qui ont les sentiments élevés et delicats... jugeront qu'un esprit à l'antiquité et un héros tel qu'Enée ne les ferait jamais tomber dans un désastre semblable à celui de Didon

(Even women...to the extent to which they have been acquainted with men endowed with refined and delicate feelings...will know that an antique attitude and a hero like Aeneas would never cause them to fall into a disaster like Dido's).

Desmarets here went on to combine his advocacy of the advancement of women and a higher appreciation of their intellectual, emotional, and spiritual capabilities, with his promotion of a modern epic which was both nationalistic and Christian. It should however be noted that Desmarets, his protector and employer Richelieu, and the other protégés of Richelieu, Huet, Charpentier, and Charles Perrault, were all anti-Cartesian. The philosophy of Descartes had been enthusiastically embraced by the literary advocates of the *modernes* only early, at the Hôtel de Lamoignon, by the Port-Royal solitaires and Arnauld, recognizing the inspiration of Bérulle and welcoming the anti-Aristotelianism, and by the early Huet, before the religious dangers of reason as an anti-religious weapon were sufficiently developed to be alarming. Nature, for Desmarets, coming from God, was perfect from the beginning, but art, of human creation, admits of and indeed requires progress.

Louis Le Laboureur's 1669 *Avantage de la langue française sur la langue latine* had already argued the view for the vernacular, and even the Jesuit Dominique Bouhours in the 1671 *Les Entretiens d'Ariste et d'Eugène* urged the superiority of French over all other languages and the equality of French literature in most of the genres with that of antiquity. Charpentier was an undistinguished incense-burner to the regime, paid for his services with an annual gratification of 1,500 livres and interested only in language, but he knew Greek. When, in 1676, the Académié des Inscriptions discussed the language of the Porte Saint-Antoine inscription, he published his 1676 *Défense de la langue françoise pour l'inscription de l'arc de triomphe*, to be followed in 1683 by *De l'excellence de la langue française*. A 1676 Jesuit discourse about the inscription was published in 1677, and answered in the same year by Marolles with a pamphlet in favour of the use of French. On the Latin side, with the Jesuits, was the *Discours en faveur des inscriptions des monuments publics faites en latin* of Amable de Bourzéys, who received an annual gratification of 3,000 livres, and who was a member, with Perrault, of Colbert's petit conseil. He successfully proposed to Colbert the recruitment to the council of Charpentier. Boileau meditated a satirical dialogue against the advocates of Latin, but he never wrote it down. The two texts we have of the brief *Dialogue des poètes* were written down by Brossette after an account by Boileau in 1702.

The achevé d'imprimer of Boileau's *L'Art poétique* is dated 10 July 1674. There were a number of incidents relevant to the *Querelle*, some perhaps coincidental, over the following six weeks. On 13 August Huet was received into the Académie française. This was the occasion on which Quinault, Charles Perrault, and Desmarets all read out triumphalist anti-*ancien* poems. A few days later Charpentier sent another to Charles Perrault. The privilège for Desmarets's reply to *L'Art poétique* is dated 25 July, and Saturday 18 August 1674, three weeks later, is the date of the achevé d'imprimer of that riposte, *La Deffense du Poëme heroïque, avec quelques remarques sur les Oeuvres satyriques du Sieur D****. *Dialogues en Vers et en Prose*. It is also the date of the first performance of Racine's delayed *Iphigénie*, at Versailles, with La Champmeslé in the lead, to celebrate Louis XIV's victory in Franche-Comté. The first public performance in Paris at the Hôtel de Bourgogne was probably before the end of December. Racine had uncharacteristically missed a season, having presented nothing new for 1673–74. It is possible that he was considering the abandonment of his theatrical career, but it seems certain that the cause of the delay, and probably of the initial presentation at Versailles rather than in Paris, had to do with the *Querelle* and the rival *Iphigénie* by Jacques Coras and Michel le Clerc, whose performance Racine had had delayed until it was put on by the Guénégaud

company on 24 May 1675. Its failure cannot have displeased him.

Much that was once taken for granted in the history of dramatic entertainment in 17th-century France has become open to question in the light of the virtually graduated distinction of genres it is becoming necessary to admit, not only between farce, comedy, tragi-comedy, heroic comedy, and tragedy, but also according to the reliance put in any particular entertainment on unscripted drama in the style of *commedia dell'arte* (q.v.), scripted drama, singing, dancing, music alone, stage "effects" contrived with or without swings, hoists, and pulleys and changes of lighting or decor, or on some mixture of any two or more of these. Where it used to be possible to think in terms of firmly compartmentalized genres, it is now necessary to recognize that there were often only graded distinctions between them (see: Georges de Scudéry).

In the immediate context of Racine's *Iphigénie*, that of Coras and Le Clerc, and the Quinault-Lulli *Alceste*, played at court from November 1673 but in Paris at the Palais-Royal only from 11 January 1674, it is not prudent to distinguish too emphatically between tragedy and opera, which may also have been an entertainment with sections of scripted drama to be spoken as well as sung. *Alceste* is often called an opera. In fact it was known as a "tragédie lyrique" or a "tragédie en musique" and, although an anonymous *Remarques sur les Iphigénies de M. Racine et de M. Coras* appeared on 26 May, apparently assuming that they were both intended to provide the same form of entertainment, the title of Pierre Perrault's 1675 (achevé d'imprimer of 2 January 1675) defence of Quinault against the animosity provoked in Lulli's rivals by the monopoly of music he had acquired implies at least here the interchangeability between tragedy and opera: *Critique de l'opéra ou examen de la tragédie intitulée Alceste ou le Triomphe d'Alcide*.

Quinault's script for *Alceste* clearly relies on stage effects and changes of scenery. There is no more striving for probability or psychological profundity than in the dramatization of a modern fairy story. There is a chorus; an oracle gives hope that the day may yet be saved; Admète, helped by Hercule, saves Alceste from her abductors, but is dying from his wounds; Alceste offers her life for his; the chorus laments; Hercule says that he loves Alceste and will go and find her in the nether world; he crosses the Styx in Charon's boat; and the entertainment ends with his triumphant return. We know that Lulli's music, following Monteverdi and Luigi Rossi, was endowing mythological subjects with emotional intensity. The script suggests a series of operatic tableaux, with not much dramatic development within scenes and almost no psychological depth at all, but too often the bare script is an inadequate guide even to what was said, as in some of Molière's plays, and only the hazards of survival which have preserved letters, diaries, chronicles, and engravings provide occasional guidance on what sort of theatrical experience was actually being offered.

The terrain is firmer if we consider subject matter. Across the genres, and however the myths were treated, there was very shortly after 1670 a movement away from political subjects towards a stronger concentration on Greek myth as the basis for new literary, dramatic, or operatic creation. Quinault and Lulli may have been inspired by movements in Italian taste, but they presented together *Les Fêtes de l'Amour et de Bacchus* in 1672 and, in 1673, *Cadmus et Hermione*. Straight scripted tragedy also appears to have turned with augmented pace to Greek themes, arousing on the whole the fury of the defenders of the anciens by introducing contemporary galanterie into the treatment of antique myth. Fleury even wanted lavishness of costume restricted with the removal of "tendernesses and sweetnesses." Rapin's views, to be developed in his *Réflexions sur la Poétique*, are already clear in the 1672 letters to Bussy-Rabutin:

C'est dégrader la Tragédie de cet air de majesté qui lui est propre que d'y mêler de l'amour, qui est un caractère trop badin et peu conforme à cette gravité dont elle fait profession

(To mingle love with tragedy is to deprive it of that air of nobility which is proper to it, imparting to it too frivolous an appearance, too little in conformity with the gravity to which it is committed).

Racine's privilège for *Iphigénie* is dated 28 January 1675; there is no achevé. The attack of the preface on Pierre Perrault's defence of Quinault is harsh, indeed arrogant. Racine, whose Greek was good, scoffs at Quinault's ignorance of the language, as at Pierre Perrault's, and makes much of the attribution to Admetus of lines allocated to Alcestis in Euripides. It was probably Charles, not Pierre, Perrault who replied to Racine in a *Lettre à M. Charpentier sur la préface de l'Iphigénie de M. Racine*, but Colbert had his second edition suppressed, not wanting one of his officials to be seen in public opposition to a protégé of Mme de Montespan, whom he much hated but whom he did not wish to offend over such a matter. It must in the meanwhile be remembered that Racine, good though his Greek was, had no monopoly of classical learning. Charpentier had started his career by translating from Greek, and Huet was a philologist.

It has been suggested that it was Boileau's posturing dogmatism which pushed Charpentier and Huet into the opposite camp. Racine's sense of drama and the Greeks' feeling for the implacable destiny against which men and women could only struggle fitted one another too closely for Racine ever not to have been destined to be on the side of the anciens, but Desmarets was still in 1670 citing him as an example of a modern poet who could rival the best of antiquity. It was Racine's inability to resist the attack on Pierre Perrault in the early 1675 preface to *Iphigénie* that crystallized the alignment into two camps, of which that supporting the anciens was much the smaller and weaker. Racine was to retire from the fight in 1677, and Boileau was not a very formidable opponent. Had he intervened in the matter of the language for the arch, it would have been on the side of the advocates of the vernacular. Was he simply, if inconsistently, swayed towards the vernacular by his dislike of the Jesuits, who believed in baroque style, baroque values, the Christian epic, but Latin? Carel de Sainte-Garde did not find it difficult in his 1675 *Défense des beaux-esprits de ce temps contre un satyrique* to teach Boileau a lesson simply by writing a eulogy of Ronsard, who was still best known for his imitation and rehabilitation of classical authors, and on whose side Boileau ought plainly to have been, if he had had any real knowledge of the Pléiade (q.v.) programme, or feeling for the history of the literature for which he pretended to legislate.

Boileau's *L'Art poétique* had been particularly savage about Claude Perrault. At this point Colbert nearly did intervene on the Perrault side, but Charles Perrault was already beginning to fall

out of favour and Colbert had not been a witness at his marriage in 1672. Claude Perrault had to content himself with circulating the satirical fable *Le Corbeau guéri par la Cigogne; ou, L'Ingrat parfait*. There was to be a lull before the next episode of the *Querelle*, but it is already clear that what was at stake was indeed deeper than personal antipathies, and had more to do with underlying values than with literary or philosophical norms. Neither advocacy nor rejection of Cartesian rationality as a criterion in philosophy, nor empirical evidence as a criterion in empirical science, nor a literary preference for primitive simplicity over degenerate refinement, nor the preferability of equality of dignity over distinctions of rank, nor the desirability of a Christian or a nationalistic epic, nor any matter of literary taste or language fully explains the alignments. What was at stake was the possibility of making the human community better and happier, whether and how the progress and perfectibility might be achieved of which the renaissance had begun to explore the possibility.

Desmarets might have been uplifted by a semi-deranged exaltation, but he was to die in 1676, just as the first flames of the *Querelle* died down. If he had put his view more soberly, universalized his vision more broadly, and eliminated the purely nationalistic elements in his thought, it might have been very difficult to disagree with him when he addressed his reader about the *Querelle*:

On te fait juge du plus grand différent qui soit maintenant au monde, et qui sera jamais, puisqu'il s'agit de juger la Grèce, Rome et la France, et les siècles passés, et le présent; et de juger encore si les Français doivent céder pour jamais la gloire du langage et du génie aux Grecs et aux Latins

(You are being made the judge of the greatest affair that is at present facing the world, or ever will. It means passing judgement on Greece, Rome, and France; on the centuries gone by, and the present; and passing judgement too on whether the French should yield for ever the glory of their language and their spirit to the Greeks and the Romans).

At issue was the question of the fundamental personal and social values of the human community. Focal points had clearly to be the relationship of human beings with God, the nature of virtue, its relationship to happiness, the reliability of human instinct as a guide, and the relationship between the sexes. All these matters were raised, alongside those of literary models and questions of language, by the *Querelle*.

The embers flared up again in the late 1680s. The alignments and the issues were now both clearer and, now that the court had moved, we hear of the division between the "gens de Versailles" and the "gens de la ville" or the "beaux esprits de Paris," the young patricians who did not relish spending their time at Versailles. The supporters of the antique had become stronger and more numerous, and now included Henri-François d'Aguesseau, to be Louis XV's chancellor, together with Condé, Conti, Arnauld, Bossuet, and those who frequented the duchesse du Maine at Sceaux. The supporters of moderne positions were grouped round Donneau de Visé and Thomas Corneille at the *Mercure galant* (q.v.) and Mme Deshoulières, and included not only Quinault, the abbé Boyer, the Tallemant family, Bensserade, Charpentier, and Perrault, but also, from Port-Royal, M. de

Saci. They were heavily aided by the thought of Malebranche and Bayle, and soon to be joined by Fontenelle and Houdar de la Motte.

The alignment remains marginally puzzling. The more open-minded partisans of the moderne positions ought, one would have thought, to have opposed the absolutist pretensions of Louis XIV. In fact the pretensions, inherited from Richelieu and Mazarin, were those of Colbert, strongly abetted by Perrault. The cultural establishment was required to sing the monarch's praises and record his deeds because, in the minds of Colbert and Perrault, the elevation of Louis XIV into the Sun King was a strategic move for the promotion of France's well-being. It was only with reluctance that Colbert allowed Louis XIV to fight the Dutch war, and built for him the preposterous palace at Versailles, although he knew France could afford neither grandiose gesture. It was La Bruyère, a supporter of the antique, and Fénelon, whose literary tastes put him on the same side, who most notoriously drew attention to the pitiful plight to which the king's unrestrained ambitions had reduced the country. Colbert's own taste, as shown by the whole pattern of his non-literary patronage, was restrained, deliberately contrasting with the flamboyance of Foucquet. In painting, Colbert promoted Lebrun, whose 1661 masterpiece *La Tente de Darius* was to be challenged by Mignard's 1689 treatment of the same subject, commissioned by Louvois. But politically, Colbert's strategy was to backfire badly after his death, when Louvois indulged the taste for glory which Louis XIV, on the pedestal designed for him by Colbert, could scarcely have helped developing.

The paradox, however, is only apparent, and resolves itself if the *Querelle* is placed in a broader context, with its literary episodes seen as surface disturbances, almost as epiphenomena, which is what they actually were, and were recognized by at least the more important participants to be. La Bruyère may have been a gloomy observer of human folly, but he deplored it and, like Fénelon or Condé, belonged on issues more important than the literary ones with the reformers, and on the side of the modernes. Perrault's orchestration of the cultural part of Colbert's strategy, as he made clear in the *Siècle de Louis le Grand* and the *Parallèle des anciens et des modernes*, went hand in hand with his strong commitment to the belief that the 17th century did mark an immense improvement in behaviour, attitudes, manners, personal and social values, religion, and relations between the sexes over the coarse roughness of Greek antiquity. Perrault was himself to publish a Christian poem, *Saint-Paulin*, in 1686, and in 1675 Desmarets had summoned him to take over the moderne torch in his *La Defense de la Poësie, et de la langue françoise. Addressée à Monsieur Perrault*:

Viens défendre, Perrault, la France qui t'appelle;
Viens combattre avec moy cette troupe rebelle,
Ce ramas d'ennemis qui, faibles et mutins,
Préfèrent à nos chants des ouvrages latins

(Come, Perrault, to the defence of France who calls out to you;/Come and fight with me this rebellious gang,/This rabble of enemies who, weak and mutinous,/Prefer to our poetry works in Latin).

Perrault, a decade or so after Desmarets, was to identify much more penetratingly the clash of values which was at issue.

In the important *De la recherche de la vérité où l'on traite de la nature de l'esprit de l'homme et de l'usage qu'il en doit faire pour éviter l'erreur dans les sciences*, of which three volumes were published in 1674 and three in 1675, the Oratorian Nicolas Malebranche identified respect for the antique among the sources of human error. The modern world, with more experience than the ancient, must also be more enlightened. In so far as the moderne party had a philosophical position in the 1680s, it was Malebranche who provided it. Bossuet was later to quarrel with him on theological grounds and, later again, Malebranche's dispute with Père François Lamy put him into a new alliance with Bossuet in Bossuet's crusade against what he regarded as quietism, but in *De la recherche de la vérité* Malebranche scarcely touches on the theology of grace to which Bossuet was to object.

None the less, until nearly the end of the century, Bossuet and Malebranche were to remain on different sides in both philosophical and theological debate, while the moderne position for which Malebranche provided the articulate philosophical foundation was to be boosted by the publication of both Bayle's 1682 *Pensées sur la comète* and three no doubt philosophically lightweight and entertainingly written, but in this context important, works by Fontenelle, the 1683 *Dialogues des morts*, the 1686 *Entretiens sur la pluralité des mondes*, which has a woman as interlocutor in dialogues about cosmology, and the 1688 *Digression sur les anciens et les modernes*.

Pierre Perrault died in 1680. In 1678 he had by implication satirized Boileau's *Le Lutrin*, itself a mock heroic poem, to which Boileau was challenged, about a trivial dispute concerning the positioning of a lectern in 1667 in the Sainte-Chapelle, removed by a dignitary who thought it concealed him from public view. Pierre Perrault had translated Alessandro Tassoni's 1622 *La secchia rapita*, a mock heroic poem about a bucket stolen by the inhabitants of Modena from a well in Bologna but, apart from the Bayle and the Fontenelle publications, there were otherwise few serious skirmishes in the literary *Querelle* between those surrounding the publication in 1674 of *L'Art poétique* and 1687. There had been the disputed elections to the Académie française. La Fontaine, in semi-disgrace after the fall of Foucquet, had gradually been readmitted to favour, but the king refused to ratify La Fontaine's 1683 election until Boileau had been elected on 17 April 1674. On the other hand, on 22 January 1685 Furetière was expelled from the Académie when, after the victory of the moderne party in imposing their vision of the Académie's *Dictionnaire*, not as defining normative usage but as encapsulating the French language as it then was, including what Furetière, Mézeray, Patru, and Richelet regarded as degenerate contemporary salon usage, he took out the privilège for a dictionary of his own.

The first really important event of the 1680s in the literary *Querelle*, however, was the sitting of the Académie on 27 January 1687 when Perrault's poem on Louis XIV's recovery after his painful operation might have been expected to contain conventional praise of the achievements of the reign. And, indeed, formally it held to the restraints demanded by convention. In content, however, *Le Siècle de Louis le Grand* went on to attack the classical heritage of humanistic education itself. Perrault had apparently for years been containing what amounted to outrage that the least work of antiquity was religiously preferred to the "plus beaux ouvrages des modernes (finest works of the moderns)."

J'avoue que j'ai été blessé d'une telle injustice, il m'a paru tant d'aveuglement dans cette prévention et tant d'ingratitude à ne pas vouloir ouvrir les yeux sur la beauté de notre siècle à qui le ciel a départi mille lumières qu'il a refusées à toute l'antiquité que je n'ai pu m'empêcher d'en être ému d'une véritable indignation. C'a été cette indignation qui a produit le petit poème du siècle de Louis le Grand

(I admit that I was wounded by such an injustice; so much blindness seemed to me to lie in the prejudice, and so much ingratitude in the refusal to recognize the beauty of our century, on which heaven has bestowed a thousand insights it refused to all antiquity, that I was not able to prevent myself from being moved to real indignation. It was that indignation which produced the little poem on the age of Louis le Grand).

Boileau occasioned a public disturbance. He did not wish to hear that Plato's dialogues were boring, that Herodotus's grasp of history was slender, or that the telescope and the microscope had rendered Aristotle's scientific views obsolete. It is important to see that Perrault's attack concentrated where it was strongest, in the empirical sciences rather than the literary achievements. He was careful to praise the oratory of Cicero and Demosthenes, although they had greater causes than modern orators to defend, but he attacked the long speeches of the Homeric heroes, their sheer brutality, cruelty and moodiness, and praised a long list of modern French authors, mentioning Régnier, Maynard, Gombauld, Malherbe, Godeau, Racan, Sarrazin, Voiture, Molière, Rotrou, Tristan, and, above all, Pierre Corneille, but pointedly omitting Racine and Boileau, before proceeding through a review of painters and sculptors to the praise of modern music and to that synthesis of all the arts, over whose gestation he does not mention that he himself had presided, the palace of Versailles. For his assertion of the superiority of Lulli's music over that of antiquity, about which virtually nothing was known, Perrault was dependent on his brother Claude, the architect who also wrote *Savoir si la musique à plusieurs parties a été connue et mise en usage par les anciens.*

Charles Perrault goes on to make much of the argument with which Fontenelle would start his 1688 *Digression.* Everything comes down to realizing that nature was no less lavish with its gifts in the 17th century than it had been in antiquity:

A former les esprits comme à former les corps,
La nature en tout temps fait les mêmes efforts,
Son être est immuable, et cette force aisée
Dont elle produit tout, ne s'est point épuisée…
De cette même main les forces infinies
Produisent en tout temps de semblables génies

(In forming minds, as in forming bodies,/Nature has in all periods made the same efforts./Its essence does not change, and the easy strength/With which it produces everything, has not been exhausted…/With the same hand the infinite forces/Produce in all periods similar manifestations of genius).

Perrault's argument was naturally strengthened by the universal agreement that everything between antiquity and the 16th century was a period of dark ages, not to be counted in any his-

tory of human progress. Then there had been the religious wars; so that contemporary cultural superiority over antiquity had very largely to have been developed within little more than the half-century preceding Perrault's poem, not much more than the life of the reigning monarch for whose image-building Perrault had largely had the responsibility and on behalf of whose minister, Colbert, Perrault, although technically only supervisor of buildings, had taken responsibility for running France's artistic life. His poem was received with applause by the assembled academicians. Boileau's instant public protest was a misjudgement. He not only alienated sympathy when he broke the procedural rules of the Académie, but implicitly claimed the high priesthood of the cult of the antique not yet conferred on him. Huet tried in vain to persuade Boileau to calm himself, and could not resist pointing out that he himself knew more about antiquity, if it should come to need defending. Racine sarcastically congratulated Perrault on the brilliance of his paradox. Boileau stormed home and immediately produced the first of a series of often witty epigrams. The applause for Perrault was warm.

Boileau's protest resolved Perrault to take matters further. On 25 August 1687 he had a poem to the king read out by his friend the abbé de Lavau. La Fontaine published his celebrated *Epître à Huet,* professing his admiration for the authors of antiquity, in an effort to reconcile the warring parties. The election to the Académie of Fontenelle in 1691, at his fifth attempt, was a victory for the modernes, while that of La Bruyère in 1693 was emphasized by his discourse on reception as a triumph for the anciens. In the meanwhile, however, Perrault used the reception of La Chapelle on 12 July 1688 to read at the Académie his poem *Le Génie,* dedicated to Fontenelle and aggressively hostile to Boileau and Racine and their "Muse stérile." By and large the public, tired of schoolmasterly lectures from Boileau and his supporters about both their taste and the artistic proprieties, were behind Perrault, who was clearly more than half right, certainly about telescopes, and probably about Plato. Perrault began to press for a decisive encounter.

The first volume of the *Parallèle des anciens et des modernes* appeared in 1688, with the second in 1690. The third and most outspoken of the four volumes extended the argument beyond the sciences and the mechanical arts, in which it was not difficult to demonstrate effective progress, to the much more difficult field of literature, which required, Perrault said in his preface, judgement in the perception of true beauty. Perrault was bringing forward his treatment of poetry in order to "donner satisfaction à mes amis et à mes adversaires (satisfy my friends and my adversaries)." He goes out of his way to say at least enough in defence of the authors maltreated by Boileau, notably Chapelain, Quinault, Saint-Amant, Cotin, and Cassagne, to make it clear that he is turning the volume into a direct challenge, and he appears to be appealing in the moderne interest to the natural sensibilities of women, of whom his spokesman, the Abbé, says,

On sait la justesse de leur discernement pour les choses fines et délicates. La sensibilité qu'elles ont pour ce qui est clair, vif, naturel et de bon sens, et le dégoût subit qu'elles témoignent à l'abord de tout ce qui est obscur, languissant, contraint et embarrassé

(The accuracy of their discernment in refined and delicate matters is well known, like the sensitivity they have to what is clear, alive, natural, and in accordance with common sense, and the instant disgust they show on coming across what is obscure, feeble, constrained, and contorted).

There is an ambiguity here. Is Perrault appealing to female taste as such, or because literate women were relatively unlikely to be instructed in or impressed by what was written in antiquity, and would on that account be on his side?

Perrault had courteously sent Boileau a copy of his third volume with a friendly letter of 25 November 1692, while Boileau was finishing his tenth *Satire*, "against women," modelled on Juvenal's sixth. Boileau was working at his satire in October 1692, but put it aside and published it only in 1694, with some vitriolic lines against Perrault, removed when the rest of the *Satire* was toned down after their reconciliation. To some extent it was intended as a composition in the traditional genre of the anti-feminist tirade. In the meanwhile Boileau had replied to Perrault's "étranges dialogues" in the 1693 *Discours sur l'ode de la prise de Namur*, as a riposte to which Perrault published the 1687 *Epître au roi*, with a preface and a *Lettre à M. D*** touchant la Préface de son Ode sur Namur*. Boileau continued with the 1694 *Réflexions critiques sur quelques passages du rhéteur Longin*, demonstrating Perrault's obvious ignorance of Pindar and of Homer, a few lines from whom Perrault did later translate by way of rather unconvincing refutation. Perrault was obviously shocked by Boileau's anti-feminism in the satire, and himself in 1694 published a popular *Apologie des femmes*. There had been sporadic defences of women over the previous decade or so, notably the 1672 *L'Egalité des deux sexes* and the ironic 1675 *L'Excellence des hommes* by Poulain de la Barre, and in 1694 alone, Boileau was also attacked for his satire by Pradon and Pierre Bellocq.

In fact, after the third volume of the *Parallèle* the 17th-century *Querelle* is simply the story of personal animosities. Then on 5 May 1694 Arnauld, still in exile, wrote to Perrault suggesting a way for Boileau and Perrault himself to climb down with dignity. It nearly did not happen. Boileau agreed, but only if Arnauld published his letter. Arnauld died, and his spiritual successor, Quesnel, tried to suppress publication. Eventually Harlay de Champvallon, the archbishop of Paris, to whom Quesnel had written, pressed by other prelates, did allow publication, although it did not occur until 1701 in Boileau's *Oeuvres*. There were meanwhile further epigrams and pamphlets on both the feminist and literary issues from both sides, but nothing else was published of real importance, and Perrault and Boileau underwent a formal reconciliation at the Académie on 30 August 1694. Boileau toned down the tenth *Satire*, and the fourth volume of Perrault's *Parallèle* was in 1697 much more moderate than the other three.

The 18th-century episode of the *Querelle* concerning the modernization of Homer took place long after the modernes had won the serious victory, and was little more than a domestic literary dispute, although it provoked a dozen or so mostly large volumes of controversy. Anne Le Fèvre was the daughter of the Protestant humanist Tanneguy Le Fèvre who taught at the Saumur academy (see: Houdar de la Motte). Encouraged by Huet, a friend of her father, and Montauzier, Chapelain employed her as an editor for the edition of the classics "ad usum Delphini (for the use of the Dauphin)," for which she produced more volumes than any other editor, including the only Greek text, Callimachus. Her scholarship was renowned throughout Europe. On 4 November 1683 she married André Dacier, a classical scholar chiefly remembered for his translations of Horace and Plutarch. The couple had a son in 1684 and in 1685, on the revocation of the Edict of Nantes, converted to Catholicism, receiving the customary royal pensions. The son died when he was 11, and of the two daughters one became a nun, while the other died at 18.

Mme Dacier's translation of the *Iliad* appeared in 1711, *L'Illiade d'Homère, traduite en français avec des remarques*. Preface and commentary justified an intense admiration for Homer, the greatest epic poet there ever was or would be, showed how he had obeyed all the rules and overcome the constraints, and lashed out at the modernes. The translation had, meanwhile, made some concessions to the proprieties (at *Iliad* V, 65–68, for instance, and later at *Odyssey* XXII, 465–73), but Mme Dacier's friend Houdar de la Motte felt himself provoked and in 1714 produced a 12-canto *Iliad*, shortened to half its length, adapted to modern taste, and prefaced with a defence of the modern position and an ode in which Homer thanked the translator for his modernization.

Houdar de la Motte had added embellishments and removed the primitive brutality from the original. Mme Dacier's reply was the 614-page *Des causes de la corruption du goût*. The cause of the corruption of taste was the neglect of the Greek and Latin classics; Homer could be reconciled with the Bible; Houdar de la Motte's abridgements were inadmissible, as was his general disparagement of the primitive qualities of the Homeric epic. Houdar de la Motte replied with the 1715 *Réflexions sur la critique*, but cut it short when Valincour gave a dinner for Mme Dacier and himself at the instigation of Mme de Lambert on Palm Sunday 5 April 1716, shortly before the appearance of the Paris edition of Anne Dacier's *Odyssey*, which does not mention Houdar de la Motte.

The controversy is interesting for technical points argued about the extent to which Mme Dacier would admit an allegorical interpretation of Homer proposed by a Jesuit, and the connection between the modernes of 1715 with the Cartesian criterion of rationality. The last word came from Fénelon in his *Lettre sur les occupations de l'Académie*, expressing admiration for Homer and the antique, but showing how completely he had assimilated the value system of the modernes. The interest of the literary dispute does not centre on the purely literary questions it raises, or even on which order of personal and social values is to be preferred, the primitive or the modern. General agreement emerged that, apart from the mechanical arts and the empirical sciences, where progress was indisputable, primitive society lacked refinement, especially in male attitudes to women, and modern society was probably elegant to the point of degeneracy, or at least threatened by a corruption seen, by the early 18th century, to be rooted in the disparity between wealth and social function.

But underneath the surface skirmishes of the *Querelle* the great insights of the renaissance had proved themselves victorious. Initiated, prompted, and fuelled by literary explorations of all sorts, the examination of French social experience had seemed to find that human society could be organized in such a way as continually to improve, and human instinct could be educated in such a way that virtue, religious perfection, and happiness did not, after all, demand its suppression or abnegation. By the beginning of the 18th century the Church, largely held back from a conceivably terminal loss of credibility by the Jesuits and their supporters, had not yet reacted in such a way as to allow atheism to become a social problem.

At every step of the way what we now regard as the period's literature, including the large proportion of it never intended for publication, or for dissemination beyond a small circle, had validated its own nature and function. Poetry, all the genres of drama, private correspondence, memoirs, fictions of all sorts, letters of spiritual direction, sermons, great treatises, epigrammatic witticisms, portraits, adventure novels, speculations, exaggerations, irony, polemic, invective, and caricature, had all tentatively been feeling towards the way ahead, the adjustments required in attitudes, values, and institutions, the possibilities of reconciliation, and the need for change. What we have retained in the literary canon are the works which made any major con-tribution to this whole complex process, those which have pierced their way through to the enrichment of the experience of a whole society. The *Querelle* opens up one particularly privileged moment which shows that great literature does not necessarily consist of great books, but of writing imaginatively powerful enough to cause a generation to change its understanding of its own experience and of the sorts of social and personal development open to it.

R

RABELAIS, François, ?1494–1553.

Novelist, satirist, doctor, and humanist.

LIFE

Our knowledge of Rabelais's life remains patchy. His father, Antoine Rabelais, was a landowner of substance at Chinon, the dean of lawyers, who occasionally replaced the lieutenant général as judge, owner of a large town house, a farm known as La Devinière, and a small château at Chavigny-en-Vallée. Rabelais had at least one sister and two older brothers. He was probably born at La Devinière, near the small Benedictine abbey of Seuillé, most probably in 1494, just possibly a year later. The date 1483, which is still sometimes given, was taken in the 18th century from the register of deaths of what had been St Paul's church in Paris, and is probably wrong. 1484 is also unlikely. It seems likely that Rabelais owed part of his education to the Seuillé monks, and virtually certain that he studied law, possibly at Angers, which he clearly knew well and where his maternal uncles lived, but perhaps at one of two major centres, Orléans or Poitiers. These centres trained Paris's civil lawyers when the Paris faculty was closed down for taking too many students away from theology and canon law.

By 1520 Rabelais was a priest at the house of the Franciscan Observants, a reformed branch of the Order, to be distinguished from the Conventuals, at Fontenay-le-Comte. He was apparently a newcomer to the house, but must somewhere have made his noviceship, graduated in arts, and attended lectures in theology. He may have done all of those things, and studied law, at the Franciscan house of La Baumette, just outside Angers, perhaps taking the habit in 1511 or 1512. At Fontenay Rabelais got to know the lawyer and humanist Pierre Amy, who had become a Franciscan and, although scarcely known to him, was in correspondence with the greatest of the living French humanists, Guillaume Budé. Amy initiated Rabelais into Greek studies and, although Amy's own letters to Budé have been lost, along probably with several of those from Budé to him, we know that Rabelais started to correspond with Budé, probably in 1520 or 1521. The earliest Rabelais text we possess is what must have been his second letter to Budé, dated March 1521. It shows that Rabelais was already a priest.

Budé's letters, which become more critical of the anti-humanist and anti-Lutheran repression imposed by the Paris theology faculty, and especially by the Franciscans, show that Rabelais knew the humanist lawyer André Tiraqueau, who lived nearby. Tiraqueau is important not only for a commitment to the *mos gallicus*, which, unlike the *mos italicus*, applied humanist learning to the interpretation of Roman law, but also because of the anti-feminism of his *De legibus connubialibus* of 1513, defending and extending the husband's rights in marriage. His book was attacked by a strongly pro-feminist Latin *Apologia for the female sex* with a Greek title (Τῆς γυναικείας ψύτλῆς apologia) of 1522 by Amaury Bouchard, prefaced by a letter from Amy to Tiraqueau, who replied with a second edition of the *De legibus* in 1524.

From this date on, the association between neoplatonism and an advanced position on the rights of women and their role in society was to be of immense significance not only in the literary exploration of social attitudes, but also in the advance in France of a whole new renaissance sensibility, clearly distinct in values, attitudes, judgements, and ways of feeling from the middle ages. It formed the background against which Rabelais's *Tiers Livre* has to be understood, and was particularly strong in the middle decades of the century and in the entourage of Marguerite de Navarre. Rabelais's association with Tiraqueau and Budé is also relevant to his later attitudes towards Hippocrates, Galen, and humanist medical studies.

When, in 1523, partly in reaction to Erasmus's publishing activities, especially in relation to the Greek text of the New Testament and his series of *Paraphrases* on the Gospels, the Sorbonne decided to forbid the study of Greek altogether, we know from a letter of Budé's that the Greek books used by Amy and Rabelais were confiscated, and that the two friars suffered some sort of confinement in their convent at Fontenay. Amy, who had become a Franciscan against his father's wishes, now left Fontenay to take refuge with the Benedictines at Saint-Mesmin, near Orléans, before going to Lyons and then on to Basle, where from early in 1525 he stayed with Conrad Pellikan, a Franciscan theologian who was later to join the Reform and is now chiefly remembered for his views on the Eucharist. Amy died shortly afterwards.

Rabelais was once more allowed access to the Greek books. The intellectual climate at Fontenay must, however, have been hostile to him. All the Franciscans, not only the Observants, were generally opposed to the new learning and to the new religious spirit it fostered, only symbolized by a devotion to Greek studies as a means of subverting the authority of the fourth-century Latin Vulgate. The Church had for centuries relied on the Vulgate, whose authority it needed to defend if it was to uphold the scriptural basis for its own teaching. Essentially the new piety, which was only just beginning to be linked to the new learning, shifted the notion of religious perfection away from the often superstitious reliance on practices extrinsic to moral achievement, and sought to rely instead on moral attitudes and religious commitment. This was in spite of the difficulties created for the theology of grace, which a reliance on inner experience seemed to make available at least to the ancient pagans of high moral stature who had had no opportunity to hear the gospel message. In the 1302 Bull *Unam sanctam* Boniface VIII had defined that there could be neither salvation nor remission of sins outside the Church.

It may well have been a desire to study medicine, prohibited to the Franciscans, as much as a reaction to the spirituality prevailing at Fontenay which caused Rabelais to seek transfer to the Benedictine Order. It was more favourable to study, and its individual houses, although loosely grouped into "congregations," were more autonomous. The Benedictines were cloistered "monks," allowed to receive revenue income, rather than "mendicant" like the Franciscan "friars," who were supposed to live uniquely from alms. While the Franciscans, unlike some other mendicant orders, were dedicated to a life of poverty, the Benedictines took a vow of stability, binding them to a single house. In 1524 or 1525 by papal indult Rabelais joined the Benedictine monastery at Maillezais, on which Seuillé depended. It was only a few miles from Fontenay. The monastery served also as a cathedral, and its abbot, Geoffroi d'Estissac, who was to become Rabelais's patron as long as he lived, was also the diocesan bishop. He made Rabelais his secretary, and it was on d'Estissac's journeys of canonical visitation that Rabelais got to know Poitou so well. Rabelais's ordinary base was with d'Estissac at the dependent priory of Ligugé, which was being restored.

Rabelais's study of medicine seems to have consisted chiefly in the study of the "humanist" Greek texts of medical theory, Hippocrates and Galen, although he was later active as a physician and was sufficiently expert in anatomy to undertake the public dissection of a human body. It is probable that he attended the university of Poitiers, and he translated the first book of Herodotus into Latin. He exchanged verse epistles with the well-known minor poet Jean Bouchet, who compliments Rabelais on his mastery in Greek and Latin letters, and wrote a few lines of Greek verse for the 1524 edition of Tiraqueau. In 1528 he left Poitou for Paris, breaking for the moment neither with the Benedictines, in whose student house he lived for a while in Paris, nor with d'Estissac, to whom he was to dedicate his 1532 edition of Hippocrates and Galen. He signed himself "doctor of medicine," and boasted of the success of the lecture-commentaries required for a higher degree, which he had the preceding year given on the Greek text of those two authors at Montpellier. He had graduated in medicine there on 1 December 1530, only weeks after matriculating (on 17 September). Bachelors of medicine usually usurped the title "doctor," and in fact Rabelais took the higher degree only in 1537.

In Paris he had abandoned the Benedictine habit in exchange, he later claimed, for the dress of a diocesan priest. He may for a period have abandoned the priesthood altogether, and even have regarded himself as virtually, if not canonically, married, but his situation was to be regularized in 1535 during his second journey to Rome, probably thanks to the intervention of d'Estissac. In January 1536 he was to be allowed to assume the Benedictine habit again, to attach himself to the monastery of his choice, and to exercise his profession as a doctor. He chose the abbey of Saint-Maur-des-Fossés, of which Jean du Bellay was the titular abbot. In August it was transformed into a community of secular canons, and Rabelais was again legitimately to wear the habit of a secular priest, which he remained.

It was probably in Paris, where we know that he left two illegitimate children, François and Junie, that Rabelais had studied medicine, and d'Estissac may have paid for his studies. A papal indult legitimizing both surviving children in 1540, well before publication of the serious satire of the Tiers Livre, was an unusual privilege and argues the exercise of strong influence on Rabelais's behalf. A third child, Théodule, died young. Rabelais

may also have travelled. His interest in medicine may have been aroused even as early as his time at Fontenay due to Tiraqueau's interest in medical studies. If it was, this strengthens the case for supposing that the continuance of medical studies was the principal reason for his change of Orders. It also seems probable that the study of medicine was the principal motive for Rabelais's move to Paris, apparently with the blessing of his abbot and bishop, d'Estissac.

In 1532 Rabelais was at Lyons, and there dedicated to Tiraqueau on 3 June an edition of the Latin letters of the Ferrara doctor Giovanni Manardi. After the Latin and Greek texts of 15 July, on 4 September he dedicated what is now known to be the inauthentic text of the Testament of Cuspidius to Amaury Bouchard. The quarrel between Bouchard and Tiraqueau at Fontenay had not healed, but Rabelais clearly hoped to keep in with both. The three works, all published by Greiff (Sebastian Gryphius), show Rabelais to have been an accomplished humanist, and the dedications show that he had in no way turned his back on his past, first as a friar and then as a monk. In November 1532 he was doctor at the Lyons hospital, the Hôtel-Dieu of Notre-Dame-de-Pitié, earning a quarter as much again as his predecessor, although only 40 livres a year. On 30 November he wrote a famous letter to Erasmus, expressing in more than just elaborately formal terms his gratitude for Erasmus's doctrine. Rabelais, at the date of Pantagruel, was a committed evangelical humanist.

Until the decree of 1564 settling the matter, French usage had erratically put the calendar beginning of the year at Easter ("old style") or on 1 January ("new style"), so that for any date before Easter it is essential for correct dating, but often impossible, to know which style is being used, and many problems of renaissance chronology are still caught up in the uncertainty of the year in which any date before Easter falls. In 1532 (new style, January–December), or just possibly before the end of 1531 (perhaps old style) the anonymous Pantagruel. Les horribles et espouetables faictz et prouesses du tresrenome Pantagruel Roy des Dipsodes, fils du grand geāt Gargantua, appeared, published by Claude Nourry. It was attributed to "Alcofrybas Nasier" and gave itself out as the continuation of the best-selling Grandes Chroniques du grand et énorme géant Gargantua, which was not written by Rabelais. Pantagruel was probably on sale for the Lyons fair on 3 November 1532. It was later generally to be printed as the second volume in Rabelais's fiction saga, since Gargantua is Pantagruel's father. There are obvious similarities but also important differences between the works, and the purely extrinsic link of recurrent, if obviously changed, characters should not mislead us into considering the "saga," if indeed it is a unified saga at all, as consisting of more than a series of works only loosely connected by the evangelical humanism under varying amounts and sorts of medieval humour.

Gargantua's date of publication is more uncertain and more important, since it has been alleged that the original text becomes much more daring in its denunciation of superstitious practices if the text appeared after the 1534 placards of 17–18 October. The placards, fly sheets written by Antoine Marcourt, pastor of Neuchâtel, and printed there by Pierre de Vingle, attacked the Mass and by implication the Church's whole sacramental system, by which rites were popularly thought to bestow grace independently of the disposition of the recipient. The placards were that night posted up and down the Loire, at Orléans,

Blois and Tours, in a concerted action of such provocation that it is difficult to know precisely what the organizers intended to achieve, and therefore who they were. The party of scholastic reaction was heavily on the defensive, and may have sought to provoke the swing in royal policy towards repression which was the actual effect of the posting of the placards, one of which was left in the king's own apartments at Amboise.

Unfortunately the title page is missing from the only surviving copy of what must be the first edition of *Gargantua*, published by another non-humanist printer, François Juste, who had also printed the *Pantagrueline prognostication* for 1533 as well as *Pantagruel* in 1533 and 1534, necessarily published before Easter of the year whose events it predicts. Rabelais had also published a popular astrological almanac, now lost, for the same year. The surviving 17th-century copy of the almanac is a manuscript which the copyist, at least, signed with Rabelais's true name, and as "doctor of medicine." The *prognostication* is signed "Maistre Alcofribas, architriclin dudict Pantagruel."

Gargantua may well have been published in 1534 old style, but the first dated edition of which a copy survives was published in 1535 old style, which suggests that the probable date for the first edition of *Gargantua* is 1535 new style, that is, early in the year, but some months after the "placards." The bibliographical problems are further confused by the way in which sheets from different printings came to be assembled, so blurring any facile distinction between separate "editions," but, printed at Lyons rather than in Paris or the Loire valley, the original text may still not have been as dangerous as has been alleged. Any religious audacity was, if not attenuated, at least counterbalanced by the scattering of asides which Rabelais flicked in, alluding to François I's hostile neighbour, the Emperor Charles V, caricatured with others as Picrochole in *Gargantua*, and in real life about to launch a campaign to extend his dominion to cover all Europe, although he started with the siege of Tunis from 20 June to 14 July 1535. Rabelais clearly had more than one Picrochole prototype in mind. The clearest allusion is to the Seigneur de Lerné, who was quarrelling with Rabelais's father, the landowner and lawyer, and many others over rights to tamper with the flow of water in the Loire. Grandgousier is a heavily stylized version of Rabelais's father.

Early in 1534 Rabelais had absented himself from Lyons to spend two months in Rome as the personal physician of Jean du Bellay, the bishop of Paris, who was travelling on an embassy from François I to the pope to try to get the effects of the excommunication of Henry VIII of England revoked. We do not know how Rabelais attracted the patronage of the powerful du Bellay family, but it was to provide him with the means he needed to keep himself, and with the humanist recognition he desired. On his return to Lyons, no later than August 1534, Rabelais edited G.-B. Marliani's recently published *Topographia antiquae Romae*, dedicated to Jean du Bellay, and again published by his humanist publisher, Gryphius. Later that year his father died, and by 14 February 1535 (new style) we know that Rabelais had quitted the Hôtel-Dieu without leave. He may have returned briefly. On 5 March the management committee noted that he had left without leave "for the second time," referring possibly to his trip to Rome a year previously, but possibly to a second, more recent sudden disappearance, which would strengthen the likelihood that Rabelais had felt endangered by *Gargantua* if it had already been published.

The placards had precipitated the immediate repression of all opinion dismissive of the Sorbonne scholasticism which underpinned what had by now become anti-Lutheran religious practice, although the reliance on direct religious experience is quite clear in Colet, Erasmus, and More, and was to be captured for an orthodox Catholic spirituality by Ignatius of Loyola, whose *Spiritual Exercises*, based on a mystical experience he underwent in 1522, certainly existed as a text in some form by 1527. It is none the less not unlikely that Rabelais was uncertain whether to disappear without notice. The probability is that he went back to d'Estissac at Maillezais. On 15 July 1535 Jean du Bellay, made a cardinal on 21 May, left again for Rome as ambassador of François I. Rabelais travelled with him, and stayed with him at the court of Ferrara, where the duchess Rénée de France held glittering court, notably protecting French exiles suspected of Lutheran tendencies, and where Rabelais met Marot. He spent some seven months in Rome, from where he reported back to d'Estissac in three surviving letters, and where his ecclesiastical position was regularized, making Jean du Bellay his new superior.

By the middle of 1535 François I had already softened the attitude adopted in the immediate wake of the placards incident towards the reformist party, partly in order to win political sympathy in the Swiss cantons. He wrote to Luther's humanist lieutenant Melanchthon on 23 June 1535, hoping to inaugurate a theological dialogue, and Jean du Bellay wrote to Melanchthon in equally conciliatory terms on 27 June. The leader of the scholastic reaction, Noël Beda, exiled after the condemnation of Marguerite de Navarre's *Miroir de l'âme pécheresse* in May 1533, had been forced to make "amende honorable" on 28 February 1535, and was still in prison. Official tolerance of reformist views had been extended again and, by the date of *Gargantua*'s second edition, still in 1535 (old style), Rabelais was carefully staying within the bounds of official tolerance in both political and religious matters.

In May 1536 Rabelais was back in Lyons with du Bellay and presumably returned to Saint-Maur-des-Fossés. In Lyons on 31 December Etienne Dolet stabbed to death the painter Compaing, in self-defence, he claimed. Dolet fled to Paris, was pardoned on 9 February by François I, and Rabelais attended the celebratory banquet with Budé, Nicolas Bérault, Pierre Danès, Salmon Macrin, Jacques Toussain, Nicolas Bourbon, Jean Dampierre, Jean Visagier, and Clément Marot. It was that May that he acquired the academic right to the title of "doctor" he had hitherto used by custom, and that summer that he dissected the corpse of a hanged man in an anatomy demonstration in Lyons. He also wrote a letter to Italy containing politically sensitive information, on account of which the cardinal of Tournon would have succeeded in having him imprisoned if Marguerite de Navarre had not afforded him her protection. At Montpellier that autumn he gave the obligatory course for newly admitted doctors, commenting again on Hippocrates, and in July 1538 he attended the meeting between François I and Charles V at Aigues-Mortes, returning to Lyons with the king's entourage.

The next thing we know for certain is that Rabelais entered the service of Guillaume du Bellay, Seigneur de Langey and brother of the cardinal, who had been appointed governor of Piedmont late in 1539. Rabelais lived with his household in Turin, making several journeys back to France, and returning there for six months with Langey, whose campaigns he chronicled in a book, *Stratagemata*, which has been lost. At around this period in Rabelais's life his third child, Théodule, was born in Lyons. We know only that he died at the age of two. In 1542 François Juste published the definitive edition of *Gargantua* and *Pantagruel*. Rabelais had toned down some of the language, for instance replacing "theologian" with "sophist" in the text of *Gargantua*. Dolet, too, printed both texts, but without modification, to Rabelais's annoyance and without his permission. From 1538 the king's policy had finally turned firmly against the reformers, and Rabelais had no wish to forfeit the considerable degree of eminent protection he enjoyed.

Rabelais returned to Turin, where Langey fell ill. He was brought back to France, and Rabelais was with him when he died near Roanne on 9 January 1543. Rabelais probably accompanied the body to Le Mans, where the funeral took place on 5 March, at which Rabelais is assumed to have met the young Ronsard, and which was also attended by Jacques Peletier du Mans. Rabelais was to write movingly about Christian death, remembering Langey, in the *Quart Livre*. It is important for an interpretation of the text of Rabelais to realize that he had by now become a considerable personage, having won recognition as a humanist, a doctor, and an administrative secretary in one of the most important households in the country. He had taken care to regularize his ecclesiastical position and, in spite of the pronounced Erasmianism of his views, had managed to contain both his opinions and his behaviour within bounds perfectly acceptable to the highest authorities, if not to the religious reactionaries, who naturally also had vested interests to protect.

On 2 March 1543 *Gargantua* and *Pantagruel* were condemned by the Sorbonne, a sign that they were not everywhere written off as popular works of bawdy entertainment for sale at the fairs, but at the same time not a sign that Rabelais himself was in any serious danger. He was to be successful in obtaining a privilège for the admittedly much more muted *Tiers Livre* during 1545, the year before it was published, and, because it was largely devoted to the revived controversy about the role of women in society, fanned again into flame by Héroët's *La parfaicte amye* of 1542, appropriately dedicated to Marguerite de Navarre. In the meanwhile, on 30 May 1543, d'Estissac had died. Another almanac, now lost, came out at the end of 1545, and the *Tiers Livre* was banned immediately on publication. Rabelais took refuge at Metz in a house belonging to his friend Etienne Lorens, Seigneur de Saint-Ayl, in whose château near Orléans he had already stayed in March 1542. Saint-Ayl used the Metz house for conferences with the German reformers undertaken on the instructions of the du Bellay family, and Rabelais was soon made the town's doctor, at a salary of 120 livres a year. That sum had to be supplemented by the Cardinal du Bellay.

François I died in April 1547, and in July Rabelais left on his third journey to Rome in the suite of du Bellay, sent to take charge of the cardinals in the French party. On his way through Lyons Rabelais gave the bookseller/publisher Pierre de Tours 11 chapters of the *Quart Livre*, which appeared in that form in 1548. Rabelais stayed two years in Rome with du Bellay. His account of du Bellay's celebration of the birth of a son to the new king was published in Lyons in March 1549 as *La Sciomachie... pour l'heureuse naissance de mon seigneur d'Orléans*. It was in the spring of 1549 that Cardinal du Bellay fell from grace with Henri II and it was also in 1549 that Gabriel de Puy-Herbaut, a monk of Fontevrault, attacked Rabelais in his *Theotimus* for his mocking effrontery and parasitic way of life. The following year, 1550, came Calvin's sharp attack in the *de scan-*

dalis, accusing Rabelais, with des Périers and Antonio de Gouvea, of having tasted the gospel, but gone back on it, led to materialist atheism by sacrilegious laughter, whereas in the same passage Dolet (in fact executed in 1546, essentially for his reformatory activities), like Agrippa of Nettesheim and Simon de Neufville, is accused of obduracy from the beginning. That year Rabelais found a new protector at Lyons, however, in Cardinal Odet de Châtillon, to whom he dedicated the full edition of the *Quart Livre*, published in February 1552 by Fezandat of Paris, where Rabelais was probably living by then. It was a travelogue, capitalizing on the interest generated by the discovery of Canada by Jacques Cartier and the possible existence of the Northwest Passage through the western hemisphere to Cathay.

In 1551 Rabelais had obtained two benefices through Jean du Bellay, Saint-Martin-de-Meudon and Saint-Christophe-du-Jambet. By the time the *Quart Livre* was published, the cardinal of Tournon had made peace between the pope and Henri II, and Rabelais's satirical allusions to Rome were regarded as misplaced. The *Quart Livre* was condemned by the Sorbonne and pursued by order of the Paris parlement. In January 1553 Rabelais resigned his benefices, and on 9 April he died in Paris. No one knows much about the final years of his life from 1549. There was a rumour in Lyons that he had been imprisoned. In 1562 a work purporting to be by Rabelais, the 16 chapters of *L'Isle sonante*, was published and the whole of a *Cinquiesme Livre* appeared in 1564. The probability is that the first 17 chapters of the final book were little more than a touched-up version of a sketch left by Rabelais. It is probable that some of the ideas in the rest of the fifth book were indeed Rabelais's own, but that what was not published in 1562 was not actually written by Rabelais himself.

WORKS

If our knowledge of Rabelais's biography is tantalizingly fragmentary, the boisterous obscenity of his ebullient but never prurient humour probably still obscures for most readers the committedly Erasmian humanist scholar, dedicated physician, historian, and administrative secretary with an exceptionally elegant renaissance hand beneath the satire, wit, and rumbustious self-mockery of the major books of fiction. Rabelais not only knew Greek and was committed to a firmly evangelical piety, but appears to have written the lost *Stratagemata* on Langey's campaigns. He corresponded with the king's ambassador in Venice, Guillaume Pellicier, the bishop of Montpellier. He employed a bewildering variety of literary registers, wrote almanacs for sale at the fairs, and tried to write a popular fairy story based on giants to raise the fast cash he evidently often needed. When that bored him, he turned *Pantagruel* from a fairy tale into an episodic satire of contemporary life, tossed great learning around for purely burlesque effect, heaped on merely to amuse himself learned allusions which no reader can have been expected to pick up, became intoxicated by the richness of his own vocabulary, and wrote in a whole spectrum of literary forms, sometimes deliberately exploiting multiple layers of meaning, at others being sharply satirical, and occasionally simply vulgar.

What has so often been missed by his commentators is the insecurity of the parodist, the underlying consciousness of inadequacy, the sadness of the clown, the uncertainty of the satirist of superstition nostalgic for the security of an early monastic piety. Rabelais clearly enjoyed playing the ribald buffoon, but went to great trouble to regularize his ecclesiastical situation and have his children legitimized. Without the unsureness which prevented him from choosing between a medley of possible personal identities his cornucopian variety of comic textures could never have been created, and without the sense of lost bearings the text could not have developed its extraordinary intensity. It is possible to be sure that, even if parts of the fifth book as we have it are very weak, or adaptations of such well-known humanist material as Franciscus Columna's *Hypnerotomachia Poliphili*, printed by Aldus at Venice in 1499, Rabelais himself must have written at least sketches for parts of the book, because there is nobody else writing in French at that date who had so resplendently riotous an imagination.

Rabelais generally wrote in energetically demotic French, could be movingly Christian, densely allusive, and vary his form from the collections of often trivially episodic contes in *Pantagruel* to short but developed dramatic comedy, as in the storm episode from the *Quart Livre*. This writing encompasses parable, fable, and myth. The *Tiers Livre* is a quest, the *Quart Livre* a travelogue, and Rabelais also wrote in refined renaissance genres like the mock encomium and the utopian satire. It seems grotesque to impose the heavy categories of the literary theoretician on so obviously spontaneous a text, but if the reader asks who is telling the story, he will quickly find an author who is also narrator, the "I" of the first sentence of *Pantagruel*'s last chapter, several non-authorial narrators, like "Alcofribas Nasier," the anagram over which the first two volumes were published, who only purport to be the author, a fictional narrator, and a set of characters who are also narrators.

Even his literary techniques betray Rabelais's uncertainty about his own identity. They include colour symbolism, allegory, riddles, acrostics, lists, litanies, and genealogies parodying those of Jesus in the Gospels without any hint of serious irreverence. Successive editions accumulate the archaisms, and the parodies include popular skits on the fancier fads to which cultivated renaissance fastidiousness gave rise, as well as a humanist transformation of traditional medieval material from the gothic world of giants and gargoyles. Humour pours out in almost unbelievable richness and density from a book which starts as the development of a traditional story about giants, whose obligatory episodes are respected and sometimes given humanist significance. As well as the huge fantasy behind the wit, there is always satire, and generally self-mockery. In imaginative power and comic vision, Rabelais may well be the single greatest author of prose fiction in the French language.

Rabelais can be taken too seriously, as well as not seriously enough. The key to understanding his text is almost always to ask what it is he is parodying, and in what tone. Throughout all four certainly authentic books, whatever their contrasts of tone, even within the same book, there lies a wonderful comic sense which expresses itself in different registers of parody, even of some of the things Rabelais was most seriously devoted to, like Erasmian evangelical humanism, medical studies, and the humanist study of Greek. In his own day Rabelais was first taken as a simple buffoon. In 1533 Jacques le Gros catalogued *Pantagruel* among his stories of adventure and chivalry. Its first condemnation was for obscenity, not for the open scorn poured in the early editions on the superstitiousness of some facets of late medieval piety and belief. But Rabelais's religious satire did not,

of course, pass unnoticed. He was notoriously to be attacked in Calvin's *De scandalis* of 1550 for having tasted the fruit of the gospel and then turned his back on it, and as early as August 1533, a year after *Pantagruel*, Antoine Marcourt was to exploit that work's success for religious purposes in a little anti-Catholic pamphlet printed "at Corinth" (Neuchâtel), *Le Livre des Marchans, fort utile à toutes gens*, written by the "sire Pantapole," said in the first edition to be the neighbour of "seigneur Pantagruel," and immediately translated into English. The open allusion to Rabelais was dropped in subsequent editions, probably at the instance of Pierre Viret.

More almost than any other of the great figures of the northern renaissance, Erasmus himself, but also Shakespeare and Montaigne, Rabelais has suffered from what is known in German as the "Kulturkampf," the battle over education between Church and state, which was particularly fierce in early 20th-century France, in which academic criticism enlisted all those authors and the renaissance itself as a movement on the side of scepticism and anti-clericalism. The pendulum swung, and it is arguable that too much attention has been paid in recent years—in the case of Rabelais since the publication in 1942 by Lucien Febvre of the book translated as *The Problem of Unbelief in the Sixteenth Century: The Religion of Rabelais*—to a Catholic orthodoxy which they all took almost for granted. On the impossibility of atheism in the 16th century, Febvre has been thought to have overstated his case, but it is primarily to him that we owe our ability today to decode Rabelais's boisterous text, with its quite serious underlying view of the major aspects of all human experience. Not even his reticence about sexual matters makes Rabelais hold back from parodying Panurge's dilemma in the *Tiers Livre* about whether or not to get married.

Pantagruel, the most loosely constructed of the books, is prefaced by Hugues Salel's "dizain" pointing to the seriousness beneath the humour, and by an author's prologue in which Alcofribas, "abstractor of the fifth essence," links his work with the popular *Grandes et inestimables Chronicques*, still containing debased elements from the Arthurian legend. The prologue lists a whole series of tales of chivalry, swears a list of horrendous mock oaths to the veracity of every word in the book, and uses for the first time a variant of the famous formula "jusques au feu exclusivement (to the point of burning, exclusively)." Very roughly the book's 34 chapters are split between Pantagruel's education and his journey with Panurge to do battle with the King of the Dipsodes. Mockery of the chronicle form starts immediately with complex confusions about ecclesiastical dates, seasons, and lengths of time.

An initial reference to Luke and Matthew was later removed, but Rabelais left in his allusion to the Creed recited at Mass, incidentally bringing in his gastronomic theme by parodying the "Patrem omnipotentem (almighty God)" with the "Ventrem omnipotentem (almighty Belly)" of the pregnant womb. A long list of physical enormities, including a penis long enough to be wrapped "five or six times" round the body, brings us to the parody of the genealogy of Jesus in Matthew's Gospel. Rabelais is already bored enough deliberately to amuse himself by extending his list of Pantagruel's forefathers to include giants and heroes from mythology, legend, Scripture, fiction, and fantasy, ending "who begat the noble Pantagruel, my master." The personal pronoun makes Nasier the implied narrator, as he is again at the end of chapter 32, when he has a conversation with "my master, Pantagruel," in whose throat he has just been sheltering.

The chapter ends with a return to the complicatedly multivalent theme of drink, the source of drunkenness, but also a metaphor of the neoplatonist prophetic "furor." This was the inspiration of Dionysus which, in Marsilio Ficino's so-called commentary on Plato's *Symposium*, the *De Amore*, elevated the mind to the penetration of the divine mysteries and was placed by such 16th-century French authors as Ronsard and Pontus de Tyard under the patronage of Bacchus. Erasmus's very serious Folly had claimed in the *Stultitiae laus* of 1511 to have been nursed by Drunkenness, daughter of Bacchus, and Ignorance, daughter of Pan. Erasmus also draws heavily on Lucian's *Icaromenippus*, mentioned by Rabelais just before the end of the first chapter. He opens the second with a reference to More's *Utopia*, meaning "Nowhere," but containing a powerful imaginative exploration of the nature of an ideal society.

Despite what is still the covert declaration of humanist affiliation, Rabelais makes uncontrollable fun with numbers, lists, incongruities, exaggerations, learned allusions, and scriptural references. The parody seeps into the style, which gets close to a pastiche of scriptural narrative while staying well clear of what could reasonably have been regarded as blasphemy. Pantagruel's name, probably taken from that of a sea devil in the 15th-century mystery plays, is given a half-crazy etymology to make it mean "consumed by thirst." The thirst theme becomes comically and metaphorically important, but may have been developed from Rabelais's own recollections of the extraordinary six-month drought in 1532. Pantagruel's mother Badebec dies giving birth to 68 muleteers with mules carrying salt, nine dromedaries with hams and salted tongue, seven camels laden with salt fish, 25 cart-loads of vegetables from the onion family, and Pantagruel himself, hairy as a bear. Gargantua, Pantagruel's father, grieves at the loss of his wife, but is overjoyed at the birth of his son. The relationship between father and son was one thing Rabelais never made fun of.

The humour returns to variations on the giant theme, which are occasionally almost surreal, as when one of the four chains used to tie down the baby Pantagruel is taken off by devils to bind Lucifer, "unchained" by the pain suffered from a colic caused by eating a fricasseed oath for lunch. As a young man Pantagruel visits many of the places associated with Rabelais's own biography, meets a Limousin scholar whose language is a satire of dog Latin, performs a giant's feats with the bells of Notre-Dame, which his father had taken to hang round his mare's neck, studies, and visits just outside the walls of Paris the famous humanist library of the abbey of Saint-Victor, a burlesque version of whose catalogue Rabelais reproduces, strengthening it with anti-Sorbonne satire in 1542. There is enough Latin in it to indicate, with the allusions, that by now Rabelais's book was bubbling with what we might regard as student humour, irreverent, sometimes clever, often deliberately offending canons of taste, sometimes weighed down with learned allusions and academic wit, and amusing only at a level above the heads of the public which had enjoyed reading or, much more often, hearing read out the *Grandes Chronicques*.

The eighth chapter consists almost entirely of a letter on study from Gargantua to Pantagruel. It is completely serious in tone, was probably written late, but creates several problems, since the 10th chapter appears directly to follow it, and there is no reason to suppose that the ninth chapter was added after the eighth. The most probable solution is that the late eighth chapter got misplaced, and should have been put after rather than before

the present ninth, which presents Panurge to the reader. Chapters 10 to 13 are devoted to a satire of legal procedures with Pantagruel as judge before Panurge reappears in chapter 14 to become Pantagruel's inseparable companion throughout the rest of *Pantagruel*, and again in the *Tiers Livre* and *Quart Livre*, although his character and role will change. The seriousness of the eighth chapter is made clear partly from the father–son relationship on which it is based.

Among God's many blessings to the human race is nature's ability to bestow in this life a sort of immortality by perpetuating a person's name "par lignée yssue de nous en mariage légitime (by a line issuing from us through legitimate marriage)," in some sort making up for the entry of death into the world with original sin. The importance attributed here to dynastic lineage helps to explain Rabelais's attitude to sex, monastic chastity, and the legitimizing of his children. The first four paragraphs of the letter contain a clear affirmation of Gargantua's devout Christian belief before he recalls his own youth at a time unpropitious to learning, "encores ténébreux et sentant l'infélicité et calamité des Gothz (still dark and smacking of the misery and catastrophe of the Goths)," who had destroyed all good literature. Now, "par la bonté divine, la lumière et dignité a esté de mon eage rendue ès lettres (by divine goodness light and dignity have in my age been restored to letters)."

Maintenant toutes disciplines sont restituées, les langues instaurées: grecque, sans laquelle c'est honte que une personne se die sçavant, hébraïcque, caldaïcque, latine; les impressions tant élégantes et correctes en usance, qui ont esté inventées de mon eage par inspiration divine, comme à contrefil l'artillerie par suggestion diabolicque

(Now all the disciplines are restored, languages taught: Greek, without which it is shameful for anyone to call themselves learned, Hebrew, Chaldaic, Latin; elegant and correct editions are in use, which were invented in my age by divine inspiration, as on the other hand artillery was invented by diabolic suggestion).

Gargantua's views on gunpowder and good literature verbally echo those of Erasmus. Women and girls have now reached out to that "heavenly praise and manna of good doctrine," while Gargantua himself has had to learn Greek and delights in Plutarch's *Moralia*, Plato, and Pausanias. Gargantua recommends Pantagruel to pay attention to his tutor, Epistémon, and to learn languages, first of all Greek, then Latin, and then Hebrew for the sacred scriptures, the programme of the newly founded trilingual colleges at Louvain, Cologne, and Oxford, of the lectureships founded in 1530 at Paris, and in general of the linguistic skills ardently promoted by Erasmus and Budé. Gargantua recommends as stylistic models Plato in Greek and Cicero in Latin, then the study of history and geography, geometry and arithmetic, and, from the liberal arts, music, with astronomy, but "laisse-moy l'astrologie divinatrice et l'art de Lullius, comme abuz et vanitéz (leave aside telling the future by astrology and the [hermetic] art of Lull, as a perversion of learning, and vain)."

Pantagruel should get to know civil law and natural history, recognize by name fishes, birds, trees, shrubs, metals, and stones, learn the medicine of Greeks, Romans, and Arabs, not forgetting the interpreters of the Talmud and the Cabbala. The New Testament is to be read in Greek, the Old in Hebrew, and

Pantagruel is to become "un abysme de science (an abyss of learning)" before learning chivalry and arms. Thinking no doubt of Pico della Mirandola, who undertook to defend his 900 *Conclusiones* against all comers at Rome in 1487, Gargantua says that Pantagruel could do no better than defend "conclusions en tout sçavoir, publiquement, envers tous et contre tous (conclusions in all disciplines, publicly, with everyone and against everyone)." He should keep learned company, and be on his guard against relying on knowledge alone:

> selon le saige Salomon sapience n'entre poinct en âme malivole et science sans conscience n'est que ruine de l'âme, il te convient servir, aymer, et craindre Dieu, et en luy mettre toutes tes pensées et tout ton espoir, et, par foy formée de charité, estre à luy adjoinct en sorte que jamais n'en soys desemparé par péché

> (according to the wise Solomon, wisdom does not enter an ill-disposed soul and knowledge without probity is only the ruin of the soul; you must serve, love, and fear God, and place all your thoughts and all your hope in him, and, through faith informed by charity, remain joined to him so that sin never separates you).

Rabelais has taken time off from the satirical comedy which started as a giant story to reveal his fundamentally Erasmian views, although he appears, whether consciously or not, to have been unable to resist allowing gigantic proportions to creep into the programme of study, pomposity into Gargantua's epistolary style, and a vulgarizing element into the presentation of the no longer excitingly new educational ideal.

Panurge in *Pantagruel* is relatively informed, the rogue reminiscent of Till Eulenspiegel rather than the weak, foolish, indecisive, and superstitious creature of the later books. In chapter nine he speaks many tongues, some of them invented, most of the others merely caricatures. This is Rabelais's clever verbal virtuosity at its least subtle, but it shows his reliance on proliferation as a comic device, and the fascination language and language jokes obviously retained for him. Panurge replies to Pantagruel in 12 languages or pseudo-languages before admitting that French is his maternal tongue. He boasts of coming from the Loire valley, where French is spoken at its purest, "car je suis né et ay esté nourry jeune au jardin de France: c'est Touraine (for I was born and brought up as a youth in the garden of France; that's Touraine)." For the rest of *Pantagruel* he is Pantagruel's pedantic, pseudo-learned companion.

Chapters 10 to 13 contain a powerful comment on legal wrangling in which Pantagruel's fair-mindedness as a judge is apparent, and there are two more episodic chapters before, in chapter 16, we are given a lifelike portrait of a non-gigantic Panurge prefacing a chapter of slapstick. The narrator uses the first-person singular "I" again at the beginning of chapter 17, in an episode that could have come anywhere, starting "One day..." and satirizing indulgences. Subsequent objects of satire include the procedures at scholastic disputations and upper-class courting procedures as Pantagruel falls in love with a Parisian woman.

From chapter 23 Rabelais returns to the giant theme, with the account of the war of the Dipsodes, who have invaded the country of the Amaurotes, as the inhabitants of More's Utopia are called. In chapter 24 there is no hint of blasphemy when the last words of Jesus on the Cross are used in an entirely secular context and, typically, Rabelais quite unnecessarily describes in detail the route taken by Pantagruel, Panurge, Epistémon, Eusthenes, and Carpalim from Honfleur to Utopia. It is the route taken by Vasco da Gama to India as given by Grynaeus in the *Novus Orbis* of 1532, topped up with three places derived from Greek words meaning "nothing" (Meden, Uti, and Udem) and one place meaning "laughable" (Gelasim) before passing near the Achorite kingdom and coming to the port of Utopia, just over three leagues from the country's capital, the town of the Amaurotes. The war is recounted farcically, but offers Rabelais the occasion to put into Pantagruel's mouth in chapter 28 another declaration of trust in God, softened in its opposition to the reactionary Sorbonne by Rabelais's later removal of what he identifies with the view of the "caphards (hypocrites)," by which he means the scholastics. Pantagruel advocates self-reliance as a means of attracting divine assistance, and thereby presupposes at least a theology that is semi-Pelagian, a term denoting the heretical view that an individual could achieve anything at all in the supernatural order unaided by grace.

Chapter 30 is noteworthy for its implied allusion to the Resurrection when Panurge sticks Epistémon's head back on, and also for the Lucianic device of recounting on earth what is going on in the underworld. Rabelais gives us a not very amusing list of how some of the well-known inhabitants are employed. Pantagruel emerges as a wise leader, and in chapter 32 Rabelais not only amuses himself by making his proportions wildly incompatible with one another, and by incorporating a traditional episode when Pantagruel harbours a whole army inside his mouth, but also mocks at his own literary activity by narrating a conversation between himself as Alcofribas and "my master, Pantagruel," from whose mouth Alcofribas has just emerged.

In the following chapter, two paragraphs are devoted to ridiculing the learned who do not know that the cause of the heat in France's hot springs is Pantagruel's infected urine. To cure his digestive tract Pantagruel swallows a dozen or so workmen of different sorts, who pitch camp within him and clean out his intestines. When they have finished Pantagruel disgorges them. All the humour is in the incongruity and the incompatibility of proportions. There is nothing here that could have been intended to produce as much as a snigger, even among the most prurient. The final chapter announces what will be the third and fourth books. *Gargantua*, without Panurge, whose age when he met Pantagruel had been given as about 35, is an interlude but, because it is about Pantagruel's father, and the action of the *Tiers Livre*, however different in tone, follows on from *Pantagruel*, *Gargantua* is always put first.

The famous last couplet of the "dizain" prefacing *Gargantua* is a complex scholastic joke:

> Mieux est de ris que de larmes escripre,

> Pour ce que rire est le propre de l'homme

> (It is better to write of laughter than of tears, because laughter is man's characteristic).

On account of the Eucharist, in which, after transsubstantiation, the "accidents" pertaining to bread and wine inhered in the "substance" of the risen Christ, scholastic logic distinguished between the "praedicamenta" (substance and accidents, like man and hair) and the "praedicabilia" in the logical order (in which accidents, like whiteness, were not essential to the definition of a thing, like hair). The standard example given for a logical "proprium" or characteristic among the "praedicabilia" was the ability to laugh, "risibilitas," thought to be unique to man, and therefore realized always and only when the definition of man as a rational animal was realized. To say that laughing was the "propre" of man simply turns a standard example from the textbooks of logic into an actual statement about human behaviour.

La Vie très horrificque du grand Gargantua, père de Pantagruel, jadis composé par M. Alcofribas, abstracteur de quinte essence; livre plein de Pantagruelisme is a more complex book to decode, but also much more integrated than its predecessor. The book grew by two chapters between 1534/5 and 1542, so that chapters cannot here be referred to by number, but the book splits into three major sections: the giant's birth and education, the Picrochole war, and the half-dozen chapters on the abbey of Thélème. The final chapter contains a long "énigme" by Mellin de Saint-Gelais, and is more pointed if publication followed the placards of October 1534, and there is an important author's prologue to the book, addressed to "Beuveurs tresillustres, et vous, Verolés tresprecieux (Most illustrious Boozers and you, most precious Pox-stricken)," which immediately connects the reader to a complex network of literary registers. The first sentence goes on to refer to Alcibiades's praise of Socrates in Plato's *Symposium*, and in particular to his comparison of Socrates to the figure of Silenus, associated in the tradition referred to by Rabelais with Bacchus, wine, and a hideous exterior which none the less hides inner wisdom and moral probity. Rabelais, as prolix as ever in his description of Silenus figures, refers to the apothecaries' boxes painted with grimacing figures outside, but used for holding precious drugs within.

Erasmus had provocatively added Christ to the list of Silenus figures in the essay "Sileni Alcibiadis" inserted into the Froben 1515 edition of the *Adagia*, adding a specifically religious dimension to the image of wisdom and virtue evoked by Socrates in Plato. Rabelais includes the prophetic neoplatonist associations of the Bacchic frenzy as well as its earthier association with alcoholic intoxication. Both in referring to the Silenus boxes, now with their added associations of Christ and Socrates, and in his play on the double significance of Bacchic alienation, Rabelais is suggesting that there is more to his book than its apparent frivolity leads the reader to expect. Socrates, "tant laid il estoit de corps et ridicule en son maintien (however ugly in body and ridiculous in demeanour he was)," "tousjours dissimulant son divin savoir (always hiding his divine knowledge)," nevertheless hid within himself not only his "entendement plus que humain, vertus merveilleuse (superhuman understanding, wondrous virtue)" but, and the stoic touch is important, "contentement certain, asseurance parfaicte, desprisement incroyable de tout ce pourquoy les humains tant veiglent, courent, travaillent, navigent et bataillent (guaranteed contentment, perfect confidence, and an unbelievable contempt for all those things on account of which humans watch, run, work, sail, and fight so much)."

Just, argues Rabelais, as the habit does not make the monk (incidentally, another favourite adage of Erasmus), so the things treated in this book "ne sont tant folastres comme le tiltre au dessus pretendoit (are not so foolish as the title above suggests)." The reader, Rabelais goes on to say, has by attentive reading and frequent reflection to "break the bone and suck the substantial marrow (rompre l'os et sugcer la substantificque mouelle)." This might, naturally, be simple self-advertisement, the mountebank beckoning the passer-by to enter the charlatan's tent. It is more probable that Rabelais's mock-serious claim that his book has a serious underlying content is a diffident way of making that claim in a truly serious sense.

Gargantua knows that he is descended from a rich line, because you never saw anyone so keen to be rich and a king, so as to make good cheer, not to work, not to worry, and to make wealthy his friends and all those of goodwill and learning. "Retournons à nos moutons (Let's get back to our sheep)," says Gargantua: his genealogy was found in a ditch, with an elaborate 16th-century riddle in decasyllables, a poem which is virtually an acrostic. His father was Grandgousier and his mother Gargamelle, who carried him 11 months in the womb. The narrator, who here plays a much greater part in the action than did the occasional commentator who was the narrator of *Pantagruel*, makes fun with a list of learned allusions to extraordinary births of great men, and Rabelais amuses himself with the academic forms his Latin references take. "ff. De suis et legit., 1. Intestato fi" is a genuine reference to the law "Intestato" from the Justinian *Digest* disallowing the legitimacy of children whose putative father died 11 months before their birth, but quite incongruously appearing in this form in what purported to be a popular fiction.

The burlesque account of the events surrounding Gargantua's birth occupies several chapters and includes "Les Propos des bien yvres (The Song of the truly drunk)," with Christ's words from the Cross "I thirst" printed in Greek. This chapter was considerably extended by Rabelais, showing that its humour went down well. It does however clearly depend on popular sayings whose associations have today been lost. Rabelais removed a satirical anti-scholastic sally of Gargamelle's, who would have preferred to hear about the life of Saint Margaret "ou quelque aultre capharderie (or some other hypocrisy)" to having the gospel quoted to her during her labour. Other satirical references to the scholastic emphasis on the arbitrary nature of, for instance, religious belief were removed from later editions of the text. Rabelais notably follows Erasmus in using the Greek to interpret Hebrews xi, 1 to the effect that faith is not simple credulity. Gargantua was born through his mother's left ear, and the narrator gives scriptural and mythological references to extraordinary births after informing his readers that Gargantua's first words were "To drink!" The humour then remains based on the giant theme, lists, and verbal abundance for several chapters, one of which incidentally ends with a passing appearance, in the book of which he is the supposed author, of Alcofribas, who has helped make Gargantua's rings.

Alciati's *Emblemata*, published in Augsburg in 1531 and 1534, by Christien Wechel in Paris in 1534, and translated into French in 1536, endowing animals, figures, and images with moral and spiritual significance, had set off a cult in the French court on which Rabelais now draws extensively. He takes very seriously the renaissance colour symbolism of Gargantua's livery, largely because of Lorenzo Valla's humanist defence of white against the 14th-century defence by Bartolo di Sassoferrato of gold as the colour of light. The Greek text of Matthew's Gospel, xvii, 2 says that at the Transfiguration Jesus's clothing became white, not as the Vulgate's "snow," but as "light," so that the emblematic significance of white became a touchstone of whether the Vulgate, as the scholastics held, or the Greek text, as the evangelical humanists held, had the greater authority. Had Bartolo been right about the colour of light, the Vulgate reading would have had to be preferred to the Greek text. There is a conventionally humanistic boutade against tyranny, and the phrase "apres la restitution des bonnes lettres (after the restoration of good learning)" was inserted in 1542. The phrase "bonnes lettres," in Latin "bonae literae," was frequently used by Erasmus to describe the object of humanist endeavour. In effect, it is an untranslatable rallying call.

Gargantua's education is a parable of the virtues of a humanist upbringing, for the most part knocking loudly on a door long since opened, and satirizing an educational system, and the textbooks it had used, whose urgent need for radical reform the schism had made apparent to everyone. The ebullient humour is still there, but it would be a mistake to regard Rabelais as a serious contributor to an educational reform well on the way to universal acceptance by 1534. He is conscious rather of braggadocio, as he is in his brusque dismissal in the best Loire renaissance tradition of all Parisians as fools. There is an almost tender relish in his references throughout *Gargantua* to the places and people he knew in his own youth. A long episode with bells leads to the final chapters on education. These are humane as well as humanist and, by cramming humorously impossible amounts of activity into each working day to avoid the great sin for all humanists of wasting time, are not without a touch of giant humour.

In the first edition Gargantua is cared for by the learned doctor Seraphin Calobarsy, an anagram of François Rabelais, and the text is loaded with polemical intent. While he is being rubbed down, Scripture is loudly and clearly read to Gargantua, leading him to "reverer, adorer, prier et supplier le bon Dieu (revere, adore, beseech, and supplicate the good Lord)," the implication being that it is not sung, so as to make it unintelligible, and that it is more likely that reading Scripture will lead Gargantua to devotion than would attendance at Mass. Then his teacher takes him over what has been read while he is on the privy, and there is time for looking at the position of the sun and any other visible astral bodies before dressing and grooming. Yesterday's lessons are repeated to Gargantua while that is going on, and he is expected to have learnt them by heart and to know how to apply them.

There is reading at table, conversation when the wine comes round, physical exercise, music, science, and there are the courtly pursuits. Gargantua excels with the lance, with the range of weapons at fencing, and at hunting, swimming, and horsemanship, and Rabelais gives a list of the technical refinements of his skills at dressage. Rabelais finds immense numbers of occasions to compile catalogues of the things to be included in this parody of a treatise on the education of a prince, a caricature only on account of the amount it contains and of Rabelais's inability to confine himself to one word where he can think of six. Most of the content is more or less serious, but there are a few boutades, and the register is amusingly light-hearted. A whole chapter is devoted to catalogues of things to be done when it is raining. Once a month Gargantua and his companions get a day off. By now the text reads as if Rabelais were making propaganda at court for the evangelical humanist beliefs which he was mixing into his apparently robust and chivalresque humour. The mixture might have been, and probably was, exactly calculated to appeal to the taste of a court which was interested in physical pursuits, hunting, and romances of chiv-

alry, but which also wanted French supremacy, the defeat of Charles V, religious peace, and a reputation for progressive educational views, cultivation especially of the decorative arts, refinement in gardening, and skills in all the leisured areas of life.

There is a totally abrupt transition to the chapters on the Picrochole war (starting with what in 1534/5 was chapter 23). The war is recounted satirically. The marvellous events of the romances of chivalry are parodied and the obsolescence of their style is exaggerated. The proceedings are localized to identifiable paths, fields, crossings, hills, villages, and vineyards which Rabelais remembered. The grape harvesters from Gargantua's territory try to buy some "fouaces," a local delicacy from Rabelais's home region made of baked dough, from some merchants of Lerné who refuse to sell, although offered the usual payment. Tempers rise; a merchant uses his whip on a harvester's legs; there is a fight; the merchants lose; their "fouaces" are taken and paid for, with something over to soothe injured pride, and the harvesters have lunch. The merchants complain to their king, Picrochole, whose name implies a superfluity of bile, about Grandgousier's shepherds and tenant farmers. Picrochole assembles an army of 16,014 harquebusiers and 35,011 adventurers, with 914 pieces of artillery, and sacks Grandgousier's peaceful territory, taking everything (18 sorts of animal) and sparing nothing and no one. At Seuillé "the poor devils of monks" do not know to which of their saints to turn. At this point Frère Jean des Entommeurs comes into the story and single-handedly saves the monastic vineyards by killing all the Lerné pillagers with the cross he takes out from under his habit. Rabelais light-heartedly catalogues the ways they die and the saints they cry out to.

Grandgousier recalls Gargantua from his studies in a letter parallel to that from Gargantua to Pantagruel in the earlier book, but now dealing with peace and social harmony. Grandgousier's style is even more old-fashioned and pompous than Gargantua's had been, conceivably a deliberate send-up of an exaggerated but ill-informed attempt to write in a Ciceronian style, and it is important that in blaming Picrochole Grandgousier says that "Dieu eternel l'a laissé au gouvernail de son franc arbitre et propre sens, qui ne peut estre que meschant si par grace divine n'est continuellement guidé (eternal God has left him to the rule of his free will and own direction, which can only be evil if it is not continually guided by divine grace)." Not only does Grandgousier see himself as a possibly elected instrument of divine wrath to punish Picrochole but, although he is later to establish free will as the essential principle of life at Thélème, he here allows that nature unaided by grace is doomed to evil, a theological view about which Erasmus (who was not to die until 1536) preferred not to make pronouncements. The letter to Gargantua is confided to Ulrich Gallet, the name of one of Rabelais's father's friends, a doctor and ally against Gaucher de Sainte-Marthe who was in fact sent to Paris to promote the lawsuit about the diversion of the river flow in the Loire.

Rabelais becomes almost didactic as Gallet harangues Picrochole, begging him to see reason, and Grandgousier prays to God to soften Picrochole's heart. He thinks Picrochole's "fouace" merchants in the wrong, but none the less restores in abundance more luxurious "fouaces," made with eggs and butter, and pays for all damage. Picrochole's evil counsellor, Toucquedillon, commander of the artillery, advises the king to exploit Grandgousier's reluctance to fight, and the narration returns to the register at once of giant story, as Gargantua brushes cannonballs out of his hair, and of evangelical humanism, as he denounces the bastion of scholastic reaction, the Collège de Montaigu. A whole chapter in which Gargantua eats six pilgrims in a salad is inspired by a reference to teeth in Psalm 123. Toucquedillon is taken prisoner and treated mercifully by Grandgousier. On his release he relates to Picrochole all that has happened to him and counsels a cessation of the war. Hastiveau contradicts him, and flatters Picrochole into carrying on. Tocquedillon draws his sword and kills Hastiveau, and the irascible Picrochole has Tocquedillon killed.

The contrast between the good, devout, peace-loving, and kind Grandgousier, who will fight only when absolutely necessary, and the irritable, greedy, and evil Picrochole is relieved by the intensity of the comic narrative, which bristles with satire, caricature, inventiveness, parable, and wit. In the end Picrochole flees and is killed. Gargantua gives a great speech, a set piece in which he is liberal, restrained, and forgiving. His own tutor, Ponocrates, is appointed tutor to Pichrochole's five-year-old heir. Rabelais allows Gargantua to name those he considers truly culpable, from the merchants of "fouaces" to Picrochole's advisers who counselled war, and only those seriously guilty are punished, and then only by being made to work Gargantua's printing presses. Those who helped in the war are all rewarded. Frère Jean refuses the abbacy of Seuillé and any other reward which would put him in charge of other monks. Gargantua offers him the country of Thélème on the banks of the Loire.

It has been suggested that the Thélème chapters were written independently of the rest of the book, but it is quite characteristic of Rabelais to switch his literary register without warning. The transition is smoother than that between the narration of Gargantua's education and that of Picrochole's invasion, and Rabelais had already shown a fascination with the courtly forms of renaissance refinement linked to an ability to make gentle fun of them. At least three clear levels of literary reference can be found in the Thélème chapters. Firstly the abbey is an anti-monastery, admitting women as well as men, prescribing not obedience, but freedom, and not poverty, but riches; not chastity, but a mixing of the sexes. Life is social, leisured, opulent, and above all free, in accordance with the abbey's only rule, "Faictz ce que vouldras (Do as you wish)."

Secondly, these chapters, like More's *Utopia*, are an imaginative dream, projecting the nature of an ideal society, given the best possible conditions for its realization. The inhabitants are young, handsome, "well born" in the Erasmian sense of naturally gifted, and surrounded by every refinement of elegance and luxury, and they please themselves without material cares about how to pass the time. Rabelais, for obvious reasons of religious prudence, turns diffidently and amusingly to the gentlest register of fantasy in order tentatively to examine the radical and daring hypothesis that a properly Christian spirituality might yet be erected on the possibility that human instinct could provide a sure guide to both virtue and happiness. This imagination obviously neglects the theological difficulties about original sin and the need for grace, and it assumes the best of all possible imaginable, if not realizable, circumstances.

Thirdly, the essential nature of Thélème is set out in a paragraph translated from Erasmus's second *Hyperaspistes* letter against Luther, part of Erasmus's controversy with Luther, against whom he had chosen the freedom of the will as the central point at issue in Luther's dispute with orthodox Catholicism.

The Thélème chapters are a programmatically anti-Lutheran declaration on Rabelais's part. Rabelais sees perfectly well, as had Erasmus, the theological implications of the possibility he wanted to examine and, however much both of them sympathized with the reformers' emphasis on the primacy of direct spiritual experience over the arbitrary religion of rites and practices extrinsic to moral stature, neither of them was prepared to sacrifice free will in the full religious sense of an autonomous human moral power to choose the good. Erasmus took refuge in satire and exegesis. Rabelais explored his optimism perhaps more recklessly in the realms of fiction taken to the point of fantasy, but where the theological issue still remained clear.

In response to Frère Jean's request for a monastery "au contraire de toutes aultres (the opposite of all others)," Gargantua, pleased, decides first that there should be no walls and no clocks, and that there should also be both women, admitted from 10 to 15, and men, admitted from 12 to 18. Rabelais amuses himself with a mock exactitude in quantities of money devoted to the endowment. The hexagonal shape of the building with its six round towers comprising six floors and a diameter of 60 feet, set 312 feet apart, suggests that Rabelais is drawing playfully on one of several possible systems of number symbolism, and therefore presupposing a readership from the closed circle of those likely to understand reasonably rarefied intellectual games, although he may also just be amusing himself with numbers. Each of the 932 rooms has its own suite, including a "chapelle," which probably means kitchen. If it means "chapel," which is the alternative, it could be taken to signify that the abbey does not have a community church for communal worship, although even private kitchens suggest that meals are, against ordinary monastic custom, not to be taken in common. Although Rabelais pays lip service throughout these chapters to the pretence that Gargantua's institution is an abbey, and its inhabitants are monks and nuns, the pretence becomes unimportant as soon as he makes it clear that he wishes to explore the possibility that the Church has got its monastic spiritualities wrong, even in their Benedictine realization, which was not lax but humane, and compatible with the new learning, if not with the full implications of the adoption of the ideology built into the new educational ideals.

The poem inscribed on the abbey gate is written in the style of the "grands rhétoriqueurs", using a complex rhyme scheme. Within the courtyard is every sort of renaissance luxury: an alabaster fountain, a manege, theatre, swimming pool, tennis court, and jousting ground. The pleasure garden stretches down to the river; the fruit trees in the orchard form a quincunx; and there are stables, archery grounds, and a falconry. The interior decoration is equally lavish, each bedroom being equipped with a full-length mirror. There are libraries and decorated galleries, splendid in their renaissance architecture. Near the women's rooms are perfumers and hairdressers. Rabelais describes the women's dresses. Total indulgence in personal preference leads, admittedly in inconceivably privileged surroundings and among unbelievably endowed youth, to complete social harmony:

Mais telle sympathie estoit entre les hommes et les femmes que par chascun jour ilz estoient vestuz de semblable parure, et pour a ce ne faillir, estoient certains gentilz hommes ordonnez pour dire es hommes, par chascun matin, quelle livrée les dames vouloient en ycelle journée porter; car le tout estoit faict scelon l'arbitre des dames

(But there was such sympathy between the men and the women that each day they dressed in similar fashion, and so that they should not fail in this, a number of gentlemen were sent each day to tell the men what dress the women intended to wear that day, for everything was done according to the women's choice).

The monks and nuns, as they continue to be called, are surrounded by a whole workforce of tailors, jewellers, dressmakers, and weavers. There is no shortage of silks, brocades, velvets, or precious metals.

In addition to its literary functions as an anti-monastery, no doubt capable of being read at the level of mere escapist fantasy, and its hint of the possibility of an ideal society created by ideal people in ideal circumstances, the word Thélème signifies free will, meaning in its original Erasmian setting the autonomous human power of self-determination to supernaturally valid innocence. This was a notion which seemed to Luther "Pelagian," and which could not in fact be reconciled with an orthodox guilt-based spirituality, or a theology of original sin and grace which did not extend the possibility of salvation to non-believers, or make divine decisions contingent on autonomous human choice. There was no Greek word for the free appetitive faculty referred to by Augustine as the will ("voluntas"), but the term "thelema" (θέλημα) is used for appetite in Scripture, and Rabelais alludes loosely in his usage of it to the faculty of the will. The scholastics of the high middle ages had used for "free will" the term "liberum arbitrium," transliterated into French as "libre arbitre (free judgement)," but in fact this term implied a contradiction because, for at least the Aristotelian scholastics like Aquinas, while the will was based on an appetite for the good, which in this life was necessarily free, the judgement was based on a natural appetite for the true, which could not be free.

Erasmus, carefully refusing altogether to deny original sin, had held that "in certain well-endowed and well-educated people there is only a minimal inclination to evil. The greatest part of the movement towards evil comes not from nature, but from bad upbringing, unsuitable food, the habitude of sinning, and evil of the will." Rabelais, who uses the term "franc vouloir" indeterminately with "franc arbitre" for free will, and insists on the day-to-day freedom of the inhabitants of Thélème, virtually translates:

En leur reigle n'estoit que ceste clause, *Faictz ce que vouldras*, par ce que gents liberes, bien nez et bien instruictz, conversans en compaignies honestes, ont par nature un instinct et aguillon, qui tousjours les pousse a faictz vertueux et retire de vice, lequel ilz nommoient honneur

(There was only this one clause in their rule, *Do as you wish*, because people who are free, well endowed, and brought up well, who mix in upright company, have by nature an instinct and a spur which continually urges them towards virtuous deeds and draws them back from vice; this they called honour).

Only the yoke of servitude can cause such people to turn away from honour. The last three lines of this chapter introduce the final "Enigme," but *Gargantua* virtually ends with the chapter from which this passage is taken. The young men and women all together do what gives pleasure to any one of their number. They

are all physically, intellectually, morally, and artistically endowed, play instruments, sing, speak half a dozen languages, are chivalrous, gallant, courteous, adept on foot and on horseback, and have all the mental, physical, and courtly skills. When one of the young men leaves, he takes with him the lady who has chosen him as her swain, in the fairy-tale language with which the chapter ends:

et, si bien avoient vescu a Theleme en devotion et amityé, encores mieulx la continuoient ilz en mariage, et autant se entreaymoient-ilz à la fin de leurs jours comme le premier de leurs nopces

(and, as they had lived well together in devotion and friendship at Thélème, so they continued even better in marriage, and loved one another at the end of their days as on the first day of their wedding).

Le Tiers Livre des faicts et dits héroïques du bon Pantagruel, signed by Rabelais under his own name and dedicated to Marguerite de Navarre, was published by Wechel before the end of January 1546, and condemned by the Sorbonne that April. The intermittent play of the earlier books with gigantic stature has been dropped. Panurge reappears but, no longer the learned companion of *Pantagruel*, is foolish, weak, and indecisive, while Pantagruel becomes the embodiment of wisdom. The prologue begins by echoing that of *Gargantua* and addressing the boozers and the gouty. It is largely concerned with Diogenes, and there is, together with an even greater luxuriance in verbal prolixity than hitherto, a new stoicism, which is important for Rabelais's now more subdued humour as well as for his attitude to life. The prologue, while emphatically patriotic, is inspired in its expressed hatred of war by Erasmus's famous 1515 essay on the subject "Dulce bellum inexpertis" ("War is sweet to those who have not tried it"), and includes a definition of "Pantagruelisme" as "une forme spécifique et propriété individuale... moienant laquelle jamais en maulvaise partie ne prendront choses quelconques ilz congnoistront sourdre de bon, franc et loyal couraige (a specific form and individual characteristic... by which [our ancestors] would never be perturbed by things which they can face with strong, fresh, and straightforward courage)."

Later on, we are told that, just as Pantagruel has been "l'idée et exemplaire de toute joyeuse perfection (the idea and exemplar of all joyful perfection)," the miraculous plant Pantagruelion contains "tant de vertus, tant d'énergie, tant de perfections, tant d'effectz admirables... (so many virtues, so much energy, so many perfections, so many admirable qualities...)." There is a final definition in the prologue to the *Quart Livre*: "C'est certaine gayeté d'esprit conficte en mespris des choses fortuites (It's a certain joyousness of mind made up of the contempt for fortuitous things)." From the somewhat passive stoicism of the cynics like Diogenes, also transmitted by Seneca and Cicero, Rabelais passes to the more active but still defensive stoicism of Epictetus, the first sentence of whose handbook holds that, since our true good is in our power, nothing which is not in our power can truly harm the wise man. The contempt of fortuitous things had in fact become a commonplace humanist topos, transmitted by several Fathers of the Church, and closely associated with both Erasmus and Budé, who wrote a treatise with that title.

The narrative of the *Tiers Livre* carries on from the end of

Pantagruel rather than *Gargantua*. Pantagruel, having conquered the kingdom of Dipsodie, transports there 9876543210 men, whose wives bear them seven children every nine months. That, however, is about the last we hear of giants, although the first chapter, mostly about how a good prince treats a defeated nation, seems to hesitate about continuing in the vein of *Pantagruel* itself. The second chapter, after some number humour of a notably simple sort, makes the decision. The narrator steps in to confirm that we must take Pantagruel seriously:

> Je vous ay ja dict et encores rediz que c'estoit le meilleur petit et grand bonhomet, que oncques ceigneit espée; toutes choses prenoit en bonne partie, tout acte interprétoit a bien; jamais ne se tourmentoit, jamais ne se scandalizoit: aussi eust-il esté bien forissu du déificque manoir de raison, si aultrement se feust contristé ou altéré, car tous les biens que le ciel couvre et que la terre contient en toutes ses dimensions: haulteur, profondité, longitude et latitude, ne sont dignes d'esmouvoir nos affections et troubler nos sens et espritz

> (But I have already told you, and tell you again, that he was the best little and big fellow ever to buckle on a sword. He took everything in good part, looked at everything in the best light, never got aggravated or scandalized; for otherwise he'd have been excluded from the divine empire of reason by becoming sad or downcast, because everything good under the skies of heaven and contained by all the dimensions of the earth, height, depth, longitude, and latitude, is not worthy of moving our emotions or bothering our reasons and our minds).

The new Panurge, the squire of Salmiguondin, had spent three years' income in less than a fortnight, not wasting it, "comme vous pourriez dire (as you might say)," by founding monasteries, churches, colleges, and hospitals, but on feasts and girls and, in a series of proverbs, "burning good wood to sell the ash," "prenent argent d'avance, achaptant cher, vendent a bon marché, et mangeant son bled en herbe (taking money in advance, buying dear, selling cheap, and eating his corn as it sprouted)." Pantagruel takes him aside and warns him gently that he won't easily get rich that way. Panurge, energetically affirming that he is doing no more than imitate the university and the parlement, now tries to justify himself in a virtuoso demonstration that he is only cultivating the four cardinal virtues, prudence, justice, fortitude, and wisdom. You can make a good green sauce from sprouting corn.

The new roles of Pantagruel and Panurge are further fixed as the conversation continues. When, asks Pantagruel, will Panurge be out of debt? Panurge replies with a string of proverbs starting with "the Greek calends," all meaning never, and launches into his famous mock encomium in praise of debt. Lucianic in origin, the mock encomium, of which Folly's praise of herself in Erasmus's satire is the best known, is a favourite renaissance genre, associated for instance also with Cornelius Agrippa of Nettesheim and Ulrich von Hütten. Panurge's version draws on Plutarch, Cicero, Augustine, and Plato, and links beauty and goodness in a characteristically neoplatonist way. Faith, hope, and charity will be abolished and debt will become the "vinculum mundi (that which binds the world together)," an allusion to Ficino's gloss on Plato's *Symposium*, in which, of course, what binds creation together is love, including God's love for man and man's for God. At the end of the fifth chapter Pantagruel indicates what he thinks by saying simply "Let's leave that subject."

Panurge now turns to marriage, the subject which will occupy most of the rest of the book, asking first why the newly married are exempted from going to war. Pantagruel says that it is to give them a chance to perpetuate their line. Then, if in the second year of marriage they are killed, at least they will have heirs. As the discussion progresses, with the register now clearly more serious than in the earlier books, Pantagruel makes a statement refusing to judge religious rights and wrongs: "Seulement me desplaist la nouveaulté et mespris du commun usage (What displeases me is only innovation, and contempt for common practice)." The exchanges continue with desultory frivolity until in chapter nine Pantagruel and Panurge begin to discuss whether or not Panurge should get married. His quest may be a metaphor of the quest for truth, but its real meaning must centre on the impossibility in life of absolute certainty. Action must be based on something less.

The humour still bubbles up everywhere, but it is more erudite, has more to do with language, and has a more profound moral: humility and trust in God. The tone is more subdued than in the earlier books and Rabelais appears more conscious of the serious implications underlying his mockery. Will Panurge be cuckolded if he marries? Pantagruel's replies are a covert allusion to Erasmus's "Echo" colloquy. As early as chapter 10 Pantagruel gives Panurge his answer. There is no choice but to decide what you want to do, and to go ahead, trusting in God:

> Aussi en vos propositions tant y a de si et de mais, que je n'y sçaurois rien fonder ne rien résouldre. N'estez-vous asceuré de vostre vouloir? Le poinct principal y gist: tout le reste est fortuit et dépendent des fatales disppositions du ciel

> (Then in what you say there are so many ifs and buts that I couldn't decide or resolve anything with them. Don't you know what you want? That's the main thing. Everything else is fortuitous and depends on the heavens and the decrees of fate).

There follow a number of chapters full of quite learned satire as Panurge and Pantagruel discuss oracles, dice-casting, divination, and the interpretation of dreams as ways of discovering whether or not Panurge should get married, and what would happen if he did. Hermetic and occult authorities and the cabbala are considered but rejected as possible sources of certainty, and at the end of chapter 14 Pantagruel touches on the problem of the discernment of spirits. There is no indication that Rabelais realized just how central to reformatory and counter-reformatory spiritualities the ability to discern whether inspiration was coming from God or from the devil was to become. Saint Paul had warned how Satan could transform himself into an angel of light (II Corinthians, xi, 15). That text gave rise to a topos used probably by Colet and certainly by More and Erasmus.

It was to become central to the spirituality of Ignatius of Loyola, whose Jesuit order had been canonically created in 1540. The recourse to direct spiritual experience it was used to justify links the evangelical humanists to the reformers, particularly Zwingli, and to the counter-reformatory spiritual currents to such an extent as to call into question the nature of any necessary opposition at all between evangelical humanist and reformed spiritualities. Rabelais, whose imaginative genres allowed him to steer clear of serious theological controversy, was, like Erasmus, certainly aware of the spiritual affinities which crossed the schism. He could not have known much about Jesuit spirituality, but he must here have been drawing on the same text by Erasmus, prefacing the 1522 *Paraphrasis* of Matthew, as Ignatius.

By this time Epistémon, the comic classical scholar and pedant, has joined the group as they consult the 16th-century equivalents of readers of palms and tea leaves, sybils, a deaf-mute, and the dying old poet Raminagrobis. At this point the satire bites very deep, as Panurge decides that the poet's soul needs saving: "Ce sera oeuvre charitable a nous faicte: au moins, s'il perd le corps et la vie, qu'il ne damne son âme (That will be a work of charity down to us: at least if he loses his body and his life, let him not damn his soul)." The physical tortures inflicted on heretics to make them recant before execution were thought to be justified precisely because life and physical wellbeing obviously counted for nothing alongside eternal salvation. To die a heretic was to go to hell for all eternity. It became a charity to extract a recantation by whatever force was necessary before executing a condemned heretic. Technically it was the Church which pleaded for the conversion, and always the secular arm in whose name the torture and execution were carried out, since the punishment, again technically, was not for the ecclesiastical "crimen" of heresy, constituted by the public dissemination of heterodoxy and considered a danger to the eternal salvation of those who listened, but for the secular crime of blasphemy. By putting those words into the mouth of Panurge, Rabelais seems to have been hinting at the exaggerated disproportion involved in totally disregarding the welfare of the body for the good of the soul.

In the quest for certainty Epistémon's classical learning is vainly called on, and the "Her Trippa" who is consulted is generally supposed to be a caricature of Cornelius Agrippa of Nettesheim, whom Rabelais is likely to have met at Grenoble in 1535, of whose *De occulta philosophia* he certainly makes fun, and whose works, including the *De incertudine et vanitate scientiarum et artium, atque excellentia verbi Dei declamatio* and the *De nobilitate et praecellentia Foeminei sexus*, he certainly knew, although it is not clear to what extent they either were, or were thought by Rabelais to be, ironic. Rabelais is in this chapter more than usually dependent on Erasmus's *Adagia*. In the next one there is an obscene litany sending up the "blasons" which had earlier in the century been used to celebrate particular parts of the female anatomy, perhaps part of a literary game whose rules have been lost. Frère Jan des Entommeurs has scriptural and liturgical tags and a clearly obscene anecdote to support his view that Panurge should marry.

In chapter 29 Panurge reports back to Pantagruel, who repeats what he had said earlier: "chascun doibt estre arbitre de ses propres pensées et de soy-mesmes conseil prendre (everyone should be the judge of his own thoughts, and take counsel with himself)." Panurge, says Pantagruel, is blinded by "philautie," the self-love of Erasmus's Folly. With the rest of the renaissance Rabelais took the blindness caused by self-love from Plutarch. It is in this chapter that the "symposium" begins. Pantagruel proposes to invite to dinner on the following Sunday a theologian, Hippothadée; a doctor, Rondibilis, whose name recalls the celebrated Montpellier doctor Guillaume Rondelet; and a lawyer,

the judge Bridoye. They represent the three graduate faculties at Paris and the professions caring respectively for soul, body, and belongings. To complete the Pythagorean tetrad, Pantagruel invites Trouillogan, the philosopher. Philosophy was the sole undergraduate discipline.

The narrative of the dinner party is an extraordinary feat of comic writing. Rabelais's skill with dialogue has advanced sufficiently for all the characters to talk in their own style, and the result is the wittily depicted failure of Hippothadée's faith and Rondibilis's reason to help Panurge. A great deal of learned play is made with humanist disputes about the nature of sperm, with Rabelais taking the Platonist side against the supporters of Galen. Trouillogan's human wisdom does not succeed in reconciling faith and reason, and Gargantua enters the room in time to hear Trouillogan say that Panurge should both marry and not marry, and that he should neither marry nor not marry.

Pantagruel gives this paradox an evangelical interpretation. Having a wife is what nature intended for the support and company she affords the husband, but not having a wife prevents any obstacle in the way of "celle unicque et suprême affection que doibt l'homme à Dieu (that unique and supreme affection which man owes to God)." Gargantua has, however, already walked out in exasperation at Trouillogan's ignorance and scepticism. Rabelais is here at his most uncertain. The balance of the argument in favour of the insuperability of human ignorance on all the important issues affecting human life seems irreversible, and from the beginning of the Sunday dinner has weighed down the text, however witty and learned, with its inevitability. The clowning has more clearly become a cover for hesitancy. Rabelais's confident optimism has given way to real hesitation and doubt.

Bridoye had not attended the dinner because he had been summoned before the senate to defend an apparently unfair judgement he had given. The next day Pantagruel attends his defence. Law, always a rich source of satire, provides Rabelais with some of the best material in the book. Bridoye decided his case after listening to all the learned arguments by throwing his dice as usual but, since the case was complicated, he used his small dice, and may have misread them. He elegantly defends the practice of allowing the litigants to tire themselves out with argument before he throws his dice to decide his cases.

Pantagruel, asked what should be done, points out that in 40 years Bridoye's decisions have always been correct. Bridoye does in fact represent the approach to life advocated all along by Pantagruel. Since certainty is unattainable, you must make up your mind and trust in God. In chapter 44 Pantagruel points out that this is precisely what Bridoye has always done although, unfortunately, Pantagruel's speech to this effect is manifestly mis-attributed to Epistémon in modern editions. Counsel is finally sought from a fool, Triboullet, but what he says is interpreted differently by Pantagruel and Panurge. The book ends with the matter undecided. Pantagruel, Panurge, Epistémon, Frère Jan and others prepare to set sail in quest of certainty from the oracle of "la dive bouteille (the divine bottle)."

A great flotilla is assembled, and four chapters, crammed with learning, much of which comes from Pliny, are devoted to the properties of the herb Pantagruelion which the travellers take with them, a symbol of the joyful, natural truth of whose discovery Pantagruel, and Rabelais, have not, in spite of the catalogue of failures in the *Tiers Livre*, yet given up hope. Pantagruelion has one wonderful property: it is indestructible. Like the salamander, the emblem of François I himself, it lives through fire. This is a compliment to the king of France, but it is also a dangerous warning that nature and truth cannot be burnt out, but will always be reborn. The reference to repression in the name of religious and political ideologies is almost palpable. This is the other, more defensive side of the moral of Thélème. Nature is an ineradicable plant. It will always assert itself, cannot be extinguished, and only through its cultivation can virtue and happiness be achieved.

Le Quart Livre des faictz et dicts héroïques du bon Pantagruel composé par M. François Rabelais, docteur en médecine lends itself more readily to an allegorical interpretation which can too easily conceal more obvious meanings, but it is undoubtedly more anecdotal than the *Tiers Livre*. Its episodes tend to comprise several chapters, and are loosely linked together by the travelogue form. Rabelais is now sufficiently conscious of the danger that his humour will be lost in learned obscurity to provide at the end of the book the "Briefve déclaration" explaining the more difficult allusions. The named members of the company blessed by Gargantua, all of whom had appeared in the *Tiers Livre*, are Pantagruel, Panurge, Frère Jan des Entommeurs, Epistémon, Gymnaste, Eusthenes, Rhizotome, and Carpalim. Rabelais cannot resist using Homer for his list of ships in the first chapter, or accounts of by then famous voyages for his route. Both legal and religious satire intensify, and the opening chapter contains a forthright if no longer particularly daring emphasis on evangelical religion, even though a psalm is quoted in the proscribed Marot translation. The third and fourth chapters contain an exchange of letters between Gargantua and his son, once more confirming the seriousness with which Rabelais takes the father–son relationship.

Panurge has a quarrel with a merchant called Dindenault from another ship and ends up playing on him an ancient trick related by Teofilo Folengo in his burlesque epic of 1517, the *Maccheronee*, published under the pseudonym of Merlin Cocai. Panurge buys a sheep from Dindenault and pushes it into the sea, where all the other sheep follow it, to be drowned with the merchant and his shepherds, who are dragged into the sea while trying to hold back the sheep. As with the shipwreck episode a little later, this time borrowed from Erasmus's *Naufragium*, Rabelais turns a dry little comic story into a brilliant miniature drama, above all by supplying appropriate language in which the stock characters express their stereotyped reactions, especially in response to danger during the storm in chapters 18 to 24. As Dindenault and his men are drowning, Panurge stops them from getting back on board. Like "un petit frère Olivier Maillard," the name of a famous 15th-century Franciscan preacher, he preaches to them

par lieux de rhétoricque les misères de ce monde, le bien et l'heur de l'aultre vie, affermant plus heureux estre les trespasséz que les vivans en ceste vallée de misère, et à chascun d'eulx promettant ériger un beau cénotaphe et sépulchre honoraire au plus hault du mont Cenis, á son retour de Lanternoys

(by rhetorical devices the miseries of this world, the goodness and happiness of the afterlife, maintaining that the dead are happier than the living in this vale of misery, and promising each of them to erect a fine cenotaph and honorific grave at the very top of Mont Cenis on his return from Lanternoys).

The name of the country of the "dive bouteille" probably conceals an obscenity; the reference to a cenotaph comes from Suetonius; and for good measure Panurge wishes those who want to go on living luck enough to meet a whale who will swallow them whole and deliver them, like Jonas, after three days to dry land.

These early chapters of the *Quart Livre* are clearly brimming with contemporary allusions, and include some irreverence about Florence: "Ce sont belles maisons. C'est tout (They're beautiful houses, that's all)." The book becomes for some chapters increasingly episodic, although without warning Rabelais slips at times into much more serious satire, particularly with Pantagruel's religious attitude during the storm, Frère Jan's practicality, and Panurge's headlong leap in the face of danger into the most superstitious and credulous type of medieval piety. Among other things it leads him to appeal to "Monsieur l'Abstracteur," who can only be his real creator, Rabelais himself in *Pantagruel*. Rabelais modified the religious implications of the comic storm narrative, partly to protect himself against the Sorbonne, and partly to emphasize against Calvin man's need to cooperate in his own salvation.

Rabelais's own religious sympathies are made even clearer in the following episode of the Isles des Macraeons in which, taking much from Plutarch and Postel, he writes of the death of Guillaume du Bellay (Langey), and of Christian death in general, at the end of the episode in chapter 28 following Postel in identifying Christ with Pan. The whole episode, whose understanding is greatly complicated by the earlier renaissance use of classical authors by Christian writers and by the existence of the numerous renaissance compilations and interpretations of signs and portents, in fact scarcely conceals Rabelais's strong affirmation of a deep and evangelical Catholic devotion.

The humour becomes lighter again, although at the end of chapter 32 through Pantagruel Rabelais throws in a growl at an assortment of hostile critics, including Calvin, the Sorbonne, and the monk of Fontevrault who had attacked him in the *Theotimus*. The humour continues to have different resonances of seriousness, and is clearly less popular in tone than it had been in *Pantagruel*. That does not mean that it is not sometimes very funny. A whale is caught and taken to the island of the Andouilles for cutting up. Whale oil was valuable, and the crew hope to cure themselves of their illness called "Faulte d'argent (Lack of money)." They find strange lands like Ruach—Hebrew for breath, soul, and wind—where everyone lives on air. The comic inventiveness is still extraordinary, as when the inhabitants discuss at their banquets the merits of the various winds as if they were wine vintages or grape varieties, and their ruler complains that even their greatest feasts can be ruined if a few drops of rain fall to spoil the winds.

Most of the names have erudite if philologically outrageous roots in learned languages, and great amusement is extracted from the "Papifigues," who despise the portrait of the pope venerated by the "Papimanes," who describe the pope in terms reserved in Scripture and the hermetic tradition for God, "He who is," a name for God used particularly by Marguerite de Navarre to describe her religious experience. In the middle of the comedy of pope-worshipping, and just before Rabelais introduces the sacred decretals, there is a sudden lurch into seriousness as Pantagruel becomes angry at the beating of small boys. Large sections of the book are in direct speech, but the narrator now and again uses the first person and occasionally, as in chapter 38, addresses the reader directly. That chapter had ended with the narrator telling the reader to believe the gospel. In chapter 53 the satire explains how, by power of the decretals, gold migrates from France to Rome, before Rabelais launches into the brilliant fantasy of the frozen words, caught by the icy winter and now, thawing out in the spring, echoing their way towards the travellers. "Messere Gaster," meaning stomach, is the first master of arts in the world, a position occupied by love in Ficino's gloss on Plato's *Symposium*. There are further short episodes after this, and occasional reference is still made to the object of the quest, that of discovering from the oracle whether or not Panurge should marry. The *Quart Livre* simply stops rather than ends. The final episode could have come almost anywhere after the storm.

The imaginative vigour is still clear in parts at least of the *Cinquiesme Livre*, whether Rabelais produced more than a sketch for at least the first part, as seems likely, or not. The episode of the Isle sonante, with its ecclesiastical hierarchy of birds headed by the single Papegault, or Pope Bird, is the equal of the episode of the frozen words in the *Quart Livre*. The birds procreate "sans compagnie charnelle, comme se fait entre les abeilles (without carnal congress, as among the bees)," but there are names for female equivalents of bishop, cardinal, and pope birds. Of the 16 chapters published in 1562, chapters two to eight are devoted to the birds. Chapters 11 to 15 constitute an episode devoted to the chats-fourrés (fur-lined cats), generally considered to be a satire of the Parlement de Paris and given their name from the ermine worn by magistrates. Pantagruel refuses to visit the island where the chats-fourrés live, and the rest of the narrator's party are taken prisoner by Grippeminault, the name of the hero of one of Marot's satires, later memorably used by La Fontaine. Panurge bribes his way out, and Frère Jehan, as he now is, plays a rather pointless trick on an old woman inn keeper who has tried to cheat the crew. The partial version ends with a chapter on the Apedeftes, a satire on the revenue office.

Whoever finished the *Cinquiesme Livre* changed the "proprium" of man to drink, and TRINCH is the oracular word of the divine bottle. The book ends strongly exploiting the ambivalence of the neoplatonist "furies" or intoxications, and an anagram tells us that the work was finished in the spirit of Rabelais. Many of Rabelais's neoplatonist themes are continued, but Pantagruel almost disappears from the book, and Panurge's question is not answered. There is less dialogue and less anecdote, but more description than is likely to have been the case if Rabelais had finished the book himself.

The real power of Rabelais's work does not reside in his defence of evangelical religion, in his frothy fun with words, or even in the pungency of his satire of what was becoming universally regarded as an old guard. It lies in the comic genius with which he linked a sane cultivation of humane values to a gay, witty, cheeky, and irreverent ability to laugh at everything in life which was exaggerated, silly, disproportionate, or plainly wrong-headed. It may still sound strange to hold up Rabelais as the patron writer of satirists defending robust common sense and moderate but intelligent views. Yet that is what he did, employing for the purpose an immense range of literary registers and comic techniques, from quite bitter invective to delicately spun fantasy, and from crude obscenity to refined wit. He was French, Chinonais, Catholic, a lawyer, and a doctor, and most of the time took himself seriously in all five capacities. He was also learned with the new humanistic learning, not at all above showing off,

demanding Greek type from printers catering for the trade generated by the book fairs, deliberately flattering a court readership, luring it well beyond its intellectual, aesthetic, and literary capacities by his chivalry, fantasy, ribaldry, cheek, and verbal acrobatics into intellectual and religious territory it wanted to be seen to occupy, but towards which it could only obscurely feel its way.

Rabelais's touch was unsure. The swings in mood are too sudden and some of the devices too crude to allow the reader to suppose that his gaze was steady and his aim certain. His immense imaginative energy was gestated largely in an effort to feel his way forward, and there are moments when he came close to settling for simple bawdiness or for the comfort of familiar medieval forms, the "blason," the enigma, fun with lists, digestive functions, dimensions, and feats of verbal ingenuity. His greatness resides in the tension he came to be able to sustain, particularly in the *Tiers Livre*, between a sad but serious view of human life and an acute sense of the ridiculousness of most of the solutions proposed to its major problems. It is not at all clear that Gargantua, Pantagruel, or Rabelais much enjoyed life. Panurge did, but in a well-ordered universe should not have done. Rabelais was always conscious that that was one of life's ironies, and his genius lay in unmaliciously pointing out its absurdity.

PUBLICATIONS

Collections

Oeuvres complètes (Pléiade edition), 1934; revised edition, 1955
Oeuvres complètes, 2 vols., 1962
Oeuvres (critical edition), 6 vols., 1912–55
The Works of Rabelais, edited by Albert Jay Nock and Catherine Rose Wilson, 2 vols., 1931
Gargantua and Pantagruel, translated by Sir Thomas Urquhart (1653) and continued by Peter Motteux (1694), edited by W.E. Henley, 1900

Fiction

Pantagruel, 1532 (possibly late 1531); edited by V.-L. Saulnier, 1965; as *Pantagruel* (in English), 1955
Gargantua, 1535 (possibly late 1534); edited by R.M. Calder and M.A. Screech, 1970; as *Gargantua* (in English), 1955
Tiers Livre, 1546; edited by M.A. Screech, 1944
Quart Livre (shorter version), 1548; full version, 1552; edited by R. Marichal, 1947
Cinquiesme Livre: L'Isle sonante, 1562
Cinquiesme Livre, 1564

Other

Pantagrueline prognostication (for 1533), late 1532?
La Sciomachie, 1549
(All three *Almanacs*, for 1533, 1535, and 1536, have been lost, as has the *Stratagemata* of 1539)
Editor, *Epistolarum medicinalium Tomus Secundus*, by J. Manardi, 1532
Editor, *Hippocratis ac Galeni libri aliquot*, 1532; revised edition, 1543

Editor, *Ex reliquis venerandae antiquitatis Lucii Cuspidii Testamentum*, 1532

Editor, *Topographia Antiquae Romae*, by J.B. Marliani, 1534

Biographical and critical studies

Plattard, J., *Vie de Rabelais*, 1928; as *Life of François Rabelais*, 1930

Lote, Georges, *La Vie et l'oeuvre de François Rabelais*, 1938

Febvre, Lucien, *Le Problème de l'incroyance au XVIe siècle: la religion de Rabelais*, 1942; as *The Problem of Unbelief in the Sixteenth Century*, 1982

Krailsheimer, A.J., *Rabelais and the Franciscans*, 1963

Kaiser, Walter, *Praisers of Folly: Erasmus, Rabelais, Shakespeare*, 1963

Krailsheimer, A.J., *Rabelais*, 1967

Bakhtin, Mikhail, *Rabelais and His World*, 1968

Frame, Donald M., *Rabelais, a Study*, 1977

Screech, M.A., *Rabelais*, 1979

Bibliography

Rawles, Stephen, and Screech, M.A., *A New Rabelais Bibliography: Editions of Rabelais before 1626*, 1987

RACAN, Honorat de Bueil, Seigneur de, 1589–1670.

Poet and dramatist.

LIFE

Racan came from the younger branch of one of France's most illustrious military families, tracing its ancestry back to the 11th century through a long line of administrators and soldiers, with 17 dead at Agincourt. A devoted disciple of Malherbe, he was able for most of his long life to enjoy the rural tranquillity which nourished his verse. Most of his relatively uneventful career was led by choice as far away from the turbulence of love and war as Racan could contrive, although his position demanded of him from time to time a show of martial endeavour. His enthusiasm for military distinction has been exaggerated, although when young he had wanted to emulate the warlike exploits of his family, and in 1608 had tried to persuade Henri IV to send him to fight with the Dutch against the Spaniards. He was, however, kept in training at Calais, and by the time he got to Holland the 1609 truce had been signed. Racan did finally appear in three campaigns, and captained a company in Effiat's army at the siege of La Rochelle. Meanwhile only a large inheritance from his cousin Anne de Bueil, the duchesse de Bellegarde and daughter of Racan's paternal uncle Honorat—eight years older than Racan's father, vice-admiral of France and lieutenant-general of Saint-Malo, where he was assassinated by the League in 1590—saved Racan from economic ruin.

Roger de Saint-Larry, duc de Bellegarde, who married Anne de Bueil in 1594, was grand écuyer de France, making Racan's cousin one of the most influential ladies of the court, at the centre, after the edict of Nantes, of a renewed social activity at court from which the later salons were to derive. Her husband was probably the queen's lover, and her relation from the other branch of the family, Jacqueline de Courcillon, comtesse de Moret, was certainly one of the king's mistresses. Racan was the only male remaining representative of her branch of the family. Tallemant, who gleefully recounts stories of Racan's ignorance of Latin and youthful poverty, and tells of a small loan from Boisrobert, and of an attempt by Conrart to find him more comfortable lodgings, originally entitled the *Historiette* devoted to him "Racan," but then added "et autres resveurs (and other dreamers)." He gives amusing examples of Racan's obviously celebrated capacity for abstraction.

Racan was born on 5 February 1589 south of Le Mans at the manoir of Champarin, which belonged to his mother, Marguerite de Vendômois, married to Louis de Bueil, a chevalier of the Order of the Holy Spirit and a maréchal de camp in Conti's army, killed in the king's service as grand master of the artillery, fighting the Spaniards still engaged in their rearguard battle for the League at Amiens in 1597. Racan's father had bought the fief from which the poet inherited his name certainly before 1569. Louis de Bueil had been born in 1544 but, although royal lieutenant of Brittany, had run into debt. In 1588 he had married the eldest daughter of the equally indebted royal lieutenant of Maine. Anne de Bueil came to the rescue and persuaded her husband to become Racan's honorary guardian.

Unfortunately the financial difficulties took some time to resolve. In 1605 Henri IV had to intervene to impose a moratorium on interest payments of 102,000 livres, and a property belonging to Racan's mother had to be sold. When Anne de Bueil died on 1 October 1631, leaving Racan 400,000 livres, everything should have been in order, but her maternal uncle, who inherited property worth only 130,000 livres, made difficulties, and Racan was involved until the end of his life in a series of court cases. Meanwhile in 1602 his mother, who had had a daughter by a first marriage, is said to have died after vainly struggling to repay her debts. Racan had for safety's sake been taken immediately after his birth to his father's more highly fortified château at La Roche-au-Majeur, near Saint-Paterne, about 30 kilometres north of Tours, where he was brought up by his mother, her sister, and his nurse, learning very little except the elements of religion and letters.

On his mother's death Racan, aged 13, was taken in by the Bellegarde family. Physically too frail for the training afforded by the royal stables, Racan became for five years a page in the royal household. He stammered, was gauche and asthmatic, and spoke French with an accent inherited from his nurse, pronouncing his name "Latan," but met Malherbe, also a member of the Bellegarde household in Paris, who is said to have envied Racan his facility at versifying, but whose devoted pupil Racan became. He was the butt of at least one practical joke which can be dated to 1626. Tallemant recounts that, when Racan had an appointment with Mlle de Gournay, Montaigne's "fille d'alliance" who did not know him but had given him her recent *L'Ombre* and invariably referred to him as "the monkey of Malherbe," two other more elegant colleagues turned up in succession rather earlier than the appointed time, pretending to the 60-year-old woman to be the Racan she was expecting. When the first one arrived, she dismissed her poetic thoughts, which might come back again, to see the handsome caller who had been announced, and who might not. Racan, untidy, out of breath, and no doubt dirty, was himself naturally taken to be one of the frauds.

As a member of the royal household, Racan was admitted without payment to the Hôtel de Bourgogne, where he enjoyed seeing Hardy's plays. Malherbe, according to Racan's later *Mémoires pour la vie de Malherbe*, would read to him from the great poets, making gruffly critical comments, before showing him how to put an ode carefully together and then harshly criticizing Racan's own efforts. Malherbe disdained most of the poets of antiquity, with Statius virtually the only exception, and almost all medieval and foreign poets, excepting only Tasso for *Aminta*. According to both Tallemant and Sorel, Racan's ignorance of antiquity was renowned, although he himself may also have exaggerated it in a celebrated later letter to Chapelain and, if he continued to take more pleasure in the poetry of Ronsard and the pastoral poems of Desportes than Malherbe thought that their impurities of diction warranted, he none the less took instruction from Malherbe in versifying. The result was Racan's peculiar blend of formal distinction with a genuine if bucolic poetic inspiration. At Malherbe's loose morals Racan merely laughed. It is unlikely to be quite true that, as he constantly gave out and as Ménage was certainly to be given to think, he could not manage Virgil without a translation.

Racan fell vainly in love with someone from his home region, and then with his distant cousin, the king's former mistress, the comtesse de Moret, the Cloris of the poems, who finally married the marquis de Vardes in 1617. In 1615 Racan had accompanied Marie de Medici and the young Louis XIII to Bordeaux to welcome to France the king's bride, Anne of Austria, infanta of Spain. It was shortly after this journey that Racan seriously considered retiring from court life altogether, and going off to marry and live at La Roche, away from intrigues and worries about money. In fact, after fruitlessly pursuing a prospective Breton bride addressed in the verse as "Amaranthe," he settled down in Paris again, spending only the summer or autumn annually at La Roche. It was probably in 1618 that he wrote for his country neighbour, René d'Armilly—"Thirsis"—what is regarded as the best of his poems, the "Stances sur la retraite," first published in 1620.

Racan, who still visited Malherbe most days, and spent much of his time with the Bellegarde family, frequented the salon of Mme des Loges, where Malherbe was regularly to be found every other day and Gombauld was the reigning celebrity, and also the chambre bleue of the Hôtel de Rambouillet, where the marquise, Catherine de Vivonne, was beginning to receive daily (see: *Guirlande de Julie*). It was there that Racan pressed his galanterie with the young and apparently experienced Catherine Chabot, married in 1615 to Bellegarde's brother, César-Auguste de Saint-Larry, the marquis de Termes and the Agénor of Madeleine de Scudéry's *Le Grand Cyrus*. Termes had been a chevalier of Malta, but had returned to secular life to marry when Bellegarde realized that he was not going to have an heir. Termes was to be killed fighting under Luynes at the siege of Clairac, dying on 23 July 1621 at the age of 40, the day after he was wounded, but he left a daughter. A month earlier, Racan had finally taken part in his own first engagement at Saint-Jean-d'Angély. He wrote consolatory verses to Bellegarde and

appears seriously to have wanted to marry the widowed Catherine Chabot, marquise de Termes. She did get married again, to Claude Vignier, seigneur de Saint-Liébault, in 1635, a président à mortier at Metz and conseiller at the parlement de Bourgogne.

Since Malherbe had broken with the vicomtesse d'Auchy and, even at 60, felt himself in need of a galant partner, he chose as the object of his attentions Catherine de Vivonne herself. Both Racan and Malherbe looked for the anagram of Catherine under which the two Catherines would be known. They rejected Enthe and Carinthée before opting for the name which was to become legendary, Arthénice. "Arthénice" was the original title of Racan's dramatic pastoral *Les Bergeries*, first played in Paris at the Hôtel de Bourgogne probably in 1619, and then in the provinces. Henriette de France played a role in a performance perhaps in 1624, before leaving for the English throne. The first edition was 1625, but there were a dozen editions in the following decade.

In 1620 Toussainct du Bray had published 60 pages of Racan's verse in *Les Délices de la poésie françoise*. From soon after 1621 and at any rate from 1625, Racan spent most of the year in the country, coming to Paris for the spring. Catherine Chabot, whose brother, the comte de Charny, had died of illness, like du Vair and Luynes himself, during the 1621 campaign, had retired to Burgundy, where she continuously received from Racan a spate of madrigals, songs, eclogues, and odes, all carefully scrutinized by Malherbe, with whom Racan kept up a frequent and intimate correspondence. Until 1636 he also corresponded regularly with Mainard. His second campaign was in 1622. Balzac congratulated him on *Les Bergeries*, and Racan began to write his first sacred poetry, with a psalm paraphrase. At the end of 1626 he could give Toussainct du Bray for a new edition of *Les Délices* the 60-odd poems which, with four more odes and a madrigal, constituted his whole output of secular lyric poetry. With seven more letters printed in 1627 by Nicolas Faret in a collection offered to Richelieu, Racan's career as a profane writer was at an end.

A neighbour, Pierre du Bois, had a daughter Madeleine, aged 15 in 1627, whom Racan now wanted to marry. Discussions were taking place when Racan was called to serve with Effiat at La Rochelle. He took advantage of the king's brief absence from La Rochelle in February 1628 to arrange his own wedding. The Bellegardes had given their consent, and Malherbe had given his. The duchesse de Bellegarde came from Paris for the wedding, held on 5 March after the betrothal ceremonies of 29 February. No doubt the duchesse was there to reassure the bride's family about Racan's eventual inheritance. Five days after the wedding, Racan left again for La Rochelle. Malherbe came, hoping in vain for vengeance for his son killed the preceding year in a duel, but died on 16 October 1628, soon after his return to Paris. Racan returned home but had soon to leave again to join the king at Grenoble. He appeared at one further campaign before settling down at La Roche. His wife bore him in November 1629 a daughter who died in infancy, and then five children in seven years, three sons and two daughters. The eldest son is squarely called a fool by Tallemant, and the second did not marry. The third died at 15. One of the daughters did not marry.

In March 1634, Racan heard that he had been appointed to the new Académie française, which had hitherto been merely one of a number of informal groups of friends, and had been coming together weekly for about five years. Racan and Balzac were the last of the initial 28 to be appointed, the canonical number of 40 not being reached until 1639. When in Paris Racan assiduously attended the meetings, held on Mondays at Desmarets's house now that Conrart had married. His discourse, read for him by the Académie's director on 9 July 1635, was entitled *Contre les sciences*, and was directed at pedantry and the imposition of rules on works of the imagination. In the same year Racan made his last military appearance, in the rearguard of Louis XIII's army in Lorraine; he resigned all his military connections in 1639.

However, Paris seems to have attracted him little after the death of Malherbe, and he went there mostly in connection with his law-suits, all of which had ultimately to do with the rich succession of Anne de Bueil. The will was disputed, and Racan was also taken to court to account for family expenditure attributable to the upbringing of his aunt Jacqueline, and for failure to pay the dowry of his elder daughter Françoise, married to sieur de La Rivière, as also over the suzerainty of Saint-Paterne. Since he was successfully rebuilding the château at La Roche, his relatives were naturally anxious to obtain from him whatever might be made out to be their due, and in 1651 he was forced for a period to settle in Paris. It was at this time that he most regularly attended the meetings of the Académie.

Racan's literary activity during the second half of his life was almost entirely sacred. The first psalm translation, the 11 stanzas of "Caeli enarrant gloriam dei," dates from 1627, and it was followed by the 600 lines of the seven *Psaumes de la Pénitence* dedicated to Anne de Bueil and published by Toussainct du Bray in 1631, just before her death. Interest in sacred poetry, already clear from the activities of Marot and then of Baïf, had markedly intensified since the end of the religious wars. In the early 1630s Racan was still sporadically writing profane odes, including one for Richelieu. Then he met the Cistercian abbot of the neighbouring monastery of La Clarté-Dieu, who asked him for a translation of psalm 26, "Dominus illuminatio mea," and then encouraged him to go on with what finally turned out to be the 32 psalm paraphrases of the 1651 *Odes sacrées*, much admired at the Académie and by Balzac. When the book was published, Racan was in Paris, at the deathbed of his 15-year-old youngest son, Honorat, who had fallen grievously ill as a page in the service of Mademoiselle.

Ménage had asked Racan for some notes on Malherbe for an edition he was preparing, and then circulated the manuscript, which was printed, although Racan had not intended to publish it, as the *Mémoires sur la vie de Malherbe*. By 1654, Racan had completed the paraphrases of the psalter, although publication was delayed until 1660, when Pierre Lamy published without Racan's consent the *Dernières ouevres et poésies chrestiennes*. The collection was considered much inferior to Racan's previous work. Racan had quarrelled with Conrart and Chapelain over the matter of Gilles Boileau's election to the Académie, the presumed reason for his non-appearance on the list of writers recommended to Colbert by Chapelain for a royal pension. Racan had also been omitted in 1657 from the list presented by Costar to Mazarin, but then it was because he was considered too rich. In fact the court settlements and the debts of his eldest son had eaten away at his revenues, and at the age of 80 Racan had to go to Paris in connection with his court cases. His death there on 21 January 1670 prevented him from seeing himself ruined, although a court decision had gone in his favour in 1667. He had four grandchildren and had lived the last decade of his life mostly at Saint-Paterne, where he established a foundation for Masses to be celebrated in perpetuity for the salvation of his soul.

WORKS

Apart from *Les Bergeries* and the psalm paraphrases, Racan's poetic output consisted of less than a score each of "Odes," "Stances," "Epigrammes," and "Sonnets," almost all of them subjected to Malherbe's scrutiny before his death. It is more than occasionally clear how Malherbe's view of poetry as a solemn and official public undertaking clashed with Racan's more lyrical, country-loving, Horatian inspiration, imposing on it artificial pomposity and inflated rhetorical locutions. Racan was not good at descriptive verse, but he does render aptly his natural indolence and its harmony with the slow rhythms of his preferred rural settings. He was impatient of Malherbe's constraints, however well he got on personally with the older poet, and however seriously he took his advice. Malherbe reproached Racan with the liberties he took in versification, and *Les Bergeries* appears almost to be a compromise. The pastoral drama in verse was a form of which Malherbe did not totally disapprove. The prefatory letter to Malherbe of 15 January 1625 is itself strongly stylized in its insistence on its author's indolence, ignorance, and enjoyment of country life.

In his 1635 discourse read to the Académie well after Malherbe's death, Racan's expression of his view is not empty of wit. Attacking those who have, he says, made a grammar, a logic, and a rhetoric "des choses les plus communes que nous avons pratiquées dès le berceau, dix ans auparavant que d'en sçavoir le nom (out of the commonest things which we did from the cradle, ten years before we knew their names)," Racan continues in *Contre les sciences*,

> ils réduiront encore en art le pleurer et le rire: ils le diviseront en plusieurs parties, comme ils ont fait de notre langage, et l'on ne pourra plus rire à propos, à leur gré, que par règles et par figures

> (they will reduce crying and laughing, too, to arts, dividing them into different parts, as they have already done to our language, and in their view we shall only be able to laugh correctly if we do it according to rules and diagrams).

When he allows himself to follow Malherbe too slavishly, he can write as bad as an ode as that to the overflowing Loir:

> Déjà, dans les terres prochaines,
> Ton courroux, enflé de boüillons,
> Traînant les arbres dans les plaines,
> Arrache les bleds des seillons;
> Déjà les peuples des campagnes
> Cherchent leur salut aux montagnes;
> Les poissons logent aux forests,
> Quittant leurs cavernes profondes,
> Et la nasselle fend les ondes
> Où le soc fendoit les guerets

> (Already, in the nearby lands,/Your anger, seething at the boil,/Dragging trees through the plains,/Tears the corn from the furrow,/Already the people from the countryside/Seek safety in the mountains;/The fish live in the forests,/Leaving behind their deep caves,/And the boat cleaves the waters/Where the ploughshare turned over the fields).

The effect Racan sought was one of almost epic dignity,

emphasizing the threat with the repeated "Déjà (already)", but the effect he achieves by perfectly respecting Malherbe's rules and rhetorical norms is merely comic, even ridiculous. He is more at home being witty, as in the ode "Vous qui riez…" in which he complains at being badly billeted, where the floor has to do service for bed, table, and sideboard.

> Nostre hoste avec ses serviteurs,
> Nous croyant des reformateurs,
> S'enfuit au travers de la crote,
> Emportant, ployé sous ses bras,
> Son pot, son chaudron et ses dras,
> Et ses enfans dans une hote

(Our host with his serving folk,/Thinking we belong to the Reform,/Flees across the filth,/Carrying off, tucked under his arms,/His pot, his cauldron, and his sheets/And his children in a basket on his back).

The lines split into sections differently, and the inclusion of the children with the pots and pans being carried off makes suddenly clear that, in spite of a reference to the Reform which might have introduced an element of terror, this is a comic picture.

Racan's most famous poem, the "Stances sur la retraite," 15 six-line alexandrine stanzas, is unfortunately too long to quote in full. It is in the end far too moralistic in its sentiments and stylized in its attitudes and imagery to be a very good poem, and its celebrity is ultimately a wrongly conceived attempt to justify Racan's reputation in terms of the gently neostoic nostalgia for the quiet life we might expect from watered-down Malherbe. After the storms of life's seas, it is time to enjoy the delights of the harbour; fortune's jade is fickle; the biggest trees fall to the storm; and kings' mansions lose their roofs before peasants' cottages. It is when the sententiousness dies down for a moment that the poetry seeps through although, amusingly and unintentionally, Racan turns the idealized peasant, king of his passions, in his hut which is his Louvre and his Fontainebleau, into someone who is at the very least a landowner with a pack of hounds for his entertainment and some real peasants to fill his barns and his vats:

> Il voit de toutes parts combler d'heur sa famille,
> La javelle à plein poing tomber sous la faucille,
> Le vendangeur ployer sous le faix des paniers,
> Et semble qu'à l'envy les fertiles montagnes,
> Les humides vallons et les grasses campagnes
> S'efforcent à remplir sa cave et ses greniers.

> Il suit aucunesfois un cerf par les foulées
> Dans ses vieilles forests du peuple reculées
> Et qui mesme du jour ignorent le flambeau;
> Aucunesfois des chiens il suit les voix confuses,
> Et voit enfin le lievre, aprés toutes ces ruses,
> Du lieu de sa naissance en faire son tombeau

(He sees his family showered on all sides with happiness,/The swathes falling in armfuls under the scythe,/The grape-picker bending under the weight of the baskets,/And it seems that the fertile mountains,/The moist valleys, and the lush meadows/Vie with each other to fill his cellar and

his lofts.//Sometimes he follows the tracks of a stag/Through the old forests far away from human beings/Where the flaming torch of which do not even know day is unknown;/Sometimes he follows the confused cries of the hounds,/And finally sees the hare, after all those deceits,/Turn the place of his birth into his tomb).

The imagery remains stylized, but whoever wrote that poem has seen hounds catch a hare, even if forests in which deer can be hunted cannot be as covered in as the one in the poem.

Les Bergeries conforms to the pastoral mode established in France and Italy, with jealous, amorous, otherwise emotionally bonded or else indifferent shepherds and shepherdesses. There are obstacles to love's fulfilment, but they are overcome. There is treachery, a magic mirror, a failed suicide, a ruse that does not work, a rapidly reversed decision to retreat to a convent, and a recognition. Love is innocent but not frivolous, and instinct can lead to virtue. All, however, is not lyrical exaltation, and there are in fact certainly events prompted by Racan's family reminiscences, as the prefatory letter to Malherbe strongly suggests. Act I, scene iii has been singled out in particular for the naturalistic delicacy of its psychology, as Arthénice is caught by her father lying about why she has got up so early. He had on the preceding day met the creature that she now maintained was a wolf, which she was afraid might be about to attack the sheep. What makes *Les Bergeries* a masterpiece is not only the sensitively observed traits of behaviour, the realism, charm, grace, and wit, but the fact that the action is not simply a dream, but forges a link between real experience and an optimistic vision of its potential.

The implausibility of the unstructured plot, which is anyway over and has to begin again at the opening of the fourth act, becomes important, because it is used as a way of indicating to the audience that the story line is not what is significant. The loose dramatic construction and the recourse to magic and to coincidence help to demonstrate that the play is about moral attitudes, examined in such a way as to suggest that true love might be relied on instinctively to find its correlative object, that the promptings of instinct, loyalty and obedience must in the end coincide, and that the reward of following the combination of instinct and virtue is bliss. That is the message which the *Astrée* was already beginning to explore, but which had not been examined in the plays of Hardy, or in anything else on the French stage before the presumed date of *Les Bergeries*, about 1620, or perhaps a year earlier. It required to be done inside a pastoral, to flaunt the implausibility of the pastoral conventions which had nevertheless to be used to assert the innocence and naturalness of a setting which everyone recognized to be entirely artificial, and to link identifiably real behaviour to an idealized vision of the meaning of human experience.

Arthénice, dedicated to and protected by a goddess, is told she may marry only someone of her native race and land, but her parents want her to marry the rich Lucidas, while she thinks the goddess wants her to marry Tisimandre, and tries to make him fall in love with her, although she actually loves Alcidor. Tisimandre loves Ydalie, and Ydalie loves Alcidor, but Alcidor himself reciprocates the love of Arthénice. Unhappily he is a stranger. Lucidas becomes jealous and employs the magician Polistène to turn Arthénice away from Alcidor. Lucidas, led on by Polistène, tries to make Arthénice believe that Alcidor and Ydalie behave as if they were already married. Tisimandre is meanwhile in despair, and still refuses to fall in love with Arthénice. Lucidas shows her in the magic mirror Alcidor kissing Ydalie. When Arthénice then meets Alcidor, she forbids him to approach her. He decides to drown himself and she resolves to retire to a convent. Alcidor, only half drowned, is picked out of the river and, when Arthénice comes to comfort his last moments, she faints. They decide to marry in spite of the goddess. Ydalie's father, touchingly called Damoclée, insists on punishing Ydalie with death for her supposed misbehaviour with Alcidor.

When act four begins, Tisimandre offers to die in her place. When the shepherd Cléante announces the imminent marriage of Alcidor and Arthénice, Lucidas is so affected that he admits to the trick he played with the magic mirror. Arthénice's father Crisante is the brother of Ydalie's father Damoclée. Tisimandre and Ydalie are now anxious to marry, as well as Alcidor and Arthénice, when the goddess now tells Crisante what she had previously told only Arthénice, that Arthénice may only marry someone of her land and race. Tisimandre is the only possibility, so the fathers agree that the children should swap partners: Tisimandre is to marry Arthénice, and Alcidor is to marry Ydalie. All four are in despair when an old man, Alcidor's guardian until he was ten, recognizes Alcidor by his bracelet, and Alcidor turns out to be Damoclée's lost son Daphnis. The goddess's prohibition of the Alcidor-Arthénice therefore no longer holds, so they marry, as naturally also do Tisimandre and Ydalie.

The verse paraphrases of the psalms are the product of very careful reflection. Racan had studied all the older versions, those of Marot, Baïf, Bertaut, Desportes, as well as Godeau's, which arrived at La Roche in 1648, Guillebert's 1620 edition, and Antoine de Laval's 1608 prose commentary. Racan's aim is to restore the full meaning of the psalms to modern readers, and he therefore updates their vocabulary, introducing what seem to us deliberate anachronisms, like "grace," "Protestant," "artillery," and "spinet." For the 32 pieces in the 1651 *Odes sacrées*, Racan uses 23 different meters. The whole psalter of 150 psalms has recently been considered the most interesting version of the psalter so far published in French. Although the interest is in the modernization and the techniques of versification, the claim is considerable without being at all absurd.

PUBLICATIONS

Collections

Les Oeuvres de M. Honorat de Bueil chevalier, seigneur de Racan, 2 vols., 1724
Oeuvres complètes, 2 vols., 1857
Oeuvres, 2 vols., 1930–37

Verse

Les Bergeries de messire Honorat de Bueil, chevalier sieur de Racan, 1625 (edited by Louis Arnould, 1937)
Recueil des plus beaux vers de messieurs Malherbe, Racan, Montfuron, Maynard, Boisrobert, etc..., 1626 (60 poems by Racan)
Les Sept Psaumes de messire Honorat de Bueil, chevalier sieur de Racan, 1631
Odes sacrées dont le sujet est pris des Pseaumes de David et qui sont accommodées au temps présent, 1651

Dernières oeuvres et poésies chrétiennes, 1660

Biographical and critical studies

Arnould, Louis, *Un gentilhomme de lettres au XVIIe siècle: Honorat de Bueil, seigneur de Racan*, Paris 1896 (2nd edition, 1901)
Camo, Pierre, *Racan: Les Bergeries et autres poésies lyriques*, preface, 1929.

RACINE, Jean, 1639–1699.

Dramatist and poet.

LIFE

Racine's biography would have been quite different if he had not been born at La Ferté-Milon, a small country town about fifty miles north-east of Paris, beyond Meaux, administratively dependent not on the capital but on Soissons. Both sides of his family had lived there for a century—local magistrates, tax officials, or artisans, ranging from the socially distinguished to small tradespeople. It seemed unlikely that Racine would ever live anywhere else. Racine's father, whose functions are differently described on different documents of roughly the same date, was certainly a minor local tax official. On 13 September 1638 he married Jeanne Sconin from the same milieu, and Racine was born in mid-December 1639. He was baptized on the 22nd. His mother died 13 months later, on 28 January 1641, after giving birth to his sister, Marie, four days previously. Racine's father married his second wife, Madeleine Vol, a lawyer's daughter, on 4 November 1642, but died on 6 February 1643 at the age of only 27. His post was sold for a very modest 350 livres to his widow's father, and she remarried in 1646. The sum did not cover his debts, and the furniture belonged to the widow, so that nothing at all was left for Racine and his sister at the ages of just three and just two. Racine was cared for by his father's family, Marie by her mother's.

La Ferté-Milon, and Racine's family, had a connection with the monastery of Port-Royal (q.v.) which went back to 1625. Suzanne, the sister of Racine's paternal grandmother, formerly Marie des Moulins, had made her profession at Port-Royal in 1625, after the death of her husband, Guillaume Passart. She was to die in 1647, but had arranged for three of the family's children from La Ferté-Milon to be educated there, including her nephew, Nicolas Vitart, born in 1624, who went to Port-Royal in 1637 when he was 13. Marie des Moulins's daughter, Agnès Racine, only 13 years older than her nephew, Jean Racine, and deeply attached to him, had been accepted as a postulant by Port-Royal, without a dowry, in 1642. She was to be professed in 1648. Her father, Racine's grandfather, died in 1649, and her mother, Marie des Moulins, together with the mother's sister, Mme Vitart, formerly Claude des Moulins, ended by retiring to the monastery, where their sister, Suzanne, had recently died.

On 2 May 1638 Saint-Cyran had been arrested, and the group of "solitaires," consisting at this time of the five sons of his penitent, Mme le Maître, together with Lancelot and Singlin, the only priest among them, were a fortnight later made by the archbishop of Paris to leave the house which Mme le Maître had had built for them near the monastery of Port-Royal in the Faubourg Saint-Jacques. They had with them a handful of children whose education had been entrusted by Saint-Cyran to Lancelot, and moved with the archbishop's permission to the dilapidated monastic buildings at Port-Royal-des-Champs, where they had spent the previous summer. There was a caretaker and a priest, but the buildings were unhealthy, surrounded by marsh. Each evening the solitaires, used to reciting matins in Singlin's room in the Paris house, now climbed the hill known as Les Granges for compline. On 14 July 1638, however, they were dispersed by Laubardemont, the Maître des Requêtes, best described as an examining judge attached to the royal household, who had been responsible for the burning of Urbain Grandier at Loudun, and who was now charged by Richelieu with the affair of Saint-Cyran.

Lancelot went to La Ferté-Milon to stay with the parents of Nicolas Vitart, taking their son back with him. There he was joined by Antoine Le Maître and his brother Séricourt, who had been turned away from other monasteries. At La Ferté-Milon the three lodged separately with branches of the Vitart family for 13 months, meeting each evening on a nearby hill for common prayer and returning through the town reciting the rosary. In summer, people sitting outside rose when they passed. In August 1639 they were allowed to return to Port-Royal-des-Champs. There was therefore already a strong connection between La Ferté-Milon, the Racine and Vitart families, and Port-Royal, when Agnès, who had virtually taken the place of Racine's mother, succeeded, no doubt on account of the multiple connection, in having him taken into Port-Royal, free, as an orphan, either in 1644–45, or when his grandmother retired there in 1649, in which case his earliest schooling was at La Ferté-Milon. The evidence is unclear, but Racine was certainly educated by Port-Royal in one of their own establishments from 1649 to 1653, and then sent by them to the house they controlled at the Collège de Beauvais from 1653 to 1655, when he was recalled to Les Granges, one the three centres of Port-Royal's famous "petites écoles (junior classes)." Had he had to pay them, the fees for Port-Royal were 500 and for Beauvais 200 livres a year.

It was at Les Granges that Racine, virtually adopted now by Antoine le Maître, in whose room he slept, acquired his excellent Greek. Le Maître also developed in his pupil the sense of harmony underlying the later verse rhythms. He was given private lessons, developed habits of intellectual rigour, and was naturally subject to the general moral intensity and spiritual austerity associated with the monastery. It also looks, however, as if Racine's teachers, who included Lancelot and Nicole, quickly discovered his prickly temperament, realising how hyper-sensitive and intense he remained, even when Arnauld d'Andilly, charged with the task, had apparently persuaded him to behave more amenably than hitherto. They thought him ill-suited to any ecclesiastical state, and gently urged him towards a career at the bar. Racine was taught elocution and rhetoric, with Hamon taking over from Le Maître when at the end of March 1656 the

solitaires again had to disperse. The education he received was unmatchable in France, and, at any rate in its entirety, could not be bought.

Racine may well have been lodged for a period after the dispersal of the solitaires with the duc de Luynes at Vaumurier, not far from Port-Royal-des-Champs. Lancelot was tutor to the Luynes's 11-year-old son, whose later title of duc de Chevreuse came from his mother's second husband's name, and Nicolas Vitart was Luynes's "intendant." Vitart was to move to the closely associated Chevreuse family, but in the meanwhile had organized from Vaumurier, where Pascal had stayed, the dissemination of the *Lettres provinciales*. In October 1658 Racine was sent to study philosophy at the Collège d'Harcourt, presumably with the idea of starting his legal studies the following year. In November 1658 Antoine le Maître died. We do not know much about Racine's activities for the next two years. He seems not to have studied law but to have undertaken work for Vitart, himself later to become rich and buy himself into the aristocracy. Racine probably supervised building activity at Vaumurier. He also, through Vitart and his wife, began to frequent galant circles. He was distantly related to La Fontaine, whom for a period early in 1661 he was seeing daily.

It would be surprising if Racine had not remained acutely conscious of the contrast between his penniless orphan background and the social privileges which adoption by Port-Royal had opened up to him. He must have known, too, how much he owed to his own talent, without which he would not have been accorded the special attention given to his education by the extraordinarily gifted teachers who devoted themselves to him, and how great was the additional advantage afforded him by the relationship of blood and friendship with Nicolas Vitart, himself also helped up socially by Port-Royal, through whom he got to know members of some of France's grandest families. It is not to be wondered at if Racine's later career showed an aptitude for social climbing and a cool detachment in pursuit of a thrusting ambition. It was not entirely due to his stage career that the Port-Royal group was later to regard him as one of their failures. They had noticed Racine's difficult temperament and aggressive tendencies, but had taught him only to dissimulate, and not to overcome them. He therefore developed an extraordinary power of adapting himself to the audience of the moment, but failed to control the attitudes and behaviour which explain some of the aesthetic, commercial, and moral resentment he was later to meet.

There is a letter of 26 January 1659, written to Arnauld d'Andilly while Racine was at Harcourt, which already surprises a little by the ease with which it slips into a pastiche of one of Pascal's *Lettres provinciales* and by its tone of familiarity with Port-Royal's grand patriarchal figure. Racine was already borrowing money from Vitart and others, and pursuing literary ambitions with some determination. In 1659 he wrote a sonnet in praise of Mazarin, and in 1660 an ode on the king's marriage, *La Nymphe de la Seine*, which, through Vitart, he submitted to Chapelain, about to become the official channel for the bestowal of the king's patronage. Vitart showed the poem to Charles Perrault, who admired it. Published anonymously, it obtained Chapelain's protection for Racine, and prepared the way for the "gratification" of 600 livres to be granted to Racine in 1663–4. Racine seems to have avoided seeking patronage in the entourage of Foucquet, the surintendant des finances, perhaps because of his protection of the Jesuits, who were intensely hostile to Port-

Royal. By the autumn of 1660 Racine had also written his first tragedy, "Amasie," of which the text has been lost. It was presented by Vitart, in an action which distanced him from Port-Royal, to the Marais company, which rejected it. In 1661 Racine also wrote the galant poem *Les Bains de Vénus*, and the Hôtel de Bourgogne turned down a play, *Les Amours d'Ovide*.

Racine by now regarded Port-Royal with ironic detachment. Its solemn attitudes had come to grate. He was no longer considered at La Ferté-Milon as belonging to the local family community, although he continued to remain in touch with his sister and her husband, Antoine de Rivière. In 1661 he fell ill. No career in literature or drama seemed assured, but his mother's brother was vicar-general of the diocese of Uzès, down in Languedoc. An ecclesiastical career with a benefice looked attractive, and Racine obtained a place in the seminary at Uzès, characteristically committing himself in November 1661 by adopting at least an external ecclesiastical discipline, hoping for his uncle's patronage. He was clearly acting under some pressure, and without having adequately prepared the ground, either by obtaining a discharge from the jurisdiction of Soissons, or by sounding out the potential extent of his uncle's good will towards him.

Racine did not pretend to have a religious vocation, but he knew that the ecclesiastical state entailed not even formal obligations, beyond celibacy and the recitation of the breviary, and that, while capable of providing an assured income, it was also even capable of being reconciled with a career writing for the stage. He was consciously playing a role, but his powers of adaptation allowed him to act it out with success. However, in spite of complicated intrigues, patience, and persistence, Racine did not succeed in acquiring a suitable benefice. Later, and certainly from 1666 to 1670, he was, to the outrage of Port Royal, to enjoy one or more benefices while also writing for the theatre. At Uzès he showed a hard head for business matters, and maintained, with what his letters show to have been some constraint, outward ecclesiastical decorum.

He had however stayed in touch with the world of galanterie up in Paris. Vitart, to whom he now owed money, continued to do what he could to help, but it quite quickly became clear that Uzès had provided only another setback, offering at best only uncertain hopes, and for the moment only a derisory benefice to which were attached conditions which Racine was bound to find too onerous. The tonsure had however made him eligible for a benefice, should one later be offered to him. A letter from Uzès of 4 July 1662 shows Racine looking for a subject for a tragedy. He was certainly back in Paris by the summer of 1663, and probably much earlier. Marie Desmoulins was to die on 12 August 1663, and Racine may well have been helped financially by Vitart and lodged at the Hôtel de Luynes. He took care to keep up a relationship with Port-Royal, although he probably by now had with him the text of the lost tragedy *Théagène et Chariclée*, which seemed to Molière at the Palais-Royal to show enough dramatic talent for him to tell Racine to come back and try again in six months.

In Paris the world of letters had changed. The fall of Foucquet in 1661 and his replacement by Colbert entailed and symbolized the change to a different style of patronage and a different set of literary and other aesthetic criteria. The mediation of Foucquet's secretary Pellisson in matters of literary patronage was to be replaced by that of Chapelain, acting on behalf of the king, but controlled by Colbert. Broadly speaking this was yet another indication that what we used to call classicism was replacing baroque, as Pascal's moral and aesthetic clash with the Jesuits in the late 1650s had already demonstrated. For about a score of years the "anciens" were to achieve important literary and religious victories over the "modernes" (see: Querelle), until styles changed again, symbolically with the death of Colbert and the replacement of his patronage with that of Louvois. A change of minister did not itself cause a change of style, and the great orchestration of the praise of the king's reign was more to the taste of the modernes with their belief in progress, than to that of the anciens, whose cooperation Colbert set about buying, but when Racine returned to Paris the brief ascendancy of the anciens was beginning to be established.

In May 1663 Louis XIV had measles, and in June Chapelain solicited from the literary world celebrations of his recovery. By about the 20th Racine had ready his *Ode sur la convalescence du roi*. He asked for and followed Chapelain's advice on presenting it, and was promised a pension. When it was not paid, he wrote in October *La Renommée aux Muses*, including an ostentatious compliment to Colbert. Boileau, who must by now have known Racine, but whose name did not figure on the first official list of gratifiés on 22 August 1664, was withering about the newcomer, "Bois-Vert," in an early version of his first satire, although Racine's long-awaited 600 livres was the lowest sum mentioned. From 1663 Racine was protected by the powerful duc de Saint-Aignan, at whose expense Boileau had imprudently permitted himself to be ironic, but who had become interested in the young author of *Le Renommée aux Muses* and was to present him to the king. When Chapelain was ridiculed in the celebrated *Chapelain décoiffé*, published in 1665, it seems likely that Racine was the only beneficiary of his patronage to have taken part.

Meanwhile the Hôtel de Bourgogne had announced a tragedy by Boyer called *La Thébaïde*. Molière, wanting to get in first, sent for the young ecclesiastic who had brought him *Théagène et Chariclée* and gave him a plan for *La Thébaïde; ou, Les Frères ennemis*. Racine, sharpening his instinct for adapting his style to whatever would please, submitted it act by act, revised it as instructed, let Molière, who was in a hurry, finish it, and saw it performed on 20 June 1664. Played a month after the original *Tartuffe*, it was only a very modest success, although Molière tried hard with it, adding a ballet for the third performance, playing a supporting farce thereafter, giving it 17 performances in its first season, presenting it again on the reopening in August, and even giving it six performances in 1665. Box office receipts for the first three performances were 370 livres, then 300, then 130. A passage said to have been closely imitated from Rotrou's *Antigone* was removed before publication in October 1664, when the piece was dedicated to Saint-Aignan, but the accusation of plagiarism was stored up and later used against Racine, among others by Pradon.

In the literary and social worlds Racine was none the less climbing fast. He had relations with Molière and, both before and after the publication of the list of gratifiés, with Boileau. He must have met Furetière and Chapelle, the writers associated with the inn La Croix-Blanche, and is known to have been admitted to the "lever du roi" in 1663, which meant at least that he was received at court. He was lodged at the Hôtel de Luynes, and frequented some of the more important salons, including the Hôtel de Liancourt and the Hôtel de Nevers. Biographically speaking, Racine's life could seem like the smooth progress of a literary courtier, starting as the composer of encomiastic odes, carrying on as a member of the Académie des inscriptions charged with having medals struck to commemorate the great events of the reign, and ending as court poet and royal historiographer, with an interlude from 1664 to 1677 during which he risked his social position and incurred sharp warnings about the spiritual jeopardy in which he was putting himself by writing for the theatre.

In fact Racine's life was dominated by an obstinate commitment to his activity as a dramatist, and the curtailment after *Phèdre* may have been a submission rather than an abandonment. He had, after all, already written his first serious tragedy by 1660, when he was 20. The great cultural revolution symbolized by the emergence of salon society from the Chambre bleue took place only in the middle third of the century. Before that the stage, in the 16th century the training ground for the declamatory exercises of grammar school boys, had not in the 17th century been considered to be a culturally serious forum much before the late 1630s, and neither actors nor even dramatists were considered to be taking part in a socially acceptable activity or anything other than popular entertainment, like that provided by the Italian players who sporadically gave a season in Paris, or were invited to perform at court.

To evaluate Racine's theatrical career, it has to be remembered that the Hôtel de Bourgogne had been used by professional actors since 1578, but the company which became the Comédiens du Roi were permanently established there only from 1628. They specialized in tragedy. Another company, associated with the director Lenoir and the actor Montdory, had played in the Hôtel, migrated to Rouen, and returned to Paris in 1634 as the company of the Marais. They were known for the complicated stage machinery required for the spectacular stage effects of many tragi-comédies. Molière's Palais-Royal company had started at the Petit-Bourbon when it opened in Paris in 1658. Although Molière was reluctant to abandon tragedy to the Hôtel, he was increasingly forced to rely on comedy, farce, and social satire. Rivalry between the companies was very strong and, while it would be absurd to speak of reviews or drama critics, Renaudot had founded his weekly *Gazette* in 1631, Sallo with Colbert's backing started the *Journal des Savants* in 1665, and in 1672 Donneau de Visé *Le Mercure galant* (qq.v.). These periodicals, with the *Gazette d'Amsterdam* and the *Gazette de Leyde*, included accounts of the literary life of Paris which quite soon started to include, alongside information, what aspired to be informed opinion about Parisian dramatic productions.

Normally, the box office receipts, after deduction of general expenses, were shared among the actors, with the author receiving perhaps two shares, but only during a play's first run, after which the author by convention could publish, but was not paid for performances. First runs were therefore kept short. With three performances a week, generally Friday, Sunday, and Tuesday, 10 to 15 performances meant a month on the bill, and success. Anything over 20 performances was a notable success. The theatre was not so much expensive as socially restrictive, with places costing from six livres or the value of two sheep for the best ones to a quarter of the value of a sheep, or 15 sous, three quarters of a livre, for standing in the parterre, sums easily enough affordable by the nobility, but unaffordable at all below the level of the upper bourgeoisie, hoping perhaps for an income of 2,000 livres a year. Prices were doubled for first nights, and sometimes also thereafter. The cost of living, which had doubled between 1590 and 1660, was to remain stable for 30 years.

Very little is known of Racine between *La Thébaïde* and his next tragedy, *Alexandre le Grand*, originally known as "Porus," created by Molière's company at the Palais-Royal in the presence of the king's brother, as well as of Condé and Henriette d'Angleterre, on 4 December 1665. A measure of the play's success is the amount of the box office takings for the first four nights: 1,294, 1,262, 943, and 1,165 livres. The leads were played by La Grange and Thérèse du Parc. However, on the evening of the sixth performance, 18 December, Racine had his tragedy played also at the Hôtel de Bourgogne, which had already given a private performance at court on the 14th, and which seems to have resurrected an *Alexandre* by Boyer of 1647 to rival Racine's play. However, Boyer's play failed. When Racine moved *Alexandre*, Floridor took over the title role, and Montfleury that of Porus. The *Gazette* made fun of Alexandre's "galanterie" and Porus's "générosité." The Préface to the published version suggests that, in spite of the immense success, public comment concentrated on the remaining strands of préciosité (q.v.) it contained. Saint-Evremond had already decided on those grounds for criticism in a letter he wrote before reading the play.

It was already not at all unknown for more than one company to stage the same play. All three Paris companies had played Pierre Corneille's *Sertorius* in 1662. It was first performed at the Marais on 22 February, and the first night at the Palais-Royal on 23 June was actually a fortnight before publication on 8 July, but the play was at any rate very close to being in the public domain. Similarly, Thomas Corneille's *Antiochus*, staged by Molière's company on the 9 January 1662, was then played at the Hôtel de Bourgogne on 25 May, but it had been published on 6 March. Racine's play was not in the public domain, and the break with custom and etiquette was so unprecedented, the connivance of the rival company so extraordinary, that there may well be something we do not know. If so, it may be bound up with another mystery. What at this date was Racine's relationship with Thérèse du Parc, who followed him to the Hôtel at Easter 1667, probably before becoming his mistress?

We do not know when they became lovers, and Thérèse du Parc may merely have been making a natural career progression, as Racine of course also was. There is no firm evidence, but a lot would be explained by the hypothesis that Racine took his play away from Molière's troupe out of pique, because, in spite of his now proven success, the leading lady, later to become his mistress, was still rejecting his advances. Historians have found it difficult to disentangle gossip, malice, and fact from the such wisps of evidence as we have been left with, but it is certain that Racine and Thérèse du Parc did become lovers, almost certain that she had a daughter by him who died at the age of eight, and perfectly possible that there was, as was certainly alleged, though it sounds doubtful, a secret marriage between them.

Thérèse Du Parc, born in 1633, was seven years older than Racine. She had married in 1653, but her husband had died in 1664, before Racine met her. She certainly gave him grounds for jealousy but, when she followed Racine to the Hôtel over a year after he had himself walked out on the Palais-Royal company, he wrote for her the part of Andromaque in the play of that name put on by the Comédiens du Roi on 17 November 1667. We know that a young nobleman, the chevalier de Genlis, was so in love with her in 1668 that he had to be restrained under guard by his family. When she died in December 1668, shortly after the success at court of Racine's *Les Plaideurs*, it was almost certainly of poison. The circumstances make it reasonable to assume that Racine had been exceedingly jealous, and was at least suspected, and quite possibly responsible. Even if we do not believe the formal testimony of 'la' Voisin, the poisoner, given on 21 November 1679, accusing Racine of murder, we know that Louvois, effectively the king's principal minister, wrote to the examining magistrate on 11 January 1680 that he could have the orders for the arrest of Racine as soon as he needed them. They were never issued, which strongly suggests that Racine was protected from proceedings by the highest intervention from the court.

Molière's company, Thérèse du Parc included, was, however, furious with Racine in December 1665, perhaps also because between 1664 and 1665 both the Corneille brothers and Quinault had moved to the Hôtel de Bourgogne, which was not only the most highly considered of the three companies, but was assuming the monopoly of the new and fashionable tragedies. Racine would no doubt have preferred the Hôtel to have taken his piece in the first place. He had almost certainly tried to negotiate with them, and he may have yielded to advances made to him after the successful premiere. His behaviour was in fact attributed to ruthless ambition, and the scandal damaged him, even if it also helped to make clear his importance.

Molière's company was under financial strain. An actor's share of the receipts in the year 1665 to 1666 was down to 2,243 livres, after 4,534 from 1663 to 1664 and 3,011 from 1664 to 1665. It was to climb again to 3,352 in the year 1666 to 1667 but Racine's share of the takings for the six performances of *Alexandre* at the Palais-Royal amounted to 564 livres, probably about a ninth of the receipts after the deduction of expenses. The money was confiscated and divided among the actors. Molière later played Subligny's *La Folle Querelle* as a satire on Racine's *Andromaque* and was never reconciled with Racine. He did play *Alexandre* three more times, but takings dropped to 112 livres on 22 December, by which date it was clearly to the Hôtel de Bourgogne that the public went to see it.

Racine's unscrupulously calculated gamble in deserting Molière's company was almost immediately followed by a movement of irritation against his Jansenist benefactors, at whose expense he had hitherto permitted himself only irony. Nicole had published his *Imaginaires* in 1664 and 1665, and was attacked by Desmarets de Saint-Sorlin in two pamphlets published late in 1665. Nicole replied on 31 December with his first *Visionnaire*, in which he described "un poète de théâtre (a dramatic poet)" as "un empoisonneur public, non des corps, mais des âmes des fidèles (a public poisoner not of the bodies, but of the souls of the faithful)," culpable of "une infinité d'homicides spirituels (an infinity of spiritual murders)." Neither Nicole nor anyone else took this very seriously. It was the traditional attack of the Church on profane theatre, expressed in the rhetorical terms of 17th-century polemic. Racine, however, took brisk exception, and in an anonymous pamphlet of January 1666, the *Lettre à l'auteur des hérésies imaginaires…*, savagely attacked Nicole, Port-Royal, and his former benefactors. He was possibly exasperated by the steady stream of disapprobation stemming from Port-Royal on account of his dramatic activities, and possibly also provoked by the element of social contempt for players and dramatists implied by Nicole. He may also have been led to hope for a benefice from the archbishop of Paris if he wrote against Port-Royal. The value of the evidence of official encouragement has been disputed. Racine's authorship of the *Lettre* seems to have been put about by d'Aubignac, also the probable

author of critical comments on *Alexandre* for its failure to adopt the more stringent norms of classical taste.

Port-Royal replied in two pamphlets of March–April 1666. Racine, who had denied the authorship of the first *Lettre*, now acknowledged it in a second. Intermediaries, certainly including Vitart, negotiated, and Racine did not publish his second letter, dated 10 May 1666, even when Nicole published the *Imaginaires* with Port-Royal's replies to Racine's *Lettre* early in 1667. Port-Royal denied responsibility for the replies, and pointed out that Racine's career would not be advantaged by pursuing his attack. Racine accepted, no doubt realizing how vulnerable his treatment first of Molière and now of Port-Royal had made him to the accusation of twice betraying benefactors for personal gain. He was received by the king's sister-in-law, Henriette d'Angleterre, the duchesse d'Orléans, but in spite of the fame brought by *Alexandre*, sent with the diplomatic courier to Holland and Rome, and read instantly by Retz and Queen Christina of Sweden, Racine had damaged his reputation badly enough for no new tragedy of his to have been presented in the season 1666–67.

Andromaque, Racine's first play to centre on the intense emotion of a strong female character, was written for Thérèse du Parc, who played the title role when the tragedy was presented at court before the king and queen on 17 November 1667. Pyrrhus was played by Floridor and Oreste by Montfleury, who died during the performance of 31 December. From 1670 the role of Hermione would be played by Marie de Champmeslé, who was to be Thérèse du Parc's successor as Racine's mistress until 1675, although their quarrelling had been the subject of gossip a year before that. In view of the possibility that by 1674 Racine may have been considering the abandonment of his dramatic career, the date of the rupture in his relationship with Marie de Champmeslé is important. Until 1673 Racine revised the balance of the parts in *Andromaque* to give greater weight to that of Hermione, and the part of Bérénice was written for La Champmeslé. Born in 1642, she began to act after the death of her first husband, remarried, and joined the Marais company in 1669, moving on to the Hôtel de Bourgogne at the resumption after Easter in 1670. She was to create the role of Phèdre in 1677.

The text of *Andromaque* appeared as early as January 1668. Success was indubitable and enormous, but the preface to the text shows Racine responding to criticism which, since it had not yet been printed, must have been going the rounds and testifies to public interest in his play. Four people sent Saint-Evremond a copy in the reliable hope of stirring up trouble. By now Racine was drawing for inspiration on live characters at court, whatever he also owed to Virgil, Seneca, and more than half a dozen modern French authors, among them Thomas Corneille, Rotrou, du Ryer, Quinault, and Boyer. He was exciting jealous hostility, still based on the reproach of galanterie, and the inability to distinguish Greece from France. The party hostile to Racine, later identifiable as the party of the *modernes*, was generally favourable to the Corneilles, and included Saint-Evremond, Boyer, and Gilles Boileau.

Molière's company gave 18 performances of Subligny's *La Folle Querelle; ou, La Critique d'Andromaque*, starting on 25 May 1668. It reproached Racine above all with breaches of the linguistic and social proprieties. Its own modest success, with box office receipts only once below 100 livres and four times above 300, testifies to the interest of Racine's tragedy on which it was obviously parasitic. Subligny, like Pradon in 1684, regards Pyrrhus's affection for Andromaque as overcultivated galanterie. It is clear from the factitious nature of the criticisms that Racine's supporters and critics were forming into hostile camps, although there were changes of side. Meanwhile Racine circulated a viciously witty quatrain in which Paris society would pick up allusions to the well-known infidelities of the husband of one of his critics, Mme d'Olonne, and the homosexuality of another, the marquis de Créqui.

Racine's next play was a comedy, *Les Plaideurs*, loosely derived from Aristophanes's *The Wasps*. It was originally inspired by the success of the Italian company, and might even have been written with it in mind, but was finally presented at the Hôtel de Bourgogne, which was on the lookout for a comedy to rival Molière's. It included a powerful satire of contemporary legal procedures and personages, and was partly inspired by jocular conversations with Boileau and Furetière, in which Boileau made fun of proceedings they had just attended at the law courts. There are allusions to events and characters likely to have been known to the prospective audience, and references to Racine's play occur in other works written shortly afterwards. In the preface Racine gratuitously includes a contemporarily current sneer at Molière for what Racine calls his "sales équivoques et…malhonnêtes plaisanteries (crude jokes and coarse double meanings)." Some lines parody well-known lines from *Le Cid*, and the play was also a reply to Subligny.

The reception was at first hesitant, perhaps on account of a court cabale. After two performances which were nearly hissed, the company refused to put the play on the bill for a third time, and a failure seemed likely until it was presented at court, where its great success with the king immediately ensured that it would subsequently go down well at the Hôtel. The first performance was in late October or November 1668, and the privilège for the printed text, technically ending the copyright, was taken out on 5 December. No doubt the text appeared very early in 1669. By the way it was placed in his collected *Oeuvres* of 1676, and then of 1697, it is clear that Racine wanted to assign it a lesser importance than his tragedies among his stage works. It has, all the same, been played more often than any other.

From 1669 to 1673 Racine, his success as an author of tragedies now firmly established, presented a play each winter. *Britannicus*, created on 13 December 1669, was not initially a success. It was a riposte to the accusations that Pyrrhus in *Andromaque* was a simpering lover, but it took a subject from Roman history, tackling Pierre Corneille on his own terrain. Its first night had to compete for public attention with the public execution of the marquis de Courboyer. The audience was dominated by Corneille's friends, and Corneille himself was present, alone in a box and noisily commenting. Robinet's *Gazette* reviewed the play on 21 December on the basis of Robinet's presence at it for the second performance on 15 December and, although Boursault's stinging criticism of the play did not appear until he wrote about the premiere at the beginning of his 1670 novel *Artémise et Poliante*, the reports of the play from others present at its performance were sufficient to kill it.

More about power struggles and jealousy with probable reference to recognizable persons and situations at Versailles than a tragedy capable of moving an audience, the play was presented only about half a dozen times, apparently either five or eight. What we know of the public reaction suggests that in the world of letters Racine's pitiless judgements, contemptuous manners, and ruthless behaviour had by now created a strong group intent on destroying him. The text's privilège is dated 7 January 1670 and Racine's preface had touches of bitterness which were toned down in the second 1676 edition. By that date he was able to bow silently to criticism and remove the appearance of Junie after the death of Britannicus, which he had previously defended. The play was dedicated to the duc de Chevreuse, and was eventually saved again by royal approval.

Bérénice was presented on 21 November 1670, a week before the premiere of Pierre Corneille's *Tite et Bérénice* at the Palais-Royal on 28 November. There has been much discussion about exactly how the choice of identical subjects arose, and there is no general agreement. It seems, however, probably that Henriette d'Angleterre suggested to Racine a subject possibly of personal significance to herself, which had already been treated by Scudéry and Segrais among others. It looks, however antecedently improbable, as if the challenge must have come from Corneille. The simultaneous treatment of one subject by different authors was itself reasonably commonplace. Thomas Corneille says he abandoned a "Stratonice" because Quinault was 200 lines further on than he was, and Racine was himself involved in three other such pairings. However, the rivalry between the two authors and the two companies was on this occasion so strident that there can be no question either of pure chance or of any cooperation simply to amuse the public, and all the evidence indicates that Racine chose first, while that is also the conclusion towards which contemporary gossip and any comparison of the two texts seems to lead.

Racine's play was the more successful. The Corneille had 21 performances, but takings at the Palais-Royal slumped while the audience for the Racine at the Hôtel de Bourgogne was as large for the 30th as for the first performance. Villars, writing from the point of view associated with d'Aubignac and Saint-Evremond, predictably attacked Racine, but the anonymous three-act satire *Tite et Titus; ou, Critique sur les Bérénices* dated Utrecht, 1673, implies that Corneille's taste had grown out of date, and Villars, against whom Racine was defended in an anonymous *Réponse* once thought to be by Subligny, went on, after Racine had published his own preface, to attack Corneille's play in a second *Lettre*. Racine's achevé d'imprimer was dated 26 January 1671, and the preface was dedicated to Colbert. Robinet wrote of the performance the day after the premiere, mentioning Racine's play on 22 and 29 November and 20 December, attributing its success to the acting of Marie de Champmeslé. Again, Racine was silently to modify his text in the light of the criticisms it received.

Bajazet was created very early in 1672, probably on 5 January. Racine was taking advantage of a fashionable interest in exotic and commercially important Turkey. There had been at least half a dozen earlier plays with Turkish settings, but Racine was stimulated by an embassy to Louis XIV in 1670, already exploited by Molière in *Le Bourgeois gentilhomme* of that year. La Champmeslé played the vacillating Atalide, with her husband as Bajazet, another of Racine's weak male characters in a play which gives all the passion to the female roles. Racine went to considerable trouble to make the atmosphere authentically Turkish, and the public reaction was favourable, although Racine was inevitably accused of putting French characters into Turkish dress, notably by Donneau de Visé in the *Mercure galant*, who remarked drily that the piece was set in Turkey, "to judge by what the author says in his preface." The preface was unusually mild, suggesting that election to the Académie française, accomplished at Colbert's insistence late in 1672 in spite of the ascendancy there of the "modernes," just before its reorganization, was already in the air.

By now even Donneau de Visé, however, was beginning to keep clear his escape routes. As early as 30 July 1672 the *Mercure* announced the likely success, in view of the author's popularity, of *Mithridate*, in fact played early in 1673, probably soon after Racine's reception into the Académie on the 12 January. The text was put on sale on 30 March, with a preface which could afford not to be polemical. The play was reviewed by Robinet after a performance at court in February, and an account of its success was also given by Donneau de Visé while reporting on the Académie admission ceremony. It was a favourite with the king and played three times before him in 1673, with La Champmeslé as Monime. It drew ostentatiously on Pierre Corneille's dramatic models, ending, like *Bérénice*, with another heroic renunciation. Corneille's friends had rallied to give exceptional advance support to his *Pulchérie*, generally felt to be his last real chance to challenge Racine. It had been read before La Rochefoucauld and then Retz, admired by Mme de Sévigné, and announced twice by Donneau de Visé and once by Robinet, but when played on 25 November 1672 it achieved no more than modest success at the Marais, and it had none at court.

Financially, Racine was now secure. He had saved prudently and could expect perhaps 2,000 livres from the company for each play, with another 200 livres from the publisher. He enjoyed gratifications ranging from 800 livres in 1667 to 1,500 livres in 1670, when the total budget for gratifications for literature and learning was regularly 100,000 livres, although it fluctuated, and was again under 60,000 in 1674. By 1672 Racine had investments of over 8,000 livres, so placed as to increase his income by perhaps 700 livres. Dedications could be worth 2,000 livres, but Racine needed no more after dedicating *Bérénice* to Colbert. By 1674 he was living in a dwelling in the Hôtel des Ursins which, to judge by an inventory surviving from 1677, he had furnished luxuriously, and he could dispose of any ecclesiastical benefice he was still holding, although it is not certain that at this date he still had one. In 1674 he became ennobled as Trésorier de France, a lucrative sinecure which he apparently owed to the patronage of Colbert. It brought in 2,400 livres a year, although the capital value of 36,000 livres at which it was assessed when Racine married has been thought generous. Normally such posts could even with official sanction only be bought. It was a munificent gift, but made to a courtier rather than a playwright. Racine's activities as a dramatist were in fact beginning to impede his social ascent. Dedications may now have been beneath him.

However, Racine's social position, which took precedence for him over his financial security and literary reputation, was also quite secure. In the literary world, of which stage activity was the least socially reputable component, he could count on the close friendship, and mostly the professional support, of Boileau, who did not however hide his dislike of *Bajazet*. He was protected by the king's favourite, Mme de Montespan. The situation was, however, rapidly changing. Since about 1670, mythical Greek subjects had been used both for opera and for nonpolitical dramas which exalted and sentimentalized human emotion, examining love primarily as a cultivated and refined feeling, a form of galanterie. Boileau and Racine held out against the new imaginative requirement, that was eventually to kill off virtually all forms of Augustinian spirituality, and in

1674 the third chant of Boileau's *Art poétique* had gone some way towards giving Racine's own concept of tragedy its canonical formulation.

The experience of human passion which Racine at that date felt the need to explore required the mythological setting of an unavoidable fate set in motion by arbitrary divinities. It accorded with Boileau's systematization of what was essentially the view of tragedy which Racine shared with Fleury and to some extent d'Aubignac, and was necessarily opposed to the galant, précieux trivialization of love in order to examine it as innocent, safe, and life-enhancing. It is difficult to suppose that it was out of loyalty to the true spirit of ancient Greece that Racine decided to write his two Greek plays, but Saint-Evremond had seen how subversive of the "moderne" position properly Greek perspectives were bound to prove. It was ultimately the need to investigate human experience in that sort of light which opposed the "anciens" as well as the Augustinians to the "modernes" as well as the Jesuits. Racine, who had not previously used Greek sources even for Greek subjects, was to be powerfully helped by his knowledge of Greek and his feeling for Greek tragedy.

In 1673 Molière died, and by order of Louis XIV his company was amalgamated with that of the Marais, to form what was soon to be known as the Compagnie de Guénégaud, henceforward the only rivals to the Hôtel de Bourgogne until, in 1680, that company amalgamated with the company of the Rue Guénégaud to produce what we still know as the Comédie-Française. Molière's widow was closely connected with Donneau de Visé and the *Mercure Galant*. In 1673, too, the literary opposition between Racine and Pierre Corneille's party, by now indistinguishible from the modernes, flared up over Boursault's *Germanicus* and, although Racine's position was secure, his personality had fuelled feelings of hostility towards him. In particular Thérèse du Parc's family were being protected by the comtesse de Soissons, a Mancini and niece of Mazarin's, hostile both to Mme de Montespan and to Henriette d'Angleterre, and closely associated with the duc de Nevers, the Vendômes, and the duchesse de Bouillon. The duc de Richelieu was also protecting a whole group of modernes, including Thomas Corneille, des Marets de Saint-Sorlin, and Michel le Clerc, who was his "intendant." Racine heard that Le Clerc, with the help of Coras, whose name was to be used but who contributed very little of the work, was preparing an *Iphigénie* to rival his own, and that the Guénégaud company, having inherited Molière's opposition to Racine, had agreed to stage it.

There seems to be no special reason, apart from diminishing financial and social pressure and the possibility that Racine may by now have been considering the abandonment of his dramatic activity, why Racine missed a season before presenting *Iphigénie*, created at Versailles for the king on 18 August 1674, after the conquest of Franche-Comté. The Hôtel de Bourgogne did not present it until late in December or early in January, perhaps as a conciliatory gesture towards Corneille, whose *Suréna* was played earlier in the season, or perhaps because Racine had found that his plays did better if not put on too close to the beginning of the season in mid-November. Racine had certainly, however, in a manoeuvre generally considered to have been too sharp, successfully intrigued to have the staging of the Le Clerc and Coras *Iphigénie* postponed, although we do not know precisely when it would have been played if there had been no court intervention to delay it for Racine's benefit until 24 May 1675, when it ran for only five performances. It was published in 1676, and its preface, while disclaiming any intention of presenting a rival to Racine's play, none the less shows the rivalry by justifying the text with reference to Racine's own norms of simplicity and unification of the action. The *moderne* party had failed in what, in retrospect, looks like a dress rehearsal for the battle over the two *Phèdres*. In the meanwhile Racine's *Iphigénie* had been a predictable success. The *Gazette d'Amsterdam*, announcing its publication on 7 March 1675, called it "la plus belle pièce qui ait jamais paru sur le théâtre français (the finest play ever to have appeared on the French stage)," and Boileau praised the performance of la Champmeslé, with whom Racine's relationship was by now deteriorating, in the seventh *Epître*.

For the first time, the text when published had an engraved frontispiece, and there were immediate Italian, Spanish, German, and Dutch translations. Racine could afford to disregard the opposition, in spite of what must be regarded as the by now expected flutter of pamphlets cautiously ironic about his achievement. However, he now did two things which spurred the opposition to regroup for what was to be a final assault. First, in the preface to the published text of *Iphigénie*, ostentatiously flaunting his ability to read the Greek text in the original, he published a coruscating attack on Pierre Perrault, who in 1675 had preferred the Quinault-Lulli opera *Alceste; ou, Le Triomphe d'Alcide* to Euripides' original which, as Racine demonstrates, he had not read in Greek. Pierre Perrault was rather feebly to attempt to turn the argument to the advantage of the "modernes" by showing that Racine's *Iphigénie* was superior to that of Euripides.

Racine had carefully abstained from mentioning the names of Quinault and Lulli, both much in favour at court. It seems likely that he was interested more in examining human experience in the light of Euripidean perspectives than in attacking the exploitation of mythological plots by such recent writers as Thomas Corneille, Quinault, and Rotrou, from all of whom he had of course himself borrowed. It is important that Racine exploits the gods primarily as the ultimate source of tragic inevitability. There could be no human appeal against their capricious decree, any more than there was against the God who, in the Jansenist tradition, arbitrarily bestowed or withheld grace. Racine does not make the analogy explicit. He would not have dreamt of profaning Augustinian spirituality by making it the subject of a dramatic performance, and it would not have been tolerated if he had, but the morality of the Greek gods is as questionable in Racine's tragedies as it was in Euripides. There are reasons for thinking that Racine himself preferred the less ironic view of the mythical Greek gods given by Euripides' contemporary, Sophocles.

On top of the assault on Perrault, he was also at least commonly thought, and not only by its author, to have intervened against the *Tamerlan; ou, la Mort de Bajazet* of Jacques Pradon, played in January 1676, as he undoubtedly had done against the other *Iphigénie*. Pradon's successful *Pyrame et Thisbé* of 1674 may have made Racine scent a new rival. Both the Pradon plays had been staged at the Hôtel de Bourgogne. For the second, Pradon had chosen Racine's Turkish subject. He was a protégé of Montauzier, husband of Julie d'Angennes, daughter of Mme de Rambouillet , and a fierce partisan of the Corneilles and the modernes. Pradon had left Rouen for Paris when Montauzier demitted the governorship of Normandy in 1668. He had also objected to the way in which Racine had had the Le Clerc-Coras

Iphigénie deferred. It was therefore Pradon whom the modernes chose to support when they heard that Racine was preparing a *Phèdre et Hippolyte*, news which in itself might have surprised them, as the ennoblement of 1674, the grand climax of *Iphigénie*, and the *Oeuvres* of 1676, whose publication had been arranged the year before, had increased speculation that Racine was beginning to regard the theatre with diminishing enthusiasm.

What we know as Racine's *Phèdre* was called *Phèdre et Hippolyte* until the collected edition of 1687. It was first played two and a half years after *Iphigénie*, on Friday 1 January 1677, at the Hôtel de Bourgogne, with La Champmeslé as Phèdre. On Sunday 3 January, Pradon's *Phèdre et Hippolyte* was staged in the Rue de Guénégaud. We know that the rivalry of the two camps did not drive them to produce any irregular pattern of box office bookings, by arranging, as has been alleged, for a hostile audience, or for empty boxes. As a matter of fact on Pradon's opening night Condé quite normally paid 110 livres for two boxes to take a party to see the Racine. Pradon had seen Racine's text, and borrowed from Racine the dramatically all-important character of Aricie, whose function for Racine had been to make Phèdre jealous. Racine's claim to have taken Aricie from Virgil (*Aeneid*, VII, 761ff) pays no more than perfunctory deference to the classical form of the myth. The introduction of Aricie meant that Racine did not therefore have to ask his audience to accept Phèdre's suicide merely on account of an incestuous and adulterous love which she did not choose and could not avoid.

The play's *achevé d'imprimer* is dated 15 March 1677. In spite of what Racine was later to write in the preface, he obviously did not in the end dare to make Phèdre merely the helpless victim of destiny and divine wrath, as Euripides's predecessors would have done. Racine in fact drove his audience to the brink of the tolerable, and first-night guffaws forced him to change Hippolyte's "chaste demeanour," which had the effect of increasing the guilt due to Phèdre's incestuous and adulterous longings, to a merely "noble" demeanour which did not affect it. In view of the closeness of the analogy with the Christian predicament as seen by the Augustinian party, it is doubtful whether the implications of the view that Phèdre incurred her self-destructive guilt merely because of her unavoidable heredity and the viciousness of Venus would have been acceptable even to the most aesthetically austere of the anciens. The Jansenists, whose views of the arbitrary bestowal and withholding of grace would have been compatible with a moral guilt from which the individual could do nothing to escape, would not anyway have come to the theatre. Arnauld did in fact criticize as unnecessary the introduction of Aricie, for which Racine provided the spurious justification in his preface.

Pradon uses the figure of Aricie, but avoids the religious dilemma posed by the possibility of atrocious moral guilt which both merits the severest punishment and derives from no avoidable choice. He simply reverted to an earlier tradition, and his Phèdre, merely betrothed and not married to Hippolyte, was not guilty either of adultery or of incest. Racine's friends had managed to get the two leading actresses of the Guénégaud company, Molière's widow and Catherine de Brie, to turn down the role of Pradon's Phèdre, but they did not succeed in getting Pradon's play banned by the king, and it was a commercial success. The nine January performances brought in 1,375, 906, 440, 860, 410, 656, 1,012, 808, and 1,362 livres. The only mystery about the January takings for the Pradon was their upward movement towards the end of the month, probably to be ascribed to public interest in the quarrel. Racine's play was eventually judged better, even by the *Mercure galant*, but for two months there was genuine indecision. Pradon had six more performances in February. The *Gazette d'Amsterdam* in a report dated 8 January had, of course, supported him, thinking his play more to the public taste, but it was played only five times after the resumption at Easter after the Lenten recess.

On the night of 1 January, after Racine's premiere, a sonnet critical of the play was composed, and by next day it was circulating round Paris, wrongly attributed to Philippe Mancini, duc de Nevers, and Mazarin's nephew. The whole Mancini family, including the sisters of Nevers, the comtesse de Soissons and the duchesse de Bouillon, to the second of whom Pradon published a dedicatory epistle with his play on 13 March 1677, were bitter opponents of Mme de Montespan, Racine's protector, and leading protagonists of the modernes. A stinging reply, with lines ending in the same words, was immediately circulated. It attacked Nevers, alluding to his cowardice, and hinting at incest with his sister, perhaps also his interest in young men, his scepticism, and his complacency at his wife's infidelities. The first sonnet was composed in the entourage of Mme Deshoulières, an ardent supporter of the modernes who, on the instructions of la Champmeslé, had been told that there was no box free when she asked for one on 1 January. The second sonnet was almost certainly the work of high-spirited young trouble-makers, perhaps inspired by Chapelle and led by Racine's supporter, Nantouillet, who had given him the subject for *Bajazet*. Racine and Boileau were blamed and had to take refuge with Condé, who smoothed things over. Damage had, however, been done, and further gleefully offensive sonnets made the rounds, almost all of them directed against Racine and, especially, Boileau, who even appears to have been the object of physical attack.

Racine's success was soon confirmed by three court performances, but we know little about the circumstances which led him at precisely this moment to abandon the theatre. It is certain that relatively soon after the decision not to publish the second letter in reply to the 1667 edition of Nicole's *Les Imaginaires* Racine began moving towards a reconciliation with Port-Royal, although not, of course, to the extent of giving up his stage career. By 1669 relationships with Arnauld d'Andilly had been re-established, and the choice of an austere Greek subject in 1674 has been seen as an indication that Racine was at least seeking to restrict his dramatic activity, and indeed his style of living, to a level at which they might be found acceptable at Port-Royal. By following Euripides, he hoped, according to his preface, to "réconcilier la tragédie avec quantité de personnes célèbres par leur piété et par leur doctrine (to reconcile tragedy with a number of people known for their piety and their doctrine)." He later spoke of his "conversion" and the role his aunt Agnès at Port-Royal had played in effecting it.

On 30 May 1677 Racine signed a marriage contract with Catherine de Romanet, aged 24 or 25, the orphan of an eminent legal family related to Vitart's wife. Her dowry was worth about 70,000 livres, roughly what Racine brought to the marriage himself. Socially his wife's aristocracy was more firmly established than his own. The signature was "witnessed" by Condé, his son the duc d'Enghien, Colbert, and the duc de Chevreuse, Luynes's son, among others, in the sense that they signed the document presented to them at home by the lawyers. The ceremony on 1 June was performed by Père Quesnel. Racine's social and

Augustinian credentials had become impeccable. His wife not only had no connection with the theatre, but she never apparently either saw or read any of her husband's plays. His marriage was a public demonstration of Racine's break with his past, due more to social than to spiritual pressures and ambitions. Thérèse du Parc, la Champeslé, and the life of the theatre to which Racine had once been so committed, could be written off. Racine in 1677 was 38. He was solidly established. It was simply time to settle down. The troubles caused by *Phèdre et Hippolyte* can only have fortified his decision. They are themselves unlikely to have caused it. In 1677 Racine, together with Boileau, was commissioned to act as a "historiographe du roi," that is, to chronicle the grand events of the king's reign, at a salary of 6,000 livres each. It is not unlikely, and was commonly assumed, that it was a condition of the commission, arranged by Mme de Montespan, that Racine should abandon the theatre, and that Boileau should cease to write satire. However, the only direct statement to that effect is in a letter of 13 October from Mme de Sévigné to Bussy-Rabutin, clearly retailing Paris gossip.

The order for the first payment, countersigned by Colbert, was received at the treasury on 11 September. It seems, however, from the *Gazettes*, the *Mercure*, and the letters of Mme de Sévigné in October and November, that a probationary appointment had been arranged after the king's campaign which had taken him away from 28 February to 31 May 1677, that the king liked whatever the two writers had produced during the summer, and that he had therefore appointed them. It is possible to see the 13 years from 1664 to 1677 as an interlude in Racine's career, which started and finished with the praise of the king. The theatre had brought him money and a social position which now required consolidating. He was thought even by contemporary opponents, to say nothing of later historians, to have sold out. That is not only anachronistically to sacralize literature, and especially drama. It is also to fail to see how Racine's dramatic exploration of the human predicament had become self-destructive. It was impossible to take the exploration of human experience any further in the direction of *Phèdre et Hippolyte* and still have a tragedy to stage. All that could have been left was the sort of invitation to submit to inevitability which was to make of Racine's later biblical pieces dramatic poems rather than tragedies.

Racine worked seriously at the task of glorifying the king's reign, and followed him in his campaigns, receiving on average 4,000 livres a year additional to his stipend from 1678 to 1688. His total income probably touched 25,000 livres a year, three times as much as would have been necessary to keep a household with 10 servants and two carriages. He also revised reprints of his tragedies, especially in 1687, when he changed the name of the 1677 tragedy to *Phèdre*. In 1680 *Phèdre et Hippolyte* was the first production of the amalgamated companies of the Comédiens du Roi and the Rue Guénégaud. Racine behaved however as if, as was indeed the case, he had graduated into being a courtier very close to the king. The history of the reign remained nevertheless unfinished, and the fragments were mostly destroyed in a fire at Valincourt in 1726.

In 1683 Racine became a founder member of the Académie des Inscriptions, charged with the striking of medals in memory of the great events of the reign, and in 1690 he was appointed a Gentilhomme ordinaire de la chambre, an office worth over 50,000 livres to those allowed to purchase it, but for which he was made to pay only 10,000 livres to the widow of his predecessor. He had some difficulty in getting the annual stipends nominally due to him, and appears to have borrowed money from Quinault's widow and from Boileau. On 2 January 1685 Racine, who had technically ceased two days previously to be director of the Académie française after his three months in office, had delivered a celebrated address of welcome to Thomas Corneille, elected in place of his dead brother Pierre, Racine's own former rival, whose work for the inauguration of drama in France as a literary genre Racine went out of his way to praise. For a brief period in 1677 Racine had assiduously attended the meetings of the Académie.

His wife bore him seven children, two boys, of whom one, Louis, born in 1692, wrote his father's life, and five girls, of whom one married, two became nuns, and two remained unmarried. Racine meanwhile became attached to the following of the new favourite, Mme de Maintenon, as the influence of his former patron, Mme de Montespan, declined. His company was genuinely enjoyed by Louis XIV, and in 1685 *L'Idylle de la paix* was commissioned from him, with music by Lulli, in honour of the king. In 1688 Mme de Maintenon, worried at the insipidly edifying or alternatively profane nature of the tragedies played by her schoolgirls at Saint-Cyr, asked Racine for a dramatic poem. He wrote *Esther* for her, and as a compliment to her. The king attended a rehearsal and, with the court, the premiere on 26 January 1689. The play's considerable success brought renewed popularity for the earlier tragedies in Paris, and court invitations to performances became a sign of social acceptability. In the end the unsettling effects dramatic success had on the young cast caused the suspension of further performances. A little later Racine was asked for *Athalie*, and performances were prepared towards the end of 1690. The king attended a rehearsal on 5 January 1691, but no proper production ever took place in Racine's lifetime. The single presentation before an audience of distinguished guests on 22 February did not use costumes or scenery, presumably on account of religious pressures. James II and Fénelon attended.

Towards the end of his life Racine's remarkably successful court career made him the object of sharp hostility. His devotion was thought suspect, although his reconciliation with Port-Royal became complete and, on Arnauld's death in 1694, almost combative. In 1694, he published his four *Cantiques spirituels* and in 1697 he wrote the history of the monastery, the *Abrégé de l'histoire de Port-Royal*, which was to remain unpublished until 1742, and in its full version until 1767. Racine spent the last five years of his life retired from court and immersed in his devotions. He may momentarily have displeased the king by a memorandum on the poverty of the French people which the king had not been supposed to see. In the spring of 1698 he fell ill, and was operated on later in the year for a large tumour. He never recovered his health, easily became exhausted, and in February 1699 fell victim to a fever. Another abscess was opened, and he suffered much pain before dying in the early hours of the morning of 21 April 1699. He left an important series of letters. Those written to his family and to Boileau are of especial interest.

WORKS

The strength of Racine's great tragedies lies in the extraordinary intensity with which he portrayed the passions that dominate his heroines. He does not attempt to depict the complexity of human affairs or the richness of experience, or to explore the social, political, economic, or metaphysical context of the individual's experience. Most of the male characters dither, a few are resolute. None is as aggressively passionate as the strongest female characters. Fierceness of passion is measured for the audience by the failure of lesser characters on the stage to understand the distortions imposed by their passions on the attitudes and actions of the principal characters. It is impossible to know whether Racine derived his inspiration for his leading female characters from his mistresses who played them, or whether they became his mistresses because of the passions he drew from them as a dramatist, but at least some connection has to be supposed between Racine's ability to create female characters of such unusual power and his relationship with the actresses who played them.

Unusually, Racine wrote out his plots in prose before putting his plays into verse. In the interests of his remarkable rhetorical fluency he composed the second line of each rhyming couplet before the first. He achieved his extraordinary range of poetic and dramatic effects while drawing on only the simplest syntactical devices and fewer than 2,000 words from a conventional but elevated vocabulary largely confined to words indicating feelings and intangible objects. For purposes of comparison, the average anglophone graduate may have an active vocabulary of up to 15,000 words. The prescribed aim for the first four years of English teaching in French secondary schools is a vocabulary of 2,000–3,000 words.

On the poetic level, therefore, Racine's effects are achieved by tension between the force of passion on the one hand and the constricting lexical and formal norms in which it is expressed on the other. "Feu" and "flamme" ("fire" and "flame") are not in this context words of insignificant embellishment, and the musicality of sounds can create vivid poetic effects, as when Phèdre exploits "m" and "n" and long "i" sounds, juxtaposing two "ire" endings signifying different meanings:

Tout m'afflige, et me nuit, et conspire à me nuire

(Everything afflicts me and harms me and conspires to harm me).

None of Racine's plays totally dispenses with a political dimension to back up the emotional drama, although *Bajazet* comes near to doing without political complications.

Dramatically, the intensity of tragic effect is achieved by the concentration of emotional impact demanded by adherence to rigorous classical conventions, like the unities. A small number of characters sufficiently high-born to be capable, on general 17th-century assumptions, of intense passion, interact at a climax of emotional tension which can, but need not, be provoked by some event reported as having occurred in the outside world.

Racine makes full use of mistaken reports and beliefs whose cancellations provoke real events in the characters' emotional reactions. The last principal character often makes a first entry at the beginning of the second act, so that the play's action is clearly separated from the exposition which has preceded it. Rhetorically Racine makes much use of very brief interruptions in a speech to draw attention to the special importance of what is coming next, and of the effects made possible in French by switching between the intimate singular and the formal plural ways of saying "you." He sometimes indicates points of high emotional tension by splitting a twelve-syllable alexandrine between up to five different speeches or using broken syntax and unfinished sentences.

La Thébaïde is the stylized but dramatically clumsy reworking of the sort of political plot which was by 1664 remote from public interest. The preface, added in 1676, attempted to lead the public to believe that Racine had modelled his play on Euripides rather than on Rotrou and Seneca, who were in fact its principal models. *Alexandre le Grand* moves the centre of interest from politics towards love, treated however in a précieux (q.v.) manner. The king accepted the dedication. The play takes a decisive step towards Racine's treatment of love itself as a tragic emotion. Pierre Corneille had in 1660 demanded for tragedy "quelque grand intérêt d'État, ou quelque passion plus noble et plus mâle que l'amour (some great interest of state or some passion more noble and more manly than love)." In Racine's play Alexandre is in love with Cléophile, sister of Taxile, one of the Indian kings Alexandre must defeat. Taxile and the other king, Porus, are both in love with Axiane. Alexandre defeats Porus and intends to reward Taxile, who had betrayed Porus out of jealousy and for the sake of Cléophile, with the hand of Axiane. Axiane, however, repudiates Taxile as a traitor, and he rushes out on to the battlefield where Porus kills him and surrenders to Alexandre, who magnanimously restores his kingdom to him, and gives him Axiane. Cléophile's last two speeches both refer to the "gloire" of Alexandre, whose passion for her takes second place to his duty to himself as warrior, king and leader. The values on which the play pivots are still half those of Corneille.

Andromaque is normally considered to be Racine's first great tragedy. In structure the plot has not advanced far beyond the tragi-comédies of an earlier generation. Oreste loves Hermione, who loves Pyrrhus, who loves Andromaque, who is faithful to the memory of her dead husband Hector, whose young son, Astyanax, is the last hope for survival of the Trojan royal line. Structurally this is a "chaîne des passions (chain of passions)" and, since the action is concentrated on the emotional interactions of the characters, everything depends on a single change of Pyrrhus's mind. As the play opens, Oreste arrives at the court of Pyrrhus to demand on behalf of the Greeks the handing over by Andromaque, held captive by Pyrrhus, of her son. Oreste is flanked by his friend Pylade, whose function, apart from enabling Oreste to let the audience know what is going on, is also to be the measure of normality against which the audience can measure the distortion imposed on Oreste by his passion for Hermione.

Racine, criticized for having introduced 17th-century galanterie into ancient Greece, still apologizes in the preface for having made Pyrrhus too brutal,—"Pyrrhus n'avait pas lu nos romans (Pyrrhus had not read our novels),"—while allowing that he has taken the liberty "d'adoucir un peu la férocité de Pyrrhus (to tone down Pyrrhus's savageness a little)." This is important because it indicates that Racine is still relying on the ethic associated with Corneille, in which the intensity of passion is justified by the merit of its object. If Pyrrhus were merely a thug, the audience, Racine silently supposes, could not sympathize with Hermione's love for him, on which the play depends. Quite late (IV,v) we learn that the betrothal of Hermione to Pyrrhus was a dynastic arrangement made by their fathers while they were infants, which at least mitigates the guilt of Pyrrhus's repu-

diation of Hermione on account of his love for Andromaque. The legend demands that Oreste should go mad. No doubt to make that resolution of the action tolerable, Racine has Pyrrhus murdered at Hermione's jealous command not by Oreste himself, but by his men. Madness seemed an adequate punishment for someone who was only almost a murderer. The first act ends, however, with Pyrrhus's offer to Andromaque to save her son, whom the Greeks for political reasons want killed, if she will marry him.

At the opening of the second act Hermione enters with her "confidente." The strength of her passion is immediately clear. She hates the Pyrrhus she also loves: "Il y va de ma gloire (my dignity demands it)." The line is important because it echoes the celebrated line of Chimène in Corneille's *Le Cid* of 1637, "Il faut que je me venge, il y va de ma gloire (I must seek vengeance, my dignity demands it)." "Gloire" in fact denotes something much stronger than dignity, or even than honour. In all the 17th-century classifications of affective states love and hate were incompatible, although from this date on their fusion with regard to the same object at the same time was sometimes regarded as constitutive of jealousy. Hermione offers her enduring love for Pyrrhus as an explanation of her present hatred,

Ah! je l'ai trop aimé, pour ne le point haïr!

(Ah! I have loved him too much not to hate him).

When Oreste enters for the second scene, another characteristic of Racinian love is made clear. It is not only irresistible, sudden, and often guilty. It is also too strong to be concealable,

L'amour n'est pas un feu qu'on renferme en une âme;
Tout nous trahit, la voix, le silence, les yeux;
Et les feux mal couverts n'en éclatent que mieux

(Love is not a fire that can be contained within the soul;
everything betrays us, speech, silence, looks; flames we try
to smother only shoot forth more strongly).

Pyrrhus, however, rebuffed by Andromaque, has decided to yield Astyanax to the Greeks. He tells Oreste, announcing, in ignorance of Oreste's feelings, that he is going to marry Hermione.

In the third act Hermione, overjoyed at Pyrrhus's decision, dismisses a dejected Oreste, and Andromaque pleads with her to intercede with Pyrrhus on behalf of Astyanax. But Hermione refuses, and Pyrrhus will not yield to his captive's own entreaties, though Andromaque—in the end, with the mad Oreste, the only character to survive—threatens suicide. She then actually makes up her mind to give in to Pyrrhus in order to save her son, and then to kill herself. Andromaque appears for the last time at the beginning of act four. Dramatically her function is over, although in the 1668 and subsequent versions she is brought back in act five to vindicate her position morally. In a confrontation between Hermione and Pyrrhus, the intensification of Hermione's jealousy is indicated first by a switch from the formal "vous" to the intimate "tu," and then by a whole series of lines beginning with "Je." By the opening of the fifth act Hermione is distracted with jealousy and furious at the report of Oreste's hesitation at turning himself into Pyrrhus's assassin on her account. When she hears that Oreste's Greeks have in fact assassinated Pyrrhus in the act of marrying Andromaque, she flies into a frenzy of grief and recrimination and kills herself over the corpse. Oreste goes mad.

Andromaque sought some support from the ethic of galanterie and gloire. The next tragedy, *Britannicus*, is based partly on a power struggle between the young Roman emperor Néron, the first two years of whose reign had been exemplary, and his mother Agrippine. Agrippine's step-son, Britannicus, who loves and is loved by Junie, might have had his claim to Néron's throne urged by Agrippine if she had not chosen to support Néron, whom she none the less mistrusts. Néron is flanked by two advisers, the wise Burrhus and the scheming Narcisse. When the play opens, Agrippine, ever perceptive of threats to her interests, has noticed the way Néron's character is starting to develop. Néron has suddenly had Junie abducted in the middle of the night to appear before him. His mother speculates that he might be politically frightened by Britannicus's claims to the imperial throne. The real reason seems more likely to be Néron's decision to stop his mother from manipulating the sources of power.

The exposition complete, Néron himself appears at the beginning of act two. Racine is making the five-act convention serve a properly dramatic purpose. Néron tells Burrhus to have one of his mother's advisers removed from his court, sends Burrhus away, and tells Narcisse of his love for Junie. Alexandrines split between characters show the importance of Néron's announcement,

... Depuis un moment, mais pour toute ma vie,
J'aime, que dis-je, aimer? j'idolâtre Junie

(Only since a moment ago, but for the rest of my life,/I love—no, not love—I idolize Junie).

Love is instantaneous as well as irresistible. Néron's political distrust of Britannicus is henceforward reinforced by jealousy. Some of the political sentiments in the play have been seen as relevant to the contemporary situation in France. Néron declares his love for Junie and orders her, in a room in which he will be a hidden watcher, to send Britannicus away. Otherwise Néron will have him killed. As Britannicus approaches, a single twelve-syllable alexandrine is split between four different speeches. Junie attempts to save Britannicus by concealing her love, upsets him, and withdraws leaving Néron determined to torment Britannicus with fresh suspicions. In the third act Junie contrives to see Britannicus again. She has been explaining her strange behaviour while Néron was eavesdropping, when Néron enters. He has them both put under house arrest. In act four there is a long confrontation between Néron and his mother, and then between Néron and Burrhus.

Néron has been won over to sparing Britannicus, when Narcisse comes in. Poison is ready for Britannicus. It has just been tried out on a slave. Narcisse urges several reasons why Néron should go ahead with his plan to kill Britannicus. He will not forgive his emprisonment, he will know poison has been prepared for him, he will continue to be loved by Junie, and Agrippine is already publicly boasting that she has regained her authority over Néron. The last reason alone is decisive, and Britannicus is poisoned offstage with the cup of reconciliation, having with further irony been hurried to his fate by an unsuspecting Agrippine. Junie escapes to become a temple virgin and

the crowd kills Narcisse, who had tried to hold her back. Racine was criticized for not ending the piece with the death of Britannicus, and the continuation beyond that point emphasizes the dependence of the tragedy on the power struggle between Néron and his mother, reluctant to surrender power to him.

It was in his preface to *Britannicus* that Racine wrote of his ideal:

une action simple, chargée de peu de matière, telle que doit être une action qui se passe en un seul jour, et qui, s'avancant par degrés vers sa fin, n'est soutenue que par les intérêts, les sentiments et les passions des personnages

(a simple action, with a small amount of matter, as an action should be that takes place within a single day and which, proceeding by steps towards its resolution, is sustained only by the interests, feelings and passions of the characters).

In *Bérénice* no one dies, although all three main characters, Titus, Bérénice, and Antiochus threaten to commit suicide. Each has an attendant, and that, apart from a messenger and a retinue, is the complete cast. Racine in his preface refers to the examples set by the writers of antiquity and declares his desire to write a tragedy with a simple action supported only "by the violence of the passions, the beauty of the feelings, and the elegance of their expression." There is no need for blood and death in a tragedy:

il suffit que l'action en soit grande, que les acteurs en soient héroïques, que les passions y soient excitées, et que tout s'y ressente de cette tristesse majestueuse qui fait tout le plaisir de la tragédie

(it is sufficient that its action should have grandeur, that its characters should be heroic, that the passions should be excited, and that everything in it be imbued with that majestic sadness which constitutes the whole pleasure of tragedy).

Titus, the successor of Vespasian as emperor of Rome, is about to marry Bérénice, who loves him, when he hears that Rome will not tolerate his marrying a foreigner. He charges Antiochus, who has secretly loved Bérénice for five years, with telling her that she must go away, but she will accept dismissal only from Titus himself. Antiochus, who had hoped to follow her into exile, is repudiated.

In the first act Antiochus resolves at last to leave Rome should Bérénice, in a last interview, tell him that she will marry Titus. Antiochus stumbles into a declaration of love, in the end incapable of being kept unavowed. He speaks a memorable line:

Titus, pour mon malheur, vint, vous vit, et vous plut

(Titus, to my sorrow, came, saw you, and was loved).

The classical resonance from Caesar's "veni, vidi, vici (I came, I saw, I conquered)" and the play on consonants and vowels are both part of Racine's poetic rhetoric. It is only after Bérénice has dismissed Antiochus that she is told by her confidente of the rumoured impediment to her marriage. She does not believe it. Titus makes his entry at the opening of the second act, and is confronted with the choice between love and duty characteristic of the tragi-comédies of a previous generation. There is an inconclusive scene with Bérénice in which occurs the famous exchange, all within twelve syllables,

Titus: Mais…
Bérénice: Achevez.
Titus: Hélas!
Bérénice: Parlez.

Titus: Rome…l'empire…

(But…/Go on./Alas!/Speak./Rome…the empire…).

In the third act Antiochus accepts the mission to confirm Titus's decision to Bérénice. The phrase "il y va de sa gloire (his honour is at stake)," is used again. A long monologue of indecision spoken by Titus leads to another confrontation between him and Bérénice. Bérénice has threatened suicide and Antiochus pleads with Titus on her behalf, a situation clearly designed to move the audience. Act five is devoted to a further confrontation between Titus and Bérénice. They are joined by Antiochus for the final three-sided heroic renunciation.

The setting of *Bajazet*, remote in place—Constantinople—if not in time, allows, as Racine notes in a 1676 addition to his preface, full scope for passionate love and jealousy. The sultan is away at war. Acomat, the grand vizier, feeling his position threatened by the absent sultan, plots his overthrow, while the sultan's favourite, Roxane, loves not the sultan but his brother, Bajazet, who himself loves and is loved by Atalide. Bajazet, however, dissimulates his affection for Atalide, and pretends to return Roxane's love in order to escape from the imprisonment ordered by his brother. He is allowed by Roxane to pretend to be in love with Atalide to protect what she takes to be his love for herself which, if it were known, would endanger both of them. Roxane is nominally in full charge in the sultan's absence, but with reason fears his spies. Her relationship with Bajazet naturally suits Acomat very well. The sultan, suspecting Roxane's love for his brother, had sent a slave with an order to have Bajazet killed. Acomat had had the slave killed. By the end of act one we know all this, and also that Roxane has told Atalide that Bajazet is going to have to marry her or die.

The second act opens with the entry of Bajazet and his confrontation with Roxane. Bajazet tries to dissuade Roxane from precipitate decisions. She switches from "vous" to "tu," as her passion overwhelms her, and then moves back to "vous" as she replaces threats with reasoning. She moves again to "tu," then back to "vous," and finally in exasperation to "tu" again before the scene ends. Atalide persuades Bajazet to save his life by appeasing Roxane's jealousy and consenting to marry her, and announces her own intention to commit suicide. Bajazet, hesitates and pretends. Roxane is perplexed and suspicious. She knows that love cannot be concealed and she tricks Atalide into revealing her concern for Bajazet by telling her that the victorious sultan is returning, and that she must now have Bajazet killed. When Atalide faints, a letter from Bajazet swearing his love for her is found on her person by Roxane's slave Zatime. Roxane breaks out into a spectacular explosion of jealous rage, full of exclamations, rhetorical questions, and unfinished sentences.

In the fourth scene of act V Roxane confronts Bajazet, start-ing with "vous," but quickly switching to "tu." Bajazet is offered his life if he will watch Atalide's execution. Finally ceasing to dissimulate, he refuses. Roxane's last command is "Go" in the "vous" form, but in the single word "Sortez." The executioners are awaiting him. Passionate love has killed its own object. The sultan has however sent an executioner for Roxane. She dies by the dagger, and Atalide kills herself. Mme de Sévigné refers to the play's end as "cette grande tuerie (that massacre)."

Mithridate returns to a more political plot. Mithridate, the aged king of Pontus, in Asia Minor, is engaged to the young Monime but is away fighting the Romans. Both his sons by different mothers, Pharnace and Xipharès, are also in love with Monime. Pharnace favours a deal with the Romans, while Xipharès, like his father, is their implacable enemy. Monime loves Xipharès. When Mithridate was thought dead, Pharnace had pressed Monime to marry him, but she sought the protection of Xipharès. Mithridate, however, returns, is immediately informed of Pharnace's love for Monime, and tests him by sending him on a mission to secure a Parthian alliance by marrying a Parthian princess. Provoked, Pharnace tells his father that Xipharès, too, is in love with Monime, and is loved by her. Mithridate confronts Monime, who, now that he knows her secret, refuses him, and Mithridate decides to rid himself of her and both his sons. At this moment, the end of act IV, Pharnace leads a rebellion against his father. Mithridate only just manages in time to countermand the order to Monime to take poison as she is about to swallow it, before, hard pressed by the Romans, he kills himself, leaving Pharnace to be dealt with by the Romans, and bestowing Monime on Xipharès. Love is not here in the end a tragic emotion at all, and the tragedy is one of heroic grandeur and renunciation. The ending, by Racinian standards, is relatively happy.

Essentially *Iphigénie* is based on a power struggle between King Agamemnon, who after vacillation consents to the sacrifice of his daughter, Iphigénie, demanded by the gods as the price of a favorable wind to Troy, and Achille, who loves Iphigénie. What decides Agamemnon is Achille's open defiance.

J'ai votre fille ensemble et ma gloire à défendre

(I have to defend your daughter and my honour at the same time).

Agamemnon's reaction is given at the opening of his brief monologue in IV, vii, "Et voilà ce qui rend sa perte inévitable (And that is what makes her destruction sure)." However, the conditions to be fulfilled by the sacrificial victim, who has to be of Helen's blood, are met by a secondary character, Eriphile, and her death by her own hand is made acceptable to the audience by the jealous love for Achille which leads her to attempt to destroy her benefactress, Iphigénie. Racine has still avoided the tragic destruction of human life simply as the result of an arbitrary fate, as he would again in Phèdre despite the preface he wrote for that play, using, as in *Iphigénie*, jealousy, acceptable as the source of tragic guilt, even if in fact unavoidable.

Phèdre, as it is now generally called, is undoubtedly Racine's masterpiece, and his most daring tragedy. It shocked in the 17th century by putting on the stage the adulterous and incestuous love of a married woman. It shocks today because of its stark examination of the possibility of a guilt, resolvable in the conventions of the society postulated by Racine only by suicide, which Phèdre had no possibility of avoiding by any choice of which she was capable.

Hippolyte, son of Phèdre's husband, King Thésée, by the queen of the Amazons is, unknown to Phèdre, in love with Thésée's enemy and captive, Aricie. Thésée has long been absent, and Phèdre loves not her husband but his son. We learn at the beginning that Thésée, reformed after a dissolute youth, has been away for six months, that Phèdre, descended from the tainted ancestry of Minos and Pasiphaé, daughter of the sun-god, had persecuted Hippolyte and had had him banished, and that Hippolyte is now frightened of his growing love for Aricie. Hippolyte, by repute untouched by love, is the charioteer who flees the light and is at home in the shade of the woods.

In the second scene we hear that Phèdre, dying, wants to see the sun for the last time. She enters. She has neither eaten nor slept for three days. Strangely and involuntarily she wishes she were in the shade of the forest. She starts when her nurse, Oenone, mentions the name of Hippolyte. She is blaming herself for something, and Racine does not make clear whether it is her love or its avowal, both involuntary, which makes her guilty. Phèdre in the same scene (I, iii) says both

Grâces au ciel, mes mains ne sont point criminelles.
Plût aux dieux que mon coeur fût innocent comme elles!

(Thank heavens my hands are not criminal./Would to the gods that my heart were as innocent!).

and

Quand tu sauras mon crime et le sort qui m'accable,
Je n'en mourrai pas moins; j'en mourrai plus coupable

(When you learn my crime and the destiny that over-whelms me,/I shall still die of it; but I shall die more guilty).

It is, however, important for an understanding of the play to know whether guilt resides in passion, or in its declaration, even if, as here and later, the declaration is as involuntary as the passion.

Cet aveu si honteux, le crois-tu volontaire?

(Do you think I made so shameful a declaration voluntarily?) (II, v).

When Phèdre tries to tell Oenone whom it is she loves, she cannot get the name out. She tries twice, breaks off each time, and has to use a periphrasis "ce fils de l'Amazone (that son of the Amazon)." In a long explanation, during which Phèdre uses the term "repos" for the absence of emotional turmoil, she explains the instantaneity and irresistibility of her love, and its conflicting physiological effects.

Je le vis, je rougis, je pâlis à sa vue

(I saw him, I blushed, I went pale at seeing him).

She saw Hippolyte everywhere, even in the face of his father.

Terrified, she obtained his exile, but had then been brought by Thésée to Trézène, where Hippolyte had gone. Her guilty passion was the revenge taken by Venus on her family.

Puisque Vénus le veut, de ce sang déplorable
Je péris la dernière et la plus misérable

(Since Venus decrees it, of this unhappy line /I die the last and most wretched),

and

C'est Vénus tout entière à sa proie attachée
(It is Venus wholly intent on her prey).

The first act ends with a report of Thésée's death.

The opening of act two sees the appearance of Aricie. Thésée's supposed death has made her love for Hippolyte innocent. He has asked to see her. Could she have touched his heart, known for its invulnerability? The pair discuss the Athenian succession. Will it fall to Hippolyte, Aricie or Phèdre's son? Hippolyte now involuntarily declares his love for Aricie, who responds favourably, and retires as the arrival of Phèdre is announced. Oenone has to prompt the Queen to say what she has come for, that is, to discuss with Hippolyte her son's claim to the Athenian throne. Phèdre loses control of what she is saying. She describes her love for her dead husband, of whom Hippolyte, to whom she is now speaking, reminds her, love not for Thésée the mature philanderer, but for Thésée young,

Mais fidèle, mais fier, et même un peu farouche,
Charmant, jeune, traînant tous les coeurs après soi,
Tel qu'on dépeint nos dieux, ou tel que je vous voi.
Il avait votre port, vos yeux, votre langage

(But faithful, proud, even a little fierce, /Charming, young, drawing all hearts after him,/As our gods are depicted, or as I see you now./He had your carriage, your eyes, your language).

Hippolyte is horrified by the unmistakable and improper declaration of love. Phèdre rebukes him for making the assumption. Hippolyte apologizes, but when, in confusion, he goes to withdraw, Phèdre, swept away, switches to "tu." "Of course you understood, only too well, what I was saying…" In the course of a magnificent tirade she blurts out her love, despises herself for it, recognizes the guilt it involves, holds that the declaration is as involuntary as the love, and asks Hippolyte to kill her. When he will not, she takes his sword. Oenone prevents her from killing herself.

In the third act Phèdre consoles herself with Hippolyte's inviolability. At least she will have no rival. She tells Venus that her triumph is complete. At this point Oenone brings news that Thésée is alive and coming back. Oenone invents the strategem of accusing Hippolyte of daring to fall in love with his father's wife. Phèdre objects. She will not do it. Oenone reassures her. Thésée will be lenient with Hippolyte. While she is talking, the king approaches. Oenone interrupts her flow to say she sees Thésée coming. Phèdre sees Hippolyte. Exhausted, she gives in.

Dans ses yeux insolents, je vois ma perte écrite. Fais ce que tu voudras, je m'abandonne à toi. Dans le trouble où je suis, je ne puis rien pour moi

(In his insolent eyes I see my ruin written./Do what you like./In the turmoil I am in I can do nothing for myself).

Hippolyte says nothing about Phèdre's declaration. Thésée is perplexed by the constrained welcome he receives.

In act four Oenone lies to him, blaming Hippolyte as she had suggested. Thésée prays to Neptune to destroy Hippolyte. Hippolyte confesses to his father his love for Aricie, but Thésée takes this for a feint, invented to cover himself against the accusation Thésée now makes of adultery and incest. Phèdre comes to Thésée to tell him the truth but, on hearing from Thésée that Hippolyte loves Aricie, can say no more. In one last interview Phèdre turns on Oenone, who drowns herself offstage. In the fifth act Aricie and Hippolyte meet for the last time. Aricie unwittingly speeds Hippolyte to his destruction by urging him to flee as Thésée approaches. She half enlightens Thésée about what has happened. He finally realizes he has been over-hasty and tries too late to recall Hippolyte. He receives instead an account of Hippolyte's death when the monster evidently sent by Neptune had frightened his horses. His chariot had overturned and he had been dragged over the rocks and killed. Phèdre comes in and confesses everything, having already taken the poison which causes her to die on stage.

In his preface as well as in the play Racine goes out of his way to exculpate Phèdre. If, as he says in his preface, she is not quite innocent, her guilt does not lie in the exhausted acquiescence in Oenone's lie, but in her jealousy—"Il faut perdre Aricie (Aricie must be destroyed),"—although even that reaction is not depicted as in any sense voluntary. It is difficult to see how Racine could have proceeded any farther in the same direction. The preface, possibly written with Port-Royal in view, makes clear that the "crimes" of Phèdre and, to a lesser extent, of Hippolyte in loving Aricie, are both involuntary and culpable. Already in *Phèdre* there is nothing that Phèdre can do apart from accepting her fate. What holds the play together is the lyrical intensity of the poetry rather than the plot.

Racine's last two dramatic pieces, being biblical poems, are devoid of intensely passionate love as well as truly tragic situations. *Esther* and *Athalie* contain some very accomplished verse, and highly elevated religious sentiment, but they were no longer intended to be the same sort of deep explorations of human experience taken to previously unknown pitches of dramatic and lyrical intensity as the earlier tragedies had been. It has been argued forcibly that *Esther* was written to be relevant to the English political situation, although the general view among historians is sceptical. It is not unreasonable to think that Racine's stature may well be higher as a poet than as a dramatist. His examination of the passions of his characters shows more power than do his dramatic situations themselves.

PUBLICATIONS

Collections

Oeuvres complètes, edited by P. Mesnard, revised edition, 10 vols., 1885
Oeuvres complètes, edited by Raymond Picard, 2 vols., 1950–2
Oeuvres complètes, edited by Jacques Morel and Alain Viala, 1980

Complete Plays, 2 vols., 1967

Plays

La Thébaïde; ou, Les Frères ennemis (produced 1664); 1664; edited by Michael Edwards, 1965; as *The Fatal Legacy*, 1723
Alexandre le Grand (produced 1665), 1666; as *Alexander the Great*, 1714
Andromaque (produced 1667), 1668; edited by R.C. Knight and H.T. Barnwell, 1977; translated as *Andromache*, 1675; as *The Distressed Mother*, 1712
Les Plaideurs (produced 1668), 1669; as *The Litigants*, 1715; as *The Suitors*, 1862
Britannicus (produced 1669) 1670; edited by Philip Butler, 1967; translated as *Britannicus*, 1714
Bérénice (produced 1670), 1671; edited by C.L. Walton, 1965; as *Titus and Berenice*, 1701
Bajazet (produced 1672), 1672; as *The Sultaness*, 1717
Mithridate (produced 1673), 1673; as *Mithridates*, 1926
Iphigénie (produced 1674), 1675; as *Achilles; or, Iphigenia in Aulis*, 1700; as *The Victim*, 1714; as *Iphigenia*, 1861
Phèdre et Hippolyte (produced 1677), 1677; as *Phaedre and Hippolytus*, 1756; also as *Phaedra*
L'Idylle de la paix, music by Lulli, 1685
Esther (produced 1689), 1689; translated as *Esther*, 1715
Athalie (produced 1691), 1691; edited by Peter France, 1966; as *Athaliah*, 1722

Verse

La Nymphe de la Seine, 1660
Ode sur la convalescence du Roi, 1663
La Renommee Aux Muses, 1663
Cantiques spirituels, 1694
Campagne de Louis XIV, with Boileau, 1730; as *Éloge historique du Roi, Louis XIV*, 1784

Other

Lettre À L'Auteur Des Hérésies imaginaires, 1666.
Abrégé de l'histoire de Port-Royal, 1742

Biographical and critical studies

Clark, A. F. B., *Jean Racine*, 1939
Brereton, Geoffrey, *Jean Racine: A critical biography*, 1939
Turnell, Martin, *Racine, Dramatist*, 1972
Lapp, John C., *Aspects of Racinian Tragedy*, 1955
Weinberg, Bernard, *The Art of Racine*, 1963
France, Peter, *Racine's Rhetoric*, 1965
——————— *Racine: Andromaque*, 1977
Mourgues, Odette de, *Racine*, 1967
Knight, R. C., (ed.), *Racine: Modern Judgements*, 1969
Knapp, Bettina, *Racine: Myths and Renewal in Modern Theatre*, 1971
Pocock, Gordon, *Corneille and Racine: Problems of Tragic Form*, 1973
Butler, Philip, *Racine*, 1974
Yarrow, Philip John, *Racine*, 1978
Barnwell, H. T., *The Tragic Drama of Corneille and Racine*, 1982

REGNARD, Jean-François, 1655–1709.

Dramatist.

LIFE

Regnard, a more interesting comic dramatist than is often supposed, was born in Paris in the quarter of Les Halles and baptized on 8 February 1655. His father was a well-to-do dealer in salted fish who died in 1657, leaving the two-year-old boy to be brought up by his mother, Marthe Gelée, and his sisters. The father had left him 120,000 livres. It is not known at which Paris college he was educated, but he later claimed in an *Epître* to have started writing verses "when he was 12," presumably an allusion to Ovid and Ronsard which may simply mean while he was still young. He also learned the fashionable accomplishments of the upper bourgeoisie, riding, fencing, and dancing.

At 15, Regnard was first sent to work for a jeweller. In 1671, when he was 16, he left Paris to travel, twice covering Italy, and apparently reaching Constantinople. His later work would show a particular affection for Venice. It is said that he returned to Paris in 1672 with a gambling profit, after paying his expenses, of 30,000 livres. There is no accurate account of where Regnard went or what he did for the next six years, although from 1676 he appears to have spent two more years travelling in Italy in company with a M. de Fercourt from Beauvais. The novel he wrote about his adventures, *La Provençale*, was published only posthumously in 1731, and we have Fercourt's less fictionalized *Relation* of their adventures, published only in 1917. Regnard apparently fell in love in Bologna with a married woman of 17 from Arles, a Mme de Prade, the model for the novel's heroine.

In September 1678 Regnard and Fercourt took an English boat from Genoa for Marseilles. It is said to have been purely by chance that the de Prades were on the same boat. It was captured on 4 October by pirates, and all four were taken captive and sold to slave merchants in Algiers in December. The three men were bought by one Achmet Thalem, and Mme de Prade by another merchant. In captivity Regnard carded the wool which Fercourt spun. Regnard gave himself credit for inventing a bird-trap which his captor sold. A Lazarist priest, Jean le Vacher, active in the ransoming of captives, managed to achieve the release of Regnard and Fercourt, negotiated at 24,000 livres. He beat the price down to 10,000 livres each, and used the rest to obtain the release of Fercourt's servant and Mme de Prade, "la Provençale." The freed captives returned to France in May 1679. In the novel, but no doubt only in the novel, M. de Prade had been thought dead, but had turned up at Arles just before Regnard was due to marry his wife. *Le Retour imprévu* (The Unforeseen Return) was to be the title of a Regnard comedy created on 11 February 1700.

On 26 April 1681 Regnard again left Paris, with Fercourt and Nicolas de Corberon, for Denmark via Holland on a mission with at least a diplomatic pretext. Regnard found all Dutch women beautiful. He was presented to Christian V of Denmark in Copenhagen, went on to Stockholm, where the party was received by Charles XI, and accepted an invitation to visit Swedish Lapland, for which they left on 23 July, returning on 27 September. Regnard left a diary of his journey, of which only the principal portion, the *Voyage de Laponie*, was published, and only in 1741, probably in reaction to Maupertuis's accounts of his scientific mission to the same region in the 1730s.

Unfortunately, much of the *Voyage* is translated from Scheffer's *Laponia*, so we do not know how personal were the responses Regnard recorded to natural grandeur, forests, boulders, mountains, and torrential rivers, in the "solitudes affreuses (frightening wildernesses)." He wrote with amused cynicism about the differences of custom and belief, edging towards the irony with which Voltaire wrote about his experience in England half a century later, but it is unlikely to have been Regnard who inscribed Latin verses at the furthest point of their journey, near Lake Tornotresch: "Hic tandem stetimus nobis ubi defuit orbis (So far had we come when we ran out of land)." He later wrote that it was improbable they would ever be seen, except by bears.

The party returned to France by Gdansk and Poland, where they were received by the king, Jan Sobieski, before continuing through Hungary, Austria, and Germany. They arrived back in Paris at the end of 1681 or the beginning of 1682. Regnard settled in the rue de Richelieu, and in 1683 bought himself the undemanding office of trésorier de France in the Paris financial administration. He developed interests in gardening and gastronomy, no doubt gambled, must have derived serious amusement from the performances of the Italian and French companies in Paris, presumably at this date wrote his novel, and probably reworked his travel notes into a diary, but appears to have had no serious occupation or ambition. He had published nothing, was unknown in the world of letters, or at court, and seems to have entertained purely out of friendship, although his guests tended a little later to be of high rank: the marquis d'Effiat, the duc d'Enghien, and the princes Sobieski. His surviving verse may date from this period, and he wrote a tragedy *Sapor*, accepted but never played by the Comédie-Française. His career as a dramatist started only in 1688. At least from the mid-1690s Regnard had a publicly acknowledged mistress, "Tontine" Loyson. His mother survived until 1693.

Regnard's indifference to any augmentation of his considerable wealth, as well as to dynastic arrangements and literary life, his exuberant and expansive outlook, his worldly success, and the myth that a great literary era had ended by the early 1680s, have all conspired to his undervaluation. What took place in the world of literature between the death of Colbert in 1683 and the revocation of the edict of Nantes in 1685 had amounted to the assured victory of the "modernes" in the cultural upheaval which lay beneath the Querelle des anciens et des modernes (q.v.). The victory of the modernes entailed, and went hand-in-hand with, the clear signs of victory of a literary exploration of values whose optimism was no doubt sometimes facile. At the same time the ruinously over-confident foreign policy of Louvois, whose effects were undoubtedly disastrous, accompanied a new flamboyance of taste and lightness of touch in architecture and the visual arts.

Drama, like the major purely literary forms, no longer needed to explore the tragic destinies of human beings, or the seriousness of a comedy which skirted pathos. Racinian tragedy had relied for its effects on declamation, and Molière's social satire was backed by strong moral vision. By the late 1680s it was no longer necessary to respond to the same constraints. Regnard was replacing Molière in much the same way, at much the same time, and for much the same reasons as Jules Hardouin-Mansart was replacing Le Vau in architecture, rebuilding his Versailles, and as Pierre Mignard was taking over from Le Brun in painting, when Louvois commissioned from Mignard his new *Tente de Darius* of 1689. The play of light against curved surfaces was succeeding monumental neoclassical façades in architecture, and in painting the stylized fantasies of Watteau's rococo were taking over from the austerities of Philippe de Champaigne and the severities of Poussin's sense of the sublime.

Historians of French literature, still partially in thrall to the era and style of Racine, may not yet have seen the aesthetic interest and social importance of what was being achieved by Regnard and his generation. Regnard himself, genial, pleasant, and easy-going, had no interest in the Académie française, whose proceedings and disputes seemed at Colbert's death already remote from the realities of cultural life. Regnard could be stirred to take a position in the cultural battle underneath the Querelle des anciens et des modernes only when Boileau published his outrageous tenth *Satire* against women in 1694, well after the definitive victory of the modernes was secure. Regnard replied with a *Satire contre les maris*, also of 1694, to which Boileau replied in his tenth *Epître*, probably first published early in 1696, warning his verses of the dreadful fate that awaited them as he grew old and the day arrived when their reputation would fall so low that they would be compared to the creations of Regnard.

Regnard's difference with Boileau was settled; he did not publish his burlesque poem *Le Tombeau de M.B.D.* on the death of a Boileau suffocated by jealousy, and he dedicated the 1705 *Les Ménechmes* to Boileau. His own name was dropped from the tenth *Epître*. But Regnard's defence of women, his delightful harlequinades, and the five-act verse comedies for the French company introduce an important new note into French drama. He was one of the generation who naturalized into French the comedia dell'arte (q.v.) of the Italian tradition when the Italian players were banned within thirty leagues of Paris in 1697. Molière's relationship with the commedia had been equivocal. He had shared a stage and scenery with Italian troupes in Paris and borrowed from their plots, but their quasi-monopoly of clowning agility and their mastery at the deployment of stereotyped characters recognizable from their masks, their incomparable buffoonery, and the light-hearted optimism of their harlequinades had forced Molière, challenged from other directions by the domination of the Hôtel de Bourgogne in simple verse tragedy without elaborate stage effects, and by the domination of the Marais troupe in drama dependent on stage machinery, swivels, cogs, hoists, and swings (see: Thomas Corneille, Desmarets de Saint-Sorlin, and Donneau de Visé), into specializing in the social satire for which he is famous.

By 1688 Molière had been dead for fifteen years, and the three French troupes of 1673, Molière's, the Marais, and that of the Hôtel de Bourgogne, had been amalgamated into the single Comédie-Française since 1680, after the Marais had on Molière's death absorbed the remnants of Molière's troupe into the Guénégaud company. The only rivals of the French company were the Italians until their expulsion, and the fairground players. By 1680 the Italian company was playing some pieces wholly in French, some traditional commedia dell'arte pieces, some comedy only partly in French and generally with farcical or burlesque elements, and some often witty, clever, and inventive harlequinades. Molière's titles had already announced the satire of generic types, "the misanthropist," "the bourgeois aristocrat," "the miser," "the hypochondriac," but his personages were still individuals, Alceste, Jourdain, Harpagon, and Argan. Regnard could take the portrayal of general characteristics a

stage further, as he was no longer subject to the pressures which had resulted in Molière's depth of comic characterization.

Regnard produced for the Italian company from 1688 a succession of prose harlequinades, often with interpolated songs in verse, and latterly, in collaboration with Charles Dufresny, *Le Divorce*, a farce first played on 17 March 1688; there followed *La Descente de Mezzetin aux enfers*, 5 March 1689; *Arlequin, homme à bonnes fortunes*, 10 January 1690; *La Critique de l'Homme à bonnes fortunes*, 1 March 1690; *Les Filles errantes; ou, Les Intrigues des hôtelleries*, 24 August 1690; *La Coquette; ou, L'Académie des Dames*, 17 January 1691; *Les Chinois*, with Dufresny, 13 December 1692; *La Baguette de Vulcain*, with Dufresny, 10 January 1693, and, later in the year, *L'Augmentation de la "Baguette"*; *La Naissance d'Amadis*, 10 February 1694; *La Foire Saint-Germain*, with Dufresny, 26 December 1695; and *La Suite de la "Foire Saint-Germain;" ou, Les Momies d'Egypte*, with Dufresny, 16 March 1696. Regnard, latterly with Dufresny, became one of the most successful as well as one of the most regular providers of material for the Italian troupe in the years before its closure on 14 May 1697.

It has traditionally been supposed that on 19 May 1694 Regnard's one-act prose play, *Attendez-moi sous l'orme*, was played by the French company, with his *La Sérénade* following on 3 July. Dufresny is said to have had his own *Attendez-moi sous l'orme* played by the Italian troupe on 30 January 1695. It has, however, been argued since 1979 that the attribution of *L'orme* to Regnard was mistaken. Regnard's *Le Bal; ou, Le Bourgeois de Falaise*, in verse, was played by the French troupe on 14 June 1696, to be followed by his first five-act verse comedy, written for the French troupe and played on 19 December 1696, *Le Joueur*. This was so successful that Regnard resigned his post as trésorier de France. In 1699 he was to buy the château de Grillon, near Dourdan, about 45 kilometres south-west of Paris and a little south-east of Rambouillet, together with the post of maître et lieutenant of the rivers and forests (lieutenance de maîtrise des eaux et forêts et des chasses de Dourdan) of the district, acquiring a number of other picturesque titles, including capitaine du château de Dourdan and bailli d'épée de Hurepoix.

Dufresny may have pillaged *Le Joueur* for the Italians, and it has been claimed that his was the better version. It was, however, also reported that it had failed. The French company read Regnard's play on 7 Šeptember 1696, and played it 18 times in Paris and once at Versailles between 19 December 1696 and 27 January 1697. Since Regnard was paid 1,317 livres it is reasonable to assume nearly 13,000 paying spectators, which made the play a respectable success. There is, however, a difficulty. At a meeting of the Comédie-Française on 24 May 1697 to decide which pieces should be kept in the repertoire for the 1697–98 season, Regnard's was marked "à corriger (to be corrected)." This may have been on account of official pressure. Gambling had become a social nuisance, and there had been a series of anti-gaming laws, culminating in a quite fierce edict of 15 January 1691, imposing fines which were, however, halved in 1694. None the less, the Sorbonne was going to produce a *Résolution* on gaming on 25 June 1697. The company may have been waiting to see what it contained. There remains none the less a mystery.

Regnard and Dufresny had been collaborating for the Italian company, and Dufresny had had a prose play turned down by the French company on 8 November 1695. If, as seems likely but cannot be proved, it was his *Chevalier joueur*, originally entitled, like Regnard's, *Le Joueur*, then the probability must be that a further collaboration of the two dramatists had broken down, that Dufresny had got in first, that his prose play had been turned down, that Regnard's verse play had been accepted and successfully played, and that Dufresny's prose play was travelling in its wake. Dufresny's piece was played at court on 26 February 1697, and in Paris by the Italian company on the following day for a large paying house of 1,247, after which it was taken off. It is clear that there was a dispute, probably involving Dufresny's observance of the proprieties, but there is no convincing explanation of what happened, although it looks as if the allegation that Dufresny's play was a failure must have been part of the propaganda issued in the course of whatever dispute took place.

Regnard's text was published with an achevé of 11 February 1697. Regnard himself failed with *Le Distrait* on 2 December 1697, written, like all his remaining dramatic work, for the French company, now that the Italians had been banished from Paris. On 23 February 1699, during the carnival, Regnard's "opéra-ballet," *Le Carnaval de Venise*, was performed, with music by Lulli's successor, Campra. In 1700 the company gave Regnard's *Démocrite amoureux* on 12 January with only mediocre success, and followed it with an adaptation from Plautus, *Le Retour imprévu*, on 11 February, for which Regnard renounced all payment. His next play was *Les Folies amoureuses* with *Le Mariage de la folie* given on 15 January 1704. *Les Ménechmes*, another Plautus adaptation, was given on 4 December 1705. *Le Légataire universel* was played with *La Critique du "Légataire"* on 9 February 1708. To have both pieces on the same bill, Regnard renounced all rights to payment for both of them.

Regnard also left three or four unplayed fragments, his novel, travel diaries, and verse. He died very suddenly on 4 September 1709. The cause of death was uncertain. For two months he had had a sore on his face, and the possibility of suicide has been discussed but generally rejected as improbable. He was buried in the chapel dedicated to the Virgin in the local church at Dourdan.

WORKS

Commedia dell'arte was generally played in front of a backdrop representing a street, with apartments and balconies above shops. The cast made entrances and exits through what appeared to the audience to be doors in the buildings. The French system at the start of the 17th century had involved a series of booths representing different settings at the back of the stage, alongside one another. A curtain was raised in front of the booth depicting the scene where, for the moment, the action played on centre stage was taking place. It was relatively easy, and lucrative, to allow seating at the side of the stage in the commercial theatre, invariably converted real tennis courts. It is partly on account of the commercial utility of the stage seating that the use of elaborate stage machinery, and the concomitant rise of opera, took place in France at first predominantly at the Italian commedia dell'arte, whose productions, relying early on the extensive use of stage effects, particularly those using fountains and fireworks, precluded stage seating, and at French entertainments not wholly dependent on a ticket-buying public and at which therefore there was no need to admit the audience to the stage—as at the Palais-Cardinal while Richelieu was alive (known as the Palais-Royal after his death in 1642), or in the Tuileries, while the court was in Paris, or at the châteaux of Fontainebleau and Saint-Germain, and finally at Versailles.

The Hôtel de Bourgogne was certainly allowing the audience on to the stage by the middle of the century, but it was too small to have made its activities commercially viable if it had done without the income generated from the extra places and installed the expensive stage machinery which was in use at the Tuileries, and from time to time during the century at the Palais-Royal, and at the Marais. The installation of expensive machinery at the Hôtel de Bourgogne would have cost money, and also prevented stage seating, compatible only with bravura tragedy. Bernini had used a stage curtain, transformation scenes, and opening lateral shutters as early as 1641 at the Palais-Cardinal. No such staging was compatible with seated members of the audience lining the sides of the stage. By the death of Molière the three French companies and the Italians had inevitably developed their own quite different house styles, partly conditioned by the size of their halls, and the consequent affordability of machinery.

The physical circumstances of dramatic presentation changed radically during the period of Regnard's dramatic activity, that is from 1688 to 1708. Mazarin had invited Bernini to Paris while Richelieu was still alive, and Bernini had used Italian machinery with the sets and lighting he devised for the first performances in Richelieu's theatre, the first one in France with a proscenium arch, where in 1641 *Mirame* was staged, followed by the spectacular ballet *La Prospérité* (see: Desmarets de Saint-Sorlin). Then Torelli had come to Paris in 1645, again at Mazarin's invitation, leaving behind him in 1662 the innovations he had brought with him from Parma and Venice, including the use of perspective in painted scenery. We have an engraving of the famous stage set which he devised for the Petit-Bourbon (see: Molière) performance of Giulio Strozzi's *La Finta Pazza* in 1645.

From 1680 to 1687 the amalgamated French companies, now the Comédie-Française, played at the Hôtel Guénégaud. On 8 March 1688 they opened in the Fossés Saint-Germain, where they were to stay until 1770. Their new hall, inaugurated on 18 April 1689, held an audience of 2,000 and was lit by 24 chandeliers. Performances now took place daily at 5.30, except in Lent. As part of the audience was seated on the stage, the curtain was never lowered, although a limited number of violins was allowed during the entr'actes, in spite of the musical monopoly accorded to Lulli's Académie royale de Musique et de Danse, which gave performances on Sundays, Tuesdays, and Fridays. From the beginning of Regnard's theatrical career, elaborate French productions requiring machinery, music, or dancing were the province of the Académie royale, installed at the Palais-Royal. Regnard's plays had to be adapted to physical theatrical constraints that had not obtained before Lulli's monopoly, granted by the letters patent of 13 March 1672, and the amalgamations starting with Molière's death in 1673.

Regnard's first five-act verse comedy, *Le Joueur*, is generally thought to be among his two or three best, although the characterization is not deep, and the structure of the intrigue is ingenious but not remarkable. Valère, Géronte's son, lives the existence of a dissolute dandy away from home. Gaming is his obsession. He is perpetually promising his mistress, Angélique, to give it up, but never does. Tired of this treatment, Angélique tries and fails to give him up, but eventually succeeds, and marries the insipid Dorante. Some of the dramatic technique is adapted from the commedia, as the ending of acts with scenes involving secondary characters, a device Regnard's comedy shares with the operas of Italian baroque.

There is a good deal of parody of lines from the great French tragedies. Valère's "que ce mot est cruel quand on aime (how cruel is that word when you are in love)" is a transposition into a comic setting of an emotional line from Racine's tragedy *Bérénice*, "Combien ce mot cruel est affreux quand on aime (How fearsome is that cruel word when you are in love)." Valère, in act IV, scene 10, praises destiny for its blows in a parody of three of Oreste's lines in Racine's *Andromaque* (act V, scene 5, lines 1614–16). The published text is prefaced by a brief but bitter paragraph attacking the plagiarist who is reading a prose piece of the same title "dans les caffez de Paris (in the cafés of Paris)," a relatively early indication that the coffee house, of which there were probably about 200 at the time in Paris (300 in 1715), was taking over a former function of the salon. In 1696 the Procope had recently opened in the rue des Fossés Saint-Germain, opposite the Comédie.

Regnard has taken care to get his setting as accurate as possible. The scene is "a furnished apartment." The play starts with Hector, Valère's valet, alone. His opening couplet sets the tone, an ordinary remark, followed by a pastiche of high lyrical style, with its inversion and elevated "ramage (warbling):"

Il est, parbleu, grand jour. Déjà de leur ramage,
Les coqs ont éveillé tout nostre voisinage

(Good heavens, it's already full daylight. Already with their warbling, / The cocks have woken our whole neighbourhood).

Hector is dreaming aloud of the sort of valet's life he would really like when Nérine, Angélique's maid, comes in demanding to see Valère. She pushes her way imperiously through, but is stopped by Hector's question, "Do you want to see my master 'in naturalibus'?" The Latin phrase means "in his natural state," that is, in the context, naked, but the phrase was widely used in a theological context for the state of man without grace. Hector the valet knows a bit of Latin, and enough theology to make that sort of joke.

Nérine is his equal. They have a furious quarrel, witty, articulate, very funny, about how awful a prospect for Angélique Valère is, with Hector confident that, however true all that Nérine says might be, although he won't admit it, Angélique is caught in Valère's nets. Nérine, who had come on her mistress's behalf to break off the relationship with Valère, still in fact out gaming from the night before, hopes that reason and herself will gain the victory for Dorante. Nérine leaves and a bedraggled Valère returns home. He has lost money, and inverts the rhetorical device used by Hector in his opening line. Valère starts with the rhetorical braggadocio, before sagging bathetically:

Tu peux me faire perdre, ô Fortune ennemie,
Mais me faire payer, parbleu! je t'en deffie,
Car je n'ay pas un sou

(You can make me lose, O hostile Destiny, / But as for making me pay, good heavens! I defy you, / As I haven't got a penny).

The comedy is in the verbal play. There is a superb scene in which briefly Valère is talking about obtaining money, but what Hector replies could be taken as a double entendre. It could also apply to obtaining Angélique. The translation code is supplied by Hector. The objects of Valère's obsession are interchangeable, Angélique and money to gamble with. If Valère says he loves Angélique, it means he has lost money. Hector asks him not about the night's gaming, but whether he loves Angélique. "I adore her," says Valère. Hector replies

…Tant pis! C'est un signe fâcheux:
Quand vous estes sans fond vous estes amoureux,
Et quand l'argent renaist vostre tendresse expire.
Vostre bourse est, Monsieur, puisqu'il faut vous le dire,
Un thermometre seur, tantost bas, tantost haut,
Marquant de vostre coeur, ou le froid, ou le chaud

(…Oh dear! That's a bad sign: / When you have no money, you're in love, / And when funds revive, your tenderness dies away. / Your purse, sir, is, since I must tell you, / A sure thermometer, sometimes low, sometimes high, / Marking the coolness or the warmth of your heart).

What turns this from light entertainment into comedy of high literary value is the inversion of class roles. Hector, the valet, is the intelligent, witty, Latin-quoting, perceptive, and sensitive character who would like to lounge in bed all day. Valère, his master, is the lout or slob who spends all night intoxicating himself irresponsibly, gambling beyond his means, and behaving disgracefully to pay for his habit. The powerful social comment is often missed, and there have been critical disputes about whether Regnard's plays are comedies of manners or of character. But it is a mistake to see Molière's practice as normative. The satirical context is now quite different.

Le Joueur merely cashes in on a topical subject. What it is about is class. When, after the opening scenes, Valère returns, Hector openly informs him that Nérine had called and that Angélique was being pressed to marry Dorante, Valère's uncle, and Hector encourages Valère to think rather in terms of Angélique's rich widowed sister, "la Comtesse," about whose mixture of prudishness and coquettishness he has some very shrewd things to say. Hector identifies himself with Valère, answers for him in the dialogue, and has a generally protective, almost avuncular attitude towards him, often taking over what should properly be his employer's role, and speaking as "we" when addressing third parties. Nérine's relationship with Angélique is analogous. Angélique, we learn, is being courted by a "marquis," formerly himself a valet, who has won a fortune gambling. He trails unmistakeable signs of fraudulence from the moment he appears, and belongs more to the burlesque of the commedia than to the French tradition of social satire. At the end of the first act, Valère's father, Géronte, comes in, and it is Hector who conducts the defence on Valère's behalf. Valère promises his father to give up gaming and goes off to see Angélique. The act ends with M. Toutabas offering to sell his services as master of gambling, not excluding a little cheating.

In the second act Angélique, still clearly in love with Valère, swears to Nérine that she will have nothing to do with him, whatever he threatens, even suicide, and agrees with her sister, the comtesse, that gambling is a worse disqualification for her future husband than being a beggar, a miser, a flirt, ill-tempered, ungainly, brutal, capricious, drunken, witless, debauched, stupid, or angry. Angélique agrees that she will not marry Valère. The comtesse then announces that, for her part, she will. There follows a brilliantly articulate wrangle. Angélique correctly says that Valère is after her sister's money. The comtesse prides herself on other charms, and derides Angélique's certainty that Valère loved her.

The "marquis" arrives, behaves abominably, almost abruptly demands to marry the comtesse, and is followed by a procession of messengers with assignations for nights of love or gambling. Like Hector, Nérine answers for her employer. Like him, she will throw in the odd educated Latin word, "optime (well done)," to cheer on Angélique as she resists Valère's protestations. Valère comes in, declaring in front of the comtesse his love for Angélique. The swiftness with which the situation changes is very reminiscent of the best commedia dell'arte scripts. The comtesse walks out; when Valère threatens suicide, and Nérine's sarcasm, Angélique softens and gives Valère her portrait in a diamond-studded frame as a token. He returns home, and notwithstanding Hector's scandalized reaction immediately pledges Angélique's portrait for 3,000 livres, which he borrows from Mme La Ressource.

In the third act Dorante proves himself a generous loser. His brother Géronte tells him he should not have tried to rival his nephew, Valère. In a comic scene Hector lists Valère's debts to Géronte. Valère comes in, his hat overflowing with his winnings. His interest in Angélique has waned sharply and, in a biting parody of much social comment from several literary traditions, Valère delivers a diatribe on the social virtues of gambling, which puts on the same level all the social classes, marquis, bourgeois, banker's wife, impoverished duchess, a clerk's domestic servant, and a duke and peer. He goes off to gamble again, refusing to take only part of his winnings, or to give Hector the wages he has not been paid since he entered Valère's employment five years previously. The non-payment of wages is not just a reminiscence of Molière's Sganarelle in *Dom Juan*. It asserts that the apparent social relationship between Valère and Hector is not the real one. Tradespeople call, to whom money is owed. The wit to send them away comes not from Valère but from Hector. The comic "marquis" comes in, boasts wildly, and there is nearly a duel between him and Valère. Valère says that as far as he is concerned the "marquis" can have the heart of the comtesse. But not, adds Hector, her purse.

In act four Nérine tries again to dissuade Angélique. Hector comes in, betrays the fact that Valère is gambling again, and then attempts to extricate himself by describing this last gambling session as if it were a duel in which Valère was fighting his compulsion to the death. The comtesse meets Dorante and immediately behaves as if he were trying to woo her. She then, to his great joy, accepts the "marquis." Valère, having lost all his money again, is in despair:

Dans l'etat où je suis, je puis tout entreprendre

(In the state I am in, I may do anything).

At the high point of Racine's *Phèdre*, Phèdre had said despairingly to Oenone,

Dans le trouble où je suis, je ne puis rien pour moi

(In my anguish I can do nothing for myself).

Regnard may have been indulging in parodic literary irreverence. Valère makes Hector read Seneca to him, finally proving his own superior education by knowing who Seneca was, but turning to burlesque in wondering which way out to take, river, gun, poison, or sword. Géronte comes in, knowing at least the title of Seneca's most famous book, the *De beata vita*. Géronte appears likely to save the day for his apparently repentant son, who goes off to Angélique.

Act five opens with a scene between Dorante, Angélique, and Nérine, gradually joined by Mme La Ressource, looking for Valère, the comtesse, and the "marquis," who turns out to owe Mme La Ressourse a great deal of money. The comtesse leaves discomfited, the "marquis" still with wild fantasies of grandeur. Mme La Ressource brings out the portrait of Angélique which Valère had pledged; Valère and Hector come in; the portrait is revealed. Angélique marries Dorante, Géronte disinherits Valère. Nérine is pleased at the outcome and finishes with a splendid double entendre about playing for high stakes. Hector goes to the library to read Seneca. Valère ends, hoping that one day

Le jeu m'acquitera des pertes de l'amour

(Gambling will repay me for my losses in love).

The wit, parody, and intrigue are all impressive, but the satire lies in the way all the characters find their own level. The ending is not happy, although the tensions of the intrigue are resolved when all the main characters end up with what they deserve, even if the fraudulent "marquis" and the self-preening comtesse are left merely to wander off to their destinies. The real question is why the obviously well-matched pair, Hector and Nérine, are not allowed to fall in love and marry. One of the clues to the nature of Regnard's achievement is that, while Molière's servants did not marry one another thirty years earlier, but Marivaux's servants did marry forty years later, it was to be almost a century before marital happiness at the social level of servants not only reflected and reinforced the unions of the minor aristocracy, as in Marivaux, but actually replaced them, as in Beaumarchais's *Le Mariage de Figaro*.

In fact Regnard does move towards Marivaux's solution. In his last play, the 1708 five-act verse comedy *Le Légataire universel*, the intrigue is led by one of the earliest resourceful valets to emerge from the commedia dell'arte into the French tradition. The plot is fast-moving and complex, but essentially concerns the will of the dying Géronte, miserly but wealthy, from the upper bourgeoisie. His nephew Eraste is in love with Isabelle, and Eraste's valet, Crispin, is in love with Géronte's maid, Lisette. Eraste has promised Crispin 300 livres a year if Crispin succeeds in getting him made Géronte's heir. Although at one point, undergoing the obligatory reversal of fortune, he was resigned to defeat, Crispin is otherwise in charge throughout, impersonating both a Norman nephew and a niece from Le Mans, in whose characters he behaves so badly to Géronte that he gets the real nephew and niece disinherited. When it seems that Géronte is on the point of death, Crispin also impersonates Géronte and dictates his will himself, pretending he is too ill to sign it. He leaves himself 1,500 livres a year and Lisette 6,000 livres. Géronte gets better and is persuaded to sign the will. In this play Eraste ends up marrying Isabelle, but Crispin also marries Lisette.

During Regnard's lifetime works of his were performed 455 times in Paris, and 22 times at court.

PUBLICATIONS

Collections

Théatre italien, edited by E. Gherardi, 6 vols., 1700; modern edition, 1981
Les Oeuvres de Mr Regnard, 2 vols., 1710–11
Les Oeuvres de Mr Regnard, 2 vols., 1714
Les Oeuvres de Mr Regnard, 5 vols., 1731
Oeuvres de Regnard, 6 vols., 1789–90
Oeuvres complètes, 2 vols., 1854
Oeuvres complètes, 1875
There are 21 known editions of the *Oeuvres* before 1800

Plays

[*Note: Not all of Regnard's plays were published outside the collected volumes. Dates of performance are given in the text above. There have been frequent translations and adaptations into English, German, and Italian*]

Le Bourgeois de Falaise, comédie (1696), 1694
La Sérénade, comédie (1694), 1695
Le Joueur, comédie en vers (1696), 1697
Le Distrait, comédie (1697), 1698
Le Carnaval de Venise, ballet (1699), 1699
Démocrite, comédie (1700), 1700
Le Retour imprévu, comédie (1700), 1700; as *The Intriguing Chambermaid*, translated by Henry Fielding, 1734
Les Folies amoureuses, comédie (1704), 1704
Les Ménechmes, comédie (1705), 1706
Le Légataire universel, comédie (1708), 1708
La Critique du Légataire, comédie (1708), 1708

Other

Satyre contre les maris, 1694; modern edition 1920
Voyage de Regnard en Flandre, en Hollande, en Danemark et en Suède, 1874
Voyage de Laponie, 1875
Voyage de Normandie, 1789–90; 1883
La Provençale, 1920

Biographical and critical studies

Calame, A., *Regnard, sa vie et son oeuvre*, 1960
Medlin, Dorothy M., *The Verbal Art of Jean-François Regnard*, 1966
Moureau, F., *Dufresny, auteur dramatique (1657–1724)*, 1979

RÉGNIER, Mathurin, 1573–1613.

Satirist and poet.

LIFE

It adds piquancy to Régnier's interest as a poet and satirist that he should both have introduced his senior, Malherbe, to his uncle, Philippe Desportes, and himself have been a supporter of the Pléiade (q.v.) and of Ronsard, against whom both Desportes and Malherbe in different ways reacted. But Régnier's relationship with Desportes remained close, while there is more than a hint of outrage in his attitude to Malherbe. He was, however, an important poet in his own right, not so much for the court poetry written for Henri IV as for the re-creation of the authentic antique inspiration of the early Pléiade, once an exultation in the optimism of the high renaissance in France and now, in Régnier, a product of the wave of cultural optimism which followed in France the end of the religious wars and the coronation of Henri IV in 1594.

Régnier's father Jacques married Philippe Desportes's sister Simone on 25 January 1573, and Régnier was born that year at Chartres on 21 December. His father, aged 27, was secretary to the chancellery of the duc d'Anjou and himself a poet, the son of an échevin of Chartres in 1552 and himself to become an échevin there in 1589. Régnier was tonsured in 1583 and educated well enough later to nourish himself on Horace and Ovid although, according to a quatrain he wrote for a 1595 Greek grammar by Jean Sursin, he still in 1594 intended, and therefore needed, to go back to the study of Greek.

Régnier joined the household of the cardinal François de Joyeuse in 1587. The cardinal was the younger son of Anne, admiral of France, Henri III's favourite mignon, who had married the sister of Henri III's queen but was killed at Coutras on 20 October 1587. François de Joyeuse had represented the interests of France at Rome from that date, and had at the request of Desportes, friend and adviser of Henri III, from 1587 incorporated Régnier into his suite as a page. Régnier certainly accompanied him in Rome from 1589 to 1596, and visited Rome with him subsequently, probably in 1598, 1603, and 1604, when Joyeuse was concerned mostly with the abjuration of Henri IV and the dissolution of his marriage to Marguerite de Valois. The fortunes of the Joyeuse family were, however, on the decline, and there are signs that Régnier did not wholly enjoy his period in the cardinal's household, where he had graduated to the position of secretary.

Desportes, abbot of Tiron, with no family responsibilities of his own, actively promoted the interests of his brothers and sisters, and during his ample periods of leisure, Régnier had the freedom of the excellent library at his uncle's country establishment at Vanves. It was when Desportes was approached by the marquis de Coeuvres, brother of Henri IV's mistress, Gabrielle d'Estrées, to sing his sister's glories for the king, that Desportes, who had by then given up profane poetry, proposed Régnier in his place. Between 1596 and 1598, encouraged by Adrien de Monluc, comte de Carmain, to whom Régnier anonymously addressed his second *Satire*, and after apparently extracting from the marquis de Coeuvres the promise of a benefice, Régnier wrote a number of elegies of which some, at least, were for Gabrielle d'Estrées. She was to die in 1599, by which time not only Régnier but also Vauquelin des Yveteaux, Rapin, and

Laugier de Porchères were writing, in her honour, works commissioned on behalf of the king.

From 1605 Régnier was in Paris, seeing much of his uncle in the months before his death on 6 October 1606. Since Desportes was to have been the dauphin's tutor, and since the king himself called on Desportes, it is unlikely that Régnier was not familiar with court society although, to judge from his dedications, he more readily frequented the humanists. The second and third *Satires* must have been written by 1598, the *Discours au Roy* and *Satires* IV-IX, with the exception of VI, probably in 1605 or 1606. We know comparatively little about Régnier's life after Desportes's death. Malherbe arrived in Paris in August 1605, and in the fourth *Satire* there is a disobliging reference to the "sauvages lois (savage rules)" Malherbe wished to impose on poetry. Malherbe may also well have been the sarcastic "mélancolique" of the seventh *Satire*. Racan recounts an incident sometime towards the end of 1605, in which Malherbe was offensively sarcastic about Régnier's poetic style during an interview of both with Henri IV. Régnier criticized Malherbe again in the ninth *Satire*, after he had first taken Malherbe to dine with Desportes, who had risen to go upstairs to get for Malherbe a copy of his *Psaumes*, only to be told by Malherbe that he had seen them, and that the stew was worth more than the book.

Malherbe regarded it as beneath his dignity to reply to attacks, and did not answer the ninth *Satire*. In the tenth, which became the twelfth in 1609, Régnier again attempted to provoke Malherbe by praising the king's painter, Fréminet, an admirer of Michelangelo whose flamboyant style was the antithesis of what Malherbe admired, and in the first, written with the tenth just before the publication of the first, 1608, edition, Régnier defended against Malherbe the Pléiade theory of poetic inspiration. Régnier continues the attack into the eleventh *Satire*, and Malherbe's distaste for Régnier can be deduced from his affectation not to know the authorship of the inscriptions which he did know Régnier had written, and by not referring to his death in his letters.

Régnier was not left anything directly by his wealthy uncle and patron, Desportes, whose benefices were re-allocated by the king within four days of his death, but Tallemant tells us that Régnier was given by the king a generous annual pension of 5,000 livres on the abbey of Vaux de Cernay, for which he expressed his fulsome thanks in the 1608 *Epître liminaire*. On 3 July 1609 Régnier became a canon of the cathedral chapter at Chartres. A well-informed article in the 1723 *Mercure* (q.v.) says that Régnier later resigned the canonry, which is not true, but that he had a pension of 2,000 livres on Vaux de Cernay, bestowed on him by the king on Desportes's death in 1606. Other references elsewhere suggest that Tallemant was wrong either about the amount of the benefice, or about the abbey from which it derived. There is documentary evidence that Régnier was still a canon of Chartres on 25 June 1612, when he had to send medical evidence from his mother's house in Paris that he was confined to bed, in order to assign to a third party some benefits in kind due to him from Beauce. That means that he had not yet spent his obligatory six months in residence at Chartres. In June 1613, within four months of his death, he was being replaced at divine office by another nephew of Desportes, so could not have resigned.

The pattern of known allusions, references, and events makes it at least probable that Régnier was trying to lead satire away from the coarse humour and more refined expressions of lust required from poets called on to sing the amours of the king, or of other grand members of the court. The steward of the king's pleasures needed a small brigade of poets to call on for this purpose. Henri IV changed his mistress five times, for instance, in the period from January 1608 to 1609, but also conceived a real and deep passion for Charlotte de Montmorency, princesse de Condé, rescued from the king by her husband and put out of harm's way at Brussels, where an ode by Régnier, "Jamais ne pourrai-je bannir...," was sent with Coeuvres in January. We find Régnier singing in the 16th *Satire*, later to raise eyebrows, of the pleasures of change. When trouble broke out openly between the counsellors of the assassinated Henri IV, Villeroy and Sully, Coeuvres supported Villeroy, and Régnier took the opportunity of congratulating Villeroy on the way he had navigated the ship of France. The 14th *Satire* was going to be dedicated to him had it been properly finished.

Whatever his poetic ambitions, Régnier was clearly therefore a court poet, expected in return for a protection which included financial provision to support the love affairs of monarchs and patrons, celebrate victories, or compose inscriptions. He took sides in literary encounters, on behalf of his uncle, Desportes, and in political debates, on the side of his patron, Coeuvres. He was available for official royal commissions. These facts give us a fair idea of his style of life. We also know that he had a refuge at Royaumont, of which Philippe Hurault de Cheverny, bishop of Chartres, held the commendatory abbacy, and where Régnier had a circle of friends, including the Dupuy brothers, Jacques-Auguste de Thou, the Sainte-Marthes, father and son, Guillaume de Baïf, and Nicolas Sanguin, who commissioned from Régnier the inscriptions for the triumphal arches for the entry of Marie de Medici into Paris in 1610. Broadly speaking, the Royaumont circle was composed of friends and successors of the Pléiade poets, and scholars, and offered a refuge from the lucrative vulgarity of court constraints.

The legend that has grown up round Régnier's name of dissolute habits, specifying all or any of atheism, sodomy, smallpox, and venereal disease, was a pure fabrication routinely released by enemies in the satirical wars of the early 17th century. Régnier's manner of life has also been misunderstood on account of the cynical exploitation of his name to boost after his death the sale of "satirical" collections of lecherous verse. It is only very recently that some certainty has been reached in the matter of false attributions.

In October 1613, gravely ill, Régnier had himself taken to Rouen to see a surgeon when on his way back from Royaumont to his mother's house in Paris. It has been conjectured that the operation was for the stone, but it failed and Régnier died, apparently on 22 October 1613, although until recently the date was given as the 13th. He was buried, as he had wished, at Royaumont.

WORKS

Régnier published 13 *Satires* (see for the meaning of the word the entry on the *Satyre Ménippée*) during his lifetime; there were 10 in the 1608 edition; 12 in 1609; 13 in 1612; all followed by the *Discours au Roi*. However, Régnier himself more or less lost interest in his book after the first two editions of 1608 and 1609, and abandoned it to the publishers, who added, extracted, and rearranged as suited them, choosing printers who were left to change spellings and correct errors. The original privilège was accorded to Toussaincts du Bray in 1608, but ran out in 1614, after which the *Satires* became the literary property of Antoine de Brueil, publisher of the *Muses gaillardes*, who in 1616 incorporated Régnier's book into a corporate collection, renaming Régnier's contribution *Satyres et autres oeuvres folastres du sieur Régnier* and following it, without transition, with often bawdy poems by such authors as Sigogne, Motin, Touvant, and Berthelot, of whom Régnier during his lifetime knew only Motin. The indignant reaction of Régnier's friends, led by the Dupuy brothers, eventually led to the edition of 1652.

Occasional pieces had from the beginning been included, but more were added in 1652, with another satire and another elegy, although not all the false attributions were eliminated. They appear now to have been satisfactorily identified, and the 1958 edition of Régnier by Gabriel Raibaud is reliable. It contains 17 satires, five elegies, and three sonnets, in addition to miscellaneous pieces. The titles by which we know the satires were added by Claude Brossette for the 1729 edition, but he did not give titles to all the satires, and the 1958 edition has re-established the original numbers, thereby making the numerical references in much critical writing obsolete.

It is necessary to know only that the original *Satire* X ("Regnier apologiste de soy mesme") was numbered XII from 1609; that the original XI ("Le souper ridicule") and XII ("Le mauvais giste") were numbered X and XI from 1609; and that Elegie I ("Non non j'ay trop de coeur...") was known as *Satire* XVII. The present *Satire* XVII is that entitled by Brossette "Ny crainte ny esperance."

The great models for the *Satires* are Horace, Ovid, and Juvenal. The metre is the alexandrine, and the outstanding characteristic is often the realistic observation and selectivity of detail in presentation. However, behind the poetry, and what elevates it, is a moral vision, an ultimately optimistic view of the world in spite of its hypocrisies, incoherences, irrationality, and follies. Régnier has above all a sense of honour, of justice, and of standards of good sense, even of the existence of absolute norms of rational taste.

The 1608 edition *Les premieres oeuvres de M. Regnier* contains the prose epistle to the king, and an ode to Régnier by Motin. The first *Satire* is that to the king, scattered with reminiscences of Ronsard, Horace, Virgil, and Theocritus. Régnier chose the alexandrine, presumably because it was by 1600 the most solemn metre, and also the nearest to the hexameter. Unfortunately the gazeteers, to say nothing of more illustrious versifiers, were to demonstrate that alexandrines, unconstrained by the mandatory schemes of vowel lengths in Latin hexameters, were long and fluid enough to be temptingly easy to write. It is immediately obvious how irritating to Malherbe this first satire must have appeared. It self-indulgently luxuriates in mythological obscurities, classical allusions, and an allegorical "Discorde." Régnier refers to his "humeur frenetique (roughly: poetic frenzy)," deliberately returning to the buoyant neoplatonism of Ronsard's poetic theory. Henri IV is greater than Aeneas and Achilles, greater than Virgil and Homer had gifts enough to praise.

The second *Satire* dates from the winter of 1597–98 and was published alone, addressed to Adrien de Monluc, comte de Caramain, one of the stewards of the royal pleasures. The allusions are to Ronsard, Baïf, Du Bellay, and Jodelle, and the poem is devoted to Régnier's years with Joyeuse and his first visits to

Vanves. The poem breaks off after 12 lines, without finishing its single sentence, after allegorizing Virtue and Vice. Régnier informs the reader in another single sentence of eight lines that he is to follow Juvenal rather than Horace. He makes much of an elaborate comparison between his anonymous verses and a foundling child, a parallel syntactically and imaginatively involved, long-winded, but forceful in the denunciation of a "sot honneur (stupid honour)" and a "batarde gloire." The poem reflects on its author's ten lost years, alluding to Régnier's service in the Joyeuse household, and begins to show some concision and selectivity. The poet travelled abroad to serve his prelate.

> J'ay changé mon humeur, alteré ma nature,
> J'ay beu chaud, mangé froid, j'ay couché sur la dure...
> En publiq', à l'eglise, à la chambre, à la table,
> Et pense avoir esté maintefois agreable

(I changed my mood, altered my nature,/I drank hot, ate cold, slept on the ground.../In public, in church, in the chamber, at table,/And think that I have often pleased).

There is in this poem the sort of baroque distortion of often stylized imagery to be found in such other major poets of the period as d'Aubigné. Régnier exaggerates the plight of poets, drunkenly obsessed with their hardships,

> ....sans souliers, ceinture ny cordon,
> L'oeil farouche et troublé, l'esprit à l'abandon

(...without shoes, belt or laces,/With fierce and troubled eye, and wild mind).

The sketches of different sorts of indigent poets are witty and amusing. If he, the writer of these lines, does not esteem their verse, he is insensitive, soulless, philistine, ignorant. Then he breaks off to sing the praises of Vanves. What makes him "et poete et satyrique (both a poet and a satirist)" is his activity

> Reglant la medisance à la façon antique

(Regulating his asperities in the antique manner).

In fact Régnier's plea against Malherbe is for a return to the learned, inspired enthusiasm of Ronsard, against the now outdated gloomy neostoicism of Malherbe, pedantically limiting his dimmed feelings, never allowed to overflow rational norms of versifying or emotion. Régnier represents the baroque reconquest of the high cultural ground from the defensive insensitiveness of the attitudes explored during the wars.

The third satire takes its tone and about 30 lines from Juvenal, and also borrows from Ariosto. There is something stylized about its lament as it deplores the state of a world in which deserts are not just and sycophancy rules, and the poet presents himself as a plain, simple, honest man without the qualities needed to succeed at court. The goods of the spirit are more important than those of the body. True goods are, as in the neoplatonist framework exploited by Ronsard, dependent on the power of knowledge to penetrate the secrets of the universe. Toned down into the direct comment on human values and behaviour which is constitutive of satire at this date, Régnier offers us a splendid restatement of the renaissance vision of early Ronsard.

The fourth satire, addressed to Motin, amusingly contrasts the poet's lot with that of the lawyer and the doctor. Régnier auto-biographically but fraudulently claims to have disregarded parental warnings against following in the footsteps of his uncle and counselling the cultivation of a warrior's skills. The fifth satire congratulates the poet and bishop of Séez, Jean Bertault, first chaplain to the queen, on the success of the second 1605 edition of his works. It contains an attack on Malherbe but, even more importantly, a reaffirmation of the renaissance values beginning to be reasserted by d'Urfé and François de Sales, after their temporary suspension during the wars. Bertault's calm mind is the consequence of sweeping imaginative visions. Régnier agrees with Ronsard

…que le chaud element
Qui donne ceste pointe au vif entendement,
Dont la verve s'échauffe et s'enflame de sorte
Que ce feu dans le ciel sur des aisles l'emporte,
Soit le mesme qui rend le poete ardent et chaud,
Suject à ses plaisirs, de courage si haut
Qu'il meprise le peuple et les choses communes
Et bravant les faveurs se moque des fortunes;
Qui le fait, debauché, frenetique, resvant,
Porter la teste basse et l'esprit dans le vent,
Egayer sa fureur parmy des precipices
Et plus qu'à la raison suject à ses caprices

(that the warm element [the blood],/Which gives a fillip to the sharp intelligence,/Whose nerve kindles and bursts into flame so/That the fire carries it on wings to heaven,/Is the same that makes the poet ardent and fiery,/Subject to the blood's pleasures, of a spirit so elevated/That he despises the multitude and lowly things,/And defying favour laughs at fortune;/Which makes the poet, unleashed, frenzied, dreamy,/Cast his eyes down and his spirit into the wind,/Enlivening his inspiration among prec-ipices/And more subject to caprice than to reason).

The point needs to be insisted on, because for so long Régnier was seen as an old-fashioned inheritor of an obsolete Pléiade tradition which required the cleansing operated by Malherbe's quasi-Cartesian (see: Cartesianism) subjection of poetry to rationally calculated norms. That interpretation of the quarrel between Régnier and Malherbe does not acknowledge the true originality of Cartesian rationality as an unprecedented act of faith in human intellectual power, and it neglects the extent to which the cultural defensiveness of the last third of the 16th cen-tury during the wars, whose neostoicism bred the attitudes and theories of Malherbe, was what had already gone out of date during the surge of cultural euphoria in the first decade of the 17th century. Régnier may have been harking back to a theoret-ical framework constituted by the early Pléiade synthesis of antique poetic models and neoplatonist poetic theory, but he was using it to reaffirm the optimistic vision of human potential which it had been constructed to support.

The sixth satire, the first to be written, is an almost conven-tional deploration of the depradations wreaked on civilized behaviour in the name above all of honour, bemoaning changes in society consequent on the building of towns and cities and on ownership, ambition, and war; it is a lament on the birth of envy, contempt, discord, fear, treason, murder, vengeance, and despair. Its occasion was the welcome to be afforded in Rome to the French ambassador in Rome from 1601 to 1605, Sully's brother, Philippe de Béthune, comte de Selles, and it is largely inspired by Mauro. The seventh satire, to Coeuvres, master of the king's pleasures, is appropriately about the irresistible attractiveness to Régnier of women. It is almost wholly a styl-ized adaptation of Ovid and starts with what must certainly be a disdainful allusion to Malherbe, "nostre Melancolique." The eighth satire, dedicated to Charles de Beaumanoir de Lavardin, abbé de Beaulieu, elevated to the see of Le Mans in 1601, when he was 15, is an adaptation of Horace, but narrates an unwel-come encounter, makes extensive use of conversation, overflows with allusions to contemporary Paris, and contains a reference to the Pont-Neuf, finished only in 1606.

The ninth satire, to Nicolas Rapin, starts with a reference to his "vers mesurés," with which others, notably Baïf, had exper-imented in the context of reinforcing the effects produced by numerically calculated poetic metres with those attributable to music. According to the neoplatonist theory elaborated, for instance by Pontus de Tyard, the elevating aesthetic effect was thereby redoubled. This satire contains Régnier's strongest attack on Malherbe, mocking his view of the great poets of antiquity as well as of Desportes and most of the poets associ-ated with Ronsard. The reproach against Malherbe and his dis-ciples is chiefly that their activity is reducible to composition according to calculated grammatical, lexical, and metrical rules, governed at best by sonority:

C'est proser de la rime et rimer de la prose

(It's making prose out of rhyme, and rhyming what is prose).

Nowhere are flights of imagination, nobility of inspiration, or elevation of feeling:

Nul eguillon divin n'esleve leur courage

(No divine stimulus exalts their spirit).

Régnier refers to the manuscript, now in the Bibliothèque Nationale, of Malherbe's comments on Desportes, a book of "fautes (errors)" as long as the original. The satire culminates in a brilliant series of sketches of types of people blinded by their passions and their interests—soldiers, lovers, misers, plough-men—and it ends by the strong declaration that what Régnier stands for in poetry is tradition: Virgil, Tasso, and Ronsard.

In spite of the interpolation of the present 11th and 12th sat-ires between the original ninth and tenth, it is clear that the orig-inal, and now restored, tenth, "A Monsieur Freminet," the painter Régnier had met in Italy, follows straight on from the ninth. Régnier here speaks affectionately of his father and seems, by writing of himself and his verse, to invite Malherbe to an altercation. After it, in the first edition, came the formally encomiastic *Discours au Roy*, a poem of 258 lines mythologiz-ing the military exploits of the king.

The 1609 edition carried two new satires, imitated respec-tively from Caporali, secretary to cardinal Aquaviva, and Berni. They are witty and amusing low-life anecdotes, "Le souper ridicule" and "Le mauvais giste," full of realistic description and conversation. The 1612 edition added the most famous of all the satires, the 13th, *Macette*, to which Brossette added "ou l'hypocrisie déconcertée (or hypocrisy surprised)." In it Régnier borrows phrases from a dozen earlier French poets, but is chiefly dependent on Ovid. It is a tour de force which describes in great detail the devout habits of a repentant prostitute.

Son oeil penitent ne pleure qu'eau beniste

(Her penitent eye weeps only holy water).

Macette knows all the technical terms—"hypostasis," used of the substantial union of two natures in Jesus, and "synderesis," normally at this date used for the mystical high-point of the soul, which is above the region of feeling—and how many days of indulgences are attached to which pious practices. She is an example of love, charity, honour, and virtue, and it has even been announced at Rome

La voyant aimer Dieu et la chair maistriser
Qu'on n'attend que sa mort pour la canoniser

(That, seeing her love God and conquer her flesh,/They are only waiting for her to die before they canonize her).

The poet thinks the change altogether too sudden. None the less, he had almost been shocked into repentance himself when, not quite having finished his business with a lady whom he sometimes visited, he was present when Macette called and, not knowing he was hidden in the room, revealed her hypocrisy, incidentally justifying herself with the view that at any rate half the malice of sin is in the scandal and

Le peché que l'on cache est demi pardonné

(The sin that is hidden is half forgiven).

a view propounded rather than defended in Marguerite de Navarre's *Heptameron*. It implies a medieval view that religious perfection can be extrinsic to interior conversion, since the sinfulness of vice is "half" dependent on whether or not there is scandal. Macette's view is a lot worse than that. Sin does not matter providing that it is hidden. Macette recommends the poet's friend to sell her favours for what she can get while they are still of value. Macette's advice is of a breath-taking cynicism, a brilliant comment on actual human behaviour,

Estimez vos amans selon le revenu

(Value your lovers according to what they bring you in).

Even in the early satires the amusing, realistic depiction of detail in traits, habits of behaviour, and characteristics is derived from Berni and his disciples, Mauro and Caporali, but it is not only the enthusiastic skill in the selection of true to life detail which marks out Régnier as a great poet, and not the poetic theory, the renewed assertion of the poetics created in the renaissance for the celebration of human dignity. The adaptations of Juvenal, Ovid, and Horace, are skilful and attractive, in spite of the baroque stylization, prolixity, and attitudinizing. What makes the poetry powerful are the underlying assumptions about humanity and its potential, the basic confidence which allows the surface cynicism.

It is difficult to maintain that Régnier is seriously undervalued, since conventional wisdom already rightly accepts now that he is one of greatest satirical writers in the history of French literature. That is certainly true, but Régnier, if not undervalued, is still generally misunderstood. Any similarity with Montaigne is on the surface only. Régnier does not plumb doubts, and was not fascinated by the need to find a response to adversity, or to overcome a fear of death. He is a great poet because very early he threw off the defensiveness of Montaigne's generation, and very early resurrected the confidence as well as the poetics of the young Ronsard, because of the power of his moral vision.

PUBLICATIONS

Les premières oeuvres, 1608
Les Satyres, 1609
Les Satyres, 1612
Les Satyres, 1613
Les Satyres et autres oeuvres, 1652
Oeuvres de Régnier, edited by C. Brossette, 1729
Oeuvres complètes, edited by J. Plattard, 1930
Oeuvres complètes, critical edition, 1958.

Biographical and critical studies

Vianey, J., *Mathurin Régnier*, 1896

Bibliography

Cherrier, H., *Bibliographie de Régnier*, 1884

RÉTIF DE LA BRETONNE, Nicolas-Anne-Edme, 1734–1806.

Novelist and prose writer.

LIFE

Rétif de la Bretonne spelt his name "Restif" only from about 1788, the date of the third edition of *La Vie de mon père*, while the rest of his family continued to omit the "s." Rétif published nothing until he was well over 30 but then, during the 40 years of his active writing career, he published some 44 titles in 187 volumes. He was born on 23 October 1734 in the small Burgundy village of Sacy, about half-way between Vézelay and Auxerre. His father, Edme Rétif, born in 1690, was a peasant who was able to buy the 50-hectare farm of La Bretonne for 5,000 livres on 12 March 1740. The cultivation was shared with a neighbor. Rétif was eight when in 1742 the family moved in. His father had had eight children by his first wife, Marie Dondaine, whom he had married on 27 April 1713 and who had died on 11 June 1730. Rétif was the first of nine children from his father's second marriage to Barbe Ferlet, three months a widow when she married Rétif's father on 25 January 1734. Rétif was later to be attached to talking of the imaginary ancient lineage of both of his parents.

In fact his mother, born in 1703 the daughter of a wine grower, had become a domestic in the bourgeois Boujat household at Auxerre, where at 20 she had had a child by the husband, Edme, whom she married on his wife's death in 1729, and who himself died in 1733, having had by her two further children who had died in infancy. Rétif was born in the house which his mother's first husband had bequeathed to the son she had had by him in 1723. Unlike Marie Dondaine, Barbe, or "Bibi" as she was known, was blonde, pretty, vivacious, and literate.

Rétif's 16-volume *Monsieur Nicolas; ou, Le Coeur humain dévoilé*, which he published himself between 1794 and 1797, and in which he plainly either lied or deceived himself when he said he was telling the unvarnished truth about himself, suggests that his pre-pubertal erotic experiences may have been particularly vivid. When later in his life he came to recount them, he switched from French into Latin, and he traces to them his later sexual tastes and ardours, both of which have been the subject of much comment. Teased and helped by a girl called Nannette who was helping in the fields, Rétif claimed that his first experience of full sexual intercourse took place before he was 11, a claim generally admitted by his biographers. Rétif does, however, clearly attempt to project an image of himself in his accounts of his childhood which suggests exaggeration when, for instance, he insists how little he learned from teachers and that, although he could read without understanding the Latin used at church, he could not at 11 read or write French.

Twice he was sent to half-sisters in neighbouring villages in pursuit of better schooling, although each time he returned to Sacy. Rétif emphasizes the robustly sexual nature of the childhood games he played with the other village children, as if to excuse in advance later excesses in his behaviour. At home his father, probably descended from a Huguenot family which had become Catholic, read out loud each day from the Bible. Rétif's later account of his reaction to birds, beasts, fields, and woods, suggest vivid reminiscences which years afterwards were given an idyllic gloss in which nature's innocence appeared both sacred and cruel. Rétif must at least have helped with the sheep, and it is possible that his upbringing left him as unshackled with shame and inhibitions as he wants us to believe. It is plain that he encouraged a precocious virility in order to dominate the nervously sensitive temperament which, for instance, led to a famous incident of bed-wetting which Rétif was unable to conceal from the girls of the family where he was lodged.

Rétif wants his readers to feel how mistaken his father had been in 1746 to send him to Bicêtre, an agglomeration only roughly separated into prison, poor-house, mental asylum, hospital, and school, catering for 3,000 inhabitants in all, mostly locked up, although subject to different regimes according to categories. Rétif's half-brother, the abbé Thomas, was employed as a schoolmaster for the paying pupils who made up the choir. The whole establishment was run by a rector, seven priests, a dozen nuns, as many lay helpers, and a staff of three bursars. Discipline was strict. Because the choirboys, known as "Frère (Brother)," already included an Edme and a Nicolas, Rétif was known as "Frère Augustin."

In July 1746 the Jansenizing (q.v.) archbishop of Paris died, and was replaced by Christophe de Beaumont, who at the end of 1747 nominated a new rector at Bicêtre with an anti-Jansenist spirituality. Rétif's half-brother, anticipating dismissal, took Rétif to stay with another half-brother, the curé of Courgis, near his native Sacy, also a Jansenist. It is plain that Rétif formed mental fixations on a number of girls of around his own age, and in one episode he threw himself at a married woman, Mme Chévrier, kissing her repeatedly, behaviour which she appears to have tolerated good-naturedly. Rétif had a liaison with Marguerite Pâris, the curé's housekeeper, and conceived an intense passion for a girl called Jeannette Rousseau.

If we can believe his diary he underwent a further initiation into sexual pleasures with a girl, Marguerite Miné, who had just got married. He also wrote an erotic poem to 12 girls, a stanza to each, which fell into the hands of his half-brother and led to a scene between Rétif and his father of which there are echoes in the 3-volume *Malédiction paternelle* in letter form, published in 1780. For eight months in 1751 Rétif stayed at Sacy, reading under the direction of a local priest. Later that year he was apprenticed to a 41-year-old printer at Auxerre, Michel-François Fournier, married to the daughter of a friend of Rétif's father, the lawyer Collet.

Mme Fournier was her husband's second wife and had four children. In Rétif's writings she is fictionalized as Mme Parangon, especially in *Le Paysan perverti* and *La Paysanne pervertie*, in which Rétif certainly also projects something of himself into the changing character of Gaudet d'Arras, and in *Le Drame de la vie*. Mme Fournier also serves as the magnetic core at the centre of the web of the sexual fantasies which are the chief subject of Rétif's writing. It would not be surprising if, in this apparently like his enemy Sade, Rétif fictionalized and dramatized his fantasies in an attempt to tame the powerful libidinous urges from which they sprang. In the memoirs out of which *Monsieur Nicolas* was to grow, Rétif declares that the four children of the Fourier household were in fact the illegitimate offspring of M. Fournier by chamber maids, and that "Colette" Fournier was still a virgin.

In fact the baptismal records have been found. Mme Fournier's children were born in 1747, 1748, 1750, and on 13 May 1751, not quite two months before Rétif started his apprenticeship. Mme Fournier had gone to rest with her parents in Paris after the birth, so that "Monsieur Nicolas," through whose person Rétif exaggeratedly claimed to be telling the true story of his life in *Monsieur Nicolas*, was in fact being truthful when narrating her absence on his arrival. Rétif can on the whole be relied on to narrate without too much fanciful distortion the details of his everyday life, many of which have been verified, but he can never be trusted to tell the truth when talking about his sexual relationships and fantasies, even when purporting to write nonfictionalized autobiography.

Auxerre had been allocated only one printing licence in 1704, with even Paris having only 36, and Fournier had had to work for the Troche family until he was 32. In 1751 he was himself employing 32 workers, and was a great deal more enterprising and intelligent than the character later depicted by Monsieur Nicolas. He wrote, and both printed and supported the clandestine Jansenist *Nouvelles ecclésiatiques*, but was delated when someone discovered his printer's sign on the forbidden periodical, and escaped through the back door which printing works were not allowed to have, since they could be used for traffic in unlicensed material. Fournier stayed away for three months. On 24 September 1751 Rétif, having passed his probation, was formally articled as an apprentice for four years. Mme Fournier returned from Paris, and Rétif claims she gave him a watch, singled him out as the son of her father's friend, and stimulated in him a vast desire for self-improvement. He also claims that his passion started by being pure, and that only later was desire mixed with worship.

It seems unlikely that the important character of the later fiction, Gaudet d'Arras, sometimes a priest and sometimes not, is inspired by any single real model. Rétif depicts himself as the disciple of this exaggerated seeker after pleasure, the upright atheist who believes in the nobility of the basest of the passions, loathes equally the states of master and slave, and the masculinity of whose reactions sometimes strike the reader as compensatory dreams in Rétif, conscious of a strongly feminine side to his character, evident in the fetishism and other perversions he was unable to overcome, even by the thoroughly masculine excesses recorded, or more likely imagined, in Latin. It is not easy to take seriously the "bis terna Venere locupletata est" during three quarters of an hour with Madelon Baron during Vespers. It is, however, extremely difficult even to guess at the autobiographical reality behind scenes fictionalized differently and from different points of view in different works, like that of 26 March 1754, which may have involved the rape of Mme Fournier, but is much more likely to have been an embarrassing and unforgotten failure.

From 1752 Rétif kept a notebook. He became a time-served printer on 8 May rather than, as originally envisaged, 1 August 1755, and Mme Fournier left Auxerre to stay with her father. Something may have happened to hasten the termination of the apprenticeship. Rétif, who had a room in the town, had been allowed to stay on with Fournier until 1 July. He apparently took his leave of Mme Fournier before departing finally for Paris on 1 September 1755. She was to die on 28 December 1757. He was to spend the next 12 years as a journeyman printer until, in 1767, the widow Duchesne bought the right to sell 2,000 copies of *La Famille vertueuse* from him for 765 livres, or 15 livres a sheet, practically a year's salary for the foreman printer he had by then become.

Rétif was sober and hard-working. His excesses of behaviour were only ever to be sexual. On arrival in Paris, he found a place at the royal press run by Anisson-Duperron, to be guillotined in 1794, and already known for his exploitation of the workforce. For the next few years he worked in Paris. There were liaisons and prostitutes, and Rétif began to write. His sister may have come to Paris. If there was a real Gaudet, he may have been there, too, and there is even a remote chance that the marriage to the English Henriette Kircher early in 1759, from the 1780 *La Malédiction paternelle*, may have derived from something other than a story Rétif was setting up in type at the time. The truth is, we can rely for this period only on the itself not necessarily insignificant biographical fact that, to judge by what he later wrote, Rétif was putting increasing weight on his fantasy world to support his everyday existence.

Rétif returned briefly to Sacy, vainly sought work in Dijon and Paris, where he was reduced to penury, and was finally invited, perhaps through the mediation of the curé of Sacy, to join Fournier in Auxerre as his foreman. He left Paris on 7 November when he received the money for the journey. On 22 April 1760 Rétif married at Auxerre Agnès Lebègue, daughter of an Auxerre apothecary apparently ruined before joining the Rhine army; he was presumed dead. Rétif's mother-in-law was mean, grasping, debt-ridden, and given to drink. Agnès herself was not the ideal welcoming home-maker of Rétif's 1777 *Les Gynographes*, but was looking towards Paris and escape from her mother.

On 10 March 1761 she bore Rétif a daughter, also called Agnès, whose story would be fictionalized in *L'Ingénue Saxancour*. After the birth Agnès went to Paris. Rétif, offered a job with Knapen, the Paris printer, and quarrelling with Fournier, willingly gave up his Auxerre job and, penniless, in June followed his wife to Paris. A daughter, Marie, was born in December 1761, but died at the age of two, and Rétif, by now writing more and more on his own account, led an almost separate life. There was enough money to live as workers in Rétif's position normally lived, but not enough to satisfy Agnès's social aspirations, and she was paying more attention to her lovers than to her husband. A third child, Elise, was born in 1763. She lived to be only seven. Sickly at birth, she had been sent out to nurse at Sacy like her sisters.

On 16 December Rétif's father died. Rétif did not have enough money for the journey home, but went down in the Lent of 1764, to find debts incurred by his mother-in-law waiting to be paid. Agnès's behaviour was so openly contemptuous of the life of a printer's foreman's wife that the marriage seemed to have broken down by 1762, the year in which Rétif sketched the first draft of what was to become *Monsieur Nicolas*. He claimed that his depiction of corruption was in the interests of encouraging his readers to virtue. Meanwhile he had moved back to the royal press, and in July 1764 was given the job of foreman by Quillau's son, himself to take over the business of his dead father. Rétif in three years increased the number of presses from four to twelve, and doubled the workforce to 70. He himself composed material in Greek and Latin. His relaxation was to write and deliver letters to pretty girls. Rétif and his wife were by now at relative financial ease. On 5 November Agnès gave birth at Sacy to "Marion," Jean-Thomas-Marie-Anne, and in February 1765 brought back the eldest child and came to live in Paris. The marriage looked again as if it might be stable.

The gestation of *La Famille vertueuse* had been slow. Rétif himself directed the printing at Quillau's for the widow Duchesne from January to May 1767, and signed the book "M. de la Bretonne." It was not to be put on sale until the autumn fair, but Rétif left Quillau's immediately the book was printed. He could set up as a man of letters. A rich cloth merchant had now fallen in love with Agnès, so Rétif's life separated again from hers. Their eldest daughter was sent to board. On 1 July Rétif returned to Sacy, but found no inspiration. By the end of September he was back in Paris. He and his wife moved frequently, sometimes living together and sometimes not. Rétif finished *Le Pornographe* but found it predictably turned down by the censor. The widow Duchesne's associate, Guy, would not buy *L'Ecole de la jeunesse*, and Rétif was lucky to sell a 200-page duodecimo *Lucile; ou, Les Progrès de la vertu*, which he took five days to write. It was an attempt to exploit a story picked up from his half-brother and told in a style derived from Voltaire. He obtained 72 livres for 1,000 copies, although he supposed 1,500 were going to be printed, and the book-seller Valade would have counterfeit editions on sale while assuring Rétif that the first edition had not yet sold out.

In the summer of 1768 Agnès's lover came back to Paris and

Rétif, who was not paying the rent, had to move out. Living on very little, he finished *Le Pied de Fanchette*, 530 pages in 11 days, which he printed himself with the help of a borrowed apprentice during September at Quillau's. It was to be a popular work, and indulges Rétif's fixation on delicate female ankles. A friend from Auxerre, Edme Rapenot, had become a book-seller and publisher, and undertook to sell the book. He also told Rétif the story of a man who gave a present to his own illegitimate daughter without recognizing her. Rétif turned it into the two volumes of *La Fille naturelle* which he set up in type as they were being written. He also sold *La Confidence nécessaire*, left unfinished after three attempts at Sacy, but completed during the winter of 1767–68 in Paris.

Rapenot, impressed by all this activity, and sniffing success, gave Rétif a free room and an advance of six livres a week to live off, and found a pension for the three daughters, since Agnès had gone off again with the silk merchant. The apprentice was devoted, and proud to marry a girl who had borne Rétif yet another illegitimate child. Valade even found a censor willing to authorize the publication of *Le Pornographe*, which proposed a reform of the laws and customs governing prostitution. *La Mimographe* of 1770 is a project for the reform of the theatre, consisting of letters advocating a realistic theatre of the people. Diderot wrote disparagingly about Rétif in Grimm's fortnightly newsletter. His attempts to reform orthography and punctuation were making his work difficult to read. Agnès had by now twice had twins by her silk merchant, who had left her and been replaced; Rétif accused her of depositing them in the public orphanage. Eventually she came with the eldest daughter late in 1679 to share Rétif's small but free room at the top of the former Collège de Prêles, put at his disposal by Rapenot. It was there that, among other things, he wrote the first two volumes of the *Le Paysan parvenu*, partly modelled on Richardson's *Pamela*.

Rétif's mother died on 5 July 1771. He never went back to Sacy again. He poured out a stream of moralizing fiction, but also had his first serious encounter with the censorship. In *Les Lettres d'une fille à son père* Rétif, in his usual way, inserted material without relevance to the central theme, thinking no doubt that he would thereby render less wearisome the reading of his text. One of the insertions was the slightly risqué conte "Il recule pour mieux sauter," but another was a sensible consideration of the role of the publisher-bookseller, strongly attacking the perpetrators of counterfeit editions. Rétif was replying to Fenouillet de Falbaire's *Avis aux Gens de Lettres*, in an insertion entitled "Contr'avis aux Gens de lettres, par un Homme de lettres qui entend ses véritables intérêts." The publisher-booksellers, who wanted a bigger literary role than Rétif thought they should have, and who also profited from counterfeited printings for which authors got paid nothing, had *Les Lettres* suppressed on the pretext that "Il recule…" was licentious. Rétif printed and bound the book himself, fifty copies without the banned conte for the censors and the police, and the rest for sale. At the same time, he went to considerable lengths to do a favour for Dhermilly, the censor appointed for *Le Paysan perverti*.

During the period from 1770 to 1775 Rétif rather naively mounted attacks on both the literary establishment, in *Le Ménage parisien*, and the medical establishment, in the "Thèse de médecine soutenue en enfer" in the 1773 novel *Nouveaux mémoires d'un homme de qualité*. The Utopian quality in his writing has often been remarked on but, even though Benjamin Franklin admired it and Schiller thought Rétif's genius extraor-

dinary, his non-fictional, non-autobiographical writing has generally been thought to remain on the level of impotent fantasy rather than constructive radicalism. In both pieces his enthusiasm considerably exceeded his acumen, and they incorporated intelligent insights insufficiently thought through to have had any other historical effect than that of an irritant. He had nowhere near the expertise necessary to put forward a serious plan to reform the administrative regulation of prostitution in France. But the need to exhort, adjust, and teach society was now sending Rétif's work into spate, and his production scarcely suffered when, one day, the free room provided by Rapenot was suddenly demolished, leaving Rétif to seek refuge with another book-seller, Valeyre. Agnès had left the Collège de Prêles in 1770, and in 1773 left Paris altogether for Joigny. She was leaving her husband, as she told a neighbour, nothing but her debts.

The eldest daughter, Agnès, was apprenticed to one of Rétif's half-sisters, a couturière married to the jeweller François Bizet and later to become a childless widow and to endow Agnès for her unhappy marriage. Rétif rented from his wife the room she had vacated, and he shared it with one of her former lovers. Rétif had sold his share in La Bretonne to his brother Pierre, and now used the money to print *Le Paysan perverti; ou, Les Dangers de la ville*, in letter form. It is the first Rétif novel to be regarded as important, and was put on sale in November 1775, although it carries the year date 1776. It was an immediate success. Grimm and Julie de Lespinasse were both enthusiastic, although both remarked on its lack of taste. It was referred to as a "pile of dung containing pearls," and the first edition was seized in March 1776, by which date counterfeit editions abounded.

In 1779 Agnès returned to Paris, having failed in her attempt to run a boarding establishment for girls. Rétif and she lived separately, but Rétif paid her for board and ate daily with her. She lived mostly by teaching dress-making. From 1 January 1780 to 1796 we have Rétif's diary, with its coy Latin phrases, not at all exclusively about sexual matters. They do, however, offer unmistakable evidence of his sexual and other obsessions and constitute a document of great psychological importance. Rétif's whole life was by now consumed by his intense devotion to his work, by the sheer need endlessly to write and to compose in type the increasingly self-revelatory products of his pen, by the satisfaction of his sexual needs, and by his financial affairs. The style of the writing, the content of the diaries, the cramped manner of setting down, and the physical way in which the documents were compiled suggest a personality obsessive to a degree which is certainly extraordinary, and may well have been psychotic. The major works can all be seen as closer approximations to authentic autobiography.

Rétif took to scratching on buildings memorable dates in his life, with an indication of his state of mind, as if to pin down the emotions he had once experienced in a way which he would always be able to recall, and which could never be erased. He had special iron instruments made for the Latin scratchings on walls and bridges of the Ile Saint-Louis in Paris, and regarded it as "a sacrilege" when asked by the web-fingered eccentric, and philosophically inclined Balthazar Grimod de la Reynière to scratch in dates which were not personal to himself. He rarely touched alcohol, was fanatically economical, and spent everything he had on the printing and illustration of his works. Occasionally he was asked out, almost exhibited, or went to the theatre. Later he was to attend and apparently enjoy the conversation at the gruesome feasts put on by Grimod de la Reynière, whom he got to know in 1782. Beaumarchais had made himself known to Rétif on the publication of *La Vie de mon Père*, and Rétif was also to get to know Sébastien Mercier, Joubert, and Fontanes.

La Malédiction paternelle, written in 1779 and published in 1780, contained something nearer to a true self-portrait than had the undisguised fiction of *Le Paysan perverti*, and can be considered a first approximation to what would be undertaken in *Monsieur Nicolas*. In 1780 the first version of *La Paysanne pervertie* took only four weeks to write. In that year Rétif conceived a strong passion for his downstairs neighbour, Sara Debée. The diary gives brief details of the physical aspects of the liaison, up to the final departure after Rétif had found her in her room, which he had entered without knocking, with two other men. He never saw her after 22 July 1782.

On 10 December 1780 Agnès Lebègue's mother died, and the next year, against Rétif's firm opposition, his daughter Agnès married a widower, Charles-Marie Augé, on 1 May. Augé was Rétif's age, and Agnès was now 20. Augé, a police spy under Sartine, had lost his job, but been taken on by the city administration. He had inherited a considerable sum from his first wife, and Agnès was being well endowed by her aunt. Augé was to marry again in January 1795 after his divorce from Agnès in 1794, and appears to have been brutal, ugly, and greedy, a dowry-hunting thug. Agnès, pregnant on marriage, was to bear him a child, Jean-Nicolas, in December. Rétif himself began to live again with his wife. She had inherited 1,388 livres, and he was now earning well, in addition to becoming known. In 1782 Rétif published the strongest statement of his political ideas in *L'Andrographe*. Although he went alone to the celebrated Grimod de la Reynière suppers where he might meet Rivarol and the Chénier brothers, it was Agnès who attracted Fontanes and Joubert to her presence.

The first version of *La Paysanne pervertie*, which cost Rétif only four weeks in 1780, was his own favourite among his books. He added some letters, started to print it himself in 1782 and issued it in 1783, having had it approved by the royal censor, the abbé Terrasson, in the usual way, that is by having a few copies bound with the cuts the censor felt obliged to make, and keeping the proscribed portions of text in the edition for sale. Unhappily for Rétif, Terrasson this time took fright. He consulted the keeper of the seals, Miromesnil, who, with Camus de Néville, director of the book trade, simply banned the whole edition. Rétif had invested very heavily in the engravings, which are indeed very fine and which he had intended to pay for out of sales.

It has been suggested that Rétif was becoming tired of passively witnessing Agnès's obsession with Joubert and Fontanes, that he confided to Fontanes that Nannette, the harvest helper, had had a child by their first meeting, that he had had a liaison with the child, Zéphire, which would be narrated in the recently begun *Monsieur Nicolas*, without knowing who she was, and that Fontanes had told the story to Joubert, but made him believe that the girl concerned was Rétif's eldest daughter by Agnès, the Agnès who had now married Augé. Whether or not that is what happened, Rétif was put under pressure from Agnès, Fontanes, Joubert, and the authorities to move away. Beaumarchais offered him the directorship of the Kehl undertaking to print Voltaire's complete works. Rétif turned the offer down, and for a moment all seemed well. He was reconciled with his daughter

Agnès, about whose unhappiness with Augé he was not at first told.

Augé's sodomizing brutality, bullying, and bare-faced grasping had reduced Agnès to a state of humiliation and panic such that she ran away three times in the first half of 1785, finally taking refuge with her father on 26 November 1785, the day after Agnès Lebègue, her mother, left Rétif for the last time. Rétif's daughter was to stay eight years, and there were renewed accusations of incest. The laconic evidence of the diaries makes it virtually certain that these were justified, and it is also not unreasonable to presume that there were incestuous relationships between Rétif and his sister Marie-Geneviève, whose unfortunate adventures made her a model for the Ursule of *La Paysanne pervertie*. If Rétif did have incestuous liaisons, it has been argued, it changes the reading of *L'Anti-Justine; ou, Les Délices de l'amour*, certainly pornographic, even if it was intended to be a book "which wives can get their husbands to read to be better helped by them." Rétif and Sade, against whose famous novel *L'Anti-Justine* was aimed, probably never met, but they disliked one another's work and each thought the other immoral. Sade had written to his wife in 1783, "Whatever you do, don't buy anything of Rétif's. He's a Pont-Neuf and Bibliothèque bleue author..." His hostility to Rétif was to grow stronger after the 1798 *L'Anti-Justine*.

Marion had come back to Paris with her mother in 1779, been sent out to board, and remained with her father when Agnès Lebègue left. Rétif continued to re-work in new forms old material from the "Cahiers" started in 1766, particularly in *Les Nuits de Paris*, started on 22 December 1786, of which six volumes (twelve parts) appeared in November 1788, two more in 1789, and the last two in 1790 and 1794. Rétif here was clearly inspired by Louis-Sébastien Mercier's *Tableau de Paris* published from 1781 until just before the Revolution. He attended the Wednesday and Saturday suppers held by Grimod de la Reynière, including that of March 1786, attempting to reproduce a famous occasion at which his host had publicly tried to humiliate his family in February 1783. Grimod de la Reynière was finally sent into exile to Domèvre on 10 April 1786 and his letters to Rétif until Rétif broke with him in 1792 are an important biographical source. Augé continued to attempt to force Agnès to return, although even the police support on which he could count proved inadequate.

The fictionalized story of Agnès's relationship with her husband, *Ingénue Saxancour*, was begun in March 1786 but not published until 1789, probably in September. On the 14 July Rétif went to view the siege of the Bastille, only to find that it was over, and to see the severed heads. Augé had seen and followed him, and realized both on that day and later that almost any delation was quite likely to result in a quasi-immediate execution. He denounced Rétif, on this occasion as an enemy of the people, but he was apparently saved by a shout from someone in the crowd, who knew him. Augé denounced Rétif again later in the year for three counter-revolutionary pamphlets. Rétif was arrested on 28 October; he reports on his own interrogation in the 15th volume of *Les Nuits de Paris*. After his domicile and a neighbouring printer's shop had been searched, Rétif was freed and Augé imprisoned for false denunciation. He was released after four days when Rétif refused to make an official complaint. Augé and Agnès were divorced on 11 January 1794 and Rétif and Agnès Lebègue were themselves formally divorced on 4 February that year.

When Grimod de la Reynière's lettre de cachet was nullified by the Revolution, he went to stay with an aunt in Béziers and wrote to express shock at *Ingénue Saxancour*. Before the Revolution Rétif had been only very moderately liberal. Since, unlike most authors, he set his own work and its revisions in type, and even acquired a small press in January 1790, it was also easily possible for him to alter a date or an attitude expressed earlier, to suit the changing tides of feeling. We cannot therefore take his published work as an indication of what it was he thought at any given date. We do, however, know that during the Revolution he suppressed the "de" and called himself simply Restif la Bretonne. He frequented the Friday salon of Fanny de Beauharnais, the "céleste Chloé," who introduced him to illuminism, to Jacques Cazotte, and to Louis-Claude de Saint-Martin, through whom he became acquainted with the philosophies of Boehme and Swedenborg.

Rétif was badly hit by the inflation of 1792–93, and seriously considered attempting to sell *Monsieur Nicolas* by subscription. Mercier had introduced him at the Café Manoury to a potential backer, Arthaud, but Arthaud's assignats lost their value too fast, even though he paid Rétif at least 19,000 livres in 1793. In 1791 Rétif's daughter Marion had married her cousin Edme-Etienne, son of Rétif's youngest brother, Pierre. Edme had died of tuberculosis in July 1794, leaving Marion with three small children. To save money Rétif moved in with Marion. Agnès meanwhile had a child, Victor, from her liaison with Louis-Claude-Victor Vignon. Rétif would have had a further incestuous liaison with Marion if she had let him. He thought seriously of trying to remarry, and was meanwhile laughed at by the Paris prostitutes who knew they could touch him for a drink by pretending to be one of his illegitimate daughters.

When the Comité d'instruction publique awarded its pensions early in 1795, Rétif was placed in the middle of three categories, with 2,000 livres, in company with Bacular d'Arnaud, Parny, and the painter Carle Vernet. A nomination for election to the Institut in 1795 resulted in failure, but Rétif was awarded for 1796 a coupon for five pounds of bread a day, a subsidy which was not negligible, and was also symbolic, since it was the rise in the price of bread that had triggered the Revolution. The bread price was the cause of much of Paris's unrest when, subsidized inside the city, it was smuggled out to the environs where it fetched double the price. In 1798 Rétif accepted a post with the censorship, and turned down the chair of history at Moulins for which, in the conditions of the Revolution, in which customary academic criteria did not necessarily count, he had applied. As a functionary he published nothing for four years, although *L'Anti-Justine* was surreptitiously sold. Agnès now married Victor Vignon, who entered the police. Rétif's own employment was discontinued in 1802, and he was obliged to make two requests to the authorities for financial help, with a further request in 1805.

Rétif, who had come to sympathize with the Revolution, was in the end ruined by the fall in the value of the assignats. He was beginning to be known outside France, particularly in Germany. His works had frequently been translated into German immediately after their appearance. *Les Posthumes*, published in 1802, was seized by the police on 2 July that year. Rétif died at home on 3 February 1806.

WORKS

It was as early as 1783 that Sade, locked up at Vincennes, told his wife on no account to send him any Rétif to read. His books belonged "to the Pont-Neuf and the Bibliothèque bleue." That means that he found them lubricious, but not of serious interest. That Rétif thought Sade a monster coming third in villainy only to his wife, Agnès Lebègue, and his son-in-law, Augé, need not surprise us. The violence of Sade's fantasies might almost have been calculated to disgust Rétif, and the strength of Sade's imagination to frighten him. Rétif's *L'Anti-Justine* tackles the problem of sexual relationships from a quite different point of view. He seeks more to encourage the timid than to tame the wild, and Sade understandably found Rétif's early work lowgrade and merely titillating pornography.

Like many others, he also found it tasteless, objecting for instance to the use of "petit Papa (little Daddy)" in connection with a 45-year-old lover as "de la dernière bassesse et du dernier commun (the ultimate in vulgarity and commonness)." Rétif's strongly attested fetishism attached to the female foot was much less dangerous to anyone that Sade's sexual need to inflict and receive pain, but it not unnaturally produced a much less sharply focused and strongly concentrated imaginative vision. The contrast and antipathy between the two offers in many ways the key to the understanding of each. Sade's problem was the more urgent, and his imaginative achievement the more vigorous.

If Sade is right about the Rétif publicly available for reading in 1783, and if therefore Rétif's texts contain too much soft pornography in bad taste, the question must be asked what is it in them that has kept interest alive, and whether the early works differ from the later ones. Sade, however, was not to revise his view. Rétif's works continually return to the same material, are often embroidered, disguised, or fictionalized autobiography, and culminate in the vast *Monsieur Nicolas*, for which Rétif claimed total autobiographical authenticity, as he had claimed for his best known work, the two-volume 1779 *La Vie de mon père*, reprinted in 1780 and 1788, that within it "tout est sans art, sans apprêt, la mémoire y tient lieu d'imagination (everything is artless, without adornment; memory takes the place of imagination)." That is not, of course, true. The work is an idealized portrait of a father whose everyday virtue was "facile, aimable,…le seul fondement solide du bonheur pour cette vie, et de la réputation qu'on laisse après sa mort (likable, attractive… the only solid foundation for happiness in this life and for the reputation left behind after death)."

The character presented in the book as Rétif's father is blamed only for wanting to advance his children in the world. He allowed only one to work in the fields. He left his whole village enriched and, it is true, recognized that "the worker is the real human being: the one who pays taxes, works, sows, reaps, trades, builds, and manufactures." Rétif turns his book into praise of the primitive idyll, in which "simple moral attitudes, like those of the early ages," are nearer innocence and rightmindedness than is thought. Rétif is in fact writing a plea for the innocence of his childhood romps in barns and fields, even for what would turn out to be later incest.

For generations of critics seeking a sense of moral restraint in works of the literary imagination, this book has seemed to be Rétif's most acceptable work. Superficially it contains all the ingredients of the late 18th-century cult of nature's beauty and innocence, although the realism of the content is a sign that Rétif's special pleading drove him to present a picture of nature which is vacuous rather than stylized. He has been thought of as in some way foreshadowing realist and naturalist modes of narration. In fact the attention focused on real objects and events in Rétif's work, limited to scenes and objects to do with rustic life at Sacy or the surroundings of a printer in Paris, are simply signs that Rétif wishes to be understood as using a literary register which is faithful to a reality whose distortion in the depiction may well not even have been noticed, let alone intended by its author.

Between 1767 and 1769 Rétif published four anonymous volumes of fiction, intended on the whole to be edifying, although urging the reader's imagination firmly in the direction of accepting as virtuous, or at least innocent, all that is prompted by nature itself: *La Famille vertueuse; Lucile; ou, Les Progrès de la vertu; Le Pied de Fanchette; ou, L'Orpheline française… Histoire intéressante et morale; La Confidence nécessaire; ou, Lettres de Mylord Austin de Norfolk, à Mylord Humfrey de Dorset*, and *La Fille naturelle*. In 1769 Rétif published *Le Pornographe*, his first work of social engineering, a project for the regulation of prostitution. In 1770 came the project for the reform of the theatre, *La Mimographe*, published as the second volume, with its immediate predecessor, of "Idées singulières." In 1770 there also appeared, still anonymously, *L'Educographe; ou, Le Nouvel Emile.*

A complete list of titles is to be found in the appended list, but Rétif was already collecting previously published material in 1772, when he also published two rejected theatrical pieces, and the essay that provoked the book-sellers to invoke the censorship. Rétif now lent his pen to people who could help him, particularly the censors Marchand and d'Hermilly, and continued to publish fiction. The next social engineering work was the 1777 *Les Gynographes* on the place of women in society. Rétif's views are frankly reactionary. In the light of his biography, that should surprise nobody. What is surprising is that Valéry, whose literary intelligence was sufficient to have been admired even by Gide, should have put Rétif in a now much-quoted but unpublished letter of 1934 "much above" Rousseau.

Rétif's first properly signed work was the four-volume 1776 *Le Paysan perverti; ou, Les Dangers de la ville*, a letter-novel of considerable technical interest and competence. It is also an early Bildungsroman in the grand style, translated into German no fewer than seven times before the end of the 18th century. There are eight letter-writers, and Rétif himself summarizes the plot. Edmond, the peasant, arrives in the town and falls into the hands of the corruptors. The letters are each prefixed by a short indication of their content written by "Pierre R***," Edmond's elder brother, who himself writes 30 of the 287 letters, and uses "I" when summarizing the contents, so that the third letter, from Pierrot to Edmond, is headed in brackets "J'encourage mon frère (I encourage my brother)." Pierre R*** lavishly uses exclamation marks, and is the narrator as well as a character. An unsigned letter to the book-seller and publisher from the "editor" accompanying the letters starts the fiction and sets the moralizing tone, summing up the moral purpose to be achieved in publishing the letters. There follows the summary of what happens in each of the eight parts and an "avis" signed Pierre R*** and declaring Pierre's intention of showing his family, and all country-dwellers, the dangers the young run in big cities.

The first part starts with an introduction setting out what those familiar with it will recognize to be Rétif's own background and early experience in a place the novel refers to as "Au**." In the avis, the narrator breaks into a lyrical apostrophe in which the dots are Rétif's:

O mes enfants! restons dans nos hameaux, et ne cherchons point à sortir de l'heureuse ignorance des plaisirs des grandes cités: le vice en donne le goût, l'irréligion excite à s'y livrer, le crime fournit les ressources; et la misère, l'infamie, le supplice des scélérats en sont quelquefois les fruits. Profitez de la lecture de ces lettres où vous pourrez suivre toute la marche de la corruption qui s'empare d'un coeur innocent et droit: vous y verrez d'abord le jeune paysan prospérer un peu; perdre enfin petit à petit ses bons sentiments, devenir libertin, criminel, et de là tomber dans l'infamie; y entraîner une malheureuse soeur; la perdre tout à fait; se relever ensuite, pour retomber plus bas. Mes enfants, un père et une mère respectables en sont morts de douleur, et toute sa famille s'est vue plongée dans l'opprobre… Le malheureux se reconnut enfin, et il se punit… mais ce fut un désespéré. Je l'ai vu, et mon coeur s'est brisé; car ce malheureux, c'était mon frère

(O my children! let us stay in our hamlets and not seek to depart from our happy ignorance of the pleasures of the great cities; vice gives the taste for them, irreligion the urge, crime provides the means; and poverty, infamy, and the punishment of villains are sometimes their fruits. Profit from the reading of these letters, in which you can follow the whole process of corruption taking hold of an innocent and upright heart. You will see the young countryman at first prospering a little; then losing by degrees his decent feelings, becoming loose-living, criminal, and then falling into infamy; dragging an unhappy sister with him; ruining her altogether, picking himself up afterwards, only to fall lower still. My children, a respectable mother and father have died of grief from what happened, and the whole family has been plunged into disgrace… The unfortunate wretch finally recognized what he had done and punished himself,… but he was in despair. I saw him, and my heart broke; for this wretch was my brother).

The fiction is over-emphatically established before the letters ever start. Everything is done to ensure that we will think the letters authentic. Rétif sets great store by his credibility, and we are firmly told how to react to the pathetic story the letters will recount. Nothing at all will stretch the reader's imagination, or stimulate any sort of reaction to the characters' behaviour other than those considerations already announced. No meaning of any kind of human experience can possibly be explored. We are being given a nursery parable, or that is what would be happening, if Rétif were not writing tongue in cheek in the knowledge that none of his readers could really be naive enough to suppose what he cannot openly admit, that we have a natural proclivity to transgress the precepts of nursery morality. But the pretence of illustrating a moral lesson, while showing by the intrigue how difficult it is to follow, would not itself necessarily constitute a literary achievement of any great interest even if it did not, as here, ring so resoundingly hollow.

In the synopsis Edmond's passions are said to be ready to second the efforts of his corruptors. Rétif's dislike of organized religion is amusingly clear from the malicious sketch of the Franciscan, Gaudet d'Arras. The highly mannered letters include long passages of quoted conversation, although the novel is essentially an adventure story. Sentiment is described rather than analysed, its motivation left too weak, and the work lacks the great penetration of Rousseau and the tight psychological organization of Laclos. The novel does not read very differently from what it actually was, a plea from Rétif, possibly to himself as well to others, to understand his personal experience as he himself would like to.

La Paysanne pervertie. Les Dangers de la ville; ou, Histoire effrayante et morale d'Ursule of 1784 shares a narrator with its predecessor. It is again a letter novel, with Ursule, sister of Pierre and Edmond, now the focus of attention, and again there are eight parts in four volumes, with the content of each letter summarized by Pierre. Both novels were also issued together in 1787, although the printed date is 1784, and a separate volume with 120 illustrations by L. Binet was also issued in 1785. Like its predecessor, *La Paysanne pervertie* combines Bildungsroman with adventure novel, and it is in epistolary form although it has a narrator. The pace of the action is erratic, and the motivation of the plot far too dependent on chance for any sort of psychological plausibility. Ursule's corruptibility is no less striking than Edmond's had been, but Rétif makes serious efforts to distinguish between the different styles of his letter-writers.

Rétif includes comments by his characters on large numbers of novels and plays, and includes little sets of rules, descriptions, depictions by the letter-writers of their feelings, attempts by them to manipulate the feelings of others, and comments on those manipulations, as if aware of the need to keep the reader's attention by an assortment of literary devices. Even the most dramatic and touching of situations, like that of Ursule's humiliation at the end of the sixth part, in letter 127, fails to move, although the laconicism of the style not infrequently elsewhere results in memorable aphorisms, as for instance in *Mon Kalendrier*:

Parler de quelqu'un c'est augmenter son existence. N'en rien dire c'est aider la mort

(To speak of someone is to extend his existence. To say nothing about him is to assist death).

Monsieur Nicolas is fascinating chiefly for the way in which it purports to be the neutral relation of Rétif's life story, when in fact it contains a strongly interpretative element. Read in the light of *Mes Inscripcions* and of the *Journal intime*, it reveals an interest of a different order from that of straight literary autobiography. Rétif's continued attempts to write decreasingly fictionalized autobiography, culminating in *Monsieur Nicolas*, reveal the impossibility for him of holding back from the self-condemnation the need for the avoidance of which drove him to write the work in the first place. It may well have been the unstated element of self-contempt, which Rétif none the less failed to suppress entirely, which attracted Nerval and, perhaps more probably, Baudelaire, to his work.

Rétif's achievement is much disputed and very differently assessed. Those critics who esteem him most highly also differ markedly in the reasons they give. The immense flow of fictionalized autobiography, the extraordinary personality it reveals, and the contrast with Sade confer an interest on Rétif which is compelling, but not strictly literary, and no case is normally made out for his literary craftsmanship, aesthetic sensitivity, imaginative ingenuity, or artistic integrity. In their place interest has been focused on the personality rather than the achievement, the psychology rather than the artistry, and the ideas rather than

the techniques. Despite the marginalization which Rétif has suffered at the hands of literary historians, critical interest in his work remains buoyant. It seems likely that in spite of excellent recent critical work Rétif's immense oeuvre still awaits its definitive assessment, and that attempts to achieve it will continue to be made.

PUBLICATIONS

[*Note: Rétif de la Bretonne's sole authorship of some of the works which carry his name is disputed. Works which are known not principally to have been by him have been omitted. Several works were re-printed with different titles, or bound with other works. The most popular works were all, and sometimes frequently, issued, often re-titled, in unauthorized editions*]

Collection

L'Oeuvre de Rétif, 9 vols., 1930

Fiction, autobiography, and pamphlets

La Famille vertueuse. Lettres traduites de l'anglais. Par M. De La Bretone, 4 vols., 1767
Lucile; ou, Les Progrès de la vertu, 1768
Le Pied de Fanchette; ou, L'Orpheline française. Histoire intéressante et morale, 3 vols., 1769
La Confidence nécessaire; ou, Lettres de Mylord Austin de Norfolk à Mylord Humfrey de Dorset, 2 vols., 1769
La Fille naturelle, 2 vols., 1769
Le Pornographe, 1769 [modern edition 1977]
La Mimographe, 1770
L'Educographe; ou, Le Nouvel "Emile," 1770
Le Marquis de T***; ou, L'Ecole de la jeunesse, 4 vols., 1771
Adèle de Com***; ou, Lettres d'une fille à son père, 5 vols., 1772 [includes *La Cigale et la Fourmi* and *Jugement de Pâris*; also *Contr'avis aux gens de lettres*]
La Femme dans les trois états de fille, d'épouse et de mère, 1773
Le Ménage parisien; ou, Délilée et Sotentout, 2 vols., 1774
Les Nouveaux Mémoires d'un Homme de qualité, 2 vols., 1774
Le Paysan perverti; ou, Les Dangers de la ville, 4 vols., 1776 [critical edition François Jost, 2 vols., 1977]
L'Ecole des Pères, 2 vols., 1776
Les Gynographes, 1777
Le Quadragénaire; ou, L'âge de renoncer aux passions, 2 vols., 1777
Le Nouvel Abeilard; ou, Lettres de deux amants qui ne se sont jamais vus, 4 vols., 1778
La Vie de mon père, 2 vols., 1779 [modern editions 1960, 1961, 1962, 1963]
La Malédiction paternelle, 3 vols., 1780
Les Contemporaines; ou, Avantures des plus jolies femmes de l'âge présent, 42 vols., 1780–85 [modern edition 1951]
La Découverte australe, 4 vols., 1781 [modern edition 1977]
L'Andrographe, 1782
La Dernière Avanture d'un homme de quarante-cinq ans, 1783
La Prévention nationale, 3 vols., 1784
La Paysanne pervertie. Les Dangers de la ville; ou, Histoire effrayante et morale d'Ursule, 4 vols., 1784 [modern edition 1972]

Les Veillées du Marais, 1785

La Femme infidelle, 2 vols., 1786

Les Françaises, 4 vols., 1786

Les Parisiennes, 4 vols., 1787

Les Nuits de Paris; ou, Le Spectateur nocturne, 16 vols., 1788–94 [modern editions 1960, 1963, 1967]; as *Les Nuits de Paris*; or, *The Nocturnal Spectator* [selection], 1964

Ingénue Saxancour; ou, La Femme Séparée, 3 vols., 1789 [modern editions 1960, 1961]

Le Thesmographe, 1789

Monument du costume physique et moral à la fin du XVIIIe siècle, ou, Tableaux de la vie, 1789; as *Pictures of Life*, 2 vols., 1790

Le Palais-Royal, 3 vols., 1790

L'Année des dames nationales, 12 vols., 1791–94

Monsieur Nicolas; ou, Le Coeur humain dévoilé [anonymous], 16 vols., 1794–97; modern edition, 6 vols., 1959; as *M. Nicolas*; or, *The Human Heart Unveiled*, 6 vols., 1930–31

Philosophie de M. Nicolas, 3 vols., 1796

L'Anti-Justine; ou, Les Délices de l'amour, 1798 [modern editions 1960, 1970]; as *The Pleasures and Follies of a Good-Natured Libertine*, 1956

Les Posthumes, 4 vols., 1802

Les Nouvelles Contemporaines, 1802

Mes Inscripcions, 1887

Journal inédit, 1972

Plays

Théâtre, 5 vols., 1789–90

Le Drame de la vie, 5 vols., 1793

Biographical and critical studies [The best bibliography is in J. Rives Childs: see below]

Childs, J. Rives, *Restif de la Bretonne. Témoignages et jugements*, 1949

Chadourne, Marc, *Restif de la Bretonne; ou, Le Siècle prophétique*, 1958

Courbin, J-C., *Le Monde de Restif*, 1961

Porter, Charles A., *Restif's Novels; or, An Autobiography in Search of an Author*, 1966

Poster, Mark, *The Utopian Thought of Rétif de la Bretonne*, 1971

Testud, Pierre, *Rétif de la Bretonne et la création littéraire*, 1977

Rival, Ned, *Rétif de la Bretonne; ou, Les Amours pervertis*, 1982

RETZ, Jean-François-Paul de Gondi, cardinal de, 1613–1679.

Writer of memoirs, historian, statesman.

LIFE

Gondi, as he must be called before his elevation to the cardinalate in 1652, came from a family of Florentine merchants who had settled in Lyons and risen to prominence under Catherine de Medici. Gondi's great–grandfather became steward of Henri II's household after his wife had attracted the patronage of Catherine de Medici, to whom she had sold some dogs which she had bred. She was called from Lyons and given charge of the royal children. She sent for her son, Albert, the eldest boy of her seven children and Gondi's grandfather, to join his parents at court. Albert married Catherine de Clermont, the widow of the baron de Retz, in 1565, and his younger brother Pierre, establishing what he did not know would become a tradition, was made bishop of Paris in 1568. Albert de Gondi, the real founder of the family's fortunes, became a maréchal de France in 1567, acted for a time as Connétable, the highest military post, never lost a battle, and was notably successful on several diplomatic missions. He became exceedingly wealthy, owned the marquisate of Belle-Ile and the county of Joigny, excited a great deal of jealousy, and was strongly disliked by Brantôme, his wife's cousin. Gondi came to belong to the noblesse d'épée.

The Retz estate was near Machecoul, south of the mouth of the Loire. It became a duchy when in 1581 Henri III made Albert a duke and peer. In 1587 Pierre became the cardinal de Gondi. In 1598 Albert's second son, Henri, succeeded his uncle as bishop of Paris, to be elevated in his turn to the sacred college in 1618 as the first cardinal de Retz. Another of Albert's sons, Jean-François de Gondi, was to take over the diocese, and to become jealous of the intellectual superiority of Gondi, his nephew and successor. It was in 1622, during the episcopacy of the extravagant, cowardly, ignorant, and promiscuous Jean-François, that the diocese of Paris was freed from its dependence on the archdiocese of Sens, making Jean-François the first archbishop of Paris. Gondi was to begin his ecclesiastical career as coadjutor to an uncle he despised.

Gondi's grandfather, the maréchal, died in 1602, followed in 1603 by his grandmother, Catherine de Clermont. She had read Greek and Latin, as well as Italian, and had been celebrated by Baïf and Jamyn. Tyard and Scévole de Sainte-Marthe had dedicated verse to her. Along with sons she had also had daughters, Gondi's aunts. One of them, Françoise, was the grandmother of Henri de Sévigné, at whose marriage to Marie de Rabutin-Chantal, marquise de Sévigné, Gondi was to officiate.

In 1598 Albert's third son, Gondi's father, Philippe-Emmanuel, comte de Joigny, became general of the galleys, that is the navy, at the age of 17. He had a genuine ecclesiastical vocation, but the careers of his two elder brothers in the church virtually forced him into military life. It was with apparent reluctance that in 1604 he married Gondi's mother, Françoise-Marguerite de Silly, daughter of the comte de Rochepot and sieur de Commercy, in Lorraine, where Retz was to spend his last years. Two years after her death in 1625, Gondi's father was to enter the Oratory. The eldest of his three sons, Pierre, comte de Joigny, born in 1602, was to be the last duc de Retz. The second, Henri, born in 1610, was the marquis des Iles d'Or, and was expected to inherit the family's ecclesiastical benefices. He had already been given the abbacies of Buzay and Quimperlé in Brittany when in 1622 he fell from his horse and was kicked to death at the age of 12. The benefices, worth 15,000 and 8,000 livres a year, were immediately passed to Gondi, the third son, who had been baptized on 20 September 1613 at Montmirail, near Joigny.

As the younger son, Gondi, aged nine, was now clearly expected to take over the family's ecclesiastical sources of income, including the archbishopric, in spite, as he later wrote, of having "l'âme peut-être la moins ecclésiastique qui fût dans l'univers (perhaps the least ecclesiastical soul there was in the whole of creation)." In fact it was at one moment thought that his father might succeed to the archbishopric. Gondi's brothers had had Vincent de Paul as a tutor, but Monsieur Vincent had left the Gondi household in 1617 to evangelize the workers on the Gondi estates. Gondi himself received the tonsure in 1623. On his mother's death he was sent to the Jesuit Collège de Clermont, where he graduated in 1631, before starting to study theology at the Sorbonne. In 1627, at 14, Gondi became a canon of Notre-Dame in Paris. He seems to have been clever, clumsy, unpopular, and arrogant at school, but then or later learnt Latin, Greek, Hebrew, German, and Spanish. His Italian was fluent. He was apparently ugly and had very poor eyesight. To avoid the nickname of Buse (simpleton) suggested by Buzay, Tallemant tells us that he called himself the abbé de Retz.

Unwilling to accommodate himself to the idea of an ecclesiastical career, Gondi loved and duelled with scandalous effrontery during his distinguished academic career as a theology student. That at least is the impression he wished to convey in what we know as the *Mémoires*. Retz himself never used that name as a title for the work, which he clearly regarded as something quite other than the history it has often been criticized for purporting to be. Both their tone and their content suggest that, although probably based on historical fact, the *Mémoires*, while presenting a heavily embroidered account of what happened, were more concerned in 1675–77, when they were written, to recall the non-ethical forms of moral grandeur fashionable a quarter of a century earlier, and explored, for instance, by Pierre Corneille; Retz sought to explain the motivation of his youthful actions and to justify attitudes he knew to have become outdated when he wrote for a close friend what he referred to as "L'Histoire de ma vie (The story of my life)." Retz claims for instance with almost unbelievable cheek to have been insolent to Richelieu, who had constrained his brother Pierre to resign the governorship of the galleys, passed on to him by Philippe-Emmanuel, in favour of Richelieu's own nephew, the marquis de Pont-Courlay.

Then Retz alleges that in 1638 he voluntarily offered to yield first place in the final exercises for the doctorate of theology to the cardinal's preferred candidate, Henri de la Mothe-Houdancourt, later bishop of Rennes and then archbishop of Auch. When Richelieu haughtily rejected the insulting offer, Gondi, knowing, as Tallemant reminds us, that the benefactions of his uncle, the cardinal Henri, to the Sorbonne would not have been forgotten, pulled every string he could. The *Mémoires* duly report that he obtained the prize with a gratifyingly large majority of 84 members of the faculty. They also say that Richelieu threatened to have pulled down the new buildings which he was having put up for the Sorbonne, and which were unfinished at Richelieu's death.

In August 1633 Gondi, attending his brother Pierre's wedding to their cousin, the daughter of Henri de Gondi, arranged as a way of reconciling two aspirations within the family to succeed to the dukedom, had attempted to elope with another cousin, Marguerite de Scepeaux, the bride's younger sister, whose duchy of Beaupréau brought her in 80,000 livres a year. A glance intercepted in a mirror by Palluau was reported to Pierre's bride, who disliked her sister and informed her father who, according to the *Mémoires*, informed Philippe-Emmanuel.

The project, which had involved considerable financial planning, was foiled. A second attempt was also foiled and, in time, Marguerite married the duc de Brissac, from whom she contracted a venereal disease which she passed on to Gondi.

Then during or soon after 1635 began Gondi's liaisons with a series of women, including Anne de Rohan, princesse de Guéméné, Marie de Cossé-Brissac, duchesse de La Meilleraye, the présidente de Pommereuil, his cousin the duchesse de Lesdiguières, and Mme de Chevreuse. Retz, who was to conduct his well-known liaisons concurrently as well as consecutively, appears to have regarded his first amorous episodes as satisfying an almost intellectual curiosity. He did not particularly care for most of the women in any sentimental way, although he concocted a plan to have the marriage of the duchesse de la Meilleraye annulled so that he could marry her. As far as we can judge, his partners seldom felt any sentimental interest in him, either, although Anne de Rohan was jealous. He may have been arrogant, but he can scarcely be said to have exploited innocent or unwilling partners. Gauche, myopic, and ugly as he was, his amorous adventures show a frenetic determination to prove to himself that he could both please and impose himself. They sometimes resulted in an almost wildly romanesque intensity of commitment.

Other sources as well as Retz's *Mémoires* and Tallemant des Réaux's tittle-tattle confirm that Gondi fought a substantial number of duels. No one took any notice of these strident proclamations, according to what Retz later gave out, of his unsuitability for the career being forced on him, but from March to December 1638 he travelled in Italy, to Florence, Venice, and Rome, in a party which included Tallemant, perhaps, as the *Mémoires* suggest, to keep him out of trouble with Richelieu. At Rome Gondi wore the soutane and prided himself on the meticulous outward observance of clerical norms of behaviour.

It was probably in 1639 that Gondi wrote *La Conjuration de Fiesque*, of which he published a revised version only anonymously and in 1665. The work shows an accomplished dramatic imagination. It is inspired notably by Plutarch and Sallust. Gondi was adapting an account of the conspiracy by Mascardi, and already shows his concern for fidelity to an order of personal merit, even at the cost of renouncing power. The manuscript was passed to Chapelain, and Boisrobert showed it to Richelieu. The *Mémoires* tell us that Richelieu said "Voilà un dangereux esprit (This is a dangerous mind)," that Gondi was unperturbed when the remark was semi-officially passed on to him through his father, and that he thenceforward behaved towards Richelieu with the distaste on his own account he had hitherto felt only on account of Mme de Guéméné's dislike of the cardinal. The incident may well be true, but Retz says that he wrote the *Conjuration* when he was 18. He flattered his own youthful precocity. He was at least 25.

Gondi's aunt, Madeleine de Silly, had retired after two scandals first to Montmirail, and then to the Carmelites, where she acquired a reputation for real devotion. When her father died, however, she left the order and married Charles d'Angennes, comte du Fargis, a member of the retinue of the king's brother, Gaston d'Orléans, and French ambassador to Spain from 1620 to 1624. In that year Mme du Fargis was appointed lady-in-waiting to Marie de Medici and reverted to a life of scandal, both amorous and political, intriguing against Richelieu, as also had Mme de Chevreuse, elder sister of the prince de Guéméné and therefore sister-in-law to Gondi's mistress. Chalais, the lover of

Mme de Chevreuse, had been executed in 1626 for conspiring with Gaston d'Orléans against the king.

Both Mme du Fargis, who had been condemned to death while safely in Lorraine in 1631 and who died in Brussels in 1639, and Mme de Chevreuse were deeply implicated in the plots against Richelieu supported by Marie de Medici and Gaston d'Orléans, and generally also by Spain. It is probable that Retz later exaggerated the part he played in the conspiracies and assassination plots but, like La Rochefoucauld, he was at least on their fringe, and may have been more deeply implicated in the plot led by the comte de Soissons in 1641. That ended when Soisson's troops were winning at La Marfée and he carelessly used his pistol to open his visor. It is usually believed that he blew out his brains, although there are lingering suspicions of murder. When Mme du Fargis's husband, also known as the comte de la Rochepot, died at Arras in 1640, he left Gondi the seigneurie of Commercy, which Gondi's aunt, his mother's sister, had brought to her marriage. Whether because of the family hostility to Richelieu or because he petitioned Richelieu for the coadjutorship of Paris for his son, Gondi's father was exiled to Lyons in 1641.

It is both exceptionally important and exceptionally difficult to know why Gondi took the next steps in his career. He has been accused of seeking power and fame through a career which "redefined the canons of hypocrisy," outwardly accepting the moral disciplines of the church whose spiritual values he rejected, and he has been praised for the lucidity of his self-analysis. Much comment ignores the nature of the *Mémoires* and the date and circumstances of their composition as a private document written for a friend. Although pious and retired from public life, Retz was still in 1675–77 concerned to justify the behaviour of his youth, assuming in the particular reader for whom he was writing an understanding of the values which had then been current. Even when composing the *Mémoires* he did, however, invent or almost wantonly exaggerate incidents and attitudes, possibly forgetting, but more probably imagining, what did happen, to fit it in with his image of himself. Everything in his youth that had gone wrong is depicted as the fault of chance, not of miscalculation. On the day of his birth a monster sturgeon had been caught in a nearby stream. It is perfectly possible to believe that the ageing Retz intended his reader to suppose that that, at any rate, is what should have happened.

Retz, who pronounced and from 1671 spelt his name "Rais," has been thought simply and cynically to have defied all that his contemporaries held sacred, and either blasphemously to have justified his behaviour or iniquitously to have deceived himself. Most commentators have thought him calculatedly wicked, whether just for his fundamental choice itself or for disguising it. Although a consideration of the *Mémoires* properly belongs later, any attempt to understand Retz himself demands some consideration at this point of what he himself wrote, since everything which subsequently took place has to be interpreted in the light of his celebrated statement:

Comme j'étais obligé de prendre les ordres, je fis une retraite dans Saint-Lazare…L'occupation de mon intérieur fut une grande et profonde réflexion sur la manière que je devais prendre pour ma conduite… Je trouvais l'archevêché de Paris dégradé à l'égard du monde, par les bassesses de mon oncle, et désolé, à l'égard de Dieu, par sa négligence et son incapacité

(Since I was obliged to take orders [to become archbishop], I made a retreat at Saint-Lazare…. My interior occupation was a serious and deep reflection on the way in which I should conduct myself… I found the archbishopric of Paris despised in the eyes of the world, on account of my uncle's demeaning behaviour, and ruined, in the eyes of God, by his negligence and incompetence).

Retz says he was quite aware of the need for properly episcopal behaviour in a bishop, and that it would for him be stricter and more indispensable than for any other because of his uncle's scandalous misconduct. At the same time he felt that he was himself incapable of what was required "et que tous les obstacles et de conscience et de gloire que j'opposerais au dérèglement ne seraient que des digues fort mal assurés (and that all the obstacles whether of conscience or of care for reputation which I would set up against disordered conduct would be but flimsy barriers)." In the passage which follows, the italicized passage is underlined in the autograph manuscript, but the underlining is unlikely to have been the work of Retz and may have been by someone who wished to draw attention to what was regarded at the unknown date of the underlining as a scandalous sentiment:

Je pris, après six jours de réflexion, le parti *de faire le mal par dessein, ce qui est sans comparaison le plus criminel* devant Dieu, mais ce qui est sans doute le plus sage devant le monde… On évite par ce moyen, le plus dangereux ridicule qui se puisse rencontrer dans notre profession, qui est celui de mêler à contretemps le péché dans la dévotion.

Voilà la sainte disposition avec laquelle je sortis de Saint-Lazare. Elle ne fut pourtant pas de tout point mauvaise; car je fis une ferme résolution de remplir exactement tous les devoirs de ma profession, et d'être aussi homme de bien pour le salut des autres, que je pourrais être méchant pour moi-même

(I decided, after six days of reflection, *to misbehave intentionally, which is incomparably worst* in the sight of God, but undoubtedly best in the eyes of the world… In that way you avoid making of yourself the most dangerous laughing-stock of which our profession admits, which is inappropriately to mix sin with devotion.

That is the holy disposition with which I left Saint-Lazare. It was however not all evil, for I made a firm resolution to fulfil exactly all the duties of my profession, and to be as much an agent of good for the salvation of others, as I might be of evil for myself).

The passage does not, in the light of the non-ethical forms of moral elevation being explored by the highest French aristocracy during the fourth and fifth decades of the century, require lengthy commentary, but Retz's taste for rhetorical antitheses should be noted. The phrase "best in the eyes of the world" is not a declaration of hypocritical intent, but a rhetorical makeweight. Knowing himself incapable of the saintly moral elevation desirable in the episcopal state, Gondi decided that the career option was the only one then open to him, and that his honour and moral dignity allowed him to keep his private behaviour separate from his public image. Whatever spiritual damage

Gondi might have been going to do to himself, he was going to avoid the scandalous flaunting of irregularity, and to work only for the spiritual good of others to whom he would present the outward appearance and edifying example of impeccable behaviour. The world has known more shocking codes of behaviour.

Even before his 1638 journey to Italy, Gondi had been at the centre of one of the small social groups like that of Conrart, from which the Académie française was formed. He received Saint-Amant, Sarrazin, Gomberville, d'Aubignac, Patru, and Scarron, then, later, Ménage and Chapelain. Some, like Marigny, were to stay close to him during the Fronde. It was after the death of Soissons in 1641 that Gondi really resolved to pursue his ecclesiastical career "parce que je crus qu'il n'y avait plus rien de considérable à faire (because I thought there was nothing else important to do)." Arnauld had converted Mme de Guéméné and taken her off to Port-Royal (q.v.) six weeks previously. The captain of the guards at the Arsenal had replaced him in the favours of Mme de la Meilleraye: "Voilà de quoi devenir un saint (That was enough to make one become a saint)." It is clear in the *Mémoires* that the ageing Retz wanted his reader to think that as a young man his real philosophy consisted in the belief that life was something not to be taken too seriously. If, as must be supposed, the *Mémoires* were addressed to Mme de Sévigné, his addressee will have understood what he meant.

Retz tells us that he did not try to pretend he was devout, but that he respected and cultivated those who were truly religious. Such behaviour is entirely in character. It implied a belief in his own superiority, and a belief in choosing the heroic, whatever the difficulty, but it was neither hypocritical nor vulgarly ambitious. It is no doubt true that Retz exaggerates the success he claims to have had in edifying the devout, and in his theological discussions with the Calvinist pastor Jean Métrezat; and no doubt his connection with Françoise de Lorraine, duchesse de Vendôme, wife of César, the illegitimate son of Henri IV, was important to him on account as much of the liaison it allowed with her daughter, later Mme de Nemours, the wife of Charles-Amédée de Savoie, as of the protection and tutelage of her influential director, Philippe Cospeau, bishop of Lisieux, which it afforded him. Gondi nonetheless began to make a name for himself as a preacher. The *Mémoires* are at this point certainly unreliable, recounting incidents involving persons known to have been somewhere other than they state and, probably in the interests of emphasizing his own daring, they exaggerate the hostility to him of Richelieu. However, Richelieu died on 4 December 1642, and the way seemed to Gondi to be open to the coadjutorship.

At first Gondi was offered only the diocese of Agde, in the south, but Louis XIII died on 14 May 1643, and his widow, Anne of Austria, duly offered the coadjutorship with right of succession. In accordance with the fiction that all episcopal jurisdiction was territorial, Gondi was given Corinth as his diocese "in partibus infidelium (in the hands of unbelievers)" and, with the bulls for which he had to borrow 48,000 livres signed on 5 October 1643 and his future now assured, he took his doctorate in theology on 19 October, preached on 1 November, the day after receiving the papal bulls, and, only in the course of November, took holy orders. He was consecrated in Notre-Dame on 31 January 1644. To the surprise of the canons and the diocese, Gondi preached frequently and won general esteem while sustaining his intimate liaison with Mme de Pommereuil, who had followed Anne de Rohan, princesse de Guéméné and,

during the Fronde, was to be succeeded in his affections by the empty-headed but exceedingly beautiful daughter of Mme de Chevreuse and granddaughter of Montbazon.

Although he kept clear of any personal involvement in the conspiracy contemptuously referred to as the "cabale des importants," about which the *Mémoires* are merely dismissive, his friends were involved, and the plot fits into the pattern of opposition first to Richelieu and then to Mazarin which was to lead to Retz's final defeat in the Fronde. The central figure was François, duc de Beaufort, of whom Retz said that he had "le sens beaucoup au-dessous du médiocre a great deal less than average good sense)," a judgement with which La Rochefoucauld and Mme de Motteville agreed. Son of César de Bourbon, duc de Vendôme, the illegitimate son of Henri IV and brother of Mercoeur, Beaufort belonged to the Vendôme family, mistrusted by Richelieu, who took away from them the governorship of Brittany, but befriended by Louis XIII's queen, Anne of Austria. Beaufort's mistress, Mme de Montbazon, the second wife of Hercule de Rohan, was 44 years younger than her husband and 12 years younger than her step-daughter, Mme de Chevreuse. She had been left by the duc de Longueville, when he married Anne-Geneviève de Bourbon-Condé, sister of le grand Condé.

The reciprocal dislike between Mme de Montbazon and Mme de Longueville was intense. Not only had Mme de Longueville taken Mme de Montbazon's lover, but her new lover, Beaufort, had himself earlier been rejected by Mme de Longueville, later to be La Rochefoucauld's mistress. Retz is contemptuous about Beaufort and his friends "who all died mad, but even then seemed to me to be scarcely sane." Mme de Montbazon had procured two letters alleged to be from Mme de Longueville to the comte de Coligny. The Condés demanded that she be silenced and when, in the end, she was exiled, Beaufort's conspiracy drove them into their alliance with Gaston d'Orléans, which was then used by Mazarin as a lever with which to establish himself as the queen's principal lieutenant. The queen was to develop a strong emotional attachment to him, and it now seems certain that he was her lover. Both Retz and La Rochefoucauld thought the Beaufort plan was to seize power without assassinating Mazarin, but Beaufort was arrested on 2 September 1643 and sent to prison at Vincennes, where he stayed until his escape on Whit Sunday, 31 May 1648. He was to play an important part as an ally of Gondi in the Fronde. Mme de Chevreuse was exiled to Tours.

Gondi started his episcopacy by trying to reform the diocesan clergy, but was thwarted by his uncle. His public conduct and pastoral concern remained exemplary, and he extended his literary patronage to include Ménage, making Sarrazin part of his household from 1644 to 1648, when he went over to Conti, leaving Gondi supported chiefly by Scarron. At first, however, Gondi succeeded in remaining on excellent terms with Mazarin, whom he none the less despised. Relations deteriorated quite slowly. Guise tried to replace Beaufort as the lover of Mme de Montbazon, insulted Mme de Longueville and killed the comte de Coligny in the resulting duel in December 1643. Guise, like Beaufort's father at Anet, the duc de Vendôme, remained a focus of opposition, hostile to the court, Mazarin, and the Condés, but an ally of Gondi.

The first brush with Mazarin came in consequence of Gondi's popular speech defending clerical immunities at the assembly of the Gallican church which opened in May 1645. Shadow boxing continued in October when courtesies and insults were exchanged over the matter of allowing the Polish bishop of Varmia to officiate at the wedding of the Polish king Ladislas VII with Marie-Louise de Gonzague, daughter of the duc de Nevers, made by Richelieu duke of Mantua. Marie-Louise had been considered a possible bride for Gaston d'Orléans. Gondi rallied clergy backing and, after a confrontation with both Mazarin and the queen, the court backed down and moved the wedding from Notre-Dame to the Palais-Royal. A trivial matter of protocol was made the pretext for another quarrel, and therefore a perceptible realignment of the political forces poising themselves for battle, when Orléans claimed and won precedence over Gondi at a ceremony in Notre-Dame. Condé's son, still duc d'Enghien until his father's death in December, rallied to Gondi, and the elder Condé brought about a reconciliation between Orléans and Gondi.

Gondi was ill late in 1646, but on his recovery began to win considerable admiration for his sermons. During the initial stages of the tension between parlement and administration, chiefly caused by the government's vacillations on the basis for taxation, as by taxing illegitimately erected buildings, wealth, and the entry of goods into Paris, Gondi retained a low profile. He spoke out in a sermon before the court on 25 August 1648, attacking the taxation of ecclesiastical property. On the following day, he presided over the formal thanksgiving for Condé's victory at Lens, a *Te Deum* after which, in spite of a plan which went wrong, Mazarin succeeded in having two leading members of the parlement arrested, one of them Blancmesnil and the other Broussel, who had to be dragged from his sick-bed. The carriage was overturned in public protest, but Broussel was taken off, and the public put barricades across the road. Gondi, still in his vestments, went to see what was happening, found La Meilleraye leading some guards and being assaulted by the mob, blessed the mob, rescued La Meilleraye, whose wife's lover he had once been, and took him to the Palais-Royal, where the queen, Mazarin, Longueville, and Orléans were meeting. The queen was obliged to release Broussel, and Retz to give the news to the crowd. He was, however, knocked over and nearly killed.

Gondi had agents in all camps, and tried to appear friendly to both court and people, while deciding which to join. The *Mémoires* are here totally unreliable. The crowd's mood changed dramatically and alarmingly almost without warning. Gondi was prepared to take over Paris, where he estimated that 1,200 barricades had been put up in two hours, but had to stand down when the queen regent was in the end forced to have Broussel released, and peace was instantly restored. Gondi, however, knew he would be blamed for having forced the queen's hand. She retired to Rueil and started to behave vindictively, anxious only to re-assert her threatened authority. From now on Condé, the easily bored, arrogant hero of the battlefield, impatient of all intrigue, held the balance between the subtle Italian-blooded Gondi, impetuous, lucid, and calculatingly in pursuit of power, and the even more Italian, patient, crafty, and infinitely patient Mazarin.

The court now moved to Saint-Germain; troops loyal to it surrounded Paris; and Condé returned from the front to find both Mazarin and his opponents soliciting his support. Quite small matters were now producing confrontatory stances in both the queen regent and the parlement, with both sides only pretending not to be provoking a now inevitable armed struggle. Condé, who despised Mazarin, dined twice with Gondi, and nearly did a deal with him involving a cardinal's hat for his brother, Conti.

Yet he wanted to avoid "sedition." Gondi feared that the parlement might act on popular dissatisfaction before Condé was committed, and Mazarin did not want civil conflict when his negotiations to end the German war seemed on the point of success. Gaston d'Orléans, Mazarin, and Condé managed to restrain Anne of Austria's hawkishness, and on 22 October signed a document allowing the parlement control over taxation. The treaty of Westphalia ending the Thirty Years' War was signed on 24 October 1648, the arrested parlementarians were released, and the court returned to Paris. Gondi refused 120,000 livres as a token of the crown's "appreciation" and turned down the possibility of the governorship of Paris, whose acceptance would have enabled Mazarin to reveal to the world the coadjutor's political ambitions.

What Gondi wanted was Mazarin's overthrow. As Orléans began to show more sympathy with the parlementaires, Condé came to side more with the queen. Gondi and his allies began to accept being called "frondeurs," after the gangs of young criminals equipped with slings, and was prepared to provoke civil war when it became clear that sentiment at the parlements of Aix and Bordeaux were as strong as they were in Paris. It is not clear how genuinely populist his feelings were, although any view of him as merely a lucidly cynical, power-hungry conspirator is certainly wrong, and his feelings of moral outrage at what he regarded as the regents's arrogant behaviour and of social and intellectual contempt for Mazarin appear to have been both genuine and understandable. Mazarin, however, now took the initiative. The court moved surreptitiously to Saint-Germain on the night of 5 January 1649, and Condé's troops blocked access to Paris. Turenne was told to prepare to return from Germany.

Gondi, ordered to join the court, pretended to be unable to get out of Paris, and the queen refused to return to Paris until the parlement had, on her orders, left for Montargis. The same afternoon, 8 January, representatives of the three sovereign parliamentary courts, also ordered to leave Paris, and of the parlement met to prepare for the defence of Paris. Retz at his own expense raised the "regiment of Corinth"; the mayor was ordered to raise 4,000 horsemen and 10,000 foot soldiers; funds were voted to be levied disproportionately from those whose offices Richelieu had created; Gondi offered the seizure of ecclesiastical silver, and the property of Mazarin's supporters was confiscated. Gondi was still short of a military leader he could trust when Elbeuf, another former lover of Mme de Montbazon who actively disliked Gondi, presented himself for the task. Fortunately for Gondi, a hesitant Longueville and a resolute Conti arrived from Saint-Germain at 2 a.m. to join him, and on 11 January Gondi had Conti named the military leader of the Fronde.

Retz reports the events of January in stirring terms, with himself as conductor of the orchestra aligning all the individual interests of his players. Beaufort now joined him, and with the reckless Elbeuf, Bouillon, a good strategist but confined to bed by gout for much of the time, Noirmoutier, a succesful field commander, and La Mothe-Houdancourt, became a lieutenant-general under Conti. Each side had about 12,000 troops, although the Fronde troops were totally untrained. One of the squadrons of Gondi's regiment was defeated on 28 January in an action known as "First Corinthians." Longueville had retired to rally the Fronde forces in Normandy, where his indifferent performance was the subject of Saint-Evremond's mocking *Retraite de Monsieur le duc de Longueville*.

The Fronde campaign was badly conducted. However,

Condé, short of troops, could not tempt the untrained Fronde forces to certain defeat in open battle, and the court, which could not count on individual regiments not to defect, had both to rely largely on mercenaries and to reserve forces to protect the Spanish border against the hostilities which were continuing there. Normandy, Poitou, Guyenne and the south were entirely disaffected. The parlements of Brittany and Languedoc followed Paris in declaring Mazarin proscribed. Gondi tried to prolong the fighting, but after the defeat of the Frondeurs on 8 February at Charenton, from which Bouillon thought they should previously have withdrawn, and the slaughter by Condé's troops of their prisoners, no route was left by which Paris could be provisioned. After Mazarin had bought over Turenne's troops with money borrowed from Condé, and Turenne, having declared himself for the Fronde, had had to flee to Holland, the peace was signed at Rueil on 11 March 1649. Gondi himself publicly accepted its provisions only in May, and on 13 July went to Compiègne to convey to the court an invitation in the name of the citizens to return to Paris. Anne of Austria returned with the young Louis XIV on 18 August to be greeted by a pale and trembling Gondi on the 19th. On 20 August Gondi made his peace with Mazarin, only to offer his support to Condé as soon as the rift between Mazarin and Condé became apparent. A convenient occasion for alliance came to hand in the again apparently trivial matter of Mme de Longueville's attempt to gain the privilege of the "tabouret" for the wife of her lover, La Rochefoucauld. Gondi persuaded Condé to withdraw his support for his sister, Mme de Longueville, against the combined wraths of the duchesses de Chevreuse, de Rohan, and de Montbazon, who threatened to have La Rochefoucauld's private parts delivered to Mme de Longueville on a silver tray, and the princesse de Guémené.

The tone of the *Mémoires* suggests that Gondi had never lost sight of his ecclesiastical career. At any rate he must have seen the prospect of political power waning, and by 1650 he was actively seeking the cardinal's hat. The difficulty is to disentangle the serious from the burlesque and the genuine from the masquerade. Apart from a reference in Saint-Evremond's *Apologie de M. de Beaufort* and at least half a dozen pamphlets which have survived, we have printed accounts from Montglas, La Rochefoucauld, Mme de Motteville, and Retz of an episode which may not have been quite so trivial as it sounds. Beaufort and a number of other former Frondeurs walked on the evening of 18 June 1649 into a restaurant in the Tuileries kept by one Renard, a valet of the bishop of Beauvais who had received his licence as a reward for preparing daily flowers for the queen, and provoked a quarrel with a group of young supporters of the court, including Souvré and Candale. Tables were overturned and swords drawn.

It seems almost certain that Beaufort and the former Frondeurs had been subjected to a series of intolerable if individually petty taunts, and were getting their own back by teaching young bloods a public lesson. All we know is that the affair attracted a surprising amount of comment for even a high-class tavern brawl, and that Beaufort, born in 1616, challenged after the incident by his cousin, the duc de Candale, born in 1627, refused him the satisfaction of a duel. The incident probably indicates continuing strong social tensions which belied the surface political alliances, but is only one of a number of what could merely have been episodes of high-spirited behaviour on both sides which we have heard about because they were thought to have got out of hand. Gondi was certainly embarrassed by the public

impropriety and sometimes sacrilegious scurrility of the behaviour of his entourage. He himself was involved in a plot to stir up Parisian feeling against Mazarin, in the course of which the marquis de la Boulaye, Bouillon's son-in-law, had Condé's empty carriage fired on while it was crossing the Pont Neuf. Gondi, Beaufort and Broussel were accused of the attempted assassination and, when reconciliation with Condé was clearly impossible, Gondi made overtures of friendship to the queen and Mazarin. An alliance formed, as it became clear that Condé, who had gone off to brood sulkily in Burgundy, offended at the lack of influence afforded to him over the queen, himself wanted to supplant Mazarin. Mazarin now put out feelers for the only alliance which would for the moment guarantee him the continued control of the regency against Condé, who was quarrelling with Gaston d'Orléans and might ally again with Gondi. Mazarin needed an alliance with Gondi, as Gondi must have supposed that eventually he would. Even in the *Mémoires* he does not show an awareness that his romanesque values would eventually ensure a victory for Mazarin's patient wiles. The real cynic in their encounter was Mazarin.

Negotiations between Gondi and the queen-regent and Mazarin were conducted privately and urgently. Gondi was to be nominated to the sacred college. Vendôme, Noirmoutier, and Brissac were to have governorships, the chevalier de Sévigné was to receive a pension, and the house of Vendôme was to get back the admiralcy it had disputed wth the Condé family. On 18 January 1650 "the princes," Condé, Conti, and their brother-in-law, Longueville, were arrested and taken to Vincennes. Gaston d'Orléans referred to them as "the lion, the monkey, and the fox." During the year, while the court was pacifying Burgundy, which disliked the replacement of Condé by Vendôme, and then repressing disturbances in Bordeaux led by Condé's wife, Bouillon, and La Rochefoucauld, Gondi, who was still contemptuous of Mazarin, cultivated Gaston d'Orléans. Neither Anne of Austria nor Mazarin trusted him, so the year passed in complicated intrigues and the cardinal's hat did not come. Mme de Longueville, having failed to rally Normandy to the defence of her brothers and her husband, had fled to Holland and joined Turenne at Stenay. La Rochefoucauld gathered forces in Poitou on her behalf.

By November 1650 Gondi was sufficiently irritated against the government openly in the parlement to take the side of the princes, for whom he demanded better conditions of imprisonment, and to attack Mazarin. He was working to ally the parlement, Gaston d'Orléans, and the princes, and had the support of Anne-Gonzague de Clèves, daughter of Nevers and now princesse Palatine, and sister of the queen of Poland, about whose wedding Gondi had been so difficult. Her mother had been Mayenne's daughter, and she may have inherited her capacity for intrigue. A formal treaty was drawn up. One of Gaston's daughters would marry Condé's son, Condé would resign the admiralcy to Beaufort, Gondi would get his red hat, and Mlle de Chevreuse, still Gondi's mistress and known as "la coadjutrice," would marry Conti. La Rochefoucauld, hearing rumours of what was proposed, suggested to Mazarin an alliance between the court and the princes, but Mazarin refused to trust him. In December Mazarin joined the royal army in Champagne. Pierre Corneille's *Nicomède* reflected the growing public sympathy for Condé.

Gondi broke openly with Mazarin on 1 February 1651. On 4 February, Gondi, against whom Mazarin was in turn exercising pressure, persuaded the parlement to insist on Mazarin's dismissal: he left Paris for Saint-Germain on the night of 6 February. Anne of Austria and Louis XIV were also about to flee the capital when Mme de Chevreuse told Gaston d'Orléans of their intention and Gondi had the city closed. The queen-regent and the king were the prisoners of Gondi and Orléans. On 13 February Mazarin personally released the princes from imprisonment at Le Havre, where they had been taken. They were met by Gondi, Orléans, and Beaufort at Saint-Denis on 16 February, while Mazarin made his way to Brühl, near Cologne, from where he pointed out to the regent that Gondi had changed sides six times in 18 months. Condé contemptuously called the scheming for the ministerial posts and the secretaryships "the war of the chamber pots."

With Mazarin absent, the regent began to make her decisions by herself, notably without consulting Gondi or Gaston d'Orléans. The alliance between Gondi and the princes soon ended, when Condé forbade the marriage between his brother Conti and Mlle de Chevreuse. For some weeks Gondi lived as a recluse in the archbishopric, preparing to separate Orléans from Condé, and in the middle of May his first pamphlet was issued in answer to a number by Condé's followers, the *Défense de l'ancienne et légitime Fronde*. Sarrazin wrote a reply from the Condé camp to a further pamphlet written in Gondi's interests in August 1651, the *Avis désintéressé*. In the ensuing pamphlet battle during August and September, largely devoted to the unmasking of Gondi's political ambitions, Patru wrote on behalf of Gondi. By the beginning of August, Gondi had come to a formal agreement with the regent, whom he would support against Condé, now seconded by La Rochefoucauld and looking for support from Bouillon and Turenne. He would also support Mazarin, and would himself be made a cardinal. The complexity of the intrigues, suspicion, and the network of agents and double agents make any intelligible summary of political events difficult, but they reached crisis point on 17 August 1651, when the regent had a series of charges against Condé read by the chancellor to deputations from the three sovereign courts and the parlement. Orléans stayed away. On 21 August, after a weekend of intense activity, both Condé and Gondi came to the parlement with an armed force.

There was uproar, and nearly an open battle. Condé sent La Rochefoucauld out to withdraw his men from the antechamber, and Gondi went out for the same purpose. As he came back, La Rochefoucauld closed the door on him and pinned him to the doorpost, calling on his assistants to stab him. Parliamentarians intervened, but Gondi, facing La Rochefoucauld's swordsmen, was also in danger from the room at the back. One of Gondi's attendants stepped between Gondi and the leader of Condé's men, and Champlâtreux, son of Molé, the chief justice, persuaded La Rochefoucauld to let Gondi go. Swords had been drawn on both sides, and only the captain of the guards prevented an affray. Gondi then accused La Rochefoucauld in the chamber of trying to murder him; La Rochefoucauld said he deserved it; Gondi replied that La Rochefoucauld was a coward and Brissac challenged La Rochefoucauld to a duel. La Rochefoucauld accepted, but Gaston d'Orléans prevented it. Battle was avoided, and the magistrates dispersed. Gondi was forbidden to return to the chamber, and Condé remained downstairs next day when the debate resumed. When he and his escort left they met Gondi leading a procession in the opposite direction. Fighting almost broke out, but Condé knelt as convention

demanded, and received Gondi's blessing. Gondi bowed deeply, and Anne of Austria held matters where they were until the king's majority was declared on 7 September, when he was 13.

Anne of Austria then resumed her rule, and Condé, accepting defeat in Paris, went to rally support in Burgundy. Gondi started to negotiate with Mazarin, offering to facilitate his return in exchange for elevation to the cardinalate, intent at all costs on keeping Gaston d'Orléans from supporting Condé, while knowing that the return of Mazarin, inevitable in view of the regent's affection for him, had also to be delayed until after his own elevation, which it would undoubtedly have compromised. Meanwhile Bouillon and Turenne defected from Condé's cause, while the princess Palatine acted as Gondi's intermediary with Mazarin. Turenne and Condé were again on opposite sides, but now it was Turenne who was serving the queen's cause.

In November 1651 two attempts to kidnap Gondi failed. They were organized by La Rochefoucauld in the interests of Condé, and were to have been executed by Condé's steward, Gourville. Purely by chance Gondi escaped the first time by taking an unusual route one evening when he had to give other people a lift home from the Chevreuse residence. On the second occasion the hired watcher, tired of waiting, had slipped off to a tavern when Gondi left Mme de Pommereuil. There is considerable evidence that Gondi was able to dispense large sums, conceivably of Spanish origin, in support of his pursuit of the cardinalate, now subject to every sort of personal, political and even ecclesiastical intrigue, at Rome, as elsewhere. Some at least of Gondi's support during the Fronde had come from Jansenist (q.v.) clerical sympathizers, a fact to which Condé now drew attention. The consistory was finally held on 19 February 1652, and Gondi heard the news on 1 March. From now on, he was the cardinal de Retz.

Retz now retired again to the privacy of the archbishopric and resumed the pamphlet battle while waiting for the king to bestow the red hat on him. His popularity in Paris had waned, but on at least one occasion he confronted a hostile crowd with a courage and dignity sufficient to win them over. They escorted him home. However, he was becoming politically isolated. Foucquet's brother, the abbé Basile Foucquet, was acting against him on Mazarin's account; Mme de Chevreuse and Noirmoutier deserted to the court, as a little later did Mlle de Chevreuse, when her affections warmed towards the abbé Foucquet and those of Retz towards Mlle de la Loupe. "La coadjutrice" was to die quite suddenly and mysteriously on 7 November. Retz himself was drawn into an alliance with Mademoiselle, Gaston's daughter, Mlle de Montpensier, "la grande Mademoiselle," who wanted to marry the king but whose policy, fiercely on the side of the princes, was opposite to that of Retz. He was also an ally of the widow of Charles I of England, Henriette-Marie, stressing to Mademoiselle the advantages of a marriage to Charles II.

The civil war in France continued. Condé instructed Nemours, at the head of a contingent of Spaniards, and Beaufort to join him in the Bordeaux region. Gaston d'Orléans wished them to stay near the Loire, where the royal troops, led by Hocquincourt and Turenne moved through Tours, Amboise, and Blois, before leaving the Loire to approach Orléans from the south. The city wanted to remain neutral, but was about to admit royal troops when Mademoiselle rowed round the barricaded city, found an open gate, entered, made her way to the central square, and governed the town for a month on behalf of her father, admitting Beaufort and Nemours. Their plan to seize the Loire bridges at Gien was foreseen by Turenne, and they were defeated at Jargeau. Condé, worried about Retz's influence over Gaston d'Orléans, left his own troops to Conti and rode with La Rochefoucauld from Agen to Orléans in nine days. He defeated Turenne at Bléneau and rode with Beaufort, Nemours, and La Rochefoucauld into Paris, where he arrived on 11 April 1652. Retz had opposed the decision to allow them in, but Condé's reputation for violence in a popular cause gave him a following in the city.

Retz's pamphlets against Chavigny, his former ally Beaufort, and Condé, and his more serious justification of his own behaviour, were on different registers, but each in its way masterly. Both Condé and Turenne, under orders from Mazarin, had at first wished not to alienate Paris opinion by campaigning too near the capital, but then saw the need to take the city by force. Only Gaston d'Orléans and Retz still realized the importance of keeping it neutral. However, Turenne's army, concentrated at Saint-Denis, resolved to trap Condé, who decided to regroup at Charenton, hoping to reach the Porte Saint-Honoré by way of the Bois de Boulogne. Gaston d'Orléans allowed Condé to send only baggage through the town. Condé's army had to pass round the walls to the Porte Saint-Antoine, where Turenne pushed it from the south into the block he had laid on the road to Vincennes. He closed the trap at dawn on 2 July, pinning Condé's army against the city walls in the Faubourg Saint-Antoine. Mademoiselle herself had the city gates opened to the wounded and had the Bastille canons fired in support of Condé to cover the operation while she allowed the remnants of his army into the city. She had one last salvo fired off in the direction of the royal party, out of range on a hill-top. She had saved Condé and ended any hopes of marrying the king.

Retz had stayed indoors all day, receiving frantic messages from Gaston d'Orléans. Condé now attempted to take control of Paris, but the mob was roused against a meeting of city notables he called; the Hôtel de Ville was fired; and several of the notables were massacred. It is unclear who roused the mob, but moderate opinion blamed Condé, and suspected he had deliberately gathered together the notables partly with the intention of provoking an assault on them which would then leave him in charge. In a duel Beaufort killed Nemours, his sister's husband, with whom he had had a serious quarrel over strategy at Orléans, and on 9 August Bouillon died. Then, on 19 August, Mazarin went again into temporary exile while order was restored. Retz stayed on in Paris, but heavily barricaded Notre-Dame against possible attack by Condé, and his popularist instinct correctly turned him into the advocate of peace. In September he went to Compiègne, invited Louis XIV to return to Paris and restore peace, and received the cardinal's hat. But he was hissed by the Paris crowd. He had not brought back peace, or established himself as the leader of the peace party. Condé, defeated, left Paris in October. The king and his court returned, and Gaston d'Orléans left in disgrace for exile to Blois. Mazarin was recalled, and insisted on the removal of Retz from Paris. Alone of the leading figures, Mazarin was victorious.

Retz's fate remained undecided for some weeks. He might have had a lucrative ambassadorship to Italy, but Servien, the minister, would do nothing for the supporters to whom Retz felt loyal. Accurate rumours reached him of orders to arrest him. He was followed and his movements were watched, but he behaved with the courageous dignity to which he always aspired and which was the ideal cultivated by his caste. There was much discussion about the mode of the arrest, but Retz was wrongly convinced that he could safely visit the Louvre on 19 December, after burning his papers, selecting some he stuffed into his pocket in case he was making a mistake.

There was something odd about the arrest, almost as if Retz had courted it and, like the rest of the cast, was acting out a choreographed role. The king was courteous, the queen frosty. He was arrested in an ante-chamber where for no obvious reason he was waiting after he had seen them both, and taken to Vincennes. Guards had been posted along the route. The ecclesiastical establishment, which anyway largely backed Retz, complained at the arrest of a cardinal, and Retz seems at first to have been maltreated by his jailers, we do not know with what complicity from above. He wrote a good deal but what he wrote has been lost. Rome's fury was assuaged with relative ease. In August 1653 Retz was offered his freedom if he would resign his coadjutorship and reside in Rome, but haughtily he turned down the proposed deal. The nuntius, Niccolo Bagni, was reproved for his part in making it.

Retz's uncle died at 4.30 a.m. on 21 March 1654. The chapter met at 5. A legal document empowering a priest to act in Retz's name was immediately used, and Retz was in titular possession of his diocese within an hour of the death. The court was furious, the see was declared vacant, and the authority of the vicars general declared null. Retz capitulated, and on 28 March resigned the archbishopric. He would reside at Nantes under the supervision of La Meilleraye, Richelieu's cousin, who was married to Retz's cousin Marie de Cossé-Brissac, maréchal de France and for a while also surintendant des finances, later a duke and peer, and father-in-law of Hortense Mancini, Mazarin's niece. When the appointment of a successor was confirmed Retz would retire to Rome with the revenues from seven abbeys.

La Meilleraye thought Retz had promised not to escape from Nantes. Retz said the promise held only for the journey there. He left Vincennes on 30 March and lived in some style at Nantes. Innocent X refused, as Retz had always supposed he would, to accept his resignation. About 5 p.m. on 8 August Retz used a rope to climb down from his apartment to a waiting horse, but fell and broke his shoulder. By 7 he had crossed the Loire. On 9 August he was received at Beaupréau by his cousin Henri de Cossé, duc de Brissac, who had married the Mlle de Scepeaux with whom the young Gondi had once wanted to elope and who was the mother of La Meilleraye's second wife. Retz wrote a letter revoking his resignation, went to Machecoul, where the duc de Brissac was frightened of receiving him, and on the night of 15 August embarked on a barge, arriving at Belle-Ile, the family fief, on 17 August.

Mazarin heard on 14 August. Machecoul was seized by La Meilleraye's troops, the court declared the see of Paris vacant and ordered the appointment of four new vicars general. Retz's father was exiled to Auvergne. Retz left Belle-Ile for San Sebastián on 9 September, was allowed to cross Spain, and embarked for Italy, arriving in Rome on 28 November 1654. A circular letter he sent to the higher clergy of France dated 14 December and not mentioned in the *Mémoires* is generally thought to have weakened his support. When Pope Innocent X died on 7 January 1655, Louis XIV forbade any French delegates to the conclave to have anything to do with Retz. Mazarin wanted the election of Giulio Saccheti. It was Retz's candidate, Fabio Chigi, who became Alexander VII.

During 1655 Retz continued to intervene in the administration of his diocese. The French court was exasperated, and Alexander VII, under constant pressure from France, grew cool, and suggested submitting Retz's position to a congregation of cardinals for consideration. Retz himself retired to an abbey at Grotta-Ferrata. Complaints were laid against him from France, and the pope suggested resignation from the archbishopric to avoid a trial. Nine cardinals and three bishops were nominated to a commission which was in no hurry to sit, while Retz, sometimes with skill but sometimes without, exacerbated sentiment against himself in both Paris and Rome by open letters, public notices, and the nomination and withdrawal of powers from his diocesan administrators. Christina of Sweden tried in vain to mediate.

From August 1656, destitute, and now friendless in Rome and Paris, Retz began a life of wandering. He was accompanied by a party of four, including his secretary, Guy Joly. In September he was at Besançon, from where he threatened to place his diocese under interdict. He disappeared for some months, although we know he travelled under false names, was at Constance, then went to Holland. Mazarin tried to have him kidnapped in Cologne. Condé helped him. Late in 1657 he published an attack on Mazarin's foreign policy and, like Condé, tried to make his peace with the French court. In November 1659 Condé, a prince of the blood, was allowed back when the peace of the Pyrenees was made. Retz tried very hard to obtain his own rehabilitation. Unsuccessful, he resumed his travels, to Hamburg and then London, where Charles II gave him money. Nothing was changed by Mazarin's death on 9 March 1661, in spite of efforts by Charles II to mediate.

Serious negotiations took place in the summer of 1661 just before the arrest of Foucquet at Nantes on 5 September. A deal was struck before the end of the year. Retz would resign and live at Commercy in exchange for a benefice of 120,000 livres, a down payment of 60,000 livres, an amnesty for his friends, and the rehabilitation of all those for whose disgrace he was responsible. The settlement was in the circumstances honorable, and Retz had provided for all those who had served him. The new archbishop died within days of receiving his bulls, and Hardouin de Péréfixe, bishop of Rodez, succeeded him. On 29 June Retz's father died at Joigny, but Retz was not allowed to attend the funeral. He was of considerable assistance to the French court in its struggles with Rome, although little gratitude was shown to him. In 1664 he was allowed back to Paris for a few days, and in 1665 spent some months in Rome smoothing out a fierce quarrel between the pope and the parlement de Paris about the Sorbonne's condemnation of a book by a Spanish Jesuit affirming papal infallibility. Retz was successful in getting the pope to acquiesce in the condemnation, but did not get the ambassadorship to Rome for which he had hoped.

He had sold Commercy, retaining only a life interest. Louis XIV thanked him coolly for his work in Rome, but sent him back there for the death of Alexander VII. Retz himself obtained seven votes at the conclave, but succeeded in getting the French candidate, Rospigliosi, elected as Clement IX. There was another frosty letter of thanks, and Retz returned to Commercy. He was allowed to visit Paris in 1667 and 1668 and was sent to Rome for the 1670 conclave. Louis XIV was behaving with what Retz rightly perceived to be intolerable arrogance, and Retz became less anxious to oblige. He did visit Paris again, however, early in 1672. He began to turn seriously towards devotion, spending more frequent periods at the Benedictine abbey of Saint-Mihiel, 18 kilometres from Commercy. He tried to resign the cardinalate and wanted to end his life as a Benedictine monk, but the resignation was refused. He none the less retired to Saint-Mihiel. In mid-1675 he began to write the *Mémoires*. He continued them in 1676, devoting himself to good works, founded an educational institution, undertook to pay his debts, and distributed pensions, much reducing the size of his household.

The conversion was regarded as play-acting by parts of Paris, although Mme de Sévigné, Turenne, and Bossuet thought it sincere, as did both the Jesuits and the Jansenists. On the death of Clement X on 22 July 1676 Retz went to Rome for his last conclave. Odescalchi was elected as Innocent XI on 20 September. Retz returned to Commercy, but was in Paris for much of 1678 and 1679, living at his abbey of Saint-Denis, but observing the monastic rule. It was there that he was taken ill on 14 August 1679. He was taken to the home of his niece, the duchesse de Lesdiguières, and died there on 24 August 1679. He was buried opposite the tomb of François I in the abbey church of Saint-Denis. Louis XIV forbade any monument or even inscription. When the royal tombs were violated in 1793, during the Revolution, no one noticed that of Retz.

WORKS

It has been established with reasonable certainty that Retz wrote his *Mémoires* between mid-1675 and mid-1677. They are the work of a man who was concerned to make his peace with God as honourably and as thoroughly as he had done everything else in his life, to right what wrongs he had done, and whose existence was now dominated by a sincere and authentic, even austere, devotion. The *Mémoires* are clearly the product of a lucidly analytic and penetrating mind, both perceptive and cynical about human ambition, the strength of the drive to pursue political power, and the mechanics of its acquisition. There is, however, also a strongly self-justificatory tendency running through the text, with the author's desire to show himself as far as possible in the light in which, at the time of writing, he wished to be seen; this involves a sometimes demonstrable attempt to conceal the truth.

It is not merely that Retz deceives himself, which he clearly does, but that he also lies. We know, although he denies it, that he distributed at Rome largesse amounting to bribes in his pursuit of a cardinal's hat, and we know that he was working for Mazarin during the summer of 1651. He wrongly affirms his participation in the Soissons plot against Richelieu, La Valette's intended assassination of himself, and Condé's plot to kidnap him on 4 July 1652. The difficulty is to reconcile not any forgetfulness, or possibly indeliberate self-deception, but the intention to deceive, with an interior conversion which Retz had already undergone when he wrote, and whose authenticity there is every reason to accept. Yet again and again he emphatically protests a veracity to which he can be shown to have been knowingly unfaithful. It would be over-ambitious to pretend that this paradox can be totally resolved in the present context, but some things do have to be said about it. No convincing reading of the *Mémoires* is possible which ignores the need to account simultaneously for all the parameters of the paradox, including the authenticity of the conversion, and the constraints on interpretation which they impose.

The first key lies in Retz's moral code, as exhibited in the biography. We do not know for whom, or at whose request, the first part of the two-part autograph *Mémoires* was so reduced in length. It seems certain that much about amorous liaisons was removed after the original composition of the *Mémoires*, but there are no apologies for what is left, nor for any of Retz's stated principles of behaviour. It is now very nearly generally agreed that the "Madame" to whom the *Mémoires* are addressed, but whose identification with the wholly probable Mme de Sévigné has seemed questionable on account of the reference near the end to "l'ordre que vous m'avez donné, de laisser des *Mémoires* qui pussent être de quelque instruction à messieurs vos enfants," must indeed have been Mme de Sévigné, or her daughter, Mme de Grignan. But it cannot have been Mme de Grignan.

Mme de Sévigné, the granddaughter of Retz's aunt, had only one son, born on 12 March 1648, and therefore also no longer a child in 1675–77, while Mme de Grignan had sons born in November 1671 and February 1676. But the *Mémoires* were clearly written throughout for someone of much the same generation as their author, as was Mme de Sévigné, born in 1626, and "messieurs vos enfants" could reasonably be taken to refer to grandchildren. Retz and the addressee of the *Mémoires* shared values, recollections, reminiscences, interests, and friends. Mme de Grignan, although Retz's godchild, did not like him, scarcely knew him, and was certainly never close enough to him to have encouraged him to write the *Mémoires*. Whoever it was must have removed the pages of the first part dealing, it may plausibly be presumed, largely with the amorous liaisons of which we know, from what has been left in, that Retz even after his conversion was not ashamed. That is not evidence, but it would have been in character for Mme de Sévigné. A few pages may also have been ripped out later on. The evidence is inconclusive. But it should not be forgotten that, whoever was the addressee, the *Mémoires* were written for the "instruction" of someone's children, no doubt when they grew up.

Retz's moral code did not, even after his conversion, dictate shame for the adulterous liaisons of a prelate vowed to chastity. What it precluded, as the passages in the biographical section make clear, was the scandal which would have resulted from the flaunting of such liaisons, and the abandonment of those not of his own class who had served him. Retz might have been bringing about his own spiritual ruin, but he was not going to do it by damaging his honour, either out of any uncontrolled inability to resist temptation or in such a way as to entail any damage to anyone else. He seriously wanted to enforce high standards of competence on the diocesan clergy. The paradox of the *Mémoires* has in fact more to do with the non-repentance of what today we regard as moral failings than with concealment of behaviour Retz in 1675–77 would clearly have preferred to have forgotten. Lying, like sexual liaisons, was nothing much to be ashamed of.

Even the veracity of which Retz so frequently boasted could be relative. He repents neither the extremes of behavior nor the integrity of the values which he wanted us to believe had guided his life. He was a man, as the conversion itself and the *Mémoires* make clear, given to going to the extreme outer limits of the values he adopted. He was capable of experiencing periods of depression and gloom, and of enduring disgrace and destitution. Occasional passages give the impression that he was not unwilling to depict himself as a martyr to the values which he must genuinely have thought had at least mostly guided his activities.

The *Mémoires* can be read partially as a compensation, much more concerned to convey a moral vision than just to tell the truth about what happened.

What counted was Retz's unflinching determination to live up to the highest ideals of personal merit, even at the cost of renouncing the power which he coveted. He disdained any compromise with honour in order to finish on the winning side, as he could so easily have done by entering into a treasonable alliance with Spain or with Condé, or by becoming a papal diplomat, or by abandoning those who had sacrificed careers or wealth to support him, or by doing a deal with Mazarin, in Retz's not unprejudiced mind cunning, mean-minded, low-born, a social climber, and tainted with the prejudices of the queen mother, of whom, however, Retz, for all his spies, can scarcely have known that he was probably the lover.

Despite the insulting contempt with which Louis XIV, inheriting his mother's attitudes, treated him, Retz scrupulously observed the terms of his resignation agreement, even working with great skill for the king when called on. Retz's populism, too, was not only a political tool. It was also sincere, like a willingness in July 1656 to return to Rome to care for those stricken with the plague, the charitable works of the end of his life, and his sincere feelings of outrage at the court's disregard for the feelings of the people. His belief that power belonged by right only to the noble and the brave explains much of the bravura of his political performance, but it also explains his readiness to spurn power if it required the sacrifice of honour. He sought in personal merit the foundation for an authority to counterbalance on the one hand the claims of the people, and on the other the tyranny of monarchs and ministers.

La Conjuration de Fiesque, an adaptation of Agostino Mascardi's 1629 *La Congiura cel conte de' Fieschi*, was written in a spirit of some animosity towards Richelieu as a result of the young Gondi's journey to Italy in 1638 undertaken, as his travelling companion Tallemant tells us, when his parents "trouverent à propos qu'il fist un voyage en Italie (found it a good idea for him to journey to Italy)" after his impertinence to the cardinal in the matter of the Sorbonne class list. Richelieu, says Tallemant, had called him "ce petit audacieux (that impertinent young man) with "une mine patibulaire (a sinister expression)." The text of the *Conjuration* was admired by Chapelain in a letter dated 6 August 1639, and had probably been composed in the early months of that year. Mascardi had already been faithfully, if poorly, translated by Jean-Jacques Bouchard, whose work, apparently finished no later than the beginning of 1636, was dedicated to Richelieu and not published until March 1639, with a privilège of 11 January.

Barbin published *La Conjuration* anonymously in 1665, with a privilège of 14 March. An unauthorized but better anonymous edition was published the same year in Cologne. There are, however, four extant manuscripts, and the editor of the critical edition, D.A. Watts, whose conclusions have subsequently been accepted by the editors of Retz's *Oeuvres* in the 1984 Bibliothèque de la Pléiade edition, has established that one pair of manuscripts represents a re-working of the other, and that the 1665 text implied a substantial revision of the original 1639 text, probably made by Retz himself. The 1665 text is more modern in language, but especially in the vigour, concision, and clarity of its style. The Barbin 1682 volume was probably the result of re-awakened public interest on account of Saint-Réal's 1674 *La Conjuration des Espagnols contre la République de Venise*. The book had been re-written, very possibly according to indications given by Retz, but is unlikely itself to have been Retz's work. The style is again modernized, notably through the replacement of long periods with short sentences.

Mascardi's treatment of the 1547 conspiracy of Gianluigi de' Fieschi against the ruling Doria dynasty in Genoa described what he depicted as essentially an irresponsible plot against a legitimate government. Gondi's elder brother had been forced by Richelieu to give up the general command of the galleys, and Gondi himself had brushed with Richelieu before leaving for Italy, where he established amical relations with the Barberini household. Maffeo Barberini as Urban VIII was hostile to Richelieu, and Bouchard, Mascardi's translator, was secretary to Francesco Barberini, the pope's nephew. Gondi's *Conjuration* was an indictment of the Doria regime, implicitly siding with the various conspirators against Richelieu. Fieschi is depicted as attempting to free the people from tyranny, although he died at the moment when his coup seemed likely to succeed with the destruction of Andrea Doria and his adopted son Jannetin. The text is notable for its interest in detailed military tactics, for its graphic reduction of the principles governing political developments to pithy aphorisms—still however a great deal more verbose than those of the *Mémoires* were to be—and for its long and careful examination of the morals to be drawn from the conjunction of personalities, events, and political forces described.

The evolution in language and style from the manuscripts to the printed editions of the *Conjuration* can obviously not be matched for the *Mémoires*, written in the last half-decade of Retz's life. The real interest of the *Mémoires* probably does lie chiefly in their awareness of the role played in the Fronde by the feelings of the people of Paris, and of the political force those feelings represented. In the years 1675–77, this awareness of popular sentiment as an unpredictable but perhaps exploitable political force was certainly new. It might reasonably be asked whether Retz, or Rais as he pronounced and, after 1671, spelt his own name, could himself have seen things from the point of view adopted in the *Mémoires* a quarter of a century earlier, when the events he narrates actually took place. Yet the 1657 *Remontrance au roi*, a maturely reflected political dissertation, unlike the earlier mocking pamphlets written during the Fronde or the defensive *Le Vraisemblable sur la conduite de Monseigneur le Cardinal de Retz*, although essentially a fiercely vicious attack on Mazarin's foreign policy, makes much of the miseries inflicted by it on ordinary people, not only of France, but of all Europe. Retz is clearly the harbinger of a new feeling that the common people are more than the passive victims of political intrigue, and is already hinting at the sort of feeling which in Fénelon was to swell into outrage.

There are three parts to the *Mémoires*. Well over half of the first part is missing from its beginning, and occasional passages are missing from later parts of the autograph manuscript, which contains only short fragments of the third part of the *Mémoires*, although the text now printed appears reliable. The work contains a remarkable political philosophy, and a real attempt to understand what happened during the Fronde, but not a reliable factual account of Retz's career, or of events outside it. No reference is made, for instance, to his inflammatory sermon against Mazarin preached on 25 January 1649 in the church of Saint-Paul, or of the defeat of his regiment on 28 January 1649, while he denies that the cardinalate was part of the deal made in January 1650. Retz also often exaggerates the importance of his

actions, as in persuading the people of Paris to lay down their arms on 26 August 1648 and then to take them up again on the next day. It is very doubtful that Retz exercised the influence he claimed over the election of Alexander VII in 1655. But he may have been the first to notice quite how far and how fast the progress of administrative absolutism begun under Richelieu and carried on by Mazarin had made the French people into a restive political force. He was certainly the first in his generation to state how much political authority rested on consent, and how fragile that consent had become under Anne of Austria and Mazarin.

The historians on whom Retz modelled himself are Tacitus and Sallust, but he adds to the larger perspectives a penetrating psychological insight to rival that of the other major moralists of his period. The *Mémoires* are strewn with portraits and brilliant observations, anecdotes and aphorisms. The tone touches the depths of defeated resignation, but can be light-hearted and good-humoured. Retz is cheerful about having had to face the prospect of becoming archbishop of Paris when his brother died, and wittily amusing about his early liaisons. He described Mlle de Scepeaux, sister of his brother's bride, with whom he fell in love, with whom he tried to elope, who became his mistress and then the wife of the duc de Brissac who sheltered Retz on his escape from Nantes:

> Je la trouvai très belle, le teint du plus grand éclat du monde, des lis et des roses en abondance, les yeux admirables, la bouche très belle, du défaut à la taille, mais peu remarquable et qui était beaucoup couvert par la vue de quatre-vingt mille livres de rente, par l'espérance du duché de Beaupréau, et par mille chimères que je formais sur ces fondements, qui étaient réels

> (I found her very beautiful, her complexion the most brilliant in the world, lilies and roses everywhere, wonderful eyes, a very fine mouth, the figure not so good, but not conspicuous and well made up for by the prospect of 80,000 livres a year, by the prospect of the duchy of Beaupréau, and by a thousand castles in the air that I built on these foundations, which were real).

We do not need to suppose that the passage cost Retz a great deal of effort, but it is cleverer than it looks. It starts in fairy-land, gets a touch realistic about the physical attractions, and turns into a witty send-up of the sentimental novel when, without any change of register, the point of view switches from that of a hot-blooded young male in pursuit of a beautiful female to parody that of a calculating planner of appropriate dynastic arrangements.

The tone continues to be that of an elderly man, laughing at his former infatuations as if in a letter to an old friend, but knowing that they involved mutual friends whose careers subsequently became famous or notorious. When Richelieu first appears in the *Mémoires*, he is furious with the young Gondi's mistress, Anne de Rohan, for having, he thought, thwarted his affection for the queen. The trouble with Richelieu is that "il avait au souverain degré le faible de ne point mépriser les petites choses (he had in the highest degree the weakness of not despising little things)." Sword fights are narrated in staccato sentences, forms of behaviour sometimes in periods reflecting the weight of observation:

Mlle de Vendôme avait très peu d'esprit; mais il est certain qu'au temps dont je vous parle, sa sottise n'était pas encore bien développée. Elle avait un sérieux qui n'était pas de sens, mais de langueur, avec un petit grain de hauteur; et cette sorte de sérieux cache bien des défauts. Enfin elle était aimable à tout prendre et en tout sens

(Mlle de Vendôme was not at all bright; but it is certain that, at the time I'm alluding to, her stupidity had not yet developed very far. She had a grave manner which stemmed not from good sense but from listlessness with a touch of disdain; and that sort of gravity covers up a lot of faults. Anyway, taking everything together, she was, in every sense, a very nice girl).

Retz recounts his glories, his galanteries, his repentances, his repartee, and his conspiracies, but always during the first part of the *Mémoires* keeps his tone entirely anecdotal. He ends the first section

Il me semble que je n'ai été jusques ici que dans le parterre, ou tout au plus dans l'orchestre, à jouer et à badiner avec les violons; je vais monter sur le théâtre, où vous verrez des scènes, non pas dignes de vous, mais un peu moins indignes de votre attention

(It seems to me that up to now I have been only in the pit, or at best in the orchestra stalls, playing and fooling with the violinists. Now I'm going to climb on to the stage where you will see scenes played, not worthy of you, but a little less unworthy of your attention).

The first section has therefore been a long introduction, and we can expect a change of tone. A good deal of comment has been devoted not only to the theatrical metaphor in this passage, but to the way Retz saw everything that happened as slightly unreal, or at least dramatized his account of the Fronde, and saw himself as having played the role of a dramatic hero. He does indeed tend to think in theatrical terms, but the dramatizing impetus of his imagination can also drop to a mere mannerism, and consideration devoted to it can easily distract attention from what is totally serious about the *Mémoires*, which is their vision of the way political forces interact, the nature of moral heroism, and the force of popular sentiment. Too many critics have given Retz bad marks for failing at the historical job he never attempted.

At the opening of the second section the tone immediately changes. The register is deeper, the sentences longer, and the anecdotal style gives way to narrative as Retz recounts his retreat at Saint-Lazare and the famous resolution he took there. Announcing how pleased Mazarin had been with him, he again addresses as "you" the person for whom the *Mémoires* were written, before giving his account of the cabale des importants, and introducing Beaufort, to become prominent in the account of the Fronde itself. It is essential to remember that, as with almost all the non-dramatic literature written under the ascendancy of Colbert, that is, between 1662 and 1683, the modern reader is eavesdropping on material either never intended for publication, or at best anonymous. Hence not only the restricted range of the experience discussed, but the tone of intimate complicity.

Retz did not expect from the addressee of his *Mémoires*, and

her friends, to whom they would no doubt be shown, more than an intimate giggle at his sweepingly outrageous sarcasms about those in high places. The two-line account of Richelieu's accomplishments, which are compared to those of the Caesars and the Alexanders, is scandalous in a dozen ways, from exaggerating the role of Retz's own family in the defeat of Protestantism to the implication that the house of Austria was half ruined. Louis XIII, "qui n'aimait ni n'estimait la Reine, sa femme (who neither loved nor esteemed his wife, the queen)," had tried to limit the power of the regency by nominating "creatures of M. le Cardinal de Richelieu," "hissed by all the lackeys on the road to Saint-Germain as soon as the king was dead," but, if Beaufort had had any common sense, or Beauvais had not been a mitred animal, or Retz's father had wanted to take a hand in things, Richelieu's creatures "would have been chased out in shame." There follow a number of disobliging comments about Anne of Austria, to become one of Retz's bitterest opponents. For example: "the queen had been seen only as persecuted, and, in people of that rank, suffering does service for great virtue." The scurrilous half-truths are sometimes brilliantly apposite and always, of course, shocking in their irreverence.

Retz gets much more serious, in giving an account, for instance, of his attempts to reform his diocesan clergy. He quite frequently inserts a "you," incidentally reminding the modern reader, for whom the text was not intended, that, however seriously it was meant, the text was also a shared intimacy and must be interpreted in that light. But Retz could also write with real perceptivity and skill, as in the famous double portrait, of Richelieu and Mazarin. The texts are too long and allusive to be fully considered here, but they are magnificently wrought, and indicate why the *Mémoires* are so important a text.

Le cardinal de Richelieu avait de la naissance. Sa jeunesse jeta des étincelles de son mérite: il se distingua en Sorbonne; on remarqua de fort bonne heure qu'il avait de la force et de la vivacité dans l'esprit…

Le cardinal de Mazarin était d'un caractère tout contraire. Sa naissance était basse et son enfance honteuse. Au sortir du Colisée, il apprit à piper, ce qui lui attira des coups de bâton d'un orfèvre de Rome…

Le dernier point d'illusion en matière d'Etat est une espèce de léthargie, qui n'arrive jamais qu'après de grands symptômes. Le renversement des anciennes lois, l'anéantissement de ce milieu qu'elles ont posé entre les peuples et les rois, l'établissement de l'autorité purement et absolument despotique, sont ceux qui ont jeté originairement la France dans les convulsions dans lesquelles nos pères l'ont vue. Le cardinal de Richelieu la vint traiter comme un empirique, avec des remèdes violents qui lui firent paraître de la force, mais une force d'agitation qui épuisa le corps et les parties. Le cardinal Mazarin, comme un médecin très inexpérimenté, ne connut point son abattement…il continua de l'affaiblir par des saignées: elle tomba en léthargie, et il fut assez malhabile pour prendre ce faux repos pour une véritable santé…Si cette indolence générale eût été ménagée, l'assoupissement eût peut-être duré plus longtemps, mais comme le médecin ne le prenait que pour un doux sommeil, il n'y fit aucun remède. Le mal s'aigrit; la tête s'éveilla: Paris se sentit, il poussa des soupirs; l'on n'en fit point de cas: il tomba en frénésie. Venons au détail...

(Cardinal Richelieu was high born. His youth emitted some sparks of his merit. His studies at the Sorbonne were distinguished. It was noticed very early that he had a forceful and vigorous mind...

Cardinal Mazarin's character was quite different. His birth was low and his childhood shameful. On leaving the Coliseum, he learned to cheat, which brought him a cudgelling from a goldsmith in Rome...

The ultimate stage of political illusion is a sort of lethargy, which is always preceded by serious symptoms. The overthrowing of ancient laws, the annihilation of their mediation between peoples and kings, the establishment of purely and absolutely despotic authority, these are the symptoms which originally threw France into the convulsions in which our fathers saw it. Cardinal Richelieu came and treated it like a charlatan, with violent remedies which made it seem vigorous, but with an agitated vigour which exhausted the body and its parts. Cardinal Mazarin, like an unpractised doctor, did not see how weak it was... he continued to drain its strength by bleedings. It fell into a lethargy, and he was sufficiently inept to take this false calm for real health. If that general coma had been carefully treated, the stupor might have lasted longer, but since the doctor took it only for a gentle sleep, he applied no remedy. The illness became worse. The head awoke: Paris recovered sensation, it let out sighs. No one did anything. It became frenzied. Let us get to the details...).

The third part of the *Mémoires* begins with the arrival in Italy, and the narrative becomes more factual, although Retz writes "I promised you some anecdotes...", and inserts some. He is fond of speculating on what might have been if something had been decided differently, or happened differently—if, for instance, Innocent X had not died when he did—mostly to illustrate what his theories of strategy and tactics meant in practice; but it is the moral vision which comes across most strongly, what constitutes heroism, what are the laws of political dynamics, what force is contained in the feelings of the people. The style strives for piquancy, is brilliant in ironic formulations, simple in its assertions, but devastating in their implications.

It must be remembered that Retz was writing with a sensibility attuned to a generation which came a quarter of a century after the events he described, that he did not write for publication, that we do not know for certain to whom his text was addressed and that, incidentally, he referred to the text as "L'histoire de ma vie (the story of my life)," which means a reflection on the events of his career. Historians might better have seized on the importance of the text if they had not started by regarding Retz as a memorialist rather than a moralist. Critics really ought to have noticed that Retz never himself pretended to have written memoirs.

PUBLICATIONS

[*Note: Retz published nothing over his own name. The text known as the* Mémoires *was not published by Retz or during his lifetime*]

Collections

Oeuvres complètes, 10 vols., 1870–96
Mémoires, Bibliothèque de la Pléiade, 1939 [2nd edition, 1956, includes the other works]
Oeuvres, Bibliothèque de la Pléiade, 1984

Prose

La Conjuration du comte Jean-Louis de Fiesque, 1665
Défense de l'ancienne et légitime Fronde, 1651
Le Solitaire aux deux désintéressés, 1651
Les Contretemps du sieur de Chavigny, 1652
Manifeste de Monseigneur le duc de Beaufort, 1652
Le Vrai et le faux de Monsieur le Prince et de M. le cardinal de Retz, 1652
Les Intérêts du temps, 1652
Le Vraisemblable sur la conduite de Monseigneur le cardinal de Retz, 1652
Trés humble et très importante remontrance au Roi, 1657
Mémoires de Monsieur le Cardinal de Retz, 3 vols., 1717; as *Memoirs of the Cardinal de Retz*, 1723

Biographical and critical studies

Battifol, Louis, *Biographie du cardinal de Retz*, 1929
Letts, Janet T., *Le Cardinal de Retz, historien et moraliste du possible*, 1966
Salmon, J.H.M., *Cardinal de Retz. The Anatomy of a Conspirator*, 1969
Bertière, André, *Le cardinal de Retz mémorialiste*, 1977
Watts, Derek A., *Cardinal de Retz. The Ambiguities of a Seventeenth-Century Mind*, 1980

RIVAROL, Antoine Rivaroli, known as **comte de, 1753–1801.**

Moralist, pamphleteer, and satirist.

LIFE

Rivarol's adult life was split very roughly in half by the outbreak of the Revolution in 1789. Before it, he was one of France's cleverest epigrammatists, writing wittily mordant reviews and developing a conversational flair for deeply bitter aphorisms, not sparing the king, the court, or the ancien régime. Then, aghast at what the Revolution had been unleashing, he became one of its sharpest and most merciless antagonists in exile in England and Hamburg, and an ardent royalist, joining with such fervent reactionaries as Peltier and Sabatier de Castres in lampooning the Revolution and its leaders.

Rivarol was born on 26 June 1753 at Bagnols-sur-Cèze, not far from Uzès. The family, originally called Rivaroli; was of Italian and noble provenance, but had become impoverished members of the bourgeoisie. It was on the way back from Spain to Italy that Rivarol's grandfather stopped in Languedoc and married a member of the Deparcieux family, whose head was a member of the Académie des Sciences. Rivarol's father would have liked to study and write, but it was presumably financial need which made him open the inn "Les Trois Pigeons." Rivarol was the eldest of 16 children, and early showed himself academically gifted. He was accordingly destined at least to test a clerical vocation and sent first to the Josephite school and then to the seminary of Sainte-Garde at Avignon. At the age of 24 he gave up and in 1777 went to Paris, where he took the name of chevalier de Deparcieux, with its touch both of social and intellectual distinction. When forced to revert to his real name, he became "le comte de Rivarol."

Details of Rivarol's life are obscure, but he was clearly easygoing. He did, however, soon find himself presented to d'Alembert, and being introduced through him to Voltaire, who apparently provoked him into translating Dante's *Inferno*. His rendering came out in two volumes in 1785. Rivarol established a reputation as a salon dilettante, indolent, and known for his acid wit and as a brilliant conversationalist, specializing in puns. He was joined in Paris by a married sister. He must have earned his living by journalism; he was certainly part of the team of regular writers for the *Mercure de France* (q.v.), as it had been called since 1724, and is the presumed author of many of its elegant and caustic reviews and accounts of social occasions. In 1778 it had been taken over by Charles-Joseph Panckoucke, who dedicated the periodical to the king while being heavily sympathetic to the philosophes (q.v.). Politically Rivarol early became a serious thinker, the theorist of counter-revolution, critical of the king, and seeking a revolution imposed by, rather than against, the monarchy.

The academy of Berlin had proposed as a subject for its prize for 1784 a *Discours sur l'universalité de la langue française*. Rivarol won the prize and was made a member of the academy. The work was praised by Frederick the Great, and Rivarol was awarded a small pension by Louis XVI. The essay, which was published, contains the memorable untruth, "Ce qui n'est pas clair n'est pas français (What is not clear is not French)," and is at the root of Rivarol's persistent desire to work on the French language and to compile a dictionary. In 1797 he was to issue his *Prospectus d'un nouveau dictionnaire* with an accompanying essay, *De l'homme intellectuel et moral*, as the *Discours préliminaire du nouveau dictionnaire de la langue française* is not quite correctly known. Rivarol's first published work had been a satirical attack on the still little-known translator of Virgil's *Georgics*, Jacques Delille, who had published a long poem *Les Jardins* in 1782, programmatically attempting to restore to noble poetic usage household names for, among other things, ordinary vegetables. In successive lines he refers to cabbages and turnips. Rivarol's riposte, also of 1782, is entitled *Le Chou et le navet* (The Cabbage and the Turnip)."

Critics and historians, on very little evidence, dispute the extent to which what one of them has called Rivarol's "dissipated worldly life" hindered his literary work, and he has been strongly defended even against accusations of indolence, for which he himself is partly responsible, made notably in a 1926 biography. It has been asserted that, on the contrary, he read widely by day and, even if he produced little, relaxed only in the evenings. He did produce a one-act verse comedy, the 1785 *L'Emprunteur* and in the same year a novel, *Isman; ou, Le Fatal-*

isme. Rivarol claimed, perhaps not entirely facetiously, that it was a great advantage for a critic to have done nothing himself.

He appears at any rate to have made enough to live on with some elegance, presumably from the anonymously published social and literary journalism but, in spite of the Dante translation and the Berlin dissertation, he first really came to public attention with another satirical attack in defence of poetry against poets with reputations which he considered overblown, the *Le Petit Almanach de nos grands hommes* for 1788, with an up-dated version for 1790. It was an incisive attack on literary pretentiousness, a mixture of epigrammatic banter and scathing analysis whose targets included many now forgotten writers as well as Delille and Beaumarchais. Rivarol's two 1788 *Lettres à Necker* on religious and moral matters are his most philosophically serious works.

If Rivarol was disillusioned with the monarchy as it was in the decade before the Revolution, he had also cultivated the ability to coin sharp, biting aphorisms at the expense of other people, to amuse by his mordant pen even when he was wrong, and to deflate with a dagger more often than with a smile. A great deal of what he wrote, except about language, is cleverly sarcastic without being either true or profound. But he had developed in himself a very sharp eye for everything—the Revolution much more than the monarchy—that was not what it pretended to be, and what its supporters took it for. By the time of the estates general of June 1789 Rivarol had begun to forecast the disasters that would pile on a France whose recent history he brought up to date in 1800, the year before his death, when he described the state of France as "violence monarchique intitulée république (The violency of a monarchy called a republic)."

Early in July 1789 the anti-encyclopédiste abbé Antoine Sabatier de Castres had sought to create a periodical to defend the crumbling ancien régime against the increasing number of pamphlets which attacked it. He first enlisted Rivarol to help him with the tri-weekly *Journal Politique National* and then emigrated, leaving Rivarol in sole charge. In fact the journal appeared irregularly for 55 numbers before it disappeared in 1790, uniquely devoted to commenting acerbically on official acts of government and administration. The criticisms were coruscating, and much admired by Burke, who said they would one day rank alongside Tacitus.

By the time the *Journal* ceased publication Rivarol was already collaborating on the satirical *Actes des Apôtres*, famous for its anti-Revolutionary violence, which appeared from 2 November 1789 until October 1791. There was an editorial team of more than a dozen "apostles" led by Jean-Gabriel Peltier, converted to counter-revolution by September 1789, but much was published anonymously, and Rivarol seems to have provided the chief impulsion. The journal contained rumour, documents, letters, and comment, but had no unified political view, containing all shades of monarchical opinion in verse and prose satire, with caricatures and long theoretical essays apparently by Rivarol. The leaders of the Revolution were attacked personally for their physical deformities, marital unhappinesses and anything, real or supposed, which could make them appear ridiculous. Targets included La Fayette, Necker, the pomposities of the royal family, Condorcet, Talleyrand, and the institutions of the Revolution.

As life in Paris became physically too dangerous, Rivarol finally left in 1792, remaining in Brussels until 1794, when he crossed over to England. He was welcomed by Pitt and Burke but disliked the social life and the weather, being uncomplimentary about the physical attractions of the women and the conversation of the men. In France he had married Louise Mather-Flint, daughter of an English teacher of grammar, but abandoned her as soon as she had borne him their son Raphael, whom he summoned to join him in exile. She wrote a brief memoir of him which was published the year after his death. Rivarol also remained close to the sister who had joined him in Paris, and to his brother Claude-François, born in 1762, who was also a writer and lived on to 1848.

Rivarol took with him from France a woman who lived with him until his death. We know only that she was called Manette. In 1795 he finally joined the refugee French colony in Hamburg, where his great dictionary was commissioned. It was to trace the development of the human mind through the development of language. Whole sections of what it might have contained have come down to us through the records of contemporaries with whom he discussed the work, but we do not know what he would finally have incorporated into his work. In spite of the support of the community there, Rivarol disliked Hamburg and moved to Berlin in 1800, hoping soon to be able to return to France. He died of pneumonia in Berlin on 11 April 1801.

WORKS

Rivarol's positive thought and political attitudes evolved and, except for the religious and moral ideas expressed in the *Lettres à Necker* of 1788 and the 1797 project for the history of the development of the human mind in the planned *Dictionnaire*, were never given systematic expression. Most of what he wrote was ephemeral, a journalistic reaction to the events, rumours, and designs of the moment, and an often anonymous if biting comment on current affairs. He is therefore known chiefly as the bitter, often ill-natured epigrammatist of the *Mercure de France*, the *Journal Politique National* and the *Actes des Apôtres*, and mostly from selections of his writings, although recently interest has been shown in the works of political theory. It is possible that his brilliant reputation as a conversationalist, recorded by Chênedollé, for whom Rivarol was "le dieu de la conversation à cette fin du siècle où la conversation était le suprême plaisir et la suprême gloire (the god of conversation at that end of a century in which conversation was the supreme pleasure and the supreme glory)," may have eclipsed the undeveloped but serious reflections on political theory, the nature of language, and the moral evolution of the human race.

That Rivarol's observations about contemporary writers, events, politicians, and institutions were venomous and brilliant should also not disguise the fact that his nose for the spurious and the pretentious was very sharp, although by no means infallible. Vicious as his comments often were, they were also sometimes based on judgements which were perceptively right. It is by them much more than by the inchoate linguistic and political philosophies which may have more lasting importance that Rivarol is at any rate still best known.

The more theoretical works do not not offer much more than starting points in their fields. The reflections about translation to which the introduction and notes to the *Inferno* gave rise are no more than intelligent and sensitive remarks about linguistic usages. About the criticism of French orthography contained in the Berlin *Discours* much the same must be said. It is a philological commonplace that written language changes according to a logic different from that affecting the development of speech, and that there is always room to make orthography better reflect the spoken tongue. When Rivarol talks in 1784 of the tyranny of etymology over orthography in French, but not in Italian, he no doubt offers us the fruit of his personal reflections, but it had all been said often enough before.

The two 1788 *Lettres à M. Necker*, "sur l'importance des opinions religieuses" and "sur la morale" reply to Necker's own 1787 *Sur l'importance des idées religieuses* advocating a liberal Protestant morality, derived from Puritanism but now vaguely deist. Rivarol's reaction shows a religious attitude that is agnostic and cynical, a starting position no doubt important for any understanding of the speed and direction of the development of Rivarol's opinions, but not otherwise of real interest. The generalizations are seldom original or pithily expressed, and are too often merely half-truths lacking either sharpness or profundity of observation. Rivarol none the less demands from Necker a greater sharpness of vision:

> Pascal vous eût rejeté bien loin avec vos preuves tirées du spectacle de la nature, lui pour qui Dieu était moins probable que Jésus-Christ, et qui concevait mieux qu'on pût être athée que déiste

> (Pascal would have rejected you in no uncertain manner, with your proofs drawn from the spectacle of nature, he for whom God was less probable than Jesus Christ, and to whom atheism was more readily conceivable than deism).

More impressive is the excellence of some of the journalism of about the same date. Of Mercier's 1781 *Tableau de Paris* Rivarol could write

> Ouvrage pensé dans la rue et écrit sur la borne; l'auteur a peint la cave et le grenier en sautant le salon

> (A work thought out in the street, and written on the milestone; the author has painted the cellar and the attic, but left out the living room).

It is one of his better remarks, but it scarcely rises above the level of good table talk. One of Rivarol's more frequently recurring targets was Mirabeau, and his assassinations of Mirabeau's character and prose style are indeed often effected with skill and economy. The dissecting scalpel can be pitilessly accurate. Rivarol's foresight, too, has been praised, as in his famous vision in 1800 of the day when Bonaparte would proclaim himself king.

His best writing, however, is surely the intensely vivid reporting for the *Journal Politique National* of the minute-by-minute events of the Revolution, in which his moral passion explodes under the severe constraints imposed on it by the need for artistic presentation, and forces Rivarol into blistering irony. The account of the storming by the crowd of the château at Versailles on 6 October 1789 is a glitteringly brilliant, meticulously precise piece of reporting, whipped along by its moral ferocity. The court, we are told, was far from sharing the confidence of La Fayette, "a general marching with the intention of doing everything his army would command him."

Sur les six heures, les différents groupes de brigands, de poissardes et d'ouvriers se réunirent, et après quelques mouvements leur foule se porta rapidement vers l'hôtel des gardes du corps en criant: 'Tue les gardes du corps, point de quartier.' L'hôtel fut forcé en un moment. Les gardes, qui étaient en petit nombre, cherchèrent à s'échapper: on les poursuivit de tous côtés avec une rage inexprimable; on en tua quelques-uns; d'autres furent horriblement maltraités et s'enfuirent vers le château, où ils tombèrent entre les mains de la milice de Versailles et de celle de Paris; quinze furent pris et conduits vers la grille, où on les retint, en attendant qu'on eût avisé au genre de leur supplice. Presque en même temps arriva le gros des brigands, hommes et femmes, qui avaient déjà pillé et dévasté l'hôtel; ils se jetèrent dans tous les cours du château....ils égorgèrent deux gardes du corps qui étaient en sentinelle, l'un près de la grille et l'autre sous la voûte. Leurs corps tout palpitants furent traînés sous les fenêtres du roi, où une espèce de monstre, armé d'une hache, portant une longue barbe, et un bonnet d'une hauteur extraordinaire, leur coupa la tête. Ce sont ces deux mêmes têtes, étalées d'abord dans Versailles, qui ont été portées sur des piques, devant le carrosse du roi, et promenées, le même jour et le lendemain, dans les rues de Paris

(At about six o'clock the different groups of brigands, fish-wives and workmen assembled, and after some shifting to and fro the crowd moved swiftly on the barracks of the body-guard, shouting, 'Kill the body-guards: have no mercy.' The barracks was taken in a moment. The guards, few in number, tried to escape: they were pursued on all sides with unspeakable fury; some were killed; others were horribly ill-treated and fled towards the château, where they fell into the hands of the Versailles militia and the militia of Paris; fifteen were taken and led to the gates, where they were kept while discussions were held about how they should be killed. At about the same time the mass of brigands, men and women, arrived, who had already pillaged and sacked the barracks; they rushed into all the courtyards of the château....they massacred two body-guards who were on sentry duty, one by the gates and the other under the archway. Their bodies, still quivering, were dragged underneath the king's windows, where some sort of monster, armed with an axe, wearing a long beard, with a cap of extraordinary height, cut off their heads. It was those same two heads, paraded at first in Versailles, which were carried on pikes in front of the king's carriage and taken that day and the next round the streets of Paris).

PUBLICATIONS

Oeuvres complètes, 5 vols., 1808

Polemical and satirical works

Le Chou et le navet, à M. l'abbé D [elille] sur son poèm des "Jardins", 1782
*Lettre à M. le Président de * * * sur le globe aérostatique, sur les têtes parlantes et sur l'état présent de l'opinion publique à Paris*, 1783

De l'universalité de la langue française, 1784
Les Chartreux, poème, 1784
L'Emprunteur, comédie en un acte, en vers, 1785
L'Enfer, poème du Dante, 2 vols., 1785
Isman; ou, Le Fatalisme, 2 vols., 1785
Première lettre à M. Necker, sur l'importance des opinions religieuses, 1788
Seconde lettre à M. Necker, sur la morale, 1788
Le Petit Almanach de nos grands hommes, 1788; "pour l'année, 1790," 1790
Les Crimes de Paris en 1789, poème, 1789
De la philosophie, 1790
Petit Dictionnaire des grands hommes de la Révolution, 1790
Une lettre à la noblesse française, 1792
Discours préliminaire du nouveau Dictionnaire de la langue française, 1797
Tableau historique et politique, 1797

Biographical and critical studies

Le Breton, André, *Rivarol, sa vie, ses idées, son talent*, 1895
Latzarus, L., *La Vie paresseuse de Rivarol*, 1926
Debidour, Victor-Henri, Introduction to *Rivarol, Ecrits politiques et littéraires*, 1956
Simon, Pierre-Henri, Introduction to *Rivarol, Maximes, pensées et paradoxes*, 1962

RONSARD, Pierre de, 1524–1585.

Poet.

LIFE

Ronsard spelt his name with a final "d" only from 1550. The family may have come from the Danube basin, and may originally have spelt their name Rosshart. Ronsard's father, Louis de Ronsart, came from the minor nobility employed by the Comtes de Vendôme as factors and wardens of the Forêt de Gastine to the north of Tours, on the plateau between the Loir and the Loire. The family had been established in the Loire valley at least since the early 14th and perhaps even since the 11th century. Ronsard's grandfather, after being in the employ of Louis XI, had died in 1493, lord of La Possonnière, the manor house where Ronsard was born during the night of 10–11 September 1524. He had fought in the Italian wars from their beginning in 1494 with the Duc d'Orléans, who became Louis XII in 1498, and later with François I, crossing the Alps 22 times in 20 years. On 2 February 1514 his eldest son, Ronsard's father, had married the more highly connected Jeanne de Chaudrier, who was to bear him a girl and four, possibly five, boys, of whom Ronsard was the youngest. As governor of the king's children, in 1526 Ronsard's father had to deliver them to Spain into the captivity of Charles V as hostages in exchange for their father. Ronsard's mother had been orphaned young. She had attempted to elope, desisted when Louis XII objected to the marriage, married Guy des Roches, and been widowed.

Ronsard's father stayed in Spain from March 1526 to June 1530, was duly rewarded by a position in the royal household, made several journeys to Italy, and had his manor refurbished by Italian workmen in the Italian style, probably with the king's aid. He wrote verse, read the classics, and protected the "rhétoriqueur" Jean Bouchet, with whom he discussed the technicalities of versification. Ronsard himself was brought up in an atmosphere impregnated with Italian renaissance values. The family was Catholic, pious, patriotic, and proud of the origins which would allow Ronsard to describe himself as "Gentilhomme vendômois" on his title pages. After being tutored at home, at the age of just nine he was sent to the Collège de Navarre in Paris, where, perhaps because he appeared better fitted to become a courtier than a scholar, he spent only six months. He appears to have caused concern to his father by taking early to writing verse. It was probably in 1535 that he inherited a considerable library from a clerical uncle, probably the one who was curé of a nearby parish, Bessé-sur-Braye.

From 1536, when he was 12, Ronsard became a page to the king's children for four years. On 10 August 1536, a few days after Ronsard's arrival, the dauphin died. His probably innocent valet, Montecuculli, was executed for poisoning him, and Ronsard passed into the service of the king's third son, the 14-year-old Charles, Duc d'Orléans. He had been briefly in Lyons with the court, had stayed in several of the Loire châteaux, and was affected to the service of Charles's sister Madeleine when the frail 16-year-old was married to James V of Scotland by Cardinal Jean du Bellay on 1 January 1537. Ronsard accompanied her to Scotland, where she was to die on 7 July. He had set out from Le Havre on 11 May, arriving at Leith on the 19th. He was still at St Andrews when, on 11 June 1538, James V married the Princesse de Guise, Marie de Lorraine, the future mother of Mary Queen of Scots. He returned to France in August 1538, but then set out from Saint-Germain on 24 December 1538 to accompany Claude d'Humières, Seigneur de Lassigny, on a mission to the Low Countries and back to Scotland, where he landed at Queensferry on 22 January 1539. He left again for France on 24 March, having been with Lassigny in London. On his return to the service of Orléans in April, Ronsard was made a "gentleman of the mews" under François de Kernvenoy, Seigneur de Carnavalet, who was just four years his senior.

The royal mews, still just outside Paris in what is now the Place des Vosges and was then soon to be amalgamated into the city as the famous and fashionable Place Royale, was a finishing school for ex-pages and provided a training for future soldiers, courtiers, and diplomats, specializing naturally in horsemanship, but also in other physical exercises and courtly pursuits. It was here that Claudio Duchi, brother of the mistress of the future Henri II and uncle of his child, inspired Ronsard to read Horace and Virgil. Then in 1540, no doubt at his father's intervention, Ronsard was sent as secretary to Lazare de Baïf, a cousin of his mother, on a diplomatic mission to Hagenau, ostensibly to conduct religious discussions. The journey lasted from 16 May to 14 August and enabled Ronsard to meet some of the principal German humanists, including Johannes Sturm, Martin Bucer, Johannes Oporin, Nikolaus Gerbel, and Johann Baptist Sleidan. It was, however, probably with Baïf in Alsace that Ronsard contracted the illness which made him arthritic and partially deaf for life, barring him from a military career. On his return from Hagenau he had to spend three or four years at La Possonnière recovering, probably until 1543. It was during this period that Ronsard started to write Latin verse and to imitate ("contrefaire") what he called Horace's "naive douceur (naive sweetness)," although probably not yet in French.

With so many obvious careers now closed to him, Ronsard decided to follow his brother Charles, now richly beneficed, into orders, and on 6 March 1543 received the tonsure, a gesture which had little effect other than to enable him to accept benefices, and which also removed him from civil jurisdiction. The matter had been arranged at the funeral of Guillaume du Bellay on 5 March at Le Mans, Ronsard's diocese, where the bishop was René du Bellay, the brother of the dead man and of the cardinal. Ronsard's mother was a cousin of the du Bellays as well as the Baïfs, and his father had served as a pallbearer. Rabelais, who had been in du Bellay's household at Turin, attended the funeral, and it must have been on that occasion, probably on the day afterwards at the Château de Touvoie, where the bishop resided, that Ronsard met Jacques Peletier du Mans, the bishop's secretary, who was seven years his senior. The two were to become firm friends. In 1541 Peletier du Mans had published a translation of Horace's *Ars poetica*. It was reprinted in 1545 and already in its preface advocated the renewal of French vernacular poetry imitated from foreign and classical sources. In 1555 he was to publish an *Art poétique* of his own, drawing on the views of Ronsard and his companions which he had earlier helped to inspire. On 6 November 1543 he became principal of the Collège de Bayeux, a position which did not suit him and which he was to resign on 7 March 1548.

Ronsard's father died suddenly in Paris on 6 June 1544. Most of the inheritance went to his elder brother, and now that an obstacle had presumably been removed, Ronsard went to Paris. He lived not far from the royal mews on the Right Bank, but called often on Lazare de Baïf. Baïf's 12-year-old son, Antoine, whose education had been begun by Jacques Toussaint, was being taught Greek by a resident tutor, the 36-year-old Jean Dorat, whose lessons Ronsard was invited to share. Early in 1545 Ronsard's mother died. In April of that year, at a ball in Blois, he met and must have been impressed by the 14-year-old Cassandre Salviati, daughter of a Florentine banker. She was to marry Jean de Peigné, Seigneur du Pré, in November 1546, but she it was whom Ronsard idealized in his first love poetry, *Les Amours* of 1552, containing four-part settings of some of the sonnets, and the augmented *Les Amours* of 1553, which suppressed the supplementary musical scores while adding a learned commentary by the humanist Marc-Antoine Muret. When Lazare de Baïf died in 1547, probably in the autumn, Dorat became principal of the Collège de Coqueret, taking with him Antoine de Baïf and Ronsard, soon to be joined by François de Carnavalet from the mews, Henri de Mesme, Nicolas Denisot, Lancelot de Carles, and Joachim du Bellay (see: Pléiade). That year Ronsard published his first poem in Peletier du Mans's *Oeuvres poëtiques* on the beauties to be desired in a mistress. It was followed by a poem by Peletier du Mans identical in form and length on the qualities required in a lover.

It is not possible to doubt the enthusiasm with which Ronsard put himself back to school at 20, even if his companion was only 12. In spite of his acquaintanceship with Horace and Virgil, his reading had centred on the medieval French romances, Lemaire des Belges, and Marot, for whom he was never quite to lose his respect, but he knew no Greek. Dorat was a gifted Latinist with wide reading also in Greek, but in spite of a certain virtuoso brilliance he was a textual scholar rather than a Latin stylist, and the desire among his pupils to imitate in French the poets of antiquity derived rather from Peletier du Mans, who appears to have met du Bellay in 1546, a year before Ronsard's famous, if possibly apocryphal, chance meeting with him in a hostelry near Poitiers. Claude Binet, Ronsard's first biographer, author of the 1586 *Discours de la vie de Pierre de Ronsard*, and Jacques Velliard, author of a funeral "laudatio" of the same date, both tell us the famous story of the shared candle, with Ronsard, having studied until two a.m., waking Baïf, who started work when Ronsard went to sleep.

In June 1548 Thomas Sébillet, a lawyer, anonymously published the *Art poetique françois*, partly codifying a usage associated largely with Marot, which Ronsard and his companions wished to discard, and partly stealing some of their thunder in proclaiming the independence of poetry from rhetoric as an elevated and autonomous art form. The reaction was a manifesto, *La Deffence et illustration de la langue françoyse*, no doubt written by du Bellay, but corporate in inspiration. The work was initialled rather than signed, but the authorship was still clear. Then in January 1550 Ronsard published his four books of *Odes*, 94 in all, in one octavo volume, together with 13 further odes in the 1550 *Bocage*. A further 12 odes, some published independently, were collected to make a fifth book together with the account of the Arcueil picnic of 1549 called "Les Bacchanales," to follow the 1552 *Amours*. It is in "Les Bacchanales" that Ronsard refers for the first time to his student colleagues as "la brigade," although not all of them belonged to the inner group of poets later to crystallize into the varying lists of seven names known as the "Pléiade."

To a new edition of Sebillet in 1551 Barthélemy Aneau added a virulent pamphlet, the *Quintil Horatian*, against the *Deffence*, strongly attacking du Bellay, but also hitting out at the obscurity of Ronsard's Pindaric odes. Ronsard had presented the volume with a prefatory Greek distich by Dorat containing an elegant anagram of the Greek for Pierre Ronsard, making him into the new Terpander, appropriately enough in view of the perhaps merely programmatic importance which Ronsard, his companions, and above all Peletier attached to music. Πέτρος ρωνσαρδος became Σως ὁ Τέρπανδρος. There were encomiastic preliminary pieces, and even a brief commentary by "I.M.P.," perhaps Jean Martin Parisian, known for his translations from Italian, to explain a dozen of the most difficult passages in the first book, more than enough to make clear the volume's polemically innovative intentions.

Ronsard was obtrusively conscious of his own originality in the preface, wrongly arrogating to himself the invention of the "ode," whether what was meant was the word, already used by Lemaire, Bouchet, Aneau, Martin, and Rabelais, or its content. Defined in any sense other than the imitation of Horace in both serious and frivolous moods, the lyrical ode was already well known in French. Du Bellay, too, was writing odes, and in spite of all he actually owed to his father's friends, Ronsard was contemptuous of "nos rimeurs, et principalement des courtizans, qui n'admirent qu'un petit sonnet petrarquizé, ou quelque mignardise d'amour (our rhymers, especially the court versifiers who admire only a trifling Petrarchized sonnet or some sentimental triviality on love)." He continued in the same vein, excoriating the "poetasters," boasting of his dependence on Pindar and "tous

les poëtes Grecs et Latins," and above all exalting the poet's moral function. Ronsard, at 25, wrote of his predecessors: "Pour telle vermine de gens ignorantement envieuse ce petit labeur n'est publié, mais pour les gentils espris, ardans de la vertu, et dedaignans mordre comme les mâtins la pierre qu'ils ne peuvent digerer (This little labour is not published for such ignorantly envious vermin, but for noble minds, burning with virtue, and disdaining to bite like mastiffs on the stone they can't digest)."

Ronsard was quickly attacked, notably by Bèze for paganism and for his Italian inspiration. The existence of a number of other hostile comments is attested, although the texts have perished. Mellin de Saint-Gelais, however, appears to have read some passages in a contemptuous tone before the king. The king's youngest sister, Marguerite de France, Duchesse de Berry, a patron of Joachim du Bellay, defended Ronsard, as apparently did her chancellor, Michel de l'Hôpital. Later in 1550 Ronsard was to write an ode to "Madame Marguerite" and one to Michel de l'Hôpital, perhaps the most famous as well as the last of the Pindaric odes, published only in 1552.

In addition to the five books of *Odes*, the 1550 *Bocage*, and *Les Amours* with their augmentation of 1553, *La Continuation des Amours* of 1555, and *La Nouvelle Continuation des Amours* of 1556, Ronsard published early in 1549 an *Epithalame*, later taken into the fourth book of *Odes*, for the marriage of Antoine de Bourbon and Jeanne de Navarre, which had taken place on 20 October 1548; a poem of 132 decasyllabic lines to celebrate the solemn entry into Paris of Henri II on Sunday 16 June 1549; and in November the *Hymne de France*, celebrating a French military victory, later, like the previous piece, to be withdrawn from the collections, as was the *Ode de la paix*, celebrating peace between France and England in 1550. Ronsard had also supplied a group of poems for the second edition (1551) of the collaborative *Tombeau de Marguerite de Valois* composed in honour of Marguerite de Navarre, the king's aunt, who had died in 1549, and in 1553 published the *Livret de Folastries* anonymously, no doubt partly on account of the obscenity of some of the poems, but also perhaps because he wanted to keep his more solemn poetry, with its highborn dedicatees, visibly separate from his frivolities. The 1554 *Bocage*, keeping only six odes from the 1550 collection, but adding about 50 other more light-hearted pieces, and *Les Meslanges* of 1554 both contain pieces predominantly dedicated to friends rather than to aristocrats and dignitaries.

In 1553 Ronsard received his first benefice, Marolles-en-Brie, to be exchanged the following year for that of Challes-au-Maine, in the gift of Jean du Bellay, and followed in 1555 by that of Evaillé-au-Maine. To the two already held were to be added Warluis-en-Beauvais (1557), Champfleur-au-Maine (1557/8), and in 1560 the archdeaconry of Château-du-Loir and canonry of Saint-Julien du Mans. When Saint-Gelais died in 1558 Ronsard replaced him as chaplain to Henri II. The post was worth 1,200 livres tournois a year and Ronsard, appointed in 1559, later kept it under Charles IX. Money was to be a constant worry for him, and it was only on the intervention of Marguerite de France with her nephew, the son of Henri II, from 1560 Charles IX, that Ronsard received the abbacy of Bellozane in 1564. He resigned it the following year, when his brother ceded to him the priory of Saint-Cosme-lez-Tours, which he was to keep until his death. He was to receive half a dozen more benefices and finally to achieve relative financial ease, mostly thanks to the patronage of Charles IX once the king (born in 1550) had reached his majority.

From certainly no later than the carnival of 1553, a close companionship had sprung up between Ronsard's group at the Collège de Coqueret and another group at the Collège de Boncourt which was trying to do for the restoration of antique drama something analogous to what Ronsard's "brigade" had done for lyric poetry. Marc-Antoine de Muret, author of a Latin tragedy, *Julius Caesar*, in which the 12-year-old Montaigne had taken the lead in 1545, when Muret was teaching in Bordeaux at the Collège de Guyenne, was the commentator of the May 1553 edition of *Les Amours*. He taught at Boncourt from 1551 to 1553, when he was joined by another author of neo-Latin tragedies once played at the Collège de Guyenne, the Scottish humanist and reformer George Buchanan. Among his pupils were Rémy Belleau, Jean Bastier de la Péruse, and Etienne Jodelle, all of whom were to become closely associated with Ronsard and the Coqueret group. It was at Boncourt, probably in the courtyard, that Jodelle's *Cléopâtre captive* was given in February 1553, with Belleau and La Péruse in the cast, probably after a performance before Henri II at the Hôtel de Reims, which belonged to Charles de Guise, the cardinal of Lorraine. The Boncourt performance gave rise to the celebrated excursion to Arcueil, probably the next day, at which a goat was caught, decorated with ivy, and offered to Jodelle in a mock Greek ceremony. Both Baïf and Ronsard wrote *Dithyrambes*, or hymns to Bacchus, to celebrate the occasion. Ronsard's poem, mentioning by name some of those present, was published in the anonymous *Livret de Folastries* of April 1553. In the bitterness of the Wars of Religion, Ronsard and his companion were to be accused of having sacrificed the goat to Bacchus, though in fact it was turned loose.

On 3 May 1554 Ronsard received the eglantine prize of the Jeux Floraux at Toulouse, an institution attacked in the *Deffence* five years earlier. At Bourgueil on 20 April 1555 he met the Marie from Anjou who was the subject of *La Continuation des Amours* of August of that year, with an inspiration altogether different from the stylized Petrarchan poetry of the earlier Cassandre cycle. In 1555 and 1556 Ronsard, visibly seeking the protection of the highest families in France, published, alongside the two new collections of *Amours*, the first and second books of *Hymnes*, elevated, high-style poetry developing the notion of the poet as seer, prophet, priest, and intermediary between man and the realm of angels, spirits, and God himself. The inspiration for poems of this sort was largely to be derived from the neo-Latin Marullus. The first book was dedicated to Odet de Coligny, the cardinal of Chastillon, whose family's patronage, like that of the Guise family, the poems show Ronsard to have been trying to attract. The second book was dedicated to Marguerite de France, the most promising of Ronsard's patrons. From 1554 to 1556 Ronsard was therefore simultaneously combining poetry of high seriousness with the love poetry he affected to despise and the simple frivolities he preferred to publish under at least ostensible anonymity. He was incidentally flattering the very great, like both the Chastillon brothers and the Guise brothers, in the single hymn the "Hymne de Pollux et de Castor."

In 1554 Ronsard had started on the great epic which would have crowned his earlier achievements, given French the poem which a great literary language required, and made Ronsard the new Homer. It was to concern the history and the lineage of the kings of France. In the end it took Ronsard 22 years from the work's conception to the publication, in 1572, of just four of the originally projected 24 cantos. The obsession with Francus is already clear in the 1549 "Hymne de France," and in April 1550

the "Ode de la paix" sketched out the epic's grand outline. There are several contemporary references to Ronsard's grand design in the early 1550s, and it seems certain that the long-awaited royal command to produce the epic was given by Henri II in 1554, when Pierre Lescot, the Louvre's architect, proposed to make an allusion to it in his stone façade. There are later plans for the poem, and published appeals to the royal purse, but Henri II appears not to have been seriously interested. Du Bellay records with obvious disappointment Ronsard's apparent abandonment of the project in 1556. He did not take it up again until the intervention of Henri II's sister, Marguerite de France, had succeeded in drawing tangible patronage from the young Charles IX in 1563 or 1564. Ronsard's enthusiasm was however again inflamed by the assignment to him of the priory of Croixval on 22 March 1566. No doubt to stimulate public interest, Lambin printed 120 lines of Ronsard's poem in the second edition of his *Horace* of 1567.

Henri II, who was married to Catherine de' Medici, died after a jousting accident in 1559, and was succeeded by his sickly son, François II, born in 1544 and married to Mary Queen of Scots, but who died a year later, in 1560. During his brief reign power was taken by Mary Stuart's uncles, the Duc and Cardinal de Guise. François II was succeeded by his younger brother, Charles IX, who had his 10th birthday in the year of his accession. The regency was held by his mother, Catherine de' Medici. In March 1560, however, the "conjuration d'Amboise" occurred, in which a group of Huguenots tried to take from the Guises the power which they had acquired under the young François II. The fierce repression which followed the failed conspiracy, when the chief instigators were left hanging from the balconies at Amboise, led directly to the religious wars, which started in 1562.

The religious discussions and theological debate led by Bèze on the Protestant side and the cardinal of Lorraine for the Catholics known as the Colloque de Poissy had failed in August 1561, and on Sunday 1 March 1562 a band of men under the Duc de Guise happened to hear Protestant hymns being sung in a barn at Wassy. They attacked the worshippers, killed 650, and wounded a further 200. The incident led directly to the first war, during which the Duc de Guise was assassinated while the Catholics were besieging Orléans and which ended with the peace of Amboise in March 1563. The series of wars, which included encounters between roving guerilla bands and disorganized military encounters as well as more formal engagements, quickly became France's last major feudal clash between its great families, ending with the abjuration of Protestantism by Henri de Navarre in 1594, although what was virtually a war against Spain continued until the Edict of Nantes of 13 April 1598, which gave a measure of toleration to the Huguenots.

These political events had a considerable impact on Ronsard, who became disconsolate at the lack of patronage towards the end of Henri II's reign, retired largely to La Possonnière, and then wrote a long series of political poems in 1558–59 when the wars with the empire were coming to their end, culminating in the treaty of Cateau-Cambrésis in April 1559. He had scarcely had time to assimilate the role of "Conseiller et aumônier ordinaire du Roi" early in 1559, taken over from Saint-Gelais, who had died and with whom he had long been reconciled, when Henri II was fatally wounded at the joust on 28 June. Ronsard had already had to change his role, however, from the rich and abundant restorer of glory to French verse to that of the propagandist spokesman for an unpalatable royal policy, for whose public relations he had partly to assume responsibility at a moment when the unpopular terms of the treaty of Cateau-Cambrésis became known in France. Worse, Ronsard had to assume responsibility for propaganda for a royal policy the king could not yet himself openly acknowledge.

The Connétable Anne de Montmorency and Gaspard de Coligny had both been captured by the Spaniards at Saint-Quentin in 1557, but François, Duc de Guise, had wrested Calais from the English on 8 January 1558 and taken the apparently impregnable Thionville on 22 June. That made Guise a threat to Henri II, who urgently needed an end to the war with Spain and the return of Montmorency. He therefore connived with Montmorency, who was already intriguing with the Spaniards for his own release in August 1558. If the attitude of Ronsard's *Exhortation pour la paix* of September/October 1558 is in direct contradiction with the patriotic stance of the *Exhortation au camp du Roy* of late August, when it looked as if there would be a pitched battle on the River Authie between the forces of Henri II and those of Philip II, it is because it had to be understood to be a declaration of a royal policy which Henri II could not yet admit to desiring to adopt, although he desperately needed peace with Spain from late August 1568. Then Ronsard found himself having to defend the terms of the peace, which included an enormous ransom paid for Montmorency, in the *Chant de liesse au Roy* and *La Paix, au Roy*, both of early 1559. Finally, Ronsard found himself obliged to defend the unpopular part of the settlement by which Philibert, Duc de Savoie, married the king's sister, Marguerite de France. He had become the voice of royal policy, and his poetic style had to change as a result.

Then, in the power struggle under François II, France's two or three remaining feudal dynasties drifted into the hostility with one another which was certainly to intensify and prolong the religious wars. Ronsard's most enthusiastic patrons, Charles de Lorraine and Odet de Coligny, a Chastillon, belonged to opposing camps. A political situation which threatened Ronsard came to reinforce a personal disillusion, and his effort was primarily directed to adjusting the balance of flattery in his verse. The 1559 pamphlet *La Paix* contained a poem to Henri II, a poem celebrating the return of Montmorency, and a poem for a tournament organized by François de Guise. The poems for the Guise family had to counterbalance poems extolling a royal policy opposed to that of the house of Lorraine.

Within a year or two Ronsard was also going to have to take sides in the religious wars. His personal friendship with the young king cannot have counted for much before the late 1560s, but any courting of Coligny, now turned Calvinist, would have brought with it the loss of Ronsard's position at court. In fact Ronsard's initial personal sympathy with the moderate policy of Marguerite de France and Michel de l'Hôpital allowed him to commit himself in the cycle of poems concerning the religious wars much more than had been possible in the peace cycle relating to Cateau-Cambrésis. His tone became harsher after Ronsard himself apparently got involved in a skirmish with marauding Protestant bands during 1562, and a hardening attitude can certainly be discerned in the *Continuation du Discours*, but real bitterness crept in only when he felt the need to reply in the anonymous 1563 *Remonstrance au peuple de France* and in the 1563 *Responce aux injures et calomnies de je ne sçay quels predicans et ministres de Geneve* to the pamphlets unleashed by his 1562 *Discours des miseres de ce temps* and *Continuation du Discours*. Ronsard's polemic was eventually halted by order of the court.

Apart from the semi-political official poetry in the plaquettes, Ronsard had written little during his period of dejection from 1557 to the death of François II. He had dedicated two further pieces to the Cardinal de Lorraine in 1558–59, and the *Chant pastoral* was published in 1559 to celebrate the wedding of Charles de Guise, Duc de Lorraine, to Claude de France, the second daughter of Henri II. Then the *Second Livre des meslanges* of 1559 had contained two poems to the Cardinal de Chastillon, nephew of Montmorency and brother of the Admiral de Coligny, the "Elegie" and the "Complainte contre Fortune," complaining of inadequate patronage. Apart from the royal Valois, there were now in France only three great dynastic families, the Guises of Lorraine, the Chastillons/Colignys, and the Bourbons/Condés of Navarre, from the first two of which Ronsard solicited patronage between 1555 and 1560. In 1560 he published the first collected edition of his works, four tiny sextodecimo volumes containing "Les Amours," "Les Odes," "Les Poëms," and "Les Hymnes." Only the third volume contains important new material, mostly elegies about the nature of poetry and poems announcing the polemical themes of the *Discours*, notably the "Elegie à Loïs des Masures" and the *Elegie de P. de Ronsard Vandomois sur les troubles d'Amboise, 1560*, as the "Elegie à Guillaume des Autelz" was called when published separately in 1562.

In 1563 and 1564 Ronsard published the *Recueil des nouvelles poësies*, a series of four plaquettes of which the first, probably published in 1563, contains some of his most elaborate and ornate mythological conceptions and the hymns to the four seasons. The 1564 edition starts with a long prose "épître" on the religious issue and includes with the hymns and mythological pieces several poems on the departure from France of the widowed Mary Queen of Scots, some new love poetry, and a begging poem, "Complainte à la Royne mere du Roy." Early in 1564 Catherine de Medici had tried to reconcile the warring parties in France at a series of court entertainments and festivities. Ronsard's poems for these occasions were published in the *Elegies, mascarades et bergerie* of July 1565, dedicated to Elizabeth of England. That year Ronsard also published a verse epistle to Catherine de Medici, *Les Nues ou nouvelles*, on political rumours which had been circulating in Paris during her absence with Charles IX on his royal progress through the kingdom, and an anonymous *Abbregé de l'art poëtique françois*. In 1567 a six-volume quarto edition of Ronsard's collected works appeared, obviously intended for the grander libraries. The third volume of that edition, containing *Les Poèmes*, is continued into the 1569 volumes the *Sixiesme Livre des poemes* and *Septiesme Livre des poemes*.

By this date Ronsard had been living in semi-retirement for some years, since being ill in Paris in 1566. He had installed himself at Saint-Cosme, just west of Tours, in March 1565, had been ordered to join the king at Bordeaux in April, but was in Paris when the humanist Adrien Turnèbe died there in June. At Saint-Cosme from 20 to 30 November he received Charles IX and his mother, who stayed a few hundred yards away at Plessis-lez-Tours. He had a house in Paris where he spent most of 1567, and on 28 January he attended Baïf's comedy, *Brave*, at the Hôtel de Guise in the presence of the king and Catherine de Medici. He acted on 15 September 1567 with the other royal lecteurs, Belleau and Baïf, as assessor for the vacancy for a royal lecturer in Greek, to which Dorat's son-in-law, Nicolas Goulu, was appointed, and then joined Charles IX at Monceaux, accompanying him back to Meaux and Paris in the face of a rumoured Huguenot plot against him. He also appears to have taken a serious interest in gardening at Saint-Cosme, where in 1565 he had installed his secretary, Amadis Jamyn, from whom he acquired the priory of Croixval on unknown terms in March 1566.

Ronsard spent most of 1568 at Saint-Cosme, where he was again ill, returning to Paris only in August 1570, after the peace of Saint-Germain had been signed on the 8th. During the second religious war, from 1567 to 1568, Montmorency was assassinated. The peace of Longjumeau was signed in March 1568, but war broke out again, and on 13 March 1569 the 18-year-old duc d'Anjou, helped by the Maréchal de Tavannes, won the battle of Jarnac against the Protestants, whose chief, Condé, was assassinated. Ronsard wrote a number of poems celebrating Anjou's victories, and at about this time some more love poetry, the "Astrée" cycle, and, perhaps not much later, the "Hélène" cycle in honour of Hélène de Surgères, a lady-in-waiting to Catherine de Medici whose name made her the suitable object of a poetic courtship by France's Homer. Both cycles were to be published only in the fifth collected edition of 1578. The third and fourth collected editions of 1571 and 1572–73 made few changes to the earlier collections.

On 24 August 1572 the St Bartholomew's Day Massacre took place in Paris. Coligny was murdered, and Henri de Béarn, son of Antoine de Bourbon and Jeanne d'Albret, who had become king of Navarre in June, on the death of his mother, had to abjure Protestantism. He was kept virtually in court captivity in Paris. It was in September 1572 that Ronsard published the first four books of *La Franciade*, which he was to continue to revise and for which he was to write a substantial new preface, first published in the posthumous collected edition of 1587. On 30 May 1574 Charles IX died, and Ronsard increasingly withdrew to his country livings, publishing however a *Tombeau* for Charles IX (1574) and a *Discours au Roi* (1575) for his successor, Henri III, duc d'Anjou, who had been the victor at Jarnac and had just returned from the throne of Poland, escaping from that country by night.

Henri spent three months in Austria and Italy before arriving on 6 September 1574 at Lyons, where Catherine de Medici, his mother, and the court were waiting to greet him. Ronsard asked Marguerite de Valois, the queen of Navarre, to present to him his *Discours*. Receiving no response, Ronsard then sent a second poem, *Les Estrennes*, for the following 1 January. He also published a *Tombeau* for the Duchesse de Savoie, his old patron, and wrote the final "Marie" poems, this time to mourn Marie de Clèves, Princesse de Condé, whose death had deeply grieved Henri III. It was in 1574, the year of his accession, that Henri founded the Académie du Palais at the Louvre in place of the old Académie de Poësie et de Musique, founded by Baïf under Charles IX. The new institution was to play an important part in the literary culture of his reign.

In the summer of 1575 Ronsard left Paris for Croixval, where he spent the winter. For all of 1576 he was at Saint-Cosme. Journeys to Paris were rare and brief, but Ronsard still published a number of court pieces and, in 1575, *Les Estoilles*, originally an ode, but later classified as a hymn. He also delivered discourses on the virtues at the Académie du Palais. Henri III continued to pay Ronsard a pension, and occasionally other sums, but he did not invite him to complete *La Franciade*. He had furthermore brought to court with him Philippe Desportes, whose Italianate culture and Petrarchan poses appealed more to him. Ronsard's poems for Marie de Clèves and the "Hélène" cycle were written in some attempt to regain the poetic primacy he had enjoyed under Charles IX. The 1578 collected edition, seven sexto-decimo volumes, not only includes the late love poetry, but also suppresses 54 sonnets and about 30 other poems, and abbreviates some of the others.

When Ronsard went to Paris now, it was to stay with Jean Galland, the principal of Boncourt, a grand-nephew of the Pierre Galland who had been principal when Jodelle and Belleau were students there. He saw his edition through the press in 1578, but was exhausted and ill as a result. Early in 1579 he returned to Croixval, which was nearer than Saint-Cosme to his native Forêt de Gastine. A *Panegyrique de la renommee* of 1579 brought back the notion of divine inspiration which had disappeared from Ronsard's verse. Ronsard prepared with great care the splendid double-column folio edition of his works of January 1584, divided into seven parts, apparently for the first time making careful arrangements about payment. The wars forced him back to Paris from February to June 1585, suffering so severely from gout that he could scarcely kneel to make his Easter Communion.

He wrote one more hymn in Marullus's style and returned with Galland at his side to Croixval, leaving Paris for the last time on 13 June 1585. In July he went to Saint-Cosme, but returned to Croixval just over a week later. In September he resigned three of his benefices, including Croixval, in favour of Galland, who heard from Ronsard on 22 October that he feared he was dying but hoped that Galland could come to console him. He confessed, heard Mass, and received Communion but, feeling better, dismissed the lawyer he had sent for and had himself taken to his priory of Saint-Gilles, where Galland joined him on 30 October. They left for Croixval again on 2 November. Ronsard found relief in writing some devotional verse and composed his own epitaph.

Galland must have returned to his college, and early in December Ronsard had himself taken to Saint-Cosme, arriving only on Sunday the 22nd. On Christmas Day he confessed again, heard Mass in his room, and communicated. On Thursday 26 December he felt a little better and dictated two last sonnets. Galland arrived for an emotional leave-taking at about midday on Friday 27 December. Ronsard died about two a.m. on Saturday 28 December 1585.

WORKS

The chronological limitation in the view that "Ronsard holds an established position as the greatest French poet of any period prior to the 19th century" may today seem timid, although it would once have been stridently challenged, and even now is more easily asserted than explained. As early as 1550 Ronsard claimed to be "le premier auteur lirique Françoys ([chronologically] the first French lyric author)." Well before he died, he knew that he had failed to crown his career by creating the national French epic he had wanted *La Franciade* to be, and which he thought necessary before any language could claim truly literary status. His achievement has long been seen as outstanding in grouping together for the first time the principal poetic genres, including the lyric, the elegy, the epic, the enco-miastic ode, official propagandist poetry, polemical invective, the mythological poem, and the cosmological hymn, as autono-mous forms of literature independent of the rules of prose and no longer merely a "second rhetoric."

Ronsard is today acknowledged as the virtual creator of what we have subsequently come to see as the French poetic tradition. This is how he would at first himself have wished to be remem-bered. What, however, is principally claimed for him now is an achievement consisting of three things: breadth of subject matter, depth of concern with life's fundamental problems, and the strictly creative ability to explore the meaning of human experience mythopoeically, so that even through the stylized pose of a love sonnet, or the frozen freshness of a conventional song of praise, a vision or a meaning which is both penetrating and universal can be communicated.

More than that of most creative artists, Ronsard's achieve-ment was floated on an almost absurdly inflated sense of his own originality and an exaggerated notion of the importance of the task he had set himself. His poetry is difficult, because it draws on a classical learning, on 16th-century political and religious quarrels, events, personages, cultural developments, philosoph-ical speculations, personal invective, and a whole spectrum of renaissance world views with different intellectual scaffoldings, as well as on a whole series of conventions, to which few modern readers have immediate access. It requires, in this like the poetry of Lamartine, another great innovator, to be judged not according to its emotional impact, but with reference to its aesthetic achievement. It gives new meaning to the old struc-tures, antique myths, or contemporary royal entertainments used by a privileged, educated, and courtly renaissance elite to inves-tigate the range of attitudes and values which it seemed open to it to adopt.

On account of the diversity of its genres, poetic registers, and themes, and of the length of some of the major pieces, Ronsard's poetry is also notoriously difficult to anthologize. Since even the minor pieces need to be understood in the context of the total oeuvre, Ronsard's full achievement is still not widely appreci-ated. More dangerously, the short pieces which recurrently appear in the anthologies, because they are taken from the total context in which perhaps a dedication or the name of a woman has been changed, almost demand to be judged as if they were straightforwardly what today they seem to be, but were never intended as. Only in the polemical poems of the early 1560s was sincerity of emotion a relevant aesthetic criterion. To understand the power of Ronsard's imagination demands an appreciation of the mastery with which he transforms the feelings, ideas, and poetic structures from which he starts.

Ronsard's contempt for his predecessors—excepting in the 1550 "Au lecteur" only, and, as it later appears, only partially, Marot, Héroët, Scève, and Saint-Gelais—his aggressive invec-tive when defending himself against Huguenot attack, and the arrogance with which he set out to make himself the creator not only of a French poetic tradition, but of French as a literary lan-guage, naturally made him enemies. Ronsard was inspired by the learned, if not exactly poetic, Erasmian humanist inheritance of Dorat, and his own disregard for what he thought of as the "petits et menus fatras come elegies, epigrames et sonnetz (slight and trivial jumble of elegies, epigrams, and sonnets)," his unhappy transformation into the propagandist court poet of the plaquettes towards the end of the war with the empire, and the

quotable nature of his anti-Huguenot polemic did not serve his reputation well. From his illness in the mid-1560s, when his only enthusiastic royal protector, Charles IX, was still in his mid-teens, Ronsard lived in at least semi-retirement. After the intense poetic activity of the years 1550–65, apart from four cantos of La Franciade and the final two of the seven volumes of Poëmes, only the important but stylized love poetry for Marie de Clèves and Hélène de Surgères was still to come. The Italian-ate taste of Henri III's court had overtaken Ronsard, and he died a disappointed poet. His reputation had already dwindled.

After his death, and the decent memorial services at Boncourt on the morning (for the university) and the afternoon (for the court) of Monday 24 February 1586, it plummeted. Malherbe is well known to have criticized Ronsard's linguistic innovations, although we have very little from his own hand except three ver-tical lines through the first 11 lines of a sonnet and a horizontal line through the 13th in one of Ronsard's printed volumes in the 1560 Oeuvres, with a remark about the grammatical impropriety of "La faute n'est de moy (The fault is not mine)," preferring one of a number of alternative constructions to make a genitive. In the first canto of L'Art poétique, Boileau assumes as a matter of course that Ronsard was nothing but an arrogant and outdated pedant, and in refined 18th-century taste Ronsard's reputation still had nowhere to go but down.

The rehabilitation was virtually spontaneous, and in retro-spect predictable, although it can accurately be pinpointed to Sainte-Beuve's two-volume Tableau historique et critique de la poésie française et du théâtre français au XVIe siècle of 1828. Interest, often historical rather than aesthetic, had been reawak-ening since the publication in 1810 of an anthology entitled Poètes du second ordre, and it was inevitable that interest in Ronsard as a lyric poet should be revived by the young genera-tion of romantics during the second half of the third decade of the 19th century. Isolated exceptions to the usual strictures based on pedantry, irregularity, archaisms, and neologisms became less infrequent after Guizot's Vie des poètes français du siècle de Louis XIV of 1813, and in 1826 an anthology was pub-lished with Ronsard's name in the title, but the Académie's prize announced in the Journal des Savants of August 1826 for an essay on the progress of French literature from the beginning of the 16th century to 1610, which produced seven entries, was won jointly by the anti-romantic critic Saint-Marc Girardin, who disparaged Ronsard, and Philarète Chasles, who, alone at that date with Sainte-Beuve, was warm towards Ronsard's poetry.

It seems that Sainte-Beuve's views, first elaborated in articles for Le Globe, owed comparatively little to any increase in inter-est stimulated by the announcement of the Académie's subject, and it is clear that his was the decisive step towards the rehabil-itation that led to ensuing glory, although occasional laudatory references to Ronsard's poetry earlier than 1828 have continued to be discovered. The young band of romantics, in many ways similar to Ronsard's own group, were virtually bound to have discovered at around that date that they had a precursor in Ron-sard. What Sainte-Beuve discovered in him was "la noblesse, la gravité et l'éclat du language (the nobility, gravity, and bril-liance of the language)," the roundness of his periods, the vivid-ness of his imagery, and the primacy he accorded to style over invention.

Ronsard's theoretical utterances, sometimes devoted to the technicalities of rhyme and orthography, do not provide a guide to his own practice or even, taken at their face value, to his intentions. The point is of importance because it leads immediately to the essential question of registers of language. Ronsard frequently states his view that the poet should be "inspired," and that inspiration, in the heady neoplatonism of the French courtly humanism of the 1540s, was often at least verbally identified with divine grace, as in Richard Le Blanc's 1546 preface to his translation of Plato's *Io*. Ronsard is also clear that the revival of French poetry and the inauguration of a grand French poetic tradition make necessary the systematic imitation of the poets of antiquity and, consequently, demand serious study. He was himself called upon to pronounce on the suitability of Goulu for the royal lecteurship of Greek. But in Ronsard inspiration and study are not conflicting requirements. Overwhelmingly the inspiration of the poet is a neoplatonist metaphor to convey the seriousness with which Ronsard, like certain of his immediate predecessors, views the poet's mission. When he writes about inspiration he uses a metaphorical register different from the serious arguments about the need to model a new French poetry on antique practice.

Marsilio Ficino, inspired by Plotinus more than by Plato, had constructed a framework, again more metaphorical than metaphysical or religious, inside which the poetic "furor," one of four, gripped the human soul and stimulated it towards a goal of moral perfection, increased unification, and growing purification, which led towards union with God. Ficino's theory is expounded by Guido Cavalcanti in the seventh "Oratio" of the *De amore*, modelled on Plato's *Symposium*, of which it is a renaissance reconstitution rather than a commentary. The theory, touched on by Rabelais among a host of Italianizing renaissance authors, is to be found in Pontus de Tyard's anonymous *Premier Solitaire* of 1552, in which, as often in Ronsard, the morally enriching effects of poetry are affirmed as being enhanced by the similar effects of music. But "inspiration," in spite of the polarity of "art" and "fureur" in Ronsard's "Ode à Michel de l'Hôpital" and du Bellay's identification of "fureur divine" with what "agite et echaufe les espris poëtiques (moves and heats poetic minds)," while it may be a metaphor of the poet's priestly status, suggests neither that poetry is the mere outpouring of strong feeling, nor that it does not require intense application to an understanding of the attitudes and values of ancient authors. The "Ode à Michel de l'Hôpital," for instance, makes quite apparent the mythologization of the role conferred on the poet by divine inspiration.

It is here that Ronsard began by almost losing his way. However brilliant his widening of the range of the Pindaric ode, originally conceived for the celebration of only athletic victors in the immensely demanding Olympic games, he was misled by Dorat into overvaluing an author whose intrinsic poetic interest Dorat probably overestimated, as he did that of Lycophron, a member of the original Alexandrian Pleiade, a copy of whose 1546 *Alexandra* Ronsard owned, and for whom Dorat's own enthusiasm had been boundless. Ronsard's critics were not altogether wrong to see in his adoption of Pindar as a model a certain pedantry and arrogance, if only because Pindar's poetic inspiration was nowhere near as close to his own as was that of Horace.

In the prefatory "Au lecteur" of 1550, Ronsard boasts of his acquaintanceship with Horace, whose "naïve douceur (sweet naturalness)" he had imitated, although in 1550 it was the 13 Pindaric odes which he put at the front of the first book of his collection. The "Ode de la paix" was integrated into the fifth book in 1552, and then put at the front of the first book of 1560, while the best of all Ronsard's Pindaric odes, the "Ode à Michel de l'Hôpital," was published in the fifth book in 1552. The Greek text of Pindar had been printed in Italy as early as 1513, and modern Pindaric odes had been written in Latin by Benedetto Lampridio, who had taught at Padua, where Michel de l'Hôpital had studied from 1526 to 1532, but whose odes were published only in 1550, and in Italian by Luigi Alamanni, seven of whose hymns in the *Opere Toscane* published in Lyons in 1533 were Pindaric in form. Dorat himself wrote Pindaric hymns in Latin.

All except one of Ronsard's Pindaric odes consist of one or more triads, each composed of strophe, antistrophe, and epode, although Ronsard does not understand the form sufficiently well to realize the relationship between antiphonal choirs at the origin of the division between strophe and antistrophe, or the essential unity of each in the Greek originals. His own strophes and antistrophes are assemblies of shorter four-, six-, or eight-line units, demarcated by their excessively complicated rhyme schemes. The first triad of the "Ode de la paix" has a rhyme scheme for strophe and antistrophe of the type aabccb/dede/ffgg/hiih. The shorter epode partly reverses the order of this scheme and runs abab/cdcd/eefggf. Ronsard extends the subjects epically glorified in his odes to royalty, and to conquerors in all types of literary, military, and personal capacities, building in like Pindar allusions to the backgrounds and birthplaces of his heroes.

It can naturally be argued that Ronsard had to adapt much less for the odes inspired by Horace. The Sabine hills could be thought of as playing in Horace's life or affections a role analogous to that of the forest in Ronsard's, and Horace's miraculous little poem to the Fons Bandusiae fitted almost like a glove the Fontaine Bellerie, on which Ronsard wrote three odes, the best known being the ninth of book two in 1550. But the imitability of Horace for Ronsard was more intimate. He shared not only the Latin poet's feeling for the fragility of life, but also his sententiousness, his fondness for nature, art, friendship, love, and wine, and his anxiety to catch the fleeting moment on its wing. "Carpe diem (Snatch at the day)" could scarcely be better rendered into French than it is by Ronsard, who rhymes internally: "Cueillez dès aujourd'hui les roses de la vie (Gather life's roses no later than today)." That line can trap a modern reader, because it is too easy to forget today what modern horticulture has done to the rose, which in the 16th century blossomed and faded in the course of a single day. In the same way a modern reader cannot be presumed to know Horace's odes, and it needs to be pointed out that when Ronsard could not re-feel the appositeness of a Horatian image, he changed or omitted it. The ode "A la fontaine Bellerie" significantly omits from Horace's ode (III, 13) the sacrifice of the goat and its blood in the water.

Ronsard's first four books of odes had originally contained 94 odes, and there were 13 more in the *Bocage*. A further 12, some new, were collected in the fifth book, added to *Les Amours* of 1552, and although in the 1550 collection the Pindaric odes were given pride of place, Ronsard wrote the Horatian odes before them. Between 1531 and 1537 Torquato Tasso's father, Bernardo, had published 18 adaptations of Horace as "inno" or "oda," so linking the titles of ode and hymn, and Ronsard must have known of them through Duchi at the royal mews. His own first imitations must date from his recuperation at La Possonnière from the illness contracted at Hagenau, since he appears to have been able to show Peletier du Mans some of his work in 1543. The first published translation of an ode of Horace is by Jean Martin and appeared in April 1544, to be followed by one by Saint-Gelais and those of Peletier du Mans in 1547, so that Ronsard may very well have been Horace's first translator in renaissance France. His first attempts are probably those published in the *Bocage*, which are all too irregular in rhyme scheme and structure to be suitable for setting to music, some drawing for their form on Marot, and many scarcely more than paraphrases of Horace's poems. Once he had become Dorat's pupil, Ronsard knew that the lyric poetry of Horace's Greek models, including Pindar, Alcaeus, and Sappho, had been written to be set to music but, although the anticipation of a musical setting may have affected Ronsard's rhyme schemes, music and its instruments remain for him chiefly a metaphor for the moral elevation which poetry was capable of mediating rather than poetry's actual accompaniment.

In view of the range of registers, genres, subjects, and techniques in which Ronsard sometimes achieved and sometimes fell short of the effects he was aspiring to attain, it seems more appropriate to draw attention to the way in which his poetic imagination worked than merely to catalogue its resources. The "Ode à Cassandre" is one of Ronsard's best known and often thought to be one of his most successful poems. Published in the May 1553 edition of the fifth book of *Odes*, it first appeared in the Veuve Maurice de la Porte edition with the 1552 *Les Amours* with Muret's commentary, but without the musical settings, since the royal printers, Adrien le Roy and Robert Ballard, had been granted the monopoly of all printing of new sheet music in Paris between the October 1552 and the February 1553 editions of *Les Amours*. It had been unusual for a poet to claim credit for his work once it had been set to music, although Ronsard had implicitly made such a claim by having the musical settings printed as an appendix. The presumption is that he caused sufficient offence for the music printers to have obtained an official monopoly.

The "Ode à Cassandre" is one of four new odes added to the collection, the first being the ode to Mellin de Saint-Gelais, with whom Ronsard had been reconciled on 1 January. Although the preceding love cycle had recalled the 14-year-old banker's daughter of the ball at Blois eight years earlier and by 1553 long since married, some of the poems in that cycle had certainly been inspired by other women, and Ronsard's affectation of intimacy with his poem's dedicatee is a simple stylization. Muret's commentary is limited to explaining that the "Plis (Folds)" of line five recall the similarity between the folds of a gown and the way rose petals fold over one another but, much more importantly, this is one of the relatively few love poems to which Ronsard made no change at all in subsequent printings. He must be supposed repeatedly to have considered it as perfect as he could make it.

The transliteration of the poem attempts no more than a rendering of the words into English.

> Mignonne, allons voir si la rose
> Qui ce matin avait declose
> Sa robe de pourpre au soleil,
> A point perdu, cette vesprée,
> Les plis de sa robe pourprée,
> Et son teint au vostre pareil.

> Las, voiés comme en peu d'espace,
> Mignonne, elle a dessus la place
> Las, las, ses beautés laissé cheoir!
> O vraiment maratre Nature,
> Puis qu'une telle fleur ne dure
> Que du matin jusques au soir.

> Donc, si vous me croiés, mignonne:
> Tandis que vôtre âge fleuronne
> En sa plus vert nouveauté,
> Cueillés, cueillés vôtre jeunesse
> Comme à cette fleur, la vieillesse
> Fera ternir vôtre beauté

(Dearest, let's go and see if the rose,/Which this morning had unfurled/Its crimson dress to the sun,/Has not this evening lost/The folds of its crimsoned dress/And its complexion like your own.

Alas, see how in a short time,/Dearest, on the spot it/Alas, alas, has let its beauties fall!/O indeed cruel stepmother Nature,/Since such a flower only lasts/From morning to nightfall.

So, dearest, if you believe me:/While your age is in flower/In its most tender freshness,/Pluck, pluck your youth/[Since] old age, as it did to that flower/Will make your beauty wither).

The ingredients of the poem are all commonplace, from the comparison of the rose with Cassandre's complexion to the brevity of beauty, the need to catch the fleeting moment when bliss may be possible, the idea that nature is cruel and uncaring, that a flower lasts only for a day, that old age is on the way, and that youth withers. They can be found throughout antiquity, in the Bible and the Fathers as well as in Homer, Theocritus, Virgil, Propertius, Tibullus, Ovid, the *Roman de la Rose*, and the Latin, Italian, and French poets of the renaissance. The immediate inspiration is clearly Ausonius, from whom Ronsard takes the direct addressing of Nature, and probably Pontano, for the comparison of the rose and the complexion in a piece paraphrased by Baïf in his 1552 Amours, "Melinelle, plus douillette..." The poem was immediately set to music, but what makes the critics unanimously declare it a masterpiece?

The answer must be its poise. The stylization is clear, delicate, and imposes a restraint on the expression of sentiment, which therefore has to be oblique and needs proper syntax. Ronsard's balance is superb. The first and third stanzas consist of a sentence each. The middle stanza has two sentences, and the syntactical break comes with a break in the flow of discourse exactly halfway through. For a stanza and a half the poet has addressed the girl. One sentence is addressed to nature, two lines of reflection to the reader, and the last stanza again to the girl, the asymmetry just enough to suggest spontaneity, but not allowed to interrupt rhythm, rhyme scheme (aabccb in each stanza), or metre. Each stanza ends with a subdued punch line, the last being the strongest.

Almost none of this can have needed conscious effort from Ronsard, any more than the other poetic effects achieved by means chiefly of repeated words ("Las, las" and "Cueillés, cueillés") and sounds, like the repeated "m" and nasalized "n" sounds of the first two lines, the cascade of "p" and "r" sounds in lines three to six, the play with "r," "m," "n," and the expostulatory "t" in lines 10 to 12, ending with the triple "q" sound of the last two lines of the second stanza. Ronsard uses a pronounced "l" consonant indulgently almost throughout, but that harsh "q" sound is taken up again in the third stanza, with "Cueillés, cueillés... Comme," as the poet, pleading again, caresses seven "v" sounds and calls for the reader's attention before delivering the final punch line. What draws attention to the superb poetic ear is the fact that only the sheer richness of sound justifies the repetition of "robe de pourpre" two lines later as "robe pourprée."

Then again the idealization is an attractive constraint. There is at least a suggestion of a garden. Such gardens as existed in the 16th century were expensive and labour-intensive luxuries, normally of the Italian variety, with patterns of low box or privet hedge rising only inches above the ground, fruit trees, and any roses trellised. Within what is at the very least a stylization, the poet pays Cassandre a forthright compliment on her physical appearance, but couches his advice to seize the pleasure of the moment offered by youth, beauty, sun, and health in quite general terms, reproaching nature for its cruelty, not here the woman for her reluctance. By showing her a rose at morning and evening, his demonstration of desire is limited to the implanting of a thought through the dramatization of the fragility and brevity of physical perfection. The idea of transience and the momentary revolt against the false mother responsible for the inevitability of decline give the idyll its necessary tinge of sadness. It is the restraint, the delicacy, and the poise imposed by the stylization which make this poem a masterpiece. The syntax, punctuation, and play of sounds then follow to express them, once Ronsard has settled on a rhyme scheme that could scarcely be simpler.

In 1555 Ronsard sought to extend his poetic range in two different directions, both of them away from the close imitation of Horace and the inspiration of Petrarch. On the one hand *La Continuation des Amours* of 1555 announces, neatly borrowing a passage from Horace, that Ronsard is accepting the criticism that his early verse was "trop obscur au simple populaire (too impenetrable to the ordinary reader)," and on the other he moves towards the imitation of Marullus in the opulent imagery of the hymns. He was never quite to move away from the rhetorical games of the "grands rhétoriqueurs" or the posturings which had come to characterize the Petrarchan tradition, but the "Marie" cycle is often more frankly sensual than anything Ronsard had previously written, and the hymns almost systematically explore, sometimes wryly, the idea that the poet holds the key to a realm beyond the merely physical, enabling him to penetrate the secrets of the cosmos. The "Hymne de la mort" is partly a mock encomium, exploiting a form much cultivated in the renaissance and used above all by Erasmus, while the "Hymne de l'or" has a connecting thread of irony. Mostly, however, the 1555 hymns establish the poet as the intermediary between man and, if not God, at least the supernatural, hermetic, esoteric world signified by such realms as those of justice, philosophy, eternity, demons, and stars, animals, and precious stones. Mostly in alexandrines, the hymns magnificently develop what has rightly been called a cornucopia of images and metaphors, so that physical luxuriance becomes the sign and counterpart of moral splendour and enhanced spiritual riches. The abandonment of the strophic form allowed Ronsard to use the longer sentences his imagery now required for its elaboration.

On the other hand, the following three lines from one of the more famous "Marie" sonnets, first published in *La Continuation des Amours*, show the way in which Ronsard can keep the stylization of the "aubade," while using the demotic "Ian (Yes)" and drawing on the tradition of "blasons" praising particular parts of the female anatomy:

Ian, je vous punirai du peché de paresse,
Je vois baiser cent fois vostre oeil, vostre tetin,
Afin de vous aprendre à vous lever matin

(So, I'm going to punish you for the sin of laziness./A hundred times I'm going to kiss your eye, your nipple,/To teach you to get up in the morning).

The tone has changed, but the "punishment" for over-sleeping is still ritualized. Ronsard referred to this style as his "beau stil bas (fine low style)," but could still use it to mourn the death of Marie de Clèves as a way of currying favour with Henri III. This is the poetic equivalent of a genre painting, with the realism and the sensuality scarcely going beyond a tease. The effect of the whole sonnet derives partly from the fact that only in this last tercet does the poem, still addressed to "Mignogne," use "I," and partly again from the use of consonants as if they were musical notes, in these three lines particularly the "p," "t," and "v" sounds.

From the beginning Ronsard wrote in a variety of metres, often using shorter lines for lighter registers, and from the later 1560s deferring to Charles IX's preference for decasyllables. But even some of the 1555 hymns, like the "Hymne de la philosophie" for Odet de Coligny, Cardinal de Chastillon, were written in decasyllabic "vers communs" rather than alexandrines, or "vers nobles." The simplification of style and relaxation of tone of 1555 were partly occasioned by the young group's discovery of the Greek anthology, first printed in Florence by Lascaris as early as 1494, and used by Ronsard particularly for two epigrams inspired by Anacreon at the end of the 1553 *Livret de folastries*. In 1554 Henri Estienne was to publish a whole volume of Anacreon, although most of the poems are now known not to be authentic. The poems, written in antiquity by an Ionian poet who died at 85, having sung of wine, roses, and love, were naturally to fill Ronsard and his companions with enthusiasm. Ronsard was himself inspired to create the "odelette" and included 31 adaptations of Anacreon in his collections of 1554 and 1555, *Le Bocage, Les Meslanges*, the third edition of the *Odes*, and *La Continuation des Amours*. Anacreon and the Greek anthology must also have been partly responsible for the new style of love sonnet of *La Continuation* and the evolution of the Pindaric ode into the hymns.

The most elaborate of the hymns include those to the four seasons, already treated by Peletier du Mans in 1547 and remodelled by him in 1555. Those of Ronsard, who probably took the idea from Folengo, were published in *Les Trois livres du recueil des nouvelles poësies* of 1563–64. In the "Ode à Michel de l'Hôpital" Ronsard had contrasted the poetic "fureur" with the "art," "sweat," and "labour" of the mere versifiers. Like Pontus de Tyard, Ronsard notes the diminishing inspiration of successive generations of poets as the Muses' grace "plus lentement agitoit (more slowly stimulated)" their fight against ignorance. Words like "fureur" and "rage" could, however, already be used in a playfully pejorative sense, as in the 1553 "Elegie à M. de Muret," but Ronsard still regards poetic inspiration, "fureur," as capable of mediating virtue, knowledge, and religious fulfilment when, for instance, the "daimons," mythological intermediaries between the human and the divine, act on the fantasy in the 1555 "Les Daimons." The "Epistre" to the cardinal of Lorraine in 1556 claims that the poet's love of the Muses

Tout furieux d'esprit me ravist nuict et jour,
Découvrant leurs secretz aux nations Françoises

(Ravished me night and day with a fury of mind,/Revealing their secrets to the peoples of France).

Ronsard's confidence in the poetic mission diminished with the onset of the religious wars. In 1559 an "Elegie" intended to preface a volume of Hamelin's translation of Livy and published in the *Second Livre des meslanges* shows it to be as strong as ever, as the poet tells of the soul's freedom when the body rests, how it talks to the gods, and, restored to the body, communicates the secrets of the heavenly movements understood during sleep. But by 1560 Ronsard regrets that the poetic "fureur" is given only in youth in an elegy dedicated originally to L'Huillier, but later changed when L'Huillier became a Huguenot. Poetic pride is presented in a markedly lower register in the 1560 "Elegie" for Pierre l'Escot, and Ronsard's elegiac mood continues through the poem for the Cardinal de Chastillon until, in the "Elegie" for Guillaume des Autels of the same year, "fureur" is what Ronsard ascribes to the Lutherans he opposes, and the "fantastique" becomes a quality of the "esprit sombre et melancolique."

Generally speaking, Ronsard's declining exploitation of an optimistic neoplatonist mythology in which, in particular, the poet's function becomes straightforwardly sacerdotal mirrors his own increasing despondency and diminishing confidence from the mid-1550s, in spite of some of the new pieces for the 1584 *Oeuvres*. In the 1563 "Hymne de l'automne," however, Ronsard joins the full panoply of one of his most splendid myths with a strong transposition into neoplatonist terms of the poetic mission, rising magnificently to celebrate one of the most potent of the myths in Western culture, the union of ripeness and fertility in the marriage of Autumn and Bacchus.

Dedicated to Claude de Laubespine, who drafted the treatise of Cateau-Cambrésis and styled himself secretary of state, the poem has 470 lines. The first 86 recount the poet's meeting with Euterpe, nymph and Muse. Then comes the story of Automne, nubile daughter of the sun and Nature, told at pubescence by her nurse to find a wind to take her to her father. Automne finds the cave of Auton, the south wind, according to Virgil wet, warm, and cloudy. Although Ronsard, like Folengo, makes Automne female, with Spring, Summer, and Winter her brothers, there is an ambiguity of gender, and for part of the poem she is androgynous. When the moon has gone off to sleep with Endymion and the rose-complexioned Aurore has opened the gates of the heavens, Automne finds the sun already in his chariot. She follows him, escapes the menacing signs of the Zodiac, and finds the palace built for Spring by Youth. Venus lives there with her swans and pigeons, but Spring has gone off to look for Zephyr, whose activities it takes Ronsard a 10-line sentence to describe.

Autumn steals flowers from Spring's palace, and goes off to find Summer, who is being feasted elsewhere by Ceres. Having stolen two rays from him to adorn her hair, she goes to find her mother, but Nature chases her off for the ruin she would cause to her other children, Winter, Spring, and Summer. At this point (line 369) she meets Bacchus and his magnificent cortège, which Ronsard describes. Love between the two is instantaneous, and by line 444 they have already lived happily ever after. Lines 445 to 446 constitute the envoi, in which the poet salutes Autumn and her husband, reserving the last four lines to say that he must now go and write a hymn to her brother, Winter. The gender of Automne is important. The French nouns for spring, summer, and winter are all masculine, which makes Spring, Summer, and Winter male. The French "automne" has now stabilized by analogy as masculine, but was still uncertain in the 16th century. Automne has of course to be a girl if we are to celebrate so potent a myth as that of her marriage to Bacchus, but Folengo was uncertain about Autumn's gender, and Ronsard several times hesitates.

The main classical sources are Hesiod and Virgil, with reminiscences also of, in particular, Ovid and, among the moderns, Michaelis Marullus, the Byzantine poet who had taken refuge in Medici Florence, where he died in 1500, leaving four books of *Epigrammata* (1490) and four of *Hymni* (1497), and who had inspired many of Ronsard's earlier hymns. In the exordium Ronsard identifies himself with the poetic "I," referring his poetic abilities to a divine gift and the guidance of the spirit ("daimon") who presides over the Muses. Ronsard is elaborating on Ovid's "deus in nobis, agitante calescimus illo (when stirred by the god within us, we burst into fire)." When humans are touched by the spur of the divinity, they can foretell events, know nature and the secrets of the heavens, rise up to be among the gods, know the virtues of herbs and plants, close up the winds, and charm the thunders. They must, however, prepare themselves "par oraison, par jeune, et penitence aussi (by prayer, by fasting, and by penitence, too)."

Before he was 15, Ronsard recounts, he would roam the countryside at nightfall to see the nymphs and fairies, the Sylvan goat-men. Following the nymphs, he was taken aside by Euterpe, washed nine times, subjected to nine spells, frightened, inspired, and promised poetic immortality. The number nine, the square of the lowest prime number after one, is of particular significance for the neoplatonist tradition. Ficino recounts how Porphyry and Plotinus celebrated the anniversary of Plato's death at 81. Euterpe tells Ronsard that he will be despised, thought mad, and cursed like all the sybils and other types of prophet, that he will be poor, but content with a forest, a meadow, a hill, a river:

Ainsi disoit la Nymphe, et de là je vins estre
Disciple de d'Aurat, qui long temps fut mon maistre,
M'aprist la Poësie, et me montra comment
On doit feindre et cacher les fables proprement,
Et à bien deguiser la verité des choses
D'un fabuleux manteau dont elles sont encloses...

(So spoke the Nymph, and from then I became/The disciple of Dorat, who for a long time was my master,/Taught me poetry, And showed me how/You had properly to make pretence and cover up in fables,/And to disguise well the truth of things/In a cloak of fable which covers them up...).

This exordium provides a neat résumé of Ronsard's neoplatonist mythologization of the poet's function, concentrating on the penetration of hidden truth, and the poet's role in presenting it to an impure and untutored people in the form first of religious fable. In the 1565 *Abbregé de l'art poëtique françois*, Ronsard was to insist that the first rule was to venerate the Muses, to hold them

> cheres et sacrées, comme les filles de Jupiter, c'est à dire de Dieu…Car la Poësie n'estoit au premier age qu'une Theologie allegoricque, pour faire entrer au cerveau des hommes grossiers, par fables plaisantes et colorées, les secrets qu'ils ne pouvoient comprendre quand trop ouvertement on descouvroit la verité

> (dear and sacred, like daughters of Jupiter, that is to say God…For in the first age Poetry was nothing other than an allegorical Theology, which allowed to enter into the brains of uncultivated men, by means of pleasing and colourful fables, the secrets which they could not understand if the truth were opened to them too directly).

The poetic qualities of the polemical verse largely derive from the much wider audience at which it was aimed. Ronsard wishes to leave theology alone, but he is the court poet, and Catherine de Medici is regent. Ronsard was being called on not to be elitist "du tout eslongné du vulgaire (as far away from the common people as possible)," as he had striven to be, just at the moment when he himself, having had the propagandist function imposed on him, was attacked by self-doubt. His whole poetic aesthetic was in conflict with the Calvinist emphasis on abstinence from all ornamentation in order to let the beauty of the gospel message impose its own force. Ronsard's solution was to write what was fundamentally still political poetry, lamenting the civil war laying France to waste, and calling for the cessation of recourse to foreign troops and for the restored unity of the kingdom.

He began with the generally non-controversial *Institution pour l'adolescence du Roy treschrestien Charles neufviesme de ce nom*, published in 1562, but written during the second half of 1561. Generally Erasmian in tone, the genre, a treatise on the education of a prince, was by this date in the renaissance already traditional. There is barely an allusion to the Huguenots, and nothing which Budé or the conciliatory chancellor Michel de l'Hôpital would not have accepted. By 1561 the popularity, even at court, of Marot's *Psalms*, was challenging Ronsard's aesthetic, and he was still hoping for one of the benefices whose abolition might well have been a chief fruit of any attempt to reform the organization of French Catholicism. The benefices Ronsard enjoyed in 1561 brought in only 1,200 livres a year, which was insufficient, and as royal almoner he could reasonably expect more. His views were diverging from the liberal opinions of the chancellor even before the end of 1561.

In 1562 the January edict authorized Calvinist religious ceremonies, but the massacre of Wassy took place none the less on 1 March. Catherine de Medici was caught between the power of the Guises, whom she disliked, and the interest of her children, which demanded peace and continuance of the dynasty at all costs. Should she not intervene to conciliate between the opposing forces of Condés and Guises massing in Paris, as her chancellor urged? François de Guise, at the head of 1,500 armed and mounted nobles, actually exchanged a polite greeting with Condé and Bèze at the head of 500 horsemen in the middle of Paris. By 29 March, Easter Sunday, there might easily have been

open warfare in the city's streets. In the end Condé withdrew on the pleas of Catherine de Medici and on the advice of his two brothers, the cardinal governor of Paris and Antoine de Bourbon, the Catholic leader. He was joined at Meaux by Coligny, and with him took the town of Orléans, from which the two Huguenot leaders threatened Paris in April and May.

Catherine obtained a conference with Condé, leaving for it on 3 June. Neither that interview nor two others in the same month were to any avail, and the royal army under Montmorency and Antoine de Bourbon was assembled at Blois. Ronsard was himself caught up in one of the many skirmishes of that year, and may almost have lost his life. It is not surprising if, following the regent's decision, he hardened the political views of his polemical writing. Both the *Discours des miseres de ce temps*, probably written in June 1562, and their *Continuation*, probably not written until about 1 October, were dedicated to Catherine. Ronsard was still carrying out a propaganda mission.

On 5 August Catherine had joined the Catholic army at the siege of Bourges, which capitulated, and by the end of September she had committed herself to establishing control over all the Normandy towns handed over during August to the English, with whom the Huguenots signed the treaty of Hampton Court on 20 September. It is at this point that the *Continuation* must have been composed, before Antoine de Bourbon was fatally wounded at Rouen on 15 October. The much fiercer *Remonstrance au peuple de France* must have been written about 1 December and printed before the battle of Dreux on the 19th although it was published anonymously and the printed date of publication is 1563. Poetically, in spite of the note of personal commitment, Ronsard was not happy writing propaganda for a mass audience and forsaking his personal and elitist aesthetic. The metaphors are too elaborate and the sentences too long to produce the sort of impact attained, for instance, by the vivid imagery of d'Aubigné's *Les Tragiques*.

Ronsard's final cycle of love sonnets has generally been considered an attempt to challenge the ascendancy of the lighter, more highly stylized register adopted by Philippe Desportes, which was popular at court. It has long been recognized that they do not represent a real love affair, or even a very serious game. Essentially they are about posthumous reputations and a poet's ability to confer lasting fame on the object of his verse. They also signify the abandonment of Ronsard's final attempt, by singing the glories of the French Helen in the amatory voice of his youth, to demand recognition as the French Homer.

Little is known about Hélène de Surgères, except that she came from a Spanish family, and that she had a brother who was a counsellor of state. Her uncle was acting governor of Piedmont, and from 1566 she had been a lady-in-waiting, or perhaps at first a maid, of Catherine de Medici. Her salary doubled to 400 livres a year when she became a lady of the chamber, a position also occupied by two of her cousins. She had a reputation for studiousness and virtue. Ronsard depicts her as unyielding and severe, and the poems have a strong current of learned humanist references flowing through them. Yet the mythologization of the deepest human emotions, particularly those occasioned by the approach of death, works astoundingly well in an almost bewildering variety of registers, courtly, humanistic, simple and rustic, stylized and quarrelsome, morally dignified, amorously casuistic, abounding in or altogether eschewing allusions and references. Again it is probably the best known which is the most nearly perfect:

Quand vous serez bien vieille, au soir à la chandelle,
Assise aupres du feu, devidant et filant,
Direz, chantant mes vers, en vous esmerveillant,
Ronsard me celebroit du temps que j'estois belle.

Lors vous n'aurez servante oyant telle nouvelle,
Desja sous le labeur à demy sommeillant,
Qui au bruit de Ronsard ne s'aille resveillant,
Benissant vostre nom de louange immortelle.

Je seray sous la terre, et fantaume sans os
Par les ombres Myrtheux je prendray mon repos.
Vous serez au fouyer une vieille accroupie,

Regrettant mon amour, et vostre fier desdain.
Vivez, si m'en croyez, n'attendez à demain:
Cueillez dès aujourdhuy les roses de la vie

(When you are really old, in the evening, by the light of the candle,/Sitting next to the fire, unravelling and spinning,/You will say, singing my verses, wondering while you do so,/Ronsard sang my praises at the time when I was beautiful.

Then you will have no servant who, hearing you say that,/Already half asleep after the day's work,/Will not start up at the sound of Ronsard,/Celebrating your name, bestowing on it immortal praise.

I shall be under the earth; a ghost without bones,/I shall be taking my rest in the shades of the Myrtle trees./You will be a bent old woman by the hearth,

Lamenting my love and your proud disdain./Live, if you believe me; do not await tomorrow./Pluck no later than today life's roses).

This is not a love poem. Despite the punch line at the end, throwing back to "Mignonne…," reinforced by its internal rhyme, it is more an elegy for approaching death, and the concentration of hope in the fading ability still to bestow poetic immortality on the object of fancy. Par excellence a genre poem, it works more by the tension between rhythm and syntax than by sound, although subdued effects are achieved, for instance by the deployment of "v" sounds in lines one and three, the "s" sounds at the beginning of the sestet, and the unleashing of the hard "c" in each of the last two lines. In the two quartets the rhythm and the sense remain in perfect harmony, a comma at the end of every line, except for full stops at the fourth and eighth. Then, however, the three two-line syntactical units conveying the sense cut right across the division between the tercets, sharpening the pace and the poem's impact.

That tension is at the heart of the poem taken as a totality, since the elegiac content is given the form of a love sonnet. The poem's message, ostensibly much the same as that of the "Mignonne…" poem, is now forlorn. The "you" should gather the rosebuds while she may, but will not. On the other hand the poet should be able to bestow immortality, but cannot. He does not give "you" a name, and it is the "you" who will in the end have bestowed immortal memory on Ronsard by thinking of him when he is dead, and reciting his verses. His name will

mean just enough to startle into wakefulness a tired, slumbering old servant. The poignancy is unmistakable. Even the "immortal praise" is a topos from Virgil.

PUBLICATIONS

Collections

Les Oeuvres de P. de Ronsard, 4 vols., 1560
Les Oeuvres de P. de Ronsard, 6 vols., 1567
Les Oeuvres de P. de Ronsard, 1571
Les Oeuvres de P. de Ronsard, 1572–73
Les Oeuvres de P. de Ronsard, 7 vols., 1578
Les Oeuvres de P. de Ronsard, 10 vols., 1587 (posthumous; last edition on which Ronsard worked)
Further collected editions were published in 1592 (5 vols.), 1597 (10 vols.), 1604 (5 vols.), 1609 (folio), 1609 (5 vols.), 1617 (5 vols.), 1623 (2 folio vols.), 1629–30 (5 vols.)
Oeuvres complètes, 8 vols., 1857–67
Oeuvres, 6 vols., 1887–93
Oeuvres complètes, 18 vols., 1914–70 (text of first editions)
Oeuvres complètes (Pléiade, edition) 2 vols., 1938 (text of 1584)
Oeuvres, 1966 ff. (text of 1587)
Les Amours, 1963
Ronsard
   1.Poems of Love, 1975
   2.Odes, Hymns and Other Poems, 1977

Verse

Les Quatre premiers livres des Odes de Pierre de Ronsard, Vandomois. Ensemble son Bocage, 1550
Ode de la Paix, 1550
Les Amours de P. de Ronsard Vandomoys. Ensemble le cinquième livre de ses Odes, 1552; augmented and revised edition, 1553
Livret de Folastries, 1553
Le Bocage, 1554 (almost totally different from 1550 volume)
Les Meslanges, 1555
Les Odes, 1555
La Continuation des Amours, 1555
La Nouvelle Continuation des Amours, 1556
Les Hymnes, 1555
Second Livre des hymnes, 1556
Exhortation au camp du Roy, 1558
Exhortation pour la paix, 1558
L'Hymne de tresillustre Prince Charles, Cardinal de Lorraine, 1559
Chant pastoral sur les nopces de Monseigneur Charles, duc de Lorraine, et Madame Claude Fille du Roy, 1559
La Paix, au Roy, 1559
Chant de liesse, au Roy, 1559
Suite de l'Hymne de tresillustre Prince Charles, Cardinal de Lorraine, 1559
Discours à Monseigneur le duc de Savoie; Chant pastoral à Madame Marguerite, 1559
Second Livre des meslanges, 1559
Institution pour l'adolescence du Roy, 1562
Discours des miseres de ce temps, 1562
Continuation du Discours des miseres de ce temps, 1562

Remonstrance au peuple de France, 1563
Responce aux injures et calomnies, 1563
Les Trois livres du recueil des nouvelles poësies, 1563–64
La Promesse, 1564
Le Proces, 1565
Elegies, mascarades et bergerie, 1565
Les Nues ou nouvelles, 1565
Sixiesme Livre des poemes, 1569
Septieme Livre des poemes, 1569
La Franciade, 1572
Le Tombeau de Charles IX, 1574
Discours au Roi, 1575
Les Estoilles, 1575
Le Tombeau de Marguerite de France, 1575
Derniers Vers, 1586

Other

Abbregé de l'art poëtique françois, 1565

Biographical and critical studies

Laumonier, P., *La Vie de Pierre de Ronsard de Claude Binet (1586)*, 1909
Laumonier, P., *Ronsard, poète lyrique*, 1909; 2nd edition, 1923
Champion, P., *Ronsard et son temps*, 1925
Chamard, Henri, *Histoire de la Pléiade*, 4 vols., 1939–40
Desonay, F., *Ronsard, poète de l'amour*, 3 vols., 1952–59
Wilson, D.B., *Ronsard, Poet of Nature*, 1961
Silver, Isidore, *Ronsard and the Hellenic Renaissance in France*, 4 vols., 1961, 1981, 1985, and 1987
Stone, Donald, *Ronsard's Sonnet Cycles: A Study in Tone and Vision*, 1966
Armstrong, Elizabeth, *Ronsard and the Age of Gold*, 1968
Silver, Isidore, *The Intellectual Evolution of Ronsard: The Formative Influences*, 1969
Cave, T.C. (editor), *Ronsard the Poet*, 1973
Silver, Isidore, *Three Ronsard Studies*, 1978
Quainton, Malcolm, *Ronsard's Ordered Chaos*, 1980
Silver, Isidore, *Ronsard and the Grecian Lyre*, 1981
Hanks, Joyce Main, *Ronsard and the Biblical Tradition*, 1982

Bibliographies

Laumonier, Paul, *Tableau chronologique des Oeuvres de Ronsard*, 1911
Raymond, Marcel, *Bibliographie critique de Ronsard en France, 1550–1585*, 1927

ROTROU, Jean, 1609–1650.

Dramatist.

LIFE

Rotrou has often been thought to rank in literary importance as a dramatist behind only Racine, Pierre Corneille, and Molière.

He was baptized on Friday 21 August 1609 at Dreux, between Chartres and Châteaudun. He came from an established bourgeois family and was to be a lawyer, as well as being contracted, probably from late adolescence, to the comédiens du roi at the Hôtel de Bourgogne as their retained playwright. In 1632 Chapelain refers to him as the company's "poète à gages (salaried dramatist)," which would mean that at that date the copyright in his plays belonged to the company, without whose permission, perhaps granted only against payment, Rotrou could not publish them. In fact the texts of only two plays have survived out of the probable 30 which he seems to assert having written before 1634.

Three generations of Rotrou's father's family had provided Dreux with mayors, and his only brother held an office in the military commissariat before becoming a tax official, a counsellor, and a maître d'hôtel in the royal household. He had three sisters and was himself from 1630 a barrister at the parlement de Paris, having studied in Paris from the age of 12 or 13. There is no record that he ever pleaded, and his livelihood came from the theatre until, no doubt aided by Richelieu, he bought an administrative charge.

The Hôtel de Bourgogne played his first piece, *L'Hypocondriaque; ou, Le Mort amoureux*, in 1628, before he was 20, and it was quickly followed by *La Bague de l'oubli*, played early in 1629 though published only in 1635. In Paris Rotrou had speedily become associated with the fringe of Du Ryer's circle, and then with Scudéry and Pierre Corneille. The seigneur of Dreux was Louis de Bourbon, comte de Soissons, to be killed at La Marfée in 1641. He was Rotrou's first patron, and it was to him that Rotrou dedicated his first play. The second was dedicated to Louis XIII himself, who had attended a performance but was well known to accept dedications only if he did not have to pay for them. It helped, however, merely to have a dedication accepted, and in 1630 Rotrou could dedicate *Diane* to the comte de Fiesque, in 1631 *L'Heureuse Constance* to the queen, and in the same year *Les Occasions perdues* to the comtesse de Soissons.

By 1632 Rotrou had met Mairet, who that year had joined Belin's household, and Fiesque had drawn Rotrou to the attention of Chapelain. It was no doubt through Chapelain that Rotrou came into the entourage of Richelieu to whom, in 1632, he dedicated his tragedy *Hercule mourant*, and one of whose five "poets," with L'Estoille, Corneille, Boisrobert, and Colletet, he became. They were to be engaged in collaborative playwriting, each being entrusted with the draft of an act before corporate revision under the cardinal's supervision, followed by sumptuous production (see: Pierre Corneille). Rotrou was, however, apparently also received at the Hôtel de Rambouillet and, through Soissons as well as the Hôtel, was loosely associated with the Condé family. His connection with the famous chambre bleue (see: *Guirlande de Julie*) was never very close.

By 1634 Rotrou's verse had appeared at the front of Pichou's *La Fillis de Scire*, Mareschal's *La Généreuse Allemande*, Scudéry's *Ligdamon et Lidias*, Cotignon de la Charnaye's *Bocages*, and the 1634 edition of Corneille's *La Veuve*. It appears to have been the patronage of Belin which rescued him from over-production. Chapelain's letter of 30 October 1632, probably to Fiesque, had spoken of his "servitude si honteuse (so humiliating an enslavement)," and of the need to set him free. It is quite likely that Rotrou had become contractually bound to the comédiens du roi immediately after Hardy's departure from the company in the autumn of 1626. From 1634 Rotrou did in fact decrease the rhythm of his output, and from that date there is no more mention of "enslavement." Belin was to die in September 1637, but Rotrou had certainly for some time been staying with him in one of his Maine estates. Unlike Mairet, another protégé of Belin, Rotrou had his own house in Paris, and did not need Belin's hospitality there.

The first edition of *Cléagénor et Doristée, tragi-comédie*, probably of 1633, was sold by Rotrou clandestinely. It was anonymous, and the publisher wrote, "This play was put into my hands some time ago by someone I did not know; he refused to name the author." In the 1634 second edition, dedicated, like the 1636 comedy *Les Ménechmes*, to Belin, Rotrou revealed his name and promised soon to publish the rest of his 30 plays. If indeed Rotrou had written 30 plays by 1634, all but *L'Hypocondriaque* and *La Bague de l'oubli*, performed respectively in 1628 and 1629 have been lost. By the date of Corneille's *Le Cid*, early in January 1637, Rotrou was sufficiently successful for Chapelain to be able casually to write, in a latter of 22 January, that the public was being entertained by *Le Cid* and by Rotrou's *Les deux Sosies* "à un point qui ne se peut exprimer (to a degree that cannot be expressed)." Rotrou who, although a friend of the innovative if spiky Corneille, was also himself a traditionalist, took no part in the famous Querelle which followed the staging and over-swift publication of *Le Cid*, Mairet's strong reaction to Corneille's *Excuse à Ariste*, and Scudéry's sycophantic manoeuvering which ended in the Académie's arbitration.

From 1634 to his death Rotrou was to write a score of plays, but from 1634 onwards Richelieu, until his death in 1642, saw to it that he had alternative administrative employment. From 1633 he had a small pension of either 600 or 1,000 livres. He was also ennobled and acquired the office of gentilhomme ordinaire de Son Eminence, lieutenant particulier du comité et bailliage de Dreux. He was never really well-to-do. Contracts of 11 March 1636 and 17 January 1637 show that he sold the rights to his first 14 plays for 2,250 livres to the booksellers Sommaville and Quinet, a sum which was generous in relation to the four livres a hundred for alexandrines and two livres a hundred for shorter lines with which du Ryer was remunerated. Gaillard's *Monomachie* refers in a famous couplet to the absence of any independent right of Rotrou to publish his plays:

Corneille est excellent, mais il vend ses ouvrages;
Rotrou fait bien des vers, mais il est poète à gages

(Corneille is excellent, but he sells his works;/Rotrou writes a great deal, but he is a salaried employee).

In 1639 Rotrou retired to Dreux, buying an office which allowed him to sign himself as "seigneur de Toisy, conseiller du roi, lieutenant particulier civil et criminel," but he continued to write for the theatre, with his best-known works dating from after Richelieu's death. Sainte-Beuve is harsh on Rotrou: "Cette noble nature avait du vulgaire, du bas (his noble nature had about it something common, vulgar)." Rotrou had in his youth a reputation for flattering on all sides, for amorous liaisons, and for gambling. By 1634, he had clearly begun to settle down. Between 1636 and 1640 he wrote only eight plays, and then only a dozen more in the decade preceding his death. After Richelieu's death, Rotrou solicited patronage from Mazarin, and the 1647 *Don Bernard de Cabrère*, published by Toussaint Quinet

in 1648 and derived from Lope de Vega, was prefaced by a dedicatory elegy to Mazarin. On 9 July 1640 Rotrou married at Mantes, near Dreux, a Marguerite Camus, born in 1615, by whom he had six children of whom only three were to survive infancy, one to become a priest, another a nun, and a third to remain a spinster.

In 1650 a form of plague broke out at Dreux. The mayor, a cousin of Rotrou, died, and the military governor remained in Paris. Rotrou thought it his duty in spite of the pleas of his brother to stay and see to the maintenance of civil order. Notes for a letter say that, as Rotrou was writing, the bells were ringing for the 22nd death that day. He himself died the day he fell ill, and was buried on 28 June 1650 at the age of 41.

WORKS

Rotrou published 35 plays, 17 entitled tragi-comédies, 12 comedies and six tragedies. We must presume that we have lost all but two of his first 30 plays, and what material we have shows some progressive seriousness of dramatic purpose, with the least perfunctory entertainments coming towards the end. Critical comment is revealing, as it concentrates almost wholly on relating Rotrou to his sources, but in ways which reveal no consistent pattern in their adaptation; to what was to follow him, which he could not have known or much cared about; to later critical categories like "baroque," which he would have found meaningless; and to contemporary debates about regularity, which did not greatly interest him, although two comedies, *Diane* and *Célimène*, and a tragi-comédie, *Amélie*, are in fact regular. Critical comment suggests, therefore, that Rotrou's interest for literary historians has been overwhelmingly historical rather than literary or dramatic. He has understandably been regarded overwhelmingly as a representative and workmanlike playwright of his generation, who himself contributed very little either to the imaginative exploration of the experience of his own generation or to the development of dramatic techniques in France.

An examination of the surviving plays does indeed show that, whatever their interest, Rotrou's plays lack imaginative depth and any seriousness of literary intention. There is much romanesque adventure; there are innumerable disguises, a dozen cases of merely apparent deaths, sword fights, and pistol fights even between characters from antique mythology; there are vast casts of up to a score, and splendidly spectacular effects; and there is embryonic analysis of sentiment and a historically important injection of realism to remind us of the connection between Rotrou, Mairet, and the patronage of Belin. But just as even when his income and social position were adequately assured and he could afford to write at greater leisure and with more concentration, Rotrou could reconcile an association with the Hôtel de Bourgogne with his work for the Marais company of which Belin was patron, so he could turn out competent drama in all three serious genres, and seek patronage, when he needed to, from milieus as generally hostile to one another as were those of Soissons and Fiesque on the one hand, and those of Richelieu and Mazarin on the other. Friendship with both Mairet and Pierre Corneille may partly explain Rotrou's abstention from any part in the Querelle which came to focus on *Le Cid*, but it is too likely as well to indicate an indifference to matters which, as we can today understand, were bound to constitute the weightiest literary concern of his generation.

What can be said of Rotrou's production, apart from noting the skill with which it is strewn with memorable aphorisms, is that he tends everywhere to emphasize the essential character of the play in hand, comic, tragi-comic, or tragic. The example of *Crisante*, played around 1635 and published in 1640, has been singled out. It is a tragedy. The Roman Cassie desires the queen Crisante. The attendant who advises her to yield is killed by Crisante. Cassie gets rid of another of her attendants by giving her to two guards to despatch. They fight over her and kill one another, bringing the corpse-count to three. Cassie rapes Crisante, is denounced, and kills himself. Crisante, to prove to her husband her own innocence, shows him Cassie's head, which she has cut off. She kills herself, and her husband then kills himself, too. A rape, a severed head, and six corpses. This is not literature but gory entertainment of no imaginative interest at all, although it is what Rotrou at his worst was fatally good at.

Hercule mourant may respect the unities, but it does not attempt a register heavier than fantasy. Hercule at one point puts his head on the lap of Iole, who continues to work at her sewing. He lets himself be consumed by the flames lit for the sacrifice he offers; there is a storm over his tomb; he comes down from the flies to deliver a last message and is then taken up again. Exuberant exaggeration makes it impossible to preserve a connection between scenes. There is sometimes as much declamation as drama; there are sustained passages of stichomythia, or one-line speeches. *L'Hypocondriaque*, which also has 613 lines of monologue, contains 36 lines of single-line speeches. *Diane* contains 25 monologues. *Les Occasions perdues* ends with four marriages. Unlike Mairet, Rotrou was writing scripts for public performance rather than for semi-private presentation among a refined elite, but he was also not writing for the fairground.

The Italians were leading the way in the no doubt affected but also refined treatment of sensuality in a pastoral setting, leading to a quite probing analysis of sentiment and the moral rehabilitation of the emotional and physical gratification of desire. In the public theatre the models were still more frequently chivalresque and Spanish, leading to the importation into France of comic realism. In tragedy Rotrou did derive his 1639 *Antigone* chiefly from Garnier and from the Italian adaptation of Sophocles by Alamanni, but mostly the sources are Spanish, including Cervantes's *Dos doncellas* for the 1639 tragi-comédie *Les Deux Pucelles*. Rotrou's comedy with its Spanish models does, however, avoid the obscenities of fairground farce, elevates the social class of his characters, and allows them to be objects of amusement while retaining a certain dignity. Historically Rotrou was a pioneer, author of more than a third of all the comedies played between 1630 and 1640. His *La Bague de l'oubli*, performed 1629, closely derived from Lope de Vega's *Sortija del Olvido* of ten years previously, about a ring which obliterates its wearer's memory, preceded such other serious comedies as Corneille's 1633 *Mélite* by four years and Mairet's 1636 *Las Galanteries du duc d'Ossonne* by seven.

The 1643 comedy *Clarice; ou, L'Amour constant*, played in 1641, contains a preface in which Rotrou praises Plautus, from whom he took three comedies, the 1636 *Les Ménechmes*, played in 1632, the 1638 *Les Sosies*, dedicated to Liancourt and played in 1636, and the 1640 *Les Captifs; ou, Les Esclaves*, played in 1638, using a subject on which Du Ryer also drew. Independently of his source, however, Rotrou makes love sudden and irresistible, as in the 1639 comedy *La Belle Alphrède*, played in 1636, with only its name taken from the *Hermosa Alfreda* of

Lope de Vega, the 1637 tragi-comédie *L'Heureux Naufrage*, and the more interesting 1639 tragi-comédie *Laure persécutée*, played in 1637, derived from Lope de Vega's *Laura perseguida* and dedicated to the celebrated beauty and friend of the marquise de Rambouillet, Mlle de Vertus, whom Rotrou appears never to have met. The historical interest of *Laure* is not, however, restricted to the irresistibility and instantaneity of the love of Laure and Orantée, nor even to the fact that it was the model for Houdar de la Motte's 1723 tragedy *Inès de Castro*, but comes also from the restored tragi-comic balance between the tragedy inherent in the situation and the comic means used to overcome it, so righting Rotrou's usual list towards the comic.

The three most important of Rotrou's plays, all written in the last five years of his life, are generally taken to be the tragedy, *Le Véritable Saint Genest*, played in 1645 or 1646 and published in 1647, the tragi-comédie *Venceslas*, played at the end of 1647 and published in May 1648, and the tragedy *Cosroès* played in 1648 and published in 1649. Before *Saint Genest*, with the exception of *Crisante*, Rotrou's tragedies had been based on antique figures. *Saint Genest*, no doubt partly inspired by Corneille's 1643 *Polyeucte*, has a Christian subject, developed from part of a play by Lope de Vega. Genest was an actor from the late third century A.D. whose story was discovered by Rotrou in the same source as that in which Corneille had discovered his account of Polyeucte, Surius's *Lives of the Saints*. Genest had been charged by Diocletian to infiltrate the Christian community in order to caricature Christian habits on the stage. As he was playing a Christian being baptized he had a vision, declared that his stage baptism was authentic, and was tortured and beheaded. There is a contamination between three different stories in the *Lives of the Saints*, and Rotrou gives his emperor the name of Maximin. In Rotrou's play, Genest acts before Maximin a play about a martyr called Adrien, borrowing copiously from a Latin tragedy written for educational purposes by the Jesuit Père Cellot.

Technically, the play within a play is too long and distracts from the principal action, which is Genest's conversion, so that Rotrou's own play does not achieve its intended tragic effect. It raises no doubt fascinating problems about levels and layers of reality and illusion, but as a play it was not possible to make it dramatically effective. In 17th-century France it was obviously impossible to put on a play which ridiculed Christian ceremony, and Rotrou's solution, of taking seriously the Adrian play acted by the Genest troupe, makes the enthusiasm of the Roman audience inexplicable. However, Rotrou is by now sufficiently able to handle the rhetorical devices skilfully, the broken lines, the interrupted syntax, the well built-up speeches, the lyrical alexandrines, and he still has his aphorisms, sententiae, and succinctly memorable phrases:

Le plus grand des larcins est celui de la gloire

(The greatest theft is that of reputation).

Qu'il cesse de m'aimer, ou qu'il m'aime chrétien

(Let him cease to love me, or love me as a Christian).

Il s'agit d'imiter, et non de devenir.

(What we must do is imitate, not be changed into).

This line from act II, scene 4, occurs at the end of a speech delivered by Genest when he is alone on the stage rehearsing his lines. As he ends, a stage direction indicates *"Le ciel s'ouvre avec des flammes, et une voix s'entend, qui dit…Tu n'imiteras point en vain (The sky opens with flames, and a voice is heard, saying…You will not imitate in vain)."*

Venceslas, played in 1647, was published in May 1648 as a tragi-comédie, but as a tragedy in the second edition published in Holland in the same year. It was Rotrou's most popular play. The sources are partly a 1640 play by Rojas, set in Poland, on the incompatibility of being both a king and a father, *No hay ser padre siendo rey*, and two plays with Hungarian settlings by Guillén de Castro. Poland and Hungary were the eastern boundaries of Christianity. For the Spaniards there was a forceful analogy with the Arabic culture threatening their Christianity from the south. Rotrou retains the atmosphere and sometimes the language of Spain, although he is obviously influenced by the wave of interest generated in France by the marriage of the king of Poland, Ladislas VII, to the daughter of the duc de Nevers, Marie-Louise de Gonzague, on 13 July 1645. Much of Rotrou's information about Poland came from Renaudot's *Gazette* (q.v.). *Venceslas* was first played at the Hôtel de Bourgogne, and then later by Molière's company, and was successful enough, after the two 1648 editions, to be re-published in 1650 and 1655. In the 18th century Marmontel, rewriting the piece at the request of the marquise de Pompadour, changed the ending. The suicide of the heroine, Cassandre, seemed more appropriate than her possible later marriage to her husband's killer. Lekain as Ladislas at first refused altogether to speak Marmontel's lines, and when finally obliged to, declaimed them with obvious bad grace. Marmontel's text was played only six times, in April and May 1759. A third compromise text was published in 1774.

The first scene, which takes up two thirds of the first act, is devoted to a long reproach delivered by Venceslas, king of Poland, to his son Ladislas, whose behaviour makes him unworthy of the succession, which in Poland was not automatic but partly elective, and to Ladislas's reply, in which he tells his father it is time he handed over power he was no longer fit enough to exercise. Ladislas is particularly bitter about his father's favourite, the duc de Curlande, and about his own younger brother, Alexandre, whom he threatens "to kill. Ladislas is insolent, foolhardy, obviously unfitted for kingship, and provokes his father, who cannot sustain his dual role as king and father, into threatening his son with death. Ladislas is obsessed by Cassandre. At the beginning of the second act Cassandre explains why she must repudiate him. Ladislas had at first pursued her simply to satisfy his desires, and at heart therefore remains for Cassandre

L'ennemi de ma gloire et l'amant de ma honte

(The enemy of my honour and the lover of my shame).

Ladislas enters brusquely, demanding that Cassandre should marry him. Otherwise he will seek death. She persists in her refusal and Ladislas, left alone with his sister, the infanta Théodore, reveals his intention to kill the duc de Curlande, whom he tells Théodore that Cassandre loves. Théodore, left alone on the stage, is confused. A 35-line monologue, with more than a dozen question and exclamation marks, trails off into generalisations about love and power. The third act opens with the

first appearance of Fédéric, the duc de Curlande, ready to renounce Cassandre for the sake of the young prince Alexandre, brother of Ladislas and Théodore. Cassandre reveals her love for Alexandre, and Ladislas, thinking her in love with Fédéric, enters and delivers an insulting tirade telling Cassandre he will have nothing more to do with her. The fifth scene of act III between Ladislas and Fédéric is doubly ironic. Ladislas pretends to favour Fédéric's marriage to Cassandre while ignorant of Cassandre's own true choice but, when Venceslas offers Cassandre's hand to Fédéric, Ladislas cannot contain himself and bursts out in fury. He will kill Fédéric if he marries Cassandre.

In the fourth act Théodore dreams of a murder, and Ladislas enters. We hear from Ladislas that Fédéric and Cassandre were privately married and were consummating the wedding the night before when Ladislas gained access, extinguished the light, and murdered Fédéric. Just as Ladislas has admitted the murder to his father, Fédéric walks in. Cassandre enters and explains that Ladislas had killed his young brother, Alexandre. She demands his death. His father deprives Ladislas of his sword, gives it to Fédéric for custody, and says he will deliver judgement. In act V Théodore is torn between sorrow for her two brothers, the murdered and the murderer. It is she with whom Fédéric is in love. She enjoins silence on him, and sends him to plead with her father for the life of Ladislas. Fédéric thinks Venceslas will not condemn Ladislas to death but, in a scene overflowing with sentiment, Venceslas forces himself to send Ladislas to execution. Théodore and Cassandre, then Fédéric and, through Octave, governor of Warsaw, the whole population, all plead for mercy, and in a final scene Venceslas hands over the crown to Ladislas:

Soyez roi, Ladislas, et moi, je serai père.
Roi, je n'ai pu des lois souffrir les ennemis;
Père, je ne pourrai faire périr mon fils.
Une perte est aisée où l'amour nous convie;
Je ne perdrai qu'un nom, pour sauver une vie…

(Be king, Ladislas, and I shall be a father./As a king, I could not tolerate the enemies of the law;/As a father, I cannot make my son die./A loss is light when love commands us;/I shall lose only a title, and will save a life…).

The play ends with the marriage of Fédéric and Théodore, and Rotrou, no doubt thinking that he will outdo Pierre Corneille, echoes of whose *Le Cid* have reverberated linguistically throughout the play, allows the curtain to fall on the possibility that one day, if not quite just yet, Cassandre will consent to marry Ladislas. Emotionally there is great tension; dramatically the technique is much improved, and stylistically Rotrou has toned down all the worst excesses. Sententiae and stichomythia are no longer abused by excessive use, and the number of asides, always a sign of dramatic weakness where not used for comic effect, is kept down. The bravura ending perfectly illustrates what limits the power of Rotrou's imagination. It offends even more against the "bienséances (decencies)" than the possible future marriage of Rodrigue and Chimène had done in *Le Cid* but it is not imaginatively daring in the way Corneille's play was, not only because the intrigue is unbelievable and the emotions of the characters too psychologically implausible for the play to be really moving, but also and chiefly because at no point before the last scene had Cassandre shown love for Ladislas, and at no earlier point had Ladislas's feelings for Cassandre transcended lust.

Cosroès is a more political play, derived from the *Annales ecclesiastici* of Baronius, just as Pierre Corneille's *Héraclius* on the same reign had been, although Rotrou also used another play by Père Cellot, written for his pupils, and a situation taken from Lope de Vega. Cosroès, king of Persia, had captured the true cross on which Jesus had been crucified, and Heraclius, defending the Christians massacred by Cosroès, had captured it back, but the religious element, important for Baronius, is eliminated from Rotrou's play. Cosroès has two sons, Syroès, lover of Narsée, by his first wife, and Mardesane by his reigning queen, Syra, who wants the throne to go to her own son Mardesane rather than to Syroès.

The play starts with a quarrel over the succession between Syra, the queen, and Syroès, the heir to her husband's throne. Mardesane himself appears and will not dispute Syroès's rights. The third scene reveals the desire of Palmyras, Narsée's father, to strengthen Syroès's indecisiveness. While Cosroès had once killed his own father, Syroès is restrained by filial affection from assuming the power of which Syra wants to see him deprived. The act ends with the news that power is about to be transferred to Mardesane.

In the second act Cosroès, eaten up with guilt at his parricide, looks forward to death, orders the arrest of Syroès and tells Mardesane he wishes him to assume power. Mardesane cannot refuse but foresees that that the transfer of power will end in disaster. In the third act, Syra thinks she has won and despatches a dagger and poison to the imprisoned Syroès to give him the choice of which way he will die. She is, however, herself immediately arrested by the captain of the guards on orders from Syroès who, it now seems, has after all assumed power. He enters, but is oppressed at the need to have taken by crime power which was rightfully to be his. The fourth act ironically starts with the arrival of the dagger and the poison sent by the queen, who is now imprisoned, to Syroès. The intrigue is unnecessarily complicated by the writing of the role of Narsée into the play. Syroès is in love with her, but she turns out not to be the daughter of Syra, as had been thought. It has been suggested that Rotrou had to create a role for an actress new to the company.

The final act starts with a confrontation between Syroès and Syra, who finishes faced with the choice of dagger or poison she had offered Syroès, if she is not to be put to death. She leaves the stage for the last time in the second scene of act V. Mardesane defies Syroès and is condemned to die before his mother's eyes. It is, however, Syroès's inability to confront his father without filial devotion that causes him to revoke the sentences passed on Syra and Mardesane. It happens too late. Mardesane, seeing the preparations being made for his death, has killed himself; his mother has swallowed the poison; and in the play's last line we hear that Cosroès himself has drained the poison from the queen's cup and is dead. We are left to assume that Syroès, who has just left the stage, will be stopped from killing himself.

Again there is much violence. In this play the stichomythia return and the play is riddled with well-turned maxims. But vacillation is not a sign of psychological complexity, Syroès is not Hamlet, and it is difficult to find in *Cosroès* more than the basis for a tragic entertainment. Only an excessive deference to formal qualities or an interest in the taste of the period could justify seeing in Rotrou more than a competent entertainer relying on violence of emotion rather than analytical depth.

PUBLICATIONS

Collections

Oeuvres, 5 vols., 1820

Plays

[The Bibliothèque de la Pléiade *Théâtre du XVIIe siècle*, vol. 1, 1975, contains *La Bague de l'oubli, La Belle Alphrède, Laure persécutée, Le Véritable Saint Genest, Venceslas*, and *Cosroès*].

L'Hypocondriaque; ou, Le Mort amoureux, tragi-comédie, (1628) 1631
La Bague de l'oubli, comédie, (1629), 1635
Cléagénor et Doristée, tragi-comédie, (1630) ?1633
La Diane, comédie, (1630) 1635
Les Occasions perdues, tragi-comédie, (1631) 1636
L'Heureuse Constance, tragi-comédie, (1631) 1636
La Célimène, comédie, (1633) 1636
Hercule mourant, tragédie, (1634) 1636; modern edition 1971
Les Ménechmes, (1632) 1636
Agésilan de Colchos, tragi-comédie, (1635) 1637
Clorinde, comédie, (1636) 1637
La Céliane, tragi-comédie, 1637
Le Filandre, comédie, (1635) 1638
L'Heureux Naufrage, tragi-comédie, (1634) 1637
L'Innocente Infidélité, tragi-comédie, (1635) 1637
La Pèlerine amoureuse, tragi-comédie (1634) 1637
Amélie, tragi-comédie, (1636) 1638
Les Sosies, comédie, (1636), 1638
Antigone, tragédie, 1639
La Belle Alphrède, comédie, (1636) 1639
Les Deux Pucelles, tragi-comédie, (1636) 1639
Laure persécutée, tragi-comédie (1637) 1639
Les Captifs; ou, Les Esclaves, comédie, (1638) 1640
Crisante, tragédie, (?1635) 1640
Iphygénie, tragédie, 1641
Clarice; ou, L'Amour constant, comédie, (1641) 1643
Le Bélisaire, tragédie/tragi-comédie, 1644
Célie; ou, Le Vice-roi de Naples, tragi-comédie, 1646
Don Bernard de Cabrère, tragi-comédie (1647) 1648
Le Veritable Saint Genest, tragédie, (1645 or 1646) 1647; modern edition 1954
La Soeur, comédie, (1645) 1647; modern edition 1970
Venceslas, tragi-comédie, (1647) 1648; modern edition 1956
Cosroès, tragédie, (1648) 1649; modern edition 1950

Verse

[*Rotrou's verse is chiefly to be found in the prefatory material to the plays.*]

Oeuvres poétiques in *L'Hypocondriaque*, 1631
Autres oeuvres in *La Diane*, 1635

Biographical and critical studies

Baelen, J. van, *Rotrou. Le Héros tragique et la révolte*, 1965
Knutson, H.C., *The Ironic Game. A Study of Rotrou's Comic Theater*, 1966

Morel, J., *Jean Rotrou, dramaturge de l'ambiguïté*, 1968

Nelson, R.J., *Immanence and Transcendence. The Theater of Jean Rotrou*, 1969

ROUSSEAU, Jean-Jacques, 1712–1778.

Novelist, autobiographer, philosopher, and political thinker.

LIFE

Rousseau was born on 28 June 1712, the second son of a quarrelsome, affectionate, unstable, but reasonably well-to-do Swiss watchmaker, Isaac Rousseau, himself the son of a politically active liberal watchmaker, David. The mother was Suzanne Bernard, who had been brought up by her respected and affluent uncle Samuel (1631–1701), a pastor who also lectured on mathematics. Her pleasure-loving father, Jacques, who had been maintaining at least one illegitimate child and had had two known mistresses, had been imprisoned for immorality before marrying Suzanne's already pregnant mother. He had died when Suzanne was nine. Rousseau's parents had married on 2 June 1704 when both were 32, a sister of Rousseau's father being already married to his mother's brother. Suzanne's mother lived with them. The first child of the marriage, François, was born on 15 March 1705. Rousseau's father was one of about 1,500 "citizens" of Geneva, the controlling centre of the Calvinist religion, who were distinguished from among some 5,000 adult males and a total population of 20,000 by this mostly inherited title, conferring status and privilege but demanding religious and social conformity. The political status of Geneva was to become important for Rousseau, even if its vaunted popular sovereignty was little more than an important myth to which the ruling patrician oligarchy was merely careful to defer.

The General Council, the "Conseil Général," had become the legislative assembly of a city-state, an independent republic, when the Catholic cantons of eastern Switzerland vetoed its incorporation into the Helvetic federation. Geneva had imported German Lutheranism from neighbouring Berne, and Calvin had devised for it a specifically Latin and humanist form of Protestantism, ambiguously fusing oligarchic elements, due in the 17th century to increase in importance, and democratic ones, which correspondingly diminished, into what he intended to be an ideal Christian state, a theocracy in which the temporal was strictly subordinated to the spiritual power. In fact power was concentrated, when necessary by force, into the hands of an aristocratic self-perpetuating executive "little council" of 25, with four "syndics."

During the seven years since François's birth, the War of the Spanish Succession had caused a slump in the export of Swiss watches, and Rousseau's father had become watchmaker to the Sultan's Seraglio in Constantinople. He was however apparently pleased to be summoned back to Geneva on the death of his mother-in-law, and arrived home in September 1711. His family was of French origin, resident in Geneva since the mid-16th century. He had been one of six surviving children out of 14 born to an active liberal opponent of the little council. Three of the survivors were sons, all watchmakers. Three were daughters, all reprimanded by the Geneva consistory for playing cards on the Sabbath; one was known, although not by Rousseau, to have given birth to a child only a day or two after her wedding. By the early 18th century Genevan Calvinism had been reduced to a system of austere and industrious social values, postponing consumption in the interests of investment, its adherents stern, unsophisticated, and plain-speaking, its dogmatic foundations virtually reduced to the proclamation of Christ as the messiah. Rousseau was for long to associate Catholicism with an openness to pleasure.

Since Rousseau's mother, the eldest of Jacques Bernard the rake's three legitimate daughters, had herself been in trouble with the authorities for defying the moral decencies by, among other things, receiving a married man, Vincent Sarasin, during her husband's protracted absence, and by dressing as a boy to attend a fair-ground performance, Rousseau himself may well have been disinclined by both sets of parental genes to pay any exaggerated respect to the social proprieties. There is no evidence, however, that he knew anything about the strain of frivolous and rebellious non-conformity which he may have inherited from both parental families, and he was to idealize the Geneva of his early youth.

The large house in which Rousseau and his brother were brought up by his father and aunts had been bequeathed by her uncle to his mother, who died of a puerperal fever at the age of 39 on 6 July 1712, a week after Rousseau's birth. She had inherited from her uncle and her mother substantial amounts of money in addition to the house, and in June 1717 the house, left in trust for the two sons until they reached their majority at 25, was sold for 31,500 florins. Rousseau eventually received only half of 13,000. The family moved to more cramped quarters by the lake in the less fashionable part of the town, where sumptuary laws still forbade any public display of luxury. Rousseau's father preferred hunting and dancing to the trade of watchmaking, even though it was reserved to "citizens" and normally lucrative, and he went so far as to become for a while a partner in a dancing school, the sort of establishment tolerated by the authorities in the 18th century in the interests of attracting to Geneva the young, foreign, Protestant nobility who were beginning to come there to finish their education and to learn French uncontaminated with Catholicism.

Rousseau was born with a deformity of the urinary tract which was later to be the cause of much pain, and of sexual humiliation. He was particularly close to his eldest aunt, "Suzon," born in 1682 and to marry only in 1730. His later recollections of childhood are idealized, but it is clear that Rousseau's father was savage and maudlin by turns, and that Rousseau was by far the favourite of the two boys. Both were beaten, and the effect on Rousseau was certainly unwholesome. What he later in several contexts regarded as a manly response to pain, in early youth at least very nearly toppled over the border into sexual deviance.

Sword-bearing in a watchmaker was something of an affectation, but Rousseau's father carried a sword, and is known four times to have drawn it. In 1722 he was shooting outside Geneva on ground belonging to a French army captain, Pierre Gautier, who objected. Four months later the two men met again in the city and renewed their quarrel. Rousseau's father suggested a duel but was told by the officer that with men like Rousseau's father he used only sticks, whereat Rousseau's father struck him with a sword. Gautier drew his, but the pair were restrained by bystanders, and two days later Rousseau's father fled Geneva, where he was sentenced in his absence to three months in prison and a fine. He settled in Nyon, on Bernese territory, married again on 5 March 1726, and lived on the income from his first wife's estate. François was apprenticed to a watchmaker, but ran away, after which we hear nothing of him. Rousseau, left in Geneva with Colonel Bernard, the brother of his mother who had married his father's sister, was sent with a cousin to board with a Calvinist country pastor, Jean-Jacques Lambercier, at Bossey, situated in Savoy but subject in spiritual matters to Geneva.

Rousseau's early education had been in the hands of his father, who had read to him Calvinist sermons, Plutarch, Tacitus and the novels of galanterie. He was now instructed by the pastor, and relished his almost total freedom, the friendship with his cousin, and idyllic country pursuits among the birds, orchards, meadows, streams, mountains, and flowers. The expression in Rousseau's later work of this delight in fresh air, walking, and the visually exhilarating phenomena of a mountainous landscape was to be the catalyst of a whole new sensibility in western Europe, although Rousseau may have had leisure to fantasize and dream too much for his own later good. He tells us in the *Confessions* that he enjoyed being spanked by the pastor's sister and, though he did not like annoying her, had to restrain himself from doing things which he knew would result in a beating from her. He had no desire to be beaten by the pastor himself and when Mlle Lambercier realized what effect her punishment was having she curtailed it. While they had hitherto slept in the same room, and in winter even in the same bed as Mlle Lambercier, Rousseau and his cousin were now put in another room together. Since sexual gratification depended on a chastisement Rousseau was naturally too timid to ask for, his satisfactions, as with some exaggeration he was later to note, were largely limited to fantasy.

The *Confessions* are not a reliable guide to the biography, although the misremembering of dates and ages, like the way in which Rousseau toned down successive versions, is often revealing. He reflects that the beatings by a 30-year-old when he was eight "determined his tastes, desires, and passions for the rest of his life." In fact Mlle Lambercier was 40 and he was 11, and the real ages make the psychology of the reactions intelligible, especially in view of the gossip occasioned locally by the display of intimacy in the pastor's domestic arrangements with his sister. Complaints had led to a reprimand for the pastor, investigation having revealed no impropriety, but obvious carelessness.

Rousseau's stay at Bossey finished sometime after the summer of 1724, when he returned to his mother's brother in the city, but the *Confessions* here confuse the dates, expanding what can only have been a few months into two or three years. By April 1725 Rousseau had been briefly articled to a prosecuting lawyer in Geneva but, quickly considered unfit for a profession, had then been apprenticed to an engraver, Abel Ducommun, on a five-year contract. Rousseau tells us that his final months at Bossey were soured on account of a severe and unjust beating from his uncle, called in by the pastor to beat both his cousin and himself, and dates from that incident his resentment at life's

injustices. It was made plain to him in Geneva that, unlike his cousin, he did not have the resources to become a military engineer, but, since he had had nothing else to do, he had in fact in the winter of 1724–25 begun to learn draughtsmanship and mathematics with his cousin. He removed from the final version of the *Confessions* the statement that his aunt, the one who had in fact given birth within days of her wedding, had, "to console herself for the infidelities of her husband," taken refuge in sanctimony.

Ducommun had been born in January 1705 and was to marry in November 1726. Rousseau regarded him as uncultivated and brutal. Fear taught the boy to lie, and hunger to steal food. He hid tools for his private use, made heraldic medallions which were taken for attempts at forged coins, was beaten, and recounts incidents showing himself to have been socially intimidated to the point almost of paranoia, as later he was in a similar way to be sexually inhibited. He visited his father, had a platonic infatuation for a girl, Charlotte de Vulson, ten years his senior, who, though in fact engaged, teased and flirted with him, and he went through a fiercely passionate relationship with a "Mlle Goton," who allowed him to take no liberties, but whipped him. One of the more remarkable qualities of the *Confessions* is the way in which they overcome the barrier against revealing what is merely silly or shameful. Rousseau tells us that other children would come up to him and tease him about being whacked by "Goton"—the name was a diminutive of Marguerite. She must have been remarkably perceptive to discern Rousseau's needs, since he added to the original manuscript of the *Confessions* that he could never bring himself to reveal his "bizarre desires" even to those who could have satisfied them, or to beg "even during the most intimate familiarities the favour that would complete all the rest." He tells us, referring to Goton, that he had the experience only once "in my childhood with a girl of my own age, and even then it was she who first proposed it."

Rousseau took refuge from the uncouth vulgarity of the Ducommun workshop by cultivating a private inner world. He read avidly and indiscriminately, turning away only from pornography. He was beaten, and his borrowed books were confiscated and destroyed, but he persisted. Reading and occasionally walking were his only recreations. It was on Sunday, 14 March 1728, when he was not yet 16, that he went for a walk outside the city and returned to find the gates already closed. That had happened twice before, and each time he had had to sleep rough and been beaten on his return in the morning. One of the officers always closed the gates early, but no one could know when he was on duty. On this occasion he was. Rousseau and his companions returned in what they took to be good time, heard the closing signal when still a mile off, ran, shouted, and watched the soldiers pull the levers to raise the drawbridge when they were within 20 paces. In the morning Rousseau's companions went in, taking a message to his cousin to say that he was running away, hoping that his cousin would join him. His cousin, later himself to run away from home, came with parting presents, and Rousseau, after spending a few nights with peasant families he had got to know on his walks, sought help in Savoy from one of the local Catholic parish priests.

Savoy, an independent duchy adjacent to Geneva whose ancient capital had been Chambéry but which was now run from Turin, was not yet part of France but was committedly Catholic. Rousseau had inherited from his father an inbred sense of superiority, and a fascination with the chivalric, the feudal, and the aristocratic. He went to a Catholic priest of noble blood of whom he must at least previously have heard, and found in him an elderly missionary scholar who was an excellent host. Rousseau was sent on to a Swiss baroness at Annecy, herself a recent convert to Catholicism and anxious to help young Protestant refugees. He took three days over the journey when he needed only one, indulged his feudal fantasies as he passed successive castles, and presented his letter to the 29-year-old Baroness de Warens, estranged from her Swiss Protestant husband, childless, in receipt of annual pensions of 1,850 livres for her missionary activities, and not unknown to make lovers of her converts, and even of her servants. Her current lover was her steward, Claude Anet, eight years Rousseau's senior, whom she had brought with her from Vevey, across the lake from Geneva.

She was generous to Rousseau, gave him hospitality and money, and arranged for his fare to Turin to be paid by the bishop. He was to go to a hospice for young converts to Catholicism. Both his father and his uncle had made only half-hearted efforts to follow him. It was cheaper for his father to compensate Ducommun than it would have been for him to keep Rousseau. Rousseau walked to Turin with a companion he had met at Annecy and his wife, having no notion, he tells us, what it was they did together during the night. He was robbed by them, but was still gay from the spring hike when he arrived at the hospice. There he determined to complete the process of his conversion as speedily as possible, was the subject of homosexual advances, had to have explained to him the mysteries of sex, and was received into the Church.

He scraped a living doing odd jobs, and was for a few months a footman and secretary to a countess dying of breast cancer. When the household broke up Rousseau stole a ribbon and accused a maid of giving it to him and then, in self-justification, of other crimes besides. Both he and the maid were dismissed, and it was partly the guilt inspired in him by this episode that finally provoked him into writing the *Confessions* 50 years later. He was helped in Turin by two priests. One was a young peasant, Jean-Claude Gaime, part model for the "Vicaire savoyard" in *Emile*, who taught him the virtues of probity and unworldliness, while the other, Carlo Vittoria de Gouvon, the younger son of a new employer to whom Rousseau was secretary, taught him Italian and rekindled his interest in Latin and literature.

Rousseau spares himself very little in the way of embarrassment in the *Confessions*. We learn of the fits of clumsiness into which the sight of an attractive woman could propel him, the humiliations of the bare-bottomed lurking in the alleys of Turin in the hope of a female spanking, with successive versions of the *Confessions* now correcting or amplifying details. The Gouvon family took an interest in his education and went out of their way to see to his proper training. A post in an embassy seemed within grasp, but Rousseau, betraying his stubborn, or perhaps wild, streak, became determined to return to Mme de Warens, to whom he had continued to write and who had warned him not to behave in any way which would damage his good fortune. When he arrived back at Annecy in June 1729, she did not seem surprised, and let him stay. Married at 14 to a 25-year-old, she had become an accomplished hostess, but had ruined her husband by the restless organization of industrial enterprises which failed. A hypochondriac, she had found the Savoy of Aix-les-Bains less stifling than Protestant Vevey, ruled from Berne, and had settled in the duchy in 1726, taking most of her husband's household property with her. Her husband divorced her, and had to sell his

barony in 1728, but Mme de Warens continued to sign herself "Baroness."

Rousseau called her "Maman" and fantasized about her, but was inhibited enough to maintain a discreet bearing in her presence, and recalls that his fantasies kept him pure. "Maman" gave him odd jobs helping Anet, and tried to complete his education. Rousseau finally consented to go to a local seminary, his training for the priesthood to be subsidized by the bishop. One of his tutors, Jean-Baptiste Gâtier, became the second model for the "Vicaire savoyard." Rousseau was dismissed after three months, apparently because his temperamental inaptitude had been discerned, but he had developed a love of music, and was now kept by Mme de Warens as a boarder in a nearby choristers' school, where he remained for six months, although he spent more of his time dreaming than learning. At Easter 1730 the choirmaster, having decided to break his contract with the Cathedral, was encouraged by Mme de Warens to take Rousseau with him to Lyons, no doubt partly to break the ascendancy over the youth gained by the Levantine musician and trickster, Venture de Villeneuve, who had caused a sensation at the choir school.

The trunk containing the schoolmaster's own music, as well as that belonging to the Cathedral, with which he had absconded, was confiscated on their arrival at Lyons, word having been sent from Annecy in advance. Rousseau then abandoned the choirmaster, returned to Annecy, and found that Mme de Warens had suddenly departed on a journey which we can now conjecture had to do with raising support in Paris for a revolution in the canton of Vaud against the domination of Berne. When she crossed the border from Savoy into France at Seyssel at the end of April, she was wearing a mask. In August the authorities in Annecy were instructed to keep her under surveillance and it was made clear that she would be wise to confine herself to missionary activities.

Rousseau immediately joined Venture de Villeneuve, staying with him at an inn. He later felt that his fastidiousness protected him from attentions which he says were lavished on him by uncultured girls. He enjoyed one celebrated day's flirtation at Thônes with two girls on horseback whom he met while walking. The pleasure which that day gave him was, he says, more intense than that afforded him by any subsequent physical satisfaction of his sexual needs. He accompanied one of Mme de Waren's maids back to Fribourg, stipulating that they should make the journey on foot. She paid his expenses, and he was presumably telling the truth when he said that she was in love with him, and that though they slept in the same room the idea of a liaison never entered his head. They had called on Rousseau's father on the way, but no real attempt was made to detain him, even for supper. A letter a year later makes clear that Rousseau's relationship with his father had deteriorated further than he admitted in the *Confessions*.

Rousseau now went to Lausanne and, in the hope of imitating Villeneuve, posed as a music master, even adopting his model's name, combined with a quasi-anagram of his own, as Vaussore de Villeneuve. The mixture of incapacity and impudence quickly led to humiliating discomfiture, but Rousseau visited Vevey, already rich in associations for him, and later to be idealized into the idyllic setting for his earthly paradise. It is at this point in Rousseau's career that the early Neuchâtel manuscript of the *Confessions* breaks off. He did however move to Neuchâtel, where he had better success as a singing instructor before becoming translator to a bogus Greek archimandrite collecting funds for the restoration of the Holy Sepulchre. After Rousseau had successfully extracted funds from the Berne senate, which he addressed, his companion was unmasked by the French ambassador at the diplomatic capital, Soleure.

Rousseau, obviously himself under suspicion, managed to make such an impression on the ambassador that, although the sequence of events is obscure and he appears to have undergone a period of greater than usual destitution, the embassy authorities arranged a post for him in Paris as tutor to a Swiss family there. Finding himself treated more as a valet than as a tutor, and friendless except for the kindly sister-in-law of the French diplomat who had arranged the appointment, Rousseau returned on foot to Lyons, hoping through a friend to effect a reconciliation with Mme de Warens, reportedly displeased with him. In Lyons, sleeping rough, he was approached by a variety of homosexuals, and finally by a monk who, having heard him singing one morning, gave him a job on the spot copying music. His transcriptions were apparently so bad that they could not be used, but the monk treated and paid him well, and news soon arrived that Mme de Warens, now at Chambéry, would be pleased for him to join her there. She sent money for Rousseau to hire a horse, but he preferred to travel again on foot.

At Chambéry Mme de Warens no longer had a beautiful house, but her connections were better, and on his arrival in the autumn of 1731 Rousseau was given a job as a clerk in the survey department of the Savoy tax office. He had to acquire mathematical skills and learn how to draw maps and to use water colours. He took up flower painting as a hobby and was tutored by Anet, whose true position in Mme de Warens's household he was told when Anet attempted suicide. The nephew of a gardener employed by her husband, Anet may have been Mme de Warens's lover before she ever left Vevey. Rousseau stayed at the survey department for eight months, not as he says two years, then left out of boredom. He devoured works on French history and literature, and appears to have tried to study music in Besançon, but to have been forced back to Chambéry to teach it. It was probably in 1733 that Mme de Warens decided Rousseau and she should become lovers and, after giving him a week's warning, she duly initiated him. Inevitably, Rousseau felt as if he had committed incest.

Anet died on 13 March 1734, just as Mme de Warens seemed likely to get him appointed curator of a botanical garden. Rousseau, whose account of Anet's fatal fever is blatantly distorted, succeeded him as her steward, but was less successful than Anet had been in curbing her expenditure, and took to hoarding and hiding money against future need, a habit which laid the foundation for his admitted future meanness. Resisting attempts to make him learn to fence and to dance, Rousseau, despite inexpertise, organized the musical activities that were the foundations for Mme de Warens's success as a salon hostess. Her fortunes were declining, but her fondness for unprofitable entrepreneurial undertakings only increased. Rousseau was later himself to send her money. In the meanwhile he became increasingly intent on a musical career, studied Rameau's *Traité de l'harmonie* of 1722, composed cantatas, and became a sort of agent for Mme de Warens, being sent by her on mysterious trips. He fell ill, almost certainly from the strain of being the lover of a surrogate mother, started on a systematic programme of self-education, and began to buy books from the Geneva bookseller and publisher Jacques Barrillot, especially works of science, philosophy and literature, and including Bayle's *Dictionnaire*.

After Anet's death Mme de Warens sold the garden plot where he had cultivated herbs, together with the garden house where she had first made Rousseau her lover. With Rousseau's encouragement she now leased the first of her summer sanctuaries in the valley of Les Charmettes, where she eventually became a tenant farmer. Rousseau's health remained poor, but his feeling of communion with nature developed during his early morning walks and he enjoyed the programme of picnics and fruit picking. Early in 1737 he nearly killed himself during a chemical experiment, when a bottle of arsenic sulphide and mercury exploded while he was following written instructions for mixing them. That year the *Mercure de France* printed a song, Rousseau's first publication, and he came of age by Genevan law. He returned to Geneva in quest of his patrimony, thinking it prudent on this occasion to observe the ban forbidding apostates to reside within the walls. He had given Barrillot power of attorney, but could not persuade the authorities that his brother was dead and had to be content with his half of the shrunken capital sum, or 6,500 florins in cash. He then entered Geneva, and was there for the liberal insurrection of 21 August.

On his return to Chambéry he found that his place as resident lover had been bestowed on another of the young men favoured by Mme de Warens, the lusty and lustful Jean-Samuel-Rodolphe Wintzenried, described by Rousseau as a hairdresser. Rousseau's reaction, encouraged by Mme de Warens, was to go to Montpellier to see a doctor she had heard about. On the journey, in the late summer of 1737, Rousseau had a passing liaison with a 44-year-old woman which prompted him to dally for three days in Montélimar. The rosy picture painted in the *Confessions* of life in Montpellier is at odds with his letters, but it appears that his illness was not taken seriously, that he was short of money, and that his relationship with Mme de Warens had deteriorated, although Wintzenried was also having a liaison with a maid, and Mme de Warens casually suggested on his return that Rousseau should continue as her lover, jointly with the newcomer. The arrangement did not appeal to Rousseau, who was then firmly quartered by Mme de Warens at a house in Les Charmettes where he lived mostly alone for two years, studied, wrote a great deal, still acted occasionally as steward and secretary to his benefactress, and further developed his love of solitude and distrust of humanity. Mme de Warens meanwhile had acquired the right to farm at Les Charmettes, and Rousseau found his rustic retreat spoiled as it became the centre of an agricultural undertaking. Mme de Warens increased the pressure on him to leave, and to support himself.

In 1738 his grandfather, David Rousseau, died a pauper at the age of 95. From Les Charmettes Rousseau published his anonymous elegy *Le Verger de Madame la Baronne de Warens* in 1739, written in 1738 and almost certainly printed at Annecy by Burdet, although purporting to have been published in London by Jacob Tomson. It was full of stilted conventions and allegorical figures. He sent begging letters seeking a pension and attempting to establish his right to his brother's unclaimed share of their joint inheritance, and tried to interest the authorities in instituting a Savoy freight service across the Alps. He finally left Les Charmettes on 20 April 1740, when Mme de Warens found him a job as tutor to the children of Etienne de Condillac's elder brother, Jean Bonnot, seigneur de Mably and Provost of Lyons, for the upbringing of whose unruly sons he wrote a rationalistic and utilitarian education treatise based largely on views later partly to be repudiated and partly to be developed in *Emile*. They were drawn from Locke, whose *Thoughts Concerning Education* (1693) had appeared in French, as *De l'Education des enfants*, in 1695, and Locke's French disciple Charles Rollin, the author of a well-known *Traité des études*. Mably, born in 1696, had in 1732 married a woman 15 years younger than he. She was to bear him 12 children, but only two were boys old enough to need a tutor in 1740, when Rousseau arrived in Lyons.

He was introduced to cultivated enlightenment society, attended the academies of sciences and of fine arts, and met Charles Bordes, a later opponent, in whose company he felt boorish, but to whom he wrote an *Epître* containing a passage in praise of industrial prosperity. Rousseau relished the role he soon found in Lyons intellectual life, compensating for being made to feel uncultivated by tingeing his appreciation of the intellectual stimulus with a touch of contempt for its social trappings. He acquired socially and intellectually influential friends like Camille Perrichon, the ex-mayor of Lyons, and attempted for the second time to finish an opera which, like the first one, he destroyed. Another *Epître*, to a famous surgeon, Gabriel Parisot, shows Rousseau still to have been anti-egalitarian as well as pro-industrial. The Mably family were kind. Rousseau was given a room of his own, but was deprived of the key to the cellar when empty bottles were found in it, and the teaching enterprise was unsuccessful. Rousseau analyses his inadequacies, not without a hint of self-satisfaction, in a *Mémoire* to his employer. He is, he says, melancholy, shy, and indifferent to the opinion of people he does not like. At the end of the year, his contract was not renewed.

Mme de Warens was starting to sell her silver, and Rousseau, whose self-dramatization is intensified at this point in the *Confessions*, had to sell books to move between Les Charmettes, where Mme de Warens was now permanently installed and where he found the maternal solicitude he still needed, and Lyons, where he was infatuated with Suzanne Serre, eight years younger than he was, and on 26 February 1745 to marry a young merchant by whom on 12 November 1744 she had already had a son. In the summer of 1742, apparently to relieve Mme de Warens of the burden of keeping him, Rousseau sold his books and possessions at Les Charmettes and Lyons and made his way to Paris, where he arrived in August. Camille Perrichon had paid his fare, and other friends from Lyons had given him letters of introduction. Rousseau had with him a scheme for a new musical notation system and his play *Narcisse*.

He found a room in the Hôtel Saint-Quentin, frequented by his Lyons friends, and was immediately introduced by another guest to Diderot, quickly to become his closest literary friend. A friend of Mably's introduced him to Réaumur, who arranged for him to present his musical notation system to the Académie des sciences, where he was congratulated on it. It was turned down, however, because its utilization of numbers, while useful for singers interested only in one note at a time, had serious drawbacks for instrumentalists needing to see large numbers of notes simultaneously. Rousseau defended himself in a long letter published by the *Mercure* (q.v.) in February 1743, and by his *Dissertation sur la musique moderne*, published by a bookseller G.-F. Quillau. Rousseau made no money out of the *Dissertation*, but lost only the publisher's licence fee. He had none the less gained a footing in cultured circles in Paris. He kept himself by giving composition lessons, and economized by going to cafés only every other day, and to the theatre only twice a week. He met Fontenelle and also Marivaux, whose exploitation of Ricco-

boni's Italian company's commedia dell'arte (q.v.) optimism, well attuned to the imaginative activities of the "modernes" camp (see: Querelle des anciens et des modernes), led Rousseau himself to espouse the Italian musical idiom in place of the rigidly rhetorical and artificial style of French music.

In Paris Rousseau was shy when Mme de Broglie, daughter of the socially important Mme de Besneval, hinted at a willingness to be seduced, but he showed himself more forward in pursuit of literary acclaim. He was well received by Mme Louise Dupin, the illegitimate daughter of the financier Samuel Bernard and his mistress, the former actress Manon Dancourt. To Mme Dupin, who appeared to have encouraged him, Rousseau made advances, but she was the surprisingly faithful wife of the immensely wealthy Claude Dupin, owner of the Hôtel Lambert in Paris and the château of Chenonceaux in the Loire valley, and Rousseau was banished from her salon, in which the rich and socially esteemed were received with the elegant, the witty, and the literary world. Later forgiven, he was very briefly a tutor in the household, and with Dupin's stepson Francueil resumed his work on chemistry, attending the courses of Rouelle, under whom Diderot had also studied. He caught pneumonia, and during his convalescence sketched out what was to become his opera *Les Muses galantes*.

Mme de Broglie obtained for him the opportunity to go to Venice as secretary to the comte de Montaigu, the new French ambassador. Rousseau haggled over money, turned the post down, demanded time to reflect when his substitute was dismissed and the terms were improved to include "expenses," and finally said he would come in a fortnight. The French minister in Genoa, Chaillou de Jonville, an efficient administrator, ambitious, generous, and with a reputation as a dandy, rescued Rousseau from solitary quarantine, imposed on all visitors to save the city from the plague, and wrote enthusiastically about him to Montaigu. Circumstantial evidence suggests that Rousseau cheated in his claim for expenses, some of which, although clearly allowable, were later contested by the ambassador and not paid. Montaigu turned out to be mean and arrogant, as well as wholly incompetent, and Rousseau was abnormally touchy about his dignity, although at first he enjoyed the work, much complicated by France's support for Spain in its war against Sardinia over the Austrian succession. Unlike the ambassador, he could speak Italian. The despatches, incoming and outgoing, had become important, and the French archives show Rousseau to have been efficient and conscientious.

His despatches run from 14 September 1743 to 25 July 1744. His disputes with the ambassador came to centre primarily on his own status. In the ambassador's opinion, Rousseau was an indispensable secretary, but also merely an elevated clerk. In his own opinion, he was a diplomat. He was to take away with him only slight comprehension of how the secretive, inquisitive, and despotic oligarchy of the Venetian "republic" actually worked, but enough to incite him to the comparison with Geneva from which *Du contrat social* was to emerge. He also came to love the gaiety of Italian life and music, taking advantage of the ambassadorial boxes at the opera, not to eat, chatter and play cards with everyone else, but to steal away to some corner where he could listen to the music. Whenever he could he also listened to sacred music. Although his salary, like Montaigu's, was hugely in arrears, Rousseau enjoyed Venice.

There were sexually curious incidents. In one, an Italian girl was scornful about Rousseau's failure to be roused by her seductive charms, of which, however, he showed himself to be fully aware. In another, he kept, jointly with a Secretary from the Spanish embassy, a 12-year-old prostitute for whom his affection remained strictly paternal. There was also the continuous battle to achieve recognition for what he considered to be his rank. The final break with Montaigu came after a quarrel about money, which had increasingly become the focal point of their clashes. The ambassador lost his temper at a claim by Rousseau for expenses. In spite of a letter to the French Foreign Office complaining of sickness, destitution, indebtedness, and over-tiredness, Rousseau lingered for some weeks in Venice after his dismissal, cared for by the French community, and especially the consul, Le Blond, who despised Montaigu and lent Rousseau the money for the return journey to Paris, over which he took seven weeks and during which, to avoid meeting his step-mother, he invited his father to dine in the inn at Nyon. The general administrative and social refusal in Paris to sympathize with Rousseau over the wrongs inflicted on him by Montaigu, whose caste privileges had to be upheld for the sake of social order, were the cause of an indignation about civil injustice which was the foundation of the *Discours sur l'inégalité*.

In Paris Rousseau stayed for some months with a wealthy Spanish aristocrat, Ignacio Altuna, whom he had met in Venice. They ate together at a lively inn, and Rousseau comments in the *Confessions* on the shyness which prevented his companion and himself from availing themselves of the girls from the dress-maker's next door. When Altuna left in the spring of 1745, Rousseau turned down the invitation to accompany him as a per-manent companion and moved again into the Hotel Saint-Quen-tin, asking his friend Daniel Roguin to try to get the tailor to take back some of the finery, still unpaid for, which Roguin had bought on Rousseau's behalf for sending out to Venice. Rous-seau worked on his opera, *Les Muses galantes*, and became the lover of Thérèse Levasseur, the illiterate laundry maid from a family which had come down in the world after the mother's bankruptcy. Thérèse was about 22. She was much teased at table by the other employees of the hotel, and Rousseau seems instinctively to have taken her side. The exact nature of their sexual and emotional relationship is disputed, but it varied. It included an element of mothering, and its closeness was clearly dependent on the modesty of Thérèse's social status and her probable willingness to cater for Rousseau's sexual needs in ways his shyness might have prevented him from seeking among the highly born. Thérèse was to bear him five children, and he was to marry her in 1768, over 20 years later.

In search of a performance for his opera, Rousseau contrived an introduction to the rich tax-farmer and music patron, Alexan-dre Le Riche de la Poplinière, who had the score played by an orchestra. The chief beneficiary of his patronage, Rameau, was not pleased, but Rousseau succeeded in having the piece given in its entirety in the house of a friend of the well-disposed duc de Richelieu. The promise of a Versailles performance was unfulfilled, but Rousseau was invited to adapt Rameau's music to a libretto by Voltaire, *Les Fêtes de Ramire*, for a court gala in December 1745. There was an entirely amicable correspon-dence between Rousseau and Voltaire, who had dashed off his text, recast from something longer. It was performed over Vol-taire's name, with neither Rameau's nor Rousseau's attached to it, but Rousseau was pleased with his overture in the Italian style. He was, however, too unwell to collect his fee before Richelieu left Paris.

From early in 1746 Rousseau again frequented the salon of Mme Dupin at the Hôtel Lambert and resumed his chemistry studies with her stepson, Francueil, still, after eight years of marriage, living in his father's house. Rousseau joined the household as a paid secretary because he had to maintain Thérèse and her mother, keeping a room near the Hôtel Lambert for himself and another at the other end of Paris for Thérèse and her mother, usually supping with them in the evening. He had still hoped to make his living as a musician or an author until its obvious deficiencies caused him to withdraw *Les Muses galan-tes* from rehearsals at the Opéra. The Italian company accepted, but neither paid for nor played, a refurbished *Narcisse*, and Rousseau was kept busy for five years by his duties as an aman-uensis to Claude Dupin, to his wife, who intended to write a book she never finished on the rights of women, and to Fran-cueil, who needed to publish a book for entry into the academy of sciences.

In the course of his duties, Rousseau read a great deal and, had it not been for the financial constraints, would have been in a situation almost ideal for him, with, on the one hand, upper-class company and luxurious surroundings, interesting books and stimulating conversation, and the exciting intellectual com-panionship of Diderot, and, on the other, the unpretentious, relaxed, lower-class domesticity of Thérèse, dim-witted almost to the point of being retarded, and her mother. He dined weekly with Diderot and Condillac, whom he had introduced to Diderot, at the Panier Fleuri, but also enjoyed the grand country-house entertainments of Chenonceaux, for which among other pieces he wrote a play, *L'Engagement téméraire*, and a poem, *L'Allée de Silvie*, as well as music for voices.

It was on his return to Paris from Chenonceaux in December 1747 that Rousseau found Thérèse pregnant with his child. He was still worldly, ambitious and quite young. Given the shortage of money and Thérèse's need to earn, it seemed perfectly normal, as Thérèse's mother also saw, to send the baby to the foundling hospital, which had received 3,274 infants in 1746, all but 950 of whom had been abandoned in the streets. There were two orphanages in Paris. Rousseau later claimed that he sent his children to one only because he could not afford to rear them, since the rich consumed too large a share of resources which were themselves adequate, and that the foundlings were well cared for. In fact, in 1741, 68% of Paris foundlings had died in infancy. In 1747 Rousseau's father died at the age of 75, and Rousseau was this time able to persuade the authorities that his brother must have died, so coming into his final inheritance from his parents of some 3,000 livres, part of which he sent to Mme de Warens, whose new loss-making industrial enterprises were dragging her ever more heavily into unrepayable debt. It was by now clear to Rousseau that he was chronically subject to inflam-mations and infections of the urinary tract, with the consequent retention of urine which was to cause him embarrassment con-stantly and misery sporadically for the rest of his life.

In his capacity as amanuensis, Rousseau was now enlisted by the Dupins in their campaign to refute Montesquieu's *De l'Esprit des lois*, which had appeared in October 1748, and with whose argument Rousseau himself much sympathized. Dupin's two-volume *Réflexions sur quelques parties d'un livre intitulé 'De l'Esprit des lois'*, published late in 1749, was immediately withdrawn. The three-volume revision entitled *Observations*, with which Rousseau also helped, was to appear late in 1751 or early the following year. By 1748, when his second child was born, Rousseau had met Francueil's mistress, the salon hostess, Mme d'Epinay, an aristocrat with literary pretensions married to a rich but of course bourgeois tax farmer, and through her the Bellegarde family of her brother-in-law, including Bellegarde's 17-year-old daughter, the future Mme d'Houdetot. Early in 1749 Diderot commissioned from Rousseau the articles on music for the *Encyclopédie* (q. v.) and he published a series of 12 songs in the Italian style. Mme Dupin raised his salary to 50 livres a month and persuaded him to accept the post of governor to her son, Chenonceaux, whom Rousseau had already briefly and unsuccessfully tutored for a week in 1743. Chenonceaux's marriage to an aristocratic young lady, then expecting to end her life a nun in her convent, had been arranged, but his character had not improved. He lost 700,000 livres gambling in one night, and the Hôtel Lambert had to be sold to pay his debts.

Diderot had found a bookseller willing to publish Condillac's *Essai sur l'origine des connaissances humaines*, but could not persuade the serious Condillac to join with Rousseau and himself in launching a review, *Le Persifleur*, on the model of that put out in England by Addison and Steele. It never appeared, although a first number was written entirely by Rousseau. Invited to meet the young Prince Frederick of Saxe-Gotha, Rousseau quickly made friends with two members of the royal party, Emmanuel Christophe Klüpfel, the founder of the *Almanach de Gotha*, and Frederick Melchior Grimm, an impoverished German baron 11 years Rousseau's junior. Rousseau never forgot the shame he felt when, after one boisterous evening, he retired to the bedroom with Klüpfel's mistress. Thérèse, herself widely believed to be unfaithful to Rousseau, was more shocked that Grimm should have told her about the incident than that Rousseau, for what he says was the last time, should have been unfaithful to her.

The unfavourable treaty of Aix-la-Chapelle in 1748 had led to increased taxation in France, publicly expressed dissatisfaction, and a harsher censorship. Diderot was incarcerated in the dungeons at Vincennes for a month from 24 July 1749, but then lavishly treated and allowed to receive visitors until his release in December. It was on the afternoon of 25 August that Rousseau set out on foot from Paris for the first of his six-mile walks to visit him. D'Alembert and a priest were with Diderot, but Rousseau was deeply affected by his visit and thereafter went "at least every other day." To slow his pace he took with him something to read, and one afternoon, while reading, was thrown into a state of violent excitement by the announcement in the *Mercure de France* of a prize to be offered the following year by the Dijon academy for an essay on the subject "Has the progress of the arts and sciences contributed to the purification of morals?" Rousseau changed the title to include the possibility that the arts and sciences had contributed more to their corruption.

In a letter of 12 January 1762 to Malesherbes, Rousseau wrote of "a sudden inspiration" in which he conceived at the same time the ideas scattered "in my three principal works," which he named at that date as the two *Discours* and *Emile*. According to the *Confessions*, he sat down under an oak tree and wrote the oration of Fabricius which ends the first part of the *Discours sur les sciences et les arts*. Diderot claims that he advised Rousseau to take the side that nobody else would, which in fact meant arguing against the enlightenment view of progress. That is what Rousseau did, although it took him some time to realize that he was pitting himself against everything which the philosophes and the *Encyclopédie* were to stand for.

The *Discours sur les sciences et les arts*, showing how culture led to slavery and vice, won the prize in July 1750. Signed by Rousseau as "A Citizen of Geneva," the *Discours* was an immediate success. Since the new chancellor of France, Lamoignon, had given charge of the censorship to his son, Malesherbes, Rousseau, who was friendly with Malesherbes, dispensed with formal permission when Diderot persuaded the book-seller Noel-Jacques Pissot to publish the pamphlet.

The *Mercure de France*, edited by the ex-Jesuit abbé Guillaume de Raynal, now publicized the *Discours*, and printed extracts from it. It also printed Rousseau's *Allée de Silvie*. By publishing attacks and criticisms, as well as a defence, Raynal kept the *Discours* at the centre of attention for over a year. Rousseau was gently rebuked by d'Alembert in the 1751 *Discours préliminaire* to the *Encyclopédie*, intended to glorify the arts and sciences. D'Alembert had built on Diderot's "Prospectus" of 1750, which had taken the view opposite to Rousseau's, although the flat contradiction between the two attitudes did not at first become apparent, perhaps because of Rousseau's deference to the authority of Bacon, acknowledged by the architects of the *Encyclopédie*, and his choice of antiquity rather than Christendom in which to find examples of moral superiority. For the moment Diderot continued to promote Rousseau's *Discours* and Rousseau continued to wish to contribute to the *Encyclopédie* and to remain on friendly terms with its editors. Only Voltaire's reaction on reading the *Discours* was immediately hostile. It was to be Rousseau's views on the corrupting influence of the arts and sciences which led towards the feeling, characteristic of the "pre-romantic" (see post-1789 volume of the Guide) generation, that moral perfection and happiness were attainable only when a harmony with nature which had been destroyed by civilization had been restored.

At the end of 1749 Rousseau set up house with Thérèse in a rented apartment, with Thérèse's numerous family under the same roof. Some of the furniture was provided by Mme Dupin. Thérèse's mother came in the morning to light Rousseau's fire and take down in writing the material on which he had meditated overnight. A third child was born during the winter of 1750–51 and sent to the foundling hospital, although Rousseau's guilt at disposing in this way of his children increased, and he was forced to justify himself in a harsh letter to Mme Francueil. It is to Mme Francueil that we owe the view, publicly espoused by her granddaughter George Sand, that Rousseau's urinary troubles made him impotent, and that he cannot have been the true father of Thérèse's children. It seems, however, certain that he was, as he himself obviously believed. The stories of Thérèse's infidelity date from a later period, when Rousseau's condition had worsened, and when impotence is to be presumed.

Meanwhile during 1750 Rousseau earned a little from the Dupins, and 100 livres owing to him from Venice was paid. On 12 March he wrote to Mme de Warens that he was in poor health, spending what leisure he had walking and going to the theatre. From early in 1751 he gave up working for Francueil and again earned his living by copying music, giving lessons, and undertaking secretarial and literary chores. He still had the fine hand of an engraver, but began to dress more simply, sold his watch, and no longer wore braid, white stockings, and a sword. The theft of his fine linen at Christmas 1751 caused him to reconsider his attitude to dress, money, and social presentation. Although wedded to the ideal of a lower-class existence, he continued to visit the Dupins, Mme d'Epinay, and the d'Holbach household, to which Diderot had introduced him. He was also visited by the rich and fashionable, but, with a touch of arrogance, appeared in society on his own terms, flaunting his contempt for the social norms with which, when he looked back, he realized he had been too ill acquainted. He dressed with deliberate shabbiness and sometimes did not shave. When those who gave him work tried to make him presents or pay him more than he charged, he accepted only his standard fee.

He joined in the debate on music which began in the summer of 1752 with the arrival in Paris of Eustachio Bambini's opera buffa company. He supported Grimm's recent attack on the French tradition of *opera seria* as represented by Destouches's *Omphale*, in which Grimm thought the disconnected arias had little relationship to the plot. Rousseau preferred French libretti but tuneful, singable Italian melodies, and in the somewhat intemperate 1753 *Lettre sur la musique française* he eventually took the lead in a frontal attack on the boorish, unpleasant, but immensely successful Rameau. The quarrel took on an ideological tinge, with the "modernes" championing the Italians in music as they already had in drama, and regarding French music as capable of neither beat nor melody nor anything except harmonic ornamentation. They considered the French tradition academic, authoritarian, and artificially constricted, but their views had deeper cultural implications in the context of the victory of an optimistic view of human experience. In the meanwhile, in the spring of 1752, staying at Passy for the mineral waters with François Mussard, a fellow-exile and lover of Italian music from Geneva, who was also a relation, Rousseau wrote his comic opera inspired partly by Pergolesi, *Le Devin du village*.

Submitted anonymously, it was accepted by the Paris opera, and played with triumphant success on 18 October before the king at Fontainebleau, and throughout 1753 at court and in Paris. The king asked for Rousseau to be presented and wanted to grant him a pension. Overcome by a mixture of diffidence and arrogance, Rousseau left Fontainebleau to return to his music-copying before the presentation could take place. The success, however, was not repeated when the Théâtre-Français presented *Narcisse*, again with no author's name attached, on 18 December 1752, and had to take it off after the second performance two days later. The play did, none the less, make some money when it ran through two editions in 1753. Rousseau gave away the royalties from the performance and publication of the play, and sent the first instalment of his advance for *Le Devin du village* to Mme de Warens. Eventually he accepted 100 louis from the king and 50 from Mme de Pompadour for *Le Devin*, and a payment from the Opéra. The piece was to become one of his most constant sources of income. The quarrel about music had made Rousseau a celebrity but had also aroused much hostility. He was attacked, notably by Fréron and stingingly by Rameau himself, and was burnt in effigy in the courtyard of the opera house. To distinguish him from J.-B. Rousseau, he was increasingly referred to simply as "Jean-Jacques." In the 1753 salon his portrait by Quentin de La Tour was exhibited.

Intellectually Rousseau's move away from the materialism of the philosophes was accompanied by a renewed interest in religion and a renewed intensity in his feelings for landscape. He submitted the most powerful of his early works, the *Discours sur les origines de l'inégalité*, for another prize announced in the autumn of 1753 by the Dijon academy, but this time, perhaps partly because his anonymity had been penetrated, he failed to win the prize. By early 1754 his relations with Grimm, Holbach,

and the other philosophes were becoming strained. He was tiring of the stresses which salon sophistication and wit imposed on him. In May he finally decided to abandon the urban corruption of Paris and leave with Thérèse for his puritanical and provincial home town of Geneva.

The second *Discours* was a manifesto dedicated not to the ruling oligarchy, but to the Republic of Geneva by its "concitoyen" who, however, prudently sent it from Chambéry, where he had stopped to see Mme de Warens, now registered as a pauper and in a state of near-destitution. Rousseau had been turned against Catholicism by the philosophes, and against them by their atheism. He had come mentally to idealize the political constitution as well as what he believed to be the direct and honest moral standards of the city of his birth, and the recovery of his citizenship would assuage what at this time were his political, religious, moral, and social needs. In 1754 Geneva welcomed him, and he mentally transformed the city-state into his ideal society, finding within it, two centuries after Calvin, the natural, deist religion which, unlike the materialism of the Paris philosophes, had established a basis for the moral standards required by his feelings of guilt. Its ecclesiastical life appeared compatible with direct religious experience without involving unnecessary or unacceptable complications deriving from dogma, rites, or superstition. External conformity to religious norms needed to be enforced in the essential interest of social order. In deference to the rules, Thérèse was officially regarded as Rousseau's nurse, and dispensed from all the tiresome rituals associated with recantation, he was re-admitted to the Lord's Supper.

He saw Mme de Warens for the last time in August 1754, just before the public sale of her goods at Chambéry on 1 September. He gave her money and was himself at this time even thinking of settling in Geneva. He was still interested in the theatre, forbidden within the city and in 1758 to be wholly condemned by Rousseau himself in the *Lettre à M. d'Alembert sur les spectacles*. However, he did not yet regard the citizens as merely "slaves of an arbitrary power, delivered up without mercy to the 25 despots of the 'petit conseil'." He was much moved by his walks in the Genevan countryside, recording later in the *Confessions* his need for landscapes with torrents, rocks, trees, and precipices, "all to make me feel fear." He did not like flat landscapes, and needed to be overawed. None the less, on his return in October to Paris, which at least offered him the possibility of earning a modest living by copying music, he began to realize that Geneva was not exactly as he had pictured it, and he was given to understand that his intention to dedicate the *Discours* to the citizens rather than the magistracy was not well regarded.

Back in Paris Rousseau and Thérèse lived more frugally than her mother would have liked. She accepted whatever gifts she could get from Rousseau's rich friends, while he prided himself on living off 1,440 livres (60 louis) a year. He frequented the salons of Mme d'Holbach and Mme Helvétius, where the entertainment was lavish, and still remained in close contact with Diderot, d'Alembert, Grimm, and Duclos. On the death of Montesquieu, regarded both by the king and by such liberal advocates of an enlightened despotism as Voltaire, deriving his theory of the state from Bacon, as a defender of aristocratic privilege, Rousseau in a letter of 20 February 1755 expressed complete agreement with him as the theoretician of social rights and obligations.

Marc-Michel Rey, a Genevan who set up his publishing business in Amsterdam, paid Rousseau 6,000 livres for the second *Discours*. Although Amsterdam was free of censorship, the importation of books into France still required a licence which, after some hesitation, Malesherbes granted. At the time, Rousseau was well pleased with the book's reception in Geneva. Even with Voltaire, who was later to annotate the text ferociously, he exchanged at the time only banter. The *Mercure* published their letters. Meanwhile Rousseau resolutely refused to earn more money by literary journalism, was content to live from copying music, prepared for the press his *Dictionnaire de musique*, which was to appear only in 1767, and published the article on "Economie politique" in the fifth volume of the *Encyclopédie* (1755). The article takes from Diderot the concept of the "volonté générale (general will)," by which each citizen desires the corporate good in a society in which the citizens freely combine to rule themselves. Laws to be enforced on all are necessary to ensure the liberty of each. In his article Rousseau uses the term "general will" in the same way as Diderot, for the collective expression of individual wills, although Diderot did not believe in the contractual basis for all human society. In his later works Rousseau would emphasize the way in which the expression of the "volonté générale" excludes that of the "volonté particulière (private will)," based on individual self-interest.

In the autumn of 1755 Rousseau spent a holiday at Mme d'Epinay's château of La Chevrette, near Montmorency to the north of Paris. Her lover, Dupin de Francueil, Rousseau's former friend and employer, was being unfaithful to her with Mlle Rose, the sister of her husband's mistress, and Rousseau himself had been ill. They got on well enough for Rousseau to accept benefactions from her. There had been accusations that Mme d'Epinay had sought to destroy evidence of a debt incurred by her husband to the heirs of her sister, who had died of smallpox at 23, and Grimm had fought a duel to defend her honour, after which he replaced Francueil as her lover, so increasing the strain on his relationship with Rousseau, whose second *Discours* Grimm had already attacked. None the less Rousseau declined an offer to obtain for him the librarianship of Geneva and eventually accepted Mme d'Epinay's gift of a cottage she had had restored for him on the estate, and in April 1756, in spite of Grimm's displeasure, Rousseau moved into "L'Hermitage" with Thérèse and her mother. Quite apart from the rent-free five-room house with a proper heating system, an ornamental and a kitchen garden, and an orchard, Mme d'Epinay found a number of other ways of surreptitiously subsidizing him. He did, however, pay for the gardener and have certain supervisory duties on the estate. Although poverty had often obliged him to walk in an age when almost everyone who travelled at all rode, drove, or was driven, he still physically enjoyed walking and was unperturbed at being 12 miles from Paris and over a mile from a road.

Thérèse increasingly became a servant. Rousseau worked long and regular hours, with an afternoon walk. He revised, he says for Mme Dupin, the pacifist writings of the abbé de Saint-Pierre, not fully published until 1782, and in the summer of 1756 wrote his letter on providence in response to Voltaire's poems on the natural law and on the Lisbon earthquake of November 1755. Relationships between the two men remained friendly until they deteriorated after Voltaire's final answer to Rousseau, which was to be *Candide*, of 1759. Meanwhile, in the summer of 1756, Rousseau began work on *Du contrat social* and on *Julie; ou, La Nouvelle Héloïse*. He saw little of Mme

d'Epinay, who spent the winter in Paris. He said later that he was glad to be spared further readings from her unfinished "novels, letters, plays, stories, and other trash."

Rousseau was annoyed to find that Thérèse's mother was seeking gifts of money in his name behind his back, and he became prickly in his relations with Diderot, feeling got at by a line of Constance's in Diderot's *Le Fils naturel* of 1757. Early in that year he fell violently in love with Elisabeth-Sophie-Françoise ("Sophie") d'Houdetot, Mme d'Epinay's sister-in-law, who was also the mistress to whom his *philosophe* friend, Saint-Lambert, turned on the death of Mme du Châtelet. She had called on foot at L'Hermitage in January 1757 with news of a friend, and had had to change her muddied clothes and borrow others from Thérèse, which she sent back with a note virtually inviting Rousseau to a relationship of some intimacy. Next time she came, it was dressed in male clothes and on horseback. Mme d'Epinay had hoped to console herself with Rousseau for the absence of Grimm, called away on military duties, but found that her husband's sister, Mme d'Houdetot, who was less rich than she but had married into the aristocracy and had a decidedly higher social position, had chosen Rousseau to console her for the absence of Saint-Lambert at the disastrous Seven Years War (1756–1763). Rousseau and Mme d'Houdetot both enjoyed their close companionship during 1757, and it is inconceivable that they did not indulge in physical intimacies. Their relationship is clearly reflected in *La Nouvelle Héloïse*, and the sudden diminution in the intensity of their friendship after Saint-Lambert's unexpected return on 12 July, on the occasion of a mission to Versailles, suggests he may rightly have suspected that Rousseau's idealization of love was having an adverse effect on his own relationship with his mistress. *La Nouvelle Héloïse* preaches the virtues of marital fidelity, strongly condemning adultery.

In the face of Mme d'Houdetot's coolness Rousseau mixed more freely with Mme d'Epinay and the guests at La Chevrette. His room there during the festivities for the opening of the refurbished chapel was moved when Grimm returned in September. Mme d'Epinay wanted Rousseau to accompany her to Geneva where she went to consult the doctor Théodore Tronchin. She may have been pregnant by Grimm, but, if she was, she will have lost the baby in an unspecified accident on 7 November at Châtillon. Meanwhile there was a succession of tensions, estrangements, and reconciliations between Sophie d'Houdetot, Mme d'Epinay, Rousseau, Diderot, Grimm, and Saint-Lambert, ending with Rousseau's final breaks first with Mme d'Epinay and Grimm, and then with Diderot when Rousseau attacked d'Alembert's article on Geneva in the seventh volume of the *Encyclopédie*, to which he had himself contributed the article on "Génie."

No doubt spurred on by Voltaire, with whom he had been staying while writing the article, d'Alembert, in addition to noting that Calvin's religion had softened into a vague and almost deist "Socinianism" in Geneva, had advocated the establishment of a theatre in the city. Rousseau sprang to the attack with his *Lettre à d'Alembert sur les spectacles*, finished in March 1758 and published in October, maintaining the immorality of the theatre, which stirred the passions, presented vice attractively, and was at best a waste of time and money. Rousseau then strongly defended the theatre of classical antiquity for its heroic themes, against the modern preoccupation with amorous ones. His pamphlet, which included an assault on *Le Mis-*

anthrope for deriding the central character, Alceste, whom Rousseau took to represent the man of forthright virtue (see: Molière), further alienated Diderot.

Until the quarrel with Hume in 1766 Rousseau did nevertheless remain friendly with d'Alembert, who for reasons of personal safety had withdrawn from the joint editorship of the *Encyclopédie* and did not object to the *Lettre*. Only later, when virtually paranoid, did Rousseau feel that d'Alembert had been machinating against him since 1758. Grimm said that the attack on the theatre provoked 300 replies within a year. Rousseau argued with skill, and may at times have been conscious of paradox in his public and private reactions but, with the spikiness to which the correspondence of 1757 begins to testify, the *Lettre* was the first clear sign that a mood could strike him violently enough to cast his mind off balance. By late in 1757 we also have the first evidence in various correspondences that a number of his friends were becoming seriously worried about his mental condition. He was involved in interminable wrangles, was absurdly touchy about trivialities at which he took unreasonable offence, and was becoming unpredictably cruel, rude, and aggressive. He wrote a series of letters to Sophie d'Houdetot which he did not send, but which sketch the ideas to be expounded in *Emile*, particularly in the celebrated "Profession de foi du vicaire savoyard." She was finally to break with him in a letter of 6 May 1758, after Diderot had revealed to Saint-Lambert the secret of Rousseau's passionate declaration of love to her. Rousseau, recognizing by whom he had been betrayed, broke finally also with Diderot, inserting an addition to the proofs of the *Lettre*'s preface unmistakably alluding to him as a traitor.

A present from Holbach replaced revenues lost from neglected music-copying, and in December 1757, the rupture with Mme d'Epinay complete on his refusal to accompany her to Geneva, Rousseau and Thérèse moved to Montlouis, nearer to Montmorency, sending Thérèse's mother back to Paris. The cottage was dilapidated but not small, and the rent was only 50 livres a year, ten livres less than Rousseau had paid the gardener at L'Hermitage. Early in 1758 Rousseau was ill, and appears to have believed that he was dying. On 8 March, to preclude any possible distraint, he drafted a declaration that everything at Montlouis belonged to "his servant" Thérèse Lavasseur, to whom he owed 13 years' unpaid wages, or 1,950 livres. An inventory was taken and notarized on 22 March. The value of the house contents was given as 300 livres. Rousseau however turned down the offer from a Genevan friend of a 1,500-livre gift and his fare to Geneva with Thérèse. He received 720 livres from Rey for the *Lettre à d'Alembert*. At midday on 29 October a famous Sunday dinner took place at La Chevrette, at which Rousseau conversed again on friendly terms with Sophie d'Houdetot and Saint-Lambert. Mme d'Epinay was still in Geneva, but M. d'Epinay had also invited the Dupins, Francueil, and Sophie d'Houdetot's husband with his sister.

It was in April 1759 that Rousseau sent Rey the final version of *Julie; ou, la moderne Héloïse*, as it was then still called. He was anxious that it should not be read in Geneva, where a book about love would give him a profile different from that he sought to acquire with the *Lettre à d'Alembert*, but Rey could not, he said, do without the Geneva market. Then the duc de Montmorency-Luxembourg, a marshal of France, came to spend Easter at his country seat. Learning that Rousseau was living on the estate, he sent an invitation to him to dine. Rousseau was hesitant. The duc himself called and persuaded him, and in the end Rousseau spent much time in the exalted social company of the château, as well as simply with the Luxembourgs, and was lodged in the Petit Château in the grounds while the roof and floors at Montlouis were being repaired. The restoration was complete by the end of the summer. By this time Rousseau's relationship with the Luxembourgs was very close. Rey was paying a little in advance for *Julie*, which he wanted Rousseau to chop into six equal parts and for which in all the author was to receive 90 louis (2,160 livres), and Rousseau was able to turn down a lucrative part-time job on the *Journal des Savants*, at 800 livres a month for what amounted to less than eight days' work. He had also given up transcribing music for the harpsichord on account of the number of notes. He was however copying out his own literary productions for various important patrons. The Luxembourgs had put rooms at his disposal in their Paris town house.

The final preparations for the illustrations, engravings, and printing of *Julie* caused Rousseau to fret at delays and fidget with changes. He was diffident about publishing a novel at all, and frightened about a pirated edition, but wanted it to be as perfect a work of art as he could make it. He would have liked illustrations by Boucher had Rey been able to afford them, but he could run only to vignettes, in the end supplied late by Gravelot and much criticized by Rousseau. Rey had enough metal type for only six or seven sheets at a time, after which the type had to be redistributed for the next set. The print-run was to be 6,000. Publication finally took place early in 1761, with the earliest editions called *Lettres de deux amans, habitants d'une petite ville au pied des Alpes*, with *Julie; ou, la Nouvelle Héloïse* the second printed title. Malesherbes, who protected both French authors and French publishers with a system of tacit permissions and blind eyes as well as the official regime of royal "privilèges," wanted Rousseau to have an edition printed in France, arguing that Rey's edition was bound anyway to be pirated. Rousseau, aware of the absurdity of the system which in principle forced French authors to seek foreign publishers who were then obliged to get licences to sell books in France, where the market was, refused to do anything to damage Rey's interest. He did however issue in France a separate second 10,000-word preface, the "préface dialoguée" or *Entretien sur les romans*, explaining why he had written a novel. It was published by Guérin on 16 February 1761.

The Rey edition was on sale in London in 1760 some weeks before Rey's agent in Paris, Etienne-Vincent Robin, received his six bales and the 60 presentation copies. Robin, however, protected by Malesherbes, who was presumably trying to play down the book's interest and therefore to diminish the public comment which was likely to cause him trouble, published the first of the innumerable French pirated editions in 1761 before releasing Rey's own "authentic" edition later in the year. Malesherbes connived at the pirated editions, since he could then more easily insist on the omission of the more daring passages, and only 2,000 copies of Rey's edition reached Paris, so that the book was mostly read in inaccurate and pirated versions. Rey none the less admits to having made 10,000 livres from the book by the end of December.

It was an immense success, easily the best-selling novel of the century, and it quickly became the foundation for a cult. We know of 72 non-pirated editions between 1761 and 1800. Rousseau's own preface had emphasized the novel's dangers, although some readers claimed that it enflamed them with a passion for virtue. In Geneva the public liked it, but not the establishment. Voltaire found it "stupid, bourgeois, impudent, and boring," and any pretence at good relations with Rousseau was terminated with the publication of Voltaire's four letters to himself purporting to come from the "Marquis de Ximénès" about the novel. In a letter of 16 February Malesherbes, acting on the advice of his new chief censor, Christophe Picquet, demanded for a "third" edition, which Malesherbes wanted the French publishers Duchesne and Guérin to bring out, nearly 50 more cuts, almost all of them in the last two parts, and almost all designed to avoid upsetting Catholic feelings.

In 1761 Rousseau was again convinced that he was dying. His illness was at last correctly diagnosed and he had to undergo a painful operation on the prostate gland. He confessed to Mme de Luxembourg the fate of his five children and asked her to see that Thérèse was looked after. She tried in vain to trace the eldest child. Rousseau kept his promise to let Rey have *Du contrat social*, for which he received 1,000 livres on delivery of the manuscript to Rey's agent, the chaplain to the Dutch embassy, on 6 November 1761, agreeing a publication date of March 1762. His uncharacteristic forbearance, though, had been exhausted and, aided by Malesherbes, he signed a contract for 6,000 livres with Duchesne for the publication of *Emile*, giving him a first option to negotiate for an "édition générale," which Rey also wished to produce. Of the 6,000 livres only half was to be in cash, and only a quarter on signature of contract.

Duchesne delayed with *Emile*, and Rousseau warmed to Rey again. He did not have to be paranoid to know that delay in setting a manuscript in type strongly suggested, if not the likelihood of cheating, then at least an increased chance of possibly pre-publication piracy. However, he suspected the Jesuits of plotting either to suppress his book or at least to give themselves time to refute it, and he wrote to Malesherbes on 18 November 1761 to say so. Two days later, learning that the Jesuits had been expelled from France, he wrote again to say that his imagination had been unhinged by solitude. Malesherbes none the less had to send an agent to supervise the printing. For a moment, in December, Rousseau appears to have contemplated suicide. In a letter written on 23 December 1761 to Paul-Claude Moultou, the Genevan pastor whom he had made his literary executor, but in the end not sent, he authorized him after his death to deal with Rey as his publisher, and affirmed that he believed there was a God and that, after death, he would find with Him "the happiness and the peace that I have not enjoyed in this world." In order to get the permission he needed for the collected works, Rey now asked Rousseau for an autobiography, and offered to pay Thérèse a pension of 300 francs a year on Rousseau's death.

Early in 1762 Rousseau wrote a series of important autobiographical letters to Malesherbes. The arrangement with Rey was modified to give the 41-year-old Thérèse 150 francs a year during Rousseau's lifetime, to be doubled after his death, and Moultou warned him that the denial of a specific revelation in the "Profession de foi" from *Emile* was bound to cause trouble. Rousseau tried to get Duchesne to get the second two parts set in Holland, but Malesherbes preferred to turn a blind eye to a French printing, although Rousseau now heard that cuts had been insisted on even in the first two parts which had already been set in type. Malesherbes wanted the text printed in France, but needed his role as virtual sponsor to be untraceable. Duchesne did set the text of *Emile* in France, but printed Néaulme's

name and "The Hague" on the title page. Rousseau felt that he was losing control, but that if Duchesne was going to lie he should at least do it convincingly, and use a different typeface for the two sections which included the "Profession de foi" and which he was going to pretend had been printed in Holland.

Du contrat social, about which Rousseau had not consulted Malesherbes, with the chapter on civil religion which gave no special status to Christianity and implied a denial of any divinely inspired scriptures, appeared in Amsterdam in April, and was shipped by Rey to Dunkirk, then taken by boat as far as Rouen. It had been pirated within a fortnight, although gradually it became clear that a licence to sell Rey's authorized edition in France would be refused. Rousseau would not have his name taken from the title page, though that, Malesherbes had indicated to Rey, might have helped. Néaulme, having actually set the text of the "Profession de foi" for his octavo Dutch edition of *Emile* before reading it, was terrified by the attack on revelation which, he thought, could not possibly be tolerated even in Holland. At least 60 presentation copies of the octavo and duodecimo of *Emile* were distributed by Duchesne in May, and the volumes were on sale at the Palais-Royal for 16 livres on 24 May, a month after *Du contrat social*, stocks of which, it was already clear, would actually be confiscated. There were none the less at least eight pirated editions of *Du contrat social* in 1762 alone.

The order banning *Emile* in Paris was signed on 31 May, but before he signed orders for seizure on 1 June, Malesherbes had warned Duchesne to remove his stock from the warehouse, where the remaining four copies were duly seized. Clandestine copies moved up to 42 livres. On 9 June the book was condemned to be shredded and burnt by the public executioner, and the judgement was executed on the 11th. There were none the less to be at least 26 authorized editions before 1788, in addition to the pirated ones. On the 19th *Du contrat social* was publicly burnt with *Emile* in Geneva, where Rousseau's arrest was also ordered. *Emile* was condemned in Holland on 30 July. Rousseau was in part the victim of a wave of intolerance which had already resulted in the hanging on 18 February 1762 of a pastor arrested by accident on 14 September 1761 in Toulouse for preaching, and indicted on the capital offence of "holding a religious assembly." Three brothers from the minor nobility who had attempted to liberate him were beheaded. Later that summer *Emile* was condemned by the Sorbonne, after having been forbidden by the archbishop of Paris.

Malesherbes, who had protected both the *Encyclopédie* in 1752 and 1755 and Helvétius in 1758, and who had been so involved in the publishing arrangements for *Emile*, now asked for his letters to Rousseau, and those to Duchesne mentioning Rousseau, to be returned. He had encouraged Duchesne to print the last two volumes in France under the pretence that they were being published in Holland, found that the deception would not work, and now sought to protect himself. He did not dare warn Rousseau, except through intermediaries, that he was in serious danger, and it took Rousseau several days to realize that neither his innocence in conscience, the legal niceties of his position, nor any patron could protect him. In the end he had to be told, for the sake of his protectors as well his own, to avail himself of the tacit promise that he would be allowed to escape, providing he had disappeared by 7 a.m. on 9 June. If he did not, an example would be made of him, if only for not concealing his authorship of *Emile*. The French authorities did not intend to make real trouble over so technical and theoretical a work as *Du contrat social* beyond merely confiscating it. *Emile* was an altogether more serious matter.

On the morning of 9 June, Mme de Luxembourg went to bed at 2 a.m. after summoning Rousseau urgently to call on her, and announcing that she would not go to sleep before he did so. The Luxembourgs took charge of Thérèse and of everything Rousseau left behind. In order to spare them embarrassment, and still without seeing that he had anything to be afraid of, Rousseau left, with little more than the papers he would need for the *Confessions*, for Yverdon in the canton of Berne, to join his old friend Daniel Roguin in his villa next to the lake at Neuchâtel. The parlement met in the morning, condemned *Emile* as subversive of religion, morals, and decency, and ordered Rousseau's arrest, imprisonment and interrogation, but the officers of the court did not arrive at Montmorency until 4 p.m. This was perhaps within an hour of Rousseau's departure, but he was allowed to leave Paris in peace, although he must have been recognized crossing Paris in Luxembourg's cabriolet and may have been saluted by the officers sent to arrest him as he passed them going in the opposite direction.

He arrived at Yverdon on 14 June, having travelled mostly in hired coaches, but was quickly expelled from Bernese territory and found refuge at Môtiers, a Prussian principality near Neuchâtel, where Thérèse joined him and where he stayed with the willing consent of Frederick the Great, was befriended by the Governor, George Keith, Earl Marischal, and got to know Boswell. In 1763 he replied in his *Lettre à M. de Beaumont* to the pastoral letter condemning him issued in August 1762 by the archbishop of Paris. After provisionally permitting its sale, the "Petit Conseil (Little Council)" of Geneva confiscated a second edition of *Emile*, and Rousseau, for some time determined to make the gesture, formally renounced his citizenship of Geneva in a letter of 12 May 1763. The resulting support for Rousseau, however inadequate, drove the Petit Conseil to veto three representations made to it, thus firmly demonstrating the real nature of Genevan government and the sham of the 1738 Mediation.

Jean-Robert Tronchin, the Genevan public prosecutor who had moved against *Emile* and *Du contrat social*, was re-elected and wrote a series of letters against Rousseau, provoking in reply Rousseau's attack on the Petit Conseil, the 1764 *Lettres écrites de la montagne*, which brought in 1,504 livres. The first five letters defend *Emile*, the sixth defends the *Contrat*, and the remaining three examine the illegitimate constitutional position of the Petit Conseil. Rousseau is at his dialectical best, but he also attacked Voltaire, exposing the open secret of Voltaire's authorship of the *Sermon des cinquante* which forthrightly attacked Christianity. Voltaire, now implacable, replied with the unpleasantly vengeful *Le Sentiment des citoyens* of 1764, revealing Rousseau's abandonment of his five infant children, and causing Rousseau to contemplate writing his *Confessions*. Voltaire's source must have been Mme d'Epinay's Genevan doctor, Théodore Tronchin.

Rousseau now entrusted the collected edition of his works to Rey. *Le Devin du village* was still a success at Versailles. Rousseau's health varied, but his income was secure, he was happy, and he resumed his botanical studies. He sketched a preamble to the *Confessions* in 1765. His *Lettres* containing the attack on Voltaire were burnt in Paris on the same fire as Voltaire's own *Dictionnaire philosophique* and he sent Duchesne the *Dictionnaire de musique*, which would be published in 1767 and for

which he received 2,400 livres. In 1765 life at Neuchâtel became more difficult, with public sentiment turning against Rousseau. The pastor who, on his arrival, had admitted him to the Lord's Supper, now preached against him, and stones were thrown at his house. He retreated to the Ile Saint-Pierre on the Lake of Bienne, but was moved on by the Bernese authorities. After considering migrating to Corsica and Berlin he went to Strasbourg. He was fêted there and granted a passport for a brief stay in Paris, where he spent the Christmas of 1765. He then left at Hume's invitation for London. Diderot had made discreet overtures, but they did not meet. Thérèse, entrusted to James Boswell, whose mistress she became, joined Rousseau in London. George III granted him a pension of £100 a year, and Hume found him a place to live in the country at Wootton in Derbyshire, where he wrote most of the *Confessions*.

He became distraught to the point of madness, perversely quarrelled with Hume, had his now paranoid imagination fuelled, and could not help savagely snapping at those who were trying to help. The skilful balance which he had needed and contrived for himself had allowed him to lead a life of unparalleled freedom from social constraint and given him the intellectual space he needed fundamentally to rethink, virtually without prejudice and with his mind unfettered, the whole of the human condition. He had written works so radical that they could have been produced only by an exceedingly powerful mind dependent, of course, on both stimulus and solitude, but virtually untrammelled by the ordinary constraints of intellectual orthodoxies, and uninhibited by the formal education and intellectual training which would have made their composition impossible. It was Rousseau's psychological need to achieve for himself the conditions which would permit the successful pursuit of his immensely courageous and compulsively committed intellectual undertaking which must have been the principal reason why he repeatedly sent his children to the foundlings' home, and why he repeatedly chose to earn so deliberately scant a living by so mindless an activity as music copying.

He had thought out almost *ab ovo* the ground rules of life, education, love, the organization of society, and the relationships between God, humanity, the arts, the sciences, nature, and civilization. The result, necessarily, was a view which, while it was in all respects linked to the society of 18th-century France, articulated patterns of thought and sensibility which were still inchoate and, by laying them clearly down, not only powerfully helped his contemporaries by expressing them, but furthered their advance. He established himself as the outstanding prophet of his generation in his attitudes to nature, both human and physical, to sentiment, to social organization, and to the foundations of civilized society. He was above all the ultimate spokesman for the view that nature and all that was natural was good, healthful, virtuous, and the foundation for happiness.

The achievement of so radical a reassessment of attitudes across so complete a spectrum of the great issues meant taking even the strongest of minds to the point of social and historical isolation at which sanity was precarious, and involved physical experience almost certain to damage a constitution even as strong, in spite of his urethral deformity, as Rousseau's. It is not at all to be wondered at that he finally succumbed to something very like clinical paranoia. What is surprising is that this was not much worse and more constant much sooner. It is difficult to measure the true extent of Rousseau's almost unbelievable and virtually unprecedented achievement without adverting to the fastidious dedication he devoted to balancing his mostly unenviable personal circumstances in such a way as to make it possible. It is the life he drove himself to lead, the persecution he almost compulsively brought down on himself, most obviously with the quite unwarranted provocation of the *Lettre à d'Alembert*, that is the key to what Rousseau tried to achieve, and very largely succeeded in accomplishing, and to the unity of his work.

It is not clear how conscious he was of the extent to which he endangered his sanity by driving his imagination so single-mindedly in order to attain to independence of vision, and how much he may have thought himself to have been playing with paradox. He was certainly at times aware of threatening mental instability, of its actual occurrence, and of his need to maintain mental vigour through the cultivation of paradox. The last confessional works allow an insight into his own mental review of his intellectual history, which is why they are so gripping. But after his departure from England in May 1767 the old vigour had gone. In France he was helped by the elder Mirabeau, father of the revolutionary, and by Conti at Trye, where for a year he lived under a false name. He visited Lyons, Chambéry, and Grenoble before settling briefly in Bourgoin in Dauphiné, where he married Thérèse in a ceremony of his own devising before two witnesses, one of whom was the mayor. Early in 1769 he moved to a farm nearby, and abandoned for a while the *Confessions*, which was virtually finished, however, by the end of the year.

In 1770 he visited Lyons, where *Le Devin* was played in his presence. To Voltaire's annoyance he subscribed to the Voltaire statue being erected in Lyons and then, in June, he returned to Paris, where he took up music-copying again, and continued his botanical studies. In September he received his collected works from Rey. The authorities caused him no more trouble, although they asked for discretion and advised him to desist from reading extracts from the *Confessions* in private houses. He moved once again in 1770, further down the same street, spending his savings on new furniture. In 1771 he began his friendship with Jacques-Henri Bernardin de Saint-Pierre. He was deliberately poor, refused to accept the back payment of his English pension, and lived off the royalties from the *Dictionnaire de musique*, a pension of 600 francs from Marshal Berwick, the former Governor of Neuchâtel, and a payment of £10 a year from the books he had sold in London. Thérèse was now receiving 300 francs a year from Rey, and Rousseau cancelled a debt of 1,600 livres a year due from Du Peyron for his collected works, since he had now quarrelled with his former agent. He needed to earn about as much again as his 1,100 francs a year. He drank wine only once a day, and even cut down on his life-long indulgence, letter-writing, to save on postage.

He had promised the authorities to stop writing, but at the request of a Polish count he did compose the nationalistic *Considérations sur le gouvernement de Pologne* (1771–72) on the understanding that it would not be published. In 1775–76 he had written the dialogues known as *Rousseau, juge de Jean-Jacques*, which he tried to lay on the altar of Notre-Dame. He found the altar closed off and physically impossible to approach and took this as a sign that God had deserted him. A month or two later he distributed a pamphlet in the street, *A tout Français aimant encore la justice et la vérité* (To all Frenchmen who still love justice and truth). The *Rêveries du promeneur solitaire*, the writing of which was largely occasioned by rumours of his death that circulated after a Great Dane had knocked him down in 1776, was intended as a sequel to the *Confessions* and, like that work and the self-justificatory *Rousseau, juge de Jean-Jacques*, was published posthumously.

Rousseau's interests in music and botany continued, and he composed operatic fragments and a duet. His *Pygmalion* was played at the Comédie-Française late in 1775. He copied music for Gluck and attended his performances, but gave this up in 1778, leaving Paris one day in spring to investigate the proffered hospitality of a former client, a financier called Girardin who offered him a cottage at Ermenonville. Two days later he sent for Thérèse and the furniture. In June he was affected by the news of Voltaire's death. His own final months were happy. He created a new herbarium, dined with his hosts, sang after dinner, talked to the villagers and their priest, and made friends with his host's 12-year-old son. He died quite suddenly on 2 July 1778, having taken his walk and breakfasted with Thérèse and their maid. The cause of death was diagnosed as apoplexy. Houdon made a death-mask.

WORKS

Rousseau never wanted to write. He had no formal education, and the consciousness of a certain lack of grace about his person, his style, his manners, and his way of life was to erode his self-confidence. This want of assurance came increasingly to be reflected in his dress, and made him feel by turns insecure, prickly, patronized, and over-assertive. It partly explains his constant need for the often ruthless but still self-justificatory analysis of his actions contained in the later confessional writings: the *Confessions* itself, but also the *Lettres à M. De Malesherbes*, the *Rêveries du promeneur solitaire*, *Rousseau, juge de Jean-Jacques*, and so much of the correspondence. What Rousseau most constantly felt was the need to think as clearly, radically and therefore independently as he could drive himself to do, about God, humanity, nature, life, art, education, love, society, and death. The results, as he was aware, while never achieved without sustained effort, were inevitably part theory, part dream, often very tentative and never really coherent. He left, apart from his letters, a long, rambling sentimental novel, speculations about the foundations of civil rights and obligations, analyses of passion and the rules which should govern its manifestations, ideas about the ways in which societies should or could enforce virtuous behaviour, and reflections about whether their existence did not itself depend on it. He elaborated views about human nature into an educational scheme and a code for the conduct of sentimental relationships.

Rousseau's writings examined principles which he himself regarded as anything between interestingly possible and perfectly certain. There were no blue-prints, only a series of suggestions, by no means always compatible with one another, and possibilities, considered through the medium of works of the imagination, concerning all aspects of emotionally inspired behaviour—instinct, passion, nobility, devotion, generosity, even criminality—and the possible institutionalization of rules of moral rectitude appropriate to any society, from a pair of lovers to an organized state. Solitude and social stimulus were both personal needs for Rousseau, neither of them necessarily desirable in themselves.

It is not surprising that Rousseau became one of the most disconcertingly powerful figures in the history of European thought, less intellectually brilliant but more radical than Erasmus. He was perhaps not a great political philosopher, as Montesquieu was, nor a great educationalist, as Fénelon had been, for his historical knowledge was too sketchy and his moral vision was too narrowly uncompromising. But he released a new sensibility, and articulated new, violent, and wholly uncompromising ways of feeling. However easily the assertions, arguments, and intensely personal lyricism of some even of the political works could momentarily be disregarded as the work of a not very dangerous crank, the sometimes contradictory modes of feeling they generated and the reactions they provoked almost swamped French political, social, and literary culture for a century.

Until 1749, when he was 37, Rousseau had written little more than libretti for his own music, memoranda, and diplomatic despatches. It was only during his experience of intense excitement on the way to visit Diderot at Vincennes that he found he had something he really wanted to write about. This realization was triggered by the notice in the *Mercure de France* about the Dijon academy's competition for an essay on the subject, "Whether the restoration of the sciences and the arts has contributed to the purification of morals." Rousseau added the phrase "or to the corruption (Si le rétablissement des Sciences et des Arts a contribué à épurer [ou à corrompre] les Moeurs)." For the philosophes, taking over from the party of the modernes, with which Rousseau's tastes in music and his early acquaintanceship with Fontenelle and Marivaux had already almost affiliated him, human nature and society were both perfectible, ameliorated with the refinement of manners and, from the mid-18th century, the progress of science. Rousseau, whether or not in order to gain the advantage of paradox in order to win the prize, demonstrated for the first time in the *Discours sur les sciences et les arts* the whole thrust of his literary imagination, which was, to promote trust in nature as a guide to virtue and happiness. He contended that luxury had always been regarded as an evil, that elegance and sophistication had always been seen to lead to vice and corruption, and that culture led necessarily to servility. The argument is based on the contrast between what is natural, plain, unaffected and what is cultivated, ornate, and luxurious.

The fall of Rome was heralded by the appointment of an arbiter of "good taste." Military discipline, agriculture and patriotism gave way to luxury, exploitation, and subjugation. The first part of the *Discours* ends with the development of an outpouring put into the mouth of Fabricius railing at the effeminacy of the Roman decadence. Rousseau, drawing on Plutarch's *Life of Pyrrhus*, was drawing a deliberate and much appreciated analogy with 18th-century France. His dialectical skill leads him in his second more theoretical part to high pitches of lyrical intensity, as he decries Hobbes and Spinoza and hears the prayer of future generations: "rends-nous l'ignorance, l'innocence et la pauvreté, les seuls biens qui puissent faire notre bonheur (give us back our ignorance, innocence, and poverty, the only possessions that can make us happy)." We are already in the presence of a strongly stylized distortion of ancient history, and a ferociously powerful moral intensity. There is also an admiration of primitive societies taken from Montaigne's chapter "Des Cannibales" (Book I, ch. xxxi), the source of the notion central to Rousseau's second *Discours*, that the beginnings of society's decline are associated with the development of agriculture and metallurgy. Meanwhile, alongside its fiercely individual reading of ancient history, the first *Discours* shows the developed forensic skills which allow Rousseau to persuade not so much by his argument, whose lack of logic and order he later deplored, as by the emotional appeal of his ringingly cadenced declamatory rhetoric.

The second "Discours" is described on its title page as *Discours sur l'origine et les fondemens de l'inégalité parmi les hommes* and is devoted, therefore, to historical development as well as to constitutional reality. It was finished by the early summer of 1754, before Rousseau went to Geneva. His opera *Le Devin du village* had been a success and his play *Narcisse* a failure, and he had abandoned his fifth child at the foundlings' hospital. He was clearly caught up in a conflict between his desire to write successful works for the stage and the views expressed in the first *Discours*, and could only plead in justification that he wrote entertainment not for advancement or money, but to distract from vice. He had published his attack on French music in the *Lettre sur la musique française*. He now used the opportunity afforded by another prize essay to elaborate his view that the constitution of a social order historically has rested, and at present still did rest, on relations of subservience among men who should be equals.

Rousseau draws heavily on Diderot, but also on Condillac, Buffon, Grotius (Huigh de Groot), Samuel von Pufendorf, Jean-Jacques Burlamaqui, Locke, and Montesquieu. He takes from the tradition established by Grotius, Pufendorf, and to some extent Barbeyrac, the idea that human liberty, unlike goods which can sold, is itself inalienable by contract. A slave's child is not a slave. He will go on to argue in *Emile* that political liberty is a natural, not a civil right, because the human being is the only natural judge of what is necessary for the preservation of life. Rousseau is seeking, the preface of the *Discours* tells us, to know what is natural and what artificial in man's present state: "ce qu'il y a d'originaire et d'artificiel dans la nature actuelle de l'homme" and "de bien connoître un Etat qui n'existe plus, qui n'a peut-être point existé, qui probablement n'existera jamais, et dont il est pourtant necessaire d'avoir des Notions justes pour bien juger de nôtre état présent (to know properly a state which no longer exists, which has perhaps never existed, and will probably never exist, but of which we must have accurate ideas in order to be able to make judgements about our present state)."

Essentially, therefore, Rousseau is writing a moral rather than a historical treatise. He acknowledges that his view of the savage innocence of primitive man has to be an extrapolation from the moral analysis of his present state. Creation itself was necessarily flawless, and the primitive state of man was pre-social and pre-moral: "les hommes dans cet état, n'ayant entre eux aucune sorte de relation morale ni de devoirs connus, ne pouvoient être ni bons ni méchans, et n'avoient ni vices ni vertus (men in that state, not having any sort of moral relationship with or known duties towards one another, could not be either good or bad, and had neither virtues nor vices)." God-given capabilities enabled humanity to reach a golden age: "un juste milieu entre l'indolence de l'état primitif et la pétulante activité de notre amour-propre (a just mean between the idleness of the primitive state and the exuberant activity of our self-love)."

The second part of the *Discours* slips into historical narrative: "Le premier qui ayant enclos un terrain, s'avisa de dire, *ceci est moi*, et trouva des gens assés simples pour le croire, fut le vrai fondateur de la société civile (The first person who, having enclosed some ground, thought of saying 'This is mine' and found people simple enough to believe him, was the true founder of civil society)." Primitive humans were solitary, mating haphazardly. Only later does Rousseau come to share Locke's view that the smallest unit in nature is the family.

The inequalities and injustices of present society stemmed for Rousseau from the development of reason to overcome primitive sentiment, from the establishment of possessions, the invention of metallurgy and agriculture, and the need for laws. Enslavement followed the replacement of the law of nature by civil law. Organized society resulted from the economic need to collaborate in groups to hunt and to cultivate the soil; so that the existence of a social condition between the state of nature and the introduction of civil order can be seen to get Rousseau round the difficulty of postulating a moral act in a pre-moral state. He clearly deplores the choices that were made, but he writes as a philosopher, starting from the impossibility that human beings have put themselves in of living according to their nature, which alone can bring happiness, true freedom, and an end to inequalities not of power based on merit, but of wealth.

The essence of the argument is the attack on Hobbes's forthright view of man in the state of nature as naturally aggressive, selfish, proud, and avaricious. Hobbes went on to argue the need for despotic rule, whereas Rousseau, whose description of man just prior to civil society does not vary very radically from that of Hobbes, was to argue more and more strongly for a republic in which no citizen could delegate his rights even to elected representatives. The other alternatives at this period were the views of Montesquieu, taken to favour a constitutional monarchy on the English model, with the exercise of sovereignty inhibited by the privileges of other groups, and the line followed by Voltaire, an advocate of enlightened despotism and a strong defender of private property.

We do not know very much about the "Institutions politiques" which Rousseau first thought about writing as a result of his experiences at Venice, except that from the early 1750s he was sporadically meditating a large-scale work on the nature of political rights and obligations, and that both the article *Economie politique*, published in November 1755 in the fifth volume of the *Encyclopédie*, and *Du contrat social* were developed from the much larger projected but abandoned work. The second *Discours* may also have drawn on notes for it. It would not have treated, as Montesquieu had done, of the positive workings of established forms of government, but of the nature of law itself, rethinking the whole natural law tradition. It is not even possible to say for certain whether the article *Economie politique*, which admits a primitive pre-civil society, but also introduces a distinction between sovereign and government, ante-dates the second *Discours* or, as most historians agree, follows it.

The *Economie politique* article starts by distinguishing its subject, the administration of the state, from domestic economy or administration, and introduces, without really explaining it, the distinction between the "volonté particulière" or self-interest of the individual, and the "volonté générale (general will)," by which the individual prefers the interest of the corporality to his own. We are told only that the distinction is "toûjours fort difficile à faire (always very difficult to make)." Only by association in civil societies can each assure the law and justice which ensures the liberty of each, but Rousseau's text turns into a lyrical celebration of the sublimity of the divine inspiration by which humanity made this step, and we are left here without any clear analysis of how the association takes place. The first duty of the legislator is to make the laws conform to the "volonté générale" of the community.

Although it was not published until 1761 as *Lettres de deux amans, habitans d'une petite ville au pied des Alpes, recueillies et publiées par J. J. Rousseau*, the novel we now know as *Julie; ou, La Nouvelle Héloïse* was written between 1756 and 1757, Rousseau having substituted "nouvelle" for "moderne" in the January of the year before publication. It was the best-selling novel of the 18th century, originally written in four parts during the period of Rousseau's intimacy with Sophie d'Houdetot, finished in the autumn of 1757, by which time the close relationship had ceased, but then continued for another two parts during 1758. Rousseau sent the manuscript in batches during 1759 to Marc-Michel Rey, the Genevan who had set up as a publisher in Amsterdam and who had published the second *Discours*.

The form is somewhat contrived. There is for instance no particular need for some of the letters ever to have been written, since the recipient was in the next room, and Rousseau could scarcely emphasize more explicitly than he does that the interest of the novel lies not in its plot, but in its exploration of the relationships between tenderness of sentiment, physical passion, and virtue. The novel, largely inspired by Richardson's *Clarissa*, published in French translation in London in 1751, and by the same author's *The History of Sir Charles Grandison*, translated by Prévost in 1755–56, contains lengthy reflections on such subjects as music, suicide, rank, husbandry, social prejudice, the theatre, duelling, atheism, and education. The story of Abelard and Heloïse was widely known from Bayle's *Dictionnaire* and Bussy's 1687 fictionalization of their relationship in the *Lettres de deux amans*. Laclos's novel *Les Liaisons dangereuses* is a much more tightly organized and executed novel, whose form as well as content are founded on a parody of Rousseau's work.

The tone of the first preface, for which Rousseau wanted eventually to substitute the *Entretien sur les romans* or "préface dialoguée," a supposed conversation between the publisher and a "man of letters", is defensive to the point of contortedness. On 14 March 1759 Rousseau had asked Rey not on any account to put *Julie* on sale in Geneva, manifestly anxious about what would be thought of him if, after his attack on d'Alembert for suggesting the inauguration of a theatre within the walls of Geneva, he published a novel about love. The depiction of honest love on the stage, he had argued, led to criminal passion. The first preface therefore starts by asserting that only in big cities are theatres necessary, and only corrupt peoples need novels. This novel, writes Rousseau, will suit very few, perhaps no one. The style will repel people with taste, the content those who are severe, and all the feelings depicted will appear unnatural to those who do not believe in virtue.

After denigrating his own work with paradox and verve at length and in detail, Rousseau contrives to commend it. Its "ton gothique (Gothic style)" will suit women better than philosophy, and it may even be useful to those, however dissolute, who still hanker after virtue. Any girl who reads a single page is, of course, lost, but it won't be the book's fault and, once she has started, she might as well finish. The coding is precise. It warns the reader to pay attention not to the story but to the literary register of the letters. Then the novel starts with the words "Il faut vous fuir, mademoiselle, je le sens bien (I must flee you, mademoiselle. I know I must)," opening a letter to Julie from someone who reminds her that he is her tutor. Rousseau thereby establishes the parameters of the fiction. The letters cannot be real love letters, since real lovers would not need to explain their circumstances to one another in this way. But because the letters, clearly fiction, purport to be love letters, Rousseau can forget about narrative, concentrate on sentiment, and exploit the ordinary advantages of Richardson's epistolary form not, as Richardson did, to depict vast scenes and detailed settings, but so that the correspondents can each comment on their emotions to one another and to third parties, digressions can be introduced, and such events as are necessary can be related from more than one point of view.

Julie d'Etanges and her tutor, Saint-Preux, who until the fourth book is known to the reader simply as "L'Amant (de Julie)," fall deeply in love. However much Saint-Preux knows he must flee he cannot bring himself to go. "Show my letter to your parents, have me refused entrance to your door, send me away if you like; I can endure anything from you. Myself I cannot leave you." The rhetoric of strong emotion is deployed with a cascade of exclamation marks, rhetorical questions, musically balanced antitheses, and a crescendo of semi-colons which finally collapses into broken syntax and staccato sentences ending in dots. The young people's feelings are of course innocent, and their inability to assuage them the fault of "les uniformes préjugés du monde (the universal prejudices of society)."

The fourth letter contains Julie's guilt-ridden but eloquent outburst admitting her own burning passion. In the novel's first ten pages the polite conventions have been shattered. Social convention will appear to win in the end, but the reader's sympathies have been commandeered on behalf of the socially unacceptable passion. Rousseau has swept his public along by daring it to condemn a burning passion, experienced as innocent, simply because social rank precludes its acceptability. It is the radical innuendo that society, which must triumph, is none the less wrong, that passion should lead both to virtue and to happiness, however absurdly optimistic or, to later generations, mawkish this may seem, that accounts for the defensiveness of the preface and the overwhelming success of the novel. The work may have lost its emotional impact, but its imaginative power, expressed in terms of such revolutionary insinuation, is obvious on nearly every page.

The first kiss takes place in the presence of Julie's cousin Claire and Julie faints (Letter xiv). The mountainous scenery, the woods, and the rest of the natural setting all underline the emotional harmony and innocence of the young couple. Julie tries to send Saint-Preux away, and Claire writes to inform him, and us, how near to death the effort has brought her. Julie's style when she writes to Claire about Saint-Preux's idea of eloping (Letter xxviii) is almost pantingly conversational, and not in the least epistolary. The following letter, much calmer, from Julie to Claire, makes it clear that it was Julie's decision that Saint-Preux and she should become lovers:

Ah! sans doute, il sait mieux aimer que moi puisqu'il sait mieux se vaincre. Cent fois mes yeux furent témoins de ses combats et de sa victoire; les siens étincelloient du feu de ses desirs, il s'élançoit vers moi dans l'impétuosité d'un transport aveugle; il s'arrêtoit tout à coup; une barriere insurmontable sembloit m'avoir entourée, et jamais son amour impétueux mais honnête ne l'eut franchie. J'osai trop contempler ce dangereux spectacle. Je me sentois troubler de ses transports, ses soupirs oppressoient mon coeur; je partageois ses tourmens en ne pensant que les plaindre. Je le vis dans des agitations convulsives, prêt à

s'évanouïr à mes pieds. Peut-être l'amour seul m'auroit épargnée; ô ma Cousine, c'est la pitié qui me perdit

(Ah, truly he loves better than I do since he is better able to control himself. A hundred times my eyes witnessed his struggles and his victory; his sparkled with the flame of his desire, he would rush towards me under the impulse of a blind emotion; suddenly he would stop; I seemed to be surrounded by an impassable barrier, and his impetuous but virtuous love would never have crossed it. I dared for too long to watch this dangerous sight. I felt myself disturbed by his emotions, his sighs weighed on my heart; I shared his torments, thinking I only sympathized with them. I saw him convulsed with anguish, ready to faint at my feet. Perhaps unmixed love might have saved me; oh, cousin! I pitied him and was lost).

Julie's father, who is a rank-obsessed baron, devoid of wealth or social function, naturally forbids the marriage of his daughter to a bourgeois, even though the English nobleman "milord" Edouard Bomston offers to set Saint-Preux up with an estate and a fortune. At the end of the first part Saint-Preux is sent away by Julie's father. In part I, Letter lxiii, in the novel's ugliest incident, her father beats her, and strikes her mother, too. Julie falls, and loses Saint-Preux's child.

In the second part Rousseau finds occasion to criticize the life of Parisian society. In the third Julie's mother dies on discovering the lovers' letters, and Saint-Preux sets out on a world journey with the British fleet. Julie forgives her father, and marries the man he has chosen for her, Baron Wolmar, recovering her lost innocence by devotion to a husband she does not love and to her children. In the fourth part Saint-Preux returns as their tutor, the ménage à trois clearly inspired by Rousseau's own hopes and experiences. Wolmar, an atheist, runs a model agricultural undertaking on strongly feudal lines. Julie and Saint-Preux do find themselves alone again, driven by a storm to shelter on lakeside rocks against a backdrop of mountains. Their feelings for one another have not changed, but they resist temptation. Rousseau himself did not know how he was going to end the novel, deciding against a conversion for Wolmar, who would remain a stern but enlightened atheist. In the end Julie dies, having saved one of her children from drowning. She wants Saint-Preux to marry her cousin, but he does not. The letter from Wolmar to Saint-Preux narrating Julie's deathbed utterances and her actual death (Part VI, Letter xi) is three times as long as any other and is a set piece. Julie's deathbed demeanour leads to the hope that Wolmar may be converted.

Du contrat social; ou, Principes du droit politique consists of four books devoted respectively to the nature of society, to the nature of sovereignty, to different forms of government, and to appropriate administrative institutions. Historians have come increasingly to regard the "Geneva" manuscript as relatively late, perhaps 1758–60, although it incorporates what had already been published in the article *Economie politique* of 1755, and probably other material prepared for the "Institutions politiques" abandoned in 1758. It contained only three books, but included the final chapter "De la religion civile", and the second chapter of the first book was devoted to a detailed refutation of Diderot's article "Droit naturel" from the volume of the *Encyclopédie* issued in November 1755. This chapter was omitted from the definitive version published in 1761, which is less logical in presentation, putting the concept of the contract before the false notions of the social bond. The final version is also harsher on Catholicism in a passage (in 1761 Book IV, chapter 8) added late to the Geneva manuscript, but placed there after the chapter on the legislator (Book II, chapter 7).

In its final state *Du contrat social* sets out from the notion that, since man is born free, his subjection to government must be the result of free assent to a social pact with his fellows. The individual, in exchange for the protection afforded by the laws of civil society, freely agrees to be bound by the conditions of association. He can never surrender his political liberty, and remains free to leave the association if he ceases to wish to observe its laws and take part in its constitutional arrangements. Book I opens with Rousseau's declaration of intention: "Je veux chercher si, dans l'ordre civil, il peut y avoir quelque règle d'administration légitime et sûre (I want to enquire whether, in the civil order, there can be any legitimate and certain rule of government)," and the first chapter opens with the famous declaration, "L'homme est né libre, et par-tout il est dans les fers. Tel se croit le maître des autres, qui ne laisse pas d'être plus esclave qu'eux (Man is born free, and everywhere he is in chains. A man may believe himself the master of others and yet be more enslaved than they are)." Rousseau says that he does not know how the change came about, but that he hopes to resolve the question of the legitimization of sovereignty.

In spite of its ringing declamatory tone, the opening sentence goes no further than such earlier political theoreticians of the "natural law" school as Pufendorf, deriving both from the sixth-century *Digest* of Justinian and from the Thomist scholastic tradition and its post-renaissance resurgence in Grotius. What was new in Rousseau was the inalienability of political liberty, which he took from the Calvinist Althusius's *Politica* of 1603. His concept of liberty clearly changes, in his second sentence, from a political to a moral one. In its moral sense Rousseau's concept of liberty is near to the Roman notion of civic virtue on which Montesquieu had depended, but the ambiguity of the meaning he created for liberty embarrassed him on at least three identifiable occasions: firstly when he came to discuss society's right to impose the death penalty: "Je sens que mon coeur murmure et retient ma plume (I feel that my heart protests and checks my pen)" (Book II, chapter 5); secondly when he could not allow that democracy was other than an unattainable ideal: "S'il y avoit un peuple de dieux, il se gouverneroit démocratiquement. Un gouvernement si parfait ne convient pas à des hommes (If there were a nation of gods, they would govern themselves democratically. So perfect a system of government is not suited to men)" (Book III, chapter 4); and thirdly when he considered civil liberties: "quiconque refusera d'obéir à la volonté générale, y sera contraint par tout le corps: ce qui ne signifie autre chose sinon qu'on le forcera à être libre (whoever refuses to obey the general will will be compelled to by the whole civil society, which means that he will be forced to be free)" (Book I, chapter 7).

Rousseau goes on to criticize Hobbes, Grotius, Pufendorf, and others, with all of whom he also partly agreed, arguing against Locke that the social pact can have only one form, in which "chacun de nous met en commun sa personne et toute sa puissance sous la suprême direction de la volonté générale; et nous recevons en corps chaque membre comme partie indivisible du tout (each of us puts in common his person and all his power under the supreme direction of the general will; and we

then as a group receive each member as an indivisible part of the whole)" (Book I, chapter 6). On the location of sovereignty, although not on the manner of its exercise and the administration of the state, Rousseau was therefore uncompromisingly and totally republican. He was conscious of his failure to find an acceptable solution to the reconciliation of liberalism and republican totalitarianism, and later considered *Du contrat social* as "une oeuvre à refaire (a book to be re-written)." After dealing with the nature of society, the second book considers the nature of the inalienable sovereignty. It is here that the difficulty is at its sharpest, and paradox takes over from logical argument:

…la volonté générale peut seule diriger les forces de l'Etat selon la fin de son institution, qui est le bien commun; car, si l'opposition des intérêts particuliers a rendu nécessaire l'établissement des sociétés, c'est l'accord de ces mêmes intérêts qui l'a rendu possible. C'est ce qu'il y a de commun dans ces différents intérêts qui forme le lien social; et s'il n'y avoit pas quelque point dans lequel tous les intérêts s'accordent, nulle société ne sauroit exister. Or, c'est uniquement sur cet intérêt commun que la société doit être gouvernée.

Je dis donc que la souveraineté, n'étant que l'exercice de la volonté générale, ne peut jamais s'aliéner, et que le souverain, qui n'est qu'un être collectif, ne peut être représenté que par lui-même: le pouvoir peut bien se transmettre, mais non pas la volonté

(…only the general will can direct the energies of the state according to the end for which it was instituted, which is the common good; for, if the clash of individual interests has made the establishment of societies necessary, it is the congruence of those same interests which has made it possible. It is what there is in common between those different interests which forms the social bond, and if there were not some point at which all those interests agree, there could be no society. It is solely according to that common interest that society should be governed.

I say then that sovereignty, being only the exercise of the general will, can never be alienated, and that the sovereign, which is only a corporate entity, can never be represented except by itself. Power can be transferred, but not the [general] will) (Book II, chapter 1).

The difficulty lies in knowing whether Rousseau regards the general will, which compels adhesion, as deriving from the concordance of individual interests, or from something in each member of a society which puts the common good above individual interest. In the fifth book of *Emile* Rousseau goes further in asserting that, in obeying the sovereign, all members of a society obey themselves. People are therefore more, not less, free under the social pact than in the state of nature. The Geneva manuscript of *Du contrat social* made clear that the cohesive force of a state declined when the general will ceased to be identical with the wills of each individual. In the published text, Rousseau writes:

Il y a souvent bien de la différence entre la volonté de tous et la volonté générale; celle-ci ne regarde qu'à l'intérêt commun, l'autre regarde à l'intérêt privé, et n'est qu'une somme de volontés particulieres...

(There is often a great difference between the will of all and the general will. The general will is concerned with the common interest alone, whereas the will of all concerns private interest, and is only the sum of individual wills). (Book II, chapter 3).

Sovereignty is inalienable, indivisible, and absolute, providing it is directed by the general will towards the common good. It logically demands the abnegation of personal and sectional interests, not their interplay. There is a link in Rousseau's mind between the education of the individual to virtue, as expounded in *Emile*, and the organization of society in such a way as to avoid the corruption of government. Like *Emile*, *Du contrat social* is developed from the moral reflections of the two *Discours*, and Rousseau is obviously concerned almost uniquely with small societies like those of Geneva and Corsica, since moral corruption is endemic in large states. Rousseau, like Machiavelli, whose republican principles he understands better than most of his contemporaries, finds the need for a disinterested legislator to guide the general will which, while always right, is not always enlightened. Rousseau regards law as a determination of the general will, and laws are properly only "les conditions de l'association civile (the conditions of civil association)." From Book II, chapter 8, after dealing with the legislator, Rousseau is obviously inspired by Montesquieu's *De l'esprit des lois*.

The third book, discussing forms of government, categorizes them in the traditional way as the democratic, which requires virtue in its citizens, the aristocratic, in which the administration is not in the hands of the sovereign, although the people remain the source of its authority, and the monarchical, the most dangerous, because it makes the public interest easiest to subvert for the sake of a single private interest. Rousseau assumes that any government which does not work for the public good forfeits its legitimacy. Censorship is defended in the interest of protecting morals. A dictatorship may be necessary in an emergency, but can have power only to suspend and not to make laws. There should be a state religion, solely concerned with spiritual matters, whose function it is to promote the fulfilment of duty. It should incorporate belief in the existence of God, in the happiness of the good and the punishment of the evil after death, and in the sanctity of the social contract and its laws. It should prohibit intolerance and cannot compel its own acceptance, although those who do not accept it can be banished as incapable of incorporation into civil society.

Emile; ou, De l'éducation is a treatise on education which turns into a Bildungsroman, and elaborates some of the ideas central to *La Nouvelle Héloïse*. The central educational idea is that a child is born innocent and is educated through its feelings, then its emotions and passions, rather than through the development of the intellect. There are five books, and again two manuscripts, of which the second, with its more elaborate but digressive developments, obscures the clearer logical lines of the first. Originally intended as "un Mémoire de quelques pages (a memoir a few pages long)," it was to be an abstract treatise on education, apparently undertaken after the series of six *Lettres à Sophie* about morality and happiness, written in the winter of 1757–58 but never sent, the most important ideas and passages

of which were incorporated into *Emile*, and particularly into the "Profession de foi du vicaire Savoyard" which its fourth book contains.

The first version of *Emile* is known as the "manuscrit Favre" after the family which owned it from 1825 and gave it to the Société Jean-Jacques Rousseau in 1915. For half of its length it refers simply to "l'élève (the pupil)," and its psychology is more purely materialistic and the tension between moral integrity and social adjustment greater than in the final version, in which the educator does not intervene so soon. As his work progressed, Rousseau obviously felt the need to write about a concrete individual rather than develop a series of abstract principles, so that the work turned itself into a novel. The first version was written between late in 1758 and the summer of 1759, and the expanded final text between late 1759 and late 1760. A good deal is owed to Fénelon.

The final version starts with another forthright paradox, "Tout est bien, sortant des mains de l'auteur des choses: tout dégénère entre les mains de l'homme (Everything is good when it leaves the hands of the author of things: everything corrupts in the hands of men)." The principles governing Emile's education are largely reducible to letting nature itself freely form the infant. The limbs should be unconstrained from birth, and the child should be breast-fed by its mother. "Observez la nature, et suivez la route qu'elle vous trace (Observe nature, and follow the path it shows you)." A hardy body avoids a precocious sensuality and leads to temperance. A child requires much attention, but it should not be pampered physically or allowed to become imaginatively fastidious. It should be brought up in the country, and allowed to play, and fall, and bruise itself, but no child should ever be beaten, because corporal punishment involves a damaging training in submission. At all stages physical and mental development should be in harmony with one another. A child should not be repressed; only when the power of abstract reasoning appears should its moral and religious education be undertaken, so prolonging the unity of reason and sentiment into adulthood and society.

The second book deals with the ages of five to twelve, when the tutor takes over from the parents. At this stage Rousseau ceases to write in abstract theoretical terms, and introduces Emile, an orphan, obviously rich, with his own ideal tutor. The text is not exempt from platitudes and prejudices. It is often speculative, and even more frequently impractical, but there are important leading principles. Emile must not be thwarted by any obvious exercise of human will, and must be guided rather than taught. The tutor must use guile. On the other hand a child's whims must not be gratified, and not everything granted that is requested. What Rousseau advocates is anything but soft, and seems indeed often cruel and humiliating. The book remains very largely an imaginative speculation about human nature, its potential, its needs, and the ways in which it can be developed or corrupted. It is not impressive as a day-to-day pedagogical manual.

Teaching must be through the handling of objects and the resolution of real problems involving, for instance, heights, distances, and the notion of property. Conventional school disciplines begin later, and not even religious education should begin before the age of 12. Thereafter a child should learn a useful trade. At 15 Emile enters the phase of social relationships, and Rousseau is at pains to keep his imagination restrained. Friendship comes before love, and history and moral science not before the age of 18. Ancient history is more important than modern, and it is best studied through biographies, preferably those of Plutarch. Apart from the few simple principles of education laid down, the book's interest lies largely in its radicalism. Right or wrong on matters of detail and principle, Rousseau has opened up the whole subject of natural potential to disturbing re-appraisal.

The most sensitive part of the book contains the sentimental deism of the "vicaire Savoyard" from Book IV, written after Rousseau had read Helvétius. It is an anti-sceptical document relying primarily on the development of a moral conscience, but also using an argument from causality for the existence of God. There must be a benevolent deity and an after-life to put right the wrongs of life on earth. There are in man innate principles of justice and virtue and, in a lyrical passage, conscience emerges as the supreme guide. The religion of the heart should be simple, humble, tolerant, and evangelical. An external cult is necessary only for social order. The "Profession de foi" allows a freedom of thought which, for political reasons, *Du contrat social* proscribed, and it dispenses with the need for any revelation. Voltaire, who thought Rousseau by now to be mad, nevertheless considered the "Profession de foi" a precious document, and we know from a great deal of external evidence that the "Profession de foi" expressed Rousseau's personal credo.

The final book deals with the education of women, which ought to be practical, avoiding the abstract and the speculative. Rousseau is less feminist in his views than Fénelon had been. Woman is born to please, flatter, and care for man. Her virtues are domestic. Sophie is treated as the counterpart to Emile, the differences of gender emphasized rather than played down. Their relationship, partly idyllic, shows the different characteristics of the sexes and their mutual need for one another in pursuit of virtue and happiness. Emile is made to wait a long time before he marries Sophie. The tutor warns them that their romantic affection is bound to cool, and in a sequel, *Emile et Sophie*, first published in 1780 in the *Collection complète des oeuvres de J-J. Rousseau*, their conjugal love does in fact break down when Sophie is unfaithful.

Emotional love results from the socializing of humanity. From haphazard mating, primitive man develops emotional bonding in early family units, and sexual drives become much stronger as mating becomes less casual. Love is a stratagem devised by the female to ensure male protection, so that sex becomes the basis for a power relationship in which the woman dominates. Female modesty is a means of strengthening male lust and transforming it into love. Surprise has often been expressed at the reactionary nature of Rousseau's views on women and female education, but surprise is misplaced. The rethinking here undertaken by Rousseau is just as radical as that which governed the rest of his views, but its conclusions are, for whatever reason, not at all what we regard as satisfactory or in the least advanced. Commentators have emphasized the extent to which Rousseau's educational principles were in advance of his time and laid the foundation for all sorts of subsequent practices and ways of looking on human nature. In fact he was, from the point of view of modern pedagogical theory, almost as wrong about male education as about female upbringing, about which however he knew less. His views must have been coloured, too, by his own attitudes to and experiences with women. *Emile*, however, remains a powerful book, not because its educational principles are right, but simply because within it

so many major assumptions about human potential are radically reappraised, without fear of the conclusions.

The later confessional writings, however fascinating, are not such great works of the imagination. *Les Confessions* was written between 1764 and 1770. The first six books were published in 1781 and the second six in 1788. Rousseau has formed the firm intention to relate even the ugly and the squalid in his behaviour, but has not quite achieved the interior freedom which would have allowed him to do that, however near he often comes to it. There are in fact self-justificatory as well as self-revelatory threads woven together, often written with lyrical intensity and offering extraordinary insights into Rousseau's own feelings and experiences up to 1766. Rousseau knew that he required to find a new language and a new style in which to narrate what *Les Confessions* contains, and he felt the need to vindicate himself for a pattern of behaviour he himself knew had had to be bizarre on account of what he had wanted it to enable him to do. He knew that only a few, particularly well-educated people could escape the corruption endemic in large societies, and then probably only at the cost of their own happiness. Rousseau's confessional writings should be seen in that light. He had imposed much misery on himself in the interests of achieving intellectual purity, and he not unreasonably wanted that fact to be known.

PUBLICATIONS

Collections to 1783

Oeuvres diverses de M. J-J Rousseau de Genève, 2 vols., Geneva 1756
Oeuvres diverses de M. J-J Rousseau, 2 vols., Amsterdam 1760; ed. augmentée, 1761
Oeuvres diverses de J-J. Rousseau, 3rd vol., Amsterdam 1763
Oeuvres diverses de Mr J-J Rousseau, citoyen de Genève, 9 vols., Amsterdam 1762–64
Oeuvres de M. Rousseau de Genève, 9 vols., Neuchâtel (Paris), 1764–68; vol. 10, 1779
Oeuvres de J-J Rousseau, 11 vols., Amsterdam 1769
Collection complète des oeuvres de J-J. Rousseau, 11 vols., Neuchâtel 1775
The Works, 10 vols., 1773–4
Collection complète des oeuvres de J-J. Rousseau, 9 vols., London (Brussels) 1774–76
Collection complète des oeuvres de J-J. Rousseau, 33 vols., Geneva 1780–89
Oeuvres, 38 vols., London (Paris) 1780–91
Oeuvres posthumes de Jean-Jacques Rousseau, 12 vols., Geneva-Neuchâtel, 1781–83
Collection complète des oeuvres de J-J Rousseau, 35 vols., Kehl 1783

Modern Collections

The Political Writings of J-J Rousseau, 2 vols., 1915 (in French) ed. Vaughan
Rousseau: Political Writings, Edinburgh 1953
Oeuvres complètes, Bibliothèque de la Pléiade, 4 vols., 1959–69

Poetry and drama

Le Verger de Madame la Baronne de Warens, (poem) 1739

Les Festes de Ramire (ballet) (produced 1745), 1745

Le Devin du village, (opera) (produced 1752), 1753; as *The Cunning Man*, 1766

L'Allée de Sylvie, (poem) 1763

Narcisse; ou, L'Amant de lui-même, (comedy) (produced 1753), 1753

Pygmalion, (incidental music by the author) (produced 1770), 1771

Other

Dissertation sur la musique moderne, 1743

Discours sur les sciences et les arts, 1750; as *A Discourse on the Arts and Sciences*, 1752; in *The First and Second Discourses*, tr. Roger D. and Judith R. Masters 1964; same title, tr. Victor Gourevitch, 1986

Discours sur l'origine et les fondemens de l'inégalité parmi les hommes, 1755; in *The First and Second Discourses*, tr. Roger D. and Judith R. Masters, 1964; same title, tr. Victor Gourevitch, 1986

Discours sur l'oeconomie politique, 1758; as *Discourse on Political Economy* in *On the Social Contract with Geneva Manuscript and Political Economy*, 1978

Lettre à d'Alembert sur les spectacles, originally *J-J. Rousseau, citoyen de Genève à M. d'Alembert...*, 1759; as *A Letter to M. d'Alembert*, 1759; as *Letter to M. d'Alembert on the Theatre* in *Politics and the Arts*, 1960

Lettre à Voltaire, 1759

Julie; ou, La Nouvelle Héloïse, 1761; as *Eloisa*, 1761; as *Julie; or, The New Eloise*, 1968

Emile; ou, De l'éducation, 1762; as *Emilius and Sophia; or, A New System of Education*; as *Emile; or, On Education*, 1979

Du contrat social; ou, Principes du droit politique, par J-J Rousseau, citoyen de Genève, 1762; as *A Treatise on the Social Compact*, 1764; as *On the Social Contract with Geneva Manuscript and Political Economy*, 1978

J-J. Rousseau, citoyen à Genève, à Christophe de Beaumont, 1763

Lettres écrites de la montagne, 1764

Dictionnaire de musique, 1767; as *A Dictionary of Music*, 1770

Rousseau, juge de Jean-Jacques: Dialogues, 1780

Considérations sur le gouvernement de Pologne, 1782; as *The Government of Poland*, 1982

Lettres à M. de Malesherbes, 1780

Les Rêveries du promeneur solitaire, 1782; as *The Reveries of the Solitary Walker*, 1979

Les Confessions, vols. 1–2, 1782, vols. 3–4, 1789; as *The Confessions*, 1783–91; same title, 1953

Botanique des enfants..., 1800; as *Letters on the Elements of Botany*, 1785

Essai sur l'origine des langues, 1976; as *Essay on the Origins of Languages* in *The First and Second Discourses*, 1986

Correspondence

Correspondance, edited by Théophile Dufour, 20 vols., 1924–34; index 1953

Correspondance, edited by R.A. Leigh, 50 vols., 1965–91

Biographical and critical studies

Starobinski, Jean, *Jean-Jacques Rosseau: La transparence et l'obstacle*, 1957

Broome, J., *Rousseau* (in English), 1963

Guéhenno, Jean, *Jean-Jacques Rousseau*, (in English), 2 vols., 1966

Grimsley, Ronald, *Rousseau: A Study in Self-Awareness*, 1969

Derathé, Robert, *Jean-Jacques Rousseau et la science politique de son temps*, 2nd ed., 1970

Masters, Roger Davis, *The Political Philosophy of Rousseau*, 1976

Cranston, Maurice, *Jean-Jacques Rousseau*
    vol. 1, *The Early Life of Jean-Jacques Rousseau, 1712–1754*, 1983
    vol. 2, *The Noble Savage, Jean-Jacques Rousseau, 1754–1762*, 1991

Miller, James, *Rousseau, Dreamer of Democracy*, 1984

Blum, Carol, *Rousseau and the Republic of Virtue*, 1986

Melzer, Arthur M., *The Natural Goodness of Man, on the System of Rousseau's Thought*, 1990

Bibliography

Senelier, Jean, *Bibliographie générale des oeuvres de Rousseau*, 1949

S

SADE, Donatien-Alphonse-François, marquis de, 1740–1814.

Novelist, writer of short stories, and dramatist.

Sade's Provençal parentage was distinguished. His ancestry could be traced back to the 12th century, and its nobility to the 15th. Among the family's better-known members had been Petrarch's Laura, wife of Hugues de Sade, glimpsed by the poet in 1327; she died of the plague in 1348. Sade's father, Jean-Baptiste-Joseph-François, was born at Avignon in 1702 and became captain of dragoons in Condé's regiment before, in 1730, being made ambassador to the czar Peter II, after whose death he was given a secret mission to London in 1733. After fighting the campaigns of 1734 and 1735 against Austria he bought for 35,000 livres the charge of lieutenant-general of Bresse, Bugey, Valromey and Gex, registered by letters patent of 29 May 1739, and on 9 November 1740 he did homage to the pope for the properties of Saumane and Mazan. He was also seigneur of La Coste, discharged further important diplomatic functions, negotiated the treaty of Nymphenburg, was promoted maréchal de camp in 1760, and died in 1767, near his estate at Glatigny. He wrote occasional verse, and plays for amateur groups.

On 13 November 1733 he married Marie-Eléonore de Maillé de Carman in the chapel of the Hôtel Condé. The bride, born in 1712, was a distant relation of the Condé family and, on marriage, was made a lady-in-waiting to the princess in succession to her mother. Her first child, Sade's elder sister, was born in 1737 but died at the age of two. Sade was born on 2 June 1740, and another sister died at birth in 1746, leaving Sade an only child. His name was intended to be Louis-Aldonse-Donatien, which is how Sade often later signed himself, thereby causing difficulties later, when he wanted his name struck off the list of émigrés. The prince de Condé, Louis-Henri, had died in January 1740, and the princess, Caroline de Hesse-Rheinfeld-Rothenburg, died in June 1741. Sade's mother appears to have helped with the education of the young prince, Louis-Joseph de Bourbon, born on 9 August 1736, married on 3 May 1752 to Charlotte de Rohan-Soubise, and then to have accompanied her husband on his diplomatic missions, leaving her son's upbringing to her mother-in-law in Avignon from 1744 and then, from 1745 or 1746, to her brother-in-law, Sade's paternal uncle, from 1744 titular abbot of Ebrueil in the diocese of Limoges. In about 1760 Sade's mother retired to the Carmelite convent of the Rue d'Enfer in Paris, where she died on 14 January 1777. Sade's early boyhood was spent in the company of the young Condé, whose seniority and superior rank and he later said he refused as a child to respect.

Sade's father had four brothers and five sisters. With the exception of Sade's youngest aunt, Henriette-Victoire, who in 1733 married the marquis de Villeneuve, by whom she had three daughters, the other uncles and aunts either died young or entered religion. Sade's uncle and guardian was a friend of Voltaire and of Mme de la Popelinière, the mistress of the maréchal de Saxe. The abbot was known for his amorous liaisons and was, indeed, imprisoned briefly in 1762 after a raid on a house where he was found with a Mme Piron, described by the police simply as a "femme de débauche (loose woman)," and a prostitute, Léonore. In 1760 the abbot leased the château de Saumane from Sade's father, although he appears to have used it at least from 1744. Sade was largely brought up there. His uncle had antiquarian interests and had worked on Petrarch, whose life he published, and on the family history.

From 1750 Sade was sent to the Paris Jesuit Collège Louis-le-Grand—the Collège de Clermont until it became a royal foundation in 1682—with a 34-year-old cleric, Jacques-François Amblet, as private tutor. While Sade was at school his father ran into financial trouble, was borrowing, and had to sell property. Sade himself was to remain on close terms with Amblet, who helped to negotiate the settlement with Rose Keller in 1768, whose guest Sade was as late as 1777, and who helped alleviate the rigours of Sade's imprisonments. In 1754, at just 14, Sade was moved to the army Ecole des Chevau-légers, having been furnished with the necessary certificate of nobility. The cost was 3,000 livres a year. In December 1755, he became a sub-lieutenant, in January 1757 a standard-bearer, and on 21 April 1759 he was bought a post as a cavalry captain for 10,000 livres. A copy exists of a letter, the earliest Sade text, perhaps of 25 April 1759, mentioning his daily quest in Paris for no doubt sexual pleasure. His behaviour in this respect and his gambling disturbed his father who in 1760 resigned his charge of lieutenant-general in favour of Sade, who succeeded to the post in 1764. In 1762 Sade had the chance of acquiring his own company, but could not afford it.

By 1763 the Seven Years War was over. Sade's father complained that Sade neglected him for balls and entertainments. From March 1763 Sade lost his post as cavalry captain, as was not unusual at the end of a war. He was allowed to return to the army in 1767. It was in May 1763 that Sade went to La Coste, where a celebration was held to receive the heir to the local title. His father, perhaps through poor administration, was by now in real financial difficulties, and was living for choice with the religious of the Missions étrangères of the Rue du Bac. Sade was himself borrowing, leading a generally debauched life, and neglecting to pay his respects at court. His behaviour was remarked on, and his father received a complaint that his son was not behaving in accordance with his rank.

Sade's reputation wrecked two possible marriage projects, but on 17 May 1763, with the king's agreement, he married Renée-Pélagie Cordier de Launay de Montreuil, the daughter of a lawyer at the cour des Aides, by whom he was to have two sons and a daughter, and who was to remain loyal to him until the outbreak of the Revolution in 1789. He already had a mistress, Laure-Victoire-Adelaine de Lauris, born on 8 June 1741 into a 13th-century family and châtelaine of Vacqueyras, whom he had hoped to marry until only a fortnight before his wedding, but whose father refused to entertain the notion. We have a passionate letter of reproach to Laure, and one to her father pleading for an invitation to a ball from the guest list for which Sade had been excluded.

The dominating figure in his wife's family was the mother, the willing dupe of her own snobbery in desiring her daughter's marriage to a young cavalry officer related by marriage to the royal family. She must positively have disregarded the danger signals and blinded herself to what was an obvious smoke screen put up by Sade's father, perfectly lucid about the character of his passionate, headstrong, and over-privileged son, with altogether too pleasure-loving and ruthless a temperament. Sade, who had been lingering at Avignon, arrived in Paris by post-chaise for his wedding. There were 85½ stages between Avignon and Paris and, even if he used only single horses, Sade will have had to pay 1 livre 5 sols per stage. Two horses cost twice as much. For the wedding his father tried to borrow 10,000 livres from his sister, the abbess of Saint-Laurent at Avignon, to clothe his son and servants, and to buy his son a carriage and a pair of horses. What came back was a page of figures and a promise, but no money. Sade's mother would not part with her diamonds. Sade's father said that to get rid of him he was doing more than he would have done if he had loved him dearly.

Permission for the marriage had been given by the necessary distinguished personages at Versailles on 1 May. They included the king and queen, the whole of the royal family, and the Condés. The contract was signed on 15 and 16 May, and on 17 May the wedding was celebrated. Sade's bride was to bring from her father the equivalent of 80,000 livres, most of it in annual payments after the death of her father and his mother, and from her mother the equivalent of 50,000 livres after her death. There was the equivalent of a further 170,000 livres to come, after various deaths, from the bride's family, who were to lodge and feed the couple with two servants for five years, after which they would give the couple 10,000 livres to set up on their own. Almost all the dowry was to come in the form of annual payments, some delayed for unpredictable periods. Sade's father contributed the lieutenant-general's post, the estates of La Coste, Mazan, Saumane, and Mas de Cabanes, less 30,000 livres to be retained, but with 10,000 livres more when the Béthunes repaid a debt to Sade's father. Sade was to pay his wife 4,000 livres a year, the capital to be passed to the children. The provisions show that Sade's father in particular was wary of entrusting his son with any large capital sum of which he could dispose freely.

The couple lived officially in the Rue Neuve du Luxembourg in Paris, or on the Montreuil estate at Echauffour in Normandy, about 150 kilometres due west of Paris. Sade's behaviour began only very gradually to become openly and arrogantly shocking. He had half a dozen apartments in Paris, Versailles, and at Arceuil, and haunted not only the more pleasure-loving of the salons, but other places where there were reasonably well brought-up girls to be found, and brothels, also the small private establishments with very restricted clienteles. Sade much preferred to use his own apartments, distinguishing between those

he kept for illegitimate but orthodox liaisons, and a "petite maison," where the acting out of fantasies and the stimulation of appetites required the presence of more than a single partner.

For some of the girls Sade appears to have felt, often simultaneously, a real infatuation. Among these must be included Mlle de Beauvoisin, famous, expensive, but seeking pleasures more than riches. Sade took her to La Coste. It is perfectly clear that his whole existence came very soon to revolve round his sex life, its only other focal points being amateur theatricals, and the difficulty of obtaining from his father the money due under the marriage contract. Sade's mother-in-law was firmly on his side, and in constant communication about money with Sade's uncle, the abbot.

Only in 1963 did a document come to light explaining what happened on the night of 18 to 19 October 1763. It is a police deposition in which a Jeanne Testard testifies that, having been sent for by a "femme du monde (lady)," she was give two louis d'or of 24 livres and taken away by someone who was certainly Sade with a coach and coachman. The deposition testifies in Sade to a mixture of ordinary atheistic affirmations with a contorted imaginative association between Jesus, his mother, and various sexual acts. Sade told her about ejaculating into a chalice used at Mass, sexually defiling with a girl consecrated hosts received at communion, and defying God to avenge himself. Thereafter, in a room in which there were religious images, particularly crucifixions, with strong sexual overtones, the girl was asked by Sade to beat him with a heated iron whip and then to choose a whip for him to use on her, some of those available liable to inflict less lasting, visible, or painful damage. She refused. According to the document, he ejaculated over a figure of Christ, made her trample on another one, uttering sexual blasphemies while she did so, and threatening to kill her if she did not, made her excrete over a figure of Christ, read to her blasphemous verses, sodomized her, and made her promise to come back the following Sunday so that they could communicate together and return to burn one consecrated host and to commit sexual blasphemies with the other.

The fundamental association of religious imagery, sexual imagery, excretion, pain, and blasphemy, with the need for strident acts of irreligion and sensual titillation is not totally uncommon although, like other psychologically urgent needs to perpetrate violent desecrations, it is plainly pathological. It had obviously taken a very strong grip on Sade by his early twenties. The girl may of course have been lying or exaggerating, but it sounds as if most of which she said was true, and similar mental patterns can be found in Sade's later works.

Sade was taken to Fontainebleau, where the king was, to be prosecuted, and then imprisoned at Vincennes on 29 October. He immediately wrote to the governor, the lieutenant of police, and his mother-in-law. To Sartine, the lieutenant of police, he was contrite, asking only to be allowed a visit from his wife, about three months pregnant. He wrote again on 2 November, asking to see a priest, and begging that his family should not be informed of the real reason for his detention. On 4 November the court arranged for a confessor to be sent to visit Sade. The king found his conduct too grave to allow him distinguished treatment, but he could have a servant, although not one of his own. His father came to Fontainebleau to intercede with the king, a journey which cost him 10 louis, "enough to live on for two months," and Sade was banished to Echauffour.

Sade's in-laws at Echauffour forgave him on a promise of

future good behaviour. He was allowed back to Paris for three months from 3 April 1764, and on 11 September for good. Meanwhile there had been amateur theatricals in April, with Sade playing the lead, at Evry, in the château belonging to his wife's uncle and aunt. Since his wife also acted, she must have had and recovered from a miscarriage earlier in the year. There was no live infant. In June Sade was invested at Dijon with the post of lieutenant-general, and appears to have done some work on local history. From July to December, he had a liaison with an actress at the Comédie-Italienne, Mlle Colet (Collet, Colette; the spelling varies). Sade was presented to her on 15 July, presumably at his own request, and next day sent an urgent, if respectful and courteous, love letter. When his servant came back empty-handed, he wrote another, more wildly exaggerated one.

By December, we know from the police inspector Marais who had been keeping a detailed watch on Sade, that he was paying Mlle Colet 25 louis a month. "La femme Brissault," Marais also tells us, nick-named "la Présidente," had told Sade to give up the actress, partly because she rightly supposed he could not afford her, and partly because, as long as he tried to, he could not use the services of her own house, of which he had been a good client. Marais had warned la Brissault, and apparently the proprietors of similar businesses, including her husband who kept a house in a different part of Paris, that it was dangerous to provide Sade with girls.

The police were keeping astonishingly well-informed files on the Paris suppliers of sexual favours. Marais's notebook for 8 February 1765 contains the information that "la Beaupré," also of the Comédie-Italienne, had turned down an offer of 20 louis a month from the marquis de Saint-Sulpice for the right to be her reserve lover, in favour of an offer of six louis from Sade, "with whom she has slept twice." On 26 April, Marais tells us that Sade is spending a good 20 louis a month on Mlle de Beauvoisin, but that both M. Douet de la Boulay and the sieur de Pienne were outpaying him. However, she went to La Coste in May with Sade, who passed her off either as his wife or as one of her relatives. Marais's notes on her are vivid enough to have been written by Mme de Sévigné. That summer at La Coste there was a whole cycle of feasts, theatricals, balls, and entertainments. Sade's uncle, the abbé, came to stay for a week, and wrote to his sister, the abbess of Saint-Benoît de Cavaillon, about the woman Sade had brought. Sade's reply to her letter of reproach made insulting remarks both about his uncle's own flagrant sexual scandals and about those of his married aunt, Mme de Villeneuve-Martignan, for whom the architect, J.-B. Franque, built the little masterpiece which now houses the Musée Calvet at Avignon.

Sade's mother-in-law got to hear of the imposture. She appears to have suppressed a scandal late in 1764 or early in 1765, and expressed horror in particular at the debts she knew her son-in-law had piled up and of which her daughter had not been informed. Sade did not reveal his return on 20 August 1765 from Provence, where he had left debts of 4,500 livres. The next day Mlle de Beauvoisin lent Sade 10,000 livres, realized partly from the sale of jewellery, and he informed his wife and mother-in-law at Echauffour that he had returned. Mlle de Beauvoisin gave birth to a child of which Sade was not the father, and was again on stage at the Comédie-Italienne in December 1765. Marais thought the child-bearing had improved her looks, and is entertaining about the young gentlemen who were paying her

court, and about whom, or how much, they had sacrificed for her favours. Sade, momentarily dropped from her list of partners, hired rooms in Versailles, and his wife came back to live with him in Paris. Her younger sister, Anne-Prospère, born between 1743 and 1745, seems already to have been attached to Sade.

The procession of women continued. We know the names and sexual aptitudes only of a handful of actresses and dancers, and we know that others were in a position to pay them more handsomely than Sade could. Sade was giving Mlle Dorville 10 louis a month, but Elchin, an Englishman who moved in the same circles, was paying her weekly visits at four louis each.

Among those of Sade's partners we know about, to many of whom he wrote in poses or outbursts of pleading or recrimination, there was a whole contingent who had also been, or were soon going to be, partners of mostly young members of the highest aristocracy or else older bourgeois from the richest financial circles. Naturally we do not know even the names of the ordinary prostitutes, except for those named on the rare occasions involving a complaint, but Sade seems to have kept his relationships, and his fantasies, compartmentalized. The anonymous participants in the episodes in which, for a variety of identifiable reasons, the fantasies required more than a single partner for their enactment, were distinguished in Sade's mind from the actresses and dancers, more expensive, sometimes the feigned or real objects of genuine affection, and treated with more social dignity than those who were casually picked up, used, paid, and discarded. It is also not unimportant to note that none of Sade's partners, as far as we know, suffered permanent physical damage as a result of the liaison. Indeed, that fact is probably the key to an understanding of the works.

A letter from the abbot to Sade's mother-in-law tells us that Sade was again in Saumane by 1 June 1766. The abbot's view is that Sade has to be quietened down gently:

Il seroit dangereux de le prendre, comme a fait son père, à rebroussepoil; il seroit capable de donner dans les plus grands écarts. Ce n'est qu'à force de douceur, d'indulgence, et de raison qu'on peut espérer de le ramener. Vous vous y êtes prise, Madame, on ne peut pas mieux. Il a pour vous beaucoup de confiance et de respect: tôt ou tard vous en ferés ce que vous voudrés

(It would be dangerous to rub him up the wrong way, as his father has done; he would be capable of going to the worst extremes. There is no hope of bringing him round except by gentleness, kindness, and reason. You have gone about it, Madame, in the best possible way. He has great confidence in and affection for you. Sooner or later you will be able to do as you like with him).

On 4 November 1766 Sade signed the lease for his "petite maison" at Arcueil. By 23 January 1767 a discontented lover complained to Marais that Mlle de Beauvoisin had taken up openly again with Sade. On 24 January Sade's father died unexpectedly. Sade's grief impressed his mother-in-law. He now inherited the title of "comte," though he did not use it, and his financial circumstances also changed. His father left debts amounting to 86,000 livres. Sade's only income independent of his wife's family was 10,000 livres as lieutenant-general, but that was now four years in arrears. In April he rejoined the army and was given the captaincy of a regiment but, presumably with leave from his colonel, he absented himself after four days. He went to join Mlle de Beauvoisin at Lyons. On 27 August 1767 Sade's wife gave birth to his first child, Louis-Marie. Sade was back in Paris by mid-October. Marais's notebook begins to show signs of outrage. He knows exactly what is going on at Arcueil, what new dancer Sade is after, and that la Brissault is refusing to supply any more girls. The Arcueil police note that Sade had become a public nuisance, had been violent in public, and was receiving parties which included boys as well as girls.

It was at 9 a.m. on Easter Sunday 3 April 1768 that Sade approached Rose Keller, the 36-year-old widow of a pastry cook, an out-of-work cotton spinner who was begging on the Place des Victoires. She agreed to follow him for three louis, not for sex but to clean his room. Had any sexual activity at all been even implicitly included in the verbal bargain, it is unlikely that there would have been a complaint. Sade made Rose Keller wait an hour in a room while he went on errands, then took her in a fiacre to Arcueil and locked her in a bedroom. That was about 12.30 p.m. She was taken downstairs, threatened with death by knifing if she did not undress, tied down, repeatedly beaten with a stick as well as with whips, and threatened with death again if she did not stop screaming. Sade stopped from time to time to rub in ointment. She asked him to spare her as she had not yet fulfilled her Easter duties. He laughed, said he would himself hear her confession, and carried on until he had an orgasm, cried out, immediately stopped, brought water for washing, brandy to soothe the lesions, food and wine, and locked the woman upstairs again. She knotted bed-covers together, escaped, and fled. There were two other girls in the house who did not know that Rose Keller had been there.

The compartmentalization and the immediate cessation of brutality on sexual relief are clearly important in any assessment of Sade's behaviour according to the conventional categories of morality, criminality, brutality, social impropriety, and mental illness. In view of the compensation extracted, no one can be entirely sure if Rose Keller exaggerated in order to increase its amount. Sade denied tying her down, and the medical reports do not confirm some parts of the story, which included incisions made with a pen-knife, which they might have been expected to corroborate if the story had been unvarnished fact.

Whatever the criminality, brutality, and morbidity involved, in some respects Sade had been unlucky, and in others stupid. It is not improbable that only the likely initial deceit about room-cleaning put his behaviour on a level all of its own. Had Rose Keller really been a prostitute, it is unlikely that the police would have acted on her complaint, backed only by nothing worse than those medical reports. However, Sade probably had picked a genuine, if foolish beggar; he had chosen respectable Arcueil, where he was a much-loathed nuisance, and Easter, which entailed the accusation, for instance in a letter of 18 April from an unidentified Mme de Saint-Germain to his uncle, the abbot, of a blasphemous mocking of the scourging of Jesus; and he had hit a moment when opinion was waiting to be outraged by any verifiable incident involving the maltreatment of a commoner by a libertine member of the court. Unlike some members of the court whose sexual tastes were known to draw much more blood, Sade was poor, notorious even outside relatively discreet court circles, and far enough from the centres of power to be made a scapegoat. He was unlucky in that his ultimate judge, Maupeou, was hostile to Sade's father-in-law Montreuil, of whose jurisdiction at the cour des Aides he was jealous. He

would be chancellor when Sade was next in serious trouble.

On the evening of 3 April Sade returned to Paris. By 7 April his wife had got hold of a lawyer and the abbé Amblet, Sade's old tutor, and sent them to Arcueil to buy off Rose Keller and remove anything compromising from the "petite maison." Rose Keller asked for 3,000 livres, was offered 1,800, and they settled for 2,400 which, later in the day, they paid. The king sent Sade, under Amblet's guard, to house arrest at Saumur. There, but for public outrage, the matter would have ended. The civil case was settled. Token criminal justice had been done. However, the criminal council of the Paris parlement insisted on its right to jurisdiction, and instructed the king's procurator general. Marais was sent to Saumur to take Sade to the prison of Pierre-Encise at Lyons. Apart from medical attention and a little accompanied fresh air, he was kept in solitary confinement. In June Marais was sent to bring him back for the formal procedure at Paris by which the king's removal of the matter from the parlement's jurisdiction by lettres d'abolition was ratified. He was then taken back to Lyons. His wife had to sell diamonds to be able to visit him in August. She stayed at Lyons. Sade was set free by order of the king on 16 November, and allowed to live at La Coste, while his wife returned to Paris, where she gave birth to Sade's second child, Donatien-Claude-Armande on 27 June 1769.

Sade returned to Paris in April 1769, having spent the winter putting on entertainments at La Coste. Since his marriage Sade had spent 60,000 livres more than his income. He was now threatened with seizure of all his possessions. The king refused to buy his mother's diamonds, or to allow the comte d'Artois to accept them as a gift. Sade was advised to stay away from court and repulsed when he tried to rejoin his regiment. He spent at least four weeks in the Low Countries, and chance later remarks suggest that he made enough money with his pen to live. He may also have spent time in England, where he claimed to have found a transcript of the trial of Joan of Arc. The later literary work utilizes what may well have been primary source material from both Burgundy and England.

Through the mediation of Condé, Sade was given an honorary military rank in March 1771, which meant that he would never again be readmitted as a serving officer. On 17 April 1771 his wife gave birth to their third child, Madeleine-Laure. In June he received 10,000 livres for his military post, but in September he was in prison in Paris at Fort-l'Evêque for eight days for debt. He was released on payment of 3,000 livres and signature of a promissory note, and spent the following year at La Coste, mostly arranging for amateur theatricals, writing and, with his wife and sister-in-law, acting. A theatre was built at the château de Mazan, and we have the intended programmes from 3 May to 22 October 1772. By the end of the winter, however, Sade was having a liaison with his wife's sister Anne-Prospère, known as Mlle de Launay. It was on account of that liaison, considered incestuous, that Sade's mother-in-law was to seek the lettre de cachet which would put him out of circulation and offer some chance of finding Anne-Prospère a husband. Anne-Prospère was certainly in love with Sade, and may well have provided him with one of his two or three experiences of real emotional dependency.

Plans were interrupted by Sade's condemnation to death on 2 September 1772. In mid-June he had gone pleasure-hunting in Marseilles, ostensibly to cash a letter of credit, and taken his valet Latour. On Thursday 25 June, Latour had found an 18-year-old in the street, Marianne Laverne, and made an assignation on Sade's behalf for 11 p.m. the next night. On the 26th she had gone boating, but she was back when Latour called at 8 a.m. on 27th. A new assignation was fixed for 10 a.m. at the house of a Mariette Borelly, aged 23, where Latour had also agreed for Mariannette Laugier and Rose Coste, both aged 20, to be present. Sade took some coins out of his pocket: whoever guessed how many would be first. It was Marianne.

Various sexual acts took place between Marianne, Latour and Sade. Marianne ate a number of chocolates which had been laced with cantharides, a poison which destroys the digestive tract but can be used medicinally in very small quantities, and was thought to irritate the erogenous parts of a woman's body and stimulate a craving for sexual satisfaction. Of the six distinct episodes, which certainly included anal and oral sex, normal copulation, flagellation by and of Sade, and acts involving Sade and Latour, five took place with more than two people in the room. Sade gave each of the four girls six livres and let them go late in the morning, making a rendezvous for the afternoon. When called for to come boating, they would not. Sade was to leave the next morning and did not intend to waste his evening. About 9 p.m. Latour picked up the 25-year-old Marguerite Coste, and took Sade to her after dinner, leaving them alone. She ate a lot of the chocolates, says she refused anal intercourse but accepted normal copulation, and was left with six livres. The sixth Marseilles girl was the 19-year-old Jeanne Nicou, whom Sade had visited several times before 25 June, but who would not come to the 10 a.m. assignation on 27 June. Marianne and Marguerite vomited with a violence proportionate to the number of chocolates they had consumed. Sade left with Latour for La Coste early on the 28 June.

It is not clear how the procureur du roi at the Marseilles sénéchaussée got to hear of Marguerite Coste's repeated vomiting and the severe gastric pains she attributed to sweets given to her by a client, or why he thought the matter required his attention, however easily any alias which may have been used by Sade would have been penetrated. It seems most likely that Sade's identity was instantly known and that his reputation was considered to warrant suspicion that he intended to poison with arsenic. The initial gastric symptoms are similar. The evidence given against Sade is tricky to evaluate, because acts of anal intercourse, even of passive participation, were capital offences, and accusations and denials therefore potent legal weapons. Five of the six girls testified that Sade had proposed such acts and maintained that they had refused him.

For literary purposes it is important to know what happened because, unless we know what Sade did and, to whatever extent possible, given his extraordinary behaviour, also what he knew, thought, and felt, we can scarcely understand how much what he wrote was simple fiction, how much self-justification, how much repressed or indulged fantasy, how much autobiography or fictionalized autobiography, and to what degree he was deranged, physiologically abnormal, arrogant, stupid, unlucky, vicious, brutal, or criminal. Whatever is to be said about his behaviour, it was not as bad as his reputation had become within a year or two of the Arcueil episode. He plainly did have a wild and uncontrolled imagination which produced erotic frenzies that limited physical capacities did not allow him to assuage. The question that has to be asked concerns the value of what he wrote when, in prison, he was forced finally to impose on his imagination the discipline to which he had been unable or unwilling to subject it between 1763 and 1777.

Sade heard that there was trouble, and fled La Coste with Anne-Prospère and Latour about 4 July 1772, the date his arrest, and that of Latour, was ordered. His wife went to Marseilles to see what could be done, but found sentiment against Sade implacable. Sentence of death was passed on Sade and Latour on 2 September, beheading for the noble, hanging for the commoner. Sentence was executed in effigy at Aix on 12 September. Since there appears to have been no complaint, and two of the girls withdrew support for the charges, it is difficult to see the legal justification for the trial. In fact the charge was virtually changed from attempted poisoning to sodomy. Public feeling was running very high, but even so, it is unlikely that the sentences would have been passed if the guilty had been available for execution. Maupeou, still jealous of the power of the cour des Aides of which Sade's father-in-law was the senior judge, was now chancellor. There was no evidence of any attempt at poisoning. The Sade of Marseilles was certainly inept and stupid, and quite possibly vicious as well, but he was not the arch-criminal the Europe-wide reputation made him sound.

By 27 October Sade, having left his luggage at Nice, was at Chambéry in Savoy, outside French jurisdiction. Anne-Prospère left, probably for La Coste. Sade's mother-in-law was now pursuing him. It was at her request that the duc d'Aiguillon requested the king of Sardinia's representative in Paris to arrange for Sade's arrest in Savoy. Sade was arrested on 8 December and taken to Miolans, 25 kilometres from Chambéry, 250 metres above the Val d'Isère, looking down on Saint-Pierre-d'Albigny. There can be few prisons in the world with a better view, and Sade got the best room, south-facing, on the fourth floor of the tower, above the governor. Minute regulation of the conditions of Sade's incarceration was overseen on orders from Turin, transmitted through Chambéry. Sade lost money gaming with his fellow-prisoner François de Songy, baron de l'Allée, who had been at Miolans from 22 February 1772 for having attempted to spring from jail at Bonneville a friend imprisoned there for debt. He was a petty aristocratic crook.

Sade and Songy nonetheless escaped on the night of 30 April 1773. Songy was re-arrested in Paris in August 1774, released in 1778, but imprisoned again in 1786. Sade tried to get to Spain via Bordeaux, where one of his plays was performed, returned to La Coste in the autumn, hid at the slightest alarm, and continued to attract his wife's support and his mother-in-law's rage. She paid very large sums of money to have him hunted down, and has been accused of wanting him killed in an affray to be caused when La Coste was raided. An expensive raid was mounted on 6 January 1774, but Sade was not there.

Late in 1774 Sade recruited five young girls for La Coste, and a complaint by at least one set of parents was laid against him. However, since his wife and sister-in-law were implicated, their mother now took very energetic and in the end successful measures to hush matters up. There were in all more than five young people at La Coste for two months that winter, but they and their families were bribed or threatened into silence. Sade's public reputation was not enhanced, but there were no vast public scandals and no further death sentences. By now Sade's uncle, the abbot, thought he should be locked up, and the danger from unpaid creditors was more pressing than the complaints of ill-treated little girls.

There was another raid in July 1775. Sade managed to hide, but then fled to Italy, crossing to Bologna, then Florence, where he was shocked by the sexual degeneracy he encountered, and

Rome, which seems from *L'Histoire de Juliette* once more to have aroused in his mind the association between sexual depravity and religious blasphemy. The openness of prostitution in Naples also horrified him. Very short indeed of money, he finally returned to La Coste late in July 1776. That November in Montpellier he negotiated to employ the 22-year-old Catherine Trillet in the kitchens at La Coste. To the establishment, from which all others had now fled, he added another kitchen girl, a chambermaid, a wigmaker, and a secretary. In January 1777 Sade's mother died. Negotiations over Catherine Trillet had been with her mother, but the father now turned up, actually shot at Sade who was trying to prevent him from removing his daughter, and by his complaint at Aix drew obvious official attention to Sade's reappearance at La Coste. Sade was again compelled to flee, and this time returned with his wife to Paris, hoping to get his mother-in-law to pay his debts and get his death sentence annulled. His wife went back to the Montreuils in the Rue Neuve du Luxembourg, and he went temporarily to the Hôtel de Danemark. His wife thought her mother now appeased.

On 13 February Marais called at the Hôtel de Danemark, having watched Sade's career with interest during the nine years since he had taken him to Pierre-Encise. He had a lettre de cachet issued at the mother-in-law's request and signed by the new king, and an armed escort. Sade was taken to Vincennes. Leave to appeal against the Marseilles sentence was granted only on 27 May 1778. Sade's uncle, the abbé, had died on 31 December. On 14 June 1778 Marais took Sade to Aix. Sade had decided not to plead temporary insanity in appealing against the death sentence. With Maupeou's dismissal on the death of Louis XV, the authority of the parlements had been re-established, which now helped Sade's case. The death sentence was replaced by a simple admonition, but Sade had not realised that he was still to be held under the lettre de cachet. He was surprised when Marais called at 3 a.m. on the morning of 15 July to take him back to Vincennes. On the night of 16 July, Sade succeeded in escaping at Valence. He got to Avignon by boat the following day. For whatever reason, Marais's pursuit had not been as determined as it might have been.

Sade was given a meal by friends, and by the morning of 18 July was at La Coste. His wife had not known of the Aix court appearance until she heard from her mother, who also informed her that she was retaining the lettre de cachet in force for the time being. Sade's wife made a scene, was forbidden by her mother to rejoin her husband, and thought it too dangerous to disobey. Sade's lawyer since early 1774, Gaspard-François-Xavier Gaufridy of Apt, was by now, as Sade suspected, in league with his mother-in-law, who renewed an earlier threat to have her daughter arrested and refused to open correspondence from her or from Sade himself. Sade felt threatened by the appearance of strangers in the village on 19 August, went to stay with a friend, then moved out into a barn, and finally came back to La Coste. On 25 August he learnt that he had been dismissed from his charge as lieutenant-general but, at his mother-in-law's instigation, received from Gaufridy reassuring news about the relaxation of his pursuit.

At 4 a.m. on 26 August 1778 Sade was arrested by a party of 10 armed men under the command of Louis Marais, the inspector's brother. He was taken back to Vincennes by Marais himself, and kept there from 7 September 1778 to 29 February 1784. From 7 December he was allowed unlimited paper and pens. His wife did everything she could, although Sade felt deserted by

her. His children were looked after by his mother-in-law, and his interests, as far as Sade would allow, by his lawyer. After the scandal of the young girls at La Coste in the winter of 1774–75, bones had been found buried in the park there. Sade had explained away their presence and it is unlikely that the authorities disbelieved him. However, it is clear from what Sade discovered at Vincennes that his public reputation now extended to child murder. Meanwhile he became extremely jealous of his wife, who in order to calm him moved to a notably austere convent in 1781. That autumn the jealousy became so bad that her visits to him had to be stopped. In August 1782, he was deprived of all books, because they over-heated his imagination and made him write what was not surprisingly considered improper. Later that month he wrote to his wife that nothing could ever change him. What he had done was the result of his physical constitution:

> Les moeurs ne dépendent pas de nous, elles tiennent à notre construction, à notre organisation. Ce qui dépend de nous, c'est de ne pas répandre notre venin au dehors, et que ce qui nous entoure, non seulement ne souffre pas, mais ne puisse même pas s'en apercevoir

> (Our morals do not depend on us, they derive from our make-up, our constitution. What does depend on us is not to spread our poison outside ourselves, and that those who surround us not only do not suffer, but do not even notice it).

In September 1782, Sade's conduct led again to the prohibition of his wife's visits. They had been permitted since the preceding January. He was sending out material he had written, but was told by his wife that from June 1783 she had no longer been receiving his letters on account of the indecencies they contained. The indecencies are mixed again with blasphemies. There are letters expressing the terrifying violence of sexual needs, and the appalling imaginative strains of attempting to satisfy them. Sade was plunged into bouts of intense depression, and there are occasional signs of manifest euphoria. We know little about exactly which of his works he composed at precise moments, but the whole documentation of his prison life makes it not unlikely that by 1783 he was sliding into a state of mental imbalance which presaged madness.

Vincennes's closure had been decided in the greatest secrecy. On 29 February 1784 Sade was moved to the Bastille. That prison, too, was scheduled for demolition, but the Revolution intervened. The food there was good, the wine drinkable, and the state paid for the prisoners in accordance with their social dignity, from three livres a day for the lowest, ten livres for judges, bankers, and writers, to 36 for marshals of France. Prisoners kept on account of a lettre de cachet were maintained at the cost of whoever was enforcing the imprisonment, and Sade was on a tariff of 800 livres a quarter, roughly on a par with the judges and bankers. He was also allowed 600 livres a year for personal expenditure. There were only 13 prisoners in the Bastille on 1 March 1784, with a staff of 15. The highest number of prisoners during the period 1782–89 was 27, some of them there for only a few days. Sade's wife was allowed a visit of three hours twice a month. However, on 2 July 1789 Sade created repeated disturbances by shouting from his window, using a metal tube as a loud-speaker, that atrocities were being committed in the prison. On 4 July he was taken to Charenton at 1 a.m. With his books, of which we have the list, he had to leave behind 15 exercise books of his own writings.

Charenton was an asylum as well as a prison, administered as a secure mental hospital by a religious order. On 9 July Sade signed the authorization for his wife to collect his papers and belongings from the Bastille, but she had not yet done so when it was overrun on 14 July. Half a dozen of its senior staff were massacred by the crowd, and Sade's old room was sacked. Nothing was salvaged. Anything he had written and not passed out of the prison has been lost. His wife succeeded in leaving Paris on 5 October. On 13 March 1790 lettres de cachet were abolished. Sade was given the news by his sons, who visited him at Charenton on 18 March, not having seen him for 15 years. Those guilty or accused of a criminal offence, or mad, were still liable to detention, and Mme de Montreuil considered appealing under one of those headings, without saying which, but decided against. Sade was released on 2 April 1790. He was given six louis by the steward of his affairs in Paris, with whom he stayed for four nights. His wife, who had now decided to separate from him, refused to see him and Sade himself, while desperately trying to sort out his affairs, seems to have been chiefly preoccupied with getting one of his plays put on, importuning the actor Molé, whom he had once known, to get him a decision about it.

The estate at La Coste had not yet been confiscated under the Revolution, but it could not be sold, so that Sade was in no position to repay his wife's dowry. The settlement was 4,000 livres a year, with whatever capital sum his estate fetched on his death. The debt was adjudicated at 160,842 livres. However, Sade could not in fact pay anything at all. He was entirely dependent on anything Gaufridy, his lawyer in Apt, sent him, and Gaufridy could not find enough money to get the sheep sheared. By the end of June Sade was again in trouble, mixed up with a cousin in a monarchist club in difficulties with its accounts, but he obtained for himself a card as an "active citizen" of the Revolution on 1 July 1790, attending the national celebration of the taking of the Bastille. On 3 August his play Le Suborneur was accepted by the Comédie-Italienne, and on 17 August his Le Boudoir; ou, Le Mari crédule was turned down by one vote at the Comédie-Française. Sade was, however, invited to present the play again after making changes. By 25 August he had formed a close liaison with Marie-Constance Quesnet, an actress deserted by her husband. He was to remain bound to her for the rest of his life. On 16 September the Comédie-Française accepted Le Misanthrope par amour; ou, Sophie et Desfrancs. It was never put on, but Sade became entitled to free seats for five years.

By 1 November he was installed with Marie-Constance and had hired a house-keeper, a cook and a lackey. He asked Gaufridy whether that was too much, and borrowed 15,000 livres from the farmer at La Coste. By 6 March 1791 Sade had had five plays accepted, of which only one would actually be performed. On the 2 May he wanted the Comédie-Française to read two or three more, and in June Justine; ou, Les Malheurs de la vertu was published. Politically Sade's position cannot easily be pinned down. He remained a monarchist, but rabidly hostile to the monarch's abuses of his privileges. We would say now that he backed a constitutional monarchy with a two-chamber parliament, but in 1791 that position could seem traitorous to almost everyone.

On 22 October 1791 Sade's play Le Comte d'Oxtiern; ou, Les Effets du libertinage was given a mixed reception in Paris. It was the adaptation of the short story Ernestine nouvelle suédoise, written in the Bastille, one of the Crimes de l'amour. On 5 March 1792 Le Suborneur failed because the audience, wearing red caps, refused to allow the performance of a play by an aristocrat. Sade's efforts to make money from the theatre were in all the circumstances futile. At La Coste revolutionary sentiment was strong. The château was sacked towards the end of September 1792, and the discovery not only of the decorations but of instruments of penance and torture fuelled the mob's anger with feelings of righteousness. Sade had in fact become secretary of the Piques section of the Paris government, was active in the reform of the hospitals, and even became a member of the national guard. In 1791 he had published a strongly republican Adresse d'un citoyen de Paris, au roi des Français.

His position was bewildering. His two sons were aristocrats and might rally to a counter-Revolution. His ex-wife and mother-in-law, against both of whom he felt grievances, were now at his mercy. His instincts were aristocratic, but his inclinations strongly iconoclastic. His interests demanded at least token adherence to the forces of the Revolution. But he was very poor, although he had estates. There seemed no way of living from his pen, or from the stage, and his mind was unstable. His actions and opinions naturally became unpredictable. His sons were listed as émigrés, and that compromised his own situation. La Coste was confiscated even though Sade himself was not an émigré. He could not afford the luxury of a consistent and thought-out position, even if he had in the circumstances been capable of formulating one. There was anyway no time to think.

To some extent, he was required to act as spokesman for sentiment within his section, shifting rapidly towards the radical step of executing the king. He was also horrified by the terrible cruelties of the Parisian mob. The September massacres of 1792 disgusted him. Few of Sade's literary texts come anywhere near dwelling on incidents as revolting as what actually happened at the Bicêtre or Salpêtrière, or to the Princesse de Lamballe's corpse during the massacres of 2, 3 and 4 September 1792. Sade was himself made a judge in April 1793. His presidency of the court sessions was characterized by a refusal as far as possible to have anything to do with delations, or cruelties undertaken in the name of justice. He was opposed to capital punishment and in fact saved the Montreuil family. He himself however became suspect of too much leniency, in spite of a speech praising the assassinated Marat and Le Pelletier, who had voted for the king's death.

On 8 December 1793 Sade was arrested and imprisoned successively in four Paris prisons, the Madelonnettes, the Carmelites, Saint-Lazare, and Picpus. He wrote to his section, which simply increased the pressures against him, until after Robespierre's fall, when again they would swim with the tide, supporting the moderation they had previously attacked, Sade wrote to the committee of public safety. He genuinely did not know on what pretext he was likely to be guillotined. Two émigré sons? Justine? Justine's publisher, Jacques Girouard, was guillotined on 8 January, perhaps on account of monarchism; the printing of Sade's Aline et Valcour was unfinished at his death. On 13 January Sade was moved to the maison des Carmes and shut up with people infected with fever. Two were to die during his eight-day stay. On 22 January he was moved to Saint-Lazare, re-opened four days earlier as a prison of the Revolution. The accusatory document of the section des Piques is entirely political. The accusation of Sade centres on his view that republican government was impractical. Sade himself denied all the accusations.

On 27 March 1794 Sade was transferred to Picpus. On 24 July his dossier was passed to the revolutionary tribunal. On 26 July Fouquier-Tinville signed a detention document with 28 names on it. The bailiff came to take the nominees to the tribunal, whose two sections were between them ordering, according to Sade, 50 executions a day, but could find only 23 of the 28 named prisoners. It seems certain that, in the administrative confusion, they had Sade's name on a list for one of the other prisons. Of the 23, one was acquitted, one had convulsions and was sent back to prison. The other 21 were guillotined. On 28 July 1794 Robespierre was himself guillotined, and the Terror was over. On 15 October Sade was released, his revolutionary orthodoxy certified by another set of colleagues from the section des Piques.

What confronted him was simple destitution. Gaufridy had been in hiding and disguise to escape death as a royalist counter-revolutionary. Sade's way of signing his name indifferently with any of his first names, and in any combination, had resulted in a confusion. His name was removed from the list of émigrés in the Bouches-du-Rhône, but not in the Vaucluse, so that none of his tenants there needed to pay rent. The winters of 1788–9 and 1794–1795 were the coldest of the century. Sade had no money for heating, and his ink froze. He managed to get access to the half-printed sheets of *Aline et Valcour* and the book was published anonymously in 1795 with Girouard's title-page. *La Philosophie dans le boudoir* came out the same year with a London imprint, purporting to be posthumous, but by the author of *Justine*. Sade was doing everything in his power to find money and employment, but pornographic literature did not much help. In the end it positively injured Sade. He was attacked for it by Rétif de la Bretonne, and then his much more innocuous work attracted attention again to *Justine*, whose authorship Sade was assiduous in disclaiming. A complete edition of the 1797 *Justine* with *L'Histoire de Juliette* was to be seized on 18 August 1800 when 14-year-old girls were found collating the sheets, including those with obscene engravings. By then, the Directoire was ushering in its new moral climate.

La Coste was eventually sold, but Sade was still being sued for debt in 1797. In order to evade his obligation to pay back his ex-wife's dowry if he sold La Coste, Sade bought two properties near Paris, at Malmaison and Granvilliers, but he did not have the money to complete the transactions, or for his own petty expenditure. In April 1797 Marie-Constance and Sade moved to a house at Saint-Ouen in northern Paris, and almost immediately went to Provence. Bailiffs were waiting for him at Mazan, but in June he was at Saumane. He was trying to sell Mas de Cabanes, too, but without success. He remained about five months in Provence, returning to Paris and even worse destitution. Marie-Constance had to stay with friends, while Sade stayed for a while with a tenant-farmer, and then took a garret at Versailles with Constance's son and a servant early in 1799. He earned a tiny pittance of 40 sols a day at the theatre. On 12 December he himself played Fabrice in his own *Oxtiern*.

On his return to Saint-Ouen, two bailiffs were waiting for him, sent by the proprietor of the restaurant at Versailles where he had eaten on credit. The police intervened and Sade was given time to pay. Meanwhile the sequestration order was lifted on Mas de Cabanes. That autumn *Les Crimes de l'amour* brought a little money. The worst seemed to be over when, on 6 March 1801, Sade called on his publisher, Nicolas Massé. The police knew they would find there both Sade and a manuscript in his writing. The tip-off may have come from Massé, somehow anxious to extricate himself from trouble. The Saint-Ouen house was also searched. Sade's study was adorned with illustrations of scenes from *Justine*. Nobody was ready to believe any longer that he was not the author, although he continued to deny it and to demand that the matter be brought to trial. He said that he was merely the copyist of *Juliette*. He was kept for 48 hours at the prefecture of police, then sent to Sainte-Pélagie.

Marie-Constance remained faithful to him and was allowed to see him every three days. In February or March 1803 Sade is said to have made indecent propositions to young men, in prison for a few days, who were on the same corridor as he was. In mid-March 1803 he was transferred to Bicêtre. For humanitarian reasons he was then transferred on 27 April to be kept in comparative comfort at his family's expense at Charenton. The director refused to treat the institution as if it were purely penal, and believed in rehabilitation, or at least therapy. The pension would be 3,000 livres a year and no requests would be made for Sade's release. He was obsessive but not mad. He still had fantasies of erotic violence. Marie-Constance would be allowed to live with him. Sade returned to the practice of religion and the frequentation of the sacraments. The police inspector was furious when he heard that Sade had been allowed to take the collection in the local parish church. He was allowed to write plays, to act, to produce stage performances, and to invite people to attend them. He began to write a rather dull historical fiction.

The end of his life was tranquil enough. He disliked police searches. He got on well with his eldest son, killed in an ambush on 9 June 1809, while serving as a lieutenant in Italy. His wife died in 1810 at Echauffour, where his daughter lived on, to die at 73 in 1844. At Charenton he was regularly visited by Madeleine Leclerc, daughter of a member of the administration, who was 12 when in 1808 she first attracted Sade's attention. Only the asylum diary first published in 1970 tells us the story of Sade's regular sexual relations with her. Marie-Constance had a bedroom of her own, so that Sade could receive Madeleine whenever he wanted. She evidently proved willing to comply with his tastes, for which she continued to cater when she was 17 and he was 74. Occasional visitors were often astounded to learn that this rather morose old man was the notorious Sade.

He was scarcely unwell the day before he died. His son had asked a doctor to spend the night in his room. Sade's breathing grew quieter, and only on going to look did the doctor discover that he had died. It was 2 December 1814. He had managed to provide for Marie-Constance, and left a will stipulating that he should be buried in an unmarked grave so that his memory would fade from the minds of society.

WORKS

The notoriety of the subject matter of Sade's fiction has led both to inflated claims for his literary importance, if sometimes only as an "influence" or a "precursor," and to an abrupt dismissiveness of his work on account of the social or moral unacceptability of the behaviour he practised, and whose implications his writings explored. In a famous test case in France which opened in December 1956 and went to appeal, it was decided in 1958 that the publication of four of Sade's works was an offence against public decency, although the legal fiction of limited editions subsequently allowed them effectively to be available to all who wanted to purchase them. The four texts were: *Les 120 Journées de Sodome; ou, L'Ecole du libertinage; La Nouvelle Justine; ou, Les Malheurs de la vertu; L'Histoire de Juliette; ou, Les Prospérités du vice*; and *La Philosophie dans le boudoir*. They are now available in paperback and in translation. The trial itself generated a relatively brief intensification of public interest in Sade, but literary interest remains sufficiently strong for it to have become scarcely possible to neglect claims made on Sade's behalf for inclusion into the French 18th-century literary canon, however tightly its boundaries are drawn.

Sade's literary reputation has also been influenced by the effect that his work is at various times alleged to have had, or to have been likely to have, on different categories of readers, so that criteria of literary importance have at times appeared to conflict with other considerations of public interest. It has also necessarily been affected by the extent to which the experiences explored in his works are thought to be fictionalizations, mythologizations, or merely exaggerated forms of quite common patterns of desire, behaviour, or fantasy. It is important for purely literary purposes to disregard the boundaries of what we may consider to be social, moral, and even medical normality, and to ask simply with what power Sade succeeds in illuminating the nature and meaning of common human experiences, including the way in which societies generate their moral norms, their margins of tolerance, and their categories of normality.

Sade, apparently overcome by overwhelming surges of physical or psychological energy, attempted at times in his life and at places in his works to dislocate certain, but never all, accepted moral values. He never, for instance, challenged the general laws of ownership, or even those concerning social rank. Yet the radical rejection of the social codes of his caste which led him partially to embrace the ideology of the Revolution, and the dislocation of values which included but were not exhausted by those concerning sexual morality, in his life as well as in his works, are plainly reflected in the way in which his cultivated and refined prose style and powers of relentlessly articulate psychological analysis are in tension with the physical and moral violence of his subject matter. He felt a psychological compulsion to reflect articulately and imaginatively about the need and possible justification for behaving as he did, and even about the connection between the way he felt and the way he behaved.

The biography makes clear that, while society may very well have needed protecting from Sade personally, and then later from the easy availability of at least some of what he wrote, his overpowering sexual drive did not make him systematically, deliberately, or more than casually cruel. He was capable of rages that took him into temporary mental imbalance, but the evidence suggests that, when not in the grip of frenzied sexual desire, he was generally moderate, and even considerate. It is apparent that his frenzies were not merely a diversion, his orgies not just amusements which got out of hand. They might easily have made him dangerously violent, but they did not. In literature his systematic pursuit of enlightenment clarity goes hand in hand with the deliberate avoidance of suspense. The probability is that he is a minor but important literary figure in the galaxy of authors from elegant and educated backgrounds whose writings, certainly built on an unusual personal experience, also examined

or somehow exemplified the explosive moral, social, and political tensions of a society on the brink of the upheaval which took place at its centre in 1789. His sexual practices, although not much was written about them for a wide mid-18th century public, were certainly not uncommon, and not even always discreet.

What he wrote that was not purely political, gothically grotesque, or historically macabre, falls into one of three categories, and it is not always easy in particular cases to know which. The first category is the cheap pornography published in the vain hope of making money at a point at which Sade was destitute. It may be thought that versions of *Justine* subsequent to the first, and *Juliette*, belong to this category. The second category contains the books which Sade did not intend anyone to read, not only the asylum diary but also *Les 120 Journées de Sodome*. The need to take into account the readership for which a text was intended in any effort to decode it is discussed in the introduction to this *Guide*. It is also important in the context of understanding certain texts of, for instance, Diderot or Stendhal. There are grounds for avoiding the literary discussion of entirely private material.

The third category into which Sade's texts can be grouped comprises the literary compositions. They show his articulate awareness of the psychological problems caused by his immense sexual drive, reflect a ferocious struggle to restrain an overpowering but wayward imagination which he assuaged only with violent practices and brutal fantasies and, at any rate at first, with blasphemy, and constitute an uncertain grappling with such major problems as those posed by the mechanisms inspiring different sorts of sexual behaviour, apparently brutal violence, and the gestation of norms of personal morality, social justice, and political organization.

We know that the first version of *Justine*, *Aline et Valcour*, and *Les 120 Journées de Sodome* were composed while Sade was imprisoned on the second floor of the Liberté tower of the Bastille, that is, between 1784 and 1788. The preliminary version of *Justine* was actually the conte philosophique "Les Infortunes de la vertu," destined for the *Contes et Fabliaux du XVIIIe siècle* and written between 23 June and 8 July 1787. Various virtuous actions are punished, as for that matter they had been in Voltaire's *Zadig*. Sade found his conte changing into a novel under his pen, and what is now known as *Justine; ou, Les Malheurs de la vertu* was finished by 1788. Sade later pretended that it was pornography written to a commission from Girouard, and he never admitted authorship. It was published anonymously in two volumes late in 1791, with a title page giving false details and a frontispiece allegorically representing Virtue between Luxury, in the sense of sexual indulgence, and Irreligion. There were six editions in ten years.

Justine, the narrator, orphaned and poor, is obliged at 14 to leave her convent, and struggles in Paris to preserve her virtue. She is wrongly accused of stealing by the money-lender Du Harpin and is committed to the Conciergerie, but at the age of 16 she escapes. She is raped in the forest of Bondy, but finds a good position employed in a nearby château. She has to leave after four years when she refuses to connive in the poisoning of the comte de Bressac's aunt, and he unleashes his mastiff at her. She is now 22 and is offered shelter by the surgeon Rodin, who brands her with a hot iron and sends her away when she refuses to help him dissect a living infant whose father he is. She goes to Sens, then Auxerre, which she leaves on 7 August 1783 on pilgrimage to the miracle-working shrine of the Virgin at Sainte-Marie-des-Bois, where she is held captive for six months by four monks. She immediately falls into the hands of the comte de Gernande, who submits her to blood-letting for a year. His wife dies of being bled.

Justine wanders down the Rhône from Lyons to Vienne, where she believes the promises of Roland, whom she helps, not suspecting that he heads a gang of counterfeiters. They treat her like an animal, and when they are all arrested and taken to Grenoble she only just escapes the scaffold. She is nearly beheaded by a bishop, and is accused of arson, theft, and murder, for which she is imprisoned at Lyons by a debauched judge. Condemned to death, she is taken to Paris to have the sentence confirmed when she meets her sister Juliette, who has married money. Justine is saved, and is on the brink of living happily ever after, when she is struck dead by lightning on 13 July 1788.

The name "Justine" is, of course, ironic. In structure the plot is a cross between *Zadig* and Laclos's *Les Liaisons dangereuses*, although the morals are quite different in each of the three. Sade adds too much gratuitous violence to leave his novel dependent on the macabre of English Gothic, and the characteristic reversal which turns virtue's reward at every step into punishment is still, in 1788, imaginatively associated in his mind with blasphemous desecration. There is no very profound statement about human nature. Justine is naturally innocent and naive, the world is a very wicked place, and if you escape its traps, there is always a thunderbolt from heaven to take care of that.

The reproach made by Rétif de la Bretonne in the 1798 *L'Anti-Justine; ou, Les Délices de l'Amour* centres on Sade's violence. Sade "ne présente les délices de l'amour, pour les hommes qu'accompagnés de tourments, de la mort même pour les femmes (only presents the delights of love accompanied by torments for men, and even death for women)," whereas Rétif wants "de faire un livre plus savoureux que les siens, et que les épouses pourront faire lire à leurs maris, pour en être mieux servis; un livre où les sens parleront au coeur; où le libertinage n'ait rien de cruel...; où l'amour ramené à la nature...ne présente que des images riantes et voluptueuses (to write a more appetizing book than his, which wives can get their husbands to read, to be served better by them; a book in which the senses will speak to the heart; in which libertinage has nothing cruel about it...; in which love, returned to nature, presents only a smiling and pleasure-loving face)." Rétif, in spite of his realism, is interested in the more conventional 18th-century refinement of a pleasure whose moral acceptability still needed to be emphasized.

Sade had his doubts, but when he himself argued in the dedication of *Justine* that his effort to show vice triumphant over virtue was a triumph of moral vision, it is difficult to take him as seriously as he appears to have been taking himself. There is always the chance of a touch of irony, or at any rate of conscious boasting. The dedication refers to virtue,

n'ayant pour opposer à tant de revers, à tant de fléaux, pour repousser tant de corruption, qu'une âme sensible, un esprit naturel et beaucoup de courage; hasarder en un mot les peintures le plus hardies, les situations les plus extraordinaires, les maximes les plus effrayantes, les coups de pinceau les plus énergiques, dans la seule vue d'obtenir de tout cela l'une des plus sublimes leçons de morale que l'homme

ait encore reçue; c'était, on en conviendra, parvenir au but par une route peu frayée jusqu'à présent

(having, in order to confront so many reversals, so many plagues, to repulse so much corruption, only a sensitive soul, a natural disposition, and great courage. To risk, in a word, the boldest depictions, the most extraordinary situations, the most frightening aphorisms, the most energetic brush strokes, simply to be able to obtain, from all that, one of the most sublime moral lessons which humanity has ever received. That, it must be agreed, is to reach the goal by a path little trodden up to now).

The disjointed way in which Sade justifies himself might reasonably be thought to indicate special pleading.

Sade also denied authorship of the 1797 version, *La Nouvelle Justine; ou, Les Malheurs de la vertu, suivie de l'histoire de Juliette, sa soeur*. The ten volumes, illustrated with 101 obscene engravings, were openly sold as pornography under the Directoire for perhaps a year before the first seizure, but the perquisitions continued, and it was probably in exchange for allowing the authorship to be pinned to Sade that Massé escaped serious trouble. Sade was arrested in Massé's offices only on 6 March 1801. In the new version Justine is no longer the narrator. The language is cruder and the psychology more meretricious. The imaginative ingenuity behind *Juliette* makes the pornographic aim even clearer. Sade is now obviously conscious as he writes of the type of impact he wants his work to make, so that, while few readers not overcome with disgust will avoid the potent feelings of revolted fascination which Sade aims at exciting, there is a strong undercurrent of macabre humour as the reader shares the author's sense of the preposterousness of what he is relating.

Juliette is a first-person narrative and deals with the sort of fantasies that people wishing to stay sane would normally never allow themselves to have. Sade forces the fantasies through the protective mechanisms of his readers, but then reduces them to merely titillating dimensions by protecting his reader with a sense of complicity in what is clearly not a credible illusion but a consciously shared fantasy. Girls are roasted on spits. The need to defile the sacred and the pure is everywhere apparent. Murder is trivial. Incest is harped on until the reader wonders distractedly if any possible incestuous combination has been overlooked. Torture is administered slowly and gruesomely. Two thirds of France is to be starved to death. A machine is invented for the decapitation or knifing of 16 people at a time. The pope celebrates black masses in Saint Peter's. The action moves all over Europe, and does not lack colour. The king of Naples has a theatre in which each spectator can pull a rope choosing a beautiful victim, male or female, and then has the choice of personally undertaking the torture or of leaving it to one of four handsome naked executioners. The king's confessor and director of orgies likes to perform his sexual acts dressed in a tiger skin and with the insane, who imagine themselves to be either Jesus or his mother.

Juliette ends with a long speech outlining what has actually been called Sade's philosophy. It makes it perfectly clear why the French authorities allowed the 74-year-old to end his days peacefully shut away, with the woman he had been living with for 25 years and a young mistress to console him, when the police authority thought it had really become too dangerous for the other inmates at Charenton to be allowed to take part in his amateur theatricals.

> Je l'avoue, j'aime le crime avec fureur; lui seul irrite mes sens, et je professerai ses maximes jusqu'au dernier moment de ma vie. Exempte de toutes craintes religieuses, sachant me mettre au-dessus des lois, par ma discrétion et par mes richesses, quelle puissance, divine ou humaine, pourrait donc contraindre mes désirs?… La nature n'a créé les hommes que pour qu'ils s'amusent de tout sur la terre; c'est sa plus chère loi, ce sera toujours celle de mon coeur. Tant pis pour les victimes, il en faut; tout se détruirait dans l'univers, sans les lois profondes de l'équilibre. Ce n'est que par les forfaits que la nature se maintient et reconquit les droits que lui enlève la vertu. Nous lui obéissons donc en nous livrant au mal; notre résistance est le seul crime qu'elle ne doive jamais nous pardonner. Oh! mes amis, convainquons-nous de ces principes; dans leur exercice se trouvent toutes les sources du bonheur de l'homme

> (I admit it, I love crime with passion; it alone stimulates my senses and I shall profess its maxims until the last moment of my life. Free from all religious fears, knowing how by using my discretion and my wealth to put myself above all laws, what power is there, divine or human, to constrain my desires?… Nature created humanity for people to enjoy everything on earth; that is its dearest law and it will always be the one next to my heart. So much the worse for the victims. They're necessary. The whole world system would destroy itself without the deep laws of equilibrium. It is only by crimes that nature maintains itself and regains the rights taken from it by virtue. We are therefore obeying it in giving ourselves over to evil. Our resistance is the only crime it should never forgive us. Oh! my friends, let us convince ourselves of these principles. It is in their exercise that all the sources of human happiness are to be found).

This is not the serious philosophy of a Nietszche, and certainly not the dangerous philosophy of a Rosenberg. What is really important is Sade's reflection on his own experience, warning of the tendency in everyone which if unrestrained would, in the words put into the mouth of Juliette, result in the absurdity of sacrificing everyone and everything to our personal pleasure, and in the lunatic nightmares which Sade allowed into his own fantasy. He used a literary discipline to tame them, in his effort to retain some grip on his mental balance, but also hoped he might sell them to keep starvation at bay. Sade never seriously proposed Juliette's philosophy. He wrote occasional essays in self-justification, mostly letters, on a fairly tentative register and not intended for publication. Some commentators have failed to identify either the potential readership or the literary register of whatever text they were dealing with, and therefore simply labelled the result as the product of evil, of genius, or of profundity. In fact there are always grounds for supposing that Sade was simply and with lifted eyebrow pointing to the logical consequences of a world erected on the laws of fantasy. There does not even seem to have been a period in his life when he would have been willing conceptually to commit himself to a position we would regard as philosophically atheistic, much as he may have wished to live in a world in which God's existence could for practical purposes have been ignored.

Les 120 Journées de Sodome; ou, L'école du libertinage cannot have been intended for publication, at least in its present form, or it would have been smuggled out of the Bastille or subsequently reconstituted. Sade had published nothing at the time of writing it, knew his text was dangerous, and before he had finished it he made a copy in minuscule handwriting on a 12-metre roll of paper which he hid in the wall of the room he occupied at the Bastille. The manuscript took 37 evenings to copy, was dated on completion 27 November 1785, and was not included in the *Catalogue raisonné* of Sade's writings which he made in the Bastille on 1 October 1788. It must have been written in an attempt to dominate his fantasies by taming them into some form of literary order. The other notable omission from the *Catalogue* was the *Dialogue entre le prêtre et un moribond* written at Vincennes in 1782, which exists in a clean manuscript copy in Sade's hand and must have been smuggled out of prison. The *120 Journées* concerns four psychopaths of immense wealth who lock themselves up in a Black Forest castle with their wives, and 38 other people to serve their terrible pleasures. The text recounts 600 perverted sexual acts in four sets of 150. There are 30 horrifyingly painful deaths, and a tightly structured framework in which the fiction of story-telling is borrowed partly from Boccaccio and partly from Marguerite d'Angoulême.

Aline et Valcour; ou, Le Roman philosophique, published in 1795, was still in draft form at the date of the *Catalogue raisonné*. It is an epistolary novel with an immensely complex plot, involving a double substitution of infants and a voyage round the world. The serious interest of the novel lies in its account of a subversive socialist utopia on the island of Tamoé, declared to be a model for European governments, in which personal and social happiness are both attainable.

In his moment of tightest control Sade could write delightful *contes*, in finely balanced periods, sometimes in the first person, often heavily dependent on dialogue, sometimes scarcely more than nudgingly naughty, and sometimes even maintaining a certain elegance of tone which allows the text to be obscene without being vulgar. Sometimes the narrator converses familiarly with the reader about the characters. The tone of light-hearted banter shows how therapeutically effective his literary activity must have proved for him, what sort of little masterpiece of irony it was capable of producing, and how dangerous it is to evaluate Sade's literary interest solely on the basis of his wilder imaginative excesses. Sometimes the realism, irony, dialogue, and pace announce Maupassant. The best Sade is to be found in pieces like this, halfway between a 17th-century portrait and a Maupassant *conte*, almost waiting for Daumier:

> Peu de gens se figurent un président au parlement d'Aix: c'est une espèce de bête dont on a parlé souvent sans la bien connaître, rigoriste par état, minutieux, crédule, entêté, vain, poltron, bavard et stupide par caractère; tendu comme un oison dans sa contenance, grasseyant comme Polichinelle, communément efflanqué, long, mince et puant comme un cadavre…On dirait que toute la bile et la roideur de la magistrature du royaume aient choisi leur asile dans le temple de la Thémis provençale pour se répandre de là au besoin, chaque fois qu'une cour française a des remonstrances à faire ou des citoyens à pendre

> (Few people know what a judge at the Aix parlement is

like: it's a sort of animal people have talked about often enough, but without really knowing it, rigorist by profession, finicky, credulous, obstinate, vain, cowardly, gossipy and stupid by character, with drawn features like a gosling's, speaking in gutturals like Punchinello, usually emaciated, tall, thin, and stinking like a corpse…You'd think all the bile and rigidity of all the country's lawyers had found sanctuary in the temple of the Provençal goddess of Justice, to issue forth from there, as required, whenever a French court had admonitions to make or citizens to hang).

PUBLICATIONS

[The principal works have been translated in *The Complete Justine, Philosophy in the Bedroom, and other Writings*, 1965, and in *The 120 Days of Sodom and other Writings*, 1966]

Collections

Oeuvres complètes du Marquis de Sade, 8 vols., 1966–68
Oeuvres complètes du Marquis de Sade, 1986–88
Oeuvres, Bibliothèque de la Pléiade, 1991–

Non-political works: early editions

Justine; ou, Les Malheurs de la vertu, 2 vols., 1791
Aline et Valcour; ou, Le Roman philosophique, 4 vols., 1795 [dated 1793]
La Philosophie dans le boudoir, 2 vols., 1795
La Nouvelle Justine; ou, Les Malheurs de la vertu, 4 vols., 1795
La Nouvelle Justine; ou, Les Malheurs de la vertu. Suivie de l'Histoire de Juliette, sa soeur, 10 vols., 1797
Oxtiern; ou, Les Malheurs du libertinage, (produced 1791), year VIII [1800]
Les Crimes de l'amour, Nouvelles héroïques et tragiques, 4 vols., year VIII [1800]
L'Auteur de "Crimes de l'amour" à Villeterque, folliculaire, year IX [1801]
La Marquise de Gange, 2 vols., 1813

Political writings

Adresse d'un citoyen de Paris, au roi des Français [1791]
Ten brochures were published over Sade's name on behalf of the Section des Piques, Paris, 1791–93

Later first editions

Dorci; ou, La Bizarrerie du sort, 1881
Les 120 Journées de Sodome; ou, L'Ecole du libertinage, 1904; 3 vols., 1931–35 [now considered the first correct édition]
Historiettes. Contes et Fabliaux, 1926
Dialogue entre un prêtre et un moribond, 1926
Correspondance inédite, 1929
Les Infortunes de la vertu, 1930
L'Aigle, Mademoiselle…, Lettres, 1949
Histoire secrète d'Isabelle de Bavière, reine de France, 1953
Le Carillon de Vincennes, 1953
Cahiers personnels, 1953
Monsieur le 6. Lettres inédites (178–84), 1954

Adélaïde de Brunswick, princesse de Saxe, 1964
Voyage d'Italie. Premières oeuvres, 1967
Le Théâtre de Sade, 4 vols., 1970
Journal inédit, 1970
Lettres et Mélanges, 3 vols., 1980

Biographical and critical studies

Gorer, Geoffrey, *The Life and Ideas of the Marquis de Sade*, 1934
Klossowski, Pierre, *Sade, mon prochain*, 1947
Blanchot, Maurice, *Lautréamont et Sade*, 1949
Heine, Maurice, *Le Marquis de Sade*, 1950
Lely, Gilbert, *Vie du marquis de Sade*, 2 vols., 1952–57; abridged version 1965, augmented 1982
The Marquis de Sade, edited by Dinnage, 1962
Barthes, Roland, *Sade, Fourier, Loyola*, 1971
Carter, Angela, *The Sadean Woman*, 1979
Pauvert, Jean-Jacques, *Sade vivant*, 1986–9
Laborde, Alice M., *Le Mariage du Marquis de Sade*, 1988
Lever, Maurice, *Donatien Alphonse François, marquis de Sade*, 1991
Thomas, Donald, *The Marquis de Sade*, 1992

SAINT-CYRAN, Jean DUVERGIER DE HAURANNE, abbé de, 1581–1643.

Spiritual director, polemicist, author of works of spirituality, letters, and theological controversy.

LIFE

Saint-Cyran, born Jean-Ambroise Duvergier, was among the younger of the at least 13 children of his father, who had married twice and was a well-to-do merchant of Bayonne. The elder Duvergier was an échevin in 1574 when only 32, and leaned strongly to the religiously uncommitted moderate position in politics. The family, like the other with which its members intermarried, was prominent in the south-west, and it was probably on account of family strategy that Duvergier was destined for the church and as early as 1591 received the tonsure. One of his nephews would be Martin Barcos. Duvergier became prebend of Bernet on 5 February 1596, and he was given a dispensation to be ordained sub-deacon on 23 January 1598, the canonical age in Bayonne being 18.

On the death of his father in 1596, Duvergier was taken into the protection of the bishop, Bertrand d'Eschaux, who was closely linked to Henri IV. He studied at the Jesuit college of Agen, and then in Paris from 1598–1600. After the expulsion of the Jesuits from France, which had taken place later in Agen than elsewhere, Duvergier followed them to their university at Louvain, where the regulations favoured speedier qualifications at lower age limits. The prefect of studies was Leonard Lessius, whose views on grace were at the centre of the Jansenist (q.v.) dispute, and the professor of scripture was the celebrated Cornelius a Lapide. Justus Lipsius was in the audience on 26 April 1604 when Saint-Cyran defended his doctoral theses.

Theologically, Saint-Cyran's training was not humanistic, based on a study of the Fathers and the Scriptures, but based on scholastic reasoning concerned at this date chiefly with the disputes about nature, grace, and free will at whose centre Lessius had become the most controversial figure. Duvergier returned to Paris and studied further scholastic theology under Nicolas Isambert before returning to Bayonne at the end of 1606, where the bishop had him made a canon, a post which allowed him to return to Paris to study further. At Paris he was not allowed to defend his theses covering the whole of scholastic theology as he had done at Louvain, but it was there that he got to know the more patristically inclined theologian Cornelius Jansen. From about 1610 Duvergier and Jansen lived and studied together in Paris and then at Camp-de-Prats near Bayonne. From December 1612 to June 1614 Jansen was principal of the college at Bayonne. Duvergier spent part of 1613 in Poitiers, but he continued to share a base with Jansen until Jansen returned to the Low Countries in 1614, after which their famous correspondence began. There is no evidence at this date that they shared theological preoccupations. Jansen was more deeply immersed in the Fathers, despising the scholastic theology which was the field of Duvergier's expertise. It must, however, have been during these years that Duvergier developed his knowledge of the history of the early Church.

His preoccupations were in fact partly determined by accusations of witchcraft alleged against his mother, his sister, and many others of his relatives in one of the not infrequent outbreaks of corporate hysteria of which an example is offered by the well-known events at Loudun, centring on the supposed diabolic possession of a group of Ursuline nuns, and the burning alive of Urbain Grandier by the magistrate Laubardemont, who was to be charged with the interrogation of Saint-Cyran and the imposition of the signature at Port-Royal. In 1609 Henri IV sent a commissioner to Bayonne with power to inflict the death penalty, and Eschaux, who had been away, managed to put a stop to his activities only after 600 burnings, including those of three priests. Duvergier plainly believed in the reality of some at least of the accusations up and down France, for instance that Antichrist had appeared. A priest, Louis Gaufridy, burnt alive at Aix on 30 April 1611, who appears to have been guilty of not much worse than seduction, was known, after all, to have admitted being Satan's precursor and the prince of magic. After the affair of Marthe Brossier's possession, which inspired Bérulle to write his *Traité des énergumènes* on diabolic possession in 1599, a Franciscan was burnt for witchcraft at Grenoble in 1608, a Norman priest in Paris in 1609, two Breton priests at Rennes in the same year, and a money-lender and his son at Vesoul in 1610. The theology of diabolic possession moved swiftly into the centre of theological discussion and, for a brief period, of Duvergier's concerns. His fundamental interest lay, however, elsewhere and, without abandoning the scholastics, he was continuing to study the early history of the Church.

Duvergier appears to have spent most of the period from 1608 to 1612 in Paris, probably introduced by his bishop as a learned cleric, not yet ordained, at a court where Henri IV once said that his Connétable, Montmorency, could not write, and that his

chancellor, Sillery, knew no Latin. Duvergier was taken up into the small circle of the comte de Cramail, grandson of Blaise Monluc, the maréchal, who had gathered round him at Toulouse a small group of educated friends, including François Mainard, and did the same at Paris, where the group is mentioned by Marolles in his *Mémoires*, published in 1656–57. Régnier had dedicated his second satire to him as early as 1603, and it was Cramail who passed on to Duvergier the king's conundrum which resulted in Duvergier's first work, the 1609 *Question royale*.

Could or should a subject sacrifice his own life if his suicide was the only way to save the life of the king? Duvergier's answer to both questions, given the right circumstances, was yes. It was the sort of playful, rather childish intellectual activity that amused Henri IV, still rebuilding his court after the religious wars, and for whom the constant menace of assassination was in the end to prove only too real. The piece allowed Duvergier to demonstrate his tact as a courtier as well as his skill in scholastic debate. On the assassination of the king in 1610 Duvergier wrote the Latin verses *Henrici magni infandum funus*, published in the 1611 *Recueil* of memorial tributes collected by the royal chaplain, G. du Peyrat. He appeared at that date, not yet ordained priest, to be on the way to becoming a court prelate, destined probably to serve some time as a chaplain while waiting for a suitable bishopric. There appears around 1610 to have been a brief and mysterious visit to England, which may have been on a political errand.

From about 1613 Duvergier was closely associated with Henri-Louis de la Rocheposay, coadjutor of Poitiers from 1608, appointed to the see in 1611 and consecrated the following year. The bishop was the son of a humanist soldier who had known Montaigne and the Pléiade, and protected J.-C. Scaliger, but who had been given the education of a nobleman and future soldier. His mother and sister were Protestants and he had remained on good terms with Scaliger, who had gone over to the reform in 1562. La Rocheposay was nevertheless a strongly counter-reformatory bishop, introducing five new religious congregations into his diocese, and reforming religious houses, as well as keeping in contact with a circle of humanists, including Balzac and the Sainte-Marthe family. When, as early as 1614, in spite of his treaty with Marie de Medici of 8 June, Condé, in alliance with the Huguenots, made an effort to seize Poitiers, it was La Rocheposay who prevented him, and whose defence of the town led to the reconciliation of Condé and Marie de Medici at Orléans on 5 July.

His combination of the roles of warrior and bishop, together with the audacity of his pacificatory gestures towards the Huguenots, made his figure controversial throughout France. Duvergier rallied to his defence with the anonymous 1615 *Apologie pour Messire H.L. Chastaigner de La Roche-Pozay, évesque de Poictiers, contre ceux qui disent qu'il n'est pas permis aux ecclésiastiques d'avoir recours aux armes en cas de nécessité*. He was particularly careful to be complimentary to Condé, to humour whom the regent was temporarily prepared to go to almost any lengths, and he argued the need for the Church to adapt its moral code to changing times. There are few laxities of which Pascal would later accuse the casuists which Duvergier did not here defend, whether they concerned the direction of intention, duels, usury, or simony.

It is of great importance for the religious and cultural history of France to note that Saint-Cyran's later rigorism was not the result of Jansen's reflections on the theology of grace. It started with his own realization that it was necessary to choose between the view that there was a strict and immutable moral law revealed in scripture and accepted by the early Church, and the view which in his defence of La Rochepposay he himself had accepted, that moral principles and prescriptions were contingent on times, places, and cultures. In 1615 Saint-Cyran stayed for six months with La Rochepposay, who provided him with a canonry at Poitiers and later a priory at Vouneuil, in return for which Duvergier daily discussed a point of theology with him. Duvergier later claimed that the social life to which he was constrained irked him. He lost his canonry at Poitiers, and his position appears not to have been welcome to the diocese's clergy. Duvergier certainly did his best to absent himself from Poitiers until he moved there sometime in the early months of 1617 for what turned out to be four years. At the end of that year his mother died, leaving difficulties about ownership of the house at Camp-de-Prats, to be ceded by Saint-Cyran to a brother in May 1622.

It may have been in order to enter into his priory on 26 October 1618 that Duvergier finally had himself ordained priest that June, celebrating his first Mass on 15 August. In view of the later stance taken against frequent communion by Arnauld and the Jansenist faction, it is an important fact that we have at least two testimonies from the 1620s to Saint-Cyran's desire to celebrate Mass with the greatest possible frequency. Accounts of a conversion before or around 1620 must be discounted. There is no reason to doubt a steady but quite normal deepening of his religious commitment, accompanied by the development of an uncertain but idiosyncratically aggressive spirituality which may have found some intellectual justification in Bérulle's development of the spirituality of Charles du Bois de Condren, in many ways Bérulle's own disciple, whom Duvergier got to know early in 1620. None the less, Duvergier plainly started to take more seriously the obligations of his state, both with regard to the pluralism of benefices and to the obstacles placed in the way of religious progress by an excess of material possessions. He never lived otherwise than comfortably.

In 1620 the quarrel in France began between the diocesan clergy and the religious orders, monastic and mendicant, exempt from episcopal jurisdiction and answerable only through their own internal superiors to the Pope. Bérulle, whose mystical theology centred on the state of priesthood and not at all on the vows of poverty, chastity, and obedience, on which the spirituality of the religious orders had been erected, was not himself in principle hostile to the religious orders. However, in 1611 he had himself founded the French Congregation of the Oratory, grouping together spiritually committed diocesan priests on the model of the congregations founded in Italy by Philip Neri, and found himself locked in a bitter dispute with the Carmelites and the Jesuits, when both strongly opposed his actually neoplatonist although in intention Christocentric mysticism. The bulls for the Congregation of the Oratory were dated 1613, the year before Bérulle was appointed Visitor of the Carmelites, who were to object vigorously to his attempt to impose on them his spirituality, with its central notion of "servitude."

The quarrel about the exemption of the religious orders from episcopal jurisdiction, which had raged since before the reformation in France, now hinged on the obligation, confirmed at Bordeaux in 1582, for the laity to attend Mass at least one Sunday in three in the parish church, rather than in one belonging to a religious order. In Poitiers everyone went to the Jesuit church, and La Rochepposay issued an instruction that the 1582 decree should be obeyed, only for the Jesuits to attack his authority. There was a considerable struggle, and the central authority intervened. Neither side won, but Duvergier seems to have been recompensed or rewarded by La Rochepposay with the abbey of Saint-Cyran-en-Brenne, with an income of 1,800 livres, and Saint-Cyran, as he now became, ceded his Bayonne canonry to one of his nephews. He does not seem to have parted with his benefactor on terms of any cordiality.

Saint-Cyran stayed on in Poitiers until the middle of 1621. Bérulle had come in the wake of the visit to the town by the king and his entourage, and Condren presented Saint-Cyran to him. Both La Rochepposay and Saint-Cyran signed the approbation to Bérulle's *Voeux de servitude* to the Virgin and to Jesus in 1620, although Lessius was to condemn the book in 1621, after which Jansen also signed an approbation. The rift between the Jesuits and those later known as Jansenists, and to whom it begs altogether too many questions to refer to as "Augustinian," was already coming into the open. Late in 1621 Saint-Cyran, having visited Louvain and resumed his discussions with Jansen about the renewal of the Church, was back in Paris, where Robert Arnauld d'Andilly, whom Saint-Cyran had met in Poitiers and to whom in Paris he was to become very close, promoted his interests strongly enough for him to have been made an honorary chaplain to Marie de Medici on 1 January 1622, a normal step towards a bishopric.

Saint-Cyran retained the same Paris address until 1628, turned down opportunities to become superior of the Daughters of Calvary, governor of Henri de Guise, future archbishop of Reims, and in 1624 first chaplain to the queen of England. For nearly a year in 1622 Saint-Cyran spent an hour a day from 6 to 7 p.m. with Bérulle discussing the basis of Bérulle's spirituality, derived from the neoplatonist *Celestial Hierarchies* of the sixth-century Pseudo-Denis, still confused with Saint Paul's first convert at Athens. Bérulle's theology was based on the *Hierarchies*, transposed into a mystical doctrine with the help of the works of the great Rhineland mystics of the late middle ages, notably Eckhart, Tauler, Suso, and Harphius, but given Condren's interpretation, calling for the "annihilation" of all that was purely human in order to procure the soul's mystical divinization, which resulted in a spirituality deeply distrustful of human nature. It was this neoplatonism, transmitted through Bérulle's Oratorian chaplain Gibieuf, which was used by Jansen for much of the underlying faculty psychology in the 1640 *Augustinus*, the great posthumous Latin folio containing the formal theology of Jansenism, although Jansen repudiated Gibieuf's terminology.

Saint-Cyran spent the period from August 1623 to June 1624 at Aire, where Sébastien Bouthillier, a friend from his student days, had just been made bishop. Bouthillier had been to Rome in 1620 in connection with obtaining Richelieu's elevation to the sacred college, and had the previous year again become very close to Saint-Cyran. He chose Saint-Cyran as his spiritual director and appears to have allowed himself to be virtually bullied by him when Saint-Cyran threatened to break off relationships if he went ahead with the proposed dismissal of a chaplain.

During 1623 Saint-Cyran had received from Jansen a score of copies of the Louvain 1555 edition of Augustine's anti-Pelagian works. Bérulle, with a privilège of 28 March 1622, had in February 1623 published his *Discours de l'état et des grandeurs de*

Jésus, dedicated to the king and with an imposing series of approbations, including those by Richelieu, d'Eschaux, now archbishop of Tours, La Rocheposay, Jean-Pierre Camus, Bouthillier, Jansen, Isambert, Richard Smith, whom Bérulle was in 1625 to have named Vicar apostolic of England, and Frère Joseph, the original "grey eminence." The Jesuit François Garasse, whose 1623 *Doctrine curieuse des beaux esprits du temps*, no doubt primarily designed to achieve the condemnation of Théophile, had strongly attacked the libertins, now produced the 1625 *Somme théologique des vérités capitales de la religion chrétienne*, largely attacking Charron. Garasse miscalculated by adopting a mockingly abusive, self-confident, and ironical tone, already out of date.

Because it had been rumoured that Bérulle was also to be attacked, but more fundamentally because he was looking for an opportunity to deal a knock-out blow against what he regarded as the humanism of Jesuit spirituality, Saint-Cyran had prepared himself to write his anonymous four-volume *Somme des fautes et faussetez capitales contenues en la Somme théologique du Père François Garassus* in refutation. Balzac admired the rhetoric of the long dedication to Richelieu. Saint-Cyran succeeded in getting Garasse's work condemned by the Sorbonne in September 1626, but his own third volume was suppressed, and only a synopsis of the fourth could be published. Saint-Cyran was incongruously involved in defending Charron, whose *De la sagesse* at this date passed for a work subversive of religious belief, "the libertins' breviary," as Garasse called it. Bérulle came increasingly to rely on Saint-Cyran, giving him a free hand for the correction of his *Vie de Jésus*. Had Bérulle not died on 1 October 1629, it is probable that he would have obtained a bishopric for Saint-Cyran. In 1625 Bouthillier died, and Saint-Cyran paid his first visits to Port-Royal-des-Champs. As well as helping Bérulle with his literary activities, Saint-Cyran was looking after the organization of the Oratory in the Low Countries.

Angélique Arnauld, born in 1591, had introduced her reform to the monastery of Port-Royal, of which she was abbess, in 1608. She had been the penitent of François de Sales but, after his death, had taken as her director the bishop of Langres, Sébastien Zamet, a friend of the Oratory whose spiritual director was Condren but who was chiefly concerned with founding a congregation dedicated to the worship of the Blessed Sacrament. He persuaded both Angélique Arnauld and Condren to agree, and succeeded in transferring Port-Royal from the jurisdiction of Cîteaux effectively to his own, ousting both Gondi of Paris and Bellegarde of Sens, who were supposed to share with him responsibility for Port-Royal. The spiritual elite were drawn to the Carmelites, whom Zamet had not admitted to his diocese, and his own new foundation was slanted to attract the well-born, those related to members of the court, "filles… polies, civiles, et d'une dévotion agréable (girls… courteous, well-mannered, and of an easy-going devoutness)," with explicit emphasis on clean ecclesiastical linen—whose laundering imposed a burden on the sacristans which was remarked on—flowers, incense, and sacred music. Corporal austerities were allowed but not imposed. The protectress was Mme de Longueville, although she did not put up any money.

Zamet's chosen superior hoped to bring with her 18,000 livres destined for her own convent, but Bérulle stopped it, deposed the sub-prior concerned, and had her kept in solitary confinement for ten months, after which she died. The new convent was, however, consecrated on 8 May 1633, and it did attract its fash-ionable clientele. Bellegarde, however, whose authority Zamet had usurped and who was a friend of the Carmelites, appears to have been jealous of Zamet's success and to have denounced Mère Agnès Arnauld's *Chapelet secret du Saint-Sacrement*, a series of accounts of religious feelings experienced in the presence of the Eucharist actually translated from the Latin six years earlier at Port-Royal. The text was kept relatively private, whence its name, but was exalted in spirit and heavily dependent on the suspect sacrificial language of Condren, extravagantly concerned with the experience of mystical self-emptying, and not at all focused on faith, hope, and charity. The *Chapelet* was therefore mildly condemned on 18 June 1633 by the superior of the Carmelites and seven of his associates, largely because its spirit clashed with that of the greatest of the Carmelite mystics and reformers, Teresa of Avila, and perhaps because it contained echoes of the two vows of servitude, to the Virgin and to Jesus, which Bérulle had tried to their fury to impose on the Carmelites.

Zamet, faced with catastrophe, turned to Saint-Cyran, who had just begun to publish his pseudonymous pamphlets under the name of Petrus Aurelius, attacking the Jesuits on political, religious, social, and theological grounds on account of another dispute over jurisdictional authority, this time in England where they were disputing the authority of the Vicar apostolic, Richard Smith. Ultimately at stake was Bérulle's spirituality, depending on the Pseudo-Denis's "celestial hierarchies" and exalting the ecclesiastical hierarchy by elevating the dignity of the priesthood, in distinction to that of those bound by religious vows who, even in male orders, were by no means all priests.

It seems as if Saint-Cyran, who might have been expected to share Bérulle's unfavourable view of Zamet, was genuinely won over by the abstract mystical exaltation of the *Chapelet*. Jansen was enlisted to take his side; Saint-Cyran wrote an *Apologie* in the autumn of 1633 which he kept unpublished but circulated in manuscript; there was a long and inconclusive controversy, involving ecclesiastical politics and the Roman curia; silence was imposed on both sides in the dispute involving the *Chapelet*; the controversy blended into that involving Richard Smith and episcopal jurisdiction in England, in which the line-up was Bérulle, the Sorbonne, and Saint-Cyran against the Jesuits; but Zamet's congregation was kept in being, and its members regarded Saint-Cyran as its saviour.

The final salvoes in the controversy had been an *Examen* of Saint-Cyran's *Apologie*, containing the only published version of that manuscript, from Bellegarde's side, to which Saint-Cyran replied in 1634 with an anonymously published *Réfutation de l'Examen*, to which the riposte was a *Discussion sommaire du…Chapelet secret*. It had so little effect that Saint-Cyran did not publish his final reply. Both the *Apologie* and the *Réfutation* had, however, strongly attacked the Jesuits, especially Etienne Binet, who had anonymously published a series of *Remarques* on Bellegarde's behalf, bringing what was to become the Jansenist-Jesuit dispute further into the open. It is important for the whole history of French culture to see that it existed as a difference of styles and religious perceptions, in some ways foreshadowing the Querelle des anciens et des modernes (q.v.) before ever it found its doctrinal focus. But in the dispute about the *Chapelet secret*, Saint-Cyran edges perceptibly nearer a definition of what came to be identified as the underlying issue, the free availability or the non-availability of the necessary justifying grace which might allow members of the fallen human race, all of whom inherited original sin, some choice under their own control which would allow them to escape hell, conceived as torture after death for unending time. Saint-Cyran's defence of Mère Agnès contains the surprising view that Christ's sacrifice had for its primary purpose not the salvation of human beings but the glory of God. Even Bossuet would still hold that Christ died to propitiate the justifiable wrath of the Father.

Saint-Cyran's prominence in ecclesiastical life had by now clearly emerged. Those who cared about such matters were not intended to be deceived by the precautionary anonymity or pseudonymity of the Latin controversial works. The two volumes of Petrus Aurelius pamphlets defending episcopal hierarchy published in 1632 were disseminated by the dean of the Paris theology faculty; a collecting box was available at the Sorbonne to help defray the costs of printing; the assembly of the clergy contributed 500 livres. Saint-Cyran's dependence on Bérulle's spirituality, from which he developed his defence of ecclesiastical hierarchy and ultimately of episcopal jurisdiction even over the exempt religious orders, sharply distanced incipient waves of Protestant sympathy, as the reaction, for instance, of Grotius showed.

Saint-Cyran was not, any more than Bérulle had been, totally hostile to the religious orders. He was himself titular abbot of a Benedictine monastery and was consulted about the reform of Maubuisson, of reformed Cistercian obedience, which was itself reformed by Angélique Arnauld. His connection with Port-Royal was first established through Arnauld d'Andilly when the community was in the Chevreuse valley, at what was to become Port-Royal-des-Champs. On 29 May 1625 Mère Angélique and 15 nuns, as many as would fit, moved into a house in the Faubourg-Saint-Jacques owned by the mother of Arnauld d'Andilly, Catherine Marion, who had borne her husband, the second Antoine Arnauld, 22 children, of whom 10 survived infancy, including Robert Arnauld d'Andilly, the oldest son to survive; Antoine "le grand" Arnauld, the youngest son to survive; Catherine, who married Isaac le Maître; the future Mère Angélique; and the future Mère Agnès; the sisters being born in that order between the two brothers mentioned. Through d'Andilly, Saint-Cyran had got to know the mother, widowed in 1619, and it was he who persuaded her to take the habit at Port-Royal herself on 4 February 1629. She chose Saint-Cyran for her confessor. He came frequently to the faubourg house, went almost never to the Chevreuse valley, and at this time scarcely knew Mère Angélique at all.

When Zamet had to go to Langres after opening his modish new Institut du Saint-Sacrement in the rue Coquillière, situated fashionably near the Louvre, he left Saint-Cyran in charge of the 10 nuns, of whom the superior was Mère Angélique, one of four Port-Royal nuns transferred physically from the faubourg Saint-Jacques house and ecclesiastically from the Cîteaux obedience. Saint-Cyran was now daily in touch with her, and preached at the convent on Sundays and feast days from early in 1634. Zamet wanted him to become the institute's spiritual director, as did Mère Angélique, but with one exception the other members of the community feared his severity and thought he might divert them from Zamet's spirituality and devotion to the Blessed Sacrament.

Nevertheless, Saint-Cyran became director in 1635, and began by making the nuns abstain from communion for a month, showing not only a change from his own attitude 20 years pre-

viously, when he wanted to celebrate Mass as often as he could, but breaking with the eucharistic spirituality which was the raison d'être of the new institute. Mère Angélique underwent one of the many spiritual crises in her life and was authorized to abstain from communicating between Easter and the feast of the Assumption on 15 August. Saint-Cyran's ascendancy over his penitents became complete, but Mère Angélique appears to have intensified the reaction against the sensuousness of Zamet's spirituality, and to have taken even further than Saint-Cyran himself Saint-Cyran's insistence on simplicity, poverty, humility, and the spirit of the primitive Church.

In September 1634 Zamet considered resigning his see of Langres and becoming an Oratorian. Condren, now superior of the Oratory, refused him, and that November Saint-Cyran turned down the coadjutorship of Langres when Zamet offered it to him. Saint-Cyran had meanwhile not neglected the convent in the faubourg Saint-Jacques. In spite of apparent success in whatever he undertook, and the general esteem in which he appeared to be held, the storm clouds were gathering. There were of course those who were jealous, and Saint-Cyran had undoubtedly appeared almost to cultivate a reputation for a high-handedness which skirted arrogance, but the root cause of the hostility he engendered must have had to do with a growing moral righteousness and a need to dominate, even to tyrannize, although apparently nearly always with charm. Those he quarrelled with, and who eventually brought about his downfall, were those who rejected his certainty that he was right and resented his assumption that he had what amounted to a divine warrant to impose his view. The difficulty is that so much that was written about him by contemporaries was either hostile polemic or hagiography.

Saint-Cyran had fuelled Jesuit hostility by signing an approbation for Gibieuf's 1630 De libertate dei et creaturae, a work aimed against the Jesuit psychology of free will. Gibieuf had been converted by Bérulle from his previous acceptance of the Jesuit position taught notably by Lessius, and the contrary view he now put forward in the De libertate was specifically attacked by the Jesuit Théophile Raynaud in the 1632 Novae libertatis explicatio, which considered it to provide the basis for an anthropology of the faculties of the soul which deprived the will of the autonomous power of moral choice. The will, that is, lost its freedom in all but some metaphysical and neoplatonist sense. Jansen himself, sharing Gibieuf's opinion that the Jesuit view of liberty implied the autonomous power of moral self-determination, none the less repudiated Gibieuf's formulations in the Augustinus as too full of a vocabulary foreign to the later Augustine, in spite of what have been shown to be his own neoplatonist assumptions.

The probability is that the years at Camp-de-Prats were devoted to study, particularly of the early Church, and possibly with the general intention of inaugurating a reformatory movement which would restore the Church to a better accord with the moral and spiritual norms of the early centuries; that until 1619 even Jansen was not aware that free will was the kernel of the dispute; and that he did not convince Saint-Cyran until the weeks they spent together in the summer of 1621.

The theology of the issue is considered in the Guide entry on Jansenism, but it is important for Saint-Cyran's biography that the Jesuits were bound to emerge as the main obstacle to the renewal envisaged, as soon as the central issue was identified as concerning the human capacity for spiritual self-determination.

A century previously the reformers had abandoned free will as necessarily entailing at least semi-Pelagian and therefore heretical consequences, but they did implicitly rely on direct religious experience as a criterion of the presence of justifying grace in the soul. Certainly Pascal and Nicole, sporadically Saint-Cyran and Jansen, and probably Antoine Arnauld attempted to erect a Christian spirituality without any possibility of reassurance on that all-important point, verifiable certainty of justification. Saint-Cyran swiftly drew the full spiritual consequences of the doctrinal position. His Christianity had to be a religion of trepidation, awareness of divine transcendance, the possibility of divine mercy, but the certainty of human guilt.

By 1635 the issues of free will and the heretical view of human powers which the Jesuit view seemed to Jansen to entail were certainly established in Saint-Cyran's mind as the hub of the dispute. As early as 1623 Saint-Cyran had sent Jansen notes for a panegyric on Augustine which, according to Saci, formed the basis for the important *Liber prooemalis* to the second volume of the *Augustinus*. Jansen was to die in 1638, and had begun the *Augustinus* no later than 1628. But the storm started to break only in 1636, with the quarrel between Zamet and Saint-Cyran involving the return of Mère Angélique to the faubourg Saint-Jacques, the intervention of the institute's titular foundress, the duchesse de Longueville, and the dismissal of an apparently unsuitable postulant, an orphan confided to Zamet's special care. Neither Mme de Longueville nor Zamet ever returned to the rue Coquillière, and the animosity of the regular clergy previously aroused by Saint-Cyran's views on episcopal jurisdiction was brought again to the boil. Circumstances conspired against Saint-Cyran. Mme de Longueville cast doubts to Richelieu on his orthodoxy. A Carmelite prior, sister of the chancellor, Séguier, was incensed against him because her niece had been enticed to the new institute, and she denounced his views on infrequent communion to her brother.

For the moment, however, the storm was averted, although Saint-Cyran now used the young Antoine Singlin to convey his spiritual instructions to the rue Coquillière. He himself appeared more frequently in the faubourg Saint-Jacques where Mère Agnès, recalled from Dijon, was installed as prior. Although he encountered some opposition from the community, particularly those members who had returned with Mère Agnès from Dijon, he quickly re-established a personal control which, by February 1638, was unquestioned. It was already producing exaggerated feelings of moral guilt in the community, typically manifested in sentiments of unworthiness at the idea of communicating.

During the regency and the early years of the reign of Louis XIII, Saint-Cyran had known Richelieu well, sometimes serving him as a personal spy. Although the anonymous *Somme des Fautes* had contained a ringingly eulogistic dedication to Richelieu, Saint-Cyran's reserves about him seem to have dated from rather earlier, probably from the time of his closer intimacy with Bérulle, who would have been exiled to Rome in 1629 had he not died that October. In November 1630 Saint-Cyran, identified with the party of Marie de Medici, would himself have been arrested if he had remained in Paris after the Journée des Dupes, and it did not help Saint-Cyran's standing with Richelieu that Jansen should in 1635 have published his strident *Mars gallicus* against the cardinal's policy in the Low Countries.

Saint-Cyran's views on attrition were merely the pretext for Richelieu to imprison him in 1638. The moral theology of the affair is much more complex than appeared at the time, or than

is now often appreciated, but the issue was thought to be whether or not for sacramental absolution regret for sin based on fear of hell, "attrition," was sufficient, or whether the motive had to be the love of God, basing repentance on "contrition." Richelieu had himself held the adequacy of attrition for sacramental absolution, as did the Jesuits. Saint-Cyran took the rigorist view, apparently against the canons of the Council of Trent.

In fact, trouble started with the conversion of the prominent barrister son of Catherine Arnauld, Antoine Le Maître, towards the end of 1637. Le Maître, who might have aspired to the highest legal offices, spent two months living an austere life of prayer in Saint-Cyran's Paris apartment while Saint-Cyran was away. On Saint-Cyran's return in December Le Maître resolved to live as a solitary, without taking orders but following an austere and devout life, a state unknown in France although not uncommon in Spain and Italy. So were born the "solitaires" of Port-Royal. He made his decision known in an open letter to chancellor Séguier, a gesture which produced its intended effect of astonishment, but worried Richelieu on account of the power Saint-Cyran was achieving, especially when Le Maître was promptly followed by his younger brother Le Maître de Séricourt, recently escaped from captivity after the 1636 battle of Philippsburg, and the young cleric Claude Lancelot.

Catherine Arnauld had a house built for her sons and Lancelot in the grounds of the monastery in the faubourg Saint-Jacques. The three were immediately joined by Antoine Singlin, the only priest; another young penitent of Saint-Cyran, Sylvain Gaudon; and the other three sons of Catherine Arnauld, so that her whole family of five were solitaires. Others came and went, and Saint-Cyran was surrounded by a small community of mostly prominent penitents. There was also an existing small group of young children from important families, the nucleus of a school which Saint-Cyran hoped to found. Singlin had taken them to pass the summer of 1637 at Port-Royal-des-Champs. Their secular instruction was entrusted to Gaudon in the autumn. Lancelot helped with the youngest, and Saint-Cyran wrote for all of them his *Théologie familière*.

Ironically for someone whose spirituality had been partly based on a defence of episcopal jurisdiction, Saint-Cyran was now, without any official position, in undisputed charge of two extremely fashionable convents, and had a collection of highborn solitaires, some of whom had renounced promising secular careers, submitting to his direction, with a group of children of leading families committed to him for instruction and moral and religious formation. He was hostile to Richelieu's foreign policy and dangerous to his domestic plans, and had been allied with Richelieu's personal enemies. His doctrine was probably suspect, his influence certainly disruptive, and his activity possibly dangerous. Ammunition collected from Zamet proved too weak, but then, in February 1638, Saint-Cyran offered Richelieu a virtual invitation to move against him by attacking Louis XIII's prayer to the Virgin for the protection of France, published on 10 February 1638.

Saint-Cyran's views on attrition had apparently been vulgarized in a series of very imprudent, even silly notes, the *Remarques*, added by the Oratorian Claude Séguenot to a translation of Augustine's *De virginitate* published on 15 March 1638. Louis XIII's Jesuit confessor, Nicolas Caussin, had had to be dismissed on Richelieu's instructions for eliciting from him acts of disinterested love of God, and Louis XIII spent three sleepless nights when he learnt that respectable teachers were still holding, in contradiction to what Richelieu had himself taught, that acts of disinterested love of God were always required of a penitent and that the requirement was not diminished even when sacramental absolution was given. Richelieu had to act swiftly or lose authority with a king frightened for his salvation.

In fact Séguenot did not personally know Saint-Cyran, but he was clearly drawing on Petrus Aurelius and repeating Bérulle's doctrine of the priesthood in such a way as to irritate the regulars, whose vows he attacked, together with the idea of self-determining human moral choice. The resultant spirituality of guilt and fear almost certainly went beyond Saint-Cyran's authentic teaching and even the exaggerations of it already current, but it none the less discredited it. Condren disowned Séguenot, who was arrested on 7 May 1638 at Saumur and taken a week later to the Bastille, where he stayed until after Richelieu's death. Saint-Cyran was taken to Vincennes on 14 May, and Séguenot's book, deemed to have been inspired by Saint-Cyran, was duly condemned on 1 July. It is conceivable that Saint-Cyran was not long expected to survive incarceration in the damp great dungeon of Vincennes, where the humidity had much abbreviated the lives of Ornano and Puylaurens, who survived only four months, and Alexandre de Vendôme, who lasted two years. Mme de Rambouillet had said the place was worth its weight in arsenic. But even if Saint-Cyran did live on, he would be out of the way.

The solitaires were first exiled to Port-Royal-des-Champs, then dispersed, most of them going to La Ferté-Milon. The children were sent away. Saint-Cyran, seriously ill, survived because Richelieu allowed him to be moved after six months. He could use the garden at Vincennes, and was allowed to have a servant and receive visitors, but was on several occasions close enough to death to have been given the last sacraments. In 1640 he was ill for several months with dysentery. His sight weakened and he could no longer say Mass. It is doubtful whether he could read much more than the table of contents when the 1641 Paris edition of the *Augustinus* appeared. He was finally released on 6 February 1643, a decent interval having been allowed after Richelieu's death on 4 December 1642. There was a solemn reception at Port-Royal. Saint-Cyran himself died of a stroke on 11 October 1643.

WORKS

It is a paradox that Saint-Cyran's most important works are his slightest: *Le Coeur nouveau*, probably written as early as 1627 for Léon Bouthillier, comte de Chavigny, who married Anne Phélypeaux on 20 May that year; the *Théologie familière*, written "on two or three afternoons" in September 1637 for the son of Jérôme Bignon, the advocate general; the letters; the short devotional treatises; and the works written when Saint-Cyran was in prison, had no books, and was nearly blind. Saint-Cyran's early works, the works of Latin controversy signed Petrus Aurelius, and the *Somme des fautes* are of considerable historical but very little literary interest. Skilful polemical writing does not require imaginative vigour, and the rhetorical sycophancy of the anonymous dedication of the *Somme des fautes*, whatever formal features may have been admired by Balzac, whose view is known only at second hand from a letter of Jansen, is no more than clever in its identification of Richelieu's interests with

those of Louis XIII, so that criticism of Richelieu's policy could be made to sound like blasphemy, the murmurs, said Saint-Cyran, of the Jews against Moses.

In the *Somme des fautes* Saint-Cyran was too thrustfully intelligent for his purposes. The work is heavy and pedantic. Garasse had been guilty of a serious misjudgement in his choice of register, and he made too many mistakes of all sorts, but it did not require a solemn four-volume book to refute him. The truth is that Saint-Cyran, trained to be a scholastic theologian, was brilliantly successful at scholastic debate, but never ceased to be a scholastic. Even after he had read the Fathers and studied the history of the early Church, read Augustine and, under the influence of Bérulle, turned against Jesuit optimism about both nature and grace, his simplest and clearest spiritual writings remain sharply aware of half a dozen distinct concepts of human nature, and as many more of divine grace. Indeed his great merit as a writer is to have produced apparently simple, metaphorical expositions of the spiritual consequences of whole lists of razor-sharp theological distinctions. How human beings should reasonably conduct their lives depended very much, after all, on what their nature allowed them to do, and what could only be achieved by a grace it was not in their power to acquire. That in turn depended on whether Adam was created in a state of pure nature or of nature in some way elevated, and whether, at the fall, what was lost was only that which had been added to nature, leaving nature itself intact, or something actually belonging to nature, so that after the fall nature could itself only be sinful and the source of sin.

Both Jansen and Saint-Cyran were convinced by Augustine's anti-Pelagian writings as they understood them. Jansen had sent Saint-Cyran a score of copies of the Louvain 1555 edition. But whereas Jansen went on to elaborate a formal treatise about the nature of fallen humanity's dependence on grace and the action of grace on the will, Saint-Cyran produced not a theology but a spirituality based on the total corruption of human nature, and the human soul's consequent total inability to contribute in any way to its eternal salvation. There were further differences. Whereas Jansen, although he repudiated Gibieuf's neoplatonist terminology in everything psychologically related to the working of grace in the will, his ontology comes very near to Gibieuf's on such matters as the divinization of the human soul, illumination, and the Christ-like state which can be substituted for fallen nature. Saint-Cyran, on the other hand, took from Bérulle the blend of Rhineland neoplatonist mysticism on divinization with the neoplatonist theology of the pseudo-Denis's *Celestial Hierarchies* which, like Bérulle, he used as a polemical weapon in defence of the diocesan clergy and the episcopal organization of ecclesiastical jurisdiction to the detriment of the exempt religious orders.

Saint-Cyran therefore was a skilful scholastically trained polemicist who, finding in Augustine a deeply pessimistic view about fallen human nature which he may temperamentally have been looking for, and which seemed to have the authority of Augustine's anti-Pelagian writings, turned it into an austere spirituality. Psychologically the pattern of his activity suggests that he must have been looking for a spirituality containing an unusually high dosage of aggressivity, and he repeatedly charmed his way into situations in which he mentally and spiritually dominated highly sophisticated disciples, who appear to have relished and depended on their discipleship. It has been accurately noticed that at exactly the right moment Jansen's theology came in the name of Augustine to justify Saint-Cyran's religion.

The matter is of importance because in no theological sense was Saint-Cyran a Jansenist, and it follows that the word Jansenism as normally used is deeply ambiguous. It is applied both to Jansen's neo-Augustinian theology and to a specific type of Oratorian spirituality, strongly coloured by the personal psychology of Saint-Cyran. He was a close personal friend of Jansen, shared with him a vision of renewing the Church in accordance with its primitive state, changed that ideal in later conversations with Jansen, but then developed his own spirituality almost irrespective of Jansen's theology, although they both shared an identical, if vulnerable, understanding of Augustine's anti-Pelagian writings. It would be tempting to reserve the term "Jansenism" for Jansen's theology and use "Augustinianism" for Saint-Cyran's spirituality. But current usage does not allow it, and it anyway suggests that Saint-Cyran's spirituality could authentically be derived from Augustine's theology, which is patently not the case. In the end Saint-Cyran, from being simply a scholastic theologian, derived the intellectual basis for a spirituality of charm, aggressiveness, austerity, and genuine charity from Bérulle.

He never quite developed the sensitivity which would have made him a great spiritual director, in the league of François de Sales or Fénelon. His letters are more interesting for their doctrinal content than for what they allow us to understand about the moral and spiritual development of their recipients. Surin was much more skilled, Jeanne-Françoise de Chantal more sensitive, and even Rancé was more subtle. Saint-Cyran always had to rein back his urge to dominate and to create dependency. Only at the end of his life, with no hope of escape except the unlikely possibility that Richelieu might pre-decease him, as in fact he did, and when he was deprived not only of dependent disciples but also of half his faculties, do the minor prison writings sometimes show the simplicity and humility of which Saint-Cyran was capable, and even then there were lapses as when he appears to be in a state of spiritual exaltation at the thought of those, like Virgil, eternally damned for the glory of God:

Il ne tombe pas une goutte de grâce pour les païens!... La colère de Dieu a paru quatre mille ans durant avant l'Incarnation, dure encore après et dans les trois parties du monde qui sont hors de l'Eglise et dans ce grand nombre de chrétiens qui sont déchus de la grâce du baptême

(Not a single drop of grace falls for the pagans!... God's wrath appeared for four thousand years before the Incarnation, and still lasts after it, both in the three quarters of the world which are outside the Church and in the large number of Christians who have fallen away from the grace of baptism).

Neither the courtly *Question royale* nor the forensically skilful *Apologie pour...La Roche-Pozay*, however central their biographical importance, is interesting for more than the expertise in largely scholastic debate to which they testify. The moral values which each work defends would no doubt later have been regarded as indefensible by Saint-Cyran himself, and the literary registers of the works do not exceed the level of skilful but morally uncommitted intellectual jousting. The behaviour of La Rocheposay, and the need to defend his protector may, of course, have shocked Saint-Cyran into his at first naive vision of restoring to the Church the evangelical values of the early centuries, but that keeps the interest of the works themselves to the level of biography.

An understanding of the later spirituality is, however, helped by an appreciation of Saint-Cyran's need both to defend La Rocheposay's repressionary use of force with reference to the standards of the Old Testament and to guard against any accusation that he was reneging on the standards preached by Jesus in the New Testament. He had impossibly to try to insist, in the company of all his contemporaries, that there had been no change, and his emphasis on the unity of the two Testaments will later allow him to find a scriptural warrant for the terrifying spirituality of fear and trembling which he was to advocate without, apparently, often provoking more than an acceptable level of moral tension.

Not much needs here to be said about the *Somme des fautes*, the attack on Garasse, part of which was suppressed and part of which had to be abbreviated. A tedious and over-lengthy demonstration of the Jesuit's fatuities and errors, the work, with its polemical back-up pieces, the *Réfutation de l'abus prétendu* and the *Advis à tous les sçavans*, is again more important for what it tells us about Saint-Cyran's spiritual development than for its actual content. Although Saint-Cyran's work did now contain genuine moral outrage, its origins may have been trigger happy. The probability is that Saint-Cyran wanted to fend off, or be ready immediately to controvert, any attack on Bérulle's *Grandeurs* or its underlying spirituality. It is in its way again ironic that it should have taken Garasse's astonishing ineptitude to shock Saint-Cyran into an awareness of the iniquity of justifying duelling on the grounds that honour might need defending, or of establishing different degrees of culpability between a nobleman who strikes a servant and a servant who strikes a nobleman.

The whole Latin controversy under the name of Petrus Aurelius consists of eight works by Saint-Cyran issued in four volumes between 1632 and 1635 except for a single work, the *Orthodoxus adversus secundum Antirrheticum* published only in 1642. The place in Saint-Cyran's life of this polemic on behalf of episcopal jurisdiction and against exemption for religious orders responsible directly to Rome is indicated in the biographical section of this entry. Its principal importance lies in its heightened antagonism towards the Jesuits on a matter removed from personal moral values or the theology of grace, and in the way in which Bérulle's reliance on the Pseudo-Denis is used by Saint-Cyran as the basis for an ecclesiastical jurisprudential view as well as a determinedly anti-naturalistic spirituality. Apart from the slight written pieces concerning the affair of the *Chapelet secret* and the letters, we are left then only with the short treatises and what was written in prison.

Le Coeur nouveau, written probably as early as 1627, certainly derives from Saint-Cyran's familiarity with Bérulle, whose own master in both theology and philosophy had been André Duval, with whom, however, Bérulle had later fallen out. Duval found him pushing and had not been pleased when his brightest pupil, Condren, had joined forces with Bérulle by joining the Oratory. Bérulle finally went too far, certainly disregarding Duval's authority when he tried to impose his vows of servitude on the Carmelites, and subsequently losing his temper with the spiritually most impressive Mme Acarie, after she had become the Carmelite Marie de l'Incarnation. Duval had identified with the heart what the mystics traditionally called the "apex mentis (high-point of the soul)," referred to in French by both François de Sales and Bérulle as the soul's "fine pointe." Bérulle translated the psalmist's "cor mundum (clean heart)" as "coeur nouveau (new heart)," and the presumption is that the opening sentence of Saint-Cyran's *Le Coeur nouveau*, referred to Ezekiel XI, 19, where the Vulgate Latin does not use "new" of the heart, derives from Bérulle:

La vie de la Grace est fondée dans l'ame, comme la vie de la Nature est fondée dans le corps: et elle commence, comme celle-là, par l'établissement du coeur, qui est une chose intérieure, et le principe de toutes les fonctions de la vie

(The life of grace is founded in the soul, as the life of nature is founded in the body: it begins, like the life of nature, by the establishment of the heart, which is interior and the principle of all the functions of life).

The probable derivation from Bérulle of what might be considered a reasonably unremarkable opening is important because of the idea common to Bérulle and Condren, and now inherited by Saint-Cyran, that fallen nature infected by sin needs not healing or restoring, but annihilating and replacing. The expression is no doubt metaphorical, but it indicates the emphatically anti-naturalistic thrust of Saint-Cyran's spirituality, as well as confirming its derivation from Oratorian neoplatonism.

The language used is also important on account of the way in which recourse to the scriptural concept of the heart avoids the scholastic dilemma that acts can come from the intellect or the will but never from both together. Both Descartes and Pascal found it impossible within the confines of that psychology of the faculties to account for acts, like the act of faith, which needed to be regarded as both rational and meritorious, intellective and volitive. Pascal's use of the term "heart" for the seat of an act which is both may owe something to Saint-Cyran, although Saint-Cyran, probably without adverting to what he is doing, constantly identifies the new heart of *Le Coeur nouveau* simply with the faculty of the will in the scholastics.

There is a further usage of the term "heart" in Saint-Cyran which may help to explain Pascal's view as expressed in *De l'art de persuader*, and strengthens the probability that the distinction between the two ways of knowing two different sorts of truth in the *Liber prooemialis* to the *Augustinus* may owe something to the sketch for a panegyric on Augustine which Saint-Cyran sent Jansen in 1623:

Il me semble qu'il y a cette difference entre les mouvemens interieurs qui naissent de la connaissance que la science aporte, et ceux qui naissent de la connoissance que donne la Foy, que les uns viennent des sens exterieurs dans le coeur, parce que les connoissances de la science des hommes passent des sens au coeur, et les autres au contraire passent du coeur dans les sens, parce que les effets de Dieu se forment premierement dans le coeur et dans la volonté, et passent ensuite dans l'entendement, et de là dans les sens...

(It seems to me that there is this difference between the interior movements deriving from the knowledge brought by learning and those which derive from the knowledge given by faith. The first sort come into the heart through the external senses because the knowledge brought by learning passes from the senses to the heart, while the other sort on the contrary passes from the heart to the senses, because the effects caused by God are felt first in the heart and the will, and then pass from there into the senses...).

That passage is unlikely either to be original or to derive from Bérulle, who does, however, in the sixth *Discours de l'Eucharistie*, mention the traditional distinction between faith, depending on authority, and the sciences which depend on reason. Saint-Cyran is probably deriving directly from Augustine.

A great deal of the later spiritual writing is still factitious, based on facile metaphors and antitheses, betraying either too much haste or inadequate thought. Carnal human beings are horrified by carnal sins, but God, who is spiritual, detests spiritual sins more. Jesus's self-abasement contrasts with Adam's self-elevation. Saint-Cyran uses the French "amour-propre" in the full sense of Augustine's "amor sui," which excludes grace from the soul at the opening of the *De civitate dei* XIV, 28 and which is so important for an understanding of Pascal, Nicole, and La Rochefoucauld. Saint-Cyran writes,

Les vertus morales sont d'ordinaire la nourriture de l'amour-propre par la complaisance et l'estime de nous-mêmes dans laquelle il nous fait entrer, et l'amour-propre est le plus grand de tous les maux, puisqu'il est comme un anti-Dieu, car il n'appartient qu'à Dieu de s'aimer soi-même, et par notre amour-propre nous devenons pires que les païens qui, adorant leurs idoles, adoraient le démon qui les animait, lequel étant un ange, quoique réprouvé, était d'un ordre supérieur aux hommes, au lieu qu'en faisant un Dieu de nous par notre amour-propre, nous nous adorons nous-mêmes

(The moral virtues are ordinarily the nourishment of self-love through the self-satisfaction and self-esteem into which it draws us, and self-love is the greatest of all evils, since it is a kind of anti-God. It belongs only to God to love himself, and by our self-love we become worse than the pagans. In adoring their idols, they were adoring what gave them life, the demon which, being an angel, even if fallen, was of a higher order than men, while we, making a God of ourselves by our self-love, are merely adoring ourselves).

The implication here, as with Pascal and Nicole, is that we cannot know whether our moral virtues are authentic or not, based on grace or based on the self-adoration which excludes grace. Everything depends on the presence or absence of grace, about which Saint-Cyran, like Pascal and Nicole, assumes that we cannot know. The result, as Saint-Cyran and Nicole make explicit, must be a spirituality of uncertainty, fear and trembling. No one can know in this life whether or not they are justified, or will persevere in justification. That is the spiritual consequence of Augustinian theology which Pascal saw and found so difficult in the *Pensées* to confront.

Saint-Cyran, however, is not consistent. Sometimes he does imply the need for intense ascetic effort, but more often he urges an interior submission, a conformity to the will of God, and an acceptance of whatever trials are imposed on us as a means virtually of meriting a heavenly reward. To one nun he wrote from prison that, having moved from the austerities of Port-Royal to the relatively relaxed tensions of Visitandine spirituality, she can expect, "if God gives you grace to spend your life there observing the rules that are kept there," no less a reward than if, apparently, "you had lived in much greater austerity." There is an almost medieval tendency at the bottom of Saint-Cyran's spiritual thinking to exult in the achievement of God's will, even when it results in eternal personal damnation. It was a dehumanized consequence of Ockhamist thought that God could make it virtuous for human beings to hate him, and the prospect of a state of damnation was one which precipitated spiritual crises for both François de Sales and Fénelon.

The most important of the minor works composed by Saint-Cyran in prison was undoubtedly that written about grace to explain to Arnauld d'Andilly, on the appearance of the *Augustinus*, exactly what, in spiritual terms, the theological dispute was about. *De la grâce de Jésus-Christ, de la liberté chrétienne et de la justification* is a short masterpiece of exposition, but also exceptionally revealing of Saint-Cyran's own thought. Human beings, he writes, have fallen not only into an abyss of mud which has filthied their bodies and their souls, but also onto the points of rocks which have bruised and broken both their bodies and their souls. By baptism we have been cleaned, not restored. Only God's grace allows the soul to produce works conducive to God's glory and personal salvation.

Disconcertingly, Saint-Cyran sometimes writes as if grace produced in us empirically verifiable effects, and sometimes as if it did not. He sometimes refuses to pander to the Christian's desperate need to know whether justifying grace is present or absent, whether our works are good or bad, because he cannot reconcile himself to the impossible uncertainty if there is no empirical criterion in the order of behaviour or experience to indicate the presence or absence of justifying grace. The result is inevitably and understandably confusing. Saint-Cyran is clear that without the active movement of grace within us we are incapable of activity that is not sinful, even if it appears to be morally good. In this treatise, he goes on to measure the growth of the love of God in empirically identifiable steps, fear of hell, a coarse movement made universally available by God which leads from attrition towards true contrition and then to baptism, or else to penance and absolution. Saint-Cyran, ever the scholastic, then distinguishes three sorts of freedom, that before the fall, that after the fall, and that of the justified. Only before the fall was it within Adam's power to choose good or evil. After the fall, all that was available to Adam and his descendants was a choice between sinful acts.

The justified, by contrast, are only notionally free to sin. Saint-Cyran is in a quandary. If grace does not compel virtuous activity, then that activity depends partly on cooperation or human choice, which for Jansen and Saint-Cyran is a heretical view. Yet if grace does compel virtuous activity, how can it be free?

La liberté des justes et des enfants de Dieu... ayant toujours le pouvoir de faire le mal... ils sont néanmoins déterminés à faire le bien, mis dans une heureuse nécessité de faire le bien seulement selon qu'il plaît à Dieu de les y pousser par les grâces actuelles qu'il donne aux justes lorsqu'il lui plaît, et qui sont si puissantes et si efficaces qu'elles charment plutôt qu'elles n'attirent la volonté qui suit avec joie le mouvement et l'inspiration de cette grâce,

qui n'est rien qu'un amour de Dieu qu'il forme dans le coeur, qui l'entraîne et lui fait faire avec un contentement et un plaisir indicibles tout le bien que la même grâce lui fait connaître

(The freedom of the justified and the children of God... retaining the power to do evil... They are nevertheless forced to do good, placed in the happy necessity of doing good only as it pleases God to force them by the actual graces which he gives to the justified when he pleases, and which are so powerful and efficacious that they charm more than they attract the will. The will joyfully follows the movement and the inspiration of grace, which is nothing other than a love of God which he forms in the heart, which draws it on and makes it, with an inexpressible pleasure and happiness, do all the good which the same grace reveals to it).

That begs the question. Does grace force the will and, if it does, how is the will free? Can the withdrawal of grace be other than a divine act of capricious arbitrariness? Saint-Cyran's language has gone into auto-register as it persuades the reader with mention of pleasure and delight not to ask the awkward questions. A little later Saint-Cyran uses the Augustinian term "délectation" which, for Augustine, is not an external constraint determining the will, as it was to become for Jansen. The language is camouflage. In the end Saint-Cyran draws the conclusion, but he was far too good a scholastic not to realize how unsatisfactory his conclusion was,

Comme le soleil fait des jours sacrés et des jours profanes, des jours de fête et des jours civils, jes jours d'été et des jours d'hiver, ainsi Dieu a fait certains hommes pour être sauvés et saints, et d'autres profanes pour être damnés, quoique Dieu ne soit pas cause de leur damnation, mais le péché qu'ils ont commis dans Adam et l'infection suivante dans laquelle ils sont nés, et la vie criminelle et dissolue qu'ils ont menée depuis

(As the sun makes days which are sacred and days which are profane, feast days and work days, summer days and winter days, so God created some men to be holy and saved, and others sinful to be damned, although God is not the cause of their damnation, but the sin they committed in Adam and the ensuing corruption into which they were born, and the criminal and dissolute life they have led since).

PUBLICATIONS

Collections

Oeuvres, 4 vols., 1679
Petri Aurelii opera, 4 vols., 1632–35

Theological and spiritual

Question royale... où il est montré en quelle extrémité, principalement en temps de paix, le sujet pourrait être obligé de conserver la vie du Prince aux dépens de la sienne, 1609

Apologie pour Messire Henry-Louis Châtaigner de la Roche-
posay...., 1615

Somme des fautes et des faussetez capitales contenues en la
Somme théologique du Père François Garassus..., only 2
vols. and abridgement of vol. 4 published, 1626

Réfutation de l'abus prétendu et le découvert de la véritable
ignorance du Père Fr. Garasse, 1626

Avis à tous les savants... touchant la réfutation..., 1626

Réfutation d'un examen naguère publié contre la réponse... aux
remarques d'un théologien contre le Chapelet secret du T.S.
Sacrement, 1634

Orthodoxus adversus secundum Antirrheticum, 1642

Maximes saintes et religieuses, 1653

Considérations sur les dimanches, 2 vols., 1670

Lettres chrétiennes et spirituelles, 1674

Lettres inédites edited by A. Barnes (*Les Origines du Jan-*
sénisme, vol. 4), 1962

Biographical and critical studies

Bremond, Henri, *Histoire littéraire du sentiment religieux en*
France, 12 vols., 1921–36

Laporte, J., *La Doctrine de Port-Royal*, vol. 1, 1923

Abercrombie, Nigel, *The Origins of Jansenism*, 1936

Orcibal, Jean, *Jean Duvergier de Hauranne, abbé de Saint-*
Cyran et son temps (*Les Origines du Jansénisme*, vols. 2 and
3), 1947–48

——————————*La Spiritualité de Saint-Cyran avec ses oeuvres*
de piété inédits (*Les Origines du Jansénisme*, vol. 5), 1962

Cognet, Louis, *Le Jansénisme*, 1964

SAINT-ÉVREMOND, Charles de Marquetel de Saint-Denis, Seigneur de, 1614–1703.

Moralist, essayist, and critic.

LIFE

Saint-Evremond appears to have been baptized on 5 January 1614 and to have been born a day or two earlier at Saint-Denis-le-Guast in Normandy. He was the younger son of Charles de Saint-Denis who, at the age of 42, had in 1608 married Charlotte de Rouville. Destined early for a military career, he was an ensign in 1629 and a lieutenant in 1632, serving at the siege of Nancy and taking part in Louis XIII's conquest of Lorraine. He was present at the French victory at Avein in 1635 and at the retaking of Corbie in November 1636, and had his own company under La Valette for the siege of Landrecies in 1637. After distinguishing himself at the siege of Arras under La Meilleraye in 1640, Saint-Evremond joined Enghien's regiment as a lieutenant in 1642, fighting with him at Rocroi in 1643 and Fribourg in 1644. We have a letter from the 26-year-old Saint-Evremond to his 74-year-old father reporting on the French pursuit of the Spanish troops on 24 June 1640 in which a number of high-ranking French officers were killed or injured. In 1645 Saint-Evremond was himself badly injured in the knee at Nördlingen.

We know relatively little about Saint-Evremond's life as an army officer before he was wounded. Six letters to one or several women tell us only that his galanterie was accomplished, and we know that his circle of aristocratic officer friends was on the whole refined and cultivated. Sometime during the winter of 1637–38, shortly after the Académie had published its *Sentiments* on *Le Cid*, Saint-Evremond wrote, perhaps with others, a satirical verse comedy, *La Comédie des Académistes*, on the attempt to reform the French language that lay close to the heart of Chapelain. The manuscript was circulated anonymously and was not published during Richelieu's lifetime. No one knew who had written it, although Mlle de Gournay thought it was Saint-Amant. Chapelain was particularly ill treated in the comedy, heading a whole list of satirized characters, including Godeau, Colletet, Gombauld, Boisrobert, Silhon, and Cerisy.

Saint-Evremond's army career continued, although he quarrelled with Condé in 1647, and unenthusiastically appeared to support Mazarin during the Fronde. He fought a duel with Louis du Vigean, marquis de Fors, almost certainly in 1647, and became very friendly with Louis de la Trémoille, comte d'Olonne, who married on 1 March 1652 the 18-year-old Catherine-Henriette d'Angennes, daughter of the seigneur de la Louppe, intimate companion of Mme de Lafayette, much admired by the future cardinal de Retz, and one of whose lovers was the duc de Candale, the duc d'Epernon's son and another of Saint-Evremond's close associates. Already in the immediate aftermath of the Fronde Saint-Evremond had therefore once been close to Condé, had supported Mazarin during the insurrection, but was also associated with what might be called the Gondi entourage. In fact it is quite difficult to be certain of his affiliations. He appears privately to have remained faithful to Condé in spite of the public quarrel and in spite of his adherence to the cause of the royal army and the leadership of Turenne. It might have been a cold calculation that finally put him on the winning side at a moment when the court appeared unlikely to prevail.

Saint-Evremond did, however, remain loyal to the royal cause. Candale wanted command of the royal forces in Guyenne, where d'Harcourt had been beaten, but Mazarin wished him to marry his niece Anne-Marie Martinozzi first. Candale, however, was appointed, and sought a cavalry regiment for Saint-Evremond. Mazarin, on his way to his second exile, gave the appropriate instructions to Le Tellier. He tried too late to change them, or so Le Tellier alleged, when he heard that Candale was too enthusiastic about Mme d'Olonne to want to marry Mazarin's niece, and that Saint-Evremond was joking with Candale at the cardinal's expense. On 16 September 1652 Candale was given command of the army in Guyenne and Saint-Evremond was made maréchal de camp, receiving from the next day a pension of 3,000 livres. Saint-Evremond had, however, played his hand too audaciously. Mazarin would have liked a niece married into the d'Epernon family, and was not going to forget his grudge against Saint-Evremond.

Saint-Evremond was by this time a friend of Foucquet. Since he paid his troops irregularly, cashing in the assignations given him on local authorities, Saint-Evremond was later able to boast that he had made 50,000 livres in two and a half years. The dates are difficult to reconcile, since peace in Guyenne was made in July 1653. Saint-Evremond may have been there since early 1651. Candale's army was doing well, and Saint-Evremond made a number of journeys to the court to further Candale's fortunes, but it was clear that Mazarin was trying to do a deal with

Conti behind Candale's back, and that it was in Candale's interests to take Bordeaux by force.

It seems clear that Saint-Evremond was responsible for having clauses favourable to the princes, Condé, Conti, and Longueville, inserted into the 1653 treaty, that jokes about Mazarin had got back to the cardinal, and that the slights offered to the cardinal in September 1652, and the opposition to Candale's marriage to his niece, had not been forgotten. Accounts may have become confused, but the probability is that Saint-Evremond was sent to the Bastille by Mazarin for some time late in 1653, before being committed there in 1658. It has been remarked that of the three most intelligent young aristocrats of their generation each had overplayed his hand at the end of 1653; Retz was in prison at Vincennes, La Rochefoucauld in exile at Verteuil, and Saint-Evremond in the Bastille. Early in 1654 Conti married Anne-Marie Martinozzi.

Whatever the ostensible reason for Saint-Evremond's imprisonment in the Bastille from June to September 1658, the real cause was Mazarin's hostility, fear, and desire ostentatiously to demonstrate his authority. Saint-Evremond's release was obtained by the 29-year-old marquis de Créquy, governor of Béthune from 1655, married to Catherine du Plessis-Bellière, daughter of Foucquet's mistress. Foucquet was by the late 1650s the focus of the opposition to Mazarin, almost symbolically taking over in the name of new money from the old aristocracy, which had seen demonstrated in the Fronde its powerlessness to contain the movement to concentrate power in the hands of a ministerial administration. Royal absolutism was, at least under Mazarin and Colbert, little more than a masquerade, which largely fobbed off the king with the outward display of power and only its more unimportant manifestations. Condé was on the verge of full rehabilitation, Conti had married Mazarin's niece, and Foucquet was preparing his defences. Pellisson was in charge of the arrangements to protect Foucquet from attack, and Créquy was in his pay.

Mazarin left for Saint-Jean-de-Luz at the end of June 1659 to negotiate the treaty of the Pyrenees and the marriage of Louis XIV with Marie-Thérèse, daughter of Philip IV. Créquy thought the provisions of the treaty dishonoured France, and Saint-Evremond who, like Créquy, travelled in Mazarin's entourage when he went to formalize what had already been agreed in Madrid and Paris, promised to send back an account of the negotiations. In fact he sent what is generally known as his *Lettre sur la paix*, a criticism of the terms of the peace, to a number of those who wanted the war to continue, and it is a pamphlet rather than a letter to a friend. According to Père Rapin, the original addressee was probably the comtesse du Plessis-Guénégaud, but it is generally supposed that the nominal addressee was Créquy.

Negotiations had been going on since 1656, and the Spanish insistence on Condé's rehabilitation had been a sticking point. The honour of the Spanish king, whom Condé had served, needed to be respected. Mazarin had mounted a pantomime proposal for the marriage of Louis XIV and the princess of Savoy, simply playing for better terms from the Spaniards, but all seemed to have been agreed by the end of June 1659. Hostilities had been suspended. The king, his mother, and the court had left Fontainebleau late in July and arrived in Bordeaux on 19 August, but the Spaniards revived the question of Condé, and Mazarin had to concede the restoration to him of the governorship of Burgundy before the maréchal de Gramont could be sent to Madrid to ask for the hand of Marie-Thérèse.

The French military establishment, in this led by Brienne, believed that France would have been better served by continuing the war, and that Mazarin had been moved by flattery, promises, and his own ambition to be seen as the architect of the peace. Foucquet no doubt thought that the continuation of the war would have further enriched him, and may well have encouraged Saint-Evremond to write his *Lettre*, probably composed in the winter of 1659–60, as a contribution to the case he was building up against Mazarin, by whom he felt threatened. The later appearance of the *Lettre* with a dedication to Foucquet suggests that the link between Saint-Evremond and Foucquet was known for certain when the *Lettre* was discovered, after the surintendant's arrest, in a locked box with other papers entrusted by Saint-Evremond to the safe-keeping of Mme du Plessis-Bellière when he left for Nantes in August 1661. It was on account of the link with Foucquet established by the letter that Saint-Evremond left France, correctly assuming that the alternative was the Bastille. The letter was itself published anonymously in the 1664 *Histoire de la paix conclue sur la frontière de France et d'Espagne... l'an 1659*, translated from the 1663 Italian original published anonymously by Gualdo Priorato.

When Foucquet was arrested on 5 September 1661, Saint-Evremond was at Nantes. Prudence kept him away from Paris, and he spent a month at Palluau with the maréchal de Clérambault, in whose coach he had probably travelled to Saint-Jean-de-Luz in 1659. Seals had been put on all Mme du Plessis-Bellière's possessions and on her house in the Rue Matignon on 8 September and were not removed until 15 October. An inventory was made starting two days later and, when the *Lettre* was found, orders were duly given committing Saint-Evremond to the Bastille. Saint-Evremond, thinking himself safe, was actually returning to Paris when he received a warning from Gourville, Condé's steward. At first he hid and waited, then he fled to Normandy, where he had to keep on the move and travel only by night. He quickly found that the pursuit would not be relaxed, and left France through Holland for London, where he had arrived before the end of November 1661.

He fully expected to be allowed to return soon to France. He enlisted the support of the French ambassador, the comte de Cominges, whom he assisted when Louis XIV ordered him publicly to assert precedence in a manner which was bound to provoke the Spaniards in London to a street brawl, like one involving Cominges's predecessor, the comte d'Estrades, which had taken place in the preceding October and in which there had been several deaths; but mentions of Saint-Evremond's repentance for the unpublished *Lettre* found in the locked box went unheeded. Further intercessions were fruitlessly made in late 1664 and early 1665 by Cominges, and by a special envoy, the comte de Ruvigny, charged to offer the services of Louis XIV as a mediator in the prospective Anglo-Dutch hostilities which would have forced France on to the Dutch side. Louis XIV was unmoved. Saint-Evremond, on whose behalf poor health and, more plausibly, indigence, had been pleaded, was in 1665 offered a pension by Charles II.

Saint-Evremond spent from July 1665 until 1670 in Holland, living a more austere life than that which he had established for himself at the English court. There was plague in London, and Saint-Evremond was depressed at not being able to return to France, but we do not really know why he went to The Hague. By 1665 war between England and Holland was inevitable, and Louis XIV was going to have to help the Dutch, however reluctantly, under the terms of an agreement of 1662. It was in Holland, where Saint-Evremond had arrived by December 1665, that he took to reading widely and writing much more; he also tried again to get back to France. It was in Holland that he much praised British maritime strength, as the commander of Dover wrote to Colbert. Praise of the British fleet will have helped British policy directed by Henry Bennet, later Lord Arlington, and done Saint-Evremond no harm in France.

In fact Philip IV died on 17 September 1665 and Louis XIV formally declared war on England on 6 January 1666. He was in no great hurry to do anything more. A secret treaty with Charles II promised the British a favourable settlement of the Dutch war, and Saint-Evremond appears to have been at Breda while negotiations were conducted there from May to July 1667. By the end of July, he had returned briefly to London. He was there again after Condé's conquest of Franche-Comté and the signing of the treaty of Aix-la-Chapelle in May 1668. His intentions seem throughout to have been to favour French interests, and he may have been involved as an agent, perhaps recompensed by the British. When Charles II let it be known that he would welcome Saint-Evremond's return to London, which duly occurred in May 1670, Colbert's brother wrote from London to Colbert himself, soliciting permission for Saint-Evremond to return to France. Louis XIV remained unmoved, and Saint-Evremond received his English pension, becoming close to Arlington, pro-Spanish, and from January 1666 husband to the Dutch Isabelle van Beverweert, the illegitimate daughter of Maurice of Nassau.

What Saint-Evremond called his "bagatelles" were taken to Barbin, who knew who their author was and published them as *Oeuvres meslées* over the initials "M.S.E." in 1668, with a privilège of 2 May. Barbin had already anonymously published some early essays in 1664, and in 1666 the *Jugement sur les sciences où peut s'appliquer un honnête homme* had also appeared in the original edition of Boileau's *Satires* (I, VII, IV, V, and II), generally thought to have been printed in Rouen. It was the appearance of that volume which Boileau said had provoked him into publishing on his own account. Then later in 1668, with a privilège of 5 August, Barbin published a duodecimo *Seconde partie des oeuvres meslées de M. D**** which he cannot at first have thought to have been by Saint-Evremond, although he attributed the four essays to Saint-Evremond in a 1689 quarto of the whole of the *Oeuvres meslées*. From this date on, the bibliographical information is complex.

Saint-Evremond never himself published anything, although he almost certainly connived at publication and subsequently sometimes acknowledged authorship. However, the texts are often corrupt, much was published in works attributed to others, or anonymously, and much that was attributed to him was not by him. The first reliable editions of the *Lettres* in two volumes and the *Oeuvres en prose* in four volumes date from the 1960s. All the works are either letters or short essays on historical, moral, or literary subjects, important for their perceptiveness, sensitivity, and the points of view they argue, as well, often, as for the information they contain. From his background, and the association with Foucquet, it is scarcely surprising that, even in exile, Saint-Evremond should have developed a pattern of attitudes identifiable as characteristic of the partisans of the "modernes" in the Querelle des anciens et des modernes (q.v.).

On 31 December 1675 the 29-year-old duchesse Mazarin, born Hortense Mancini, the cardinal's niece, arrived in London, where she was an instant success at court, and became Saint-Evremond's close companion and the object of his galant attentions. When she was 15 the cardinal had married her to the marquis de la Meilleraye, whom he had made duc Mazarin. The duchess had left him in 1668 to join her sister Marie, connétable Colonna, in Italy. She was an adventurer, had to leave Rome in 1672, travelled, and spent three years at Chambéry with her elder sister, the comtesse de Soissons, at the court of Savoy. It may be it was hoped by those who wished to ruin the credit of the duchess of Portsmouth that Charles II would make her his mistress. The duke of York, later James II, brother of Charles, whose second wife and queen, Mary of Modena, was the granddaughter of one of Mazarin's sisters and therefore the daughter of Hortense's cousin, Laura Martinozzi, bought her a house, but money was short, and a liaison with the marquis de Courcelles ended unhappily. Hortense's desire to retire to a French convent seems to have been more a form of blackmail than the result of genuine devotion.

As late as 1685 Saint-Evremond, living modestly but happily in London, was seeking to return to France, but permission came only in 1689, when it was too late. The French expatriate colony in London had expanded, while the ascendancy of Louvois, the death of Colbert, the revocation of the edict of Nantes, and the removal of the court to Versailles all made life at the French court seem less attractive. Saint-Evremond stayed in England where, in 1698, he was made governor of Saint James's park. Although he was fascinated by religious attitudes, he scandalized the society in which he moved by his apparent unconcern about the possibility of an after-life, his religious uncertainties, and his Epicurean inclinations. He had known Spinoza, Heinsius, and Vossius in Holland. His interests were never sufficiently serious to make him a scholar, and he enjoyed good living. He was one of the "costeaux," so-called after the three vineyards in the champagne region of whose wines alone they approved, but total immersion in the elegant and foppish amusements of life in London also made him chafe. He was neither heroic nor committed to any ideology or ideas, and he never composed a major work. He seems to have been easy-going, but his imagination was potent, his intelligence sharp, his psychological perceptivity acute, and his reputation as a major author seems unlikely yet to have reached its peak.

Hortense Mazarin died in 1699. Towards the end of Saint-Evremond's long life he became friendly with Pierre Silvestre, a Bordeaux-born Protestant doctor who knew Bayle, came to England with William of Orange in 1688, followed Schomberg to Ireland, and returned when Schomberg was killed in 1690 to join Montagu's household. Saint-Evremond was delighted when Silvestre brought back Corelli's latest sonatas from a journey with Montagu's son to Italy, and was to leave him his books and manuscripts. With Pierre Desmaizeaux, also a friend of Bayle, a pastor's still youthful son who had himself studied theology, Silvestre was to edit Saint-Evremond's work in 1705. Desmaizeaux, who knew Saint-Evremond much later and less well, also produced the 1706 Amsterdam edition, and another volume including false attributions and his own life of Saint-Evremond, who had died on 20 September 1703, probably within a few months of his 90th birthday, and sufficiently distinguished to have been buried in Westminster Abbey.

WORKS

Saint-Evremond's writings were all occasional and generally short. In spite of connivance at publication, they were mostly intended to be neither completely private, like a diary, nor completely public, like a book, but generally designed for a restricted circle within which Saint-Evremond supposed that they might circulate or, as chiefly the historical works make clear, for a slightly wider but cultivated public with sophisticated tastes and a background of formal education. Many of them show a brilliant mind and a refined taste, but it is frequently important to distinguish their tone, which can be lighthearted or frivolous, from their register, which varies, but can be deeply committed and is almost never totally unserious.

The comte d'Olonne had married the 18-year-old Catherine-Henriette d'Angennes on 1 March 1652. She at first established a reputation for prudishness, to the frustration of the future cardinal de Retz, but from 1656 her licentious conduct had become notorious, and much is made of it by Bussy-Rabutin in the *Histoire amoureuse des Gaules*. She is La Bruyère's "Messaline," and was the subject of an outrageous comedy, of which a printed version is kept in the pornographic collection of the Bibliothèque Nationale. After Beuvron, her publicly acknowledged lover was Candale, who died of venereal disease in 1658. Her closest friends included Gilonne d'Harcourt, comtesse de Fiesque, an intimate of Mademoiselle, who counselled a decent period of mourning, but Mme d'Olonne managed only three or four days. Vineuil published her portrait in the 1659 *Divers Portraits* dedicated to Mademoiselle, and a few months later Saint-Evremond wrote to her, sending a caractère which was published in Barbin's 1659 *Recueil des Portraits et Eloges en vers.*

There are several reasons why this apparently slight piece is interesting, the chief of which is the fundamental seriousness of the character analysis masquerading as a caractère, and therefore nominally confined to external characteristics. The semi-formal caractère contains a penetrating edge of good-natured malice, softened by the different register of the accompanying letter, which yet takes nothing back. It was intended to admonish as well as to flatter its recipient and, read together, the caractère and the letter make a brilliant miniature.

The opening flattery is delicate and elegant, pointedly different from the comparisons of eyes and sun, complexion and flowers, which would have characterized such galanterie before the Fronde. In Mme d'Olonne are united the "charmes divers des diferentes beautez: ce qui surprend, ce qui plaist, ce qui flate, ce qui pique, ce qui touche (separate charms of the different beauties: what surprises, what pleases, what flatters, what stimulates, what moves)." Then come the appropriately veiled admonitions. Mme d'Olonne's sentimental indifference must derive from the absence "des sujets dignes de vous (of subjects worthy of you)." In other words she would do well to attach herself to her lovers by ties other than those binding her merely to sources of sexual gratification. There are also elegant but frank criticisms, as of her poor judgement:

> Je vous ay veuë souvent estimer trop des gens médiocres; et dans certaines docilitez, qui veritablement ne vous durent gueres, soûmettre votre jugement à celuy de Personnes peu éclairées.
>
> Il me semble aussi que vous vous laissez trop aller à l'habitude: ce que d'abord vous avez jugé grossier fort sainement, vous paroist à la fin délicat sans raison; et quand vous venez à guerir de ces erreurs, c'est plustost par un retour de vostre humeur, que par les reflexions de vostre Esprit

(I have often seen you over-estimate second-rate people, and in moods of acquiescence, which actually do not last very long with you, submit your own judgement to that of the ignorant. It seems to me, too, that you let yourself be too swayed by habit: what at first you very reasonably judged vulgar in the end appears to you without reason to be refined; and when you recover from these aberrations, it is on account more of a change of mood than of a mental process).

Mme d'Olonne's actions, too, neglect the "petites formalitez, qui sont de véritables gesnes dans la vie (little proprieties, which constitute real constraints in life)", so that she has "to fear the opinion of the stupid, and the annoyance of those whom your merit has made your enemies." Saint-Evremond implies a compliment to Mme d'Olonne's physical attractiveness by telling her that women are her declared enemies, but he adds that she could show more respect for their feelings. The accompanying letter, full of further compliments, also makes open the admonitory intention: "si vous suivez mon conseil (if you follow my advice)."

For reasons we do not know, two pieces by Saint-Evremond, the *Retraitte de Monsieur de Longueville en son gouvernement de Normandie pendant la guerre de Paris, 1649* and the *Apologie ou deffence de Monsieur le duc de Beaufort contre la Cour, la Noblesse et le Peuple*, were published with the first clandestine edition as part of La Rochefoucauld's *Mémoires* in 1662. The first attributions to Saint-Evremond date from 1689 and 1690. Both pieces are among the controversial political writings of Saint-Evremond, giving slanted accounts of personalities and events connected with the Fronde. The *Lettre sur la paix*, probably of 1659–70, which seems to have established the link between Saint-Evremond and Foucquet's milieu, and therefore to have led to his exile, is an anti-Mazarin pamphlet denouncing the peace of the Pyrenees in 1659.

The probability is that the four pieces by Saint-Evremond published by Barbin in 1664—*Sur Seneque, Plutarque et Petrone*; *Sur Petrone*; *Sur Alexandre et Cesar*, and *La Matrone d'Ephese*—were left behind by him when he went into exile. They may have been written considerably earlier, perhaps even during the three months Saint-Evremond had spent in the Bastille in 1653, shortly after Desmarets de Saint-Sorlin's publication of *Les morales d'Epictète, de Socrate, de Plutarque et de Seneque*. They are partly reflections stimulated by Amyot's translation of Plutarch, by Petronius, and by Montaigne. They give radical and penetrating analyses of their subjects, showing clearly that, at the date at which they were written, Saint-Evremond's sympathies lay with Seneca's personality rather than his works, and with Plutarch's *Lives* rather than his moral works. Saint-Evremond writes not as a scholar, but engagingly as an amateur who enjoys reading Tacitus and admires the cultivated intellect and taste of the sceptical and imperturbable Petronius, whose death was "the finest in all antiquity."

The *Jugement sur les sciences où peut s'appliquer un honneste homme* was probably written between 1655 and 1661 and is again of interest primarily for the values which it reflects. Saint-Evremond appears not to write affectedly when he declares, "Je n'ay jamais eu de grands attachemens à la lecture (I have never been greatly drawn to reading)," preferring enjoyable company—a remark repeated in later essays. He deals with theology in a page inspired by Sorbière's 1649 and 1652 translations of Hobbes and, like Montaigne, regards the subject as one unsuitable for female study: "il est ridicule que les femmes mêmes osent agiter des questions qu'on devroit traiter avec beaucoup de mystere et de secret (it is ridiculous that even women should dare to discuss questions which should be treated as mysteries and in private)." This is an unusually reactionary position for any associate of Foucquet's circle. Theology, Saint-Evremond argues, depends on authority, and its discussion can lead only to desacralization and doubt. Although attracted by some aspects of Christian spiritualities, and increasingly by the social utility of religion, Saint-Evremond always found it difficult intellectually to accept the metaphysical foundations for Christian belief.

Saint-Evremond said that he preferred philosophy to theology, as it left the mind more freedom, but he relates how doubt had entered his own mind, once filled with certainty, and how Gassendi, "le plus éclairé des Philosophes et le moins presomptueux (the most enlightened and least presumptuous of philosophers)," in a series of conversations had convinced him that the human mind's unbounded quest for knowledge was combined with only a tiny area of certainty. A discipline which led to so restricted and precarious a reliable intellectual conviction seemed to Saint-Evremond not worth pursuing. But he differs from Gassendi in his resignation to metaphysical uncertainty, and in his solution to the problems arising from it, replacing the avoidance of pain, "l'indolence," as the end of life, with a more positive pursuit of such refined, varied, and balanced pleasures as friendship.

Neither his doubts nor his hedonism were in the least aggressive or, indeed, other than resigned. "Nous passons notre vie à croire et à ne croire point, à nous vouloir persuader et à ne pouvoir nous convaincre (We spend our lives believing and not believing, trying to persuade ourselves, and not convincing ourselves)." Saint-Evremond's attitude to life was in consequence pragmatic and, while he might have been attracted towards Spinoza's views, his reliance on personal experience perpetually prevented him from adhering to any philosophical system. His stance could be described as tolerant and Christian, but he was not convinced by Descartes's great effort to establish the spirituality, and therefore the immortality, of the soul.

Mathematics was too difficult, and only its applications were important to him, "car à parler sagement nous avons plus d'interest à jouïr du monde qu'à le connoître (because, if we are to talk sensibly, it is more in our interest to enjoy the world than to know it)." The only disciplines which have any interest for "les honnêtes gens (people of the world)" are "la Morale, la Politique et la connoissance des Belles Lettres," by which Saint-Evremond understands the practical aphorisms of moral teaching by which we learn "to govern our passions," statecraft, and the knowledge not of what we call "belles lettres" but of something nearer to what Erasmus and the renaissance humanists had called "bonae literae (good learning)," which had also had a clearly moral dimension. Saint-Evremond concludes by commending the relaxed philosophy of the Epicureans, which he understands in the light of Gassendi's Christian adaptation of Epicurus. Gassendi had taken his view largely from Diogenes Laertius, whose version of Epicurus's moral teaching is practically stoic and notably more austere than that of Lucretius, but Saint-Evremond is inclined to prefer the interpretation which makes of the sovereign good a more active pursuit of refined pleasure.

Saint-Evremond's letters to Joachim de Lionne, cousin of the minister Hugues de Lionne, show that Barbin's duodecimo *Oeuvres meslées* of 1668, signed simply "M.S.E." was published with his connivance. Racine's *Alexandre le Grand*, played at the end of 1665, was printed in January 1666. Saint-Evremond read the play and found it mediocre. He then re-wrote his criticisms in 1666–67, and prepared a third version. We do not know if the attenuated version printed by Barbin was this third version, or a fourth, written after Saint-Evremond had received copies of Racine's *Andromaque* and Pierre Corneille's *Attila* very early in 1668. Barbin's privilège is dated 2 May 1668. Saint-Evremond did see some merit in *Andromaque*, but always preferred the heroic values of Corneille to the analysis of passion in Racine, for reasons which perhaps had more to do with his military career than his sympathy for the aesthetic values of Foucquet's entourage, or for those of the partisans of the "modernes" in the Querelle des anciens et des modernes (q.v.). Corneille thanked him for his views.

Barbin's editions are very unreliable, of interest chiefly for the eagerness they demonstrate in the publisher to get hold of Saint-Evremond's material. The second part of the *Oeuvres meslées* of 1668 contains slight pieces, probably written, at least in first draft, before 1650. After 1668 there appeared a series of reprints and counterfeit editions stretching over a dozen years. *Les divers génies du peuple romain*, of which the first fragment was published in 1668 and whose publication was completed with Barbin's five anonymous volumes of 1684, started with an interest primarily in Hannibal and moved on towards a concern with the way in which Roman society's values had developed and with the history of conspiracies. The final work reflects Saint-Evremond's reactions to life in Holland, considering forms and styles of government, as well as Roman moral attitudes. Saint-Evremond's interest in classical antiquity had been stimulated in Holland by his friendship with Isaac Vossius, whose views can also be discerned behind Saint-Evremond's intervention in what he regarded as the futile dispute between Antoine Arnauld and Pastor Claude in 1669.

The 1684 volumes also contained a number of literary and moral essays probably written between 1665 and 1668. In "L'Interest dans les Personnes tout-à-fait corrompuës," Corruption is placed in opposition to duty, friendship, and gratitude, and is identified with "le vray genie de l'interest, que j'ay cultivé par l'estude, et fortifié par l'experience (the true spirit of self-interest, which I have cultivated by practice and strengthened by experience)." It is important that here, as elsewhere in Saint-Evremond, the French word "intérêt" has kept the strongly pejorative overtones it acquired in the theological contexts of the Jansenist (q.v.) and quietist disputes, although it is now being used outside any reference to Christian spiritual doctrine, and in La Rochefoucauld, unlike "amour-propre," had already lost them. Sometimes it is necessary, says Corruption, out of self-interest to affect disinterest. Corruption preens itself on preferring the useful to the upright, the "utile" to the "honnête."

S'attacher à l'utile, c'est suivre le dessein de la nature, qui par un secret instinct nous porte à ce qui nous convient, et nous oblige de ramener tout à nous-mesmes. L'honneur est un devoir imaginaire, qui pour la consideration d'autruy, nous fait abstenir des beins que nous pourrions avoir, ou nous deffaire de ceux que nous devrions garder

(To become attached to what is useful is to follow the design of nature, which leads us by a secret instinct towards that which suits us and makes us refer everything to ourselves. Honour is an imaginary duty which out of concern for other people makes us abstain from gratifications which we could have, or renounce those we should keep).

"La Vertu trop rigide (Too rigid Virtue)," whose name also implies a repudiation of the views expressed by the character, counsels the moderation of desires and the good utilisation of whatever fortune sends. It also praises the "repos (peace of mind)" brought by reason's conquest of "la fantaisie," here to be understood in its technical sense, as the faculty on which the passions depend. There is an implicit reference to Pierre Corneille and the ethical ambiguity of the character Cléopâtre's evilly directed moral grandeur in *Rodogune* in the view put forward by Virtue that

On trouve d'illustres scelerats, mais il ne fut jamais d'illustres avares. La grandeur de l'Ame ne peut compatir avec les ordures de l'avarice

(There are illustrious rogues, but there have never been illustrious misers. Greatness of soul is incompatible with the base actions of avarice).

The dispute between complete corruption and exaggerated virtue is resolved in "Les Sentimens d'un honneste et habile Courtisan," which may be supposed, even if not in any properly thought-through manner, to present an approximation to Saint-Evremond's own tentative view. What it most importantly contains is the essence of the "moderne" position, linking the attraction of Petronius and the *Divers génies* to the later moral and critical pieces.

Je sçay que la raison nous a esté donnée pour regler nos moeurs; mais la raison, autrefois rude et austere, s'est civilisé avec le temps, et ne conserve aujourd'huy presque rien de son ancienne rigidité. Il luy a falu de l'austérité pour établir des loix qui puissent empescher les outrages et les violences; elle s'est adoucie pour introduire l'honnesteté dans le commerce des hommes; elle est devenuë delicate et curieuse dans la recherche des plaisirs, pour rendre la vie aussi agreable qu'elle estoit des-ja seure et honneste

(I know that we were given reason to regulate our behaviour; but reason, once rough and harsh, has become civilized with time, and today keeps almost none of its former inflexibility. It needed harshness to establish the laws which could prevent aggression and violence; it softened to introduce polish into human intercourse; it has become delicate and cultivated in the quest for pleasure, to make life as enjoyable as it was already regulated and polished).

Merit, argues the courtier, now includes "la politesse, la galanterie, la science des voluptez (good manners, galanterie, the science of pleasure)." Pleasure can now be morally good, and virtue no longer consists solely in the effort needed to contain the desires which natural savagery imposed on the first generations. This is precisely the view to be endorsed a quarter of a century later in Perrault's still daring *Parallèles des anciens et des modernes*. Saint-Evremond's courtier now goes on, more delicately, to argue that Cato's virtue was too absolute. He might have saved his country had he been less exigent.

Une probité moins entiere, qui se fust accommodée aux vices de quelques particuliers, eut empesché l'oppression generale

(A less total probity, ready to tolerate the vicious conduct of a few, would have prevented the oppression of all).

A partly corrupt republic would have been the result, but that would have been better than the tyranny which in fact took its place. Did La Bruyère know that Saint-Evremond's courtier advised not so to envisage the world as it should be, as not to be able to endure it as it is, when he famously used the same antithesis, comparing Corneille and Racine in *Les Caractères*? Saint-Evremond's courtier suggests that the ungrateful and the miserly can be cured by an appeal not to their better natures, but to their own interests. Self-interest is beginning to point the way to virtue. The whole thrust of the courtier's argument is that the establishment of well-ordered social intercourse is itself a good to be cultivated, and a goal more important to achieve than confronting everybody with the highest requirements of austere virtue. Besides, argues the courtier, in each of us there is some mixture of the bad with the good, and we each have different virtues and vices.

Apart from two prose comedies *Sir Politick Would-be*, written with English friends, and *Les Opera*, published in 1705, and the *Conversation du Maréchal d'Hocquincourt avec le P. Canaye*, published in a Dutch collection of 1687, most of the authentic works of Saint-Evremond which Barbin did not publish in the series of volumes ending in 1684 are contained in the quarto *Oeuvres meslées* in the two volumes of 1689 and 1692. The date of publication is not, however, generally related to the date of composition, which often precedes publication by anything up to 20 years, and Barbin's 1689 text is often faulty. A reading from one or other of the surviving manuscripts has often rightly been preferred by René Ternois, the editor of the critical edition of 1962–69, whose cautious dating of the individual essays is here being followed.

Most of the essays on literary topics date from before the arrival in London of the duchesse Mazarin in whose salon, Saint-Evremond complained, gaming soon made serious conversation impossible. Some of the literary essays date from as early as 1669, and occasionally references to works published afterwards were subsequently inserted. Saint-Evremond preferred his own century to the age of Sophocles, and also Pierre Corneille to Racine, although his taste was partly conditioned by the English stage, where he preferred the strength of the passions displayed to the galanterie of Quinault, while still remaining attached to the French "bienséances (proprieties)" and regularities.

Saint-Evremond's literary essays include those on comedies, French historians, taste, opera, and translators. *Sur les tragédies* extols Corneille above Sophocles, whom Saint-Evremond must have read in Latin, and Euripides, a little of whose work was available in French. Corneille is praised for his understanding of the emotions and his judicious use of love to soften the horrors of antique tragedy without, however, abandoning pity and terror for "de petits soûpirs ennuieux (tedious little sighs)." Saint-Evremond lists other plays which have moved him, and names tragedies by Tristan, Mairet, Du Ryer, Rotrou, Thomas Corneille, and Racine, although letters to Lionne of March–April 1668 and March–April 1670 make it clear that Saint-Evremond can only hope the Racine of *Britannicus* will one day equal the achievements of Corneille. Saint-Evremond has nothing good to say about the Italian plays he has been to, and would like the English plays he has seen to be made more regular, to accord more with the bienséances and the unities, confining the more violent actions to a "récit," or messenger's report.

The *Conversation de M. le Maréchal d'Hocquincourt avec le Père Canaye*, perhaps the most celebrated of Saint-Evremond's pieces, must date from about 1669, although it did not become widely known until about 1686 and was published only in the Dutch collection of 1687, *Le Retour des Pièces choisies*. Although the characters represent real people, the *Conversation* certainly misrepresents the views of Père Canaye, if he was the actual Jesuit whose pupil Saint-Evremond may conceivably have been, rather than a random representative of the order, and it cannot be a reliable guide to Hocquincourt, a maréchal in charge of royal armies during the Fronde, who was the lover of Mme de Châtillon, was—not only on that account—mistrusted by Mazarin, and was persuaded by Mme de Châtillon to desert to Condé and the Dutch, for whom he subsequently fought. He died in battle on 12 June 1658. The last 30 lines were clearly added to the body of the text to link it to the *Conversation de M. d'Aubigny* of much the same date.

The Hocquincourt piece is quite short, a sparring match between the blustering free-thinking soldier and the astute Jesuit. Hocquincourt must be careful, warns Père Canaye, of the devil seeking whom he may devour or, "pis que devorer (worse than devour)," make into a Jansenist. Saint-Evremond's mockery of the Jesuit is on a light-hearted register. It is innocent to love war, "Aller à la guerre est servir son Prince; et servir son prince est servir Dieu (To go to war is to serve your sovereign; and to serve your sovereign is to serve God)." It is however sinful to covet Mme de Montbazon, notoriously the mistress of Rancé who, after her death in 1657, had become seriously devout, reformed the abbey of La Trappe, and by the date of the *Conversation* was well known for the terrifying austerities he imposed on his monks. The lightness of the irony is remarkable. The Jesuit thanks God for the way in which Hocquincourt, jealous of Rancé's success with Mme de Montbazon, is moved away from Jansenism, and subsequently away from rational argument to true belief. The final, added section is much heavier and clumsier but, although the *Conversation* makes fun of the Jesuit, it does not go beyond amusing irreverence. Of itself it tells us nothing about Saint-Evremond's beliefs.

The *Conversation avec M. de Candale* was written at least in part by 1668, although the text we have cannot have been finished before 1670. Saint-Evremond remembers here, as in some other pieces, incidents from his life twenty years previously. The *Conversation* is virtually a series of portraits combined into a memoir. The short moral treatises, often perceptive and always intelligent, are sometimes also revealing about moral attitudes and values, although too slight to warrant detailed individual consideration here. They are much more than merely charming and delicate. Saint-Evremond is in full reaction against the excesses of the galanterie of the pre-Fronde period, and continues to uphold the heroic values of Corneille. On love and friend-

ship he emphasises in the text *Sur l'amitié*, composed of fragments written at different moments between 1668 and 1678, the by then old-fashioned up-grading of instinctive love by reference to a judgement about the merit of its object:

> Ce que je veux dans les Amitiés, c'est que les lumières précédent les mouvemens, et qu'une estime justement formée dans l'Esprit, aille s'animer dans le Coeur, et y prendre la chaleur nécessaire pour les Amitiés, comme pour l'Amour. Aimez donc, Madame, mais n'aimez que des Sujets dignes de vous

> (What I am looking for in friendships is that knowledge should precede affections, and that an esteem formed for good cause in the mind should go to be quickened in the heart, and find there the warmth necessary for friendships, as for love. Love, then, Madame, but love only subjects worthy of you).

In *Sur les caractères des tragédies*, Saint-Evremond carefully defines the terms used of loving, "aimer (to love)," "brûler (to burn)," and "languir (to languish)," which he regards as the finest of love's movements. He blames the diminution of the popularity of Corneille on an excessive refinement in his analysis of sentiment.

> Aprés avoir comme usé les passions ordinaires dont nous sommes agités, il s'est fait un nouveau merite à toucher des tendresses plus recherchées, de plus fines jalousies et de plus secretes douleurs; mais cette étude de penetration étoit trop delicate pour les grandes assemblées, et une decouverte si pretieuse luy a fait perdre quelque estime dans le monde, au lieu qu'elle devoit luy donner une nouvelle reputation

> (Having as it were used up the ordinary passions by which we are moved, he achieved a new merit in reaching more refined sentiments, sharper jealousies, and more private griefs; but this effort towards greater penetration was too delicate for large audiences, and so precious a discovery caused him to lose some of the world's favour when it should have won him a new reputation).

Most of the remaining treatises reiterate what has been said before. *Sur les anciens*, of very uncertain date, reaffirms the changes in moral attitudes with the evolution of human society and prefers the sublime to the mythical, the bare truth to the fables in which it had traditionally had to be wrapped for the earliest generations. Aesthetically, there are very few enduring principles. The *Réflexions sur la religion*, probably written soon after 1675, show a subtlety of psychological analysis unsurpassed by any other moralist and equalled by very few. Saint-Evremond delicately points to the satisfaction to be gained from self-mastery and abstinence before giving his criteria for authentic devotion and re-emphasizing the uncertainty we suffer as our minds move back and forth between religion and nature, just as our senses, when gratified, send us back to religious solace, which itself makes us feel the need for sensual satisfaction. "Dans la plûpart des chrétiens, l'envie de croire tient lieu de créance (In most Christians, the desire to believe takes the place of belief)." It is even possible to love God sincerely without believing in him. God alone can give us a firm, sure faith. All we can do is compel our minds to belief in spite of natural reason, and do what is prescribed. Saint-Evremond does not enter here, with Pascal and Nicole, into the relationship between belief, behaviour, grace, and justification.

In a text for Ninon de Lenclos, *Sur la morale d'Epicure* of perhaps 1684, Saint-Evremond discusses the nature of Epicurus's "volupté," at this point rejecting the earlier attempts which had been made to reduce it to mere stoicism. In a young person, the sovereign good has to mean more than mere tranquillity. There are further delicate passages of psychological analysis, for instance in *Sur la complaisance qu'ont les femmes en leur beauté*. The long essay *A Monsieur le Maréchal de Créqui*, composed between 1669 and 1671, is prefaced by a lengthy introduction written much later, probably in 1685–86, in the relaxed tone of a man who was over 70. The whole work is a reflection on moral attitudes and literary experiences, modelled on Montaigne, containing a large number of fascinating reflections and judgements, scarcely related to one another, and offering a mellow but fundamentally unchanged series of views.

In the end Saint-Evremond's interests are more socially orientated than is often assumed. It is for its its social utility above all that he warms to Christianity, and it is social considerations which underpin his aesthetic criteria. His short discourses were immensely popular. There were innumerable counterfeit editions and inauthentic works printed over his name. He spoke to France from the freedom of exile and was avidly read. Although quite clearly of his own age, his works mark him out as not so much a precursor as an early author of the French enlightenment.

PUBLICATIONS

[*Saint-Evremond himself published nothing, but connived at some publication. Spurious and counterfeit editions are not listed*]

Collections

Oeuvres meslées de Mr de Saint-Evremond, 2 vols., 1705
Oeuvres meslées de Mr de Saint-Evremond, 5 vols., 1706
Mélange curieux des meilleures pièces attribuées à Mr de Saint-Evremond, 1706
Oeuvres en prose, 4 vols., 1962–69
Lettres, 2 vols., 1967–68

Early Barbin editions [including many texts not by Saint-Evremond: items 2–8 give the appearance of a single duodecimo edition of 11 volumes, although signed differently or not at all]

Jugement sur Sénèque, Plutarque et Petrone, 1664
Oeuvres meslées, 1668
Seconde partie des Oeuvres meslées de M. D***, 1668
Oeuvres meslées de M. de S.E., vol. 3, 1670
Oeuvres meslées de M. D*** vol. 4, 1670
Oeuvres meslées de M.S.E., vol.5, [reprint of 1664 volume] 1678
Oeuvres meslées, vol. 6, 1680
Réflexions sur les divers génies du peuple romain, 5 vols., 1684
Oeuvres meslées, 2 vols., 1689, 1692 [quarto]

Translations of collections into English

Miscellany. Essays by Monsieur de St. Evremont, vol. 2, 1694
Mixt Essays … by the Sieur de Saint-Euvremont, 1685
Miscellanea … by the Sieur de Saint-Evremont, 1686
Miscellaneous Essays, by Monsieur Saint-Euremont, 1692

Biographical and critical studies

Schmidt, A.-M., *Saint-Evremond; ou, L'Humanisme impur*, 1932
Spalatin, K., *Saint-Evremond*, 1934
Ternois, René, Introductions and notes in the *Oeuvres en prose* and the *Lettres* (see above under Collections)

SAINT-SIMON, Louis de Rouvroy, duc de, 1675–1755.

Author of memoirs.

LIFE

Saint-Simon was born vidame de Chartres in Paris on 5 January 1675, the only son of a 68-year-old father and a 31-year-old mother. His father, Claude de Saint-Simon, had been made a duke and peer by Louis XIII whose first écuyer and favourite he was. By a first marriage the father had had a daughter who became duchesse de Brissac and died without issue in 1684, leaving as her residuary legatee Saint-Simon, as it is simpler to call him from the outset to avoid confusion with Philippe d'Orléans, still duc de Chartres. His mother, Charlotte de Laubespine de Châteauneuf d'Hauterive, was a cousin of Mme de Maintenon and friend of Mme de Montespan. Saint-Simon was her only child, constantly warned by his mother that his elderly father and her own lack of worldly accomplishments meant that he would have to make his own way in the world. Saint-Simon tells us that his great fondness for history, especially French memoirs since François I,

> me firent naître l'envie d'écrire aussi ceux de ce que je verrois, dans le désir et dans l'espérance d'être de quelquechose et de savoir le mieux que je pourrais les affaires de mon temps

> (bred in me the desire to write those [memoirs] of what I would myself see, in the desire and hope of counting myself for something in, and knowing as well as possible, the affairs of my time).

He began these "memoirs" after reading Bassompierre when he was a maître de camp, roughly the equivalent of a colonel, of his own regiment at Guinsheim on the Rhine in 1694.

Saint-Simon tells us that in 1691 he was in the top class at the small private school for nobles in the rue des Canettes. He was already friendly with Philippe d'Orléans, still known as the duc de Chartres, the king's nephew and the future regent, Saint-Simon's senior by eight months, whom Saint-Simon wanted to join in the army. Saint-Simon's early education had been broad but good, in the hands of a tutor from whom he learnt Latin, German, and history, but who also instilled into him a serious Christian piety. School, with its emphasis on cadet-like military training and horsemanship, had the predictable and probably desired effect, and Saint-Simon persuaded his father to arrange for him in 1691 to become a musketeer, a necessary preliminary to the captaincy of cavalry or the artillery commission required before an officer was allowed to buy a regiment of which he would be colonel.

In 1692, when he was 17, Saint-Simon fought at Namur, and the following year was given a captaincy in the cavalry. On 2 May 1693 his father, whose memory haunts the *Mémoires*, passed over to Saint-Simon his offices and possessions, so preserving them from creditors when, later the same day, he died. Saint-Simon was in the victorious French army at Neerwinden in 1693, and in due course was bought his post as colonel of the regiment of Paul of Lorraine, killed at Neerwinden, over whose standard of discipline Saint-Simon was taken to task by Louis XIV. Like his marriage, Saint-Simon regarded his military career firstly as a duty imposed on him by his standing as a duke and peer in succession to his father.

In 1692 the future regent, the king's nephew, had married the youngest of the king's daughters by Mme de Montespan, the 15-year-old Mlle de Blois. Saint-Simon, who recounts how the king's decision was made known to all the parties concerned, including bride and groom, was himself urged by his mother early in 1694 to marry and makes clear that his first consideration was his high aristocratic station. With his mother's approval he sought to marry the eldest daughter of Paul, duc de Beauvillier, son of a friend of his father, like him a duke and peer, married to Colbert's second daughter, minister of finance from 1685, then minister of state in succession to Louvois in 1691, and himself charged with supervising the education of the dauphin's three children, the ducs de Bourgogne, d'Anjou and de Berry. Beauvillier was therefore Fénelon's immediate superior in his post as tutor.

He had two sons and eight daughters, of whom seven became nuns, including the eldest, whom Saint-Simon had never seen, and who was 14 when Saint-Simon sought her hand. Told by her father that she wanted to be a nun, and that the second daughter was not marriageable, Saint-Simon asked for the third, who was 12. Saint-Simon's account of the interview is delightful, if self-congratulatory, but Beauvillier, who said that nobody had ever argued with him as Saint-Simon had just done and who asked Saint-Simon to treat him as a father, told him to come back the next day, when the answer was a regretful negative. There were too many complications, mostly caused by the potential religious vocations and, although Saint-Simon persisted, nothing except protestations of good will came of the approach.

Before rejoining the army, Saint-Simon went to see Rancé at La Trappe. He was to remain friendly with Rancé until Rancé's death, and was inclined like Rancé to austerity in matters of religion, if only because of Louis XIV's general hostility to Jansenist (q.v.) spirituality as well as to what he regarded as its insubordination in matters of theology. Saint-Simon's Jansenist sympathies waned somewhat during the regency when some informal collusion between the Jansenists and the parlement could be discerned. It was at this point that occurred the clash with the Luxembourgs which occasioned what Saint-Simon in his important letter to Rancé of 29 March 1699 thought the most bitter passage of the *Mémoires* as they then existed. The affair blocked Saint-Simon's career, cost him the king's confidence, and demonstrated his pertinacity in defence of the established order and traditional privilege, as well as a certain bad-tempered obstinacy and an aristocratic disdain for the proprieties. The immediate occasion of his intransigence was the desire of the duc de Luxembourg to be raised in order of precedence among the peers from eighteenth to second. Luxembourg was a Montmorency, the brilliant, slightly hunch-backed marshal and general of the army in which Saint-Simon was serving, son of the comte de Bouteville whom Louis XIII had had executed for duelling in 1627, and known as the "tapissier de Notre-Dame" from the number of enemy colours he captured and hung in the cathedral.

A peerage or "pairie" in France was not precisely personal. It came with a fief which was erected into a comté-pairie or duché-pairie and the group of dukes and peers, which had once exercised the original functions of the parlements, was being again conceived, in reaction to the king's absolutizing of power, as an inchoate grand council of state, to which Saint-Simon wanted more power to be given. That was the background to his clash with Louis XIV. However, the quarrel with Luxembourg was neither trivial nor merely symbolic. Luxembourg's intimate association with Condé during the Fronde did not subsequently endear him to Louis XIV, and when in 1661 he married Madeleine de Luxembourg-Piney, princesse de Tingry, the greatest heiress in France, his patent as duke and peer ranked Luxembourg 18th. After Neerwinder he claimed second place by virtue of his wife's family's elevation in 1571. He was supported by Harlay, the premier président, by Racine, and by the king, grateful to Harlay for smoothing the way for the marriages of the king's children by Mme de Montespan and their legitimization. The upset caused by Luxembourg's claim seemed to give the king an opportunity to have his illegitimately born children raised in precedence above the other peers, and finally made able to succeed to the throne. Saint-Simon's vigorous advocacy, and the succession of legal cases he brought on behalf of the peers of France against Luxembourg, did his career much immediate damage, but Luxembourg's precedence was not altered. The "royal bastards" were deprived of their precedence after their father died and Saint-Simon triumphed at the Regent's side, to the relief of the country's ancient nobility.

After the dispute, Saint-Simon moved away from Luxembourg's command to serve in Germany under the maréchal de Lorges, whose eldest daughter, Gabrielle de Durfort, aged 17, he married at midnight on 8 April 1695. He was 20. The match was not at all dynastically orientated, but dictated by prudent bourgeois financial considerations. Saint-Simon said of his mother-in-law "Qu'elle avoit fait oublier ce qu'elle était née (that she had made people forget what she had been born)." Bussy called her the daughter of a servant. The bride was presented to the king, who immediately invited her to sit, that is to use the privilege of the tabouret accorded to the wife of a duke and peer. His wife was to bear Saint-Simon three children, Charlotte, the future duchesse de Chimay, Jacques-Louis, duc de Ruffec and father of the comte de Valentinois, and Armand-Jean, marquis de Ruffec, named after the abbé de Rancé. Saint-Simon and his wife became renowned for the strong affection which developed between them.

In the January 1702 promotion Saint-Simon was not made a brigadier, and immediately, in accordance, he says, with the unanimous advice of his father-in-law, Choiseul, and a host of other prominent acquaintances, resigned from the army, a move which increased the disfavour in which the king held him. He remained assiduous in his attendance at court, however, intensely curious about its workings, drawing information from a series of highly placed friends, and observing very closely. There was some question of an ambassadorship to Rome to which the marquis de Torcy persuaded Louis XIV to appoint Saint-Simon in 1705, but it was cancelled before anything happened. Discouraged and bitter, Saint-Simon was tempted to give up his court life and retire to his country estates, but his mother and his wife managed to dissuade him, and in 1710 his wife was made duchess-in-waiting to the duchesse de Berry, daughter of the future regent and of one of Louis XIV's daughters by Mme de Montespan. Saint-Simon had himself grown close to the duc de Bourgogne before his death in 1712, and was to succeed in getting his friend Philippe d'Orléans to break with his mistress, Mme d'Argenton.

Just as he wrote with seigneurial disdain for rules and purity of language, so also he disdained the ordinary rules of prudence by forcing an interview with the king to find out where exactly he stood. Louis XIV told him that he was too flamboyant and too critical, "c'est que vous parlez et que vous blâmez; voilà ce qui fait qu'on parle contre vous (it's because you speak too openly, and you criticize; that's what makes people speak ill of you)." Saint-Simon was, however, accorded a warmer mix of those minute signs by which favour and disfavour could be measured at Versailles, the most important of which was an apartment in the château.

Soon, however, Saint-Simon's importance shot upwards. The deathbed scene of the dauphin in 1711 is one of Saint-Simon's more masterly set pieces, and the dauphin's death also made the duc de Bourgogne successor to the throne. For a short period Saint-Simon and his young protégé, pupil of Beauvillier and Fénelon, planned together the future of France, naming names. Saint-Simon wanted a constitutional monarchy, but with the ancient aristocracy forming a council of state. He was promised the governorship of the young duc de Bretagne. Then in 1712 the duc de Bourgogne, his wife, and the elder of his two surviving children, all died in an epidemic, leaving only the future Louis XV. Of the duc de Bourgogne's brothers, the duc d'Anjou had become Philip V of Spain and had solemnly renounced for himself and his heirs all right to the French succession in the 1713 treaty of Utrecht, and the duc de Berry was to die in 1714, the year before his grandfather, Louis XIV. In 1714 Louis XIV was 76 and his successor was two. The regent was to be Saint-Simon's childhood companion and lasting friend, Philippe d'Orléans. Mme de Maintenon's attempt to ensure that real power was held by the duc du Maine failed.

Saint-Simon appeared to have a real political future. He declined the post of governor of Louis XV and says he turned down the post of first minister. It is more likely that he stopped it from being given to Noailles. He defeated the machinations of the duc du Maine, whose precedence he so fiercely resented, and he was a close adviser to the regent. He was a member of the council of regency, but he was given no real power. He had declared too many of his cards too far in advance, and he was too impulsive, determinedly aristocratic, and committed to a France ruled by the seven councils now instituted, which, in his view, should have been exclusively composed of nobles. The nobles, however, as well as the parlements, resented the high-handedness of the peers, even to the extent of siding with the legitimized princes; and the astute, ambitious, and unscrupulous commoner Cardinal Dubois, the regent's old tutor, now fresh from his diplomatic alliances with Britain and Holland on 4 January 1717, was soon to impose himself as the real source of political authority. Dubois, by far the more intelligent of the two, and the better politician, disliked Saint-Simon, and was despised by him.

Dubois's policies succeeded in enticing Spain into cooperation with what became in 1720 the quadruple alliance of France, England, Holland, and Austria. Philip V had conspired with the duchesse du Maine to undo the provisions of the treaty of Utrecht, but now wanted to abdicate, as in 1724 he briefly did, and sought to regain the French succession for his son. In the interest of securing strong French protection, he now offered the infanta's hand to Louis XV and asked for the hand of the regent's daughter, Mlle de Montpensier, for his own heir. In July 1721 Saint-Simon was appointed ambassador extraordinary to organize the exchange of the princesses, which took place on 9 January 1722. He had arranged for modest recompense for services rendered to the regent by assuring the succession of his inherited governorships for his sons and the repayment of his father's debts to the state. His emoluments as governor of Senlis were increased, and his sister-in-law was given an abbey. The somewhat perfunctory ceremonial duties of the ambassador extraordinary were the subject of equally perfunctory Spanish honours and a great deal of protocol, to whose exact observance Saint-Simon clearly attached great importance. Both sons, but not his wife, accompanied him, and although he caught smallpox and his elder son a bad fever, he was made a grandee, and his elder son a member of the Order of the Golden Fleece. There were, by Saint-Simon's own account, petty but imperious exhibitions of tantrums when things went wrong.

Saint-Simon stayed in Madrid from 21 November 1721 to 24 March 1722. When he returned to Paris he found himself deprived by Dubois of all real influence. He had warned the regent against Law's financial system which collapsed in 1720. By the end of the preceding year Law's banknotes had become indistinguishable from share certificates, and were trading well above their face value, with 500-livre notes trading as high as 15,000–18,000 livres by November 1719. The dividend of 40% declared that year on the face value represented a real return of under 1½%, and payment against the notes was suspended on 1 November 1720. Saint-Simon escaped personal loss, but the crippling of France's economic power and colonizing ability was to reverberate for a century. On Law's collapse, d'Aguesseau was brought back. His Jansenist leanings commended him to the parlement. Dubois was elevated to the sacred college of cardinals in July 1721 and had himself named first minister, ousting d'Aguesseau, whose Jansenist sympathies displeased Rome. The council had lost its power, and Saint-Simon resigned from it in favour of his elder son, who was not, however, admitted to the parlement until Saint-Simon's formal retirement from it in 1733. Saint-Simon's seven councils were replaced by a revival of the old secretaries.

The king was consecrated at Reims, and a 13-year-old boy became ruler of France. The regent resigned on 16 February 1723, and Louis XV appointed as first minister the duc de Bourbon, grandson of le grand Condé, who immediately repudiated the Spanish marriage and sent the infanta back to Spain. Saint-Simon had already retired from the court, but on 10 August Dubois died, and for a brief period that autumn Saint-Simon was again influential, until the ex-regent died of a heart attack on 2 December.

From now on little is known of Saint-Simon's activities in retirement. He exchanged over 1,000 letters with Cardinal Gualterio and spent most of his time on his estates at La Ferté-Vidame, near Chartres. From 1714 to 1746 he had a large house in Paris. He moved about for four years, and spent the last five years of his life from May 1750 in Paris, in a house in the rue de Grenelle. The *Mémoires* were written between 1739 and 1751. Saint-Simon's wife died on 21 January 1743, then his two sons. He himself died on 2 March 1755, and was buried alongside his wife at La Ferté-Vidame.

WORKS

On Saint-Simon's death no one knew of the existence of his carefully written out *Mémoires*, to which a supplement, going to the death of Fleury, has been lost. Saint-Simon died heavily indebted, and there was an immediate quarrel among his heirs about the 277 bound manuscript volumes in the inventory, some of which were relevant to the country's administration. A court decree entrusted the manuscripts to a notary, until in 1760 they passed definitively into the archives of the ministry of foreign affairs. Choiseul, the minister, had them abridged by Voisenon, and the resulting nine volumes were all that the 18th century ever knew of the *Mémoires*. Copies of the manuscript quickly circulated, and it was partially published around 1780. Further editions followed swiftly, at least seven in 10 years, with that of 1788 the first to bear its author's name. The first complete edition was that of 1829–30.

There is no real evidence that Saint-Simon ever intended his *Mémoires*, as they were written between 1739 and 1751, for publication. In his concluding chapter after having reached the death of the regent in 1723, Saint-Simon reaffirms once more what has been his intention throughout, "J'ai préféré la vérité à tout, et je n'ai pu me ployer à aucun déguisement (I have preferred truth to everything, and I have not been able to bend myself to any concealment)," before going on to say that impartiality was an impossible ideal to which he did not aspire. However, he holds to the exactness of the facts, while realizing that "si ces Mémoires voient jamais le jour (if these Mémoires ever see the light of day)," what he has in 1751 just finished writing would still be likely to cause strong feelings, "une prodigieuse révolte (enormous revulsion)."

If there is no evidence that he then expected them to be published, it seems almost certain from the fact that his will, dated 26 June 1754, does not mention the manuscript, and from its subsequent history, not only that he did not, but that their final redaction had taken this fact into account. It is full of vivid, cruel, violent lampoons, ungrammatical and maliciously expressive coinages, and wonderfully unfair caricatures. The text, nearly 7,500 pages in the modern Bibliothèque de la Pléiade edition, was also too long for publication to be seriously envisaged. Half a century earlier, on 29 March 1699, when Saint-Simon had written to the abbé de Rancé, he had had about five years' worth of records of personal impressions, started in 1694, which he referred to as "des espèces de Mémoires de ma vie (a sort of memoir of my life)," on which he said he had been working. There were two versions, that in the first person making clear who the author was and that in the third at least quasi-anonymously referring to himself as to any other person appearing in the pages.

At about the date of the letter to Rancé, Saint-Simon appears to have abandoned the writing up of his impressions, and even to have wondered whether the way he had "satisfied his inclinations and passions" in speaking about other people did not mean that he should burn the text. He asked Rancé for advice about how he should write, sending him examples, including a copy of what he had written about M. de Luxembourg and his son, which he thought "faithful to the most exact truth," but considered to be that part of the text which was "[le] plus âpre et [le] plus amer (most harsh and most bitter).

The publication of Retz's *Mémoires* in 1717 had caused a sensation, and a whole series of memoirs published between 1717 and 1720, including those of Retz, Mme de Motteville, Gourville, Brienne, and Joly, must have encouraged Saint-Simon to think of writing again himself, perhaps for posthumous publication, but it was not until 1729, when the duc de Luynes communicated to him in his retirement the manuscript of Dangeau's *Journal*, on which Saint-Simon compiled comments, that he thought of giving final form to the *Mémoires*, and not until 1739 that he started work. Dangeau's *Journal*, Saint-Simon said, was "d'une fadeur à faire vomir (dull enough to make you sick)," however much he relied on it. The *Mémoires* as we know them were probably the product of a conversation of Saint-Simon with himself, and probably belong to the long list of major literary works whose authors are the subject of entries in the *Guide* but which were never intended by their authors to be published.

Major works by Pascal, Retz, La Rochefoucauld, Saint-Evremond, Mme de Sévigné, Boileau, Diderot, and Sade are among those whose writers did not mean them to be put into public circulation. Many other writers published with what were clearly varying gradations of anonymity and pseudonymity, which is a somewhat different matter, but sometimes the works of the authors mentioned were clearly not intended for any eyes but those of their writers. Of these only some were meant to be copied and shown to a selected group of friends, and perhaps a few were disseminated in manuscript in the hope that publication would take place in circumstances which would allow authorship subsequently to be disavowed.

With Saint-Simon, writing about relatively recent history, trying to be accurate, but aware of the strength of feeling he was stirring up in himself, the interpretation of the work hinges, more than with most of the others, on the existence or absence of any intention to publish. Was he essentially a chronicler, too indisciplined not to interpolate vast surveys, flash-backs, and summings-up, carefully prejudiced, arresting set pieces, combining amused detachment of language with real emotion? or a historian whose view of what had happened a third of a century earlier was distorted by prejudice, spite, and narrowness of intelligence? Was he simply a purveyor of elevated but well out-of-date gossip? Or was he writing an interpretation of his career for his grandchildren, or for self-vindication, or re-writing the past either to comply with his strong sense of nostalgia, or to mediate to himself, and perhaps others, some understanding of the present and the future?

Did he compile an account of the court from 1691 to 1723 for the purposes for which people keep snapshot albums, selecting and rejecting entries for much the same variety of reasons? Was he at heart more of a moralist than a politician, anxious to understand the interplay of motivations, appearances, personalities, and situations from which emerge policies and the exercising of power, and from which enduring political laws can be induced? What kept him trying to recreate the court as it actually was, dealing out some sort of aristocratically offhand justice when, for his own private purposes, particularly after the death of his wife and his two sons, he might simply have indulged the malicious, prejudiced, vindictive recollections of his career as a failed grandee?

He might, after all, have broken the rules of his own game, and merely have comforted his old age with the warped satisfaction which comes from elegantly assuaging a life-time of resentment, disdain, and sheer spite. He does not write as if he supposed in 1751, or a little earlier, that anyone would any longer be interested in the minor part he had played in public affairs, or as if he was in quest of posthumous fame or pecuniary reward, or even the satisfaction of creating what he felt was a literary masterpiece by flouting all the established rules of good writing. The point about the *Mémoires* which is often missed is that their literary quality derives precisely from the tension between the desire to move and the need to parody, the urge to be fair and the need to be vindictive, the nostalgia for what never happened and the disdain for what did.

"Il faut que celui qui écrit aime la vérité jusqu'à lui sacrifier toutes choses (Whoever wants to write must love truth to the point of sacrificing everything to it)," wrote Saint-Simon, meaning surely that the memorialist must present what happened as it happened, but as he himself sees it. It is true that Saint-Simon did not have Retz's intelligence or lucidity, but he was not writing for the same reasons. He did not write as well as Chateaubriand, but his purposes were different. Saint-Simon was well aware that his wickedly malicious remarks about people and events would amuse, but also argue a point of view, that he could afford to indulge crusty animosities and a fascination with protocol only because he was genuinely capable of being moved.

Easiest to savour, even extracted from the long, meandering, and syntactically involved sentences in which they are often embedded, are the pungent phrases: "cuistres violets (purple prigs)" for bishops; "mine de chat fâché (expression of an angry cat)," to describe a politician; "un quart de femme, une espèce de biscuit manqué (a scrap of a woman, a sort of sponge cake that did not rise)" of Mme de Castries; "après avoir rougi de la sorte (after having gone red like that)" of a newly created cardinal; "une manière d'éléphant pour la figure, une espèce de boeuf pour l'esprit (the appearance of some sort of elephant, the mind of a kind of ox)" for Bélébat; "un soldat aux gardes, et même un peu suisse, habillé en femme (a guardsman, with a touch of Swiss mercenary, dressed as a woman)" for the duchesse de Cheaulnes. Of Harlay we are told that "il portoit sous son manteau toute la fatuité que le maréchal de Villeroy étaloit sous son baudrier (he carried under his cloak the stupidity which the marshal de Villeroy exhibited under his sword–belt)," while Villeroy had a face "exactly like a fat parrot," and as for others, "l'odeur de la Ligue leur sortait par les pores (they sweated the stench of the League)."

Some of Saint-Simon's best expressions do violence to the language, as when he mentions the "tout permis au gendre du tout-puissant ministre (the all-permitted to the son-in-law of the all-powerful minister)," or writes with simple negligence, taking no notice of agreements, or loading sentences with unrelated pronouns. The striving for vivid terseness occasionally dips into obscurity, although the metaphors are often striking, and the effect is varied artlessly as Saint-Simon slips into the first-person reaction of someone whose reactions he is describing, or announces a set piece by an exclamation: "Quel spectacle! (what a sight!" or comically switches tenses to exaggerate the effect on Charost of a remark which Saint-Simon has just made.

> Voilà Charost qui chancelle (nous étions debout), qui veut répondre, et qui balbutie: la gorge s'enfle, les yeux lui sortent de la tête, et la langue de la bouche: Mme de Nogaret s'écrie; Mme du Châtelet saute à sa cravate qu'elle lui défait, et le col de sa chemise; Mme de Saint-Simon court à un pot d'eau, lui en jette, et tâche de l'asseoir et de lui en faire avaler

> (Now Charost is reeling (we were standing). He wants to reply, and stammers. His throat swells, the eyes come out of his head and the tongue from his mouth: Mme de Nogaret screams; Mme du Châtelet leaps at his cravate, which she undoes, and his shirt collar; Mme de Saint-Simon runs to a jug of water, throws some at him, and tries to sit him down and get him to swallow some).

The high-point of the text is the 1718 lit de justice at which the late king's illegitimately born children were stripped of their special prerogatives, but the set pieces also include portraits, summaries, descriptions, assessments of achievements, scores of portraits, and a number of death scenes. Louis XIV cannot have been as fully employed in controlling the niceties of social distinctions and behaviour marked by his favour or disfavour as Saint-Simon makes out, but the insight into the way in which Versailles was designed to fulfil its various, and in Saint-Simon's view often nefarious functions fascinated him, as it continues to fascinate modern readers. How did Versailles work? That is one of the principal questions addressed by the *Mémoires*, although Saint-Simon is really interested in only some of its functions. But what deviousness of mind, Saint-Simon reflects, went into the creation of the court, the power centre, the military headquarters, the pleasure palace, the administrative complex, the espionage service, and the hunting lodge at Versailles, through which Louis XIV contrived to rule his large country, control his court, and indulge his private pleasures and extravagant tastes? Did Saint-Simon really so deplore the loss of the view at Saint-Germain, where members of the court had had to take lodgings in town, and were the difficulties in the water supply system at Versailles as difficult as he pretended, or did he resent the augmented power and additional control Versailles gave the king in the conduct of his business and his pleasures? Did the royal apartments back as closely as he said on to a courtyard without light, offering for view only the privies on a facing wall, and were the buildings as unplanned as he suggests?

However, it is not merely political curiosity or Saint-Simon's nose for gossip, his eye for telling detail, his interest in the microscopic social event as well as in the panoramic overview, and his ear for arresting language which make the *Mémoires* a masterpiece. The literary power comes from the tension in Saint-Simon between the need to be fair and the urge to indulge his pent-up savagery, between the urge to make mordant moral and critical judgements and the intention to chronicle accurately, between the desire to give an amused, detached, and cynical account of the workings of Versailles and his personal compulsion to form an authoritative view of its functioning as a social entity. What constitutes the *Mémoires* as a literary monument is above all the tension in Saint-Simon between his role as largely moral commentator on events which had taken place up to half a century before, and his readiness, when writing about them, still to be moved by a vanished world in which he had taken part.

In particular when he comes to an important death, Saint-Simon sums up. He records the event, and describes his subject's physical appearance and moral characteristics before assessing the achievement. On Friday 12 February 1712 the duchesse de Bourgogne died. Since the death of the dauphin, her father-in-law, in April of the preceding year, she had expected to become queen of France. Born Adélaïde de Savoie in 1685, she had been married to the dauphin's eldest child in 1697 and was, as even Saint-Simon admits, childish and more than a little silly. Both she and her husband almost certainly died of measles and medical maltreatment, but Saint-Simon thought that both had probably been poisoned.

The king had left the duchesse de Bourgogne at Versailles only shortly before she died. He drove to Marly. On the morning of Saturday 13 February the duc de Bourgogne was persuaded to follow his brother, the duc de Berry, from Versailles to Marly. He left at 7 a.m., heard Mass, went to his apartments, where Mme de Maintenon immediately came to see him, and the princes and princesses called briefly to offer condolences on his bereavement. The duchesse de Berry called, attended by Saint-Simon's wife, and the duc de Bourgogne then talked to his brother, the duc de Berry. Saint-Simon joined the three pages who came to announce that it was time to go to the king's réveil, and was rewarded with "a touchingly gentle and affectionate look," although the duc de Bourgogne had a wild look, seemed ill, and his face was covered in spots.

Saint-Simon relates what happened, speaking of the heir to the throne just after the king's réveil has been announced:

> ...les larmes qu'il retenoit lui rouloient dans les yeux. A cette nouvelle il se tourna sans rien dire, et demeura. Il n'y avoit que ses trois menins et moi, et Du Chesne; les menins lui proposèrent une fois ou deux d'aller chez le roi, il ne remua ni ne répondit. Je m'approchai et je lui fis signe d'aller, puis je le lui proposai à voix basse. Voyant qu'il demeuroit et se taisoit, j'osai lui prendre le bras, lui représenter que tôt ou tard il falloit bien qu'il vît le roi; qu'il l'attendoit, et sûrement avec désir de le voir et de l'embrasser; qu'il y avoit plus de grâce à ne pas différer; et en le pressant de la sorte, je pris la liberté de le pousser doucement. Il me jeta un regard à percer l'âme, et partit. Je le suivis quelques pas, et m'ôtai de là pour prendre haleine. Je ne l'ai pas vu depuis. Plaise à la miséricorde de Dieu que je le voie éternellement où sa bonté sans doute l'a mis!

> (...his eyes were filled with pent-up tears. At the announcement he turned round without speaking, and stayed still. There were only his three pages and me, and Du Chesne; the pages suggested once or twice that he should go to the king, but he did not move or reply. I went up to him and made him a sign to go. Then I suggested it in a low voice. Seeing that he remained still and silent, I went so far as to take him by the arm and point out to him that he would sooner or later have to see the king, that the king expected him and certainly wanted to see and embrace him; that it would be more gracious not to defer things, and while urging him in this way I took the liberty of pushing him gently. He gave me a heart-rending look and went. I followed him a few paces, then took myself off to draw breath. I never saw him again. May it please God's mercy that I should see him eternally where God's goodness has no doubt placed him).

Saint-Simon now recounts what happened. On the next day the duc de Bourgogne's illness had got worse. He died on the morning of the Thursday, which was 18 February. "These *Mémoires* are not written to give an account of my feelings. If they appear, a long time after me, the reader will feel my sentiments only too well."

Saint-Simon now inserts a set piece, sketching the prince's character, neutrally listing such matters as his temper, his tendency to cruelty, his ambiguous sexuality, his stubbornness, and his love of hunting, of music and of winning at cards. Then comes his physical appearance, an account of his upbringing, an account of his views, which makes them sound suspiciously like Saint-Simon's, and a final panegyric spattered with exclamation marks.

Saint-Simon was not a dispassionate observer, a chronicler, nor even just a vivid, malicious and amusing analyst of the court of a quarter of a century before. He was also giving an account to himself of events in which he had participated, and of people he had known. If he had not once been so committed to the world he describes he would not have needed to write the *Mémoires*, and it is the review of his commitment, its wisdom and its effects, which gives the work its principal literary value.

PUBLICATIONS

[The abridgement of the manuscript of the *Mémoires* made by Voisenon for Choiseul soon after 1760 was used as the basis for extracts which were circulated in manuscript, and some portions of the text were published from 1780. The list below starts with the first signed edition, itself made from Voisenon's Abridgement and very imperfect]

Collections

Mémoires de M. le duc de Saint-Simon, 3 vols., 1781
Oeuvres complettes de L. de Saint-Simon, 13 vols., 1791
Mémoires complets et authentiques du duc de Saint-Simon, 21 vols., 1829–30
Mémoires complets et authentiques du duc de Saint-Simon, 20 vols., 1856
Mémoires complets et authentiques du duc de Saint-Simon, 20 vols., 1856–58
Mémoires du duc de Saint-Simon, 22 vols., 1873–86
Mémoires de Saint-Simon, 43 vols., 1879–1930
Mémoires, Bibliothèque de la Pléiade edition, 7 vols., 1947–61
Oeuvres complètes, 1964ff.
Ecrits inédits, 8 vols., 1880–93

Journal du marquis de Dangeau, 19 vols., 1854–60 [with notes by Saint-Simon]

[A large number of extracts from the *Mémoires* has been published in French and English, including the English translation by B. St John, 4 vols., 1857]

Biographical and critical studies

Fatta, C., *Esprit de Saint-Simon*, 1954
Bastide, F.R., *Saint-Simon*, 1957
Coirault, Y., *L'Optique de Saint-Simon*, 1965
——*Les manuscrits du duc de Saint-Simon*, 1970

SALES, François de, 1567–1622.

Author of spiritual treatises and spiritual director. Bishop. Canonized saint and Doctor of the Church.

LIFE

The literary importance of François de Sales derives chiefly not from his status as one of the greatest writers of baroque prose in the French language, in spite of allegations of mawkishness alleged against him, nor from his theological knowledge, nor his expertise as a spiritual director, but from his spiritual doctrine itself, based on the central and theologically revolutionary view that human beings have a natural desire to love God. Sales was the first Doctor of the Church systematically to weld the often disparate elements of earlier mystics, theologians, and moralists into a spirituality based on redeemed nature's inclination to love God, which made its promptings, safeguarded by the adequate direction necessary to avoid self-delusion, a reliable guide to spiritual perfection.

It is true that his most striking gifts were those of a spiritual director, and then more generally as a pastor. All his spiritual treatises were written, like his letters, with individual "penitents" in mind, so that the doctrine was never expressed otherwise than as a form of spiritual direction, however generalized from the original advice to individuals. As a director, he was most strikingly successful in helping to spiritual maturity women with strong personalities, and it is clear from his works that he gradually became aware of a markedly feminine element in his own temperament, and also that he was disinclined to write any form of abstract treatise, or to formulate his views otherwise than in relation to the practical requirements preferably of individuals, but never of more than small groups.

His preaching, letters, exhortations, and books all derive from the desire to give practical advice, while even the early and short of works of controversy are reducible to not much more than a lawyer's argument on a controverted point. But more even than contemporary novelists and dramatists, François de Sales revealed to a whole generation during the first two decades of the 17th century a view of human nature which was both rigorously orthodox and unprecedently optimistic, it mixed the close fidelity to Augustine of the opening chapter of the *Traité de l'amour de Dieu* with a considered confidence in human instinct, as it also mixed the austere ascetic norms of Sales's direction of saint Jeanne-Françoise Frémyot de Chantal, cofounder with him of the Visitation Order, and incidentally grandmother of Mme de Sévigné, with the cultivation of a relaxed peace of soul.

Sales was beatified on 28 December 1661 and canonized—his feast-day is 29 January—on 19 April 1665, at a time, that is, when authentic Augustinianism was thought to be represented by the repressive and anxiety-inducing spirituality of the Port-Royal (q.v.) directors. Armand-Jean le Bouthillier de Rancé was about to impose, from 1664, on the monks of his Cistercian reform at La Trappe the stultifying mortifications which hastened the deaths of an embarrassingly large number of them. Beatification and canonization, however, primarily concerned Sales's personal sanctity. By raising him to the status of Doctor of the Church on 16 November 1877, Pius IX officially endorsed the compatibility and perhaps even the congruence of his doctrine itself with the most rigorous norms of Catholic orthodoxy. Since the whole of Salesian spirituality is erected on the natural human desire to love God, the Church, however tardily, assented to that massive upgrading of the moral stature of properly directed human instinctive drives which was virtually constitutive of the seismic adjustment of cultural values which took place in Europe during the period from the renaissance to the enlightenment.

The Sales family belonged to the noblesse d'épée, and could trace back its connection with Thorens, of which it later acquired the château and the jurisdiction, to the 14th century. On 12 May 1560 François de Nouvelles, the younger son of Jean de Sales, was betrothed to the seven-year-old Françoise de Sionnaz, whose dowry included the seigneurie of Boisy, about an hour and a half from Sales. The territory belonged to the sovereign state of Savoy, and in 1565 the Sales were made gentilshommes ordinaires de sa chambre by the duc de Savoie. The wedding of François de Nouvelles, now M. de Boisy, and Françoise de Sionnaz took place in the spring of 1566 when the bride was 14, and on 21 August 1567 Sales was born two months prematurely at the fortified château de Sales near Thorens. Sickly as an infant, he was taken by his godmother to Monthoux, where the air was better and where he remained until 1573. On his return in that year to Sales he was sent with three cousins to board at the Collège de La Roche, and then for the three academic years from 1575 to 1578 to the Collège chappuysien at Annecy.

The minute scrutiny to which every detail of Sales's life was subjected during the canonization process has left us exceptionally well informed about him. His family had destined him for the magistracy, but in September 1578 he was tonsured and sent with his cousins to Paris with the not very gentle abbé Déage as his guardian. Deterred by its reactionary reputation, he was unwilling to attend the Collège de Navarre, and went for four years to the newly opened humanities classes of the Jesuit Collège de Clermont. There followed the liberal arts and philosophy courses from 1582 to 1588, although Sales quickly developed a serious interest in theology, using notes passed to him by Déage from his own courses at the Sorbonne, and an antipathy to the career anticipated for him in the magistracy. At the end of his humanities or shortly thereafter Sales had undergone a feeling of revulsion against the authors of pagan antiquity. By late adolescence his religious commitment was already becoming intense. Then in 1584 he made his initial acquaintance with mystical theology at Clermont under Gilbert Génébrard, the commentator on the *Song of Songs*.

Déage saw to it that Sales's physical development was cared for. He became an expert dancer and an accomplished horseman, learned to fence, and later distinguished himself among the episcopacy by visiting his parishes not in a carriage but on horseback. It is quite possible that, as the early biographers relate, he had occasion a little later on, while studying at Padua for three years from December 1588, to fight two duels. His skills at rowing and climbing, useful enough in his mountainous diocese, are also mentioned in the early accounts of his life but, although his health later became robust enough to sustain a life in which both nourishment and sleep were kept to a minimum, and although he was able to survive both typhoid at Padua in 1590–91 and the plague at Annecy in 1597–98, he was in youth nervous and prone to obsessive anxieties.

It has been suggested that the serious personal crisis Sales underwent in Paris in December 1586 and January 1587 may have been precipitated by the repression of strong sexual desires, to which his companions, sharing the same age, gender, and social background, normally gave rein. Sales at this time frequented the passably dissolute court of Marie de Luxembourg, duchesse de Mercoeur, married to Philippe-Emmanuel de Lorraine, governor of Brittany and one of the leaders of the League, and was on terms of friendship with a number of the mignons of Henri III, including Joyeuse and d'Epernon. The alternative hypothesis is that what amounted to a nervous breakdown originated in religious difficulties deriving from the doctrine of predestination, met with no doubt in the generally Thomist teaching on grace transmitted in Déage's notes.

For six weeks Sales was convinced that he was going to be damned. He compiled a collection of obsessive ejaculatory prayers, threw himself into his work, and tried to cultivate an attitude towards God so purely motivated as to be independent of any hope of eternal reward, and a love of God which could survive the certainty of unending agony as the result of an arbitrary divine decree. The spiritual dilemma consequent on any real assent to the dogma of predestination had sporadically caused acute personal suffering since the late middle ages and had at least contributed to the outbreak of schism at the Reformation. It was to be at the centre of the Jansenist (q.v.) controversy and its anguished spiritual repercussions in the 17th century; produced often bitter theological controversy in attempts within the Catholic Church to reconcile the doctrines of predestination and free will; and was at the heart of the "pure love" controversies between Antoine Sirmond and Jean-Pierre Camus, and then between Fénelon and Bossuet later in the century. Bossuet was to think Sales's doctrine on the natural inclination to love God Pelagian, to repudiate his authority in matters of dogma, and to erect his own religious teaching on virtually opposed spiritual principles. Sales's personal experience was no doubt fundamental to the central place he thereafter accorded in his spirituality to the cultivation of peace of soul. During the crisis Sales lost all appetite, could not sleep, and became pale, thin and physically ill for about six weeks.

The crisis was resolved not by exasperated revolt but by religious submission:

Quoi qu'il en soit, Seigneur, pour le moins que je vous aime en cette vie, si je ne puis vous aimer en l'éternelle, puisque personne ne vous loue en enfer

(However it may be, Lord, at least let me love you in this life, if I cannot love you in eternity, since no one sings your praises in hell).

Sales had gone to pray at the chapel of the Blessed Virgin in the Dominican church of Saint-Etienne–des–Grès in very similar terms, although at slightly greater length, ending with the petition "Allow me at least not to be among those who curse your name even 'si meis exigentibus meritis maledictus de maledictorum numero sum futurus' (if because of my just deserts I am to be cursed among the number of the accursed)."

He then devoutly read a short prayer to the Virgin available for public use, and the anguish dropped from him, never to return, although the intellectual resolution of the dilemma continued to occupy him, and at Padua, where he was supposed to be studying law but also devoted much of his time to theology, he filled six exercise books with notes on grace, predestination, and reprobation, ending with huge emphasis on the universality of God's will to save men, commonly based on the phrase "who willeth that all men should be saved" (I *Timothy*, ii, 4). It was on this text that Sales based his later Molinism, clearly teaching the autonomy of the human power of moral self-determination to good or evil in both the fifth chapter of the third book of the *Traité de l'amour de Dieu*, and in his letter to Lessius of 26 August 1618 congratulating him on his celebrated treatise on predestination, the *De gratia efficaci, decretis divinis, libertate arbitrii et praescientia Dei conditionata, disputatio apologetica* written in 1601, approved in 1608, and published in 1610.

In Padua he later wrote, "I studied law to please my father, and theology to please myself." He chose the Jesuit Père Possevin as his spiritual director. Typhoid brought him near to death in Padua in January 1591, but on 5 September he obtained his doctorate "in utroque iure," that is, both canon law and civil law. His Italian was by now as fluent as his French and Latin, and he had acquired an adequate knowledge of Greek and Hebrew. On 8 October he left Venice, still with Déage, to visit Ancona and Loreto. The party was unable to get to Rome, and Sales spent the two months from 20 November 1591 to 21 January 1592 in Venice before returning to the château de la Thuile in Savoy through Mantua, Milan and Turin. He was 25. During the next few months his activities were still characterized by a temperamental hesitancy he was only later to overcome.

Sales's father wanted him to have a career in the magistracy, bought for him the title of seigneur de Villaroget, and was irritated at his reserved behaviour on two visits to the bride chosen for him, Françoise Suchet de Mirebel. Sales became a member of the Chambéry bar on 24 November 1592, and was to leave his name on the list until 1597. In the meanwhile he declined the exceptional offer from the duc de Savoie of letters patent making him a senator, but could not bring himself to inform his father of his firm intention to become a priest. He entrusted that task to his cousin, Canon Louis-Amédée de Sales who, with the support of Monsignor de Granier, bishop of Geneva, successfully undertook the necessary steps at Rome to ensure that the vacant post of prévôt of the chapter, the second rank in the diocese, was conferred on him. The post was compatible with a seat on the senate and conferred the right of nomination to a third of the cures in the diocese. The bulls were signed at Rome on 7 March 1593 and were brought to Annecy on 7 May. Only then was Sales's father informed. He gave his consent.

During May Sales renounced the seigneurie of Villaroget, took the soutane, entered into possession of his ecclesiastical office and made an ordination retreat prior to receiving minor orders on 9 June, then the sub-diaconate (18 June), the diaconate (18 September), and the priesthood (18 December). He celebrated his first Mass on 21 December. From September 1594 to October 1597, he was in charge of the mission to the Chablais region, where Calvinism had been imposed partly by force and whose inhabitants were forbidden by their ministers to listen to Sales. The mission, undertaken with his cousin, was dangerous and at first fruitless. It was impossible to find listeners. Sales eventually conceived the idea of posting fly-sheets and getting them circulated clandestinely. They were written at the Catholic citadel of Allinges about two kilometres south of Lac Léman and the first was ready on 25 January 1595. Known today as *Les Controverses*, although originally gathered together as *Le Mémorial*, the fly-sheets are penetrating and direct, showing the clear legal mind behind them.

Sales was writing controversy, and the serenity characteristic of his later style was not yet even called for. The technique, if more expository than polemical, is pointed and ardent, although never ill-humoured, and the mission itself finally ended in success. By 1598, when Sales was recalled and the mission confided to the Capucins, most of the Chablais had been reconverted to Catholicism. Sales's opposition to Calvinism naturally derived in part from the emphasis strict Calvinist teaching was still putting on the doctrine of predestination, which had so troubled Sales spiritually, but was also at least tinged with nationalistic feeling. Calvinist hegemony on Savoy territory meant acquiescence in the political ascendancy of Geneva.

Political unity was fractured by religious division. Notes taken in Padua in 1591 already show that Sales had nationalistic as well as religious and personal reasons for his desire to re-convert the Chablais, and had at the very end of 1593 devoted his sermon at his enthronement as prévôt to the need to "reconquer" Geneva. His weapons, he wrote to Antoine Favre on 27 November 1594, were "prayer, alms, and fasting," which he considered to be rope to bind his opponents which it would be difficult for them to break. Although his resources were meagre, he gave what he had to the poor and lived with striking frugality. He learned, in the course of his mission, how essential it was actually to like those whom he wished to convert, but he was also much concerned to be seen to be acting with the authority of the duc de Savoie as well as with that of his ecclesiastical superiors.

Sales's properly mystical experiences, that is, extraordinary experiences in the context of prayer inexplicable alone in terms of any then, or perhaps even now, known psychological mechanisms, have been incontrovertibly attested. After Easter in 1595 he had returned for a few weeks to Annecy and taken part in the synod there; an extraordinary experience in prayer is recorded on the feast of Corpus Christi that year. By June he was back at Thonon, on the south bank of Lac Léman. During 1597 he had three discussions with the Calvinist theologian Théodore de Bèze, with Louis de Sales present on 9 April and Antoine Favre on 3 July, when the Genevan police nearly succeeded in apprehending him. We do not know the date at which the third meeting took place. Sales made no impact in theological argument with Bèze, but as early as April 1597 was urging that pressure

be put on Henri IV to get freedom of worship allowed in the parts of the Chablais under his control, so contributing to the forces which resulted on 13 April 1598 in the then still controversial promulgation of the edict of Nantes which, for instance, was regarded as lamentable by Clement VIII.

An important meeting to discuss missionary tactics was held at Annemasse, about six kilometres east of Geneva, on 29 July, with the result that a "Forty hours" religious celebration was held there on 7 and 8 September. There were bonfires, lights, music, and musket salvoes, the whole thing culminating in a triumphant procession and the erection of a huge cross facing Geneva. The Calvinists replied with a day of penitence at Geneva on 14 September and an anonymous pamphlet against image worship by the minister Antoine de la Faye, the *Bref traité de la vertu de la Croix et de la manière de l'honorer*. Sales prepared his reply, *La Défense de l'étendard de la Sainte Croix*, whose publication, however, was delayed until 1600.

At the end of 1597 Sales was recalled to Annecy. He was ill from October to February 1598 and had to put off his departure for Rome with Granier. The "Forty hours" celebration was renewed after some delay, on an even grander scale at Thonon, under the presidency of Granier, on 19–20 September. Both the duc de Savoie and the papal legate, the cardinal of Florence, visited Thonon before the end of the month. There were thousands of converts to Catholicism, and here too a large cross was erected. The duc de Savoie, inclined to severity towards the Protestants, was in no way discouraged in the harshness of his attitude by Sales, now for the first time regarded by the crowd as a miracle-worker. Sales demanded the exile of the Calvinist minister Viret and the exclusion of Protestants from public office, still on the grounds that religious schism was politically divisive, while intervening personally to mitigate the economic and other distress of those who finally preferred exile to abjuration.

From the end of 1598 to the end of March 1599 Sales was at Rome, where he was nominated bishop of Nicopolis "in partibus infidelium" and coadjutor to Granier as bishop of Geneva. He supported in vain a request that the episcopal residence should now be transferred from Annecy to Thonon, and various other measures designed to reinforce Thonon's position as a bastion of Catholicism, although a split now appeared in the Catholic position. While Sales wanted a college, seminary and religious foundations at Thonon, his lieutenant, the Capucin Père Chérubin, and a majority of Catholics wanted to establish a supremacy that was also political and jurisdictional.

While at Rome Sales must have been consulted by Clement VIII about the celebrated "de auxiliis" (see: Jansenism) dispute between the Jesuits and the Dominicans concerning grace and free will. When, after the 18th session of the congregation on 28 August 1607, Paul V imposed silence on both sides, he was taking Sales's advice, for which both orders showed him their gratitude. Clement VIII attended his episcopal examination by Borromeo, Bellarmine, Baronius, Borghese, and others, and Sales communicated at the pope's Mass on 25 March 1595 and himself celebrated Mass at Saint Peter's before leaving on 31 March for Annecy, travelling via Loreto and Turin during April and May.

On 6 April 1601 his father died. After a visit in June to the Chablais, Sales left with Déage and Antoine Favre for Paris on a journey concerned with the administration of the bailliages of the Gex region, just north of the western corner of Lac Léman.

They set out on 2 January 1602, arriving on the 22nd. Sales was immediately introduced by the young Bérulle, engaged in negotiating the introduction of the Carmelites into France, to the circle of the mystic, Barbe d'Acarie, later Marie de l'Incarnation. She lived in a vast house and received the capital's principal religious figures. In spite of his intellectual brilliance, Sales was immediately conscious of his provincial background. He apologized for his gaucheness, and cultivated the art of classical allusion and the wit which, ten years later, he was to regret. He had not yet overcome the diffidence which had prevented him from himself informing his father of his intention to become a priest and whose signs in his life do not really disappear until after his confidence had been boosted by the patent success of his spiritual direction.

He remained silent before the reforming abbess of Montmartre, Marie de Beauvilliers, to whom he would merely counsel gentleness with the older members of communities to be reformed, and he visibly shrank from taking on the spiritual direction of Mme Acarie. He did nonetheless accept at short notice an invitation to give the Lenten sermons preached before the queen in the Louvre, and met with such success that Henri IV, who had withdrawn to Fontainebleau over Easter, invited him to preach on Low Sunday and pressed him in vain to accept the coadjutor see of Paris, an offer which was to be renewed by Cardinal de Gondi in 1619. Sales's sermons, of which he preached about a hundred during seven months or so in Paris, swiftly became celebrated, and his political skills were sufficiently developed for him to refuse a pension from the king without offending him, and to preach at Notre-Dame on 27 April 1602 the funeral oration of the duc de Mercoeur, leader of the League after the death of the Guise brothers, in such a way as to please both the king and the family.

On his way back from Paris, Sales learned at Lyons in late September of Granier's death. After making his retreat under a Jesuit, Père Fourier, Sales was consecrated bishop of Geneva at Thorens on 8 December, the occasion of a further extraordinary experience in prayer. In 1603 he made a protracted visit to Turin, staying with the papal nuntius, and became busy with the administration and reform of his diocese. He also wrote his first letters of spiritual direction. Then in 1604, he preached the Lenten sermons at Dijon, where business had brought him, starting on Ash Wednesday, 3 March. It was on Friday 5 March that he noticed in his congregation the attentive Jeanne-Françoise Frémyot de Chantal, later to be his co-founder of the Visitation Order, herself canonized in 1767.

Tortured and ardent, she had bound herself by four vows, of obedience to her director, not to change him, not to reveal what he said to her, and not to discuss her interior life with anyone else. After the sermon Sales met her at the house of her brother, André Frémyot, archbishop elect of Bourges. She was immediately attracted by his obvious devoutness, although he remained reserved and discreet. She was a widow, and Sales told her that, if she did not wish to marry again, she should "pull down the sign," objecting to the superfluous lace she was wearing. That evening, she herself unpicked the stitching.

On 14 April she was violently troubled by the habitual obsessive anxieties occasioned by the quadruple vow, and after a somewhat anguished dinner began to confide to Sales in a corner of the room. He consoled her without committing himself. Next day at table, she proposed in his presence to go on pilgrimage to Saint-Claude, and Sales agreed to bring his mother to meet her

party. After Easter he heard her confession and exhorted her to obey her usual director, who may have been well intentioned but was clearly domineering. He must also have been stupid. Not only on the spiritual level were those four vows clearly an obstacle to his penitent's attainment of spiritual maturity and peace of soul but, as two outside opinions subsequently confirmed, they were sufficiently imprudent to have been canonically invalid. Sales left Dijon on 26 April, writing a note after dinner, "God, it seems to me, has given me to you; I am more convinced of it every hour. That is all I can say to you." Further letters of encouragement followed, attempting to appease renewed scruples about the vows. Sales was being provoked by the sheer absurdity of the situation to overcome his own diffidence and to take control.

Finally on 24 August Sales, his mother and his sister Jeanne, the baronne de Chantal, the présidente Brûlart, and her sister Rose Bourgeois de Crépy, abbess of Puy-d'Orbe, all met at Saint-Claude. Sales took the baronne aside, listened to an account of her already extraordinary and intense interior life, but did not reply. Only the next morning did he come to her "very early," not having slept. "It is indeed true that it is God's will that I should charge myself with your spiritual direction and that you should follow my advice…all your four vows can result only in destroying your peace of conscience… Do not be surprised if I have delayed so long in giving you a decision. I wanted to be sure about God's will and that there should be nothing in this affair except what his hand directed."

Of the estimated 20,000 letters written by Sales, only 2,000 survive. The letters of direction are the masterpiece of that genre in a century which has left us, among others, the remarkable collections of Surin, Saint-Cyran, Saci, Rancé, and Fénelon. Since religious experience had been widely adopted on both sides of the schism in the 16th century as the criterion of spiritual stature, it had become essential to distinguish between what was authentically religious experience and what was self-delusion. It was generally agreed that this discernment required recourse to a spiritual director, who ideally combined a developed psychological sensitivity with a sound grasp of the principles of what came to be called ascetical and mystical theology. Inexpert and inexperienced directors, of whom there were many, did a great deal of damage, but Sales's gifts could scarcely be excelled.

His letters of direction are characterized by a slow, measured, prudence, and the unremitting insistence on mortified purity of intention. Advice is always tailored in the first instance to the immediate needs of the recipient. It is often severe without ever being harsh, emphasizing the absolute primacy of the love of a God whose qualities included what Sales was not afraid to call "mignardise" and, as Sales's own experience had copiously taught him, the need for liberation from scruples, inhibitions, and obsessive constraints, for what he was often to sum up in the word "débonnaireté". There is very little insistence on definite practices, although Sales does not shrink from suggesting them, but a desire to cultivate in the recipients above all the complete dedication of which only a mature and self-possessed personality is capable. Ardour without tranquillity will not suffice. The message is epitomized in a letter of October 1604 to Mme de Chantal: "Here is the general rule of our obedience in capital letters: We must do everything out of love, nothing by force; we should love obedience more than we fear disobedience. I leave you the spirit of liberty."

Later, on 24 January 1622, when Angélique Arnauld was

hoping to resign as abbess of Port-Royal in order to enter the Visitation, Sales wrote to her:

> Il faut donc attendre le mot de Rome, et cependant demeurer en paix; et quand le mot sera venu, demeurer en paix; et quoique l'on réponde, demeurer en paix, et toujours demeurer en paix, de tout notre pouvoir

> (We must therefore await word from Rome, and in the mean time remain at peace; and when it arrives, still remain at peace; and whatever the answer is, remain at peace, and always remain at peace, with all our power).

Sales had very early seen the damaging tensions at work in that intense and aristocratic personality. In a letter of 14 May 1620 he referred to Angélique Arnauld's chief spiritual obstacle as her "promptitude naturelle," her touchy proclivity to sharp overreaction, and to her need to cultivate "modestie, douceur et tranquillité (modesty, gentleness, peace)," and thereby "to calm her external behaviour, her demeanour, her gait, her bearing, her hands;" he foresaw that it would take years. "Would it not be better," he once said to her, "not to catch such big fish, but to catch more of them?" It was he who finally refused to accept Angélique Arnauld into the Visitation Order, and it is difficult to see how, in spite of her extraordinary gifts, she would have fitted in there.

Mme de Chantal came to stay at Sales for ten days from 21 May in 1605, otherwise remaining in Burgundy while Sales himself was in Savoy. We have 43 letters he wrote to her at that time, enough only to form a sound understanding of his doctrine, and of the developing relationship of relaxed intimacy, intense only in the purity of its common dedication to the perfection of the love of God, between the two saints. Similarly, we have not enough of the sermons to give us a full idea of Sales's pulpit achievement. He is said to have preached every day in 1619, when he was in Paris, and for most of his active episcopal life three or four times a week. He almost always preached spontaneously or from scrappy notes in a mixture of French and Latin. Although some sermons have been reconstructed, we know only that he gave the contents a strongly religious emphasis, stripping his sermons of ornamentation and erudition, and doing away with the geometrical divisions and sub-divisions, as well as the violence of tone, of the sermons of the late 16th century. Such texts as we possess scarcely explain the effect we know that they had. He preached Advent and Lenten courses most years, including five at Annecy. In 1603 he had shared the Lenten sermons at Annecy, and after the 1604 Lent at Dijon, preached Lenten courses in successive years at La Roche-sur-Foron, Chambéry, Annecy, Rumilly, and Annecy.

During the winter of 1606–07 he succeeded, with Antoine Favre, in realizing a dream inspired by the Italian academies and the Paris Académie du Palais by establishing the Académie florimontane, open to artisans but not heretics, and partly political as well as religious in inspiration. It lasted only from 1607 until 1610, when Antoine Favre had to move to Chambéry as president of the senate and made his large house over to Sales, but it swiftly became famous. Sales intervened personally to defend one of its members, Don Redente Barranzano, a Barnabite supporter of the already suspect Galileo, who was to be in trouble over his 1617 *Uranoscopia seu de coelo*, inviting the general of the Barnabites to leave Don Redente at Annecy. Sales had

reacted against an excessively erudite classicism, but he remained humanist in the sense that he never doubted that revelation and the created cosmos, the work of the same God, had to be in harmony. There could be no conflict between science and religion, and no reason to fear the conclusions of empirical scientific investigation.

It was in the April of 1607 that Louise du Chastel, lady-in-waiting to Catherine de Clèves and married since 1600 to Sales's cousin, Claude de Charmoisy, seems formally to have put herself under Sales's direction. Sales was already director of Rose Bourgeois, abbess of Puy-d'Orbe, the baronne de Chantal, Mme Brûlart, président Frémyot, Antoine Favre, his wife, and their children René, Claude, Claude de Quoex, Jacqueline, and Philippe. Mme de Charmoisy had to attend to a case she had before the senate at Chambéry, and was away six months. Sales advised her to put herself under the direction of Père Fourier, to whom she showed some "Mémoires" written for her by Sales. Fourier wrote to Sales on 25 March 1608, urging him to publish them. Sales wrote a preface dated 8 August 1608, and the *Introduction à la vie dévote* was published by Rigaud at Lyons in 1609. It quickly sold out.

In February 1609, Sales wrote to Mme de Chantal asking for all the letters he had ever sent her, using the material he then received to enlarge his text, which he also changed and re-ordered, and from which he also dropped material. To a reference to the reader's husband is added "or wife," thereby generalizing the advice to include men. This second edition of the *Introduction* was published in or just before September 1609, also by Rigaud of Lyons. Three chapters had been dropped "by mistake" from the second edition, so Sales prepared a third. There had already been counterfeit editions and translations, and the 1610 edition continued to contain mistakes. There was another edition in 1616, still too careless, and Sales had the definitive edition published in Paris by Joseph Cottereau in 1619. He had made more than 1,000 purely stylistic emendations to his text since the first edition. By that date seven unauthorized editions are also known, with translations into Italian, English, Flemish, and Spanish.

On 8 October 1607, Sales's sister had died in the arms of Mme de Chantal, whom Sales himself was not to meet again until August 1608. He had already begun work on what was to become the *Traité de l'amour de Dieu*, and Mme de Chantal, who inspired parts of the work, most notably the ninth book, attended the Lent sermons preached by Sales in 1609 at Annecy. It was her third visit to Annecy. On 13 October 1609 Sales's brother Bernard married Marie-Aimée de Chantal, the elder of the two surviving daughters of Mme de Chantal and consequently aunt to the future Mme de Sévigné, the daughter of Marie-Aimée's elder brother. Sales had himself a month earlier been able to ride through Geneva with an escort without being molested.

On 1 March 1610, his mother died. On 29 March, Mme de Chantal left Dijon with Jeanne-Charlotte de Bréchard for Savoy. Sales, with an escort of 25 companions, went to meet her and conduct her to Sales, where she stayed several weeks. Sales had announced in 1607 his intention of founding a religious order, and on Trinity Sunday, 6 June 1610, Mme de Chantal, Charlotte Bréchard, Marie-Jacqueline Favre, and Anne-Jacqueline Coste as a lay sister went to live in a small house La Galerie, in the faubourg Perrière at Annecy. The Visitation Sainte-Marie had been founded, a new religious congregation to care for the sick in their homes, a community in which even the least robust could dedicate themselves to God.

The visiting of the sick began in 1612, when the small community moved inside the town on 3 October, to the house of a lawyer called Nicollin, while their convent was being built. The *Introduction* had stridently declared that sanctity was quite independent of physical circumstances, compatible with any social rank or civil status, with marriage, and with the career of a merchant, soldier, valet, or courtier. The book was a practical spiritual guide for persons whose vocations were neither religious nor even lay contemplative. Its text was sufficiently emphatic on the point to contain a chapter (III, 39) "De l'honnêteté du lit nuptial (On the moral acceptability of marital relations)," normally omitted as too forthright by the 19th-century editions. Of very considerable spiritual and imaginative daring in its treatment also of such subjects as dancing and make-up, the work showed how the devout life could be practised according to the "strength, business, and duties" of each, even in the middle of a developed social life. The Visitation Order derived from an extension of the same line of thought to those who felt further called to a religious life according to the evangelical counsels of poverty, chastity, and obedience.

It was to differ from earlier monastic foundations by the absence of any prescribed corporal penances of the sort on which Rancé, for instance, was going to rely so heavily. There were to be no barriers of wealth or social standing, such as were effectively still sometimes imposed through the requirement of a dowry. "This congregation," Sales wrote, "has been instituted so that no great harshness should prevent the weak and sick from entering it to cultivate there the perfection of the love of God." The spirit of the new congregation is clear from the series of *Entretiens spirituels* given informally by Sales on innumerable occasions between certainly no later than 1611 and his death. Some of these have come down to us, reconstituted from notes and memory by the nuns, possibly but not certainly shown to Sales for authentication, and published in 1628 in an unauthorized but authentic text as "Colloques spirituels". Mère de Chantal sought to have the edition destroyed and replaced by an authorized but polished and less authentic text published in 1629 as *Les Vrays Entretiens spirituels du Bien-Heureux François de Sales, Evesque et Prince de Genève, Instituteur et Fondateur de l'Ordre des Religieuses de la Visitation Sainte Marie*. The work is now usually referred to as *Entretiens spirituels*, and the best edition is undoubtedly that by Roger Devos in the first volume of Sales's *Oeuvres* (1969) in the Bibliothèque de la Pléiade collection.

The actual institution came to diverge from the initial vision from 1615, when a second house was founded at Lyons on 2 February at the request of the archbishop, Denis-Simon de Marquemont. Sales visited the new house from 25 June to 10 July 1615, and the archbishop then came to Annecy at the end of October. In a Mémoire which he subsequently sent to Sales, he insisted on changes in the Visitation's way of life if the congregation was to be established in his archdiocese. He required the formal approbation of the Holy See for the new foundation, solemn vows, the monastic rule of Saint Augustine, and strict enclosure, which precluded the visiting of the sick. In the end Sales had to give way on all these points, and even to forbid the provision of facilities for women who wanted to make retreats in the Visitation's houses, withdrawing for short periods from the world. Sales wrote new constitutions for the Visitation

during the second half of 1616. He was able to salvage from the original project only its name, the "Visitation," and its essence, a forum in the centre of towns for the free cultivation of the love of God with as little constraint as possible. By his death, 12 convents had been founded outside Annecy: Lyons in 1615, Moulins in 1616, Grenoble and Bourges in 1618, Paris in 1619, Montferrand, Nevers, and Orléans in 1620, Valence in 1621, and Dijon, Belley, and Saint-Etienne in 1622. From 1610 Sales devoted most of his time to the administration of his diocese, visiting its parishes and nursing the order he had founded, and to writing, incessant preaching, and spiritual direction.

Mme de Chantal had asked Sales to write the life of a recently deceased poor village girl. We have a reply from Sales to Mme de Chantal of 11 February 1607 excusing himself with a joke. He was writing the life of a saint Mme de Chantal had never heard of, called "la sainte charité (holy charity)." It was his way of announcing the *Traité de l'amour de Dieu* and, at that date, he thought he might still find in it a corner for the life of "our villager." By early in 1609, a letter of 15 February to Monseigneur Pierre de Villars, archbishop of Vienne, suggests that the projected "livret de l'Amour de Dieu (short book on the love of God)" had split into two smaller works with pastoral aims,

> Je médite donc un livret de l'Amour de Dieu, non point pour en traiter spéculativement, mais pour en montrer la pratique en l'observation des commandements de la première Table. Celui-ci sera suivi d'un autre, qui montrera la pratique du même amour divin en l'observation des commandements de la seconde Table

> (I'm thinking of writing a short book on the love of God, not treating it speculatively, but showing how it should be practised in the observance of the first commandment. It will be followed by another showing the practice of the same divine love in the observance of the second commandment).

The first book was hugely expanded and the second never written, although Sales makes clear in the *Traité* that "le comble de l'amour de la divine bonté du Père céleste consiste en la perfection de l'amour de nos frères et compagnons (the summit of the love of the divine goodness of the heavenly Father consists in the love of our brethren and companions)" (Book X, chapter 11).

It was no doubt the foundation of the Visitation and the requirements imposed by the direction of its early members which made Sales realize that a short practical guide would not fulfil his aims, and that what was being demanded from him was a full-scale spiritual treatise. On 14 December 1610 a letter to Rigaud, who was pressing for his manuscript, foresees some further delay, and references to the *Traité de l'Amour de Dieu* appear sporadically in the correspondence until finally a letter of 7 November 1614 to Mme de la Fléchère announces its completion, although it still needed to be transcribed several times. In fact, Sales continued to work on his text. Rigaud obtained a permit to print it on 28 March 1616, but Michel Favre, Sales's secretary and chaplain, without whom he never visited the nuns, did not deliver the manuscript until about the beginning of May. Favre oversaw the printing. The work's ecclesiastical approbation is dated 20 May, the final permission to print 25 May, and the achevé d'imprimer 31 July 1616. Sales himself always preferred the 1616 edition to those which appeared subsequently, several in 1617, and others in 1618 and 1620, with increasing numbers of printing and other errors. There may have been an Italian translation of 1620, although the first known translation into Italian is that of 1642. There were translations into English (1630), Latin (1643), Spanish and German (1661), and Polish (1751). Vaugelas was to call the work a chef-d'oeuvre, admired by all those capable of judgement, but was also to say that to estimate it at its true value required both learning and devotion, two qualities rare on their own but even rarer in conjunction.

Sales's model for the reorganization of his diocese had been the work of Milan's reforming archbishop, Charles Borromeo, later to be canonized, who had died in 1584 and to whose tomb Sales made a pilgrimage in the spring of 1613, when in Turin and Milan arranging for the installation of the Barnabites at the Collège d'Annecy. After his return from Lyons in 1615 he scarcely travelled again except to preach Advent at Grenoble in 1616 and Lent there in 1617 and 1618, and for his visit to Paris from October 1618 to October 1619. His brothers died, Gallois in 1614 and Bernard in 1617. In 1618 the Visitation was given the canonical status of religious order, rather than congregation. This bestowed on it a number of privileges, and exemption from diocesan jurisdiction. Its houses became convents.

Sales travelled to Paris in the suite of Cardinal Maurice de Savoie to seek the hand of Christine de France, daughter of Henri IV, for Victor-Amadeus, prince of Piedmont and later to become duc de Savoie. The visit is characterized by incessant preaching, including Lent in Paris in 1619. The marriage took place on 10 February 1619, and Christine chose Sales as her grand aumônier. He had a number of discussions with Angélique Arnauld at Maubuisson (5 April, 11 June, 1 July, 25 August, and 2 September), founded the Paris Visitation, went to Port-Royal, and joined the court in the Loire valley before returning to Annecy on 31 October. In 1620 he preached Lent there. On 17 January 1621 his brother Jean-François was consecrated bishop and became his auxiliary. Sales himself thought of retiring.

In 1622, however, at the request of Gregory XV, Sales presided over the general chapter of the Feuillants, a branch of the Cistercians, and then visited Turin, later on going to Avignon where the duc de Savoie was congratulating Louis XIII on his victory over the Protestants. He returned through Valence to Lyons, where he was present for the solemn entry of Louis XIII on 8 December 1622. In spite of many offers of hospitality from the highest-ranking members of the community, he insisted on staying in the cottage of the Visitation's gardener. It was there that he had his first stroke. Three days later he saw Mère de Chantal for the first time in three years. It was to be their last meeting.

On 24 December 1622 Sales felt unwell during a religious ceremony but could say his three Christmas Masses and preach on Christmas Day. On 27 December he gave his last conference to the nuns of the Visitation. That night he was taken ill, had a further stroke, and received the last sacraments. He died at about 8 p.m. on 28 December 1622.

WORKS

Handbooks of piety for lay-people, aids to prayer, subjects for meditation, and manuals to prepare for confession were not unknown during the 15th and 16th centuries. Thomas More translated Pico della Mirandola's *Twelve Rules* into English, and Erasmus also used them for the *Enchiridion militis christiani*, written in 1501 although published only two years later. There were were also the four mid-15th century treatises of Thomas à Kempis, gathered together as *The Imitation of Christ*, the works this had inspired, and the less generally influential handbooks of simple piety by Gerson, which were clearly discernible in the gestation of Sales's ideas; so that the idea of a spiritual guide for lay-people was not original in the early 17th century.

When Sales first formulated his powerfully original spiritual doctrine in his notes for Louise de Charmoisy, and then added to them some of the contents of the letters of direction he had written to Mme de Chantal, before generalizing his material into the practical advice contained in the *Introduction à la vie dévote*, he none the less drew on a number of established traditions and specific sources. The passive note especially, and the striving for tranquillity from the tumult of the passions, later to be transformed into the quest for peace of soul, develop the teaching of the neostoic moral treatises written during and just after the religious wars, notably by Guillaume du Vair and Pierre Charron.

The concept of the spiritual life as a battlefield was channelled through the 1589 *Spiritual Combat* of the Theatine priest, Lorenzo Scupoli, a book which Sales recommended more frequently than any other work, in which he read daily, and which he kept on his person for 18 years. Scupoli himself had used Pico's *Twelve Rules*. Sales also takes much from the Spanish Dominican, Luis de Granada, whose *Oeuvres spirituelles et dévotes* were published in Paris in 1602. Granada's guides to lay piety were opposed by his Dominican colleague, the inquisitor Melchior Cano, also a strong opponent of the Jesuits, but had been strongly defended by Charles Borromeo, whose uncle, the pope, had upheld Granada's views.

The strands of properly mystical theology can be traced back to the writings of the great Flemish mystics and the tradition deriving from Eckhart, Tauler, and Suso. Various texts of the Flemish mystics had appeared in Paris in the last years of the 16th century, but the channel of transmission to Sales was the Carthusian, Richard Beaucousin, at Vauvert, to whom Sales was introduced in 1602 and who helped Bérulle to publish his youthful and abstract *Bref discours de l'abnégation intérieure*. Beaucousin helped the Capucin, William Fitch, known as Benoît de Canfeld, whose manuscripts were written to circulate among a restricted circle from 1592, and the first two parts of whose *Règle de Perfection contenant un abrégé de toute la vie spirituelle réduite à ce seul point de la volonté de Dieu*, although not intended for publication, were in fact published in 1608, followed by the third part in 1610.

From Benoît, Sales took the fusion of the divine and human wills as the summit of religious perfection, so by-passing the mediation of Jesus's humanity in the soul's ascent to mystical union with God. Beaucousin also translated Ruysbroeck and drew on Harphius, from whom derived Sales's teaching on the "fine pointe," usually known as the "high point," of the soul. Beaucousin's group, whose views dominated Mme Acarie's circle, were also devotees of the Pseudo-Denys, translated into French in 1608 by Jean de Saint-François Goulu, as also of Theresa of Avila, reformer of the Spanish Carmelites, and John of the Cross, from whom came the notion of the dark nights successively of the spirit and of the soul.

A further clear and dominating source for Sales's spiritual

doctrine was the Jesuit spirituality of Ignatius of Loyola, which also mediated the 14th-century meditations on the life of Jesus known as the *Vita Christi* by Ludolph the Carthusian and Garcia de Cisneros's *Ejercitatorio de la Vida espiritual*. It was from the Jesuits that Sales took not only the fusion of methods of prayer built on the examination of conscience and on meditations on incidents from Jesus's life recorded in the Gospels, but also the resolution of the difficulties about predestination and freedom, raised in the dispute "de auxiliis," in favour of man's autonomous power of moral and religious self-determination.

In the *Introduction à la vie dévote* inspiration from all these sources is fused together into a forcefully practical and imaginative spirituality for devout lay persons. The system is not at all lax, but realistically envisages the need for guidance of those who cannot entirely forsake the obligations of their state in life, who are called on to pursue their religious perfection without a vow of poverty or chastity but as married persons or as property owners, with ordinary needs, obligations, and duties in the world. In the process Sales finds it possible to trust human nature to a degree never hitherto explicit in a major spiritual authority, simply by stripping his doctrine of all that is merely theoretical, and attempting to write a ruthlessly practical guide to religious progress in the everyday world. He never doubted that it was desirable to be as gentle as was compatible with necessary singleness of purpose. This is his leading principle. He found it possible to be more gentle and more practically explicit than any of his predecessors, while sacrificing nothing at all of the rigour necessary for the pursuit of complete purity of intention.

The advice sent to Louise de Charmoisy was already to some extent generalized, and probably included separate sets of notes—on mental prayer, on perseverance in devotion in the middle of life at court, and on the annual renewal of her devout resolutions—already communicable to a wider readership. Sales was writing the *Traité de l'amour de Dieu* at much the same time as he was putting together the *Introduction*, and on at least two occasions in 1604 he explicitly asked Rose Bourgeois to pass letters on to or to receive letters from her sister, Mme Brûlart. In one letter he mentions "quelques points que je désire vous être particuliers (some points I am making for you personally)."

The *Introduction* as we have it starts with an "Oraison dédicatoire" to Jesus. It was dated 1609 but almost certainly published before the end of 1608. The Préface starts with a magnificently baroque comparison taken from Pliny the Elder and intended to communicate the author's intention simply to rearrange the same flowers used by others, but so as to make the bouquet look different. Sales writes in the first person, alluding directly, although not by name, to Mme de Charmoisy and to Père Fourier. He is addressing not those who have withdrawn from the world, but those who live "ès villes, ès ménages, en la cour, et qui par leur condition sont obligés de faire une vie commune quant à l'éxtérieur (in towns, in households, at court, and who by their social situation have externally to live as part of a group)." Sales then goes on to announce how his work is divided into five parts: firstly, he will try to turn the pious desire of his penitent Philothée into a firm resolution, leading to confession, communion, and life lived within the ambit of her saviour's love; secondly, he intends to show how to make progress with the sacraments and the use of prayer; thirdly, he will suggest means of practising the virtues that will help; fourthly, he wishes to uncover certain traps and to teach how to bypass them; and fifthly, he will take his penitent aside for her to get back her

breath and restore her strength for further progress in the devout life. The preface then has further recourse to the examples from natural history, taken from Pliny, of which Sales is so fond.

The work itself begins with a definition of true devotion, starting from another reference to Pliny. True devotion does not consist in fasting if there is bitterness in the heart. It is possible for someone not to dare to soak the tongue in wine, or even water, from abstinence, while soaking it in a neighbour's blood "par la médisance et calomnie (by back-biting and calumny)." Sales gives a list of apparently devout forms of behaviour which can be accompanied by others which show the impurity of the motivation. Then comes, still in the first chapter of the first part, the apparently straightforward but in fact audacious definition of "la vraie et vivante dévotion (true and living devotion)," which is nothing other than "un vrai amour de Dieu (a true love of God)," which can be seen in different lights:

> en tant que l'amour divin embellit notre âme, il s'appelle grâce, nous rendant agréable à sa divine Majesté; en tant qu'il nous donne la force de bien faire, il s'appelle charité; mais quand il est parvenu jusques au degré de perfection auquel il ne nous fait pas seulement bien faire, ains nous fait opérer soigneusement, fréquemment et promptement, alors il s'appelle dévotion. Les autruches ne volent jamais; les poules volent, pesamment toutefois, bassement et rarement; mais les aigles, les colombes et les arondelles volent souvent, vitement et hautement

> (in so far as divine love adorns our soul, it is called grace, making us acceptable to his divine Majesty; in so far as it gives us strength to act well, it is called charity; but when it has arrived at the degree of perfection at which it causes us not only to behave well, but to act carefully, frequently, and promptly, then it is called devotion. Ostriches never fly; hens fly, but clumsily, low, and seldom; but eagles, doves and swallows fly often, fast, and high).

The baroque imagery at the end serves a number of purposes. It is, to start with, an apt way of categorizing those who are or should be pursuing the life of devotion. The images from natural history are of course striking. But above all, they alter the register, making it seem as if Sales was almost amusingly just seeking to illustrate an obvious truth.

There was nothing at all obvious about the view Sales had just expressed. It implied that devotion was as natural and instinctive to man as flying to birds although, like birds, human beings could be bad at it. It emphasized heavily that sanctity was the result of a continuation of ordinary religious practice taken seriously, implied that it sprang from an interior attitude, the love of God, which was alone essential, that it bore fruits in behaviour, even if it had earlier been made clear that apparently virtuous behaviour could be counterfeited, and that progress was achievable, but demanded effort. It is the continuity of properly motivated religious practice with sanctity that is again emphasized as the chapter ends.

The work proceeds, piling analogy on extended metaphor, its tone of cheerful optimism overflowing into the irresistible charm of the prose style. Devotion is the perfection of charity:

> Si la charité est un lait, la dévotion en est la crème; si elle est une plante, la dévotion en est la fleur; si elle est une

pierre précieuse, la dévotion en est l'éclat; si elle est un baume précieux, la dévotion en est l'odeur, et l'odeur de suavité qui conforte les hommes et réjouit les Anges

(If charity is the milk, devotion is its cream; if it is a plant, devotion is its flower; if it is a precious stone, devotion is its sparkle; if it is a valuable oil, devotion is its odour, and the odour of sweetness which comforts men and rejoices angels).

Sales goes on in his third chapter happily to apply to Christians the snippet from *Genesis* (I, xi) about God's command that the fruits of the earth should produce seed "each according to its kind". Each should produce the fruits of devotion "selon sa capacité et vacation (according to ability and occupation)."

La dévotion doit être différemment exercée par le gentil-homme, par l'artisan, par le valet, par le prince, par la veuve, par la fille, par la mariée; et non seulement cela, mais il faut accommoder la pratique de la dévotion aux forces, aux affaires et aux devoirs de chaque particulier… La dévotion ne gâte rien quand elle est vraie, ains elle perfectionne tout, et lorsqu'elle se rend contraire à la légitime vacation de quelqu'un, elle est sans doute fausse

(Devotion should be practised differently by the noble, by the artisan, by the servant, by the prince, by the widow, by the unmarried girl, by the wife; and not only that, but the practice of devotion must be adjusted to the strength, business, and duties of each individual… Devotion when it is genuine conflicts with nothing but perfects everything and, when it becomes incompatible with anyone's legitimate occupation, it is doubtless inauthentic).

The danger is that the genial and apparently artless style should lead us to overlook the audacity of the content. Sales and his readers knew perfectly well that, however true, his statement was not a legitimate inference from *Genesis*, but Sales uses it to make it sound as if he is playing a game, although he intends it to be understood that he is not. What Sales was providing was the radically new spirituality needed and devoured by the hope-filled generation which had seen the religious wars resolved. But he is conservative enough to maintain in the third part of the *Introduction* that even devout lay-people should live according to the spirit of the evangelical counsels of poverty, chastity, and obedience.

The work now insists on the individual's need for guidance, and for a director capable of being both trusted and revered, implying the quasi-certainty of delusion without a director, and the extreme difficulty of finding a director with the necessary charity, learning, and power of discernment. For the rest of the first part Sales stays on more traditional ground, insisting, however, not only on abstinence from what is externally sinful, but also on the eradication of sinful desires. The devout individual must no longer look longingly on forms of behaviour which are sinful. Sales proposes a series of meditations directly inspired by those in the *Spiritual Exercises* of Ignatius of Loyola. The second part continues in the same tradition, with practical advice on the necessity and conduct of mental prayer and the frequentation of the sacraments, recommending frequent communion. The third part, on the practice of virtue, again insists on the primacy of interior attitudes over external acts and personal preferences. The role of the director remains paramount, but it is especially in this part that the work shows its seams. Sales moves disconcertingly between advice of an extremely detailed and practical nature to much wider considerations of spiritual principles.

It is in the 11th chapter of the third part that he comes back to his fundamental distinction between lay and monastic spirituality.

La seule charité nous met en la perfection; mais l'obéissance, la chasteté et la pauvreté sont les trois grands moyens pour l'acquérir. L'obéissance consacre notre coeur, la chasteté notre corps et la pauvreté nos moyens à l'amour et service de Dieu: ce sont les trois branches de la croix spirituelle, toutes trois néanmoins fondées sur la quatrième qui est l'humilité

(Charity alone confers perfection on us; but obedience, chastity, and poverty are the three great means to acquire it. Obedience consecrates our heart, chastity our body, and poverty the means of which we dispose for the love and service of God. They are the three branches of the spiritual cross, but all three are founded on the fourth, which is humility).

In spite of the experience of Mme de Chantal, Sales does not necessarily disapprove of a vow of obedience to the spiritual director, although he is not warm about it. What is important is the acceptance of guidance, especially in anything to do with attempts to tame the appetites of the body by physical austerities and mortifications.

On the subject of social conduct, Sales warns expressly against speaking ill of one's neighbour, the "médisance" that is to be of such concern to the moralists half a century later. Gambling at games of chance is condemned, dancing considered dangerous but allowable. Modesty, dignity, and a pure intention are called for, and Sales recommends some vivid reflections to help keep temptation at bay while you dance. However, both gambling and dancing are, in moderation, acceptable forms of recreation. It is noticeable that, at this level of specificity, Sales is more tentative than when he was gaily discussing the general principles of devotion in the first part. It is also clear that, however carefully the language has been emended, the assumption in Sales's mind is that his advice is addressed to women, and that the director is likely to be male.

In marriage the bodily union of husband and wife is not so important as the affective union of the two hearts, whose product is fidelity. There is a robust good sense about the role of physical intercourse in the chapters on marriage and the duty of spouses to accommodate themselves to one another's desires. Intercourse should not be conducted differently just because on a particular occasion conception might be impossible. Sexual congress can become blameworthy in the measure in which demand for it is excessive or "lorsque l'ordre établi pour la production des enfants est violé et perverti (when the order established for the production of children is violated or perverted)." That, Sales goes on to point out, does not mean during pregnancy or in cases of known sterility. The chapters make interesting social as well as spiritual history in what they plainly presuppose about marital attitudes and practices.

Sales has gone a long way forward for a book of spiritual guidance, as he actually had to if he wished his work to be seriously helpful in offering spiritual guidance to those who were married, or were going to be married. But the hierarchy of fruits of marriage, first the union of hearts, then fidelity, then the production of offspring, does not prevent reference a chapter later to the primary "end" of marriage itself, although not of each individual act of "commerce corporel (sexual intercourse)," which appears to remain procreation. At the end of his two chapters on the subject (III, xxxviii and xxxix) he becomes almost coy: "I think I have said everything I wanted to say, and allowed to be understood without saying it what I did not want to say." The following two chapters are addressed to those widows who do not contemplate remarriage, and to virgins, whom Sales tells "gardez jalousement votre premier amour pour votre premier mari (keep your first love jealously for your first husband)."

The work's fourth part contains, as well as some particularly acute psychological observation and a view of the emotions already quite close to that which Descartes was to systematize half a century later, a strong attack on anxiety. "L'inquiétude est le plus grand mal qui arrive en l'âme, excepté le péché (Anxiety is the greatest evil that can occur to a soul except sin)." Sales defines it as "un désir déréglée d'être délivré du mal que l'on sent (a disordered desire to be delivered from a felt evil)." "Tristesse" is simply discouragement, and Sales's advice on both spiritual joys and spiritual dryness goes little further than the classical teaching to be found, for instance, in most of the important 16th-century Jesuit authors. In the very short fifth part, he does not do much more than summarize and wind up what he has already said, encouraging his Philothée to make progress in the devout life.

The *Traité de l'amour de Dieu*, contemporary with the *Introduction*, while equally written for individuals, the sixth, seventh, and eighth books for Mère Anne-Marie Rosset as well as the ninth for Mère de Chantal, is much more theoretical than the *Introduction*. Its preface warns the reader that some effort has been made at systematizing the birth, progress, and characteristics of the love of God, and it is also now addressed to "Théotime," which in verbal form is masculine. Written "entre plusieurs distractions (amidst many distractions)," it was conceived in 1607 and its plan was becoming clear in 1609. A first draft was not completed until 1614, and it was extensively revised before publication in the summer of 1616. There are 12 books which admirably provide the theoretical foundation for the trust in human nature which informs the *Introduction*. The first four books constitute systematic philosophical and theological introductions to the practical considerations which follow.

The *Traité* begins by establishing the framework of psychology of the faculties, inside which the later teaching is to be understood. Technically speaking, what has happened is that elements of Platonism and neostoicism have been incorporated into what is essentially the Augustinian view. Augustine himself had radically modified neoplatonist psychology in the light of the Christian theology of the Incarnation and the Trinity, as it had been recently defined by the early Councils of the Church, and it was the systemization of Augustine by Aquinas that the Platonism and neostoicism of the renaissance had distorted. It is unlikely that Sales thought that he was modifying the Thomist view when he attempted to establish the supremacy of the will over the other faculties in man, the will's "naturelle monarchie," over "l'innumérable multitude et variété d'actions, mouve-

ments, sentiments, inclinations, habitudes, passions, facultés et puissances (the innumerable multitude and variety of actions, movements, feelings, inclinations, habits, passions, faculties and powers)" of the soul, but his argument is coloured by echoes of Ficino's *De amore*. He also relies on the fourth chapter of the Pseudo-Denys's neoplatonist *De divinis nominibus* in distinguishing between goodness and beauty. That text was to become important in the history of 17th-century spirituality. The authenticity of the pseudo-Denys's writings, thought to be those of Saint Paul's first convert at the Areopagus in Athens, had recently been defended against Valla, Erasmus, and Cajetan by Martin Delrio in his *Vindiciae Areopagiticae* of 1607, and by Dom Jean de Saint-François Goulu in his 1608 *Apologie*.

There are over 70 quotations from Augustine in the early portion of the *Traité*, with five reference to Augustine's *De civitate dei* in the third chapter, which lists twelve passions and thereby shows that Sales has not understood the principles of Aquinas's own classification, which he intended to follow, but which could yield only eleven different affective states. Augustine is closely followed in his rejection of the stoic view that, because the passions were false judgements of value, the wise man was without them. The mixture of ingredients is important, because it was Augustine who introduced the will ("voluntas") as a faculty into western thought, and its relationship to the intellect has been the subject of philosophical and theological dispute ever since. In the 13th century Aquinas had attempted, but in fact failed, to establish the hegemony of the intellect, making the will a "rational" appetite.

For Sales the "delectation" (see: Jansenism) attracts but does not determine the will, and it is not rational at all. The will is not itself a rational appetite, as it was for Aquinas, and the moral qualities of the passions stem not, as in Aquinas, from their accordance with "right reason," but from the quality of the love in the will, notoriously in the end deriving either from the virtuous love of God "usque ad contemptum sui (taken as far as the contempt of self)" or from sinful "amor sui usque ad contemptum dei (self-love taken as far as contempt for God)." Sales is not concerned by his lack of consistency when he holds at the same time, with Aquinas, that the "sensitive appetite," the passions or affective movements of the soul, escape the complete control of the will and, with the Jesuit Molinist tradition, that our love should be entirely in our power, "d'autant que la volonté n'ayme qu'en voulant aymer (because the will loves only because it chooses to love)." Sales happily endorses the view, no doubt derived from the first sentence of Epictetus's *Enchiridion*, translated in 1609 by Dom Jean de Saint-François Goulu, that our true good is in our power, and he follows Augustine in regarding the love of God, or charity, as the infused "habitual" or "sanctifying" grace which produces in the soul the state of justification.

In the fifth chapter of Book III, Sales accepts the Molinist view that predestination occurs only "post praevisa merita (after the prevision of merits)." He writes of God,

Il voulut premièrement, d'une vraie volonté, qu'encore après le péché d'Adam 'tous les hommes fussent sauvés' [I *Timothy* ii, 4], mais en une façon et par des moyens convenables à la condition de leur nature, douée de franc arbitre; c'est-à-dire, il voulut le salut de tous ceux qui voudraient contribuer leur consentement aux grâces et faveurs qu'il leur préparerait, offrirait et départirait à cette intention. Or, entre ces faveurs, il voulut que la vocation fût la première, et qu'elle fût tellement attrempée à notre liberté, que nous la puissions accepter ou rejeter à notre gré. Et à ceux desquels il prévit qu'elle serait accepté, il voulut fournir les sacrés mouvements de la pénitence; et à ceux qui seconderaient ces mouvements, il disposa de donner la sainte charité; et à ceux qui auraient la charité, il délibéra de donner les secours requis pour persévérer; et à ceux qui emploieraient ces divins secours, il résolut de leur donner la finale persévérance et glorieuse félicité de son amour éternel

(He first wanted, with a firm will, that even after Adam's sin 'all men should be saved,' [I *Timothy* ii, 4], but in a way and by means appropriate to their nature, which is endowed with free will. That is to say, he desired the salvation of all those willing to contribute their consent to the graces and gifts which he would prepare for them, would offer, and would bestow to that end. But, among those gifts, he desired that membership of the elect should be the first, and that it should be so attuned to our freedom that we could accept or reject it at our will. And on those by whom he foresaw that election would be accepted, he desired to bestow the sacred movements of penitence; and to those who would cooperate with these movements, he decreed the gift of holy charity; and to those who had charity, he decided to give the assistance necessary for perseverance; and to those who would use this divine assistance he resolved to give final perseverance and the glorious beatitude of his eternal love).

A score of years later the theologians associated with Port-Royal, also writing in the vernacular, would take a quite opposite view. Before Sales, the dispute, however monumental its religious consequences had already been, had on the level of technical theology itself been conducted in Latin. Sales not only opened up the theological dispute, but his insistence jointly on the universality of the divine will to save men and on the autonomous power of human spiritual self-determination also entailed the unusually optimistic view of human nature which he held, no doubt for reasons which were not either purely theological or even purely connected with his own spiritual crisis when, in Paris, he thought for six weeks that he was going to be damned.

Sales had already established his high estimation of the capacities of human nature in chapter 16 of the first Book, "Que nous avons une inclination naturelle d'aimer Dieu sur toutes choses (That we have a natural inclination to love God above all things)." Before Adam's sin, the natural inclination in human beings to love God above all things corresponded to what is theologically known as the "elevated" state of nature in which Adam was created. After Adam's sin, the natural inclination remains but (chapter 17), since the will was more greatly damaged than the intellect, Sales holds that it cannot be given effect without the aid of grace. At this point Sales inserts a paragraph on his admiration for "le pauvre bon homme (that unfortunate good fellow)" Epictetus, who could speak of God "avec tant de goût, de sentiment et de zèle (with so much desire, feeling, and ardour)" that you would take him for a Christian emerging from some holy and deep meditation. Yet Epictetus speaks of the gods as a pagan. The implication is that pagans are excluded from

grace, which is limited to believers as defined, in particular, by the 1302 bull *Unam sanctam*, and by the decree of the Council of Florence for the Jacobites, of 4 February 1441.

Something effectively like Sales's solution, that Adam's fall has left human nature with a natural instinct towards virtue which can, however, be given effect only with the aid of supernatural grace, eventually won the theological battle, although it was to be strongly contested by Jansenist theology in France. Doctrine is now differently interpreted. But as Sales expressed his view in the vernacular in 1616, his position remained theologically vulnerable. However, he was writing not theology but the theoretical basis for generalized spiritual advice for the religiously advanced, and in upgrading the moral and religious promptings of human nature as it existed he was responding to the imaginative constraints imposed by the whole thrust of French culture in the early years of the 17th century. God's own "infinie débonnaireté (infinite kindliness)" did not allow him to be as rigorous with humanity as it deserved. Chapter 18 of Book 1 reaffirms the utility of our natural inclination to love God, who will give us the means to put it into effect if we cooperate with his grace.

The theological minefield created by the concepts of nature and grace was actually more dangerous than it has been necessary to indicate here, where the points to be made concerned Sales's optimism and his audacity in their literary and generally cultural settings. He did not himself write as if he had been aware quite how controversial his stance was, and he coated the pill of the somewhat abstract argument with an elaborate analogy taken from the life of the partridge chick which, even when hatched in an alien nest (*Jeremiah* xvii, 11), instantly recognizes the first call of its real mother, just as our natural inclination directs us to our true end, however we might have been disorientated or incapacitated by Adam's sin.

The bulk of the *Traité*, while less abstract, uses a vocabulary which is just as technical, although the work's content is chiefly exhortatory. The language is still often figurative, even when no longer dependent on analogies from classical history, myth, or natural history, but occasionally Sales changes the register, as from the metaphorical to the psychological when, for instance, he acknowledges (Book IX, chapter 13) that our wills cannot truly be said to die.

Certes, notre volonté ne peut jamais mourir, non plus que notre esprit, mais elle outrepasse quelquefois les limites de sa vie ordinaire, pour vivre toute en la volonté divine... Elle ne périt pas tout à fait, mais elle est tellement abîmée et mêlée avec la volonté de Dieu, qu'elle ne paraît plus et n'a plus aucun vouloir séparé de celui de Dieu

(Certainly, our will can never die, any more than our mind, but it sometimes goes beyond the limits of its ordinary life to live entirely in the divine will... It does not altogether perish, but it is so engulfed and blended with the divine will, that it no longer appears and has no desire other than that of God).

This union of wills, manifested in obedience and, necessarily, the abnegation of all purely personal desire, is the summit of the love of God, as was shown on Calvary.

The *Entretiens* as we have them cannot be considered to be Sales's works, although they certainly contain his doctrine and may have been revised by him from notes taken by the nuns and written up after his talks. His spiritual teaching can perhaps best be summed up from the final *Entretien*, given two days before his death:

> Car enfin il ne faut rien désirer ni rien refuser, mais se lais- ser entre les bras de la Providence divine, sans s'amuser à aucun désir, sinon en ce que Dieu veut faire de nous... Toute notre perfection dépend de ce point

> (For in the end we should desire nothing and refuse noth- ing, but leave ourselves in the arms of divine Providence, without distracting ourselves by any desire, except what God wants of us... Our whole perfection depends on that attitude).

PUBLICATIONS

[*There were innumerable unauthorized editions of individual works and of selections, and a large number of selections not listed here have also been published in English translation*]

Collections

Les Oeuvres de Messire François de Sales, 1637
Les Oeuvres du Bien-heureux François de Sales, 2 vols., 1641 (edition supervised by Mère de Chantal)
Oeuvres de François de Sales, 27 vols., 1892–1964
Oeuvres, Bibliothèque de la Pléiade, vol. 1, 1969

Works

Défense de l'étendard de la Sainte Croix, 1600
Introduction à la vie dévote, 1609, 1616; as *An Introduction to a Devoute Life*, 1613
Traité de l'Amour de Dieu, 1616; as *A Treatise on the Love of God*, 1630
Les Entretiens, [1628] (unauthorized); as *Les Vrays Entretiens spirituels*, 1629
Les Controverses, 1672 (in re-edition of *Les Oeuvres* of 1641)

Biographical and critical studies

Goulu, Dom Jean de Saint-François, *La vie du bien-heureux Messire François de Sales*, 1624
La Rivière, P. Louys de, *La Vie de l'Il. et Rev. François de Sales*, 1624
Longueterre, de, *La vie de tres illustre Messire François de Sales*, 2 vols., 1624
Philibert (de la Bonneville), *Vie du bienheureux François de Sales*, 1624
Sales, Charles-Auguste de, *Histoire du bienheureux François de Sales*, 1634
Camus, Jean-Pierre, *Esprit du bien-heureux François de Sales*, 6 vols., 1641; edited by J.-I. Depéry, 3 vols., 1840; as *The Memoirs of Saint Francis of Sales*, 1814; as *The Mind of Saint Francis of Sales*, 1868
Sainte J.-Fr. de Chantal, 7 vols., 1876–90
Bremond, Henri, *Histoire littéraire du sentiment religieux en*

France, 12 vols., 1916–36
Trochu, F., *Saint François de Sales*, 2 vols., 1941–6
Liuima, A., *Aux Sources du Traité de l'Amour de Dieu de saint François de Sales*, 2 vols., 1959–60
Lemaire, Henri, *Les Images chez saint François de Sales*, 1962
Ravier, A., and Devos, R., *Saint François de Sales*, 1962
Lajeunie, E., *Saint François de Sales*, 2 vols., 1966

Bibliography

Brasier, V., Morganti, E., and M. St Durica, *Bibliografia salesi- ana, opere e scritti riguardanti S. Francesco di Sales (1623–1955)*, 1956.

SATIRE MÉNIPPÉE, La, 1594.

Satirical pamphlet by Pierre Leroy, Jacques Gillot, Nicolas Rapin, Pierre Pithou, Jean Passerat, and Florent Chrétien.

The *Satire Ménippée* was never intended to be a book. It is a col- lection of satirical writings loosely connected to the general theme of the 1593 Estates General of the Catholic League. The texts have different literary registers, use different sorts of irony, or dispense with irony altogether. They circulated with other similar texts now excluded from the collection, which was printed with different titles, and at different stages of the texts' development. All the pieces in what is currently known as the *Satire Ménippée* did however, originate from the same group, and all purport to be earlier and more daring than they actually were. The Catholic League, which the work attacks, had already been defeated when it was published.

In 1588, most of the population of France, and virtually all the major towns except Bordeaux and the towns of the Loire valley, but especially Paris, were in favour of the Catholic League, founded in 1576 partly on account of the indignation felt at the concessions made to the Protestants by King Henri III at the peace of Beaulieu the preceding year. Both Henri III's elder brothers, François II and Charles IX, had died, and in 1575 Henri III had married Louise de Vaudémont of the house of Lor- raine. Since there was no issue from that marriage, the heir pre- sumptive was the King's only younger brother, the duc d'Anjou. When the duc d'Anjou died in 1584, genealogically, and if females were excluded, the heir presumptive became Henri de Navarre, a Protestant, the great grandson of Louise de Savoie but also husband of Marguerite de Valois, the youngest of the three daughters of Henri II. The eldest daughter of Henri II, Elisabeth de Valois, had married Philip II of Spain, by whom she had a daughter, Isabella.

It is too often overlooked that the genealogical tables on their own left some room for discussion about the legitimacy of the succession, that the "Salic law," in fact no more than a series of Frankish codes invoked in the middle ages to exclude claims to succession based on a female line, had no other force than that of debatable ancient custom, and was called into use as a manifestation not of constitutional propriety but of political will, and that the only realities which counted in the imposition of a solution were ultimately not religious, or even national, but simply political and military. Independence from Spain seemed by no means inevitable and probably to entail a Protestant France.

Behind the bitterness which made the hostilities of the religious wars become almost continuous from 1584 until their resolution in 1593 was the apparent inevitability of a united France ruled by a Protestant, a situation wholly unacceptable to most of the kingdom; or an equally unacceptable united France, Catholic but dominated by the Guise family and relegated to the status of a Spanish satellite; or a France splintered again into fragments such as those from which it had only quite recently been forged, which seemed at moments the most likely and not necessarily the least tolerable result. The emergence of an independent and reasonably united France under the monarch whose claims to legitimacy of succession were highest, but who was Catholic, and also willing to enact what we know as the edict of Nantes, did not in 1584 seem probable.

When "La Sainte Ligue" was founded in 1576 to defend Catholicism against Calvinism in France, Henri III had put himself at its head in an attempt to pre-empt leadership of the Catholic party. But by 1585 the League had become completely dominated by the three sons of the Guise family: the duc Henri de Guise, known as le Balafré, the cardinal de Guise, and the duc de Mayenne. On 2 January 1585 Philip II had pledged support at Joinville for the claims of the cardinal archbishop of Rouen, Charles de Bourbon, to the French throne, and Catherine de Medici was forced that summer to surrender all north-east France to the Guise interests. The king and Henri de Navarre moved closer to one another, while Paris under the revolutionary government of the "Seize (sixteen)," that is the 50 or so individuals, representatives of the 16 Paris quartiers of 1587, but not themselves 16 in number, delivered the city to the Guise family. Catherine de Medici was attempting to temporize, but her son was facing demands from Henri de Guise early in 1588 which were calculatedly insolent and, when the king forbade him to enter Paris, Guise not only ignored him, but called on Catherine de Medici there.

When the king posted Swiss mercenaries all over the town on 12 May 1588, the Parisians put up the celebrated barricades to isolate the Swiss units from one another. On 13 May, the king quietly galloped off to Chartres, leaving his wife and his mother to mediate. In October the king summoned the Estates to Blois, the speakers for all three estates or orders being strongly pro-League. On 23 December the king summoned the duc de Guise and the cardinal, and had them killed on successive days. The bodies were burned and the ashes thrown into the Loire in case relics were sought. Among the members of the League arrested were the cardinal de Bourbon and the archbishop of Lyons. Catherine de Medici died on 5 January and the pope, who disliked having his prelates imprisoned and was now confronted by the king alone, threatened excommunication. Then, just as Henri III was preparing to take Paris, he was assassinated on 2 August 1589. The *de iure* king of France was a Protestant who hated Spain and commanded no allegiance at all in most parts of the country.

It is essential to appreciate the popularity of the League, the liberal and democratically advanced ideas it propagated on sove-

reignty, its notion of a pact between king and people, which could be regarded as broken if dishonoured, the manifest inadequacy of Henri III as a political leader, and the daunting challenge which faced Henri de Navarre, in order to understand texts like the *Satyre Ménippée*. The pamphlet could simply not have scoffed in that way, or advocated the policies it did, before the League had discredited itself, and it was not clear before late in 1592 how that could happen. An instant conversion of Navarre would have alienated his supporters without satisfying the League. He decided to move slowly, and in fact exercised extraordinary skill. He promised in due course to take "instruction" in the Catholic religion, and waited for the League to overreach itself.

Meanwhile he did not even dispose of enough troops to take Paris, but Mayenne went too far when he gambled by proclaiming the imprisoned cardinal de Bourbon as Charles X. Navarre slowly built up support, holding his own at Arques on 21 September, and routing Mayenne at Ivry on 14 March 1590. On that occasion, the order was given to spare French troops, but Mayenne's mercenaries were massacred. On 10 May the old cardinal de Bourbon died, leaving the League without a figurehead, and Navarre began the siege of Paris. Only Parma's skill relieved the beleaguered city early in September, and only at the end of 1590 could a handful of "politiques" even begin to dream of the final reconciliation.

Parma, whose generalship constantly outwitted his opponents, died in 1592, and it gradually became clear that France could be united under Navarre if he became a Catholic. There was a serious chance of attaining the ideal solution, and the more realistic it became, the quicker support for the League was dissipated and the stronger the support for the politiques. Still the League was too strong, however, to be treated as dismissively as in the *Ménippée*. Its victory was not just a bad dream, and its rump was too strong to laugh at. By mid-1592 serious negotiations were taking place between moderates who had supported the League and Huguenots prepared to envisage Henri's conversion to Catholicism. When news reached Paris on 4 December that Parma had died, the League could no longer look to a military victory to save them. Mayenne immediately called a meeting of the Estates in Paris for January 1593. The Spanish delegation urged the appointment of the Infanta as queen. She was, after all, the daughter of the eldest child of Henri II to leave issue. The "Salic law" excluded her on grounds of gender, but the *Ménippée* heavily exploits anti-Spanish feeling. Religion was no longer really the issue.

By 29 April 1593, representatives of the League and the king were with Mayenne's encouragement having serious discussions at Suresnes. On 18 May the king expressed his willingness to be "instructed." On 25 July he received absolution and heard Mass. On 18 September Lyons rose against the pro-Guise duc de Nemours, but the League was still strong, especially in Toulouse. In Brittany, Picardy, the north and east, its authority was not yet seriously challenged. There were major changes in the winter of 1593–94, but the coronation of 27 February 1594 had to take place at Chartres. The traditional stage for coronations, Reims, was still in League hands.

The *Satyre Ménippée* as we have it, is at least the third revision of a series of satirical documents, drawn up by different pens and at different times, with additions, changes of emphasis, and adaptations made as events progressed, but always in the same milieu. Parts of the original text may antedate the Suresnes conference, while other passages cannot have been written before the spring of 1594. Henri IV's entry into Paris took place on 22 March. The text shows obvious signs of patching and stitching, reflecting the year-long process of up-dating. Since it certainly started by circulating in manuscript, and probably went through innumerable manuscript versions, we can go for its content only on what must be regarded as a series of definite but perhaps arbitrary points in the text's development at which it has been printed, starting with the *Abbregé et l'Ame des Estatz convoquez à Paris en l'an 1593, le 10 de febvrier*, which has 12 leaves, making 24 pages, and no verse. While this document is little more than a first sketch, the order of subsequent editions is still disputed.

The book purports to be an account of the Estates written by Mlle de la Lande, known to be employed by Mme de Nemours, and by "Messieurs Domay et Victoon, penitens blancqs." The first printed version may have been available in 1593. It was certainly circulating in manuscript before Henri de Navarre formally asked for instruction. There are innumerable variants in the early printed copies, and it is not entirely certain, although it is probable, that the next clear stage of the text, dated 1593, but not available until 1594, was *La Vertu du Catholicon d'Espagne. Avec un Abrégé de la tenue des Estats de Paris convoques au X de febvrier 1593 par les Chefs de la Ligue*. This version, in which Henri is actually receiving instruction, is said to be taken from Mlle de la Lande's memoirs and from her secret conversations with a Jesuit, Père Comme-laid ("How-Ugly"), swiftly changed to a neutral Commelet. The text normally regarded as definitive is the "editio princeps," *La Satyre Ménippée; ou, La Vertu du Catholicon*, published by the royalist printer, Jamet Mettayer, at Tours at the beginning of 1594, but not called *Satyre Ménippée* until the second or third 1594 edition, printed in Paris. From very early on the text was augmented by the addition of Jean de la Taille's *Les Singeries de la Ligue* and of the anonymous *Le Supplement du Catholicon; ou, Nouvelles des regions de la lune*, a parody of Lucian's satire the *Icaromenippus* and of Rabelais, which was attributed to "a Jesuit" and dedicated to the king of Spain.

The reworking of the original text was extensive, and clearly drew piecemeal on other contemporary attacks on the League as they began to circulate, notably F. Cromé's *Dialogue entre le maheustre et le manant* (Dialogue of the Courtier and the Commoner). The non-ironical oration of d'Aubray for the third estate, written by Pierre Pithou, was more than quadrupled in length, turning the pamphlet into something much more than a mocking caricature of the League. It was strengthened to include a serious analysis of recent events, piling discredit on to Mayenne, and pointing out the way in which the title conferred on him in 1589 by the League, "Lieutenant de l'Estat et Couronne," allowed him to usurp royal power without incurring the opprobrium of using the designation of king. The title is unheard-of, foreign, "and has a great long tail, like an unnatural monster, to frighten children." The tone becomes altogether more serious, too, when an attempt is made by in d'Aubray's oration to see the importance for Spain of control of French territory, given Philip's need for constant movement of goods and troops between the kingdom itself and the Spanish Netherlands.

An anti-Spanish addition to Rose's oration reflects an actual and unexpected invervention by the real Rose at the Estates which apparently stunned the assembly. The *Ménippée* also exploits the increasing hostility of the Seize to Mayenne, who was notoriously furious at the pamphlet's publication. The ora-

tion put into the mouth of Mayenne himself, as "Monsieur le lieutenant," now satirizes his cowardice and military failures, while multiplying boasts about his intrigues. Rose's oration is lengthened to harden the case against Mayenne, accusing him of offering the throne of France to the highest bidder, pointing to the way he had undermined the young duc de Guise's hopes for the crown. which for a moment had seemed close to being realized, and double-dealt with Henri, trying in Rome to prevent the absolution which was expected automatically to follow the abjuration of Protestantism while negotiating to hand over Paris and make peace at the same time.

The satire as we have it therefore changes its purpose as it goes along. From the original mockery, celebrating and intensifying the discomfiture of the League as a result of its loss of support and the failure of its final bid, the January 1593 Estates, it develops into a pamphlet concerned with ancient custom in matters of succession, the perils of an elected sovereign, and the dangers of democracy. The democracy envisaged by the Seize is indeed likely to have been dictatorial, and it may be that readers were expected to realise that fact. But by 1594, readers were complaining of the tedium of d'Aubray's harangue, and the printer, whose second "Discours" may have been by Passerat or Pithou, tied himself in knots trying to explain both the "Satyre" and the "Ménippée" of the title.

In view of the manner of its gestation and its continued fame, the text has to be taken exactly as it now stands. It is impossible to distinguish within the printed text what, at any give date, was ancillary to the intentions of the many people concerned in its composition and dissemination. As first printed in its present state, the pamphlet was scarcely intended to move opinion, except possibly about the high constitutional principles which it argues were at stake. As a pamphlet it does not so much write history from the victors' point of view as justify what had happened by recourse to yardsticks of sanity, expediency, constitutional argument, and divine authority. It also at least implicitly attempts to justify the use of coarse exaggeration and often grotesque caricature in the interests of pouring ridicule on defeat, and presents itself to the public as a document with an internal unity and coherence it manifestly does not possess.

It is possible to give some indications about those concerned in its composition. We know from internal and different sorts of external evidence that the serious constitutional thought, contained in the original and then massively enlarged "Harangue de Monsieur d'Aubray pour le tiers estat," came from Pierre Pithou (1539–96), theologian, constitutional historian, and author of the *Traitez des droits et libertez de l'Eglise gallicane*. Born at Troyes and a close friend of the executor of Pierre de la Ramée, Antoine Loisel, he studied law with Cujas, following him, with Loisel, from Bourges to Valence. He became a Calvinist, took refuge at Sedan, moved on to Basle, and returned to Paris after the 1570 edict of pacification, miraculously escaping the Saint Bartholomew's Day massacre by climbing out of an attic window and over roof-tops. Loisel hid him. In 1573 he abjured, became a bailli at Sancerre, and a substitute procureur in 1579. He married, was procureur in Guyenne, wrote in favor of French episcopacy's power to absolve Henri IV without recourse to Rome, maintained the liberties of the Gallican church, and was appointed Procureur général of the parlement de Paris.

The original parody appears to have been thought up in the milieu of Jacques Gillot (?1550–1619), dean of the chapter at Langres, then a canon of the Sainte Chapelle, who received at his house on the Quai des Orfèvres well-known scholars, lawyers, and poets, including J.-J. Scaliger and Desportes and was, from 1573, a conseiller-clerc at the parlement de Paris. In January 1589 he was put in the Bastille with Achille de Harlay, and hastened on his release to Tours, where he remained faithful to the cause of Henri de Navarre. The "Harangue de Monsieur le Légat" has been attributed to him.

Of the others taking part, Nicolas Rapin (?1540–1608), born at Fontenay-le-Comte in Poitou, was a poet imitator of Ronsard who fought as a captain for Henri IV at Ivry. He studied law at Poitiers, married in 1565 and had a large family, complained of the burden of seven, then nine, children and a hundred creditors, and attempted, like Baïf, to write quantitative verse. He managed to buy the office of prévôt des maréchaux de France in Poitou, became mayor of Fontenay, and in 1584 was promoted to Paris. Protected by Harlay, he became lieutenant criminel, or chief of police, and a grand-prévôt, and strongly defended the legitimacy of Henri de Navarre's claim to be heir presumptive at the Estates of 1588. He was driven from Paris by the Seize, but must have returned to write the verses and the orations attributed to him in the *Ménippée*, those of Monsieur de Lyon and Monsieur le recteur Rose. He finally acquired property near Fontenay, retired there, and died on his way to Paris in 1608. His manners were rough, and he was at heart a soldier as well as a poet. He wrote verse in Latin and Greek, and translated from the Italian, and the psalms from Latin. He disliked what was new, whether Calvinism or the League, but was not given to lofty speculation of any sort.

Jean Passerat (1534–1602), who composed most of the verse, could be witty as well as indignant. For the last five years of his life he was blind, having lost one eye in childhood playing tennis. He ran away from the pension where he had been sent to school, took service with an army marshal, finished his studies at Paris, and became professor of humanities at the Collège du Plessis before going to Bourges to study with Cujas. Back in Paris in 1569, he became friendly with Henri de Mesmes and lived in his household for 29 years. After the murder of Pierre de la Ramée, Passerat succeeded to his chair. Both a philologist and a wit, he was a firm Catholic. Unpaid during the League's control of Paris, Passerat claims to have re-read Plautus 40 times, deriving an inspiration which has been enough to suggest that he may have written the oration of Rieux, normally unattributed. Some of his poetry is graceful and witty.

Florent Chrétien (1540–96), born at Orléans, son of the Breton doctor of François I and of Henri II, was a Calvinist and tutor to the future Henri IV, translator into Latin of Pibrac's famous quatrains, after attacking Ronsard for his anti-Calvinist poetry and Pibrac as an apologist for the Saint Bartholomew's Day massacre. De Thou knew him well. Chrétien became a Catholic, and was a scholar, who translated several texts of Aristophanes into Latin verse. He is reputed to have written the oration of the cardinal de Pelvé. Henri IV ransomed him when he was a League prisoner at Vendôme, but is thereafter thought to have neglected him.

Finally Pierre Leroy, a canon of Rouen and chaplain to the young cardinal de Bourbon, is said by de Thou to have inspired the whole project. All we know of him is the half-dozen lines in de Thou's history.

As the text now stands it consists of two very unequal parts, with appendices, of which the first is the prefatory burlesque account by the printer, written from the point of view of a fanatical adherent of the League, of how the text came into his hands; this was removed after the first five editions. The first part proper starts with the title *Satyre Ménippée*, best considered with the final "Discours de l'imprimeur," in which the printer tries to explain it. This is followed by the first section "La Vertu du Catholicon," depending for its effect on rather crudely farcical language, as if the stylistic model had been the Rabelais of *Pantagruel*, on which Passerat had written a commentary which his confessor had made him burn. Rabelais is in fact quoted several times, particularly in those parts of the work probably or certainly attributable to Passerat.

As the deputies assemble in the Louvre for the first session of the Estates, two charlatans vaunt their wares. The Spanish charlatan is offering a "Catholicon" much more effective than the Roman sort, which prepares souls for salvation and beatititude in only the other world. We are given 20 items from a list of 50 miraculous effects of the drug which protects from the effects of irreligion and can turn its wrapping into a cardinal's hat. The Lorraine charlatan is much poorer, offering a less ambitious Catholicon. He is identified as Pelvé, the anti-Gallican cardinal archbishop of Reims. The effects of the drugs offer much scope for allusive topical scurrilities, often trading on gossip about well-known figures, and the text depends on the age-old technique of attributing claims and statements in the manner of a cartoonist putting into the mouth of a character what the cartoonist wishes to suggest the character might really be thinking behind the smiling front.

Then comes the "Abrégé" itself, describing first the procession, and then the tapestries of the room prepared for the meetings. The procession alludes to that of 17 January 1593 in Paris, to pray for the Estates, but perhaps also to other League processions which had been held in Paris. The date mentioned in the text is 10 February. The technique depends on ridicule by exaggeration, but the comedy is no longer so extravagantly burlesque as in the earlier section. Humour is extracted, for instance, from the lists of religious orders to which the monks belonged, and the motet is called after the psalm verse "How full of delights are thy dwellings," but omits the final reference to God, whose dwelling, the Sainte Chapelle, they were in. The humour of the tapestry subjects is very subdued indeed. The assassination of Henri III is represented, and the promotion of Aumale to Connétable after he had fled from the battlefield at Senlis is no more than an ironic topical allusion.

The much longer second part of the text starts with the order of precedence according to rank of those taking part. There follow the various orations. The first is Mayenne's self-condemnation, "I have always preferred my own interest to that of God who can look after himself." Mayenne remembers the thousands of French martyrs who have died for the League, "by the sword, of hunger, of flame, of rage, of despair...?" "Must I recount to you the base and servile submissions I made...?" The author deploys the crudest forms of sarcasm in depicting Mayenne's self-pity and in making him discredit himself with references to his own self-interest. No-one who was going to read the text needed convincing of Mayenne's misdeeds. This speech was merely a celebration by his opponents of Mayenne's accomplished defeat, in which the authors gloated over what the piece regarded as Mayenne's own self-destruction.

The papal legate speaks half in comic but comprehensible Italian, denouncing peace with heretics, and half in Latin, urging the claims to the French throne of the Spanish infanta, Henri II's granddaughter. Pelvé speaks partly in Latin about electing a king, since the pope has declared that Henri de Navarre has already been damned to hell. The harangue of Pierre d'Espinac, archbishop of Lyons, invites the company to celebrate the wonders worked by the League. As Jesus humbled the mighty and lifted up the poor, so, too, all the villains are now transformed into members of our party. Rose's oration is a quite funny parody of academic rhetoric, leading everywhere to obviously absurd conclusions. Choosing the King is going to be difficult. Mayenne wants the job, but so does his nephew, and his brother, and then there are the dukes of Savoy and of Lorraine to think about. Each has as much right as the others.

In fact the very weakness of the League orations shows that the *Ménippée* is ritually burying a lost cause. There is no need any more to produce real arguments to counter, but Rose produced an open attack on Mayenne which went too far for some even of his colleagues. Rieux, here speaking for the nobility, was in fact a petty thief who was caught and hanged in 1594. Into his mouth is put an apologia for thievery and, if it comes to electing a king, he does not see that he is inferior to any of the other candidates. It was a reproach made against the Seize by its enemies that they were very largely small merchants and petty villains.

Claude d'Aubray was a real person, considered to be head of the "politiques," and driven out of Paris early in 1594. He had refused to negotiate with any member of the Seize. In life, he was much more violent against the League than in the speech the *Ménippée* puts into his mouth. His long harangue for the third estate is full of serious argument and enlightened and elevated discourse, but it is not a unified oration in the classical style. It is not well constructed, but meanders from one topic to the next. It starts by denouncing the Catholicon as an imposture. France is ruined. The text breaks into apostrophe, and the tone is moving as d'Aubray addresses Paris:

Te voilà aux fers! Te voilà en l'inquisition d'Espagne, plus intolérable mille fois, et plus dure à supporter aux esprits nez libres et francs, comme sont les François, que les plus cruelles morts dont les Espagnols se sauroyent adviser.... tu endures qu'on pille tes maisons, qu'on te rançonne jusques au sang, qu'on emprisonne les senateurs, qu'on chasse et bannisse tes bons citoyens et conseillers: qu'on pende, qu'on massacre tes principaux magistrats: tu le vois, et tu l'endures: tu ne l'endures pas seulement, mais tu l'approuves, et le loues, et n'oserois et ne sçaurois faire autrement

(You are in chains! You are under the Spanish inquisition, only a thousand times more intolerable, and harder to bear for spirits born free and unconstrained, like the French, than the cruellest deaths the Spaniards could think of.... you put up with having your houses sacked, with suffering extortion until you bleed, with having your senators imprisoned, with having your good citizens and counsellors driven away and banished, with having your chief magistrates hanged and massacred. You see it, and you put up with it. You not only put up with it, but you approve of it, and praise it, and haven't the courage or the power to do otherwise).

The references are to the parlementarians taken to the Bastille

on 16 January 1589, and to the execution of Barnabé Brisson, hanged with two others by the Seize on 16 November 1591 for being insufficiently anti-royalist. D'Aubray exaggerates the benefits Henri III has brought to Paris and uses a more highly charged, emotional style than, for instance, du Vair in his speech to the parlement de Paris of 28 June 1593, which makes much the same point more forcibly. His classical periods were needed because, unlike the *Ménippée*'s d'Aubray, who could afford the rhetorical histrionics, the lengthy succession of rhetorical questions, du Vair actually made his speech, and wanted to convince.

D'Aubray condemns the 1559 treaty of Cateau-Cambrésis which had ended the Italian wars, "ceste miserable paix qui fut sellee, et signalee de la mort de nostre bon roy Henri II (that wretched peace which was sealed and signalled by the death of our good king Henri II)." It is of course true that Cateau-Cambrésis was a victory for Philip II, who sold the English short by giving Calais back to the French, but also himself got back everything Spain had lost to France; but to blame the Spaniards even by association for the death of Henri II, killed by accident at the tournament to celebrate the double marriage called for in the treaty, makes clear the impassioned appeal to the emotions on which d'Aubray is made to rest his case.

D'Aubray is on stronger ground when he points to the way in which Philip fostered internal dissension within France, and to Philip's obvious need to preserve communications between his territories.

Premièrement je diray avec preface d'honneur que le roy d'Espagne est un grand prince, sage, caut, et advisé: le plus puissant, et le plus grand terrien de tous les princes chrestiens: et le seroit encore davantage si toutes ses terres et royaumes se tenoyent, et estoyent joincts à l'approche l'un de l'autre: mais la France qui est entre l'Espagne et les Pays-Bas, est cause que ses seigneuries separees lui coustent plus qu'elles ne luy valent... C'est pourquoy il a tasché de semer la division et la discorde parmi nous mesmes... car toutes les sanglantes tragédies qui ont depuis esté jouees sur ce pitoyable eschafaut françois, sont toutes nees et procedees de ces premieres querelles: et non de la diversité de religion, comme sans raison on a faict jusques icy croire aux simples et idiots

(Firstly, let me acknowledge by way of preface that the king of Spain is a great prince, wise, prudent, and shrewd: the most powerful of all the Christian princes, with the most territory; and he would be even more so if all his lands and kingdoms were joined together, and connected with one another: but France, which is between Spain and the Low Countries, makes these territories cost him more than they are worth... That is why he has tried to sow division and discord among us... for all the blood-letting tragedies which have since been played on this pitiable French stage were all born and have been generated from these first disputes, and not from the diversity of religion, which is what until now the simple and the foolish have been made without reason to believe).

The line of argument, obvious enough, is taken from the advice of François de Noailles to Henri III in 1585, as we know from de Thou. D'Aubray then launches into a long, detailed history of various disputes and claims which had split the great French families. The passionate reading of history leads naturally to the call to rally to the position whose victory was at any rate certain by the time the pamphlet was read, the unification of France under a converted Henri de Navarre.

Of the miscellaneous ancillary material, the only piece of real importance in a literary context is the "Discours de l'imprimeur" added to the Paris edition, and addressed to Mettayer at Tours. The Paris printer's discourse states in 1595 that the text was given to him at the coronation of Henri IV at Chartres, which took place on 27 February 1594. The word used is "sacre," only ever otherwise used of the consecration of a bishop, traditionally the highest degree of the sacrament of "holy orders," the other two forms being the deaconate and the priesthood. Just as the notion of temporal and spiritual powers, and indeed of jurisdiction, were not yet clearly and systematically separated by the end of the 16th century, so the word used here betrays the dual secular and religious nature of the anointing of a king, and explains much about the constitutional impossibility in Catholic France of a Protestant successor to Henri III. In the late 16th century sacred and civil terms and systems were still often interchangeable, so that, for instance, the penalty for contempt of court blended into that of excommunication for contempt of ecclesiastical authority. In the 16th century prelates like Wolsey still exercised both secular and ecclesiastical jurisdiction. Penalties for both excommunication and contempt of court were at least until recently never imposed for a fixed period, but only until the offence was "purged."

The printer maintains that the original "Avis" was wrong. The text cannot have been written in Italian. It comes not from "Italie" but from "Alethie (truth)," part of the town of "Eleuthere (free)," built and inhabited by Parisians. After continuing the burlesque for some pages, the printer comes to the title "Satyre Ménippée." The "y" is important. According to the printer, all those "nourris aux lettres (humanistically educated)" know that the word "satyre" means

(1) *not only* "un poeme de mesdisance, pour reprendre les vices publics ou particuliers de quelqu'un, comme celles de Lucilius, Horace, Juvenal, et Perse (a poem of invective attacking the public or private vices of someone, like the satires of Lucilius, Horace, Juvenal, and Persius)."

(2) *but also* "toute sorte d'escrits, remplis de diverses choses et de divers arguments, meslez de proses, et de vers entrelardez, comme entremets de langues de boeuf salees. Varron dit qu'on appelloit ainsy anciennement une façon de pastisserie, ou de farces, ou l'on mettoit plusieurs sortes d'herbages et de viandes (all sorts of writings, filled with different matters and arguments, with prose mixed up with verse, like a galantine of salted beef tongues. Varro said that this was what people used to call a sort of pastry, or stuffing, in which were put several sorts of herbs and meats)."

But (3) "j'estime que le nom vient des Grecs, qui introduisoyent sur les eschafauts, aux festes publiques, des hommes deguisez en Satyres qu'on feignoit estre demi-dieux lascifs et folastres par les forests (I think that the name comes from the Greeks, who introduced on to their platforms at public feasts men disguised as Satyrs, who were supposed to be lascivious and joyous half-gods inhabiting the forests)."

Since the term "satire" is so important not only for the *Ménippée* but in a quite general 16th-century French literary context, a contamination of meanings and models needs to be unscram-

bled. Firstly, however, it needs to be noticed that satire does not imply irony. It had to do with an attack on public or private behaviour, but includes polemic and invective without implying the stating of things known not to be true, innuendo, superciliousness, or anything other than what is actually said. The word does not mean "satire" in the modern sense.

The Greeks knew Satyrs and Sileni, half men and half goats or horses, with the Sileni becoming old and ugly, while the satyrs were young and lecherous. Only one satyr play has survived, Euripides's *Cyclops*, but that was transmitted by a Latin satirist, Lucilius, and that is the origin of the printer's confusion. The Latin word "satura," meaning full, has actually no relationship with the Greek word Satyr, in spite of what the *Ménippée*'s printer thought, or with Greek Old Comedy, the forerunner of Greek tragedy, but the persistence of the "y" spelling indicates that the 16th century wrongly thought that the word did come from the Greek.

Horace is responsible for some of the confusion, by dissociating from satire the idea of mixture in his compendious guide to literary genres, the *Epistula ad Pisones*, more widely known as the *Ars poetica*, which discusses at some length the satyr play, but in which the word was also taken to refer to his own "satires". Horace also relates Lucilius to the Old Comedy (*Satire*, I, iv). Various 5th-century A.D. glosses show that by then Horace was thought to have said that Lucilius derived his idea of satire from Greek Old Comedy, so that the original Latin meanings of "mixture" and "filling" were conflated by the renaissance grammarians with the comic Greek predecessors of tragedy, and with the burlesque satyr plays. Indeed, Roman ignorance of Greek is ultimately responsible for the whole inadequate system of tenses, conjugations, declensions, and moods we have ourselves inherited from the renaissance.

In 1531 Robert Estienne's important *Thesaurus Latinae Linguae*, depending on Diomedes's and Donatus's readings of Horace and codifying renaissance understanding of much more than word meanings, wrongly gives the Greek etymology for "satire," and makes the word mean both abundance and mixture, and the genre "satire" of its essence defamatory. He alludes to Varro, who wrote 150 "Menippean" dialogues, of which we have only titles and fragments, attacking the luxury and follies of his contemporaries, and he ends with a reference to dirty and impudent satyrs. Our printer, or Passerat or Pithou if one of them wrote the "Discours," must have been aware of the renaissance popularity of the Lucianic dialogue, and of Lucian's dependence on the mixture of verse and prose in the cynic philosopher Menippus of Gadara, alluded to in the title of his own *Icaromenippus*, but Estienne, who naturally uses the "y" form, is the source for our printer, his confusion, and the intended significance of the title of the *Satyre Ménippée*.

Estienne's *Thesaurus* had instantly become the basis for the standard school edition of Juvenal and Persius, and even J.-C. Scaliger accepted the nonsensical conflation of meanings, all of them still non-ironic, of the word "satire." He was already out of date. By then Denys Lambin and Isaac Casaubon in the 1699 edition of his earlier *De Satyrica*, had subjected the etymology to critical examination, and shown the fallacies. But "Satyre" in the 16th century was a literary genre. Marot's coqs-à-l'âne may have been "satyres" according to Sebillet and du Bellay, but Rabelais did not write "satire," and there was no French verb to "satirize." It is not without literary importance that there still isn't.

PUBLICATIONS

Abbrégé et l'Ame des Estatz convoquez à Paris en l'an 1593, le 10 de febvrier; as *Le Texte primitif de la Satyre Ménippée*, edited by Read, 1878
Le premier texte manuscrit de la Satyre Ménippée, edited by Giroux, 1896
Satyre Ménippée du Catholicon d'Espagne, 1594 [later editions bear the earlier date of 1593]
La Satyre Ménippée; ou, La Vertu du Catholicon selon l'édition princeps de 1594, edited by Read, 1892
La Satyre Ménippée, 3 vols., 1726
Satyre Ménippée..., edited by Labitte, 1874

Critical Studies

Lenient, Charles, *La Satire en France; ou, La Littérature militante au XVIe siècle*, 2 vols., 1877
Jolliffe, J.W., *Satyr: Satura: —a study in confusion* in *Bibliothèque d'Humanisme et Renaissance*, 18 (1956), pp. 84–95
Salmon, J.H.M., *French Satire in the late sixteenth century* in *Sixteenth Century Journal*, 6 (1975), pp. 57–88; reprinted in *Renaissance and Revolt*, 1975, pp. 73–97
Zsuppán, C.M., *From Abbrégé des Estats to Catholicon d'Espagne* in *Forum for Modern Language Studies*, 21 (1985), pp. 349–361

SCARRON, Paul, 1610–1660.

Burlesque poet, dramatist, and novelist.

LIFE

Scarron, born on 4 July 1610, was the seventh of eight children born to his mother, Gabrielle Goguet, of whom only two others, Anne and Françoise, survived childhood. His mother died in 1613, and his father, Paul, who came from an old and aristocratic Italian family which had been in France since the 15th century, married again in 1617. Scarron's stepmother, the Breton Françoise de Plaix, about whose gambling and whose mean, domineering, and avaricious behaviour colourful anecdotes have survived, bore her husband further children, of whom three survived childhood.

Scarron's father, Paul, was known as "l'apôtre (the apostle)" because, according to Tallemant des Réaux, he was for ever quoting Saint Paul. He was seigneur of Beauvais and of La Guespière, dressed in a style half a century out of date, and was a counsellor at the cour des comptes of the Paris parlement and a member of the noblesse de robe. He was dismissed by Richelieu in 1640, largely for resisting him in the creation of 16 new treasury posts, and then disgraced for the sharpness of his reac-

tion. Although Richelieu, certainly touched by Scarron's *Requeste du petit Scarron au Grand Cardinal*, referring to Scarron's slightness of stature, announced a pardon in October 1642, he died before it could be implemented. When, after Scarron's *Requeste au Roi*, it was made official, Scarron's father had already died in exile.

Scarron was disliked by his step-mother. He plainly had a lively and cheerful temperament, which enabled him to protect himself with a mocking playfulness in the face of whatever life was offering and, although his formal upbringing involved a turbulent succession of educational establishments, and a period with relatives at Charleville when he was 13 and 14 while his father, helplessly divested of any say in the organisation of his domestic and financial affairs, tried to re-establish domestic harmony, he learned enough Greek, Latin, and Spanish to appear in the world with a lettered plumage. At 19, he could dance and play the lute, and had started to versify, balancing refined accomplishments with low-life tastes.

His step-mother's dislike for him was venomous, and his father despaired of anything but an ecclesiastical career for so frivolous a male heir. Scarron at first resisted, preferring the uncircumscribed joys of the companionship of Scudéry and Tristan to the relative respectability of incipient salon society, but he accepted the tonsure in 1629 without ceasing to womanize, versify, and drink. Probably as early as this, and certainly later, he knew Marion Delorme, also Gondi, another ecclesiastic without a clerical vocation, assiduously attended stage performances, and may have studied theology. His first published piece was a poem to preface the 1631 tragi-comedy of Georges de Scudéry, *Lygdamon et Lydias*.

About this date, Scarron's father tried to get for him the vacant priory of Rumilly, which was in Richelieu's gift and, when that failed, turned for help to his cousin, Pierre Scarron, bishop of Grenoble. It was probably thanks to help from Grenoble that in 1632 Scarron joined the household of Charles de Beaumanoir-Lavardin, the elegant and witty bishop of Le Mans, with the promise of the first vacant canonry in the diocesan chapter, to which he was duly appointed in 1636, although the appointment was disputed by the heirs of his predecessor, and it took until January 1640 for the case to be decided in his favour by the ecclesiastical courts. We hear more of Scarron's role as amusing guest at the various houses of the Lavardin family than we do of his ecclesiastical functions, but it is to be presumed that from 1636 he attended a decent minimum of the canonical hours with the cathedral chapter.

Although he plainly amused himself and others at the expense of the more solemn members of the episcopal household, including Ambroise Denisot, the bishop's secretary and probable model for Ragotin in *Le Roman comique*, Scarron was much more than its resident jester. Underneath his early delight in what may to some extent have been a protective burlesque, he was developing a discerning and intelligent literary taste. His life at Le Mans, to judge from his verse and references left by his contemporaries, was dominated by the joyous, refined, but more or less dissolute company he kept. He wrote exaggerated love poems, and enjoyed tavern life, popular entertainments, and light-hearted festivities in the houses of the grander local gentry. When his rowdiness attracted the attention of authorities charged with keeping order in public places, Scarron was protected by his bishop.

In 1635 he was taken to Rome for five months by Beaumanoir

in the entourage of Alphonse de Richelieu, the cardinal's elder brother who, after having been a Carthusian, became archbishop of Aix. Gaston d'Orléans, the king's brother, had secretly married Marguerite de Lorraine in January 1631. The marriage did not at all suit Richelieu, who needed the ability to control Lorraine, where Marguerite's brother was in league with the emperor, and he sought to have it annulled at Rome. He argued that, although the marriage had been validly contracted and consummated, the king's brother did not have the right to marry without the king's consent, a view upheld in 1635 by the parlement de Paris and the assembly of the clergy, but far too Gallican to prove acceptable at Rome, where Richelieu had vainly sent his brother to negotiate.

In Rome Scarron met Mainard and Poussin, whose work he much admired, but whom he also teased. Poussin found Scarron's liking for caricature distasteful and was later to ask him to stop sending him his books. For Scarron, Rome was enjoyable. It has a serious background role in *Le Roman comique*, but offered Scarron much in the way of diversions, especially, it seems, female and gastronomic. The *Gazette* gives an account of a sybaritic feast given by the French ambassador before the party left in September. It was apparently very hot; dinner was served in a grotto with twelve fountains, and snow had been fetched from the mountains to chill the wine. The social implications of any ability to cool wine with mountain snow at the end of a hot Roman summer can scarcely be overlooked.

In Le Mans Scarron resumed his active social life on both of its levels, high society and low tavern. At the more elevated end of the social spectrum, he was taken up by both the comtesse de Soissons at Bonnétable, celebrated for her stage entertainments, and the pleasure-loving François d'Averton, comte de Belin, with seigneurial houses on his domains of Milly, Le Plessis, Averton, and Orgery, where he entertained to balls, hunts, firework displays, and gourmet meals. He was a strong patron of letters generally, but especially of the nascent theatre, in which his interest resembled and rivalled that of Richelieu. His mistress was an actress. He supported Montdory, from time to time invited Parisian troupes to perform, had helped both Rotrou and Mairet, and took sides against Corneille in the controversy occasioned by *Le Cid* in 1637. He may have encouraged Scarron to write for the theatre, and certainly incited him to write against Corneille, the amateur from Normandy who was challenging his own protected dramatic authors.

Scarron's poetic production at this time, in spite of the prebendary status not yet adjudicated to him, was partly scatological, and the two pamphlets he wrote against Corneille were devoted more to replying to Corneille's sneer at Mairet's poor origins than to any discussion of the dramatic proprieties. Mairet had been staying with Belin when he published his attack on Corneille in April 1637, *L'Auteur du vrai Cid espagnol*, and it was in answer to Corneille's May *Lettre apologétique* that Scarron wrote in prose the *Apologie pour monsieur Mairet contre le calomnies du sieur Corneille de Rouen*, followed by his outraged *La Suite du Cid en abrégé* in verse that June, suggesting that the proper "suite (continuation)" to *Le Cid* would be 50 blows with a bludgeon. He was later to regret his part in the polemic.

At the end of 1637 Beaumanoir died, followed within weeks by Belin, and in 1638 Scarron began to become a victim of the terrible disease which, presumably rheumatoid or tubercular in origin, was to end by totally crippling him. At first, by early in

1640, he could manage with a cane to support him, but in time he became totally deformed. There was some slight remission, but two visits to the waters at Bourbon-l'Archambault did no good, the pain was intense, and Scarron spent the rest of his life unable to move from the chair which became celebrated. He was impotent from 1640, his legs totally paralyzed, his neck unbendable. He was later to describe himself as "Z-shaped," his legs at first at an obtuse angle to his thighs, then a right angle, and finally an acute angle. His thighs made another with his body, and his head was bent over his stomach. He managed to laugh at the wretchedness of his condition, eventually petitioning leave to have himself known as "the queen's invalid." Anne d'Autriche gave him a pension of 1,500 livres a year.

It was, however, as Scarron later said, his illness which drove him to serious writing. Tallemant tells us that Scarron's paralysis resulted from treatment for what was thought to be a venereal infection. Another account of the origins of the deformity, that Scarron, disguised during the carnival of 1638 with feathers glued with honey to his skin had to dive into the Sarthe and stay there, to avoid being mobbed by girls intent in ripping the feathers off the naked canon, is wildly improbable, but it does say something about the sort of anecdote to which Scarron's lifestyle gave rise.

In late December 1639 Marie de Hautefort, born on 5 February 1616, was exiled by Richelieu to Le Mans on account of the closeness of her relationship with the king, to whose attention she appears to have come as early as 1630. She had the right to be called Madame before she was married, and Scarron came to adore "Madame Sainte Hautefort." She helped him to come to terms with his misfortune. Then in 1641 Scarron returned to Paris, where he succeeded in amusing Richelieu into pardoning his father, whose disgrace had taken place early in 1640, and who was living at La Guespière, near Amboise. Scarron spent the rest of his life in Paris surrounded by close friends. He was to sell his canonry for a derisory 3,000 livres to a friend when he decided to marry, earned a little from his writing, but had a long legal battle with his step-mother for his inheritance. It has been alleged that he was in semi-permanent financial distress, but the evidence points to reasonable ease, presumably from the "marquisat de Quinet," the cash-box of his publisher, Toussainct Quinet, after whose death Scarron changed to Quinets son-in-law Guillaume de Luyne, who paid 1,000 livres for the second part of *Le Roman comique*. It was in the context of his case against his step-mother that in 1652 Scarron published his *Factum ou Requête, ou tout ce qu'il vous plaira pour Paul Scarron, doyen des malades de France*.

In 1641 and 1642 he had commemorated his two journeys to the waters with a first and second *Légende de Bourbon*, verse epistles addressed to Marie de Hautefort. At Bourbon Scarron had met Gaston d'Orléans, another patron of actors and their troupes, who was to become an important protector. Meanwhile in 1643 Scarron issued his first volume, the *Recueil de quelques vers burlesques*, and in 1644 the first poem of the French burlesque, *Le Typhon; ou, La Gigantomachie*, in a genre visibly derived from Marot, whose poetry was much admired at the Hôtel de Rambouillet (see: *Guirlande de Julie*), and from Voiture, who had drawn on Marot. Mazarin disdained the offer of the dedication. Scarron's third major poem, *Léandre et Héro* was published in 1656, with further collections of short pieces of *Oeuvres burlesques* in 1646, 1647, and 1651. In March 1651 Scarron suddenly produced his anonymous but virulent attack on Mazarin, the *Mazarinade*, which cost him the pension Anne d'Autriche had been paying him, and which he was to have real cause to regret. The manuscript had been leaked from Holland. After this, Scarron rallied to Foucquet, the court, even Mazarin, and the party of power and reward. He was to have a serious quarrel with Gilles Boileau and to be attacked by Cyrano de Bergerac. Foucquet paid him a pension of 1,600 livres from 1653, and Scarron dedicated to him his 1655 play, *Le Gardien de soi-même*, and his poem *Léandre et Héro*, and to Foucquet's wife the second part of *Le Roman comique*.

Marie de Hautefort had been recalled to Paris by Anne d'Autriche on the death of Louis XIII on 14 May 1643, and it was through her that Scarron became well known at court, a curiosity on account of his deformity, but also cultivated for his wit and still extravagant humour. Among those whose acquaintance he made were Ninon de Lenclos, Sarrazin, and Ménage. Later on his circle widened to include Vivonne, d'Elbène, and Mancini. Gondi was close to him, and from 1656 his friendship with Pellisson was intimate. Segrais said of Scarron that he dedicated his poems for reward. Among the personages to whom dedications are recorded, like Condé and Pompone de Bellièvre, Scarron was closest to Foucquet himself, and the members of his circle.

The probability is that *Jodelet; ou, Le Maître valet*, drawing on Spanish comedy and using the stage name of the character already created by Julien Bedeau at the Marais, was already successfully played in 1643, although a later date used to be assumed, no doubt on account of the privilège of 25 April 1645. Its successor of 1645 was "Les Trois Dorothées; ou Jodelet souffleté," with a privilège of 17 July 1646, which became *Jodelet duelliste*. It, too, was a box office success, but Scarron then abandoned the Marais, and necessarily changed the name of his valet for *L'Héritier ridicule*, which was another resounding success in 1649. Bedeau was to leave the Marais in 1657 for Molière's company, where Molière created for him the Jodelet of *Les Précieuses ridicules*. Bedeau was to die in 1660, a year later. Scarron had a further brilliant success with *Dom Japhet d'Arménie*, probably with Villiers in the lead at the Hôtel de Bourgogne in 1651 or 1652, later than used to be thought. Molière's troupe was to play it 34 times, as it played the first Jodelet play over 30 times with Gros-René in the lead. Scarron's *Le Gardien de soi-même*, dedicated to Foucquet, was less successful than the rival play by Thomas Corneille, *Le Geôlier de soi-même*, probably in 1655, and was to be the cause of a dispute with Boisrobert.

Scarron's theatre developed away from the burlesque towards the romanesque. *L'Ecolier de Salamanque; ou, Les Ennemis généreux*, whose privilège is dated 4 December 1654, was already called a tragi-comedy, and the *Marquis ridicule; ou, La Comtesse faite à la hâte* of 1656 is a satire whose humour is quite removed from burlesque valets. Of the last two plays, published only posthumously, *La Fausse Apparence* has been thought already to announce Racine's treatment of love, while *Le Prince corsaire* returns to the romanesque themes already treated by Du Ryer and Scudéry.

By 1648 Scarron was working on *Le Roman comique*, of which the first part was to appear in 1651 and the second in 1657. The third part, unfinished at his death, had been started by 1659. Meanwhile, Anne d'Autriche had come to rely increasingly on Mazarin, and Marie de Hautefort, who had married Charles de Schomberg, duc d'Halluin, on 24 September 1646, again went into exile. Scarron, no doubt inspired by G.B. Lalli's

recent *Eneida travestita*, published his completed seven books of the *Virgile travesti* from January 1648 until July 1652, although in the dedication of the fifth book, in 1649, he attacks his imitators, and expresses real doubts even about the burlesque genre itself, understood in its proper sense of that which explains what is serious in terms of the absurd, and not in its then currently debased form of coarse vulgarity. Sarrazin had reimported the word from Italy. It implies something like systematic desolemnization.

Pellisson condemned burlesque in the sense of an attack on reason and common sense in a digression in his 1652 *Histoire de l'Académie*, and Scarron was actually in a letter to Pellisson to agree with the Jesuit Père Vavasseur's compendious condemnation of the whole burlesque style, the *De ludicra dictione* of 1658. Madeleine de Scudéry was to introduce another condemnation into the eighth volume of *Clélie* in 1660. From 1658 Scarron had already clearly turned away towards satire composed in alexandrines, virtually clearing the way for Boileau, as *La Fausse Apparence* had tentatively moved towards the path to be trodden by Racine.

In April 1652 Scarron married. Françoise d'Aubigné, born on 17 November 1635, later to become Mme de Maintenon, then tutor to the king's children by Mme de Montespan, and finally to be privately married to Louis XIV himself after the death of Marie-Thérèse, was the impoverished daughter of Agrippa d'Aubigné's son, in 1635 in prison at Niort, where he seduced and then married the daughter of the prison governor. He had died at Orange on 31 October 1647, after living with his wife and children for a while in Martinique. In 1650 Scarron was introduced to the barely adolescent Françoise by Esprit Cabart de Villermont, who lived next door to him at the Hôtel de Troyes and who had been to Martinique, where he had met her.

Françoise had supposed that her fate would be a convent. Scarron apparently offered her a dowry which she refused. The marriage was private and may not have been in Paris. The contract was signed on 4 April at the residence of a neighbour and witnessed only by the neighbour, his brother, and Villermont. Ostensibly to seek a cure for his illness, but probably in order to escape from Mazarin, who was about to return to Paris in 1653 after the Fronde, Scarron considered taking his bride to America. In fact he spent over a year in Touraine, and by February 1654 he and his wife were back in Paris at the Marais du Temple in the Rue Neuve Saint-Louis. There they received Scarron's friends, now including Boisrobert, Chapelain, and La Calprenède as well as Mignard—who painted Françoise—Segrais, and Madeleine de Scudéry. The couple appeared in *Clélie* as Scaurus and Lyriane, and they figure in Somaize's *Dictionnaire des précieuses* as Straton and Stratonice.

There was a complicated quarrel with Boisrobert who may have adapted a plot for a play which Scarron was using for *L'Ecolier de Salamanque*. A third play with a similar plot appeared, this time by Thomas Corneille, and all three were played in the same season. Scarron then attacked Boisrobert, whose brother Antoine le Metel, sieur d'Ouville, then accused Scarron of borrowing without acknowledgement from Maria de Zayas for his collection of *Nouvelles tragi-comiques tournées de l'espagnol en français*, published in the course of 1655 and 1656. D'Ouville himself translated María de Zayas, also in 1655, and in 1657 Boisrobert continued the quarrel with the *Nouvelles héroïques et amoureuses*.

In 1657 Scarron met Queen Christina of Sweden in Paris. He

is said to have experimented with alchemy. In 1655 the publisher Alexandre Lesselin had suggested to him the publication of a *Gazette burlesque* for which a privilège was taken out on 9 January. It was meant to rival Loret's *Muse historique*, but ran, from 14 January, for only 15 numbers. The most obvious reason for discontinuance was lack of subscribers, but there have been other conjectures, especially from historians who take the view that Scarron lived in a state of constant financial crisis, and from others who believe that he was the author of the anonymous but pornographic 1655 *L'Escolle des filles* of which a copy which he had given to Foucquet was found in a locked drawer at Vaux after Foucquet's arrest.

From 1659 to 1660 Scarron retired to the country to stay with his sister Françoise at Fontenay-aux-Roses, where he finished his last two plays. In 1660 he returned to Paris, and on 5 or 6 October that year, after a score of years of intense pain, he died. His libertin friends were with him until the end. It seems to have been under pressure from his wife that he received the last sacraments. Tallement says it was "for appearances' sake."

WORKS

The fundamental techniques of burlesque verse as practised by Scarron are neither coarse nor vulgar. They were perceived by his contemporaries as refined and witty, and were capable of being subtle as well as elegant. Essentially that which is held in awe is treated as if it were ordinary and unremarkable. In this way the strength of the giants led by Typhon is demonstrated in their use of huge rocks, the size of the bell-tower at Strasburg, to play skittles. Obviously, the desacralization process is hugely aided by the twin ridicules of incongruity and anachronism. Rabelais is not a burlesque writer in the 17th-century sense, because Gargantua and Pantagruel are not taken from a tradition which inspired awe.

The Greek and Roman gods not only did once inspire awe, but they continued to impose their grandeur by the solemnity with which the 17th century reverenced their treatment by Homer and Virgil. Malherbe had thought the renaissance pretentions of Ronsard to rival the poets of antiquity almost a blasphemy. Burlesque was a strong reaction. There was in mid-17th century France even an anonymous, and admittedly impertinent *Passion de Notre-Seigneur en vers burlesques*, probably by Lignières. It was possible, if dangerous, to write burlesque verse about Mazarin, or even the king. The deities of classical mythology were safer targets. Scarron took *Le Typhon; ou, La Gigantomachie* from Noël Conti's *Traité de mythologie*, translated from the Italian in 1641. If the poem were not sustained and its plot resolved, it would scarcely be more than a schoolboy joke. In fact Scarron did touch the peak of an understandably short-lived fashion. The gods behave like ordinary people, and the giants like children. Typhon loses his temper, and hurls his rocks into the air where they hit, and practically destroy, Olympus, where no attack had currently been anticipated:

> Jupiter le lance Tonerre
> Dormoit ayant bu trop d'un verre
> Et Junon qui n'avoit moins bû
> Dormoit sur un lit à cul nu

(Jupiter, the hurler of thunderbolts/Was asleep, having had too much to drink/While Juno who had drunk no less/Was on a bed asleep with no clothes on).

By the time he reached the fifth book of *Virgile travesti* in 1649, Scarron was getting unsurprisingly tired of the joke, and the fashion was suitably interred with the ponderous Vavasseur volume of 1658.

Scarron's theatre more importantly exploits the same vein of inspiration, and evolves more clearly. "Jodelet" was the stage name of an actor as well as the name of the character he played, a boastful, cowardly, greedy valet from the Spanish tradition, only distantly related to the lithe, agile, scheming rogues of Italian comedy although, like them, made up with flour, the heavy white make-up denoting the clown's role, as in the circus it still does. The Jodelet of Scarron's two titles was Bedeau, who played at the Marais. When Scarron moved his productions to the Hôtel de Bourgogne the lead was played by Claude Deschamps, known as Villiers, whose stage character was often called Philippin, a rival to Jodelet, particularly in cowardice. All Scarron's plays, like his fiction, depend heavily on Spanish originals from which they are often closely derived.

Jodelet; ou, Le Maître valet, probably first played in 1643, was a popular success. It is alluded to in *La Boutade des comédies*, a "ballet de cour" of about 1646 which mentions the half-dozen most fashionable recent productions, and there are a score of lines on it in Sarrazin's *Epître à M. le comte de Fiesque*, proclaiming its superiority over the Italian comedies. Scarron's source is Francisco de Rojas Zorrilla's *Donde hay agravios no hay celos, y amo criado*, published in the first volume of his theatre in 1640. A "gracioso," the clowning valet, points out to the audience the absurdity of the highly romantic plot in which two well brought-up girls risk their lives for their loves. Vengeful brothers are preoccupied with family honour, galant lovers are cynical, and a willingness to duel is a sign of caste. Scarron follows his source scene by scene. The first "day" and the third "day" of the Spanish comedy become the first two and last two of Scarron's five acts, the names are Gallicized, and Sancho becomes Jodelet. Scarron carefully keeps in his characters the original balance between nobility and absurdity, the senility of Dom Fernand coupled with attributes of a young hero, and high moral ideals mixed with boorishness in Dom Louis.

Nothing else is Gallicized as it was, for instance, in *Le Menteur*, adapted by Pierre Corneille from a Spanish original in 1643. Scarron keeps the Madrid setting and exploits the Spanish local colour. He suppresses some of the loftier and more moving passages of the Spanish play, and some of the open expression of female emotion, and he introduces an element of parody. He adapted the valet's part for Bedeau's loquacious, greedy, pompously uncomprehending stage persona, modelling himself on "Madame Nature", and attempting with comic effect to ape the manners of his social superiors. Molière uses the same basic traits of the Jodelet persona. Scarron is not even anti-précieux (q.v.), although his Béatris makes some fun of the fashion for over-utilizing diminutives and superlatives. He takes the high style of Corneille's heroes with perfect seriousness, and we know from the opening of the 18th chapter of the second part of *Le Roman comique* that by 1657 Scarron was prepared to make amends to Corneille by expressing his narrator's unstinted admiration for *Nicomède*.

That does not stop Scarron from being playful at Corneille's expense, putting a famous line into slightly more ordinary grammar, or modifying a line of Corneille while also parodying its solemnity:

Je le ferais encor, si j'avais à le faire (Corneille, *Le Cid*, III, iv and *Polyeucte*, V, iii)

Je le ferais encor si je l'avais à faire (Scarron, *Jodelet*, V, iv)

(I would do it again, if I had it to do).

and

Pleurez, pleurez, mes yeux, et fondez-vous en eau

(Weep, weep, my eyes, and melt into water) (Corneille; *Le Cid*, III, 3).

parodied as

Pleurez donc, ô mes yeux; soupirez, ma poitrine

(Weep then, my eyes; sigh, my breast) (Scarron, *Jodelet*, II, iii, and see the opening of V, i).

The key to Scarron's work, and to 17th-century French burlesque of which he is the supreme representative, is precisely the tension kept between elevated nobility and elegant refinement on the one hand, and a mockingly cynical realism on the other, and the ease with which Scarron moves between the two perfectly serious extremes, alighting at any point in the spectrum, to the bewilderment more of modern critics than of his 17th-century contemporaries.

In Scarron's work nobility of emotion coexists with an ironic reflection about it, and amusement is not incompatible with a sense of the sublime as, for instance, it had been for Poussin. Scarron's imagination is now mimicking the high-life and low-life realities of his painless golden years, the Le Mans period, even if he gradually came to regard it as inapposite to mock at the refinement of taste associated with Foucquet's circle, and became tired of parody. The relationship with Poussin in Rome was symbolic. The painter would not use living models, but pinned miniature dresses on the wax ones from which he painted in order not to disturb his sense of the sublime. Scarron understood Poussin, but Poussin could not fathom Scarron.

The second Jodelet play, adapted from two Spanish originals, was less successful than the first, and it is difficult to know whether the move to the Hôtel de Bourgogne was the cause or the effect of Scarron's movement from burlesque to satire. *L'Héritier ridicule* of 1649 was again an overwhelming box office success but, although written for Philippin, its comedy did not depart from the original Jodelet model as far as its equally successful satirical successor, *Dom Japhet d'Arménie*, of either 1651 or 1652. Scarron derived his play from *El Marqués del Cigarral*, a comedy in three "days" by Alonso Castillo Solórzano, from whom Scarron also took the model for *L'Héritier* and for three of the four stories intercalated into *Le Roman comique*. The adaptation is now much freer, with new scenes added, like the burlesque reception of Dom Japhet in the third act, and Scarron complicates the amorous intrigue, adding another couple. There is now no real effort to integrate the love

interest with the comedy. Dom Japhet could almost be said simply to have provided comic interludes in a drama of romance, except that they are so long, and in their way as serious as clowning as the heroic gestures and attitudes of the other characters are serious at the level of dramatic romance. Dom Japhet is not merely mad, he is also the professional fool of Charles V. He is rich as well as ridiculous, witty as well as pedantic, and skilled in the use of words, as well as clumsy about their contexts, meanings, and usages. The intention is satirical.

Le Roman comique, Scarron's best-known work, purports to narrate the adventures of a troupe of actors. It is more a series of episodes than a continuous story, with four interpolated short stories, three from Solorzano and one from Dona María de Zayas, as well as numerous anecdotes. It is realistic in the sense of describing scenes and events with the immediacy of direct observation, it parodies the epic style and the 17th-century adventure novel, and yet it derives part of its interest from imitating them, and from the seriousness of its idealistic vision. Scarron digresses, writes without discipline, lingering or speeding on as the fancy takes the author, but not necessarily his reader. Nonetheless he fascinates with wit, is often amusing, describes vividly what he has seen, and writes with unusual vigour and liveliness. The narratorial "I" frequently intervenes, overwhelming the reader with his sheer breathlessness, conveyed by a disjointed style, often breaking in to tell the reader that he does not know about this or that, or saying that he does think it important enough to delay over, and suggesting that we should get back to the story, on some occasions putting the first pronoun subject into the plural "We," or "Let us…": This is part of Scarron's technique for breaking the novel's illusion and thereby parodying the novel form itself. The narrator's style continually switches register, from real admiration to vivid description, to sarcastic quips about characters or classes of people, to narrative accounts that are almost never without ironic comment on who characters are, or what is only to be expected of them, or what they are up to.

The troupe consists of three actors, Le Destin, L'Olive, and the embittered, malevolent, and appropriately named La Rancune, with their valets, three actresses, the poet Rocquebrune, and the unfortunate lawyer Ragotin, who has attached himself to the company and is their butt. The female characters include La Caverne, her daughter Angélique, and l'Etoile. The company is paid to stay in Le Mans for a fortnight. Scarron describes how the young men of the town crowded into the room of the actresses, how they set up stage in private houses, how they were received. We are given accounts of inns, brawls, practical jokes, of conversations about drama, actors, patrons, novels, and provincial society generally. The romantic interpolations are quite serious, as are the flattering references to a personage who is intended to be recognizable as Belin.

The novel starts with the arrival of part of the troupe in Le Mans. The pace of the first chapter is very slow as Scarron sets the tone.

Le soleil avait achevé plus de la moitié de sa course et son char, ayant attrapé le penchant du monde, roulait plus vite qu'il ne voulait. Si ses chevaux eussent voulu profiter de la pente du chemin, ils eussent achevé ce qui restait du jour en moins d'un demi-quart d'heure; mais au lieu de tirer de toute leur force, ils ne s'amusaient qu'à faire des courbettes, respirant un air marin qui les faisait hennir et les avertissait que la mer était proche, où l'on dit que leur maître se couche toutes les nuits. Pour parler plus humainement et plus intelligiblement, il était entre cinq et six quand une charrette entra dans les halles du Mans

(The sun had finished more than half his course, and his chariot, having passed the apex of the world, was travelling faster than he wanted. If his horses had wanted to take advantage of the slope of the path, they could have finished what remained of the day in less than a half-quarter of an hour; but instead of pulling with all their strength they were just curvetting, breathing in a sea breeze which made them neigh and told them that the sea was near, where it is said their master sleeps every night. To speak more humanly and more clearly, it was between five and six when a cart came into the market place at Le Mans).

La Caverne is sitting on top of the pyramid of trunks, parcels, and packages, dressed "half country, half town," and on foot alongside are Le Destin "as poorly clad as he was richly countenanced," carrying a gun "with which he had assassinated several magpies, jays, and crows," and La Rancune. Accosted by the lieutenant du prévôt (officer of the constabulary) called La Rappinière, Le Destin said they were "Français de naissance, comédiens de profession (French by birth, players by calling)," a description to be borrowed and polished by Voltaire and applied to Saint Dunstan, "Irish by nation and saint by profession."

Here is the farcical mixture of a high-style mythological description of the sun in his chariot with the practical problems of controlling horses going downhill and getting skittish at the sniff of the air from the sea where, incongruously, the sun appears to spend the night. We then move to the comic realism with which the entry into Le Mans of the troupe is described, a grotesque parody of a solemn triumphal entry.

The interpolated stories are important as examples of the nouvelle, later to be developed by Segrais and to provide a fictional form alternative to the great adventure novels of Scudéry and La Calprenède. Scarron was to publish a series of five nouvelles translated, adapted, or at least closely derived, from Spanish originals, the *Nouvelles tragicomiques tournées de l'espagnol en français*.

PUBLICATIONS

Collections

Oeuvres, 7 vols., 1786
Oeuvres diverses, 1948ff.

Verse

La Suite du Cid en abrégé, 1637
Recueil de quelques vers burlesques, 1643
Le Typhon, ou, La Gigantomachie, 1644
Suite de la première partie des Oeuvres burlesques, 1646
Suite des Oeuvres burlesques, 2e partie, 1647
Troisième partie des Oeuvres burlesques, 1651
Virgile travesti, 7 vols., 1648–52; as *Scarronides*, 1854
Léandre et Héro, 1656

Fiction

Le Roman comique [1st part], 1651
Nouvelles tragi-comiques tournées de l'espagnol en français, 5 vols., 1655–56; as *Scarron's Novels*, 1694
Le Roman comique. Seconde partie, 1657; as *The Comical Romance*, 1968
Le Roman comique edited by E. Magne, 1955; in *Romanciers du XVIIe siècle*, Bibliothèque de la Pléiade, 1958

Plays

Jodelet; ou, Le Maître valet, 1645; in *Théâtre du XVIIe siècle*, Bibliothèque de la Pléiade, 2 vols., 1986
Les trois Dorothées; ou, Jodelet souffleté [*Jodelet duelliste*], 1646
Les Boutades du capitaine Matamore et ses comédies, 1646
L'Héritier ridicule; ou, La Fame intéressée, 1649
Dom Japhet d'Arménie, 1653; edited by R. Garapon, 1967; in *Théâtre du XVIIe siècle*, Bibliothèque de la Pléiade, 2 vols., 1986
L'Ecolier de Salamanque; ou, Les Ennemis généreux, 1654
Le Gardien de soi-même, 1655
Le Marquis ridicule; ou, La Comtesse faite à la hâte, 1656
La Fausse Apparence, 1662
Le Prince corsaire, 1662

Other

Apologie pour M Mairet, 1637

Biographical and critical studies

Morillot, P., *Scarron*, 1888
Magne, E., *Scarron et son milieu*, 1924
MacCurdy, Raymond R., *The Theater of Paul Scarron and the Spanish Comedia*, 1941
Phelps, Naomi, *The Queen's Invalid, a Biography of Paul Scarron*, 1951
Berens, Robert, *Aspects of Literary Satire in Sorel, Scarron, and Furetière*, 1966
Armas, Frederick A. de, *Paul Scarron*, (in English), 1972

Bibliography

Magne, E., *Bibliographie générale des oeuvres de Scarron*, 1924

SCÈVE, Maurice, ?1501–1564.

Poet.

LIFE

Scève was the most important of the Lyons poets of the French renaissance, and the first French poet to write a "canzoniere," a sustained cycle of love poems addressed to one real or imaginary woman. He came from a rich family of merchants and law-yers, several of whose members had been or were to be active in the administration of a town which was near Italy, had easy access to the reformed cantons of what is now Switzerland, and was on the road and river routes from Paris to Rome, and whose largely Italianate cultural life was untrammelled by the exist-ence either of a university or of a parlement.

Lyons was also a printing centre, in which perhaps 13,000 books were published in the 16th century, probably just over half as many as in Paris. Sébastien Gryphius was active there from 1528 to his death in 1566, and from about 1527, when informal teaching was put under municipal administration and the Ecole, later Collège, de la Trinité was founded, Lyons must be regarded for perhaps a score of years as the principal centre of literary humanism in France. Barthélemy Aneau, an impor-tant humanist as well as du Bellay's adversary, was professor of rhetoric there from 1529, also principal from 1529 to 1550 and again from 1558 until his death in a riot in 1561.

Lyons had once sought freedom from ecclesiastical govern-ment by becoming incorporated into France, where the kings welcomed it as a bastion against the imperial threat from the south and east, but its spirit of independence was shown by an openness throughout the 16th century to technological, finan-cial, intellectual, artistic, religious, scientific, and literary inno-vations, and appeared as much in the relative protection it afforded to evangelical humanism during the second third of the century as later in its whole-hearted support of the Catholic League against the king. The "Vêpres lyonnaises" of 24 August 1572 echoed at Lyons the St Bartholomew massacre in Paris, but on the whole Lyons was independent enough to make up its cor-porate mind on religious, political, and cultural issues in ways which did not invite interference from Paris.

The arrival of the French court on 17 February 1536 had brought with it a temporary influx not only of important states-men and ecclesiastics, but a host of minor mostly neo-Latin poets, court composers of encomiastic verse. Politically, the position of François I was at that date for once strong, and he was able to use Lyons as a base from which temporarily to con-solidate his power, and from where he could confront the emperor in Provence. François I spent much of 1536 in Lyons, returning there on 20 May and 4 August after only brief absences and leaving victorious, thanks to Montmorency's strategy, in October. It was to be an important year for Scève.

It is generally thought that Scève had three sisters, two of whom played some part in the town's literary life. One, Clau-dine, married the eldest son of another grand Lyons family, Mat-thieu de Vauzelles, who studied law at Pavia. A cousin, Guillaume, appears to have been a patron of neo-Latin poets, and certainly corresponded with Dolet and Boissonnée. Scève's father, who must have died about 1522, was an elected échevin in 1504 and 1508, a delegate deputed to offer the town's alle-giance to François I in 1515, and a royal judge hearing appeals to the crown from decisions of the local judiciary until he resigned his post in favour of Matthieu de Vauzelles in 1517. He owned two town houses, woodland, a number of farms with houses on them, and an estate with a château. The young Scève was brought up in the fashionable quarter between the Saône and Fourvière.

Paradoxically, it constitutes a biographical fact about Scève's own life that we know so little about it. He never put his name to his works, although he did not hide his identity; none of his works contains any information about himself; he printed no dedications and can have solicited no patrons; and he did not print the customary tributes from other poets which inform us about the lives of so many 16th-century authors. Yet he appears to have been confident of poetic immortality, and his works are signed, sometimes with his initials "M.SC. L[yonnais].," and sometimes with a motto, in his youth "souffrir non souffrir," implying some moral victory over the experience of pain, and later "Non si non la," both intentionally enigmatic in meaning, but used as a claim to authorship. The first edition of the *Délie* even carried Scève's head represented on a medallion.

Even this alone adds up to enough biographical fact to war-rant a suspicion of hauteur, possibly even of arrogance, an impression which the range, tone, and style of his published verse does not dispel. Unfortunately the parish and municipal records which must have contained Scève's name are known to have been destroyed, and no trace of his career has been found before 1533. He may have attended an Italian university, prob-ably accepted at least the tonsure, and is referred to as "docteur" in a document of 1540. The first we hear of him is in the com-pany of a Florentine nobleman and of the grand vicar of the car-dinal de Medici in early 1533 at Avignon, where he was looking for the burial place of Petrarch's Laura, traditionally supposed to have been close to the Sade family, who had a chapel there. Under a tombstone with an indecipherable inscription, Scève found some bones, a whole jaw, and a lead box. Inside the box were an Italian funeral poem on parchment, whose fifth line could allude to a Laura and whose style suggests a 15th-century origin, and a bronze medallion inscribed "M.L.M.J." and show-ing a woman uncovering her breasts.

Scève thought he had discovered Laura's grave, that the poem must be by Petrarch, and that the initials stood for "Madonna Laura Morta Jace," which for a whole variety of reasons, includ-ing the Latin, is unlikely. The probable meaning is "Mariam Laudate Matrem Jesu (Praise Mary the mother of Jesus)," and from Bembo onwards no one has thought it possible that the extended sonnet could have been written by Petrarch. Bar-thélemy Castellano, an Avignon deacon, wrote to Bembo to ask his opinion, and Bembo's negative reply is dated 24 April 1533. Nonetheless, the tomb became a place of literary veneration. François I made the pilgrimage with Sadoleto on his way to Marseilles to see Clement VII later that year. Petrarch was held in extraordinary veneration, and it looks as if Scève had con-ceived the ambition of becoming the French Petrarch. He wrote a canzoniere, and went out of his way to import Italian Petrarchism into his poetry.

He was probably back at Lyons by the summer of 1534, but was certainly there in 1535 when he published *La deplourable fin de Flamete*, a prose translation of the Sevillian Juan de Flo-res's adaptation of Boccaccio's tale, in Spanish *Grimalte y Gradissa*. The work was signed simply "souffrir se ouffrir," sug-gesting much but meaning nothing. The type was carelessly set by François Juste, a book-seller who catered for the popular trade. He got some of the initial characters upside down, and used the same characters as he used for the 1534/5 *Gargantua* of Rabelais. Juste and Claude Nourry had already each pub-lished different French versions of the Boccaccio conte, made from the Italian, in 1532 in Lyons, probably for the book fair. Scève's first publisher was not therefore aiming at the humanist market, and his first publication belonged not to the tradition of idealized neoplatonist love, but to the chivalric treatment of adultery which traces its ancestry to Ovid. Scève's introduction, the "Epistre proëmiale" treats love as art which can be learned, and speaks of his own escape from the shipwrecks of love's sea. There was a second edition in 1536.

It was in 1535 that Marot disseminated his descriptive "Blason du beau tétin" from his exile in Ferrara, and incited the Lyons poets to emulate him with poetic descriptions of parts of the female body. The response suggests that the challenge was taken up with some relish. Blasons were written by Victor Brodeau on the mouth, Jean de Vauzelles on the hair, Eustorg de Beaulieu on the cheek, the tongue, and the nose, Lancelot Carles on the foot and the knee, Michel Amboise on the tooth, Mellin de Saint-Gelais on trimmed hair and the eye, Claude Chappuys on the hand and the stomach, and Héroët on the eyes. Scève wrote on the forehead, the eyebrow, the tear, the sigh, and the neck. Renée de France and the French ladies of her court at Ferrara awarded the prize to the unknown Scève for his piece on the female eyebrow.

Marot had never even heard Scève's name, although it now quickly became celebrated. Lyons was on the whole behind Marot in his quarrel with Sagon, and both Marot and Sagon now took care not to alienate Scève. Both associated him in verse with other well-respected Lyons poets, like Chappuys, Héroët, and Saint-Gelais. A collection of blasons was published by Juste, in a volume in which they followed a French translation of Leon Battista Alberti's *Hécatomphile*, deriving from neoplatonist inspiration on love. Marot started a new competition for "contreblasons," with poets describing the ugliness of that part of the body of whose beauty they had previously sung, and so parodying themselves. He himself began again with the "Blason du laid tétin," but satire gave way to indecency, and a reaction set in against the whole fad. Scève did not take part in the second round. From 1539 blasons were published on domestic interiors, rings, hearts, pins, birds, and a variety of other subjects less highly charged than parts of the female anatomy.

The court arrived at Lyons in 1536. The edict of 31 March allowed Marot to return from exile, although he had to make his abjuration from heresy to the cardinal de Tournon in Lyons. It is there that Marot later that year got to know Scève, certainly sufficiently well for Scève to have encouraged him to take up the study of music. A short poem of Marot suggests that Scève was an accomplished musician, and clearly implies friendship. Dolet, whom they both knew, had finally got permission to print his *Commentarii linguae latinae*, in whose second volume of 1538 a short digression is devoted to Scève and Marot. It was Dolet who, on the sudden death of Francois I's 18-year-old son at Tournon on 10 August, had organized the poetic tribute which included eight pieces by Scève, among them a Latin poem, two eight-line French poems and an eclogue, "Arion," imitated from a piece by Marot written as an epitaph for Louise de Savoie, and again signed "Souffrir Se Ouffrir." This time Juste used better paper and took more trouble. He was publishing the work of a dozen of France's best humanist poets.

The dauphin had been playing tennis in the Provençal sun and became ill after drinking cold water handed to him by his steward Montecuculli. He died after four days, and François I commanded the court, the ambassadors, the prelates, and the Lyons nobility to attend Montecuculli's appallingly cruel execution on 7 October. He was almost certainly innocent, and it is now accepted that the dauphin died from natural causes. Scève had meanwhile, during the course of 1536, become one of France's

foremost poets, his eminence both achieved and proclaimed by the pride of place given to him by Dolet in the *Recueil de vers latins et vulgaires de plusieurs Poëtes françois composés sur le trespas de feu M. le Dauphin*. References to Scève in letters and verses from poets outside Lyons as well as within it begin to become abundant, not only from Marot and Dolet, but also from Visagier, Bourbon, and Charles de Sainte-Marthe.

By the end of 1536 it is at least probable that Scève had started the *Délie*, and virtually certain that some emotional experience not much after the beginning of that year had jolted him into a reflection about love, reminded him of amorous episodes in his life going back as far as 15 years before, and started him off on his unusually intense and extraordinarily dense canzioniere, whose name, form, structure, and meaning are all the result of complex but enigmatic codification. The fact that Scève knew Pernette du Guillet, probably 20 years younger than he was, and that the *Délie* contains, as well as much else, a dialogue with her, since some of her poems answer some of Scève's dizains, tells us nothing about the nature of their relationship, beyond the possibility that Scève's dizains were sometimes so angled as to provoke her replies.

Scève and Pernette may have been playing an elaborate game with verse, or using one another to stimulate their poetic endeavours, but even that is not necessarily the case. If they were, Scève put a lot more ingenuity into his poetic statements, with their complicated patterns of emblems, mottoes, dizains, and unspoken questions than she into her more open and ardent responses, and they could either still have been in love with someone else or have been using an idealization of someone quite different in their imaginations, while at the same time playing a poetic game with each other. There is actually no evidence for the physical existence of any single "Délie." Indeed, there is no external evidence at all about Scève's emotional life, and the internal evidence suggests, but does not compel belief in, no more than some complicatedly stylized set of poetic poses.

The sheer complexity of Scève's poetic imagination virtually precludes any possibility that the *Délie* is straightforwardly addressed to a woman for whom Scève had a physical passion, and that conclusion is confirmed by the probable length of time taken for the poem's gestation, its variation not only in the quality but also in the intensity of the emotional content, and its use of reminiscence. The *Délie* cannot be understood at all without reference to its cultural context, which sets it, in the form in which we know it, firmly in Lyons in the 1540s. For a huge number of reasons, the cycle as it exists could have been written at substantially no other time and in no other place, but it tells us nothing about Scève's emotional relationships, and anything we knew about his love life would not help us to understand the poem.

We possess very little information about Scève's biography between 1536, when he must be assumed to have started to think seriously about the *Délie*, and 1544 when he published it in Lyons, with a privilège of 30 October 1543. The second edition was to appear in Paris in 1564, and the third not until 298 years after that, in 1862. Scève's name is mentioned in a Latin poem in connection with annual municipal festivities on the Ile Barbe in the Saône in 1537 to venerate the relics of St Anne, and the organization of the solemn entry into the town on 17 May 1540 of Ippolito d'Este, from 1539 cardinal of Ferrara and archbishop of Lyons. On 17 July 1545 Pernette du Guillet died, and early the next year Scéve's cousin Guillaume also died, probably in a Paris prison, awaiting the definitive resolution of a court case against a colleague from the newly founded parlement of Chambéry, where he had been a counsellor since 1539. He had accused the colleague of negligence and was in prison as a result of counter-accusations. Scève appears for a while to have retired from active participation in city affairs, and in 1547 published the melancholy eclogue on the solitary life, the *Saulsaye, Eglogue de la vie solitaire.*

François I died on 31 March 1547. A year later it was anticipated that his successor, Henri II, would visit the eastern provinces, and naturally come to Lyons. Scève, aided by the historian Guillaume de Choul, by Barthélemy Aneau, and others not named, was entrusted with the organization of the solemn entry, and an account has been left of some of the preparations—commissions to painters, goldsmiths, architects, engravers, swordsmen, and boatmen, for gifts, decorations, and entertainments. The entry took place from 23 September 1548. Various accounts of it were published, but burnt as defamatory on the orders of the town's elected consulate, which entrusted Scève "qui a conduicte la dicte entrée (who was in charge of the aforementioned entry)" to draw up an authentic account. Scève's French text and an Italian translation were both published by the town in 1549. The march past included 333 butchers, stationers, and clothesmakers, 685 dyers, weavers, and goldsmiths, 592 carpenters, saddlers, and masons, and 413 printers. Those numbers must presumably include the workforce employed by each artisan. The expense of the magnificent horses, apparel, and general accoutrements, most of it borne privately, was obviously prodigious. There were 9,000 Lyonnais in the procession, all in new satin or silk embroidered costumes and carrying gilded implements, naturally outshone by the great Florentine merchants and bankers, with even the pages who preceded them mounted on Turkish horses.

Scève, entrusted with the organization of all the pomp, clearly revelled in the reproduction of aspects of antique, particularly Roman, skills and accomplishments among the tournaments, river displays, and human tableaux, and it is obvious that the citizens of Lyons thought, no doubt rightly, that they could rely on what must have been his quite exceptional taste, knowledge, and organizational skill, outstanding even in the Italianate Lyons of the high renaissance, wishing to show itself off in the most opulent style and with the most sumptuous refinements of taste and elegance it could muster.

From 1548 onwards Scève's reputation was at its zenith. He was asked for complimentary verses, forewords, prefaces. He was looked up to by both Sebillet and the nascent Pléiade (q.v.) poets, as well, of course, as by the Lyonnais. Marguerite d'Angoulême asked him to write preliminary sonnets for her two books of *Marguerites*, and Jean de Tournes dedicated to him an edition of Petrarch's *Rime* and in 1547 of Dante's *Divina commedia.* He may have travelled, although even in the context of the effort to reconstruct Scève's biography, to conclude that he did from the knowledge he shows of Spain in the *Microcosme*, and from the advantages he imputes to the experience of travel in the preliminary sonnet, is far too speculative. He appears to have got on well enough with Aneau, the author of the *Quintil Horatien*, who was heavily inclined towards the reform, against the Italianization of French culture, and towards the reinstatement of the late medieval poetic forms of the rhétoriqueur tradition. He was in frequent contact towards 1550

with both Pontus de Tyard and the young Guillaume des Autels, with both of whom he was publicly associated in an epigram by Charles Fontaine.

After the Protestant influx of the 1550s Lyons, without abandoning allegiance to the king, was in Protestant hands from 30 April 1562 until, a few months later, it fell to Catholic forces in 1563, in which year it was also ravaged by plague. Eventually it became a stronghold of the League. No one knows what happened to Scève. He may have died of the plague, and it has even been suggested that he went to Germany or became a Protestant. He had friends like Jean de Tournes who became Protestants, and others whose sympathies were strongly evangelical. He himself never mentions his religion, and from his works it is difficult to guess at the degree of evangelical sentiment which privately informed it. In public allegiance he was, at least in the 1550s, certainly Catholic, and the *Microcosme*, probably written towards the end of 1561 and at the beginning of its year of publication, 1562, suggests that no great change had taken place by that date, but it is conceivable that Scève lived on during the religious wars following the massacre of Wassy, on 15 March 1562. The argument that he did not is based only on a single reference by him to feeling old, on statistical averages, and on the absence of any of the explicit allusions or references we might otherwise have expected.

The solemn entry of Charles IX to Lyons on 13 June 1564 makes a sad contrast with what had happened in 1548. The *Microcosme* was published anonymously at Lyons in 1562. Scève may even have been dead. The balance of probability, in the absence of any firm evidence, suggests that Scève died in 1564, if not the year before, still in Lyons, and still a Catholic.

WORKS

Delie, object de plus haulte vertu is, strictly speaking, a book which contains a text. After the printer's preliminaries comes an eight-line stanza "A sa Délie," followed by the motto "Souffrir non souffrir," then five 10-line stanzas ("dizains"), then a series of 50 woodcuts in the form of emblems, each with a motto or proverb, and each except the 50th and last followed by nine dizains. The 50th emblem is followed by only three dizains. The dizains are in decasyllables, and an overwhelming majority follow the same unremarkable rhyme scheme (ABABBC-CDCD). Two other schemes are occasionally employed, one 11 times (ABBAACCDCD), and one four times (ABABBC-CDDC). The total pattern of dizains is therefore 5 + (49 × 9) + 3. There has been endless speculation about the caballistic or neoplatonist significance of the numbers. Ficino had solemnly repeated as historical fact the death of Plato on his birthday at the age of 81, which is the square of the square of the magic number 3. The other number of special significance because it is a prime is 7. If from the *Délie's* 449 dizains we subtract the introductory five and the concluding three, we are left with 49 sets of 9, the product of the squares of the two magic numbers, 7 and 3.

If Scève adverted to the implications of his square roots at all, he did not attach any importance to them. The emblems divide the text into arbitrary groupings of 9 which are not linked thematically within each group, but which do cross boundaries between groups. So D203 and D205 are linked poetically, but separated by an emblem, as are D347 and D349. It is not certain where the emblems came from, what they meant, or how they are related to their mottoes, although the relationship between picture and title is normally obvious enough; but it is clear that neither the emblems, nor their titles, nor their mottoes, can be specifically related to the group of 9 dizains following each emblem except the 50th, because there is no thematic link binding each group of 9 dizains together, and separating each of them from the others.

The very strong likelihood is that Scève found a "set" of 50 emblems somewhere, as Aneau found a set for his 1552 *Picta poesis* whose number he had to make up to 100. Scève's emblems appear originally to have been assembled more or less at random, and to have been put together as carvings for misericordes or gargoyles. They were then presumably used primarily to upgrade his book's presentation, with the eight numerically superfluous dizains split to go before the first and after the 50th emblem. The titles of the emblems generally state quite simply what the picture is, perhaps implying references or meanings, some of which may have yet to be elucidated. Scholars dispute such matters as the relationship between emblem 26, the unicorn seeing its own image, and Luca Pulci's 1489 *Driadeo*. The mottoes often form the last line of the first dizain of the set of nine which follow each emblem, and there is sometimes a very loose connection between either picture or motto—as in the case of the woman churning butter, whose motto, "The more I soften it, the more I harden it" can be given an obvious relevance to love—and one or more of the dizains in the following set. But some of the emblems had been used in earlier emblem books, sometimes with different mottoes, and at least four of the dizains are re-worked from earlier published poems by Scève. The book was partly forged from assembled elements, not originally generated as a unity.

In view of the apparently arbitrary selection of a set of 50 heterogeneous emblems, not obviously connected either to one another or to their mottoes, or to the dizains which follow them, and of the haphazard way the emblems or their mottoes are related to the groups of dizains, the most probable and certainly the safest assumption is that the *Délie* is essentially a poem, arbitrarily split into nine-stanza segments by a set of almost unrelated emblems, themselves not clearly related to their mottoes, but with some effort sometimes made to integrate the different elements of the book, emblems, titles, mottoes and groups of dizains, to give meaning to what remains essentially a decorative device, to which the mottoes may add a teasing puzzle.

It remains true that some of the emblems, like the saw, represent obviously useful handcrafts, or domestic objects, like the clock or the lamp, or insects, like the spider or the fly, or vaguely resonant folk symbols, like Orpheus, or Leda and the swan, which had ceased to have any precise reference to Jupiter's courtships, or the viper killing itself to give life to its children, which can be traced back to Pliny but had in the meanwhile been appropriated by medieval Christianity, which transformed the viper into the pelican and used the life-conferring self-immolation as a symbol of Jesus. Too much scholarly ingenuity has gone into finding appropriate things for Scève's emblems to symbolize, perhaps because they are rendered enigmatic by their apparently random mottoes. The result has too often been another attempt to give the poem an esoteric significance and to deflect attention from the poetry of the text.

The first problem posed by the text of the canzoniere is its title. It is unlikely that the anagram of "L'idée (the idea)" is

important, and difficult to see how it would connect the poems to any authentic neoplatonic tradition even if it were. On the other hand the general reference to the moon goddess, the chaste huntress, and the goddess of the underworld is exploited, although the various roles of the Delian goddess are too nonspecific to confer on the canzoniere's addressee more than the suggestion of unattainability and extensive but capriciously exercised powers. The poem is placed under the direction protection of Petrarch, both starting and ending with direct references to him, although otherwise referring directly to him on less than a score of occasions. There are half a dozen allusions to Serafino, but very few to any other single modern or antique author. However, apart from the last dizain, which is the most important of all and contains a clear reference to Petrarch, and those which refer to recent events, the last 25 dizains depend heavily on the first of Speroni Speroni's 1542 *Dialoghi d'Amore*. The fact that this reliance on a recent work comes at the end of the sequence confirms the suggestion that much of the rest was composed earlier.

The organizational principle unifying the poem is the poet's reflection on his own experience. It is easily the most important poetic reflection on love to come out of its milieu, but its central concern is not very far removed from those of Héroët and Tyard. Essentially Scève's reflection is on the relationship between the emotional experience of loving, in all its moments of intensity and insouciance, exhilarating reciprocation and frustrated longing, desire and despair, and a perfective aspiration to moral self-transcendance. He reflects on his past experience of love, and a present or very recent emotional obsession, and explores the possibility that the physical and emotional reality of love might mediate the moral fulfilment of the lover, and even that emotional rejection might be the condition that it should.

The poem is not a narrative. The initial eight-line dedicatory stanza tells us that much: the poem is about the re-kindling in the poet by Délie of the embers of dead love. She may find harsh what he has to say, but Love, seeing him write it for her, has passed it through his flames. That stanza was printed in front of the poem in 1544, but after its end in 1564, as if Scève were uncertain whether to ensure that the reader understood the poem's register before he began reading or after he had finished. Wherever the stanza goes, what it tells us is that the poem is a reflection on the poet's experience of love, written for someone he loves to think about. Has he correctly understood his experience? Is the experience of loving like this? Does it have these effects, consequences, peaks, troughs, moments of intensity and of slackness, satisfaction and frustration? Does it justify Scève's conclusion? Before ending the last dizain of the *Délie* with a couplet affirming that the poet's evergreen love, symbolized by the juniper tree, will never, in words taken from Petrarch's *Trionfo del Tempo*, "succumb to earthly oblivion," Scève concludes,

Aussi ie voy bien peu de difference
Entre l'ardeur, qui noz coeurs poursuyvra
Et la vertu, qui vive nous suyvra
Oultre le Ciel amplement long, et large

(I therefore see very little difference/Between the passion which will pursue our hearts,/And living virtue which will follow us/Further than the sky whatever its length and breadth).

The conclusion to the poet's reflection on love, made on the basis of his past and present experience, is that, in its pursuit of us into eternity, earthly love, passionate emotion, will be followed by virtue itself. Scève has concluded that love, as it has been depicted in the poem, is in the ordinary, earthly sense, morally elevating.

We know from his activities in 1533 that Scève had somehow felt the importance of Petrarch's love for Laura. When he imitated Petrarch by writing his own very different canzoniere, having thought he had found Laura's grave, Scève placed it under Petrarch's protection from the very beginning, the remark about his "youthful errors" constituting an unmistakable allusion to the opening of the *Rime*. The Petrarch he was thinking of was the real poet who had looked on his own experience in a way wholly different from the way of earlier generations, articulating with intense power for the first time what we have come to regard as a renaissance sensibility. When, therefore, Scève uses "Petrarchan" themes like the basilisk and the life-death antithesis, we should not think of him as simply reorganizing traditional poetic material, or handed-down images, but as attempting to renew Petrarch's actual vision, whose originality had been eroded into affectation in Italy and whose imagery had often been plundered for merely decorative exploitation in France.

Scève's 15th emblem was a weathervane (girouette). In the poem's first dizain he creates a verb out of the word. The first dizain runs,

L'Oeil trop ardent en mes ieunes erreurs
Girouettoit, mal cault, a l'impourueue:
Voicy (ô paour d'agreables terreurs)
Mon Basilisque auec sa poingnant' veue
Perçant Corps, Coeur, et Raison despourueue,
Vint penetrer en l'Ame de mon Ame.
Grand fut le coup, qui sans tranchante lame
Fait, que vivant le Corps, l'Esprit desuie,
Piteuse hostie au conspect de toy, Dame,
Constituée Idole de ma vie

(My eye, too fiercely in my youthful indiscretions/Swung like a weathervane incautious and unpredictable:/Now (Oh dread of terrors of delight)/My basilisk with its murderous look/Piercing body, heart, and reason overcome,/Came and penetrated into the soul of my soul.//Severe was the blow which, with a blade that left no wound/Makes, while the body lives, the spirit depart life,/Pitiful victim at the sight of you, my Lady,/You, made into the idol of my life).

The basilisk, whose look was lethal, looks at himself in the mirror in the 21st emblem. "L'âme de mon âme" is a technical term in mystical theology normally translated as "the highpoint of the soul." It means innermost essence, that unreachable part of the personality which, derived from the stoic "divine spark" in man, is beyond the realms of activity and passivity. Scève's verse does in fact assemble traditional elements, the conjunction of terror-delight, the blade that leaves no blood, the antithesis living/departing life, the conquest of reason, and the basilisk, but the organization is strongly personal enough to convey that, behind the verse, lies at least the memory of a strong emotional experience.

Scève draws eclectically on a number of different philosophical systems, and has not yet by any means got away from the rhétoriqueur reliance on puns and other forms of word play, on affected forms of poetic debate, and on the rhetorical flourish at the end of a stanza. The stanzas often make the same points as one another; the suddenness of love, the totality of its impact, the destruction of the lover's liberty, the enjoyable but ruinous dependence to which it reduces the lover. The tension is often relaxed by the introduction of references to mythological or real places, people, and events, distracting from the intensity of the analysis of the lover's experience. In D22 Délie is explicitly compared to the goddesses Hecate and Diana, as well as the moon.

Most of the canzoniere is given over to interrogating the experience of love about the meaning of sometimes relatively trivial emotional events in the central relationship. Why, asks the poet, does it happen like this? What does it mean? The poem does not progress in the sense that the reader would feel something was wrong if sizeable sections of the text were moved around, although the sequence would lose its questing, tentative, inquiring register if any real attempt were made to re-arrange the dizains in some order thought to be more logical. That would also obscure the principle of unification, which is the poet's attempt, caught on the wing, to understand his own present experience in the light of his past. No single dizain, or even handful of dizains, illustrates all the techniques, variations of mood, or types of answer the poet expects to his implied questions. The moments of rapture are rare, but one occurs in D136. Perhaps the best way to illustrate the type of poetry Scève is writing, and the way the canzoniere makes its effect, is to quote the eight-line stanza by Pernette du Guillet, "Epigramme 13," together with Scève's dizain thought to be a reply to it,

Pernette du Guillet:
    L'heur de mon mal, enflammant le desir,
    Feit distiller deux cueurs en un debvoir:
    Dont l'un est vif pour le doulx desplaisir,
    Qui fait que Mort tient l'aultre en son povoir.
    Dieu aveuglé, tu nous a faict avoir
    Du bien le mal en effect honnorable:
    Fais donc aussi, que nous puissions avoir
    En noz espritz contentement durable.

Scève:
    L'heur de nostre heur enflambant le desir
    Unit double ame en un mesme pouoir:
    L'une mourant vit du doulx desplaisir,
    Qui l'autre viue à fait mort receuoir.
    Dieu aueuglé tu nous as fait avoir
    Sans aultrement ensemble consentir,
    Et posseder, sans nous en repentir,
    Le bien du mal en effect desirable:
    Fais que puissions aussi long temps sentir
    Si doulx mourir en vie respirable.

(Pernette du Guillet: The joy of my sorrow, inflaming desire,/Had two hearts distilled into a single willing:/Of which one is alive from sweet torment/Which means that Death holds the other in its power./Blinded God, you have given us/What is in fact the ennobling evil from what is good:/Grant, too, that we may have/In our minds a lasting happiness.

Scève: The joy of our joy inflaming desire/Unites a double soul in a single power:/One dying lives on by this sweet torment,/Which makes the other, living, become the victim of death.//Blinded God, you have granted us/Without otherwise consenting together,/To possess, without regret/What is in fact the good from the evil that is desirable:/Grant that we may also long be/Able to breathe in life so sweet a death).

Here the debate is between Pernette and the poet of the *Délie*. Mostly the poet's debate is conducted within himself, but here the externalization of the verbal casuistry makes clear what is going on in Scève's poem, and what extraordinary intensity the abstract vocabulary is made to convey. The satisfaction that yet inflames desire is a medieval topos, a metaphor for heaven, and much is of course made of the contrasts of pleasure/pain, good/evil, and two/one. The word "God," is in each case at the beginning of a line, and is therefore capitalized. Is the blinded God just the lower case god Cupid, or the upper case Christian God, allowing the moral uprightness of a technically illicit union or, most daringly of all, is there a hint that Cupid's activities are not so dissimilar from those of the Christian God? Are we, the readers, asked to choose which reference to make?

It is true that the last Speroni-inspired dizains of the *Délie* do tell of an effort to spiritualize the poet's affection, but the insistent theme breaks in again as the poet repeatedly refuses to repent of his love, or to regard it as illegitimate. There is a moment when the poet wonders if he is wrong, in D441. Then in D442 he strongly maintains that no God could wish to cause so bitter a life as his would be, deprived of its love, "Amour si sainct, et non point vicieux (so holy a love, and not a vice)." Death will be a relief from the interior struggle, but Scève has already resolved it. The *Délie* certainly contains the most powerful moral rehabilitation of physical passion in poetry to come out of the first half of the 16th century in France, and its power is intensified by the anguish of the internal conflict which the poet makes articulate.

La Saulsaye recounts the myth of the nymphs transformed into willow trees. Two shepherds, Antire and Philerme, praise the solitary life and the charms of nature, but the poem contemplates a withdrawal from active participation in affairs and is tinged therefore with sadness. *Le Microcosme*, on the other hand is a major epic poem on the progress of humanity, a celebration of the creation, and of the human role in imitating the role of God by participating in it. Human potential is infinite. Already in the *Délie*, singing the praises of François I in D253, Scève had demonstrated his belief in the new culture, "ce Siecle aux precedantz barbares,/S'enfle du bien, que par toy luy abonde (this age, compared with the previous barbarian ages,/Swells up with the greatness which through you abounds in it)." Now, in *Le Microcosme* he celebrates the greatness of humanity.

Unhappily the poem, like so much of what has been called the "scientific" verse of the renaissance, presents problems of access to the modern reader, still accustomed to anchor the varied splendours of renaissance culture in a revival of interest in antiquity. In consequence, both the evangelical aspects of the northern renaissance, and the frankly anti-intellectual developments which arose out of the Franciscan scholastic tradition of Bonaventure, have been overlooked. Together with various forms of late medieval mysticism, they found expression in the "devotio moderna" in north Europe east of the Rhine, and in the

tradition centring on the semi-mystical philosophy and theology of Nicholas of Cusa in France, Italy, and south Germany. Cusa in particular, followed in early 16th-century France by Jacques Lefèvre d'Etaples, for instance, and then by Symphorien Champier, Charles de Bouelles, and Guy Lefèvre de la Boderie, used strands of neoplatonist and Pythagorean thought which are fundamental to the imagery and poetic expression of *Le Microcosme*. The same Cusan inspiration can also notably be found, no doubt mediated by Lefèvre and Briçonnet, in the spiritual works and letters of Marguerite d'Angoulême.

Scève took his Cusan thought patterns and imagery from the encyclopedic 1503 *Margarita philosophica* of Gregor Reisch, from 1502 prior of the Carthusian monastery at Freiburg. The fundamental image of God deriving from the spirituality of Cusa and immensely important for a whole range of French renaissance authors, including Ronsard in the "Hymne de l'Eternité" and Du Bartas in the first *Sepmaine*, is expressed by Scève at the beginning of his poem:

Premier en son Rien clos se celoit en son Tout,
Commencement de soy sans principe, et sans bout,
Inconnu, fors à soy connoissant toute chose,
Comme toute de soy, par soy, en soy enclose:
    Masse de Deïté en soymesme amassee,
Sans lieu, et sans espace en terme compassee,
Qui ailleurs ne se peut, qu'en son propre tenir
Sans aucun tems prescrit, passé, ou avenir,
Le present seulement continuant present
Sans estre de jeunesse, et de vieillesse exent:
    Essence pleine en soy d'infinité latente,
Qui seule en soy se plait, et seule se contente
Non agente, impassible, immuable, invisible
Dans son Eternité, comme incomprehensible,
Et qui de soy en soy estant sa jouïssance
Consistoit en Bonté, Sapience, et Puissance

(First sealed in his nothing, concealed in his all,/Commencing of himself without start and without end,/Unknown, but knowing all outside himself,/Totally of himself, by himself, and in himself enclosed://Mass of divinity massed in himself,/Without place, and contained in no space,/Who cannot exist except contained within himself,/Bounded by no time, past or future,/The present alone continuing present/Without coming from youth or going to age;//An essence complete in itself, with latent infinity,/Whose joy is in itself alone, and alone is joyous/Not active, not passive, immutable, invisible/In its eternity, and unintelligible,/And which of itself and in itself being its joy,/Consisted of goodness, wisdom, and potency).

God is all and nothing, and exists neither in time nor in space. He is unknowable. The doctrine is Cusan, but the exploitation of it by Scève, that God contains all things within himself, knows all things in himself, and creates all things by knowing them as they are within him, is developed from a famous chapter (VII, 2) of the Pseudo-Denis's *De divinis nominibus*. The principle is momentous. If God creates by knowing the essences contained within himself in his own all-sufficient self-knowledge, then the way is open to Platonic ideas, creation according to the *Timaeus*, considered as a philosophical counterpart to the theology of

Genesis, and both to the late Greek Christian theology of the Trinity and the Platonist theory of the demi-urge.

Pico della Mirandola's *Oratio de dignitate hominis* shows how Cusa, building on the Pseudo-Denys, provided the renaissance with one of its singularly powerful myths, inside which it could glorify man within the bounds of Pauline theology and Christian orthodoxy. That is what Scève undertakes to do in *Le Microcosme*. He has impeccable scriptural authority for regarding man's goodness, wisdom, and potency as attributes of God, made by later theology characteristic respectively of Father, Son, and Holy Spirit, and shown by John of Salisbury in his 12th-century *Polycraticus* (VII, 5) to be characteristic, too, of the three first causes in the *Timaeus*, the demi-urge, the archetypes, and the supreme good. The fusion of Platonism and Christian theology goes back, as usual, to Augustine, this time to the 25th chapter of the 11th book of the *De civitate dei*.

Human knowledge, in a fashion analogous to divine knowledge, is itself creative. The human mind generates concepts. It is important for a proper understanding of Descartes to see the staging post for his innate ideas, marked by Cusa's neoplatonist and Pythagorean spirituality, developed by the learned poets of the 16th century. It is difficult to avoid the impression that Scève's poetic adaptation of Reisch's popularization of Cusa is at least historically a great deal more important than has been thought. In its all-embracing cosmic enquiry into the universe and the nature of human existence, its scale is altogether grander and its aspirations are more ambitious than those of the *Délie*. It is more abstract, and lacks the earlier poem's emotional intensity, but its great mythological account of the universe and of the role within it of human knowledge, and its optimistic celebration of unlimited human potentiality make *Le Microcosme* an immense poetic achievement.

PUBLICATIONS

Collections

Oeuvres poétiques complètes, edited by B. Guégan, 1927
Le opere minori di Maurice Scéve, edited by E. Giudici, 1958
Oeuvres poétiques complètes, edited by H. Staub, 1970

Verse

Délie, object de plus haulte vertu, 1544; 2nd ed. 1564, 3rd ed. 1862; edited by I. McFarlane (critical edition), 1966
Saulsaye, Eglogue de la vie solitaire, 1547; edited by M. Françon, 1959 *Le Microcosme*, 1562

Prose

La déplourable fin de Flamete, 1535
La Magnificence de la superbe et triumphante entrée... à Lyon faicte au... Roy... Henri II, 1549

Biographical and critical studies

Baur, Albert, *Maurice Scève et la renaissance lyonnaise*, 1906
Saulnier, V.-L., *Maurice Scève*, 2 vols., 1948–49
Falbe, A., *Die Dichtung Maurice Scèves: Komposition, Struktur, Bilder*, 1964

Giudici, E., *Maurice Scève Bucolico e Blasonneur*, 1865
Staub, Hans, *Le curieux désir*, 1967
Coleman, Dorothy Gabe, *Maurice Scève, Poet of Love: Tradition and Originality*, 1975
Fenoaltea, Doranne, *"Si haulte architecture:" The Design of Scève's "Délie"*, 1982

SCUDÉRY, Georges de, 1601–1667.

Dramatist, poet, and novelist.

LIFE

Georges and Madeleine (see next entry) de Scudéry were the only two surviving children out of five born to Georges I de Scudéry, captain of the port of Le Havre, and Madeleine de Martel de Goutimesnil. There is no archival record of the Italian ancestry of which Scudéry boasted, although the family can be traced back to Apt in Provence in the 14th century. Scudéry's father was born at Gap into a noble family "d'épée et de robe (of the military and the magistracy)," fought for the League in the religious wars, and followed André de Brancas, duc de Villars, first to Lyons, where Brancas was governor, and then to Normandy, where on Brancas's behalf he became commander of the fort of Sainte-Catherine in Rouen and, when Brancas was made admiral and governor of Le Havre, Scudéry's father became his assistant as captain of the port. It was there that he married in November 1599. Scudéry was baptized on 12 August 1601, and his sister Madeleine on 1 December 1608.

Scudéry's father's captaincy was not quite the licence to practise piracy that he made of it, and he was imprisoned and ruined for pillaging and sinking a Dutch ship. Released in 1610, he died in 1613, followed a few months later by Scudéry's mother. The two orphaned children were put into the care of an uncle, who was certainly lettered and probably lived at Rouen. Not a great deal is known of the children's youth, except that both had an excellent education. Scudéry certainly visited Rome before taking up a military career. Most of what is known about his young adulthood can be traced back to himself, and he exaggerated his military experience, so that what he says about himself is unreliable. Tallemant tells us he boasted that he had his own regiment, which is certainly untrue. Tallemant also had, presumably from Conrart, the information, if that is what it is, that Scudéry's father's ruin was the result of the jealousy of the admiral's daughter-in-law, sister of the duchesse de Beaufort, who had once loved him. Conrart can only have heard that from Scudéry himself.

Scudéry was in Paris in July 1627, undoubtedly served in the Piedmont campaigns under the duc de Longueville and the prince de Carignan, although probably not for the seven years he claims, and took part in the retreat at the Pas de Suze in 1629. In 1630 he is to be found in the world of the theatre in Paris. His military career appears to have been honourable, and to have lasted, possibly with a brief interruption, from about 1623 until 1629. At some time he almost certainly spent long enough in Apt to have a liaison. From the circumstantial evidence of her first novel, it is likely that his sister was with him. Some care is called for in any attempt to assess his later literary standing. It is possible that his celebrated attack on Pierre Corneille's *Le Cid* has distorted a proper understanding both of his achievement, imposing on it an interpretation which sees it in the perspective of neo-classical norms, and of his relationship to Richelieu, which may have been seen as closer than it was.

Scudéry had already made his literary début with an ode in defence of Théophile de Viau, accused of obscenity and atheism on account of the 1622 collection of verse *Le Parnasse satyrique* for whose publication he is alleged to have been responsible, and imprisoned from 1623 to 1625 while awaiting trial. Théophile was exiled, which meant in fact only that he was obliged to stay away from Paris for some months until he received tacit permission to return, but Scudéry's ode is violently hostile to the Jesuits responsible for the prosecution, although it takes care to affirm his belief in God. Théophile was to die on 25 September 1628 and, although Scudéry never met him, he was to edit Théophile's works in 1632 with an aggressive preface, perhaps aimed at Balzac.

Meanwhile, early in 1630, the first of Scudéry's 16 published plays was staged, *Ligdamon et Lidias; ou, La Ressemblance*, a tragi-comedy with its subject taken from *L'Astrée*, like that of its three immediate successors, the 1631 *Le Trompeur puny; ou, L'Histoire septentrionale*, the 1632 *Le Vassal généreux*, and the 1633 *Orante*. The next tragi-comedy was *Le Prince déguisé* of 1634. The first certain performance of the comedy *La Comédie des comédiens* was at the Arsenal before the queen on 28 November 1634. Before the intervention against Pierre Corneille in 1637 which gave Scudéry, already widely known, much greater authority in the world of letters, he had also staged a comedy in 1634, *Le Fils supposé*, and two tragedies, *La Mort de César* in 1635 and *Didon* in the 1635–36 season. The distinction between tragi-comedy and tragedy became fluid, particularly in the wake of the Querelle du *Cid* in 1637, after which tragi-comedy began to accommodate itself not only to the unities, but also to the "bienséances (decencies)," avoiding duels, deaths on stage, extravagant stage settings, and the more violent features of the romanesque. Scudéry published 12 of his plays as tragi-comedies, and two with subjects drawn from the antique as tragedies, with only *Le Fils supposé* actually published with the qualification comédie added to the title. *La Comédie des comédiens* was originally called a "poème de nouvelle invention (a newly conceived creation)," no doubt because it is an unconventional stage discussion, partly in prose, between actors, who give a demonstration which convinces an uncle that the stage is a fit place for his nephew to make a career.

Scudéry's last play, *Arminius; ou, Les Frères ennemis*, normally considered in spite of its title a tragedy, a failure in 1643 following the unsuccessful *Axiane* of the preceding season, led Scudéry to announce that he would abandon the stage altogether, although on 29 June 1642 he had, through the good offices of Cospeau and Mme de Rambouillet, been appointed governor of the tiny fort of Notre-Dame-de-la-Garde at Marseilles, for which he left with his sister in November 1644. In the printed preface to *Arminius* Scudéry reviews his career as a dramatist. The Marseilles post was a sinecure and less well paid than Scudéry had hoped, although it seems unlikely that the governor was actually required to reside. It may well be that the failure of the final two plays did determine Scudéry and his sister, comfortably living in the fashionable Marais district, to move for a period to Marseilles, or that decision, and the one to abandon the stage, may have had something to do with the death of Richelieu, to whom Scudéry's role in the dispute with Corneille must have brought him closer.

It seems likely that his first plays were staged by the Marais company, and it is certain that Montdory, who played with the troupe under Lenoir from 1629 to 1634 and from 1634 until 1637 was its director, himself acted some of Scudéry's leading roles. Scudéry's role with the Marais company was not that of employed playwright, as was Rotrou's at the Hôtel de Bourgogne, but the relationship between him and the company was close until 1635, when Montdory played Scudéry's Brutus in *La Mort de César*. When Montdory, playing Tristan l'Hermite's Hérode in *La Marianne* before Richelieu in 1637, had his stroke and was forced to retire, Scudéry switched to the Comédiens du roi at the Hôtel de Bourgogne under Bellerose.

In the background of the commercial and professional rivalry between the two companies, it must be remembered that Louis XIII had in 1634 simply removed Charles Lenoir from the Marais to the Hôtel de Bourgogne probably to annoy Richelieu, who much favoured the troupe which settled at the Marais. The Hôtel de Bourgogne troupe played Scudéry's *Le Trompeur puny* on 12 December 1634, soon after the Marais company lost the copyright on its publication, and Floridor took it to Drury Lane in 1635. The theatre was becoming fashionable, almost respectable, and the rivalry between the two companies early gave rise to the simultaneous staging by each of a series of plays on the same subject. Scudéry's *La Comédie des comédiens* was doubled in the same year, 1632, by a piece by Gougenot on the same general theme and with the same title. Scudéry's 1636 *L'Amant libéral*, taken from a short story by Cervantes, was staged at the Marais, but doubled by a play with the same title and from the same source written by Guérin for the Hôtel de Bourgogne. Scudéry, like Tristan, also drew heavily on Italian sources, notably sharing the French enthusiasm for Marino, from whose *Adone* he derived his own 1634 *Le Prince déguisé*.

Scudéry was also a lyric and an epic poet, publishing his lyric verse mostly at the end of the volumes containing his plays. The 11,000 lines of the 12 books of *Alaric; ou, Rome vaincue*, Scudéry's epic poem on the king of the Visigoths, were dedicated to Christina of Sweden, the "Queen of the north," but unhappily for their author the poem was published only in 1653, the year before her abdication. The printed date of publication is actually 1654. There were seven editions during Scudéry's lifetime. As a dramatist Scudéry was undoubtedly a popular success in the early 1630s. He says so himself, but so, for instance, does Rotrou, and his first play was given three times at Fontainebleau. He himself affected a bombastic style, and was blusteringly hearty in manner, rather over-ready to play the fool. Tallemant is disdainful, treating him like a buffoon. But it may possibly have been early that he was introduced to the Hôtel de Rambouillet, where he became known as "le généreux Astolphe" and joined in the games of madrigals, sonnets, and gifts of verses; after 1637, he was mentioned in the correspondence of both Chapelain and Balzac.

Early in his career as a dramatist, Scudéry was an ally of Pierre Corneille, who contributed, with du Ryer and Rotrou, preliminary compliments for the published versions of Scudéry's early plays, as Scudéry himself had for Corneille's *La Veuve*. Scudéry was not an intimate of Richelieu, not one of his five poets, nor even a member of his new academy drawn from Conrart's circle. Yet Scudéry at least started a lost or abandoned epic in praise of Richelieu, the "Discours de la France à Mgr le Cardinal de Richelieu après son retour de Nancy" in 1635, and dedicated to the cardinal his first tragedy, the 1636 *La Mort de César*. It may have been simply on account of jealousy at the success of a rival, borrowing, as Scudéry himself had done, from Spanish sources; or possibly because of Corneille's own not unaffectedly dismissive attitude towards those who made their living from the stage; or from irritation at the way Corneille's *L'Illusion comique* for the 1635–36 season had borrowed from Scudéry's own *La Comédie des comédiens*, first certainly played before the queen at the Arsenal on 28 November 1634; or out of annoyance at Corneille's arrogant and niggardly behaviour over *Le Cid* and the unfortunately timed publication of his *Excuse à Ariste*—the most generally accepted reason; or, perhaps most likely of all, on account of Scudéry's desire to curry favour with the increasingly powerful minister with a passion for the theatre; but in any case Scudéry broke suddenly with Corneille in 1637 to draw up his *Observations sur Le Cid*. Unlike Mairet, Scudéry was not personal in his attack. He appears to   e envisaged an academic debate to centre on the worthlessness of Corneille's subject, the cavalier attitude to the dramatic rules, the lack of judgement in the play's execution, the poor quality of some of the lines, the derivative nature of what was good in it, and the inappropriateness of the esteem accorded to the play.

The *Observations*, improbably for their romanesque author basing itself on a list of high academic authorities, Aristotle, Horace, Heinsius, and Scaliger, appeared about 1 April 1637, at roughly the same moment as Mairet's pamphlet but independently of it. It was when, six weeks later, Corneille replied with his *Lettre apologétique* that Scudéry knew he had drawn blood, and towards the end of the first half of June he appealed to the academy. Richelieu saw the chance to establish its authority, a chance which Scudéry may have intended to set up for him, and was helped by the general outrage felt at Corneille's vicious attacks on his assailants. Scudéry was again to put forward his views on the subject of drama in his 1639 *L'Apologie du théâtre*. Years later the breach was closed, and Corneille's 1663 *Avis au lecteur* published at the head of *Sophonisbe* again complimented Scudéry. Scudéry's follow-up to the *Observations* was his brilliantly successful tragi-comedy *L'Amour tyrannique*, dedicated to the duchesse d'Aiguillon, Richelieu's favourite niece, and published with a prefatory eulogy by Sarrazin to the plaudits of Balzac. It was to be singled out and admired by Sorel in the 17th century and Voltaire in the 18th.

From 1637 Scudéry and his sister gave up moving between Rouen and Paris and settled in the Marais district. The fort at Marseilles of which Scudéry was nominated governor was manned by five only intermittently paid men. Bachaumont and Chapelle in their 1656 *Voyage en Provence et Languedoc* claimed that all the fort needed for its protection was a Swiss Guard with a halberd painted on the gate. For a period, while Scudéry claimed he was on leave, the fort is said to have been taken and Scudéry was dismissed, though he was later reinstated, signing himself as governor until 1661 but doing nothing beyond drawing the salary. The dismissal in 1652 had almost certainly been on account of despatches sent from Paris to Condé during the Fronde. In a way, Scudéry's faithfulness to

Condé, incidentally helping to explain his access to the Hôtel de Rambouillet, is reminiscent of his equally obstinate defence of Théophile against the tide of official policy.

Scudéry had returned with Madeleine to Paris in 1647, and in 1648 published his *Discours politiques des Rois*, wrongly dated 1647, dedicated to Mazarin, followed in 1649 by his *Poésies diverses*. Further small volumes of verse followed. In 1650 he succeeded Vaugelas to the Académie française, but had to leave Paris as a result of the Fronde, in which he was closely linked to Condé. Madeleine did not accompany him into exile in Normandy, where he married the 27-year-old Marie-Madeleine de Montcal de Martinvast, who was apparently in the course of writing a lengthy novel. The contract is dated 14 June 1654, and both Tallemant and Somaize suppose that the uniting factor between the 53-year-old ex-dramatist and his youthful bride was an interest in fiction. Scudéry went back to Paris only after the return of Condé in 1660 and the death in 1661 of Mazarin. He had a son in 1662.

When his sister first started to receive at her famous "samedis (Saturdays)," Scudéry took no part. He had, however, signed her first novel *Ibrahim; ou, L'Illustre Bassa*, which had appeared in 1641 and from which Scudéry derived a play of the same title for the 1641–42 season. Scudéry is said to have contributed the battle scenes to his sister's novels, and to have touched up the portraits to make them unidentifiable, although contemporaries generally recognized her sole authorship of *Ibrahim*, as well as of the others. Scudéry may have been responsible for the overall plans. His wife was well connected and presented her husband at court. He died in Paris on 14 May 1667. His widow kept up a fascinating correspondence with Bussy-Rabutin, and survived until 1711.

WORKS

The external evidence suggests that Madeleine de Scudéry was the sole author of the novels. Tallemant tells us that the 1641 *Ibrahim; ou, L'Illustre Bassa* is entirely her work. We know that Madeleine must herself have written *Clélie* virtually without her brother's involvement, since he was not with her in Paris. We therefore have internal evidence, drawn from Madeleine's interests, style, and whole approach to the writing of fiction—particularly her descriptions—in *Clélie*, which strongly confirms that the 1641 novel was at least principally written by his sister, even if signed by Scudéry. Since the literary register of *Le Grand Cyrus* changes from that of a romanesque adventure story, with most of its intrigue, incidents, and style borrowed from La Calprenède's *Cassandre* and the earlier parts of *Cléopâtre*, to that of an analysis of sentiment, and since a change of style accompanies the change of register to the style and register adopted in the *Clélie* we know to have been written by Madeleine, it is reasonable to assume that in the novels only the romanesque parts of *Le Grand Cyrus* are at all likely to have been written by Scudéry rather than his sister.

For Scudéry himself to have produced either the style or the content of the final volume of *Le Grand Cyrus* is not possible, and the internal evidence is strong enough to suggest that his role progressively diminished from the fifth volume. Costar is quite formal in asserting that Madeleine wrote both the later novels. It remains possible that Scudéry did sketch outline plots, touch up portraits, and contribute battle scenes and other adventurous episodes, but it seems appropriate to consider the novels, whatever Scudéry's contribution, as overwhelmingly the work of his sister, and they are therefore treated in the *Guide* under her name.

Any assessment of Scudéry's role in the Querelle du *Cid* surrounding Corneille's play must be more conjectural. We know from Chapelain's letter of 22 January 1637 that *Le Cid* had been created a fortnight before. Opening nights were invariably Fridays or Sundays, and in 1637 the 4 January was a Sunday. The presumption is that the first night was the 4 January, with 2 or 9 January as second guesses. The privilège for the publication of the text, taking it out of the copyright of the company which created it, is dated 21 January 1637, scandalously soon after the first performance, and the achevé d'imprimer is dated 23 March. Corneille had already a well-attested and public reputation for being mercenary about his theatrical activity, and about 20 January, on account of the play's exceptional success, had asked the Marais company for an extra 100 livres.

What was taken to be the offensively arrogant *Excuse à Ariste* was published about 20 February. When Corneille's proclamation that he had no superior was published in the *Excuse*, Scudéry is unlikely to have felt aggrieved. Mairet, perhaps especially because he had at least reason to feel that his creative powers were declining, would scarcely have been human not to. Mairet was at the château de Belin in Maine, and there was almost certainly no collusion between him and Scudéry, who was in Paris, although his pamphlet *L'Auteur du vrai Cid espagnol* and Scudéry's *Observations sur Le Cid*, much less personal, and indeed surprisingly academic in tone, appeared together at the very beginning of April.

Given what we know about the lost or abandoned epic Scudéry had written in praise of Richelieu, his semi-exclusion so far from the inner circle of Richelieu's literary entourage, both the circle of five authors and the incipient academy, and Richelieu's public and obvious desire to see his academy properly established, it is difficult not to accept the probability that, while Mairet's pamphlet was an act of personal hostility occasioned by the *Excuse*, Scudéry either on his own initiative or because it was suggested to him, set up what we know as the Querelle du *Cid*. He uncharacteristically showed a scholarly interest in the nature of tragedy by making what was effectively a challenge to Corneille, with whom his relations had always been friendly, to debate in a reasonable manner the rules which should govern tragedy. He knew that Corneille had published *Le Cid* as a tragi-comedy, and had himself presented at least five works he had called tragi-comedies and two he had called tragedies, but may still have been uncertain about the lines of demarcation between tragi-comedy and tragedy, and consistently referred to *Le Cid* as a tragedy. A public discussion of Corneille's attitude to the rules of tragedy was just the sort of debate that clearly called for an authoritative solution to be imposed by the new academy which, as we know, was reluctant to assume the authority Richelieu wanted for it.

Nettled by Mairet, but not rising to Scudéry's bait, Corneille duly replied with much personal animosity towards Mairet in his mid-May *Lettre apologétique*, but it was enough for Scudéry, who had a formal appeal to the academy by letter in the arena sometime between 4 and 13 June. On 13 June Corneille tacitly, if ungraciously, accepted that he had fallen into a trap, and agreed to submit to the academy's ruling. If that is a true reading of what took place, then Scudéry's rambling *Observations* are of no real intrinsic importance. The treatise constitutes a move in a well-conducted and victorious skirmish in what was to turn under Colbert into a full-scale war to bring the country's cultural life under the control of its central administration.

No historian or critic has sought to make out a case for the rarefied nature of Scudéry's poetic talent. However, since the volume of his production was considerable, since the processes of repeated selection by which historians, compilers, critics, and anthologizers sieve out the best are normally reliable, and since "L'incrédule" is a better than average example of what was acclaimed in galant circles in the mid-17th century, it is worth while observing its stylized poses, its affectedness, its exaggerations of language, and its repertoire of rhetorical devices on which it depends:

Connaissez vos attraits, adorable incrédule,
Et lors assurément vous me connaîtrez mieux;
Remarquez le beau feu qui brille dans vos yeux
Pour juger de l'ardeur de celui qui me brûle.

Quand je fais des soupirs, c'est que je dissimule;
Quand je parle, je mens; je suis malicieux;
Quand je ne parle point, mon sort n'en va pas mieux,
Et bien loin d'avancer, mon espoir se recule.

Etrange aveuglement qu'on ne peut trop blâmer!
Philis, vous peut-on voir et ne vous pas aimer?
Vous outragez mon coeur, vous choquez votre gloire.

O bizarres effets de mon sort inhumain!
Quand je dis que je meurs, vous ne me pouvez croire,
Et quand je serai mort, vous me croirez en vain

(Know your own attractions, adorable unbeliever,/And then certainly you will know me better;/Look at the fine fire which shines in your eyes/To judge the heat of that which burns in me.//[You say that] whenever I sigh I am just pretending;/Whenever I speak, I am lying; I am teasing;/When I do not speak, my fate is no better,/And far from going forward, my hope is in retreat.//Strange blindness that cannot be adequately blamed!/Philis, can you be seen without being loved?/You insult my heart you wound your own glory.//O strange effects of my inhuman fate!/When I say that I am dying, you cannot believe me,/And when I am dead, you will believe me in vain).

As a dramatist, Scudéry's chosen form was the tragi-comedy. Corneille was in the end to designate *Le Cid* a "tragédie" from 1648, but Scudéry's *Observations* refer to it as a "tragédie" even in 1637. There is no established criterion in use among modern critics to distinguish between tragedies and tragi-comedies when discussing the dramatic works of this period in France, although there is a natural tendency to regard the pastoral as determined by its setting, whatever the intrigue, and to distinguish tragedy from tragi-comedy in one of three ways, all of which can be shown to yield an unsatisfactory basis for classification. Authentic tragedy is distinguished sometimes by its adherence to the unities and the "bienséances," sometimes by its selection of subject matter from authentic events or characters from ancient history or legend, and sometimes by its avoidance of the spectacular and dramatic in favour of the declamatory and the rhetorical, making the criterion the movement of the audience's emotions, so that the psychological plausibility of the characters' reactions on stage become all-important. In spite of what the renaissance theorists had said, it was not generally assumed in roughly the two centuries between the age of Corneille and that of Goethe, that is between the renaissance and the romantics, that tragedy could not have a happy ending.

Often in the 17th century regarded as Scudéry's best play, and extravagantly admired, *L'Amour tyrannique* of 1638 was called by its author a tragi-comédie, although Sarrazin's eulogy regrets that classification and his prefatory discourse refers to the piece as a tragedy. Since Corneille and Scudéry disagreed about the classification of one play, and Sarrazin and Scudéry about that of another, and since Scudéry was certainly aware that there was a distinction, using both classifications for different plays of his own, it is clear that in the 1630s there was no rigid distinction in the minds of French writers between the pastoral, which often merged into the tragi-comedy, tragi-comedy, and tragedy itself.

L'Amour tyrannique was intended as a counterpart to *Le Cid*, to illustrate how Corneille should have gone about his task, particularly in confining passion to legitimate limits within marriage, which would, of course, have taken all the point out of Corneille's play, which explored the possible legitimacy of a love in which one partner had just killed the other's father in a duel. The two plays have in common that in 1638 their authors thought that each was a tragi-comedy, but that in each case other serious critics were describing them as tragedies. Not surprisingly, Richelieu disliked *Le Cid*, if only for the concept of honour which legitimized duelling. He was notoriously enthusiastic about *L'Amour tyrannique*, the play through which his rehabilitation of Pascal's father was arranged, partly no doubt on account of the way it makes private emotion subservient to the interests of state, but also because it emphatically demands that an absolute monarch be virtuous. Imaginatively, it is not in any way at all daring.

Ormène, married to Tiridate, the king of Pontus, is the daughter of Orosmane, king of Cappodoccia. She deeply loves her husband, and seeks to end her life when Tiridate falls in love with Polyxène, wife of her brother Tigrane, and wins his war against her father. In the second scene Tiridate bursts with pride and showers the audience with aphorisms about the importance of the "raison d'état" when talking to his ancient governor, Pharnabase. Orosmane comes in to beg for a refuge for his son Tigrane, the brother-in-law Tiridate has vanquished. Tiridate replies scornfully to his request,

Tiridate veut vivre ainsi qu'il a vécu;
Ne vaincre qu'à demi c'est n'avoir pas vaincu

(Tiridate wants to go on living as he has lived;/Only half to conquer is not to have conquered at all).

The declaration is hubristic, but also aphoristic and euphonious. Tiridate is consistently given verse of this quality, perhaps repetitive, possibly exaggerated, but theatrically effective. The language, however, is recognizably a take-off of Corneille. The unity of place is almost comically observed by putting a wall between the two opposing armies of Tiridate, confident of winning, and Tigrane, whose father, Tiridate's prisoner, is brought out to speak to him across the wall. Tiridate's lieutenant is holding a dagger at Orosmane's back, and Tigrane, echoing Rodrigue in the famous stances from *Le Cid*, defines his conflict

Que dois-je devenir? Nature, Honneur, Amour...

(What is going to happen to me? Nature, honour, love...).

Orosmane exhorts Tigrane to be "généreux," in a further pastiche of Rodrigue's attitude in the stances. In spite of his father's insistence on saving his honour, Tigrane surrenders to save his father's life. Tiridate's plan has worked, and the first act ends with the assault by Tiridate's army on Tigrane's forces. There is no intrigue to be resolved. Appropriate attitudes have been taken up, and the play virtually has to start again in the second act. The last lines of the first act, spoken by Orosmane, are still Corneille pastiche. Orosmane says to Tigrane

...Meurs en fils d'Orosmane,
Comme je vais mourir en père de Tigrane

(...Die like a son of Orosmane/As I shall die like the father of Tigrane).

With the beginning of the second act, the meaning of the title begins to become more clear. Tiridate's appalling heartlessness continues as he reproaches his wife with fidelity to her brother rather than to himself. Orosmane's ex-subjects come and beg to be allowed to die with him, so that the pathetic runs at full tilt into melodramatic implausibility. Tiridate treats Orosmane's ex-subjects with such contempt that even Pharnabase warns him against the hubris of excessive confidence in his own invulnerability to fate and fortune, giving an edifying lecture to his ex-pupil on the prince's need for virtue, an issue already forcing itself on public attention as Richelieu began to build up monarchical absolutism. Only a prince seen to be just and virtuous could hope to increase royal power and keep its hereditary transmission intact, but in 1638 what was to happen in 1789 did not yet seem inevitable.

Tiridate himself reveals that his sole motivation is love for Polyxène. She restrains Tigrane from killing himself, but asks him to kill her to solve her dilemma. The second act ends as Tigrane's fortress is assaulted. As the third starts, we learn that Tiridate's lieutenant has a plan which involves contriving his master's defeat. Tigrane appears in disguise and with a dagger. He believes he has killed Polyxène at her request made out of love for him. Tiridate, in the face of further frightened warnings from Pharnabase shows in himself the result of power without virtue:

Il n'est point d'autre loi que le vouloir des Rois.
C'est de nous qu'elle vient, tout-puissants que nous sommes;
C'est nous qui sommes Dieux, qui la donnons aux hommes;
Mais bien que les mortels la doivent respecter,
Celui qui fait un joug ne le doit pas porter

(There is no other law than the desire of kings./It is from us that it comes, all-powerful that we are;/It is we who are gods, who give it [law] to men;/But although mortals must respect it,/He who imposes a yoke does not have to carry it).

When Tigrane threw Polyxène in the river, her wound was only superficial, and she reproaches Tiridate, who has now openly declared his love for her, above all for his treatment of

Orosmane, ending with an attempt at physical assault on him, which is thwarted. In the fourth act the plan of Tiridate's lieutenant becomes clear and Tiridate is given a set of "stances" modelled on those of Rodrigue. He remembers a famous line from Corneille when he says "Il y va de leur gloire et de leur renommée (Their glory and their renown are at stake)," and Ormène suddenly suggests to Polyxène that she should surrender herself to Tiridate, her captor. There is a long scene between Tigrane and his sister, Ormène, Tiridate's wife, in which she justifies to her brother her love for her husband, in spite of the long series of crimes listed by Tigrane. The reminiscences of Rodrigue's stances are by now almost obsessive:. "Plutôt que de souffrir sa haine et son mépris... (Rather than suffer his hatred and contempt...)," and Ormène almost casually mentions to Tigrane that his wife is still alive, "Non, sans doute elle vit, / Elle est dans notre camp (No, she is certainly still alive, she is in our camp)."

In the final act Tigrane, recognized, is taken captive, and writes to Polyxène asking her to send him poison. Orosmane urges her to do so, and gives her the poison the kings of Cappadoccia always carry about their person. Tiridate intercepts it; Tigrane, Orosmane, Polyxène, and Ormène all in turn tell Tiridate to kill them, but his lieutenant's ruse has succeeded, and Tiridate is personally saved as a human being by his defeat as a prince. There are further echoes of Rodrigue—"O désespoir! ô rage! (Oh despair, oh rage!),"—and Tiridate tells his rebellious subjects to kill him. Orosmane is made king, and Ormène pleads for Tiridate. Tiridate says he has been conquered by reason, Orosmane insists on forgiving him, and there is general happiness and reconciliation as tyrannous love gives way to reasonable love, the implication being that Tiridate's enslavement by love has led to the enslavement of others. Good sense wins.

In some ways, there is nothing at all to be said in favour of what is at best acceptably undemanding low-brow entertainment, with wild and wholly unmotivated changes of fortune, disguises, daggers, imprisonments, poisons, and mistakes, psychological and dramatic implausibility of a quite high order, heart-rending scenes of psychologically unprepared and therefore arbitrary pathos, lectures on the need for virtues in princes, and an obsessive pastiche of Corneille's style with no shred of his imaginative vigour. No light is shed on the significance of any human experience, and neither values nor attitudes are ever other than plainly good or plainly bad. Nothing is tentative, exploratory, or evaluative. For good measure, one might add, the dramatic thread keeps snapping. Why do Orosmane's ex-subjects come in and demand to die with their king?

And yet it is an important play. It shows what Richelieu, the real founder of the French dramatic tradition, found acceptable, and its multifarious weaknesses, coupled with its public and official success, provide a yardstick by which much greater achievements than those of Scudéry can be measured. Scudéry is historically important on account of his verse, his association with his sister's novels, his role in the Querelle du Cid, his idea of what Corneille ought to have done to make Le Cid acceptable in place of what he did do, his general dramatic activity, and the link he provides between the entourage of Richelieu, the circle of Théophile, the chambre bleue of Mme de Rambouillet, and the Condé family, with all of which he had a loose association.

The very modesty of his successes elevates his work in several genres and contexts into series of controls which demarcate the norms, even if he believed in them no more strongly than he did in his own criticisms of Le Cid, which must surely have been

a try-on to bring the important issue of theatrical norms in a newly important art form before the new academy. The point of Scudéry's uncharacteristic challenge to an academic debate issued to Corneille seems likely to have been to force the young academy to take seriously the responsibilities Scudéry knew Richelieu wanted to give it. Of no very great literary achievement, Scudéry is a singularly important figure not only for the history of the literature of France, but for the understanding in a whole variety of fields of writers whose work was much more imaginatively powerful than his own.

PUBLICATIONS

Plays

Lygdamon et Lidias; ou, La Ressemblance, tragi-comédie, (1630) 1631
Le Trompeur puni; ou, L'Histoire septentrionale, tragi-comédie, (1631) 1633
La Comédie des comédiens, poème de nouvelle invention (1634) 1635; modern edition 1975
Le Fils supposé, comédie, (1634) 1636
La Mort de César, tragédie, (1635) 1636
Orante, tragi-comédie, (1633) 1635
Le Prince déguisé, tragi-comédie, (1634) 1636
Le Vassal généreux, poème tragi-comique (1632) 1636
Didon, tragédie, (1635–36) 1637
L'Amant libéral, tragi-comédie, (1636–37) 1638
L'Amour tyrannique, tragi-comédie, (1638) 1639; in *Théâtre du XVIIe siècle,* vol. 2, Bibliothèque de la Pléiade, 1986
Andromire, tragi-comédie, (1640) 1641
Eudoxe, tragi-comédie, (1639) 1641
Ibrahim; ou, L'Illustre Bassa, tragi-comédie, (1641–42) 1643
Axiane, tragi-comédie en prose, (1642–43) 1644
Arminius; ou, Les Frères ennemis, tragi-comédie, (1643) 1644

Verse

Elégie sur l'arrest de Théophile, 1623
Le Temple, poème à la gloire du Roi et de M. le cardinal de Richelieu, 1633
Discours de la France à Mgr le cardinal duc de Richelieu après son retour de Nancy, 1635
Epitaphe sur le Roi Louis XIII, 1643
L'Ombre du grand Armand, 1643
Le Cabinet de M. de Scudéry, 1646
Le Grand Exemple. A Mgr le duc de Richelieu, 1647
Poésies diverses, 1649
Salomon instruisant le Roi, par de Scudéry, 1651
Alaric; ou, Rome vaincue, poème héroïque, 1654
Ode sur le retour de M. le Prince, 1660
Poésies nouvelles, 1661

Fiction

[in collaboration with Madeleine de Scudéry]

Ibrahim; ou, L'Illustre Bassa, 4 vols., 1641
Artamène; ou, Le Grand Cyrus; 10 vols., 1649–53; English translation 1653–77

Clélie, histoire romaine, 10 vols., 1654–60; English translation, 1655–61
Almahide; ou, L'Esclave reine, 8 vols., unfinished, 1660–63

Other

Observations sur Le Cid, 1637
Lettre de M. de Scudéry à l'illustre Académie, 1637
La Preuve des passages allégués dans les Observations sur le Cid. A Messieurs de l'Académie, 1637
L'Apologie du théâtre, 1639
Les Femmes illustres; ou, Les Harangues héroïques, 2 vols., 1642–44
Discours politiques des rois, 1647

Biographical and critical studies

Clerc, Charles, *Un matamore des lettres: la vie tragi-comique de Georges de Scudéry*, 1929
Dutertre, Eveline, *Scudéry dramaturge*, 1986

SCUDÉRY, Madeleine de, 1608–1701.

Novelist and poet.

Scudéry, on whose background see the previous entry on her brother, was baptized in Le Havre on 1 December 1608. Orphaned in 1613, Scudéry, who was to make a fortune put at 300,000 livres for the publisher of her novels, Courbé, was the first woman in the history of French literature to live by her pen. She was brought up by an uncle, who may have been an ecclesiastic, probably at Rouen. She plainly had an unusually good education, learned at least to read Italian and Spanish as well as Latin, and was taught music, drawing, and dancing. We know that she was much attached to reading novels. Tallemant tells us that a lawyer, of whom we know that he came to Paris from Rouen in 1635, used to lend them to her. At some time before she came to settle in Paris with her brother in 1637 it seems clear from the virtually certain attribution to her of the 1641 *Ibrahim; ou, L'Illustre Bassa*, although it was signed by her brother, that she spent what must have been at least a matter of months in the south of France, near the Mediterranean coast, from where her father's family originated. A stray masculine past participle in the text incidentally shows that her brother probably did have some part in composing the final text of *Ibrahim*.

By 1637 Scudéry's brother, Georges, was well known in Paris as a dramatist. It was in that year that he produced his criticisms of Pierre Corneille's *Le Cid*, over which he was to appeal for a ruling to Richelieu's new academy. Scudéry had been spending much of her time in Rouen, but now came to instal her brother and herself in the Rue Vieille-du-Temple in the Marais district of Paris, the fashionable new quarter built up in the very early years of the century near the Place Royale (now the Place des

Vosges) which, until about 1600, had still been an orchard outside the city boundary. It was probably through her brother that, very soon after her arrival in Paris, Scudéry was invited to the celebrated chambre bleue of Mme de Rambouillet. Chapelain notes her presence there in 1638. Her role, however, appears to have been less central than that of her brother.

Tallemant, who returned from Italy at the very end of 1638 and appeared at the Hôtel de Rambouillet at about the same time as Scudéry, compared her with her brother in a "historiette" which, with Conrart's *Mémoires*, is the source of much of the little we know about her before 1647, but which cannot have been written until some time between 1654 and 1659.

> Sa soeur a plus d'esprit que luy, et est tout autrement raisonnable. Mais elle n'est guères moins vaine: elle dit tousjours: "Depuis le renversement de nostre maison." Vous diriez qu'elle parle du bouleversement de l'empire grec. Pour la beauté il n'y en a nulle; c'est une grande personne maigre et noire, et qui a le visage fort long. Elle est prolixe en ses discours, et a un ton de voix de magister qui n'est nullement agréable

> (His sister is more intelligent than she is, and much more reasonable. But she is scarcely less vain. She always says "Since the fall of our house." You'd think she was talking of the overthrow of the Greek empire. As for beauty, she is without it. She is a tall, thin, dark woman, with a very long face. She is prolix in conversation, and has a schoolmasterish tone of voice which is not at all pleasant).

It is Tallemène who tells us what is amply confirmed by the internal stylistic evidence, that it was Scudéry herself who wrote "all of *L'Illustre Bassa*," referring to *Ibrahim; ou, L'Illustre Bassa*, dedicated to Mlle de Rohan, the only daughter of Henri de Rohan and Marguerite de Béthune, with a privilège dated 6 November 1640 and an achevé d'imprimer of 20 March 1641, and "une partie des harangues des (part of the harangues of) *Femmes illustres*," referring to the gallery of speeches and portraits of that title published in 1642, like *Ibrahim*, over her brother's name. The reason for publishing over her brother's name is given by Tallemant as either modesty, or the commercial advantage of exploiting her brother's high literary reputation. What he did, says Tallemant, "quoyque assez meschant, se vendoit pourtant bien (although rather poor, none the less sold well)."

According to Tallemant, Scudéry's brother was excessively jealous of his literary reputation and violently defended his authorship of what she had written. It is from Tallemant, too, that we know about Georges de Scudéry's aversion to Paul Pellisson, later to become his sister's close friend, his dislike of her Saturday receptions from 1653, and the detail that Georges, when correcting his sister's proofs, deliberately rendered the portraits unrecognizable. Offence was being taken by some of those who no doubt correctly recognized themselves even in the novel *Artamène*. It was only in 1857, when Victor Cousin published in the *Journal des Savants* (q.v.) notes on a key he had found in the Bibliothèque de l'Arsenal to the portraits in *Le Grand Cyrus*, that the compelling interest of the portraits for Scudéry's contemporaries became apparent.

Georges de Scudéry was appointed to the sinecure governorship of the minuscule fort of Notre-Dame de la Garde in June

1642, but Scudéry and he were still in Rouen in September 1644. In November they travelled to Bourg-la-Reine by coach, then down the Rhône from Lyons, arriving at Avignon on 27 November and at Marseilles on 8 December. They came back to Paris at the end of 1647. Scudéry, who found that three plays had been taken from the now fashionable *Ibrahim*, did not immediately meet Paul Pellisson, and did not begin to receive at her famous "samedis (Saturdays)" in the Rue de Beauce until after the Fronde. The overwhelming probability is that, together with her brother, Scudéry now undertook the ten-volume *Artamène; ou, Le Grand Cyrus*, commonly referred to by its sub-title, in rivalry and imitation of La Calprenède, whose ten-volume *Cassandre* appeared from 1644 to 1650, and whose twelve-volume *Cléopâtre* began to appear in 1647.

It seems likely that the overall conception of *Le Grand Cyrus*, its preface and the first four books, all closely modelled on La Calprenède, were essentially the work of Georges de Scudéry, to which Scudéry contributed only episodes, mostly a portrait or an incident leading to an analysis of sentiment. The completed work is well over twice the length of d'Urfé's *L'Astrée*. Its first volume appeared on 7 January 1649, and two further volumes appeared later that year; volumes four and five appeared in 1650; six and seven in 1651; eight in 1652; and nine and ten in 1653, with the final achevé d'imprimer dated 13 September 1653. A second edition of the first three volumes appeared with the fourth and fifth in 1650; the first two volumes were again reprinted, and new editions of all ten volumes appeared in 1654 and 1656. An English translation appeared from 1653 to 1677, and there was an Italian translation in 1682. The hero, Artamène, is generally taken to have represented Condé, and Mandane, Mme de Longueville.

By 1653 the Fronde was over. The final volume of *Le Grand Cyrus* had explored a radically new form of love, which focused on the emancipation of the woman from a totally subordinate role, and heavily emphasized her right to freedom from male sexual domination. The sexual freedom of the woman, together with the refinement of manners, language, and standards of behaviour, were to be the serious platforms on which the civilizing function of préciosité (q.v.) was to be based. As salon life began to resume, Scudéry frequented the salons of other hostesses, and began herself to receive one of the intimate groups she frequented at her own house on Saturdays. The Saturday meetings in fact started at the residence of Mme Aragonnois, widow of a rich financier, subsequently known as the "ancienne ville (old city)," and then moved to the "Nouvelle ville (new city)" of Mme Bocquet before being removed to Scudéry's residence in the Rue de Beauce. The apartment was leased for 300 livres, and there was a coach entrance, court, and garden, but the only way to the apartment was through an ugly hall and up a dark staircase.

The samedis themselves were much less exclusive and more bourgeois gatherings than had been those of the Hôtel de Rambouillet, now in decline, although assiduously attended by Georges de Scudéry until his departure from Paris. At the Hôtel de Rambouillet the presence of gay and pretty girls had encouraged a galanterie not obvious at the graver samedis, centring on a much smaller group of ladies more advanced in years. There were a dozen intimates including, among the males, Pellisson, Conrart, and Sarrazin, whose salon names appear in the novels. Pellisson had several, but notably Acante; Conrart was Théodamas; and Sarrazin was Polyandre. Scudéry herself was

Sapho; Mme Aragonnois, Philoxène; and her sister, Mlle Legendre, mistress of the bishop of Langres, La Rivière, who was to leave her 20,000 livres, was Cléodore. If there were no longer the practical jokes of the Hôtel de Rambouillet, there was still much versifying. Pellisson and Scudéry sent one another madrigals all day on 20 December 1653, but the fact that they were collected suggests a lack of spontaneity; there were *Chroniques du samedi*; and there was a *Gazette de Tendre*. The frivolity had become self-conscious, earnest, and chronicled. Although Scudéry kept the Rue de Beauce apartment for the rest of her life, the samedis were virtually over as soon as Pellisson ceased in 1657 to be able to attend regularly.

In 1653 Scudéry's famous close Platonic friendship with Pellisson, her "tendre ami," had begun. She had met Pellisson through Conrart, with whom she was then closely linked, in the summer of 1653, on a famous excursion to Romène, where Mme Aragonnois had a country retreat near Yerres, then frequently at Conrart's, and with Godeau. Pellisson, who came from Castres, had arrived in Paris for a second time to stay briefly in 1650, but in July that year had become permanently disfigured by smallpox, had bought the office of sécretaire du roi in 1652, and stayed permanently in or near the capital, entering Foucquet's service in 1657, becoming his principal confidant, and being sent to the Bastille on his fall. His *Histoire de l'Académie* of 1652, not intended to be a history in the modern sense, acquired him membership of that organization, but alienated Pierre Corneille and Sorel as well as Georges de Scudéry.

Scudéry explained to Pellisson, at whose yellowish colouring after his disfigurement Boileau was later to make a cruel quip, the notion of love examined in the last volume of *Le Grand Cyrus*, and put forward in November 1653 the distinction between a friendship which was "particulier," such as she had for him, and one which was "tendre," such as she had for very few. There were also friendships which were half-friendships, new friendships, old friendships, and solid friendships. She had imposed on Pellisson a six-month probation, at which he fretted, in September, before constituting him her "tendre ami" in February 1654, the date of the *Carte de Tendre* inserted into the first volume of Scudéry's ten-volume *Clélie, histoire romaine*, whose achevé d'imprimer was 31 August 1654. It was through Scudéry that Pellison met Suzanne de Bruc, marquise du Plessis-Bellière, through whom he was taken into Foucquet's service. The "Bélisanthe" of *Clélie*, she was a close friend of Scudéry and Foucquet's mistress who also organized his social life and artistic patronage.

Geographies of love, epiphenomena of the increasing interest in the analysis of the affections within progressively more refined galant society, were becoming popular games. For 1654 alone we have, in addition to the *Carte de Tendre*, d'Aubignac's *Relation du Royaume de Coquetterie*, the *Carte du Royaume des Prétieuses* attributed to Maulévrier, the *Carte du Royaume d'Amour* attributed to Tristan l'Hermite, and Bussy-Rabutin's *Carte géographique de la Cour*, better known as the *Carte du pays de la Braquerie*. In fact Scudéry was much criticized for the pedantry of a map of love, and had repeatedly to explain that it was half an hour's joke "intended for half a dozen people with intelligence, not for two thousand who had none." The *Carte de Tendre*, which will be considered in the context of *Clélie*, is for various reasons peculiarly important, although perhaps less directly influential than the galleries of portraits whose vogue was inaugurated by *Le Grand Cyrus* and *Clélie*. Segrais, collecting with Huet the 57 portraits for the princesse de Montpensier, daughter of Gaston d'Orléans, for the *Galerie des portraits*, of which not many more than 30 copies were printed in Caen in 1659, explicitly acknowledges the inspiration of *Le Grand Cyrus* and *Clélie*. Scudéry was therefore at the origin of the sudden vogue for the portrait in the second half of the century which led to the fictional exploration of personal characteristics and emotional profiles, to fill so important an imaginative function for at least a quarter of a century.

Georges de Scudéry was deprived by Mazarin of his post as governor of the Mediterranean fortress in 1652. By June 1654 letters of his to Condé had been discovered, and he found it expedient to leave Paris, roughly at the moment of increased intimacy between Scudéry and Pellisson, and of the commencement of *Clélie*. From this time on Scudéry's relations with her brother were more or less strained. He was not always made welcome when he wanted to come and stay, and any little he had to do with the composition of *Clélie* must have been confined to the beginning, and perhaps to the overall plan although, in spite of its plot, the novel is little more than a long succession of portraits. Its conception of love owes something to Pellisson who, although associated with préciosité and with Foucquet, was none the less a devotee of Homer, whose *Odyssey* he translated. In spite of his advocacy of purity of language, he admired Ronsard, and his 1656 preface to the poems of Sarrazin explains much about the true nature of the balanced values governing cultivated behaviour and, subordinately, linguistic usage at the heart of préciosité.

Although there is a relatively uncomplicated plot at the heart of *Clélie*, its contemporary popularity can be explained only in terms of the numerous portraits. The novel, only just over half as long as *Le Grand Cyrus*, may well have been begun before its predecessor was finished. After the first volume on 31 August 1654, Courbé published the different parts fairly regularly, although nothing appeared for the first time in either 1656 or 1659. The final parts of the tenth volume appeared on 1 March 1660, and reprints of the earlier parts were issued before the novel was ever finished. An English translation appeared from 1656–61 and a German translation in 1664. There were at least projects for Italian and Arabic translations. Like the two earlier novels, *Clélie* was signed by Scudéry's brother.

The fourth novel, *Almahide; ou, L'Esclave reine*, remained unfinished. It was a failure. Only eight volumes were published between 1660 and 1663. Signed, like the other three, by Scudéry's brother, *Almahide*, like them, has usually been attributed to Scudéry herself, but the very active participation of Georges de Scudéry, if not his sole authorship, was cogently argued by J.W. Schwitzer in 1939, and has since gained strong support. By 1983 it was being argued that Scudéry herself cannot even have collaborated in the composition of the work.

Scudéry was attacked, notably by Antoine Furetière in his 1658 *Nouvelle allégorique; ou, Histoire des derniers troubles arrivés au royaume d'éloquence*, as later by Boileau in his *Dialogue des héros de roman*, of which a first draft was probably composed in 1666. Furetière was a friend of Gilles Boileau, and a lawyer who apparently lost his job for too openly accepting bribes. A satirist, friend also of Pellisson, in his allegory he puts Scudéry on the side of Prince Galimatias in his war against Rhétorique and its prime minister Bon Sens (Good Sense). The samedis may have continued, even without Pellisson, until the autumn of 1661 and the fall of Foucquet, but they did not survive

that event, and may not have lasted until it. Préciosité itself, in the full sense, did not last much longer. Meanwhile Scudéry received a whole catalogue of presents, including a large diamond from Christina of Sweden in 1662, 1,200 livres from the king in 1663, and later a pension of 2,000 livres in 1683. The list of extravagant gifts from wealthy admirers is long, and has been used to discredit Scudéry's non-aristocratic character. In 1671, she was to win a prize from the Académie française for her *Discours de la louange et de la gloire*.

From 1680 to 1692 Scudéry published a series of *Conversations* and *Entretiens*, essentially extracted from *Le Grand Cyrus* and *Clélie*, although given new introductions. They were much admired by Mme de Sévigné, sent by Mme de Maintenon to Saint-Cyr, and read to the king at Versailles. There are tributes to them in the *Journal des Savants* for 20 September 1688, and from Bayle and Mme Dacier. Scudéry is also the author of an entertaining correspondence, especially with Bussy-Rabutin. She died peacefully in Paris on 2 June 1701.

WORKS

It does no special service to Scudéry to quote her merely gracious and competent verse. Better than her brother's, her poems, to be found only in anthologies, remain none the less essentially salon pieces, of no real significance, whereas other salon frivolities, like the *Carte de Tendre* and some of the portraits from the two major novels, apparently of no real consequence, have in their social context a very considerable importance.

The first novel, *Ibrahim; ou, L'Illustre Bassa*, relies notably more than the others on description. Its preface announces guiding principles analogous to the unities, specifying unity of action, a start *in medias res* with the intrigue already approaching its climax, and a respect for "vraisemblance (plausibility)." There is also a clear movement towards interest in the analysis of sentiment. The framework of plot concerns the slave Justinian who under the emperor Soliman becomes grand vizir with the name of Ibrahim. He receives permission to leave Constantinople for six months in order to see Isabelle, the princess of Monaco he loved, but wrongly thought was married. He returns alone, since he will not take Isabelle to a country where he is a slave. The generous Soliman has her sent for, but falls in love with her himself. Finally, his generosity wins, and he frees them both.

Essentially this is an unremarkable romanesque adventure story, no more than adequately cliff-hanging, exalting true love, fidelity, perseverance and generous renunciation: with four storms, two shipwrecks, four naval battles, three duels, two escapes, and four disguises. That actually means a relative dearth of suspense, and more concentration than usual on interior debates and exterior descriptions, with a quite strong emphasis on Scudery's psychological interest at the expense of her brother's preference for violent incident and nail-biting adventure. Georges de Scudéry's participation in the redaction of the text has been cogently argued from an inexplicable lapse into the authorial masculine "si je n'estois persuadé… (if I were not persuaded…)" in the third book (p. 505).

In *Artamène; ou, Le Grand Cyrus*, the portraits emerge as a compromise. Scudéry progresses slowly from the adventure story to the novel of psychological analysis, with a probable change at least of principal author from the fifth volume. Written after the return from Marseilles, the novel starts in almost crude, quasi-plagiaristic rivalry with La Calprenède. The plot concerns Cyrus, son of the king of Persia and disguised as Artamène, and his love for Mandane, daughter of the Médes, whom he pursues through successive abductions, first by Labinet, then by Mazare, and finally by Aryande. Cyrus throws down his disguise, allies himself first with Labinet, then with Mazare, and re-conquers Mandane. She is again abducted, and Cyrus has to rid himself of Thomiris, who has fallen in love with him. He is victorious in battle; his principal rivals are dead; Thomiris is forced to flee, and Cyrus marries Mandane.

The novel makes constant use of the term "galant" and its cognates, always denoting the need for patience and restraint in the implementation of male sexual desire and for reticent reserve in the female. There is now much more analysis of affective states. In spite of the crude story of adventure and lust, there is a powerful undercurrent of imaginative investigation into the rules for distilling from crude passion a cultivated and morally enriching as well as emotionally fulfilling affection. At the end an ideal of love is examined which is so palpably unrealizable as to appear mere exaggeration, fantasy, or dream. The dream loses power by its rarification, but it has a serious core of interrogative aspiration.

The prolixity with which possible manifestations of true galanterie are probed also detracts from the power of the investigation, which none the less, written during the Fronde with a hero obviously representing Condé, had necessarily to be tentative in order to avoid excessive political provocation. The casuistry of love, and the discussion of its signs, conduct, nature, and potential begin already in *Le Grand Cyrus* to move into the areas of subtlety and over-refinement associated with the excesses, although not the kernel, of later préciosité. Should you seek to inspire love in those for whom you do not wish to harbour it? Can you legitimately accept expressions of a passion you do not wish to return?

Ten years later salon society would be awash with such discussions. Indeed the questions would become neatly tabulated, and ten years later still even provincial bourgeois readers of *Le Mercure Galant* (q.v.) would have the socially acceptable answers to such problems provided for them. But there is a powerful sense of new ground being at least assayed by Sapho's delicate tentacles, however long-winded her prose. The portraits, too, are prolix, spattered with superlatives, too slackly achieved for effective quotation in the present context, although the portraits of Voiture, of Mme de Rambouillet and Julie d'Angennes, of Condé and Mme de Longueville, and Sapho's own self-portrait make up in discerning sensitivity and their ability to distinguish strengths and weaknesses much of what they lack in concentration and selectivity.

Most important are Sapho's views on love expressed to Cydnon. Gently utopian, they nevertheless articulate not only the desire to free women from sexual tyranny, but also the need to find some way of turning the crudely passionate into the morally enriching without at the same time sacrificing the claims of emotional relationships. There is also the beginning of a reaction against the baroque exuberance of a d'Urfé. Sapho's imagination probes less confidently than his into the possibility of grafting moral enrichment on to sexual fulfilment, but she seeks to point out what would happen if that possibility did not exist. Is celibacy too high a price to pay for freedom from the demands of male passion?

Je veux qu'on espère d'être aimé, mais je ne veux pas qu'on espère rien davantage, car enfin c'est, selon moi, la plus grande folie du monde de s'engager à aimer quelqu'un si ce n'est dans la pensée de l'aimer jusques la mort. Or est-il que, hors d'aimer de la manière que je l'entends, c'est s'exposer de passer bientôt de l'amour à l'indifférence, et de l'indifférence à la haine et au mépris.... J'entends qu'on m'aime ardemment, qu'on n'aime que moi et qu'on m'aime avec respect. Je veux même que cette amour soit une amour tendre et sensible, qui se fasse de grands plaisirs de fort petites choses, qui ait la solidité de l'amitié et qui soit fondée sur l'estime et sur l'inclination. Je veux de plus que cet amant soit fidèle et sincère; je veux encore qu'il n'ait ni confident ni confidente de sa passion et qu'il renferme si bien dans son coeur tous les sentiments de son amour, que je puisse me vanter d'être seule à les savoir. Je veux aussi qu'il me dise tous ses secrets, qu'il partage toutes mes douleurs, que ma conversation et ma vue fassent toute sa félicité; que mon absence l'afflige sensiblement; qu'il ne me dise jamais rien qui puisse me rendre son amour suspecte de faiblesse; et qu'il me dise toujours tout ce qu'il faut pour me persuader qu'elle est ardente et qu'elle sera durable. Enfin je veux un amant sans vouloir un mari, et je veux un amant qui, se contentant de la possession de mon coeur, m'aime jusqu' à la mort, car si je n'en trouve un de cette sorte, je n'en veux point

(I would like him to hope to be loved, but I would not like him to hope for anything more, because in my view it is the silliest thing in the world to commit yourself to love someone except with the intention of loving him until death. But unless you love in the way I'm talking about, you will be exposed to passing soon from love to indifference, and from indifference to aversion and contempt.... I want to be loved ardently, to be loved exclusively, and to be loved with respect. Indeed, I want that love to be gentle and feeling, deriving great pleasures from small things, to have the solidity of friendship, and to be based on esteem and liking. What is more, I want this lover to be faithful and sincere; I further want him to confide his passion to no one, male or female, and I want him to keep all his feelings of love concealed in his heart so that I can pride myself on being the only one to know of them. I want him to tell me all his secrets, and to share all my sorrows. I wish my conversation and my presence to be all his happiness, and my absence to afflict him painfully; that he should never say anything which allows me to suspect his love of weakness, and that he should always tell me everything necessary to persuade me that his love is ardent and will endure. In brief, I want a lover without wanting a husband, and I want a lover who, being content with the possession of my heart, will love me until death, because, if I don't find one like that, I don't want one at all).

This entirely unrealistic utopian dream is intended to be understood as just that. Sex subjects the female to tyranny. Utter male devotion, entirely private but absolute, is the ideal I want, says Sapho, and if I can't have I'll do without anything. She goes on to make the point even clearer:

...de la manière dont j'ai le coeur, si j'aimais, j'aimerais si tendrement et si fortement qu'il serait difficile qu'on me rendît l'amour avec usure. Cependant je suis persuadée que, pour être heureuse en aimant, il faut croire qu'on est pour le moins autant aimée qu'on aime, car autrement on a de la honte de sa propre faiblesse et du dépit de la tiédeur d'autrui. C'est pourquoi, bien je sois persuadée qu'on peut aimer innocemment, et que je le sois aussi bien que Phaon est aimable et qu'il a quelque disposition à m'aimer, je ne laisse pas d'être résolue de faire ce que je pourrai pour ne l'aimer point

(...my heart being as it is, if I were to love, I would love so tenderly and strongly that it would be difficult to return my love with interest. However, I am convinced that, to love happily, you must believe that you are at least as much loved as loving, as otherwise you are ashamed at your own weakness and angry at your lover's lukewarmness. That's why, although I'm convinced that it is possible to love innocently, and that Phaon is lovable and is disposed to love me, I'm none the less resolved to do what I can not to love him).

The ideal, therefore, is self-defeating. There are no circumstances in that philosophy in which a woman can happily love. This is kite-flying, not rule-making, but it does insist that our love must remain in our power.

There is already incipient anxiety about the situation Racine and Mme de Lafayette will feel called on to examine. Where will love take us if it is not in our power? For d'Urfé it did not matter, since it would be proportionate to the merit of its object, and therefore morally up-lifting. Descartes had not yet written *Les Passions de l'âme* to show that love, like all the other affections, was still in our power. But Jansenist (q.v.) spirituality was already loud and clear about our impotence to control our ultimate, and therefore only really important, destiny. Scudéry has provided an exceedingly sensitive indicator to the strength with which the dilemma was being felt in salon society as it was renewed after the Fronde.

Understood as an entirely comprehensible cry of protest, Sapho's attitude not only makes sense, but it points to the female need for equality, emotional satisfaction, and emancipation from sexual subservience to the male. It is too obviously absurd to be taken as a blueprint for ideal relationships, however restrained and refined the social ambience. Understood as it must be, it is a powerful protest and a clear pointer to the direction in which values and behaviour patterns seemed to Scudéry's alter ego, Sapho, to need moving.

However hastily put together, the view of love in the *Carte de Tendre*, perhaps because more corporate in its conception, is also more nuanced. Scudéry was probably telling the truth when she said it was run up by a few friends in half an hour when she finally admitted Pellisson to the status of "tendre ami" in February 1654. It was published in the first volume of *Clélie, histoire romaine* on 31 August 1654. Essentially, it indicates three possible routes from "Nouvelle amitié (new friendship)" to love, now called "tendre", with its implications of galanteries, rather than "amour," to which still clung overtones of passion. Scudéry comes quite near to trying on exorcism by euphemy. There is an overland route through various hamlets—Complaisance, Soumission, Petits Soins, Assiduité, Empressement, Grands Services, Sensibilité, Tendresse, Obéissance, and Constante

Amitié—which takes the new friend to Tendre-sur-Reconnoissance (Love-on-Gratitude) on the Reconnoissance Fleuve (River of Gratitude). If you lose your way, you risk ending on the mountainous cliff of Orgueil (Pride) or going through Indiscretion, Perfidie, Médisance, and Méchanceté to drown in the Mer d'Inimitié (Sea of Enmity).

There is another overland route through Grand Esprit, Joli Vers, Billet Galant, Billet Doux, Sincérité, Grand Coeur, Probité, Générosité, Exactitude, Respect, and Bonté, which takes the new friend to Tendre-sur-Estime (Love-on-Esteem). If you lose the way, you pass through Négligence, Inégalité, Tiédeur, Légèreté, Oubli (Forgetfulness), and end at the Lac d'Indifférence (Lake of Indifference). But there is an alternative to the land routes. You can take the river Inclination, which takes you to Tendre-sur-Inclination, or love based on passion. However, the map does not indicate how you stop when you get there, and you can be carried on to La Mer dangereuse (the Sea of Danger), beyond which lie the Terres Inconnues (Unknown Country).

There is no gradation in the affective names of the hamlets on the overland routes, and the names could be exchanged without damaging the fundamental conception. Passion is dangerous because it cannot be controlled. What can be controlled leads only to the safe destinations of love based on esteem or gratitude, the two feelings the princesse de Clèves was to have for her husband in Mme de Lafayette's novel. What she had for Nemours was "inclination," which here means passion. What is serious about the *Carte de Tendre* is its fear of loss of control, and consequently of any emotional involvement which is not rationally controlled. If it is rationally controlled, based on esteem or gratitude, you can at worst lose your way into hostility or indifference. The Sea of Danger is depicted with lots of obviously perilous rocks.

The novel itself has a token plot about Aronce and Clélie who are separated by an earthquake just before their marriage. Clélie is imprisoned with Horace in Ardée, besieged by Tarquin. There is an uprising at Rome when the republic is inaugurated, Tarquin is overthrown by Clelius, whose prisoner Clélie becomes and with whom, after various peripeteia, Aronce is reconciled. He marries Clélie. This time, however, the romanesque adventure element comes near to fading away before the portrait gallery and the analysis of emotion. But, although the social setting, feasts, entertainments, and characters are all heavily idealized, the novel is by no means just escapism. Its fundamental interest is in the notion of love which underlies the escapist elements, as well as the teasing 17th-century game of putting real names to the fictional characters. There is also a deliberate attempt at education in the ways of sophistication and refinement, kept from being too patronizing by the idealization itself. The reader is gently instructed in polite behaviour by this account of a country celebration. The weather is naturally as well behaved as the cast:

...toutes les Femmes destinées à porter les Festons estoient belles, propres, et bien faites; il y eut une quantité prodigieuse de Fleurs,... l'ordre de la Cérémonie fut soigneusement observé; le jour mesme fut favorable à cette Feste champestre, le Festin s'en fit sous un grand Berceau de Jasmin à un costé du Parterre, au milieu duquel est une Fontaine qu'on avoit toute couverte de ces Festons de Fleurs: et le reste du jour se passa en promenade, et en conversation agréable

(…all the women charged with carrying the garlands were beautiful and elegant, with a good figure; there was a huge quantity of flowers,… the order of ceremonies was carefully observed; even the weather was favourable to the fête champêtre. The feast itself took place under a large canopy of jasmin on one side of a plot in the middle of which is a fountain covered with these garlands of flowers, and the rest of the day was spent in strolling and in pleasant conversation).

In a sense the jumble of tenses denotes careless writing, just as the idealization might seem puerile. That is to miss the underlying strength, which becomes clear only when the literary register is correctly identified—adventure story, social gossip, and a delicate, immensely tentative, and rather long-winded but very radical investigation into the ideals which should govern social behaviour and erotic relationships.

PUBLICATIONS

Fiction

Ibrahim; ou, L'Illustre Bassa, 4 vols., 1641
Artamène; ou, Le Grand Cyrus, 10 vols., 1649–53; English translation 1653–77
Clélie, histoire romaine, 10 vols., 1654–60; English translation 1655–61
Almahide; ou, L'Esclave reine, 8 vols., unfinished, 1660–63, probably by Georges de Scudéry
Célinte, nouvelle première, 1661
Mathilde, 1667
La Promenade de Versailles, 1669
Conversations sur divers sujets, 2 vols., 1680
Conversations nouvelles sur divers sujets, 2 vols., 1684
Conversations morales, 2 vols., 1686
Nouvelles conversations de morale, 2 vols., 1688
Entretiens de morale, 2 vols., 1692

Other

Discours de la louange et de la gloire, 1671
Lettres de Mlle de Scudéry à M. Godeau, 1835
Lettres inédites de Mlle de Scudéry à Pierre-Daniel Huet, 1902

Biographical and critical studies

Magendie, Maurice, *La Politesse mondaine et les théories de l'honnêteté en France au XVIIe siècle, de 1600 à 1660*, 2 vols., 1925
Magne E., *Le Salon de Mlle de Scudéry; ou, Le Royaume de Tendre*, 1927
Mongrédien, Georges, *Mlle de Scudéry et son salon*, 1946
Nunn, R., *Mlle de Scudéry's "Clélie"*, 1966
Niderst, A., *Madeleine de Scudéry, Paul Pellisson et leur monde*, 1976
Godenne, René, *Les Romans de Mademoiselle de Scudéry*, 1983

————————

SEDAINE, Michel-Jean, 1719–1797.

Dramatist and librettist.

LIFE

Sedaine was born in Paris on 4 July 1719, the son of an architect working for the bâtiments du roi. His father died when Sedaine was 13, and Sedaine's schooling at the Ecole des Quatre-Nations had to be interrupted. In order to assist his mother, Sedaine worked as a stone-mason, and his situation was brought to the attention of Buron, the architect, whose employee Sedaine became and of whose architectural business he later became manager, having apparently terminated his education without further formal study. He was later to repay Buron's kindness when in turn he adopted Buron's grandson, the painter David. It was probably Buron who found Sedaine a patron in Le Comte, a lawyer, who paid Sedaine a pension of 1,200 livres.

We know little of Sedaine's circumstances for the years during which he was a stonemason, but as a young man he was able to indulge a dedicated interest in the theatre, particularly in what was available at the fairs and from the Italian company. He was able to frequent café society, met d'Alembert and his protégé, Charles-Simon Favart, a brilliant librettist for light entertainment and later director of the Opéra comique, and mixed with the future philosophes (q.v.). Sedaine got to know Diderot well and, had he been younger, would have been welcomed by Diderot as a son-in-law. Sedaine discovered in himself a talent for writing amusing lyric verse, and began to compose the pieces compiled in the *Pièces fugitives* of 1752. The earliest to which a date can be assigned is the 1745 "L'Epître à son habit."

It was in 1752 that Rousseau's *Le Devin du Village* was played before the court, and that the first Italian opera buffa company visited Paris. Paris already knew the "pièces en vaudevilles" put on by the Italian company, with spoken dialogue and, with Rousseau's importation of the style of the Italian intermezzi, opéra comique had virtually been created. The comic dramatists found themselves increasingly facing the choice of writing either "comédie larmoyante," serious but sentimental bourgeois comedy, or what amounted to libretti for comic operas, such as were to be produced by Favart, Louis Anseaume, and Sedaine, and to be set to music by such composers as François-André Philidor, André Grétry, and Pierre-Alexandre Monsigny.

The Italian company, re-established in Paris under Riccoboni from 1716, had used the Hôtel de Bourgogne, and in the summer of 1721 leased the newly built Théâtre de la Foire de Saint-Laurent. That theatre replaced the wooden shacks used by the visiting companies during the Foire Saint-Laurent, whose season had already been extended from late June until October. From 1723, on the Regent's death, the Comédie Italienne had a public subsidy, and could again use the Hôtel de Bourgogne. Sedaine's 1761 *On ne s'avise jamais de tout* was the last light opera given at the Théâtre de la Foire before the theatre was closed and the resident fairground company absorbed into the Comédie Italienne, at that date still in the hands of a company of Italians.

By 1779 Grimm could write that the company was relying on comedies from its former French repertoire, and that there were no foreign actors left except Carlin Bertinazzi and his understudy, who played the Harlequin roles in the French pieces. In

April 1783 the company left the Hôtel de Bourgogne for the new theatre in the Boulevard des Italiens, to be known during the Revolution as the Théâtre Favart. Its amalgamation with the company at the Théâtre de Monsieur, later the Théâtre Feydeau, which was to produce the Opéra-Comique company, took place in 1801. The building known as the Opera-Comique was built after the Théâtre des Italiens had been destroyed by fire in 1835.

From about 1756, Sedaine was a professional dramatist and librettist writing almost exclusively for the Théâtre de la Foire or the Théâtre-Italien. He started with the 1756 *Le Diable à quatre; ou, La Double Métamorphose*, published in 1757 as a three-act "opéra-comique," of which Sedaine published five up to *On ne s'avise…* of 1761. The music was invariably by Philidor or Monsigny. After the closure of the Théâtre de la Foire came the 1762 *Le Roi et le fermier*, a "comédie en trois actes, mêlé de morceaux de musique (three-act comedy with musical interludes)," derived from Robert Dodsley's 1737 *The King and the Miller of Mansfield* by way of Charles Collé's *La Partie de chasse de Henri IV*, still suppressed for showing the king on familiar terms with the less socially exalted of his subjects. In 1764 came an "opéra-comique" and Sedaine's own favourite among his libretti, the "bergerie" *Rose et Colas*, described on publication as a "comedy in one act, prose and music."

Then in 1765 Sedaine presented to the Comédie-Française a riposte to Palissot's satire on the philosophes, the 1760 *Les Philosophes*. The first night of what was then called "Le Duel" was scheduled for 21 October 1765, but the censors intervened, and the central character had to forbid his son from fighting the duel which is the point of the play, and which as a noble he was bound in honour to fight. The re-written play was passed by the censors on 10 November, by the lieutenant of police on 13 November, and on 29 November had to be run through in front of a commission from the Châtelet, much to Grimm's derision. On 2 December the Comédie-Française played it under the title *Le Philosophe sans le savoir*, but its success was only mediocre and the text had to be changed for further performances. It was only after the sixth performance, postponed until 12 January 1766 on account of the dauphin's death, that there was any public enthusiasm, and the first run was a respectable 21 performances.

In 1766 *Aline, reine de Golconde* with music by Monsigny was put on at the Opéra. Sedaine described it on first publication in 1766 as a "ballet héroïque," but in 1771 as an "opéra." The light one-act comedy of manners *La Gageure imprévue* was presented at the Comédie-Française in 1768. In 1769 Sedaine married Marie-Madeleine Sérigny, who bore him three children. He adopted not only Buron's grandson, but also other children, and was now comfortably off. The marquis de Marigny, director-general of the bâtiments, had Sedaine made permanent secretary of the Académie des Beaux-Arts, which brought him a pension of 1,800 livres and an apartment in the Louvre, and Catherine of Russia sent him gifts of money, with which he bought a small estate at Saint-Prix near Montmorency. Marie-Antoinette played at Versailles in rehearsals of his pieces where, in 1780, *Aucassin et Nicolette; ou, Les Moeurs du bon vieux temps* with music by Grétry was to be given before transfer to the Théâtre des Italiens. Sedaine described it simply as a comedy in four acts and in verse.

Mingling with the light musical entertainments were occasional excursions into other genres. *Thémire* of 1770 was a one-act pastoral played before the court at Fontainebleau, no doubt

with music. A five-act prose tragedy of 1770 *Maillard; ou, Paris sauvé*, set in 1358, was played in 1777 before being suppressed by the censorship, and not published until 1788. In 1784 *Richard coeur de lion* with music by Grétry was sufficiently successful with the Italian company to ensure Sedaine's election to the Académie française in 1786 at the fifteenth attempt. In 1786 *Amphitrion* with music by Grétry was described simply as an opera and played by the opera company. The next year, as well as *Raoul Barbe-Bleue* with music by Grétry at the Théâtre des Italiens, Sedaine presented a five-act prose comedy *Raymond V, comte de Toulouse; ou, Le Troubado[u]r* at the Comédie-Française.

Although favourable to the Revolution, Sedaine took no part in it, broke with the Jacobins, and occasionally helped its victims. Bernardo Porta wrote music to two of Sedaine's later libretti. The Revolution impoverished him when his pension ceased, and he was omitted when the Académie was suppressed and replaced by the Institut in 1795. He died after a long illness on 18 May 1797, having apparently read his own obituaries after his death had prematurely been reported.

WORKS

Sedaine would not be remembered except as a popular librettist of his time whose success was due entirely to the composers with whom he collaborated, were it not for one play, *Le Philosophe sans le savoir*, of interest chiefly because it is a reply to Palissot, because it had to be re-written to be acceptable to the censorship, and because it was a systematic attempt to put into practice Diderot's dramatic theories. Its ending needed modification after the first performance to tone down the expectation of a strong emotional reaction in the audience, and even then its success was only modest.

Sedaine has been sharply criticized for platitudinous dialogue and generally inept writing. Neither his situations nor his characters are alive, and there is a certain earnestness which takes him too easily into pomposity and rather clumsily skirts the beginnings of melodrama. Sedaine's purely dramatic works derive perhaps too obviously from the principles enunciated by Diderot. There is a mixture of the humorous with the emotional, a concern for the details of bourgeois life distilled into too emphatic a concentration on small realistic details, and a greater interest in the social roles and domestic obligations of the characters than in their individual personalities, which never become the focus of interest. However, as with the work of such contemporaries as Favart—more effective and less pretentious as a librettist and nearer to an authentic popular folk-culture—Sedaine's production, however sentimental its emotions, strained its effects, and contrived its devices, was for the most part intended to be sung, and was clearly effective once the pastiche was transformed into stylized and undemanding operetta.

The single work of purely verbal drama for which Sedaine is remembered is *Le Philosophe sans le savoir*, interesting among other things for the way in which it can still rely on the old aristocratic duelling ethic and the obligations of honour while exalting the bourgeois values on which the philosophes believed domestic bliss to be based. The list of characters itself almost stridently proclaims what sort of play it precedes. It shows that M. Vanderk has to be a rich bourgeois, who employs an "homme de confiance," what we might indeterminately call an agent, and that he has a daughter, Sophie, whose "futur époux (future husband)" is "un président," an anonymous judge who, therefore, has not purchased an office conferring titles of nobility. The wedding is to take place the day after the play opens. Vanderk's wife has a sister who is a marquise. The cast list also contains a former officer and his son, "a cavalry officer," and there are servants. We are in the immediately sub-aristocratic social zone of the professional and possibly also mercantile bourgeoisie.

The play opens when the agent, Antoine, finds his own daughter, Victorine, in tears:

Quoi! je vous surprends votre mouchoir à la main, l'air embarrassé, vous essuyant les yeux, et je ne peux pas savoir pourquoi vous pleurez?

(What, I find you with your handkerchief in your hand, looking embarrassed, wiping your eyes, and you won't tell me why you're crying?).

To open a play with those lines demonstrates Sedaine's essential weakness, the over-statement of the obvious. The over-emphasis on the ordinariness of what everyone feels and says actually denies theatre its principal operative mode, and goes with a constant straining for effect, no longer achieved by the theatrical transposition of the everyday into the extraordinary. Everything that Antoine says in those two lines should be obvious before he ever opens his mouth. It was naturally the very ordinariness of the lines, their complete lack of ornamentation or obvious rhetorical embellishment, which so recommended the play to Diderot, who wrote in lengthy praise of it to Grimm on the day after the first performance.

It turns out that Victorine unreasonably but rightly suspects that a conversation she has overheard concerns a duel to be fought between Vanderk *fils*, brother of the next day's bride, and the cavalry officer d'Esparville *fils*. The rest of the first act is devoted to presenting Vanderk as an idealized businessman. At the wedding the next day the servants must be served the same food as their masters; there must be no drunkenness; doors must be carefully locked; financial affairs are treated with scrupulous reverence. Sedaine is following Diderot in systematically refusing any mythical status to what is being enacted. As in real life, characters come in and leave without adequate motivation.

The second act reveals that Vanderk *père* once fought a duel, and he and his son are in fact both of noble birth, and consequently with an aristocratic code of honour to uphold. Vanderk *père* has adopted a mercantile profile because he was helped, supported, and cared for by a merchant whose business he inherited and naturally regards as a trust. His sister, however, is exceedingly attached to her nobility of birth, and presented as obviously ridiculous, particularly in her grudging acceptance of the groom's noblesse de robe as a reasonable substitute for authentic noblesse d'épée. In the third act we learn that Vanderk *fils* is fighting his duel because of a quarrel following an insulting remark made by an officer about the whole merchant class. Originally Vanderk *père* reproached him with silliness, but acknowledged that he had a duty to fight. The censors forced Sedaine to have Vanderk *père* forbid the duel. Sedaine made the son crawl across the stage to get out of the house.

The text is now presented as Sedaine originally wrote it. Vanderk *père* agrees that honour demands his son should fight the duel, even on his sister's wedding day, and takes the practical

precautions required to save his son from the law if he should kill his opponent. Relays of horses and bills of exchange are made available on the route to Calais. The fourth act is filled with domestic emotions, and some fun at the expense of Vanderk's sister. In the fifth act the father of his son's opponent, d'Esparville, calls on Vanderk on a matter of business, and they discover that they are the fathers of the two opponents. The business was to cash a bill so that d'Esparville's son could flee if he was victorious in the duel. Antoine gives a pre-arranged sign that Vanderk *fils* has been killed, but turns out to be mistaken. The two duellists have been reconciled, and the Esparvilles are invited to join the wedding company.

PUBLICATIONS

[*Most of the libretti have been published in English translation, but only with the music.*]

Collections

Oeuvres dramatiques, 4 vols., 1776
Théâtre, 1877
Théâtre, 1878

Plays

Le Diable à quatre; ou, La Double Métamorphose, opéra-comique en trois actes, (1756) 1757 [music by Philidor]
Blaise le savetier, opéra-comique, suivi de La Noce de Nicaise, intermède, (1759) 1759 [music by Philidor]
L'Huître et les plaideurs; ou, Le Tribunal de la chicane, opéra-comique en un acte en prose, (1759) 1761
Le Jardinier et son seigneur, opéra-comique en un acte en prose, mêlé de morceaux de musique, (1761) 1761 [music by Philidor]
On ne s'avise jamais de tout, (1761) 1761 [music by Monsigny]
Le Roi et le fermier, comédie en trois actes, mêlé de morceaux de musique (1762) 1762 [music by Monsigny]
L'Anneau perdu et retrouvé, opéra-comique en deux actes, mêlé de morceaux de musique, 1764
Rose et Colas, comédie en un acte, prose et musique (1764) 1764 [music by Monsigny]
Aline, reine de Golconde, ballet héroïque en trois actes (1766) 1766 [music by Monsigny]
Le Philosophe sans le savoir, comédie en prose et en cinq actes (1765) 1766
La Gageure imprévue, comédie en prose et en un acte (1768) 1768
L'Isle sonnante, opéra-comique en trois actes (1768) 1768
Les Sabots, opéra-comique en un acte mêlé d'ariettes (1768) 1768
Le Déserteur, drame en trois actes, en prose, mêlé de musique (1769) 1769 [music by Monsigny]
Thémire, pastorale en un acte 1770
Le Faucon, opéra-comique en acte en prose mêlé d'ariettes (1771) 1771 [music by Monsigny]
Le Mort marié, comédie en deux actes, en prose (1771) 1771 [music by Bianchi]
Le Magnifique, comédie en trois actes, en prose et en vers (1773) 1773 [music by Grétry]

Les Femmes vengées, opéra-comique en un acte et en vers
(1775) 1775 [music by Philidor]

Félix; ou, L'Enfant trouvé, comédie en trois actes, en prose et en vers mis en musique (1777) 1777 [music by Monsigny]

Aucassin et Nicolette; ou, Les Moeurs du bon vieux temps, comédie en quatre actes et en vers (1780) 1780 [music by Grétry]

Amphitrion, opéra en trois actes (1786), 1786 [music by Grétry]

Richard coeur de lion, comédie en trois actes en prose et en vers mis en musique (1784) 1786 [music by Grétry]

Le Comte d'Albert, drame en deux actes en prose et en vers, mis en musique (1786), 1787 [music by Grétry]

Maillard; ou, Paris sauvé, tragédie en cinq actes et en prose, (1777) 1788

Raoul Barbe-Bleue, comédie en prose, en trois actes mêlé d'ariettes (1789) 1791 [music by Grétry]

Guillaume Tell, drame en trois actes, en prose et en vers (1791) 1794 [music by Grétry]

Other

Pièces fugitives, 1752

Le Vaudeville, poème didactique en quatre chants, 1756

Biographical and critical studies

Guieysse-Frère, E., *Sedaine*, 1907
Gunther, L., *L'Oeuvre dramatique de Sedaine*, 1908
Arnoldson, L.-P., *Sedaine et les musiciens de son temps*, 1934

Bibliography

Brenner, C.D., *A Bibliographical List of Plays in the French Languages 1700–1815*, 1947

SÉVIGNÉ, Marie de Rabutin-Chantal, marquise de, 1626–1696.

Letter-writer.

LIFE

Marie de Rabutin-Chantal, born on 5 February 1626 in the fashionable newly built Place Royale in Paris, the present Place des Vosges, was the only surviving child of Celse-Bénigne de Rabutin-Chantal, who was born in 1596 and killed fighting the English at the Ile de Ré on 22 July 1627, when his daughter was one year old. Celse-Bénigne's father, Christophe de Chantal, had been killed in a hunting accident in 1600. In 1610 Christophe's widow, Marie's grandmother, Jeanne-Françoise Frémyot, baronne de Chantal, had left her children to found the Order of the Visitation under the direction of François de Sales. She was to be canonized in 1767. Celse-Bénigne, the son of the future saint, was 14 when his mother left home. This marriage

to Marie de Rabutin's mother, Marie de Coulanges, was regarded as a regrettable mésalliance by the Rabutin family, which could trace its ancestry back 500 years to 1147. A prospective marriage in 1618 had fallen through for want of money and, although the noble Rabutin branch of Celse-Bénigne's family boycotted the wedding arrangements, his mother and her brother, André Frémyot, the former archbishop of Bourges, both supported Celse-Bénigne's marriage to the wealthy Marie de Coulanges on 14 May 1623.

Marie de Coulanges came of a family which belonged to the magistracy until her father acquired a contract to supply bread to the army, and then became a tax farmer, which made him sufficiently wealthy to endow his daughter with 90,000 livres, enough for her to marry an impoverished Rabutin, and to promise to provide the young couple with board, lodging, and service for two years. In fact they were still living on the second floor of the large Coulanges house in the Place Royale when Celse-Bénigne was killed. On his marriage to Marie de Coulanges, his uncle André Frémyot, who was himself to retire from the archbishopric of Bourges in 1621 to another house in the Place Royale, paid Celse-Bénigne's debts and guaranteed his nephew an annual income of 1,000 livres.

An elder brother and sister of the future marquise had died in infancy in 1624 and 1625. Then, already fatherless in 1627, she lost her mother on 21 August 1633 and, an orphan at seven, her maternal grandparents in 1634 and 1636. When she was 10, her remaining grandparent was the future saint. Marie had lived on in the house in which she had been born with her mother's father until his death in December 1636, after which it was her uncle, her mother's eldest brother, Philippe II de Coulanges, and his wife, Marie Lefèvre d'Ormesson, who looked after her. They, too, had come to live in the Coulanges hôtel in the Place Royale on their marriage in the year of Marie de Rabutin's birth, 1626, and soon had a family of their own.

The future marquise was brought up in a house she knew, and in a household whose head, born in 1595, was only 31 years her senior. The household also included four of Philippe II's brothers, her uncles Antoine, Louis, Charles, and Alexandre, respectively 14, 12, 10, and 8 years older than Marie. Between Philippe and Antoine, there was another uncle, Christophe, born in 1607 and since 1623 abbot of Livry. Her senior uncle's first child was born in 1633 and baptized two days after her mother's funeral. Marie de Rabutin fitted neatly into a large and wealthy family, although the Rabutins, as well as Celse-Bénigne's sister, who also wanted her Coulanges money, tried to reclaim charge of her. She might well have ended up in a convent if the Frémyots, the retired archbishop and his nephew, Jacques de Neuchèze, bishop of Chalon, had not sided with the Coulanges. The arrangement nominating Philippe de Coulanges and his wife as guardians was then legally confirmed.

Marie de Rabutin's early upbringing was liberal, but fears expressed on that account by her grandmother, the religious foundress, were quickly assuaged by her brother, the ex-archbishop. In view of Sévigné's later movement towards a committed piety often too lightly associated by commentators with Port-Royal (q.v.), it must be remembered that the distinguishing qualities of the spiritualities of both Jeanne-Françoise and her director, François de Sales, included an unusual gentleness. The Visitandines, as they are known, were expressly founded for those women with a religious vocation who could not support the rigours of conventional monastic life.

On the death of Marie's Coulanges grandfather, the Coulanges family decided to divide the inheritance, and Marie received her mother's share, less the dowry she had already inherited, when the division was made on 14 January 1638. Alexandre, Marie's youngest uncle, had died at 18 in 1637, and in July 1638 her mother's sister, Henriette de la Trousse, lost her husband at the siege of Saint-Omer. The family house was sold. Two of the Coulanges uncles, Louis and Charles, now shared a house, while Christophe and Antoine shared another, both still in the Marais district. Louis and Antoine both served as army officers and attended court until Antoine died as the result of a duel in 1639. Both Andre Frémyot and his sister, Jeanne-Françoise de Chantal, died in 1641. After two years in a nearby house, Philippe de Coulanges moved to a vast residence in the Rue Francs-Bourgeois. He stayed there until his death in 1659, and Marie until her marriage in 1644. Christophe joined his elder brother there in 1643.

Philippe, whose wife had also brought him a dowry of 90,000 livres, had rapidly ascended the social hierarchy, reaching the post of treasurer of France in 1624. He had had a child by Jeanne de Montluc in 1617. He appears in Sévigné's letters as the abbé de la Mousse, was for a time her daughter's tutor, and seems to have been adopted by the Coulanges family as one of themselves. Philippe was able to buy his eldest son the judicial post of maître des requêtes at the Paris parlement in 1658. After Philippe-Emmanuel, born in 1633, Philippe and Marie Lefèvre d'Ormesson had other children, Anne-Marie in 1639, Marie-Madeleine in 1642, and Alexandre in 1643. Philippe also acquired a vast estate at Sucy-en-Brie, about 12 kilometres east of Paris, where Marie de Rabutin spent much time. It was near Amboille, an estate belonging to his wife's brother, Olivier Lefèvre d'Ormesson, and not 20 kilometres from Livry to the north, whose abbacy was held by Christophe de Coulanges. The social life was not restricted to the family.

Marie de Rabutin mixed with a cheerful band of young people, and learnt above all in the country the arts of conversation and of presenting herself socially, at which, whenever she was not overawed by courtly grandeurs, she came to excel. She later said that she read much, mostly the plays and novels reflecting the increasing refinement of social life, regarding them as incorporating models of elegant behaviour. She also learnt to read Italian, but not Latin. The family formally allocated money to pay for tutors for her, 1,200 livres as against the 800 allotted to expenditure on upkeep, augmented to 1,800 livres annually in 1642. As an adolescent, therefore, she was used to practising her religion, to moving in cultivated social circles, to joining in educated discussion of worldly matters, to being part of an extended family with friends of her own age, and to spending part of her year in the country and part in Paris.

The Rabutin family had two branches, the seigneurs de Chantal, called Rabutin-Chantal, to which Marie belonged, and the junior branch, the seigneurs de Bussy, called Bussy-Rabutin. The common ancestor was Celse-Bénigne's great-grandfather. Léonor de Bussy-Rabutin, the junior of his two grandsons, was one of the Rabutins who had refused to sign Celse-Bénigne's marriage contract with a Coulanges. Léonor's son, Roger de Bussy-Rabutin, one of Sévigné's most frequent correspondents, conscious enough of his lineage to write a *Histoire généalogique de la maison de Rabutin*, was also linked to Sévigné through his first marriage to Gabrielle de Toulongeon, daughter of Celse-Bénigne's sister Françoise, the aunt who had

wanted to get her hands on the money the Coulanges marriage had brought to her spendthrift brother.

It is difficult for today's readers to understand exactly what 17th-century French society thought was at stake in their social arrangements, although the need for an impoverished aristocracy to "fertilize" its estates by intermarriage with new bourgeois money, discreetly laundered through purchased titles, is not difficult to grasp. In the present context the importance of dynastic marriages and the process of social ascent by which the richer bourgeoisie could, with requisite permissions, purchase the ennobling offices of the magistracy, or "noblesse de robe," is threefold. It explains the subject matter of a great deal of 17th-century French literature; it partly explains the sensibility behind the writing of many of the greatest names, certainly including Sévigné; and it explains the tortuous relationships between the old aristocracy, on the one hand, and the writers, scholars, clerics, merchants, tax farmers, and administrative officials on the other. The social ascent of the Coulanges family and the tensions in Sévigné herself are characteristic enough to be virtually a paradigm. Philippe I, from an already honourable position in the magistracy, had risen, through a monopoly in provisioning the army, tax farming, and property speculating, to a position in which he was able to marry his eldest daughter to a Rabutin-Chantal. Her only surviving child took the Coulanges to the summit of social success when, at midnight on 4 August 1644, Marie de Rabutin-Chantal, aged 18, married Henri, marquis de Sévigné, aged 21.

The service was conducted by the bishop of Chalon, Jacques de Neuchèze, nephew of André Frémyot, the late archbishop of Bourges. Apart from the officiant, the couple, and three Coulanges uncles, only Jean-François Paul de Gondi, archbishop of Corinth and coadjutor bishop of Paris, signed the act. He was to be the Cardinal de Retz from 1652, and it is he who appears to have arranged the marriage. There had been an earlier project to marry Marie to Jacques-Auguste de Thou, son of the famous historian. It fell through in 1642 when de Thou's brother François was arrested with Cinq-Mars and executed by Richelieu. That made it impossible for a rich member of the noblesse d'épée to marry into a family from the noblesse de robe, one of whose members had recently been the subject of an act of political vengeance, even though Richelieu, its perpetrator, had died three months later.

The marriage to Henri de Sévigné was first mentioned as a possibility in his diary for 7 March 1644 by Olivier Lefèvre d'Ormesson. Henri de Sévigné had lost his mother at eight months and his father in January 1635, when he was 12. During his adolescence at a family estate, Les Rochers, about six kilometres from Vitré, he appears to have been left in the charge of the servants. A delay of four months from its serious consideration to the date of the wedding was rather longer than was usual and, had she disliked the proposed marriage, Marie might have drawn back, although the grace to love one's partner was naturally supposed to be conferred with the nuptial blessing. There was some consternation when the future groom was seriously injured in the leg and thigh in a duel on 29 May, and his survival was momentarily in doubt. For a month the Coulanges could reasonably have turned away, but agreement was confirmed between all the parties, including the spouses, on 7 July. The duel had probably made the groom a more exciting prospect for the novel-reading heiress. Her grandfather, the saint's husband, said to have been a mild man, had been victorious in 18 duels, and her father, Celse-Bénigne, was not only an inveterate dueller but was saved only by flight from being hanged for duelling after church on Easter Sunday 1624. The groom had actually wanted to bring forward the marriage in order to take part in what was to prove the successful engagement led by the duc d'Enghien, the future Condé, at Friburg.

The contract was signed on 1 August, three days before the wedding. There were the same signatures, but for the bride additionally three Lefèvre d'Ormessons, and this time those of Léonor and Hugues de Bussy-Rabutin, grand prior of France. For the groom there were also the signatures of René-Renaud de Sévigné, whose subsequent marriage to Isabelle Péna, mother of Marie-Madeleine Pioche de la Vergne, later to become Mme de Lafayette, was to deprive Henri de Sévigné of part of the inheritance he had come to expect; of Charles de Schomberg, duc d'Alluin, peer and maréchal; of Jacques Hurault, marquis de Vibraye, and his wife Anne de Vassé; of Louis de Cossé, duc de Brissac, and his wife, Marguerite de Gondi; and of four other members of the Gondi family, including Henri, duc de Retz, and Pierre, duc de Beaupréau, both peers, Philippe-Emmanuel de Gondi, general of the Oratory, and the coadjutor bishop's uncle, Jean-François de Gondi, archbishop of Paris. The list extended to paternal relatives in the higher Breton clergy and magistracy, and the Retz connection explains the link henceforward between Sévigné and her close friend, Marie-Madeleine de Lafayette.

The Sévigné family was not more ancient than the Rabutin family, but it was more prominent. Henri de Sévigné's father, Charles, elder brother of René-Renaud, had in 1621 married Marguerite de Vassé, daughter of Lancelot and Françoise de Gondi, one of Retz's aunts. Marie de Rabutin took with her into marriage 40,000 livres in cash in addition to promises of legacies, including an inalienable 30,000 livres from Jacques de Neuchèze, and various other rights amounting to a huge 330,000 livres in all. Sévigné herself miscalculated on 10 June 1671 when she wrote that on marriage she had been worth 530,000 livres. In fact, from 1653, her actual disposable wealth was not much above 250,000 livres, and Colbert's effective devaluations of rates of return were to make very considerable inroads in that. Sévigné's husband, of whom much ill has unjustifiably been spoken, and who appears to have been witty, good-looking, and a man of some distinction, also brought to the marriage more than double as much as his bride, mostly in estates in Brittany. In spite of her lineage, Marie de Rabutin was an orphan, and the Sévignés were protected by the Gondis. The Coulanges may have promoted themselves, but they did not neglect Marie's interests. In the accepted sense, she made a good marriage. We know that the marriage was satisfactorily consummated on the night of the wedding.

Sévigné's husband tried to buy himself a commission in the royal guards, commanded by Charles de Schomberg, whose family, linked by marriage to the Gondis, protected the Sévignés. The Coulanges, watchful of Sévigné's interests, refused to guarantee the necessary loans, and her husband had to continue to fight as a volunteer. It left him more freedom, but gave him less responsibility. The couple lived in the Marais at a rent of 1,050 livres a year, which meant comfort without ostentation, although the marriage contract had provided for a life style that was luxurious, with a budget seven or eight times higher than the value of Celse-Bénigne's household possessions, horses, and carriage at his death, which was less than 5,000 livres. Sévigné and her husband were kept within the

40,000 livres cash content of the dowry, but explicitly allocated a further 36,000 livres, subsequently increased to 40,000 livres, for setting up house.

Sévigné and her husband led a lively social life, largely centred on the Condé circle, which included Sévigné's impoverished cousin, Roger de Bussy-Rabutin ("Bussy"), Pierre Lenet, procurator-general at the parlement of Bourgogne, and the poet Marigny, famous for his attacks on Mazarin. The princesse de Condé was a Montmorency, the daughter of one of Celse-Bénigne's greatest friends. While the friends of Enghien, the future "grand" Condé, were not exactly debauched, they were loose-talking, fairly loose-living, and not given to excess in the matter of austerity. Sévigné learnt quickly to fit in well, while her husband scarcely needed to learn.

The Fronde put an end to the parties at the beginning of 1649. Condé was at first with the queen and Mazarin, while his brother, Conti, and sister, Anne-Geneviève de Bourbon, duchesse de Longueville, were with the Frondeurs and Retz, to whom the Sévignés remained closely attached (see: Lafayette). Bussy hastened back to Condé's army and wrote to Sévigné saying that he did not know if she was now his enemy or still his good cousin. Henri de Sévigné was with Longueville in Normandy, first at the capture of Evreux, and then at Rouen, cultivating his cynical reputation and indulging in coarse jokes. Bussy and Sévigné remained on opposing sides during the renewal of the Fronde in 1650, although each had changed sides with respect not to the king, but to Mazarin, momentarily allied with Retz.

As Bussy wrote to Sévigné, her choice of sides at least meant that she could stay in Paris, while his camps were always outside it. On 7 June 1650 Henri de Sévigné acquired a less important office than that to which he had previously aspired, becoming for 60,000 livres governor of Fougères. The king made him maréchal de camp. The boisterous behaviour of both Sévigné and her husband was the subject of unpleasantly ribald comment in Loret's rhymed *Gazette burlesque* for 16 July 1650, which had become *La Muse historique* and insinuated that the comte d'Harcourt, who had commanded the royal troops, had had to think of closing his house to the overdone galanteries of Sévigné, the comtesse de Fiesque, and Mme de Montglas. On 10 September Sévigné appointed her uncle Christophe de Coulanges her procurator at Paris, and the Sévignés gave up their Paris residence, which the abbé sub-let for them.

The presumption is that what persuaded the couple of the wisdom of lying low was Loret's public comment in the gossip verses and the general aura of scandal surrounding Sévigné's determination to amuse herself and her husband's notorious liaisons, rather than the coming break between Retz and the court, which was to lead to the second Fronde and the arrest of Condé and Conti. The governorship of Fougères offered a reasonable pretext for retiring to the Brittany Estates. Henri de Sévigné had to return to Paris from time to time on official business. On 4 February 1651 he fought a duel with Miossens, the chevalier d'Albret, over Mme de Gondran, known as "Lolo." He died two days later. Sévigné spent her period of mourning in Brittany, giving as her Paris address the Hôtel de Retz. On 19 November the *Muse historique* noted her return to Paris.

There had been six and a half years of marriage. On 10 October 1646 Sévigné had given birth in Paris to a daughter, Françoise-Marguerite, later to become the comtesse de Grignan, and on 12 March 1648 to a son, Charles de Sévigné, at Les

Rochers. Most women in her position conceived more frequently. Her marriage into the Sévigné family had opened the court to her, but she rarely attended and, when she did, was sufficiently over-impressed to betray her bourgeois Coulanges upbringing in spite of her pride in her Rabutin ancestry. She visited her husband's estates with him soon after the wedding, with Christophe de Coulanges in attendance, and was away from Paris for almost four months.

In the spring of 1645 Sévigné, who had inherited the title "demoiselle de Bourgogne," appears to have visited the Rabutin estates in Burgundy. The family house at Bourbilly was deserted, and Sévigné and her husband were probably looking for a tenant farmer. They went on with Bussy at the end of April to the Nivernais, whose lieutenancy he had just inherited. In May Sévigné was in Brittany to take over the administration of her husband's estates while he attended to other matters in Paris or with the army. In June her mother's sister, Henriette de Coulanges, who had married François le Hardi, seigneur de la Trousse, in 1631, was with her at Rennes, where she stayed at the Hôtel de Brissac, and that October her husband joined them at Les Rochers. In February 1646, by this time pregnant, she was again with her husband and aunt at Nantes, probably having wintered there. Back in Paris in June, she gave birth to Françoise-Marguerite, astonishingly for the period, in the presence only of d'Ormesson's wife and mother. There was a strangely long delay before the baptism, and no Coulanges were present at either the birth or the baptism. The name Françoise-Marguerite came from the Rabutins and the child's godparents were a Frémyot and a Gondi. Not even Mme de la Trousse was to hand. There must have been strained relationships between Sévigné and the family which had adopted her.

The Sévignés spent the winter of 1646–47 in Paris, and then seem to have been in Brittany from April 1647 to December 1648. Charles was baptized on the day of his birth, although he did not receive his name from his godfather, Charles de Schomberg, maréchal de France and son of the godfather of Henri de Sévigné, until after Henri's death in 1652. Sévigné gloated over his birth to Bussy, who only had three girls. She was in Paris during the 1649 Fronde while Henri was in Normandy, but they both returned to Les Rochers after the peace in December, were in Paris in the spring of 1650, and retired to Les Rochers after the scandal stirred up by Loret. Sévigné was at Les Rochers when she heard of her husband's death and did not return to Paris with her children until November 1651.

Now began her period of great social success. Among her admirers were Foucquet, Conti, and Turenne. Her reputation was again endangered, and a number of scandalous asides about her are recorded, including a manuscript jotting, "If you're afraid of the leaves, don't go into the wood." The likelihood, borne out by Sévigné's subsequent letters to her daughter, is that she felt that she had acquitted her duty by bearing two children, including a male heir, and disliked the risk to her health and beauty which further pregnancies would have entailed. Bussy is entirely open about what amounted to her aversion to physical sexual relations in L'Histoire amoureuse des Gaules, and it was well known to both her children, as were her daughter's opposite feelings in the matter.

There are hints of Sévigné's distaste, no doubt fuelled by the refinements of préciosité (q.v.), throughout the letters, especially in the advice given to her daughter in the matter of sexual relations with her husband, and Sévigné's attitudes to the physical aspects of love go some way to explaining her husband's conduct, particularly the notorious affairs with Ninon de Lenclos, later publicized by Bussy, and with Mme de Gondran, a lawyer's wife and tax farmer's daughter whose sister was married to Tallemant's elder brother. Both relationships, which must date from 1650, may well stem from Sévigné's own preference for abstinence after the birth of her children. It is difficult to resist the impression that she was complacent about, or may even have connived at, her husband's liaisons. It was incidentally for Mme de Gondran that Henri de Sévigné in a famous episode borrowed the duchesse de Chevreuse's earrings during the carnival of 1650 on the pretext that Marie-Madeleine Pioche de la Vergne, the future Mme de Lafayette, wanted to wear them. The duchesse naturally got to hear about it, and Marie-Madeleine had to go and thank her for the loan.

Sévigné had recently given the dinner for Mme de Chevreuse which had led to one of the damaging gossip rhymes in the *Muse historique*. Licence was not, however, allowed to interfere with codes of honour, as Henri de Sévigné's fatal duel attests. Sévigné's husband had denied impugning Albret's honour with Mme de Gondran. The denial was accepted, and they embraced, but the code demanded that they should none the less fight. Sévigné sent back to Mme de Gondran her letters to her husband, and is even, reports Tallement, acknowledging hearsay, said to have asked Mme de Gondran for a portrait of her husband, or a lock of his hair.

On the death of her husband and following family agreement, Sévigné was officially appointed the guardian of her children and administrator of their inheritance. On her visit to Paris after the duel she had stayed at the Hôtel de Retz. Mazarin had fled Paris on the day of her husband's death and, with the king and queen virtually prisoners, Condé had returned to Paris and broken with Retz, who, for his part, was negotiating with Mazarin and the queen. Retz agreed with Mazarin to lead the fight against Condé in exchange for a ministerial post and a cardinal's hat. Retz might have been killed by La Rochefoucauld when Retz and Condé met on 21 August 1651. He remained publicly aligned with Mazarin, and was duly rewarded with the cardinalate on 19 February 1652. Sévigné had negotiated a lease at 1,200 livres a year for a large Paris residence, to be shared with her aunt Henriette, and her aunt's children, a son and two daughters. She was to stay there until her own daughter's wedding in 1669.

On 18 June 1652 Tonquedec, who had once promised to raise a regiment for the duc de Rohan on behalf of Condé before finally rallying to the support of Mazarin, was sitting in a chair near the head of Sévigné's bed when Rohan called. The degree and motivation for Tonquedec's impertinence in merely half rising can only be guessed but, several days and visits later, Rohan ordered Tonquedec to leave and Tonquedec drew a sword. The episode drew the unwanted attention of the *Muse historique* on both 23 and 30 June, Loret naturally implying that the motivation for the dispute had not been primarily political. It did not help that René-Renaud de Sévigné, the comte de Lude, the duc de Brissac, and Chavagnac all challenged Rohan in support of Tonqueduc. Sévigné herself went to spend the summer and autumn in Brittany, and no doubt found it prudent to stay there when Retz was imprisoned on 19 December and his closer supporters, including René-Renaud de Sévigné, were exiled from Paris. She did not herself return until the early summer of 1653. Peace had been established late in 1652 with the return of the king, the exile of Gaston d'Orléans, his brother, and the condemnations of Condé and Conti. Mazarin returned on 3 February 1653.

Social life resumed, and with it a relationship with Bussy more playful than formerly. Bussy later claimed that the discovery of an indiscreet letter had led Sévigné's husband to forbid him access for the six months before the duel. Sévigné herself now delighted in playing the unique but unyielding object of Bussy's worship, and the relationship plainly cooled when Bussy took Mme de Montglas as his mistress some time after 1653. Sévigné warned Bussy that his letters were to be read by her aunt, Henriette de la Trousse, on whom she does appear to have relied to protect her from any over-enthusiastic reactions to her playfulness.

Her husband had proved inept at handling his family affairs and had left a number of debts, which Sévigné now cleared, obtaining much help from Christophe de Coulanges. Lawsuits dragged on well into the 1660s. Marie Lefèvre d'Ormesson had died on 5 July 1654 and Philippe de Coulanges, Sévigné's former guardian, in 1659. From her husband's properties Sévigné had chosen Les Rochers, where she had spent the most peaceful and perhaps the happiest days of her marriage. Visits to Brittany did, however, become rarer. After her return in 1651 she is known to have been there only in 1652, 1656, and 1658, and during the next 13 years only twice, in 1661 and 1666. She looked after business matters, went less and less often and for increasingly brief periods to the country, and enjoyed the social life of Paris and now, increasingly, of the court. She had got to know Ménage, and in 1655 signed the marriage contract of René-Renaud de Sévigné's stepdaughter, Mme de Lafayette. Ménage's relationship with Mme de Lafayette had been closer, but he played her off against the more daringly flirtatious Sévigné in an elaborately galant charade, about which malicious remarks were made, but which took in nobody very much.

In the third part of *Clélie*, which appeared in February 1657, Madeleine de Scudéry accurately portrayed Sévigné as Clarinte. Chapelain, as well as Ménage, contributed to her tardy intellectual formation. Chapelain, occurs in the correspondence first in 1654, and was known to Sévigné principally as the former tutor of Henriette de la Trousse's husband, although he had long seemed the only poet capable of restoring its glory to French poetry by writing a modern epic. His opinion is quoted by Sévigné on matters naturally more of taste than of scholarship, but Bussy seems occasionally to feel that Chapelain was usurping a literary authority over her to which he presumed himself. Sévigné's culture, however, was so resolutely contemporary that Bussy need not have worried. Sévigné's taste had in fact essentially been formed in the Hôtel de Rambouillet, especially after the Fronde, when the atmosphere had become more scholarly and when Conrart and Chapelain reigned there supreme, although she must have frequented the Chambre bleue with Condé's friends in the early years of her marriage, while the accent was still on frivolity and madrigals (see: *Guirlande de Julie*).

Sévigné's charms, first sung in print by Ménage in 1652, were the subject of two poems written by Jacques de Marigny, author of the 1658 *Lettres en prose et en vers*, and Mathieu Montreuil in the anthology of *Poésies choisies* published by Charles Sercy in 1653. Then, after the portrait in *Clélie*, her formal consecration occurred when she was mentioned by name in a quatrain from a madrigal in *La Lyre du jeune Apollon; ou, La Muse nais-*

sante du petit Beauchâteau, which appeared in April 1657, prepared by Mainard, and whose pretended author was only nine at the time. Thereafter the tributes flowed, notably from Saint-Gabriel, Pélisseri, and Segrais, in a portrait in a collection published three times in 1659, from Costar, and in Somaize's *Grand Dictionnaire* of 1661. Bussy notes that Foucquet, Surintendant des finances from 1653, changed his affection from passion to friendship in 1657. La Fontaine confirms Sévigné's influence in Foucquet's entourage, and we learn of other admirers, Turenne, Noirmoutier, Lesdiguières, and, above all, the comte de Lude. Testimony comes down heavily in favour of regarding Sévigné, in spite of her preference for physically restrained male devotion, as anything but an adherent of the préciosité which began to be spoken of, although not yet by name, in 1652. From all that the memorialists tell us, her mind was almost bawdy.

Bussy continued to serve in the army. He had bought a commission as "maître de camp général de la cavalerie" in 1653 and been short of money ever since. Foucquet was failing to pay him, and Mazarin had not rewarded him after the Fronde. When peace with Spain was made with the 1659 Treaty of the Pyrenees, he had broken with Sévigné, who had been dissuaded in 1658 by Christophe de Coulanges, her informal business manager, from lending him money without security. Bussy had hoped vainly that, as a last resort, she might have exerted influence on Foucquet. Briefly to be exiled to the country for riotous behaviour during the 1659 carnival, Bussy had been too hard up to take part in the Spanish campaigns of 1658–59. He later recognized that he had been wrong to be so bitter with Sévigné, but it was he who broke off relations, although he defended her when she was embarrassed by the discovery of her letters to Foucquet.

Relations, briefly restored in 1663, when Sévigné did guarantee a loan for Bussy, were ruptured again by the harsh portrait of her written after the quarrel but which circulated in manuscript before being published in the unauthorized edition of the *Histoire amoureuse des Gaules* early in 1665. Mme de Montglas had tried to mediate, but the friendship was fully restored only after Bussy's release in August 1666 from the Bastille, to which he had been sent for the audacious *Histoire amoureuse* on 17 April 1665, to the ensuing exile to his Burgundy estates, which lasted until 1682. Although long delays were imposed, the reconciliation dated effectively from 16 May 1666, when Bussy had to be cared for in hospital by the surgeon Dalancé, and Sévigné was the first to call on him. From 1668 there was an epistolary fight to establish responsibility for the break.

Sévigné was herself in need of money and had borrowed from the Lafayettes in June 1658, her loan guaranteed by Christophe de Coulanges. By 1660 she could no longer rely on the favours of the disgraced Retz, or on her husband's family, or on the Rabutins, Bussy having by now been exiled to the country. We do not know how close she was to Foucquet, to whom she was tenuously connected through the Foucquet family's multiple membership of the Visitation Order. Only La Fontaine mentions her presence in Foucquet's entourage in 1657. The evidence suggests strongly that Sévigné's letters to Foucquet, found on his fall in 1661, were innocently, if imprudently, galant. They were not found with the business correspondence, however, and naturally again gave rise to comment. Adultery was frequent enough in Sévigné's circle, but "médisance (malicious gossip)" was also common, universally regarded as a plague, and social hypocrisy at the higher social levels demanded the avoidance of scandal and the integrity of reputations. Much higher standards of behaviour were required from women. It was part of Molière's brilliance to ally Alceste's detestation of hypocrisy with its logical consequence, médisance, in *Le Misanthrope*.

There is a striking lack of evidence of any particularly strong maternal affection in Sévigné before her daughter's marriage and separation unleashed the flood of remarkable letters for which she is known. She kept her children by her side for some years, but from 1657 Françoise-Marguerite was boarded at a Paris convent and then, when Sévigné was again in Brittany, at the Visitation convent at Nantes in 1658. The nuns noticed there that Sévigné had a deep affection for her daughter, but it does not appear to have been extraordinary, despite what has been read into later documents. All that can be said is that Sévigné's daughter was sent to a convent rather late, and left for the private tuition of a great-uncle rather early. He initiated her into the philosophy of Descartes. Sévigné and her son, Charles, got on together unusually well. Her intense affection for her daughter dates from about 1663, when Françoise-Marguerite, at 17, more reserved and withdrawn than her mother, began to react against her emotionally.

From 1663 to 1665, the graceful, poised, distant, and beautiful Françoise-Marguerite shone in the court ballets, and in 1663 she was universally admired dancing in Bensserade's *Ballet des Arts* in the company of Henriette d'Angleterre, wife of the king's brother, Françoise-Athénaïs de Mortemart, Madame de Montespan, Mlle de la Vallière, shortly to be the king's mistress, and Mlle de Saint-Simon, the future duchesse de Brissac. The *Muse historique* was duly complimentary on 20 January. Françoise-Marguerite was invited to dance again in 1664. This time the king himself also danced in Bensserade's *Ballet des Amours déguisés*, with Mme de Montespan, Mme de Vibraye, Gaston d'Orléans, alongside the best professional actors in Paris, Floridor and Montfleury. This time Loret openly insinuated that Françoise-Marguerite was worthy of becoming the king's mistress. Sévigné and her daughter continued to be invited to the court celebrations at Versailles, although Sévigné's well-known sympathies for Foucquet, imprisoned but not sentenced until December 1664, made her position delicate. Françoise-Marguerite, however, danced again in January 1665. Bensserade's ballet was *La Naissance de Vénus*, and Loret's comment on 31 January in the *Muse historique* was directed at the way Françoise-Marguerite shared her mother's ability to resist male advances, jocularly pleading with her to forget her "courage inhumain (inhuman inflexibility)," which works "Au détriment du genre humain (To the disadvantage of the human race)."

The life which had come to involve masked balls, fancy dress, court entertainments, and the social round of the highest aristocracy suddenly stopped. There is a hint of a fall from grace in Loret's piece in January 1665, and it can only be Bussy's disgrace, buttressed perhaps by the association with Foucquet and possibly by an association which had sprung up with the Duplessis-Guénégauds, that prevented invitations for the three following years. Sévigné and Françoise-Marguerite were back in high favour at the king's own table at the Versailles celebrations on 18 July 1668. On 22 August Sévigné's son Charles, who was about to depart in a vain attempt to lift the Turkish siege on Candia (Iráklion) in Crete, delegated authority for a signature to be given on his behalf to any marriage document. Something was in the air.

By 6 October a marriage project had been provisionally arranged. The document of that date was signed only by the future spouses, Sévigné, Christophe de Coulanges, Mme de Lafayette, the comte de Brancas, a former associate of Foucquet and perhaps the instigator of the marriage, and d'Harouys, the treasurer of the Brittany Estates. It was unusual for a minor of such distinction, daughter of a widow, to have her marriage arranged with so little representation of the various branches of her family. The contract was signed on 27 January 1669, and the marriage took place on 29 January. The groom, François Adhémar de Monteil, comte de Grignan, twice a widower, was 36. In 1658 he had married Madame de Rambouillet's third daughter, Angélique-Clarisse d'Angennes, who died in 1664, and in June 1666 Marie-Angélique du Puy-du-Fou, who had died on 30 May 1667. Françoise-Marguerite was 22.

Negotiations for three earlier prospective marriages, to Juste-Joseph Cadar d'Ancézune, duc de Caderousse, who married a Duplessis-Guénégaud, to Charles Moustiers de Mérinville, and to the comte d'Etauges, had been broken off, apparently on Sévigné's initiative, and Grignan, although apparently rich, later turned out to be crippled with debts. There is every sign that Sévigné, if she did not actually suspect that Grignan was bringing financial trouble from his previous marriages, was not interested in finding out, and so risking the failure of a fourth projected marriage. The marriage, in prospect in August, was originally intended to take place before the end of 1668, and the final date represents a postponement. Sévigné was in a hurry, and may have had a number of reasons for wishing to conclude her daughter's marriage without any risk of further delay.

Firstly, Françoise-Marguerite was getting old. Four years were knocked off her age on the wedding contract. The match looked suitable, as the Grignans were unsurpassed in nobility and antiquity, finding an ancestor as far back as the late seventh century, and the indebtedness was not immediately apparent. The signatories to the contract for Grignan represented the finest families of the very old feudal aristocracy. Secondly, the Sévignés had been friendly with too many of those who had been in disfavour at court or in opposition to the king, Retz, Bussy, Foucquet, the Duplessis-Guénégauds. The seriously ambitious might want to avoid a Sévigné match. Thirdly the failure of three prospective matches meant that a fourth failure at 22 would begin to make everyone wonder whether and why Françoise-Marguerite was unmarriageable.

Fourthly, however, and most preposterously, although not least probably, it was thought at court, and may have been true, that the king himself had his eye on the pretty and graceful young Sévigné. Bussy plainly thought so, and there is a strong innuendo in the positioning and title of the first fable of La Fontaine's fourth book, published on 31 March 1668, "Le Lion amoureux. *A Mlle de Sévigné*." If it was true, Sévigné needed to act quickly to prevent her daughter, more than once referred to as "la belle Lionne (the beautiful Lionness)," from becoming the royal mistress or, because everyone knew of the king's desires and the possibility of his bitterness, unmarriageable to anyone else. Both fates would have inspired Sévigné with understandable horror on her daughter's behalf.

What is clear is that Sévigné went as near as possible towards concluding the marriage agreement before allowing the proposed match to be known to those, like Retz and Bussy, who might, on grounds of financial prudence, have wanted to make further financial enquiries. There seemed to be no need. Grignan's uncles included Jacques Adhémar, bishop and count of Uzès and peer, and François Adhémar, archbishop of Arles, with one of the husband's brothers, Jean-Baptiste de Grignan, his coadjutor and successor. Two other brothers held army commands, and Grignan, who had been a colonel, was now the king's lieutenant-general for Languedoc, a post which had cost him 213,000 livres in 1663. The family château was vast, and Grignan himself had just inherited. He was also, however, slowly drowning in debt.

There are unambiguous signs that the couple were very soon in love with one another, he with her first. The wedding night was a farce but, if the brilliant social surface was scarred for contemporaries by financial cracks, by any modern standards the arranged union of Françoise-Marguerite and François Adhémar de Grignan was a very good marriage. In March 1669 Charles de Sévigné returned from Crete, where less than half of his elite company had survived, and Sévigné, who had had to borrow heavily again to find her daughter's dowry, had to produce 75,000 livres to buy him a regular army commission. His promotions were to cost another 70,000 livres in the eight years which followed. Sévigné herself moved within the Marais, sharing a Paris house with separate entrances with her daughter and son-in-law, who paid half the 3,000 livres rent.

At first not much changed. Françoise-Marguerite and her husband were under the same roof as herself, and they shared a more or less common social life. On 4 November 1669 at Livry Mme de Grignan was out riding when her brother-in-law fell from his horse. She suffered shock and lost the child she was carrying. A male, he was born prematurely and lived only four hours thereafter. The baby was buried on 5 November. The accident may only have been the occasion for the miscarriage. The Grignans must already have heard that on 29 November the count was to be made lieutenant-general of Provence, effectively governor in succession to Mérinville, the father of Mme de Grignan's former suitor. Vendôme, the governor, had died on 6 August and his son, the new duc de Vendôme, was only 16 and not yet able to take over. The post of lieutant of Provence, which cost 300,000 livres, was much more important than that of lieutenant-general of Languedoc, where the post had been one of three, but it entailed residence. There may even have been an element of royal revenge. Grignan was anyway going to have be a long way away for a long time. Sévigné was to lose her daughter, although for what turned out to be comparatively few long periods, to Provence, and her letter writing career proper was to begin.

Whether or not Charles-Philippe's fall, or the emotional state of Mme de Grignan at the thought of leaving Paris, and the knowledge of the effect it would have on her mother, was the cause or occasion of the miscarriage, it is from about this time that dates the gossip about Sévigné's excessive attachment to her daughter, considered almost morbid. That there was gossip, that Sévigné was wounded by it, and that it regarded her attachment to Françoise-Marguerite, is quite clear from the content and tone of the correspondence with Bussy during 1670. Sévigné was 44 when, on 6 July 1670, she wrote a remarkable letter to Bussy defending herself against the gossip of which he had warned her. She pretended to misunderstand. "Ma vie est toute unie; ma conduite n'est pas dégingandée (My life is not split; my behaviour is not loose)"; she had a "bonne réputation (blameless reputation)," was nearly a grandmother, had white hair, was no longer young or pretty; "c'est un état où l'on n'est

guère l'objet de la médisance (it is a situation in which you are not made the subject of wagging tongues)." Bussy disillusions her on 10 July: "I wasn't lying when I said I knew you had enemies." It is only Sévigné's modesty that makes her say she is no longer young or beautiful. She could still misbehave, but "That's not what people are saying about you."

It took time to sell the Languedoc post and make other appropriate arrangements, but when Grignan himself left Paris on 19 April 1670, he left his wife behind, because she was again pregnant. Given the arduous journeys to which even the most high-born subjected their pregnant wives and mistresses, and the journeys undertaken during later pregnancies by Mme de Grignan herself, it seems certain that the 1670 pregnancy, even given the earlier miscarriage, was used merely as an excuse for Sévigné to keep her daughter in Paris. There had been gossip about the possibility of an emotional bond between Mme de Grignan and her brother-in-law before the accident. Remaining in Paris could only provoke more rumour. Bussy called it a "comédie (farce.)" It had not escaped notice how much more time, attention, and money had been spent on Françoise-Marguerite than on Charles. Both Sévigné herself, in her letters to her son-in-law Grignan, and her daughter, who refused to appear in public and dressed only in black, went to elaborate lengths to allay public suspicions of any sort of social or emotional excesses, so that even Sévigné herself became aggravated by her daughter's "ugly black coat." The baby, Marie-Blanche, was born in Paris on 15 November, and on 4 February 1671, already impatient at the delay caused by that winter's floods, Mme de Grignan left for Provence. There followed the first separation from Sévigné.

Exactly at the right moment for Sévigné's correspondence to begin, the French postal system was properly organized in December 1668, one month before her daughter's wedding. Louvois had been running the postal service, in fact, but he was appointed its surintendant only on 24 December 1668. Even under the early days of Richelieu, private letters were dependent on the irregular departure of courriers, although Madeleine de Scudéry's Paris correspondents in 1644 could count on regular Friday afternoon departures for Marseilles. In 1671 departures for Provence were on Wednesdays and Fridays, then from 17 March 1672 on Mondays and Fridays, changing back in 1675. A third weekly post was established in 1683. Sévigné could then write her conversational letters at odd periods during the days, knowing that they could be terminated and sent on Mondays, Wednesdays, and Fridays, the postal organization having virtually made possible, if not inevitable, the creation of a new literary form, the chatty, anecdotal letter. Sévigné would often start a "reply" knowing that, before she added the final paragraphs, she would have received the letter to which she was beginning a response. The letters she sent on Wednesdays are on average much longer than those dispatched on Fridays.

Mme de Grignan could from the beginning commit letters to the post on Wednesdays and Saturdays, the closer proximity of Grignan to Paris being compensated by the distance to be travelled on foot from Montélimar, which had its first post office in 1670. From Paris to Vitry there was a bi-weekly service from 1654, but letters posted on Wednesdays from Vitry sometimes missed the Friday departure from Paris to Provence. Similarly a Saturday letter from Grignan missed the following Saturday's post from Paris to Vitry except in summer, leaving Paris only on Wednesday, catching the same post to Vitry as the next letter, so that two letters would normally arrive on Fridays. Sévigné gave tips to ensure a quick transfer on the arrival of post at Paris. The post chaise, with a leather trunk full of mail, galloped between post stages, where horses were changed at roughly seven-kilometre intervals, there being 35 between Paris and Rennes, 88 from Paris to Aix. Letters from Aix to Paris, if not delayed, took six days. Town gates had to be kept open for the post, all night if the post was late.

From 1676 to 1703 a single letter of one folded sheet cost 5 sols, Paris–Aix, 6 if in an envelope; it cost 8 for two sheets, or 15 an ounce if more. From Paris to Vitry the prices were respectively 4,5,6, and 12 sols, all postal fees payable by the addressee, with 20 sols to the livre. Sévigné's life, and that of her household, was organized to fit in with the departure, but much more the arrival, of the post. Mother and daughter had agreed to write with each post, so that a gap meant either a treason in the relationship or a serious illness. A perfectly ordinary mishap, like a mis-routing, was never assumed, and Sévigné was more dependent on receiving letters than on writing them, especially when absence from Paris removed the possibility of using the exchange of gossip as an excuse for such regular and lengthy letters. Reading what her daughter actually put in her letters was of secondary importance to receiving them. Françoise-Marguerite, herself, able to write from a distance and with more time for reflection, gradually outgrew the need to defend her independence which she had felt during the brisk and often sudden flareups that had occurred while they were together. Her affection for her mother flourished more when she was not being overwhelmed by her crushing personality.

A male child, Louis-Provence, was born on 17 November 1671, and on 13 July 1672 Sévigné herself left for a visit to Grignan, arriving on 30 July. Mme de Grignan had a stillborn child on 27 March 1673, and her mother did not return to Paris until October of that year, when she travelled back via Burgundy. Mme de Grignan came to Paris in February 1674 and gave birth to a daughter, Pauline, on 9 September. The second long separation took place from the parting of mother and daughter at Fontainebleau on 24 May 1675 until Mme de Grignan returned to Paris on 22 December 1676. Sévigné had been ill in Brittany, and had gone to Vichy to take the waters. Mme de Grignan gave birth prematurely to a son, Jean-Baptiste, on 9 February 1676. He was to live only 16 months. The third separation lasted from June to November 1677. During that autumn Sévigné was to take a second cure at Vichy, and in October she was to move to the Hôtel de Carnavalet. She would live there until she died.

From 1671 Sévigné disappeared from the centre of social life in Paris. Mme de Grignan had left on 4 February 1671, exactly 20 years after her father's fatal duel. On 5 February Sévigné was 45. On 6 February the first letter to her daughter began: "My sadness would be of little account if I could describe it to you…" It was carnival week, and Sévigné went only to daily Mass, having Mass said daily, too, for her daughter. She visited Mme de Lafayette, attended sermons, decided to make a spiritual retreat at Livry over Easter, and organized her whole life obsessively round the absence of her daughter. The letters reveal her inner struggle as, both in grief and in guilt, she turned her attention to God and to spiritual matters.

After Easter social duties reasserted their claims, then neglected business in Brittany. Charles accompanied her, taking his mother into his confidence about his adventure with Ninon and his dealings with la Champmeslé. She recounted everything to Mme de Grignan, was naturally touched by the souvenirs she found everywhere at Les Rochers, but found that she had become too important a figure not to be drawn into the social life of Brittany, where the Estates were being held. Charles left on 4 July, but Sévigné stayed on, supervising the construction of her chapel, having alleys replanted, and reading, often material associated with Port-Royal, Arnauld d'Andilly's *Instructions chrétiennes*, extracted from Saint-Cyran's letters, and the *Essais de morale* of Nicole, whose spirituality partly centred on submission to the will of God, an equally Jansenist (q.v.) and Jesuit Christian adaptation of stoicism which assuaged Sévigné's feelings of loss. She returned to Paris on 18 December, but was immediately put in a new residence by Christophe de Coulanges, the son of the new tenant of the Grignan flat having contracted smallpox. She lunched daily with Mme Scarron the future Mme de Maintenon, went to *Bajazet*, attended a reading of Pierre Corneille's *Pulchérie* at La Rochefoucauld's, and frequently saw Retz. Some of her social sparkle and spirit of fun returned in relationships with the queen and with Monsieur. Then on 26 June her aunt, Henriette de la Trousse, her mother's sister, and at one time her own quasi-chaperon, died.

In May 1672 Sévigné moved to a small house, still in the Marais, giving a small celebratory dinner there on 12 May. She had only once received while staying at the house provided by the Coulanges, and indeed almost never entertained, by far preferring to be invited elsewhere. In July, she left for Grignan. She had begun to be worried about her daughter's financial situation and took Coulanges with her. Visiting relations on the way, she took 17 days, making the last part of the journey by river down the Rhône. She found her daughter pregnant for the fourth time, and herself became ill. The trouble was plainly menopausal. She went to consult members of the medical faculty at Montpellier and, since she could not now bring her daughter back to Paris with her as she had hoped, decided to stay the winter with her in Aix, and over Christmas at Lambesc, 20 kilometres away. Grignan himself, the king's representative, was indulging in a power fight with the Forbin family, which had two episcopal members. Everywhere Sévigné was treated with great honour, but towards the end of the pregnancy she was taken away by her son-in-law, who had business at Marseilles and Toulon, to afford mother and daughter a respite from one another, which had plainly become necessary.

Mme de Lafayette supported a request from Charles for more money for the Dutch campaign, which dragged on. Sévigné borrowed 6,000 livres for him. The stillbirth on 27 March 1673 took two days of labour, required surgical assistance, and nearly cost Mme de Grignan her life. Sévigné stayed on, waiting until her daughter could come back with her. Finally, they quarrelled, and Mme de Grignan told her mother she thought it her duty to stay with her husband. On 5 October Sévigné left for Paris. The same day the Grignans went to the annual Provence assembly at Lambesc. Political troubles in Provence, and their eventual appeasement after a brief military episode at Orange, brought the Grignans to Paris in February 1674. They stayed with Sévigné, and on 9 September another child, Pauline, the future marquise de Simiane, was born. Grignan himself had had to leave in May. He had won his political struggle against the Forbins, but royal absolutist ambition was now eating away at his power, and he was proving unable to pay the pensions representing the repayment to his daughters of his first wife's dowry. The situation became grave and was resolved only when, against the advice of Coulanges and Retz, Mme de Grignan took on joint responsibility for all her husband's debts, so compromising her own position if, as was likely, he pre-deceased her. It was the only way of preventing the need to sell her husband's office.

On 24 May 1675 Mme de Grignan, accompanied by her mother as far as Fontainebleau, left for Provence. Charles had been slightly wounded in September 1674. Louis de Coulanges, Christophe's brother and Sévigné's uncle, died on 10 May 1675. Christophe, 68, who had shared a lease with him, now came to live with his niece. That year, there was an uprising in Brittany. Sévigné quite naturally sympathized with authority. She felt no incongruity in merely wishing to enjoy her tranquillity and prosperity in the peace of her woods. She had, however, to stay on in Brittany to economize. There was little or no money from the harvest. From September to January she went only twice as far as Vitré, and then on 11 January her right side was paralysed. She was in pain, feverish, and swollen, unable even to turn over in bed. She recovered only slowly, could totter to Mass on 9 February, and by 15 February could walk a little. The problem seems to have been a form of generalized dropsy, cured essentially by suppressing the evening meal. There had been a night disturbed by an overflow of maternal affection, manifesting itself in a dream and sleeplessness, and Sévigné had taken to walking outside in the cold Brittany winter evenings rather than risk weeping alone in the house, with the result that her health had briefly given way.

Sévigné had recovered by mid-April. Meanwhile, on 9 February, Mme de Grignan gave birth to Jean-Baptiste. It was her sixth and last pregnancy. It is again possible that the premature birth had been due in part to the emotional disturbance caused by news of her mother's state. Sévigné left Les Rochers on 24 March 1676, still unable to use her right hand. The letters had henceforward to be dictated, but the signs are that everyone near her knew how important to Sévigné the correspondence was, and her life continued to be organized round it. In May she went to Vichy for the waters, drinking 12 glasses at dawn each day, the unpleasant hot showers in a hole in the ground, and a cure of sweating. Vichy, like Bourbon, was fashionable, and Sévigné found a number of friends among the clientele. After seven more days of waters, she returned to Paris, the usage of both hands almost restored.

Mme de Grignan arrived in Paris on 22 December, having been bullied and morally backmailed by her increasingly egocentric and frightened mother. Her husband could only come a month later. A new three-year lease was taken on the vast next-door property, which would also accommodate Grignan's daughters by his first marriage. Notice was almost immediately given to terminate on the following 1 October. Sévigné planned to travel with her daughter to Vichy, and return alone after the cure, but mother and daughter were too plainly destroying one another. Grignan, Coulanges, and Mme de Lafayette stepped in to separate them. Mme de Grignan returned to Provence in June, and Sévigné left for Vichy with Coulanges on 16 August. In August 1677 Montauzier consented to allow his nieces, Grignan's daughters by his first marriage, Louise-Catherine, aged 16, and Julie-Françoise, aged 13, to stay with their father. They were boarded at the Reims convent of Saint-Etienne, whose reverend mother was their aunt Louise-Isabelle d'Angennes, third daughter of Mme de Rambouillet.

Mme de Grignan arrived back in Paris towards the end of November 1677. Her mother and she had arranged to share with Coulanges a three-year lease at 2,500 livres a year on the Hôtel de Carnavalet. There was much power play between mother and daughter over who should use which rooms for what, important only because it makes clear that neither mother nor daughter really understood the motivations of the other. When Mme de Grignan had left Paris in June, she had not been well. She had, surprisingly, not recovered at Grignan, away from her mother, but now found her mother's solicitude unbearable. She tried to get back to Grignan for the summer, but circumstances of all sorts were against her, her mother, her two stepdaughters, the likelihood of the end of the war. She was happy only with her husband, with whom her understanding appears to have been near flawless, but the Grignans endured the unavoidable separations, and did not finally leave Paris until 13 September 1679, with Louis-Provence and Mme de Grignan's stepdaughters.

Sévigné had scarcely attended court since 1670, and only rarely in the letters are there reports of the social activities of either court or town. She was flattered to be invited by Mme de Maintenon to Racine's *Esther* at Saint-Cyr, was lent a carriage for the occasion, and was absurdly impressed when the king murmured half a sentence to her. Her spirituality deepened at Les Rochers in the summer of 1680, although it still scarcely went beyond an aspiration to accept in everything the operations of the divine will. The elder of Mme de Grignan's stepdaughters wanted to become a nun, which conveniently cancelled the debt she represented and entailed the return of Mme de Grignan to Paris. Louise-Catherine did become a Carmelite, although she had to leave the Order for health reasons. The Grignan debt was none the less cancelled in return for a pension of 1,200 livres, and Louise-Catherine continued to lodge in a convent, opposite her former Carmelite monastery. A projected marriage for Grignan's other daughter from his first marriage fell through on Montauzier's opposition, and Julie-Françoise left the Hôtel Carnavalet to stay with the duchesse d'Uzès, her cousin and Montauzier's daughter. She awaited her majority and finally married the marquis de Vibraye. There was no opposition, but neither Montauziers nor Grignans attended.

Charles de Sévigné appeared more attracted to the life of a country gentleman in Brittany than to life at court. He had caught gonorrhoea from a duchess—not, as his mother rightly pointed out, that it made any difference from whom he had caught it—and wanted to sell his army commission. Marriage projects were entertained, showing that a large dowry was to be preferred to a noble name. The marriage finally arranged was with Jeanne-Marguerite de Bréhant de Mauron, once the difficulties of Jeanne-Marguerite's large endowment had been overcome. The wedding took place at Rennes on 8 February 1684. Charles was 37, his bride 26, and an account of the ceremony was given in the *Mercure galant* (q.v.). Sévigné did not attend.

The abbé de Coulanges died on 29 August 1687, a year after Olivier Lefèvre d'Ormesson. Condé had died in December 1686, and Sévigné had attended the funeral oration preached by the Jesuit Bourdaloue. Unhappily one very important letter which has not survived is that to Mme de Lafayette of July 1685, in which Sévigné explained why she would not, at 59, marry Louis-Charles Albert, the 65-year-old duc de Luynes and friend of Port-Royal. It would have conferred on her, along with the financial security, an even more elevated social position, the right of the "tabouret" allowing princesses and duchesses to remain seated in the presence of the king and queen. Luynes was twice a widower and a close friend of Port-Royal, but Sévigné had no longer the courage, energy, or appetite for the style of social life such a marriage would have entailed.

Mme de Grignan returned to Paris in 1680. The lease on the Hôtel de Carnavalet had been renewed for a further four years, and the house restored and redecorated. After Coulanges's death it was Sévigné who went to eat with her daughter rather than the other way round. From 1680 they lived quite happily under the same roof, and often in one another's company. It is conventional to speak of Sévigné's Jansenist conversion in 1680. What happened is little more than the gilding in religious language of the realization that she had been too possessive in her maternal affection for her own happiness. Controlling her passions, suppressing her amour-propre, and asking God's forgiveness were not specifically Jansenist ways of behaving but the religious terminology of a mature wisdom, accompanied by a Chrisian view of the need to prepare for death. Sévigné was reading Augustine in 1680, but the spiritual treatises of Augustine are not at all what the 17th century knew as Jansenism. The spirituality of abandonment to divine providence which characterized the Christianity of Sévigné's later years was developed from renaissance neostoicism largely by François de Sales, who took the Jesuit side on grace but was also highly regarded by the Port-Royal directors. Its classical statement was to be made by the Jesuit de Caussade in his treatise on abandonment, but it also had affinities with Fénelon's quietism.

Mme de Grignan returned to Provence in October 1688, having been with her mother for eight years, detained in Paris largely by an inherited lawsuit, except when her mother spent a year from 1684 to 1685 in Brittany, and when she was briefly absent in 1687, taking the waters at Bourbon. In 1684 Chrétien-François de Lamoignon bought the house near the Hôtel Carnavalet which henceforward bore his name. There were mutual visits, and a friendship developed. Mme de Grignan records the presence of the Jesuits Rapin and Bourdaloue. Her only son appears to have been educated by the Jesuits at the Collège de Clermont, renamed Louis-le-Grand from 1682. His first appearance at court for the carnival was in 1685. He was not quite 14. By the time his mother left for Provence in 1688, Louis-Provence was in the army. The war of the League of Augsburg was about to begin, and Louis-Provence was to be slightly injured at Mannheim, escaping with more glory than pain.

From the departure of her daughter in 1688 to her own visit to Brittany in April 1689, Sévigné led an active social life. From Les Rochers, where she had taken her great friend Mme de Chaulnes, with whom she shared the grand social life pertaining to governors of Brittany, she went directly to Grignan in October, returning to Paris with the Grignans in 1691. Mme de Lafayette and the Chaulnes had tried to tempt her back to Paris, offering horses, and money if required, in the autumn of 1689, but Sévigné preferred her rocks and woods. She was living economically, struggling with debts, and trying to salvage something for Charles, who came with his wife from Rennes to spend much of the winter with her. The bankruptcy of her once rich friend d'Harouys, from whom she had borrowed so much, made matters worse. Treasurer of the Estates of Brittany, he was sent to the Bastille owing 6,600,000 livres, and Sévigné still owed interest on old debts. On 18 September 1689 she wrote a relaxed, happy, and informative letter about her daily routine with Charles and his wife. She was neither lonely nor bored, and it did not much matter whether anyone came to call. She was now well enough to cross France and arranged to leave Les

Rochers on 3 October 1689 to arrive at Grignan on the 22nd.

Life in Provence was pleasant. Charles came in 1691, and sometime between mid-November and mid-December Sévigné was back in Paris, with the Grignans or shortly to be followed by them. Mme de Lafayette and then Bussy died in 1693. Mme de Grignan, retained by lawsuits, was not to leave Paris again until March 1694. Her mother followed her to Grignan in May. Her social life had continued after her daughter's departure, although in the few letters written during the brief separation of 1694 there is a stronger accent than previously on hearing Mass, going to hear fashionable preachers, and reading books of spiritual edification, especially those concerned with morality.

In late 1689 Jean Le Blanc de Valfère, treasurer of the Estates of Provence, from whom the Grignans were accustomed to borrow, was declared bankrupt and from 1690 the Grignans' own financial situation became increasingly serious. Grignan's debt was about 45,000 livres or over twice his annual income of 18,000 livres as lieutenant-general. Repayment over 10 years was arranged, with interest of 8,000 livres. The normal rate of interest for all official and semi-official loans in 17th-century France was five per cent. Since agricultural yields were not above three per cent, even in good years, it often paid to sell land rather than increase debt. It did not help that there was a real shortage of credit to be had, and that Sévigné had incidentally, in an effort to avoid leaving her family to settle personal debts incurred by herself, ruined tenant farmers whose leases she had refused to renew. Their goods were sold up, and they fell from bourgeois affluence to poverty, but the proceeds from the sales did not cover the debts, which had to be written off, and the new farmers could not increase the yield. The king, pressed for money to fight the war, had similarly applied too much pressure, and the royal coffers did not swell as a result of the ruin of the treasurers. It was the war, too, which increased the burden on the families supplying the officers who had troops to maintain and regiments to run.

By 1692 the Grignan debt to the younger daughter of the first marriage had risen to 128,346 livres. Grignan could find only 2,000. Almost all of Mme de Grignan's income went on debt repayment, leaving 5,500 disposable income from a revenue of 46,000 livres over two years. On concluding with the elder daughter for a modest pension, Sévigné had said: "That's the sauce, now for the fish," hoping for a similar arrangement with the younger daughter. She was disappointed. Louis-Provence had speedily to be married to a rich wife. The wedding to the 18-year-old Anne-Marguerite de Saint-Amans, daughter of a tax farmer whose dowry included 300,000 livres in immediate cash, took place on 2 January 1695, a number of other families having turned down marriage into such considerable ruin. There were to be no children. The marriage of 1695 was implicit, it has been said, in that arranged without too close a financial inspection by Sévigné for her daughter in 1669. While that is true, it is also possible to take the view that, in the circumstances, she had made a remarkably good bargain for her daughter.

On 19 November 1695 Pauline de Grignan married Louis de Simiane de Truchenu. A simple calculation of dates makes clear that her mother's famous aphorism, as reported by Saint-Simon, that "il fallait bien de temps en temps du fumier sur les meilleures terres (from time to time even the best land needs manure)" cannot, in the way Saint-Simon reports it, ever have been uttered, or had the consequences normally imputed to it, including the removal of Saint-Amans's daughter from Grignan. It may well be true that Saint-Amans was not being paid the agreed 15,000 livres a year interest on that part of the dowry used to pay off the Grignan debts, and that Louis-Provence was not receiving the 10,000 livres a year laid down in the contract, but it was perfectly normal for Louis-Provence and his wife to live in Paris, where Saint-Amans provided accommodation for them. Moreover, the Grignans were to present their daughter-in-law at court, and there is historical evidence that Saint-Amans, after the supposed rupture, provided the 30,000 livres cash content of Pauline's dowry, with the promise of 30,000 livres on decease. The groom's nobility was without suspicion, and his considerable estates neighboured those of the Grignans. His mother gave him 30,000 livres, his aunt made him the beneficiary of her will, and he had 25,000 livres a year of his own. He was a good match for Pauline.

Mme de Grignan was severely ill in 1695 with trouble of menopausal origin, but including severe bleeding, which ceased, and an inability to digest, which became dangerous. It was chiefly on account of her inability to travel to Paris that Saint-Amans took the young couple back with him on 1 September. After Pauline's wedding, when Mme de Grignan seemed out of danger, Sévigné went away for a fortnight, visiting Marseilles, Lambesc, and the Visitation at Aix, where the 25-year-old Marie-Blanche had now been a nun for eight years, and where the community was delighted to receive their foundress's granddaughter. Mme de Grignan's health had deteriorated a little, but then recovered. Sévigné had been back at Grignan for Christmas. On 10 January she wrote a letter in which it is clear that she felt her life was over. She fell ill on 6 April and died on 17 April 1696, almost literally of exhaustion, and of fear for her daughter's health. She was just 70, and the immediate cause of death was almost certainly pneumonia. It is possible that Mme de Grignan was not physically present, and even that Sévigné preferred to die without her beloved daughter as onlooker. She insisted on receiving the last sacraments on the fifth day of her illness. She had composed herself to die, consciously or unconsciously unwilling to watch her daughter precede her. She may well have wanted to avoid the agony of an emotional parting. We do not know. Mme de Grignan records the suddenness of the final sickness and death. As Sévigné had written in 1680, it was natural that she should die before her daughter.

In fact Mme de Grignan died of smallpox on 13 August 1705. Louis-Provence had died at Thionville of the same disease on 10 October 1704. Charles was to die in 1713, and Grignan himself on 31 December 1714.

WORKS

Sévigné wrote nothing for publication, and left only her correspondence, 1,372 letters, of which less than 250 were written to her rather than by her. Her stature as one of the greatest writers of 17th-century France derives primarily not from the great panoramic view the letters afford us of the golden age of French culture at its peak, or from their interest either as social history or even as self-analysis, but from the fact that, in desperate psychological need of the affection of the daughter to whom most of her letters were addressed, Sévigné wrote an intimate episodic monologue with the intention of diverting, informing, and guiding her daughter, and of retaining or regaining her love and sympathy. Since she had no public end in view, Sévigné wrote with a singleness of private purpose which neither demanded nor even allowed the observance of ordinary literary norms, although the letters do in fact show much effort at conscious restraint, and they do contain some set pieces. In them, Sévigné unintentionally developed a personal style of such self-revelatory power as to swamp even the letters' enormous intrinsic social and literary historical interest.

The sheer bulk of the correspondence and its fragmented nature have forced commentators to concentrate on its small vignettes, on the unrevised page or so which often vividly sketches an impression, a scene, an event, or a mood. It is true that some of these impressionistic evocations are brilliantly successful, but the real power lies in the whole, not the parts, in the spontaneity of an active, sensitive, cultivated, and alert female mind tumbling together all manner of concerns, which are organized only by their chronology as mental events. Sévigné's mind is always struggling to master its material, the potent mixture of relaxed gossip, informed comment, solicitude, description, news, reflection, and business, interrupted whenever it was time to catch the post.

The chief purpose of the letters was to get back missives as often as possible. The content of what was received mattered much less than the fact that tokens of affection were sent back whenever possible, which was a reasonably convenient twice a week. Too much has been made of the way in which Sévigné vicariously lived her daughter's life, imagining it, going over souvenirs of it, and sharing its concerns. She certainly did all those things, self-indulgently, guiltily, and with an increasing awareness of the damage she was doing herself. But what counted for her was not living her daughter's life, or even knowing about it, so much as receiving expressions of her affection.

Again, it did not much matter to her what she herself wrote about, unless occasionally when overcome by maternal anxiety about the possibility of a pregnancy or a malady, or overwhelmed by the vividness of an impression or the depth of a mood. Sévigné needed to send the letters to communicate her strongest and most intimate feelings not to the person she got on best with, which was her son, but to the person she loved the most, which was her daughter, and to elicit the tokens of affection she needed to assure her that the strength of her affection was being perceived. Naturally that affection overwhelmed its recipient. Mme de Grignan loved her husband and had her own life to lead and social duties to fulfil which she found both important and agreeable. There were flare-ups when the exigence of maternal solicitude and intimacy became too crushing and, underlying the correspondence, there is the search for an equilibrium which Mme de Grignan's husband helped his wife to find, as Sévigné's own son and friends helped her. Sévigné sometimes found it easier to write than to talk.

Since she had to send letters, irrespective of their content, she used them as a way of focusing her mind, much as other people use diaries. Sévigné was sharply observant and often wryly amusing, but she was not consciously employing stylistic devices or striving to achieve any particular effect. She needed, almost before she needed to communicate, to pin down, articulate, and understand her own experience. Montaigne reflected slowly on the philosophical implications of his own experience, similarly trying to grasp an imagination spinning riotously out of control, but he was not sending bi-weekly missives, and his chapters score for depth of intelligence, whereas Sévigné's letters score for vividness of impression, but Sévigné, like Montaigne, and like successful diarists, cannot present a finished literary work. That is what Proust so admired about her.

The whole interest lies in the spontaneity, the scarcely ordered jumble of remembered experience. Had she done things in order to be able to have something to write to her daughter about, the effect would have been ruined. She lived her life first, and then jotted down the things in it which struck her, or which she felt the need to articulate in order to understand, or which she especially wanted to communicate in the course of protecting her intimacy with her daughter. Her letters to other people are witty, informative, and amusing. Something of the private rhetoric of the letters to Mme de Grignan overflows, and there is the same inner effort to pin down a flighty mind, but they lack the compulsive urgency which makes Sévigné's letters to her daughter the real masterpiece.

There were about 100 months of separation during the 27 years from the wedding to Sévigné's death. In 1670, when her daughter is still with her after Grignan's departure for Provence, Sévigné, no doubt remembering her own marriage, is at pains to reassure her son-in-law both of his wife's affection and of her careful conduct. She sympathizes with him at having to read such long letters from her: "There is no hope that it is me who can teach you that she loves you. All her actions, all her behaviour, everything she does, all her sadness tell you enough about that" (15 August 1670). The first letter after her daughter's departure assuages the grief by expressing it. Sévigné went to the convent which her daughter had for a while attended, as she would do again on 29 January 1672, the third anniversary of the wedding. Two days before departure she had given her daughter one of her very few gifts of any value, a diamond, "que jamais je ne le voie en d'autres mains que les vôtres. Qu'il vous fasse souvenir de moi et de l'excessive tendresse que j'ai pour vous (may I never see it in any hands but yours. May it make you remember me and the overflowing love I have for you)."

Then, on the Friday after the Wednesday departure, Sévigné wrote to Françoise-Marguerite about how she had felt. There was the sense of loss, of increasing distance as her daughter's journey progressed, the visit to the convent "toujours pleurant et toujours mourant (crying all the time and dying all the time)," the need to be alone, foreseen and prepared for: "on me fit du feu. Agnès me regardait sans me parler; c'était notre marché (they lit a fire for me. Agnès watched me without talking to me. That's what we had agreed)." Agnès was a Visitation nun who knew Françoise-Marguerite. Sévigné stayed at the convent until five, wrote to her son-in-law, then went to see Mme de Lafayette, "qui redoubla mes douleurs par la part qu'elle y prit (who doubled my sorrow by sympathizing with it)." Mme de Lafayette lived a short walk away from the convent, across the Luxembourg gardens, at the opposite end of Paris from Sévigné. La Rochefoucauld called. They talked about Mme de Grignan, and Sévigné stayed until eight.

On returning home and going upstairs to her apartment she passed the open door through which she could see her daughter's baby. The next day she received a letter, "qui me remit dans les transports (which plunged me back into my first grief)." Sévigné does not even thank her daughter for the letter, which must have been sent off at the first stop. Part of the effect of the letters is the way they communicate how ordinary social constraints can simply be dissolved in moments of strong emotion. Then on Friday evening Sévigné writes as much again, perhaps 400 words, a paragraph of news, the agreed pretext for the cor-

respondence, a paragraph of solicitude ("I beg you to look after yourself for my sake"), a paragraph of general social information, and a final paragraph with a piece of amusing gossip about Mme d'Heudicourt's liaison and médisance.

Monday's letter tells of Sévigné's fears. She thinks her daughter will have written hurtfully, or that she must be ill, or have had an accident. Then letters arrive "and it's the exact opposite. You love me, my dear one, and you say it in a way I can't stop crying at." She realizes vaguely that she thinks continuously about her daughter in the way religious people are supposed continuously to think about God, and then the outpouring changes into an account of how she cannot yet face people who are trying to be kind, except for Mme de Villars, who let her cry. She recounts her attendance at a sermon, at Benediction, and mentions three social calls. It is carnival. She is going to dine with Mme de Lafayette, and she has a Mass said daily for her daughter. Then comes a paragraph about Grignan's brother, a plea to her daughter to look after her health, to sleep well, drink soup "et servez-vous de tout le courage qui me manque (and serve yourself with all the courage I can't find)." Then comes a paragraph mentioning Mlle d'Harcourt's wedding and the ball given by the Guises and attended by the king, and then another returning to the story of Mme d'Heudicourt, almost certainly exiled not for a liaison but for virtual spying at court. That evening Sévigné wrote another 400 words between receiving a visitor who must have brought more news and going to dine with Mme de Lafayette. She reports almost graphically on the scene at the Guise ball she had not attended, and sends a good deal more gossip.

What these two letters reveal is Sévigné's attempt to gain control of her mind, while reporting on her attempts to achieve control over both her emotions and her behaviour. It is the unconcealed and unconstrained nature of the first of these three attempts which makes the letters into a literary work of the highest order. The wit, gossip, malice, and developed eye for the vivid detail make the text instructive and entertaining, but it is the attempt to set down what has happened to her, and what is going on within her, which takes Sévigné to literary heights touched in the 1670s perhaps only by her close friend Mme de Lafayette, and by Racine. All three, and surely not by coincidence, explored the near-impossibility of imposing rational order on human experience, and of subjecting personal behaviour to rational control.

On 18 February, exactly a fortnight after Mme de Grignan's departure, Sévigné is at her most self-revelatory. The first paragraph has 30 lines asking her daughter to remember the effect on her mother of "la petite circonstance d'être persuadée que vous m'aimez (the small matter of being convinced that you love me)" and culminating in an account of the unconscious workings of memory, guaranteed to interest any reader of Proust:

Je suis présentement assez raisonnable. Je me soutiens au besoin et, quelquefois, je suis quatre ou cinq heures tout comme un autre, mais peu de chose me remet à mon premier état, un souvenir, un lieu, une parole, une pensée un peu trop arrêtée, vos lettres surtout, les miennes même en les écrivant, quelqu'un qui parle de vous, voilà des écueils à ma constance, et ces écueils se rencontrent souvent

(At the moment I'm quite calm. I can hold myself together if necessary, and sometimes I can go four or five hours like anyone else, but it doesn't need much to send me back where I started, a memory, a place, a word, a thought lingered over too long, your letters especially, mine even while I'm writing them, someone who mentions you, those are the reefs for my self-control, and those reefs often crop up).

After that paragraph there immediately follows one recounting how she has heard a new song from *Psyché* sung by a famous singer at the comtesse de Lude's, which her daughter will have to sing for herself, with the implication that Sévigné herself would be too sad, and another giving news of herself, and of how that Lent Mascaron and Bourdaloue are surpassing one another as preachers. Then she switches to how she has followed her daughter's route, knowing each night where she slept, but which route would they take from Lyons, she wonders, and then follows a paragraph about the king at a carnival mascarade, and a famous quotation from Voiture to Julie d'Angennes, "nobody has yet died of your absence except me." The letter continues, switching the whole time between Mme de Grignan's conjectured doings and feelings, Sévigné's own feelings, and gossip.

On 18 February there was a fire next door but one. On 20 February Sévigné wrote first that she was starved of news from her daughter. Then she describes what happened. It is a witty past tense account, in which Sévigné comments on how she started her story: "I came home and went to bed. That's not extraordinary, but what is, very, is that at three am I heard shouts of thief, fire…" She was sure it was her granddaughter, but, no, it was at the Guitauts: "C'étaient des cris, c'était une confusion, c'étaient des bruits épouvantables, des poutres et des solives qui tombaient (There were shouts, there was confusion, there were terrible noises, beams and joists falling)." Looking back, she writes almost amusedly. They saved a jewel or money box, some silver tableware, a few furnishings, but Guitaut's wife, five months pregnant, held him back: "Il faisait pitié. Il voulait aller sauver sa mère, qui brûlait au troisième étage (We were sorry for him. He wanted to go and save his mother, who was burning on the third floor)." Sévigné had to keep hold of his wife, but happily Guitaut found that his mother had escaped. There was no fire brigade until 1705, but the neighbouring Capucins isolated the fire. No pertinent detail goes unobserved: an estimate of the damage at 30,000 livres, not too far off the finally agreed 23,000, a rough inventory of what was lost, the bleeding of Mme Guitaut in the hope of preventing a miscarriage.

Then Sévigné gives in to the incongruity: Guitaut naked under his nightshirt, with shoes; Mme Guitaut with naked legs and one slipper; Mme de Vauvineux in a short nightdress without a dressing gown; all the servants and all the neighbours in night bonnets; the Venetian ambassador in dressing gown and wig, perfectly preserving the dignity of the Most Serene. But you should have seen his secretary. "What a chest. You could see it all, white, fat, plump, and above all with no shirt. The cord that should have done it up had been lost in battle." There is a lot more gossip, and there are witticisms at the expense of a well-known cuckold: "I can't do justice to everyone who sends greetings. The crowd is enormous, it's Paris, it's the court, it's the universe. But La Troche wants to be singled out, and Lavardin."

The letters continue in much the same way, varying in tone between intense emotion and light-hearted fun, with business, news, gossip, and the eye-catching descriptions of people, places, and events, at which Sévigné plainly realized she was outstandingly good, the stock in trade of a brilliant conversationalist. Although she jumps from topic to topic disconcertingly for those trying to follow particular threads or registers, Sévigné achieves sufficient control for it very rarely to seem as if she is wondering what to say next, and she rarely fails to reduce mental confusion to often graphic verbal order, sometimes switching to the present tense in the middle of an anecdote to make her point. She writes, she says on 30 July 1677, without knowing where she is going to go, "if my letter is going to be long or short. I write at my pen's pleasure. That's what governs everything." In other words she sits down to recapture her experience, to crystallize it in words, stimulated by the thought of her daughter and the reward to be expected, which is the letter in return.

Among the most famous letters are those devoted to "relations," more carefully prepared narrative accounts. Sévigné wrote one on 30 March 1671, a single paragraph using the narrative present, devoted to the smallest of social gaffes, when a pretty woman suffered the discomfiture of taking off her gloves to serve a princess of the blood when she was not the person of highest rank present, who de-gloved herself and got in front: "Ma bonne, je suis méchante; cela m'a réjouie (My dear, I'm wicked; I was delighted)." Much better known is the "relation" of Vatel's suicide: "ce n'est pas une lettre, c'est une relation (this isn't a letter, it's an account)." Sévigné had written on Friday 24 April 1671. It is fine, after the rain. Her daughter does not tell her enough about herself. She met an amusing abbé and has bought some material for a robe de chambre, "like your last skirt… a little green, but with mauve predominating." Mme de Grignan's baby daughter is flourishing. Then she adds a postscript from La Rochefoucauld's about the suicide of Condé's maître d'hôtel, Vatel, because the fish had not arrived. Two days later she wrote the famous "relation."

Condé had invited the king to a two-day entertainment from Thursday to Saturday at Chantilly, whose cost, carefully given by Sévigné as 50,000 écus, was actually over 60,000, or more than 180,000 livres, according to Gourville's accounts. Vatel was well known and had been Foucquet's maître d'hôtel before he became Condé's. Not surprisingly, commentators have found the motivation for the suicide, not mentioned in the *Gazette* (q.v.), which devotes much space to an account of the celebration, difficult to believe. It is also impossible to commit suicide in the manner recounted by Sévigné's set piece, as she must have known. It has been conjectured that Gourville, recently returned from exile as Condé's intendant, or steward, had discovered irregularities in Vatel's accounts. Sévigné gives snippets of conversation, important details, like the dismaying cost of the fireworks (16,000 livres), which failed on account of the cloud, and switches into the present tense. Vatel was disturbed. He had not slept for 12 nights, he had told Gourville, and then there had been more guests than expected, and not enough roasts to go round the bottom tables. The next day was the Friday, hence meatless, and Vatel had ordered fish from all the ports. At four in the morning Vatel, unconsoled even when Condé had come into his room to reassure him, had found only two parcels of fish. He waited, and no more came. He told Gourville that he could not survive the blow to his reputation:

Gourville se moqua de lui. Vatel monte à sa chambre, met son épée contre la porte, et se la passe au travers du coeur, mais ce ne fut qu'au troisième coup, car il s'en donna deux qui n'étaient pas mortels; il tombe mort. La marée cependant arrive de tous côtés. On cherche Vatel pour la distribuer. On va à sa chambre. On heurte, on enfonce la porte, on le trouve noyé dans son sang… On loua et blâma son courage… Cependant Gourville tâche de réparer la perte de Vatel; elle le fut. On dîna très bien, on fit collation, on soupa, on se promena, on joua, on fut à la chasse. Tout était parfumé de jonquilles, tout était enchanté

(Gourville laughed at him. Vatel goes to his room, puts his sword against the door, and runs it through his heart, but that was only at the third thrust, as he gave himself two which were not fatal. He falls to the floor, dead. Then the fish arrives from all sides. They look for Vatel to share it out. They go to his room. They knock, they break down the door, they find him drowning in his own blood… His courage was disparaged and praised… But Gourville tries to repair Vatel's loss. That was done. They lunched well, they took refreshments, they dined, they went for walks, they played games, they hunted. Everything was scented with daffodils, everything was magic).

Equally famous is the series of letters of July 1676 on the torture and execution on 17 July of the celebrated poisoner the marquise de Brinvilliers, which left Sévigné aghast, and the moving passage in the letter of 20 June 1672 in which Mlle de Vertus recounts to Mme de Longueville the death of her son at the crossing of the Rhine.

Sometimes the writing is careful and the vignettes are contrived. Sometimes there is a jumble of verbs and nouns, concrete and abstract, jotted down as a series of impressions, like touches of paint flicked on to an impressionist canvas. The more vivid passages are often composed of lists: "Elle fait cent petites choses, elle parle, elle caresse, elle bat, elle fait le signe de la croix, elle demande pardon (She does a hundred little things, she talks, she strokes, she fights, she makes the sign of the Cross, she says she's sorry)." The images can be striking. Charles can "avaler le péché comme de l'eau (swallow sin like water)." There is little sympathy for the Breton peasants in the 1675 uprising, an increasing preoccupation with spiritual and religious matters, as Sévigné learns to dominate the suffocating expressions of affection, and, if not most importantly, then most famously, spontaneous verbal skill, at its most brilliant in this description of the Louvois wedding sent on 19 November 1679:

J'ai été à cette noce de Mlle de Louvois. Que vous dirai-je? Magnificence, illustration, toute la France, habits rabattus et rebrochés d'or, pierreries, brasiers de feu et de fleurs, embarras de carrosses, cris dans la rue, flambeaux allumées, reculements et gens roués; enfin le tourbillon, la dissipation, les demandes sans réponses, les compliments sans savoir ce que l'on dit, les civilités sans savoir à qui l'on parle, les pieds entortillés dans les queues

(I was at Mlle de Louvois's wedding. What shall I say? Magnificence, glorification, all France, clothes lined and braided in gold, jewels, braziers full of fire and of flowers, jostling of carriages, shouts in the street, lighted torches, throngs pressed forwards and backwards; then the whirling crowds, the relaxing, the questions without replies, compliments made without knowing what you were saying, politenesses without knowing who you were talking to, feet wound round tails).

PUBLICATIONS

Works

Lettres choisies de Mme la marquise de Sévigné…, 1725
Lettres de Marie Rabutin-Chantal, marquise de Sévigné, 2 vols., 1726
Lettres de Mme de Sévigné, de sa famille et de ses amis, 14 vols., 1862
Lettres inédites de Mme de Sévigné, 2 vols., 1876
Correspondance de Mme de Sévigné (Pléiade edition), 3 vols., 1972–78

Biographical and critical studies

Fitzgerald, Edward, *Dictionary of Mme de Sévigné*, 2 vols., 1914
Tilley, Arthur, *Mme de Sévigné: Some Aspects of Her Life and Character*, 1936
Stanley, Arthur, *Mme de Sévigné: Her Letters and Her World*, 1946
Allentuch, Harriet Ray, *Mme de Sévigné: A Portrait in Letters*, 1963
Nicolich, Robert, *Mme de Sévigné and the Problem of Reality and Appearance*, 1965
Duchêne, Roger, *Réalité vécue et art épistolaire: Mme de Sévigné et la lettre d'amour*, 1970
Avigdor, Eva, *Mme de Sévigné: un portrait intellectuel et moral*, 1975
Duchêne, Roger, *Madame de Sévigné; ou, La Chance d'être femme*, 1982
Duchêne, Jacqueline, *Françoise de Grignan; ou, Le Mal d'amour*, 1985

SOREL, Charles, sieur de Soigny, ?1599–1674.

Satirist, novelist, historian, and critic.

LIFE

It is claimed of Sorel that, although he wrote half a hundred volumes, he is the author of only one book, the *Histoire comique de Francion*, first published anonymously in 1623, augmented and toned down in 1626, then finished and published pseudonymously in 1633. Sorel was by trade a historian, but by taste and inclination a novelist, parodist, and critic. Both his satirical parody of the *Astrée*, the 1627 *Le Berger extravagant*, and his critical account of earlier French writers, *La Bibliothèque française* of 1664, have had a bad press, but both contributed something to the formation of at least the aesthetic canons required of the authors to receive official patronage under Colbert, and Sorel's encyclopedic compilations still offer a valuable key to the understanding of the imaginative needs and endeavours of the generation that flourished during Colbert's ascendancy, as well as to those of the subjects of Louis XIII who immediately preceded them. *La Bibliothèque françoise* is actually a critical assessment of earlier authors, remarkable for its accuracy, sensitivity, and malicious sparkle.

Very little is known of Sorel's life, except that in 1635 he bought the charge of historiographe du Roi which had belonged to Charles Bernard, his mother's brother. After 1663 the pension was no longer paid, interest payments on what amounted to municipal bonds fell off, and Sorel had to sell his house. He was to die in poverty, cared for by the nephew, Simon de Riencourt, his sister's son, into whose house his sister and he had both moved. His father, Nicolas Sorel, although not noble, could trace his ancestry back to 13th-century Sézanne, about 100 kilometres east of Paris, and had fought during the religious wars. He subsequently bought the charge of procureur. Sorel, called "sieur de Soigny" in the privilège of his 1666 *Droits du Roi*, after a small estate he possessed near Sézanne, had only one sister, Mme Parmentier, who later married a procureur who conspired with Retz against Richelieu.

The register of burials at Saint-Germain-l'Auxerrois says that Sorel was 72 when he died on 7 March 1674, but that is virtually impossible, since in 1616, when on that reckoning he would have been 14, he published his *Epithalame* for the marriage of Louis XIII. Guy Patin, his close companion for most of his life, said in 1653 that Sorel was 54, which sounds possible, but 1597 is also alleged for his date of birth, as indeed is 1582, although we would have heard more about it if Sorel had lived to be 92. It needs from time to time to be recalled that in the 17th century only notaried documents, not even registers of births, baptisms and deaths, can be trusted as accurate sources for dates.

Sorel studied at the Collège de Lisieux in Paris, and went on not very enthusiastically to study law. He said he wanted to study science and philosophy, and to write verse, and his biographer conjectures that he kept himself by what we would call journalism, the paid confection of pamphlets, popular handbooks, of which *La louange et l'utilité des bottes par le chevalier de Rozandre* of 1622 is a send-up, and light-weight fiction, like his anonymous *L'Histoire amoureuse de Cléagénor et de Doristée*, published by Toussainct du Bray in 1621, which Rotrou later dramatized. This narrative fiction, written to pander to the least sophisticated taste in the literate classes, is naturally full of facile incidents, abductions, violence, and strong passions, although from the beginning Sorel is marked out by his realism, not only in his settings, but above all in the accuracy with which he reproduces different types of language, as used by different sorts of people. As a writer Sorel was precocious and exceptionally fluent, with a gift for mimicry which he used for parody, composing satirical versions of adventure novels, of pieces in précieux (q.v.), picaresque, or baroque style, and of pastorals. In appearance he was short and stout. Furetière, with whom he quarrelled, said that his long pointed red nose was invariably red.

On the libertin edge of the court, Sorel collaborated with Théophile, Saint-Amant, Boisrobert, and Claude de l'Estoile, writing libretti for stage entertainments, but appears then to have been dropped by his more highly born acquaintances. A novel, the 1622 *Palais d'Angélie*, dedicated to the king's sister, is alleged to have been stolen from him, or at any rate signed in his place without payment, by Marcilly, who had a reputation for cheating at cards. Sorel may simply have published it pseudonymously. Some months later, in 1623, Sorel published *Les Nouvelles françoises*, not to be confused by the more famous work of the same title put out by Segrais in 1656. The characters have real-sounding names rather than stylized ones, and the action takes place in recognizable places. In 1623 Sorel also collaborated with Boisrobert on *Les Bacchanales*.

Sorel may have been the secretary of the comte de Cramail, the former friend and patron of Mainard and Régnier. It is the libertin elements in his work, which their company would have encouraged Sorel to cultivate, which were dropped from the 1626 edition of *Francion* after Théophile's condemnation at the end of his second trial, which started in October 1623 and ended on 1 September 1625. Sorel himself says that parts of his work, particularly *Francion*, are autobiographically based, and it is certain that he deliberately if parodically took himself for his own hero, and decided apparently for the first time to write without any model in mind. Some autobiographical details are deliberately disguised, and the original text is seasoned with a number of salacious episodes. The coarse licentiousness of tone is a deliberate reaction against the encroaching reforms of linguistic usage and the inchoately but increasingly refined social behaviour associated with Malherbe's group and with the Hôtel de Rambouillet.

The 1623 novel *Francion* in seven books was an immediate success, and not merely on account of the parodic elements it contained. The privilège was dated 5 August 1622, and there is no achevé d'imprimer, but by 9 September 1623 Jean de Lannel had obtained a privilège for his long *Le Roman satyrique*, obviously modelled on Sorel. There were more than 30 editions of *Francion* before 1700. Although Sorel's 1626 edition, now extended to 11 books, removed the realistic coarseness of language, carefully reproduced from the real life speech patterns of the Parisian people, though not of the upper bourgeoisie, he made some effort to keep his irreverent public amused. Balzac had been incautious enough to compare in a letter to Boisrobert of 28 September 1623 his own epistolary art with the novel's vulgarity. In 1626 Sorel's pedant, the gluttonous and lecherous Hortensius, is given all the choicest locutions from Balzac's *Lettres* from 1622 to 1625, and plunged into absurd and ridiculous adventures. The 1633 version has 12 books, finishes the plot, and is signed with the name of an obscure and deceased Norman author, Moulinet du Parc.

Sorel certainly had the idea of basing plots on subjects other than love and war, like the law, finance, and commerce. He put the notion into the mouth of Hortensius, but did not himself go on to invent modern bourgeois fictional plots. His own later comic or realist novels do not follow Hortensius's programme, and sometimes simply return to the romanesque. The 1627 *Le Berger extravagant*, inspired by Cervantes, is too thickly weighed down by commentaries on the satire for the humour to escape being smothered. Sorel went on publishing novels until the 1648 *Polyandre*, in fact probably written at least in part some years before, and never finished. When published, the first part was not a success, in spite of the compliments Sorel paid it in *La Bibiothèque françoise*.

It is likely that at around the time of his break with the libertin court group Sorel had considered the possibility of suicide. His temperament seemed melancholy, although in his letter of 25 November 1653 Patin said it was not. Sorel, however, was quite cynical about the society in which he lived, and he felt pessimistic about its follies, but by the time of the Fronde he had settled down to a celibate existence, shared with his sister the inheritance left by his parents, by 1653 was living in the house he now shared with her and her family, and had abandoned pretensions to nobility and aspirations to take part in life at court. As early as 1634 he was writing works of piety, the *Pensées Chretiennes sur les Commandements de Dieu*, and there is even a manuscript of perhaps 1638, dedicated to Richelieu, entitled *Discours du Courtisan chrétien*.

Sorel took Corneille's part in the Querelle du *Cid* and mocked the nascent Académie française, as with all the rest of Paris he attacked Mazarin. It is not really surprising that Sorel should also have taken the précieux (q.v.) movement seriously, using his acute ear to note ways of speaking and new modes of expression in the salons as well as in the streets, and giving pieces to Sercy and others for their anthologies or "recueils." His *Lois de la galanterie* and *Connaissance des bons livres* are still important sources for the history of préciosité. The enormously ambitious *La Science universelle* reviewing all the scientific and philosophical systems from late antiquity to the 17th century is normally considered to be too loose, dilettante, and ill-informed to be of serious interest, with the works of moral philosophy and theology even emptier. The picture of Sorel left by Furetière and Patin suggests that his driving force was economic need, particularly after the suppression of the historiographer's salary by Colbert in 1663. Sorel's sister's family had also had to sell their house, as Sorel, his sister, and her family moved in with Sorel's Riencourt nephew. The cause of the quarrel between Sorel and Furetière is not clear, although the satirical portrait of Sorel in the 1666 *Le Roman bourgeois* is clear and cruel.

WORKS

Francion, on its first appearance, was a coarse book, full of obscene language and low-life episodes, intended to be amusing, but also seriously satirical in intention, and penetrated by a deep pessimism. Its coarse realistic hedonism in the world of students and prostitutes is outspoken without being dangerous. The boldness comes from crossing the dividing line between the drunken and promiscuous fraternity of the tavern community, the libertins, and the serious religious doubters, responsible for blasphemies and brutalities, those to whom Garasse refers in the 1623 *Doctrine curieuse des beaux esprits de ce temps* as "impies et Atheistes." Although the most audacious ideas in *Francion* are tentatively suggested in a delirious and erotic dream sequence near the beginning of the third book (pp. 252–62 of the 1623 edition), they became dangerous, and were removed after the Théophile trial. Only one copy of the 1623 edition has survived what must have been systematic suppression. Happily it has been copied and was published, with an indication of the original page numbers, in the 1924 critical edition.

The original version is too emphatically insistent on the use of magic in order to achieve sexual stimulation, too obviously unheroic in its characters and events, and altogether too heavily weighed down by its realism to produce today the effect for which its author clearly hoped, and which it may have had in 1623, if only for the unsophisticated readership at which it was obviously aimed. The parody of the picaresque and chivalresque, however, is probably too crass to have constituted much more than bawdy amusement even in 1623, and the

replacement of the inspiration to virtue, heroism, and self-transcendence by the difficulty of attaining sufficient vigour to manage ordinary sexual intercourse must even then have seemed too laboured. But the novel did plainly succeed in getting its belly laughs, and the depiction of the sordid, mean, and unheroic is arrestingly well contrived,

The "plot" is merely a framework into which are inserted incidents, almost as if the novel were a series of episodes from a comic strip based on a central character with obvious and systematically emphasized recurring characteristics. Magic, sexual potency, and their combination, together with extreme superstition, recourse to diabolic aid, mistaken identities, burglary, robbery, rope ladders, and travesty, all jammed into half a dozen laconic pages, set the novel in motion. The nearest it comes to pornography is the mention of Laurette's view that what the candle will allow her to see will make love-making a more enjoyable experience than it would have been in the dark. What she sees is the wrong man. Historically, this is quite important. The 17th-century reader of this type of fiction would instantly recognize the relationship of the text of *Francion* to that of the medieval contes of lechery, to their prettification in renaissance clothing by Boccaccio and Marguerite d'Angoulême, and to the contemporary fiction which sought to examine love as primarily an emotional phenomenon which, dignified by the merit of its object, might lead to spiritual perfection, a point of view observable but also mocked in Marguerite's *Heptaméron* and more thoroughly examined, without being mocked, in d'Urfé's *Astrée*, still unfinished, but whose third volume had appeared in 1619.

At the beginning of the fourth book Sorel changes tack. Francion says to the reader that he must redeem his promise and, instead of continuing with his "advantures courtisanes (adventures as a courtier)," turn to his academic experience, his "advantures scholastiques." The jokes tend to be complex and the "intertextual" allusions to works with which barely literate 17th-century schoolboys (the gender assumption is Francion's) must have had some nodding intimacy not always simple to explain. There is both an imitation and a parody of Rabelais, and it is supposed that the reader will have enough Latin to know that the etymology of the Latin for moon, "luna," cannot possibly be explained from the phrase "quasi luce lucens aliena ("as if by light illuminating other things," if it means anything at all), any more than the French word for shirt, "chemise," can come from "sur chair mise (put on the flesh)," which was a traditional example.

Since the jokes are too feeble to bear much explaining, the allusions to early 17th-century life too complicated, and the historically interesting thing about the book is its style, a brief, relatively simple passage about Francion in the classroom is enough to show the tone of the narrative. He describes himself as badly dressed, unkempt, with ill-fitting clothes, and

tousjours j'avois un Roman caché dessus moy, que je lisois en mettant mes autres livres au devant, de peur que le Regent ne l'apperceust: Le courage m'estant alors creu de beaucoup, je souspirois en moy mesme de ce que je n'avois encore faict aucun exploit de guerre, bien que je fusse a l'aage où les Chevaliers errans avoient desja defaict une infinité de leurs ennemis.... Ne vous estonnez point si j'aymois mieux lire que d'escouter mon Regent, car c'estoit le plus grand asne qui jamais monta en chaire. Il ne nous con-toit que des sornettes, et nous faisoit employer nostre temps en beaucoup de choses inutiles, nous commandant d'apprendre mille grimauderies les plus pedantesques du monde

(I always had a novel hidden about me, which I read putting my other books in front, in case the teacher saw. My Courage having much increased, I sighed within myself at not yet having performed any martial exploit, although I was at the age when knights errant had already defeated an infinite number of enemies…. Don't be surprised if I preferred reading to listening to my teacher, for he was the greatest dolt who ever climbed on to a rostrum. What he told us was just a load of nonsense, and he made us spend our time on lots of useless things, ordering us to learn by the ton the most pedantic childish rubbish you could think of).

The style is relaxed and colloquial without being particularly lively. Sometimes Sorel uses language too obscene to be found in the dictionaries. What is interesting about this passage is its unwarranted assumption of boldness. Francion can scarcely have been of an age even to dream of knight errancy, and "chevalier errant" had already been relegated to child's language; and yet he can have had no choice but to attend class, to have been afraid of the schoolteacher, and to seem to suppose it daring both to read a novel in class and to call his teacher a pedant and a fool. Francion is being ironic about his own dreamt-up courage as a knight errant, in view of his fear of his teacher. The reactions in the paragraph are those, perhaps, of a modern 12-year-old, and it is impossible not to see ineptitude in Sorel's apparently indeliberate confusions of viewpoint and attitude in Francion's narration of his comic ups and downs.

Le Berger extravagant contains more of the same, but is rather less amusing or convincing. Lysis has read too many pastorals and takes to the way of life of a fictional shepherd, wearing shepherd's clothes and adopting a shepherd's lifestyle. His friends flatter his illusion, and he is involved in another series of grotesque comic-strip adventures. In the end his friends take pity on him and restore him to normal life. Sorel himself explains the title "Anti-roman" given to *Le Berger* in his review in the 1664 *Bibliothèque françoise* of his own anonymous and pseudonymous works "attribuez a l'autheur de la *Bibliotheque françoise* (attributed to the author of the *Bibliothèque françoise*)":

en effet c'est un Anti-Roman; et si vous voulez c'est une Histoire Comique et Satyrique, où toutes les sottises des Romans et des Fables Poëtiques sont agreablement censurées. En ce qui est de ce livre il peut avoir de l'approbation, puis que dans le Christianisme on a interest de combattre toutes les Fables des Payens, et que mesmes plusieurs Peres de l'Eglise, se sont employez à les rendre ridicules au Peuple. L'Histoire du Berger Extravagant décrivant un Homme qui est devenu fou pour avoir leu des Romans et de Poesies, et qui se fait Berger à la maniere de ceux de l'ancienne Arcadie, cela pouvoit divertir assez de Gens, mais ce n'estoit pas là le seul dessein. Il y a des *Remarques* jointes à cette Histoire, lesquelles donnent de l'instruction sur plusieurs choses, et ne sçauroient estre desagreables, estans aussi gayes que serieuses

(in fact it is an anti-novel; and if you like it is a comic and satirical story in which all the stillness of novels and poetic fables is amusingly censured. As regards this book, it can be approved because, within Christianity it is important to combat all the fables of the pagans, and even several Fathers of the Church have applied themselves to making the fables ridiculous to the people. The story of the crackpot shepherd, describing a man who has gone mad through reading novels and poetry, and who turns himself into a shepherd like those of ancient Arcadia, might amuse a lot of people, but that was not its only purpose. There are *Remarks* added on to the story which teach important lessons, and are not unpalatable because they are as humorous as they are serious).

That paragraph is important for a number of reasons. Partly, of course, because it draws attention to the use of the term "anti-novel" in what was in fact 1633, but also because Sorel indicates that he never expected his anonymity to be more than a polite veil; he dreams up a serious purpose for a frivolous book, and that purpose is said in 1664 to have been Christian, by implication in 1627; and there is a traditional connection made between fable and primitive theology, with the discrediting of pagan fables openly discussed 30 years before Fontenelle wrote on the subject.

For the intelligence of its critical comments as well as the quality of its literary gossip the *Bibliothèque françoise* offers very good value. Sorel clearly knows in 1664 who wrote the 1662 *La Princesse de Montpensier*, pokes delicious fun at Balzac, offers an intelligent resumé of what has been said for and against Montaigne's *Les Essais* before giving his own remarkably judicious opinion, is far more sensitive than any of his contemporaries to the achievement of Ronsard, and ably and knowledgeably recounts the Querelle du *Cid*. The 1666 edition gives an up-to-date list of the 40 members of the Académie, together with a list of all deceased members. Sorel does not make it easy to gauge precisely how ironic is the attitude he may be taking to the Académie.

On sçait qu'une partie de nos bons Autheurs, sont de l'Academie Françoise, tellement qu'on se peut bein rapporter à leurs écrits pour l'excellence du Stile et pour la force du Discours… Si quelques-uns des Academiciens n'ont pas tant écrit que les autres, ou n'ont mis aucun Ouvrage en lumiere, il faut croire qu'ils ne sont pas d'humeur de publier ce qu'ils font, ou que leurs affaires ne leur donnent pas le loisir de s'occuper à ce travail, et qu'ayant esté jugez dignes de leur place, ils servent à examiner les écrits des autres, et à leur donner de bons Conseils touchant la maniere de bien écrire; et comme il se trouve entre eux des Personnes de haute condition, ils honorent fort la Compagnie par leur dignité et par leur merite propre

(We know that some of our good authors belong to the French Academy, so that we can rely on their writings for excellence of style and force of argument… If some of the Academicians have not written as much as the others, or have published nothing at all, we must suppose that they have no inclination to publish what they write, or that their affairs leave them no time to devote to such work, and that having been judged worthy of their place, they can be used for the examination of the works of others, and to give good advice about how to write well. Since there are among them persons of high condition, they much honour the company by their rank and their own merit).

PUBLICATIONS

[*Since so many of Sorel's works are anonymous or pseudonymous, or were written in collaboration, no complete list of publications can be drawn up*]

Fiction

Histoire amoureuse de Cléagénor et de Doristée, 1620
Le Palais d'Angély, par le sieur de Marzilly, 1622
La Louange et l'utilité des bottes, 1622
Les nouvelles françoises, où se trouvent divers effects de l'amour et de la fortune, 1623
Histoire comique de Francion..., 1623; modified 1626 and 1633; English translation 1655
Les avantures satyriques de Florinde habitant la basse région de la lune, 1625
Le Berger extravagant, 1626
L'Orphyse de Chrysante; ou, L'Ingratitude punie, histoire cyprienne, 1626
La vraie suite des aventures de la Polyxène du feu sieur de Molière, 1634
La Solitude et l'amour philosophique de Cléomide, 1640
La Maison des jeux, 2 vols., 1642 (continuation, 1645)
Les nouvelles choisies, 1645
Polyandre, 1648

Other

Epithalame, 1616
Advertissement sur l'histoire de la monarchie françoise, 1628
Tombeau de l'orateur françois, 1628

Histoire de la monarchie françoise, 1630
Pensées chrestiennes sur les commandements de Dieu, 1634
La Science des choses corporelles, 1635
Des talismans, 1636
Le Jugement du Cid, 1637
La Science universelle, 3 vols., 1641 (vol. 4, 1664)
La Deffence des Catalans, 1642
La Fortune de la Cour, 1642
Histoire du roi Louis XIII, 1646
Discours sur l'Académie françoise, 1654
De la perfection de l'homme, 1655
La Description de l'Ile de Portraiture, 1659
Relation de ce qui s'est passé au royaume de Sophie depuis les troubles excités par la Rhétorique et l'Eloquence, 1659
Oeuvres diverses, 1663
La Bibliothèque françoise, 1664; revised 1666
La Science de l'histoire, 1665
Les Droits et les prérogatives des rois de France, 1666
Remarques sur la Lorraine, 2 vols., 1666
De la connaissance des bons livres, 1671
De la prudence; ou, Les Bonnes Règles de la vie, 1673

Biographical and critical studies

Roy, Emile, *La Vie et les oeuvres de Charles Sorel*, 1891
Lyons, J.C., editor, *Charles Sorel and his Bibliothèque françoise*, 1950
Emont, L., *Seventeenth-century French Society in the Novels of Charles Sorel*, 1958

T

TALLEMANT DES RÉAUX, Gédéon, 1619–1692.

Memorialist and moralist.

LIFE

As an observer of his times and as a moralist, Tallemant belongs in the same league as La Rochefoucauld, Retz, and Saint-Simon. As a chronicler of the recent past, his painstaking research puts him on the level of such serious historians as de Thou. As a moralist he must very nearly have invented the portrait, and he certainly turned it into a developed literary genre, dependent on the selection of characteristic details as well as on anecdote, and informed by a tolerant, cynical, and amused, but clearly identifiable set of moral values. Unlike La Rochefoucauld and Retz, Tallemant was clearly writing sketches or drafts for something he hoped would be published. Unlike Saint-Simon, he probably at one time hoped that publication would occur in his lifetime. Unlike any of them, he did not leave his work in a state which in any sense he regarded as final. While, in view of the history of the manuscript, his neglect is understandable, the 1961 publication for the first time of the full text of the *Historiettes*, by Antoine Adam in the Bibliothèque de la Pléiade, leaves no further possible doubt about Tallemant's status as a major author.

There are three Tallemants called Gédéon: Tallemant's grandfather's fourth son, and therefore his uncle; his uncle's second son, and therefore his cousin; and Tallemant himself. The family came from Tournai, in the Spanish Netherlands. In 1561 Tallemant's grandfather, François, had taken refuge in La Rochelle, where he started a business as a ship's chandler, married well, equipped boats for the Newfoundland pelt and cod-fishing trade, and rose to become a member of the town council from 1590, and in 1600 one of the mayor's two assessors. Of his two daughters and four sons, one son, Pierre, took over his father's business before joining in 1604 with his brother, Gédéon, and brother-in-law Paul Yvon, to found a bank.

In 1605 Pierre married Elisabeth Bidault and in 1615 he became mayor of La Rochelle. In 1617 his wife died and Pierre remarried in 1618. His new wife, Marie Rambouillet, unrelated to the celebrated marquise, was the sister of a Rouen banker with whom Pierre Tallemant did business. Tallemant himself, the second son of the second marriage, was born on 2 October 1619. Four years later the family moved to Bordeaux, where Pierre established a bigger branch of the bank, a maritime insurance company, and, in 1632, five tax farms, for which he paid no less than 2,640,000 livres. By 1634 he realized that he could direct his affairs only from Paris, where he therefore moved, buying a house in the Rue des Petits-Champs, in a section of the town favoured by the business community, among whose Protestant members Pierre speedily became prominent.

The sons took the names of estates acquired by their father without waiting for the conferment of titles of nobility. The eldest became Tallemant de Boisneau, the writer became Tallemant des Réaux, after a property near Montluçon, and the third Tallemant de Lussac. Tallemant, while young, learnt Greek, Latin, Italian, and Spanish and from youth was attracted to reading chivalresque novels. At home, he began to collect books and was teasingly known as "le Chevalier (the knight)," and in Paris he early had a series of amorous adventures, feeling strong attraction for a cousin, Madame Harambure, and for a young widow, Marie le Goux, both of whom inspired him to put lofty sentiments into verse. As an adolescent his social life was developed, and at the age of 19 he was invited to accompany the abbé de Retz to Rome. The journey took almost the whole of 1638 and included travelling by boat from Lyons down the Rhône, with stops at Avignon, Vaucluse, Aix, and then Marseilles. The party visited Venice and Florence before going on to Rome, where Tallemant became friendly with Voiture and with Claude Quillet, doctor to the French embassy.

On his return Tallemant resisted all attempts to make him a lawyer and buy him a legal office, preferring a life of leisure, pretty girls, books, and companions who interested him. His brother François had become a convert to Catholicism and a priest devoted to letters, eventually to be rewarded by membership of the Académie, but Tallemant, after some years of the life of dissipation not uncommon among the rich young Protestants of his generation, appears to have fallen in love with the daughter of his cousin Nicolas, Elisabeth Rambouillet, born on 6 May 1633, whom he married on 14 January 1646, while she was still only 12. Tallemant and his young wife went straight away to an apartment in the Pré aux Clercs. She was to bear him four daughters.

The rich Protestant bourgeoisie included several important patrons, among them Tallemant's cousin Gédéon, on the way to ruining himself, whose wife, a well-known salon hostess, appears both in Madeleine de Scudéry's *Le Grand Cyrus* and Somaize's *Dictionnaire des Précieuses*, and it is noticeable from the *Historiettes* that this is the society Tallemant knew best—the rich, cultivated, leisured, artistically inclined, Protestant bourgeoisie. The attribution to Tallemant of a madrigal in the *Guirlande de Julie* (q.v.) is simply impossible if the poem was in the 1633 manuscript, although the poem with his name attached might have been added for the calligraphed version of 1641. We do not know whether additions were made or, if so, which poems were added.

Even if by then he was sufficiently close to the inner circle of the Hôtel de Rambouillet to have been invited to contribute to the *Guirlande*, and the poem is in fact by him, Tallemant cannot have felt completely at ease with the duc d'Enghien and his "petits maîtres," his foppish cronies at the Hôtel during the period of the Condé ascendancy there, before Julie d'Angennes's wedding, the death of the marquise's only surviving son at

Nördlingen in 1645, and Enghien's succession to the Condé title in 1646. For Tallemant, who was probably collecting material for some form of memoirs by the time he went to Rome with Retz, the Hôtel represented a rich source of material, to be drawn not only from the people he observed there, especially the older generation of Conrart and Gombauld to which he rallied, but also from the information confided to him by the marquise herself, particularly during the early years of her widowhood, which dated from 1652, and certainly including confirmation of the publicly known fact that Madame la Princesse was the mistress of the cardinal de la Valette. When the marquise herself died at the end of 1665, Robinet's *Gazette* mentions the names only of Tallemant and his brother François as still close to her.

From about 1645 Tallemant was associated with the circle of Olivier Patru, the "Table Ronde," with its chivalresque connotations in which, as at the Hôtel de Rambouillet, the company, which included Perrot d'Ablancourt, Maucroix, Pellisson, Furetière, and La Fontaine, parodied itself by investing its members with mythological names and in this case pseudo-Arthurian identities. Tallemant and his wife were known as Astibel and Rosaliane, and Tallemant became noted for his satires and other verses. It was here, above all, that he acquired gossip and more serious information, not only about his own contemporaries, but about Louis XIII and Richelieu and their protégés, friends, enemies, and entourages. Boisrobert was of particular help. It was about 1657 that, encouraged by the marquise de Rambouillet, Tallemant began the composition of the freely judged and openly expressed portraits, some chronologically anterior and some contemporary, but all historical, which Tallemant called *Les Historiettes*. They were intended to be part of some compilation of obviously portrait-based memoirs, to go with, or be part of, a series of "Mémoires de la Régence."

Most of Tallemant's sources were written, although not necessarily printed. With respect to oral sources, in addition to confidences from the marquise de Rambouillet and her daughter Julie, from Boisrobert and from Tallemant's friends of La Table Ronde, material came from a fistful of informants whose names we know: Maucroix for the personalities of Champagne; Nyert on the delicate subject of Louis XIII's homosexual inclinations for Cinq-Mars; Tallemant's cousin Gédéon for the Bordeaux region; Le Pailleur for Brittany; Patru for lawyers; and there are portraits of several clients of one or other of the Tallemant and Rambouillet banks. The written sources include above all de Thou's *Historia sui temporis*, the *Thuana*, Sully's memoirs, the *Economies royales*, and Grammond's *Historiae Galliarum libri*.

Tallemant mentions recent biographies of Lesdiguières and d'Epernon, and had clearly studied the pamphlet material aimed against Richelieu and the regime of Louis XIII, particularly Mathieu de Mourgues's venomous attacks on Richelieu. Something came from a lost memoir by Racan, from the then still unpublished *Mémoires* of Montglas, and from a text of La Rochefoucauld's *Mémoires* first published in 1817. Tallemant must also have known in manuscript the *Mémoires* of Mlle de Montpensier, and we simply do not know by what chance or industry Tallemant got hold of some other written source material. He ferreted out, came across, or had his attention drawn to a whole range of obscure and unpublished political or legal documents we know about only from other historians who named their sources.

In 1651 Tallemant had bought the fine renaissance château du Plessis-Rideau near Chouzé-sur-Loire in Touraine. His father

died in 1656, and his elder brother, Boisneau, took over the bank. It was doing well, working for Mazarin, financing the colonization of the Indies and the pelt trade. However, Tallemant's cousin Jacques Bibaud, who had become Tallemant's father's close associate and was in charge at La Rochelle, had decided to open his own bank, and in 1658 moved to Paris. When he left, the La Rochelle branch owed the Paris branch of the Tallemant bank 3,000,000 livres which Bibaud would do nothing about. Disaster hit when Boisneau died in 1661 and the bank went bankrupt in the sum of 4,000,000 livres. Tallemant's wife left him for a convent, where in 1665 she abjured Protestantism, and was duly awarded the statutory pension of 2,000 livres. Tallemant meanwhile faced a tax bill of 400,000 livres.

The difficulties were slowly sorted out after much litigation. Tallemant's wife returned, and in 1670 a decree of the parlement finally relieved Tallemant of the burden of his debt. In about 1680 he and his wife were living in Paris in a three-storey house with a domestic staff of five. Tallemant abjured Protestantism in July 1685, three months before the revocation of the edict of Nantes. His still had his château, and increasingly disliked the oppressive conformity imposed by Louis XIV and his ministers. His third daughter, Charlotte, refused to abjure, but was given the opportunity to emigrate to London. The oldest daughter and Tallemant's ultimately frivolous and unintelligent wife rallied strongly to the support of Louis XIV, about whom Tallemant was deeply sceptical. He died on 10 November 1692.

WORKS

Tallemant left nothing in print. A privilège for an edition of pieces by and about Voiture was withdrawn at the demand of a bookseller, and all that is left are two volumes of Voiture's works annotated by Tallemant. His poems have disappeared, but a draft of a tragedy and much else in manuscript still exists in La Rochelle. A draft of the *Historiettes* still exists and it may once have been considered complete, but Tallemant then marked the margins with so much new material for incorporation into the text that it must be supposed the original manuscript either never had or soon lost any definitive status.

In fact the original manuscript clearly once ended with "Naifvetez, bons mots, reparties, contes divers," a blank sheet, and a table in which that is the title of the last historiette. On the blank sheet Tallemant wrote the historiette of Mme de Langey, but could not fit it on to the two sides, although he resorted to using double columns and leaving no margin. It is finished on the space beneath the end of the table of historiettes. Since it mentions the arrest of the marquis de Langey, which took place on 8 February 1659, but Tallemant did not know when he wrote it about the marriage on 17 February 1661 of Anne-Magdelaine de L'Isle-Marivaux and Jean-Louis de Louet, marquis de Calvisson, it is reasonable to assume that it was written after the bulk of the historiettes, but before the last four we now have. What we do not know is when the material contained in the margins of the manuscript was added. It may well have been before the historiette of Mme de Langey. At any rate, the bulk of the work dates in its present form from the period 1657–59, and it is possible, but not certain, that nothing was added after that date. At some point Tallemant clearly abandoned *Les Historiettes* and whatever other project was connected with them.

There are certain hints in *Les Historiettes* which suggest that the "Mémoires" themselves may have been started before *Les Historiettes* was dropped, although nothing of them survives. In 1659 Tallemant had another 33 years to live. *Les Historiettes* as we have it is therefore an abandoned enterprise, on which Tallemant is virtually certain to have ceased work before or during his epic financial crisis of 1661. The manuscript passed to Tallemant's widow's heirs and was forgotten until the end of the 18th century, when it was sold at auction for 20 livres. Eventually its interest not as literature but as historical gossip was realized, and a six-volume edition appeared in 1834–35, with the more scandalous revelations removed. A slightly expanded edition appeared in 1840, and another in 1854–60. Even as recently as 1989, in spite of the eight-volume edition of the *Historiettes* by Georges Mongrédien (1932–34), the two post-war Bibliothèque de la Pléiade volumes, and the established fact that the number of factual errors is tiny, of the order of less than a dozen in 3,000 pages, with a relatively low number of inadvertences and confusions, historians of literature have either totally ignored him, like the editors of the 1969 Oxford series *French Literature and its Background* and the 1989 Harvard *A New History of French Literature*, or rather grudgingly admitted, like the 1969 edition of *The Oxford Companion to French Literature* that, even if Tallemant was "pre-eminently a scandal-monger,… many of his statements are borne out by independent evidence."

The slow recognition of Tallemant in France, in spite of a few brilliant pages by Sainte-Beuve, can no doubt be explained by the venerable myths with which France for so long invested the history of what used to be regarded as "le grand siècle." Once it became impossible to maintain that Tallemant's text was either a forgery or a fantasy, what he revealed made it necessary for him to be regarded as a subversive, whether or not one approved of subversion. English-language critics have been slow to follow the lead of Edmund Gosse, who wrote as far back as 1925 that Tallemant was "the inventor of the miniature biography." In 1954 even Georges Mongrédien devoted three times as much space to defending Tallemant's accuracy as a historian as he did to proclaiming his literary merits, to which however attention has now been properly drawn at last, not least in the US in 1969 and in Franco Simone's 1972 Italian *Dizionario critico della letteratura francese*.

As a portraitist Tallemant came early, although just later than Madeleine de Scudéry, than whom he is a great deal more vivid. More importantly, the reader of the 376 historiettes catches quite seriously informed narrative history at the moment of its transformation into a 17th-century literary gallery of historical portraits. Not only are the historiettes often brilliantly conceived and executed, although much less taut, succinct, and logically coherent than La Bruyère's shorter pieces, but *Les Historiettes* as a work systematically displays a new concept of history. It is true that there is much gossip, scandal in the sense of revelation of what lies beneath the public image, although not more than is acceptable in lively historical journalism, but Tallemant is firmer on fact than all but the best of what is today published as popular historical biography. Tallemant is indeed longer on amusing anecdote than on serious reflections about historical motivation. But the essential purpose of the anecdotes is to show that great battles are fought, great kingdoms ruled, and great power exercised by ordinary people with ordinary reactions and individual weaknesses, tastes, quirks, whims, fancies and commitments.

The anecdotes, which catalogue pleasant and unpleasant personal traits, foibles, appearance, and characteristics, are often amusing but are generally informative. We learn about love affairs, law suits, sexual proclivities, and aspirations, and Tallemant, like most good literary portraitists, feels moral indignation not so much at bad behaviour as at hypocrisy. He is also restrained, refraining from repeating unfounded but popular gossip about Richelieu and Marion de l'Orme, for instance, discreet about the behaviour of the cardinal de la Valette, less biting than he might have been about Julie d'Angennes. Just occasionally Tallemant would, had he published the text as it stood, have been regarded as obscene. But he did not publish the text as it stood. Having presumably lost the appetite for continuing it, he chose not to publish it at all, however anonymously.

Tallemant tells us a great deal that we would not otherwise know. Even what can be discovered elsewhere is seldom to be found narrated with Tallemant's mixture of verve, wit, irony, malice, and indulgence. He has a very sharp eye for visual detail, a sensitive ear for witty remarks of all sorts, and an extraordinary nose for what reveals the ordinariness of even the grandest characters in his cast. But Tallemant seldom or never writes about people who are merely dull. We should be more astonished than we are that his judgement in that respect has been so generally endorsed by posterity, quite independently of any impact which could be attributed to *Les Historiettes* itself. It says a great deal about French society that so many of its liveliest minds even at that date knew one another.

The difficulty in the present context is that what Tallemant tells us about those whom posterity has deemed the most important and interesting figures from his own generation and that immediately preceding it, that is from about 1600 to nearly 1660, in addition to those destined by birth for grandeur, is so gripping as to make it difficult to concentrate on how well the historiettes are done, on the literary qualities of the text as distinct from its riveting historical fascination, and its captivating gossip about the apparently great and good, the strong, the noble, the rich, and even the pious.

The book as we have it starts with a short note about the meaning of the title *Les Historiettes*, "petits Mémoires qui n'ont aucune liaison les uns avec les autres (short memoirs which have no connection with one another)." Tallemant announces a roughly chronological order and continues:

> Mon dessein est d'escrire tout ce que j'ay appris et que j'apprendray d'agreable et de digne d'estre remarqué, et je pretens dire le bien et le mal sans dissimuler la vérité, et sans me servir de ce qu'on trouve dans les histoires et les mémoires imprimez. Je le fais d'autant plus librement que je sçay bien que ce ne sont pas choses à mettre en lumière, quoyque peut-estre elles ne laissassent pas d'estre utiles

> (My intention is to write down everything I have learnt and that I shall learn which is pleasant and worth remarking on, and I intend to tell what is good and bad without hiding the truth, and without using what can be found in printed histories and memoirs. I shall do it the more freely because I know that these are not things one should bring to light, although perhaps they are none the less useful).

Since Tallemant did use printed sources, which anyone could have checked, and since this preface is clearly addressed to prospective readers, it must be taken as an honest declaration of intention written at the outset, which adds interest to the fact that

Tallemant was obliged to change his mind later and hunt in printed sources, while from the start professing his intention of revealing what was not publicly known. He intends, he says, frequently to refer to the "mémoires que je pretens faire de la Régence d'Anne d'Autriche (the memoirs I intend to write on the regency of Anne of Austria)." To start with something illustrious, the first historiette will be "Henry le Grand et sa cour (Henry the Great and his court)."

The first paragraph on Henri IV starts perceptively, and immediately sets the tone of almost impertinent irreverence.

Si ce prince fust né roy de France et roy paisible, apparemment ce n'eust pas été un grand personnage; il se fust noyé dans les voluptez, puisque malgré toutes ses traverses, il ne laissoit pas, pour suivre ses plaisirs, d'abandonner ses plus importantes affaires

(If this prince had been born king of France and had had peace, it does not look as if he would have been a great man. He would have sunk himself in pleasure since, in spite of all his tribulations, he would abandon his most important business to satisfy his desires).

There follows an account of a pair of well-known occasions when Henri risked the outcome of wars by dallying with mistresses. Then the second paragraph:

Il n'estoit ny trop liberal ny trop reconnoissant. Il ne louoit jamais les autres et se vantoit comme un gascon. En recompense, on n'a jamais veu un prince plus humain ny qui aimast plus son peuple

(He was neither too generous nor too grateful. He never praised others and boasted like a Gascon. On the other hand, no more humane prince was ever seen, nor one who loved his people more).

That is a reasonable summary of Henri IV's character. By the third paragraph Tallemant is back to the king's sex life. D'Aubigné, a Protestant source, hints strongly that Zamet, highly rewarded by Henri IV for notable services, may well have poisoned Gabrielle d'Estrées, duchesse de Beaufort, whom Henri IV used to visit at Zamet's house. She died suddenly after 30 hours of pain on 10 April 1599. De Thou, Bassompierre, and L'Estoile say nothing. Tallemant simply says that if Zamet did have her killed, he was doing Henri IV a favour. The note is Tallemant's, included here to show that he regarded his work as serious:

Si Sebastien Zamet, comme quelques-uns ont dit, donna du poison à Mme de Beaufort, on peut dire qu'il rendoit un grand service à Henri IV, car le bon prince alloit faire la plus grande folie qu'on pouvoit faire; cependant il y estoit resolu*. [* Voyez-en les raisons dans les mémoires de M. de Sully]

(If Sebastien Zamet, as some people have said, did give poison to Mme de Beaufort, you could say that he was rendering Henri IV a great service, because the good prince was going to commit the greatest folly you could think of; still he was determined to do it*. [* See on this matter the *Mémoires* of Sully]).

This first historiette meanders on about the remarkable quality of the love lives of the female members of the Estrées family, quotes a satirical quatrain, reports a short narrative in direct speech showing what was throughout the work a lively interest in financial matters, takes us through the eight members of Mme d'Estrées family, and is clearly amused by the story that, to stop the king from marrying Gabrielle d'Estrées, the captain of the bodyguard offered to show the king Mme d'Estrées in bed with Bellegarde, but

quand il fallut entrer dans l'appartement de la Duchesse, le Roy dit: 'Ah! cela la fascheroit trop.' M. le mareschal de Praslin a conté cela à un homme de qualité de qui je le tiens

(when the time came to go into the duchess's room the king said, 'No. It would annoy her too much.' M. le maréchal de Praslin told that to a person of quality from whom I have it).

It is slightly engaging that Tallemant should preen himself on the back-stairs quality of that sort of informed tittle-tattle whose real purpose, of course, is to keep us from taking Henri IV too seriously. We are given a higher than usual density of scabrous material in the first historiette, almost all of it recounted with malicious amusement.

Les Historiettes would be a major work of literature, even if the characters were all made up, although its actual piquancy derives from the coordinated demythologizing of the revered. They felt, thought, and were motivated to behave as they did, just like everyone else. Salon gossip or back-stairs chatter about the personal hygiene of princes is too tawdry a way to describe the quizzical, cynical, but often indulgent debunking, generally built on to the skeleton of a curriculum vitae, which constitutes the major part of the historiettes, but it closely enough describes the way in which substantial portions of the text achieve their effect.

There is a deliciously waspish fairly short historiette on Conrart, whose circle became the Académie. Conrart's father would not let him study and that is why Conrart did not know Latin. He was made to keep his hair short; he was not allowed garters, or buckles on his shoes, so he had to wait until he got to the corner of the street before putting them on. Once when his father found him doing it, "il y eut bien du bruit au logis (there was a great row at home)." The style is now equal to the best of Molière, and the character of the ploddingly ambitious non-scholar, eager to please, over-anxious to help, offering his friendship round the street to anyone who would take it, is a merciless but amusing piece of character assassination. Conrart is made out to be an errand-running, would-be light of the literary world, who would still correct your proofs in exchange for a dedicatory letter. The cause of the trouble, Tallemant lets drop, is Conrart's jealousy when Tallemant's friendship with Patru grew to exclude Conrart. But throughout the historiette there remains an undercurrent of affectionate indulgence, which turns the piece from merely clever satire into something with perfect literary tensions.

The snap character judgements are almost always right, and the understanding of motivation often acute. Tallemant goes out of his way for an amusing anecdote, but he is a serious historian with a firm sense of right and wrong, a dislike of pretence and humbug, and a dry quizzical humour which makes him immensely readable. He is also very informative indeed about the outstanding military, aristocratic, and literary figures of his age.

PUBLICATIONS

Les Historiettes, 6 volumes, 1834–35; augmented 1840
Les Historiettes, 8 volumes, edited by G. Mongrédien, 1932–34
Les Historiettes, 2 vols., edited by A. Adam, Bibiothèque de la
    Pléiade edition, 1960–61

[The verse, other prose, and drama have not yet been published]

Biographical and critical studies

Magne, E., *La Joyeuse Jeunesse de Tallemant des Réaux*, 1921
—— *La Fin Troublée de Tallemant des Réaux*, 1922
Gosse, E.W., *Tallemant des Réaux*, (in English) 1925
Wortley, W. Victor, *Tallemant des Réaux. The Man through his
    Style*, 1969

THÉOPHILE de VIAU: see VIAU, Théophile de

**TRISTAN L'HERMITE (François l'Hermite, known as),
    ?1601–1655.**

Dramatist, poet, and novelist.

LIFE

Tristan's descriptive poetry about nature and love is itself sufficiently unusual in the audacity of its imagery, the concreteness of its vocabulary, and its sensuousness to arouse the justified expectation that the poet's life must have been lived on the margin of any organized literary activity. He was a friend of Théophile de Viau, but of his contemporaries only Saint-Amant came near to him in poetic style. Little is known directly of his early biography, but Toussainct Quinet published Tristan's autobiographical novel *Le Page disgrâcié*, dated 1643, relating the adventures of its narratorial author up to the age of 19. We are told that it was to be followed by two further volumes, but they never appeared. The fictionalized autobiography was once taken

as a historical record of Tristan's career, so that legends prompted by it have accumulated, although it contains a good deal that cannot possibly have happened. The difficulty lies in disentangling what in it did pertain to Tristan's actual experience and what was romanticization or fantasy. The work itself is a delightful mixture of realism and idealization.

François Tristan l'Hermite de Souliers was born in the château du Solier at the north-west corner of the Massif Central, about halfway between Moulins and La Rochelle. There is no documentary evidence of the year, but 1601 is more likely than any later date. Tristan and his contemporaries were convinced he was descended from the Pierre l'Hermite who preached the first crusade in 1097. His family was certainly very old, and came from the more barren part of the Massif Central. It is likely that *Le Page disgrâcié* provides an accurate account of Tristan's childish naughtiness, his precocity, and his adventurousness. His grandmother appears to have taken him to Paris when he was three, and a little later he seems to have been made a page of Henri de Bourbon, marquis de Verneuil, the illegitimate son of Henri IV by Henriette d'Entragues.

It is relatively certain that Tristan developed very young a passion first for gaming and then for drinking. He appears to have drifted from place to place, picking up jobs, quarrelling, and falling in love, even if the details of duels, flights, and travels given in *Le Page disgrâcié* are certainly fiction. It is unlikely that Tristan killed an adversary in a duel when he was 13, or that he then fled to London or even to Norway. It is on the other hand not at all unlikely that he acted for short periods as secretary to the great, or as tutor to their children. At Poitiers, at the age of about 17, Tristan entered the service of Nicolas de Sainte-Marthe, a man of letters interested in drama who passed Tristan on to his venerable uncle, the 82-year-old poet Scévole de Sainte-Marthe, whose reader and librarian at Loudun Tristan became. After 15 months with the older Sainte-Marthe, Tristan joined the household of the marquis de Villars-Montpezat near Loches. He was taken by him to join the entourage of Marie de Medici in Bordeaux in 1620.

After the submission of the princes, that is Condé, Conti, Bouillon, Longueville, Nemours and Vendôme, Louis XIII took Tristan to Paris, as gentilhomme of his household. Like Théophile de Viau, Tristan took part in the campaign of 1621 against the Protestants. He was ill for three months when he was with the besieging force at the siege of Montauban, and seems to have had little enthusiasm for military life. Finally, in 1621 or 1622, Tristan entered the household of the king's younger brother, Gaston d'Orléans, who became 14 in 1622. Tristan was to survive for 20 years with him, through a series of dismissals and rehabilitations; to be with him at La Rochelle in 1627, during the Lorraine campaign of 1631, and in exile in Flanders in 1632; and to dedicate to him his first tragedy, *La Marianne*, originally played in the spring of 1636. In 1634 Tristan had left Flanders for England, where he may have become acquainted with *Romeo and Juliet* and *Hamlet*, both apparent sources for his *La Folie du sage*, unpublished until 1645, although probably played in 1642.

At the end of 1634 Gaston d'Orléans made his submission to his brother, Louis XIII, and returned to Paris, where Tristan joined him. There followed a relatively stable period in Tristan's life, during which he flattered Richelieu and established himself as a dramatist. In 1636 Montdory played Herod in Tristan's *La Marianne* at the Théâtre du Marais, and the success reverberated for decades. Tallemant lavishly praised the performance of Montdory, calling it his chef d'oeuvre and attributing the heart attack which ended his career to the effort he exerted in playing it. Rapin still spoke with admiration of Montdory's performance in his two volumes of *Réflexions sur la Poétique d'Aristote et sur les ouvrages des poètes anciens et modernes* of 1674–75:

> Quant Montdory jouait *La Marianne* de Tristan au Marais, le Peuple n'en sortait jamais que rêveur et pensif, faisant réflexion à ce qu'il venait de voir et pénétré à même temps d'un grand plaisir

> (When Montdory played Tristan's *La Marianne* at the Marais, the audience never failed to come away dreamy and reflective, meditating on what it had seen and permeated at the same time with a great pleasure).

La Calprenède wrote a follow-up play, the *La Mort des enfants d'Hérode; ou, La suite de la "Marianne,"* of 1639, and Scarron described a performance of *La Marianne* in the second chapter of *Le Roman comique*. Tristan's play was quickly taken up by the Hôtel de Bourgogne, which commissioned an appropriate decor, while the third Parisian troupe, that of Molière, took it into the repertoire as soon as it returned to Paris, playing it on 30 September 1659 and a score of times during the 1660s. Published in 1637, with a privilège of 14 June 1636 and an achevé d'imprimer of 15 February 1637, there are 13 known 17th-century editions and 13 from the 18th century.

The year after *La Marianne* Tristan published a *Panthée* which did not succeed, and which provoked Richelieu to ask urgently for a *Jugement* from the abbé d'Aubignac, which was finally published in 1657, appended to d'Aubignac's *La Pratique du théâtre*. D'Aubignac, who had been asked to strengthen Tristan's fourth act and his denouement, had found the whole piece irredeemable, requiring to be rewritten from beginning to end. Tristan, however, went on to write *La Folie du Sage, tragicomédie*, probably in 1642, to be published only in 1645; *La Mort de Sénèque, tragédie*, played in 1644 and published in January 1645 with a privilège of 17 October 1644; *La Mort de Chrispe, tragédie*, probably played in the 1644–45 season and published in 1645; *La Mort du grand Osman, tragédie*, played in 1646 or 1647 and published by Quinault only in 1656, although Tristan had taken out a privilège of 17 June 1647; *Amaryllis, pastorale*, played in 1652 and published in 1653; and *Le Parasite, comédie*, played in 1653 and published in 1654.

After Richelieu's death in 1642 Tristan sought new protectors, and wrote for the Illustre Théâtre, created by Molière on 30 June 1643, which was protected by Gaston d'Orléans and opened on 1 January 1644. The approach had probably come from the new company, since Madeleine Béjart, Molière's principal associate in the enterprise, had an aunt, Marie Courtin, who in 1636 had married Tristan's brother, Jean-Baptiste l'Hermite. Tristan became an equerry of the duchesse de Chaulnes, but when her husband was made governor of Auvergne in 1645, Tristan, pleading ill health, having probably for some time already suffered from tuberculosis, left her service and stayed in Paris. His final protector from 1646 was Henri II of Lorraine, the fifth duc de Guise (1614–1664), whose loves he sang. He lived in a fourth-storey apartment in the Marais, and wrote at the same time as his Turkish tragedy, *La Mort du grand Osman*, an *Office de la sainte Vierge* in verse and prose published in the same volume at the end of 1646. Guise went to help the Neapolitan rising against Spain in 1647 in the hope of regaining the throne of Sicily, to which he thought himself entitled, but was taken prisoner by the Spaniards. He was released and returned to Paris in 1652; Tristan then went to live in the Hôtel de Guise. Meanwhile, in 1649, Séguier, the chancellor, had had Tristan elected to the Académie française.

During the Fronde Tristan did not take sides, although he tried to regain the favour of Gaston d'Orléans and to acquire that of Christina of Sweden and of the young Louis XIV. Quinault, whose literary beginnings Tristan protected, was his valet-secretary. Tristan died of his chest infection in the Hôtel de Guise on 11 September 1655. There has been much speculation about his religious beliefs, and it has been argued from his lack of commitment that he had no convictions or was positively a sceptic, as also that he started as a sceptic but gradually took a more conformist position. It is clear that his inclination to rebelliousness was prudently restrained in the service of a number of protectors when, if Tristan had allowed it to, it would have compromised him.

His Office of the Virgin Mary may not have implied a deep religious commitment, but it is not easy to find it compatible with outright scepticism. Even during his lifetime, his views and circumstances were not clear. He admired Théophile de Viau, and was admired by Mainard and Cyrano de Bergerac, but he himself never urged any religious doubts or disbelief, and he was accepted not only by the Académie française but into a closer association with the admirers of Malherbe and with Conrart, Chapelain and Balzac. On the other hand Tristan's name appears with those of Scarron, Cyrano de Bergerac, and La Mothe le Vayer at the head of d'Assoucy's 1648 *Jugement de Pâris*, which suggests a religious attitude of some detachment. Tristan's literary originality is clearer in his poetry than in his drama, and it seems certain that he also left burlesque verses, published only anonymously and after his death. Sorel says that he was also the author of the *Carte du royaume d'amour*, published in the 1658 *Recueil des pièces en prose* (see: Préciosité).

In spite of the protection of Guise, who lodged him, Scarron tells us that Tristan died poor. According to Brossette, Boileau was thinking of Tristan when he wrote the original version of his first satire, probably as early as 1657, although it was not published until 1666 and was unrecognizably transformed by the time it reached its final form in 1701. The portrait suggests that Tristan had become a legend very soon after his death and is, of course, stylized. We have to rely on Brossette for the identification.

> Cet Autheur si fameux dont la Muse fertile
> A charmé tant de fois et la Cour et la Ville,
> Mais qui n'étant vétu que d'un simple bureau,
> Passe l'Esté sans linge, et l'Hyver sans manteau;
> Et dont le corps tout sec et la mine affamée
> N'en sont pas mieux refaits pour tant de renommée;
> Las de perdre en rimant et sa peine et son bien,
> D'emprunter en tous lieux et de ne gagner rien,
> Sans habit, sans argent, ne sçachant plus que faire,
> Sort de Paris chargé de sa seule misère

> (This famous author whose fertile Muse/So often charmed both the court and the town,/But who, dressed only in simple rough wool,/Spends the summer without linen, and

the winter without a coat;/And whose skinny body and hungry look/Are none the better for all that renown;/Tired of losing by rhyming his trouble and his livelihood,/Of borrowing everywhere but earning nothing,/Without clothes, without money, no longer knowing what to do,/Leaves Paris taking with him only his poverty).

WORKS

Tristan published five volumes of non-religious poetry: *La Mer* of 1627, dedicated to Gaston d'Orléans; *Les Plaintes d'Acante* of 1633, containing "Le Promenoir des deux amants," addressed to "Silvie," who was Elisabeth, comtesse de Bergh, a niece of the prince of Orange, on behalf of "Acante," who was Frédéric Maurice de la Tour, duc de Bouillon; *Les Amours* of 1638; *La Lyre* of 1641; and the *Vers héroïques* of 1648. *La Mer* combines the personifications of natural phenomena, like the sun, with mythical creatures, like nymphs and Tritons, and with evocative descriptions of the sea at various times of day and in different weather conditions, calm and windless at dawn and sunset, or raging in a gale and a thunderstorm, then calm again. In much the same way, a new sensuousness intrudes into conventional love poetry, and a real feeling for natural objects into stylized images of nature's harmonies. Occasionally the imagery tips over into a fascination not only with the real, but with the macabre:

Il tenait un poignard pour ouvrir son cercueil,
Et la nuit déployant sa robe de ténèbres,
N'attendait que sa mort pour en prendre le deuil

(He held a dagger to open his coffin with,/And the night, unfolding its robes of darkness,/Awaited only his death to start mourning).

Some of Tristan's images and procedures either are taken from a common stock, like some of his images and his way of making rhetorical points, or could at any rate have gone unremarked in the work of his contemporaries. Part of Tristan's audaciousness has to do with his almost systematic exploitation in French verse of Marino's Italian conceits, and with his choice of Théophile de Viau's open sensuousness as a poetic model. What is different about Tristan's verse concerns the way in which images and descriptions, whether of the experience of love or of the observed physical phenomena of nature, like light and darkness, convey an intensity of personal perception or experience which is too vivid to be accommodated by the perfunctory techniques of versification to be found, for instance, in the contemporary *Guirlande de Julie* (q.v.). Tristan has been thought as important a poet as La Fontaine in the French 17th-century poetic expression of feelings stimulated by nature.

In spite of its meticulous symmetry, this description of a forge in "Les Forges d'Antoigné" from *Les Plaintes d'Acanthe* shows how Tristan's vivid images can overcome the tendency of his period towards an allegorization in which objects or living creatures represent human experiences or abstract qualities:

Le fer dont la masse allumée
Rougit les objets d'alentour,
C'est une image de l'amour

Qui gêne mon âme enflammée.
Cette enclume en sa dureté
Représent ma fermeté.
Cette rivière fond mes larmes,
Ce brasier ardent, mes désirs,
Ces marteaux, mes vives alarmes:
Et ces soufflets ont moins de vent que mes soupirs

(The iron whose glowing mass/Reddens the objects around,/Is an image of the love/Which distresses my inflamed soul./This anvil in its hardness/Represents my steadfastness./This molten flow melts my tears,/This burning brazier, my desires,/These hammers, my starts of alarm:/And these bellows force out less air than my sighs).

Le Page disgrâcié belongs to one of the fictional genres whose popularity owed something to the need to counterbalance the exaggeration of heroic perfection utilized in the mainstream fiction of Georges and Madeleine de Scudéry and La Calprenède, issuing from d'Urfé's *L'Astrée*, to achieve its function of exploring the vast moral and physical potential of human nature. Sorel used the cumbersome but not inept description, "roman vraisemblable et divertissant (credible and diverting fiction)," to describe the genre to which Tristan's short fictionalized autobiography might be thought to belong. Some of the episodes are clearly autobiographical, while others are equally clearly taken from mostly Italian renaissance collections like those of Boccaccio, Poggio, and the 1596 *Fuggilozio* of Tommaso Costo. The blending of fictionalized autobiography with borrowed material already fictionalized into a narrative presented as a true personal history is neither a new nor at this date a surprising genre.

Tristan's hero's improbable peregrinations take him to Normandy and Norway, England and Bordeaux. He undoubtedly gives us some idea of a court page's life and its vivid contrasts with the ordinary existence of peripatetic alchemists, English aristocrats, soldiers, and peasants. The descriptions are brisk and unemotional, the incidents without any moral, and the details selective, without any lingering over love or war. The model used is the picaresque novel, and the text is episodic, held together only by its central character, who narrates it, and depicts himself as incapable of resisting gambling and women.

La Marianne, with which Tristan made his dramatic debut in the early months of 1636, had much in common with Pierre Corneille's *Le Cid*, including immediate, resounding, and enduring public success. It is, however, not possible to assume that, had it not been for the helpful publicity generated for *Le Cid* by the offence taken in 1637 by Mairet at Pierre Corneille's publication subsequent to *Le Cid* of his early love poem, and for Georges de Scudéry's desire to curry favour with Richelieu, Tristan's play could have been as famous as Corneille's (see: Pierre Corneille and Mairet). Tristan lacks Corneille's imaginative daring in exploring the possibility that the outstanding merit of love's object can justify a love which clearly transgresses the boundaries of propriety.

Tristan's play was clearly inspired by Mairet's *La Sophonisbe*, with which it shares not only a historical subject, but also the concentration of the action into a few hours, and a tragic intensity. Tristan appears not to have known the treatment of his subject by Ludovico Dolce, whose *Marianna* was published in Venice in 1565, but he clearly did know the *Mariamne* of Hardy, on whose adaptation of the plot Tristan to some extent relies, while replacing the ghost used by Hardy with Hérode's dream at the opening of the play, and much strengthening the play's emotional impact.

The principal source of *La Marianne* is Flavius Josephus, whose *Jewish Antiquities* was the basis for the section "Le Politique malheureux" in the 1624 *La Cour sainte* of the Jesuit Nicolas Caussin, in 1637 briefly the king's confessor, on which Tristan drew, and about which he expresses himself enthusiastically in his avertissement. It is from Caussin that Tristan derives his mixture of jealous cruelty and devouring passion. Tristan's avertissement draws attention to his desire to present what is in effect a psychologically compelling heroization of Herod's actions, creating, as Corneille was notoriously to create in *Rodogune*, a form of moral grandeur which was ethically evil:

> Je me suis efforcé de dépeindre au vif l'humeur de ce Prince sanguinaire, à qui la Nature avait fait assez de grâces pour le rendre un des plus grands hommes de son siècle, s'il n'eût employé ces merveilleux avantages contre sa propre réputation, en corrompant des biens si purs par le débordement d'une cruauté sans exemple, et des autres vices qu'on a remarqués en sa vie... j'ai seulement voulu décrire avec un peu de bienséance les divers sentiments d'un tyran courageux et spirituel, les artifices d'une femme envieuse et vindicative, et la constance d'une Reine dont la vertu méritait un plus favourable destin

> (I have tried to depict vividly the temperament of this bloody prince, whom nature had endowed with enough advantage to make him one of the greatest men of his age, if he had not employed these marvellous favours against his own reputation, corrupting such pure gifts by the excesses of an unexampled cruelty and of the other vices which have been noticed in his life... I wanted only to describe with some propriety the different feelings of a tyrant who was brave and intelligent, the artifices of a woman who was envious and vindictive, and the constancy of a queen whose virtue deserved a kinder fate).

The precise mixture of psychological credibility striven for, the neostoic sentiment, the ethically ambiguous nature of moral heroism, and the heroization of stature is by itself sufficient to situate the play clearly within its period. It is in the interests of psychological realism that Tristan points out how he is turning his back on recent affected Italian models in the depiction of passion. There are 16 characters, all played by three actors in the manner prescribed by Jean de la Taille in the performance fictionally mentioned in Scarron's *Le Roman comique*.

There is a manuscript version of the play which gives precise names to the characters referred to in the printed text only by their functions, like judge, captain, cup-bearer, or prévôt; it incidentally also includes more stage directions than are printed. The play starts with Hérode's awakening after a frightening dream predicting unspecified disasters, a baroque device for announcing the initial situation from which the intrigue sets out. There is some discussion about the vanity of dreams before Hérode, reassured, complains to his brother and sister, Phérore and Salomé, of the reluctance of his wife, Marianne, to return his passion. Both Phérore and Salomé speak ill of Marianne, for whom Hérode sends.

Almost anticipating the usage to be systematized by Racine, Tristan brings in a major character, Marianne, at the beginning of the second act. Marianne cannot love Hérode, a "monstre abominable," responsible for the destruction of her family. Her lady-in-waiting and confidente, Dina, advises her to pretend to love Hérode, and Marianne's sense of personal merit is outraged.

> Moi? que je me contraigne? étant d'une naissance
> Qui peut impunément prendre toute licence,
> Et qui sans abuser de cette autorité,
> Ne règle mes désirs que par l'honnêteté?

> (I? I, force myself? when my birth/Allows me full licence to act as I please with impunity,/And when, without abusing that power,/I govern my desires only in accordance with probity?).

We learn from Marianne that Hérode had once given orders that she should be killed by his servant Soême if he did not return from his interview with Auguste at Rhodes, and she resolves never to see her husband again. Dina sees that Marianne has been overheard by Salomé, with whom Marianne has a scene, including an exchange in stichomythia. Salomé conspires with the cup-bearer that he should go to Hérode to tell him that Marianne had asked him to put a love potion into Hérode's drink so that Hérode should love her more, but that he, the cup-bearer, knowing his master's feelings, thought it appropriate to tell Hérode rather than execute the command. The cup-bearer was obviously to imply that he believed the potion was a poison.

Marianne has come to Hérode as he had commanded, and is now told by him that his thwarted passion for her is turning to rage. He then tells Salomé that his love has turned to hatred. He is informed by the usher that the cup-bearer wishes to see him with news of a plot against him. He summons the queen, and in the third act accuses her of attempting to poison him. Tristan in his "argument" says that she defends herself with more courage than intelligence, but the queen does break down on thinking of her children, as Hérode presses the two judges for the death sentence. Hérode is moved, but Marianne reproaches him with having ordered her execution if he had not returned from Rhodes. Hérode has both Soême and the queen's eunuch executed in spite of their pleas.

In the fourth act Hérode is torn by fear of another attempt by Marianne at his assassination, and by desire for her. While his mind, "troubled by fear and love, hesitates between mercy and justice," Phérore and Salomé urge him to rigour. Marianne shows an example of constancy. Her mother, Alexandra, tells Marianne that her fate serves her right, hoping thereby to exculpate herself from complicity in her daughter's supposed crime. Caussin in particular is outraged, in his account from Josephus, at Alexandra's behaviour. In the fifth act Marianne's death is reported. Hérode changes his mind about the execution too late—

> La constance et l'honneur, comme la piété
> Viennent de rendre l'âme avec cette Beauté

> (Constancy and honour, together with piety/Have just breathed their last along with that beauty).

Hérode faints, becomes demented, stabs himself with the sword of Narbal, the nobleman who narrates Marianne's death and, in a splendid guilt-ridden tirade, curses the Jews. His mind is confused, divided between distress and images of love. He fancies that he sees Marianne's soul ascending to heaven, and faints.

Tristan's "arguments" before each act are as interesting as his script itself. He is in style, in violence of imagery and language, in daring in the psychological authenticity of Hérode's deranged emotional conflict, and in the grandeur of Hérode's jealous cruelty, clearly exhibiting characteristics which can reasonably be referred to as baroque. The arguments make clear what emotions he is trying to depict, what sudden changes of mood, and what conflicts, but the intention rhetorically to move the audience, however effectively executed, went back to La Taille's conception of tragedy of 1572, and the emphasis on Marianne's heroic but neostoic constancy also returned to a system of moral values which had reached the peak of an ascendancy promoted by the religious wars more than a quarter of a century previously. Tristan's language and style are vivid. Rhetorical verse is skilfully and poetically deployed to demonstrate the full power of conflicting and changing passions. But Tristan's poetry is fresher and more imaginatively compelling than his drama, because the values on which the dramatic oeuvre relied were out of date, no longer imaginatively in tune with the needs of a generation which had less than a year to wait for the immensely powerful moral daring of Le Cid.

La Mort de Sénèque was no doubt the first play commissioned by the Molière-Béjart Illustre Théâtre, and was certainly written in response to an invitation from the new association. Néron is a revitalized Hérode. Tristan is relying on Tacitus, Caussin's La Cour sainte again, and the 1637 La Mort et les dernières paroles de Sénèque by Mascaron, the barrister from the parlement de Provence who was the father of the celebrated preacher, Jules de Mascaron. We are again concerned with moral grandeur which is ethically evil, and love, in La Marianne reduced to the crude physical passion, here plays virtually no part at all. Tallemant says that the role of the freed female slave Epicaris was Madeleine Béjart's chef-d'oeuvre. The play, first given at the beginning of 1644, was a success. Tristan placed his next play, La Mort de Chrispe, with the same company, and on 17 September 1644 Gaston d'Orléans, long Tristan's protector, allowed the players to call themselves the "comédiens de Son Altesse Royale." La Mort de Sénèque was dedicated to François Honorat de Beauvilliers, comte, then from 1663 duc, de Saint-Aignan, and published in 1645 with a privilège of 17 October 1644 and an achevé d'imprimer of 10 January 1645.

As the play opens, Néron is rejoicing with Sabine, to whom he is now married, at the death of his repudiated former wife, Octavie. Sabine tries to make Néron suspicious of his former tutor, Sénèque, who, knowing that he is in danger from those who envy him his wealth, offers to return to Néron everything he has been given by him. Néron refuses. In the second act the three conspirators against Néron, Pison, Rufus, captain of the guards, and Sévinus, plot together, and are encouraged by Lucain, Sénèque's nephew, and the freed slave Epicaris. Lucain tries in vain to draw Sénèque into the conspiracy, and Procule, captain of the navy in whom Epicaris has confided, denounces her. In the third act Epicaris is sent to be tortured. Sabine, after a bad dream, warns Néron and presents to him Milicus, an ex-slave of Sévinus, who confirms to Néron the existence of a plot against him. Sévinus is summoned and, confronted with Néron's

suspicions, allays them, but is to be interrogated separately from his conspirator Natalis.

In the fourth act Pison is terrified by what Epicaris will say under torture. Rufus informs him that Sévinus has been arrested. Sévinus is pressed by Rufus in front of Néron to name the other conspirators, and accuses Rufus himself. He gives Néron the list of conspirators in the hope of attracting mercy for himself. Néron has the suspects arrested, and Sabine ensures that Sénèque is included. Sénèque opens the last act with a series of stances. He is offered the choice of death by fire, water, sword or poison. Epicaris dies defiantly, refusing to reveal anything. Sénèque leaves all he has to Néron and has his veins slit in the bath, his wife Pauline being already dead from poison she has taken. Tristan's tragic formula has not changed. His characters still react to extraordinary situations in such a way as to allow them to move the audience to different emotions by extraordinary rhetorical feats. Apart from the irony that it is the freed slave who shows more courage than the Roman conspirators, and except for Pauline's tender insistence on sharing Sénèque's death, the attitudes exhibited are those most admired some decades previously, although now taken to heroic extremes.

Tristan's drama has been compared to that of Rotrou. La Mort de Chrispe draws in 1644 on the plot of Rotrou's 1643 Bélissaire. Tristan's La Folie du sage depends partly on Rotrou's Célie. Behind the plot is a fascination with alchemy. The daughter of a learned father loves a young man, but is loved by a prince. To rid herself of him she takes poison, but recovers. While her father thinks she is dead, he delivers a long tirade cursing learning and books. He then pronounces a singular speech in which he enumerates everything that has to be known for the curing of maladies. When his daughter recovers from the sleeping draught, her father recovers his sanity, the prince withdraws, and she can marry the man she loves.

Le Parasite, Tristan's verse comedy, is also dependent on a Rotrou play, the comedy La Soeur, played in 1645 and published in 1647, although it derives in much greater detail from the 1635 Angelica of Fabricio de Fornaris. Tristan's play, in its turn, was undoubtedly the proximate source for Molière's L'Etourdi. Tristan's Le Parasite was given in the course of 1653, and was published with a privilège of 13 March 1654 signed by Conrart, and an achevé d'imprimer of 19 June. It was dedicated to Charles Albert d'Ailly, duc de Chaulnes, and is structurally very near to being a perfunctory farce on to which is grafted a character representing greed, with a name actually taken from Rabelais, Fripesauces. Lisandre, son of Lucille, is in love with, and at the end of the play marries, Manille's daughter Lucinde. Fripesauces is modelled on the Mastica of the Italian play, a valet, and the comedy ends with the revelation of a long-lost relationship making the denouement possible. Its interest lies primarily in the context of the derivation of French comedy of character from Italian commedia dell'arte (q.v.).

PUBLICATIONS

Collections

Le Théâtre complet de Tristan l'Hermite, 1975
[*La Marianne* and *La Mort de Sénèque* are printed in the second volume of the Bibliothèque de la Pléiade *Théâtre du XVIIe siècle*, 1986]

Poetry

La Mer, 1627
Les Plaintes d'Acante, 1633
Les Amours, 1638
La Lyre, 1641
Vers héroïques, 1648

Plays

La Marianne, tragédie (1636), 1637
Panthée, tragédie (1637), 1639
La Folie du sage, tragi-comédie (?1642), 1645
La Mort de Sénèque, tragédie (1644), 1645
La Mort de Chrispe, tragédie (1644 or 1645), 1645
La Mort du grand Osman, tragédie (1646 or 1647), 1656
Amaryllis, pastorale (1652), 1653
La Parasite, comédie (1653), 1654; modern edition 1934

Fiction

Le Page disgrâcié, 1642; modern edition, 1898

Biographical and critical studies

Bernardin, N.M., *Un Précurseur de Racine. Tristan l'Hermite, sieur du Solier (1601–55), sa famille, sa vie, ses oeuvres*, 1895
Carriat, Amédée, *Tristan; ou, L'Eloge d'un poète*, 1955
Guillumette, Doris, *La Libre Pensée dans l'oeuvre de Tristan l'Hermite*, 1972

TYARD, Pontus de, 1522–1605.

Poet.

LIFE

The biographies of early sixteenth-century poets have normally to be reconstructed from poetic greetings or autobiographical fragments published in their early collections, or else from the haphazard survival of documentary or other evidence. Although he was clearly a literary figure of some importance, very little has been discovered about Tyard. He was named by Ronsard, whom he did not meet before 1575, in each of the lists of seven "premiers et plus excellens (first and most excellent)" poets, headed by himself, referred to by him as the Pléiade (q.v.), and enumerated in the 1553 "Elegie de Jean de la Peruse," the 1555 "Hymne de Henri II," and the definitive list printed by Binet in the 1597 edition of his *Vie de Ronsard*. The pen portrait by de Thou in his *Historiarum sui temporis ... libri* is more extended than that of most of the other poets, although it concentrates chiefly on Tyard's vast size and his huge appetite for books, food, and wine with which, de Thou solemnly notes in a work not intended to purvey gossip, Tyard did not mix water. It also expresses surprise that Tyard, living so heartily, should have slept so well and enjoyed such sound health of mind and body until he was 84.

A cousin of Guillaume des Autels, Tyard was born into the old aristocracy at the family's feudal château at Bissy-sur-Fley, a dozen kilometres from Chalon-sur-Saône. His uncle, a chevalier of the Order of Alcantara, belonged to the household of the Emperor Charles V; his mother, Jeanne de Ganay, was the niece of the chancellor of France; and his father, Jean, seigneur de Bissy, was lieutenant-général of the royal baillage of Mâcon. Tyard was early destined for an ecclesiastical career and we know that he studied in Paris, returning to Burgundy probably in 1537, when he was 16. He was left a canonry in the chapter of Mâcon cathedral in his father's will, and became a protonotary apostolic in 1553 before eventually being made bishop of Chalon by Gregory XIII on 16 June 1578. With the permission of Henri III he resigned his bishopric in favour of his nephew Cyrus on 29 July 1589, and in his later years abandoned his interests in mathematics, philosophy, and literature to give himself to the study of theology.

Tyard's literary career had been concentrated in the period between 1549 and 1555. He was commissioned to compose for the château d'Anet, which Henri II was having built for Diane de Poitiers in 1556, a set of a dozen designs for paintings of mythological rivers, for each of which he also composed an epigrammatic sonnet, making up the *Douze fables de fleuves ou fontaines*. The paintings were probably executed, but later destroyed, perhaps to be replaced in 1698 by the château's famous mirrors. Tyard's text, frequently inspired by the pseudo-Plutarchan *De fluviis* as well as by Ovid, was printed against his will in 1585, when he considered such concerns frivolous, by his admirer Etienne Tabourot. In the 1550s Tyard had published not only verse, but also important works about poetry, music, the calender, and astrology, to be gathered together as half a dozen *Discours philosophiques* in 1587; he also devoted himself to the study of mathematics and philosophy. From 1558 he enjoyed the wealth left by his mother, living the life of a feudal seigneur and country aristocrat at Bissy, and spending much of his time on study.

He was back in Paris towards 1568–69, and again in 1572–73, frequenting the salon of Claude-Catherine de Clermont-Dampierre, the widowed maréchale de Retz, whose husband had been killed at Dreux in 1562. In 1565 she had married again, this time Albert de Gondi, sieur du Perron, from a rich Florentine family with a bank at Lyons, bringing with her as a dowry the Retz property, whose name Gondi took. By 1581 he was a duke and peer. She received in her "salon vert" or "cabinet de Dictynne" poets and musicians as well as the court, its great ladies as well as the young ladies-in-waiting of Catherine de Medici. Pasquier, Belleau, Jodelle, Jamyn, and Desportes, among others, came to her gatherings.

It was this company, in which he must have felt rather old, which encouraged Tyard to take up poetry again. The 1573 *Oeuvres poetiques* may well have been dedicated to Mme de Retz, although the person to whom the dedication is addressed is called a "damoiselle." The second edition of the *Solitaire premier* was certainly dedicated to the comtesse de Retz in 1575, and we know from d'Aubigné that Tyard attended Baïf's Palace Academy, whose Letters Patent date from 1570, as late as 1576, after which there is no further sure record of his presence in Paris. Tyard certainly travelled from time to time, at least once to Dieppe, and probably from time to time to court on the Loire.

Amyot describes Tyard discoursing on the movements of astral bodies to Henri III, who made him a counsellor, and we have a long and amusing letter to him from the humanist lawyer and historian, Etienne Pasquier, of about 1585. Pasquier's letter is mostly about how to get away with plagiarism, the virtue of copying Italian and Spanish authors, and how to pretend you have read books whose covers you have never even set eyes on. From October 1588 to January 1589 Tyard represented the Burgundy clergy at the estates at Blois, where he defended the record and political stance of Henri III.

The 1573 volume of *Oeuvres* was printed not, like the earlier works, at Lyons, but in Paris, and Tyard tells tells us in the dedicatory letter that he had started to write verse some 30 years earlier. There is some confirmatory evidence that he did in fact start writing his *Erreurs amoureuses*, clearly inspired by Scève, in about 1543. We now know that there was a real "Pasithée" at the latest from 1548, but we know of her only that she was then about 18 and married, that she played the lute, danced, and wrote verse, and that her social status was high even for Tyard. When Pasquier later doubted whether good love poetry could be based on an authentic passion, Denys Sauvage wrote to him to tell him how displeased Tyard had been by what he had written. The first volume of the *Erreurs* was published in 1549, followed by a *Continuation* in 1551, and a third part, preceding the *Vers liriques*, was printed in the cumulative collection of 1555 *Erreurs*. The 1573 dedication may be thought to betray a hint of resentment that Tyard's own originality had been challenged by Ronsard and du Bellay at around the time he had first published his verse, however sincere his admiration for them also was, as it was for Scève.

In 1549 Tyard had also started the translation he was to publish in 1552 of the 1535 *Dialoghi d'amore* by Leone Ebreo, derived from Ficino and exceedingly important for its definition of love as an "affection volontaire de jouir avec union de la chose estimee bonne (an affection in the will to enjoy union with something judged to be good)." From that definition, making love in the will dependent on an interpolated judgement of value in the intellect, depends the casuist calculus which served a whole century for the up-grading of instinctive love. Tyard saw very well that, by having recourse to the merit of its object, as perceived in a necessarily intellectual judgement, Ebreo, also translated by Denys Sauvage in 1551, had derived from Ficino a way of indicating how the emotional and passionate basis for love could be made compatible with a moral enrichment which it mediated.

Tyard's views about love, poetry, and music, and his whole exploitation of the Ficinian legacy must owe something to discussions with Scève and later, but only after publication of the *Solitaire premier*, with Jacques Peletier du Mans, who was in Lyons for some years from 1553 and may partially be represented by the Mantice of the two *Curieux* dialogues, as des Autels partially was by "Le Curieux" himself. Judging by the preface to the 1578 edition of *Le premier Curieux* and the manuscript of the manual of rhetoric which Tyard drew up for the king, his duties as counsellor were deemed to have included those appropriate to an academic adviser. It is at any rate plain that Tyard's relationship with Henri III could not endear him to the League, especially powerful in Burgundy. The château de Bissy was in fact sacked by the League in 1591, but Tyard had already left and was staying with his nephew Héliodore near Verdun. He could not get a passport from the League when summoned by Henri IV to Paris for his abjuration of Protestantism in 1593. He spent his final years in his house near Bragny-sur-Saône, working on translations and his religious writings. Héliodore's wife died in 1594, and Héliodore himself in 1595. Tyard wrote epitaphs in French and in Latin, in which language he had also previously published other verse. He died on 23 September 1605, and was buried at Bragny.

WORKS

It is so antecedently probable that a poet in the Petrarchan tradition writing in the 1540s, modelling himself on Scève, borrowing from Tebaldeo, Serafino, and Chariteo, yet remaining faithful to the versification of Marot, Salel, and Saint-Gelais, would be content to write amorous verse of elegant refinement without any real emotional content, that it is comes as a surprise to meet Tyard's insistence on the fleshly reality of his "Pasithée." This name, that of the extra fourth Grace in addition to the traditional three in Gyraldi's 1548 *De deis gentium*, which we know Tyard was using, was commonly given to Catherine de Retz. The name Pasithée, authentically Homeric, is introduced only in the 1552 *Solitaire premier*, and occurs only once in the *Erreurs amoureuses*, but Tyard was insistent, and the poetry occasionally bears out the idea that the three books were addressed to a real woman.

> Amy, dit elle en visage amoureux,
> Je mettray fin à tes jours langoureux,
> Pour commencer tes bien-heureuses nuits

> (Friend, she said looking amorously at him,/I'll put an end to your languishing days,/To start your blissful nights).
> (*Erreurs*, I, 44)

It is at least probable that the attachment celebrated in all three collections of *Erreurs* was to only one woman, and the relationship was the subject of gossip.

As Tyard said in the 1573 dedication, he had not 30 years previously been able to find French poems "respondans à l'elevation de mes passionnées conceptions (corresponding to the intensity of my passionate ideas)," and had had to rely alone on "la force de la beauté qui me commandoit (the strength of the beauty which compelled me)" to "embellir et hausser le stile de mes vers plus que n'estoit celuy, des rimeurs qui m'avoient precedé (embellish and elevate the style of my verse more than that of the rhymers who had gone before me)."

After mentioning Ronsard and du Bellay, Tyard goes on in his dedication to single out Baïf, Belleau, and Jodelle, distinguishing three sorts of poets, those notable for their "docte substance (learned content)," those who are "riches inventeurs, et admirables en l'embellissement de la disposition (rich in invention, and admirable in ornamenting the construction [of their verse])," and those who are "subtils imitateurs (refined imitators)." He shows more tolerance in his classification than du Bellay's intransigent *Deffence et illustration de la langue françoise* had done 24 years earlier. Tyard does in fact use commonplace neoplatonist imagery in a way which keeps him close to Scève, although these are sonnets, not dizains, and poems, not epigrams on an acrostic pattern in a book of emblems, like Scève's *Délie*.

The first approach to Tyard from Ronsard's group came when

du Bellay mentioned him, as a champion against ignorance, in the *Musagnoeomachie* of the end of 1550. Du Bellay was responding to the first edition of the *Erreurs*, in which the sonnet form predominated but was not exclusively employed, as it had been in du Bellay's *L'Olive*. Then in 1551 Tyard, in the opening sonnet of the *Continuation des Erreurs amoureuses* mentions Scève, des Autels, du Bellay, and Ronsard. Ronsard and du Bellay are again mentioned together in Tyard's "Chant en faveur de quelques excellens poëtes de ce tems" from the same collection, and Tyard's compliments are acknowledged by Ronsard in sonnet lxxiii of the 1552 *Amours*. In 1553 Tyard's name is in the list of seven poets in the "Elégie à Jean de la Peruse," and early in 1552 du Bellay had already set out to rival Tyard in his *XIII Sonnets de l'honneste amour*, published with the translation of the fourth book of the *Aeneid*. From the *Continuation* there is a move markedly nearer to Ronsard, too, as Tyard began to draw heavily on the mythology he absorbed from Gyraldi.

Technically the poems of the first *Erreurs*, all devoted to love, are interesting for the particular features of the Petrarchan tradition which they exploit and the range of emotions—fear, hope, frustration, and jealousy—on which they draw. They are notable also for the adoption of Marot's sonnet form, for the techniques of the blason and those from the rhétoriqueurs which they employ, the frequent allusions to other arts—especially significant in the light of the theoretical links which Tyard envisaged between them—and an apparent weakness in sustaining images and tensions for the length of a sonnet. It is important that, however philosophically audacious the Platonism of the prose works, even if the register is still partly imaginative, the love poetry steps back from Héroët in separating the beatifying love between human beings from emotional or physical entanglements. The first *Erreurs* ends with a "chant de chaste amour," which, perhaps perfunctorily, keeps the two loves apart:

Noz deux esprits d'une complexion,
Sont eslongnez de toute passion,
   Passion qui tourmente:
Vivans ainsi en ce mortel sejour
Avec espoir, qu'au Ciel leur grande amour
   Sera du tout contente

(Our two minds with a single feeling,/Are distant from all passion,/Passion which tortures:/Thus living in this mortal realm/With the hope that in heaven their great love/Will be wholly bliss). (Lines 127–132)

The 1551 *La Continuation des Erreurs* starts with a poetic allusion to the opening of du Bellay's *L'Olive*, and the second sonnet of du Bellay's *Les Regrets* will take up the mythological allusions in the second sonnet of Tyard's *Continuation*. The *Continuation* also takes up primarily from Ronsard the idea that the poet confers immortality on the person loved,

Si ne dois-tu despriser la louange,
Que tu reçois de moy: car l'escriture
Plus que beauté mortelle, beaucoup dure

(So you should not despise the praise/Which you receive from me, for the written word/Lasts long; longer than mortal beauty). (II, ix)

The myths chosen by Tyard are not the best-known ones, but are

employed to transmit enduring status to fleeting moments of actual enchantment or distress. Singing becomes important for Tyard because it unites music and poetry. Natural settings begin to appear in the verse, as do objects belonging to, or physically enhanced by the touch of, the loved one. The 1555 third part of the *Erreurs* has an almost elegiac tone, with that part of the material in the *Vers liriques* which is new being a collection of odes covering a deliberately wide range of subjects and tones. In seeking inspiration above all from Horace and Propertius, these odes follow much more clearly the work of Ronsard and du Bellay than anything by Tyard which had preceded them. Tyard stays too close to his early Platonism to follow Horace and Ronsard in their poetic advice to take advantage of the sensual delights offered by the passing present.

Les Nouvell' Oeuvres poétiques of 1573 contains some material which probably dates from the mid-1550s. Tyard starts, however, with a sonnet announcing that he is no longer singing the praises of his "premiere beauté (first beauty)," who had no difficulty in wounding his heart when he was still young, but has now found a new perfection. The mythology is now less obscure. Tyard uses terza rima, and he includes an "Elégie à Pierre de Ronsard," which appears to date from some time previously.

It is, however, for his prose works that Tyard is chiefly of importance in the history of literature. He builds in them a philosophical structure which appears rationally, or at any rate imaginatively, to justify and link all artistic, scientific, and speculative intellectual endeavour. The framework is generally Ficinian, and the later texts have much in common with the views of Jacques Peletier du Mans, especially as put forward in his celebrated lecture at Poitiers in 1579.

The 1552 *Solitaire Premier; ou, Prose des Muses, et de la fureur poetique* was on its first appearance dedicated to the "doctes, gentilz et gracieux espritz françois (learned, noble, and refined minds of France)," and in 1575 to the comtesse de Retz. It contains ten numbered sections. It is of the greatest interest for the establishment of an intellectual framework linking all the arts and sciences, its importance lying not in the stringency of the argument but in the imaginative thrust of the endeavour. Man is weak, ignorant, and needy, but distinguished from the beasts nonetheless by "la providence, la raison, et l'entendement (foresight, reason, and understanding)." Some men have lodged their supreme good, the "souverain bien," in earthly benefits, while others have put it in the enjoyment ("jouissance") of eternal light, raising aloft their reason, like the stoics, trying to apprehend the immutable angelic essence, like Anaxagoras, or, like Plato and Pythagoras, seeking their good in the source of goodness, beauty, and wisdom, the unique divine sun. Through human knowledge, that is the sciences, are provided the steps for the acquisition of the knowledge of divine things and the object of eternal joy.

Already, in this first section, the study of the sciences has been elevated from an inquiry into the causes of events to the ladder of knowledge leading to the knowledge of God in which, for the more intellectualist tradition of scholastics, but also for Ebreo's intellectualist interpretation of Ficinian Platonism, human beatitude consisted. "Travail littéraire (the study of letters)" can therefore be undertaken for the love of virtue, whether it concerns itself with the individual sciences or with the "spherique Enciclopedie," the circle of disciplines mentioned by Quintilian, Martianus Capella and Vitruvius, and in the renaissance among others by Budé, Melanchthon, Nizolio, Guy Le Fèvre de la Boderie, Scève, and, Tyard's certain direct source, Gyraldi, drawing on Martianus Capella and Vitruvius. In the château of Ancy-le-Franc, built from about 1546, the circular organization of the disciplines is depicted through the symbolism of Apollo, the Muses, and the Graces, of whom the additional fourth, Pasithée, symbol for Pontus of the union of poetry and music, appears to encompass all the rest.

In the second section the solitaire is sent into ecstasy by the sound of Pasithée harmonizing her voice to the strings of a lute, and singing an ode in French. The humanistic significance of the ode had become clear with Ronsard's 1549 volume, and the importance of the vernacular in du Bellay's *Deffence et illustration* of the same year. The union of music and poetry was another important Pléiade theme, to be explained notably by Peletier du Mans in terms of the numerical ratios underlying measures, quantitative verse, and the division of the octave into chords, as well as the mathematics of planetary orbits and the harmony of the spheres. The four principal aspects of Pasithée's activity—measured verse, its harmonization to chords, the ode, and the vernacular—enhance one another's significance. Tyard is creating a semi-mythological structure intended to emphasize the moral and spiritual significance of the intellectual and artistic activities which he mentions, but into which others can also be inserted.

The second section leads to what is virtually a lecture to Pasithée by the solitaire, in which he distinguishes in an already traditional renaissance way between the two sorts of "alienation," that proceeding from illness or madness, and that

engendrée d'une secrette puissance divine, par laquelle l'ame raisonnable est illustrée: et la nommons, fureur divine, ou, avec les Grecs, Enthusiasme

(engendered by a secret divine power by which the rational soul is illuminated, and which we call divine fury or, with the Greeks, enthusiasm).

This is one of the four divine furies or frenzies by which the soul is elevated to the ecstatic contemplation of God in Ficino's celebrated *In Platonis de amore Symposium commentarium*, the *De amore*.

Ficino's "Platonism" is in fact structurally more dependent on Plotinus than on Plato. The fiction is that God, who is one, is immanent in his creation in concentric circles, those of angels, who are minds without bodies, of men, of irrational animals, and of brute matter. Human beings themselves seek, with the help of one or more of the four furies, to reacquire their own unity, fractured in the present state of the cosmos, and thereby acquire the beatifying union with God. The erotic fury, in particular, raises the soul from physical attraction to the body of the beloved, through love of the mind, then of the angelic idea of truth itself, culminating in the knowledge of God which confers on the soul beatification and reunification.

Ficino himself allowed the compatibility of physical love on earth with the culmination of the morally perfective ascent of love to its divine object. Most of his immediate successors, including Ebreo and Castiglione, were not so audacious. The intellectual scaffolding was nonetheless in place for the up-grading of instinctive love, already at Tyard's date clear in Héroët and Marguerite d'Angoulême, as well as for perspectives

inside which study, contemplation, and the cultivation of any of the arts were given a moral dimension. Tyard does not achieve perfect internal coherence for the intellectual structure any more than Ficino had, but the point of the immensely powerful myth is quite clear. The third section starts:

Les Philosophes Platoniques tiennent que l'ame descendant en ce corps distribuée en diverses operations perd l'unité tant estimée, qui la rendoit cognoissante, et jouissante du souverain *Un*, qui est Dieu: tellement qu'en ceste division, et separation de son unité, ses parties superieures endormies, et ensevelies en une lente paresse, cedent l'entier gouvernement aux inferieures touchées sans cesse des perturbations: et ainsi demeure tout l'ame remplie de discordes, et desordres difficiles à rapointer. Aussi c'est là, où gist l'oeuvre: c'est là, où consiste le labeur à tirer l'ame embourbée hors de la fange terrestre, et l'eslever en la conjonction du souverain *Un*, à fin qu'elle mesme soit remise en sa première unité. Or, pource que l'ame en descendant, et s'abismant dans le corps, passe par quatre degrez, il est pareillement necessaire, que par quatre degrez son elevation de ça bas en haut, soit faite. Quant aux quatre degrez de la descente, le premier, et plus haut, est l'Angelique entendement, le second la Raison intellectuelle, le tiers l'Opinion, et le quart la Nature

(The Platonic philosophers hold that the soul, descending into the body, is distributed between different operations [and] loses the much prized unity which allowed it to know and enjoy the sovereign *One*, which is God: so that, in this division and diffusion of its unity, its higher parts, asleep and buried in a slow indolence, yield the whole direction to the lower parts, that are subject to the ceaseless promptings of the passions: so the whole soul remains filled with discords and disorders difficult to repair. So it is there that the work lies: it is in that that the labour consists: in lifting the embedded soul out of the earthly mud and raising it to unification with the sovereign *One*, so that it should itself be restored to its former unity. But, because in its descent and sinking into the body, the soul passes through four steps, it is similarly necessary that by four steps its elevation to high from low should be accomplished. As to the four degrees of the descent, the first, and highest, is angelic intelligence, the second rational intellect, the third opinion, and the fourth nature).

The four steps in Ficino's Latin were "mens," "anima", "natura," and "materia." In the *Solitaire Premier* the single means available to the soul to make its ascent back to unity, and to union with God, is the "fureur divine" (divine fury)." Pasithée, the solitaire informs us, was still agog after he had given a lengthy disquisition on the four steps, which are also the concentric circles of creation and divine immanence. He continues:

En quatre sortes peut l'homme estre espris de divine fureur. La premiere est par la fureur Poëtique procedant du don des Muses. La second est par l'intelligence des mysteres, et secrets des religions souz Bacchus. La troisiesme est par ravissement de prophetie, vaticination, ou divination souz Apollon: et la quatriesme par la violence de l'amoureuse affection souz Amour et Venus

(The human being can be possessed in four ways by the divine fury. The first is by the poetic fury proceeding from the gift of the Muses. The second by the understanding of the mysteries and secrets of religions under Bacchus. The third by the ecstasy of prophecy, fore-telling, or divination, under Apollo: and the fourth by the violence of amorous affection under Love and Venus).

Apart from the substitution of Bacchus for Dionysus, this passage is a straight translation from Ficino's *De amore*. These four furies are each capable of taking us through the four steps, leading through a knowledge of the disciplines and the practice of the virtues to beatitude, unity, and the knowledge of God. The solitaire goes on to expound in greater detail the action of poetry and music in restoring harmony to the soul, in which dissonant discords are driven out by harmonious chords, introducing a "certaine egalité bien et proportionnément mesurée (certain equality well and proportionately measured)." The solitaire goes on to show Pasithée how each of the furies achieves its effect.

The fourth section of the *Solitaire Premier* starts by again following Ficino, although on poetic inspiration it later follows Ronsard, and not du Bellay (in the third chapter of book II of the *Deffence*), on the primacy of inspiration over art. Tyard, also an outspoken advocate of the vernacular, here makes his solitaire proscribe translation, gives an account of the history of poetry and of the names of the Muses, and discusses the principal musical chords. In a long commentary on the traditional three Graces, their names, and the way they are depicted naked, Pasithée turns out by implication to be herself the fourth Grace. Much of the rest of the text consists in a learned disquisition on mythology, ending in the tenth section with a poem and an encomium of poetry, especially when supported by music.

Music is the subject of the *Solitaire Second; ou, Discours de la musique*, also first published in 1552. The *Solitaire Premier* had been virtually a dialogue between the solitaire and Pasithée. The second dialogue introduces the character of Le Curieux. We are given the usual renaissance list of the remarkable effects achieved by music. It is now clear, if only from the passages quoted, how music, like poetry, leads to virtue. The mutual reinforcement of the two was by now a commonplace, derived from both Plato and Plutarch, and its promotion was the purpose of Baïf's academy, the precursor of the Palace Academy founded by Henri III, but the relationship between the basic chords, the notes appropriate to the elements, and the to us inaudible music of the spheres is worked out by Tyard with great ingenuity. Earth, water, air, and fire are related like the notes of a major chord.

In 1556 Tyard published the *Discours de temps, de l'an, et de ses parties*, again drawing on a treatise of Gyraldi. In 1557 appeared *L'Univers; ou, Discours des parties et de la nature du Monde*, which brings in the character of Le Curieux alongside Hieromnime, the theologian, and the solitaire, who always speaks in the first person. The text is devoted to the praise of science, notably astronomy, but also physics and metereology, sometimes in distinctly poetic prose. In 1578 Tyard split the text into the two dialogues, *Le premier Curieux* and *Le second Curieux*. The prologue to the second dialogue contains Tyard's strongest piece on the vernacular, and there is an important preface by Jacques Davy du Perron. In 1558 came Tyard's final dialogue, *Mantice; ou, Discours de la vérité de divination par astrologie*. Mantice is the advocate of divination, with the author and Le Curieux as the other characters.

The *Curieux* dialogues attempt a synthesis of all scientific and of all religious knowledge. Like the other philosophical prose works, they are fascinating not only for their ingenuity, and for what they tell us about how it was possible to look on the world in 16th-century France, but chiefly because of their huge imaginative thrust towards a synthesis which would serve also as a basis for a moral and orthodoxly religious view of human activity, heavily underlining the importance of all artistic, scientific, and speculative activity. Tyard may not be a great philosopher, although without his idea of a possible unification of the disciplines there could have been no Descartes, but he was a writer of imaginative prose works of the greatest cultural if not exactly literary importance.

PUBLICATIONS

Collections

Les Nouvell' Oeuvres poetiques, 1573
Les Discours philosophiques, 1587
Oeuvres poétiques complètes, 1966
Les Oeuvres poétiques, 1875

Verse

Erreurs amoureuses, 1549
Continuation des Erreurs amoureuses, 1551
Erreurs amoureuses, augmentées d'une tierce partie. Plus un livre de vers liriques, 1555
Erreurs amoureuses, 1967
Douze fables de fleuves ou fontaines, 1586
Tumuli duo, 1594

Other

Leon Hebrieu de l'amour, 1552
Solitaire Premier; ou, Prose des Muses, et de la fureur poetique, plus quelques vers lyriques, 1552; edition critique 1950
Solitaire Second; ou, Discours de la musique, 1552
Discours du temps, de l'an et de ses parties, 1556
L'Univers; ou, Discours des parties de la nature du Monde, 1557; as *The Universe*, 1950
Mantice; ou, Discours de la verité de divination par astrologie, 1558
Ephemerides octavae spherae, 1562
Homilies sur l'oraison dominicale, 1585
Homilies sur la première table du Decalogue, 1588
Extrait de la genealogie de Hugues surnommé Capet, roy de France, 1594
De recta nominum impositione, 1603
Maximes d'estat tirées d'Aristeas et d'Agapet, 1604

Biographical and critical studies

Chamard, Henri, *Histoire de la Pléiade*, 4 vols., 1939–40
Yates, Frances A., *The French Academies of the Sixteenth Century*, 1947
Hall, Kathleen M., *Pontus de Tyard and his "Discours philosophiques,"* 1963
Lapp, J., Introduction to the *Oeuvres poétiques complètes*, 1966

U

URFÉ, Honoré d', ?1568–1625.

Novelist, moralist, and poet.

LIFE

D'Urfé is a still under-valued writer of enormous imaginative power whose importance derives not, as has been thought, from his development of the pastoral or his place in the history of the novel, but from the exceptional intensity with which he examined a quite new vision of human potential. He was a witness of the process by which the gloomy neostoicism of French cultural attitudes during the religious wars gave way to the exuberant and sometimes even light-headed optimism about human nature which swept like a tidal wave through roughly the first quarter of the 17th century, the period which can reasonably be regarded as lying at the heart of French "baroque."

His achievement, to which the establishment of the pastoral in France and d'Urfé's place in the development of the novel from a simple collection of *contes* was scarcely more than incidental, was to undertake a thorough imaginative exploration of the morally enriching capacities of human affective relationships and the possibility of some congruence between an affection which was erotically satisfying and one which was spiritually fulfilling. For it to be properly understood, d'Urfé's literary attainment needs to be compared with the parallel developments accomplished by François de Sales in spirituality and Descartes in philosophy. The work of all three authors is based on an exhilarating confidence in human nature undreamt of even at the height of the renaissance in France, and simply unthinkable during the blood-letting of the religious wars.

Reaction was to set in as early as the 1620s in the spirituality of Condren and Bérulle at the Oratory, at first unimportantly, but then spreading to the theological neoplatonism of Gibieuf, the form of Augustinianism specific to the Jansenists (q.v.), and the spirituality of Saint-Cyran and Port-Royal (q.v.). Nonetheless d'Urfé's great novel, the *Astrée*, is the monument to the confidence and hope which permeated French cultural activity from the end of the religious wars, through the period of the ascendancy of Mme de Rambouillet (see: *Guirlande de Julie*) and Pierre Corneille's great plays, to Descartes's commitment to the view that the achievement of personal happiness could be engineered by a proper understanding of ethics, which presaged the general victory in the 18th century of the belief in human perfectibility and in the possibility of social progress.

D'Urfé's life covered the crucial years of cultural change, from his young manhood during the religious wars until his death at a moment when, even if it was already undermined, cultural optimism had not yet reached its first major peak. He was baptized at Marseilles on 11 February, and must have been born on that day or the day before. The certificate is dated 1567 but, since d'Urfé later claimed to have been 26 on 1 October 1594, it should be regarded as probable that the certificate's date is given in the "old style," according to which the new year 1568, would start only at Easter. He was the fifth of six boys from a family of 12 born into an ancient and aristocratic family of soldiers, diplomats, and administrators. The family, of remote but perhaps 12th-century Germanic origin, had established itself in a mountain château between Feurs and Montbrison in the Forez, in the upper Loire valley about 60 kilometres west of Lyons; Jean d'Urfé is said to have been murdered there by his servants in about 1418. In the 15th century the family took over the château de la Bastie, in the nearby Lignon valley, which they eventually transformed into an elegant renaissance villa with a loggia wing in the Italian style associated with d'Urfé's grandfather, Claude.

The office of *bailli de Forez* which became hereditary in the family was first held by an ancestor named Guichard in 1410. His son, Pierre I, was grandmaster of the crossbowmen of France and died in 1444. Guichard's grandson, Pierre II, was a distinguished brigand who, having been an enemy of Louis XI, grand écuyer of France under Charles VIII, knight, counsellor, royal chamberlain, sénéchal of Beaucaire and Nîmes, and bailli of the Forez, finally died at La Bastie on 10 October 1508 more piously than he had lived. His son, Claude, was the family's first diplomat, serving as ambassador of François I to Rome from 1549 to 1553 and to the Council of Trent when it moved to Bologna. He was a member of the privy council of Henri II, governor of his children, and designated by him on 15 August 1553 to be part of Catherine de Medici's council of regency. He amassed a huge collection of 4,600 books, including 200 vellum manuscripts. D'Urfé's own father, Jacques, Claude's son, took a lesser part in the affairs of the kingdom, but was nonetheless counsellor of state, royal chamberlain, and bailli and lieutenant-general of the Forez. At the outbreak of the religious wars 800 people were massacred at Montbrison as early as 14 and 15 July 1562. Jacques d'Urfé defended the Forez in the Catholic interest and in 1570 prevented Coligny from crossing the Loire.

D'Urfé's father was to die on 23 October 1574, 20 years after his marriage to Renée de Savoie-Tende, a member of the house of Savoy and descended from the Lascaris of Constantinople. A woman of extraordinary vigour, she wrested power in the comté de Tende from her uncle and did not avoid brutality in establishing her dominion. She was responsible for that part of the Italianate culture acquired by her husband and inherited by her children which her husband had not already acquired from his father. Of her six male children, one died young. Anne was born in 1555, wrote verse from his early youth, composed a collection of 140 sonnets in 1572, was a member of a group of Forez poets surrounding Loys Papon and his two brothers, to which Etienne du Tronchet, Antoine du Verdier, and Jean du Crozet also belonged, and was to publish a book of hymns in 1608.

Anne d'Urfé visited Italy, was heavily influenced by contemporary Italian literature, as his grandfather had been, and became bailli and lieutenant-general of the Forez. His marriage contract with Diane de Châteaumorand, born on 30 November 1561, was signed on 22 October 1571, although the wedding was deferred for three or four years on account of the bride's youth. The marriage was to be formally annulled in 1598. In 1600 Diane de Châteaumorand was to marry d'Urfé, whose sister-in-law she would once have have been if her marriage had ever been valid. There is a tradition among historians, but no evidence, that d'Urfé had been more or less in love with Diane, whom he had naturally regarded as his brother's wife, since shortly after he had left school. She was a rich only child, brought up a Protestant. She became a Catholic before, or shortly after her wedding to Anne d'Urfé, although the contract catered for the difference of religion.

When Anne d'Urfé took orders he was succeeded at La Bastie by his brother Jacques. Christophe, seigneur de Bussy, comte de Pont-de-Veyle and Châtillon, died before 2 December 1597 in the service of the duc de Savoie. D'Urfé's only younger brother, Antoine, acquired a reputation for learning "comme vray filz ayné de l'Anciclopédie (as a true elder son of the encyclopedia)," became prior of Montverdun, abbot of Chaise-Dieu, and bishop elect of Saint-Flour. He published a Platonist dialogue on honour in 1592 and a second dialogue on valour in the same year. He was killed by mistake at the age of 23, by one of his brother Honoré's troops outside Villerêt on 1 October 1594.

D'Urfé was at first brought up by a family tutor at home. The family, although wealthy, had debts, and it was decided that d'Urfé should become a knight of Malta and his brother Antoine an ecclesiastic. D'Urfé's mother insisted that he should take his vows and wear the habit from the canonically irregular age of 13, although the required proofs of nobility appear to have been furnished only a decade later. The profession made little difference to the way he was living, and like at least two of his brothers, d'Urfé attended the recently established and heavily endowed Collège de Tournon, founded by the cardinal of Tournon and approved by François I in 1542, made into a university in 1552, and given to the newly founded Jesuit order to run in 1561.

About half the 1,500 pupils were noble, but they included substantial numbers of students who were poor, Protestant, or foreign. D'Urfé must have attended from about 1577 to 1583 or 1584 and when, on 24 April 1583, Madeleine de la Rochefoucauld, recently married to Just-Louis de Tournon, the founder's nephew, made a triumphal entry into the city, the Jesuits, displeased by accounts of the occasion which failed in their view to do justice to the college, gave d'Urfé the task of writing something more adequate. The dedication to the bridegroom of the 130-page volume, signed "Honoré d'Urfé, chevalier de Malte," is dated 2 July 1583. The enthusiastic and unreliable Jean-Pierre Camus, when bishop of Belley, noted in L'Esprit du bienheureux François de Sales that d'Urfé had acquired, with Latin and Greek, a knowledge of German, Italian, and Spanish.

It seems probable that d'Urfé had written the "Moresque," or comedy involving Moors, of which La triomphante entrée gives an account. We know from Jean du Crozet's 1593 La Philocalie, mainly a series of dialogues on love with interpolated poems and contes, whose first book was dedicated to d'Urfé, with the second to Anne's wife, Diane de Châteaumorand, that its author had already seen a sketch for the Astrée which seems to have inspired his own work, itself probably written after the 1590

siege of Espaly but before that of 1591. Since d'Urfé was also fighting continuously for the League from 1589, it is most likely that it was during the period more or less immediately after his return from school to La Bastie that he wrote the sketch. Patru, whose account is shot through with demonstrable inaccuracies, claims not altogether implausibly to have had it on d'Urfé's own authority that d'Urfé spent "several years" in Malta at what can only have been this period.

It was in 1584 that the death of the duc d'Anjou, on 10 June, made Henri de Navarre, a Protestant, the legitimate heir to the French throne. The Catholic League, founded by the duc de Guise in 1576 and strongest in Picardy, suddenly took on a quite different order of importance, especially when Sixtus V, on the papal throne since the spring of 1585, finally issued a bull on 9 September 1585 declaring Navarre and Condé incapable of succeeding to the throne and releasing all their vassals from their allegiance. In 1587, retreating Huguenot forces under Châtillon crossed part of the Forez. The king left Paris to the League in 1588, and in December had the duc and cardinal de Guise murdered. On 5 January 1589 Catherine de Medici died, and every important town in France outside the lower Loire valley, except only Caen and Bordeaux, declared itself for the League; Lyons, which began to behave like an independent state, declared itself on 24 February, and the Forez swiftly followed, its noble families solid in their support.

From 1587 Anne d'Urfé had played a leading part in directing the military effort of the Forez League, on whose behalf d'Urfé himself for a time held Saint-Etienne. D'Urfé was committed to the duc de Nemours, who raised troops and money for the League but behaved like an independent prince. D'Urfé had to surrender Saint-Etienne to the king's troops on 6 May 1590, and pillaged the château of Essalois, near Saint-Etienne, brutally enough to draw down on himself later a civil claim, although what was alleged was only damage to the furniture. By then enough amnesties had been ganted to make the whole case futile, and d'Urfé was in due course acquitted. In both 1590 and 1591 the château d'Espaly, near Le Puy, had held out against the League, and d'Urfé probably took part with his brother in both sieges. After the final capitulation most of the defenders were massacred, and on 25 September d'Urfé was rewarded by Nemours with the lordship of Châtelard.

In December 1592, after a year of relative calm, Nemours took over Montbrison from Anne d'Urfé's troops. He was encircling Lyons to take it for himself. Lyons, still behind the League but by now opposed to Nemours, erected barricades against him and imprisoned him on 18 September 1593. Anne d'Urfé, however, had already deserted his cause and was finally to rally to Henri IV; he was made governor of the Forez by the Lyons authorities in 1594. D'Urfé himself had seemed to follow the predominating sentiment at Lyons, although less committedly than his brother, but when, on 26 July 1594, Nemours escaped, d'Urfé joined him. On 30 September 1594 Nemours made him lieutenant-general of the government of the Forez. It was in consequence of d'Urfé's subsequent military activities that his young brother Antoine was shot by mistake by one of d'Urfé's men, and that his elder brother Anne withdrew from military activity, not without feeling embittered towards the king, who had failed to reward or support him.

On 16 February 1595 d'Urfé was taken prisoner at Feurs. What happened next is unclear, but he was released on the payment or promise of a ransom by Diane de Châteaumorand, borrowed by his brother Jacques, to be deducted from d'Urfé's patrimony on his marriage. Whatever they were, the financial arrangements were not entirely disentangled when, after Nemours's mysterious illness and his death at Annecy on 15 August, at which d'Urfé was present, d'Urfé was again taken prisoner in what must have been a last-ditch military action at Montbrison. From his second imprisonment, only six weeks after Nemours's death, he signed the first book of his *Epistres morales* on 24 September 1595. It was to be published only in 1598. D'Urfé himself blurs together his two imprisonments, tells us that each was the result of a betrayal, one by enemies, and one by false friends, and that the second imprisonment had not awaited the entire resolution ("issuë") of the first one, athough it must have entailed a physical release.

He was released for the second time early in 1596. Feeling too compromised to stay in France, he bought the small property of Senoy, near Virieu-le-Grand, on Savoy territory, and based himself there until his marriage. He had been defeated and impoverished, and his hopes of a military or political career had been destroyed. His protector was dead, he was obliged to live in exile, had acquired the reputation of an adventurer, and was thought foolish or worse by family and friends. He continued to fight in 1597 and 1598, now for the duc de Savoie, against the royal army under Créquy. On 24 November 1596 he had finished his pastoral poem *Le Sireine*, started soon after he had left school and very largely derived from Montemayor's pastoral novel *Diana*, published in 1559 and in French translation in 1578. By 25 August, he had finished the first book of his epic poem *La Savoysiade*. It is probably during the period shortly after his second release from prison that d'Urfé wrote most of the religious poems published, perhaps without his permission, in a 1618 edition of *Le Sireine*, of whose first edition, probably between 1600 and 1604, we have no record. The first known edition is dated 1606, and the poem became a popular success only in the wake of the first volume of the *Astrée*, published in 1607.

Whatever may have been the earlier emotional relationship between d'Urfé and his sister-in-law, if any, in 1597 Diane de Châteaumorand applied to Clement VIII for the annulment of her marriage to Anne d'Urfé on the grounds of her husband's impotence. The pope referred the matter to the archbishop of Lyons by a rescript of 5 January 1598. Evidence was taken, a number of witnesses questioned, and the decree of nullity granted on 18 May 1599. On 28 May 1599 the d'Urfé brothers split their patrimony in view of d'Urfé's own proximate marriage to Diane. The complex arrangements involved liquidating the ransom paid earlier and the accompanying mortgage on La Bastie. D'Urfé acquired Virieu and a house at Châteauneuf. The humiliated Anne, his marriage declared invalid, retired to ecclesiastical life, saying his first Mass on 29 September 1603, and was content to be dean of Montbrison until 1611, then prior of Montverdun and canon of Lyons until his death on 23 June 1621. In 1608 he published a volume of hymns.

D'Urfé, who had had the necessary papal rescript since 1592, on 28 June 1599 obtained a dispensation from his solemn vows of poverty and chastity in the order of Malta, on the dual grounds that his mother had forced him to make them and that he had made them before the canonical age of 16. He married Diane at Châteaumorand on 15 February 1600. No relations signed the contract, only the necessary witnesses. The d'Urfés must have felt that Diane had dishonoured them, the Châteaumorands presumably that it was they who had been dishonoured

by the d'Urfés. In the 17th century it was thought by Huet, and in the 18th by others, too, not necessarily mistakenly, that d'Urfé had married Diane so that the property she had brought with her should remain in d'Urfé hands.

The matter is not unimportant when one tries to discount the effect of d'Urfé's personal experience in the attempt to evaluate the power and intensity of his imaginative vision. His affairs took such a pronounced turn for the better at the turn of the century, and there are in the *Astrée* so many wisps of the certain recollection of youthful happiness, probable reminiscences of young love, possible allusions to real people, places, and events, and perhaps fictionalized autobiography, that it is tempting to play down the imaginative achievement. What analysis of the text reveals might have to be understood partly in autobiographical terms. Literary historians, until recently too inclined to write off the novel's eroticism as merely playful and its flamboyant imaginative euphoria as insufficiently austere, have been reluctant to believe in its simple audacity. Its overwhelming imaginative energy is not entirely surprising when seen against the background of the energetic personal and military career.

By the treaty of Lyons on 17 January 1601, Virieu was reincorporated into France. D'Urfé now lived at Virieu and at Châteaumorand, not quite a kilometre from Saint-Martind'Estreaux, which was on the royal route from Paris to Lyons, at the northern tip of the Forez, on the knife edge separating the north of France from the south by custom, law, and language; in principle, from Saint-Martin d'Estreaux to the south written Roman law obtained, instead of the customary law to the north. The Forez itself and its river, the Lignon, now became for d'Urfé merely the setting for the novel. Slowly he renewed relations with the French court, but without breaking with Savoy. In the capital, Turin, Charles-Emmanuel, duc de Savoie, came to rely on him.

When Biron was executed in July 1602, the duc de Savoie was still, as a matter of fact rightly, suspected of unadmitted complicity in his plot, and d'Urfé's arrest was ordered. He was away, was obliged to present himself at Lyons, and probably had to go to Paris to clear himself, but by 1603 the former adherents of the League were returning to favour. D'Urfé generously guaranteed the payment of a debt for which the owner of a neighbouring château in the Forez was imprisoned in the Conciergerie, was soon made a gentilhomme ordinaire du roi, little more than a declaration that public disgrace was withdrawn, and in 1603 the second volume of the *Epistres morales* was published together with a new printing of the first volume, no longer at Lyons but at Paris. During the next decade d'Urfé became an important channel through which Henri IV and the duc de Savoie could communicate.

During a grievous illness, probably in 1597 during his first withdrawal to Savoy, d'Urfé had confided the manuscript of the first book of the *Epistres morales* to the celebrated lawyer and close friend of François de Sales, Antoine Favre, who dedicated the volume to the duc de Savoie on 6 April 1598. The third volume would first appear, together with the other two, in Paris in 1608. While the first volume, written during the religious wars and in prison, is conventionally neostoic, the 1603 volume, largely written by 1597, while still largely devoted to the uses of adversity, already contains a defence of the passions and suggests the discreet but certain inspiration of the Florentine neoplatonism of Ficino, while the third volume openly embraces the Ficinian view of love. When based on beauty and goodness, love cannot be sinful, and necessarily leads to self-transcendence.

By the end of 1603 d'Urfé had returned to Châteaumorand, where he stayed for over two years. He almost completed *La Savoysiade*, the heroic poem about Savoy's mythical founder, Bérold, whose first book was finished at Senoy on 25 August 1599, and whose last and ninth book was finalized at Virieu on 29 August 1606. Copying of the complete manuscript was finished on 29 December. Whether because he realized that the poem had not succeeded, or because publication had become politically inexpedient after the renewed relationship with Henri IV and the French court, d'Urfé did not publish *La Savoysiade*, although a section of the second book was to appear in the 1609 *Nouveau recueil des plus beaux vers de ce temps*, probably included without his knowledge.

At this time d'Urfé was also writing the third volume of the *Epistres morales* and the first volume of the *Astrée*. D'Urfé and Diane went on pilgrimage to Loreto. In all but name they had adopted as their own Eléonore de Calvacque, the daughter of d'Urfé's sister Madeleine, whose marriage contract with Diane's cousin, Pierre Lelong, seigneur de Chenillac, was dated at Châteaumorand on 25 June 1605. D'Urfé and his wife then consented to found a college "for the advancement and propagation of the Catholic, apostolic, and Roman religion" at Moulins, to be entrusted to the Jesuits, recalled to France in September 1603 after their brief expulsion. The project appears to have come to nothing on account of Diane's insistence that the institution should be known as the "Collège de Châteaumorand." From 1606, d'Urfé was also for at least a few months a member of the "Académie Florimontane" founded at Annecy as an assembly of scholars and creative artists by François de Sales, whom d'Urfé knew well. The purpose was literary and scientific study, and the first president was Antoine Favre, to whom d'Urfé was much closer than to François de Sales. It is unlikely that the academy survived by long Favre's move to Chambéry in July 1610.

From now on d'Urfé left his wife alone at Châteaumorand for increasingly long periods, while he himself, certainly from about 1614, in the immediate aftermath of a somewhat laughable quarrel between Diane and Saint-Géran, governor of the Bourbonnais, preferred to live at Virieu, although often writing to and sometimes spending a whole season with her. They were together in Paris from the autumn of 1605 until the end of 1606, when Diane may have accompanied d'Urfé to Virieu, where he spent that winter. In 1607 d'Urfé was certainly in Paris, where he took out a privilège for the first 12 books of the *Astrée* on 18 August. The volume, in spite of a confident dedication to "Astrée," was published anonymously. For the winter of 1607 Diane and d'Urfé were together at Châteaumorand, returning together in February 1608 to Paris, where they took and furnished an apartment and stayed two years, leaving Châteaumorand in the hands of a steward, whose accounts were signed by Diane on her return on 20 January 1610.

The literary life of Paris during the first decade of the century was exiguous, but d'Urfé certainly met and probably frequented Malherbe, who found d'Urfé's versifying artistically inferior and socially demeaning for someone in d'Urfé's position. He also met the aged Pasquier and the young Racan, du Perron, Mlle de Gournay, probably the Jesuits Sirmond and Coton, and the circle surrounding Marguerite de Valois, the repudiated first wife of Henri IV back in 1605 from exile at Usson, which included Desportes, Mainard, Scipion Dupleix, Coëffeteau, des Yveteaux, and Vital d'Audiguier. Van Dyck painted a portrait of d'Urfé looking strikingly elegant, sensitive, and physically vigorous, and d'Urfé ceased to have his Savoy titles printed on his title pages, no doubt in deference to the French court.

The second part of the *Astrée* was dedicated to the king in 1610, and after the assassination of Henri IV on 14 May 1610, d'Urfé's prestige continued to grow. Marie de Medici sent him on a delicate mission to Savoy, indicating France's continued agreement to the marriage between the elder daughter of Henri IV, Isabelle, and Victor-Amédée of Piedmont, but in such a way as to indicate that the bride's age demanded a delay. D'Urfé may have believed this, although it should have been obvious to him that French policy had actually changed, and that the projected marriage would now be blocked. Isabelle was needed as a pawn in the Franco-Spanish rapprochement, and had to marry Philip IV of Spain. The duc de Savoie either failed to understand what was happening or pretended to fail, but the manors of Châteauneuf and Virieu were made into the marquisate of Valromey, and d'Urfé, after a number of intricate land deals involving Diane's money, received the marquisate of Bâgé en Bresse, near Mâcon. It was Diane, however, who saw to the administration of the new property. She was thrusting, energetic, and capable as well as intransigent, unintelligent, and quarrelsome.

D'Urfé had probably left Paris early in 1611, collecting his wife at Châteaumorand and dropping her off at Virieu. He had arrived at Turin on 13 February 1611 and did not come back until mid-April, when he returned to Paris, perhaps picking his wife up on the way. They spent the summer together at Châteaumorand, and the following winter was partly taken up with legal squabbles. Diane claimed a percentage of the proceeds of corn sold by the Carthusians in her new marquisate, and they appealed to a charter of 1231 exempting them. That matter ended in a friendly settlement, but Diane's litigious temperament was bound to bring her into collision with others claiming rival or higher jurisdiction in her domains. Not only were legal battles over property rights endemic in the French nobility, but there was also a serious conflict of jurisdictions in many important areas of law. In particular, the bourgeois legal administrators and local judges much disliked the feudal rights of the old aristocracy to dispense justice on its estates.

In 1601, when Bresse, Bugey, Valromey, and Gex had been incorporated into France, a "présidial" had been created at Bourg, to which appeal appeared to be allowed from seigneurial justice. The nobles protested and the king declared their rights undiminished, virtually coming down on both sides at once. About 1612, however, the Bourg présidial moved to the attack. D'Urfé held that, as marquis de Bâgé, he was an appeal judge from whom further appeal could be only to the parlement, not the présidial. His relationship with the bourgois administrators of justice, that is the lawyers who made money out of squabbles about property and the outward manifestations of aristocratic privilege, was always difficult and sometimes grievously strained.

One quarrel, not this time involving the présidial, but provoked by D'Urfé's wife, while petty enough, is here important for the light it sheds on the lingering glamour of feudal supremacy at the beginning of the 17th century. It concerns Jean-François de la Guiche, comte de Saint-Géran and governor of the Bourbonnais, notable for imposing his will by military force, running a private army, wresting a pardon from the king, and flouting the law as he pleased. He was an aristocratic brigand left over from the private armed bands which marauded during the religious wars. His brother, Godefroy, was seigneur de Chitain and of similar temperament. The unpleasantly spirited Saint-Géran disliked Diane de Châteaumorand, and was apt to be spiteful about her acceptance of admiration. His governorship had come from his reckless support for the king while d'Urfé had been fighting for the League.

Saint-Géran and his brother belonged to the Vitri family which owned a château and estate at Lalière, and a chapel, built about 1500, in the church at Saint-Martin-d'Estreaux. The quarrel was fundamentally about local jurisdiction, but came picturesquely to centre on ownership of the chapel. The interest of the story derives from the way in which buccaneering was bounded by a certain anxiety for legality; the connivance of the authorities in feudal misbehaviour could no longer quite be taken for granted.

It started when Diane, relying on a decree of 1468 which limited the lords of Lalière to jurisdiction in cases of only petty crime, demanded release from their custody into hers of prisoners held in their dungeon. They replied that the prisoners came from parts of the Lalière estate over which the lords of Châteaumorand held no higher jurisdiction. Diane then absurdly demanded to assert rights of ownership over the chapel in virtue of a document of 1446, pre-dating the chapel's construction, and ignoring the fact that the chapel had been paid for and built by the Vitri family, carried their arms, contained one of their tombs, and was named after them.

In the late summer of 1613 the Guiche grandmother died at the château de Lalière. Saint-Géran and his brother had had her buried in their chapel, adorning the tomb with four columns carrying the gravestone. D'Urfé was away when Diane de Châteaumorand had the pillars removed and the gravestone symbolically lowered to the chapel floor level. She swore there would be no customary ceremony to mark the 40th day after the death, though one had been fixed for Monday 11 November 1613. On 9 November she sent a messenger to the prévôt of the maréchaussée of the Forez, Guillaume de la Chaize, appealing to royal jurisdiction to impose civil order on what she wanted to be seen as aristocratic piracy, inviting him with assumed coyness to inquire into the behaviour of a horde of armed men wreaking mischief on her estate. The prévôt duly set out at 2 p.m. with his lieutenant, a bailiff, and a dozen archers, arriving at Châteaumorand at 6 a.m. on Sunday morning. De la Chaize managed to penetrate to the château and to persuade an ill-tempered Saint-Géran to accompany him, only to find an emissary from the governor of Lyons sent to mediate. Legitimate authority might not yet be ready to intervene, but it was going to observe. The ceremony was duly held on 11 November and the prévôt's enquiry began.

Saint-Géran had raised an army of several hundred men intending to take by force from Châteaumorand the document proving its superior jurisdiction to that of Lalière. Part of the siege force asked to be allowed in at night, counterfeiting the voices of the relations of Diane they pretended to be, but the ruse was spotted. They could merely hurl insults, shoot at windows, and do some damage to a plantation. For two or three days the Châteaumorand vassals were terrorized. Crops were destroyed, provisions stolen, stores pillaged, a barn was burnt, some geese and chickens were shot, and some lambs slaughtered. One old man was knocked down and severely hurt, and a rape was narrowly avoided.

On the evening of 7 November Saint-Géran had taken possession of the church as if he were conducting a military operation, and there was much desecration, with a fire in the nave. Everyone kept cool enough to have every sacrilege, blasphemy, and act of aggression committed by either side certified by a notary in front of witnesses. Everyone was armed at the ceremony, and a magnificent new set of pillars was installed to hoist the gravestone to a much higher position than that it had previously occupied. The Vitri family had saved its honour. In spite of the imprecations that had been uttered, civilization kept a sufficiently tight control to limit actual damage, and after the ceremony Saint-Géran's riff-raff fired two salvoes of greeting and disbanded.

The incident, in itself trivial enough, derives its importance from the backdrop it forms to one of the most forthrightly civilizing works in the canon of French literature. It may be that Diane de Châteaumorand and the comte de Saint-Géran are spectacularly vivid examples of the potential readership of the *Astrée*, but the achievement of d'Urfé's novel, of Mme de Rambouillet's chambre bleue (see: *Guirlande de Julie*), of François de Sales and the early Pierre Corneille can only begin to be understood if the still atavistic behaviour of substantial parts of the potential readership is constantly kept in mind. The incident shocked the court. On 12 November D'Urfé was gently summoned to a discussion with Marie de Medici, then less gently on 16 November, after he had made clear that he had felt it his prior duty to rush back to deal with Saint-Géran; Diane was written to quite firmly by the regent on 12 November; and Saint-Géran was told to take his men away and to restore peace.

The matter did not end quite so easily. It looks as if there may well have been a duel between d'Urfé and Saint-Géran on 25 January 1614, and d'Urfé certainly complained to the parlement de Paris, on the basis of de la Chaize's enquiry, that Saint-Géran had armed troops without royal authority. The parlement, no doubt in response to pressure from court, issued a decree of 27 February 1614, refusing to press the serious accusation of usurping royal authority, although it summoned Saint-Géran and his brother to appear on civil charges concerning damage to property. The matter was finally settled when the privy council ordered two years later, on 27 February 1616, that all criminal charges be dropped. Effectively the crown, in the person of the regent, had simply stepped in to settle a squabble between feudal aristocrats and had overridden statutory process. The civil case against Saint-Géran dragged on, but in the name of Diane alone. D'Urfé had dropped out. A friendly resolution of 22 June 1620, by which date Saint-Géran was a marshal of France, almost ended the matter, but Diane de Châteaumorand's heir, Jean-Claude de Lévis, finally killed Chitain, Saint-Géran's brother, in a duel on 15 January 1627.

It is possible that Diane de Châteaumorand's arrogance had something to do with d'Urfé's preference for Virieu. Much of what we know of her character comes only from her enemies among the d'Urfés, retailed by Charles-Emmanuel, son of d'Urfé's brother Jacques, to Huet, who related it in a letter to Madeleine de Scudéry. Diane is said to have been wildly jealous, and to have tried almost paranoiacally to protect her complexion from wind and sun, staying in her room for days on end, or only coming out of it wearing a mask. Charles-Emmanuel said that she had had repeated pregnancies, but that no live-born infants had survived. If that is true, it could account for a conflict of evidence about her obesity, but she was 38 when she married d'Urfé, and certain provisions of the marriage contract, excluding legitimate heirs in favour of one another, suggest that they did not expect to have children. It is also quite believable that she was intolerably high-handed, and not at all unlikely that, as her nephew alleged, she took her dogs to bed with her, and was offensively unclean.

From Virieu, after he had more or less retired there in 1614, d'Urfé travelled frequently to Turin, but also to Venice, Milan, and in 1615, Rome, as well as to Paris. In 1616 he was at Parma. He was acting chiefly in the interests of Savoy, dangerously going so far in 1615 as to accept a mission to Paul V from Condé and Nevers, who were openly attempting to regain power from the queen regent and the court, and recruiting troops for the duc de Savoie, at that moment France's unreliable ally who faced a possible clash with Spain. D'Urfé was certainly attacked in the pamphlet war which broke out between the court and the princes, and may himself have been the author of at least one pamphlet arguing the case for a close alliance between France and Savoy. Towards the end of his life, at any rate from 1619, d'Urfé was to regard himself as a Savoyard, and was not from that year to visit Paris more than very briefly again.

In 1616 Diane came to Virieu, where she still was in November. D'Urfé had been sending troops to Savoy from early August, and himself arrived at Chambéry on 26 August, moving on to meet the duc de Savoie at Annecy on 28 August. In his own generation he was as well known for his military as for his literary exploits, and indeed, it was his military glory which ensured such overwhelming and immediate success for the Astrée. It has been suggested that it was the contrast between the colonel-general of the French cavalry of Savoy and the author of the idyllic pastoral fiction which was the cause of the fascination. It is much more likely that d'Urfé's contemporaries understood the boldness of the imaginative vision as an extension of the military prowess of its author as, for instance, we know that Sorel and Scudéry did. The Astrée is not, of course, an idyll.

D'Urfé fought the winter campaign of late 1616 for the duc de Savoie. In July 1617 he inspired, if he did not write, at least one account of the failure of his expedition to relieve Vercelli, on the Milanese side of Piedmont. Don Pedro, the governor of Milan, lost 6,000 men before the town was taken on 26 July. D'Urfé was on the point of raising reinforcements near Lyons when the united troops of Savoy and France began to be victorious, and peace was signed on 9 October at Pavia. D'Urfé was speedily rewarded with lands and honours, although his companies were not disbanded until February 1618. On 5 January 1618, visiting, near his headquarters on the lake of Annecy, the shrine at Villaret which had been erected by popular demand at the birth-place of Pierre Favre, one of Ignatius of Loyola's earliest companions and the first Jesuit priest, d'Urfé was overwhelmed by an intense religious experience. Each year thereafter he made an anniversary pilgrimage on foot to the same shrine, once in thanksgiving for the cure of a condition that had threatened his sight. François de Sales had consecrated the altar of the chapel, probably on 7 October 1607, and d'Urfé had a painting of the beatified Jesuit executed and installed above it. He also founded in 1618 the celebration in perpetuity of two annual solemn high Masses.

D'Urfé probably spent 1618 at Virieu, but was back in Turin that December. After a period at Virieu, he spent the summer of 1619 at Châteaumorand, probably after a final visit to Paris to obtain the privilège, dated 7 May, for the third part of the Astrée,

whose achevé d'imprimer was dated 3 June. The three first books of the third part had been published without his knowledge at Arras in 1617. The fourth part, although not published until 1627, two years after his death, is wholly by d'Urfé. Four books of the fourth part, plus a few pages of the fifth book, were the subject of a privilège obtained by d'Urfé's niece, Gabrielle, on 20 November 1623, and were then published without his authorization. The achevé d'imprimer was 2 January 1624, and d'Urfé had what was left of the partial edition seized and destroyed by a judgement of 24 May.

The authentic fourth part was published in 1627 by d'Urfé's secretary, Balthazar Baro, who complained much about the two counterfeit volumes of a Pseudo-Astrée, written by Borstel de Gaubertin and Marin Le Roy de Gomberville, published in Paris by Robert Fouet in 1625 and 1626, although probably printed in Holland. Baro himself, invited by the Princess of Piedmont and d'Urfé's niece—Geneviève, daughter of Jacques, the widowed duchesse de Croy—used d'Urfé's notes to write a conclusion to the novel, which he published in 1628. D'Urfé's own Paris publisher had been Toussainct du Bray, together with Jean Micard for the second part and with Olivier de Varennes for the third. Baro had the fourth volume published by Toussainct du Bray and three other publishers, with his own Conclusion by François Pomeray and two others.

The work's immense popularity, which led to the naming of colour shades as "Céladon" and "Astrée," and the slowness of the publication of its constituent parts, generated a continuation by La Motte du Broquart and a vast number of unauthorized printings of the various parts. The novel's vogue was quite without previous parallel, as was its traceable effect on all centres of the process of social refinement in 17th-century France. Large numbers of plays and paintings were inspired by its pages, although it did not inspire much pastoral fiction, and quickly itself became the object of sometimes malicious satirical attack, usually on the ground of incongruity, by critics who took, or more often pretended to take, its pastoral conventions as something other than the stylized pantomime trappings they were intended to be. The only two early editions of the whole novel are those of 1632–33 and 1647. Most extant sets are made up of different printings, and many single volumes are older impressions with new title pages, or even new impressions with old title pages.

The anonymity of the first part was not intended as serious camouflage and disappeared in the second part, whose 1610 privilège covered both the first two parts for six years. Although a 1612 quarto edition of the first part announced that the novel would be in three parts, and the second part was published in the same quarto edition in 1616, the edition was then dropped. D'Urfé almost ostentatiously regarded his writing as a pastime, and it looks as though he kept it for moments of leisure, or even boredom, when he was not occupied negotiating royal weddings, fighting, arguing about leases, raising troops, administering his estates, or running diplomatic errands. The background story of the novel's composition helps to explain its mixture of escapist dreaming, imaginative daring, and personal reminiscence.

In a letter of 1 March 1624 no less than 48 German aristocrats, who had formed an "Académie des Parfaits amants," wrote to d'Urfé from the "Carrefour de Mercure" saying that, between them, they could now if necessary have re-written the first three parts from memory, and asking him what was going to happen next. They had each appropriated the name of a character, although none had dared to assume that of the hero, Céladon, which they offered to d'Urfé himself. The letter took a year to arrive, and d'Urfé's polite but slightly satirical reply, written at Châteaumorand on 10 March 1625, was his last literary act. He was more concerned with joining Lesdiguières and the duc de Savoie to defend the Valtellina pass against the Spaniards. It was the only land route between France and Venice that did not pass through Spanish-dominated Milan, and the only route joining the Spanish troops in Milan with the imperial forces in Austria. The situation was made more complicated by the persecution the Catholic population of the valley had endured at the hands of the Protestants of Grisons (Graubünden), which dominated it.

From about 1619, and especially after the marriage of Chrétienne, daughter of Henri IV and Marie de Medici, to Victor-Amadeus, prince of Piedmont, d'Urfé used his Savoyard titles rather than French ones on official documents. He saw much more of his wife again, and was at Châteaumorand in 1621, for the summer and autumn of 1623, and again, ten weeks before his death, in 1625. He made his wife the administrator of all his goods, and they appeared together in public. Together they arranged for various testamentary dispositions, the foundation of Masses, and the dowry of Charlotte-Emmanuelle, daughter of d'Urfé's brother Christophe, who had lived much of her life at Virieu and whose marriage contract with Henri de Maillard, marquis de Saint-Damien, was signed at the château de Bâgé on 11 January 1621.

A privilège of 3 February 1625 for a *Berger désolé* by d'Urfé may refer to a conte by him in a volume not actually published until 1628. Another privilège, of 12 April 1625, for a pastoral play, *Sylvanire; ou, La Morte-vive*, refers to the dramatization of an episode in the fourth part of the *Astrée*, although there is some dispute about whether or not the episode in the novel derives from the pastoral play or whether it was the other way round. The play has five acts, with a prologue and a chorus, but is far too long ever to have been intended for the stage and is an experiment in blank verse.

The commission to raise a regiment for the Valtelline war was dated 29 April 1625. The valley was easily taken by the marquis de Coeuvres for the French, while Lesdiguières and the duc de Savoie prepared to attack the republic of Genoa. There was a quarrel about strategy, in which a compromise was reached between the duc de Savoie, who wanted to march on Genoa, and Lesdiguières, who thought that that would be altogether too dangerous. It was resolved first to take Savona. D'Urfé's role in the 20-day campaign was outstanding. He led the avant-garde of the duc de Savoie's successful army, taking a number of important towns and forts, ending with Oneglia. There he suddenly fell grievously ill. He was taken the 60 or 70 kilometres to Villefranche, where he died on 1 June 1625. There is evidence that he had been ill for some time, and that he died of a disease of the lung, its terminal attack brought on by strenuous physical exertion as he literally climbed into Oneglia on 15 February. The funeral took place at Turin, but the body was brought back to the Forez. Diane, having settled her affairs, died at Châteaumorand on 8 March 1626.

WORKS

It is doubtful whether d'Urfé's work would have shown its

redoubtable imaginative vigour if it had not been the work of an off-duty military captain and country landowner, intended for no particular readership, and written without concern for any effect it might produce. A fervent Catholic, heavily committed to the League, fiercely partisan, loyal to the interests of his family, a rural gentleman content, on the whole, to let his energetic wife walk the dogs, run the farms, and administer the estates, d'Urfé knew more success as a soldier than as a diplomat, but was more successful as a writer than as a feudal overlord. He was easily moved to pity but quite fearless, pious, seriously interested in moral and spiritual problems, with a strong poetic vein, and totally incapable of writing the charming sickly-sweet pastoral romance for which the *Astrée* was for so long taken.

The main value of the religious verse lies in its value as a source for d'Urfé's spiritual biography and ultimately, therefore, in its importance not only in tracing his spiritual and imaginative evolution, but also indirectly for its bearing on the interpretation of the *Astrée* itself. It was first published in the Micard edition of *Le Sireine* of 1618 and was probably written in 1596 or 1597, mostly at Senoy in the months following the two imprisonments. It is optimistic enough to include a paraphrase of the *Song of Songs*, but can also be seen against a whole background of Christian stoicism characteristic of the piety of the moderates, often drawn from the magistracy, during the religious wars. It has much in common with the attitudes of the early Montaigne, but there are also plain efforts to overcome some bitterness at the "betrayals" which d'Urfé thought put him in prison, and to further the affirmation of himself against the overbearing figure of his brother Anne, from whose political tutelage he was to emerge when Nemours escaped from Lyons, and whose former bride he was himself to marry.

The *Epistres morales* themselves need to be understood not only against the background of the Christian stoicism of the late sixteenth century in France, but with the frequent attempts to christianize the moralists of antiquity, particularly Plutarch, Seneca, and Epictetus, also in mind. It must be remembered too that what we can distinguish as stoicism and scepticism were often confused in the later sixteenth century. There is an intrinsic connection even in antiquity between scepticism, based on the notion of our incapacity for knowing the real world as it is, and stoicism, understood as an acceptance of whatever fate has in store, changed in late 16th-century French moralists into the advocacy of "constancy." Pyrrho, the best-known of the antique sceptics who, according to Diogenes Laertius, believed chiefly in the suspension of judgement or "epokè ($\dot{\epsilon}\pi o\chi\dot{\eta}$)," was presented by Cicero uniquely as a stoic, and the connection between stoicism and scepticism is made quite explicit in the first years of the 17th century by the Belgian moralist, Justus Lipsius, who published a *De constantia* in 1583 and in 1604 a *Manuductio ad stoicam philosophiam* and a *Physiologia stoicorum*.

D'Urfé in the *Epistres morales* was not so much sceptical as uncertain. His stoic moral stance was merely defensive. He derived it less from Cicero and Seneca, as christianized for instance by Pierre Charron at about the same time, or by Montaigne a little earlier, than from the very different "stoicism" of Epictetus, based on the opening affirmation of his *Enchiridion* that our true good must be in our power, the foundation for Guillaume du Vair's 1585 *Philosophie morale des stoïques* and near to the core of the devout humanism of François de Sales. At the date of the *Epistres morales* there is no clash at all between the moral attitudes of antique stoicism and the Christian spirituality of abandonment to the will of God as developed by the Jesuit Sirmond in his 1640–41 controversy with Jean-Pierre Camus, later by another Jesuit, de Caussade, and by Fénelon in the *Maximes des saints* to a degree felt by Bossuet to be dangerously quietistic. Gassendi was shortly to attempt the much more improbable christianization of Lucretius.

D'Urfé would later move on from the position he takes in the series of letters about the reaction to adverse fortune, the crucible of virtue, in the first volume of the *Epistres morales*, but there is already a strong sense of his own personal merit, proved by the fact that it was he whom fortune had chosen to attack, and also by the fact that his spirit had survived fortune's hostility. Like Charron, d'Urfé praises ambition as "un grand esguillon de la vertu (a great spur to virtue)." In the second volume there is less emphasis on personal misfortune and more on the general use of time, on death, and on contentment. There is an early defence of the "passions et affections," and now a firmly Ficinian neoplatonist link is established between love and virtue, goodness and beauty. The fourth letter, "Que l'amour naist de surabondance de vertu," argues after Ficino's *De amore*,

L'amour est un désir de beauté, la beauté et la bonté se confondent ensemble; car rien ne peut estre beau qui ne soit bon, ny bon qui ne soit beau, ainsi que Platon nous enseigne dans le *Sympose*. Or la bonté, c'est Dieu; car Dieu seul est bon, lequel ne se pouvant diviser, il s'ensuit que désirer la beauté, c'est désirer la bonté, et désirer la bonté, c'est désirer Dieu... Ce qui est seul aymable, c'est la vertu; donc, pour estre aymé, le vray amant se rendra vertueux

(Love is a desire of beauty, beauty and goodness are inseparable; for nothing that is not good can be beautiful, or good which is not beautiful, as Plato teaches us in the *Symposium*. But goodness means God, for God alone is good, and since he cannot be divided, it follows that to desire beauty is to desire goodness, and that to desire goodness is to desire God... What alone is lovable is virtue; so, to be loved, the true lover must make himself virtuous).

This exploitation of Ficino's *De amore* has a renewed note of buoyancy absent from all the moral writing of the religious wars, when none of the moralists had been much concerned with the perfective aspects of human affection. It is noteworthy that d'Urfé is again, after the wars, able to have renewed recourse to Ficino, but also that he should justify his emotional love by pointing to the merit of its object. Above all, d'Urfé interpolates into the instinctive, emotional experience the intellectual judgement of merit inherited from Leone Ebreo and characteristic of the strong literary movement to build into any discussion of love a personal moral enrichment which it was thought capable of mediating. When love is defined by Silvandre in the *Astrée* as

un acte de volonté qui se porte à ce que l'entendement juge bon

(an act of the will towards what the intellect judges to be good).

d'Urfé is establishing or echoing the content of a whole tradition of apparently anodyne scholastic formulations of different

degrees of conceptual commitment to be found in authors writing in genres as different as those of Pierre Charron, Guillaume du Vair, François de Sales, and Jean-Pierre Camus. Descartes himself was to regard what was for him the immensely important passion of "générosité" as the resolution in the will to undertake whatever is judged to be best, "ce qui est suivre parfaitement la vertu (which is what the perfect following of virtue is)." D'Urfé differs from all of them in the effervescent optimism with which he uses the intellectual judgement of merit.

If there is any single source for d'Urfé's immensely important formulation of the definition of love, it is the gloss on Ficino by Leone Ebreo, who defines love as "une affection volontaire, et deliberée de jouir par union d'une chose estimée bonne (an affection of the will based on a judgement to enjoy union with an object considered good)." In the *Epistres morales* d'Urfé is almost elaborating a series of abstract, philosophical answers which resolve in advance the problems of amorous casuistry which the *Astrée* will explore imaginatively:

D'autant que celuy est blasmable qui, pouvant faire deux louables actions, se contente de la moindre (car c'est tesmoignage ou de peu de courage ou de peu de prudence), celuy aussi qui s'arreste entierement aux beautez du corps sans s'eslever à celle de l'âme ne peut estre excusé de l'un de ces deux deffaux...

(Since he is blameworthy who, of two praiseworthy actions, is content with the less good, because that shows either a want of courage or a want of prudence, so he who stops completely at bodily beauty without lifting himself up to the beauty of soul cannot be excused from one or other of these faults).

Every "honneste homme (upright man)" must be in love, because not to love that which is lovable can only proceed from a defect of judgement, but the lover, in making himself lovable, must avoid that austerity of over-concentrated virtue which is perceived as intimidating:

cette moderation doit venir de l'amour, pour ce qu'il ne desire rien que d'estre aymable, et ce desir doit addoucir en quelque sorte l'aspreté de la pure vertu

(that moderating impulse must come from love, because it desires nothing except to make itself lovable, and this desire has as it were to soften the asperity of pure virtue).

Love based on beauty and goodness cannot lead to sin. Human affection is the start of a movement towards religious beatitude. D'Urfé's brother Antoine, in the 1592 dialogue *L'Honneur*, had added a letter to d'Urfé on the preference to be given to the Platonists over other philosophers, and Anne had already written sonnets on "L'Honneste amour." D'Urfé is rather clumsily arguing out with himself moral principles on the basis of what we could regard as no more than a good school grounding in the classical moral principles of antiquity and of the moral outlook of the modern authors he had read, often Italian or Spanish. The mistake would be to take his amorous casuistry too seriously as moral philosophy. None the less it should not be taken too unseriously. It was not merely a complicated game striving for a logical consistency which belonged to the realm of idealization and remained remote from what happened in the real lives of real people.

The insight of the *Epistres* and the power of the novel both lie in d'Urfé's determined effort to use the calculus of Ficinian neo-platonism in order to interpret the everyday experience of ordinary human affection, with all it entails in the physical and emotional realms, in the light of the spiritually enriching experience he believes it should be. The possibility that the exploration of ordinary affective experience needed to be undertaken in neo-platonist terms had been poetically touched on in such authors of the high French renaissance as Marguerite d'Angoulême, Antoine Héroët, Maurice Scève, and Pontus de Tyard. It had been defensively dropped during the afflictions of the religious wars, but with d'Urfé's generation, and above all in d'Urfé himself, it now became the leisurely subject of an exhaustively detailed imaginative investigation covering the whole range of possible forms of not only heterosexual love between human beings.

Le Sireine, no doubt later touched up for publication, was substantially finished at Chambéry on 24 November 1596. It was based on Montemayor's pastoral novel *Diana*, having probably been at least begun a decade previously. In six-line stanzas of octosyllabic verse of a sometimes astonishing ineptitude, the poem is made up of dialogue, monologues, letters, and speeches, and concerns the mutual love of Diane, forced by her mother to marry the rich shepherd Délio, and Sireine, who has had to leave the country of Léon to go and look after his master's sheep on the banks of the Eridan. He returns immediately when he receives the despairing message from Diane about her marriage, but arrives too late. She is dragged to the altar and, although she still loves Sireine, will not see him. This is the imaginative world of the early sketch for the *Astrée* as known from du Crozet. Diane's love is allowed to conflict with a higher duty instead of itself constituting the highest duty of all. To suffer in silence is presented as the only honourable conduct, but the psychology is still rudimentary, and the ethics insist on external conformity to accepted social pressures from outside, whatever the inner feelings. The public success of the poem, most of whose 11 editions came out between 1615 and 1619, is certainly attributable to d'Urfé's renown as author of the *Astrée*.

When, in 1593, du Crozet published the four books of *La Philocalie*, dedicated to d'Urfé, but with its second book especially dedicated to Diane de Châteaumorand, whose marriage to Anne d'Urfé had not yet been annulled, the character, Athille, sings some verses he has composed on the *Bergeries* of d'Urfé. *Bergeries* was presumably an early manuscript title of what was to become the *Astrée*, which was passed round or from which readings were given. The novel then centred according to Athille on Céladon's resistance to Queen Galathée, and Astrée's regret at her severity for so faithful a lover as Céladon, whom she believed dead and whom she did not wish to survive. The theme of jealousy did not arise, the male chauvinist character of Hylas does not appear yet to have been invented, and Achille foresees not the marital happiness of Astrée and Céladon, but the granting to Céladon of only spiritual satisfaction.

From the beginning of the novel as we have it, d'Urfé goes to extraordinary lengths to make clear that it contains personal reminiscences and fictionalizations of real, if perhaps composite, characters, and that the fifth-century pastoral setting is a simple stylization designed to isolate from everyday cares the emotional entanglements of the plainly contemporary charac-

ters who are the subject of the novel. They merely posture as shepherds. When he sent the first part to Pasquier, d'Urfé wrote that "Ceste bergère que je vous envoye n'est véritablement que l'histoire de ma jeunesse, sous la personne de qui j'ay représenté les diverses passions, ou plutost folies, qui m'ont tourmenté l'espace de cinq ou six ans (This shepherdess I'm sending you is really the story of my youth; in her person I've depicted the different passions, or rather follies, which tormented me for five or six years).

Pasquier chided him for not delivering the copy himself in case he should be seen blushing as he handed over "vostre beau livre d'*Astrée*" because it is "l'histoire de vos jeunes amours, que vous appelez folies (your beautiful book, the *Astrée*...the story of your young love, which you call folly)." Pasquier goes on to allude to d'Urfé's intention "de célébrer sous noms couvers plusieurs seigneurs, dames et familles de vostre païs de Forest... Je voy un Céladon, qui estes vous mesmes, esperdu de la belle Astrée, se laisser emporter à la mercy de vostre Lignon...[et] accueilli par la nymphe Galatée (to celebrate under fictitious names several gentlemen, ladies, and families of your country of Forez...I see a Céladon who is you, in love with the beautiful Astrée, letting yourself be swept away at the mercy of your [river] Lignon...[and] given shelter by the nymph Galathée)."

That there is somewhere a semi-biographical inspiration is certain, and there was probably even a sort of key to the real people stylized to the point of caricature under the names of the shepherds. Pastorals very often had keys, and finding such keys for the *Astrée* became a social preoccupation in the 17th-century salons, although today the real interest for us would be more likely to reside in any symbolic allusion in the narrated events. The point, however, is that the novel was announced and received as something much more important than escapist fantasy. D'Urfé also gives it an actual setting in time and place, describing precise locations, recognizable geographical features, and acknowledged historical circumstances, even to the extent in 1619 of expressing in the dedication of the third part his gratitude to the river Lignon and to the region in which he had experienced the joys of his youth.

He addresses Astrée at the beginning of the first part: if people say you don't talk in patois and don't smell of sheep and goats, tell them that you and your companions are not "de ces bergères nécessiteuses qui pour gagner leur vie, conduisent leurs troupeaux aux pasturages, mais que vous n'avez toutes pris cette condition que pour vivre plus doucement et sans contrainte (among those needy shepherdesses who lead their flocks to the pastures to earn their living, but that you have all taken to that way of life only to live more pleasantly and freely)." In the novel the nymph Galathée says to Léonide that the characters are shepherds by choice, not because they cannot live otherwise, but "pour s'achetter par cette douce vie un honneste repos (to obtain for themselves by so gentle a life a real peace)."

It is not made clear whether the peace is social, or interior, or both, but the fictionalized Forez of the novel is partly a utopian dream world, and partly a place which makes possible escape from life's more sordid preoccupations. The Forez might even be taken to represent an inner self in which external events, when they occur, are incidental to and precipitated by the effects of interior emotions. Some of the characters are noble, with their châteaux in the hills. They live in comfortable cottages in the valley but, when Amasis's capital Marcilly is threatened by the treacherous Polémas—who had been turned down by Amasis's daughter, Galathée—and his ally Gondebaud, king of the Burgondes, the shepherds instantly revert to being warriors. It cannot have been unintended that the verbal assonances Marcilly/Marseilles and Burgondes/Bourgogne have suggested a further link with the real world, and had the ideas and language of his characters been those of ordinary shepherds, said d'Urfé, nobody would have listened to them with enjoyment. They differed from d'Urfé's contemporaries and social equals only in the way they dressed up, the life-style they chose, their developed intellectual curiosity, and the detailed analyses of their emotional lives to which their disguise allowed the author, occasionally using the first person, to subject them.

D'Urfé eventually planned five parts for his novel, each with twelve books. There is a central narrative concerning the couple Astrée-Céladon. Céladon was 14 or 15, Astrée 12 or 13 when they fell in love instantaneously and irresistibly at a feast of Venus. Their love for one another was all-absorbing, but had to be dissimulated on account of the enmity of their parents. Astrée has ordered Céladon to pretend to be in love with Aminthe but, as the novel starts, Astrée has come to think that Céladon really does love Aminthe. We are told only much later that it is in tricking her into this belief that the treachery of the jealous Sémire consists. Astrée bans the perplexed Céladon from her presence. He throws himself into the Lignon and, when his hat floats down the river, is presumed dead. Astrée faints, falls into the Lignon, and is saved. She does not know that Céladon had been rescued by three nymphs—the princess Galathée and her attendants Sylvie and Léonide—plainly representing the highest aristocracy among d'Urfé's contemporaries. Galathée falls in love with Céladon, but Léonide helps him escape.

He lives in a cave on plants and fruit, erects to Astrée altars and a temple of foliage in which he hangs the twelve tablets of the laws of love, carves his grief on the barks of trees, and puts a letter "to the most loved and the most beautiful shepherdess of the universe" into the hands of the sleeping Silvandre. The chief druid, Adamas, then contrives the expedient whereby Céladon is passed off as his absent daughter, Alexis. With this new identity, Céladon/Alexis can appear before Astrée without violating her original prohibition against appearing in her presence without her permission, and until the beginning of the final dénouement of the novel Céladon is dressed in travesty as Alexis, of whom Astrée makes a close friend in a relationship whose sexual equivocalness is certainly intentional. When in the end Céladon reveals himself, Astrée is ashamed at the intimacies she has permitted him, and banishes him again. Céladon, Astrée, and two others, Silvandre and Diane, all go to the Fontaine de vérité d'amour which once had the property of reflecting the image of the person loved, with that of the lover when the love was returned, or with the image of his rival if it was not. The fountain had lost its power, and the two unhappy couples go to seek death from the lions and unicorns which protect it.

There is a storm with thunder and lightning, the lions and unicorns become marble statues, Céladon sees Astrée's image reflected with his own, Silvandre sees Diane's, and even Hylas sees his Stelle's. The novel closes with rejoicing at the three weddings. The ending alters the pace and balance, and Baro's conclusion is more concerned with the narrative lines than with psychological analyses. But it is not untrue to d'Urfé's essential aim. The essence of the novel is the convergence of the three couples, Céladon-Astrée, Silvandre-Diane, and Hylas-Stelle

into the acceptance of a normal marital relationship. Silvandre had started the novel as the spokesman for a neoplatonist view of love which wrongly understood Ficino, from whom his view is directly taken, as having excluded physical and emotional relationships between human beings from the spiritually satisfying affection which transforms itself into the love of God. In the ninth book of part two he had emphatically denied that love was a form of desire. By the third book of part four he admits that love is the desire "de ce qui est jugé bon ou beau (of what is judged to be good or beautiful)."

Hylas had started as Silvandre's opposite number, from Céladon's other flank, regarding love as reducible to lust, and finding no virtue in fidelity. Silvandre tells Hylas

> Non, non, Hylas, il n'y a que cette différence: ceux qui aiment comme je fais, ils n'ont les désirs desquels tu parles que par ce qu'ils aiment, mais ceux qui aiment comme toi, ils n'aiment que parce qu'ils ont ces désirs

> (No, no, Hylas, there is only this difference: those who love as I do have the desires you speak of only because they love, but those who love as you do, love only because they have those desires). (Part 3, Book 10)

Céladon himself had regarded love as servitude, its own reward, with death preferable to its betrayal or even diminution, and not necessarily dependent on reciprocation or on emotional or physical fulfilment. In the end the wisdom is that of Adamas. True and faithful commitment to a loved one is not exclusive of ordinary physical and emotional bonds, but is none the less spiritually enriching and religiously fulfilling. In spite of Baro's somewhat hasty ending, it is important not to miss d'Urfé's elaborate signals that he was not writing a fairy story. In case it has been missed, his educative intention is emphasized in the preface of the second part "L'Auteur au berger Céladon (The author to the shepherd Céladon)," in which the author points out how ridiculous Céladon's behaviour seems to "our own century."

> Ne dis-tu pas que ton amour ne peut jamais estre sans le respect et l'obéissance? Que la fortune te peut bien priver de tout contentement, mais non pas te faire commettre chose qui contrevienne à la volonté de celle que tu aimes ou au devoir de celui qui veut se dire amant sans reproche? Que les peines et les tourmens que tu souffres ne sont que des témoignages glorieux de ton amour parfaite? Qu'au milieu des plus cruels supplices tu jouys d'un bien extrême, sachant que tu fais ce que doit faire un vrai amant?...
>
> Ah! Berger, que l'âge où nous sommes est bien contraire à ton opinion!... on tient aujourd'hui des maximes d'état d'amour bien différentes, à savoir qu'aimer et jouir de la chose aimée, doivent estre accidens inséparables

> (Do you not say that your love can never exist without respect and obedience? That fortune can deprive you of all happiness, but not make you do anything which goes against the will of the person you love, or against the duty of whoever wants to be called a lover without reproach? That the pains and torments which you suffer are only glorious testimonies to your perfect love? That in the middle of your cruellest sufferings you enjoy an extreme pleasure, knowing that you are behaving as a perfect lover should?

Ah! Shepherd, how different from your attitudes are those of our age… Ideas are held today about love which are quite different, namely that love and enjoyment of the object of love should go inseparably together).

The author ends with a panegyric of Céladon's love and the hope that one day his attitude will be restored. But if the aim is educative, and the author is here taking sides with Céladon against Hylas, he does not in the total context endorse the view of Silvandre, as expressed especially in Silvandre's long discourse in the first book of the second part, that the absence of the loved person is necessary to remove distractions from the perfection of love, and that for its spiritual perfection love should therefore actually exclude the enjoyment of its physical object. It needs incidentally to be noted that, in the novel, the word "honneste" is used in its bourgeois, moral sense, rather than for the quality of worldliness, sophistication, and polish in which it was current in aristocratic, courtly circles.

Structurally the main Astrée-Céladon narrative is entwined with an almost indeterminate number of sub-plots and narrative episodes exhibiting possible varieties of affective relationships. Lycidas is Céladon's brother and Phillis is Astrée's cousin. They, too, attempt to keep their relationship secret, but Lycidas becomes jealous of Céladon, with whom it is agreed that Phillis should merely pretend to be in love. In fact, it is Lycidas who is momentarily unfaithful with Olimpe, who becomes pregnant. Phillis forgives him, but his self-confidence is undermined by his second jealous conviction that Silvandre is in love with Phillis.

Silvandre, who has always, previously to the novel's action, regarded love as no more than a spiritual ladder to moral perfection, and who does not know his parenthood, accepts a wager that he will be seen to be the most perfect in the service of Diane. She has loved once only and then sworn allegiance to her Filandre, who had died rescuing her from the hands of a Moor. Only very slowly do Silvandre and Diane feel the power of love engulfing them, with Diane agreeing to accept the devotion of Silvandre just as long as she can regard his affection as feigned. In book nine of part three Phillis is actually declared to have served Diane better, taking the role of the chaste male servant and playing a role analogous to that of Astrée in her quasi-male relationship with Alexis. D'Urfé was not uninterested in exploring the difference between gender and sex.

The doubling up of relationships and roles in the novel allows d'Urfé scope for analyzing the most sophisticated psychological variations. Just as Sémire had made Astrée think that Céladon really was in love with Aminthe, so the treachery of Laonice persuades Diane that Silvandre really loves Madonte, but whereas Astrée banished Céladon, Diane makes up her mind to go further by actually marrying someone else, Adamas's son, Pâris. One of the weaknesses of Baro's conclusion is the facile substitution: Silvandre turns out to be Adamas's son, Pâris, while the shepherd who was thought to be Pâris turns out to be ineligible as a spouse for Diane, since he is her brother. Baro also brings about too speedily the transformation of Galathée from a totally self-absorbed creature of high social rank to a less imperious and self-willed friend of Astrée and Céladon.

Hylas, who comes not from the Forez, but from Provence, is reminiscent of Hircan in Marguerite d'Angoulême's *Heptameron*, the lustful, unfaithful male, earthy, charming, and cynical, who sees infidelity as a positive virtue. Together with his dozen or so named partners, he is drawn to Alexis, but finally falls in love with the young widow, Stelle. As a result of permitting one another infidelities they grow obsessed only with each other, and in the end Hylas commits himself to fidelity. In another secondary story both Thamire and the younger Calidon, whom he has raised as a son, fall in love with Célidée, who wants to marry Thamire. Twice when that seems likely Calidon falls grievously ill. In the end Célidée destroys her beauty by making deep marks on her face with a diamond, although she had earlier cried when being scratched by the stone. Calidon's love, which was "selon le désir (according to desire)" evaporates, but that of Thamire, "selon raison (according to reason)," endures, although it had admitted a great deal of fondling and kissing, and had also been said to proceed from "inclination (passion)." When she has proved the authenticity of Thamire's love, Célidée's face is healed again with a "powder of sympathy."

The centrally important metaphysical disquisitions on the nature of love are largely confined to two characters, Adamas and Silvandre. Silvandre is normally thought to represent the "neoplatonist" position, but in spite of the clear reference he makes to Ficino, in fact represents the hypostasization of a spiritual ideal in which the aspiration is not to union but to service, as in those forms of medieval "courtly" love which, on account of their spiritually perfective function, automatically excluded the lover's wife from the possible objects of his courtly devotion. Medieval authors almost generally regarded passionate love as morally deviant, and the later attempts of the courtly tradition to accord instinctive affection with moral elevation were always seen as emanating from an exalted cultural level and met with widespread suspicion in the name of established ethical norms.

Silvandre's philosophy of love not only refracts Ficino's views in the *De amore* through the prism of Leone Ebreo's intellectualist vulgarization, but it also tinges them with the stoicism popular in the religious wars, and such commonly held "Aristotelian" notions as the primacy and anteriority of knowledge over love in the pursuit of beatitude, and the possibility of the soul's becoming the object of its own love. It is not rare for characters in the *Astrée* to proclaim that love is, or at least can be, spiritually enriching—"L'amour a cette puissance d'ajouter de la perfection à nos ames (Love has the power of adding [spiritual] perfection to our souls),"—and it is not normally, except for the early Silvandre, exclusive of the manifestation of sensual desire. On the other hand it is, except for the early Hylas, certainly more complex than simple physical passion.

Jealousy, which plays so great a part in the novel and, in Astrée's original banishment of Céladon, provides the springboard for the plot, is resolutely rejected as a legitimate emotion. The narrator points out that jealousy is a perversion of love, drawing to itself the sap that ought to nourish the "bonnes branches et bons fruits," and Silvandre naturally agrees with the narrator. According to Léonide, jealousy "rend preuve d'une amour malade (demonstrates a sickness of love)," while Lycidas early in the novel bitterly reproached Astrée for the jealousy which set off the whole plot. There is some distinction between the spiritually and morally enriching love and the physical passion. Léonide, recognizing that the heart can contain only one love and that Céladon's love is for Astrée, says "donc n'ayant plus d'amour à me donner comme à maistresse, je vous demande votre amitié comme à votre soeur (so, having no more love to give me as to a mistress, I ask for your friendship as to a sister)." D'Urfé is concerned to promote neither the simple glorification of passion nor the idealized and spiritually enriching affection which excludes physical relationships. What he is exploring is the relationship between an affection that is instinctively based and the spiritual perfection it may be capable of mediating.

Adamas goes so far as to hold that there is no sort of virtue with which love is incompatible, not even chastity, and he quotes the example of Endymion, presumably from Apollodorus. But Adamas does not yield to the tendency obvious in Silvandre and Diane to over-intellectualize the affection of love. Silvandre explains how love can arise through the mediation of the senses, but insists that

il faut bien quelque chose de plus ferme et de plus solide pour la rendre parfaite, et cela ne peut estre que la connoissance des vertus, des beautés, des mérites

(there has to be something firmer and more solid to make it perfect, and that can only be the knowledge of virtues, beauties, and merits). (Part 2, book 1)

For Silvandre the sensuous passion is necessarily opposed to the interior emotional love which has to be rational. The intellectual equation is perfect. Love is based on a knowledge of value. It follows for Silvandre that

plus nous avons de connoissance de la perfection de la personne aimée, plus aussi notre amour s'augmente

(the more knowledge we have of the perfection of the loved one, the more our love increases). (Part 2, book 1)

Diane affirms roundly "il est impossible d'aymer ce qu'on n'estime pas (it is impossible to love someone whom one does not esteem), and Silvandre's view is printed in capital letters in book nine of the second part, "que l'amant croit toutes choses tres parfaites en la personne aimée (that the lover thinks everything most perfect in the loved one)."

Silvandre is not, however, merely mouthing neoplatonist common-places. D'Urfé uses Adamas to transfer the discussion to a more serious philosophical plane. Silvandre's love based on an intellectual judgement of merit is of itself equivocal. François de Sales uses the same equation to account for the love of God in chapter 11 of the first book of the *Traité de l'amour de Dieu*: "Nous avons une volonté par laquelle nous sommes portés a la recherche du bien, selon que nous le connoissons ou jugeons estre tel par le discours (We have a will by which we are drawn to seek the good, as we know or judge it to be so by the intellect)," and Pierre Corneille exploits it to justify the clearly instinctive reciprocal love of Rodrigue and Chimène in *Le Cid*. In the *Astrée*, as expressed by Silvandre, the justification of love in terms of the merit of its object would demand that every shepherd should be in love with the most virtuous woman, and that the most virtuous woman was also the most beautiful.

Adamas in his long and important discourse in the fifth book of part three goes some way towards agreeing.

La raison nous enseigne que tout ce qui est aimable se doit aimer selon les degrés de sa bonté, et...il s'ensuit que, plus

le bon est reconnu, plus aussi doit-il estre aimé... Mais puisque toutes les bonnes choses ont l'amour pour leur but,...de toutes l'amour est la meilleure

(Reason teaches us that all that is lovable should be loved according to the degree of its goodness, and...it follows that, the more the good is known, the more, too, it must be loved... But since all good things have love as their end, of all things love is the best). (Part 3, book 4)

But the important discourse of Adamas in the fifth book of the third part comes to grips with the irrationality of instinctive love, however unsatisfactorily, by having recourse to the neoplatonist doctrine of sympathy:

qui est cette conformité que nous rencontrons d'avoir les uns avec les autres, et laquelle est la véritable source de l'amour

(which is that conformity which can exist between people, and which is the true source of love).

This is not on any serious level a satisfactory solution to the problem, since it appears to destroy the idea that love is justified by the intellectual perception of merit, but it shows that d'Urfé is sensitive to the nature of the problems involved in applying Ficinian categories to real emotional relationships.

Love is not the only subject of the novel. There are chivalresque as well as pastoral episodes, and not all the episodes take place in the Forez. Alongside the Astrée-Céladon narrative there are half a dozen other main stories with shared characters or incidents, and numerous other subsidiary contes, perhaps 30, according to how they are split. What is truly remarkable is the psychology of the affections which allows d'Urfé to provide, along with customary fictional entertainment, necessarily episodic in a work of this length, a minute analysis of amorous states indicating how, when, and why ordinary affective relationships can be morally elevating, and under what circumstances human instinct can be trusted as a guide to virtue. The possibility had been at least hinted at by Erasmus and the neoplatonist poets of the high renaissance in France, then left unconsidered during the wars. At Ficino, Montaigne only laughs (*Les Essais*, Book III, chapter 5). What is new in d'Urfé, and without parallel among his immediate contemporaries, is the minuteness of his psychological analyses, the implied and explicit comparisons of attitudes, feelings, and temperaments involved in affective relationships.

It is difficult to see how critics who have understood what is happening in the text have been able to pronounce it boring, repetitious, or improbable. There are tiny inconsistencies, it is true, and for less baroque tastes there are too many concessions to the merely panoramic. The text is profligate with yet further instances of amorous attitudes to be analyzed, and it is too complex for easy comprehension, but it is simple to see why it seemed so important a text to a whole century obsessed by the affective states of which the human heart was capable, by their capacity for further refinement, and by their ultimate significance for human moral stature.

It seems likely that d'Urfé started out on a unified collection of contes, or a single fiction on the Spanish or Italian models, with Montemayor's *Diana* specifically in mind, although he introduced from the beginning a much greater degree of realism. D'Urfé no doubt hoped to promote the refinement of manners, perhaps even what he imagined to have been a reversion to the ideal which the author associates with the knights of the round table in his letter to Céladon at the beginning of the second part. The framework was then probably enlarged to take in elements of the adventure novel, with its duels, disguises, and recognitions, some of which fit only incongruously and perfunctorily into the pastoral setting. D'Urfé gets far enough away from sheep to include the siege of Marcilly, home of Galathée's mother, Amasis, by the rejected Polémas. The narrative skill remains, however, considerable. The novel starts, for instance, with the dramatic banishment of Céladon by the jealous Astrée long before we know how or why Sémire made her jealous, who the two lovers are, or why and how they needed to disguise their love. The sustained use of flashback, growing out of the renaissance drama's preoccupation with starting "in medias res," that is as near the climax of the action as possible, marks an advance in narrative technique, as does the exploitation of such devices as overhearing and watching without being seen.

The *Astrée* is no exception to the general rule that renaissance neoplatonism always leads to advanced positions about the social role of women. The justification of love in terms of the beauty and goodness on which it is based puts a premium on the traditionally feminine attribute of beauty. Women, the narrator perhaps inadvertently implies, therefore have a status to which men cannot aspire, although even in the male, according to Silvie, speaking to Galathée, "ce qui rend aimable, est cela mesme qui rende honneste homme (what makes them worthy of love is their moral probity)."

D'Urfé has written a novel, not a treatise. He cannot be said to have provided a solution to the problem of producing a coherent framework which makes clear how the actual phenomena of affective relationships are spiritually elevating and morally enriching. If love is based on a judgement, then it cannot be free. Yet if it is to be morally perfective, it must be the result of free choice. There is a whole catalogue of conquests by the will in the novel, although love's irresistibility is not menacing when, as here, its instinctive basis is being explored for its morally enriching, not its potentially sinful repercussions. The possibility that love was irresistible seemed threatening only after the century had run a third of its course.

How can love be based both on judgement and on instinctive sympathy? The endless analyses of the *Astrée* do not resolve the difficulties. Indeed, the conceptual framework within which they could have been resolved was simply not capable of being erected within the psychological categories based on the separate faculties of intellect and will available to d'Urfé, or even Descartes. The final vision remains unclear, but the whole thrust of d'Urfé's imagination in his novel, confirmed by the evolution of his creative writing from the first volume of the *Epistres morales* is, however, clear. Somehow the physically and emotionally based human affective relationship known as love, even when reduced to the eroticism of the beauty contest in which Céladon, disguised as Alexis, gives the prize to the naked Astrée, has to be not only compatible with, but positively to lead towards, a state of moral elevation and religious fulfilment. Ficino's *De amore* had edged the Platonic love-myth somewhere near to parable, while d'Urfé wants to make easier the transfer of the myth's reference to actual human psychology.

The strength of the *Astrée* lies in the minute examination of ways which would allow the psychological possibility that ordinary human love was spiritually enriching to become manifest at a properly conceptualized level, upgrading instinctive behaviour by showing its link with spiritual perfection. It is d'Urfé's pertinaceous and even partly successful effort to find the necessary articulate psychological analyses connecting instinctively governed behaviour and deliberately directed moral aspiration into a single converging movement of human endeavour which gives the *Astrée* its prodigious imaginative strength, and makes it one of the half-dozen major staging posts in the central movement linking the development of European culture from the renaissance to the enlightenment.

PUBLICATIONS

Non-fiction and verse

La triomphante Entrée de tresillustre Dame Madame Madeleine de la Rochefocaud, 1583; edited by Maxime Gaume, 1976
Le Sireine: 1st edition lost; 2nd edition 1606; augmented with religious verse, 1618; edited by Marcos, 1979
Les Epistres morales,
vol. 1, 1598
vol. 2, 1603
vol. 3, 1608
La Sylvanire; ou, La Morte-vive, 1627

Fiction

Les douze livres d'Astrée, 1607
Astrée: seconde partie, 1610
Astrée: troisième partie, 1619
La vraye Astrée (authentic fourth part, finished by Baro), 1627
La Conclusion et dernière partie d'Astrée, (by Baro), 1628
Les tristes amours de Floridon, 1628
L'Astrée, edited by H. Vaganay, 5 vols., 1925

Excerpted editions of the *Astrée*

edited by Magendie, Maurice, 1928
edited by Genette, Gérard, 1964
edited by Gaume, Maxime, 1981

Biographical and critical studies

Reure, O.-C., *La Vie et les oeuvres d'Honoré d'Urfé*, 1910
Magendie, Maurice, *Du Nouveau sur l'Astrée*, 1927
L'"Astrée" d'Honoré d'Urfé, 1929
Ehrmann, Jacques, *Un paradis désespéré: l'amour et l'illusion dans l'"Astrée"*, 1963
McMahon, Mary Catherine, *Aesthetics and Art in the "Astrée" of Honoré d'Urfé*, 1969
Gaume, Maxime, *Les Inspirations et les sources de l'oeuvre d'Honoré d'Urfé*, 1977
Horowitz, Louise K., *Honoré d'Urfé*, 1984

V

VAUVENARGUES, Luc de Clapiers, marquis de, 1715–1747.

Moralist.

LIFE

Vauvenargues is a small village about 15 kilometres from Aix. Above it on a rocky hill is the 14th-century château owned by the Clapiers family since the 16th century, and by the counts of Provence before that. The Clapiers belonged to the relatively impoverished but ancient Provençal aristocracy, but also had a 15th-century town house in Aix. The future Vauvenargues, born on 6 August 1715 of a mother about whom nothing is known and a 24-year-old father, Joseph de Clapiers, was the eldest son of a family of three boys and a girl. His father was first consul of Aix when a ship from Sidon brought the plague to Marseilles, from where it spread to Aix, killing 7,500 people in 1720 and 1721. Joseph de Clapiers, with one colleague, refused to flee, carried on the town's administration, and was long remembered for heroic efforts to check the spread of the disease. Louis XV erected Vauvenargues into a marquisate and gave Joseph de Clapiers a pension of 3,000 livres with the title which his son was the first person to use.

All three sons took up military careers, and Vauvenargues's sister became a Carmelite. He himself had poor health and seems not to have attended much the Jesuit school at Aix where he was sent. He never learnt to read Latin or Greek fluently, and had difficulty even with correct French. He did not get on well with his energetic and vigorously philistine father, although he inherited from him staunch family pride. In his writings Vauvenargues's remarks about childhood are all coloured by reminiscences of repression. At 25 he remembered being deeply impressed by Plutarch and Seneca when he was 16.

In 1733 Vauvenargues, aged 17, joined the king's regiment when, after 18 years of peace, the army under Villars crossed the alps to re-take for France's allies, Sardinia and Spain, parts of the Austrian possessions in Lombardy. France was acting in pursuit of the claim of Stanislas Leszczynski, father-in-law to Louis XV, to the throne of Poland. On 15 March 1735 Vauvenargues became a sub-lieutenant and on 22 May a full lieutenant. After the peace of 1736 he remained with the army, spending the next five years garrisoned in various towns of the north-east. Letters survive from 1737, making it possible to know some details of his life and circumstances. He had poor eyesight and was incompetent in practical matters, so had no real prospect of military advancement, even if his family had had the money to purchase him a colonelcy. He was bored by trying to lead the social life of an itinerant garrison officer, and by 1739 heavily in debt. He did not gamble, but it was the custom for young officers to entertain well. The army had actually had to issue edicts limiting the number of courses served at meals and forbidding the use of valuable glass and crockery.

Introverted, shy, lacking in the social graces, Vauvenargues began to despise the frivolities in which his companions passed their time, and realized that he was becoming withdrawn. He appears to have read a good deal, almost systematically going through the French classics, early Voltaire, Pope and Locke. By 1737 he was himself writing a treatise on free will. Letter-writing became a cultivated hobby, and what has survived from the period 1737–1740 allows us to trace Vauvenargues's friendship with Victor Roquetti, marquis de Mirabeau, like himself a member of the Provençal aristocracy. Mirabeau, author of a treatise on political economy, father of the revolutionary orator, was irascible enough to be responsible during his lifetime for around 50 lettres de cachet issued against members of his family. He inherited the family fortune in 1737 when he was 22.

Vauvenargues and his father were in Paris for two or three months in 1738 and then spent the winter in Aix. His letters to Mirabeau become more self-revelatory from that Christmas. By April 1739 Vauvenargues was back with his regiment at Arras, and Mirabeau was pushing him to become a professional writer, just as he would soon urge him to leave the army. Vauvenargues was in fact writing, but only in the hope of acquiring the skills necessary for a diplomatic career. In an important 3,000-word letter from Paris, of 16 January 1740, Vauvenargues wrote to Mirabeau, explaining that, if it were possible, he would really like to seek prestige at Versailles. He knew the ambition was hopeless, but the disappointments and frustrations of his life constitute an important background to the moral writing. Later in 1740 the correspondence became less intimate and, although it continued, no letters survive after 21 August.

There is another correspondence, with Jules François-Paul Fauris de Saint-Vincens, a future magistrate and antiquary who was a 21-year-old law student when it began in 1739. In 1746 he was to marry a 15-year-old girl who was, it appears, wrongly acquitted of forgery in 1774. Vauvenargues and Saint-Vincens use "tu" to each other, and Saint-Vincens lent Vauvenargues money. He proposed to lend him some more in 1740, when Vauvenargues was contemplating the then culturally fashionable journey to England, but nothing came of the project and Vauvenargues spent the second half of 1740 at Aix, where he was seriously unwell. On recovery he felt constrained at living with his family, but needed money, which he did not have, for any other existence. He did spend from December 1740 to February 1741 in Paris, but apparently did not much enjoy it.

The immediate future was settled by the death of the emperor Charles VI in Vienna, which left the kings of Prussia, Poland, and Spain, as well as the duke of Bavaria, claiming the inheritance of Maria Theresa, the Austrian succession. Frederick II of Prussia successfully invaded Silesia, and Vauvenargues, who had rejoined his regiment at Metz, heard that his brother Antoine had been killed in Corsica. He was himself ill again in May, and took the waters at Plombières in the Vosges until the end of June. In July he left France with the army under the command of Belle-Isle, put at the disposal of the elector of Bavaria. With the Bavarians the French moved from Linz not, as expected, on Vienna, but on Prague, crossing the Danube for the northward march in November. Vauvenargues never forgot the extreme cold. Prague was taken on 25 November and Vauvenargues was among those sent to Vietach in pursuit of the retreating Austrians.

Vauvenargues was ill, but could not return to Prague until 2 March. Both of his legs were severely frost-bitten, probably during this winter rather than the next. Frederick II and Maria Theresa made peace, leaving the French in Prague besieged by the Austrians, who held the surrounding countryside. By August 1742 the French were killing their horses for food. On 22 August Vauvenargues's commander, the duc de Biron, was wounded in a sortie and, on the following day, Vauvenargues was made a captain. That year he had composed a group of works, including the two *Discours sur la gloire*, the *Discours sur les plaisirs*, and the *Conseils à un jeune homme*, for a 17-year-old officer, Paul-Hippolyte-Emmanuel de Seytres, to whom he had become deeply attached in what was the strongest emotional experience of his adult life, but who had died in April. Vauvenargues then wrote a lyrical *Eloge funèbre*.

The military situation became hopeless and, in the intense cold of 16 December 1742, Belle-Isle and 14,000 men broke out of Prague, leaving behind 5,800 of whom 4,000 were ill. It seems almost certain that Vauvenargues was among those who left. Belle-Isle skilfully managed to avoid an encounter and reached Eger in ten days, but he had lost large numbers to the cold. Although Vauvenargues survived, and reached Amberg in Bavaria with the remnants of the army on 6 January 1743, his health had been ruined by the retreat and he had contracted the illness, either pleurisy or consumption, from which he was eventually to die young, in 1747, not yet 32.

After six weeks at Nancy the king's regiment was sent to join the campaign in east Germany which culminated in the battle of Dettingen. In the meanwhile there were interest payments to Saint-Vincens to meet. Vauvenargues was reduced to asking his father for help. He had decided to leave the army if he could obtain a diplomatic posting or a position at court. In the remote hope of launching himself on a literary career he also on 4 April 1743 sent Voltaire a copy of an essay he had written comparing Racine with Pierre Corneille, already a standard exercise. Voltaire liked what he read more for what it promised than for what it contained, was flattered at being regarded as an arbiter on a matter of taste, genuinely wanted to be helpful, made enquiries, approved of what he heard, and replied charmingly, sending Vauvenargues a copy of his works. Vauvenargues sent back more of his own work, heard again from Voltaire, and left for the war.

He was not harmed during the defeat of the French by the English at Dettingen, and spent most of 1743 in Alsace, augmenting his literary output. He wrote a round of letters soliciting, for the second time, a court or diplomatic post, and resigned his commission on 14 January 1744. It has been conjectured that it was the intervention of Voltaire which brought the real hope of a diplomatic appointment now offered by the administration. Vauvenargues was very short of money indeed, but managed to travel to Paris where for the first time he met Voltaire, who was

charmed by him. Vauvenargues's father ordered him back to Aix just as he had been given an interview with Amelot, the minister for foreign affairs. His father appears not to have believed in Vauvenargues's career hopes, and he threatened to cut off further subsidies. We know that Vauvenargues did stay in Paris and that Voltaire became very enthusiastic about him, and it seems that an agreement was reached between Vauvenargues and his father whereby he would return home and study diplomatic history while waiting for a post. Amelot must more or less have committed himself.

It was at Aix, in the late summer or autumn, that Vauvenargues fell seriously ill with smallpox. His frostbite had probably made him lame, the smallpox had damaged his eyesight, and the chest illness contracted on the retreat from Prague was giving trouble. From 1744 until the end of his life he underwent a long-term physical degeneration, interspersed with bouts of recovery and effervescent spirits. There is evidence that his appearance changed. Marmontel, his friend for his last years, tells us that Vauvenargues, realizing how infirm the smallpox had made him, felt obliged to write to Amelot thanking him for his help and informing him of his unsuitability for a diplomatic post. He also determined to try to get to Paris and, with Voltaire's help, to launch himself on a literary career, which no longer seemed quite so impossible now he had the backing of France's most famous writer. Voltaire, whose literary reputation as a poet and dramatist was at its peak, was preparing at Versailles for *La Princesse de Navarre*, but found time to read further essays which Vauvenargues sent him, and to reply courteously. The exchange of letters, after an interruption of 18 months, became cordial again.

In May 1745 Vauvenargues arrived in Paris and took lodgings for what were to be the last two years of his life. He never again returned to Aix or saw his family. He continued to work, and his health continued to decline. He took up his intercourse with Voltaire again, and with Voltaire's friends, and he was obviously in constant financial need. It was Voltaire who introduced to him another young protégé, Jean-François Marmontel, born in 1723, who had failed to win a prize at the Toulouse Jeux in 1743, had won one in 1744, and had carried off three in 1745. Voltaire had treated him almost exactly as he had treated Vauvenargues, but without quite the same respect for literary promise. Like Vauvenargues, Marmontel was poor, but unlike Vauvenargues he managed to pay off his debts and was later to live the pleasant life of a man of letters. It is to his *Mémoires d'un père pour servir à l'instruction de ses enfants*, and to one or two of his *Contes*, that we owe his reminiscences of Vauvenargues.

Vauvenargues became Marmontel's idol. Marmontel set up house opposite him with an unsuccessful writer called Jean-Grégoire Bauvin, with whom he also edited a new literary weekly in which Voltaire took a warm interest, *L'Observateur littéraire*. It died after eight numbers. Vauvenargues was not well enough to join Bauvin and Marmontel at the famous café, the Procope, in the evenings, but he did meet Marmontel frequently at Voltaire's, and Voltaire not infrequently called on him. It was in the literary company of Voltaire and his friends that Vauvenargues came out of his shell, and lost his shyness sufficiently to share the dominant role with Voltaire in the conversation. Vauvenargues was also one of those from whom Voltaire welcomed detailed criticism of his work.

In 1745, Vauvenargues had brought with him to Paris the draft of a treatise which was to cover all moral, religious, and political questions. He must have realized that he could not write it as planned, or perhaps that it could not be written. In the event he published with Briasson reworked parts of it, as *Introduction à la connaissance de l'esprit humain*, in February 1746. The text was followed by that of a series of *Réflexions critiques sur quelques poètes* and a selection from Vauvenargues's shorter writings, including the *Conseils à un jeune homme* and the *Méditation sur la foi*, with fragments gathered together as *Réflexions, Paradoxes*, and *Maximes*.

Vauvenargues's health improved a little and he anticipated returning to Aix to visit his family. In the winter of 1746–47 the south of Provence was threatened by the troops of the duke of Savoy, in league with the Austrians, but the Vauvenargues estate escaped. Vauvenargues himself, in one of his periodic bouts of elation, had volunteered to join in the fighting. But early in 1747 his health collapsed, and by February he was house-bound. He intended, should he ever recover, to return permanently to Aix. In fact he never did recover, and died in Paris on 28 May 1747 at the age of 31. He does not appear to have received the last sacraments, although there is little foundation for the rumour that he refused them.

WORKS

Vauvenargues published only one volume during his lifetime. Printed by Antoine-Claude Briasson in 1756, it did not carry Vauvenargues's name, was in the convenient small duodecimo format, and had not quite 400 pages. It contained a number of "works," including the principal one, the *Introduction à la connaissance de l'esprit humain*, twenty-two *Réflexions sur divers caractères*, eleven *Conseils à un jeune homme*, five *Réflexions critiques sur quelques poètes*, two *Fragments sur les Orateurs et sur la Bruyère*, and a *Méditation sur la foi*, followed by a *Prière*. Since the volume was not long enough Vauvenargues had added a series of *Maximes* which he had not originally intended for publication.

We know from Vauvenargues's life that he had envisaged a literary career only from two years earlier, that he had put together a volume of pieces varying in literary finish and in place, date, and circumstance of origin, but that they formed a selection, operated by himself, from among the material he had written. He was preparing a second edition when he died, and his work was completed by the abbé Trublet, still friendly with Voltaire, and the abbé Séguy, the king's preacher. There were corrections, additions, and omissions, and a preliminary *Discours* by Vauvenargues. This second edition was published in the year of Vauvenargues's death and can be considered as having been sanctioned by him.

We also know from a crucial passage in Vauvenargues's long letter to Mirabeau of 16 January 1740 what at that time seemed to Vauvenargues to be a legitimate aspiration. After listing some ambitions as unworthy, Vauvenargues continued,

...mais de souhaiter, malgré soi, un peu de domination, parce qu'on se sent né pour elle; de vouloir plier les esprits et les coeurs à son génie; d'aspirer aux honneurs pour répandre le bien, pour s'attacher le mérite, le talent, les vertus, pour se les approprier, pour remplir toutes ses vues, pour charmer son inquiétude, pour détourner son esprit du sentiment de nos maux, enfin, pour exercer son génie et son talent dans toutes ces choses; il me semble qu'à cela il peut y avoir quelque grandeur

(…but to desire in spite of yourself some domination, because you feel born for it; to want to bend minds and hearts by your brilliance; to aspire to honours in order to spread good, in order to attract merit, talent, and virtue and appropriate them to yourself, to carry out all your ideas, to appease your anxiety, to turn your mind from the consciousness of our ills, in brief, to exercise your gifts and your talent in all these things; it seems to me that there can be some grandeur in that).

A number of points need to be made about that passage: it contains a sense of superiority which many may feel but few would care to reveal; it was not intended for us to see and, if reading it allows us some insight into a self-knowledge unusually deep and unusually honest and helps us to understand the published work, we have none the less, by reading it, been prying into what Vauvenargues wrote to an intimate friend in a privileged moment of self-analysis.

Secondly, the passage is poorly written. A quick glance at the punctuation and syntax makes it obvious that that passage is not the work of an educated pen. Indeed, Voltaire's copy of the 1746 edition of Vauvenargues's book, now in the Bibliothèque Mejanes at Aix, shows phrases inked out in Voltaire's handwriting which were replaced by more polished substitutes in the 1747 edition, suggesting that Voltaire helped Vauvenargues to improve his expression. The phrase "hors son nom qu'on veut nommer (except his name which you want to name)" was scratched out by Voltaire and replaced by "hors son nom qu'on ne peut rappeler (except his name which you have forgotten)." Voltaire instantly saw that Vauvenargues had brilliant analytic powers, and no real ability to express himself. We are therefore left with the possibility that in Vauvenargues's process of selecting from his output that part of it of which he felt confident enough to allow himself to be judged by, he may have been too eager to pick on that which had literary polish and too reluctant to publish his deepest but perhaps badly expressed insights. Vauvenargues may be one of those rare writers to whom critics do not risk doing an injustice by ignoring the distinction between published and suppressed material.

How far should we go towards the other extreme? Two-volume editions of Vauvenargues in 1797 and 1806 each added unpublished material, and a three-volume edition in 1821 added a whole new volume of unpublished writing. Then in 1857 came the definitive two-volume edition by D.-L. Gilbert, based on Vauvenargues's own 708 pages of notebooks, not all of the same format, which occasionally contained six or eight versions of the same material, sometimes with different titles as well as variants and drafts. The Gilbert edition therefore contains much raw material, the result of the first stage of the literary process actually to involve pen and paper, of which it can be said with certainty that Vauvenargues would never have published all of it as it stood. Gilbert's edition is excellently comprehensive but necessarily conjectural. The fascination of such an edition is, of course, the opportunity it gives the modern reader to watch the creative process at work, but we have to make up our own minds which are the finished literary artefacts. To some extent the literary critic ought to discount the rest, or at least take into account the reasons why it was not published.

Vauvenargues's notebooks were burnt in the Louvre fire on the night of 23 May 1871, so that, unless new letters appear, or manuscripts in private hands are revealed, what we now have is all that we will ever have, chiefly an arrangement a century later of just over 700 inaccurately numbered pages of writings that Vauvenargues collected together. We are left with only speculation about what, or how, or in what form, he might have published their contents. Gilbert tells us that one piece, which started on page 564 of the manuscript, ended on page 541. The manuscript leaves were in confusion when they were numbered. Additional manuscript material existed and was incorporated into the three-volume 1874 edition. But in seeking to know what Vauvenargues thought, and by what writing he would have wished to be remembered, we clearly have little choice other than to go by the 1746 and 1747 editions. The best modern edition, dated 1968, preserves at least the most interesting of the comments made by Voltaire on his copy of Vauvenargues's works, which still exists, and also divides the individual pieces into those which appear finished and those which are more clearly raw material in an unworked state.

Mostly because too little account has been taken of the differences of status between the different works, critical comment offers little sure guidance to the nature of Vauvenargues's achievement. What interests him is human motivation. He wrote in different ways for different readerships, and probably, in spite of one or two occasions on which he held stoutly to his own views, deferred too much to Voltaire. But it is noticeable that his boldest thoughts and fantasies, those, for instance, which justify violence and intrigue, were among those he never published. In the unpublished *Essai sur quelques caractères*, for instance, there is a passage from "Lentulus; ou, Le factieux" which undoubtedly betrays a tendency in Vauvenargues, although not only was "Lentulus" never published by him, but this revealing passage was demoted to a note even in the now incinerated manuscript:

Mais, l'ambition, la hauteur, et plus que tout cela, les grands talents, révoltent aisément la multitude; le soupçon et la calomnie suivent le mérite éclatant, et le peuple cherche des crimes à ceux qu'il estime assez courageux pour les entreprendre, et assez habiles pour les cacher

(But ambition, elevation, and more than all that, great gifts easily provoke the crowd; suspicion and calumny dog outstanding merit, and the people looks for crimes in those it thinks courageous enough to undertake them and skilful enough to conceal them).

In fantasy Vauvenargues could undoubtedly sympathize with, or possibly even share, Lentulus's aristocratic contempt for the crowd left to admire the courage of his evil deeds and the skill deployed in their concealment, but it was more than another century before Nietzsche could seriously argue that there existed a moral grandeur which transcended the distinction between good and evil. Part at least of Vauvenargues's power resides in the way he admits such fantasies into his consciousness but rejects them. His greatness as a moralist may well depend on the chance circumstances that have fixed for us what values, late in 1746 or early in 1747, he was in the process of examining, accepting and rejecting.

Among the constants of his thought are the characteristic

expressions of indignation, particularly at the frivolity of ordinary social intercourse, at which he so conspicuously failed to excel and yet which exercised for him the fascination summed up in the hidden ambition to succeed at court. We catch him wrestling with himself, analysing himself, fascinated more by the way people behave than by the moral judgements it might be appropriate to make on their behaviour. There is something like exasperation in this advice to Hippolyte de Seytres:

La frivolité anéantit les hommes qui s'y attachent; il n'y a point de vice peut-être qu'on ne doive lui préférer; car encore vaut-il mieux être vicieux que de ne pas être

(Frivolity annihilates those who devote themselves to it; there is perhaps no vice that should not be preferred to it; because it is better to exist with vices than not to exist at all).

The central detestation of dehumanizing frivolity runs right through the *Essai sur quelques caractères* and is brilliantly caught, for instance, in the caractère of Thersite, the cultivated and effeminate sycophantic officer, better at salon conversation than at fighting wars, but it is not Vauvenargues's only target. There is Masis, who never finds anything admirable in anyone:

Il ne loue aucun homme vivant, et on lui parle d'aucun misérable qui n'ait mérité son malheur; il est dispensé par ses maximes d'aimer, d'estimer ou de plaindre qui que ce soit

(He praises no living person, and you can speak to him of no wretch who has not deserved his misfortune; he is dispensed by his principles from loving, esteeming or sympathizing with anyone at all).

It is not at all a paradox that Vauvenargues's dislike of frivolity on the one hand and rigour or severity on the other should have given him that sensitive and indulgent understanding of human beings on which fed what has often been acclaimed as his optimism. He was of his century, and it was very difficult then to have a view of human nature as wholly bad. By 1746 Jansenism was spiritually a spent force, reduced to the status of a religious prop to political Gallicanism. Calvin's understanding of predestination had been carefully extracted from the sorts of Calvinism left to flourish. Vauvenargues's vision of a heroic ideal remained quite compatible with his sympathy for human weakness. Its appearance, however, in published and unpublished work alike, was sporadic. No synthesis of Vauvenargues's view is possible, and it is clear from the quality of his jottings that not all the insights are of equal power. Some are short developments which do not really work. What remain remarkable are the individual insights into the motivation of his own behaviour and that of others.

In the *Discours préminaire* to the 1747 edition, in which Vauvenargues added Quinault and J.-B. Rousseau to the subjects of the *Réflexions critiques sur les poètes*, he acknowledged retouching his style and correcting the "fautes de language (errors of language)" which had been brought to his attention in the first edition. He also attempted to define his aim. He was struck that every principle could be confronted with its contradiction, but that life could be lived only if a knowledge of truth could be attained. He did not, however, know how to escape from the uncertainties which surrounded him. He himself expressed the unifying principle of his writings:

Alors j'écoutai cet instinct qui excitait ma curiosité et mes inquiétudes, et je dis: Que veux-je savoir? Que m'importe-t-il de connaître? Les choses qui ont avec moi les rapports les plus nécessaires, sans doute? Or, où trouverai-je ces rapports, sinon dans l'étude de moi-même et la connaissance des hommes, qui sont l'unique fin de mes actions et l'objet de toute ma vie? Mes plaisirs, mes chagrins, mes passions, mes affaires, tout roule sur eux; si j'existais seul sur la terre, sa possession entière serait peu pour moi: je n'aurais plus ni soins, ni plaisirs, ni désirs; la fortune et la gloire même ne seraient pour moi que des noms; car il ne faut pas s'y méprendre: nous ne jouissons que des hommes, le reste n'est rien. Mais continuai-je, éclairé par une nouvelle lumière: qu'est-ce que l'on ne trouve point dans la connaissance de l'homme? Les devoirs des hommes rassemblés en société, voilà la morale; les intérêts réciproques de ces sociétés, voilà la politique; leurs obligations envers Dieu, voilà la religion

(Then I listened to that instinct arousing my curiosity and my anxieties, and I said: What do I want to know? What do I need to understand? Those things doubtless which most closely concern me? But where do I find them, except in the study of myself and the knowledge of others, which are the sole end of my actions, and the object of my whole life? My joys, my sorrows, my passions, my affairs all centre on them. If I existed alone on earth, my possession of it all would matter little to me; I should have neither cares, nor pleasures, nor desires; fortune and glory even would be mere names for me; for there should be no mistake: we enjoy only other people, the rest is nothing. But, I continued, enlightened by a new insight: what is there which is not found in the knowledge of others? Their duties when they are gathered into a society, that is morality; the mutual interests of those societies, that is politics; their obligations towards God, that is religion).

Everything that Vauvenargues wrote is governed by this statement of his intention. His texts often lack concrete details, colour, variety, and vivacity, but their value lies in the flashes of penetrating insight with which he put his intention into execution, whether in descriptive portraits, literary criticism, imaginary conversations, maxims, or the formal consideration of the values he had observed at work in human motivation in a range of situations which nobody could consider unremarkable.

PUBLICATIONS

Collections

Introduction à la connaissance de l'esprit humain, suivie de Réflexions et de Maximes, 1746; revised and augmented 1747; as *Maxims*, 1903; as *Reflections and Maxims*, 1940
Oeuvres complètes, 1781
Oeuvres de Vauvenargues, 2 vols., 1797
Oeuvres de Vauvenargues, 1806
Oeuvres de Vauvenargues, 1818

Oeuvres posthumes de Vauvenargues, 3 vols., 1821
Oeuvres complètes de Vauvenargues, 3 vols., 1823
Oeuvres de Vauvenargues, 2 vols. (D.-L. Gilbert edition), 1857
Oeuvres morales de Vauvenargues, 3 vols., 1874
Oeuvres de Vauvenargues, 1975
Oeuvres de Vauvenargues, 3 vols., 1929
Oeuvres complètes de Vauvenargues, 2 vols., 1968

Biographical and critical studies

Wallas, May, *Luc de Clapiers, marquis de Vauvenargues* (in English), 1928
Richard, P., *La Vie de Vauvenargues*, 1930
Rocheblave, S., *Vauvenargues; ou, La Symphonie inachevée*, 1934
Vial, F., *Une philosophie et une morale du sentiment, Luc de Clapiers, marquis de Vauvenargues*, 1938
Sacy, S. de, *Vauvenargues; ou, Qui perd gagne*, 1956
Coulet, H., *Le Succès et l'échec dans la morale de Vauvenargues*, 1965

VIAU, Théophile de, 1590–1626.

Poet and dramatist.

LIFE

Théophile de Viau, invariably known simply by his forename, was born in April 1590 at Clairac, near Agen, of a strongly Protestant family from the minor aristocracy. His literary reputation has much increased with the general acceptance of the historical category of "baroque," as also with the concentration of interest in cultural history on the early free-thinking milieux with which Théophile was associated. His career has been read in very different ways, and the free-thinking elements in his thought may have been exaggerated. It is certain at least that he rebelled against his strict Protestant upbringing and that for a period he was welcome and trusted at court, and it is normally supposed that he had at least two homosexual relationships, one with a shadowy figure who made an accusation against Théophile at his trial, and the other with Guez de Balzac, with whom Théophile was at the university of Leiden. It was common gossip that there was a homosexual relationship between Théophile and his close friend Des Barreaux around 1622.

Théophile studied at Nérac, then Montauban, and finally at the Collège de Médecine at Bordeaux. He may then have gone on to Saumur. Thereafter, although it has been conjectured that he had some contact with a travelling group of players, we know very little before 1615, except that Théophile was registered as a student at Leiden with Guez de Balzac. They caroused and quarrelled, and Théophile returned to Paris where, in 1615 he joined the household of Henri de Nogaret d'Epernon, comte de Candale, for whom he wrote love poems and with whom he fought in Condé's second rebellion during the fighting of 1615–1616 in the south-west. Candale was appointed general of the Protestant armies in the Cévennes, and abjured Catholicism in the church of Alais on 10 January 1616.

Immediately thereafter he continued to write verses for Candale addressed to Marguerite de Béthune, wife of the duc de Rohan who, judging from the content of the verses, appears to have yielded to Candale in 1617. However, in December 1617 his wife demanded a separation on grounds of his impotence, and the formal test of "congrès" took place on 11 March 1618, without doctors, but with Séguier and Bérulle for judges. Candale was victorious, and had his wife imprisoned. They were in the end legally separated. Théophile lived under Candale's protection until about 1619, well known at the court of the young Louis XIII, highly regarded for his poetic skills, irreverent wit, and sacrilegious attitudes by the more educated members of the young aristocracy.

There was clearly a private as well as a public style of behaviour, and the most likely resolution of the biographical problems is that Théophile permitted himself too incautiously to do and say in private things which became the subject of public knowledge, or at least speculation. He was certainly well protected, after he had broken with Candale, by Liancourt, perhaps even by Luynes, and then certainly by Montmorency. In 1618 he was not only pardoned for his rebellious activities on behalf of the Huguenots, but given a royal pension. In 1619 he was exiled. It seems certain that he had been caught up in the Vanini affair.

Vanini had arrived in Paris in 1615 and stayed until 1617, when he went to Languedoc. Accused of spreading blasphemous views, he was arraigned before the parlement of Toulouse and condemned to have his tongue torn out before being strangled and then burnt at the stake on 9 February 1619. Vanini did not write with rigour, but with a wild intensity, and may have been more of a crank than a true "atheist," in the sense of anti-Christian apologist. He wrote one book against atheism and a second on natural providence, the *De admirandis naturae reginae deaeque mortalium arcanis*, was approved by the Sorbonne before being re-examined and burnt. His views were alarmingly naturalist in a way not expressed but possibly supposed in Théophile's poetry.

At Théophile's trial it was testified that he had spent three months of 1615 in Saint-Affrique, due north of Narbonne and about 90 kilometres north-west of Montpellier, and had spoken not only blasphemously but also obscenely about the Virgin. The witness said that the Huguenot ministers themselves would have raised the people against him, if the town's governor, a certain Panat, had not saved him. That testimony is suspect for a number of reasons. The date is certainly wrong, and two Panat brothers have been confused with each other. The involvement of Huguenot ministers suggests that the cult of the Virgin was not what was at stake. However, the testimony confirms that Théophile was indeed suspected of holding a Vanini type of naturalism, and suggests that he was compromised by Vanini's trial, so providing a clear reason for the decree of exile in 1619, officially explained in terms partly of Théophile's expressed views about religion, and partly of the "saletés (filthinesses)" of his language about religious matters. At his first interrogation in 1623, Théophile was accused of teaching that "no God should be recognized but nature, to which entire abandon should be made and which the individual, forgetting Christianity, should follow like an animal."

Théophile went to Spain, but soon returned and in 1620 was fighting under Luynes in the royal army. It was at this time that he met the man who became his closest friend, Jacques Vallée des Barreaux. In 1621 Théophile's *Oeuvres* were published by Billaine and Quesnel. There were to be further editions in 1623 and 1624, showing a move away from Malherbe, whose advice Théophile had once sought and taken, towards a relaxed and self-revelatory style of versifying. There are 93 known 17th-century editions of Théophile's works. It seems most likely that Théophile's single play, *Pyrame et Thisbé*, published in 1623, was first played in 1621. That year Théophile returned to the army, now fighting the Protestant separatists of the south-west. The following year, after his father had died in June 1622, Théophile became a Catholic. Both Liancourt and Montmorency appear to have entrusted Théophile with important diplomatic missions in Holland and England. In Paris he mixed with Lhuillier, Mainard, Boisrobert, Saint-Amant and Tristan as well as with Des Barreaux. A ballet on which Théophile collaborated with Saint-Amant, Boisrobert, Duvivier, and Charles Sorel, *Les Bacchanales*, danced before Louis XIII on 26 February 1623, alluded to Montmorency's love for the queen, Anne of Austria, in too open a manner for the king not to understand.

On 13 April 1623 a volume had appeared entitled *Le Parnasse satyrique*, containing audacious and partly licentious poems, including a section signed by Théophile. The volume was condemned on 11 July by the Paris parlement, which also ordered Théophile's arrest. He was in hiding with Montmorency at Chantilly when, on 19 August, he was burnt in effigy with his works, including *Pyrame*. On 25 August the Jesuit Père Garasse published his *Doctrine curieuse des beaux esprits de ce temps*, one of the early salvoes in the great campaign to penalize non-conformity of thought and behaviour which was to gain momentum during the decade, but primarily directed against Théophile, by now a symbol of all that was subversive of orthodoxly organized dogmatic thought and Christian religious attitudes.

Théophile immediately took fright and left for England, but was arrested near the Belgian frontier at Le Catelet, south of Cambrai, and brought back to Paris with an unnecessarily large military escort, to be imprisoned in the Tour Montgomery, where Ravaillac had been detained. It is normally supposed that the devout party, mobilized by the Jesuits for the court, worked for a death penalty. Théophile put up a determined defence. In the end he was sentenced to a diminished form of exile, and on his release on 1 September 1625 after nearly two years, his health broken by the incarceration, he was allowed to move about between the Ile de Ré, Selles in Berry, Champsaume, and Chantilly, where he was based. He finally died in Paris on 25 September 1626.

Théophile had been accused of denying the resurrection of the dead because, in *Pyrame*, Thisbé had said that her Pyrame "est mort sans espoir qu'il retourne (was dead without hope of his return)." We know that *Pyrame* was played at court, but it may have been late in 1621. Théophile had undoubtedly been indiscreet, provocative, and too cocksure of his own charm, skill, and influence. Everything about him was fresh, natural, and spontaneous. His arrest and detention, no doubt triggered by the publication of *Le Parnasse satyrique*, set off a leisurely hunt for pretexts for interrogations, and provided the efficacious deterrent which the authorities were looking for. The warning to incautious tongues and indisciplined attitudes had been sharp and clear. A death penalty for Théophile in Paris was never as likely as has been suggested. It would have served no purpose, would by 1625 have seemed incommensurate with any allegeable offence, and would have been quite uncharacteristic of Richelieu's administration, which was merciless, but which reserved the enforcement of the death penalty by the central authorities for very clear categories of offence.

WORKS

While Théophile under interrogation undoubtedly denied writing some things he must have written, like the first satire, published anonymously in the 1620 collection *Délices satyriques*, then signed in the second book of the *Délices* of the same year and in the first edition of his *Oeuvres* in 1621, it is normally accepted that he is at least unlikely to have written the scabrous pieces attributed to him in the 1623 *Le Parnasse satyrique*. Because attributions and dates are so uncertain, it is difficult to be specific about dates of compositions of Théophile's verse, but it is generally agreed that the early poems are the lively, spontaneous pieces, negligently written and full of archaisms, including *Le Matin*, *La Solitude*, and *L'Hiver*.

It was under the influence of Malherbe that Théophile went back to his early work and corrected it. Not only was Théophile's verse thereby improved, but the utility of Malherbe's reform was demonstrated. However silly Malherbe's pedantic comments on Ronsard and Desportes can be made to look, however closer to being right Régnier was on everything about which they disagreed, however ungracious his personal behaviour and however hostile he was to the reality and the theory of poetic inspiration, Malherbe insisted that writing poetry should be difficult. No doubt he went too far in excluding everything personal, fresh, lyrical, and satirical from his elegiac pieces, but he also excluded another danger less often remarked on, which is that of assuming that it takes no more than rhyming every twelfth syllable to turn prose into poetry. Malherbe felt strongly that poetry had to be constrained by difficult rules to give prose the density required by poetic intensity. Théophile in his early work, indeed in the whole way he lived his life, seems to have been looking for the right constraints to funnel his creative energy into formal art works.

Later, the pieces written to further Candale's amorous objectives were professionally adequate. About 1618 Théophile wrote an *Elégie à M. de C...* The poet talks about "la divinité (the divinity)" who "formed" Candale's "essence" rather than the God who created his soul. That might be regarded as poeticization, as might the rest of the first four lines which say that, when Candale was born, the divinity put a fine mind into a well-formed body. The difficulty arises over the next eight lines, which have been read as implying Vanini's naturalism, or as being the normal way of expressing elegiac sentiments in verse about the lot of human beings:

La trempe que tu pris en arrivant au monde
Estoit du feu, de l'air, de la terre et de l'onde,
Immortels élémens, dont les corps si divers
Estrangement meslez, font un seul univers,
Et durent enchaisnez par les liens des âmes,
Selon que le destin a mesuré nos trames:
Triste condition que le sort plus humain
Ne nous peut asseurer au soir d'estre demain!

(The temper you took on arriving in the world/Was of fire, air, earth, and water,/Immortal elements, of which the very different bodies/Strangely mingled make a single universe,/And chained together by the bonds within [between?] souls, last/For as long as destiny has fixed our life-spans:/[How] sad [is our] condition, that fate, more humane,/Cannot promise us tonight that we shall still exist tomorrow!).

If those lines were simple metaphor, they would be harmless, and there is only the slightest hint in the consistency of the metaphor that Théophile might be going beyond a commonplace lament that life carries on only for as long as fate has preordained that it should. If he has gone beyond simple metaphor, there is still no need to see the wilder side of Vanini's naturalism altogether dispensing with divine providence. A corpuscular universe, in which the duration of a life is limited and which is made of the four traditional elements, in any case more easily fits Gassendi's dangerous but perfectly orthodox views. Yet it is difficult to avoid the impression that Théophile was indeed insinuating a naturalism which simply confronted a Christianity based on a false understanding of the nature of things, while doing it in such a way as to allow him, if challenged, to draw back in wide-eyed innocence at the possibility of inferring any such intention.

What the prosecutor did pick on was a few lines from the first *Satyre* published in 1620. The poet is lamenting the human condition. You are born wailing and hungry, naked too,

Ton esprit ignorant encor ne forme rien
Et moins qu'un sens brutal sçait le mal et le bien.
A grande peine deux ans t'enseignent un langage,
Et des pieds et des mains te font trouver l'usage.
Heureux au prix de toy les animaux des champs!
Ils sont les moins hays comme les moins meschans

(Your mind, ignorant as yet, can form no idea/And less than the senses of an animal knows evil from good./With great difficulty two years teach you a language,/And allow you to find the use of your hands and your feet./Happier than you are the animals in the fields!/They are less cursed and less evil).

There follows a long development about how on birth birds fly and fishes swim. The prosecuting commissioners were thinking of the lines above when they reproached Théophile with despising man, and "praising the animals who follow nature." The question again is whether Théophile in 1620 was maliciously going beyond the permitted bounds of metaphor. The probability is that, not expecting his text to be so closely analysed, Théophile was a little more provocative than was prudent. The penalty inflicted had to deter well-educated patrician rebels from indisciplined public behaviour, and its severity may have been miscalculated. To assume that the two-year-long interrogation about the propriety of stretched metaphors was other than ritual postulates an unlikely degree not only of malevolence but also of stupidity in the prosecuting authorities.

It is true that the accusation was blasphemy which, for technical reasons to do with the barbaric Roman legal enactment "Quisquis" punishing the crime of "laesus maiestatis," was known as "lèse-majesté divine" and punishable by death, and that Théophile was kept in the cell once occupied by Ravaillac in the Tour Montgommery of the Conciergerie, part of the Palais de Justice on the Ile de la Cité. But in Paris by this date capital punishment was normally reserved for infanticide, bigamy, robbery, treason, political crimes, and crimes involving death. Toulouse, where Vanini was executed, was notoriously quite the most religiously intolerant jurisdiction in France. It is more likely that the authorities realized, too late, that they had let Théophile's case drag on too long, and that his health had broken down. Prisoners were not as well treated in the Conciergerie as in the Bastille, but they were not expected to die there. For death by incarceration Vincennes was normally used. A token sentence of banishment immediately commuted was too late to save Théophile.

The early *Le Matin* contains 16 four-line stanzas, tight arrangements of sound—evoking scenes very loosely linked to the central theme of dawn. It was a poem much rewritten, and much parodied for its clichés, not least by Théophile himself. The eighth line has been commended for the unusual transitive use of "ronfler (here: neigh/whinny)," but it is in fact the sound values which turn the assembled images into poetry. The sense is clearly sacrificed to them. The first stanza, perfectly keeping the rules of prose syntax, has vivid imagery and a possibly indeliberate lingering for effect on the long o/or/aur/ur/our/oire sounds nine times, with no fewer than nine pronounced "l" sounds, all within 32 syllables:

L'aurore sur le front du jour,
Sème l'azur, l'or et l'ivoire,
Et le soleil, lassé de boire,
Commence son oblique tour.

Ses chevaux, au sortir de l'onde,
De flamme et de clarté couverts,
La bouche et les naseaux ouverts,
Ronflent la lumière du monde

(Dawn on the brow of day,/Sows blue, gold, and ivory,/And the sun, weary of drinking,/Starts his ecliptic course./ /His horses, on leaving the wave,/Covered with flame and brightness,/With mouth open and nostrils flared/Whinny the light of the world).

Théophile genuinely admired Malherbe, although he did not follow his reform very far or for very long and personally delighted in goading him. There is a quatrain against Malherbe, and in his own poetics, as formulated in the *Elégie à une dame* of late 1620, Théophile wrote,

Je veux faire des vers qui ne soient pas contraints,
Promener mon esprit par des petits desseins,
Chercher des lieux secrets où rien ne me déplaise,
Méditer à loisir, rêver tout à mon aise,
Employer toute une heure à me mirer dans l'eau,
Ouïr, comme en songeant, la course d'un ruisseau,
Ecrire dans le bois, m'interrompre, me taire,
Composer un quatrain sans songer à le faire

(I want to write verses which are not constrained,/To take my mind through small projects,/To look for hidden retreats where there is nothing to displease me,/To meditate at leisure, to dream at my ease,/To spend a whole hour looking at myself in the water,/To hear, as if in a dream, the rushing of a stream,/To write in the woods, to pause, to be silent,/To compose a quatrain without thinking about it).

In this passage Théophile is writing expository verse, telling us something, and the poetic sound effects are less central to his purpose, but they are still there, a v-f-v in the first line, four "p" sounds in the second, three "m" consonants in the fifth, the sibilant "s" sounds of lines six and eight, and the three related vowels immediately succeeding one another in line six, "en songeant."

The alternative to sound patterns as an intensifying and organizing principle in Théophile's verse is the rhetoric of persuasion. The first *Satire* is a long hymn to following personal inclination, to resisting pressures to conform:

Qui suyvra son génie et gardera sa foy,
Pour vivre bienheureux, il vivra comme moy

(Those who follow their inspiration and keep faith with themselves,/To live blissfully happy, will live as I do).

The best of the lyric poetry is probably contained in the ten odes written for "Sylvie," the duchesse de Montmorency, in the cycle called *La Maison de Sylvie*, the house being Chantilly. The odes, begun before the troubles of 1623 and finished in prison, delicately mythologize the house and park at Chantilly, and mix the mythological with the real in such a way as to elevate the everyday into the magical.

It is normally accepted that Théophile had already had some experience of writing theatrical entertainments, although the evidence is scant and the dates very uncertain. Whatever audacities it may have contained, the tragedy *Pyrame et Thisbé* is elevated in tone, goes out of its way to preserve the unity of place and the 24-hour rule, and aspires to nobility of style. It was written probably in 1621, certainly for the court, and the performance which took place before the king is more likely to have been given during the carnival of 1621 than at any later date. The piece was first published in 1623, and later, in 1627, played at the Hôtel de Rambouillet, which guarantees that it was acceptable in circles which did not welcome licentiousness, or its purveyors. The Hôtel de Bourgogne put it on the bill, and Scudéry in 1635 said that everyone knew it by heart.

The dramatic construction is undoubtedly weak, but Théophile was not interested in drama. Characters enter and exit simply to deliver their speeches; there is no link between scenes; and the fifth act is composed only of two monologues. The play is a simple panegyric of love, its story based on Ovid and well enough known already to have been treated parodically in the comic context of Shakespeare's *A Midsummer Night's Dream* of perhaps 1595. The interest is concentrated entirely on the emotional content of the intrigue. There is no real context. The geographical localization is a conventional "Babylone" and the obstacles to love are the age-old ones, parents, kings, and natural hazards which here come in the form of lions. That *Les Amours tragiques de Pyrame et de Thisbé, tragédie* kept its popularity is shown by the existence of 73 editions between 1626 and 1698.

The piece opens with an impassioned diatribe by Thisbé proclaiming that love is of the very essence of life. Before it, we do not live, and without it, life is a living death. Without love we would be lower than the animals, like trees. The ensuing conversation with Bersiane, the old lady, makes clear that Thisbé is marked out as a tragic heroine. She likes to be alone, to be silent, to dream, to flee noise. Even a sunbeam can irritate her, a leaf falling, a breeze, an atom. We learn that there is enmity between the houses of Pyrame and Thisbé. Pyrame's father, Narbal, who has listened to the diatribe, is resolved to concede nothing. If Thisbé has absolutized love, Narbal absolutizes parental authority, second in the moral hierarchy only to the king's incarnation of absolute power.

The king, jealous of Pyrame, intends to have him killed, in the hope of subsequently attracting Thisbé's affection. Syllar, his minister, asks him whether he would go so far as to violate the law. When the king replies, "Tu sais que la justice est au-dessous du Roi (You know that justice is beneath the King)," the context of the play's composition argues strongly against reading into the line some form of personal protest by Théophile against the encroaching absolutism of Louis XIII, and similarly some profession of anti-Christian sentiment. Théophile is not balancing the rights of the tyrant against those of his subjects; he simply needs absolute positions and inflexible attitudes to show the strength of the passion opposed to completely implacable power. He therefore endows his characters with extraordinary powers of resolution, unappeasability, until they personify only their principal obsession.

The second act starts with Pyrame affirming the absolute nature of his devouring passion for Thisbé to his friend Disarque. Pyrame well knows that his passion must lead him to death, but demands support from Disarque in the conservation of his malady. The scene simply allows Pyrame to reinforce the total concentration of Pyrame in his passion. In the act's second scene Pyrame and Thisbé are together, lamenting their fate in comparison with that of the birds, the breezes, and the rivers, who can sing "la fureur qu'Amour leur a donné (the madness which Love has inspired in them)" as long as they like.

The central point of the tragedy is rammed home again in the third act, when Syllar's servant Deuxis has doubts about the murder of Pyrame on which they are embarked. Syllar points out that the king's will is absolute, and that, once they are involved in the king's plan, disobedience would certainly mean death. Deuxis is less impressed by the promise of reward, "L'or, ce métal sorcier, corrompt tout par ses charmes (Gold, that spell-casting metal, corrupts everything by its charms)." He attacks Pyrame and just has time to tell him that Syllar and he have been ordered by the king to assassinate him before dying from a blow struck by Pyrame to defend himself. Syllar, wounded, returns to the king, whose messenger has been rebuffed by Thisbé. The king's resolution is only fortified by her resistance.

Pyrame and Thisbé come together again in the fourth act. Thisbé is jealous of the air Pyrame breathes and the flowers he treads on. Her mother rallies to her side and Thisbé, alone, in true baroque style, addresses the moon. She hears a lion coming. In act five, Pyrame arrives and delivers himself of a love poem of delicate intensity and, when he sees traces of blood, deduces that Thisbé has been killed by a lion. At the end of his 170-line monologue, during which he has moved round the stage following the traces of blood and during which wild fancies have passed through his mind of adoring the lion which has devoured Thisbé, he kills himself. The idea of adoring the lion that had eaten Thisbé is grotesquely baroque in its cavalier exaggeration and distortion of feeling, as is the conclusion, in which Thisbé comes in and, after her 120-line monologue, dies.

The play is not so much a tragedy as a poetic dialogue in which Théophile, who has no interest in credibility, does give the expression of ferociously intense love a cloak of sometimes exquisite poetry which elevates it. Love, as here poetically expressed by Théophile, is an ennobling emotion. In its absolute form it ennobles absolutely, so that there can be no excess. The play is not about virtue and happiness. It is about the potential nobility of natural and instinctive passion:

Mais je me sens jaloux de tout ce qui te touche,
De l'air qui si souvent entre et sort par ta bouche

(But I feel jealous of everything that touches you,/Of the air which so often goes in and out of your mouth).

Théophile did leave a fragment of a novel, and it has been conjectured that his prose might have been even better than the best of his verse. His poetic gift was for the evocation and description of intense emotion, and there is not enough of the *Fragments d'une histoire comique* to judge. He was certainly a free spirit, imprudent, delighting in provocation and in all that was natural, confident to the point never of arrogance, but of mocking cockiness. It is easily possible to understand why his generation regarded him as a leader in its quest for a refreshing liberty, naturalness, and lack of constraint in belief and behaviour and why, for that matter, Julie d'Angennes enjoyed playing not Thisbé, the free but submissive woman, but Pyrame, the free spirit of natural man. There is in Théophile an incipient refusal of the sexual values traditionally associated with female gender which can reasonably be said to anticipate the précieuses (q.v.).

PUBLICATIONS

[*Much of Théophile de Viau's work was published first in collective volumes*]

Collections

Oeuvres, 1621; also 1622, 1623, 1625, and 1626; modern edition 2 vols., 1855–56
Oeuvres poétiques, 2 vols., 1651–58
Oeuvres complètes, 3 vols., 1978–

Plays

Les Amours tragiques de Pyrame et de Thisbé; first published in the 1623 *Oeuvres*; separate publication 1626; modern edition 1968, in *Théâtre du dix-septième siècle*, Bibliothèque de la Pléiade, vol. 2.

Biographical and critical studies

Lachèvre, Frédéric, *Le Libertinage devant le parlement de Paris: le procès du poète Théophile de Viau*, 2 vols., 1909
——*Une second révision des oeuvres du poète Théophile de Viau*, 1911
Adam, Antoine, *Théophile de Viau et la libre pensée française en 1620*, 1935
Impiwaara, Heikki, *Etudes sur Théophile de Viau, auteur dramatique et poète*, 1963

VISÉ, Jean DONNEAU DE: see **DONNEAU DE VISÉ, Jean**

VOITURE, Vincent, 1597–1648.

Poet and man of letters.

LIFE

Voiture was born at Amiens and baptized on 24 February 1597. His father, also called Vincent, was a wine merchant, a well-known card player after whom both Pellisson and, depending on him, Tallemant des Réaux, tell us that a particular configuration of gaming chips at piquet was named. On 18 July 1580 Voiture *père* had married Voiture's mother, Jeanne de Collemont, who bore him seven children, one of whom died in infancy. Since the fourth of Voiture's elder sisters was born on 3 January 1590, and his younger brother Florant was born in Paris on 22 September 1605, her confinements must have stretched for 25 years after her marriage. Trade was prospering sufficiently to warrant a move to the capital, where the family settled in the Rue Saint-Denis.

Two of Voiture's elder sisters married merchants, and two married husbands with administrative charges. Voiture was sent to school at the Collège de Boncourt, where he may already have begun to form his later friendship with Claude de Mesmes, comte d'Avaux. He studied law in Orléans, civil law not yet having been brought back to Paris. Florant pre-deceased Voiture fighting in the army of the king of Sweden. A contract has survived whereby Voiture's father, in 1609 already one of a dozen privileged suppliers of wine to the court, undertook to supply the household of Marie de Medici for the year 1615 with as much "vin de bouche (fine wine)" at 80 livres and as much "vin commun" at 40 livres as it wanted, and wherever it was needed. Voiture came therefore from a prosperous merchant family, from which the female children might aspire to marry into, and the male children to acquire minor posts in, the magistracy. Voiture was to achieve a very high income, to lose heavily at gambling, but in adult life never to drink wine.

We know from the books he left—as well as those in Latin and Greek many in Gothic type—that Voiture's tastes were not entirely humanist, and that he early developed a serious interest in Spanish literature, which his later activity suggests must initially have been stimulated by the *Amadis de Gaule* romances, whose first eight books had been translated by Herberay des Essarts between 1540 and 1548, and whose final volumes appeared in French adaptation as late as 1615. But the split in the literary habitués of Catherine de Rambouillet's Chambre bleue (see: *Guirlande de Julie*) between those surrounding Montauzier, like Chapelain, Conrart, and Balzac, whose tastes were formal and whose intentions serious, and those who shared Voiture's taste for practical jokes, galanterie, the lighter verse forms, and frivolous literary pastimes, cannot simply be explained in terms of attitudes to Spanish or Italian literature, or a preference for one over the other.

Personal friendships and antipathies disturbed tidy ideological line-ups as they always do. Despite the delight in pastiche, the posturing, the gaming, and the womanizing, there was an underlying seriousness about Voiture. He was small, witty, very conscious of his non-aristocratic origins, and he knew that he depended for the success he enjoyed on charm and an ability to amuse. He has lent himself to too many of Tallemant's frothy and entertaining anecdotes for some literary historians to have regarded his slight production as much more than a pretext for enlivening their narrative with amusing historical gossip, but what joined and what separated the two literary groups, known as "le corps" and "l'anticorps," at the Hôtel de Rambouillet clearly prefigured the Querelle des anciens et des modernes (q.v.) and is of fundamental importance for any real understanding of 17th-century French literature. For a moment, at least, Voiture was to be the centre of the group out of which would eventually emerge the partisans of the "modernes" in the Querelle.

Tallemant, a principal source for our knowledge of Voiture, recounts with relish the stories behind the four duels he attributes to him, what, using Ariosto's words, he calls his "arme e l'amori (arms and loves)." The first, in Orléans over a girl, was with Des Hameaux, later a président in the Rouen parlement, and Voiture was wounded in the fingers; the second was against La Coste-Montbrun, an officer in Enghien's regiment, who had apparently attempted to cheat at cards; the third, fought in moonlight against a Spaniard in Brussels, was over a girl; and the fourth and last was in the garden of the Hôtel de Rambouillet, in the light of flares, against Jean Chavaroche, the intendant of the household. This last fight, between two beneficed clerics who, as Mme de Rambouillet said, ought to have been reciting their breviaries, when Voiture was about 50, was finally provoked by rivalry for the coquetteries of Angélique-Clarice d'Angennes, later a précieuse (q.v.) and a prude. The fight came as the culminating point of all sorts of rivalries and dislikes. There had always been ill feeling between Montauzier, from 1645 the husband of Julie d'Angennes, the eldest daughter of the house and the recipient of the *Guirlande de Julie*, and Voiture, who had been allowed to play the distant galant before the betrothal was announced, but had once been banished for a fortnight for touching Julie's arm with his lips.

On Voiture's return from Orléans, he had a liaison with Madeleine de la Touche, by whom he had a daughter, Madeleine, whom he later acknowledged, and who entered religion after coming into her inheritance of one sixth part of what Voiture left. She had passed for a period into the service of Mme de Sablé, whom Voiture knew well, having at one time affected an unrequited passion for her, a posturing recorded by Madeleine de Scudéry in the sixth part of *Le Grand Cyrus* under the guise of Callicrate's attitude to Parthénie.

Tallemant's well-informed but colourful *Historiettes* are too full of gossip to be relied on for accurate historical detail but, according to him, Voiture's dalliance with Madeleine de la Touche took place while his friend d'Avaux was with his mistress, Marguerite Vion, wife of the reputedly jealous Pierre de Saintot, the trésorier de France at Tours, to whose household Voiture's social status was not considered exalted enough to warrant admittance. Marguerite Vion, the sister of Charles Vion d'Alibray, the close friend of Saint-Amant and himself a knowledgeable translator, was the daughter of the correcteur des comptes, Nicolas, seigneur d'Oinville. After being d'Avaux's mistress, she did become Voiture's, but it was one of the many originalities of Mme de Rambouillet that, so early in the century, she received together the highest aristocracy and the liveliest as well as the more solemn men of letters, providing a social forum which worked to the advantage of both groups.

Towards 1623 Voiture had sent Marguerite Vion his translation of Ariosto's *Orlando furioso* as a prelude to becoming her lover. Tallemant's invaluable gossip relates that it was Voiture's refinement of manner, his galanterie, which attracted the attention, at what must have been about this time, of Claude d'Urre du Puy-Saint-Martin, seigneur de Chaudebonne, attached to the household of Gaston d'Orléans's first wife, and a close friend of Mme de Rambouillet. Chaudebonne had had a reputation for unbelief until Condren, aided by Balzac, converted him not just to belief, but to devotion. We are told that he said to Voiture, "Monsieur, vous êtes un trop galant homme pour demeurer dans la bourgeoisie; il faut que je vous en tire (Sir, you are too refined a person to stay in the bourgeoisie, I must get you out of it)," and it was through Chaudebonne that Voiture entered the service of Gaston d'Orléans and became an habitué of Mme de Rambouillet's salon, where his presence is attested from about 1625, soon after its inception. Tallemant confirms Sarrazin's reports about Voiture's reputation as a galant, and Voiture himself did whatever he could to encourage it.

He had, however, also met Malherbe and Balzac, and frequented the salon of Marie Bruneau, Mme des Loges, associated with the circle of Gaston d'Orléans and with Malherbe and, like the chambre bleue, too worldly not to be hostile to academic pedantry. Voiture was always complaining about his colds, and it was Mme des Loges who initiated the 1628 "Portraict du pitoyable Voiture," composed entirely of octosyllables ending in "-ture," naturally not omitting "roture (of common birth)," to which a malicious conclusion, probably by Malleville, was later added, after Mme des Loges, fearing suspicion of complicity in anti-Richelieu plots, had left Paris, remaining away from 1629 to 1636. Had she not absented herself, nor died in 1641, her salon might well have rivalled that of Mme de Rambouillet as the forcing ground for literary talent as well as the nursery for patronage in Paris during the second quarter of the century. The Voiture "Portraict" was published in the 1654 *Nouveau Recueil des plus belles poésies*.

By 1626 Voiture was a conseiller du roi, and towards the end of 1627 he became "introducteur des ambassadeurs," a steward in the household of Gaston d'Orléans's, which brought him another 2,000 livres a year. He was obliged to travel with his somewhat light-headed master, who was also sporadically disaffected towards his brother, the king. In 1629 Voiture joined Orléans in Lorraine, a rallying point for conspirators against the crown and Richelieu, returning to Paris after Orléans's submission early in 1630. He joined Orléans again in Brussels after his marriage in 1632 to Marguerite de Lorraine, and followed him on his long journey of rebellion across France in June, before going to Madrid in July, to accompany the marquis du Fargis, the representative of the Orléans interest. Orléans himself abandoned to Richelieu's vengeance the defeated Montmorency, duly executed in 1632, whose defection to him had been a final, futile and, as it turned out, fatal attempt to reassert feudal autonomy, and made his peace, retiring to Blois, while du Fargis left an unwilling Voiture as Orléans's resident representative in Madrid. Voiture was actually on the way home when, in December 1632, he heard at the French frontier that Orléans had fled again to the Low Countries, and himself returned to Madrid, where he was joined by the comte de Maure, representative of the queen mother.

After having been ill in 1632, Voiture appears to have enjoyed Madrid in 1633, although he became short of money and was subsidized by the Spanish government. From March 1633 he was free to return home, but feared the consequences of his alignment with Orléans, whom he did not want to join in Brussels. He therefore stayed in Spain a further three months, and visited first Africa, then Portugal, embarking in Lisbon in October for London. He then crossed from Dover to Dunkirk in December 1633, to join Orléans in Brussels. After he had reconciled himself in 1634 with his brother, Louis XIII, Orléans retired to Blois, where Voiture joined him in November. Although Voiture made brief stays in Paris, his real return there, according to Chapelain, coincided with that of Orléans in October 1636. However, he had been careful enough to act in the interests of Richelieu's favourite niece, Mme de Combalet, when Orléans wanted to take her captive, so that he had kept a powerful protector in Richelieu's camp. To Mme de Combalet he owed his membership of the nascent Académie française from its inception in 1634. Meanwhile he became maître d'hôtel, that is, head of household, to Gaston d'Orléans's new wife, not properly constituted Madame until the marriage was recognized in 1643. Voiture, his income now considerably augmented, also wrote a much admired letter in November 1636, defending Richelieu's policy after the French had retaken Corbie from the imperial troops.

In 1637 Voiture became paymaster of the présidial of Beauvais, and journeyed with Orléans to Tours, from where he visited Mme de Combalet at what must have been Richelieu's château at Rueil, that at Richelieu itself having being left empty and unfurnished after its rebuilding. Then in 1638 he was sent as extraordinary ambassador to the Grand Duke of Tuscany to announce the birth of the new heir, the future Louis XIV. On the way he visited Marie-Christine de France and Louis, from 1621 cardinal de la Valette, brother of the military leader and third son of the duc d'Epernon, much famed at the Hôtel de Rambouillet for his ugliness. Voiture travelled by sea from Genoa to Livorno. After Florence came Rome, then back by sea to Marseilles. Voiture was in Paris again on 1 January 1639. That year he also returned to visit La Valette in Piedmont for three months. The cardinal was to die on 28 September.

In 1640 Voiture accompanied Orléans to Amiens for the siege of Arras, captured on 9 August, and became a gentilhomme ordinaire to Orléans on 19 February 1642. In 1643 he was confirmed as maître d'hôtel ordinaire of Louis XIII, a post he had actually held since 1639 and was to keep, in spite of the deaths of Richelieu in December 1642 and then of the king on 14 May 1643. He had followed the king round the south of France during the winter. He celebrated Enghien's victory over the Spaniards at Rocroi on 19 May, just days after the king's death, and became premier commis to the comte d'Avaux, appointed surintendant des finances by the queen. Mazarin continued to pay Voiture in the hope that he would be useful in controlling the wayward Orléans, and Voiture was appointed maître d'hôtel to the party accompanying Marie-Louise de Gonzague as far as Péronne on her journey to meet her new husband, the king of Poland, Vladislas VII.

On average Voiture was earning 18,000 livres a year, far more than any other writer. The tally is Tallemant's. He lists the sources, but seems to have underestimated the income, noting, however, that Voiture ate at the Hôtel de Rambouillet and that his great expense was gambling. It had been hazard that had introduced Voiture to the entourage of Gaston d'Orléans, where he saw the possibility of being useful to Richelieu, and then Mazarin. His career argues considerable political skill, although no great addiction to principle. His addictions were to women, but even more to gaming, after each session of which he was so drenched in the sweat of excitement that he had to change his shirt. Mme Saintot, who truly loved him, called him "son desloyal (her disloyal one)," and was treated off-handedly by him. He finally ruined himself for Angélique-Clarice d'Angennes, and had to withdraw from the Hôtel de Rambouillet. He died comforted by two ex-mistresses, Mme Saintot and a daughter whose name we do not know of the gazetteer Théophraste Renaudot.

Voiture was capable of sparkling wit, but also of withdrawal to the point of sulkiness. He liked fine clothes, yet behaved in grand company with the boorishness of a peasant and, conscious of his bourgeois origins, was plain-speaking with the great to the extent of downright rudeness. Tallemant tells us that once at the Hôtel de Rambouillet he kicked off his galoshes to warm his feet. To start with, he should have been wearing shoes: "C'estoit desjà assez de familiarité que d'avoir des galoches; mais, ma foy, c'est le vray moyen de se faire estimer des grands seigneurs que de les traiter ainsi … il leur parlait assez librement (Wearing galoshes was already informal enough; but really, that's the right way to get yourself well thought of by the high-born, to treat them like that … [and] he was pretty free in his speech with them)."

The portrait given by Tallemant, although naturally spiced with scandal and mockery, is quite different from the picture of a spinner of facile verse compliments, the light-weight epigrammatist, that has been handed down, and much easier to reconcile with the serious gamer, the political operator, the skilful diplomat, and the passionate flirt, who exploited his humble origins by stopping just short of unacceptable effrontery. Tallement says he thinks it was Enghien who said, "Si Voiture estoit de nostre condition, il n'y auroit pas moyen de le souffrir (If Voiture was of our rank, there would be no way of tolerating him)." It is Tallemant, too, who says that Voiture was small but good-looking, that he was amiable, fascinated women, much entertained the more fastidious of them, and seemed to be laughing at everybody he talked to, while actually everywhere seeking his own advantage.

His social skill lay in the ability to observe amusingly what everyone else missed. He was entertaining when he stuck to galanteries. When he was in love he became a bore, "stupide," says Tallemant. The balance between the ardent womanizer and the sighing galant, the wit and the buffoon, the administrator and the salon entertainer, the employee of Gaston d'Orléans and the servant of Richelieu and Mazarin, was sufficiently precarious for Voiture inevitably from time to time to have lost it—not only in the final duel, in the occasional exaggeration, sulk, or social miscalculation, but also when, for instance, a carriage overturned on a bumpy ride, and he caused embarrassing concern by pretending to have broken a leg. Angélique Paulet suspected the charade, but had to send for a doctor before Voiture revealed his bluff. There are comments about ungainly efforts to dance to his own string-playing which he would have been wiser to avoid. Mme de Rambouillet, who could manage to accept the dreaminess and the occasional pouting, complained of his "suffisances et négligences (conceited ways and casual behaviour)." An indiscreet letter, leaked by Mme de Sablé, nearly ruptured Voiture's relationship with Cardinal de la Valette; a misunderstanding of the earnestness with which Richelieu wanted the Académie française to be taken precipitated not only sudden assiduous attendance, but also the occasion for Chapelain to be sardonic at Voiture's expense.

He was known at the Hôtel as "El rey chiquito (the tiny king)," an allusion to the Spanish novels he was fond of, as well as to his stature. As early as 1630 the habitués of the Chambre bleue at the Hôtel de Rambouillet had taken to using names taken from old novels, particularly the 14th-century *Roman de Perceforest*; Renée-Julie Aubry, daughter of the seigneur du Troussay, at his death the senior conseiller d'Etat, was known as "la Pucelle Priande." Voiture wrote verses in old French, including some to Saint-Aignan, "Chevalier de l'Isle invisible." Invented by Voiture, the game caught on, and the company played at being knights errant and damsels in distress, at taking part in a chivalric world with its mixture of feudal courage and refined dedication to heroic ideals. The point was the exorcism of bawdiness and brutality in the relationship between the sexes, and its replacement at first by galanterie and coquetterie. The reign of the précieux and the prudes was to signal the arrival of a brief but strong reactionary wave during the literary ascendancy of Racine and Boileau.

When Voiture came into a room, people stopped talking to listen, although the performance was not as spontaneous as it seemed. "C'est le père de l'ingénieuse badinerie (He was the father of clever teasing)," says Tallemant, to whom Voiture was, it appears, never very civil. He was not pretentious. "You will see," he said to Mme de Rambouillet, "that one day there will be people stupid enough to go and look here and there for what I have done, and they will have it printed." That pronouncement is often quoted, but sounds like false modesty, part of the performance, which mockingly pandered to the stupidity of Montauzier, who lacked the wit to see Voiture's jokes, and of whom Voiture's pretended jealously over Julie d'Angennes was half real. It was Montauzier who did not invite Voiture to contribute to the *Guirlande de Julie*. Voiture knew very well what real achievement underlay the playfulness, the exaggerations that occasionally went awry, the delight in allegory, mystification, and especially the serious business of pretending that life was lived in fairyland.

Then there were the high spirits, practical jokes, the vaudevilles, the follies, the disguises, the games of literary gazettes, the correspondence conducted in common, with Angélique Paulet the corporate letter-writer, the joint outings, the sense of fun. Voiture surprised Mme de Rambouillet by surreptitiously bringing a couple of bears into the room where she was reading. She got her own back by having a Voiture sonnet printed and stuck into an old book for Voiture to think that the poem he had invented had already been previously printed. The literary division into the corps and anti-corps started as a joke between Voiture and his great friend Pisani, the marquise's son, whom Voiture made much play of teasing for his ignorance. It ended by pitting Chapelain and Voiture against one another with real malice. The Querelle des anciens et des modernes had virtually begun.

Voiture's final duel with Chavaroche displeased his friends, and Mme de Rambouillet above all. Excluded from the Hôtel, he also lost his pension from Mazarin. He was ill for only four or five days before he died on 26 May 1648. Sarrazin wrote a fittingly ironic *Pompe funèbre*.

WORKS

It is not difficult to argue that the enormous historical importance of Voiture for the development of literature in France was not matched by any great work he composed. His prose, particularly the letters, may represent a greater achievement than the verse. The sheer ingenuity, the inventiveness which characterizes both is impressive. In verse Voiture inaugurated vogues for the rondeau, the epigram, the madrigal, the triolet, the ballade, and the gazette galante, in prose for the metamorphosis and a new style of letter. His real poetic originality lay in the slightly mocking tone of his sentimental poetry, which allowed the introduction of very free metres and rhythms, the elimination of rhetorical pomposity, and the relatively elevated galanteries that made room for amusement, and especially erotic innuendo, without lowering the tone.

We owe the letters partly to the fact that Voiture's position as the established poet and jester to the Hôtel de Rambouillet did not go unchallenged. While he was in Spain and Morocco conducting his amusing semi-public correspondence with Angélique Paulet, he feared that Godeau would take his position. He had already died when the "Sonnet d'Uranie" was plucked from his work as an example with which to challenge Bensserade's "Sonnet de Job," but while he was still alive Sarrazin, who rarely appeared at the Hôtel, was encouraged to challenge him, and both Claude Malleville and Tristan l'Hermite wrote rival sonnets on the theme of "La belle matineuse (The beautiful early riser)," a well-known Italian theme used by du Bellay and Ronsard and imitated by Voiture from the 16th-century Annibale Caro, although Voiture imported into his sonnet "Des portes du matin l'amante de Cephale (From the gates of morning the lover of Cephale)" lines imitated from the Spanish Gongora. Voiture's dependence on Spanish sources for some of his most delicately achieved effects, for instance in the "stances" "Je me meurs tous les jours en adorant Sylvie (Each day I die adorong Sylvia)," has been minutely documented. His verse is remarkable, too, for its mixture of sensuality and grace. Underneath the frivolity and the pastiche, the affectations and the occasional simple miscalculation of a joke, is a real layer of humanist competence as well as a sense of fun.

Surprised by Anne d'Autriche while dreaming beside a fountain at Rueil, Voiture was asked what he was dreaming about. Mme de Motteville, through whom the quite long poem was passed on, tells us that Voiture wrote it on the spot. It is exquisitely calculated to flatter with audacity, but without offence, and goes out of its way to draw attention to what a humble poet might be permitted to aspire to in the presence of a queen. There is a repeated "Je pensois (I thought)," and towards the end the poet thinks

> A la ravissante merveille
> De cette taille sans pareille,
> A la bouche la plus vermeille,
> La plus belle qu'on vit jamais,
> A deux pieds gentils et bienfaits...

> Devinez sur cela, Madame,
> Et dites à qui je pensois

(Of the ravishing miracle/Of that figure beyond compare/Of the most crimson mouth,/The most beautiful that was ever seen,/Of two delicate, well-formed feet.../Then guess, Madame, after this,/Who I was thinking of).

That degree of barely stylized refinement was unknown in earlier French verse. Elegance and delicacy have replaced both passion and Petrarchism.

There are party games in Voiture's verse, and much that is not at all poetic, but simply modish, or witty, like the pieces on the water-drinker he was:

> D'un buveur d'eau, comme avez debatu,
> Le sang n'est point de glace revestu,
> Mais si bouïllant et si chaud, au contraire
> Que chaque veine est en eux une artere
> Pleine de sang, de force, et de vertu

(Of a drinker of water, as you have thought,/The blood is not full of ice,/But on the contrary so boiling and so hot/That each of the veins is an artery/Full of blood, strength, and power).

A great deal is charming and clever, and much else just a trivial society pastime. One poem, however, deserves special attention, less for its intrinsic merit than because it was not only admired by Malherbe but also chosen by the critics of Bensserade as an example of a better sonnet than the "Sonnet de Job" which he had sent with the 1648 edition of his *Paraphrases sur les IX leçons de Job*, no doubt to Charlotte Saumaise de Chazan, former lady-in-waiting to Anne d'Autriche, and not yet separated from the comte de Brégy. Bensserade's sonnet is given in the entry devoted to him.

Mme de Brégy, who had been pregnant when she married in 1637 and later became famous for her denunciation of too-frequent pregnancies, showed Bensserade's sonnet around, and his enemies, spear-headed by Anne-Geneviève de Bourbon-Condé, Condé's sister and later Mme de Longueville, chose Voiture's "Sonnet d'Uranie" to oppose it. The Querelle des deux sonnets was over at the end of 1649. Voiture had died in 1648, but his sonnet must have been written before Malherbe's death in 1628. Its importance lies chiefly in its choice by Voiture's champions. They presumably wanted to find a sonnet, and Voiture had written only half a dozen.

> Il faut finir mes jours en l'amour d'Uranie,
> L'absence ni le temps ne m'en sçauroient guerir,
> Et je ne voy plus rien qui me pût secourir,
> Ni qui sçeust r'appeler ma liberté bannie.
>
> Dés long-temps je connois sa rigueur infinie,
> Mais pensant aux beautez pour qui je dois perir,
> Je benis mon martyre, et content de mourir,
> Je n'ose murmurer contre sa tyrannie.
>
> Quelquesfois ma raison, par de foibles discours,
> M'incite à la revolte, et me promet secours,
> Mais lors qu'à mon besoin je me veux servir d'elle;
>
> Apres beaucoup de peine, et d'efforts impuissans,

Elle dit qu'Uranie est seule aymable et belle,
Et m'y r'engage plus que ne font tous mes sens

(I am going to have to end my days in love with Uranie,/
Neither absence nor time will be able to cure me,/And I
can see nothing that could help me,/Or that could bring
back my banished freedom.// For a long time I have
known her infinite severity,/But thinking of the beauties
for which I must perish,/I bless my martyrdom, and happy
to die,/I do not dare to murmur against her tyranny.//
Sometimes my reason, with weak arguments,/Provokes
me to rebellion and promises me help,/But when I want to
use it to help myself,// After much trouble, and fruitless
efforts,/It says that Uranie alone is lovable and fair,/And
binds me again to her more closely than all my senses do).

This is a formally stylized love sonnet, in alexandrines full of
abstract words and conventional sentiments about love, rigour,
tyranny, martyrdom, death, almost to any woman from any poet
writing in the wake of the later Ronsard and Desportes. It may
well have been written to flatter Malherbe's known ambitions to
purify the language and solemnify its usage. It is in the style Voiture had not yet broken away from when he wrote it, not the one
he was to invent in much freer verse forms for the delicate and
refined expression of playfully erotic sentiment. It is none the
less a good deal better than Bensserade's.

Even at its best, Voiture's poetry is often not exempt from the
witty rhetorical flourish of the rondeau. It is impossible not to
find amusing the trivial "stances" in which the poet, once prisoner to a yellow and black slipper, is now in thraldom to one of
black and blue, like some prisoner conducted from the country
surroundings of the awesome Vincennes to the frightening
Bastille. Prose is better suited to his playfulness. Mme de Rambouillet and Angélique Paulet had given him a limited period in
which to make Anne de Bourbon laugh, when she was ill once.
He related to her the penalty inflicted on him for failure—he was
tossed in a blanket.

Ce que je puis dire, Mademoiselle, c'est que jamais personne ne fut si haut que moi et que je ne croyais pas que la
fortune me dût jamais tant élever. A tous coups ils me per-
daient de vue et m'envoyaient plus haut que les aigles ne
peuvent monter. Je vis les montagnes abaissées audessous
de moi; je vis les vents et les nuées cheminer dessous mes
pieds; je découvris des pays que je n'avais jamais vus et
des mers que je n'avais point imaginées. Il n'y a rien de
plus divertissant que de voir tant de choses à la fois et de
découvrir d'une seule vue la moitié de la terre

(What I can tell you, Mademoiselle, is that never did any-
body go as high as I did, and that I never thought fortune
would raise me up so far. At every toss they lost me from
sight and sent me higher than eagles can fly. I saw the
mountains, small in the distance beneath me; I saw the
winds and clouds moving along beneath my feet; I discovered countries I had never seen, and seas I had not imagined. There is nothing more entertaining than to see so
many things at once and to discover at a single glance half
of the world).

Voiture has created a convention of light-hearted pastiche, but it
is more than that. The sprightliness of fancy and the spontaneity

of the letters are delightful, and the diversity of his relaxed literary devices, poses, flourishes, openings, mockeries, and even
allegories has understandably been noticed, although their real
significance has seldom been remarked on.

There is a famous letter from Voiture to Enghien, later Condé,
who had left for what was to be his great victory at Rocroi,
alluding to some parlour game in which Enghien had been a pike
and Voiture a carp. The letter, from the carp to the pike, is to
modern taste a terribly over-extended allegory, exploiting the
gender of the French words for various sorts of fish. The pike
(brochet), being masculine is male, like the bass, while tench,
perch, and trout are all feminine and female. Voiture hopes that
Enghien will soon be home to enjoy female company again. The
enchanting, if over-complex allegorization is more than just a
literary device: it reflects a refining of sentiment, as does the
allegorical siege of the Paris citadel "which even Piccolomini
would not prevent me from taking," of which Voiture writes to
Cardinal de la Valette, referring to a woman he was going to capture, even if the Austrian general tried to stop him.

Voici le Lion du Nord et ce conquérant dont le nom a fait
tant de bruit dans le monde qui vient mettre à vos pieds les
trophées de l'Allemagne et qui, après avoir défait Tilly et
abattu la fortune d'Espagne et les forces de l'Empire, se
vient ranger dans le vôtre

(This is the Lion of the North, and the conqueror whose
name has resounded so loudly through the world, come to
place at your feet the trophies of Germany; having defeated
Tilly and demolished the fortunes of Spain and the forces
of the Empire, he comes to put himself in yours).

Finally there is one genre in Voiture's repertoire, the metamorphosis, obviously classical in origin, of which an example
should be given. He wrote a number of them, the "Métamorphose de Lucine en rose" for Mme de Rambouillet, and the
"Métamorphose de Léonide en perle" for Angélique Paulet, as
well as that given below, the "Métamorphose de Julie en diamant" for Julie d'Angennes, then already Mme de Montauzier.
They share some of the best characteristics of his prose and
poetry, and are important for a variety of reasons. They give an
example of the light-hearted non-pedantic humanism admissible
at the Hôtel; they show the early semi-permanent attribution to
living people, in a tightly closed but immensely important society, of mythological or allegorical names, or those taken from
medieval or modern romances; they inaugurate the vogue for
portraits; and they are written in fairy-tale form, always starting
with an adverbial clause followed by a narrative verb in the past
tense, the pattern of "Once upon a time…went/did…"

This is Julie's metamorphosis into a diamond. The allusion is
to the probably false etymology whereby the word diamond is
derived from "Adamas," meaning "the invincible" or, as here,
"the unique." From "Adamas," too, by way of medieval misunderstanding, comes the French use of "aimant"—also the
present participle of the verb "to love"—for "magnet." Hence
Voiture's complicated joke towards the end about knowing and
loving. The primacy between the two was the subject of serious
medieval philosophical debate. Voiture adds a stiffening of
irony. Diamonds are hard:

En la partie du monde où le soleil se lève et où le ciel

engendre les pierres précieuses, naquit par miracle une Naïade, la plus accomplie que les Dieux eussent jamais faite. Et la Mer n'avait jamais rien vu de si beau, non pas le jour même qu'elle fit naître Vénus. Neptune, pour l'amour d'elle, donna de la jalousie à Thétis et à toutes les Nymphes de l'Océan. Mais, lassé de ses mépris, il la changea en une pierre que les Grecs appellent Unique ou Diamant. Comme elle fut incomparablement belle, d'un esprit divin, insensible, opiniâtre et impérieuse, cette pierre a une beauté qui efface toutes les autres, un feu qui semble venu du ciel. Elle ne se peut rompre par nulle force. Elle résiste au fer et au feu et elle monte jusque sur la tête des Rois. Comme elle fut aimée de tous ceux qui la connurent, les Grands et les petits l'aiment encore, et elle est désirée de tout le monde. Enfin le Ciel et la Terre ne font rien de si parfait, et les hommes ne connaissent aucune chose de si grand prix

(In the part of the world where the sun rises and where the sky produces precious stones, there was born by a miracle a Naiad, the most exquisite that the gods had ever made. And the sea had never seen anything so beautiful, not even on the day it gave birth to Venus. Neptune, for love for her, made Thetis and all the nymphs of the ocean jealous. But, tired of her indifference, he changed her into a stone which the Greeks call Unique or Diamond. As she [Voiture plays here again on the feminine pronoun, indicating both the Naiad, "she," and the precious stone, "it"] was incomparably beautiful, of a divine intelligence, unfeeling, obstinate, and imperious, this stone has a beauty which eclipses all others, a fire that seems to have come from the skies. No force can break her. She resists forge and fire and climbs up to the forehead of kings. Since she was loved by all who knew her, great and small still love her, and she is desired by everyone. In short, heaven and earth make nothing so perfect, and men know nothing so precious).

Enabled and encouraged by Mme de Rambouillet and her lively young aristocratic friends, Voiture created a refined banter sufficiently sophisticated to bring within range the sort of alliance between the top social levels of society and its imaginatively powerful literary figures which was the necessary and sufficient condition for the serious examination and eventual reform of personal and social values in French society. The cultivation of grace and elegance, of galanterie and coquetterie, were to be taken to absurd lengths and provoke strong and even violent denunciations. In spite of his duels, Voiture's taming of the brutalities of passion, with the restraints of wit and elegance but without simply negating their reality by empty stylizations, was a key part of the process by which French culture civilized its feudal worship of male dominance, strength and martial feats. Between them Mme de Rambouillet and Voiture produced the social milieu and the literary convention that, bringing together male and female, the aristocratic and the bourgeois, created the first tentative realization of what for the high renaissance had remained merely a dream.

PUBLICATIONS

Collections

Les Oeuvres de Monsieur de Voiture, 1650; revised 1650; revised 1652

Les Lettres et les Poésies de Monsieur de Voiture, 1654
Recueil des Oeuvres de Monsieur de Voiture, 2 vols., 1695
Lettres et autres oeuvres de Monsieur de Voiture, 2 vols., 1697; as *Works*, 2 vols., 1705
Oeuvres de Voiture, Lettres et Poésies, 2 vols., 1855
Poésies, critical edition, 2 vols., 1971

Poems

Hymnus Virginis, seu Astraeae, 1612 [Either the date is wrong or the poem is wrongly attributed]
Mars, A Monseigneur Frère unique du Roy. Stances, 1614 [Attribution possible, but uncertain]
Estraines célestes au Roy, no place or date [?1615]

[Most of Voiture's poems were first published in the following collections: the number of Voiture's poems published in each collection is given in brackets]

Les Poésies et Rencontres, 1630 (2)
Recueil de divers rondeaux, 1639 (26)
Nouveau recueil des bons vers de ce temps, 1646 (1)

Biographical and critical studies

Magne, E., *Voiture et les origines de l'Hôtel de Rambouillet*, 1911
——*Voiture et les années de gloire de l'Hôtel de Rambouillet*, 1912

VOLTAIRE, pseudonym of AROUET, François-Marie, 1694–1778.

Philosophe, satirist, moralist, historian, dramatist, poet, and pamphleteer.

LIFE

Voltaire's mother, Marie-Marguerite Daumard, was born into the minor aristocracy. Her father was an official of the Paris parlement, whose jurisdiction extended over half of France. On 5 June 1683 she married François Arouet (c.1650–1722), a senior administrative official in the tax-office. Voltaire was convinced that his father was a certain Rochebrune, about whom we know nothing. Of the six children born to his mother, Voltaire, as he was to call himself, was the youngest of the three who survived infancy. Armand (1685–1745) was to be sent to the Oratorian school at Saint-Magloire and to become a devout Jansenist (q.v.), and Marie-Marguerite (?1691–1726) was to marry another civil servant, Pierre Mignot, and become the mother of Voltaire's nieces and nephew. The family was well off, with a 14-room house about six miles away from the capital, at Châtenay, near Sceaux, as well as one in Paris, where Voltaire was born. Both houses were expensively equipped, but in 1701, when Voltaire was six, the family moved to an official residence in the Palais de Justice with about 10 main rooms. Voltaire's mother died in the same year.

Voltaire was fragile as an infant, often ill, and later never robust, although also a hypochondriac. His godfather, François de Châteauneuf, a worldly priest, claimed to be Ninon de Lenclos's last lover. Voltaire was presented to her, and she left him a not inconsiderable 1,000 francs to buy books. From 1704 to 1711 he attended the college of Louis-le-Grand, where he was a boarder, and afterwards he remembered his Jesuit teachers with some gratitude. It may well have been their confident spirituality tinged by immersion in the classics which started Voltaire on the road to deism. He was to be followed by such other fellow-pupils as Diderot, Helvétius, Malesherbes, Choiseul, Maupeou, and both the d'Argenson brothers—René-Louis, who became minister for foreign affairs, and Marc-Pierre, who became the minister for war and to whom the *Encyclopédie* was to be dedicated. The catechism taught at Louis-le-Grand insisted heavily on hope, forgiveness, and the efficacy of repentance, while skating over the doctrines of hell and original sin, and over the spiritual implications of the cross and the sacrificial basis of the Eucharist.

Voltaire was at school during France's multiple defeats in the War of the Spanish Succession (1701–13), the politically and economically disastrous end of the reign of Louis XIV, and the legendary cold of the 1709 winter. His ability and impetuous temperament were remarked on, and he wrote what, for schoolboy exercises, was distinguished verse. When he left school, in spite of a clearly literary inclination, he was sent to study law, with a view no doubt to buying one of the offices whose multiplication and sale were among the many fiscal expedients to which Louis XIV was obliged to resort. Among the verses composed by Voltaire as a student was one expressing indignation at the unfair way in which the tax system weighed on the poor.

While still at school, the bright 17-year-old Arouet had been introduced to the free-thinking, high-living, cultivated group which met at the Temple, the headquarters of the old "Templars," now the knights of St John. Its informal leader was the charming poet and hedonist abbot, Chaulieu, charged with managing the affairs of the prior, Philippe, the younger son of the duc de Vendôme. The company included the poet La Fare, the abbé Servien, who openly flaunted his homosexuality and was later to go to prison, and Bussy, the future bishop of Luçon, to whom Voltaire is said to have written verses to console him for the loss of his mistress. It was in this rather dissipated company that Voltaire first got into debt, and composed the draft of his tragedy *Oedipe*. He wanted to write and was indeed, in his own lifetime, chiefly to be renowned for his poetry and drama.

In 1713 Voltaire's family, alarmed at the life of debauchery he seemed to be leading, sent him to Caen, and then to The Hague, where his late godfather's brother had been made ambassador in September 1713, a few months after the treaty of Utrecht had put an end to the war. The Hague was overrun with refugee families from France, some of whom had fled as a result of the revocation of the Edict of Nantes. Voltaire frequented the emigré French community and had his first love affair with Olympe du Noyer, whose mother had had an adventurous background, but retained social pretensions. She complained to the ambassador, who put Voltaire under house arrest. Olympe dressed up as a man and attempted to elope with Voltaire, but the attempt was

foiled, and he was sent back to France. Although Olympe was almost illiterate, Voltaire was genuinely fond of her, would at 19 willingly have married her, and stayed in touch with her until at least 1754.

He reached Paris on Christmas Eve 1713, not much more than eight weeks after arriving in Holland. Threatened with arrest, imprisonment, and exile if his supposed father executed the legal order he had obtained, Voltaire agreed to be articled to a lawyer, with whom he also boarded. It was in the lawyer's office that he met his life-long friend Nicolas Thieriot. He had several love affairs, generally remaining on excellent terms with his ex-mistresses, frequented the Temple group again, some of whose members had incurred exile for exceeding permissible bounds of behaviour, and wrote a number of stingingly satirical poems, most of which amused the dissipated Philippe d'Orléans, Regent from the death of Louis XIV on 1 September 1715. Voltaire, never sensitive to where the boundaries were drawn, was none the less lucky to escape so lightly when he alluded in a lampoon to persistent gossip about incest between the Regent and his daughter, the duchesse de Berry. The Regent laughed, and Voltaire was given token banishment to the Loire house at Sully belonging to his friend of that name from the Temple. A gracefully repentant verse epistle brought him forgiveness from the Regent in October 1716 after a summer as Sully's guest in the country, although Arouet senior remained implacable.

Voltaire's literary reputation had started to spread in fashionable Paris, but he lay low that winter until, while living in a Paris inn, he was arrested on the night of 16 May 1717, this time for a Latin lampoon, again on the Regent's alleged incest, which he probably did not write. He made light of his imprisonment in the Bastille, a fate sometimes imposed for trivial insolence and which he shared with other fashionable young men who had been too bold. At least once he dined with the governor, and while in prison he lost his current mistress without rancour to a friend. It was while in prison that he began the *Henriade*, redrafted *Oedipe*, and changed his name from Arouet to its near anagram. Voltaire, to get away from the association of "à rouer (to be beaten)." The first letter using the new name is signed "Arouet de Voltaire." He must have been kept short of writing materials, as he had to memorize his poem.

Released after 11 months, Voltaire was exiled to Châtenay but permitted to spend increasingly long periods in Paris, where he was allowed to remain from October 1718. On 18 November *Oedipe* was given by the Comédie-Française to great acclaim. Its initial run of 30 performances was not surpassed by any other 18th-century tragedy, and Voltaire earned 3,000 francs. Unusually the censor, Houdar de la Motte, on whom Voltaire had looked down, had eulogized the piece, seeing in its author a worthy successor to the brothers Corneille. The play in fact contained a systematic de-sacralization of all authority, but the Regent had the tragedy played at court, permitted its dedication to his mother, and awarded Voltaire a gold medal and a pension of 1,200 livres, to which he was soon to add another 2,000. George I sent a gold medal and a watch. The female lead was played by the mistress who had deserted Voltaire while he was in prison, and the play was published in 1719. Voltaire's portrait was painted by Nicolas Largillière.

For all his combative vigour Voltaire always remained modest and self-critical. He did not enjoy personal criticism, but welcomed criticism of his work. When his next play *Artémire* failed to please at its opening on 15 February 1720, he withdrew it after its first performance. M. Arouet died on 1 January 1722, somewhat reconciled to Voltaire after the success of *Oedipe*, and leaving him what in the end amounted to 150,000 livres in trust. This provided insufficient means for Voltaire's tastes, although he did have his pension and some money put aside, perhaps from his mother, as well as what he had earned from *Oedipe*. He spent much time as a guest in grand houses, and had a liaison with the 35-year-old Mme de Bernières, wife of a président à mortier of the Rouen parlement, with whom there was also talk of a business venture connected with the salt tax. Ineffectually Voltaire attempted to find a diplomatic post, and in July 1722 he travelled with a new mistress, the widowed Mme de Rupelmonde, to Cambrai, where the peace congress was to be celebrated and where *Oedipe* and a parody of it were played, then to Brussels, where he rode, played tennis, visited a brothel, and felt unusually well. Meeting by chance the spy who had had him arrested in 1717, he had insulted him, and was then waylaid and beaten by him. Thereafter he spent time and money tracking him down until he got him imprisoned.

For Mme de Rupelmonde he wrote his first long declaration of his beliefs in *L'Epître à Uranie*, also known as *Le Pour et le contre*, a poem vaunting the virtues of natural religion against what he took to be the unjust God of Christian, and especially Jansenist, superstition. Up to the time it was published clandestinely in 1732, the poem was kept locked away and it was not included in any edition of Voltaire's works until 1772. From Brussels Voltaire moved on to The Hague. The *Henriade*, which was still known as *La Ligue*, was now printed, but not published, as the French authorities withheld permission. On his return to France Voltaire made another round of country houses, and it was Bolingbroke, exiled to La Source, near Orléans, who encouraged Voltaire to decide on clandestine publication. Manuscript copies had already been circulating for some time. He was still to add the sixth book, and the poem, beginning with a direct allusion to the *Aeneid*, was to be much revised and reprinted fifty times during Voltaire's lifetime. Devoted to the siege of Paris during the religious wars, although in fact a depiction of the whole spectrum of religious fanaticism, the poem of 10 books and about 4,300 lines is about a third of the length of Virgil's epic. It was enthusiastically admired, although not chiefly for its epic qualities and, during his life, was regarded as Voltaire's chief claim to fame. It was almost immediately pirated by Desfontaines, to whom Voltaire behaved at first magnanimously, but of whom he later became the confirmed enemy.

Voltaire had spent most of the winter of 1722 at Ussé, where he no doubt worked on his new tragedy *Mariamne*. Late in 1723 he was seriously ill with smallpox at Maisons-Lafitte, in the famous house designed by François Mansart and belonging to his young friend, de Maisons. *Mariamne* was withdrawn after failing at a single performance in March 1724. Another play of the same name by Augustin Nadal was booed a few months later by a public calling for Voltaire's piece, and when Nadal published his, Voltaire was attacked in the preface. It looks as if Voltaire had mounted a successful claque, as Nadal claimed. Voltaire rewrote his own play, called it *Hérode et Mariamne*, and succeeded with it in May 1725. A few weeks later his one-act comedy *L'Indiscret* was also successfully played, followed by the further light-hearted *La Fête de Bélébat*, played at Bélébat and written for Mme de Prie, the prime minister's mistress, whose lover Voltaire became. Late in 1725 the queen, too, granted Voltaire an annuity.

Then, a few weeks later, he let his tongue run away with him, and replied too woundingly to a taunt about his bourgeois origins by the Chevalier de Rohan, whom he had known for a long time and whose effeteness was a commonplace. While dining with Sully some days later, Voltaire was called to a coach at the door where he was beaten with clubs on the shoulders in front of Rohan by his servants. When he returned dishevelled upstairs, Sully, constrained by the laws of caste and kinsmanship, could only shrug. Voltaire appeared so intent on pressing the matter to a duel that the Rohan family had him put in the Bastille in April 1726. He was deserted by his friends among the nobility, but released after a fortnight on condition that he left Paris. He went to England and remained there, apart from one brief and secret return to Paris, until the winter of 1728–9. He was well received by English society.

The principal literary fruit of his visit was the *Lettres philosophiques*, published in England in 1733 as *Letters concerning the English Nation*, and in French simultaneously at London and Rouen in 1734. There are three pirated French editions of the same year, but the genuine Rouen edition included the commentary on selections from the *Pensées* of Pascal. The *Lettres* contain a trenchant criticism of French institutions under the guise of an introduction to liberal English religious, philosophical, and scientific thought, although they also show bewilderment at the irregularity of English literary canons, to which Voltaire preferred those of late 17th-century France. By 1734, in spite of the incendiary content of the *Lettres*, Voltaire wanted above all to escape renewed incarceration in the Bastille. He narrowly missed it. Maurepas ordered his arrest but Voltaire prudently escaped to Lorraine before his rooms were searched, his papers seized, and the *Lettres* ordered to be burnt by the public executioner.

While in England Voltaire also drafted the *Histoire de Charles XII, roi de Suède*, the history of the Swedish king, published surreptitiously in 1731 at Rouen over a fictitious Basel imprint. This was a new form of characteristically irreverent history, in which the great are called on to give an account of their actions, on which the biographer then feels free to comment as he chooses. Finally, in England Voltaire also wrote his tragedy *Brutus*, showing the influence of English drama, but played with only moderate success in Paris in 1730, with the 15-year-old Marie-Ange Dangeville as Tullie, the female lead. It outspokenly attacked the arbitrary exercise of authority, was later to gain in popularity, and was prefaced by a "Discours de la tragédie" registering the impact on Voltaire of his contact with Shakespeare.

It was in fact the *Lettres philosophiques* which first introduced Shakespeare to the literate French public. It is not until 1680 that a Shakespeare volume is first recorded in a French library catalogue, but the first translations of Shakespeare plays into French filled four volumes of the eight-volume *Théâtre anglais* of P.-A. de Laplace (1745–8), and from 1769 to 1792 Jean-François Ducis, who did not know English but worked from the earlier translations, was to produce, with plots altered to suit 18th-century French taste, a series of adaptations: *Hamlet* (1769), *Roméo et Juliette* (1772), *Le Roi Léar* (1783), *Macbeth* (1784), and *Othello* (1792). Letourneur was still to produce his prose translation in 20 volumes from 1776 to 1783. In 1776, the year of Letourneur's first volume, containing *Othello, The Tempest*, and *Julius Caesar*, d'Alembert read to the Académie on 25 August a discourse by Voltaire accentuating the criticisms of

Shakespeare's roughness of style already made in the *Lettres*. Voltaire's attitude to Shakespeare had hardened in the intervening forty years, and was perhaps part of the reaction against the praise of all things English which he had himself helped to inaugurate, but against which he had turned by 1761, the date of his manifesto in favour of the French stage, the *Appel à toutes les nations de l'Europe*.

On his return to France, one of Voltaire's first preoccupations had been to establish financial security for himself. He had lost money on the default of a banker and by buying Paris bonds on which the city had defaulted. In public, he made light of his financial misfortune, but he successfully set about putting it right. Together with the mathematician, La Condamine, Voltaire cornered the lottery tickets by which the city decided each month which of the bonds on which it had defaulted it would reimburse. The lottery tickets were on sale at one franc per 1,000-franc bond held, giving a yield of nearly half a million francs per month to be shared between the winners. By organizing various block purchases, Voltaire's syndicate made six or seven million francs within a year, of which Voltaire's share was about half a million. He also made a lot of money from a loophole in an issue of Lorraine bonds, and within a year was much more than comfortably off for life, although he maintained armies of dependents, and spent a great deal indulging his whims. Then on 1 March 1730 his inheritance was released to him. In 1732, when he lost 12,000 francs at cards, he took in good part the frustration of his desire to become a landowner, but there seems to be little doubt that his financial security encouraged him to be more outspoken that he might otherwise have dared to be.

As early as March 1730, indignant at the refusal to give an ecclesiastical burial to Adrienne Lecouvreur, whose lover he had been, who had played Mariamne and whose last role had been as Jocaste in a revival of *Oedipe*, Voltaire wrote and daringly published a fiercely outspoken ode attacking the Church's prejudices against the stage. His devotion to the theatre lasted throughout his life. He never ceased to write for it and was himself a reasonable actor, although not all his plays were staged, even in the private theatres he had built for himself. In 1731–2 there was an *Eriphyle* of which he thought so little that he never published it. Then in 1732 he wrote in three weeks the highly successful *Zaïre*, produced on 13 August. It owes a good deal to *Othello* as well as to Racine.

From 1731 Voltaire had shared accommodation with Mme de Fontaine-Martel, although they were never lovers. When she died in January 1733, Voltaire moved, and it was in his new residence that Emilie du Châtelet with her friend, the duchesse de Saint-Pierre, first called on him in November 1733. He had known her as a child and met her again that June. They now soon became lovers, openly acknowledging their liaison only from 1734, when they both attended a marriage which Voltaire had arranged between the duc de Richelieu and the Princesse de Guise. Voltaire, fleeing possible arrest after the publication of the *Lettres*, then followed Richelieu to the army camp at Philippsburg to try to prevent a duel between Richelieu, descended from the du Plessis family ennobled only by marriage in the 15th century, and a member of the bride's family, Henri Jacques de Lorraine, Prince de Lixin, who regarded the marriage as a mésalliance and had flagrantly provoked Richelieu by making his view clear. The duel was not prevented, and Richelieu killed the prince.

Voltaire returned not to Paris but to Mme du Châtelet's château at Cirey in independent Lorraine. He did not take advantage of the permission to return to Paris granted in 1735. Born in 1706, Gabrielle-Emilie Le Tonnelier de Breteuil, marquise du Châtelet, had studied the Latin classics, English and Italian, and was interested in mathematics, metaphysics, music, and drama. She had married at 18, had three children and several lovers, including Richelieu and Maupertuis, and was finally to fall in love with Saint-Lambert. She also published a number of books on scientific subjects, living with Voltaire until her death in 1749, although their physical liaison had ceased when Voltaire was dropped for Saint-Lambert. Mme du Deffand notoriously wrote bitter comments about her.

In 1733 Voltaire anonymously published *Le Temple du goût*, an essay in a mixture of prose and verse which attempted to refine the criteria of good taste, and outspokenly attacked a number of the painters, musicians, and writers who sought admission to the temple of taste. He believed that there were rules for the creation of aesthetic masterpieces, which he sought to purify, partly by eliminating the irregular and the Gothic. It was at remote and inaccessible Cirey that Voltaire wrote many of his plays. *Adélaïde du Guesclin* was the first play to put a French historical subject on the stage, but it failed after two performances in 1734. Rewritten as *Amélie* it was a success 18 years later, and 13 years after that was even more successful in its original form and with its original title, a circumstance which afforded Voltaire considerable amusement. In 1735 *La Mort de César* provided an interesting comparison with Shakespeare's *Julius Caesar*. Voltaire's play was naturally more regular, and had many fewer characters and an action more concentrated on their psychological confrontation than on the power struggle between them. From now on, however, Voltaire often used an opposition of principles rather than hopeless emotional entanglements as the basis for his plots. *Alzire*, a political play set in Peru, dedicated to Mme du Châtelet and prefaced by a discourse in praise of natural religion, and *L'Enfant prodigue*, a five-act comedy in octosyllabic verse, were both successful in 1736.

During the early years at Cirey Voltaire also wrote, in addition to the plays, the *Traité de métaphysique* of 1734 in which he doubts the immortality of the soul and which Mme du Châtelet kept locked in a desk; the 1736 poem in praise of luxury, *Le Mondain*, after which he took refuge for some weeks in Holland; the verse sequence of the *Discours sur l'homme*, written in 1737–8 although later augmented, suggested by Pope's optimistic *Essay on Man* of 1733 and influenced by Locke; and the immensely successful, popularizing *Eléments de la philosophie de Newton* of 1738. Voltaire had dabbled in even experimental physics. The *Eléments* ran into the now familiar difficulties. The Chancellor, d'Aguesseau, refused a licence to print, and Voltaire finally gave the manuscript to a Dutch publisher, who printed it without Voltaire's authorization and with additional chapters by different hands. It was largely on account of the *Eléments* that Voltaire was later to his great gratification to be elected to the Royal Societies of London and Edinburgh.

It was in 1736 that Voltaire first heard from the Francophile Frederick, later "the Great," born in 1712, and from 1740 to be king of Prussia. It seems unlikely that Voltaire really intended to accept a not wholly realistic invitation to visit Frederick at the end of 1736, when he left Cirey to distribute his defence of *Le Mondain*, which had caused predictable trouble. He apparently got no nearer Sans-Souci than Amsterdam and was back at

Cirey by 1 March 1737, but that year he exchanged 30 letters with Frederick, mostly about literature and philosophy. He spent much time arranging his affairs. His correspondence, especially with his Paris business agent, canon Bonaventure Moussinot, shows that, aware of the constant danger from repressive governments in view of his own determination to speak his mind openly, he was putting his finances in order and ensuring a secure income for life as well as a large supply of ready cash. He needed to safeguard his mobility. He also concerned himself with scientific experiments and with the decoration of Cirey, provided dowries for his nieces, and undertook journeys to Brussels for the affairs of the du Châtelets. After the accession of Frederick the Great, Voltaire also undertook diplomatic missions to Potsdam on behalf of the French foreign minister, Cardinal Fleury.

Voltaire's sister had died in 1726 and her widower in 1737. Voltaire's nieces, Marie-Louise, born in 1712, and Marie-Elisabeth, born in 1724, lived in Paris with an aunt and were invited to Cirey. Voltaire tried to arrange two marriages for Marie-Louise, offering a dowry, but she had fallen in love with a lawyer connected with the army commissariat, Nicolas-Charles Denis, and married him on 25 February 1738. Marie-Elisabeth married Nicolas-Joseph de Dompierre de Fontaine on 19 June of the same year. In 1739 Voltaire travelled with the du Châtelets to Brussels and Paris, where there was rejoicing at the wedding of the king's daughter to the son of the King of Spain. Voltaire met the young and wealthy tax collector, Helvétius, and warmly invited him to Cirey.

He returned to drama, attaching much importance to an opera, *Pandore*, first mentioned in 1740 but never performed, and adapted *La Prude*, at first called "La Dévote," from Wycherley's *The Plain Dealer* of 1674, while also writing *Mahomet*, subtitled "Le Fanatisme," which alluded in the plot to the dangers of superstition and religious fanaticism. Conceived early in 1739, it was thought by Voltaire to be his best play. It was triumphantly played at Lille in 1741 and in Paris in 1742, but fell there after its third performance on account of a cabal organized against it when the censor, Crébillon the elder, had failed to prevent its performance. Although the underlying theme of the play was anti-Jansenist and there was a reference to the Jansenist convulsionaries in the cemetery of Saint-Médard in the years following 1727, and although the play certainly contained an attack on the corruption of the innocent by religious fanaticism, Voltaire gave a copy to Cardinal de Fleury, and eventually dedicated the play to Benedict XIV.

In 1743 the tragedy, *Mérope*, based on the Latin version of a Greek legend, adapted from a play by Maffei, and without a love interest, was an immediate triumph. For the first time a Parisian audience called for an author after the curtain had come down. Voltaire's answer to Crébillon was to take the subjects of six of his plays and treat them himself. He was to give *Sémiramis* in 1748, using lavishly spectacular effects, which finally drove the audience off the stage, where the best seats were still aligned along the sides, and followed it in 1749 by *Nanine*, derived from Richardson's *Pamela*. *Oreste* and *Rome sauvée* of 1750 stimulated Crébillon, now over 70, into renewed dramatic activity after an interval of 22 years. Voltaire's last Paris tragedies were to be *L'Orphelin de la Chine* (1755), *Tancrède* (1760) and *Irène* (1778).

He was to write five more tragedies and four comedies, of which two were played in Paris. *L'Ecossaise* of July 1760 is important as a response to Palissot's *Les Philosophes*, performed in May of that year. Palissot's comedy lampooned Helvétius, Mme Geoffrin, Duclos, and Diderot, with some rough treatment for Rousseau and the actress Mlle Clairon, perhaps the greatest of her generation, who appeared in a number of Voltaire's plays and, like the celebrated actor Lekain, who performed with her in *Tancrède*, was to come to Ferney to act in Voltaire's private theatre there. Palissot spared Voltaire and d'Alembert, but Diderot was badly upset. Voltaire also replied to the implied request from the encyclopédistes (q.v.) with a mild letter of expostulation to Palissot and a fierce attack on his ancient enemy, the critic Elie Fréron, a disciple of Voltaire's enemy and favourite target, the abbé Desfontaines, whom he had once helped. Desfontaines had turned against his benefactor and finally published, in answer to *Le Préservatif*, Voltaire's self-defensive expostulation against him, the scurrilous *Voltairomanie*. Fréron had praised *Les Philosophes* in the *Année littéraire* and was now depicted as the repulsive villain of *L'Ecossaise* under the name of Frelon, grafted on to a character from the existing draft of a comedy.

Voltaire and Frederick the Great finally met in September 1740, when Frederick used the meeting to camouflage his aggressive intentions towards Liège. Mme du Chatêlet, who was not received, began a new flirtation with her former lover, Richelieu. Then in April 1744 Marie-Louise's husband died, and Voltaire's affection for his niece became openly passionate. They had already become sporadic lovers and, apart from a brief interval, were to remain together until Voltaire's death. Mme Denis was apparently ill-favoured as well as greedy, grasping, and spendthrift. Voltaire's affection for Mme du Châtelet was waning, and his life-style was changing.

In 1745, following the death of his brother on 18 February, Voltaire's wealth increased, and he began to win at court the favour to which he aspired. His entertainments and congratulatory verse won him an established social position, in spite of attempts to discredit him, connived at by Frederick, who wanted him at Potsdam. On 25 April 1746 he was also, after several efforts, elected to the Académie française, and he was a member of several other academies in France and abroad. He could write letters in English, Latin, German, Italian and Spanish, and was clearly Europe's most outstanding man of letters. On 1 April 1745 he had been appointed historiographer of France, and on 22 December 1746 he was made a gentilhomme ordinaire du roi, a title he was allowed in 1749 to sell for 53,000 francs, although he continued to be allowed to use it. In 1745 he first heard from Jean-Jacques Rousseau, who wanted to make some changes in the libretto of a court entertainment, *La Princesse de Navarre*, which Voltaire had written.

Late in 1747 Mme du Châtelet lost heavily at cards, apparently to cheats, and Voltaire hurried her away to stay with the duchesse du Maine at Sceaux. In order to amuse the company, he wrote his first contes, *Babouc*, *Le Crocheteur borgne*, *Cosi-sancta*, and the *Memnon* which was later to become *Zadig*. From Sceaux the pair went on to Lorraine, where Mme du Châtelet, now a 41-year-old grandmother, fell in love with Saint-Lambert, later to rival Rousseau for the affection of Mme d'Houdetot. Voltaire remained gracious to Saint-Lambert, but Mme du Châtelet died giving birth to Saint-Lambert's child on 10 September 1749. Voltaire, unsettled, set up house in Paris with his niece, but in 1750 left without Mme Denis for a three-year stay in Berlin, not to return to Paris for 28 years. The French authorities were not displeased by his departure, but took from him the post of royal historiographer.

At first all went well in Berlin, but Voltaire was too restless, touchy, and self-important, Frederick too possessive, demanding, and devious. Voltaire helped Frederick with his literary work, worked on his own *Siècle de Louis XIV*, which French disapproval forced him to publish in Prussia, started to write satirical prose dialogues and other short pieces, including the *Eloge historique de Madame la marquise du Châtelet* and his *Pensées sur le gouvernement*, and carried on with the preparation of a new edition of his own *Oeuvres* brought out by Georg Conrad Walther. He also wrote his conte *Micromégas*. Frederick had Voltaire's correspondence intercepted and read his letters, and was provoked by the manner in which Voltaire made an illegal deal with Abraham Hirschel, a "protected" Jew, for whom Voltaire used his privileged position to hold Saxon bonds which under a 1745 settlement had to be honoured in full when owned by a Prussian citizen. Voltaire ended up by suing Hirschel, but for Frederick Voltaire remained an intimate companion and an excellent literary guide. Meanwhile the *Siècle de Louis XIV*, the history of the reign, was an immense success. It virtually created the myth of the "grand Siècle" and went immediately to a dozen editions. It was instantly pirated, compelling Voltaire to overtrump the pirates with ever more augmented and revised authentic editions.

At Potsdam Voltaire formed a close friendship and probably had a liaison with the high-born Charlotte Sophie, countess Bentinck, whose husband, son of the Earl of Portland, had been made a count of the Holy Roman Empire to render the marriage acceptable. The pair had separated in 1740, creating complicated if shallow political repercussions on account of various royal families involved, and there was a long drawn-out lawsuit. Voltaire also helped the young abbé Jean Martin de Prades, whose sceptical thesis had run him into trouble in Paris. He turned out to be untrustworthy, but Voltaire had got Frederick to find him employment. Voltaire's removal expenses had been reimbursed, and he was given 20,000 francs a year, plus a modest allowance of 4,000 francs. He now also invested the money he had brought with him to buy an annuity secured on properties in Württemberg.

By the middle of 1752, however, it became clear to him that his presence had begun to outlive its usefulness to Frederick. La Mettrie had reported to him the previous year Frederick's statement, "Quand on a sucé l'orange, on jette l'écorce (When you have sucked the orange dry, you throw away the peel)." Voltaire was also jealous of the importance of the twin leaders of the Potsdam academy, the irascible Maupertuis, with whom he fell out, and Baculard d'Arnaud, whose exile he contrived. He quarrelled with Lessing. Trouble finally culminated when he took the part of Samuel König, a disciple of Wolff who had been Mme du Châtelet's mathematics tutor, against Maupertuis in a dispute about the authenticity of some Leibniz letters in which König was right but Frederick supported Maupertuis. Voltaire composed at Leipzig his biting satire, the *Diatribe du docteur Akakia*, which owed something to Boileau's *Arrêt burlesque* and which Frederick enjoyed, but whose manuscript he had burnt.

Permission for Voltaire to leave, sought at first informally, was requested on 1 January 1753, and in the end granted with some reluctance on 15 March. He left on 26 March. After Leipzig he visited Gotha and Cassel, reaching Frankfurt on 29 May, where he was joined by his niece. Frederick sent after him,

and secured his arrest. His baggage was searched, but on 7 July, on the intervention of the civic authorities, he managed to flee with his niece penniless across the Rhine to Mainz. From the summer of 1753 Voltaire was taken up, for about a year at Strasburg and then, from October to June, in Colmar, with a number of minor literary tasks. He published the much-pirated *Abrégé de l'histoire universelle*, a contribution to the later *Essai sur les moeurs*. He had written a burlesque epic poem of some 8,300 decasyllabic lines in 21 books, *La Pucelle d'Orléans*, of which the first authentic edition is that of 1762. The unauthorized 1755 edition of *La Pucelle* and of his historical works caused him considerable annoyance, and he returned to the theatre with *L'Orphelin de la Chine*, successfully performed in Paris in August 1755.

He was banned throughout Germany, as well as in Paris, at Frederick's request, and now also in Lorraine, but he sub-let part of his Paris house, sold some paintings, silver, and books, and, in spite of difficulties with the Württemberg annuity, was rich enough to settle where he wanted. He was also by now experienced enough to realize that, for the full exercise of the intellectual independence to which he was dedicated, he needed the easy ability to put himself outside the reach of authority. After some difficulties on account of his nominal Catholicism, and the purchase of a property he found too big—the château de Prangins, overlooking the Lake of Geneva just north of Nyon—Voltaire was allowed to buy for 77,200 francs the life-time use of a house just outside Geneva and close to four frontiers. He was to call it "Les Délices" and was to live there until in 1758, unhappy with his Calvinist environment, he bought in his niece's name just inside the French border the substantial property of Ferney, and a lease on Tournay, just outside France but only four miles away. He later failed in a bid to buy the Tournay house outright, but built theatres at all three residences.

On 1 November 1755 occurred the famous Lisbon earthquake in which 20,000 people died. Voltaire was profoundly moved and his reaction to the optimism of Leibniz's 1710 *Essais de théodicée* crystallized. Leibniz, whose view had been reflected by Pope, had held that God had created the least imperfect world possible, a position which Voltaire now dismissed as absurd in the *Poème sur le désastre de Lisbonne*, finished before the end of November. It was published in 1756, importantly in conjunction with the *Poème sur la loi naturelle*, defending man's innate sense of justice and attacking the evil done in the name of religion. The Lisbon poem brought a letter defending the beneficence of providence from Rousseau, who had already supported the Calvinist ban on attendance at Voltaire's theatre at Les Délices. Voltaire's sense of disillusion now deepened and provoked from him the most famous and densest of all his philosophical contes, the anonymous 1759 *Candide; ou, L'Optimisme*.

In 1756 Voltaire finally published the seven-volume work on universal history on which he had been working for over 20 years, the *Essai sur l'histoire générale et sur les moeurs et l'esprit des nations*, into which the 1765 *Philosophie de l'histoire*, dedicated to Catherine II, was to be incorporated as an introduction from 1769. Although the work was printed in Geneva and Voltaire had intended to compliment Geneva on what he took to be its current liberal tolerance, his strictures on Calvin's fierce intransigence none the less gave great offence. Geneva also upheld its ban on theatrical performances, and Voltaire persuaded d'Alembert to attack the prohibition in the article

"Genève," published in 1757, which he wrote for the *Encyclopédie* while staying at Les Délices in 1756. It was that article which drew from Rousseau the famous *Lettre à d'Alembert sur les spectacles* for which Voltaire never forgave him.

Voltaire's own attitude to the *Encyclopédie*, to which he contributed articles on only relatively uncontroversial subjects (such as "Esprit," "Finesse," "Français," "Grâce" in the non-theological sense, "Heureux," "Histoire," and "Idole") remained equivocal. For Voltaire, the *Encyclopédie* was too long and ponderous to be the propagandist weapon he sought, and his own *Dictionnaire philosophique, portatif* of 1764 was in a sense to be an attempt to do the job more economically. For his part Diderot, with much the more profound mind, distrusted the brilliant dramatist, poet, historian, and wit with wealth and influence, more concerned to keep open his escape routes than radically to attempt to undermine established beliefs and attitudes.

Voltaire was not originally a subscriber to the *Encyclopédie*, although his initial praise of the enterprise was characteristically hyperbolic. By the late 1750s Voltaire had become seriously critical of some of the articles already published and although, when d'Alembert withdrew from co-editorship after the trouble caused by the "Genève" article, Voltaire urged him to persevere, he changed his mind when he learnt that the anonymous 1757 attacks on the philosophes (q.v.), the *Premier Mémoire sur les Cacouacs*, which appeared in the *Mercure de France* (q.v.), and the *Nouveau Mémoire pour servir à l'histoire des Cacouacs* probably had the backing of the court. The "Cacouacs" were described as monsters with tongues incapable of not emitting poison, who rejoiced in doing evil. Voltaire himself then withdrew and urged others to do likewise, or to transfer the whole operation from Paris, where Diderot tenaciously fought on, to Switzerland.

Both the Lisbon poem and the 1755 *La Pucelle* had been the subject of very wide public interest. Voltaire said that there were 6,000 manuscript copies of *La Pucelle* circulating in Paris in 1755, and there were over 20 non-authorized editions before Voltaire finally released the much-revised authentic 1762 text. In 1759 he published his *Histoire de l'empire de Russie sous Pierre le Grand*. By that date he was directing most of his literary energies according to his new motto, "écrasez l'infâme (crush the object of infamy)," although it is unclear whether the symbolic "l'infâme," first used in this context in a letter by Frederick, with whom sporadically courteous relations had again been re-established and then for a while broken off again, meant superstition or supernatural religion in general. Not long after this date, perhaps inspired by the state of social misery to which the peasants on the Ferney estates had been driven by mismanagement and administrative policy, Voltaire started his famous campaign to right judicial wrongs, while issuing a number of lampoons whose anonymity was scarcely more than a perfunctory pretence for the avoidance of prosecution.

Candide was written at Schwetzingen where Voltaire, on one of his increasingly rare journeys, was staying with the Elector Palatine. It was published anonymously and in several places simultaneously, was immediately condemned, and sold 6,000 copies within weeks in Paris alone. Later in the year Voltaire produced a précis in verse of the biblical books of *Ecclesiastes* and the *Song of Songs*. While waiting for the production of *Tancrède* on 3 September 1760, he wrote and published the satirical comedy *L'Ecossaise*, a slight burlesque which might well never have been staged although, directed against Voltaire's opponent Fréron, depicted as "Frelon (hornet)," it was in fact produced in 1760, ran for 16 performances, and occasioned the revival of four other Voltaire plays. *Tancrède*, endlessly discussed in the correspondence and tested at Tournay, was taken off after only 13 performances, although the houses were good, never below 816, with 1,205 paid admissions for a single performance on 26 January 1761, and over 1,200 for each of the first two performances of the second run in March 1761. During the season 1761–2 the Comédie-Française gave 16 performances of five Corneille plays with an average attendance of 705, 18 performances of six Racine plays, with an average attendance of 672, but as many as 76 performances of 16 Voltaire plays with an average attendance of 557.

Voltaire also defended the philosophes against the satirical attack in Palissot's 1760 play *Les Philosophes*. Now very rich, he spent vast sums rebuilding first the gardens at Les Délices which he was about to leave, then the house at Ferney, where the theatre was finally ready in 1761. In 1760 he virtually adopted an impoverished great-granddaughter of a cousin of Pierre Corneille, and furthered his own ambition of publishing the great 17th-century classics by editing Corneille's works for the French academy in a 12-volume annotated edition of 1764, producing a dowry of nearly 100,000 francs for the young girl. His niece, Mme Denis, normally ungracious, and extravagant at Voltaire's expense, almost uncharacteristically helped in the upbringing of Marie Corneille. After further expenditure of 1,000,000 francs in 10 years, Voltaire pruned back the Ferney budget to 40,000 francs a year, which allowed for 60 servants and 12 horses. At his death his revenues certainly exceeded 200,000 francs a year.

From 1761 Voltaire was much occupied by a series of at first minor disputes involving social injustices, his feelings often inflamed by the same passions as those which inspired the satirical contes. Then on 9 March 1762, shortly after the Protestant pastor François Rochette, arrested by accident, had been executed for preaching, the Protestant Jean Calas was condemned to death and broken on the wheel for the murder of his son, suspected of wishing to become a Catholic. In fact the son had committed suicide, and Voltaire eventually succeeded in having the verdict overturned in 1765. His *Traité sur la tolérance*, written in 1762, was published in 1763, and the matter created great popular interest as well as absorbing much of Voltaire's enormous energies for three years. 1764 was the date of the anonymous first edition of the *Dictionnaire philosophique, portatif*. Voltaire often published short pieces of philosophical prose as leaflets or pamphlets, but the *Dictionnaire* is really a series of miscellaneous alphabetically-arranged essays, later revised as *La Raison par alphabet* and *Questions sur l'encyclopédie*.

The second of the legal cases made famous by Voltaire concerned Pierre Paul Sirven and his wife, Protestants accused of the murder of their daughter Elisabeth, who had been confined to a convent after an attempt to convert her to Catholicism. She escaped and, said to be deranged, drowned herself in 1765. The two remaining daughters were condemned to watch their parents' execution, but all four escaped to Ferney. Voltaire published his *Avis au public sur les parricides* in 1766, and an acquittal was procured in 1771. The third well-known case was that of the Chevalier de la Barre who once, at the age of 18, had failed to kneel or remove his hat when a religious procession carrying the consecrated Host passed by. He was convicted, without evidence, of a number of other small blasphemies and, although his companions were allowed to flee, or let off because they were younger still, local jealousies saw to La Barre's conviction, even though the bishop tried to have the charges dismissed. He was condemned to have his hand cut off and his tongue torn out before being burnt alive. What shocked all Europe was that on appeal the sentence was confirmed, to stem the spirit of the philosophes which was spreading through France. The mutilations were remitted, but La Barre was executed in July 1766. The ferocity of La Barre's sentence weighed more heavily on Voltaire than had the injustice of the earlier condemnations, but he also felt strongly on issues that were not religious, and succeeded in having the reputation of General Lally-Tollendal rehabilitated after his execution for having surrendered Pondicherry in spite of heroic efforts on behalf of France.

In 1765 Voltaire had sold Les Délices. The four years between the Lisbon earthquake and *Candide* had confirmed his inability to believe in human progress. This was the fundamental point underlying his reservations about the views of Diderot and at issue in his later attitude to Rousseau. In 1766 he published *Le Philosophe ignorant*, urging toleration and inaugurating a final series of works varying in tone from frustration to resignation at man's inability to resolve the great metaphysical questions. They were to include *L'ABC* of 1768, *Dieu et les hommes: Oeuvre théologique mais raisonnable* and the commentary on Malebranche, *Tout en Dieu*, both of 1769, and *Les Dialogues d'Evhémère* of 1777. From about 1750 Voltaire had ceased to believe in free will, but in his last years, fearful of the social effects of the atheistic materialism of La Mettrie and d'Holbach, he insisted increasingly on the need to preach immortality and the belief in the "Dieu rémunérateur et vengeur (God who rewards and avenges)."

In religion Voltaire's distaste for rites and dogmas was based on the superstitions and intolerance to which they respectively gave rise. In politics, as late as 1766 he emphatically reaffirmed his belief in absolute monarchism, believing in the social need for a single source of absolute political power, although his social thought was otherwise advanced. He was himself an enlightened landlord and an excellent manager of his estates. Although it concentrates on legal and penal matters, Voltaire's commentary on Cesare Bonesana Beccaria's 1764 *Dei delitti e delle pene*, the *Commentaire sur le livre 'Des délits et des peines'*, published in 1766, provides a good example of his sometimes radical, if also randomly applied liberalism. In 1768 he published in dialogue form *L'Homme aux quarante écus*, a story containing a serious discussion of political economy, dealing with agriculture, education, luxury, and war, and *La Princesse de Babylone*, sometimes considered to be among the best of the philosophical contes, and based as earlier contes had been on a voyage which allowed Voltaire to satirize a wide spectrum of social institutions and customs, again exploiting a naive central figure whose common sense is confounded by what he finds going on. *L'Ingénu* had been published in 1767, and then in 1775 came the *Histoire de Jenni*, part fiction, part dialogue, part drama, in which an atheist unconvincingly allows himself to be converted by a liberal Anglican priest.

In 1768 Mme Denis, who had enjoyed the revenues from Les Délices and then Ferney, and had had vast sums from Voltaire, acting in complicity with La Harpe, who had been protected by Voltaire and formed part of his household, stole a manuscript from Ferney containing an attack on Genevan Calvinism which, to Voltaire's embarrassment, was printed without his authoriza-

tion. On 1 March he sent his niece away, although it distressed him, and he continued to care for her financial and physical wellbeing, while also upbraiding her for her extravagance. By then rather against his will, she returned to Ferney on 27 October 1769, having been away 18 months. Voltaire's allegorical play on Geneva, *Les Scythes*, privately printed on his own press and played at Ferney, was finally performed without great success in Paris in 1767. In 1769 he published a further two-volume historical work, the *Histoire du Parlement de Paris*, arguing as usual for reform. His final years at Ferney were passed largely in business, although he returned to writing narrative and satire in verse. In 1774 his *Sophonisbe* failed in January, but in May his hopes of being allowed to return to Paris were—vainly—revived by the death of Louis XV.

The autobiographical *Commentaire historique sur les oeuvres de l'auteur de l'Henriade*, whose title indicates Voltaire's own estimation of the public view of his claim to fame, appeared in 1776, with the two volumes of *La Bible enfin expliquée*, and the anti-Shakespearean defence of the classical French theatre. Voltaire's niece left Ferney for Paris on 3 February 1778 charged, among other business, with discovering how unwelcome a visit by Voltaire to Paris would be to the authorities. That evening he decided not to wait to hear, and himself left on 5 February. The populace gave him a warm welcome; there were hundreds of callers; and both the Académie française and the Comédie-Française sent deputations of welcome. On 30 March a bust of Voltaire was crowned with laurel on the stage, and he himself attended the sixth performance of his *Irène* at the end of March. He died just before midnight on Saturday 30 May 1778 in his 84th year. His body was taken secretly, but with the probable connivance of the authorities, to Scellières, of which his nephew was the abbé commendataire, to ensure burial in consecrated ground.

WORKS

When Voltaire died, Diderot had been dead for four years and Rousseau, who was by 18 years Voltaire's junior, had less than five weeks to live. The contrast between Voltaire and Rousseau has for long been a historical and critical commonplace, but the differences between them can still illuminate the ultimate significance of the works of each, if not quite in the way which has become traditional. It is true that Rousseau, in spite of his fear that the process of industrialization was corruptive, and the nostalgia he cherished for the smallest of possible communities living as closely as possible to nature, none the less believed in nature's and man's perfectibility, whereas Voltaire came sharply to disbelieve even in rational progress as an agent in the process of perfecting humanity, shrugging his shoulders at the metaphysical puzzles, and seeking only increasingly social solutions to human problems. That has always appeared to be the principal difference between them, and to lie at the root of their personal antipathy.

But the similarities are important, too. Both Voltaire and Rousseau were simultaneously enthusiastic about and distrustful of the 18th-century world of scientific progress and rational enlightenment. Each tried hard to admire post-Calvinist Geneva, only to find too much of Calvin's spirit lingering within its confines, capable of being exploited by the ruling oligarchy as a basis for power, wealth, and privilege. Both were, with differing degrees of commitment at different times, deists, and both, even in maturity, had lived within or just outside the boundaries of some form of organized Christianity. Both had advanced social views. Voltaire at Ferney behaved in perfect accordance with the ideal of the landed proprietor envisaged by Rousseau in *Julie; ou, la Nouvelle Héloïse*, and Voltaire's ideal clergyman would have believed much the same as Rousseau's vicaire savoyard in *Emile; ou, De l'éducation*, even if his recourse would have been more to his reason and less to his feelings.

The real contribution of the comparison to the understanding of the texts of each author lies elsewhere. Both dedicated themselves totally to their chosen tasks, carefully selecting environments, life-styles, and virtually careers so as to permit the achievement of the different tasks to which they had devoted themselves. Both needed a certain sort of freedom, and each attained it. But Rousseau, the radical re-thinker of the nature and meaning of virtually all human activity, succeeded in achieving an almost total independence of social constraints, keeping only the patronage and the intellectual stimulus he needed, while living a life of humdrum poverty, mind-chillingly dull professional activity, and barely middle-class ordinariness. Voltaire, the waspish, sarcastic propagandist, needed freedom to ridicule, to caricature, to influence, and to wound. He chose to be rich, elegant, and mobile, and was witty and powerful enough to escape the serious persecution which anyone prosecuting his objectives and propagating his views from a more lowly status could not intellectually have survived.

As a result, we have two immensely important lives, the one on the whole unhappy, but scattered with half a dozen masterpieces of radical thought, the other, no doubt more enjoyably lived, with a fragmented literary achievement of drama and verse that did not have the imaginative vigour to withstand changes of taste, fashion, and social experience, and of fiction and loaded propagandist history which contains no single great unified masterpiece, but whose impact on the social life of 18th-century France was quite immeasurable. Rousseau was an unpolished, unrigorous, but deeply radical thinker who doubted the stability of the foundations on which any part of his culture was erected. He was a committed republican. Voltaire was fundamentally an elegant and witty conservative who wanted to reform the existing order but despairingly doubted the possibility of serious progress anywhere except in the growth of tolerance and the abolition of superstition. He believed in the sting of ridicule as the weapon of reform, and in an absolute monarchy.

Both the plays and the poems of Voltaire are loaded with ideological squibs, but must here be considered in isolation from the history, fiction, and other genres. A year by year examination of Voltaire's works, many of which are minor but stake out important positions, and to which the 20,000 surviving letters provide a continuous but coded descant, would demand a vast intellectual and literary history of a long life and an enormous production, too complex yet to have been properly undertaken anywhere. In fact, problems of multiple piracy and forgery led Voltaire continuously to revise his work in the interests of making pirated editions out of date. For this reason among others, and because he so much enjoyed the posturing which prevented too many people from pinning down his opinions even in his correspondence and the often merely pseudo-anonymous works, it seems unlikely that a full account even of his literary activity will ever be written.

Voltaire is the author of over forty separately published plays,

the first begun when he was 18 or 19, the last performed for the first time when he was 83. He took his dramatic activity with great seriousness, built private theatres at each of his principal residences, occasionally acted himself, was quite clear about the ways in which he wanted the various parts played, and endlessly discussed with his actors and others the precise dramatic effects he was trying to achieve. His first play, *Oedipe*, a tragedy in alexandrines, was instantly successful and was immediately parodied by the Italian company in Paris. Its antique subject, its use of a chorus, the request for advice from André Dacier, husband of the famous protagonist of the "anciens" in the Querelle des anciens et des modernes (q.v.), and the renunciation of a love interest, all suggest that Voltaire not only wished to follow in the classical tradition of 17th-century French drama, but also shared the inclination of the "ancien" partisans of that drama to explore the less immediately gratifying and more obviously tragic aspects of human experience.

Jocaste, who had loved Philoctète, prince of Euboea, had been made instead to marry Laius, the king of Thebes. As the play opens, Philoctète is told that Laius has been killed four years previously, and that Jocaste has now married Oedipe, the new king of Thebes. In Thebes a plague is raging which can be ended only if the killer of Laius is discovered. Jocaste tells Oedipe that she is hiding Phorbas, suspected of the murder, because she thinks he was innocent. When Philoctète is suspected, Jocaste confesses her love for him, maintaining that her previous affection for Laius, like her present feelings for Oedipe, were less deep. When the High Priest accuses Oedipe of the crime, he slowly recognizes his guilt and asks to be executed, but is defended by Jocaste on the grounds that he did not know the victim's identity. The death of Polybe, king of Corinth and Oedipe's presumed father, is now reported, and it becomes clear that Oedipe is in fact the son of Laius and Jocaste. The pestilence ends, and Jocaste, finding herself unwittingly married to her own son, stabs herself to death.

Voltaire later wrote that the play derived from his reading of the Greek tragedians and from the grounding in the classics given him by the Jesuit Charles Porée. Its success must have been due to something other than the scarcely embroidered re-working of the Oedipus myth, and has been attributed to the anti-authoritarianism of some of its lines, with the desacralizing of the king as "un homme ordinaire (an ordinary man)," demonstrations of the failures of human justice, and the assertion of the dependence of sacerdotal authority on human credulity:

Nos prêtres ne sont pas ce qu'un vain peuple pense,
Notre crédulité fait toute leur science

(Our priests are not what the thoughtless crowd believes. It is our credulity which creates their knowledge).

Like Racine's Phèdre, Voltaire's Jocaste, if less powerfully, is seen as the victim of the gods, incurring a guilt she could not avoid:

J'ai fait rougir les dieux qui m'ont forcé au crime

(I have made the gods blush for forcing me to this crime),

although unlike Phèdre, whose jealousy renders her death acceptable to the audience because it makes her psychologically guilty, Jocaste's guilt, like Oedipe's, is in no sense the result of a personal choice, and the tragedy becomes more a parable of misfortune than a myth about guilt. In this sense, the play betrays Voltaire's underlying optimism. His imagination virtually blocks out the examination of any properly moral guilt in his tragic victim. The myth is exploited instead to tilt at the unfairness of fate, destiny, and perhaps God.

While Voltaire's sense of the tragic is constantly undermined by an inability, not unlike that to be found in Pierre Corneille, to envisage a destiny without achievement, as well as by his equivocal admiration for Shakespeare, he almost invariably keeps to the external conventions of classical tragedy, retaining the unities, the five-act structure, and the alexandrine. There are, however, too many weak lines in the plays. The language is stiff, clumsy, sometimes even bathetic. He himself came to realize that the strength of his dramatic writing lay in the clash of ideas. *Artémire* failed and was withdrawn after one performance in 1720, and it seems likely that the failure of the original *Mariamne* in March 1724 cannot wholly be blamed, as Voltaire later maintained, on the audience's laughter when Adrienne Lecouvreur drank poison and died on the stage. There may have been a war of claques between Voltaire and Augustin Nadal, whose own *Mariamne* was booed off the stage when it replaced that of Voltaire, whose own less histrionic version, more attuned to public taste, was successful in May 1725.

Voltaire's drama was transformed when he visited England and got to know the works of Shakespeare. *Brutus*, started in England and finished by the end of 1729, was clearly inspired by Shakespeare's *Julius Caesar*. Staging was for some reason delayed, perhaps on account of the play's outspokenly pro-democratic lines. Performed in 1730, the tragedy concerned an earlier Brutus than Shakespeare's. On publication in 1731, it was prefaced by the important *Discours sur la tragédie*, introducing Shakespeare to the French public. The plot is complex and hinges on a conflict between Titus's love of Tullie and his loyalty to Rome, whose defence against the tyranny of Tarquin, Tullie's father, is to be led by his own father, Brutus. Titus does in the end betray Rome, urged on by his friend Messala. The plot to betray Rome is discovered. Both Messala and Tullie take their own lives. Titus's brother Tibérimus, who was ready to betray Rome, is killed, and Titus is condemned to death.

Voltaire's best-known tragedy is probably *Zaïre*, written in three weeks and played on 13 August 1732. It brought Voltaire an ovation, had an initial run of 31 performances, and has been revived in France more often than any other Voltaire play. A purely incidental interest of the text is the introduction into French spelling of "ai" for the very common vowel sound pronounced like that by the 18th century but, until *Zaïre* was printed, still written "oi." By using the new spelling Voltaire was in fact publicizing the text of his play, into which he also introduced religion and a much stronger love interest than usual. The result owes something to *Othello*, but the point of Voltaire's play is that adherence to a religion is dependent on the accident of birth and upbringing rather than on the acceptance of a revealed and universally knowable truth:

J'eusse été près du Gange esclave des faux dieux,
Chrétienne dans Paris, musulmane en ces lieux

(By the Ganges I would have been the slave of false gods,/
In Paris a Christian, and here a Moslem).

Zaïre, a Christian child carried off by the Turks at the capture of Caesarea, is a slave of Orosmane, the sultan of Jerusalem, whom she loves and by whom she is loved in return. A former companion in captivity, the Christian Nérestan, had been ransomed and had promised to bring back from France the means to ransom 10 knights. He arrives back at the seraglio just as Zaïre and Orosmane are to marry, and pays the ransom but, his resources exhausted, surrenders himself again as a prisoner. Orosmane generously refuses the ransom and tells Nérestan to leave with 100 prisoners he has set free, although he is retaining Zaïre and the aged but politically dangerous Lusignan, the last of the French kings of Jerusalem. Zaïre obtains from Orosmane the release of Lusignan, who is brought from his dungeon to be presented to her and to Nérestan. Various signs enable the dying Lusignan to recognize in Nérestan and Zaïre his own lost children and he begs Zaïre, who has been brought up a Moslem, to become a Christian. She agrees, and her relationship to Nérestan, who urges her to accept secret baptism, is concealed. Orosmane becomes jealous of Nérestan when Zaïre asks for a postponement of the wedding, but suspicions are allayed until a letter to Zaïre from Nérestan asking for a meeting is intercepted. Orosmane attends the meeting place and knifes Zaïre. When he hears the truth from Nérestan, Orosmane releases the Christian captives and kills himself.

La Mort de César, written in 1731 but first produced only on 11 August 1735, contains no female character and, although modelled on Shakespeare, confines the action within the unities. Brutus, who does not at first know that he is César's natural son, has been replaced as his heir by the adopted Octave, and accuses his father of tyranny on account of César's desire to be king. He leads the senate in its proposal to assassinate César, and is held to his conspirator's oath even when he informs the senators that he has learnt that he is César's son. He fails to dissuade his father from appearing before the senate. Cassius, dagger in hand, announces César's death, and Antoine pronounces his funeral oration. The style throughout is noble, flat, stilted, and undifferentiated between characters. The only real reminiscence of Shakespeare's colourful tragic panoply is the climax of the bare action.

Voltaire himself thought *Mahomet*, entitled in 1743 *Le Fanatisme; ou, Mahomet*, his best play. From 1745 it was dedicated to Benedict XIV after first having been dedicated to Frederick the Great. The setting is Mecca. Mahomet, depicted as an unscrupulous impostor, has established his power at Medina. The two captive children Séide and Palmire, in love with one another, have been brought up in his camp, but Palmire has been recaptured from him and is looked after in Mecca by Zopire, the sheik who, unknown to Séide and Palmire, is in fact their father. Mahomet, attracted to Palmire, demands her return. He comes to Mecca and arranges that Séide shall kill Zopire as a condition of securing Palmire, persuading him that it is an act of legitimate religious vengeance; Séide himself will then be poisoned. Séide therefore, after hesitation and amid much open theatricality and some contrived dramatic climaxes, unwittingly murders his own father and, when he discovers what he has done, rouses the citizens against Mahomet, not knowing that he has already swallowed the poison that will kill him. Mahomet points to Séide's death as a proof of divine support, but Palmire kills herself.

Mérope is a re-working of Hyginus's version of the legend of Merope inspired by Maffei's *Meropa* which had been played in Paris in 1717. Voltaire's play, conceived in 1736 and continuously revived for several years, was produced on 20 February 1743. Immensely successful in spite of the absence of any love interest, it was turned into an opera by Frederick the Great, broke records for revenue and attendance, and caused the audience to call for the first time for the appearance of the author when the curtain was lowered. Matthew Arnold discussed Voltaire's treatment of the theme in the introduction to his own *Merope* of 1858.

Cresphonte, king of Messenia, has been killed by Polyphonte, who aspires to the throne and wants to strengthen his claim by marrying Cresphonte's widow, Mérope, and killing her surviving son, Egisthe, if he can be found. He has in fact been brought up by the elderly Narbas in rustic simplicity and ignorance of his parentage. Mérope refuses Polyphonte. A youth is brought before her who has killed another youth, he says in self-defence. Mérope wonders if he could be Egisthe, but it seems more likely that Egisthe was the young man he killed. She consents to marry Polyphonte if she can herself with her own hand execute the murderer of her son, intending to kill herself immediately afterwards. When the captive is brought to the altar Narbas comes forward to declare that the youth is in fact Egisthe, and Polyphonte the killer of Cresphonte. Egisthe then wields the axe against Polyphonte, and is enthusiastically recognized as king.

It is almost coincidental that *Mérope* has a happy ending, although a tragedy with a happy ending, such as Corneille allowed for and Goethe indulged in, has invariably made for a popular success. Voltaire's plays are not great drama. The succession of unmotivated and psychologically unprepared climaxes comes over as contrived in a way which contrasts to Voltaire's disadvantage both with Shakespeare and with Racine. The characters too often suffer not from any inner compulsion, but from one which seems affected, or is exploited to demonstrate symbolically the effects of tyranny or intolerance. The sentiment is frequently histrionic in display rather than deep in feeling, and much of the language is too flat to lift the alexandrines to the poetic level which that verse form requires. The unities, used by Racine to intensify the focus on the passions of the characters, clash in Voltaire with the crowded incidents, mistakes, and recognitions on which he has to rely. His theatrical output is none the less important, not only as the historical foundation for his reputation in the world of letters, but because its whole thrust demonstrates his imaginative inability to shake off the irrepressible quest for an optimism whose intellectual justification increasingly eluded him. His drama came more and more to centre on the clash of ideas rather than of characters.

The earliest of Voltaire's major poetic works is *La Ligue; ou, Henri le Grand: poème épique* of 1723, known since the 1728 edition as *La Henriade*. It was probably begun in 1717 while Voltaire was staying near Fontainebleau with the marquis de Saint-Ange, Louis Urbain Lefèvre de Caumartin, one of the most revered of the group associated with the Temple. Voltaire composed and memorized several hundred lines of it while in the Bastille, and for some years gave occasional readings at country houses and in salons. He claims once to have thrown the manuscript into the fire, from which Charles Hénault retrieved it, and he later became dismissive of the version which he published surreptitiously in 1723. He was continuously to revise the work, adding for instance what became the sixth book. Over 50 editions appeared in his lifetime.

The hero is Henri IV, and the poem incidentally praises Protestant leaders in the Wars of Religion, and deals at length with the siege of Paris by Henri III and Henri de Navarre, eventually to become Henri IV. The work recounts the story of the St Bartholomew massacre, the assassination of Henri III, and the defeat of the League, and culminates with the abjuration of Protestantism by Henri on his accession. It is panoramic rather than epic, and the most effective lines are epigrammatic. Its popularity derived from the way in which no religion was conceded a special status as divinely instituted, but only the law which God has revealed to all: "La simple loi qui parle à tous les coeurs (The simple law which speaks to every heart)." The passage from which that line is taken was later toned down.

La Pucelle is a mock-heroic burlesque, in parts licentious, a narrative in parody of the life of Joan of Arc, with long satirical digressions. Only the light-hearted literary register prevents the blasphemy from being too sharp, allowing, for instance, the consignment to hell of Socrates, Solon, Homer and Cicero, "Tous malheureux morts sans confession (Unhappy wretches all, dead without confession)." A whole list of Voltaire's enemies is attacked, and the pseudo-subject at the poem's centre is the religious importance which really was attached to the virginity of the national heroine and saint. In the last line a member of the crowd "Criait encore: 'Anglais! elle est pucelle' (Still cried out, 'Englishmen! she is a virgin')." Work on the poem must have started by 1730, and it was the proliferation of manuscript copies which forced publication of the unauthorized text in 1755.

The *Poème sur le désastre de Lisbonne*, written swiftly and begun immediately on reception of the crushing news of the earthquake and its effects, is an elegiac attack on the notion that the world is governed by a free and benevolent providence. Why Lisbon rather than London or Paris? Could God not have made an earth without earthquakes? The attack on Leibniz is factitious. Voltaire blames Leibniz for failing to solve the problems of moral and physical evil in the world, as he would otherwise have to blame God directly, which he refuses to do:

Humble dans mes soupirs, soumis dans ma souffrance,
Je ne m'élève point contre la Providence

(Humble in my sighs, submissive in my suffering, I do not raise my voice against Providence).

There is no intellectual basis for optimism, but Voltaire's optimism remains irrepressible. The alternative to optimism was simply unbearable.

Three years later *Candide* momentarily goes as far as to explore the possibility that the universe may actually have been abandoned by God to the control of "quelque être malfaisant (some evil-wreaking being)," as the Manichean Martin thinks. But even then the register is light-hearted; Eldorado is a privileged exception; and Martin merely provides the point of view opposite to that of Pangloss, equally caricatured, equally incapable of providing an adequate explanation of human experience, and not therefore seriously denying the possibility of mindless hope with which that work, like the *Poème*, ends. In 1755, in spite of the weight on his mind brought about by pity for those who suffered at Lisbon, Voltaire ends on an irrationally defiant note of hope; in later editions he follows the word with a question mark:

Un jour tout sera bien, voilà notre espérance [?];
Tout est bien aujourd'hui, voilà l'illusion

(One day all will be well, that is our hope[?]./Today everything is well, that is the illusion).

The *Poème sur la loi naturelle*, written for Frederick before the Frankfurt episode although published only afterwards, none the less provides a counterpart of optimism to the mood of bleakness prevailing in the Lisbon poem with which it was published. There is a natural law underlying all religion. Notions of justice and duty are innate. Upbringing alone accounts for differences of religious sect. The attack on intolerance, fanaticism, and persecution is strident. All subjects of all states have the right to peace, order, and safety, and all are equal before the universal law.

Voltaire's first important prose work was the *Histoire de Charles XII, roi de Suède*, published surreptitiously at Rouen over a Basel imprint in 1731. Although it was banned, there were at least 10 editions in two years. Charles XII had died young in 1718, and Voltaire drafted his book in England in 1727, finishing it in 1729. Its daring can be exaggerated. Kings had been criticized before, and their actions evaluated even outside the bounds of a strict narrative of events. What Voltaire introduces is the generalized principle of public accountability of the great for their actions: "being public men, they owe the public an account of their actions." Voltaire also here uses the mock-naive style he was later to develop to such effect in the contes. Nothing in the style betrays the breath-taking cynicism or sarcasm of the content, as Voltaire perfects the art of the poisoned adverb: "He almost never attended the Council except to cross his legs on the table"; "he did not believe that there was a prince so enslaved to his promises as not to sacrifice them to his greatness."

The *Lettres philosophiques* is a heterogenous collection of miscellaneous letters criticizing French institutions under the guise of an introduction to religious, social, philosophical, scientific and literary life in England. The work appeared first in English in 1733. The Thieriot London edition of 1734 has a Basel imprint; and of the four 1734 editions bearing the title *Lettres philosophiques par M. de V**** the authentic Rouen edition by Jore of which Voltaire corrected the proofs and which was burnt by the Parlement de Paris is the 387-page duodecimo purporting to be by E. Lucas of Amsterdam. There are 24 letters, plus the "Anti-Pascal." Seven deal with religion and religious toleration:

S'il n'y avait en Angleterre qu'une religion, le despotisme serait à craindre; s'il y en avait deux, elles se couperaient la gorge; mais il y en a trente, et elles vivent en paix, heureuses

(If there were only one religion in England, there would be a danger of despotism; if there were two, they would cut each other's throats; but there are 30, and they live in peace, happily).

Four deal with institutions, including inoculation against smallpox, six with philosophers and science, and seven with literature and the arts.

In religion Voltaire prefers the Quakers although, having used them as a stick with which to beat other Christian bodies, he then holds them up to ridicule themselves. It is here that his religious position clearly emerges as dominated by a hatred of rites, because they lead to superstition, and a hatred of dogmas, because they lead to intolerance. His attitudes already flow outwards, rippling away in concentric but weakening circles of disbelief. He sees quite clearly what is obviously wrong, but becomes progressively more uncertain as clarity dissolves into doubt about the solutions to the great problems. At this date the Quakers seemed to offer Voltaire the best balance between tolerance and minimal dogmatic commitment on the one hand, and the institutional organization of Christianity to guarantee the fabric of society on the other. The *Lettres* contains more than one echo of Fénelon.

English democracy is similarly idealized and used as a weapon against the French ancien régime. The importance of trade is emphasized. Bacon and, above all, Locke are praised for their devotion to empirical investigations into science and philosophy. The letter on Locke, which alludes to Locke's diffident suggestion that matter might be so organized as to be endowed with mental processes, so blurring the distinction between a body destined to corruption and a spiritual soul which, the repository of knowledge, was independent of it and could be eternal, was the only one to which the censor objected. It shows Voltaire's polemical style at its lapidary best. Locke's "flambeau de la physique (torch of physics)" is contrasted with the "roman de l'âme" of Descartes, "né pour découvrir les erreurs de l'antiquité, mais pour y substituer la sienne (romance of the soul… born to uncover the errors of antiquity only to substitute its own)."

Immortality cannot be demonstrated and has to be revealed, but "le bien commun de tous les hommes demande qu'on croie l'âme immortelle; la foi nous l'ordonne, il n'en faut pas davantage, et la chose est décidée (the common good of all men requires that the soul should be thought immortal; faith ordains it, nothing else is necessary, and the matter is settled)." The *Lettres* is a work of propaganda, not of argument. Its literary technique introduces the pose of disinterested naivety and largely derives from Pascal's *Lettres provinciales*, which Voltaire called "le premier livre de génie qu'on vit en prose (the first work of genius to be seen in prose)," and on which he would continue to draw heavily for the philosophical contes. He took from it the mocking send-up of some absurdity, often by the use of strikingly inappropriate adverbs or conjunctions, and the reduction of major issues to trivial disputes, apparently self-evident affirmations, or innocuous-looking irrefutabilities. The Pascal attacked in the "Anti-Pascal" is primarily the gloomy protagonist of the Jansenist attitude to the effects of original sin on human nature. Voltaire was always to loathe Jansenism and its sister spirituality, Calvinism, both ironically attacked in *Mahomet*:

Qu'on adore mon Dieu, mais surtout qu'on le craigne

(Let my God be adored, but above all let him be feared).

In 1741 Voltaire was still an unrepentant intellectual optimist.

The 15th, 16th, and 17th of the *Lettres* are largely devoted to Newton and demonstrate not only Voltaire's ability to reduce complex matters—without distortion when he wished—to easily intelligible statements, but also his remarkable gift for seizing on the essence of an advance in experimental science, mathematics, or theoretical physics. The *Eléments de la philosophie de Newton* exploits both these gifts. Its great popularity is also a useful reminder of how imaginatively stimulating to Voltaire's contemporaries were the scientific discoveries of the 18th century. From time to time, as when considering Voltaire, it is salutary to be reminded that at no time in the history of European literature has it really been possible to isolate from scientific and technological advance, or indeed from progress in the other arts disciplines, the focuses of the literary imagination.

Voltaire always wrote disparagingly about his contes, today generally regarded as his most important writings. He can reasonably be said to have invented the conte philosophique, of which *Zadig* and *Candide* are examples, which must however be distinguished from such works as *L'Ingénu*, which is practically a nouvelle, and which Voltaire himself preferred to them. Voltaire makes his ironic points with the aid of multiple incongruities which, like the episodic form of the contes, their brevity and rapidity of action, and their tongue-in-cheek narrative style, must be understood in the light of the fact that he started to write them for reading aloud in country houses. The first to be published, *Zadig; ou, La Destinée. Histoire orientale*, appeared as *Memnon. Histoire orientale* in the summer of 1747. It was printed in Amsterdam under a London imprint, and appeared before the author's flight late in 1747 from Paris court life to Sceaux, where it may well have been the three extra chapters added for the 1748 edition which were read out to amuse the company. Voltaire was to write three further chapters, two of which he did not himself publish, and he had the September 1748 edition printed in separate halves by different printers. A second 1748 edition must have been later than September. The form often comes near to dialogue, and it is certainly true that the succession of contes, considered with their dates, constitutes a series of interior monologues in which Voltaire amusingly externalizes his serious intellectual preoccupations. The very short piece of 1749 now known as *Memnon* was not published separately.

For the sub-title of *Zadig* Voltaire says he would have used "providence" instead of "destinée" if he had not been writing "a work of pure amusement," and while the conte is undoubtedly a brilliantly written small comic masterpiece, its parodically light-hearted literary register must be respected. It does not set out to discuss any problem seriously. What it achieves is the frivolous discussion of an issue Voltaire knew to be gnawingly serious. The elaborate precautions about publication were taken only partly to elude the counterfeiters and pirate publishers. They needed to be taken also because the implications of the text, particularly in the characters' intepretations of events, were too pointedly incompatible with intellectual, devotional, and social orthodoxies to be allowed, even under the cloak of frivolity. Anonymity was abandoned for publication in volume eight of *L'Oeuvre de M. de Voltaire* published by Walther in 1748.

Like Montesquieu, from whose *Lettres persanes Zadig* must have derived, Voltaire gives his text an exotically oriental setting. Zadig undergoes a long series of misfortunes. The point, made clear in a list of his adventures at the end of the chapter entitled "Les Rendez-vous," is that he is always punished when he ought to be praised, but rewarded when something goes wrong, and the conte is a light-hearted reflection on the inadequacy which leads to the punishment of good deeds and the rewarding of error. Voltaire, happily, cannot resist pillorying the representatives of any sort of authority. In what is now the penultimate chapter, "L'Hermite," much fun is made of popular debasements of Leibniz's philosophy. Zadig promises to stay

with the hermit for a few days whatever the hermit does, and the hermit burns down a house in which they had just slept, and then drowns a 14-year-old boy, explaining that underneath the ashes of the house their host would discover a great treasure and that the boy, had he lived, would have killed his aunt in a year's time, and Zadig the year after that.

The hermit then turns into the angel Jesrad mouthing pseudo-Leibnizian explanations of evil. The wicked are there to sharpen the virtue of the good; without evil this would be a different world, with causes and effects different, and earth would be heaven; there has to be a variety of worlds to manifest divine omnipotence; nothing is fortuitous, "tout est épreuve, ou punition, ou récompense (everything is trial, or punishment, or reward)." The ending of the parable is similar to that of *Candide*. Here Jesrad says to Zadig,

"Faible mortel! cesse de disputer contre ce qu'il faut adorer."

"Mais," dit Zadig...

Comme il disait *mais*, l'ange prenait déjà son vol vers la dixième sphère. Zadig, à genoux, adora la Providence, et se soumit

("Weak mortal! stop arguing with what should be adored."

"But," said Zadig...

As he said *but*, the angel had already taken off for the tenth sphere. Zadig, on his knees, worshipped Providence, and submitted).

There are no real answers to the serious metaphysical or religious problems which are compatible with religious belief, but that innuendo is cloaked in an amusingly absurd fantasy.

The next fiction to be published was *Micromégas. Histoire philosophique*, published in 1752, although probably a re-working of a piece called "La Relation du voyage...de M. le baron de Gangan" sent by Voltaire to Frederick in June 1739. Considerable amusement is derived from measurements, astronomy, and mathematics, and the old device of extra-terrestrial visitors to the earth is exploited with economy and verve. The ideas made fun of are, naturally, serious ones, from Aristotle, Descartes, Malebranche, Leibniz, and Locke, for instance. Pedantry is sent up by alluding to Aristotle *On the Soul* in a specified edition (du Val, 1619). After 1752, Voltaire emphasized his point by introducing into the text first two words of Greek, Εντελεχια εστι (it is an entelchy: a technical term in Aristotle for the force directing vital processes towards their goal), before, in a later edition wrongly dated "Berlin 1750," he puts in a whole line of Aristotle in Greek. The caricatures of philosophical notions and the absurd conclusions legitimately drawn from their mis-statements are crass enough to have been hilarious to any 18th-century audience educated to the standards of sophisticated salon literacy. Voltaire is merely being wittily epigrammatic when he writes, "The Cartesian started to speak, and said 'The soul is a pure spirit which received all the metaphysical ideas while in its mother's womb and which, on leaving it, has to go to school to learn again what it once knew so well, and what it will never know again.'"

Candide; ou, L'Optimisme was anonymously published in Geneva and elsewhere, probably in February 1759, with the note that it had been translated from the German of "M. le docteur Ralph." The central character, as his name implies, is a naive young man. In search of his lost beloved, the once beautiful Cunégonde, he travels through the world undergoing grotesque and unpleasant adventures, with everything that happens the subject of a caricature of a Leibnizian gloss from the obstinately sanguine "docteur Pangloss," and then also, after the first third of the book, of a gloss in the opposite sense from Martin the Manichean, who believes that the universe is in the hands of an evil spirit. The title of the first chapter deliberately recalls Rabelais, of whom the reader is constantly put in mind. The unsubtlety of the caricature and of some of the humour can be gauged from the introduction of Pangloss. The text is pantomime.

Pangloss enseignait la métaphysico-thélogo-cosmolonigologie. Il prouvait admirablement qu'il n'y a point d'effet sans cause, et que, dans ce meilleur des mondes possibles, le château de monseigneur le baron était le plus beaux des châteaux, et madame la meilleure des baronnes possibles

(Pangloss taught metaphysico-theologico-cosmolonigology. He proved admirably that there is no effect without a cause, and that, in this best of all possible worlds, M. the baron's château was the finest of châteaux, and Madame the best of possible baronesses).

The technique of reducing complicated issues to the level of farce again derives from Pascal's *Lettres provinciales*. The imaginative projection of a perfect society in the Eldorado chapters constitutes the weakest part of the book. But Voltaire's wit pricks like a foil, and he is at his best when poking fun or animosity at doctrines, habits, attitudes, or people to whom he has taken a dislike, not when examining possible solutions. It is for this reason that he never thinks as radically as Rousseau, however much readier his wit and sharper his eye for abuse. It is in this work that Voltaire coined his famous epigram about Byng's execution, "Il est bon de tuer de temps en temps un amiral pour encourager les autres (It is a good thing to kill an admiral from time to time to encourage the others)."

It is not easy to demonstrate that the sparkling *Candide* is a work of disillusion, burying the possibility of intellectual optimism, except that the satire of facile solutions to the problem of the existence of evil is now more concentrated than previously, and more bitter. The reiterated attack, and the fact that Martin is more obviously reasonable than Pangloss, do however suggest that an intellectual crisis was taking place underneath the surface froth. In the final chapter Voltaire teases the reader by suggesting that at last everything had come right, and that Candide, Cunégonde, the philosophe Pangloss, the philosophe Martin, the prudent Cacambo, and the old lady could live happily ever after. But Candide was "cheated by Jews," his wife daily became uglier, the old lady became ill and bad tempered, Cacambo was overworked and cursed his fate, Pangloss was in despair at not being a brilliant philosopher in a German university, and only Martin, realizing that things were equally bad everywhere, was happy. Two further characters reappear, Frère Giroflée and Paquette, they, too, having failed to find happiness.

At the end they go and consult a dervish, the best philosopher in Turkey, who asks what it has got to do with them if there is good and evil in the world. When his Highness the Sultan sends a ship to Egypt, does he worry whether or not the mice are comfortable?

"Que faut-il donc faire?" dit Pangloss.

"Te taire," dit le derviche.

"Je me flattais," dit Pangloss, "de raisonner un peu avec vous des effets et de causes, du meilleur des mondes possibles, de l'origine du mal, de la nature de l'âme, et de l'harmonie préétablie."

Le derviche, à ces mots, leur ferma la porte au nez

(What should we do then?' said Pangloss.

"Keep quiet," said the dervish.

"I had hoped," said Pangloss, "to have some discussion with you about effects and causes, the best of all possible worlds, the origin of evil, the nature of the soul, and pre-established harmony [Leibniz's term for the relationship of knowledge to events outside the mind]."

At these words the dervish slammed the door shut in their faces).

They meet a Turk who is happy. He cultivates a little land with his children. Work keeps three great causes of unhappiness away: boredom, vice and want. Candide has cause for thought. Pangloss, the unrepentant pedant, recites a long and learned list of unfortunate monarchs.

"Vous savez…"

"Je sais aussi," dit Candide, "qu'il faut cultiver notre jardin."

"Vous avez raison," dit Pangloss; "car quand l'homme fut mis dans le jardin d'Eden, il y fut mis *ut operaretur eum*, pour qu'il travaillât: ce qui prouve que l'homme n'est pas né pour le repos."

"Travaillons sans raisonner," dit Martin; "c'est le seul moyen de rendre la vie supportable."

("As you know…"

"I know also," said Candide, "that we must cultivate our garden."

"You're right," said Pangloss; "since when man was put in the garden of Eden, he was put there *in order to work it*, so that he would work: which proves that man is not born for rest."

"Let's work without thinking," said Martin; "it's the only way to make life bearable").

The naive figure occurs again in *L'Ingénu* of 1767, its famous opening in fact a strong reminiscence of Saint-Evremond:

Un jour saint Dunstan, Irlandais de nation et saint de profession, partit d'Irlande sur une petite montagne qui vogua vers les côtes de France, et arriva par cette voiture à la baie de Saint-Malo. Quand il fut à bord, il donna la bénédiction à sa montagne, qui lui fit de profondes révérences et s'en retourna en Irlande par le même chemin qu'elle était venue

(One day Saint Dunstan, Irish by nation and saint by profession, left Ireland on a little mountain which floated towards the coast of France, and arrived in this conveyance at the Bay of Saint-Malo. When he was on land he gave his blessing to the mountain, which bowed deeply to him and returned to Ireland by the same route as that by which it had come).

This is actually an anti-Jansenist nouvelle, although purporting to come from the papers of the Jansenist Père Quesnel, and devoting amusing attention to a sketch of the Jesuit Père Tout-à-tous (everything to everybody). It spills over with irreverence, profundity, and wit, keeping up the same breathless narrative pace as the more philosophical contes, but developing the usual subjects with the usual dry wit a little less episodically. The "Ingénu" is a young Huron, another Voltaire character whose apparently unprejudiced observations the author uses to satirize everything he wishes, and through whose ways of behaving and moral attitudes he examines a state of uncorrupted natural innocence. The Huron could have found a place in Rousseau, but not as the object of everyone's flippant curiosity. On landing from an English boat in Brittany, at which Voltaire pokes much fun, the Ingénu rushes towards a prior and his sister who turn out to be his uncle and aunt. The sentence recounting the recognition has clipped clauses, 10 semicolons and 13 verbs in the imperfect tense. Even the style is a caricature of the emotional peak of an adventure narrative.

The Ingénu's encounters with Christianity, from the early discovery that the first step to conversion is circumcision, are predictably amusing. Voltaire pretends to record meticulously the Ingénu's surprise as he compares the practice of Christianity with what it says in the New Testament they had given him. His previous reading had been limited to Shakespeare and Rabelais. When he goes missing at the triumphalist ceremony his baptism was to be, he is found standing up to his neck freezing in a river waiting for the baptismal cortège. He asks the bishop to show him where, in the New Testament, anyone was ever baptized anywhere other than in a river. Inevitably a novel of such concentrated boutades leaves no room for characterization. The characters are wittily caricatured stereotypes, and the novel is still so disconnected that it must necessarily be short. The Ingénu falls in love with his godmother and naturally protests that the New Testament says nothing about a pope who must give a dispensation for a union between godmother and godchild.

Only 10 years or more later does the style change. *L'Histoire de Jenni* is scarcely a conte at all, but an intellectual confrontation in which Voltaire, frightened by the radical atheism of Holbach and La Mettrie, cannot find the intellectual arguments he needs to support organized Anglicanism as a necessary prop to the social order. It is a novel entirely of ideas and religious arguments in which the Anglican wins because the atheist, who has the better of the argument on points, throws in the towel.

The historical writings shade into the contes, since both include essays on the theological and philosophical background to religious and social topics and treat themes which they both also have in common with the philosophical dictionary and the philosophical dialogues like *L'ABC* and the *Dialogues d'Evhémère*. Although Voltaire rallies to a form of social conformity for which he explores the possibility that loosely organized Christianity might provide the best adhesive, and although he sustains his merciless satirical attack on philosophical, theological, and religious absurdities, as on superstition and intolerance, he can neither solve nor leave alone the fundamental problems to which he perpetually returns. The later treatment of the old themes—immortality, the problem of evil, heaven, hell, the soul, nature, virtue, and happiness—is less flippant, less amusing, and less irreverent but no less obsessive.

Even the historical works, although often painstaking in their documentation, are nowadays of interest primarily for the comments they contain on the attitudes and actions of the great, and on the events they caused, prevented, or failed to prevent. The width of interest again invites comparison with Rousseau, although the focuses are different, and the styles of treatment quite dissimilar. Prejudices abound, and the sharp, elegant wit can seldom resist wielding the weapon of ridicule. Not even on the stage does Voltaire attempt to abstain from implied moral judgements. The range, however, like the wit, is extraordinary, and there are few major subjects of interest to any section of the educated public of his day on which an anthology of Voltaire's comments could not be produced. He is at his best in light, darting pricks of irony, over-histrionic and sometimes overtly didactic in his drama, and weak at sustained philosophical argument. He shaped a new literary form to his own requirements, and made the episodic conte into the perfect vehicle for the wry, humorous comment on his own interior dialogue which lies at the core of his literary achievement.

PUBLICATIONS

Collections

Oeuvres complètes, 40 vols., Geneva 1775 [The last of 13 editions of complete works published in Voltaire's lifetime]
Oeuvres complètes [Kehl edition], 70 vols., 1784 and 1785–9
Oeuvres complètes [Moland edition], 52 vols., 1877–85
Complete Works (in French) [Besterman edition, Geneva/Toronto: includes second, definitive edition of *Correspondence*], 135 vols., 1968–

Verse

La Ligue; ou, Henri le Grand: Poème épique, 1723; as *La Henriade*, 1728; as *Henriade* (in English), 1732
Le Temple du Goût, 1733; revised as *Le Temple de l'amitié et le temple du goût*, 1733; as *The Temple of Taste*, 1734
Le Mondain, 1736
La Pucelle d'Orléans, 1755 [constantly augmented during Voltaire's lifetime]; as *La Pucelle; or, The Maid of Orleans*, 2 vols., 1785–6
Poème sur le désastre de Lisbonne, 1756

Poème sur la loi naturelle, 1756

Précis de l'Ecclésiaste en vers, 1759

La Cantique des cantiques en vers, 1759

Contes de Guillaume Vadé, 1764

La Guerre civile de Genève, 1767; as *The Civil War of Geneva*, 1769

Epîtres, satires, contes, odes, et pièces fugitives, 1771

Poèmes, épîtres, et autres poésies, 1777

Plays

[*During his lifetime Voltaire published his collected dramatic works, progressively augmented, in 1753, 1762, 1764, 1768–70, and 1772. Items not in italics in the list below were not published as separate volumes in Voltaire's lifetime*]

Oedipe (produced 1718), 1719

Artémire (produced 1720)

Mariamne (produced 1724); as *Hérode et Mariamne* (produced 1725), 1725

L'Indiscret (produced 1725), 1725

Brutus (produced 1730), 1730

Eriphile (produced 1732), 1732 [published, as noted on title page, against Voltaire's will]

Zaïre (produced 1732), 1733; as *Zara*, 1776

Les Originaux (produced 1732)

Adélaïde du Guesclin (produced 1734)

La Mort de César (produced 1735), 1735 (clandestine), 1736

Alzire; ou, Les Américains (produced 1736), 1736; as *Alzira, Or Spanish insult repented: a tragedy*, 1755

L'Enfant prodigue, comédie en vers (produced 1736), 1738

Les échanges, ou quand est-ce qu'on me marie? comédie en deux actes (produced 1734); as *Le comte de Boursoufle; ou, Les Agréments des droits d'afnesse*, 1826; also as "comédie-bouffe"

Zulime (produced 1740), 1761

Mahomet (produced 1742), 1742 (clandestine); as *Le Fanatisme; ou, Mahomet le prophète*, 1743; as *Mohamet, the Imposter*, 1744

Mérope (produced 1743), 1744; as *Merope* (in English), 1744

La Princesse de Navarre, comédie-ballet (produced 1745), 1745

Le Temple de la gloire, (music by Rameau, produced 1745), 1745

La Prude; ou, La Gardeuse de cassette, comédie en vers en cinq actes, (produced 1747)

Sémiramis (produced 1748), 1749; as *Semiramis* (in English), 1760

Nanine, comédie en trois actes en vers (produced 1749), 1749

Oreste (produced 1750), 1750

Samson, tragédie lyrique, 1750

Catalina; ou, Rome sauvée (produced 1750), 1752; as *Rome Preserved*, 1760

Le Duc de Foix (produced 1752), 1752; also as *Amélie; ou, Le Duc de Foix*; as *Matilda* (in English), 1811

L'Orphelin de la Chine (produced 1755), 1755; as *The Orphan of China*, 1756

Saül, [1764: *hyper-drame héroï-comique en cinq actes*], 1755; as *Saul* (in English), 1820

La femme qui a raison, comédie en trois actes, en vers (produced 1758), 1759

Tancrède, tragédie en vers et en cinq actes (produced 1760), 1761; as *Almida* (in English), 1771

Le caffé, ou, L'Ecossaise, comédie par M. Hume traduite en françois (produced 1760), 1760; as *The Coffee House*, 1760

Le Droit de Seigneur, comédie en vers (produced as *L'Ecueil du sage* 1762), 1763; three-act version for Vienna, 1764

Olimpie (produced 1764), 1763

Octave et le jeune Pompée, ou, Le Triumvirat (produced 1764), 1767

Les Scythes (produced 1767), 1767

Charlot; ou, La Comtesse de Givri (produced privately 1767), 1767

Le baron d'Otrante, opéra bouffe (produced 1768)

Les Guèbres; ou, La Tolérance, 1769

Sophonisbe (produced 1774), 1770

Les Pélopides; ou, Atrée et Thieste, 1772

Le Dépositaire, comédie en vers et en cinq actes (produced 1772), 1772

Les Lois de Minos; ou, Astérie, 1773

Don Pèdre, roi de Castille, 1775

Agathocle (produced 1777)

Irène (produced 1778), 1779

Le Duc d'Alençon; ou, Les Frères ennemis, 1821

L'Envieux, comédie en trois actes et en vers, 1834

Fiction

[*During his lifetime Voltaire published his collected contes in 1764, 1771, and 1775. A six-volume edition appeared in 1780. Many of the works of fiction and other works were first published under false imprints, giving spurious authors and places of publication*]

Romans et contes, 2 vols., 1978

Memnon. Histoire orientale, 1747

Zadig; ou, La Destinée. Histoire orientale, 1748 [Same work as above]; as *Zadig and Astarte*, 1810

Micromégas, 1752; as *Micromegas* (in English), 1753

Candide; ou, L'Optimisme, 1759; as *Candid*, 1759

Le Monde comme il va. Vision de Babouc, 1759

Jeannot et Colin, 1764

L'Ingénu, 1767; as *The Pupil of Nature*, 1771; as *The Sincere Huron*, 1786

La Princesse de Babylone, 1768; as *The Princess of Babylon*, 1927

L'Homme aux quarante écus, 1768; as *The Man of Forty Crowns*, 1768

Les Lettres d'Amabed, 1769

Le Taureau blanc, traduit du syriaque, 1774; as *The White Bull*, 1774

Le Crocheteur borgne, 1774

Histoire de Jenni; ou, Le Sage et l'athée, 1775

Other

Essai sur les guerres civiles de France, 2 vols., 1729; as *Essay upon the Civil Wars in France*, 1727

Histoire de Charles XII, roi de Suède, 2 vols., 1731; as *The History of Charles XII*, 1734

Letters Concerning the English Nation, 1733; as *Lettres écrites de Londres sur les Anglais*, 1734; as *Lettres philosophiques*, 1734

Elémens de la philosophie de Newton, mis à la portée de tout le monde, 1738

Histoire de la guerre de mil sept cent quarante et un, 2 vols., 1745; as *The History of the War of Seventeen Hundred and Forty-one*, 1756

Le Siècle de Louis XIV, 2 vols., 1751; *Supplément*, 1753; as *The Age of Louis XIV*, 2 vols., 1752; revised 1753

Annales de l'Empire, depuis Charlemagne, 2 vols., 1753

Essai sur l'histoire générale et sur les moeurs et l'esprit des nations, 7 vols., 1756; revised, 8 vols., 1761–3; as *The General History and State of Europe*, 1754; as *An Essay on Universal History*, 1759

Histoire de l'empire de Russie sous Pierre le Grand, 2 vols., 1759–63; as *The History of the Russian Empire under Peter the Great*, 1763

Appel à toutes les nations de l'Europe, 1761

Traité sur la tolérance, 1763; as *A Treatise of Religious Tolerance*, 1764

Dictionnaire philosophique, portatif, 1764; revised 1765 and frequently thereafter, including *La Raison par alphabet* (2 vols., 1769) and *Questions sur l'Encyclopédie*, (9 vols., 1770–72); as *The Philosophical Dictionary for the Pocket*, 1765

La Philosophie de l'histoire, 1765

Collection des lettres sur les miracles, 1765; the 20 letters were also published separately in 1765, and as *Questions sur les miracles*, 1765

Le philosophe ignorant, 1766; as *The Ignorant Philosopher*, 1767

Les Honnêtetés littéraires, 1767

Examen important de milord Bolinbroke, 1767

Lettres sur Rabelais, 1767

Homélies prononcées à Londres en 1765, 1767; *fifth homélie*, 1769

Le Dîner du comte de Boulainvilliers, 1767

Les Singularités de la nature, 1768

L'ABC, 1768

Histoire du parlement de Paris, 2 vols., 1769

Collections d'anciens évangiles; ou, Monument du premier siècle du christianisme, 1769

Dieu et les hommes: oeuvre théologique, mais raisonnable, 1769

Tout en Dieu, 1769

Les Adorateurs, 1769

Précis du siècle de Louis XV, 2 vols., 1769; as *The Age of Louis XV*, 2 vols., 1774

Fragments sur l'Inde, 1773; augmented with *Fragments sur l'histoire générale et sur la France*, 1774

Commentaire sur le livre 'Des Délits et des peines', 1776; as ancillary material to English edition of Beccaria, 1801

Commentaire historique sur les oeuvres de l'auteur de la Henriade (autobiography), 1776; as *Historical Memoirs of the Author of the Henriade*, 1977

La Bible enfin expliquée, 1776

Lettre à l'Académie française, 1776

Dialogue d'Evhémère, 1777

Commentaire sur l'Esprit des Lois de Montesquieu, 1778

Prix de la justice et de l'humanité, 1778

Traité de métaphysique, 1937

Translator

Thomson, James, *Socrate*, 1759

Shakespeare, *Julius Caesar*, 1764

Calderon, *L'Héraclius espagnol; ou, Dans cette vie tout est vérité et tout mensonge*, 1764

Editor

Extraits des sentiments de Jean Meslier, 1762

Biographical and critical studies

Desnoiresterres, G., *Voltaire et la société au XVIIIe siècle*, 8 vols., 1869–76

Naves, R., *Le Goût de Voltaire*, 1938

Pomeau, R., *La Religion de Voltaire*, 1956

——————*La Politique de Voltaire*, 1963

Brumfitt, J., *Voltaire Historian*, 1958

Gay, P., *Voltaire's Politics*, 1959

Crocker, Lester G., *An Age of Crisis*, 2 vols., 1959–63

Otieux, Jean, *Voltaire*, 1966

Wade, Ira O., *The Intellectual Development of Voltaire*, 1969

Besterman, Theodore, *Voltaire* (in English), 1969

Ridgway, R.S., *Voltaire and Sensibility*, 1973

Mason, Haydn, *Voltaire*, (in English) 1975

——————*Voltaire, a Biography*, 1981

Bibliography

Barr, Mary Margaret, *A Bibliography of Writings on Voltaire, 1825–1926*, 1929

——————————————*Quarante années d'études Voltairiennes: Bibliographie analytique des livres et articles sur Voltaire, 1926–65*, 1968

Bengesco, Georges, *Voltaire. Bibliographie de ses oeuvres*, 4 vols., 1882–90 (Index by John Malcolm, 1953)

[Bibliographical information appears regularly in *Studies on Voltaire and the eighteenth century*, 1955ff]

[This glossary is intended for quick reference: some of the information it contains is given more fully in the General Index, which also offers access to types of technical information which cannot be accommodated in a glossary.]

Abolition, lettres d'	Letters signed by the king to "abolish" serious crimes, granting a complete pardon, or at least removing them from the jurisdiction of the parlements
Absolution	The sacramental forgiveness of the guilt of sin
Achevé d'imprimer	Date at which a work's printing was finished. Books were frequently put on sale the same day by the printer, who was often also publisher and bookseller
Aides, cour des	Court with jurisdiction in tax matters. Because nobles were exempt from the taille, these courts also pronounced on claims to nobility
Alexandrine	A 12-syllable line in poetry
Amant	The word does not necessarily mean lover in the modern sense. It can refer merely to any man who pays court, in however stylized a fashion, to a woman
Amende honorable	Public humiliation and apology for a crime, to which the guilty could be sentenced, sometimes before the infliction of more severe penalties. Abolished 1791
Amiral de France	Important office conferring the right to exercise royal powers over all ships and maritime matters, and lucrative jurisdiction over ports and coastal territories
Anciens	Those defending the superiority of antique over modern culture in the Querelle des anciens et des modernes (q.v.)
Angelus	The brief thrice-daily devotion commemorating the Annunciation by the angel Gabriel to the Virgin Mary, imposed in France by Louis XI in 1472. Church bells were rung at about 6 a.m., midday, and 6 p.m.
Archers	Originally the bowmen of small military groups; the term came to denote foot-soldiers generally
Arrêt	Decree
Arsenal	The Paris munitions factory and warehouse which was turned into a library in the 18th century. Confiscated during the Revolution, it was opened to the public in 1797, and then restored to its owner, the comte d'Artois
Assignats	Negotiable bonds, issued during the Revolution, backed by state-owned real estate, much of it confiscated. Fell speedily in value
Attrition	Sorrow for sin based on the fear of hell. Some theologians were alleged to have taught that, either with or without the sacrament of penance, attrition was sufficient to remove the guilt of sin, while others insisted on the necessity of contrition, motivated by the love of God. There were technical but bitter controversies on the issue from the 13th to the 17th centuries
Augustinian(ism)	The view alleged to have been held by Saint Augustine that human nature was so damaged by original sin as now, without grace, to be incapable of any non-sinful act; also any analogous doctrine, or view tending towards it
Bailli	The bailli was a royal officer, a noble charged with supervision of the prévôts and with holding a court over which his lieutenant, a lawyer, presided. Answerable to provincial governors, baillis, like them, rarely resided. Baillis were also employed by the great landowners
Bailliage	The basic administrative division, more often known as sénéchaussée in the south. Their number varied from about 100 to about 300
Ballade	A poem, usually in octosyllables or decasyllables, of three stanzas, usually of eight or ten lines, and a half-stanza, or envoi
Ballet	An entertainment involving dance, created in France under Italian influence in the later 16th century. At first individual dancers were not singled out, and formations were the chief source of visual effect. Court nobles danced some scenes, and normally the "grand ballet" finale
Ballet-comique	The ballet-comique, based on a continuous, often mythological plot, was historically followed by the ballet-mascarade, with burlesque scenes or entrées, often comic and containing allusions to contemporary life. The texts began to be sung rather than declaimed, a trend reversed in Molière's comédies-ballets. Ballet merged in France with what became opera under Lulli at the Académie royale de Musique
Baptism	The sacrament of Christian initiation. It was normal to administer baptism on the day of birth, and birth dates are often dubiously based on surviving baptismal registers. Baptism was sometimes

	delayed for months after birth, and socially elevated godparents were seldom present
Barnabites	A religious order of clerks regular founded at Milan in 1538
Baroque	A term primarily used of architecture, apparently deriving from the Spanish barrucco for a large irregularly-shaped pearl. The term is often used in French literary history of all or part of what was written between about 1580 and about 1660, but there is no consensus as to its meaning
Benedictines	The monastic order founded by Saint Benedict early in the sixth century
Bienséances	Decencies, proprieties: technical term for what decencies and proprieties had to observed in presentation of on-stage action
Blason	Poem minutely describing some physical animate or inanimate object and its properties
Blasphemy	The civil crime for which heretics were normally condemned by the civil powers
Brethren of the Common Life	Devotional communities inspired by the evangelical spirituality of Geert Groote (1340–1384) which flourished chiefly in the Low Countries and north Germany in the 15th century. There were about 50 houses for males. There was also a sisterhood whose history is less well documented
Brevet	Military commission, or generally any official document conferring rank or title
Breviary	Liturgical book containing all the movable and immovable parts of the divine office to whose daily recitation all priests were held
Brief	A papal document, often of appointment or condemnation, more solemn than a "rescript," but less than a "bull"
Bull	The most solemn form of papal pronouncement
Caesura	Pause in a line of verse
Canzone/ Canzoniere	A poetic form associated as the canzone with Dante, and as the canzoniere with Petrarch. In French literature the term, associated with Scève, denotes a cycle of love poems
Capucins	Franciscan breakaway order of mendicant friars founded about 1520
Caractère	Prose genre which flourished in the late 17th century, largely replacing the portrait and depicting externally visible characteristics
Cardinal	In origin the cardinals were parish priests of the Roman diocese, whose bishop, the pope, they elect. In time a grade of cardinal was established which did not presuppose priesthood. Unlike bishops, cardinals did not necessarily have territorial jurisdiction, although some French cardinals held territorial titles because, often by inheritance, they also possessed seigneurial rights. Some bishops were cardinals, and the other cardinals were chiefly papal administrators and diplomats. Their number was limited to 72; they met in a "consistory" to elect a new pope whenever necessary; were known collectively as the "sacred college," appointment to which was colloquially referred to as elevation "to the purple," or being given the "red hat"
Carmelites	Mendicant, then contemplative religious order, founded in the 12th century, but virtually re-founded in the 16th century by Saint Teresa of Avila (1515–1582) and Saint John of the Cross (1542–1591)
Carthusians	A contemplative religious order founded in the 11th century with a strict rule. The monks live almost like a community of hermits
Celestines	A religious order founded in the 13th century
(Grand') Chambre	Appeal court of the Paris parlement
Chancelier	Chief legal and legislative officer, of similar rank to military Connétable. The lucrative post normally involved custody of the seal, for whose application to a document a charge was levied. The Chancellor could not be dismissed, but the seal could be entrusted to someone else, then known as the Garde des Sceaux
Chant royal	Complex form of ballade cultivated by the "grands rhétoriqueurs" and consisting of five stanzas and a final half-stanza or envoi
Châtelet	The "Grand Châtelet" was the headquarters of Paris's criminal investigation department. The "petit Châtelet" was a prison
Chevalier	The lowest rank of the higher level of nobility, above the mass of écuyers. By the 18th century the younger male members of titled families were called chevalier
Chiasmus	Figure of speech in which the second part of an antithesis is expressed in reverse order to the first
Collège de France	The royal foundation which grew out of the project for a French trilingual college, scaled down to the royal lecturerships of 1529–30 partly on account of opposition from the university. There were 17 lecturerships under Henri III, but no special building was finally undertaken until 1610
Collet	Collar. The "petit collet" was worn by tonsured clerics

Commendatory | Word applied to lay, temporary or secular abbots, priors and other holders of ecclesiastical office who received the income from the benefice without themselves exercising the office

Connétable | The king's chief military officer. The appointment was made only intermittently until it disappeared under Richelieu

(Grand) Conseil | The most important of the special courts, dispensing justice in the name of the king in cases he removed from the jurisdiction of the parlement

Conseil d'état | Principal council of Louis XIV, meeting three times a week, and consisting of only four or five persons. Louis XIV presided in his own apartments and no minutes were kept

Conseil des dépêches | Louis XIV's council for internal affairs. Held in the king's presence in the private apartments

Conseil des finances | Louis XIV's council concerned with financial affairs. Met in private apartments, attended by the king

Conseiller | An honorific title attaching to an increasing number of non-remunerated posts

Constitution | France had no constitution before the Revolution. The word invariably referred in the 18th century to the anti-Jansenist bull *Unigenitus* of 18 September 1713

Deniers extraordinaires | Revenues raised for special needs, normally wars

Devotio moderna | A term first used in Pomerius's *Life of John Ruysbroeck*, written between 1414 and 1421, where it describes the evangelical spirituality of Geert Groote, concentrating on religious and moral experience and attaching diminished importance to the rites and dogmas imposed by the Parisian scholastics

Director of conscience | Not necessarily the confessor, or a priest. The director's function was to interpret the religious experience of the "penitent" and to guide the penitent's devotional practices

Dominicans | Religious order, founded by Saint Dominic in the early 13th century, to which Saint Thomas Aquinas belonged

Echevin | Members of a town's executive committee appointed by the king through the intendant or a local seigneur

Ecuyer | A title any noble was free to assume

(Grand) Ecuyer | Master of the king's horses, who also ran what amounted to a junior military academy for royal pages, and took charge of the royal postal service

Election | The process by which God destines an individual for salvation, decreeing the graces necessary both for justification and for perseverance. Opposite of reprobation

Elections | Territorial sub-divisions of the généralités for paying purposes, usually co-terminous with dioceses, but confined to provinces which had no estates through which taxes were paid

Elu | Official charged with assessing the taille in an élection. The office was venal, although the élus had originally been elected

Enclosure | That part of a religious house to which persons of the opposite sex are not admitted

Enjambement | The holding over to a following line of words which complete the sense of the foregoing line in French verse

Epée, noblesse d' | Also known as noblesse de robe courte, nobility of military origin

Epithalame | Poem composed to honour a wedding

Estates General | Composed traditionally of the three orders of nobility, clergy, and people, they were called only when the king thought it expedient to consult his subjects

Estates (regional) | Provinces entitled to hold estates in 1661 were Brittany, Navarre, Languedoc, Provence, Burgundy and Bresse, and Artois. These provinces paid their direct taxes through their regional administration

Exempt(ion) | Apart from the often complex rules for exemption from various forms of taxation, the word is used for the exemption from episcopal or diocesan jurisdiction enjoyed by the ancient religious "orders," but not the newer "congregations"

Feminine ending | Used of lines in verse which end in mute "e," "es," or "ent"

Feuillants | Religious order, male and female, observing rule of Saint Bernard

Feuillants, Club des | Political association of moderates which broke away from the Club des Jacobins on 16 July 1791. The name survived the club

Foires (fairs) | Originally the Foire Saint-Germain was held in early spring and that of Saint-Laurent in late summer, but the seasons became extended, and the companies of travelling players who performed at the fairs established permanent theatres

Franciscans | Religious order which split into several branches. Their medieval theological tradition, different from that of the Dominicans, was represented by Saint Bonaventure and Scotus

Friars | Generic name for members of the mendicant religious orders

Gabelle | Tax on salt, a royal monopoly often levied by compulsory purchase, and sometimes also by a tax on consumption computed from a notional normal household requirement

Galant(erie)	Socially cultivated male or his behaviour showing generally stilted and sometimes exaggerated respect for one woman, or for women generally. One galant could have several maîtresses in the same group. The relationship was often affected
Gardes du corps	The four companies of officers who formed the king's bodyguard
Généralité	One of 34 areas into which France was divided for administrative purposes
Girondins	Party of moderate republicans during the Revolution, opposed to Robespierre and the Terror
Gloire	Regarded in the early 17th century as the most distinguished of moral qualities, it involved integrity, honour, and self-respect, but not necessarily external recognition
Grace	Supernatural gift of God justifying the soul after sin, and enabling it to perform meritorious works
Grammar	Lowest class of humanities in Jesuit colleges
Gratification	Financial payment made on king's behalf to writers and other creative artists
Greffier	Court officer in charge of records and registrations
Hell	The state of physical and mental torment to which the majority of the human race was thought to be eternally damned on death, unless justified by grace. Eternity was conceived as never-ending time. Reconciliation of the eternity and possible inevitability of hell with God's justice and mercy was a principal cause of religious controversy
Heresy	The ecclesiastical crimen of publicly disseminating heterodox doctrine. It involved repudiation of the Church's teaching magisterium and not its jurisdiction. Jansenism was a heresy which did not lead to schism, Lutheranism a schism which did not necessarily involve heresy. To suppress heresy, the ecclesiastical courts handed individuals to the civil courts, where they were normally prosecuted for the civil crime of blasphemy
Historiographer	The officer(s) charged with recording the glorious events of the reign and deeds of the monarch
Huissier	Court usher whose functions were gradually extended to the collection of fines and external execution of the court's orders
Indulgence	A papal grant, in exchange for money, of the same spiritual effect as would be achieved by a given number of days spent in penance. Indulgences could be applied to the souls of named or

	unnamed dead who might be undergoing the purification of purgatory prior to admission to the beatitude of heaven
Intendants	Royal officers appointed generally from the upper bourgeoisie to govern administrative units, so by-passing the governors and the parlements. They became the administrators of direct taxation, responsible for the suppression of rebellions
Jacobins	The extreme party of Robespierre during the Revolution
	Also name given to Paris Dominicans after their studium generale in the Rue Saint-Jacques, founded in 1221
Jesuits	Religious order founded 1540 by Ignatius Loyola, as he came to be called. The order quickly became powerful, and was celebrated for its schools
Lecteurs royaux	Humanist lecturers appointed by François I from 1529–30 in place of the trilingual college originally contemplated
Lettres de cachet	Royal letters to private persons often issued at the request of officials or heads of households to obtain arrests
Lettres de jussion	Royal orders to the parlements demanding immediate registration of legislation
Lieutenant	A senior officer assisting a bailli or a sénéchal
Lit de justice	Procedure whereby the king removed all delegated sovereignty from the parlement, assuming all authority himself
Livre	Monetary unit, of which three made an écu, until Richelieu made the écu worth 4 livres 14 sols. The livre was divided into 20 sols, and each sol into 12 deniers
Maîtres des requêtes	Originally judges with jurisdiction over the royal household, then judges directly accountable to the king whose status as one of the five sovereign courts was disputed by the Paris parlement
Maîtresse	Lady to whom a galant—often affectedly—paid court
Malta, Knights of	Members of the crusading order of the Knights of Saint John to which Malta was granted by Charles V in 1530. The knights, who had to prove nobility and vowed celibacy, came to be dominated by the French
Maréchal de camp	The lowest rank of general. Required nobility
Maréchal des logis	Officer in charge of organization of encampments, chief of staff
Mestre de camp	Commander of the second company in a regiment, and the regiment's second-in-command
Mignons	Generally derogatory term for young nobles surrounding Henri III, many of whom showed much courage and skill in battle, but with some of whom a

strongly emotional relationship with the king was the subject of contemporary comment

Modernes   Defenders of the superiority of modern culture in the Querelle des anciens et des modernes (q.v.)

Nature   There are four concepts of human nature which must be borne in mind in the context of the religious disputes of the 16th and 17th centuries:

i) "Pure" human nature before original sin but without Adam's supernatural gifts

ii) Elevated human nature with which Adam was endowed before original sin

iii) Human nature after original sin

iv) Fallen human nature as affected by the redemption

What the capacities and exigences of nature were in each of these four senses was hotly disputed and logically accompanied very different sorts of religious behaviour

New style   The dating system which started the year from 1 January, instead of Easter (generally)

Nobility   The fiscal privileges of the French nobility added considerably to the attractions of membership of its ranks

Nominalism   A position taken in the medieval dispute about the nature of universal ideas, leading in the late middle ages to a theological position emphasizing divine transcendance and the arbitrary nature of divine revelation and law

Old style   The dating system which faded out in the first half of the 16th century by which the new year did not start generally until Easter. 1 February 1520 (new style) was therefore 1 February 1519 (old style)

Oratory   A congregation of priests founded by Saint Philip Neri in Rome in 1564 and brought to France by Bérulle in 1611

Parlement   The French parlements lost a long struggle to be more than courts of justice. The jurisdiction of Paris included the whole of the north outside Normandy, and stretched as far south as Lyons. Quasi-parlements in Normandy and Brittany developed into full parlements and others briefly came and went. In 1561, there were eight: Paris, Toulouse, Grenoble, Bordeaux, Dijon, Rouen, Aix, and Rennes. Pau and Metz were to be added. Each parlement had several sets of courts. Paris had the Grand' Chambre, the court of appeal which also heard all cases directly relevant to the monarchy, whose judges (présidents) wore the mortier, a crimson and gold cap, and over which the king sometimes presided. There were also the Chambres des

Enquêtes, dealing with lesser cases pertaining to the jurisdiction of the Grand' Chambre, the Chambres des Requêtes, dealing with cases passed up from non-parliamentary tribunals by lettre de committimus and the criminal court, La Tournelle

Parties casuelles   After the explosion in the number of hereditary offices for sale under Henri III, Sully imposed an annual tax of one sixtieth of the value of the office, the parties casuelles also known as the paulette after the first tax farmer to sign the receipts

Prebendary   Synonym for canon: beneficed member of a cathedral chapter constrained for a period to sing divine office, or to pay for a replacement

Premonstratensians   An order of Augustinian canons founded in the 12th century

Président   A presiding judge of one of the five sovereign courts. See Parlement

Présidiaux   A new tier of courts instituted by Henri II between the bailliages and the parlements for the sake of the new offices made available for sale

Prévôt   Lowest-ranking royal judge hearing cases not reserved to the bailliage or sénéchaussée

Prévôt des marchands de Paris   Head of the Paris municipal government

Privilège   At first a protection against pirate editions granted to a printer or to an author for a prescribed period, but later denoting a censor's permission

Procureur   Either prosecutor, or legal representative, or proxy

Protestant   The word is not attested in French until 1546 as an adjective and 1586 as a noun, in English not before 1539 as an adjective and 1553 as a noun. The Protest itself took place at Speier on 19 April 1529, when six princes and 14 cities repudiated the majority view upholding "the most worthy sacrament of our Lord Jesus Christ's Body and Blood"…"nor shall the celebration of the Mass be done away…"

Récit   The account delivered by a messenger or witness of an event too violent to be presented on stage

Régale   The royal right to the benefices from vacant episcopal sees, bitterly disputed because the king had the power to protract vacancies

Rentes   Annuities or interest-bearing bonds

Reprobation   The divine decree by which justifying grace, or perseverance in a justified state, was denied to the individual soul

robe, Noblesse de   The nobility acquired by lawyers and other administrative office-holders, socially inferior to the noblesse d'épée

Schism	The repudiation of the primatial jurisdiction claimed by the Roman see. See Heresy
Secrétaire du roi	Office in the chancellor's department conferring noble status. There were some hundreds of secrétaires
Sénéchaussée	See Bailliage. Sénéchaussée was normally used for the territorial unit in the south but, where there was also a bailli, the sénéchaussée was the larger.
Septuagint	The authoritative Greek Bible in use in the Hellenistic Jewish community in Alexandria
Sorbonne	University college teaching only theology which, in the 16th century, became the meeting place for the faculty of theology, with which the college then became popularly identified
Sovereign courts	The Requêtes, the Grand Conseil, the parlements, the Cours des Aides, of which at one period there were five, and the Cours des Comptes, of which there were five
Stances	The term, deriving from stanza, came to mean a poem similar to the ode
Stichomythia	A series of conversational replies of regular length in tragedy, often of one line each, opposing contradictory sententiae, and contrasting with the tirade or monologue
Surintendant des finances	The supreme financial officer, whose title changed to contrôleur général des finances after the downfall of Foucquet
Tabouret	A stool: the rare right to sit in the queen's presence
Taille	The principal form of direct taxation
Terza rima	An Italian verse form rhyming aba bcb cdc....
Tombeau	A verse collection commemorating a death
Tonsure	The initiation into clerical status implying celibacy, but conferring the right to accept benefices and to be tried in ecclesiastical courts. The minimum age varied, and the ecclesiastical status was easily dispensed
Tontine	A system of inheritance whereby all goes to the last surviving heir
Trésoriers de France	Officials responsible for collecting the king's ordinary household revenue, the finances ordinaires. Their responsibilities were later extended to the collection of the finances extraordinaires including the taille
Unities	Arose from the view partly derived from Aristotle that a play should concentrate on one principal action which should not occupy more than 24 hours (unity of action, 24-hour rule). The unity of place was introduced into France a little later
Ursulines	Religious congregation for women founded in 1535, most of whose French members took solemn vows, turning that part of the congregation into a religious order
Valet de chambre	Purely honorific title entailing no duties inside or outside the royal household. Frequently bestowed on writers, artists, or merchants
Visitation	Religious order for women founded in 17th-century France by Sainte Jeanne-Françoise de Chantal and her director, Saint François de Sales

TITLE INDEX

The following index includes the titles of books—both in French and in English—listed in the Fiction, Verse, and Plays sections of the Publications lists for each writer. These abbreviations are used:

f	fiction
v	verse
p	play

A selection of titles from other sections (Works, Prose, Other, etc.) are listed; in these cases no abbreviation appears before the author's name.

Initial articles are omitted in all titles, whether French or English.

A Monseigneur le cardinal de Richelieu (v Malherbe)
A Monsieur de Verdun (v Malherbe)
ABC (Voltaire), 1768
Abrégé de l'histoire de Port-Royal (Racine), 1742
Acajou et Zirphile (f Duclos), 1744
Achilles (p Racine), 1700
Acteurs de bonne foi (p Marivaux)
Adam (Perrault), 1697
Adélaïde de Brunswick (Sade)
Adélaïde du Guesclin (p Voltaire), 1734
Adèle de Com*** (f Rétif de la Bretonne), 1772
Adolescence clementine (v Marot), 1532
Adonis (v La Fontaine), 1825
Adresse d'un citoyen de Paris, au roi des Français (Sade)
Adventures of Gil Blas of Santillane (f Lesage), 1749
Adventures of Telemachus (Fénelon), 1742
Aenéide travestie (v Furetière), 1649
Aesop at court (Bensserade), 1768
Agathocle (p Voltaire), 1777
Age of Louis XIV (Voltaire), 1752
Agésilan de Colchos (p Rotrou), 1635
Agésilas (p P. Corneille), 1665
Agioteurs (p Dancourt), 1710
Agreeable Surprise (p Marivaux), 1766
Ah! quel conte! (f Crébillon *fils*), 1754
Aigle, Mademoiselle (Sade)
Alaric (v G. Scudéry), 1654
Alcione (Houdar de la Motte), 1706
Alexander the Great (p Racine), 1714
Alexandre le Grand (p Racine), 1665
Aline (p Sedaine), 1766
Aline et Valcour (Sade), 1795
Allée de Sylvie (Rousseau), 1763
Almahide (f G. & M. Scudéry), 1660
Almida (p Voltaire), 1771
Alzire (p Voltaire), 1736
Amadis de Grèce (Houdar de la Motte), 1699
Aman (p Montchrestien)
Amant libéral (p G. Scudéry), 1636
Amants magnifiques (p Molière), 1670
Amaryllis (p Tristan l'Hermite), 1652
Amélie (p Rotrou), 1636
Amélie (p Voltaire)
Amorous Quarrel (p Molière), 1762
Amour à la mode (p T. Corneille), 1651
Amour castillan (p Nivelle de la Chaussée), 1747
Amour des amours (v Peletier du Mans), 1555

Amour échappé (f Donneau de Visé), 1669
Amour et la vérité (p Marivaux), 1720
Amour médecin (p Molière), 1665
Amour pour amour (p Nivelle de la Chaussée), 1742
Amour tyrannique (p G. Scudéry), 1638
Amours (v Ronsard), 1552
Amours (v Tristan l'Hermite), 1638
Amours d'Hippolyte (v Desportes)
Amours de Diane (v Desportes)
Amours de Jan-Antoine de Baïf (v Baïf), 1552
Amours de Psyché et de Cupidon (La Fontaine), 1669
Amours de Vénus et d'Adonis (p Donneau de Visé), 1670
Amours du Compas et de la Règle (v Desmarets), 1637
Amours du Soleil (p Donneau de Visé), 1671
Amours et nouveaux eschanges des pierres precieuses, vertus et proprietez d'icelles (v Belleau), 1576
Amours tragiques de Pyrame et de Thisbé (p Viau), 1623
Amphion au roi (v Malherbe)
Amphitrion (p Sedaine), 1786
Amphitryon (p Molière), 1668
Ample discours au Roy sur le faict des quatre estats du royaume de France (v Du Bellay), 1567
Andrographe (f Rétif de la Bretonne), 1782
Andromache (p Racine), 1675
Andromaque (p Racine), 1667
Andromède (p P. Corneille), 1650
Andromire (p G. Scudéry), 1640
Angélique et Médor (p Dancourt), 1685
Anneau perdu et retrouvé (p Sedaine), 1764
Année des dames nationales (f Rétif de la Bretonne), 1791
Annibal (p Marivaux), 1720
Anti-Justine (f Rétif de la Bretonne), 1798
Antigone (p Garnier), 1580
Antigone (p Rotrou), 1639
Antiochus (p T. Corneille), 1666
Apollon menteur (Palissot de Montenoy), 1748
Apologie des Femmes (Perrault), 1694
Argument de la pierre philosophale (p Donneau de Visé), 1681
Ariadne (p T. Corneille), 1982
Ariana (f Desmarets), 1636
Ariane (f Desmarets), 1632
Ariane (p T. Corneille), 1672
Aristippus (Balzac), 1659
Arlequin poli par l'amour (p Marivaux), 1720
Arminius (p M. Scudéry), 1643
Arrêt rendu à l'amphithéâtre de l'Opéra (Diderot), 1753
Art poëtique (v Peletier du Mans), 1555

GENERAL INDEX

In order to provide as helpful a thematic index as possible while keeping to manageable length, a sharp distinction has been made between those authors, reviews, institutions or movements with their own main entries in the body of the *Guide*, and all other indexed names and themes. **Where an index entry also has a main entry, the fact is indicated in the index by bold type but, to avoid replication of the contents of the *Guide* in its index, none of the indexed references under such an index entry refers to the main entry concerned**. To discover what the *Guide* contains about Molière, to whom a main entry has naturally been devoted, the main entry itself should be consulted. Indexed under his name are only references to him in other entries. Some major authors are referred to relatively seldom outside the main entries devoted to them, and have in consequence only short index entries. But for example Lulli, who was a composer, and Colbert, who was a minister, have no main entries under their own names, and as many references to them are indexed, with their thematic contexts, as seemed practicable and useful.

To avoid unwieldy length, names that are specific to a single author, like those of husbands, wives, antecedents, relatives, and close associates, are not indexed unless they have an importance outside the immediate context of the author concerned. Lazare de Baïf, for instance, is indexed, but on account of his role in the literary culture of France, and not simply because he is the father of the poet Jean-Antoine. The index does not contain names from antiquity unless in a specific context they have a particular importance, as Cicero has in the context of the 16th-century debate about how normative his Latin style was. Kings, queens, ministers, and generals have indexed references only when there is a special reason, as the award of a promotion or a pension, and not when they are used merely to identify a period, or situate an event against a political background, as in 'the Dutch wars of Louis XIV' or 'during the ascendancy of Colbert.'

The alphabetical convention noted in the Preface (p. xlvi) has been followed in the index, but although cross-referencing has been provided where it seemed necessary, users of the *Guide* may need to be warned that many of the persons whose names occur in the index had different names at different dates, or were known indifferently by their family name or the name of their property. In the body of the text the same person is normally referred to as Henri de Navarre and Henri IV according to the date, but he appears in the index as Henri IV. The sister of François I, correctly known as Marguerite de Navarre no earlier than 1528, was born Marguerite d'Angoulême, under which title her name appears in the index. In the main entries she is at the appropriate dates also known as Marguerite d'Alençon. Inherited titles, particularly important when the duchies of royal princes changed from Alençon to Anjou, and then from Anjou to Orléans, generally because elder brothers had died, mean than total provision could scarcely be made for all changes of an individual's name. It should, however, be noted that different titles, like 'marquis,' 'comte,' and 'duc,' can distinguish between contemporary brothers, like the duc de Créquy and the marquis (later duc) de Créquy, and that some titles travelled through the female line, so that the duchy of Retz, for instance, passed into the Gondi family through the second marriage of Claude-Catherine de Clermont-Dampierre, who acquired it from her first husband, Jean d'Annebault. These examples are adduced not because they need to be remembered, but merely to illustrate the complexities of identifying in the index an individual mentioned in the text.

However, doubtless the most important preliminary note concerns the index entry 'nature and instinct.' Any attempt to provide a thematic index must necessarily rely on semi-arbitrary key words for purposes of alphabetical arrangement. The *Guide* contains a very large number of references to attempts to explore the possibility of upgrading natural and instinctive human activity by suggesting or doubting its connection with an elevation which is morally enriching and religiously virtuous, and with happiness. 'Nature and instinct' has been chosen as the key general term to indicate all such efforts, although much more specific references can also be found under such thematic keywords as 'freedom of the will,' 'will, faculty of,' or 'grace, theology of.' or simply 'merit.' There is an entry in the Glossary on the theological concepts of nature.

belonged to a group round Ménage and Retz, and was close
to Saint-Amant, and it was through him that Pascal's scientific friends acquired their knowledge of Bruno

> challenges Mairet by adapting Bonarelli's *Solyman*,
> 462–63

allegory: a 17th-century dispute divided the protagonists of allegory, including d'Aubignac, Cotin, Gilles Boileau, and
Furetière, from its opponents, including those, like Ménage
and Huet, referred to as pedants, those in the entourage of
Foucquet concerned with the analysis of sentiment, and the
authors of portraits and caractères, including Madeleine de
Scudéry and Anne de Montpensier

Alphonso IV d'Este (1634–62)

> Bensserade's ballet for wedding of, 59

Althusius (Althaus), Johannes (1557–1638), Calvinist author of
a detailed political system making sovereignty the inalienable
prerogative of the people and incapable of delegation, the
Politica methodice digesta (1603)

> opposed to Bodin, 69
> Rousseau takes inalienability of sovereignty from, 754

Altuna y Porta, Don Manuel Ignacio (1722–62), Spanish noble
Rousseau invited to become permanent companion of, 743

Amadis de Gaule (Les), chivalresque Spanish romances, possibly of 14th-century Portugese origin, related to the Arthurian
legend and considered to derive from Old French sources.
Four books were printed in 1508, with the others in 1519 from
a Spanish literary redaction by Garcia Ordonez de Montalvo.
Nicolas d'Herberay des Essarts published eight volumes of a
French adaptation (1540–48). The 'translation' was continued. Twelve books were published in French in 1556, and 12
more between 1571 and 1615. Bernardo Tasso published an
Italian translation in 1535. The book was immensely popular
in France, generated large numbers of derivatives, and came
to be regarded as a guide to elevated conduct. Amadis
avenged the oppressed and was a model of fidelity in love,
depicted as the source of all virtue and the most noble of all
motivations, although not every action it inspires is innocent,
and there is an inconstant lover, Galaor. Calvin, Brantôme,
and La Noue considered the work corrupting

> Voiture nourished on, 889

Amboise, Georges d' (1460–1510), opposed to regency of Anne
de Beaujeu and imprisoned for two years; recalled to court
from diocese of Montauban as adviser to Louis XII; archbishop of Narbonne (1492) and Rouen (1493). He got permission from Alexander VI for Louis XII to marry the widow of
Charles VIII and obtained a cardinalate for himself (1498).
He brought sculptors, painters, and architects to France from
Lombardy, and was noted for his practical concern for the victims of plague and famine

> Budé heavily critical of, 100

Amboise, Jacques d' (died 1516), brother of the above. He was
a Benedictine, abbot of Cluny (1485) and bishop of Clermont
(1505), a reformer and artistic patron who protected Clichtove and in 1506 made him tutor of his nephews, François, for
whom Clichtove wrote the *De vera nobilitate* (1512), and
Geoffroi, for whom he wrote the *De laude vitae monasticae*
(1513)

> Clichtove dedicates the *Opera* of Hugh of Saint-Victor to
> in 1506, 445

Amelote, Deny (1606–79), superior of Oratorian mother-house
in Paris

closely associated with dissemination of spirituality of
Bérulle, 468

Amerbach, Basile (1488–1535), second son of Johann Amerbach, the printer; graduated B.A. at Paris in 1505 and studied
law at Freiburg; did not get on with Froben

> hopes to study with Lefèvre d'Etaples, 445

Amerbach, Bruno (1484–1519), eldest child of Johann; studied
in Paris at same dates as Basile; returned there in 1506;
entered family printing house, where he works on Erasmus's
edition of Jerome. He retained an interest after his father's
death, when it was taken over by Froben

> proposes to study with Lefèvre, 445–46

amour-propre, self-interest, and disinterest: cluster of words
important when used in any of four distinct ways

> a) in context of the traditional power of blinding attributed
> to self-love ('philautia/philautie') in Plutarch, Erasmus,
> and Rabelais, 666
>
> b) in context of dispute about whether the highest form of
> the love of God ('charity') was necessarily 'pure' in the
> sense of discounting any hope of reward; the central
> issue, analogous to one raised by Ockham, between
> Camus and Sirmond, then between Bossuet, Fénelon,
> and Malebranche, centring on the 33rd article d'Issy, and
> involving Molinos, quietism, Mme Guyon, and philo-
> sophical discussions about the nature of the will as a fac-
> ulty, all individually indexed
>
>> see entries on Bossuet and Fénelon, passim François
>> de Sales; his experience and spirituality, 791–92
>>
>> Malebranche's views on Fénelon doctrine, especially
>> 471 and 473
>>
>> Richelieu's dismissal of king's confessor on this
>> issue, 774–75
>
> c) in any context which exploits the derivation of 'amour-
> propre' from Augustine's 'amor sui,' which necessarily
> involves sin, that is the absence of justification, and
> excludes its irreconcilable opposite the 'amor dei (love
> of God).' The importance of the theological usage of the
> terms 'amor sui' and 'amour-propre' in 17th-century
> France was immense, particularly for Saint-Cyran, the
> Jansenist disputes, Nicole, Pascal, debates about semi-
> Pelagianism, the freedom of the will and the theology of
> grace, all of which are individually indexed Nicole's
> spirituality and amour-propre, 560–61
>
>> Pascal's use of the term, 576
>>
>> Saint-Cyran and, 777
>
> d) the secularization of the concept of self-interest, exploit-
> ing the pejorative overtones of 'amour-propre' (but not
> necessarily the psychological motivation of self-inter-
> est), in a purely non-theological context
>
>> La Rochefoucauld and, 433, 435–36, and 560–61
>>
>> Saint-Evremond and, 783–84
>>
>> satirical usage, 569

Amy, Pierre (died c1525), Franciscan observant at Fontenay-le-
Comte who before 1522 fled to the Benedictine abbey of
Saint-Mesmin. Virtually all that is known about him is in the
entry on Rabelais

> Amy and Rabelais; corresponds with Budé, 654

Amyot, Jacques (1513–93), bishop who studied Greek at Cardinal Lemoine, graduating in 1532; private tutor to nephews of
Jacques Colin and lecturer in Greek at Bourges (1535);
charged in 1547 by François I with translating Plutarch; vis-

ited libraries at Rome and Venice, and was sent to Council of Trent by Henri II; tutor to his sons (1557); made grand almoner by 10-year-old Charles IX in 1560; bishop of Auxerre (1570); loyal to Henri III when Auxerre went over to the League. His translations include works by Euripides and Sophocles, Heliodorus's *Théagène et Chariclée* (1548), Diodorus Siculus (1554), and Longus's *Daphnis et Chloë* (1559). The translation of Plutarch's *Vies* appeared in 1559, and the *Oeuvres morales* in 1572

> Belleau draws on, 53
> du Vair uses Plutarch translation of, 270
> present at death of Charles IX; the *Tombeau* and *Vray discours*, 316
> Huet relies on *Daphnis et Chloë* translation, 360
> Plutarch translations of, 379; and Montaigne's admiration for, 539
> Saint-Evremond draws on, 782
> describes Tyard discussing astronomy with Henri III, 863

Amyraut, Moses (1596–1664), controversial theology professor at Saumur, author of first original Protestant ethical system, *La morale chrestienne* (1625–60), who narrowly escaped condemnation for liberal views on universal grace at Synod of Alençon in 1637

> Arminianism of, 30–31
> Cartesianism of, 122

Anacreon: Greek poet of sixth century B.C. notable for relatively simple verse forms and witty celebration of pleasure. In 1554 Henri Estienne published the Greek text of a manuscript he had found in 1549, with a Latin translation of what he took to be Anacreon's poems, although few were authentic. Belleau translated it in 1556, while Ronsard, who had clearly had access to the manuscript before publication, drew extensively on it for the collections of 1554 and 1555

> Baïf inspired by, 20
> Balzac on Ronsard's treatment of, 28
> Belleau's translation of, 51–52

Andelot, Charles d' (1565–1632), eldest son of Coligny, imprisoned by League in 1590 and converted to Catholicism

> Protestant leader in 1567, 92

Andilly, Robert Arnauld d': see Arnauld

Andouins, Diane (1554–1620), vicomtesse de Louvigni, who in 1567 married Philibert de Gramont, comte de Guiche; was widowed in 1580 and became the mistress of Henri IV; known as 'la belle Corisande;' to whom Henri IV wrote and signed a promise of marriage in his blood

> La Boétie's sonnets dedicated by Montaigne to, 380

Andreini, Francesco, an actor from about 1558, he was from 1600 at the latest leader of I Gelosi, Flaminio Scala's commedia dell'arte company, having in 1578 married the 16-year-old Isabella. He played the vainglorious military captain and created the character of the Sicilian doctor, Falsirone, as well as the magician and the shepherd Corinto; was an accomplished performer on a variety of instruments, and spoke Italian, French, Greek, Slavonic, and Turkish. A poet and writer, member of the religiously committed actors' guild, the Spensierati, in Florence, he had been a soldier, spent seven years in Turkish captivity, and escaped still young enough to play the young lover for I Gelosi

> I Gelosi in France, 150

Andreini, Isabella (1562–1604), married to above, actress, scholar, member of several academies, honoured by Tasso and du Ryer. Henri IV wrote to Villeroy, governor of Lyons, that the troupe would be passing through and, on Isabella's death there of a miscarriage, she was given a solemn funeral. Her inamorata was the idealized woman, never the subject of stage obscenity. It was Catarina Biancolelli who turned the character into the flirtatious boyish tyrant of parents and lovers alike. Isabella used her own first name for the inamorata stage character

> and court of Marie de Medici, 150

Andrelini, Fausto (c1462–1518), Italian poet protected by the Mantua family of Gonzagas, allowed with Balbi and Vitelli to teach poetry in Paris for an hour a week from 1489. Balbi, ferociously jealous, obtained Vitelli's departure and quarrelled viciously with Andrelini, who finally forced Balbi out, not before reciprocal accusations of sodomy. He gained illustrious patrons, became a royal poet, and helped Erasmus

> dedicated *De influentia syderum* to Budé, 96
> and group of Italian humanists in Paris, 444

Aneau, Barthélemy (c1500–c1565), studied under Wolmar at Bourges; from 1529 teacher of rhetoric at new Collège de la Trinité at Lyons. Suspected of Protestantism, he was killed during an uprising. Among numerous works of poetry, satire, and natural history, he left a book of Latin and Greek emblem verses *Picta poesis* (1552) which, along with other works, including Alciati's *Emblemata* and More's *Utopia*, he translated into French. He is best remembered for the 1550 *Le Quintil Horatien sur la Deffence et illustration de la langue françoyse*, a defence of traditional French poetic practice against du Bellay

> and defence against Du Bellay, 257
> helps Scève organize entry of Henri II into Lyons, 817
> adds *Quintil* to new edition of Sebillet, 722
> emblems for *Picta poesis*, 818

Angennes, Angélique-Clarisse d' (died 22 December 1664), known as Mlle de Rambouillet, sixth child of the marquise; married François-Adhémar de Monteil, comte de Grignan, later the husband of Mme de Sévigné's daughter, on 27 April 1658

> one of the original group who acknowledged the name of précieuses, 127–29, 627
> Voiture's duel over, 889; and its consequences, 891
> borrows money from Chapelain, 130

Angennes, Julie d' (1607–71), eldest daughter of the marquise de Rambouillet, and later herself marquise de Montauzier, the Julie of the *Guirlande de Julie* q.v.

> see entry on *Guirlande de Julie*, passim
> plays in amateur production of Mairet's *Sophonisbe*, 462
> marriage to Montauzier on 4 July 1645, 627
> teases Mme de Sablé about her hypochondria, 630
> and Voiture, and the chambre bleue, and its amusements, 131, 328, 889
> Chapelain's letter to Montauzier on death of, 134

Angran, Mme, later, probably from 1674, marquise de Roucy, whose first husband, 'le licencié Angran,' was sent to Rome to plead the cause of the Augustinian bishops in 1649. Sainte-Beuve, nettled by an attack, has pages of notes distinguishing three ladies sometimes referred to by the same name. This one was prominent in the underground network which hid Arnauld and Nicole in Paris in the early 1660s

> Nicole lodged by, 557

Anjou, duc d' (1683–1746): see Philip V of Spain

Bacon, Francis (1561–1626), Lord Chancellor of England (1618), author of attempt to inaugurate renovation of knowledge in the *Advancement of Learning* (1605), the *Novum Organon* (Latin, 1620), and the *De dignitate et augmentis scientiarum libri ix* (1623)

see indexed references under 'disciplines'

d'Alembert and, 5

Descartes inspired by, 210

Diderot accused of plagiarizing, 231; but models himself on, 232

possible derivation of *L'Encyclopédie* from, 274

Rousseau's deference to authority of; divergence from d'Alembert, 744

Baculard d'Arnaud, François-Thomas-Marie de (1718–1805), novelist, dramatist, and poet, was recommended to Frederick the Great by Voltaire, with whom he quarrelled, returning in 1755 from Potsdam to live in poverty in Paris, where he was briefly imprisoned during the Revolution. He excelled in the depiction of horror, tormented characters, and mysterious, gloomy settings in which gruesome forces are at work; is best remembered for his plays, including the tragedy *Coligny* (1740), *Euphémie* (1768), set in a crypt, the medieval tragedy *Fayel* (1770), in which the Lady of Fayel is supposed to eat the heart of the châtelain de Coucy, *Mérinval* (1774), and *Le Comte de Comminges* (1765), based on a novel by Mme de Tencin and the only one to be staged (in 1790), set in the burial crypt of a Trappist monastery.

Baculard was a committed Catholic. He clearly anticipated aspects of romantic melodrama and the grotesque. He also left *Les Epreuves du sentiment* (6 vols., 1806) and the *Délassements de l'homme sensible* (12 vols., 1783–87). His reputation as a poet, based on several odes and *Les Lamentations de Jérémie*, and as a novelist (*Les Epoux malheureux*, 1746; *Fanni; ou, L'Heureux Repentir*, 1764; *Sidnei et Silly*, 1766; and *Zénothémis*, 1733) was never high

recommended to later Frederick II as Paris correspondent, 333–34

Voltaire imposes Raynal on Frederick to succeed as his Paris literary correspondent, 301

Voltaire expresses bitterness about Crébillon *père* in letter to, 187

awarded middle class of pension in 1795, 702

removal from Berlin contrived by Voltaire, 899

Bade, Josse (c1461–1535), scholar-printer educated by Brethren of the Common Life, who visited Italy, worked for Trechsel at Lyons, married Trechsel's daughter, moved to Paris in 1499, and opened his own press in 1507. Known as Jodocus Badius Ascensius, he acquired Greek type in 1520

published Budé, 97

Erasmus's implied comparison of Budé with, 98

on tragedy, 439

Baïf, Jean-Antoine de (1532–89)

Life, 16–20; Works, 20–22; Publications, 22–23

see Introduction xl

early education of with Ronsard under Dorat; move to Coqueret; study of Greek; *Dithyrambes* for Arcueil picnic; on Binet's list of Rondsard's chosen associates, 582, 610, 721, 723

Le Brave of performed 1567; verses recited by to Catherine de Medici in interval; Ronsard attends, 222, 724

pall-bearer at Belleau's funeral, 52, 223

Ariosto adaptation; contributes to tombeau of L'Aubespine, 222

Desportes stays with on death of Joyeuse, 224

and Garnier, 314, 315

associated by Muret with Jodelle; sole reference to Jodelle's *Didon* in, 371–73

esteem for La Boétie, 378; includes La Boétie pieces in *Euvres en rime*

measured verse of related to Peletier's theory of memory, 586

receives pension and patronage, 316

joins La Péruse in Poitiers, 611

celebrates Catherine de Clermont-Dampierre, 705

paraphrases Pontano, mediating to Ronsard inspiration of Ausonius, 728

reflects intensified interest in religious poetry, 671

helps appoint Dorat's son-in-law as successor in Greek chair, 724–25

Baïf, Lazare de (1496–1547), father of the poet; with Longueil studied Greek in Italy under Musurus and Lascaris; shared the archaeological fascinations of the French humanists, writing about antique clothes, vases, and boats; translated the first four *Lives* of Plutarch and Sophocles's *Electra*.

From 1529 he was French ambassador in Venice, where the illegitimate Jean-Antoine was born. Recalled in 1534 he discharged diplomatic functions and was sent on the 1540 mission to Hagenau, taking Ronsard in his suite, ostensibly to work for religious conciliation, but in fact to subvert the emperor's influence with the six princes and 10 cities forming the Schmalkaldic league of 1531

early career of, Longueil, Musurus, Lascaris, and Robert Estienne; dedications of to Jean de Guise, Antoine du Bourg, and François I; admired by Erasmus; translations of Sophocles in verse and of Plutarch by; member of household of first cardinal de Guise; employed Pierre Bunel; communication between mansion of and Ronsard dwellings; legal and diplomatic career and mission to Hagenau, 16

praised by du Bellay, 256; and Peletier, 587

treatise of tragedy by, 439

Baillet, Adrien (1649–1706), conscientious biographer of Descartes (1691), ascetic, historian, and critic, employed as librarian by Lamoignon

provides only evidence for Descartes's intellectual experience near Ulm, 201–202

see entry on Descartes, passim

thought Pradon's *Tamerlan* preface aimed at Racine, 623

Baius (Michel du Bay), 16th-century Louvain theologian, whom Jansen partly set out to defend

teaching of on nature and grace, 365–68

Balbi, Giovanni Battista, choreographer of Strozzi's 1645 *La Finta Pazza*

cooperation with Torelli, 151

Balbi, Girolamo (born 1454), Italian teacher of poetry in Paris, fled in 1491 to Vienna after accusations of sodomy and bitter dispute with Andrelini. Forced to flee Vienna for the same reasons in 1493, settled in Hungary, found favour at court, enjoyed benefices, was sent on diplomatic missions, became a bishop, then papal chaplain to Adrian VI. He was still living in 1520 and group of Italian teachers of literature in Paris, 444

VIII, whose help François I needed, preferring the risk of another schism to any dilution of doctrine, and was in 1533 finally exiled as a result of the condemnation of the king's sister's *Miroir de l'âme pécheresse*. Recalled from Montargis for investigation, Beda led the attack on the new royal lecteurs, was imprisoned for some months in 1534, sentenced to a public degradation on 31 January 1535, and exiled to Mont Saint-Michel. In 1536 he provided for six scholarships at Montaigu

> Principal of Montaigu, 111
> and Roussel, Marguerite d'Angoulême, Cop, and Calvin, 112
> hostile to Lefèvre d'Etaples, 447–48
> role in condemnation of the *Miroir*, 485
> amende honorable (see Glossary) and exile, 656

Bedeau, Julien: see Jodelet

Beeckman, Isaac, principal of the college of Dordrecht
> Descartes and, 202
> persuades Gassendi to widen his objectives, 322

Béjart, Madeleine (1618–72), one of at least 10 children of a minor legal official. With Molière she founded L'Illustre Théâtre in the October of 1643. The members of the family associated with Molière were:

> Joseph Béjart (1616–59), actor for L'Illustre Théâtre with stammer
> Madeleine Béjart (1618–72), co-founder, signed 1643 act, actress
> Geneviève Béjart (1624–75), signed act of 1643, actress, married 1664 and again in 1672
> Louis Béjart (1630–78), limped in right leg, played minor parts (the limping La Flèche in *L'Avare*), retired 1670
> Armande Béjart (c1643–1700), wife of Molière, mother of his three children, remarried on his death, retired 1694; joined the Guénégaud troupe on Molière's death
> see entry on Molière passim
> according to Tallemant, Madeleine's finest role was Epicaris in Tristan's *La Mort de Sénèque*, 862

Bélébat, Charles-Paul Hurault de l'Hospital, seigneur de
> Saint-Simon comments on, 790

Belin, François d'Averton (died 1637), comte de, son of the governor of Paris, patron of Scarron, Rotrou, Mairet, and the Marais troupe of actors, of whose manager's wife, Isabelle Mestivier, Mme Lenoir, he was the lover, and for whom he had created the leading roles in Mairet's *Sophonisbe* and *Virginie*.

It was largely through Belin's connections, notably with Cardinal de la Valette, Fiesque, and Mme de Rambouillet, that a close relationship was established between members of the aristocracy and the leading figures of the theatre. It was Belin who arranged for Montdory to play Mairet's *Virginie* at the Hôtel de Rambouillet. The cardinal was impressed enough to give Montdory a pension. The two plays dedicated to him did not observe the unities

> see Introduction xxxvi, xlii
> attends Hôtel de Rambouillet, 460
> patron of Mairet; career and character of Belin, 460–61, 465
> patron of Rotrou; and receives dedications from, 733
> frequented by Scarron; sided with Mairet against Pierre Corneille in Querelle du *Cid*; incites Scarron to write against Corneille, 810

Bellarmino, Roberto (1542–1621), Jesuit and cardinal, author of theologies of political sovereignty and of the action of grace; his defence of the temporal power of the papacy caused offence in France by its strength, and in Rome by its weakness

> read by d'Aubigné, 8
> theory of grace, 366
> examines François de Sales for episcopacy, 794

Belleau, Rémy (1528–77)
> **Life, 51–52; Works, 52–53; Publications, 53–54**
> member of Boncourt group under Muret, 723
> Baïf's *Méline* and, 18
> and appointment of Dorat's son-in-law to succeed him, 25, 724
> writes ode for Garnier, 314, 315
> Jodelle associated with, 371; played in *Cléopâtre* of, 257, 371
> replaces La Péruse on Ronsard's list of seven poets, 610
> recites verses to Marguerite, youngest sister of Henri II, 222
> frequents maréchale de Retz, 862
> coffin carried by Baïf, Desportes, Jamyn, and Ronsard, 223

Bellefonds, Bernardin de (1630–94), maréchal de
> protector of Pierre Corneille, 165

Bellegarde, Octave de, archbishop of Sens, designated co-superior of Port-Royal, but effectively bypassed by Zamet, of whose success Bellegarde, a friend of the Carmelites, was jealous

> denounces the *Chapelet du Saint-Sacrement*, 772
> alliance with the Jesuits against Saint-Cyran, 772

Bellegarde, Roger de Saint-Lary (1586–1646), duc de, Grand Ecuyer, joined entourage of Gaston d'Orléans; disgraced for opposition to Richelieu; rehabilitated after cardinal's death. Replaced as lover of Gabrielle d'Estrées by Henri IV, was made governor of Burgundy. In 1620 Louis XIII erected his property into a duchy, making Bellegarde a peer. He married Anne de Bueil; she was cousin to Racan, whose education he saw to in the Ecurie. Publicly thought to be homosexual

> Balzac becomes secretary to, 23
> patronage and protection of Malherbe, 475–76
> Racan member of household of, 477
> Racan and, 669
> anecdote from Tallemant concerning, 856

Belle-Isle, Charles Foucquet de (1684–1761), maréchal, led withdrawal from Prague, 880

Bellerose, Pierre le Messier, known as (c1600–70), notable member of the troupe that became the 'comédiens du roi,' which took over the Hôtel de Bourgogne and of which he became director soon after 1630. His acting was quieter and less declamatory than that of Montdory at the Marais, and his most celebrated role was the lead in Pierre Corneille's *Le Menteur*. He married Nicole Gassot, the widow of an actor

> probably urges Bensserade to take Mairet subject, 462
> and Hardy, 346–48
> Georges de Scudéry switches his company to that of, 822

Bellièvre, Pompone de (1529–1607), chancellor (1599–1605)
> leaves Cracow, 223
> complaint about Montchrestien's *L'Ecossaise* made to, 542
> dedication by Scarron to, 811

Bellocq, Pierre (1645–1704), poet, friend of Boileau, from whom a piece against Boileau's *Satire* against women, *Lettre à Mme de N...* briefly estranged him

examine them. On 24 June François I moved the examination into the hands of the chancellor Duprat, endowed with both ecclesiastical and civil jurisdiction, but the Sorbonne, having already come to a decision, had passed the matter to the parlement. The faculty had recommended a prohibition from translating or writing anything prejudicial to faith, and the parlement handed the affair to the bishop of Paris. Berquin apparently declined the bishop's invitation to apologize, was imprisoned on 1 August, and indicted for heresy by the bishop of Paris on 5 August. He was released on orders from the king; the trial was dropped, but the books were burnt on 8 August.

Arrested again during the king's Madrid captivity in January 1526, Berquin was sent by the commission of Juges-délégués, two theologians and two members of the parlement's courts, but with special delegated ecclesiastical powers from Clement VII as well as civil jurisdiction, to be sentenced by the parlement which, however, held back from sentence on hearing of the release of the king who, in spite of obstructive tactics, had Berquin freed again.

In 1528 the king agreed to an examination of Berquin by a commission of 12 laymen appointed by the pope, but the laymen were denounced by the faculty as 'Lutheran,' and the king protested uselessly, since his army in Italy had surrendered and he could no longer move the pope. He in fact appears mentally to have written off Berquin who now faced again the same judges as previously, and was sentenced to life imprisonment on 15 April 1529, two days before the rash appeal
  Budé and, 98
  Marguerite d'Angoulême and, 484–85
Berry, Charles (1686–1714), duc de, grandson of Louis XIV, and third son of the dauphin Louis; married Marie-Louise-Elisabeth (1686–1714), the eldest daughter of Orléans, later the regent
  see Chronology 1715
  Fénelon's tutorship extended to, 282
  death of, 788, 791
Berryer, Nicolas-René, lieutenant-general of police,
  interrogates Diderot, 230
  authorizes the prospectus for *L'Encyclopédie*, 231
  decrees mild conditions for Fréron in Bastille, 302
  Voltaire approaches for suppression of Fréron journal, 301
Bertaut, Jean (1552–1611), court poet under Henri III and Henri IV, from 1606 bishop of Séez, a reliable poet for official occasions, with verbal skill, elegant, pointed, without strong emotion. His occasional poetry was published in 1601; the love poems in 1602; and Bertaut also left religious verse, including translations and paraphrases, and a collection of sermons
  poems of edited by Gomberville, 328
  Régnier dedicates *Satire* to, 696
Berthelot, René (died 1664), actor and acrobat husband of Thérèse du Parc
  taken on by Molière, 151
Berthier, Guillaume-François (1704–82), Jesuit, director of *Journal de Trévoux*, later royal librarian
  controverts *Encyclopédie* prospectus, 231
Bertier, David de (1652–1719), bishop of Blois (1693), member of family associated with Compagnie du Saint-Sacrement which had provided three bishops of Rieux
  member of Fénelon's mission to La Rochelle, 280

Bérulle, Pierre de (1575–1629), cardinal, active in promoting the French branch of the Carmelite order, on which however he wished to impose his own spirituality based on vows of servitude to Jesus and Mary; founder of the French congregation of the Oratory, instituted on the analogy of Saint Philip Neri's Italian foundation. Bérulle was the protagonist of a neoplatonist spirituality, chiefly developed by his lieutenant and successor, Condren, based on the *Hierarchies* of the Pseudo-Denis, and intended to elevate the significance of priesthood and to dignify the role in the church of the diocesan as opposed to the regular clergy. As an ecclesiastical diplomat Bérulle had negotiated in 1624 at Rome the dispensation for Henriette de France, daughter of Henri IV, to marry the Protestant English prince, the future Charles I. Politically identified with the pro-Spanish party
  see Introduction xliii
  overtures to Angélique Arnauld of; and alliance with Zamet, 615
  defends diabolic possession of Marthe Brossier against medical evidence, 770
  judge in congrès between Candale and his wife, Anne d'Halluin, 885
  opposition of Carmelites to vows of servitude of, 772
  neoplatonism of pseudo-Denis developed into anti-naturalist spirituality of annihilation, 775
  encourages Descartes, 122, 203
  derives vocabulary from Duval; literary source for Saint-Cyran, 777
  Gibieuf and; bridge between his spirituality and that of Jansenism, 210
  publishes *Grandeurs* in 1623; list of approbations, 771
  and Jansenism, 76
  Malebranche and neoplatonist spirituality of, 468
  visits Marie de Medici at Angoulême
  spirituality of and Saint-Cyran, 771; on whom he increasingly relies; spirituality at stake in Saint-Cyran's disputes, 771–72
  introduces François de Sales to Mme Acarie, 795
  deposes superior chosen by Zamet for new Institut, 772
  reactionary nature of spirituality of, 645, 867
  increasing political influence of, 773
Berwick, James Stuart (1671–1734), duke of, illegitimate son of James II, naturalized French, maréchal (1706) and duc de Fitzjames
  Montesquieu and circle of, 548
Bessarion (of Trebizond, 1403–72), ordained 1431, studied at Mistra under Plethon, diplomat, bishop of Nicea (1437), spokesman at Florence for the Greek church, cardinal (1439), and subsequent holder of a number of Italian bishoprics. In 1463 he became patriarch of Constantinople, was legate to Bologna (1450–55), and was principally concerned with the organization of a crusade which did not take place. Briefly in France in 1472, he left as his most important work the defence of Plato against George of Trebizond, the *In calumniatorem Platonis libri IV* (1469)
  Pico lends Lefèvre d'Etaples Aristotle translation by, 444
  Lefèvre d'Etaples edits Aristotle translation by, 447
Beuvron, François d'Harcourt (1598–1658), marquis de. After the famous duel of 14 May 1627 he fled France, and hoped to rehabilitate himself by leading the French garrison at Montferrat in 1629. In 1626 he had married Renée

Scève's victory in Marot's competition, 816

failure of the contreblasons, 816

Blégny, Nicolas de (c1646–1722), Catholic doctor, editor of the first medical journal, went to prison for innovatory medical methods

project of a cooperation with Desbordes and Bayle on a new journal, 32

Blondel, David (1590–1655), Protestant pastor who succeeded Vossius at Amsterdam (1659)

re-opens debate on pagan oracles, 297

Boccaccio, Giovanni (c1313–75), author of *Il Decamerone*, written against the background of the Florentine epidemic of plague in 1348, translated into French in 1545

source for Brantôme, 94–95; and Desmarets, 219; and La Fontaine, 423, for whose *Contes* Boccaccio provides model, 428; and for La Taille, 438; and for *Heptaméron* of Marguerite d'Angoulême, 491; and Montaigne's taste leads him to, 539; and Sade uses fictional techniques of, 768; and Scève publishes story by, 815; and source for Tristan's *Le Page disgracié*, 859

and the prettification of medieval stories of lechery, 850

Bochert, Samuel (1599–1667), Protestant pastor and scholar

introduces Huet to court of Christina of Sweden, 360

Bodin, Jean (1529/30–1596)

Life, 65–67; Works, 67–70; Publications, 70

see Introduction xxxii

Charron meets, 137

Garnier's early politics similar to those of, 316

attitude of Montesquieu towards, 550, 553

Boerhaave, Herman (1668–1738), Dutch doctor/botanist of international fame

Jaucourt studies under, 274

La Mettrie works with, 606

Boileau, Gilles (1631–69), elder brother of Boileau-Despréaux, with whom, after mixing constantly in the same literary company, he was to break. He was finally elected to membership of the Académie française in 1659, when he was only 28, through the patronage of Colbert and Séguier. He had translated the *Tableau de Cébès* (1653) and the *Vie d'Epictète* (1655), flattered d'Aubignac's taste for irony, gained fame with the *Avis à M. Ménage* (1655), was jealous of his younger brother, and tempered his judgements and literary activities to suit his ambitions. He broke successively with Ménage, Costar, and Scarron, and sharply criticized Balzac, Chapelain, and Ménage, while still accepting their patronage, or publicly professing admiration for them

career and literary relationships of, 71–72, and (especially) 308–310

and the *Chapelain décoiffé*, 75

relationship of with Colbert; possible authorship of *Dissertation sur Joconde*, 76

election to the Académie, blocked by Ménage, imposed by Chapelain, and consequent literary alignments, 133

satire on Ménage's relationship with Mme de Lafayette, 410

association with comtesse de la Suze group, 518

Perrault returns to controversy about allegory; and duplicity of, and new alignments, 590–91

hostile to Racine, 677

Scarron quarrels with, 811

Boileau, Jacques (1635–1716), dean of Paris theology faculty

career of; friendship with Loménie de Brienne, 71

Boileau-Despréaux, Nicolas (1636–1711)

Life, 70–74; Works, 74–78; Publications, 78

see Introduction xlii and Preface xlv

early literary alignments of; the *Chapelain décoiffé*, 310

involvement in literary politics, 361–62

dismissive of Bensserade, 56

close to Bossuet, 82

see Chapelain entry, passim

uses term 'siffler (hiss/whistle),' 153

dislike of sumptuous dramatic entertainment, 177

thinks Crébillon *père* even worse than the Pradons and Boyers, 187–88

Cyrano anticipates burlesque treatment of Aristotle by, 195

attacks Desmarets, 218

Donneau de Visé replies to anti-feminist *Satire X*, 252

dependence of *Art poétique* of on Fleury, 646–47

attacks 'Molinosism,' 283

association of with Hôtel de Lamoignon, 289

dedicates *Epître V* of 1674 to Guilleragues, 338

and incidents surrounding Racine's *Phèdre et Hippolyte*, 338, 621

pension from privy purse; then general list, 360

La Bruyère calls on to read 'maxims,' 383

circulates *Dialogue des Héros de roman*, 417

La Fontaine and, 422, 425, 428

and the 'badinage élégant' of Marot, 505, 509

and changing relationship with Molière, 165, 518, 521

quarrel with Perrault, its incidents and alignments, 590, 594–96

hostilities with Pradon, 621–24, 626

Madeleine de Scudéry defended against, 626

see entry on Querelle des anciens et des modernes, passim

and Racine, 675, 679–82

and Regnard, 689

strictures on Ronsard of, 726

satirical style of anticipated by Scarron, 811

original *Satire I* may have had Tristan in mind, 858

historiography appointment, 253

Boindin, Nicolas (1676–1751), lawyer and dramatist

frequented Café Procope, 263

Boisrobert, François le Métel de (1589–1662), poet, virtually Richelieu's secretary in literary matters, later protected by Mazarin. Born a Protestant, he became a Catholic and a priest; received benefices, and letters of nobility for his father (1636); published paraphrase of penitential psalms (1627); entered Richelieu's entourage from service of Marie de Medici; and went on diplomatic missions to England (1625) and Rome (1630).

His verse was light, encomiastic, published in the *Récit des plus beaux vers* (1627) and the *Epîtres* of 1646 and 1659. He specialized in libretti for court entertainments, wrote numerous plays, was one of Richelieu's 'five authors,' and published narrative fiction (*Histoire indienne d'Anaxandre et d'Orazie*, 1629, and *Nouvelles héroïques et amoureuses*, 1657). Allowed indulgence for unecclesiastical behaviour, he nonetheless exceeded the bounds of tolerance and in 1655 was exiled from court, returning only in 1658. Quarrelsome by temperament, he had personal disputes particularly with such former friends as Scarron, Ménage, and both Corneille brothers

Ethics in 1704, was sympathetic to Spinoza, and popularized his views in France. Boulainvilliers drew on Descartes and Locke, but held that animals could think, and that the laws of nature admitted neither of exceptions nor of miracles. At death the soul remains as spirit, and can be restored to matter
  attacks Bossuet for absolutism
Boulainvilliers, Philippe de, comte de Dammartin
  protector of Jodelle, 372
Bourbon, Anne de: see Longueville, Mme de
Bourbon, Antoine de (1518–62), duc de Vendôme, king of Navarre from 1533, brother of Louis I, prince de Condé, husband of Jeanne d'Albret, queen of Navarre, which she inherited from her mother Marguerite d'Angoulême. Wounded at Rouen and died on 17 November 1562
  see Chronology 1548, 1560
  killed fighting in Catholic army, 6
  marriage to Jeanne d'Albret, 487
  Ronsard's poem for wedding, 722
  death of, and chronology of Ronsard's polemical poems, 731
Bourbon, Catherine de, 'Madame,' sister of Henri IV, married duc du Bar
  d'Aubigné writes to, 10
Bourbon, Charles de (1523–90), Cardinal, named king by the League
  arrested by Henri III; proclaimed king by Mayenne, given into d'Aubigné's charge, and death of, 9
  1588 arrival in Paris and imprisonment, 266–67, 804
Bourbon, Charles, duc de Vendôme (1489–1537), from 1527 duc de; father of Antoine de Bourbon, king of Navarre, of Charles, Cardinal de Bourbon, and of Louis I, prince de Condé [no specific reference in *Guide*]
Bourbon, Charles III (1490–1527), duc de, Connétable de France, owner of large compact territory round Moulins. Rift with François dates from death of Bourbon's wife in 1521, when the rapacious queen-mother, Louise de Savoie, and François I first claimed, then appropriated, the inheritance. Bourbon may have been rejected suitor of the queen-mother; allied himself with Charles V; vacillated; broke with François I on 7 September 1523. The ill-organized rebellion attracted massive public support against the chancellor, Duprat; the courts imposed provocatively lenient sentences; Bourbon, wronged, was none the less anachronistically defiant in defence of feudal rights. He died scaling the walls of Rome with the imperial troops in the Sack of 1527
  joins imperial forces, 484
  possibility of marriage to Marguerite d'Angoulême, 484
Bourbon, Louis I de (1530–69), prince de Condé, father of Henri I, prince de Condé, of François, prince de Conti (1558–1614), and of Charles, comte de Soissons (1566–1612). Youngest brother of Antoine de Bourbon, father of Henri IV; brother of Cardinal Charles de Bourbon
  see Chronology 1560
  political and military career of in 1562; capture and release, 6
Bourbon, Louis-Henri (1692–1740), duc de, grandson of le grand Condé, from 1686 duc d'Enghien, minister in 1723, personally subservient both to his mistress, Mme de Prie, and to the youngest of the Pâris Duverney brothers, who had profited much from Law's bankruptcy. Disgraced in 1726, Mme de Prie was sent to exile in Normandy and Pâris Duverney to the Bastille

  La Bruyère tutor to, 382–83
  appointment of as first minister, 788
Bourbon, Louis de (1661–1711), le grand Dauphin, only son of Louis XIV and Marie-Thérèse
  see Chronology 1715
Bourbon, Nicolas (1503–after 1549), poet latterly protected by Marguerite d'Angoulême and tutor to her daughter, Jeanne d'Albret
  and Marguerite d'Angoulême, 485
  mentions Scève, 816
Bourbon, Nicolas (1574–1644), neo-Latin poet and royal lecturer in Greek, enlisted by Balzac in his dispute with Goulu, brother of Bourbon's predecessor
  Balzac's break with, 25
Bourbon-Montpensier, Marie de, princesse de Dombes, then duchesse d'Orléans, the heiress courted by Soissons whom Richelieu forced Gaston d'Orléans, the heir presumptive, into marrying in August 1626. She died giving birth to the princesse de Montpensier, '(la grande) Mademoiselle,' on 4 June 1627
  see Chronology 1626, 1627
  Mairet's allusion to marriage of, 460, 465
Bourdaloue, Louis (1632–1704), Jesuit preacher widely regarded by his contemporaries as the greatest of his generation. He appears to have memorized his sermons, to have delivered them rapidly and authoritatively, with eyes frequently closed, to have gesticulated violently, and to have fascinated his congregations with allusions precise enough to allow speculation about their reference to actual people. He preached Lent or Advent courses before Louis XIV ten times between 1672 and 1697. Unhappily very few authentic texts survive
  visited Huet regularly until his death, 362
Bourgogne, duc de (1682–1712), grandson of Louis XIV, and briefly heir apparent to the throne of France
  see Chronology 1682, 1715, Introduction xxxi
  Beauvillier made governor of, 280, 282
  Fénelon tutor to; works written for, 277, 288; fidelity of to Fénelon, 285
  La Fontaine writes fables for, and receives pocket money from, 426
  future of discussed by and with Saint-Simon; death of, 788, 791
Bourgoing, François (1585–1662), general of the Oratory
  Bossuet preaches funeral oration of, 80
  Bérulle's disciple and successor
Boursault, Edme (1638–1701), literary journalist, novelist, and dramatist, employed and then dismissed by the king as editor of a rhymed gazette. His patrons included Pierre Corneille and Montauzier. He is best known for the 1663 *Le Portrait du peintre; ou, Le Contre-critique de 'L'Ecole des Femmes*, attacking Molière's *L'Ecole des Femmes*, played at the Hôtel de Bourgogne, and for the 1668 *Satire des satires* against Boileau. His name is strongly associated with the *modernes*, but he was later reconciled with Boileau
  hostile to Boileau, 72
  and circle of Pierre Corneille, 164
  attack on Molière, and dispute over *L'Ecole des Femmes*, 250, 518
  re-groups supporters of the *modernes* in the Querelle, 310
  forced to change title of parody of *Mercure Galant*, 513

the king's preacher (1608). He left an important anti-stoic *Tableau des passions* (1620), and works of anti-Protestant controversy

Balzac reacts against, 25

Coeuvres, marquis de: see Estrées, François-Annibal d'

Colasse, Pascal (1649–1709), composer, assistant to Lulli, for whom he is said to have written the parts between treble and bass

La Fontaine wrote a libretto for, 426

Colbert, Charles (1625–96), marquis de Croissy, brother of Jean-Baptiste; minister for foreign affairs

Fénelon submits memoir to on Franco-papal dispute, 282

Colbert, Jean-Baptiste (1619–83), contrôleur général des finances, surintendant des bâtiments (1664), was in possession of all the important portfolios, including culture, and the architect and chief practitioner of administrative, financial, and cultural absolutism, designer of the Sun King's thurification, commissioning orchestrator of the chorus celebrating his mythologization; personally austere, with a streak of populism but cold, incorrupt, highly intelligent, low-born but sensitive to elegance and refinement, the most professional European statesman of his century.

In 1662, soon after Colbert came to power, Claude le Petit, a 23-year-old lawyer, was executed for disrespect and irreverence. For 10 years Colbert's power was supreme. Thereafter he had more difficulty in restraining the royal grandiosity for which he was partly responsible. His eirenic policies, based on wealth-producing activities at home, were increasingly swept aside in favour of the bellicose strategies of territorial conquest advocated by Louvois, who displaced him.

Mazarin's successor, Colbert began by overturning Foucquet, whose condemnation to death he failed to achieve, and about 4,000 lesser tax farmers, some of whom were condemned to death, though none was actually executed, and almost all of whom were very heavily fined. He created a powerful navy, encouraged trade, advocated indirect taxation, and fostered industrial growth. With the crown virtually the sole remaining source of artistic patronage, Colbert reorganized France's cultural life; he enhanced the status of craftsmen by a system of academies of which they became socially upgraded associates, but of which he was the paymaster. He believed in public access to the arts, was a dedicated, almost artistic manipulator of power, and turned artistic patronage on a grand scale into an instrument of government policy.

He invented the system of gratifications, administered chiefly by Perrault, initially on the advice of Chapelain. He turned the Gobelins into a school for training young painters and sculptors in the styles of which Lebrun approved, with every design requiring official sanction, so that the institution was able to provide everything necessary for the creation of a royal palace except the carpets. These were made at the Savonneries

see Chronology 1661, 1683, Introduction xli, xlii, xliii, Preface xlv

for the cultural organization of France under, see entries on Chapelain and Perrault, passim; in context of Huet, 360–61; Perrault and, 592; policy backfires, 650; concentration of power, 591; dissolution of 454

and attitude to Foucquet: supported by Boileau, 71; contrast of styles, 179; and reform of tax system, 592; hatred of Foucquet explains advancement of Chapelain, 591

and the theatre, amalgamations of 1673 and 1680, 152–53

hostility to and from La Fontaine, 423–34; La Fontaine admitted to Académie only after death of; enmity of explains La Fontaine's conjunction of pro-Foucquet and pro-Augustinian attitudes, 424

and Sallo and *Journal des Savants*, 374–75

and other individuals: Bensserade, 56; Bernier, 324; Gilles Boileau, 71–72, 76; Boileau-Despréaux, 72; Bussy, 107; Desmarets, 218; Guilleragues, 338–39; and Ménage, 71; and Molière, 518–20; and Racine, 595, 649, 678–79, 681

fondness for fairy-tales, 601

marriages of daughters, 277

Colet, Claude, 16th-century poet, died between 1553 and 1555

associated with Jodelle, 371

on Ronsard's 1553 list of poets, 611

Colet, John (1467–1519), theologian, dean of Saint Paul's, London, and founder of the famous school; turned from a neoplatonist enthusiasm to evangelicalism; encouraged Erasmus and More, and acted as spiritual director to both

see Introduction xl

inspired Erasmus to learn Greek, 97

dispute with Erasmus about suffering of Jesus, 447

and spiritual dilemma imposed by theology of grace, 558

reliance on direct interior experience, 656

and 'discernment of spirits,' 665

Coligny, Gaspard de (1519–72), admiral, leader of Huguenot party in religious wars. His assassination was attempted by a Guise supporter on eve of Saint Bartholomew Day massacre. Henri III sent his own physician, the Protestant Ambroise Paré, to attend him. It was the successful attempt to assassinate him the following day that triggered the massacre. His corpse was exhibited on the gibbet at Montfaucon

see Chronology 1572

d'Aubigné given commission in army of, 7

role in religious wars, 92

murder of defended by Jodelle, 373

captured in 1557, 724

held back by Jacques d'Urfé from crossing Loire, 867

Colin, Jacques (died 1547), appointed to royal household in 1526, sent on diplomatic missions to Savoy, Italy, the Swiss cantons, and the German states, royal almoner to 1537

supervises foundation of first royal lecturerships, 98

translates Castiglione's *Il Cortegiano*, 351

Collé, Charles (1709–83), dramatist and diarist admired by Sainte-Beuve

disliked Chamfort's plays, 126

helped found the 'dîners du Caveau,' 182

diary entry on Henrietta Stafford, 183

adapts fairground material for country-house entertainments, 562

epigram against Nivelle de la Chaussée, 565

little enthusiasm for Palissot's *Les Philosophes*, 568

Collège de France, Collège royal only from 1610, grew out of the royal lecturerships first established by François I in 1529, outside the university and in place of the trilingual college originally projected on the model of those at Louvain, Alcala, Oxford, and Cambridge, and Leo X's foundation for Greek studies in Rome. The first lecturers were appointed to teach the ancient languages, Pierre Danès and Jacques Toussaint for Greek, François Vatable and Agathias Guidacerius for

see Chronology 1610, 1614

military and political activity and imprisonment of, 10, 460, 543, 770

attitude to Gaston d'Orléans's marriage, 460; reconciles Orléans and Retz, 709

Mairet's sympathy for, 460, 465; Montchrestien's tragedies dedicated to (1601 and 1604), 542–43; will not receive Théophile de Viau, 359

Condé, Henri-Jules de Bourbon, duc d'Enghien, prince de, known as 'Monsieur le Duc,' then 'Monsieur le Prince,' son of le grand Condé and father of La Bruyère's pupil

and La Bruyère's post, 382–83

frequents Mme de Lafayette, 413

signs Racine's wedding contract, 681

Condé, Louis I de Bourbon, first prince de (1530–69), became a Protestant, was implicated in the Conjuration d'Amboise (1560), and was condemned to death for treason on 26 November 1560. The intervening death of François II on 5 December saved him from the execution scheduled for 10 December. Released on 13 June 1561, he was killed at Jarnac. He left three sons, Henri I prince de Condé (1552–88), François, prince de Conti (1558–1614), and Charles, comte de Soissons (1566–1612)

see Chronology 1559, 1560, 1563, 1569

military and political activity of, 6, 92, 315

execution of cancelled, 91

Belleau celebrates release of, 52

Condé, Louis II (1621–86), duc d'Enghien until 1646, then prince de, 'le grand Condé.' Son of Henri II, married Richelieu's niece, Clémence de Maillé-Brézé, on 11 February 1641; celebrated for his series of victorious military engagements during the Thirty Years War (1618–48). When still 22, his generalship virtually destroyed the Spanish infantry at Rocroi, and he was later active in the German campaign. He led the royal troops against the parlementaires in 1648, but was later imprisoned by Mazarin. After release he sought Spanish aid, but was defeated by Turenne after being severely wounded in an attempt to capture Paris. Later restored to his command of the royal troops, he fought in the Dutch war.

His role in the literary culture of France arises not only from his political importance and his relationship with such figures as La Rochefoucauld and Retz, but also because his apparent arrogance towards established authority and accepted restraint on behaviour, joined to his military exploits, commended him to a series of authors for whom he was a hero model, who had the added advantage of defending traditionally aristocratic attitudes in the face of the centralization of political power and its delegation away from the old feudal families. He became an important patron, notably of Molière, Boileau, and Racine, by whose *Alexandre* he felt flattered, and from about 1638 had come increasingly with the petits-maîtres to dominate the Hôtel de Rambouillet

see Chronology, 1643, each year from 1648 to 1653, 1659, 1672–78

political and military career, arrest and imprisonment 1650–51, 164, 217, 337, 343, 407, 431–32, 709–13, 787, 837–38

accusation of incest against, 71, 74

relationship with Boileau and Racine, 72–3, 676, 680–81

and other major authors: Bossuet, 80, 82; Bussy, 105–107; Chapelain, 130, 132; Desmarets, 216–17; Donneau de Visé, 250; Gomberville, 329; La Calprenède, 392; Mme de Lafayette, 408; La Fontaine, 425; La Rochefoucauld's *Mémoires*, 433; Molière, 519, 521; Saint-Evremond, 729, Scudéry, 823

and Hôtel de Rambouillet, 627

Condé, Louis-Joseph (1736–1818), married in 1752 to Charlotte de Rohan-Soubise, emigrated in 1792 and founded army at Koblenz

awarded Chamfort 2,000 livres for *Mustapha* and household position, 126

companion of young Sade, 758

assists Sade in later life, 761

Condillac, Etienne Bonnot de (1714–80), abbé de Mureaux, took orders in 1740, and frequented philosophe circles. Tutor to the duke of Parma, grandson of Louis XV (1758–67), he retired in 1773. His life was as austere as his style was dry

see entry on Philosophes, 605–606, 608

one of like-minded group elected to Académie with help of d'Alembert, 1

relationship with Diderot and Rousseau, 229; weekly dinner, 743

reaction to Cheselden's operation on blind boy, 242

does not write for *L'Encyclopédie*, 272

career of, disciple of Locke, 605; debate with Diderot, 242, 606

received by Mme Helvétius, 607

Rousseau draws on for second *Discours*, 751

Condorcet, Marie-Jean-Antoine-Nicolas Caritat, marquis de (1743–94)

Life, 155–56; Works, 156–57; Publications, 157–58

one of like-minded group elected to Académie with help of d'Alembert, 1

d'Alembert received by Mme Condorcet, 3

employed by Beaumarchais on Voltaire edition, 43

and 'Société de 1789,' 127

and Chénier, 143–44

and physiocrats, 238

writes for *Mercure*, 514; and attacked by *Actes des Apôtres*, 718

Condren, Charles de (1588–1641), general of the Oratory (1629) in succession to Bérulle, and chief author of its spirituality

see Introduction xliii

and Jansenism, 76; and Cartesianism, 122

reactionary spirituality of, 867; and Bérulle and Malebranche, 468; and Angélique Arnauld, 615, and neoplatonism, 645; and Saint-Cyran, 771 and Zamet, 773, 775

converts Chaudebonne, 890

Conflans, Henri de (c1618–1639), marquis d'Armentières

intimate of Bensserade, 54

Confrérie de la Passion

commercial organization by 1548; rights over Hôtel de Bourgogne, 149

see entry on Commedia dell'arte, passim

monopoly of, 345–47, and dissolution in 1667, 152

and renaissance drama generally, 439

Conrart, Valentin (1603–75), Huguenot, cousin of Godeau, close associate of Chapelain and Balzac; host at regular gathering of friends, nine of whose names we know, meeting to

wrote between 1670 and 1672 and then between 1701 and 1702 two volumes of *Mémoires*

> recommends Guilleragues to Conti, negotiates for Conti and acts as his principal adviser, 337–38

Cospeau (Cospéan), Philippe (1571–1646), bishop of Aire (1607), Nantes (1621), and Lisieux (1636), a well-known preacher who gave Henri IV's funeral oration and assisted Louis XIII on his deathbed

> copy of Balzac's letter to du Vair sent to, 26
>
> joke played on by Marquise de Rambouillet, 342
>
> helps Georges de Scudéry, 822

Cossé, Artus (1512–82), maréchal, aligned behind 'politique' forces advocating reconciliation in the religious wars in 1574, jailed for complicity in the plot to remove Alençon and Navarre from court surveillance, and released to negotiate on court's behalf

> imprisoned, 8, 92; and released, 92
>
> political background, 315

Cossé, Louis III de (1625–61), duc de Brissac, married Marguerite-Françoise de Gondi, the cousin of Retz, who had been her lover; afforded Retz assistance, brief asylum, and financial aid for his escape from Nantes. In search of adventure, he attached himself to Orléans during the Fronde

> signs Mme de Sévigné's wedding contract, 836

Cossé-Brissac, Marie de, married to the widower, the maréchal de la Meilleraye, in 1637. She died aged 89 in 1710, and was the daughter of François de Cossé, duc de Brissac (1585–1651), lieutenant-general of Brittany (1515), whose first wife, Anne de Schomberg, had successfully petitioned for dissolution of the marriage on grounds of his impotence, but who had five sons and four daughters by his second. Marie, the eldest daughter married Charles de la Porte, duc de la Meilleraye, and should not be confused with her sister, who married Charles de la Porte, marquis de Vezins

> liaison with 'the coadjutor', later Cardinal de Retz; Retz's cousin, and wife of his captor, 712

Cossé-Brissac, Timoléon de (1545–69), son of Charles de Cossé, maréchal de Brissac (1506–63/4); a colonel and grand falconer, killed at Mussidan three weeks after his 24th birthday after an already brilliant military career. His tutors included Buchanan

> Peletier tutor to, 583

Costar, Pierre (1603–60), an excellent linguist, ally of Voiture, bon viveur, canon of Angers, who lived with Charles de Beaumanoir-Lavardin, bishop of Le Mans, and was never forgiven by Chapelain, who had him excluded from the Hôtel de Rambouillet, for criticizing his *Ode à Richelieu*. Two apologias for Voiture (1653 and 1655) also offended Balzac, and Costar also briefly quarrelled with Boisrobert. He was a supporter and former secretary of Ménage and left his *Lettres* (1658), and the *Entretiens de M. Voiture et de M.Costar* (1654)

> ostentatiously abstains in quarrel of sonnets, 56
>
> recognizes portrait of Mme de Sévigné in *Clélie*, 108
>
> consulted by Colbert on recruitment to choir of royal encomiasts, 133
>
> and literary alignments and quarrels of mid-1650s anticipating the Querelle, 309, 590; see 361
>
> and friendly relations with Mme de Lafayette, 408–10
>
> alignment with La Mesnardière, Pinchesne, and Ménage, 591

Coste, Pierre (1668–1747), translator of Locke

Essay concerning Human Understanding translated by, 242, 604

> extract from published by Fréron, 302; imprisoned, 302

Cosway, Richard (1742–1821) and Marie Hadfield, his wife, miniaturist painters

> Chénier and, 142

coteaux (hillsides: vineyards): Tallemant's *historiette* of Boisrobert of about 1658 relates Boisrobert's anecdote that Beaumanoir-Lavardin, bishop of Le Mans, had complained that three of his companions at table, the comte d'Olonne, Sablé-Bois-Dauphin, son of Mme de Sablé, and Saint-Evremond, had such delicate palates that there were not four vineyards in France of whose wines they approved. They became known as the three coteaux, and their principal maxim was not to eat sucking pig. In the popular songs, the list of names subsequently changed, and the three vineyards which did produce acceptable wines were identified as Ay, Haut-Villiers, and Avenoy, all now producing champagne grapes. There is a 1665 one-act comedy *Les Costeaux; ou, Les Marquis frians*

> Saint-Evremond among, 781

Cotignon de la Charnaye, Pierre de, belonged to circle of 'illustres bergers', published an *Ouvrage poétique* in 1626, and was still active in 1638. Knew Colletet, Rotrou, and du Ryer

> Rotrou write prefatory verses for, 733

Cotin, Charles (1604–81), abbé, priest, and satirist on friendly terms with Chapelain and Gilles Boileau, but an ally of Pure, Quinault, and Boursault in the Querelle des anciens et des modernes (q.v.). With Furetière and Gilles Boileau, he upheld the purist tradition of Malherbe against the madrigalists, and wrote a particularly harsh attack on Ménage, which also involved Scarron and Madeleine de Scudéry.

Himself attacked by Boileau in 1666, he was probably concerned with Pure and Quinault in the *Bastonnade* (1666) replying to Boileau. The probable author of the *Critique désintéressé* (1666), attacking the violence of Boileau in literary matters, Cotin also attacked Molière, and was in turn recognizably caricatured as Trissotin in *Les Femmes savantes*. He left the *Regrets d'Aristée sur le trépas de Daphnis* (1631), many poems, a *Traité de l'âme immortelle* (1655) and his *Poésies chrétiennes*. His *Oeuvres mêlées* appeared in 1659, and the *Oeuvres galantes* in 1663

> Voted for election to Académie of Bensserade, 56
>
> belonged to Marolles circle, 71, 309; position in changing literary alignments of the mid-1650s, and hostility to Boileau, 71, 72, and see 77; defends Gilles Boileau, and attacks Ménage, 361, 413, 591
>
> gratification, 360
>
> inaugurates vogue for riddles at Hôtel de Rambouillet, 342
>
> inspiration necessary for poetry; poem read by at Huet's Académie reception, 361
>
> Molière and, 518, 521, 527
>
> defended by Perrault, 651

Cottin, Jean (died 1569), Protestant tutor of d'Aubigné

> madness and burning of, 6

Coucy, edict of, 16 July, 1535: the edict affirmed that heresy had been wiped out, ordered the release of religious prisoners, halted persecution, and allowed the exiles home providing they abjured within six months. The edict excluded sacramentarians, who allowed only a figurative function to the sacred species in the eucharist, but was extended to them on 31 May 1536. The penalty for relapsing remained hanging

Calvin took advantage of, 114; and Marot, 507

Coulanges, Christophe de (1607–87), abbé de Livry, Mme de Sévigné's uncle and principal adviser on business matters
see entry on Mme de Sévigné, passim
advises Mme de Sévigné to refuse loan to Bussy, 106

Coulanges, Philippe II de (1595–1659), married in 1626 to Marie Lefèvre d'Ormesson; became maître des comptes in 1632, and brought up the orphaned Marie de Rabutin-Chantal, later the marquise de Sévigné
poem of satirized by Guilleragues, 338

Courcelles, marquis de, married in 1666 to Maria Sidonia de Lenoncourt, whose behaviour soon became publicly scandalous
Hortense Mancini, close friend of Saint-Evremond, has liaison with, 781

Le Courrier Français, founded by the two doctor sons of Renaudot, Isaac and Eusèbe, to defend the position of the Paris parlement during the Fronde. It appeared only 12 times from 5 January to 7 April 1649, when Théophraste Renaudot succeeded in reaffirming his privilège against the *Courrier* and a host of imitations, including a weekly burlesque of it in verse. The 13th number was seized
publication of, 326

Court, the: the French sovereign's entourage, a formally defined body, some of whose members belonged by right of birth; a centre more of privilege than of power. There were degrees of both membership and exclusion. Presentation was necessary, although it did not lead automatically to the right to attend the 'lever du roi' or, after the move to Versailles, to the coveted right to living apartments in the palace, just as exile was a form of exclusion graduated in duration, distance, and rigour of enforcement. Court favour, indicated in the most trivial of ways, like a placing at table, could lead to immense social prestige, to heritable titles, to offices and to property, but the real power lay neither with the members of court, nor with the newly enriched financiers, but with the professional administrators who controlled internal affairs, did the political deals across Europe, and plighted royal troths for the political alliances with which they intended to shape Europe's future.

There were about 10,000 members of court, obviously not all in permanent or regular attendance, when it moved to Versailles in 1682. Security was very lax. As late as 1757 there was a serious attempt on the life of Louis XV, and Louis XIV complained of the ease with which outsiders could wander into the palace. Only a knowledge of the internal geography of the Luxembourg saved Richelieu on the Day of Dupes, when he found a door he knew Marie de Medici would have forgotten to lock.

Both ministers and monarch used the court to control the noblesse d'épée, who nurtured lingering feudal pretensions. The grandeur of the state apartments and the monarch's appurtenances kept the nobility from forgetting its allegiance and its place, while court ritual, etiquette, and diversion were calculated to be demanding enough to keep its members harmlessly employed.

In 1696 a decree was formally passed allowing the purchase of offices which admitted to noble rank, although the practice had been steadily accelerating for decades. Under Colbert's regime, major writers and musicians could become at least courtiers

see especially the entries on Bussy and Saint-Simon, passim

Courville, Joachim-Thibault de (died 1581), composer
association with Baïf, 20

Cousin, Louis (1627–1707), editor of *Journal des Savants*
editorial activity, 375

Cousin, Victor (1792–1867), minister and philosopher, see indexed references in post-1789 volume of *Guide*
on Fénelon, 281
and Pascal, 579 and Introduction xxxi

Coustel, Pierre (1621–1704), after teaching at the 'petites écoles' of Port-Royal became tutor to the nephews of Cardinal Furstemberg, and then taught at the Collège des Grassins
shares with Fénelon ideas on education, 288

Coypel, Charles-Antoine (1696–1751), painter from illustrious family of artists, and successful administrator
friend of Duché-Lemarchant, 563

Cramail, Adrien de Monluc (?1571–1646), prince de Chabanois, comte de, also baron de Montesquiou, comte de Monluc, grandson of the maréchal; married Jeanne de Foix on 22 September 1592. He was at the centre of a literary group including François Mainard in Toulouse, and another including Marolles in Paris, in spite, according to Tallemant, of his scant natural aptitude. He wrote, perhaps with help, a series of anonymous works, *Pensées du solitaire* (1629), *Jeux de l'inconnu* (1630), a *Comédie des proverbes* (1633), and *Les jeux de jour et de nuit*, later published by Cotin. He asked Saint-Cyran for the *Question royale*, appointed Vanini tutor to one of his nephews, was exiled for his relationship with Mme du Fargis, sent to the Bastille in 1635 for his hostility to Richelieu's policies, and liberated on the cardinal's death, but found himself without political support, since Anne of Austria had made peace with supporters of Richelieu's policies
persuades Mairet to adopt regularity for French pastoral, 460–61
Régnier dedicates second *Satire* to, 693, 695
Saint-Cyran joins circle of; puts to Saint-Cyran conundrum of *Question royale*, 770
Sorel likely to have been secretary of, 849

Cramoisy, Sébastien (c1585–1669), from a family of printers, printer and book-seller in Paris from 1606, royal printer from 1633 to 1664, and director of the Imprimerie royale (1640–69)
printer of works praising Louis XIII and Richelieu, 132

Creation, date of, formerly computed from the number of generations recorded in the Bible between Adam and Jesus
Bossuet and, 89
Buffon estimates in public 60,000 years, in private, 3,000,000, 103

Crébillon, Claude-Prosper Jolyot de (1707–77), known as Crébillon *fils*
Life, 182–83; Works, 183–85; Publications, 185
as censor passes Beaumarchais's *Barbier*, 42
defended by Grimm against Fréron, 301
organizes hostility to Marivaux, 497

Crébillon, Jolyot, sieur de (1674–1762), known as Crébillon *père*
Life, 185–87; Works, 187–89; Publications, 189–190
and Marivaux; witness at wedding, 495; critical of drama of, 496; signed privilège for, 498; more highly regarded than Marivaux by Italian company, 498

and Voltaire; Crébillon obituary part of anti-Fréron hostilities, 303;

cabal of successful against Voltaire, 301; feud with, 898

Créquy, Armande de Saint-Gelais de Lusignan de Lausac, married in 1653 to Charles, duc de Créquy; improbably rumoured in July 1664 to have had a liaison with the nuntius Chigi. Her husband ordered her to retire to Boulogne

mention of rumours confirms that interpolations were made in Bussy's 1660 text, 107

Créquy, Charles III (1624–87), marquis, then duc de, French extraordinary ambassador in Rome in 1662. Eldest of three sons of maréchal Charles I, duc et pair (1652), married preceding, 1653; underwent short period of disgrace in Bastille for 'disrespect.' Attacked by Racine in an epigram for a quip at *Andromaque*, publicly renowned for mental incapacity. Governor of Paris and ambassador extraordinary to London. Dies in disgrace 13 February 1687, a few days after his brother, below. Saint-Simon judges him severely

Bensserade's allusion to stupidity of, 59

Racine alludes to homosexuality of, 678

allows drunken guard to set in train important diplomatic crisis, 619

Créquy, François de Blanchefort de (1629–87), youngest brother of Charles III above, and of the comte de Canaples, his military career was distinguished. He died a maréchal on 3 February 1687. From 1649 loyal to Mazarin and the court, he later quarrelled with Turenne. In 1657 married Catherine du Plessis-Bellière and took title marquis. Severely damaged financially, and exiled from court for six years on disgrace of Foucquet, he was recalled when required to command the army of the Rhine

probable addressee of Saint-Evremond's *Lettre sur la paix*, 780

in pay of Foucquet (10,000 livres a year, and 200,000 needed in July 1661 to pay for the generalship of galleys), 780

Croismare, Marc-Antoine-Nicolas (1694–1722), whose friendship was cultivated by Mme d'Epinay at the suggestion of Grimm. He shared with Rousseau an interest in music

hoax played on, 235

Diderot's letters to in his newsletter, 244

Crosilles (Croisille), Jean-Pierre (died 1651), abbé, friend of Marolles, imprisoned for 10 years on suspicion of attempted marriage

attacks Balzac, 25

Croy, Guillaume de: see Vives

Cujas, Jacques (1522–90), legal theorist and professor of law opposed to Bartolist jurisprudential casuistry, arguing the mos gallicus (see Glossary), that the Roman codes should be stripped of glosses, and the enactments situated in their original social contexts

dispute with Forcadel, and role of Bodin, 66

dispute with Bodin, 68–69

teaches at Toulouse, 529

Cureau de la Chambre, Marin (1586–1669), doctor and moralist, protected by Séguier; early member of the Académie française, and founder member of the Académie des Sciences (1666). He frequented the samedis of Madeleine de Scudéry and the salon of Mme de Sablé, was admired by Boisrobert and Balzac, and advised Séguier, whose doctor he was, on suitable recipients of his patronage. He projected a grandiose

work on the passions, virtues, vices, and customs of men, relating physical characteristics to moral tendencies, to be called *L'Art de connoistre les hommes*, but published only five volumes of *Les Caractères des passions* (1640, 1645, 1659, 1659, and 1662) and some treatises of scientific speculation, some letters, and *Le Système de l'âme* (1664)

and Cartesianism, 122

popularizes word 'caractères', 384–85

Cusa, Nicolas of (1401–64), brought up by the Brethren of the Common Life at Deventer, he was sent by a patron to study law at Padua, abandoned law as a profession, took orders, and became archdeacon of Liège. His *De concordantia catholica* had maintained the superiority of councils over popes, but Cusa was to reverse that position. He was a legate four times between 1441 and 1446, cardinal (1448), and reforming bishop of Brixen (1450). Both his theology and his spirituality are based on the pseudo-Denis's neoplatonism, and the negative knowledge of God which in the *De docta ignorantia* emerges as alone possible

see Introduction, xl

Lefèvre d'Etaples nourished on spirituality of, and edits 443, 446

Reuchlin sends Lefèvre Cusa manuscript, 448

spirituality of and Marguerite d'Angoulême, 489

image of circularity applied to God and to knowledge, 585, 587

Scève's dependence on, 820; and others sharing the Cusan spiritual tradition, 820

Cyrano de Bergerac, Savinien de (1619–55)

Life, 190–91; Works, 191–96; Publications, 196

see Introduction xxxiv

Scarron attacked by, 811

admired Tristan, 858

Dacier, André (1651–1722), classical scholar and translator who on 4 November 1683 married the future translator of Homer. He was the son of a Protestant lawyer, and with his wife became a Catholic on the revocation of the edict of Nantes, translated Horace in 10 volumes, wrote on Longinus, and published several minor classical texts. After his conversion he translated Marcus Aurelius (1691), edited Aristotle's *Poetics* (1692), the *Oedipus* and *Electra* of Sophocles (1693), Hippocrates (1697), several of Plato's dialogues (1699), and the *Life of Pythagoras* with his works. His most important translation, however, was of Plutarch's *Lives* in eight volumes, finished in 1721. In 1694 he became keeper of the king's books, and in 1713 permanent secretary of the Académie française

collaboration with wife, Anne Dacier, 356

and Voltaire, 902

Dacier, Anne le Fèvre (1647–1720), translator of Homer, and author of a defence of the primitive qualities of the Homeric ethic, and their consonance with the Christian tradition. Daughter of the liberal Protestant scholar Tanneguy Le Fèvre (died 1672), she was recommended to Chapelain, and edited between 1674 and 1684, for the 'dauphin' series of classical editions commissioned with the dauphin in mind, more texts than any other editor, and the only Greek author, Callimachus. She also translated poems by Sappho and Anacreon, in 1683 three comedies of Plautus, in 1684 two comedies of Aristophanes, and in 1688 the six comedies of Terence. She had a son who died at 11, and two daughters, one of whom became a nun. The other died at 18.

The prose translations of the *Iliad* (1699) and the *Odyssey* (Amsterdam 1708, then Paris 1716 with polemical preface) provoked the abbreviated and edulcorated verse *Iliad* by Mme Dacier's friend, Houdar de la Motte, prefaced by the *Discours sur Homère* of 1714. Mme Dacier replied with *Des causes de la corruption du goût*, to which Houdar de la Motte cut short his reply, *Réflexions sur la critique*, when he was reconciled with Mme Dacier at a dinner given by Valincour at the instigation of Mme de Lambert on Palm Sunday, 5 April 1716, shortly before the Paris edition of the *Odyssey* which does not mention La Motte.

Mme Dacier's final work, *Homère défendu contre l'Apologie du R.P. Hardouin* (1716), was a defence of Homer against one of his apologists, the Jesuit Père Hardouin, who allegorized the *Iliad*, interpreting it as a poem about the fall of the house of Priam. The Daciers frequented the salon of Mme de Lambert, and in 1720 Mme Dacier was given the right to succeed her husband as keeper of the king's books at the Louvre. She predeceased him, however, and died in August 1720, after an illness of three months

Damiens, Robert-François (1715–57), attempted on 5 January 1757 to assassinate Louis XV, with the consequence of a considerable swell of cultural reaction and tightening of restrictions on dissidence. Damiens was pulled apart by horses attached to his limbs

Dampierre, Jeanne de Vivonne, Mme de (died 1583)

Damville (d'Anville), Henri de Montmorency (1534–1614), second son of Anne de Montmorency, who succeeded to title on death of his brother, François, in 1579; governor of Languedoc (1563), maréchal de France (1565), connétable (1593)

Danchet, Antoine (1671–1748), opera librettist

Dancourt, Florent Carton, sieur d'Ancourt, known as **(1661–1725)**

Dangeau, Philippe de Courcillon (1638–1720), marquis de, Catholic, converted like his brother Louis (1643–1723) by Bossuet, and military captain close to Louis XIV; elected to the Académie in 1668, diarist

Danton, Georges-Jacques (1759–94), Revolutionary orator; guillotined

Da Ponte, Lorenzo (1749–1835), librettist used by Mozart

Daubenton, Louis (1716–1800), French naturalist

Daunon, Pierre (1761–1840), archivist

David, Jacques-Louis (1748–1825), well-known painter with strong Revolutionary sympathies

Delbene, Bartolomeo, 16th-century Florentine who lived at the French court, father of the more famous Alphonse (1538–1608), bishop of Albi, poet, and historian

'delectation,' term used by Augustine himself, and in 17th-century Jansenist disputes, in which a 'victorious delectation' occasioned by the presence of grace or alternatively the attraction of what was sinful was sometimes seen as a force external to the will, which destroyed the individual's autonomous power to choose how it was determined between grace-inspired and sinful activity. Some authors wrote as if they thought that the delectation could be felt (see: ontology). See in general Fénelon; freedom of the will; grace, theology of; and Jansenism

Deleyre, Alexandre (1726–97)

Delille, Jacques (1738–1813), abbé, prolific, facile, and popular lyric poet, much scorned by critics, written off by Baudelaire as 'méprisable (contemptible),' and regarded by Sainte-Beuve as having written 'à froid et par système (coldly, and by system),' possessing 'ni l'art, ni le style poétique (neither poetic art, nor poetic style).' Within 15 years of his death, Delille's reputation had sunk apparently beyond any hope of recovery, but interest has recently been aroused by the historical phenomenon of his former popularity.

Delille taught Latin at Beauvais, professed humanities at Amiens and in Paris and, after translating the *Georgics* in only just over 200 lines more than the original (1770) was elected to the Académie française at the insistence of Voltaire, although the king delayed admission from 1772 to 1774, in case he was a philosophe (q.v.). He was later given the royal chair of Latin poetry, published the successful *Jardins; ou, L'Art d'embellir les paysages*, and was given the abbacy of Saint-Séverin without needing to take holy orders. He followed Choiseul-Gouffier in his embassy to Constantinople,

ages de Gulliver, 1727), and author or editor of a number of well-known gazettes, the *Le Nouvelliste du Parnasse* (December 1730 to March 1732, 52 numbers), the *Observations sur les écrits modernes* (March 1735 to August 1743, 34 volumes), and the *Jugements sur quelques ouvrages nouveaux* (1744–45). From 1723 he helped to save the *Journal des Savants*, a monthly from 1724, and he edited Prévost's *Le Pour et le Contre* from October 1733 until February 1734.

An ex-Jesuit, he apparently pirated an edition of Voltaire's *Henriade*. Voltaire, at first indulgent, intervened to secure his release when Desfontaines was imprisoned for the capital offence of homosexual practices, but a year later Desfontaines appears to have intrigued against Voltaire, reviewing him anonymously and unfavourably, and Voltaire developed in return one of his obsessive hatreds. To his invective in *Le Préservatif* (1738), Desfontaines replied with two scurrilous attacks, *La Voltairomanie* (1738) and *Le Médiateur* (1739)

Beaumarchais's censor, 48; Diderot writes for, 229; and Fréron, 300, 305; source for Houdar de la Motte, 357; hostile critic of Marivaux, 496; who takes notice in subsequent portion of *La Vie de Marianne*, 501; won over to Nivelle de la Chaussée, 565; writes warmly of Prévost, 636; and Voltaire's hostility mentioned, 896

rewrites Laclos's *Ernestine* as comic opera, 399

editorial activity and monopoly of *Journal des Savants*, 375

translator of *Gulliver's Travels*, 496

Deshoulières, Antoinette Ligier de la Garde (1637/8–1694), Mme de, poet renowned for friendship with partisans of modern culture in the Querelle des anciens et des modernes (q.v.), and for her central role in the attack on Racine's *Phèdre et Hippolyte*. The offensive sonnet was written in her drawing room. Her poems were published in the *Mercure Galant* and later in two collected volumes. Towards the end of her life she wrote impressively meditative verse inspired by the prospect of death

friendship of Bensserade for, 57

salon of frequented by Fontenelle, 294

associated with Marolles circle, 309

role in the anti-Racine camp, 621; introduces Pradon to Nevers milieu, 623

anti-Racine sonnet, and refusal of admission to *Phèdre et Hippolyte*, 681

Desjardins, Marie-Catherine: see Villedieu, Mme de

Des Loges, Marie Bruneau (c1585–1641), Mme, from a rich Huguenot family, married Charles de Rechignevoisin and made a strong impression at court. Her salon was attended not only by Gombauld and Malherbe, but also by Protestants like Turenne and Conrart. The Catholics included Racan, Godeau, Voiture, and Gaston d'Orléans. Mme Des Loges gained a reputation for wit, intelligence, and political power. Tallemant, who clearly admired her, says she was pregnant before she married. She wrote stylishly, was always available, had a sense of humour, and was never out of countenance. She had nine children. The hostility between Orléans and Richelieu persuaded her to retreat quietly to the country in 1629

salon of attended by Racan, 670; and Malherbe and Voiture, 890

absents herself from Paris, 1629–36, 890

Desmaizeaux, Pierre (1666–1745) Protestant biographer of Bayle

Bayle's relationship with, 29, 33

editor of Saint-Evremond, 781

Desmarets, Jean, sieur de Saint-Sorlin (?1600–1676)
Life, 213–18; Works, 218–21; Publications, 221

see Introduction xlii

votes for Bensserade's election to Académie française, 56

laughs at Boileau, 72; and is attacked by him, 73; and Desmarets's riposte, 77; and renewed attack by, 361; and new riposte, 648

appointed to Académie française, 131; and given gratification, 360

Richelieu real author of *Mirame*? 152; provides plots for, 160; and Desmarets's role in Querelle du *Cid*, 161

further positions of: ardent moderne partisan at Académie, 361, 648; and quarrel with Nicole, 557, 677; and role in dispute with Port-Royal, 619; supports Le Clerc-Coras *Iphigénie*, 621; dispute over superiority of vernacular, 644, 646; on what was at stake in the Querelle, 649

appeal to female taste of, 647; increase of licentiousness over d'Urfé, 395

Biblical poems of, 645

Chapelain on *Clovis* of, 136

name of associated with Cyrano de Bergerac, 190

contributes to *Guirlande de Julie*, 343

possible inspiration for Saint-Evremond pieces, 782

Desmasures, Louis (1523–74), neo-Latin poet belonging to the circle of Salel, Peletier, and Ronsard's 'brigade' who became a Huguenot, and is remembered for his trilogy of sacred tragedies from the life of David (1563). He translated the *Aeneid* for the Cardinal of Lorraine (probably 1547, but 1552–60 is the oldest surviving edition), and in 1557 published his *Carmina*, his lyrical *Oeuvres poétiques*, and some psalm translations. He did not return to France after 1562, wrote a violent satirical poem, *Babylone*, attempted an epic, *Borbonias*, on the religious wars, and published a Protestant morality, the *Bergerie spirituelle*

played by Le Conte, 345

scriptural tragedies of, 439

Desmolets, Pierre-Nicolas (1678–1760), Oratorian librarian who helped shape Montesquieu's serious interests while he was studying law in Paris

Desmoulins, Camille (1760–94), moderate Revolutionary leader, guillotined

Marie-Joseph Chénier and, 143

Des Oeillets, Alix Faviot (1621–70), actress

changes companies with admired performance in Pierre Corneille's *Sertorius*, 164

Despautère, familiar name for universal 16th-century grammar by van Pauteren

Cyrano de Bergerac character parodies, 192

Des Périers, Bonaventure (c1510–c1543), poet and classical scholar who collaborated at Neuchâtel with Olivétan on his Bible (1535) and with Dolet at Lyons on the *Commentarii linguae latinae* (1536), was employed by Marguerite de Navarre, moved to an apparently syncretist position in the Lucianic dialogue *Cymbalum mundi* (1537), and is perhaps best remembered for his collection of contes, the posthumous *Nouvelles récréations et joyeux devis* (1558). In the quarrel with Sagon, he took Marot's side. Des Périers also translated Plato's *Lysis* for Marguerite de Navarre, and was a poet of genuine lyrical and satirical gifts in the tradition of Marot.

Henri Estienne reports in 1566, perhaps correctly, that Des Périers killed himself in a fit of madness, although his account must have been coloured by the horror of the *Cymbalum*'s 'atheism' felt by Postel, and by Calvin's reaction in the *Traité des scandales* (1550). However, even the Paris theology faculty, while condemning the *Cymbalum* in 1538, held that, although pernicious, the work did not contain errors of faith.

The *Cymbalum* consists of four short dialogues satirizing aspects of human behaviour and such traditional social vices as greed, vanity, egoism, and belligerence, but allowing itself a religious reference, suggesting a preference for a morally elevated and spiritualized Christianity. The first dialogue satirizes the substitution of the human for the divine in human religious affairs, and in the second Mercury listens to three philosophers, representing Luther, Bucer, and possibly Erasmus, each of whom claims to possess the true philosopher's stone, which is however fragmented in the sands of the earth. The fourth dialogue between two dogs suggests that a dog's life would not necessarily be improved by the power of rational argument.

protected by François Olivier, 352

taken into service of Marguerite d'Angoulême, 486

Joyeux devis posthumously published by Peletier, 584

attacked by Calvin, 657

Desportes, Philippe (1546–1606)

Life, 221–25; Works, 225–27; Publications, 227

see Introduction xxxi

Baïf, the Académie du Palais, and, 18, 19–20, 140

attends Belleau's funeral, 52; entertains, 316; associated with Gillot, 806; and frequents duchesse de Retz, 862

loses Jeux Floraux award to Baïf, 20; with whom he celebrates wedding and mourns death of Anne de Joyeuse, 20

Malherbe's attitude to, 476, 478; nevertheless admired by Racan, 670

Malherbe introduced to by Régnier, 693

Italianate culture of, and displacing of Ronsard, 725, 731

Desportes, Thibault, younger brother of the poet

administrative and diplomatic careers of, 224

marries, 225

Destouches, André Cardinal (1662–1749), French composer of opera, ballet, and church cantatas. His 1697 *Issé* was a 'pastorale héroïque'

Omphale of occasions pamphlet from Grimm, 333

writes music for Houdar de la Motte libretti, 355

hostile critic of Marivaux, 496

Rousseau supports attack of Grimm on, 745

Destouches, Louis Camus, chevalier, father of d'Alembert, 1

des Touches, Pelletier (?1622–1703), early devotee of Saint-Cyran, and his secretary when he was released from prison. He was rich. In 1644 he sheltered the pupils of the 'petites écoles' of Port-Royal on an estate at Chesnay, near Versailles, later sold to Charles Maignart de Bernières (1616–62), another close friend of the movement and the monastery. About a score of pupils appear to have been lodged in the left wing of the house

and the 'petites écoles' of Port-Royal, 556

devotio moderna: see Brethren of the Common Life

Diane de Poitiers (1499–1566), mistress of Henri II and duchesse de Valentinois, daughter of the comte de Saint-Vallier and widow of Louis de Brézé. Henri II built the château of Anet for her

see Chronology 1547

present at Paris reception for Henri II in 158, 372

ascendancy of as mistress of Henri II, 488

Henri II commissions château d'Anet for; sonnets commissioned from Tyard, 862

Diane de Salviati, niece of Ronsard's Cassandre, and daughter of sieur de Talcy

d'Aubigné meets, 7

Diderot, Denis (1713–84)

Life, 227–40; Works, 240–48; Publications, 249

see Introduction, xxix, xliv; Preface xlv

see entries on *L'Encyclopédie*, Grimm, and Rousseau, passim

d'Alembert and: co-editors of *L'Encyclopédie*, 1–5; *Rêve de d'Alembert* of, 2; introduces Condorcet to, 155

Beaumarchais inspired by, 39, 40, 46

relationship with Fréron, 301–304

joined by Condillac at Panier Fleuri meetings with Rousseau, 605; debate with Condillac, 606

writes, but does not publish, refutation of Helvétius, 608

role in 1752 conflict about Italian music, 333

and Marivaux: Diderot dismissive of, 498; invents term 'Marivaudage'

and Palissot: attacked by, 567; *Les Philosophes* of, and Diderot's *Père de famille*, 568

definition of 'philosophe' in *L'Encyclopédie*, 603

accused of stealing Réaumur's plates for *L'Encyclopédie*, 603

writes disparagingly about Rétif de la Bretonne, 700

linked by Rousseau with d'Holbach, 609

not welcome in grander salons, 607

Sedaine knows, 832; applies dramatic theories of, 833

distrust of Voltaire, 900; Voltaire's doubts about progress, 901

death of respectfully reported in *Mercure*, 514

Didot, François (1689–1757), together with François-Ambroise (1730–1804), Pierre-François (1732–95), Pierre (1761–1853), Henry (1765–1852), and Firmin (1790–1876), members of an outstanding and characteristically close-knit family of Parisian printers, publishers, and book-sellers. François, apprenticed in 1698, set up as a book-seller in 1713 and became 'syndic de la communauté des Libraires (President of the Association of Book-sellers).' He married the daughter of a book-seller, herself a member of the guild. His sister and three of his 11 children also married book-sellers. His son, François-Ambroise, is acknowledged to have printed the best colour plates in late 18th-century France, while Firmin engraved and cast a new type-face, invented a new form of press, and had vellum manufactured to his own specifications. Pierre-François printed several famous editions before founding paper factories, to be taken over by his son, Henry

Bernardin de Saint-Pierre and Félicité Didot, 62

Prévost faithful to, 635

Diodati, Elie, close friend of Galileo and in correspondence with most of Europe's leading scientists, regarded by Patin as having constituted a quartet ('tétrade') with Naudé, Gassendi, and La Mothe le Vayer; principally important here for having converted Gassendi to Galileo's theories during a stay in Grenoble in June 1625

Gassendi meets in 1625, 322; and is associated with, 324

presses Gassendi to reply to Descartes's replies to his original *Dubitationes*, 323

du Crozet, Jean, late 16th-century poet of whom almost nothing is known beyond his connection with d'Urfé, and his publication of *La Philocalie du Sieur Ducroset Foresien, divisée en quatre livres*, important for the account it gives of an early sketch for *L'Astrée*. The first edition was printed at Lyons in 1593, and the sub-title shows an early resurgence of the optimistic view of human experience whose exploration had ceased with the religious wars: *Où sont introduicts six Bergers maistrisez de l'Amour de six Pucelles, lesquelles apres plusieurs Discours, non moins beau que graves et delectables, accompagnez d'Elegies, Odes, Chansons, Sonnets et Stances, recitent quatre Histoires convenables à ce temps. Plus une Eclogue qui exprime naïfvement et les miseres de la guerre, et la force de l'Amour.* A second edition appeared at Rouen in 1600 entitled *L'Amour de la beauté, divisée en quatre livres*, augmented with miscellaneous verse

 early account of plot of *L'Astrée* in, 875

du Deffand, Marie de Vichy-Chamrond (1697–1780), marquise, salon hostess celebrated for her beauty, influence, cynical wit, for her 1764 quarrel with Julie de Lespinasse, but chiefly for her letters to Hénault, Voltaire, the duchesse de Choiseul, and Horace Walpole. She was niece of the duchesse de Luynes, married at 22 the lieutenant-general of the Orléans district, and was separated after four years, during which she was fleetingly the regent's mistress. It is she who is credited with the aphorism, on hearing that the beheaded Saint Denis had walked for some miles carrying his head, that she did not find it difficult to believe, 'il n'y a que le premier pas qui coûte (it is only the first step that is difficult).' Her salon attracted d'Alembert, Montesquieu, Fontenelle, Marmontel, Marivaux, Sedaine, Condorcet, and many members of the nobility, but she was not generally favourable to the philosophes (q.v.)

 salon of: d'Alembert centre of, 1–2; quarrel with d'Alembert involving Voltaire, 2; break with Julie de Lespinasse, 1; company in salon of, 155; salon frequented by Marivaux, 498; and Montesquieu, 550, 551; and role of, with other salons, 607

 applauds Chamfort, 126; offended by tactlessness of Fréron, 303

 bitterness towards Mme du Châtelet, 897

duelling: the first really serious attempt to suppress the practice was made under Richelieu, whose elder brother, Henri du Plessis-Richelieu, was killed in a duel by Charles de Lauzières, marquis de Thémines, in April 1619. Although Richelieu later put Thémines forward for promotion, his brother's death caused him much grief. The Catholic revival of the 1620s strengthened Richelieu's hand in condemning the practice and, when on Saturday 14 May 1627 the severe edict of 1626 was flaunted at midday by the return of the exiled duellist, the comte de Montmorency-Bouteville, to fight the marquis de Beuvron in the new, ultra-smart Place Royale, the provocation could scarcely be ignored. Bussy-d'Amboise, a fanatical duellist, was killed by Rosmadec des Chapelles, one of Bouteville's seconds. Bouteville and Chapelles were beheaded on 22 June. The inheritors of the aristocratic ethic had goaded the authorities too far.

 The importance of duelling in the context of the *Guide* is its almost symbolic place in the struggles of the old noblesse d'épée to retain something of their position by reaffirming their ethic, which made the willingness to duel into a criterion of social distinction. Corneille in *Le Cid* was clearly correct

in assuming that his audience in 1637 would admire Rodrigue's acceptance of the obligation to fight Chimène's father but, as late as the first quarter of the 18th century, of the 44 duellists brought before the Paris courts, 12 were acquitted, 26 released for a fictitious lack of evidence and, of the six sentenced, one had to pay expenses, one was exiled, one was hanged in effigy, and one was sent to the galleys. None was executed. Loret was regularly reporting duels in the *Muse historique* during the 1650s. At least a dozen authors with main entries in this volume of the *Guide* are known to have duelled

du Fail, Noël (c1520–1591), lawyer from a Breton family of country squires, published a substantial legal work, but is remembered only for three collections of contes, the *Propos rustiques* (1547), the *Baliverneries; ou, Contes nouveaux d'Eutrapel* (1548), both published over the anagrammatic name 'Leon Ladulfi,' and *Les Contes et discours d'Eutrapel* (1585), a mixture of anecdotes and conversations, with material from du Fail's youth apparently weighed down with later satirical and didactic accretions. The stylized treatment of country bliss often derives from Guevara's *Mespris de la Cour*. The five *Baliverneries* are more directly modelled on Rabelais than the *Propos*, a series of sessions devoted to story-telling between four village characters, but the work was less tightly organized, and proved less popular

du Fargis, Mme: see Silly

du Fossé, Pierre-Thomas (1634–98), the youngest of the three sons of the Rouen maître des comptes, whose correct name according to Sainte-Beuve was Gentien Thomas, and who was converted to serious piety by Saint-Cyran after losing his parish priest to a life of devotion. Of the three sons he sent to be educated at Port-Royal, two died young. Pierre-Thomas left memoirs

 and the 'petites écoles', 556

Dufresne (Abraham-Alexis Quinault) (1693–1767), actor and brother of the three Mesdemoiselles employed, as he was, with the Comédie-Française. One of the sisters was Nivelle de la Chaussée's mistress. Dufresne himself created Voltaire's Oedipe

 in Nivelle de la Chaussée's *La Fausse antipathie*, 564

Dufresny, Charles Rivière (1648–1724), dramatist, novelist, and from 1710 to 1713 director of the *Mercure Galant*; started in business, held an appointment at court, and was for a time in charge of the royal gardens. He collaborated with Regnard and wrote numerous comedies of which the most famous are *Le Joueur* (1696), which directly rivalled a piece of the same title by Regnard and caused their rupture, and *L'Esprit de contradiction* (1710). Nine were performed by the Italian company in Paris before its expulsion, after which Dufresny had his comedies played by the French theatre. His series of dialogues, anecdotes, and observations, *Amusements sérieux et comiques d'un Siamois à Paris* (1699), anticipated, and may have been known to, Montesquieu

 and Gherardi's *Théâtre italien*, 153

 and market for popular stage entertainments, 455

 appears in Lesage novel, 457

 Marivaux draws on, 495

 editor of *Mercure Galant*, 513

 cooperation and rivalry with Regnard, 689–90

Dugast, Robert, titular owner of Collège de Coqueret when, on Lazare de Baïf's death, Dorat was made principal

 Coqueret and, 17

vius, 3, 19; also used by des Autels, 256, 612; Melanchthon, Scève, 865; analogous implications in Descartes,
121, 866; and Peletier, 585; avoided by Amyot translating Plutarch, 3

    in Quintilian and Budé, 100–101; for Cartesianism and
    Nizolio, 121; and Rabelais, 121; and Tyard, 864; and his
    source Gyraldi, 865

    term used in modern English sense, 4, 16

    neoplatonist context of, and suggestions of moral elevation
    implied by, 19–21

    symbolized at Ancy-le-Franc, 865

    word used in connection with learning of Antoine d'Urfé,
    868

L'Encyclopédie, 272–76

    see entries on Diderot and Philosophes, passim

    contributors to: d'Alembert, 1–5; Buffon, 103; Daubenton,
    103; Condorcet, 155; Grimm, 333, see 335; Montes-
    quieu, 549; d'Holbach, 608; Rousseau, 744; Voltaire,
    900

    reception: Fréron's constant hostility, 301–302; Palissot's
    attack, 567–68; article 'Genève' attacked, 302

    Malesherbes and, 302; suppression of, 302

    ideology of propagated by Grimm, 332

    article 'Philosophe' in, 603

    source for treatment of philosophers, 604

    Rousseau uses Diderot's concept of general will in article
    for, 746

Enghien: see Condé; Louis II, prince de; and Henri-Jules, prince
de

Enlightenment: history and meaning of term, 602–603

Entresol, club de l', founded in 1724 by the abbé Pierre-Joseph
Alary (1690–1770), tutor of Louis XV, in four entresol rooms
in the house of Président Hénault, where some of the greatest
names of France came to tea on Saturdays from 5.0 to 8.0 to
discuss papers presented on controversial political and historical topics. The club also met at the Tuileries, had d'Argenson
for secretary, and Montesquieu, Pomponne, Bernardin de
Saint-Pierre, and Bernis among its frequenters. It was suppressed by Fleury in 1731. D'Argenson tried unsuccessfully
to revive it in 1734, and left accounts of its proceedings in his
nine-volume *Journal et Mémoires* (1859–67)

    Montesquieu attends, 549

Epernon, Bernard de Nogaret (1591–1661), duc d', son of following, governor of Burgundy, then of Guyenne

    quarrels with du Vair, 267

Epernon, Jean-Louis de Nogaret de la Valette (1554–1642), duc
d', mignon of Henri III, colonel-general of infantry (1584),
admiral (1587), rebelled against Henri IV in 1595, governor
of Annis and Saintonge in 1616, of Guyenne in 1622

    see Chronology 1585, 1620

    withdraws forces on assassination of Henri III, 9

    Desportes assumes charge of further education of, 223

    Balzac in service of; and quarrel with Luynes and du Vair
    of; and godfather to Balzac's niece, 23–24

    political background to activities of, 27

    military opposition to and literary satire of by d'Aubigné, 10

Epictetus, Greek stoic philosopher of first century A.D. who
asserted that the achievement of our true good had to within
our own power, and that we should therefore remain indifferent to everything that was not. Developed notably by du Vair,
a Christianized version of Epictetus anticipated Descartes's

methodic doubt, and lay behind not only the more passive
spiritualities of the 17th century, but also that of François de
Sales (q.v.), who firmly believed in an autonomous human
power of moral self-determination, and in a Molinist theology
of grace

    see entry on du Vair, passim

    translation by Baïf seen by du Verdier, 19

    source for Budé, 100

    source for Descartes's ethic, 209; and see 210–12

    source for François de Sales the Dom Jean de Saint-
    François Goulu translation, 1609, 801

Epicurus, Athenian philosopher of fourth and third century B.C.
associated with the view that pleasure is the principal end of
life, and known to the 17th century in France largely through
Lucretius. Thought to have been an 'atheist,' and his adherents were not infrequently referred to as pigs

    see entry on Gassendi, passim

    Christian rehabilitation of Gassendi's life-work, 322

    Héroët and Epicurean 'volupté (pleasure),' 354

    Saint-Evremond and, 783

Epinay, Louise de la Lire (1726–83), Mme d', closely associated
with Rousseau, and with other philosophes. She was Grimm's
mistress, related by marriage to Sophie d'Houdetot

    see entry on Grimm, passim

    Buffon frequents, 102; Galiani writes to, 126; Dupin de
    Francueil lover of, 746; possibly satirized by Palissot,
    568

    Diderot stays with, 236

    Grimm's duel on behalf of, 746; her possible pregnancy by,
    746; Grimm tires of, 236

    Rousseau lives on estate of, 233; role of in Diderot-Rous-
    seau quarrel, 233; Rousseau and, 744, 746; refuses to
    accompany her to Geneva, 747

    autobiographical novel published with real names, 239

epistemology: see knowledge

Equicola, Mario, Italian author of 1525 work on love deriving
from Ficino

    Héroët's derivation from, 352

Erasmus of Rotterdam, Desiderius (c1468–1536), best-known
of all the evangelical scholars who proclaimed and promoted
the cause of 'bonae literae'

    see Introduction xxxviii, xxxix, xl

    see entries on Budé and Lefèvre d'Etaples, passim

    attitudes of: denounces flattery, 13; admires Lazare de Baïf,
    16; ostentatiously Greek-based scholarship, 16; Bayle
    does not go beyond, 37; concern with pagan virtue, 490;
    central dilemma of grace and free will, 558; reliance on
    direct spiritual experience, 579, 656, 665–66; allows
    link between instinct and virtue, 878

    works of: letters, 24; Lucian translations, 97; ambivalence
    of Bacchus in, 659; Pico's *Rules* and, 798;

    reactions to: Marguerite d'Angoulême's failure to reply to,
    481; d'Aubigné and exegesis of New Testament verse,
    13; Calvin and, 118; Clichtove's hostility to, 482; used
    by Cop, 112; Dorat's Coqueret group and, 260; read by
    Gassendi, 321; study of Greek considered subversive on
    account of, 654; Rabelais writes to, 655, and is heavily
    dependent on, 659–61, and borrows passage from for
    Thélème, 663, and shares pacifism of, 664, and further
    borrows from 664, 665, 667; and Rousseau compared
    with, 750

Cartesianism of, 122; Descartes and Malebranche, 468; and Newton, 650; and d'Alembert, 3; piece for *L'Encyclopédie*, 232; Fénelon inspired by, 288; target of Fréron, 300; Houdar de la Motte ode to; signs privilège for Marivaux novel, 495; enthusiasm for Montesquieu, 551; attack on by Nivelle de la Chaussée, 564; probably meets La Mettrie, 607; Rousseau meets, 742

Forcadel, Etienne (1534–73), professor of law opposed to Cujas's textual criticism of Roman legal codes

 dispute with Cujas, and role of Bodin, 66

Fortuné, Robert (died 1528), taught rhetoric and philosophy at the Collège du Plessis

 Lefèvre d'Etaples dedicates Aristotle translation to, 446–47

Foucher, Simon (1644–96), admirer of Descartes and Leibniz, but opponent of Malebranche

 instant reaction of to *Recherche de la vérité*, 469

Foucquet, Basile (1622–80), abbé, brother of the surintendant, who broke with his brother, but shared his disgrace. He managed a group of spies and thugs for Mazarin during the Fronde. Gourville says that his private organization ran to 50 or 60 heads, 'la plupart gens de sac et de corde (most of them men of the sack and the rope, i.e. gallows birds).' He is known to have had liaisons with the duchesse de Châtillon and the comtesse d'Olonne

 acts for Mazarin against Retz, 711

Foucquet, Nicolas (1615–80), surintendant des finances; immensely rich with wealth subsequently judged to have been acquired corruptly, although certainly with Mazarin's connivance; generous patron who built the magnificent palace of Vaux-le-Vicomte, and sympathized with the nascent group of the modernes. He thought he had bought the protection he needed, worked largely through Pellisson, but was toppled by Colbert on Mazarin's death with 4,000 other financiers. Colbert sought the death penalty, and the court's relatively lenient sentence had to be stiffened to life imprisonment by using royal authority. Arrested in September 1661, Foucquet was sentenced in 1664 and died in prison at Pignerol. He had married Louise Fourché and then Marie-Madeleine de Castille Villemarenil. His mistress was Suzanne de Bruc, marquise du Plessis-Bellière

 see Chronology 1653, 1661, and Introduction xxviii, xliii

 career: disgrace, Vaux celebration of 17 August 1661, and arrest on 5 September, 133, 361, 422, 517, 592, 645; Colbert fails to obtain death penalty, 76

 and Mme de Sévigné: letters from 106, 108, 838–39

 literary relationships: hostility of Boileau, 71; of Chapelain, 133, 591; patron of Pierre Corneille, 164; and Thomas Corneille, 176; and generally, 308; and La Fontaine, 310, 422, 424; friendship for Jesuits, 73; invites Mme de Lafayette, 411; pays 10,000 livres to La Rochefoucauld, 432; patron of Molière, 517; Perrault in circle of, 590, 597; literary alignment of, 591; Racine avoids circle of, 674, 782; Saint-Evremond's links with, 779, 780; Scarron rallies to, 811; and Madeleine de Scudéry and literary portraits, 108

Fragonard, Jean-Honoré (1732–1806), virtuosic painter of versatility, verve, charm, and skill

 Diderot on, 244

François I (1494–1597), king of France (1515), son of Louise de Savoie, and brother of Marguerite d'Angoulême. Heir presumptive from accession of Louis XII on 8 April 1498; the possibility of actual succession seemed remote, but he was given an annuity of 8,000 livres, and Valois was erected into a duchy. When in spite of repeated pregnancies the king's young second wife produced only a daughter, Claude (1499–1524), it became clear that the unity of France could be hoped for only if Claude were married to the heir presumptive, an arrangement first made in 1500, reaffirmed in Louis XII's will of 1505, and confirmed with a solemn betrothal on 21 May 1506. Louis XII's second queen, Anne de Bretagne, died on 9 January 1514, and the marriage of François and Claude took place on 18 May.

François settled at court in August 1508, aged nearly 14. A second daughter, Renée, was born to the queen on 25 October 1510, and a still-born son in 1512. To the pleasure of his ambitious mother, François began to be treated as dauphin. Louis XII married Mary Tudor, sister of Henry VIII, on 9 October 1514, but died on 1 January 1515. The new king was crowned on 25 January as soon as it was clear that Mary Tudor was not pregnant. The duc de Bourbon (1490–1527) had already been declared Connétable. The nature of the king's contract with towns, corporations and individuals was disputed, but in practice François relied on the Conseil étroit for making policy, the Grand Conseil as chief judicial body, and the parlement de Paris, a set of law courts, but also with not always clearly defined administrative and executive functions.

François was outbid by Charles I of Spain in his attempt to have himself made emperor. His reign was marked by an initial victory at Marignano, the Concordat of Bologna (1516), a vain effort to ally with England in 1520, and the struggle against the powers of Spain and Austria united in the person of the emperor, now Charles V. Defeated at Pavia in 1525, François was imprisoned at Madrid, and finally withdrew from Italy, buying back Burgundy. The famous emblem of the salamander in the midst of flames had been used by his father and grandfather. The motto, 'Notrisco al buono, stingo el reo' means 'Feed on the good [fire], and extinguish the evil one.'

 see Chronology, 1498 and passim 1515 to 1547; Introduction, xxviii

 see entries on Budé, Lefèvre d'Etaples, and Marguerite d'Angoulême, passim

François II (1544–60), eldest son of Henri II and Catherine de Medici, betrothed in 1548 to Mary, queen of Scots; acceded to French throne on death of Henri II in 1559 at 15. In spite of his technical majority, his weakness of mind made a council of government necessary, and France was in fact ruled by the Guise family, the queen's maternal uncles, François de Lorraine, second duc de Guise (1519–63), and Charles de Guise, cardinal de Lorraine (1524–74)

 see Chronology 1533, 1548, 1559, 1560

 accession of, 258, 315

 and Guise ascendancy, 91

 provides Baïf with pension, 18

Franklin, Benjamin (1706–90), American statesman and physicist

 Diderot takes up conclusions of, 232

 work of on electricity discussed by Diderot, 243

 received by Mme Helvétius, 607

 admires style of Rétif de la Bretonne, 700

Frederick II ('the Great') (1712–86), king of Prussia from 1740, patron of writers and thinkers, whom he gathered to his resi-

made superior of Port-Royal in Paris by Urban VIII, 615;
effectively ousted as part superior of Port-Royal de Paris
by Zamet, 772
uncle of 'the coadjutor' Retz, 705

Gondi, Philippe-Emmanuel de (1581–1662), third son of
Albert, married, obtained the lucrative senior maritime command of general of the galleys, then entered the Oratory in
1627 and became Père de Gondi. He was father of 'the coadjutor' Retz, of Henri, and of Pierre, the last duc de Retz,
whose daughter Paule-Marguerite was to marry in 1675
François de Créquy, from 1677 duc de Lesdiguières
father of 'the coadjutor' Retz, and of two other sons, 705
Commery enters family through, 705
exiled to Lyons in 1641, 706

Gondi, Pierre de, son of Philippe-Emmanuel and elder brother
of 'the coadjutor,' was left the generalship of the galleys by
his father but, according to Retz, forced to resign the post in
favour of Richelieu's own nephew, Pont-Courlay
account in Mémoires of Retz, 706

Gondi, Pierre de, brother of Albert, duc de Retz, and son of
Henri II's steward; cardinal (1587), and first member of the
family to be bishop of Paris (1568). In 1596 he resigned in
favour of his nephew, Albert's son, Henri de Gondi (died
1622), who passed the bishopric on his death to his brother
Jean-François de Gondi, under whom the see became an archbishopric (1523) no longer dependent on the archiepiscopal
see of Sens
great-uncle of 'the coadjutor' Retz , 705
offers coadjutorship of Paris to François de Sales, 795

Gondran, Charlotte Bigot, Mme de, known as 'Lolo,' about
whose numerous liaisons Tallemant and Conrart are malicious and amusing
Henri de Sévigné lends Mme de Chevreuse's earrings to,
407
Henri de Sévigné killed in duel concerning, 837
his liaison with, 838

Gongora y Argote, Luis de (1561–1627), Spanish ecclesiastical
administrator, poet and wit
Voiture imitates from, 892

Gonzague, Louise-Marie de (1612–67), later to be queen of
Poland. Gaston d'Orléans fell in love with her after the death
in childbirth of his first wife
marriage of to Ladislas VII, and wedding ceremony, 709
wedding stimulates French interest in Poland, 736
Mairet supports Orléans in his marriage project, 460

Gosselin, Jean (?1504–1604), librarian successively of Charles
IX, Henri III, and Henri IV
succeeded by Casaubon, 225

Gottsched, Johann Christoph (1700–66), Francophile German
poet, professor of philosophy (1734), author of project to
establish Saxon linguistic usage as the educated German
norm and to reform the German stage. His imperious attitude
cost him influence, and his reputation waned from about 1740
Grimm's discipleship of, 333

Gougenot, dramatist from Dijon, author of the 1632 Comédie
des comédiens for the Hôtel de Bourgogne, with three acts
devoted to actors discussing their professional activity, and
three to a tragi-comédie they give. Scudéry immediately produced a play of the same title for the Marais troupe, and Pierre
Corneille's L'Illusion comique (1635) is a reply to both
Gougenot's play, 161, 170

early example of 'doubling' in 1632, 822

Goujet, Claude (1697–1767), abbé, author of an unreliable life
of Nicole
need none the less to rely on Goujet, 506

Goulart, Simon (1543–1628), Genevan pastor who left France
after Saint Bartholomew's Day massacre with difficulty and
for good. He published much, but most notably the three-
volume Mémoires (1576), including material from numerous
pamphlets, tracts, and treatises, almost all translated where
necessary into French
La Boétie's Mémoires first fully published in Mémoires of,
377, 380, 536

Goulu, Jean (1576–1629), son of the royal lecturer in Greek who
was married to Dorat's daughter; superior of the Feuillants
from 1624, also known as Dom Jean de Saint-François
dispute with Balzac, 25
source for François de Sales; translates Epictetus; defends
authenticity of pseudo-Denis, 801; first biographer of
François de Sales, 803

Goulu, Nicolas (1530–1601), son-in-law of Dorat, appointed
royal lecturer in Greek in succession to his father-in-law by a
committee of his father-in-law's ex-pupils and friends
knows Monantheuil, 269
appointment of by Ronsard, Baïf, and Belleau, 727

Gourmont, Gilles de, scholar-printer active in first third of 16th
century, the first in Paris to use Greek (1507) and Hebrew
(1508) type. He was already selling books printed in Antwerp, and had his own bookshop in Louvain
Budé's letter to Lupset printed by as preface to More's
Utopia, 100

Gournay, Marie Jars de (1566–1645), learned but self-taught
admirer of Montaigne, whom she got to know, with whom she
exchanged visits, and whose adoptive daughter she became.
She supervised and introduced the posthumous editions of
Les Essais from the Bordeaux 1595 folio, with the preface
withdrawn in 1598, to the definitive 1635 folio. Her
Promenoir de Montaigne was frequently reprinted
makes contact with Montaigne; defends Montaigne and
Ronsard against Malherbe, 533
intimate of Montaigne's last years, and editor of 1635 folio
edition which established his reputation, 534
Racan calls on, 669–70; meets d'Urfé, 870

Gourville, Jean Hérault de (1625–1703), steward to the La
Rochefoucauld family, exiled for his role in the Fronde but
used by both Mazarin and Foucquet; officially condemned to
death, no doubt because unavailable for execution, but given
confidential missions, refused to pay a large fine, pardoned,
and appointed steward to the Condé household
provides refuge for Boileau and Racine, 73
mission on behalf of Mazarin to Conti, whom Guilleragues
advises; negotiates 1653 peace of Bordeaux; friendship
with Guilleragues; employment with Condés, 337
social courtesies to La Bruyère respected, 383
Mme de Lafayette and La Rochefoucauld have use of
house at disposal of, 413–14
may have helped La Rochefoucauld, 432
and plan to kidnap 'the coadjutor' Retz, 711
warns Saint-Evremond of dangers of return to Paris, 780
publication of memoirs of stimulates Saint-Simon, 789

Gouvea, Andrea de, (c1470–?1557) nephew of Diego de
Gouvea, principal of Collège de Sainte-Barbe, whom Andrea

replaced for most of period 1529–33. Unlike his uncle, an anti-Erasmian disciple of Standonck and Beda, Andrea was an evangelical reformer. After Cop's sermon of 1 November 1533, left Paris and was made principal of Bordeaux Collège de Guyenne from which, in 1547, he took a team of teachers to found the college at Coimbra

  see Chronology 1533

  leaves Sainte-Barbe, 113, 486

  principal of Collège de Guyenne, 378, 529

Gouvea, Antonio de (1505–66), Portugese jurist of the school of Cujas who sought to reconstruct Roman law in its historical context; cousin of Andrea. His legal treatises included *De iure accrescendi* (1549) and *De iurisdictione* (1550)

  attacked by Calvin in *De scandalis*, 657

Gouvea, Diego de, (c1470–?1557) titular head of Collège de Sainte-Barbe, known for its Iberian connections, in fact chiefly occupied as a travelling inquisitor for the king of Portugal, rooting out Erasmianism, then dean of Paris theology faculty (1544–50) 113, 486

grace, theology of: It was impossible to import the notion that Adam had fallen into a state of fallen but retroactively redeemed nature (see 'nature' in glossary) without allowing that grace was available, by virtue of their redeemed nature, also to the pagans, and therefore that salvation was not dependent on Christian belief, a view regarded as heretical from the high middle ages to the late 17th century, although the evangelical scholars of the early 16th century certainly edged towards it. Of the innumerable efforts to reconcile a real autonomous human power of self-determination to good (free will in the fullest sense) with a non-Pelagian account of the gratuity of grace, none was successful. Among the most serious failed attempts were those of the Ratisbon diet of April–May 1541, the Council of Trent's decree on justification (13 January 1547), the 'de auxiliis' congregations held at Rome between Dominicans and Jesuits from 1598 to 1607, and the discussions held in Paris between Jesuits and Jansenists 1662–63

  see entries on Calvin and Jansenism, passim, indexed entries on freedom of the will, Molinism, will, and semi-Pelagianism

  general: uncertainty about salvation and, 579; and need to make religious perfection intrinsic to moral attainment, 654; free availability of justifying grace underlying issue in religious disputes, 772–73, 794

  individual authors and: Marguerite d'Angoulême, 489–90; Nicole's theory non-Jansenist, 557, 559; constraints on Pascal, 577; half metaphorically used by Prévost, 637ff; Rabelais and 660, 662, 664; and Racine's theatre, 680; Saint-Cyran and, 770, 775, 778;

  Pascal's view that Jesuit moral teaching is cause of their theology of grace, 578

  not at stake in Port-Royal disputes after 1656; Saint-Cyran's spiritual rigorism independent of, 771ff

  effect on François de Sales of Thomist teaching on, 793

Graffigny, Françoise d'Issembourg d'Happancourt de (1695–1758), great-niece of the engraver Jacques Callot, for some weeks in 1738–39 close to Voltaire, about whose private life she wrote a series of colourful and conversational letters. She probably left Cirey because a former lover flirted too openly with Mme du Châtelet, lived for a while in poverty, but finally had great success with the sentimental *Lettres d'une Péruvienne* (1747) after the unsuccessful *Recueil de ces Mes-*

sieurs. Her sentimental comedy *Cénie* (1750) was a success, admired by Diderot

  Beaumarchais acknowledges drawing on, 46

  Fréron's release organized in salon of, 305

  unkind about Helvétius, 607

Gramont, Antoine (1604–78), comte de, maréchal (1641), until 1644 known as Guiche, but duc de Gramont from erection of Gramont into a duchy in 1663. He was the elder son of his father's first marriage, to Louise de Roquelaure, and the elder brother of Roger, comte de Louvigny. Minister in 1653, he left *Mémoires* published in 1716. Tallemant quotes a malicious popular song about his sexual habits; admirer of Gillonne d'Harcourt de Fiesque

  aligns with Voiture and Pisani at Hôtel de Rambouillet, 131; butt of practical joke, 342

  sent formally to ask for hand of Marie-Thérèse for Louis XIV, 780

Gramont, Armand de (1638–73), comte de Guiche, son of Antoine; exiled on account of a plot with Vardes to inform the queen about the king's liaison with Mme de la Vallière; himself probable lover of the king's sister-in-law, Henriette de France. Known to have been effeminate, a favourite of Philippe d'Orléans and friend of Manicamp

  and Henriette de France, 88

Gramont, Philibert de (died 6 August 1580), whose widow, Diane d'Andoins (1554–1620) soon became the mistress of the future Henri IV and was known as 'la belle Corisande.'

  Montaigne witnesses fatal wounding of, 531

Grandier, Urbain (1590–1634), parish priest of Loudun, accused of causing possession of Ursuline nuns, condemned by Laubardemont and burnt alive

  prosecution of threatens Renaudot, 326

  Saint-Cyran's family threatened by Loudun hysteria, 770

Granet, François (1692–1741), ordained deacon, but never priest. He came to Paris in 1723, and from 1735 until his death collaborated with Desfontaines on the *Observations sur les écrits modernes*

  and Desfontaines, 300

Grandval, Marc de, entered the abbey of Saint-Victor about 1496, doctor of theology in 1513, whose attempts at reform were strongly resisted. Author of one of the dozen or so treatises in the controversy about the three Marys

  view of hostile to that of Lefèvre d'Etaples, 448

'gratifications,' or pensions, awarded by Colbert, advised by Chapelain and the petit conseil, and used largely in the context of orchestrating the mythologization of the monarch

  regime of instituted, 592; first list of, 75, 360; Chapelain and administration of, 133–34

  exclusion of Boileau brothers, and subsequent inclusion of Gilles, 71–72

Gravelot, Hubert-François Bourguignon (1699–1773), designer and engraver who introduced his style into Britain with engravings for Richardson's *Pamela* and Fielding's *Tom Jones*

  Rousseau critical of engravings by for *Julie*, 747

Gravina, Gian Vincenzo (1664–1718), Italian jurist, author of a celebrated *Origines iuris civilis libri III*

  relates histories of politics and institutions, source for Montesquieu, 550

Greek Anthology, a collection of Greek poetic epigrams known as the palatine anthology because the only manuscript of the

10th-century rearrangement of the many antique collections by Cephalas was found in the palatine library at Heidelberg. The epigrams go back to the fourth century B.C., but the only manuscript known before 1606 was that dating from 1301 by the monk Planudes, who had removed many of the poems, although he does include epigrams from a lost book of Cephalas. The *Anthology*, of great importance for Ronsard and his contemporaries, was published by Lascaris in Florence in 1494 and by Bade in Paris in 1531. There are eight known 16th-century printings of the Planudean text, frequently drawn on by neo-Latin poets, by Ronsard, notably in the 1553, 1554, and 1555 collections, and by Baïf from the *Amours de Méline* of December 1552 to the Latin *Carmina* of 1577

    used by Baïf, 18, 22

    discovery of by Ronsard's group, 729

Gregory XIII, Ugo Buoncompagno (1502–85), pope (1572) who regarded schism as rebellion and still favoured military solutions to religious problems, but who reformed the calendar, rewrote canon law, built the Quirinal, and put the fountains in the Piazza Navona

    Baïf dedicates psalm translation to, 19

Grétry, André-Ernest-Modeste (1741–1813), composer, mostly of comic opera

    and opéra comique, 832

    writes for Sedaine, 833

Greuze, Jean-Baptiste (1725–1805), painter specializing in modern subjects from middle-class life

    praised by Diderot, 236; whose admiration shows his sentimentality, 241

Grévin, Jacques (1538–70), doctor, poet, and dramatist, whose conversion to Calvinism occasioned a break with Ronsard, and prudent exile, ultimately in Turin. He left two comedies, *La Trésorière* (1559) and *Les Esbahis* (1561), and a tragedy *Jules César* (1561), played in the Paris colleges. A third comedy, *La Maubertine*, is either lost or, less probably, is identical with one of the other two. His most important verse collections were *L'Olimpe* (1560) and a satire on ecclesiastical abuse, *La Gélodacrye* (1560–61). *Jules César* is prefaced by an important *Bref Discours* defining tragedy and comedy. In the play itself the presence of the chorus on stage is justified by putting it into soldiers' uniforms

    met, or knew du Bellay, 258; La Taille, 438; Peletier, 584

    on tragedy, 439, 441

Grignan, Angélique-Clarisse d'Angennes (died 1664), Mme de: see Angennes

Grignan, Charles-Philippe de, one of the younger brothers of the husband of Mme de Sévigné's daughter, Françoise-Marguerite. The rumours of her attachment to her brother-in-law were probably irresponsible or malicious

    fall of from horse, and Françoise-Marguerite's miscarriage 841

Grignan, François-Adhémar de Monteil (1632–1714), comte de, married (1658) the youngest daughter of the marquise de Rambouillet, Angélique-Clarisse d'Angennes (died 1664), one of the original précieuses (q.v.) who affected to be averse to all physical relationships on account of the sexual tyranny they involved, by whom he had two children, born in 1660 and 1663. On the death of his first wife, he remarried (1666) Marie-Angélique du Puy-du-Fou (died 1667), by whom he had a child who died in infancy, and on the death of his second

wife he remarried (1669) Françoise-Marguerite de Sévigné (1646–1705), by whom he had five children

    marriage to Angélique-Clarisse d'Angennes, 341

    marriage to Françoise-Marguerite de Sévigné, and circumstances of, 840–41ff

Grignan, Françoise-Marguerite de Sévigné (1646–1705), comtesse de, married 29 January 1669 to preceding

    birth of, 837; education of, and relationship with mother, 840

    success at court, possible admiration of king for, and mysteries surrounding marriage of, 840–42 passim

    relationship with Montauzier, guardian of Grignan's daughters by first marriage, and with her mother, 843

    Retz's '*Mémoires*' not written for, 713

Grimarest, Jean-Léonor le Gallois (1659–c1715), Molière's first biographer (*Vie de M de Molière*, 1705; *Additions à la vie de M. de Molière*, 1706)

    unreliable as biographer, 515, 516

Grimm, Friedrich Melchior, Baron von (1723–1807)
Life, 332–35; Works, 335–37; Publications, 337

    see Introduction xliv

    see entry on Diderot, passim

    remark of about Buffon's discourse on style, 103

    mixed views on Chamfort, 126

    remark on Condorcet's Académie election, 155; frequents salon of, 156

    and *L'Encyclopédie*: critical of d'Alembert's 'Genève' entry, 2, 4; close to centre of enterprise, 232; helps with proofs, 234; signs only two articles for, 274

    and '*Correspondance littéraire*': includes Diderot pieces in, 236; hostile comment on Laclos's *Ernestine*, 399; and disparaging on Rétif de la Bretonne, 700

    Fréron's view of, 300; defends Crébillon *fils* against Fréron, 301; satirized by Fréron, 304; but shares approach with, 304

    hostile to Marivaux, 496, 498; caricatured by Palissot, 568; knows Helvétius, 607

    relationship with Rousseau: friendship with, 744; supports attack of on Destouches's opera seria, 745; strain in relationship, 745, attack on second *Discours* of, 746; final break with, 746; Mme d'Epinay's possible pregnancy by, 746; on Rousseau's attack on d'Alembert, 747

    on Italian theatre, 832; derisive of censorship, 833

Grimod de la Reynière, Balthazar (1758–1838), eccentric, gourmand, and dramatic critic. Imprisoned on a lettre de cachet at his father's request, he became for a period destitute. After the Revolution he re-established both his fortunes and his eccentricities

    and Chénier, 142

    and Rétif de la Bretonne, 700–701

    lettre de cachet against, 702

Grocyn, William (died 1519), divinity reader at Magdalen College, Oxford, before spending two years from 1488 in Italy, where he was joined by Linacre and Latimer. From 1491 he lectured on Greek at Oxford until he moved to Saint Lawrence Jewry in London. He taught Richard Croke and Thomas More, and introduced Erasmus to William Warham, his future patron, in 1506. He left some 105 books and 17 manuscripts, published nothing, was conservative in religious outlook, preferred Aristotle to Plato, and did not believe that the author of the *Hierarchia ecclesiastica* was Saint Paul's first convert (see pseudo-Denis)

Budé and English group of, 100

Gros-Guillaume, an early player of farce, whose real name was Robert Guérin and who played serious roles as La Fleur. He died in 1634. Like Turlupin he played the character with his own name in *La Comédie des comédiens*. He used heavily floured white make-up, and was a favourite of Henri IV and early 17th-century theatre, 347

Grotius, Hugo (Huigh de Groot) (1583–1645), Dutch jurist
notion of law of attacked by Bossuet, 83, 89
Montesquieu derives material from, via Pufendorf, 549; develops natural law theory of, 554–55
Rousseau draws on for second *Discours*, 751; his attitude to in *Contrat*, 754
alienated from Saint-Cyran by underlying spirituality of Bérulle, 773

Gruget, Claude (died before 1561), poet and translator, in particular of Speroni's *Dialogi* (1555)
named by Ronsard on 1551 list of poets, 611

Grynaeus, Simon (c1494–1541), Swabian friend of Melanchthon who studied in Vienna and taught at Buda. From 1523 he was at Wittenberg and in 1524 was appointed to teach Greek at Heidelberg, where he had to supplement his stipend by teaching mathematics and Latin. His views of the figurative nature of the eucharist were near those of Zwingli, and he moved to Speier before accepting the chair of Greek offered jointly by civil and ecclesiastical authorities at Basle, where he spent most of the rest of his life. He visited England, however, and with difficulty obtained leave to attempt to reconstitute the university at Tübingen in 1534. In 1537 he retained Calvin's confidence while defending Strasbourg's concessions to the Lutherans, but failed to persuade the Basle authorities to admit to the ministry pastors without university degrees. Only in Strasbourg did he find any balance between civil and ecclesiastical authority. Elsewhere the question was only who would be victorious
cooperation of with Calvin, 113; and Berne conference, 115
publishes the *Novus orbis*, 660

Gua de Malves, Jean-Paul de (c1712–86), abbé, mathematician and philosopher, originally commissioned to translate and edit a French edition of Chambers's *Cyclopaedia*. He failed to reach an understanding with the publishers, and was gradually replaced by d'Alembert and Diderot as editors of *L'Encyclopédie*. Thereafter he mostly earned a living by translating but, after a lawsuit with his family, died close to poverty
d'Alembert and, 1–2
and *L'Encyclopédie*, 229–30

Guarini, Giambattista (1538–1612), author of the pastoral drama called by its author a tragi-comedy, *Il pastor fido* (1590), deriving from Tasso's *Aminta*

Guasco, Ottaviano di (1712–81), abbé, close friend of Montesquieu
translates *De l'Esprit des lois*, 551

Guémené, Anne de Rohan, princesse de, ally and defender of the Port-Royal community who died in 1685. In 1617 she had married her cousin Louis de Rohan, prince de Guémené, duc de Montbazon (died 1667)
residence of within the precincts of the Paris monastery, 616
presence at Port-Royal on 21 August 1644, 619

liaison of with Retz, 'the coadjutor,' 706, 708

Gueullette, Thomas-Simon (1683–1766), published the three-volume collection of 'Parades,' known as *Théâtre des boulevards; ou, Recueil des parades* (1756)
Beaumarchais caters for public of Gueullette's authors, 45
fairground plays and parades published by, 153
adapts fairground material for country-house entertainments, 562
Nivelle de la Chaussée borrows from, 565

Guiche, Antoine: see Gramont

Guichet, Journée du, at Port-Royal-des-Champs, 25 September 1609, 614

Guilleragues, Gabriel-Joseph de Lavergne, vicomte de (1628–85)
Life, 337–39; Works, 339–44; Publications, 344
Boileau's *Epître V* dedicated to, 73
Montesquieu's *Lettres persanes* draws on, 552
participates in sonnet against Nevers, 73, 621

Guirlande de Julie (La), 340–44 The collection of madrigals presented to Julie d'Angennes and composed by some of those who frequented the salon, known from its decoration as the 'chambre bleue,' of her mother, the marquise de Rambouillet. Indexed under this heading are important references in the *Guide*'s main entries to 'Hôtel de Rambouillet' and 'chambre bleue,' other than those in the *Guirlande* entry itself
see entries on Chapelain and Voiture, passim
mentioned casually as received in chambre bleue: Balzac, 26; Bensserade, 55; Bossuet, 79; Desmarets, 216; Huet, 360; Cardinal de la Valette, 460; comte de Belin, 460; Mairet, 460; Malherbe, 477; Racan, 670; Rotrou, 733; Madeleine de Scudéry, 827; Georges de Scudéry, 827; Tallemant, 853–54
social and literary alignments: the 'corps' of Voiture, Pisani, Guiche, Vaillac, and the 'anti-corps' of Montauzier, Chapelain, the Arnauld family, Conrart, and Balzac, 131, 889; division anticipates Querelle des anciens et des modernes (q.v.), 889, 891
atmosphere of chambre bleue, 853; more scholarly after Fronde, 839
vogue for taking names from *Perceforest*, 891
Boileau and, 75
no uniformity of alignment in the Fronde among habitués, 343

Guise, House of: younger branch of the Vaudémont house of Lorraine, a strongly Catholic independent duchy outside French jurisdiction. The ascendancy of the Guises was promoted by Diane de Poitiers, the 27-year-old beauty who was the mistress of Henri II on his accession, during the palace revolution which followed the death of François I.
The first duc de Guise was Claude (1496–1550), the younger son of René II, duc de Lorraine, and elder brother of Jean de Guise (1498–1550), Cardinal de Lorraine. Claude's sons included François de Lorraine, second duc de Guise (1519–63), whose men were responsible for the massacre of Huguenots at Wassy on 1 March 1562, and who was assassinated by Poltrot de Méré on 18 February 1563; and Charles de Guise (1524–74), also Cardinal de Lorraine. It was the eldest son of François, Henri (1550–88), known from his wound as 'le Balafré,' and passionately attached to avenging his father, who momentarily aspired to take over the throne

to culminate in a new crusade against the Turks. Although party to the anti-Venetian League of Cambrai, Julius made peace with Venice and turned against France. He lost Bologna, and had to endure the rebel council of Pisa and Milan in November 1511, but came to be seen as Italy's liberator, and himself convoked the fifth Lateran council. He was undoubtedly coarse-tongued and given to irrational outbursts of rage; remembered as Erasmus's warrior pope

Julius III (Giovanni Maria del Monte) (1487–1555), pope (1550)

    du Bellay on mission from Henri II to, 257

Jurieu, Pierre (1637–1713), Calvinist controversialist and political activist who from Holland ran what amounted to a small spy-ring in France. Once a friend and benefactor, he became an enemy of Bayle, who hoped that the Calvinists who had fled France on the revocation of the Edict of Nantes might yet be allowed to return

    and Bayle 30–33; and support for enemies of Louis XIV, 32–33

    political activity of, 33; and the *Avis important* attributed to Bayle, 33

    Le Clerc hostile to, 34

    like Bayle, did not penetrate the irony of Fontenelle's *Relation sur l'île*, 295

Justel, Henri (1620–93), a Protestant who, until he left Paris for religious reasons in 1681, was the centre of a lively scientific and philosophical circle of Paris intellectuals and scholars; librarian after his exile of the royal library in London

    and circle of, 294

Justus Lipsius (1547–1606), Belgian scholar, translator and devotee of Seneca. Originally a Catholic, he taught as a Calvinist at Leiden from 1579 until 1591, when he became a Catholic again and taught at Louvain. He adapted Senecan stoicism to Christian usage in three major works, the 1583 dialogue, *De constantia*, the 1604 *Manuductio ad stoicam philosophiam*, and the *Physiologiae stoicae libri III* of the same year. Lipsius makes clear the internal connections between antique scepticism and stoicism, which again becomes characteristic of the French moralists during the religious wars. Stoicism provides the only rational ethical attitude in the face an unknowable world. What is clearly known to be good should be embraced; what is clearly evil should be avoided; in everything else the only rational behaviour lies in the sceptical suspension of judgement

    see Introduction xli

    accepts the suspension of judgement, deriving it from Seneca, 321; and connects stoical ethical attitudes with intellectual doubt, 873

    source for Descartes, 121; connection with du Vair, 139, who draws on Lipsius, 269; is in 1621 among Gassendi's favourite authors, 321

    Balzac on, 268; Lipsius's enthusiasm for Montaigne shared with Marie Jars de Gournay, 533

Kempis, Thomas à (1379–1451), canon regular of the Windesheim congregation, long considered the author of the four treatises known corporately as *The Imitation of Christ*, which was certainly a product of the spirituality of the 'devotio moderna,' and which he may have indeed have written

    the *Imitation* translated by Pierre Corneille, 164; and Desmarets, 216;

    the *Imitation* an early spiritual handbook for the laity, 798

Kepler, Johannes (1571–1630), German astronomer

    Cyrano de Bergerac mentions in burlesque context, 194

    theory of planetary revolutions opposed by Fontenelle, 295–96

    predicted path of Mercury experimentally confirmed by Gassendi, 322

Klüpfel, Emmanuel Christophe, founder of the *Almanach de Gotha*, and member of the household of the young prince of Saxe-Gotha

    Rousseau's friendship with, 744

knowledge, theory of

    see entries on Cartesianism and Descartes, passim, also indexed references to Condillac, Locke, and ideas

    d'Alembert and, 4; Descartes's, especially 210; Locke's criticized in *Journal des Savants*, 231; Malebranche and, 469; theory of Malebranche about attacked by Fontenelle, 295

    role and combination of sense data in, 242; and dispute about universal ideas, 364

    whether knowledge precedes or follows love, 353; and see indexed references under 'will'

König, Samuel (1712–57), mathematician friend of Voltaire with whom Maupertuis quarrelled at Potsdam

    quarrel with Maupertuis, 605

    Voltaire sides with on the authenticity of Leibniz letters, 899

La Barre, François Poulain de (1649–1723), doctor of theology who left the Church in 1688, and from 1700 lived in Geneva; the author of strongly pro-feminist treatises

    the pro-feminist works of 1672 and 1675, 652

La Baume, Catherine de Bonne, marquise de, confined by her husband to the convent of La Miséricorde at Lyons by lettre de cachet. Her liaison with Candale had been publicly notorious

    Bussy lends manuscript of the *Histoire amoureuse* to, 106–107

    interest of Bussy's portraits for, 110

Labé, Louise (?1520–65) called 'la belle cordière' after her husband's trade, poet whose reputation for great beauty, wide culture, and martial skills encouraged a legend about her life. Her *Euvres* (1555) contain three elegies, two dozen sonnets, and a prose *Débat de folie et d'amour* in which Folie, having blinded Amour, is finally condemned by Jupiter to be Amour's guide. The *Débat*, although medieval in form, contains a warm neoplatonist defence of love by Apollo, and in the defence of Folie by Mercury there are elements of a mock encomium clearly reminiscent of Erasmus. The sonnets evoke with intensity an old passion, and draw heavily on the Petrarchan tradition for its expression

    salon of frequented by Peletier, 583

La Boétie, Etienne de (1530–63)

    Life, 377–79; Works, 379–81; Publications, 381

    see Introduction xxxv, xli

    relationship with Montaigne, 529; and death of, 530

    Montaigne's intentions to publish, 536

La Borderie, Bertrand de (c1507–?1550), author of *L'Amie de Court* (1541) which cynically argues for the galanteries condemned by Castiglione's *Il Cortegiano*. The *Amie de Court* attacks not only the Petrarchan tradition, but also the idealiza-

lent *Ménagerie*. The fault would widen into the abyss which was on serious grounds to separate the defenders of the antique from the believers in progress and perfectibility during the Querelle des anciens et des modernes, but in the meanwhile La Mesnardière became a leading member of Pinchesne's group, forerunners of the modernes, with Charpentier, the abbé Tallemant, Ménage, Pellisson, and, until his death, Costar.

La Mettrie, Julien Offroy de (1709–51), doctor who studied under Boerhaave at Leiden, visited China, and became a military doctor. In 1745 he published the provocatively subversive but not yet purely mechanistic *Histoire naturelle de l'âme*. It was burnt and he prudently moved to Holland in 1746, where he satirized the Paris medical faculty and published the not entirely committed *L'Homme machine* (1748), dedicated to the Bernese Protestant doctor and historian A.E. von Haller, and *L'Homme plante* (1748). La Mettrie's views were now dangerously materialistic when taken as seriously as they were by the Dutch Calvinists, and he was forced into further exile, accepting the asylum offered through Maupertuis by Frederick II in Berlin. Haller refused the proffered dedication, and was attacked by La Mettrie in *Le petit homme*.

La Mettrie died of food poisoning from pheasant pâté, having published translations and works of medical vulgarization. His works include *Les Animaux plus que machines* (1750), a *Discours sur le bonheur* (1748), *Système d'Epicure* (1750), *L'Art de jouir* (1751), and *Vénus métaphysique; ou, Essai sur l'origine de l'âme humaine* (1751), alluding in its title to a work by Maupertuis. La Mettrie was inclined to think that psychological events in the mind might originate in organic changes in the brain. Criminality might well have physiological roots, and education might be the sole way to make society moral. La Mattrie's friends did not take him very seriously, although he can be seen as having offered a flamboyantly radical challenge to established norms, erected partly on the basis of the philosophies of Locke and Condillac. He preceded more important philosophers like Helvétius and was a distant precursor of positivism

Lamoignon, Chrétien-François de (1644–1709), son of Guillaume, and himself avocat général (1674) and président à mortier (1698)

Lamoignon, Guillaume de (1617–77) premier président in the Paris parlement who presided over Foucquet's trial. From 1667 he held a small salon limited to 18 members, including Guy Patin, Père Rapin, Pellisson, Rohault, Clerselier, Cordemoy, Fleury, and Boileau. Papers were read on Mondays from 5 to 7 p.m.

Lamoignon, Guillaume-Henri de (1683–1772), father of Malesherbes and chancellor of France, grandson of Guillaume

La Môle, Joseph de Boniface, seigneur de (died 1574), lover of Marguerite de Valois, wife of Henri de Navarre; tortured and beheaded for complicity with the duc de Montmorency and the maréchal de Cossé-Brissac in a plot to enable Alençon (future duc d'Anjou) and Henri de Navarre (future Henri IV) to escape from court and join Ludovic of Nassau and the Dutch insurgents at Sedan. The plot was mixed up with astrologers and alchemists. After the execution, Marguerite de Navarre bought the head from the executioner and had it embalmed, while the duchesse de Nevers did the same for his colleague, Coconnato

La Mothe-Houdancourt, Henri de, bishop of Rennes (1642), archbishop of Auch (1662), died in 1684

La Mothe le Vayer, François de (1588–1672), abbé, given by later intellectual historians an ill-founded reputation for religious cynicism. He studied law, frequented the Dupuy circle, formed with Diodati, Gassendi, and Naudé what came to be known as the 'tétrade,' and only with a false date and a pseudonym published in 1630, when he was over 40, the *Quatre dialogues faits à l'imitation des anciens*. They point to the infirmity of reason, the power of prejudice, and the futility of arguments from universal consent. In 1631 five more dialogues sharpen the tone, pointing to apparent contradictions in Christian teaching between divine foreknowledge and human liberty, and reaffirming the need for faith to resolve them. Dogma becomes a means of protecting the moral rules needed for life in society.

For the next 10 years La Mothe le Vayer was employed by Richelieu. He wrote a series of impeccably orthodox works, including a *Petit discours chrétien de l'immortalité de l'âme* (1637), an anti-Jansenist treatise *De la vertu des païens* (1642), and *Considérations sur l'Eloquence française de ce temps* (1637), attacking excessive linguistic purism, but also affirming the authority of the learned against the salon amateurs in matters of language. On Richelieu's approval of his *De l'instruction de M. le Dauphin* La Mothe le Vayer was recommended to Anne of Austria as tutor to the future Louis XIV. At first given charge only of her second son, he succeeded well enough to be given charge from 1652 to 1660 of the education of Louis XIV, for whom he wrote a number of pedagogical treatises.

On Richelieu's death he published further reflective *Opuscules* (1643), followed by works sharply conscious of the limits of what could be based on scientific method and historical evidence (1668), and in 1670 appeared the brief but morally relaxed *Hexaméron rustique*. He clearly reined in a sharp and wide-ranging intelligence to a role which compromised neither his career nor his social standing, but it is doubtful whether much genuine scepticism underlay an obviously attractive cynicism

> Bayle and, 35; and Boileau's fourth *Satire* addressed to, 71; name of Cyrano de Bergerac associated with, 190, 191, and Cyrano makes fun of, 195; associated with Gassendi, 322, 324, and Dupuy group, 324; accuses Gomberville of grammatical purism, 328; and Furetière's references to, 311
>
> gratification granted, 360
>
> argues authenticity of pagan virtue, 435
>
> character in work of argues superiority of modern culture, 646

Lamy, Bernard (1640–1715), Oratorian mathematician and theologian

> dismissed for Cartesianism, 122

Lamy, François (1636–1711), Dom, became a Benedictine after a military career. A Cartesian, he controverted Bossuet, Arnauld, Fontenelle, Leibniz, Nicole, Rancé, and the Jesuits on different issues, and wrote polemical material in favour of the disinterested love of God against Bossuet and Malebranche, although his tone was always eirenical

> Fénelon endorses refutation of Spinoza by, 284; he supports Fénelon's view, 285
>
> shows Bossuet draft of Malebranche text, 470; and takes Malebranche's side in dispute, 470; Malebranche's *Lettres* to Lamy, 471

Lancelot, Claude (1619–95), solitaire at Port-Royal (q.v.) from January 1638, moving that summer to the Paris monastery, where he taught Greek and mathematics. He moved back to Port-Royal-des-Champs where, in 1653, he had five pupils. In 1656 he became tutor to the eldest son of the duc de Luynes, later duc de Chevreuse. From 1669 until their mother's death in 1672, he was tutor to the children of the prince de Conti. Lancelot retired to the abbey of Saint-Cyran, became a subdeacon (1673), and a professed monk (1674). In 1679, in the course of the administration's anti-Jansenist measures, he was sent by lettre de cachet to the Benedictine abbey of Sainte-Croix-de-Quimperlé. He wrote grammars of Latin and Greek, with the rules in octosyllabic verse, possibly by Sacy, a *Nouvelle Méthode* for Spanish with Chapelain, and with another unknown collaborator a manual for Italian

> introduced to Port-Royal by Saint-Cyran, 615; and moves in with Antoine Le Maître as solitaire, 774; goes with group of solitaires to La Ferté in 1638, 616; stays with Vitart family, 674; finds Racine a prickly pupil, 674; tutor to Racine and Luynes's son, 674
>
> and the petites écoles, 556
>
> calls on archbishop of Paris, 1664, 619

Languet de la Villeneuve de Gergy, Jean-Joseph (1677–1753), doctor of theology, bishop of Soissons (1715), archbishop of Sens (1731), councillor of state (1747), anti-Jansenist, apparently of no distinction, and famous only for being ritually rude on account of the stage connection when receiving Marivaux into the Académie. Buffon, who succeeded him, did not mention him in the accustomed manner when he succeeded to his place

> receives Nivelle de la Chaussée into the Académie française, 563

Lannel, Jean de, sieur de Chanteau et de Chambort, écuyer, author of a *Roman satyrique* (1624). He defended Théophile de Viau

> praises Balzac's letters, 25

La Noue, François de (1531–91), Huguenot military leader who left a series of *Discours politiques et militaires* (1587), written in captivity, which advocate tolerance and include the author's own memoirs together with more general reflections, notably attacking *Les Amadis de Gaule* as morally corrupting

> refuses to take Catholic oath of allegiance in 1562, 66
>
> early member of Politique movement, 315
>
> fights alongside d'Aubigné, 8
>
> Brantôme, friend of son of, 92, treats with on behalf of Henri III, 92

Lanson, Gustave (1857–1934), French critic and literary historian

> and Nivelle de la Chaussée, 564

La Pérouse, Jean-François de Galaup (1741–88), comte de, explorer who circumnavigated the globe

> Laclos draws up account of the 1785–88 voyage of, 402

La Péruse, Jean de (1529–54), poet mentioned by Ronsard as one of his group of seven in the *Elégie à Jean de la Péruse* (1553); took part in the Boncourt production of Jodelle's *Cléopâtre*, and in 1553 composed his own posthumously published *Médée*. His premature death the following year drew a tribute from Ronsard

> see 611–12
>
> belongs to Boncourt group under Muret, 723; plays in *Cléopâtre*, 51, 257, 371, 611
>
> Baïf joins in Poitiers, 17; replaced by Belleau in Ronsard's list, 51; La Taille knows, 723

La Pinelière, Guérin de, author of two or three plays 1634–35. Died 1642 or 1643

> early use of mythological subject for *Hippolyte* 1634

La Poplinière, Alexandre-Jean-Joseph Le Riche de (1693–1762), financier and well-known literary patron

> Buffon and, 102
>
> maréchal de Saxe lover of wife of, 758
>
> has Rousseau's *Les Muses galantes* played through, 743

La Porte, Joseph (1713–79), abbé de, former Jesuit, indefatigable compiler who published in 1776 a three-volume *Dictionnaire dramatique*. He quarrelled twice with Fréron, with whom, after the reconciliation, he collaborated on the *Année littéraire* until 1754. After the second quarrel, he became an ally of the philosophes (q.v.), and edited the monthly *Observateur littéraire* from 1758 to 1761. From 1760 the *Observateur* became a supplement to the *Mercure*, to which La Porte moved before giving up in December 1761

> collaborates with Chamfort, 126
>
> reviews Diderot coolly in *Observateur*, 244
>
> collaborates with Fréron, 300; and allies himself with Fréron's alienated publisher, 302

La Ramée, Pierre de (1515–72), educated as a poor scholar at the Collège de Navarre, later principal of the Collège de Presles, noted more for the pedagogy of his *Dialecticae institutiones* (1547) than for his neoplatonist philosophical critique of Aristotelian psychology. He became a Protestant and perished in the Saint Bartholomew's Day massacre.

> Knowledge for La Ramée was the rediscovery of the divine truth existing in the universe and reconstituted in the mind by a process of dialectical invention. Teaching involved scientific descent from general principles to specific facts or propositions by bipartite division, and the pedagogy was sufficiently developed for La Ramée to be able to boast that

There were two ways of paying lip service to the binding legislation of antiquity while making its application to 16th-century circumstances possible, reflected in two different ways of teaching the subject: the 'mos italicus' associated with Bartolo di Sassoferrato, which openly adapted the law in applying it to new situations, and the 'mos gallicus' of the 16th-century French jurists, which attempted to relate antique legislation to the social circumstances which had given rise to it, strip away the glosses, and attend to the intention of the lawgiver.

However, since Roman law in any form could be used to favour imperial authority, its study was not favoured by either the papal or the French courts. A series of decrees starting in 1218 banned the teaching of civil law in Paris. By the 14th century the ban had been tightened because the academic system depended on arts graduates for the bulk of the teaching, and civil law could be studied without a previous arts degree. It also enticed too many students from the study of theology. The ban was fully and permanently lifted only in 1679, with the result that the universities of Orléans, Poitiers, Bourges, and Toulouse flourished more than they might otherwise have done, and that they also became important cultural centres on the teaching of law, see entries on Bodin and Budé and also 90–91, 96, 97–99, 112, 486, 529, 589, 654

2. For most of the period with which this volume is concerned the appropriate authorities were acutely conscious of the distinction between civil and ecclesiastical jurisdiction, even when it was still regarded as axiomatic that the civil power had every right to impose religious conformity. However, there were two sources of civil jurisdiction, the parlements and the crown, frequently in conflict, although a compromise was worked out whereby each became dependent on the other. Only rarely did the crown suspend the jurisdiction of a parlement, although individual cases such as some of those of the evangelical reformers were occasionally removed from a parlement's jurisdiction. The parlements were normally allowed to exercise considerable powers of obstruction in refusing or delaying the registration of administrative edicts.

More complex was ecclesiastical jurisdiction, which has to be distinguished from the Church's power of binding and loosing from sin, and from the Church's teaching authority, whose seat was disputed and whose function more than sporadically usurped by the Paris theology faculty, which could not itself impose even spiritual penalties. It could however 'condemn,' and in 1589 even declared that the king had forfeited any right to the allegiance of his subjects. Since there was never schism in France, all ecclesiastical jurisdiction always derived finally from the pope, just as all civil jurisdiction derived in theory from the crown. Among the ways found round the distinction of jurisdictions were the uniting of papal and royal jurisdictions in chancellors who were also papal legates, like Duprat in France and Wolsey in England. The formal appointment in 1525 of the 'juges délégués' endowed with full jurisdiction by pope and parlement alike included a right of appeal to the parlement, which therefore gave that body the final authority

to judge any bishop indicted for heresy. In the religious disputes of the 16th century, and the Gallican confrontations and Jansenist condemnations of the 17th, it is essential for the modern reader to keep in mind the power struggles involving jurisdiction which were taking place behind public events

see Introduction xxxviii; also entries on Bossuet, Lefèvre d'Etaples, Marguerite d'Angoulême, and Port-Royal, passim, and indexed references to Berquin, Briçonnet, Dolet, and Roussel civil and ecclesiastical jurisdictions, 808, 810

3. The literary culture of France in the period covered by this volume of the *Guide* resounds with assumptions and discussions about the nature of divine, natural, and civil law, and the nature of legitimate political authority, or 'sovereignty.' 'Natural law' theory, antique in origin, was developed notably by Aquinas, and made dependent on the promulgation of an ordination of divine reason in which human reason derivatively participated. At all stages of the evolution of this theory the law-giver, even God, whose nature was rationality, was subject to law. The alternative scholastic theory preserved an apparently threatened divine transcendance, but made law entirely dependent on a promulgation of the divine will, and therefore at least potentially arbitrary

see entries on Bodin, Budé, Montesquieu, and Rousseau, passim, and also indexed entries on Althusius, Aquinas, Grotius, Hotman, Ockham, Pufendorf, and Scotus

legal studies as human discipline, 67

Bossuet and natural law theory, 83, 89; Fénelon and the underlying problems, 290; Lefèvre d'Etaples and nominalist view of law, 443; and on natural law, 452; Malebranche and obligation, 472

satirical treatment of law, 661, 666

Leibniz, Gottfried Wilhelm (1646–1716), German Protestant philosopher and mathematician who explored with Bossuet the possibility of ending the schism between Catholics and Protestants

philosophy of: and d'Alembert, 3; Buffon sides with Newton against, 102; and Cartesianism, 122; admired by Condorcet, 157; published in *Journal des Savants*; Malebranche's theory of ideas and, 469; and his debate with 471–72; Bayle sees little difference between the positions, 604; and points to materialistic implications of Newton, 605

Bossuet's discussions with, 83–84

saw last text of Descartes on 1619 experience, 202

satirized by Diderot, 247

Voltaire's reaction to optimism of, 899

Le Jeune, Claude (c1529–1600), co-founder with Baïf of his academy

setting of Baïf published by, 20

Lekain, Henri-Louis (1729–78), celebrated actor whose career Voltaire much advanced

refuses to speak Marmontel's lines in Rotrou's rewritten *Venceslas*, 736

Le Laboureur, Louis (died 1679), Cartesian and author of an epic poem *Charlemagne* (1664), both patriotic and Christian, which takes the side of the advocates of modern culture, and maintains that the function of art is to express nature. In 1667 he published the *Avantages de la langue françoise sur la langue latine*

published in 1659 some of Brantôme's manuscripts to be used by Mme de Lafayette, 93

on poetry as imitation of nature, 361; and dispute over supremacy of vernacular, 644; on language to be used for triumphal arch, 648

Lemaire de Belges, Jean (1473–?1515), nephew of Jean Molinet and himself a court poet in the rhétoriqueur tradition. He was alert to newly imported Italian culture and composed *Le Temple d'Honneur et de Vertu* (1503) and *La Plainte du Désiré* (1504) on the deaths in 1503 of two early patrons, Pierre de Bourbon and the comte de Ligny, showing some emancipation from the stilted 'déploration,' while still exploiting allegorical characters. The further elegy for Philibert de Savoie, the *Couronne Margaritique*, mourns with wit and grace in prose and verse the death of a parrot, in whose name Lemaire went on to write *Les Epîtres de l'amant vert*, 'vert (green)' standing in medieval colour allegory for passionate love. Further deaths made of Lemaire primarily an elegiac poet, but he also wrote polemical prose, attacking Venice in *La Légende des Vénitiens* (1509) and Julius II in *La Différence des schismes et des conciles* (1511). The 1511 *Concorde des deux langages* celebrates mostly in verse the spiritual unity of the French and the Florentines, while the prose *Illustrations de Gaule* (1510–13) is a romanticized history showing the Trojan origins of the French

spared criticism by du Bellay, 261

Ronsard's early reading includes, 721

Le Maître, Antoine (1608–58), eldest son of Isaac and Catherine Le Maître, lawyer and the first Port-Royal solitaire

moves to Port-Royal as solitaire, 615

goes with solitaires to La Ferté in 1638, 616, 674

special relationship with young Racine, 674

conversion of; and Saint-Cyran, and open letter to Séguier, 774

Le Maître, Catherine Arnauld (1590–1651), daughter of Antoine 'l'avocat'; her five sons became solitaires at Port-Royal, where she herself took the veil on the break-up of her marriage. She had in 1605 married Isaac Le Maître, who in 1615 became a Protestant. Within days 'l'avocat' had obtained seven decrees against him and taken back his daughter and her children. Catherine lived with her mother, took her vow of chastity on 17 July 1619, and made her profession as a nun in 1644

vow of chastity of; and religious profession, 612

Le Maître de Saci, Isaac (1613–84), third son of Isaac Le Maître and Catherine Arnauld; Port-Royal solitaire

life: lives in Saint-Cyran's house, 616; at 'petites écoles', 556; imprisoned, 213, 620; conversation with Pascal and reserve at Pascal's impetuosity, 572; unofficial historian of solitaires, 613; effective superior of Port-Royal, 620; contributes to Arnauld's *Apologie* for Saint-Cyran, 368; school edition of Phaedrus by, 424; on which La Fontaine relies, 428; supports Arnauld's intransigence on grace 1662–63, 559; Nicole writes preface to liturgical works by, 557

source of information that Liber Prooemalis to volume II of the *Augustinus* is based on notes by Saint-Cyran, 774

Le Maître de Séricourt, Simon (1611–50), second son of Isaac and Catherine Le Maître

moves in with his elder brother, Antoine, as solitaire, 615, 774

goes with small group to La Ferté in 1638, 616, 674

Le Mercier de la Rivière, Pierre-Paul-François-Joachim-Henri (1720–94), economist and physiocrat whose *L'Ordre naturel et essentiel des sociétés politiques* (1767) antedates the work of Dupont de Nemours

recruited by Diderot for Catherine II, 238

helps Diderot with project for reform, 239

Lémery, Nicolas (1645–1715), doctor and chemist from Rouen prominent in Justel's circle, 294

Le Moyne, Pierre (1602–71), Jesuit poet, moralist, essayist, author of *Saint Louys; ou, La Sainte Couronne conquise sur les infidèles* (1653)

mentioned as author of Christian epic, 217

uses term 'caractères' in 1640 *Peintures morales*, 384

Lenclos, Ninon de (1620 or 1623–1705), famous for her beauty, her salon, her freedom of spirit, and her many amorous episodes with the highest nobility

on the précieuses, 432, 630

received by Mme de la Sablière, 423; satirized by Lesage, 454; Saint-Evremond writes for, 786; Scarron knows, 811; Henri de Sévigné's liaison with, 838; and Voltaire's godfather, 'her last lover,' and Voltaire, 895

Lenglet-Dufresnoy, Nicolas (1674–1755), journalist, historian, and critic

attacks Prévost, 634

Lenoir, Charles, actor-manager who formed the Marais troupe with Montdory and Viliers in 1624. Lenoir was transferred by Louis XIII at the same time as Jodelet in December 1634 to the Hôtel de Bourgogne and Bellerose's company, leaving Montdory at the Marais. Lenoir was survived by his wife, but is not mentioned after she retired in 1637. The comte de Belin had been her lover, and Mairet wrote roles for her

Belin and Lenoir, 461

the 1634 move to the Hôtel de Bourgogne, 822

and Montdory, 676

Lenôtre, André (1613–1700), garden designer, responsible for Vaux-le Vicomte and Versailles, the greatest master of the layout of the French formal garden

Versailles maze of, 57

La Fontaine and removal of exotic trees from Vaux to Versailles, 424

Perrault complains of being cheated in favour of, 595

Leo I, Saint Leo the Great, pope from 440 to 461, chiefly important for the definitive Latin formulation of the doctrine of the Incarnation adopted by the Council of Chalcedon in 451 A.D.

Lefèvre d'Etaples and, 447

Leo X (1475–1521), ordained priest after election as pope on 11 March 1513, concluded Concordat of Bologna with France, and issued the bull condemning, although not as heretical, 40 propositions of Martin Luther

his Roman college for Greek studies, 97

Lutheran dispute appealed to, 111

patron of Vitalis, 261

contributes to Boisrobert's 1633 anthology, 215

Sorel collaborates with, 849

Leonardo da Vinci (1452–1519), Italian painter, musician, and engineer; in France 1516–19

Diderot assimilates aesthetics of, 237

Lépine, Madeleine-Françoise, Beaumarchais's sister

grandson of Louis XIV; see details of succession in Chronology for 1715. The new king was five and his great-grandfather, correctly estimating the undesirability of conferring power, as distinct from the unavoidable external appearance of authority, on his brother's son, had made provision for a council of regency. The nephew, Philippe III d'Orléans, unambitious for power, disliked the affront to his character, and, having bought sight of his uncle's will, had an intelligently conceived coup in place, immaculately executed within 24 hours of his uncle's death, remaining regent until the king's majority was declared when he reached 13. He was also for the time being heir presumptive.

A project for Louis XV to marry the Spanish infanta and for the regent's daughter to marry the heir to the Spanish throne led to the exchange of the princesses in 1722. Louis, although healthy, occasionally overtaxed his strength while hunting, and his serious illness in 1725 hastened the decision to abandon the Spanish marriages. The infanta was sent home, stones were thrown at Frenchmen in the streets of Madrid, the first bullfight for 20 years was authorized by the Spanish court, and the lumpish Bourbon, grandson of the 'grand Condé' and now first minister, selected with the approval of his slim, beautiful and power-hungry mistress Mme de Prie, Maria Leszczynska as wife to Louis XV. The proxy marriage was consummated on 5 September 1725, and in 1729, after three daughters, a male heir was born, father of Louis XVI

see Chronology 1715, 1722, 1723, 1725, 1757, 1774
see entry on Saint-Simon, passim, for succession of Louis XV and preparation for Spanish marriages
cultural effect of attempted assassination of, 272–73, 302
Beaumarchais's friendship with daughters of, 39, 41
Buffon printed at imprimerie royale, 103
patronage of Crébillon père, 187
pays Rousseau for Le Devin du village, 745

Louis XVI (1754–93), grandson of Louis XV, son of the dauphin and Maria Josepha of Saxony. The dauphin himself had died in 1765, and in 1770 his third son and successor married Marie-Antoinette of Lorraine, arch-duchess of Austria, becoming Louis XVI in 1774. At the date of his accession, some radical reform of the political and social life of the nation was clearly inevitable, although the grosser violences of the Revolution in Paris were still avoidable. Such reforms as had already been begun had been largely the work of the professional administrators, particularly away from Paris, although at the centre the counsels of Malesherbes, Turgot, and Necker might have led to greater liberalization and less turbulence than actually ensued. In fact the resistance of the privileged classes to change, and the burdensome irrelevance of king and court to the real needs of the nation, were such as to make the challenge of 1789, if not the actual course of subsequent events, ineluctable

see Chronology 1725, 1754, 1770, 1774
personally censors Le Mariage de Figaro, 43
moved to tears by Chamfort tragedy, and bestowal of pension, 126
and mission of Orléans to London, 401
pension awarded to Rivarol, 718

Louis de France, duc de Bourgogne (1682–1712), son of the 'grand Dauphin,' (see below), put at the age of seven in August 1689 under the governorship of Beauvillier, with Fénelon for tutor; Fénelon's preceptorate was extended to Bourgogne's brothers, the duc d'Anjou in 1690 and the duc de Berry in 1691. Bourgogne could normally expect one day to succeed his father as king of France. In 1689 Louis XIV became 51 and Bourgogne's father 28. However the grand Dauphin died in 1711, leaving Bourgogne heir apparent until his own death the following year. He had married Marie-Adélaïde de Savoie in 1697. His first son had died in 1705 and the second, the duc de Bretagne, died in 1712 with his father and mother in a mysterious fever. The future Louis XV had been born in 1710

and Fénelon, 280, 285, 287–90; Saint-Simon on, 791

Louis, the 'grand Dauphin,' (1661–1711), the only one of Louis XIV's five children by Marie-Thérèse to survive infancy. His education, entrusted to Bossuet, was at best ineffectual. He married Maria-Anna, sister of the elector of Bavaria, on 28 January 1680, and she bore him three sons:

Louis, duc de Bourgogne (1682–1712)
Philippe, duc d'Anjou (1683–1746), who became Philip V of Spain and renounced rights to the French crown
Charles, duc de Berry (1686–1714)
see Chronology 1661, 1715
Bossuet accepts tutorship of, 81

Louise de Lorraine (or de Vaudémont) (1553–1601), queen of France, married to Henri III on 14 February 1575, the day after his coronation as king of France. On his death she retired to Moulins, and died without issue

Louise de Savoie (1476–1531), comtesse, then duchesse d'Angoulême, daughter of Marguerite de Bourbon and Philippe, comte de Bresse, later duc de Savoie, and niece of Louis XI. She was brought up after her mother's death when she was herself seven by Anne de Beaujeu, daughter of Louis XI, and on 16 February 1488 was married at the age of 12 to the 28-year-old Charles d'Angoulême, nephew of Charles d'Orléans, who had taken part in the 1487 insurrection led by the future Louis XII against the regency of Anne de Beaujeu. Widowed on 1 January 1496, Louise brought up her own children, Marguerite d'Angoulême (q.v., born 11 April 1492) and the later François I (born 12 September 1494) with her husband's three illegitimate daughters, two by Antoinette de Polignac, whom she took as a lady-in-waiting, and one by Jeanne Comte.

Although Louise was only 19, and 25 was the legal age for guardianship outside Angoulême, where customary law allowed guardianship at 14, she was granted limited custody if she did not remarry, although important decisions had to be referred to Louis d'Orléans, the nearest male relative of the children. Orléans succeeded to the throne as Louis XII when Charles VIII died childless and, although it seemed likely that Orléans would in due course have a male heir, Louise's son was for the time being heir presumptive. Louise did not hide her satisfaction, as the years progressed, at Orléans's failure to produce a male heir.

Louise and her children were kept virtual prisoners at Blois and then Amboise until François was sent to court in 1508. Louise backed the promotion of Duprat as chancellor on her son's accession in 1515, and François raised Angoulême to a duchy, giving his mother also the duchy of Anjou, the comtés of Maine and Beaufort-en-Vallée, and the barony of Amboise. Her daughter's husband was made governor of Normandy and given second rank in the kingdom. Regent during her

Charles Perrault, 594; allusion in Guilleragues, 338–39; Donneau de Visé and, 251, 254; and La Fontaine, 425

and interest in Turkey, 622

and 18th-century dispute about French and Italian styles, 232, 242

Luneau de Boisgermain, Pierre-Joseph-François (1732–1801), journalist, producer of manuals and compendia, involved in legal disputes with Le Breton, publisher of *L'Encyclopédie*

Diderot takes side of, 238; and against, 239

Lupset, Thomas (1498–1530), English scholar who entered the household of Colet and went to Cambridge, where he met Erasmus, whom he helped with the New Testament and the edition of Jerome's letters. Lupset probably accompanied Richard Pace to Italy, and certainly went to study in Paris in 1517, supervising the printing of two of Linacre's translations from Galen as well as the second edition of More's *Utopia*. The introduction to Budé was probably through Linacre

visits Budé, 100

Luther, Martin (1483–1546): see Lutheranism

see Chronology 1517, 1520, Introduction xxxviii, xxxix, xl

see entry on Calvinism, passim

Bayle's article on, 37; Budé on, 101; and Lefèvre d'Etaples, 443

scholastic dilemmas and, 365; recourse to direct spiritual experience in, 579; and attribution of *Corpus Dionysiacum*, 445

excommunication of, 482

satire on in Rabelais, 663–64

'Lutheranism:' neither the doctrinal nor the spiritual content of what in the France of the 1520s was known as 'Lutheranism' has ever been adequately defined, and discussion of subversive religious tendencies has widely suffered from inadequate historical awareness of the often disputed limits on the powers of the French crown, the Paris theological faculty, the parlement de Paris, and the pope. It was not until well into the 1540s that there was a body of doctrine commonly held by schismatic Christian communities that could clearly be seen to be heretical, openly at variance with the teaching of the Church, and not until the middle of the century that the reactionary but penetratingly clear definitions of the Council of Trent made plain what the boundaries of orthodoxy actually were, even on such central points as the seven sacraments and the sacrificial nature of the Mass.

The dogmatic authority of the Paris theological faculty was self-proclaimed, and the faculty needed the support of the Paris parlement or the court for its views to have any civil consequences. The crown, concerned with its political relationship with Rome, was as wary of the parlement's attempts to cut back royal authority as Rome was of the theology faculty's attempts to usurp its teaching authority. It was only from 1538, when there appeared to be real danger of schism, that François I started to transfer stronger powers to the parlement. Before about 1538 'Lutheranism' in France was a simmering of religious discontent and provocation, not easily distinguishable from evangelicalism, and linked to learning only by a desire to subvert the authority of scholastic religious teaching by recourse to scripture in the original languages. The focus of attack was superstition and all rites, practices, and observances which divorced religious stature from interior moral conversion

see entries on Marguerite d'Angoulême, Budé, Calvin,

Lefèvre d'Etaples, Marot, and Rabelais, together with indexed references, especially under Beda, Berquin, Briçonnet, Bucer, Caroli, Dolet, Farel, Roussel, and Zwingli

Luxembourg, François-Henri de Montmorency-Bouteville (1628–95), duc de, son of the duellist beheaded in 1627; brilliant military tactician, captain of the bodyguard in 1673, maréchal in 1675

Saint-Simon and dispute over precedence of, 787

Luxembourg-Piney, Madeleine de, princesse de Tingry, married in 1661 to above, who took her name after registration in 1662 as duc et pair

husband of claims new precedence derived from the marriage, 787

Luynes, Charles d'Albert (1578–1621) duc de, connétable (1621), elder companion of Louis XIII under whose tutelage the king assumed the government of France and was forced to consummate his marriage

see Chronology 1617, 1621

political role: d'Aubigné joins 1620 uprising against, 110; quarrel with Epernon, 24; relationship with Louis XIII, 24, 268, 460; and political alignment, 27

marriage to Marie de Rohan-Montbazon, 24

Balzac returns to Paris after death of, 25; Malherbe writes satirical verses about, 476

Luynes, Louis-Charles d'Albert de (1620–90), son of the connétable and the future duchesse de Chevreuse, married first to Louise-Marie Séguier, daughter of Pierre Séguier, marquis d'O, who died in 1651 leaving her husband five children. He retired to Lésigny, then to Liancourt. Turned Jansenist, he sold Lésigny and built Vaumurier, very close to Port-Royal-des-Champs. In 1661 Luynes married his beautiful but feather-brained aunt, Anne de Rohan, born 1640, 20 years after her nephew, who now became her husband. She died in 1684 and Luynes married Marie d'Aligre in 1685

translated Descartes's *Meditationes*, 205; has Le Maître's *Office du Saint-Sacrement* translated into French

Arnauld's second *Lettre* addressed to, 370, 573

father of duc de Chevreuse, 574; unrealized project of marriage to Mme de Sévigné, 843

Pascal stays with early in 1655, 575; building of Vaumurier and rebuilding of Port-Royal-des-Champs, 617; Racine may have lodged with, 674

Mabillon, Jean (1632–1707), Dom, Benedictine of the Saint-Maur congregation who became at Saint-Germain-des-Prés the centre of a small Benedictine academy devoted from 1668 to compiling the *Acta sanctorum*, attempting to remove the accretions of legend from the lives of the saints, justifying his critical method in the 1681 *De re diplomatica*, with rules for establishing the age, provenance, and authenticity of manuscripts. He travelled widely in search of manuscripts, publishing a series of travel journals and spending more than a year in Italy (1685–86), and also edited the works of Saint Bernard, wrote the history of his order, the *Annales* of 1703ff, published works of piety, composed a *Traité sur les études monastiques* (1691) which gave rise to a dispute with Rancé, and left a vast correspondence. He refused a pension offered by Colbert

attended Bossuet's study group at Versailles, 82

Huet close to before Mabillon's death, 362

fied as a doctor in England, and left medical works as well as the egalitarian *Les Chaînes de l'esclavage* (1774), a three-volume work on the interaction of mind and body, and an *Eloge de Montesquieu* (1785). He had returned to France in 1775, and his daily pamphlet during the Revolution was very largely composed of diatribes demanding violence. Charlotte Corday was guillotined for his murder. Jacques-Louis David (1748–1825) considered his famous painting of the assassination, which took place while Marat was having a bath, to be one of his two best. Chénier wrote a celebrated ode to Charlotte Corday

    attacked by Beaumarchais, 44

    opposed by Chamfort, 127

    Chamfort and, 143

Marbeuf, Pierre de (1596–1645), magistrate, co-pupil of Descartes at La Flèche, published a *Psaltérion chrétien* (1618) and a *Recueil de vers* (1628)

    Tallemant asserts deliberate misattribution by Boisrobert of Desmarets piece to, 215

Marcellus II (Marcello Cervini) (1501–55), elected pope 9 April 1555, died 21 days later on 30 April; his reign was sandwiched between those of Julius III and Paul IV

    reign of, 257

Marchand, A.-Prosper (c1675–1756), Protestant bookseller who moved to Leiden, having sold books in Paris and then (1711) in Amsterdam

    and Challe, 123–24

Marchand, Jean-Henri (died c1785), lawyer, censor, author of amusingly witty collections of prose and verse

    helped by Rétif de la Bretonne, 703

Marcourt, Antoine, a French Zwinglian who became the first pastor of Neuchâtel in 1530. Author of the 'placards' (on which see index entry) against the Mass distributed in France on the night of 17–18 October 1534

    authorship of placards and subsequent *Traité*, 486

    capitalizes on Rabelais's success, 658

Mareschal, André, dramatist, active 1630–35

    Vendôme patron of, 159

    attacks regularity in tragi-comédie, 461

    Rotrou writes preliminary verses for *La Généreuse Allemande* of, 733

Marguerite d'Angoulême, duchesse d'Alençon, reine de Navarre (1492–1549)

    Life, 480–88; Works, 488–94; Publications, 494

    see Chronology 1494. 1548, Introduction xl

    imagination and spirituality of: Platonism of and upgrading of instinctive love, 351; Briçonnet, Lefèvre d'Etaples, and, 446; Lefèvre's spirituality behind Briçonnet's letters to, 448; shelters Marot, 506; religious troubles of 1533 and, 112–13

    protects university of Bourges, 112; and Héroët, 350; receives La Taille dedication, 439; Marot enters service of, is protected by, 504; protects Rabelais, 656, and receives dedication of *Tiers Livre*, 664; invites Scève to write preliminary verses for *Marguerites*, 817

    Brantôme brought up at court of, 90; and draws on *Heptaméron* as source, 94; Challe uses form of, 124; Sade draws on fictional techniques of, 768; Hircan in *Heptaméron* of, and d'Urfé's Hylas, 877

    and prettification of medieval tales of lechery, 850

    Montaigne amusingly dismissive of, 539

Marguerite de France (1523–74), duchesse de Berry, daughter of François I, later, under the terms of the treaty of Cateau-Cambrésis, married to Emmanuel-Philibert (1528–80), duc de Savoie from 1553

    see Chronology 1545, 1559

    receives Brantôme, 91

    du Bellay dedicates *Recueil de poésie* to, 256; and marriage of, 258

    Peletier at Annecy court of, 584

    defends Ronsard against Melin de Saint-Gelais, 722; and obtains benefice for him, 722; Ronsard's second book of *Les Hymnes* dedicated to, 723

Marguerite, princesse de Lorraine (1613–72), sister of Charles, duc de Lorraine; became second wife of widowed Gaston d'Orléans in 1632, while he was still heir presumptive. Marguerite joined him in Brussels, travelling in male dress in the cardinal de Lorraine's carriage. A horse, a companion, and two servants were waiting for her in a wood near the border, which she successfully crossed. The secret marriage was publicly recognized by Louis XIII, Orléans's brother, shortly before his death in 1643, by which date a direct heir had been born, and Richelieu was dead.

    see Chronology 1632

Marguerite de Valois (1553–1615), daughter of Catherine de Medici and Henri II, known as 'la reine Margot,' who married Henri de Navarre on 18 August 1572 and agreed to be repudiated by him only in 1599, after the death of his mistress, Gabrielle d'Estrées. From 1583 to 1605 she was obliged by her husband, who had meanwhile become Henri IV, to live at Usson

    see Chronology 1599

    gathering of Huguenot notables in Paris for wedding of occasion for massacre of Saint Bartholomew's Day, 7

    consents to annulment, 10

    takes Brantôme into her circle, 92; dedicates her memoirs to him, 93; Charron preaches for, 137; Desportes presses suit of Bussy-d'Amboise with, 223; Montaigne visits on 8 February 1582, 532

    Paris circle on return from Usson, 870; and is known by d'Urfé, 870

Mariana, Juan de (1536–1624), Spanish Jesuit and historian, notorious as a protagonist of the view that, under circumstances involving the forfeiture of legitimate authority, a sovereign could behave in such a way as to legitimize tyrannicide. Montaigne sardonically notes that the argument changed sides during the religious wars when, on the death of Anjou in 1584, the heir presumptive became a Protestant

    the 20-volume *Historiae de Rebus Hispaniae* (1592) of, to which was added a 10-volume supplement in 1605, establishes the historicity of the Rodrigue-Chimène marriage in Pierre Corneille's *Le Cid*, 170

    condemnation of *De Rege* of, 369

    used by Mme de Lafayette, 417

Maria-Anna-Victoria (1660–90), sister of the elector of Bavaria, married the 'grand Dauphin', Louis, the heir of Louis XIV, in 1680

    see Chronology 1681, 1715

    and Italian theatre company, 153

Marie-Antoinette de Lorraine (1755–93), archduchess of Austria, married the future Louis XVI in 1770. Noted for her

removes Frederick of Bohemia, 206

Mayenne, Charles de Lorraine (1554–1611), duc de, brother of Henri, third duc de Guise, and Louis, second cardinal de Guise, both killed at Blois on the orders of Henri III in December 1588; took over the leadership of the League, was defeated by Henri IV at Arques (September 1589) and Ivry (14 March 1590). He made his submission during a celebrated interview in 1595. Created a duke and peer in 1573, he led successful military actions against the Huguenots, accompanied the future Henri III to Poland, was made governor of Burgundy, which he raised for the League in 1585, and was at Lyons when his brothers were killed. He organized the administration of Paris, adding representatives of the trades and professions to dilute the pro-League fervour of the representatives from each of the 16 districts, thereby constituting the body known as the 'seize.' He was himself on the moderate wing of the League, hostile to the Spanish domination of France. On his submission to Henri IV, he was allowed to keep Chalon-sur-Saône, Seurre, and Soissons for three years, was made governor of the Ile-de-France, and was paid a huge indemnity

    see Chronology 1577, 1585, 1589, 1590, 1592, 1594

    see entry on *Satire Ménippée*, passim

    leader of League, 9; proclaims cardinal de Bourbon king, 9

    supported by du Vair against the seize, 265

    career, and relationship to house of Guise, 266–67

    and siege of Paris, 269

Mayenne, Claude (1526–73), duc d'Aumale, marquis de, uncle of preceding, brother of François de Guise, married Louise de Brézé, daughter of Diane de Poitiers, which partly accounts for the family's ascent under Henri II

    see Chronology 1547

Mayenne, Henri de Lorraine (1578–1621), duc de (1611), son of Charles, showed some lingering loyalty to the League. Peer and chamberlain of France, he had sympathized with Marie de Medici and the disaffected aristocracy in the movement which led to the skirmish of 1619 at Ponts-de-Cé, but was made governor of the south-west, and was killed at the unsuccessful siege of Montauban fighting for Louis XIII

    see Chronology 1620

Mazarin, Hortense Mancini (1646–99), duchesse de, Mazarin's niece and a woman of proverbial beauty, married to Armand-Charles de la Meilleraye. Mazarin left the couple the bulk of his estate on condition that they took his name. Her husband was jealous to the point of derangement, and she at heart an adventuress. The marriage broke down, and Hortense went to Italy, Savoy, and England, where she achieved much social success and was a close friend of Saint-Evremond

    marriage of, 73; father-in-law of and Retz, 712

    London salon of, 784; and Saint-Evremond, 781

Mazarin, Jules (1602–61), cardinal and minister who succeeded Richelieu, wily, astute, of very high intelligence and immensely patient, he survived intense unpopularity with bewildering skill. His political manoeuvres were less ruthless than those of Richelieu, who preceded him, and more successful than those of Colbert, who took over from him.

Born Giulio Mazarini, he entered the papal army and then, as an unordained ecclesiastic, the papal diplomatic corps, negotiating a truce beteen France and Spain. Made nuntius to Louis XIII in 1634, he entered French service in 1636, became a naturalized French citizen in 1639, was made a car-

dinal in 1641, and was almost certainly the lover and very probably the secret second husband of the regent, Anne of Austria, widow of Louis XIII. He notoriously enriched himself to an extent which must have involved at least the connivance of Foucquet, and emerged successful from the twin challenges from parlements and aristocracy in the Fronde.

As in public life Mazarin was even closer to Anne of Austria than anyone realized, so in the arts his inclinations were largely opposed to those of Richelieu before him and those of Colbert, who was to replace him and to overthrow Foucquet, with whom Mazarin must to his enrichment have connived, and to impose central control where Mazarin had welcomed diversity. Against Richelieu's nationalistic preferences, Mazarin brought back commedia dell'arte, and bestowed pensions on Ménage and Costar, while Colbert was to revert to Richelieu's preference for what was French, to rely on Chapelain, and to believe above all in centralizing control of the nation's cultural life. Mazarin's patronage was also bestowed on authors like Naudé and La Mothe le Vayer, with the possible exception of Cyrano all orthodox enough but with proven independence of mind. Mazarin's spectacular library was opened to the public in 1643, sold off during the Fronde, but subsequently reconstituted and, left to the nation, forms the nucleus of the library of the Institut. Naudé was Mazarin's librarian

    see Chronology 1641, 1643, 1649, 1650, 1651, 1652, 1653, 1661, Introduction xliii

    career, and Fronde: marriage of duc de Richelieu and Anne Poussart de Fors, its alignments and consequences, 217; imprisonment and release of Condé, Conti, and Longueville, 217, 709–12; negotiations with Conti, 337–38; conduct of during Fronde, 431ff, and in particular for relationship with Retz, 708–16, 837; double exile, 58, 408, 432; and Saint-Evremond and peace of Pyrenees, 780, 782; relations in 1651 with Condé and Retz, 838; Bussy joins forces of, 106; administrative legacy of, 591

    cultural: and Bensserade, 55–56; Italian opera and, 59; suppresses Compagnie du Saint-Sacrement, 79; see entry on Chapelain, passim; accords gratification to Pierre Corneille, and receives dedication of *Pompée*, 163; and of Thomas Corneille's *Stilicon*, 180; Cyrano de Bergerac and, 190–91; Descartes receives pension from, 204; Desmarets loses favour under, 213; Fénelon and, 286; uses and censors the *Gazette*, 326, 338; and Furetière, 309; and La Fontaine's dislike of, 421; attacked in *Livre abominable*, 519; and Scarron, 589, 810–11; hostility of to Port-Royal, 617; attacked by Sorel; continues to employ Voiture, 890

measured: see vers mesurés

Meaux, reform of diocese of: see indexed references under Briçonnet and main entries on Lefèvre d'Etaples and Marguerite d'Angoulême

Medici: see under first names for Catherine de Medici and Marie de Medici

Medici, Cosimo de (1389–1464), ruler of Florence and founder of Platonic academy entrusted to Ficino. Huge artistic patron

    Catherine de Medici reminded of relationship to, 18

    Ficino edition of *Corpus hermeticum* dedicated to, 445

Medici, Lorenzo de (1449–92), succeeded Cosimo as ruler of Florence

execution of 486, 816

Montemayor, Jorge de (c1520–61), Portuguese author of the
Spanish *Los siete libros de la Diana* (?1559), completed or
more probably answered by the *Los cinco libros de la Diana
enamorada* (1564) of Gaspar Gil Polo (c1519–85), and partly
inspired by Sannazaro's *Arcadia*
> and d'Urfé's *L'Astrée*, 869
> source for *Le Sireine*, 875; and *L'Astrée*, 878

Montespan, Françoise-Athénaïs de Rochechouart-Mortemart
(1641–1707), marquise de, married in January 1663 Louis-
Henri de Pardaillan de Gondrin, a year younger than she was,
by whom she had two children. She was also the mistress of
Louis XIV from 1667 and mother of seven of his children, of
whom the first, Louis-Auguste, duc du Maine, his father's
favourite, was born in 1669. Her husband caused surprise by
publicly objecting, and was briefly imprisoned and compelled
to exile himself in Spain pending an official separation procured by Achille de Harlay in 1674. Montespan accused Mme
de Montauzier of acting as a go-between for his wife and the
king in order to secure the Normandy governorship for her
husband.

Mme de Montespan was certainly a client of La Voisin,
from whom she at least acquired potions to rekindle the king's
waning interest in her. In 1675 she was refused communion
on grounds of flagrant adultery, but the subsequent public
separation from the king, stage-managed by Bossuet, was
only brief. In 1679 she was relegated to the supervision of the
queen's household when Marie-Angélique de Scorraille de
Roussille (1661–81), Mlle de Fontanges, became the king's
mistress in April 1679. From 1680, it is clear that the extent
of the involvement with La Voisin of Mme de Montespan and
others in high places was being hushed up in a conspiracy to
which the king, Louvois, Colbert, and Mme de Maintenon
were privy. Louis XIV continued to spend time with Mme de
Montespan, but she was allowed to retire to a convent in 1691
with a pension of 500,000 livres. She became converted to a
life of devotion and good works, and was an important protector of Racine and Boileau
> see Chronology 1684
> relationship with Louis XIV; Mme de Ludres, 56; refusal
> of communion to Mme de Montespan 81; position at
> court, 787, 788
> involved in affair of poisons, 252
> and Boileau, 72–73; and Racine, 679; and both together,
> 681
> Colbert wary of offending, 595, 649
> Huet's relationship with, 361
> and Mme de Lafayette, 413; and Saint-Simon's mother,
> 786
> La Fontaine respected by, 424; and dedicates *Fables* to, 429

**Montesquieu, Charles-Louis de Secondat, baron de
(1689–1755)**
> **Life, 547–52; Works, 552–55; Publications, 555**
> see Introduction xxxi, xxxv, xliv
> works stimulating interest in east, 548, 553
> article for *L'Encyclopédie* on taste contains material from,
> 274
> Fénelon admired by, 289; and Helvétius liked by, 607
> rational explanation for sacred history in, 297
> dismissive of Marivaux, 498
> pamphlet in praise of by Palissot, 567

celebrated judgement of on Prévost's *Manon*, 638
> Rousseau's complete agreement with in 1755, 745; Rous-
> seau draws on for second *Discours*, 751; and distances
> himself from Montesquieu's preferred constitutional
> model, 752; and in *Contrat* closely follows *De l'Esprit
> des lois* from II, viii, 755

Monteverdi, Claudio Giovanni Antonio (1567–1643), Italian
priest, composer of sacred and secular music, author of three
surviving operas of which the first, *Orfeo*, was staged at
Mantua in 1607. The other two complete operas, *Il ritorno
d'Ulisse in patria* (1641) and *L'incoronazione di Poppea*
(1642), were performed in Venice
> Mazarin fails to get music of accepted in Paris, 520

Montfleury, Antoine Jacob (1639–85), lawyer and dramatist,
son of following, who satirized the Palais-Royal company in
an attack on Molière's *L'Impromptu de Versailles*. He married
Floridor's daughter and supplied the Hôtel de Bourgogne
with farces and comedies intended to rival those of Molière
> continues attack on Molière, 250
> > Donneau de Visé provides rival for *Gentilhomme de
> > Beauce* of, 251
> joins attack on Molière, 518; who parodies title of play by,
> 523

Montfleury, Zacharie Jacob (1600–67), father of above; actor at
Hôtel de Bourgogne known for the obesity, loudness, and
pomposity satirized by Molière in *L'Impromptu de Versailles*,
and author of the formal accusation of incest against Molière,
whom he disliked. Said to have been a fine tragic actor, he created the role of Prusias in Pierre Corneille's *Nicomède* and
was esteemed by Richelieu and Saint-Evremond. He played
the lead in his own tragedy, *La Mort d'Asdrubal*
> Cyrano de Bergerac quarrels with, 191
> rivalry with Molière, 516; and allegation of incest against,
> 517, 518
> plays in Racine, 676, 677

Montglas, Cécile-Elisabeth Hurault de Cheverny, born 1618,
married in 1645, and noted for her long liaison with Bussy.
She is said to have been the only woman he ever loved. She
herself had other liaisons, with the duc d'Elbeuf and the abbé
Bullion, as well as La Tour-Roquelaure, which has raised
questions about her taste
> boisterous conduct of remarked on by the *Muse historique*,
> 837
> > Bussy's liaison with, 106, 839; loan to Bussy by, 106;
> > estrangement from and reconciliation with him, 108;
> > Bussy's desire to entertain with the *Histoire amoureuse*

Montglas, François de Paul de Clermont (1620–75), marquis de,
author of *Mémoires militaires* (1727)
> Bensserade's ballet role for, 58
> one account of 1649 incident in Tuileries in *Mémoires* of,
> 710
> source for Tallemant, 854

Montgolfier brothers, Joseph (1740–1810) and Etienne
(1745–99), inventors of early hot air balloons
> Beaumarchais present at ascents, 42

Montgomery, Gabriel de Lorges, comte de (1530–74), captain
of Scotch guards of Henri II; he accidentally inflicted a fatal
wound with a broken lance above the king's right eye at a
joust during the celebrations in honour of the double marriage
agreed at Cateau-Cambrésis in July 1559. Fighting on the
Protestant side, Montgomery was in 1574 captured in Nor-

Rousseau's cordial relationship with, 747

Montpensier, Anne-Marie-Louise d'Orléans (1627–93), duchesse de, daughter of Gaston d'Orléans and his first wife, Marie de Bourbon-Montpensier, who died giving birth to her. Known as '(la grande) Mademoiselle,' she was active on behalf of Condé during the Fronde and was thereafter based for many years at Saint-Fargeau, finally at 42 marrying in secrecy the comte de Lauzun (1633–1723)

see Chronology 1627

non-literary connections: role in Fronde 711–12; Retz and, 711–12; opens gates of Paris to remnants of Condé's army, 432; exiled to Saint-Fargeau for refusing to marry king of Portugal, 412; marries Lauzun, 413

the *Divers portraits*: the vogue for portraits and the Saint-Fargeau house party, 108; publication of the *Divers portraits*, 108, 361, 383, 411; containing La Rochefoucauld's self-portrait, 433; and Perrault, 590; and relationship of volume to préciosité, 629, 630

literary connections: friendship for Bussy, 106; and his admiration for her, 110; protects Cotin, 413; Segrais in service of, 361; *Mémoires* of a source for Tallemant, 854

Montpensier, Henri de Bourbon (1573–1608), duc de, prince de Dombes, member of the League, and one of the first to submit to Henri IV on his accession

du Vair dedicates *De la constance* to, 266

Montpensier, Louis II de Bourbon (1512–82), duc de, Catholic leader victorious at Jarnac in 1569, although not by his own generalship, and in charge of royalist forces in the west in 1574

Montaigne joins army of, 531

Montreuil, Mathieu de, abbé and secretary of Daniel de Cosnac, the bishop of Valence, then of Aix

publishes in 1653 madrigal to Mme de Sévigné (in which she is named only in 1666), 839

Monvoisin, Catherine Deshayes (executed 1680), Mme, known as 'la Voisin,' implicated in the outbreak of poisoning in 1672, arrested on 12 March 1679 for the crime not of witchcraft, which had been abolished by Colbert in 1672, but for multiple infanticide, multiple abortions (more than 2,000, she thought), and complicity in poisoning. She certainly sold love philtres and lockets purporting to promote potency and bind affections, dabbled in forms of magic, and was associated with the provision of infant corpses for black masses. She was not tortured, presumably out of fear of what she might reveal, and a number of highly placed persons were implicated, and others protected. The scandal certainly reached as far as Mme de Montespan. Mme Monvoisin was strangled before being burned on 22 February 1680. Mme de Sévigné, in spite of some often-quoted passages, was not an eye-witness, but merely went with other grand ladies to watch the tumbril pass. The famous account of the burning was one of the more formal set pieces inserted into the apparently domestic correspondence

arrest of, 252

subject of Thomas Corneille-Donneau de Visé *La Devineresse*, 152

Moore, Edward (1712–57), English playwright

The Gamester of translated by Diderot, 235

Mora, marquis de (1744–74), Spanish officer

Julie de Lespinasse's love for, 2

More, Saint Thomas (1478–1535), Lord Chancellor of England

see Introduction xxxix

theology and spirituality: and theology of grace, 558; and reliance on direct spiritual experience, 579, 656; and discernment of spirits, 665; translates into English Pico's *Twelve Rules*

literary: translates Lucian, 97; Budé writes to, 96; admires Budé's style, 99; and community of property in *Utopia*, 100; use of Budé letter to preface *Utopia*, 100; Rabelais's references to *Utopia*, 659–60; a source for Cyrano de Bergerac, 194

at Field of Cloth of Gold, 98

Moreau, Jacob-Nicolas (1717–1803), Marie-Antoinette's librarian and royal historiographer who took the initiative in amassing an immense number of copies of documents relevant to the history of France. Hostile to the philosophes (q.v.), for whom he coined the derisory term 'cacouacs,' Moreau wrote verse and history, including the 21-volume *Principes de morale publique et du droit public; ou, Discours de l'histoire de France* (1777–89)

attacks d'Alembert, 3, 302

meaning of 'cacouacs', and pamphlet war involving, 234

Voltaire's reaction to the cacouac mémoires

Morel d'Embrun, Jean de (1511–81), seigneur de Grigny, scholar, courtier, and patron who, after travelling in Italy and visiting Erasmus, at whose deathbed he assisted, returned to keep an open house in Paris for French and foreign scholars. He helped first such neo-Latin poets as Macrin, Bourbon, and Buchanan, and then Ronsard and, especially, du Bellay on his return from Rome. The intellectual abilities and personal refinement of his three daughters, Camille, Lucrèce, and Diane, often occasioned comment

du Bellay's dedication to, 257, and feelings for, 258

knows du Vair, 265

and literary activity in Paris, 316

Morellet, André (1727–1819), abbé, contributed theological and metaphysical articles to *L'Encyclopédie* (q.v.), remaining within the group until 1752. He belonged to the circle of Mme Geoffrin, wrote a *Petit écrit* on tolerance, and was renowned for intelligence and wit. A biting anonymous *Préface de la comédie des philosophes* (1760) directed against Palissot landed him in the Bastille for two months, after which Rousseau instigated his release. He was a well-known translator and theoretical economist whose projected *Prospectus d'un nouveau dictionnaire du commerce* was suspended only on account of the Revolution, which he at first supported, but came to detest.

Morellet went to England in 1772, visited Voltaire, and came to know Marmontel. In 1784 he received a pension of 4,000 livres from Louis XVI. In spite of a serious fall in 1815 he produced in 1818 his four-volume *Mélanges de littérature et de philosophie*

Beccaria translated by, 236; Galiani defended by Diderot against, 238; supports project for Voltaire statue, 238; writes for *L'Encyclopédie*, 274; imprisoned for anonymous preface to Palissot play, 568, 609–10

and Chamfort, 127; and Condorcet salon, 156; Grimm meets, 333; received by Mme Helvétius, 607; attends d'Holbach's dinners, 609; niece marries Marmontel, Morellet frequents Mme Geoffrin, 609–10

Moreri, Louis (1643–80), priest and doctor of theology who published his *Grand Dictionnaire historique* in 1674

Racinian tragedy and Jansenist spirituality clearly explore the reactionary possibility that human instinct cannot or should not be relied on. Rousseau raises the question whether the proper exercise of sovereignty must not demand the constant participation of all citizens of the democratic state, perhaps not realizing he had implied that the inalienable sovereignty of the people was at best an impossible dream. There has to be representation, with whatever necessary checks and balances. Descartes thought that he could demonstrate philosophically the path to both virtue and happiness in a way compatible with orthodox Catholicism. This index entry is concerned with a rough categorization of the imaginative and other structures used in authors, movements, and works considered in the main entries to explore the personal and social values generated by the attempt of a whole culture to take an enthusiastic view about the potential of human nature and instinct

> see Introduction xxvii, xxxiv, xxxviii, entry on Querelle des anciens et des modernes, passim, Glossary entry on 'nature,' and index entries on grace, free will, semi-Pelagianism, pagan virtue, ethical ambiguity, and perfectibility

1. Upgrading of instinctive love by recourse to Plotinian context of Ficino's *De amore*: Héroët, 351, 352–54; in Marguerite d'Angoulême, 493; Peletier's development of Ficino's myth, 585; Scève and the Petrarchan tradition, 818; separation and continuity of instinctive affection and spiritual love in Tyard, 864, 865, 867; d'Urfé's return to Ficinian vision after religious wars, 874–75, 876–78

2. Justification of instinctive love by insistence on merit of its object: suggestion in Brantôme, 95; systematic in Pierre Corneille, 159, 171–72, 173, 174; Thomas Corneille and, 179; moral merit foundation for passion in Gomberville, 330–31; merit of object of love in La Calprenède, 394–96; and in Mme de Lafayette, 416; Mairet, types of audience, genres, and treatment of love, 462; Pradon's renewed recourse to Corneille's moral equation, 625; softening in Racine's *Andromaque* of Pyrrhus's demerit, 683; Tyard's development of Ebreo, 863; d'Urfé's dependence on Ficino, 870, 874

3. Continuity between instinctively-based physical and spiritually perfective affection: in Crébillon *père*, 186; rehabilitation of passion culminating in Descartes, 211–12; and Desmarets's mythologization of love, 213, 216; the success of Houdar de la Motte, 357; imaginative thrust of Marivaux, 499, 501; ethical implications of Perrault's position in the Querelle, 597, 599; Prévost challenges reader to condemn passion, 636, 638; instinct leading to virtue in Racan, 672; Rousseau's strong invitation to condone Saint-Preux's passion, 753; instinct as guide to happiness and virtue in Saint-Evremond, 784–85; continuity of human affection and divine love implied by François de Sales, 800–801

4. Refinement of which love is capable, and danger if unrefined: explored at Hôtel de Rambouillet (see entry on *Guirlande de Julie*, passim); and Perrault, 599; and entry on préciosité, passim; and Madeleine de Scudéry, 830–31; see index entry under Petrarchism

5. Virtue determined by force with which will pursues intellectually perceived good: in Charron, 140; and du Vair, 269; and joined to happiness by Descartes, 209, 211–12; in Ebreo and Tyard, 863; in François de Sales, 878, and d'Urfé, 874, 878

mythologization of passion in Donneau de Visé, 251, 253

Duclos's treatment of love, 264; for an exploration of the destructive potential of female passion, see the entry on Racine, passim

for intense, but disguised and often satirically projected exploration of human perfectibility, see entries on Rabelais, passim, and on Rousseau, especially 749

for the theology of human nature, see Glossary entry on nature; Fénelon's concept of nature, 282; see entry on Jansenism, passim; assumptions made by Montaigne, 539; Nicole and concept of redeemed nature, 558; on concept of nature as flawed, see entry on Saint-Cyran, especially 777, and indexed references to Bérulle, Condren, and Gibieuf

Naudé, Gabriel (1600–53), doctor and Mazarin's librarian, who sold his own collection to the minister. One of the 'tétrade' with Diodati, La Mothe le Vayer, and Gassendi; there is no evidence that he held religiously subversive views, as used to be believed

on Charron's *De la sagesse*, 139

association with Gassendi, 322–24

Naugerius (Andrea Navagero) (1483–1527), Italian poet, scholar, historian, and diplomat. His metrical innovations were taken up in Spain

Belleau inspired by *Damon* of, 52

Desportes sonnet derives from, 226

Navarre, Collège de, one of the four colleges of the University of Paris at which the graduate discipline of theology could be studied in the 16th century

skit on Marguerite d'Angoulême at, 112

and Bossuet's involvement in college's dispute with Sorbonne, 79

attended also by Bensserade, 54; Chénier, 142; Condorcet, 155; Guilleragues, 337; Peletier du Mans, 582

Necker, Jacques (1732–1804), Swiss Protestant financier, shrewd reformer as finance minister after Turgot's fall (1776–81, 1778–79, and 1789–90). Father of Mme de Staël

see Chronology 1776, 1781

puts up money for prize given to Chamfort, 126

attacked by Turgot and Condorcet, 155

delicacy of Diderot's relationship with, 239

object of satirical attack, 718; and Rivarol, 719

Necker, Suzanne Curchod (1739–94), Mme, in her Swiss youth sought in marriage by Gibbon, married Swiss banker Jacques Necker in 1765, and welcomed most of the more serious liberal thinkers to her salon, including Marmontel, Dorat, Buffon, Diderot, Grimm, d'Alembert, Galiani, Morellet, and Raynal. Bernardin de Saint-Pierre's *Paul et Virginie* was first read there. She was the mother of Mme de Staël, and retired to Geneva during the Revolution

d'Alembert and salon of, 3

Buffon and, 102

and project for Voltaire statue, 238

Nemours, Charles-Amédée de Savoie (1624–52) duc de, second son of Henri (1572–1632); succeeded to the Nemours title after the death of his elder brother Louis in 1641; and passed it on to his younger brother Henri (1625–59), with whom Charles-Amédée is often confused. Any reference to the duc de Nemours between 1641 and 1652 can only correctly be understood of Charles-Amédée. It was for him that Mme de Longueville deserted La Rochefoucauld, it was he who had the famous liaison with the duchesse de Châtillon, who lost him to and won him back from Mme de Longueville, and finally it was he who fought with Condé during the second Fronde and was killed in the famous duel on 30 July 1652 by his wife's brother, François

of her that before her marriage 'elle estoit précieuse par son air et par sa modestie (she was a précieuse in her bearing and in her modesty),' he was using the word 'précieuse' in the sense it acquired only in 1654

> Bussy's interest in, 108, and remarks on, 110; lists lovers of, 782
>
> and Retz and the future Mme de Lafayette, 408, 711
>
> one of the original précieuses, 628, 630; La Bruyère's Messaline, 782
>
> Saint-Evremond's essay on, 782

Olonne, Louis de la Trémouille (1626–86), comte d', married to Catherine-Henriette d'Angennes de la Louppe (above)

> marriage of on 1 March 1652, 782
>
> Racine's quatrain on infidelities of, 678

ontological order, or order of being, frequently confused in major religious texts with the psychological order, or order of experience. For scholastic theology, justification is a grace-elevated state which, if obtaining at the moment of death, entitles the individual soul to salvation, a state of fully satisfying never-ending joy. It is not on earth an empirically verifiable psychological experience, although sometimes the vocabulary used suggests that it might be. Jansenist theologians sometimes regarded what Augustine had termed the 'victorious delectation' of grace, or alternatively of sin, as belonging to the realm of experience. In a similar way, the French word 'amour-propre' could in the 17th century refer either to a state of non-justification, if used as Augustine had used the Latin 'amor sui,' in which case its presence was not empirically verifiable, as it was not for Nicole, or it could simply refer to the psychological motive of self-interest, not at all necessarily sinful. The arguments about the possibility of a disinterested love of God in which Fénelon and Malebranche were concerned were caught up in the same sort of confusion between ontological and psychological orders

> distinction fundamental to Fénelon-Bossuet dispute, 282, 291
>
> ambiguity built into condemnation of Fénelon, 285–90
>
> and Jansenist dispute, 366, 775

ontological argument: for existence of God

> in Descartes, 210–11

opera

> see index entry on Pierre Perrin
>
> dispute about French and Italian styles in, 232
>
> opera buffa and comédie-ballet, 520; and Paris dispute on 1752 visit of Bambini's opera buffa company, 745
>
> graded difference between tragedy and, 648
>
> creation of comic opera, 832–33

Oppian, Greek poet of the late second century A.D.

> translated by Bodin, 66

oracles: whether or why they ceased on the birth of Christ was the subject of a lively debate with serious religious implications. Attitudes on the subject could for instance serve as a guide to scepticism about prophecies in scripture, and therefore about scriptural inspiration

> Fontenelle and van Dale on, 297–98
>
> and Cyrano de Bergerac, 192

Orbay, François d' (1631–97), architect who collaborated closely with Le Vau, and whose part in Le Vau's later designs, greater than used to be thought, is disputed

> and the east colonnade of the Louvre, 594

orient: France's literary culture reflected and stimulated interest in the exoticism and commercial importance for France of the east, directed at first chiefly towards the accessible eastern Mediterranean, with Turkey of special importance during the 17th century, then much further east with Raynal and Montesquieu in the 18th

> plays with Turkish backgrounds, 622; background works relevant to Montesquieu's *Lettres persanes*, 548; see also Racine's *Bajazet*, 678–79

Origen, early third century Greek Father of the Church, immensely influential in later centuries. His theology, essentially, gives a Christian interpretation to stoic and neoplatonist forms of antique culture centring on the spirituality, eternity, and immutability of God and all spiritual essences. For the early 16th century his view entailed the ultimate restoration of all things in God, the freedom of the will, and the non-eternity of hell. A serious effort was made, at least not obstructed by Erasmus, to replace the authority of the pessimistic Augustine of the late anti-Pelagian works with the buoyant optimism of Origen's Christianity

> see Introduction xl and index entry on Merlin
>
> attacked by Calvin on free will, 119

Orléans, Charles d' (1522–45), third son of François I and, after the death of François the dauphin in 1536, his father's favourite son. He was firmly of the party of the king's sister and his mistress, Marguerite d'Angoulême and Anne d'Heilly, and opposed to that of the connétable, Montmorency, to whom his brother, the future Henri II, was attached. The rivalry between the brothers made each the focus of a political faction. The king's foreign policy was partly aimed at retaining Milan for Charles

> see Chronology 1545

Orléans, Gaston (1608–60) d'Anjou, then duc d' (1626), son of Henri IV and Marie de Medici, brother of Louis XIII and, from the death of his brother Philippe duc d'Orléans (1607–11) until 1638, heir presumptive to the throne of France. Married Marie de Bourbon-Montpensier, princesse des Dombes, on 6 August 1626, was widowed when his wife died giving birth to her first child, and secretly married Marguerite, younger sister of Charles, duc de Lorraine, in 1632

> see Chronology 1610, 1622, 1626, 1631, 1632, 1642, 1651, 1652, 1660
>
> see Introduction xlii and Preface xlv
>
> political: rebellion after Day of Dupes, 215; Mairet's allusion to marriage of, 460, 465; intrigues against Richelieu, 707; effective dissolution of marriage to princesse de Lorraine, 215; wins dispute with Retz about precedence, 709; crisis meeting with Mazarin and Anne of Austria 26 August 1648, 707; role in Fronde, 707–12; 1652 exile of, 839
>
> literary: protected Balzac, 25; Boileau's brother, Pierre de Puymorin, in household of, 71; entertainment given for by Richelieu, 214; Desmarets loosely connected with circle of, 215; present at private performance of *Sophonisbe*, 462; titular patron of Molière's Illustre Théâtre, 515; and of his Paris company, 516; three-act *Tartuffe* played for on 25 September 1664, 519; protector of Scarron, 819; Tristan taken into service of, 857; employs Voiture, 890

Orléans, Philippe II (1640–1701), duc d', brother of Louis XIV, also known as 'Monsieur,' married Henriette d'Angleterre and then Charlotte-Elisabeth de Bavière, the princess palatine see Chronology 1638

invites Mme de Lafayette to lunch, 411

attends first night of unknown Racine's *Alexandre le Grand*, 676

Orléans, Philippe III (1674–1723), duc d', son of Philippe II; regent during minority of Louis XV

see Chronology 1661, 1715, 1717, 1722, 1723

friend of Saint-Simon, 786, 788

favourable to Fénelon, 285; lodged Fontenelle, 296; intervenes on behalf of Lesage, 455; and Voltaire, 895

Orléans, Louis-Philippe-Joseph (1747–93), duc d', known as Philippe-Egalité, strong adherent of the Revolution who voted for the death penalty for his cousin, Louis XVI, and was himself guillotined

Laclos and party of, 399–401

Ormesson, Olivier III Lefèvre d' (1616–86), lawyer, diarist, joint president of Foucquet enquiry in 1662, and brother of Marie de Coulanges, wife of Philippe, the uncle and guardian of the future Mme de Sévigné. It was Ormesson's increasing awareness of the irregularities in Colbert's preparation of the case against Foucquet that saved Foucquet's life, if only at the cost of Ormesson's own later career

association with Hôtel de Lamoignon, 289

and marriage of future Mme de Sévigné, 836

Ormesson, Marie Lefèvre d' (1595–1654), wife of Philippe II de Coulanges; took the orphaned future Mme de Sévigné into her own family, and brought her up with her own children. She had married in 1626, and had five children. She died on 5 July 1654

wife of Philippe II de Coulanges, 835

Ornano, Jean-Baptiste (1581–1626), governor of the future Gaston d'Orléans (1619), maréchal (1620), sent to the Bastille in 1624 for disrespectful letter of protest to the king, exiled, allowed to return, but opposed Richelieu's intention to marry Gaston to the princesse de Montpensier. Louis XIII called for him, and had him arrested at Fontainebleau on 4 May 1626 and consigned to the dungeon at Vincennes. He died on 2 September, one of its early victims. The cause of death was 'retention of urine, dysentery, and fever'

and the Vincennes dungeon, 775

Pace, Richard (c1483–1536), impressed Thomas Langton, bishop of Winchester, by his musical ability, and was enabled by him to study in Italy, where he was to be found in Padua, Bologna, and then Ferrara. Pace entered the service of Cardinal Bainbridge, Henry VIII's representative in Rome until he died in 1514, when Pace transferred to Wolsey's service. He was in England again in the service of Henry VIII from 1517 to 1519, when he succeeded Colet as dean of Saint Paul's. He was at the Field of the Cloth of Gold

Budé's correspondence with, 100

Paets, Adriaan van, (died 1686), Dutch ambassador to London

Bayle and, 31–32; Jurieu and, 31

pagans, salvation of: one of the crucial subjects in the history of western Christian theology. Any assertion that pagans might be saved appeared to put into question the mediating role of membership of the church in the bestowal of grace, while any denial appeared to imply that God created some individuals who would never be offered the possibility of salvation and who must therefore be condemned to perpetual suffering through no individual choice of their own. If pagans could be

saved, there would be little point in the church's immense missionary activity, or in the definition and enforcement of a tight intellectual orthodoxy, while the obstacle to reconciling true freedom of the will with the gratuity of grace would also be removed. If the bestowal of justifying grace was not dependent on orthodox belief, then nature itself could be regarded as redeemed, and therefore capable of accepting proffered grace without semi-Pelagian implications.

The western church in the wake of Augustine and, especially, Fulgentius certainly believed that heterodoxy of belief blocked the bestowal of justifying grace, and the matter appeared to be settled by the famous 1302 bull *Unam sanctam* defining that there was no salvation outside the church. None the less the reaction against late medieval nominalism represented by such figures as Erasmus and Lefèvre d'Etaples notoriously edged towards acceptance of authentic pagan virtue. The question was at the heart of the religious life of the 16th and 17th centuries, and was pin-pointed in the Jesuit-Jansenist debate. La Mothe le Vayer's *De la vertu des païens* was written at Richelieu's instigation

see Introduction xl, main entry on Jansenism, passim, Glossary entry on nature, and index entries on freedom of the will, grace, theology of, perfectibility, and semi-Pelagianism

historical importance of debate, 365–66, 368, 558

dilemma resulting from disbelief in pagan virtue, 435

salvation of pagans admitted by Lefèvre d'Etaples, 452, denied, then affirmed, by Marguerite d'Angoulême, 490

implications about in Montaigne, 539; and Montesquieu, 548; and the problem of extrinsic perfectibility, 654; and François de Sales, 802

Saint-Cyran's exultation in damnation of pagans; and view of purpose of Christ's death

Paine, Thomas (1737–1809), English writer on jurisprudence who went to America in 1774, returning to Europe in 1787. He published *The Rights of Man* (1791–2), defending the French Revolution in answer to Burke. He was declared an outlaw, took refuge in France, and was nearly executed. He returned to America in 1802

view derived from that of Montesquieu, 551

Paisiello, Giovanni (1740–1816), Italian composer

turned Beaumarchais's *Barbier* into an opera in 1782, 43

Palaprat, Jean de Bigot (1650–1721), author of witty light-hearted plays for the Italian company

exploited popular taste in stage entertainment, 455

Palatine, Princess (Anne de Gonzague de Clèves, known as) (1616–84), younger daughter of duc de Nevers, destined for a convent. Henri de Guise, cardinal archbishop of Reims, fell in love with and secretly married her, probably in 1639. Hostile to Richelieu, Guise, head of the family in 1640, allied himself with Soissons and Bouillon, and went to Holland. The princess, in male attire, followed in 1641, but was stopped at the frontier. She learnt that her husband had married elsewhere and in 1645 she herself married the duke of Bavaria, prince palatine

favoured Bensserade in quarrel of the sonnets, 56

supports Retz, 710

Palissot de Montenoy, Charles (1730–1814)

Life, 567–68; Works, 568–70; Publications, 570

d'Alembert alleges to Voltaire Mme du Deffand's support for *Les Philosophes*, 2; replies with lampoon to d'Alem-

fessor of theology, moved into schism and went to Zürich. He had a bitter dispute with Erasmus

Amy stays with in Basle, 654

Pellisson, Paul (1624–93), who replaced Conrart as the 'tendre ami' of Madeleine de Scudéry; friend of La Fontaine, trusted adviser of Foucquet, his principal private agent and the administrator of his patronage; and the author of galant verse. He had organized what Foucquet had hoped would if necessary be his safe withdrawal to the west coast as, in spite of the magnificent celebrations at Vaux on 17 August 1661, Colbert's hostility intensified. The death of Mazarin had freed it from constraint. Pellisson was himself arrested with Foucquet at Nantes on 5 September 1661, imprisoned in one of the towers of the château, and moved to the Bastille, where he continued to defend Foucquet in two *Discours au roi* when he was allowed pen and ink. He was released in January 1666; made royal historiographer early in 1670, he abjured Protestantism that October, and was rewarded with a post of maître des requêtes.

Pellisson had been part of the circle of Maucroix and Furetière before returning to the south in 1648. He was deformed by smallpox in 1650, established himself again in Paris, purchased in 1652 the office of sécretaire du roi, which he filled with distinction, and seriously committed himself to the role of frustrated galant in which Madeleine de Scudéry finally consented to cast him. His critical *Histoire de l'Académie française* (1653) in letter form made him some enemies, but so pleased the Académie that Pellisson became the only member in its history to be elected to it when no chair was vacant. In 1656 he composed an important preface to Sarrazin's verse. On entering Foucquet's service in 1657, he committed himself to the aesthetic as well as the political values to which Chapelain, now securing his position as Colbert's cultural lieutenant, was opposed. He had effectively joined the ranks of the protagonists of the modernes, leaving behind Gilles Boileau, Cotin, and Furetière

> votes for Bensserade's election to Académie française, 56; early career of, 828; intimate friendship with Scarron, 811; subject of Boileau's quip, 71, 828; attends Bossuet's study group at Versailles, 82; initially blocks Académie election of Gilles Boileau and breaks with Chapelain and Conrart, 133, 591; link with Foucquet established, and alignment with moderne party, 133; Chapelain's subsequent favourable assessment of, 218; Pierre Corneille meets Foucquet through, 164; source for list of Conrart's circle, 215; records existence of last Desmarets comedy, 216

> see 301–309 for changes of literary alignment involving Pellisson's relationship with Patru, Furetière, the Marolles circle, Ménage, Gilles Boileau; and Ménage, 361; and Table Ronde, 421, 854; introduces La Fontaine to Foucquet; relationship with Habert de Montmort circle, 645; and Lamoignon circle, 646; alienation of Pierre Corneille and Sorel, 828

> Madeleine de Scudéry and, 629, and 20 December 1653 exchange of madrigals, 828; and préciosité (q.v.), 629; disliked by Georges de Scudéry, 827

> contributes to Molière's *Les Fâcheux* at Vaux on 17 August 1661, 517; arrest with Foucquet, 422; in charge of projected defences on Belle-Isle to protect Foucquet if arrested, 780; historiographer, converted to Catholicism,

dedicates himself to promoting conversions, 595; death of, and Fénelon's discourse of reception into Académie française, 291

penal code: official enforcement was cruel, but precisely regulated, and penalties were generally lighter and fewer than the code allowed for, except for such crimes as attempts on royal lives. Investigations were in secret; the accused were confronted by witnesses only after depositions had been taken which they could not without penalty change. In the 18th century the death penalty was execution by hanging or, for nobles, beheading; for crimes of violence it was breaking on the wheel; for poisoning, sodomy, and sacrilege, it was burning. Torture was used to extract an avowal of guilt ('la question préparatoire'), or the names of accomplices ('la question préalable'), and both could be 'ordinaire' or 'extraordinaire,' with very precise regulations for each, stipulating the angles of wedges, amounts of water, and its temperature, the height of trestles and the tightness of ropes. In practice there was usually a reasonable effort to fit the penalty to the crime. About a third of the 23,000 convicts in 1660 had been sentenced for failure to pay tax. The branding of those sentenced to the galleys was discontinued only when it was understood how it affected subsequent performance at the oars.

Death sentences were more freely passed when the condemned had fled, and they could be executed only in effigy, but the general ferocity of sentencing reflected more the inadequacy of policing than social vindictiveness. There were for instance only 70 gendarmes in Bordeaux for a population of perhaps 45,000 by 1650. The public often refused to testify. Evidence was invariably withheld to shield military deserters, of whom there were thousands, and for whom the death penalties seemed so harsh that even the authorities often executed only one in three, unless they had formed marauding bands of brigands.

Diderot thought that there were 300 executions a year in France. In theory absolute physical certainty of guilt was required, and the judges generally added a 'retentum' to the arrêt, revealed only to the executioner, stipulating after how many blows, or minutes, the condemned was to be strangled before a burning or a breaking on the wheel. As early as the 16th century most of those condemned to burning were strangled first. Executions, like floggings, were public, and could attract crowds of thousands. Doctors had to be present, with the power to bleed to death, and every detail of the ritual was specified in minute detail. Very often the issue of letters of remission after condemnation was automatic although, before 1788, the penalty was normally inflicted on the day of sentencing. In 1665, out of 347 death sentences pronounced at the Grands Jours of Auvergne, 324 were executed in effigy

> on the imposition of sanctions to enforce authority, see especially 304–305 and 886–87 as well as the entry on Sade, passim

pénitents bleus, pious association of lay persons

> Fénelon's family belong to, 278

Pepys, Samuel (1633–1703), English diarist

> reads Bussy's *Histoire amoureuse des Gaules*, 108

Péréfixe, Hardouin de Beaumont de (1605–70), bishop of Rodez, then archbishop of Paris, tutor of Louis XIV

> Bossuet made personal assistant to, 80

> forbids readings of 'Panulphe,' attenuated version of *Tartuffe*, 520

gained control of secular power. His wife had earlier been arrested for dancing, and Perrin's party was to lose power altogether when in 1557 Berne and Geneva united against Savoy. As a political opponent of Calvin, Perrin was condemned to death when, in 1555, Calvin consolidated his political victory

    and the political struggle in Geneva, 115–16

Perrin, Pierre (c1620–75), a former protégé of Montauzier, obtained on 28 June 1669 a privilège for an Académie d'opéras. In association with the composer Cambert (c1628–77), Perrin staged *Pomone* on 3 March 1671, and then seems to have gone to prison for debt. A new association with two rivals who had put on a court pastoral appears to have been formed but not yet to have become active when, prompted by Colbert, Lulli acquired the privilège from Perrin in prison. It was that privilège which enabled Lulli to obtain the letters patent on 13 March 1672 creating his celebrated monopoly. Molière's opposition, signified on 29 March, made Colbert hesitate, but the king stepped in, Perrin's new hall was closed, and Lulli opened a new jeu-de-paume decorated by Vigarani. It was after the Quinault-Lulli-Vigarani *Cadmus et Hermione*, played before the king on 27 April 1673, that Lulli was given the Palais-Royal. All other companies were in principle limited to two singers and six violins

    signs the *Bastonnade* against Boileau, 72

    conditions in which monopoly privilège passed to Lulli, 520

Petau, Denys (1583–1652), Jesuit classical scholar, anti-Jansenist controversialist and theologian,

    Huet in contact with, 360

Peter of Spain, later pope John XXI, medieval dialectician of vast importance

    Summulae logicales of, 450

Petit (Parvy), Guillaume (c1470–1536), Dominican inquisitor-general in France, king's confessor from 1509 and from accession of François I also royal librarian at Blois, overseeing the publication of numerous manuscripts. At least 21 dedicatory epistles were addressed to him. His influence was conservative but not reactionary in the religious disputes which came to centre on Lutheranism. He denounced Michel d'Arande, discouraged attempts to censure Luther and Erasmus, and was used by both sides in disputes between the king and the theology faculty

    attempts to get François I to found a tri-lingual college, 98

    Lefèvre d'Etaples dedicates anti-Muslim works to, 446

    publishes Sebond's *Theologia naturalis*, 446

    favours Lefèvre's view of scripture, 447

    denounces Michel d'Arande, and backs down, 484

Petit-Bourbon, hall known on account of its use by Molière until the 1660 demolition. It was the hall of the Paris palace of the Montmorencys, with a stage at one end, and had long been used for court ballets. The Gelosi had performed there in 1577. In 1647 Torelli was invited by Mazarin to oversee the production there of *Orphée*, and in 1658 Molière's troupe was given the extraordinary days, with the Italians under Fiorillo playing on the ordinary days. On its demolition, Molière had the seating and boxes moved to the Palais-Royal, but Vigarani, court architect and scene-painter, claimed Torelli's machinery and scenery for his new Salle des Machines, and burnt it out of jealousy

    demolition of, and Molière's move, 516–17

petits-maîtres, name given to swaggering, often arrogant and loudly behaved young nobles associated with the early entourage of the grand Condé. They were regarded as a social pest, and were a recurrent subject of annoyance, parody, and satirical attack

    Marivaux satirizes, 497

    Tallemant in company of, 853

petites écoles of Port-Royal: the term is used in the sense of 'junior classes'

    see index entry on Pelletier Destouches

    organization of, 556

Petrarch (Francesco Petrarca) (1304–74), Italian poet, moralist, and scholar

    Budé and the theme of contempt for the world in, 100

    drawn on directly by Desportes, 223; du Bellay, 256, 259–61; and Marot, 504, 508, 509

    at beginning of movement to upgrade instinctive love, 351; *Trionfi* of represented in tapestry, 482; and Griselda figure, 601; translated by Peletier, 585

    Ronsard moves away from 729

    Scève and what he took for Laura's tomb, 815; allusions to Petrarch in *Délie*, 818–19

Petrarchism: name given to a poetic tradition sometimes only distantly related to Petrarch, relying on refined but stylized conceits to express emotions, particularly love, and including a repertoire of images and devices often employed by court poets, and by those hired to sing the loves of social superiors who commissioned or employed them

    see entry on Desportes, passim

    examples in d'Aubigné, 11; and du Bellay, 255, 257; cultural importance of in du Bellay, 259–60; and renunciation of by du Bellay, 261; cultivation of by Marot, 504; in Peletier, 586; and in Scève, 815

    inadequacy of the Petrarchan tradition, 354

Pfefferkorn, Johannes, the converted Jew, friend of the Cologne Dominicans, who in writings between 1507 and 1509 violently called for the suppression of the Talmud (*Mischna* and *Guemara*), elaborated from the second to the fifth centuries, and the 13th-century *Cabala*, whose anti-Christian inspiration he thought was preventing the conversion of the Jews. The doctrine of the *Cabala* had been expounded by the highly distinguished Hebraist Reuchlin in his *De verbo mirifico*

    hostility to of Lefèvre d'Etaples, 447

Phaedrus, Roman fabulist of first century A.D.

    vogue for fables of, 424; school edition by Le Maître de Saci, 424

    La Fontaine's reliance on, 428

Pharès, Simon de, son of the astrologer of Charles VIII, was condemned by the Paris theology faculty for divinatory astrology in February 1494

    Lefèvre d'Etaples and, 444

Philidor, François-André Danican (1726–95), prolific composer, famous for his skill at chess. His half-brother, Anne Philidor (1681–1728) had founded the 'concert spirituel' in Paris in 1725, for the public performance of music other than that written for church or stage

    early composer of works for opéra comique, 832

Philip II (1527–98), king of Spain, married to Elisabeth de Valois, daughter of Catherine de Medici and Henri II

    see Chronology 1555–56, 1559

population: probably approaching 20,000,000 in early 14th-century France, it must have fallen back to not much more than half that figure in the second quarter of the 15th century. It climbed again between 1450 and the outbreak of the religious wars soon after 1560. The figure faltered during the wars, but may have reached 19,000,000 by 1600.

Estimates suggest that Paris in 1600 had a population of some 200,000, rising to 500,000 sometime between 1660 and 1700. Marseilles and Lyons may have increased to 100,000 at the same date, followed by Rouen, which may have reached 80,000. The only other towns with 40,000 inhabitants in the late 17th century were Rennes, Nantes, Toulouse, Orléans, and Bordeaux (45,000?), with less than 20% of the population living in towns, and only 2% in Paris. Infant mortality was high, but the average 10-year-old could expect to reach 40.

Between 1700 and 1790 the population appears to have risen from just above 20,000,000 to just below 30,000,000, with fewer than 20% living in towns of 2,000 people or more, as against 10% in the late middle ages. The rough and vari-

ances with the power centres, the other two involving the Epernon and the Grammont families. It looked as if there was no height to which Puylaurens could not now aspire. He had however made himself dispensable. He was arrested on 14 February 1635, confined to the infamous dungeon at Vincennes, so damp that, as Tallemant tells us, saltpetre formed in it, and died of the predictable infection on 30 June 1635, 'ex fluxu dyssenteretico et atrabiliario,' dropsy, and continuous fever, as Guy Patin wrote on 4 July

> wedding of, 214
>
> Mairet's *Sophonisbe* played privately for, 462

Pyrrho(nism): see suspension of judgement

Pythagoras, philosopher and mathematician of sixth century B.C. important for French educational reform of 16th century. He held that the spirit was purified by study, turned the investigation of nature into a religious activity, regarded the soul as imprisoned in the body and condemned to a cycle of reincarnation, and discovered the numerical ratios determining the principal musical intervals. The universe was governed by mathematical proportions, which ruled even moral qualities. The movements of the heavenly bodies generated a harmony of the spheres, formed from sounds which accorded on account of the numerical ratios governing their orbits. The earth and the universe, a product of the infinite and the void, were spherical

> Bardi's *Discorso* and, 18

Quatre Nations, Collège des, founded by Mazarin in 1661 for the instruction of 60 nobles from different countries. The college, which eventually established a reputation for Jansenism, inherited Mazarin's books. It was suppressed at the Revolution. The building, by Le Vau, with the library, now belongs to the Institut de France

> d'Alembert sent to, 1

Querelle des amyes, the specific agglomeration of poems both continuing and challenging the traditional medieval anti-feminist satire in the light of Castiglione's *Il libro del Cortegiano* (original Italian edition, 1528); this widened into the much more general controversy, about the status of women in society and the moral qualities attaching to the different sorts of love, usually known as the Querelle des femmes. In the narrow debate, not without affectation on both sides, Antonio de Guevara's paradoxical but austere *Mespris de la cour* (*El menosprecio del corte*), to be translated by Alaigre in 1543, was brought forward against Castiglione's manual of courtly behaviour for the French, available only in Italian until the 1537 translation by Jacques Colin d'Auxerre (died 1547).

As early as 1537 Almanque Papillon had issued his *Victoire et triumphe d'Argent contre Cupido Dieu d'Amours*, to which Charles Fontaine had replied in the same volume with a 'débat' ending with a judicial decision. Then in 1542 Bertrand de la Borderie took the anti-feminist stance in his *Amye de Court*, put into the mouth of a woman boasting of the lucrative seductive powers which she could exercise without compromising herself morally. This provoked a *Contr'Amye de Court* from Fontaine, attacking both Castiglione and La Borderie, as well as Héroët's *La parfaicte amye*, whose spokeswoman does not belong to the court, and for whom the highest love is not an aristocratic privilege, but a perfective human bond. Fontaine was directly inspired by Plato, and

strongly urges that love is the 'fruition de la beauté (enjoyment of beauty).'

The narrower Querelle des amyes culminates in the collective volume of 1547, *Opuscules d'amour*, in which there are further pieces by Papillon, Paul Angier, and La Borderie after contributions to the half-playful game by Antoine du Moulin, who in 1545 published a satire on Héroët, *L'Amante loyalle qui depuis a esté variable*, Gilles d'Aurigny, whose *Tuteur d'Amour* dates from 1546, the *Compte du rossignol* of 1547, probably by Gilles Corrozet, and François Habert's *Nouvelle Vénus* of the same year.

> For the wider Querelle des Femmes, see the main entries on Marguerite d'Angoulême and Rabelais
>
> see Introduction xl, and the indexed references under Fontaine and Bertrand de la Borderie
>
> see entry on Héroët, passim (especially 351)

Querelle des anciens et des modernes, 644–53

> build-up to: opposing groups develop, 28; career of Bensserade and, 55–59; and Fontenelle on Bossuet's Versailles group, 82; Cartesianism, Malebranche, and, 122; Chapelain and, 132; entourage of Foucquet and, 133; Querelle du *Cid* precursor of, 158, 162, 164; severity of public taste round 1660 prepares for, 167; and Pierre Corneille and baroque, 167; Descartes's position with respect to, 208; Hôtel de Rambouillet and, 307, 343, 889, 891; quarrel over Académie election of Gilles Boileau and, 309; Boursault's rallying of the modernes, 310; partisans of moderne and Foucquet's entourage, 361; Molière, préciosité and, 517; alignments about 1660, 590; relevance of préciosité to, 627; and attitudes to authority, 644
>
> climax of, 1670–94: relevance of issue of Bensserade's nobility, 54; see entry on Boileau, passim; arguments of modernes taken over by Protestants, 83; see entry on Thomas Corneille, passim; Desmarets on moderne side, 213, 217–18, 219; events of August 1674 and, 218; see entry on Donneau de Visé, passim; Huet's efforts at mediation, 360; and Huet Académie reception, 361, and Huet's position, 361, 417; and La Bruyère's *Les Caractères*, 384, 387; La Bruyère's Académie election and all 1691–93 elections; see also Fontenelle and Mercure, 385; Mme de Lafayette on, 410–12; non-alignment of La Fontaine in, 422, and his 1674 letter to Huet, released 1687, 425; further definition of alignments, 425; and *Mercure Galant* supporting modernes, 513; see entry on Perrault, passim; the Perrault Académie interventions 1687–88, 595; dispute over language for Porte-Saint-Antoine arch, 647; society support for modernes, Soissons, Nevers, Bouillon, Richelieu, 679; role of Montauzier, 680; see entries on Pradon and Racine, passim
>
> later episodes: see entry on Houdar de la Motte, passim; position of Fénelon, 289, 291, 356; and Fontenelle, 293, 295, the *Digression*, 298; Fréron's sympathies with anciens, 306; victory of modernes apparent by 1700, 186; supporters of the modernes and Italian theatre, 355; Mme Dacier and, 356; Marivaux and the moderne position, 495, 499; and Regnard, 688; and Saint-Evremond, 781
>
> fundamental issues, 578, 649, 650

Querelle du *Cid*: the issues and attitudes of those principally involved in the debate to which Pierre Corneille's *Le Cid* gave rise are in clear need of reassessment, as the main entries on Pierre Corneille, Jean de Mairet, and Georges de Scudéry make clear. In addition the usage of the terms 'tragédie' and 'tragi-comédie' in the dispute, and the successive changes made to his text by Corneille suggest that the history of French drama, and indeed French cultural history generally in the first half of the 17th century, require re-appraisal, a view confirmed notably by the *Guide*'s main entries on Descartes, Cartesianism, François de Sales, and d'Urfé, but also by several others

In 1660 he had married Louise Goujon, a rich widow with whom he had been in love before her marriage to the merchant Jacques Bonnet, and bought the office of valet de chambre ordinaire to the king. The court commissioned a pastoral allegory commemorating the peace of the Pyrenees and the king's marriage, *Les Amours de Lysis et d'Hespérie*, played in November 1660. In 1661 he was given a 3,000-livre present, and, with Floridor, the Paris-Cahors parcels monopoly. By 1670 his successful dramatic production also included the tragedy *La Mort de Cyrus* (1656), the tragi-comedy *Amalasonte*, (produced 1657 and dedicated to Mazarin), *Stratonice*, played at the Hôtel de Bourgogne on 2 January 1660, the tragedy *Agrippa, roi d'Albe; ou, Le Faux Tibérinus*, dedicated to Louis XIV and played late in 1662, and the tragedy *Pausanias* played on 11 November 1668. Like Racine, he was not committed to a career as a dramatist. By the date of his Académie reception in 1670, he was already thinking of abandoning the theatre, and would no doubt have done so when in 1671, soon after his tragedy *Bellérophon* had been successfully staged, he at length achieved his ambition of becoming an auditeur at the chambre des comptes. It may have been the king himself who pressed him to cooperate with Lulli.

Quinault had already worked with Pierre Corneille and Molière on the 1671 *Psyché*, given on 17 January, the anniversary of Bensserade's 1656 *Ballet royal de Psyché*, and taking up again the theme from La Fontaine's 1669 *Amours de Psyché et de Cupidon*. *Psyché* was first performed in the Salle des Machines reopened on 7 February 1662 with the *Ercole amante* of Buti and Cavalli, whose celebrated decor by Vigarani the new *Psyché* was to re-utilize, the hall in between having been used only for Molière's 1668 *Amphitryon*.

The collaboration with Lulli, who was the dominant partner and paid Quinault 4,000 livres a year, was not easy. Quinault had a relatively free hand with the dialogues, but was sometimes made to rewrite the divertissements a score of times. In 1674 there was a four-month break when Lulli abandoned Quinault for La Fontaine after the half-failure of the *Alceste* mauled by Racine in the *Iphigénie* preface, and in 1677 Quinault had made an allusion in *Isis* to the persecution of Mlle de Ludre, with whom the king had had a liaison, by Mme de Montespan, who had made him break it off. Mme de Montespan forced Lulli to exchange Quinault for Thomas Corneille, who wrote the 1678 *Psyché*, but the king, beginning to tire of Mme de Montespan, brought back Quinault three years later, and he now allowed himself more openly satirical allusions to Mme de Montespan, who had even made Racine and Boileau cooperate with Thomas Corneille on the 1679 *Bellérophon*, so deeply were they in her debt.

Quinault's dramatic works filled the Hôtel de Bourgogne, and his tragédies lyriques with Lulli pleased the court. Chapelain, Boileau, Scarron, and Somaize were severe, but after the *Fêtes de l'Amour et de Bacchus*, played on 11 November 1672, and the brilliantly successful *Cadmus et Hermione* of 27 April 1673, Quinault wrote the libretti for four more tragédies lyriques to Lulli's music at the Palais-Royal before 1677, *Alceste* (19 January 1674), *Thésée* (12 January 1675), *Atys* (10 January 1676), and *Isis* (5 January 1677). After the renewal of the partnership with Lulli came *Proserpine* on 3 February 1680, *Le Triomphe de l'Amour* of 21 January 1681, a simple ballet with assistance from Bensserade, *Persée et Andromède* on 18 April 1682, *Phaéton* for Versailles on 9

Pièces de clavecin was influenced by Couperin and the 1722 *Traité de l'harmonie* became a standard work, emphasizing the importance of key centres, of a fundamental bass, and of the roots and inversions of chords, so establishing the elements of modern harmony. His overtures go beyond Lulli's innovations to set the musical context for the following act or entrée, and he gave much less importance than hitherto to long set-piece arias, using shorter 'petits airs (short tunes)' to break up the recitatives.

In 1726 he published the *Nouveau système de musique théorique*, and in 1733 had his first great theatrical success with *Hippolyte et Aricie*. As a composer of opera he was often dissatisfied with his librettists, of whom the principal was Louis de Cahusac (1706–59), who was successful with his own tragedy *Pharamond* (1736) and comedy *Zénéide* (1742), neither of them published, although Rameau also set Bernard's *Castor et Pollux* (1737) and two texts of Voltaire, *Les Fêtes de Ramire* and *La Princesse de Navarre*. He was given a pension by Louis XV, was strongly opposed by Rousseau, and was at the centre of the disputes which pitted French music, centring on harmony and suitable for tragedy, against the more fluently melodic and lighter Italian style.

Of about 25 stage works Rameau's greatest operatic successes included *Dardanus* (1739) with a libretto by Le Clerc de la Bruyère, the opera-ballet *Les Indes galantes* (1735), satisfying the fashion for exoticism, unrequited love, and noble savages, *Les Fêtes d Hébé* (1739), *Le Temple de la gloire* with libretto by Voltaire (1745), and the ballet-bouffon *Platée* (1745), whose revival in 1754 marked the triumph of the French style over the Italian intermezzo. In 1741 Rameau published another book of *Pièces de clavecin* which contained trio sonatas with combinations for different instruments, and in 1750 a *Démonstration du principe de l'harmonie*. In 1749 he presented the successful *Zoroastre* with libretto by Cahusac

    Rousseau, Diderot, Grimm, and dispute with: Diderot popularizes theories of, 230; irritated by Rousseau's *Encyclopédie* articles, 232; annoyance of Diderot with, 232, contrasted with Lulli by Diderot, 242; treatment of in pamphlet by Grimm, 333, and in quarrel about Italian music, 333; Rousseau studies harmony of, 741, displeased when La Popelinière shows favour to Rousseau, 743; Rousseau invited to adapt music of, 743; Rousseau's attack on, and sharply hostile counter-attack by, 745

    d'Alembert develops musical theory of, 3; attends dîners du Caveau, 182; partisans of in opera, 232; Fréron's nationalistic preference for, 305

Ramus: see La Ramée, Pierre de

Rancé, Armand-Jean le Bouthillier de (1626–1700), reforming abbot of the Cistercian abbey of La Trappe and the author of an unmitigatedly penitential spirituality which he defended in a series of mostly non-literary controversies. Both parents came from families belonging to the magistracy, and Rancé's first name came from his godfather, Richelieu. Destined for an ecclesiastical career on the death of his elder brother, and tonsured in 1635, Rancé held five family benefices by the time he was 12. The Greek commentary on Anacreon presented to Richelieu in 1637 over his name cannot have been his own work. His mother died in 1638; brought up by private tutors, he graduated from the

Collège d'Harcourt in 1643, and became the lover of the duchesse de Montbazon (?1612–57), whose husband was 44 years older than she was and who was mistress successively to the ducs de Longueville and de Beaufort. Rancé contracted a passion for horsemanship and hunting. He lost his father in 1650, was ordained in 1651, became a noted preacher and doctor of theology, was a delegate to the 1655 Assemblée du clergé, and loyally supported Retz against Mazarin.

His life changed on the sudden death of Mme de Montbazon. He sought serious spiritual advice, from Arnauld d'Andilly among others, lived austerely and read widely in the history of the church. He visited the houses of which he was commendatory abbot or prior, decided to settle at one of them, La Trappe, going to Perseigne, another monastery of the reformed Cistercians, for his year's noviceship in 1663. He broke down during its course, and had to return for several months to La Trappe, on which he subsequently imposed a radical reform, creating as a context for a life of prayer a minimal diet, hard physical work, corporal mortification, deprivation of sleep, and the infliction of arbitrary humiliations. Intellectual activity was normally banned. Much of Rancé's later life was taken up with defending this interpretation of Cistercian spirituality and fighting for the administrative arrangements which would ensure its survival within the order. His opponents notably included Mabillon.

Rancé had no shortage of candidates for La Trappe, although he was embarrassed by the alarming death rate in the community. His personality was combative, and his rigorism clearly attracted Jansenist sympathizers, although he carefully avoided taking sides on the doctrinal issues. Rancé's success is largely attributable to the way in which, outside his monastery, he tempered his spiritual severity to suit his judgement about the spiritual gifts and secular responsibilities of his different correspondents

    comes first in his graduating year, 79

    Fénelon and, 280; sends Houdar de la Motte away from, 355; conversion after death of Mme de Montbazon, 785; friendship with Saint-Simon, 787, 789; visited by Bernardin de Saint-Pierre, 62; canonization of François de Sales pointed comment on spirituality of, 792

    Mme de Lafayette corresponds with, 414; Mme de la Sablière becomes penitent of, 425; literary interest of letters on, 620; lack of subtlety in direction of, 776

Rapin, Nicolas (?1540–1608), lawyer, poet, and translator, chiefly celebrated for his anti-League contributions to the *Satire Ménippée*, but also a captain in the army of Henri IV, author of Greek, Latin, and French verse (*Les plaisirs du gentilhomme champestre, 1581*), who paraphrased the penitential psalms, and composed vers mesurés

    Hardy calls on, 346; Henri IV commissions love poetry from, 693; Régnier dedicates a *Satire* to, 696

    part author of *Satire Ménippée*

Rapin, René (1621–87), Jesuit who played a leading role in the literary life of Paris, frequented the Hôtel de Lamoignon, and left a series of *Réflexions sur la poétique d'Aristote et sur les ouvrages des poètes anciens et modernes* (1674), upholding classical aesthetic principles and affirming notably that what is true is to be found only in the ideal and universal orders, 'dans

Richelieu went outside France only once, to obtain in 1608 a dispensation for appointment to the see of Luçon, for which to the apparent amusement of Paul V, he lied about his age. He achieved prominence at the Estates General of 1614–15, and attached his fortunes to those of Marie de Medici, becoming chaplain to Anne of Austria on her marriage to Louis XIII in 1615. On Concini's death in 1617, Richelieu followed Marie de Medici into exile at Blois before being exiled to Avignon in 1618 from what he had hoped was retirement to Luçon. He was brought back to the entourage of Marie de Medici to provide a moderating influence to counterbalance that of such semi-rebellious nobles as Epernon, and was in Angoulême by 17 March 1619. It was when his oldest brother Henri was nominated governor of Angers that Thémines, hostile to the Richelieu influence, challenged Henri to the duel in which he killed him.

Richelieu's personal arrangements were remarkably fastidious, marked by meticulous organization rather than ostentation or lavishness. Outside the theatre, his aesthetic tastes were more concerned with architecture and, above all, gardens, than with the beautiful objects bought by his agents to

Séguier. She frequented the Hôtel de Rambouillet and, in spite of sympathies for Jansenist spirituality, but not theology, she characteristically had a Jesuit spiritual director, Père de Sesmaisons, whose advice, passed on by Mme de Sablé to the princesse de Guémené, indirectly led to Arnauld's composition of *De la fréquente communion*.

In 1654 Mme de Sablé was forced to sell the marquisat of Sablé, and in 1656 she retired to Port-Royal, having moved near the monastery in 1652. She had a celebrated glass partition separating her from the monastery church so that she could hear Mass without coming into contact with the germs of other worshippers. When the community was banished to Port-Royal-des-Champs in 1664–65, she remained in Paris, keeping close contact with the conforming remnant as well as with the exiles. Pascal was among those who brought aphorisms for discussion, and a joint volume of maxims by La Rochefoucauld, Mme de Sablé, and Jacques Esprit was at one time envisaged. It was Mme de Sablé who had multiple copies of the manuscript of La Rochefoucauld's *Maximes* made and circulated for comment among friends from 1661. It was one of those copies which was leaked and published without authorization in Holland in the Jansenist interest. Arnauld consulted Mme de Sablé on the *Logique de Port-Royal*, and she left a number of short treatises in addition to her own *Maximes*

    career: favoured Voiture in quarrel of sonnets, 56; relationship with Bossuet, 81; and Guilleragues, 339; frequented Hôtel de Rambouillet, 343; Jansenism of not doctrinal, 436; takes up residence in Paris Port-Royal monastery, 616; and removed by police in 1661, 618; and préciosité and career, 630; takes Voiture's daughter into her household, 889; and leaked Voiture letter, 891

    aphorisms, friends: and moral maxims as literary form, 383; possible jealousy at losing company of La Rochefoucauld to Mme de Lafayette, 412; Mme de Lafayette's relationship with, 414; La Rochefoucauld and, 432–33; other members of circle of, 432; *Maximes* of, and article in *Journal des Savants*, 433; close cooperation with La Rochefoucauld and Jacques Esprit, 433, 630; circulates La Rochefoucauld's maxims for comment, 433

Sablier, Charles (1693–1786), tutor (1744) to the duc d'Aumont, friend and editor of Nivelle de la Chaussée, translator of Goldoni, author of occasional literary works
    association of with Nivelle de la Chaussée, 562

Saci, Isaac Le Maître de: see Le Maître de Saci

Sacrobosco, John of, first half of 13th century, taught mathematics at Oxford and Paris. The *Tractatus de sphaera* on spherical astronomy, printed in 1472, went to 24 editions before 1500, with 40 more in the next half-century. He also wrote a work pointing out the increasing error in the Julian calendar
    Lefèvre d'Etaples writes commentary on, 445

Sacy, Louis de (1654–1727), translator who adapted Cicero's *De amicitia* and dedicated it to Mme de Lambert
    rehabilitates amour-propre, 436

Sade, Donatien-Alphonse-François, marquis de (1740–1814)
Life, 758–65; Works, 765–69; Publications, 769
    see Introduction xliv
    possible derivation of from Duclos, 263–64
    mutual antipathy between Rétif de la Bretonne and, 701, 702

Sadoleto, Jacopo (1477–1547), after Ferrara studied for 12 years in the household of Oliviero Carafa, then dean of the sacred college. Promoted to apostolic secretariat (11 March 1513) on election of Leo X, Sadoleto was given a dozen benefices and in 1517 the diocese of Carpentras in the papal state of Avignon, the comtat Venassin. He was an early genuine believer in the power of liberal studies to lead to moral elevation. His commentary on *Romans*, arguing the inherent goodness of human nature, published in 1635, was censured by the Paris theology faculty. He was recalled to Rome, made a cardinal on 22 December 1536, and set to work on the commission of nine to produce the *Consilium de emendenda Ecclesia*, a project for reforming the Church presented to Paul III on 9 March 1537. Sadoleto's own minority report appears to have been too radical for his colleagues. He left a liberal work of educational theory *De liberis recte instituendis*, felt that the unity of Christendom should be reinstated by discussions with moderates like Bucer and Melanchthon, and in March 1539 wrote a celebrated letter to the Genevans to which Calvin, although in exile, was invited to reply
    letter to the Genevans of, 115
    visits with François I what purported to be grave of Petrarch's Laura, 815

Sagon, François, 16th-century French poet of whom little more is known than the facts about the dispute with Marot given in the text
    see 506–507, 816

Saint-Aignan, François de Beauvillier (1610–87), comte, then duc de, as maître de camp (1644) headed a cavalry regiment; was close to Louis XIV, a patron of letters, and a close friend of Bussy. In 1633 he married Antoinette Servient, daughter of Nicolas, cousin of Abel, who shared the title of surintendant des finances with Foucquet, and was himself treasurer of France at Rouen and tax farmer for the Paris parties casuelles. After his wife had died at 63 on 22 January 1680, Saint-Aignan married Françoise de Géré de Rancé on 8 July 1680. She bore him a daughter in April 1681, a first son, the future bishop of Beauvais, in October 1682, and a second, born on 25 November 1684, who inherited the title in 1711
    choreographs 1654 royal ballet, and designs costumes, 59
    friendship for Bussy, mediation on behalf of, 107, 110
    protection of young Racine, 675
    Tristan's *Mort de Sénèque* dedicated to, 861

Saint-Amant, Marc-Antoine Girard de (1594–1661), poet chiefly noted for the visually descriptive elements in his verse, whose merits, overlooked in the wake of strictures by Boileau, were the subject of a famous essay by Gautier. A Protestant, son of a naval officer, he fought several campaigns, travelled widely between 1627 and 1642, often in the entourage of Harcourt, and acquired a reputation for roisterous living, writing verse evoking life's more robust pleasures. Converted to Catholicism, he became the principal poet in the Liancourt circle. He knew neither Latin nor Greek, but had Spanish, English, and Italian.

Saint-Amant relied on Gongora, but more heavily on Marino, whose richness of imagery he justifies in a preface to the *Passage de Gibraltar* (1640). From 1627 his purpose was often to amuse, as in such pieces as 'Le melon,' 'Le fromage,' 'La vigne,' and 'Le poète crotté.' There are love poems and satire, with a sense of humour leading to the creation of a new form of often melancholy burlesque. His own luxury of fantasy and vocabulary represents a tradition alien to Malherbe's reform. His most famous poems include those on the four sea-

Paris in 1635, entered the service of Léon de Bouthillier, comte de Chavigny, son of the surintendant, whom in 1639 he accompanied to Italy, where he got to know Voiture. From 1644 he was employed in the household of Retz, where he met Ménage, who introduced him into the Dupuy circle. He met Chapelain and Patru, and frequented the Hôtel de Rambouillet. In 1648 he left Retz for Conti, and in the Fronde was therefore on the opposite side from his former employer. After the restoration of peace he frequented the samedis of Madeleine de Scudéry. He died in December 1654, having followed Conti to the Pyrenees. He may earlier have been imprisoned by Mazarin for diverting official funds, dissipated with a woman. Both sexually and financially Sarrazin appears to have taken a somewhat cavalier attitude to the prevailing norms.

His most famous work is the *Pompe funèbre* (1648) in prose and verse, a form which is itself discussed in the 1649 *Lettre écrite de Chantilly à Mme de Montauzier* and was exploited again in the delicate *Voyage de Chapelle et de Bachaumont*. While witty, his poetry was strictly organized, and rarely trivial. It was posthumously published by Pellisson and Ménage, and bore a relationship to both Malherbe and Voiture, to the protagonists of the epic, and to the salon poets, which made clear Sarrazin's efforts to bridge the gulf opening between the two factions later to be known as 'anciens' and 'modernes'

    see Introduction xxxvii

    career: Gourville claims that Sarrazin advised Conti to have him drowned, 337; death of affects position of Guilleragues, 338; delights with Ménage in salon literature, 361; dines with Retz on first day of barricades, 328; and belongs to entourage of Retz, 708; attends Hôtel de Rambouillet, 343; knows Scarron, 811; attends samedis of Madeleine de Scudéry, 828; on Bensserade, 55; favours Voiture in quarrel of sonnets, 56

    'Sarasin' a character in Chapelain dialogue, 136; named by Perrault among modern authors whose fame might grow, 651; allusion to in Pure's *La Prétieuse*, 631

Sartine, Antoine de (1729–1801), comte d'Alby, lieutenant-general of police, then naval minister

    director of book trade, 236

    asks Diderot's advice, 238; and Diderot writes to, 238

    Sade writes to, 759

Sasso de' Sassi (1455–1527), Italian poet

    Desports and, 223

    du Bellay draws on, 261

satire: 16th-century confusion about meaning of term, 808

Satire Ménippée (La) 803–809

    du Vair complimented in, 265

Saunderson, Nicholas (1682–1739), English mathematician blinded by smallpox at age of one

    Diderot draws on for theory of senses, 242

Sauvage, Denys (c1520–c1587), translator and historiographer of Henri II

    used by Peletier as character in dialogue, 586

    mentioned by Ronsard in 1553 list, 611

    writes to Pasquier about Tyard, 863; translates Ebreo, 863

Sauval, Henri (1623–died between July 1671 and mid-1673), son of a merchant and brother of a financier, barrister and author of the posthumously published *Histoire et Recherches des Antiquités de Paris* (1724). His name was linked with that

of Mlle Desjardins, and he was a friend of Furetière, the Boileau brothers, and Cassandre. Pellisson, Patru, Sorel, and Costar all expressed admiration for him. There is an unexplained but offensive reference to him in Boileau's seventh *Satire*

    the mocking reference in Boileau, 71

Sauveur, Joseph (1653–1716), mathematician and physicist, tutor to the grandson of the grand Condé

    attends Bossuet's Versailles study group and owes post to him, 82

    tutor to duc de Bourbon, 382–83

Savonarola, Girolamo (1452–98), Italian Dominican, prior of Florentine convent of San Marco, denouncer of corruption and luxury, attempted to establish in Florence a semi-theocratic and semi-democratic regime. He was hanged, then burnt, for heresy

    Lefèvre d'Etaples attends sermon of, 444

Saxe, Maurice de (1696–1750), comte, maréchal, illegitimate son of Augustus II of Saxony, the colourful general naturalized French in 1746, lover of Mme de la Popelinière and, on account of his military victories, given the château at Chambord, where he died of multiple excesses

    Grimm enters service of nephew of, 744

    Sade's uncle and tutor, 758

Scaliger, Joseph Justus (1540–1609), Italian scholar, tenth child of Julius Caesar (below), educated at the Collège de Guyenne until the outbreak of plague in 1555. He then spent his father's last years with him, studied in Paris, learnt Greek, and travelled in Italy and then England as companion to Louis de Chasteignier, duc de La Rocheposay (died 1595). He became a Protestant, studied law with Cujas, and was appointed professor in Geneva. In 1574 he returned to live with the La Rocheposay family and began to produce his editions and his celebrated work on the calendar and the measurement of time, the *De emendatione temporum* (1583). He spent the last 13 years of his life at Leiden, with the second half of that period marred by bitter conflict, notably with Gaspar Scioppius

    associated with Gillot and Desportes, 806

    Charron meets, 137

    protected by La Rocheposay, 770

Scaliger, Julius-Caesar (1484–1558), father of Joseph Justus (above); Italian doctor who wrote against Erasmus and composed a treatise on poetics introducing Aristotelian theory into France, the 1561 *Poetices Libri septem*

    publication of the *Poetics*, 439–41; edition admired by Chapelain, 130

    model for La Boétie, 378

    on meaning of term 'satire,' 808

Scarlatti, Alessandro (1660–1725), Italian musician and prolific composer of opera; father of Domenico (1685–1757), who composed mainly for the harpsichord

    Bambini company play Alessandro opera in Paris in 1752, 333

Scarron, Paul (1610–60)

    Life, 809–12; Works, 812–14; Publications, 814

    see Introduction xxxvii

    career: favours Bensserade in sonnet quarrel, 56; supports Mazarin, changes sides, 191; and dispute with Cyrano de Bergerac, 191; laughs at Belin and supports Mairet in quarrel following Pierre Corneille's *Le Cid*, 461; Scarron's *La Précaution inutile* challenged by Molière's

Seize, council of the, governed Paris from 1586 in the interests of the League, although its corporate policy was more extreme than that of the League's political leaders. Two representatives from each of the 16 Paris administrative districts had been secretly elected in 1585, to which for the sake of moderation the League's political leaders added a sprinkling of merchants and others, making probably 40 or 50 members of the council in all
 see Chronology 1586
 policy of, 265–68, 804, 805, 807
 La Bruyère's family and, 381
Semblançay, Jacques de Beaune (c1457–1527), baron de, général des finances and a private financier, blamed in 1522 for the loss of Milan for failing to send 1,200,000 livres to the army. An enquiry cleared him, but in 1524 his accounts were again examined with those of many lesser officials. The only fault found was the mingling, at their own request, of credits and debits belonging to François I with those belonging to his mother, Louise de Savoie. The king owed Semblançay 480,000 livres more than Semblançay owed Louise de Savoie. His arrest on 13 January 1527, after transacting no important crown business since 1525, was due to his efforts to recover money due to him from the crown. At a rigged trial, with his known enemies appointed to replace a first set of judges, he was accused of bribery, corruption, maladministration, and misappropriation of royal funds, and on 9 August he was sentenced to death. He was hanged on 11 August after waiting six hours at the Montfaucon gallows
 see Chronology 1527
 execution of 489
 Marot's poems for, 504
semi-Pelagianism, a heresy which differs from full Pelagianism, the view that human nature (see Glossary) can merit salvation, by affirming pure or fallen nature's ability in some way to initiate, persevere in, or autonomously either to accept or to cooperate with proffered justifying grace. To avoid making salvation available outside the Church, a view certainly heretical at least from the beginning of the 14th until the end of the 17th centuries, it was universally necessary to assume a concept of nature within which it was a corollary that it was going to be simply impossible to reconcile any doctrine of free will, in the sense of an autonomous human power of self-determination to good, with a theory of grace that was not at least semi-Pelagian, as the religious controversies of the 16th and 17th centuries make abundantly clear
 see entry on Jansenism, passim
 Jansenist view of Molinism as semi-Pelagian, 279
 Malebranche on semi-Pelagianism of Fénelon, 290; and Malebranche's own dilemma, 469; and that of Nicole, 559; and of Pascal, 577, 579; and of François de Sales, 793; and in the Jansenist-Jesuit disputes, 773–74
 Rabelais's assumptions, 660, 662, 664
Senault, Jean-François (1601–72), Oratorian preacher who published, in addition to his sermons, a moral work contributing to the rehabilitation of the passions at the peak of the early 17th-century confidence in human nature
 publication of *De l'usage des passions* in 1641, 435
 use of term 'paresse,' 576
Senneterre, Antoine de (died 1592), bishop of Le Puy (1561)
 employs Desportes, 222
Serafino dei Ciminelli, Aquitano (1466–1500), Italian poet

Desportes dependent on, 223; Marot draws on, 504; Scève's use of, 818; Tyard uses as model, 863
 goes out of fashion in Italy, 507
Sercy, Charles de, Parisian printer and bookseller, publisher of the five-part *Recueil de pièces en prose, les plus agréables de ce temps, composées par divers autheurs* (1658, 1660, 1660, 1661, 1663), containing much that had been published before, and some verse, and of the 1661 *Recueil des plus beaux vers qui ont esté mis en chant*, as well as of the five-part *Poésies choisies* known as the *Recueil Sercy* (1653–60)
 relies for material on Bensserade, 57; publishes Cyrano de Bergerac, 191; La Rochefoucauld on amour-propre, 433; and his self-portrait, 434, the 1659 *Recueil des portraits*, 108, 411; and caters for vogue for maps of love, 629
 the five-part *Recueils* of, 629
 Mme de Sévigné praised in 1653 *Poésies choisies*, 839
Servet, Miguel (c1511–1553), from the old Catalonian nobility, studied law, accompanied the emperor to coronation in Bologna (24 February 1530), and then stayed for more than six months with Oecolampadius before visiting Bucer at Strasbourg. In 1531 he published his *De Trinitatis erroribus libri septem*, condemned in Switzerland and the cause of inquisitorial proceedings at Saragossa and Toulouse. In 1532 he published a less plainly anti-Trinitarian *Dialogorum de Trinitate libri duo* in 1532. He changed his name to Villanovanus (Villeneuve), travelled, worked for Lyons printers, edited Ptolemy, defended the neoplatonist doctor Symphorien Champier, lectured on astrology, and practised medicine.
 The theological exchange with Calvin begins in 1539–41 and is recommenced in 1546. Servet published his *Christianismi restitutio* in 1552 or 1553; it also contained an account of the circulation of the blood, but was intended to oust Calvin's *Institutio*. Servet was denounced as a heretic by a close friend of Calvin, imprisoned at Vienne, escaped, fled to Geneva where he was arrested on 13 August, was tried, convicted of spreading heresy, and burnt. Calvin's position was considerably strengthened as a result
 and Calvin's pursuit of, 114–15
 possible reason for Bodin's departure from Geneva, 66
Servien, Abel (1593–1659), name more correctly spelt Servient; diplomat and financier. Secretary of state for war from 1630, Servien was entrusted with various diplomatic missions by Richelieu, but was exiled to Angers from 1636 to 1643. When he was appointed surintendant des finances on 18 February 1653, he was only nominally on a par with Foucquet. On his death he was not replaced
 on death of, Colbert warns Mazarin about financial administration, 591
 antagonistic to Retz supporters, 712
Sesmaisons, Pierre de (1588–1648), Jesuit, author of a guide for Mme de Sablé, his penitent, recommending frequent communion. Mme de Sablé showed it to the princesse de Guémené, who sought comments from her own confessor. The slight notes of Sesmaisons circuitously led to Arnauld's massive *De la fréquente communion*
 the provocation for Arnauld's work, 368
Sévigné, Charles de (1648–1713), son of Mme de Sévigné
 see entry on Mme de Sévigné, passim
 views of Mme de Sévigné on a prospective bride for, 279

stage machinery and changes of scenery: It may be unsafe to assume that the declamatory tragedy relying chiefly on a verse text and a rhetorical delivery which culminated in Racine was what chiefly attracted the more sophisticated 17th-century audiences. There is some evidence to suggest that the tragi-comedy and the pastoral, and then the prototype operas—plays with music, singing, stage effects, and changes of decor—were regarded as catering for the more refined tastes, that the vogue for mythological subjects may have been seen as a way of elevating tragedy out of early entertainments relying on the perfunctory plots and corpse-strewn denouements of Hardy, and that more attention needs to be paid by historians to the Italian companies, who appear to have been the main force behind the introduction of complicated stage effects and multiple changes of decor.

Richelieu allowed no Italian company in Paris, strongly encouraged French theatre, believed in regularity and the 24-hour rule, but also magnificently equipped the larger theatre in the Palais-Cardinal with theatrical machinery. As soon as he was dead, Mazarin brought back the Italians—Torelli, Vigarani, to be joined by his son, and the commedia dell'arte (q.v.). Both under Marie de Medici and under Mazarin and Colbert, the social standing of the Italian companies was high. Royal godparents do not seem to have been difficult to arrange for the infants of heads of troupes, and there is a puzzling absence of difficulty about ecclesiastical burials for Italian actors. It is hard to think of a valid ecclesiastical reason which would allow different rules for the burial of French and Italian actors.

The introduction into France of complex stage machinery capable of producing effects to be marvelled at is no doubt due to Richelieu, who may have spent 100,000 livres installing the equipment needed to play what may largely have been his own *Mirame* in 1641. Richelieu died at the end of 1642, Mazarin was confirmed in power by Anne of Austria on the death of Louis XIII in 1643, and within 18 months there was an Italian troupe back in Paris. By 1645 Mazarin had brought over Torelli. Elaborate machinery had long been used in Italy, and it was needed for such pieces as *La Finta Pazza*, played by the Bianchi company in 1645, *Rosaura*, *Orfeo*, and *Ercolano Amante*. *La Finta Pazza* was played without music, just 'little drums' for the ballet (choreographed by Balbi) for four bears and four monkeys with which the first act ends.

Olivier d'Ormesson describes the five decors used, marvelling at the perspectives and at the speed with which Aurora flies over the stage in her chariot before four zephyrs descend and rise again with the same speed. *Orfeo*, played early in 1647 and also at the Petit-Bourbon, requires 12 settings without lowering any curtain which may have been installed. The cost of *Orfeo* is stated to have been 500,000 livres. The play failed. It might be noted in comparison that in the peak year,

theory of grace of, 366

treatise on angels of importance for Malebranche, 469

Subligny, Adrien Perdou de (?1636–96), chiefly famous for his parody of *Andromaque*, played by Molière in 1668, after Racine had created the principal role of *Andromaque* for Thérèse du Parc at the rival company, having already transferred there his successful *Alexandre*. Subligny had already praised Molière in *La Muse dauphine* (1666–67), and may have been the author of *Le Désespoir extravagant* played by Molière's company in 1670–71, of a *Déroute des précieuses* and a novel *La Fausse Clélie* (1671)

> thought Pradon's *Tamerlan* preface aimed at Racine, 623
>
> *La Folle Querelle* of satire on *Andromaque*, 677
>
> Racine's reply in *Les Plaideurs*, 678

Sully, Maximilien de Béthune (1560–1641), baron de Rosny, duc de, Protestant who fought with and administered for Henri IV, in charge of France's economic organization. He was supported by the Guise family, but opposed by the Condés and the Soissons. Capable, but domineering and imperious, he retired in 1611, after the assassination of Henri IV, to great personal wealth. He left *Mémoires*, fascinatingly written, and of great importance to historians

> Régnier supports Villeroy against, 694
>
> important source for Tallemant, 854

Surin, Jean-Joseph (1600–65), Jesuit spiritual director, exorcist from 1634 of the Ursulines of Loudun, important for an insistence on the interior virtues of freedom from inner constraint, purity of heart, and peace of soul, developing the doctrine of his director Lallemant in a way which conflicted with emergent Jansenism in Saint-Cyran and which reacted against the earlier Jesuit baroque tradition.

Surin restored to sanity the Ursuline prioress, Jeanne des Anges, after the hysterical exhibitions which previous exorcists, like the ill-named Père Tranquille, had provoked. His reaction against earlier Jesuit insistence on external asceticism made him suspect to Roman superiors, and his experience as an exorcist made him subject to schizoid depressions, plunging him into serious mental illness. He attempted suicide in 1645. He left some 600 letters, edited in 1966, almost 150 written before 1639, and about 450 after his recovery in 1657. About a third were to Jeanne des Anges. He also wrote a series of *Cantiques spirituels* (1660), a *Catéchisme spirituel* (1663), and some posthumous works, including *Le Triomphe de l'amour* (written 1636), *Dialogues spirituels* (1655–57), *Fondements de la vie spirituelle* (1667), and the *Guide spirituel* (1660)

> Fénelon submits doctrine of to Issy commissioners, 283
>
> and 17th-century letters of spiritual direction, 612, 620
>
> skill as director, 776

Suso, Heinrich (1300–66), Rhineland ascetic and mystic who developed his doctrine from Eckhart

> source for Bérulle, 771

suspension of judgement: or εποχὴ, associated with sceptics of antiquity, particularly Pyrrho, but also with Sextus Empiricus, and with the stoics, with whose doctrine antique scepticism had logical affinities and with which it was anyway confused in transmission through Cicero, who makes Pyrrho a stoic, and through Diogenes Laertius, who insists on Pyrrho's association with the suspension of judgement. In late 16th-century France the intellectual suspension of judgement is strongly linked to Christian neostoicism through the work of the Belgian scholar Justus Lipsius, important for Montaigne, du Vair,

and Charron among others. Descartes's methodic doubt, which is a suspension of judgement until metaphysical certainty is achieved, originates, like his definition of générosité, in du Vair

> see Introduction xli
>
> and Charron, 139; and Gassendi, 321; and Montaigne, 537
>
> and Justus Lipsius, 121, 873; and Descartes, 209

Table Ronde: the Round Table of Arthurian legend, and name adopted by a loose association of like-minded young writers, whose names are given in the entries on La Fontaine (p. 421) and Tallemant des Réaux (p. 854). They heavily parodied themselves by giving each other pseudo-Arthurian identities

> source of information for Tallemant, 854

tabouret: the privilege accorded to ladies of only the highest aristocracy of remaining seated in the presence of the queen. It was intensely coveted and bitterly disputed as a mark of social rank, especially in 1649 when Mme de Chevreuse obtained the privilege for Mme de Guémené and it was given also to Mlle de Montbazon (Anne de Rohan) before she married the duc de Luynes. Condé wanted it withdrawn from Anne de Rohan in a move seen as part of the class struggle between the house of Condé, with its princes of the blood, and Longueville against the houses of Rohan and Chevreuse

> bestowed on Julie d'Angennes, 343; La Rochefoucauld and, 431–32; accorded to Saint-Simon's wife, 787; and turned down by Mme de Sévigné when, at 59, she refused to marry the 65-year-old Luynes, 843
>
> squabble over occasion for real political manoeuvre, 710

Tabourot, Etienne (1549–90), known as 'Tabourot des Accords,' lawyer, adherent of the League, poet, historian, and author of prose contes. *Les Bigarrures* appeared from 1572 to 1585, treating a series of frivolous and serious but unconnected subjects, and forming a collection of miscellaneous essays. The *Touches* (1585–88) is a series of commonplace epigrams. The *Apothegmes* (1585) and the posthumous *Escraignes dijonnoises* (1603) contain crude popular tales, drawing on Rabelais and some Italian models

> publishes *Douze Fables* of Tyard, 862

tacit permissions: semi-formal permissions to publish constituting a private agreement between publisher or author and the authorities. They fell short of a full privilège, recorded and printed, but did not involve the same degree of censorship and could be withdrawn or have their existence denied if, for instance, the director of the book trade found himself in political difficulties, but they offered a measure of security to publishers and authors, and kept the printing and publishing in France

> see the entry on Fréron, passim
>
> see also 231, and on Malesherbes's use of the system, 747

Tahureau, Jacques (1527–55), Le Mans poet who died very young, having published his *Sonnets, odes et mignardises amoureuses de l'Admirée* in 1554, and a discourse on the excellence of the French language in 1555. Two popular satirical dialogues attacking pretentiousness were published posthumously in 1556

> Baïf's friendship with, 17; and joins La Péruse in Poitiers, 611
>
> interests of promoted by Saint-Gelais, 18; among poets mentioned by Ronsard, 611; writes poem to Jodelle, 371; meets Garnier, 314

Baïf present at final sessions, 18; Baius sent as theologian to, 366; a d'Urfé present at, 867; dictates papal political strategy, 487

refuses to reconcile free will with gratuity of grace, 365, 559

and Pascal, 577

Tressan, Louis-Elisabeth de la Vergne (1705–83), comte de, governor of Toul (1750). Close to the Polish court at Nancy, he moved after the death of Stanislaus Leszczynski to Champagne, then Paris, and finally Franconville, adapting or modernizing many chivalresque works and adventure novels, and he wrote an original paper on electricity. He remained on good terms with both the Polish court and the philosophes (q.v.)

organizes Fréron's release from prison, 305

protests at Palissot's lampoon of Rousseau, 567

Tristan l'Hermite (François l'Hermite, known as) (?1601–1655)

Life, 857–59; Works, 859–61; Publications, 861–62

see Introduction xlii

Cyrano de Bergerac and, 190–91, 193, 195; writes to order for Molière, 515; named by Perrault among authors whose fame might increase, 598, 651; Scarron enjoys company of, 809; Théophile mixes with, 885; involved in sonnet rivalry with Voiture, 892

Osman and interest in Turkey, 622; cartographer of love, 629; admired by Saint-Evremond, 785

Tronchin, François (1710–93), younger brother of Jean-Robert (below); lawyer, member of Geneva's grand conseil, and its public prosecutor who roundly condemned Voltaire's *Dictionnaire philosophique* of 1764, holding that some of the Bible passages quoted were unworthy of God, although he did not deny the divine inspiration of scripture, or the unchristian sentiments it sometimes contained

Diderot's letters to, 2

Tronchin, Jean-Robert (1702–88), brother of above; banker and lawyer at Lyons, and later a tax farmer in Paris, who helped Voltaire with his installation at Les Délices, supplied him with wines, cloth, plants, paint, a carriage, and a collection of precious objects. He mediated the finance for the whole installation

letters of against Rousseau, 749

Tronchin, Louis, liberal Calvinist theology professor at Geneva, uncle of Chouet

and Bayle, 30

Tronchin, Théodore (1709–81), cousin of Jean-Robert and François; Voltaire's doctor, who accompanied him on his last journey to Paris, and Europe's most celebrated physician. He fuelled the mutual antagonism of Voltaire and Rousseau and was well known for his treatment of nervous troubles by exercise and fresh air

Diderot friendly with, 230; defends Geneva against d'Alembert, 234; source of Voltaire's information about Rousseau, 749; consulted by Mme d'Epinay, 746

advocate of inoculation, 236; writes entry on inoculation for *L'Encyclopédie*, 274

Tronson, Louis (1622–1700), superior of the congregation of Saint-Sulpice and Fénelon's early spiritual director

spirituality of, 278

appointed to Issy commission to consider writings of Mme Guyon, 84, 283

Fénelon's early director, 278ff, consulted on suitability of Fénelon for tutorship, 282; commends *Maximes des saints*, 284; Fénelon reads *Mémoire* to, 284

Trublet, Nicolas-Charles-Joseph (1697–1770), abbé and apologist against the philosophes (q.v.), but editor of Maupertuis's *Essai sur la formation des corps organisés* (1754). He is chiefly known for Voltaire's persecution of him. Educated by the Jesuits at Rennes, took the side of the modernes in the Querelle des anciens et des modernes (q.v.), and was ordained in 1723. A disciple of Fontenelle, he frequented Mme de Tencin, entered the service of her brother the cardinal, and moved after Mme de Tencin's death to the salon of Mme Geoffrin. He became archdeacon of Dinan, treasurer of Nantes, and editor of the *Journal des Savants* (1736–39), but was made to appear ridiculous by his literary ambitions, and annoyed Voltaire. From 1758 to 1760 he worked for the *Journal chrétien*. The Goncourts thought his critical writings the most discerning of his century. He left nearly a dozen works, notably including the four-volume *Essais sur divers sujets de littérature et de morale* (1735–60)

career: proposed for Académie by duchesse de Chaulnes, 1; passes Diderot unacceptable Fontenelle piece for *L'Encyclopédie*, 232; biographer of Fontenelle, 293–94; succeeds Morand as censor, and defends Fréron, 302; lifts suspension of *L'Année littéraire*, 301; resigns as censor, 302; meets Maupertuis, 607; prepares posthumous second edition of Vauvenargues, 882

thought indulgent to Fréron by Malesherbes, 234; depicts Marivaux as edgy, 498; attack on by Nivelle de la Chaussée, 564

Tunstall, Cuthbert (1474–1559), an Oxford contemporary of More, Grocyn, Colet, and Linacre. He moved to Cambridge, then Padua, where he stayed six years, learnt Greek and probably Hebrew, and graduated in law. In 1506 he acquired four rectories, but was ordained subdeacon only in 1509 and priest in 1511. He became master of the rolls and bishop of London before translation to the more lucrative see of Durham. A conservative theologian, he was an able diplomat and spent much time abroad negotiating on behalf of the king. An opponent of the royal annulment, Tunstall none the less accepted Cranmer's decision and attended the coronation of Anne Boleyn. In 1535 he acknowledged the king as the supreme head of the Church in England

Budé's correspondence with, 100

Turenne, Henri de la Tour (1555–1623), vicomte de, Protestant from 1576, later duc de Bouillon and sovereign prince of Sedan by virtue of his first marriage to Charlotte, the only daughter of Henri-Robert de la Marck. Turenne was a maréchal from 1592, compromised in the conspiracy for which Biron was beheaded in 1602, and a member of the dissident Protestant aristocracy with Lesdiguières, Sully, his son-in-law Rohan, and Rohan's brother, Soubise

d'Aubigné's advice prevails over that of, 9

an early 'politique', 315

Turenne, Henri de la Tour d'Auvergne (1611–75), vicomte de, maréchal, second son of above, and brother of the successor to the Bouillon title. His military training took place in the bodyguard of his uncle, Maurice of Nassau, but he entered French service in 1630. His military career during Richelieu's ministry showed distinguished generalship, and in spite of his religion before Bossuet converted him to Catholicism in

1668, and the political complications caused by the relationship between Sedan and France, Turenne was made a maréchal in 1643. After his victory against the imperial forces at Summerhausen in 1648 Turenne, no doubt partly on account of an attachment to Mme de Longueville, joined forces with the princes in 1649, but failed to carry with him his army, apparently bribed by Mazarin, and had to take refuge in the Netherlands.

Had he not fled again in time to hold Stenay with the duchesse de Longueville against royal forces, he would probably have been arrested at the same time as Condé, Conti, and Longueville in January 1650. In fact Turenne, defeated at Rethel, returned to the allegiance of Mazarin and the court, commanding the royal troops which pinned down Condé's forces in the Faubourg Saint-Antoine. Turenne continued his successful military career after the Fronde, and was killed by a chance bullet during the Alsace campaign of the Dutch war on 27 July 1675

see Chronology 1641, 1648, 1649, 1650, 1651, 1652

career: summons back from Germany signals outbreak of Fronde, 709; and conduct during Fronde, 710; takes refuge in Netherlands, and returns, 432; flight to Stenay and subsequent conduct, 712

personal: converted to Catholicism by Bossuet, 80; Bussy serves under and does not get on with, 106; accepts sincerity of Retz's conversion, 713; admirer of Mme de Sévigné, 838

Turgot, Anne-Robert-Jacques (1727–81), marquis de l'Aulne, one of France's most original finance ministers and economic theoreticians, loosely associated with Quesnay and physiocratic ideas, whose views had much in common with those of Adam Smith, and proved too radical to prevent his fall. His views on human progress and perfectibility inspired Condorcet, who wrote his life, and whose *Esquisse* develops many of Turgot's ideas. A maître des requêtes, then intendant of Limoges, Turgot became controller-general of finance in 1774. His translations of Virgil, Horace, and Pope had been little more than literary exercises, but he frequented the salons of Mme du Deffand and Julie de Lespinasse, was a friend of d'Holbach and Helvétius, and wrote five important essays for *L'Encyclopédie* (q.v.), including 'Existence,' 'Foires,' 'Marchés,' and 'Fondations' which, together with those of Quesnay on 'Grains' and 'Fermiers' virtually founded the science of economics in France. Turgot's article on 'Etymologie' was a serious step towards a proper philology.

Among the reforms to which Turgot was most dedicated were those to trade freely in corn and to import it, to suppress the restrictive industrial corporations, to reform the fiscal system, estimating taxable wealth by property and agricultural yield, and to abolish the 'corvée' by which labour was conscripted for the upkeep of roads. He also abolished the state monopoly of salt, strongly favoured the cultivation of the newly introduced potato, and envisaged a reorganization of the tiered system of local government. His work was hampered by rocketing food prices. Its principles were laid out in his *Réflexions sur la production et la distribution des richesses* (1766) and the *Valeurs et monnaies* (1769)

see Chronology 1774, 1776

see entry on Condorcet, passim

and *L'Encyclopédie*, 2, 274; ceases to contribute to, 236; and Galiani, 238; and Diderot's relations with, 239

and Mme du Deffand and Julie de Lespinasse, 2; effect of dismissal of on Chamfort, 127; and liking for Helvétius, 607

Turnèbe, Adrien (1512–65), royal lecturer in Greek, father of following

épître of, 258

protected by François Olivier, 352

teaching at Toulouse, and praised by Montaigne, 529

Turnèbe, Odet de (1553–81), son of preceding, dramatist

knows du Vair, 265

Tyard, Pontus de (1522–1605)

Life, 862–63; Works, 863–66; Publications, 866

see Introduction xl

career: and Académie du Palais, 19, 140; du Bellay meets, 257; friend of Peletier, 584; and vernacular and orthography, 584; dedicates piece to Catherine de Clermont, 705; associated with Scève, 817; named in Ronsard's list of seven poets, 610, 862; cousin of Guillaume des Autels, 862

views of: Baïf's community of inspiration with, 16–18; and morally elevating effects of music and poetry, 20–21, 727; in du Bellay's list of poets hostile to ignorance, 256; belief that mathematical ratios underlie memory and universe, 585, 586

Unigenitus, anti-Jansenist constitution of bull signed at Rome on 8 September 1713 listing errors of Pasquier Quesnel

see Chronology 1713

suppression of *L'Encyclopédie* entry on, 232

causes Fénelon to issue *Instruction pastorale*, 291

unities: of time (24-hour rule), place, and action, were not one and indivisible, but extensible and not even always clearly discernible. They were the chief ingredients of a 'regularity' which also included observance of often ill-defined rules about the avoidance of on-stage violence, of monologues by female characters on an empty stage, and other variable conventions which could purport to trace their ancestry, if not through Scaliger to Aristotle, at least to Italy and Castelvetro. Efforts to observe the unities were, at least in the beginning, announcements of seriousness of dramatic purpose, introduced first in the imaginatively demanding pastorals and tragi-comedies, rather than in tragic melodrama or fairground burlesque. The imaginative concentration of regular dramas naturally led towards an intensity of psychological interest not easily attainable in dramatic entertainments covering huge time spans and large distances or involving emotionally traumatic events occurring on stage

see entries on Mairet and Rotrou, passim

Mairet, Rotrou and regularity, related to genres and audience types, 460–62; unities imposed by actors as box-office draw, 132; Richelieu, Chapelain and, 132, 135; origin of in France, 149; Corneille's third *Discours* and, 169; need for to generate psychological intensity, 177; imported from Tasso and Guarini, 405; Saint-Evremond finds English stage too irregular, 785; La Taille and, 440–41

24-hour rule in Pierre Corneille's *Clitandre*, 160; unity of place and dramatic genres in Scudéry, 825; for distinction between tragédie and tragi-comédie, see also

Houdar de la Motte draws on, 357

Lesage's *Le Diable boîteux* inspired by, 454

Veliard, Jacques, preached Ronsard's funeral oration at the Collège de Boncourt on 24 February 1586

source for anecdote of candle shared by Ronsard and Baïf, 722

Vendôme, Alexandre de (1598–1629), grand prior of the knights of Malta. Briefly imprisoned in 1626 for complicity in the treasonable plot for which Chalais was executed

see Chronology 1626

Vendôme, Antoine de: see Bourbon

Vendôme, César (1594–1665) duc de, illegitimate son of Henri IV and Gabrielle d'Estrées, married in 1609 Françoise de Lorraine, duchesse de Mercoeur, d'Etampes, et de Penthièvre, who bore him a daughter, later Mme de Nemours, wife of Charles-Amédée de Savoie (1624–52), and a son, François de Bourbon, duc de Beaufort. Vendôme and Retz were in command of the small force of 3,000 infantry and 400 cavalry which rallied to Marie de Medici at Ponts-de-Cé in August 1620, and Vendôme was stripped of his governorship of Normandy for his part in the conspiracy for which Chalais was in 1626 the sacrificial victim. Vendôme was implicated again in the 1641 uprising, with Turenne's elder brother Bouillon, Guise, and Soissons, in which Soissons died at La Marfée

see Chronology 1626, 1641

relationship of the 'coadjutor' Retz with, 708

Vendôme, Charles (1489–1537), duc de: see Bourbon

Vendôme, Philippe de (1655–1727), younger brother of the duc Louis-Joseph, nephew of the duchesse de Bouillon, and grand prior of the knights of Malta (1678), who presided over the liberal and no doubt modestly dissolute group known as the Société du Temple. His distinguished military career was accompanied by a social life often referred to as debauched, in the course of which he lost a vast fortune. Louis XIV obliged Vendôme to break with the abbé de Chaulieu (1639–1720), who was then taken into the household of Philippe's brother

presided over Société du Temple, 454

protector of the moderne faction, 679

and Voltaire, 895

Vêpres lyonnaises: see p. 815

Vergèce, Ange (c1505–c1514), Greek scholar and calligrapher tutor to Baïf, 17

Vernes, Jacob (1728–91), Genevan pastor and friend of Rousseau

Palissot writes to about Rousseau, 567

Vernet, Antoine-Charles-Horace ('Carle') (1758–1835), French naturalistic painter chiefly associated with large battle-pieces awarded middle category of pension in 1795, 702

Vernet, Jacob (1698–1789), Calvinist minister

engaged by Montesquieu to see *De l'Esprit des lois* through the press, 551

Verneuil, Henri de Bourbon (1601–82) comte de, the son of Henri IV and Henriette de Balzac d'Entragues, who was bishop of Metz and abbot of Saint-Germain-des-Prés before, at the age of over 60, returning to the lay state. In 1668 he married Charlotte Séguier, widow of Sully's grandson. He was a duke and peer from 1661, and ambassador to England in 1665. On 12 December 1622 his sister, Gabrielle-Angélique, close friend of the young queen, married Bernard

de la Valette, son of the duc d'Epernon; she died giving birth to his child in April 1627

helped Furetière to obtain two priories, 307

Tristan probably a page to, 857

Verneuil, Henriette de Balzac d'Entragues. Daughter of Marie Touchet, who had borne a child to Charles IX, and her husband, François de Balzac, seigneur d'Entragues, she was herself a publicly acknowledged mistress of Henri IV, to whom she bore two children (see above, Henri de Bourbon, comte de Verneuil)

Luynes's failure to marry Gabrielle-Angélique, 24

Gabrielle-Angélique and Anne of Austria's miscarriage, 24

Versailles: the small château built there in 1624 for Louis XIII consisted of three wings surrounding a courtyard. Louis XIV had two wings added by Le Vau, and for a period contemplated pulling everything down to start again. In 1669 it was however decided to envelope the existing château in a new building, leaving only the old courtyard façades exposed, but covering the garden front. Its recessed centre had left room for a terrace, but that was subsequently filled in by the galerie des glaces started in 1678, and the whole scale has been ruined by the addition of the vast wings to north and south, trebling the length of the garden front. Le Nôtre planned and created the gardens in the 1660s. By 1664 they could be used for the three-day *Plaisirs de l'île enchantée* fête, and by 1674 for the even more remarkable celebrations in honour of the re-taking of Franche-Comté. From 1678 Jules Hardouin-Mansart was in complete charge of the architecture, and in 1682 the court finally moved in, although Colbert would much have preferred to allow the previous arrangements centring on the Louvre to stand

first big event attended in May 1664 by Mme de Lafayette, 412

Molière play in 1668 for inauguration of gardens, 520

Perrault's description of the gardens, 594

court moves to in 1682, 595

Vertus, Catherine-Françoise de Bretagne (1617–92), demoiselle de, daughter of Claude de Bretagne (1582–1635), comte de Vertus, and of Catherine Fouquet (1590–1670), who never married. She was a seriously devout supporter of Port-Royal (q.v.), one of a family of eight daughters, sister of Mme de Montbazon, close to both La Rochefoucauld and to Mme de Longueville, and was directed by Singlin, then by Saci. She lived first with the comtesse de Soissons, then from 1650 in the Place Royale with the duchesse de Rohan, before becoming virtually a companion of Mme de Longueville, for whom she procured Singlin as director. Mazarin paid her a pension, and she spent the last 11 years of her life confined to bed. For her consolation she was allowed to undergo a modified form of clothing at the monastery on 11 November 1674

lives at Port-Royal-de-Paris, 620

Viau, Théophile de (1590–1626)

Life, 884–86; Works, 886–88; Publications, 888

see Introduction xlii

career: Balzac and, 23, 25, 27, 28; 1618 exile, 24; Liancourt patron of, 159; refers to 'Marets,' court fool of Louis XIII, 214; performance of *Pyrame* at Hôtel de Rambouillet, 342; temporarily replaced by Mairet in Montmorency household, 459; imprisoned September 1623 to September 1625, 459

reputation: taken as model by Gomberville, 328; Mairet inherits papers of, 460; Pradon draws on, 622; Georges de Scudéry writes in defence of, and edits, 822; Sorel associates with, 849; and emends *Francion* text after trial of, 850; friend of Tristan, 857; and admired by him, 858; and used by him as poetic model, 859

Vicentini, Tomasso Antonio ('Thomassin') (1683–1739), played tragic and, when young, female parts in Rome. He was the Arlequin of Riccoboni's troupe re-established in Paris in 1716, with Biancolelli as Trivelin. His French debut was as the harlequin in *L'Inganno fortunato* on 18 May 1716. In the summer the troupe played at the Foire Saint-Laurent, in the winter at the Hôtel de Bourgogne
  the return of the Italians to Paris, 154

Vico, Giovanni Batista (1668–1744), Italian philosopher, historian, and jurist, who developed a theory of natural law in the *Scienza nuova* (1725). His earlier history of law developed into a philosophy of history
  Galiani derives from, 238
  Montesquieu's derivation from, 553

Victor-Amadeus I, prince of Piedmont, then duc de Savoie (1630), who married Christine of France (1606–63), daughter of Henri IV and Marie de Medici. His reign was brief, but the renewed alliance with France sealed by his marriage enabled him to regain for Savoy most of the territories lost when French policy had forced his father to submit to Spanish domination. Savoy remained an important buffer for France, protecting it from immediate contiguity with imperially controlled territory in Lombardy, and the reign of Victor-Amadeus resulted in an arrangement which was in the interest of France as well as of Savoy. Victor-Amadeus died in 1637
  François de Sales and, 798

Victorines, theologians associated with the abbey of Saint-Victor outside the walls of Paris, belonging to the Augustinian canons. The principal theologians were Hugh of Saint Victor (1096–1141) and Richard of Saint Victor (died 1173)
  seen as predecessors of Descartes, 210

Vigarani, Gaspare (1586–1663), and his son Carlo, whose dates are uncertain but who worked with his father, were designers of stage settings and stage machinery for the production of astonishing theatrical effects. Gaspare was called to Paris by Mazarin, possibly in connection with preparations for the celebrations in honour of the wedding of Louis XIV in 1660, as is sometimes asserted, but more probably earlier. Carlo became a naturalized Frenchman, was frequently employed by Lulli, lived in an apartment in the Louvre, and was certainly still living in 1693. His widow was alive in 1716. It seems clear that it must have been Carlo who was primarily concerned with the installation of the Salle des Machines in the Tuileries, and who was responsible for the destruction of Torelli's sets and machinery when the Petit-Bourbon was knocked down, and it is certain that it was Carlo who arranged for the effects at Versailles during the *Plaisirs de l'île enchantée* in 1664
  burning of Torelli's settings, 151

Vigean, Anne de Neubourg (1600–82), marquise du, was married to François Poussart, marquis du Vigean, on 25 July 1617, and bore him four children, Louis in 1620, Anne and Marthe in 1622, and François in 1623. She was celebrated for her passionately affectionate relationship with the duchesse d'Aiguillon, Richelieu's niece and heir, and malicious satirical verses circulated about her relationships with both Mme de Puisieux and the prince de Guémené.

Condé, who in 1644–45 had been in love with Mme du Vigean's daughter Marthe, gained more than a social victory by successfully defending against the duchesse d'Aiguillon the marriage on 29 December 1649 of the duchesse's nephew, Armand-Jean de Vignerot du Plessis, duc de Richelieu, with the 27-year-old widowed daughter of Mme du Vigean, Anne Poussart de Fors. Mme du Vigean took the side of her friend, the duchesse d'Aiguillon, against her daughter. Condé's successful protection of the marriage incorporated into his entourage Richelieu's politically, socially, and militarily useful great-nephew in the teeth of the opposition of the groom's aunt, Richelieu's heir, and the bride's mother. Mazarin thought carefully before no doubt skilfully allowing the marriage to stand, rightly seeing where his long-term advantage lay. The imprisonment of the princes, Condé, Conti, and Longueville, during the Fronde was partly the result of the provocation they had offered to the court in abetting the Richelieu-Neubourg wedding
  Desmarets's relationship with, and with the Richelieu family, 213–14
  imprisonment of princes possibly result of marriage, 217
  duchesse de Richelieu and Desmarets, 219; reception given by, 342; bridge between Richelieu and chambre bleue, 343

Vigean, Anne Poussart du: see Poussart du Pons, Anne de

Vigean, François Poussart, baron de Fors, sieur de, from old Protestant La Rochelle family
  dances at court ballet, 214

Vigneul-Marville, pseudonym of Bonaventure d'Argonne (c1640–1704), essayist, critic
  on Pierre Corneille, 158

Villars, André de Brancas (died 1595), seigneur de, governor of Le Havre, member of the League, successfully defended Rouen against the siege by Henri IV in 1592, making peace only in 1594, when he was appointed amiral de France. He was killed at Doullens
  see Chronology 1594
  Desportes negotiates for Villars with Mayenne, 224

Villars, Nicolas-Pierre-Henri de Montfaucon (1635–73), abbé de, attended the seminary at Alet and the university of Toulouse and spent most of 1661 in the Bastille for unknown reasons. He was assassinated, leaving *Le Comte de Gabalis; ou, Entretiens sur les sciences secrètes* (1670) as well as his attacks on both Racine's *Bérénice* and Pierre Corneille's *Tite et Bérénice*. Mme de Sévigné approved of Villars's criticisms of Racine
  Villars on the two Bérénice plays, 678

Villayer, Jean-Jacques Rebouard (1605–91), seigneur de, depicted by La Bruyère as 'Hermippe,' inventor of a mechanical lift
  and La Bruyère, 385

Villedieu, Marie-Catherine-Hortense Desjardins (?1632–83), Mme de, poet, dramatist, novelist, and a leader in the move away from adventure novels to those based uniquely on galanterie. Born at Alençon, she was a noted beauty. She joined the household of Mme de Rohan when she came to Paris. In 1658 the *Muses illustres* published a sonnet and in 1659 she wrote three portraits for the *Galerie* of Segrais. Her defence of Molière's *Les Précieuses ridicules* and her association with Mme de la Suze, Sauval, Patru, Boileau, and d'Aubignac suggest that she was siding against the more vapid excesses

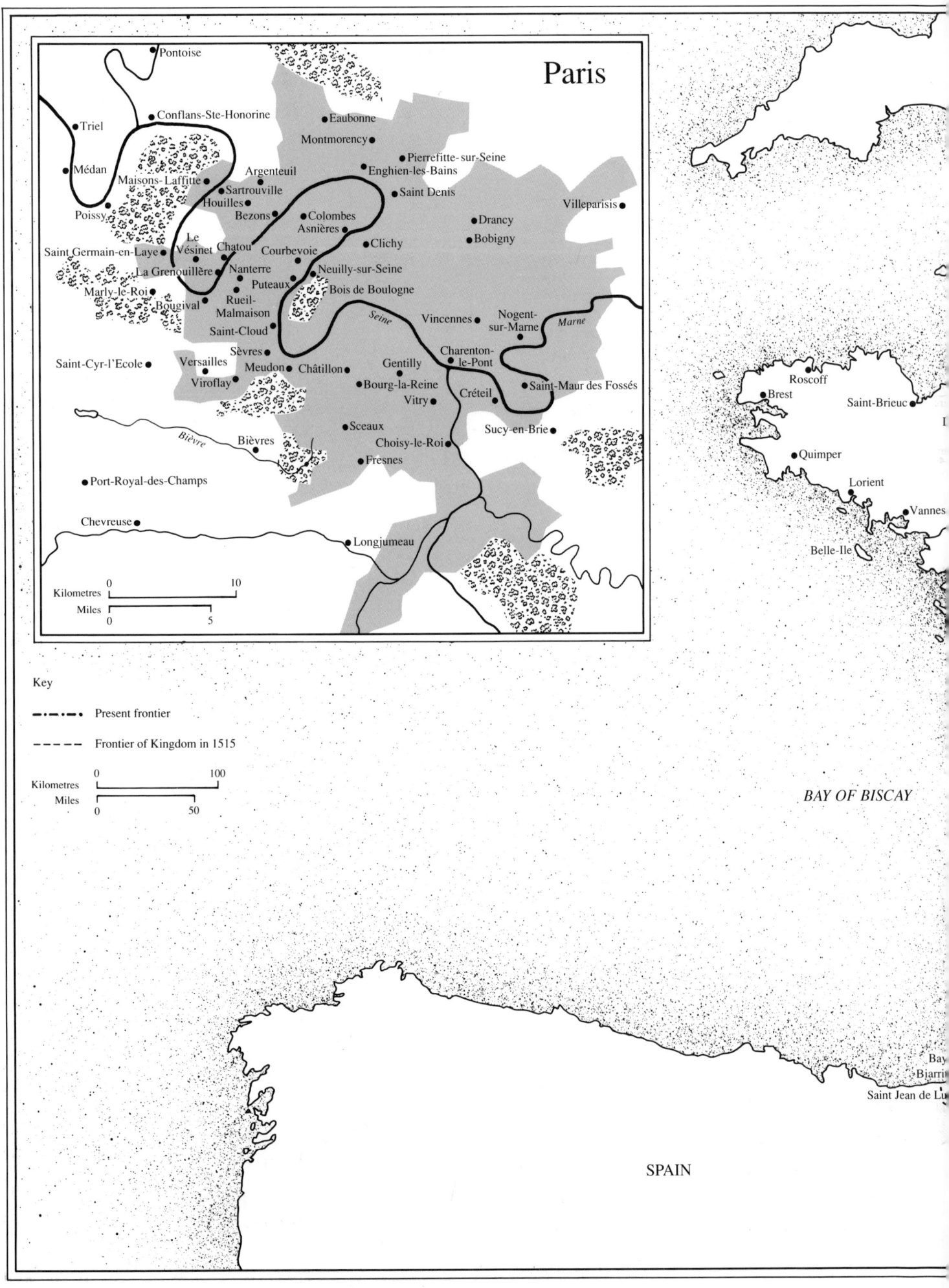

Paris

Pontoise

Triel

Conflans-Ste-Honorine

Médan

Maisons-Laffitte

Poissy

Saint Germain-en-Laye

La Grenouillère

Marly-le-Roi

Bougival

Saint-Cyr-l'Ecole

Chevreuse

Port-Royal-des-Champs

Eaubonne

Montmorency

Pierrefitte-sur-Seine

Argenteuil

Enghien-les-Bains

Sartrouville

Saint Denis

Houilles

Bezons

Colombes

Villeparisis

Asnières

Drancy

Le Vésinet

Chatou

Clichy

Bobigny

Courbevoie

Nanterre

Neuilly-sur-Seine

Puteaux

Bois de Boulogne

Rueil-Malmaison

Seine

Vincennes

Nogent-sur-Marne

Marne

Saint-Cloud

Sèvres

Charenton-le-Pont

Versailles

Meudon

Châtillon

Gentilly

Viroflay

Bourg-la-Reine

Créteil

Saint-Maur des Fossés

Vitry

Bièvre

Sceaux

Sucy-en-Brie

Bièvres

Choisy-le-Roi

Fresnes

Longjumeau

Kilometres 0 10

Miles 0 5

Key

—•—•—• Present frontier

— — — Frontier of Kingdom in 1515

Kilometres 0 100

Miles 0 50

Roscoff

Brest

Saint-Brieuc

Quimper

Lorient

Vannes

Belle-Ile

BAY OF BISCAY

Bay

Biarri

Saint Jean de Lu

SPAIN